The Eerdmans
Dictionary *of* Early Judaism

The Eerdmans
of

Dictionary Early Judaism

Edited by

John J. Collins *and* Daniel C. Harlow

William B. Eerdmans Publishing Company

Grand Rapids, Michigan / Cambridge, U.K.

Published 2010 by
Wm. B. Eerdmans Publishing Co.
2140 Oak Industrial Drive N.E., Grand Rapids, Michigan 49505 /
P.O. Box 163, Cambridge CB3 9PU U.K.
www.eerdmans.com

Printed in the United States of America

15 14 13 12 11 10 7 6 5 4 3 2 1

Library of Congress Cataloging-in-Publication Data

The Eerdmans dictionary of early Judaism / edited by John J. Collins and Daniel C. Harlow.
p. cm.
Includes bibliographical references.
ISBN 978-0-8028-2549-0 (cloth: alk. paper) 1. Judaism — History — Post-exilic period, 586 B.C.–210 A.D. — Dictionaries. 2. Jews — History — 586 B.C.–70 A.D. — Dictionaries. I. Collins, John Joseph, 1946–. II. Harlow, Daniel C.
BM176.E34 2010
296.09′0103 — dc22

2010037935

Maps on pp. 317, 538, 564, 706, 725, 730, 732, 989, 1028, 1046, 1118, 1155, and 1213 by International Mapping, Ellicott City, Maryland

Contents

Preface

The field of Second Temple Judaism has emerged as a major area of study only in this generation. In large part, the flowering of the field has been due to the discovery of the Dead Sea Scrolls, which made available for the first time a wealth of primary sources for the period between the Bible and the Mishnah. There has also been a resurgence of interest in the Pseudepigrapha, the large and loosely defined corpus of literature transmitted by Christians that includes many works of Jewish origin. Despite the proliferation of studies, however, there has not hitherto existed a major reference work devoted specifically to this period. At the beginning of the twenty-first century, the time is ripe to take stock of this burgeoning field.

Naming and delimiting the field have been a problem. The old German label *Spätjudentum* ("Late Judaism") had pejorative connotations, and in any case was largely based on the rabbinic literature, from a later period. Second Temple Judaism, strictly defined, includes most of the Hebrew Bible, while several major nonbiblical, nonrabbinic works were composed after the destruction of the Temple in 70 C.E. (e.g., the writings of Josephus, some of the apocalypses). "Early Judaism" has been the accepted name for the Judaism of the Hellenistic and early Roman period in the Society of Biblical Literature for some time, and that is the name we have adopted here. The boundaries of the period are admittedly fuzzy. The primary focus falls on the period between Alexander the Great in the late fourth century B.C.E. and the Roman emperor Hadrian and the Bar Kokhba Revolt in the early second century C.E. It is impossible to study this period, however, without taking some account of the Persian period and the postexilic biblical books, on the one hand, and of the subsequent development of rabbinic Judaism, on the other.

This Dictionary has two parts. The first part contains thirteen major essays that attempt to synthesize major aspects of Judaism in this period. The second, substantially longer part offers 520 entries arranged alphabetically. Many of these entries have cross-references, and all have select bibliographies. Equal attention is given to literary and nonliterary evidence. The New Testament writings are included, as evidence for Judaism in the first century C.E. This volume does not attempt full treatment of the Hebrew Bible or rabbinic Judaism, but it does contain some entries on these areas that provide the reader with at least initial reference information.

The volume is intended to meet the needs of scholars and students, but also to provide accessible information for the general reader. It is ecumenical and international in character. Two hundred and sixty-six authors, from as many as twenty countries, have contributed. These include Jews, Christians, and people of no religious affiliation. Naturally, the opinions of these authors are diverse, but all are competent scholars with expertise in the subjects they address.

The completion of this Dictionary would not have been possible without help from several quarters. At Eerdmans Michael Thomson first broached the idea and asked us to undertake it. Klaas Wolterstorff oversaw the volume's production at every stage with great care and expertise. Tim Straayer did the laborious work of electronic compositing. Nancy Collins was a great help with researching illustrations. Willem Mineur came up with a fetching cover design. Milton Essenburg put our pages through several rigorous rounds of proofreading. And Tracey Gebbia produced the ancient city maps. Calvin College provided Dan Harlow with a sabbatical in January and Spring 2005 so that he could lay the groundwork for this project. Several contributors went above and beyond the call of duty by providing replacement articles on short notice as the project drew to a close. To these, and to all our colleagues who took the time to write articles for this volume, we are deeply grateful.

JOHN J. COLLINS — DANIEL C. HARLOW

Consulting Editors

Contributors

Martin G. Abegg Jr. Professor of Religious Studies, Trinity Western University, Langley, British Columbia
War, Book of

Samuel L. Adams Assistant Professor of Old Testament, Union Theological Seminary and Presbyterian School of Christian Education, Richmond, Virginia
Proverbs, Book of; Qoheleth

William Adler Professor of Early Christianity and Judaism, North Carolina State University, Raleigh, North Carolina
Chronography; Demetrius the Chronographer

Patricia Ahearne-Kroll Assistant Professor of Religion, Ohio Wesleyan University, Delaware, Ohio
Joseph and Aseneth

Dale C. Allison Jr. Errett M. Grable Professor of Early Christianity, Pittsburgh Theological Seminary, Pittsburgh, Pennsylvania
Abraham, Testament of; Elisha; Kingdom of God

David Amit Deputy Director, Department of Excavations and Surveys, Israel Antiquities Authority, Jerusalem, Israel
Aqueducts; Cisterns and Reservoirs

Randal A. Argall Associate Professor of Religion, Jamestown College, North Dakota
Persecuted Righteous Person

Daniel Assefa Assistant Professor of Sacred Scriptures, Capuchin Franciscan Institute of Philosophy and Theology, Addis Ababa, Ethiopia
Dreams, Book of (1 Enoch 83–90); Ethiopic

Kenneth Atkinson Associate Professor of Religion, University of Northern Iowa, Cedar Falls, Iowa
Gamla; Masada; Solomon, Psalms of

Harold W. Attridge The Reverend Henry L. Black Dean and Lillian Claus Professor of New Testament, Yale Divinity School, New Haven, Connecticut
Greek Religions

David E. Aune Professor of New Testament, University of Notre Dame, Indiana
Miracles and Miracle Workers; Prophecy

Alan J. Avery-Peck Kraft-Hiatt Professor in Judaic Studies, College of the Holy Cross, Worcester, Massachusetts
Neusner, Jacob

Daniel P. Bailey Adjunct Professor of New Testament and Greek, Northern Seminary, Lombard, Illinois
Arch of Titus; Atonement; Suffering Servant

Carol Bakhos Associate Professor of Near Eastern Languages and Cultures, University of California at Los Angeles
Midrash, Midrashim

Elitzur Avraham Bar-Asher Lecturer, School of Linguistics and Department of the Hebrew Language, The Hebrew University of Jerusalem, Israel
Hebrew

John M. G. Barclay J. B. Lightfoot Professor of Divinity, University of Durham, England
Assimilation, Acculturation, Accommodation; Apostasy; Grace; Josephus, Against Apion

Albert I. Baumgarten Professor of Jewish History, Bar-Ilan University, Ramat-Gan, Israel
Bickerman, Elias; Smith, Morton

David Bernat Assistant Professor of Bible, Hebrew College, Newton, Massachusetts
Adiabene; Circumcision

Shani Berrin Tzoref Lecturer in Hebrew, Jewish, and Biblical Studies, University of Sydney, Australia
Pesharim

Jonathan Ben-Dov Lecturer in Bible, Haifa University, Israel
Babylonian Culture; Calendars; Mishmarot

Beth A. Berkowitz Associate Professor of Talmud and Rabbinics, Jewish Theological Seminary, New York
Babylonian Talmud

Katell Berthelot Chargée de recherche au Centre National pour la Recherche Scientifique, Aix-en-Provence, France; Centre de Recherche Français de Jérusalem, Israel
"Early Jewish Literature Written in Greek"; Hecataeus of Abdera; Universalism

René S. Bloch Research Fellow, University of Lausanne, Switzerland
Orpheus, Pseudo-

Gideon Bohak Senior Lecturer in Jewish Philosophy and Religious Studies, Tel Aviv University, Israel
Amulets; Divination and Magic; Gematria; Gentile Attitudes toward Jews and Judaism; Heliopolis; Oniads

Marianne Palmer Bonz Independent Scholar, Plymouth, Massachusetts
Sardis

Oded Borowski Professor of Middle Eastern Studies, Emory University, Atlanta, Georgia
Agriculture in Palestine

Alejandro F. Botta Assistant Professor of Hebrew Bible, Boston University School of Theology, Boston, Massachusetts
Elephantine, Elephantine Papyri; Sanballat; Slaves, Slavery

Raʿanan Boustan Assistant Professor of History, University of California at Los Angeles
Hekhalot Literature; Ishmael b. Elisha; Yoḥanan b. Zakkai

Beverly A. Bow Assistant Professor of Religious Studies, Cleveland State University, Ohio
Birth, Miraculous

James E. Bowley Professor of Religious Studies, Millsaps College, Jackson, Mississippi
Abraham; Apollonius Molon; Aristobulus; Artapanus; Berossus; Cleodemus Malchus; Justus of Tiberius; Nicolaus of Damascus

Monica Brady Research Associate, Department of Theology, University of Notre Dame, Indiana
Prophets, Pseudo-Texts

George J. Brooke Rylands Professor of Biblical Criticism and Exegesis,University of Manchester, England
Genesis and Exodus, Commentary on (4Q422); Florilegium (4Q174); Genesis Apocryphon; Testimonia (4Q175)

Magen Broshi Curator Emeritus, Shrine of the Book, Israel Museum, Jerusalem
Diet in Palestine

Joshua Ezra Burns Assistant Professor of Theology, Marquette University, Milwaukee, Wisconsin
Conversion and Proselytism; God-fearers

David Carr Professor of Hebrew Bible, Union Theological Seminary, New York
Literacy and Reading; Pentateuch; Writing

Mark A. Chancey Associate Professor of Religious Studies, Southern Methodist University, Dallas, Texas
Jotapata; Romanization; Sanders, E. P.; Stone Vessels; Temple Tax

David W. Chapman Associate Professor of New Testament and Biblical Archaeology, Covenant Theological Seminary, St. Louis, Missouri
Family

James H. Charlesworth George L. Collard Professor of New Testament, Princeton Theological Seminary, New Jersey
Serpent

Esther G. Chazon Senior Lecturer in Hebrew Literature, Hebrew University of Jerusalem, Israel
Words of the Luminaries (4Q181)

Randall D. Chesnutt William S. Banowsky Chair in Religion, Pepperdine University, Malibu, California
Solomon, Wisdom of

Kelley Coblentz Bautch Associate Professor of Religious Studies, St. Edward's University, Austin, Texas
Geography, Mythic

Shaye J. D. Cohen Nathan Littauer Professor of Hebrew Literature and Philosophy, Harvard University, Cambridge, Massachusetts
Ioudaios; Judaizing; Mishnah; Tosefta; Yavneh

John J. Collins Holmes Professor of Old Testament Criticism and Interpretation, Yale Divinity School, New Haven, Connecticut
"Early Judaism in Modern Scholarship"; Apocalypse; Apologetic Literature; Canon; Death and Afterlife; Enoch, Ethiopic Apocalypse of (1 Enoch); Eschatology; Exodus, the; Hecataeus, Pseudo-; Philo the Epic Poet; Tcherikover, Victor (Avigdor)

Edward M. Cook Associate Professor of Semitics, Catholic University of America, Washington, D.C.
Aramaic

Mary Rose D'Angelo Associate Professor of New Testament, University of Notre Dame, Indiana
Sexuality

James R. Davila Professor of Early Jewish Studies, St. Mary's College, University of St. Andrews, St. Andrews, Fife, Scotland
Liturgical Works from Qumran; Pseudepigrapha, Old Testament

Roland Deines Professor and Reader in New Testament, University of Nottingham, England
Pharisees

Pascale Derron Librarian, Bibliothèque Cantonale et Universitaire de Lausanne, Switzerland
Phocylides, Pseudo-

Devorah Dimant George and Florence Wise Professor Emerita of Judaism in the Ancient World, University of Haifa, Israel
Pesher on the Periods (4Q180); Wicked and Holy (4Q181)

Lorenzo DiTommaso Associate Professor of Theology, Concordia University, Montréal, Québec
Daniel, Additions to; Daniel, Book of; Daniel, Pseudo-Texts; Jerusalem, New; New Jerusalem Text; Sibylline Oracles

Robert Doran Samuel Williston Professor of Greek and Hebrew, Amherst College, Massachusetts
Antiochus IV Epiphanes; Eupolemus; Eupolemus, Pseudo-; Thallus; Theodotus

Henryk Drawnel Assistant Professor of Old Testament, Catholic University of Lublin, Poland
Amram, Visions of; Elect of God (4Q534-536); Qahat, Admonitions of

Jean Duhaime Professor of Biblical Interpretation, Faculté de Théologie, Université de Montreal, Montréal, Québec
War Scroll (1QM)

James D. G. Dunn J. B. Lightfoot Professor of Divinity, Emeritus, University of Durham, England
Jesus Movement

Yaron Eliav Jean and Samuel Frankel Associate Professor of Rabbinic Literature and Jewish History of Late Antiquity, University of Michigan, Ann Arbor, Michigan
Baths; Medicine and Hygiene

Peter Enns Senior Fellow, Biblical Studies, The Biologos Foundation
Lives of the Prophets

Tali Erickson-Gini Archaeological Inspector, Southern Negev District, Israel Antiquities Authority, Jerusalem
Pottery

Esther Eshel Senior Lecturer in Bible, Bar-Ilan University, Ramat-Gan, Israel
Demons and Exorcism; Genesis Apocryphon; Jonathan the King Text (4Q448); Self-Glorification Hymn

Hanan Eshel† Professor of Land of Israel Studies and Archaeology, Bar-Ilan University, Ramat-Gan, Israel
Bar Kokhba Caves; Bar Kokhba Revolt; Naḥal Ḥever; Murabbaʿat, Wadi

Craig A. Evans Payzant Distinguished Professor of New Testament, Acadia Divinity School, Wolfville, Nova Scotia
Elders; Joshua, Apocryphon of; Mark, Gospel of; Sanhedrin; Tanḥumim

Daniel K. Falk Associate Professor of Religious Studies, University of Oregon, Eugene
Festivals and Holy Days; Moses; Moses Texts from Qumran; Rule of Blessings (1QSb); Sabbath

David A. Fiensy Professor of New Testament, Kentucky Christian University, Grayson
Homily

Stephen Finlan Adjunct Professor of Religious Studies, Manhattan College, New York
Atonement

Frances Flannery Associate Professor of Religion, James Madison University, Harrisonburg, Virginia
Dream and Vision Reports

Peter W. Flint Professor of Religious Studies, Trinity Western University, Langley, British Columbia
Papyri from Qumran Cave 7; Psalm 151; Psalms Scrolls

Michael F. Fox Halls-Baxcom Professor of Hebrew Emeritus, University of Wisconsin, Madison, Wisconsin
Esther, Book of; Esther, Greek Version of

Steven D. Fraade Mark Taper Professor of the History of Judaism, Yale University, New Haven, Connecticut
Targum, Targumim

Jörg Frey Professor of New Testament, University of Zurich, Switzerland
Essenes; Hengel, Martin; Schürer, Emil

Sean Freyne Director of Mediterranean and Near Eastern Studies, Emeritus Professor of Theology, Trinity College, Dublin, Ireland
Galilee; Iturea

Deirdre N. Fulton Lecturer in Classics and Ancient Mediterranean Studies, Pennsylvania State University, University Park, Pennsylvania
Esdras, First Book of; Genealogies

Katharina Galor Adjunct Professor of Art History, Rhode Island School of Design and Adjunct Assistant Professor of Judaic Studies, Brown University, Providence, Rhode Island
Tiberias

Sandra Gambetti Associate Professor of History, College of Staten Island, New York
Diadochi; Ptolemies; Roman Emperors; Seleucids

Simon Gathercole Lecturer in New Testament Studies and Fellow, Fitzwilliam College, Cambridge University, England
Covenantal Nomism; Election; Wisdom (Personified)

Susan Gelb Rosenberg Research Fellow in Classics, University of Texas at Austin
Transjordan

Gary Gilbert Associate Professor of Religious Studies, Claremont McKenna College, Claremont, California
Aphrodisias; Gentiles, Jewish Attitudes toward

Yonder M. Gillihan Assistant Professor of Theology, Boston College, Chestnut Hill, Massachusetts
Associations

Haim Gitler Curator of Numismatics, Israel Museum, Jerusalem
Coins

Matthew Goff Associate Professor of Religious Studies, Florida State University, Tallahassee, Florida
Beatitudes (4QBeatitudes); Instruction (4QInstruction); Wisdom Literature; Wisdom Texts at Qumran

Robert Goldenberg Professor of History and Judaic Studies, Stony Brook University, New York
Pagan Religions

Roger Good Editor, Living Stream Ministry, Anaheim, California
Jacob

Lester L. Grabbe Professor of Theology, University of Hull, England
Babylonians; Mesopotamia, Media, and Babylonia; Parthians; Persian Period; Popular Religion

David F. Graf Professor of Religious Studies, University of Miami, Coral Gables, Florida
Nabatea

Deborah A. Green Greenberg Assistant Professor of Hebrew Language and Literature, University of Oregon, Eugene, Oregon
Tales of the Persian Court (4Q550)

Leonard J. Greenspoon Klutznick Chair in Jewish Civilization, Creighton University, Omaha, Nebraska
Septuagint

Bradley C. Gregory Assistant Professor of Theology and Religious Studies, University of Scranton, Scranton, Pennsylvania
Wealth and Poverty

Andrew David Gross Assistant Professor of Semitic Languages, Catholic University of America, Washington, D.C.
Oaths and Vows; Temple Scroll (4QTemple)

Erich S. Gruen Gladys Rehard Wood Professor of History and Classics, Emeritus, University of California, Berkeley
"Judaism in the Diaspora"; Hellenism, Hellenization

Oren Gutfeld Lecturer in Archaeology, Institute of Archaeology, Hebrew University of Jerusalem, Israel
ʿAraq el-Amir; Jericho

Noah Hacham Lecturer in Jewish History, Hebrew University of Jerusalem, Israel
Fasting

Rachel Hachlili Professor of Archaeology, University of Haifa, Israel
Architecture; Art; Burial Practices

Gideon Hadas Director, Ein Gedi Oasis Excavations, Kibbutz Ein Gedi, Israel
ʿEin Gedi

Robert G. Hall Elliot Professor of Religion, Hampden-Sydney College, Virginia
Isaiah, Ascension of

Betsy Halpern-Amaru Professor Emerita of Religion, Vassar College, Poughkeepsie, New York
Judith, Book of; Land, Concept of

Daniel C. Harlow Professor of Religion, Calvin College, Grand Rapids, Michigan
"Early Judaism and Early Christianity"; Abraham, Apocalypse of; Ascent to Heaven; Baruch, Third Book of; Demons and Exorcism; Fortresses and Palaces; Joseph, Prayer of; Messianic Apocalypse (4Q521); Phoenix

Daniel J. Harrington, S.J. Professor of New Testament, Boston College, Chestnut Hill, Massachusetts
Apocrypha; Baruch, First Book of; Ethics; Jeremiah, Letter of; Maccabean Revolt; Paul

Hannah K. Harrington Professor of Old Testament, Patten University, Oakland, California
Holiness; Purity and Impurity; Sin; Tohorot

Charlotte Hempel Birmingham Fellow, Department of Theology and Religion, University of Birmingham, England
Damascus Document

David Henshke Professor of Talmud, Bar-Ilan University, Ramat-Gan, Israel
Tithing

Matthias Henze Watt J. and Lilly G. Jackson Associate Professor of Biblical Studies, Rice University, Houston, Texas
Baruch, Second Book of; Nebuchadnezzar; Syriac

Jens Herzer Professor of New Testament Exegesis and Theology, University of Leipzig, Germany
Baruch, Fourth Book of

Karina Martin Hogan Assistant Professor of Theology, Fordham University, New York
Ezra, Fourth Book of

Anders Hultgård Professor Emeritus of the History of Religions, University of Uppsala, Sweden
Persian Religion

Larry W. Hurtado Professor of New Testament Language, Literature, and Theology, School of Divinity, New College, University of Edinburgh, Scotland
Mediator Figures; Monotheism

Tal Ilan Professor of Jewish Studies, Institut für Judaistik, Freie Universität, Berlin, Germany
Women

David Instone-Brewer Research Fellow, Tyndale House, Cambridge, England
Marriage and Divorce

Matt Jackson-McCabe Associate Professor of Religious Studies, Niagara University, New York
James, Epistle of; Jude, Epistle of; Peter, Epistles of

Naomi Jacobs Postdoctoral Fellow in Hebrew Bible and Biblical Hebrew, Washington University in St. Louis, Missouri
Tobit, Book of

Sara Raup Johnson Associate Professor of Classics, University of Connecticut, Hartford
Court Tales; Maccabees, Third Book of; Novels

Jutta Jokiranta Lecturer in Old Testament, University of Helsinki, Finland
Sectarianism

Christine E. Joynes Associate Director, Centre for Reception History of the Bible, University of Oxford, England
Elijah

Richard Lee Kalmin Theodore R. Racoosin Professor of Rabbinic Literature, Jewish Theological Seminary, New York
Rabbis

John I. Kampen Academic Dean and Professor of New Testament, Methodist Theological School in Ohio, Delaware, Ohio
Hasideans

Ranon Katzoff Professor of Classical Studies and General History, Bar-Ilan University, Ramat-Gan, Israel
Babatha Archive; Contracts from the Judean Desert

Allen Kerkeslager Associate Professor of New Testament, Saint Joseph's University, Philadelphia, Pennsylvania
Athletics; Cyprus; Cyrenaica; Gymnasium

Angela Kim Harkins Assistant Professor of Religious Studies, Fairfield University, Connecticut
Hymns, Prayers, and Psalms

Michael A. Knibb Samuel Davidson Professor Emeritus of Old Testament Studies, King's College London, England
Enoch, Similitudes of (1 Enoch 37–71)

James L. Kugel Professor of Bible and Director, Institute for the History of the Jewish Bible, Bar-Ilan University, Ramat-Gan, Israel
"Early Jewish Biblical Interpretation"

Robert A. Kugler Paul S. Wright Professor of Christian Studies, Lewis and Clark College, Portland, Oregon
Aaron; Dead Sea Scrolls; Herakleopolis Papyri; Levi; Naphtali, Testament of (4Q215); Priests; Testaments

David A. Lambert Assistant Professor of Religious Studies, University of North Carolina, Chapel Hill, North Carolina
Repentance

Jonathan D. Lawrence Associate Professor of Religious Studies and Theology, Canisius College, Buffalo, New York
Washing, Ritual

Kyong-Jin Lee Assistant Professor of Biblical Studies, Spring Arbor University, Spring Arbor, Michigan
Almsgiving; Righteousness/Justice

Keith,

w/ love,

Agnes

Mary J. W. Leith Associate Professor of Religious Studies, Stonehill College, Easton, Massachusetts
Seals and Seal Impressions; Daliyeh, Wadi ed-

Tracy Lemos Assistant Professor of Hebrew Bible, Rhodes College, Memphis, Tennessee
Intermarriage

Jutta Leonhardt-Balzer Lecturer in New Testament, King's College, University of Aberdeen, Scotland
Dualism

Dan Levene Senior Lecturer in History, University of Southampton, United Kingdom
Magic Bowls and Incantations

Lee I. Levine Professor of Jewish History and Archaeology, Institute of Archaeology, Hebrew University of Jerusalem, Israel
Caesarea Maritima; Jerusalem; Synagogues; Temple

John R. Levison Professor of New Testament, Seattle Pacific University School of Theology, West Seattle, Washington
Adam and Eve; Spirit, Holy

Bert Jan Lietaert Peerbolte Professor of New Testament, University of Amsterdam, The Netherlands
Antichrist

Timothy H. Lim Professor of Hebrew Bible and Second Temple Judaism, New College, University of Edinburgh, Scotland
Multilingualism

James M. Lindenberger Professor of Hebrew Bible, Vancouver School of Theology, British Columbia
Letters

Marilyn J. Lundberg Associate Director, West Semitic Research Project, Rolling Hills Estates, California
Leviticus Targum (4Q156); Paleo-Hebrew Scrolls

Daniel A. Machiela Assistant Professor of Religious Studies, McMaster University, Hamilton, Ontario
Babel, Tower of; Flood; Noah

Jodi Magness Kenan Distinguished Professor for Teaching Excellence in Early Judaism, University of North Carolina at Chapel Hill, North Carolina
ʿEin Feshka; Qumran

Christl E. Maier University Professor of Old Testament, Philipps-Universität Marburg, Germany
Ruth, Book of; Song of Songs

Paul Mandel Lecturer in Hebrew and Comparative Literature, University of Haifa, Israel
Hillel; Shammai

Adam Marshak Lecturer in Classical Studies, Gann Academy, Waltham, Massachusetts
"Jewish History from Pompey to Hadrian"; Fortresses and Palaces; Herod the Great; Herodian Dynasty; Idumea

John W. Marshall Associate Professor of Religion, University of Toronto, Ontario
Revelation, Book of

Eric Mason Associate Professor of Biblical Studies, Judson University, Elgin, Illinois
Hebrews, Epistle to the; Melchizedek Scroll (11Q13)

Steve Mason Professor of Humanities & Ancient History and Canada Research Chair in Cultural Identity and Interaction, York University, Toronto, Ontario
Josephus; Josephus, Jewish Antiquities

Byron R. McCane Albert C. Outler Professor of Religion, Wofford College, Spartanburg, South Carolina
Miqvaʾot; Ossuaries

Carmel McCarthy Professor Emerita of Hebrew and Syriac, University College Dublin, Ireland
Peshiṭta

James S. McClaren Senior Lecturer in Theology, Australian Catholic University, Fitzroy, Victoria
Imperial Cult, Jews and the; Josephus, Jewish War; Resistance Movements

Steven L. McKenzie Professor of Hebrew Bible, Rhodes College, Memphis, Tennessee
Deuteronomistic History

Doron Mendels Max and Sophie Mydans Professor of Humanities, Hebrew University of Jerusalem, Israel
Alexander Polyhistor; Historiography

Sarianna Metso Professor of Hebrew Bible, University of Toronto at Mississauga, Ontario
Rule of the Community (1QS + Fragments)

David P. Moessner Professor of Biblical Theology, University of Dubuque Theological Seminary, Iowa
Luke-Acts

David G. Monaco Ph.D. Candidate, University of Chicago Divinity, Chicago, Illinois
Menander, Sentences of the Syriac

Stewart Moore Ph.D. Candidate in Religious Studies, Yale University, New Haven, Connecticut
Moore, George Foote

Frederick J. Murphy Professor of Religious Studies, College of the Holy Cross, Worcester, Massachusetts
Biblical Antiquities (Pseudo-Philo)

Hindy Najman Associate Professor of Jewish Studies, University of Toronto, Ontario
Decalogue; Torah and Tradition

Gordon D. Newby Professor and Chair, Department of Middle Eastern and South Asian Studies, Emory University, Atlanta, Georgia
Arabian Peninsula

Judith H. Newman Associate Professor of Old Testament, Emmanuel College, University of Toronto, Ontario
Psalms, Book of; Worship

Carol A. Newsom C. H. Candler Professor of Old Testament, Candler School of Theology, Emory University, Atlanta, Georgia
Job, Book of; Songs of the Sabbath Sacrifice; Theodicy

George W. E. Nickelsburg Daniel J. Krumm Professor Emeritus of New Testament, University of Iowa, Iowa City
Charles, Robert Henry; Resurrection; Son of Man

Maren Niehoff Senior Lecturer in Jewish Thought, Hebrew University of Jerusalem, Israel
Joseph; Philo, Allegorical Commentary; Philo, Exposition of the Law

Bilhah Nitzan Associate Professor of Hebrew Culture, Tel Aviv University, Israel
Berakhot (4Q286-290)

Brent Nongbri Postdoctoral Fellow in Classics, Macquarie University, New South Wales, Australia
Bousset, Wilhelm; Greek Authors on Jews and Judaism

David Noy Lecturer in Classics, University of Wales, Lampeter Ceredigion, United Kingdom
Alexander the Great; Egypt; Papyri

Gerbern S. Oegema Professor of Religious Studies, McGill University, Montréal, Québec
Creation; Zephaniah, Apocalypse of

Saul M. Olyan Professor of Religious and Judaic Studies, Brown University, Providence, Rhode Island
Sacrifices and Offerings

Aharon Oppenheimer Professor of Jewish History, Tel Aviv University, Israel
People of the Land

Andrei Orlov Associate Professor of Theology, Marquette University, Milwaukee, Wisconsin
Enoch; Enoch, Slavonic Apocalypse of (2 Enoch); Melchizedek; Metatron; Slavonic

J. Andrew Overman Professor of Classics, Macalester College, St. Paul, Minnesota
Matthew, Gospel of

Alexander Panayotov Leverholme Postdoctoral Research Fellow, School of Divinity, University of St. Andrews, Scotland
Greece and the Aegean

Donald W. Parry Abraham O. Smoot Professor of Hebrew Bible, Brigham Young University, Provo, Utah
Isaiah Scrolls

Joseph Patrich Professor of Archaeology, Institute of Archaeology, Hebrew University of Jerusalem, Israel
Entertainment Structures; Samaria-Sebaste

Michael Peppard Assistant Professor of Theology, Fordham University, New York, New York
Music

Dorothy M. Peters Assistant Professor of Biblical Studies, Trinity Western University, Langley, British Columbia
Joseph, Apocryphon of (4Q371 and 4Q342)

Jean-Pierre Pettorelli Independent Scholar, Port-Louis, France
Adam and Eve, Life of

Stephen J. Pfann President, University of the Holy Land, Jerusalem, Israel
Scripts and Scribal Practices

D. Nathan Phinney Associate Professor of Biblical Studies, Malone College, Canton, Ohio
Ezekiel, Book of

Michele Piccirillo† Professor of Archaeology, Biblical Geography and History, Studium Biblicum Franciscarum, Jerusalem, Israel
Mosaics

Chad Pierce Assistant Professor of New Testament, Central College, Pella, Iowa
Satan and Related Figures

Kenneth E. Pomykala Professor of Religion, Calvin College, Grand Rapids, Michigan
Catenae (4Q177, 4Q182); David; David Apocryphon; Judah; Kingship; Messianism

Mladen Popović Director, Qumran Institute, University of Groningen, The Netherlands
Astronomy and Astrology; Determinism; Horoscopes; 'Otot; Sun and Moon

Jonathan J. Price Professor of Classics and Ancient History, Tel Aviv University, Israel
Revolt, First Jewish

Miriam Pucci Ben Zeev Professor of Jewish History, Ben Gurion University, Beersheva, Israel
"Jews among Greeks and Romans"; Diaspora Uprisings

(116-117 C.E.); Manetho; Rights of Jews in the Roman World

Reinhard Pummer Professor of Religious Studies, Ottawa University, Ottawa, Ontario
Gerizim, Mount; Samaria; Samaritan Pentateuch; Samaritanism

Rebecca Raphael Assistant Professor of Religious Studies, Texas State University, San Marcos, Texas
Healing; Sickness and Disease

Uriel Rappaport Professor of Jewish History, University of Haifa, Israel
Judas Maccabaeus; Maccabees, First Book of

Annette Yoshiko Reed Assistant Professor of Religious Studies, University of Pennsylvania, Philadelphia
Fallen Angels; Jewish Christianity; Job, Testament of; Parting of the Ways

John C. Reeves Blumenthal Professor of Judaic Studies, University of North Carolina at Charlotte
Enosh; Giants; Gnosticism; Seth

Eyal Regev Senior Lecturer, Land of Israel Studies and Archaeology, Bar-Ilan University, Ramat-Gan, Israel
Boethusians

Adele Reinhartz Associate Vice-President of Research, University of Ottawa, Ontario
John, Gospel of

Benjamin E. Reynolds Honorary Research Fellow in Divinity and Religious Studies, University of Aberdeen, Scotland
Faith/Faithfulness

James N. Rhodes Visiting Assistant Professor of Religious Studies, Saint Michael's College, Colchester, Vermont
Adversus Judaeos Literature; Allegory

Jason Ripley Assistant Professor of Religion, St. Olaf College, Northfield, Minnesota
Aqedah; Isaac

Deborah W. Rooke Lecturer in Old Testament Studies, King's College London, England
Joshua (Jeshua), the High Priest; Zadokites

Renate Rosenthal-Heginbotton Independent Scholar, Grossolt, Germany
Jewelry

David Rothstein Assistant Professor of Bible, Bar-Ilan University, Ramat-Gan, Israel
Phylacteries and Mezuzot

Christopher Rowland Dean Ireland's Professor of the Exegesis of Holy Scripture, Queen's College, University of Oxford, England
Apocalypticism

David T. Runia Master of Queen's College and Professorial Fellow, University of Melbourne, Australia
Philo, Questions and Answers on Genesis and Exodus

Leonard V. Rutgers Professor of Late Antiquity, Institute of History, Utrecht University, The Netherlands
Catacombs; Rome

E. P. Sanders Arts and Sciences Professor of Religion Emeritus, Duke University, Durham, North Carolina
Jesus of Nazareth

Joachim Schaper Reader in Old Testament, University of Aberdeen, Scotland
Levites

Lawrence H. Schiffman Ethel and Irvin A. Edelman Professor of Hebrew and Judaic Studies, New York University
"Early Judaism and Rabbinic Judaism"

Alison Schofield Assistant Professor of Hebrew Bible and Judaic Studies, University of Denver, Colorado
Exile; Wilderness

Eileen M. Schuller Professor of Religious Studies, McMaster University, Hamilton, Ontario
Hodayot (1QH and Related Texts); Psalms, Apocryphal

Daniel R. Schwartz Professor of the History of the Jewish People, Hebrew University, Jerusalem
Tobiads; Maccabees, Second Book of

Joshua J. Schwartz Professor of Historical Geography of Ancient Israel, Bar-Ilan University, Ramat-Gan, Israel
Judea; Pilgrimage

Adiel Schremer Professor of Jewish History, Bar-Ilan University, Ramat-Gan, Israel
Celibacy

Steven Schweitzer Academic Dean and Associate Professor of Old Testament, Bethany Theological Seminary, Richmond, Indiana
Chronicles, Books of; Cyrus the Great; Sheshbezzar; Tobiah; Zerubbabel

James M. Scott Professor of Religious Studies, Trinity Western University, Langley, British Columbia
Covenant; Restoration

Judith Lynn Sebesta Professor of Classics, University of South Dakota, Vermillion, South Dakota
Clothing and Dress

David Rolph Seely Professor of Ancient Scripture, Brigham Young University, Provo, Utah
Barki Nafshi (4Q434-438)

Chris Seeman Assistant Professor of Religion, Coe College, Cedar Rapids, Iowa
"Jewish History from Alexander to Pompey"; Phoenicia

Alan F. Segal Professor of Religion and Ingeborg Rennert Professor of Jewish Studies, Barnard College, Columbia University, New York
Mysticism

Arthur Segal Professor of Archaeology, Zimman Institute of Archaeology, University of Haifa, Israel
Decapolis; Theaters

Michael Segal Senior Lecturer in Bible, Hebrew University of Jerusalem, Israel
Jubilees, Book of

Alexei Sievertsev Assistant Professor of Religious Studies, DePaul University, Chicago, Illinois
Family Religion

Carolyn Sharp Associate Professor of Old Testament, Yale Divinity School, New Haven, Connecticut
Jeremiah and Lamentations

Israel Shatzman Professor of History, Hebrew University of Jerusalem, Israel
Military, Jews in

Aharon Shemesh Professor of Talmud, Bar-Ilan University, Ramat-Gan, Israel
Legal Texts; Ordinances (4QOrdinances)

Joseph Sievers Professor of Jewish History and Literature in the Hellenistic Period, Pontifical Biblical Institute, Rome, Italy
Hasmoneans

Dennis E. Smith Professor of New Testament, Philipps Theological Seminary, Tulsa, Oklahoma
Meals

Daniel L. Smith-Christopher Professor of Old Testament, Loyola Marymount University, Los Angeles, California
Ezra, Book of; Nehemiah, Book of; Peace

Benjamin D. Sommer Professor of Bible, Jewish Theological Seminary, New York
Isaiah, Book of

Günter Stemberger Professor of Jewish Studies Emeritus, Institut für Jüdaistik, University of Vienna, Austria
Sadducees

Gregory E. Sterling Professor of Theology, University of Notre Dame, Indiana
Philo, Apologetic Treatises

Ryan Stokes Ph.D. Candidate in Religious Studies, Yale University, New Haven, Connecticut
Belial; Evil; Sons of God; Watchers, Book of the (1 Enoch 1–36)

Michael E. Stone Gail Levin de Nur Professor of Religious Studies and Professor of Armenian Studies, Hebrew University of Jerusalem, Israel
Aramaic Levi Document; Armenian

James F. Strange Distinguished University Professor, University of South Florida, Tampa
Sepphoris

Loren T. Stuckenbruck Richard J. Dearborn Professor of New Testament, Princeton Theological Seminary, New Jersey
"Apocrypha and Pseudepigrapha"; Enoch, Epistle of (1 Enoch 91–108); Giants, Book of

David W. Suter Professor of Religious Studies, Saint Martin's University, Lacey, Washington
Hermon, Mount; Paneion

Marvin A. Sweeney Professor of Hebrew Bible, Claremont School of Theology and Graduate University School of Religion, California
Minor Prophets

Joan E. Taylor Adjunct Senior Lecturer, University of Waikato, New Zealand
John the Baptist; Therapeutae

D. Andrew Teeter Assistant Professor of Hebrew Bible, Harvard Divinity School, Cambridge, Massachusetts
Scribes and Scribalism

Eibert Tigchelaar Research Professor, Faculty of Theology, Katholieke Universiteit, Leuven, Belgium
"The Dead Sea Scrolls"; Job Targum (4Q157, 11Q10)

Samuel Thomas Assistant Professor of Religion, California Lutheran University, Thousand Oaks
Goodenough, Erwin Ramsdell; Mystery; Mystery Religion, Judaism as

Thomas H. Tobin, S.J. Professor of Theology, Loyola University, Chicago, Illinois
Logos

Pablo A. Torijano Associate Professor of Hebrew Philosophy, Universidad Complutense de Madrid, Spain
Solomon; Solomon, Testament of

Paul Trebilco Professor of New Testament Studies, University of Otago, Dunedin, New Zealand
Antioch (Pisidian); Asia Minor

Julio Trebolle Barrera Professor of Hebrew and Aramaic Studies and Director, Instituto de Ciencias de las Religiones, Universidad Complutense, Madrid, Spain
Latin Versions of the Hebrew Bible

Johannes Tromp Professor of the History and Literature of Early Judaism, Leiden University, The Netherlands
Cain and Abel; Idols and Images; Latin; Moses, Assumption of

Fabian E. Udoh Visiting Professor of New Testament, McGill University, Montréal, Québec
Economics; Tribute and Taxes

Eugene Ulrich John A. O'Brien Professor of Hebrew Scriptures, University of Notre Dame, Indiana
"The Jewish Scriptures: Texts, Versions, Canons"

Jan Willem van Henten Professor of New Testament, Hellenistic-Jewish, and Early Christian Literature, University of Amsterdam, The Netherlands
Maccabees, Fourth Book of; Martyrdom

Jacques van Ruiten Senior Lecturer in Old Testament and Early Jewish Studies, University of Groningen, The Netherlands
Garden of Eden — Paradise

Annewies van den Hoek Lecturer in Greek and Latin, Harvard Divinity School, Cambridge, Massachusetts
Philo, Philosophical Works

Pieter W. van der Horst Professor of Early Judaism and Ancient Christianity, Universiteit Utrecht, The Netherlands
Ezekiel the Tragedian; Greek; Inscriptions

James C. VanderKam John A. O'Brien Professor of Hebrew Bible, University of Notre Dame, Indiana
"Judaism in the Land of Israel"; Enoch, Astronomical Book of (1 Enoch 72–82); High Priests

Marjorie Venit Professor of Art History and Archaeology, University of Maryland, College Park, Maryland
Alexandria

Benedict Thomas Viviano, O.P. Professor of New Testament, University of Fribourg, Switzerland
Education

Hanne von Weissenberg Lecturer in Biblical Studies, University of Helsinki, Finland
Miqṣat Maʿaśê ha-Torah

Rodney A. Werline Senior Minister, First Christian Church, Greensboro, North Carolina
Manasseh, Prayer of; Penitential Prayer

Steven Weitzmann Professor of Jewish Studies, Stanford University, California
Copper Scroll (3Q15); Violence

L. Michael White Ronald Nelson Smith Chair in Classics and Director, Institute for the Study of Antiquity and Christian Origins, University of Texas at Austin
Ostia

Sidnie White Crawford Professor of Hebrew Bible, University of Nebraska, Lincoln
Reworked Pentateuch (4QRP)

K. William Whitney, Jr. Independent Scholar, Arlington, Massachusetts
Behemoth; Leviathan

Margaret H. Williams Research Fellow in Classical Studies, The Open University, Milton Keynes, England
Julius Caesar, Gaius; Latin Authors on Jews and Judaism; Roman Generals; Roman Governors

Lawrence M. Wills Ethelbert Talbot Professor of Biblical Studies, Episcopal Divinity School, Cambridge, Massachusetts
Asceticism

David Winston Professor Emeritus of Hellenistic and Judaic Studies, Graduate Theological Union, Berkeley, California
Greek Philosophy; Wolfson, Harry Austryn

Michael O. Wise Professor of Hebrew Bible and Ancient Languages, Northwestern College, St. Paul, Minnesota
Archives and Libraries; Bar Kokhba Letters; Crucifixion

Archie Wright Associate Professor of Biblical Studies, Regent University, Virginia Beach, Virginia
Angels; Michael, the Archangel

Benjamin G. Wright III Professor of Religious Studies, Lehigh University, Bethlehem, Pennsylvania
Aristeas, Letter of; Ben Sira, Book of

J. Edward Wright Professor of Hebrew Bible and Early Judaism, University of Arizona, Tucson
Cosmology; Heaven; Stars

Jed D. Wyrick Associate Professor of Religious Studies, California State University, Chico
Animal Worship; Pseudepigraphy

Geza Xeravits Professor of Bible, Sapientia Theological College, Budapest, Hungary
Rule of the Congregation (1Q28a); Son of God

Azzan Yadin Associate Professor of Jewish Studies, Rutgers University, New Brunswick, New Jersey
Akiba (Aqiva)

Adela Yarbro Collins Buckingham Professor of New Testament Criticism and Interpretation, Yale Divinity School, New Haven, Connecticut
Blasphemy

Kent L. Yinger Associate Professor of New Testament, George Fox University, Newberg, Oregon
Judgment

Molly Zahn Lecturer, Religious Studies, University of Kansas, Lawrence, Kansas
Text Types, Hebrew

Jürgen K. Zangenberg Professor of New Testament Exegesis and Early Christian Literature, Leiden University, The Netherlands
"Archaeology, Papyri, and Inscriptions"

Magnus Zetterholm Adjunct Associate Professor of Culture and Communication, Linköping University, Sweden
Antioch (Syrian); Damascus; Syria

Alphabetical List of Entries

Topical List of Entries

Primary Languages of Jews in the Second Temple Period
Aramaic
Greek
Hebrew

Secondary Languages in Which Early Jewish Literature Is Preserved
Armenian
Ethiopic
Latin
Slavonic
Syriac

Literary Genres
Adversus Judaeos Literature
Allegory
Apocalypse
Apologetic Literature
Calendars
Chronography
Contracts from the Judean Desert
Court Tales
Dream and Vision Reports
Gematria
Genealogies
Historiography
Homily
Hymns, Prayers, and Psalms
Legal Texts
Letters
Novels
Testaments
Wisdom Literature

Biblical Texts, Versions, and Canon
Canon, Canonization
Latin Versions of the Hebrew Bible
Peshiṭta
Samaritan Pentateuch
Septuagint
Text Types, Hebrew

Hebrew Bible
Chronicles, Books of 1-2
Daniel, Book of
Deuteronomistic History
Esther, Book of
Ezekiel, Book of
Ezra, Book of
Isaiah, Book of
Jeremiah and Lamentations
Job, Book of
Minor Prophets
Nehemiah, Book of
Pentateuch
Proverbs, Book of
Psalms, Book of
Qoheleth
Ruth, Book of
Song of Songs

Apocrypha
Apocrypha, Old Testament
Baruch, First Book of
Ben Sira, Book of
Daniel, Additions to
Esdras, First Book of
Esther, Greek Version of
Ezra, Fourth Book of
Jeremiah, Letter of
Maccabees, First Book of
Maccabees, Second Book of
Maccabees, Third Book of
Maccabees, Fourth Book of
Manasseh, Prayer of
Psalm 151
Solomon, Wisdom of
Tobit, Book of

Pseudepigrapha and Hellenistic Jewish Texts
Abraham, Apocalypse of
Abraham, Testament of
Adam and Eve, Life of
Aristeas, Letter of
Aristobulus

Artapanus
Baruch, Second Book of
Baruch, Third Book of
Baruch, Fourth Book of
Biblical Antiquities (Pseudo-Philo)
Cleodemus Malchus
Demetrius the Chronographer
Dreams, Book of (1 Enoch 83–90)
Enoch, Astronomical Book of (1 Enoch 72–82)
Enoch, Epistle of (1 Enoch 91–108)
Enoch, Ethiopic Apocalypse of (1 Enoch)
Enoch, Similitudes of (1 Enoch 37–71)
Enoch, Slavonic Apocalypse of (2 Enoch)
Eupolemus
Eupolemus, Pseudo-
Ezekiel the Tragedian
Gabriel, Vision of
Hecataeus of Abdera
Hecataeus, Pseudo-
Isaiah, Ascension of
Job, Testament of
Joseph and Aseneth
Joseph, Prayer of
Jubilees, Book of
Lives of the Prophets
Menander, Sentences of the Syriac
Moses, Assumption of
Orpheus, Pseudo-
Patriarchs, Testaments of the Twelve
Philo the Epic Poet
Phocylides, Pseudo-
Pseudepigrapha, Old Testament
Sibylline Oracles (Jewish)
Solomon, Psalms of
Solomon, Testament of
Thallus
Theodotus
Watchers, Book of the (1 Enoch 1–36)
Zephaniah, Apocalypse of

Dead Sea Scrolls
Dead Sea Scrolls
Liturgical Works from Qumran
Paleo-Hebrew Scrolls
Pesharim
Wisdom Literature at Qumran
Documents arranged here by cave number are arranged by document title in the A–Z entries
1QapGen (Genesis Apocryphon)
1QH and Related Texts (Hodayot)
1QIsa^{a,b} (Isaiah Scrolls)
1QM (War Scroll)
1QS (Rule of the Community)
1Q21 etc. (Aramaic Levi Document)
1Q22, 2Q21 etc. (Moses Texts from Qumran)
1Q23-24 (Giants, Book of)
1Q26 etc. (Instruction)
1Q28a (Rule of the Congregation)
1Q28b (Rule of Blessings)
1Q32 etc. (New Jerusalem)
2Q22 (David Apocryphon)
3Q15 (Copper Scroll)
4Q156 (Leviticus Targum)
4Q157, 11Q10 (Job Targum)
4Q158, 364-367 (Reworked Pentateuch)
4Q159 etc. (Ordinances)
4Q174 (Florilegium)
4Q175 (Testimonia)
4Q176 (Tanḥumim)
4Q177, 182 (Catenae)
4Q180 (Pesher on the Periods)
4Q181 (Wicked and Holy)
4Q186, 534, 561 (Horoscopes)
4Q215 (Naphtali, Testament of)
4Q242-245, 246 (Daniel, Pseudo-Texts)
4Q252-254 (Genesis Commentaries)
4Q265-273, etc. + CD (Damascus Document)
4Q274 etc. (Tohorot)
4Q285, 11Q14 (War, Book of)
4Q286-290 (Berakhot)
4Q319 (ʾOtot)
4Q320 etc. (Mishmarot)
4Q371-373 (Joseph, Apocryphon of)
4Q378-379 (Joshua, Apocryphon of)
4Q380-381 (Psalms, Apocryphal)
4Q385-390 (Prophets, Pseudo-)
4Q394-399 (Miqṣat Maʿaśê ha-Torah)
4Q400-407 etc. (Songs of the Sabbath Sacrifice)
4Q422 (Genesis and Exodus, Commentary on)
4Q434 etc. (Barki Nafshi)
4Q448 (Jonathan the King Text)
4Q491 etc. (Self-Glorification Hymn)
4Q504-506 (Words of the Luminaries)
4Q521 (Messianic Apocalypse)
4Q525 (Beatitudes)
4Q534-536 (Elect of God)
4Q542 (Admonitions [Testament] of Qahat)
4Q543-548 (Amram, Visions of)
4Q550 (Tales of the Persian Court)
7Q1 etc. (Papyri from Qumran Cave 7)
11Q11 etc. (Psalms Scrolls)
11Q13 (Melchizedek Scroll)
11Q19 (Temple Scroll)

Philo of Alexandria
Philo
Philo, Allegorical Commentary
Philo, Apologetic Treatises
Philo, Exposition of the Law
Philo, Philosophical Works
Philo, Questions and Answers on Genesis and Exodus

Josephus
Josephus
Josephus, Against Apion
Josephus, Jewish Antiquities
Josephus, Jewish War

Greek and Latin Authors on Jews and Judaism
Greek Authors on Jews and Judaism
Latin Authors on Jews and Judaism
Alexander Polyhistor

Mythological and Primordial Figures, Places, and Events

Religious Beliefs and Influences

Practices

List of Maps

Chronology

B.C.E.	
538-332	Palestine ruled by the Persians
before 525	Jewish Temple erected at Elephantine in Egypt
516/515	Jerusalem Temple rebuilt (traditional date)
458-445	Careers of Ezra and Nehemiah in Jerusalem
332-323	Conquests of Alexander the Great
322-301	Wars of the Diadochi
301-198	Palestine ruled by the Ptolemies
259-258	Zenon, secretary to a finance minister of Ptolemy II, visits Palestine
ca. 250	Translation of Torah into Greek
222-187	Antiochus III rules the Seleucid Empire
198-142	Palestine ruled by the Seleucids
190	Battle of Magnesia: Antiochus III defeated by Rome
ca. 180	Hyrcanus ben Joseph of the Tobiad family builds a palatial estate at ʿAraq el-Emir in Transjordan
177-164	Antiochus IV Epiphanes rules Seleucid Empire
175	High Priest Onias III deposed by Antiochus IV and replaced by Jason, who establishes a gymnasium in Jerusalem
172	Menelaus outbids Jason and is appointed high priest
170	Onias III killed by Menelaus
169	Antiochus IV's first Egyptian campaign; plunder of the Jerusalem Temple
168	Antiochus IV's second Egyptian campaign (aborted); founding of the citadel in Jerusalem
167	Desecration of the Jerusalem Temple and persecution of Judeans: beginning of the Maccabean Revolt
164	Rededication of the Temple; death of Antiochus IV
162	Menelaus executed; Alcimus appointed high priest
161	Judas defeats Nicanor and makes treaty with Rome
160	Battle of Elasa; Judas killed; Jonathan assumes leadership
ca. 160	Onias IV builds temple at Heliopolis in Egypt
159	Death of Alcimus
159-152	Jewish high priesthood vacant
157	Treaty between Jonathan and Bacchides; Syrians withdraw from Palestine
152	Jonathan appointed high priest by Alexander Balas
142	Death of Jonathan and accession of Simon
141	Conquest of the Jerusalem citadel
140	Simon confirmed as high priest, commander, and ethnarch
139	Expulsion of Jews from Rome
134	Death of Simon and accession of John Hyrcanus; Antiochus VII invades and besieges Jerusalem; John Hyrcanus comes to terms with Antiochus VII; Judea temporarily under Seleucid domination
129/128	Antiochus VII dies; Judea is *de facto* independent; Hyrcanus campaigns in Transjordan
126-104	Hasmonean expansion into Samaria, Idumea, and Galilee
112/111	Samaritan temple on Mt. Gerizim destroyed by John Hyrcanus
104-103	Aristobulus I high priest and king
103-76	Alexander Jannaeus high priest and king
76-67	Shelamzion Alexandra rules Judea as queen
67-66	Hasmonean civil war breaks out; Hyrcanus II abdicates to Aristobulus II

65	Hyrcanus and Aretas the Nabatean besiege Aristobulus; Romans halt siege
64	Pompey annexes Syria: end of Seleucid rule
63	Pompey captures Jerusalem: end of Hasmonean rule
58-49	First Roman Triumvirate (Pompey, Crassus, Julius Caesar)
49-45	Roman civil war between Julius Caesar and the *optimates* (conservative republicans), initially led by Pompey
48-47	Antipater enlists Jewish support for Julius Caesar in Alexandria
47	Phasael and Herod appointed *stratēgoi* in Galilee and Judea, respectively
44	Assassination of Julius Caesar
44-31	Second Roman Triumvirate (Marc Antony, Lepidus, Octavian)
42	Phasael and Herod appointed tetrarchs by Marc Antony
40	Parthians and Mattathias Antigonus invade Judea and besiege Jerusalem; Herod proclaimed King of Judea by Roman Senate
37	Herod defeats last Hasmonean ruler, Mattathias Antigonus, and captures Jerusalem
31	Battle of Actium: Octavian defeats Marc Antony
30	Roman conquest and annexation of Egypt
27	Octavian given titles *Augustus* and *Princeps;* rules as *de facto* emperor until death in 14 C.E.
4	Herod the Great dies
4 B.C.E.–6 C.E.	Archelaus rules Judea, Idumea, and Samaria; Antipas rules Galilee and Perea; Herod Philip II rules area northwest of Galilee until 34 C.E.
6	Judas the Galilean and Zadok the Pharisee found the "fourth philosophy" and lead a revolt in protest of the Judean census
6-41	Judea made a Roman province ruled by prefects
14-37	Tiberius, emperor
26-36	Pontius Pilate, prefect of Judea
27-30	Public career of Jesus of Nazareth
34-64	Missionary career of Saul of Tarsus (Paul)
37-41	Gaius Caligula, emperor
38	Anti-Jewish pogrom in Alexandria, Egypt
40	Caligula orders a statue of himself to be installed in the Jerusalem Temple
41	Edict of Claudius confirms rights of Jews in Alexandria but warns them not to strive for more than they have
41-44	King Agrippa I rules most of Palestine
41-54	Claudius, emperor; expels Jews from Rome
44-66	Roman procurators govern most of Palestine
54-68	Nero, emperor
60-66	Roman procurators Festus, Albinus, and Florus deal with brigands and popular uprisings in Judea
62	Roman governor Flaccus seizes Jewish Temple tax from Apamea, Adramyttium, Laodicea, and Pergamum in Asia Minor
64	Fire in Rome
	Death of James (brother of Jesus), Paul, and Peter
66	Anti-Jewish riots in Alexandria; Tiberius Julius Alexander enforces reprisals
66-70	First Jewish Revolt against Rome
68-69	Year of the four emperors (Galba, Otho, Vitellius, and Vespasian)
69-79	Vespasian, emperor
70	Jerusalem Temple destroyed by Romans; *fiscus Iudaicus* imposed on Jews in lieu of Temple tax
73/74	Masada, the last refuge of Jewish rebels under Eleazar ben Ya'ir, falls to Romans
	Oniad temple at Leontopolis in Egypt destroyed by Romans
79-81	Titus, emperor
80-90	Beginnings of rabbinic academy at Yavneh (Jamnia)
	House of Hillel gains ascendancy over the House of Shammai
	Yoḥanan ben Zakkai is the leading rabbinic sage in Palestine
81-96	Domitian, emperor
90-115	Gamaliel II is the leading rabbinic sage
96-98	Nerva, emperor
98-117	Trajan, emperor
100-135	Ishmael ben Elisha and Akiba ben Joseph are the leading rabbinic sages
116-117	Diaspora Jewish uprisings in Egypt, Cyprus, and Cyrene
117-138	Hadrian, emperor
132-135	Bar Kokhba Revolt
200	Rabbi Judah the Patriarch edits the Mishnah

Abbreviations

ABD	*Anchor Bible Dictionary*, ed. D. N. Freedman
ʿAbod. Zar.	*ʿAboda Zara*
ʾAbot. R. Nat.	*ʾAbot de Rabbi Nathan*
Abr.	*De Abrahamo*
Ach74	Achaea inscription no. 74
Add. Esth.	Additions to Esther
AE	*Année Epigraphique*
Aet.	*De Aeternitate Mundi*
Ag. Ap.	*Against Apion*
Agr.	*De Agricultura*
AJA	*American Journal of Archaeology*
AJS Review	*Association for Jewish Studies Review*
ANET	*Ancient Near Eastern Texts Relating to the Old Testament*
Anim.	*De Animalibus*
ANRW	*Aufstieg und Niedergang der römischen Welt*, ed. H. Temporini and W. Haase
Ant.	*Antiquities of the Jews*
AOT	*The Apocryphal Old Testament*, ed. H. F. D. Sparks
ap	Apocryphon (e.g., 1QapGen)
APAT	*Die Apokryphen und Pseudepigraphen des Alten Testmanents*, ed. E. Kautzsch
Apoc. Abr.	*Apocalypse of Abraham*
Apoc. Mos.	*Apocalypse of Moses*
Apoc. Sedr.	*Apocalypse of Sedrach*
Apoc. Zeph.	*Apocalypse of Zephaniah*
APOT	*The Apocrypha and Psuedepigrapha of the Old Testament*, ed. R. H. Charles
ar	Aramaic (e.g., 4QMess ar)
ʿArak.	*ʿArakin*
Aram.	Aramaic
As. Mos.	*Assumption of Moses*
Asc. Isa.	*Ascension of Isaiah*
ASTI	*Annual of the Swedish Theological Institute*
b.	Babylonian Talmud tractate
B. Bat.	*Baba Batra*
B. Meṣ.	*Baba Meṣiʿa*
B. Qam.	*Baba Qamma*
BA	*Biblical Archaeologist*
BAR	*Biblical Archaeology Review*
Bar.	Baruch
2 Bar.	*2 Baruch (Syriac Apocalypse)*
3 Bar.	*3 Baruch (Greek Apocalypse)*
4 Bar.	*4 Baruch (Paraleipomena Jeremiou)*
Barn.	*Barnabas*
BASOR	*Bulletin of the American Schools of Oriental Research*
B.C.E.	Before the Common Era
BCH	*Bulletin de correspondance hellénique*
Bek.	*Bekorot*
Benj.	*Benjamin*
Ber.	*Berakot*
BGU	*Berliner Griechische Urkunden* (Ägyptische Urkunden aus den Königlichen Museen zu Berlin), Berlin, 1895-1912
Bib	*Biblica*
Bib. Ant.	*Biblical Antiquities (Liber Antiquitatum Biblicarum)* of Pseudo-Philo
Bik.	*Bikkurim*
BIOSCS	*Bulletin of the International Organization for Septuagint and Cognate Studies*
BJRL	*Bulletin of the John Rylands University Library*
BR	*Biblical Research*
BSOAS	*Bulletin of the School of Oriental and African Studies*
ca.	circa
C. Ord. Ptol.	Corpus des Ordonnances des Ptolémées
C.E.	Common Era
Cant.	Canticles
CAP	*Aramaic Papyri of the Fifth Century* B.C., ed. A. E. Cowley, Oxford: Oxford University Press, 1923 (cited by document number)
CBQ	*Catholic Biblical Quarterly*
CBR	*Currents in Biblical Research*
CCSG	Corpus Christianorum: Series Graeca

CD — Cairo Genizah copy of the *Damascus Document*
chap(s). — chapter(s)
Cher. — *De Cherubim*
CHJ — *Cambridge History of Judaism*
Chron. — Chronicles
CIG — *Corpus Inscriptionum Graecarum*, ed. A. Boeckh, 4 vols., Berlin, 1828-1877
CIJ — *Corpus Inscriptionum Judaicarum*, ed. J.-B. Frey, Vatican City: Pontificio istituto di archeologia cristiana, 1936-52
CIL — *Corpus Inscriptionum Latinarum*, 18 vols., Berlin, 1862-1989
CIS — *Corpus Inscriptionum Semiticarum*
CJZC — *Corpus jüdischer Zeugnisse aus der Cyrenaika*, ed. G. Lüderitz, Wiesbaden: Reichert, 1983
1 Clem. — *1 Clement*
2 Clem. — *2 Clement*
cm(s). — centimeter(s)
col(s). — column(s)
Col. — Colossians
Conf. — *De Confusione Linguarum*
Congr. — *De Congressu Eruditionis Gratia*
Cont. — *De Vita Contemplativa*
Cor. — Corinthians
CPJ — *Corpus Papyrorum Judaicarum*, ed. V. Tcherikover and A. Fuks, 3 vols., Cambridge: Harvard University Press, 1957-1964
Dan. — Daniel
Decal. — *De Decalogo*
Dem. — *Demai*
Det. — *Quod Deterius Potiori Insidiari Solea*
Deus — *Quod Deus Sit Immutabilis*
Deut. — Deuteronomy
Dial. — *Dialogue with Trypho the Jew*
DJD — Discoveries in the Judaean Desert
DSD — *Dead Sea Discoveries*
DSS — Dead Sea Scrolls
Ebr. — *De Ebrietate*
Eccl. — Ecclesiastes
ed. — edited by, edition
e.g. — *exempli gratia* (for example)
ʿEd. — *ʿEduyyot*
Egyp. — Egyptian
EncJud — *Encyclopedia Judaica*
Eng. — English
ep. — epistle
Ep. Arist. — *Epistle of Aristeas*
Ep. Jer. — Epistle of Jeremiah
Eph. — Ephesians
ʿErub. — *ʿErubin*
Esdr. — Esdras
esp. — especially
et al. — *et alii* (and the others)
etc. — *et cetera* (and the rest)
EvT — *Evangelische Theologie*
Exod. — Exodus
ExpTim — *Expository Times*
Ezek. — Ezekiel
f(f). — following pages, lines, verses, etc.
fl. — flourished
Flacc. — *In Flaccum*
fol(s). — folio(s)
frg(s). — fragment(s)
Frg. Tg. — Fragment Targum
Fr. — French
Fug. — *De Fuga et Inventione*
Gal. — Galatians
GCS — Die griechische christliche Schriftsteller
Gen. — Genesis
Geog. — *Geography*
Ger. — German
Gig. — *De Gigantibus*
Giṭ. — *Giṭṭin*
GLAJJ — *Greek and Latin Authors on Jews and Judaism*
Gr. — Greek
Hab. — Habbakuk
Hag. — Haggai
Ḥag. — *Ḥagiga*
Ḥal. — *Ḥallah*
Heb. — Epistle to the Hebrews
Hebr. — Hebrew
Hekh. Rab. — *Hekhalot Rabbati*
Her. — *Quis Rerum Divinarum Heres Sit*
Ḥev. — Naḥal Ḥever
Ḥev/Se — Naḥal Ḥever documents earlier attributed to Seiyal
Hist. Eccl. — *Church History* of Eusebius of Caesarea
Hom. adv. Jud. — *Homiliae adversus Judaeos*
Hos. — Hosea
HSCP — *Harvard Studies in Classical Philology*
HTR — *Harvard Theological Review*
HUCA — *Hebrew Union College Annual*
Ḥul. — *Ḥullin*
Hypoth. — *Hypothetica*
ICS — *Illinois Classical Studies*
i.e. — *id est* (that is)
IEJ — *Israel Exploration Journal*
IGRR — *Inscriptiones Graece ad Res Romanas Pertinentes* (1901-1927)
IJO — *Inscriptiones Judaicae Orientis*, ed. D. Noy et al., 3 vols., Tübingen: Mohr-Siebeck, 2004
ILS — *Inscriptiones Latinae Selectae*, ed. H. Dessau, 3 vols. in 5 pts., Berlin, 1892-1916
INJ — *Israel Numismatics Journal*
Int — *Interpretation*
IOS — *Israel Oriental Society*
Isa. — Isaiah
Issa. — *Issachar*
JAAR — *Journal of the American Academy of Religion*
JANES — *Journal of the Ancient Near Eastern Society*

JAOS	*Journal of the American Oriental Society*
Jas.	James
JBL	*Journal of Biblical Literature*
JBT	*Jahrbuch für biblische Theologie*
JDS	Jewish Desert Studies
Jdt.	Judith
JECS	*Journal of Early Christian Studies*
Jer.	Jeremiah
JIGRE	*Jewish Inscriptions of Graeco-Roman Egypt*, ed. W. Horbury and D. Noy, Cambridge: Harvard University Press, 1992
JJS	*Journal of Jewish Studies*
JNES	*Journal of Near Eastern Studies*
Jos.	*De Josepho*
Jos. & Asen.	*Joseph and Aseneth*
Josh.	Joshua
JQR	*Jewish Quarterly Review*
JR	*Journal of Religion*
JRA	*Journal of Roman Archaeology*
JRRW	*Jewish Rights in the Roman World: The Greek and Roman Documents Quoted by Josephus Flavius*, ed. M. Pucci Ben Zeev, Tübingen: Mohr-Siebeck, 1998.
JSHRZ	Jüdische Schriften aus hellenistisch-römischer Zeit
JSJ	*Journal for the Study of Judaism*
JSJSup	Journal for the Study of Judaism Supplement
JSNT	*Journal for the Study of the New Testament*
JSOT	*Journal for the Study of the Old Testament*
JSP	*Journal for the Study of the Pseudepigrapha*
JSQ	*Jewish Studies Quarterly*
JSS	*Journal of Semitic Studies*
JTS	*Journal of Theological Studies*
Jub.	*Jubilees*
Jud.	*Judah*
Judg.	Judges
J.W.	*Jewish War*
Ker.	*Keritot*
Ketub.	*Ketubbot*
kg.	kilogram
Kgdms.	Kingdoms
KhQ	Khirbet Qumran
km(s).	kilometer(s)
Kourion	*The Inscriptions of Kourion*, T. B. Mitford, Philadelphia: American Philosophical Society, 1971
LAB	*Liber Antiquitatum Biblicarum*
Lam.	Lamentations
Lat.	Latin
LCL	Loeb Classical Library
Leg. Alleg.	*Legum Allegoriae*
Legat.	*Legatio ad Gaium*
Lev.	Leviticus
lit.	literally
Liv. Pro.	*Lives of the Prophets*
LXX	Septuagint
m.	meter
m.	Mishnah tractate
Maʿaś.	*Maʿaśerot*
Maʿaś. Š.	*Maʿaśer Šeni*
Macc.	Maccabees
Magn.	*To the Magnesians*
Mak.	*Makkot*
Makš.	*Makširim*
Mal.	Malachi
Mart. Isa.	*Martyrdom of Isaiah*
Mart. Pol.	*Martyrdom of Polycarp*
Mas	Masada
MasŠirŠabb	*Songs of the Sabbath Sacrifice* fragments from Masada
Matt.	Matthew
Meg.	*Megilla*
Mek.	*Mekilta*
Menaḥ.	*Menaḥot*
mg.	margin
Mic.	Micah
Mid.	*Middot*
Midr.	*Midraš (Midrash)*
Migr.	*De Migratione Abrahami*
Miqw.	*Miqwaʾot*
Mird	Khirbet Mird
MMT	*Miqṣat Maʿaśê ha-Torah* or *Some of the Works of the Law*
Mos.	*Moses*
ms(s).	manuscript(s)
Mt.	Mount
MT	Masoretic Text
Mur	Murabbaʿat
Murray	*Excavations in Cyprus*, A. S. Murray et al., London: British Museum, 1900
Mut.	*De Mutatione Nominum*
n.	note
Nah.	Nahum
Naph.	*Naphtali*
Ned.	*Nedarim*
Neg.	*Negaʿim*
Neh.	Nehemiah
Neotest	*Neotestamentica*
Nez.	*Neziqin*
NHC	Nag Hammadi Codex
Nid.	*Niddah*
NJPS	*Tanakh: The Holy Scriptures.* New Jewish Publication Society Translation
nos.	numbers
NovT	*Novum Testamentum*
N.S.	new series
NTS	*New Testament Studies*
Num.	Numbers
O.	Ostracon
Obad.	Obadiah
OG	Old Greek
OGIS	*Orientis Graeci Inscriptiones Selectae*, 2 vols., ed. W. Dittenberger, Leipzig: Hirzel, 1903-1905
Ohol.	*Oholot*
OL	Old Latin

OLP	Orientalia Lovaniensia Periodica
Opif.	*De Opificio Mundi*
Opusc. Arch.	*Opuscula Archaeologica*
ʿOr.	*ʿOrlah*
OTP	*Old Testament Pseudepigrapha,* 2 vols., ed. J. H. Charlesworth
p(p).	page(s)
P.	Papyrus
P.Dion.	*Dionysios Papyri = Les archives privés de Dionysios, fils de Kephalas,* ed. P. W. Pestman and E. Boswinkel, Leiden: Brill, 1982
P.Harris	*The Rendell Harris Papyri of Woodbrooke College, Birmingham,* ed. J. E. Powell, Cambridge: Cambridge University Press, 1936
P.Teb.	*The Tebtunis Papyri,* ed. B. P. Grenfell, A. S. Hunt, and J. G. Smyly, London: Henry Frowde, 1902
PAAJR	*Proceedings of the American Academy of Jewish Research*
paleo	Paleo-Hebrew (e.g., 11QpaleoLev)
PAM	Palestine Archaeological Museum
Pan.	Epiphanius of Salamis, *Panarion*
pap.	Papyrus (e.g., 4QpapParaExod gr)
Bib	Biblica
para.	paraphrase
par(s).	parallel(s)
PEQ	*Palestine Exploration Quarterly*
Pesaḥ.	*Pesaḥim*
Pesiq. R.	*Pesiqta Rabbati*
Pesiq. Rab Kah.	*Pesiqta de Rab Kahana*
1 Pet.	1 Peter
PG	*Patrologia Graeca*
PGM	*Papyri Graecae Magicae,* 3 vols., ed. K. Preisendanz, Leipzig: Teubner, 1928-1941
Phil.	Philippians
Phld.	*To the Philadelphians*
Pirqe R. El.	*Pirqe Rabbi Eliezer*
PL	*Patrologia Latina*
pl(s).	plate(s)
Plant.	*De Plantatione*
Post.	*De Posteritate Caini*
Pr. Azar.	Prayer of Azariah
Pr. Man.	Prayer of Manasseh
Praem.	*De Praemiis et Poenis*
Praep. Evang.	*Praeparatio Evangelica*
Prob.	*Quod Omnis Probus Liber Sit*
Prov.	*De Providentia*
Prov.	Proverbs
Ps(s).	Psalm(s)
Ps.-	Pseudo-
Ps.-Clem. *Hom.*	Pseudo-Clementine *Homilies*
Ps.-Clem. *Recog.*	Pseudo-Clementine *Recognitions*
Q	Qumran
1Q, 2Q, etc.	Numbered caves of Qumran
1QapGen	*Genesis Apocryphon*
1QH	*Hodayot* or *Thanksgiving Hymns*
1QIsa^{a,b}	Isaiah Scrolls
1QM	*Milḥamah* or *War Scroll*
1QpHab	*Habakkuk Pesher*
1QS	*Serek Hayaḥad* or *Rule of the Community*
1QSa	*Rule of the Congregation*
1QSb	*Rule of Blessings*
4QMMT	*Miqṣat Maʿaśê ha-Torah* or *Some of the Works of the Law* from Qumran Cave 4
11QMelch	*Melchizedek Scroll*
11QPs^{a}	*Psalms Scroll*^{a}
11QTemple	*Temple Scroll*
Qidd.	*Qiddušin*
QE	*Quaestiones et Solutiones in Exodum*
QG	*Quaestiones et Solutiones in Genesim*
Qod.	*Qodašin*
Qoh.	Qoheleth
Rab.	*Rabbah*
RB	*Revue biblique*
REJ	*Revue des études juives*
Reub.	*Reuben*
Rev.	Revelation
rev. ed.	revised edition
RevQ	*Revue de Qumran*
RHPR	*Revue d'histoire et de philosophie religieuses*
Rom.	Romans
Rom.	*To the Romans*
Roš Haš.	*Roš Haššanah*
rpt.	reprint
RQ	*Römische Quartalschrift*
RSR	*Recherches de science religieuse*
S. ʿOlam Rab.	*Seder ʿOlam Rabbah*
Šab.	*Šabbat*
Sacr.	*De Sacrificiis Abelis et Caini*
Salamis	*The Greek and Latin Inscriptions from Salamis,* ed. Terence B. Mitford and Ino K. Nicolaou, Nicosia: Department of Antiquities, 1974
Sam.	Samuel
Sanh.	*Sanhedrin*
SB V	*Sammelbuch griechischer Urkunden aus Ägypten,* vol. 5, ed. E. Kiessling, Wiesbaden, 1950
SBLSP	*Society of Biblical Literature Seminar Papers*
sc.	*scilicet* (namely)
SCI	*Scripta Classica Israelica*
Šeb.	*Šebiʿit*
Šebu.	*Šebuʿot*
SEG	*Supplementum Epigraphicum Graecum*
Šeqal.	*Šeqalim*
Sib. Or.	*Sibylline Oracles*
Sif. meṣ. zab.	*Sifra meṣoraʿ zabim*
Sim.	*Simeon*
Sin.	Sinaiticus
Sir.	Sirach
ŠirŠabb	*Šîrôt ʿÔlat Haššabbat (Songs of the Sabbath Sacrifice)*
SJOT	*Scandinavian Journal of the Old Testament*

SJT	*Scottish Journal of Theology*
Sobr.	*De Sobrietate*
Somn.	*De Somniis*
Sop.	*Soperim*
SP	Sacra Pagina
Spec. Leg.	*De Specialibus Legibus*
SPhA	*Studia Philonica Annual*
SR	*Studies in Religion*
Sukk.	*Sukka*
Sus.	Susanna
SVF	*Stoicorum Veterum Fragmenta,* 4 vols., ed. H. F. A. von Armin, Leipzig: Teubner, 1902-1904
t.	Tosefta tractate
T.	*Testament*
T. 12. Patr.	*Testaments of the Twelve Patriarchs*
Ta'an.	*Ta'anit*
T. Abr.	*Testament of Abraham*
TAD	*Textbook of Aramaic Documents from Ancient Egypt,* ed. B. Porten and A. Yardeni, Jerusalem: Hebrew University, 1986-1999 *TAD* A = vol. 1, *Letters* *TAD* B = vol. 2, *Contracts* *TAD* C = vol. 3, *Literature and Lists* *TAD* D = vol. 4, *Ostraca and Assorted Inscriptions*
TBT	*The Bible Today*
TDNT	*Theological Dictionary of the New Testament,* 10 vols., ed. G. Kittel and G. Friedrich, Grand Rapids: Eerdmans, 1964-1976
Ter.	*Terumot*
tg	Targum (e.g., 11QtgJob)
Tg. Jer.	*Targum Jeremiah*
Tg. Neof.	*Targum Neofiti*
Tg. Onq.	*Targum Onqelos*
Tg. Ps.-J.	*Targum Pseudo-Jonathan*
Thess.	Thessalonians
Tim.	Timothy
Tob.	Tobit
Tohor.	*Tohorot*
trans.	translated by, translation
TS	*Theological Studies*
TZ	*Theologische Zeitschrift*
USQR	*Union Seminary Quarterly Review*
v(v).	verse(s)
VC	*Vigiliae Christianae*
VF	*Verkundigung und Forschung*
Virt.	*De Virtutibus*
vol.	volume
vs.	versus
VT	*Vetus Testamentum*
WDSP	Wadi Daliyeh Samaria Papyri
Wis.	Wisdom of Solomon
y.	Palestinian (Jerusalem) Talmud tractate
Yad.	*Yadayim*
Yebam.	*Yebamot*
ZAW	*Zeitschrift für die alttestamentliche Wissenschaft*
Zeb.	*Zebulun*
Zebaḥ.	*Zebaḥim*
Zech.	Zechariah
Zeph.	Zephaniah
Zer.	*Zera'im*
ZNW	*Zeitschrift für die neutestamentliche Wissenschaft*

Early Judaism in Modern Scholarship

JOHN J. COLLINS

Judaism in the period between the conquests of Alexander the Great in the fourth century B.C.E. and the last Jewish revolt against Rome in the early second century C.E. has been characterized in various ways. For German scholars of the late nineteenth and early and mid-twentieth century, such as Emil Schürer and Wilhelm Bousset, this was *Spätjudentum,* "Late Judaism." The "lateness" was relative to the teaching of the prophets, and bespoke decline as well as chronological sequence. The decline reached its nadir in rabbinic Judaism, understood as a religion of the Law.

After the Holocaust, this way of characterizing ancient Judaism was widely (but not universally) recognized as not only offensive but dangerous. It was also inaccurate. On any reckoning, the history of Judaism since the Roman period is longer than the preceding history. Moreover, it is now increasingly apparent that the religion of ancient Israel and Judah before the Babylonian conquest was significantly different from the "Judaism" that emerged after the Exile. It has often been assumed that the reforms of Ezra in the fifth century marked the beginning of Judaism, but in fact we have little historical knowledge about these reforms, or indeed about Ezra himself. Shaye Cohen has argued persuasively that the Greek word *Ioudaios* originally meant "Judean," a usage that never disappears, but that "in the latter part of the second century B.C.E. is supplemented by a 'religious' or 'cultural' meaning: 'Jew'" (Cohen 1999: 3; Mason 2007 disputes the supplementary meaning). The word "Judaism" derives from the Greek *Ioudaismos,* which first occurs in 2 Maccabees (2:21; 8:1; 14:38), as does its counterpart *Hellenismos* (4:13). The Jewish, or Judean, way of life was certainly recognized as distinctive before this. It was noted by Hecataeus of Abdera at the beginning of the Hellenistic period (ca. 300 B.C.E.). The right of Judeans, even communities living outside of Judah, to live according to their ancestral laws was widely recognized by Hellenistic rulers, who were probably continuing Persian policy. But there are good grounds for regarding "Judaism" as a phenomenon of the Second Temple period. Accordingly, the period under review in this volume belongs to the early history of Judaism, even if the beginnings should be sought somewhat earlier.

While some biblical books (Daniel and probably Qoheleth) date from the Hellenistic age, the primary evidence for Judaism in this period lies in literature and other evidence dated "between the Bible and the Mishnah" (Nickelsburg 2005). Accordingly, this has sometimes been called the "intertestamental" period. While this term does not have the derogatory character of *Spätjudentum,* it does reflect a Christian perspective. Moreover, it obscures the fact that the New Testament itself provides evidence for Judaism in this period, and that some of the important Jewish writings (e.g., Josephus, *4 Ezra, 2 Baruch*) are contemporary with or later than some of the Christian Scriptures. In recent years, it has become customary to use the label "Second Temple Judaism" for this period (Stone 1984). Again, several relevant Jewish authors (most notably Josephus) worked after the destruction of the Second Temple, but the inaccuracy can be excused on the grounds that many of the later writings are still greatly preoccupied with the Temple and its destruction, and that the restructuring and reconceptualizing of the religion that we find in rabbinic literature did not occur immediately when Jerusalem fell. The Second Temple period, however, must begin with the Persians, and includes the editing, if not the composition, of much of the Hebrew Bible.

In this volume, we are mainly concerned with the evidence for Judaism between the Bible and the Mishnah. There is still overlap with the later biblical books, and the rabbinic corpus, compiled centuries later, also contains material relevant to the earlier period. No characterization, and no exact delimitation, is without problems, but "Early Judaism" seems the least problematic label available. (The designation "Middle Judaism," suggested by Gabriele Boccaccini [1991], might be applied more appropriately to the Middle Ages. It is hardly appropriate for prerabbinic Judaism.) The conquests of Alexander are taken as the *terminus a quo,* on the grounds that they marked a major cultural transition. Several extant postbiblical Jewish writings date from the third or early second century B.C.E., prior to the Maccabean Revolt, which has often served as a marker for a new era (e.g., in Schürer's *History*). The reign of Hadrian (117-138 C.E.) and the Bar Kokhba Revolt (132-135 C.E.) are taken to mark the end of an era, but not the end of Judaism by any means. The rabbinic literature, which later tradition would take as normative, took shape in the following centuries, but it did so in conditions that were very different from those that had prevailed before the great revolts.

The Recovery of the Pseudepigrapha

For much of Western history, there were relatively few sources for Judaism between the Bible and the Mishnah. The Apocrypha, or deuterocanonical books, were traditionally (and still are) part of the Bible of the Catholic Church. This is a very small selection of Jewish literature from the period 200 B.C.E. to 100 C.E. It includes the books of Maccabees, major wisdom books (Ben Sira and Wisdom of Solomon) and pious tales (Tobit, Judith), but apocalyptic writings are conspicuous by their absence. (2 Esdras, which includes the apocalypse of *4 Ezra,* is included in the Apocrypha but not in the deuterocanonical books that are part of the Catholic Bible.) The history of the period was well known because of the books of Maccabees and the writings of Josephus. In recent years these sources have been supplemented by archaeology, but few additional literary sources have come to light. Also, the great corpus of Philo of Alexandria's works was transmitted by Christians, because of its similarity to the writings of the church fathers. The Hellenistic Jewish literature was of marginal interest for orthodox Jewish scholarship in the nineteenth century, but it was the subject of some important studies, notably in the work of Jacob Freudenthal (1874-1875; see Niehoff in Oppenheimer, ed. 1999: 9-28).

There exists, however, an extensive class of writings attributed to Old Testament figures that is not included in the Apocrypha. These writings are called "pseudepigrapha" (falsely attributed writings). There is also a small number of pseudepigraphic writings attributed to figures of pagan antiquity, most prominently the Sibyl. Most of the Greek and Latin writings relating to the Old Testament, such as the *Testaments of the Twelve Patriarchs,* were collected by J. A. Fabricius in his *Codex Pseudepigraphus Veteris Testamenti* in 1713. But many important works were preserved only in less widely known languages, such as Ethiopic, Syriac, and Old Church Slavonic. The translations from Ethiopic of the *Ascension of Isaiah* (1819) and *1 Enoch* (1821) by Richard Laurence inaugurated a new era in the study of ancient Judaism. During the latter half of the nineteenth century, several more important pseudepigrapha came to light — *Jubilees, 2* and *3 Baruch, 2 Enoch,* the *Apocalypse of Abraham,* and the *Testament of Abraham.* These discoveries greatly enlarged the corpus of apocalyptic works from around the turn of the era and potentially provided resources for a new view of ancient Judaism. At the beginning of the twentieth century, there were landmark editions of the collected Pseudepigrapha in German (Kautzsch 1900; Riessler 1928) and English (Charles 1913), but editions of the individual books had been available from the late nineteenth century.

The Relevance of Rabbinic Writings

This newly available material was not immediately integrated into the study of ancient Judaism. Emil Schürer's *Geschichte des jüdischen Volkes im Zeitalter Jesu Christi* (1886-1890) included surveys of Jewish literature (divided between "Palestinian Jewish" and "Hellenistic Jewish" literature), but his depiction of Jewish religion is drawn heavily from rabbinic writings. This is especially true of his treatment of "Life under the Law," in which he drew primarily from the Mishnah, but even his account of messianic belief integrated data from the Pseudepigrapha with rabbinic beliefs. In the judgment of George Foote Moore, the chapter on the Law "was conceived, not as a chapter of the history of Judaism but as a topic of Christian apologetic; it was written to prove by the highest Jewish authority that the strictures on Judaism in the Gospels and the Pauline Epistles are fully justified" (Moore 1921: 240). Schürer's work was a mine of information and historical detail. Its enduring value can be seen in the degree to which its structure, and much of its detail, are retained in the English edition revised by Geza Vermes and his collaborators. The revisers "endeavoured to clear the notorious chapter 28, *Das Leben unter dem Gesetz* — here re-styled as 'Life and the Law' — and the section on the Pharisees . . . of the dogmatic prejudices of nineteenth-century theology" (Vermes et al. 1973-1987: 2:v; cf. 464 n. 1). Nonetheless, Schürer's introductory claim is repeated: "The chief characteristic of this period was the growing importance of Pharisaism . . . the generalities of biblical law were resolved into an immense number of detailed precepts . . . this concern with the punctilious observance of the minutiae of religion became the hallmark of mainstream Judaism" (Vermes et al. 1973-1987: 1:1). Likewise, the section on messianism retained the systematic presentation, which synthesizes data from rabbinic sources and the Pseudepigrapha.

The first scholar to offer a reconstruction of Jewish religion based primarily on the Pseudepigrapha was Wilhelm Bousset, whose *Religion des Judentums im neutestamentlichen Zeitalter* first appeared in 1903. It was greeted by a storm of criticism from Jewish scholars (Wiese 2005: 159-215). Bousset's view of Judaism was more differentiated than that of Schürer. In addition to the legalistic aspect of Pharisaism, he also detected a universalistic strand on which the teaching of Jesus could build. Some of his Jewish critics objected to "this dogmatic reduction of Judaism to a 'praeparatio evangelica'" (Wiese 2005: 180). But there was also a fundamental disagreement on the question of appropriate sources. Felix Perles praised Bousset's treatment of the piety of apocalyptic and Hellenistic Judaism but objected to the prominence accorded to this material and the lack of a systematic description of "normative Judaism," as represented by rabbinic literature. Bousset, he claimed, had missed the "center of the Jewish religion" (Perles 1903: 22-23; Wiese 2005: 181). Bousset responded that one must differentiate between "the scholarship of the scribes," which became normative after 70 C.E., and the more diverse "popular piety" of the earlier period, and he charged that Perles was "incapable of understanding the richer and more diverse life of Jewish popular religion before the destruction of the Jewish nation, because he is focused on the Mishnah and the Talmud and the entire later history of the scribes" (Bousset 1903b; Wiese 2005: 186). Few scholars would now accept Bousset's characterization of the Pseudepigrapha as "popular religion" without qualification, but the issue of the relevance of rabbinic literature for the Second Temple period persists as a live issue down to the present.

R. H. Charles, the scholar who did most to advance the study of the Pseudepigrapha, did not attempt a comprehensive study of ancient Judaism. While his own work focused largely on the apocalypses, he held that "Apocalyptic Judaism and legalistic Judaism were not in pre-Christian times essentially antagonistic. Fundamentally their origin was the same. Both started with the unreserved recognition of the supremacy of the Law" (Charles 1913: vii). Charles viewed the apocalyptic material positively, as a bridge between the prophets and early Christianity. His view of Judaism in this period as comprising two main strands is one of the major paradigms that has been adapted with various nuances in later scholarship (see VanderKam in Boccaccini and Collins 2007).

Perles's criticisms of Bousset were echoed almost two decades later by the American Christian scholar, George Foot Moore:

> The censure which Jewish scholars have unanimously passed on *Die Religion des Judentums* is that the author uses as his primary sources almost exclusively the writings commonly called Apocrypha and Pseudepigrapha, with an especial penchant for the apocalypses; and only secondarily, and almost casually the writings which represent the acknowledged and authoritative teachings of the school and the more popular instruction of the synagogue. This is much as if one should describe early Christianity using indiscriminately for his principal sources the Apocryphal Gospels and Acts, the Apocalypses of John and Peter, and the Clementine literature. (Moore 1921: 243)

While acknowledging the problem of the date of the rabbinic material, Moore insisted: "it is clear that the author ought not to have called his book *Die Religion des Judentums,* for the sources from which his representation is drawn are those to which, so far as we know, Judaism never conceded any authority, while he discredits and largely ignores those which it has always regarded as normative" (244).

But as F. C. Porter pointed out in his review of Moore's own masterwork (Moore 1927-1930), "When Moore speaks of the sources which Judaism has always regarded as authentic, he means 'always' from the third century A.D. onward. . . . Was there then no other type of Judaism in the time of Christ that may claim such names as 'normative,' 'normal,' 'orthodox'?" (Porter 1928; cf. Neusner 1981: 9). More fundamentally, one might question whether notions of normativity are appropriate to a discussion of the history of a religion at all. As Jacob Neusner, with all due appreciation for Moore's goodwill, pointed out: "Moore's is to begin with not really a work in the history of religions at all. . . . His research is into theology. It is organized in theological categories, not differentiated by historical periods at all" (Neusner 1981: 7). Neusner was no less critical of Jewish scholarship at the beginning of the twentieth century. The attempt to draw a direct line from the Hebrew Bible to a "normative" Judaism defined by the rabbis was an anachronism, motivated by apologetics (Neusner 1984: 101; Wiese 2005: 213).

The mantle of Moore was taken up half a century later by E. P. Sanders, with some qualifications. Sanders recognizes that the tannaitic literature (i.e., literature traditionally ascribed to the period between 70 and 200 C.E.) cannot be assumed to provide "an accurate picture of Judaism or even of Pharisaism in the time of Jesus and Paul, although it would be surprising if there were no connection" (Sanders 1977: 60). He also recognizes that Jewish literature from this period, including the tannaitic literature, is very varied. Yet he argues that "a common pattern can be discerned which underlies otherwise disparate parts of tannaitic literature" (Sanders 1977: 70), which he describes as "covenantal nomism." The Law must be seen in the context of election and covenant. It provides for a means of atonement, so that the covenantal relationship can be reestablished or maintained. All who are maintained in the covenant will be saved. Salvation, then, does not depend on purely individual observance of the Law. Sanders finds this pattern not only in tannaitic literature but also in the Dead Sea Scrolls, Apocrypha, and Pseudepigrapha, with the single exception of *4 Ezra* (Sanders 1977: 422-23). He concludes that his study "lends no support to those who have urged that apocalypticism and legalism constitute substantially different religious types or streams in the Judaism of the period" (Sanders 1977: 423) and denies that apocalypticism constituted a distinct type of religion (Sanders 1992: 8). The case for the compatibility of concern for the Law with apocalyptic beliefs finds strong support in the Dead Sea Scrolls.

In Sanders's view, "covenantal nomism does not cover the entirety of Jewish theology, much less the entirety of Judaism" (Sanders 1992: 262). It is nonetheless an aspect of "common" or "normal" Judaism. Mindful of the criticism directed at Moore, Sanders is careful to qualify the word "normative": "whatever we find to have been normal was based on internal assent and was 'normative' only to the degree that it was backed up by common opinion — which has a good deal of coercive power, but which allows individuals who strongly dissent to break away" (Sanders 1992: 47). The pillars of common Judaism were the belief in one God, the Scriptures, especially the Torah, and the Temple. Within a common framework, considerable variation was possible. Sanders's approach is focused on practice rather than belief. Even when he draws his data from Josephus or other Second Temple sources, the kinds of issues on which he focuses are generally similar to those that predominate in the Mishnah. Apocalyptic speculations about the heavens or the end of history tell us little about the authors' daily observances.

Sanders's portrait of common Judaism is less vulnerable to critique than Moore's normative Judaism, and it enjoys wide acceptance (see, e.g., Goodman 2002: 38). It does not deny that diversity existed but places the emphasis on what all (or at least most) Jews had in common. One could also place more emphasis on diversity with equal validity. The other end of the spectrum from Sanders is occupied by Jacob Neusner, who insists on speaking of "Judaisms" rather than "Judaism" (e.g., Neusner, Green, and Frerichs 1987: ix). The plural has been adopted by some scholars (e.g., Boccaccini) but is infelicitous: to speak of "a Judaism" requires the overarching concept of "Judaism" in the singular. While Neusner's insistence that each corpus of Jewish literature (say, the Dead Sea Scrolls) be analyzed in its own right and not read through the lens of another corpus (say, the Mishnah) is salutary, it does not follow that each corpus represents a distinct religious system. Insistence on radical diversity distorts the data just as much as an essentialist approach that would exclude ostensibly Jewish material that does not conform to a norm (see the remarks of Green 1994: 298 on Sanders's *Paul and Palestinian Judaism:* "Paul's writings are analyzed in juxtaposition to Judaism rather than as part of it").

In his recent attempt at a sweeping characterization of early Judaism, Seth Schwartz is sharply critical of Neusner: "I reject the characterization of Judaism as multiple, as well as the atomistic reading of the sources that justifies it" (Schwartz 2001: 9). He continues: "The notion that each piece of evidence reflects a discrete social organization is obviously wrong." It is not apparent, however, that Neusner associates his different "Judaisms" with "discrete social organizations." Schwartz goes on to distinguish broadly between "apocalyptic mythology" and "covenantal ideology" (Schwartz 2001: 78-82). He regards these as "incongruous systems": "The covenant imagines an orderly world governed justly by the one God. The apocalyptic myth imagines a world in disarray, filled with evil; a world in which people do not get what they deserve. God is not in control in any obvious way; indeed the cosmology of the myth is dualist or polytheist. . . ." The accuracy of this sketch of "the apocalyptic myth" might be questioned, especially with regard to whether God is in control, but there is no doubt that there are real differences here. Schwartz notes "the repeated juxtaposition of the covenant and the myth in ancient Jewish writing" and infers that "though the systems are logically incongruous, they did not for the most part generate social division." Thus he agrees with Sanders that "apocalyptic Judaism" was not a separate entity. He is also dubious about "covenantal Judaism." Rather, he supposes that "the apocalyptic myth" was "a more or less fully naturalized part of the ideology of Judaism." Insofar as he recognizes "incongruous systems," Schwartz may not be as far removed from Neusner as he thinks, although the latter would surely insist on a greater variety of systems. At the same time, Schwartz can avoid the impression of fragmentation that is conveyed by Neusner's insistence on multiple Judaisms.

The Place of the Pseudepigrapha

In his critique of Bousset, Moore acknowledged that critical use of the rabbinic writings is difficult, but he argued that the critical problems presented by the Pseudepigrapha are no less difficult: "How wide, for example, was the currency of these writings? Do they represent a certain common type of 'Volksfrömmigkeit,' or did they circulate in circles with peculiar notions and tendencies of their own? How far do they come from sects regarded by the mass of their countrymen as heretical?" (Moore 1921: 244). Perhaps the most fundamental question to be asked about the use of the Pseudepigrapha in the reconstruction of ancient Judaism is whether they are in fact Jewish at all. Most of these texts were preserved by Christians, not by Jews. Robert Kraft has argued repeatedly that these texts should first be understood in their Christian context (Kraft 1994; 2001). At the same time, it is incontrovertible that some pseudepigraphic writings which were preserved only by Christians were composed by Jews in the centuries around the turn of the era. Fragments of most sections of *1 Enoch,* and of *Jubilees* were found in Aramaic and Hebrew, respectively, among the Dead Sea Scrolls. It does not necessarily follow that all pseudepigrapha attributed to Old Testament figures are of Jewish origin. Since most Christian literature refers explicitly to Christ, and Christians often added references to Christ to Jewish writings, the tendency has been to assume that any Old Testament pseudepigraphon that has nothing explicitly Christian in it is in fact Jewish.

This tendency has recently been challenged by James Davila (2005). We have a considerable corpus of writings from antiquity that are indisputably Jewish, because of their language or the context of their discovery (most notably, the Dead Sea Scrolls). On the basis of these texts Davila attempts to identify "signature features" that can reliably indicate the Jewish origin of a work:

- substantial Jewish content, and evidence of a pre-Christian date;
- compelling evidence that a work was translated from Hebrew;
- sympathetic concern with the Jewish ritual cult;

- sympathetic concern with Jewish Law/Torah and halakah;
- concern with Jewish ethnic and national interests. (Davila 2005: 65)

These "signature features" are not necessarily foolproof, but they can help establish a balance of probability. They enable Davila to authenticate as Jewish a work like *2 Baruch,* which was clearly written by a Torah-observant Jew, against the objections of Rivkah Nir (2003), who argues that several of its apocalyptic motifs are typical of Christianity rather than Judaism (Davila 2005: 131). He rightly argues that Nir's concept of ancient Judaism is "narrow to the point of being procrustean," as she does not even include works like *1 Enoch* and *Jubilees* in her control corpus of Jewish material. He also defends the Jewish origin of the *Similitudes of Enoch* (*1 Enoch* 37–71), which shows no interest in Torah observance, and which was regarded as a late Christian work by J. T. Milik (1976: 89-98). In this case the conclusive consideration is the apparent identification of Enoch, not Jesus, with the Son of Man in *1 Enoch* 71:14 (Davila 2005: 134). The identification, though, is not as unambiguous as Davila claims (Collins 1998: 187-91), but it is inconceivable that a Christian author would have allowed any ambiguity as to the identification of the Son of Man. Other cases are more difficult to decide. The Jewish origin of *Joseph and Aseneth* has been questioned forcefully by Ross Kraemer (1998). Davila fails to detect either Jewish or Christian signature features that would decide the issue (Davila 2005: 193). Neither does the *Testament of Job* offer any decisive evidence, although it fits quite comfortably in the context provided by the oldest attestation, in Christian circles in Egypt in the early fifth century C.E. He also finds the *Testament of Abraham* congenial to a late antique Christian setting. Less plausibly, he finds nothing in the Wisdom of Solomon "that prohibits or even renders unlikely its having been written by a gentile Christian in the second half of the first century CE" (Davila 2005: 225). But there is no parallel for Christian composition of a pseudepigraphic writing in the name of an Old Testament figure at such an early date, and the retelling of the exodus story in Wisdom of Solomon 11–19 surely meets the criterion of concern for Jewish ethnic and national interests. Davila's reasoning is not persuasive in every instance, but he has advanced the discussion by showing that the evidence for Jewish origin is much clearer in some instances than in others.

There is plenty of evidence that Christians sometimes composed works in the names of Old Testament figures (e.g., Isaiah, Ezra, Elijah, Daniel). It is also plausible that they inserted explicit Christian passages into Jewish works to render them more suitable for Christian devotion (see, e.g., Harlow 1996 on *3 Baruch;* Collins in Charlesworth 1983: 330-53 on *Sibylline Oracles* 1 and 2). The more extensive the Christian redaction, the more hazardous the reconstruction of the underlying Jewish work becomes. The most celebrated problem case in this regard is the *Testaments of the Twelve Patriarchs.* This collection is clearly Christian in its present form. One of its distinctive features is the expectation of a messiah from Levi and Judah, who is evidently identified as Christ. He will be priest and king, God and man (*T. Sim.* 7:2). He is referred to as "the lamb of God" (*T. Jos.* 19:6). *Testament of Judah* 24 speaks of a man from the tribe of Judah, for whom the heavens will be opened and in whom no sin will be found. Scholars have argued that each of these references can be justified in a Jewish context, or that they are Christian insertions in a text that is basically Jewish (Charles 1913: 291). The cumulative evidence, however, is far more easily explained on the assumption of Christian authorship (de Jonge 1953).

Nonetheless, there are good reasons to think that the *Testaments* draw heavily on Jewish traditions. The association of the messiah with both Levi and Judah inevitably recalls the two messiahs of the Dead Sea Scrolls. Partial parallels to the *Testament of Levi,* in Aramaic, and to the *Testament of Naphtali,* in Hebrew, have been found among the Dead Sea Scrolls. It is possible, however, that these were source documents used by the Christian authors of the *Testaments* (de Jonge 2000). We do not have conclusive evidence for a Jewish *Testaments of Twelve Patriarchs* (as distinct from apocryphal writings associated with individuals such as Levi). The ethical teachings of the *Testaments* can be explained satisfactorily in the context of either Hellenistic Judaism or early Christianity.

In cases where the Christian elements are not extensive, and somewhat incongruous, a stronger case can be made for Jewish authorship. The fifth *Sibylline Oracle* contains only one overtly Christian verse (arguably two) in a composition of 531 verses. Verse 257 qualifies the "exceptional man from the sky" with the line "who stretched out his hands on the fruitful wood." The following verse says that he will one day cause the sun to stand. Most commentators excise either one or both verses as an interpolation (Collins in Charlesworth 1983: 399). The reference to causing the sun to stand could be regarded as part of the interpolation because of a play on Jesus/Joshua). Davila allows that this is possible, but finds it unnecessary: "Sibylline Oracles 5 as a whole reads comfortably as a work by a Jewish-Christian who was outraged by the Roman destruction of Jerusalem and who put after-the-fact prophecies in the mouth of the Sibyl both to condemn the Romans and the other polytheistic nations and to predict the coming of Jesus as the eschatological redeemer" (Davila 2005:189). But while the outrage over the destruction is loud and clear in this work, the identification of Jesus as the eschatological redeemer is perceptible only in this one passage, and is not very explicit even there. Davila notes that *Sibylline Oracles* 5 shows no interest in circumcision, dietary laws, or the Sabbath, and virtually reduces the Law to idolatry and sexual sins. But this is quite typical of Jewish writings from the Hellenistic Diaspora (Collins 2000: 155-85). As this example shows, the identification of a given text as Jewish depends on the profile of Judaism one is willing to accept. In some cases, arguments against Jewish provenance reflect a narrow, normative view of Judaism (Efron 1987: 219-86 on the *Psalms of Solomon;* Nir on *2 Baruch*). This is not true of Davila, however, and the questions may be justified in some cases. The boundaries of Judaism cannot be restricted to concern for the Torah or covenantal nomism. Conversely, arguments for Jewish diversity based on pseudepigraphic texts of uncertain origin cannot bear the full weight of evidence unless they are supported by parallels in texts that are clearly Jewish.

The Place of Apocalypticism

The controversy over the use of the Pseudepigrapha in the reconstruction of early Judaism is due in large part to the prominence of apocalyptic literature. Even pseudepigraphic books that are not formally apocalypses, such as the *Sibylline Oracles,* the *Psalms of Solomon,* or the *Testaments of the Twelve Patriarchs* have much in common with them, especially in their view of history and eschatology. Only one apocalyptic writing, the book of Daniel, was included in the Hebrew Bible, and the apocalyptic tradition was rejected by rabbinic Judaism. The noncanonical apocalypses were transmitted by Christians, and were not preserved in Hebrew or Aramaic, although Aramaic fragments of *1 Enoch* and Hebrew fragments of *Jubilees* have been found in the Dead Sea Scrolls. It has been said that apocalypticism is the mother of Christian theology. R. H. Charles saw it as the link between biblical prophecy and early Christianity, and the view that it was "the child of prophecy" has always been popular in English-language scholarship (Rowley 1944). Bousset, in contrast, attributed its rise to Zoroastrian influence. Other sources, both biblical (wisdom literature, von Rad 1965: 2:315-30) and foreign (Babylonian traditions, e.g., Kvanvig 1988) have occasionally been proposed. Only in the last quarter of the twentieth century has apocalypticism been recognized as a phenomenon in its own right rather than as a mutation (or degeneration) of something else (Collins 1998: 26-42).

After the great burst of creative energy expended on the Pseudepigrapha in the late nineteenth and early twentieth centuries, this literature received little scholarly attention for more than half a century. (This neglect must be seen in the context of a general shift in focus from history of religion to biblical theology in this period.) Many of the more influential scholars who addressed it, such as Rowley and von Rad, were biblical scholars who naturally enough tried to assimilate the strange noncanonical material to biblical categories. Much of the scholarship that purported to deal with "apocalyptic" actually dealt with postexilic prophecy or with the letters of Paul. The discovery of the Dead Sea Scrolls, however, led to renewed interest in Judaism between the Bible and the Mishnah. From the 1970s onward there was extensive work on the Pseudepigrapha both in the United States and in Europe, which bore fruit in the two-volume translation of Old Testament Pseudepigrapha edited by Charlesworth (1983-1985), which included much more material than the older edition of Charles, and the German series of fascicles *Jüdische Schriften aus hellenistisch-römischer Zeit.* Now the apocalypses came to be studied in the context of the contemporary pseudepigraphic literature and the Dead Sea Scrolls. This in turn led to a change in focus from "apocalyptic" as a kind of theology, usually studied with an eye to its relevance for the New Testament, to the literary genre apocalypse (Koch 1972; Collins ed. 1979).

Three results of the study of the genre are noteworthy. First, apocalypses are not only concerned with historical eschatology (the end of the present age) in the way familiar from Daniel and the book of Revelation. They are also, even primarily, revelations of heavenly mysteries (Rowland 1983). A whole subtype of the genre is concerned with otherworldly journeys, and this material is important for the early history of Jewish mysticism (Himmelfarb 1993). Second, since only one book in the Hebrew Bible, Daniel, could be said to exemplify the genre, discussion of "apocalyptic" or "protoapocalyptic" in the prophetic literature became increasingly dubious. Third, the genre is not peculiar to Judaism and Christianity, but has important parallels in Persian tradition and throughout the Greco-Roman world, especially in the case of the heavenly journeys (Hellholm 1983).

Another byproduct of the focus on the genre apocalypse and on the context of the Pseudepigrapha was increased interest in the collection of writings known as *1 Enoch*. Charles had already realized that some parts of *1 Enoch* were older than Daniel. Interest was greatly increased by the publication of the Aramaic fragments found among the Dead Sea Scrolls (Milik 1976). The Italian scholar Paolo Sacchi argued that the root of apocalypticism should be found in the *Book of the Watchers* (*1 Enoch* 1–36), one of the earliest segments of the tradition (Sacchi 1997). The generative question was the origin of evil, and the answer was that it was brought to earth by fallen angels. Sacchi tended to identify apocalypticism with the Enochic tradition, in contrast even to the book of Daniel. His student, Gabriele Boccaccini, has proceeded to argue, in Neusnerian fashion, that *1 Enoch* testifies to "Enochic Judaism," which he further identifies with the Essenes, whom he regards as the parent movement of the Qumran sect (Boccaccini 1998).

Even if one were to grant that the *Book of the Watchers* is the earliest Jewish apocalypse, the whole phenomenon cannot be defined only on the basis of its earliest exemplar. The differences between Daniel and Enoch show only that there was some diversity within apocalypticism, and that it should not be restricted to a single social movement. Again, while the books of Enoch were preserved at Qumran (except for the *Similitudes*), they were not the only, or even the primary source of sectarian ideology, and there is no evidence whatever that would warrant identifying them with the Essenes. Nonetheless, the early Enoch books attest to a kind of Judaism that is significantly different from the covenantal nomism of "common Judaism." As George Nickelsburg has argued, "the general category of covenant was not important for these authors" (Nickelsburg 1998: 125). Enoch rather than Moses is the mediator of revelation. Unlike the book of *Jubilees*, which is closely related to Enoch in some respects, there is no attempt to read back Mosaic legislation into the primeval period. Even the *Animal Apocalypse*, which touches on the exodus and the ascent of Mt. Sinai in the course of a "prophecy" of the history of Israel, conspicuously fails to mention either the making of a covenant or the giving of the Law. In all of this there is no polemic against the Mosaic Torah, but the Torah is not the explicit frame of reference. Moreover, the Enoch literature attests to a soli-lunar calendar different from the lunar calendar that was observed in the Jerusalem Temple (at least in later times), but similar to the one found in *Jubilees* and the Dead Sea Scrolls.

The idea of a movement within Judaism that is not centered on the Mosaic Torah may seem anomalous in the context of the Hellenistic age, but it was not without precedent. The biblical wisdom literature is distinguished precisely by its lack of explicit reference to either the Mosaic Torah or the history of Israel, and it retains this character as late as the book of Qoheleth, which may be roughly contemporary with the early Enoch literature. Charles, then, was not correct when he claimed that "apocalyptic Judaism" "started with the unreserved recognition of the supremacy of the Law." At least in the case of the early Enoch literature, this was not the case.

What is true of the Enoch literature, however, is not necessarily true of all the Pseudepigrapha, or even of all apocalyptic literature. The book of *Jubilees* adapts the myth of the fallen angels from *1 Enoch* (Segal 2007: 103-43), and shares with it the solar (364-day) calendar. It can be viewed as an example of "rewritten Bible," or biblical paraphrase, but it is also an apocalypse, in the sense that it is a revelation mediated by an angel. But the recipient of the revelation is none other than Moses, and the content is a paraphrase of the book of Genesis. Moreover, this paraphrase is informed throughout by a keen interest in halakic issues. The sectarian writings of the Dead Sea Scrolls are at once apocalyptic and focused on the exact interpretation of the Law of Moses. The Torah also plays a central role in the apocalypses of *4 Ezra* and *2 Baruch,* which were composed after the destruction of the Temple, at the end of the first century C.E. The relationship between apocalyptic literature and the Torah is illustrated most vividly by *4 Ezra.* At the end of the book, Ezra is commissioned to replace the books of the Law that had been burnt. He is given a fiery liquid to drink, and inspired to dictate the books. In all, ninety-four books are written. Of these, twenty-four are made public so that the worthy and unworthy may read them. But the seventy others are kept secret, in order that they may be given to the wise among the people. The extra or hidden books contain "the spring of understanding, the fountain of wisdom and the river of knowledge." *4 Ezra* is neither critical of the Torah nor opposed to it, but it claims to have further revelation, which provides the context within which the Torah must be understood. This claim of higher revelation is one of the defining characteristics of apocalyptic literature. In the words of Seth Schwartz, "it was a way of compensating for the deficiencies of the covenantal system" (Schwartz 2001: 83). The covenant promised life and prosperity to those who observed it and threatened disaster to those who did not, but life evidently did not work this way. One of the major topics of apocalyptic revelation was judgment after death and the contrasting fates of the righteous and wicked in the hereafter. Belief in life after death was not confined to apocalyptic literature; the immortality of the soul was widely accepted in Greek-speaking Judaism, and the Pharisees, who may have subscribed to apocalyptic ideas to various degrees, believed in resurrection. But belief in the judgment of the dead and a differentiated afterlife is first attested in Judaism in the books of *Enoch* and Daniel, and it is the primary factor that distinguishes apocalyptic eschatology from that of the prophets (Collins 1997b: 75-97).

The Dead Sea Scrolls

The most important development for the study of early Judaism in the past century was undoubtedly the discovery and eventual publication of the Dead Sea Scrolls. The scrolls were found in proximity to a ruined settlement at Khirbet Qumran, south of Jericho, by the Dead Sea. Cave 4, where the main trove of texts was found, is literally a stone's throw from the site. Most scholars have assumed that the texts constituted the library of a sectarian settlement at Qumran (VanderKam 1994: 12-27). The Roman writer Pliny says that there was an Essene settlement in this region (*Natural History* 5.73), and there are extensive parallels between the rule books found at Qumran, especially the *Serek Ha-Yaḥad,* or *Community Rule,* and the accounts of the Essenes by Philo and Josephus (Beall 1988). Both the association with the site and the identification with the Essenes have been contested, often vociferously, in recent years (Galor, Humbert, and Zangenberg 2006). Norman Golb has insisted that such an extensive corpus of scrolls could have come only from the Jerusalem Temple, and that the multiplicity of hands belies composition in a single community (Golb 1995). With regard to the identification with the Essenes, the main point in dispute has been the issue of celibacy, which is noted by all ancient writers on the Essenes but is never explicitly required in the scrolls. Also, the accounts of the Essenes do not hint at messianic expectation or at the kind of apocalyptic expectations found in the *War Scroll* and other texts at Qumran.

The discussion has been obscured by a tendency among scholars to think of Qumran as a single, monastery-like institution. In fact, the rule books make clear that there was a network of communities, which could have as few as ten people, at various locations. The accounts of the Essenes (other than Pliny) also emphasize that they had many settlements. Josephus notes that there were two orders of Essenes, one of which accepted marriage. One of the rule books found at Qumran, the so-called *Damascus Document,* also appears to distinguish between "those who live in camps and marry and have children" and others who presumably do not. It is unlikely that all the scrolls were copied at Qumran. An alternative scenario is that Essenes from other settlements fled to Qumran in face of the advancing Romans in 68 C.E. and brought their scrolls with them. This would account for the high number of sectarian texts and also for the presence of different editions of the rule books in the caves.

In any case, it is clear that the corpus of texts found at Qumran includes many that were not sectarian in origin, although they may been used in a sectarian context. These include the biblical books, but also compositions like the books of *Enoch* and *Jubilees,* which apparently were composed before the formation of the sect in the middle or late second century B.C.E. and circulated more widely. But also many texts that were not known before the discovery of the scrolls may have been in broader use in the Judaism of the time. Yet the scrolls cannot be taken as a random sampling of Second Temple literature. On the one hand, the proportion of clearly sectarian texts, including sectarian rule books, is too great. On the other hand, several important writings from this period are conspicuously absent from Qumran. These include 1 Maccabees, the propagandistic history of the Hasmonean family, and the *Psalms of Solomon,* which has often been suspected of Pharisaic ideology. Nothing in the Dead Sea Scrolls can be identified as Pharisaic, and only one text (4Q448, the *Prayer for King Jonathan*) can be read as supportive of the Hasmoneans. The corpus is not narrowly sectarian, in the sense of containing only sectarian literature, but it is nonetheless selective and excludes some literature for ideological reasons.

The first scrolls were discovered on the eve of the Arab-Israeli war that led to the division of Palestine. When partition occurred, Qumran was on the Jordanian side of the border. The seven scrolls originally found in Cave 1 (*Community Rule, War Scroll, Hodayot, Habakkuk Pesher, Genesis Apocryphon,* and two copies of the book of Isaiah) were acquired by Eliezer Sukenik and his son Yigael Yadin, but Jewish scholars would have no access to the rest of the corpus until after the Six-Day War in 1967. The international team appointed to edit the fragments included no Jewish scholars. The first phase of scholarship on the scrolls, then, was dominated by Christian scholars, and Christian interests took priority. There were many comparisons of the community behind the scrolls to early Christianity, and such matters as eschatology and messianism received great attention (see, e.g., Cross 1995). In 1967, however, both Qumran and the Rockefeller Museum where the scrolls were stored came under Israeli control. This did not at first lead to any change in the editorial team, but it had a profound impact on scholarship in another way. Yadin, who was a general in the Israeli army, appropriated a long text, known as the *Temple Scroll,* from the antiquities dealer Kando, and he published it a decade later (Yadin 1977, 1983). This scroll contains a rewriting of biblical laws, and its interests are primarily halakic. Its publication aroused new interest in the aspects of the scrolls that were continuous with rabbinic rather than with Christian interests. Even more revolutionary was the disclosure in 1984 of a halakic work known as 4QMMT (Qimron and Strugnell 1994). This document is apparently addressed to a leader of Israel, and it outlines the reasons for the separation of a sectarian group from the majority of the people. The reasons had to do with issues of calendar and purity, and the scroll shows that halakic issues (issues of religious law) were vital to the raison d'être of the sect. The positions taken on these issues typically disagreed with those associated with the Pharisees in rabbinic literature and agreed with those of the Sadducees on some points. The scroll showed beyond any doubt that the kinds of issues debated in the Mishnah and Talmud were of great concern already in the late Second Temple period (Schiffman in Oppenheimer 1999: 205-19), and that in this respect any account of Judaism based only on the Apocrypha and Pseudepigrapha would be incomplete.

A third phase in the study of the scrolls began when the entire corpus became generally available in the early 1990s, and the editorial team was greatly expanded under the leadership of Emanuel Tov. It is now possible to get a more balanced view of the entire corpus.

Whatever their relation to "Enochic Judaism," the scrolls testify to the pervasive authority and influence of the Mosaic Torah. They provide important evidence about the development of the biblical text. The majority of the textual witnesses are close to the Masoretic Text, but there were also other textual forms in circulation. In some cases it is difficult to decide whether a given text is a variant form of the biblical text or a deliberate adaptation of it, in the manner of "rewritten bible," such as we find in *Jubilees*. The *Temple Scroll* reinterprets the legal traditions of Leviticus and Deuteronomy by presenting them in rewritten form as a revelation to Moses. In this way the writer's interpretation of the biblical laws is invested with the authority of the revelation at Sinai. Some scholars have argued that the *Temple Scroll* was intended to replace the Torah as the definitive law for the end of days (Wacholder 1983; Wise 1990: 184). It is more likely, however, that it presupposes the authority of the biblical text and is intended as a companion piece and guide to its interpretation (Najman 1999). The scrolls also contain many examples of explicit commentary, most notably in the pesharim, which date from the first century B.C.E. and are the oldest extant formal biblical commentaries. The commentaries are primarily on prophetic texts, including Psalms, and relate them to the history of the sect and the "end of days." Especially interesting is the so-called *Pesher on Genesis* (4Q252), which combines a paraphrase of the flood story with a pesher-style interpretation of the Blessing of Jacob in Genesis 49.

The scrolls also provide ample evidence for an extensive literature associated with biblical figures, in the manner of the Pseudepigrapha (Dimant 1994; Flint in Flint and VanderKam 1998-1999: 2:24-66). Since most of this literature is fragmentary, it is difficult to be sure of literary genre of many compositions. Related to the Enoch literature is a fragmentary *Book of Giants.* Possible apocalypses found at Qumran include the *Visions of Amram,* which describes dualistic angelic-demonic powers, the so-called *Aramaic Apocalypse* or *Son of God* text (4Q246), the *New Jerusalem* text (a vision in the tradition of Ezekiel 40–48), and a "four kingdoms" prophecy where the four kingdoms are symbolized by four trees (4Q552-553). There are also prophecies after the fact attributed to Daniel (4Q243-244, 245) and a similar text, 4Q390, variously identified as *Pseudo-Moses* or *Jeremiah Apocryphon.* There are Aramaic texts relating to *Levi* and *Qahath,* and an Aramaic *Genesis Apocryphon.* The Aramaic literature found at Qumran is not perceptibly sectarian.

Since so many of the scrolls are dependent on biblical texts, there is a tendency to assume derivation from biblical prototypes. In some cases, this is justified. There are Targums of Leviticus and Job, and the *Genesis Apocryphon* and *Aramaic Levi Document* are obviously related to the biblical text. But this literature is not all derivative. The *Prayer of Nabonidus* may have been a source for the book of Daniel, but it does not depend on it, and at least some of the pseudo-Daniel literature also appears to be independent. The text sometimes known as *Proto-Esther* (4Q550) is related to Esther only insofar as both are tales set in the Persian court. The book of Tobit, which is included in the Apocrypha and is found at Qumran in both Hebrew and Aramaic, is another example of a narrative work that is not derived from a biblical story, although it draws on various biblical motifs. The scrolls also expand significantly our corpus of nonbiblical wisdom literature, including an extensive and important text, 4QInstruction (Goff 2007). Fragments of Ben Sira were also found. The corpus of liturgical texts is also enlarged (Nitzan 1994; Falk 1998). The sapiential and liturgical texts are in Hebrew, but in many cases they are not necessarily sectarian. The scrolls, then, support the view that Jewish literature in the late Second Temple period was quite diverse. Some of it certainly shared the halakic interests of the later rabbis, but much of it also exhibited concerns similar to those attested in the Apocrypha and Pseudepigrapha.

The most distinctive literature found in the scrolls consists of sectarian rule books (Metso 1998). The *Community Rule* and *Damascus Document* describe a complex sectarian movement that had more than one form of community life. They exhibit important parallels with Greek voluntary associations (Weinfeld 1986), but they are conceived in terms of membership in a new covenant. These rules show extensive similarity to the descriptions of the Essenes in Philo and Josephus, with regard to admission procedures, common property, and community life. The Essenes were not the only sectarian movement to emerge in Judaism in the last centuries before the turn of the era. Rather, sectarianism was a feature of the age, and the scrolls are an important witness to the phenomenon (Baumgarten 1997).

The movement described in the scrolls has often been called an "apocalyptic community," with good reason (Collins 1997c). The *War Scroll* and the Treatise on the Two Spirits in the *Community Rule* are prime examples of what Seth Schwartz has called "the apocalyptic myth" (Schwartz 2001: 74-82). Yet the community does not seem to have used the literary form of apocalypse to any significant degree. In this case, the Torah of Moses was unequivocally regarded as the primary source of revelation. Moreover, the figure called the Teacher of Righteousness was revered as the authoritative interpreter, and rendered pseudonymous mediators such as Enoch or Daniel superfluous. In this respect, the sect was quite unique. It shows, however, that there was no necessary conflict between the veneration of the Torah and interest in apocalyptic revelations.

Judaism and Hellenism

Throughout the period under consideration in this volume, Jews lived in a world permeated by Hellenistic culture. The pervasiveness of Hellenistic influence can be seen even in the Dead Sea Scrolls (where there is little evidence of conscious interaction with the Greek world), for example, in the analogies between the sectarian communities and voluntary associations.

Modern scholarship has often assumed an antagonistic relationship between Hellenism and Judaism. This is due in large part to the received account of the Maccabean Revolt, especially in 2 Maccabees. The revolt was preceded by an attempt to make Jerusalem into a Hellenistic *polis.* Elias Bickerman (1937) even argued that the persecution was instigated by the Hellenizing high priest Alcimus, and in this he was followed by Martin Hengel (1974). Yet the revolt did not actually break out until the Syrian king, Antiochus IV Epiphanes, had disrupted the Jerusalem cult and given the Temple over to a Syrian garrison. The revolt was not directed against Hellenistic culture but against the policies of the king, especially with regard to the cult. Judas allegedly sent an embassy to Rome and availed of the services of one Eupolemus, who was sufficiently proficient in Greek to write an account of Jewish history. The successors of the Maccabees, the Hasmoneans, freely adopted Greek customs and even Greek names. Arnaldo Momigliano wrote that "the penetration of Greek words, customs, and intellectual modes in Judaea during the rule of the Hasmoneans and the following Kingdom of Herod has no limits" (Momigliano 1994: 22; see also Hengel 1989; Levine 1998). Herod established athletic contests in honor of Caesar and built a large amphitheater, and even established Roman-style gladiatorial contests. He also built temples for pagan cults, but not in Jewish territory, and he had to yield to protests by removing trophies, which involved images surrounded by weapons, from the Temple. In all cases where we find resistance to Hellenism in Judea, the issue involves cult or worship (Collins 2005: 21-43). Many aspects of Greek culture, including most obviously the language, were inoffensive. The revolt against Rome was sparked not by cultural conflict but by Roman mismanagement and social tensions.

Because of the extensive Hellenization of Judea, the old distinction between "Palestinian" Judaism and "Hellenistic" (= Diaspora) Judaism has been eroded to a great degree in modern scholarship. Nonetheless, the situation of Jews in the Diaspora was different in degree, as they were a minority in a pagan, Greek-speaking environment, and the Greek language and cultural forms provided their natural means of expression (Gruen 1998, 2002). The Greek community in Alexandria, the Diaspora community of which we are most fully informed, regarded themselves as akin to the Greeks, in contrast to the Egyptians and other *Barbaroi*. The Torah was translated into Greek already in the third century B.C.E. Thereafter, Jewish authors experimented with Greek genres — epic, tragedy, Sibylline oracles, philosophical treatises (Goodman in Vermes et al. 1973-1987: 3:1.470-704; Collins 2000). This considerable literary production reached its apex in the voluminous work of the philosopher Philo in the early first century C.E. This Greco-Jewish literature has often been categorized as apologetic, on the assumption that it was addressed to Gentiles. Since the work of Victor Tcherikover (1956), it is generally recognized that it is rather directed to the Jewish community. Nonetheless, it has a certain apologetic dimension (Collins 2005: 1-20). It is greatly concerned to claim Gentile approval for Judaism. In the *Letter of Aristeas*, the Ptolemy and his counselors are greatly impressed by the wisdom of the Jewish sages. *Aristeas* affirms that these people worship the same God that the Greeks know as Zeus, and the roughly contemporary Jewish philosopher Aristobulus affirms that the Greek poets refer to the true God by the same name. The Sibyl praises the Jews alone among the peoples of the earth. Philo, and later Josephus, is at pains to show that Jews exhibit the Greek virtue of *philanthrōpia*.

To some degree, Hellenistic Jewish authors wrote to counteract perceptions of Jews that circulated in the Hellenistic world (Berthelot 2003). Already at the beginning of the Hellenistic era, Hecataeus of Abdera wrote that Moses had introduced "a somewhat unsocial and inhospitable mode of life." He told a garbled story of Jewish origins which conflated the Jews with the Hyksos, the Syrian invaders of the second millennium B.C.E. whose memory in Egypt was accursed. The story was elaborated by the Egyptian historian Manetho. It is unlikely that either Manetho or Hecataeus knew the exodus story in its biblical form, or that either had more than an incidental interest in the Jews. The association of the Jews with this tradition was highly negative. Many of the negative stereotypes and calumnies of the Jews were collected by the Alexandrian grammarian Apion in the first century C.E. We owe their preservation, ironically, to the refutation by Josephus, in his tract *Against Apion*.

There has been a tendency in modern scholarship to find in this material the roots of anti-Semitism (Gager 1983; Schäfer 1997). But the portrayal of Jews was not uniformly negative (Feldman 1993: 177-287). Moses was often praised as a lawgiver, even already by Hecataeus. Moreover, we should bear in mind that the Jews were by no means the only ethnic group in the Hellenistic world who were subjected to ridicule (Isaac 2004). In the first century C.E., however, antagonism moved beyond ridicule to violence, in the form of a virtual pogrom in 38 C.E. Violent conflict would eventually consume the Jewish Egyptian community in the revolt under Trajan (Pucci ben Zeev 2005). The alleged anti-Semitism in Alexandria must be seen in the concrete historical and social circumstances of this conflict

Jews had prospered in Egypt in the Ptolemaic period, despite occasional tensions. Some had served as generals in Ptolemaic armies. Philo's family became wealthy bankers. In the Roman era, however, their fortunes declined, and there were pogroms in Alexandria in the time of Caligula and again in 66 C.E. The classic explanation of this conflict was offered by Tcherikover, who made good use of papyrological evidence (1959: 296-332; Tcherikover and Fuks 1957-1964; cf. Modrzejewski 1995). For purposes of taxation, the Romans drew a sharper line between citizen and noncitizen than was the case the Ptolemaic era. Jews responded by trying to infiltrate the gymnasium, as a way of attaining citizenship. The Alexandrians resisted, and conflict ensued. The evidence for this construction of events is admittedly fragile, as Erich Gruen especially has pointed out (Gruen 2002: 54-83). It is doubtful whether the Jews actually sought citizenship, which would presumably have entailed some acknowledgment of the Greek gods (Kasher 1985). Rather, they wanted a status equal to that of citizens. What is apparent is that the Roman conquest of Egypt intensified ethnic rivalry in Alexandria. The Alexandrian citizens were jealous of their diminished status. Jews resented being classified with Egyptians. The role of the Roman governor in manipulating the conflict for his own ends is less than clear. The details of the case are a subject of ongoing debate (Collins 2005: 181-201).

Diaspora Judaism, no less than its counterpart in the land of Israel, had its frame of reference in the Torah, which in its Greek translation is the great wellspring of Greco-Jewish literature. Many of the fragmentary writings can be described as parabiblical, even if they are cast in Greek forms. The retelling of the exodus in the form of a Greek tragedy by one Ezekiel is a case in point. There has been growing appreciation in recent years of the role of exegesis of the Torah as a unifying element across the full spectrum of ancient Judaism (Kugel 1998).

Egyptian Judaism, however, was distinctive in important ways. Philo, the greatest exegete of Alexandrian Judaism, viewed the Torah through a prism of Greek philosophy, which led to a very different understanding from anything we find in Hebrew or Aramaic sources. Few Alexandrian Jews would have shared Philo's philosophical sophistication, but virtually all the writings we have from this community use Greek literary forms and categories to appropriate the biblical tradition. In contrast to the Dead Sea Scrolls, the Diaspora literature makes minimal reference to halakhic issues or purity laws. It does, however, insist on Jewish monotheism, and frequently ridicules pagan idolatry. It also insists on the superiority of Jewish sexual ethics and the fact that Jews refrain from infanticide. These were matters which enlightened Greeks could, in principle, appreciate, and they are indicative of the self-image cultivated by Diaspora Jewry. Complete assimilation to the Gentile way of life certainly occurred. (The most famous example is Philo's nephew, Tiberius Julius Alexander, who became prefect of Egypt and assisted in putting down the Jewish revolt against Rome.) But the Jewish community as a whole preserved a distinct identity, even while embracing most aspects of Hellenistic culture other than idolatry. (On the degrees of assimilation and acculturation, see Barclay 1996.)

Conclusion

The story of modern scholarship on early Judaism is largely a story of retrieval. None of the literature of this period was preserved by the rabbis. The Greek literature of the Diaspora may not have been available to them. Much of the apocalyptic literature and of the material in the Dead Sea Scrolls was rejected for ideological reasons. The recovery of this literature in modern times presents us with a very different view of early Judaism than was current in the nineteenth century, and even than more recent accounts that impose a rabbinic paradigm on the period in the interests of normativity.

No doubt, our current picture of early Judaism is also incomplete. Despite the important documentary papyri from the Judean Desert dating to the Bar Kokhba period (Cotton in Oppenheimer, ed. 1999: 221-36), descriptions of the *realia* of Jewish life still rely heavily on rabbinic sources that are possibly anachronistic. The overdue study of women in this period is a case in point (Ilan 1995). One of the salutary lessons of the Dead Sea Scrolls is that they revealed aspects of Judaism that no one would have predicted before the discovery. And yet this was only the corpus of writings collected by one sect. To do justice to early Judaism we would need similar finds of Pharisaic, Sadducean, and other groups, and further documentary finds similar to those that have shed at least limited light on Egyptian Judaism and on Judah in the Bar Kokhba period.

BIBLIOGRAPHY

Barclay, John M. G. 1996. *Jews in the Mediterranean Diaspora.* Edinburgh: Clark.

Baumgarten, Albert I. 1997. *The Flourishing of Jewish Sects in the Maccabean Era: An Interpretation.* Leiden: Brill.

Beall, Todd S. 1988. *Josephus' Description of the Essenes Illustrated by the Dead Sea Scrolls.* Cambridge: Cambridge University.

Berthelot, Katell. 2003. *Philanthropia Judaica: Le débat autour de la 'misanthropie' des lois juives dans l'antiquité.* Leiden: Brill.

Bickerman, Elias J. 1937. *Der Gott der Makkabäer.* Berlin: Schocken.

Boccaccini, Gabriele. 1991. *Middle Judaism: Jewish Thought, 300 B.C.E.–200 C.E.* Minneapolis: Fortress.

———. 1998. *Beyond the Essene Hypothesis: The Parting of the Ways between Qumran and Enochic Judaism.* Grand Rapids: Eerdmans.

———, ed. 2005. *Enoch and Qumran Origins: New Light on a Forgotten Connection.* Grand Rapids: Eerdmans.

Boccaccini, Gabriele, and John J. Collins, eds. 2007. *The Early Enoch Literature.* Leiden: Brill.

Bousset, Wilhelm. 1903a. *Die Religion des Judentums in neutestamentlichen Zeitalter.* Berlin: Reuther und Reichard.

———. 1903b. *Volksfrömmigkeit und Schriftgelehrtentum: Antwort auf Herrn Perles' Kritik meiner 'Religion des Judentums im N.T. Zeitalter.'* Berlin: Reuther und Reichard.

Charles, R. H., ed. 1913. *The Apocrypha and Pseudepigrapha of the Old Testament.* 2 vols. Oxford: Clarendon.

Charlesworth, James H., ed. 1983-1985. *The Old Testament Pseudepigrapha.* 2 vols. New York: Doubleday.

Cohen, Shaye J. D. 1999. *The Beginnings of Jewishness: Boundaries, Varieties, Uncertainties.* Berkeley: University of California Press.

Collins, John J., ed. 1979. *Apocalypse: The Morphology of a Genre.* Semeia 14. Missoula, Mont.: Scholars Press.

———. 1997a. *Jewish Wisdom in the Hellenistic Age.* Louisville: Westminster John Knox.

———. 1997b. *Seers, Sibyls and Sages in Hellenistic-Roman Judaism.* Leiden: Brill.

———. 1997c. *Apocalypticism in the Dead Sea Scrolls.* London: Routledge.

———. 1998. *The Apocalyptic Imagination: An Introduction to Jewish Apocalyptic Literature.* Rev. ed. Grand Rapids: Eerdmans.

———. 2000. *Between Athens and Jerusalem: Jewish Identity in the Hellenistic Diaspora.* Rev. ed. Grand Rapids: Eerdmans.

———. 2005. *Jewish Cult and Hellenistic Culture: Essays on the Jewish Encounter with Hellenism and Roman Rule.* Leiden: Brill.

Cross, Frank Moore. 1995. *The Ancient Library of Qumran.* 3d ed. Sheffield: Sheffield Academic Press.

Davila, James R. 2005. *The Provenance of the Pseudepigrapha: Jewish, Christian, or Other?* Leiden: Brill.

Dimant, Devorah. 1994. "Apocalyptic Texts at Qumran." In *The Community of the Renewed Covenant: The Notre Dame Symposium on the Dead Sea Scrolls.* Ed. Eugene Ulrich and James VanderKam. Notre Dame: University of Notre Dame Press, 175-91.

Efron, Joshua. 1987. *Studies on the Hasmonean Period.* Leiden: Brill.

Fabricius, J. A. 1713. *Codex Pseudepigraphus Veteris Testamenti.* Leipzig: Liebezeit.

Falk, Daniel K. 1998. *Daily, Sabbath, and Festival Prayers in the Dead Sea Scrolls.* Leiden: Brill.

Feldman, Louis H. 1993. *Jew and Gentile in the Ancient World: Attitudes and Interactions from Alexander to Justinian.* Princeton: Princeton University Press.

Flint, Peter W., and James C. VanderKam, eds. 1998-1999. *The Dead Sea Scrolls after Fifty Years: A Comprehensive Assessment.* 2 vols. Leiden: Brill.

Gager, John G. 1985. *The Origins of Anti-Semitism: Attitudes toward Judaism in Pagan and Christian Antiquity.* Oxford: Oxford University Press.

Galor, Katharina, Jean-Baptiste Humbert, and Jürgen Zangenberg, eds. 2006. *Qumran: The Site of the Dead Sea Scrolls: Archaeological Interpretations and Debates.* Leiden: Brill.

Goff, Matthew J. 2007. *Discerning Wisdom: The Sapiential Literature of the Dead Sea Scrolls.* Leiden: Brill.

Golb, Norman. 1995. *Who Wrote the Dead Sea Scrolls? The Search for the Secret of Qumran.* New York: Scribner.

Goodman, Martin. 2002. "Jews and Judaism in the Second Temple Period." In *The Oxford Handbook of Jewish Studies.* Ed. M. Goodman. Oxford: Oxford University Press, 36-52.

Green, William S. 1994. "Ancient Judaism: Contours and Complexity." In *Language, Theology and the Bible: Essays in Honour of James Barr.* Ed. S. E. Balentine and J. Barton. Oxford: Oxford University Press, 293-310.

Gruen, Erich S. 1998. *Heritage and Hellenism: The Reinvention of Jewish Tradition.* Berkeley: University of California Press.

———. 2002. *Diaspora: Jews amidst Greeks and Romans.* Cambridge: Harvard University Press.

Harlow, Daniel C. 1996. *The Greek Apocalypse of Baruch (3 Baruch) in Hellenistic Judaism and Early Christianity.* Leiden: Brill.

Hellholm, David. 1983. *Apocalypticism in the Mediterranean World and the Near East.* Tübingen: Mohr-Siebeck.

Hengel, Martin. 1974. *Judaism and Hellenism: Studies in Their Encounter in Palestine in the Early Hellenistic Period.* 2 vols. Philadelphia: Fortress.

———. 1989. *The Hellenization of Judaea in the First Century after Christ.* Philadelphia: Trinity Press International.

———. 1990. "Der alte und der neue Schürer." *JSS* 35: 19-64.

Himmelfarb, Martha. 1993. *Ascent to Heaven in Jewish and Christian Apocalypses.* New York: Oxford.

Ilan, Tal. 1995. *Jewish Women in Greco-Roman Palestine: An Inquiry into Image and Status.* Tübingen: Mohr-Siebeck.

Isaac, Benjamin. 2004. *The Invention of Racism in Classical Antiquity.* Princeton: Princeton University Press.

Jonge, Marinus de. 1953. *The Testaments of the Twelve Patriarchs: A Study of Their Text Composition and Origin.* Assen: van Gorcum.

———. 2000. "The Testaments of the Twelve Patriarchs and Related Qumran Fragments." In *For a Later Generation: The Transformation of Tradition in Israel, Early Judaism and Early Christianity.* Ed. Randall A. Argall, Beverly A. Bow, and Rodney A. Werline. Harrisburg, Penn.: Trinity Press International, 63-77.

Kasher, Aryeh. 1985. *The Jews in Hellenistic and Roman Egypt.* Tübingen: Mohr-Siebeck.

Kautzsch, Emil. 1900. *Die Apokryphen und Pseudepigraphen des Alten Testaments.* Tübingen: Mohr.

Koch, Klaus. 1972. *The Rediscovery of Apocalyptic.* Naperville, Ill.: Allenson.

Kraemer, Ross S. 1998. *When Aseneth Met Joseph: A Late Antique Tale of the Biblical Patriarch and His Egyptian Wife, Reconsidered.* Oxford: Oxford University Press.

Kraft, Robert A. 1994. "The Pseudepigrapha in Christianity." In *Tracing the Threads: Studies in the Vitality of Jewish Pseudepigrapha.* Ed. John C. Reeves. Atlanta: Scholars Press, 55-86.

———. 2001. "The Pseudepigrapha and Christianity Revisited: Setting the Stage and Framing Some Central Questions." *JSJ* 32: 371-95.

Kugel, James L. 1998. *Traditions of the Bible: A Guide to the Bible As It Was at the Start of the Common Era.* Cambridge: Harvard University Press.

Kvanvig, Helge S. 1988. *Roots of Apocalyptic: The Mesopotamian Background of the Enoch Figure and of the Son of Man.* Neukirchen-Vluyn: Neukirchener Verlag.

Laurence, Richard. 1821. *The Book of Enoch the Prophet.* Oxford: Oxford University Press.

Levine, Lee. I. 1998. *Judaism and Hellenism in Antiquity: Conflict or Confluence?* Seattle: University of Washington Press.

Mason, Steve. 2007. "Jews, Judaeans, Judaizing, Judaism: Problems of Categorization in Ancient History." *JJS* 38: 457-512.

Metso, Sarianna. 1997. *The Textual Development of the Qumran Community Rule.* Leiden/New York: Brill.

Milik, J. T. 1976. *The Books of Enoch.* Oxford: Clarendon.

Modrzejewski, Joseph Mélèze. 1995. *The Jews of Egypt: From Rameses II to Emperor Hadrian.* Princeton: Princeton University Press.

Momigliano, Arnaldo. 1994. *Essays on Ancient and Modern Judaism.* Chicago: University of Chicago Press.

Moore, George Foote. 1921. "Christian Writers on Judaism." *HTR* 14: 197-254.

———. 1927-1930. *Judaism in the First Centuries of the Christian Era: The Age of the Tannaim.* 3 vols. Cambridge: Harvard University Press.

Najman, Hindy. 1999. *Seconding Sinai: The Development of Mosaic Discourse in Second Temple Judaism.* Leiden: Brill.

Neusner, Jacob. 1981. *Judaism: The Evidence of the Mishnah.* Chicago: University of Chicago Press.

———. 1984. *Das pharisäische und talmudische Judentum.* Ed. Hermann Lichtenberger. Tübingen: Mohr-Siebeck.

Neusner, Jacob, William S. Green, and Ernst Frerichs, eds. 1987. *Judaisms and Their Messiahs at the Turn of the Christian Era.* Cambridge: Cambridge University Press.

Nickelsburg, George W. E. 1998. "Enochic Wisdom: An Alternative to the Mosaic Torah?" In

Hesed ve-emet: Studies in Honor of Ernest S. Frerichs. Ed. Jodi Magness and Seymour Gitin. Atlanta: Scholars Press, 123-32.

———. 2005. *Jewish Literature between the Bible and the Mishnah.* 2d ed. Minneapolis: Fortress.

Nir, Rivkah. 2003. *The Destruction of Jerusalem and the Idea of Redemption in the Syriac Apocalypse of Baruch.* Atlanta: Society of Biblical Literature.

Nitzan, Bilhah. 1994. *Qumran Prayer and Religious Poetry.* Leiden: Brill.

Oppenheimer, Aharon, ed. 1999. *Jüdische Geschichte in hellenistisch-römischer Zeit: Wege der Forschung, Vom alten zum neuen Schürer.* Munich: Oldenbourg.

Perles, Felix. 1903. *Bousset's* Religion des Judentums im neutestamentlichen Zeitalter *kritisch untersucht.* Berlin: Peiser.

Porter, F. C. 1928. Review of *Judaism in the First Centuries of the Christian Era: The Age of the Tannaim* by G. F. Moore in *Journal of Religion* 8: 30-62.

Pucci ben Zeev, Miriam. 2005. *Diaspora Judaism in Turmoil, 116/117 CE: Ancient Sources and Modern Insights.* Leuven: Peeters.

Qimron, Elisha, and John Strugnell. 1994. *Qumran Cave 4, V. Miqṣat Maʿaśê Ha-Torah.* DJD 10. Oxford: Clarendon.

Rad, Gerhard von. 1965. *Theologie des Alten Testament.* 4th ed. Munich: Kaiser.

Riessler, Paul. 1928. *Altjüdisches Schrifttum ausserhalb der Bibel.* Augsburg: Filer.

Rowland, Christopher. 1983. *The Open Heaven: A Study of Apocalyptic in Judaism and Early Christianity.* New York: Crossroad.

Rowley, H. H. 1944. *The Relevance of Apocalyptic.* London: Athlone.

Sacchi, Paolo. 1997. *Jewish Apocalyptic and Its History.* Sheffield: Sheffield Academic Press.

Sanders, E. P. 1977. *Paul and Palestinian Judaism.* Philadelphia: Fortress.

———. 1985. *Jesus and Judaism.* Philadelphia: Fortress.

———. 1990. *Jewish Law from Jesus to the Mishnah.* London: SCM.

———. 1992. *Judaism: Practice and Belief, 63 BCE–66 CE.* Philadelphia: Trinity Press International.

Schäfer, Peter. 1997. *Judeophobia: Attitudes toward the Jews in the Ancient World.* Cambridge: Harvard University Press.

Schiffman, L. H. 1999. "Halakha and History: The Contribution of the Dead Sea Scrolls to Recent Scholarship." In *Jüdische Geschichte.* Ed. A. Oppenheimer. Munich: Oldenbourg, 205-19.

Schürer, Emil. 1886-1911. *Geschichte des jüdischen Volkes im Zeitalter Jesu Christi.* 2 vols. Leipzig: Hinrichs (1886-1890; 3d ed., 3 vols., 1898-1901; 4th ed., 1901-1909, with index volume, 1911; English translation of 3d ed.: *A History of the Jewish People in the Time of Jesus Christ,* 3 vols., Edinburgh: Clark, 1890-1893).

Schwartz, Seth. 2001. *Imperialism and Jewish Society, 200 B.C.E. to 640 C.E.* Princeton: Princeton University Press.

Segal, Michael. 2007. *The Book of Jubilees: Rewritten Bible, Redaction, Ideology and Theology.* Leiden: Brill.

Stone, Michael E., ed. 1984. *Jewish Literature of the Second Temple Period.* Assen: Van Gorcum; Philadelphia: Fortress.

Tcherikover, Victor. 1956. "Jewish Apologetic Literature Reconsidered." *Eos* 48: 169-93.

———. 1959. *Hellenistic Civilization and the Jews.* Philadelphia: Jewish Publication Society.

Tcherikover, Victor, and Alexander Fuks. 1957-64. *Corpus Papyrorum Judaicarum.* 3 vols. Cambridge: Harvard University Press.

VanderKam, James C. 2010. *The Dead Sea Scrolls Today.* Rev. ed. Grand Rapids: Eerdmans.

Vermes, Geza et al., eds. 1973-1987. *The History of the Jewish People in the Age of Jesus Christ (175 B.C.–A.D. 135) by Emil Schürer: A New English Edition Revised and Edited.* 3 vols., vol. 3 in 2 parts. Edinburgh: Clark.

Wacholder, Ben Zion. 1983. *The Dawn of Qumran: The Sectarian Torah and the Teacher of Righteousness.* Cincinnati: Hebrew Union College.

Weinfeld, Moshe. 1986. *The Organizational Pattern and the Penal Code of the Qumran Sect.* Göttingen: Vandenhoeck & Ruprecht.

Wiese, Christian. 2005. *Challenging Colonial Discourse: Jewish Studies and Protestant Theology in Wilhelmine Germany.* Trans. B. Harshav and C. Wiese. Leiden: Brill.

Wise, Michael O. 1990. *A Critical Study of the Temple Scroll from Qumran Cave 11.* Chicago: Oriental Institute.

Yadin, Yigael. 1977. *Megillat ha-Miqdash.* 3 vols. Jerusalem: Israel Exploration Society.

———. 1983. *The Temple Scroll.* 3 vols. Jerusalem: Israel Exploration Society.

Jewish History from Alexander to Hadrian

From Alexander to Pompey

CHRIS SEEMAN

The conquests of Alexander the Great had far-reaching consequences for the Jews. In the course of a single decade (334-324 B.C.E.), Jewish communities everywhere found themselves subjects of a new world empire ruled by Macedonians and connected with Greek culture. Macedonian monarchs would continue to dominate the Near East for the next three centuries, while Hellenism itself would cast a still longer shadow over the region and its peoples.

These new realities carried with them both peril and prospect for the Jews of Asia Minor, the Levant, Egypt, Mesopotamia, and Iran. The inability of Alexander's successors to hold together his far-flung dominions condemned those lands to chronic interstate warfare and incessant dynastic instability. Physical displacement, economic hardship, political factionalism, enslavement, and other woes are prominent themes of this era. But Jews could also benefit from the opportunities created by so volatile an environment. Some found ready employment in the military and bureaucratic sectors of the Hellenistic states. Others engaged in interregional trade networks and participated in the cosmopolitan life of Greek cities. By the second half of the first century B.C.E., the Hasmoneans were able to forge a sovereign, Jewish state in Palestine — the first in almost 500 years. The Hellenistic age brought Jews into contact with a wider world; it also brought them to the notice of that world. When the Roman general Pompey set foot in Palestine in 63 B.C.E., the Jews had become a people to be reckoned with.

Before Alexander

Before the conquests of Alexander, all Jews (so far as we are aware) resided within the confines of the Persian Empire. Stretching from Anatolia in the west to Afghanistan in the east and from the Caspian steppe in the north to Upper Egypt in the south, the multiethnic domain of the Achaemenid dynasty sustained numerous Jewish communities. Most of these are known to us only through indirect or retrospective testimony. Thus, our present understanding of Jewish life on the eve of Alexander's conquests is imperfect, especially outside of Palestine.

An obscure biblical allusion and a stray Aramaic inscription *may* attest to a Jewish presence in Asia Minor before Alexander, but their interpretation and dating are contested. In the absence of stronger evidence, it is more defensible to treat the Jewish settlement of western Anatolia as a Hellenistic development.

The Babylonian Diaspora is a major focus of the prophetic corpus of the Hebrew Bible. The later flowering of talmudic culture in that region spawned a wealth of traditions concerning the Jews of Mesopotamia. But the historicity of the latter is often suspect, and the former deals mostly with the Neo-Babylonian period. This gap in reliable testimony is partly remedied by economic documents that locate individual Jews (as well as at least one predominantly Jewish town) in the Babylon-Borsippa and Nippur regions. As yet, there is no cuneiform evidence for a Jewish presence in the city of Babylon itself during Achaemenid times.

Less certain still is the extent of pre-Hellenistic Jewish penetration of lands of the Zagros arc — Armenia, Adiabene, Media, Elam — or the vast Iranian plateau beyond. Late antique sources attest to an Achaemenid deportation of Jews to distant Hyrcania around 340 B.C.E., and the subsequent appearance of "Hyrcanus" as a Jewish name has been cited as corroboration for this tradition. It is possible, however, that the alleged deportation has been chronologically misplaced and that it actually happened six centuries later.

The geopolitical situation of Palestine has traditionally linked it with Egypt. The Bible is rife with references to pro-Egyptian factions collaborating with allies on the Nile. Such interstate cooperation appears to have supplied the occasion for the emergence of a Jewish military colony at Elephantine (Yeb) in Upper Egypt. Although there were certainly other Jewish settlements in Egypt, the Elephantine garrison is the only one whose persistence into Achaemenid times has been verified by papyri. Unfortunately, this documentation peters out by the end of the fifth century B.C.E. One Hellenistic text, the largely fictional *Letter of Aristeas,* claims additional colonists settled in Egypt with the advent of Persian rule, but no precise chronology is offered. Still, it is a reasonable inference that there were Jews living in Egypt at the time of Alexander's capture of that country in 332 B.C.E. The pattern of military settlement certainly continued under Macedonian rule.

We are better informed about Palestinian Jewry than any other, though the picture remains woefully incomplete. Survey archaeology has revealed a gradual demographic expansion during late Achaemenid times, as well as significant commercial involvement with the Greek world via the Phoenician coast. Recent excavations on Mt. Gerizim have firmly dated the construction of a Samaritan temple there to the mid-fifth century, though it remains unclear whether or to what extent this event reflects the developed Jewish-Samaritan rivalry of the Hellenistic period.

The wars of Alexander and his successors undoubtedly disrupted Jewish life in the late fourth century, but the core areas of Jewish settlement persisted and, in time, expanded. By the time of Pompey, Jews could be found not only within the lands of the former Persian Empire, but also in the Aegean, the Greek mainland, North Africa, even the city of Rome. The consolidation of the Hasmonean state in the late second and early first centuries extended Jewish settlement (or at least control) over much of Palestine, transforming Judea from a minute, land-locked, temple community into a major regional power. In Achaemenid times, many Jews — perhaps a majority — inhabited the hinterlands of the great urban centers of the Near East. This was to change during the age of Alexander. In the course of the Hellenistic period, many Jews would be drawn to the Greek *polis* and would absorb and appropriate its culture (selectively) as their own. This development, more than any other, propelled the creative genius of early Judaism.

Alexander and the Diadochoi

The principal Greek and Roman historians who chronicled the campaigns of Alexander make no mention of the Jews, who appear to have played little or no active role in the titanic clashes of that decisive decade. The first-century-B.C.E. Jewish historian, Flavius Josephus, conjures up a very different picture. In his account, Alexander visited Jerusalem after his capture of Gaza in 332, attributed his victories to the favor of the Jewish god, guaranteed all Jews the right to live by their ancestral laws, and invited any who wished to join the Macedonians in their war against Persia (*Ant.* 11.325-39). Hecataeus of Abdera (or, more likely, a Jewish pseudepigrapher writing in his name) preserves episodes involving Jewish soldiers in Alexander's forces (*apud* Josephus, *Ag. Ap.* 1.192, 200-204). Although judged to be fictional by most scholars, these and other imaginative reconstructions reflect the fact that Jews did serve in the armies of the Hellenistic monarchies.

Alexander died in 323 without a viable heir and apparently without any clear instructions for choosing one. The result was a series of ultimately unsuccessful attempts by his former companions to prevent the fragmentation of Alexander's realm. The rival maneuverings of these generals, collectively dubbed the Diadochoi ("Successors") by later historians, turned the lands of the Near East into an incessant battleground. The loss of Alexander's natural kin to attrition removed the Macedonian royal house as a putative object of common allegiance, impelling each of the Diadochoi in turn to proclaim himself king. The failure of the strongest of these to achieve ascendancy over his rivals at the Battle of Ipsus in 301 B.C.E. precipitated a division of territory that would eventually harden into three relatively stable monarchies: Antigonid Greece, Seleucid Asia, and Ptolemaic Egypt.

References to Jewish fortunes during the early wars of the Diadochoi are sparse. The Alexandrian historian Agatharchides of Cnidus relates that Ptolemy I captured Jerusalem, probably in 312 B.C.E. (*apud* Josephus, *Ag. Ap.* 1.209-11; cf.

Ant. 12.6). The *Letter of Aristeas* states that Ptolemy enslaved some of its inhabitants and relocated others to Egypt, absorbing roughly a third of the latter into his defense forces. *Aristeas'* numbers (100,000 deportees) are clearly exaggerated; but even if the story oversimplifies a more complicated series of population transfers, it surely reflects at least one source of Egypt's Jewish population during the early Hellenistic period. Josephus also claims Jews served in the armies of Seleucus I (ruled 305-281) and were rewarded with citizenship in the cities he founded (*Ant.* 12.119). As with the Ptolemaic tales, this tradition smacks of retrospection by later Jewish inhabitants of these cities — especially those of the Seleucid capital at Antioch (*Ant.* 12.120-24). A precise chronology of early Jewish settlement within the Ptolemaic and Seleucid realms is not recoverable.

The Third Century

The Ptolemaic Empire dominates the historical record of Jewish life in the third century B.C.E. From the Battle of Ipsus until the Seleucid seizure of Palestine in 198, roughly half the world's Jews were subjects of the House of Ptolemy. (Of the other half, we possess virtually no evidence for this period.) From an Egyptian core, centered on the maritime metropolis of Alexandria, the Ptolemies projected their power across the eastern Mediterranean. Cyrenaica, Cyprus, Crete, the islands of the Aegean, the coasts of Anatolia and the Levant, along with much of the Syrian and Palestinian hinterlands, all felt the hand of Ptolemaic rule.

Egypt itself provides the greatest wealth of documentation for Jews in the Ptolemaic realm. Third-century papyri reveal Jewish military settlements in the Fayyum, while funerary inscriptions from the vicinity of Alexandria indicate an early concentration of Jews there. This picture is reinforced by inscriptions from Schedia and Arsinoe-Crocodilopolis dedicating prayer houses to Ptolemy III (ruled 246-221 B.C.E.). The presence of one such building at Schedia on the Nile may also lend some credence to Josephus' claim that Jews had been involved in official oversight of river traffic (*Ag. Ap.* 2.64).

The vexed and ultimately insoluble problem of dating the *Letter of Aristeas* need not detain us. Most scholars conjecture a late second- or early first-century-B.C.E. setting; but whatever the date of its creation, *Aristeas* must have postdated (probably by several generations) the actual event of the Pentateuch's translation into Greek. Since there is no convincing reason to question Alexandria as the site of the translation, we may infer that, by the end of the third century, the Ptolemaic capital supported a Greek-speaking Jewish population numerous enough to warrant such an extensive undertaking. It is unnecessary to account for the existence of this community by any single event or cause. A century of Ptolemaic rule, along with the city's economic importance, is sufficient grounds for Alexandria's reputation as the largest urban Jewish settlement of the Hellenistic age.

The Libyan pentapolis of Cyrenaica was incorporated into the Ptolemaic realm already by the late fourth century. Predictably, Josephus attributes the origins of Jewish presence there to an act of Ptolemy I, bent on consolidating his hold over this tenuous frontier (*Ag. Ap.* 2.44). More substantial testimony for Jewish habitation of North Africa emerges only in the first century B.C.E., and so can tell us little about its possible beginnings two hundred years earlier (*Ant.* 14.115).

As for Jewish settlement elsewhere in the Ptolemaic Empire (apart from Palestine), we have no direct third-century evidence. The book of 1 Maccabees, probably composed in the late second century B.C.E., contains a list of cities and countries, including Cyrene and many other communities that fell within the zone of Ptolemaic hegemony (1 Macc. 15:22-23). This list, which refers to a Roman request that the addressees extradite any Jews who may be seeking asylum among them, has sometimes been construed as evidence for Jewish habitation in those places. This, however, is neither stated nor implied in the passage, which is itself historically suspect. It is possible that Jews penetrated the islands and coasts of the Ptolemaic-controlled Mediterranean by this time or earlier, but firmer statements to this effect must await new discoveries.

Our two primary sources for the history of Ptolemaic Palestine itself are Josephus and the so-called Zenon Papyri. Numismatic and archaeological data contribute to the assessment of this written testimony but also complicate its interpretation. Josephus' narrative focuses upon the fortunes of the Tobiads, a clan of Jewish notables who achieved prominence as collaborators and mediators of Ptolemaic rule. These colorful tales depict Judea as a distinct ethnic unit within Palestine whose tributary relations with Alexandria are mediated by the high priest in Jerusalem — until, that is, this role is transferred to the Tobiads. Tensions with his countrymen (possibly coincident with the conquest of Palestine by the Seleucids) eventually prompt Hyrcanus, one scion of the family, to withdraw to Transjordan, where he establishes himself as an independent strongman (*Ant.* 12.154-222).

Josephus' account suffers from historical inaccuracies, and many features of the Tobiad cycle are patently folkloric. The Zenon Papyri, a dossier detailing the economic activities of an agent of the chief finance minister for Ptolemy II, reveals a much more centrally controlled fiscal regime than that envisioned by Josephus. Being occasional by its very nature, Zenon's correspondence can offer only vignettes of Ptolemaic Palestine, not a comprehensive panorama. No reference is made in them, for example, to the high priest (or the Tobiads) as the nexus of Ptolemaic administration. Strikingly, though, one papyrus does verify a Tobiad military presence in Transjordan a half century prior to Hyrcanus' settling in that region. Excavations have positively identified 'Araq el-Emir and its environs with the fortified estate Josephus attributes to Hyrcanus (and possibly with the military colony of Hyrcanus' ancestor, Tobias, associated by Zenon with "Birta in Ammanitis"). But scholarly consensus on the chronology of the surviving structures has yet to be achieved. What does emerge with certainty is that the institution of military settlement continued to be an important anchor for Macedonian control in the region, and that Jews could and did acquire power and prominence in other areas of life through that initial channel.

Another avenue of inquiry into the history of third-century Palestine is afforded by coinage. A series of small silver denomination, dubbed by numismatists "Yehud coins," crosscuts the boundary between the Persian and Hellenistic eras, and is coextensive with the period of Ptolemaic rule. Two features of these coins have attracted historical notice. The first is the fact that the name of the local governor (who apparently had acted as the minting authority under the Persians) disappears from the third-century issues. This absence, combined with the centrality of high priests in the literary sources, has led many to the conclusion that the Jewish high priest assumed an enlarged secular role under the Ptolemies. In addition to the *Letter of Aristeas* and the Tobiad romance, other texts referential to this period (1 Macc. 12:20-23; Sirach 50; 3 Maccabees 2; Hecataeus *apud* Diodorus 40.3.5-6) are unanimous in presenting the high priest as representative and leader of the Jewish people. These portraits may well be idealized, but the presumption that they reflect some degree of reality remains a defensible hypothesis. The modification of the coin legend *Yehud* to *Yehudah* on the later groups may indicate an administrative reorganization (perhaps during the reign of Ptolemy II). Advocates of the high priest-as-political-leader thesis often see the coins as indirect corroboration that the office was melding into a combination of cultic, diplomatic, and municipal roles. Enticing as these theories are, the numismatic evidence remains mute and therefore amenable to other interpretations. Whatever else they may point to, the coins do reveal that the coming of Ptolemaic rule did not involve a total break with existing institutions.

But Ptolemaic rule was not to last. Seleucus I's claim upon the lands of the Levant was never forgotten by his heirs, who, over the course of the third century, launched no fewer than five successive campaigns to recover the region. The last of these, fought between 202 and 198, definitively wrested Palestine from the Ptolemies, ushering in a century of Seleucid dominance.

Antiochus III

With the reign of Antiochus III (223-187 B.C.E.), Jewish history became inextricably bound up with the fortunes of the Seleucid dynasty. When he came to power, Antiochus presided over a failing empire. Challenged internally by secessionist forces and confined from without by Ptolemy IV, the young monarch spent the better part of two decades reconsolidating Seleucid hegemony over Syria, Asia Minor, Mesopotamia, Iran, and central Asia. Jews appear to have played some role in this process. Josephus reproduces the text of a letter announcing Antiochus' decision to transplant 2,000 Jewish families from Mesopotamia and Babylonia to western Asia Minor, in hopes of establishing a loyalist presence in the rebellious satrapies of Phrygia and Lydia (*Ant.* 12.148-53).

The letter is not dated but cannot have been penned earlier than 213, the year Antiochus completed his reduction of Anatolia and began turning his attention to eastern affairs. If authentic, it supplies the earliest unambiguous testimony for Jewish settlement here. It also implies that Antiochus had reason to trust the Jewish communities of Babylonia and Mesopotamia. The justifications offered in the letter, however, are less than convincing (devotion to their God and loyalty toward the king's forefathers), prompting some to regard the document as a pious fiction — but one undoubtedly concocted by Jewish inhabitants of the regions mentioned. (Other documents in Josephus relating to Asia Minor in the late second and mid-first century B.C.E. provide ample evidence for Jews living there.)

The death of Ptolemy IV in 204 B.C.E. offered Antiochus a window of opportunity to recapture the southern Levant (which he had been forced to evacuate after an abortive conquest a decade and a half earlier). The details of the Fifth Syrian War that followed are imperfectly known. For the Jews of Palestine, the decisive turning point was the Battle of Panion (200 B.C.E.), which put Ptolemaic forces on the run. Subsequent coastal victories over Sidon (199) and Gaza (198) sealed Seleucid control over the region. According to Polybius (*apud* Josephus, *Ant.* 12.136), Jerusalem was captured soon after Panion, the Jews having assisted Antiochus in dislodging the city's Egyptian garrison (*Ant.* 12.138).

Josephus adduces two documents of Antiochus regarding Jerusalem and its people in the aftermath of Panion. The first promises royal financial underwriting for the Temple service and its physical repair from damages suffered in the conflict, mandates restoration to their homes of war captives and other displaced persons, guarantees the Jews shall live according to their traditional laws, exempts Temple personnel and other notables from certain taxes, and offers partial remission of tribute until the city and its hinterland recover from the ravages of war (*Ant.* 12.138-44). The second document asserts the sanctity of the Temple and its city, upholding purity regulations defined by "the ancestral law" and prescribing a fine to be paid in the event of their violation (*Ant.* 12.145-46).

The first of these documents is presented as a letter from Antiochus to a "Ptolemy" (probably to be identified with the Seleucid governor of Coele-Syria and Phoenicia attested in other contemporary sources). Its historicity is today generally accepted on the grounds that it conforms in most respects to known patterns of Seleucid beneficence. The second document is more problematic because it lacks a preamble identifying the king as its author. Some of the prohibitions it mandates find echoes in the *Temple Scroll* from Qumran (thought to have been composed half a century later). If Antiochus did promulgate such a decree, its stipulations were clearly governed by Jewish conceptualities, rather than conventional Hellenistic notions of temple inviolability.

Having secured his southern frontier against Egypt, Antiochus trained his gaze westward to the remaining Ptolemaic dependencies along the coasts of Anatolia. But his ambitions went beyond neutralizing the Ptolemaic Empire. In that same year (197), the Romans defeated Philip V of Macedon, erstwhile hegemon of Antigonid Greece. Stepping into this political vacuum, Antiochus crossed the Hellespont in 196 and began projecting Seleucid power into Europe. Four years later, the king's involvement in Greece precipitated war with Rome. Repulsed by Roman arms, Antiochus withdrew to Asia, where he was defeated at the Battle of Magnesia late in 190. Two years later, the humbled monarch ratified the Peace of Apamea, whose terms included a sizable war-indemnity, the transfer to Rome of royal hostages as surety for the king's good behavior, and a total ban on military involvement in Anatolia or Europe.

Antiochus himself died the following year on campaign in the east. But the terms of Apamea remained in force, and would have a significant impact on Seleucid relations with Judea for the next twenty-five years. The imperative to raise money to pay off annual installments of the indemnity frequently strained Seleucid resources. It may be that the attempt by Seleucus IV (Antiochus' son and successor) to plunder the Jerusalem Temple treasury a decade after Apamea reflects these pressures (2 Maccabees 3). The shadow of Apamea undoubtedly also increased the willingness of Antiochus' descendants to accept monetary bribes from rival Jewish aspirants to the high priestly office, setting a precedent that would persist even after the indemnity was paid off. Another long-term effect of Apamea on Jewish-Seleucid relations was the political instability it engendered. The treaty's stipulation that a scion of the House of Seleucus be held hostage in Rome created, in effect, a potential usurper "waiting in the wings." Dynastic rivalry resulting from this heightened the claimants' need to solicit support from their subjects. The factionalism fueled by this dynamic would prove to be one of the central engines of Jewish history during the second half of the second century B.C.E.

Antiochus IV

Upon the death of Seleucus IV, his younger brother Antiochus IV seized power. Our principal source for Jewish history during the early years of the new Antiochus' reign is 2 Maccabees, which focuses on events in Palestine. Central to this narrative is the Seleucid-backed acquisition of the high priesthood by two successive candidates, and the civil strife ensuing from their rivalry. The first of these, Jason, secured not only the high priesthood but also the king's permission "to establish, through his authority, a gymnasium and an *ephebeion,* and to enroll the Antiochenes in Jerusalem" (2 Macc. 4:9). Having been granted these requests in exchange for a hefty donation to the royal coffers, Jason proceeded to promote a Greek way of life in Jerusalem among "the noblest of the young men" and among his fellow priests (2 Macc. 4:11-15).

No scholarly consensus exists as to the meaning of the petition concerning "the Antiochenes in Jerusalem." This group is mentioned on only one other occasion, in the context of a delegation sent by Jason to an athletic competition held in the Phoenician city of Tyre (2 Macc. 4:19). The dominant view is that Jason was requesting a Greek city to be founded within Jerusalem ("Antioch in Jerusalem"), and that the ephebic institutions he established were intended for the training of a citizen body for the new *polis.* This interpretation trades on Antiochus' attested reputation elsewhere in the empire as a *ktistēs* (city-founder). However, given its unusual wording, other readings of this line are possible. Whatever the nature of Jason's actions as high priest, the key historical issue is whether these actions contributed to the political strife that erupted a decade later.

It is not at all obvious that they did. When Jason's high-priestly tenure was terminated three years later by the bribe of one Menelaus, the author of 2 Maccabees attributes this to the latter's corruption, not to any dissatisfaction with Jason's policies (4:23-25). Having lost royal support, Jason took refuge in Transjordan, leaving Menelaus in possession of the high priesthood. For his part, Menelaus, finding himself unable to pay off his royal patron by legitimate means, consolidated his position (so the hostile narrative claims) by doling out Temple vessels as gifts to

Seleucid officials and neighboring cities, and by engineering the murder of Onias when the ex-high priest threatened to expose his sacrilege (2 Macc. 4:32-34). Nefariousness, not Hellenism, appears to have motivated Menelaus' behavior.

During the winter of 170/169, Antiochus invaded Egypt, preemptively halting Ptolemaic designs to recapture his Levantine possessions. By the following summer, the king controlled most of Lower Egypt and had installed a pliant youth on the throne. But this détente swiftly deteriorated, prompting a second Seleucid invasion in 168. Though victorious in battle, Antiochus was compelled to call off the campaign under threat of Roman intervention.

In the course of his contest with Egypt, Antiochus paid two visits to Jerusalem that seriously tried the allegiance of his Jewish subjects. The first involved a fleecing of the Temple's adornments, probably with a view to replenishing the king's war chest in the wake of his Egyptian expedition. The second visitation came in response to a violent upheaval among the Jews themselves. While the king was occupied with Egypt, the ex-high priest, Jason, marched against Jerusalem at the head of an army, intent on deposing Menelaus and his supporters (an objective he failed to achieve). Antiochus, unable or unwilling to discriminate aggressors from defenders, brought down bloody slaughter upon Jerusalem. Not long after this debacle, the king dispatched a sizeable force to garrison Jerusalem indefinitely, an event (according to our hostile sources) accompanied by gratuitous violence and brutality. Menelaus remained in power, guarded by the Seleucid garrison (the "Akra"), which also came to serve as a place of refuge for Jewish loyalists of Antiochus' regime.

Some scholars are skeptical of the Maccabean narrative, contending that the king's repressive measures are unintelligible, unless the Jerusalemites as a whole had in fact attempted to cast off Seleucid rule. The absence of direct testimony for such a revolt necessarily renders any speculation moot. Yet even if the revolt hypothesis were substantiated, it would not account for Antiochus' actions following his installation of the Akra: the suppression of Judaism itself. A litany of horrors describing this unparalleled persecution are paraded in both Maccabean accounts: the Temple and its worship were profaned in every conceivable way, its altar rededicated to Olympian Zeus; other altars were erected throughout Judea and cultic celebrations prescribed in honor of Dionysus and the king's birthday; Torah scrolls were burned, and anyone found in possession of one or abiding by its laws was put to death (1 Macc. 1:41-61; 2 Macc. 6:1-11). According to 2 Maccabees, similar resolutions were adopted by the neighboring coastal town of Ptolemais (2 Macc. 6:8-9).

The Maccabean tradition offers no credible explanation for this unprecedented revolution in Seleucid policy. Second Maccabees simply casts Antiochus into the biblical mold of the arrogant tyrant who unwittingly executes God's judgment upon rebellious Israel. First Maccabees alleges a royal decree, addressed to all Seleucid subjects, demanding "that all become one people, and that each abandon his [own] customs" (1 Macc. 1:41-42). If Antiochus ever issued such a decree, its implementation is nowhere in evidence (except, of course, in Judea itself). In fact, nowhere in either account is there any insinuation that the king's suppression of Judaism extended to Jews living elsewhere in the Seleucid realm. Whatever the motivation for the Antiochene persecution, Palestine was its sole focus.

The persecution itself lasted approximately three years. Jewish responses ranged from outright collaboration with (or acquiescence in) the king's policies, to passive noncooperation, to willing martyrdom or militant resistance. The last of these take center stage in the Maccabean accounts, making it difficult to analyze the others. In particular, the tradition downplays the role of Menelaus and his supporters in bringing the persecution to an end through negotiation, a development attested in a dossier of letters preserved in 2 Maccabees. The Maccabean narrative focuses instead upon the purification and rededication of the Temple half a year later and continued Jewish (i.e., Maccabean) dissatisfaction with the Seleucid-backed high priesthood.

Antiochus himself did not personally preside over the Judean theater for long. Financial pressures and the imperative to reassert Seleucid sovereignty over the eastern satrapies drew him away in 165; he named his under-aged son, Antiochus V, coruler under the supervision of a guardian, Lysias. Cuneiform sources confirm that Antiochus IV died on campaign in the east near the end of the following year. News of the king's death precipitated the first of many succession struggles that would influence Judean affairs for the next half century.

The Maccabean Revolt

Armed resistance to Antiochus IV's decrees quickly gravitated around the priestly family of Hashmonay (hence, "Hasmoneans"). Following the death of the family's patriarch Mattathias in 166, his son Judas Maccabaeus assumed leadership of the insurgency. Over the next two years, Judas distinguished himself in battle against local Seleucid commanders. But it was not until 164 that Lysias himself undertook a full-scale expedition to stamp out the revolt. The Seleucid vizier combined his military efforts against Judas with diplomatic overtures toward other Jewish groups. In spite of the success of these negotiations, Judas fought on.

On the military front, Lysias' expedition failed to achieve its goal. He besieged Judas in the strategic town of Beth Zur, but withdrew to Antioch before taking it. This withdrawal enabled Judas to enter Jerusalem and take control of the Temple Mount, which he appointed priests to cleanse and rededicate. The joint decision by "Judas and his brothers and all the assembly of Israel" (1 Macc. 4:59) to commemorate the event as an annual festival, and his garrisoning of Jerusalem and Beth Zur, indicate that by the end of 164 Judas had acquired recognition by a significant segment of his countrymen.

The death of Antiochus IV constrained Lysias to devote the better part of the following year to consolidating his power as guardian of the royal heir. This respite gave Judas and his brothers an opportunity to launch expeditions into the surrounding territories where Jews were a vulnerable minority in need of protection. One result of these raids was the relocation of Jewish refugees to Judea, thus increasing Judas' reservoir of potential recruits for his growing forces. Early in 162, Judas felt his position strong enough to launch a direct attack against the Akra.

This bold move provoked Lysias to lead a substantial force into Judea in May of that year with the boy-king Antiochus V in tow. Judas' forces were overwhelmed and forced to retreat, while Lysias and the king pressed on to Jerusalem and besieged the Temple Mount. Within two months, however, news of an insurrection at Antioch by a rival general brought the siege to a standstill. A truce with the Temple's defenders was affected, but Judas' fortifications were demolished. The absence of Judas from 1 Maccabees' narrative of events following his defeat by Lysias is conspicuous. Second Maccabees claims he was received by the king in conjunction with the truce; but this account also denies that Judas was defeated, thus casting suspicion on its reliability. Either way, the events of 162 were a setback for the Maccabean movement.

The deterioration of Judas' position continued. Later that same year, a new aspirant to the Seleucid throne, Demetrius I, seized power in Syria and executed Lysias along with Antiochus V. This abrupt regime change prompted an embassy from the Jews led by one Alcimus, who obtained from Demetrius the high priesthood (Menelaus having been done away with by Antiochus V). Alcimus received military assistance in subjugating Judas and his agitators. This precipitated a series of military engagements between Syrian forces and Alcimus' Jewish opponents, culminating in Judas' death in the spring of 161.

It was in the midst of these campaigns, immediately following a dramatic victory over Demetrius' general, Nicanor, that Judas is said to have sent an embassy to Rome seeking friendship and alliance. According to 1 Maccabees, the Senate acceded to Judas' request, conferring a treaty of mutual assistance and delivering a heated letter of condemnation to Demetrius (1 Macc. 8:23-31). The authenticity of the treaty and its attendant letter has had its share of detractors, but there are no persuasive reasons for rejecting either document out of hand. The more pertinent question is why Judas would have appealed to Rome in the first place. Second Maccabees reports the involvement of Roman envoys in negotiations conducted between Lysias and the Jews three years earlier, but their role appears to have been marginal (2 Macc. 11:34-38); it supplied no obvious precedent for Judas' action in 161. Nor is it likely that Judas seriously expected Roman arms to defend the Maccabean cause. A more plausible interpretation would see the overture as a propaganda ploy on Judas' part to shore up his claim to act as representative and defender of the Jewish people. Conversely, a senatorial rebuke of Demetrius, casting him in the role of aggressor, would serve to discredit Alcimus' regime. Whatever its intent, Judas' Roman mission had no tangible impact on the ground. It did, however, set in motion a tradition of diplomacy that Judas' successors would intermittently draw upon as part of their arsenal of legitimation.

Alcimus died (seemingly of natural causes) not long after Judas' own demise. Demetrius made no move to appoint a new high priest, and apparently no candidates stepped forward. This anomalous state of affairs would persist for seven years, indicating that the contending Jewish factions had reached some kind of stalemate. During this period, Judas' surviving supporters gathered around his brother Jonathan, who continued to agitate the status quo. The stalemate broke down around 158, when Jonathan's enemies summoned a Seleucid force to eliminate his guerilla band. The plan backfired when the commander of this force made peace with Jonathan and returned to Antioch. But the position of the Maccabean group did not change dramatically until 153.

In that year, the rule of Demetrius was challenged by a pretender, Alexander Balas, who established himself at Ptolemais. This development strategically positioned Judea as a potential asset to both contenders. Jonathan exploited the situation, eventually siding with Balas, who appointed him high priest and friend of the king. Alexander's final victory over Demetrius in 152 or 151 further strengthened Jonathan's authority as a Seleucid appointee, securing him immunity from domestic rivals. Subsequent struggles for the Seleucid throne over the next decade replayed this scenario. For Jonathan, the downfall of one monarch merely meant the prospect of new honors from the next. Local "renegades" occasionally attempted to stir up trouble for him, but they could be dealt with by bribery. In short, Jonathan maintained his legitimacy through exactly the same methods employed by his high-priestly predecessors — Jason, Menelaus, and Alcimus. Jonathan is often thought to be the "Wicked Priest" referred to in the biblical commentaries *(pesharim)* from Qumran. The "wickedness" in question, however, has to do with his opposition to the sectarian leader known as the Teacher of Righteousness, not with his political machinations.

In 143, Jonathan fell victim to the game of kings in which he had embroiled himself. His brother Simon took up his mantle by rejoining the fray, obtaining the high priesthood from Demetrius II, son of the monarch whom Judas had fought against. Like other Seleucids before him, Demetrius sweetened the deal with numerous concessions, releasing Judea from tribute, acknowledging Simon's possession of all Maccabean strongholds, and inviting Jewish troops to enroll in the royal forces. For these achievements, Simon was credited with the "removal of the yoke of the Gentiles" (1 Macc. 13:41). Notably though, Demetrius' concessions did not cede control over the Akra. But by June of 141, Simon had starved its inhabitants into submission, thus bringing all of Jerusalem under his power. The last memorial of Antiochus IV's infamy had been swept away.

The following year, a great assembly of the Jewish people commemorated Simon, who had "fought off the enemies of Israel and established its freedom" (1 Macc. 14:26). In recognition of these achievements, a resolution was passed that Simon

> . . . should be their leader and high priest indefinitely (until a trustworthy prophet should arise), and that he should be their general, and that he should be given custodianship of the sanctuary and that he should appoint men over its functions and over the countryside and over the weapons and over the fortresses, and that he should be obeyed by all, and that all contracts in the country should be written in his name, and that he should wear purple and gold. And it shall be forbidden for anyone of the people or of the priests to abrogate any of these things or to oppose things said by him or to convene an assembly in the country without him or to wear purple or to put on a golden buckle, and whoever acts contrary to these things or abrogates any of them shall be liable for punishment. (1 Macc. 14:41-45)

The pro-Maccabean narrative in which this decree is embedded presents it as a spontaneous, voluntary, unanimous expression of the popular will. The dictatorial character of the privileges bestowed upon Simon belie that image, indicating the presence (or prospect) of significant internal challenges to his leadership. Simon's death at the hands of a would-be usurper half a decade later lends weight to this interpretation, as does the extradition clause in a Roman diplomatic missive penned on his behalf (1 Macc. 15:16-21). The Simon decree signals a shift in the orientation of the Maccabean movement toward *de facto* monarchy.

Beyond the cleansing of the Temple, the repeal of Antiochus IV's decrees, and the removal of the Akra garrison, it is notoriously difficult to discern what the ultimate aims of the Maccabean revolt actually were. Resistance to Seleucid authority cannot be disentangled from the Maccabees' struggles against native rivals who enjoyed Seleucid support. Once the possibility of negotiation with the Macedonian overlord had become a viable option, Judas and his brothers embraced it wholeheartedly as a tool of entrenchment against their Jewish adversaries. In time, the descendants of Simon would achieve enduring political independence from Seleucid suzerainty; but this achievement was ultimately a function of Seleucid weakness, not of Hasmonean strength.

The Oniads in Egypt

Another Jewish family narrative surfaces during the latter half of the second century. Excluded from office by the upheavals of the Seleucid-backed high priesthood, Onias IV, son of the murdered high priest of the same name, fled to Egypt. There he obtained a land grant and permission from the reigning monarchs (Ptolemy VI and Cleopatra II) to erect a temple modeled on that of Jerusalem in the eastern Nile Delta. Conflicting sources obscure the precise timing and intent of this undertaking, but it is evident that (as so often with Jewish settlement in the Hellenistic age) the Oniad district and its temple functioned as a military colony, providing internal security for Lower Egypt, as well as supplying manpower for the Ptolemaic army when called upon.

Although Jewish inhabitants of the region embroiled themselves in Egyptian conflicts as late as Julius Caesar's Alexandrine War (48 B.C.E.), testimony for the career of the Oniad family itself is confined to the period of the dynastic intrigues of Cleopatra II and Cleopatra III (145-102 B.C.E.). In his refutation of Apion's diatribe against the Jews of Alexandria, Josephus tells of two Jewish generals, Onias and Dositheos, who supported Cleopatra II's claim to the throne against her brother, Physcon, and his Alexandrian partisans, following the death of her husband in 145 (*Ag. Ap.* 2.49-56). Although Josephus does not explicitly connect this Onias with the expatriate Jerusalemite, the probability of their identification seems quite strong. (The identity of Dositheos and his relationship to Onias cannot be determined with certainty.) Two sons of Onias IV — Chelkias and Ananias — likewise emerge as generals during the reign of Cleopatra III (whose titulature and propaganda reveal a consistent effort to win over and maintain the allegiance of her mother's traditional support base). In 103, Chelkias and Ananias led an Egyptian army into Palestine against the queen's would-be usurper, her elder son Ptolemy Lathyrus. Chelkias fell in battle, but Ananias (if Josephus is to be believed) influenced Cleopatra's decision to forge an alliance with the Judean king, Alexander Jannaeus (*Ant.* 13.324-55).

After this episode, information on the Oniads dries up. But epigraphic evidence testifies to the continued vitality of the community Onias founded. More than seventy Jewish funerary inscriptions have been recovered from Tell el-Yahudiyya (ancient Leontopolis) dating as late as the early second century C.E. One epitaph explicitly names the "Land of Onias" as the patrimony of the deceased (*JIGRE* 38). Like the Maccabean narrative, the Oniad saga illustrates the capacity of Jews to operate within the framework of the Hellenistic monarchies. But whereas the Oniads were absorbed into the Ptolemaic hierarchy, the relationship of the Hasmoneans to the Seleucid state was to develop along quite a different path.

The Hasmonean Dynasty

Seleucid interference in Judean affairs was not ended. But unlike earlier ventures, which had as their goal the elimination of the Maccabean insurgents, containment or curtailment of Hasmonean power now became their prime objective. Ongoing dynastic quarrels were complicated by an increasingly belligerent Parthian menace. The Parthian annexation of Babylonia in 140 posed a major threat to the coherence of Macedonian rule in the east, and the invaders' readiness to play off one Seleucid against another compounded the crisis. The diversion of energies to meet these pressing new problems loosened the Seleucids' grip on their ambitious Jewish clients. In response, Simon's successors applied themselves to the pursuit of Hellenistic statecraft.

Territorial acquisition commenced in earnest under Simon's son, John Hyrcanus I (ruled 135/134-104), who extended Hasmonean hegemony into Idumea, Samaria, and Galilee. Aggrandizement accelerated during the tenure of Hyrcanus' own sons, who pushed their conquests as far north as Iturea, while absorbing much of the Transjordanian and coastal zones. The transition to Hasmonean rule was not a smooth one. The Samarian campaign resulted in the demolition of the temple on Mt. Gerizim, intensifying Jewish-Samaritan animosity. Circumcision and adherence to Jewish laws became mandatory for continued residence within the newly subjugated Idumean and Iturean domains. Pompey's later liberation of Greek cities controlled by the Hasmoneans signals both the extent of their military success and the unwelcome, imposed character of their rule.

Militarism demanded manpower, which in turn required money. Hyrcanus is said to have plundered the tomb of David in order to buy off Antiochus VII and to supplement his own force with mercenaries. His son, Alexander Jannaeus (ruled 103-76), is known to have continued this practice, his territorial gains doubtlessly enhancing his purchasing power. With the development of standing armies beholden to their Hasmonean paymaster rather than to their fellow countrymen came overt monarchic assertion. Hyrcanus' son, Aristobulus I (ruled 104-103), was the first to claim royal honors, and Jannaeus followed suit. And with kingship came dynastic struggles whose divisive potential and destructive impact was only amplified by the resources at each side's disposal. Between 67 and 63 B.C.E., the sons of Jannaeus — Aristobulus II and Hyrcanus II — became embroiled in a contest for the kingship that ultimately terminated the career of the Hasmonean state.

Already under Hyrcanus I, Hasmonean pretensions met with Jewish resistance. Internal opposition reached its apogee during Jannaeus' reign. So intense was their detestation of the king that his enemies actually appealed to the reigning Seleucid monarch for assistance in ousting him. The ouster failed. But the brutality of Jannaeus' repressive regime thwarted any possibility of peace between himself and his alienated subjects. (Qumran texts remember him as the "Lion of Wrath.") A more conciliatory situation appears to have developed under Jannaeus' wife, Shelamzion (Salome) Alexandra, who succeeded him (ruled 76-67).

According to Josephus, a key ingredient in Alexandra's success was her cultivation of the Pharisees, a group whose existence is first mentioned in the context of the time of Jonathan. Josephus himself ascribes anti-Hasmonean activity to Pharisaic instigation, a thesis that gains some plausibility from his claim that Jannaeus crucified 800 members of the sect. Alexandra, at any rate, placated the populace by involving the Pharisees in her administration. It is clear, however, that for some Jews, the excesses of Jannaeus and the sectarian flip-flopping of Hyrcanus were symptoms of a more fundamental wrong: monarchic rule itself. When the contentious sons of Alexandra appealed to Pompey for arbitration of their competing claims in 63 B.C.E., they were challenged by a third party, comprising more than 200 of the most prominent men of Judea. Virulently opposed to both Hasmoneans, these Jewish notables demonstrated to the Roman general that their own forebears

> had negotiated with the Senate, and had received the leadership of the Jews as a free and autonomous people — the title of king not having been taken, but with a high priest set over the nation. But that now these men [Aristobulus II and Hyrcanus II] were holding power by virtue of the fact that they had annulled the ancestral laws and had unjustly reduced the citizenry to slavery; for by a mass of mercenaries and by outrages and by many impious murders they had acquired royal power for themselves. (Diodorus 40.2)

The significance of this indictment, delivered at so pivotal a moment in Jewish history (the eve of Rome's first direct intervention into Judean affairs), lies not in the historical veracity of its claims (which are debatable). Its importance lies rather in the contrast it draws between two visions of early Judaism: the ideal temple-community, governed by the Torah and presided over by a high priest; and the historical contingencies of a sovereign state, struggling to maintain its independence amidst the successor-kingdoms of Alexander the Great. In 63 B.C.E., both the Hasmonean princes and their aristocratic opponents viewed Rome as the key to preserving their vision.

From Pompey to Hadrian

Adam Kolman Marshak

The period from the conquest of Jerusalem by Pompey the Great in 63 B.C.E. to the violent repression of the revolt under the emperor Hadrian in 135 C.E. was one of both tremendous accomplishments and incredible setbacks for the Jews as a people and Judea as a kingdom. This period began with the violation of the Jerusalem Temple and ended with the expulsion of the Jews from Jerusalem, during which the city morphed from the Jewish city of Jerusalem to the Roman *polis* Aelia Capitolina. At the same time, Hadrian changed the name of the province from Judea to Syria Palestina.

This is not to say that life for Jews in Judea during this period was a perpetual nightmare. Indeed, for the majority of the 200 years from Pompey's conquest to Bar Kokhba's revolt, Jews in Judea lived in peaceful coexistence within the Roman Empire. Moreover, during this period, Jews were spreading all over the Diaspora and settling in or expanding within the major cities of the empire. Significant populations of Jews could be found in Egypt, Asia Minor, Syria, the Greek islands, and even Rome itself. Thus, although many of the major events in this period were ruinous for the Jews, there were prolonged periods of peace and prosperity.

The End of Hasmonean Rule and the Rise of the Antipatrids

The twenty-year period from Pompey's siege of Jerusalem to the accession of Herod the Great was one of almost constant civil war between two factions of the Hasmonean family led by John Hyrcanus II and Judah Aristobulus II, the sons of Alexander Jannaeus and Salome Alexandra. Both sides appealed to Rome for support. Pompey sided with Hyrcanus, and in response Aristobulus and his supporters barricaded themselves within fortresses and the Temple itself. Pompey and his army besieged Jerusalem and the Temple, and in the ensuing siege, the city was badly damaged. Aristobulus' faction was massacred inside the Temple precinct itself, and Pompey himself violated the sanctity of the Temple by entering the Holy of Holies. After establishing order in the city, Pompey restored Hyrcanus to the high priesthood but stripped him of his royal title and political authority.

During the next nine years, an Idumean family of courtiers, the Antipatrids, rose to preeminence in the Hasmonean court. They first achieved prominence during the reign of Alexander Jannaeus when he appointed an Idumean noble named Antipas as *stratēgos* of Idumea. It is likely that Antipas' son, Antipater, succeeded him. Antipater quickly became the real power behind the Hasmonean throne. He was a consummate politician who excelled at cultivating and exploiting friendships with local rulers as well as with leading Romans. Antipater first secured the friendship of Pompey and then of Julius Caesar when he eclipsed Pompey. In 48 B.C.E., Julius Caesar found himself besieged in Alexandria by native Egyptians. Antipater came to his aid by enlisting the support of local rulers as well as personally leading an army into Egypt. In recognition of his support, Caesar bestowed Roman citizenship on Antipater and his family (*J.W.* 1.187-94; *Ant.* 14.127-39).

Although Antipater was now clearly the main man at court, he still had powerful enemies, who assassinated him in 43 B.C.E. (*J.W.* 1.225-26; *Ant.* 14.280-84). Herod and his brother Phasael, who had been appointed *stratēgoi* of Galilee and Judea respectively (47 B.C.E.), assumed the leadership of their family as well their father's position as the dominant courtiers in the Hasmonean court. Their power and influence increased further in 42, when Marc Antony appointed them tetrarchs (*J.W.* 1.244; *Ant.* 14.326). However, in 40 the Parthians and their ally, the Hasmonean Mattathias Antigonus, the son of Aristobulus II, invaded Judea and besieged Jerusalem. While on a diplomatic mission to the Parthians, Phasael and Hyrcanus were arrested and imprisoned. Phasael chose to commit suicide by dashing his head against a rock. Herod, on the other hand, fled to Rome to secure its support against the Parthians and Antigonus. With the support and lobbying of the triumvirs Antony and Octavian, the Roman senate proclaimed Herod King of Judea and promised him military aid in his war against Antigonus (*J.W.* 1.282-85; *Ant.* 14.381-89). It took Herod three years to defeat Antigonus and capture Jerusalem, but in Spring 37 B.C.E. he entered Jerusalem as both *de jure* and *de facto* King of Judea (*J.W.* 1.349-57; *Ant.* 14.476-91).

Herod, King of Judea and Client of Rome

Herod the Great was arguably the most powerful and influential Jewish monarch in history. During his long reign (40-4 B.C.E.), he amassed extraordinary wealth, implemented an elaborate and comprehensive building program, and transformed Judea from a small petty kingdom into an economic center of the Eastern Mediterranean. Jerusalem, too, changed from a crowded and dilapidated provincial city into a major pilgrimage site and tourist attraction of the Greco-Roman world. Despite his significant achievements, Herod's reign was not a smooth one. In his early years, one of his major concerns was establishing and maintaining his own legitimacy. As a usurper who had risen to power through Roman support, his claims to legitimacy were somewhat suspect. In addition to legitimacy issues, he also had to contend with the ambitions of Cleopatra, who wanted to reclaim the Ptolemaic Empire and annex Judea to her kingdom. Through astute political maneuvering, he was able to keep Cleopatra at bay and rule in relative security until 30 B.C.E. In that year, Herod's patron Antony, along with Cleopatra, was defeated by Octavian Caesar at the Battle of Actium. Like his father before him, Herod wisely saw the benefit of switching loyalties, so he quickly sailed to Rhodes to persuade the victorious Octavian that he could fit well into his new regime as a loyal and friendly client king. Octavian confirmed Herod's position and enlarged his kingdom (*J.W.* 1.386-97; *Ant.* 15.187-201). For the next twenty-six years, Herod provided a stable and friendly ally on the eastern border and promoted economic development and Romanization in Judea. As a reward for his services, Octavian, who after 27 B.C.E. was known as Augustus, bestowed upon Herod additional territories such as Trachonitis, Batanea, and Auranitis in 24/23 B.C.E. and Ulatha and Paneas in 20. He also ceded Herod control of the copper mines on Cyprus and half of their revenue. Thus, by the end of his reign, Herod ruled over a kingdom that rivaled all previous Jewish monarchies in size, wealth, and importance within the Mediterranean world.

Despite his numerous political and economic successes, Herod's reign was also marked by considerable domestic difficulties. His relationship with his Jewish subjects was periodically strained partially due to his somewhat ambiguous attitude toward Judaism. Internal dissension among his own family also caused Herod numerous problems and resulted in the execution of three sons and one wife as well as several other relatives and friends. Finally, a series of riots and disturbances broke out after his death in 4 B.C.E. Such social disorder suggests considerable dissatisfaction with the regime among many of his subjects. Despite these failings, Herod achieved enough legitimacy and security during his reign to rule without any significant threat to the stability of his kingdom. Furthermore, he was able to bequeath his kingdom to his three chosen successors, his sons Herod Archelaus, Herod Antipas, and Herod Philip.

Herod's Sons and Successors

After Herod's death, there was a struggle among his sons over who was going to succeed him, and the rival delegations traveled to Rome to solicit the princeps' opinion. In the end, Augustus chose to honor Herod's last will and divide the kingdom among the three named sons. Archelaus received Judea, Samaria, and Idumea, but only the title of ethnarch instead of king. Herod Philip, who became a tetrarch, received Batanea, Trachonitis, Auranitis, and other nearby territories. Finally, Galilee and Perea went to Herod Antipas, who received the title of tetrarch (*J.W.* 1.14-15, 20-38, 80-100; *Ant.* 17.219-49, 299-320). These three brothers ruled Herod's territory with varied success for the next thirty years.

Archelaus' short reign was a disaster from the beginning. His cruelty and oppressive measures enraged his subjects, and in 6 C.E. Augustus banished him to Vienne in Gaul. Judea then became a province governed by a procurator (*J.W.* 1.39-79, 111-17; *Ant.* 17.250-98, 339-55). His half-brother Herod Philip, on the other hand, ruled in relative peace for approximately thirty-eight years, and although little is known of his reign, it seems to have been successful and benign. Jews were a minority in his kingdom, and most of the inhabitants were of Syrian or Arab descent. During his reign, he rebuilt the city of Paneas and renamed it Caesarea Philippi in honor of himself and Augustus. He also expanded and embellished Bethsaida, renaming it Julias, in honor of Augustus' daughter Julia (*J.W.* 1.168; *Ant.* 18.28). When Philip died childless in 34 C.E., the emperor Tiberius attached his realm to the province of Syria (*Ant.* 18.106-8).

Of the three successors to Herod the Great, Herod Antipas is the one about whom we know the most. He reigned for more than forty years, longer than either of his brothers, and throughout his reign he was a valuable ally and client king to Rome. He rebuilt Sepphoris in Galilee and Betharamphtha in Perea, renaming them Autocratoris and Livias, respectively (*J.W.* 1.168; *Ant.* 18.27). His most expansive urban project, however, was the construction of a new capital city, Tiberias, in honor of the emperor Tiberius. According to coin evidence, this city was dedicated in the twenty-fourth year of Antipas' reign (19/20 C.E.). Although pious Jews initially refused to live in the city because of its construction atop a graveyard, eventually it became a center of Jewish learning and study (*J.W.* 1.168; *Ant.* 18.36-38).

As with his father, Antipas' personal life was less stable than his political rule. After several years of marriage, he abandoned his first wife Phasaelis, the eldest daughter of King Aretas IV and married his niece, Herodias, who had also been married to two of Antipas' half-brothers, Herod Philip and Herod son of Mariamne, the daughter of Simon Boethus. As a result, he incurred the wrath of both his former father-in-law and the charismatic preacher John the Baptist (Mark 6:14-29; Matt. 14:1-12; Luke 3:19-20; *Ant.* 18.116-19). Antipas' defeat in battle against Aretas and his army was seen by his subjects as just punishment from God for the execution of John (*Ant.* 18.113-16).

Despite his defeat by the Nabatean army, Antipas' positive relationship with Tiberius enabled him to survive on his throne. However, upon the death of Tiberius in 37 C.E. and the accession of Gaius Caligula, Antipas' status severely declined. One of Gaius' early acts was to appoint Antipas' nephew Herod Agrippa, who was also Herodias' brother, king in the territory of Herod Philip. Herodias, who was supposedly jealous of her brother's rise in power, believed that her husband also should receive the royal title. She therefore urged him to go to Rome and petition the new emperor. However, because of the machinations of Herod Agrippa, who disliked and distrusted his uncle, Gaius decided that Antipas was a traitor and exiled him to Lugdunum in Gaul (present-day Lyon). Because of her status as Agrippa's sister, Gaius was willing to permit Herodias to retain her property and not go into exile with her husband. Nevertheless, she voluntarily chose to share Antipas' fate (*J.W.* 1.181-83; *Ant.* 18.237-54).

Judea under Roman Rule (6-41 C.E.)

Meanwhile, since Archelaus' deposition in 6 C.E., a Roman prefect or procurator had governed Judea and Samaria, beginning with Coponius. Josephus' narratives provide most of the information about this period in Judean history, although the Gospels also provide some information, specifically about Pontius Pilate. Coin evidence and some archaeological material supplement Josephus' testimony, but for the most part scholars rely upon Josephus' account. In general, his depiction of the Roman administrators is decidedly negative, and he asserts that their mismanagement played a fundamental role in the downward spiral of the relationship between Rome and its Judean subjects. In this first stage of Roman occupation, however, Josephus' narrative is rather neutral, and the majority of these early governors receive minimal mention, which suggests somewhat peaceful interactions (*Ant.* 18.2, 29, 31-35). The sole exception to this is the tenure of Pontius Pilate (26-36 C.E.).

Outside of literary sources such as Philo, Josephus, and the Gospels, the name Pontius Pilate appears in only one inscription, which records his dedication of a

Tiberieum and was discovered in the theater at Caesarea. In the literary sources, two main images appear. In the Gospels, Pilate is depicted as the blameless instrument of Roman justice. In both Philo and Josephus, however, he appears as a ruthless administrator who openly offended Jewish sensibilities and reveled in brutal methods of suppressing dissent. Philo calls him "a man of inflexible, stubborn and cruel dispositions" whose tenure was characterized by "venality, violence, robbery, assault, abusive behavior, frequent executions without trial, and endless savage ferocity" (*Legatio* 301–2). On more than one occasion, Pilate blatantly disrespected Jewish religious sensibilities, and his response to their complaints was often to resort to violence (*J.W.* 2.169-77; *Ant.* 18.55-62, 85-87). Finally, in ca. 36/37 C.E., he was recalled by the governor of Syria, Lucius Vitellius, and ordered to return to Rome to explain his conduct to the emperor.

Things were relatively quiet in Judea until the Winter of 39/40 C.E., when the non-Jewish minority of Jamnia erected an altar to the imperial cult, which the Jewish inhabitants of the town promptly destroyed. The imperial procurator in Jamnia, Gaius Herrenius Capito, reported the incident to the new emperor, Gaius Caligula, who was enraged at the supposed insult to his majesty. He ordered the new governor of Syria, Publius Petronius, to march into Judea with two of the four legions stationed in Syria and to erect a golden statue of Gaius in the Temple. If the Jews resisted, Petronius was ordered to suppress them by force (*J.W.* 2.184-85; *Ant.* 18.261-62; Philo, *Legatio* 198–207). Realizing that Jewish resistance was inevitable, Petronius attempted to delay constructing the statue.

Herod Agrippa I

In the midst of Petronius' delaying tactics, Herod Agrippa, the grandson of Herod the Great and ultimately his successor as King of Judea, also took up the Judean cause. He had been educated in Rome alongside the imperial family, in particular the future emperor Claudius (*Ant.* 18.143, 165). With the rise of Gaius to the throne, Agrippa finally achieved prominence. He had become close friends with Gaius, and his friendship was rewarded with the tetrarchy of his recently deceased uncle Herod Philip (*J.W.* 2.181; *Ant.* 18.237). After the banishment of Antipas in 39 C.E. Caligula enlarged Agrippa's kingdom by annexing Galilee and Perea (*Ant.* 18.252).

Agrippa arrived in Italy in the midst of the statue crisis. Through either a letter (*Legatio* 261–334) or a banquet (*Ant.* 18.289-301), Agrippa successfully persuaded Gaius to forgo his plans for the statue, at least temporarily. However, both Philo and Josephus describe Gaius reneging on his promise not to place the statue in the Temple, and only the emperor's assassination saved the Jews from open conflict with Rome (*Legatio* 337–38; *J.W.* 2.202-3; *Ant.* 18.302-9). This incident only increased tensions between Rome and Judea.

Shortly before the assassination of Gaius, Agrippa returned to Rome, and after the emperor's murder, Agrippa was a crucial advisor to his successor, Claudius, and helped to secure his accession as emperor (*J.W.* 2.204-13; *Ant.* 18.236-67). As a reward for his services, Claudius appointed Agrippa king over the territory once ruled by his grandfather. Claudius also appointed Agrippa's brother Herod as ruler of Chalcis in Lebanon (*J.W.* 2.215-17; *Ant.* 18.274-77).

Herod Agrippa returned to Judea and governed it for the next three years (41-44 C.E.). He sought to further enhance the prestige of Judea. To this end, he initiated a building program around the Levant that, while not equaling his grandfather's, still enabled him to enhance his status and that of his kingdom. Among other projects, he built a theater in Berytus and a new city wall in Jerusalem across the northern edge of the city that enclosed the suburb of Bezetha. This wall, however, was not completed during Agrippa's reign because the governor of Syria, Vibius Marsus, was suspicious of Agrippa's intentions and persuaded Claudius to prohibit its completion. Jewish rebels hastily completed this wall after the outbreak of revolt in 66 C.E.

As part of this campaign to aggrandize his position within the Eastern Mediterranean, Herod Agrippa called together a meeting of the region's rulers at Tiberias, including the kings of Commagene, Emesa, Armenia Minor, and Pontus, as well as his brother, the ruler of Chalcis. Although Marsus feared that Agrippa was planning a revolution at this meeting, this is extremely unlikely. More likely, Agrippa was seeking to establish himself as the preeminent client king of the Eastern Mediterranean. His efforts, therefore, were directed more toward his neighbors than toward Claudius.

During Passover in 44 C.E., Agrippa traveled to Caesarea to attend the games being held there in honor of Claudius. According to Josephus, in the midst of the festival, Agrippa fell ill with violent pains and died five days later (*Ant.* 19.343-52; Acts 12). At the time of his death, Agrippa's heir and namesake, Herod Agrippa II, was approximately seventeen. Because of the age and inexperience of the younger Agrippa, Claudius returned Judea to the rule of a Roman procurator (*J.W.* 2.220; *Ant.* 18.362-63).

The Road to Revolution (44-66 C.E.)

Despite its size and importance to both the Roman economy and political system, when Judea again became a Roman province following the death of Agrippa I, it was not upgraded to proconsular status. Instead, as before, an equestrian procurator governed from Caesarea under the supervision of the governor of Syria. For the next twenty years, these procurators would govern a province that became increasingly unstable and hostile to Roman rule. Ultimately, their mismanagement of the province would be one of the major causes of the outbreak of the Great Jewish Revolt in 66 C.E. Josephus attributes the outbreak of revolution in 66 C.E. to the following other factors: Roman oppression, socioeconomic tensions, religious incitement, and quarrels with local Gentiles. Some scholars have added another factor ignored by Josephus: the failure of the Judean elite to control the province and its restive population (Goodman 1987). As with any complex event, it is more likely that the culmination of these factors, as opposed to one or another, caused the revolt.

The First Jewish Revolt

Revolution broke out in Judea in the early summer of 66 C.E. Some Jewish young men had parodied the greed and stinginess of the procurator Florus. In response, he marched to Jerusalem and demanded that the elders of the city hand over the youths for punishment. The local authorities refused to comply, and Florus let loose his soldiers upon the city. According to Josephus, he even crucified some Jewish *equites* (*J.W.* 2.294-308). Some members of the Jerusalem ruling elite attempted to defuse the situation, but this proved impossible. Florus made the situation more volatile by demanding a public display of submission and ordering the Jewish populace to greet the two cohorts he had sent to Jerusalem as reinforcement of the city garrison. However, the soldiers of these cohorts behaved so arrogantly toward the populace that more riots broke out, forcing Florus to withdraw to Caesarea. Meanwhile, Herod Agrippa II and his sister Berenice, who had heard about the disturbances in the city, tried to appeal for calm. Nonetheless, their efforts ultimately failed, and they were expelled from the city (*J.W.* 2.309-14, 334-35, 343-406). In May/June 66 C.E., some of the young priests, incited and led by the captain of the Temple, Eleazer ben Ananias, terminated the sacrifices offered daily at the Temple on behalf of the emperor. In essence, this served as an open proclamation of revolution and war.

Fighting broke out between various factions over both control of the city and the resumption of the daily sacrifices. This internecine fighting became even more violent when *sicarii* led by a certain Menahem ben Judah entered the city and joined with Eleazer. Eleazer's father and uncle, who were the leaders of the faction trying to avoid war with Rome, were murdered by Menahem and his men, and the soldiers sent into the city by Agrippa II to restore order either joined the rebels or were driven out of the city. A small contingent of Roman auxiliaries, who found themselves trapped inside the city, tried to escape, but were killed by Eleazer's men. The rebellion thus quickly became unavoidable and irrevocable.

Given this situation, Jews from all over Judea took the opportunity to rise up against their non-Jewish neighbors and vice versa. Seeing that the situation had gotten out of control, the governor of Syria, Cestius Gallus, collected a large army including the Twelfth Legion and some auxiliaries supplied by Agrippa and began marching south to Judea. Gallus reached Ptolemais in September and secured Galilee with little opposition. However, in October, his forces met Jewish resistance, which plundered his baggage train before he had even reached Jerusalem. Nevertheless, Gallus marched his army to Jerusalem and seized the northern suburbs, especially the district of Bezetha, with little difficulty. Despite this success, Gallus quickly determined that he could not take the city that year, so he ordered a retreat to the coast, but this withdrawal was completely disorderly, and the Jewish army took the opportunity to inflict heavy casualties on the retreating Roman forces.

At this point, the Jewish rebels now began to organize themselves as a revolutionary government. Joseph ben Gurion and Ananus ben Ananus became joint leaders of the provisional government, and they appointed generals to conduct the war. Josephus himself was selected to be the general of the forces in Galilee. In Rome, Nero dispatched Titus Flavius Vespasianus, who had distinguished himself in the invasion of Britain during the reign of Claudius. By June 67 C.E., Vespasian reached Galilee with his army, which had secured the region through brutal tactics. Josephus, who lacked proper troops and armaments, was reduced to protecting little more than small hilltop fortresses and was finally captured at the siege of Jotapata. He managed to ingratiate himself with Vespasian by hailing him as the next emperor of Rome. The other Jewish resistance fighter in the region, John of Gischala, attempted to continue the war against Vespasian, but he was forced to flee to Jerusalem in late summer 67.

Back in Jerusalem, the situation was becoming increasingly unstable. The population was dissatisfied with the provisional government because of its inability to hold Galilee. Dissatisfaction only increased in the spring of 68 when Vespasian began to march toward and encircle Jerusalem. Opposition to Ananus was bolstered partially by rural peasants, who had fled into the city because their homes and farms had been captured or threatened by the Roman army. In this hotbed of factionalism rose a new group of elite priests, who described themselves as Zealots because of their zeal for the Temple and its cult. These Zealots accused the provisional government of not prosecuting the war with enough enthusiasm. Such a charge may have been unfair, but it was strengthened by the reality that many original members of Ananus' faction, including Josephus, had by this time defected to the Roman side. Regardless, the Zealots ultimately barricaded themselves within the Temple, where they were soon joined by John of Gischala and his men as well as a large force of Idumeans who had come to Jerusalem to defend the city. This new faction was able to overthrow the provisional government and execute Ananus and his closest supporters, including Josephus' friend and patron Joshua ben Gamala. Now firmly in power, John and the Zealots began a bloody purge of their enemies within the city.

Meanwhile, back in Rome Nero committed suicide, and with his death ended Vespasian's mandate as imperial legate. Because of this development, Vespasian suspended his campaign and waited to see what would happen. His campaign resumed in May/June of 69, and by the time that he was proclaimed emperor in July, his army had recovered the land previously conquered and just finished encircling Jerusalem again. For a second time, the Roman campaign against Jerusalem was suspended as Vespasian turned to securing control of the empire.

While the Romans were engaged in a civil war known as the "Year of the Four Emperors," the Jews in Jerusalem were involved in their own civil war. In the year 68 some of the factional leaders, whom John and the Zealots had ousted from power, left the city and joined the army of Simon bar Gioras, a commander in the battle against Cestius Gallus who had been sidelined by Ananus' government. With Ananus now dead, Simon entered the fray, again capturing Hebron in spring 69 and then camping outside of Jerusalem. With the help of the Idumeans, who had become disenchanted with the Zealots and John, Simon was able to seize control of all of Jerusalem except the Temple itself. John eventually split from the Zealots and occupied the outer precincts of the Temple, while the Zealots holed up in the inner Temple. This tripartite division of the city lasted until Vespasian's son Titus and his army arrived before the walls of Jerusalem in March 70 and began to besiege the city. With the arrival of the Roman army, the three factions set aside their differences and began coordinating their defenses.

Titus could have tried to starve the city into submission, but the new Flavian regime needed a magnificent victory, and so he determined to take the city by force. By May 70, the Romans had captured the third wall. The Antonia fortress fell in June, and by August the Romans had captured and burned the Temple itself. As autumn began, the Roman army focused its attention on crushing any pockets of resistance that remained in the Upper City. It then turned its attention to the handful of Herodian fortresses occupied by Jewish resistance. The most famous of these, Masada, was not taken until 73/74, after its defenders committed mass suicide.

Judea was placed under the control of a praetorian legate, and a legion was permanently stationed in Jerusalem. Vespasian also established a veteran colony at Emmaus to keep the peace (*J.W.* 7.217). The Temple was not rebuilt, and its plundered riches were transported to Rome, where they played a central role in the Flavian triumph. Simon Bar Gioras, who had been captured in the siege, was also taken to Rome, forced to march in the triumph, and then ritually executed (*J.W.* 7.153-55). The Jewish political state ceased to exist. With the loss of the Temple, the people of Judea were forced to survive in radically different circumstances.

The Jewish Diaspora from Pompey to 70 C.E.

The late-Hellenistic and early Roman periods saw a tremendous expansion of the Jewish Diaspora. By the first century C.E., large and prosperous Jewish communities existed all over the Mediterranean from Syrian Antioch to Asia Minor and from Greece to Alexandria in Egypt. There was some settlement in Italy and in Rome, but there is no evidence for Jews in the Western Mediterranean until the Late Roman period. Although there were some Jews living in the countryside, in general during the Roman period, the Diaspora was an urban phenomenon. In cities such as Alexandria, Jews lived in self-regulating communities, which were isolated either by law or by custom.

The heart of any Diaspora community was the synagogue, and each Jewish community had at least one, although larger communities had several. These synagogues evolved into more than just meeting places. Especially after the destruction of the Temple in 70, they became the main location for religious expression and communal interaction. The Septuagint, a Greek translation of the Hebrew Bible composed in Alexandria, was the most standard version of Scripture in the Diaspora. Indeed, for Jews such as Philo, the Septuagint had divine authority.

In terms of religious practice, there was a certain amount of regional variation among Diaspora communities. Nevertheless, according to the often-negative comments by non-Jewish authors, the religious practices of Diaspora Jews were quite similar to those in Judea. Diaspora Jews practiced circumcision, kept kosher, and observed the Sabbath. During the reign of Herod the Great, an embassy of Ionian Jews appealed to the king to intercede with Marcus Agrippa on their behalf. One of their complaints was that their Gentile neighbors were dragging them into court on Shabbat and their other holy days (*Ant.* 16.27). Such an incident attests to the importance of Sabbath observance for Diaspora Jews. The Diaspora also supported the Temple in Jerusalem by paying the half-shekel tax incumbent upon all Jewish men. In the Ionian Jews' petition to Herod, another of their complaints was that the money they had raised to be sent to Jerusalem was being unlawfully seized by the non-Jewish government (*Ant.* 16.28). Further evidence of this practice appears in a speech by Cicero in 59 B.C.E. in which he defended the proconsul of Asia, Lucius Valerius Flaccus (Cicero, *Pro Flacco* 28.66-69).

In general, Diaspora Jews seem to have coexisted peacefully with their non-Jewish neighbors. The massacres and violence perpetrated by both sides in the wake of the First Revolt probably reflect local conflicts and disputes that had originated years before and about whose causes and origins we can only speculate. Roman officials usually protected Jewish rights and interests, and a number of edicts and letters that appear in Josephus' narratives show Roman leaders such as Caesar, Antony, Augustus, and Agrippa upholding Jewish rights and condoning their religious, political, and social distinctiveness (*Ant.* 14.186-267, 306-23; 16.166-73). Violations did occur, but in most cases the Roman government quickly remedied the situation. When Marcus Agrippa heard about the offenses against the rights of the Jews of Ionia, he immediately ruled in their favor (*Ant.* 16.58-61). When the Jews of Asia and Cyrenaica again experienced discrimination and the confiscation of the money they had raised for the Temple tax, they complained directly to Augustus, who ruled in their favor (*Ant.* 16.160-65). Although these incidents testify to periodic tension between Jews and non-Jews, in general Diaspora Jews were tolerated by their pagan neighbors.

The Diaspora community about which we know the most is Alexandria. The Jewish community of this city had thrived under the later Ptolemies because of direct royal patronage. During this period, the Jews enjoyed a civil status almost equal to that of their Greek neighbors. However, the situation changed with the end of the Ptolemaic dynasty. When Augustus took control of the country, he demoted them to a status equivalent to that of the native Egyptians because it was consistent with his policy of entrusting the government and political power to the Greeks of the Eastern Mediterranean. Such relegation was extremely irksome to many Alexandrian Jews, who felt themselves to be fully immersed within the wider Greco-Roman culture, despite maintaining their distinct Jewish identity. The history of Alexandrian Jewry during the Roman period is marked by a consistent drive to remove the ignominious burden of the *laographia* (poll tax) and achieve *isopoliteia* (political autonomy).

The troubles of the Alexandrian Jews reached a dangerous level in 38 C.E., when the newly appointed King Herod Agrippa I visited Alexandria on his way to Judea. His presence in the city stirred up an unruly mob of non-Jews, who publicly insulted him by parading a local madman into the arena and using him to parody Agrippa. Then the mob started calling for graven images to be placed within the synagogues of the city. As a result, the mob attacked and desecrated the synagogues and eventually started attacking the Jews themselves, shutting them off into one section of the city and causing hundreds of casualties. Homes were ransacked and businesses were destroyed (Philo, *In Flaccum* 25–85, 95–96). In his *Em-*

bassy to Gaius, Philo again describes the anti-Jewish riots of 38, but in this text he blames the violence on Emperor Gaius and the anti-Jewish Alexandrians rather than on the Alexandrians and Flaccus.

Once peace had been restored to the city, both sides sent embassies to Gaius in order to exonerate themselves of blame for the riots and to seek an imperial edict codifying the position of the Jews within the city. According to Philo, the emperor was stirred against the Jews by a small group of Alexandrian advisors, especially a certain Helicon. Ultimately, neither embassy achieved its goal of receiving an official answer from Gaius. At the time of his murder, the issue was still open. Claudius finally settled the matter when he ordered both sides to behave but telling the Jews that they lived in a city not their own, and warning them not to aim for more than what they had (*CPJ* 153; the edict of Claudius, as reported by Josephus in *Ant.* 19.280-91 is much more positive toward the Jews than the papyrus, and is of doubtful authenticity).

Roman Jews also experienced mixed relations with their non-Jewish neighbors. The Jewish community in the city of Rome was composed mostly of the descendants of slaves brought to the capital after Pompey's conquest in 63 B.C.E. and that of Gaius Sosius in 37. This community had expanded during the early Principate, and under Augustus many of these slaves received their freedom. Despite their new liberty, these Jews largely remained within the lower classes of the city, living across the Tiber in Trastevere. Yet even in the face of the usual toleration granted by the government, the Jews of Rome periodically experienced official persecution, such as their expulsion under Tiberius (Tacitus, *Annales* 11.85; Suetonius, *Tiberius* 36; Josephus, *Ant.* 18.65-84) and later under Claudius (Acts 18:2; Suetonius, *Claudius* 25; Dio 60.6). During both expulsions, it is unlikely that many Jews actually went farther than Rome's suburbs. Even if they did, the Jewish community quickly returned. By the end of the Roman period, as evidenced by the catacombs in Rome, a large Jewish population inhabited the city.

Judea between the Revolts

The tragic outcome of the Great Revolt substantially changed life in Judea, but it also had a strong ripple effect on the Diaspora as well. Jerusalem and the Temple were destroyed and the priesthood disbanded. The Sanhedrin ceased to function, and the old ruling class vanished. Although Herod Agrippa II was rewarded for his loyalty in 75 C.E. with additional territory in Lebanon and the *ornamenta praetoria,* he received no new territory in Judea. And yet, Jewish life managed to continue. The prestige of the priesthood persisted, and individual priests were still receiving tithes, but as their religious utility declined, so too did their influence and power. It is highly likely that the Jews of this period continued to hope for a restoration of the Temple. Both Josephus and the author of *1 Clement* write under the assumption that the Temple would be rebuilt and the priesthood restored. In practice, however, Judaism became localized and centered on the village synagogue. The local scribes, whose skill at interpreting Torah had made them influential, filled the power vacuum, and some of these scribes ultimately became the rabbis.

Rabbinic tradition tells of the fortuitous escape and surrender of Yoḥanan ben Zakkai during the siege of Jerusalem. According to the story, while other rabbis such as Simon ben Gamaliel participated fully in the revolt and defense of Jerusalem, ben Zakkai decided that resistance was futile. He therefore smuggled himself out of the city as a corpse and then surrendered to the Romans. He impressed Vespasian by predicting his accession as emperor. Vespasian therefore granted ben Zakkai's request to found a new center of Jewish law at Yavneh (Jamnia). In the generations following ben Zakkai, the rabbis continued to study Torah and attempt to rebuild Jewish religious and cultural life. It is not entirely clear how much political or religious power the rabbis actually possessed during this early period, and it is likely that acceptance of their leadership by Jews was gradual and perhaps only in its infancy when rebellion again broke out in Judea in 132 C.E.

The Diaspora between the Revolts

Few Jews in the Diaspora had been inspired to join in the revolt of 66. There was a brief uprising in Alexandria, but it was short-lived. Roman retaliation against the Jews also included the forced closure of the Oniad temple at Leontopolis in 72 and its precincts in 73, even though it had never been a center of unrest or disloyalty since its foundation in the mid-second century B.C.E. Titus' destruction of the Jerusalem Temple in 70, however, severely strained Diaspora Jews' loyalty. Further complicating matters was the imposition after 70 of the *fiscus Iudaicus,* an annual payment made to Jupiter Capitolinus by all Jews, regardless of gender, in lieu of payment of the Temple tax. This tax weighed heavily on the Jews, especially the poorer ones with large households, and its rigorous application by the emperor Domitian only made conditions worse (Suetonius, *Domitian* 12).

In Alexandria, local conditions and grievances made the status of the Jewish community quite unstable. A single papyrus, the *Acta Hermaisci,* recounts rival embassies from Alexandria to Emperor Trajan only a decade before the outbreak of another uprising. Although the account has been heavily fictionalized, it speaks to the tensions between Alexandrian Jews and non-Jews. Some scholars have argued that there were additional factors leading up to the rebellions (Pucci Ben Zeev 2005). In particular, rebels who had fled Judea after the suppression of the First Revolt continued to cause problems, which only heightened tensions between Jews and non-Jews. There was a general rise in messianic aspirations and expectations of Rome's collapse, especially after an earthquake that occurred in Antioch during a visit of Emperor Trajan in 115.

In 115/116, these tensions exploded into full-scale revolt in Egypt, Cyrene, Cyprus, and Mesopotamia. This revolt, also called the War of Quietus after the general Lusius Quietus who suppressed the revolt in Mesopotamia, raged until 117. In Egypt, the Jewish rebels managed to take over much of the countryside including the Athribite district, the Fayum, Oxyrhynchus, and the nome of Herakleopolis. To the south, fighting broke out in the districts of Apollinopolis Magna, Hermopolis, Kynopolis, and Lycopolis. In Alexandria itself the rebellion seems to have involved destruction of pagan shrines, such as the shrine of Nemesis near Alexandria and the tomb of Pompey (Appian, *Bella Civilia* 2.90). In Cyrene, the rebels, who were led by a certain Andreas (Dio 68.32.1) or Lukuas (Eusebius, *Hist. Eccl.* 4.2.3), killed several thousand non-Jews and destroyed several statues of the gods as well as several temples and sanctuaries, including the temples of Zeus and Hecate and parts of the sanctuaries of Apollo and Asclepius. Finally, perhaps in fear of a Roman military arrival by sea, the rebels smashed up the road connecting Cyrene to its port (*CJZC* 24-25). In Cyprus, a man named Artemion led an attack on the Gentile population and razed the city of Salamis. Not much information is known about the uprising in Mesopotamia except that Trajan sent Lusius Quietus to suppress the rebellion. It is possible that the Jews were simply one part of a general anti-Roman revolt within the region, and that the inhabitants there preferred Parthian control to Roman.

The Roman response to the uprisings in Cyrene, Cyprus, and Egypt was swift and brutal. Trajan sent two forces to put down the rebellion: the VII Claudia legion to Cyprus and Quintus Marcius Turbo, with a large fleet and a number of legions, to Egypt and Cyrene. Egyptian papyri also indicate that local non-Jewish militias fought alongside the legions. Turbo sailed into Alexandria and defeated the rebels over the course of several battles in which his army killed several thousand Jews.

The results of the war were cataclysmic for the Jewish populations of Egypt, North Africa, and Cyprus. Jews were banished from Cyprus and were prohibited from stepping foot on it on pain of death. After the revolt, there is no more evidence for Jewish settlement in the countryside of Egypt or Cyrene. Tragically, the great Jewish community of Alexandria disappeared and seems to have been destroyed, although there are a few traces of Jews left in the city afterward. Outside of the region under revolt, however, there does not seem to have been any anti-Jewish backlash. In the following years, large swaths of North African territory needed to be resettled and repopulated. Trajan and his successor Hadrian used confiscated Jewish property to fund the reconstruction efforts, especially the rebuilding of pagan temples.

The Bar Kokhba Revolt

After suppressing the Jews of Mesopotamia, Lusius Quietus was elected consul, and Trajan then appointed him governor of Judea. There are no specific details concerning any war in Judea related to the Diaspora uprisings of 115-117, and none of the Greek or Latin sources refers to fighting in Judea during this period. Rabbinic sources (*Seder ʿOlam Rabbah* 30; *m. Soṭah* 9:14) do mention a "War of Kitos" that occurred fifty-two years after Vespasian's war and sixteen years before the Bar Kokhba Revolt. Like these two wars, the "War of Kitos" saw the passage of sumptuary laws by the rabbis and a prohibition of teaching Greek. Nevertheless, the rabbinic sources are ambiguous at best. Rabbinic tradition preserves an account of two martyrs, Julianus and Pappus, who supposedly died under Trajan, but these deaths could have taken place anywhere (*m. Soṭah* 9:14; *Megillat Taʿanit* 29).

However, war and rebellion soon came to Judea, led by a charismatic leader, Shimon ben Kosiba. Later rabbinic sources claim that Ben Kosiba received the support of Rabbi Aqiba, who renamed the revolutionary leader Bar Kokhba (Aramaic for "Son of the Star") in reference to the prophecy in Num. 24:17 ("A star will come out of Jacob; a scepter will rise out of Israel"). Bar Kokhba does not make any messianic claim in his letters, but on his coins he is called "prince *(naśi')* of Israel," a title that had a long history of messianic associations.

The immediate causes of the war are unclear because we lack a detailed narrative of its course. It is likely that economic distress, hatred of the Romans, and anger over the destruction of the Temple played major roles in inciting Jews to rebel. Further, land confiscations probably exacerbated economic hardship, and religious factors also seem to have been influential. According to the *Historia Augusta*, the revolt began because Hadrian issued an edict prohibiting circumcision (14.2). The ban was part of a wider, empire-wide prohibition on mutilation, including castration, but Hadrian must have known how the Jews would respond. Dio suggests that the emperor also had decided to turn Jerusalem into a new pagan city, Aelia Capitolina (Dio 69.12.1-2), and perhaps this prohibition was connected to that larger plan.

The rebellion's territorial extent is also unclear, but most evidence suggests a concentration in the part of Judea closest to Jerusalem and the Dead Sea. The Jews seem to have had some success in the beginning, but it is not clear if the Jewish rebels ever managed to seize Jerusalem. The rebel letters found in the desert refer to Herodion and not Jerusalem as the insurgent headquarters, and their last stronghold was Bethar, not Jerusalem.

The Romans responded seriously to this new threat, and Hadrian sent Gaius Julius Severus from Britain to take over command of Judea in 134 C.E. Dedicatory inscriptions indicate that legions from all over the empire were sent to Judea, but otherwise there is no indication of troop size or makeup. The paucity of evidence from Greco-Roman authors suggests hesitancy on the part of the imperial government to mention a brutal suppression of rebellion, which did not fit well with Hadrian's image of benevolent patronage of the provinces.

According to Dio, the Romans killed more than 500,000 Jews and destroyed 50 towns and 785 villages in the suppression of the revolt. He also claims that they enslaved many of the survivors (Dio 69.14.3). Although these numbers likely are inflated, the bones discovered in the Judean Desert caves testify to Roman thoroughness and ruthlessness. Rabbinic sources state that many sages were martyred, including Rabbi Aqiba, and a period of strict persecution followed in which Jews could not practice many facets of their religion, including studying Torah, observing the Sabbath, and circumcising their sons. Indeed, Jews did not receive permission to circumcise their sons until after Hadrian's death. Perhaps the most long-lasting and devastating result of the war, however, was the expulsion of the Jews from Jerusalem (now called Aelia Capitolina) and its territory (Justin, *Apology* 7.6). Hadrianic coins celebrated the new city with a Greek figure representing it, and a temple dedicated to Hadrian was constructed atop the Temple Mount itself. Thus, what began as an attempt to liberate the Jews of Judea ultimately led to their death and to the enslavement and expulsion of Jews from their Holy City. With the failure of the Bar Kokhba Revolt, a major period of Jewish history comes to an end.

BIBLIOGRAPHY

Bagnall, Roger S. 1976. *The Administration of the Ptolemaic Possessions outside Egypt.* Leiden: Brill.

Bar-Kochva, Bezalel. 1989. *Judas Maccabaeus: The Jewish Struggle against the Seleucids.* Cambridge: Cambridge University Press.

Barclay, John M. G. 1996. *Jews in the Mediterranean Diaspora.* Edinburgh: T&T Clark.

Ben Zeev, Miriam Pucci. 2005. *Diaspora Judaism in Turmoil, 116/117 CE: Ancient Sources and Modern Insights.* Leuven: Peeters.

Berlin, Adele M., and J. Andrew Overman, eds. 2002. *The First Jewish Revolt: Archaeology, History, and Ideology.* London: Routledge.

Bickerman, Elias J. 1980. "La Charte séleucide de Jérusalem." In *Studies in Jewish and Christian History (Part Two).* Leiden: Brill, 44-85.

———. 1979. *The God of the Maccabees: Studies on the Meaning and Origin of the Maccabean Revolt.* Leiden: Brill.

Bouché-Leclercq, Auguste. 1903-1907. *Histoire des Lagides.* 4 vols. Paris: Leroux.

———. 1913-1914. *Histoire des Séleucides (323-64 J.-C.).* 2 vols. Paris: Leroux.

Brutti, Maria. 2006. *The Development of the High Priesthood during the pre-Hasmonean Period: History, Ideology, Theology.* Leiden: Brill.

Cohen, Getzel M. 2006. *The Hellenistic Settlements in Syria, the Red Sea Basin, and North Africa.* Berkeley: University of California Press.

Eshel, Hanan. 2008. *The Dead Sea Scrolls and the Hasmonean State.* Grand Rapids: Eerdmans.

Fischer, Thomas. 1980. *Seleukiden und Makkabäer: Beiträge zur Seleukidengeschichte und zu den politischen Ereignissen in Judäa während der 1. Hälfte des 2. Jahrhunderts v. Chr.* Bochum: Studienverlag Dr. Norbert Brockmyer.

Gafni, Isaiah. 1984. "The Historical Background." In *Jewish Writings of the Second Temple Period.* Ed. Michael E. Stone. Assen: Van Gorcum; Philadelphia: Fortress, 1-31.

Gera, Dov. 1998. *Judaea and Mediterranean Politics, 219 to 161 B.C.E.* Leiden: Brill.

Goodblatt, David. 2006. *Elements of Jewish Nationalism.* Cambridge: Cambridge University Press.

Goodman, Martin. 1987. *The Ruling Class of Judea: The Origins of the Jewish Revolt AD 66-70.* Cambridge: Cambridge University Press.

Grabbe, Lester L. 1992. *Judaism from Cyrus to Hadrian.* 2 vols. Minneapolis: Fortress.

Grainger, John D. 1997. *A Seleukid Prosopography and Gazetteer.* Leiden: Brill.

Green, Peter. 1990. *Alexander to Actium: The Historical Evolution of the Hellenistic Age.* Berkeley: University of California Press.

Gruen, Erich S. 1993. "Hellenism and Persecution: Antiochus IV and the Jews." In *Hellenistic History and Culture.* Ed. P. Green. Berkeley: University of California Press, 238-55; 256-74.

———. 2002. *Diaspora: Jews amidst the Greeks and Romans.* Cambridge: Harvard University Press.

Hengel, Martin. 1989. *The Zealots: Investigations into the Jewish Freedom Movement in the Period from Herod I until 70 A.D.* Trans. David Smith. Edinburgh: T&T Clark.

Hoehner, Harold. 1972. *Herod Antipas.* Cambridge: Cambridge University Press.

Hölbl, Günther. 2001. *A History of the Ptolemaic Empire.* London: Routledge.

Johnson, Sara R. 2004. *Historical Fictions and Hellenistic Jewish Identity.* Berkeley: University of California Press.

Jones, A. H. M. 1938. *The Herods of Judea.* Oxford: Clarendon.

Kasher, Aryeh. 1985. *The Jews in Hellenistic and Roman Egypt.* Tübingen: Mohr-Siebeck.

———. 1990. *Jews and the Hellenistic Cities in Eretz-Israel: Relations of the Jews in Eretz-*

Israel with the Hellenistic Cities during the Hellenistic and Roman Era (332 BCE–70 CE). Tübingen: Mohr-Siebeck.

Kokkinos, Nikos. 1998. *The Herodian Dynasty: Origins, Roles in Society and Eclipse.* Sheffield, England: Sheffield Academic Press.

Lipschits, Oded et al., eds. 2007. *Judah and the Judeans in the Fourth Century B.C.E.* Winona Lake: Eisenbrauns.

Lüderitz, Gert, ed. 1983. *Corpus Jüdischer Zeugnisse aus der Cyrenaika.* Wiesbaden: Reichert.

Mendels, Doron. 1992. *The Rise of Jewish Nationalism: Jewish and Christian Ethnicity in Ancient Palestine.* New York: Doubleday.

Meshorer, Yaʿakov. 2001. *A Treasury of Jewish Coins: From the Persian Period to Bar Kokhba.* Nyack, N.Y.: Amphora.

Modrzejewski, Joseph Méléze. 1995. *The Jews of Egypt: From Rameses II to Emperor Hadrian.* Princeton: Princeton University Press.

Mørkholm, Otto. 1966. *Antiochus IV of Syria.* Copenhagen: Nordisk Forlag.

Netzer, Ehud. 2006. *The Architecture of Herod, the Great Builder.* Tübingen: Mohr-Siebeck.

Neusner, Jacob. 1969. *A History of the Jews in Babylonia,* vol. 1, *The Parthian Period.* Leiden: Brill.

Price, Jonathan. 1992. *Jerusalem under Siege: The Collapse of the Jewish State 66-70 C.E.* Leiden: Brill.

Rajak, Tessa. 2002. *Josephus: The Historian and His Society.* 2d ed. London: Duckworth.

Richardson, Peter. 1996. *Herod: King of the Jews and Friend of the Romans.* Columbia: University of South Carolina Press.

Rooke, Deborah W. 2000. *Zadok's Heirs: The Role and Development of the High Priesthood in Ancient Israel.* Oxford: Oxford University Press.

Schäfer, Peter, ed. 2003. *The Bar Kokhba War Reconsidered.* Tübingen: Mohr-Siebeck.

Schalit, Abraham. 1969. *König Herodes: Der Mann und sein Werk.* Berlin: de Gruyter.

Schürer, Emil. 1973-1987. *The History of the Jewish People in the Age of Jesus Christ.* Rev. and ed. G. Vermes, F. Millar, and M. Goodman. 3 vols. Edinburgh: Clark.

Schwartz, Daniel R. 1990. *Agrippa I: The Last King of Judea.* Tübingen: Mohr-Siebeck.

Schwartz, Seth. 2001. *Imperialism and Jewish Society, 200 B.C.E. to 640 C.E.* Princeton: Princeton University Press.

Shatzman, Israel. 1991. *The Armies of the Hasmonaeans and Herod.* Tübingen: Mohr-Siebeck.

Sievers, Joseph. 1990. *The Hasmoneans and Their Supporters.* Atlanta: Scholars Press.

Smallwood, E. Mary. 1976. *The Jews under Roman Rule: From Pompey to Diocletian.* Leiden: Brill.

Tcherikover, Victor. 1959. *Hellenistic Civilization and the Jews.* New York: Jewish Publication Society. (Reprint: Peabody, Mass.: Hendrickson, 1999, with a preface by John J. Collins.)

Trebilco, Paul R. 1991. *Jewish Communities in Asia Minor.* Cambridge: Cambridge University Press.

VanderKam, James C. 2004. *From Joshua to Caiaphas: High Priests after the Exile.* Minneapolis: Fortress.

Wilker, Julia. 2007. *Für Rom und Jerusalem. Die herodianische Dynastie im 1. Jahrhundert n. Chr.* Frankfurt am Main: Verlag Antike.

Yadin, Yigael. 1963-2002. *The Finds from the Bar Kokhba Period in the Cave of Letters.* 3 vols. Jerusalem: Israel Exploration Society.

———. 1966. *Masada: Herod's Fortress and the Zealot's Last Stand.* New York: Random House.

Judaism in the Land of Israel

James C. VanderKam

Judaism as a designation for the entire phenomenon of the Jewish ways of living and believing is a Greek term *(Ioudaismos)* first attested in 2 Macc. 2:21; 14:38. It is related to the name for the land where many Jews lived — the land of Judah or Judea — and seems to have been coined as a way of contrasting traditional Jewishness with Hellenism (*Hellenismos;* see 2 Macc. 4:13). This essay will focus on Judaism as it came to expression in the land of Israel.

The Land of Israel

The Scriptures repeatedly mention God's promise that the descendants of Abraham and Sarah would possess the land (Gen. 12:7; 13:14-17; 15:7, 17-21; etc.), and the book of Joshua shows how that promise came to fruition (e.g., Josh. 21:43-45). The people of Israel lived in the promised land for centuries, but finally their sins, according to the Deuteronomistic History (2 Kings 21:10-15; etc.), so sorely tried the divine patience that YHWH invoked the curses of the covenant upon them, and gave them into the power of their enemies, who torched Jerusalem and the Temple and exiled many from the land. Decades later a return to the land began and a new temple was constructed on the site of the old one. Though a large number of Jewish people by this time lived in the various diasporas, the land of Israel remained a powerful symbol for them, although this spiritual and national force did not necessarily impel them to live there. The Temple was a center for pilgrimages and gifts in addition to being the place where sacrifices were continually offered. The prophets had looked forward to a day when the dispersed people of God would be gathered to their home (e.g., Isa. 11:10-16; Ezek. 37:15-28), and that longing comes to expression in some of the literature written when the Second Temple stood, although the vast majority of Diaspora Jews remained where they were.

The Temple

One phenomenon related to and underscoring the centrality of the land of Israel, one that exercised a strong attraction for Jews everywhere, was the Temple in Jerusalem. Other Jewish temples existed — one at Elephantine in Egypt and later one in Leontopolis, also in Egypt — but the sanctuary in Jerusalem held a special place. Ezra 6:13-18 dates the completion and dedication of the Second Temple to the sixth year of King Darius (515 B.C.E.); that building complex (with repairs) apparently lasted until 20 B.C.E. when King Herod began completely rebuilding it on a grander scale. Herod's temple was to be destroyed with the city of Jerusalem in 70 C.E.

If the Second Temple followed the structural plan of Solomon's temple (see 1 Kings 6:2-6), the building itself would have had three rooms — the nave or vestibule, the Holy Place, and the Holy of Holies — along with several altars. These would have been set within at least two large courts and would have been surrounded by other structures required for the personnel and materials of sacrificial worship and other sanctuary-related activities. The Herodian temple area (see Josephus, *Ant.* 15.391-420; *Ag. Ap.* 2.102-4) included four courts with ever greater degrees of holiness: one accessible to all, including non-Jews, one for all Jews including women, one for Jewish men, and one for priests only. At various places there were marble columns and porticoes with steps and walls between enclosures. Only the high priest, on the Day of Atonement, could enter the Holy of Holies, the innermost room of the Temple itself.

Because of the central place occupied by the Temple in Jerusalem, the priests who served there exercised important functions in society, and some of them became its leading officials. According to the scriptural genealogies and laws, all qualified males of the tribe of Levi were clergy, but only the members of this tribe stemming from Aaron's line were priests (Num. 8:5-26; see also Exod. 28:1-3; 29:1-37). The Levites performed other duties at the sanctuary and served the priests, the sons of Aaron (Num. 18:1-7; 4:46-49). At the head of the body of priests stood the high priest, who, in the early centuries of the Second Temple period, came from the family of Joshua/Jeshua (the first high priest of the Second Temple) and held the post in hereditary succession (Neh. 12:10-11). The high priest seems at times to have exercised political power as well, serving as the chief national official in the absence of a governor. Those Hasmoneans who held the high-priestly office from 152 until the Roman conquest in 63 B.C.E. were not only heads of the cultic establishment but also chiefs of state and commanders of the army. During the years of Roman rule and before the defeat and destruction of Jerusalem in 70 C.E., the high priests continued to be influential leaders in dealing both with Jewish and Roman officials.

There were too many priests to allow all of them to serve at the Temple complex at the same time. 1 Chronicles 24:7-18 contains a list dividing the priests into twenty-four groups, one of which served at the Temple for a week, after which it was replaced by the next group on the list (Josephus, *Ant.* 7.365-66; *Ag. Ap.* 2.108). In this system, therefore, most of these divisions of priests were on duty at the Temple for only two weeks each year (twenty-four groups each serving two weeks would fill forty-eight weeks so that four would have to serve a third week) and at the great festivals when more of them were needed because of the large numbers of people bringing offerings. The Levites may have been organized in a similar way; from among their ranks came the singers and gatekeepers at the Temple (1 Chronicles 25–26; *Ant.* 7.367).

Worship at the Temple followed and built upon the prescriptions in the Mosaic Law. Animal and grain offerings with their libations were regularly made there. Each day, as the Law prescribed, there were two sacrifices of a lamb with accompanying grain and liquid offerings — the morning and evening sacrifices described in Exod. 29:38-42; Num. 28:3-8 (see 1 Chron. 15:40; 2 Chron. 8:11; 31:3). There were other mandated sacrifices for the Sabbaths, the first of each month, and for the festivals (Numbers 28–29), and passages such as Leviticus 1–7 describe the many kinds of sacrifice — their contents, who offers them, and the occasions for them. The priests were the ones who performed the procedures carried out at the altar (Num. 18:1-7; 1 Chron. 6:49-53), and for their support priests received prescribed parts of offerings other than the whole burnt offering (e.g., Lev. 2:3, 10; 5:13; 6:16-18, 26, 29; 7:6-10, 14, 31-36; Num. 18:8-20) as well as other gifts.

The festivals constituted an important if less frequent part of worship at the Temple in Jerusalem. The Law of Moses commanded that an Israelite male was to present himself before the Lord three times each year: at the Festival of Unleavened Bread, the Festival of Weeks, and the Festival of Tabernacles (Exod. 23:14-17; 34:18-24; Deut. 16:1-17). It came to be understood that the Jerusalem Temple was the place where one appeared before YHWH; as a result, thousands of Jews would travel to Jerusalem to celebrate those holidays, whether from the land or the Diaspora. Deuteronomy also stipulated that Passover be held at the sanctuary; consequently, large crowds converged on Jerusalem on the prescribed date (1/14); they could remain there for the Festival of Unleavened Bread, which followed immediately (from 1/15 to 1/21). The Day of Atonement (7/10) involved elaborate rites at the Temple, including several trips in and out of the Holy of Holies by the high priest (Leviticus 16). During Hasmonean times another Temple-related festival — Hanukkah — was added to the list in the Hebrew Bible; it celebrated and remembered the reconsecration of the Temple in 164 B.C.E. after it had been defiled.

Worship at the Temple also involved music. There are references in the literature to the singing of the Levites, with the books of Chronicles being especially rich in passages relating to this levitical function. They present the Levites as singers at the time of David and his royal successors, but these books may reflect more of the situation in Second Temple times when they were compiled. In 1 Chron. 6:31-48 David appoints Levites to provide music at the house of the Lord; among them are Asaph and Kohath, whose names are found in the titles of some psalms (sons of Korah: Psalms 42, 44–49, 84–85, 87–88; Asaph: Psalms 50, 73–83; in 1 Chron. 16:7-36 Asaph and his kin sing from Psalms 105, 95, and 106; see also 2 Chron. 29:25-30; 35:15). The king ordered the singers and instrumentalists to perform at the times of sacrifice, Sabbaths, and festivals (1 Chron. 23:30-31). When Jews presented their Passover offerings, the Levites sang the Hallel psalms (Psalms 113–18; *m. Pesaḥ.* 5:7).

The large costs incurred in connection with the forms of worship at the Temple and the maintenance of the structures were met through different means. As noted, support for the priests, who had no land to supply them with their needs, came from the parts of sacrifices allotted to them by the Law, and they also received one of the tithes mentioned in the Scriptures. The Law provided that the Levites, who also lacked land, should receive tithes from the Israelites (cf. Deut. 14:28-29), and they in turn were to give a tithe from their tithe to the priests (Num. 18:21-32). Tobit 1:6-7 gives a summary of the firstfruits contributions and the clerically related payments as the protagonist describes his religious practice before he was exiled from his land: "I would hurry off to Jerusalem with the firstfruits of the crops and the firstlings of the flock, the tithes of the cattle, and the first shearings of the sheep. I would give these to the priests, the sons of Aaron, at the altar; likewise the tenth of the grain, wine, olive oil, pomegranates, figs, and the rest of the fruits to the sons of Levi who ministered at Jerusalem."

In addition to these means of support for the clergy, the sources disclose other revenues. First, several foreign monarchs who ruled Judea made contributions to the Temple. This is attested for three Persian kings (Ezra 6:1-5 [Cyrus], 8-10 [Darius I]; 7:15-23 [Artaxerxes I]) and for the Seleucid rulers Antiochus III (Josephus, *Ant.* 12.138-44) and Seleucus IV (2 Macc. 3:2-3; cf. 1 Macc. 10:40). The passage from 2 Maccabees claims: "it came about that the kings themselves honored the place and glorified the temple with the finest presents, even to the extent that King Seleucus of Asia defrayed from his own revenues all the expenses connected with the service of the sacrifices." Ezekiel had envisaged that the prince in Jerusalem would pay for the sacrifices on holidays and Sabbaths (45:17; see also 45:22–46:15), but in reality it was foreign rulers who did so. Second, the Jewish populace worldwide supported the Temple through a tax. Exodus 30:11-16 records an imposition of one-half shekel that each Israelite male twenty years of age and above was to pay as an atonement; YHWH ordered Moses: "You shall take the atonement money from the Israelites and shall designate it for the service of the tent of meeting" (30:16; 38:25-28, where it is apparently for construction of the tabernacle; see also 2 Chron. 24:4-14; Josephus, *Ant.* 3.194-96). Exodus attaches the payment to a census Moses was to take and does not say how often the Israelites were supposed to pay it. In the time of Nehemiah the people not only pledged to bring wood for the offerings at the Temple, the firsts of the crops and herds, and the tithes (10:34-39), but also obligated themselves to pay an annual tax of one-third of a shekel "for the service of the house of our God: for the rows of bread, the regular grain offering, the regular burnt offering, the Sabbaths, the new moons, the appointed festivals, the sacred donations, and the sin offerings to make atonement for Israel, and for all the work of the house of our God" (Neh. 10:32-33). The reader does not learn why the amount of this levy differed from the one in Exodus 30, but later one finds references in the sources to an annual half-shekel payment (see Matt. 17:24-27; *m. Šeqal.* 4:1-5) — one that Josephus mentions several times and indicates that it applied to Jews in the Diaspora as well as those in the land (*Ag. Ap.* 2.77; *Ant.* 16.163; 18.312-13 [Babylon]; see Philo, *Spec. Leg.* 1.76-78). After Jerusalem was destroyed in 70 C.E., the Romans redirected the tax monies to the temple of Jupiter Capitolinus in Rome (*J.W.* 7.218). It is interesting that a text from Qumran decrees that the tax be paid only once in a person's lifetime (4Q159 1 ii 6-7) — perhaps a polemical view based on Exod. 30:11-16.

Festivals

Besides the daily and other sacrifices and ceremonies performed regularly at the Temple in Jerusalem, the cycle of festivals was centered there. As noted above, the Passover (1/14) and the three pilgrimage festivals took place at the sanctuary as the Mosaic Law directed. For the Passover, the representative of each household presented the paschal lamb at the Temple, where it was sacrificed. The Festival of Unleavened Bread, lasting from 1/15 to 1/21, coincided with the barley harvest; the Festival of Weeks, occurring at some unspecified point in the third month, marked the wheat harvest; and the Festival of Booths, celebrated on 7/15-21, came at the end of the entire harvest season. Each of the three pilgrimage holidays was also a firstfruits festival that required presentation of a part of the relevant crop at the sanctuary. The two additional firstfruits festivals mandated in the *Temple Scroll* (of wine and oil) would have taken place at the Temple, if they were ever implemented (11QT[a] 19:11–23:2). The Second Passover (2/14; for individuals who, for certain legitimate causes, were not able to celebrate the Passover in the first month [see Num. 9:16-14]) also was a Temple festival, while the ceremonies for the Day of Atonement (7/10) necessarily took place at the Temple (Leviticus 16). The book of Esther provides the dramatic story that gave rise to the holiday called Purim (lots), but there was no requirement that it be observed at the sanctuary. And Hanukkah, an eight-day festival commemorating and celebrating the rededication of the Temple in 164 B.C.E. (1 Macc. 4:36-59; 2 Macc. 10:1-8), was by definition associated with the Temple, but there was no requirement that one had to travel there to mark it properly.

Each of the festivals summarized in Leviticus 23 and Numbers 28–29 required sacrifices at the Temple beyond the daily ones offered, and the firstfruits holidays, as noted, involved the appropriate offering from the harvest of that season. This entailed that the Temple became a very busy and crowded place on these occasions. As a result, the priests who happened to be on duty at the Temple at the time of a major festival were not able to handle the large increase in sacrifices and related activities; they were augmented by priests from the other rotations.

It is not possible to infer from the way in which the Pentateuch dates festivals the nature of the calendar by which they were calculated. In the priestly portions of the Torah, the months are designated with ordinal numbers and the days are, of course, numbered as well. But no text indicates whether a solar calendar, a lunar calendar, or a combination of the two was used as the system in Second Temple times for the very practical issue of determining when public festivals occurred. Exodus 12:1 identifies the month of the Passover as the first month of the year; hence, for dating festivals, a Spring inception of the year was assumed. Psalm 104:19 could be taken as an indication that lunar considerations were involved in dating festivals (as they were later): "You have made the moon to mark the seasons [or: the festivals]; the sun knows its time for setting." But nothing specific should be inferred from the verse. Sirach 43:6-8, after a section extolling the wonders of the sun, has been adduced as evidence that by the early second century B.C.E. the moon determined festal dates. Note in particular 43:6-7: "It is the moon that marks the changing seasons, governing the times, their everlasting sign. From the moon comes the sign for festal days, a light that wanes when it completes its course." One prominent trait of *1 Enoch* 72–82, *Jubilees,* and the sectarian literature from Qumran is the prominence of a solar year lasting 364 days; the festival dates are determined according to it.

It is appropriate to append a short reference to synagogues to this survey of information about the Temple and worship in the land of Israel. It would seem that having only one temple could prove inconvenient for those who lived some distance from it, even though the area of Jewish settlement was not very large and a person was not often required to be at the Temple. Also, the traditional form of sacrificial worship at the Jerusalem Temple (the only place where it could be effected) may not have met all the religious needs of Jewish people. Whatever the reasons may have been, at some point or very gradually in the Second Temple period, synagogues, local places for worship and study, began to appear, perhaps at first in the Diaspora (there are third-century-B.C.E. references from Egypt), but also in the land of Israel (the earliest evidence is from the first century B.C.E.). The Gospel of Luke documents the presence of a synagogue at Nazareth and the importance of Scripture reading and exposition in the Sabbath service there (Luke 4:16-30; notice that 4:15 refers to *synagogues* in Galilee). Others are known from Herodium, Masada, and Gamla, and there are references to synagogues in Jerusalem (e.g., Acts 6:8-9). The synagogue was a place for communal activities (see the Theodotus Inscription) including reading, studying, and expositing the Scriptures and prayer. Synagogues appear not to have been seen as rivals in some sense to the Temple but rather as complements to it.

Institutions

The Temple was a dominant institution in the Judaism as practiced in the land, and later in the period synagogues served key functions, but there were other institutions that played central roles in society. Some information has survived regarding the political organization of the Jewish people in their land. A fundamental fact of life throughout the centuries of early Judaism was that Judah/Judea was under foreign control (Persia, the Hellenistic kingdoms of the Ptolemies and Seleucids, Rome), with the exception of a few decades when the Hasmoneans controlled the state and were somewhat independent of the Seleucid administration.

There was a governor in Jerusalem at a number of times, although the evidence is insufficient to show that there was always an office of this sort. Sheshbazzar (Ezra 5:14) and Zerubbabel (Hag. 1:1), perhaps both descendants of David, are called governors in the late sixth century, and Nehemiah, who refers to his predecessors in the office (Neh. 5:15), served in the same capacity in the second half of the fifth century. An official named Bagohi/Bagoas/Bigvai was the governor at the end of the century according to one of the Elephantine papyri (*TAD* [*Textbook of Aramaic Documents from Ancient Egypt*] A4.7 = *CAP* [Cowley, ed., *Aramaic Papyri of the Fifth Century*] 30), and a certain Hezekiah is called governor on some coins from the end of the Persian and perhaps the beginning of the Hellenistic periods. After this, there is a lengthy gap in attestations of a governor, and it may be that the high priest became the chief of state. This appears to be the case in the Tobiad Romance and also in Jerusalem as pictured at the beginning of the historical account in 2 Maccabees (3:1–4:6). In all of the narratives in 1-2 Maccabees, there is no mention of a governor other than a member of the Hasmonean family (the governor Philip in 1 Macc. 5:22 is a foreigner imposed from without for a short time).

When the Hasmoneans became high priests (starting in 152 B.C.E.), they also served as political leaders and army commanders. Beginning either in the short reign of Aristobulus I (104-103 B.C.E.) or in that of Alexander Jannaeus (103-76), these rulers called themselves kings. They retained that office (with one queen, Salome Alexandra) until the Roman conquest of the area in 63 B.C.E. Yet, even after this date a high priest such as Hyrcanus II enjoyed very high positions in society and is still called *king* a few times, and Antigonus briefly claimed the royal office (40-37 B.C.E.). Josephus indicates that in the first century the aristocratically constituted state of the Jews was led by the high priests (*Ant.* 20.251), although this was done under Roman supervision.

Herod's appointment as king by the Roman senate profoundly changed the political landscape. From the time of his reign (37-4 B.C.E.) until the destruction of Jerusalem (and beyond), he and his descendants were dominant rulers among the Jews in the land. Herod held the office of king, as did two of his sons (Antipas [4 B.C.E.–39 C.E.] and Philip [4 B.C.E.–33/34 C.E.]) in parts of their father's realm, while Archelaus (4 B.C.E.–6 C.E.), who inherited the rule of Judea, served as ethnarch until he was deposed for his incompetent and violent rule. In Judea the Romans then assumed more direct control by appointing prefects (from 6 to 41), among whom the best known is Pontius Pilate (26-36/37). King Agrippa I briefly reunited the kingdom of his grandfather Herod the Great (between 37 and 44) before dying at a young age. Following his death in 44 C.E., the Romans again assumed closer control by appointing procurators, an arrangement that lasted until the end of the revolt. During this latter period, Agrippa's son Agrippa II came to have a significant influence in Jewish political and religious affairs.

A second institution that seems to have occupied an important place in Jewish society was the council of elders (*gērousia* in Greek) or Sanhedrin, if, as seems likely, the two terms refer to the same type of body. There are references in Ezra to "the elders" as an influential group, but whether they constituted a ruling body is not said (Ezra 5:5, 9; 6:7, 14; in these passages they are involved in rebuilding the Temple and negotiations about it). Apart from the book of Judith (e.g., 4:8), which has a weak claim to historicity, the earliest mention of a council of elders is in Josephus' citation of the letter issued by Antiochus III (223-187 B.C.E.) regarding the Jewish people: he says they with their senate *(gērousia)* greeted him when he visited the city (*Ant.* 12.138); later the king mentions the Jewish form of government and lists the senate among the groups exempt from three taxes (12.142). In 2 Macc. 4:4 the senate is the body that sends representatives to King Antiochus IV to press a case against the actions of the high priest Menelaus (vv. 43-50). In subsequent times the term continues to be used in official letters in which the leaders of the Jews are listed (e.g., 2 Macc. 1:10) or addressed (2 Macc. 11:27; 1 Macc. 12:6; 13:36 [where they are called "the elders"; see also 11:23; 12:35]; 14:20, 28 [in the section regarding the decree honoring Simon]). Josephus reports that Gabinius, a

Roman official, set up five sanhedrins in Jewish territory in the 50s B.C.E. (*Ant.* 14.91), but not long afterward the historian relates the story of young Herod's trial before the Sanhedrin (14.165-79). From this episode the judicial nature of the group's work is clear, although it was definitely intimidated by the military power of Herod. The Sanhedrin as a judicial body is also evidenced in the trial of Jesus (Mark 14:53-65, where the members are identified as the high priest, the chief priests, elders, and scribes; Matt. 26:59-68; Luke 22:66-71) and that of his brother James (*Ant.* 20.199-203). The book of Acts, among several references to the council, includes Paul's appearance before it; there the members are the high priest along with representatives of the Pharisees and the Sadducees (22:30–23:12). Rabbinic sources know of a Sanhedrin that was a gathering of scholars who, among other activities, discussed matters of religious law. How that picture relates to the earlier references in Josephus and other Greek sources is not entirely clear.

Groups

As in any society, there were various groups among the Jewish people in the land of Israel. The sources for the earlier centuries of the period are sparse, but they indicate differing perspectives on some issues. So, for example, Ezra stands as a representative of a separatist point of view, one absolutely opposed to intermarriage with people of other races and nationalities; the book that bears his name includes information about many who had felt free to engage in exogamy and who were forced to dismiss their families. A number of scholars have argued that a fundamental tension in Judean society in the early Second Temple period was between those who found fulfillment of promises in the restored community and Temple and those of a more visionary bent who looked for more spectacular realizations of God's plans for his people. Those expectations found expression in some late prophetic literature and perhaps in some texts with traits that would later characterize the apocalypses.

During the early Hellenistic period there is evidence for some Jewish people who had greater ties with the Ptolemaic government (the Tobiad family, for one), while others seem to have favored the Seleucid administration (note the friendly reception of Antiochus III at Jerusalem). But the most famous division in Jewish society, one that became unmistakable in the early second century B.C.E., is the one between those Jews who were more open to aspects of Greek culture and those who opposed the adoption of Greek ways. The contrast should not be pictured as absolute, since Hellenistic influence, such as the spread of the Greek language, was multifaceted and in part religiously neutral. But 2 Maccabees describes a situation in which a group of Jews, led by the usurping high priest Jason and with the approval of the Seleucid monarch Antiochus IV (175-164 B.C.E.), introduced into Jerusalem the central institutions of Greek education and citizenship — a gymnasium and an ephebate. 1 Maccabees 1:11 presents the perspective embraced by such people in these words: "In those days certain renegades *(paranomoi)* came out from Israel and misled many, saying, 'Let us go and make a covenant with the Gentiles around us, for since we separated from them many disasters have come upon us." The author adds that not only was the gymnasium built in Jerusalem but these people "removed the marks of circumcision, and abandoned the holy covenant. They joined with the Gentiles and sold themselves to do evil" (v. 15). Later, when the worship of a different god was set up in the Jerusalem Temple, not all Jews were opposed to the innovation although some, under Hasmonean leadership, violently fought it.

In the context of the early Hasmonean period, specifically in his account of the reign of Jonathan as high priest and leader, Josephus (*Ant.* 13.171-73) reports that there were three sects or schools of thought *(haireseis)* among the Jews and lists them as the Pharisees, the Sadducees, and the Essenes. Josephus mentions members of these groups in various places in his narratives and devotes a couple of sections to describing them, especially in *J.W.* 2.119-66 (see also *Ant.* 18.11-22). The information from Josephus regarding these groups can be supplemented from the Dead Sea Scrolls and from the New Testament. Rabbinic literature, too, refers to Pharisees and Sadducees.

About the Pharisees Josephus reports that they were known for their skill and accuracy in interpreting the Law of Moses (*J.W.* 2.162), and to this he adds that "the Pharisees had passed on to the people certain regulations handed down by former generations and not recorded in the Laws of Moses" (*Ant.* 13.297 [trans. R. Marcus]). This appears to be the oral Torah known from other sources, a tradition of commentary and interpretation that allowed the Pharisees to apply the ancient law to changed circumstances. Josephus, who mentions this Pharisaic trait while describing disagreements between Pharisees and Sadducees at the time of John Hyrcanus (134-104 B.C.E.), says that these regulations of the Pharisees were not accepted by the Sadducees, who insisted "that only those regulations should be considered valid which were written down (in Scripture), and that those which had been handed down by former generations need not be observed" (13.297). The meaning of this distinction in views between the two groups has received much scholarly discussion, but it is clear enough that at issue between the two was the proper way for interpreting and applying the Mosaic Law, which both of course accepted as authoritative for practice. A number of the controversies between Jesus and the Pharisees reported in the Gospels present a similar picture of the Pharisees. When the "Pharisees and scribes" asked Jesus why his disciples "break the tradition of the elders" since they did not follow the practice of washing their hands before they ate, he answered: "And why do you break the commandment of God for the sake of your tradition?" (Matt. 15:3; see also v. 6; he cites their view about identifying goods as an offering and thus not using them to support parents as a violation of the fourth commandment).

Josephus identifies the Pharisees as an influential group within Jewish society. He claims that there were some 6,000 of them (*Ant.* 17.42) but says they were able to bring the masses to their side and even compel rulers to act in accord with their teachings (*Ant.* 13.288, 298; 18.15). Whether that was always true may be debated, but Josephus does tell about two periods when the Pharisees were especially influential with Hasmonean rulers and thus in the state. The background to his story about John Hyrcanus' break with the Pharisaic party is that they were in his favor before this. In fact, Josephus calls John Hyrcanus a disciple of theirs; how long this relationship had existed and whether it obtained in the time of his predecessors is not said. When Hyrcanus, convinced they had maligned him by telling him he should give up the high priesthood, changed to the side of the Sadducees, the Pharisees lost power and Jews were forbidden to practice their regulations. The dominance of the Sadducees with the Hasmonean rulers continued through the violent reign of Alexander Jannaeus, who apparently killed many Pharisees, but with his successor, his wife Salome Alexandra (76-67 B.C.E.), the situation was reversed and the Pharisees regained a position of dominance. After this time the evidence becomes sketchy, and it is not apparent whether Pharisees continued to enjoy political as well as religious prominence.

Regarding their beliefs, Josephus mentions their moderate position on the issue of what he calls fate: they believed that both divine and individual human aspects were involved in human actions so that people had a measure of responsibility for what they did. According to him, they also anticipated a resurrection for the righteous and eternal punishment for the wicked. There is support for some of this description in Acts 23, where the Pharisees are identified as the members of the Sanhedrin who accept the belief that a resurrection would occur. It adds that they also believed there were angels and spirits.

The next group in Josephus' list, the Sadducees, he describes generally in contrast to the Pharisees. Their view of fate, for example, was not the moderate or balanced approach of the Pharisees: the Sadducees are supposed to have denied there was any thing such as fate that influenced human behavior, explaining rather that people are responsible for what they do. As noted above, the Sadducees rejected the validity of the tradition adopted by the Pharisees and insisted that the scriptural law alone was valid. It is difficult to imagine that the Sadducees had no tradition of how to interpret or apply scriptural law; whatever their way of interpreting may have been, it must have been different from the Pharisaic one. Acts 23:8 summarizes some of their theological disagreements with Pharisees in this way: "The Sadducees say that there is no resurrection, or angel, or spirit; but the Pharisees acknowledge all three." In his appearance before the Sanhedrin, Paul, who identifies himself as a Pharisee, exploits the difference by appealing to the resurrection.

Josephus adds that, while the Pharisees were influential among the masses of the people, the Sadducees, whose number he does not estimate (although he says there were few of them), appealed to the wealthy. In the episode in which John Hyrcanus broke with the Pharisees, he is said to have gone over to the Sadducean side. As a result, the Sadducees were not dominant in the period before this time in his reign, but they retained their position of influence throughout the rest of Hyrcanus' reign and apparently through that of Aristobulus I (104-103 B.C.E.) and of Alexander Jannaeus (103-76), before the Pharisees returned to their previous status. Josephus presents, for later times, a strange situation: the few Sadducees were people of the highest rank, but when they assumed an office, they were compelled to follow the dictates of the Pharisees because the people otherwise would refuse to tolerate them (*Ant.* 18.17). The point is related to the question whether the high priests — people who enjoyed the very highest rank — were Sadducees. The name Sadducee many be related to the Zadok, the leading priest in the time of David and Solomon, and an ancestor of the Second Temple high priests. John

Hyrcanus, a high priest, became a devotee of the Sadducees, and his sons Aristobulus I and John Hyrcanus may have been as well. But here the evidence grows very thin. In fact, the only other high priest who is identified as a Sadducee is Ananus ben Ananus who briefly held the office in 62 C.E. Josephus says that Ananus, followed the Sadducean school and that Sadducees were noted for being harsher than others in judgment (*Ant.* 20.199). A high priest is mentioned in connection with Sadducees in Acts 5:17, but he is not identified as a Sadducee.

The Essenes, Josephus' third group, are the one he describes at the greatest length (*J.W.* 2.119-61), perhaps because his source material was more complete or because their unusual character made them more interesting. He estimated there were some 4,000 of them throughout the land (*Ant.* 18.21) and describes them as living a very disciplined form of life and gathered into communities of self-help and support. In their communities the members gave up their private property to the group so that the needs of all could be met. They avoided marriage, although there was a type of Essenes who did take wives and have children. They worked hard and were frugal in their ways; they were also known as the strictest in their keeping of the Sabbath. One of the topics regarding the Essenes that Josephus describes at some length is the process, several years in length, of admission into the group. He also notes their meetings and the rules that prevailed at them. Their view of fate, he reports, was that it determined everything — exactly the opposite of the view he attributes to the Sadducees; they also studied the writings of the ancients and were accurate predictors of events.

Scholarly interest in the Essenes increased with the discovery and study of the Dead Sea Scrolls. Most experts have identified the group responsible for the scrolls at Qumran as a small band of Essenes, so the scrolls can now fill in the information from Josephus and elsewhere regarding the Essenes. It may be that Josephus' comment about the Essenes' view regarding fate is exemplified in 1QS 3:13–4:26, where the divine governance of the universe and human actions through two opposing spirits is the subject. The scrolls community also practiced a community of goods, and their entry procedures very much resemble the ones noted by Josephus.

The scrolls probably allow us to see some of the controversies that separated the Essenes and the Pharisees. Several writers refer to their opponents as "the ones who look for smooth things," probably a punning allusion to the Pharisees. These writers accuse them of taking a more relaxed approach to the Law of Moses and thus of violating the covenant. Some scrolls, especially the copies of 4QMMT, express some legal positions that are attributed to the Sadducees in rabbinic sources. This does not mean that the authors of the Scrolls were Sadducees, since they disagree with the Sadducees on basic theological points (e.g., fate); it probably means that both the Essenes and the Sadducees adopted conservative, stricter understandings of the Law.

The community of the Dead Sea Scrolls illustrates the fact that the social makeup of early Judaism was more complex than our other sources suggested. Before they were discovered between 1947 and 1956, there was only a hint or two in the literature that such a group existed; there was no indication that it had a large library indicative of extensive study and much more. The scrolls reveal a community that had in protest separated itself physically from other Jews and that apparently did not participate in worship at the Temple in Jerusalem. In the wilderness of Judea they pursued the way of life they thought was revealed in the Scriptures and looked to the day when, in a final war between the sons of light and the sons of darkness, the former would win a great victory and a new age would dawn.

These were not the only groups in the land of Israel in the later Second Temple period. Josephus also speaks of the Zealots as people who refused to accept human rule, although in other respects they agreed with the Pharisees (*Ant.* 18.23). Josephus considered them and their violent ways instrumental in causing the revolt against Rome in 66 C.E. (*Ant.* 18.6-10).

Literature

There is no doubting that Jews in the land of Israel wrote a sizable literature in the centuries when the Second Temple stood, and a considerable amount of it has survived to the present in one form or another, that is, in whole or in part, in the original language or in translation. Rarely is there information about exactly when a book was written or who wrote it, but texts of a variety of literary genres were composed in the period. A number of those works are now incorporated into the Hebrew Bible, although it is not always certain which books date from the Second Temple era. There would be a large amount of agreement among experts about the following as coming from the postexilic age:

Final form of the Pentateuch
1-2 Chronicles
Ezra
Nehemiah
Esther
Many of the psalms
Ecclesiastes
Daniel
Third Isaiah (Isaiah 56–66)
Joel
Haggai
Zechariah
Malachi

Perhaps there are other books or parts of books in the Hebrew Bible stemming from the years after the initial return from exile.

In the later centuries of the period, Jews continued to write, and many of their compositions have survived to the present. One difficulty is that it is not always clear which books were written in Israel and which in the Diaspora. A possible indicator of location is language (if we happen to know the original language of the work): a book written in Hebrew or Aramaic is more likely to have been written in Judea (or Babylon) than in Egypt, while a work in Greek has a better chance of coming from Egypt or some other part of the Hellenistic world. But one should not exclude the possibility that a Greek work comes from Israel. One other note should precede the survey of Jewish literature from Israel: in a sense Josephus, a prolific author whose works are invaluable for understanding early Judaism, is a writer from Israel. He spent the first thirty years or so of his life in Judea, where he was a prominent priest and occupied important positions. But the Judean Jew Josephus actually wrote his histories *War* and *Antiquities* and his *Life* and *Against Apion* while he was living in Rome after the end of the Jewish revolt in 70 C.E. In that sense he is a Diaspora writer. He seems to have composed *War* in a Semitic language, but only the Greek version exists today.

It is convenient to divide the books and other works that were probably written in Israel into different, rather general literary categories.

History

An important component of the Hebrew Scriptures is the set of histories that trace the great events of Israel's sacred and not so sacred past (Genesis, Exodus, Numbers, Joshua, Judges, 1-2 Samuel, 1-2 Kings, 1-2 Chronicles, Ezra, Nehemiah). Writing in this vein continued in early Judaism. The most prominent example is 1 Maccabees. It is likely that the work was written in Hebrew. It presents a historical review of the period from Alexander the Great to the death of the Hasmonean Simon (from the late fourth century to 134 B.C.E.), but it covers the first centuries of this period in a few sentences and concentrates its attention on the approximately thirty years from about 175 to 134. The author is an advocate of the Hasmonean family, beginning with Mattathias, who sounded the call to revolt against the policies of Antiochus IV Epiphanes, and continuing with his sons Judas, Jonathan, and Simon, who led the nation in its struggle for the right to practice their traditional religion and to freedom from foreign rule. At first they led forces that were opposed to the suppression of ancestral religious practices and to the desecration of the Temple. After regaining the Temple Mount from Seleucid and renegade Jewish control, they purified the Temple and inaugurated the festival of Hanukkah to commemorate the event (it lasts eight days, beginning on 9/25). After Judas died in battle, leadership of the Hasmonean forces fell to Jonathan, who, in 152 B.C.E., was appointed the high priest. He held the office until his capture and death in 142, when his brother Simon assumed the leadership and the high priesthood. Simon was killed in 134, and the book ends with a notice about the reign of his son John Hyrcanus I. Despite its strong pro-Hasmonean bias, the book is a profoundly important history for the period covered. The author quotes official documents and offers a careful chronology of events. The book was written no later than 104 B.C.E. (the death of John Hyrcanus); it was translated into Greek and became a part of the Greek Bible (it is in Roman Catholic and Orthodox Bibles today but is considered apocryphal by Protestants and Jews).

The other major histories of the period that are extant are Josephus' *War* and *Antiquities*, although, as indicated above, they were not written in Judea. *War* is primarily an account of the First Jewish Revolt against Rome (66-70 C.E.) with a long prologue beginning just before Hasmonean times. *Antiquities* begins with the scriptural stories (from the beginning of Genesis) and follows them to the end (Esther, Ezra-Nehemiah material) before continuing with events until Josephus' own time. His coverage of large parts of the post-Hebrew Bible period is sketchy because of inadequate source material, but he offers extensive accounts from the Hasmonean period to the mid-first century C.E. and is often the only source of information about these times.

Stories

A number of narrative works that do not appear to be historical in intent express, often in highly entertaining ways, the theological and ethical views of the authors.

The book of Tobit may have been written in Israel, although it is not impossible that it comes from somewhere in the eastern Diaspora. The Aramaic work (copies of it have been found at Qumran [4Q196-199 in Aramaic, 4Q200 in Hebrew]) tells the parallel stories of two pious Jews whose lives had become tragedies, although they maintained their religious fidelity in dire circumstances, and who were delivered through the agency of the angel Raphael. The book commends pious deeds by Diaspora Jews such as almsgiving, care for fellow Jews, praise of God, prayer, and endogamy.

The book of Judith was written in Hebrew, although it is available only in a Greek translation. The author paints a confusing situation blending Babylonian, Persian, and perhaps other times, but its aim is to describe the deliverance God gave to his beleaguered people through the hand of a woman named Judith, whose extraordinary piety and remarkable bravery and cleverness brought about victory for the Jews in the land when the great general Holophernes and his massive army wished to destroy them. The book also presents an interesting example of a proselyte in the form of Achior the Ammonite.

Legal Texts

From early in the Second Temple period there is little evidence of legal literature in the sense of laws such as those in the Pentateuch. Those books may have reached their final form early in the period, but from the centuries that followed no such texts are attested until the literature found at Qumran. Among the scrolls are different sorts of works that deal with and expound the law of Moses; these are in addition to the numerous copies of the pentateuchal books found there. Examples are 4QMMT, which lists more than twenty legal points on which the group differs from those whom they address; and the *Temple Scroll,* which describes a grand future temple and all that will accompany it, such as the festivals, and represents and paraphrases a large part of the material in Exodus 25 through Deuteronomy. Additional texts, only fragmentarily preserved, deal with various aspects of the Law (e.g., ones that treat issues of purity and impurity [4Q274-279]; calendar texts [4Q317-330]). Other sorts of legal texts, ones that supply laws specifically for the group, are the *Rule of the Community* and the *Damascus Document,* the latter of which includes a lengthy halakic section. The legal texts from Qumran show that the kind of reflection that was later codified in the Mishnah and the Talmuds was at home in a much earlier time and was practiced by a group representing a very different point of view from the one found in the rabbinic works.

Wisdom Literature

A major sapiential work, the Wisdom of Ben Sira, was written in Hebrew (more than half of which has been recovered) at some time in the early second century B.C.E. The lengthy book (51 chapters) stands in the tradition of Proverbs, offering wise teachings on a range of practical issues. It marks an additional step in the sapiential tradition by teaching that the place where wisdom is to be found is in the Law of Moses (see also Bar. 3:9–4:4) and that the essence of wise behavior is to fear God. Ben Sira also differs from earlier wisdom literature by surveying Israel's history and the divine guidance in it. The Hebrew work was rendered into Greek by the author's grandson, whose preface explains the situation, purpose, and time of the translation.

A second example of a wisdom text is 4QInstruction, a work represented in several copies among the Dead Sea Scrolls (4Q415-418, 423; 1Q26). It offers prudent instructions to a younger person on familiar topics, but it also has characteristics which distinguish it from its predecessors in the wisdom tradition. One expression that appears a number of times is "the secret of what is/will be" — apparently meaning the secret teaching about the true character of the creation and of history. The work also incorporates eschatological teachings into a wisdom work.

Scriptural Interpretation

Throughout early Judaism, interpretation of older scriptures was an important exercise. This is evident in the Hebrew Bible (e.g., Daniel 9) and outside it. Among the most interesting examples are a series of commentaries found at Qumran. These pesharim or interpretations offer comments on scriptural prophetic texts; they cite a passage and then explain it before proceeding to the next passage in the book (occasionally more than one book is involved). The best-preserved examples are the commentaries on Nahum (4Q169) and Habakkuk (1QpHab); altogether seventeen copies of pesharim have been identified (1QpHab; 1Q14-16; 4Q161-71, 173), treating Isaiah, Hosea, Micah, Nahum, Habakkuk, Zephaniah, and several Psalms. These lemmatized commentaries allow the reader to see how the Qumran community understood the ancient prophecies to be coming true in their own day; they also disclose some information about that time and important characters in their world. Other types of commentaries are not tied to particular texts but are more thematic and thus treat texts from various places in the scriptures. Among them are the *Florilegium* (4Q174) and the *Melchizedek* text (11Q13).

Scriptural interpretation may be the rubric under which to survey a set of works called by scholars Rewritten Bible or, better, Rewritten Scriptures. These texts take the contents of an older scriptural work, in whole or in part, and re-present them. At times the representation is so close to the original that the difference is practically negligible (*Reworked Pentateuch* from Qumran is an example), while in others there is a wide difference (such as in the *Book of the Watchers* [*1 Enoch* 1–36]). The representation can accomplish several goals, such as clarifying obscure passages, adding to or subtracting from the older text in various ways to communicate the old message in a new form. Familiar examples that fall into this broad and diverse category are parts of *1 Enoch,* the *Aramaic Levi Document,* the *Genesis Apocryphon,* the *Book of Jubilees,* and the *Temple Scroll. 1 Enoch* 1–36 (the *Book of the Watchers*) in part treats passages about Enoch and the immediate pre-flood period in Genesis 5–6 but expands considerably through an elaborate story of angels who descend, marry women, and have gigantic children whose misdeeds, with the illicit teachings of the angels, cause the flood. Enoch is presented as a mediator between God and the sinful angels and also as a traveling companion of angels on a tour of the world. The *Aramaic Levi Document* takes the rather problematic scriptural character Levi and greatly exalts him as a divinely appointed priest, the ancestor of a priesthood, and the recipient of revelations. The Aramaic *Genesis Apocryphon* offers stories from the early chapters of Genesis until chap. 15 (where the manuscript breaks off). The book of *Jubilees* more closely adheres to its scriptural base as it retells the stories from Genesis 1 to Exodus 24, all of which was revealed to Moses on Mt. Sinai. It packages them in its theologically eloquent chronology of fifty jubilee units and emphasizes the one, frequently renewed covenant between God and the chosen line, the importance of separating from the nations, the need to keep the Sabbath properly, and the significance of following the correct calendar of 364 days in a year. The *Temple Scroll* is a rewriting of the remaining parts of the Pentateuch (beginning with Exodus 24), while the *Reworked Pentateuch* is at times classified as scriptural and at times as Reworked Scripture.

Also within the area of scriptural interpretation are targums, Aramaic translations and interpretations of the Hebrew Scriptures. Although the major targums *(Onqelos* and *Jonathan)* date from much later times, the presence of Aramaic renderings of Job (4Q157; 11Q10) and apparently Leviticus (4Q156) at Qumran illustrate that this type of exercise has ancient roots.

Apocalypses

Several works give an account of revelatory experiences given to exemplary leaders; the revelations to them disclose information about the future and the heavenly world. Among the apocalypses, perhaps the oldest is the Enochic *Apocalypse of Weeks* (*1 Enoch* 93:1-10; 91:11-17), which divides all of history and the future judgments into ten "weeks" (long units of time). Other early instances are the various revelations in Daniel 7–12, which "predict" the attacks on Jews and Judaism by Antiochus IV as the climax of evil and distress before the deliverance of the people of God. The *Animal Apocalypse* (*1 Enoch* 83–90) may come from nearly the same time. It surveys scriptural history, symbolizing almost all characters as various kinds of animals, and pictures a new age after the final woes caused by the nations that rule Israel and the judgment on the sinners. A number of other works fit in this category: the *Similitudes of Enoch* (*1 Enoch* 37–71), the *Testament of Moses*, *4 Ezra*, and *2 Baruch*. The first two of these may have been written around the turn of the eras, while the latter two offer apocalyptic reflection upon the destruction of Jerusalem and the Temple. In some of the apocalypses a messianic leader plays a role in the final drama (e.g., *Animal Apocalypse*, *Similitudes of Enoch*, *4 Ezra*, *2 Baruch*).

It is generally agreed that there was no canon of Scripture until perhaps the very end of the Second Temple period, but it is evident that there were ancient writings that exercised considerable influence and were acknowledged to contain God's words. Those books would have included Genesis through Deuteronomy and the prophetic works and Psalms and probably more, but it is not possible, given the evidence at hand, to decide exactly which books were considered authoritative and by whom.

Poetic and Liturgical Works

The Psalms incorporated into the Hebrew Psalter served various functions in Temple worship and presumably in other settings as well, but these 150 poems hardly comprise the totality of poetic writing in the period. Again, the Qumran texts have offered abundant examples of such compositions. The *Hodayot* or *Thanksgiving Hymns* are sectarian poetic compositions which celebrate the greatness of God and his goodness to those whom he has chosen and other teachings of the group (such as divine predestination of events). Another set of poems has been labeled *Noncanonical Psalms* (4Q380-381). Among the scrolls are also texts that contain prayers for certain occasions (daily [4Q503] and festival [4Q507-509] prayers) and blessings for each day (4Q504-506; see also the *Berakhot* or *Blessings* texts, 4Q286-290). Considerable interest attaches to the *Songs of the Sabbath Sacrifice* (4Q400-407; 11Q17), which describes the heavenly worship on the first thirteen Sabbaths of a year and assumes a unity between the angelic worship offered in the celestial sanctuary and the worship offered by humans on earth. Poetry of a different nature is found in the *Psalms of Solomon*, a first-century-B.C.E. work that, among other topics, speaks bitterly about the Hasmonean rulers and about Pompey, the Roman general who took Jerusalem in 63 B.C.E. *Psalms of Solomon* 17 and 18 also offer some important statements about a Davidic messiah.

Other texts were written, but the above survey should suffice to give an idea of the range of Judean literature written in the period of early Judaism.

Commonalities

The surviving evidence exhibits a richness and diversity in Judaism of the Second Temple era, a diversity so great that some have resorted to the neologism "Judaisms" to express it. Yet, despite the undoubted diversity present in the texts, there are fundamental beliefs and practices that would have been accepted by virtually all Jews during those centuries and that justify retaining the singular noun Judaism.

Monotheism

There were some Jews who rejected this doctrine, but the data, both Jewish and foreign, indicate that belief in one God was a defining characteristic of Judaism. Jews confessed that God was one and that he was the creator and sustainer of all, and non-Jews recognized monotheism as a trait that made Jews different from most others. In obedience to the second commandment, Jews made no representation of the God they worshiped, and in this regard, too, they were distinctive. The Temple in Jerusalem was unusual in that it contained no visible representation of the deity; he was thought to be enthroned upon the Ark of the Covenant between the cherubim, but there was no object representing him.

Covenant

The one God had entered into a covenant with Abraham, the ancestor of the Jews and, later, with his descendants, the people of Israel. The covenant remained valid and binding; it not only defined a relationship between YHWH and his people but also took the concrete form of stipulating the way of life that the descendants of Abraham were to follow in order to remain in covenantal fellowship with him. The most specific form of that definition was the Law of Moses, which therefore had to be obeyed and interpreted as new situations arose. Among the laws that regulated the covenantal behavior of Jewish people, several stood out as particularly important and known to non-Jews: an aniconic worship of the one God and rejection of all other deities and idols associated with them, Sabbath observance, circumcision, food laws, festivals, and separation from others because of the theological danger of intermarriage and impurity.

The history of the covenantal relationship that obtained between God and Israel took on special importance as evidence of divine election and guidance and as a source of lessons to be learned about the consequences of obedience or disobedience. Covenant violation was regarded as the root cause for catastrophes such as the destruction of Jerusalem and the Temple; the wise could learn from such instances and act accordingly. Amid disaster, Jews entertained hopes for a restoration of grander times; one such hope was for a messianic leader from David's line.

With the loss of the center — Jerusalem and the Temple — in 70 C.E. and carnage and loss throughout the land, an era in Jewish history ended and a new one began. Of necessity, the leadership of the nation changed, with no Jewish political leader and no class of priests in influential positions, but so rich was the heritage of Judaism that other aspects of it came to the fore as it moved into the age of the Tannaim and their work. Even the brutal Roman quashing of the Bar Kokhba Revolt (132-135 C.E.), another disaster for the land and its populace, did not prevent the Jewish people from surviving, from continuing to believe in the one God, and from adhering to the covenant and the way of life entailed in it.

BIBLIOGRAPHY

Ådna, Achim. 1999. *Jerusalemer Tempel und Tempelmarkt im 1. Jahrhundert n. Chr.* Wiesbaden: Harrassowitz.

Charlesworth, James H., ed. 1983-1985. *The Old Testament Pseudepigrapha.* 2 vols. Garden City, N.Y.: Doubleday.

Collins, John J. 1998. *The Apocalyptic Imagination: An Introduction to Jewish Apocalyptic Literature.* 2d ed. Grand Rapids: Eerdmans.

Falk, Daniel K. 1998. *Daily, Sabbath, and Festival Prayers in the Dead Sea Scrolls.* Leiden: Brill.

Grabbe, Lester L. 1992. *Judaism from Cyrus to Hadrian.* 2 vols. Minneapolis: Fortress.

———. 2000. *Judaic Religion in the Second Temple Period: Belief and Practice from the Exile to Yavneh.* London: Routledge.

Hengel, Martin. 1974. *Judaism and Hellenism.* 2 vols. London: SCM.

Kugel, James L. 1998. *Traditions of the Bible: A Guide to the Bible As It Was at the Start of the Common Era.* Cambridge: Harvard University Press.

Levine, Lee I. 2002. *Jerusalem: Portrait of the City in the Second Temple Period (538 B.C.E.–70 C.E.).* Philadelphia: Jewish Publication Society.

Mantel, Hugo. 1961. *Studies in the History of the Sanhedrin.* Cambridge: Harvard University Press.

Mendels, Doron. 1987. *The Land of Israel as a Political Concept in Hasmonean Literature.* Tübingen: Mohr-Siebeck.

Murphy, Frederick J. 2002. *Early Judaism: The Exile to the Time of Jesus.* Peabody, Mass.: Hendrickson.

Nickelsburg, George W. E. 2005. *Jewish Literature between the Bible and the Mishnah.* 2d ed. Minneapolis: Fortress.

Rajak, Tessa. 2002. *Josephus: The Historian and His Society.* 2d ed. London: Duckworth.

Richardson, Peter. 1996. *Herod: King of the Jews and Friend of the Romans.* Columbia: University of South Carolina Press.

Rubenstein, Jeffrey L. 1995. *The History of Sukkot in the Second Temple and Rabbinic Periods.* Atlanta: Scholars Press.

Safrai, Shmuel. 1965. *Pilgrimage at the Time of the Second Temple.* Tel-Aviv: Am Hassefer (in Hebrew).

Sanders, E. P. 1992. *Judaism: Practice and Belief 66 BCE–66 CE.* London: SCM; Philadelphia: Trinity Press International.

Schiffman, Lawrence H. 1991. *From Text to Tradition: A History of Judaism in Second Temple and Rabbinic Times.* New York: KTAV.

———. 1998. *Texts and Traditions: A Source Reader for the Study of Second Temple and Rabbinic Judaism.* New York: KTAV.

Schürer, Emil. 1973-1987. *The History of the Jewish People in the Age of Jesus Christ.* Rev. and ed. G. Vermes, F. Millar, and M. Goodman. 3 vols. Edinburgh: Clark.

Segal, Judah Benzion. 1963. *The Hebrew Passover from the Earliest Times to A.D. 70.* Oxford: Oxford University Press.

Sievers, Joseph. 1990. *The Hasmoneans and Their Supporters: From Mattathias to the Death of John Hyrcanus I.* Atlanta: Scholars Press.

Stone, Michal, ed. 1984. *Jewish Writings of the Second Temple Period: Apocrypha, Pseudepigrapha, Qumran Sectarian Writings, Philo, Josephus.* Assen: Van Gorcum; Philadelphia: Fortress.

Ulfgard, Håkan. 1998. *The Story of Sukkot: The Setting, Shaping, and Sequel of the Biblical Feast of Tabernacles.* Tübingen: Mohr-Siebeck.

VanderKam, James C. 2001. *An Introduction to Early Judaism.* Grand Rapids: Eerdmans.

———. 2004. *From Joshua to Caiaphas: High Priests after the Exile.* Minneapolis: Fortress.

VanderKam, James C., and Peter W. Flint. 2002. *The Meaning of the Dead Sea Scrolls: Their Significance for Understanding the Bible, Judaism, Jesus, and Christianity.* San Francisco: HarperSanFrancisco.

Judaism in the Diaspora

Erich S. Gruen

A Roman army destroyed the Temple in Jerusalem in 70 C.E. For the Jews of antiquity the loss of the Temple not only constituted a devastating blow but signaled an enduring trauma. The reverberations of that event still resonate. The day of the Temple's destruction, which, by a quirk of fate or (more probably) fabrication, coincides with that on which Jerusalem fell to the Babylonians six and a half centuries earlier, continues to receive annual commemoration in Israel. For many it shaped the consciousness of the Jewish Diaspora through the centuries to follow. The eradication of the center that had given meaning and definition to the nation's identity obliged Jews to alter their sights, accommodate to a displaced existence, and rethink their own heritage in the context of alien surroundings.

The Extent of the Jewish Diaspora

The focus on the consequences of the Temple's destruction, however, overlooks a fact of immense significance: the Jewish Diaspora had a long history prior to Rome's crushing of Jerusalem. Indeed, the notion of removal from the homeland is lodged deeply in the mythology of the nation. The curse of Cain, condemned to perpetual wandering over the earth, symbolizes it. So do the years of enslavement and oppression in Egypt prior to the exodus, followed by years of meandering in the wilderness. And that was just the beginning. The record of Jewish experience included the "Babylonian captivity" in the sixth century B.C.E., ostensibly a serious dislocation from the homeland. The story may contain exaggeration and embellishment but does not deliver pure fiction. And, whatever the historicity of the "Return" from that displacement, the Diaspora was already a fact, not to be reversed. Jews dwelled in Egypt in the sixth century, as papyri from a Jewish military colony at Elephantine reveal. And an archive of documents from Babylon attests to Jews in a variety of trades and professions even after their supposed restoration to Judah.

The pace quickened, however, and the scattering multiplied from the late fourth century B.C.E. The conquests of Alexander the Great sent Greeks into the Near East in substantial numbers. The collapse of the Persian Empire prompted a wave of migration and relocation. New communities sprang up, old ones were repopulated or expanded. Mobility increased, and a host of settlements beckoned to the restless and the adventurous. As Greeks found the prospects abroad enticing, so also did the Jews. A burgeoning Jewish Diaspora, it appears, followed in the wake of the Greek Diaspora.

Precise numbers elude us. But they were clearly substantial. By the late second century B.C.E., the author of 1 Maccabees could claim that Jews had found their way not only to Egypt, Syria, Mesopotamia, and the Iranian plateau, but to the cities and principalities of Asia Minor, to the islands of the Aegean, to Greece itself, to Crete, Cyprus, and Cyrene. We know further of Jewish communities in Italy, including large settlements in Rome and Ostia. The Greek geographer Strabo, writing at the end of the first century B.C.E. (and he had no axe to grind on the subject), remarked that there was hardly a place in the world that did not possess members of this tribe and feel their weight. And all of this occurred well before the demolition of the Temple. Even without explicit figures we may be confident that Jews abroad far outnumbered those dwelling in Palestine — and had done so for many generations.

The fact needs to be underscored. Diaspora life in the Second Temple period was no aberration, not a marginal, exceptional, temporary, or fleeting part of Jewish experience. In important ways it constituted the most characteristic ingredient of that experience. The Temple stood in Jerusalem. Yet the vast majority of Jews dwelled elsewhere. The physical and emotional world of the Jews cannot be grasped without placing the Diaspora under scrutiny.

What motivated the mass migration? Some of it, to be sure, was involuntary and unwelcome. Many of those who found themselves abroad had come as captives, prisoners of war, and slaves. Conflicts between the Egyptian and Syrian kingdoms in the third century B.C.E. caused periodic dislocation. Internal upheavals in Palestine in the following century created some political refugees and forced settlements. Roman intervention in the Near East temporarily accelerated the process. Pompey's victories in Judea in 63 B.C.E., followed by battles on Palestinian soil over the next three decades, brought an unspecified number of Jews to Italy as human booty, the victims of conquest.

Compulsory displacement, however, cannot have accounted for more than a fraction of the Diaspora. A host of reasons could motivate Jews to migrate voluntarily. Overpopulation in Palestine may have been a factor for some, indebtedness for others. But more than hardship was involved here. The new and expanded communities that sprang up in consequence of Alexander's acquisitions served as magnets for migration. In a mobile society, a range of options presented themselves. Large numbers of Jews found employment as mercenaries, military colonists, or enlisted men in the regular forces of Hellenic cities or kingdoms. Others seized opportunities in business, commerce, or agriculture. All lands were open to them.

The Jewish Conception of Diaspora

How did Jews conceptualize the Diaspora? What sort of self-perception shaped the thinking of those who dwelled in Antioch, Alexandria, Rome, Cyrene, Ephesus, or anywhere outside Judea? The biblical reverberations of the scattering of Israel possessed a decidedly somber character, a dark cloud cast upon Jews whose memories of the homeland grew ever dimmer. The book of Leviticus had declared that divine retaliation for their sins would disperse Israelites among the nations. The anger of YHWH, so one reads in Deuteronomy, would pursue them in foreign lands where they would worship false gods and idols. Jeremiah's pronouncements reinforced the message: the Israelites who turn their backs on YHWH will live as slaves of alien lords in alien parts, scattered among strange peoples where they will endure God's punishment until their destruction. And Daniel warns that failure to heed divine commandments will provoke God to order the dispersal of Israel. Diaspora thus appears to emblematize enforced expulsion from the homeland, a condemnation for wickedness, with sinners languishing abroad in distant parts under the oppressive sway of hostile strangers.

Yet dire biblical forecasts may bear little relevance to Diaspora life in the Hellenistic and Roman periods. Historical reality stands in the way. Can one plausibly conceive of Jews living abroad in countless numbers over many generations mired in misery and longing for the land of their forefathers? The scenario is preposterous. A sense of displacement did not dominate Jewish consciousness in communities strewn around the Mediterranean. It is noteworthy that Jews seem to have felt no need to fashion a theory of Diaspora. Those who inhabited a world of Greek culture and Roman power did not wrestle with or agonize over the fact of dispersal. It was an integral part of their existence and a central element of their identity.

The very term "Diaspora" is a Greek one. It rarely appears as a noun in Hellenistic Jewish authors. And it nowhere serves as a translation of *galut* or *golah* with the connotation of "exile." In fact, the authors of the Septuagint normally rendered such terms as "colony" or a version of "colony." In normal Greek usage the word carried no negative overtones and, in fact, Hellenic colonies generally developed fully independent existences. The founding of Jerusalem is ascribed to Moses by a Greek author who labels it a "colony" and gives it a positive meaning. Jews evidently picked up this phraseology from the Gentiles. Philo alludes to the Hebrews led out of Egypt by Moses as a "colony." And movement in the other direction receives the same designation: the Jews of Palestine sent out colonies to places all over the Mediterranean and the Near East. The migration generated a sense of pride, not an embarrassment or a lament. Jewish intellectuals did not fill their writings with complaints about being cut off from the center and confined to a truncated, isolated, and subservient existence. One hears no agonizing rationalizations, justifications, or apologias for Diaspora. That itself is telling.

Just how the Jews did feel about their circumstances abroad escapes direct notice. Indirect evidence has to suffice. And generalizations that encompass the Mediterranean world would be hazardous, if not downright misleading. The experience of Jewish communities in Asia Minor may have little bearing on that of the Jews in Babylon or Cyrene or Rome. The very notion of "Diaspora Judaism" suggests a uniformity that is unlikely to have existed. Circumstances differed and reactions varied. It would be an error to imagine that Jews everywhere faced a choice of either maintaining tenacious adherence to a segregated existence or assimilating fully to an alien culture. There was much room in between, and Jews doubtless ranged themselves on all parts of the spectrum. Each individual area struck its balance differently and constructed its own peculiar mixture. It was rarely a conscious or calculated process.

Synagogues in the Diaspora

But common ground did exist. Substantial evidence attests to the near ubiquity of synagogues. The term itself, *synagōgē,* may not always have been applied. Other designations like *proseuchē* (prayer house) or *hieron* (holy place) also appear. And the reference may be to a gathering or an assemblage rather than to a building. No model or pattern held throughout. A diversity of functions, physical characteristics, and institutional structures preclude any notion of uniformity. But impressive and widespread testimony demonstrates that the synagogue (in whatever form) could serve as a means to promote communal activity among Jews and advance a sense of collective identity. The evidence comes from literary texts, inscriptions, papyri, and archaeological finds that disclose outlines of the structures themselves. The bulk of it dates to the period after destruction of the Temple. But ample attestation in the Second Temple era shows the broad geographical range of the synagogue.

A sanctuary at Elephantine in Upper Egypt served a Jewish military colony as early as the sixth century B.C.E. That may have been exceptional, but it signals the natural inclination of Jews, wherever they were, to find a medium for expressing common interests. By the mid-third century, inscriptions reveal synagogues (termed *proseuchai*) in Middle Egypt, dedicated by Jews in honor of the Ptolemies, the ruling family of the land. Royal favor extended to the Jewish *proseuchai,* even to the extent of granting the formal status of places of asylum, commonly accorded to pagan temples, a notable mark of official approval. A plethora of synagogues stood in Alexandria, noted by literary sources and epigraphic texts. The latter provide the standard formulas whereby the dedicators establish their *proseuchē* on behalf of Ptolemy and his household. Egyptian Jews were fully comfortable in hailing the Gentile rulers while simultaneously dedicating their synagogues to the "Most High God." No tension or inconsistency troubled the two concepts. Jewish synagogues were a familiar part of the Egyptian landscape.

Jews also settled in Cyrenaica in significant numbers. Synagogues clearly sprang up. One inscription honors donors whose gifts helped to repair the synagogue in a Cyrenaic town. That a graphic declaration of gratitude to benefactors should be put on public display, in addition to the structure itself, which they hoped to refurbish, demonstrates that Jews took open pride in the maintenance of their own institutions and in announcing that maintenance to any interested party in the larger community.

Jews were to be found all over Asia Minor. The travels of Paul and his colleagues brought them regularly to Jewish synagogues of that region. And Roman pronouncements, collected through the documentary researches of Josephus, guaranteed the rights of Jews to construct and assemble in synagogues.

The institution surfaces quite strikingly in Greek cities on the north and east coasts of the Black Sea. A remarkable group of documents from the first century C.E. records the emancipation of slaves by Jews in the synagogues of those cities and provides for the continued association of the freedmen with the Jewish community, which took responsibility for their guardianship — a clear sign of collective solidarity.

Numerous other examples can illustrate the geographic spread of the synagogue. Paul's journeys, for example, took him to synagogues in various cities of Macedon and Greece. An actual structure, almost certainly a synagogue, emerged from excavations at the island of Delos in the Aegean. That a Jewish community settled in that holy site, the legendary birthplace of Apollo, dramatically attests to the comfort of Jews and their own institutions even in a key center of pagan religion. Jews indeed went as far from the homeland as Italy to establish thriving communities. The presence of Jews in Rome is well attested not only by literary texts but by funerary epitaphs from the Jewish catacombs that convey the names of at least eleven synagogues in the city. And archaeologists have unearthed the remains of a synagogue in Ostia, the principal harbor of Rome, situated near the bank of the Tiber. Here, as often elsewhere, the finds disclose characteristic Jewish features like an apsidal structure for Torah scrolls and images like the menorah, lulav, shofar, and ethrog, thus making the identification clear. Jewish synagogues of the Second Temple period stretched from the Black Sea to North Africa, and from Syria to Italy.

The synagogue supplied a vehicle for a wide range of activities that promoted the shared interests of Jews. These included study and instruction; discussion of the Scriptures, traditions, law, and moral teachings; prayers, rituals, and worship; communal dining, celebration of festivals, and commemoration of key events in Jewish history; adjudication of disputes, passage of decrees, meetings of members; maintenance of sacred monies, votive offerings, dedicatory inscriptions, and archives of the community. To be sure, not all synagogues performed all these functions. Local circumstances doubtless dictated numerous divergences. But the spectrum of services was broad. And they did not occur in hidden enclaves. Synagogues stood in public view; congregations had their own officialdom, leaders, and representatives; Gentiles frequently remarked about Sabbath services; inscriptions announced decisions of the membership; and the letters and decrees of Roman spokesmen gave public sanction to Jewish practices, most of which took place in the synagogue. The impressive testimony demonstrates the existence of thriving and vigorous Jewish communities, self-assured in the exhibition of their traditions and their special character.

The Jews' Participation in Social and Political Life

Explicit testimony on how Jews led their lives in the scattered cities of the Diaspora is hard to come by. But most of the fragmentary indications, clues, and indirect signs suggest circumstances in which they could both partake of the social and cultural environment and maintain a separate identity. These were not mutually exclusive alternatives.

One might note, for example, the gymnasium, that most Hellenic of institutions. The gymnasium was a conspicuous feature of Greek education, at least for the elite, in communities throughout the Mediterranean. It catered to the corps of ephebes, the select youth of upper-echelon families, the training ground for generations of Hellenic leadership in the urban centers of Greek migration. That institution would appear to be the last place available to Jews. Yet unmistakable traces of their participation in gymnasia do exist. Ephebic lists include Jews in places as different as Alexandria in Egypt, Cyrene in North Africa, Sardis in western Asia Minor, Iasos in southwestern Asia Minor, and Korone in southern Greece. So even the preeminent bastion of Hellenism, the gymnasium, was, at least in several sites, open to Jews.

The fullest information on Jewish life abroad (and it is very skimpy) comes from Egypt, where the papyri allow us to peer selectively into some corners of social and economic experience. The evidence, reinforced by some literary and epigraphic testimonia, shows that Jews served in the Ptolemaic armies and police forces, reached officer rank, and received land grants. Inscriptions in Aramaic and Greek from Alexandrian cemeteries disclose Jews, evidently mercenary soldiers, buried alongside Greeks from all parts of the Hellenic world. Jews had access to various levels of the administration as tax-farmers and tax-collectors, as bankers and granary officials. They took part in commerce, shipping, finance, farming, and every form of occupation. And they could even reach posts of prestige and importance. Juridically, the Jews, like other Greek-speaking immigrants to Egypt, were reckoned among the "Hellenes" — not singled out for prejudicial discrimination.

The nature of Jewish civic status remains obscure and controversial. The Jews did have an established place in Alexandria by the end of the first century B.C.E. Strabo, who had no Jewish agenda, reports that the Jews had a large portion of the city allotted to them, and had their own official, an ethnarch, to govern them, decide disputes, and oversee contracts and decrees. He plainly implies that Jews governed their own internal affairs but also took part in a larger Alexandrian entity to which they owed allegiance. Other evidence shows that they lived in all parts of the city, not restricted to a ghettoized existence. They could label themselves "Alexandrians," a term that carried more than geographic designation. The Roman emperor Augustus, in fact, referred to them on a bronze stele as "citizens of the Alexandrians." Whatever that means, it signals an acknowledged role in the political process of the city, a feature independently attested by Philo, who notes that Alexandrian Jews "shared in political rights." Although we lack precise data, Jews clearly had some claim on civic prerogatives, just as they had on the social and economic life of the city.

Elsewhere, the political status of Jews receives only occasional mention. At Herakleopolis in Egypt, recent papyrological finds reveal the existence of a Jewish *politeuma,* a self-governing body that could, among other things, adjudicate cases involving both Jews and non-Jews. A comparable *politeuma* existed in Cyrenaica, and we possess evidence indicating that Jews could serve in the governing body of the larger Cyrenaic community as well. Citizen privileges of some sort also belonged to the Jews of Antioch, as they did for those in Sardis and the Ionian cities of Asia Minor. Moreover, Jews were eligible for Roman citizenship, well outside the city of Rome. Paul, a Jew from Tarsus and a Roman citizen, is only the most celebrated example. Just what prerogatives this involved and how far they were exercised remain controversial. But no barriers, it appears, excluded Jews from becoming full-fledged beneficiaries of Roman power.

The Jews' Participation in Cultural and Intellectual Life

One can go further. Jews had access even to cultural life in the upper echelons of Hellenistic society. Jewish authors were well versed in most, perhaps all, forms of Hellenic writings. Those conversant with the conventions included epic poets like Theodotus and Philo, tragic dramatists like Ezekiel, writers of history like Demetrius and Eupolemus, philosophers like Aristobulus, composers of novellas and historical fiction like the authors of the *Letter of Aristeas,* 3 Maccabees, and *Joseph and Aseneth,* and those who engaged in cosmology and mythography like Pseudo-Eupolemus, and the authors of the *Sibylline Oracles.* The capacity to produce such works demonstrates that the writers could partake of higher education and engage deeply with Hellenic cultural traditions. They were themselves an integral part of the intelligentsia. Most of the names known to us come from Alexandria. But, as we have seen, gymnasium education was available to Jews elsewhere and doubtless spawned writers whose reputations do not survive.

Jewish writers clearly showed a wide familiarity with the genres, forms, and styles of Greek literature. They wrote in Greek and they adapted Greek literary modes. But they employed those conventions to their own ends. Jewish intellectuals may have embraced Hellenic canons of literature, but they had no interest in recounting the tale of Troy, the labors of Herakles, the house of Atreus, or the Greco-Persian wars, let alone the myths of the Olympian gods. Their heroes were Abraham, Joseph, and Moses. They appropriated Hellenism to the goals of rewriting biblical narratives, recasting the traditions of their forefathers, reinvigorating their ancient legends, and shaping the distinctive identity of Jews within the larger world of Hellenic culture. The challenge for the Jews was not how to surmount barriers, cross boundaries, or assimilate to an alien society. In a world where Hellenic culture held an ascendant position, they strove to present Judaic traditions and express their own self-definition through the media of the Greeks — and even to make those media their own.

A particularly striking example can illuminate the point. Tragic drama is perhaps the quintessential Greek medium. This did not render it off limits to the Jews. The Alexandrian writer Ezekiel, working within the tradition of classical tragedy, produced a play, the *Exagōgē,* based on the story of Moses leading the Israelites out of Egypt. Ezekiel hewed closely to the narrative line contained in the book of Exodus, while employing the conventions of the Greek theater. But he inserted some creativity of his own. This included a remarkable scene in which Moses recounts a dream vision of God sitting on a throne, summoning Moses to him, handing over his diadem and scepter, and departing. The dramatist here not only exalts the grandeur of Moses but reconceives Moses' relationship with God. The celestial realm appears as analogous to royal governance on earth. Moses' ascension to the throne and acquisition of kingly emblems signal his appointment as YHWH's surrogate in governing the affairs of men. This had clear resonance to the contemporaries of Ezekiel. Moses' role as executor of God's will on earth, with absolute authority, reflected royal rule in the Hellenistic realms. The author thus reinvents the position of Moses on the model of Hellenistic kingship while making him the precursor of Hellenistic kingship itself. Moses as supreme judge would expound the Law for all nations. The Israelite hero becomes a beacon for humankind, a representative of the divinity, described in phraseology that struck responsive chords among Ezekiel's Hellenic or Hellenized compatriots. The tragic poet had effectively commandeered a preeminent Greek genre and deployed it as a source of esteem for his Jewish readership.

Another celebrated composition illustrates both the intersection of Jew and Gentile in the Diaspora and the emphasis on the special qualities of the Jews. The *Letter of Aristeas* was drafted by a Hellenized Jew from Alexandria, probably in the second century B.C.E. It purports to recount the events that led to the translation of the Hebrew Bible into Greek. That undertaking came about in Alexandria around the middle of the third century, an episode of the highest importance for Diaspora Jewry. The need for a Greek Bible itself holds critical significance. It indicates that many Jews dwelling in the scattered communities of the Mediterranean had lost their mastery of Hebrew but nonetheless clung to the centerpiece of their tradition. If they were to read the Bible, it would have to be in Greek. The initial rendering or renderings eventually congealed into what became known as the Septuagint. For the vast majority of Jews living in the Greco-Roman period, it *was* the Bible.

The *Letter of Aristeas* ascribes the translation's origin to the initiative of the court of Ptolemy II, ruler of Egypt in the mid-third century. As the narrative has it, the impetus came from the chief librarian in Alexandria, who persuaded King Ptolemy to authorize the addition of "the laws of the Jews," evidently the Pentateuch, to the shelves of the great library. This required translation, for the available Hebrew texts were carelessly and improperly drawn up. Ptolemy composed a letter to the high priest in Jerusalem, requesting translators. The high priest graciously complied and selected seventy-two Jewish scholars, six from each tribe, experts in both languages, to do the job. The Jewish sages reached Alexandria, where they were warmly welcomed, Ptolemy himself paying homage to the sacred scrolls that they had conveyed from Jerusalem. Indeed, he went beyond that to organize a seven-day banquet (serving kosher food!), during which the king put a different question to each of his seventy-two guests, largely concerning the appropriate means of governing wisely, and found reason to praise every one of them for his sagacity. The translators then repaired to the island of Pharos, where they went to work, periodically comparing drafts, agreed upon a common version, and completed their task in precisely seventy-two days. The priests and leaders of the Jewish community in Alexandria pronounced it a definitive version, not a line of it to be altered. Ptolemy joined them in admiration, paid reverence to the new Bible, and lavished gifts upon the Jewish scholars.

Such is the gist of the tale. None can doubt that it issued from the pen of a Jewish author cloaked in the garb of a learned official at the court of Ptolemy II. The particulars, of course, are largely, if not entirely, fictitious. But the author's creation holds high significance. The *Letter of Aristeas* offers a showcase for the familiarity of Jewish intellectuals with diverse features and forms of Greek learning from ethnographic excursuses to textual exegesis and allegorical interpretation. The author is plainly steeped in Hellenic literature. On the face of it, this treatise would seem to be the most telling attestation of a cultural convergence between Judaism and Hellenism — at least as viewed from the Jewish side. The Hellenistic monarch promotes the project, and the Jewish scholars carry it out. The translators act at the behest of the king to enhance the pagan library, while the king pays deep homage to the sacred books of Israel. The pseudonymous narrator, Aristeas, even declares to Ptolemy that the Jews revere God, overseer and creator of all, who is worshipped by everyone, including the Greeks, except that they give him a different name, Zeus.

Yet cross-cultural harmony and blending do not tell the whole story. Another dimension carries equal importance. The *Letter of Aristeas,* while fully conversant with Hellenic literary genres, adapted that knowledge to advertise the advantages of Jewish tradition. The distinctiveness of the Jews is never in question. The god to whom all bear witness, even though the Greeks may call him Zeus, is the Jewish god. The high priest happily sends Jewish scholars to Alexandria to render the Bible into Greek, but he reminds the Greeks of the superiority of the Jewish faith, ridiculing those who worship idols of wood and stone fashioned by themselves. He insists that Mosaic Law insulated the Hebrews from outside influences, erecting firm barriers to prevent the infiltration of tainted institutions. And the high priest observes that the Jews offer sacrifice to God to insure the peace and renown of the Ptolemaic kingdom — a neat reversal of the patron-client relationship.

One can go further. The seven-day symposium may have been a fundamentally Hellenic practice, but the Jewish sages answered every query by the king with swift and pithy answers, adding a reference to God in each response, and earning the admiration not only of Ptolemy and his courtiers but of all the Greek philosophers in attendance, who acknowledged their inferiority to the sagacity of the guests. Ptolemy applauds and commends every answer by a Jew, no matter how commonplace and banal. The king hardly emerges as discerning or discriminating. The *Letter of Aristeas,* to be sure, portrays Ptolemy as a wise, gentle, and generous ruler, a man of deep cultivation and learning. But the author carries his portrait somewhat beyond the sober and the plausible. He makes Ptolemy deferential to a fault. The king bows no fewer than seven times to the Hebrew scrolls upon their arrival in Alexandria, even bursts into tears at the sight of them, and then proclaims that the date of their arrival would henceforth be celebrated as an annual festival. The author extends this form of caricature to the Greek philosophers as well, turning them into awestruck witnesses of the superiority of Jewish learning. In short, the *Letter of Aristeas,* that quintessential text of harmony and collaboration between Jew and Gentile in a Diaspora setting, simultaneously underscores the distinctive character — and the precedence — of Jewish values.

The very idea of rendering the Hebrew Bible into Greek has profound significance for the Diaspora. The historicity of the tale in the *Letter of Aristeas* is a secondary issue. Ptolemy II may or may not have had a hand in its creation. His reputation for learning made him a logical figure to whom a later writer could ascribe such an initiative. The need of Jews abroad to comprehend the holy books and laws of their tradition in the language that was now their own played a greater role. And, more fundamentally, the work of translation represents a signal instance of Jewish pride and self-esteem. It signified that the Jews had a legitimate claim on a place in the prevailing culture of the Mediterranean. Their Scriptures did not belong to an isolated and marginal group. They contained the record and principles of a people whose roots went back to distant antiquity but who maintained their prestige and authority in a contemporary society — and in a contemporary language. That may be the clearest sign that the Jews perceived themselves as an integral part of the Hellenistic cultural world.

Maintaining Jewish Identity

Jewish comfort and familiarity with the Hellenistic world in no way entailed abandonment or compromise of their distinctive identity. Terms like "assimilation" and "accommodation" deliver misleading impressions that are best avoided, suggesting that the Jews needed to transform themselves in order to fit into an alien environment. On the contrary, they unabashedly called attention to their own characteristic features.

The issue of endogamy, for instance, recurs in Second Temple literature. The book of Tobit, among other things, exhorts those dwelling in the Diaspora to adhere to the teachings of their fathers, to hold their coreligionists to the highest ideals, and to reinforce the solidarity of the clan. The work enjoins Jews in the lands of the Gentiles to maintain their special identity through strict endogamy, a theme that runs throughout the tale, thus assuring survival of the tribe. The author of Tobit may indeed take the point too far, deliberately so, with a touch of irony. He has almost every character in the narrative, even husbands and wives, greet one another as brother and sister, with numbing repetition. This is endogamy with a vengeance, perhaps a parody of the practice — but also testimony to the practice. The author himself is evidently not partial to clannishness. He has Tobit's deathbed speech offer a broader vision in which Jerusalem will eventually encompass Jew and Gentile alike, attracting all the nations of the world to its light.

The matter of endogamy surfaces prominently also in the Jewish novella, *Joseph and Aseneth,* a grandiose elaboration on the brief scriptural notice of Joseph's marriage to the daughter of an Egyptian priest. The romantic story underscores in no uncertain terms Joseph's unbending resistance to marriage outside the clan, relenting only when Aseneth abandons all her heresies, smashes her idols, and seeks forgiveness through abject prayers to the god of Joseph. The author here too, by exaggerating Joseph's priggishness and Aseneth's debasement, may suggest the disadvantages of taking endogamy to extremes. But the importance of the practice as highlighting Jewish particularity is plain.

Jews seem quite uninhibited in displaying in the Diaspora traits peculiar to their ancestral traditions. One need only think of those practices remarked upon most often by Greek and Roman authors: observance of the Sabbath, dietary laws, and circumcision. The institution of the Sabbath frequently drew comment, generally amused comment. Pagan writers found it quite incomprehensible that Jews refused to fight on the Sabbath — thus causing Jerusalem to fall on three different occasions. And even if the prohibition did not cause disaster, it seemed a colossal waste of time: why did Jews waste one-seventh of their lives in idleness? Comparable mirth directed itself against the abstention from eating pork. Even Emperor Augustus, in reference to the notorious intrigues and murders that took place in the household of Herod, famously observed that "it's better to be Herod's pig than his son." That quip implies that the Jewish dietary restriction was well known among the Romans. Satirists indeed had a field day with it. Petronius, author of the *Satyricon,* concluded that, if Jews don't touch pork, they must worship a pig-god. And Juvenal characterized Judea as a place where a long-standing indulgence permits pigs to reach a ripe old age. As for circumcision, it provided much grist for the jokesters' mill. Philo reports that circumcision called forth considerable ridicule from non-Jews. Among the instances of this was Juvenal's claim that Jews are so exclusive that they would not even give directions in the street to anyone who was not circumcised. None of this amounts, as has often been thought, to "anti-Semitism." It represents mockery rather than animosity. But it demonstrates that Diaspora Jews had no qualms (and no fears) about practicing their conventional customs, thereby denoting their differences from Gentiles.

In fact, what struck pagan writers most was not Jewish assimilation but Jewish separateness. That emerges in Juvenal's quip noted above. It recurs also in a comment by his contemporary, the historian Tacitus, who claimed that Jews took up circumcision precisely in order to express their distinctiveness from all other people. The impression of Jewish separatism appears, in fact, as early as the first extant Greek writer to take note of the Jews, Hecataeus of Abdera, a historian of the late fourth century B.C.E. Hecataeus, in an account generally favorable to Jews, indicates that they tended to keep to themselves and shun the company of others.

The uncommon character of their customs both provided bonds among Diaspora Jews everywhere and announced their differences from other peoples. The surviving evidence underscores this again and again. The collection of an annual tax to be sent to the Temple from Jewish communities throughout the Mediterranean exemplifies it. So does the regular celebration of festivals that mark major milestones in the history of the nation. The Jews of Egypt kept the Passover at least as early as the fifth century, as the Aramaic papyri from Elephantine attest. Scattered testimony reveals observance of Shavuot, Sukkot, and Yom Kippur in Jewish communities outside Palestine, conspicuous links to ancient tradition. Later feasts have strong Diaspora connections. The Purim festival began in the Persian period, according to the book of Esther, and was celebrated annually by the Jews of Persia. A comparable anniversary occurred in Alexandria to celebrate a Jewish triumph, according to the narrative of 3 Maccabees. And the Jews of Jerusalem invited their compatriots in Egypt to commemorate the purification of the Temple in their own Diaspora location.

As noted earlier, the structures in which Jews of the Diaspora met often carried the designation of *proseuchai* or prayer houses. That term applies regularly to Jewish meeting places in Egypt but also in the Bosporan region, in Delos, in Halicarnassus, and doubtless in other communities where the evidence fails us. The implication seems clear enough: such gatherings included prayers, acts of worship of some sort that gave voice to the particular Jewish relationship with the divinity. Such places of assemblage, whether called *proseuchē* or *synagōgē,* served also as a site for collective Torah study and for other instructional activity that reinforced the continued commitment to Jewish tradition.

Philo, the learned Alexandrian Jew, places particular emphasis upon this aspect of synagogue activity, noting that the laws were read out to weekly meetings on the Sabbath. Priests or elders, according to Philo, took responsibility for reading and commenting on the sacred laws, even keeping the congregation at it for hours, and providing them with great impetus toward piety. In Philo's portrayal, perhaps somewhat shaped by his own philosophic proclivities, congregants sit in their synagogues, read their sacred books, and discuss at length the particulars of their ancestral philosophy. He reckons the synagogue as a Jewish replica of a philosophical academy. The presentation may be slightly skewed but surely not far off the mark.

The book of Acts portrays Paul repeatedly entering Jewish synagogues in various cities of the Diaspora, in Thessalonica, Athens, Corinth, and Ephesus, and arguing with Jews about the meaning of the Scriptures. Close attention to holy writ obviously remained central to Jewish activity outside Palestine — and to Jewish self-perception. The vitality of the Torah was undiminished. The stimulus for translation into Greek suffices to establish that. And, as Philo reports, the completion of the project receives annual celebration on the island of Pharos, where the translators allegedly worked, a strong signal of Jewish pride in the heritage that marked them out from others.

The tenacious adherence to signature principles occurred perhaps most obviously in the Jewish insistence upon rejecting idolatry. The affirmation did not consist, strictly speaking, in pitting monotheism against polytheism. Jewish intellectuals recognized that Greek philosophic thinking often expressed itself in terms of a supreme deity or a single divine principle. What Jews resisted unequivocally was the worship of deities in the form of images. Such practice they reckoned as profaning the spiritual essence of God. The stance, of course, derives from the biblical commandment against graven images, and the struggle against idolaters fills the pages of the Torah and the Deuteronomistic history. The principle retained its power in the Second Temple. As we have seen, even the *Letter of Aristeas,* a prime document for accord between the Jewish and Hellenic worlds, draws the line firmly at idolatry, denouncing in harshest terms those who fashion their own gods in wood or stone and thus fundamentally misconceive the nature of divinity. Aseneth's acceptance of Joseph's god could come only when she pulverized every idol in the household. And the assault on idolatry gains voice also in the *Sibylline Oracles,* composed by Jews who emphasized the failings and offenses of Gentiles. The incorporeal character of God represented an unshakable principle. Jewish aniconism was conspicuous and widely acknowledged by non-Jews. Some found it peculiar and puzzling, even akin to atheism. Others admired it. The Roman historian Tacitus held up the Jewish practice as a worthy contrast with animal worship indulged in by Egyptians and with emperor worship, which Tacitus deplored. Indeed the most learned of Romans, the great scholar Varro, in the late first century B.C.E., praised the imageless conception of the deity, likening it to ancient Roman custom as genuine piety before the Romans began to set up images and adulterate their creed. But whether questioning or admiring, pagan references to Jewish aniconism make clear that perseverance in this principle that set Jews apart from their neighbors received widespread notice. They erected no façade of assimilation.

Gentile Attraction to Judaism

The insistence on distinctiveness, however, did not entail a closed society. Indeed the accessibility of Judaism to the outsider, a striking feature often overlooked, merits attention. A considerable number of non-Jews found Judaism enticing. We can no longer recover the reasons, and they doubtless varied from place to pace, and person to person. Some may have been attracted by its great longevity, by the ethical precepts, by the rigorous adherence to the Law, by the discipline demanded in its practices, by the social bonding of the synagogues, by the celebration of its festivals, or by the reputation not only for Eastern wisdom but for skills in both the practical and the occult sciences. We can only speculate on the motives. But the fact of Gentiles entering into Jewish society in some fashion is incontrovertible. This did not require conversion — nor necessarily an abandonment of previous identity and associations. It might take the form of imitating the Jewish way of life up to a point, like observing the Sabbath, or adopting certain codes of behavior, or taking part in synagogue activities, or providing material support for the Jewish community. The Jews did not turn such people away.

We hear of several non-Jews who held Judaism in high esteem and showed genuine interest in it. The Gospel of Luke mentions a Roman centurion at Capernaum as one who loved Jews and had built them a synagogue. According to Philo, the Roman prefect of Syria had gained familiarity with Jewish philosophy and piety. Josephus indicates in several contexts the attraction of eminent women to Judaism, including even the wife of the emperor Nero. Gentile reverence for Jewish laws and mores appears with some frequency in Josephus' works.

Indeed, if Josephus is to be believed, pagans everywhere included observers of the Sabbath, people who adopted Jewish dietary practices, or those who attempted to imitate the Jews in their internal concord, their philanthropy, their skill in the crafts, and their adherence to the Law even under duress. Philo makes a similar claim, asserting that almost all people, especially those who place a premium upon virtue, pay homage to Jewish laws. The Jewish authors, to be sure, are hardly unbiased witnesses. But their statements, however exaggerated and embroidered, do not arise out of the void.

Non-Jewish sources supply corroboration. The Roman satirist Juvenal, writing in the early second century C.E., refers in sardonic fashion to the appeal that Jewish practices have in Rome. He alludes to fathers who revere the Sabbath and follow Jewish dietary restrictions. Their sons then go further: they worship a deity of the sky, draw no distinction between consuming swine's flesh and cannibalism, and even engage in circumcision. A very different text, the Christian book of Revelation, composed about the same time, denounces those who falsely claim to be Jews but are not so. This may refer to Gentiles who have adopted Jewish behavior and institutions — without becoming Jews.

Such persons seem even to have a name. "God-fearers" serves as the conventional designation (even if not technical terminology) for Gentiles seriously drawn to an association with Judaism or the Jewish community. The Acts of the Apostles contain several references to "those who fear God" or "those who revere God," denoting Gentiles who were closely and sympathetically involved with the Jewish community and who lived in accord with at least some of its precepts. The terminology has a parallel in Josephus, who attributes the wealth of the Temple to contributions both from Jews and from "those who worship God" all over the world. Closely comparable phrases appear in inscriptions of somewhat later periods from a wide variety of regions ranging from Italy to the Black Sea. Gentiles in substantial numbers participated in some fashion (doubtless in diverse fashions) in Jewish synagogues and communities — and they were clearly welcomed.

Relations with the Homeland

An important question remains. How did Diaspora Jews relate to the homeland? Did the land of Israel beckon to those dwelling in distant places, a prime objective of the displaced, the principal means of realizing the destiny of the people for whom the "Return" represented the fulfillment of Yahweh's promise? Or had the Jews instead assimilated to life abroad, finding gratification in the concept that their identity resided in the "Book," not in any territorial legitimation. For such Jews, restoration to the homeland was irrelevant and superfluous; the land of their residence rather than the home of the fathers constituted the cardinal attachment.

The dichotomy misleads and deceives. The whole idea of valuing homeland over Diaspora or Diaspora over homeland is off the mark. Second Temple Jews need not have faced so stark a choice.

The Bible, of course, has YHWH promise eventually to return the children of Israel from the most remote regions to the land of their fathers. And similar comments recur in Jewish Hellenistic writers who deplore the dispersal and forecast the ingathering of the exiles, as in the book of Tobit, the *Psalms of Solomon*, and *Jubilees.* But in each instance the termination of exile and the return to the homeland are connected to the reconstruction of the Temple. As a symbol of the faith, its demolition at the hands of Babylon had caused heartbreak and longing. But a comparable condition did not hold in the Hellenistic Diaspora. The Temple stood again in Jerusalem. And few Jews abroad were held there by constraint.

The generally satisfactory circumstances of the Diaspora defused any widespread passion for the "Return." Jews, as we have seen, generally formed stable communities at places quite distant from Judea, entered into the social, economic, and political life of the nations they joined, and aspired to and obtained civic privileges in the cities of the Hellenistic world. Josephus maintains that Jews have every right to call themselves Alexandrians, Antiochenes, or Ephesians. And Philo refers to his home as "our Alexandria." An inscription from the Phrygian city of Acmonia, set up by a Jew or group of Jews, alludes to the fulfillment of a vow made to the "whole *patris.*" This records a conspicuous and public pronouncement of local loyalty. Philo confirms the sentiment in striking fashion: Jews consider the holy city as their "metropolis," but the states in which they were born and raised and which they acquired from their fathers, grandfathers, and distant forefathers they adjudge to be their *patrides.* That fervent expression denies any idea of the "doctrine of return." Diaspora Jews, in Philo's formulation at least, held a fierce attachment to the adopted lands of their ancestors.

None of this, however, diminished the sanctity and centrality of Jerusalem in the Jewish consciousness. The city's aura retained a powerful hold on Jews, wherever they happened to reside. Even the pagan geographer Strabo observed the Jews' devotion to their sacred "acropolis." Numerous other texts characterize Palestine as the "Holy Land." That designation appears in works as different as 2 Maccabees, the Wisdom of Solomon, the *Testament of Job,* the *Sibylline Oracles,* and Philo. Most, if not all, of those texts stem from the Diaspora. They underscore the reverence with which Jews around the Mediterranean continued to regard Jerusalem and the land of their fathers. But the authors who speak with reverence do not demand the "Return." Commitment to one's local or regional community was entirely compatible with devotion to Jerusalem. The two concepts in no way represented mutually exclusive alternatives.

What meaning, then, did the notion of a homeland have for Jews dwelling in scattered Mediterranean communities? They never yielded the principle. Jewish attitudes here, as in many other regards, corresponded with those of their pagan neighbors. Loyalty to one's native land represented a frequent sentiment in the rhetoric of the Hellenistic world. Philo more than once endorses the idea that adherence to one's native land held singular power. He puts failure to worship God on a level with neglecting to honor parents, benefactors, and native land. It does not follow, however, that Diaspora Jews set their hearts upon a return to the fatherland. Broad pronouncements about love of one's country accord with general Hellenistic expressions. They do not require that those native environs be reinhabited for life to be complete.

Jerusalem as concept and reality remained a powerful emblem of Jewish identity — not supplanted by the Book or disavowed by those who dwelled afar. It appears again and again in the texts of Second Temple authors as a symbol of the highest appeal. Yet this tenacious devotion did not entail a widespread desire to pull up stakes and return to the fatherland.

Jews reminded themselves and others every year of their commitment to Jerusalem. The reminder came in the form of a tithe paid to the Temple annually by Jews all over the Mediterranean. The ritualistic offering carried deep significance as a bonding device. That fact is vividly illustrated by an episode in the mid 60s B.C.E. A Roman governor of the province of Asia (essentially northwestern Asia Minor) banned the sending of gold by the Jews of the region to Jerusalem. This was part of a broader Roman policy and did not apply to Jews alone. But the solidarity of Jewish reaction was impressive. Word got back in great haste to the Jewish community in Rome. Demonstrations mobilized and strong pressure mounted on the Roman government by Jews in the city expressing concern in unequivocal terms for their compatriots abroad. The event underscores the importance of Jewish commitment to provide funds annually to the Temple from Italy and from all the provinces of the Roman Empire. Clearly the plight of Asian Jews who were prevented from making their contributions had powerful resonance among fellow Jews far off in Rome. The latter expressed their sentiments in no uncertain terms. Jerusalem and the Temple remained emblematic of their common purpose across the Mediterranean.

References to the gravity of the tithe abound. Josephus proudly observes that the donations came from Jews all over Asia and Europe, indeed from everywhere in the world, for countless years. When local authorities interfered with that activity, Jews would send up a howl to Rome — and usually get satisfaction. Areas beyond the reach of Roman power also tithed consistently. Jewish communities in Babylon and other satrapies under Parthian dominion sent representatives every year over difficult terrain and dangerous highways to deposit their contributions in the Temple. The value of paying homage to Jerusalem was undiminished. That annual act of obeisance constituted a repeated display of affection and allegiance, visible evidence of the unbroken attachment of the Diaspora to the center.

The remittance, however, did not imply that Jews viewed the Diaspora as no more than a temporary exile to be terminated by an ingathering in Jerusalem. Indeed, it implied the reverse. The yearly contribution proclaimed that the Diaspora could endure indefinitely — and quite satisfactorily. The communities abroad had successfully entrenched themselves; they were now mainstays of the center. Their fierce commitment to the tithe did not signify a desire for the "Return." It rendered the Return unnecessary.

A comparable institution reinforces that inference: the pilgrimage of Diaspora Jews to Jerusalem. Major festivals could attract them with some frequency and in substantial numbers. According to Philo, myriads came from countless cities for every feast, over land and sea, from all points of the compass, to enjoy the Temple as a serene refuge from the hurly-burly of everyday life abroad. Josephus informs us that the women's court at the Temple was large enough to accommodate those who resided in the land and those who arrived from abroad — a clear sign that numerous female pilgrims came with some regularity.

The Holy City was a compelling magnet. But the demonstration of devotion did not entail a desire for migration. Pilgrimage, in fact, by its very nature, signified a temporary payment of respect. Jerusalem possessed an irresistible claim on the emotions of Diaspora Jews, forming a critical part of their identity. But home was elsewhere.

The self-perception of Second Temple Jews projected a tight solidarity between center and Diaspora. Images of exile and separation did not haunt them. What affected the dwellers in Jerusalem affected Jews everywhere. The theme of intertwined experience and identity recurs with impressive frequency and variety in Second Temple literature. The two letters affixed to the beginning of 2 Maccabees illustrate the point. The Jews of Jerusalem take for granted the intimate relationship that exists with their brethren in Egypt. The preamble of the first letter greets them as "brothers" to "brothers" and alludes to their common heritage: God's covenant with Abraham, Isaac, and Jacob. And the concluding lines of the second letter make reference to the desired reunion of all Jews in the holy site. The latter delivers a summons to Egyptian Jews to attend the newly instituted festival, thus to celebrate the purification of the Temple, a reaffirmation of the solidarity among Jews everywhere. It reflects the practice of pilgrimage, not a program to dissolve the Diaspora.

The *Letter of Aristeas* makes an equally forceful statement about the connection between Jerusalemites and other Jews. King Ptolemy's missive to the high priest in Judea asserts that his motive in having the Hebrew Bible rendered into Greek is to benefit not only the Jews of Egypt but all Jews throughout the world, including those yet unborn. One may legitimately question whether the king ever made such a statement. But the Jewish author of the *Letter* conceived or conveyed it. And that is the point. At the conclusion of the work, when the scholars from Jerusalem complete their translation and have it read out to the Jews of Egypt, the large assembly bursts into applause, a dramatic expression of the unity of purpose.

Historical events reinforce the evidence of literary creations. As we have seen, the demonstrations of Roman Jews on behalf of their compatriots in Asia whose contributions to the Temple were in jeopardy reveal a strong sense of Jewish fellowship across the Mediterranean. Another, very different, episode adds conformation. At the height of the Roman civil war, Julius Caesar found himself besieged in Alexandria in 48/47 B.C.E. A troop of three thousand Jewish soldiers marched to his rescue. But Egyptian Jews who dwelled at Leontopolis, site of a long-standing Jewish enclave, blocked their path. The stalemate, however, was swiftly broken. The Jewish commander overcame the resistance of the Leontopolitans by appealing to their common nationality and their common loyalty to the high priest in Jerusalem. No further persuasion proved necessary. The Jews of both Leontopolis and Memphis declared themselves for Caesar and helped to turn the tide of war. The connection between Judea and Diaspora held firm.

A similar conclusion derives from quite a different occasion. The death of Herod the Great in 4 B.C.E. prompted a major discussion in Rome on the future of the regime. Fifty envoys came to Rome from Judea urging Emperor Augustus to put an end to the rule of the Herodian family. And 8,000 Jews resident in Rome, so we are told, joined their fellow Jews in this lobbying effort. A network of connections across the Mediterranean made it possible. And the interests coincided. When a pretender to the throne of Herod emerged, claiming to be a reincarnation of one of Herod's sons, he found widespread support from Jews in Crete, in Melos, and in Rome itself. The network was extensive. Such events provide a revealing window upon the lively interest and occasionally energetic engagement of Diaspora Jews in the affairs of Palestine.

The affiliations emerge most dramatically in the grave crises that marked the reign of the emperor Caligula (37-41 C.E.). Bitter conflict erupted in Alexandria, bringing harsh sufferings upon the Jews of that city. And a still worse menace loomed over Jerusalem when the eccentric and unpredictable Roman emperor proposed to have a statue for pagan worship installed in the Temple. When Alexandrian Jews were attacked, says Philo (a contemporary of the events), the word spread like wildfire. Reports swept not only through all the districts of Egypt but from there to the nations of the East and from the borders of Libya to the lands of the West. Philo's claims of such speedy communications may stretch a point, but the concept of tight interrelationships among Jews of the Diaspora is plain and potent. With regard to news of Caligula's decision to erect a statue in the Temple, Philo's description is telling: the most grievous calamity fell unexpectedly and brought peril not to one part of the Jewish people but to the entire nation at once. The disaster was averted, thanks in part to a letter of the Jewish prince Agrippa I, a friend of the emperor and recent recipient of a kingdom among the Jews. Agrippa urgently alerted Caligula to the gravity of the situation. He made it clear that an affront to Jerusalem would have vast repercussions: the Holy City was not merely the metropolis of Judea but of most nations in the world since Jewish colonies thrived all over the Near East, Asia Minor, Greece, Macedon, Africa, and the lands beyond the Euphrates. The image of Jerusalem binding together Jews everywhere in the world remained central in the self-perception of the Diaspora.

A moving passage elsewhere in Philo encapsulates this theme. Although he thrived in the Diaspora, enjoyed its advantages, and broadcast its virtues, Philo nevertheless found even deeper meaning in the land of Israel. He interprets the Shavuot festival as a celebration of the Jews' possession of their own land, a heritage now of long standing, and a means whereby they could cease their wandering. Philo saw no inconsistency or contradiction. Diaspora Jews might find fulfillment and reward in their communities abroad. But they honored Judea as a refuge for those who were once displaced and unsettled — and the prime legacy of all.

Josephus makes the point in a quite different context but with equal force. In his rewriting of Numbers he places a sweeping prognostication in the mouth of the Midianite priest Balaam. The priest projects a glorious future for the Israelites: they will not only occupy and hold forever the land of Canaan, a chief signal of God's favor, but their multitudes will fill all the world, islands, and continents, outnumbering even the stars in the heavens. That is a notable declaration. Palestine, as ever, merits a special place. But the Diaspora, far from being a source of shame to be overcome, represents a resplendent achievement.

The respect and awe one paid to the Holy Land stood in full harmony with a commitment to the local community and allegiance to Gentile governance. Diaspora Jews did not bewail their fate and pine away for the homeland. Nor, by contrast, did they shrug off the homeland and reckon the Book as surrogate for the Temple. Palestine mattered, and it mattered in a territorial sense — but not as a required residence. Gifts to the Temple and pilgrimages to Jerusalem announced simultaneously one's devotion to the symbolic heart of Judaism and a singular pride in the accomplishments of the Diaspora.

None of this, of course, suggests that the experience of Jews in the Diaspora was everywhere and always untroubled, serene, and harmonious. Outbursts of violence and turbulence occasionally shattered their existence. Most notoriously, tensions among Greeks, Egyptians, and Jews in Alexandria, exacerbated by insensitive Roman overlordship, resulted in a bloody assault on Jews in 38 C.E. A quarter century later, the outbreak of Jewish rebellion against Roman rule in Palestine also had reverberations in the Diaspora. The Jews of Alexandria were victimized by a riot in 66 C.E. and, when they retaliated, encountered fierce Roman reprisals administered by Tiberius Julius Alexander, himself a Jew now in Roman service. The temple at Leontopolis in Egypt, which had stood for more than two centuries, also suffered destruction in that upheaval. A still wider Diaspora rebellion occurred in 116 C.E., involving Jews in Cyrene, Egypt, Cyprus, and possibly Mesopotamia. What caused these uprisings remains unknown. But the Roman crackdown, ordered by the emperor Trajan, was harsh, terminating the existence of many Jewish communities in these regions.

Episodes of this sort cause little surprise in the circumstances of rivalries and tensions in multiethnic societies. What is noteworthy, however, is their remarkable rarity. Given that our sources dwell on violence and upheaval when they can, the relative absence of such turmoil in our evidence is particularly significant. Even in Egypt, over a period of four centuries, the outbreak of hostilities is very much the exception rather than the norm. Elsewhere in the Diaspora, in Italy, mainland Greece, Asia Minor, and Babylon, no serious disquiet stands on record — and Jewish communities continued to thrive.

BIBLIOGRAPHY

Applebaum, Shim'on. 1979. *Jews and Greeks in Ancient Cyrene.* Leiden: Brill.

Barclay, John M. G. 1996. *Jews in the Mediterranean Diaspora.* Edinburgh: Clark.

———, ed. 2004. *Negotiating Diaspora: Jewish Strategies in the Roman Empire.* London: Clark.

Bartlett, John R. 2002. *Jews in the Hellenistic and Roman Cities.* London: Routledge.

Cappelletti, Silvia. 2006. *The Jewish Community of Rome from the Second Century B.C. to the Third Century C.E.* Leiden: Brill.

Cohen, Shaye J. D., and Ernest S. Frerichs, eds. 1993. *Diasporas in Antiquity.* Atlanta: Scholars Press.

Collins, John J. 2000. *Between Athens and Jerusalem: Jewish Identity in the Hellenistic Diaspora.* 2d ed. Grand Rapids: Eerdmans.

———. *Jewish Cult and Hellenistic Culture.* JSJSup 100. Leiden: Brill, 2005.

Feldman, Louis H. 1993. *Jew and Gentile in the Ancient World.* Princeton: Princeton University Press.

Gafni, Isaiah M. 1997. *Land, Center, and Diaspora.* Sheffield: Sheffield Academic Press.

Goodman, Martin, ed. 1998. *Jews in a Graeco-Roman World.* Oxford: Clarendon.

Grabbe, Lester L. 2000. *Judaic Religion in the Second Temple Period: Belief and Practice from the Exile to Yavneh.* London: Routledge.

Gruen, Erich S. 2002. *Diaspora: Jews amidst Greeks and Romans.* Cambridge: Harvard University Press.

———. 1998. *Heritage and Hellenism: The Reinvention of Jewish Tradition.* Berkeley: University of California Press.

Hachlili, Rachel. 1998. *Ancient Jewish Art and Archaeology in the Diaspora.* Leiden: Brill.

Honigman, Sylvie. 2003. *The Septuagint and Homeric Scholarship in Alexandria.* London: Routledge.

Horbury, William, and David Noy. 1992. *Jewish Inscriptions of Graeco-Roman Egypt.* Cambridge: Cambridge University Press.

Kasher, Aryeh. 1985. *The Jews in Hellenistic and Roman Egypt: The Struggle for Equal Rights.* Tübingen: Mohr-Siebeck.

Levine, Lee I. 2000. *The Ancient Synagogue.* New Haven: Yale University Press.
Linder, Amon, ed. 1987. *The Jews in Roman Imperial Legislation.* Detroit: Wayne State University Press.
Modrzejewski, Joseph M. 1995. *The Jews of Egypt from Ramses II to the Emperor Hadrian.* Philadelphia: Jewish Publication Society.
Overman, J. Andrew, A. Thomas Kraabel, and Robert S. MacLennan, eds. 1992. *Diaspora Jews and Judaism.* Atlanta: Scholars Press.
Pucci Ben Zeev, Miriam. 1998. *Jewish Rights in the Roman World: The Greek and Roman Documents Quoted by Josephus Flavius.* Tübingen: Mohr-Siebeck.
———. 2005. *Diaspora Judaism in Turmoil, 116/117 CE.* Leuven: Peeters.
Rajak, Tessa. 2001. *The Jewish Dialogue with Greece and Rome: Studies in Cultural and Social Interaction.* Leiden: Brill.
———. 2009. *Translation and Survival: The Greek Bible of the Ancient Jewish Diaspora.* Oxford: Oxford University Press.
Rutgers, Leonard V. 1995. *The Jews in Late Ancient Rome.* Leiden: Brill.
Smallwood, E. Mary. 1976. *The Jews under Roman Rule.* Leiden: Brill.
Tcherikover, Victor. 1961. *Hellenistic Civilization and the Jews.* Trans. S. Applebaum. Philadelphia: Jewish Publication Society of America.
Trebilco, Paul R. 1991. *Jewish Communities in Asia Minor.* Cambridge: Cambridge University Press.
Williams, Margaret H. 1998. *The Jews among the Greeks and Romans: A Diaspora Sourcebook.* London: Duckworth.

The Jewish Scriptures: Texts, Versions, Canons

EUGENE ULRICH

The texts that eventually came to constitute the canonical books of the Hebrew Bible or Old Testament display a pattern of developmental growth in their composition. Like a cross-section of a tree with multiple rings, they show repeated stages of new growth from their beginnings, which are usually lost in the darkness of history, continually until the end of the Second Temple period. This developmental growth did not cease until some time after the destruction of the Temple in 70 C.E., when it halted rather abruptly.

The Composition of the Scriptural Texts

The popular imagination, formed as early as rabbinic times, envisioned a few holy men (e.g., Moses, Samuel, Isaiah, Daniel) as the authors of the books that bear their names, similar to classical or modern authors who individually compose and publish books under their own name. Prior to the Enlightenment, however, several attentive readers began to raise suspicions about those views of authorship, and buoyed by the Enlightenment, questions concerning authorship gained momentum, resulting in sustained, critical analysis of the literary character of the biblical books. The overwhelming conclusion of this international and interconfessional scholarship was that the books of the biblical anthology were composed in stages. Small units of what usually began as oral material — stories, laws, songs, proverbs — were gathered into larger, growing literary complexes. Earlier source materials were brought together into a unified work by an anonymous person who is usually labeled an editor or redactor. Tradents and scribes passed on the traditions, faithfully retaining the earlier message, and at times creatively adapting them to address newer concerns that affected the successive communities. Textual critics detected further minor developments within the major stages of the compositions, noting additions to, losses from, and errors in the text of each book after it had been composed and as it continued to be recited or copied from generation to generation.

Thus the Scriptures were seen to be composed over the course of approximately a millennium, from source materials in the premonarchic and monarchic periods to within a generation or so of the fall of the Second Temple in 70 C.E.

No manuscript evidence survives from the early centuries to provide clear details for a reconstruction of the history of Israel's religious and cultural literature. The scholarship described above was theoretical, based not on manuscripts but on literary clues embedded within the works themselves. But the general results of that vast modern library of theoretical scholarship have now been solidly confirmed by abundant documentary evidence provided by the biblical manuscripts from Qumran.

Thus there are two distinct periods in the history of the biblical text: a formative period of developmental growth and pluriformity until the time of the Jewish revolts against Rome, eclipsed by the period of a uniform text tradition since the second century C.E. The dynamics of these two periods account for the character of the textual witnesses preserved and the transmission history of these books.

The Texts in the Early Second Temple Period

As the liberated Judean exiles returned from Babylon to Jerusalem and environs, they gradually rebuilt the Temple, the walls, and the city. Religious leaders also assumed the responsibility of reconstituting the literary heritage from the monarchic culture as well as producing new religious works that attempted to help the people refocus their understanding of their relationship with God after the disaster.

The literary heritage from the monarchic era — which would have been primarily transmitted orally, even if priests or scribes possessed written copies — was rich and diverse. Early Israel in all likelihood had some kind of oral accounts of its formation as a people; it seems inconceivable that they lacked any traditional accounts of their origins. Martin Noth posited five themes of oral traditions that were eventually woven together to form what became the Tetrateuch or Hexateuch: the promise to the patriarchs, the guidance out of Egypt, the wandering through the wilderness, the revelation at Sinai, and the occupation of the land. Historically it is unlikely that any single group experienced the events behind all five of these traditions. Rather, different groups experienced different events which eventually were memorialized in these themes, and some individuals wove the themes together, probably adding new insights and commentary, to form what could be called a national epic. As the unity among the disparate groups developed, all groups increasingly accepted all components of the tradition as "our" story, giving it a pan-Israelite significance.

In addition to the origins narratives, various preexilic traditions would have survived in the memory of the people, including the Deuteronomistic History, or at least many of the tribal, royal, military, and religious traditions which served as the sources of that History. Included also in that early heritage were collections of sayings of and stories about prophets, such as Elijah, Elisha, Amos, Hosea, and Isaiah of Jerusalem, as well as collections of priestly rituals, liturgical hymns, and wisdom instructions.

For the most part Second Temple tradents or scribes assiduously recited or recopied those traditions as accurately as they could, but occasionally there were creative minds that sought to revise and expand the texts with insights addressing new situations and making the works meaningful to the current generation. A priestly edition of the Torah was produced and interwoven into the earlier origins traditions to help the people understand that the ancient covenant was not ephemeral and did not necessarily rest on land, autonomous kingship, and the historical process, but rather was eternal and rested on theocracy, Temple liturgy, and adherence to Torah. The Deuteronomistic History was also updated, putting heavier emphasis on the curse which would result in war, defeat, and exile from the land flowing with milk and honey. In contrast, certain prophetic collections with oracles of judgment were supplemented with much-needed oracles of salvation or consolation (e.g., Amos 9:11-15, and Isaiah 40–55 joined to Isaiah 1–33).

New compositions were also produced in reaction to the shocking loss of independence, land, king, and temple. In addition to the expanded and retheologized editions of the Torah and the Deuteronomistic History, Second Isaiah joyously trumpeted the exiles' imminent and glorious return to Jerusalem, typologically promising a new creation, new exodus, new covenant, and new Jerusalem. Job may be seen as an attempt to understand and deal with life and the God-human relationship after the Exile. New psalms emphasized themes of lament and the ideal of Torah as wisdom. New works, such as Chronicles and Ezra, Haggai and Zechariah, also depicted the efforts at restoring the Temple, the religion, and the people.

Recognition of the Literature as Scripture

Many if not all of these works originated as, and were generally viewed as, humanly produced literature; indeed, Sir. 44:1-15 could be seen as an ancient witness to this view. There is a spectrum of theological views concerning the divine origin of the Scriptures, but here the focus must be on how the human community came to recognize these books as divinely authored. They served a variety of purposes: the early narrative strands of the Pentateuch and the Deuteronomistic History served as a national epic and national history; Leviticus, Psalms, and Esther were used for the liturgy; *Jubilees,* the Deuteronomistic History, Proverbs, Job, Qohelet, and Ben Sira contributed to religious, moral, and practical education; the Song of Songs, Tobit, and Ruth were models for human love and loyalty; and Daniel provided a model for courage in perilous times. The literature grew as community literature, and countless tradents and copyists contributed to its dynamic development from its earliest origins as sayings, reports, songs, and other materials into books sufficiently well known and treasured to assure that they would be transmitted as important for successive generations. Just as the community formed the literature, so too the literature formed the community as it moved through history.

Of the many works produced, some came to be regarded as sacred Scripture; that is, they were regarded as in some sense having God as author. There is little evidence for reconstructing this important transition, but certain contributing factors can be proposed.

First, God was increasingly understood to be speaking through the texts to the people. For the Greeks the *Iliad* and the *Odyssey* held essential religious importance, but they were principally seen as national epics. Similarly, the early hexateuchal narratives originally would likely have been perceived more as a national epic than as "Scripture." Just as the gods spoke in the Homeric poems, so too did God speak in Israel's texts. But once the priestly portions were incorporated, especially the legal materials listed as divinely spoken on Sinai, and insofar as the divine source was reinforced by the preaching of the Torah as articulating God's will, it is quite easy to understand how God came to be viewed as the author. Already by the early second century B.C.E., *Jubilees* clearly attests this: "The LORD revealed to him . . ." (*Jub.* 1:4), and "The angel of the presence spoke to Moses according to the word of the LORD, saying: 'Write the complete history of the creation . . .'" (*Jub.* 2:1).

The divine authorship envisioned on Sinai was extended to material that had presumably been simply the priests' ritual handbook for Temple sacrifices. It is quite plausible that editorial framing in the Second Temple period transformed the priests' handbook of directions for performing the various offerings. The directions in Leviticus 1–7 may at an earlier point have begun with "When any of you bring an offering of livestock to the LORD, you shall . . ." (1:2b), proceeded with the detailed sacrificial directions, and then ended with "This is the ritual of the burnt offering, the grain offering, the sin offering, the guilt offering, the ordination offering, and the sacrifice of well-being" (7:37). The editorial framing of those priestly directions would then have introduced the section with "The LORD called Moses and spoke to him from the tent of meeting, saying, 'Speak to the people of Israel and say to them'" (1:1-2a), and concluded it with "which the LORD commanded Moses on Mount Sinai, when he commanded the people of Israel to bring their offerings to the LORD, in the wilderness of Sinai" (7:38; cf. also 4:1-2a; 5:20; 27:1-2a, 34). According to this view, the priestly ritual handbook was transformed into a divinely authored book.

Just as Moses relayed God's word in the Torah, certain prophets were seen to deliver God's message to the king and people. But eventually the entire prophetic book, including stories about the prophets and the full editorial framework, was considered divine revelation. With the passage of time a book containing God's word became a divinely revealed book.

Similarly, the Psalms, which originated as humanly composed hymns to God, were elevated to the status of divinely authored Scripture. The largest Psalms scroll from Qumran states explicitly the divine source of David's Psalter: "All these he spoke through prophecy that was given to him from the Most High" (11QPs[a] 27:11). The divinely inspired prophetic nature of the Psalms is echoed in the Acts of the Apostles: "Since he was a prophet. . . . Foreseeing this, David spoke of the resurrection of the Messiah . . ." (Acts 2:30-31).

Second, additions that enhanced the theological, pious, or festival nature of a text seem to have been influential in considering a book as Scripture. For example, the theological material in Proverbs 1–9 may well have been the factor that achieved scriptural status for that book. The older section starting in chapter 10 had probably been much more regarded as a collection of commonsense folk wisdom and pithy sayings. But the additions — such as "the LORD created [Wisdom] at the beginning" (8:22) and she was beside him "When he established the heavens . . . , when he made firm the skies above" (8:27-30) — helped transform the collection so that one could seek and "find the knowledge of God" (2:5). The not-excessively pious Qohelet may have gained scriptural status once the more traditional appendix, urging the reader to "fear God and keep his commandments" (Eccl. 12:9-14) was added. The same status may have been gained for the book of Esther with the institution of the feast of Purim (Esth. 9:18-32).

Third, hermeneutical innovation also contributed to sacralization. The Song of Songs, which like the Psalms originated as human literature, was sublimated through a hermeneutical lens into a meditation on God's love for Israel.

The book of Daniel also provides an interesting example. There was a growing cycle of Danielic materials, which perhaps drew on the righteous figure of Dan(i)el, laconically mentioned in Ezek. 14:14, 20, and which attached his name to traditions such as the anonymous Jewish healer in the Prayer of Nabonidus (4Q242). The cycle (1) achieved the form of a small literary collection of wisdom tales during the Persian period (Daniel 2–6); (2) developed into a larger collection due to the persecution of Antiochus IV (Daniel 1–12) and yet a larger collection with the Additions (1–14); and (3) continued to emerge in the form of other Pseudo-Daniel traditions (4Q243-245). Out of that developing cycle, the collections of chapters 1–12 and of 1–14 were accepted by different communities as Scripture, though not the earlier or later materials.

Other factors that may also have contributed to the recognition of Israel's literature as divinely authored Scripture were the increasing antiquity of a work, the educational or liturgical settings in which this literature was proclaimed to be speaking in the name of God or articulating the will of God, and the "resignification" or adaptability of the texts to the current community's ongoing life, whereby they could readily identify their situation with one in which God had favored Israel in the past.

Religious leaders and pious people sincerely trying to understand and articulate the divine will produced the religious classics of Israel. As generation after generation pondered their religious traditions in light of their current historical, political, and social reality, in one sense, the word *about* God became the word *of* God. The communities continued to hear it repeated as such, and eventually they recognized and described it explicitly as such.

Early Translations: Aramaic and Greek

Another possible indication that the Torah was considered authoritative Scripture before the middle of the Second Temple period is the translation of those texts into the vernacular languages. The *Iliad* and the *Odyssey,* despite their central cultural importance when the Romans took over the Greek culture, were apparently never translated into Latin in antiquity. A summary of the *Iliad* is attributed to Baebius Italicus in Nero's time, but it is a brief (only 1,070 hexameters) pedestrian version of the majestic original. By contrast with the Homeric poems, which were not translated, the Torah was translated in subsequent centuries into languages that the people could understand. The texts were important not only for the educated and cultured, and spoke not only of the past; they were central to the ongoing life of the whole community and had to be applicable to the future situations that the people might encounter. So the Scriptures were translated into Aramaic and Greek, the respective languages of the Persian Empire and the Jewish community in Babylon, and of the Hellenistic Empire and the Jewish community in Alexandria.

The Babylonian destruction and exile caused many fractures in Israel's life, including that of language. Aramaic was the imperial language of the Persian Empire, and Greek the language that the successors of Alexander attempted to impose upon their conquered territories. Though there was resistance to Greek culture, an increasing number of Jews became Aramaic or Greek speakers, creating a need for translations. Because the texts were important for community identity and had to be applicable to the future situations and foreign surroundings in which the Jewish people would find themselves in the Diaspora, the Scriptures were translated into languages that the people could understand.

There is no early evidence, but it seems likely that by the third century B.C.E. the Jewish community in Babylon had begun to translate the Torah and possibly also prophetic books into Aramaic. We do not know whether these were complete, written translations or oral, functional explanations of the Hebrew. The latter scene is mirrored in Neh. 8:8, narrated probably in the fourth century: accompanying a public reading from the Hebrew scroll, the Levites translated it and gave the sense, so that the people could understand. The earliest extant manuscripts are a Targum of Leviticus (4QtgLev) from the late second or early first century B.C.E. and two of Job (4QtgJob, 11QtgJob) from the middle of the first century C.E. Apart from these Qumran texts, the witness of the Targums for text-critical purposes is reduced, however, irrespective of the date when complete Targums of the Torah and other books were finally written down, since all preserved Targum texts have subsequently been revised to agree with an early form of the Masoretic Text (MT). It is difficult to have confidence that any specific readings provide premishnaic evidence.

Unlike the nebulous situation regarding early Aramaic translations, the probability is strong that the Jewish community in Alexandria had translated the Torah into Greek during the third century B.C.E. The legendary *Letter of Aristeas* elaborately narrates such an early translation, though it is generally believed to have been written in support of a version making claims for hegemony about a century later. Nevertheless, plausible examples of quotations in the late third and the second century B.C.E. as well as manuscript evidence make a third-century date for the translation close to certain. Demetrius the Chronographer already in the late third century quotes the Greek Genesis, and Eupolemus in the mid-second century uses the Greek Chronicles, which probably means that the more important Prophets had already been translated as well. Moreover, in the last third of the second century Ben Sira's grandson translated his grandfather's work and only casually mentions the translation of the Torah and the Prophets and other books, which suggests that those translations were not recent but had become widely known. Finally, the discovery of second-century manuscripts of Greek Pentateuchal books both in Egypt and in Palestine (already showing noticeable development) makes a third-century translation probable. Again, this unprecedented fact of translation may be a strong indicator that the Torah had become regarded as authoritative Scripture.

The Value of the Early Versions

The Targums generally do not help penetrate to ancient forms of the text other than those inherited in the MT collection. The Old Greek (OG) translation, on the other hand, provides for many books an invaluable witness to Second Temple textual forms that have otherwise perished. Whereas prior to the middle of the twentieth century the value of the LXX for text-critical purposes was often denigrated, the discovery of Hebrew manuscripts from Qumran vindicated the veracity of the LXX. Scrolls such as 4QDeut^{q}, 4QSam^{a,b}, and 4QJer^{b,d} display in Hebrew the type of texts from which the OG had been faithfully translated.

Those manuscripts have illuminated the first of four levels that must be taken into account when dealing with the individual Hebrew parent text from which the original translation was made. Previously, it had mainly been presumed that the parent text was virtually identical with the form in the MT, but the abundant variant editions unearthed at Qumran have freed critics from that myopic vision. One must seriously consider that the Greek is a witness to a Hebrew text that may simply be no longer available.

The second level is that of the act and product of the translation itself. Due to the many sources of possible variation from the parent Hebrew, the Greek often presented a text at odds even with the parent Hebrew it did use. Those sources included, for example, errors or damaged spots in the Hebrew manuscript, the uncertainty involved in understanding an often ambiguous Hebrew, misreading or misunderstanding of the Hebrew on the part of the translator, and different division of sentences due to lack of punctuation. Thus, though the translator was usually attempting to translate the Hebrew source text faithfully, unintended variants were inevitable. It is often declared that every translation is an interpretation. In a restricted sense that is correct; of course, the translator must interpret what the meaning of the original is. But the degree of interpretation is at times exaggerated to include theological *Tendenz,* or even "actualizing exegesis," whereby the translator deliberately changed the ancient text to highlight some current event or view. Despite the attractiveness and relatively heightened significance of such theological interpretation — if it were correct — the creative exegesis is usually to be assigned to the scholar proposing it. In light of the pluriform Hebrew and Greek manuscripts from Qumran, a Herculean burden of proof falls on one who would claim that the translator saw and understood one message in the Hebrew and deliberately produced a different message in the translation. A distinction must also be made between the meaning that the translator produced and diverse possible interpretations of that wording later.

Messages different from the Hebrew could and did result from a third level. Roughly six centuries of copyists' transmission elapsed between the original translation and the earliest full copies of the LXX dating from the fourth century C.E. It must be presumed that textual variants, both inadvertent errors and intentional corrections or supplements, began to affect the Greek texts from the earliest copies that scribes attempted to produce, just as happened with the Hebrew. Some variants entered the text through cross-fertilization from variant Hebrew formulations. Theological changes also occasionally occurred during the transmission process, clearly exemplified in passages such as LXX Ps. 13:3, with a long insertion quoted from Rom. 3:3-10, and other patently Christian additions in the transmitted texts at Pss. 50:9 and 95:10. Variants at the transmission level multiplied voluminously over the centuries and are seen now flooding the critical apparatus of the Göttingen Septuagint editions.

A fourth level visible in LXX manuscripts took the texts in a different direction. While variants multiplied in the LXX transmission, Jewish scholars labored to unify the developing LXX text, revising it toward conformity with what they presumed was the "original" Hebrew text, which for them happened to be the collection of texts now in the MT. This recensional process — seen primarily in the work of Aquila, Symmachus, and (proto-)Theodotion, and culminating in Origen's Hexapla — instead of unifying the ongoing Greek manuscript tradition, rather infiltrated and complicated it. To use the LXX critically, it is important to work with the first and second levels, sifting out influence from the third and fourth levels.

In addition to serving as a valuable window into ancient Hebrew text forms, the LXX also provides luminous witness to the understanding of the Scriptures in late antiquity. The Greek texts also developed a life of their own, soon no longer moored to the precise meaning of the Hebrew originals, becoming the Scriptures of both Christian and Greek-speaking Jewish communities. The Old Latin and the "daughter versions" (e.g., the Armenian, the Bohairic, etc.) were translated from the LXX and serve indirectly as witnesses to possible alternate Hebrew texts, but all the remaining versions witness uniformly to the MT collection.

Surprising Texts from the Late Second Temple Period

Starting in the latter half of the third century B.C.E., light begins to shine on the textual landscape, thanks to the discovery of more than two hundred biblical manuscripts in caves near Qumran and at other sites along the western side of the Dead Sea. The biblical scrolls provide a wide-ranging parade of textual surprises that deserve close review.

Exodus

An extensively preserved manuscript of Exodus written in the Paleo-Hebrew script and dated to approximately the middle of the first century B.C.E. surprised scholars shortly after the discovery of Cave 4. 4QpaleoExod^{m} routinely displayed the expanded text edition that was well known from the Samaritan Pentateuch (SP). In every instance where it is preserved, it displays the major expansions beyond the

MT and the LXX that are exhibited by the SP. Where it is not extant there is also no reason to suspect that it did not agree with other SP expansions, except for one instance. It apparently did not have space to contain the lengthy extra commandment added in the SP at Exod. 20:17b after the traditional commandments. That specifically Samaritan commandment (though taken from Deuteronomy 11 and 27, common to MT, SP, and LXX) to build an altar at Mt. Gerizim evidently was not in 4QpaleoExod[m], just as it is lacking in the MT and the LXX. It seems clear, then, that there were at least two variant editions of the text of Exodus in circulation within Jewish circles during the first century B.C.E. Evidently both were used and enjoyed equal status. 4QpaleoExod[m] was damaged at one point, and someone carefully sewed a patch over the large hole and reinscribed the lost words. The Samaritans made use of that secondary, expanded edition and apparently made only one theological change in two forms: they added the commandment that Israel's central altar was to be built on Mt. Gerizim, and in the recurring formula they stressed that God had chosen Mt. Gerizim, not Jerusalem, as that central shrine where his name should dwell. Thus, the "Samaritan" Exodus was mainly a general Jewish text of Exodus. And that secondary, expanded edition that lacked the two specifically Samaritan changes continued to be used by Jews and was still being copied around the middle of the first century B.C.E. There does not appear to be any evidence that the Jews and Samaritans were aware of or concerned about the specific text-type.

Numbers

Scholars were generally slow in digesting and accepting that new evidence from 4QpaleoExod[m], but the most extensively preserved scroll of the book of Numbers provided confirmatory evidence with a profile similar to that of the Exodus scroll. 4QNum[b], written in the Jewish script and dating from the latter half of the first century B.C.E., also exhibits agreement with the additions in the SP beyond the traditional text as in the MT and LXX. But like 4QpaleoExod[m], it does not have the specifically Samaritan readings. It thus confirms the pattern seen in Exodus, that Palestinian Judaism knew at least two editions of the book of Numbers, and that the Samaritans used the secondary, already expanded Jewish tradition exemplified in 4QNum[b]. Again, both editions of Numbers were apparently in use by Jews in the late Second Temple period.

Joshua

The oldest manuscript of Joshua also provided a surprise, but in a different direction. 4QJosh[a], from the latter half of the second or the first half of the first century B.C.E., presented a sequence of important episodes that was strikingly at variance with the order of events in the traditional MT. In the scroll, Joshua evidently builds the first altar in the newly entered land at Gilgal, immediately after he has traversed the River Jordan and led all the people safely across. That is, the episode occurs at the end of chapter 4, thus prior to the circumcision and then the ensuing conquest. The scroll's sequence seems natural and logical, and one might expect that the sanctification of the land — by the building of the first altar, the recitation of the Torah, and the rite of circumcision — would be the inaugural episode of the occupation of the promised land. In contrast, the MT locates the building of the first altar at the end of chapter 8, placing it on Mt. Ebal, which causes numerous problems. Commentators have had to struggle with that odd location, for it requires a march of twenty miles from Ai up to Ebal, the construction of the altar, then a return march south, back to Gilgal. Meanwhile, Joshua would have left that important altar abandoned in enemy territory, and, whereas Gilgal remained an important shrine (1 Sam. 11:14-15; 2 Kings 2:1), Mt. Ebal is otherwise insignificant. The problem is worsened since Josh. 9:1 logically and syntactically follows 8:29, not 8:35, suggesting that the insertion of vv. 30-35 at the end of chapter 8 is secondary. Moreover, the LXX presents yet a slightly different order, though it is in basic agreement with the MT regarding the location of the altar. But perhaps the strongest confirmation of the sequence in 4QJosh[a] is provided by Josephus, who also places the altar at Gilgal (*Ant.* 5.20) and who must have used as his source a biblical text that agreed with the Qumran scroll. He even adds further support (*Ant.* 5.45-57) insofar as he does not narrate a building of the altar where the MT places it, between the conquest of Ai (8:1-29) and the Gibeonites' ruse (Joshua 9). An additional piece of the puzzle is provided by the SP, which reads "Mount Gerizim," in agreement with the Old Latin, which reads "Garzin," at Deut. 27:4, the command that is the basis for this episode in Joshua. Thus 4QJosh[a] evidently provides a more original form of the narrative. The placement of that first altar in the land has serious consequences, of course, and the most plausible reading of the textual evidence is that 4QJosh[a] has the earliest sequence and that a northern faction (Samarians or Samaritans) secondarily rearranged the location of the altar at their sacred shrine on Mt. Gerizim. At a third stage, in counterreaction, southerners (Judeans or rabbis), due to religious polemics, simply changed the name of the mountain from Gerizim to Ebal, despite the anomaly created.

Judges

The oldest manuscript of the book of Judges (4QJudg[a]), dating from about 50-25 B.C.E., survives in but a single small fragment. It contains Judg. 6:2-6 followed directly by vv. 11-13. It lacks 6:7-10, a separate unit whose style differs from the preceding and following verses and appears to be a later theological insertion. Thus, again, the Qumran text of Judges exhibits an early, short form of Judges 6, and the MT has a secondary, theologically expanded version.

Samuel

4QSam[a], dating from near the mid-first century B.C.E., contains a form of text that included a complete paragraph that is not present in the MT, the LXX, or any other extant version. It narrates the oppression by Nahash the Ammonite that introduces the material now found in 1 Sam. 11:1 in the MT and other texts. The fragment itself contains a case of a scribal skip of the eye (parablepsis), which lends support to the probability that the passage was lost in the MT tradition through the same kind of error. Parallel to Josephus' agreement with 4QJosh[a], he also shows he used a text of Samuel like 4QSam[a], since he also narrates the content, details, and wording of that otherwise lost paragraph (*Ant.* 6.68-69).

Isaiah

The Great Isaiah Scroll (1QIsa[a]) was the first and most dramatic biblical manuscript to gain widespread fame. Especially because the text displays multifaceted disagreement with the traditional MT, the assumption was made that it was a Qumran text of Isaiah, that is, that its unusual features were specifically due to the "sect" that lived at Qumran and copied it there. A second Isaiah scroll (1QIsa[b]) was also found in Cave 1 and by contrast was nearly identical with the MT. It did indeed show that the medieval MT of Isaiah had been copied with great accuracy over the intervening thousand years. But whereas the two scrolls were first categorized as one authentic text and one "vulgar" Qumran text, in fact they demonstrated — though scholars could not yet realize it — the two principal lessons for the biblical text from the new discoveries. The MT is, for the most part, an accurate copy of some ancient text for each book; but importantly, there were also valuable variant editions of many books in antiquity that had been lost, discarded, or rejected. Though the linguistic and orthographic profile of 1QIsa[a] is generally secondary to that of the MT, its textual profile is earlier in numerous cases. 1QIsa[a] demonstrates that the MT displays a recurring pattern of a sentence or more added to the text; in seven instances the MT inserts secondary expansions of up to four verses where 1QIsa[a] preserves the earlier short text.

Jeremiah

While several scrolls show that the edition they represent is at variance with the MT, the scrolls of Jeremiah provide an example of two variant, successive editions of the book visible among the scrolls themselves. Small fragments of two manuscripts, 4QJer[b] and 4QJer[d], both from the second century B.C.E., display in Hebrew the earlier, shorter edition with one arrangement of the book that formed the basis of the OG translation. In contrast, both 4QJer[a], from ca. 225-175 B.C.E., and 4QJer[c], from the latter part of the first century B.C.E., have the later, more expanded edition with a variant arrangement in agreement with the MT. Just as 4QJer[b] and the OG witness to the secondary addition of vv. 6-8 and 10 into chap. 10 in the MT, 4QJer[a], though it agrees with the MT in its overall edition, nonetheless exposes a large secondary addition of seven verses in the MT at Jer. 7:30-34; 8:1-3. The original scroll, copied ca. 225-175 B.C.E., lacked this lengthy pair of passages; but a later scribe, palaeographically dated a century or more later, about 100-50 B.C.E., inserted them into the old text. He squeezed three lines of tiny script into a horizontal space in the text, continued with four lines written down the left margin, and, since there was yet more text, wrote a final line upside down in the bottom margin (DJD 15: 155 and plate 24). That this two-part passage was not part of the original Jeremiah text is suggested by the fact that it is not closely related to the context, that the prose insertion interrupts the flow of the poetic verse 7:29 into another logically following poetic verse 8:4, and that the original scribe's omission of it would have required an unparalleled parablepsis involving about twelve lines of text.

Psalms

The evidence from Qumran and Masada also demonstrates that there were at least two editions of the Psalter in antiquity. One manuscript from Masada has Psalm 150 followed by a blank sheet, showing that it represented the same edition handed down in the MT. Cave 11, however, held a beautiful and generously preserved scroll with Psalms that was so different from the MT that many scholars, especially in the early decades, considered it as nonbiblical. 11QPs[a] contains thirty-nine Psalms known from the MT plus ten additional compositions. Shortly after it was published, there was a vigorous debate concerning its nature, whether biblical or not. Its editor, James A. Sanders, considered it a biblical scroll and thus listed "Ps" in the title, but other major scholars challenged this classification. Their challenges included the following reasons: (1) the psalms that are familiar as biblical psalms are presented in a sequence that differs repeatedly from that of the MT; (2) it includes additional "nonbiblical" psalms not found in the MT; (3) it was characterized as "liturgical," because even within the biblical Psalm 145 an antiphon is repeatedly added in contrast with the MT; (4) it includes in the midst of the Psalms a prose piece, "David's Compositions"; and (5) the tetragrammaton is written in the Paleo-Hebrew script, not in the normal Jewish script used for the remainder of the scroll.

But in light of the accumulating evidence from the biblical manuscripts, each of those objections collapsed, and the scroll is being increasingly acknowledged as an alternate edition of the biblical Psalter in ancient Judaism. (1) The MT Psalter does not have a rigorously or clearly intentionally arranged sequence to its psalms; some deliberate groupings can be postulated, but there is no discernible comprehensive plan. (2) Four of the so-called noncanonical compositions are in fact psalms found in the Greek and Syriac Psalters, and two others are found at other places in the MT or LXX, namely, 2 Sam. 23:1-7 and Sir. 51:13-30. The remaining psalms were hitherto unknown but had been composed in the ancient style of the biblical psalms, not in that of the later Qumran *Hodayot.* They were clearly originally Hebrew psalms, even if not eventually accepted into the MT edition of the Psalter. (3) 11QPs[a] is indeed a liturgical scroll, but so is the MT Psalter by its very nature. The antiphon interspersed in Psalm 145, "Blessed be the LORD, and blessed be his name forever and ever," is totally derived from verse 1 of Psalm 145, and it is systematically repeated in the identical manner in which the antiphon

"For his faithfulness endures forever" is repeated in Psalm 136 in the MT. (4) "David's Compositions" stakes an explicit claim for prophetic inspiration and thus scriptural status of the Psalter. It may have originally been positioned not *within* the collection but at the *end* of an earlier edition of the collection (before Psalms 140, 134, and 151 were appended), thus functioning as a quasi-colophon with the claim for scriptural status. (5) The use of the Paleo-Hebrew script for the divine name in a text written in the Jewish script had earlier been considered an indication that the text was not biblical, but several other biblical scrolls in the Jewish script have also been identified that write the tetragrammaton in the Paleo-Hebrew script. Two additional manuscripts (11QPs^{b} and 4QPs^{e}) apparently witness to the 11QPs^{a} edition, whereas none of the ancient manuscripts found at Qumran unambiguously supports the MT sequence of Psalms against the 11QPs^{a} sequence.

The (Reworked?) Pentateuch

Four sets of fragments, three of them containing text from four or all five books of the Pentateuch, still pose challenges that deserve exploration. First, it remains undecided whether 4Q364-367, to which yet a fifth manuscript (4Q185) has been linked, represent copies of the same composition or only similar variant forms of pentateuchal development. Second, the classification is still debated. In large part the fragments present a running text of the Pentateuch but have frequent additions, a few omissions, and alternate sequences. Accordingly, they were first published as "4QReworked Pentateuch"; that is, the variants were deemed to outweigh the agreements, and thus they were not the Pentateuch but beyond the Pentateuch. A number of scholars, having digested the lessons from the many variant, developing editions of the biblical books — that additions, omissions, and altered sequences are characteristic of the biblical text in the Second Temple period — have begun to see these texts as a yet later form (or forms) of the Pentateuch, and thus refer to it as 4QPentateuch. It seems to be moderately developed beyond the expanded Jewish version used by the Samaritans; in fact, many of its variants agree with the SP, though none are sectarian. Other scholars remain somewhere in a middle position between "Pentateuch" and "reworked," searching for a proper category and term.

Similar Examples from the MT, SP, and OG

Once taught by the variant editions posed by the biblical scrolls, scholars could recognize similar examples long available in familiar sources. The MT was recognized as containing revised and expanded editions when compared with the OG, in the Tabernacle account (Exodus 35–40), the account of David's induction into Saul's service (1 Samuel 16–17), and the book of Jeremiah. The SP was recognized as witnessing the already expanded Jewish editions of the pentateuchal books with only slight theological changes. The OG of Daniel was seen as an expanded form of the edition in the MT — the reverse process compared with the situation in Jeremiah.

The Greek papyrus 967 may well also display an edition of Ezekiel that is earlier than the edition now attested by the MT and the LXX. It has the order of chapters as 36, 38, 39, 37, and 40, and lacks 36:23c-38. Analysis suggests that this was the early form translated from a Hebrew text with that order. A later Hebrew editor transposed chap. 37 into its present (MT) position and added the last section of chap. 36 (vv. 23c-38) at the same time as a suitable eschatological introduction into chap. 37. Other ancient sources join the biblical texts in adding their witness. Josephus, for example, as seen above, used biblical texts similar to 4QJosh[a] and 4QSam[a], rather than the forms in the MT, for his *Jewish Antiquities.*

Lessons from the Biblical Scrolls

After reviewing the parade of biblical manuscripts from Qumran and the major variants in the MT, SP, and OG that can be seen and appreciated in clearer focus due to the Qumran scrolls, what lessons do they offer? The first headline that immediately flashes is "textual pluriformity." The pluriformity, however, is not chaos but shows patterns that can be clearly seen and intelligibly classified. There are four principal categories of variation detectable through comparison of the Qumran manuscripts, MT, SP, and OG: (1) orthography, (2) individual textual variants, (3) isolated interpretive insertions, and (4) revised and expanded editions. Studies show that these four types of variation operate on different levels unrelated to each other.

Orthography

The six centuries of the Second Temple period saw noticeable development in the Hebrew language, and especially its spelling practices. Scribes, through the insertion of *matres lectionis,* made early contributions to the interpretational process that concluded with the Masoretes' vocalization of the texts. Since the text was sometimes ambiguous, the tendency toward fuller spelling was helpful for correct reading and preservation of correct understanding. The *matres* were inserted at times unintentionally, at times intentionally, insofar as the source text may have had one spelling, but the scribe nonetheless inadvertently or consciously wrote the word as he customarily spelled it, regardless of the source text. Usually the fuller form simply indicated the correct form more clearly and involved no change in meaning. For example, in Isa. 8:19 the ambiguous *ha-'bwt,* which could mean "ancestors," was correctly vocalized in 1QIsa[a] as *ha-'ôbôt,* "ghosts," and similarly in the MT as *ha-'ōbôt.* But in Isa. 40:6 the ambiguous *w'mr* was interpreted in the MT as third person, whereas it was clarified as first person in 1QIsa[a].

Individual Textual Variants

The human difficulty in accurately copying large amounts of complicated text resulted in readings that differed from the parent text for virtually every ancient manuscript. Many variants were unintentional (e.g., numerous types of errors, inadvertent substitution of *lectiones faciliores,* loss of letters, loss of one or more words through inattention or parablepsis); others were intentional (clarifying insertions, scribal correction [whether correct or not], additional information, linguistic smoothing, euphemistic substitutions, literary flourishes, theological ideas). This general phenomenon is well known, and the traditional handbooks on textual criticism primarily deal with this level, describing general rules of thumb that remain well founded for judging variants.

Isolated Interpretive Insertions

Learned scribes occasionally inserted into the text they were copying what they considered an appropriate piece of additional material. Comparisons between the Scrolls, the MT, the SP, and the LXX highlight insertions of up to eight verses now in one text, now in another. Depending upon the genre of book being copied, the insertions provided information (2 Sam. 5:4-5 in MT vs. 4QSam^{a}), offered instruction (Isa. 2:22 in 1QIsa^{a} MT vs. LXX), solved nomistic inconsistencies (Lev. 17:4 in 4QLev^{d} SP vs. 11QpaleoLev^{a} MT), stemmed from piety (Isa 2:9b in 4QIsa^{a} 4QIsa^{b} MT LXX vs. 1QIsa^{a}), added prophetic apparitions (Judg. 6:7-10 in MT vs. 4QJudg^{a}), introduced apocalyptic tendencies (Isa. 2:10 in 4QIsa^{a} 4QIsa^{b} MT LXX vs. 1QIsa^{a}, plus many "on that day" passages in Isaiah), or simply added similar material (Isa. 34:17b–35:2 in MT LXX vs. 1QIsa^{a}; Jer. 7:30–8:3 in MT 4QJer$^{a\ 2m}$ vs. 4QJer^{a*}) or contrasting material (Jer. 10:6-8, 10 in MT vs. 4QJer^{b} LXX). The prophetic books especially are replete with such expansions, and results of this activity have penetrated all texts; indeed, it seems to have been a widespread factor in the development of all the biblical books. If such interpretive insertions are isolated and not linked as part of a series, they are classified in this category. If there are a number of coordinated patterned sets showing substantial harmonizations, revisions, or insertions, these would form a new edition of a book.

New and Expanded Editions of Biblical Books

The most influential method by which the texts developed in major ways was through successive revised and expanded editions of each book. From their earliest, shadowy beginnings the texts solidified and developed by faithful repetition but also by occasional creative, updated editions to form the books as we begin to see them when manuscript evidence becomes available. Source-critical examples, such as the retheologizing of the older monarchic traditions in light of the destruction and exile (traditional P), and more specifically the insertion of the P flood story into the older J story in Genesis 6–9, help illustrate the phenomenon. Those new editions were achieved not through displacement of the old but through combination of the new with the old. A more sustained and documented example is the four or five successive editions of the book of Exodus. Exodus 35–40 is preserved in two successive editions; the OG is presumably the earlier edition (edition $n + 1$) and the MT the later (edition $n + 2$), developed from the Hebrew parent text used by the OG. Then 4QpaleoExod^{m} displayed an expanded edition (edition $n + 3$) based on but expanding the edition as in the MT, while the SP exhibited the same general edition as 4QpaleoExod^{m} but with such significant theological changes (albeit not significant quantitative changes) that it could be regarded as a fourth edition (edition $n + 4$). There is now even a fifth, if 4QRP is considered 4QPentateuch (edition $n + 5$). A similar pair of successive editions for Numbers was seen in 4QNum^{b}, while for Genesis the MT, SP, and LXX all clearly show intentionally revised editions of the two extended passages in chaps. 5 and 11.

The Nature of the Biblical Text

Before the discovery of the scrolls in 1947, scholars generally viewed the MT, the SP, and the LXX as three main, but not equal, text types. The MT, in a purified form, was seen as the "original" Bible; Gesenius had shown that the SP was derivative from the MT and thus farther from the "original," and the LXX was usually denigrated as an inaccurate translation where it disagreed with the MT. The SP and the LXX were occasionally helpful, to be sure, but the prevailing mentality was that the MT represented the closest extant form of the *Urtext.* The *Urtext* theory was championed by Paul de Lagarde in the late nineteenth century. It envisioned a single original Hebrew text that was no longer extant in its pure form but that could largely be recovered through the MT with comparative analysis of the SP, the LXX, and the versions. Paul Kahle in the middle of the twentieth century unsuccessfully challenged it with his *Vulgärtexte* theory, seeing a plethora of variant texts overshadowed by the MT, the SP, and the LXX; but the genetic relationship between all texts argued strongly against it. The *Urtext* theory probably emerged from three factors: (1) the absence of evidence, because only a single Hebrew text form had been transmitted to posterity after the Second Jewish Revolt in 132-135 C.E.; (2) the traditional religious view, that the biblical text was the word that God spoke to Moses and the Prophets and the Sages, and thus was unique; and (3) early scholarly views, that the books were "documents" or major written compositions by single authors or compilers. Thus, the purified MT was ultimately God's word, and the diverse manuscripts that survive attest to the errors that human scribes have allowed to penetrate it.

But just as the invention of the telescope and accurate observation of astronomical data allowed the Copernican heliocentric cosmology to eclipse the unquestioned Ptolemaic-medieval geocentric cosmology, so too the discovery of the biblical scrolls and accurate observation of the data they provide have eclipsed the view of the MT as the textual center of the Hebrew Bible. Though the biblical scrolls from the Judean Desert were early assumed to be sectarian, the more they are studied, the more it is obvious that there is nothing sectarian about them; they constitute the most ancient and authentic witness to what the texts of the Jewish Scriptures were like at the time of the origins of Christianity and rabbinic Judaism.

The Qumran biblical manuscripts — and in their light, the LXX, the expanded Jewish text used as the basis for the SP, the biblical texts used by Josephus, and citations in the New Testament and rabbinic writings — make it clear that the MT was not the textual center. A number of lessons have emerged. First, the scrolls did confirm that the medieval codices of the MT had for over a millennium been very accurately hand-copied from texts like 4QGen[b], 1QIsa[b], and 4QJer[a,c]. But they also confirmed that the SP (in light of 4QpaleoExod[m] and 4QNum[b]) and the LXX (in light of 4QDeut[q], 4QSam[a,b], and 4QJer[b,d]) preserved equally important witnesses to alternate ancient forms of the biblical text otherwise lost.

Second, scholars realized not only that the MT is not "the original text" or the *Urtext* of the Hebrew Bible, but that it is not "a text" at all. Like the LXX, it is a varied collection of texts — a different type of text for each of the books — each being simply a copy of one of the editions of that book that was circulating in late Second Temple Jewish circles. Again, the MT is not "the original text"; it is rather the only collection of texts in the *original language* that had been preserved (beyond the Samaritan community) since the second century C.E.

Third, there was a revival of theories making major advances in charting the history of the biblical text. The discoveries at first supported the position of the three main text types, since various scrolls agreed with the MT, the LXX, and the SP. Large fragments of 4QSam[a,b] (agreeing with the LXX) and 4QpaleoExod[m] (agreeing with the SP) were published early, and thus W. F. Albright and, more substantially, Frank Moore Cross posited three localities as producing the three local text types, seeing a textual development of "one-into-three" — the presumed original into the MT, the LXX, and the SP. But numerous differences in the scrolls from these three types led to further theories. Shemaryahu Talmon, noting the pluriformity, saw rather a "many-into-three" situation, noting that out of the many textual traditions only three survived. Socio-religiously only three communities survived the Roman destruction: the rabbis, the Samaritans, and the Christians, each preserving their own set of texts. But the numerous disagreements in the scrolls also dethroned the LXX and the SP from their positions as the other two "main text types." Seeing the numerous disagreements as well as the agreements, Emanuel Tov expanded the view, proposing two other types of "nonaligned" texts and "texts written in the Qumran practice."

Prior to the Jewish revolts against Rome, however, there was no "standard text" — whether MT, LXX, or SP — with which texts should be "aligned" or judged "nonaligned," and thus those four categories appeared anachronistic for classifying the scrolls. Furthermore, some texts in "the Qumran practice" (e.g., 1QIsa[a]) may well have been copied prior to the settlement at Qumran and may simply exhibit late Second Temple scribal practice. Thus, the present author proposed a series of successive revised and expanded editions of each of the biblical books, noting that the pluriformity and great variation in the texts were not chaotic, but patterned in the four principal categories of variation discussed above. Each book had its own history and developed along its own trajectory. The main lines of development resulted from the creative revised and expanded editions of each book. Each copy of whichever edition displayed its own particular individual textual variants, and further copies would either reproduce the orthographic profile of the source text or show modernizing tendencies in spelling practices. Occasionally, scribes would put into the text isolated interpretive insertions that had become either customary oral supplements or marginal glosses, and these would become an accepted part of the transmitted text. Each of the four kinds of variation took place independently of the other three. The MT, the LXX, and the SP should not be regarded as "the three main text types" but are merely manuscript copies for each book in their collection, each copied more or less accurately from one or other of the available editions of that book. Thus, the Masoretic texts must be judged on a par with and according to the same criteria by which the LXX, the SP, the scrolls, the versions, and all other texts are judged, word by word.

From Collection of Scriptures to the Canon of Scripture

The discussion thus far has centered on individual texts, since the books developed separately and were written on separate scrolls during the Second Temple period. By the third or fourth century C.E., however, the collection of texts coalesced into a single text. Books considered to have divine authority formed a special group distinct from other works. The group of five books seen as the revelation to Moses became "the book of Moses" (4QMMT C10), though the authoritative status of *Jubilees* in certain circles raises the question whether the category of Torah was strictly confined to the five books. The book of Moses together with an undefined collection of prophetic books (including, for most Jewish groups, Psalms and Daniel) formed a special collection of authoritative Scripture — "the Law and the Prophets" — during the late Second Temple period. Many other works, some of which would, and others of which would not, become part of the Writings, or Poetic and Wisdom books, were still finding their place in the first century C.E. By approximately the third century, though the scroll format apparently continued in Jewish circles, at least for Christians the codex gradually supplanted the scroll as the preferred form, and the texts that had been placed only in a mental category were now transformed into a physical unity, a single text: the Old Testament. Thus, the idea of a collection of sacred texts originated in Judaism, but explicit discussion of a canon of sacred Scriptures and physical reproduction of it apparently arose in Christian circles.

"Canon" is a theological *terminus technicus* denoting the definitive, official list of inspired, authoritative books that constitute the recognized and accepted body of sacred Scripture which forms the rule of faith for a major religious group, that definitive list being the result of inclusive and exclusive decisions after serious deliberation. Jews, Catholics, Protestants, Orthodox, and others have differing lists of books as their canon, but the definition of "the canon of Scripture" remains the same for all, and the process leading up to the establishment of the canon was an analogous process for each.

There is no solid evidence from the Second Temple period regarding the specific books in the canon and at best inconclusive evidence for anything beyond "the Law and the Prophets." The Prologue to Ben Sira is clearest with "the Law and the Prophets and the other books of our ancestors" (8–10; cf. 1–2, 24–25). But this could mean either a tripartite or a bipartite collection: either (1) the Law, (2) the Prophets, and (3) the Writings; or (1) the Scriptures (i.e., the Law and the Prophets) and (2) other important religious literature helpful toward instruction and wisdom. Whereas both the bipartite and the tripartite (albeit quite vague for the third category) positions are defensible, in contrast, the oft-cited reference to a tripartite canon in 4QMMT C 10 ("in the book of Moses [and] in the book[s of the P]rophets and in Dav[id . . .]") requires serious scrutiny. The DJD editors' interpretation as an attestation of a tripartite canon is highly dubious on at least five levels: questionable placement of a fragment (4QMMT^{d} frg. 17), paleographic transcription of several letters, reconstruction of the composite text in light of disagreements between the manuscripts, awkward syntax, and the content denoted by the last phrase (*wbd??*[ ]). That is, two of the three sections, "the book[s of]" the Prophets, and "David," may well disappear from the alleged tripartite reference. Appeals to other biblical references — such as in Ben Sira's own work and 1 and 2 Maccabees — are likewise unpersuasive, unless one takes a maximalist approach in which mere knowledge of or allusive mention of a book means that it, or even its entire category of books, was already considered canonical. Only toward the end of the first century C.E. does Josephus write of an exclusive twenty-two-book collection, and *4 Ezra* mentions a set of twenty-four books for the public alongside seventy to be distributed among the wise. Thus, the absence of any clear mention of a tripartite collection of Scriptures prior to the late first century C.E. weighs in favor of a bipartite collection envisioned in the Prologue to Ben Sira.

Terminological Distinctions

For clarity and to avoid maximalist overinterpretation, it is essential to distinguish between terms or realities that are closely associated with the concept of canon but are not identical with it. An *authoritative* work is one which a group, whether secular or religious, recognizes and accepts as determinative for its conduct, and as of a higher order than can be overridden by the power or will of the group or any member. An example would be a constitution or law code. A book of *Scripture* is a sacred authoritative work believed to have God as its ultimate author, which the community recognizes and accepts as determinative for its belief and practice; it is not necessarily a fixed text but may be still developing and circulating in several textual forms. *A collection of authoritative Scriptures,* as opposed to a canon, is an open collection to which more books can be added. Certainly such a collection was recognized as fundamental to the Jewish religion from sometime in the first half of the Second Temple period; at that time it was probably confined to the Law of Moses, as attested by the OG translation of the Pentateuch and the Samaritan canon. According to the distinction between "a collection of authoritative books" and "an authoritative collection of books," throughout the Second Temple period the collection was growing and thus there was not yet a canon.

A *canon,* as defined above, is a religious body's official, definitively debated and permanently decided, exclusive list of inspired, authoritative books that constitute its recognized corpus of sacred Scripture. The *Bible,* in the singular, denotes a textual form of the collection of canonical books. In contrast to the canon, which is the normative list of the books, the Bible is the text of that collection of books, conceived of as a single anthology, and usually presented physically as such. Thus, the term is probably anachronistic prior to the codex format of the collection. "The Scriptures" can be an open collection, but the "Bible" connotes an already closed collection.

The *canonical process* is the journey of the many disparate works of literature within the ongoing community from their early stages when they began to be considered as somehow authoritative, through the sifting and endorsement process, to the final judgment concerning their inspired character as the unified and defined collection of Scripture — that is, until the reflective judgment of recognition that officially constituted the canon. *Canon* as such is a static concept, the result of a retrospective conclusion that something has come to be. Until that final decision is reached, *process toward canon* or *canonical process* is preferable. Some speak of an "open canon" or of "adaptability" as the primary characteristic of the canon; but the canon is by definition closed, and so an "open collection" is preferable; and adaptability is a function, not the essence, of the canon — how it is used, not what it is.

The Evidence from Qumran for the Process toward Canon

In the absence of clear early written discussion, surveying the Qumran evidence can be somewhat illuminating, especially since it generally agrees with the New Testament evidence. Criteria of varying strengths for canon or scriptural status would be: (a) a title of the canon or its parts, or a list of its books; (b) formulas that introduce explicit quotations of Scripture; (c) books explicitly quoted as Scripture; (d) multiple copies of a book; (e) books on which commentaries were written; and (f) books that were translated into the vernacular languages.

Unfortunately, the Dead Sea Scrolls provide no conclusive evidence for determining the exact contents of the collection that the covenanters considered the authoritative books of Scripture or whether they even discussed the question. But that they regarded the Law and the Prophets as divinely revealed Scripture is clear from statements such as "[God] commanded through Moses and all his servants the prophets" (1QS 1:1-3), "As you said through Moses" (1QM 10:6), and "As God said through Isaiah the prophet" (CD 4:13). Thus, there is (a) no clear evidence for a canon of Scripture, but (b) certitude regarding the Law and the Prophets as Scripture. (c) Isaiah and the Minor Prophets are quoted nine times, pentateuchal books (but not Genesis) and Ezekiel 1–5 times; the only others are Psalms and Daniel 2, and one each for Jeremiah, Proverbs, and *Jubilees.* The Former Prophets and the remainder of the Writings are never quoted (except for the prophetic oracle in 2 Samuel 7). (d) There are thirty-six Hebrew copies of the Psalms, thirty of Deuteronomy, twenty-one of Isaiah, twenty of Genesis, seventeen of Exodus, fourteen of *Jubilees,* thirteen of Leviticus, twelve (or twenty?) of *1 Enoch,* eight of the Minor Prophets and

Daniel, seven of Numbers, six of Jeremiah and Ezekiel, and five of Tobit. The Former Prophets and the Writings all have four or fewer copies — fewer than the *Community Rule,* the *Damascus Document,* the *Hodayot,* and the *War Scroll.* (e) Exegetical commentaries treat only the Law and the Prophets (Isaiah, the Minor Prophets, and Psalms). Finally, (f) the Qumran texts show only the Torah (and possibly *1 Enoch*) translated into Greek, while Aramaic targums were rare: one for Leviticus and two for Job. The Greek Minor Prophets scroll from Naḥal Ḥever, however, adds valuable evidence. Since this scroll from the turn of the era is already in revised Greek form, it indicates that the original Greek translation of the main prophetic books had also been accomplished at least by the first century B.C.E.

Admittedly, the evidence for each criterion is only suggestive; but the combination is quite persuasive. It is clear that the books of the Torah and the Prophets (including Psalms and Daniel) were considered Scripture. *Jubilees* and *1 Enoch* have a strong claim. Job and possibly Proverbs might qualify. But regarding the Former Prophets and the remainder of the Writings, it can only be claimed that the literature was known to the Qumran covenanters; it may or may not have been considered Scripture, though the presence of four copies of Canticles presumably indicates that it was read at least as spiritual allegory.

Shifts in the Process toward Canon

While the terminology regarding the canonical process may be clarified, and the evidence from Qumran may witness to certain Scriptures but no canon yet, the waters remain largely uncharted for the more important and intriguing issue of the socio-political struggles and theological debates that formed the path to the eventual canon. A few turns in the path, however, can be seen.

First, there was a shift from national literature to sacred Scripture, described above. Some works of Israel's literature became recognized as having divine origin and thus were regarded as sacred Scripture.

Second, there was a shift in the understanding of revelation. Whereas revelation had been seen as dynamic and a continuing possibility, gradually it was viewed as verbal and recorded in the distant past. This gets expressed in the ancient (and a lingering modern) conviction regarding the cessation of prophecy.

Third, there was a shift from a religion centered primarily on the Temple and its rituals to a religion centered on its texts. This was a result of the destruction of the Temple and the ability of shared texts to function as a unifying force even for a people spread throughout Diaspora communities.

Fourth, vague consciousness had to give way to clear decisions regarding the scriptural status of books toward the periphery. The new focus on sacred texts as Judaism's centripetal force required new questions, scrutiny, debate, and decisions about the relative status of various texts. While all Jews recognized the sanctity of the Torah and most recognized divine revelation in a collection of prophetic books, now decisions had to be made concerning which books belonged in the "Prophets" collection and whether extra books might also deserve to be accorded supreme authority.

Fifth, a dramatic shift replaced textual pluriformity with uniformity. Throughout the Second Temple period, the texts were characterized by fluidity, pluriformity, and creativeness in composition. But the shocks of the two revolts and the increased importance of the texts precluded further development. This shift, which froze each book in a single textual form, happened quite abruptly in the late first or early second century C.E.; it is often referred to as "stabilization," but "freezing" or "termination of development" is more accurate, since it was not a textual process but simply a cessation.

Sixth, the format of the books of the Scriptures shifted from individual scrolls to codex. Whereas a scroll usually contained one or at most two books, a codex could contain a large number of books. Thus, decisions whether a book was recognized as sacred Scripture were more pressing when considering its inclusion in, or exclusion from, a single collection between front and back covers.

At the end of the lengthy process of composition and development of the Scriptures from their beginnings and through the late shifts just described, came the Romans. After two failed revolts by the Jews, the Qumran covenanters were no more; the Samaritans remained apart; the Jewish followers of Jesus inherited a large, not yet delimited collection of Scriptures emphasizing the prophetic writings. The rabbis eventually restricted the collection to twenty-four books, rejecting *1 Enoch,* Ben Sira, and others; de-emphasizing certain apocalyptic and messianic aspects; and focusing on the sapiential rather than prophetic character of the Psalms and Daniel.

BIBLIOGRAPHY

Abegg, Martin, Peter Flint, and Eugene Ulrich. 1999. *The Dead Sea Scrolls Bible: The Oldest Known Bible Translated for the First Time into English.* San Francisco: HarperSanFrancisco.

Auwers, J.-M., and H. J. De Jonge, eds. 2002. *The Biblical Canons.* Leuven: Leuven University Press and Peeters.

Cross, Frank Moore, and Shemaryahu Talmon, eds. 1975. *Qumran and the History of the Biblical Text.* Cambridge: Harvard University Press.

Fernández Marcos, N. 2000. *The Septuagint in Context: Introduction to the Greek Versions of the Bible.* Trans. W. G. E. Watson. Leiden: Brill.

Flint, Peter W., and James C. VanderKam, eds. 1998. *The Dead Sea Scrolls after Fifty Years: A Comprehensive Assessment.* 2 vols. Leiden: Brill.

Harl, Marguerite, Gilles Dorrival, and Olivier Munnich. 1988. *La Bible grecque des Septante: Du judaïsme hellénistique au christianisme ancien.* Paris: Cerf and C.N.R.S.

Herbert, Edward D., and Emanuel Tov. 2002. *The Bible as Book: The Hebrew Bible and the Judaean Desert Discoveries.* London: British Library and Oak Knoll Press.

McDonald, Lee M., and James A. Sanders, eds. 2002. *The Canon Debate.* Peabody, Mass.: Hendrickson.

Mulder, Martin Jan, ed. 1988. *Mikra: Text, Translation, Reading and Interpretation of the Hebrew Bible in Ancient Judaism and Early Christianity.* Assen: Van Gorcum; Philadelphia: Fortress.

Purvis, James D. 1968. *The Samaritan Pentateuch and the Origin of the Samaritan Sect.* Cambridge: Harvard University Press.

Sanderson, Judith E. 1986. *An Exodus Scroll from Qumran: 4QpaleoExod^{m} and the Samaritan Tradition,* Atlanta: Scholars Press.

Schiffman, Lawrence H., and James C. VanderKam, eds. 2000. *The Encyclopedia of the Dead Sea Scrolls.* 2 vols. New York: Oxford University Press.

Shepherd, David. 2004. *Targum and Translation: A Reconsideration of the Qumran Aramaic Version of Job.* Assen: Van Gorcum.

Sokoloff, Michael. 1974. *The Targum to Job from Qumran Cave XI.* Ramat-Gan: Bar-Ilan University.

Tov, Emanuel 1999. *The Greek and Hebrew Bible: Collected Essays on the Septuagint.* Leiden: Brill.

———. 2001. *Textual Criticism of the Hebrew Bible.* 2d ed. Minneapolis: Fortress; Assen: Royal Van Gorcum.

Trebolle Barrera, Julio. 1998. *The Jewish Bible and the Christian Bible: An Introduction to the History of the Bible.* Leiden: Brill; Grand Rapids: Eerdmans.

Ulrich, Eugene. 1999. *The Dead Sea Scrolls and the Origins of the Bible.* Grand Rapids: Eerdmans; Leiden: Brill.

Van der Ploeg, J. P. M., and A. S. van der Woude. 1971. *Le Targum de Job de la Grotte XI de Qumrân.* Leiden: Brill.

VanderKam, James C., and Peter W. Flint. 2002. *The Meaning of the Dead Sea Scrolls: Their Significance for Understanding the Bible, Judaism, Jesus, and Christianity.* San Francisco: HarperSanFrancisco.

Early Jewish Biblical Interpretation

JAMES L. KUGEL

Scripture was, by all accounts, a major interest, if not to say an obsession, among a broad spectrum of Jews in the Second Temple period. People argued, sometimes violently, about the meaning of this or that verse in the Torah (Pentateuch), or about the proper way to carry out one or another of its laws. People also *wrote* a great deal about Scripture: numerous compositions that have survived from the Second Temple period seek to explain various scriptural prophecies and songs and stories, and even those books that are not explicitly exegetical are usually replete with allusions to Scripture and scriptural interpretation. Moreover, a whole new institution emerged in this period, the synagogue, a place where people might gather specifically for the purpose of studying Scripture; indeed, the synagogue went on to become a (one might even say *the*) major Jewish institution, both within the land of Israel and in the Diaspora.

But perhaps the most striking evidence of Scripture's importance comes from the Dead Sea Scrolls, a collection of writings found at Qumran, south of Jericho. This library, apparently the possession of a particular Jewish community that flourished at the end of the Second Temple period, is itself a most impressive thing, consisting of roughly 800 individual manuscripts. (It was no doubt still larger at one point: some of its original contents have certainly been lost to the depredations of nature or human hands.) The library contained not one or two copies of what was to become our Hebrew Bible, but, for example, thirty-six different manuscripts of the Psalms, twenty-nine copies of Deuteronomy, and so forth. In all, these scriptural manuscripts made up a little more than a quarter of the library's total contents. But the remaining three-quarters were scarcely less tied to Scripture: nearly all of these other compositions seek, in one way or another, to explain, allude to, or expand upon things found in biblical books. Indeed, the rules governing the daily life of the community that lived at Qumran specify that the study of Scripture is to be a steady, ongoing activity: "Anywhere where there are ten people, let there not be lacking a man expounding the Torah day and night, continuously, concerning the right conduct of a man with his fellow. And let the [Assembly of the] Many see to it that in the community a third of every night of the year [is spent] in reading the Book and expounding the Law and offering blessings together" (1QS 6:6-8).

In short, Scripture was on nearly everyone's mind. The words of Ps. 119:97 — "How I love your Torah; I speak of it all day long" — might have served as the motto of *all* the different Jewish communities and sects in Second Temple times. Now when one stops to consider this state of affairs in its larger context, it should appear more than a little strange. After all, religious piety elsewhere in the ancient Near East consisted principally of the offering of animal sacrifices at one or another sanctuary, participation in mass religious revels with singing and dancing, or solemn rites to ward off evil and demonic forces. None of these elements was absent from Second Temple Judaism, but along with them, and ultimately displacing them, was the oddest sort of act: reading words written centuries earlier and acting as if they had the highest significance for people in the present age. How did this come about?

The Rise of the Bible

The idea of a specific set of writings called the Bible did not exist before the end of the Second Temple period. Before that, there existed a somewhat inchoate group of books considered sacred by one or more of the various religious communities that flourished during this period. The heart of Scripture, all communities agreed, was the Torah or Pentateuch, that is, the biblical books of Genesis, Exodus, Leviticus, Numbers, and Deuteronomy. These books were attributed to the authorship of Moses, and from an early time their laws in particular were looked to for guidance in matters of daily life. Along with them were other works — historical writings covering the period from the death of Moses to later times; prophetic books and visions associated with various figures from the past; psalms, hymns, and similar works, many attributed to King David; wise sayings and other wisdom writings, some attributed to King Solomon; and so forth. Some of these texts were actually composed within the Second Temple period, but many went back far earlier, to the time before the Babylonian exile in the sixth century B.C.E. For example, most modern scholars agree that large parts of our biblical books of Isaiah, Hosea, Amos, and Micah go back to the eighth century B.C.E.; to a still earlier period belong a number of other texts — for example, some of the songs and psalms found in the Bible, along with a portion of the historical and legendary material later included in different books.

If these texts had thus been preserved for hundreds of years before the start of the Second Temple period, they must have played some active role in the lives of those who preserved them. After all, the parchment or papyrus on which texts were generally written begins to disintegrate after a century or so; recopying books was a tedious, and expensive, process. If these writings were nonetheless saved and recopied, it seems likely that, far back into the biblical period, people were using them for some purpose. Ancient laws were no doubt written down to preserve their exact wording, so that they might be explicated and applied to real-life cases; if psalms and hymns were similarly recorded, it was probably because they were an actual part of the liturgy in use at one or another ancient sanctuary; tales of past heroes and their doings were written down to be read in court or at festive occasions; and so forth.

Nevertheless, it is only some time after the return from the Babylonian Exile at the end of the sixth century B.C.E. that we begin to find frequent reference to the Scripture (principally the Pentateuch) and its interpretation. This is truly the time when these ancient texts begin to move to center stage in Judaism. Several factors combined to make Scripture so important.

One of these is a rather universal phenomenon. Scripture may have come to play a particularly important role in Judaism, but in many religions and civilizations (some of them quite unrelated to Judaism), writings from the ancient past also play a special role — the Vedas in Hinduism, the Zoroastrian Avesta, the writings of Confucius, and so forth. What is behind this phenomenon? With regard to premodern societies, our own view of knowledge as a dynamic, ever-expanding thing is rather inappropriate. In such societies people generally conceived of knowledge as an altogether static, unchanging thing, and they therefore tended to attach great significance to the wisdom found in writings from the ancient past. Indeed, as the chronological distance between such writings and themselves increased, so too did the esteem in which these ancient pronouncements were held. After all, what the ancients knew, or what had been revealed to them, was timeless truth, part of that great, static corpus of knowledge; it could never be displaced by later insights (nor would anyone want it to be).

Israel's ancient writings had no doubt long enjoyed a similar cachet. But added to this were several more specific things that heightened the role of Scripture in the early postexilic period. The first was the fact of the Babylonian Exile itself. Though it lasted scarcely more than half a century, it profoundly disrupted things for the exiled Jews. Institutions like the royal court, the Jerusalem Temple, and other formerly crucial centers were no more; soon, the traditions and ways of thought associated with them began to fade. Instead, the exiles' heads were now filled with foreign institutions, a foreign language, and a way of thinking that hardly bothered to take account of the tiny nation from which they had come. Under such circumstances, Israel's ancient writings offered an island of refuge. Here, the royal court and the Jerusalem Temple still lived in their full glory; here the God of Israel still reigned supreme, and His people and their history occupied center stage; and here was the exiles' old language, the Judean idiom, written down in the classical cadences of its greatest prophets and sages. It seems altogether likely that, during those years in Babylon, such writings as had accompanied the Judeans into exile only grew in importance — if not for all, then at least for some significant segment of the population. And once the exile was over, these same ancient texts continued in this role: they were the history of the nation and its pride, a national literature and more than that, a statement about the ongoing importance of the remnants of that kingdom, for its God, and for the world.

The Mode of Restoration

When the Babylonian Empire collapsed and its conqueror, the Persian king Cyrus, issued his famous decree (538 B.C.E.) allowing the exiled Judeans to return to their homeland, the ancient writings took on an additional, and still more central, role. After all, not all the exiles took up Cyrus' offer. Some had settled into life in Babylon, whatever its hardships, and were loath to make the long trek back to an uncertain future in their ancestral home. The returnees were thus a self-selected group. All of them had, in one way or another, resolved to go back to the place of an earlier existence. No doubt their motives varied, but this *mode of restoration,* of going to back to what had been before, was common to all.

But how exactly could one know what had been before? The landscape itself was mute; one could not pick up a rock or interrogate a tree to find out. The past lived only in those same ancient writings, and to the extent that the returnees sought consciously to restore their land and themselves to a former way of being, their first point of reference was necessarily what those texts said or implied about how things had been before the Exile. Israel's ancient writings thus acquired a potentially *prescriptive* quality. What they said about the past could easily be translated into a potential program for the future.

Of course, the returnees were not all of one mind. Some wished only to settle down to life as residents of an obedient province in the Persian Empire, while others clung to the hope that their nation would soon find the opportunity to shake off foreign rule and return to political independence, indeed, to regain the political and military preeminence that had existed in the days of David and Solomon. Descendants of the former power elites — members of prominent families and clans, not to speak of the royal dynasty and the hereditary priesthood — must have hoped that the old social order would be re-created. Others — visionaries, prophets, reformers of various allegiances — saw in the return from exile just the opposite prospect, an opportunity to reshuffle the social deck. But precisely because all were in this *mode of restoration,* they all sought to use accounts of the past to justify their own plans for the future.

One of the most striking illustrations of this mentality is the biblical book of Chronicles, composed, according to most scholars, relatively early in the postexilic period. Although much of this book simply repeats material narrated in the biblical books of Samuel and Kings, modern scholarship has revealed subtle changes introduced here and there by the author of Chronicles, changes that embodied his own definite program for the future. He believed, for example, that the Davidic monarchy should be restored, and he looked forward to a day when the inhabitants of Judah would join forces with their northern neighbors in Samaria to form a great, United Kingdom as in days of old. He also had his own ideas about the Temple, the priesthood, and the very nature of God. Yet he did not put these ideas forth in the form of a political manifesto or religious tract. Instead, he presented them as part of a history of preexilic times, in fact, a crafty rewriting of that history that would stress all that he believed in while suppressing everything else. Why did he do so? The apparent reason is that he, and the rest of his countrymen, looked to the past for guidance about what to do in their own time.

The Laws of the Pentateuch

Of all the writings that made up Israel's Scripture, it was probably the laws of the Pentateuch that played the most important role in restored Judea. These laws covered all manner of different things: civil and criminal law, Temple procedure, ethical behavior, ritual purity and impurity, proper diet, and so forth. Nowadays, a country's laws do not play a very active part in most people's lives — certainly not in their religious lives. Someone who breaks the law may have to pay a fine or even go to prison, but this in itself has no particular spiritual dimension. Likewise, someone who upholds the law may be proud to be a good citizen, but nothing more. In restored Judea, by contrast, the laws of the Pentateuch were held to come from God, and this automatically gave them a wholly new significance. To break a law ordained by God was not merely to commit a crime; it was to commit a sin. Likewise, observing the laws and doing what they said was not merely good citizenship but a form of divine service, a way of actively seeking to do God's will. This view of things may have existed in preexilic times, but it became particularly prominent after the return from exile.

Perhaps it was the very course of recent events that made Second Temple Jews so concerned with biblical law. Many of them must have asked themselves why their homeland had been conquered by the Babylonians, and why the Babylonian Empire had in turn collapsed shortly thereafter. Some, no doubt, gave to these questions a purely practical answer: the Babylonian army was simply stronger than that of little Judah, so it won; similarly, once the Medes and the Persians had combined forces, they easily overcame the Babylonians and took over their whole empire. But the Bible contains a different, more theological explanation: God *allowed* His people to be conquered as a punishment for their failure to keep His laws, the great covenant He had concluded with their ancestors. "Surely this came upon Judah at the command of the LORD" (2 Kings 24:3). By the same token, lest anyone think it was by any merit of the Babylonians that Judah had been overcome, He subsequently dispatched the Persian army to reduce them to ruin. So now, returned to their ancient homeland, the Judeans (or at least some of them) set out to draw the obvious theological conclusion and avoid repeating their ancestors' mistake. This time they would scrupulously obey all of God's commandments; this time, everyone would be an expert in the application of divine law, so that there would be no mistakes (Jer. 31:31-34).

There was probably another, more practical side to the importance attributed to these ancient laws. The Bible reports that the Persian administration actually adopted them as part of the Israelite legal system to be instituted in their new colony. The Persian king Artaxerxes I is thus reported to have written a letter to Ezra, a Jewish priest and sage who took over as a leader of the reestablished community:

> "And you, Ezra, according to the God-given wisdom you possess, appoint magistrates and judges who may judge all the people in the province [of Judah] who know the *laws of your God;* and you shall teach those who do not know them. All who will not obey the law of your God and the law of the king, let judgment be strictly executed on them." (Ezra 7:25-26)

It may always be, of course, that one or another element in the Bible is the result of exaggeration or wishful thinking on the part of the biblical historian, but skepticism in this case is probably unwarranted. Other, extrabiblical sources have shown the Persians to have generally been enlightened rulers who sought to accommodate their subject peoples by, among other things, maintaining the local legal system; it would simply have been good sense to adopt such an approach with the Judeans as well.

The Rise of Biblical Interpreters

For all such reasons, Scripture came to be a major focus of attention in the Second Temple period. But Scripture needed to be interpreted in order to be understood. So it was that a new figure emerged in Judean society, the biblical interpreter, and he would soon become a central force in postexilic society.

One of our first glimpses of this new figure at work is found in the biblical account of Ezra's public reading of the Torah to the assembled returnees in Jerusalem:

> When the seventh month came — the people of Israel being settled in their towns — all the people gathered together into the square before the Water Gate. They told the scribe Ezra to bring the book of the Law of Moses, which the LORD had given to Israel. Accordingly, the priest Ezra brought the Law before the assembly, both men and women and all who could hear with understanding. This was on the first day of the seventh month. He read from it facing the square before the Water Gate from early morning until midday, in the presence of the men and the women and those who could understand; and the ears of all the people were attentive to the book of the Law. The scribe Ezra stood on a wooden platform that had been made for the purpose. . . . And Ezra opened the book in the sight of all the people, for he was standing above all the people; and when he opened it, all the people stood up. Then Ezra blessed the LORD, the great God, and all the people answered, "Amen, Amen," lifting up their hands. Then they bowed their heads and worshiped the LORD with their faces to the ground. Also Jeshua, Bani, Sherebiah, Jamin, Akkub, Shabbethai, Hodiah, Maaseiah, Kelita, Azariah, Jozabad, Hanan, Pelaiah, the Levites, *helped the people to understand the law,* while the people remained in their places. So they read from the book, from the Law of God, *with interpretation.* They gave the sense, so that the people understood the reading. (Neh. 7:73b–8:8)

A few things stand out in this account. It is not at Ezra's initiative, but that of the people, that this great public reading is said to have taken place. Apparently, "all the people" knew that this great book of law (presumably our Pentateuch) existed, but they were still somewhat fuzzy about its contents. So they willingly stood for hours, "from early morning until midday," in order to hear its words firsthand. It is remarkable that this assembly included "both men and women and all who could hear with understanding," that is, children above a certain age: the Torah's words were, according to this passage, not reserved for some elite, or even for the adult males of the population, but were intended for the whole people to learn and apply. But — most significantly for our subject — this public reading is accompanied by a public *explanation* of the text. The Levites "helped the people to understand the Law, while the people remained in their places"; thus, "they read from the book, from the Law of God, *with interpretation.*"

Why should Scripture have needed interpreters? No doubt the need began with very down-to-earth matters. After all, every language changes over time, and by the Second Temple period some of the words and expressions used in preexilic texts were no longer understood. Even such basic concepts as *get, take, need, want, time,* and *much* were expressed with new terms by the end of the biblical period; the old words had either shifted their meaning or dropped out of the language entirely. Under such circumstances, some sort of interpreter would be necessary to make the meaning of the ancient text comprehensible. The same was true with regard to other things — names of places that no longer existed or historical figures or events long forgotten or social institutions that had ceased to be.

In addition to such relatively mundane matters, however, interpreters ultimately came to address far broader and more consequential questions. As already discussed, the returning exiles had looked to texts from the ancient past in order to fashion their own present, and this way of approaching Scripture as *prescriptive for the present* went on long after the return from exile was an established fact; interpreters continued to look to these ancient writings for a message relevant to their own day. But at first glance, at least, much of Scripture must have seemed quite irrelevant. It talked about figures from the distant past: what importance could their stories have to a later day other than preserving some nostalgic memory of people and events long gone? Why should anyone care about laws forbidding things that no one did any more anyway, indeed, things that no one even understood anymore? Part of the interpreter's task was thus to make the past relevant to the present — to find some practical *lesson* in ancient history, or to reinterpret an ancient law in such a way as to have it apply to present-day situations, sometimes at the price of completely distorting the text's original meaning. It appears that interpreters only gradually assumed these functions, but as time went on, they became more daring in the way they went about things while, at the same time, settling into a more important and solid niche in Judean society.

In the case of Ezra's reading, we have no way of knowing what sort of interpretation was involved. Was it a matter of explaining an odd word or phrase here or there? Or were the interpreters (as one ancient Jewish tradition has it) actually translating the whole text word-for-word, presumably into Aramaic, then the *lingua franca* of the Near East? Or did they go beyond even this, explaining how this or that biblical law was to be applied — what was involved in "doing no work" on the Sabbath, for example?

Interpretation inside the Bible

If the Bible provides no solid leads in the case of Ezra's reading, it does offer a number of other examples of ancient biblical interpretation; in fact, the most ancient examples of biblical interpretation that we have are found within the Bible itself, where later books explain or expand on things that appear in earlier books. Often, the things that ancient interpreters felt called to comment upon were apparent inconsistencies or contradictions within the biblical text. Take, for example, the law in Exodus about the Passover meal:

> Tell the whole congregation of Israel that on the tenth of this month they are to take a lamb for each family, a lamb for each household. If a household is too small for a whole lamb, it shall join its closest neighbor in obtaining one; the lamb shall be divided in proportion to the number of people who eat of it. Your lamb shall be without blemish, a year-old male; you may take it from the sheep or from the goats. . . . They shall eat the lamb that same night; they shall eat it roasted over the fire with unleavened bread and bitter herbs. Do not eat any of it raw or boiled in water, but roasted over the fire, with its head, legs, and inner organs. (Exod. 12:3-9)

This passage could hardly be less ambiguous: the Passover meal was to feature the meat of a lamb (though, apparently, goat meat was also acceptable, "from the sheep or from the goats"), and it was not to be boiled, but roasted. But if so, then how is one to explain this passage from Deuteronomy?

> You shall offer the Passover sacrifice to the LORD your God, from the *flock and the herd,* at the place that the LORD will choose as a dwelling for his name. You shall *boil it* and eat it at the place that the LORD your God will choose; the next morning you may go back to your tents. (Deut. 16:2, 7)

The phrase "from the flock and the herd" presumably means that a calf or a bull would be just as acceptable as a lamb or goat, and whichever animal was chosen, its meat was apparently to be boiled — precisely what the earlier passage had forbidden. What was a person to do?

The author of the book of Chronicles, an early postexilic work, seems to have been aware of the contradiction between these two texts, since he addressed at least part of it in his own history:

> They [the Israelites] slaughtered the Passover offering, and the priests dashed the blood that they received from them, while the Levites did the skinning. . . . Then they *boiled the Passover offering in fire* according to the ordinance. . . . (2 Chron. 35:13)

"Boiled" — the same word used earlier by Deuteronomy — need not necessarily mean "boiled in water," this passage suggests; instead, it might just be a circumlocution for roasting, that is, "boiling in fire." If so, then there really was no contradiction between the Exodus and Deuteronomy passages — both of them really meant "roast"; it was just that Deuteronomy had, for some reason, not used that word explicitly.

Another little problem found within an early book of the Bible was addressed by a later one; this time, the issue concerned the inheritance rights of the firstborn son. According to biblical law, the firstborn son was to receive a larger portion of his father's estate — just because he was the firstborn. But what happened if the father had two wives and wished to give precedence to the son of his other wife, even though that son was not his first? This was probably not an uncommon situation, since the law in Deuteronomy is quite emphatic:

> If a man has two wives, and one of them is favored over the other, and if both the favored one and the other have borne him sons, the firstborn being the son of the disfavored one; then on the day when he wills his possessions to his sons, he is not permitted to grant the son of the favored wife preference over the son of the other, who is the firstborn. Instead, he must acknowledge as firstborn the son of the one who is not favored, giving him a double portion of all that he has; since he is the first issue of his virility, the right of the firstborn is his. (Deut. 21:15-17)

The firstborn son is to get the double portion no matter how the father feels about the boy's mother. But if so, then how does one explain what happened in the biblical story of Jacob and his sons? Jacob marries Leah and Rachel, but it is clear from the start that Rachel is his favorite (Gen. 29:17-18). Nevertheless, Reuben, Leah's son, is Jacob's oldest boy, so by rights the double portion is to be his. As things turn out, however, Reuben gets pushed aside: it is Joseph, Rachel's son, who effectively ends up with the extra inheritance (Gen. 48:5-6). To later readers of Scripture, this surely seemed to be a blatant violation of biblical law. To make matters worse, Reuben kept being referred to as Jacob's "firstborn" (Exod. 6:14; Num. 1:20; 26:5; etc.). Was he — and if so, why did he lose his inheritance?

Once again, the author of Chronicles went out of his way to explain an apparent contradiction in the text:

> The sons of Reuben, the firstborn of Israel [that is, Jacob]. (He *was* the firstborn, but because he defiled his father's bed, his birthright was given to the sons of Joseph son of Israel, so that he is not enrolled in the genealogy according to the birthright.) (1 Chron. 5:1)

In Reuben's case, the Chronicler explains, an exception was made to the general rule because of Reuben's egregious sin with his father's concubine (Gen. 35:22). He was still, in genealogical terms, the firstborn, but the firstborn's special inheritance (the "birthright") was given instead to Joseph, Rachel's son.

Interpretations outside the Bible

Biblical scholars have been diligent in uncovering little spots of interpretation such as these within the Hebrew Bible itself: later versions of earlier laws sometimes modify their wording or reconfigure their application; original biblical prophecies are sometimes supplemented or rearranged to stress the new interpretation now given to them; later editors sometimes inserted phrases that glossed earlier texts whose wording was no longer understood. But considered as a whole, these inner-biblical interpretations pale before the great body of ancient interpretation that has been preserved outside of the Jewish Bible, in works composed from about the third century B.C.E. to the second century C.E. and beyond. This was the golden age of biblical interpretation, the period in which various groups of (largely anonymous) interpreters put their stamp on the Hebrew Bible and determined the basic way in which the Bible would be interpreted for the next 2,000 years.

The writings in which their interpretations are attested are quite varied. Some of them are originally Jewish compositions included in Christian Bibles — identified there as "Deuterocanonical Books" or "Old Testament Apocrypha" — works such as the Wisdom of Jesus Ben Sira (second century B.C.E.) and the Wisdom of Solomon (first century B.C.E. or C.E.). Others are categorized as "pseudepigrapha," compositions falsely ascribed to ancient figures from the Bible but actually written in a later period — works such as the book of *Jubilees* (early second century B.C.E.) or the *Testament of Abraham* (first century B.C.E. or C.E.). Much ancient biblical interpretation is also preserved in the Dead Sea Scrolls; some of these texts go back to the third century B.C.E. or earlier. Ancient translations, such as the Old Greek (Septuagint) translation of the Pentateuch (third century B.C.E.) or various targums, translations of the Bible into Aramaic (probably originating in the first century C.E. or earlier, though later material was often added in the process of transmission), also contain reflections of ancient biblical interpretation. Hellenistic Jewish writers such as Philo of Alexandria (ca. 20 B.C.E.–ca. 50 C.E.) and Josephus (ca. 37 C.E.–100 C.E.) also present a great deal of biblical interpretation — part of it entirely of their own fashioning, but much else gathered from or influenced by the work of earlier interpreters. Christian writings of the first two centuries C.E., including the New Testament and other early compositions, also contain a good deal of biblical interpretation — much of it rooted in the pre-Christian exegesis. Finally, later Jewish writings such as the Mishnah (put in its final form around 200 C.E.), along with the Tosefta and the tannaitic midrashim (both from roughly the same period), contain a great deal of exegetical material, much of it continuing the line of earlier biblical interpretation. Considered together, this is a vast body of writings, many times greater than the Hebrew Bible itself. In studying it, scholars are able to piece together a developmental history of how the Bible was understood starting early in the second B.C.E. or so and continuing through the next three or four hundred years — a crucial period in the Bible's history.

A note about the form of biblical interpretation: relatively few of the abovementioned texts are written in the form of actual *commentaries,* that is, writings that cite a biblical verse and then explain what the interpreter thinks the verse means. Such commentaries did exist — they were the preferred genre of Philo of Alexandria, and commentary-like texts have been found as well among the Dead Sea Scrolls. But the favorite form for transmitting biblical interpretation in writing was the *retelling.* Most writers simply assumed that their readers would be familiar with the biblical text, indeed, familiar with the exegetical problems associated with this or that verse. So he or she would retell the text with little interpretive insertions: a word no longer understood would be glossed or replaced with a word whose meaning everyone knew; an apparent contradiction would be resolved through the insertion of an explicative detail; the retelling would take the trouble to explain *why* A or B had done what they did, or *how* they did it, thereby answering a question left open in the laconic biblical version of the same story. Such retellings are a common phenomenon in ancient interpretation: the book of *Jubilees,* the *Genesis Apocryphon* from Qumran, and Pseudo-Philo's *Book of Biblical Antiquities* are good examples of compositions that are, from start to finish, interpretive retellings. So, in a sense, are Aramaic targums such as that of *Pseudo-Jonathan* or *Neofiti;* they "translate" the Pentateuch into Aramaic, but with so many interpolations that they are actually more like retellings than real translations.

The Four Assumptions

Why was this a crucial period? Because, as already mentioned, these interpreters established the general way in which the Bible was to be approached for the next two millennia — indeed, to a certain extent, their approach is still with us to this day. Their way of reading and explaining texts was anything but straightforward — it was a highly ideological (and idealistic) form of exegesis, one that relied on a somewhat idiosyncratic combination of very close reading and great exegetical freedom. The interpretations these ancient sages came up with soon acquired the mantle of authority; they were memorized and passed on from generation to generation, sometimes modified in one or more detail, but basically maintained as *what the Bible really means* for hundreds and hundreds of years.

As best we can tell, the ancient interpreters were a highly varied lot. Some lived in the land of Judea and were steeped in the Hebrew language and traditional Jewish learning. A few others, however, seem to have lived elsewhere and had a thoroughly Hellenistic education and orientation — for example, the author of the Wisdom of Solomon or Philo of Alexandria, both of whom wrote in Greek, alluded to Greek philosophical ideas, and generally cited Scripture in its Septuagint translation. (Some contemporary scholars doubt that Philo was even competent to read the Hebrew Bible in the original.) And even among those interpreters who inhabited Judea there was great variety: the author of *Jubilees* was a would-be religious innovator and a bit of a rebel; his contemporary, Ben Sira, was quite the opposite, a creature of the establishment who would probably have refused to sit at the same table with *Jubilees'* author. Pharisees battled with Sadducees over matters of interpretation, and the proprietors of the Dead Sea Scrolls (most likely to be identified with a third group, the Essenes) disagreed with both these other groups; some of them, having withdrawn to the desert, vowed to keep their own interpretations of Scripture hidden from all but the members of their own community, meanwhile waiting for the "day of vengeance" when God would strike down the other groups for their false teachings and errant practices.

And yet, for all their diversity, all these ancient interpreters went about the business of interpreting in strikingly similar fashion. It seems as if they all had, as it were, the same general set of marching orders; or, to put it differently, they all shared the same basic assumptions about *how* Scripture is to be interpreted and what its message ought to be. This is most surprising. It would appear likely that if they all shared the same basic approach — one which, as we will see, was very much influenced by the ancient Near Eastern concept of "wisdom" — this was because they were all descended, directly or otherwise, from a "wisdom"-influenced way of thinking about Scripture that existed even before these various groups of interpreters developed.

However these groups of ancient interpreters came to exist, modern scholars can, in examining their writings, deduce the basic assumptions underlying their way of explaining biblical texts. These assumptions may be broken down into four fundamental postulates:

1. All ancient interpreters assumed that scriptural texts were basically *cryptic;* that is, while the text may say A, often what it really means is B.
2. They also assumed that, although most of Scripture had been written hundreds of years earlier and seemed to be addressed to people back then, its words nevertheless were altogether *relevant* to people in the interpreters' own day — its stories contained timeless messages about proper conduct; its prophecies really referred to events happening now, or in the near future; its ancient laws were to be scrupulously observed today, even if they seemed to refer to situations or practices that no longer existed; and so forth. In a word, the basic purpose of Scripture was to *guide* people nowadays; although it talked about the past, it was really aimed at the present.
3. On the face of it, Scripture included texts written by different prophets and sages, people who lived hundreds of years apart from one another and who came from different strata of society. Nevertheless, these diverse writings were assumed to contain *a single, unitary message.* That is to say, Scripture's different parts could never contradict one another or disagree on any matter of fact or doctrine; indeed, what Scripture taught would always be perfectly consistent with the interpreters' own beliefs and practices, whatever they might be (Greek philosophical doctrines; common historical or geographical lore; the halakic teachings of later postbiblical teachers). In short, Scripture was altogether *harmonious* in all its details and altogether true; carried to its extreme, this approach postulated that there was not a single redundancy, unnecessary detail, or scribal error in the text: everything was perfect.
4. Some parts of Scripture directly cite words spoken by God, "And the LORD said to Moses . . ." and so forth. Other parts, however, are not identified as divine speech — the whole court history of King David and King Solomon, for example, or the book of Psalms, whose words are addressed *to* God. Nevertheless, ancient interpreters came to assume that all of Scripture was *of divine origin,* that God had *caused* ancient sages or historians or psalmists to write what they wrote, or that their writings had somehow been divinely guided or inspired. In short, all of Scripture came from God and all of it was sacred.

How Interpretation Worked

To see how these assumptions combined to shape the way in which interpreters interpreted, it might be appropriate to consider an actual text from the Bible, the biblical account of Abraham's near-sacrifice of his beloved son Isaac:

> And it came to pass, after these things, that God tested Abraham. He said to him, "Abraham!" and he answered, "Here I am." He said, "Take your son, your only son Isaac, whom you love, and go to the land of Moriah. Then sacrifice him there as a burnt offering on one of the mountains that I will show you." So Abraham got up early in the morning and saddled his donkey. He took two of his servants with him, along with his son Isaac; he cut the wood for the burnt offering and then set out for the place that God had told him about. On the third day, Abraham looked up and saw the place from afar. Abraham told his servants, "You stay here with the donkey while the boy and I go up there, so that we can worship and then come back to you."
>
> Abraham took the wood for the burnt offering and put it on his son Isaac; then he took the fire and the knife, and the two of them walked together. But Isaac said to his father Abraham, "Father?" and he said, "Here I am, my son." And he said, "Here is the fire and the wood, but where is the lamb for the burnt offering?" Abraham said, "God Himself will provide the lamb for the burnt offering, my son." And the two of them walked together.
>
> When they came to the place that God had told him about, Abraham built an altar and arranged the wood on it. He then tied up his son Isaac and put him on the altar on top of the wood. Abraham picked up the knife to kill his son. But an angel of the Lord called to him from heaven, and said, "Abraham, Abraham!" And he said, "Here I am." He said, "Do not harm the boy or do anything to him. For now I know that you fear God, since you have not withheld your son, your only son, from me." And Abraham looked up and saw a ram caught in a thicket by its horns. Abraham went and took the ram and sacrificed it as a burnt offering instead of his son. (Gen. 22:1-13)

Ancient interpreters were no doubt troubled by a number of elements in this story. Did not the very fact of divine omniscience seem to make this divine "test" of Abraham unnecessary? Surely God knew how it would turn out before it took place — He knew, as the angel says at the end of the story, that Abraham was one who "fears God." So why put Abraham through this awful test? Equally disturbing was Abraham's apparent conduct vis-à-vis his son. He never tells Isaac what God has told him to do; in fact, when Isaac asks his father the obvious question — "I see fire and the wood for the sacrifice, but where is the sacrificial animal?" — Abraham gives him an evasive answer: "God Himself will provide the lamb for the burnt offering, my son." This actually turns out to be true; God does provide a ram at the last minute — but Abraham had no way of knowing this at the time. Along with this is Abraham's problematic coldness. God orders him to sacrifice his son, who, God reminds him, is "your son, your only son Isaac, whom you love," and Abraham does not utter a word of protest; in fact, the text says explicitly that Abraham "got up early in the morning," as if eager to carry out the deed.

Such problems were clearly on the minds of ancient interpreters when they commented on this story, and they did their best to find a solution to them. It is important to stress that ancient interpreters generally were not out to arrive at a modern-style critical or objective reading of Scripture's words. In keeping with Assumption 2, they began with the belief that Scripture had some important lesson to teach *them,* and in the case of this story, it had to be a positive lesson about all concerned — not only Abraham and Isaac, but about God as well. If that lesson was not immediately apparent, then it had to be searched for through a careful weighing of every word, since, in keeping with Assumption 1, the meaning of any biblical text could be hidden: it might say A when it really meant B.

With regard to the first question mentioned above — why should God need to test anyone if He is omniscient? — interpreters set their eye on an apparently insignificant detail, the opening clause of the passage: "And it came to pass, after these things. . . ." Such phrases are often used in the Bible to mark a transition; they generally signal a break: "The previous story is over, and now we are going on to something new." But the word "things" in Hebrew *(dĕbārîm)* also means "words." So the transitional phrase here could equally well be understood as asserting that some words had been spoken, and that "it came to pass, after these *words,* that God tested Abraham." What words? The Bible did not say, but if some words had indeed been spoken, then interpreters felt free to try to figure out what the words in question might have been.

At some point, an ancient interpreter — no one knows exactly who or when — thought of another part of the Bible quite unrelated to Abraham, the book of Job. That book begins by reporting that Satan once challenged God to test His servant Job (1:6-12; 2:1-6). Since the story of Abraham and Isaac is also described as a divine test, this interpreter theorized that the "words" mentioned in the opening sentence of the passage ("And it came to pass, after these *words,* that God tested Abraham . . .") might have been, as in the book of Job, words connected to the hypothetical challenge spoken by Satan to God: "Put Abraham to the test and see whether He is indeed obedient enough even to sacrifice his own son." If one reads the opening sentence with this in mind, then the problem of why God should have tested Abraham disappears. Of course God knew that Abraham would pass the test — but if He nevertheless went on to test Abraham, it was because some words had been spoken leading God to take up a challenge and prove *to Satan* Abraham's worthiness. One ancient interpreter who adopted this solution was the anonymous author of the book of *Jubilees.* Here is how his retelling of the story begins:

> There were *words* in heaven regarding Abraham, that he was faithful in everything that He told him, [and that] the Lord loved him, and in every difficulty he was faithful. Then the angel Mastema [i.e., Satan] came and said before the Lord, "Behold, Abraham loves his son Isaac and he delights in him above all else. Tell him to offer him as a sacrifice on the altar. Then you will see if he carries out this command, and You will know if he is faithful in everything through which you test him." Now the Lord knew that Abraham was faithful in every difficulty which he had told him. . . . (*Jub.* 17:15-16)

Here, the "words" referred to in Gen. 22:1 are words of praise uttered by the other angels. "And it came to pass, after these *words*" were uttered, that Satan felt moved to challenge God concerning his faithful servant. God takes up the challenge, but the author of *Jubilees* goes to the trouble to assure his readers that there was really no need for the God to test Abraham, since "the Lord knew that Abraham was faithful in every difficulty which he had told him" and would certainly pass this test as well.

As noted, this revised version of the biblical story contains a lesson for today (Assumption 2): Abraham was faithful to God, even when put to a very difficult test; you should be too, and you will be rewarded as Abraham was. It also illustrates Assumption 3, the idea that the Bible is not only internally consistent, but that it agrees with the interpreter's own beliefs and practices — in this case, the belief that an all-knowing God would have no need to put Abraham to the test. (As a matter of fact, however, the idea of divine omniscience is never stated outright in the Hebrew Bible — apparently, this notion did not come into existence until later on.) Finally, it is thanks to Assumption 1, that the Bible speaks cryptically, that this interpretation was possible: When the Bible said "after these things," although this looked at first glance like a common transitional phrase, what it really meant was "after these words," and it thereby intended readers to think of the book of Job and the divine test with which that book begins.

All this was well and good, but interpreters still had not completely resolved the matter of what God knew beforehand. They were still troubled by the way the test ended:

> The angel of the LORD called to him from heaven and said, "Abraham! Abraham!" and he said, "Here I am." He said, "Do not put your hand on the boy or do anything to him; for *now I know* that you fear God, since you have not withheld your son, your only son, from Me." (Gen. 22:12)

"*Now* I know" certainly seems to imply "I did not know before." Why should God say such a thing if He was really omniscient? To this problem, too, the book of *Jubilees* had an answer:

> Then I [the angel who narrates the book of *Jubilees*] stood in front of him [Abraham] and in front of Mastema [Satan]. The Lord said: "Tell him not to let his hand go down on the child and not to do anything to him, because I know that he is one who fears the Lord." So I called to him from heaven and said to him: "Abraham, Abraham!" He was startled and said, "Yes?" I said to him, "Do not lay your hands on the child and do not do anything to him, because now I know that you are one who fears the Lord. You have not refused me your firstborn son." (*Jub.* 18:9-11)

This passage is basically a rewording of the biblical verse cited above, Gen. 22:12, but the author of *Jubilees* has done something that the biblical text did not: he has supplied the actual instructions that God gave His angel before the angel cried out to Abraham. God instructs the angel, "Tell him not to let his hand go down on the child and not to do anything to him, because I know that he is one who fears the Lord."

The author of *Jubilees* loved little subtleties. God's instructions to the angel are identical to what the angel says in Genesis — except for one word. God does not say "*now* I know"; He simply says, "I know." For the author of *Jubilees,* such a scenario explained everything. The angel may not have known how the test would turn out, but God certainly did. "I *know* that he is one who fears the Lord," He tells the angel in *Jubilees* — in fact, I've known it along! Thus, the words that appear in Genesis, according to *Jubilees,* do not exactly represent God's command, but the angel's rewording of it. It is the angel who only now found out what God had known all along.

As for Abraham's hiding his intentions from Isaac — once again it all depends on how you read the text. Ancient interpreters noticed that the passage contains a slight repetition:

> Abraham took the wood for the burnt offering and put it on his son Isaac; then he took the fire and the knife, *and the two of them walked together.* But Isaac said to his father Abraham, "Father?" And he said, "Here I am, my son." And he said, "Here is the fire and the wood, but where is the lamb for the burnt offering?" Abraham said, "God Himself will provide the lamb for the burnt offering, my son." *And the two of them walked together.* (Gen. 22:6-8)

Repetition is not necessarily a bad thing, but ancient interpreters generally felt (in keeping with Assumption 3) that the Bible would not repeat itself without purpose. Between the two occurrences of the clause "and the two of them walked together" is the brief exchange in which Abraham apparently hides his true intentions from Isaac. Here Abraham's words were, at least potentially, ambiguous. Since biblical Hebrew was originally written without punctuation marks or even capital letters marking the beginnings of sentences, Abraham's answer to Isaac could actually be read as two sentences: "God Himself will provide. The lamb for the burnt offering [is] my son." (Note that Hebrew has no verb "to be" in the present tense; thus, this last sentence would be the same whether or not the word "is" is supplied in translation.) Read in this way, Abraham's answer to Isaac was not an evasion but the brutal truth: "You're the sacrifice, Isaac." If, following that, the text adds, "And the two of them walked together," this would not be a needless repetition at all: Abraham told his son that he was to be the sacrifice, and Isaac agreed; then the two of them "walked together" in the sense that they were now of one mind to carry out God's fearsome command. Thus, in keeping with Assumptions 1 and 3, the apparent repetition was no repetition at all, and Abraham's apparent evasion was actually an announcement to Isaac of the plain truth. The conduct of both Abraham and Isaac was now above reproach: Abraham did not seek to deceive his son, and Isaac, far from a mere victim, actively sought to do God's will no less than his father did. Indeed, their conduct might thus serve as an example to be imitated by later readers (Assumption 2): even when God's decrees seem to be difficult, the righteous must follow them — and sometimes they turn out merely to be a test.

But did interpreters actually believe their interpretations? Didn't they know they were distorting the text's real meaning? This is always a difficult question. It seems likely that, at least at first, ancient interpreters were sometimes quite well aware that they were departing from the straightforward meaning of the text. But with time, that awareness began to dim. Biblical interpretation soon became an institution in ancient Israel; one generation's interpretations were passed on to the next, and eventually they acquired the authority that time and tradition always grant. *Midrash,* as this body of interpretation came to be called, simply became what the text had always been intended to communicate. Along with the interpretations themselves, the interpreters' very *modus operandi* acquired its own authority: this was how the Bible was to be interpreted, period. Moreover, since the midrashic method of searching the text carefully for hidden implications seemed to solve so many problems in the Bible that otherwise had no solution, this indicated that the interpreters were going about things correctly. As time went on, new interpretations were created on the model of older ones, until soon every chapter of the Bible came accompanied by a host of clever explanations that accounted for any perceived difficulty in its words.

Words and Verses

One final point about the "how" of ancient biblical interpretation: it always worked via a scrupulous examination of the precise wording of the biblical text. Even when the issues addressed by interpreters were broader — divine omniscience, Abraham's character, Isaac's apparent passivity — these were always approached through the interpretation of a specific verse, indeed, sometimes through a single word in the verse. "Do you want to know what 'after these things' means in the story of Abraham and Isaac? It means *after these words.*" "Do you know why *the two of them walked together* is repeated? The second time is a hint that Abraham had just told Isaac he was to be sacrificed, and he agreed." It was always from such precise points of wording that larger issues were approached.

Ancient biblical interpretation was thus, no matter how broad its intentions, formally an interpretation of single verses. And this is what enabled specific interpretations to travel so widely. Teachers in school as well as preachers in synagogue or church would, in the course of explaining a biblical text, inevitably pass on an insight into this or that verse: "Here is what it is really talking about!" Thereafter, all the listeners would know that such was the meaning of that particular verse, and they would think of it every time the verse was read in public; indeed, they would pass on the explanation to others. Since the biblical text was known far and wide and often cited — the Torah, in particular, was learned by heart at an early age — a clever answer to a long-standing conundrum would circulate quickly throughout the population.

Nowadays, such verse-centered interpretations are known as *exegetical motifs* — "motifs" because, like musical motifs, they were capable of being inserted into different compositions, reworked or adapted, and combined with other motifs to make a smooth-running narrative. After a while, retellers sometimes did not even bother to allude to the particular biblical verse in question, but simply incorporated the underlying idea into their retelling. Thus, for example, the idea that Abraham had explained to Isaac that "the lamb for the burnt offering [is you,] my son," and that Isaac, far from fleeing, had willingly embraced his martyrdom, shows up in a variety of retellings, some of them terse, but others lovingly expanding on the basic idea:

> Going at the same pace — no less with regard to their thinking than with their bodies . . . they came to the designated place. (Philo, *On Abraham* 172)

This is indeed intended as a precise explanation of the two occurrences of "and the two of them walked together" in the Genesis tale; the first refers to their physical walking (what Philo designates as the motion of "their bodies"), whereas the second refers to their agreement that Isaac should be sacrificed (Philo's "with regard to their thinking").

> Remember . . . the father [= Abraham], by whose hand Isaac would have submitted to being slain for the sake of religion. (4 Macc. 13:12)

> When the altar had been prepared (and) he had laid the cleft wood upon it and all was ready, [Abraham] said to his son: "My child, myriad were the prayers in which I beseeched God for your birth, and when you came into the world, I spared nothing for your upbringing. . . . But since it was by God's will that I became your father and it now pleases Him that I give you over to Him, bear this consecration valiantly. . . ." The son of such a father could not but be bravehearted, and Isaac received these words with joy. He exclaimed that he deserved never to have been born at all if he were to reject the decision of God and of his father. . . . (Josephus, *Ant.* 1.228-32)

> And as he was setting out, he said to his son, "Behold now, my son, I am offering you as a burnt offering and I am returning you into the hands of Him who gave you to me. But the son said to the father, "Hear me, father. If [ordinarily] a lamb of the flocks is accepted with sweet savor as a sacrifice to the Lord, and if such flocks have been set aside for slaughter [in order to atone] for human iniquity, while man, on the contrary, has been designated to inherit this world — why should you be saying to me now, 'Come and inherit eternal life and time without measure?' Why if not that I was indeed born in this world *in order to* be offered as a sacrifice to Him who made me? Indeed, this [sacrifice] will be the [mark of] my blessedness over other men. . . ." (Ps.-Philo, *Bib. Ant.* 32:2-3)

The Wisdom Connection

It was suggested above that the common ancestor of all the diverse biblical interpreters of ancient Judaism and Christianity was the ancient Near Eastern sage, who pursued what the Bible calls "wisdom." Wisdom was an international pursuit, and a very old one; some of the earliest texts that we possess from ancient Sumer and

Babylon and Egypt are collections of proverbs, the favorite medium for transmitting wisdom. What wisdom was is not given to easy summary, but its basic premise was that there exists an underlying set of rules (including, but not limited to, what we would call "laws of nature") that governs all of reality. The sage, by studying the written words of earlier sages as well as through his own, careful contemplation of the world, hoped to come to a fuller understanding of these rules and, hence, come to know how the world works. His wise counsel was therefore sought by kings and princes, and he was often a teacher who trained the next generation of sages.

At a certain point in Second Temple times, the job description of the Jewish sage was changed. Now, instead of contemplating the proverbs of previous generations, it was the Torah that occupied the sage's attention: he became a biblical interpreter. In a sense, this transformation takes place before our eyes, in books like the Wisdom of Ben Sira (or: Sirach). The second-century-B.C.E. author is, in many ways, a traditional sage: his book is full of clever, pithy proverbs, many of them his own rewording of the insights from earlier generations and centuries. But along with this traditional sort of wisdom writing, Ben Sira also explains laws and stories from the Bible; indeed, his book concludes with a six-chapter review of biblical heroes and the lessons their stories are designed to impart. This is because, for him, it is the Torah that is the great repository of wisdom. Indeed, he says as much in an extended paean to wisdom in the middle of his book, in which Wisdom (here personified as a woman) tells of her own existence.

> "I came forth from the mouth of the Most High, and covered the earth like a mist. I dwelt in the highest heavens, and my throne was in a pillar of cloud. Alone I compassed the vault of heaven and traversed the depths of the abyss." (Sir. 24:3-5)

But God then orders Wisdom to transfer her headquarters out of heaven and take up residence on earth:

> He said, "Make your dwelling in Jacob, and in Israel receive your inheritance. . . ." [So] I took root in an honored people, in the portion of the Lord, His heritage. (Sir. 24:8, 12)

In recounting this, Ben Sira is not merely being a proud Jew who asserts that wisdom is the peculiar possession of his own people. Rather, he has something more specific in mind:

> All this is the book of the covenant of the Most High God, the Torah that Moses commanded us as an inheritance for the congregations of Jacob. (Sir. 24:23)

In other words, Wisdom *is* the Pentateuch, "the book of the covenant of the Most High God." Thus, if you wish really to know how the world works, to know about the underlying set of rules that God established for it, then the Pentateuch is your basic resource.

The wisdom connection apparent in Ben Sira explains much about the character of ancient biblical interpretation — not only for him, but for his contemporaries and predecessors as well. For when these sages-turned-exegetes approached the Pentateuch, they brought to their reading of it many of the same expectations and interpretive techniques that they had used in reading collections of proverbs and other wisdom compositions. Thus, the full meaning of a proverb was not immediately apparent; its words had to be studied and sifted carefully before they would yield their full significance. So too did all of Scripture have to be scrutinized, since the meaning of a particular word or phrase or prophecy or story might similarly be hidden from view. And just as proverbs were full of lessons for today, so biblical texts, even though they seemed to talk about the past, were likewise understood to have a message for the present; indeed, those two favorite opposites of ancient wisdom, the "righteous" and the "wicked," might turn out to be embodied in a biblical narrative about the (altogether righteous) Abraham or Jacob, and such (altogether wicked) figures as Lot or Esau. The insights of wise proverbs were part of a single weave of divine wisdom, the great pattern underlying all of reality; even when one proverb seemed to contradict another (see Prov. 26:4-5), there really was no contradiction. Similarly, the Bible, the great compendium of divine wisdom, could contain no real contradiction; careful contemplation of its words would always show that they agree. Finally wisdom, although it was transmitted by different sages in different periods, truly had no human author; these tradents were merely reporting bits and pieces of the great pattern that had been created by God. Similarly, the books of Scripture may be attributed to different authors, but all of them, since they are full of divine wisdom, truly have only one source, God, who guided the human beings responsible for Scripture's various parts. The various characteristics mentioned here are, it will be noticed, none other than the Four Assumptions shared by all ancient interpreters. It seems likely, therefore, that these common elements all derive from the wisdom heritage of the earliest interpreters, going back at least to the time of Ezra, "a *sage* skilled in the law of Moses" (Ezra 7:6). Although Scripture's interpreters included people from many different orientations and walks of life, wild-eyed visionaries, priests and temple officials, experts in law and jurisprudence, and so forth — *all* appear to have been touched by this crucial consilience of scriptural interpretation and ancient Near Eastern wisdom.

* * *

Such was biblical interpretation in early Judaism. To modern eyes, some of it may not appear to be interpretation at all; certainly some of the claims made about the meaning of this or that verse or passage seem to us highly fanciful, if not patently apologetic or forced, though in fairness one ought to note that modern biblical commentaries are themselves not entirely free of such traits, even if they are usually more subtle about their intentions. But whatever one's judgment of the work of these interpreters, their importance can scarcely be gainsaid. It is not just that, as mentioned earlier, they determined the basic way that the Bible would be approached for the next two millennia. Their Four Assumptions continued to be assumed by all interpreters until well after the Renaissance and the Protestant Reformation of the sixteenth century; indeed, they are, to a great extent, still with us today. But still more important was the effect that these ancient interpreters had on their own contemporaries. Had they not succeeded in persuading their listeners that biblical texts did indeed have a message vital to people in their own day; and that the biblical corpus was perfectly consistent and harmonious, free of any error or defect; indeed, that these texts had been given by God for the purpose of guiding humans on their path, if only they were clever enough to understand the hidden meaning of many of its verses — had they not succeeded in getting these basic ideas and this basic approach across through myriad examples of actual interpretations, it seems quite unlikely that the writings of ancient Israel would ever have become what they did, the centerpiece of two great biblical religions, Judaism and Christianity.

BIBLIOGRAPHY

Anderson, Gary. 2001. *The Genesis of Perfection: Adam and Eve in Jewish and Christian Imagination.* Louisville: Westminster John Knox.

Borgen, Peder. 1997. *Philo of Alexandria: An Exegete for His Time.* Leiden: Brill.

Campbell, Jonathan G. 2004. *The Exegetical Texts.* Companion to the Qumran Scrolls. London: T&T Clark.

Charlesworth, James H., and Craig A. Evans, eds. 1994. *The Pseudepigrapha and Early Biblical Interpretation.* Sheffield: Sheffield Academic Press.

Endres, John C. 1987. *Biblical Interpretation in the Book of Jubilees.* Washington, D.C.: Catholic Biblical Association of America.

Evans, Craig A., ed. 2004. *From Prophecy to Testament: The Function of the Old Testament in the New.* Peabody, Mass.: Hendrickson.

Feldman, Louis H. 1998. *Josephus's Interpretation of the Bible.* Berkeley: University of California Press.

Fishbane, Michael. 1985. *Biblical Interpretation in Ancient Israel.* Oxford: Clarendon.

Henze, Matthias, ed. 2005. *Biblical Interpretation at Qumran.* Grand Rapids: Eerdmans.

Hirschman, Marc G. 1996. *A Rivalry of Genius: Jewish and Christian Biblical Interpretation in Late Antiquity.* Albany: SUNY Press.

Kugel, James L. 1990. *In Potiphar's House: The Interpretive Life of Biblical Texts.* San Francisco: HarperSanFrancisco.

———. 1998. *Traditions of the Bible: A Guide to the Bible As It Was at the Start of the Common Era.* Cambridge: Harvard University Press.

———. 2001. *Studies in Ancient Midrash.* Cambridge: Harvard University Press.

———. 2006. *The Ladder of Jacob: Ancient Interpretations of the Biblical Story of Jacob and His Children.* Princeton: Princeton University Press.

Kugel, James L., and R. A. Greer. 1986. *Early Biblical Interpretation.* Philadelphia: Westminster.

Mulder, M. J., and H. Sysling, eds. 1988. *Mikra: Text, Translation, Reading and Interpretation of the Hebrew Bible in Ancient Judaism and Early Christianity.* Assen: Van Gorcum; Philadelphia: Fortress.

Najman, Hindy. 2003. *Seconding Sinai: The Development of Mosaic Discourse in Second Temple Judaism.* Leiden: Brill.

Najman, Hindy, and Judith Newman, eds. 2004. *The Idea of Biblical Interpretation.* Leiden: Brill.

White Crawford, Sidnie. 2008. *Rewriting Scripture in Second Temple Times.* Grand Rapids: Eerdmans.

Zakovitch, Y. 1992. *An Introduction to Inner-Biblical Interpretation.* Even-Yehudah: Reches (in Hebrew).

Apocrypha and Pseudepigrapha

LOREN T. STUCKENBRUCK

The terms "apocrypha" and "pseudepigrapha" mean, respectively "hidden things (books)" and "books falsely ascribed/inscribed." However, under the problematic headings of "Old Testament Apocrypha" and "Old Testament Pseudepigrapha" they have come to designate collections or groups of ancient Jewish writings which were either composed during the Second Temple period or which preserve traditions that arguably go back to that time. Thus these designations, as conventionally used today, are not descriptive and do not always reflect the way they (and the concepts underlying them) were sometimes used in antiquity. It is the ancient background, especially as now informed by the writings preserved among the Dead Sea Scrolls, which may suggest that what "apocrypha" and "pseudepigrapha" appropriately signify may need to be rethought. Since the contemporary use of these terms is largely determined by developments after the Second Temple period, the present discussion will review their use in Christian and Jewish tradition from late antiquity through the post-Reformation and then consider how they were being applied by some of the Jewish writers who composed them.

Apocrypha

Apocrypha during and since the Reformation and Counter-Reformation

Most commonly, the term "Apocrypha" refers to a collection of writings that fall outside the canons of the Hebrew Bible (Old Testament) and New Testament, but that are nonetheless included in some modern Christian translations of the Bible, usually between the Old and New Testaments. In modern translations this group of writings consists of the following: 1 Esdras (= *3 Ezra*), 2 Esdras (= *4, 5,* and *6 Ezra*), Tobit, Judith, Additions to the Book of Esther, Wisdom of Solomon, Sirach (or Ecclesiasticus), Baruch and Letter of Jeremiah, the Prayer of Azariah and the Song of the Three Young Men, Susanna, Bel and the Dragon, Prayer of Manasseh,

1 Maccabees, and 2 Maccabees. However, traditional Protestant and Catholic definitions and judgments of the value of these writings have diverged.

Among the Protestant Reformers, the value attributed to the "Apocrypha" was not entirely uniform. Martin Luther, whose translation of the Bible (completed in 1534) did not include 1 and 2 Esdras among the Apocrypha, defined Apocrypha as "books which are not considered equal to the Holy Scriptures" while being "profitable and good to read." Other reformers, such as Oecolampadius, adopted a similar view, while translations such as the Dutch Bible (1526) and the Swiss-German Bible (1527-1529) preface the "Apocrypha" with statements, respectively, that these books, which are not found in the Hebrew Bible of the Jews, are "not in the canon" and "are not reckoned as biblical." A more discriminating statement about their value was offered in 1520 by Andreas Bodenstein of Karlstadt *(De Canonicis Scripturis Libellus):* some works (Wisdom of Solomon, Sirach, Tobit, Judith, 1 and 2 Maccabees) outside the Hebrew canon are "holy writings" and their content "is not to be despised" (sections 114, 118), while others (1 and 2 Esdras, Baruch, Prayer of Manasseh, Prayer of Azariah, Song of the Three Young Men, Susanna, Bel and the Dragon) are so problematic that they are "worthy of a censor's ban." Thus, despite the inclusion of "Apocrypha" in a number of Protestant translations, sentiments comparable to those of Karlstadt were widely held (e.g., the Belgic Confession 1561, the Synod of Dort 1618-19, Westminster Confession 1647) and have led to the removal of these writings in many translations of the Bible until today.

The widespread criticism of the Apocrypha among Protestant Reformers led the Roman Catholic Church to a response during the first Council of Trent. In Session VI of the deliberations in 1546, the delegates pronounced a curse against any who were not prepared to recognize all those books contained in the Latin Vulgate Bible. (Although many Latin manuscripts had also included 1 and 2 Esdras and the Prayer of Manasseh, the Council denied them the canonicity accorded to the other books. These were reinstated as appendices to the New Testament in the Clementine Bible published in 1592.) Since Sixtus of Sienna (1566), many Roman Catholic scholars have referred to Old Testament writings not included in the Jewish Hebrew Bible as "Deuterocanonical," a term that is meant not so much to imply their secondary or inferior status as rather to acknowledge that their canonicity had not been formalized by ecclesiastical authorities until a more recent time.

Apocrypha in Orthodox Traditions

It is important to remember that the term "Apocrypha," while playing an important role in Protestantism, has been of only little significance in other traditions. In this respect, we may draw attention to eastern Orthodox confessions, such as the Greek, Russian, Syriac, and Ethiopic churches, which have defined their biblical canons in a way that includes some of the "Apocrypha" and, indeed, even further writings (which vary in each tradition). Each of these ecclesiastical traditions includes a core of these writings within their Bible, while the determination of what constitutes Scripture as a whole varies, depending on factors such as the form and shape of traditions received into their respective languages, use in liturgy, other issues in emerging self-definition, and the understanding of "canon."

Among the Orthodox traditions, some thirteen writings regarded by the Council of Trent as "Deuterocanonical" have acquired some form of biblical status. While five of these appear as material attached to the end of other books (Psalm 151, Letter of Jeremiah [to Baruch], Additions to Esther, and Additions to Daniel in Prayer of Azariah, Song of the Three Young Men, Susanna, and Bel and the Dragon), the remaining seven have been transmitted as free-standing works (Tobit, Judith, Wisdom of Solomon, 1 and 2 Maccabees, Sirach, and Baruch).

In the Greek Orthodox Church, after some debate, these writings were labeled as "Deuterocanonical" during the Synod of Jerusalem of 1672; however, they are more often referred to as "things which are read" (Gr. *anagignōskomena*). Not found in the Hebrew Bible, but transmitted as part of the Greek Old Testament, this group of books also includes Prayer of Manasseh, 1 Esdras, and 3 Maccabees (while 4 Maccabees, transmitted in a more limited number of biblical manuscripts, is now placed in an appendix). The affirmation of the validity of the "Deuterocanonical" writings by the Synod was more a commendation than a dogmatic pronouncement, so that opinion regarding their canonical status in the Church has varied.

Beyond the core list, the Russian Orthodox Church, drawing on a tradition that received the Greek Bible, included in its first published Bible in Old Church Slavonic (in Ostrog 1581) a list of writings that differs slightly from that of Greek Orthodoxy: Prayer of Manasseh, 2 Esdras (= 1 Esdras), 3 Esdras (= 2 Esdras), and 3 Maccabees. Here one may notice not only the difference in nomenclature for the Esdras books but also the complete absence of 4 Maccabees. The status of these books, however, has not been rigorously maintained in subsequent centuries, so that they now have an ambivalent place and function within the biblical canon.

The Ethiopian Orthodox Church has an understanding of canon that has not operated with the same degree of fixedness as found in other traditions. Moreover, unlike most of the Orthodox churches, the Ethiopic tradition did not inherit the Greek Bible. Many biblical manuscripts copied in Classical Ethiopic (Geʿez) tradition contain Prayer of Manasseh (where it follows immediately upon 2 Chron. 33:12), 1 Esdras, 2 Esdras 3–14 (= *4 Ezra,* without the Christian additions in chaps. 1–2 and 15–16), *1 Enoch,* and *Jubilees.* The degree of recognition accorded the latter two works and, indeed, a number of books in the Old Testament may have varied during the early stages of their reception and consolidation into the Ethiopic tradition. For example, while there is little or no evidence that the scriptural status of *Jubilees* was ever questioned, other works could be regarded as "disputed" (Chronicles, Esther, Job, Proverbs, Ecclesiastes, Song of Songs), while some of these and even others could be labeled as "noncanonical" (Ezra-Nehemiah, 1 Esdras, 2 Esdras, Tobit, Judith, Wisdom of Solomon, Ecclesiastes, Baruch, *1 Enoch, Ascension of Isaiah, 4 Baruch*).

It is not clear whether the West-Syrian Orthodox traditions (e.g., Syriac Orthodox and Monophysite Orthodox churches), such as the Ethiopian, initially received an Old Testament based on the Hebrew Bible or derived it from the Greek. Although the Peshiṭta, the standardizing Syriac translation of the Bible, transmitted the Jewish Bible as its Old Testament, the Old Testament writings not in the Hebrew Bible were soon added to this tradition. Not only did the fourth-century fathers Aphrahat and Ephrem treat them as part of their Bible, but these writings are copied in the earliest complete Syriac Bibles whose manuscripts may date back as early as the sixth century. Significantly, one of these early manuscripts, designated *7a1*, even contained *2 Baruch*, *4 Ezra*, and 4 Maccabees. Moreover, the oldest Syriac version of the Psalter from the twelfth century (now in Baghdad, the Library of the Chaldaean Patriarchate) includes five additional psalms (Psalms 151–155), of which Psalm 151 corresponds to the same document by that name in the Greek Psalter and, together with Psalms 154 and 155, is preserved in Hebrew among the Dead Sea manuscripts (11Q5). In addition, a fourth-century document called *Canons of the Apostles*, the Syriac text of which goes back to at least the seventh century, includes Judith, Tobith, and Ben Sira in its list of "accepted books."

Apocrypha in Greek Codices of the Bible

The "Apocrypha" are sometimes casually defined as those books or parts of books found in the Septuagint but not in the Jewish Hebrew Bible. If we consult the three prominent Greek codices that contain the Old Testament writings — Codices Sinaiticus (fourth century), Vaticanus (fourth century), and Alexandrinus (fifth century) — the following books come into view:

Sinaiticus	**Vaticanus**	**Alexandrinus**
Greek Esther	Greek Esther	Greek Esther
Judith	Judith	Tobit
Tobit	Tobit	Judith
1 Maccabees		1 Maccabees
		2 Maccabees
		3 Maccabees
4 Maccabees		4 Maccabees
Wisdom of Solomon	Wisdom of Solomon	Wisdom of Solomon
Sirach	Sirach	Sirach
		Psalms of Solomon
1 Baruch	1 Baruch	1 Baruch
Epistle of Jeremiah	Epistle of Jeremiah	Epistle of Jeremiah
	Susannah	Susannah
	Bel and the Dragon	Bel and the Dragon
		Psalms and Odes (including Prayer of Manasseh)

In addition, two somewhat later biblical codices preserve copies of several of these writings: Marchalianus (sixth/seventh century) includes 1 Baruch, Epistle of Jeremiah, Susannah, and Bel and the Dragon, while Venetus (eighth century) has Greek Esther, Judith, Tobit, 1-4 Maccabees, Wisdom of Solomon, Sirach, 1 Baruch,

Epistle of Jeremiah, Susannah, and Bel and the Dragon. Furthermore, the partially preserved Cologne–Chester Beatty Papyrus 967 (second-third century) contains fragmentary versions of Susannah and Bel and the Dragon alongside several biblical books (Esther, Ezekiel, Daniel). Finally, like Codex Alexandrinus, the seventh-century Codex T transmits the Prayer of Manasseh among the Odes appended to the Psalms.

The manuscript tradition thus reflects a fluid understanding of where the boundaries for the literature not preserved in Hebrew lie. The manuscripts attest the following works, which are omitted from modern collections of the "Apocrypha" or "Deuterocanonicals": *Psalms of Solomon,* 3 and 4 Maccabees. This fluidity is echoed by the Syriac manuscript *7a1* (see above) and, of course, the Ethiopic Orthodox tradition.

At the same time, two works not found in the Greek but preserved in many Latin manuscripts have found their way into this collection: 2 Esdras (chaps. 3–14 of which = *4 Ezra*) and the Prayer of Manasseh (first attested in Syriac manuscripts in the ninth century and in Latin manuscripts from the thirteenth century, but also found in the Cairo Geniza).

"Apocrypha" in Antiquity

Luther's view of "apocrypha" as profitable to read without being Scripture goes back to Jerome. The prefaces to his Latin translations of Jewish and Old Testament writings (ca. 405 C.E.) make it clear that for Jerome "apocrypha" such as Wisdom of Solomon, Sirach, Tobit, Judith, and 1 and 2 Maccabees could be read for edification in the church; however, the church does not receive them "among the canonical books," and they should not be used to establish doctrine (so Jerome's prologues to the book of Kings [= *Prologus Galeatus*], Judith, Tobit, and the books of Solomon).

Jerome's use of the term "apocrypha" was, however, not consistent. He not only could admit in the translation prefaces a certain overlap between what he called "apocrypha" and "pseudepigrapha" (e.g., in the case of Wisdom of Solomon), he could even appear to equate the two terms altogether. In a letter (107.12) written in the year 403, he instructs a certain Laeta to have her daughter "avoid all apocryphal writings" because they cannot be read for "the truth of the doctrines they contain," they "are not actually written by those to whom they are ascribed," and they have "many faults" that "have been introduced into them." This negative assessment of "apocrypha" did not mean Jerome denied them all religious value; but it takes "great prudence *(grandis . . . prudentiae)* to find gold in the mire *(in luto)*."

This last-mentioned understanding of "apocrypha" was a widely held view among Jerome's contemporaries and is reflected in the later Roman Catholic tradition. For example, Cyril of Jerusalem (mid-third century) had applied the term to "disputed" works that are not acknowledged by all; the church should neither study nor read them, so that they are best avoided altogether. For Cyril of Jerusalem Scripture consists of "twenty-two books of the Old Testament that were translated by the seventy-two translators" of the Septuagint, though both this numeration and his description of the individual books themselves makes it clear that, except for 1 Baruch (regarded as an appendix to Jeremiah), this did not include any of the works that Jerome would have called apocrypha in any sense (*Catechetical Lectures* 4.33). Rufinus, an older contemporary of Cyril, was more explicit in distinguishing between three groups of writings (*Expositio Symboli* 34): (a) "canonical" works, that is, the "twenty-two" books of the Old Testament; (b) "ecclesiastical" books — Wisdom of Solomon, Sirach, Tobit, Judith, 1-2 Maccabees — that may be read but not in order to confirm faith; and (c) "Apocrypha," that is, falsely ascribed writings (pseudepigrapha) and heretical books that should not be received in the church at all, as indicated in the preface to a list of "apocrypha" in the Gelasian Decree (fifth century). This last use of the term is aptly illustrated as early as the late second century C.E. by Irenaeus who, in his *Against Heresies* (1.20.1), referred to the existence of "an unspeakable number of apocryphal and spurious writings" that confuse the foolish and ignorant. Similarly, Origen in the third century C.E. declared that certain writings are called *apocryphae* because "many things in them are corrupt and contrary to true faith" (*Commentary on Song of Songs;* cf. also *Commentary on Matthew* 10.18.13.57). The equation of "secret" books with deception, though applied by Irenaeus (and Origen) to inauthentic traditions about Jesus, would in time be applied to "pseudepigraphal" Jewish compositions as well.

In summary, Jerome's twofold use of "apocrypha" would be picked up, respectively, in the Reformation (Luther) and Counter-Reformation (Council of Trent). The Protestant "Apocrypha" had their counterpart in the Roman Church's "Deuterocanonicals," while the latter has regarded "Apocrypha" as the remaining (mostly pseudepigraphal) religious writings from Jewish antiquity.

The reason for the use of "apocrypha" to designate noncanonical works during the fourth century may be found in the widespread notion of "hidden" or "sealed" books in Greco-Roman and especially Jewish antiquity (Dan. 8:26; 12:4, 9-10; *Sib. Or.* 11.163-71; *4 Ezra* 12:37; 14:5-6; 14:44-47; *2 Bar.* 20:3-4; 87:1; implied in *Jub.* 1:5; *1 Enoch* 82:1-3; 107:3; *2 Enoch* 35:1-3). In a number of Jewish apocalyptic writings, authors sometimes presented themselves (or, rather, those ancient figures whose names they were using) as having been instructed by God or an angel to "seal" or "hide" their works. This fictional instruction functioned as a way of explaining how such works attributed to such ancient authors had not been in circulation until the present. The existence of these books was a "secret" until the time when they actually appeared. A closely related idea is the instruction that a writer "seal" the book so that its contents will not be accessible until the appropriate time.

In this regard, three texts in particular seem to have exercised some influence: Daniel, *4 Ezra,* and *2 Baruch.* (a) The book of Daniel presents itself as an apocryphal work. The writer is told to "seal up the vision" given to him, "for it refers to many days from now" (8:26). This instruction is then echoed in 12:4 ("keep the words secret and the book sealed until the time of the end"), while according to 12:9-10 the seer, who has completed writing down his revelations, is to consign his work "to remain secret and sealed until the time of the end." This self-presentation of Daniel is closely bound up with the view that the special revelation in this book will be comprehended only by the wise (12:10). (b) *4 Ezra* picks up similar ideas in several passages. In 12:37-38 the command that the seer record his visions is accompanied by the directive that he deposit them "in a hidden place"; similar to Daniel, the hidden status of the writing establishes its contents as teaching for "the wise . . . whose hearts . . . are able to comprehend and keep these secrets." In a later passage (14:5-6) the figure of Moses himself is presented as having been the recipient of a double revelation (cf. Deut. 29:29), one being open and available to all, the other being secret and restricted in access. While the generally available teaching refers to the Mosaic Torah, the esoteric teaching involves "the secrets of the times" and "the end of the times." Near the end of the book (14:44-47), the seer, who patterns himself after Moses, claims to have been given, along with five men with him, ninety-four books to record during forty days of revelation. Of these books, the twenty-four to be made public are to be read by "the worthy and unworthy," while the remaining seventy are to be given to "the wise" in whom there are "the springs of understanding," "the fountains of wisdom," and "the river of knowledge." The association of esoteric revelation with more discerning readers is reminiscent of Daniel. It is tempting to see here a distinction between "canonical" and "noncanonical" writings. However, the force of the passage emphasizes that both groups of writings, though distinct, are equally revelatory. Indeed, if from *4 Ezra* 12:37-38 one has the impression that the activity behind *4 Ezra* itself is "hidden," in 14:37-48 the writer presents himself as the primary mediator among those who produced all ninety-four books (without even mentioning Moses). It was only later, for example, in the fourth century C.E., that Epiphanius of Salamis (*De Mensuris et Ponderibus* 10, Armenian), perhaps influenced by *4 Ezra* 14, turned the partition of the same number of writings into a classification of first- and second-rank books in the Septuagint: twenty-two works of the Old Testament and seventy-two "apocryphal" works. This ranking, however, says less about *4 Ezra* itself than about ideas of canonicity that had developed by Epiphanius' time. (c) In *2 Baruch* the seer, having been instructed to seal divine commands given to him (20:3-4), concludes his work by saying, "I folded it, sealed it cautiously, and bound it to the neck of the eagle. And I let it go and sent it away" (87:1).

The passages just cited from Daniel and *4 Ezra* make clear that their intended reception among a more exclusive class of "wise" readers underscores their special value rather than having anything to do with any measure of inferiority later associated with the term "apocrypha" as, for example, would later be the case with Rufinus and Jerome. Instead, revelation for a privileged group would have underscored its particular value. An analogy for this may be detected in Jesus' exclusive teaching of parables to his disciples preserved in the Synoptic Gospels (see Mark 4:10-11; Matt. 13:10-11; Luke 8:9-10).

The self-presentation of Daniel, *4 Ezra*, and *2 Baruch* as "hidden" works shows the degree to which the term "apocrypha" does not describe the character of those books that would later be collected under this designation. Indeed, while Daniel came to be understood as "biblical," *4 Ezra* was treated as "deuterocanonical" or "apocryphal," and *2 Baruch* was assigned to the "pseudepigrapha."

Recent Use of "Apocrypha" as a Title for Ancient Documents

Whereas the notion of "hiddenness" is part of the literary technique employed by the authors of Daniel, *4 Ezra,* and *2 Baruch,* the term "apocryphon" has more recently been applied more loosely to those writings that represent or contain traditions whose existence was unknown before they were discovered in modern times. This is the case with a number of documents from the Dead Sea Scrolls, of which the more prominent examples would be *Genesis Apocryphon* (1Q20), *Apocryphon of Moses* (1Q22, 1Q29, 2Q21, 4Q375, 4Q376, 4Q408), *Apocryphal Prophecy* (1Q25, 2Q23, 6Q12), 2QApocryphon of David (2Q22), 4QApocryphal Lamentations (4Q179, 4Q501), 4QApocryphal Daniel (4Q246), 4QApocryphal Pentateuch A (4Q368), 4QApocryphon of Joshua (4Q378), 4QApocryphon of Jeremiah (4Q383, 4Q385a, 4Q387, 4Q387a, 4Q388a, 4Q389-390), 4QApocryphon of Elisha (4Q481a), 4QApocryphon of Malachi (5Q10), and 11QApocryphal Psalms (11Q11). While the titles assigned to some of these works have varied, here "apocryphon" has functioned as a designation for a previously unknown tradition related to a biblical book or figure. As such, the term could be a source of confusion, since it has been made to refer to neither "apocrypha" in the senses it has acquired in Catholic and Protestant circles nor to works which formally use "hiddenness" as a way of presenting themselves.

Coherence of the "Old Testament Apocrypha"

If neither the technical nor ecclesiastical usage is properly descriptive, how are the books called "apocrypha" in Protestant tradition to be characterized? First, we may recognize that the great codices from the fourth and fifth centuries as well as the Protestant "Apocrypha" or Roman Catholic "Deuterocanonicals" include very different kinds of literature: (a) Several works were composed as supplementary materials to already existing biblical books: Esther (expansions with further chapters in Greek); additions to Daniel (Prayer of Azariah, Song of the Three Young Men, Susannah, and Bel and the Dragon); and 1 Baruch and the Epistle of Jeremiah. (b) Two of the works are historiographical: 1 and 2 Maccabees. (c) Two may be classified as literary tales: Tobit and Judith. (d) Liturgical prayer is also included: Prayer of Manasseh (see also *Psalms of Solomon,* Psalms and Odes, and Psalm 151). (e) The sapiential or wisdom literature is represented by Ben Sira and Wisdom of Solomon. Finally, (f) *4 Ezra* is an apocalyptic vision. The only sense in which these diverse compositions are all "apocrypha" is if one eschews any etymological meaning and simply regards them as a modern (and somewhat fluid) collection of books.

Second, these writings were originally composed in different languages. For several of the documents an original composition in Hebrew or Aramaic is confirmed through the evidence from the Dead Sea Scrolls. Most chapters of Tobit are found in fragments from one Hebrew manuscript (4Q200) and in four Aramaic manuscripts (4Q196-199); Hebrew texts of Ben Sira exist in two manuscripts from the Qumran caves (2Q18 [from 6:14-15 or 1:19-20 and 6:20-31]; 11Q5 21:1–22:1 [from Sirach 51]) and the Ben Sira scroll from Masada (fragmentary text of 39:27–

44:17); Psalm 151 is found in 11Q5 col. 28, though, unlike in the Greek Orthodox Psalter, it is divided into two psalms separated by a *vacat* and carrying their own superscriptions (151A in 11Q5 28:3-12; 151B in 28:13); and, finally, Hebrew texts for Psalms 154 and 155 from the Syriac Psalter are preserved, respectively, in 11Q5 18:1-16 and 24:3-17.

In addition, linguistic studies have made it likely that several documents preserved only in Greek or Latin versions derive from now-lost Semitic versions: Judith, 1 Esdras, Epistle of Jeremiah (preserved in a Greek fragment from Qumran, 7Q2), Prayer of Azariah, the Song of the Three Young Men, Bel and the Dragon, and 1 Maccabees. Interestingly, Jerome claims to have known Semitic versions of Tobit (Aramaic), Ben Sira (Hebrew), and Judith (Hebrew). Less certain is whether and to what extent a Semitic version lies behind the Greek texts of 1 Baruch, Prayer of Manasseh, and Susanna. On the other hand, several of the works were originally composed in Greek. These are Greek Esther, Wisdom of Solomon, 2 Maccabees, and 3-4 Maccabees.

Third, though it is impossible to be precise about the date of composition for each of the Protestant "apocrypha," it is at least certain that they emerged during the period between Alexander the Great's conquests in the fourth century B.C.E. and the Bar Kokhba Revolt in 132-135 C.E. The writing of Tobit, Ben Sira, and Epistle of Jeremiah falls within the early part of this period, that is, from 300 B.C.E. until the Maccabean crisis in 175-164 B.C.E. Most of the books derive from the time between the Maccabean wars until the turn of the Common Era: 1 Esdras, Judith, Greek Esther, Prayer of Azariah, the Song of the Three Young Men, Susannah, Bel and the Dragon, 1 and 2 Maccabees, and possibly Prayer of Manasseh. The latest composition is *4 Ezra* (ca. 100 C.E.), which addresses circumstances arising from the destruction of the Second Temple in Jerusalem by the Romans.

The diverse linguistic origin, literary genre, and date of these works indicate why it was that they would not become a collection of books during the Second Temple period. Only with the development of the codex (which made larger collections of books possible) and only when decisions came to be made about canonicity were they formally brought together in different forms, first in Greek and then in Latin. Far from descriptive, then, the term "apocrypha" is anachronistic, and it remains a problem to find terminology that more accurately accords with the respective ways the books present themselves while at the same time recognizing their history of reception among Jews and Christians during the last two millennia.

The "Outside Books" in Jewish Tradition

A related problem to the early development of classifications for "Scripture," on the one hand, and books deemed heretical or rejected, on the other, is found in the rabbinic designation "outside books" *(sĕfārîm ha-ḥîṣōnîm),* which first occurs in *m. Sanh.* 10:1, where a saying attributed to R. Akiba states that those who have no place in the World to Come include anyone "who reads the outside books." The Babylonian and Palestinian Talmud commentaries on this passage single out "the books of Ben Sira" as a poignant example. However, this condemnation is not unequivocal. For example, in the Babylonian Talmud (*b. Sanhedrin* 100b), after R. Akiba's condemnation is endorsed by a ruling of Rabbi Joseph, the latter himself is nonetheless made to permit the use of Ben Sira for instruction. This tension is underscored in the number of instances in which the Rabbinate continued to cite Ben Sira with the same respect shown to biblical works (*b. Berakot* 48a; *y. Berakot* 11b; *y. Nazir* 54b; *Bereshit Rabbah* 91:3; *Qohelet Rabbah* 7:11), presumably because its teaching could be seen as consistent with the Torah. In its condemnation of readers of Ben Sira, the Palestinian Talmud (*y. Sanhedrin* 10a) adds those who make use of the books of a so-called "Ben Laana." The text, however, states that a further category of literature, enigmatically called "the books of *hamiras*" (Homeric works?), is not problematic at all: "the one who reads them is like one who reads a letter" *(ha-qōrêʾ bā-hen kĕ-qōrêʾ bā-ʾigeret).* Crucially, then, the text leaves the impression that the danger of Ben Sira consists in its potential for being confused with Torah, while no such difficulty exists for ancient literature held to be nonreligious. While it may be misleading to generalize from Ben Sira to other books, this broad classification suggests that for the rabbis the "outside books" would have at least consisted of the sort of Jewish writings that later Christian tradition would regard as "Old Testament Apocrypha" and "Old Testament Pseudepigrapha."

Apocryphal Collections in Medieval Jewish Manuscripts

The comparative devaluation of "outside books" in Jewish tradition did not mean an avoidance of them altogether. A number of Aramaic and Hebrew Jewish manuscripts from the Middle Ages contain short collections of works that to some extent resemble what would become the Protestant "apocrypha." Here, the texts for each of the works were either secondary versions (e.g., Tobit and Judith, translated from Latin and/or Greek; Epistle of Jeremiah), summaries (e.g., Baruch, Ben Sira, Esther, 1-4 Maccabees, Susanna, Prayer of Manasseh), or adaptations (Bel and the Dragon), related materials (to Esther: The Dream of Mordecai and the Books of Ahasuerus), and often additional obscure pieces (with titles such as the Book of Yashar, Proverbs of Solomon, the Book of Enoch [neither *1* nor *2 Enoch*], the Fables of Aesop, the Proverbs of Sandabar, The Deed of the Jerusalemite, The Speech of Aphar and Dinah, and so forth). The reason for such collections within manuscripts — that is, whether they were driven by an internal Jewish dynamic or in some sense were meant as counterparts to existing Christian compilations — has yet to be studied properly.

Pseudepigrapha

The Problematic Term "Pseudepigrapha"

The difficulties described above in relation to the use of "apocrypha" apply to "pseudepigrapha" as well. First, if "pseudepigraphon" refers to a work falsely ascribed to a figure who is not the real author, then it does not pertain to a discrete collection of works. Indeed, several books in the Hebrew Bible are arguably pseudepigrapha (e.g., Deuteronomy, Proverbs, Qoheleth, Daniel, and the Davidic Psalms), while the same may be said regarding "apocrypha" such as 1 Baruch, Epistle of Jeremiah, Prayer of Manasseh, Psalm 151 (and Syriac Psalms 154–155), Wisdom of Solomon, and *4 Ezra*. Second, as already noted, in Roman Catholic tradition it is pseudepigraphal works outside the "Deuterocanonicals" that are called "Apocrypha"; this accords with ancient usage of the term "apocrypha." Third, since the term does not describe a set of writings that can be distinguished from other existing collections (e.g., "biblical," "apocryphal"), it often refers today to an ever-growing and fluid corpus of documents preserved from antiquity. In this latter sense, the narrow definition of "pseudepigrapha" does not describe all documents which have occasionally been collected under this heading. A good case in point is James H. Charlesworth's edition of *The Old Testament Pseudepigrapha* (1983-1985), which, for example, includes a number of works or parts of works associated with their real authors' names (e.g., Aristeas the Exegete, Aristobulus, Artapanus, Cleodemus Malchus, Demetrius the Chronographer, Eupolemus, Ezekiel the Tragedian, and Theodotus).

Several considerations make a more precise understanding and definition of an ancient Jewish "pseudepigraphon" possible. (a) The designation is formally a subset of "anonymous" writings, that is, those compositions for which the historical author's identity remains unknown. This means that any information about the writers depends on what they reveal about themselves in the texts. (b) Following from this, a "pseudepigraphon" usually takes one of two basic forms: a writer either (i) communicates in the first person by directly taking on the name of an important or ancient paradigmatic figure (e.g., *1 Enoch, 2 Baruch, Testament of Job, Sibylline Oracles*); or, more loosely, (ii) composes a third-person account that attributes revelatory knowledge, instruction, or activity to such a figure (e.g., *Jubilees* [Moses], *Life of Adam and Eve, Proverbs of Ahiqar, Testament of Abraham*). (c) Thus, while the assumption of an ancient ideal figure's name is fictive in itself, it does not follow that ancient novella or legendary stories such as Tobit, Judith, *Joseph and Aseneth, Book of Giants,* or 11QMelchizedek are "pseudepigrapha" in the strict sense. (d) Sometimes ancient compositions combine these literary forms. Several examples illustrate this point. In the *Genesis Apocryphon* (1Q20) an anonymous author strings together a series of smaller first-person accounts attributed to different patriarchs such as Lamech, Noah, and Abraham to form a larger work that as a whole is not a pseudepigraphon. While the macro-genre of Tobit is that of a tale, part of it is presented as the words of the protagonist, Tobit; in this case, the first-person idiom, the extent of which differs among the versions of the book, forms a relatively small part of the work. Finally, in a number of works the predominant first-person discourse is introduced or framed by a brief third-person narrative that provides a setting (e.g., *Testament of the Twelve Patriarchs, Testament of Job, Testament of Moses, Ladder of Jacob*). It is not always clear in these cases whether the use of the third person is secondary or original to a given work.

Why "Pseudepigraphal" Writings?

To today's readers the notion of a falsely ascribed literary work can carry with it the connotation of "forgery." It is precisely this caricature that has made it difficult for religious communities to value "pseudepigrapha" for their theological ideas. To be sure, in antiquity a writer's use of another name was sometimes criticized, and the criterion of authenticity or nonauthenticity could be invoked as a reason, respectively, for a book's inclusion or noninclusion among sacred traditions. Josephus in the first century C.E., for example, treated the book of Daniel as written during the Babylonian exile by a prophet of that name; since what he prophesied about the Greeks' accession to power came true through the conquests of Alexander the Great, the "books" of Daniel (i.e., including the additions preserved in Greek) are to be found "among the sacred writings" (*Ant.* 10.210; cf. 10.190-281; 11.337-38; 12.322). Furthermore, insofar as *1 Enoch,* for example, was treated as coming from the patriarch Enoch himself, it could be regarded as scripture (*Epistle of Barnabas* 4:3; 16:5-6; Tertullian, *De Cultu Feminarum* 3, *De Idololatria* 4; cf. Jude 14-15) or at least highly valued (Irenaeus, *Adversus Haereses* 4.16; Clement of Alexandria, *Eclogae Prophetarum* 2 and 53; Anatolius of Alexandria, *Paschal Canon* 5; Ethiopic Orthodox tradition), even though the main criterion for value was based more on the importance accorded to the contents of the book. On the other hand, as noted above, spuriousness was frequently held out by Jews and Christians as a reason to reject the use of certain writings (Tertullian, *De Cultu Feminarum* 3; cf. Origen, *Contra Celsum* 5.54; Augustine, *De Civitate Dei* 18.38).

For all the growing worry about pseudepigraphy expressed by Jewish and Christian writers during the first centuries of the Common Era, it remains true that the phenomenon itself was not only widespread but also widely received. This was so much the case that the notion of false ascription to authors could not be applied as a criterion for rejection in every case; the use of some books in faith communities had, for various reasons, gained an irreversible momentum. The main question to ask, however, is why pseudepigraphy was so popular, that is, why so many in antiquity were prepared to write under the name of an important personage. To this question several answers may be given.

First, libraries such as the great one in Alexandria were keen to collect copies of works by well-known writers. In response to such advertising, a supply of writings could be produced for purchase that met this demand. Not only was the Greek translation of the Jewish Torah reportedly produced for such a reason during the third century B.C.E. (see the *Letter of Aristeas*), during the first several centuries many "heretical" works of suspicious value were brought to the Library of Alexandria, which perhaps on that account was subjected to destructive activities in 48 B.C.E. (Julius Caesar), 270-275 C.E. (Aurelian), and especially 391 C.E. (the decree by the emperor Theodosius) and 634 (by the order of the caliph Umar).

Second, writing under the name of someone important frequently served to gain a hearing for one's own views. Thus the analogies between the time of the real author and the ancient figure invoked could not always hide the very real and immediate concerns behind the composition. Examples of this abound, more obviously in pseudepigraphal documents that contain historical allusions to present or more recent events (so the *post-eventum* prophecies of *1 Enoch* 85–90 and 91:11-17; 93:1-10; Daniel 8-11; *2 Baruch*). For example, where the biblical book of Ezra is associated with the return from exile, the erection and rededication of a new Temple, and the reestablishment of the Torah among the people, *4 Ezra* is concerned more immediately with the aftermath of the destruction of the Second Temple by the Romans. Thus the affinities between biblical context and the time of writing were overwhelmed by the real author's pressing interests. Moreover, the process of transmission attempted to reshape or redirect received pseudepigraphal traditions to address new circumstances and theological issues; this can be observed in the later activities of Christian scribes who edited and even interpolated into the texts (e.g., *Testaments of the Twelve Patriarchs, Testament of Job, Testament of Abraham, 3 Baruch, 4 Baruch, 2 Enoch, Apocalypse of Zephaniah*).

Third, in some streams of tradition, such as philosophical schools or apocalyptic circles, the notion of writing in one's own name could simply be regarded as unethical. This was the case during generations subsequent to Pythagoras and Plato among students who produced a vast number of writings in the names of their teacher. Such a practice was regarded by the writers as a reasonable way for them to express their humility, indebtedness, and devotion in relation to the received tradition.

A fourth reason is related to the previous two: the name of a famous teacher or well-known figure of the past could be invoked in order to combat or refute other interpretations or views of the same tradition. This was especially true, again, in the literary output of philosophical schools and in the reception, transmission, and reappropriation of earlier pseudepigraphical tradition. An example of this is provided in the second-century-B.C.E. *Epistle of Enoch* at *1 Enoch* 104:10-11, a passage preserved in Ethiopic and Greek texts:

Ethiopic	**Greek**
(10) And now I know this mystery, that many times the sinners will alter and pervert the word of truth; and they will speak evil words, and lie, and make big works and write my books in their own words.	(10) . . .] of truth they will alter; and the sinners co[py] and change many things, and lie and fashion great works and w[rit]e down books in their own names.
(11) And would that they would write down all the words accurately in their languages and neither pervert nor omit (anything) from my words, but accurately write down everything which I have testified before concerning you.	(11) An[d] would that [they wou]ld write all my words accurately in their names and [nei]ther omit nor change these words, but write all things accurately which I testify to them.

It has argued by some, especially on the basis of the Greek version, that the writer of this passage is engaged in a defense of his own work as a pseudepigraphon. If this is so, the possible charge of writing under someone else's name is met by reversing the accusation: those who write "in their own names" are the ones who perpetrate falsehood and corrupt the truth. It is not clear, however, that this reading reflects the sense of the text in its entirety. The emphasis in both versions on "my words" in verse 11 suggests that the writer's attack is predominantly concerned with those who, from his point of view, have subverted or misrepresented the Enoch tradition they have all received. The writer, in using Enoch's name, claims to be the authentic interpreter and transmitter of Enochic revelation and shows that he is aware of others who have deliberately taken it upon themselves to make improper use of it. While the polemic here may be directed against the construals of the figure of Enoch in works such as Ben Sira, *Jubilees,* or *Pseudo-Eupolemus,* the fictive character of the *Epistle of Enoch* momentarily gives way to an admission that the real author is not, in fact, Enoch himself. If this admission is sufficiently plain, then the text assumes a reception among its readers as a pseudepigraphon.

One should, of course, be cautious in regarding *1 Enoch* 104:10-11 as paradigmatic for how other pseudepigraphal authors understood what they were doing. In almost all the extant literature, the writers offer little or no direct hints about their *own* persona, and it is notoriously difficult to identify the context of origin and the groups for which they were writing. Nevertheless, from the perspective of the authors themselves, "pseudepigrapha" is a misleading label. They presented their works as divine revelation that is binding on its readers. "Truth" in content was more important than the literary genre or idiom chosen to convey it. By attributing the instructions and story lines to remote figures, the writers of pseudepigraphal works contextualized their messages within or in relation to master narratives that had been circulating widely and for a long time. Thus the effectiveness of their communication may have depended on what readers could be expected to be already familiar with from ancient tradition and, on the basis of such familiarity, be able to draw inferences from the analogies for themselves. On the other hand, the pseudepigraphal writings set their own terms of reference and already filtered through the ancient traditions in particular ways (as in the historical apocalypses or in reviews of the sacred past), so that direct acquaintance with such traditions would not have been necessary. To this extent, the implied readers are drawn into the sacred world being set before them: stark distinctions drawn between the faithful pious and the disobedient apostates in narratives and between divine or heavenly wisdom and errant knowledge in instructions invite readers, especially if they are ideally aligned with an author's intentions, to participate imaginatively in the religious *truths* being revealed to them. In those apocalyptic works that anticipate eschatological judgment, readers are presented with a decision: whether to align themselves with the way the righteous are described in the book and be rewarded or to reject the author's message, knowing that for this they will suffer the consequences of punishment. Thus, at the behest of the fictive protagonist, readers are transported into a "biblical" world that has extended into and beyond their time. Problems that beset the readers in the present — whether religious marginalization, social and political oppression, apostasy, or some other form of religious disorder — are resolved by an appeal to a paradigm in the remote past and imminent future. The pseudepigraphal idiom would have reminded readers that divine activity on behalf of the pious lies essentially outside the time in which they live. Now is the time for action, for a clear-cut decision to be faithful, whatever the circumstances.

Pseudepigrapha since the Enlightenment and the Dead Sea Scrolls

Since the beginning of the nineteenth century there has been a significant growth in textual witness to a number of pseudepigraphal writings. Many of these texts survive in the following languages: Latin, Greek, Old Slavonic, Armenian, Georgian, Rumanian, Coptic, Syriac, and Ethiopic; as such, they demonstrate how much the preservation of Jewish traditions composed during or derived from the Second Temple period depended on the activity of Christian writers, translators, editors, and copyists through many centuries since the first century C.E.

The discovery of the Dead Sea Scrolls in eleven caves from 1947 to 1956 made a significant impact on the study of ancient pseudepigraphy. This is so in two main respects. First, the Dead Sea materials have yielded non-Christian Jewish evidence for at least some of this literature. Among the previously known pseudepigrapha (if we take the technical meaning of the term as the point of departure), the following works have been confirmed as present at Qumran:

- *1 Enoch* (Aramaic)
    - *Book of Watchers* (chaps. 1–36): 4Q201, 4Q202, 4Q204, 4Q205, 4Q206, XQpapEnoch
    - *Astronomical Book* (chaps. 72–82): 4Q208, 4Q209, 4Q210, 4Q211
    - *Animal Apocalypse* (chaps. 85–90): 4Q204, 4Q205, 4Q206, 4Q207
    - *Exhortation* (91:1-10, 18-19): 4Q212
    - *Apocalypse of Weeks* (93:1-10; 91:11-17): 4Q212
    - *Epistle of Enoch* (92:1-5; 94:1–105:2): 4Q204, 4Q212
    - *Birth of Noah* (chaps. 106–7): 4Q204

- Daniel (Aramaic): 1Q71, 1Q72, 4Q12, 4Q13, 4Q14, 4Q15, 4Q16, 6Q7

- *Jubilees* (Hebrew): 1Q17, 1Q18, 2Q19, 2Q20, 3Q5, 4Q176 frgs. 17-19, 4Q216, 4Q217, 4Q218, 4Q219, 4Q220, 4Q221, 4Q222, 4Q223-224, 11Q12

- Materials related to *Testaments of the Twelve Patriarchs*
    - *Testament of Judah* [?]: 3Q7 Hebrew, 4Q484 Aramaic
    - *Testament of Naphtali:* 4Q215 Aramaic
    - *Aramaic Levi Document* (Aramaic): 1Q21, 4Q213, 4Q213a, 4Q213b, 4Q214, 4Q214a, 4Q214b

- Psalms 151, 154, 155: 11Q5

- Related, though not formally a pseudepigraphon, is the Aramaic *Book of Giants* (1Q23, 1Q24, 2Q26, 4Q203, 4Q206a, 4Q530, 4Q531, 4Q532, 4Q533, 6Q8).

Second, pseudepigraphal documents for which there has not been previous evidence have come to light through fragments from the Dead Sea:

- Traditions related to the biblical book of Daniel (Aramaic)
  - *Prayer of Nabonidus* (4Q242)
  - *Four Kingdoms* (4Q552, 4Q553)

- Testamentary material (Aramaic)
  - *Testament of Jacob* (4Q537)
  - *Testament* (or *Apocryphon*) *of Judah* (4Q538)
  - *Testament* (or *Apocryphon*) *of Joseph* (4Q539)
  - *Testament* (or *Apocryphon*) *of Levi* (4Q540, 4Q541)
  - *Testament of Qahat* (4Q542)
  - *Visions of Amram* (4Q543, 4Q544, 4Q545, 4Q546, 4Q547, 4Q548)
  - *Genesis Apocryphon* (Aramaic) (1Q20)
  - *New Jerusalem* (Aramaic) (1Q32, 2Q24, 4Q554, 4Q555, 5Q15, 11Q18)

Again, related materials to these include a number of documents which, in their preserved forms, show no evidence of being pseudepigrapha: *Pseudo-Daniel* (4Q243, 4Q244, 4Q245); *Aramaic Apocalypse* (4Q246); *Apocalypse?* (4Q489, 4Q490); *Noah* (4Q534, 4Q535, 4Q536; and 1Q19, 1Q19 bis); *Daniel Susanna?* (4Q551); and *Four Kingdoms* (4Q552, 4Q553).

While these materials, preserved in manuscripts dating from the third century B.C.E. until the first century C.E., both confirm and augment the existence of pseudepigraphal writing in Second Temple Judaism, two points should be noted. First, none of them are documents whose origins can be traced to the Qumran community, whose extant literature was invariably composed by (formally) anonymous writers. This means that, while the collection and, possibly, copying of these materials imply that the Qumran community did not reject them, the phenomenon of pseudepigraphy was fairly widespread among Hebrew and especially Aramaic-speaking Jews of the time. Second, these texts, especially those which can be said to pre-date the Maccabean revolt *(Book of Watchers, Astronomical Book)* or contain pre-Danielic tradition *(Aramaic Levi Document, Prayer of Nabonidus, Visions of Amram, Testament of Qahat),* demonstrate that the practice of attributing wisdom and speech was well established during the third century B.C.E. This undergirds our confidence that a number of other works showing little or no overt sign of Christian editorial intrusion are originally Jewish and were composed during the Second Temple period (or at least before the Bar Kokhba Revolt): examples of this include *1 Enoch* 108 *(Eschatological Admonition), 4 Ezra, 2 Baruch, Apocalypse of Abraham, Testament of Abraham, Letter of Aristeas, Pseudo-Philo* (= *Liber Antiquitatum Biblicarum*), *Psalms of Solomon, Similitudes of Enoch* (= *1 Enoch* 37–71), *Testament of Job, Testament of Moses, Joseph and Aseneth, Life of Adam and Eve, Pseudo-Phocylides,* 3 Maccabees, 4 Maccabees, and Prayer of Manasseh.

But for all their importance, the manuscripts from Qumran should not mislead one to assume that many or most of the "Old Testament" pseudepigrapha not attested at Qumran were also composed during the Second Temple period. To begin with, many of these compositions are simply Christian or contain very little trace of direct borrowing from non-Christian Jewish tradition (*Sibylline Oracles* books 6–8, *5 Ezra, 6 Ezra, Questions of Ezra, Greek Apocalypse of Ezra, Vision of Ezra, Apocalypse of Elijah, Apocalypse of Zephaniah, Apocalypse of Sedrach, Apocalypse of Daniel, Testament of Adam, Testament of Isaac, Testament of Jacob, Testament of Solomon, Ascension of Isaiah, Odes of Solomon*).

A number of others seem to be so predominantly Christian in outlook and tone that indicators of Jewish tradition seem best explained as a matter of reception or borrowing by Christian or Jewish-Christian writers (*Lives of the Prophets, Sibylline Oracles* books 1–2 and 14, *History of the Rechabites*).

More Jewish in outlook, several documents may derive from at least some Jewish written sources that have been edited, supplemented, or interpolated by Christian scribes (so, e.g., *Sibylline Oracles* books 3, 4 and 5; *3 Baruch; 4 Baruch;* the *Hellenistic Synagogal Prayers;* and *Testaments of the Twelve Patriarchs*). Here, some of the Christian interpolations are easy to identify (*4 Bar.* 8:12–9:32; *Sib. Or.* 1.324-400; *Sib. Or.* 3.776; *T. Levi* 4:4; 10:2-3; 14:2; 16:3, passim; *Hell. Syn. Prayers* 5:4-8 and 20-24; 7:4, etc.). Finally, some writings may have circulated in both Jewish and Christian circles, but show very little direct influence from either *(Ahiqar Proverbs, Sentences of the Syriac Menander).* These classifications are not clear-cut; it sometimes remains difficult, if not impossible, to determine whether a given document or one of its passages without obviously Christian ideas therefore stems from a non-Christian Jewish tradition (e.g., many parts of *Testaments of the Twelve Patriarchs*).

Nevertheless, when non-Christian Jewish and Christian traditions have come together in a composition, scholarship in recent years has begun to shift from the assumption that a Jewish source has been reworked by Christians to a default view that attributes the essential form of the document to Christians who were inspired by Jewish traditions. Such a shift has been noticeable in recent treatments of *Testaments of the Twelve Patriarchs* (de Jonge, in numerous works from 1953 to 2003), *Ascension of Isaiah* (Norelli 1995), *Lives of the Prophets* (Satran 1995), *3 Baruch* (Harlow 1996), and *Joseph and Aseneth* (Kraemer 1998). A methodological corollary to this shift is that, when the earliest evidence for such documents exists in Christian manuscripts, it is these Christian contexts that should provide the point of departure for study and analysis (Kraft 2001; Davila 2005). With regard to Early or Second Temple Judaism, then, it becomes crucial to identify and make use of criteria which might (or might not) assist in determining the extent to which pseudepigraphal writings originated among Jewish (or Jewish-Christian) groups. Scholars will continue to debate about how far each of these writings can be classified in precisely the ways outlined above. However, the different possibilities listed here illustrate (a) the complexities students of the materials face when attempting to determine their date and religious provenience, (b) the occasionally stark differences between Jewish and Christian tradition, and yet (c) how similar and, indeed, often indistinguishable, Jewish, Jewish-Christian, and non–Jewish-Christian traditions could be.

Conclusion

Today the terms "Apocrypha" and "Pseudepigrapha" refer to collections of writings of which many do not strictly reflect the literal meaning of these terms. The Apocrypha (or, for Roman Catholicism, Deuterocanonicals) is a fluid collection if one compares the lists of them among the different ecclesiastical traditions. However, within each ecclesiastical tradition, their identification has been remarkably stable. These writings may be confidently regarded as Jewish in origin; in addition, they all date to before the Bar Kokhba Revolt (132-135 C.E.) and, except for *4 Ezra*, were all originally composed before the destruction of the Second Temple (70 C.E.). At the same time, the free use of the term "apocryphon" for a number of documents discovered among the Dead Sea Scrolls reflects the ancient meaning of "hidden" traditions without, however, being "hidden" in the more technical sense found in Daniel, *4 Ezra*, and *2 Baruch*.

By contrast, collections of "pseudepigrapha" (or "apocrypha" in Roman Catholic tradition) have been anything but stable. This is due to a number of factors: (a) The term "pseudepigraphon" has often not been applied in its narrow meaning of a writing falsely ascribed. Instead, it has sometimes served as a broad category that refers to religious Jewish and Christian writings that are neither found in the "Bible" nor included in a church's list of "Apocrypha." (b) Since the beginning of the nineteenth century, when entrepreneurs and collectors brought ancient manuscripts to Europe from monasteries in Africa and the Middle East, and until the present, as manuscripts for new documents from Ethiopia, Armenia, and the Dead Sea have continued to come to light, collections of pseudepigrapha (however the term is defined) have been growing in number. (c) Modern collections of translated works — here we may take German and English publications since 1900 as an example — have each differed from one another in what to (and not to) include. Some of these differences can be attributed to nomenclature, that is, whether or not a given editor focused on "pseudepigrapha" per se (Kautzsch 1900, Charles 1913, Charlesworth 1983-1985, Sparks 1984: "apocryphal Old Testament"), more generally on works "outside the Bible" (Riessler 1927), or on Jewish writings from the Greco-Roman period (the series Jüdische Schriften aus hellenistisch-römischer Zeit [JSHRZ] 1973-present). These more widely disseminated collections, however, have fluctuated greatly on the number and selection of documents: Kautzsch (thirteen documents), Charles (seventeen), Riessler (sixty-one, including *Shemoneh Esreh, Megillat Taʿanit,* Heraclitus of Ephesus, Theodotus, *Caves of Treasures*), Sparks (twenty-five), Charlesworth (sixty-five, though ten nonpseudonymous works are included within a supplementary section entitled "Fragments of Lost Judeo-Hellenistic Works"), and JSHRZ (fifty, including "Apocrypha").

Beyond the writings included in these collections, a number of further documents could be included. The significance of the Dead Sea Scrolls has been noted for the addition of new materials, and there is little doubt that these materials were composed during the Second Temple period. A further project entitled *More Old Testament Pseudepigrapha* (MOTP), based at the University of St. Andrews under the direction of James Davila, is seeking to supplement the Charlesworth edition with an additional fifty pseudepigraphal writings, plus nearly thirty more that are found either in fragments or in quotations. The MOTP collection is casting its net more widely to include pseudepigrapha composed by Jews and Christians all the way up to 600 C.E. and the rise of Islam. With some notable exceptions (e.g., *Aramaic Levi Document, Book of Giants, Hebrew Naphtali, Balaam Text* [from Deir Alla], *Hebrew Apocalypse of Elijah, Geniza Wisdom Text, Sword of Moses, Massekhet Kelim, Midrash Vayissa'u, Eighth Book of Moses, Sepher ha-Razim, Sepher Zerubbabel*), many of the additional works in MOTP are Christian compositions and face the same issues regarding the relation between Jewish and Christian tradition outlined above. Accordingly, the net has been cast more widely here to include some pseudepigraphal documents in the Dead Sea Scrolls, but also works composed until 600 C.E. Thus the significance of each work for the Second Temple period varies widely and will require analysis on a case-by-case basis.

The problems that beset the terms "Apocrypha" and "Pseudepigrapha" have not prevented scholars from applying them to discrete collections of ancient works that stand alongside other recognized collections of works such as the Dead Sea Scrolls, rabbinic literature, the Hekhalot texts, the Nag Hammadi Library, and the works of Philo and Josephus. These different, though sometimes overlapping classifications of texts cannot hide the fact that in order to be interpreted, they need to be read together for a more comprehensive understanding of the diversities of Judaism that flourished during the centuries leading up to and after the turn of the Common Era.

BIBLIOGRAPHY

Baum, Armin Daniel. 2001. *Pseudepigraphie und literarische Fälschung im frühen Christentum.* Tübingen: Mohr-Siebeck.

Charles, Robert H., ed. 1913. *The Apocrypha and Pseudepigrapha of the Old Testament.* 2 vols. Oxford: Clarendon.

Charlesworth, James H., ed. 1983-1985. *The Old Testament Pseudepigrapha.* 2 vols. New York: Doubleday.

Chazon, Esther G., and Michael E. Stone, eds. 1997. *Pseudepigraphic Perspectives: The Apocrypha and Pseudepigrapha in Light of the Dead Sea Scrolls.* Leiden: Brill.

Collins, John J. 1998. *The Apocalyptic Imagination: An Introduction to Jewish Apocalyptic Literature.* 2d ed. Grand Rapids: Eerdmans.

Davila, James R. 2005. *The Provenance of the Pseudepigrapha: Jewish, Christian, or Other?* Leiden: Brill.

de Jonge, Marinus. 2003. *Pseudepigrapha of the Old Testament as Part of Christian Literature: The Case of the Testaments of the Twelve Patriarchs and the Greek Life of Adam and Eve.* Leiden: Brill.

DeSilva, David. 2002. *Introducing the Apocrypha: Message, Context and Significance.* Grand Rapids: Baker.

Flint, Peter W. 1999. "'Apocrypha,' Other Previously-Known Writings, and 'Pseudepigrapha' in the Dead Sea Scrolls." In *The Dead Sea Scrolls after Fifty Years.* 2 vols. Ed. Peter W. Flint and James C. VanderKam. Leiden: Brill, 1:24-66.

Harlow, Daniel C. 1996. *The Greek Apocalypse of Baruch (3 Baruch) in Hellenistic Judaism and Early Christianity.* Leiden: Brill.

Harrington, Daniel J. 1999. *Invitation to the Apocrypha.* Grand Rapids: Eerdmans.

Hollander, Harm W., and Marinus de Jonge. 1985. *The Testaments of the Twelve Patriarchs: A Commentary.* Leiden: Brill.

Kautzsch, Emil, ed. 1900. *Die Apokryphen und Pseudepigraphen des Alten Testaments.* 2 vols. Tübingen: Mohr.

Kraemer, Ross S. 1998. *When Aseneth Met Joseph: A Late Antique Tale of the Biblical Patriarch and His Egyptian Wife, Reconsidered.* Oxford: Oxford University Press.

Kraft, Robert A. 2001. "The Pseudepigrapha and Christianity Revisited: Setting the Stage and Framing Some Central Questions." *JSJ* 32: 371-95.

Nickelsburg, George W. E. 2001. *1 Enoch 1.* Philadelphia: Fortress.

———. 2005. *Jewish Literature between the Bible and the Mishnah.* 2d ed. Philadelphia: Fortress.

Norelli, Enrico. 1995. *Ascensio Isaiae,* vol. 1, *Commentarius.* Turnhout: Brepols.

Riessler, Paul. 1927. *Altjüdisches Schrifttum ausserhalb der Bibel.* Heidelberg: Kerl.

Satran, David. 1995. *Biblical Prophets in Byzantine Palestine: Reassessing the "Lives of the Prophets."* Leiden: Brill.

Sparks, H. F. D., ed. 1984. *The Apocryphal Old Testament.* Oxford: Clarendon.

Stone, Michael E. 1990. *Fourth Ezra.* Minneapolis: Fortress.

———. 1996. "The Dead Sea Scrolls and the Pseudepigrapha." *DSD* 3: 270-96.

Stuckenbruck, Loren T. 2007. *1 Enoch 91–108.* Berlin: de Gruyter.

Wyrick, Jed. 2004. *The Ascension of Authorship: Attribution and Canon Formation in Jewish, Hellenistic, and Christian Traditions.* Cambridge: Harvard University Press.

The Dead Sea Scrolls

Eibert Tigchelaar

In a comprehensive sense, the Dead Sea Scrolls include all texts from Wadi Daliyeh, Ketef Jericho, Qumran, Wadi en-Nar, Wadi Ghweir, Wadi Murabbaʿat, Wadi Sdeir, Naḥal Arugot, Naḥal Ḥever/Wadi Ṣeiyâl, Naḥal Mishmar, Naḥal Ṣeʿelim, Masada, as well as Khirbet Mird. In common usage, and in this essay, the term "Dead Sea Scrolls" refers specifically to the texts found between 1947 and 1956 in the caves near Qumran, close to the northwestern shore of the Dead Sea. Some fragments that are reported to have been found in caves near Qumran may in fact stem from other sites that were discovered by the Bedouin in the same period, notably Wadi Murabbaʿat and Naḥal Ḥever/Wadi Ṣeiyâl. Likewise, the origin of some fragments in private collections is unknown.

The importance of the Dead Sea Scrolls for the history of early Judaism lies in the combination of the size, the antiquity, and the nature of the corpus. The scrolls are by far the largest collection of Jewish religious texts from the Second Temple period, preserving fragments of more than a hundred different religious compositions, most of which were hitherto unknown. For many different aspects of Judaism, the Dead Sea Scrolls provide the first literary evidence. Thus, for example, the corpus contains the oldest Hebrew and Greek biblical manuscripts, the first Aramaic translations of biblical books, the oldest *tefillin,* the earliest liturgies for fixed prayers, the oldest nonbiblical halakic works, as well as the oldest exorcistic prayers. In many cases we find hitherto-unknown precursors to or roots for phenomena found in rabbinic Judaism, such as the hymns embedded in the Hekhalot literature. At the same time, some scrolls attest to Second Temple practices and beliefs that did not become part of later normative Judaism, which is why they sometimes are called sectarian. This goes, for example, for so-called rule texts that discuss the membership of the movement of the "renewed covenant," exegetical works that apply scriptural prophecies to the contemporary history and future of the group, eschatological works dealing with the final war, and religious calendrical texts based on a 364-day calendar.

Because of the content of so-called sectarian texts, especially the *Rule of the*

Community, scholars in the 1950s framed the Qumran-Essene hypothesis of the provenance of the Dead Sea Scrolls, which at the end of that decade had become the paradigm of scrolls scholarship. The scrolls were assumed to be the remnants of the library of an Essene, or Essene-like, sectarian community that dwelt at Qumran, composed and copied texts, and hid their manuscripts in various caves before the Romans conquered the site in 68 C.E. At present there are many different modifications of this paradigm. Most importantly, there is a broad recognition that not all the compositions and scrolls can be attributed to this one "sectarian" group, and that many texts may have been composed or written somewhere else, before they were brought to Qumran. Some archaeologists even deny that Qumran would have been a religious center and therefore assume that all the scrolls were brought from elsewhere. The following survey offers an overview of the corpus, a description of the texts and their contribution to our knowledge of Judaism in the Second Temple period, and critical reflections on the nature of the corpus.

The Contours of the Corpus

Although generally the Dead Sea Scrolls are discussed as one corpus, they comprise the inscribed material from eleven different caves in the vicinity of the ruins of Qumran. The finds in the caves share many commonalities but also differ in important respects. Largely or partially intact scrolls have been found only in Caves 1 and 11. The completely preserved Cave 3 *Copper Scroll* stands out because of its material, contents, and language. Cave 4, which yielded more than 15,000 fragments that can be assigned to at least 700 different manuscripts, surrendered far more manuscripts than all other caves together. In Cave 7 only fragments of Greek texts were found, and Cave 6 produced a relatively large number of papyrus texts. According to the current paleographical dating, the texts from Caves 1 and 4 are on average considerably older than those from Caves 2, 3, 5, 6, and 11. Caves 9 (one shred of papyrus with a few letters) and 10 (a shard of pottery with two letters) can be ignored in this overview.

The most characteristic feature of both the entire corpus and the collections of the individual caves is that virtually all the manuscripts contain texts of a religious nature or touching upon religious issues. Only a few, badly preserved fragments are the remnants of nonliterary texts such as letters, accounts, or deeds, and it cannot be excluded that some of those actually stem from Naḥal Ḥever.

The present inventory of Dead Sea Scrolls lists around 930 items. In most cases one item corresponds to one manuscript, but in view of the many unidentified fragments that have not been included in the lists, it is plausible that the materials known to us stem from more than a thousand different manuscripts. Only in a few cases do substantial parts of manuscripts remain, and often a manuscript consists of no more than a few identified fragments.

Most Dead Sea Scrolls were written on skins of domesticated goats and ibexes. Some exceptionally thick scrolls, like 11Q5, might be calfskin. Ten to fifteen percent of the manuscripts were written on papyrus. The Cave 3 *Copper Scroll* is the only text written on metal. Both in and near the caves (Caves 4, 6, 7, 8, and 10), and at the site of Qumran, jars and shards with inscriptions or incisions were found. Notable are the ostraca found at Qumran, as well as a small limestone plaque of five lines with what may be a literary text (KhQ 2207). Some fragments, both of skin and of papyrus, were found to be written on both sides.

The majority of the manuscripts are written in Hebrew. About 12 percent (or 17 percent of the nonbiblical, nondocumentary texts) are written in Aramaic. Almost 3 percent of the inventory items are written in Greek, but the percentage drops to less than 1 percent if we bracket out Cave 7. All but two Aramaic manuscripts and most Hebrew ones are written in the so-called square or Aramaic script. Two Aramaic manuscripts are written in a Nabatean script. Some Hebrew texts use the Paleo-Hebrew script, or several kinds of so-called cryptic scripts, the most common one being referred to as Cryptic A. The square script is attested in formal, semiformal, and semicursive hands, and a few of the documentary texts are written in a cursive hand. Some Hebrew texts display the orthography and morphology known from the Masoretic manuscripts of the Hebrew Bible; others have a distinct full orthography and special morphological features that are unattested or rare in Hebrew texts outside the corpus. Many manuscripts with those morphological features also have specific nontextual scribal features, so Emanuel Tov has proposed that we have within the corpus a large group of documents written according to a special "Qumran scribal practice."

The traditional paleographic dating of the manuscripts ranges from the mid-third century B.C.E. to the end of the first century C.E., but the vast majority of the manuscripts date to the first century B.C.E. Radiocarbon analysis of manuscripts by and large gives date ranges from the late third century B.C.E. to the early second century C.E., even though for specific samples paleographic and radiocarbon datings disagree. No manuscripts are internally dated, and the few texts that mention identifiable historical persons refer to figures that lived in the second century and especially in the first half of the first century B.C.E.

The near completion of the publication of all materials in the 1990s has enabled new approaches to the corpus, by allowing scholars to correlate different kinds of subsets within the corpus. For example, one may contrast collections from different caves, compare "biblical" texts written in the so-called Qumran scribal practice to other "biblical" texts, or use the date of the hands of manuscripts in order to trace chronological developments in the corpus.

Scholarly Categorizations Old and New

Classifications of the different kinds of Dead Sea Scrolls have shifted over time, as more scrolls became known, and as scholarly concepts, terminology, and interpretations changed. Initially, on the basis of the Cave 1 finds, the scrolls were roughly classified in three categories: (1) biblical or canonical; (2) apocryphal and/or pseudepigraphal; and (3) sectarian or Essene. This old categorization was partly based on genre and content of texts but also implied a historical view according to which (with the exception of Daniel) canonical books preceded apocryphal and pseudepigraphal ones, which in turn were older than the sectarian texts. At the same time, this three-part division was thought to reflect the literature of respectively all Jews, some Jews, and only the Dead Sea Scrolls sect. Gradually, the problematic categories of apocrypha and pseudepigrapha were subsumed in a broader general category of "parabiblical texts," and the initial tripartite scholarly categorization was in practice limited to two sets of oppositions, "biblical" versus "nonbiblical," and "sectarian" versus "nonsectarian," which influence scholarship up to the present.

The publication of all the Cave 4 materials and their subsequent analysis has required a thorough revision of those earlier classifications. The corpus does not conform to anachronistic assumptions connected to the term "biblical." This realization has provoked discussions of whether texts like the *Reworked Pentateuch* manuscripts are biblical, or whether *Jubilees* or the *Temple Scroll* had scriptural status for the group that collected the scrolls. Also, consideration of the corpus as a whole challenges the view that all the hitherto-unknown texts were written by only one group and suggests that they originated in different movements at different times. The result is that the sharp contrasts between the two sets of oppositions, "biblical" versus "nonbiblical" and "sectarian" versus "nonsectarian," has broken down; scholars now allow for different degrees of authoritativeness of scriptures and varying kinds of sectarianism. From a practical view, a classification with two sets of oppositions also has limited value, since most newly published manuscripts should have been assigned to the categories "nonbiblical" and "nonsectarian." The large increase in known materials does, however, enable one to classify the materials differently, according to literary form, content, or function of compositions. Such new classifications of the material can be found in the translations of García Martínez and Vermes, and in a more elaborate form in Lange's overview in DJD 39. In Lange's classification of the nonbiblical texts, which has been adopted by the *Dead Sea Scrolls Reader,* we find categories such as "parabiblical," "exegetical," "concerned with religious law," "calendrical," "poetical," "liturgical," "sapiential," "historical," "apocalyptic," "eschatological," and more.

The Texts and Early Judaism

The present survey does not aim at a strict categorization of the manuscripts but rather discusses the corpus and the most important texts thematically. It aspires to relate the materials to present scholarly discussion and to clarify what they contribute to the knowledge of early Judaism.

Authoritative Scriptures and the Formation of the Bible

In general the term "biblical" is used, anachronistically, but for practical reasons, for those scrolls which contained the text, or part of the text, of one or more compositions that would later be included in the Tanak. Altogether, the corpus contains more than two hundred Hebrew and Aramaic "biblical" manuscripts," five manuscripts with Greek translations of pentateuchal books, three with Aramaic translations *(targumim),* and thirty-three phylacteries and *mezuzot.* In addition, many of the "nonbiblical" manuscripts are in various ways intertextually related to the "biblical" books. While the "biblical" manuscripts give direct witness to the forms of the biblical books and their text in the period just before the final stage of the formation of the Hebrew Bible, the corpus as a whole gives indirect witness to those compositions and their text, but also sheds light on the authoritativeness of scriptures for the group(s) behind the corpus.

The "biblical" Dead Sea Scrolls reflect a wide diversity of textual variants and recensions. Whereas many manuscripts present a text that stands fairly close to the Masoretic Text (MT), there are also scrolls that preserve variants and even recensions that correspond to those of the Old Greek (e.g., 4QJer[b]), or to the Samaritan Pentateuch (4QpaleoExod[m], 4QNum[b], and 4QDeut[n]). But many other "biblical" manuscripts do not closely correspond to any of those three texts, since they either have multiple unique variant readings, or have readings that cannot be aligned with only one of the traditional texts. Therefore, with regard to textual readings, we do not have a limited number of text types but multiple texts. With regard to recensions, the manuscripts generally correspond with the types of recensions found in the MT or the LXX (where book by book the one or the other may be older), or with the harmonizing kind of recensions that are also found in the Samaritan Pentateuch (SP). Famous is the case of 4QJer[b], which displays the recensional differences in which the LXX differs from MT. But here again, some scrolls preserve recensions that are independent from other known texts (e.g., 4QJudg[a]). None of the variants or recensions has a clearly "sectarian" concern, though some of the 1QIsa[a] variants have been interpreted as expressing the self-understanding of the Dead Sea Scrolls community.

For the assessment of the LXX and the SP, the scrolls are invaluable because they demonstrate that divergent readings and recensions of the Old Greek (OG) often go back to a Hebrew *Vorlage* and are not tendentious innovations of the translator, and that the harmonizations in the SP were already present in the text the Samaritans chose. The variety of the "biblical" manuscripts from Qumran may be contrasted with the homogeneity of the post-70-C.E. "biblical" manuscripts found at Wadi Murabbaʿat, Wadi Sdeir, and Naḥal Ḥever/Wadi Ṣeiyâl, which preserve a text that is virtually identical to the MT. This contrast has been explained chronologically and sociologically: the Qumran "biblical" manuscripts, the majority of which stem from the first century B.C.E. and the early first century C.E., reflect the textual variety before the post-70-C.E. move toward textual standardization that influenced the other Judean Desert "biblical" manuscripts; or, mainstream (Pharisaic, proto-rabbinic) Judaism promoted a standardized text, whereas the group who collected or copied the Dead Sea Scrolls did not. The pre-73-C.E. "biblical" manuscripts found at Masada make the issue even more complex, since they are found at the same site as "nonbiblical" manuscripts comparable to those from Qumran but seem to display a text that is arguably closer to the MT than the "biblical" Dead Sea Scrolls are.

Equally important is the phenomenon of multiple, probably successive, recensions and rewritings of "biblical" books. For several biblical books, the LXX and the MT preserve two different recensions, and for the Pentateuch we have the systematically harmonizing recension of the SP. Yet another recension is found in the so-called *Reworked Pentateuch* manuscripts (4Q158; 4Q364-367), which contain editions of the Pentateuch characterized by harmonizations and relocations of materials, but also by additions of new text relating to, for example, the festival laws. Discussions of whether these manuscripts should be called biblical or authoritative scripture relate both to the analysis of the manuscripts and to suppositions regarding the concepts "biblical" and "authoritative." From a literary point of view, the recension in the *Reworked Pentateuch* goes one step beyond that of the SP by adding new materials, generally based on exegesis of the text. The techniques used in this recension are comparable to those used in some of the LXX recensions, for example, 3 Kingdoms and Esther. Whether these expansionist *Reworked Pentateuch* texts were biblical in the precanonical sense of authoritative depends on whether one assumes a strict boundary between texts or recensions of texts that were regarded as authoritative and those that were not.

From the perspective of the later canon, one may ask to what extent the books of the Tanak already were scriptural among the Dead Sea Scrolls. The partially reconstructed reference in 4QMMT to "the book of Moses, the books of the prophets, and David (?)" has been taken to refer to a threefold structure of scriptures, but this is only one of several possible readings, reconstructions, and interpretations of this passage. Copies of all books of the Hebrew Bible have been identified among the scrolls, with the exception of Esther (though the status of one fragment with a section of Chronicles and of another text is unclear). The quantity of preserved scrolls per book differs considerably, and one may contrast the large number of copies of the books of the Pentateuch, Isaiah, and Psalms (several of which are attested by twenty copies or more) with the small number of preserved copies (three or less) of Joshua, Judges, Kings, Proverbs, Qohelet, Ezra, and Chronicles. There are no *a priori* grounds for assuming that all the later biblical books of the Tanak were already scriptural or authoritative to the same degree. It seems that a core group of scriptures (Pentateuch, Isaiah, the Minor Prophets, and Psalms), were differently transmitted, interpreted, and granted a different degree of authority than other scriptures. For example, the textual transmission of Isaiah and the Minor Prophets is fairly stable: we have only one major recension. Also, there are pesharim interpreting those books, which indicates that the contents were seen as authoritative but in need of interpretation. In contrast, there are different recensions of Jeremiah and Ezekiel, and instead of pesharim we find parabiblical literature connected to those books. Some of the Ketuvim are extensively used in other Dead Sea Scrolls, such as the Psalms, Daniel, Proverbs, and Lamentations. Other Ketuvim, like Canticles, Ruth, Ecclesiastes, Esther, and Ezra, are not known to have been used or referred to in other texts.

Criteria that may cumulatively indicate the importance or authority that a group attached to a text include (a) the number of preserved copies of a composition, (b) the existence of commentaries on those works, (c) quotations or references to a text in other compositions, (d) the existence of translations of those texts, (e) implicit or explicit claims to authority in a work, and (f) attribution of a text to preexilic authors. Hence, it has been suggested that *Jubilees* and (some of) the books of *Enoch,* but possibly also texts like the *Aramaic Levi Document* and the

Apocryphon of Joshua, may have been authoritative scriptures for groups behind the Dead Sea Scrolls. But here, too, the question is whether one should assume a sharp distinction between scriptural and nonscriptural.

Extending Scriptures by Interpretative Rewriting

Since the 1990s, the term "parabiblical" has gained popularity in Dead Sea Scrolls studies as an umbrella term for a large variety of texts that are closely related to texts or themes of the Hebrew Bible. This category includes both those texts that were formerly described as "rewritten bible" or "biblical interpretation," and those compositions that are attributed or connected to biblical figures and that often were characterized as pseudepigraphal and apocryphal. Even though there sometimes is an overlap, as in the case of rewritings attributed to Moses or Ezekiel, these are two distinct types, and the general but vague term "parabiblical" obfuscates the differences.

The first type consists of interpretative rewritings of earlier scripture, in the form of "rewritten scripture," or as a paraphrase or retelling of either entire books, or sections of books, or even as a pastiche of different passages. These rewritings sometimes have expansions that may go back to older sources or traditions, or derive from the interpretation of the author. The best-preserved examples of the first type are the book of *Jubilees* and the *Temple Scroll,* both of which contain extensive interpretative rewritings of parts of the Torah, as well as parts that have no direct correspondence in the Torah and that may have been taken from other sources or traditions. Less well-preserved examples are the *Apocryphon of Joshua* and many other fragmentary manuscripts that deal with events from the Torah and Joshua. These include some parts of the *Genesis Apocryphon,* some of the Moses Apocrypha, notably *Words of Moses* (1Q22) and *Apocryphal Pentateuch A* (4Q368) and *B* (4Q377). A few texts are related to the books of Samuel and Kings, such as *Vision of Samuel* (a misnomer for 4Q160) or *Paraphrase of Kings* (4Q382), and to the prophets, especially the *Pseudo-Ezekiel* manuscripts. We also find works of this type relating to the books later collected as Ketuvim, for example *Apocryphal Lamentation A* (4Q179), which rewrites parts of Lamentations, and *Wiles of the Wicked Woman* (4Q184) and *Beatitudes* (4Q525; 5Q16), which are copies of one or two works closely related to the text of Proverbs 1–9.

These compositions represent different degrees and kinds of rewriting. In the case of *Jubilees* and the *Temple Scroll,* the compositions both rewrite Torah and claim to be Torah themselves. They complement the pentateuchal Torah as its valid and authoritative interpretation. For other rewritten Mosaic texts, a similar relation to the Pentateuch may be assumed but cannot be established because the texts are too fragmentary. The *Apocryphon of Joshua* is a good example of different aspects of the process of rewriting: the author tackles exegetical problems in the scriptural book of Joshua, reworks Joshua according to his own agenda (the centrality of Jerusalem and the status of the land of Israel), and provides an interpretation of the prophetic curse in Josh. 6:26. In cases like this, it is not clear whether the *Apocryphon* intended to complement or supplement the book of Joshua. In any case, the preserved manuscripts of the *Apocryphon of Joshua* outnumber those of the scriptural Joshua. On the other hand, it is not clear to what extent the extensive use and reworking of Proverbs 1–9 in 4QBeatitudes and 4QWiles of the Wicked Woman was meant as authoritative interpretation of scripture, or rather as imitation of a scriptural example.

In a few cases it is demonstrable that such rewritings of scriptures actually gained, at least in some circles, some kind of scriptural status. The quotation of Josh. 6:26 in *Testimonia* (4Q175) follows the text of the *Apocryphon of Joshua.* A series of fragmentary manuscripts called *Pseudo-Jubilees* (4Q225-227, but also 4Q217 and perhaps 4Q228) are new rewritings based on the text of *Jubilees.*

This phenomenon of interpretative rewriting sheds an interesting light on the issue of scriptures in the second and first century B.C.E. The very act of interpretation and rewriting endorses the authoritative and foundational character of "biblical" scriptures, but at the same time extends this authority to the interpretative reworking of those scriptures.

Expanding Scripture by Ascribing Traditions to Foundational Figures

Apart from new scriptures that are primarily based on interpretative rewriting of a scriptural text, there is a group of largely or entirely new compositions attributed or closely related to scriptural authors or figures. This second type is not based primarily on the text of Scripture but consists largely of a series of compositions, written in Aramaic, and ascribed to pre-Mosaic figures, from Enoch through Amram. Included in this category are several books of *Enoch,* the *Aramaic Levi Document,* the Lamech and Noah sections of the *Genesis Apocryphon,* a series of very fragmentary works that have been described as testaments of Jacob and several of his sons *(Testament of Qahat,* the *Visions of Amram,* and possibly the *New Jerusalem).* Also relevant here were compositions written in Hebrew that are attributed to Moses (especially the *Apocryphon of Moses* texts) and to Jeremiah *(Apocryphon of Jeremiah C),* and perhaps also those attributed to David (noncanonical psalms in 11Q5; the *Apocryphal Psalms* of 11Q11).

The Aramaic texts ascribed to Enoch, Noah, and the pre-Mosaic patriarchs should be considered a separate group of compositions. Here we find first-person narrative, generally with ancestral instruction, sometimes visionary reports, and, more rarely, exegetical expansions of scriptural narrative. The use of first-person narration is a feature common to other Aramaic literature (Ahiqar, Tobit) and may be regarded as a stylistic preference. The contents of these Aramaic texts suggest that some might have a pre-Maccabean origin in priestly-Levitical circles who had knowledge of Mesopotamian lore and science. They were influenced by Persian ideas and emphasize revelation through dreams and visions, as well as the transmission of ancestral traditions above or alongside the interpretation of the Scriptures. Though some of these Aramaic texts include interpretative or paraphrastic sections, the main link is with the ancestral "scriptural" figure, not with the scriptural text.

The Hebrew examples of new writings attributed or connected to Moses, Jeremiah, and David belong to a somewhat different category than the Aramaic examples. The former may be seen as foundational figures according to the functions ascribed to them in the Scriptures. All the new texts attributed to Moses belong to a Mosaic discourse in which specific interpretations of the Law were regarded as divine revelation to Moses on Sinai. Likewise, the *Apocryphon of Jeremiah C* is based on the image of Jeremiah being the leader and teacher of the nation after the destruction of the Temple.

Most of these texts have in common that their ascription to ancestral patriarchs or foundational figures may be seen as an expansion of Scripture, although only in some cases is there evidence that they achieved scriptural status in some circles. This goes for the Enochic writings, the *Aramaic Levi Document,* and perhaps the *Apocryphon of Jeremiah C,* if 2 Macc. 2:1-4 is connected to that text.

More importantly, the Dead Sea Scrolls call for a more sophisticated approach toward the phenomenon of pseudepigraphy, which ranges from no more than a purely literary device in some texts (like the *Genesis Apocryphon*) to attribution of one's traditions to ancestral figures to an authority-conferring strategy of presenting one's new interpretation of authoritative Scripture.

Expounding Scripture in Commentaries and Pesharim

Whereas rewritten texts and paraphrases are implicitly interpretative, a special category of texts makes an explicit distinction between scripture and commentary. The clearest examples are the so-called continuous pesharim, such as the *Habakkuk Pesher* and *Nahum Pesher* and the pesharim on Isaiah, some Minor Prophets, and some of the Psalms. They feature a quotation of one or more verses from a "prophetic" Scripture, a commentary on the quoted verse(s), a quotation of the next verses, its interpretation, and so on. Characteristic is the explicit introduction of the commentary by means of the term *pišrô,* "its interpretation" (or *pešer ha-dābar,* "the interpretation of the passage"), which often involves the identification of the subject of the scriptural verse with subjects that were active just before or during the author's time, or expected to become active in the near future. Other commentaries, like *Florilegium* (4Q174) and *Catena A* (4Q177), which probably are two copies of one and the same composition *Eschatological Midrash,* as well as *Melchizedek* (11Q13), have been called either midrash (on the basis of the use of the term in 4Q174), or "thematic pesharim," since they do not interpret a running scriptural text but rather select different verses which, according to the interpretation, relate to the same theme. A special case is *Ages of Creation* (or *Pesher on the Periods;* 4Q180), which includes a series of notes commenting on the text of Genesis and explaining problematic issues in the text.

Some manuscripts seem to combine rewritten scripture with implicit exegesis and commentary with explicit exegesis. This holds, for example, for *Commentary on Genesis A* (4Q252), which starts out with a rewriting of the flood story in Genesis 7–8, consisting mainly of scriptural verses and chronological additions, continues with a discussion of problematic sections of Genesis, and ends with a commentary of Jacob's blessings, including the technical *pišrô* phrase. These different kinds of interpretative writing in 4Q252 may owe to a compilation of various sources. Or they may reflect the gradual transition from implicit interpretative rewriting (down to the first century B.C.E.) to explicit commentaries, which came into existence in the first half of the first century B.C.E. However, the explicit *pišrô* (and *pešer ha-dābar*) formula is used specifically with regard to "prophetic" texts, including Psalms and Jacob's prophecies in Genesis 49, which would explain the different exegetical techniques used in the same text. In 4Q180, and probably also in the fragmentary *Exposition on the Patriarchs* (4Q464), we find a different use of the phrase *pišrô ʿal,* "interpretation concerning," as a section heading for new topics. The official title of 4Q247, *Pesher on the Apocalypse of Weeks,* is misleading in at least two aspects. First, the sparse text of the extant fragment does not use the term *pesher,* nor are there any other indications that the text is exegetical. Second, though the scheme of weeks corresponds to that also found in the *Apocalypse of Weeks,* there is no indication that the fragment rewrites or interprets that specific text.

These different forms of extending, expanding, and expounding Scripture underline how by the early second century B.C.E. at the latest Judaism had become thoroughly scripturalized, even though the borders between scripture and interpretation may have been somewhat shifting, since some interpretation itself claims revelation and hence authoritativeness. Also fluid are the transitions from interpretative rewriting to explicit commentary, and from exegesis of texts to attribution of nonscriptural materials to foundational figures. The Dead Sea Scrolls therefore illustrate various kinds of exegetical techniques, as well as different strategies for conferring authority in early Judaism.

Special attention should be given to *Jubilees,* which combines rewritten Scripture, the adaptation of other traditions, and the attribution of the text to the founding figure of Moses. More importantly, *Jubilees* is related to many other texts in the corpus. It includes material found in the oldest Enochic books and in the *Aramaic Levi Document;* it shares halakic traditions with the *Temple Scroll;* it is in its turn imitated or rewritten in the *Pseudo-Jubilees* manuscripts; and diverse texts such as the *Words of Moses* and the *Apocryphon of Jeremiah C* are dependent on it.

Interpreting the Law in Legal Works

Some interpretative works deal partly or exclusively with the interpretation of the Law of Moses. But whereas the corpus includes much legal material, only a few texts are primarily focused on legal questions. Without a doubt, the two most important legal texts are the *Temple Scroll* and the so-called *Halakic Document,* now known as MMT for *Miqṣat Maʿaśê ha-Torah,* one of the phrases in the text. Other legal texts include the legal section of the *Damascus Document,* the remnants of different *Tohorot* compositions, the Moses Apocrypha (including *Apocryphal Pentateuch A*), and compositions referred to as *Ordinances* (4Q159; 4Q513-514), *Halaka A* (4Q251) and *B* (4Q264a), and *Miscellaneous Rules* (4Q265).

The *Temple Scroll,* which is based on Deuteronomy but presented as God's word spoken in the first person at Sinai, contains the most extensive collection of legal material. It also discusses the construction of the sanctuary, its altar, and its courtyards, the festival calendar and festal sacrificial offerings; and purity laws. And it engages in a rewriting of Deuteronomy 12–23, into which are inserted the so-called Law of the King and other regulations regarding the Levites and crucifixion. The composition has been described as a utopian vision of the present age, and a polemic against Hasmonean policies and Pharisaic rulings.

MMT is as an epistolary treatise of which the central part (called B by the editors) consists of a survey of legal issues. They deal mainly with the purity of the sanctuary. The authors ("we") apparently disagree (sometimes with a direct appeal to Scripture) with either contemporary Temple practices or their opponents' views. In several cases, the points of discussion are known from rabbinic literature, where the "we" position of MMT is ascribed to the Zadokites/Sadducees and the opposite position to the Pharisees.

The publication of both texts and their subsequent study had a large impact on Scrolls studies. It became clear that the *Temple Scroll* did not fit in with the then known "sectarian" texts, and this confirmed the suspicion that the corpus contained works from different, albeit related, groups. MMT has been interpreted as a foundational document, summing up the calendrical and legal disputes with the Jerusalem priests and the Pharisees.

For the study of early Judaism, the legal texts confirm that the rabbinic descriptions of legal discussions between Sadducees and Pharisees were not anachronistic inventions but debates already current in the Hasmonean era. Also, the legal texts attest to practices that are much earlier than the rabbinic texts in which they are recorded. This goes, for example, for the *minyan* (minimum of ten men) described in *Rule of the Congregation* (1QSa), the *Rule of the Community* (1QS), and the *Damascus Document* (CD). More generally, the mere existence of written law codes in Second Temple Judaism is at odds with the Pharisaic-rabbinic rule that extrabiblical legal traditions should remain oral.

The topics under discussion in the legal texts shed light on issues that had become important in the second and first century B.C.E., such as Sabbath and purity. This holds for purity concerns in general, and for the purity of the Temple and Jerusalem in particular, an issue that may reflect a reaction to the defilement of the Temple by Antiochus Epiphanes. Typical of the purity laws included in the corpus is that they are in general more stringent than the later rabbinic purity laws. Some texts extend the concept of purity from ritual to moral issues.

Harmonizing Times and Festivals: Calendrical Documents and Annals

The corpus contains a small amount of generally badly preserved calendrical documents, most of which are actually lists. These lists include enumerations of the number of days per month, registers of the holy festivals on their respective dates in a 364-day year, registers of the priestly watches or *mišmārōt* related to this calendar, lists relating phases in the monthly revolution of the moon to corresponding dates of the 364-day year, and the so-called *'Otot* list synchronizing the six-year *mišmārōt* cycles with the seven-year *shemitah* and the forty-nine-year jubilee cycle.

In some cases calendrical lists are part of larger documents. For example, *'Otot* (4Q319) is actually the end of one of the Cave 4 copies of the *Rule of the Community* (4Q259), and a calendrical list is found at the beginning of one of the MMT manuscripts (4Q394). A special, related case is the two very fragmentary works (*Historical Texts D* and *E;* 4Q332 and 4Q333) that list historical events, including proper names, in relation to dates and priestly watches.

Virtually all the calendrical documents attest to the 364-day calendar defended in the Enochic *Book of the Luminaries* and in *Jubilees,* and implied in most other texts in the corpus — exceptions could be *Daily Prayers* (4Q503) and *Zodiology and Brontology* (4Q318). These documents are the result of exegetical activity and try to harmonize the different scriptural prescriptions for Sabbaths and dates of festivals, as well as priestly watches and larger cycles, into a coherent system. Many of the liturgical texts are based on this calendrical system, and the lists can therefore be seen as the legal basis for the priestly service and the liturgical and festal year. The difference between the 364-day calendar and the 354-day calendar known from other Jewish sources is crucial, since it implies a different festival calendar and would have provoked a major schism in early Judaism.

Performing Scripture: Liturgical and Poetical Manuscripts

Some poetical manuscripts in the corpus have explicit markers that indicate an intended liturgical or ritual use; other collections of poems lack such evidence. A large number of texts may be categorized as hymns and prayers. These include liturgies for evening and morning blessings for all days of the month, prayers for the days of the week, songs for the Sabbath sacrifice, and festival prayers. All of these texts are the oldest liturgies for fixed prayer times on record. Scholars are divided on two questions. First, whether these liturgies for fixed prayers were specifically sectarian or were rather representative of liturgies of Second Temple Judaism at large. Second, how these prayers relate to rabbinic prayer material. Because of the paleographic dating of *Words of the Luminaries*[a] (4Q504) around 150 B.C.E., and the lack of explicit sectarian terminology, it has been suggested that *Words of the Luminaries (Divre Ha-me'orot)* may plausibly be presectarian. The composition apparently utilized the same periodization of history found in the Enochic *Apocalypse of Weeks,* which may indicate a provenance in groups with affinities to the Enochic writings. Many thematic and vocabulary correspondences between the prayers in the Scrolls and rabbinic prayers have been adduced, but only very rarely are they unique. More generally, the vocabulary and character of both groups of prayers are dependent on Scripture, and specific shared features should probably be attributed to common streams of tradition rather than direct literary dependence. Even though there is no direct relation between the two corpora, the scrolls demonstrate that the fixation of prayer after Yavneh was not a new invention but the institutionalization of practices that already existed in Second Temple times.

Similar issues of comparison may be made for the *Songs for the Sabbath Sacrifice,* the *Blessings* (4Q286-290), and the hymnic material in *Mysteries*[c] (4Q301), which have been characterized as mystical due to the language of awe and mystery.

Even though the medieval Hekhalot literature attests to a different kind of mystical practice, the style of the hymns in the Hekhalot seems to go back to such Second Temple precursors.

Whereas a specific ritual is assured for the *Blessings,* the *Purification Liturgies,* and the prayers and songs with an exorcistic character, it is disputed whether, for example, the *Hodayot,* the *Bless My Soul,* and the *Noncanonical Psalms* were composed for private prayer or reading or for communal recitation. The different collections of *Hodayot* from Caves 1 and 4 stand apart in the corpus on account of the highly unique and personal songs in the middle of the large Cave 1 *Thanksgiving Scroll.* These songs have been read as autobiographical expressions of a leading figure praising God for release from affliction, for the revelation of his wonders, and for having placed hymns in his mouth to instruct the lowly. More than other hymns, they contrast God's greatness to human smallness. The suggestion that the author may be the Teacher of Righteousness mentioned in the pesharim (hence the name "Teacher Hymns") is attractive but remains hypothetical. Some *Hodayot* collections also contain community hymns in which the "I" of the hymn may refer to individual members of the group.

Whereas older scholarship generally referred only to the anthological style of the hymns and prayers, it has become clear that they are often scripturalized in multiple respects. They use scriptural language but often interpret and allude to specific passages; they sometimes use scriptural patterns but also emulate or rework specific biblical sections, such as Psalm 18 in 1QH^{a} XI and in the *Prayer of the Man of God* in *Noncanonical Psalms B* (4Q381).

Understanding All There Is: Sapiential Texts

The term "wisdom literature" is used in a general way for those texts that have several, but not necessarily all, of the following characteristics: instructional or admonitory style; practical, proverbial, or didactic advice; intellectual reflection on the order of creation, human nature, and society; a concern with the meaning of human life and fate after death; and overtly sapiential terminology. The most substantial wisdom texts in the corpus are three very different works, 4QInstruction, the *Book of Mysteries,* and *Beatitudes.* 4QInstruction combines practical advice on many different matters of life with descriptions of eschatological judgment. The work contains discourses on the predestined order of creation and the nature of human beings. It is based in part on exegesis of Genesis and displays an interest in the angelic world. The multiple levels of discourse in the text and the different topics and addressees suggest that the composition may have been a handbook for a specific group of religious teachers, who in their turn had to instruct others.

The *Book of Mysteries* comprises many diverse materials, ranging from depiction of the eschatological judgment based on interpretations of the prophets, proverbial riddles, taunts of opponents, legal discussion of Temple issues, to a Hekhalot-like hymn in 4Q301. *Beatitudes* (and *Wiles of the Wicked Woman*) can be characterized as an eschatologizing rewriting of Proverbs 1–9 and is more homogeneous than the other sapiential works.

4QInstruction, and to some extent also *Mysteries,* attest to a transformation of older wisdom traditions. These works appropriate originally non-Jewish scientific concepts (such as the horoscope and Platonic ideas about the spirit) and expand the topic of wisdom to include not only earthly but transcendent realities. The acquisition of insight depends both on the pursuit of truth (including the exegesis of Scripture) and on divine enlightenment, which allows one to have insight into transcendent secrets. One may refer to this phenomenon as the apocalypticizing of wisdom. A less speculative concern with transcendent realities, but nonetheless a concern with divine judgment, is also found in wisdom texts such as *Sapiential Work* (4Q185) and *Beatitudes.* The connection of practical and religious instruction with eschatology may have a parenetic function, but it seems to reflect the status of specific scribes or teachers as knowledgeable of everything.

Such scribal sapiential interest also explains the presence of various scientific texts in the corpus, such as 4QHoroscope (4Q186), 4QPhysiognomy (4Q561), 4QZodiology and Brontology (4Q318), and perhaps also the various astronomical texts, such as *Astronomical Enoch* and 4QLunisolar Calendar (4Q317).

The major contribution of the Dead Sea Scrolls sapiential texts is that they illustrate the merging of many different kinds of knowledge, including the appropriation of non-Jewish concepts, and the fusion of diverse literary genres. This is turn suggests the rise of a new kind of Jewish scholarship that tried to integrate all available disciplines and fields of knowledge.

Envisioning the End: Apocalypses and Other Eschatological Texts

The corpus contains a variety of texts that are in some way focused on the future. Those include many Aramaic apocalyptic and visionary texts, such as the texts assigned to *Enoch* and the *New Jerusalem* text, which may be a vision of Jacob, as well as texts related to the figure or the book of Daniel, such as *Apocryphal Daniel* (4Q246), the pseudo-Danielic compositions (4Q243-245), and perhaps the *Four Kingdoms* (4Q552, 4Q553, and 4Q553a). One may add the *Words of Michael* (4Q529, 4Q571, and 6Q23) and other small fragmentary visionary or prophetic Aramaic manuscripts. It is remarkable that most apocalyptic and visionary works are written in Aramaic, which may reflect a literary preference or a special provenance for those texts.

With the possible exception of *Vision and Interpretation* (4Q410) and *Narrative A* (4Q458), eschatological texts written in Hebrew rarely have a visionary form. Instead, there are poetic descriptions of the eschatological period, such as *Time of Righteousness* (4Q215a), *Renewed Earth* (4Q475), and *Messianic Apocalypse* (4Q521), a composition on the messianic period and resurrection, as well as rules for the congregation and blessings for the "last days" (1QSa, 1QSb). The corpus includes a series of related but different manuscripts on the eschatological war. They describe the final war between the children of light and the children of darkness, assisted by the angels and the troops of Belial, respectively, and prescribe the prayers to be said at different stages of the war. Other works, like the sapiential texts and the "Treatise of the Two Spirits" (1QS 3-4), contain eschatological sections.

These eschatological texts do not present a homogeneous worldview. For example, they do not seem to share the same messianic expectations. Three general aspects of the eschatological texts illustrate their contribution to the study of early Judaism. First, most Hebrew eschatological works are based on interpretation of Scripture, including perhaps the books of *Enoch.* For example, the rules for purity in the *War Scroll* are modeled on the prescriptions in Numbers, whereas the prayers in the scroll refer to other victories described in the Scriptures (e.g., David beating Goliath). Further, both *Time of Righteousness* and *Renewed Earth* are based on prophetic texts. Second, the fusion of descriptive and prescriptive elements in the war scrolls, 1QSa, and 1QSb — which include instructions for purity and other legal issues, as well as hymns, prayers, and blessings — suggests that these texts may have had a performative use. Third, these eschatological works attest to a series of different apocalyptic themes, such as the periodization of history, expectation of the end, communion with the heavenly world, and the eschatological war. These themes are also found in other works in and outside the corpus and may therefore be seen as reflecting a broader apocalyptic mentality.

Returning to the Law: Community Rules and Related Texts

The corpus contains several so-called community rules, the most important ones being the *Serekh ha-Yaḥad (Rule of the Community),* and especially its core as found in 1QS 5–9 and in 4Q256 and 4Q258; the so-called *Damascus Document;* and the *Serek ha-Edah (Rule of the Congregation).* Each of these documents gives rules pertaining to the entry into a specific group, the organization and officials of the group, responsibilities of the members, and organization of its meetings. The *Damascus Document* and *Rule of the Community* discuss such issues as transgressions and punishments, and they describe in some detail the aims of the groups. In general terms, these rules can be compared to other rules for ancient voluntary associations. These two large rules each contain sections not preserved in the other one. Thus, the *Damascus Document* has a large admonitory review of history and a substantial legal section, including Sabbath and purity laws. Some versions of the *Rule of the Community,* including 1QS, include a description of an annual covenant ceremony and the "Treatise on the Two Spirits," and end with a thanksgiving hymn, whereas the version preserved in 4Q259 ends with a calendrical text *(ʾOtot).*

The groups depicted in the main rules differ in various respects. The *Damascus Document* describes different groups but focuses on the congregation of those Israelite households or families who lived in cities and camps throughout the land, and who committed themselves to return to the Law of Moses as it should apply to all Israel, according to its correct interpretation. The *Rule of the Community* uses another word, *yaḥad,* to refer to groups at different locations. It never refers to women or families but only to the "men of the community." The work mentions an oath to return to the Law of Moses, stresses communal activities, emphasizes the handing over of one's property to the inspector, and describes a complex admission procedure. Both rules refer to a subgroup that aspires to a higher degree of holy perfection, but whereas this is mentioned only in passing in CD 7, the *Rule of the Community* discusses at length a real or ideal subgroup of twelve men and three priests who in some way had a higher degree of holiness. The example of the *Rule of the Congregation,* which refers to both "the congregation" and "the council of the *yaḥad,*" cautions that one cannot make an easy distinction between the congregation and the *yaḥad.*

Several manuscripts in the corpus may be directly connected to the *Damascus Document* or the *Community Rule,* due to shared organizational expressions that are not found elsewhere. Thus, for example, the term "the Community" is very rare outside of the *Rule of the Community* and the *Rule of the Congregation,* and the few other manuscripts with this term would seem to refer to the same group. This goes for several of the pesharim, for legal texts like *Miscellaneous Rules* (4Q265) and *Harvesting* (4Q284a), and for the liturgical text *Blessings,* which includes blessings and curses that are very similar to those mentioned in 1QS 2. Another document, *Rebukes of the Overseer* (4Q477), records rebukes as described both in the *Damascus Document* and the *Rule of the Community,* and mentions the *yaḥad.* The Teacher of Righteousness appears in the *Damascus Document* and has a special role in several pesharim, specifically the *Habakkuk Pesher,* which also refers to the *yaḥad.* The fragmentary manuscripts *Communal Ceremony* (4Q275) and *Rule* (5Q13), which mention the "overseer" and refer to an annual ceremony, may be connected to either of the main rules.

Taken in themselves, these different rules give an unprecedented insight into aspects of the formation, organization, practices, and beliefs of early Jewish groups or movements on the basis of their different interpretation of the Law.

The Nature and Significance of the Corpus

Apart from specific organizational expressions, the rule scrolls attest to communal ritual, disagreements about calendrical matters, legal rulings with regard to everyday practices, a cosmological and ethical dualistic worldview, apocalyptic or eschatological expectations, and views on Scripture and authority. Many other texts in the corpus reflect the same or similar interests or views, sometimes expressed in identical formulations. For example, the introduction of 1QS is directly connected to 1QM since both oppose the "sons of light" to the "sons of darkness." Or, with hindsight, now that we know all the Cave 4 calendrical texts, it is easy to recognize how both the *Damascus Document* and the *Hymn of the Maskil* at the end of the *Rule of the Community* put forth a 364-day calendar, a point which is made even more explicit by the inclusion of the *'Otot* in one of the *Rule of the Community* manuscripts. A third example — in various compositions, including the two rules — is the attribution to the *maśkîl* of laws, hymns, and instructions, which probably indicates that this sage was to recite or teach them. In other cases, connections between texts consist of multiple shared locutions, such as those between the *Apocryphon of Jeremiah* and the *Damascus Document.*

Such connections illustrate that many works in the corpus are interlinked and should be related to a current in early Judaism that comprised the movements described in the *Damascus Document* and the *Rule of the Community,* and probably also to the circles responsible for *Jubilees* and the *Temple Scroll.* It is a challenge for scholarship to unravel the precise relationships among different texts and groups. However, the different versions of both the *Damascus Document* and the *Rule of the Community,* and the likelihood of different layers in those works, show that within this current the different movements and their compositions were in flux and that they changed and influenced one another. Likewise, manuscripts of other compositions may have been edited or revised in order to appropriate them, or to adjust them to the interests of specific copyists or movements, a phenomenon which can be seen, for example, in the Cave 4 versions of the *Aramaic Levi Document.*

There is no evidence that before their deposit in the caves all the manuscripts of the corpus were together as a single collection. Nor can one know, for that matter, whether all those manuscripts that were together at a certain time in the same place were actively read and studied or were merely deposited. Even the status of Cave 4 — as a library, repository, temporary place of concealment, or perhaps even a genizah — is unclear. And we do not know the precise historical events that led to their deposit in different caves near Qumran. But from the contents of the manuscripts, we may conclude that the corpus is not a random reflection of all kinds of available Jewish texts of the time but representative of a specific current in early Judaism.

Two vital perspectives are constitutive of the corpus. First, the corpus as a whole — from *Jubilees* and the *Temple Scroll* to the pesharim, legal texts, and Moses apocrypha — attests to a variety of strategies for interpreting Scripture, ranging from reworking and various degrees of rewriting, to expansion with new scriptures, exegesis, and commentary. Some texts in the corpus imply, others indicate explicitly, that the correct interpretation of Scripture is attained by exegesis, which may be confirmed by divine revelation of those things that hitherto had been hidden (i.e., not included in the Scriptures). The authority of interpreted Scripture may also go beyond the traditional "rewritten Scripture" texts and hold true for hymns and prayers like the *Hodayot.* For the study of the corpus, this perspective demands a more sophisticated approach in differentiating between the Scriptures and other writings, between revelation and interpretation.

Second, by and large the corpus represents a legal interpretive tradition that can be related to both *Jubilees* and the *Temple Scroll* (notwithstanding differences between those two works). The most decisive element is the 364-day calendar as the basis for the religious festival calendar, which is either stated explicitly or implied in a variety of texts of the corpus (e.g., *Jubilees, Temple Scroll, David's Compositions* in the Cave 11 *Psalms Scroll, Commentary on Genesis A, Songs of the Sabbath Sacrifice,* as well as a variety of calendrical texts). It is moot to what extent this 364-day festival calendar was actually designed on the basis of scriptural exegesis, or was practiced in some form in pre-Seleucid times. In both cases, the adherence to a 364-day calendar, as opposed to the one observed in the Temple, links the different circles and movements represented in the corpus.

From this perspective, and with the limited undisputed historical data we have, it makes most sense to study the corpus primarily as the product of a specific early Jewish current consisting of different interlinked groups and movements with a common interpretative approach to Scripture and a shared legal tradition.

BIBLIOGRAPHY

Alexander, Philip. 2006. *The Mystical Texts: Songs of the Sabbath Sacrifice and Related Manuscripts.* London: T&T Clark.

Collins, John J. 2002. *Apocalypticism in the Dead Sea Scrolls.* London: Routledge.

———. 2007. "The Nature and Aims of the Sect Known from the Dead Sea Scrolls." In *Flores Florentino: Dead Sea Scrolls and Other Early Jewish Studies in Honour of Florentino García Martínez.* Ed. Anthony Hilhorst et al. Leiden: Brill, 31-52.

Duhaime, Jean. 2004. *The War Texts: 1QM and Related Manuscripts.* London: T&T Clark.

Falk, Daniel K. 2007. *The Parabiblical Texts: Strategies for Extending the Scriptures among the Dead Sea Scrolls.* London: T&T Clark.

Flint, Peter W., and James C. VanderKam, eds. 1998-1999. *The Dead Sea Scrolls after Fifty Years: A Comprehensive Assessment.* 2 vols. Leiden: Brill.

García Martínez, Florentino. 1996. *The Dead Sea Scrolls Translated.* 2d ed. Grand Rapids: Eerdmans.

———. 2008. "¿Sectario, no-sectario, o qué? Problemas de una taxonomía correcta de los textos qumránicos." *RevQ* 23/91: 383-94.

Goff, Matthew J. 2007. *Discerning Wisdom: The Sapiential Literature of the Dead Sea Scrolls.* Leiden: Brill.

Jokiranta, Jutta. 2005. "Identity on a Continuum: Constructing and Expressing Sectarian Social Identity in Qumran Serakhim and Pesharim." Dissertation, University of Helsinki.

Lange, Armin, with Ulrike Mittman-Richert. 2002. "Annotated List of the Texts from the Judaean Desert Classified by Content and Genre." In *The Texts from the Judaean Desert: Indices and an Introduction to the Discoveries in the Judaean Desert Series.* Ed. Emanuel Tov. Oxford: Clarendon, 115-64.

Lim, Timothy H. 2002. *Pesharim.* Sheffield: Sheffield Academic Press.

Parry, Donald, and Emanuel Tov, eds. 2004-2005. *The Dead Sea Scrolls Reader.* 6 vols. Leiden: Brill.

Reed, Stephen A. 2007. "Find-Sites of the Dead Sea Scrolls." *DSD* 14: 199-221.

Schiffman, Lawrence H. 2008. *The Courtyards of the House of the Lord: Studies on the Temple Scroll.* Leiden: Brill.

———, and James C. VanderKam, eds. 2000. *Encyclopedia of the Dead Sea Scrolls.* 2 vols. New York: Oxford University Press.

Tov, Emanuel. 2004. *Scribal Practices and Approaches Reflected in the Texts Found in the Judean Desert.* Leiden: Brill.

Ulrich, Eugene. 1999. *The Dead Sea Scrolls and the Origins of the Bible.* Grand Rapids: Eerdmans.

Vermes, Geza. 1997. *The Complete Dead Sea Scrolls in English.* New York: Lane.

White Crawford, Sidnie. 2008. *Rewriting Scriptures in Second Temple Times.* Grand Rapids: Eerdmans.

Early Jewish Literature Written in Greek

Katell Berthelot

A large number and great variety of early Jewish works were composed in Greek, but many of them survive only in excerpts quoted by church fathers. Our knowledge of Jewish thought and literature in the Greek-speaking Diaspora therefore depends to a large extent on the care with which Christian authors and scribes quoted and copied their Jewish sources. Yet the selective interests and apologetic agendas of the Christian transmitters means that they handed on only what was of use to them. These works not only enriched Judaism but also engaged Hellenism. Taken together, they demonstrate that Jews were able to embrace several aspects of Hellenistic culture while maintaining their Jewish identity in a creative, critical, and at times even subversive appropriation of Greek literary genres, mythological figures, and philosophical concepts. Many of these works take their inspiration from biblical traditions and attempt to solve exegetical problems or else refashion them. Others celebrate the superiority of Judaism over pagan religions in an attempt to strengthen the identity of their Jewish readerships.

The Nature of the Corpus

Several Greek texts will be set aside here, either because their original language was Hebrew or Aramaic (e.g., 1 Maccabees and Tobit), because their Jewish origin is uncertain (e.g., Thallus and Theophilus, who were probably pagan writers), because they have been significantly altered or perhaps even composed by Christians (e.g., *3 Baruch, 4 Baruch, Testament of Abraham*), or because their original language of composition is uncertain (e.g., *2 Enoch, Life of Adam and Eve*). The decision to put aside Greek translations of texts originally written in Hebrew or Aramaic means that we will not deal with the Septuagint as such. We will, however, discuss writings in the Septuagint that were composed in Greek and have occasion to emphasize that many Jewish authors writing in Greek used the Septuagint and were influenced by its terminology.

Jewish writings composed in Greek are not the only documents to qualify as Hellenistic Jewish literature or Judeo-Hellenistic literature. Every piece of Jewish literature produced during the Hellenistic and early Roman periods may be labeled "Hellenistic" regardless of the language in which it was written. For this reason, "Hellenistic" is too vague a term, except as a chronological label for the period extending from the conquests of Alexander the Great in the fourth century B.C.E. to the end of the first century B.C.E. It is also somewhat problematic: for those who think that "authentic" Judaism necessarily expressed itself in Hebrew or Aramaic, the term "Hellenistic" carries strong pejorative connotations. More to the point, Hellenism was itself a mingling of different cultures, that of the Greco-Macedonians and that of the Eastern peoples whom they conquered. To single out some Jewish texts written in Greek as "Hellenized" implies that Hellenism and Judaism are two different and intrinsically antagonist cultural phenomena, a view that is certainly advocated by the author of 2 Maccabees but that does not necessarily reflect the historical reality of that time. The relationship between Greek and Jewish culture was far more complex.

Since some of the relevant texts adapt distinctively Greek genres, such as tragedy (Ezekiel the Tragedian) and epic poetry (Theodotus), one might well speak of Greek literature that is Jewish instead of Jewish literature written in Greek. When the latter expression is used, the focus is laid right from the start on the Jewish character of this literature, implying that the linguistic dimension is secondary. But how are we to define Jewish literature in antiquity? What makes an ancient text Jewish? Scholars have traditionally appealed to two criteria: (1) content based on biblical tradition or containing distinctively Jewish themes or terminology; (2) the Jewishness of the author, which may be attested by reliable external sources or inferred from his name or from the topic (which takes us back to the first criterion). These criteria have their limits in some cases. The *Sentences* of Pseudo-Phocylides offers a good example. For centuries this text was regarded as an original composition of Phocylides, a sixth-century-B.C.E. Greek poet, and not as a Jewish text. It was only in the sixteenth century that Joseph Scaliger pointed up its Jewish origin. The content is not so distinctively Jewish as to allow the reader to identify its author as a Jew. This interesting example should warn us that a Greek text attributed to a Greek philosopher or historian may be a Jewish text. Not all Jewish literature is "obviously Jewish."

Due to a lack of information, we must exclude from the corpus texts written by Jews who either had no commitment to their cultural heritage and religious tradition, or who chose to express themselves on topics that had little or nothing to do with the characteristic features of Judaism. Conversely, we will mention in passing authors who are not Jewish but who excerpted Jewish writings (e.g., Alexander Polyhistor) or who mentioned Jews and Judaism in a way that invited a response from early Jewish authors (Manetho, Apion).

One more reason to be cautious is that nearly all the Jewish texts written in Greek have been transmitted to us through Christian channels. Moreover, some of the church fathers — Clement of Alexandria and Eusebius, in particular — depended on Alexander Polyhistor, a Greek historian active during the first century B.C.E. The evidence we have is thus indirect, and it should not been taken for granted that we have the *ipsissima verba* of the Jewish authors whose works are now lost. What is more, the church fathers who quoted early Jewish writers such as Aristobulus, Eupolemus, and Artapanus did not attempt to preserve Jewish literature as such. They were looking for proofs of the antiquity of biblical revelation, in order to respond to pagan critics such as Celsus and Porphyry. What they ultimately wanted to show was that Christianity was not a new cult but a respectable religion with very ancient roots, even older than Greek civilization itself. Since Jewish authors had taken pains to demonstrate the antiquity of the Jewish people and the influence Moses exercised on Homer, Pythagoras, Plato, and others, their writings represented a providential pool of arguments for the church fathers. In Josephus, they also valued references to events contemporary with Jesus' life and the view that the Jewish defeat in the First Revolt was a punishment for the sins of the Jewish people, the Christian interpretation of what Josephus wrote being that the Jews had sinned in rejecting Jesus. The case of Philo is different, since many church fathers sincerely admired his work and took inspiration from his allegorical exegesis. Nevertheless, they used Jewish literature written in Greek with their own agenda in mind, an agenda that was clearly apologetic. They frequently manipulated the works they were quoting, either by omitting the context or by modifying the text. In short, the preservation and transmission of early Jewish literature written in Greek is itself problematic. This, in turn, helps explain why so many of the texts rewrite, explicate, or refer to the Bible: the corpus itself reflects to a great extent the church fathers' selective interests.

The Use of Biblical Traditions

Most early Jewish works composed in Greek that have come down to us deal with biblical topics. Obviously, in the case of works that survive only in fragments, we do not know exactly what topics were dealt with in the sections that have not been preserved. At any rate, the evidence we have looks roughly as follows: ten works deal partly or exclusively with the book of Genesis and eight with the book of Exodus; one is based on a story from the book of Judges; two refer in some way to the history of the kings of Judah (roughly 2 Samuel through 2 Kings); one is based on the book of Jonah; and two retell the story of Job. The works of Philo and Josephus, which are particularly long and well preserved, deal with a greater variety of biblical texts: the whole Pentateuch and even, in the case of Josephus, most of the books eventually included in the Masoretic canon, plus a few others.

Writings Based on Genesis

Among the Jewish writers who wrote about Genesis, Demetrius probably comes first. He evokes the episode of Isaac's sacrifice, the fate of Jacob, his two wives and his twelve sons, and the story of Joseph, focusing on chronological issues (frgs. 1 and 2). Then we have Artapanus, who recalls Abraham's descent to Egypt, mentions that he taught Pharaoh astrology, and retells the story of Joseph, attributing to him agricultural reform as well as the invention of measures (frgs. 1 and 2).

Other creative rewritings of the Genesis account include fragments of two authors known through Polyhistor: Cleodemus and Pseudo-Eupolemus. Cleodemus freely elaborates upon Gen. 25:1-4, which lists Abraham's offspring by his wife Keturah. He imagines that two sons of Abraham helped Heracles fight Antaeus, and that one of them, called Aphran, even gave him his daughter in marriage. Pseudo-Eupolemus, who probably was a Samaritan, and who seems to have used Berossus' *Babyloniaca,* focuses on Abraham's discovery of astrology and astronomy, a science that he taught to the Phoenicians. He further refers to the war Abraham waged to free his nephew Lot, to the way he was welcomed in the sanctuary located on Mt. Gerizim (hence the identification of Pseudo-Eupolemus as a Samaritan), and to his encounter with Melchizedek. Like Artapanus, Pseudo-Eupolemus also mentions Abraham's stay in Egypt and says that he taught astrology and other sciences to the Egyptian priests. The first discovery of astrology is said to go back to Enoch, whereas the Babylonians attributed it to Belus and the Greeks to Atlas.

From a completely different perspective, the exegete and philosopher Aristobulus treats the significance of the Sabbath, which he connects to the creation account in Genesis 1 rather than to the liberation from Egypt, as in Deuteronomy 5. The epic poet Philo deals with the Binding of Isaac in Genesis 22 (frgs. 1 and 2), evidently construing it as a ritual that was pleasing to God. He also mentions the patriarchs Abraham, Isaac, Jacob, and Joseph (frg. 3). The epic poet Theodotus focuses especially on the story of Dinah and the vengeance against Shechem (Genesis 34), at least in the forty-seven lines that have come down to us from Eusebius, who took his excerpts from Alexander Polyhistor.

Philo of Alexandria deals at length with the book of Genesis in several of his works, especially in the allegorical commentary and in his *Questions and Answers on Genesis.* Josephus rewrites Genesis at the beginning of his *Jewish Antiquities.* Finally, the anonymous work entitled *Joseph and Aseneth* tells the story of the conversion of Aseneth, the daughter of an Egyptian priest, to Judaism, and of her marriage to the patriarch Joseph. Other texts allude here and there to characters or episodes from the book of Genesis — for instance, 4 Maccabees 13:12 and 16:20 refer to the *Aqedah* — but these matters do not constitute the main topic of the book.

Writings Based on Exodus

The book of Exodus is well represented too, sometimes in the same works. Demetrius addresses chronological as well as exegetical issues concerning the exodus (frgs. 3-5). Artapanus rewrites not only the story of Joseph but also that of Moses, whom he presents as the teacher of Orpheus and the inventor of several branches of learning, including philosophy. According to Artapanus, Moses was a great cultural benefactor who gave Egypt its political and religious institutions. Artapanus also retells the story of the exodus.

Eupolemus (frg. 1) writes that Moses was the first wise man as well as the first lawgiver and that he invented the alphabet and gave it to the Jews, who then passed it down to the Phoenicians, who in turn taught it to the Greeks. Aristobulus tries to explain some anthropomorphisms in the book of Exodus, such as the expression "the hand of God" (frg. 2), and addresses the issue of the date of the Passover (frg. 1).

A certain Ezekiel wrote a whole tragedy based on the story of the Exodus, in which he recalls the events from Moses' birth until the destruction of the Egyptian army. Fragment 16 mentions the arrival of the Hebrews at Elim (Exod. 15:27), and fragment 17 describes the extraordinary bird known as the phoenix. The Wisdom of Solomon also deals at length with the story of the exodus and the fate of the Egyptians, in order to demonstrate the perfection of God's justice.

Philo of Alexandria probably examined every verse of the book of Exodus in his *Questions and Answers on Exodus,* most of which is now lost. He also comments on the exodus in his *Life of Moses* and in several passages throughout his corpus. Josephus rewrites Exodus in the *Jewish Antiquities* and also deals with the historical accuracy of the biblical account in his apologetic book *Against Apion,* in which he tries to refute slanderous accounts of the origins of the Jewish people.

To this list one may add the *Letter of Aristeas* and 3 Maccabees, insofar as the biblical story of the exodus constitutes an implicit background for both. However, apart from very limited references, the exodus is not explicitly dealt with in these two works, which are concerned with more recent "historical" events.

Writings Based on Other Biblical Books

The other books of the Torah — Leviticus, Numbers, and Deuteronomy — were apparently given much less attention, but this is probably a misleading picture. The church fathers who quoted Jewish authors were not interested in their interpretation of specific commandments but were looking for testimonies about the patriarchs — hence their interest in passages from Genesis and the beginning of Exodus. However, the Wisdom of Solomon (chap. 12) alludes to specific passages from Deuteronomy (and perhaps from Joshua) that refer to the fate of the Canaanites. The works that deal most extensively with Leviticus, Numbers, and Deuteronomy are Philo's *On the Special Laws* and Josephus' *Jewish Antiquities* (3.208–4.331).

Occasionally, other biblical books inspired works written in Greek. Demetrius' work was actually entitled *Concerning the Kings in Judea,* and the sixth fragment is a chronological summary of Israel's history based on material from 2 Kings. One of Eupolemus' works is also known as *Concerning the Kings in Judea.* Fragments 2 to 4, which refer to another book by Eupolemus entitled *Concerning the Prophecy of Elijah,* rely on the Deuteronomistic History in general, especially 2 Samuel though 2 Kings, and perhaps Jeremiah as well. Eupolemus (frg. 5) also attempted chronological calculations, from Adam to the reign of Demetrius I Soter (162-150 B.C.E.). He seems to have been followed by Justus of Tiberias, who apparently wrote a *Chronicle of Jewish Kings* (from Moses to Agrippa II), perhaps a comprehensive world chronicle, which was used by later Christian chroniclers but has not survived. In his *Jewish Antiquities,* Josephus rewrites the history of the Jewish people from Adam to the time of Nero and therefore uses a great diversity of biblical books, including ones written in the Hellenistic period like Daniel and Esther. He also uses Jewish books that were not included in the rabbinic canon, such as the *Letter of Aristeas* and 1 Maccabees.

Among the Jewish authors quoted by the church fathers is a certain Aristeas, often called "the Exegete" to distinguish him from the narrator of the *Letter of Aristeas.* He wrote the book *On the Jews* and summarized the story of Job, probably at the end of his account of Genesis (since Job is presented as a son of Esau). The pseudepigraphic *Testament of Job* rewrites more extensively the story of this pious character, presenting him as a convert who purifies a nearby temple from its idolatrous cult and as a consequence is persecuted by Satan. Finally, two Jewish synagogal sermons originally written in Greek and wrongly attributed to Philo have been transmitted to us in an Armenian translation. The first one is based on the book of Jonah, the second on the story of Samson in the book of Judges.

Writings with Little or No Basis in Biblical Tradition

Before we turn to a different aspect of Jewish literature written in Greek, a few words should be said about the works that do not evoke biblical characters and topics in an explicit or significant way. To this category belong several pseudepigrapha: the Pseudo-Orphic verses, Pseudo-Hecataeus, the Jewish *Sibylline Oracles,* and Pseudo-Phocylides. To this group we may add the *Letter of Aristeas,* which is not a pseudepigraph *stricto sensu,* since no famous Greek writer named Aristeas is known to us, but which pretends to be written by a Greek instead of a Jew. That no reference to the Bible should be found in texts purportedly written by non-Jews comes as no surprise. However, there are biblical expressions or implicit references to biblical texts in works like the *Sibylline Oracles* and the *Sentences* of Pseudo-Phocylides. Sometimes explicit references can be found too, as in the *Letter of Aristeas,* in which the dietary laws of Leviticus 11 are openly discussed along with other biblical and Jewish notions. But even in the case of the *Letter of Aristeas,* the topic of the work does not come from a biblical book. Other works that do not have their point of departure in biblical tradition include those that deal with religious persecutions (2, 3, and 4 Maccabees), with Jewish history during the Hellenistic and Roman periods (Philo's *In Flaccum* and *Legatio ad Gaium,* Justus of Tiberias' history of the Jewish war, Josephus' *Jewish War* and the final part of his *Jewish Antiquities*), and with apologetics (Josephus' *Against Apion*).

The Literary Genres Represented

Jewish texts composed in Greek employ a great diversity of literary genres. The texts can be classified most broadly as poetry or prose. To the first category belong Philo the Epic Poet, Theodotus, Ezekiel the Tragedian, the *Sibylline Oracles,* Pseudo-Orpheus and other forged verses of Greek poets, Pseudo-Phocylides, and the Wisdom of Solomon. To the second belong Demetrius, Artapanus, Aristobulus, the *Letter of Aristeas,* Eupolemus, Pseudo-Eupolemus, Aristeas the Exegete, 2 Maccabees, Pseudo-Hecataeus, the Prologue to Ben Sira, Cleodemus Malchus,

3 Maccabees, Philo of Alexandria, Justus of Tiberias, Josephus, *Joseph and Aseneth,* 4 Maccabees, the *Testament of Job,* and the synagogal sermons *On Jonas* and *On Samson.* These texts can be further classified according to literary genre, even though one work may blend together several genres. The *Letter of Aristeas,* for instance, is a good example of the Hellenistic taste for *poikilia* — literary and stylistic diversity within a single work.

Prose Works Dealing with the Past

Several Jewish works composed in Greek are prose literature about the past, a rather loose category that includes genres such as chronography, historiography, and ethnography but also historical fiction *(Joseph and Aseneth).* Several authors and texts belong to this group: Demetrius, Artapanus, the *Letter of Aristeas,* Aristeas the Exegete, Eupolemus, Pseudo-Eupolemus, Cleodemus Malchus, Pseudo-Hecataeus, 2 Maccabees, 3 Maccabees, Philo's *In Flaccum* and *Legatio ad Gaium,* Justus of Tiberius, Josephus' *Jewish War* and *Jewish Antiquities,* and *Joseph and Aseneth.* The term "history" has completely different meanings from one text to another. In several cases, history means biblical history, and the work may not look like history at all to the modern reader, who would classify it either as rewritten Bible (a rather anachronistic label) or as midrashic literature. However, these ancient writers certainly thought that they were writing history. Moreover, when dealing either with biblical history or with events more or less contemporaneous with the author, many texts contain sometimes glaring inaccuracies and frequently describe miracles and interventions by angels, so that the distinction between historiography and legend is blurred. Obviously, ancient texts should not be judged according to modern historiographic standards, especially given the variety of genres represented, from the nearly classical historiography exemplified by Josephus' *Jewish War,* to the very creative rewriting of Exodus by Artapanus, to the highly fictional story told in 3 Maccabees.

Sapiential and Parenetic Works

Sapiential and parenetic literature comprise a second group of texts, to which the following works belong: Prologue to Ben Sira, Pseudo-Phocylides, Wisdom of Solomon, *Testament of Job,* 4 Maccabees, and the synagogal sermons *On Jonas* and *On Samson.* Once again, nearly every text belongs to a specific subgenre, such as gnomic poetry (Pseudo-Phocylides), sermon, testament, and so on. The Prologue to the Wisdom of Ben Sira, written by Ben Sira's grandson, is not a sapiential work in itself but merely introduces the Greek translation of Ben Sira's ethical teaching, which closely resembles the biblical book of Proverbs. The Wisdom of Solomon is also strongly reminiscent of Proverbs (especially Proverbs 8) but is much more concerned with the fate of the righteous after death. 4 Maccabees can be considered both a diatribe and a panegyric, but it aims at religious edification. The work may have been delivered orally at some unknown commemorative festival.

Although most Jewish texts written in Greek deal with biblical traditions, there are very few exegetical works. Demetrius addresses the origin of the weapons held by the Israelites in the desert (frg. 5); because they departed from Egypt unarmed, the question of how they acquired weapons naturally presented itself. Similarly, in his *Jewish Antiquities* Josephus implicitly or explicitly deals with exegetical problems. But in neither case is the prime focus of the work on exegesis as such. Rather, the use of scriptural material for the purpose of historiography prompts the writer to analyze problematic aspects of the biblical text. In contrast, Aristobulus and Philo focus on the explanation of the biblical text as such and read the texts at different levels, both literally and symbolically or allegorically.

Philosophy

Philosophical treatises in the strict sense of the term are even rarer. Philo of Alexandria is the only early Jewish author known to have written whole treatises dedicated to philosophical questions (e.g., *De Aeternitate Mundi* and *Quod Omnis Probus Liber Sit*). The use of philosophical concepts or vocabulary in exegetical treatises such as Aristobulus' work, or in sapiential or parenetic texts such as the Wisdom of Solomon and 4 Maccabees, does not allow us to characterize these works as philosophical treatises *stricto sensu.*

Apology

There are at least two Jewish apologetic works written in Greek, Philo's *Hypothetica* (preserved only in part in Eusebius' *Praeparatio Evangelica*), and Josephus' *Against Apion.* However, there are many apologetic passages in the rest of Philo's and Josephus' works. Furthermore, Jewish works written in Greek often emphasize the superiority of Judaism over Greek culture and are therefore not devoid of apologetic overtones.

Autobiography

Josephus produced a work belonging to yet another literary genre, the *Life,* which is the fullest surviving example of Roman autobiography before Augustine's *Confessions.* It was appended to the *Jewish Antiquities* and was often read as an integral part of the latter but nevertheless remains an early example of personal memoir.

Epic Poetry and Drama

Epic poetry is represented by Philo the Epic Poet and Theodotus. Other poetic texts belong to different categories. The *Sibylline Oracles,* for instance, represent a specific type of oracular poetry. Finally, we have one Jewish tragedy on the exodus, written by an Egyptian Jew named Ezekiel who wrote in Alexandria in the middle of the second century B.C.E. He wrote his play in iambic trimeters, the standard meter used in Greek drama. He relied on the Septuagint but introduced several interesting haggadic embellishments. The most famous and debated scene has Moses report a dream that he had in which he was enthroned in heaven. His drama was certainly performed for a Jewish audience, perhaps in a synagogue.

The Influence and Reshaping of Greek Ideas

In most cases, the Jewish authors writing in Greek show a great familiarity with Greek literary themes and ideas, not only from the classical period but also from the Hellenistic age. This is especially true of the poetic texts. Theodotus uses Homeric expressions in a very skillful way, so that the fight of Simeon and Levi against Shechem and Hamor is reminiscent of Homeric battle scenes. In particular, the image of Shechem on his knees, clutching at the knees of Levi, recalls the image of Lycaon clutching the knees of Achilles, who slays him (*Iliad* 21.65). But Theodotus also uses non-Homeric terms that occur in Hellenistic epic poetry. Philo the Epic Poet's language is notably obscure, and his style has been characterized as pretentious, but it is actually quite typical of this form of Hellenistic epic. Pseudo-Phocylides was clever enough for his dactylic hexameters written in the old Ionic dialect to be considered authentic for many centuries.

Not only were Jewish authors writing in Greek able to imitate the styles and literary models of well-known Greek poets and tragedians, but they were also very familiar with Greek mythology, historiography, and philosophy. The Jewish "historians" were able to connect biblical figures to Greek, Babylonian, and Egyptian divine or heroic figures. For instance, Pseudo-Eupolemus identifies Bel with Cronos and presents him as the grandfather of Canaan, whom he considers the ancestor of the Phoenicians. He also equates Atlas with Enoch. In the *De Praemiis et Poenis* (23), Philo of Alexandria writes that Noah and Deucalion are the same person. At the beginning of his *Jewish Antiquities,* Josephus allusively establishes a relationship between the Nephilim (Gen. 6:4) and the giants, probably with reference to Hesiod's *Theogony* (*Ant.* 1.73). This is not unparalleled in Hebrew or Aramaic literature; both *1 Enoch* (10:2) and *Jubilees* (5:6) implicitly link the Watchers (the angels who mated with women) to the Titans bound in Tartarus. Josephus also endeavors to compare biblical chronologies with those of other cultures.

Although Justus of Tiberias' work has not been preserved, he seems to have made use of the Hellenistic universal chronicles even more intensively than Josephus did. Josephus himself was inspired by Greek precursors to a considerable extent, and he mastered the conventions of Greek historiography. He seems to have been particularly influenced by Thucydides and Dionysius of Halicarnassus. Before Josephus, Jewish authors who produced historiographical works or historical fiction, such as Eupolemus and the author of 3 Maccabees, also displayed great ability in imitating the language used in official Hellenistic and Roman documents.

Greek philosophy was also relatively well known by several Jewish authors, even if they generally did not write philosophical treatises. Aristobulus is introduced by Clement of Alexandria as a Peripatetic philosopher (*Stromateis* 1.15.72.4), whereas the fragments quoted show that he was well acquainted with Stoic allegorical readings of Homer and with Pythagorean theories of numbers. Philo's command of Greek philosophy and of the debates among the different philosophical schools of his time is remarkable and ranks far beyond that of any other Jewish author writing in Greek. Yet the way in which the author of 4 Maccabees freely presents Stoic notions such as the mastery of reason over the passions in Jewish garb also shows a familiarity with Hellenistic philosophical teachings.

In short, Jewish texts written in Greek are especially interesting for their complex intertextual relationship with biblical or Jewish literature on the one hand and with Greek literature on the other. Jewish authors had a rather good knowledge of Greek literature and philosophy, and even quoted Greek texts along with biblical ones to illustrate a specific point. Their efforts to adapt biblical narratives to Greek literary forms such as poetry and drama also led to significant literary achievements. Thus, Hellenistic culture was also the culture of these Jewish authors, especially in the case of Aristobulus, Theodotus, Pseudo-Phocylides, and Philo. It was *theirs,* even if not in the same way as biblical traditions were. Obviously, Jewish culture had its own integrity, whereas Greek culture was originally foreign to Judaism. But in Jewish authors writing in Greek, we may indeed speak of Greek-Jewish culture because both cultures were closely intertwined. The use of the Greek language was not a mere stopgap to make up for a deficient knowledge of Hebrew or Aramaic but an intrinsic part of the identity and worldview of early Jewish authors. And since words do not convey meanings in a neutral way, even the simplest statement of Jewish beliefs and customs in Greek took on a slightly different meaning than one formulated in Hebrew or Aramaic and gave birth to a different kind of Judaism. This is not to say that early Jewish writings composed in Greek did not share common themes or characteristics with their counterparts in Hebrew or Aramaic. A closer look at the issues tackled by the former will help us evaluate their connections with the latter.

Some Important Themes

Regardless of their literary genre, all early Jewish works composed in Greek convey a religious message at one level or another. Even Josephus' *Jewish War* contains considerable theological interpretation, and Philo's arguments against the rationality of animals in *De Animalibus,* to cite but one example, have an implicit biblical background: the first chapters of Genesis, which establish the superiority of human beings over animals. So there is no "profane" Jewish literature written in Greek, even if many texts perform functions besides religious edification and even aim at entertaining their audience. Humor, pleasure, aesthetics, polemics, and religious or moral instruction are not mutually exclusive goals.

Jews and Foreign Rulers

Beyond this general statement, several key issues can be emphasized. First, a strikingly recurrent theme of Jewish literature written in Greek consists in reflections about the relationship between the king or the emperor and his Jewish subjects. It represents a major topic in the *Letter of Aristeas,* 2 Maccabees, 3 Maccabees, Philo's *In Flaccum* and *Legatio ad Gaium,* Josephus' *Jewish War* and part of his *Jewish Antiquities.* It also appears, though to a lesser extent, in 4 Maccabees. All these works convey a certain vision of what a good king or emperor should be. The good monarch is the one who protects the Jews and grants them the right to live according to their ancestral laws and customs. In the *Letter of Aristeas,* the king even bows down in front of the Mosaic law and gives orders for the banquet to be prepared according to Jewish dietary laws. Moreover, he is willing to take advice on how to rule from the Jewish sages who come from Jerusalem. In works that describe a historical or fictional religious persecution, either perpetrated or only planned — Antiochus IV in 2 Maccabees and 4 Maccabees, Ptolemy IV in 3 Maccabees, Ptolemy VI in Josephus, *Against Apion* 2.51-55, Caligula, and Flaccus — a negative portrait of the ruler is drawn that helps to define what a good and just sovereign should be. In many instances, the monarch or his representatives repents of his wicked ways and recognizes the greatness of the God of Israel. This is the case with Heliodorus and Antiochus IV in 2 Maccabees and with Ptolemy IV in 3 Maccabees. The alternative scenario is the death of the impious ruler, as in the case of Flaccus and Caligula. However, a quite different picture emerges from Josephus' writings, due to his perspective on the First Revolt and his position as a protégé of the Flavians. In the *Jewish War,* he is at pains to describe Vespasian and Titus in a positive light, even if he is not as uncritical as some commentators have thought. In the *Antiquities,* he also insists on the "privileges" granted to the Jews by the Roman senate and the Roman emperors, who generally allowed the Jews to live according to their ancestral traditions. In this respect, Josephus' conception of the just ruler is similar to that of his predecessors from Alexandria.

Another leitmotiv in these texts is the Jews' faithfulness to the king. It is stressed again and again that the Jews are loyal subjects. According to these texts, the normal or ideal relationship between Jews and Hellenistic or Roman rulers is one of mutual trust and collaboration: the king protects the Jews and grants them the right to live according to their laws, at least in certain matters, and the Jews serve the king, pray for his welfare and that of his kingdom, dedicate *proseuchai* (houses of prayers) to him and his family, and even offer sacrifices at the Jerusalem Temple on his behalf. The same theme also appears in works composed in Hebrew and Aramaic, such as Daniel, Esther, and 1 Maccabees. Yet these works tend to depict non-Jewish sovereigns in a harsher light than do the Jewish texts written in Greek, and to present a less optimistic vision of the relationship between Jews and foreign rulers. There is no Hebrew or Aramaic counterpart of the *Letter of Aristeas.* This fact likely owes to the different ways in which Ptolemaic and Seleucid rule were experienced by Jews in Eretz Israel and in the Diaspora.

Jews and Non-Jews

A second issue is the relationship between Jews and non-Jews. Especially prominent is the topic of endogamy, the prohibition against marrying non-Jews. It is not always stated explicitly but can arise from small modifications to the biblical narrative. For instance, in Demetrius' account of the life of Moses (frg. 3), Zipporah, Moses' wife, whom the biblical text describes as a Midianite (Exod. 2:21), becomes a descendant of Abraham. Theodotus is more straightforward; when retelling the rape of Dinah, he omits Jacob's condemnation of his sons' violence. Moreover, the Shechemites are depicted as utterly wicked and are denied the possibility of joining the people of Israel through circumcision and of marrying the daughters of Israel. Philo is also quite explicit about the prohibition of marriage to foreigners (*Spec. Leg.* 3.29), but since he is merely paraphrasing Deut. 7:4, which refers to the Canaanites, it is not clear how he understood this interdiction in his own context. From the rest of his work, one may guess that he accepted intermarriage only with non-Jews who converted to Judaism. The synagogue sermon *On Samson* uses the example of Samson's unhappy relationship with Delilah (Judges 14–16) to insist on the danger represented by a union with a foreign woman (see especially §§22-23, 33). Similarly, in his *Jewish Antiquities* Josephus paraphrases the biblical account of the reign of Solomon and condemns his passion for foreign women (*Ant.* 8.190-96). In the *Testament of Job* (45:3), Job exhorts his children not to marry foreign women. Like Demetrius, the author of *Joseph and Aseneth* addresses a problem that stems from the biblical text: the reference to Joseph's marriage to the daughter of an Egyptian priest (Gen. 41:45). The author could have solved the problem by noting that Joseph lived before the Law was given at Mt. Sinai and therefore did not know the Mosaic legislation concerning forbidden unions, but he took a different approach. One passage in *Joseph and Aseneth* (8:6) bluntly emphasizes that Joseph hated foreign women. Aseneth therefore becomes a convert, an outcome that the very beginning of the work foreshadows by stating that she did not look like the daughters of the Egyptians but rather like the daughters of the Hebrews, and even like Sarah, Rebecca, and Rachel (1:7-8).

Jewish authors writing in Greek, then, seem unanimous in their condemnation of exogamy. However, there are a few exceptions. Artapanus and Ezekiel the Tragedian do not seem to have been bothered by the foreign wives of Joseph and Moses. Moreover, Artapanus apparently had a very open definition of the descendants of Israel. According to him, Joseph anticipated the conspiracy of his brothers and willingly traveled to Egypt with the help of the kings of the Arabs, who were "sons of Abraham and brothers of Isaac" and, as such, "descendants of Israel" (Eusebius, *Praep. Evang.* 9.23.1). Whereas the condemnation of forbidden unions can also be found in Jewish literature written in Hebrew (e.g., in *Jubilees*), Artapanus' and Ezekiel's lenient attitude is peculiar to Jewish literature written in Greek.

Circumcision is an issue closely connected with endogamy and with the preservation of Jewish identity, but it is not mentioned that often in Jewish texts written in Greek. Apart from Theodotus' epic poem, it is referred to in 2 Maccabees, in the context of the persecution ordered by Antiochus IV. The author tells us that circumcision was prohibited but that pious Jews resisted and even died rather than give up circumcising their children (2:10). 4 Maccabees also reports the fact, without building upon it except to introduce the story of the martyrs. Philo justifies the commandment of circumcision at some length at the beginning of the *Special Laws,* whereas Josephus refers to it only briefly in his retelling of the life of Abraham (*Ant.* 1.192) and mentions it again in connection with the conversion of non-Jews to Judaism (especially in *Ant.* 20.38-48, the story of the conversion of King Izates).

The dietary laws constitute yet another frequent theme pertaining to the general issue of the relationships between Jews and non-Jews. In the *Letter of Aristeas,* the high priest Eleazar explains the dietary laws in a symbolic way and emphasizes that they are supposed to lead to justice in social relationships (§§143-69), but he also states that they belong to the purity laws that are meant to separate the Jews from people who practice idolatry (§§139, 142). 3 Maccabees tends to equate faithfulness to the Torah with observance of the dietary rules. Moreover, its author acknowledges that these laws separate the Jews from their non-Jewish neighbors, and that this social *amixia* is perceived as a mark of hostility by those who are themselves hostile to the Jews. He does not give the commandments up for all that, but rather affirms that Jews have won for themselves a good reputation in social intercourse thanks to their righteousness (3:4-7). The issue of the dietary laws is found in the most dramatic way in 2 and 4 Maccabees, where it is linked to the story of the prohibition of Judaism by Antiochus IV. The old Eleazar, the seven brothers, and their mother are all put to death because they refuse to eat pork (2 Macc. 6:18–7:42; 4 Maccabees 5–18). Both Philo and Josephus frequently refer to the Jews' faithfulness to their ancestral laws, including the dietary laws. Philo explains them in a symbolic or allegorical way (*Spec. Leg.* 4.100-118) but also insists on the necessity of putting them into practice (*De Migratione Abrahami* 90–93). Finally, in *Joseph and Aseneth,* Joseph refuses to kiss Aseneth because she worships idols and eats impure food (8:5). Jewish texts written in Hebrew and Aramaic take up the issue of dietary laws too, but they tend to focus on halakic aspects rather than on the question of the laws' implications for the relationship with pagans. And in comparison with 2 Maccabees, 1 Maccabees is much less concerned with the dietary laws.

To conclude on the theme of the relationships between Jews and non-Jews, a few words should be said about the issue of conversion. Interestingly enough, converts and conversions appear in rather late texts. Philo praises proselytes who abandon idolatry or wrong conceptions about God and join Israel (see especially *De Virtutibus* 179, 182, and 219). In the *Antiquities,* Josephus reports the story of the conversion of the king of Adiabene, and mentions other cases as well. In *Against Apion,* he follows Philo in stating that Judaism's openness to proselytes is a mark of *philanthrōpia* (2.261). But in the *Antiquities* and the *Life,* Josephus also confronts the issue of forced conversions to Judaism, in the context of the Hasmonean wars and the war against Rome (see *Ant.* 13.257-58; 318-19; *Life* 112–13). Other texts that refer to proselytes are *Joseph and Aseneth* and the *Testament of Job,* whose main characters are converts. They both date from the first century C.E. (if not later). This list probably reflects the fact that the very notion of conversion and the ritual surrounding it — which should be distinguished from mere recognition of the God of Israel as the one true God — emerged and developed only at the end of the Hellenistic period. Among Greek translations of Jewish texts originally written in Hebrew or Aramaic, Esther LXX (8:17) and Judith (5:5–6:20) allude to or explicitly deal with conversions, but these translations are late as well (and the original version of Judith itself only dates from the second century B.C.E.).

Judaism's Superiority over Paganism

A third theme frequently found in Jewish texts written in Greek, perhaps the most widespread of all, is the superiority of Judaism over paganism. This theme has important biblical roots but received a new impetus in the Hellenistic age. On the one hand, as in biblical texts, idols are condemned and mocked as handmade objects with no power to save, and those who worship them are depicted as foolish, wicked, or abominable. This is the case in several texts, including the *Letter of Aristeas* (134–38 in particular), Pseudo-Hecataeus (who, through the story of Mosollamus, mocks pagan superstitious belief in omens), 3 Maccabees (4:16 in particular), Wisdom of Solomon, Philo, Josephus, *Testament of Job,* and *Joseph and Aseneth.* On the other hand, a monotheistic creed is attributed to well-known figures much admired by the Greeks, such as Orpheus, Homer, Hesiod, Pythagoras, Plato, and a few others, but they are said to have been inspired by Abraham, Joseph, or Moses. Thus, even if Greek culture is not utterly rejected as vile paganism, it is still considered inferior to Judaism since it derives its truth and its beauty from Judaism — hence the efforts of Josephus and others to demonstrate the great antiquity of the Jewish people and of the Mosaic revelation, which in their view predated the beginnings of Greek civilization. Hence, also, the use of pseudepigraphy in the pseudo-Orphic poem and the other verses attributed to famous Greek poets, and in the *Sibylline Oracles.*

All these works were conceived of as pagan testimonies to the truth and superior wisdom of Judaism. Even Artapanus, who presents Moses as the founder of Egyptian animal cults, was motivated by a sense of Judaism's superiority to Egyptian paganism. True, his perception of the latter is not as negative as in other Jewish texts (especially the *Letter of Aristeas* and Philo, who abhor Egyptian animal cults). But Moses' role as cultural benefactor in Egypt is still a mark of the superiority of Judaism over the culture of the natives. And the worship of animals is explained euhemeristically, implying that they are only animals that Moses judged to be useful. Moreover, Moses is identified with Mousaeus, the teacher of Orpheus. Thus, Artapanus celebrates the superiority of Judaism over both Egyptian and Greek culture, which is why his work can be considered an example of "competitive historiography."

The Mutual Faithfulness of God and Israel

A fourth theme prevalent in Jewish literature written in Greek is the mutual faithfulness of God and Israel. Several texts highlight God's justice and his providential care for Israel or reward of the righteous. For instance, in contrast to 1 Maccabees, 2 Maccabees introduces the episode of Heliodorus and of God's miraculous intervention to preserve the Temple in Jerusalem (chap. 3) and describes Antiochus IV's agony at length (chap. 9). Similarly, 3 Maccabees celebrates God's intervention at the Jerusalem Temple but also at the hippodrome in Alexandria (1:8–2:24 and 5:46–6:29, respectively). Philo makes it very clear that Flaccus' disgrace was a divine punishment (*In Flaccum* 180–91). Even Artapanus gives an example of divine retribution when he writes that, because of his treatment of the Jews, the Egyptian ruler Chenephres was the first man to contract elephantiasis (frg. 3 in Eusebius, *Praep. Evang.* 9.27.20). The Wisdom of Solomon also recalls God's intervention in favor of Israel and his chastisement of the Egyptians and the Canaanites. Yet it argues first and foremost that the righteous will be blessed with eternal life, whereas his adversaries will be punished and disappear forever. Similarly, the *Testament of Job* describes the righteous hero who suffers but is finally rewarded and achieves immortality, in contrast to the wicked Elihu, who is condemned to permanent destruction. In all cases, what is at stake is divine justice and the ways it manifests itself, either in this world or in the afterlife, at a collective or individual level. In the latter, eschatological concerns lead to the belief in bodily resurrection (2 Maccabees, *Sibylline Oracles* 4) and the immortality of the soul (Wisdom of Solomon, Philo, *Testament of Job*). Messianic expectations do not figure prominently in Jewish literature written in Greek, although some hints may be found in Philo, Josephus, and *Sibylline Oracles* 5.

To God's faithfulness toward Israel corresponds Israel's faithfulness to God and his Law. Jewish texts written in Greek tend to present the Jewish people as pious. Apostates are few. In 2 Maccabees, impious Jews in Jerusalem try to introduce a Greek way of life and to alter the ancestral customs, thus causing the wrath of God to fall on the Judeans (4:7-17). In 3 Maccabees, some Jews yield to Ptolemy's threats and promises, and apostatize through their initiation into the Dionysian mysteries (2:31-33). However, in both these books the vast majority of the Jews remain faithful to the covenant. At a more individual level, Aristeas and the *Testament of Job* retell the story of Job, the righteous man who continued to trust in God despite his great hardships. Particularly interesting are the stories of martyrdom or readiness to undergo martyrdom in 2, 3 and 4 Maccabees, as well as in several passages in Philo and Josephus (though martyrdom should be distinguished from noble death and suicide). Martyrdom is the supreme expression of the Jews' faithfulness to God's laws. Jewish readiness to die for the Law is emphasized by several authors, including Philo and Josephus. Conversely, apart from allusions in Daniel and 1 Maccabees (whose account is much shorter than that of 2 Maccabees and does not promote martyrdom), this theme does not appear frequently in Jewish literature written in Hebrew or Aramaic, even if apocalyptic literature often refers to a period of trials before the final reward of the elect. However, the more general issue of God's justice and Israel's faithfulness to the covenant is a recurring topic in Jewish literature written in Hebrew or Aramaic too.

This list of themes is not exhaustive; Jewish texts written in Greek engage other issues as well. But some themes are strikingly absent or marginal: messianism and cultic prescriptions, to name just a few. If one were to add to the corpus texts such as *3 Baruch, 4 Baruch (Paraleipomena Jeremiou), Testament of Abraham,* and *2 Enoch,* heavenly visions and angelic revelations would feature more prominently in the general picture. The Jewish or Christian provenance of these works, though, continues to be disputed. Also conspicuous is the lack of liturgical and halakic texts. Here again, though, the shape of the corpus likely reflects the selective interests of the church fathers.

Ideological Features

Jewish works composed in Greek do not display uniform ideological features. For instance, Theodotus' epic poem reflects a nationalistic and exclusive conception of Judaism. As mentioned above, he completely omits Jacob's condemnation of the aggression perpetrated by Simeon and Levi against the Shechemites (Gen. 34:30). By contrast, the author of 4 Maccabees refers to this condemnation and even quotes Gen. 49:7: "Cursed be their anger, for it is fierce, and their wrath, for it is cruel." According to him, the very fact that Jacob says about Simeon and Levi "May their anger be cursed" means that reason is able to restrain anger (4 Macc. 2:19-20). The violence with which the two brothers avenged their sister, which seemed so praiseworthy to Theodotus that he presented it as the fulfillment of an oracle from God, is depicted as a reprehensible passion by the author of 4 Maccabees. The same degree of disagreement can be noticed concerning other issues. For example, as we noted above, not all Jewish authors writing in Greek condemned marriages to foreign women. Moreover, had the writings of extreme allegorizers of Scripture (criticized by Philo in *De Migratione Abrahami* 89–90) been preserved, we would probably have an even more diverse picture.

The use of the Greek language and the mastery of Greek literary forms, then, does not in itself predetermine the ideological or philosophical orientation of the writer. In particular, writing in Greek is not synonymous with openness to Gentiles or universalism. Still, in Second Temple literature the most universalistic texts are indeed to be found among those written in Greek, especially those of Aristobulus and Philo. Universalism, though, is not based primarily on a willingness to welcome proselytes but rather on a broad understanding of God's law and of the cult at the Jerusalem Temple. Some Jewish authors writing in Greek boldly conceived of the Torah as a universal law that could appeal to every human being, mainly through reason. Philo goes so far as to present Israel as a priest offering sacrifices and prayers to God for the sake of all human beings (*Spec. Leg.* 2.163-67). It is especially in Jewish literature composed in Greek, then, that the relationship between Israel and the rest of humankind is thought out in its deepest and most positive way.

Scholars debate whether Jewish works composed in Greek should be labeled "apologetic" literature. On the one hand, this is not a missionary literature, even if the evidence shows that proselytes and God-fearers were welcome in the Jewish communities of the Diaspora. On the other hand, although the intended audience of the vast majority of these texts was Jewish, apologetic interests are not to be denied in some cases. To claim the superiority of Judaism over paganism and Greek philosophy, or to provide a rationale for dietary laws and circumcision, is to engage in apologetics. But the apologia was an affirmation of the superiority of Judaism directed in most cases to Jews themselves, to help them face the challenges of their Greco-Roman environment and to strengthen and comfort them in their religious and cultural identity.

Significance

Jewish literature written in Greek is significant for several reasons. First, it constitutes the main literary testimony to the ways people in the ancient Near East rose to the challenge of Hellenism. Although other cultures produced important works in Greek, these works have not survived, or only in fragments, as in the case of Manetho's *Aegyptiaca,* which is known mainly through Josephus' *Against Apion.* Jewish literature written in Hebrew or Aramaic during the Hellenistic and early Roman periods also offers important testimony to the encounter of Judaism with Greek civilization, at least in some cases. Moreover, the archaeological and documentary evidence (inscriptions, papyri, coins, and other artifacts) sheds crucial light on the processes of acculturation that took place during the Greco-Roman period. However, Jewish works composed in Greek remain our main and most explicit evidence for the Jewish engagement with Hellenism.

This literature documents a remarkable attempt to embrace Greek culture while maintaining a distinctive Jewish identity. On the one hand, it demonstrates the huge interest that Greek culture aroused among Jewish elites, and how much they could feel at home in the Greek-speaking world. On the other hand, it also shows that Jews remained very much aware of their distinctive cultural and religious identity. Admittedly, some Jews abandoned the ancestral customs of their people. We know, for instance, of Dositheos son of Drimylos and of Philo's nephew, Tiberius Julius Alexander. "Apostasy," if we may call it that, was probably more common among the elites than among the ordinary people. But in the case of Greco-Roman Egypt, which we know better than other places in the Diaspora, both the literary and the papyrological evidence show that, in general, Jews who expressed themselves in Greek did not indulge in religious paganism or give up the commandments of the Torah. Their culture and identity were bipolar and their relationship to Hellenism selective. They showed a great deal of creativity and boldness in appropriating Greek literary genres, Greek mythology, and Greek philosophical concepts, but used them for their own purposes. In other words, their relationship with Greek culture was not passive but active — and critical. Even when dealing with the biblical or Jewish traditions they inherited, however, they showed great exegetical freedom (a freedom not unparalleled in Hebrew and Aramaic compositions).

That Jews in the Hellenistic and early Roman eras borrowed concepts, literary motifs, and vocabulary from the surrounding culture was nothing new or exceptional. The biblical texts already attest many borrowings from Canaanite, Babylonian, and Persian cultures. Whatever its stage of development, Judaism was never impermeable or completely inward-looking. What was new was the attempt to translate the tradition into a language and cultural idiom that were not Semitic. Obviously, for texts to be translated one first needed to have them reach a certain state of completion. This was achieved in the course of the Hellenistic period, as the collection of manuscripts from Qumran shows. This was a major historical and cultural phenomenon that would leave important marks on the cultural history of the world.

This process of translation was not merely a linguistic one. Even the Septuagint — a collection of Hebrew and Aramaic texts translated into Greek — represented a *cultural* translation, an endeavor to transpose Jewish beliefs and traditions into a different key. Since Jewish beliefs and traditions were not set once and for all, this transposition also gave birth to new ways of expressing Jewish identity and faith. However, the term "syncretism," which is sometimes used in connection with Jewish texts written in Greek, is generally ill chosen. In most Jewish works composed in Greek, there is no syncretism at all, even if Greek terminology is used and Greek gods or heroes are referred to. For instance, that the narrator of the *Letter of Aristeas* compares the God of Israel with Zeus (16) is no proof of syncretism on the part of the real author of the *Letter,* since the narrator is a Greek. The comparison is part of playing the game of pseudonymous attribution. But even if "Aristeas" had been a Jew, the comparison with Zeus would still not count as religious syncretism but remain an example of cultural translation: in the mind of a Greek living in the second century B.C.E., the name "Zeus" did not necessarily conjure up all the mythological tales told by the poets. It could be used in a more philosophical way and refer to a more sophisticated conception of the divine. So an imperfect correlation could indeed be established between the God of Israel and what "Zeus" represented from a Greek philosophical perspective. Accordingly, "Aristeas" defines Zeus as the universal source of life and being, a definition not completely inappropriate to the God of Israel.

Above all, one should bear in mind that Jews writing in Greek frequently used Greek terminology in a subversive way. The use of a Greek term did not necessarily imply that the writer accepted the traditional Greek meaning of the word or all of its cultural implications. For example, the author of 3 Maccabees uses features of the Hellenistic kings to describe the God of Israel. One could argue that he was thoroughly Hellenized. His command of Greek and his knowledge of the language of the Ptolemaic court are certainly beyond doubt. However, the vocabulary he chose to use also conveys the idea that God alone is the true king of the world, above all human kingships. Similarly, the Wisdom of Solomon uses the term *mystēria* to designate both the holy revelations of Wisdom (2:22) and the abominable ceremonies of the Dionysian cult (14:23). Yet the use of the term *mystēria* in connection with Judaism is not a mark of religious syncretism but a way to oppose Judaism to pagan mysteries and to celebrate the superiority of the former. At a more distinctly philosophical level, Philo sometimes uses the Stoic term *oikeiōsis* ("appropriation"), which carried philosophical implications quite contrary to Jewish ethical principles. But he subverts its meaning by endowing it with the sense of *homoiōsis tō theō,* the Platonic "assimilation to God," which could easily be linked with the Jewish ideal of the imitation of God.

The encounter with Greek culture certainly represented a challenge to Jews in the Hellenistic and early Roman periods. But it also prompted them to explore new ways of expressing their identity and to elaborate the very notion of *Ioudaismos.*

BIBLIOGRAPHY

Bar-Kochva, Bezalel. 1996. *Pseudo-Hecataeus on the Jews: Legitimizing the Jewish Diaspora.* Berkeley: University of California Press.

Barclay, John M. G. 1996. *Jews in the Mediterranean Diaspora.* Edinburgh: Clark.

Burchard, Christoph. 2003. *Joseph und Aseneth.* Leiden: Brill.

Collins, John J. 2000. *Between Athens and Jerusalem: Jewish Identity in the Hellenistic Diaspora.* 2d ed. Grand Rapids: Eerdmans.

———. 2005. *Jewish Cult and Hellenistic Culture: Essays on the Jewish Encounter with Hellenism and Roman Rule.* Leiden: Brill.

Davila, James R. 2005. *The Provenance of the Pseudepigrapha: Jewish, Christian, or Other?* Leiden: Brill.

Denis, Albert-Marie. 1970. *Introduction aux pseudépigraphes grecs d'Ancien Testament.* Leiden: Brill.

———. 2000. *Introduction à la littérature religieuse judéo-hellénistique.* 2 vols. Turnhout: Brepols.

Herr, Moshe D. 1990. "Les raisons de la conservation des restes de la littérature juive de l'Époque du Second Temple." In *La fable apocryphe I.* Ed. P. Geoltrain, E. Junod, and J.-C. Picard. Turnhout: Brepols, 219-30.

Goodman, Martin. 1986. "Jewish Literature Composed in Greek." In E. Schürer, *The History of the Jewish People in the Age of Jesus Christ (175 B.C.–A.D. 135).* Vol. 3, Part 1. Rev. and ed. Geza Vermes, Fergus Miller, and Martin Goodman. Edinburgh: Clark, 470-704.

Gruen, Erich S. 1998. *Heritage and Hellenism: The Reinvention of Jewish Tradition.* Berkeley: University of California Press.

Holladay, Carl. 1983-1996. *Fragments from Hellenistic Jewish Authors.* 4 vols. Atlanta: Scholars Press.

Honigman, Sylvie. 2003. *The Septuagint and Homeric Scholarship in Alexandria: A Study in the Narrative of the Letter of Aristeas.* London: Routledge.

Inowlocki, Sabrina. 2006. *Eusebius and the Jewish Authors: His Citation Technique in an Apologetic Context.* Leiden: Brill.

Johnson, Sarah R. 2004. *Historical Fictions and Hellenistic Jewish Identity: Third Maccabees in Its Cultural Context.* Berkeley: University of California Press.

Lanfranchi, Pierluigi. 2006. *L'Exagoge d'Ezéchiel le tragique: Introduction, texte, traduction et commentaire.* Leiden: Brill.

Motzo, Raimondo Bacchisio. 1977. *Ricerche sulla letteratura e la storia giudaico-ellenistica.* Roma: Centro Editoriale Internazionale.

Walter, Nikolaus. 1976. *Fragmente jüdisch-hellenistischer Historiker.* JSHRZ I, 2. Gütersloh: Gerd Mohn, 89-164.

———. 1983. *Fragmente jüdisch-hellenistischer Epik: Philon, Theodotos. Pseudepigraphische jüdisch-hellenistische Dichtung: Pseudo-Phokylides, Pseudo-Orpheus, Gefälschte Verse auf Namen griechischer Dichter.* JSHRZ IV, 3. Gütersloh: Gerd Mohn.

———. 1989. "Jewish-Greek Literature of the Greek Period." In *The Cambridge History of Judaism,* vol. 2, *The Hellenistic Age.* Ed. W. D. Davies and L. Finkelstein. Cambridge: Cambridge University Press, 385-408.

Archaeology, Papyri, and Inscriptions

Jürgen K. Zangenberg

Next to literary texts, the remains of material culture are an essential source for understanding Jews and Judaism in the Second Temple period. This article surveys archaeological, epigraphical, and papyrological material from Palestine and the Diaspora in chronological order. The criteria for defining an object as "Jewish" and for including it in this discussion are deliberately broad. Religion does not play the decisive role. While there can be no doubt that material culture can serve religious functions in a given society, many archaeologists rightly warn not to overemphasize the religious character of artifacts. Not all artifacts had a religious meaning, and religion was not the only meaningful component even of a religious artifact like an altar or a temple. Moreover, the question is often not whether an object can be identified as Jewish, but *what type* of Judaism it might reflect.

Ancient cultures, and among them early Judaism, were constantly in contact with each other. Responses to the "other" were never uniform but complex and diverse, dependent on prevailing regional and social conditions. Boundaries were often blurred. Some elements of material culture reflect no particular religious affiliation, others acquired different meanings according to the cultural context in which they were used, and still others are regional phenomena that would be absent if the same religious group had lived elsewhere. A large part of material culture sits right on the margins, where clear "decoding" is difficult. Consequently, this survey will discuss not only material that reflects early Judaism — that was made for and used by Jews to practice their religion — but also elements of material culture that were commissioned or built by Jews even if these structures had no particular religious functions. The survey will also touch on non-Jewish material culture if it influenced developments and trends in the Jewish world or illustrates the conditions under which Jewish material culture developed.

Palestine in the Hellenistic Period (ca. 320-164 B.C.E.)

Although we have substantial material evidence for Jews and Judaism from the Persian period both from Palestine and the Diaspora (especially Egypt), the conquests of Alexander and their aftermath initially left no deep traces in the material record of early Judaism.

The situation in Palestine at the end of the Persian period is reflected through excavations and surveys in areas such as Galilee and Judea. Excavations in Jerusalem indicate the small size of the city, and seal impressions give evidence of administration. Among the remains in Samaria are fortifications, coins, and seal impressions. Excavations on Mt. Gerizim have revealed the beginnings of a large sanctuary on the acropolis. Papyri provide interesting details about social and legal conditions during the second half of the fourth century B.C.E. From Wadi ed-Daliyeh come fragments of about thirty-eight documents and ninety-seven legible seal impressions. From Jericho coins and stamped handles have been found, and from Idumea around 800 Aramaic ostraca (potsherds) have been uncovered.

Although Palestine was strategically important to Alexander the Great as a bridge between Egypt and Asia, he left few archaeological traces in the region. Andromachos, the first Macedonian governor, was killed by Samarians, but the revolt was quickly put down and a new governor installed. While few of the excavated structures in Samaria can be safely associated with the earliest Macedonian inhabitants (the three round towers on the acropolis being the most likely candidates), the skeletons and documents from Wadi ed-Daliyeh may represent remains of some of the insurgents.

For the first hundred years after the wars among Alexander's successors, the Diadochi, Palestine belonged to the Ptolemaic kingdom. It is symptomatic of the situation in the first half of the third century B.C.E. that fortifications are among the best-known structures. The most impressive one is in Dor, but others are located in Ptolemais, Straton's Tower, Philoteria, Gaza, Shechem, and elsewhere. Ptolemaic rule was tolerant and did not interfere with local matters. The papyri archives of a Ptolemaic official named Zenon (260/59 B.C.E.) give insight into the mechanisms of economic exploitation in Palestine and the way local elites were used by the king to secure regular taxation.

From the second half of the third century B.C.E., both the growing contacts between the coastal cities and the larger Greek world and the rapid development of cities in Transjordan increasingly influenced the cultural context of the traditionally Jewish regions in central Palestine. From then on, the hill country of Judea, Samaria, and the Galilee was sandwiched between areas deeply influenced by Hellenism.

The Coastal Plain

Particularly important were developments in the coastal plain. The region functioned as a starting point for more permanent settlement of Phoenician colonists in the agricultural hinterland. In the south, Khirbet el-Qom and Aderet are good examples of rural sites having contacts with the coast. The hinterland provided agricultural goods (mostly wine and oil) that were consumed in or exported from the coastal cities. In turn, the inhabitants of settlements in the hinterland (above all, cities like Samaria) bought goods that had entered the country through the coastal plain harbors. Small amounts of Greek luxury ceramics had already served local elites since the fourth century B.C.E. Now, stamped amphorae indicate a growing demand for imported goods. Although perhaps only a few Jews lived in cities like Gaza, Ashkelon, Ashdod, Dor, and Ptolemais (Akko), the old cultural demarcation between coastal plain and hill country gradually decreased.

The Transjordan Plateau

The systematic reurbanization of the Transjordanian plateau created markets east of central Palestine that were to a large extent supplied by the cities on the coast. The exact circumstances of the transformation of older settlements into new, Hellenized urban centers during the first half of the third century B.C.E. are not entirely clear, but they quickly constituted an ever-growing cultural and economic factor. In cities like Gadara, Pella, Gerasa, Philadelphia, and Scythopolis (Beth Shean), which later combined with others to form the Decapolis, a lively blend of Greek and local pagan-Semitic culture developed.

Jerusalem

In contrast to these urban centers, only one place in Judea deserved the label *city:* Jerusalem. Its only source of income and status was the Temple. Early Hellenistic Jerusalem was fairly small (basically only the City of David was inhabited) and quite poor. Only the small priestly aristocracy enjoyed moderate wealth, mostly based on income from the Temple and revenues as landowners. Most people had access only to local goods. Handles of storage vessels stamped with YHD indicate taxation in kind, probably managed by authorized tax collectors or (in the case of stamps with YRSLM and a star) by members of the priesthood. These stamps first appear in the Persian period and were used well into the Ptolemaic age.

The situation in the hill country and especially in Jerusalem changed after 200 B.C.E. when Antiochus III defeated Ptolemy V Epiphanes in the battle of Paneion and the Seleucids took control of the region. The Seleucids supported the Temple out of their own politically inspired agenda, via members of the local elite who supervised the implementation of Seleucid policy.

The spectrum of finds from Jerusalem is notably different from that of the previous period. Now, large amounts of stamped amphora handles from Greek islands like Rhodes and Kos indicate frequent imports from the Aegean to meet the demands of elite who became increasingly attracted to Greek culture and had the means to acquire luxury goods. Few archaeological remains have survived from the pre-Hasmonean period. No remains of Seleucid Akra have been identified securely, and only some stretches of the city walls in the City of David and around the citadel may date to the pre-Hasmonean period. Arrowheads and inscribed lead projectiles from the second century B.C.E. were found in Hellenistic layers at the citadel and probably belong to the siege by Antiochus VII in 133/32 B.C.E.

All other settlements in Judea were even smaller than Jerusalem. Bethel was a large village and Qalandiya no more than a large farmstead specializing in the production of wine. Fortresses continued to be built (e.g., at Maresha, Samaria, Beth-Zur, and Gebel Sartaba near Pella).

Samaria

In the region of Samaria, at least three sites can be called cities. The city of Samaria, the former seat of the Persian governor and later a Macedonian garrison, was certainly more important and cosmopolitan than Jerusalem. Several periods of excavation have uncovered substantial remains from the third century B.C.E., among them houses with painted stucco, Greek inscriptions, and imported Greek pottery. It seems that the population was largely pagan.

The second, certainly smaller city was the old site of biblical Shechem (Tell Balata), which was resettled at the end of the fourth century B.C.E. Contrary to many scholars who suppose that the new city was inhabited by Samaritans, the evidence points in the opposite direction. If Josephus is right (*Ant.* 11.344), we can assume that Shechem was a settlement of Sidonian colonists who wanted to control the strategically important valley between Mt. Gerizim and Mt. Ebal and the traffic crossing the fertile al-Askar plain. Material culture from Hellenistic Shechem was considerably poorer than from Samaria. All earlier structures on the Tell were covered by a thick layer of fill; the Middle Bronze Age city wall was used as a foundation for new fortifications; and the interior was filled with regularly built private houses. 2 Maccabees 6:2 mentions a temple dedicated to Zeus Xenios on Mt. Gerizim, probably on Tell er-Ras, the eastern summit of Mt. Gerizim, which served as an acropolis for Shechem.

Around 200 B.C.E. at the latest, a third city existed on the summit of Mt. Gerizim, surrounding an older sanctuary. The sanctuary consisted of a large open courtyard measuring about 90 by 90 meters that was accessible over large stairways and surrounded by halls, rooms, and massive fortifications. Unlike the situation in Jerusalem, the sacred precinct does not seem to have housed a temple building but a large open altar. The remains of the altar were later obliterated by the construction of a Byzantine church. Outside the sacred precinct, archaeologists have excavated parts of a large city that, together with the sanctuary, was protected by a wide city wall. The houses were all very well built; many had large courtyards and rooms for processing agricultural produce (oil presses). Greek style bathtubs in some houses indicate a high standard of living. Many inscriptions in a recently published corpus of some 400 fragments (most of them dating to the third and second century B.C.E.) contain dedicatory formulae and mention names and titles of cultic personnel in Aramaic and Paleo-Hebrew. Although found in secondary use, it is possible that the inscriptions were once on display somewhere in the sacred precinct. On the basis of the epigraphic evidence, there can be no doubt that the city was the main settlement of the Samaritans, and that the sanctuary was their central place of worship, which included sacrifices and pilgrimages. Due to the lack of a natural spring on the summit, the city was not easy to defend despite strong fortifications (including chamber gates very much in the Iron Age tradition). Both city and sanctuary were destroyed by John Hyrcanus around 112/111 B.C.E. (Josephus, *Ant.* 13.254-57). Greek inscriptions from the second to fourth century C.E. witness to Samaritan pilgrimage to Mt. Gerizim long after the temple there had been destroyed.

The Galilee

Settlement activity in the Galilee seems to have been low and sparse before 100 B.C.E., but this impression will probably change as a result of more intensive surveys. Around the mid-third century B.C.E. veteran settlements were established at Philoteria, et-Tell (Bethsaida), and Gamla to guard the traffic arteries between the coast (especially Tyre) and the eastern plateau. A large public building at Hamath Tiberias dates from the later Seleucid period. Apart from that, there is growing material evidence of an indigenous, Semitic population in the hills of Upper and northern Lower Galilee. Some elements of its material culture seem influenced by the Phoenicians; others stand in the late Iron Age tradition. The sanctuaries at Dan and Paneion had regional importance in the second century B.C.E. A Phoenician presence itself is evident in the administrative center at Qedesh, the mountain sanctuary at Mitzpe Yamim, and the emporium at Tell Anafa. A fortification on the acropolis at Sepphoris, probably dating to sometime during the second half of the second century B.C.E., guarded the traffic route running inland from Ptolemais. The fort reflects the strategic value of the Galilee as a geographical link between harbors on the Mediterranean and the cities of western Syria.

Perea

Ever since the Persian period, Jews had lived in Perea east of the Jordan. Here the Ptolemies confirmed the descendants of the Persian governor "Tobiah the Ammonite" as landholders. Ptolemy III Euergetes appointed Joseph son of Tobiah as the highest civil functionary of the entire Ptolemaic province. He resided in ʿAraq el-Amir, a palace in a large estate seventeen kilometers west of Amman. The beginnings of the estate date back to the late Iron II period. The famous Tobiah inscriptions at the entrance to two caves date to the fifth century B.C.E., and a gateway was added in the late third century B.C.E. In the early second century B.C.E., the famous palace at Qasr el-Abd was built with monolithic columns, window fronts, and lion reliefs (Josephus, *Ant.* 12.230-33). The size of the estate and the lavish decoration of the palace, which shows a fine blend of Greek and oriental styles, offers a good indication of the Hellenizing tendencies of many members of the landowning Jewish upper class.

The Early Hellenistic Diaspora

Jewish communities in Egypt and Mesopotamia date back to the sixth century B.C.E. In the fourth century B.C.E. Jews are attested at Kition in Cyprus; epitaphs in Phoenician script mention names with a YHWH component. With the expansion of Hellenistic kingdoms and with Rome eventually controlling vast territories and connecting regions, Judaism reached Asia Minor, the Greek islands, mainland Italy, the area around the Black Sea, North Africa, Spain, and southern Gaul.

Although the origins of many of these Diaspora communities predate the Hasmonean period, most of our material dates to the late second century B.C.E. Inscriptions survive in sometimes great variety but are often distributed very irregularly. Jews generally enjoyed the protection of the rulers, but individual communities lived under very different cultural, legal, and social conditions. They took part in public life and used regionally available material culture.

Palestine in the Hasmonean Period (164-40 B.C.E.)

Antiochus IV Epiphanes' ill-fated attempt to forcibly stabilize Palestine around 167 B.C.E. with the help of the deeply Hellenized faction of the Jerusalem elite eventually resulted in the violent overthrow of Seleucid rule and the establishment of an independent Jewish state in Palestine under the Hasmoneans, a priestly family from rural Modein in Judea. The Hasmonean takeover of Palestine was a protracted process lasting well over two generations until John Hyrcanus' (134-104 B.C.E.) large-scale occupations in Samaria, Perea, the Galilee, and Idumea.

Hasmonean restoration did not mean the end of Hellenization. It was during the Hasmonean period that Judaism developed a distinct variant of eastern Hellenistic material culture. Hellenism became indigenous to Jewish Palestine, embedded in its culture and in the self-definition of its ruling dynasty. Symptomatic of that process is how Simon Maccabee (high priest and ethnarch 142-134 B.C.E.) integrated elements of Greek architecture into his renovated family tomb in Modein (1 Macc. 13:23-30; Josephus, *Ant.* 13.210-12).

Until well into the second century B.C.E., there are no criteria to distinguish a Jewish site from a non-Jewish one apart from general geographical considerations, inscriptions (still very rare), and textual information. Both Jewish and non-Jewish populations to a very large extent used the same pool of material culture, which often followed regional rather than religious patterns.

The Seleucid garrison in the Akra of Jerusalem was captured by Simon in 141 B.C.E. (1 Macc. 14:49-52). The subsequent territorial acquisitions by Simon, Hyrcanus, and Alexander Jannaeus followed a religiously inspired agenda. Pagans were expelled from cities such as Joppa and Gezer and repopulated by Jews; strongholds like Beth-Zur were destroyed and neutralized by settling Jews in the vicinity; and in the rural hinterland new, small settlements were established that guarded the hills and exploited regional agricultural resources.

Alexander Jannaeus (103-76 B.C.E.) undertook an aggressive expansion that brought about much destruction especially in Samaria (Gerizim, Samaria, Shechem) and in the Galilee. Often the new settlements were oriented toward new markets and therefore lacked luxury pottery that had often abounded before (as in Gezer). The presence of *miqva'ot* (ritual baths) in houses signals new religious practices, as in Gezer and the Sepphoris acropolis. Next to expansion, Jannaeus' activities were directed toward internal consolidation. Strongholds were erected at Masada, Machaerus, Hyrcania, and Alexandrion. Although these fortresses lack the highly complex palace structures characteristic of the subsequent Herodian period, they were not only intended for purely military purposes.

Palace Architecture

Palace architecture was not confined to fortresses, as the palace in Jericho demonstrates. Jannaeus integrated the residential complex there into a large estate and built a highly effective water supply system. The palace consisted of a fortified section situated on a moat overlooking Wadi Qelt, as well as several huge pools surrounded by gardens, pavilions, and storage facilities. Remains of stucco and wall paintings show that sumptuous decoration was already present in the initial phase of the palace. The ceramic profile, however, demonstrates that until the beginning of the Herodian period few foreign imports reached the palace; the residents used mainly local ware. Another, earlier example of Hasmonean palace architecture can be found in the second-century-B.C.E. phase of the Qasr el-Abd palace at ʿAraq el-Amir. Here, unlike west of the Jordan, free use was made of figurative art on a truly monumental scale.

Architecture in Rural Contexts

Architecture in rural areas was far less lavish than in the palaces of the ruling elite and more or less followed traditional lines. Typologically, houses in Hellenistic Palestine fell into two types: (1) polygonal courtyard complexes separated from each other by irregular streets; and (2) rectangular courtyard houses integrated into square neighborhoods in classical Greek, "Hippodamic" style. Towns and villages mostly followed traditional, irregular plans, as in Shechem, Shiqmona, and Bethel. At the end of the second century B.C.E., a new type of rural settlement made its appearance: the fortified farmstead consisting of rooms and installations arranged around an usually rectangular courtyard with a tower in one corner. The building type is similar to that of Hellenistic farmsteads in Asia Minor and the Black Sea area. It made its way into late Hellenistic and early Roman Palestine, in upper-class agricultural sites such as Ramat ha-Nadiv.

From around 100 B.C.E. onward settlement intensified in various regions. On the Dead Sea, ample evidence attests a systematic integration of the once rather thinly populated area. Settlements at Qumran, Khirbet Mazin, Qasr et-Turabe, Masada, and Machaerus signal growing interest in the region. After 100 B.C.E. settlement activity also dramatically increased in the Galilee and the Western Golan. Due to the destruction and abandonment of some sites (e.g., at Anafa and Qedesh) and the foundation of new settlements (e.g., at Gamla and Yodefat), settlement patterns and the flow of household goods changed. On Tel Anafa a small village with square houses of similar size was built a couple of years after the destruction of the large stuccoed building. The once fortified site on et-Tell was now built up with irregularly oriented, large farmhouses. New regional types of common ware developed (e.g., Kfar Hananiah ware), but the region was not entirely cut off from outside influence, as glass and some imported ware in the fishermen's village on et-Tell show.

Burial Practices

Burial practices offer a good example of how Jewish culture was susceptible to symbiosis with surrounding cultures. Mourning and burial were family affairs in both the Jewish and non-Jewish worlds. Among the common elements were preparing the body of the deceased for burial, wailing, playing music, marching in procession, and observing purity taboos. Early Hellenistic burial culture followed late Persian traditions for the most part. Sometimes single shaft tombs were used (e.g., in Dor and Atlit) along with chamber tombs (e.g., at Bat-Yam, Tell en-Nasbe, el-Azariye, and Lachish). Sometimes a cemetery was made up of one type alone. Architectural decoration is largely unknown, and grave goods are both poor and scarce.

The general situation changed in the first half of the second century. Traditional chamber tombs (e.g., at Maresha in about 200 B.C.E.) came under Hellenistic influence: funeral benches inside the burial chamber were replaced by longitudinal receptacles for the corpse hewn into the rock called *loculi* or *kokhim,* and the interior layout became more regularized. Tombs were sometimes painted, and architectural decoration such as columns, capitals, and pilasters were used on façades. About two generations later the new style was adopted in Jerusalem's upper-class tombs, and from there it was taken over by more and more families. Especially famous is Jason's Tomb, one of the oldest and most elaborate upper-class tombs in Jerusalem, built around 100 B.C.E.

Funeral culture demonstrates that traditional clan structures underwent a process of differentiation during the first century B.C.E. and C.E. in which individuals and smaller family units acquired a greater role. Instead of continuing the old Iron Age tradition of indiscriminate secondary burial in bone chambers, small limestone receptacles known as ossuaries became fashionable in the last decades of the first century B.C.E. and allowed for families to be buried in separate niches within the same tomb. About a third of these ossuaries bear names of the individuals buried in them, sometimes revealing information about the origin or the occupation of the deceased. Archaeologists debate whether ossuaries reflect particular beliefs about the afterlife such as resurrection of the body.

Pottery

Pottery is by far the most frequent type of material artifact and therefore extremely important for archaeological analysis. The question of how far pottery can directly define or identify the ethnicity of a given population is particularly controversial. Jews, like others, mostly used pottery that was produced locally, and in regions predominately populated by Jews, such as Palestine, Jews produced their own pottery, which was then regionally distributed. There is no such thing as explicitly and exclusively "Jewish pottery." Of course, pottery forms changed over time. Some early Hellenistic types developed from forms of the late Persian period; this was true of cooking pots and storage vessels. Others adapted and further developed Hellenistic forms, as is evident in the making of bowls and flasks. Apart from the coastal region, imported ware was very rare until the second half of the second century B.C.E. From then on, larger amounts of imported wares such as Eastern red-slipped pottery *(terra sigillata)* and mold-blown glass from Phoenicia became available and were readily absorbed by local customers.

Coins

The first clearly identifiable Jewish elements of material culture are coins. It is commonly accepted that John Hyrcanus I (134-104 B.C.E.) was the first ruler to issue coins. He did so under his Hebrew name, *Yehohanan.* Hasmonean minting started at around 120 B.C.E., when autonomous cities in the vicinity of Palestine also began issuing their own denominations. Hasmonean coins were issued in huge numbers only in bronze and are an important sign both of the independence of the Hasmonean state and of how firmly the realm was integrated into the material and political developments of the eastern Mediterranean. Human and animal imagery was strictly avoided. Especially under Alexander Jannaeus (103-76 B.C.E.) and Mattathias Antigonus (40-37 B.C.E.), Hasmonean coins used generic Hellenistic symbols of prosperity and legitimate rule: cornucopias, pomegranates, stars, anchors, helmets, wreaths, and diadems. Many coins are decorated only on the margins and focus primarily on the title of the ruler ("priest"; "high priest"; "king") and of the ruled ("council of the Jews"). Legends are mostly written in Paleo-Hebrew, but Aramaic and later even Greek were used (e.g., one of Jannaeus' coins has the Greek legend *Alexandrou basileōs*). Due to limited variation in iconography and nomenclature, many questions about precise chronology and iconographical development of specific types are still open.

Stepped, Plastered Pools

The earliest finds with a clear connection to Jewish religious practices are stepped, plastered pools. The earliest examples are attested in Sepphoris, where such pools were built into a former cistern sometime in the first half of the first century B.C.E., and in the palaces at Jericho. The houses of the new Jewish settlers in Gezer also had stepped pools, as did the palace-fortress of Masada, the wealthy mansions and small houses in Jerusalem, and the earliest phase of the settlement at Qumran. The evidence from Qedumim in Samaria shows that Samaritans also built stepped pools in the first century C.E. Although many of these installations served as ritual baths *(miqva'ot),* it is far from certain that all stepped, plastered pools had ritual purposes or that their form was standardized.

The Late Hellenistic Diaspora

Archaeological evidence for Jewish life in the Diaspora during the second and first centuries B.C.E. is limited. While we know from numerous written sources that Judaism considerably expanded in the eastern Mediterranean basin during the Ptolemaic and Seleucid periods, no architectural structures and only a few inscriptions are known. Jewish "identity markers" such as *miqva'ot,* stone vessels, and ossuaries are virtually absent from the Diaspora.

Alexandria

Egypt must come first in our survey. One of the most influential events for Diaspora Judaism was the foundation of Alexandria at the mouth of the Nile in 321 B.C.E. Jews soon became a large and influential part of the city's inhabitants and enjoyed its economic opportunities, far-reaching contacts, and famous centers of Greek learning. Because few large-scale excavations have been carried out in the area of the ancient city, and because many older excavations in the surrounding necropolises remain poorly published, we know little about the actual living conditions of the city's Jewish community. The magnificent synagogue of Alexandria is known only from first-century-C.E. literary texts (Philo, *Legatio ad Gaium* 134; cf. the legendary version in *t. Sukkah* 4:6; *y. Sukkah* 5:1 [55ab]; *b. Sukkah* 51b). Its construction date is unknown, but its importance as a civic center for Alexandrian Jews is beyond doubt. It was destroyed during the uprisings under Trajan (116-117 C.E.).

Many Alexandrian Jews are attested in necropolises either through inscriptions (few of them *in situ*) or *in natura.* No separate cemeteries were used. Only the treatment of the corpse was somewhat different. Unlike the Egyptians, Jews did not practice embalming, and grave goods were rare. A number of decorated ossuaries indicate the sporadic practice of secondary burial.

Given the sprawling cultural interaction and the long tradition of Jewish life in Egypt, it is no surprise that the earliest evidence for a crucial Jewish institution comes from Egypt instead of Palestine: the dedication of a "prayer house" *(proseuchē)* by the *Ioudaioi* of Schedia, a suburb of Alexandria, from the time of Ptolemy III Euergetes (246-221 B.C.E.; *CIJ* 1:440). Because the building itself has not been found (indeed, no synagogue building has been excavated at all in Egypt), nothing is known about its shape and architectural context. Altogether, fifteen inscriptions and a number of papyri from the third century B.C.E. to the first century

C.E. mention a synagogue (almost all use the term *proseuchē;* the term *synagōgē* is rare).

Leontopolis

Around 160 B.C.E. Ptolemy VI Philometor and Cleopatra III granted permission to the Jewish priest Onias IV to build a temple and a town at Leontopolis, a site in the Heliopolite nome thirty-two kilometers northeast of Cairo in the southeastern Nile delta (Josephus, *Ant.* 12.388; 13.63, 67, 285; *J.W.* 1.31-33; 7.427). The temple apparently flourished until the Roman prefect Lupus (71-73/74 C.E.) was instructed by Vespasian to destroy it (*J.W.* 7.421), an order that only Paulinus, Lupus' successor, followed (*J.W.* 7.433-35). Although it is disputed whether Onias' temple has indeed been identified at Tell el-Yehudiyyeh (it was excavated in 1887 and in 1906), a large number of tombs appear to have been used by Jews. As in Alexandria, the tombs usually follow contemporary forms. All of them are *hypogea* (underground chambers), most of them used for an entire family. The bodies were placed in *loculi* or *kokhim* (niches) hewn into the rock rectangular to the tomb's inner chamber. The head was often placed on an earthen "cushion," and the body received no embalming or decoration. More than eighty Greek tombstones (few found *in situ*) may be Jewish, but identification is notoriously difficult. The earliest inscription dates to 117 B.C.E., but most belong to the first century C.E. Both the size of the cemetery and the shape of the graves suggest that the population was well established and organized until its end in the uprisings of 116-117 C.E.

Other Sites in Egypt

Through inscriptions, ostraca, papyri, and burials, Jewish communities are also attested in many towns and villages in the Delta (Schedia, Athribis, Nitriai) and in Middle Egypt and the Fayyum (Arsinoe, Alexandrou Nesos, Oxyrhynchus, Hermoupolis Magna, Edfu, Sedment el-Gebel).

Greece

Archaeological evidence from Greece is scant before the second century C.E. Delos plays an especially prominent role. 1 Maccabees 15:23 attests a Jewish community there in 140 B.C.E. One building, built as a private home in the second century B.C.E., was rebuilt as a local assembly hall in two phases, first between the late second century B.C.E. and 88 B.C.E., and then in the first century B.C.E. The identification as a synagogue is based on the existence of a large assembly room and five dedicatory inscriptions mentioning *Theos Hypsistos* (the Most High God) and another inscription nearby mentioning a *proseuchē.* A cistern nearby could have been used as a *miqveh,* and a seat may have represented the "seat of Moses." Like synagogues in pre-70 Palestine, the assembly hall at Delos has a simple architecture and little decoration. The translation of *epi proseuchē* in the inscription as "house of prayer" is uncertain, since the phrase can mean "in (fulfillment of) a prayer/vow" (*IJO* 1:227). Several lamps with pagan motifs were also found in the house. The building itself followed the pattern set by other Delian associations, whose structures had a porticoed courtyard and a marble chair. The "mixed" profile of material culture leaves two alternatives: either a synagogue for a Jewish community deeply assimilated to local pagan culture (if so, then it would be the earliest one excavated in the Diaspora), or the assembly hall of a pagan guild. At present both options appear equally viable.

Two inscriptions from an unexcavated building near the possible synagogue demonstrate that Jewish communities were not the only ones to spread across the eastern Mediterranean; Samaritan communities did as well. Interestingly enough, the self-designation of the Samaritan community on Delos was "the Israelites in Delos who pay tribute to the holy sanctuary Argarizim," and they called their assembly hall a *proseuchē*. Two epitaphs inscribed before 88 B.C.E. were found on Rhenaia, the burial island of Delos. Each mentions the violent death of a woman and calls upon "*Theos Hypsistos*, Lord of the spirits and all flesh" to send "the angels of God" to avenge the crime. The terminology seems to indicate a Jewish milieu.

Evidence from other places in Greece is sparse. The second-century-B.C.E. date of an epitaph mentioning a certain Sim(e)on son of Ananias from Athens is debated (*IJO* 1:156-57). Especially interesting are two inscriptions incised on the polygonal wall of the temple of Apollo at Delphi dated to 163/62 and 158/57 B.C.E., respectively. The inscriptions document the manumission of a male slave named Ioudaios and a female slave named Antigone. In another inscription from Delphi from the second to first century B.C.E., Ioudaios son of Pindaros declares his slave Amyntas free (*IJO* 1:173-76). The oldest manumission inscription mentioning a *Ioudaios* ("Jew" or "Judean") comes from the Amphiareion at Oropus and is dated to 300-250 B.C.E. Here Moschus son of Moschion obeyed a dream sent by the gods Amphiaraos and Hygieia commanding him to erect an inscription documenting his manumission from an unknown master (*IJO* 1:177-80). On an inscription from Iasos, a certain Niketas son of Iason from Jerusalem is listed as one of two *metoikoi* (resident foreigners) who have together donated 100 drachmas for an unnamed pagan festival. If Niketas was indeed a Jew, the inscription, dated after 150 B.C.E., documents participation of Jews in public life. Another list of names from Iasos, dated to the early first century B.C.E., may also include Jews since the names Judas and Jason are mentioned (*IJO* 2:129-31). A list of benefactors from Smyrna dated 123/24 C.E. mentions that "a group of former Jews" pledged to give 10,000 drachmas. The phrase *hoi pote Ioudaioi* is unique and enigmatic: does it refer to inhabitants of Smyrna who used to live in Judea or who were apostate Jews? The term *Ioudaios* can indicate both regional origin and religious affiliation. Also unclear is whether the phrase is a self-definition or a label applied to them by the city officials who commissioned the inscription (*IJO* 2:177-79).

Asia Minor

For the growing Jewish communities in Asia Minor, literary texts are virtually our only sources before the second century C.E. Here the fragmentary nature of our archaeological material is especially deplorable.

Palestine in the Herodian Period (40 B.C.E.–39 C.E.)

The separation of the Hasmonean from the Herodian period is to a large extent artificial and follows historical rather than archaeological categories. In many respects, Herodian material culture not only builds upon earlier developments and inventions but also intensifies and differentiates them.

Herod's grandiose building projects put him in the first rank among his fellow eastern regents. Usually, three phases of construction are distinguished. The first phase lasted from his accession to power in 40 B.C.E. to the Battle of Actium in 31 B.C.E. and comprised fortresses (the refurbishment of older ones at Alexandrion, Machaerus, and Masada and the construction of new ones at Antonia, Hyrcania, and Cyprus) and palaces (the western palace at Masada, the first palace at Jericho, and perhaps the palace at Callirhoe).

The second phase, which extended from the Battle of Actium until the visit of Augustus' friend Marcus Vipsanius Agrippa to Judea in 15 B.C.E., saw the most numerous and largest of Herod's building projects. Military architecture decreased; the focus now lay on development of the realm through cities, palaces, and buildings for entertainment and cult. After the construction of the theater and amphitheater in Jerusalem, Herod founded Sebaste, the Herodion, and Caesarea Maritima; built the sanctuary in Paneas, his palace in Jerusalem, the second palace in Jericho, and the northern palace in Masada; and started expanding the Temple in Jerusalem.

The third phase of Herod's building program extended from the visit of Agrippa until Herod's death in 4 B.C.E. Few new accents appear in this phase. Many of the projects started in the second phase were continued. Complementary initiatives were the embellishment of David's tomb in Jerusalem, the foundation of military colonies in Trachonitis and Batanea, the construction of the third palace in Jericho, and the addition of the casemate wall at Masada. It is not clear if the sanctuaries in Mamre and Hebron and the foundation of the cities of Phasaelis, Antipatris, and Livias belong to the second or third phase. In addition to being enterprising in Palestine, Herod was an eager benefactor and donated money or commissioned buildings in many places around the Mediterranean.

Herod's sons readily followed their father, albeit on a lesser scale. In the southern Jordan Valley, Archelaus founded Archelais to better exploit the date palm groves; in Galilee, Antipas rebuilt Sepphoris and founded Tiberias in 18 C.E. as his two residential cities; and Philip refounded Bethsaida as Julias.

Herod's Building Style

Herod's building style mirrored the shrewdness of his political sensibilities and the multiethnic nature of his realm. He avoided almost entirely the use of figurative art in public and private contexts in regions where Jews were the predominant inhabitants. Here he brought the Hasmonean material culture to a new climax. This restriction went hand in hand with the intensified development of an alternative architectural and decorative idiom that had already begun in Hasmonean times. As before, the new style is inconceivable without contemporaneous architectural and decorative models borrowed from outside Palestine.

Herod's builders adapted building types and architectural models such as hippodromes, amphitheaters, Roman-type baths, domes, arches, vaults, triclinia (dining rooms with couches on three sides), gardens, peristyle courts (courts surrounded by a row of columns), and large piscinae (fish ponds). Huge fortresses at Masada, Machaerus, and Herodium, palaces in Jericho and Jerusalem, and cities like Sebaste and Caesarea show new styles of wall construction, including *opus reticulatum:* the use of pyramidal blocks laid out diagonally with their bases facing outward. The delicate geometrical patterns displayed on polychrome aniconic mosaics and on architectural elements of the Temple were based on Hellenistic and Roman decorative patterns of the first century B.C.E. but did not simply copy them. The same trend seems to be evident in Herodian-period painting. There is evidence that Herod had some of his walls painted by artisans from Italy. Much of the new style also appears outside the court, as in the mosaics in the Upper City of Jerusalem and the wall paintings at Yodefat and Gamla.

The temples that Herod had built offer good examples of the complex blend of Hellenistic and indigenous traditions. The general layout of the Jerusalem Temple precinct resembles other contemporaneous sanctuaries in Heliopolis (Ba'albek), Damascus, and Palmyra. The porticoes and stoa around the platform followed the best of Greek style and employed lavish classical decoration with meanders, rosettes, and floral designs. The sanctuary provided space for thousands of pilgrims, scores of cultic officials, and numerous installations. Although the Temple itself was built in centuries-old oriental fashion, the entire sanctuary reflected Herod's participation in the cultural koine of his time.

Herod's outlook is also visible in the promotion and architectural embellishment of traditional Semitic cult centers in Mamre, Hebron, and Paneion. In Mamre and Hebron the old cultic installations were surrounded with a monumental perimeter wall made in the same style as the Temple platform in Jerusalem. In Paneion the traditional cave sanctuary was embellished with a temple building directly placed in front of the grotto.

Settlement Activity

The Herodian age brought an intensification of settlement activity that was connected to and enabled a rise in population. Surveys in the Galilee have demonstrated that the decades after the turn of the era produced the greatest density in settlement before the Byzantine period. The same can be said of the area around the Dead Sea. Here, old structures were expanded (Qumran) and new ones added (ʿEin Feshkha). Entirely new settlements (e.g., Livias and Callirhoe) filled gaps in the regional infrastructure. Even the most luxurious palaces, such as those at Callirhoe and Jericho, were not isolated but integrated into large complexes.

Qumran

One of the most famous and controversial sites is Khirbet Qumran, located about fifteen kilometers south of Jericho on the western shore of the Dead Sea. Excavated by Roland de Vaux between 1949 and 1956, the site was soon identified as a settlement for a group of Essenes who had already been linked to scrolls found in a nearby cave in 1946/47. More caves and scrolls were discovered over the next decade. Due to the lack of a detailed report on the stratigraphy of the site and a complete presentation of finds, the history of the buildings and the stages of occupation are still not entirely clear. Many scholars accept the following chronology: after an initial phase of settlement in Iron Age II that lasted from about 630 to 580 B.C.E., a second phase of occupation began around 100 B.C.E. and lasted until about 9/8 B.C.E. or shortly thereafter (Period I). After a brief period of abandonment, the site was reoccupied from around 4 B.C.E. until it was destroyed by the Romans in 68 C.E. (Period II). A small Roman garrison was then stationed at Qumran until 73 or 74 C.E. (Period III).

More disputed is the function of the site in Periods I and II. While most scholars still more or less accept de Vaux's view that a sectarian community of Essenes inhabited Qumran during these phases, a significant minority regard Qumran as part of the economic infrastructure of the Dead Sea region. Advocates of the Essene hypothesis point to several features of the site that suggest its use as a religious community center: the high number and large size of the stepped pools, interpreted as *miqvaʾot* (ritual baths); the distinctive cylindrical jars, thought to have been used to store scrolls and other valuables; the high number of ink wells, indicative of scribal activity; the animal bone deposits, suggestive of kosher communal meals; the communal dining rooms, with adjacent pantries containing more than a thousand dishes; the numerous workshops, including a kiln for the production of ritually pure pottery; and the large cemetery nearby that is hard to explain unless a community used it over time. Proponents of the Essene hypothesis also point to the nearby caves with scrolls, several of which describe the beliefs and practices of a sectarian group that resembles the Essenes as described by Pliny, Philo, and Josephus.

Several alternative identifications of the site have been proposed in recent years: a military fortress, a country villa, a commercial entrepôt, a fortified farm, or a center for ritual purification used by various Jewish groups. Most of these proposals doubt that there was a connection between the scrolls and the site. Some of them maintain that the pottery repertoire at Qumran is not distinctive and that neither the settlement's layout and location nor the nearby cemetery is unique or indicative of a religious community.

ʿEin Feshka

In an oasis only two kilometers east of Qumran lies ʿEin Feshkha. The ceramic data indicate that the settlement was contemporaneous with Qumran Period II and was likewise destroyed in 68 C.E. ʿEin Feshkha is a good example of the continuity of traditional architecture in a rural context: a rectangular courtyard was surrounded on all sides by rooms; an industrial installation for processing dates or balsam lies immediately north of it, and stables to the south. Other sites such as Rujm el-Bahr, Qasr et-Turabe, and Khirbet Mazin show that the vicinity of Qumran was intensively used between 100 B.C.E. and 68 C.E.

Synagogues

In the Herodian period we find the oldest synagogues in Palestine. While the synagogue at Gamla may slightly predate the Herodian period, the ones at Qiryat Sefer and Horvat Etri and the added synagogues in Masada and Herodion are Herodian or later. The character of the "synagogue" in Jericho is uncertain. Since none of these buildings is explicitly identified as a synagogue through inscriptions, definition is a matter of conjecture based on form and functionality. All the structures have various shared architectural features: long halls divided by rows of columns into a central nave with surrounding aisles and stepped benches along all four walls. The earliest epigraphic evidence for synagogues in Judea is a building inscription in Greek found in a secondary context on Mount Ophel. No remains of the building itself have survived, but the inscription, which dates to the first decades of the first century C.E., names the dedicator of a synagogue, a man named Theodotus:

> Theodotus, son of Vettanos, a priest and an *archisynagōgos,* son of an *archisynagōgos* grandson of an *archisynagōgos,* built the synagogue for the reading of Torah and for teaching the commandments; also the hostel, and the rooms, and the water installation for lodging needy strangers. Its foundation stone was laid by his ancestors, the elders, and Simonides.

Stone Vessels

Apart from *miqvaʾot* and synagogues, two other types of objects connected to Jewish religiosity came into use during the later first century B.C.E.: stone vessels and ossuaries. Stone vessels are now known from more than sixty sites in ancient Palestine. They first appeared around 50 B.C.E. in Jerusalem and during the following decades flooded the market in an ever growing variety of forms, peaking just before the First Revolt and declining until the Bar Kokhba Revolt. After 150 C.E. they disappeared. Most widely used were small mugs with a handle (sometimes also with a lid) and round bowls mass produced by turning blocks of soft limestone on a lathe. Since the raw materials were especially easy to find near Jerusalem and in the vicinity of Nazareth, these two locations served as production centers. At the turn of the era, large crater-like vessels imitating luxurious Hellenistic marble ware were added to the repertoire of Jerusalem workshops, as were trays, tabletops, decorative elements, small columns, and sundials. It is conceivable that the rapid distribution of simple stone vessels in first-century-B.C.E. and -C.E. Judea was inspired by stricter purity regulations, but it would go too far to link all products of the growing stone industry to religious attitudes or practices. Many products were simply fashionable, practical, and available in sufficient numbers to be successful on the market.

Ossuaries

Ossuaries are another product of the limestone industry. They came to be used only during the later decades of the first century B.C.E., starting in Jerusalem. They peaked just before the First Revolt and gradually disappeared in the second century C.E. Most of the ossuaries found in Jerusalem are not decorated, but most in Jericho are. The latter were ornamented with architectural, geometric, and plant motifs. The most frequent type of decoration involved incising or chip-carving a series of zigzag lines within two straight lines. As noted above, some ossuaries have the names of the deceased inscribed on them and at times add details about the origin or the occupation of the deceased.

Menorahs

One of the most prominent symbols of Jewish culture and identity is the menorah, the seven-branched candelabrum. Originally part of the inventory of the Second Temple, the menorah came to be adopted in other contexts as well. The only archaeological witness to the Temple menorah itself is the famous relief on the Arch of Titus in Rome (81 C.E.). There the candelabrum is depicted among other spoils of war, including the showbread table and trumpets, being presented in triumph by the victorious Roman army. The oldest depictions of the menorah, however, date to shortly before the Herodian period. In his struggle against Herod, Mattathias, the last Hasmonean king and high priest, minted coins depicting the menorah on the reverse and the showbread table on the obverse as the most prominent cultic objects in order to emphasize his priestly lineage and the legitimacy of his rule. Later, menorahs were found incised on walls of rooms (the most famous from a wall in a house of the Upper City in Jerusalem dated to the first century C.E.), on a sundial found in the vicinity of the Temple (its original context is unknown but it is dated to the first century B.C.E./C.E.), in tombs (the eastern wall of the porch of Jason's tomb from around 30 C.E.), on ossuaries (one example comes from the Goliath family tomb in Jericho), and on a cistern wall in a refuge cave in Naḥal Mikhmas. None of these contexts has a particularly cultic character. Evidently, the menorah was on its way to becoming a more generic symbol of the Jewish religion. The number of menorahs depicted before the second half of the second century C.E. is very low, and there are no depictions from the Diaspora before the third century C.E., except in the Arch of Titus.

Glassware

During the Herodian period, Palestine benefited from the stable political conditions in the early Empire and enjoyed unprecedented economic growth and prosperity. Consequently the variety of small objects, both locally produced and imported, grew considerably. Glass from the Lebanese coast and fine ware from Syria, Cyprus, and Italy were increasingly imported into Palestine, where they supplemented traditions of local pottery production. From the second century B.C.E. onwards, molded glass bowls, later complemented by beakers, were imported into Palestine. Blown glass quickly spread after its invention somewhere on the Phoenician coast in the very late first century B.C.E. or early first century C.E. Imported ware from Italy became available during the middle and latter part of the first century C.E. That glass is almost ubiquitous in first-century contexts indicates that it quickly lost its status as a luxury item and became a fairly common commodity. From the Herodian period onward, Palestine was firmly integrated into the empire-wide glass market, and its inhabitants showed no qualms in acquiring affordable vessels of the latest fashion, such as "Ennion" beakers in Jerusalem's Upper City and pieces of imported Italian glass found at Qumran. Some common household glass was even produced in local workshops in the Upper City of Jerusalem (including tools for blowing) before 70 C.E., but no large-scale glass factories are known from Palestine before the fourth century C.E.

Coins and Weights

Coins and weights provide important evidence about Herodian administration. Apart from one group (the Year 3 coins), Herod's coins are all undated. Minting took place first in Sebaste and then in Jerusalem. New imagery appeared, partly imitating Roman coins; among them was the *caduceus* (winged staff with two snakes wrapped around it), the ceremonial cap of an *augur* (Roman priest who specialized in divination), and the *aphlaston* (fan-like ornament at the stern of ancient galleys). But sometimes these images were balanced by a more traditional one on the reverse. One coin even shows an eagle. It is likely that Herod's Jerusalem mint copied Tyrian silver shekels after the completion of the Temple.

Of special importance is an Aramaic inscription on a stone weight, excavated in one of the houses in the Jewish quarter. It mentions "Bar Kathros," possibly the name of one of the four high-priestly families who according to the Mishnah (*m. Pesaḥ.* 57:1) oppressed the people.

Inscriptions and Funerary Epitaphs

The number of inscriptions in both public and private contexts rose dramatically during the Herodian period. The rise no doubt owes to increased building activity especially under Herod himself, but it is particularly notable in the private sector connected with burial. One third of ossuaries are inscribed.

A number of inscriptions illustrate aspects of worship in the Jerusalem Temple and deserve particular attention. One of them was set up on the platform on the Temple Mount and threatens with death every foreigner who dares to enter the courtyard reserved for Israelites. Josephus reports that such warnings were set up in Greek and in Latin (*J.W.* 5.194; *Ant.* 15.417). A Greek specimen of the inscription was found in 1896, a second, fragmentary one in 1935.

Another fragmentary inscription was found in 1968 in the debris filling a pool south of the Temple Mount. It gives in Greek the name "[S]paris son of Akeson . . . in Rhodes," a man who donated an unknown number of drachmas for a floor dated to the twentieth year of Herod (18-17 B.C.E.). Despite its fragmentary state, the inscription indicates that private donations from the Diaspora played some part in erecting and decorating the Temple, and that donors did not have to be Jewish.

A third monumental inscription, found incomplete in the debris and written in square script is read by excavator Benjamin Mazar as "to the place of trumpeting to pr[oclaim the Sabbath]" (*lbyt htqy'h lhk*[]). On another fragment only the Hebrew word "elders" *(zqnym)* is readable. Yet another, written in Paleo-Hebrew letters (only the word *bn* is discernible), was found in the fill below an Umayyad floor. It indicates that Paleo-Hebrew was still used for monumental inscriptions in Second Temple Jerusalem. It is impossible to say whether the use of Paleo-Hebrew reflects a special political or ideological intent. In any case, the material on which the inscription was made was marble imported from Greece or Italy.

Funerary epitaphs grant insight into the society of late Second Temple Jerusalem. Many of them are written in cursive Hebrew script, some in Aramaic, others in square script, still others in Paleo-Hebrew. Several ossuaries found in the burial complexes at Aceldama south of the Temple Mount demonstrate that Greek was also used. Monumental inscriptions on tomb façades are still rare, but inscriptions are numerous and instructive. Many of them mention the occupation or origin of the deceased, and several demonstrate that many Diaspora Jews wanted to be buried in Jerusalem. Some of the names on ossuaries have been identified with persons known from the New Testament: James the brother of Jesus (unprovenanced and highly disputed), Nicodemus, and Caiaphas (reading not entirely certain). Others name individuals who are otherwise unknown: "Simon the Temple builder," apparently one of the artisans who worked on the Temple; "Nicanor who made the Gates"; and Yehohanan from Giv'at ha-Mivtar, a man who was crucified. The longest inscription from a chamber tomb comes from the Giv'at ha-Mivtar neighborhood of Jerusalem. It was placed on the wall opposite the entrance of the tomb and written in Aramaic using Paleo-Hebrew script. It is inscribed, very unusually, in the first person by the man who buried the deceased:

> I, Abba, son of the priest Eliez[ar] son of Aaron the Great; I, Abba, the oppressed, the pursued, who was born in Jerusalem and went into exile in Babylonia and (was) carried up (for interment), Mattathi[ah] son of Yud[ah], and I buried him in the cave that I purchased by the writ.

The Diaspora in the Early Roman Period

Compared to Palestine, the archaeological evidence for Jewish life in the Diaspora in the first century B.C.E. and C.E. is slim.

Inscriptions

In the first century B.C.E. the number of inscriptions from the Greek Diaspora in Achaia and Ionia grew. Between 37 and 27 B.C.E. the people of Athens honored King Herod (titled *philorhōmaios* [friend of the Romans] and *philokaisar* [friend of Caesar]) with at least two inscriptions for his benefaction *(euegersia)* and goodwill *(eunoia)*. A similar inscription was set up somewhere in the propylon (monumental gateway) of the temple of Apollo in Delphi by the "Athenian people and those living on the islands" in honor of the "Tetrarch Herod son of King Herod" (Herod Antipas). Obviously the Herodian family showed particular sympathy towards Apollo. A certain Justus son of Andromache from Tiberias is mentioned in an epitaph from Taenarum on the Peloponnesus dated to the first century C.E. or later.

Jews moved not only from the Diaspora to Palestine and especially Jerusalem but also in the opposite direction. A Greek epitaph from Smyrna dated to the early Imperial period mentions a certain Lucius Lollius Justus, "secretary of the people in Smyrna" *(grammateus tou en Zmyrnē laou)*. The word *laos* may refer to the Jewish people, but judging from the tripartite name Justus was a Roman citizen. During the first century C.E., Jews probably originating from Egypt began to leave traces in North Africa; evidence for this comes in two honorary inscriptions of Jews from Berenike in Cyrenaica. Although literary testimony leaves no doubt that Jews lived in Rome at least since the first century B.C.E., archaeological evidence there is rare. Most catacombs date to the second to fourth century C.E.

Synagogues

Archaeological evidence for Diaspora synagogues in the first century C.E. comes only from Ostia, beneath later building phases. There was a main hall with benches along the walls. Another first-century-C.E. synagogue is attested at Acmonia in Phrygia by its building inscription. Its socio-historical significance can be compared with the famous Theodotus inscription from Jerusalem. The inscription reads:

> the lifetime *archisynagōgos* P. Tyrronius Klados and the *archisynagōgos* Lucius son of Lucius, and the *archōn* Popilius Zotikos restored with their own means

> and those of the congregation the house that Julia Severa had built. They had the walls and ceilings painted, the safety of the windows restored and all the other decoration. They were honored by the congregation *(synagōgē)* through a gilded shield. (*IJO* 2:348-55)

Since the patron of the first synagogue, Julia Severa, belongs to the first century, the original synagogue must as well. The renovation may have been carried out in the second or third century C.E. Yet Julia Severa and her family are often mentioned in connection with the Imperial cult in Acmonia; she herself served as a priestess, so it is unlikely that she was Jewish. Judging from their names, the two *archisynagōgoi* and the *archōn* were Roman citizens. Honoring benefactors with a precious shield was not unusual in Greek cities but is unattested elsewhere in a synagogue context. The vast majority of Diaspora synagogues date to the later Roman period, a few to the late second or third century C.E. Again, Asia Minor is deeply underrepresented in the archaeological record.

Palestine before the First Revolt (ca. 6-66 C.E.)

Direct Roman rule in Palestine began after Archelaus was exiled from his ethnarchy Judea and replaced by a governor of equestrian rank in 6 C.E. From then on, Caesarea Maritima functioned as the capital of what was now a largely independent subunit of Syria under a subordinate official: a prefect of Judea *(praefectus Iudaeae)*. The other parts of Herod's former kingdom came under direct Roman administration only after their rulers Antipas and Philip had died, but they were not added to Judea. Only between 41 and 44 C.E. were all parts reunited under the Jewish king Agrippa I.

Few material remains can be securely attributed to the Romans, among them mostly inscriptions or building projects relating to infrastructure such as the aqueducts at Caesarea Maritima and Jerusalem. Caesarea is the only city where some building activity from the post-Herodian and pre-Revolt period can be observed. The governor probably resided in Herod's promontory palace, not far from the hippodrome. Administrative buildings were erected and the large storage vaults used for trade. Especially famous is an inscription discovered in 1961 that mentions Pontius Pilate (re)erecting a building dedicated to Tiberius (probably a lighthouse): *Tiberieum [Pon]tius Pilatus [Praef]ectus Iuda[eae].* Large estates that formerly belonged to members of the Herodian family were now administered by *procuratores* of the emperor, who were mostly freedmen. A small garrison was stationed on Masada.

The First Revolt (66-73/4 C.E.)

The outbreak of the Jewish Revolt in 66 C.E. interrupted most integrative trends in Palestinian Jewish culture. Archaeological evidence for the activities and ideology of the insurgents is strong and varied. Coins serve as direct evidence of the ideology of the insurgents and their efforts to set up an effective administration. The Jewish population was mobilized and cities, especially in the north, were fortified. Many of these fortifications are known from Josephus, only a few from the archaeological record. Apart from the wall surrounding Itabyrion (Mt. Tabor), it is especially the Zealot occupation at Herodion and Masada that has triggered the interest of scholars. Both strongholds and their supplies were seized from the Romans in the year 66. At Herodion and Masada, triclinia were converted into assembly rooms (synagogues) by changing the layout of the room (Masada) and adding benches around the walls (Herodion and Masada). The casemate walls at Masada were subdivided into workshops, and living quarters for families and headquarters were set up in the western palace. According to the excavators, the construction of numerous stepped pools *(miqva'ot)* and the use of special types of pottery ("dung ware" made from a mixture of animal dung and clay) testify to the purity concerns of the inhabitants. Toward the end of the revolt, many people fled to caves in the Judean desert or took refuge in underground hideouts. The coins from Sepphoris with their blunt designation as NEPWNIA CPFW . . . EIPHNOPOLI ("Neronias-Sepphoris, city of peace") are a rare indication of refusal to join the revolt.

Archaeology also allows detailed insight into the tactics and skills of the Roman occupational force, further illustrated by detailed descriptions in Josephus. Among the best-preserved archaeological remains of Roman battlefields are the breach in the wall of Gamla and the destruction of its main tower, and the siege works at Narbata, Yodefat, Machaerus, and Masada. Weapons such as arrowheads, swords, *ballistae* (heavy missile weapons), and parts of military equipment such as catapults have been found at Gamla and Masada.

Qumran provides a good example of the destruction of a smaller settlement. Remains of the Jewish defenders are rare but telling. In the Burnt House in Jerusalem, a spearhead and a severed arm of a woman were found, as were two skulls in the Kenyon excavations in the City of David. The famous skeletons discovered by Yadin on Masada, however, belonged to the occupants of the post-revolt garrison.

Excavations in the Old City of Jerusalem show signs of profound destruction. The sanctuary was damaged during the siege and the Roman assault. The Temple had gone up in flames. Large blocks tumbled from the platform and covered the paved streets west and south of the sanctuary. All shops were destroyed, many showing signs of burning. In the city, entire residential quarters were destroyed. The Burnt House in the Lower City and the area around the Palatial Mansion in the Upper City are telling witnesses of the devastation. From then on, the *Legio X Fretensis* (Roman Tenth Legion) guarded the interests of Rome in the region. The Romans celebrated their victory by issuing the famous IVDAEA CAPTA (Judea Captured) coins, dedicating monuments like the Arch of Titus and the Coliseum, and setting up inscriptions, some of which are known from Rome and Jerusalem.

Palestine between the Two Revolts (73/74-132 C.E.)

Archaeological evidence for Roman influence after 73/74 is continually growing. While only little research has been carried out in Joppa (Jaffa) and Nikopolis, second-century-C.E. Neapolis is much better known. A theater, a hippodrome, and a temple dedicated to Zeus on Tell er-Ras and parts of the necropolis have been excavated. Caesarea Maritima continued to flourish as governor's seat and mercantile center, with the Latin presence becoming even more prominent. Soldiers built a new aqueduct and repaired the old one. Tombstones and military diplomas attest many of the auxiliary units stationed in the region along with the *Legio X Fretensis,* and they provide prosopographic and administrative information. The first governor of Judea after the conquest of Jerusalem, Sextus Lucilius Bassus, governor from 71-73 and conqueror of Herodium, is mentioned in a fragmentary building inscription found in the vicinity of Abu Ghosh at the Roman road from Joppa to Jerusalem. Lucilius Bassus also seems to be named on a milestone reused as support for a pillar in an Umayyad palace.

In Jerusalem, many remains of the Herodian city were gradually removed. Remains of the Temple were completely obliterated from the platform, and large parts of the *temenos* (Temple precinct) walls were torn down. Herod's palace on the western side of the city in today's Armenian quarter was completely razed to make room for the camp of the *Legio X Fretensis.* Parts of the Ophel/City of David were used as a dump and a quarry. In other areas, especially in the northwest and northeast, the Romans slowly began to rebuild the city. Pottery workshops at the outskirts of Roman Jerusalem mass-produced building material for the army, including tiles with the stamp of the Legion. A bakery built into former shops at the southwestern corner of the Temple Mount catered for the army. Roman soldiers introduced cremation to the region. Although Jerusalem's population gradually became pagan, the city retained its old name, Hierosolyma, until 130/131 C.E. Foreign cults must have found their way into the city after 70 C.E., providing the basis for the second-century paganization under Hadrian.

Archaeological traces of a Jewish presence in the decades between the two revolts are scant. Often tendencies and impulses from the late Herodian period continued, such as the first display of the menorah on lamps dating to the early second century C.E., and of grapes, fruit, and other symbols. Similar designs were used on ossuaries.

The Diaspora between the Revolts

The First Revolt had little direct support from the Diaspora, and the devastating uprisings in Egypt, Cyprus, Cyrenaica, and Mesopotamia during the reign of Trajan in 115/116-117 C.E. evidently had little effect on Palestine. Archaeological evidence for these uprisings remains extremely scarce, but papyri do shed some light. One dated to 19 June 116 indicates that the *stratēgos* Apollonios, who took part in the conflict, had requested the purchase of new arms (P. Gissenses 47), and another shows that at the beginning of September Apollonios' wife Aline was deeply concerned for his safety (*CPJ* 2:436). Epigraphic evidence indicates that Jews attacked temples and other centers of Greek civic life. In the city of Cyrene, in the sanctuary of Apollo, the baths and other neighboring buildings were burned to the ground. The temple of Hecate was also destroyed, as were the Caesareum and the temple of Zeus. Papyri from Egypt show that the uprising spread over vast sections of the country and that Jews won some early victories. Eventually, though, the uprisings brought total disaster on the Jews. In Egypt, Jewish property was confiscated by the Roman government (*CPJ* 2:445, 448; P. Berolensis inv. 7440; P. Berolensis inv. 8143), and evidence for Jewish life in Egypt, Libya, and Cyprus virtually disappears after 117 C.E.

A number of inscriptions shed light on some aspects of Jewish life in the late first and early second century C.E. Manumission inscriptions from the first to second century C.E. in Pantikapaion, Phanagoria, and Gorgippia on the Black Sea mention a "community of the Jews" (sometimes the phrase *theon sebōn* — "who worship God" — is added) that served as the slaves' guardian upon their manumission (*IJO* 1:268-86, 295-301, 303-19). In that respect, the "prayer house" *(proseuchē)* functioned like pagan temples.

The Bar Kokhba Revolt (132-135 C.E.)

Unlike the First Revolt, which was documented in great detail by Josephus, the history of the Second Revolt is not well known. When Hadrian set off for his famous oriental journey and traveled to Egypt through Judea in 130 (Cassius Dio, *Epitome* 69.11.1), many local councils took the chance to demonstrate their loyalty by renaming their city and commissioning public buildings in honor of the emperor. Coins proclaimed the ADVENTVS AVGusti IVDAEAE ("Arrival of Augustus in Judea") and inscriptions were erected. Hierosolyma was renamed Aelia Capitolina in honor of Aelius Hadrianus and the Capitoline Trias. With it came a prestigious building program: an equestrian column was erected on the Temple platform, other sanctuaries were founded or refurbished, and public buildings erected or commissioned. Coins announced the new city: COLonia AELia CAPITolina CONDita ("Founding of the Colony of Aelia Capitolina"). Before many of these building projects could be implemented or even completed, the Second Revolt broke out in 132.

As in the First Revolt, coins provide the most prominent evidence of the ideology of the Jewish insurgents. All coins refrained from displaying offensive images but deliberately used traditional imagery with clear religious connotations: the façade of the Temple, grapes, the four species (lulav, ethrog, willow, myrtle), Temple vessels, palm tree, and musical instruments (lyre, harp, trumpets). The only symbol that has classical predecessors is the wreath. The titulature of the coins expressed hope for the liberation of Jerusalem and the restoration of the Temple and its cult. The leader of the revolt, Shimon bar Kosiba (nicknamed Bar Kokhba, "Son of a Star," after Num. 24:17), is designated "prince *(naśi')* of Israel." As in the previous revolt, years were counted from the beginning of the insurgency (year one to four of the "redemption"). The coins were struck in bronze and silver and were inscribed in square or Paleo-Hebrew script. Often Roman coins were simply overstruck. In caves by the Dead Sea, refugees hid precious goods (documents, keys, textiles, basketry, coins) that they had either brought from their own homes or, as in the case of incense shovels, plundered. Some of the bronze jugs even had pagan images defaced.

Initially, Roman resistance was uncoordinated, and the revolt spread through various parts of central Palestine. Three very different kinds of archaeological sources can be used to reconstruct the geographical range of the rebellion: the distribution of rebel coins, the distribution of characteristic hiding places, and place names mentioned in documents written by insurgents. The focus of the revolt clearly was Judea, including the Judean Desert, and the Jewish-populated hill country to the west, east, and south and ʿEin Gedi. New papyrological evidence suggests that Jerusalem was under the control of the insurgents at least for a short period, but this is not yet corroborated by coin finds. Jewish communities in western Transjordan were also affected. Material evidence from Galilee is not yet sufficient to determine whether the region actively took part in the revolt. The final battle at Bethar, west of Jerusalem, is documented by archaeological remains (siege works, military equipment).

The results of the Second Revolt probably were even more devastating for the Jews than those of the First. Judea was renamed Syria Palestina to erase the rebellious Jews' name from memory. The plans to rebuild Hierosolyma as Aelia Capitolina were carried out. A large arch was built north of the city (Damascus Gate), and in the second half of the second century C.E. another arch was built to demarcate the civil and military parts of the city (Ecce Homo Arch). The chance find of a cuirassed bronze torso of Hadrian in 1975 near Tel Shalem, twelve kilometers south of Scythopolis, and the results of subsequent excavations (more bronze fragments, a bronze head of a boy, and a fragmentary inscription) throw fascinating light on one particular victory celebration. Both the statue and the inscription belonged to a triumphal arch that was erected by the senate and people of Rome after the fighting had ended in early 136, to commemorate Hadrian's personal efforts in suppressing the revolt and to celebrate the reorganization of Judea as Syria Palestina.

The surviving Jewish population shifted south to Darom and north to the Galilee, where Jewish cultural life was gradually reconstituted along new lines that included prayer in synagogues and study of religious law. Material traces of the revival do not begin to appear until one or two generations after the crushing of the Second Revolt, so they fall beyond our chronological scope.

It is significant that Hellenization did not end during the period of Jewish reconstruction but was resumed and even intensified by the new elite comprised of rabbis and other scholars. Crucial institutions were directly continued (above all the synagogue), while other elements of material culture, such as stone vessels and ossuaries, gradually disappeared. Elements of Hellenistic art and architecture played a much greater role than before the revolt. Late Roman and Byzantine synagogues are a good example; they were lavishly decorated with mosaics representing complex theological concepts and central scenes of salvation history, but the frequent use of animals and human figures goes well beyond the limits of what most Jews would have considered tolerable before the year 70.

Textual Discoveries from Palestine

Apart from Egypt, where large numbers of texts on perishable material such as papyrus, leather, and wax tablets made of wood have been found, the Judean Desert, especially its caves on the western side of the Dead Sea, has proved the major source for such texts since the late 1940s. Popularly known as the Dead Sea Scrolls, they are more properly referred to as documents from the Judean Desert. The texts were found at different places, come from different periods, and fall into various categories.

Qumran

Undoubtedly the most famous and most widely discussed texts among the Dead Sea Scrolls are those found between 1946-1947 and 1956 in eleven caves near Qumran. As noted above, most scholars regard the texts as remains of a library associated with a group of Essenes. Discovered were around 100,000 fragments of approximately 800 to 900 manuscripts representing some 350 literary compositions, penned between the third century B.C.E. and around 50 C.E. The distribution of manuscripts between the caves is very uneven. No less than 70 percent of the manuscripts were found in Cave 4, while the most complete ones come from Caves 1 and 11. Caves 2, 3, 5, 6, 8, 9, and 10 produced very few texts. In Cave 7 only Greek papyrus fragments were found.

The Qumran texts differ from all other manuscript finds from the Judean Desert by their number and their religious character. About a quarter of the corpus, around 220 manuscripts, are multiple copies of biblical works, though Nehemiah and Esther are apparently lacking. The biblical manuscripts not only throw important light on the development of the biblical text and the history of the Jewish canon, but they also allow new insights into techniques of copying and transmitting biblical manuscripts. Another quarter of the corpus, close to 200 manuscripts, represents a wide variety of religious texts, a few previously known but most heretofore unknown. Slightly more than a third of the corpus, around 250 manuscripts, are recognized by most scholars as documents that reflect the ideology and practices of a particular sect, usually identified as Essene. This category includes such works at the *Rule of the Community* (1QS), the *Rule of the Congregation* (1QSa), the *Rule of Blessings* (1QSb), the *Thanksgiving Hymns* (1QH), the *War Scroll* (1QM), and the pesharim (e.g., 1QpHab).

The great majority of books from the Qumran corpus were written in Hebrew, only a few in Greek, among them copies of LXX manuscripts in Cave 4 and a small number from Cave 7. Aramaic is represented by a significant minority of texts, among them reworkings and expansions of biblical traditions (e.g., *Genesis Apocryphon; Aramaic Levi Document)* and apocalyptic works, mostly from the Enoch cycle. Most of the texts use the square Aramaic script regardless of whether their language is Hebrew or Aramaic. Paleo-Hebrew appears in a small number of copies of pentateuchal books (e.g., 4Q11; 4Q22), Job (4Q101), and theological texts (4Q123). In some manuscripts Paleo-Hebrew is used only for the Tetragrammaton.

Besides square script, Paleo-Hebrew, and Greek, a small number of texts were written in three types of a "cryptic" Hebrew script attested nowhere else.

Seventeen documentary texts from Cave 4 written in Hebrew, Aramaic, Greek, and Nabatean probably did not originally come from Qumran. The Aramaic economic list 4Q355, Hebrew documentary texts 6Q26-6Q29, and Hebrew ostraca KhQ 1-3, however, are connected to the site.

Several graffiti and ostraca (fifty-one in Hebrew and Aramaic, eleven in Greek, and three in Latin) were found at Qumran and at ʿEin Feshkha, in addition to seven graffiti of uncertain content and ten recently discovered ones. The vessels used for the graffiti are of various origins and document the connection between settlement and the Dead Sea region, not only the caves.

Wadi Murabbaʿat

Many other texts of a different character were found south of Qumran in caves perched in the eastern cliffs of the Judean Desert. Apart from traces of habitation from the Chalcolithic, Bronze, and Iron Ages and the Arab period, the four caves in Wadi Murabbaʿat (Naḥal Dargah) examined in 1952 yielded important finds from the late Second Temple period to the time of the Bar Kokhba Revolt (pottery, coins, textiles, Roman military equipment, and documents). The oldest document from Murabbaʿat dates to the Second Temple period and is a record of a court decision (Mur 72; paleographically dated to between 125 and 100 B.C.E.). A few private legal documents suggest that refugees from the Jerusalem area fled to the region at the end of the First Revolt; these include an acknowledgment of debt (Mur 18); a writ of divorce dated to "year 6" (Mur 19); deeds of sale of land (Mur 21, 23, 25); and a marriage contract (Mur 20)

The majority of texts, however, date to the Bar Kokhba period when refugees brought private documents on papyrus (letters as well as legal documents) and religious texts on scrolls with them. The private documents cover a wide range: marriage contracts, a certificate of remarriage, farming contracts, and fiscal and administrative documents. Two letters are directly written by Bar Kokhba to Yeshua Ben Galgula (Mur 43-44). Mur 29 and 30 are especially important because they indicate that Jerusalem recognized the authority of a Jewish state as late as September-October 135.

Naḥal David

Apart from a number of graves dated to the Hasmonean and Herodian periods in caves in and around Naḥal David (Wadi Sudeir), one cave was used as a place of refuge during the Chalcolithic and Iron Age and especially the Bar Kokhba period. During their treasure hunt through caves in the ʿEin Gedi area in 1952 and 1953, the Bedouin took the remains of at least three manuscripts from the Cave of the Pool (named after a large pool at the entrance similar to the ones in Cave 1 in Wadi Murabbaʿat and Cave 40 in Naḥal Harduf): fragments of a Genesis scroll on leather and remains of two fiscal documents on papyrus, one in Greek and the other in Aramaic dated to 134 C.E. In 1961/62 Yoḥanan Aharoni and Nahman Avigad found pottery, glass vessels, combs, food remains, and a bow and arrowheads in the same cave.

Naḥal Ḥever

When Naḥal Ḥever (Wadi Habra) was surveyed by Yohanan Aharoni in 1953, ten caves were discovered, and three of them were examined in 1953 and 1955. In 1960 and 1961 intensive excavations were conducted by Yigael Yadin. It turned out that these caves were primarily used as shelter by refugees during the Bar Kokhba period. Two Roman camps, one on each side of the wadi, show that the Romans besieged the caves. Unfortunately, the manuscript caves had been searched by Bedouin before Aharoni and Yadin arrived. Three of the caves in Naḥal Ḥever proved especially important.

In a large cave with two openings, located under the northern bank of the wadi (5/6Ḥev, called the Cave of Letters), Yadin discovered a burial chamber in 1960 that contained skeletons of nineteen individuals, coins, pottery, a fragment of a Hebrew Psalms scroll (5/6Ḥev 1b), a couple of bronze objects, and a leather flask with fifteen letters written by Shimon Bar Kosiba and his comrades. A year later, Yadin found more pottery, glass vessels, metal objects, fragments of a scroll of the book of Numbers (5/6Ḥev 1a), and again a large number of papyrus documents. In all, the papyri from 5/6 Ḥev (now named P. Yadin) represent four separate archives.

The first of these archives, the Bar Kokhba Archive discovered in 1960, is especially famous (P. Yadin 49–63). Most of these letters were addressed to Yehonatan ben-Beʾayan and Masabala, two of Kosiba's commanders from ʿEin Gedi who took refuge in the cave (P. Yadin 49–56, 58–60). Only four of the documents were written in Hebrew (P. Yadin 49, 51, 60, 61), two in Greek (P. Yadin 52, 59), the rest in Aramaic. These letters give interesting insight into the legal authority of Bar Kokhba and the social and economic implications of his command.

The second archive is hardly less famous. It consists of thirty-six legal documents written in Aramaic (P. Yadin 7–8, 10), Greek (P. Yadin 5, 11–35), and Nabatean (P. Yadin 1–4, 6, 9; also P. Yadin 36, originally published as XḤev/Se nab 1) that date from between 11 August 94 and 19 August 132 C.E. They belonged to a Jewish woman named Babatha, who had fled from her hometown Maḥoz Eglatain on the eastern shores of the Dead Sea to the region of ʿEin Gedi.

Five other documents, belonging to Eleazar ben-Samuel, a farmer from ʿEin Gedi, were also found; these include private legal deeds, mostly leases and receipts from the time of Bar Kokhba (P. Yadin 42–43 in Aramaic, P. Yadin 44–46 in Hebrew, and P. Yadin 47a/b in Aramaic), possibly belonging to the same archive. These texts offer important insights into the land administration in ʿEin Gedi by Bar Kokhba.

Other documentary texts written in Hebrew, Aramaic, and Greek come from a fourth archive, one belonging to the family of Salome Komaise, daughter of Levi: P. Ḥever 12 (Aramaic) is a receipt for dates; P. Ḥever 60-64 (Greek) are deeds; P. Ḥever 65 (Greek) is a marriage contract. The Nabatean document catalogued as XḤev/Se nab. 1, first published by Jean Starcky in 1954 and now called P. Yadin 36, may also come from this archive, as may the rest of the Nabatean documents from XḤev/Se. Salome came from the same town as Babatha. Her archive contained deeds of sale and of gifts, petitions, land registrations, receipts, mortgages, promissory notes, and marriage contracts covering a period from 30 January 125 until 7 August 131 C.E.

Six papyrus documents written in Nabatean (XḤev/Se nab. 1-6), most of which were found by Bedouin, and one document in Greek probably belonging to the archive of Salome Komaise (P. Yadin 37) were also found in the Cave of Letters, as were two fragments that were wrongly assigned to the Qumran corpus but match texts from Naḥal Ḥever (4Q347 and 4Q359). All these texts — the documents from the Bar Kokhba circle, the archives of private persons, and documents concerning property — closely resemble text finds from Wadi Murabbaʿat and Wadi Seiyal.

A second cave on the southern bank, designated 8Ḥev and also known as the Cave of Horror, was excavated by Aharoni in 1961. It contained more than forty skeletons together with three ostraca with names of the deceased and Hebrew scroll fragments (8Ḥev 2). The nine fragments from a Greek scroll of the Minor Prophets found in 8Ḥev (8ḤevXIIgr) matched fragments already handed over by the Bedouin to the Rockefeller Museum in 1952 and 1953. Two fragmentary personal documents in Greek and Aramaic complement the textual finds from this cave.

Also found by Bedouin was another group of documents that probably originated from a cave further up the wadi. The documents evidently belonged to refugees from neighboring villages in the Judean Desert. This cave was excavated in 1991 by Hanan Eshel and David Amit (P. Ḥever 9 and 69).

Naḥal Mishmar

After three very badly fragmented documents and two ostraca, all probably from the Bar Kokhba period, entered the antiquities market with documents said to have come from Naḥal Se'elim (Wadi Seiyal) in 1952 and 1953, the Israel Exploration Society launched the Judean Desert Expedition in 1960 and 1961. Expedition B, directed by Yohanan Aharoni and Nahman Avigad, concentrated on several caves in Naḥal Se'elim and Naḥal Harduf (Wadi Abu Maradif), about four kilometers north of Masada. Four caves on the northern bank, one in Naḥal Harduf (Cave of the Reservoir) and three in Naḥal Se'elim (Cave of the Arrows, Cave of the Skulls, Cave of the Scrolls), yielded remains from the Bar Kokhba period. In addition, four Roman forts that guarded the area were identified.

Although most of the caves had been pillaged by Bedouin, they fortunately missed a small cave on the northern bank of the wadi (Cave 34). Here, eight written documents were found (34Se 1-8), together with a couple of personal objects, among them a coin from the Severan period. Among the texts are two phylacteries on parchment with passages from Exodus (34Se1 frgs. A and B), one fragmentary legal papyrus in Aramaic, and remains of two others in Greek. Fragments of a census list (34Se 4) and an account in Greek (34Se 5) complement the collection from Seiyal and were published in DJD 38.

A number of other caves yielded additional documents from the time around the First and the Second Revolt. Many of these documents are still unpublished; others have been collected and made accessible in DJD 38 (among them nineteen papyri from Jericho). The excavation of the large cave complex (Cave VIII/9) and the Cave of Avior (Cave VIII/10) during an expedition in 1993 yielded nine additional documents in Aramaic, six in Greek, and four in Hebrew. Five as yet unpublished Greek and Semitic documents on parchment and papyrus are listed in the PAM archives (Palestinian Archaeological Museum, now the Rockefeller Museum) as coming from Wadi en-Nar (Kidron Valley).

Masada

The last site in the Dead Sea area that has yielded written documents is Masada, excavated by Yigael Yadin between 1963 and 1965. The character and composition of the Masada finds reflect the turbulent history of this stronghold from its construction in the second century B.C.E. to the deposition of Archelaus in 6 C.E. Masada was the location of a Roman garrison until the outbreak of the First Revolt (4 B.C.E./6 C.E. to 66). It offered the last refuge for Zealots during the First Revolt (66-73/74 C.E.) and again housed a Roman garrison guarding the eastern flank of *Provincia Iudaea* from 73/74 to around 112/113 C.E. Centuries later, it was used as the site for a small Byzantine monastery.

All the Latin *tituli picti* (labels on amphorae written in ink, nos. 795-850) and Latin amphora stamps (nos. 946-51) belong to the Herodian period. The dated ones come from the period between 27 and 14 B.C.E. Stamps and labels represent large shipments of imported wine and luxury goods, mostly from Italy, such as apples and garum (a Roman fish sauce), for the court of Herod, who appears with his official title REX IVDAICVS (King of Judea).

It is unlikely that any of the Latin, Greek, and Semitic documents can be associated with the first Roman garrison, given the widespread nature of the destruction and cleaning up in 73/74 and the lack of supporting dates on any of the documents. It can be assumed, however, that during the first half of the first century a peaceful coexistence between Roman soldiers (all of them auxiliaries) and local Jews developed; some Greek ostraca written by Jews and mentioning deliveries (nos. 772-77) and Greek *tituli picti* (nos. 854-914) may indicate as much, if the latter are not to be dated to the Herodian phase of the site. The only Latin document to be dated to before or during the siege is P. Masada 722, a legionary pay record brought by its owner to the site.

Several biblical scrolls, including fragments of Genesis, Leviticus, Deuteronomy, Ezekiel, and Psalms, were discovered at Masada, as were fragments of other religious texts that include Ben Sira, the *Genesis Apocryphon,* the *Joshua Apocryphon, Jubilees,* and *Songs of the Sabbath Sacrifice.* These texts were probably brought to Masada by refugees before the Roman siege had the fortress effectively closed off. Seven fragments were found in casemate room 1039, which apparently was used as a garbage dump by the Romans. All fourteen literary texts are written in Hebrew (one in Paleo-Hebrew on papyrus) with one possible exception in an Aramaic text that remains unclassified.

A second class of finds from Masada is comprised of ostraca that are usually associated with the Sicarii. Among them are shards inscribed with letters, personal names including the famous "lots," and lists of priestly shares. The ostraca are written in Hebrew or Aramaic cursive script; twenty are in Paleo-Hebrew script. Some of them can be connected to the internal administration of the fortress by the Sicarii, such as the distribution of provisions; others mention names of owners of store jars (O. Masada 462) or give instructions for supplying bread (O. Masada 557-84). Still others may have been used as food coupons, as tags for a "population registry," or as lots for watch duties. A somewhat more intimate view of those who occupied Masada is given by three personal letters on ostraca, one of them written with charcoal. All other texts are written in ink.

After the siege, a small Roman garrison remained on Masada. No Greek documents date to the period after 73/74. The Latin papyri and ostraca written by members of the Tenth Legion do not provide an official archive but a random collection that affords insight into the life and duties of Roman soldiers. Among these items are a line from Virgil, a legionary pay stub, and a list of hospital supplies.

Jewish Papyri from Egypt

Among the tens of thousands of papyri found in Egypt are many that were written by Jews or refer to Jews. These papyri come from all regions of Egypt and document all phases, areas, and aspects of Jewish presence along the Nile. Among the most important corpora are the Elephantine Papyri, written by members of a Jewish military colony that lived on the island of Elephantine between 495 and 399 B.C.E. and even ran their own temple. Also important are the papyri in the Zenon Archive. Zenon was a Ptolemaic official who toured Palestine in 260/59 B.C.E. The documents in his archive, which include accounts, lists, receipts, and memoranda, provide valuable information on the social and economic situation. There are also many papyri from Alexandria reflecting various private and public affairs such as private letters, requests directed to city officials, pagan warnings against Jewish moneylenders, a letter of Claudius to the city of Alexandria demanding peace and unity between pagans and Jews, and documents connected to the revolt of 116-117.

One unique document from Egypt is the Nash Papyrus, which contains the Hebrew text of the Decalogue with wording drawn from both the Exodus and Deuteronomy versions. It was acquired by an antiquities dealer but may have come from the Fayum. Its first editors dated it to the first or second century C.E., but recent studies date it to the second century B.C.E. A fragmentary Hebrew prayer after meals found at Dura-Europos in Mesopotamia (P. Dura 10) joins the Nash Papyrus in providing rare evidence for the use of Hebrew as a liturgical language in the Diaspora.

We also have papyri from the Jewish *politeuma* (a council of an acknowledged ethnic community) of Herakleopolis dating to 143-132 B.C.E. That Jews in Herakleopolis apparently enjoyed as high a degree of autonomy as their fellows in Alexandria and Leontopolis is attested in literature and papyri. They yearly elected their officials *(archontes)* under a *politarchēs* and were allowed to run their own internal affairs. Many aspects of the privilege of living according to their ancestral customs are addressed in the papyri; these include civil law, synagogue courts, oaths, Sabbath, and pilgrimage.

Papyri also attest various practical and legal aspects of Jews living together with Greeks, Egyptians, and members of other ethnic groups. Many legal practices documented in Jewish papyri from Egypt are reminiscent of issues and formulas in papyri from the Judean Desert.

Ostraca

As a special case of written documents, a few notes on ostraca are appropriate. Ostraca are texts incised on pottery shards or written on them with ink. In Hellenistic and Roman Palestine, the same languages appear on ostraca as on papyrus and in inscriptions. The variety of texts on ostraca is notably broad, although they are usually short and confined to mundane matters. Especially frequent are writing exercises or abecedaries, written in Hebrew and Aramaic in square script; several of these are known from Qumran, Wadi Murabbaʿat, Masada, and other sites. A few are written bilingually in Greek and Latin. In many cases ostraca provided a good and cheap alternative to papyrus. Texts on ostraca were not necessarily less carefully written in terms of grammar or orthography, and they are a good indication that writing was widespread and even employed for the most profane purposes.

Often single personal names or lists of names in Hebrew or Aramaic appear on ostraca (Mur 74-77), sometimes also in Greek (Mur 165-76) or Latin (Mur 168). The earliest examples come from second-century-B.C.E. Gezer. The most famous corpus of this kind is the more than 700 shards from Masada bearing names, single letters, or combinations of letters on them.

A clearly economic purpose is evident in a list scratched onto the lid of an ossuary found in 1910 in a tomb at Bethpage. The lists gives twenty-three names along with sums of money. It is evidently a roster of workers in an ossuary workshop and indicates their daily wages. It was found only 1.5 kilometers from the large limestone quarries of Hizma.

Other ostraca parallel papyrus documents. One of the most famous and controversial examples is KhQ 1, the largest of three ostraca found in 1996 atop Roland de Vaux's excavation dump at Qumran. This Hebrew ostracon is probably the draft of a deed documenting the sale of an orchard by a certain Honi to Eleazar son of Nahmani. The deed was written in Jericho and is dated to "year two," which for paleographical reasons must refer to the First Revolt (67 C.E.). Unfortunately, the text is fragmentary. It gained some attention when the first editors read a partial word in line 8 as *yaḥad* and interpreted the ostracon as another link between the Qumran settlement and the texts from the caves. This reconstruction has rightly been rejected by several specialists. An Edomite ostracon from Maresha dated to summer 176 B.C.E. is also documentary in nature and represents so far the only marriage contract on an ostracon from ancient Palestine. One of the very few examples of a "narrative" text on an ostracon from the Hellenistic and Roman periods is Mur 72, which describes the activities of a certain Yoḥahan. Unfortunately, the fragmentary nature of the text provides little information on the context and purpose of the narrative passage.

BIBLIOGRAPHY

General

Berlin, Andrea M. 2005. "Jewish Life before the Revolt: The Archaeological Evidence." *JSJ* 36: 417-70.

———, and J. Andrew Overman, eds. 2002. *The First Jewish Revolt: Archaeology, History, and Ideology.* London: Routledge.

Binder, Donald D. 1999. *Into the Temple Courts: The Place of the Synagogues in the Second Temple Period.* Atlanta: Scholars Press.

Chancey, Mark Alan, and Adam Lowry Porter. 2001. "The Archaeology of Roman Palestine." *Near Eastern Archaeology* 64, 4: 164-203.

Hachlili, Rachel. 1988. *Ancient Jewish Art and Archaeology in the Land of Israel.* Leiden: Brill.

———. 1998. *Ancient Jewish Art and Archaeology in the Diaspora.* Leiden: Brill.

———. 2005. *Jewish Funerary Customs, Practices and Rites in the Second Temple Period.* Leiden: Brill.

Levine, Lee I. 2000. *The Ancient Synagogue: The First Thousand Years.* New Haven: Yale University Press.

———. 2002. *Jerusalem: Portrait of the City in the Second Temple Period (538-70 C.E.).* Philadelphia: Jewish Publication Society.

Magen, Yizhak, Haim Misgav, and Levana Tsfania. 2004-2008. *Mount Gerizim Excavations I: The Aramaic, Hebrew and Samaritan Inscriptions,* vol. 2, *A Temple City.* Jerusalem: Israel Antiquities Authority.

Netzer, Ehud, with R. Laureys-Chachey. 2006. *The Architecture of Herod, the Great Builder,* Tübingen: Mohr-Siebeck.

Pucci Ben-Zeev, Miriam. 2005. *Diaspora Judaism in Turmoil, 116/117 CE: Ancient Sources and Modern Insights.* Leuven: Peeters.

Richardson, Peter. 2004. *Building Jewish in the Roman East.* Waco, Tex.: Baylor University Press.

Schäfer, Peter, ed. 2003. *The Bar Kokhba War Reconsidered: New Perspectives on the Second Jewish Revolt against Rome.* Tübingen: Mohr-Siebeck.

Egypt

Porton, Bezalel, and Ada Yardeni, eds. 1986-1999. *Textbook of Aramaic Documents from Ancient Egypt,* 4 vols. Jerusalem: Hebrew University (vol. 1 = *Letters;* vol. 2 = *Contracts;* vol. 3 = *Literature and Lists;* vol. 4 = *Ostraca and Assorted Inscriptions*).

Masada

Yadin, Yigael, Joseph Naveh, Yaacov Meshorer, et al., eds. 1989-2006. *Masada I-VII: The Yigael Yadin Excavations 1963-1965. Final Reports.* Jerusalem: Israel Exploration Society. (A final volume is in preparation.)

Qumran

Galor, Katharina, Jean-Baptiste Humbert, and Jürgen Zangenberg, eds. 2006. *Qumran: The Site of the Dead Sea Scrolls: Archaeological Interpretations and Debates.* Leiden: Brill.

Hirschfeld, Yitzar. 2004. *Qumran in Context: Reassessing the Archaeological Evidence.* Peabody, Mass.: Hendrickson.

Humbert, Jean-Baptiste, and A. Chambon, eds. 1994. *Fouílles de Khirbet Qumrân et de Aïn Feshkha I: Album de photographies, repertoire du fonds photographique, synthese des notes de Chantier du P. Roland de Vaux OP.* Fribourg: Editions Universitaires.

———. 2003. *Excavations of Khirbet Qumran and Ain Feshka: Synthesis of Roland de Vaux's Notes.* Trans. S. J. Pfann. Fribourg: Academic Press (Eng. trans., with corrections, of the French ed.).

———, and Jan Gunneweg, eds. 2003. *Khirbet Qumran et ʿAin Feshkha II: Studies of Anthropology, Physics and Chemistry.* Fribourg: Academic Press.

Magness, Jodi. 2002. *The Archaeology of Qumran and the Dead Sea Scrolls.* Grand Rapids: Eerdmans.

Vaux, Roland de. 1973. *Archaeology and the Dead Sea Scrolls.* Rev. ed. London: Oxford University Press.

Coins

Meshorer, Ya'akov. 1989. *The Coinage of Aelia Capitolina.* Jerusalem: Israel Museum.

———. 2001. *A Treasury of Jewish Coins from the Persian Period to Bar Kokhba.* New York: Amphora Books.

———, and Shraga Qedar. 1999. *Samarian Coinage.* Jerusalem: Israel Numismatic Society.

Inscriptions

Ameling, Walter. 2004. *Inscriptiones Judaicae Orientis.* Vol. 2. *Kleinasien.* Tübingen: Mohr-Siebeck.

Boffo, Laura. 1994. *Iscrizioni Greche e Latine per lo Studio della Bibbia.* Brescia: Paideia Editrice.

Frey, Jean-Baptiste. 1936-1952. *Corpus Inscriptionum Judaicarum: Recueil des inscriptions juives qui vont du IIIe siècle avant Jésus-Christ au VIIe siècle de notre ére.* 2 vols. Rome: Pontificio istituto di archeologia Cristiana.

Horst, Pieter W. van der. 1991. *Ancient Jewish Epitaphs: An Introductory Survey of a Millennium of Jewish Funerary Epigraphy (300 BCE–700 CE).* Kampen: Kok Pharos.

Lüderitz, Gert, with Joyce M. Reynolds. 1983. *Corpus jüdischer Zeugnisse aus der Cyrenaika.* Wiesbaden: Reichert.

Noy, David. 1993-1995. *Jewish Inscriptions of Western Europe.* 2 vols. Cambridge: Cambridge University Press.

———, and William Horbury. 1992. *Jewish Inscriptions of Greco-Roman Egypt.* Cambridge: Cambridge University Press.

———, Alexander Panayotov, and Hanswulf Bloedhorn. 2004. *Inscriptiones Judaicae Orientis.* Vol. 1. *Eastern Europe.* Tübingen: Mohr-Siebeck.

———, and Hanswulf Bloedhorn. 2004. *Inscriptiones Judaicae Orientis.* Vol. 3. *Syria and Cyprus.* Tübingen: Mohr-Siebeck.

Textual Discoveries from Palestine

The manuscripts from Qumran Caves 1-11, Wadi Murabbaʿat, Jericho, and Wadi Seiyal, as well as many texts from Naḥal Ḥever, are presented in the series Discoveries in the Judean Desert (DJD), published by Oxford University Press. Another large part of the Naḥal Ḥever corpus is available in the series Judean Desert Studies (JDS).

Papyri from Palestine

Cotton, Hannah M., and Ada Yardeni, eds. 1997. *Aramaic, Hebrew and Greek Documentary Texts from Naḥal Ḥever and Other Sites, with an Appendix Containing Alleged Qumran Texts.* DJD 27. Oxford: Clarendon.

Lewis, Naphtali, Yigael Yadin, and Jonas C. Greenfield, eds. 1989. *The Documents from the*

Bar Kokhba Period in the Cave of Letters: Greek Papyri, Aramaic and Nabatean Signatures and Subscriptions. Jerusalem: Israel Exploration Society.

Yadin, Yigael. 1963. *The Finds from the Bar Kokhba Period in the Cave of Letters.* Jerusalem: Israel Exploration Society.

———, Jonas C. Greenfield, Ada Yardeni, and Baruch Levine, eds. 2002. *The Documents from the Bar Kokhba Period in the Cave of Letters: Hebrew, Aramaic and Nabatean-Aramaic Papyri.* Jerusalem: Israel Exploration Society.

Yardeni, Ada. 2000. *Textbook of Aramaic, Hebrew and Nabataean Documentary Texts from the Judaean Desert and Related Material.* Jerusalem: Hebrew University.

Papyri from the Diaspora

Cowey, James M., and Klaus Maresch, eds. 2001. *Urkunden des Politeuma der Juden von Herakleopolis (144/3-133/2 v. Chr.) (P. Polit. Iud.): Papyri aus den Sammlungen von Heidelberg, Köln, München und Wien (Gebundene Ausgabe).* Wiesbaden: Westdeutscher Verlag.

Porten, Bezalel, et al., eds. 1996. *The Elephantine Papyri in English.* Leiden: Brill.

Tcherikover, Victor, and Alexander Fuks, eds. 1957-1963. *Corpus Papyrorum Judaicarum.* 3 vols. Cambridge: Harvard University Press. (A fourth volume is in preparation by I. Fikhman.)

Jews among Greeks and Romans

MIRIAM PUCCI BEN ZEEV

The relations of Jews with Greeks and Romans during the Second Temple period were complex. On the one hand, a variety of source materials including inscriptions, papyri, and formal documents quoted by Josephus show that Jews were thoroughly integrated into the economic, social, and political life of Hellenistic cities, that they embraced several aspects of Greco-Roman culture, that they enjoyed certain rights and privileges pertaining to the practice of their ancestral customs and laws, and that they even attracted the admiration of non-Jewish sympathizers, adherents, and converts. On the other hand, these same sources indicate that Jews frequently encountered competition, resentment, and even overt hostility from their non-Jewish neighbors and at times ran afoul of their Greek and Roman overlords. They also suggest that Jewish rights were neither permanent nor inherently stable. Greek and Roman rulers could rescind those rights or simply choose not to enforce them. When the government did intervene in support of the Jews, oftentimes little was done to solve the underlying problems. On a few occasions, direct intervention actually exacerbated the problems, not least when rulers sided with the Greeks against the Jews.

At the root of these sometimes tense relations was Jewish exclusiveness or separatism: Jews not only formed their own communities and practiced a measure of political autonomy, but they refused to participate in the cults of the patron deities of Greek cities. Precisely because religion was an integral part of civic identity in the Greco-Roman world, Jewish nonparticipation was felt keenly. Jewish monotheism and aniconism led to pagan accusations of atheism and misanthropy. As a result, Jewish life in the Greco-Roman world was somewhat precarious even as it flourished.

The Jews under Hellenistic Rule

The Legal Status of Jews under the Ptolemies and Seleucids

Already in the Persian period (539-332 B.C.E.), the Torah was officially recognized as the law to which the Jews of Judea had to conform their lives and by which their judicial cases were to be adjudicated (Ezra 7:25-26). The same probably applied to Jews living in other provinces of the Persian Empire, namely, in Egypt and in Babylon. It was not that the Persians had a special regard for the needs of the Jews; they simply found it useful to codify the laws of subject peoples in order to consolidate their control. Thus, for example, Darius ordered that "the law of Egypt that had formerly been valid" be written down. The codified law, written in Aramaic and in Demotic, was thereby introduced as the provincial law of Egypt. The same policy was implemented after the conquests of Alexander the Great. Josephus has Alexander grant the Jews of Judea the right "to observe their country's laws" (*Ant.* 11.338), which was probably extended, *de iure* or *de facto,* also to Jews living in the Diaspora.

In third-century-B.C.E. Egypt, the Greek translation of the Torah was officially recognized by its integration into the judicial system created by King Ptolemy II. It became a statute *(nomos)* to which Ptolemaic judges had to accord their official sanction, in conformity with a royal decree directing them to render judgments when a matter was not dealt with in the royal legislation. In other words, the Greek Torah, as part of the legal system of Ptolemaic Egypt, became one of the political laws, a kind of "civic law for the Jews of Egypt." In return, the Jews stressed their loyalty to the government by dedicating their houses of worship *(proseuchai)* to the king, his wife, and their children (*JIGRE* 9, 13). In all the countries under Ptolemaic rule — Judea, Libya, Cyprus, and Egypt — the Jews were free to live according to their ancestral laws.

Evidently no major changes took place when Judea came under Seleucid rule at the beginning of the second century B.C.E. A document quoted by Josephus states that King Antiochus III allowed the Jews "to have a form of government in accordance with the laws of their country" (*Ant.* 12.142); and in Asia Minor, too, the Jews seem to have had the right "to use their own laws" (*Ant.* 12.150). Yet there was probably no binding royal legislation, and so Jewish rights could be revoked at any time for any reason. In the first half of the second century B.C.E., when internal Jewish struggles for power in Judea were interpreted by King Antiochus IV Epiphanes as a rebellion against Seleucid rule, this provoked not only a military reaction but also an enforced Hellenization. Jews were compelled "to depart from the laws of their fathers and to cease living by the laws of God. Further, the sanctuary in Jerusalem was to be polluted and called after Zeus Olympius" (2 Macc. 6:1-2). This forced Hellenization lasted only a few years, but it made clear that Jewish freedom always depended on the personal goodwill of the ruler who happened to be in power.

Cultural Antagonism between Jews and Greeks in Egypt

Since the beginning of their settlement in Egypt early in the third century B.C.E., the Jews were active in most branches of economic activity. Extant papyri show them as farmers, artisans (*CPJ* 1:33-47), tax farmers and tax collectors, bankers, granary officials (*CPJ* 1:48-124, 127, 132, 137), and soldiers, even officers, in the Ptolemaic army (*CPJ* 1:18-32; Josephus, *J.W.* 1.175, 190-92; *Ant.* 14.99, 131-32; *Ag. Ap.* 1.200-204; 2.64). The Jews were a strong presence in the economic life of the country, a fact that created competition and perhaps friction between them and their Greco-Egyptian neighbors. This was all the more the case because the Jews insisted on forming their own separate communities and refused to participate in the religious activities of the Greek cities. The issue was particularly problematic because these activities often had civil and economic underpinnings; identification with the gods of one's city was a fundamental aspect of civic identity, as in the cases of the cult of the deified Alexander and Ptolemies and of the patron deities of the Greek city.

Cultural antagonism may have developed in the third century B.C.E. also on account of the translations of the Pentateuch into Greek that were circulating in Egypt — the best known was the Septuagint — which made generally known the account of the Exodus, with its strong anti-Egyptian bias. No source tells us how extensively it may have been read and known, but there are a number of parallels between the biblical account of the Exodus and its counter-version in the work of Manetho, a priest of the Greco-Egyptian god Serapis who was influential in the court of Ptolemy Philadelphus. One of the two passages of Manetho quoted by Josephus associates the Jews with the tyrannical Hyksos regime, a foreign dynasty that had ruled Egypt harshly. After five hundred years of domination, they left Egypt "with their possessions . . . and journeyed over the desert into Syria. . . . There . . . they built in the land now called Judea a city . . . and gave it the name of Jerusalem" (*Ag. Ap.* 1.73-91).

The other account of Manetho quoted by Josephus draws on popular legends and recounts the segregation of a crowd of lepers, led by a priest named Osarseph, identified with Moses, who advocated social isolation and taught them not to worship the Egyptian gods but rather to sacrifice the Egyptian sacred animals. In the end, the Egyptian king defeats the lepers and expels them from Egypt, pursuing them to the frontiers of Syria (*Ag. Ap.* 1.228-52). Similar stories with different details were recounted between the second century B.C.E. and the first century C.E. by other Greco-Egyptian authors such as Lysimachus, Chaeremon, Ptolemy of Mendes, and Apion. Written in Greek, these accounts deeply influenced public opinion even outside Egypt, as the later Roman *Histories* of Tacitus witness (5.3.1–5.4.2).

These are not the only manifestations of antagonism preserved by our sources. 3 Maccabees reflects memories of a conflict between the Jews and the Egyptian ruler — a persecution sparked by Jewish religious practices that was thwarted thanks to divine intervention. The conflict probably belongs to a later historical period, but it remains significant that the author of the book places it in the Hellenistic age, at the time of Ptolemy IV Philopator in the third century B.C.E. (Josephus dates the event to the reign of Ptolemy Physcon [Euergetes II] in the second century B.C.E.)

Toward the end of the Ptolemaic period, the rule of the kings weakened under the strain of dynastic strife, and the security that the Jews had enjoyed in the early period could no longer be taken for granted. In the first half of the first century B.C.E., a papyrus dealing with commercial issues warns that in Memphis "they loathe the Jews" (*CPJ* 1:141).

Jewish Engagement with Hellenism

At the end of the fourth century B.C.E., the conquests of Alexander the Great brought a real revolution not only on the political level but also in the cultural sphere. All over the Near East, people came in close contact with the thought, cultural values, and institutions of the Greeks; among them, a special role was played by the gymnasium, where people trained in physical exercises and devoted themselves to letters, music, rhetoric, and philosophy. Through the medium of a common language — the Hellenistic form of Greek, the so-called *koine,* which soon became the lingua franca of the East — Greek culture spread widely and reached all the countries under Hellenistic governments, influencing every aspect of life. The world became a small world — the "inhabited world" *(oikoumenē)* — where each people followed their own traditional customs and beliefs, participating at the same time in the new common supernational culture, which was open to everybody since it was based not on birth but on education.

The Jews, too, participated in this formidable movement of peoples and ideas. In Egypt, they learned to speak and write in Greek, appealed to Greek tribunals when the need arose, and gave Greek names to their children. The onomasticon attested by the papyri shows that Jewish names amount to no more than 25 percent; most names are Greek. Literary works composed by Jews in Egypt also attest a high degree of integration between Greek culture and traditional Judaism, and similar developments may well have characterized other Diaspora communities. Scholars emphasize the appropriation of Hellenistic themes, genres, forms, and styles for Jewish purposes. The Jews appropriated Hellenism to the goals of rewriting biblical narratives, recasting the traditions of their fathers and shaping their distinctive identity within the larger world of Hellenic culture. In a world where Hellenic culture held an ascendant position, they strove to present Judaic traditions and express their own self-definition through the media of the Greeks. Literary models and rhetorical devices were often Greek, while the content related specifically to Jewish interests.

An author such as the epic poet Theodotus (second to first century B.C.E.) writes on biblical themes, while his language betrays Homeric influences. The tragedy composed by Ezekiel (second century B.C.E.) is based on the biblical story of the Exodus but reflects Euripides' influence. Aristobulus, the second-century-B.C.E. philosophic writer and supposed teacher of Ptolemy VI, maintains that Greek philosophy is to be found in the Pentateuch, which he interprets allegorically. The same line of thought is followed by the author of the *Letter of Aristeas,* who strives to demonstrate that Hellenistic and Jewish traditions are only two different expressions of the same metaphysical reality. He, too, gives an allegorical interpretation to the text of the Pentateuch that explains the Jewish law according the principles of Greek thought and presents Judaism and Hellenism as two different forms emanating from the same divine entity, venerated under different names.

Historical works composed by Jews also reflect the influence of Greek literary models while centering on Jewish cultural and theological values. In 2 Maccabees, which deals with the history of the Jewish people in Judea at the time of Antiochus IV Epiphanes (175-164 B.C.E.), history is presented according to a Jewish interpretative scheme in which the causes of events are sought in the spiritual rather than the political realm. Accordingly, the religious persecution is regarded as punishment for the sins committed by the Jews, sins which are identified with the extreme Hellenization of those Jews who had been ready to give up the exclusivity of Judaism in order to become an integral part of the Hellenistic world. From a theological point of view, this book is a distinctly Jewish work, while formally and literarily it is completely Greek.

Yet there are early Jewish works that reflect cultural antagonism of one sort or another. One of them is the Wisdom of Solomon, in which considerable learning, sophisticated vocabulary, developed rhetorical features, and Hellenistic philosophical influences are employed not to integrate Judaism with its environment but to construct a sophisticated attack upon it, focusing on worship of animals and idolatry, which are presented as the height of folly and the root of immorality. Another case is that of 3 Maccabees, where the narrative centers on the hostility between Jews and Gentiles, and *Joseph and Aseneth,* a work fiercely antagonistic to all non-Jewish religion. Similar features are displayed by the third book of the *Sibylline Oracles,* which may reflect a revival of Jewish nationalistic sentiment in the wake of the Maccabean revolt. Directed against the unjust regimes of Greece, Macedonia, and Rome, it predicts woes and cosmic disasters, followed by visions of worldwide repentance and the worship of all nations at the Temple of God.

In the practical domain, too, Hellenism influenced Jewish life in different ways. Recent scholarship distinguishes between assimilation (social integration) and acculturation (linguistic, educational, and ideological integration). At one end of the spectrum, we find a complete submersion of Jewish cultural uniqueness, well illustrated by the cases of Dositheos son of Drymilos in the third century B.C.E. and of Tiberius Julius Alexander in the first century C.E. Both of these men abandoned Jewish ancestral traditions and made brilliant carriers in the Ptolemaic and Roman administrations. At the other end of the spectrum are the Therapeutae, who closely resembled the Essenes while including women; they were an ascetic Jewish community living in the vicinity of Alexandria who devoted themselves to study and contemplation. Philo calls them "the citizens of heaven and of the universe." In the middle between these extremes, there were "mainstream" Jews whose cultural identity was well defined and who adhered to Jewish practices. Hybrid cases are also attested, as that of a certain Moschios, son of Moschios, who is mentioned in an inscription erected at Oropus, Greece, in the temple of Amphiaraos (*CIJ* 1:82); he calls himself a Jew but mentions the instructions he received in a dream from the gods Amphiaraos and Hygieia. For Jews to live in a deeply Hellenized milieu and maintain their Jewish identity over generations was certainly a challenge.

The Jews under Roman Rule

Religious Freedom

No significant change took place when the Romans conquered the East. The Roman government had a conservative character that tended to preserve the existing frameworks. In Judea, a decree issued by Julius Caesar allowed the Jews to live according to their ancestral laws and customs (*JRRW* 1), possibly confirming a decree issued by Pompey after the conquest of Jerusalem in 63 B.C.E. that has not been preserved.

Religious freedom was also granted to Diaspora Jews. From Josephus' narrative and from a number of documents quoted by him, we learn that in different centers of the Mediterranean the Jews were allowed to follow Jewish law, assemble, perform their rites on Sabbaths and festivals, send their contributions to the Temple in Jerusalem, have autonomous internal administration and jurisdiction, build sacred and profane buildings, and have kosher food in the local markets.

The right to follow Jewish customs and laws, however, was by no means stable or permanent. In 38 C.E., Emperor Caligula's desire to impose his own worship on all his subjects encouraged the Gentile population of Yavneh (Jamnia) in Judea to set up an altar to him. This altar was promptly destroyed by the Jews, an act to which Caligula responded by ordering a golden statue of himself to be set up in the Jerusalem Temple. His purpose was probably to stress his power over the Judean population, but for the Jews it was a serious infringement of religious freedom; a statue in the Temple would have polluted it and automatically suspended its cult. Thanks to the successful delaying tactics of the local Roman governor and to the assassination of the emperor early in 41 C.E., the statue was not set up, but the incident shows that Jewish religious rights were intrinsically precarious.

The Jews in Rome

Even though a foreign labor force had increasingly become a necessity in the Roman economy, the Romans did not particularly enjoy the presence of foreigners in their city. They feared that foreign manners, customs, and cults — which often differed significantly from their own — might influence their society negatively and contaminate Roman values and ancestral traditions, the so-called *mores maiorum.* Between the second century B.C.E. and the first century C.E., foreigners were periodically expelled from Rome. In the second century B.C.E., the Jews were kicked out along with the astrologers, who were accused of disturbing fickle and silly minds with a fallacious interpretation of the stars, while the Jews were accused of "infecting" the Roman customs with their cult (Valerius Maximus, *Facta et Dicta Memora-*

bilia 1.3.3). In the early years of Tiberius' reign, a strong reaction occurred against foreign cults, and the Jews were expelled along with the adherents of the Egyptian cult of Isis (Josephus, *Ant.* 18.81-84; Cassius Dio, *Roman History* 57.18.5a).

The attitudes toward Jews preserved in Latin literature are not particularly friendly. In the middle of the first century B.C.E., some years after the conquest of Jerusalem by Pompey, Cicero, the well-known Roman politician, lawyer, and statesman, held that, since they resisted Pompey's troops, the Jews were to be regarded as enemies. He stressed the great cultural discrepancy between the Roman and the Jewish people: even "when Jerusalem was still standing and the Jews were at peace with us, the practice of their sacred rites was at variance with the glory of our empire, the dignity of our name, and the customs of our ancestors" (*Pro Flacco* 28, 69). Poets such as Tibullus, Horace, and Ovid were less interested in political issues; what provoked their satire and ridicule were Jewish customs such as observance of the Sabbath, circumcision, and abstinence from pork. Pompeius Trogus, the first historian to deal at some length with the past history of the Jewish people, displays a rather objective tone but quotes anti-Jewish Egyptian sources that were percolating into Roman consciousness, thereby making them more widely known in the capital.

The attitude of the Roman upper classes became more rigid and hostile in the course of the first century C.E., perhaps as a result of the spread of Jewish customs in Roman society and of the intensified rebel movements in Judea. Seneca resented the popularity of Jewish customs in Rome, singling out for adverse comment especially the observance of the Sabbath and the custom of lighting Sabbath lamps, a visible and apparently attractive feature of Jewish observance. Caustic comments on the Jews appear in the work of Juvenal, in a combination of cultural and class snobbery. In the second century C.E., Tacitus, a Roman senator and historian, wrote extensively about the Jews, calling their rites "base and abominable" and declaring that they "owe their persistence to their depravity. . . . the Jews are extremely loyal toward one another . . . but toward every other people they feel only hate and enmity." In particular, Tacitus lamented their influence on Roman society, since they teach converts "to despise the gods, to disown their country, and to regard their parents, children, and brothers as of little account." His account of Jewish customs ends with the observation: "the ways of the Jews are preposterous and mean" (*Histories* 5.5.1-5).

On the other hand, extant sources show that the Jews of Rome also attracted sympathy, winning admirers and imitators among ordinary citizens and even, in certain cases, among the higher echelons of society. We hear of notable figures who supported the Jews, among whom was Nero's wife, Poppaea Sabina, who exerted her patronage on behalf of Judean priests who had been sent to Rome on trial.

Concerning the social integration of the Jews in Roman society, we know very little. They left no written records at all, a fact for which different explanations have been put forward in contemporary research, all of them speculative. Philo and Josephus tell us that the bulk of the Jewish population of the capital descended from Jewish prisoners brought to Rome and sold as slaves after the conquest of Pompey in 63 B.C.E. Other slaves arrived after the numerous failed revolts that followed, and a conspicuous number reached Rome after the defeat of the Judean rebellion in 70 C.E. In time, many Jews gained their freedom. Josephus was certainly not the only Jew granted Roman citizenship (*Vita* 423). Many Jews were entitled to the corn dole (Philo, *Legatio ad Gaium* 158) and may have gained citizenship on manumission. Yet, on the whole, it appears that Jews did not achieve leading positions in Roman society. Philo states that in the reign of Augustus Jews were settled mainly on the right bank of the Tiber, in an area of generally poor residences, far from the heart of Rome, a location that suggests a generally humble mode of life. That Jews were not an economically and socially significant presence in the city may explain why we do not hear of episodes of tension or conflict between them and their neighbors. The case of the relations between the Jews and their neighbors in the eastern parts of the Mediterranean, however, is different.

Jews and Greeks in the Eastern Mediterranean Diaspora

A Problem of Sources

We have far better information concerning the relations between Jews and Greeks in the eastern Mediterranean Diaspora. The problem is that our sources — a few papyri and inscriptions, quoted fragments of several Greek and Roman documents, and literary records — always concentrate on a given place at a given time and fail to provide a comprehensive historical context. Moreover, we often get the impression that our literary sources — mainly the narratives of Philo and Josephus — omit as much as they include, so that we have to read between the lines. Great caution is required when drawing general conclusions from our scraps of evidence. Nevertheless, all of our sources clearly point both to the integration of Jews in society and to controversies between Jews and Greeks.

Social and Economic Integration

Josephus tells us that in Cyrene there were three thousand well-to-do Jews (*J.W.* 7.445). The numbers are certainly exaggerated, but the existence of a high Jewish society is confirmed by the epigraphic material, which attests the presence of Jews among the ephebes of Cyrene, in the highest rank of the administration (*CJZC* 6 [late first century B.C.E.] and 7 [3/4 C.E.]). A Jew named Eleazar son of Jason is found in the list of the "guardians of the law" *(nomophylakes)* (*CJZC* 8 [60/61 C.E.]), a position that entailed considerable responsibility and required education, experience, and the confidence of the civic leaders. At Teucheira, among the names scratched on the walls of the gymnasium are some that are probably Jewish (*CJZC* 41), and an inscription attests the rise of individual Jews into positions of civic responsibility (*CJZC* 36). Josephus mentions that wealthy Jews in Asia Minor were required to perform liturgical duties (*Ant.* 16.28), a role that suggests a high degree of civic responsibility. At Iasos there was at least one and probably several Jewish ephebes, and an inscription from Hypaepa indicates the existence of an association of Jewish youths, apparently ephebes, who had graduated from the gymnasium while retaining their Jewish identity (*CIJ* 755).

In Alexandria, Egyptian Jews actively participated in the economic life of the city. Philo mentions Jewish shipowners, merchants, and moneylenders (*In Flaccum* 57). Alexander the Alabarch, Philo's brother, belonged in the highest stratum of Jewish society and held an important administrative role probably connected with customs collection on the Nile. He was rich enough to donate nine massive gates of silver and gold to the Jerusalem Temple (Josephus, *J.W.* 5.205). Philo himself no doubt received a thorough training in a gymnasium, and his familiarity with theatrical and sporting events suggests that he enjoyed the regular entertainments of Alexandrian citizens.

Cases of local inhabitants being attracted to Judaism are also well attested. According to Josephus, each city in Syria had its "Judaizers" (*J.W.* 2.463); at Damascus, many women had "submitted to the Jewish religion" (*J.W.* 2.559-61); at Antioch, the Jews were constantly attracting to their religious practices "a considerable body of Greeks, whom they had in some measure made a part of themselves" (*J.W.* 7.45). Attraction to Judaism may have taken various forms, from a general interest and sympathy to real adherence to Jewish practices. The statement of the New Testament that the Pharisees "compass sea and land to make one proselyte" (Matt. 23:15) may be exaggerated, but the testimony of later Jewish sources — which take pride in the claim that some of the greatest Jewish figures descended from proselytes — suggests a policy of acceptance.

Friendly relations, however, are not attested always and everywhere. Josephus also reports that serious controversies and disputes arose between the Jews and their Greek neighbors in various places around the Mediterranean. A reconstruction of these episodes and their causes is extremely difficult, since we get only the Jewish point of view. Even when Josephus quotes non-Jewish documents, for example, his choice is always subjective and leads him to cite only those texts attesting favorable decisions concerning the Jews.

Controversies between Jews and Greeks

Mesopotamia

Jews arrived at Seleucia in the first part of the first century C.E., having escaped from Babylon, where they had been always "quarreling with the Babylonians because of the contrariety of their laws" (*Ant.* 18.371). In Seleucia they got caught up in conflicts between Syrians and Greeks. An armed attack against the Jews ensued in which an enormous number of Jews were killed (*Ant.* 18.372-76). Those who managed to escape fled to Ctesiphon, a Greek city near Seleucia, but there too the local Greek population did not receive them favorably, so they had to leave and take refuge at Nearda and Nisibis (*Ant.* 18.377-79).

Syria

According to Josephus the Jews in Syria enjoyed "the protection of the Seleucid kings" (*J.W.* 7.43) and were granted citizen rights "on equality with the Greeks" (*J.W.* 7.44), a claim that is difficult to accept at face value. In any case, the resentment of the Greek population reached its peak in 66 C.E. when the Jewish rebellion started in Judea and "hatred of the Jews was everywhere at its height" (*J.W.* 7.47). Josephus writes that at Antioch a Jew named Antiochus approached the Greek magistrates and accused his fellow Jews of conspiring to burn the whole city to the ground. Then a real fire broke out that destroyed the market square, the magistrates' quarters, the record office, and the basilicas. The Greeks "rushed for the Jewish masses, believing the salvation of their native place to be dependent on their prompt chastisement." Antiochus sought to furnish proof of his conversion and of his detestation of Jewish customs by sacrificing after the manner of the Greeks. He recommended that other Jews be compelled to do the same. As a result observance of the Sabbath was prohibited not only in Antioch but also in other cities (*J.W.* 7.46-62). Possibly in this context, efforts were made to abolish the privileges of the Jews to get their own non-Gentile oil (Josephus, *Ant.* 1.120).

Another episode reported by Josephus took place in Damascus. Learning of the disaster that had befallen the Romans at the beginning of the Jewish revolt in Judea, the Greeks "were fired with a determination to kill the Jews who resided among them. As they had for a long time past kept them shut up in the gymnasium . . . they fell upon the Jews, cooped up as they were and unarmed, and within one hour slaughtered them all with impunity, to the number of ten thousand five hundred" (*J.W.* 2.559-61). Then, at the end of the war, the Greeks of Antioch asked Titus to expel the Jews, or at least to have their rights abolished (*J.W.* 7.100-111).

Asia Minor

In Asia Minor Jewish settlements were apparently a conspicuous element of the local population. The Jews had formed vital and influential communities dating back to the third century B.C.E., but on several occasions the Greeks prevented the Jews from observing their traditional customs. We learn about these incidents from a number of documents quoted in part by Josephus. The authenticity of these texts has often been challenged in modern scholarship, and Josephus has even been accused of forging the documents in order to prove that the Jews had always been held in high esteem by Rome. This view, however, is not tenable. Parallels in structure, phraseology, and content can be readily found in authentic contemporary Greek and Roman documents preserved on stone, bronze, and papyrus. Moreover, if the documents were forgeries they would not contain so many errors; an informed forger would have taken pains to replicate standard formulas and conventional structures correctly. Paradoxically, the textual corruptions and factual errors constitute the strongest argument for authenticity and indicate that the original texts had probably been copied several times before they reached Josephus.

From these documents, which date to the second half of the first century B.C.E., we learn that at Delos the Jews were denied religious freedom by a decree issued by the Greek city (*JRRW* 7). In Laodicea, the Greek magistrates wrote to the Roman proconsul agreeing to let the Jews observe their Sabbaths and rites in accordance with their native laws, but that the people of Tralles were dissatisfied and would not easily comply with the Roman requests (*JRRW* 17). At Miletus, the Roman governor resented that, "contrary to our expressed wish, you are attacking the Jews and forbid them to observe the Sabbaths, perform their native rites, and manage their produce in accordance with the laws" (*JRRW* 18). At Halicarnassus, Roman pressure forced the Greek city to issue a decree allowing the Jews to follow their customs (*JRRW* 19). That the Jewish observance of the Sabbath was liable to a fine we learn from another decree, issued this time at Ephesus, where, again under Roman pressure, the Greeks agreed that "no one shall be prevented from keeping the Sabbath days nor be fined for so doing" (*JRRW* 21). Kosher food also represented a problem; special permission was necessary at Sardis for "having suitable food for them [the Jews] brought in" (*JRRW* 20).

Not surprisingly, the Roman letters and decrees were not very effective. A few generations later, during the reign of Augustus, some of the same issues were still pending. Quoting the work of Nicholas of Damascus, Herod's secretary, who personally witnessed the episode, Josephus presents us with two reports of a visit to Ionia in 14 B.C.E. by the Roman statesman Agrippa and King Herod. In the first report (*Ant.* 12.125-27) the Ionians are said to have requested from Agrippa that the citizenship *(politeia)* granted by Antiochus Theos should be restricted to them alone and should not include the Jews, who declined to worship the gods of the Ionians. This statement is illuminating: the Jews are not entitled to the same rights of the Greeks since they refuse to acknowledge the city's gods. Economic and religious issues were intermingled because religion was central in the maintenance of civic patriotism. A local cult with a world-famous temple, for example, was vital to a city's identity and crucial to its economy.

The second report (*Ant.* 16.27-28) centers on Jewish claims. The Jews do not mention civic rights and the city's gods, but rather their mistreatment by the Greek cities, which forbade them to observe their religious laws, compelled them to attend judicial hearings on their holy days, stripped them of the monies destined for the Temple in Jerusalem, pressed them into military service, and forced them to spend their income on unwanted civic duties "although they had been exempted from these duties because the Romans had always permitted them to live in accordance with their own laws." These "unwanted civic duties" may have been liturgies, that is, public services assumed by, or rather imposed upon, the wealthier citizens as a compulsory duty toward the community. In the difficult economic situation following the Roman civil struggles of the last years of the Republic, which had drawn heavily on Asian resources, liturgies had become a problematic feature in the life of Greek cities in the East. The Jews of Ionia based their refusal to participate in these duties on their religious freedom, which was legally recognized by the Roman government. But why did they justify their refusal on religious grounds and expect Agrippa to agree with them? Their appeal makes sense only if the liturgies in question were somehow incompatible with Jewish religious scruples. The obligations may have included something like underwriting the cost of pagan festivals or the expenses of the local gymnasium.

The same issues may have been at stake in an episode reported by Josephus, in which the Jews complained that the Greeks "were persecuting them to the extent of taking their sacred monies away from them and doing them injury in their private concerns" (*Ant.* 16.160-61). In hard times, the Greeks may have resented that the Jews made no contribution to renovate the dilapidated temples in their own cities but sent their monies to a temple way off in Jerusalem. They therefore took steps to rectify this lack, which was felt as injustice, and seized the monies that the Jews had collected to be sent to the Jerusalem Temple. The situation must have been grave, since Augustus had to provide a special penalty for those caught stealing Jewish sacred monies or sacred books (*JRRW* 22).

Libya

In Libya as well we hear of friction between Jews and Greeks over taxation. Josephus quotes a letter in which Agrippa, Augustus' best general and son-in-law, writes to the magistrates of Cyrene: the Jews complain that "they are being threatened by certain informers and prevented (from sending their monies) on the pretext of their owing taxes, which are in fact not owed" (*Ant.* 16.170). Scholars suggest that this statement may refer to the *metoikion,* which all noncitizens had to pay. If so, the claim would have been that some or all of the Jews of Cyrene had the same (or equivalent) rights as those of the members of the Greek city, the *polis,* and therefore did not have to pay the taxes owed by noncitizens. But other suggestions may be offered too. For example, the taxes here may have been related to pagan worship, as was the case in Ionia in the same period. In any case, attempted tax evasion was apparently a common feature of the time. During Augustus' reign, the Greek cities also appealed to the emperor against Roman citizens who claimed exemption from taxation and liturgy duties (*SEG* 9, 8, section III). Moreover, since the Greek cities were engaged in a war against native tribesmen, economic pressure may have exacerbated financial disputes.

Egypt

Theoretically, there was no dramatic change when Egypt fell under Octavian's control in 31 B.C.E. after the Battle of Actium. Octavian, now Augustus, implemented the traditional policy of the Ptolemies toward the Jews and confirmed their traditional rights. The testimonies of Josephus (*J.W.* 2.488; *Ant.* 14.282) and Philo (*Legatio ad Gaium* 159, 291; *In Flaccum* 50) are confirmed by a Greek papyrus that mentions the religious freedom enjoyed by Alexandrian Jews "in the time of the god Augustus" (*CPJ* 2:153).

Yet significant changes, both good and bad, occurred in other areas. The abolition of Ptolemaic monopolies opened new possibilities in the local economy, so that a few generations afterward we find wealthy Jews living in Alexandria as shipowners, merchants, and moneylenders (Philo, *In Flaccum* 57). This status may well have increased the competition that already existed between the Jews and the upper strata of the Greek population.

Not all Jews, however, benefited from the change in rule. Jews serving in the Ptolemaic army, for example, lost their source of income when it was disbanded. Jews working in the administration simply disappear from the papyri of the Roman period, a fact that scholars relate to the preference now accorded to Greeks.

Frustration on both sides may have exacerbated underlying competition. The Greeks resented the loss of their political freedom when Augustus abolished their civic council, the *boulē*. They regarded this act as an injustice, especially in view of the confirmation of Jewish religious rights. Other changes of policy were resented by the Jews, among them the special status granted to the Greek cities *(poleis),* which allowed them a kind of fictitious freedom. Alexandria, for example, was called *Alexandria ad Aegyptum* — "by Egypt," not "in Egypt" — as if to underline its (obviously fictitious) independent status. More significantly, the Greek cities received economic privileges such as exemption from the poll tax *(laographia),* which all Egyptians had to pay on the principle that a conquered people should render tribute. Descendants of mixed marriages had to pay the tax at reduced rates. To obtain an exemption, it was necessary to demonstrate one's right to citizenship in one of the country's Greek cities.

No legal source tells us whether the Jews were considered Greeks or Egyptians, but from the very beginning of the Roman period Jews began lodging complaints. In a petition written to the prefect of Egypt under Augustus (*CPJ* 2:151), a Jew named Helenos son of Tryphon complains of an injury done to him by a financial office of the government. Helenos contested the decision, which evidently concerned payment of the poll tax, and asserted his right to be exempt since his father was an Alexandrian citizen and he himself had always lived in the city of Alexandria and received "the appropriate education" as far as his father's means allowed. Helenos styled himself "an Alexandrian," but the scribe who wrote the letter for him struck out this word and in its place wrote "a Jew from Alexandria." This is an extremely significant change, since "Alexandrian" meant a citizen of the Greek city, while "a Jew from Alexandria" meant a person who lived in the city as a simple resident. The scribe's rewording may well indicate that a legal dispute lay behind the issue.

A generation later, Philo observes that the Jews were "anxious to obtain equal rights with the burgesses and are near to being citizens because they differ little from the original inhabitants" (*Mos.* 1.34-35) — a claim strongly rejected by the Greeks. From a Greek papyrus we learn that Isidorus, one of the fiercest Alexandrian leaders in the time of Caligula, accused the Alexandrian Jews of being of the same character as Egyptians because both nations had to pay the poll tax (*CPJ* 2:156c). Scholars have debated whether these rights had to do only with membership in the Greek *polis* or included additional rights for the Jewish community. The scarcity of the sources, their fragmentary state, and their obvious bias make it extremely difficult to reach a definitive conclusion. Yet one thing clearly emerges from all the sources: Jewish claims were strongly contested by their Greek neighbors.

The reasons for these objections may have to do with Jewish religious separatism. Josephus puts an important question in the mouth of Apion, a grammarian and Homeric scholar of Egyptian origin who played a prominent part in the cultural and political life of the first century C.E.: "Why, then, if they are citizens do they not worship the same gods as the Alexandrians?" (*Ag. Ap.* 2.65). This may be a rhetorical question intended to conceal more practical concerns. Recent scholarship emphasizes that it may represent a maneuver to limit other Jewish rights. By focusing on religious issues, the Greeks would have pushed the Jews on the most sensitive matters. If the Jews insisted on maintaining their practices, as of course they would, the municipal governments could regard this as their opting out of civic responsibilities and debar Jews from the services and benefits of the community.

In any case, Jewish refusal to participate in the cult to the gods of the city may have been difficult for Greeks to understand in a syncretistic world where cults and mythologies freely intermingled. Moreover, this refusal was made in the name of the Jewish god, who could not be seen or represented in the form of a statue or image. This aniconism made the Jewish god a nonentity in Greek eyes — hence the accusation of atheism found in Apollonius' work (*De Iudaeis* in Josephus, *Ag. Ap.* 2.148). A cult in a temple that had no image in its inner sanctum was also difficult for Greeks to understand. Apion claimed that the Jews worshiped the head of an ass in their temple. In this accusation he was relying on a supposed relation of the Jews with Seth, the god of evil, chaos, and confusion who was often identified with the donkey, an animal abhorred by the Egyptians (*Ag. Ap.* 2.79-80).

Another feature of Judaism criticized in Egypt from the time of Hecataeus in the third century B.C.E. was its social separateness: "The sacrifices he [Moses] established differ from those of the other nations, as does their way of living, for as a result of their own expulsion from Egypt he introduced an unsocial and intolerant mode of life" (*Aegyptiaca,* apud Diodorus Siculus, *Bibliotheca Historica* 60.3.4). In time, Jewish separateness was interpreted as misanthropy — hence the accusation of hatred of humanity and of ritual murders. Its first formulation is found in the work of Apion, who claims that the Jews used to "kidnap a Greek foreigner, fatten him up for a year, and then convey him to a wood, where they slew him, sacrificed his body with their customary ritual, partook of his flesh and, while immolating the Greek, swore an oath of hostility to the Greeks" (*Ag. Ap.* 2.91-95).

Intellectual antagonism materialized at the time of Emperor Caligula. In the year 38 C.E., the arrival of King Agrippa in Alexandria was the occasion of a popular riot, described at length in Philo's *Against Flaccus.* Stirred up by a group of extremists, the Alexandrians installed images of the emperor in the synagogues, so that the Jewish cult automatically ceased. Jews were proclaimed "foreigners and aliens" (*In Flaccum* 54) and shut up in one quarter of the city. When forced by the scarcity of food to leave the quarter and to appear in the marketplace, they were pursued and slaughtered; their houses were plundered and their goods stolen or destroyed. Members of the Jewish senate were flogged with whips in the theater. Jewish traditional autonomy was officially abolished. Seeking reconciliation, the Jewish aristocracy sent a delegation to the emperor in Rome, but it failed in its purposes. As soon as Caligula was killed in 41 C.E., Jews in Alexandria rose in arms and retaliated against the Greeks. Josephus tells us that "upon the death of Gaius, the Jews, who had been humiliated under his rule and grievously abused by the Alexandrians, took heart again and at once armed themselves." Claudius commanded the prefect of Egypt to put down the uprising (*Ant.* 19.278-79). Peace was restored but the dispute was not solved; there were continuous clashes between Jews and Greeks in which each crackdown by the authorities further exacerbated the quarrel between the two sides (*J.W.* 2.489).

Two generations later, amidst the prevailing anti-Jewish attitudes at the time when the First Jewish Revolt broke out in Judea in 66 C.E., another episode of violence took place in the theater of Alexandria (*J.W.* 2.487-98). And some years later, in the aftermath of the First Revolt, the citizens of Alexandria appealed to Titus to strip the Jews of their rights (*Ant.* 12.121-24)

Two additional episodes of conflict in Alexandria took place at the beginning of Trajan's reign, about which we learn from Greek papyri. One of them (*CPJ* 2:157) belongs to the so-called *Acts of the Alexandrians,* which deal with historical facts by inserting them in a fictional framework and manipulating them with strong political bias. Precise historical details are impossible to reconstruct, but a conflict between Jews and Greeks had taken place, probably at some point between 110 and 113 C.E. Another episode of strife between the Greeks and the Jews occurring a couple of years later is reported by an official Roman document written in October 115 (*CPJ* 2:435). The Jews complain about "fire and weapons" prepared against them, and a Roman authority, possibly the Roman prefect, displays a critical attitude towards the Greeks. Obscure references are made to disorders and to a demonstration held in the theater of the city, and the arrival of a judge sent by the emperor to investigate is noted. Other fragmentary papyri appear to allude to the eventual condemnation of those responsible for the disorders: sixty Alexandrians were exiled and their slaves beheaded (*CPJ* 2:158a, 158b).

Some months later, in the spring of 116 C.E., there was an uprising of Jews not only in Egypt but also in Libya, Cyprus, Mesopotamia, and Judea. The catalyst for the uprisings has unfortunately left no trace in extant sources. In Libya, Egypt, and Cyprus, the Jews attacked their Greek and Roman neighbors, destroying temples, statues of gods, and centers of Greek civic life (*CJZC* 17-23). The attacks were led by Andreas (according to Dio), or by Lukuas (according to Eusebius), to whom Eusebius ascribes the title "king," a fact that has led some scholars to assume that the uprising had a messianic background. The evidence, however, is scanty. In Cyprus, the Jews were led by a certain Artemion (Dio 68.32.2), and here too we get an impression of great destruction. In Egypt, where the local Jews acted in cooperation with those of Libya (*Hist. Eccl.* 4.2.3), the uprising covered large sections of the country, and for a while Jews had the upper hand (*CPJ* 2:438). The Greeks fought back, led by their *stratēgoi* — the most well known is Apollonios — and helped by the Egyptian peasants and the Romans. The Jewish uprisings were crushed only when Trajan decided on a massive intervention. Order was restored by the autumn of 117 (*CPJ* 2:443), and at Oxyrhynchus the victory over the Jews was commemorated by a festival that was still observed some eighty years later (*CPJ* 2:450).

Assessment

These long-running disputes could arise only if the Jewish communities were a significant presence in the cities concerned. In Asia, for example, a small and insignificant community would have been ignored by the city magistrates or coerced into submission. But in the extant documents and in Josephus' narrative, one senses the presence of Jews sufficiently prominent in city life for their refusal to attend court or do business on the Sabbath to be deemed highly awkward if not even offensive. Some modern interpreters consider Jewish integration as the dominant reality and treat controversies as minor episodes, while others suggest the opposite. In fact, however, no real contradiction exists when social, cultural, and political integration, on the one hand, and antagonism and conflicts, on the other, are regarded as two sides of the same coin.

Jews, Greeks, and Roman Policy

In the regions under their rule, the Romans always tried to pursue a policy that would give them full control but allow the inhabitants to remain reasonably satisfied. That is why the existing organizational framework was usually preserved and the local laws typically endorsed. The status quo of the Jews was likewise preserved and their traditional rights endorsed. All the decrees and edicts quoted by Josephus that were issued between the middle of the first century B.C.E. and the middle of the first century C.E. by Roman commanders, the Roman senate (the so-called *senatus consulta*), Roman governors, and Roman emperors point in the same direction. They all proclaim that the Jews are free to follow their traditional laws and customs: to assemble, to feast and hold common meals, to perform their cult, to have a measure of internal administration and jurisdiction, to build sacred and profane buildings, and to have kosher food in the markets of their cities. It was not a pro-Jewish policy per se; inscriptions and papyri attest that permission to follow local laws was usually granted to conquered peoples by the Romans.

From these same documents quoted by Josephus, however, we also understand that Roman grants had a somewhat theoretical character. Asians, Libyans, Alexandrians, and perhaps other Greeks had their own good reasons for ignoring the Roman ordinances and for preventing the Jews from following their traditional customs and laws. The Jews requested Roman support and, as far as we can judge from the evidence quoted by Josephus, they often got it, but the new letters and the new decrees issued by the Roman government did not get better results, and few practical consequences followed.

This somewhat apathetic attitude on the part of the Romans should occasion no surprise since it was a common feature of Roman politics. The Romans seem to have had a very limited interest in what happened in the provinces and perhaps did not even expect their decisions to be implemented. It was therefore only theoretically that the Romans sided with the Jews and only, it must be emphasized, when religious issues were at stake.

In other areas, the situation was ambiguous. The issue of taxation provides a case in point. Several times the Jews appealed to the Roman authorities, claiming that they did not have to pay the taxes imposed upon them by the Greek cities. In spite of the Jewish sources' desire to present the Romans as generous partners, it appears that the Romans simply refrained from dealing with the matter. A dispute concerning taxes owed to a Greek city took place in Asia in the time of Augustus. Josephus tells us that the emperor granted the Jews "the same equality of taxation as before" (*Ant.* 16.161), but this is not confirmed by the edict quoted immediately below (*JRRW* 22), which deals only with Jewish traditional rights and does not mention taxation at all. Josephus' remarks, therefore, are misleading. In Libya, too, a letter written by Agrippa to the magistrates and the people of Cyrene (*JRRW* 25) mentions the Jewish claim to the effect that they do not owe the taxes imposed upon them by the Greek city. Agrippa's own statement, however, concerns only the Jewish sacred monies, not taxes.

Philo and Josephus would often like us to believe that the Romans sided with the Jews, but this was not always the case. When the Alexandrians introduced images of the emperor Caligula into Jewish synagogues in the city — effectively terminating the Jewish religious cult, in open violation of their traditional rights — the Roman prefect Flaccus could have ordered the statues removed, but he did not, possibly out of fear that his act might be interpreted in Rome as hostility toward the emperor. Whatever the reasons, Flaccus sided with the Greeks, had the leaders of the Jews taken and publicly scourged in the theater, and issued an edict proclaiming that Alexandrian Jews were "foreigners and aliens" in the city (Philo, *In Flaccum* 54). Modern scholars have labored to explain and even justify Flaccus' behavior in an attempt to counterbalance the perspective of Philo and Josephus. But the fact remains that Flaccus was either unwilling or unable to stop the anti-Jewish pogrom, and that is why he was later condemned for his behavior, exiled, and then put to death (*In Flaccum* 109–115, 121–26, 147–51, 169–70, 181, 185–91).

When the next emperor took power, the need to settle the Alexandrian question on a more stable base was urgent, and this time we are fortunate enough to have a reliable document. Preserved in a Greek papyrus (*CPJ* 2:153), it is a letter written by Emperor Claudius to the Alexandrians showing that the situation was far less complimentary to the Jews than Josephus would like us to believe. Again, an apathetic attitude emerges: Claudius states right away that he does not wish "to make an exact inquiry" into what transpired and limits himself to ordering the two parties "to keep peace": "I adjure the Alexandrians to behave gently and kindly towards the Jews who have inhabited the same city for many years . . . [and] . . . to allow them to keep their own ways." The Jews, on the other hand, are ordered not to aim at more than they have previously had "since they enjoy what is their own, and in a city which is not their own they possess an abundance of all good things" (*CPJ* 2:53). This statement is amazing. The claim of Alexandrian Greeks that the Jews were strangers in Alexandria, which had been accepted by the prefect Flaccus some years before, is now endorsed for the first time by a Roman emperor.

Obviously, Claudius' policy did nothing to solve the underlying conflict. Two generations later, when a violent clash took place in Alexandria in the theater of the city, the Roman prefect, Tiberius Julius Alexander, a nephew of Philo and a renegade Jew who had made a brilliant carrier in Roman administration, seems to have crushed the disturbance with ruthless cruelty (*J.W.* 2.487-97).

When public order was menaced, the Roman response was typically immediate and harsh. This happened also when the Jews took up arms during the reign of Trajan in 116 to 117. The Roman prefect, Rutilius Lupus, seems to have participated in the engagements, and Trajan took serious measures to suppress Jewish disorder by sending his best generals: Caius Valerius to Cyprus, with a detachment of soldiers on a military expedition (*ILS* 3:9491), and Marcius Turbo to Egypt, with land and sea forces including cavalry. Turbo "waged war vigorously . . . in many battles for a considerable time and killed many thousands of Jews, not only those of Cyrene but also those of Egypt" (Eusebius, *Hist. Eccl.* 4.2.3-4). In Libya, during the war against the Jews, a Roman *praefectus castrorum* mentioned by Artemidoros Daldianus (*Oneirocriticon* 4.24) was killed. In Egypt, a victorious battle against the Jews took place in the vicinity of Memphis (*CPJ* 2:439), and the Roman historian Appian states that in his day Trajan "exterminated" the Jewish race in Egypt (*Bella Civilia* 2.90). As always, maintenance of peace and order was the main goal Roman policy.

BIBLIOGRAPHY

Barclay, John M. G. 1998. *Jews in the Mediterranean Diaspora: from Alexander to Trajan (323 BCE–117 CE).* Edinburgh: Clark.

Bartlett, John R. 2002. *Jews in the Hellenistic and Roman Cities.* London: Routledge.

Berthelot, Katell. 2003. *Philanthropia Judaica: Le debat autour de la "misanthropie" des lois juives dans L'antiquite.* Leiden: Brill.

Cappelletti, Silvia. 2006. *The Jewish Community of Rome: From the Second Century BCE to the Third Century BCE.* Leiden: Brill.

Collins, John J. 2005. *Jewish Cult and Hellenistic Culture: Essays on the Jewish Encounter with Hellenism and Roman Rule.* Leiden: Brill.

Feldman, Louis H. 1993. *Jew and Gentile in the Ancient World.* Princeton: Princeton University Press.

Goodman, Martin. 1994. *Mission and Conversion: Proselytizing in the Religious History of the Roman Empire.* Oxford: Clarendon.

Gruen, Erich S. 2002. *Diaspora: Jews amidst Greeks and Romans.* Cambridge: Harvard University Press.

Horbury, William, and David Noy, eds. 1992. *Jewish Inscriptions of Graeco-Roman Egypt.* Cambridge: Harvard University Press.

Lüderlitz, Gert, ed. 1983. *Corpus jüdischer Zeugnisse aus der Cyrenaika.* Wiesbaden: Reichert.

Modrzejewski, Joseph M. 1995. *The Jews of Egypt: From Rameses II to Emperor Hadrian.* Philadelphia: Jewish Publication Society.

Pucci Ben Zeev, Miriam. 1998. *Jewish Rights in the Roman World: The Greek and Roman Documents Quoted by Josephus Flavius.* Tübingen: Mohr-Siebeck.

Rajak, Tessa. 2001. *The Jewish Dialogue with Greece and Rome: Studies in Cultural and Social Interaction.* Leiden: Brill.

Schäfer, Peter. 1997. *Judeophobia: Attitudes toward the Jews in the Ancient World.* Cambridge: Harvard University Press.

Smallwood, E. M. 1981. *The Jews under Roman Rule from Pompey to Diocletian.* Leiden: Brill.

Stern, Menahem. 1972-1984. *Greek and Latin Authors on Jews and Judaism.* 3 vols. Jerusalem: Israel Academy of Sciences and Humanities.

Tcherikover, Victor. 1979. *Hellenistic Civilization and the Jews.* New York: Atheneum.

Tcherikover, Victor, and Alexander Fuks, eds. 1957-1964. *Corpus Papyrorum Judaicarum*. 3 vols. Cambridge: Harvard University Press.

Trebilco, Paul. 1991. *Jewish Communities in Asia Minor*. Cambridge: Cambridge University Press.

Williams, Margaret H. 1998. *The Jews among Greeks and Romans: A Diasporan Sourcebook*. Baltimore: Johns Hopkins University Press.

Early Judaism and Early Christianity

Daniel C. Harlow

Today it is a commonplace to acknowledge that Jesus and his first followers were Jews thoroughly embedded in the Judaism of their day. But this has not always been the case. Well into the twentieth century, New Testament scholarship tended if not to separate Jesus from his Jewish milieu then at least to view him as transcending its "legalism" and "ritualism." Only in the post–Holocaust era have Christian scholars overcome the negative caricature of ancient Judaism and reckoned with the essential Jewishness of Jesus. The group he inspired began as a movement within Second Temple Judaism, so for much of the first century C.E., the term "Christianity" is inappropriate if taken to suggest a non-Jewish religion. The term itself (Gr. *Christianismos*) was invented in-house in the early second century (Ignatius, *Rom.* 3:3; *Magn.* 10:3; *Phld.* 6:1; *Mart. Pol.* 10:1), while the epithet "Christian" *(Christianos)* was coined by outsiders several decades before (Acts 11:26, 28; 1 Pet. 4:16). Initially, though, even "Christian" did not designate adherents of a non-Jewish faith but followers or partisans of *Christos* the Jew.

Our main sources for the early Jesus movement are the New Testament writings, which were composed over the course of about seventy years, from roughly 50 to 120 C.E. These documents provide valuable historical evidence not only for Jesus and his first followers but also for the wider Jewish world they inhabited. Apart from the ancient Jewish historian Flavius Josephus, the apostle Paul — the earliest and major writer of the New Testament — is the only (former) Pharisee to have left behind a literary legacy. The Synoptic Gospels are a mine of information about first-century Palestinian Judaism: they mention such figures as Herod the Great and his son Antipas, the tetrarch of Galilee; they witness to the beliefs and practices of various Jewish groups; and they supply evidence for Jewish institutions like Temple and synagogue, Jewish rituals like hand washing and kosher table fellowship, Jewish festivals such as Passover, and Jewish theological ideas like angelology, eschatology, and messianism. They also offer examples of Jewish modes of scriptural interpretation and of early Jewish exegetical traditions. The Gospel of Luke and its sequel, the book of Acts, are especially rich in details of Jewish tradition. The third gospel gives the earliest narrative portrait of pilgrimage to Jerusalem and of synagogue worship in the land of Israel. For its part, Acts mentions Gamaliel, Theudas and "the Egyptian," Judas the Galilean, and Agrippa I, and describes a communal organization for the Jerusalem congregation of Jesus' followers which has some points of similarity with that of the Qumran sect. It also distinguishes the Pharisees and Sadducees in their beliefs concerning angels and resurrection, and affords insight into synagogues in the Jewish Diaspora, including the presence there of God-fearing Gentiles. Of course, this material has to be evaluated critically, but it remains nonetheless important.

Any attempt to discuss the relation between early Christianity and early Judaism must confront two main difficulties. The first is the sheer variety that characterized both of them, a variety so pronounced that some scholars prefer to speak of "Judaisms" and "Christianities." Nothing like an official or normative Judaism existed in the earliest centuries of the Common Era; it was probably not until the fourth century or later that the rabbinic movement could lay serious claim to be the dominant form of Judaism. The same is true, *mutatis mutandis,* of early Christianity. Although the New Testament writings do not fully reflect the range of diversity that characterized Christianity in the first century, they still reveal considerable variety and tension.

The second difficulty lies in the recognition that in some settings the boundaries between "Judaism" and "Christianity" were fluid even after the latter had become overwhelmingly non-Jewish in its ethnic composition. Among Jews and Christians, there was considerable overlap in areas of theological identity owing in part to their common scriptural heritage, and to the Christian preservation and transmission of most of the extant literature of Second Temple Judaism. There is also some evidence that Jews and Christians interacted with one another in social and even liturgical contexts into late antiquity and beyond.

Despite these difficulties, it is still meaningful to speak of early Judaism and early Christianity. For all the manifest variety in Second Temple Judaism, a set of core beliefs and practices characterized the piety of most observant Jews. This "common Judaism" centered on the exclusive and imageless worship of the one God, the notion of covenant election, reverence for the Torah, and devotion to the Jerusalem Temple; it included practices such as circumcision for males, Sabbath and festival observance, and kosher diet. To be sure, groups like the Essenes at Qumran defined election in narrow sectarian terms, and in the Hellenistic Diaspora Jews had to negotiate their Jewish identity rather differently than did their compatriots in the homeland. It is also true that in some early apocalypses neither covenant nor Torah is constitutive of Jewish identity. But even these caveats do little to erase the impression of a common Judaism, which receives confirmation in archaeology and in the observations of Greek and Latin authors who wrote about Jews and Judaism. Likewise, all varieties of early Christianity shared in revering Jesus, even if their doing so took on different forms, from simply remembering him as a miracle worker or venerating him as a great teacher to worshiping him as the incarnate Son of God. Further, although "Judaism" and "Christianity" were never airtight categories, the initially Jewish Jesus movement did eventually become a non-Jewish religion, not least in the sense that most of its adherents were Gentiles who did not observe Torah.

In order to highlight some of the major areas of continuity and discontinuity between Second Temple Judaism and early Christianity, it will be useful to examine Jesus in his Jewish context, the Jewish character of the early Jesus movement, and the relation of Paul to Judaism. From there the discussion will proceed to the range of perspectives on Jews and Judaism reflected elsewhere in the New Testament, and conclude with some reflections on the "parting of the ways" between Judaism and Christianity.

Jesus within Judaism

A critical sifting of the Synoptic Gospels of Matthew, Mark, and Luke, our principal sources for Jesus of Nazareth, reveals that he fits securely within Second Temple Judaism. He was an apocalyptic prophet who proclaimed and symbolically enacted the imminent arrival of God's kingdom on earth. In his prophetic role, he bears some resemblance to Jesus ben Hananiah, Theudas, and other popular prophets in first-century Palestine mentioned by Josephus. In his reputation for performing healings and exorcisms, he shows certain affinities with charismatic holy men like Hanina ben Dosa and Honi the Circle Drawer recalled in rabbinic tradition. Scholars debate whether and in what sense Jesus called himself the "Son of Man" and whether he accepted the titles "Messiah" or "Son of God" (in its royal, messianic sense). But he almost certainly regarded himself as God's final envoy to the people of Israel, urging his countrymen to heed his message and calling on some of them to follow him. That both Jesus' former mentor John the Baptist and the movement Jesus left behind were steeped in apocalyptic eschatology argues strongly in favor of seeing him as an apocalyptic figure. The point bears emphasizing since some scholars construe Jesus as a nonapocalyptic sage and social reformer, an understanding of him that is suspect on several counts (see below).

Jesus symbolized the eschatological restoration of Israel by calling twelve disciples to represent the twelve tribes of Israel (Mark 1:16-20 pars.), and he dramatized the eschatological reversal of fortunes by sharing table fellowship with the outcast, including prostitutes, tax gatherers, and other "sinners" — those who lived in flagrant violation of the Torah. He believed that he and his disciples would have places of leadership in the coming kingdom (Mark 10:29-31, 35-40; Matt. 19:28-29) and that those who accepted his message would be included in it. He also predicted the destruction of the Temple (Mark 13:1-2 pars.), having symbolically enacted its demise in a provocative demonstration within its precincts (Mark 11:15-17 pars.), probably on the conviction that God would establish a new temple for the new age.

Careful analysis of the Synoptic tradition shows that Jesus was an observant Jew who did not directly oppose any significant aspect of the Torah. He was circumcised, he observed the Sabbath, he attended the synagogue, he taught from the Torah, he went on pilgrimage to Jerusalem and celebrated the Jewish festivals, and he accepted the atoning efficacy of sacrifice at the Temple (Mark 1:44 pars.; Matt. 5:23). When asked about the greatest commandment, he affirmed the Shema and the obligation to love one's neighbor, innovatingly combining the two

(Mark 12:28-34 pars.). He never denounced Moses or the Law and never denied the covenant election of the Jewish people. The Synoptics portray him in conflict with scribes and Pharisees over such halakic matters as healing on the Sabbath, fasting, tithing, food purity and meal practices, oath taking, and divorce. On at least one occasion he debated with some Sadducees about the resurrection of the dead (Mark 12:18-27 pars.). But these issues were commonly disputed among Palestinian Jews, and since no group represented the "official" position on any matter — there was none — Jesus cannot be said to have opposed the Judaism of his day.

Unfortunately, the original contexts of these disputes were soon forgotten as oral traditions about Jesus began to circulate, so it is impossible to gain a full sense of his attitude toward aspects of Torah piety. Nevertheless, even granting the historicity of the halakic disputes in the Synoptics (which stand in some doubt), the positions attributed to Jesus fall within the bounds of acceptable behavior. Healing on the Sabbath, for instance, was not considered a violation of Sabbath law in pre-70 Judaism (at least no pre-70 Jewish text indicates that it was), and Jesus' stance on marriage and divorce (Mark 10:2-12 pars.) was not less but more stringent than what the Torah requires. Although his disciples were allegedly criticized by some Pharisees for plucking grain on the Sabbath and not washing their hands before meals (Mark 2:23-28 pars.; Mark 7:1-23/Matt. 15:1-20), these perceived infractions would have been relatively minor. The single major infringement of Jewish halakah attributed to Jesus comes with the statement in Mark that "he declared all foods clean" (Mark 7:19b). But this is the evangelist's editorial comment and reflects an attitude that probably goes beyond Jesus' own position. It is quietly dropped in Matthew's redaction of the passage (Matt. 15:17-18).

Whence then the opposition? What Jesus' Pharisaic and Sadducean interlocutors found most objectionable was probably not so much his particular stance on matters of Torah praxis but the way he articulated his stance. He propounded his views by uttering authoritative pronouncements in the first person, and not by entering into debate in the style of a contemporary scribe or rabbi. Instead of citing the opinions of revered teachers, he went straight to the Scriptures. This practice appears most dramatically in the series of antitheses that now make up the Sermon on the Mount, which are introduced with the formula "You have heard it said to the men of old . . . but I say to you . . ." (Matt. 5:21-48). Some of the antitheses are polemical and go beyond the literal meaning of the Torah, but they effectively intensify Torah commandments by trying to get at their root intention. The formula "You have heard it said . . . but I say to you" does not imply a demotion — far less a rejection — of the Torah but only a challenging of traditions of scriptural interpretation. An analogous formula, "You know . . . but we say," features in the halakic document from Qumran (4QMMT). On occasion, Jesus also pronounced sins forgiven when he healed people (Mark 2:1-12 pars.), but the passive verb form he used, "Your sins are forgiven," bears the implication "by God." In making such statements he certainly invited censure, but he was not necessarily claiming divine status for himself, only an authority that relativized the prerogative of the priests. That in itself would have made him plenty controversial.

No doubt Jesus *was* controversial in his day, but it seems unlikely that it was anything that he said or did during his Galilean ministry that got him killed. This suspicion is confirmed by the observation that in the gospel passion narratives it is not the Pharisees who have him arrested and handed over to Pilate but the Jerusalem Temple leadership. Some of his parables, notably the Vineyard and Tenants (Mark 12:1-12 pars.), imply criticism of the Jerusalem priesthood, but the critique is scarcely harsher than what we find in the sectarian writings from Qumran. Jesus' proclamation of the coming kingdom of God might have been regarded by Pilate as politically subversive if he had ever gotten wind of it, since it implicitly challenged the kingdom of Rome. More likely, however, it was the messianic enthusiasm of large crowds that greeted him on his entry into Jerusalem and his attack on the Temple that brought him to the lethal attention of the chief priests and the Romans. Both of these incidents are reported in the Synoptics and independently in John with a thick overlay of interpretation (Mark 11:1-10 pars. and John 12:12-19; Mark 11:15-17 pars. and John 2:13-25), but there is no good reason to doubt their essential historicity. What prompted Jesus' demonstration in the Temple is unclear. Perhaps his ire was aroused by Herod's remodeling program, which had transformed the Temple's outer court from a sacred space into a commercial venue. Equally offensive to him, perhaps, was the type of coinage required to pay the half-shekel Temple tax: Tyrian silver issues that bore the image of the Canaanite god Melqart. Whatever prompted his gesture, he probably intended it to symbolize the Temple's impending doom and eschatological replacement. This understanding of the event finds support in the tradition of his predicting the Temple's destruction, a prediction that need not be taken as an *ex-eventu* prophecy (Mark 13:1-2 pars.).

The Markan trial narrative and its parallel in Matthew depict false witnesses offering conflicting testimony before the Judean council that Jesus threatened to destroy the Temple himself (Mark 14:57-58/Matt. 26:60-61; cf. Jesus' symbolic threat in John 2:19). The charge is not sustained but replaced with the accusation of blasphemy (Mark 14:64). What actually transpired at Jesus' interrogation by the high priest is beyond recovery. In the Markan account he is accused by Caiaphas of blasphemy after confessing to be the messiah and declaring, "You will see the Son of Man seated at the right hand of Power and coming with the clouds of heaven" (Mark 14:62). Among Jews claiming to be the messiah was not a blasphemous assertion, but the Son of Man saying as Mark words it implies that Jesus arrogated divine power and status to himself. Had Jesus made such a claim, it would indeed have been regarded as blasphemy. But again, what he actually said cannot be known.

The clearest indication of why Jesus was crucified comes from his Roman executioners, in the *titulus* that Pilate had affixed to Jesus' cross: "King of the Jews" (Mark 15:26 pars.). With mocking irony, the inscription suggests that he was executed on grounds of political sedition. This does not mean that Pilate regarded Jesus or his followers as a real political threat to the Roman Empire, only that Jesus' provocative demonstration in the Temple had to be dealt with so as to quell potential unrest in Jerusalem during the politically charged atmosphere of Passover, a Jewish festival celebrating liberation from foreign domination. In turning him over to Pilate, the chief priests no doubt sought to avoid the vigorous police action from the Romans that any further disturbances in the city would have risked (cf.

John 11:48, "If we let him go on like this, everyone will believe in him and the Romans will come and destroy both our holy place and our nation" — a statement attributed to the chief priests apropos of the raising of Lazarus that would make excellent historical sense in relation to the Temple incident). Indeed, the chief priests may have been working with Pilate to preserve public order and may have arrested Jesus with Pilate's approval.

The Early Jesus Movement(s)

Within a few weeks of Jesus' death around the year 30, several of his followers began boldly proclaiming that he had appeared to them risen from the dead. Over the next months and years, their reflection on Jesus' life, their study of the Jewish scriptures, and their experience of his spiritual presence in their midst led them to elaborate on their core proclamation: God had sent Jesus to redeem all humankind; his death was necessary to inaugurate God's sovereign rule in the earth; and faith in the saving death and resurrection of the one now exalted to God's right hand would prepare all who turned to him for the coming judgment and grant them eternal life in the coming kingdom.

Initially the members of "the Way" or "the Assembly" *(ekklēsia),* as the group called itself, would have appeared to outsiders as yet one more messianic movement within Palestinian Judaism. In their social organization and religious practice, they resembled other Jewish groups: they met in one another's homes for table fellowship, prayer, and study, in the manner of the later Pharisaic *havurot;* some continued to worship in the Temple and to participate in the life of their local synagogue communities.

The early years of the Jesus movement in Palestine remain sketchy because of the sparse quantity and apologetic nature of the source material. The book of Acts is the principal source for the first three decades, but its narrow focus and idealizing tendencies present some obstacles. Acts portrays the movement having its center in Jerusalem under the aegis of the Twelve and expanding under their auspices, with Peter and James, the brother of Jesus, as the chief leaders. In itself the account is credible, but it probably does not tell the whole story, and for many historians it fits too neatly with Luke's understanding of salvation history. It is also countered by the putative existence of other groups in other locales. Independent traditions in the Gospels of Mark and Matthew and in the epilogue of John point to appearances of the risen Jesus in Galilee. Moreover, a small handful of passages in the Synoptic Gospels (e.g., Matt. 10:5-15) seem to reflect the interests and lifestyle of traveling bands of miracle-working teachers and prophets in Galilee, Syria, and the Decapolis, figures attested more clearly at the end of the first century in the *Didache.* These wandering charismatics would have been active alongside more settled clusters of followers in towns and villages, relying upon them to support their itinerant, mendicant existence.

Some scholars have posited the existence of a Galilean community on the basis of the Q document, a Greek source for Jesus' sayings adapted by the Gospels of Matthew and Luke. Recent reconstructions suggest that the group revered Jesus as a countercultural wisdom sage and attached no redemptive significance to his death and resurrection. These reconstructions, though, are as problematic in their own way as the idealized picture in Acts. Some literary stratifications of the Q source rely on dubious assumptions regarding the generic incompatibility of the wisdom sayings (supposedly early) and apocalyptic sayings (allegedly later) attributed to Jesus. Just as questionable is the notion that Q exhausts everything that its author(s) and community believed about Jesus. Most speculative of all is the correlation of Q's alleged literary layers with stages in the history of the "Q community."

The Jesus movement likely did take root in different places rather quickly, assuming different forms in a variety of social settings. But the fact remains that no significant community is attested for Galilee in the early decades. After Jesus' death and resurrection, the principal Galilean disciples either remained in or relocated to Jerusalem, which became the effective center of the movement. The city's status as such receives independent confirmation from the letters of Paul, whose relations with the Jerusalem church were often tense but who shows no awareness of any other major community in Palestine. There were many locales but only one true center.

For several decades, the ethos of the Jerusalem community remained Jewish. According to Acts, its members sacrificed in the Temple and experimented with a communal sharing of goods now seen to resemble the organizational life of the Qumran sectarians (Acts 2:44-45; 4:32-35; cf. 1QS 6:19-20, 22). They also attracted priests and Pharisees to their ranks, and three decades later were still "all zealous for the law" (Acts 21:20). Until the First Jewish Revolt disbanded the community, it practiced traditional forms of Jewish piety such as fasting, almsgiving, Torah study, and observance of holy days.

One thing that did distinguish the early Jesus movement from other forms of Second Temple Judaism was its strong missionary impulse. Initially, it evangelized other Jews and not Gentiles, but as it extended into urban areas of Palestine and neighboring regions, contact with Gentiles became inevitable. According to Acts, the impetus for expansion beyond Jerusalem came as an unforeseen but providential consequence of the stoning of Stephen, a leader of the movement's Hellenist wing comprised of Greek-speaking Jews from the Diaspora who were critical of the Temple (Acts 6:8–8:1a). After his martyrdom, Stephen's fellow Hellenists were driven from the city, taking their message about Jesus with them into wider Judea and Samaria, to Phoenicia, and as far as Cyprus and Syrian Antioch (Acts 8:1b–11:27). Several early evangelists and apostles in the movement were Diaspora Jews. Acts names Philip, Barnabas (from Cyprus), Paul (Tarsus), Prisca and her husband Aquila (Pontus), and Apollos (Alexandria). All but Philip are mentioned in Paul's letters as well. In addition, Acts refers to several unnamed men from Cyprus and Cyrene as the first to proclaim the new message to Gentiles in Antioch.

An important focus of missionary effort centered on Jewish synagogues in cities of the Mediterranean Diaspora, whose Gentile attendees and benefactors were open to embracing the new, multiethnic variety of Judaism on offer. Diaspora synagogues supplied the Jesus movement not only with potential Gentile converts but with religious resources and models of communal organization. Early Christian hymns and prayers probably borrowed freely from the liturgies of synagogues, and

Christian house churches imitated the social intimacy, international networking, and practice of hospitality that characterized synagogue communities. Perhaps most importantly, the Diaspora synagogues bequeathed to early Christianity a massive literary and theological legacy in the form of the Septuagint, alongside numerous other works written in an astonishing range of genres that today make up the Old Testament Pseudepigrapha — histories and novellas, apocalypses and testaments, philosophy and wisdom, drama and poetry.

As increasing numbers of non-Jews joined the movement, their table fellowship with Jewish believers raised a critical issue: whether Gentile converts should be required to accept kosher food restrictions. The matter was pressing because early Christian worship took place in the context of a communal meal. To most Jewish believers and to many Gentile converts as well, both this requirement and that of circumcision would have made obvious sense; after all, they were mandated by Jewish Scripture, had the weight of tradition, and were sanctioned by the example of Jesus and his disciples. Others disagreed, however. The best known and most controversial dissenter was Saul (Paul), a Diaspora Jew who joined the Hellenist wing of the movement after his persecuting it was brought to an abrupt end by a vision of the risen Jesus. Both Acts and Paul's letter to the Galatians indicate that the issue came to a head in Antioch and was settled at a meeting of the Jerusalem apostles (ca. 49 C.E.) in a way that did not require circumcision of Gentile converts (Acts 15:1-35; Gal. 2:1-10). Beyond these bare facts, the two sources disagree over several details. Most notably Acts reports that, although Gentiles did not have to be circumcised, they were expected to "abstain from idol meat, from sexual immorality (possibly including close kinship marriages), from what has been strangled, and from blood" (Acts 15:20, 29). According to Galatians, however, no such ritual restrictions were imposed. In any case, the accommodation opened the way for increasing numbers of Gentiles to enter the movement without adopting the traditional sign of covenant membership. It was a fateful development and had a major impact on the Christian movement's eventually becoming a religion separate from Judaism.

Paul

Next to Jesus, Paul was the most significant figure in the movement during the first century. In some respects, he was even more controversial than Jesus. We know a lot more about him thanks to the second half of Acts and to some letters of his that survive. (His authoring seven of them is undoubted, but the other six were probably written in his name by his associates in the decades after his death.) The two sources are not completely at odds, but they do present rather different portraits of Paul's relation to Judaism. Acts depicts him as an observant Jew even after he joined the Jesus movement. He continues to follow Jewish laws and observe Jewish customs. He has Timothy circumcised, frequents Diaspora synagogues, gets his hair cut to fulfill a vow, travels to Jerusalem to give alms to his nation and offer sacrifices, undergoes ritual purification in the Temple, pays the expenses of a Nazirite ceremony for four men, and announces before the Sanhedrin that he is a Pharisee. For Luke, then, Paul was basically a Jew who added faith in Messiah Jesus to his Judaism.

Paul's letters (which Acts nowhere mentions) confirm several elements of this profile. In them he claims to be a Hebrew born of Hebrews who was circumcised on the eighth day (Phil. 3:5). He proudly calls himself an Israelite and a descendant of Abraham (Rom. 11:1). He concedes that circumcision is of value if one practices the Torah (Rom. 2:25). He speaks of the Jewish people as his "kinsmen according to the flesh" and avers that "to them belong the adoption, the glory, the covenants, the giving of the Law, the worship, and the promises"; they are beloved for the sake of the patriarchs, and to them belongs the messiah (Rom. 9:3-5; 11:28). And he staunchly insists that even though Christ came to save Gentiles, God has not abandoned the Jewish people; in fact, their election is "irrevocable" and all "Israel will be saved" (Rom. 11:26, 29). He pronounces the Torah "holy, just, and good" (Rom. 7:12) and protests that faith in Christ does not abrogate the Law but establishes it (Rom. 3:31). "It is not the hearers of the Law who are righteous before God but the doers of the Law who will be counted righteous," he writes to Christians in Rome (2:13). Indeed, the "just requirements of the Law" (the moral demands of the Torah) are to be fulfilled in the lives of believers as they cooperate with the Spirit of God at work within them (Rom. 8:4).

These strong affirmations of Jewish identity, however, reveal only part of the picture. Most of Paul's positive statements about the Torah appear in a single letter, Romans, his last; and they look like strategic backpedaling, written out of deference to Jewish believers in Rome and with an eye toward his upcoming visit to Jerusalem. His letter to the Galatians is far more negative. There Paul speaks of his "former life in Judaism" in a way that distances him from it (Gal. 1:13). In lines written to believers in Thessalonica so harsh that many regard them as an interpolation, he says of the Jews in Judea that they "killed both the Lord Jesus and the prophets and drove us out; they displease God and oppose all people, hindering us from speaking to the Gentiles so that they may be saved, so as to fill up constantly the measure of their sins. But God's wrath has come upon them at last!" (1 Thess. 4:15-16). As for circumcision, it ultimately counts for nothing (Gal. 5:5; 6:15; 1 Cor. 7:19). More, if his Gentile converts have their foreskins cut off under compulsion, they will cut themselves off from Christ (Gal. 5:4). The Jew is one whose Jewishness is "inward" *(en tō kryptō),* and real circumcision is a matter of the heart, spiritual not literal (Rom. 2:29; Phil. 3:3). The Torah presided over a ministry of condemnation (2 Cor. 3:9) as an unwitting ally of Sin (understood as a cosmic power) that brought only death (Rom. 7:9-11). Because it cannot "make alive" (Gal. 3:21), its fading glory has been set aside in Christ (2 Cor. 3:10-11), who is the "end" but also "goal" *(telos)* of the Law (Rom. 10:4). "No one is counted righteous by works of the Law [i.e., by observing the Torah's ritual commandments] but by faith in Jesus Christ [or: the faithfulness of Jesus Christ]," and all who rely on works of the Law, especially circumcision, are under God's curse (Gal. 2:16; 3:10).

For Paul, Jesus' himself is more than just the messiah of Israel; he is the universal Savior and Lord. In a proto-binitarian rewriting of the Shema, he includes Jesus in the life of the one God and identifies him as the divine agent in creation: "for us there is one God, the Father, from whom are all things and for whom we exist, and one Lord, Jesus Christ, through whom are all things and through whom we exist" (1 Cor. 8:6). Christ's preexistence, divinity, and incarnation are also alluded to in the statement that, though he was in the form of God, he emptied himself by being born in human likeness (Phil. 2:6-11). Like Paul's midrash on the Shema, this poem (probably of pre-Pauline origin) effectively identifies Christ with heavenly Wisdom. Here messianism encroaches on monotheism.

It is important to note that Paul addressed none of these letters to Jews or Jewish believers in Jesus but to his Gentile converts (though the non-Pauline congregations in Rome probably numbered some Jews), so in none of them does he engage Judaism directly. Even the Judaizing advocates of Gentile circumcision whom he attacks in Galatians and Philippians — he calls them "the dogs, the evil workers, the mutilation" (*katatomē,* a wordplay on *peritomē,* "circumcision"; Phil. 3:2) — may have been Gentile, not Jewish, believers. Nevertheless, Paul's statements regarding covenant election and salvation being possible only in Christ clearly apply to both Jews and Gentiles ("two-paths-to-salvation" interpretations of Romans 9–11 notwithstanding). He does not seem to have objected to Torah observance as such, and evidently had no problem with Jewish believers in Jesus abiding by Jewish laws and customs. It is even conceivable, though very unlikely, that he would not have objected to Gentile converts doing so as long as they did not regard such observance as necessary for inclusion in the covenant or salvation. As a practical missionary expedient, he himself could live as a Jew under the Torah in order to win Jews (1 Cor. 9:19-21). In spite of all this, he considered himself free from the Law and wanted his Gentile congregations to do the same.

Except for their worshiping the God of Israel and adopting the Bible's sexual ethics, the communities that Paul founded and nurtured in Asia Minor and Greece were not Jewish in their ethos. True, the theological motivation for his mission to them was thoroughly Jewish, being predicated upon the biblical vision of the Nations worshiping the God of Israel in the last days. But the Hebrew prophets who envisioned the inclusion of Gentiles in the eschatological restoration of Israel had been rather vague, mentioning no entry requirements beyond worshiping God (e.g., Isa. 60:8-12; Mic. 4:1-2). Paul concluded that there were not to be any — except faith in Christ. Significantly, there is no hint in his letters that his Gentile congregations had social contacts with Diaspora synagogue communities, even though in his three-decade mission he himself visited synagogues often enough to receive the "forty lashes less one" on five occasions (2 Cor. 11:24). So in their *ethnos* and *ethos,* the Pauline churches were not Jewish.

If with E. P. Sanders we agree that Judaism's "pattern of religion" in the first century can be characterized as "covenantal nomism," what can be said of Paul's pattern of religion? The essential components of covenantal nomism look like this:

God's gracious election of Israel at Sinai → Israel's grateful response of obedience to the Torah → final judgment with rewards and punishments

The basic structure of Paul's religion looks very similar:

God's gracious act in Christ → grateful response of "the obedience of faith" in Christ → final judgment with rewards and punishments

It is not that Paul's theology reflects a fundamentally different pattern of religion than Judaism, as Sanders maintains. The pattern is the same, but its crucial element — Christ instead of Torah — differs. Christ is the only true offspring of Abraham and sole heir to God's promises, and only those who have faith in him — who are united to him by being baptized into his death and having his life formed in them by the Spirit — become fellow heirs to those promises. This notion, that the Abrahamic covenant and faith in the messiah trump the Sinai covenant and living by Torah, has no precedent in early Judaism. And there is nothing in early Jewish thought to account for why the coming of the messiah should dethrone the Torah. (Paul, of course, would protest that he and his Gentile converts were indeed living by Torah, in accord with its true intention. He says as much in Rom. 3:31, "Do we then nullify the Law through faith? Absolutely not! Rather, we uphold the Law.")

Since Paul was a Jew who regarded faith in Christ as the fulfillment of Judaism, it is wrong to call him "anti-Jewish." It is also unfair to call him an "apostate" since he considered his Gentile mission to be a prophetic vocation within his native religion, not the consequence of a conversion to a new one. But in redefining the notion of covenant election so radically, he struck at the heart of the Jewish identity of most Jews. Disagreement over who is elect was certainly part of intra-Jewish debate in the Second Temple period. This is clear enough from the sectarian Dead Sea Scrolls. Paul, however, went a step beyond the covenanters at Qumran: for them not all Jews are elect, but all the elect are still Jews. Not so for Paul: only those in Christ are in the covenant and among the elect. In his vision of a new humanity destined for a new creation, ethnicity — so essential to Jewish identity — disappears. If his theology implies no wholesale rejection or supersession of Israel, it does imply a new definition of "Israel" and a displacement of historic Israel's covenantal self-understanding as a community formed by physical descent and ritual observance.

Other New Testament Perspectives on Jews and Judaism

Paul's theology is the most complex — and on the subject of the Law, the most convoluted — in the New Testament. The rest of the corpus presents a range of attitudes toward Jews and Judaism. At one end of the spectrum are writings that engage in a constructive and relatively positive appropriation of Jewish scripture and tradition without vilifying or even referring directly to Jews or non-Christian Judaism. At the other end are those that were written to communities of believers who were in competition with Jewish communities and that therefore reflect varying degrees of polemic, separation, and supersession.

The General Epistles and Revelation

Representative of the more irenic end of the spectrum are the "general" or "catholic" epistles of James, Peter, Jude, and Hebrews. Although Acts and Galatians remember James as an advocate of ritual Torah observance, the epistle that bears his name deals only with the ethical teachings of the Torah. It is a fine specimen of Hellenistic Jewish wisdom literature, addressed to "the twelve tribes of the Diaspora" (Jas. 1:1), a designation that ostensibly suggests Jewish believers. The body of the letter consists of a series of short aphorisms and admonitions followed by a sequence of mini essays that pick up and elaborate on the key themes of the sayings. The work contains no Christology to speak of — and in fact mentions Jesus only twice — but it does contain echoes of Jesus' teachings. It understands the "royal law" or "law of liberty" (1:24; 2:8, 12) not as a body of instruction distinct from the Torah but as the Torah's command to love God and neighbor, now ratified, at least by implication, in the teaching and example of Jesus. All of this is stated with absolutely no polemics against Jews or non-Christian Judaism.

The epistles attributed to Peter and Jude also arrogate Jewish tradition to themselves without indulging in anti-Jewish invective. The latter is attributed to "Jude a servant of Jesus Christ and brother of James" (Jude 1) and addressed to believers whose location is not specified, though if the attribution is genuine a Palestinian provenance would be likely. As with James, the authorial attribution to a brother of Jesus is regarded by many scholars as pseudonymous. The body of this short document condemns false teachers, evoking various figures and groups in the Jewish Scriptures as examples of wickedness that merited divine punishment. Among its accusations is that the ungodly teachers "slander the glorious ones" (v. 8), a charge that occasions mention of an extrabiblical tradition about the angel Michael disputing with Satan over the body of Moses (v. 9; cf. *Assumption [Testament] of Moses*). It also quotes *1 Enoch* as Scripture (vv. 14-15; *1 Enoch* 1:9).

Most of Jude was taken up into 2 Peter, a letter almost universally regarded as a pseudonymous writing of the early second century. Like Jude, 2 Peter shows no concern with Jews or Judaism as it co-opts Jewish tradition. So also with 1 Peter, a circular letter from Rome (called "Babylon," 5:13) sent to Gentile believers in Asia Minor who are addressed as "exiles in the Diaspora" (1:1). Composed by a disciple of Peter (or perhaps of Paul) in the late first century, it is a letter of moral exhortation designed to bolster its audience in the face of slander and ostracism from their pagan neighbors. One of its major means of identity formation is to confer on its Gentile readers the prestige of Israel's sacred rites and institutions. The readers are "living stones" being built into a "spiritual house" in which they serve as members of a "holy priesthood" and offer "spiritual sacrifices" (2:5). They are a "chosen race," a "holy nation," and "God's own people" (2:9; cf. LXX Exod. 19:6; Isa. 43:20; Hos. 2:25). Again, not a single reference to non-Christian Jews surfaces.

Falling roughly at the same point on the continuum of positive appropriation to negative engagement is the Epistle to the Hebrews. The traditional title is a complete misnomer. With epistolary features coming only in the closing lines, it is more a sermon than a letter. It was directed not to Hebrews but Christians, perhaps from a Jewish background but possibly from a Gentile one. Rome may be the intended destination. The addressees have experienced persecution, though of what sort and by whom are not specified. They have grown weary in their commitment to Christ and are in danger of falling away. There is no clear support in the text for the traditional view, frequent among commentators, that the author wrote to dissuade a Jewish-Christian audience from reverting to Judaism. The homily's poetic prologue contains some of the highest christological affirmations in the New Testament: Christ as divine Son is mediator, heir, and Lord of the entire cosmos. He is "the exact imprint of God's very being" — an honorific that early Jewish tradition conferred on the figure of divine Wisdom personified (Heb. 1:3; Wis. 7:26). Hebrews asserts Christ's superiority to angels, to Moses, and, most extensively, to the levitical priesthood, employing a variety of sophisticated rhetorical devices and frequent exposition of passages in the Psalms and other Jewish Scriptures (e.g., Gen. 14:17-20; Jer. 31:31-34; Pss. 2:7; 8:4-6; 95:7-11; 110:4). Its signal contribution to New Testament Christology is its designation of Jesus as an eternal, heavenly priest in the line of Melchizedek whose atoning death has established a new covenant ratified in the heavenly sanctuary (chaps. 7–10). Strikingly, though, the author of Hebrews never so much as glances at a living Judaism or at the Jerusalem Temple and priesthood of the first century. The points of comparison, contrast, admonition, and warning are made rather with respect to the newly formed levitical priesthood in the days of Moses and Aaron, the desert tabernacle, and the Israelites of the exodus generation. The author is familiar with interpretive traditions concerning Melchizedek, Moses, and angels known from a variety of Second Temple texts, and his Platonism has affinities with the thought of Philo of Alexandria. He engages in typological, midrash-like, and promise-and-fulfillment exegesis of the Scriptures. His acquaintance with Jewish tradition seems to be pure book learning.

All these so-called general epistles virtually ignore Jews and Judaism of the first century, either because their social settings were distant from Jewish communities or because their authors' varied agendas simply required no direct engagement. The same is true of the Deutero-Pauline and Johannine epistles. Ephesians, for instance, has a moving statement about how in Christ Gentiles have been brought near to the "commonwealth of Israel" and the "covenants of promise," and how the "dividing wall" of hostility between Jews and Gentiles has been torn down. Yet the union of Jew and Gentile in one new humanity is bought at the price of Christ's nullifying the "law [made up] of commandments in decrees" (Eph. 2:11-22; cf. Col. 2:16-19 for a disparaging reference to Jewish dietary practices). It is a unity that effectively erases Jewish distinctiveness. Nevertheless, Ephesians and the other epistles appropriate early Jewish tradition mostly by treating it as a resource for constructing and strengthening Christian identity. Their authors ransack the Septuagint for self-defining language in order to forge a link with Israel's sacred past and to write Christian believers into her story. To judge only by what they wrote, the Christians reflected in these documents look less like competitors of Jews than aspiring imitators and heirs.

With a few notable exceptions, the situation is largely the same in the book of Revelation, an apocalypse with an epistolary framework written by a Jewish prophet of Christ named John, and dispatched to seven communities in as many cities in Asia Minor. It was probably written (in an often awkward Semiticizing Greek) during the reign of the emperor Domitian (81-96 C.E.). It calls for radical cultural disengagement, urging Asian Christians not to assimilate to the idolatrous political, economic, and religious system of the Roman Empire, and preparing them for the prospect of persecution. The work has a high Christology:

although it does not explicitly assert Christ's preexistence or divinity, Jesus nevertheless shares completely in the sovereignty of God. Unlike angels (Rev. 19:10; 22:8-9), Jesus *legitimately* receives worship in a heavenly throne room scene precisely parallel to one focused on God (4:1–5:14; cf. 7:10; 11:15; 12:10-12; 19:6-8). He also shares with God the title "the alpha and omega" (1:8 and 22:13; cf. 1:17 and 21:6) and is petitioned in prayer (22:20). Virtually every line of the work is steeped in the language of Jewish scripture, though never by way of direct quotation; and at more than one point, the full complement of God's faithful people is defined in terms of the twelve tribes of Israel (7:4-8; 21:12). The apocalyptic visions in chapters 4–22 — the bulk of the book — do not mention Jews or attack non-Christian Judaism, but early on, in the proclamation to the congregation in Smyrna, John has the exalted Christ say, "I know the slander *(blasphēmia)* on the part of those who say they are Jews *(Ioudaioi)* and are not, but are a synagogue *(synagōgē)* of Satan" (2:9). The message to believers in Philadelphia includes a similar statement (3:8). The word *Ioudaioi* here is a positive epithet with a negative thrust. The Jewish author thinks highly of it, so highly as to imply that he and his fellow believers have exclusive claim to it. The Jews down the street have forfeited their right to the title, having rejected the proclamation about Jesus while enjoying the legal privileges and exemptions that the Romans granted the Jewish people. It may be that these Jews were denying the title to partisans of Christ, and perhaps taking measures to exclude Christian believers from access to the privileges it afforded by denouncing them before Roman authorities. But this is not clear. In any event, this sort of name-calling was typical in intra-Jewish conflicts, as in the Qumran sect's labeling its opponents the "congregation of Belial."

The Gospels and Acts

At various points along the negative part of the spectrum of attitudes toward Jews and Judaism are the Gospels and Acts. The Gospel of Mark and Luke-Acts are the least vituperative, while Matthew and John are at once the most "Jewish" and "anti-Jewish." The anonymous Gospel of Mark was written either just before or (less likely) just after the destruction of Jerusalem and the Temple in 70 C.E. It is traditionally assigned a provenance in the city of Rome but more likely stems from somewhere in the Roman East, perhaps in close proximity to the Jewish homeland. The closest Mark comes to reflecting a supersessionist stance toward Judaism is in the Parable of the Vineyard and the Tenants (12:1-12). There he invites his readers to regard the chief priests, scribes, and elders of the people as the landlords of God's vineyard (Israel) who seized and killed Jesus, God's "beloved son." "What will the owner of the vineyard do?" the Markan Jesus asks. "He will come and destroy the tenants and give the vineyard to others." It is not clear who Mark means by "the others" who inherit the vineyard — that is, the patrimony of Israel in the coming kingdom of God. On Jesus' original telling of the parable, the "others" were probably to be understood as himself and the Twelve, who would be the nation's new leaders. Mark, however, may have in mind the leaders of his own and other largely Gentile communities who accept Jesus as the messiah. This acceptance may not imply the rejection of Israel as a whole, but it would exclude most of ethnic Israel.

Luke-Acts was composed around 80-90 C.E. using Mark, Q, and other sources. Its place of composition is unknown; Antioch is often suggested on the basis of tradition, but almost any major city around the Mediterranean is possible. The two-volume work stresses the salvation-historical continuity between Israel and the Christian movement more explicitly and extensively than any other New Testament writing. Luke alone among the evangelists has a positive attitude toward the Temple: his gospel both begins and ends there (Luke 1:5-23; 24:52-53); Jesus does not abandon it after cleansing it but teaches there (19:47; 20:1; 22:53); in Acts the apostles continue to worship and teach within its precincts (Acts 3:1-8; 5:21, 25). His attitude toward Jerusalem is more ambivalent. On the one hand, it symbolizes positively God's relationship with the people of Israel. On the other, it is the place of Israel's rejection of its Prophet-Messiah. Like Joseph and Moses, Jesus is at first rejected by his brethren but eventually vindicated by God (in the resurrection and outpouring of the Spirit on his followers) in a way that empowers him to save the very ones who rejected him. In Acts, the apostles are the new leaders of Israel, but God has not written off the Jewish people. The history and story of Israel are continued and fulfilled in the work of Jesus and the community he formed, which is not a renegade sect but the authentic form of the restored people of God. In Luke's view, membership in the people of God is no longer limited to those who are Jews by birth but open to "anyone in every nation who fears him and does what is right" by "believing in Jesus and receiving forgiveness of sins through his name" (Acts 10:34, 43). To be a part of the "people" *(laos)* of God, Gentiles do not have to convert to the "nation" *(ethnos)* of the Jews by following their "custom" *(ethos)* of circumcision. Yet the inclusion of Gentiles in the restored people of God does not mean the replacement of Israel but its expansion. And the exemption of Gentiles from circumcision does not trumpet the dismissal of the Torah but the fulfillment of its true, prophetic intention "made known from long ago."

The most negative portrait of Jews in Luke-Acts comes in the account of Paul's missionary journeys in Asia Minor and around the Aegean rim. Jews in synagogues of the Diaspora treat him to the ancient equivalent of tar and feathering, sometimes stalking him from city to city. When he gets to Jerusalem, a number of Jews from Asia accuse him of defiling the Temple and almost beat him to death before he is taken into Roman custody (Acts 21:27-31). Soon after, more than forty Jews swear an oath to assassinate him (23:12-15). At the end of Acts, the leaders of the Jewish community in Rome greet him coolly but ask to hear more about "this sect *(hairesis)* . . . everywhere spoken against" (28:22). The response of Jews to Paul's message about Jesus is mixed; some accept it, but most reject it. Throughout Luke-Acts, Israel remains divided. Is the work "anti-Jewish"? The label is no less dubious than when applied to Paul. Yet, although there is no overt supersession of Israel by Gentiles, no "true" or "new" Israel to replace the old one, there is a supersession of Israel's ethnically exclusive covenantal election.

The Gospel of Matthew was written around the same time as Luke-Acts and draws on Mark and Q as the two-volume work does. It was composed in and for a community of believers in Jesus that considered itself Jewish in every respect —

ethnic, cultural, religious. Located perhaps in Antioch or a city such as Caesarea, Sepphoris, or Scythopolis, it was in fierce competition with Pharisaic Judaism in a nearby synagogue community. The Jewishness of the Matthean community is reflected in several subtle but noticeable ways, such as the omission of Mark's explanation of Jewish customs and of the Markan narrator's comment that Jesus "declared all foods clean." More overt examples of Matthew's limning of Jesus' Jewishness include a genealogy that traces his ancestry to Abraham (Matt. 1:1-17) and an extensive typological correspondence between Jesus and Moses drawn in the infancy narrative, the Sermon on the Mount, and other passages. Like Moses in the books of Exodus and Deuteronomy, Jesus is a liberator who has come to set his people free from their bondage and to give them the Torah anew. The Matthean Jesus does not nullify the Torah; he is its true and final interpreter. In a saying unique to Matthew, Jesus says,

> "Do not think that I have come to abolish the Law or the Prophets; I have come not to abolish but to fulfill. For truly I tell you, until heaven and earth pass away, not one letter, not one stroke of a letter, will pass from the Law until all is accomplished. Therefore, whoever breaks one of the least of these commandments, and teaches others to do the same, will be called least in the kingdom of heaven. For I tell you, unless your [Torah-based] righteousness exceeds that of the scribes and Pharisees, you will never enter the kingdom of heaven." (Matt. 5:17-20)

On the negative side, Matthew underscores the distinction or even separation of his community from Pharisaic Judaism by referring to "*their* synagogues" and having Jesus speak of "*your* Law" when debating with Pharisees. He also darkens the Markan portrait of the Pharisees in his Galilean section and the profile of the Jerusalem authorities in his passion narrative. Most notoriously, he has "the people as a whole" tell Pilate, "His blood be on us and our children!" (27:25).

Even so, Matthew's community represents a type of Judaism. It was comprised largely of Jews who continued to observe Sabbath (12:1-8; 24:20), to practice tithing (23:23), and to engage in almsgiving, prayer, and fasting (6:1-19) — and who were not ready to dispense completely with ritual purity concerns such as kashrut even though they set a priority on matters of moral purity (15:17-18; contrast Mark 7:19b). It is not Judaism that Jesus' followers are to reject but the hypocrisy, the burdensome halakah, the casuistry, the ostentatious piety, and the status-seeking of the Pharisees (Matthew 23). But they must also recognize that ethnic Israel no longer holds exclusive elect status since God's plan of salvation now includes the Nations as well. The Matthean community's debate with Pharisaic Judaism can be seen in large part as an intra-Jewish argument, but the community reflected in this gospel pushed the boundaries of the common Judaism of the day to the breaking point.

The Gospel of John vies with Matthew for the distinction of being the most "Jewish" and "anti-Jewish" of the Gospels. Like the Matthean community, the Johannine community pitted itself against Pharisaic Judaism. By the time the Fourth Gospel was written (ca. 90-100 C.E., somewhere in the Diaspora, possibly Ephesus), it had broken off all contact with the synagogue and was so deeply alienated from its formative roots in Judaism that it called Jesus' opponents (and its own) "the Jews." The term does not refer to all Jews in all times and places but primarily to the Jewish leadership, who in this Gospel are identified, anachronistically, with the Pharisees. (In a few passages, *hoi Ioudaioi* is a neutral designation for the inhabitants of Judea, and in 4:22 it is used positively in Jesus' remark to a Samaritan woman that "salvation is from the Jews.") In the narrative, the Jews function as a dramatic foil to Jesus and in symbolic terms are equivalent to "the world" in its ignorance, unbelief, and rejection of him.

The Fourth Gospel was written independently of the Synoptics, though its author knows some Synoptic traditions and was probably aware of one or more of the other gospels. Although it has some affinities with them, especially in its passion narrative, and though it shares half a dozen episodes from Jesus' public ministry with them, it is largely unique in content, style, and theology. Its Jewishness is evident in its regard for major marks of Jewish identity such as Torah, Temple, Sabbath, and Festivals. But in John Jesus fulfills and replaces these key institutions. And it alone among the gospels has an explicit Christology of pre-existence, divinity, and incarnation — not only in its prologue ("In the beginning was the Word, and the Word was with God, and the Word was God. . . . And the Word became flesh and dwelt among us," 1:1, 14) but on Jesus' own lips: "No one has ascended to heaven except the one who descended from heaven. . . . Before Abraham was I am. . . . The Father and I are one. . . . Whoever has seen me has seen the Father" (3:13; 8:58; 10:30; 14:9). Jesus is the one and only path to God and to eternal life: "I am the way, the truth, and the life; no one comes to the Father except through me" (14:6).

Instead of teaching in parables and aphorisms, the Johannine Jesus delivers long monologues. Their subject is not the kingdom of God but Jesus' identity as the only Son of the Father come down from heaven to reveal and to save. In dialogues with his opponents, which frequently turn into monologues, the subject of controversy centers not on aspects of Jewish halakah but on Jesus' identity and self-claims. Gone in John are debates over fasting, tithing, food purity, oath taking, and divorce. Instead, Jesus' healing on the Sabbath quickly provokes the charge that he makes himself out to be "equal to God" (John 5:18; cf. 10:33). When the Jews assert their Abrahamic paternity and deny Jesus' divine paternity, he replies, "You are of your father, the Devil" (8:44). Though he submits to the Father's will and declares "the Father is greater than I" (14:28), he does not hesitate to claim unity with God (e.g., 10:30, 38; 14:10-11; 17:21). From the narrator's point of view, though, this is not blasphemy, since Jesus is no mere man but the Logos incarnate. Doubting Thomas does well to bow before Jesus and call him "My Lord and my God!" (20:28).

The most revealing passage in the Fourth Gospel for the Johannine community's separation from the synagogue comes in the story of the man blind from birth in John 9. The passage starts off as a Synoptic-like healing story, but after he heals the man Jesus is absent for most of the chapter, so that the focus falls on the man. He is hauled before "the Jews" twice and interrogated. The more they pressure him to denounce Jesus as a sinner, the higher and bolder his claims about Jesus become. In the scope of some twenty verses, he goes from referring to him as "the man called Jesus" to saying "he is a prophet" to declaring "he is from God." His Pharisaic interrogators expel him from the community, "for the Jews had already agreed that anyone who confessed Jesus to be the messiah would be put out of the synagogue (*aposynagōgos,* 9:22; cf. 14:42; 16:2). When Jesus later finds him and elicits faith in himself as the Son of Man, the fellow replies, "'Lord, I believe.' And he worshiped him" (9:38). This remarkable passage seems to telescope a years-long process of conflict in a synagogue community. In a narrative palimpsest, the conflict has been inscribed onto the story of Jesus. Debates over whether Jesus was the messiah had escalated into heated arguments over claims about his divine status, claims forged in the fires of the conflict itself. The Fourth Gospel is not anti-Jewish — far less anti-Semitic — in any ethnic sense, but in it Judaism without Jesus is no longer a viable path to God.

The Parting of the Ways

Without question the Christian movement began as a messianic renewal movement within Judaism and for several generations retained much of its Jewish character. Yet the seeds for a gradual distancing and eventual separation from Judaism were planted early on with the movement's high Christology, which led to veneration of Jesus in a way that infringed on Jewish monotheism, and in its outreach to Gentiles, which led to a demotion of the Torah and a dismantling of covenant election by descent or conversion. Both of these developments were underway within a few years of Jesus' death and resurrection, though certainly not in every quarter.

In the last two decades, the leading metaphor for Christianity's separation from Judaism has been the "parting of the ways." The metaphor is salutary insofar as it grants Judaism its own integrity, but it is also problematic because it conjures up images of two neat and tidy religious groups who began as happy siblings but ended completely estranged. When, why, and how the separation took place remains contested. Some see it occurring, at least *in nuce,* as early as Jesus' own career; others date it to the time of the First Jewish Revolt in 66-73 or to the Bar Kokhba Revolt of 132-135 C.E. More recently some have pushed it as late as the fifth and even sixth century. Decisive historical moments have been sought in the Apostolic Council around the year 49, the alleged flight of the Jerusalem congregation to Pella in Transjordan in the mid 60s, the destruction of Jerusalem and the Temple in 70, the convening of a rabbinic summit at Yavneh around 90 and the supposed promulgation there of the *Birkat Ha-minim* (a formal curse designed allegedly to expel believers in Jesus from Jewish synagogues), or the failure of the Bar Kokhba Revolt in 135. Others have focused less on historical factors than theological ones, such as the Gentile-inclusive tendencies of Jesus' ministry, the Law-free gospel of Paul and other Hellenist believers, and the high Christology evident in several New Testament writings.

Both the historical and theological factors invoked as determinative for the separation entail difficulties. In the theological domain, the downplaying of the ritual aspects of the Torah has some precedent in Diaspora Judaism, and high Christology has parallels in early Jewish logos and wisdom theology and in ideas about divine mediation centered on principal angels like Yahoel and Metatron and on human figures like Enoch and other exalted patriarchs. Some of the historical arguments are equally shaky. The earliest mention of the Pella tradition comes from the fourth-century church father Eusebius and stands in some doubt. Similarly, the traditions concerning Yavneh and the *Birkat Ha-minim* date to the Talmudic period. The rabbis at Yavneh did not have the Christian movement on their agenda, and the *Birkat Ha-minim* was not current in the first century in a form that would have targeted believers in Jesus; indeed, it may not have been added to the *Amida* or *Eighteen Benedictions* until the third century. There are also indications of ambiguity, contact, and overlap between "Judaism" and "Christianity" in the second through fifth centuries, factors that to many interpreters are most evident in the phenomena of "Judaizing" and "Jewish-Christianity."

The verb "Judaize" — "to live like a Jew" — is used in several Christian sources for Gentile believers in Jesus who adopted Jewish practices like circumcision, Sabbath observance, and kosher diet (e.g., Gal. 2:14; Ignatius, *Magn.* 10:2-3). Yet in the patristic literature, the label just as often has nothing to do with following Jewish customs. In some of the church fathers it is a polemical label for Christians whose Christology is too "low" or who interpret the Old Testament literally instead of figuratively. Like the phenomenon "anti-Judaism," "Judaizing" need not imply direct contact with or influence from Jews or Judaism. More often it reflects intra-Christian theological disputes and seems not to have been encouraged by non-Christian Jews.

The category "Jewish-Christianity" is no less slippery, complicating rather than clarifying the parting of the ways. The ambiguous label is a modern creation that can refer either to ethnic Jews who believed in Jesus or to people of any ethnicity — Jew and non-Jew alike — whose devotion to Christ included aspects of Torah observance. Jewish-Christianity in both these senses is attested in the New Testament and other early Christian sources. Further muddying the waters, some scholars use the label "Jewish-Christian" loosely to describe Christian writings that draw extensively on Jewish scripture and tradition, regardless of whether their settings reflect Jewish ethnicity or practice. Others restrict the designation to groups such as the Ebionites and Nazoreans, marginal groups regarded as heretical sects by church fathers like Eusebius and Epiphanius whose members occupied a shrinking no-man's-land between emergent orthodox Christianity and ascendant rabbinic Judaism.

There can be no denying that the borderlines between Judaism and Christianity were not clear-cut everywhere in the early centuries of the Common Era, or that the separation between them was uneven and complex. It was at least *possible* to live both as a Jew — a member of a Jewish synagogue — and as a believer in Christ until Theodosius I made Christianity the only religious option in the Roman Empire (380 C.E.). Nevertheless, Christianity did separate from its Jewish matrix in substantive ways already in the first century. Because early Christianity was characterized by considerable diversity, speaking constructively about the parting of the ways requires precision about whether one has ethnic-demographic, sociological-cultural, or theological-religious factors in view, and which regions, settings, and times one is investigating. Some generalizations in each of these three areas, however, are inevitable and even necessary.

(1) In sheer demographics, the Jesus movement was overwhelmingly non-Jewish in its constituency by the end of the first century, and in that sense was a largely Gentile religion. Since ethnic descent was a fundamental identity marker in early Judaism (except for proselytes), this datum is significant.

(2) In terms of social identity, Pauline and other congregations of the middle and later decades of the first century were separate from Jewish synagogue communities. Although Jewish and Christian individuals continued to interact with one another for centuries, by the second half of the first century Jews and Christians as social groups were going their separate ways, organizing themselves around distinctive beliefs and practices. Then, too, by the latter decades of the first century, the Romans seem to have begun distinguishing Christians (Lat. *Christiani*) from Jews, as the Neronian persecution in Rome in 64 C.E. and the imposition of the *fiscus Iudaicus* ("Jewish tax") after the First Revolt suggest. This is undoubtedly the case by the time of the Pliny-Trajan correspondence ca. 110 C.E. (*Epistles* 10.96, 97). Further, the evidence for contact between Jews and Christians in the patristic period is almost exclusively literary, and most of it comes from the Christian side. To be sure, church fathers like Justin, Origen, and Jerome had scholarly exchanges with learned Jews, and several patristic sources gladly incorporate Jewish exegetical and haggadic traditions. But on the whole the rabbis simply ignored Christianity. It is also true that Judaism continued to be a vital religion that continued to attract Christian believers into late antiquity. This is most evident in fourth-century Antioch, where John Chrysostom preached a series of homilies against the Judaizing proclivities of Christians in the city who were consulting with rabbis, attending synagogue services, and participating in Jewish festivals. This sort of evidence, however, is not abundant in late antiquity and has no counterpart on the rabbinic side.

(3) Finally, although early Christianity is unthinkable apart from its reliance on Jewish scripture, theology, and ethics, there remain two crucial areas in which the Jesus movement diverged from the rest of Judaism at a very early date: covenant election and monotheism. The moment Gentiles began to be welcomed into the Jesus movement without being required to adopt the chief ritual marks of Jewish identity — especially circumcision — the Jewish notion of covenant election was radically spiritualized, and the defining role that Torah observance had for most Jews was effectively demoted. Further, the moment that Jesus began to be identified so closely with the one God as to be petitioned in prayer and worshiped, Christian messianism collided with Jewish monotheism. It is not that high Christology did not build upon early Jewish logos and wisdom theology (it did), or that the worship of Jesus was not prepared for by the veneration of mediator figures like exalted patriarchs or principal angels (it was). But the worship of the crucified and risen Jesus — a man of living memory and not a figure of hoary antiquity — as the incarnation of a preexistent divine being represents a quantum leap beyond any form of Second Temple Judaism. Neither of these theological developments nor their sociological corollaries are late phenomena but early realities that can be dated with some precision to the 30s and 40s C.E. in texts like the pre-Pauline Christ hymn in Philippians. If a definitive separation between Rebecca's children was long in the making, the seeds for it were sown very early on.

BIBLIOGRAPHY

Barclay, John, and John Sweet, eds. 1996. *Early Christian Thought in Its Jewish Context.* Cambridge: Cambridge University Press.

Bauckham, Richard. 2008. *Jesus and the God of Israel.* Grand Rapids: Eerdmans.

Becker, Adam H., and Annette Yoshiko Reeds, eds. 2003. *The Ways that Never Parted: Jews and Christians in Late Antiquity and the Early Middle Ages.* Tübingen: Mohr-Siebeck.

Boyarin, Daniel. 1994. *A Radical Jew: Paul and the Politics of Identity.* Berkeley: University of California Press.

———. 2004. *Border Lines: The Partition of Judeo-Christianity.* Philadelphia: University of Pennsylvania Press.

Brooke, George J. 2005. *The Dead Sea Scrolls and the New Testament.* Minneapolis: Fortress.

Cohen, Shaye J. D. 1999. *The Beginnings of Jewishness: Boundaries, Varieties, Uncertainties.* Berkeley: University of California Press.

Dunn, James D. G. 2003-2008. *Christianity in the Making.* 2 vols. Grand Rapids: Eerdmans. (A third volume is forthcoming.)

———. 2006. *The Parting of the Ways between Christianity and Judaism and Their Significance for the Character of Christianity.* 2d ed. London: SCM.

Fredriksen, Paula. 1999. *Jesus of Nazareth, King of the Jews: A Jewish Life and the Emergence of Christianity.* New York: Knopf.

Hengel, Martin, with Anna Marie Schwemer. 2007. *Geschichte des Frühen Christentums I: Jesus und das Judentum.* Tübingen: Mohr-Siebeck.

Hurtado, Larry. 1998. *One God, One Lord: Early Christian Devotion and Ancient Jewish Monotheism.* 2d ed. Edinburgh: Clark.

Jackson-McCabe, Matt, ed. 2007. *Jewish Christianity Reconsidered: Rethinking Ancient Groups and Texts.* Minneapolis: Fortress.

Jossa, Giorgio. 2006. *Jews or Christians? The Followers of Jesus in Search of Their Own Identity.* Tübingen: Mohr-Siebeck.

Lieu, Judith M. 2005. *Neither Jew nor Greek? Constructing Early Christianity.* Edinburgh: Clark.

McCready, Wayne O., and Adele Reinhartz, eds. 2008. *Common Judaism: Explorations in Second-Temple Judaism.* Minneapolis: Fortress.

Meier, John P. 1991-2009. *A Marginal Jew: Rethinking the Historical Jesus.* 4 vols. New Haven: Yale University Press.

Mitchell, Margaret M., and Frances M. Young, eds. 2006. *The Cambridge History of Christianity,* vol. 1, *Origins to Constantine.* Cambridge: Cambridge University Press.

Murray, Michelle. 2004. *Playing a Jewish Game: Gentile Christian Judaizing in the First and Second Centuries* C.E. Waterloo, Ont.: Wilfrid Laurier University Press.

Nickelsburg, George W. E. 2003. *Ancient Judaism and Christian Origins: Diversity, Continuity, and Transformation.* Minneapolis: Fortress.

Sanders, E. P. 1977. *Paul and Palestinian Judaism.* London: SCM.

———. 1985. *Jesus and Judaism.* London: SCM.

———. 1990. *Jewish Law from Jesus to the Mishnah.* London: SCM.

———. 1992. *Judaism: Practice and Belief 66 BCE–66 CE.* London: SCM.

Sandmel, Samuel. 1978. *Anti-Semitism in the New Testament?* Philadelphia: Fortress.

Schiffman, Lawrence H. 1985. *Who Was a Jew? Rabbinic and Halakhic Perspectives on the Jewish-Christian Schism.* Hoboken, N.J.: Ktav.

Segal, Alan F. 1990. *Paul the Convert: The Apostolate and Apostasy of Saul the Pharisee.* New Haven: Yale University Press.

Setzer, Claudia. 1994. *Jewish Responses to Early Christians: History and Polemics, 30-150* C.E. Minneapolis: Fortress.

Simon, Marcel. 1986. *Verus Israel: A Study of the Relations between Christians and Jews in the Roman Empire AD 135-425.* London: Littman Library of Jewish Civilization.

Taylor, Miriam S. 1994. *Anti-Judaism and Early Christian Identity.* Leiden: Brill.

Tomson, Peter J. 2001. *'If This Be from Heaven': Jesus and the New Testament Authors in Their Relationship to Judaism.* Sheffield: Sheffield Academic Press.

Udoh, Fabian E. et al., eds. 2008. *Redefining First-Century Jewish and Christian Identities: Essays in Honor of Ed Parish Sanders.* Notre Dame: University of Notre Dame Press.

Vermes, Geza. 1993. *The Religion of Jesus the Jew.* Minneapolis: Fortress.

Wilson, Stephen G. 1995. *Related Strangers: Jews and Christians 70-170 C.E.* Minneapolis: Fortress.

Yarbro Collins, Adela, and John J. Collins. 2008. *King and Messiah as Son of God: Divine, Human, and Angelic Messianic Figures in Biblical and Related Literature.* Grand Rapids: Eerdmans.

Early Judaism and Rabbinic Judaism

Lawrence H. Schiffman

One of the central issues of the history of Judaism is the periodization of its early history. Behind this issue lurks a much more central question: To what extent may we trace continuity between the various bodies of Jewish literature and the religious ideas that they embody? When we study the development of Judaism from the late books of the Hebrew Bible, through the texts of the Second Temple period, into rabbinic literature, to what extent do we observe continuity and to what extent do we see change? This question is made more complex by the variegated nature of Second Temple Judaism, to the extent that some would prefer to use the designation "Judaisms." At issue, then, is not only the fact of historical change but also competing forms of Judaism at various times — a phenomenon best documented and understood for the Hasmonean period but no doubt also present at other times. Within this complex framework, one may ask how Judaism in the Second Temple period as represented in the Apocrypha, Pseudepigrapha, Philo, Josephus, and Dead Sea Scrolls relates to the Judaism of the Mishnah, Talmud, and Midrash, that is, to the rabbinic or talmudic tradition. What has been continued, and what has been changed; what is old and what is new?

To a great extent this question is complicated by a related issue. In the transition from the period of the Hebrew Scriptures to Second Temple times, the earlier period bequeathed a massive literary legacy to the subsequent history of Judaism: the Hebrew Bible. This religious, literary, and historical legacy remains a permanent, indeed formative, ingredient in all subsequent Jewish development. Yet although Second Temple Judaism passed the Bible on to rabbinic Judaism, it did not pass on its own literary productions. There is only one text from the Second Temple period that fell into the hands of the talmudic rabbis in its entirety: Ben Sira. Beyond that, they did not have, or perhaps did not want to read, the Dead Sea Scrolls or the writings that now comprise the Apocrypha and Pseudepigrapha, nor the works of Philo and Josephus. This hiatus in culture, indeed an abyss from a literary point of view, remains largely unexplained. This gap is not unique; after all, some twenty-two books are mentioned in the Hebrew Bible that did not survive into later periods. Still, that virtually nothing passed from Second Temple times to the talmudic era stands in stark contrast to the large body of Israelite literature that was transmitted to Second Temple Judaism.

If there was no direct literary influence, we will have to content ourselves with seeking common ideas and approaches that were passed down as part of a general religious ambience. Because the halakic and theological forebears of the rabbis were the Pharisees, we have to expect that rabbinic literature and rabbinic Judaism are dependent primarily on the Pharisaic teachings. But here we have no existing Second Temple texts written by Pharisees. This situation most probably owes to the penchant for oral tradition among the Pharisees, as known from Josephus, even if the ideological notion of oral revelation and transmission was actually articulated only in the tannaitic period. At the same time, some Pharisaic texts may have lost popularity as oral tradition came to dominate Pharisaic Judaism. Obviously, such texts would not have been preserved in the Qumran sectarian collection, since the sect was so anti-Pharisaic. In any case, the Pharisees bequeathed no literary materials to the talmudic enterprise but only extensive oral traditions. It is possible that as Pharisaic Judaism emerged as the only real survivor of the Second Temple period, the other books were ignored or suppressed, under the category of "outside (apocryphal) books."

Indirect Influences and Continuities

There are very few explicit references to apocryphal works in rabbinic literature. In fact, rabbinic texts mention only two such works, one being Ben Sira, which the rabbis apparently knew and quoted. Another is Sefer ben La'ana (*y. Sanhedrin* 10a), of whose contents nothing is known. The rabbis explicitly prohibit the reading of such books, but there is some uncertainty regarding the meaning of this prohibition. On the one hand, it might be a blanket prohibition forbidding the reading of these texts under any circumstances. The assumption would be that it is forbidden to write, and therefore to read, any books other than those of Scripture. On the other hand, the prohibition may have extended only to the public reading of these books as part of the lectionary. In this case, it would be permitted to read such books privately. Such an approach would explain the use of Ben Sira by the rabbis.

An interesting example of the indirect influence of Second Temple books on the rabbis comes in their fundamental agreement with a theme central to the book of *Jubilees,* that the patriarchs observed all of the laws later to be given at Sinai. Apparently, this notion was part of the common heritage of Second Temple Judaism and was taken up by some rabbis.

Numerous sectarian groups are in fact mentioned in rabbinic literature. These groups, however, while apparently practicing modes of piety similar to those known from the Dead Sea Scrolls, seem in no way to be identifiable with the specific literary works of the Second Temple period. Rather, it appears that the later rabbis were aware of the general nature of Judaism in the period before 70 C.E. Indeed, they blamed the phenomenon of sectarianism for the disunity that led to the destruction of Jerusalem and the Temple. However, none of the reports that they preserve can be directly associated with the textual materials from Second Temple times. We can only assume, again, that they did not or would not read these texts.

The sect of the Essenes is not mentioned by name in rabbinic literature. Attempts to identify the Essenes with the Boethusians *(baytôsîn* or *baytûsîn)* have failed to garner significant support because of the philological difficulties involved. While it is possible that some practices of the Essene sect might be described somewhere in rabbinic literature, it is more likely that the Essenes described by Philo and Josephus shared the Sadducean-type halakic tradition polemicized against in rabbinic texts.

One area in which rabbinic literature provides fruitful parallels to sectarian organization is the system of entry into the sect and the close link between purity law and sectarian membership. A similar system was in effect for the *havurah,* a small group that practiced strict purity laws, extending Temple regulations into private life even for non-priests. Scholarly literature has tended to associate this group with the Pharisees, most probably correctly, but the textual evidence seems to separate these terms. In any case, the detailed regulations pertaining to entering the *havurah* (*m. Dem.* 2:3-4; *t. Dem.* 2:2–3:4) are more closely parallel to the initiation rites of the Qumran sect (1QS 6:13-23) than they are to the descriptions of the Essenes in Josephus, with which they also share fundamental principles.

Some practices typical of the Qumran sect are indeed mentioned in rabbinic polemics against heterodoxy, termed *derek aḥeret.* But these practices are too few to indicate any kind of real knowledge of the Qumran sect or its practices or of other sectarian groups.

One interesting area is that of calendar disputes. Alongside the calendar of lunar months and solar years used by the Pharisaic-rabbinic tradition, other groups, including the Dead Sea sectarians and the authors of *1 Enoch* and *Jubilees,* called for use of a calendar of solar months and solar years. Although numerous problems still beset study of the calendrical situation in Second Temple Judaism, some part of it was clearly known to the rabbis. Rabbinic sources report that certain sectarians, Sadducees, and Boethusians practiced such a calendar, insisting that Shavuot fall on a Sunday and, hence, that the start of the counting of the omer commence on a Saturday night. If indeed these rabbinic notices refer to the calendar controversy known from the Scrolls and pseudepigraphal literature, then it seems that the rabbis' knowledge was quite fragmentary or that they chose to pass on only a small part of the picture. From rabbinic sources alone one would never have gathered that this sectarian calendar was based on solar months and that it represented an entirely alternative system. All we would have known is that they disagreed on the date of Shavuot.

Rabbinic Engagement with Second Temple Issues

From what we have said so far, one would assume that there simply is very little relationship between the literature of Second Temple Judaism and the rabbinic corpus. Yet when we examine the Judaism of the Dead Sea Scrolls sect and of the literature they preserved, we find both similarity to and interaction with views preserved in rabbinic texts. Further, fundamental ideas preserved in the Apocrypha and Pseudepigrapha found their way into the rabbinic tradition. And still to be fully explained, rabbinic literature preserves a variety of reflections on historical data preserved by Josephus, either in his words or those of his sources. In what follows, we will concentrate on examples illustrated by materials preserved in the Qumran corpus, including some that stem from books otherwise preserved in the Apocrypha and Pseudepigrapha.

Jewish Law

Qumran sectarian law was characterized by a clear distinction between the "revealed law" — that is, the written Torah — and the "hidden law" derived by sectarian exegesis and known only to the sectarians. This concept is clearly different from the rabbinic concept of a dual Torah, which includes a written law and an oral law. Further, the sectarian view makes no attempt to trace its second Torah to divine revelation at Sinai, seeing it rather as something that emerged with divine inspiration from the life of the sect and its leadership. At the same time, the sectarian system and the Pharisaic-rabbinic dual Torah both provide for a supplement to the fundamental written Torah, solving in slightly different ways the difficult problem of applying the written Torah to the life of the community. Further, both groups share the notion that the second Torah was divinely inspired. True, the *Temple Scroll* seems to be based on a very different approach; it assumes that only one Torah was revealed at Sinai, and it enshrines the author's interpretations in his law. Such a one-Torah system is at serious variance with that of the rabbis, but the revealed/hidden approach more broadly typical of the Qumran texts seems to share some of their fundamental concepts.

As is well known, tannaitic literature contains two kinds of halakic texts: collections of apodictic laws arranged by subject matter (mishnah) and those organized according to Scripture (midrash). The Qumran legal materials display both of these options in a "proto-rabbinic" mode. Laws such as those pertaining to the Sabbath, to courts and testimony, and to forbidden sexual unions often appear as a series of apodictic laws organized by subject and titled accordingly. These collections parallel in form the mishnaic tractates and even have similar titles. Further, texts like the *Temple Scroll* and certain fragments of legal texts indicate that some authors chose to express their legal views in the context of Scripture. There is one essential difference, though. Whereas in rabbinic literature midrashic exegesis maintains a strict distinction between the words of the Bible and the words of the rabbinic explanations, the *Temple Scroll* freely rewrites the biblical text in accord with sectarian assumptions. Such an approach would have been anathema to the rabbis. A further difference involves the very apodictic statements preserved in Qumran texts. Whereas in rabbinic literature such statements are composed in mishnaic Hebrew, and therefore are linguistically distanced from the biblical texts upon which they might depend, many Qumran apodictic laws make use of the language of the Bible and even allow us to determine their biblical midrashic basis from their phraseology.

When we come to the actual subject matter of the laws, the situation is also complex. Some laws and their derivation from Scripture seem to be virtually the same, as, for example, the statement that the Sabbath begins on Friday at sunset. Although some of the laws are very similar, such as the requirements to wear clean clothes on the Sabbath, others differ more extensively, such as the establishment of two separate Sabbath limits or the setting up of courts of ten for judging issues of Jewish civil law. These differences almost always derive from differing interpretations of Scripture. This is certainly the case with the *Temple Scroll,* whose laws and interpretations are often at variance with those of the rabbis.

Nevertheless, these differences often constitute a conceptual link between the Second Temple texts and the rabbinic corpus. In many cases, it is only the alternative interpretations in the Dead Sea Scrolls that allow us to understand the intellectual world within which the talmudic views were being put forth. Much research remains to be done in this area, and one example must suffice here: It is clear that rabbinic laws pertaining to ritual purity and prayer are closely linked to Temple purity laws preserved in the *Temple Scroll* and other Qumran documents. There is simply no other way to understand these laws, even as presented in the Babylonian Talmud.

It is generally accepted that ancient Judaism knew two separate approaches to Jewish law, that of the Zadokite priestly tradition and that of the Pharisees and rabbis. The former approach typifies the codes of the Qumran sect and such works as *Jubilees* and the *Aramaic Levi Document.* These trends were opposed by the Pharisaic-rabbinic approach preserved for us in talmudic literature. Due to the strictures of the Pharisees against writing down their traditions or other vicissitudes of preservation, the Pharisaic-rabbinic tradition is represented only in the later corpus of the talmudic rabbis. Nonetheless, it is possible to reconstruct the early layers of that material and in so doing often to reconstruct the Pharisaic views that were opposed, explicitly or implicitly, by the authors of the Dead Sea Scrolls. The Scrolls have enabled us to uncover an earlier layer of history in which the approach later ensconced in rabbinic works competed with the priestly approach for dominance in the halakic market. The importance of this perspective in understanding rabbinic literature cannot be overestimated.

This is especially the case when rabbinic literature itself preserves evidence for the content of the Zadokite tradition. After the removal of those references to Sadducees *(Ṣĕdûqîm)* that owe to scribal alterations, there remains a series of passages that seem to describe this alternative halakic tradition and that stand in general agreement with the information available from the Scrolls and other Second Temple texts. In this manner, some sense of the general authenticity of rabbinic materials that report on the Second Temple period has been gained, and scholars have begun to discard more skeptical approaches of the last generation. This situation is exemplified, perhaps exceptionally, by the collection of Pharisaic-Sadducean disputes in Mishnah *Yadayim* and the parallel collection in the halakic document found at Qumran, *Miqṣat Maʿaśê ha-Torah* (MMT). What is astounding here is the presence of a group of traditions in both places, of course stated from the opposing perspectives. In general terms, the rabbinic literature and Second Temple texts often represent opposite sides of the same coin, that is, two separate approaches to the same set of problems. Without the Second Temple materials, we would never have known this.

Phylacteries, Mezuzot, and "Bibles"

Scribal practice constitutes a distinct area of halakah. Here it seems clear that much of the scribal art transcended sectarian religious affiliation. This would explain why scribal law in rabbinic texts and indeed in later Jewish tradition is so close to that found in the Dead Sea Scrolls and other biblical texts from the Judean desert. Rabbinic Judaism received a scribal tradition from the earlier Jewish community and, for the most part, simply passed it down, following virtually the same mechanics for the preparation and production of hides, writing, and the storage of scrolls. Further, in the case of mezuzot and phylacteries, there is an intersection of the common scribal arts with the varying interpretations of the contents. Apparently, the sectarians were willing to include passages from the previous and following literary context, beyond those required by the Pharisaic-rabbinic tradition, which limited itself and did not allow any additional material. But the commonality in the preparation and construction of phylacteries and in the practice of mezuzot shows clearly that these were elements inherited from the common Judaism of Second Temple times. This is the case even though rabbinic traditions connect these religious objects closely to oral law, an approach eschewed by the Qumran sectarians and other priestly groups.

However, the Second Temple biblical materials contrast greatly with rabbinic statements on the subject and with what seems to be the evidence of Pharisaic influence at Masada and in the Bar Kokhba caves. Rabbinic texts assume a much greater standardization of the biblical text than what is in evidence in the Qumran texts and in the secondary use of biblical material in the Scrolls. Further, the Septuagint and the use of biblical materials in the Apocrypha and Pseudepigrapha often support the looser construction of biblical texts known to us from Qumran, where a variety of texts and text types coexisted. While this stands in contrast with rabbinic texts, despite some textual variants in biblical materials preserved there, we cannot be totally certain that Pharisaic Jews in Second Temple times would have had "Bibles" as standard as those assumed by the Mishnah and Talmud. Josephus writes as though this was the case at the end of the first century C.E., but we cannot be certain about the Pharisees of the earlier period.

Biblical Exegesis

Despite the absence of direct literary influence, and all the fundamental historical changes, a central aspect of continuity between Second Temple Judaism and rabbinic Judaism may be seen in the area of biblical exegesis. But even here, the issues are complex.

The translation of the Scriptures represents one area of continuity. The two translations at issue are the Greek (Septuagint) and the Aramaic (Targumim). Regarding the Greek, one might gather from the tannaitic parallel to the account of the seventy-two elders in the *Letter of Aristeas* (*b. Megilla* 9b; *y. Meg.* 1:9) that the rabbis saw the translation as a tragic step in the Hellenization of the Jews and yet approved of the actual translation, at least of the modifications supposedly made by the elders for polemical reasons. However, scholarly investigation of these variants shows that the account reflects no actual familiarity with the Septuagint, which, like the rest of Greek Jewish literature, was apparently lost to the rabbinic Jewish community. This is the case even though additional Jewish translations (Theodotion, Aquila, and Symmachus) were created or adapted after the Septuagint to bring the Greek closer to the Masoretic Text, which became the standard for Jews. The Greek Bible simply became identified with Christianity, despite the use of the Septuagint by Josephus and/or his assistants. Even so, rabbinic texts attribute special status to the Greek language and its use in Bible translation — clearly an echo of its former status.

With Aramaic translation the situation is more complex. Although the fragmentary Qumran Leviticus targum has exegetical parallels with the later Leviticus targums and rabbinic exegesis, the actual text from Qumran was not taken up by the rabbis. Nor was the Job targum found at Qumran. Like the targum to Job preserved by the rabbinic community, this is a very literal translation. Rabbinic tradition (*t. Šabb.* 13:2) mentions that both Rabba Gamliel I and II buried Job targums in the belief that translation was part of the oral law and so should not be written down. No mention of sectarian provenance appears, and in any case there is nothing at all sectarian about the (pre-) Qumran Job targum. Yet there is no literary relationship between the two Job targums. The Second Temple version apparently fell into disuse and was replaced later by a much younger one, probably dating to the Byzantine period. The rabbinic tradition, then, continued the pattern of translation but initially rejected putting it in writing. All pre-70-C.E. targums were lost, and later texts, composed or at least recorded after the rabbis, loosened up their prohibition of writing down the oral law and replaced the old, lost ones.

Another type of biblical interpretation that deserves mention has come to be called "rewritten Bible." Some of the exegetical presumptions of these texts are similar to those of rabbinic aggadah. Here we need to distinguish form from content. Whereas the Second Temple texts among the Pseudepigrapha and numerous Dead Sea Scrolls allow the authors to invade the actual biblical texts, as is done in the *Genesis Apocryphon*, *Jubilees*, and for halakah in the *Temple Scroll*, it seems that the barrier between written and oral tradition for the rabbis meant that such books were totally forbidden.

The rabbis maintained this distinction strictly, even with the gradual abeyance of the prohibition of writing down the oral law, with the result that not a single literary connection can be established between these early Jewish texts and rabbinic literature. However, parallels are also evident in the specific units of interpretation and sometimes in the actual content. In general terms, specific passages in the Second Temple texts use exegetical techniques similar to those of the rabbis. The interpretations of the rabbis are often quite different, though. At times there are common interpretations, and these were no doubt part of the traditions inherited by the rabbis from Second Temple times, but more often rabbinic tradition directly contradicts the interpretations found in earlier books.

One type of exegesis found in the Dead Sea Scrolls with no real resonance in rabbinic literature is the pesher. This form of contemporizing exegesis assumes a two-step process of prophecy and fulfillment, on the conviction that the Hebrew prophets did not really speak to their own times but to Second Temple circumstances. Parallels between pesher and rabbinic exegesis usually concern only the basic interpretation of the text, and not the pesher form itself. The theological presumptions of pesher exegesis were not in agreement with rabbinic notions of prophecy, and the rabbis tended in general to minimize apocalyptic trends.

Sectarian versus Rabbinic Theology

Both Second Temple texts and rabbinic literature were heir to the complex and often contradictory theological views of the various biblical books. Both corpora also share basic Jewish theological ideas such as belief in God the creator, the revelation of the Torah, and hope in a coming redemption. An important question is whether ideas in Second Temple texts that differ substantially from the biblical tradition were taken up in rabbinic Judaism. The extreme dualism and determinism taught in the sectarian Dead Sea Scrolls offers an interesting case in point. This set of beliefs assumes that God has preplanned the entire course of the cosmos and certainly of humans, who are divided into two lots, as are the heavenly beings, who struggle eternally against one another. Individual actions, for good or evil, seem in this system to be beyond one's own power, and yet individuals are punished for transgressing God's law, even including prescriptions that are not known beyond the sect. There is no basis for such ideas in the Hebrew Scriptures, and it is widely assumed that these concepts are somehow influenced by Persian dualism. In the rabbinic corpus, predestination is not accepted, although human free will can be countermanded by God. There is no cosmic dualism but rather an inner spiritual dualism of the good and evil inclination *(yeṣer)* in each person. Later, this concept merged with Hellenistic notions so that the two inclinations came to be identified closely with the spiritual and physical aspects of humanity. But free will is the basis of God's judgment of people, and all are responsible for their actions.

Another notion found in the Scrolls and other Second Temple texts but at variance with rabbinic theology is that prophetic or revelatory phenomena did not end with the story line of Scripture ca. 400 B.C.E. but rather continued into Greco-Roman times. This point of view underlies a lot of Second Temple literature but is virtually absent in rabbinic texts. The rabbis state explicitly that prophecy ended with the last of the Hebrew Bible prophets — Haggai, Zechariah, and Malachi. In fact, the end of Malachi is probably an addition emphasizing the completion of the prophetic canon. The only remnant of prophecy, the *bat qol,* some kind of echo of a divine voice, is explicitly declared to be null and void. Clearly the system of Oral Torah obviated the need for direct divine inspiration. Perhaps most importantly, the rise of Christianity seems to have confirmed the rabbis in their belief that the end of the biblical period meant the end of prophecy and the end of writing scriptural books.

A few words need to be said about eschatology and messianism. Both of these themes are very important in rabbinic literature, with extensive materials devoted to them. This is not to speak of the apocalyptic-type messianic materials that appear in posttalmudic writings and that resemble such texts as the Qumran *War Scroll*. Here we must distinguish as two separate issues the nature of the messianic figure or figures and the nature of the messianic expectations. We need to ask first how many and what kinds of messiahs are expected and then what kind of events are expected to lead up to the messianic era and what its nature will be.

Second Temple texts contain three different types of messianism. Some texts make no explicit mention of any messiah. We cannot be certain that in these instances no such leader is expected; it is simply that no messianic figure appears in the texts. A second variety, perhaps the most common, awaits a Davidic messiah. The third approach, known to us from certain Qumran sectarian texts and from the *Testaments of the Twelve Patriarchs*, is the notion of two messiahs, one of Aaron and one of Israel. Many scholars simply assume that the messiah of Israel is Davidic, but this may not be the case. In any event, rabbinic Judaism assumes that there must be a messianic figure, even though some rabbis argued that the messiah had already come. The dominant expectation centers on one messiah, a scion of David. No serious rabbinic parallel at all can be adduced for the notion of a priestly messiah. Talmudic tradition does, however, speak of a second messiah, a messiah son of Joseph. This Josephite messiah (referred to in some later apocalyptic texts as a son of Ephraim) may be mentioned in a recently published stone inscription dated to the late first century C.E. known as the *Vision of Gabriel*, which refers to Ephraim in a messianic context (A. Yardeni and B. Elizur in *Cathedra* 123 [2007]: 155-66). However, such a figure is otherwise not found in any Second Temple text. The upshot of this is that the dominant notion in Second Temple times, carried over into rabbinic tradition, was the expectation of a Davidic messiah who would bring about the redemption and rule over Israel as the messianic king. While this approach has extensive rabbinic parallels, other competing approaches seem to have become extinct and not to have crossed the literary abyss that separates Second Temple from rabbinic tradition.

A significant difference of opinion among Second Temple texts regarding the onset of the messianic era itself is carried over into rabbinic texts. Two trends have always been observable in Jewish messianism: the first trend, the restorative trend, assumed that the messianic era would constitute a return to the great glories of the ancient Jewish past. A second trend, the catastrophic or utopian, assumed that the messianic era would usher in an era of total perfection, one that never had existed before, in which all evil and suffering would be eradicated. While the restorative approach assumed that the messianic era could be created by the gradual improvement of the world, the catastrophic one assumed that a great war, often termed the Day of the Lord, would lead to the total destruction of the wicked and the onset of the eschaton. Both of these views existed in Second Temple times, but the Dead Sea Scrolls particularly emphasize the apocalyptic belief that a great war between the sons of light and the sons of darkness, in which all but the sectarians would be destroyed, would bring on the messianic era. These two trends are reflected in rabbinic texts and constitute an aspect of the common Judaism of the Greco-Roman period that passed, with no literary framework, into the thought of the rabbis. In the aftermath of the Great Revolt (66-73 C.E.) and the Bar Kokhba Revolt (132-135

C.E.), the rabbis tended toward more quietist types of messianism. The militant apocalyptic notions, however, resurfaced in amoraic times and were further ignited when the Byzantine period gave way to the Moslem conquest.

There was also a debate during Second Temple times about the nature of the messianic age. On the one hand, Jews who awaited a Davidic messiah expected him to restore Jewish national independence and to rebuild the Temple. On the other hand, those who expected two messiahs and who believed that the messiah of Aaron would have precedence over the messiah of Israel anticipated the restoration of the Temple to the standards of holiness and sanctity that it deserved. In the aftermath of two Jewish revolts, the rabbis longed for a restoration of the Davidic glories of old, of a political entity secure and independent. Apparently, in their view this would insure the proper rebuilding of the Temple. Yet they did not see the Temple as the central act in the messianic drama but as only a part of the process. For this reason, the Aaronide messiah has no parallel in rabbinic literature. This is the case even though Eleazar the Priest appeared with Bar Kokhba on coins, conjuring up the messianic pair of the *naśi* ("prince") and *kōhēn* ("priest").

Prayer and Poetry

Prayer was a significant part of the individual piety of a fair number of Israelites in First Temple times. Individual prayer was accompanied apparently by poems written for the collective people of Israel. Such prayers seem definitely to have attained a place in the psalmody of the Temple by the Second Temple period. In various Second Temple texts there are individual and collective prayers, and toward the end of the Second Temple period, prayer was becoming institutionalized increasingly, at least as appears from the tannaitic evidence. From the set liturgical texts preserved at Qumran, it seems that daily statutory ritual had become part of the life of the sectarians, who had separated from the Temple, which they regarded as impure and improperly conducted. These texts appear not to be of sectarian origin and may typify wider trends in the Jewish community. Further, the Dead Sea Scrolls give evidence of the twice-daily recital of the Shema and the use of mezuzot and phylacteries, some of which were prepared in a manner similar to that required by Pharisaic-rabbinic tradition.

Some tannaitic practices may have derived from those in evidence in Qumran liturgical texts. Both corpora require that a benediction of lights be part of the service each morning and afternoon-evening. This seems to be the only required benediction in the daily prayer texts preserved at Qumran. However, it seems to be equivalent to one of the two blessings before Shema required by the rabbis.

Qumran liturgical texts include also supplication texts similar to later rabbinic propitiatory prayers, and festival prayers seem to share similar motifs. However, not a single prayer preserved in the Scrolls is part of the rabbinic liturgy, and no text of rabbinic prayer was found in the sectarian collection. Again, the parallels in practice seem to derive from the common Judaism of Second Temple times, not from any literary or other direct connection.

Second Temple literature also seems to have played a major role in the development of the Jewish religious poetry known as piyyut. Before the discovery of the Dead Sea Scrolls, the evidence for Hebrew poetry in the postbiblical period was ignored. The poems in 1 Maccabees, for example, and even in the New Testament, not to mention early Jewish liturgy preserved in rabbinic texts or capable of being reconstructed from the later prayer texts, went largely overlooked. It was assumed that biblical psalmody was a dead-end tradition to be continued only later by a new form of Hebrew liturgical poetry that developed virtually *ex nihilo*. When the first scrolls were discovered, the *Hodayot* were taken to be an inferior version of Psalms poetry. No one seemed to realize that we were dealing with the next stage in the history of Hebrew poetry. Indeed, elements of Qumran religious poetry point in various directions toward the style, though not the content, of the later piyyut. This is clear now especially in the reuse of biblical material to form postbiblical poems and in the tendency to create grammatical forms not previously known. Yet, as a corpus related closely to rabbinic literature, the piyyut takes the rabbinic liturgical calendar and its content as a starting point and is suffused with rabbinic midrashic material and legal rulings, even if some of them are at variance with those taken as normative in the rabbinic legal texts.

Conclusion

How can we explain the contradictory observations that we are making here? On the one hand, we have emphasized the lack of a literary pipeline from early Judaism into rabbinic Judaism, beyond that of the Hebrew Scriptures themselves. On the other hand, we have pointed to rich parallels and apparent intellectual interaction between those who left us Second Temple texts and those who were apparently the spiritual ancestors of the Tannaim, namely, the Pharisees. It would seem that the existence of a "common Judaism" provides the answer.

As we have noted, Pharisaic-rabbinic Judaism was at odds with sectarian and apocalyptic trends, both in Second Temple times and after the destruction. The relationship between early Judaism and rabbinic Judaism, then, is characterized not by dependence but dialogue, disputation, and sometimes polemic. We lack adequate documentation of the Pharisaic side of the debate beyond reconstructing it on the basis of rabbinic literature. However, the license to perform such a reconstruction is inherent in the anti-Pharisaic polemics of the Second Temple texts, especially the Dead Sea Scrolls. The texts hint at a rigorous debate replete with polemics back and forth. This polemic must have been quieted greatly in the aftermath of the destruction of the Temple, when the Pharisaic-rabbinic approach gradually emerged as the consensus. From this point on, in an atmosphere of rabbinic debate, various aspects of the common Judaism of Second Temple times were preserved in the rabbinic movement and its literature. All kinds of ideas crossed the literary abyss without the rabbis having read Second Temple texts. It is these ideas that constitute the heritage of Second Temple literature and the Dead Sea Scrolls for the rabbis, but they were vastly outnumbered and overpowered by the Pharisaic heritage, which was transmitted as an unwritten tradition and served as the real basis of rabbinic Judaism.

BIBLIOGRAPHY

Cohen, Shaye J. D. 2006. *From the Maccabees to the Mishnah.* 2d ed. Philadelphia Westminster John Knox.

Collins, John J. 2010. *The Scepter and the Star: The Messiahs of the Dead Sea Scrolls in Context.* 2nd ed. Grand Rapids: Eerdmans.

Edrei, Aryeh, and Doron Mendels. 2007-2008. "A Split Jewish Diaspora: Its Dramatic Consequences." *Journal for the Study of the Pseudepigrapha,* vol. 16, no. 2: 91-137; vol. 17, no. 3: 163-87.

Jaffee, Martin S. 2001. *Torah in the Mouth: Writing and Oral Tradition in Palestinian Judaism 200 BCE–400 CE.* Oxford: Oxford University Press.

Neusner, Jacob. 1994. *Introduction to Rabbinic Literature.* New York: Doubleday.

Nickelsburg, George W. E., and Robert A. Kraft, eds. 1986. *Early Judaism and Its Modern Interpreters.* Atlanta: Scholars Press.

Reif, Stefan C. 1993. *Judaism and Hebrew Prayer: New Perspectives on Jewish Liturgical History.* Cambridge: Cambridge University Press.

Sarason, Richard S. 2001. "The 'Intersections' of Qumran and Rabbinic Judaism: The Case of Prayer Texts and Liturgies." *DSD* 8: 169-81.

Schiffman, Lawrence H. 1989. *From Text to Tradition: A History of Judaism in Second Temple and Rabbinic Times.* Hoboken, N.J.: Ktav.

———. 1994. *Reclaiming the Dead Sea Scrolls.* Philadelphia: Jewish Publication Society.

———. 1998. *Texts and Traditions: A Source Reader for the Study of Second Temple and Rabbinic Judaism.* Hoboken, N.J.: Ktav.

Shanks, Hershel S., ed. 1992. *Christianity and Rabbinic Judaism: A Parallel History of Their Origins and Early Development.* Washington, D.C.: Biblical Archaeology Society.

Urbach, Ephraim E. 1987. *The Sages: Their Concepts and Beliefs.* Cambridge: Harvard University Press.

VanderKam, James C., and Peter W. Flint, eds. 1998-1999. *The Dead Sea Scrolls after Fifty Years: A Comprehensive Assessment.* 2 vols. Leiden: Brill.

Dictionary Entries

A–Z

A

Aaron

A descendant of Levi and brother of Moses (Exod. 6:20; Num. 26:59; 1 Chron. 6:3 [MT 5:22]), Aaron was Israel's first high priest and the ancestor of its priestly line. During the exodus and wilderness sojourn, Aaron shared leadership with Moses and their sister Miriam. The biblical account of Aaron as an individual is ambiguous: while the Chronicler and the so-called Priestly tradition in the Pentateuch make him the progenitor of the high priesthood (e.g., 1 Chron. 23:13; 24:19; Exodus 28–29), elsewhere he is depicted less sympathetically as a sponsor of Israel's idolatry (Exodus 32; Deuteronomy 9) and a rebel against Moses' authority (Numbers 12). Moreover, in Ezekiel his priesthood is eclipsed by the line of Zadok (Ezek. 40:46; 44:15). Unlike his ancestor Levi, though, Aaron's double image in the biblical tradition did not inspire a substantial exculpating literature in early Judaism; instead, Scripture's exaltation of him as the first high priest is largely assumed and his moral failings virtually overlooked.

If we count the Chronicler and Ezra-Nehemiah as early Jewish literature, we find the solution to the dilemma posed by Ezekiel's favoring Zadokites: Zadok is made a descendant of the line of Aaron (1 Chron. 5:27-34; Ezra 7:1-6). This maneuver renewed Aaron's reputation as the originator of the high priesthood and altar priesthood, and if we accept early Jewish literature's silence regarding him until the second century B.C.E. as reliable evidence, this solution must have been satisfactory enough to relieve any concern to tell stories that would legitimate claims for the Aaronite origin of altar and high priests.

Indeed, when Aaron does return to the spotlight in early Jewish literature, his appearances are spare and assume the ascendancy of his line among priests. To validate Hasmonean claims to the high priesthood, 1 Maccabees assigns to Mattathias Aaronite ancestry (1 Macc. 2:26, 54); Mattathias' zeal for Israel is like that of Phinehas, grandson of Aaron (Num. 25:6-13, esp. v. 7). A handful of other passages in the Greek pseudepigrapha (of varying date) likewise mention Aaron honorifically, demonstrating the uncontested character of his line's ascendancy (e.g., *Liv. Pro.* 2:11, 14; 4 Macc. 7:11; Ezekiel the Tragedian, *Exagōgē* 116).

The tendency to reconcile the line of Zadok with that of Aaron and to assume the ascendance of Aaron's direct descendants among claimants to the altar and high priesthood are most obviously united in the Dead Sea Scrolls. To be sure, the handful of references to the person of Aaron (see CD 5:18 and the fragmentary references in the *Visions of Amram*) underscore his role as the source of all high and altar priests, but much more telling are the myriad references to the Aaronites, "the sons of Aaron." Particularly the sectarian scrolls, ones whose authorship we attribute to the members of the Qumran community, attest to the group's unquestioned assumption that the title "Aaronite" belongs naturally to pure priests — whom they imagine themselves or their idealized selves to be (e.g., 1QS 9:6, 7) — and is more or less equivalent to the title "Zadokites" (see, e.g., the references to both in 1QS 5 and 9).

Probably to stress his own priestly lineage (see *Life* 1.2), Josephus attributes Aaron's initial appointment to the high priesthood to his being virtuous and gifted with prophecy (*Ant.* 3.188, 190; Exodus 28–29); he also retells the story of Korah's rebellion as proof that Aaron was appointed to the high priesthood not by a nepotistic act of Moses, but on God's authority (*Ant.* 4.54-66; Numbers 16).

Lastly, Philo extends the early Jewish tradition of assuming Aaron's ascendancy and essential purity, but with some small exceptions and variations. In general he is exalted not so much for his priesthood as for his association with speech and reason (and the latter's concomitant restraint), and with prophecy, largely on the basis of his appointment as Moses' voice (*Leg. Alleg.* 3.45, 119, 123, 125, 128, 131; *De Migratione Abrahami* 78; 84; *De Mutatione Nominum* 208; cf. Exod. 4:14). Philo is unusual in offering brief, mostly exculpatory reflections on the episode of Aaron and Miriam (*Leg. Alleg.* 1.76; 3.103; cf. Numbers 12), and in twice stressing Aaron's descent from Levi (*Quod Deterius Potiori Insidiari Soleat* 132; 135; cf. Exod. 4:14).

BIBLIOGRAPHY
J. L. KUGEL 1998, *Traditions of the Bible: A Guide to the Bible As It Was at the Start of the Common Era*, Cambridge: Harvard University Press.

See also: High Priests; Levi; Priests

ROBERT A. KUGLER

Abraham

The presentation of Abraham, supreme patriarch of Jewish tradition, in Second Temple literature reflects the values and interests of the authors and their communities. These values and interests do not neatly divide into Judean versus Diaspora camps, but there are definitely divergent portraits of Abraham among Second Temple authors.

Israelite Literature

The book of Genesis contains a lengthy narrative focused on the patriarch, beginning with an account of his calling by YHWH with a promise of great blessing while in Mesopotamia, his movement to Canaan and continued loyalty to his God, God's provision of an heir, and ending with Abraham's eventual death in old age (Gen. 11:26–25:10). When Abraham is mentioned in other biblical texts, it is usually in formulas and divine appellations invoking the name of the ancestors Abraham, Isaac, and Jacob (e.g., Exod. 2:4; 3:6). He is mentioned in only four of the prophetic writings (four times in Isaiah and once in Jeremiah, Ezekiel, and Micah). Some of the postexilic literature written after Genesis, such as the book of Nehemiah (9:7), is clearly aware of traditions narrated in the book.

There are passages in which passing references to Abraham demonstrate that there were other traditions about him current in ancient Israel not derived from Genesis (e.g., Josh. 24:2; Isa. 29:22; 41:8; 2 Chron. 20:7). Exilic and postexilic texts (e.g., Isa. 51:2) make most use of Abraham as patriarchal ancestor, recipient of the divine covenant, and father of Israel even though he is not the eponymous ancestor.

The Book of Jubilees

The second-century-B.C.E. book of *Jubilees,* a work presented as a revelation to Moses, spends roughly a quarter of its narrative on Abraham (*Jubilees* 11–23). Most important for this author is Abraham's rejection of idolatry in Mesopotamia (a theme related to Joshua 24 but not to Genesis) and of other practices such as astrology and sexual immorality. Positively, Abraham and his descendants are to maintain the eternal covenant with God through circumcision (chaps. 14–15), justice, fidelity to the Jewish purity and sacrificial rules (chaps. 20–21), and obedience to all of God's commands. For *Jubilees* Abraham represents the supreme example of one who practiced and advocated holiness, maintained separation from noncovenant (read non-Jewish) people, and was rewarded by God for doing so. Similar themes associated with Abraham are found in *2 Baruch* 57, *Testament of Benjamin* 10, and CD 3:2.

Dead Sea Scrolls

The Aramaic *Genesis Apocryphon* discovered among the Dead Sea Scrolls was composed around the same time as *Jubilees* and also includes a large section (cols. 19–22) that narrates part of Abraham's life corresponding to Genesis 12–15. Like Genesis and *Jubilees,* the author is eager to show Abram (never Abraham) as recipient of divine promises and blessings. Unlike Genesis, though, the author is eager to explain and justify Abram's apparently selfish deception of the Egyptians that put his wife at risk in an effort to save his own skin. It is also important to the author that Sarai, Abram's wife, was preserved from the sexual advances of the Egyptian king.

Another Dead Sea Scroll (4Q225) also parallels *Jubilees* in making the evil angel Mastema responsible for Abraham's near sacrifice of his son (Genesis 22). In other Scrolls that speak of the patriarch, the theme of Abraham as the initial recipient of God's covenant is often encountered. It is found, for example, in texts such as the *Damascus Document* (12:11), the *Psalms of Joshua* (4Q378 frg. 11 line 3; frg. 22 col. i line 4), *Pseudo-Jubilees* (4Q225 frg. 1 line 2), and *Pseudo-Ezekiel* (4Q388 1 ii 2; 4Q389 1 ii 8). Sometimes this theme includes the promise of land to Abraham (4Q378 11 3) or an emphasis on the longevity of the covenant with contemporary implications.

Abraham Pseudepigrapha

Among the Old Testament Pseudepigrapha is a work called the *Apocalypse of Abraham* that dates to the first or second century C.E. The revelations granted to Abraham in this document stress God's exclusive choice of Abraham and his descendants for an eternal covenant and for their deliverance from the destiny of the wicked (*Apoc. Abr.* 9:1-10; 14:3; 20:5; 23:3-5; 24:1; 31:1-8). The first six chapters tell the story of the young Abraham and his insightful recognition of the falseness of idolatry. This story and motif will flourish especially in later rabbinic literature.

Another pseudepigraph of the first or second century C.E. is the *Testament of Abraham.* Despite its title, the work is not a testament but an entertaining tale of Abraham's last days when God sends the angel Michael to prepare Abraham for his imminent death. Abraham requests and is granted a tour of the world; along the way, he is taught to have compassion on all, even as God does. Clearly, the overriding religious concern of this work is Abraham's piety, but in contrast to writings about Abraham that stress Jewish separation and fidelity to the covenant, the *Testament of Abraham* has universal appeals to compassion for all and lacks emphasis upon distinctly Jewish concerns.

Jewish and Non-Jewish Writings in Greek

The image of Abraham shifts again in the works of authors who wrote in Greek, many of whose writings are preserved only in later quotations. Among them are Demetrius (third century B.C.E.), Pseudo-Eupolemus (ca. second century B.C.E.), Artapanus (second century B.C.E.), and Cleodemus Malchus (second or first century B.C.E.). They present the patriarch in ways that appeal to their Hellenistic audiences. The same can be said for the writings of Philo of Alexandria and Josephus from the first century C.E. The Jewish poet Philo of the second century B.C.E. labels Abraham "famous."

Remarkably, Abraham is also referred to by non-Jewish authors. In contrast to Moses and other figures of Jewish tradition, he is always presented positively. He appears in the pages of the Babylonian Berossus (third century B.C.E.), Apollonius Molon of Rhodes (first century B.C.E.), Pompeius Trogus of Gaul (first century B.C.E.), and Nicolaus of Damascus (first century B.C.E.). In all these writings Abraham is first and foremost the patriarch of the Jews. In line with a popular Hellenistic ethnographic trend, these authors link Abraham to other peoples. Thus, according to the last two authors he was at one time king of Damascus. According to Cleodemus, Abraham is linked to the Greek hero Heracles through the marriage of his daughter. Abraham's children turn out to be ancestral founders of nations in Africa and Arabia (so Demetrius, Cleodemus, and Josephus). Similarly, 1 Macc. 12:20-21 contains the tradition that the Jews and Spartans are both descendants of Abraham.

Among these authors Abraham stands out as a member of the class of international intelligentsia. Most of them present him as having studied astronomy in his native Chaldea, and for some he is also a teacher of astronomy to the Egyptians and indirectly of the Greeks (so Pseudo-Eupolemus, Artapanus, Josephus). At least one astrological work was composed and credited to Abraham; it was known to the second-century-C.E. author Vettius Valens and the fourth-century writer Firmicus Maternus. In more general terms, Abraham is often depicted as a great sage with remarkable intellectual skills. Philo and Josephus hold him up for his philosophical skills and, to a lesser extent, for his religious virtues. As one would expect, Philo interprets the life of Abraham philosophically and allegorically in his *On Abraham*.

It is not possible to determine the precise intentions of all of these authors, especially those that are fragmentarily preserved. In some cases it appears that they were seeking to convey historical information or, in the case of Philo, philosophical enlightenment. For other authors it may well be that entertainment, literary creativity, or ethnic pride were the prime motivators.

Early Christian Literature

Given the importance of Abraham as the chief patriarch of the covenant in Second Temple traditions, it is not surprising to find that he plays an important polemical role among early Christians, whose religious life centered on the significance of Jesus, often with covenantal themes. Abraham is adduced as a model of faithful endurance (Heb. 11:4-12) and of faith showing itself through works (Jas. 2:21-24). According to Paul, Abraham's faith made him the covenantal father of Jews and Gentiles who put faith in Abraham's "seed," Christ. Gentiles are made members of the covenant not by observing the "works of the Law" (the Jewish identity markers of circumcision, Sabbath, and food restrictions) but by their faith in Jesus Christ (Galatians 2–3; Romans 3–4). The Fourth Gospel depicts Jesus asserting that Abraham recognized that Jesus was greater than he and accusing "the Jews" as being "of your father, the Devil" (John 8:31-59). The attempt to claim that believers in Jesus are Abraham's legitimate and exclusive heirs, and to disinherit unbelieving Jews from Abraham's patrimony, became a foundational idea in several early Christian writers, as seen in second-century works like the *Epistle of Barnabas* (13:6-7) and Justin Martyr's *Dialogue with Trypho* (119:3-6; 120:2; cf. Siker 1991).

Rabbinic Literature

Rabbinic literature continues weaving and expanding some, but not all, of the threads of Abrahamic traditions from the Second Temple period. The importance of Abraham as covenantal patriarch continues, and he is especially praised for his faithful obedience. This obedience is seen in the ten trials of Abraham (*m. 'Abot* 5:3; *Midr. Ps.* 18:25) and in God's confidence in Abraham's faithful deeds (*Gen. Rab.* 55:1-2). Abraham "obeyed the entire Torah, even before it was written" (*m. Qidd.* 4:14). The stress on obedient deeds may be partly in reaction to Christian emphasis on Abraham's faith. His early and wise recognition of the one true God led him to oppose idolatry, even though his own father was a maker and seller of idols (e.g., *Gen. Rab.* 38:13). For speaking against idols, Abraham was thrown in a fire by King Nimrod but rescued by the true God and sent to Canaan. Though Abraham is not above critique (e.g., *Gen. Rab.* 42:8; *b. Šabbat* 89b), it is not surprising to read that on account of his merit the world is preserved (*Midrash Tanḥuma* Exodus 34).

BIBLIOGRAPHY

J. E. BOWLEY 1992, "Traditions of Abraham in Greek Historical Writings," Dissertation, Hebrew Union College. • J. E. BOWLEY 1994, "Compositions of Abraham," in *Tracing the Threads: Studies in the Vitality of Jewish Pseudepigrapha,* ed. J. C. Reeves, Atlanta: Scholars Press, 215-38. • L. H. FELDMAN 1987, "Hellenizations in Josephus' *Jewish Antiquities:* The Portrait of Abraham," in *Josephus, Judaism, and Christianity,* ed. L. H. Feldman and G. Hata, Detroit: Wayne State University Press, 133-53. • D. J. HARRINGTON 1976, "Abraham Traditions in the Testament of Abraham and in the 'Rewritten Bible' of the Intertestamental Period," in *Studies on the Testament of Abraham,* ed. G. W. E. Nickelsburg, Missoula, Mont.: Scholars Press, 165-71. • J. L. KUGEL 1998, *Traditions of the Bible: A Guide to the Bible As It Was at the Start of the Common Era,* Cambridge: Harvard University Press, 243-350. • J. SIKER 1991, *Disinheriting the Jews: Abraham in Early Christian Controversy,* Louisville: Westminster.

See also: Abraham, Apocalypse of; Abraham, Testament of; Aqedah; Isaac JAMES E. BOWLEY

Abraham, Apocalypse of

The *Apocalypse of Abraham* narrates the Israelite patriarch's conversion from idolatry and his ascent to heaven. Preserved only in late Slavonic manuscripts, the work addresses the problem of evil in the world, the interplay of predestination and free will, and the suffering of Israel at the hands of the nations. It is generally regarded as an early Jewish composition, written in response to the destruction of Jerusalem and its Temple in 70 C.E., and is widely recognized as one of the earliest examples of merkavah mysticism, the interpretations of the heavenly chariot in Ezekiel 1–2 that became prominent in the later Hekhalot literature.

Contents

The *Apocalypse of Abraham* begins with a haggadah on Abraham's renunciation of idolatry (chaps. 1–8), followed by an account of his ascent to heaven (chaps. 9–32). Abraham's father Terah is a priest and maker of idols, and Abraham begins to doubt the efficacy of idols when some of them fall and are broken or burnt beyond repair (chaps. 1–3). After a series of episodes and disputations with his father, Abraham comes to reject the idea of idolatry. His reflections end with a monotheistic confession and an appeal that the true God reveal himself (chaps. 4–7), whereupon God commands him to leave his father's house, which is immediately destroyed by fire (chap. 8).

The biblical account of the covenant between the pieces in Genesis 15 provides both the occasion and the framework for Abraham's heavenly ascent. The angel Yahoel (Iaoel), who bears the divine name (YHWH), comes and serves as Abraham's guide and instructs him about sacrifice, joining him in a forty-day fast. The angel Azazel appears as a bird of prey and tries to keep Abraham from offering sacrifice on Mt. Horeb and ascending to heaven, but Yahoel assists Abraham by giving him an exorcistic formula to drive Azazel away (chaps. 9–14). Abraham is then taken to heaven on the wing of a pigeon, one of the birds left from the sacrifice (chaps. 15–16), and has a vision of God enthroned, worshiping the deity with a song that Yahoel has taught him (chaps. 17–18).

God proceeds to grant Abraham a series of visions. From the highest heaven, he looks down on the seventh, sixth, and fifth heavens, which are full of different classes of angels but empty of any gods. He sees in turn the stars (chaps. 19–20), the earth, and the place of torment under the earth (chap. 21). He also watches the events of history played out in series of vignettes framed in a great picture that is divided into a left side, inhabited by Gentiles, and a right side, inhabited by the people of Israel. The first scenes within the picture depict the sin of Adam and Eve in the Garden of Eden (cf. Genesis 3), the murder of Abel, and a variety of human transgressions (chaps. 23–24). Abraham also sees a vision of the Temple and its altar desecrated by cultic abominations epitomized by an "idol of jealousy" (a phrase taken from Ezekiel 8) that is worshiped and before which children are slaughtered (chaps. 25–26). Abraham then witnesses Gentiles burning and plundering the Temple and its holy things; he is told by God that the devastation will happen because his descendants have provoked God with their idolatry and other abominations (chap. 27). When Abraham asks how long the punishment will last, he is given two symbolic periodizations of history; he sees four entrances into (or hosts/armies entering) the Temple (27:3) and is told that they represent four 100-year periods (28:4-5), each of which is also one of twelve hours allotted to the impious age (28:5; 29:1-2).

Chapter 29 then describes the advent of a "man going out from the left, the heathen side." People from the heathen side go out to worship him, while people from the right side insult him, some striking but others worshiping him. As they worship the man, Azazel runs and worships him, kissing his face. This rather obscure passage (29:4-13), which is probably textually corrupt, is usually identified as an interpolation made by the Bogomils. However, much of the passage may be original (Hall 1988; Harlow, forthcoming).

At the end of chap. 29 God tells Abraham that ten plagues will come upon the entire creation, but "the righteous men of your seed" will be protected and live, "being sustained by the sacrifices and the gifts of justice and truth in the age of justice." The righteous will destroy and rebuke those who have destroyed and rebuked them (29:14-21).

In chaps. 30–31, Abraham is back on earth, where God describes for him the ten eschatological plagues, which will be followed by the appearance of "my chosen one," who will gather the dispersed people of God from the nations. Those who have mocked God and followed idols will be consigned to eternal punishment, rotting in the belly of the crafty worm Azazel and burned with the fire of his tongue (chap. 30). The final, brief chapter (chap. 32) predicts Israel's slavery in Egypt and the exodus, which is the same point where the covenant of pieces ceremony in Genesis 15 ends (Gen. 15:13-14).

Manuscripts

The *Apocalypse of Abraham* survives in six Old Church Slavonic manuscripts copied in Russia from the fourteenth to seventeenth centuries. Four of the six manuscripts are included in the *Explanatory Palaea (Tolkovaja Paleja)*, a Slavic compendium of biblical and other materials. The oldest manuscript, itself incomplete and defective in places, comes from the fourteenth-century Codex Sylvester, which includes the work alongside the lives of various saints. The best witness is manuscript B (Sin 211, fols. 76-90) from the sixteenth century. The East Slavic manuscripts go back to a South Slavic parent text (translated from Greek) that may date to the tenth to eleventh centuries. An intermediate Greek stage of transmission is not only *a priori* likely, since most early Slavic documents were translated from Greek, but also suggested by numerous Hellenisms in the text, including graphic misinterpretations and both morphological and semantic calques. Some passages in the narrative have been identified as Christian glosses (e.g., 20:5, 7; 22:5) and interpolations (e.g., 29:3-13) because they seem to ally God with Azazel. If so, they were likely made by the Bogomils, a medieval, dualistic sect that flourished in the Balkans. Yet since they allow a different interpretation, they may be original.

Authorship, Language, Date

Although the *Apocalypse of Abraham* is preserved in Christian manuscripts and may contain Christian passages, its original Jewish authorship is suggested by its concern with the destruction and eschatological restoration of the Temple, and its likely composition in a Semitic language. The second feature in particular seems determinative. Several Semitisms in the work suggest that its original language was either Aramaic or, more likely, Hebrew (Rubinkiewicz 1980; Lunt 1985; Kulik 2004). Although Semitisms are not in themselves sufficient to establish that a work was composed in Hebrew (since many Jewish and Christian authors writing in Greek could and did imitate the Semitic idiom of the Septuagint), recent research has shown that many obscure passages in the *Apocalypse* make sense only when they are retroverted into Hebrew (Kulik 2004). If the work was composed in Hebrew, then it was almost certainly written by a Jew, and its place of origin was almost certainly the land of Israel.

Because the *Apocalypse of Abraham* responds to the destruction of the second Jerusalem temple in 70 C.E., it is usually dated to the end of the first or beginning of the second century C.E. An upper limit for its composition is hard to come by. Several dateable Christian sources mention various apocryphal works attributed to Abraham, but there is no certainty that any of them has this *Apocalypse* in view. The most compelling potential allusion comes in the Pseudo-Clementine *Recognitions* (ca. 200 C.E.), which says of Abraham that "an angel standing by him instructed him more fully about those things that he was beginning to understand. And he also showed him what was in store for his race and posterity" (Ps.-Clem. *Recog.* 1.32).

Character and Affiliations

The *Apocalypse of Abraham* is an important example of early Jewish midrashic exegesis (Kugel 1998), mystical speculation (Halperin 1988), and apocalyptic conceptuality (Collins 1998). The patriarch's rejection of idolatry has no basis in Genesis but was evidently inferred from Josh. 24:2-3, "From of old your ancestors — Terah, the father of Abraham and of Nahor — lived beyond the River [Euphrates] and worshiped other gods. And I took your father Abraham from beyond the River and led him through all the land of Canaan." The notion that Abraham renounced his father's idolatry and converted to worship of the one God became a subject of popular speculation and is developed in various early Jewish writings (*Jub.* 12:1-8, 12-14; Philo, *Migr.* 1.176-86 and *Abr.* 66–68; Josephus, *Ant.* 1.154-57; Ps.-Philo, *Bib. Ant.* 4:16–7:5). As in them, so in the *Apocalypse* many narrative details depend on creative interpretations of biblical texts. The parody of idols in chaps. 1–8 is ultimately rooted in biblical polemics against idolatry, especially the satire in Isa. 44:9-20. Abraham's leaving his father's house takes its inspiration from Gen. 12:1, and his escape from Ur develops traditions known from *Jubilees* 12 and Pseudo-Philo's *Biblical Antiquities* 6, which in turn work from Gen. 15:7 ("I am YHWH, who took you out of Ur [read as Hebr. *'ûr,* "fire"] of the Chaldeans" (cf. Isa. 29:22, which says that God *rescued* Abraham). Abraham's heavenly ascent has its point of departure in Gen. 15:5, where God takes Abraham outside and bids him look to heaven and count the stars. This verse, along with Gen. 22:17, inspired Pseudo-Philo to speak of Abraham's being "lifted above the firmament" (*Bib. Ant.* 18:5).

The song that Abraham sings in chap. 17 reflects the idea of apocalyptic visionaries joining the angels in heavenly singing (e.g., *1 Enoch* 71:1; *3 Enoch* 1:11-13; *Hekh. Rab.* 24:1). The text of such a song is preserved elsewhere in Second Temple texts only in *1 Enoch* 39:10-14, and a song of Abraham himself is mentioned in *Genesis Rabbah* and *Haggadat Šir ha-Širim.* The exegetical stimulus for the song may be an apocalyptic rewriting of Gen. 14:22 (Weitzmann 1994).

Abraham's angelic guide Yahoel, who plays a role that Hekhalot literature assigns to Enoch-Metatron (e.g., *3 Enoch* or *Sefer Hekhalot;* cf. *b. Sanhedrin* 38b), is described on the basis of biblical passages like Exod. 24:10, Ezek. 1:26, and Daniel 7. For Yahoel's wicked counterpart Azazel, the work is indebted to the *Book of the Watchers* (*1 Enoch* 1–36), and for Abraham's vision of the throne in chaps. 18–20 it draws on Ezekiel 1, 10 and *1 Enoch* 14.

Among early Jewish apocalypses, the *Apocalypse of Abraham* is unique for combining a review and periodization of history with a heavenly ascent. Among ascent apocalypses, it is exceptional for not describing a tour of the heavens but instead placing the visionary directly in the highest heaven. As a response to the destruction of the Temple in 70 C.E., the work invites comparison with *4 Ezra* and *2 Baruch,* apocalypses written around the same time. These works lack the *Apocalypse of Abraham*'s emphasis on worship, while it lacks their emphasis on the Torah (though see *Apoc. Abr.* 31:4, which refers to keeping the commandments). All three writings share a concern for theodicy, but *4 Ezra* and *2 Baruch* develop it at much greater length.

The *Apocalypse of Abraham* epitomizes evil in the world as idolatry. Evil in its various forms amounts to false worship. Only when Abraham has renounced idolatry and been ritually separated from it on Mt. Horeb, and only once he has overcome and even usurped Azazel as a heavenly priest and been taught proper worship by Yahoel, is he ready for a vision of God and of history's course and climax. When Israelites [Jews] engage in idolatry, they align themselves with the very Gentile nations that have oppressed them, and will be subject to the same judgment awaiting the heathen.

The work relates these issues in turn to the even larger one of free will and predestination, affirming that the two coexist (26:1-7). Sin is a matter of human choice, but human life and history nevertheless proceed according to God's plan. The course and climax of history are built into the fabric of the cosmos from the time of creation. The problem of evil, then, is ultimately rooted in false worship, and its final solution will come with eschatological judgment and true worship centered on a restored Temple.

Setting and Function

There are no indications in the book of its compositional setting. The apocalypse obviously values the Temple but is also critical of the Temple cult, yet the priesthood is not indicted overtly. The story of Abraham's renunciation of idolatry may have been intended, or read, as a manifesto against Jewish artisans and merchants participating in the growing idol trade in Palestine after 70 C.E. Its polemic against the idolatry and murder perpetrated on the altar of the Temple may reflect inner-Jewish struggles and assassinations associated with the Zealot occupation of Jerusalem at the end of the First Revolt. But it is risky to see in such symbolic images reflections of specific incidents. The most that can be said is that the work was composed in an apocalyptically and mystically oriented circle, in which biblical tradition and apocalyptic speculation were put to haggadic and hortatory use.

BIBLIOGRAPHY

Editions

B. PHILONENKO-SAYAR AND M. PHILONENKO 1981, *L'Apocalypse d'Abraham, Semitica* 31, Paris: Librairie d'Amérique et d'Orient Adrien-Maisonneuve. • R. RUBINKIEWICZ 1987, *L'apocalypse d'Abraham en vieux slave: Introduction, texte critique, traduction et commentaire,* Lublin: Catholic University of Lublin.

English translations with introductions and notes

G. H. BOX AND J. I. LANDSMAN 1918, *The Apocalypse of Abraham,* London: SPCK. • A. KULIK 2004, *Retroverting Slavonic Pseudepigrapha: Toward the Original of the Apocalypse of Abraham,* Atlanta: Society of Biblical Literature, 1-35. • R. RUBINKIEWICZ AND H. G. LUNT 1983, "The Apocalypse of Abraham," in *OTP* 1: 681-705. • H. F. D. SPARKS AND A. PENNINGTON 1984, "Apocalypse of Abraham," in *AOT* 361-91.

Studies

J. J. COLLINS 1998, *The Apocalyptic Imagination,* 2d ed., Grand Rapids: Eerdmans, 225-32. • R. G. HALL 1988, "The 'Christian Interpolation' in the Apocalypse of Abraham," *JBL* 107: 107-10. • D. J. HALPERIN 1988, *The Faces of the Chariot,* Tübingen: Mohr-Siebeck, 103-13. • D. C. HARLOW FORTHCOMING, "Idolatry and Alterity: Israel and the Nations in the *Apocalypse of Abraham,*" in *The "Other" in Second Temple Judaism: Essays in Honor of John J. Collins,* ed. D. C. Harlow et al., Grand Rapids, Eerdmans. • J. L. KUGEL 1998, *Traditions of the Bible,* Cambridge: Harvard University Press, 244-74. • A. KULIK 2004, *Retroverting Slavonic Pseudepigrapha: Toward the Original of the Apocalypse of Abraham,* Atlanta: Society of Biblical Literature, 36-94. • H. G. LUNT 1985, "On the Language of the Slavonic Apocalypse of Abraham," *Slavica Hierosolymitana* 7: 55-62. • J. R. MUELLER 1982, "The Apocalypse of Abraham and the Destruction of the Second Jewish Temple," *SBLSP* 21: 341-49. • A. ORLOV 2008, "Praxis of the Voice: The Divine Name Traditions in the Apocalypse of Abraham," *JBL* 127: 53-70. • R. RUBINKIEWICZ 1979, "La vision de l'histoire dans l'Apocalypse d'Abraham," *ANRW* II.19.1: 137-51. • R. RUBINKIEWICZ 1980, "Les sémitismes dans l'Apocalypse d'Abraham," *Folio Orientalia* 21: 141-48. • J. C. POIRIER 2004, "The Ouranology of the Apocalypse of Abraham," *JSJ* 35: 391-408. • A. RUBINSTEIN 1953, "Hebraisms in the Slavonic 'Apocalypse of Abraham,'" *JJS* 4: 108-15. • S. WEITZMAN 1994, "The Song of Abraham," *HUCA* 65: 21-33. • É. TURDEANU 1972, "L'Apocalypse d'Abraham en slave," *JSJ* 3: 153-80, rpt. in idem, *Apocryphes slaves et roumains de l'Ancien testament* (Leiden: Brill, 1981), 173-200.

DANIEL C. HARLOW

Abraham, Testament of

Contents

The *Testament of Abraham (T. Abr.)* first came to the attention of Western academics in 1892 with the publication of the critical edition of M. R. James. In contrast to the meager report in Gen. 25:7-10, the book imaginatively recounts the dramatic and humorous circumstances of Abraham's death. When the day for the patriarch to die draws near, God sends the archangel Michael to tell the patriarch to set his affairs in order and otherwise prepare to die. When Michael descends and greets the virtuous man, the latter fails to recognize his heavenly visitor, although he was one of three angels who formerly announced the birth of Abraham's beloved son, Isaac (Genesis 18). The earthly host shows such hospitality to his mysterious houseguest and is so good-natured and pious that the angel cannot bring himself to deliver his message. Excusing himself, Michael returns to heaven, from which God sends him once again to tell Abraham that his end is near.

Returning to Abraham, Michael eventually reveals his true identity and his mission. Abraham, however, refuses to cooperate. The man who in the Bible is the paradigm of submission to God's will here disobeys his Lord. Eventually the patriarch proposes a bargain: he will relinquish life if he can first see all the creation. God agrees, and Abraham travels upon a cloud to behold the world. But God, who is far more compassionate than the sinless saint, has to bring the tour to a premature halt when the patriarch begins calling down death upon the people he sees sinning.

Abraham is next taken to the place of judgment, where he witnesses the postmortem weighing of souls and learns compassion for sinners. Upon returning to earth, however, he reneges on his deal and again refuses to give up his soul. At this point God retires the archangel Michael and, in his place, commissions Death to take the patriarch's life. Although Abraham likewise refuses to cooperate with this new visitor, his obstinacy does not matter. Death, after revealing his terror and decay, manages to trick him and draw forth his soul anyway. And so the book ends with Abraham never having composed a will or accepted his own death.

Relation to Biblical Tradition

In the *Testament of Abraham,* God is the Jewish God of the Bible. Yet the work is not concerned with the Jewish people as such. Nor does it mention specifically Jewish practices such as circumcision and Sabbath keeping. The land of promise is not emphasized, and the eschatology concerns individuals, not the nation. The judgment is, further, according to good and bad deeds in general, not works of Torah in particular. Thus the book is interested in broad religious ideas rather than the traditional markers of Jewish identity. God is the God of all humanity, and the relevance of specifically Jewish practices and beliefs, while perhaps assumed, is unspoken.

The *Testament of Abraham* regularly quotes, refers to, and otherwise borrows from Genesis and other parts of the Tanak and traditions dependent upon them (e.g., *T. Abr.* 3:3 draws upon Isa. 6:6; *T. Abr.* 4:6 makes use of Job 1:1, 8; 2:3; *T. Abr.* 10:6-7 uses the language of 2 Kings 2:23-25; *T. Abr.* 10:8-9 alludes to Numbers 16; *T. Abr.* 10:10-11 echoes 2 Kings 1:9-12; and *T. Abr.* 10:14 repeats a refrain from Ezek. 18:23, 32; 33:11). In its first half especially, *T. Abr.* constantly weaves into its narrative dozens of words and phrases from the LXX story of Abraham, especially from Genesis 18 and 22.

Yet despite its keen knowledge of and interaction with Scripture, the *Testament of Abraham* does not promote a canon-centered piety. Not only are central scriptural themes conspicuously absent but the story itself does not follow the Bible. *T. Abr.* makes its main points not through exegesis but through a new, imaginative narrative. Moreover, it does not scruple to contradict the Bible itself, as when Abraham lives to be 995 (1:1), or when Sarah is alive at his death (20:6). Beyond such blatant contradictions is also the implicit criticism of the behavior of Moses, Elijah, and Elisha in chap. 10. So while it regularly echoes and finds inspiration in the Bible, *T. Abr.* feels perfectly free to go its own way. It does not make Scripture the last word but creatively exploits it for novel ends.

Versions and Recensions

The *Testament of Abraham* circulated in Greek, Coptic, Arabic, Ethiopic, Slavonic, and Romanian versions. The Greek, which appears to lie behind all the other versions, is extant in two very different recensions, a long recension (with three subgroups) and a short recension (with two subgroups). Although the two recensions regularly recount the same events with different words, the overlap in vocabulary that does exist shows that they go back to the same Greek exemplar, not to translations of a Semitic original.

Some have argued for the priority of the long recension, others for the priority of the shorter one. Those urging the latter can appeal to its language being more Semitic and less ecclesiastical. But the evidence seems to favor the originality of the longer recension. The manuscripts of both recensions as well as the versions exhibit a very strong tendency toward deliberate abbreviation. Comparison reveals that, time and again, words, phrases, sentences, and even whole sections have been omitted, and yet the remaining text is intelligible. The shorter recension seemingly reflects a desire to abbreviate, to reduce contradictions with the Bible, and to polish Abraham's character so that he becomes again the obedient figure of Genesis (the upshot being exclusion of many of the comedic elements).

Jewish or Christian Provenance

M. R. James characterized the *Testament of Abraham* as Christian. Most have disagreed (but see recently Davila 2005). The book is full of Jewish ideas, Jewish idioms, and Jewish lore, and positing a non-Christian *Urtext* is natural. The telling point is not the overwhelming number of verses whose language or thought has Jewish parallels but rather the places that have no Christian parallels and indeed clash with what we otherwise know of Christian beliefs. The soteriological optimism that evidently characterized an early form of our work does not seem at home in the church, which is presumably why the recensions have countered it. Even universalists such as Origen and Isaac of Nineveh would have had trouble with a prayer that brings unbaptized sinners into eternal life in an instant, without some purgation through postmortem suffering (see chap. 14). Also lacking are Christian parallels for the idea, expressed in 14:15, that retribution in this life can cancel retribution in the next. Some Jews, by contrast, did teach that earthly suffering atones and brings redemption in the world to come. It is, finally, suggestive that a book concerned above all with death and the hereafter nowhere even so much as alludes to the resurrection of Jesus or his salvific descent into hell.

Jewish Character

As to the sort of Judaism the *Testament of Abraham* might represent, the book fails to take a defensive stand over against pagan society or to speak against assimilation to the pagan world. It neither indicts idolatry nor teaches the superiority of Judaism. It is rather consistently cosmopolitan. Despite its focus on Abraham, the book has almost nothing to say, even indirectly, about the Jewish people. Apart from 13:6, which may be from a Christian hand, Israel plays no role. Indeed, the repeated reformulation of God's foundational promise in Gen. 22:17 has no reference to the land; nor do the stars and sand represent the number of Abraham's descendants, that is, the multitude that is Israel, but his own physical possessions and wealth, which are beyond counting (1:5; 4:11; 8:5). The soul's destiny in the afterlife, moreover, appears to be wholly independent of one's religious affiliation (chaps. 11–14). Descent from Abraham and membership in the covenant made with him are unrelated to salvation. Sabbath, circumcision, and Torah observance play no role.

Place of Origin and Date

The most common theory about local origin is that the Greek text appeared first in Egypt, perhaps Alexandria. The closest parallels to the postmortem judgment as the *Testament of Abraham* recounts it are in Egyptian sources, and the depiction of Death personified has its closest parallels in Christian writings from Egypt. It is also suggestive that both Greek recensions share much vocabulary with several books often reckoned to come from Egypt, including Wisdom, 2 Maccabees, 3 Maccabees, and 4 Maccabees. To all this one can add that there are striking similarities between *T. Abr.* and the *Testament of Job* and the fragments of Artapanus. All three are Greek Diaspora texts that entertain with humor, wit, and irony, and they do not expound the biblical text but rather find in it inspiration for their own fictional creations. This matters because Artapanus almost certainly wrote in Egypt, and the *Testament of Job* is most often assigned to the same place.

As for the date, since we have a Sahidic fragment from the fifth century, a Greek version of the *Testament of Abraham* must have been in circulation in Egypt before then. There is also a series of books likely indebted to the work — the Coptic Enoch Apocryphon catalogued as "Pierpont Morgan Library. Coptic Theological Texts 3" (from fifth-century Egypt), the *History of Joseph the Carpenter* (fourth or fifth century, probably from Egypt), the *Discourse on Abbaton* (fourth century?), the *Apocalypse of Paul* from Nag Hammadi (NHC V,2 17.19–24.9; probably third century), the *Testament of Isaac* and the *Testament of Jacob* (third or fourth century?), and the *Visio Pauli* (third or late second century).

So the external evidence strongly suggests that some form of the *Testament of Abraham* was already in circulation by the third century. This is consistent with the generalization that Jewish books adopted by Christians were, as a rule, known no later than the second century C.E. Moreover, if the book originated among Egyptian Jews, we should date it before 115-117 C.E. This is because the revolt of those years left Egyptian Jewry, especially in Alexandria, decimated, and thereafter Egyptian Jewish literature almost dries up until the late third or early fourth century. This inference is all the more sure because *T. Abr.* reflects no hostility between the Jewish and Gentile worlds, which is hard to imagine after the revolt. As for a *terminus a quo,* both recensions know the LXX, so *T. Abr.* in anything like one of its present forms must have come into existence after the LXX established itself, which means one cannot hazard a date before the second century B.C.E.

The Focus on Death

The central issue in the *Testament of Abraham* is death, the focus on Abraham being ultimately incidental. The patriarch is not, so to speak, his biblical self but rather the human being faced with death who, no matter how pious, is anxious. Abraham is in fact denial incarnate. He is tardy to recognize Michael and fathom his mission. Then he refuses to cooperate. Then he makes a deal on which he reneges. Then he delays the inevitable by quizzing Death about multiple matters. And when slipping away at the end, he is still telling Death to depart. Indeed, at his dying moment he is fantasizing about getting well (20:8-9). So from beginning to end Abraham runs from reality. He never comes to terms with the fact that his death is at hand.

Although the *Testament of Abraham* candidly displays the human denial of death, it does so with humor and sympathy, and it is ultimately optimistic, at least for all those whose bad deeds do not exceed their good deeds. Abraham may, like everyone else, fear death, but wisdom recognizes that the world is ultimately "futile" (1:7) and that leaving it is, for the redeemed, to exchange suffering, grief, and groaning for peace, fervent joy, and eternal life (20:15). Death has hideous faces, but they soon fade. *T. Abr.* copes with death-related anxiety by teaching that death is not the end but instead the beginning of a better existence.

BIBLIOGRAPHY

D. C. ALLISON, JR. 2003, *The Testament of Abraham,* Berlin: de Gruyter. • J. R. DAVILA 2005. *The Provenance of the Pseudepigrapha: Jewish, Christian, or Other?* Leiden: Brill, 199-207. • M. DELCOR 1973, *Le Testament d'Abraham,* Leiden: Brill. • M. R. JAMES 1892, *The Testament of Abraham,* Cambridge: Cambridge University Press. • E. JANSSEN 1975, *Testament Abrahams,* JSHRZ 3: 193-256. • J. W. LUDLOW 2002, *Abraham Meets Death: Narrative Humor in the Testament of Abraham,* London: Sheffield Academic Press. • G. W. E. NICKELSBURG, ED. 1976, *Studies in the Testament of Abraham,* Missoula, Mont.: Scholars Press. • N. RODDY 2001, *The Romanian Version of the Testament of Abraham: Text, Translation, and Cultural Context,* Atlanta: Society of Biblical Literature. • F. SCHMIDT 1986, *Le Testament grec d'Abraham: Introduction, édition critique des deux recensions grecques, traduction,* Tübingen: Mohr-Siebeck. • M. E. STONE 1972, *The Testament of Abraham: The Greek Recensions,* Missoula, Mont.: Scholars Press. • E. TURDEANU 1981, "Le Testament d'Abraham en slave et en roumain," in *Apocryphes slaves et roumaines de l'Ancien Testament,* Leiden: Brill, 201-18, 440.

DALE C. ALLISON, JR.

Adam and Eve

All of the ancient pseudepigraphical writings that were attributed to Adam have been lost to the vagaries of historical accident (see Stone 1992). There exist, nonetheless, important extant references to Adam and Eve that underscore their significance in antiquity. Some of these references are scant and void of detail. A wedding-night prayer in Tob. 6:8 cites Gen. 2:24. In *1 Enoch* 32:6, the angel Raphael identifies for Enoch a marvelous tree of wisdom "from which your old father and mother . . . ate and came to know wisdom; and [consequently] their eyes were opened and they realized they were naked and [so] they were expelled from the garden." The primeval pair are included in the allegory of the animals in *1 Enoch* 85:3-10 and 90:37-38. And a Jewish sibyl declares that God "fashioned Adam, of four letters, the first-formed man, fulfilling by his name east and west and south and north" (*Sib. Or.* 3.24-26).

Wisdom Literature

Authors in the wisdom tradition tend to shift the focus away from Adam as an Israelite patriarch and toward an interpretation that understands him as characteristic of the human race in general. (Eve is not mentioned as an individual.) Although the early second-century-B.C.E. Jerusalem sage Ben Sira makes a passing reference to the glory of Adam in his praise of famous men (49:16) and, slightly at odds with this reference, to the first man's inability to grasp wisdom (24:28), he tends otherwise to focus upon those dimensions of the creation narratives that underscore human mortality in general (15:9–18:14; 33:7-13; 40:1-11, 27). The need for wisdom prompted by human mortality, which he discovers in Genesis 1–3, dominates the teaching this scribe imparts to his protégés.

The author of the Wisdom of Solomon, writing perhaps nearly two centuries later, probably in Alexandria, refers to the "earthborn protoplast" of whom Solomon, in his shared mortality with all humans, is the descendant (Wis. 7:1-6). This protoplast is a type of the just person whom wisdom aids to avoid sin (10:1-2) and, with the help of the divine spirit's inspiration, to exercise dominion (9:1-3). God's inbreathing (Gen. 2:7) is universal as well; it is the implantation of an immortal soul into every human being (2:23-24). Another Alexandrian author, Philo Judaeus, universalizes this inbreathing as well: God breathes into Adam's face the divine spirit in order to impart a conception of God and a capacity for virtue (*Leg. Alleg.* 1.36-38). Philo's interpretations, however, reach so far beyond this that he deserves to be treated in his own right.

Philo Judaeus

Philo devotes substantive discussions to Adam and Eve. Although in *De Opificio Mundi* 24–25, 64–88, 134–50, and 151–69, he interprets Genesis 1–3 in standard commentary form, verse by verse, his interpretations are anything but pedestrian. For example, he interprets Adam, Eve, and the Serpent according to a complex but consistent allegory of the soul: "Pleasure does not venture to bring her wiles and deceptions to bear on the man, but on the woman, and by her means on him. . . . For in us mind corresponds to man, the senses to woman, and pleasure encounters and holds parley with the senses first, and through them cheats with her quackeries the sovereign mind itself" (165). In his explicit allegorical interpretation of Scripture, *Legum Allegoriae* (1.31-42 and 2.4), Philo creatively resolves the presence of two creation accounts in Genesis 1–3. He explains that the heavenly man of Genesis 1 represents both the superior mind (an anthropological category) and the person who lives exclusively according to that mind — or reason (an ethical category). Similarly, the earthly man of Genesis 2 represents both the mortal mind, which lies between the immortal mind and the body (an anthropological category), and the person who lives according to this mind (an ethical category) and who may succumb to the flesh or rise to the life of the immortal mind. Once again, a component of Genesis 2 comes, in Philo's interpretative scheme, to represent anthropology and ethics.

What is perhaps of singular importance is the realization that Philo, a first-century Jewish philosopher cum interpreter, joins Ben Sira and the author of the Wisdom of Solomon when he interprets Adam and Eve — and other elements of Genesis 1–3 — in terms of human existence, as a repository of anthropological and ethical insight, rather than exclusively as individual historical figures. In *De Virtutibus* 199–205 he interprets the primeval flood as a second creation and Noah as a second Adam.

Josephus

In the late first century C.E., in Rome, Josephus molded Genesis 1–3 to conform to the primary lesson of his *Antiquities of the Jews,* which he clarifies in its proem: "God, as the universal Father and Lord who beholds all things, grants to such as follow him a life of bliss but involves in dire calamities those who step outside the path of virtue" (Preface 20). In his revision of Genesis 3, Josephus, not unlike other Roman historians, inserts a speech, this time in the mouth of God, who says, "Nay, I had decreed for you to live a life of bliss," with the luxury of spontaneously sprouting plants (a Stoic detail), in a beautiful earthly garden. Instead, the man and woman forfeited this earthly bliss (not immortality) because they sinned. The primeval fall from bliss to catastrophe, then, precisely illustrates Josephus' thesis that those who disobey God fall from bliss into dire calamities.

Rewritten Bible

Jubilees

The book of *Jubilees* offers a thoroughgoing transformation of Genesis 1–3 that engages in an anachronistic reading of Genesis 1–3 in light of Israelite laws. For example, according to *Jubilees,* Adam and Eve were created in the first week, though Eve was not shown to him until the second because Lev. 12:2-5 demands a period of (maternal) seclusion of seven days for a male child and fourteen — that is, an additional seven — for a female child. Further, the angels brought Adam into Eden after forty days and Eve after eighty, in conformity with the same levitical text. The consequences of disobedience are also transformed. Adam acted as priest by offering incense in front of Eden, which in *Jubilees* is probably the Holy of Holies (2:1–3:32), after covering his nudity in accordance with the strictures for priests in Exod. 28:42-43. In other words, a clear sign of shame in Genesis 2–3 becomes in *Jubilees* Adam's virtuous priestly activity that accords with specific laws.

Liber Antiquitatum Biblicarum

The *Biblical Antiquities* of Pseudo-Philo rewrites a lengthy swath of Scripture. Written perhaps in the first century C.E., it offers a very different portrait. Adam is a negative figure (apart from a neutral genealogy in 1:1). Adam transgressed, persuaded by his wife who was deceived by the serpent, so that death was ordained for the human race (13:8-9). He lost access to precious stones that, presumably, had existed in paradise (26:6, 13) and, perhaps, later appeared in Israelite priestly clothing. What Adam exemplifies in *Jubilees* — the priesthood — he loses in Pseudo-Philo. Yet all is not lost. Although Adam lost all, what he lost was restored to Israel at Sinai, where paradise gave off the scent of its fruit (32:7, 15).

Apocalypses

The apocalyptic authors of *4 Ezra* (3:4-11, 20-27; 4:26-32; 6:45-59; 7:11-14, 62-74, 116-31) and *2 Baruch* (4:1-7; 14:17-19; 17:1–18:2; 19:8; 23:4-5; 48:42-47; 54:13-19; 56:6-10), during the decades following the destruction of Jerusalem in 70 C.E., accentuate the effects of the sin of Adam — and Eve in *2 Baruch* — by viewing him as the inaugurator of the present evil age. *4 Ezra* contains the indictment: "And you laid upon him one commandment of yours; but he transgressed it, and immediately you appointed death for him and for his descendants" (3:7). *2 Baruch* laments, "For when he transgressed, untimely death came into being, mourning was mentioned, affliction was prepared, illness was created" (56:6).

These authors are not satisfied with an explanation of Adam's effects upon the present age. They also question Adam's (and Eve's for *2 Baruch*) place in the problem of ongoing moral depravity. The author of *4 Ezra* appears to blame Adam: "O Adam, what have you done?" Yet there is a measure of ambivalence when he continues, "For what good is it to us, if an eternal age has been promised to us, but we have done deeds that bring death?" (7:117-20). Ultimately, the angel lays responsibility at the individual's feet: "This is the meaning of the contest which every person who is born on earth shall wage" (7:127-28). Although the question in *2 Baruch* is the same — "O Adam, what did you do to all who were born after you?" (48:42) — the answer is crisper than in *4 Ezra*. While Adam brought physical death to the present evil age, individuals have the capacity to determine their destinies in the age to come: "For, although Adam sinned first and has brought death upon all who were not in his own time, yet each of them who has been born from him has prepared for himself [herself] the coming torment" (54:15). In other words, "Adam is, therefore, not the cause, except only for himself, but each of us has become our own Adam" (54:16).

Dead Sea Scrolls

The Dead Sea Scrolls are deeply, though not overtly, indebted to Genesis 1–3. The book of *Jubilees,* which was valued highly by the community that preserved the Scrolls, tends to exonerate Adam. In 1QS 3–4, the "Teaching on the Two Spirits" is undoubtedly a reflection upon the inbreathing of the first man; the belief that two spirits, good and evil, coexist within a person from the beginning derives from Gen. 2:7. The *Hodayot,* or *Thanksgiving Hymns,* contain countless Job-like reflections upon mortality that pick up the language of Genesis 2–3, such as, "I know that there is hope for someone you fashioned out of dust for an everlasting community" (11:20). Despite the unavoidable mortality of individuals formed from dust, the community nonetheless claims residence in Edenic paradise (e.g., 1QH 14:15-17; 16:4-13). This community expects, further, to receive in the age to come "all the glory of Adam" (though the word *ʾādām* could refer to humankind). The reflections on human nature in the wisdom text 4QInstruction are also based on interpretations of the story of Adam (4Q417 1 i 16-18; 4Q423 1-2).

Life of Adam and Eve

Several fascinating revisions of Genesis 1–4 are extant in Greek, Latin, Georgian, Armenian, and Slavonic. The Greek version of the *Life of Adam and Eve* (which exists in no less than three distinct text forms or recensions) reflects perhaps an early Jewish original (Dochhorn 2005), though this is debated. Notwithstanding these questions, the Greek *Life of Adam and Eve* is significant by dint of its creativity and its indirect influence upon subsequent Western conceptions of Adam and Eve. Among its salient extrabiblical features are Eve's vivid dream in which Cain drinks Abel's blood and then vomits it; several references to Adam's pain and disease; Seth and Eve's unsuccessful return to paradise to obtain the oil of mercy for Adam and an encounter along the way with a beast (Satan in other versions) that excoriates Eve but turns away at Seth's command; and a unique testament of Eve (chaps. 15–30) where a testament of Adam might be expected. This *Life* is a remarkable showcase of the metamorphosis of Adam and Eve during the Greco-Roman era.

BIBLIOGRAPHY

G. A. ANDERSON AND M. E. STONE, EDS. 1999, *A Synopsis of the Books of Adam and Eve,* 2d ed., Atlanta: Scholars Press. • G. A. ANDERSON, M. E. STONE, AND J. TROMP, EDS. 2000, *Literature on Adam and Eve,* Leiden: Brill. • D. A. BERTRAND 1987, *La vie Grecque d'Adam et Ève,* Paris: Maisonneuve. • J. J. COLLINS 2004, "Before the Fall: The Earliest Interpretations of Adam and Eve," in *The Idea of Biblical Interpretation: Essays in Honor of James L. Kugel,* ed. H. Najman and J. H. Newman, Leiden: Brill, 293-308. • M. DE JONGE AND J. TROMP 1997, *The Life of Adam and Eve and Related Literature,* Sheffield: Sheffield Academic Press. • J. DOCHHORN 2005, *Die Apokalypse des Mose: Text, Übersetzung, Kommentar,* Tübingen: Mohr-Siebeck. • J. FRISHMAN AND L. VAN ROMPAY, EDS. 1997, *The Book of Genesis in Jewish and Oriental Christian Interpretation,* Louvain: Peeters. • J. R. LEVISON 1988, *Portraits of Adam in Early Judaism,* Sheffield: Sheffield Academic Press. • D. T. RUNIA 2001, *Philo of Alexandria: On the Creation of the Cosmos according to Moses: Introduction, Translation and Commentary,* Leiden: Brill. • M. E. STONE 1992, *A History of the Literature of Adam and Eve,* Atlanta: Scholars Press.

See also: Adam and Eve, Life of

JOHN R. LEVISON

Adam and Eve, Life of

The *Life of Adam and Eve* is a narrative about the first humans after their expulsion from the Garden of Eden. It survives in several versions — Greek, Latin, Slavonic, Armenian, Georgian, and Slavonic — and the versions themselves exist in different forms. The work was copied very often, both in the Byzantine and Middle Eastern countries and in the Latin world, as the many manuscripts that transmit it prove. It was popularized in the West through five incunabula editions in Rome at the beginning of printing between 1475 and 1500. Then it was ignored for more than three centuries, even in the early collections of apocrypha by J. Fabricius in 1713 and 1723.

Editions

The first edition of the Greek version was published in 1866 by Konstantin von Tischendorf. He called the work

ADAM AND EVE, LIFE OF

Apocalypsis Mosis because one of his manuscripts bore the title "The Narrative and Life of Adam and Eve the Protoplasts or First Ones, Revealed by God to Moses His Servant." In 1878 W. Meyer published the first critical edition of the Latin version based upon several manuscripts. Convinced that the Greek *Life* and the *Vita Adae et Evae* were pieces *(Stücke)* of an original text *(Urtext)*, which he entitled *The Hebrew Book of Adam*, he published the Latin text and included the Greek pericopes that the Latin ignores. In 1893 V. Jagic edited the Slavonic. In 1896 H. S. Yovsēpʿiancʿ published an Armenian translation of the Greek *Life* that was translated into English by J. Issaverdens in 1934.

The Greek, Latin, and Slavonic versions initially appeared to represent more or less independent traditions, but further textual discoveries opened up new prospects. In 1929 J. H. Mozley published a distinctive form of the Latin text from manuscripts in Great Britain with unknown variants in the first chapters. In 1964 C. Kʿurcʿikidze published a Georgian version with a different narrative structure. In 1974 M. Nagel presented a synthetic study of all the known versions in which he analyzed their relations to the Greek, of whose priority he was convinced. In 1981 M. E. Stone edited the *Penitence of Adam*, a new Armenian form of the apocryphon with the same structure as the Georgian version. In the same year, J.-P. Mahé presented a French translation of the latter. In 1994 the publication of a synopsis of the books of Adam and Eve by G. A. Anderson and M. E. Stone provided visual evidence of the relationship of all of the versions. In 1998 J.-P. Pettorelli discovered a Latin text-form quite close to the Armenian and Georgian versions. In 2005 J. Tromp presented a long-awaited critical edition of the Greek form based upon witnesses already analyzed by Nagel. Most recently, in 2007, Pettorelli published a complete edition of the Latin manuscript tradition in which he distinguished two forms: one (lat-V for Vulgate) is represented in more than 100 witnesses that can be arranged in seven families; the other (lat-P for Paris) survives only in one almost complete manuscript and in one containing the narrative's first part.

The latest research suggests that all the versions come from a single narrative, itself the work of a single author who organized a variety of original traditions according to his own plan. During its transmission, certain elements of this tale were alternately enriched and impoverished, some even disappearing completely. Nonetheless, the original plot underlying all forms known today can still be discerned.

Contents

The Search for Food and Satan's Jealousy

After their expulsion from the Garden, Adam and Eve weep for nine days. They become hungry and cannot find any food except grass suitable for animals. Eve, aware of her guilt, begs Adam to kill her so that he may return to Paradise to find angelic food. Adam refuses and decides that they should do penance, he in the Jordan River, Eve in the Tigris (chaps. 1–8). Determined to prevent their return to Paradise, Satan tempts Eve to break off her penance, to Adam's great disappointment (chaps. 9–10). Satan explains that this ploy avenges him for having been expelled from his celestial abode because he and angels who followed him had refused to bow before Adam. Adam prays to God to deliver him, and Satan leaves him (chaps. 11–17).

Adam and Eve's Children

Ashamed, Eve departs westward to await death. Suffering unexplained pains, she prays to the stars to inform Adam. In response to Adam's prayer, celestial powers explain that she will give birth, and they help her deliver Cain, her firstborn (chaps. 18–21). Adam takes Eve and his son eastward. Michael brings him seeds and teaches him how to cultivate the earth. Thus the problem of human food is resolved (22:1-2). Eve gives birth to Abel and has a dream in which Cain sucks Abel's blood. God sends Michael to tell Adam that Cain will kill Abel but that God will give him another son, in God's image. Separating them does not prevent Cain from killing his brother (22:3-23). Adam and Eve give birth to Seth and then to thirty sons and as many daughters. Adam lives 930 years (chap. 24).

Adam's Sickness; Eve and Seth's Mission to Paradise

Stricken with pain, Adam calls for his sons. He refuses Seth's suggestion to obtain curative oil from Michael and confesses that he and Eve have eaten of the forbidden fruit of the Tree of Life. (In their present state, chaps. 32–33 tell virtually the same story twice.) Therefore God struck him with seventy-two blows (chaps. 30–34). Feeling guilty, Eve offers herself to bear half of Adam's pains. He agrees to send her and Seth to seek the oil of mercy from Michael (chaps. 35–36). On their way, Seth is attacked by a beast, an attack that shows Eve that she and Adam have lost power over the animals through their sin. Seth curses the beast, which leaves him with a scar from a bite (chaps. 37–40). At the gates of Paradise, Seth and Eve beg Michael to bring them the oil. Michael responds with the promise that God's son will come to earth after 5,500 years and that, after being baptized in the Jordan River, he will anoint Adam and the faithful with the oil of mercy (chaps. 40–43). On Eve's return with Seth to her husband, Adam blames her and obliges her to tell her sons how she caused their misfortune (chap. 44).

[In what follows, chaps. 45–73 of the Latin-P, Armenian, and Georgian versions are indicated by adding 30 to the numbering of the Greek *Life* starting from chap. 15.]

Eve's Confession

Adam and Eve divided the animals according to sex (chap. 45), and Satan hid in the snake that tempted Eve (chap. 46). Satan appeared briefly as an angel and invited her to taste the fruit of the Tree of Life; she was convinced to eat it and swore to offer it to Adam. Discovering her nakedness, she dressed herself with fig leaves (45:1–50:5a). She then tempted Adam, who ate the fruit and hid himself (50:5b-51). God descended on his chariot throne to judge Adam (chaps. 52–54) and then Eve and the snake (chaps. 55–58). God ordered angels to expel them from Paradise. Adam prayed to the angels to bring three petitions for forgiveness; he was allowed to take only some fragrant herbs (chap. 59). The section concludes with the statement, "We were expelled from Paradise and came to the earth" (59:6-60).

The Death of the Protoplasts

Eve worries about Adam's death and her own future, so Adam comforts her and gives her his last will. Eve confesses her sin (61:1–62:2), and then Adam dies (62:3-4). Eve and Seth witness an angelic liturgy without understanding it. God descends on the merkavah surrounded by angels who pray that God will forgive Adam. A seraph carries Adam to Lake Acheron and places him in Paradise, whereupon the angels thank God for forgiving Adam (chaps. 63–67). Then a second liturgy begins: Gods descends to Paradise to the place of Adam's body and promises forgiveness, commanding the archangels to enshroud Adam and Abel and to bury them near Paradise. He promises Adam's resurrection and that of all mankind (68:1–72:2). Eve asks her sons to bury her near Adam so that she will not be separated from him in death. She gives up the ghost, and her sons bury her near Adam and Abel (72:3–73:1). A brief epilogue concludes the narrative (73:2-4).

An Anthropological Tale

The book of Genesis and the *Life of Adam and Eve* offer very different portraits of the first humans. Whereas Gen. 2:4–5:5 is a treatise of theological anthropology, focusing on the primordial couple's creation and fall but without expatiating upon the situation that ensued, the *Life* seeks to describe the main characteristics of the human race as encountered in daily life: hunger, temptation, pain in childbirth, jealousy between brothers, sickness, and death. The "anthropologist" who first wrote the *Life of Adam and Eve* was also a teller of tales. The first sentence of the narrative is quite typical of these two aspects: "When Adam and Eve were expelled from Paradise, they made a tent for themselves and spent nine days mourning and lamenting in great sadness. But after nine days they began to be hungry. . . ." Isn't that how the life of every human child begins? No such idea occurs in Genesis 1–5. A fondness for this sort of narration appears in the account of Adam and Eve's penance (chaps. 7–9), in the setting of the first son's birth (18–21), in Abel's murder (22–23), in the encounter with the beast (37–39), and in the first temptation (45–59).

The Textual Traditions

The following analysis of the different textual traditions of the *Life of Adam and Eve* is based on the hypothesis that its original structure is that described above. It favors those traditions that transmitted the work in its entirety: Latin-P, Armenian, and Georgian.

The Common Tradition Attested by the Armenian, Georgian, and Latin-P Versions

Latin-P is distinguished by a simpler structure of the common tradition, particularly in chaps. 55–59: it lacks the curses on Eve and Satan (the Armenian and Georgian add Gen. 3:14-15 in reverse order) and Adam's first two requests before the expulsion (chap. 59). Even more remarkably, it lacks the second funerary liturgy (chaps. 68–69). The fact that Latin-P's only witness dates from the mid-twelfth century, and that the Latin-V version from England and the tenth-century Old Irish poem *Saltair Na Rann* (Greene, Kelly, and Murdoch 1976) preserve Latin-P readings, proves its antiquity. Based on the rule that narratives tend to expand with time, it seems that Latin-P in its simplicity brings us close, at least in these sections, to the original structure of the *Life*.

There is no doubt that the Georgian and Armenian depend on the same source as Latin-P, but the witnesses that transmit them, which are much later (fifteenth and sixteenth centuries) than the only witness of Latin-P (twelfth century), tend to introduce explanatory or wordy expansions (e.g., 20:2b). Only further analysis will enable us to get closer to the initial form.

The Georgian version is clearly closer to the Greek version, and both transmit two funerary liturgies. The Georgian tends to expand the narrative (e.g., 20:2; 56:1-2). The Armenian, on the contrary, has suffered in transmission or was made from a partly corrupt source (see chaps. 63–68).

The Greek Tradition: Three Families

In a Strasbourg doctoral dissertation presented in 1972, M. Nagel (1974) studied twenty-three Greek manuscripts of the twenty-nine inventoried and identified three families (cf. Tromp 1997: 31-35). The second family (manuscripts R and M) adds a condensed narrative of the first eight chapters of the common tradition at the end of Eve's first temptation narrative. The third family is only a rewriting of the first. Nagel's classification and the form of the original Greek text are still debated (cf. Eldridge 2001: 75-100; Tromp 2005: 67-105).

Nagel concluded that the Greek version represents the original form of the *Life of Adam and Eve,* a thesis still defended by some scholars (de Jonge and Tromp 1997; Tromp 2005: 96-102). According to Tromp, the other versions "do not represent an archetype other than the one that can be reconstructed on the basis of the extant Greek manuscripts" (Tromp 2005: 97), but he does not give a clear demonstration of this claim.

Many clues suggest another hypothesis (Pettorelli 2003). All surviving Greek witnesses contract chaps. 1–22 of the narrative presented above in a unique sentence, combining its first and last clauses: "After they had gone out of Paradise" (1:1), "Adam took Eve his wife and went to the East" (22:1). This curtailment can only be deliberate, since several of these chapters were known by the Greek tradition in the witnesses R and M. Likewise, to describe Adam's reaction to Abel's murder, the Greek version uses a sentence that expresses his response when Eve's pain comes to him, even though the Greek ignores this pericope (Greek 2:4 = Latin-P 20:1-2).

This curtailment might have two causes. First, most of the Greek manuscripts are anthologies of liturgical texts, so a long narrative could have been shortened for ceremonial use. Second, from the seventh century on, the Byzantine church rejected the ancient belief in Satan's jealousy toward Adam that lies at the heart of the first part of the book (cf. Anastasius Sinaïta, *Questiones et Responsiones*, ed. J. Munitiz, CCSG 59, p. 130).

Acknowledging that the Greek is a shortened version need not lead to undervaluing the Greek text it preserves. Two issues must be distinguished: the original structure of the work (and in this, the Greek version is not preferable) and the value of the surviving Greek text. Where it exists, the Greek version is the most reliable witness to the original Greek text of the *Life*, even if further research may prefer other versions in certain passages.

The Latin-V Tradition

Latin-V transmits the first three parts of the *Life* fully, but sometimes the text is abridged. Although it keeps the introductory sentence of Eve's confession attested in other traditions, it ignores the rest and then gives a very condensed form of Adam's death in which some parts of the detailed narrative can be recognized. However, rather than seeing this as a summary, it is better to view it as a more ancient form of the narrative, because it transmits some sentences that better accord with the work's general content. Thus in Lat-V 46:2 the command given to Seth — "Arise from the body of your father and come with me and see what the Lord God has arranged for him" — is spoken by Michael, Seth's usual chief interlocutor in the *Life of Adam and Eve*, but in the Greek (34:2) and Georgian it is implausibly attributed to Eve.

Other probably secondary passages have been inserted into Latin-V:

(1) Adam's speech to Seth, including (1a) the narrative of his ascent to the merkavah, during which God reveals to Adam his fate and Adam begs for mercy, for himself and his offspring (25:1–29:1); and (1b) the revelation of the future history of God's people, centered on the Temple (chap. 29).

(2) A section (chaps. 50-53) relating to the inscribed tablets, in two parts: (2a) Eve's order to her sons to engrave their parents' history (i.e., the narrative we have just read) upon clay and stone tablets, to be transmitted to their descendants; and (2b) the further history of these tablets, engraved by Seth under angelic guidance: rescued from the flood, the stone tablets were found by Solomon's servants, and an angel revealed to him that he must build the Temple in the same place where Seth deposited the tablets, in Adam's chapel. This revelation links the tablet story (chaps. 50–53) to that of the Temple (chap. 29), perhaps a separate, older story that is no longer attested. The origin of the idea of the two judgments, of water and of fire, which is also attested by Josephus (*Ant.* 1.2), remains obscure.

Latin-V was transmitted from the tenth to the fifteenth century. The hundred witnesses known can be sorted into six families that separate into two groups. The first group transmits Latin-V as described above and is composed of four families. The oldest witnesses of families A, R, and B come from German abbeys created by the "Scots." Family A differs from R in its simpler syntax, B in its more learned rewriting. The E family (for "English," because its manuscripts were found in libraries in England), preserve the Latin-V form but adjust it to Latin-P in the first twelve chapters.

The second group, the T (= tardy) family, combines the former narrative with the medieval Holy Rood legend. This group begins with a very condensed form of the *Life of Adam and Eve* and their sons and then tells how, instead of fragrant herbs, Eve and Seth took back from their pilgrimage to Paradise three cuttings that Seth planted at the head of Adam's grave. From these cuttings grew the wondrous forest from which King Solomon would take the beams used in the building of the Temple, except one that would become the horizontal beam of Christ's holy cross. First written separately in several thirteenth-century manuscripts, the two traditions were combined, the legend of the Holy Rood taking the place of the story of the tablets in the *Life*. This is also the text form that printers in Rome used in their five incunabula editions, both simplifying it and prefacing it with a narrative of Satan's fight against our first parents.

Conclusions and Unanswered Questions

The foregoing analysis yields two conclusions: (1) The relationship between the Latin-P, Armenian, and Georgian versions suggests that their narrative structure was the original form of the tradition. (2) The absence of the first part of the narrative from the Greek version therefore looks like the result of a shortening of it in the Byzantine tradition. Yet several questions remain unanswered: Was the doubling of Adam's funeral narrative in the Greek and Georgian versions, of which the Armenian is a truncated transcription, the initial form, or should we prefer Latin-P, which has only one? What is the origin of the inserted traditions in Latin-V? Can the much simpler funeral narrative in Latin-V be considered an earlier form of it? How are we to explain the double writing of chaps. 32–33 in the Latin-P, Armenian, and Georgian versions?

Provenance, Language, and Date

The Jewish or Christian origin of the *Life of Adam and Eve* is another subject still being debated among scholars. In spite of some Christian elements (the Jordan and not the Euphrates as the site for Adam's penitence in chap. 8, and the expectation of the Son of God in chaps. 42–43), there is no compelling reason to deny the narrative a Jewish origin. Today the debate is centered on the origin of traditions concerning Adam and Eve as they appear in *Pirqe de Rabbi Eliezer* (20–22) and *Genesis*

Rabbah (8–24). A future critical edition of these two works would probably bring an answer to the question.

The original language and date of the *Life of Adam and Eve* also remain uncertain. There are no convincing indications of a language other than Greek, even though Adam's history was highly esteemed in the Syriac tradition. The earliest manuscripts of the various versions, as well as the Old Irish transcription of Latin-P, date from the tenth or eleventh century. The shortening of the Greek version is attested by Anastasius Sinaïta about 780. Therefore, one can set the *terminus post quem* in the seventh century. Yet even though the tradition of Satan's jealousy of Adam is attested by Irenaeus at the end of the second century, there are no decisive criteria to establish the original date of composition.

BIBLIOGRAPHY

General

G. A. ANDERSON AND M. E. STONE 1999, *A Synopsis of the Books of Adam and Eve*, 2d rev. ed., Atlanta: Scholars Press. • A.-M. DENIS 2000, *Introduction à la littérature religieuse judéo-hellénistique*, vol. 1, Turnhout: Brepols, 3-58. • J.-C. HAELEWYCK 1998, *Clavis Apocryphorum Veteris Testamenti*, Turnhout: Brepols, 1-12. • M. E. STONE 1992, *A History of the Literature of Adam and Eve*, Atlanta: Scholars Press.

Editions of the Greek

C. TISCHENDORF 1866, *Apocalypses Apocryphae*, Leipzig: Mendelssohn (rpt. Hildesheim: Olms, 1966). • D. A. BERTRAND 1987, *La vie grecque d'Adam et Eve: Introduction, texte, traduction et commentaire*, Paris: Librairie d'Amérique et d'Orient, Adrien-Maissonneuve. • A.-M. DENIS 1987, *Concordance grecque des pseudépigraphes d'Ancien Testament*, Louvain-la-Neuve: Université catholique de Louvain, 815-18. • J. TROMP 2005, *The Life of Adam and Eve in Greek: A Critical Edition*, Leiden: Brill.

Editions of the Latin

W. MEYER 1878, "Vita Adae et Evae," *Abhandlungen der königlichen Bayerischen Akademie der Wissenschaften: Philosophisch-philologische Classe* 14: 185-250. • J. H. MOZLEY 1929, "The 'Vita Adae,'" *JTS* 30: 121-49. • J.-P. PETTORELLI 2007, *Vita Adae et Evae*, Turnhout: Brepols.

The Holy Rood Legend

W. MEYER 1882, "Die Geschichte des Kreuzholzes vor Christus," *Abhandlungen der königlichen Bayerischen Akademie der Wissenschaften: Philosophisch-philologische Classe* 16: 103-66.

Armenian Life

M. STONE 1981, *The Penitence of Adam*, Louvain: Peeters, 429-30. • H. S. YOVSĒP'IANC' 1896, *Uncanonical Books of the Old Testament*, vol. 1, Venice: Mechitarist Press, 1-26 (an Armenian translation of a manuscript of the *Apocalypsis Mosis*). • J. ISSAVERDENS 1934, "The Book of Adam," in *The Uncanonical Writings of the Old Testament Found in the Armenian Mss. of the Library of St. Lazarus*, 2d ed., Venice: Mechitarist Press, 23-42 (a different work from *Penitence of Adam*).

Georgian Life

C. K'URC'IKIDZE 1964, "Adamis Apokrip'uli C'xovrebis K'art'uli Versia," *P'ilologiuri Dziebani* 1: 97-136. • J.-P. MAHÉ 1981, "Le Livre d'Adam Géorgien," in *Studies in Gnosticism and Hellenistic Religions*, ed. R. van den Broek and M. J. Vermaseren, Leiden: Brill, 227-60. • J.-P. MAHÉ 1983, "Notes philologiques sur la version géorgienne de la *Vita Adae*," *Bedi Kartlisa* 41: 51-66.

Slavonic Life

V. JAGIC 1893, "Slavische Beiträge zu den biblischen Apocryphen. I: Die altkirchenslavischen Texte des Adambuches," *Denkschriften der kaiserlichen Akademie der Wissenschaften, philosophisch-historische Classe* 4: 1-104.

Translations without Text

English

M. D. JOHNSON 1985, "Life of Adam and Eve: A New Translation and Introduction," in *OTP* 2:249-95. • L. S. A. WELLS 1913, "The Books of Adam and Eve," in *APOT*, 123-54.

German

C. FUCHS 1900, "Das Leben Adams und Evas," in *APAT*, 506-28. • O. MERK AND M. MEISER 1998, "Das Leben Adams und Evas," *JSHRZ*, II/5: 737-870.

Spanish

N. FERNANDEZ MARCOS 1987, "Vida de Adan y Eva (Apocalipsis de Moises)," in *Apocrifos del Antiquo Testamento*, vol. 2, ed. A. Diez Macho, Madrid: Ediciones Cristiandad, 316-52.

Gaelic Poem

D. GREENE, F. KELLY, AND B. O. MURDOCH 1976, *The Irish Adam and Eve Story from Saltair Na Rann*, 2 vols., Dublin: Dublin Institute for Advanced Studies.

Studies

M. D. ELDRIDGE 2001, *Dying Adam with His Multiethnic Family: Understanding the Greek Life of Adam and Eve*, Leiden: Brill. • M. DE JONGE AND J. TROMP 1997, *The Life of Adam and Eve and Related Literature*, Sheffield: Sheffield Academic Press. • M. NAGEL 1974, "La Vie grecque d'Adam et éve," Ph.D. dissertation, Strasbourg-Lille. • J.-P. PETTORELLI 2003, "Essai sur la structure primitive de la Vie d'Adam et éve," *Apocrypha* 14: 237-56. • M. E. STONE, G. A. ANDERSON, AND J. TROMP, EDS. 2000, *Literature on Adam and Eve: Collected Essays*, Leiden: Brill.

See also: Adam and Eve

JEAN-PIERRE PETTORELLI

Adiabene

Adiabene (*Hadyab* or *Hedayab* in rabbinic and Syriac texts) was a small Mesopotamian kingdom on the northern Tigris. Its import for Jewish history lies in the supposed conversion of the royal family to Judaism during the early part of the first century C.E. Primary accounts of the Judaization of Adiabene are found in Josephus' writings and in rabbinic literature, and the respective versions are congruent in their broad strokes and in many details. Adiabene is mentioned in contemporaneous sources (Tacitus, *Annales* 12.13-14; 15.1-14), with key figures and political events in synchrony with Josephus' reports. However, there is no corroboration of the conversion or Jewish identity of the royals. Due to this lack, and the legendary character of the Adiabene episodes, historians are skeptical as to their veracity. Conversely, there is no contradictory evidence, and the absence of corroboration is to be expected. The internal religious dynamics of a minor principality, over one or two generations, would not have garnered wide notice, inasmuch as they had little or no impact upon events concerning the imperial powers of the day, Rome and Parthia. Thus, it is plausible that a matter of particular interest to Jews, with at least a legitimate historical "kernel," would be preserved exclusively in Josephus and rabbinic writings, two principal sources of late Second Temple Jewish historiography. Questions of historicity aside, the Adiabene conversion pericopae have significant implications for the study of early Judaism.

Josephus

The core Adiabene episode is contained in one sustained unit (Josephus, *Ant.* 20.17-96) that can be summarized as follows: Late in his life, Monobaz, king of Adiabene, falls in love with a woman named Helena, marries her, and they have a son, Izates. Izates is favored by God and by his father, who designates Izates for royal succession though he is not the eldest. As a young man, before he is ready to assume the throne, Izates resides in Charax Spasini, a neighboring principality. There, he embraces Judaism under the tutelage of Ananias, a Jewish merchant who had been teaching Judaism to the king's wives. Izates returns home with Ananias to find that his mother Helena had also embraced Judaism. Izates desires to adopt more fully Jewish norms and customs, especially circumcision, but is counseled against such an undertaking by his mother and Ananias, who fear that his public display of Judaism will alienate Izates' subjects. Ananias argues that one can serve or worship God *(theon sebein),* and be fully devoted to Judaism, without circumcision. While Izates initially accedes to this advice, he is subsequently persuaded to undergo circumcision by Eleazar, a Jew of Galilean origin who appeals to the authority of the Torah, which Izates had been studying. Later, Izates' kin, influenced by the king's piety, also become Jewish. During the balance of his rule, Izates faces challenges from his court, and from foreign enemies, and fends them off successfully, due to his own character and capability, and to divine providence *(pronoia).* Grateful for God's protection of Izates, Helena travels to Jerusalem to sacrifice at the Temple and finds the city in the throes of a famine. She and Izates provide financial support for Jerusalem and purchase vast quantities of food to alleviate the starvation. The Adiabene story concludes with the death of Izates and Helena, both of whose bones are brought to Jerusalem and interred in the monuments that had been earlier commissioned by Helena.

The narrative bears several ideological and stylistic hallmarks of Josephus' writings. Notable examples include emphasis upon the efficacy of petitionary prayer (*Ant.* 20.89-91) and the significance of *pronoia* (*Ant.* 20.18, 49, 91). Also typical of Josephus' writings, the account is replete with biblical motifs. Monabaz' favor for his youngest son, resulting in filial strife (*Ant.* 20.17-38), reflects the Joseph story (Genesis 37; *Ant.* 2.7-10), while Izates' success against the Parthian Volgoses' military campaign (*Ant.* 20.81-91) echoes the deliverance of Hezekiah's Jerusalem from Sennacherib's siege (2 Kings 18:13–19:27; Isa. 36:1–37:38; 2 Chron. 32:1-23; *Ant.* 10.1-23; *J.W.* 5.387).

Besides the *Antiquities* narrative, the *Jewish War* has several scattered references to the Adiabene royals and their deeds. These include references to Jews in Adiabene generally (*J.W.* 1.6); to Adiabenian participation in the revolt against Rome (*J.W.* 2.388, 520; 5.474); and to Helena's monument, and other structures, built by members of the royal family in greater Jerusalem (*J.W.* 4.567; 5.147, 252-253). Eusebius (*Eccl. Hist.* 2.12), citing Josephus, alludes to two elements of the account: Helena's monument in Jerusalem, and the queen's provision of food to Judea during the famine under the reign of Claudius. Eusebius coordinates this famine (*Ant.* 20.51-53) with the famine mentioned in Acts 11:27-30, where the Antiochene church community sends relief to Judea through the agency of Barnabas and Saul.

Rabbinic Literature

References to Adiabene in rabbinic writings are diffuse and chiefly concerned with the piety of Helena and Monobaz, and their commitment to Jerusalem, the Temple, and its ritual functions. *M. Yoma* 3:10 (cf. *t. Yoma* 2:3; *y. Yoma* 3:8; *b. Yoma* 37a-b) describes monuments erected by Helena and Monobaz. *M. Nazir* 3:6 (cf. *b. Nazir* 19b) recounts a Nazirite vow undertaken by Helena, culminating in a visit to Jerusalem, and interaction with sages from the school of Hillel. *T. Sukkah* 1:1 (*b. Sukkah* 2b) alludes to a very tall sukkah erected by Helena, and the halakic validity of its height. *T. Megillah* 4:30 (cf. *b. Menaḥot* 32b) attributes to Monobaz the practice of affixing a mezuzah on temporary dwellings during his travels. *T. Pe'ah* 4:18 (*y. Pe'ah* 1:1; *b. Baba Batra* 11a) highlights Monobaz' generosity in that he depletes the royal storehouse during lean years, presumably to benefit the poor. This particular tradition dovetails, in some respects, with Josephus' assertion of Helena's and Izates' aid to Judea during the "Claudian" famine.

The only discrete, albeit short, rabbinic Adiabene narrative is in *Gen. Rab.* 47:10. Izates and his brother, while studying Torah, read Gen. 17:11, God's circumcision command to Abraham. Both are distressed about their own intact foreskins, and are independently circumcised. They reveal their act to their mother Helena, who is anxious about the reaction of their father (here inexplicably named Ptolemy). She suggests that they justify their actions by declaring that their circumcision was recommended by a physician to remedy a dermatological outbreak. The passage concludes with the question, "How does God reward the piety of Monobaz and Izates?"

While some details of the *Genesis Rabbah* and *Antiquities* versions of the tale are at odds with each other, they do align in that the initial "Judaization" of Izates did not involve circumcision. Only later does he undergo the ritual. It is noteworthy, and pertinent to the question of historicity, that in the rabbinic sources cited above, the names of the key actors, Helena, Monobaz, and Izates, are mentioned consistently but are never explicitly associated with Adiabene. The name Adiabene in rabbinic and targumic sources appears in geographic contexts (*b. Qiddušin* 72a; *b. Yebamot* 16b; *Tg. Jer.* 51:27; *Tg. Ezek.* 27:23) but never in connection to a Judaized royal house. Additionally, as noted above, in *Genesis Rabbah,* Izates is named as a son of Ptolemy.

Implications

The Adiabene conversion story has important ramifications for questions about Jewish identity, Jewish proselytism, and the nature of Diaspora Judaism. The rabbinic and Josephan material accords with other testimony in describing vital Jewish Diaspora communities that maintained ties to Jerusalem and supported the Temple economically (Josephus, *Ant.* 18.312-13; Philo, *Legatio ad Gaium* 156; Tacitus, *Historiae* 5.5; Cicero, *Pro Flacco* 66–69). While there is no evidence of concerted, systematic, Jewish missionary campaigns, the data suggest that individual Jews did actively proselytize and that Jewish tenets and practices were attractive to many pagans, especially affluent, aristocratic, women (Josephus, *Ant.* 18.65-84; Dio Cassius, *Historiae Romanae* 57.18; Tacitus, *Annales* 2.85). The Adiabene accounts add to our picture of the "God-Fearers" (Gr. *sebomenoi, theosebeis, phoboumenoi;* Lat. *metuens*), those who may have adhered to Jewish forms of monotheism and worshiped the God of Israel but did not uphold many Jewish customs and were not identified as Jews or as converts.

While conversion was a recognized phenomenon, there is no indication of a fixed or standard ritual process by which a Gentile's entry into the community was ratified or solemnified. The rabbis legislated immersion and sacrifice for all proselytes, and circumcision for all male converts (*Sifre Numbers* 108; *b. Keritot* 9a). Still, the extent to which this mandate was in force during the first century C.E. in Israel or the Diaspora is unknown, and the Adiabene accounts are completely silent regarding any conversion procedures. In this regard, however, the Adiabene material does underscore the importance of circumcision, both from an internal Jewish perspective as a sign of piety, and externally as a distinctive mark of Jewish identity. Further, the texts substantiate the notion that circumcision was viewed with contempt in the Roman world but was also regarded in some circumstances to have medical utility.

Finally, it should be noted that archaeologists have attempted to link Helena's burial monuments with the so-called Tombs of the Kings in Jerusalem. Of interest in the same locale is an ossuary with the Aramaic inscription "Sarah the Queen." It has been suggested that this is Helena's own ossuary, Sarah being her "conversion" name. This identification is attractive yet tenuous.

BIBLIOGRAPHY

B. BROOTEN 1982, *Women Leaders in the Ancient Synagogue,* Chico, Calif.: Scholars Press. • N. P. CLARKE 1938, "Helena's Pyramids," *PEQ* 70: 84-104. • G. GILBERT 1991, "The Making of a Jew: 'God-Fearer' or Convert in the Story of Izates," *USQR* 44: 299-313. • R. JACOBY 1993, "The Decoration and Plan of Queen Helena's Tomb in Jerusalem," *Qadmoniot* 26: 62-63 (in Hebrew). • S. MATTHEWS 2001, *First Converts: Rich Pagan Women and the Rhetoric of Mission in Early Judaism and Christianity,* Stanford: Stanford University Press. • J. NEUSNER 1964, "The Conversion of Adiabene to Judaism: A New Perspective," *JBL* 83: 60-66. • J. NEUSNER 1966, "The Conversion of Adiabene to Christianity," *Numen* 13: 144-50. • L. H. SCHIFFMAN 1987, "The Conversion of the Royal House of Adiabene in Josephus and Rabbinic Sources," in *Josephus, Judaism, and Christianity,* ed. L. H. Feldman and G. Hata, Detroit: Wayne State University Press, 293-312. • D. R. SCHWARTZ 1996, "God, Gentiles, and Jewish Law: On Acts 15 and Josephus' Adiabene Narrative," in *Geschichte, Tradition, Reflexion: Festschrift für Martin Hengel,* ed. H. Cancik et al., Tübingen: Mohr-Siebeck, 263-82.

See also: Aphrodisias; Circumcision; Conversion and Proselytism; God-Fearers DAVID A. BERNAT

Adversus Judaeos Literature

Adversus Judaeos literature as a category customarily refers to writings of church fathers whose purpose is to demonstrate the superiority of Christianity to Judaism.

The "Parting of the Ways"

Early Christian writing "against the Jews" emerged as part of a process frequently referred to as the "parting of the ways" between Judaism and Christianity. How and when this separation became more or less complete is a subject of intense scholarly debate (see, e.g., Lieu 1996; Becker and Reed, eds. 2003; Boyarin 2004; Dunn 2006). While some would see this separation as substantially complete by the end of the first or the middle of the second century C.E., others would point to the fourth century with the accession of Constantine, the first Christian emperor, or even later. As a result, scholars disagree on the extent to which *Adversus Judaeos* literature itself bears witness to a *de facto* separation between Jews and Christians, or to precisely the opposite.

Adolf von Harnack (1908) argued that the separation between Judaism and Christianity was effectively complete by the end of the first century C.E. Harnack's perspective was tainted by his view of "late Judaism" as a moribund religious tradition, superseded by the vigorous and superior Christian message. This led Harnack to conclude that Judaism simply retreated within itself after the destruction of the Second Temple. As a result, the Jews one encountered in the writings of the church fathers were inevitably "straw men" whose presence served the ideological interests of the Christian

ADVERSUS JUDAEOS LITERATURE

author and scarcely reflected ongoing social interaction with real "flesh-and-blood" Jews.

Harnack's view was challenged in 1948 by Marcel Simon (1986), who argued that the situation was precisely the opposite of what Harnack had envisioned. According to Simon, the evidence suggests that Gentiles (including Gentile Christians) were often attracted to the synagogues and perhaps did not see a categorical distinction between Judaism and Christianity. The ongoing vitality of Judaism was perceived as a threat by the church fathers as the two communities competed for the same Gentile converts. The *Adversus Judaeos* literature thus bears witness not to a *de facto* separation between church and synagogue — and still less to a moribund Judaism — but to two communities in frequent contact and ongoing rivalry.

Simon's view has been influential among scholars working on the *Adversus Judaeos* tradition, and has put to rest the notion that Judaism in the pre-Constantinian era was lacking in vitality, or simply retreated in the face of Christian expansion. However, the tendency of Simon and others to equate "vitality" with "missionary zeal" has recently been challenged by Miriam Taylor (1995). According to Taylor, such an equation not only imposes a distinctively Christian notion of religious vitality (thus measuring Judaism against Christianity, by Christian standards), it allows the *Adversus Judaeos* tradition to be explained away and excused as a regrettable but perhaps inevitable product of social conflict. Taylor thus presses for a reconsideration of the *Adversus Judaeos* literature as the product of internal forces inherent in early Christian self-definition. On such a view, the vitality of non-Christian Judaism belongs with greater certainty to the background of the *Adversus Judaeos* tradition than to the foreground of a particular text.

Ultimately, much depends upon whether one thinks of the "parting of the ways" between Judaism and Christianity in demographic, ideological, or sociological terms — in other words, whether the key measurement of separation is ethnic composition, theological self-identity, or social interaction. Each of these measurements is potentially meaningful but will yield different results. There is growing recognition that such assessments cannot adequately be made from the *Adversus Judaeos* literature alone, but that these texts must be read in conjunction with material evidence. Similarly, there is growing awareness that a grand hypothesis that imposes a single theoretical model of Jewish-Christian relationships on a wide range of historical contexts is unlikely to reflect reality. Individual texts may yield differing conclusions, or refuse to yield firm conclusions at all, notwithstanding the scholarly tendency to force them into one theoretical model or another.

Literary Genres

For the sake of simplicity, the patristic *Adversus Judaeos* literature may be grouped broadly into three basic types: (1) testimony collections, (2) dialogues, and (3) argumentative monologues (treatises, epistles, and homilies).

Testimony Collections

The most basic form of Christian literary activity that would later give rise to *Adversus Judaeos* literature in the proper sense was the accumulation of scriptural proof texts adapted to Christian apologetic needs. The beginnings of this development are evident in the New Testament itself: Psalms 22 and 68 were influential in shaping the ways that Jesus' followers interpreted and retold the story of his passion, while Pss. 110:1 and 2:7 are cited several times each in reference to Jesus' resurrection and divine sonship, respectively. Isaiah 6:9-10, Ps. 118:22, and Dan. 7:13 rapidly became proof texts used to explain the rejection of Jesus and to claim his (eventual) vindication. These developments ostensibly gave rise to collections of *testimonia,* organized by topics and keywords (often without regard to their original historical context) and reproduced with little or no interpretation. Already in 1 Pet. 2:6-8 one finds a catena of proof texts clustered around the keyword "stone" (Isa. 8:14; 28:16; Ps. 118:22).

In the early twentieth century, J. Rendel Harris (1916-1920) argued that an original collection of OT *testimonia,* compiled and circulated by the apostle Matthew and subjected to numerous additions and revisions, was the authoritative source at the root of most, if not all, patristic testimony collections. Although the theory of a single "original" source is widely rejected, there is general agreement that testimony collections are one of the foundations on which subsequent *Adversus Judaeos* literature is built. Among the extant literature, Cyprian's *To Quirinius: Testimonies against the Jews* (third century) and Pseudo-Gregory of Nyssa's *Testimonies against the Jews* (fourth century) are the best examples of patristic testimony collections in "pure" form.

Dialogues

A second major genre of Christian controversial literature is the dialogue. The earliest known example of this genre is the *Dialogue of Jason and Papiscus,* composed in the mid-second century by Aristo of Pella, but now lost. Origen of Alexandria knew the dialogue and defended it against Celsus, who viewed it as manifestly absurd and unworthy of refutation (Origen, *Against Celsus* 4.52). Although little is known of its contents, it apparently advocated a christological interpretation of Gen. 1:1 ("In the *beginning* God created . . .") as "In the *son* God created. . . ."

Far better known to posterity is Justin Martyr's *Dialogue with Trypho,* often considered the classic example of the genre. Justin purports to recount for the reader an extended conversation he had with a Jew named Trypho some twenty years prior, at the time of the Bar Kokhba revolt. Composed of 142 chapters, the *Dialogue* is longer than the four New Testament gospels combined and focuses on three major themes characteristic of *Adversus Judaeos* literature: the abrogation of the Jewish law, the messianic status of Jesus, and the Christian claim to supersede the Jews as the "true" Israel. Justin's argumentation is primarily scriptural in nature, emphasizing the fulfillment of prophecy in a way that often fails to see beyond its own Christian presuppositions. By contrast, Trypho's replies usually attempt an interpretation closer to the original historical context of a passage. Thus, while Justin sees Isa. 7:14 as fulfilled only in Jesus, Trypho regards Hezekiah, son and successor of Ahaz, as the one to whom the prophecy refers (*Dialogue with Trypho* 66–67).

Much ink has been spilled over the way Trypho is portrayed in the *Dialogue.* Is Trypho a literary "straw man" whose sole purpose is to facilitate the progression of a debate that Justin must necessarily win? Or does he represent with some accuracy the types of arguments that second-century Christians met in day-to-day encounters with Jews? While the dialogue is certainly not a transcript, and Trypho's views are rarely given equal time, recent scholars have found more verisimilitude in the exchange than earlier generations had allowed. Unlike the more stereotyped figures in later examples of the genre, Trypho does not become a Christian at the end of the debate.

Subsequent examples of the genre surviving from the fourth or fifth century include the *Dialogue of Athanasius and Zacchaeus,* the *Dialogue of Simon and Theophilus,* and the *Dialogue of Timothy and Aquila.* Scholars continue to speculate on the possibility that one or more of these may reflect material inherited from the lost dialogue of Aristo of Pella.

Argumentative Monologues (Letters, Treatises, and Homilies)

The majority of anti-Jewish literature falls into a third general category, whose developed argumentative structure distinguishes it from the testimony collection and whose rhetorical mode of presentation distinguishes it from the dialogue. These include letters *(Epistle of Barnabas),* treatises (Irenaeus, *Demonstration of the Apostolic Preaching;* Tertullian, *Against the Jews;* Eusebius, *Demonstration of the Gospel*), and homilies (Melito of Sardis, *On the Passover;* Aphrahat, *Demonstrationes;* John Chrysostom, *Discourses against Judaizing Christians;* Augustine, *In Answer to the Jews*). It is not always clear which of these genre classifications best describes a particular text; the *Epistle of Barnabas,* for example, has been identified variously as a homily and a doctrinal treatise in epistolary form. Although the examples offered above are by no means exhaustive, they illustrate well the geographical spread of the tradition, stretching from Persia (Aphrahat) to Gaul (Irenaeus), and including Palestine (Eusebius), Asia Minor (Melito), and North Africa (Tertullian, Augustine).

The *Epistle of Barnabas* (ca. 135), perhaps the earliest example of patristic *Adversus Judaeos* literature, is also among the harshest in its assessment of the Jews. *Barnabas* claims (perhaps with intentional hyperbole) that Israel lost its covenant at Sinai after the episode of the golden calf. Although the New Testament itself places responsibility for the death of Jesus on the Jews, Melito of Sardis (ca. 180) is the first known writer to explicitly charge the Jews with "deicide" (*On the Passover* 96). The most comprehensive literary effort remains that of Eusebius of Caesarea, whose *Demonstration of the Gospel* (in twenty books, ten of which are extant) was part of an exhaustive apologetic for the church's providential supersession of Jewish and Hellenistic precursors. In the late fourth century, the apex of patristic invective is reached with John Chrysostom's *Discourses against Judaizing Christians.* Chrysostom charges the Jews with the death of Christ, denies that they worship God, calls the synagogue a brothel and a lair of demons, and speaks of his hearers' attraction to Judaism as a "disease" from which they must be cured.

The Hermeneutics of the Literature

Patristic *Adversus Judaeos* literature is typified by the presumption that those who follow Jesus as messiah are heirs to the promises made to historical Israel, and that Christians therefore supersede contemporary non-Christian Jews as the "True *(Verus)* Israel." It therefore draws heavily on the Jewish Scriptures both to establish its own claims of continuity with the sacred past and to marginalize Jewish claims to the same historical and scriptural legacy. It is important to point out that such an agenda serves both internal (legitimating) and external (polemicizing) apologetic needs; by itself, the presence of such argumentation neither demands nor excludes explanation in terms of active social conflicts or "religious rivalry." A variety of hermeneutical strategies was brought into play, including historical (and metahistorical) arguments, typology, allegory, and prophetic proof-texting.

Prophetic Proof-texting

As has already been noted, the most basic hermeneutical activity consisted of accumulating scriptural proof texts in support of Christian claims. These included positive "proofs" relating to Jesus (virgin birth: Isa. 7:14; divine sonship: Ps. 2:7; vicarious suffering: Isaiah 53; death and resurrection: Ps. 16:9; Hos. 6:2) and the call of the Gentiles (Hos. 1:10; Isa. 49:6). Equally important were negative "proofs" that appeared to devalue cultic dimensions of the Jewish law such as sacrifice (Jer. 7:22-23), fasting (Isaiah 58), and circumcision (Jer. 9:25-26). Of particular importance were passages that criticized Israel for disobedience to God (Isa. 6:9-10) or seemed to speak of its "rejection" (Hos. 1:9). The Deuteronomistic tradition, which charges Israel with the persistent rejection of God's prophets, was a rich quarry from which Christian polemicists frequently drew ammunition. In this way the Jewish tradition's inherent capacity for self-criticism (evident in its preservation of such texts) was co-opted and used against it.

The ability to read the OT christologically was facilitated in part by use of the Septuagint, where the translation of the Tetragrammaton YHWH via the Greek *kyrios* enabled one to find references to "the Lord (Jesus)" whenever the text permitted such a meaning in the mind of the Christian interpreter. Similarly, the emerging "logos" Christology of the church allowed references to Jesus to be found whenever prophets spoke of receiving "the word (logos) of the Lord." Justin Martyr went so far as to argue that all the theophanies in the OT (appearances of "the Lord" or the "angel of the Lord")

ADVERSUS JUDAEOS LITERATURE

were in fact references to Jesus, the preincarnate logos (*1 Apology* 63). The dark side of this hermeneutical maneuver is that it permits Justin to argue that the Jews who rejected Jesus failed to recognize the God who had appeared to their own forefathers.

Christian reliance on the Septuagint led to its subsequent rejection by the Jews in favor of more literal Greek versions (Aquila, Symmachus, Theodotion), with the result that polemical exchanges sometimes focus on the validity of the text being cited. Thus, for example, Justin and Trypho spar over whether Isa. 7:14 properly refers to a "virgin" (LXX: *parthenos*) or merely a "young woman" (Aquila: *neanis*) (*Dialogue with Trypho* 67). Due perhaps to their use of independent collections of *testimonia*, the church fathers sometimes err in identifying the author of a scriptural quotation, or even cite "proofs" that depend upon defective textual readings. Isaiah 45:1, for example, is frequently cited as "Thus says the Lord to my messiah *the Lord,*" reading *kyriō,* "Lord," for *kyrō,* "Cyrus" (*Barn.* 12:11). Similarly, Ps. 96:10 is frequently cited as "the Lord reigns *from the tree*" (*Dialogue with Trypho* 10). Where such discrepancies emerge, Justin accuses the Jews of tampering with the text (*Dialogue with Trypho* 71–73).

Typology and Allegory

A second strategy of scriptural interpretation in the *Adversus Judaeos* literature involves the use of typology and allegory. The term "typology" generally refers to the identification of a pattern or similarity between two elements (e.g., people or events) that is deemed to be historically or theologically significant. By contrast, allegory (or allegoresis) refers to the more or less arbitrary imposition of a symbolic meaning upon a text. Although the distinction is not absolute, typological thinking generally preserves the independent significance of the realities being compared, while allegoresis tends to collapse the two into one and the same thing. Both rely on a sort of "associative" logic.

The *Epistle of Barnabas,* for example, dismisses Jewish cultic practices *in toto* by allegorizing the laws of Moses. Thus, circumcision is strictly a matter of the heart, true fasting signifies social justice, and the dietary laws symbolize types of behavior to be emulated or avoided. Although later church fathers sometimes relativize Jewish cultic practices in similar language, what distinguishes the allegorism of *Barnabas* is the author's insistence that such laws never had any literal significance.

Church fathers frequently adduce both Isaac and Joshua as "types" of Jesus: the binding of Isaac, Abraham's beloved son, prefigures the sacrificial death of Jesus, God's beloved son (*Barn.* 7:3). Joshua, the successor of Moses, prefigures Jesus, who leads God's people into the *true* Promised Land (Tertullian, *Answer to the Jews* 9). Here again, a typological connection was facilitated by the Greek Old Testament, which renders the name "Joshua" as *Iēsous* ("Jesus"). Such typologies often give way to more elaborate allegorizations.

Patristic writers saw the brothers Esau and Jacob (or Manasseh and Ephraim) as types of Israel and the church, since the one to whom the rights of the first-born son naturally belonged was made subservient to a younger (chosen) brother (e.g., Cyprian, *To Quirinius* 1.21). Perhaps most important of all was the impulse to see a typological relationship between the destruction of the First and Second Temples. If Scripture laid the blame for the prior destruction on the nation's failure to heed God's prophets, early Christian writers had no qualms about blaming the second destruction on Israel's rejection of Jesus (e.g., Tertullian, *Answer to the Jews* 13). Typological arguments of this nature pervade the patristic literature.

History and Metahistory

If the arguments made by the patristic writers exhibit a certain recognizable logic, and reflect, in many cases, interpretive techniques shared with contemporary Jewish exegetes, they nevertheless also evince an inherent theological bias. This is evident both from some of the conclusions drawn and from the inconsistency of some of the arguments made. Justin, for example, argues that circumcision can have nothing to do with righteousness since women cannot be circumcised, nor can it be a sign of God's covenant since Egyptians and other nations also practice it. Later, when he wants to argue that circumcision is a sign intended to mark out the Jews for punishment, Justin conveniently overlooks the objections that half of all Jews are not circumcised and that circumcised men are not all Jews (*Dialogue with Trypho* 16). The common denominator in such arguments is simply the conviction that physical circumcision is of no significance for Christians. Similarly, after the Romans destroyed the Second Temple in 70 C.E., both Jews and Christians found it natural to interpret this event in typological relation to the loss of the First Temple in 587 B.C.E. However, whereas Jewish exegetes found within this comparison a reason to hope for future restoration, patristic writers typically saw it as proof that God had abolished the Mosaic covenant and abandoned the Jews for good.

At the end of the day, most (if not all) of the arguments brought forward by the church fathers — from the simple citation of proof texts to more sophisticated forms of argumentation — are part of a larger metahistorical framework in which the life, death, and resurrection of Jesus are collectively seen as the climactic moment in a providential history rapidly approaching its dénouement. Although the beginnings of such a metanarrative are found in Paul (Gal. 4:4-7; 1 Cor. 15:1-58), he was able to hold this view in tension with the theological metanarrative he knew instinctively as a Jew: God had made a covenant with Israel and would never utterly forsake them (Rom. 11:29). By the early second century, the leaders of a predominantly Gentile church found it increasingly difficult to imagine the conversion of Israel that Paul seems to have envisioned (Rom. 11:25-26). As a result, even though the Christian metanarrative grew out of the Jewish one, it no longer seemed possible to the church fathers to affirm Israel's chosenness when the Jews refused to assimilate their own self-understanding to the Christian vision. The patristic *Adversus Judaeos* literature thus reflects a clash of metanarratives about God's purposes in history and the respective roles of Israel, the Mosaic Law, and Jesus of Nazareth.

Social Context and Theological Legacy

Among the most debated issues pertaining to the *Adversus Judaeos* literature is the extent to which it bears witness to ongoing social contact and conflict between Christians and Jews — and consequently how one explains (or inadvertently excuses) the persistence throughout the patristic age of a tradition whose presuppositions and rhetoric remain deeply troubling. Is the very existence of the literature *prima facie* evidence in favor of extensive Jewish-Christian interaction? And does "interaction" necessarily imply "missionary rivalry" or "active hostility" on the Jewish side? Or is the literature a by-product of Christianity's internal struggle to define itself (1) in relation to a scriptural past it simultaneously claimed as its own but rejected as normative on cultic matters, and (2) in relation to a community whose ongoing vitality seemed to place an inherent question mark over Christian truth claims? To put the matter bluntly, was it the actions of a rival community or the mere presence of such a rival that the church fathers perceived as a threat?

In some cases, such as the *Discourses* of Chrysostom, the text points clearly to the presence of a Jewish community perceived as a formidable rival. In other cases, such as the *Epistle of Barnabas*, scholars remain divided. In still others, such as Irenaeus' *Demonstration of the Apostolic Preaching*, negative statements about the Jews are subservient to more general theological and catechetical purposes. If Simon and others have shown convincingly that Judaism remained a vital religious presence throughout the patristic age, Taylor has argued persuasively that such a fact does not by itself account for the persistence of Christian anti-Judaism or the consistency of its motifs. It bears noting that "rivalry" itself is an explanatory construct whose causes may be attributed to internal, psychological, and ideological forces as well as external, social ones. If the disturbing legacy of Christian anti-Judaism is sufficiently clear, its precipitating causes are still widely debated.

BIBLIOGRAPHY

M. ALBL 1999, *'And Scripture Cannot Be Broken': The Form and Function of the Early Christian Testimonia Collections*, Leiden: Brill. • M. ALBL 2004, *Pseudo-Gregory of Nyssa: Testimonies against the Jews*, Atlanta: Society of Biblical Literature. • A. H. BECKER AND A. Y. REED, EDS. 2003, *The Ways That Never Parted: Jews and Christians in Late Antiquity and the Early Middles Ages*, Tübingen: Mohr-Siebeck. • D. BOYARIN 2004, *Border Lines: The Partition of Judaeo-Christianity*, Philadelphia: University of Pennsylvania Press. • J. D. CROSSAN 1995, *Who Killed Jesus? Exposing the Roots of Anti-Semitism in the Gospel Story of the Death of Jesus*, San Francisco: Harper. • N. DE LANGE 1976, *Origen and the Jews: Studies in Jewish-Christian Relations in Third-Century Palestine*, Cambridge: Cambridge University Press. • J. D. G. DUNN 2006, *The Partings of the Ways between Christianity and Judaism and Their Significance for the Character of Christianity*, 2d ed., London: SCM. • A. VON HARNACK 1908, *The Mission and Expansion of Christianity in the First Three Centuries*, trans. J. Moffatt, New York: Putnam. • J. R. HARRIS 1916-20, *Testimonies*, Cambridge: Cambridge University Press. • J. LIEU 1996, *Image and Reality: The Jews in the World of the Christians in the Second Century*, London: Clark. • M. MURRAY 2004, *Playing a Jewish Game: Gentile Christian Judaizing in the First and Second Centuries CE*, Waterloo, Ont.: Wilfred Laurier University Press. • J. NEUSNER 1971, *Aphrahat and Judaism*, Leiden: Brill. • J. N. RHODES 2004, *The Epistle of Barnabas and the Deuteronomic Tradition: Polemics, Paraenesis, and the Legacy of the Golden-Calf Incident*, Tübingen: Mohr-Siebeck. • D. ROKEAH 2002, *Justin Martyr and the Jews*, Leiden: Brill. • R. RUETHER 1974, *Faith and Fratricide: The Theological Roots of Anti-Semitism*, New York: Seabury. • H. SCHRECKENBERG 1999, *Die christlichen Adversus-Judaeos-Texte und ihr literarisches und historisches Umfeld (1.-11. Jh.)*, 4th ed., Frankfurt am Main: Peter Lang. • J. S. SIKER 1991, *Disinheriting the Jews: Abraham in Early Christian Controversy*, Louisville: Westminster John Knox. • M. SIMON 1986, *Verus Israel: A Study of the Relations between Christians and Jews in the Roman Empire (AD 135-425)*, Oxford: Oxford University Press (trans. of 2d French ed. 1964). • O. SKARSAUNE 1987, *The Proof from Prophecy: A Study in Justin Martyr's Proof-Text Tradition: Text-Type, Provenance, Theological Profile*, Leiden: Brill. • M. TAYLOR 1995, *Anti-Judaism and Early Christian Identity: A Critique of the Scholarly Consensus*, Leiden: Brill. • A. L. WILLIAMS 1935, *Adversus Judaeos: A Bird's Eye View of Christian Apologiae Until the Renaissance*, Cambridge: Cambridge University Press. • W. VARNER 2004, *Ancient Jewish-Christian Dialogues: Athanasius and Zacchaeus, Simon and Theophilus, Timothy and Aquila: Introductions, Texts, and Translations*, Lewiston, N.Y.: Edwin Mellen. • R. L. WILKEN 1983, *John Chrysostom and the Jews: Rhetoric and Reality in the Late Fourth Century*, Berkeley and Los Angeles: University of California Press.

See also: Judaizing; Parting of the Ways

JAMES N. RHODES

Agriculture in Palestine

The cultivation of the soil and related activities in order to grow food and to provide other useful products did not come to an end in the land of Israel with the destruction of the kingdom of Judah and Jerusalem in 587/6 B.C.E. by Nebuchadnezzar. According to 2 Kings 25:12, "the captain of the guard left some of the poorest people of the land to be vinedressers *(kôrĕmîm)* and tillers of the soil *(yôgĕbîm)*." While Jerusalem and other urban centers were destroyed, rural life continued in the exilic and postexilic periods. The indigenous means of livelihood that had been practiced in this region for the past millennia continued throughout the Second Temple and later periods. Comparison of agricultural practices from the Israelite period (ca. 1200-586 B.C.E.) with those of later periods, including that of preindustrial Palestine, suggests very strongly that not much had changed. The similarities include methods and tools of cultivation; installations for processing the harvest;

and the species of field crops, fruit trees, and vegetables that were cultivated. Such a comparison can be carried out through the study of material culture provided by archaeological explorations and by anthropological investigations. Furthermore, written sources such as the Mishnah and the Talmud are replete with information related to agricultural tools, methods, species, and the like. The relevant data are embedded in discussions related to the observances of biblical laws. The lack of change in the agricultural practices throughout the ages suggests that there were no major climatic changes or changes in the diet of the local population.

Plowing

The most important agricultural activity was plowing, because it not only made planting possible but enhanced the fertility of the soil and improved the crop yield. That is why the early Jewish sources devote so much space to it and provide a great deal of information (Feliks 1963: 25-89). Accordingly, there were different types of plowing, each identified by a different term. Some farmers elected to plow soon after ending the harvest to open the ground for rainwater. Others would plow after the first rain, when the ground had been softened, to accommodate the following rains. Not only timing but also distances between furrows were different for these two types. Before planting, deep plowing that could reach three *tĕphāḥîm* (27 cm.) was practiced to uproot weeds and after-growth and to prepare the ground for the new planting. Since most planting was done by broadcasting, a second plowing was necessary to cover the seed. When planting seed was done with a funnel attached to the back of the plow, no second plowing was needed to cover the seed. Plowing was done also as part of the agricultural cycle of leaving the field not sown for at least one season, thus enabling the soil to rejuvenate. Other types of plowing were done for summer planting, between rows, and in orchards and terraces.

Animals used for plowing were mostly cattle (oxen, cows). In the fields, plowing was usually done with a pair of animals; however, since not everyone had a second animal, farmers had to cooperate. Under certain field circumstances, in orchards, terraces, or gardens, conditions dictated that plowing would be done with one animal only. At times, when space was even narrower, hoeing was required.

The number of animals harnessed to the plow dictated the harnessing equipment (Feliks 1963: 56-72). Different yokes were used with a pair of animals and with a single one. There was a special, narrow yoke (two *'āmôt* = 112 cm.) used for plowing with one animal in vineyards. A pair's yoke was connected to the plow with a beam that ran between the two animals, while that of a single animal was attached by ropes. To prod and direct the animals, the farmer used an ox goad *(malmad).* This instrument was made of three components: a cane two meters in length with a small metal shovel (15-20 cm. long x 15 cm. wide) on one end for cleaning the plow point and a metal nail-like piece at the other for prodding the animals (Feliks 1963: 69-70; Sass 2004: 2018).

The plow maintained its same basic structure from earliest times in Mesopotamia (ca. 3500 B.C.E.) till the modern age (Feliks 1963: 72-89). The Mishnah describes its parts in detail. The body was made of wood with a point for penetrating the soil that was mostly made of iron attached to its bottom. Unlike the Mesopotamian plow, which had two handles and required two people — one to control the animals, the other to plow — the Palestinian plow had only one handle so one plowman could exert pressure on the plow while controlling the animals with reins and a goad (Borowski 1987: 52).

Fertilizing

Fertilizing was often practiced as part of the agricultural cycle. It was carried out mostly in orchards and row planting and in unirrigated fields where it was plowed over. Fertilizing was discussed at length by the Jewish sages (Feliks 1963: 91-115). The most common matter used as fertilizer (cf. Luke 13:8-9) was dung produced by cattle and other domestic animals. An efficient way of spreading dung involved bringing the herds to the field. Dung was supplemented with organic matter such as house refuse used for compost. In certain cases, wine was added as well for enhancing the flavor of fruit. During the period of the Second Temple, blood was sometimes applied to certain fruit trees. Other substances used as fertilizer were ash from ovens, burnt straw, and dirt from ruins. Dung was collected and sold as fertilizer. It was kept in specially designed places either built or dug in the ground.

Cultivated Plants

The deep concern of the Jewish sages with mixed planting *(kil'āyîm)* provides, through lengthy discussions in the Mishnah and Talmud, detailed information enumerating the field crops, fruit trees, and garden plants cultivated during that period (Feliks 1963:117-65). Additionally, these sources provide information concerning planting times and growing periods.

Winter crops (cereals) were the most important produce because they provided the raw material for making bread. Wheat was planted before barley because it takes longer for wheat to ripen. The sages provide information concerning planting times for grain, flax, legumes, summer crops, and vegetables and discuss rates of sowing. All this information comes in the context of the ongoing discussions about observing religious laws.

According to mishnaic and talmudic sources, plants cultivated in late antiquity were varied and plentiful (Feliks 1983: 15-198). These included winter and summer crops (cereals and legumes), vegetables, herbs and spices, plants for making perfumes, oil, medicines, dyes, summer and winter fruit, nuts, and plants for the manufacture of ropes and textiles. Remains of some of these plants have been recovered in archaeological excavation, as for example at 'Ein Gedi (Melamed and Kislev 2005)

Harvesting and Threshing

Harvesting and threshing of winter crops was not different than in biblical times (Feliks 1963: 187-289; Borowski 1987: 57-69). Harvesting of cereals was done with a sickle. The sheaves were transported to the threshing floor and processed, as in biblical times, by a threshing sledge and then winnowed in the wind with a winnowing fork and a wooden shovel. This was followed by sifting with a variety of sieves. Fruit and vegetables were also harvested and processed by the old methods.

Viticulture and Olive Growing

As the late books of the Hebrew Bible show (e.g., Prov. 31:16; Cant. 1:6; 6:11), vine-dressing was of major concern. The main change between the early biblical and later periods came in the volume of the produce of certain cultivars, mostly grapes and olives, and the amounts of their by-products, that is, wine and oil. These developments can be followed because of the richness of archaeological evidence, both in the form of the installations for the production of wine and oil and in artistic representations such as mosaics, coins, wall paintings, and reliefs (Borowski 1996).

The size of installations suggests whether they were individually owned or operated by a larger entity. Through archaeological excavations, many installations of different sizes from this period have been recovered. Based on size and design, smaller installations seem to have belonged to individuals, while a substantial number of large ones appear to have been operated either by large landowners, a group of cooperating landowners, or the central government.

Irrigation

In biblical times, irrigation in Palestine was not very well developed (Feliks 1963: 291-345; Borowski 1997). Whereas Deut. 11:10-12 describes Canaan as a land watered only by rain and dew, Deut. 8:7 maintains that Canaan has rich water resources — "a land with flowing streams, with springs and underground waters welling up in valleys and hills." Written sources indicate that, in the Second Temple period and later, irrigation of fields and gardens was very common.

Josephus describes irrigation in Jericho (*J.W.* 4.83) and in the Gennesaret area (*J.W.* 3.10.7). The *Letter of Aristeas* also talks about land fertility and the Jordan as a water source (112, 115). In arid regions, runoff agriculture was developed and utilized in the desert during the Roman period, possibly by the Nabateans or their successors.

Basically, there were two approaches to irrigation: continuous and intermittent (supplementing the rain). Continuous irrigation would require intensive work but would yield two harvests. However, this required the protection of the water rights of the local inhabitants. Irrigation was mostly used for vegetables and herbs (Cant. 6:2). The most irrigated field crop was rice, which was also exported. With fruit trees, only the young plants were watered using channels, furrows, and other means. Many cultivars benefited from preplanting watering. Water was directed with a *magrepha,* a hoe-like tool that could be used for many other jobs like digging channels. Archaeological remains related to irrigation have been discovered in ʿEin Gedi and its environs (Porath 2005). There were different methods of irrigation: by gravitation using channels, by flooding, and by fashioning an *ʿarugah* (square dish), mostly for vegetables and rice, or an *ʿugit* (round dish). When gravitation could not be used, water was transported from lower sources by employing a jar attached to a wooden arm (*qilôn*). Another mechanical device was the *galgal* (Eccl. 12:6), a wheel with a rope around it and a vessel tied to its end, known also in Hebrew as *ʿantiliya.* A highly developed apparatus was Archimedes' Screw (Sperber 1993: 38-41), known in Hebrew as *naʿorah;* in the Mishnah it is also mentioned as *agtargatiya* (Sperber 1993: 42-45).

Irrigation Rights

Water rights for agricultural use during the Roman period in Palestine were carefully guarded and recorded, as is evidenced in the documents from the archive of Babatha, a Jewish woman from ʿEin Gedi who hid during the Bar Kokhba Revolt in a nearby cave. The rights for irrigation were enumerated according to days of the week, number of hours, and water sources (see P. Yadin 7, lines 6-7, 9-10, 38 in Yadin, Greenfield, et al. 2002: 80-81, 84-85, 95-96).

Artistic Representations

The richness of agriculture and its central place in the economy of the land of Israel during the Second Temple period are well illustrated in various artistic creations. Mosaics as well as tombs and stone sarcophagi were decorated with motifs of the grape vine or bunch. Vine tendrils and leaves provide the frameworks for mosaic designs. Similar motifs appear on coins struck by Herod the Great, Herod Archelaus, and the Jewish rebels against Rome.

Bibliography

O. Borowski 1987, *Agriculture in Iron Age Israel,* Winona Lake, Ind.: Eisenbrauns. • O. Borowski 1996, "Viticulture," in *Dictionary of Judaism in the Biblical Period,* vol. 2, ed. J. Neusner and W. S. Green, New York: Macmillan, 660-61. • O. Borowski 1997, "Irrigation," in *The Oxford Encyclopedia of Near Eastern Archaeology,* ed. E. M. Meyers, vol. 3, New York: Oxford University Press, 181-84. • J. Feliks 1963, *Agriculture in Palestine in the Period of the Mishnah and Talmud,* Jerusalem: Magness (in Hebrew). • Y. Feliks 1983, *Plants and Animals of the Mishnah,* Jerusalem: Institute for Mishnah Research (in Hebrew). • Y. Melamed, and M. Kislev 2005, "Remains of Seeds, Fruits, and Insects from Excavations in the Village of ʿEn Gedi," *ʿAtiqot* 49: 89*-102* (in Hebrew); English summary 139-40. • J. Porath 2005, "Survey of the Ancient Agricultural System at the ʿEn Gedi Oasis," *ʿAtiqot* 50: 1*-20* (in Hebrew); English summary 239. • B. Sass 2004, "Iron Age and Post-Iron Age Artifacts, Section A: Vessels, Tools, Personal Objects, Figurative Art and Varia," in *The Renewed Archaeological Excavations at Lachish (1973-1994),* vol. 4, ed. D. Ussishkin, Tel Aviv: Tel Aviv University and Marco Nadler Institute of Archaeology, 1983-2057. • D. Sperber

1993, *Material Culture in Eretz-Israel during the Talmudic Period,* Jerusalem: Yad Izhak Ben-Zvi and Bar-Ilan University Press. • Y. YADIN, J. C. GREENFIELD, ET AL. 2002, *The Documents from the Bar Kokhba Period in the Cave of the Letters: Hebrew, Aramaic and Nabatean-Aramaic Papyri,* Jerusalem: Israel Exploration Society; Institute of Archaeology, Hebrew University; and Shrine of the Book, Israel Museum.

ODED BOROWSKI

Akiba (Aqiva)

Rabbi Akiba (Aqiva) ben Yosef (ca. 50-135 C.E.) is one of the best-known figures in rabbinic history. He was active in the land of Israel in the late first and early second centuries, during the period leading up through the Bar Kokhba Revolt. His renown stems from two main sources that need to be differentiated. The first is Rabbi Akiba's centrality to the formation of the early rabbinic corpus, the second, his representation in posttannaitic literature, particularly in the Babylonian Talmud.

Tannaitic sources attest to Rabbi Akiba's importance to the two main branches of early rabbinic literature — the corpora that present legal statements as extrascriptural teachings anchored in rabbinic authority (the Mishnah and the Tosefta), and those that present their legal conclusions as a result of scriptural engagement (the Halakhic Midrashim). In the Mishnah, Rabbi Akiba is regularly represented as an important recipient of traditions from his masters, particularly Rabbi Eliezer and Rabbi Yehoshua. In *m. Maʿaś. Š.* 5:8 Akiba overturns an existing tradition, apparently on the authority of the traditions he possesses. The same authority appears to be at work when Rabbi Akiba's mishnah — a discrete set of received legal traditions — supersedes "the first mishnah" (or "the earlier mishnah"), as happens in *m. Sanh.* 3:4. To Rabbi Yoḥanan, the great Palestinian Amora who lived at the time of the redaction of the Mishnah (ca. 200 C.E.), is attributed the statement that "the unattributed sections of the Mishnah are from Rabbi Meir, those of the Tosefta are from Rabbi Nehemiah, of the *Sifra* from Rabbi Yehudah, and of the *Sifre* from Rabbi Shimon — and all follow Rabbi Akiba" (*b. Sanhedrin* 86a). Setting aside the question of the precise identification of the individual corpora referred to in this statement, it is clear that the entirety of tannaitic literature is being traced back to the teachings (or, perhaps, editorial work) of Rabbi Akiba.

Rabbi Akiba's importance as a master of extrabiblical halakot is evident even when the Mishnah lauds him as an interpreter of Scripture. For often what is praised is his ability to provide *ex-post-facto* scriptural support for an existing legal decision. Thus, in *m. Soṭah* 5:2 Akiba finds a scriptural anchor for a legal decision regarding the transmission of impurity that has already been established by no less an authority than Yoḥanan ben Zakkai, who "used to say that a future generation will declare the third-level loaf clean since it is not scriptural — but your disciple Rabbi Akiba adduced a scriptural proof text for its impurity."

Interestingly, the same attitude is evident in many passages of the *Sifra,* the legal midrash most closely associated with Rabbi Akiba. Moreover, like the Mishnah, the *Sifra* represents Akiba at his interpretive best when he grounds an existing halakah in Scripture (rather than establishing a novel legal conclusion on the basis of Scripture). Thus, after his midrash clarifies a question regarding the laws of sacrifice, his older contemporary Rabbi Tarfon addresses Rabbi Akiba and says: "It was I who received the oral tradition but was unable to explain while you explicate *(doresh)* and agree with the oral tradition" (*Sifra Nedava, parshata* 4.5; Weiss 6a). The *derashah* is valid because it "agrees[s] with the oral tradition."

Recognizing the role and scope of Rabbi Akiba's interpretive activities in tannaitic sources throws into stark relief the profound difference in the way he is represented in posttannaitic sources. In the famous story of Moses' visit to Akiba's *bet midrash* (*b. Menaḥot* 29b), Akiba has almost oracular interpretive abilities that allow him to midrashically derive rulings from the (nonsemantic) adornments God placed on the letters of the Torah. Elsewhere Akiba is described as being able to interpret particles such as *'ak, raq, 'et,* and *gam.* Here, Rabbi Akiba's midrash is understood as deriving new legal conclusions rather than buttressing existing halakot.

The sharp break between the earlier and later sources regarding Rabbi Akiba is in further evidence with regard to his haggadic biography. Though the sources differ on a number of important details, both Talmuds, the minor tractates, and *'Abot de Rabbi Nathan* (much of which is demonstrably posttannaitic) say that Akiba was an *ʿam ha-'āreṣ* — an ignoramus — in his youth. The most important of these are *b. Ketubbot* 62b–63a and *b. Nedarim* 50a, both of which recount the famous tale of Akiba's youth as a shepherd, his love for Rachel, the daughter of his landlord, and his eventual ascent to the summit of Torah scholarship. But the tannaitic sources do not refer to this dramatic life change, and there may even be evidence that they have no knowledge of it. The Tosefta refers to Yehoshua, the son of Rabbi Akiba, who "married a woman and agreed with her that she be responsible to support him and his Torah study" (*t. Ketub.* 4:5). The use of the Yehoshua story as a paradigm of wifely devotion to her husband's Torah study suggests the Tosefta did not know the biographic traditions associated in Amoraic and later sources with Akiba's youth. This possibility is strengthened by the confusion surrounding Akiba's youth in *Sifre Deuteronomy* §357, with some manuscript witnesses even suggesting that he spent his youth in study — a stark contrast to the testimony of the Talmudim.

The break between early rabbinic sources and later elaborations and, perhaps, outright inventions is evident in other aspects of Rabbi Akiba's life. According to a passage in the Jerusalem Talmud (*y. Taʿan.* 4:7, 68d), he hailed Bar Kokhba as messiah. He was also said to have been martyred by the Romans. Recent scholarship casts doubt on these traditions. But the specific details are less important than the general need to distinguish different strata when examining the figure of Rabbi

Akiba, who was transformed in more ways than one by later rabbis.

BIBLIOGRAPHY

L. FINKELSTEIN 1936, *Akiba: Scholar, Saint, Martyr,* New York: Athenaeum, rpt. 1981. • S. FRIEDMAN 2004, "A Good Story Deserves Retelling — The Unfolding of the Akiva Legend," *JSJ* 2: 55-93. • W. S. GREEN 1978, "What's in a Name? — The Problematic of Rabbinic 'Biography,'" in *Approaches to Ancient Judaism,* vol. 1, ed. W. S. Green, Missoula, Mont.: Scholars Press, 77-96; P. SCHÄFER 1980, "Rabbi Aqiva and Bar Kokhba," in *Approaches to Ancient Judaism,* ed. Green, vol. 2, 113-30.

AZZAN YADIN

Alexander the Great

Alexander's reign (336-323 B.C.E.) and the Macedonian conquest of the Persian Empire probably involved little direct contact with Jews and Judaism, but the effects that these events had were profound for the Jews who lived under the rule of the Ptolemies and Seleucids, the successor dynasties based respectively in Egypt and Syria. Alexander's conquests changed Jerusalem from being an eastward-looking part of the Persian world to a westward-looking part of the Mediterranean world, facilitating (if not actually causing) the spread of the Greek language and associated culture to Aramaic-speaking regions, and creating the conditions for the expansion of the Jewish Diaspora in Syria, Asia Minor, and Egypt.

A silver tetradrachma from the time of Ptolemy I (ca. 300 B.C.E.) depicting Athena Promachos and Alexander the Great *(Richard Cleave)*

Legendary Visit to Jerusalem

The story of Alexander the Great's visit to Jerusalem in late 332 B.C.E. is told by Josephus (*Ant.* 11.326-38), but its reliability has been dismissed by nearly all scholars. The context is that Alexander, besieging Tyre, called for Jewish help, but the high priest Yaddua said that he would not break his oath to the Persian emperor Darius, whereas the Samaritans gave Alexander their support and received his endorsement for building their temple on Mt. Gerizim. After capturing Tyre and Gaza, Alexander made his way to Jerusalem with the intention of punishing the Jews for their lack of support. However, he was so impressed by the procession that came to meet him, led by the high priest in his full regalia, that he changed his mind and said that he had already seen the high priest in a dream promising him victory over Darius. Josephus even says that Alexander worshiped the name of God on the gold plate on the high priest's forehead; he uses the Greek verb *(proskynēsen),* which can mean to bend the knee or even to prostrate oneself. He went to the Temple and offered sacrifice under the high priest's direction. As a result, he allowed the Jews in Judea and Babylonia to live by their own laws and gave them exemption from tribute every seventh year.

The most obvious anomaly in the story is that, according to Josephus, Alexander was shown the book of Daniel and found a reference to himself in it (presumably in Dan. 7:6; 8:3-4; or 11:3), even though the book is generally thought to date from the time of the Maccabean Revolt nearly two centuries later. The story as recorded by Josephus contains elements from various sources: *adventus* stories, in which a conqueror is impressed by a defeated city and its gods; stories of Alexander's interest in and visits to local deities (particularly Ammon at Siwah); and stories involving foreign generals such as Pompey making offerings at the Temple. There is no reference to the visit to Jerusalem in any of the main sources on Alexander. Arrian (3.1) and Quintus Curtius Rufus (4.7.2) say that he made for Egypt immediately after the sack of Gaza, and there would have been no strategic reason for him to postpone his main goals in order to visit Jerusalem. The visit is also not mentioned in the brief and generally hostile summary of Alexander's life in 1 Macc. 1:1-9. Josephus places the visit between two mutually contradictory stories about the Samaritans: Alexander giving permission for them to build a temple, and then being invited to go from Jerusalem to visit their already fully functioning temple.

Cohen (1982) argues that the part of the story concerning the Jews' surrender to Alexander comes from the period when Jerusalem was under the control of his Ptolemaic or Seleucid successors, whereas the part con-

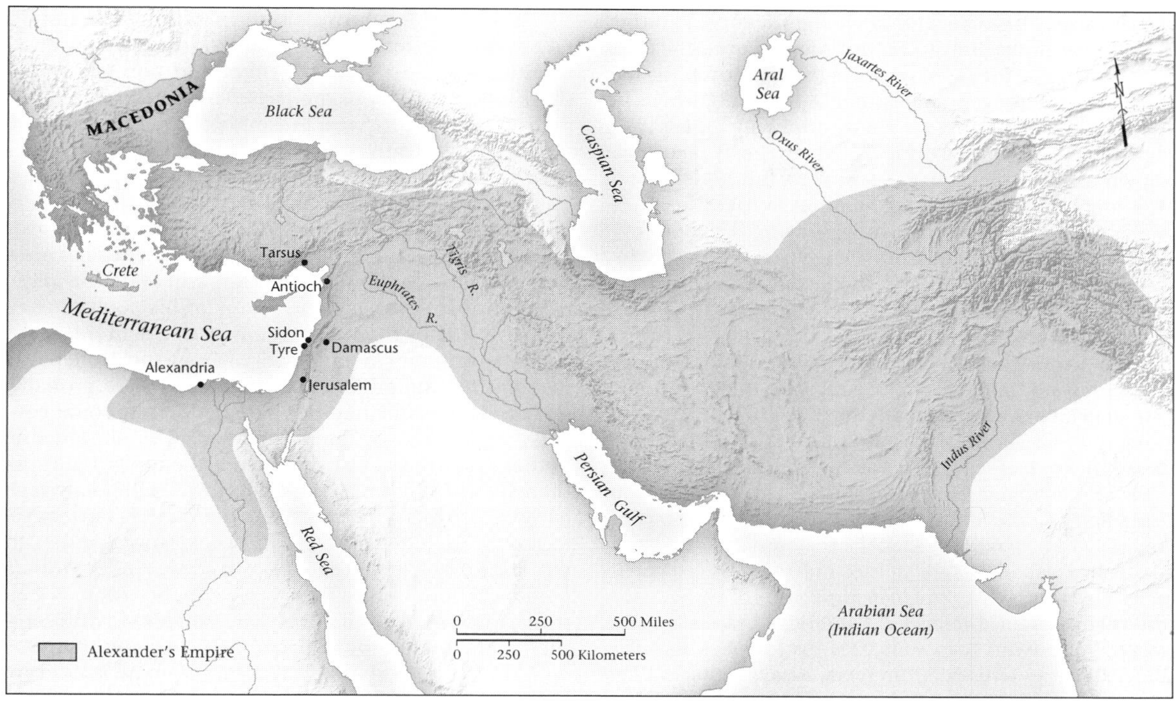

THE EXTENT OF ALEXANDER'S EMPIRE

cerning Alexander's acknowledgment of God is from the Maccabean period. Momigliano (1994) suggests that the whole story could have been created in Egypt rather than Jerusalem, since the image of Macedonians and therefore of Alexander did not suffer among Egyptian Jews as it did in Judea during the Maccabean period.

Some details may reflect reality, however. The Jews, or at least the Temple authorities, had no reason initially to throw off their allegiance to Darius, but Jerusalem had no choice, in view of the fate of Tyre and Gaza, other than to accept Alexander. Someone on Alexander's behalf probably offered sacrifice at the Temple as part of the process of pacifying the occupied region. Jerusalem under Alexander retained the limited autonomy that the Persians had allowed. Some Judeans must have enrolled in Alexander's army, since at Babylon they refused to join the other soldiers in rebuilding the temple of Bel (Josephus, *Ag. Ap.* 1.192). The building of the Samaritan temple on Mt. Gerizim probably happened in Alexander's time. The city of Samaria rebelled against Alexander's governor Andromachus in 331 B.C.E. and was destroyed in reprisal, being refounded as a Macedonian colony (Curtius 4.8-10). The Wadi Daliyeh papyri found near the River Jordan along with about 200 skeletons seem to have been left by the refugees. The monotheistic population of the region regrouped at Shechem, and that is the time to which the building of the temple can be attributed.

The Alexander Romance

The ancient work known as the *Alexander Romance* (sometimes called Pseudo-Callisthenes) existed in many forms, combining historical details about Alexander with activities from the world of myth such as meeting the Amazons. One version includes Alexander's visit to Jerusalem and tries to give it a context, saying that he went from there to Egypt. Some other stories from the *Alexander Romance* found their way into rabbinic literature (e.g., *b. Tamid* 32a). The visit is also found in a talmudic version (*b. Yoma* 69a), with some of the same details as Josephus, particularly Alexander bowing down before the high priest (there called Simeon the Just). However, this tradition puts the episode in the context of a Samaritan attempt to get Alexander's support against the Jews. A medieval Jewish version (Josippon 10) has all Jewish boys born that year being named Alexander, perhaps in an attempt to explain the popularity of the name among Jews.

Other Legends

Alexander is not an important figure in rabbinic tradition, but he is shown on one occasion siding with the Jews against their enemies (*b. Sanhedrin* 91a). There was a legend (*Life of the Prophet Jeremiah* 5–6), probably of Jewish origin, that he removed the bones of Jeremiah to Alexandria in Egypt to provide supernatural protection for his new city. Josephus credits Alexander with giving the Jews of Alexandria equal rights with the Greeks (*Ag. Ap.* 2.43). This is clearly not historical, since any Jewish population of the city before Alexander's death cannot have been of such significance. It rather represents an attempt to recruit Alexander to the later Jewish struggle for equal rights in the city. Josephus has one other reference to Alexander (*Ant.* 2.348), where he mentions the Pamphylian Sea withdrawing for him as a sign that God wanted him to defeat the Persians (as shown also by Alexander's dream of the high priest); this incident is mentioned by other sources less dramatically as a favorable wind allowing Alexander to march along the coast from Phaselis to Perge on the Pamphylian coast.

BIBLIOGRAPHY

E. BICKERMAN 1988, *The Jews in the Greek Age*, Cambridge, Mass.: Harvard University Press, 1-12. • S. J. D. COHEN 1982, "Alexander the Great and Jaddus the High Priest according to Josephus," *AJS Review* 7: 41-68. • C. H. T. FLETCHER-LOUIS 2004, "Alexander the Great's Worship of the High Priest," in *Early Christian and Jewish Monotheism*, ed. L. T. Stuckenbruck and W. E. S. North, London: Clark, 71-102. • M. HENGEL 1989, "The Political and Social History of Palestine from Alexander to Antiochus III (338-187 BCE)," in *Cambridge History of Judaism*, vol. 2, *The Hellenistic Age*, ed. W. D. Davies and L. Finkelstein, Cambridge: Cambridge University Press, 35-78. • A. MOMIGLIANO 1994, "Flavius Josephus and Alexander's Visit to Jerusalem," in idem, *Essays on Ancient and Modern Judaism*, Chicago: University of Chicago Press, 79-87.

DAVID NOY

Alexander Polyhistor

Lucius Cornelius Alexander Polyhistor (ca. 105-35 B.C.E.) was a Greek philosopher, geographer, and historian whose fragmentary writings provide valuable information about the ancient world. In the study of early Judaism, he is best known for having written a book, *On the Jews (Peri Ioudaiōn)*, that presented excerpts from Hellenistic Jewish writers whose works no longer survive.

Alexander was born in Miletus in Asia Minor. He was taken prisoner by the Romans during the war against Mithridates VI (88-84 B.C.E.) and brought to Rome as a slave. There he was manumitted by Sulla in 82 C.E. and remained in Rome, probably for the rest of his life. He was so prolific that he received the surname "Polyhistor," but his work survives only in quoted excerpts. Alexander may be numbered among those writers in antiquity who had no ambition to produce original compositions but who compiled a great deal of information about many regions of the world. His most notable work consisted of forty-two books of historical and geographical material concerning nearly all the countries of the ancient world.

As an epitomist, Alexander's main interest was in geography and the *ethnē* of the Roman Empire, apparently especially the eastern part. In line with this interest, he also collected material about the Jews. To judge from the remaining identifiable fragments of his book *On the Jews*, he wished to present his sources more or less verbatim (here and there switching to indirect speech and providing some connecting sentences).

Alexander Polyhistor's work constituted an important source for some of the church fathers who wanted to cite Hellenistic Jewish writers and non-Jewish authors who wrote about the Jews. Thus Clement of Alexandria (ca. 200 C.E.) and Eusebius of Caesarea (ca. 300 C.E.) took derivative excerpts from Alexander rather than drawing directly on authors such as Eupolemus, Theodotus, and Artapanus. Unfortunately, the fathers used these authors for their own theological purposes and thus picked up very little of them. Their use of Alexander Polyhistor shows that he was still available in the first centuries C.E. and that many of his sources were probably lost by then. Indeed, most of the literature of Hellenistic Judaism vanished early in the Hellenistic era, and Alexander Polyhistor's extracts were probably one of the reasons that they perished. If one could consult his shortened "encyclopedia," why should one bother reading the full versions of the quoted authors themselves? What has survived of the Hellenistic Jewish writers, then, reflects what the church fathers selected for their own limited purposes. However, we can still get some clue to the interests of Alexander and his audience; both he and they were probably interested in the anthropology of the Jews, their ancient history, and their contribution to the pagan world around them.

Most of the existing fragments from Alexander relating to Jews and Judaism derive from Eusebius' *Praeparatio Evangelica* 9.17-39. At the beginning of chap. 17, in a section concerning Abraham's visit to Egypt, Eusebius cites "Alexander Polyhistor, a man of great intellect and much learning, and very well known to those Greeks who have gathered the fruits of education in no perfunctory manner; for in his compilation *Concerning the Jews* he records the history of this man Abraham in the following manner word by word: 'Eupolemus in his book *Concerning the Jews of Assyria* says . . .'" (here Eusebius presents a long quotation). Later (chap. 18) he adduces Artapanus' *Jewish History*, and in chap. 19 he quotes from Apollonius Molon's work *Against the Jews* and other sources. He continues with quotations from Cleodemus Malchus, Demetrius, Theodotus, and others.

Alexander's books probably disappeared for two main reasons: he was certainly not an original thinker, and his work was cannibalized by later authors to such an extent that those who quoted him had a greater chance than he did of surviving in independent volumes.

BIBLIOGRAPHY

J. FREUDENTHAL 1875, *Alexander Polyhistor und die von ihm erhaltenen Reste jüdaischer und samaritanischer Geschichtswerke*, Breslau: Skutsch. • C. R. HOLLADAY 1983, *Fragments from Hellenistic Jewish Authors*, vol. 1, *Historians*, Chico, Calif.: Scholars Press. • F. JACOBY 1964, *Die Fragmente der Griechischen Historiker*, vol. 3A, Leiden: Brill, 262-296, 96-126 (text); 262-296 (commentary), 248-313. • D. MENDELS 2004, *Memory in Jewish, Pagan and Christian Societies of the Graeco-Roman World*, London: Clark, 1-29. • M. STERN 1976, *Greek and Latin Authors on Jews and Judaism*, vol. 1, Jerusalem: Israel Academy of Sciences and Humanities, 157-64.

See also: Apollonius Molon; Artapanus; Berossus; Cleodemus Malchus; Demetrius the Chronographer; Eupolemus; Greek Authors on Jews and Judaism; Philo the Epic Poet; Theodotus DORON MENDELS

Alexandria

Almost from its foundation in 331 B.C.E. until the devastating battles of 115-117 C.E., Alexandria in Egypt stood as the most vibrant intellectual center of the Jewish Diaspora. It was the birthplace and home of Philo, the great Hellenistic Jewish philosopher; the city in which the Pentateuch was translated into Greek; and, if current consensus holds, the urban center inhabited by more Jews than any city in the ancient world.

History

Founded by Alexander the Great on the north coast of Egypt, Alexandria emerged as the most luminous city in the Hellenistic world. After the Roman conquest and annexation of Egypt in 30 B.C.E., Alexandria counted as the greatest city in the Roman Empire, second — or, perhaps, even equal — to Rome. And until the Arab conquest, Alexandria was numbered as one of the great cities of the Christian East. After Alexander's death, Egypt was seized by Alexander's Macedonian schoolmate, Ptolemy, and his name — which was also adopted by the other male rulers of the dynasty — provided the adjective 'Ptolemaic' for the period from 302 to 31 B.C.E.

The capital of Egypt in the Ptolemaic period and the seat of the prefecture after the Roman conquest, Alexandria was a Greek city. It was in Egypt but not of Egypt. In antiquity it was called *Alexandria ad Aegyptum* (Fraser 1972: 1:107), "Alexandria by or near Egypt," and the title of its Roman prefect was *praefectorus Alexandriae et Aegypti* (Gambetti 2003: 42). A city without a past, Alexandria sought aggressively to be Greek.

Topography and Urban Planning

Set on a strip of limestone between the Nile-fed Lake Mareotis to the south and the Mediterranean to the north, Alexandria was auspiciously situated to command trade between eastern emporiums and the Mediterranean world. "Among the happy advantages of the city," says Strabo (*Geography* 17.1.13), "the greatest of all is that it is the only place good by nature for both things from the sea, because of its good harbor, and those from the countryside, because the river easily carries and brings together everything into such a place,

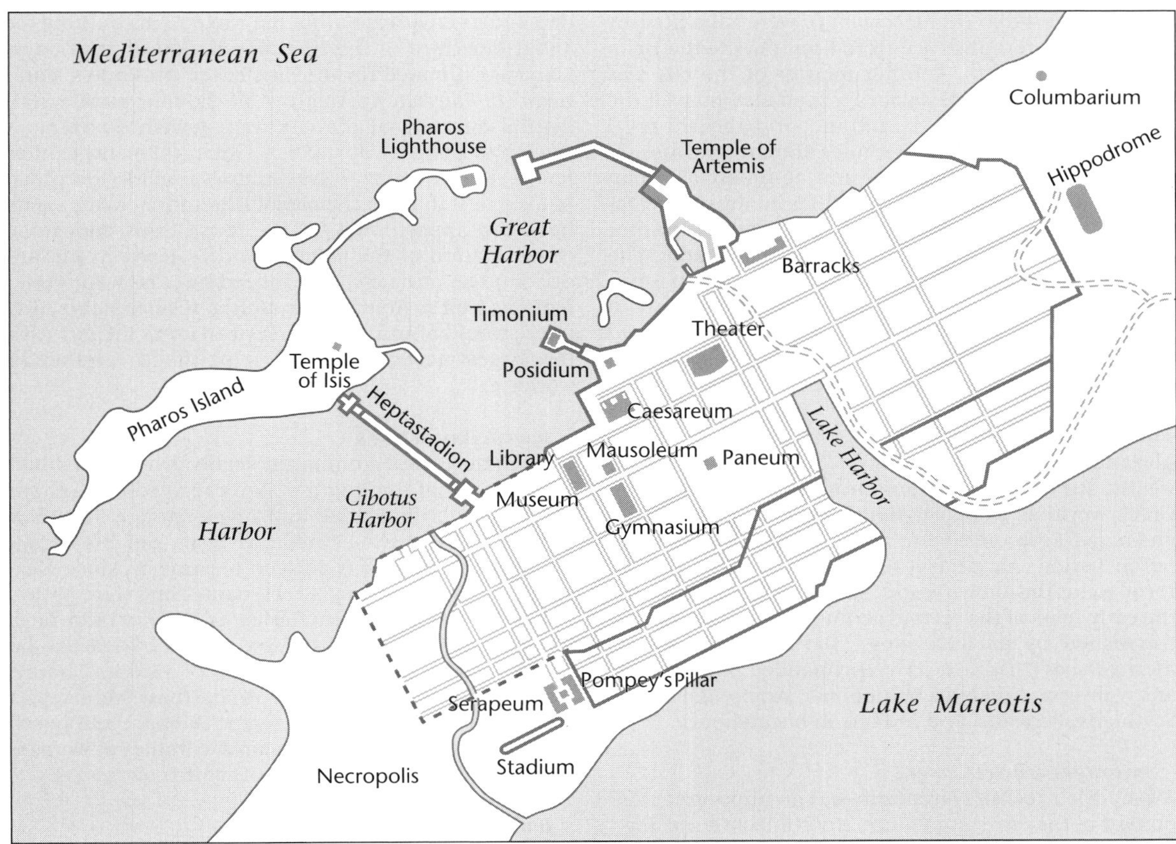

ALEXANDRIA IN THE EARLY ROMAN PERIOD

which indeed is the greatest emporium of the inhabited earth." Its strength and defining factor was its geographical position, which opened it to Egypt and located it as a key crossroad between east and west, attracting both wealth and a polyglot community (Venit 2002:10).

The city was laid out on a Greek Hippodamian plan, with broad streets and avenues that opened it to the Etesian breezes from the north and rendered it unusually salubrious (Strabo, *Geog.* 17.1.7-8). From its foundation, Alexandria was constitutionally fashioned on the Greek *polis,* with the political machinery of a democracy accompanying the autocratic reality of regal power. It had a citizen body *(demos),* a civic law-code, an assembly *(ekklēsia),* a council *(boulē),* a board of magistrates *(prytaneis),* and a body of elders *(gērousia)* (Fraser 1972: 1:93-96). Its citizens were accorded a fictive past by their division into townships *(demes)* and family groups (*phratries;* cf. Fraser 1972: 1:38-48). The city harbored all the physical elements necessary to administer a Greek constitutional government: an agora, a council house, a city hall, and law courts. It also had other amenities that characterize Greek cities, such as athletic fields, gymnasiums, stadiums, theaters, and a hippodrome (Strabo, *Geog.* 17.1.10; Fraser 1972: 1:30).

The city was divided into five quarters named for the first five letters of the Greek alphabet, two of which, according to Philo (*In Flaccum* 55), were inhabited by Jews, though Josephus seems to limit Jews to the Delta quarter (*J.W.* 2.495). Another quarter of the city was given over to the royal palaces, which also housed the Mouseion (Strabo, *Geog.* 17.1.8) and, probably, the royal library (Fraser 1972: 1:335). Under Roman rule, Alexandria remained a lively social and commercial urban center (Strabo, *Geog.* 17.1.7), adding an amphitheater (Strabo, *Geog.* 17.1.10), and through its double harbor passed the wheat that fed the populace of Rome. The city must have shone resplendent in the brilliant Egyptian light. Strabo (*Geog.* 17.1.8) celebrates the glory of its public precincts and, in his novel *Leucippe and Cleitophon,* Achilles Tatius eulogizes the beauty of Alexandria as "beyond [his] eyes' scope."

The Jewish Community

Alexandria's location, its power, its learning, and its wealth attracted immigrants from the breadth of the Greek world as well as Syrians, Persians, Gauls, Jews, and native Egyptians (Venit 2002: 10). By the Roman Imperial Period, Alexandria was home to peoples from throughout the known world. Speaking in Alexandria in the early years of the second century C.E. to a crowd distinguished by its unruliness, Dio Chrystostom (*Ad Alexandrinos* [*Discourse* 32]) reprimanded, in turn, Syrians, Libyans, Cilicians, Ethiopians, Arabs, Bactrians, Scythians, Persians, and Indians in his audience.

Initial Jewish Settlement

Alexandria's Jewish community was an important component of the city's population. Josephus (*Ag. Ap.* 2.43) relates that Alexander himself invited Jews to settle in his eponymously named city, but this account emerges from Josephus' glorification of the Jews and should be discounted (Gruen 2002: 71; 1998: 189-200, esp. 199). Epigraphic and archaeological evidence, however, from the early Alexandrian cemeteries at Chatby and Hadra (Horbury and Noy 1992: 1-13, nos. 1-8; 15-19, nos. 10-12; Venit 2002: 20-21) testify to Jewish burials dating possibly as early as the early third century B.C.E., which indicate substantial Jewish settlement in Alexandria at least as early as the turn of the fourth to the third century.

Ancient sources provide conflicting explanations to account for the initial Jewish presence in the city. The *Letter of Aristeas* (4; 12–13; 23; 35–36) relates that Ptolemy I deported Jews from Jerusalem, but Hecataeus of Abdera, as reported by Josephus (*Ag. Ap.* 1.186-89), and Apion (*Ag. Ap.* 2.33) say that Jews emigrated freely. Josephus (*Ant.* 12.7-9) accepts both accounts, and he may be correct. Since the Ptolemies were intermittently engaged in wars in the Levant beginning in 312 B.C.E., and since much of the Levantine coast was part of the Ptolemaic Empire throughout the third century B.C.E., Jews conceivably entered Alexandria both as captives of war and as newly minted Ptolemaic subjects.

Jewish Population

Diana Delia (1988: 287) tentatively proposed that in the early Roman period the Jewish population in Alexandria and its environs numbered 180,000, accounting for about one-third of the total population of 500,000 to 600,000 estimated for the city. Based on Philo's statement (*In Flaccum* 55) that two of the four private residential quarters of the city were Jewish quarters — though Josephus (*J.W.* 2.488; *Ag. Ap.* 2.35) seems to allot Jews a single quarter — and Strabo's remark (Josephus, *Ant.* 14.117) that "in the city of Alexandria, a large part has been apportioned to [the Jews]," this enormous concentration of the ancient world's Jewry in Alexandria (and its environs) may indeed be correct for Ptolemaic, as well as Roman, Alexandria. If sustainable, this figure would afford Alexandria primacy as the city with the largest Jewish population in the Greco-Roman world.

Jewish Burial Sites

Though the Jewish community seems to have inhabited two (or one) of the quarters, Jews resided throughout the city, according to Philo (*In Flaccum* 55), and their burials in the city's cemeteries bears out his claim. Though the evidence is difficult to come by, since Alexandria's Jews often bore Greek names and were always buried in the same cemeteries as Greeks (and later Romans), relatively well-attested Jewish burials can be noted for the eastern cemeteries of Hadra, Chatby, Ibrahimiya, and Moustapha Pasha (now Moustapha Kamel), in the western cemetery at Gabbari, and possibly at the Roman-period catacomb complex at Kom el-Shoqafa to the south of the city (Venit 2002: 20-21).

Jewish Civic Status

In the Ptolemaic period, the Jewish community held a special place in the city. Along with other foreigners, a small number of Jewish residents were possibly granted Alexandrian citizenship as early as the third century (see Fraser 1972: 1:49-50) but, as important, those resident in Alexandria were counted among the Macedonians (Josephus, *J.W.* 2.488), which located them below the Greeks, but of higher status than Egyptians. Uniquely for Alexandria, the Jewish community probably constituted a *politeia* — a corporate body of citizens comprised of residents from a foreign country — at least as early as the mid-second century B.C.E. (see Fraser 1972: 1:85). According to Strabo (Josephus, *Ant.* 14.117) "an *ethnarch* of [the Jews] is appointed, who governs the ethnic group and arbitrates disputes and oversees contracts and ordinances (?), as if ruling an autonomous state." Under Ptolemy VI Philometor, at least two Jews, Onias and Dositheos, served as generals (Josephus, *Ag. Ap.* 2.49), and Jews occupied the highest offices of the state (Fraser 1972: 1:83-84, 688).

Under Roman rule, it is likely that a few Jewish families retained Alexandrian citizenship. In the first century C.E., members of Philo's family seem to have held Alexandrian citizenship; his brother Alexander held the office of *alabarch,* one of the highest offices in the city; and, under the Roman emperor Nero, Alexander's son Tiberius Julius Alexander became the "Prefect of Alexandria and Egypt."

During the Ptolemaic period and under Roman rule, Jewish religious practice was countenanced. Philo (*Legat.* 20.132) notes a great many synagogues throughout the city, and inscriptions bear him out (see Fraser 1972: 1:84; Horbury and Noy 1992: 13-15, no. 9; 19-21, no. 13; 23-26, nos. 16 and 17; 30-32, no. 19; cf. Gruen 2002: 283, note 109). One of these synagogues was so large and so splendidly appointed that it is mentioned in the Jerusalem Talmud (*y. Sukk.* 5:1, 55 a-b; cf. Modrzejewski 1997: 91).

Jewish Social Life

Alexandria's Jewish population was integrated into all aspects of the everyday life of the city. Jews served in the Ptolemaic army as soldiers, officers (Josephus, *Ant.* 13.284-87), and at least twice as generals as well as traders, farmers, ships' captains, merchants, and artisans (Philo, *In Flaccum* 56–57). Philo (*Legat.* 7.45) speaks familiarly of the theater, the gymnastic games, and contests at the hippodrome, and though the gymnasium and the education it provided would have been off-limits to Jews who were not citizens, Jews appear to have enjoyed theatrical performances and games. Their Hellenization may be further measured by the relatively few assuredly Jewish burials that have come to light in Alexandria in great contrast to the size of the Jewish population of the city. The burial customs of Alexandria's Jewish inhabitants followed those of Alexandrians.

Jewish Literature

Much of Alexandria's Jewish population regarded Greek as their mother tongue (Sterling 2001: 273-74), and it is quite likely that the Pentateuch was translated into Greek, not for the edification of Ptolemy II Philadelphus as vaunted in the *Letter of Aristeas,* but in order to instruct Alexandrian Jews, who no longer easily read Hebrew. Alexandria's Jewish intelligentsia, some of whom like Philo must have had a Greek education, were conversant with Greek literature and Greek literary forms. Alexandria was an especially important center of learning in the Hellenistic world and, among all the cities of the Diaspora, it is in Alexandria that Hellenistic-Jewish literature most greatly flourished. In addition to the translation of the Septuagint, and the writings of the philosopher Philo, Alexandria may be credited with the *Sibylline Oracles* and the *Letter of Aristeas* and perhaps with the writings of the chronographer Demetrius, the historian Artapanus, and the playwright Ezekiel. The Wisdom of Solomon was almost certainly written in Alexandria, while the novels *Joseph and Aseneth* and 3 Maccabees both come from Egypt, though probably not from the city itself (Bartlett 1985: 5; Sterling 2001: 288-89)

Jewish Relations with Greeks

Until Roman intervention in Egypt, Greeks and Jews coexisted relatively peacefully in Alexandria. 3 Maccabees tells a story of horrific anti-Jewish activity under the reign of Ptolemy IV Philopator (221-203 B.C.E.). Josephus (*Ag. Ap.* 2.49-56) ascribes it to Ptolemy VII Physcon (146-117 B.C.E.), but this dating is questionable. The story has legendary qualities in any case. Both the remote and immediate causes for the anti-Jewish outbreak in 38 C.E. are subjects much debated in modern scholarship. Josephus (*J.W.* 2.487) notes a growing tension that culminated in the anti-Jewish riots of 38-41 C.E. Sandra Gambetti (2003: 129-45) has suggested that ancient Egyptian enmity toward Jews, documented since the history of Egypt written by Manetho for Ptolemy I in the third century B.C.E., coupled with Greek assimilation of this anti-Jewish Egyptian literature, contributed to the contempt for Alexandria's Jews from the late Ptolemaic period onward.

Pieter W. van der Horst (2003: 24-33) has recently argued for a long-standing Greek hatred of Alexandrian Jews; others have tempered that assessment (e.g., Collins 2005: 191-97). Nevertheless, Greeks could only have resented Jewish support of the Roman invaders, for the Jewish community had sided with the Romans in 57 B.C.E. and again in 48-47 B.C.E. (Kasher 1985: 12-18; Smallwood 1961: 11; van der Horst 2003: 20-21). Further, the rift between the two groups must have deepened with the Roman conquest of Egypt in 30 C.E., which changed the status of both Alexandria's Greek population and its Jewish community. Alexandria's Greeks lost their council (the *boulē*) (Fraser 1972: 1:94) and, most importantly, the sovereignty they had enjoyed for three centuries. The capital of Ptolemaic Egypt became part of a Roman province and was ruled by a prefect chosen by the emperor in Rome. Concurrently, with the Roman conquest of Egypt, Alexandria's Jews retained their "autonomous state," with only the replacement of the *ethnarch* (Strabo, quoted by Josephus *Ant.* 14.117) by a council of elders *(gērousia)* (Philo, *In Flaccum* 74), but lost their position in the ethnic hierarchy. No longer "Macedonians," Jews could not aspire to Alexandrian citizenship nor the Greek education that opened portals to a rich political and social life. Further, like Egyptians (from whom they assiduously tried to distance themselves), they were forced to suffer the financial burden and social indignity of a poll tax (though this is disputed by Kasher 1985: 19; Gruen 2002: 75-77).

Anti-Jewish Outbreak in 38 C.E.

In 38 C.E., two events coalesced to upset the tenuous status quo between the two communities. Herod Agrippa I, who had been appointed king of Syria by the Roman emperor Gaius (Caligula), visited Alexandria, and Flaccus, the Roman prefect, rescinded the special privileges held by Jews. Nationalistic Greeks resented the elevation of a Jewish king and, repudiating any vestige of loyalty to the emperor in Rome, they openly mocked Agrippa. Jews were devastated by both the seemingly officially condoned behavior of the Greeks and by their own loss of status. During the riots, Jews were confined by Flaccus to the Delta quarter; the quarter(s) of their own that had formerly been considered an entitlement now served as a restriction (Fraser 1972: 1:56). These events are described most fully in *In Flaccum* (17–96) and the *Legatio ad Gaium* (120–36) by Philo, who lived through the riots and participated in the embassy to Gaius intended to restore the Jewish privileges.

The Letter of Claudius

After the death of Gaius in 41 C.E., as recorded in the *Letter of Claudius to the Alexandrians* (P. London 1912), the new emperor Claudius did restore the old privileges to Alexandria's Jews, but he "explicitly order[ed] the Jews not to agitate for more privileges than they formerly possessed," which presumably maintained their poll tax. At the same time, he urged that "the Alexandrians show themselves forbearing and kindly towards the Jews who for many years have dwelt in the same city, and dishonor none of the rites observed by them in the worship of their god, but allow them to observe their customs." In the years between 41 and 66 C.E., little hostility between Greeks and Jews is recorded in Alexandria.

The Riot in 66 C.E.

In 66 C.E., Tiberius Julius Alexander was appointed prefect of Egypt by Nero, and that year witnessed another confrontation between Greeks and Jews. Josephus (*J.W.* 2.490-98) is the single source for the event, which began during an assembly in the amphitheater and then spilled out into the city. "Recognizing that nothing but a major catastrophe would stop the revolutionaries" (*J.W.* 494), Tiberius Alexander called upon his legions, both those stationed in Alexandria and those arrived by chance from neighboring Libya, to quell the rioters. The legions set upon the Jews, who were concentrated in the Delta quarter, plundering their possessions, burning down their houses, and killing with "no pity toward the infants [and] no reverence for the old" (*J.W.* 2.496). Josephus reports, with possible exaggeration, that 50,000 Jews were killed during the massacre.

The Diaspora Uprisings

Ancient Alexandria's Jewish community, however, suffered its most severe blow — and one from which it would never recover — during the revolt of 115/116-117 C.E. Jews in Cyrene and Cyprus rose up against Roman rule, and they were shortly followed by those in Egypt. The uprisings were crushed by the Roman legions and, though Alexandria retained a Jewish presence (Horbury and Noy 1992: 22-23, no. 15 and 23-25, no. 16, for example, note two late-Roman synagogue dedications from the city), the vibrant intellectual life that distinguished Alexandria's Jewish community was extinguished.

BIBLIOGRAPHY

J. R. BARTLETT 1985, *Jews in the Hellenistic World: Josephus, Aristeas, The Sibylline Oracles, Eupolemus,* Cambridge: Cambridge University Press. • J. J. COLLINS 2005, "Anti-Semitism in Antiquity: The Case of Alexandria," in idem, *Jewish Cult and Hellenistic Culture: Essays on the Jewish Encounter with Hellenism and Roman Rule,* Leiden: Brill. • D. DELIA 1988, "The Population of Roman Alexandria," *Transactions of the American Philological Association,* 118: 275–92. • D. DELIA 1991, *Alexandrian Citizenship during the Roman Principate,* Atlanta: Scholars Press. • P. M. FRASER 1972, *Ptolemaic Alexandria,* 3 vols., Oxford: Clarendon. • S. GAMBETTI 2009, *The Alexandrian Riots of 38 CE and the Persecution of the Jews: A Historical Assessment,* Leiden: Brill. • E. S. GRUEN 1998, *Heritage and Hellenism: The Reinvention of the Jewish Tradition,* Berkeley: University of California Press. • E. S. GRUEN 2002, *Diaspora: Jews amidst Greeks and Romans,* Cambridge, Mass.: Harvard University Press. • W. HORBURY AND D. NOY 1992, *Jewish Inscriptions of Graeco-Roman Egypt,* Cambridge: Cambridge University Press. • P. W. VAN DER HORST 2003, *Philo's* Flaccus: *The First Pogrom,* Leiden: Brill. • A. KASHER 1985, *The Jews in Hellenistic and Roman Egypt: The Struggle for Equal Rights,* Tübingen: Mohr-Siebeck. • J. M. MODRZEJEWSKI 1995, *The Jews of Egypt from Rameses II to Emperor Hadrian,* trans. R. Cornman, Philadelphia: Jewish Publication Society. • D. I. SLY 1996, *Philo's Alexandria,* London: Routledge. • E. M. SMALLWOOD 1961, *Philonis Alexandrini: Legatio ad Gaium,* Leiden: Brill. • G. E. STERLING 2001, "Judaism between Jerusalem and Alexandria," in *Hellenism in the Land of Israel,* ed. J. J. Collins and G. E. Sterling, Notre Dame: University of Notre Dame Press, 263-301. • V. TCHERIKOVER 1959, *Hellenistic Civilization and the Jews,* Philadelphia: Jewish Publication Society. • V. TCHERIKOVER AND A. FUKS, EDS. 1957-64, *Corpus Papyrorum Judaicarum,* 3 vols., Cambridge: Harvard University Press. • M. S. VENIT 2002, *Monumental Tombs of Ancient Alexandria: The Theater of the Dead,* Cambridge: Cambridge University Press.

See also: Diaspora Uprisings; Egypt; Philo of Alexandria MARJORIE S. VENIT

Allegory

Allegory as a literary genre should be distinguished from allegory as a hermeneutical tool. Allegory proper is a literary form in which a web of intratextual relationships both intends and invites a transferred interpretation through the use of overt symbolism. As a mode of interpretation, allegorism (or allegoresis) refers to the *imposition* of transferred senses upon a text, either naïvely or self-consciously.

Allegory as Literary Genre

Allegory in the most basic sense is a form of extended metaphor, closely related to the parable. Early twentieth-century biblical scholarship encouraged a distinction between parable and allegory on the grounds that the former necessarily presupposes a singular point of comparison. This insistence is now generally abandoned in recognition that parable and allegory represent a continuum rather than a rigid categorical distinction. The Hebrew term *māšāl* covers both.

Allegory in the strict sense is comparatively rare in the Jewish Scriptures. Among the possible examples — some perhaps better seen as parable — are Nathan's prophetic *māšāl* against David (2 Sam. 12:1-4) and Isaiah's *māšāl* of the vineyard (Isa. 5:1-6). Several passages in Ezekiel come closer to allegory proper. These include treatment of Samaria and Jerusalem as two adulterous sisters (Ezekiel 16, 23) and the story of the vine and two eagles (Ezekiel 17).

A long history of interpretation saw in the Song of Songs an allegory of God's love for Israel. Modern scholars rightly see the Song as love poetry without inherent allegorical intention. This tradition may have been spawned by the influence of other scriptural texts (e.g., Hosea, Jeremiah) where a spousal relationship serves as an extended metaphor for the covenant between God and God's people. By its very nature, intertextual interpretation invites the transposition of meaning (*allēgorein* = *alla agoreuein,* "saying something else").

Apocalyptic literature poses a special problem. Here one finds an extensive web of symbolism that borders on the allegoristic insofar as it relies on a set of stock images (e.g., beasts as nations; horns as rulers), is frequently transparent in its context (e.g., the "historical" apocalypses), and serves a larger narrative goal. At the same time, unnatural and violent combinations of images effect a surrealism quite foreign to allegory in its more familiar didactic forms.

An example of the allegoristic tendency in apocalyptic literature is the so-called *Animal Apocalypse* (*1 Enoch* 85–90). Composed during the Maccabean Revolt, this text offers a symbolic narrative of biblical history from Adam to the coming of the messiah. The chosen nation is represented as a flock of sheep, its patriarchs and heroes as rams and bulls, its enemies as wild beasts (dogs, wolves, lions), fallen angels by stars, and the messiah by a white bull.

Allegorism as Hermeneutical Tool

The adoption of allegorical hermeneutics by Jewish authors in the Hellenistic period should be seen against the backdrop of contemporary allegorical readings of Homer and Hesiod. Such readings served the dual purpose of saving the Greek myths from their anthropomorphic portrayal of the gods and giving newly minted philosophical doctrines an appropriately ancient pedigree. This development also reflects the inherent tension that arises when a text attains sacred or quasi-sacred ("culture-defining") status: the "truth of the text" and the "truths of the culture" must coinhere in such a way that "new" truths can be accommodated and new "problems" can be neutralized. Allegorical interpretation is ideally suited to this task, for it reads into the text the very truths it subsequently claims to find.

Aristobulus and *Letter of Aristeas*

The fragments of Aristobulus and the *Letter of Aristeas,* both dating to the second century B.C.E., are the earliest surviving examples of Jewish allegoresis. In two of five fragments preserved by Eusebius of Caesarea, Aristobulus shows special concern to explain some of the more anthropomorphic images of God in the Jewish Scriptures. Thus, references to God's "hand" designate God's power; God's "standing" and God's "voice" refer to establishing the created order; and the theophany at Sinai revealed God's majesty without requiring a literal and local "descent" (frgs. 2, 4).

The *Letter of Aristeas,* best known for its legend of the origin of the Septuagint, uses allegory to show that the distinctive dietary customs of the Jews have a logical underlying rationale (§§128-71). To this end, anatomical and behavioral traits of animals are viewed as symbols of human behavior to be imitated or avoided. Thus the prohibition of predatory or carnivorous birds teaches one to reject violent behavior. Various domestic ruminants are permitted for food because rumination symbolizes the remembrance of God. The divided hoof, moreover, symbolizes the ability to make moral distinctions and the separation of Jews from the nations. According to *Aristeas,* the dietary laws are not arbitrary but intended to mold human conduct to just ends.

Philo of Alexandria

The use of allegory as a hermeneutical tool is most clearly attested in the writings of the first-century-C.E. philosopher and exegete Philo of Alexandria, whose name is often simplistically equated with the allegorical method itself. It is therefore important to note that Philo frequently refers to predecessors from whom he has inherited certain interpretations (*De Abrahamo* 99), as well as contemporary allegorists with whom he disagrees (*De Posteritate Caini* 41–42). Philo thus stands within a tradition that was both broader and deeper than the extant literature permits us to trace.

Although Philo occasionally rejects the literal interpretation of Scripture entirely (e.g., *Somn.* 1.92-95), more typically he finds both literal and figurative meanings, and he positions himself against those who favor an exclusive allegiance to one or the other. He expresses impatience both with those who disbelieve miraculous events (*Mos.* 1.212) and with those who fail to see beyond literal interpretations (*De Confusione Linguarum* 190). He criticizes those for whom literalism is an excuse to ridicule the text as absurd (*De Mutatione Nominum* 60–61), as well as those whose devotion to spiritual mysteries leads them to neglect the letter of the Law entirely (*De Migratione Abrahami* 89–93). In short, not all allegory is Philonic, and Philonic exegesis is not exclusively allegorical.

Like Aristobulus, Philo is sensitive to anthropomorphic and anthropopathic descriptions of God, which he seeks to neutralize (*De Confusione Linguarum* 134–36). Philo allegorizes the dietary laws in a manner similar to Aristeas but places this tradition in a larger philosophical framework, focusing on the dangers of passion and pleasure (*Spec. Leg.* 4.79-118). On occasion Philo even adapts contemporary Homeric allegory. His equation of Hagar, the handmaid of Sarah, with education, the handmaid of virtue (*De Congressu* 23), presupposes a Stoic topos about Penelope (= philosophy) and her suitors.

The methods employed by Philo include numerology, associative logic, etymology, and paronomasia. Thus, for example, the number four might evoke the four cardinal virtues or vices (*Leg. Alleg.* 1.63); the number five, the five senses (*De Opificio Mundi* 62). The trees of Paradise symbolize virtues planted in the soul (*De Plantatione* 36–37), while the serpent, which crawls on its belly, symbolizes a life devoted to pleasure (*De Opificio Mundi* 157–59). In a pseudo-etymology worthy of Plato's *Cratylus*, the name "Aaron" is interpreted as "mountainous," playing on the Hebrew word *har* (*De Ebrietate* 128). A superfluous word or unusual expression was a clue to dig for deeper significance, and Philo often finds meaning in the subtle differentiation of synonyms (e.g., *Quod Deterius* 104).

Early Christian Writings

Examples of allegory in the New Testament are relatively few. In 1 Cor. 10:1-4 Paul argues that the Israelites in the wilderness enjoyed spiritual food and drink, and the spiritual "rock" from which they drank was Christ (cf. Philo, *Leg. Alleg.* 2.86, who identifies the rock as "wisdom"). In Gal. 4:21-31 Paul treats Sarah and Hagar as symbols of two covenants, one based on promise, the other bound by the Law. Elsewhere, Paul explains Jewish rejection of the gospel by comparing Israel to an olive tree from which some branches have been pruned so that others (= Gentile Christians) might be grafted in (Rom. 11:17-24).

Jesus' parable of the sower illustrates well the continuum between parable and allegory. In the Synoptic Parable of the Sower, each seed is equated with a specific type of response to the message of Jesus (Mark 4:3-9, 14-20 and pars.). Scholars debate whether such specific details are secondary developments (cf. the shorter version of the parable in *Gospel of Thomas* 9). Other Synoptic parables that approach the allegorical include the parable of the weeds, the parable of the tenants, and the parable of the wedding banquet (Matt. 13:24-30, 36-43; 21:33-45; 22:1-14). At the far end of this spectrum one finds the second-century *Shepherd of Hermas*, whose "similitudes" border on full-fledged allegory.

The *Epistle of Barnabas* (ca. 130-135 C.E.) illustrates the growing Christian tendency to allegorize parts of the Jewish Scriptures whose literal interpretation was perceived as problematic. Whereas Aristeas and Philo had used allegory to clarify and support the observance of Jewish cultic practices, Barnabas turns this tradition on its head and spiritualizes these practices completely. For Barnabas, circumcision is strictly a matter of the heart, true fasting signifies social justice, and the dietary laws merely symbolize types of behavior to be emulated or avoided.

The subsequent history of allegorism among Christian writers reflects in large measure the reception and transmission of the writings of Philo. Philonic influence is particularly strong in the works of Clement, Origen, Eusebius, Gregory of Nyssa, and Ambrose of Milan.

Bibliography

Y. Amir 1988, "Authority and Interpretation of Scripture in the Writings of Philo," in *Mikra: Text, Translation, Reading, and Interpretation of the Hebrew Bible in Ancient Judaism and Early Christianity,* ed. M. J. Mulder and H. Sysling, Assen: Van Gorcum; Philadelphia: Fortress, 421-53. • J. D. Crossan 1973, "Parable as Religious and Poetic Experience," *JR* 53: 330-58. • R. P. C. Hanson 1959, *Allegory and Event: A Study of the Sources and Significance of Origen's Interpretation of Scripture,* London: SCM. • J. N. Rhodes 2004, *The Epistle of Barnabas and the Deuteronomic Tradition: Polemics, Paraenesis, and the Legacy of the Golden-Calf Incident,* Tübingen: Mohr-Siebeck. • D. T. Runia 1993, *Philo in Early Christian Literature: A Survey,* Assen: Van Gorcum; Minneapolis: Fortress, 1993. • F. J. Siegert 1996, "Early Jewish Interpretation in a Hellenistic Style," in *Hebrew Bible/Old Testament: The History of Its Interpretation,* vol. 1, ed. M. Saebo, Göttingen: Vandenhoeck & Ruprecht, 130-98.

James N. Rhodes

Almsgiving

Hebrew Bible

Early Jewish practice of almsgiving is typically associated with two of the most fundamental principles in the Israelite religious thought — *ḥesed* (mercy) and *ṣedeq* (righteousness). Charitable giving became such an important expression of the divine and human quality of mercy and righteousness that several modes of its observance were listed in the Torah. There is no singular term in classical Hebrew, however, that precisely embodies the act of charitable giving to the poor and the marginalized of the society.

The Mosaic Law presumes an agricultural, rural, and independent community for the inhabitants of the land. Customary charitable gifts entailed permission to the needy to access cultivated lands for the produce. According to Lev. 19:9-10, "When you reap the harvest of your land, you shall not reap to the very edges of your field, or gather the gleanings of your harvest. You shall not strip your vineyard bare, or gather the fallen grapes of your vineyard; you shall leave them for the poor and the alien." Landowners are also commanded every seventh year to let the crop "rest and lie fallow, so that the poor of your people may eat" (Exod. 23:11). The Deuteronomist stipulates a generous and compassionate credit system on behalf of the members of the community in need even when the Year of Remission may be drawing near (Deut. 15:7-15). It is not clear, however, whether and to what extent these ordinances were actually fulfilled. Communal and individual care for the poor might have been considered a voluntary contribution rather than a practice to be enforced by the law.

In the postexilic period, the Diaspora and urbanization made tithing and jubilee no longer applicable. The previously pastoral and agricultural economy was now joined by a fast-growing population of merchants and artisans — a significant shift away from patrimonial lands to towns and cities. Consequently, donations for the poor were also made in the form of money.

The concern for the welfare of the poor was not solely financial. Financial plight was often accompanied by deprivation of justice. The Hebrew prophets lambaste the corrupt and greedy elites of the Israelite society (i.e., judges, nobles, landholders, and bureaucrats) for taking advantage of the poor (Isa. 3:14-15; 10:1-2; Jer. 5:28; Amos 8:4-6). There are a number of prohibitions against perverting the justice due to the poor in lawsuits. There are also warnings that ultimately YHWH maintains the cause of the needy and executes justice for the poor (Exod. 23:6; Lev. 19:15; Pss. 72:2; 140:12; Qoh. 5:8; Isa. 10:2). Hence, an ideal king is described as one who hearkens to the cause of the poor and afflicted (Psalm 72; Prov. 29:14; Jer. 22:15-16; Dan. 4:24).

Apocrypha and Pseudepigrapha

Apocryphal books commonly explore the themes of mercy and righteousness. There is an expressed desire to adhere to the Mosaic commandments, including provision for widows and orphans. Tobit and Ben Sira recommend almsgiving for its pragmatic value for Jews displaced from the land of Israel since almsgiving is the equivalent of sacrifice (Sir. 3:30) and saves from physical death (4:8-11). There is no promise of eternal rewards or resurrection in exchange. Other apocryphal books, such as the Wisdom of Solomon, still feature mercy and righteousness prominently. Yet they do not specifically refer to almsgiving. The Pseudepigrapha stress the eternal consequences of almsgiving. They promise rewards in heaven for the righteous (*2 Enoch* [J] 9:1; 51), while proper retribution awaits those who oppress the poor (*2 Enoch* 10:5). The *Sibylline Oracles* attest to the benevolent "share of the harvest" by some wealthy Jews with the poor (3.234-47).

New Testament

The Gospels regularly depict Jesus showing and calling for preferential concern for the welfare of the poor (Matt. 11:5; 19:21; 26:9-11; Mark 10:21; Luke 4:18; 6:20-21; 7:22; 14:13, 21; 18:22; 19:8; John 12:5-6). Examples on how to care for the poor are listed in Matt. 25:31-46. Here those who feed the hungry, practice hospitality to strangers, and visit the sick and the imprisoned are extolled as the "righteous" who will enter into eternal life. Jesus' ministry is prominently associated with beggars, lepers, and widows; and presumably he made occasional monetary donations to the poor (John 13:29). Acts of mercy attain eternal reward in heaven (Luke 14:13-14; Mark 10:21). The polemical edge in Matt. 6:1-5 suggests that almsgiving was viewed as an expression of religious piety. This passage also demonstrates that spontaneous gifts to the poor in public spaces were practiced. Acts 3:2-3 indicates that begging alms from the people going into the Temple was common in the late Second Temple period. Both the book of Acts and Paul's letters depict the apostle reminding his Gentile converts of their obligation to help the needy: "In all this I have given you an example that by such work we must support the weak, remembering the words of the Lord Jesus, for he himself said, 'It is more blessed to give than to receive'" (Acts 20:35; cf., e.g., 1 Thess. 5:12; on Paul's collection for the poor saints in Jerusalem, see 1 Cor. 16:1-12; Gal. 2:10; 2 Corinthians 8–9; Rom. 15:25-29).

Rabbinic Judaism

In the aftermath of the destruction of the Temple in 70 C.E., Rabbi Yoḥanan ben Zakkai and his colleagues inaugurated a new chapter in Judaism. The rabbis implemented a kind of "emergency" ruling that essentially redefined Jewish piety as the study of Torah, the act of prayer, and the practice of charity. R. Yoḥanan reinterpreted the meaning of sacrificial atonement; in a famous tradition, he consoled a grieving rabbi at the ruins of the Temple, "Be not grieved; we have another atonement as effective as this. And what is it? It is acts of loving-kindness, as it is said, 'For I desire mercy *(ḥesed)* and not sacrifice' [Hos. 6:6]" (*ʾAbot R. Nat.* 34). According to the Mishnah, Shimon HaṢaddik declared that the world stood on three pillars: Torah, Temple service, and acts of loving-kindness (*m. ʾAbot* 1:2). Rabbis used the Aramaic term *ṣdq* to mean "almsgiving," affirming the fundamental truth that *ṣĕdāqâ* or righteousness is simply doing the right thing.

BIBLIOGRAPHY

R. B. BECKNELL 2000, "Almsgiving: The Jewish Legacy of Justice and Mercy," Dissertation, Miami University. • C. BOERMA 1980, *The Rich, the Poor — and the Bible,* Philadelphia: Westminster Press. • G. CLARK 1993, *The Word Ḥesed in the Hebrew Bible,* Sheffield: Sheffield Academic Press. • Z. FALK 1992, "Law and Ethics in the Hebrew Bible," in *Justice and Righteousness: Biblical Themes and Their Influence,* ed. H. G. Reventlow and Y. Hoffman, Sheffield: JSOT Press, 82-90. • E. FRISCH 1924, *An Historical Survey of Jewish Philanthropy,* New York: Macmillan. • N. LOHFINK 1991, "Poverty in the Laws of the Ancient Near East and of the Bible," *TS* 52: 34-50. • F. ROSENTHAL 1950-51, "Sedaka, Charity," *HUCA* 23: 411-30. • E. P. SANDERS 1977, *Paul and Palestinian Judaism: A Comparison of Patterns of Religion,* Philadelphia: Fortress Press.

KYONG-JIN LEE

AMRAM, VISIONS OF

ʿAm Ha-ʾAretz → People of the Land

Amram, Visions of

The Aramaic *Visions of Amram* is a fragmentary pseudepigraphic text from Qumran Cave 4. Together with the *Visions of Levi* (or *Aramaic Levi Document*), *Admonitions* (or *Testament*) *of Qahat,* and the Aramaic *Astronomical Book,* it forms a corpus of priestly didactic literature (Drawnel 2004, 2006b). This priestly literature grew out of the experience of levitical priestly teachers and, in the case of the *Visions of Levi* and the Aramaic *Astronomical Book,* is unquestionably influenced by the didactic practices of Babylonian school tradition and scribal arithmetical knowledge (Drawnel 2006a).

The *Visions of Amram* is preserved in five manuscripts that by overlapping indicate their mutual relationship (4Q543, 4Q544, 4Q545, 4Q546, 4Q547). Two other manuscripts (4Q548, 4Q549) do not overlap with the rest of the composition but have been added to it on the basis of paleographical similarities and thematic parallels; hence, their connection to the composition remains hypothetical.

The manuscripts date paleographically from different periods: 4Q543, 4Q544, and 4Q547 were written in the second half of the second century B.C.E.; 4Q545 and 4Q546 were copied in the first half of the first century B.C.E.; and 4Q548 and 4Q549 are dated to the second half of the first century B.C.E. (Puech 2001: 285-87). All the manuscripts are copies of the Aramaic text, while the composition of the pseudepigraphon is tentatively dated to the third century B.C.E., but not later than the first half of the second century B.C.E. The work must have been written before the book of *Jubilees,* usually dated to the middle of the second century B.C.E., since the latter knows about the war between Egypt and Canaan at the time of the burial of the patriarchs in Hebron (*Jub.* 46:9-11). The same event is mentioned in the *Visions of Amram* (4Q544 frg. 1 lines 1-9).

Like his grandfather Levi and father Qahat, Amram does not fulfill any priestly duties in the Hebrew Bible, which gives only a few details of his life. The Pentateuch says that Amram was the son of Qahat (Exod. 6:18; Num. 3:19; 26:58) and that he took to wife his father's sister Jochebed, who bore him Aaron, Moses, and Miriam (Exod. 6:20; Num. 26:59). The postexilic book of 1 Chronicles mentions Amram among the sons of Qahat (1 Chron. 5:28; 6:3; 23:12) and cites his own descendants (1 Chron. 5:29; 23:13) in the context of levitical genealogies.

Although the manuscripts of the *Visions of Amram* are very fragmentary, a succession of events may be hypothetically reconstructed. The beginning of the book is well preserved, but the end is lacking. The preserved text can be divided into two parts: a narrative framework and an autobiographical account in the first-person singular. The two sections can be outlined as follows:

- I. Narrative framework
  - A. General presentation of the content and chronological details (4Q543 1 1-4a (= frg. 1, lines 1-4a); 4Q545 1a i 1-4a (= frg. 1a, col. i, lines 1-4a)
  - B. Marriage of Amram's brother Uzziel to Amram's daughter Mariam (4Q543 1 4b-7a; 4Q545 1a i 4b-7a).
  - C. Meeting with Aaron (4Q543 1 7b-9a)
- II. Autobiographical account
  - A. Amram's speech to Aaron
    1. Direct call on Aaron to gather all the brothers (4Q543 1 9b-10; 4Q545 1a i 9b-10).
    2. Aaron's wisdom and glorious future as God's messenger/angel and judge (4Q545 1a i 11-13; 4Q543 2a-b).
  - B. Sojourn in Hebron
    1. Travel to Hebron in the company of the sons of Amram's uncles (4Q544 1 1-2a; 4Q545 1a-b ii 11-15a).
    2. Return of the company to Egypt; Amram remains in Hebron to build the tombs for the sons of Jacob (4Q544 1 2b-4a; 4Q545 1a-b ii 15b-18).
    3. Canaan and Philistines fight against Egypt, while Amram stays in Hebron (4Q544 1 4b-8; 4Q545 1a-b ii 19).
    4. Return of Amram in Egypt foretold (4Q544 1 9a).
  - C. Amram's vision of two angelic beings
    1. Dialogue between Amram and the two angels/judges (4Q544 1 9b-12).
    2. Description of the angel of darkness and angel of light (4Q544 1 13-15; 4Q543 frgs. 5-9, 4-8; frgs. 10 and 14).
    3. Dialogue with the angel of light (4Q544 frgs. 2 and 3).
    4. Glorious future of Aaron and Moses (4Q545 4; 4Q546 7-12).
    5. Sacrifice at Sinai and glorious future of a priest (Aaron?) (4Q547 9 1-7).
    6. End of Amram's vision (4Q547 9 8-11).
  - D. Amram's speech to Aaron and all his descendants
    1. Instruction concerning Aaron and Amram's visions (4Q546 13-15).
    2. Sacrificial instruction (4Q547 frg. 8; frgs. 3-7?).
    3. Sons of light and sons of darkness (4Q548 1 ii 2)
  - E. Concluding section (?)
    1. Death of patriarch (?) (4Q549 2 1-6)
    2. Descendants of Uzziel and Mariam and the marriage of Hur (?) (4Q549 2 7-11).

The didactic character of the work is palpable in the narrative introduction, where the narrator tells the reader that the copy of the writing of the visions of Amram contains everything that the latter transmitted to and taught his sons on the day of his death. The content of the work allows the assumption that Amram speaks not only to Aaron but to Aaron's descendants (4Q546 14 4) and priests in general (4Q543 1, 10; 4Q545 1a i 9). In his speech to Aaron, Amram stresses Aaron's wisdom and judgment. Amram's second speech to Aaron and his sons contains fragments of a teacher's opening formula: "And now, my sons, listen to what [I am instructing you about]" (4Q546 14, 4; cf. 4Q548 1 ii–2 9). The next fragmentary verse contains a verb, "I saw" (4Q546 14 5), which suggests that the visionary material in the pseudepigraphon should also be considered didactic. Thus the dualistic realm of angelic powers finds its reflection in human behavior that decides whether one is to be called son of light or son of darkness (4Q548 2). The autobiographical section indicates Amram's piety towards his ancestors, a virtue strongly recommended in the *Admonitions of Qahat* (4Q542 1 i 7–1 ii 1). Scholarly study of this composition has focused on the metaphysical dualism in the angelic world (Milik 1972; Kobelski 1981; García Martínez 1987).

BIBLIOGRAPHY

H. DRAWNEL 2004, *An Aramaic Wisdom Text from Qumran: A New Interpretation of the Levi Document,* Leiden: Brill. • H. DRAWNEL 2006A, "Priestly Education in the *Aramaic Levi Document (Visions of Levi)* and *Aramaic Astronomical Book* (4Q208–211)," *RevQ* 22/4: 547-74. • H. DRAWNEL 2006B, "The Literary Form and Didactic Content of the Admonitions (Testament) of Qahat," in *From 4QMMT to Resurrection: Mélanges qumraniens en hommage Émile Puech,* ed. F. García Martínez et al., Leiden: Brill, 55-73. • F. GARCÍA MARTÍNEZ 1987, "4QʿAmram B 1, 14: Melki-rešaʿ o Melki-sedeq?" *RevQ* 12: 111-14. • P. KOBELSKI 1981, *Melchizedek and Melchirešaʿ,* Washington, D.C.: Catholic Biblical Association of America. • J. T. MILIK 1972, "4QVisions de ʿAmram et une citation d'Origène," *RB* 79: 77-97. • J. T. MILIK 1978, "Écrits préesséniens de Qumrân: d'Hénoch à ʿAmram," in *Qumrân: Sa piété, sa théologie et son milieu,* ed. M. Delcor, Paris: Duculot; Leuven: University Press, 91-106. • É. PUECH 2001, *Qumrân Grotte 4. XXII: Textes araméens, Première partie: 4Q529–549,* DJD 31, Oxford: Clarendon.

HENRYK DRAWNEL

Amulets

Amulets are small protective objects and devices worn on a person's body to protect him or her from disease, the evil eye, demons, or similar dangers. A recurrent phenomenon in all human societies and cultures, amulets may be divided into two distinct types: those consisting of natural or man-made substances and objects (corals, roots, seashells, stones and minerals, cords, knots, and so on), and those consisting of a material on which a text, an image, or both have been inscribed. In the Jewish world, the early use of both types of amulets is attested in the Hebrew Bible (e.g., Isa. 3:18-23) and by archaeological finds. Especially notable are the two inscribed silver amulets found at Ketef Hinnom (Jerusalem), which date to the late seventh or early sixth century B.C.E. and contain the Priestly Blessing (Num. 6:24-26) and perhaps an even longer apotropaic text, written in the paleo-Hebrew script that was in use among Jews at the time (Barkay et al. 2004). In this case, the nature of the inscribed text, the fact that both silver sheets were rolled after being inscribed, and their location in a family tomb all argue for the amuletic use of these two objects, whose Jewish origins can hardly be in doubt.

While the Jewish production and use of some written amulets is attested in the First Temple period, in the Second Temple period we have evidence for the Jewish use of nontextual amulets, but no real evidence for the use of written ones. Several early Jewish texts refer to amuletic substances and devices, including the amuletic and prophetic cords described in *Testament of Job* 47, and the numerous mishnaic references to the amuletic uses of knots, coins, and such rarer items as the egg of a locust, the tooth of a fox, or a nail from a crucifixion (*m. Šabb.* 6:6, 9-10). The use of such amulets by ancient Jews is confirmed by a child's linen T-shirt found in the Cave of Letters, where some Jews took refuge during Bar Kokhba's disastrous revolt. The shirt displays several knotted "pouches" containing an assorted mixture of seashells, salt crystals, seeds, and some unidentified materials. Whereas such amulets certainly were deemed harmless from a Jewish perspective, other ancient Jewish texts display an awareness of the use by some Jews of "pagan" amulets produced by their non-Jewish neighbors (2 Macc. 12:39-42; cf. Pseudo-Philo, *Biblical Antiquities* 25–26), a practice sharply condemned by the authors of these texts.

Moving to a later period, we find a growing body of evidence relating to the Jewish use of amulets (due in part to the predilection of rabbinic literature to discuss such things at great length), and clear proof, from the third or fourth century C.E. onward, that Jews were once again producing and using textual amulets. Among the rabbis there were frequent discussions of amulets that had proved their efficacy, or that had been produced by an amulet maker who had proven the efficacy of his amulets (*m. Šabb.* 6:2; *t. Šabb.* 4:9; *y. Šabb.* 6:2 [8b]). The Babylonian Talmud preserves an interesting story of a rabbinic disciple who wrote his (non-Jewish?) client an amulet that proved ineffective against the sixty demons who were pestering him, and thus put him in great danger — until another rabbinic disciple wrote out the appropriate amulet and the boisterous demons fled the scene (*b. Pesaḥim* 111b).

On the archaeological side, dozens of Jewish amulets written in Aramaic, Hebrew, and Greek have been found in Israel, Egypt, Turkey, Syria, and elsewhere. Most of these are incised into thin sheets of bronze, silver, gold, or other metals, and some are incised on semi-precious gems or on other objects (presumably, amulets written on papyrus and vellum simply did not survive). All are characterized by a typically Jewish mixture of prayers to God and the adjuration of angels, peppered with biblical verses and with magical signs and words borrowed by their Jewish producers from their non-Jewish colleagues. That they are sometimes found in tombs, and that one cache of nineteen amulets was found in the apse of a synagogue at Ḥorvat Maʿon, clearly demonstrates the wide use and general acceptance of amulets in late-antique Jewish society.

BIBLIOGRAPHY
G. BARKAY, M. J. LUNDBERG, A. G. VAUGHIN, AND B. ZUCKERMAN 2004, "The Amulets from Ketef Hinnom: A New Edition and Evaluation," *BASOR* 334: 41-71. • L. BLAU 1898, *Das altjüdische Zauberwesen,* Strasbourg: Trubner, 1898 (2d ed., Berlin: Lamm, 1914). • G. BOHAK 2007, *Ancient Jewish Magic,* Cambridge: Cambridge University Press. • R. KOTANSKY, J. NAVEH, AND S. SHAKED 1992, "A Greek-Aramaic Silver Amulet from Egypt in the Ashmolean Museum," *Le Muséon* 105: 5-26. • J. NAVEH 2001, "An Aramaic Amulet from Bar'am," in *Judaism in Late Antiquity,* Part III, vol. 4, ed. A. J. Avery-Peck and J. Neusner, Leiden: Brill, 179-85. • J. NAVEH 2002, "Some New Jewish Palestinian Aramaic Amulets," *Jerusalem Studies in Arabic and Islam* 26: 231-36. • J. NAVEH AND S. SHAKED 1993, *Magic Spells and Formulae: Aramaic Incantations of Late Antiquity,* Jerusalem: Magnes. • J. NAVEH AND S. SHAKED 1998, *Amulets and Magic Bowls: Aramaic Incantations of Late Antiquity,* 3d ed., Jerusalem: Magnes. • Y. YADIN 1971, *Bar-Kokhba,* London: Weidenfeld & Nicolson, 79-82.

See also: Demons and Exorcism; Divination and Magic; Magic Bowls and Incantations

GIDEON BOHAK

Angels

Angels are spiritual beings that serve a variety of functions in the literature and piety of early Judaism. They are mentioned in the Hebrew Bible and received increasing attention in the Second Temple Period.

Terminology

Běnê (ha) 'Ĕlōhîm

Any discussion of "angels" in early Judaism must begin in the Hebrew Bible. One of the more significant terms used of them is *běnê (ha) 'ĕlōhîm* (Gen. 6:2, 4; Job 1:6; 2:1; 38:7; Pss. 29:1; 89:7), a phrase translated most often as "sons of God." The idiom "sons of" does not imply genealogical relationship with the God of Israel but functions merely to mark membership in a group, in this case the order of "divine beings" or *ĕlōhîm.* The *běnê 'ĕlōhîm* fall into three main categories in the Hebrew Bible: angels, minor deities, and god-like men (Wright 2005: 62). The LXX translates *běnê (ha) 'ĕlōhîm* as *hoi huioi tou theou* or *angeloi tou theou* (cf. Philo, *Gigantibus* 6; Josephus, *Ant.* 1.73; Ps.-Philo, *Bib. Ant.* 3:1). These "sons of God" are understood as part of the heavenly council or court of YHWH. It is possible that they may have been identified as minor deities at some point in the history of Israel (e.g., Ps. 82:1), but it is fairly clear that following the Babylonian Exile, the sons of God came to be understood as angels of God.

Mal'āk/Angelos

The most commonly used term for angels in the Hebrew Bible is *mal'āk* or "messenger," rendered in the LXX as *angelos* and often translated into English as "angel." Because the term can be used of either a heavenly or human messenger, it is unclear in some passages which type of being is in view (e.g., Judg. 2:1; Mal. 3:1). The term *angelos* is used in the LXX to translate the Hebrew terms *'ĕlōhîm,* "god(s)" (Pss. 8:6; 97:7; 138:1) and *śar* or "prince" (Dan. 10:21; 12:1, both times referring to the archangel Michael).

The Development of Angelology

Angels were very much a part of the religious and theological world of ancient Israel; how well they were defined is a different question. They appear in some of the earliest stories of the patriarchal narratives in Genesis (chaps. 16, 21, 22, 31) and also in Exodus and Numbers. Both here and throughout the Tanak, the most common usage is "angel of the LORD."

Exilic and postexilic canonical texts witness to an increased interest in the activities and figures of the heavenly realm. Why this increase occurred in early Judaism is not fully comprehended. Some scholars suggest that close contact with Babylonian and Persian belief systems is one factor in the emergence of a developing angelology, but precise parallels are hard to come by, and most Persian texts are quite late. Further, as many have noted, there is evidence of an established angelology of some sort already in the religion of preexilic Israel. The notion of a heavenly council or court is reflected, for example, in Gen. 28:12; 32:1-2; Pss. 29:1; 82:1; 89:6-9; 2 Sam. 14:17, 20; 19:28; 1 Kings 22:19-22. Deuteronomy 32:8 (LXX) suggests that each nation has an angel or minor deity to govern its activities. Reference to the heavenly "host" is made in Deut. 33:2 and Josh. 5:14. The "angel/messenger of the LORD" features in Gen. 16:11-12; 19; 22:11-12; Exod. 3:2; Num. 22:31-35; Judg. 13:3-5; 2 Samuel 24; 1 Kings 13:18; 2 Kings 1:3; Pss. 35:5-6; 78:49; and Isaiah 6. It appears that the important factor in this early angelology is not the heavenly being itself but the deeds that the angel executes on behalf of YHWH. Michael Mach (1992) has suggested that the messenger of the LORD and the divine council were originally distinct concepts. It was the combination of these two conceptions that came to typify postexilic angelology and is evident already in late biblical books such as Job, some of the Psalms, Daniel, and Zechariah.

Significant to this discussion is the relationship of the "angel of the LORD" to YHWH himself. On more than one occasion (e.g., Gen. 16:7-11; 21:15-21; Exod. 3:2-6; Judg. 6:11-24), this heavenly being is identified as YHWH. While the most likely explanation of this usage is that a mediator was required between YHWH and humanity, it is possible to account for it by recognizing that the identity of the sender has been granted to the messenger in order to establish the divine authority of the message. Whether the heavenly being is identified as an angelic messenger or as YHWH seems incidental; more important is that the presence of the angel of the LORD affirms the continued involvement of YHWH in the life of Israel.

Angels in Postexilic Biblical Books

Job and Zechariah

Alongside the angel of the Lord, we find a second notable angelic figure, the *śāṭān* or "adversary." This shadowy figure, which evolves into the cosmic opponent of

YHWH in later Jewish and Christian angelology and demonology, stands in the divine council to accuse those whose devotion to God might be questioned. Job 1–2 reintroduces this figure, which receives its first mention in Num. 22:22 and appears later in Zechariah 3 and 1 Chron. 21:1. In each of these passages, the *śāṭān* functions under the auspices of YHWH with a limited autonomy granted to him. Also emerging in the book of Job is the concept of "guardian" angels (Job 33:23-26). On occasion, these angelic beings protect or speak up for individuals so that they may stand before YHWH, as in Zechariah 3 (cf. 2 Kings 19:35).

The Book of Daniel

A similar theme is assumed in the book of Daniel. In Dan. 3:25 we find the *bar 'ĕlāhîn* who intercedes and protects Shadrach, Meshach, and Abednego in the furnace. This term is the Aramaic equivalent of *bĕnê 'ĕlōhîm,* which, as is evident from other literature of the period (e.g., *1 Enoch* 6:2; Tobit), certainly would have been understood by some Jews in the Second Temple period as an angel of God. Daniel 6:22 presents an analogous situation in which Daniel is protected and delivered by a *mal'āk* sent by God. The identity of the being is clarified by Daniel as "his [God's] *mal'āk*" and is perhaps the equivalent of "the angel of the LORD."

The book of Daniel reflects the increasingly complex angelology that developed in the Second Temple period. It also portrays an angelic hierarchy that includes the naming of particular angels (e.g., Dan. 8:15-16; 10:13) and the assigning of an angelic prince to each of the nations of the earth (Daniel 10; cf. Deut. 32:8 LXX). The tendency to assign angels proper names evidently had one of its main impulses in the exegesis of older biblical passages, particularly those that feature hierophanies, military terminology, textual cruxes, and rare words (see Olyan 1993).

Angels in Other Early Jewish Literature

The writings in the Apocrypha, Pseudepigrapha, and Dead Sea Scrolls attest a heightened awareness and importance of the role of angels in the worldview of early Judaism. Angels are identified as "spirits" (*1 Enoch* 15; 1QS 3:18-19, 25; CD 12:2-3; 1QH 3:21-23; 11:13; 1QM 13:2, 11-12; 14:10; 4Q403 1 i 35). They are closely associated with heaven and most often described as "holy" (1QS 11:8; 1QH 3:22; 1QM 7:6; 4Q401 frg. 16 line 3; 1QSa 2:8-9).

Appearance of Angels

Since angels are thought to be spiritual beings, it is not surprising that the appearance of these creatures is often described in terms closely related to the depiction of the glory of YHWH (e.g., *2 Enoch* 1:3-5; *Apoc. Abr.* 11:1-3; 2 Macc. 3:25-26; *Apoc. Zeph.* 6:11-15). These physical descriptions usually include phenomena such as light, fire, or precious stones and metals (e.g., 4Q377; 4Q301; 4Q416 frg. 1 line 7; 4Q405 15 ii 16). Some scholars suggest that these depictions are based on the portrait of God's glory in Ezekiel 1. Despite their close affinity to the glory of God, angels are nevertheless regarded as created beings, although in most cases this status is only implied (e.g., *Jub.* 2:2; *1 Enoch* 9:5; 1QH 10:6; 4Q405 frg. 4 line 12; 1QS 3:15-21; 1QM 13:10-12). Some scholars think that there are texts which imply that angels played a part in the creation of the cosmos (Fossum 1985: 192-213); however, the relevant texts appear rather to depict angels praising the work of God in creation (*Jub.* 2:3; Job 38:7; 11QPs[a] 26:12).

Surrogates for God

Various texts categorized as "rewritten Bible" depict angels as agents of God's will. In some contexts, they perform an action that biblical tradition ascribed to God (e.g., Gen. 11:6 and *Jub.* 10:22-23; Gen. 15:17 and *Jub.* 14:20; Genesis 22 and *Jub.* 17:15-18; Num. 14:10-12 and Ps.-Philo, *Bib. Ant.* 15:5; 1 Sam. 17:47 and *Bib. Ant.* 61:5).

Intercessors

The role of intercessor is also brought to the forefront. In various sections of *1 Enoch* and the *Testaments of the Twelve Patriarchs,* we find angels bringing the prayers of the righteous before the Lord in an attempt to help and protect them (e.g., *1 Enoch* 100:5; 1QM 13:10; 4QTobit; *T. Dan* 6:5; *T. Naph.* 8:4; *T. Jud.* 3:10; see also Ps.-Philo, *Bib. Ant.* 38:3; 59:4; 3 Macc. 6:18).

Teachers and Tour Guides

In some Second Temple texts, we also find angels being identified as teachers or mediators of God's will (e.g., of punishment: 4Q197; *T. Naph.* 8:6; *1 Enoch* 56; 4Q390; 4Q*Pseudo-Moses;* of revelation to humans: *Jub.* 1:27-29; 10:10-14; 4Q216; *1 Enoch* 7; 8; 89:61-77; 90:14-20; *T. Levi* 9:6; *T. Reub.* 5:3; *T. Jos.* 6:6; 4Q169 3-4 ii; 4Q180). In addition, the *angelus interpres* functions as dialogue partner and heavenly tour guide in apocalyptic literature (e.g., *1 Enoch* 17–36; *Apocalypse of Abraham* 10–18; *4 Ezra* 3–14; *3 Baruch*).

Hierarchy of Angels

A distinct hierarchy of both good and bad angels becomes increasingly evident as the Second Temple period progresses. Within this hierarchy certain angels of both types are given a personal name or task (*1 Enoch* 6; 8; 4Q204 col. ii [= *1 Enoch* 6:7]; 4Q206 frg. 2 col. ii [= *1 Enoch* 22:3-7]; 4Q216 col. v [= *Jub.* 2:1-4]; 4Q287 frg. 2; 4Q403 [*ŠirŠabb*[d]]). In many cases the incorporation of the divine name into an angel's name (e.g., Yahoel in the *Apocalypse of Abraham*) makes it clear that these heavenly beings are acting as agents of YHWH.

The angels Michael, Gabriel, Raphael, and Uriel, who came to be identified as "archangels," are most often seen in the role of intermediaries between the righteous and YHWH (Tob. 12:15; Dan. 9:21; 10:13; *1 Enoch* 9:1; 21:10; *4 Ezra* 4:1; *Sib. Or.* 2:215; 1QM 9:15-16; 4Q285 frg. 1). In certain texts the number of archangels is seven, and they are at times identified as "angels of the presence" (e.g., Tob. 12:15; *T. Levi* 8:2; *Jub.* 1:27; *1 Enoch* 9:1; 1QM 9:15-16; 1QSb 4:25; 1QH 6:13)

The primary leader of the righteous angels is Michael, the patron angel of Israel (Dan. 12:1). He seems to be the one who in the Qumran texts is called the Angel of Truth (1QS 3:24), Prince of Light (CD 5:18; 1QS 3:20; 1QM 13:10; 17:6-8; 11QMelch 8, by implication), and perhaps also Melchizedek (11QMelch; 4QAmram).

In addition to the archangels, there are various other classes or ranks of angels found in several early Jewish sources. The "Watchers" of *1 Enoch* are a special class of angels who were sent to the earth to watch over the development of humanity (e.g., 4Q201 col. i; 4Q204 col. i; 4Q206 frg. 2 col. ii; 4Q212 col. iii; 4Q227 frg. 2; 4Q266 frg. 2 col. ii). In texts of the Enoch tradition, the Watchers lead humanity astray by teaching them illicit knowledge and skills.

There are seven chief and deputy angels in 4Q403 (*ŠirŠabb*[d]) 1 i 1-29 and 4Q405 (*ŠirŠabb*[f]) 13:4-7, and a variety of angelic beings is found in *1 Enoch* 61:10 (cherubim, seraphim, ophanim, angels of principalities; see also 4Q286 frg. 1 col. ii; 4Q287 frg. 2; 4Q405 frgs. 20-22; 11Q17 col. vii; 11Q19 col. vii). These different classes of angels are found in the different levels of the heavens. *2 Enoch* 20, for instance, identifies several classes of angels in the seventh heaven and ten ranks of angelic armies in the tenth heaven with God (cf. *T. Levi* 3). It should also be noted that these angels are assigned tasks related to the orderliness of the cosmos, including the movement of the sun, moon and stars, and to the proper functioning of the elements of nature (e.g., *1 Enoch* 60:16-22; 82:9-20; *2 Enoch* 19; 1QH 1:10-11).

Angelic Warriors

One of the primary actions of angels in early Jewish literature is their involvement as warriors in the defense of Israel (e.g., 4Q434 frg. 1 col. i) and in the eschatological battle of the cosmos. Particularly in the Qumran *War Scroll,* we find angels active in the eschatological battle (1QM 17:6-8; cf. *T. Mos.* 10:1-10; Daniel 12). Within this eschatological battle, we find a dualistic angelology which pits the "good" angels of God and the righteous of humanity against the "evil" angels (or spirits) and the wicked (although there is some argument whether or not these angels are operating under the sovereignty of God; cf. Wright 2005: 166-90). A cosmic dualism is explicit in various texts from the Qumran library. There are clear lines set that depict the angels of light (and the sons of light) versus the evil agents who operate under the direction of Mastema (*Jub.* 10:8; 17:15-18; 1QM 13:11; 4Q271 frg. 4 col. ii; CD A 16:1-18). This leader of the forces of darkness appears under a variety of other names: *Satan* (*Jubilees* 10; 1QH 12:6; CD 5:17-19; *Jub.* 17:15-18; 48:2, 9, 12, 15, 17); *Belial* (1QM 1:1; 13:11; 1QS 2:4-5; CD 5:17-19); *Beliar* (*Jub.* 1:20; *T. Reub.* 2:2; *T. Jud.* 25:3); and *Melchiresha*ʿ (4QAmram; 4Q280 frg. 1 line 2).

Angels in the Heavenly Temple/Court

In a variety of texts, angels function as priests in the heavenly sanctuary. They observe the Sabbath and other commandments of Torah (e.g., *Jub.* 2:17-18; 6:18; 15:27; 30:18; *T. Levi* 3:5-6; 1QSb 4:24-26). Several apocalyptic texts offer detailed descriptions of the heavenly court, with angels playing deliberative, judicial, revelatory, or liturgical roles (Dan. 7:9-10; *1 Enoch* 14:19-23; 40:1-7; 60:2-6; 61:9-13; *2 Enoch* 20:4–21:1; *4 Ezra* 8:21-22; *Apoc. Abr.* 10:9; 18:11-14; Ps.-Philo, *Bib. Ant.* 18:6; *Apoc. Zeph.* 8:4; *T. Job* 48–50).

Communion with the Angels

Apocalyptic texts also describe a close communion of the righteous with the angels. The Enochic tradition, for instance, reflects the expectation that the righteous will be transformed into an "angelic" state of the sort attained by Enoch and other heavenly sojourners (*2 Enoch* 22; 1QS 4:6-8; 11:7-8; 1QSa 3:3-11; 1QH 3:21-22; 6:12-13; 11:10-14).

Angels in the New Testament

The New Testament writings offer few new elements in their depiction of angels. They perform many of the same functions that they do in the Hebrew Bible and are described as creatures that radiate the glory of God in a great light while robed in white garments (Matt. 28:3; Luke 2:9; 9:26; 24:4; John 20:12; Acts 1:10; 10:30; 12:7; 2 Pet. 2:10; Jude 8; Rev. 10:1; 15:6; 19:14). Angels are also spoken of as performing tasks that in the Hebrew Bible are attributed to God. Thus, an angel spoke to Moses from the burning bush (Acts 7:30, 35) and gave the Law to him (Acts 7:38, 53; Gal. 3:19; Heb. 2:2). The transfer of these actions from God to angels reflects midrashic traditions of the Second Temple period.

The authors of the New Testament certainly recognize the existence of angels, but the heavenly beings play a relatively minor role in their writings. The Gospels refer to the "angel of the Lord" (Matt. 1:20, 24; 2:13, 19; 28:2, 5; Luke 1; 2:9, 10, 13, 21; 22:43; in John 12:29 the people think they hear an angel speaking). In the book of Acts they appear as the "messenger of the Lord" or as defenders of the righteous (Acts 5:19; 6:15; 7:30, 35, 38; 8:26; 10:3, 7, 22; 11:13; 12:7, 8, 10, 11, 15). In other passages, they dispense divine revelation in dreamlike visions (Matt. 1:20-21; 2:13, 20; Luke 1:11-20, 26-38; Acts 8:26; 10:3-6; 27:23-24; Rev. 1:10). Acts 12:15 presents the notion that humans have an angel (perhaps a guardian angel), but the meaning of the reference is unclear.

Angels are conspicuously absent in the Gospel of Mark. Their absence may owe in part to the lack of a nativity story. Mark makes two references to the existence of angels, but they do not actually appear in the narrative (Mark 8:38; 13:32). There is also a possible reference to an angel in Mark 16:5 if read alongside Matt. 28:3, although Mark describes the figure as a "young man."

Angels play a significant role in the Synoptic Gospel accounts of Jesus' ministry. They protect Jesus during his wilderness temptation and minister to him afterward (Mark 1:13; Matt. 4:6-11; Luke 4:10-11). They are also present during Jesus' agony before his arrest (Luke 22:43). Twelve legions of angels stand ready to rescue him during his trial (Matt. 26:53), and one or more angels are said to have rolled away the stone from his tomb (Matt. 28:2).

Matthew 25:41 and Rev. 12:7-9 pose the difficulty of "evil" angels on the earth. These angels may be those who fell and committed sin, as in *1 Enoch,* though the

Enoch tradition does not identify Satan as their leader. Some suggest that the war between the two groups of angels reflects the religious and political struggles portrayed in a variety of texts from the period (cf. Daniel 10–12; 1QM 13:9-13; 17:5-8; 1QS 3:20-25; *T. Levi* 5:3-6; *1 Enoch* 56:5-6; *Jub.* 35:17; *2 Bar.* 13:1; *2 Enoch* 19:4; *T. Joseph* 6:7; Matt. 18:10; Acts 12:15). In any case, the increased recognition of angels during this period clearly reflects the desire to separate God from evil while still affirming that God remains active in the world.

There are only a few references to angels in the New Testament epistles; in several of them, it is unclear whether the author is describing angels or some other power or authority. Nevertheless, it is clear from these passages that there was a strong belief in the existence of an angelic host, both good and evil (1 Pet. 1:12, angels long to know the things that have been revealed to humans through the gospel; 2 Thess. 1:7, angels will accompany Jesus at his Parousia; 1 Cor. 4:9, angels are observing what is happening on earth; 13:1, angels have a language; 1 Tim. 5:21, Jesus has chosen angels; Heb. 1:7, angels are serving God; 12:22, there are myriads of angels in the heavens; Jude 14, angels are the holy ones of the Lord; Gal. 1:8; 4:14, angels are messengers from heaven or God and can take on human form).

There are two clear references to the concept of archangels in the New Testament: 1 Thess. 4:16 (the archangel sounds the trumpet) and Jude 9 (the archangel Michael battles the devil for the body of Moses). Mention of an archangel may indicate a hierarchy of angels, as may references to "principalities and powers" (1 Cor. 15:24; Eph. 1:21; 2:2; 3:10; 6:12; Col. 1:16; 2:10, 15; 1 Pet. 3:22; Rom. 8:38). However, these texts offer no clear indication that the beings represented are heavenly beings; they may be part of established earthly authority, or perhaps the evil spirits created by the "sons of God" and the "daughters of men" known from the Enochic tradition.

Some New Testament passages may reflect a hierarchy of "evil angels" on the earth under the rule of Satan, but the texts are ambiguous. Jude 6 and 2 Pet. 2:4 clearly describe the angels who committed sin in Gen. 6:1-4 and subsequently *1 Enoch* 6–16; as in *1 Enoch* and *Jubilees,* so here the wicked angels are held in a pit (likely Tartarus) until the Day of Judgment. These same angels may also be in view in 1 Cor. 6:3.

In various New Testament passages, angels carry out God's judgment. In Acts, the angel of the Lord strikes down the murderous and vainglorious Herod Agrippa I (Acts 12:20-23). Angels will descend at the Parousia with Christ (Matt. 16:27; Mark 8:38; 1 Thess. 4:16; 2 Thess. 1:7; Jude 14-15) and will be involved in separating the wicked from the righteous at the Last Judgment, when they will also observe Christ's denial of the wicked (Matt. 13:39-42; Luke 9:26; 12:8-9; Rev. 3:5).

The Apocalypse of John contains numerous references to angels. They function in Revelation 2 and 3 as "angels over the seven churches." This notion may relate in some way to the "angels of the nations" or else to guardian angels (cf. Acts 5:19-20; 12:6-11, 15). In Revelation 8–11, 14, and 16–19, angels act as agents of God's wrath when they perform tasks that help bring about the final destruction of evil and the restoration of the cosmos. In Revelation 20–22 they serve as heavenly guides to the author of the Apocalypse.

Angels in Early Rabbinic Writings

Angels play a much less prominent role in rabbinic literature than they do in Second Temple writings. Even so, there are a vast number of references concerning angels in the rabbinic corpus. There is a growing interest in rabbinic literature attributing the actions of God found in the Hebrew Bible to angels (e.g., *Deuteronomy Rabbah* 9; *Gen. Rab.* 31:8; *b. Sanhedrin* 105b). The idea of a guardian type angel as seen in some NT writings also occupies a significant place in rabbinic angelology. Some texts introduce the idea that angels have no free will and exist to perform a sole task (*b. Šabbat* 88b; *Gen. Rab.* 48:11; 50:2). Others state that angels are subordinate to righteous humans (*Genesis Rabbah* 21; *Deuteronomy Rabbah* 1) and are capable of committing errors (*b. Sanhedrin* 38b; *Midr. Ps.* 18:13). The naming of angels continues in rabbinic writings; in particular, the biblical figure of death is identified as the "Angel of Death" (e.g., *Pirqe Rabbi Eliezer* 13).

BIBLIOGRAPHY

W. CARR 1981, *Angels and Principalities,* Cambridge: Cambridge University Press. • M. J. DAVIDSON 1992, *Angels at Qumran,* Sheffield: Sheffield Academic Press. • J. E. FOSSUM 1985, *The Name of God and the Angel of the Lord,* Tübingen: Mohr Siebeck. • D. D. HANNAH 1999, *Michael and Christ: Michael Traditions and Angel Christology in Early Christianity,* Tübingen: Mohr Siebeck. • M. MACH 1992, *Entwicklungsstadien des judischen Engelglaubens in vorrabbinischer Zeit,* Tübingen: Mohr-Siebeck. • A. Y. REED 2005, *Fallen Angels and the History of Judaism and Christianity,* Cambridge: Cambridge University Press. • S. M. OLYAN 1993, *A Thousand Thousands Served Him: Exegesis and the Naming of Angels in Ancient Judaism,* Tübingen: Mohr-Siebeck. • L. T. STUCKENBRUCK 1995, *Angel Veneration and Christology: A Study in Early Judaism and in the Christology of the Apocalypse of John,* Tübingen: Mohr-Siebeck. • K. P. SULLIVAN 2004, *Wrestling with Angels: A Study of the Relationship between Angels and Humans in Ancient Jewish Literature and the New Testament,* Leiden: Brill. • A. T. WRIGHT 2005, *The Origin of Evil Spirits,* Tübingen: Mohr Siebeck.

See also: Fallen Angels; Michael, the Archangel; Satan and Related Figures; Sons of God

ARCHIE T. WRIGHT

Animal Apocalypse → Dreams, Book of

Animal Worship

Animals played an important role in the symbolism of the despised Canaanite religions: the calf was connected with YHWH, Baal, El, and Dagon, the cow with Astarte, and the lion with Asherah. Nevertheless, few biblical prohibitions single out the worship of animals from among the general critiques of idolatry and polytheism, indicating that animal worship was not deemed as a specific threat to the Israelite population. It is probably to combat idolatry rather than animal worship that Hezekiah destroys Moses' brazen serpent, to which the Israelites had been burning incense (2 Kings 18:4). Similarly, the episode of the Golden Calf in Exod. 32:1-8 may be a veiled polemic against the images of the royally sponsored shrines at Dan and Bethel (1 Kings 12:28; 2 Kings 10:29) rather than a depiction of the lure of Canaanite worship. In these shrines, YHWH was likely conceived as standing on the back of the calf pedestal, much as he was viewed as enthroned on the cherubs of the Jerusalem Temple (Zevit 2001: 317).

Animal worship was a prominent feature of the religion of ancient Egypt, where divinities were represented in images with animal features and animals were considered sacred through their relationship with a particular divinity. In Egypt, animals could also be worshiped as divinities in their own right (e.g., the Apis or Mnevis bulls and the Mendesian goat).

Anti-Jewish Accusations

During the Persian period, the Passover sacrifice of a lamb at the Jewish temple located at Elephantine in Upper Egypt was likely viewed as sacrilege by priests of the neighboring temple of Khnum, the ram god, and may have led to their destruction of this temple in 410 B.C.E., one of the first instances of anti-Judaism on record (Porten 1968: 284-98). In the Greek and Roman periods, Egyptian animal reverence inspired a number of anti-Jewish accusations. Manetho claimed that Moses made it a law that the Jews should kill and eat the sacred animals. Mnaseas, Damocritus, and Apion alleged that the Jews worshiped a golden image of the head of an ass placed in the Jerusalem Temple. The charge drew on the Egyptian legend of the ass as the sacred animal of the demonic Seth or Typhon, declared by Manetho and others to be the divinity of the Asiatic Hyksos invaders as well as that of the Jews. Similarly, belief that Jews abstained from and therefore held sacred the pig may have encouraged the charge that the Jews were psoriatic heretics of Egyptian descent, since pigs were connected to both skin ailments and Seth by Manetho and others. Manetho also claimed that Moses made it a law that the Jews should kill and eat the sacred animals. Later authors such as Tacitus (*Historiae* 5.4.32) continued to promulgate the connection between Jewish sacrifice and their alleged derision for Ammon and Apis worship. However, a less disparaging version of Jewish opposition to animal worship was also possible; according to Strabo (*Geographica* 16.2.35), Moses left Egypt because he opposed animal worship.

Early Jewish Views of Animal Worship

The Egyptian Jewish writer Artapanus (third century B.C.E.) asserts that Moses made ibises, dogs, and cats sacred for the Egyptians, in part in recognition of their usefulness to man, and in part to organize Egyptian society and military. Artapanus also states that Moses revealed the usefulness of oxen, prompting the pharaoh to divinize the Apis bull. But the destruction of the sacred animals at the parting of the Red Sea is implied in Artapanus' account, perhaps indicating his view of their ultimate powerlessness.

Growing distaste in the Greco-Roman period for the practice of animal worship encouraged Jewish writers to lambaste it as a crucial element in their campaign against Egyptian anti-Jewish calumny (Smelik and Hemelrijk 1984: 1910-20). The Septuagint mocks the cult of Apis in LXX Jer. 26:15 (although this may reflect an authentic Hebrew variant to MT). The *Letter of Aristeas* (late second century B.C.E.) ridicules the foolish Egyptians who place their reliance on beasts and creeping things (138). The Wisdom of Solomon (first century B.C.E.) states that the witless thoughts of the Egyptians led them astray to worship irrational serpents, worthless beasts, and creatures of the most hateful and unintelligent sort; moreover, through the plagues, the Egyptians were punished by these very creatures (11:15; 15:18-19). While Philo of Alexandria (ca. 20 B.C.E.–ca. 40 C.E.) admits that Moses had been instructed in the regard the Egyptians paid to animals (*Mos.* 1.23) and partially excuses the worship of useful animals such as bulls, rams, and goats (*De Decalogo* 76–80), he states that the souls of the Egyptians are transformed into beasts by their worship of the most savage and untamable of wild animals. Moreover, the willing participation of the Alexandrian Greeks in animal deification explains their willingness to deify Caligula as well as their lack of respect toward divinity itself. Philo frequently describes the worship of the golden calf as a revival of Egyptian animal worship.

Building from Exod. 8:26, where Moses points out to Pharaoh that it is not wise to sacrifice what is detestable to the Egyptians in their sight, midrashic and targumic texts portray the sacrificial practices of the Israelites as an offense to the Egyptians and an unmasking of "the abomination of Egypt" that teaches the inefficacy of animal deities to Egyptians and Israelites alike (*Targums Onqelos* and *Yerushalmi* Exod. 8:22; *Exod. Rab.* 16:2-3). In turn, Egyptian abhorrence of the Israelite practice of animal sacrifice explains their revulsion for the Hebrews in Genesis (*Targum Onqelos* Gen. 43:32; Smelik and Hemelrijk 1984: 1907-10). It is notable that the prevalence of animal worship among the enslaving Egyptians is used by Moses as an excuse for the Israelites' worship of the golden calf (*Exod. Rab.* 43:7). In the Babylonian Talmud, questions explored include whether an animal that had been worshipped is fit for secular use, since all parties agreed that it was unfit for ritual purposes (*b. Qiddušin* 57b). It is also determined that benefit may be derived from the specific animal involved in animal worship and that it should not be put to death (*b. Sanhedrin* 55a).

BIBLIOGRAPHY

B. PORTEN 1968, *Archives from Elephantine,* Berkeley: University of California Press. • K. A. D. SMELIK AND E. A. HEMELRIJK 1984, "'Who Knows Not What Monsters Demented Egypt Worships?' Opinions on Egyptian Animal Worship in Antiquity as Part of the Ancient Conception of

Egypt," *ANRW* II.17.4, 1852-2000. • K. VAN DER TOORN ET AL., EDS. 1999, *Dictionary of Deities and Demons in the Bible*, Grand Rapids: Eerdmans. • Z. ZEVIT 2001, *The Religions of Ancient Israel: A Synthesis of Parallactic Approaches*, London: Continuum.

See also Gentile Attitudes toward Jews and Judaism; Gentiles, Jewish Attitudes toward; Pagan Religions

JED WYRICK

Antichrist

Antichrist is a Christian conception found in writings from the latter part of the first century onward (1 John 2:18-22; 4:1-6; 2 John 7; Polycarp, *Phil.* 7:1). The term is used of an eschatological opponent of Jesus Christ who is expected to act as deceiver in order to lead believers astray. The figure numbers among several eschatological opponents mentioned in early Christian writings as antagonists of Jesus Christ destined to appear prior to Jesus' second coming. Other characters with similar functions are described as "false prophets" and "false messiahs" (Mark 13 and pars.; *Apoc. Peter* 2:7-13); the "man of lawlessness" (2 Thess. 2:1-12; Justin, *Dialogue with Trypho* 32; 110); the dragon, the beast, the false prophet, and other personifications of evil in the book of Revelation (Revelation 12–13; 17); the "deceiver of the world" (*Didache* 16); an eschatological tyrant depicted in Danielic terms (*Epistle of Barnabas* 4); and Beliar (*Ascension of Isaiah* 4). From the late second century onward, the Antichrist features prominently in Christian writings (e.g., Tertullian, *Resurrection* 24.60.24; 27.64.76; 27.65.10; *Against Marcion* 1.22.1; 3.8.2; 5.16.4; Hippolytus, *Antichrist* and *Commentary on Daniel* 4.24.7-8).

In his reconstruction of the history of the Antichrist legend, Wilhelm Bousset (1895) argued that the concept originated in an esoteric Jewish oral tradition. This view was taken over by many scholars (e.g., Friedländer 1901; Charles 1920) and was held as *communis opinio* until the late twentieth century. Today the scholarly consensus has moved away from this position and regards the figure of Antichrist as a Christian development rooted in earlier Jewish traditions. Further, the early Christian period did not have one single concept of an eschatological adversary of Jesus Christ. According to this position, the character of Antichrist was molded on the basis of a christological reinterpretation of a number of traditions found in early Jewish sources (Ernst 1967; Jenks 1991; Lietaert Peerbolte 1996; a more critical position is taken by Horbury 1998; a less than critical exception is Lorein 2003, who speaks about "The Antichrist in the Qumran Writings").

The constitutive Jewish traditions include the climax of evil that was expected to take place preceding God's ultimate intervention in history; the expected appearance of false prophets; the coming of an eschatological tyrant; the final defeat of Belial/Beliar and of the chaos monsters Leviathan and Behemoth; the tradition of the final assault of Gentile nations; and the legend of *Nero redivivus*. Many early Jewish sources depict the period immediately preceding God's ultimate intervention in history as a period of general upheaval in which the social, natural, and even cosmic order will be inverted. This disturbance of order can be characterized as a general climax of evil. Descriptions of this kind are found in early Jewish apocalypses such as Daniel (chaps. 7–8 and 11–12); *Jubilees* (23:13-21); *1 Enoch* (80:2-7; 91:6-7, 11; 93:9-10; 99:4-8; 100:1-4); *Assumption of Moses* (7–8); *4 Ezra* (5:1-12; 6:18-24; 8:49-50; 9:3-6; 14:16-18); *2 Baruch* (48:26-41; 70:2–71:11; 89:9-21); and the *Sibylline Oracles* (3.635-651, 796-806; 4.152-61). Within this expected climax of evil, various figures are described as personifications of the power of evil.

Given the prominent position of false prophets in early Christian writings, one would expect that early Jewish sources would also feature this character in a distinctive way, but this is not the case. The characteristics of eschatological false prophets as described in Christian texts are found only in the picture of Beliar in *Sib. Or.* 3.66-68. Apparently, the concern with false prophets and false teachings was peculiar to the early Christian movement.

More prominent in Jewish sources that anticipate eschatological upheavals before God's ultimate intervention in history is the political figure of an eschatological tyrant. The book of Daniel apparently introduced this characterization, as a way of depicting the Seleucid king Antiochus IV (Dan. 7:8, 20-27; 8:9-12, 23-25; 11:21-45). After Daniel, other sources mention similar characters (*As. Mos.* 8:1-3; *4 Ezra* 5:6; 11:29-35; 12:23-31; *2 Bar.* 36:7-11; 40:1-3). In *Sib. Or.* 3.75-92; 3.611-615 the portrait of the eschatological tyrant is so detailed that it probably also reflects a contemporary figure.

The one personality that is described mostly as a superhuman instigator of evil is Belial, mentioned in Greek sources as Beliar. Especially in Qumran writings Belial is seen as a leader of the forces of evil. Thus, Belial heads the army of the "sons of darkness" and as such forms a counterpart to Michael, who is presented as the head of the forces of the "sons of light" (1QM *passim*). This Belial is thought to rule until God's final intervention in history, and he will not be defeated before that moment (e.g., 1QM 14:8-10; 1QS 4:18-23). This view is taken up in the Christian *Testaments of the Twelve Patriarchs*, where Beliar is presented in similar fashion (*T. Benj.* 3:8; *T. Dan* 5:10-11; *T. Jud.* 25:3; *T. Levi* 3:3; 18:12; *T. Zeb.* 9:8). One passage in the Qumran writings hints at an eschatological advent of Belial (CD 8:2), whereas this expectation is described explicitly in *Sib. Or.* 2.154-73 and *Sib. Or.* 3.63-74.

Several passages in early Jewish sources speak of the eschatological defeat of the two chaos monsters God has created, Leviathan and Behemoth (*1 Enoch* 60:7-8, 24-25; *4 Ezra* 6:49-52; *2 Bar.* 29:4). An important part of the expectation of the climax of evil preceding the final intervention of God or his envoy in history is an assault on Jerusalem and Palestine by the Gentile nations. Descriptions of this final assault are found in *Jub.* 23:22-25; *1 Enoch* 56:5-8; 90:13-19; 4Q246; *4 Ezra* 13:5-38; *Sib. Or.* 3.657-68. The Qumran community apparently interpreted Psalm 2 and the raging of the nations it describes as a prediction of its own present (see 4Q174).

ANTIOCH (PISIDIAN)

One special feature that is found in the *Sibylline Oracles* is the legend of the return of Nero (*Sib. Or.* 3.63-74; 4.119-224; 4.137-39; 5.28-34; 5.137-51; 5.214-27; 5.361-71). Apparently Nero is seen as an eschatological tyrant who will come back in order to avenge himself. A striking parallel with the opposition of Christ/Antichrist in Jewish sources is the depiction of Melchizedek and Melchiresha' found in a number of Qumran texts (cf. 11QMelch; 4QAmram; 4Q280). In these texts Melchiresha' is described as the leader of the evil spirits, whereas Melchizedek is his positive counterpart.

The one view all eschatological scenarios in early Jewish sources hold in common is that God will ultimately intervene in history. The means through which he is expected to do so may differ, but ultimately God is regarded as the highest authority who holds power over all human, natural, and cosmic events. The expectation of a climax of evil before God's ultimate intervention in history may take many forms. The various expressions of this expectation all share the thought that this climax of evil is the necessary, but final attempt of all forces hostile to God to grasp hold of the created world. This attempt is, however, considered as doomed to fail.

BIBLIOGRAPHY

W. BOUSSET 1895, *Der Antichrist in der Überlieferung des Judentums, des Neuen Testaments und der alten Kirche,* Göttingen: Vandenhoeck & Ruprecht; Eng. ed.: *The Antichrist Legend: A Chapter in Christian and Jewish Folklore,* Atlanta: Scholars Press, 1999. • R. H. CHARLES 1920, *A Critical and Exegetical Commentary on the Revelation of St. John,* 2 vols., Edinburgh: Clark, 76-87. • M. FRIEDLÄNDER 1901, *Der Antichrist in den vorchristlichen jüdischen Quellen,* Göttingen: Vandenhoeck & Ruprecht. • J. ERNST 1967, *Die eschatologischen Gegenspieler in den Schriften des Neuen Testaments,* Regensburg: Pustet. • W. HORBURY 1998, "Antichrist among Jews and Gentiles," in *Jews in a Graeco-Roman World,* ed. M. Goodman, Oxford: Oxford University Press, 113-33. • G. C. JENKS 1991, *The Origins and Early Development of the Antichrist Myth,* Berlin: de Gruyter. • B. J. LIETAERT PEERBOLTE 1996, *The Antecedents of Antichrist: A Traditio-Historical Study of the Earliest Christian Views on Eschatological Opponents,* Leiden: Brill. • G. W. LOREIN 2003, *The Antichrist Theme in the Intertestamental Period,* London: Clark. • B. MCGINN 1994, *Antichrist: Two Thousand Years of the Human Fascination with Evil,* San Francisco: Harper.

BERT JAN LIETAERT PEERBOLTE

Antioch (Pisidian)

The City

The city of Pisidian Antioch, which was 3,600 feet above sea level, was one of sixteen cities to bear the name Antioch. It was actually in Phrygia, but in order to distinguish it from other cities (especially from the Antioch on the Meander River and so also in Phrygia), it was called "Antioch on the Pisidian border" or "Antioch towards Pisidia" (see Strabo 12.569, 577) and hence is generally referred to by scholars as Pisidian Antioch. The city was officially called Colonia Caesarea Antiocheia (Pliny, *Naturalis Historia* 5.94), and was in the Roman province of Galatia.

The city was founded by Greek colonists, and moved there from Magnesia on the Maeander, probably by either Antiochus I (281-261 B.C.E.) or Antiochus II (261-246 B.C.E.). Augustus refounded the city as a Roman colony and settled a group of Latin-speaking veterans there around 25 B.C.E.; the descendants of these veterans became the dominant group in the city. In the first century C.E. the city was the civil and administrative center for the southern part of the province of Galatia. Latin was used for official functions rather than Greek, and many of the inscriptions from the city are in Latin.

The Origin of the Jewish Community

The origins of the Jewish community in Pisidian Antioch probably lie in the actions of Zeuxis in 210-205 B.C.E. According to Josephus, Antiochus III ordered Zeuxis to transfer two thousand Jewish families from Mesopotamia and Babylonia to Lydia and Phrygia as military settlers (*Ant.* 12.147-53). Although doubts have been raised about the authenticity of this passage, we can have confidence in the veracity of Josephus' report. Given that he speaks of two thousand families being settled in Phrygia and Lydia, and that Pisidian Antioch was a significant city in Phrygia, it seems very likely that some of these Jews were settled in Pisidian Antioch. As Seleucid military settlers, these Jewish families would probably have been established on reasonable terms in Pisidian Antioch. According to Josephus, they were also allowed to use their own laws, which would have given them the opportunity to maintain their Jewish identity.

The Jewish Community according to Acts

The only literary text that speaks explicitly of Jews in Pisidian Antioch is Acts 13:14-50; 14:19. Although there is no other evidence for the events spoken of here, Paul's mission in southern Galatia is likely historical (so, e.g., Lüdemann 1989: 157-58). The events described in this passage probably occurred sometime between 45 and 48 C.E. (Mowery 2006). The passage gives us five key points of information about the Jews in Pisidian Antioch.

First, the passage shows that there was a Jewish synagogue building in the city in the time of Paul (Acts 13:14) and that in Pisidian Antioch, as elsewhere, public reading of the Law and the Prophets followed by exposition was customary on the Sabbath (Acts 13:15).

Second, according to Acts 13:15, the *archisynagōgoi* ("rulers of the synagogue") are said to have sent a message to Paul and his company, saying, "Brothers, if you have any word of exhortation for the people, give it." The plural "rulers of the synagogue" has been a puzzle to interpreters, since elsewhere we do not explicitly hear of more than one "ruler of the synagogue" serving at the same time. However, two people who held the office, one "for life," are mentioned in an inscription from nearby Acmonia (*IJO,* vol. 2, no. 168), so it is possible that more than one person could bear the title concurrently. The passage also shows that the rulers of the synagogue, at least in this city, fulfilled a role in the worship of the community that included inviting visitors to address the gathering.

Third, in Acts 13:43 we read that "many Jews and devout proselytes followed Paul and Barnabas." Although this group of proselytes is not mentioned elsewhere in the passage (in 13:16 and 13:26 they seem to be included among the Jews), there is no reason to doubt their existence, and we know of a number of Jewish proselytes from other places. In Acts 13:43 Luke uses the word "worshiping" or "devout" *(sebomenoi)* in application to proselytes; normally *prosēlytoi* and *sebomenoi* are used of two different groups.

Fourth, the passage speaks of the presence of "God-fearers" in the synagogue. In Acts 13:16 Paul addresses those present in the synagogue as "You Israelites, and others who fear God *(hoi phoboumenoi ton theon),*" and in 13:26 he addresses the group again as "Brothers, you descendants of Abraham's family, and others who fear God *(hoi . . . phoboumenoi ton theon).*" Again, in 13:50 we are told of "the devout women *(tas sebomenas gynaikas)* of high standing" whom the Jews are able to call upon to assist in driving Paul and Barnabas out of their region.

Here the two terms *(hoi phoboumenoi ton theon* and *tas sebomenas)* are used of non-Jews who in some ways can be said to fear or worship the Jewish god. They are generally called "God-fearers" and are understood to be Gentiles who could be formally associated with the Jewish community, were involved in at least some facets of synagogue life, and adopted some Jewish practices without becoming proselytes. Although doubts have been expressed about the existence of God-fearers, we have sufficient evidence for them from a range of sources and can be confident that they are a historical phenomenon. Most notable is an inscription from Aphrodisias, probably to be dated in the fourth century C.E., that lists fifty-four God-fearers. There are also other inscriptions from Tralles, Sardis, and Miletus in Asia Minor in which there is a strong probability that *theosebēs* designates a God-fearer (Trebilco 1991: 145-66; Snyder in Drew-Bear et al. 2002: 46-49). The existence of God-fearers in Pisidian Antioch highlights the attractiveness of the Jewish community to Gentiles and the openness of Jews to the involvement of Gentiles in their community.

Fifth, in Acts 13:50 we read: "But the Jews [of Pisidian Antioch] incited the devout women of high standing and the leading men of the city, and stirred up persecution against Paul and Barnabas, and drove them out of their region." Here, then, the Jews of the city are able to enlist some high-standing women (probably God-fearers) and some influential men of the city in their campaign to drive Paul and Barnabas out. It seems possible that some of the "leading men of the city" were husbands of some of the "devout women of high standing." Again, we have no corroborating evidence for this event, but we do have evidence for the attraction of women, including women of high standing, to Judaism (see, e.g., Acts 17:4, 12; Josephus, *J.W.* 2.559-61; Cassius Dio 67.14.2), and we have no reason to reject the account. R. L. Mowery (2006: 232) comments, "Most of the women of high standing in first-century Pisidian Antioch would have been descendants of Augustus' Italian veterans, as would most of the leading men of the city." Hence it seems that the Jewish community was attracting support from among the aristocracy of the city. C. K. Barrett (1994: 660) also notes that "some of the leading families are known to have been associated with the cult of the god *men* and may have attacked Paul and Barnabas because they were a threat to the cult."

The evidence given here for proselytes and God-fearers, and for the influence of the Jewish community among high-status Gentiles, combines to suggest that the Jewish community in Pisidian Antioch generally enjoyed good relations within the wider city, where it had a measure of influence and respect. The combined impression we get from these passages also indicates a Jewish community of some size.

An Inscription

There is only one Jewish inscription that may give evidence for Jews in Pisidian Antioch. This inscription comes from the end of the second or beginning of the third century C.E. (Schürer 1973-1987: 3.1.32) and was found in nearby Apollonia. It speaks of a woman named Deborah, who is from a city called "Antioch." It reads: *[kleinēs A]ntiochissa patrēs goneōn polyteimōn ounoma Debbōra,* "[A]ntiochian from the famous fatherland, of highly honored parents, named Deborah" (*CIJ*, no. 772; *IJO*, vol. 2, no. 180). It has been thought that Deborah was Jewish because of her name; this is likely but not certain. It has also been suggested that she was from Pisidian Antioch, because of the proximity of that city to Apollonia, where the inscription was found. However, it has been noted that "The tone of the epitaph nevertheless strongly suggests that she had come from an Antioch more distant than this one [i.e., Pisidian Antioch], perhaps the Carian Antioch on the river Meander" (Schürer 1973-1987: 3.1.32; see also Levick 1967: 128; *IJO*, vol. 2, p. 385). But it is also possible that she came from Antioch in Syria (see Mitchell 1993: 2:8-9). Thus, although some scholars think of her as from Pisidian Antioch (Conzelmann 1987: 103), this seems doubtful.

The Debate over Galatians

There is continuing debate about whether Paul's letter to the Galatians was written to churches in the *territory* of Galatia, which would be central Anatolia around Ankara (the so-called North Galatian theory) or to the Roman *province* of Galatia (the so-called South Galatian theory). If it is to the latter, then it would include the churches mentioned in Acts 13–14: Derbe, Lystra, Iconium, and Pisidian Antioch. In this case, Christians in Pisidian Antioch would be included among the addressees of Galatians. Paul's letter would then give evidence for Jewish-Christian teachers in the area, since at the time of writing these teachers were evidently attempting to persuade the Gentile Galatians to undergo circumcision. However, the actual destination of Galatians remains uncertain, and in any case the letter provides evidence for traveling Jewish-Christian teachers (probably from Jerusalem) rather than for the Jewish community in the area.

BIBLIOGRAPHY
W. AMELING 2004, *Inscriptiones Judaicae Orientis,* vol. 2, *Kleinasien,* Tübingen: Mohr-Siebeck. • C. K. BARRETT 1994, *The Acts of the Apostles,* vol. 1, Edinburgh: Clark. • H. CONZELMANN 1987, *Acts of the Apostles,* Philadelphia: Fortress. • T. DREW-BEAR, M. TASHALAN, AND C. M. THOMAS, EDS. 2002, *Actes du Ier Congres International sur Antioche de Pisidie,* Paris: Boccard. • B. LEVICK 1967, *Roman Colonies in Southern Asia Minor,* Oxford: Clarendon. • I. LEVINSKAYA 1996, *The Book of Acts in Its Diaspora Setting,* Grand Rapids: Eerdmans. • G. LÜDEMANN 1989, *Early Christianity according to the Traditions in Acts: A Commentary,* London: SCM. • S. MITCHELL 1993, *Anatolia: Land, Men and Gods in Asia Minor,* 2 vols., Oxford: Clarendon. • S. MITCHELL AND M. WAELKENS 1998, *Pisidian Antioch: The Site and Its Monuments,* London: Duckworth. • R. L. MOWERY 2006, "Paul and Caristanius at Pisidian Antioch," *Bib* 87: 223-42. • J. REYNOLDS AND R. TANNENBAUM 1987, *Jews and Godfearers at Aphrodisias: Greek Inscriptions with Commentary,* Cambridge: Cambridge Philological Society. • E. SCHÜRER 1973-1987, *The History of the Jewish People in the Age of Jesus Christ,* 3 vols., rev. and ed. G. Vermes et al., Edinburgh: Clark. • P. R. TREBILCO 1991, *Jewish Communities in Asia Minor,* Cambridge: Cambridge University Press. • B. WANDER 1998, *Gottesfürchtige und Sympathisanten: Studien zum heidnischen Umfeld von Diasporasynagogen,* Tübingen: Mohr-Siebeck.

See also Aphrodisias; Asia Minor; God-fearers

PAUL TREBILCO

Antioch (Syrian)

History

According to the sixth-century chronicler John Malalas (*Chronographia* 199-201), the Hellenistic king Seleucus I Nicator founded Antioch-on-the-Orontes in May 300 B.C.E. Together with Apamea and Laodicea-on-the-Sea, Antioch and Seleucia constituted a strategically important area by linking each coastal city with an inland city, securing northwestern Syria.

Located in the fertile land of the southwest corner of the Amuk Plain and the Orontes Valley, on a navigable river about one day's sail from the coast, Antioch enjoyed excellent strategic and economic conditions. The location was, however, not entirely ideal, being prone to earthquakes and flooding and difficult to defend where it expanded up the slopes of Mt. Silpius.

The city followed the typical layout for Hellenistic cities of the period. Malalas (*Chronographia* 200) reports that Seleucus built a temple to Zeus, who together with Apollo was considered to be the founder and protector of the Seleucid dynasty. It is reasonable to assume, even though the evidence is scanty, that this temple was located at the *agora* together with other public buildings, such as various shrines and military and administrative buildings. There is no evidence of a stadium (apart from one in Daphne, which was in existence in 195 B.C.E.), but it is generally assumed that Antioch had a stadium or a hippodrome. The city was adorned with different monuments, such as a statue of Zeus that Seleucus erected outside the city in honor of Zeus' eagle, and a statue of Tyche wearing a turreted crown, which represented the city wall, and at her feet a youthful body representing the river Orontes.

During the period of the immediate successors of Selecus I Nicator, one of the main events was the transference of the capital from Seleucia Pieri to Antioch. This was of great importance for the further development of the city, especially during the reign of Antiochus IV Epiphanes (175-163 B.C.E.), when Antioch turned into one of the greatest cities of antiquity, which occurred, paradoxically, during a period when Seleucid power was in general decline.

After Antiochus' death, the decline of the Seleucid kingdom continued until the conquest by the Romans in 64 B.C.E. During the Roman occupation, especially after Julius Caesar brought an end to civil war, and during the *Pax Romana,* Antioch flourished as the capital of Roman Syria. During the first centuries C.E., Antioch continued to be an important religious, economic, and cultural center but suffered from several devastating earthquakes and plagues. In 638 C.E., Roman Antioch came to an end with the surrender of the city to the Arabs.

The Jewish Community in Antioch

It is likely that Jews were among the first inhabitants of Antioch, since Josephus twice claims that Seleucus I Nicator granted them certain privileges (*Ant.* 12.119; *Ag. Ap.* 2.39). This indicates that Jews already from the beginning were recognized as an identifiable ethnic group. While there may have been Jews among the native Syrians, the majority of the first Jewish settlers were probably retired soldiers from Seleucus' army (see, e.g., 2 Macc. 8:20). Apparently, the Jewish population increased significantly during the following centuries. Josephus reports (*J.W.* 7.43) that while Jews were found in large numbers all over Syria, they were particularly numerous in Antioch. As for the first century C.E., estimations of the Jewish population vary between 20,000 and 40,000, which means that Jews probably made up five to ten percent of the population.

The relation between the Jewish community and the *polis* of Antioch has been a much-debated issue. In three texts Josephus seems to claim that the Jews of Antioch were given rights of citizenship. In *Ag. Ap.* 2.39, he states that Seleucus I granted *politeia* to the original settlers, and in *Ant.* 12.119, he emphasizes that the Jews were given *politeia* equal to that granted to the Macedonians and Greeks. A similar statement is made in *J.W.* 7.44, where the equality with the Greeks is again underlined, but the privileges are now said to have been granted by the successors of Antiochus IV Epiphanes.

It is clear that the Jews of the Diaspora usually enjoyed certain privileges, such as permission to assemble (Josephus, *Ant.* 14.260), to observe dietary laws and Jewish festivals (e.g., *Ant.* 14.226), to collect a temple tax to be sent to Jerusalem (*Ant.* 16.169-70), and to be ex-

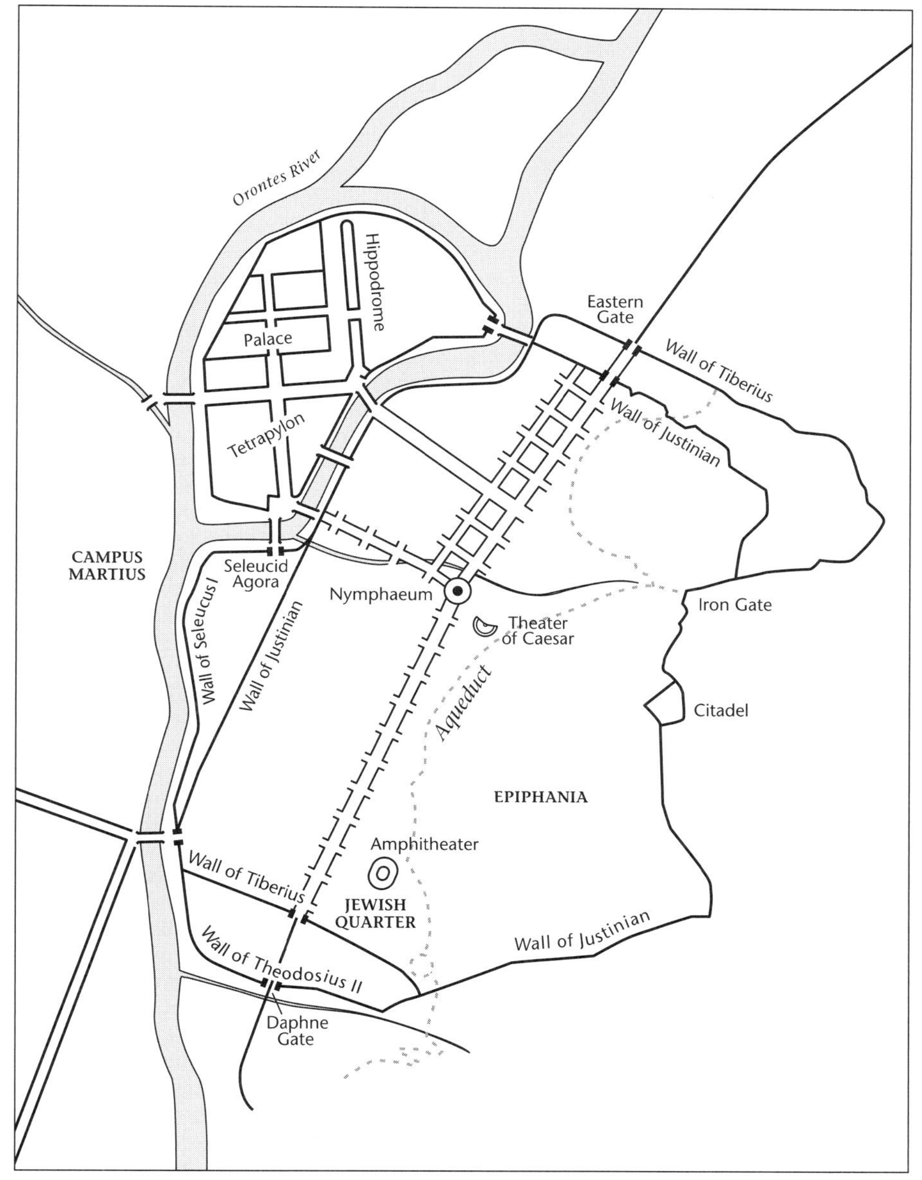

Ancient Antioch (in Syria)

empt from participation in the official Greco-Roman cult (*Ant.* 19.280-85). It is, however, unlikely that the Jewish community as a group was given citizenship in any *polis,* since this would have entailed worship of the city gods. It is therefore more probable that Josephus refers to the right of the Jewish community to practice its religion and to live in accordance with its own legislation. Thus, the Jews of Antioch were most likely not part of the same *politeia* as the Greeks, but of another one, of the same kind. This does not exclude the possibility that some prominent Jewish families were granted citizenship in the *polis* of Antioch and were able to combine this with a Jewish identity without being compelled to worship the city gods (cf. Josephus, *Ag. Ap.* 2.65).

The Jewish community of Antioch was divided into several subcommunities. Even though there is evidence of only three synagogues (all literary — no Jewish remains were found during the excavations), one outside Daphne, the suburb of Antioch, one in the city, and one east of the city, the existence of many more must be taken for granted. It is reasonable to assume an ideological division as well. There is evidence of a strong Torah-oriented tendency in the city that partly seems to have been connected to the tradition of the Maccabean martyrs (2 Maccabees 6–7; 4 Maccabees), whose remains are reported to have been kept in a synagogue in the city (e.g., Malalas, *Chronographia* 206-7). The Maccabean revolt in Judea during the reign of Antiochus IV Epiphanes probably reinforced general anti-Hellenistic tendencies among some Jewish groups in Antioch, and indirectly affected the relations between Jews and non-Jews. The city, which was not immediately affected by the Maccabean uprising, was certainly drawn into the aftermath of the more acute conflict. When internal struggles over the Seleucid throne resulted in a rebellion of his own troops, Demetrius II appealed for help from the Hasmonean leader Jonathan, who sent 3,000 Jewish soldiers to the city. With help from the Jewish militia, Demetrius was able to suppress the revolt, but the soldiers also plundered and burned the city and returned to Jerusalem with their spoils (1 Macc. 11:41-51; Josephus, *Ant.* 13.135-42).

Josephus mentions an incident during the First Jewish Revolt against Rome that also reveals a strong commitment to traditional Jewish values. Faced with either sacrificing to the Greek gods or being executed, a few Jews submitted to sacrificing "after the manner of the Greeks," but some chose death rather than abandon their devotion to the God of Israel (*J.W.* 7.50).

There is further evidence of strained relations between some Jews and non-Jews, especially during the reign of Gaius Caesar Germanicus, better known as Caligula (37-41 C.E.), and during the First Revolt (e.g., Josephus, *J.W.* 7.46-53; Malalas, *Chronographia* 244-245).

It is likely that certain anti-Jewish feelings arose when the authorities, whether Greek or Roman, confirmed Jewish privileges, sometimes against the will of some members of the non-Jewish population. Josephus mentions (*J.W.* 7.96-111) that in the aftermath of the First Revolt, the non-Jewish population wanted to have the Jews of Antioch expelled. Titus, however, refused and confirmed the Jewish rights. A similar incident occurred when a copy of Claudius' edict (Josephus, *Ant.* 19.280-85; *CPJ* 153), which primarily dealt with the situation in Alexandria, was also sent to Syria, stating that the Jews were again free to follow their own customs (*Ant.* 19.279).

However, Antioch was also the setting of positive interaction between Jews and non-Jews. While non-Jewish interest in Judaism during the first centuries C.E. is generally well attested (see, e.g., Murray 2004), Josephus reports that the non-Jews of Antioch were especially attracted by Judaism (*J.W.* 7.45). It is probably in the context of participation by non-Jews in the activities of the synagogues that the apparent success of the Jesus movement among non-Jews in Antioch should be viewed (Acts 11:19-21). Yet, as is evident from Acts 15 and Gal. 2:11-14, the issue of the status of the non-Jews within the Jewish Jesus movement also gave rise to intra-Jewish conflicts.

While contacts between Jews and Christians continued after the emergence of Christianity as a non-Jewish religion early in the second century, the Jewish community of Antioch gradually lost its former grandeur and suffered from several devastating pogroms during the fifth, sixth, and seventh centuries.

BIBIOGRAPHY

J. M. G. BARCLAY 1996, *Jews in the Mediterranean Diaspora: From Alexander to Trajan (323 BCE–117 CE),* Edinburgh: Clark, 242-58 • G. DOWNEY 1961, *A History of Antioch in Syria from Seleucus to the Arab Conquest,* Princeton: Princeton University Press. • G. HADDAD 1949, *Aspects of Social Life in Antioch in the Hellenistic-Roman Period,* Chicago: University of Chicago Press. • C. KONDOLEON, ED. 2000, *Antioch: The Lost Ancient City,* Princeton: Princeton University Press. • C. H. KRAELING 1932, "The Jewish Community at Antioch," *JBL* 51: 130-60. • S. KRAUSS 1902, "Antioche," *REJ* 89: 27-49. • W. A. MEEKS AND R. L. WILKEN 1978, *Jews and Christians in Antioch in the First Four Centuries of the Common Era,* Atlanta: Scholars Press. • M. MURRAY 2004, *Playing a Jewish Game: Gentile Christian Judaizing in the First and Second Centuries CE,* Ontario: Wilfried Laurier University Press. • M. ZETTERHOLM 2003, *The Formation of Christianity in Antioch: A Social-Scientific Approach to the Separation between Judaism and Christianity,* London: Routledge.

See also: Damascus; Syria

MAGNUS ZETTERHOLM

Antiochus IV Epiphanes

Antiochus IV (ruled 175-164 B.C.E.) was the youngest son of Antiochus III, possibly by adoption. After the defeat of Antiochus III by the Romans and as part of the Peace of Apamea (189/188 B.C.E.), the Romans took this son as a hostage to Rome, where he remained until replaced by the son of Seleucus IV in 178 B.C.E. During his stay in Athens on his slow return to Antioch, his elder brother Seleucus IV was assassinated by Heliodoros in 175 B.C.E. With the help of Eumenes II, Antiochus gained the throne, had Heliodoros executed, and took Seleucus' younger son, Antiochus, as coregent. By 173 B.C.E., Antiochus IV had officially taken the epithets *Theos* (God) and *Epiphanēs* (Manifest), thereby heightening the dynastic cult that Antiochus III had introduced, and had his nephew killed in July/August 170 B.C.E.

The empire taken over by Antiochus IV had several problems requiring his attention. One of his first endeavors was to secure the recognition of his position by the Romans and the Greek cities. He secured recognition by the Roman Senate in 174 B.C.E. and in 173 paid off the last portion of the indemnity remaining since the Peace of Apamea. He was also active diplomatically and gave major benefactions and gifts to many Greek cities. He made major economic reforms, particularly of the coinage, to undergird the empire's financial security. His concern for local activity appears to include concern for the maintenance of local cults, as reflected in his continuing the gifts of earlier Seleucid kings to the temples in Babylon. While he did not want to confront Rome, he actively sought to rebuild the prestige of the Seleucid Empire.

When the Ptolemies made threatening overtures, Antiochus IV sent ambassadors to Rome to complain. He had already secured the southern border with Egypt through a journey into the southern part of Coele-Syria in 173 or 172 B.C.E. When hostilities broke out in 170 B.C.E., he quickly gained control of Egypt outside of Alexandria, installed his nephew Ptolemy VI as king while he himself was most likely crowned Pharaoh, and, without capturing Alexandria, left Egypt with much booty in 169 B.C.E. After his departure, however, the Ptolemaic rivals made peace. When Antiochus IV demanded from Ptolemy VI that he be given control of Cyprus and Pelusion, hostility resumed. Once again, Antiochus easily entered Egypt in 168 B.C.E. However, this time a Roman legate, C. Popilius Laenas, met him. The Romans had just ended the Third Macedonian War at Pydna in 168 B.C.E., and Popilius Laenas, in a scene known as the "Day of Eleusis," demanded that Antiochus withdraw from Egypt. Antiochus did so. He regrouped, however, and staged a major procession of his troops in Daphne near Antioch in 166 B.C.E. to proclaim his triumph over Egypt.

In spring 165 B.C.E., Antiochus set out to show his authority over his eastern provinces. First, he reclaimed his power over Armenia, before setting out for the Persian Gulf, and for Elymais and Persis. During this time he died, most likely while attempting to extract money from the temple of Artemis at Elymais, in November/December 164 B.C.E.

Antiochus IV was thus an energetic and capable leader, who lived in a time of Roman ascendancy and who tried to restore the prestige and fame of the Seleucid Empire. Yet he is considered very differently by his enemies. The Ptolemies, followed by Polybius, made a wordplay on his epithet *epiphanēs* and said that rather he was *epimanēs* (mad). This seems to make fun of Antiochus' attempts to introduce some Roman-style leadership behavior that went against the grain of traditional kingly conduct. He is also described as a temple robber, a *topos* used of tyrants, but this appears to refer to his attempts to collect taxes and money owed him by temple states.

Antiochus IV had a particularly bad reputation among Judeans. He was the defiler of the Temple, the king who ordered Geron the Athenian to Jerusalem to abrogate the ancestral laws of the Jews in Judea. Gruesome tortures were inflicted on those who did not comply with his edict, including the martyrdom of a mother and her seven sons. Why Antiochus acted in this way is a puzzle. His plunder of the Jerusalem Temple after his first invasion of Egypt could be seen as an attempt to recover the money owed him by the high priest Menelaus. His abrogation of the ancestral laws of the Judeans after his loss of prestige at the hands of the Romans during his second invasion of Egypt might have been caused by his wish to show that he was still a force to be reckoned with. The author of the epitome of the events found in 2 Maccabees says that Antiochus thought the city of Jerusalem was in revolt against him and so took it at spear point (2 Macc. 5:1-16). As conqueror, he could allow the Judeans to keep their ancestral laws or not. He chose not to. The author of 2 Maccabees uses the persuasive power of the term "ancestral laws" to depict Antiochus as an arch tyrant, one who fights against God. The success of the Maccabean uprising in response to his decision is celebrated in the Feast of Hanukkah. However, the decision seems not to have been one of much concern to the king. When, some time later, either in Spring 165 or Spring 164 B.C.E., the high priest Menelaus told him of the unrest that his decision had provoked, he had no qualms about granting the Judeans permission to use their own customs and laws as formerly (2 Macc. 11:31).

In sum, Antiochus IV was an energetic and able leader who sought to reinvigorate the Seleucid Empire, but whose decision to abrogate the ancestral laws of the Judeans led to unexpected consequences and the blackening of his name.

BIBLIOGRAPHY

E. S. GRUEN, 1993, "Hellenism and Persecution: Antiochus IV and the Jews," in *Hellenistic History and Culture,* ed. P. Green; Berkeley: University of California Press, 238-69. • C. HABICHT 1989, "The Seleucids and Their Rivals," in *Cambridge Ancient History,* 2d ed., vol. 8, *Rome and the Mediterranean to 133 B.C.*, ed. A. E. Astin et al.; Cambridge: Cambridge University Press, 324-87. • P. F. MITTAG 2006, *Antiochos IV. Epiphanes: Eine politische Biographie,* Berlin: Akademie. • O. MØRKHOLM 1966, *Antiochus IV of Syria,* Kopenhagen: Gyldendal.

See also: Seleucids ROBERT DORAN

Aphrodisias

The ancient city of Aphrodisias lies in southwest Asia Minor (modern Turkey), in the region of Caria. Little is known of the city and its history in the pre-Roman period. Aphrodisias gained prominence in the second half of the first century B.C.E., largely as the result of a fortuitous connection, exploited by the city, between the eponymous civic deity, Aphrodite/Venus, and the claim of the Julian family (e.g., Julius Caesar, Augustus) to be descended from the same goddess. The nexus led Rome to bestow upon Aphrodisias special recognition and privileges, such as autonomy, exemption from taxes, and designation as an asylum site. By the early imperial period, Aphrodisias had developed into a flourishing city with impressive civic institutions, including agora, temples, council chamber *(boulēterion),* theater, odeon, baths, basilica, and stadium. In the first century the city erected an imperial temple *(sebasteion),* accompanied by a portico lavishly decorated with mythological, allegorical, and imperial images in high relief. By the third century Aphrodisias had become the provincial capital of Caria, and remained a leading city of the region throughout the late Roman and Byzantine periods. Aphrodisias produced or was home to several prominent literary figures, such as the novelist Chariton and philosopher Alexander of Aphrodisias, one of the most important ancient commentators on the writings of Aristotle. Aphrodisias was also highly regarded as a major center of finely crafted marble work and expert sculptors.

The Aphrodisias Inscription

The Jewish community of Aphrodisias is known from the remains of a handful of inscriptions and carvings in stone. Jews in Aphrodisias marked their presence through the use of highly identifiable and traditional symbols — menorahs, rams' horns, citrons, and palm branches — that were common among Jews throughout antiquity both in the Diaspora and the land of Israel. None of this material can be dated with any certainty, although most if not all comes from the fourth century and later. No literary text mentions, much less describes, the community, nor has a synagogue been located, although some of the material remains may have come from such a building.

In 1976 archaeologists uncovered the single most important source of information, a marble pillar almost three meters in height with writing on two sides. The stone provides a fascinating glimpse into the Jewish community and its relations with non-Jews in the late Roman period. Face *a* records the activity of a Jewish organization calling itself a *dekany* and the names of its donors, including its presiding official *(prostatēs)* Jael, three proselytes, two men identified as *theosebēs* (often translated as "God-fearer"), and possibly a priest. The top portion of face *b* lists the names of fifty-five members of the Jewish community, and in some cases their occupations. Below this comes a second list of fifty-two men designated as *theosebeis.*

The donative inscription has been the subject of considerable analysis and controversy. Much about it remains uncertain, including whether the pillar contains one or two inscriptions, the date of the inscription(s), the nature of the Jewish organization, and the type of involvement by non-Jews exhibited in the text(s). A plausible reconstruction suggests that the pillar records two related inscriptions, both written in the fourth or perhaps early fifth century, that relate to an alimentary project, sponsored by the Jewish organization, providing food relief to the people, both Jews and non-Jews, of Aphrodisias.

The Jewish Community

While the extant materials offer little information on the religious life of the Jewish community, a few generalizations can be made. Jews in Aphrodisias worshiped God, studied biblical texts, engaged in prayer, and supported charitable projects. These activities were probably not uniformly observed throughout the community. Most Jews listed as members of the *dekany,* for instance, possessed biblical names, such as Judas, Joseph, and Samuel. By comparison, both Jews on face *b,* who may have been supporters but not members of the *dekany,* and their fathers infrequently bore such names. The wide disparity suggests that some Jews in Aphrodisias were drawn to more active engagement in Jewish life through membership in Jewish organizations and regular study and prayer.

Communal and religious leadership is represented by several positions including head of the *dekany (prostatēs),* ruler *(archōn),* archdeacon *(archidekanos),* psalm-singer *(psalmologos),* and possibly "teacher of friends" *(didaskalos philōn),* although the identity of M. Aurelius Leontius Auchenius is not certain. One member, Samuel, is identified as an elder *(presbeutēs)* and possibly a priest, although this term was erased and replaced with Perge, an indication of his place of origin or residence. The presence of Jael, who was most likely a woman, as a leader of the *dekany* indicates that this Jewish community, like Jewish communities elsewhere, welcomed women in leadership positions.

In two graffiti from the odeon, Jews designated themselves as Hebrews *(Hebraioi).* It is not clear why this term rather than Jew *(Ioudaios)* or Israelite *(Israelitēs),* was chosen, and whether it implies a particular understanding of Jewish identity. Jews of Aphrodisias seem to have been in contact with Jews from other cities of Asia Minor and possibly beyond. Although we cannot reconstruct the exact lines of communication, the interaction is evident in the presence of a Jewish elder *(presbeutēs)* from Perge, 200 km. to the southeast, and in the religious activities and symbols shared by Jews in other communities.

Jews in Civic Life

Jews were actively involved not only in their own community but also in the civic life of Aphrodisias. They attended events in the odeon and were recognized as supporters of the Blues, one of the major circus factions of the Byzantine period, although in this context the term is more likely a reference to the faction's involvement in the production of theatrical and other forms of entertainment. Jews participated in the economic life of the city as metal smiths, animal dealers, confectioners, and grocers. Several Jewish symbols appear in the stone work of the shops adjacent to the, by then, defunct imperial temple *(sebasteion),* indicating that Jews conducted their business activities alongside non-Jewish citizens of Aphrodisias. One of the *dekany's* leading members, Theodotus, served as *palatinos,* a high-ranking official in the administration of the Roman Empire.

Jews and Non-Jews

The Jewish community enjoyed respect from many non-Jews of Aphrodisias. The attitude manifested itself in close associations between Jews and Gentiles. Three of the eighteen persons listed as contributing to the *dekany*'s project were proselytes, each one taking a biblical name and one of them, Samuel, serving as an officer of the organization. Two other members along with the fifty-two men, including nine city councilors *(bouletēs),* in some fashion joined with or supported the Jewish community. The exact nature of their involvement remains unclear. One possibility would be that these men, designated as *theosebeis,* were God-fearers similar to the persons in the Acts of the Apostles, such as the Roman centurion Cornelius, who were drawn to Judaism out of a compelling interest in Jewish ideas, texts, and religious practices. It seems more likely, however, that the Aphrodisians engaged with the Jewish community less from religious motivations and more in an effort to support the civic activities of the *dekany.* The presence of such notable Gentile interest in the Jewish community, including three converts and fifty-four Gentile supporters, raises the question whether the Jewish community engaged in any form of missionary activity. Again, the evidence is inconclusive, but close personal, professional, and civic connections alone could account for the Gentile interest in and support of the Jewish community. Regardless of the exact nature of the involvement and its causes, the evidence from Aphrodisias demonstrates strong positive interactions between Jews and non-Jews, similar to the relations that existed in neighboring cities, particularly Sardis.

Jews and Christians

By the early fourth century, the Jews of Aphrodisias existed alongside a growing Christian community. Hagiographical traditions report the martyrdom of two Christians in the third century. In the early fourth century, Bishop Ammonius attended the Council of Nicea. The appearance of crosses in the shops of the former *sebasteion* indicates that Jews and Christians worked side by side. During the fourth and fifth century, the Christian population grew, although Christians did not come to dominate the civic and religious life of the city until perhaps the end of the fifth or early sixth century. At this time the temple of Aphrodite, the city's main sanctuary, was converted into a church, a monastery was founded nearby, and the majority of civic leaders were now Christian. Sometime in the early seventh century, the official name of the city was changed to Stauropolis (City of the Cross), in an effort to remove the pagan identification that several centuries earlier enabled the city to rise to prominence. No explicit information exists on relations between Jews and Christians. The seats in the odeon reserved for Jews, however, suggest that Jews continued to enjoy participation in public life into late antiquity, a time when Christianity exerted a strong if not dominant presence.

BIBLIOGRAPHY

M. P. BONZ 1994, "The Jewish Donor Inscriptions from Aphrodisias: Are They Both Third-Century and Who Are the *Theosebeis?*" *HSCP* 96: 281-99. • A. CHANIOTIS 2002, "The Jews of Aphrodisias: New Evidence and Old Problems," *SCI* 21: 209-42. • G. GILBERT 2004, "Jews in Imperial Administration and the Dating of the Aphrodisias Inscription," *JSJ* 35: 1-16. • G. GILBERT 2006, "Jewish Involvement in Ancient Civic Life: the Case of Aphrodisias," *RB* 113: 18-36. • J. REYNOLDS AND R. TANNENBAUM 1987, *Jews and Godfearers at Aphrodisias,* Cambridge: Cambridge Philological Society.

See also: God-fearers GARY GILBERT

Apocalypse

"Apocalypse" (Gr. *apokalypsis*) means "revelation," but the word is used to refer to works like the Book of Revelation or Apocalypse of John. This kind of revelation describes the reception of the revelation by a human being, and its interpretation by an angel or other heavenly figure. In Jewish apocalypses, the recipient is always a famous ancient figure (such as Daniel or Enoch; this is called pseudepigraphy). The revelations are of two types: (1) The recipient has symbolic dreams or visions, or is directly addressed by a heavenly being. This type typically involves a prediction of the course of history, often divided into periods, and ending with resurrection and judgment (e.g., Daniel 7–12). (2) The visionary is taken on an otherworldly journey, with an angelic guide, and sees the abodes of the dead, the place of judgment, and even the divine throne (e.g., the *Book of the Watchers* in *1 Enoch* 1–36).

Daniel

Daniel 7–12 is a series of four revelations preceded by a collection of stories about Daniel and his friends at the Babylonian court. In Daniel 7, Daniel sees in a dream four great beasts coming up out of the sea. The fourth has ten horns, and then an additional "little horn" sprouts up. Then Daniel sees "one like a son of man" coming on the clouds and being presented to the Ancient of Days, who is enthroned, surrounded by holy ones. The imagery is drawn from old mythic traditions, which are known most fully from the Ugaritic tablets from the second millennium B.C.E. and are partially known from the Hebrew Bible. These myths tell of a conflict between the unruly powers of the Sea and the storm god who rides on the clouds (Baal in the Ugaritic myths), but is distinct from the supreme god (El). The kingdom is awarded to this "son of man," and the beasts are destroyed. An angel explains to Daniel that that the four beasts are four kingdoms, and that "the holy ones of the Most High" and "the people of the holy ones" will receive the kingdom.

Chapter 8 provides another symbolic vision about the destruction of a beast with a little horn that rebels against heaven. In chap. 9, an angel explains to Daniel that Jeremiah's prophecy that Jerusalem will be desolate for seventy years actually means seventy weeks of years.

In the final revelation, in chaps. 10–12, an angel explains to Daniel that there is a struggle in heaven between angelic princes who preside over the different nations. He then predicts the course of history in the Hellenistic period. This history is accurate down to the time of the persecution of the Jews by Antiochus Epiphanes, but predicts the death of the king incorrectly. The accurate part of the prophecy was written after the fact *(ex eventu).* In the time of persecution, a group of "wise" people *(maśkilîm)* emerges, who defy the persecution and instruct the common people. At the end, the archangel Michael, prince of Israel, will arise victorious. Then the righteous dead will be raised, and the wise teachers will shine like the stars. The wicked will rise to everlasting shame. Michael should also be identified with the "one like a son of man" in chap. 7. The holy ones are the angelic host, and the people of the holy ones are Israel.

There was a tradition of symbolic visions in the Hebrew prophets, beginning with Amos. Closest to Daniel are the visions of Zechariah, which are also interpreted by an angel. (Some prophetic texts that are commonly called "apocalyptic" do not describe revelations at all. The so-called "Apocalypse of Isaiah" in Isaiah 24–27 uses mythological language similar to Daniel 7 and describes the dissolution of the cosmos, but in form it is an oracle, not an apocalypse.) Several features of Daniel's visions, however, are not attested in the older prophets. These include the device of pseudepigraphy, extended *ex eventu* prophecy, the division of history into periods (four kingdoms, seventy weeks of years), and, most importantly, the resurrection and judgment of the dead. Daniel is also distinguished from the older prophets by the prominence of angels. Many of these features can be paralleled in other cultures in the Hellenistic period. There are several examples of extended *ex eventu* prophecy from Babylon, and this motif is also found in the *Sibylline Oracles,* in Greek. The schema of four kingdoms, followed by a definitive fifth one, is attested in several Roman authors but is thought to derive ultimately from Persia (since Media is typically listed as one of the four). Full-blown apocalypses, with the division of history into periods, and resurrection and judgment at the end, are found in the Persian tradition. (Note especially the *Bahman Yasht,* which takes the form of a symbolic vision.) The Persian apocalypses survive in Pahlavi, and date from the sixth century C.E. or later, but they may be based on older traditions. Daniel's visions are a response to the persecution in the Maccabean period and can be dated to the years 167-164 B.C.E.

The Book of the Watchers

A different kind of apocalypse is pioneered in the *Book of the Watchers* in *1 Enoch* 1–36. This work survives in full only in Ethiopic, but Aramaic fragments have been found in the Dead Sea Scrolls. It takes its name from the story of the Watchers, recounted in *1 Enoch* 6–11, which in turn is based on the enigmatic passage about the descent of the sons of God in Genesis 6. The Watchers are heavenly beings who sin by taking human wives but also by imparting to humans forbidden knowledge. They beget giants, who cause chaos on earth. Eventually God orders the archangels to cleanse the earth and imprison the Watchers under it. The Watchers appeal to Enoch to take a petition up to God on their behalf, and this becomes the occasion of his ascent on the clouds. He has a vision of the divine throne, which is quite similar to that in Daniel 7. The petition of the Watchers is rejected. They are condemned because they had forsaken the spiritual life of heaven in order to mate with human women. Enoch, in contrast, is a human being who ultimately forsakes the earthly life to commune with the angels.

In the later part of the *Book of the Watchers,* Enoch is given a tour of the ends of the earth with an angelic guide and sees, among other things, the abodes of the dead and the places prepared for judgment. While much of his tour is concerned with cosmology, the fate of the dead and the final judgment provide the central focus. The ascent apocalypses do not usually engage in reviews of history, but eschatology, primarily the judgment of the dead, is of central importance. The *Book of the Watchers* is a composite work that was compiled gradually. The finished work is probably a little older than Daniel, but parts of it may date from the third century B.C.E. Journeys to the other world are widely attested in the ancient Near East and also in the Greco-Roman world.

Other Enochic Apocalypses

Astronomical Book

The *Book of the Watchers* now serves as the introduction to *1 Enoch,* a collection of apocalyptic writings preserved in Ethiopic and partially in Aramaic and Greek fragments. The oldest of these, the *Astronomical Book* (*1 Enoch* 72–82), is atypical, as it is primarily an instruction about the movements of the heavenly luminaries, with a view to supporting the 364-day calendar. It is given an apocalyptic frame insofar as the heavenly bodies are shown to Enoch by the angel Uriel, and there is a brief prediction of a time of sin and punishment in chap. 80, with a hint at personal afterlife in chapter 81. More typical of the genre is the *Animal Apocalypse* (*1 Enoch* 85–90), a symbolic vision in which the whole course of history, from Adam to the final judgment, is described. The angels lift Enoch up to a high place from which he can view the course of history, but he is not given a tour. Human beings are depicted as animals, while angels are represented as men. A few humans (Noah, Moses) are transformed into "men" or angels. This apocalypse alludes to the Maccabean Revolt, and seems to endorse the militancy of the Maccabees. The heroes of the story are "lambs," who grow horns. Judas Maccabee is depicted as a sheep with a great horn.

Apocalypse of Weeks

Another apocalypse from this period is the *Apocalypse of Weeks* (*1 Enoch* 93:1-10 + 91:11-17). Here Enoch reports "that which appeared to me in the heavenly vision, and (which) I know from the words of the holy angels and understand from the tablets of heaven." His vision is not described. History is divided into ten "weeks." (The tenfold division is also found in the *Sibylline Oracles* and may reflect the Persian idea of the millennium.) The crucial transition takes place in the seventh week, when a group called "the chosen righteous" arises. In the eighth week a sword will be given to the righteous to execute judgment. In the tenth, the first heaven will pass away, and a new heaven will appear. This is one of the few apocalypses that actually envision an end to the present world, although time will continue thereafter ("after this there will be many weeks without number"). The *Apocalypse of Weeks* is also exceptional for not speaking explicitly of resurrection. It is embedded, however, in a longer composition, the *Epistle of Enoch,* which attaches great importance to the hope for a blessed afterlife with the stars or heavenly host.

Several of these apocalypses (Daniel, *Apocalypse of Weeks, Animal Apocalypse,* also *Jubilees* 23) speak of elect groups that arise toward the end of history, shortly before the divine intervention. The apocalypses describe the revelations that strengthened these groups in the time of crisis and assured them of angelic assistance and of the hope for fellowship with the angels in the hereafter.

Other Pre-Christian Apocalypses

Jubilees

Daniel and several of the Enochic apocalypses were written in the first half of the second century B.C.E. We have only a few apocalypses from the following two centuries. The book of *Jubilees* represents a borderline example of the genre. It is introduced as a revelation that God tells the angel of the presence to write for Moses, encompassing history from the beginning of creation "till the time when my sanctuary shall be built among them for all eternity, and the Lord appear in the sight of all." In fact, it is a paraphrase of Genesis and the early chapters of Exodus. One of the innovations, over against the biblical account, is the introduction of the figure of Mastema, leader of the demons. There is also an eschatological prediction in chap. 23 that speaks of a time of tribulation followed by a time when "the children will begin to study the law" and lives will grow longer in peace and joy. It is said of the righteous that "their bones will rest in the earth, and their spirits will have much joy," apparently referring to a form of immortality other than bodily resurrection. *Jubilees,* then, has the framing elements of an apocalypse, but the content is atypical and is better described as a form of "rewritten Bible." *Jubilees* dates to the second century B.C.E.

Testament of Levi 2–5

There is a brief apocalypse involving an ascent through numbered heavens in the *Testament of Levi* 2–5. The *Testaments of the Twelve Patriarchs* have a complicated history; they are Christian in their present form, but they contain much Jewish material. Initially, in chapter 2, Levi appears to ascend through three heavens, but chapter 3 begins, "hear, then, about the seven heavens." It likely that an old account of an ascent through three heavens was later expanded. The idea of seven heavens became standard only in the first century of the Common Era. There is a very fragmentary account of an ascent of Levi in the *Aramaic Levi Document* found at Qumran, but the number of heavens is not mentioned in the extant fragments.

Similitudes of Enoch

A major apocalypse, the *Similitudes of Enoch* (*1 Enoch* 37–71), dates from the first half of the first century C.E. This is the only part of *1 Enoch* that has not been found in the Dead Sea Scrolls. It consists of three "parables" (chaps. 38–44, 45–57, and 58–69) and a double epilogue in chaps. 70 and 71. The revelation begins with the ascent of Enoch to "the end of heaven." There he sees "the dwelling of the righteous and the resting places of the holy" with the angels and holy ones. A major part of the revelation, however, consists of visions that are clearly indebted to Daniel 7. In chap. 46, Enoch sees "one who had a head of days" and with him "another whose face had the appearance of a man, and his face (was) full of grace, like one of the holy angels." The angelic interpreter explains: "This is the Son of Man who has righteousness." Henceforth the latter figure is referred to as "that Son of Man." Later, in chaps. 61 and 62, he is seated on the throne of glory and presides over the judgment. This figure cannot be identified with the archangel Michael, who appears separately. We are told that his name was named before the sun and stars were created. This apocalypse does not have any extended *ex eventu* prophecy or review of history, such as we find in Daniel, but it is concerned not only with individual eschatology but also with the judgment of the kings and the mighty.

1 Enoch 70:1 describes, in the third person, how Enoch was taken up "into the presence of that Son of Man and into the presence of the Lord of Spirits." A second epilogue, in chap. 71, is in the first person. In 71:14, when Enoch ascends to heaven he is greeted by an angel who tells him, "You are that Son of Man who was born for righteousness" (or perhaps "you are a son of man . . ."). There is no indication in the rest of the *Similitudes* that "that Son of Man" is Enoch. It is likely that this second epilogue was added secondarily, perhaps to counter the Christian identification of the Son of Man as Jesus. In later Jewish tradition *(3 Enoch* or *Sefer Hekhalot)* Enoch becomes Metatron when he ascends to heaven and is enthroned, at least for a time.

The Dead Sea Scrolls

Apart from the books of Daniel and Enoch, no texts that can be clearly identified as apocalypses have been found among the Dead Sea Scrolls. There are several fragmentary texts that could be apocalypses, but crucial parts (such as the beginning and the end) have not been preserved. 4Q246 (the Aramaic "Son of God" text), of which the beginning is fragmentary and the end is missing, was dubbed "the Aramaic Apocalypse" by its editor. It apparently involves the interpretation of a vision, but the interpreter seems to be human rather than angelic. This is also true of the other Pseudo-Daniel texts from Qumran (4Q243-244; 4Q245). The Aramaic "New Jerusalem" text is also too fragmentary to admit of a clear identification of its genre.

The books of Daniel and Enoch were found at Qumran, and the sectarian scrolls were influenced by them at many points. The sect known from the Scrolls, however, derived its revelation from the interpretation of the Torah of Moses and looked to the Teacher of Righteousness as the authoritative mediator of revelation. There was no need, then, to compose revelations in the name of Daniel or Enoch.

4 Ezra and 2 Baruch

An important cluster of Jewish apocalypses can be dated to the end of the first century C.E., after the destruction of Jerusalem. *4 Ezra* (= 2 Esdras 3–14) was probably composed in Hebrew but is extant only in Latin, Syriac, and other secondary versions. It begins with three extended dialogues between Ezra and an angel (Uriel). Ezra presses the question of theodicy, or the justice of God, in light of the destruction of Jerusalem, in a manner reminiscent of Job. The angel deflects his questions and talks about the wonderful things that are to come. In chap. 7, the angel explains how the messiah will come and rule for 400 years and then die, and creation will be returned to primeval silence for seven days. Then the resurrection will follow. In chap. 10, Ezra is told to eat "the flower that is in the field," after which he has a vision of a woman grieving for her son. He begins to chide her and tells her that she should "let herself be persuaded" that if she accepts the judgment of God she will receive back her son in due time. While he is speaking, she is transformed into a city, and he recognizes that she is Zion. Henceforward, Ezra lets himself be persuaded too. He then has two dream visions, each of which is clearly influenced by Daniel. In the first, Daniel's fourth kingdom is identified as Rome, although it was not so explained to Daniel. In the second he sees a human figure come up from the sea on a cloud. The figure takes his stand on Mt. Zion and repels the nations, in a passage that combines the traditional imagery of the Davidic messiah with that of the Son of Man. In the final chapter (14), Ezra is inspired to dictate to scribes a total of ninety-four books, twenty-four of which replace the Scriptures that had been lost, and are made public, while seventy are reserved for "the wise among the people."

Closely related to *4 Ezra* is *2 Baruch,* which is preserved in Syriac. This apocalypse is also a meditation on the fall of Jerusalem and is structured in seven sections like *4 Ezra.* Baruch also has symbolic visions, which express messianic and eschatological expectations. One of these visions concerns a cloud that rains alternately black and white waters, symbolizing twelve periods of history. But where Ezra took a very pessimistic view of fallen human nature ("Oh Adam, what have you done?"), Baruch is more confident of the possibility of keeping the Law ("each of us is Adam to his own soul"). *2 Baruch* appears to be written as a rejoinder to *4 Ezra,* telling people to trust in the Almighty and his Law, and that vindication will follow.

Ascents to Heaven

Apocalypse of Abraham

The *Apocalypse of Abraham* also dates from the period after the fall of Jerusalem. It is preserved in Slavonic, which was translated from Greek, but was probably composed in Hebrew or Aramaic. It falls into two sections: chaps. 1–8 recount the story of Abraham's conversion from idolatry. Chapters 9–32 describe the revelation. Abraham's sacrifice in Genesis 15 provides the point of departure. An angel takes Abraham up to heaven on the wing of a pigeon and assists him in uttering celestial songs. Abraham has a vision of the divine throne and is shown a picture of the course of history, divided into twelve hours, beginning with Adam and culminating with the destruction of the Temple. The picture of the world is highly dualistic. (The satanic figure is called Azazel.) There are some Christian interpolations, possibly by Bogomil scribes in the early Middle Ages.

3 Baruch

Some other ascent apocalypses are thought to have been composed in Greek and originated in the Diaspora, probably in Egypt. *3 Baruch* is preserved in a Greek version (Greek was the original language) and in a Slavonic version. Baruch is weeping over the destruction of Jerusalem. An angel tells him not to trouble himself so much about it: "Come, and I will show you the mysteries of God." The angel then guides him upward through five heavens. It is likely that the standard number of seven heavens is presupposed but that Baruch's ascent is aborted so that he does not come directly into the presence of God. He sees the abodes of the dead, both blessed and damned. The gate of the fifth heaven is closed until Michael opens it to receive the prayers and merits of humans and take them up to a higher heaven. Unlike many heroes in ascent apocalypses, Baruch makes no speech when he returns to earth. The lessons of his tour are implied in lists of vices associated with the damned. Some verses in chap. 4 and especially in chaps. 11–15 are clearly Christian, but the Christian redaction appears to be a secondary development. The apocalypse reflects its Diaspora situation in being willing to let go of Jerusalem and focus instead on individual eschatology.

2 Enoch

2 Enoch is the most elaborate ascent apocalypse transmitted from antiquity. It is preserved in Slavonic, and its provenance is uncertain. It is usually assumed to be Jewish because of the lack of explicit Christian elements, but much of its content could be affirmed by Christians as well as by Jews. It is certainly influenced by *1 Enoch.* It describes Enoch's ascent through seven heavens. He sees both the workings of the cosmos and the abodes of the dead. In the seventh heaven, he is transformed to an angelic state in the presence of God. The angel Uriel dictates to him all things in the cosmos and in history, and he writes them down in 360 books so that they can survive the flood. When he returns to earth, he instructs his children and the assembled multitude on the basis of his experience.

Testament of Abraham

Also of debated origin is the Greek *Testament of Abraham.* Abraham is reluctant to die, so the archangel Michael is commissioned to take him on a tour of the world. In the course of his tour he witnesses a judgment scene presided over by Abel, son of Adam. Some motifs betray Egyptian provenance, notably the weighing of the souls at the judgment. Abraham learns from the judgment that he has been overly zealous in condemning sinners. Despite the title of the work, he makes no testament. The *Testament of Abraham* is exceptional among the apocalypses because of its humor. There is nothing in it that is distinctively Christian, but nothing that is distinctively Jewish, either.

Later Transmission

As will be apparent, most of the Jewish apocalypses were transmitted by Christians, including the books of Enoch, whose Jewish origin is confirmed by their discovery in the Dead Sea Scrolls. Rabbinic Judaism seems to have repudiated apocalyptic revelation, on the Deuteronomic principle that revelation is "not in heaven" but on earth, in the Torah. The apocalyptic heritage lived on, however, in the mystical strands of Judaism, known as merkavah mysticism. A fine example of a late Hebrew apocalypse (fifth-sixth century C.E.?) is the work known as *3 Enoch,* or *Sefer Hekhalot,* which describes the ascent of Enoch and his (temporary) enthronement as Metatron in heaven. The genre flourished in Christianity down to the Middle Ages.

Forms and Functions

It is also apparent that there was considerable variety within the genre. But there were commonalities, too: the appeal to heavenly revelation, the importance of angelic mediators, and the expectation of a judgment of individuals beyond death. The function of the literature varies, from encouragement in time of crisis to consolation in the wake of disaster. Most fundamental, perhaps, is the attempt to view life in light of the impending judgment and to adapt one's values and lifestyle accordingly.

BIBLIOGRAPHY

J. J. COLLINS, ED. 1979, *Apocalypse: The Morphology of a Genre,* Semeia 14, Missoula, Mont.: Scholars Press. • J. J. COLLINS 1997, *Apocalypticism in the Dead Sea Scrolls,* London: Routledge. • J. J. COLLINS 1998, *The Apocalyptic Imagination,* 2d ed., Grand Rapids: Eerdmans. • J. J. COLLINS, ED. 1998, *The Encyclopedia of Apocalypticism,* vol. 1, *The Origins of Apocalypticism in Judaism and Christianity,* New York: Continuum. • I. GRUENEWALD 1980, *Apocalyptic and Merkavah Mysticism,* Leiden: Brill. • D. HELLHOLM, ED. 1983, *Apocalypticism in the Mediterranean World and the Near East,* Tübingen: Mohr-Siebeck. • M. HIMMELFARB 1993, *Ascent to Heaven in Jewish and Christian Apocalypses,* New York: Oxford University Press. • H. KVANVIG 1988, *Roots of Apocalyptic: The Mesopotamian Background of the Enoch Figure and of the Son of Man,* Neukirchen-Vluyn: Neukirchener Verlag. • C. ROWLAND 1982, *The Open Heaven: A Study of Apocalyptic in Judaism and Early Christianity,* New York: Crossroad. • P. SACCHI 1996, *Jewish Apocalyptic and Its History,* Sheffield: Sheffield Academic Press • J. C. VANDERKAM AND W. ADLER, EDS. 1996, *The Jewish Apocalyptic Heritage in Early Christianity,* Assen: Van Gorcum; Minneapolis: Fortress. • A. YARBRO COLLINS 1996, *Cosmology and Eschatology in Jewish and Christian Apocalyptic Literature,* Leiden: Brill.

See also: Apocalypticism; Ascent to Heaven; Eschatology

JOHN J. COLLINS

Apocalypticism

The term "apocalypticism" comes from the Greek term *apokalypsis,* meaning "revelation," "unveiling," or "disclosure." In modern scholarship, it is a used to designate a pattern of religion found in different forms in a variety of religious traditions (Collins, McGinn, and Stein 2000). It is frequently employed to describe a religious outlook claiming to derive from dreams, visions, or otherworldly journeys, modes of revelation that convey insight into mysteries of the heavenly world and/or the course and climax of history. Within Judaism and Christianity, apocalypticism has played a significant part in both mainstream and fringe religion. It is rooted in the prophetic and wisdom books of the Hebrew Bible and, according to some scholars, also indebted to the blending of religious ideas that became prominent in the early Hellenistic period. For the sake of clarity, it has become common in recent years to distinguish between "apocalypticism" as a broad worldview or pattern of religion based on revelatory experience; "apocalyptic eschatology" as a set of beliefs regarding such "last things" as the climax of history, the salvation of Israel, the renewal of the cosmos, and the fate of the individual dead; and "apocalypse" as a genre of revelatory literature in which the former two phenomena are to be found in their fullest form.

Defining Apocalypticism

Distinguishing Feature

What distinguishes apocalypticism as a religious outlook is its peculiar hermeneutical basis. In apocalypticism, theological understanding does not come by the exercise of established methods of reading and interpretation but by supernatural revelation. Revelation is not dependent on ingenuity or the interpretation of tradition but is in some sense given from beyond. The closest analogy is the dream, which the dreamer does not create, even if the components of the dream may themselves be contingent upon past experience, whether religious or otherwise (Flannery-Dailey 2005). The mode of reception is passive, which is to suggest not that there is any lack of preparation on the part of the recipient conducive to the reception of a dream or vision (such as fasting or study of sacred texts) but that the moments of revelatory insight come by way of divine initiative (cf. Dan. 10:1-3; *4 Ezra* 6:35; 9:26). Although Scripture might be a launching pad for what comes to the reader of sacred texts, it is clearly not the only medium of understanding. The method outlined in Sirach 38, for example, in which the insightful interpreter looks for meaning, is different from the situation that the apocalyptic writers describe.

The Synthesis of "Apokalyptik"

Although apocalypticism has always been a significant factor in Judaism and Christianity, it became central to scholarly concerns in the nineteenth century, when the word *Apokalyptik* came to be used as a way of systematizing a pattern of religion found not only in Daniel and the book of Revelation but also in other, recently rediscovered Jewish texts. Foremost among these texts was the Ethiopic *Apocalypse of Enoch,* or *1 Enoch,* which was published in 1821. The concept of *Apokalyptik* has had enormous influence. This religious perspective, characterized by an expectation of the imminent end of the age, a radical contrast between present and future, the hope for another world breaking into and overtaking this world, the activities of angels and demons, and complex visionary imagery, came to be treated as distinct from the types of Judaism based on careful interpretation of the law of Moses.

A good example of this kind of approach is reflected in the following statement of Philip Vielhauer (1965): "We may designate apocalyptic as a special expression of the Jewish eschatology which existed alongside the national eschatology represented by the rabbis. It is linked with the latter by many ideas, but is differentiated from it by a quite different understanding of God, the world, and humanity." While Vielhauer recognized that the world of ideas typical of apocalypticism is far from uniform, he listed the following as characteristic features: a contrast between the present age, which is perishable and temporary, and the age to come, which is imperishable and eternal; a belief that the new age is of a transcendent kind, which breaks in from beyond through divine intervention and without human activity; a wider concern than merely the destiny of Israel; an interest in the totality of world history; the belief that God has foreordained everything and that the history of the world has been divided into epochs; and finally, an imminent expectation that the present unsatisfactory state of affairs will only be short lived.

Subsequent study has shown that this neat distinction of *Apokalyptik* from other strands of Judaism is fallacious (Stone 1991). Not only is eschatological expectation a key aspect of most varieties of ancient Judaism, but a work like *4 Ezra* indicates that the law of Moses could play a key part in apocalyptic literature. Apocalyptic elements are endemic to several varieties of Second Temple Judaism, with proto-rabbis and eschatological prognosticators alike drawing on a common stock of imagery rooted in the prophetic books of the Bible. A glance at the activity of the scribe as set out in one of the supposedly least apocalyptic books of the Second Temple period, the Wisdom of Jesus ben Sirach, proves the point. In chap. 38 Ben Sira has the scribe engaged in the kind of deep exegesis of scriptural texts that is typical of the wise men as represented in the book of Daniel. It is true that the Enochic literature has relatively little to say about the Law of Moses, and, indeed, has an alternative description of the origin of evil in *1 Enoch* 6–18 compared with what we find in the book of Genesis. But this should remind us that apocalyptic literature represents a very heterogeneous collection not neatly attached to specific groups or sects within early Judaism.

Two Major Approaches

There have been two major approaches to the understanding of apocalypticism. One concentrates on the *contents* of early Jewish texts and attempts to construct some kind of synthesis of religious ideas. More or less continuing the synthesis typical of *Apokalyptik,* it understands apocalypticism as basically an eschatological belief system characterized by dualism and expectation of a new and better world breaking into this world from beyond and swamping this age with its glory. The other approach starts from consideration of the *fact and form of revelation* described in the relevant texts, whether the disclosure comes through vision, audition, or dream. It regards the claim to transcendent, revealed knowledge as central and emphasizes that eschatology is not the sole focus of apocalyptic literature but only one emphasis alongside others such as cosmology.

Both content and form are important for the understanding of apocalypticism, and few would deny that the visionary component is central. The content of many (though not all) of these visions is eschatological in orientation, but we need to be careful not to assume that there was a radical, and widespread, shift from "this-worldly" to "otherworldly" in the eschatology of the apocalypses. The apocalypses largely reflect the biblical hope for fulfillment in this world, even if *4 Ezra* and Revelation also have a replacement of this world at the end of a temporary messianic kingdom. Further, a few ascent apocalypses such as *3 Baruch* and the *Testament of Abraham* focus only on matters of "personal" eschatology — the individual judgment of the dead — and give little or no attention to national, political, or corporate eschatology of the sort that would involve the restoration of Israel and the judgment of the nations. Most apocalypses, though, do expect a new age or world order of some sort but envision it being fulfilled precisely in this world. This is true even of texts that narrate otherworldly journeys (e.g., *1 Enoch, T. Levi,* and *2 Enoch*) and of those that expect a new transcendent order after a temporary messianic kingdom on earth (e.g., *4 Ezra* and Revelation).

Apocalyptic Literature

A variety of texts have given shape to the discussion of apocalypticism. In addition to the major apocalypses of *1 Enoch,* Daniel, *4 Ezra,* and Revelation, others include the *Apocalypse of Abraham, 2 Enoch,* the *Testament of Abraham,* the Greek *Testament of Levi* (chaps. 2–5), *2 Baruch, 3 Baruch,* and the Christian *Ascension of Isaiah* and *Shepherd of Hermas.* All these works evince a pattern of religion in which the revelation of divine secrets enables those privileged to read the book to discern the mysteries of the cosmos and/or the future and to fathom some of the unexplained mysteries of human life such as the problem of evil. The latter is most clearly seen in *4 Ezra,* which offers less an answer than the assertion that humans cannot comprehend the answer, a strategy familiar from the book of Job.

Among the Dead Sea Scrolls are copies of previously known apocalypses *(1 Enoch)* and works with apocalyptic features *(Jubilees)* as well as newly discovered works with revelatory contents, such as the *War Scroll,* the *Temple Scroll,* the *Testament of Amram,* the Pseudo-Daniel fragments (4Q243-245), the pseudo-prophetic texts (4Q385-330), the Aramaic Son of God text (4Q246), the New Jerusalem text (1Q32; etc.), and the so-called *Messianic Apocalypse* (4Q521). The fragmentary character of the Cave 4 texts makes it impossible to know whether those with apocalyptic features and eschatological contents formed part of larger apocalypses. We thus have no clear example of a full-blown apocalypse composed and not just copied at Qumran.

Biblical Roots

Apocalyptic literature has obvious links with the prophetic texts of the Hebrew Bible, particularly with the future hope of the prophets. The eschatological concern in apocalypses with human history and the vindication of Israel's hopes echoes prophetic themes in the books of Ezekiel (esp. chaps. 38–39), Isaiah (esp. chaps. 24–27; 55–56), and Zechariah (esp. chaps. 9–14). Apocalyptic visions and their interpretations are influenced by the "mantic" wisdom of dream interpreters like Joseph and Daniel. The angelic tour guides and interpreters prominent in otherworldly journeys have a precedent in Zechariah 1–6. There are also some features in the apocalypses that have parallels in the wisdom literature. In particular, the catalogues of natural and cosmic phenomena in some wisdom texts (e.g., in Job 28 and 38–39) resemble the lists of revealed things in apocalypses like *1 Enoch, 4 Ezra,* and *2 Baruch* (Stone 1991: 379-418).

Social Settings

The social settings of apocalypticism are difficult to specify, given that most apocalypses are written under the pseudonym of a revered figure of the past, and that their contents cannot always be linked with particular historical events. Because apocalyptic texts are oriented toward the future and often critique the present, apocalypticism is often regarded as the product of a marginalized minority whose concerns could find expression only in visions of a different and better world. In this view, marginality is linked with a despair of political change and a consequent retreat from hope in the fulfillment of the divine promises in history. However, while postexilic Judaism was indeed characterized by a polarization between a powerful hierarchy of priests and other, less powerful groups (Hanson 1979), the origins of apocalypticism cannot be attributed to a specific protest movement. It appears rather that a variety of groups used apocalyptic ideas and expected their eschatological hopes to be fulfilled on this earth.

Since apocalyptic ideas came to be linked in the early modern and modern periods with sectarian traditions, it is easy to see why many commentators suppose that the apocalypses must stem from marginalized groups. Nevertheless, these works contain a vast array of different subjects that do not always reflect the experience of ostracism, oppression, or persecution: the future purposes of God; astronomical and other cosmic mysteries; descriptions of heaven and angels; the question of theodicy raised by the destruction of Jerusalem and the Temple or by the universality of sin; and the postmortem fate of the individual dead. All these topics were of concern to various learned groups within Second Temple Judaism. Even if some of the apocalypses may have been written by the marginalized, the character of these books indicates that they were not written by the uneducated. In the Dead Sea Scrolls, it is apparent that we have the ideology of a group whose origin at least was among some of the most self-consciously elite members of Second Temple Jewish society, the priests.

Seeing and Writing Visions

Over the years in his work on *4 Ezra,* Michael Stone has repeatedly suggested that pseudepigraphy has too often been a reason for not taking seriously the experiential basis of the visions described in some of the apocalypses (Stone 2003; cf. Stone 1991: 21-28). There is a wealth of cross-cultural evidence from different periods of history suggesting that visionaries or seers of various kinds felt themselves to be not just recipients but mediums of the communications that came from heavenly or distinguished "others." The notion of "automatic writing," possibly prepared for by ascetic practices or other means, has a long history down to the present, and its role is not to be discounted as a way of explaining the complex problem of pseudepigraphy in writings that claim visionary authority.

Yet it is unclear how ancient visionaries received their revelation. Did they sit down like a poet and exercise that mixture of imagination and attention to form which is characteristic of poetry? Or did they have visions akin to the experience of dreams? Granted that vision reports are not raw, undigested transcripts of such experiences, how may we discern genuine religious experience at the basis of these literary compositions? Many commentators suppose that apocalypses are the result of a conscious attempt to weave together Scripture and contemporary challenge in a way not dissimilar from the way in which Paul wrote his epistles. But there are many signs in works like the book of Revelation of a dream-like quality in which the visionary not only sees but also is an active participant in the visions he sees (e.g., Rev. 1:12, 17; 5:4; 7:13; 11:1; 17:3; cf. 1:10 and 21:10).

The Influence of Ezekiel 1

In several places in apocalyptic literature there is also evidence that the apocalyptists were, like the merkavah mystics of later rabbinic tradition, interested in the first chapter of Ezekiel (e.g., Dan. 7:9; *1 Enoch* 14:20; Revelation 4; 4Q 405 20 ii 21-22; *Apocalypse of Abraham* 17–18) and the first chapter of Genesis (e.g., Pseudo-Philo, *Biblical Antiquities* 28; *4 Ezra* 6; *Jubilees* 2; and *2 Enoch* 25–26). In some interpretations of Ezekiel 1, the meaning of the text may have come about as the result of "seeing again" what Ezekiel saw. The visionary's own experience of what had appeared to Ezekiel would itself have been the context for a creative interpretation of the text. For these apocalypticists, Ezekiel 1 was therefore probably not just the subject of learned study but a catalyst for visionary experience, in which expounders saw again what had appeared to the prophet, but in their own way and in a manner appropriate for their own time. Three aspects of Ezekiel's vision are often dwelt upon in later interpretations of the vision: the prominence of color; the difficult word *hašmal* (Ezek. 1:4, 27 and 8:2); and the human-like figures mentioned in the vision. It is the term *hašmal* (usually rendered with the phrase "gleaming amber" or the like) which is of particular interest. In one of the passages that discuss it (*b. Ḥagigah* 13a; cf. *y. Ḥagigah* 77a), there is evidence that an experiential element was involved in meditating upon the meaning of this word and that doing so could harm inexperienced individuals.

The New Testament

Although the book of Revelation is the only apocalypse in the New Testament, most of its other documents are pervaded with language and passages that may be termed apocalyptic or revelatory. Visionary material is central to the representation of Christian origins in these texts, whether it be Paul's own testimony to his apostleship in Gal. 1:12 and 16, or the Acts of the Apostles, where the role of the visionary is stressed in the unfolding of the divine economy in this highly selective account of Christian history. Apocalyptic eschatology is also a major leitmotif in the Gospels and Acts, the Epistles, and the book of Revelation. Those texts that became foundational for the early Christian movement place the events in Galilee, Judea, and Jerusalem within an overarching eschatological framework, which in the language of Paul and his successors may be characterized as the revelation *(apokalypsis)* of the ultimate mystery. This eschatological outlook in no way distinguishes Christianity from other parts of Judaism. Indeed, much of what we find in the New Testament has its analogues scattered among Jewish texts of the Second Temple period or later. In this respect the New Testament offers a rich resource for understanding religious developments in Judaism during the closing years of the Second Temple.

Rabbinic Judaism and Later Christianity

The meditative visionary practice based on Ezekiel's call vision played an integral part in the emergence of rabbinic religion at the beginning of the second century C.E. Sages like Rabban Yoḥanan ben Zakkai and Rabbi Akiba were both linked in the tradition with merkabah mysticism. Yet in circles influenced by rabbinic Judaism, reading Ezekiel 1 was severely restricted because of its use by visionaries and the dangers to faith and life that visionary activity posed (*m. Meg.* 4:10; *t. Meg.* 4[3]: 31ff.; *b. Megillah* 24ab). After the failure of the Second Revolt under Simeon bar Kosiba in 132-135 C.E., in which messianism played a significant role, there is evidence of a growing reluctance in Jewish circles to countenance apocalyptic eschatology.

This waning of eschatological belief coincided with a suspicion of apocalyptic elements in second-century Christianity. The perceived excesses of the ecstatic prophecy of the Montanist movement in Asia Minor had a widespread dampening effect on late second-century Christianity, even though one of its major writers, Tertullian, ended up as part of that movement. At the same time, however, in some Christian circles there was a widespread appeal to visionary inspiration linked to apostles in writings that are usually given the term "Gnostic" because of their claim to offer access to esoteric divine knowledge *(gnosis)* about the secrets of God and the universe. Thanks to the Nag Hammadi discoveries, we know much more about this kind of religion. Among these texts are several works with apocalyptic features, but they are largely devoid of revelations concerning the future of the cosmos such as we find in early Jewish apocalyptic literature. Instead, they set out ways of understanding cosmogony in order to determine one's position in the universe and one's existential destiny.

BIBLIOGRAPHY

J. J. COLLINS 1997, *Apocalypticism and the Dead Sea Scrolls*, London: Routledge. • J. J. COLLINS 1998, *The Apocalyptic Imagination: An Introduction to Jewish Apocalyptic Literature*, 2d ed., Grand Rapids: Eerdmans. • J. J. COLLINS, B. MCGINN, AND S. STEIN, EDS. 2000, *The Encyclopedia of Apocalypticism*, 3 vols., New York: Continuum. • S. L. COOK 1995, *Prophecy and Apocalypticism: The Post-Exilic Social Setting*, Minneapolis: Fortress. • F. FLANNERY-DAILEY 2004, *Dreamers, Scribes, and Priests: Jewish Dreams in the Hellenistic and Roman Eras*, Leiden: Brill. • I. GRUENWALD 1988, *From Apocalyptic to Gnosticism: Studies in Apocalypticism, Merkavah Mysticism and Gnosticism*, Frankfurt: Peter Lang. • P. D. HANSON 1979, *The Dawn of Apocalyptic: The Historical and Sociological Roots of Jewish Apocalyptic Eschatology*, rev. ed., Philadelphia: Fortress. • M. HIMMELFARB 1993, *Ascent to Heaven in Jewish and Christian Apocalypses*, Oxford: Oxford University Press. • D. HALPERIN 1988, *The Faces of the Chariot: Development of Rabbinic Exegesis of Ezekiel's Vision of the Divine Chariot*, Tübingen: Mohr-Siebeck. • D. HELLHOLM, ED. 1989, *Apocalypticism in the Mediterranean World and the Near East*, 2d ed. Tübingen: Mohr-Siebeck. • H. S. KVANVIG 1988, *Roots of Apocalyptic: The Mesopotamian Background of the Enoch Figure and the Son of Man*, Neukirchen-Vluyn: Neukirchener Verlag. • J. R. LEVISON 1999, *Of Two Minds: Ecstasy and Inspired Interpretation in the New Testament World*, North Richlands Hills, Tex.: Bibal. • M. LIEB 1991, *The Visionary Mode: Biblical Prophecy, Hermeneutics, and Cultural Change*, Ithaca, N.Y.: Cornell University Press. • C. ROWLAND 1982, *The Open Heaven: A Study of Apocalyptic in Judaism and Early Christianity*, London: SPCK. • C. ROWLAND, P. GIBBONS, AND V. DOBRORUKA 2006, "'A Door Opened in Heaven': An Essay on the Character of Visionary Experience," in *Paradise Now: Essays on Early Jewish and Christian Mysticism*, ed. A. DeConick, Leiden: Brill. • M. E. STONE 1991, *Selected Studies in Pseudepigrapha and Apocrypha with Special Reference to the Armenian Tradition*, Leiden: Brill. • M. E. STONE 2003, "A Reconsideration of Apocalyptic Visions," *HTR* 96: 167-80. • J. C. VANDERKAM AND W. ADLER, EDS. 1996, *The Jewish Apocalyptic Heritage in Early Christianity*, Assen: Van Gorcum; Minneapolis: Fortress. • P. VIELHAUER 1965, "Apocalypses and Related Subjects: Introduction," in E. Hennecke and W. Schneemelcher, *New Testament Apocrypha*, 2 vols., London: Lutterworth, 2:581-642.

See also Apocalypse; Ascent to Heaven; Cosmology; Death and Afterlife; Dream and Vision Reports; Eschatology; Heaven; Hekhalot Literature; Mysticism; Pseudepigraphy CHRISTOPHER ROWLAND

Apocrypha, Old Testament

The term "Apocrypha" is customarily applied to early Jewish writings included in the Greek (Septuagint) and Latin (Vulgate) Old Testament manuscripts but not in the Hebrew (Masoretic) Bible. The word derives from the Greek term for "hidden away, kept secret." In 2 Esdras *(4 Ezra)* 14:45-46 a distinction is made between the twenty-four books that can be made public and read by the worthy and unworthy (Hebrew Bible), and seventy other books "that were written last" and given only to the wise (Apocrypha). Today Jews and Protestants follow the canon of the Hebrew Bible, while Catholics and Orthodox Christians include several additional Old Testament books in their canons of Scripture.

Most modern Bible versions now include the Apocrypha. Catholic Bibles intersperse them among the Old Testament books, while Protestant Bibles place them in a separate section between the Old Testament and the New Testament. The New Revised Standard Version divides them into four sections: (1) books that are in the Roman Catholic, Greek, and Slavonic Bibles (Tobit, Judith, Additions to Esther, Wisdom of Solomon, Sirach, Baruch, Letter of Jeremiah, Additions to Daniel, 1 Maccabees, and 2 Maccabees); (2) books in the Greek and

APOCRYPHA, OLD TESTAMENT

Slavonic Bibles but not in the Roman Catholic canon (1 Esdras, Prayer of Manasseh, Psalm 151, 3 Maccabees); (3) a book in the Slavonic Bible and in the Latin Vulgate appendix (2 Esdras); and (4) a book in an appendix to the Greek Bible (4 Maccabees).

The Old Testament Apocrypha constitute only one, very disparate corpus in the much larger body of Second Temple Jewish literature. However, since these books appear in most Christian Bibles today, they can be a convenient and accessible starting point for the study of early Judaism. The Old Testament Apocrypha add considerably to the inventory of literary genres and rhetorical techniques employed in ancient Jewish literature. The corpus includes histories (1 and 2 Maccabees), historical novels (Tobit, Judith), wisdom instructions (Sirach, Wisdom of Solomon), prayers (Prayer of Manasseh, Additions to Esther), and even the first detective stories (Susanna, Bel and the Dragon).

Variety of Literary Genres

The books of Tobit and Judith, which tell good stories about (mostly) edifying characters, develop their plots by a sophisticated shifting of scenes from one place to another. The book of Sirach is a huge wisdom instruction in which Jesus Ben Sira, a Jewish teacher in Jerusalem in the early second century B.C.E., expresses opinions on practically every imaginable topic. In doing so he uses the rhetorical forms typical of ancient Near Eastern wisdom literature (numerical sayings, beatitudes, maxims, prohibitions, etc.), as well as various poetic devices (chiasms, inclusions, acrostics, etc.). The Wisdom of Solomon and 4 Maccabees combine Greek rhetorical and philosophical concepts in the service of Jewish theology. The Jewish apocalypse preserved in 2 Esdras 3–14 (also known as *4 Ezra*), which is roughly contemporary with the New Testament book of Revelation, uses dialogues and dream visions to raise questions about Jerusalem's destruction in 70 C.E. and to provide encouragement about Israel's future.

The history of Israel in Judea during the second century B.C.E. is greatly illumined by 1 and 2 Maccabees. Both works approach the events from distinctive ideological perspectives. Second Maccabees has been described as "temple propaganda" (because it focuses on the defense of the Jerusalem Temple) and "pathetic history" (because it appeals to the emotions, or *pathē* in Greek). Nevertheless, it provides important and generally reliable information about the events and characters leading up to the Maccabean Revolt and the early successes as its leader, Judas Maccabaeus. First Maccabees is sometimes called "dynastic propaganda" (because it describes three generations in the history of the Maccabee family). Its thesis is that deliverance was given to Israel through this family (see 5:61-62). It describes the crisis under Antiochus IV Epiphanes and the resistance begun by the priest Mattathias (1:1–2:70), as well as the military and political exploits of Judas (3:1–9:22) and his brothers Jonathan (9:23–12:53) and Simon and Simon's son, John Hyrcanus (13:1–16:24). These two books describe how Judea became an independent state with a national identity based on Temple, land, and Torah. They also describe how the Romans entered into Jewish history, thus providing the context for Judea's incorporation into the Roman Empire and setting the stage for the events described in the Gospels.

Divine Providence

In the area of theology the Old Testament Apocrypha also have much to contribute. They describe God's care for righteous persons (Tobit, Susanna), his use of weak instruments (Judith), love for and protection of Israel (3 Maccabees, Judith), and defense of the Temple (2 Maccabees). Since there is only one God (monotheism), the worship of other gods (idolatry) is the height of folly and brings about evil effects (Wisdom 13–15, Bel and Dragon, Letter of Jeremiah).

The Figure of Wisdom

Several of these books give special attention to how God works in the world through the figure of Wisdom. According to Sirach 24, Wisdom makes her dwelling place in the Jerusalem Temple and is the Torah ("the covenant of the Most High God, the Law that Moses commanded us," 24:23). Likewise, according to Baruch, wisdom is "the book of the commandments of God, the law that endures forever" (4:1). In the book of Wisdom, the figure of Wisdom functions as the equivalent of the world soul of Stoic philosophy, filling the world and holding all things together (1:7). Wisdom animates all creation with "a spirit that is intelligent, holy, unique, manifold, subtle, mobile, clear, unpolluted . . ." (7:22).

Theology of Suffering

If any theme unites these very disparate books, it is suffering. In some works (Baruch, Letter of Jeremiah, 1 and 2 Esdras) Israel's sufferings, especially the destruction of its Temple and the Exile, are presented as just punishments for the people's sins and as warnings to return to the way of righteousness (the Torah). In 2 Maccabees Israel's sufferings are explained as due to divine discipline, while in several other books the fidelity of key characters (Tobit, Judith, Daniel, Judas Maccabaeus, etc.) moves God to act on his people's behalf and to rescue them from danger. Several books (Wisdom, 2 and 4 Maccabees, 2 Esdras 3–14) present life after death and/or the full coming of God's kingdom as the time when God's sovereignty will be fully manifest, and when the righteous will be vindicated and the wicked will be punished. With the help of concepts from Greek philosophy, 4 Maccabees develops the idea of the expiatory or atoning value of the Maccabean martyrs' deaths on behalf of God's people.

Their History

Formation of the Canon in Judaism and Christianity

From the ancient witnesses, two clear tendencies emerge: There was a movement within Judaism in the late first century C.E. toward a three-part canon of twenty-four books in Hebrew as the Jewish canon of Scripture; and there was an acceptance of a wider and more inclusive Old Testament canon by most Christians by the late fourth and fifth centuries C.E. (if not much earlier). These two tendencies have often been explained somewhat simplistically as due to the Jewish Council (or Synod) of Jamnia/Yavneh in the late first century C.E., and to the Christian adoption of a more inclusive Old Testament canon current in the Jewish community at Alexandria. But neither hypothesis can be proved, and the historical realities were very likely more complicated.

Fragments among the Dead Sea Scrolls

The earliest Jewish manuscripts of the Hebrew Bible and some of the Old Testament Apocrypha are from Qumran. They range in age from the third century B.C.E. to the first century C.E. Every book in the Hebrew Bible except Esther is represented in some way. There are also fragments of some "apocryphal" books (Sirach, Tobit, Letter of Jeremiah, and Psalm 151) among the Dead Sea Scrolls.

There is no list of canonical books from Qumran. However, from the biblical and nonbiblical texts found there it appears that the Pentateuch, the Former Prophets (historical books), Latter Prophets (including the Twelve), and the Psalms were used in ways (that is, copied, commented upon, appealed to in arguments) that suggest that they possessed a high degree of authority. But there is no way to know which writings (if any) were regarded as canonical at Qumran. Indeed, if the number of manuscripts is any indication, it would appear that *1 Enoch* and 4QInstruction were considered more authoritative than many "biblical" books. *Jubilees* and the so-called *Reworked Pentateuch* probably also had scriptural status at Qumran.

Use in Jewish Tradition

The earliest Jewish reckonings of canonical books come from the late first and second centuries C.E. In *Against Apion* 1.37-43 Josephus claims that there are twenty-two "justly accredited books" and sets the time of "Artaxerxes who succeeded Xerxes as king of Persia" as the cutoff point for inclusion. Since there are twenty-two letters in the Hebrew alphabet, Josephus' number may suggest that all truth is contained in these books. The number twenty-four given in 2 Esdras 14:45-46 probably reflects a different and more common way of combining and numbering certain books. A Jewish tradition *(baraita)* in the Babylonian Talmud (*b. Baba Batra* 14b–15a) from the second century C.E. also gives the number of books as twenty-four and divides them into the Torah, Prophets, and Writings. In the early rabbinic period there were disputes about whether certain books (Ezekiel, Proverbs, Ecclesiastes, Song of Songs, and Esther) belonged in the canon of the Hebrew Scriptures. In any case, the restriction to twenty-two or twenty-four books left no room in the Hebrew canon for the inclusion of what came to be known as the "apocryphal" books.

Use in the New Testament

The evidence for the direct use of the Old Testament Apocrypha by New Testament writers is slim. While there are many parallels, there are few, if any, direct quotations or allusions. The best examples are Matt. 11:25-30 (Sir. 51:1-30?), Rom. 1:18-32 (Wisdom 13–15?), and Heb. 1:3 (Wis. 7:26?). However, all these texts have been explained in other ways. Moreover, even if one could prove that they were direct quotations, this would not prove that the New Testament writers regarded their sources as canonical.

Inclusion in Greek Bible Manuscripts

The oldest (fourth-fifth centuries C.E.) and most important Christian manuscripts of the Greek Bible show an openness to the Old Testament Apocrypha. Codex Vaticanus contains Wisdom, Sirach, Judith, Tobit, Baruch, and the Letter of Jeremiah. Codex Sinaiticus has Tobit, Judith, 1 and 2 Maccabees, Wisdom, and Sirach. Codex Alexandrinus includes Baruch, Letter of Jeremiah, Tobit, Judith, 1 and 2 Maccabees, 3 and 4 Maccabees, Wisdom, Sirach, and Psalms of Solomon. These books are interspersed among the "canonical" books and not placed in a separate section. The order of books in each manuscript is different. These facts indicate that there was some fluidity around the edges of the early Christian Old Testament canon, and that the core "Apocrypha" were included in some Christian biblical manuscripts.

Use by Patristic Writers

The evidence for the use of the Old Testament Apocrypha by patristic writers is stronger. Early Christian writers frequently appealed to characters such as Tobit and the Maccabean martyrs in these books as examples of morality or courage. They also found in them relevant material about angels (Tobit), immortality and resurrection (Wisdom, 2 Maccabees), and the doctrine of *creatio ex nihilo* (2 Macc. 7:8). Material from the book of Sirach was often quoted and adapted by Greek and Latin Christian writers, because that book was regarded as a repository of human wisdom and as relevant for Christians as well as Jews.

Use in the Eastern and Western Churches

The lists of canonical Old Testament books from the Eastern churches tend to support a more restrictive canon, like that of the Hebrew tradition. The lists from the Western churches were more expansive and inclusive. In both areas, there were also those who expressed doubts about or objections to certain books or to the Apocrypha as a whole. The most important objector was Jerome (ca. 340-420 C.E.), the most competent and famous biblical scholar of the patristic period.

Jerome As Jerome made progress in his study of Hebrew and began using the Hebrew text rather than the Greek Septuagint as the basis for his Latin translation (Vulgate), he became increasingly convinced that the Christian Old Testament should be restricted to the books of the Hebrew Bible and that the other books should be set apart among the Apocrypha. He correctly perceived that Sirach and 1 Maccabees had been composed in Hebrew, and he claimed to have translated Tobit and Judith from Aramaic. While Jerome had great respect for the Apocrypha and encouraged their reading, he argued that these books should be read for the edification of the people but not for establishing the authority of church doctrines.

Augustine In responding to Jerome, Augustine (354-430 C.E.) did not deny the value of the Hebrew texts. However, he argued in favor of basing the new Latin Version (Vulgate) on the Greek Septuagint in the hope that it would promote greater unity between the Latin-speaking churches of the West and the Greek-speaking churches of the East. In his list of Old Testament books, Augustine included Tobit, Judith, 1 and 2 Maccabees, Wisdom, Sirach, and Baruch (as part of Jeremiah). Augustine won the day, and these Old Testament Apocrypha plus the Additions to Daniel and Esther became part of the Vulgate Bible tradition. There were still, however, occasional opponents like Hugh of St. Victor (d. 1142), who did not regard the Old Testament Apocrypha to be canonical, though he allowed them to read in church.

Luther With respect to the Old Testament Apocrypha, the judgment of Martin Luther (1483-1546) was shaped to some extent by theological controversies about purgatory and prayers for the dead, and their alleged basis in 2 Macc. 12:45-46. He picked up on Jerome's hesitation about basing church doctrines on the Old Testament Apocrypha. In his German translation of the Bible, Luther included the Old Testament Apocrypha in a separate section with the heading: "Books which are not held to be equal to Holy Scripture, but are useful and good to read."

Protestant Bibles Luther's practice of including the Old Testament Apocrypha in a separate section along with but apart from the undisputed Old Testament books became common in Protestant Bibles. Their gradual omission was prompted first by the practical decision of some publishers, since their inclusion added to the size and price of Bibles. In the nineteenth century, however, some Protestant publishers began to omit these books on theological grounds because they were "extracanonical" and therefore not inspired.

Roman Catholic Bibles In the fourth session of the Council of Trent (1546), the Roman Catholic Church rejected the distinction proposed by Luther, and ultimately by Jerome, between the canonical (Hebrew) Old Testament books and the Old Testament Apocrypha. Its definitive list of canonical books was the first to be issued by an ecumenical council. It included the core books (Tobit, Judith, Wisdom, Sirach, Baruch, and 1 and 2 Maccabees) and placed them among the other Old Testament books without distinction. It declared "anathema" those who might think otherwise. Bibles produced under Roman Catholic auspices therefore include the so-called Old Testament Apocrypha as integral parts of the Old Testament.

BIBLIOGRAPHY

F. F. BRUCE 1988, *The Canon of Scripture,* Downers Grove, Ill.: InterVarsity. • D. A. DESILVA 2002, *Introducing the Apocrypha,* Grand Rapids: Baker. • D. J. HARRINGTON 1999, *Invitation to the Apocrypha,* Grand Rapids: Eerdmans. • L. M. MCDONALD 1995, *The Formation of the Christian Biblical Canon,* Peabody, Mass.: Hendrickson. • L. M. MCDONALD AND J. A. SANDERS, EDS. 2002, *The Canon Debate,* Peabody, Mass.: Hendrickson. • S. MEURER, ED. 1991, *The Apocrypha in Ecumenical Perspective,* New York: United Bible Societies. • A. C. SUNDBERG 1964, *The Old Testament in the Early Church,* Cambridge, Mass.: Harvard University Press.

DANIEL J. HARRINGTON, S.J.

Apollonius Molon

Apollonius Molon was a Greek author and a prominent orator and teacher who came to the island of Rhodes from Alabanda during the first half of the first century B.C.E. His skills brought him renown in Rome, and according to the biographer Plutarch (early second century C.E.), among his pupils were Cicero and Julius Caesar. Apollonius also spent time in Rome, serving as ambassador of Rhodes and arguing in Roman court. He is not to be confused with another rhetor in Rhodes, the slightly older Apollonius Malacus (Strabo 14.2.13, 24-26), nor with Apollonius of Rhodes, the poet of *Argonautica* (third century B.C.E.).

No writings of Apollonius Molon have survived directly, but fragments exist through citations in other writers. Strabo credits Apollonius with a work he calls *Against the Caunians,* the people of Caunus, a city of Caria once subject to the Rhodians. This work apparently dealt with the origin and customs of the Caunians; such a work seems congruous with what is known of Apollonius' writing concerning the Jews.

Josephus refers frequently to Apollonius in his *On the Antiquity of the Jews,* better known as *Against Apion* (2.16, 79, 145, 148, 236, 255, 258, 295). However, he does not provide quotations, except as Apollonius' words and phrases may have been incorporated into Josephus' summaries and remarks. There is one citation of Apollonius preserved in *Praeparatio Evangelica* (9.19.1-3) by the Christian apologetic historian Eusebius. Eusebius cites Apollonius through the intermediate work of Apollonius' contemporary, Alexander Polyhistor of Rome, who produced an abridgement of Apollonius. It is from Eusebius that we learn the name of Apollonius' work, *Against the Jews (kata Ioudaiōn).*

Josephus considered Apollonius a malicious writer — "partly from ignorance, mostly from ill will" — against Jews. He puts him in the company of Apion as a symbol of those writers who "delight in lies" against the Jews — so much so that others who write against Jews are dubbed "Apions and Molons" (*Ag. Ap.* 2.295). We are told that Apollonius scattered his accusations throughout his work and reviled the Jews as atheists, misanthropes, cowards, and "the most witless of all non-Greeks," who had contributed nothing to civilization (*Ag. Ap.* 2.148).

Josephus otherwise provides little specific narrative information from Apollonius. Josephus thought Apollonius was one of the sources for Apion's shocking story about the Jews keeping and worshiping the head of an ass in their Temple, and the gruesome claim that in Jerusalem a Greek was kidnapped, fattened, slaughtered, and eaten as part of an annual festival (*Ag. Ap.* 2.79-96). Of course, without an actual text of Apollonius, this is impossible to confirm, though it is plausible. The same is the case for another charge, namely, that "Apollonius Molon, Lysimachus, and others" malign Moses as a "charlatan and imposter" who taught vice instead of virtue (*Ag. Ap.* 2.145).

The closest text we have to an actual fragment of Apollonius, the indirect-speech quotation from Eusebius (*Praep. Evang.* 9.19.1-3), is a seemingly confused and highly condensed history of Jewish ancestors from the generation of the flood to Moses. Here the flood survivors leave Armenia and travel to Syria. Abraham, whose name meant "father's friend," was born three generations later. He became wise and traveled to the desert, where he married two wives, one a relative and one an Egyptian. With the Egyptian he fathered twelve sons who moved to Arabia and became the twelve kings of the Arabs. With his other wife he had a son whose name in Greek means "laughter." To Laughter were also born twelve sons, the last being Joseph, whose great-grandson was Moses.

However conflated or confused this text may be, it is clear that Jewish traditions, such as those preserved in Genesis, likely in Greek, stand behind Apollonius' account, but stark differences also show that he did not depend directly on the book of Genesis. There are also indications of Semitic etymology and of materials not found in Genesis. This is easy to explain since in the first century B.C.E., according to 1 Macc. 15:22-24, numerous Jewish communities lived in the region of Apollonius' native Caria and on the islands of Cos and Rhodes. Apollonius could have learned Jewish traditions from any number of sources, and the kind of information he gives fits well with the ethnographic and genealogical interests of Hellenistic writers, both Jewish and non-Jewish. Furthermore, Apollonius was likely influenced by the prolific author and philosopher Posidonius (135-51 B.C.E.), his older contemporary from Rhodes, who also wrote negatively about the Jews (*Ag. Ap.* 2.79).

Apollonius' recounting of Abraham stands in stark contrast to Josephus' remarks; Apollonius seems positive only regarding Abraham and the generations after him. At the same time he seems completely ignorant of the traditional role of Abraham as the Jewish ancestor who settled in Palestine after leaving Babylonia. Abraham's Chaldean origins are conspicuous and important in Genesis and in Hellenistic authors such as Pseudo-Eupolemus, Nicolaus of Damascus, Philo, and Josephus.

Apollonius represents a different view of the historical development of the Jews, namely, that Jewish ancestry was laudable until Moses. Such a view contrasts with texts of Hecataeus of Abdera and Strabo, who admired Moses but thought that Jewish practices were corrupted after him. Apollonius, whose contempt for contemporary Judaism is clear, seems to blame Moses for the corruption.

BIBLIOGRAPHY

J. G. GAGER 1972, *Moses in Greco-Roman Paganism,* Nashville: Abingdon. • F. JACOBY 1958, *Die Fragmente der griechischen Historiker,* 3C: 687-89. • M. STERN 1976, *Greek and Latin Authors on Jews and Judaism,* vol. 1, Jerusalem: Israel Academy of Sciences and Humanities, 148-56.

See also: Alexander Polyhistor; Greek Authors on Jews and Judaism JAMES E. BOWLEY

Apologetic Literature

"Apologetic literature" is literature that seeks to refute criticism and defend a person or people. In the late nineteenth and early twentieth century, it was customary to classify most of the Jewish literature written in Greek as apologetic literature in this sense, or alternatively as missionary propaganda. That view of the literature was undercut by Victor Tcherikover in a famous essay in 1956. More recently, Martin Goodman (1994) has shown that there was no organized missionary or proselytizing movement in ancient Judaism. It is now accepted that the Jewish literature written in Greek was intended primarily for Jewish consumption, and served as a means of self-expression in a Hellenized environment.

Explicitly Apologetic Works

There are some admitted examples of Jewish apologetic literature. The clearest is the tract of Josephus, *Against Apion,* written in Rome toward the end of the first century C.E., which cites and refutes anti-Jewish claims by a wide array of Hellenistic authors. It is mainly from Josephus that we know that such anti-Jewish literature existed, but since he quotes passages out of context it is often difficult to know whether Judaism was a central or a peripheral concern for many of these authors. Josephus is especially concerned to affirm the antiquity of the Jewish people, to claim that it has always been held in high regard, and to rebut the charge of misanthropy, or anti-social attitudes. In the process, he responds to derogatory accounts of Jewish origins and customs. The philosopher Philo also wrote an *Apologia pro Iudaeis,* probably to be identified with the *Hypothetica,* which is preserved only in part in Eusebius' *Praeparatio Evangelica* (8.6-9). This work seems to be a defense of the excellence of the Jewish law and way of life. Much of Philo's writing has an apologetic purpose in this sense.

While explicitly apologetic Jewish writings are rare in the Hellenistic and early Roman periods, much of the Jewish literature written in Greek has an apologetic aspect, even if it was addressed to a Jewish audience. It is often at pains to praise the Jews and their way of life, and to rebut implicitly the caricatures and derogatory accounts circulated by some Gentile writers.

Gentile Pseudonyms

One strategy for doing this was to put the praise of the Jews on the lips of a pagan. The *Letter of Aristeas* is ostensibly a report written by one Gentile courtier to another. Aristeas was not the name of an especially famous person. It was sufficient that he was a Greek and could supposedly report how Judaism and its law were perceived at the Ptolemaic court. At no point does he say anything even mildly critical of Judaism. The Jewish priest Eleazar, in contrast, is quite critical of Greek and Egyptian religion, but his criticisms are reported with apparent admiration by Aristeas. These even include criticism of polytheism and idolatry. It is implied that the best and most cultured Greeks share or at least appreciate the Jewish position on these issues, even if the rank and file do not. A major theme of this writing is Gentile respect for Jews. In the table talk toward the end of the book, the Jewish sages respond to questions posed by the king and are rewarded with the approval of king, courtiers, and philosophers. Throughout, the Greeks concede the superiority of everything Jewish, and this assessment acquires validity from the fact that it is rendered by Greeks. The Greeks at the royal court constitute an implied audience, whose judgments confirm the value and excellence of Judaism. The *Letter* also provides an explicit defense of the Jewish food laws, by providing an allegorical interpretation for them. "Do not take the contemptible view that Moses enacted this legislation because of an excessive preoccupation with mice and weasels or suchlike creatures. The fact is that everything has been solemnly set in order for . . . the sake of righteousness" (144).

The *Sibylline Oracles* purport to be the inspired utterances of a pagan prophetess. The leitmotif of these oracles is the prediction of divine judgment on various peoples and places. Nonetheless, she has nothing but praise for the Jews: "There is a city . . . in the land of Ur of the Chaldeans, whence comes a race of most righteous men. They are always concerned with good counsel and noble works" (*Sib. Or.* 3.218-20). Their conduct is contrasted with the foolish pursuits of the Gentiles, including the study of the heavens and divination. Again, the Jews are "a sacred race of pious men" who honor God and the Temple (3.573-600). The Greeks are exhorted to offer sacrifice to the true God. The fact that such praise of Judaism, and criticism of pagan religion, is ostensibly uttered by a pagan prophetess makes its witness all the more compelling.

Competitive Historiography

Several of the Hellenistic Jewish historical works, which have survived only in fragments, can be considered examples of "competitive historiography," which claims for its national heroes what other peoples claimed for theirs. A colorful example is provided by Artapanus, who credited Moses with establishing the Egyptian animal cults. This claim effectively countered that of the Egyptian historian Manetho, who alleged that Moses forbade his people to worship the gods or abstain from the flesh of the sacred animals. Manetho claimed that Moses had invaded Egypt. Artapanus countered that Moses restrained the Arabs from invading. In Manetho's account, the pharaoh sought refuge in Ethiopia when Moses invaded. In Artapanus, Moses conducted a campaign against Ethiopia on behalf of the pharaoh. In all of this, Artapanus was defending the Jewish lawgiver against Gentile attack. Beyond this, he and several other Hellenistic Jewish writers claimed that the heroes of their tradition were the founders of culture. Abraham taught the Egyptians astronomy. Joseph organized the division of the land and discovered measurements. Moses was known to the Greeks as Mousaeus and was the teacher of Orpheus. Aristobulus, a Jewish philosopher in the second century B.C.E., claimed that Plato and other Greek philosophers borrowed from Moses.

Excellence by Greek Standards

In claiming antiquity and priority for Abraham and Moses, the Jewish writers were claiming that the heroes of Jewish tradition excelled by Greek standards and should therefore be admired by the Greeks. Aristobulus writes, "All philosophers agree that it is necessary to hold devout convictions about God, something which our school prescribes particularly well. And the whole structure of our law has been drawn up with concern for piety, justice, self-control, and other qualities that are truly good" (frg. 4). The treatise known as 4 Maccabees is an extended argument that obedience to the Torah is in conformity with reason. Philo is at pains to show the philanthropic character of Jewish law (a motif also found in the Wisdom of Solomon), thereby implicitly refuting those who say that it is anti-social or misanthropic.

The Use of Greek Literary Forms

To some degree, the use of Greek literary forms can be seen as an exercise in apologetics. One Ezekiel wrote an account of the Exodus in the form of a tragedy. One Philo, not the philosopher, wrote an epic poem about Jerusalem, incorporating material from Genesis. No doubt these poets were expressing their identity in the forms that were familiar to them from their environment. But they were also making the claim that the Jews could produce literature by Greek literary standards. Jewish readers were probably more impressed by this claim than were the Greeks.

A Postcolonial Perspective

None of this requires that the Jewish literature was written primarily for Gentile readers. Diaspora Jews regarded themselves as culturally Greek and admired Greek values except in matters that involved polytheism and some (un)ethical practices such as homosexuality and the exposure of infants. The ethical/sapiential treatise ascribed to Phocylides is so thoroughly Hellenistic in form and content that it was recognized as a Jewish composition (on the basis of biblical allusions) only in the sixteenth century. But Jewish self-perception as cultured Hellenes was contested. In Hellenistic and Roman Egypt, the area of the Diaspora that is best documented, ethnic polemics raged, and Alexandrian Greeks looked with disdain on Jews as on native Egyptians. Consequently, Jews needed to be assured that they did measure up by Greek standards. Much of the corpus of Jewish literature written in Greek can be seen to provide that assurance, sometimes putting it in the mouths of Greeks or pagans, and sometimes simply asserting the superiority of the Jewish way of life. In the categories of modern postcolonial analysis, we might say that the Jewish authors adopt the discourse of the hegemonic culture, and to a great degree adopt its values. At the same time, they use the discourse of the dominant culture to affirm and maintain the excellence — and even superiority of — Judaism and its values.

BIBLIOGRAPHY

J. M. G. BARCLAY 2002, "Apologetics in the Jewish Diaspora," in *Jews in the Hellenistic and Roman Cities,* ed. J. Bartlett, London: Routledge, 129-48. • J. M. G. BARCLAY, ED. 2004, *Negotiating Diaspora: Jewish Strategies in the Roman Empire,* London: Clark. • K. BERTHELOT 2003, *Philanthrôpia Judaica: Le débat autour de la "misanthropie" des lois juives dans l'Antiquité,* Leiden: Brill. • J. J. COLLINS 2005, "Hellenistic Judaism in Recent Scholarship," in idem, *Jewish Cult and Hellenistic Culture,* Leiden: Brill, 1-20. • M. GOODMAN 1994, *Mission and Conversion: Proselytizing in the Religious History of the Roman Empire,* Oxford: Clarendon. • G. E. STERLING 1992, *Historiography and Self-Definition: Josephos, Luke-Acts and Apologetic Historiography,* Leiden: Brill. • V. TCHERIKOVER 1956, "Jewish Apologetic Literature Reconsidered," *Eos* 48: 169-93.

See also: Aristeas, Letter of; Josephus, Against Apion

JOHN J. COLLINS

Apostasy

"Apostasy" is a loaded, not neutral term indicating a judgment that another's behavior (and/or belief) constitutes a fundamental desertion from the ranks of one's own group. The Greek term *apostasia* and its cognates are used occasionally in this sense in early Jewish literature (e.g., 1 Macc. 2:15), deriving from its more general political meaning of "defection" or "revolt." But a variety of other terms and phrases is also used to convey what the speaker/author considers abandonment of the Jewish way of life or of the Jewish people (e.g., "abandoning the ancestral laws"; "neglecting the ancestral customs"). It is crucial to recognize that there is no objective measure by which this can be assessed; although it normally relates to some form of "assimilation," the judgment of what counts as apostasy is always a relative one: apostasy is in the eye of the beholder. Following the "interactionist" perspective on deviance, one may observe that groups not only define their own norms and boundaries but also select and stereotype those they choose to mark as deviant. We should expect that different Jewish groups, in different social and cultural circumstances, might vary in their definition of norm-breaking, and especially in what they consider a step "too far" — the step from relatively "casual" or "harmless" nonobservance of Jewish norms into what they consider outright apostasy. Whenever we find such labels or judgments in our sources, we should ask whose definition is operative, and whose interests it serves.

Palestinian Judaism

Given the factional (even sectarian) nature of Palestinian Judaism in the Hellenistic and Roman eras, it is not surprising to find numerous examples of Jews who accused others of committing apostasy in one form or another. A vivid expression is found in the heavily slanted accounts of the Maccabean crisis, where the authors of the Maccabean literature accuse those who complied with the Hellenizing movement of outright apostasy (e.g., 1 Macc. 1:11-15, 41-53). Critical issues here were the use of Greek religious rites, diet (consumption of pork), Sabbath observance, and male circumcision. From a partisan standpoint, the author of *Jubilees* polemicizes against any who break the Sabbath (*Jub.* 2:27-33), eat blood (6:12), fail to keep the solar calendar (6:32-35), or intermarry with foreigners (30:7-10). In each case there is the drastic threat of death or "uprooting from the midst of all Israel." From another perspective, the *Psalms of Solomon* constantly criticizes "sinners" in Israel whose "lawless actions surpassed the Gentiles" (*Ps. Sol.* 1:8); defilement of the Temple and its sacrifices (2:3; 8:12-13) are among its most virulent charges. Perhaps the fullest and most dramatic evidence of such accusations is found in the Dead Sea Scrolls, where the sectarian texts regularly treat all Israelites who are not members of the sect as "traitors" and people from "the lot of Belial"; they have broken the covenant and wandered off the paths of righteousness (e.g., CD [A] 1:12-21; 1QS 2:4-10; 1QpHab 2:1-7). Here the fundamental issues concern the calendar, religious leadership, and the interpretation of the Torah. The question of loyalty inevitably came to a head for Palestinian Jews at the time of the Judean War (66-70 C.E.), when they were forced to take sides. Just as Josephus reports Jews in Scythopolis being accused of apostasy (i.e., defection from the Jewish community, *J.W.* 2.466-76), so he himself, after surrendering to the Romans and assisting their siege of Jerusalem, was accused of being a traitor to the Jewish cause (*Vita* 140; *J.W.* 3.438-42; 5.541-47).

Diaspora Judaism

In the context of the Diaspora, Jews judged variously the reaction of their fellow Jews under the cultural and social pressures to assimilate. Philo, a highly acculturated Alexandrian Jew, indicates the pressure on Jews to "lose their footing" and "change to alien ways" (*De Iosepho* 254); he criticizes those who gain social success by gradual disaffiliation from their Jewish communities, "transgressing the laws according to which they were born and bred and subverting the ancestral customs" (*Mos.* 1.31). He is particularly aware of the danger of intermarriage, with the resulting drift into "alien" religious customs (e.g., *Spec. Leg.* 1.54-58; 3.29). Philo also repudiates those who abandon the practice of the laws, observing only its allegorical meaning (*De Abrahamo* 89–93), and those who "reject the sacred writings" by moral or intellectual critique of the Torah (*QG* 3.3; *De Confusione Linguarum* 2–13). Josephus uses the story of the Midianite women (Numbers 25) to dramatize the dangers of exogamy (leading to the adoption of others' religious rites and the abandonment of Jewish dietary laws, *Ant.* 4.126-55). In the course of his work, he describes a number of individuals who "abandoned their native customs": Herodians brought up in Rome (*Ant.* 18.141), Antiochus in Antioch at the start of the Judean War (*J.W.* 7.46-62), and, most famously, Tiberius Julius Alexander, the Jewish governor of Egypt whom Josephus describes in his later (not his earlier) work as "not abiding by his ancestral customs" (*Ant.* 20.100). In all such cases, political, social, and religious factors are interwoven in their changes of lifestyle. It is probable that in these named cases the individuals concerned recognized themselves to have left the Jewish community and abandoned its customs, but in the absence of this consent it was always possible for individuals to deny that they were apostates, even if others so labeled them. Where the author of 3 Maccabees, for instance, labels as "apostates" those who accepted Alexandrian citizenship (3 Macc. 2:28-33; 7:10-15; cf. 1:3), there were undoubtedly some Jewish Alexandrian citizens who considered themselves, and were considered by other Jews, faithful members of the Jewish community (cf. Josephus, *Ag. Ap.* 2.65).

Jewish Christianity

This inevitable element of relativism meant that the status of early Jewish Christians was often ambiguous and contested. In his Pharisaic days, Paul obviously considered some of these worthy of physical and legal punishment (Gal. 1:13), but after his "call" he was himself subject to similar treatment (Gal. 5.11). While his reputation for apostasy (Acts 21:21, persuading Jews against circumcision) was not always fair, the fact that he was repeatedly given the thirty-nine lashes in synagogues (2 Cor. 11:24) suggests that he was often accused of serious breaches of the Law and, despite his protestations of Jewish identity, may have been frequently considered an apostate. Similarly clashing opinions seem to have surrounded the status of those Jewish Christians addressed by the Gospel of Matthew (cf. Matt. 5:11, 17-20; 23:34), while Johannine Christians, and those mentioned by Justin Martyr, experienced some kind of expulsion from Jewish synagogues (John 9:22; 12:42; 16:2; Justin, *Dialogue with Trypho the Jews* 16; 95–96; 110).

Rabbinic Judaism

In the rabbinic literature we find several discussions of *minim,* a flexible term used to cover various forms of belief and practice considered dangerous to the Jewish community (e.g., *m. Meg.* 4:8-9; *m. Ber.* 9:5; *t. Ḥul.* 2:22-23; *t. Šabb.* 13:5), usually eliciting severe condemnation and threats of Gehenna. Such accusations sometimes took specific form in the figure of Elisha ben Abuyah (known as Aḥēr, "the other"); it is hard to identify historical reality under this heavily fictionalized figure, but he clearly served as a rhetorical conduit for the fears of some rabbinic circles.

The common thread that unites these various charges is the notion that the individuals concerned have abandoned the Jewish people, its customs, and its traditions; socio-political and religious factors are interlinked, and beliefs sometimes named alongside practices. Regular engagement in "idolatry" appears to have been sufficient to gain this reputation, or repeated infringement of distinctive Jewish laws (e.g., those regarding food and circumcision). But the definition of "idolatry," the identification of "infringement," and the level of seriousness attached to each, could vary in different times and locations. In defining its boundaries and maintaining its identity, each Jewish community had to set its own limits, even if the contacts between Jewish communities and their general attachment to ancestral customs undoubtedly gave to such limits some commonality and some continuity over time. But in the last resort, apostasy always remained a matter of local judgment, and it is impossible to construct any objective or impartial measure by which we can identify who were apostates in early Judaism.

BIBLIOGRAPHY

J. M. G. BARCLAY 1995A, "Deviance and Apostasy: Some Applications of Deviance Theory to First-century Judaism and Christianity," in *Modelling Early Christianity,* ed. P. F. Esler, London: Routledge, 114-27. • J. M. G. BARCLAY 1995B, "Paul among Diaspora Jews: Anomaly or Apostate?" *JSNT* 60: 89-120. • J. M. G. BARCLAY 1998, "Who Was Considered an Apostate in the Jewish Diaspora?" in *Tolerance and Intolerance in Early Judaism and Christianity,* ed. G. N. Stanton and G. S. Stroumsa, Cambridge: Cambridge University Press, 80-98. • G. FORKMAN 1972, *The Limits of the Religious Community: Expulsion from the Religious Community within the Qumran Sect, within Rabbinic Judaism, and within Primitive Christianity,* Lund: Gleerup. • A. GOSHEN-GOTTSTEIN 2000, *The Sinner and the Amnesiac: The Rabbinic Invention of Elisha Ben Abuyah and Eleazar Ben Arach,* Stanford: Stanford University Press • J. T. SANDERS 1993, *Schismatics, Sectarians, Dissidents, Deviants: The First One Hundred Years of Jewish-Christian Relations,* London: SCM Press • S. STERN 1994, *Jewish Identity in Early Rabbinic Writings,* Leiden: Brill • S. G. WILSON 2004, *Leaving the Fold: Apostates and Defectors in Antiquity,* Minneapolis: Fortress Press.

See also: Assimilation, Acculturation, Accommodation; Blasphemy JOHN M. G. BARCLAY

Aqedah

The binding ("Aqedah") and near sacrifice of Isaac in Genesis 22 was the subject of much interpretive creativity in the literature of Second Temple Judaism. Though the Aqedah's definition and scope is debated, references to Genesis 22 are found throughout the chronological and ideological spectra of early Judaism.

Second Temple Texts

Cultic Concerns

Cultic issues dominate many interpretive expansions. Several texts locate the near sacrifice of Isaac on the site of the future Jerusalem Temple (2 Chron. 3:1; Philo the Epic Poet's "On Jerusalem"; *Jub.* 18:13; Josephus, *Ant.* 1.226). Philo exploits the spatial ambiguity expressed in

Abraham's arriving at the place *(topos)* only to look up and see it from afar (Gen. 22:3-4) to expound the immanence and transcendence of God (*De Posteritate* 14–21; *Somn.* 1.61-71). *Jubilees* 17:15 integrates the event into a solar calendar, correlating the near-sacrifice to Passover. Abraham and Isaac are both stylized as prototypical priests (Philo, *De Abrahamo* 198; Josephus, *Ant.* 231; cf. *Jub.* 21:7-24; *T. Levi* 9:1-14), with 4Q225 inserting a genealogy connecting Levi directly to Abraham and Isaac. Josephus' designation of Isaac's age as twenty-five (*Ant.* 1.227), presented in the context of Isaac's construction of the altar (contra Gen. 22:9), further connects Isaac with the levitical priesthood, whose service began at age twenty-five (Num. 8:24; cf. LXX Num. 4:3 *passim*) and involved setting up the Tent of Meeting. Isaac is also stylized as the incarnate paradigm of the whole burnt offering (Philo, *Sacrificiis* 109; cf. *Abrahamo* 198). The depiction of Isaac as a cognizant, willing participant (4 Macc. 13:12; 4Q225; Ps.-Philo, *Bib. Ant.* 32:3) — a psychological explication of Abraham and Isaac walking "as one" (Gen. 22:6, 8) — likely reflects in part the ancient insistence upon the animal victim's "willing" participation in the sacrifice.

Angelic Opposition

Such theological sensibilities arguably inform another addition: angelic opposition. *Jubilees* 17:15-18 (cf. 4Q225) envisions the test arising from the opposing angel Mastema, who questions whether Abraham's pleasure with Isaac exceeds his faithfulness to God; thus, God's directive intends to shame Mastema through Abraham's piety (*Jub.* 18:12). In a variation of this theme, Pseudo-Philo imagines God's command as a response to angelic jealousy over Abraham's miraculous gift of a son (*Bib. Ant.* 32:1-2).

The Morality of the Episode

Other possible explanations for God's directive are also examined. Josephus implies that God's directive is neither arbitrary nor senseless, but rather a reasonable public manifestation of piety commensurate with the favor provided by the divine patron (*Ant.* 1.223-24; cf. Philo, *Abrahamo* 177). Lack of divine knowledge regarding Abraham's response is ruled out; instead, the episode is understood as "making known" to others that Abraham is faithful (*Jub.* 18:16; *Bib. Ant.* 32:4; cf. *Gen. Rab.* 56:7). Any hint of God's thirst for human blood is explicitly denied (*Ant.* 1.233; Philo, *Abrahamo* 179–81; *Sacrificiis* 110; though cf. *Abr.* 192), and the love that exists between all involved is repeatedly stated (Philo, *Abrahamo* 168–70, 198; Josephus, *Ant.* 1.222-25; cf. *Jub.* 17:15, 18). In sum, these developments likely reflect sensitivity to the questionable moral character of this episode, resulting in various interpretive and apologetic frameworks capable of making hermeneutical, ethical, and theological sense of the Aqedah.

The Faithfulness of Father and Son

This anxiety did not prevent exegetes from lauding the faithfulness of Abraham and Isaac. Philo goes so far as to characterize the Aqedah as greater than all other actions of piety put together (*Abrahamo* 167). Some contextualize the Aqedah within a series of faith challenges. *Jubilees* 17:17-18 delineates seven tests, beginning with Abram's call (Gen. 12:1); the list extends to ten after Sarah's death (*Jub.* 19:2-8; cf. *m. 'Abot* 5:3). Both texts psychologize Abraham's faithfulness, highlighting the self-control of his spirit and resultant lack of impatience and anxiety. Abraham's mastery over his parental affection is a model for the mother of the seven martyrs in 4 Macc. 15:23-28 (cf. 18:1-2), and Abraham's zeal to sacrifice Isaac is a spiritual paradigm for the seven brothers to emulate in the midst of their suffering for the sake of God (16:16-24). Pseudo-Philo also suggests that Abraham's willingness rendered the deed an acceptable, completed offering, and the unelaborated mention of blood could hint that the sacrifice came closer to physical consummation than Scripture lets on (*Bib. Ant.* 18.5).

Isaac's consenting faithfulness, unstated in Genesis 22, is also celebrated. Judith 8:26-27 identifies Isaac as a subject in the test. 4 Maccabees 16:20 asserts that Isaac did not cower at the descending knife but provided a model of self-controlled reason for the martyr Eleazar (4 Macc. 7:12-14). Josephus (*Ant.* 1.232) and Pseudo-Philo (*Bib. Ant.* 32:2-3) insert a speech in which Abraham informs Isaac that he is the one to be offered, followed by a statement of joyful consent by Isaac (cf. *Bib. Ant.* 40:2; *Frg. Tg.* Gen. 22:10; *Exod. Rab.* 44:5). 4Q225 most probably contained Isaac's request to be bound (attested in the targumim). Josephus, however, omits the potentially shameful, slave-like binding (cf. *J.W.* 7.385) altogether, depicting Isaac rushing delightedly to the altar for sacrifice (*Ant.* 1.232).

Application to Jewish-Gentile Relations

Much contested are the conceptions of righteousness believed to be exhibited in the Aqedah, especially concerning their application to Jewish-Gentile relations. The appeal to Abraham's testing in 1 Macc. 2:52 employs the logic of disregarding one's life and one's kinship bonds to support executing the idolatrous fellow Jew and laying down one's life in struggle against oppressive Gentile rulers. Judith 8:26 appeals to Isaac's testing as a model of hostile resistance to Gentile encroachment (Jdt. 7:27), with an emphasis on the promise in Gen. 22:17 that Abraham's seed shall conquer their enemies (cf. Jdt. 5:18, 13:4-5). The priestly warrior Josephus adds an explicit anti-Canaan, militaristic interpretation of that biblical blessing (*Ant.* 1.235). By way of contrast, 4 Maccabees eliminates the militaristic dimension altogether, insisting that Jewish conquering is achieved by steadfast endurance even unto death, namely, the "reason of Isaac" (4 Macc. 7:14; cf. 18:1-4). Cultic metaphors of atoning sacrifices are thus applied to the nonviolent resistance of the martyrs (4 Macc. 17:21-22), in place of martial configurations (e.g., 1 Macc. 3:8). Sirach 44:21-23 configures the land blessing universally, to the ends of the earth, and emphasizes the blessing of all peoples rather than the promise of triumph over enemies.

Early Christian Texts

New Testament appropriation of Genesis 22 shows a similar distancing from violent applications. James uses Abraham's near sacrifice in support of joining faith and works (2:21-23), defining true piety as caring for orphans and widows (1:27), seeking peace (3:18), and suffering with steadfast endurance (5:10-11). Hebrews asserts Abraham's faith in a heavenly city built by God (11:8-10, 13-16), effectively redirecting any potential zeal for establishing by force an earthly kingdom. It exalts Isaac's near sacrifice as an act that affirms resurrection (11:17-19), in stark contrast to the realized eschatology of the Maccabean kingdom. The Gospel of John configures the "only son" as an idealized martyr like Isaac (John 1:14, 18, 29; 3:16; 10:11-18; 18:12, 24; 19:17), one advocating a nonviolent path to freedom rather than armed resistance (8:31-59; 18:10-11, 36). In a slightly different fashion, Paul employs the Aqedah as an expression of God's self-sacrificing faithfulness in creating a covenant community that includes Jew and Gentile alike (Rom. 3:32-39; cf. 15:8-9a).

Early Christian writings outside the New Testament tilt toward a typological reading of Genesis 22, seeing a type of Christ in either Isaac, the beloved son carrying the wood to slaughter (*Barn.* 7:3) or the ram who was actually slaughtered (Augustine, *Civitas Dei* 16.31-32). Many interpreters join together Isaac and the ram as an illustration of Jesus' dual nature, which in its divinity did not suffer death but in its humanity did suffer and die (Origen, *Homiliae in Genesim* 8.6-9; cf. Tertullian, *Against Marcion* 3.18.2; *Adversus Judaeos* 13.636; Clement of Alexandria, *Paedagogus* 1.5.21.3–1.5.23.2).

Rabbinic Texts

Rabbinic developments further the theological creativity already discussed, and while many of the details likely date from the Second Temple period, it is difficult to establish with confidence the date of traditions that are otherwise uncorroborated by Second Temple texts (Vermes 1961). *Targum Neofiti* and the *Fragmentary Targum* to Genesis 22 include Abraham's informing of Isaac and the latter's consent, including the admonition to bind his hands properly lest the offering be rendered unfit. Isaac is given a heavenly vision, and Abraham prays that his obedience and Isaac's willingness be remembered by God on behalf of their descendants. Several texts include reference to a vision of cloud, variously indicating the mountain to which Abraham should journey, attributing the leaving behind of the servants to their inability to see this cloud, or asserting that Isaac's ability to see the vision was a divine indication that he — rather than Eliezer or Ishmael — was the lamb of the sacrifice. The Palestinian targumim to Exod. 12:42 also mention the sacrifice of Isaac in their discussion of the night of Passover, which is a fourfold memorial to creation, Abraham and Isaac, deliverance from Egypt, and eschatological salvation. Eventually the Aqedah became linked with the appeals to mercy and salvation in the blowing of the ram's horn on Rosh ha-Shanah.

BIBLIOGRAPHY

R. DALY 1977, "The Soteriological Significance of the Sacrifice of Isaac," *CBQ* 39: 45-75. • P. DAVIES AND B. CHILTON 1978, "The Aqedah: A Revised Tradition History," *CBQ* 40: 514-46. • R. HAYWARD 1981, "The Present State of Research into the Targumic Account of the Sacrifice of Isaac," *JJS* 32: 127-150. • J. L. KUGEL 1997, *The Bible as it Was,* Cambridge: Belknap/Harvard University Press, 165-78. • J. D. LEVENSON 1993, *The Death and Resurrection of the Beloved Son,* New Haven: Yale. • A. SEGAL 1987, "The Sacrifice of Isaac in Early Judaism and Christianity," in idem, *The Other Judaisms of Late Antiquity,* Atlanta: Scholars. • J. SWETNAM 1981, *Jesus and Isaac: A Study of the Epistle to the Hebrews in the Light of the Aqedah,* Rome: Biblical Institute. • J. C. VANDERKAM 1997, "The *Aqedah, Jubilees,* and Pseudo-Jubilees," in *The Quest for Context and Meaning,* ed. A. Evans and S. Talmon, Leiden: Brill, 241-61. • G. VERMES 1961, *Scripture and Tradition in Judaism,* Leiden: Brill, 193-227. G. VERMES 1996, "New Light on the Sacrifice of Isaac from 4Q225," *JJS* 47: 140-46.

See also: Isaac JASON J. RIPLEY

Aqueducts

An aqueduct is a water carrier, either built of stone above ground or cut as a channel in rock, through which water flows from one place to another. By its very definition, it is not an independent installation but has a water source at its beginning and facilities for collection, purification, regulation, and distribution at its end. These auxiliary installations were built in accordance with the type of the aqueduct's source and destination. An aqueduct could supply water to many diverse possible destinations: cities, palaces, fortresses and army encampments, ritual baths, and monasteries. The water source had to be higher than its destination, since aqueducts act by force of gravity. The source was either a spring, floodwaters, runoff water, or water from a cistern or well drawn and brought to the aqueduct. At times several types of water sources were combined. Some aqueducts included different installations in order to overcome topographical difficulties, such as retaining walls on parallel slopes, stone ramparts for crossing streams, arched bridges and siphons for crossing valleys, and tunnels for crossing mountain ridges and spurs.

A Roman aqueduct leading to Caesarea on the coast of Palestine

Water was always scarce in the land of Israel, a fact already recognized by the biblical authors, who described the land as one of springs and rainwater, unlike Mesopotamia and Egypt (at the two extremities of the Fertile Crescent), whose wide rivers provided them with abundant water. Deuteronomy describes the promised land as "a land with streams and springs and fountains issuing from plain and hill" (8:7) and "a land of hills and valleys [that] soaks up its water from the rains of heaven" (11:11). These descriptions of the land's geographical and hydrological conditions are repeated by later authors and remain valid to the present. The mean annual precipitation in the land of Israel varies from some 1,000 mm. in the north to less than 100 mm. in the southern part of the Negev. Rain falls only in the winter, and there are no large rivers.

During the Bronze and Iron Ages, cities relied primarily on the local water supply from pools, cisterns, wells, and springs within their walls or in their immediate vicinity. In the Hellenistic, and especially, the Roman period, new standards and techniques for the building of cities were introduced, and aqueducts began to be built in the land of Israel.

Aqueducts initially developed in Mesopotamia and in the Greek world. For the first time, large-scale planned irrigation systems were established in the valleys of the major rivers, as the basis for urban culture. The earliest testimony to the transition from irrigation with buckets to water flowing through aqueducts appears in an inscription from Mari (eighteenth century B.C.E.).

The hydraulic and engineering knowledge acquired in the river valleys resulted in the construction of complex and sophisticated water systems in the Assyrian Empire (first millennium B.C.E.), mainly during the reign of Sennacherib (eighth century B.C.E.). The aqueduct of Nineveh, for example, extended for 55 km. and included a dam and an arched bridge; the one at Erbil incorporated a shaft tunnel some 15 km. long.

The use of pipes developed in the Greco-Roman period, with improved water supply to cities and fortresses. The supply of water through aqueducts reached its greatest development in the Roman world. The Roman authorities considered aqueducts to be part of the basic services they were to provide for inhabitants of a city. The leading technological innovations of the period were invested in aqueducts: the arch, the vault, and the use of cement. The writings of the architect Vitruvius Pollio (first century B.C.E.) and Frontinus, a water commissioner of Rome (first century C.E.), contain a wealth of material on the planning, construction, and operation of aqueducts. Thanks to this literary material, together with the data collected in surveys and excavations of Roman-period waterworks, our knowledge of ancient aqueducts is one of the richest in archaeological research. This is true for all the lands of the Roman world, including the land of Israel.

Recent research has identified about thirty Greco-Roman water systems in Israel. Of these, eleven are urban, three supplied palaces and estates, five fed Hasmonean-Herodian desert palace-fortresses, three served fortified hill towns or villages, two led to Roman camps, and two were monastic. An additional two agricultural water systems date to the medieval period. Many of the systems, and particularly the urban ones, comprised several aqueducts.

The geomorphological conditions of a site and the surrounding terrain dictated the course of an aqueduct and its installations and components. The Jordan Rift Valley contains many springs adjacent to sites such as Panias (Banias) or Jericho, but at a lower elevation, and aqueducts were required to bring water from different sources to these higher elevations. In the case of the cities situated along the central mountain ridge, such as Jerusalem and Samaria, or Sepphoris in Galilee, water had to be delivered from distant springs to the required elevations. Topographical obstacles necessitated winding routes and the frequent use of tunnels or bridges. For the abundant springs on the western side, at the foot of the mountain ridge, gravitational flow sufficed. Thus, relatively short aqueducts led to Emmaus and Eleutheropolis (Beth Govrin), located in the lowlands at the foot of the mountains, and to Dor and Caesarea, located on the Mediterranean coast. Further south, the coastal plain expands and the springs at the foot of the mountains are more remote, while underground water is easily accessible. Remains of aqueducts have not been discovered in cities to the south of Caesarea, such as Appolonia, Jaffa, Azotos, Ascalon, or Gaza. It seems that these cities received their entire water supply from cisterns and wells.

The best known and best preserved of the urban water systems are those of Jerusalem and Caesarea. The Jerusalem system comprised four separate aqueducts that reached the city from springs south of Bethlehem. Caesarea's system was no less elaborate: the upper-level aqueduct, renowned for its long double arcade, reached the city from the north, as did the lower-level aqueduct, while a single terra-cotta pipe came from the south. Sebaste was fed by four lines: two terra-cotta pipes and two aqueducts; Hippos-Susita had three aqueducts; Sepphoris had two; Dor also had two aqueducts, as did Emmaus and Beth Govrin; while Acre, Banias, and Tiberias relied on a single aqueduct each.

Bibliography

D. Amit, J. Patrich, and Y. Hirschfeld, eds. 2002, *The Aqueducts of Israel,* Portsmouth, R.I.: Journal of Roman Archaeology. • A. T. Hodge 1992, *Roman Aqueducts and Water Supply,* London: Duckworth. • Vitruvius (Marcus V. Pollio) 1934, *On Architecture,* vol. 2, Book VIII: *Water-Supply,* trans. F. Granger, LCL, Cambridge, Mass.: Harvard University Press, 131-93.

See also: Cisterns and Reservoirs David Amit

Arabian Peninsula

The Arabian Peninsula has been a part of Jewish legendary imagination and history from biblical times to the present. In spite of this long association, Arabia has been poorly understood and even more poorly documented. The two best-recorded periods are the time around the rise of Islam in the sixth and early seventh centuries of the Common Era, and the modern period, particularly in the area of the Yemen. In addition, past eras have defined the geographic limits of Arabia differently from our present political borders.

Geography

Arabia is a quadrilateral plateau resting on the Arabian tectonic plate that extends and is moving northward toward Anatolia and the Eurasian plate. It has a spine of mountains on its western side, averaging 5,000 feet, with the highest peak rising to 12,336 feet in Yemen. The center of the peninsula is hard desert with oases, but no permanent watercourses. Around this central desert are soft, sandy areas that have acted as effective barriers for the interior. The most well known of the sandy deserts are the Nafûd in the north and the Rubʿ al-Khâlî in the south. These areas have no accessible water, and travelers must carry water for themselves and for their animals in order to cross. At the perimeter are areas of rocky steppe, ancient lava fields, and mountains. The steppe areas possess the greatest populations, but even here there are no rivers or permanent streams, only oases tapping ancient groundwater. Temperatures have been recorded over 120 degrees Fahrenheit and below zero and can range from freezing to over 100 degrees in a single day. The ancient geographers referred to the area as *natura maligna,* "malignant nature," and regarded the more hospitable southern tip as *Arabia Felix,* "happy" Arabia, only with some irony. Yet, despite the forbidding nature of the land, it was an area of opportunity and refuge.

Legends of Jewish Settlement

According to Islamic legendary traditions, the original inhabitants of Arabia were the Amalekites. In this legend, Moses sent Jewish soldiers to kill all the Amalekites, but they spared a single youth. For this they were banished and settled in the Ḥijâz, becoming the first Jews to settle in Arabia. This foundation legend, based on Num. 24:20 and 1 Samuel 15, is linked with a second legend, which holds that the Jews, after the destruction of the Second Temple, fled to Arabia, and lived among and married into those original Jewish families. The Jewish tribes, the B. Qurayẓa and the B. an-Naḍîr, were held to be "priestly" tribes from a migration of priests after the destruction of the Second Temple. It is most likely that these and other foundation legends were promulgated by Arabian Jews from around the time of the rise of Islam and adopted by some Arabs to connect themselves with biblical histories and genealogies. The Jewish communities of the Yemen claimed ancestry from Jewish settlers who had left Jerusalem forty-two years before the destruction of the First Temple. When Ezra called on them to return from exile, they refused, because they foresaw the destruction of the Second Temple.

Modern scholarship has seen various theories, including the desiccation theory, which asserts that Arabia, once verdant, was the Semitic homeland, and that the drying dispersed the Semites, leaving a remnant of Jews and Arabs. Another theory, based on scanty epigraphic evidence, attributes the origins of the Jews in Arabia to the last king of Babylon, Nabonidus (556-539 B.C.E.), who conquered the Ḥijâz and resided there for ten years. He was supposed to have taken a Jewish advisor with him who started the community.

Jews in the Pre-Islamic Period

We see somewhat more solid historical evidence of Jews in Arabia as a result of the Jewish wars with Rome and the movement of Jews away from persecution and Hellenization. Archaeological evidence shows that some Jews settled in Arabia Nabatea and farther south, along the trade routes from the Yemen. We know that the apostle Paul started his mission in Arabia (Gal. 1:17) and would have known of the Jews of Arabia present at the Pentecost mentioned in Acts 2, but more certain evidence comes from the fifth and sixth centuries C.E. Beginning in the fifth century, Arabia came under intense missionary pressure from various Christian groups, Nestorians, Jacobites, Coptic Monophysites, among others, as well as Jews. All of these groups represented or were reacting to the imperial ambitions of the Roman (Byzantine) and Persian (Sassanian) Empires, which used these religious groups as clients. In the Ḥijâz, the Jewish tribes were established as "kings" of the Ḥijâz to collect taxes for the Persian "king of kings," while in the Yemen we learn of the Jewish king Yûsuf Dhû Nuwâs, also a client of the Persians. Yûsuf Dhû Nuwâs, in defending his kingdom, encountered Coptic Monophysite Christian soldiers from Abyssinia who, allied with Byzantine imperial forces, defeated him and occupied southern Arabia. When they pushed north to capture Mecca, their general, Abraha, and his troops were miraculously decimated according to traditions associated with Qur'an 105, the chapter called "The Elephant." Supposedly, this took place in the year 570 C.E., the year of Muhammad's birth. In spite of successes by Jews and Christians in converting groups of native Arabians to forms of rabbinic Judaism and varieties of Christianity, those religions' conflicts with each other, each religion's claim to absolute truth, and their association with the imperial ambitions of the major empires led many Arabians to seek religious answers independent of either of the older two religions.

At the time of the birth of Muhammad in 570 C.E., Jewish economic and political fortunes were in decline in Arabia, but the Jewish communities of the Ḥijâz were vital and thriving. Jews were members of all aspects of Arabian society. There were Jewish merchants, warriors, farmers, Bedouin, and poets. Jews spoke Arabic, including an early form of Judeo-Arabic, Hebrew, and Aramaic and were in touch with the major religious centers in Babylonia and Palestine. Like many Jewish communities at the end of the sixth century C.E., they represented a variety of beliefs and practices, some of which were or would become condemned as the authority of the Babylonian Talmud became predominant under the Islamic Empire. Jewish clans were present in many

Arab tribes, whether urban or pastoral, and intermarriage and conversion to Judaism were regular. The famous pre-Islamic Jewish poet as-Samaw'al typified the martial values of Bedouin Arabia, but it is through the urban, literate Jews of the Ḥijâz that much biblical, midrashic, and mystical material became known among Muhammad's contemporaries. The Qur'an is replete with discussions of biblical figures, with Moses dominating all other figures. Islamic traditions commenting on the Qur'an draw heavily from haggadic and midrashic materials, some of which were available to Muhammad and his companions. While the split between Rabbanite Jews and Karaite Jews would happen after Muhammad's death, it is clear that some of the elements of the controversy were present among the Jews of Arabia.

Islamic Period

In the year 622 C.E., twelve years after Muhammad received his first revelation that would begin the religion of Islam, opposition to his message forced him and his small number of followers to migrate from Mecca to Medina. Known as the Hijrah, this migration marks the beginning of the political establishment of Islam and the beginning of Muhammad's close encounter with the Jews of Yathrib, better known as *al-Medînah,* "the City." This was a city in conflict, with Jews and Arab polytheists fighting among themselves for limited resources. The conflict was, however, not chiefly along sectarian lines, although certain prominent Jewish tribes were central to the strife. Muhammad was invited in by two of the Arab tribes as a mediator. In a document known in modern scholarship as the "Constitution of Medina," Muhammad declared Jews and Muslims in the city as members of the same community, each with their own religious laws. While this notion was modified in later Islamic history, Muhammad's vision of a multiconfessional community became a model for Muslim–non-Muslim relations until modern times. When the Muslim community was attacked by the opposition forces from Mecca, some Jews sided with the Meccans and, after Muslim victory, were expelled, with some sold into slavery or, in the case of prominent warriors, executed.

At the time of Muhammad's death, however, many Jews remained in Medina and elsewhere in the Ḥijâz. Twenty years after the Hijrah, the Caliph ʿUmar I is said to have promulgated an order expelling all Jews from the Ḥijâz, but documents from the Cairo Geniza indicate that Jews still lived in the Ḥijâz and corresponded with coreligionists in Palestine. And, as late as the eighteenth century, reports circulated that Jewish Bedouin regularly attacked Muslim pilgrimage caravans, terrifying the travelers and giving rise to tales of giant Jewish warriors. After the rise of the Wahhabi-backed Saudi tribe's takeover of Arabia, reports of Jews in northwest Arabia end. Jewish presence in the Yemen continued strongly until the 1950s, when the majority of the Yemenite Jewish community was brought to the State of Israel, leaving fewer than 500 families of the once robust community.

BIBLIOGRAPHY

B. AHMAD 1979, *Muhammad and the Jews: A Reexamination,* New Delhi: Indian Institute of Islamic Studies. • J. ʿAlî 1950-1953, *Ta'rîkh al-'Arab Qabl al-Islâm,* 3 vols., Baghdad: Tafîd. • M. J. KISTER 1990, *Society and Religion from Jâhiliyya to Islam,* Aldershot: Variorum. • M. LECKER 1998, *Jews and Arabs in Pre- and Early Islamic Arabia,* Aldershot: Ashgate. • I. LICHTENSTADTER 1940, "Some References to Jews in Pre-Islamic Arabic Literature," *PAAJR* 10: 185-94. • G. D. NEWBY 1988, *A History of the Jews of Arabia: From Ancient Times to Their Eclipse under Islam,* Columbia: University of South Carolina Press. • G. D. NEWBY 1989, *The Making of the Last Prophet: A Reconstruction of the Earliest Biography of Muhammad,* Columbia: University of South Carolina Press. • C. C. TORREY 1933, *The Jewish Foundation of Islam,* New York: Jewish Institute of Religion Press.

GORDON DARNELL NEWBY

Aramaic

Aramaic, like Hebrew, is one of the Northwest Semitic languages. The earliest attestations of Aramaic are inscriptions from the ninth to seventh centuries B.C.E. from Syria and Upper Mesopotamia. It began to be used as a *lingua franca* in the Neo-Assyrian period (745-609 B.C.E.) and reached its zenith during the time of Persian supremacy in the Near East (539-332 B.C.E.), as the chancelleries of the Achaemenid kings used Aramaic for legal and diplomatic correspondence. This increased use of "official" or "imperial" Aramaic parallels the spread of the vernacular Aramaic dialects in western Asia, which replaced or were used alongside the regional languages.

After the conquests of Alexander (333-323 B.C.E.), Greek became a principal language of government and commerce in the Near East, but Aramaic did not cease to be used. The regional dialects of Aramaic continued to be spoken and written with other indigenous tongues. This produced a complicated linguistic situation throughout the Near East, but especially in Palestine, where, by the time of the Roman takeover in 63 B.C.E., Greek, Aramaic, and Hebrew were all used in various spheres of life and among various ethnic groups.

Jewish Use of Aramaic in the Hellenistic Period (332-165 B.C.E.)

Ostraca from Gaza, Tel Ira, Tell el-Fara, and Jerusalem from the third century B.C.E. containing lists of names and commodities show that Aramaic was still used in administration and commerce. Nevertheless, the new language situation is apparent in a bilingual Greek-Aramaic ostracon from Khirbet el-Kom, dated to 277 B.C.E., and in a Greek-Aramaic pagan votive inscription from the third century B.C.E. from Tell Dan. In Egypt, Jewish Aramaic tomb inscriptions from Alexandria and Edfu from the third century B.C.E., as well as a list with Jewish Aramaic names from around 300 B.C.E. found at Elephantine (*CAP* 81) show that Aramaic was used within some Diaspora Jewish communities. Note also the occasional Aramaisms in the Septuagint, e.g., Exod. 12:19 *geiôras* = Aram. *giyyôrâ,* "proselyte."

The book of Tobit was probably composed in the Hellenistic period, in the Diaspora, either in Aramaic or Hebrew. The Persian court story discovered at Qumran (4Q550) may also have originated in this era, if not earlier, as well as the *Prayer of Nabonidus* (4Q242). The canonical Aramaic tales of Daniel in Daniel 2–7 certainly belong to Hellenistic times, although they probably were composed earlier than the final redaction of the book as a whole in 165 B.C.E. The "son of God" text (4Q246) may be contemporary with the Aramaic sections of Daniel. The origins of the early Enochic literature, such as the *Book of the Watchers* (chaps. 1–36 of *1 Enoch*), may belong to the third century B.C.E., along with the Enochic *Astronomical Book* (chaps. 72–82) and the Enochic *Book of Giants.* Aramaic fragments of all these have been found at Qumran.

Hasmonean Period (165-63 B.C.E.)

Aramaic was used on the coinage of Alexander Jannaeus, along with Hebrew and Greek, and a series of Greek-Aramaic boundary markers from Gezer may belong to this period. But public inscriptions of any kind are rare: a fragmentary funerary inscription from Khirbet Mird (Hyrcania) is the only certain example, and possibly a charcoal inscription on the Tomb of Jason in Jerusalem. The only legal text is a fragmentary ostracon from Murabbaʿat (Mur 72) containing a legal deposition.

Literary texts, however, are abundant. The Enoch literature continued to grow with the addition of the *Dream Visions* (*1 Enoch* 83–90). And most of the Qumran Aramaic texts belong to the Hasmonean period; the *Genesis Apocryphon* (a retelling of the patriarchal narratives in popular style) and the *Targum to Job* (translation of Job into Aramaic) are the most notable. The testamentary genre probably originated in this period, and fragments of visionary works relating to Levi (4Q213-214, 540-541), Amram (4Q543-548), and Qahat (4Q542) were found at Qumran, as well as texts possibly relating to Judah (4Q538) and Joseph (4Q539). Visionary-apocalyptic writings such as the *Four Kingdoms* (4Q552-553), the *New Jerusalem* (1Q32, 2Q24, 4Q554-555, 11Q18), the *Elect of God* (4Q534-536), and others (4Q529, 556-558), as well as divinatory writings such as a brontologion (4Q318), a physiognomic horoscope (4Q561), and an incantation against demons (4Q560), show that Aramaic literary culture was rich and diverse, although poetry, theology, religious law, and biblical commentary were written in Hebrew.

Roman Period to the First Revolt (63 B.C.E.–74 C.E.)

The entry of Roman power into the Near East meant an increased role for Greek (and Latin) and a diminishing one for Aramaic as the official language. Nevertheless, Aramaic continued to be the vernacular of many, if not most, Jews. It was still publicly used, as in many of the inscriptions on ossuaries (bone boxes), a popular means of reburial of human remains; they bear the names of the deceased, their kin, profession, and sometimes other details. Other funerary inscriptions are known, including a plaque describing the reburial of the bones of King Uzziah. Another "royal" inscription on a sarcophagus refers to "Sarah (*or:* Sadah) the queen," in both Aramaic and early Syriac script (Estrangela), probably referring to Helena, the queen of Adiabene, who converted to Judaism in the first century C.E. (Josephus, *Ant.* 20.17; *J.W.* 5.147).

Aramaic was also used in legal and economic documents. At the Wadi Murabbaʿat were discovered texts on papyri from the first century C.E. such as deeds (Mur 23, 25, 27, 28), marriage contracts (Mur 20, 21), a divorce settlement (Mur 19), a ration list (Mur 8), and a debt acknowledgment (Mur 18), the latter dated to the "second year of Nero Caesar" (56 C.E.). In addition, a few documents from Naḥal Ḥever may date to this period (Ḥev/Se 9 [deed], 9a, 10 [receipt]). The legal texts 4Q344-346 stem from the first century C.E., as does the letter fragment 4Q342. Many brief Aramaic epigraphs on ostraca were uncovered at Masada, the last stronghold of the Jewish rebels of the First Revolt.

Finally, the New Testament has a number of transliterated Aramaic words and sentences, such as *talitha koum(i),* "O lass, stand up!" (Mark 5:41); *ephphatha,* "be opened!" (Mark 7:34); *golgotha,* "skull" (Mark 15:22; Matt 27:33); *eloi eloi* (or: *eli eli*) *lema sabachthani,* "My God, my God, why have you forsaken me?" (Mark 15:34, Matt 27:46); *maranatha,* "Our lord, come!" (1 Cor. 16:22); and *kephas,* "rock (Peter)" (John 1:42) as well as Aramaic names with the element *bar-,* "son of," such as Barabbas, Bartholomaios, Bariesus, Bariona, Barnabas, Barsabbas.

Roman Period to the Second Revolt (70-135 C.E.)

From Naḥal Ḥever the legal archive of Babatha, a propertied woman from Judea, dates from 94-132 C.E. and includes only three Jewish Aramaic (and six Nabatean Aramaic) documents out of thirty-five; the rest are in Greek, although many of the signatures of witnesses are in Aramaic. The smaller archive of Salome Komaise from Naḥal Ḥever has one Aramaic document, six in Greek. Both women lived within the sphere of the Greek-speaking Roman provincial court. Other documents from Naḥal Ḥever and other sites include deeds of sale, marriage contracts, receipts, and signatures in Aramaic, as well as Greek and Hebrew. Many documents from the Second Revolt are either Aramaic or Hebrew, including nine letters in Aramaic from Bar Kokhba, leader of the revolt, to his commanders.

The Influence of Aramaic

The influence of Aramaic was felt in other languages. Besides the Aramaic words in the NT, scholars have detected Aramaic influence on its Greek syntax and vocabulary (e.g., the idiomatic use of "before" in Matt. 11:26 par.). The same is true of the Septuagint; for example, LXX Isa. 53:10 translates the Hebrew word meaning "bruise" as if it were the Aramaic soundalike "purify." The Hebrew Bible texts themselves were not immune; one of the Qumran Isaiah scrolls (1QIsa[a]), for instance, has the Aramaic form for "solemn meeting" at 1:13 instead of the Hebrew (the same form cited by Josephus, *Ant.* 3.252). Finally, the Hebrew of the Qumran texts and the Mishnah is heavily influenced by Aramaic idioms and vocabulary.

The Language Situation in Palestine and the Diaspora

Although the importance of Aramaic is undisputed, its exact social relationship to Greek and Hebrew is debated. Purely by chance, most of the Aramaic literary texts that survive from the Second Temple era are from the late Hellenistic or Hasmonean period, and it is not clear, for instance, whether its "minority" relationship to Hebrew in the Qumran finds is typical. Greek is well represented as a Jewish literary language in the Diaspora (e.g., Philo), and it was necessarily used in Palestine when Jews and Gentiles communicated. However, intra-Jewish use of Greek in Palestine seems to have been infrequent; even Jews educated in Greek culture often preferred to speak Hebrew or Aramaic. Paul gains a hearing from the crowd in Acts 22:2 by speaking "the Hebrew dialect," and Josephus, a cultivated man, admits his knowledge of Greek was not refined enough to write his works unaided by assistants (*Ag. Ap.* 1.50). In one of the Greek Bar Kokhba letters, the writer feels obliged to give a reason (not clear, the text being damaged) for not using Hebrew. Greek loanwords are rare in Hebrew and Aramaic texts until after the First Revolt, as are Greek documentary texts, and there may have been in Palestine a nationalist resistance to the use of Greek that did not fully subside until after the Second Temple period (cf., e.g., *m. Soṭah* 9:14).

Aramaic and Hebrew were jointly used outside the Gentile sphere. Although some texts refer to Aramaic words as "Hebrew" (John 5:2; 19:13, 17; 20:16; *Ant.* 3.252), most writers properly differentiate them (e.g., Rev. 9:11; 16:16; Josephus, usually). The *Letter of Aristeas* says that the Jews use "a peculiar dialect. . . . They are supposed to use the Aramaic language, but this is not the case; their language is quite different" (*Letter of Aristeas* 11). This refers to the language of the Bible, not of daily life, but it does confirm that people distinguished the languages. In nonbiblical texts, Hebrew, we may assume, was especially favored for poetry, liturgy, and theology, and in some locations, such as Jerusalem, it may have been the vernacular as well. Aramaic, however, seems to have been the "default" language for most communication between Jews. In sociolinguistic terms, there was a condition of *diglossia,* the coexistence of "high" and "low" (vernacular) languages within Judaism in Palestine:

	Within Palestinian Judaism	*Gentile-Jewish Interaction*
High	Hebrew	Greek
Low	Aramaic	

In particular cases, the terms of the diglossia may have changed; for instance, communication between Palestinian Jews and Diaspora Jews (or Jews living in Hellenized cities in Palestine) will have used the vernacular of the addressees. We find Paul speaking in "Hebrew" in Jerusalem (Acts 22:2) but writing letters to the Diaspora churches in Greek. According to rabbinic tradition, Gamaliel II (end of first century C.E.) wrote epistles to Jewish communities in Lydda, Galilee, and the eastern Diaspora in Aramaic (*t. Sanh.* 2:5-6).

For some, the existence of the targums (Aramaic translations of the Bible) settles the question in favor of Aramaic as the dominant tongue. The extant rabbinic targums, however, clearly date from after the Second Temple period, and their use in the synagogue belongs to a later time. The Qumran Job Targum (4Q157) and Leviticus Targum (4Q156) were used by a group that certainly knew Hebrew well, judging by the rest of their library; these "targums" must have been study aids for scholars rather than renderings for those who knew little or no Hebrew.

Bibliography

J. Barr 1989, "Hebrew, Aramaic and Greek in the Hellenistic Age," in *Cambridge History of Ancient Judaism,* vol. 2, *The Hellenistic Age,* ed. W. D. Davies and L. Finkelstein, Cambridge: Cambridge University Press, 79-114. • K. Berthelot and D. Stökel, eds. 2010, *Les textes araméens de Qumrân,* Leiden: Brill. • K. Beyer 1984, 2004, *Die aramäischen Texte vom Toten Meer,* 2 vols., Göttingen: Vandenhoeck & Ruprecht. • J. Fitzmyer and D. Harrington 1978, *A Manual of Palestinian Aramaic Texts,* Rome: Biblical Institute. • A. Millard 2000, *Reading and Writing in the Time of Jesus,* New York: New York University. • U. Schattner-Rieser 2005, *Textes Araméens de la Mer Morte,* Brussels: Safran. • M. Sokoloff 2003, *Dictionary of Judean Aramaic,* Ramat-Gan: Bar-Ilan University. • A. Yardeni 2000, *Textbook of Aramaic, Hebrew and Nabataean Documentary Texts from the Judean Desert and Related Materials,* Jerusalem.

See also: Greek; Hebrew; Multilingualism

Edward Cook

Aramaic Levi Document

The *Aramaic Levi Document (ALD)* is a fragmentary narrative concerning the Israelite patriarch Levi's consecration to the priesthood and his teaching to his children. It was composed in the Aramaic language at the latest in the third or the early second century B.C.E. and most likely in Judea. This writing, which has not survived in its entirety, is also sometimes known confusingly as "Aramaic Testament of Levi" or "Aramaic Levi." Since neither the beginning nor the end of the work has survived, it is not clear that it was a testament; its literary genre remains unknown. Moreover, *ALD* must be distinguished from the Greek *Testament of Levi (T. Levi),* which is one of the *Testaments of the Twelve Patriarchs.*

Significance

The *Aramaic Levi Document* is one of the earliest extrabiblical writings, and it is highly significant as such. More or less contemporary with the oldest parts of *1 Enoch,* it contributes to our understanding of Judaism in a period of which we know little, the third century B.C.E. *ALD* deals with a number of interesting

ARAMAIC LEVI DOCUMENT

subjects. One substantial part, presented as Isaac's instruction of the newly ordained priest, Levi, is composed of cultic regulations specifying the different sacrifices and the amounts of incense, oil, fine flour, and salt to be used with each type of sacrificial animal. The order of butchering of the sacrificial beast is given, and the types of wood to be burnt on the altar are listed. Most of this cultic material is neither drawn from pentateuchal law nor paralleled by rabbinic regulations. The question arises whether it reflects the practice of the Temple (or of some sectarian group) at the time or whether it is ideal and theoretical. Equally intriguing is the mystery of the identity of the work's author(s).

The Solar Calendar

The *Aramaic Levi Document* uses a 364-day solar calendar of the type promoted by *Jubilees* and the Enochic *Book of the Luminaries.* Later, the same calendar was also advanced by the Dead Sea sect. Where it originated is still a mystery, as is the question of its social location. Calendar has considerable sociological ramifications, and acceptance or rejection of a particular calendar signifies adherence to a particular religious group or acceptance of a particular religious authority. In contrast to *Jubilees, ALD* does not make any polemical point about the use of this calendar. This might indicate that, while *Jubilees* was directed toward adherents of other calendars, *ALD* was not. How that is to be explained remains unknown, but it is surely related to *ALD*'s social context and function.

Relation to the Book of Jubilees

A third significant point in the *Aramaic Levi Document* is its narrative structure and the chronological lists of events that are introduced into the work. These cohere for the most part with those in *Jubilees.* From a comparison of the events narrated and their dates with the corresponding events in *Jubilees,* it emerges that *ALD* is prior to, and probably served as a source of, *Jubilees.* The *Aramaic Levi Document* is also cited in the *Damascus Document* known from the Cairo Geniza and Qumran, and seems to be a source of the *Testament of Levi* as well. The oldest of these three writings is *Jubilees,* composed in the first third of the second century B.C.E. The date of *ALD* can be inferred, then, from the fact that it is a source of *Jubilees.* Its Aramaic language also indicates (but does not prove) an early date.

Messianism

The messianism of the *Aramaic Levi Document* is also of very great interest. That many Jews expected a future messiah, a descendant of David, is well known. Less widely familiar, but nonetheless broadly recognized, is that in certain texts and according to some groups, the restoration of the ideal polity of Israel will involve the reestablishment of both anointed offices, the high priesthood and the monarchy. Such texts are Zechariah (Zech. 4:3, 11-13), the *Community Rule* from Qumran (1QS), and the *Damascus Document* (12:23–18:1). Now it can be shown from various statements in *ALD* that its author(s) expected only one messiah, son of Levi — that is, a priestly messiah — to whom it attributed both kingship and priesthood (Stone, Greenfield, and Eshel 2004: 35-39).

The Prominence of Joseph

In the *Aramaic Levi Document* Joseph is of great paradigmatic prominence. He is a wise and righteous man, and Levi calls on his offspring to model themselves on Joseph (13:6). Later, in the Christian *Testaments of the Twelve Patriarchs,* Joseph serves as a type of Christ and a figure whom one should strive to emulate. The description of Joseph in *ALD* shows that his special role antedates the Christian interpretation. A wisdom tradition is connected with Joseph and is joined in *ALD* to the priestly.

Manuscript Discoveries

The *Aramaic Levi Document* has reached us in a very complex way. At the end of the nineteenth century, two Aramaic sheets of it were discovered among the manuscript fragments from the Cairo Geniza. Soon after, it was observed that one of the manuscripts of the *Testament of Levi* in Greek included some additional passages that overlapped with the Geniza *ALD* fragments and supplemented them. A small extract in Syriac also turned up.

Finally, among the Dead Sea Scrolls seven fragmentary manuscripts of *ALD* were discovered, one from Qumran Cave 1 and six more from Cave 4. The oldest of these date to the Hasmonean period. The work reconstructed from these fragments (which were published separately) has recently been edited and translated as a whole, and now joins the corpus of early Jewish apocryphal writings.

Bibliography

Editions

M. E. Stone, J. C. Greenfield, and E. Eshel 2004, *The Aramaic Levi Document: Edition, Translation, Commentary,* Leiden: Brill. • M. E. Stone and J. C. Greenfield 1996, "Aramaic Levi Document," in *Qumran Cave 4, XVII, Parabiblical Texts, Part 3,* DJD 22, Oxford: Clarendon Press, 2-72.

Published Fragments

R. H. Charles and A. Cowley 1907, "An Early Source of the Testaments of the Patriarchs," *JQR* 19: 566-83. • J. T. Milik 1955, "Le Testament de Lévi en araméen," *RB* 62: 398-408. • H. L. Pass and J. Arendzen 1900, "Fragments of an Aramaic Text of the Testament of Levi," *JQR* 12: 651-56.

Studies

H. Drawnel 2004, *An Aramaic Wisdom Text from Qumran: A New Interpretation of the Levi Document,* Leiden: Brill. • J. C. Greenfield and M. E. Stone 1979, "Remarks on the Aramaic Testament of Levi from the Geniza," *RB* 86: 214-44. • M. de Jonge 1988, "The Testament of Levi and 'Aramaic Levi,'" *RQ* 13: 376-85. • M. de Jonge 1999, "Levi in Aramaic Levi and in the Testament of Levi," in *Pseudepigraphic Perspectives: The Apocrypha and Pseudepigrapha in Light of the*

Dead Sea Scrolls, ed. E. G. Chazon and M. E. Stone, Leiden: Brill, 71-89. • J. KUGEL 1993, "Levi's Elevation to the Priesthood in Second Temple Writings," *HTR* 86: 1-64. • R. KUGLER 1996, *From Patriarch to Priest: The Levi-Priestly Tradition from Aramaic Levi to Testament of Levi,* Atlanta: Scholars Press. • J. TROMP 1997, "Two References to a Levi Document in an Epistle of Ammonas," *NovT* 29: 235-47.

MICHAEL E. STONE

ʿAraq el-Amir

ʿAraq el-Emir is located some 29 km. east of Jericho and 17 km. west of Amman, atop a hill overlooking the western bank of Wadi es-Sir. Scholarly interest in the site began in 1817, after Irby and Mangles identified it with the city of Tyros mentioned by Josephus (*Ant.* 12.230-233). Among the various explorers who later visited the site were de Vogüé (1864), de Saucy (1868), Conder (1881), and Butler (1907).

The site was surveyed in 1904-1905 by the Princeton University Archaeological Expedition to Syria. Further research was carried out by Lapp in 1961-1962. A French expedition under the directorship of Villeneuve and Larché, with the assistance of Zayadin from the Jordanian Department of Antiquities, carried out extensive excavations between 1976 and 1985, along with undertaking the reconstruction of the remarkable Qasr al-Abd ("Palace of the Slave"), which was built — but apparently never completed — by the governor Hyrcanus ben Joseph.

Covering an area of some sixty hectares, the site comprises the following: an archaeological tell containing six occupation strata ranging from the Early Bronze Age to the Hellenistic period; cliffs and both natural and carved caves, of which two feature the inscribed name "Tobias" at their entrance; a villa or palace situated at the foot of a cliff; remains of an earthen embankment that may have supported a man-made lake; a monumental building (Qasr al-Abd) with a large entrance complex; a square-shaped structure north of the entrance complex; remains of aqueducts and various structures; and plots of land leveled for the construction of structures or gardens. The villa, built during the third century B.C.E., was significantly enlarged ca. 180 B.C.E. by Hyrcanus, who built other structures at the site as well. Today, much of the villa's remains are covered by the modern village of ʿAraq el-Amir.

The well-preserved structure of Qasr al-Abd has been securely dated to the early second century B.C.E. on the basis of the Hellenistic pottery found adjacent to it, originating in the sole occupation stratum found between the Early Bronze and the Byzantine strata. Until the latest excavations, scholars argued that this was either a fortress, temple, palace, or mausoleum. According to Villeneuve's and Larché's reconstruction, Qasr al-Abd was a rectangular building that measured ca. 38 × 19 m. and 12 m. high. Its entrance was from the north, through a portico, by which one could reach the center of the ground floor. An impressive staircase ascended to the upper floor. A second portico led also to the building from the south, and Netzer (1999) argues that its primary purpose was to create architectural symmetry. Four rooms stood in the center of the ground floor, each about 7 × 3.5 m., surrounded by corridors. The corridors, ca 3.5 m. wide, were well illuminated by seventeen large windows, which also served as the light source for the internal rooms. Villeneuve and Larché suggested that the second floor contained dwelling rooms.

The structure was built of megalithic ashlars and featured carved animal reliefs (lions, panthers, and eagles) that surrounded the building on all four sides. Most of the reliefs were on the level of the second floor, but two panthers, which apparently served as fountains, are seen on each side of the ground floor. Two additional fountains, though of different animals, were found: one in the western wall and one, of red and white dolomite, in the eastern wall.

Villeneuve and Larché proposed that this was either a palace or manor house built in the center of a palatial estate. Its ground floor contained agricultural installations, such as storerooms for grains and facilities for animals, and the second floor, as mentioned above, contained dwelling rooms. However, Netzer (2000) argues that the massive construction coupled with the adjacent land development, primarily the man-made lake that covered an area of six hectares, is not in keeping with the modest agricultural installations. He believes that this was a pavilion, intended from the very beginning to stand in the center of the lake. The architect's goal was to impress: the buildings and its carved reliefs would reflect in the water, creating the illusion of a floating ship — similar to the *thalamegos,* a floating palace of Ptolemy IV. Visitors could enjoy the sight from boats, as well as from the promenade that ran along the lake. According to Netzer, this structure served as a major source of inspiration for the Hasmonean and, later, Herodian palaces.

BIBLIOGRAPHY

M. J. B. BRETT 1963, "The Qasr el-Abd: A Proposed Reconstruction," *BASOR* 171: 39-45. • H. C. BUTLER 1907, *Ancient Architecture in Syria,* Leiden: Brill. • C. R. CONDER 1889, *The Survey of Eastern Palestine,* vol. 1, London: Palestinian Exploration Fund. • D. K. HILL 1963, "The Animal Fountain of ʿAraq el-Amir," *BASOR* 171: 45-55. • C. L. IRBY AND J. MANGLES 1823, *Travels in Egypt and Nubia, Syria and Asia Minor,* London: Darf. • N. L. LAPP 1983, "Excavation at Araq el-Emir," *BASOR* 47-48: 1-74. • P. W. LAPP 1962, "Soundings at Araq el-Emir," *BASOR* 165: 16-34. • P. W. LAPP 1963, "The Second and Third Campaigns at Araq el-Emir," *BASOR* 171: 8-39. • F. LARCHÉ 2005, *ʿIraq al-Amir, Le château du Tobiade Hyrcan,* vol. 2, *Restitution et Reconstruction,* Beyrouth: Institut français du Proche-Orient. • F. LARCHÉ, F. VILLENEUVE, AND F. ZAYADIN 1981, "Recherches archaelogiques à ʿIraq al-Amir," *Liber Annuus* 31: 333-42. • F. LARCHÉ, F. VILLENEUVE. AND F. ZAYADIN 1982, "Recherches archaelogiques à ʿIraq al-Amir," *Liber Annuus* 32: 495-98. • E. NETZER 1999, *The Palaces of the Hasmoneans and Herod the Great,* Jerusalem: Yad Ben Zvi. • E. NETZER 2000, "Tyros, the Floating Palace," in *Text and Artifact in the Religions of Mediterranean Antiquity,* ed. S. G. Wilson and M. D. Desjardins, Waterloo: Wilfrid

Laurier University Press, 340-53. • S. G. ROSENBERG 2006, *Airaq al-Amir: The Architecture of the Tobiads*, Oxford: Hedges. • M. DE VOGÜÉ 1864, *Le Temple de Jérusalem, monographie du Haram-ech-Chérif, suivie d'un Essai sur la topographie de la Ville-sainte*, Paris: Noblet & Baudry, 34-38; pls. 34-35. • E. WILL ET AL. 1991, *'Iraq al-Amir: Le château du tobiade Hyrcan*, Paris: Geuthner.

See also: Tobiads; Transjordan OREN GUTFELD

Architecture

The architecture of the Second Temple period begins with remains of Hasmonean architecture encountered in sites and structures that were later reconstructed or completely renewed by the Herodian architectural projects.

Hasmonean Architecture

Hasmonean architecture survives mostly in the remains of fortifications, desert fortresses, funerary art, and water systems. The sole architectural structure exhibiting features that can be related specifically to the Hasmoneans is the Jericho winter palace complex.

The development of the Jericho Valley probably began in the reign of John Hyrcanus I (135-104 B.C.E.). The availability of water and land as well as the mild climate enabled the development of agriculture, including date palm and balsam cultivation, which caused economic growth. This brought about the building of winter palaces, first by the Hasmoneans and later by Herod. Jericho was a garden city and royal estate that flourished during the first century B.C.E.

The Hasmonean palace complex (fig. 1) was built at the outlet of Wadi Qelt on a hill overlooking the Jericho Valley (Netzer 2001: 15-42). The first palace built by John Hyrcanus I was only partly preserved and integrated an earlier watchtower, later covered by an artificial mound

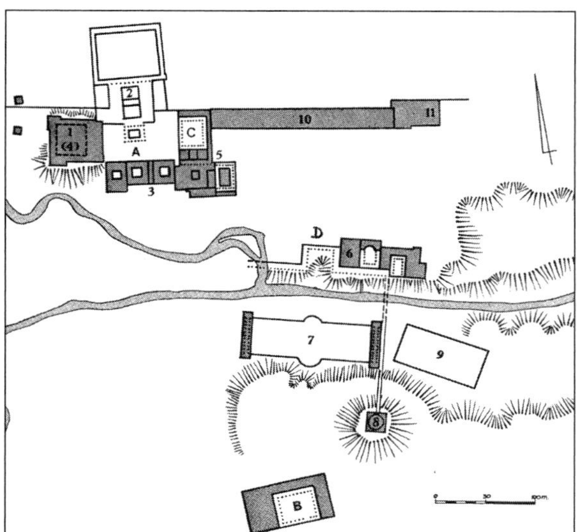

Figure 1. Site plan of the Hasmonean and Herodian palaces at Jericho

constructed by Herod. The palace consisted of an inner court with a large north wing including living quarters and service rooms; some of the rooms were decorated with stucco and fresco. Remains of a storage hall, bath, and *miqveh* (ritual bath) have been uncovered. A system of pipes and channels brought water from the aqueduct to the palace. The remains indicate that the palace was probably two stories high and contained about forty to fifty rooms. The south wing most likely was used for ceremonies and receptions. Two small swimming pools were built on the west, and the floor surrounding them was paved with mosaic and the walls decorated with frescoes. A fortified palace surrounded by a moat, a swimming pool complex, and a pair of pools were erected by Alexander Jannaeus (103-76 B.C.E.). It was constructed to the northwest and adjacent to the central building. The area was built with a court serving as a garden, probably surrounded by columns that have not survived. South of the pools and on the same axis, the pavilion was erected with columns and entablatures shaped in Doric style. This complex probably served the inhabitants for reception and leisure purposes; it had a magnificent view of the valley and Wadi Qelt. It probably was destroyed by an earthquake; only its foundations, columns, and architrave survive. The drowning of Aristobulus III, as described by Josephus in *Ant.* 15.53-56, may have occurred in one of the pools.

At a later period, the complex was extended to the south by the addition of twin palaces erected during the reign of Queen Alexandra, Shlomzion (76-67 B.C.E.). Each of the twin palaces has a central open court surrounded by rooms, a hall, a bathhouse, a *miqveh*, and gardens (fig. 1). The palaces were decorated with frescoes; each had an adjacent court with a small swimming pool. Sometime later an additional swimming pool was built onto the eastern palace, and some other buildings, houses, installations, and *miqveh* complexes were built around the palaces. The Hasmonean palace complex probably continued to be in use until its destruction by the earthquake of 31 B.C.E.

Herodian Architecture

The sources relating to the construction of monumental building projects that commenced during Herod's reign (37-4 B.C.E.) are literary and archaeological. The major literary sources are the works of Josephus, *Jewish Antiquities* 15–17 and *Jewish War* 1, 2, and 5. Extensive archaeological excavations add information that both corresponds and conflicts with the literary sources. Herod built three new towns: Antipatris, Caesarea, and Sebaste (Samaria). Two new towns were built by Herod's sons: Tiberias was founded by Herod Antipas in 18 C.E.; and Paneas, which was built by Herod, was extended by his son, Herod Philip.

Thirty-three building projects are mentioned by Josephus, twenty of which were within the borders of Herod's kingdom and thirteen of which were in other countries. The list of Herodian architectural projects includes mention of the erection, extension, and reconstruction of towns, fortresses, and palaces as well as of the Temple in Jerusalem, the royal stoa, the large palace at Herodium, and, at Caesarea, one of the largest harbors ever constructed in antiquity. Most of these structures were built during Herod's reign, but renovations and reconstructions were undertaken during the first century C.E. until the destruction of the Second Temple in 70 C.E.

Herodian architecture was based on inheritance from the Hasmonean buildings and the influence of the surrounding Hellenistic cultures, especially in the ornamentation of the buildings — wall paintings, stucco on walls, columns, ceilings, and mosaic pavements. The incorporation of *triclinia* (Roman-style dining rooms with couches or a platform on three sides of an open area or low table), peristyle courts, gardens, bathhouses, and pools is similar in some ways to the *domus* and villa type of house.

The typical features of Herodian architecture include high-level planning with the selection of natural or artificial topographical locations. The complexes with a commanding architectural focal point contain buildings, open spaces, pools, and gardens. A variety of functional purposes for the structures integrate residence, administrative, leisure, and entertainment structures within a palace. The building techniques included the use of simple and local materials such as stone and sun-dried bricks, and the plastering of exteriors and interiors with high-quality plaster. Ashlar stones were sometimes used on some walls and were a type of ornamental motif in Second Temple period art. At Jericho Palace III and Paneas, some walls were covered with *opus quadratum* (rectangular blocks of stone set without mortar) and *opus reticulatum* (small tufa blocks placed diagonally), which were Roman masonry techniques. Barrel-vaulting was employed for some roofing. An interesting feature of Herodian architecture is the naming of public and private structures for Herod's relatives and Roman patrons, as mentioned by Josephus.

Netzer maintains (1981b: 52-54; 2001: 133-34) that these projects involved innovative and original planning by King Herod as well as his personal involvement. An ostentatious attitude is indicated by the proportions of the huge podium and monumental stones of the Temple mount and its royal stoa, and in the Herodium palace-fortress. Herod's main venture was conducted primarily in his capital city of Jerusalem, where he built his chief palace and the Temple, which was most likely the largest temple built in antiquity. At Jericho, Herod built three winter palaces, presumably to serve his family and court for residence, entertainment, and leisure. Other extensive architectural projects included the structures at Masada, which was his major desert fortress and winter palace. Herodium was probably Herod's major summer palace, and at Caesarea Maritima he built a palace and harbor.

Palaces

The Herodian palace, which followed the common plans of the Roman *domus* and villa, was typically an elaborate building with a main wing containing a triclinium consisting of a large hall with three rows of columns parallel to three walls and a wide entrance open to the landscape or an inner court. The palace in-

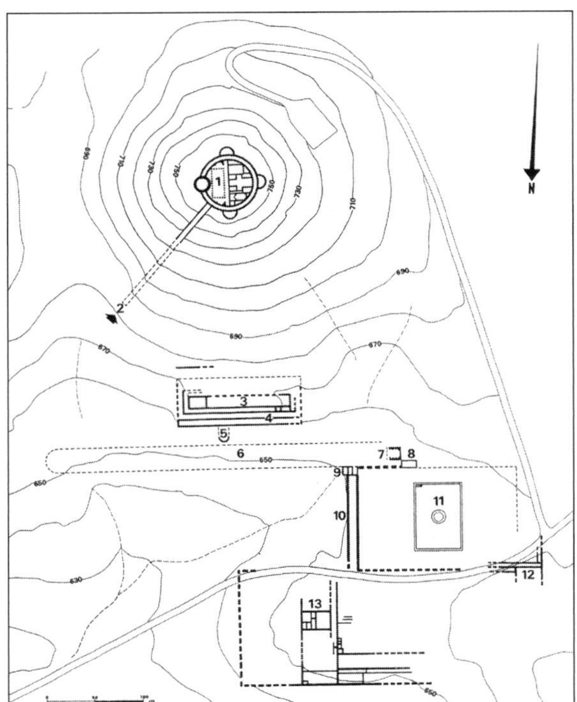

Figure 2. Site plan of Greater Herodium

cluded a peristyle court with rows of columns and double columns in its corners; it had an inner garden, a bath house, and dwelling rooms. The extended palace complex frequently included entertainment facilities: pools for swimming and sailing boats; elaborate gardens; and water installations, channels, and aqueducts to bring water to the residential wings, the pools, and the gardens.

Jericho Three Herodian winter palaces at Jericho (fig. 1) were built on both sides of Wadi Qelt (Netzer 2001:40-63, fig. 42). *Winter Palace I* ("Gymnasium") at Jericho is dated to the early years of Herod's reign. The Herodian palace, a grand villa, was built south of Wadi Qelt. It was a rectangular building with a central peristyle court, a triclinium, a peristyle hall, a bath house, and a pair of pools that may have functioned as a ritual bath *(miqveh)* and served for residential and ceremonial purposes.

Winter Palace II was a rebuilding and extension of the palace complex that included several wings. The south wing was erected over an artificial platform under which the Hasmonean palace was buried, probably serving as Herod's private residential villa. The two pools retained from the Hasmonean complex were now combined into one large swimming pool, and extended by another, smaller pool surrounded by gardens planted over the remains of the destroyed Hasmonean twin palaces. The eastern wing was constructed on two levels and served recreational purposes.

The enlarged *Winter Palace III* was built by Herod on both sides of Wadi Qelt. It consisted of a northern wing, a sunken garden, a large pool, and an artificial mound with a building on the south bank of the wadi.

Herodium Herod built the *Herodium palace-fortress,* named it after himself, and chose it as the site of his burial. Sources for this palace-fortress are the writings of Josephus (*Ant.* 14.359-60; 15.323-25; *J.W.* 1.265, 419-21) and extensive excavations (Netzer 1981a; 2001: 98-116, fig. 138). Greater Herodium (fig. 2) consists of an upper mountain palace-fortress and a lower area containing a building complex.

The mountain palace-fortress was built on top of a hill and was the first building constructed at Herodium; it was erected in the shape of a cylinder and consisted of two concentric circular walls with a corridor. Four towers were built outside the walls, three of which were semicircular. The fourth, eastern tower was the tallest and was probably multi-storied. The structure was five to six stories high and contained rooms. Netzer (1981a: 100-101) asserts that the prototype for the Herodium palace-fortress was the Antonia fortress in Jerusalem. Within the encircling fortress walls and towers, Herod built a palace to serve as a residential villa; it was divided into eastern and western wings.

Below the mountain palace-fortress and at the foot of the mountain, *Lower Herodium* consists of a large central palace built on an elevated platform; at its western end stand the remains of a monumental building connected to the course and a pool complex surrounded by formal gardens, with a circular colonnaded pavilion at its center. The pool was used for swimming, sailing boats, and storing water. The monumental building contained a hall with niches once covered by frescoes. This building with the course may have formed part of a burial complex. The northern wing was used for dwellings for Herod's family and court, for service facilities, or for residences for the administrative staff. The aqueduct built by Herod brought water from Urtas to the Lower Herodium complex.

Masada The isolated and easily defendable rock upon which *Masada* is built provided excellent conditions for a fortress-palace (fig. 3). Masada had three major building phases during Herod's reign (Yadin 1966; Netzer 1991; 2001: 79-97, figs. 99, 110, 123, 124). The first phase (ca. 35 B.C.E.) included the nucleus of the western palace, similarly planned palaces 11, 12, 13, and the early stages of buildings 7 and 9. The second, main phase (ca. 25 B.C.E.), concentrated on the north and center, included three major projects: the northern palace and adjoining bathhouse, the storerooms complex, and a water system. The third phase included the extensions to the western palace and storerooms and the casemate wall around the whole mountain.

The northern palace-villa at Masada is an unusual structure consisting of three terraces, one above the other, built on the northern edge of the rock. The entrance was on the east side of the upper terrace. The upper terrace consisted of rooms along the sides of an open court, living quarters, and a semicircular balcony that probably had two rows of columns. The middle terrace contained a circular pavilion structure with two rows of columns. South of the circular building was a

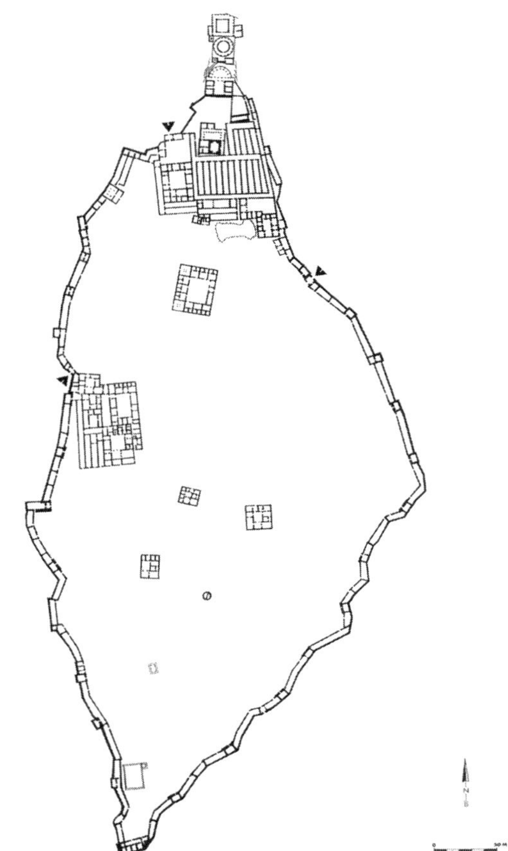

Figure 3. Site plan of Masada showing the western palace and the northern palace-villa with adjoining facilities

staircase connecting the upper and middle terraces. A large hall on the east was decorated with a colonnade, a "false façade," and fresco imitating marble. The lower terrace was constructed on a raised area of supporting walls. The central area was porticoed, consisting of a double colonnade of half-columns made of sandstone plastered with colored Corinthian capitals. The lower parts of the portico walls were decorated with fresco imitating marble. Behind the porticoed area was a "false façade" wall with half-columns attached to the rock and fresco panels between them. On the east was a small bathhouse, and on the west was a staircase leading from the middle terrace to the lower terrace. This palace had only a few living rooms on the upper terrace and was intended mostly for leisure.

The western palace at Masada, built close to the western gate, is the largest of all the palaces and contains four parts: the southeast section including the royal apartments, the northeast service wing and workshop, the southwest storerooms, and the northwest administrative wing and residence for palace officials. Several smaller palaces with a similar plan served the royal family and were utilized as residences for high officials and as administrative centers.

The Masada palaces differ in plan from the Herodian palaces of Jericho and Herodium. They are characterized by a simple, central court and by halls each with two columns in antis, leading to a triclinium, usually in the southern part of the court. The plan of the Masada palaces follows basic elements of Hellenistic architecture. However, it is possible that Herod, when building the Masada palaces, utilized a plan that had also been used earlier by the Hasmoneans.

Hebron Herodian in plan and ornamentation, the *palace of Hilkiya* has been uncovered in the Hebron area. The palace was a rectangular building with a peristyle court and an open triclinium at its center. The palace contained mostly rooms around the courts, some of which had barrel vaults and were decorated with stucco. A bathhouse was found in the northern wing. In the west a tower was constructed. The palace was named after a Greek inscription on a limestone slab that mentions Hilkiye, son of Simon.

Caesarea The *promontory palace at Caesarea-Maritima* was a two-story structure. It contained a swimming/bathing pool at its center with a peristyle surrounding it, and an east wing with five rooms, some paved by mosaics (Netzer 2001: 117-22, figs. 155, 162).

Fortresses

Seven fortresses built in the Judean desert — at Alexandrium, Cypros, Doq, Herodium, Hyrcania, Machaerus, and Masada — constitute an important component of Herodian architecture. Located in the desert, the fortresses were isolated and autonomous but within view of each other. Built on mountain tops, they were strongly fortified and had extensive systems for the entrapment and storage of water (Tsafrir 1982). The history of the fortresses begins in the Hasmonean period. Upon establishing his rule in about 30 B.C.E., Herod rebuilt and refortified all the existing fortresses and also established Herodium. The fortresses functioned as military bases, border controls, and places of refuge. They also served as administrative centers for important routes and for agricultural and royal farm areas. They even served as burial places both for the Hasmoneans and for Herod. Elaborate palaces were constructed on their premises. The fortresses were also extensively used in the First Jewish Revolt against the Romans (66-73 C.E.), especially those at Masada, Herodium, and Machaerus, which still stood after the fall of Jerusalem (70 C.E.).

In Jerusalem two important fortresses or citadels were built. One was the Antonia, which commanded the Temple Mount, and the other was the citadel near Herod's palace.

Caesarea Harbor

Herod's most important undertaking in Caesarea was the harbor named Sebastos. It boasted a warehouse and shipping installations built along the harbor front.

Entertainment Structures

The hippodrome at Jericho (located at Tel el-Samarat, south of ancient Jericho) is a unique complex in the Greco-Roman world (fig. 4); it is a combination hippodrome (racetrack for horse and chariot racing) and theater at the rear of which a building is attached (Netzer 2001: 64-67, figs. 80, 81). The hippodrome course has a rectangular shape. The spectators presumably sat in the theater-like structure at the northern end of the course. A large building was found behind the theater surrounding a large court. The building may have served as a royal reception wing or a gymnasium, or possibly a combination of both.

The hippodrome of Caesarea includes remains of granite *metae,* turning posts for chariot races, and fragments of an obelisk that stood in the center. *The theater at Caesarea* built by Herod indicates that it is of Hellenistic type, particularly in its *cavea* (subterranean cells where animals were confined before combat), seats, and gangway. *The stadium of Samaria-Sebaste* was built probably by Herod. The stadium was surrounded by four porticos with Doric columns, and its walls were plastered. *Colonnaded streets* were built by Herod in several towns including Antipatris (Aphek), Caesarea, and Samaria. Several *aqueducts* were constructed by Herod in Caesarea, Herodium, Jerusalem, and Samaria.

Jerusalem

The construction of the Jerusalem Temple is described at length by Josephus (*Ant.* 15.380-425; *J.W.* 5.184-227). There are also several references in the Mishnah (tractates *Middot* and *Tamid*) and a few citations in the New Testament (e.g., Mark 13:1; Luke 21:5). Archaeological excavations around the Temple area tend to confirm the literary sources (Ben-Dov 1983). The renovation and expansion of the Temple under Herod probably began in the year 20-19 B.C.E. and officially took nearly ten years to complete, but most likely building continued for many more years until 62-64 C.E.

The plan of the Temple consisted of a rectangular *temenos* or precinct surrounded on all four sides by porticos. The inner Temple was erected in the center, close to the western porticos. The earlier one was destroyed and a new one was erected on its site by the Herodian builders (*Ant.* 15.390-91; *b. Zebaḥim* 62a). Herod's renovations included doubling the size of the mount with the addition of a platform and retaining walls, and building porticos and bridges. The height of the Temple itself was raised and the façade was ornamented. The upper parts of the western and southern walls were decorated with a row of projecting pilasters. An important find is a stone inscribed in Hebrew: "To the place of trumpeting." This stone had fallen into the street and was probably located originally at the southwestern corner of the uppermost wall, marking the spot where the priest blew his trumpet every Friday evening to mark the beginning of Sabbath (Josephus, *J.W.* 4.582). The Temple's inner and outer courts were surrounded by porticos and were separated by a low boundary wall *(soreg)* that bore an inscription warning Gentiles from entering the inner court (Ben-Dov 1982: fig. on p. 102). Beyond this barrier a flight of either twelve or fourteen steps that surrounded the Temple led up to a rampart *(ḥel)* separate from the Temple's inner walls. This wall

ARCHITECTURE

was a fortress with gates and towers. Some new insights into the form and function of the gates and courts surrounding the Temple have been proposed by Netzer (2005). The Temple *temenos* was divided into three parts: the outer, women's court; the inner court of the priests with the court of the Israelites; and the sanctuary. The sanctuary was itself divided into three parts: (1) the porch; (2) the sanctuary proper, with outer and inner doors housing the sacred golden vessels (the menorah, the showbread table, and the altar of incense); and (3) the Holy of Holies, which occupied the western part of the Temple, with its entrance through two curtains. It contained no objects, whereas that of the Solomonic Temple contained the ark of the covenant. The high priest alone was allowed to enter once a year on the Day of Atonement.

Herod's Temple in Jerusalem was the focal point for the Jewish nation, the center for worship, and the place where political, economic, and spiritual affairs of world Jewry could be discussed and determined. As the destination for pilgrims during the feasts, it influenced the economic and social life of the city and therefore needed to accommodate thousands of people who gathered there to celebrate.

The *royal stoa,* a magnificent basilica-type structure, was built along the entire length of the southern wall (*Ant.* 15.411-12) and served as an assembly hall before, during, and after the Temple services. Fragments of this portico found toppled down during the course of the excavations are ornamented by geometric and floral motifs.

Sections of *Jerusalem's walls* have been uncovered in excavations (Avigad 1983: 65-74). The Hasmoneans began to fortify the city of Jerusalem, and the extensive excavations revealed three walls. The first wall encompassed the whole western hill and encircled the upper and lower cities; the northern line of the first wall ran from the Herodian palace towers in the area of the present-day citadel to the Temple Mount. The reconstruction of the second wall's line is subject to controversy. According to Josephus it ran from the "Gennath Gate" in the first wall to the Antonia fortress. It had only twelve towers, probably due to its fairly short course. The remains of the Herodian gate foundation under the Damascus gate are considered part of this wall, which is ascribed to Herodian city fortifications. The third wall was built by King Agrippa I (41-44 C.E.), Herod's grandson. Its construction ended abruptly and was renewed only during the First Revolt in 67 C.E.

Herod's palace in Jerusalem was situated close to three towers in the area of the present-day citadel. Josephus' description of it (*J.W.* 5.176-82) is substantiated by the Jericho palaces, which contain architectural features such as triclinia and gardens that are mentioned as having existed in the Jerusalem palace as well. Archaeological excavations conducted south of the present-day citadel have revealed remains of this palace.

Residential houses of the Herodian period are mostly known from those uncovered during the excavations of the upper city, the Temple Mount area, and the Armenian quarter outside the Zion gate. Each house was usually structured around a central court. Rooms were decorated with mosaic floors, wall paintings, and stucco, and had elaborate water installations (Avigad 1983: 83-98; Ben Dov 1983: 149-53).

The archaeological excavations in Jerusalem have yielded important data concerning the areas of the Temple Mount gates and the areas outside the west, south, and east retaining walls. Streets, arches, interchanges, squares, and monumental passageways have been uncovered.

Second Temple Synagogues (fig. 5)

The public structures at the fortresses of Masada, Herodium, and Gamla served as local assembly halls during the years of the First Revolt against Rome, when it was extremely difficult to travel to Jerusalem to participate in Temple worship. Recently uncovered public structures at Hasmonean Jericho (Netzer et al. 1999) and in several Jewish villages — Kiryat Sefer (Magen et al. 1999: 27-30); Horvat ʿEtri, dated to the end of the first or early second century B.C.E. (Zissu and Ganor 2002); and Modi'in (Onn and Weksler-Bdolah 2005) — are also thought to be synagogues of this period.

Common architectural features of these structures are (a) their construction as oblong halls; (b) the division of the hall by rows of columns into a central nave and surrounding aisles; (c) stepped benches erected along the walls of the hall facing the center; and (d) a ritual bath *(miqveh)* next to the building. These local structures existed as community assembly halls with a focal point in the center of the hall, which would explain the function of the benches lining the walls: the congregation would

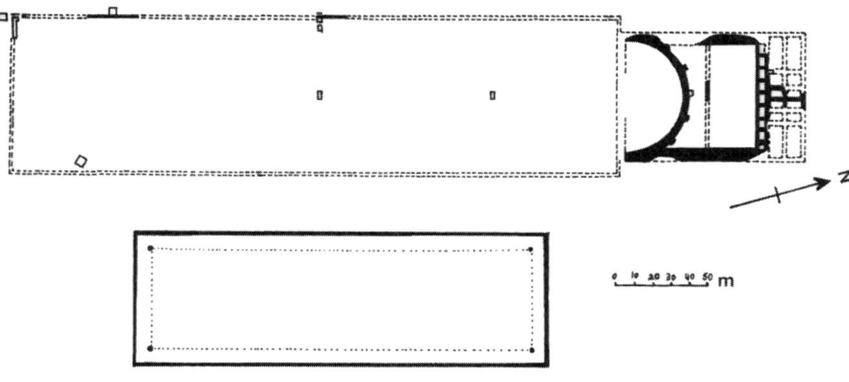

Figure 4. Site plan of the hippodrome at Jericho

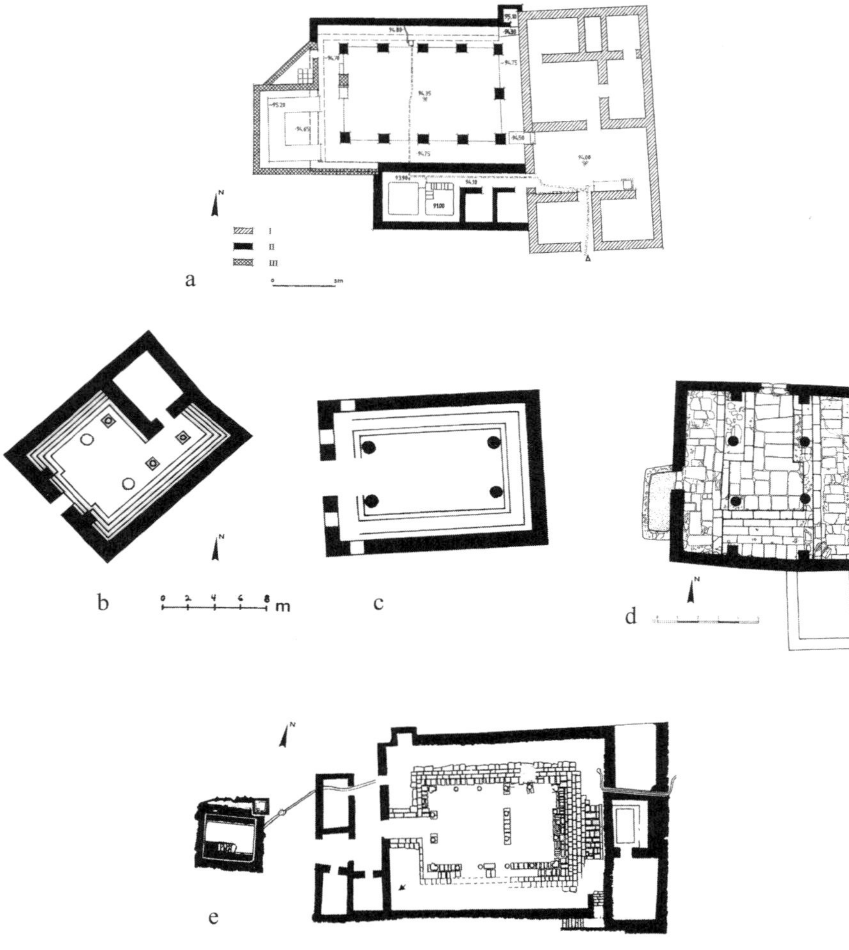

Figure 5. Synagogues of the Second Temple period

have faced inwards. They ostensibly served didactic purposes. Services might have been conducted on Sabbaths and feast days, but they were not places of cult or worship. These structures are assumed by scholars to be synagogues because of the circumstantial evidence of similarity in architectural plan, hence in function, even though no actual proof has been uncovered. As long as the Temple existed in Jerusalem, Jews were careful to avoid any competition with it. The existence of synagogues in the first century C.E. functioning as centers of Scripture reading and studies is also attested by epigraphic and literary sources such as Josephus, the New Testament (Josephus, *Ag. Ap.* 2.175; Acts 15:21), and the Theodotus inscription from Mount Ophel, which records a synagogue in Jerusalem.

Architecture in the Bar Kokhba Period

Caves in the Judean Desert were used as places of refuge from the Romans. The main occupation in these caves seems to have been during the Second Jewish Revolt against the Romans, the Bar Kokhba War (132-135 C.E.). Excavations in the caves revealed documents, artifacts, and remnants of cloth and leather.

In the Judean foothills and the Hebron Mountains, about 150 cave complexes have been discovered at seventy sites (Kloner 1983). These were a series of caves hewn into the limestone and connected by tunnel-like passages. Each complex had its own individual water source. Several characteristic features indicate that the cave complexes were places of hiding and refuge: the entrances are small, low, and intentionally concealed; and they could be closed and defended from the inside. Tunnel-like passage or burrows, which were cut low and narrow so that passage was possible only by crawling on all fours, connected the various rooms of the complexes. They could be completely or partly sealed off for defensive purposes. Some passages served variously as storage space, water reservoirs, ventilation areas, and escape routes. In many of the rooms and burrows, lamp niches are hewn at various levels into the walls.

Two types of cave complexes have been classified: small groups for families and large public complexes. A cave could hold from twenty to forty people, probably several families. The public complexes were much larger and included halls and long passages. The complexes are dated to the first and second centuries C.E., in the period following the destruction of the Second Temple. Advance planning and construction of the subterranean hiding places is attested by the fact that the Judean foothills were under the control of Bar Kokhba; by the similarity in plan, method, and technique; and by the defense installations found in the complexes. They were used by the fighters and served as temporary hiding places where weapons and provisions could be stored in preparation for the revolt.

BIBLIOGRAPHY

N. AVIGAD 1983, *Discovering Jerusalem*, Jerusalem: Shikmona Publishing and Israel Exploration Society. • N. AVIGAD

1954, *Ancient Monuments in the Kidron Valley,* Jerusalem: Bialik Institute (in Hebrew). • M. BEN DOV 1983, *In the Shadow of the Temple: The Discovery of Ancient Jerusalem,* Jerusalem: Keter. • R. HACHLILI 1988, *Ancient Jewish Art and Archaeology in the Land of Israel,* Leiden: Brill. • A. KLONER 1983, "The Subterranean Hideaways of the Judean Foothills and the Bar Kokhba Revolt," *The Jerusalem Cathedra* 3: 114-35. • Y. MAGEN, Y. ZIONIT, AND E. SIRKIS 1999, "Kiryat Sefer: A Jewish Village and Synagogue of the Second Temple Period," *Qadmoniot* 117: 25-32 (in Hebrew). • E. NETZER 1981A, *Greater Herodium, Qedem* 13, Jerusalem: Institute of Archaeology, the Hebrew University of Jerusalem. • E. NETZER 1981B, "Herod's Building Projects: State Necessity or Personal Need? A Symposium," *The Jerusalem Cathedra* 1: 48-80. • E. NETZER 1991, *Masada III,* Jerusalem: Israel Exploration Society. • E. NETZER 2001, *The Palaces of the Hasmoneans and Herod the Great,* Jerusalem: Yad Ben-Zvi and Israel Exploration Society. • E. NETZER 2005, "The Form and Function of Courts and Gates that Surrounded the Second Temple," *Qadmoniot* 130: 97-106 (in Hebrew). • E. NETZER, Y. KALMAN, AND R. LAUREYS 1999, "A Synagogue from the Hasmonean Period Recently Exposed in the Western Plain of Jericho," *IEJ* 49: 203-21. • A. ONN AND S. WEKSLER-BDOLAH 2005, "Khirbet Um el Umdan: A Jewish Village with a Synagogue from the Second Temple Period in Modiin," *Qadmoniot* 130: 107-16 (in Hebrew). • P. RICHARDSON 2004, *Building Jewish in the Roman East,* Waco, Tex.: Baylor University Press. • D. W. ROLLER 1998, *The Building Program of Herod the Great,* Berkeley: University of California Press. • Y. TSAFRIR 1982, "The Desert Fortresses of Judea in the Second Temple Period," *The Jerusalem Cathedra* 2: 120-45. • Y. YADIN 1966, *Masada: Herod's Fortress and the Zealots' Last Stand,* London: Weidenfeld and Nicolson. • B. ZISSU AND A. GANOR 2002, "Horvat ʿEtri: The Ruins of a Second Temple Period Jewish Village on the Coastal Plain," *Qadmoniot* 123: 18-27 (in Hebrew).

See also: Aqueducts; Art; Bar Kokhba Caves; Caesarea Maritima; Domestic Dwellings; Entertainment Structures; Fortresses and Palaces; Herod the Great; Jerusalem; Jerusalem Temple; Mosiacs; Romanization; Synagogues; Theaters RACHEL HACHLILI

Archives and Libraries

The terms "archive" and "library" have more than one meaning in common parlance; they can refer either to the building or room in which a collection of texts is stored, or to the collection itself. Here the focus is on the second meaning. Further, the terms frequently are used with a certain overlap or imprecision that is best considered head-on. Following the usage suggested by Olaf Pedersén, "archive" will be understood as referring to a collection of documents: letters, legal and economic materials, and administrative texts. Normally, an archive will store only a single copy of each text, although exceptions are known. "Library" will denote a collection of literary texts, works of the human imagination, which may include historical, religious, and "scientific" writings. Multiple copies of the same text are frequent in such collections.

Occasionally archives are found to include literary works, or libraries of documents. One might, with Pedersén, label such discoveries "archive with library" or "library with archive." Yet for the study of early Judaism, this distinction is not very useful, since while archives are sometimes found *in situ* with literary works, and vice versa, it is never clear that the same owners are involved. Thus it is uncertain that these actually are mixed collections, as opposed to two or more collections of different character. Accordingly, Pedersén's further refinement shall not be followed, but possible mixture will be noted where relevant. We shall proceed chronologically, by considering not only collections gathered by Jews, but also non-Jewish collections that are especially important for what they can tell us about Jewish history in the Second Temple period and its aftermath.

Elephantine

During the nineteenth and early twentieth centuries, occasional finds and, eventually, concerted archaeological digs led to the discovery at and near Elephantine, Egypt — an island at the first cataract of the Nile — of Official Aramaic materials related to a Jewish military colony that once inhabited the island. The original provenance of these Jews is unknown; they may have derived from the northern kingdom of Israel, fleeing to Egypt with the fall of Samaria to the Neo-Assyrians in the late eighth century B.C.E. Much more likely, however, they fled Judah at or about the time of its fall to the Neo-Babylonians and Nebuchadnezzar in the early sixth century. The earliest document dates to 495 B.C.E., but the earliest dateable historical reference in the materials is to the invasion of Egypt by Cambyses in 525 B.C.E. By that date the settlers claim already to have been present and to have been worshiping Yahweh (and possibly, various texts suggest, other gods) in a temple they had built there. Three archives are prominent among the Elephantine Papyri, and two literary texts also require mention.

The Archive of Mibtaḥiah Daughter of Maḥseiah

The archive of Mibtaḥiah comprises eleven legal documents spanning the years 471 to 410 B.C.E. Mibtaḥiah was a Jewish woman whose father, Maḥseiah, bequeathed to her a house-plot. Four of the documents concern issues related to this bequeathal. Another four documents concern her spouses and marriages (she was married three times), from which important facts about marriage law can be learned. The last grouping of documents in her archive involves the estate of her deceased parents.

The Archive of Anani

The archive of Anani includes thirteen documents concerning two related Jewish families, and dates to the years 456-402 B.C.E. The texts deal with legal matters of property, marriage, and divorce, and a peculiar form of manumission.

The Communal Archive of the Elephantine Jews

The ten documents from the communal archive are the

ARCHIVES AND LIBRARIES

most important of the Elephantine discoveries for the understanding of Jewish history. The central personality is Jedaniah the son of Gemariah, the communal leader and, apparently, high priest of the local temple to Yahweh. He engaged in correspondence that sheds considerable light upon important issues of biblical and historical understanding. One letter, dated 419/418 B.C.E., arrives to inform him of a directive from Darius II that includes instructions about the required observance of Passover. The letter's instructions make it debatable whether and to what degree the Elephantine Jews were already familiar with the festivals of Passover and Unleavened Bread, with conclusions impinging on issues of pentateuchal criticism. Several other letters revolve around the destruction of the Jews' temple in 410 B.C.E. and their efforts to get permission to rebuild it. Here correspondence includes letters to the Jerusalem high priest, Jehohanan; to the governor of Yehud, Bagohi; and to Delaiah son of Sanballat in Samaria. The Elephantine temple's existence, its practices, and the appeal to Delaiah all have notable potential implications for issues of biblical criticism and Jewish history in the early Second Temple period.

Notable also among the finds from Elephantine are an Aramaic copy of the Besitun inscription of Darius I, evidencing the circulation of that political propaganda as a literary text à la Augustus' *Res Gestae;* and an Aramaic copy of the *Proverbs of Ahiqar,* the oldest known version of the work, having considerable significance for the understanding of ancient Aramaic poetry and the development of the Ahiqar legend that came to intersect the book of Tobit.

Samaria Papyri

Alexander the Great conquered Tyre in 332 B.C.E. and as a consequence annexed Palestine, including Samaria. No sooner did Alexander leave for Egypt than the Samarians rebelled, burning alive his prefect in Syria. Alexander took vengeance, marching on the city of Samaria, from which the leaders of the revolt fled with their families south into the wilderness, ultimately taking refuge in a cave in the Wadi Daliyeh. Discovered there by the Macedonians, all were slaughtered. They had, however, brought with them among their possessions a considerable number of legal documents, which were discovered by Taʿamireh Bedouin exploring the cave in 1962. Archaeological explorations of the cave in 1963-1964 gave a context to the finds and added modestly to the materials.

The finds include eighteen papyri that to various degrees can be reconstructed and read, and 128 clay sealings that were once attached to the documents. How many archives are here represented is uncertain, but it is clearly more than one. The majority of the documents concern the sale of slaves. Dating between 375 and 335 B.C.E., they are composed in Official Aramaic in a script intermediate between that of Egyptian Aramaic materials and the earliest of the Dead Sea Scrolls; accordingly, they are important for an understanding of the development of Jewish scripts and thus for biblical studies. Otherwise their greatest importance is for the history of Jewish law, for they demonstrate developments of terminology and concepts originally borrowed from Neo-Babylonian practices, here seen midway toward the stage attested later in the Bar Kokhba contracts.

The sealings imply a Samarian culture that was highly syncretistic; they borrow elements from the ancient Near East along with Jewish and Attic Greek motifs. The latter were probably mediated through Phoenicia before the coming of Alexander. Only two of the bullae can be paired with extant papyri, but these two are notable for the information they provide. WD (Wadi Daliyeh) 22 and 23 utilize the Paleo-Hebrew script, thereby apparently implying a cult of Yahweh in Samaria at this date. WD 22 reads "Yeshayahu," perhaps to be equated with WD 23, "Belonging to Yeshayahu the son of Sanballat." The mention of the Sanballatids suggests that this was a dynastic name and that members of the clan ruled the region for a long period of time, stretching back at least to the Sanballat who was an opponent of Nehemiah.

Zeno Papyri

Extensive Greek archives belonging to Zeno, an official who served under Apollonius, finance minister to Ptolemy II Philadelphus, came to light in 1915 in the ancient village of Philadelphia, in the Fayum. Zeno was charged with managing the large estate belonging to Apollonius in that village, but earlier in his life he had carried out various missions for his superior, including a trade journey through Palestine in the year 259 B.C.E. Afterward he returned to Egypt and archived documents and letters produced during that year. From time to time he added new letters from his correspondents in Palestine. Only about forty of the 1,200 documents of the Zeno Papyri relate to that trip, but these notes, accounts, letters, and memoranda are extremely important for understanding Jewish affairs during the mid-third century B.C.E., a time for which there are otherwise virtually no certainly dated sources.

The Dead Sea Scrolls

Approximately 930 manuscripts comprising both biblical and nonbiblical writings (by the canonical standards of later Judaism) were discovered between 1947 and 1956 in eleven caves, located north and south of a site known today as Qumran. The ancient name of the site is uncertain, but it may have been Sekakah. The works are largely in Hebrew (about five-sixths) and Aramaic (one-sixth), with about twenty manuscripts composed in Greek.

Whether the caches derived directly (or indirectly) from Qumran or from elsewhere is debated, but most scholars think that they do. Most scholars think that the inhabitants of the site were a group of Essenes and that the Dead Sea Scrolls are an Essene library. Only about 15 to 20 percent of the manuscripts are identifiably sectarian, but these sectarian works do have notable connections with Essene ideas as known from Josephus. Notable points of disagreement with Essene ideas or reported practices also exist, and these incline some scholars to reject the "Essene hypothesis." Further

ARCHIVES AND LIBRARIES

clouding the issues, it is arguable because of differences in the contents and methods of the cave deposits, and the scribal characteristics of the manuscripts themselves, that they represent not a single large collection but rather a number of smaller libraries, including individual, noncommunal collections.

Only one or two documentary texts (nonliterary works) were certainly found in the caves: 3Q15, the *Copper Scroll;* and a very fragmentary apparent contract, 6Q26. Some seventeen additional documentary texts (4Q342-360a) were believed in the 1950s to derive from Cave 4, but it is now known that at least four, and quite possibly all, of these texts actually come from other sites in the Judean Desert, principally Naḥal Ḥever and Murabbaʿat.

The biblical manuscripts number between 209 and 211, with 144 to 146 coming from Cave 4 alone (the numbers are uncertain because of their fragmentary state). Every book of the Bible apart from Esther is represented, many in several or even multiple copies (Psalms, 36 copies; Deuteronomy, 31; Isaiah, 21; Genesis, 19-20; Exodus, 15). The approximately 720 "nonbiblical" manuscripts constitute some 360 separate literary works, about 300 of which are nonsectarian. Most frequent are Enochic works (24 copies), *Jubilees* (16), the *Community Rule* (12; sectarian), the *War Scroll* (11; sectarian), the *Damascus Document* (10; sectarian), *Aramaic Levi* (9), *Songs of the Sabbath Sacrifice* (9; possibly sectarian), *Instruction* (8), *Thanksgiving Hymns* (8; sectarian), *MMT* (7; probably sectarian), *New Jerusalem* (7), *Visions of Amram* (6), *Apocryphal Jeremiah* (6), *Proto-Esther* (6), and *Pseudo-Ezekiel* (6).

The Dead Sea Scrolls have revolutionized the study of various aspects of the Hebrew Bible's formation and transmission. They have further revolutionized understanding of early Jewish thinking and society more generally.

Masada

Excavations conducted under the leadership of Yigael Yadin in two seasons between 1963 and 1965 yielded fifteen fragmentary literary works as well as hundreds of Jewish documentary materials including tags, jar inscriptions, letters, supply instructions, ostraca and *tituli picti* (commercial labels stamped on amphorae and other vessels) in Hebrew, Aramaic and Greek. It is reasonable to see at least some of the literary works as comprising a collection, probably associated with the synagogue built by the Sicarii on the site. Further, it appears that at least one archive is represented by the documents.

The Masada Synagogue Collection

The fifteen literary works were discovered in seven different loci on the site, but two were especially prominent. At Locus 1043, an inner room of the synagogue, two biblical scrolls, of Deuteronomy and Ezekiel, were found buried under the floor. This may have been a genizah, a storeroom for worn manuscripts. Nearby, in locus 1039, a private family dwelling in the casemate wall, seven additional manuscripts were found. These manuscripts comprised copies of Genesis, Leviticus, Psalms, *Songs of the Sabbath Sacrifice, Apocryphal Joshua,* a "Samaritan" work of some kind, and an Aramaic text too fragmentary to be identifiable. All of these materials had been gathered in this locus and piled among much other potential plunder, probably by the Roman soldiers of the Tenth Legion in the aftermath of Masada's fall. Accordingly, whether and how many of these works came from the synagogue is uncertain, but since it is known that ancient Jewish synagogues often had collections of books, at least some of these writings likely originated in locus 1043. The remaining literary works were found scattered throughout the site, mostly in public locations, but two were discovered in family dwellings within the casemate wall. A copy of Ben Sira (Ecclesiasticus) originated in locus 1109, one of these family apartments, and was found beneath a niche in the wall that may have been its home. Since the site of Masada was plundered in antiquity, one may reasonably suppose that additional scrolls, valuable as they were, may have been removed. Thus the defenders of Masada may have held additional private library collections.

The Masada Military Archive

Of the many ostraca bearing Hebrew and Aramaic inscriptions found on the surface of Masada, about 60 percent seem to have originated in room 184, an erstwhile tower that stood near the Water Gate. Most came to light in storeroom 113. This tower was arguably where registration of arrivals occurred and the general registry of inhabitants was kept. The many tags were used to regulate daily life, such as guard duty, and for drawing lots. Thus these materials shed much light on daily life at Masada during the years of its occupation by the Sicarii. Further, analysis of the lots by Ehud Netzer has suggested that they lend considerable support to Josephus' account of the Masada episode, including his rendition of the drawing of lots among rebel leaders for the purpose of assisted suicide on the night before the Romans breached the wall.

Murabbaʿat

Materials later traced to caves in the Wadi Murabbaʿat came on the antiquities market in 1952; subsequent exploration by archaeologists located additional materials and verified the point of origin for documents that had been purchased. Study of the materials in recent years has determined that these texts represent two distinct periods in the site's habitation, one associated with the First Revolt, the other with the Second Revolt. In addition, several literary works surfaced, including remnants of what may once have been a complete Torah scroll, Genesis through Deuteronomy (Mur 1), and significant portions of a scroll of the Minor Prophets (Mur 88). The question of association of the literary works with owners of the archives is, as usual, moot.

Archives of the First Revolt

At least a dozen of the documents are possibly to be dated to the time of the First Revolt on the basis of dating formulas, content, and paleographic analysis. Since it is known that people took entire archives to the Judean caves in times of emergency, it is reasonable to attempt to find connections among these dozen documents, and to query whether they may represent several larger archives rather than single texts, each belonging to one person. Naturally, the results of such analysis will be more or less speculative at points, and conclusions must be considered tentative. Nevertheless, arguably two significant archives are included among the First Revolt materials, one possibly brought to the cave by the woman Salome daughter of Honi (Mur 25, 27, 28, 30, 31, and 32), and the other perhaps brought by Shapira the daughter of Jesus (Mur 26 and 29). These documents are all deeds of purchase or sale except for one bill of loan. They are written in Hebrew or Aramaic, but signatures include a third language, Greek. Several of them state that they were produced in Jerusalem, thus providing a kind of window into the city at the very time of the war with Rome — even, perhaps, after the city was surrounded by Roman forces.

The Archive of the Bene Galgula Family

Of the documents dateable to the period of the Second Revolt, most of the Bar Kokhba letters, and one remarriage contract (Mur 115) seem to have been cached by a single family, two sons and a daughter of Yoḥanan Galgula. One son, Jesus, was a military commander under Bar Kokhba in the area of Herodium; seven letters either certainly or probably belonged to him (Mur 42-45, 47, 51-52). Two other letters from ʿEin Gedi appear to have been addressed to his brother, Jose (Mur 46, 48), who was also either a commander or an official. The remarriage contract, a type of document known from elsewhere, belonged to Salome, who was either their sister or their niece. Elsewhere it is known that women brought archives to the caves, the men in the family presumably having died; all family documents would fall to this survivor, who may have been Salome in this case.

Naḥal Ḥever

In the 1950s and early 1960s a large group of documents and a few significant literary works (principally a Greek version of the Minor Prophets, 8ḤevXIIgr) originating in caves in the Naḥal Ḥever came to light, either through purchase from the Bedouin of the region, or through archaeological explorations. Israeli archaeologists under the leadership of Yigael Yadin conducted two seasons of exploration at Naḥal Ḥever focused especially on the so-called Cave of the Letters in 1960-1961. The manuscript discoveries of these excavations, combined with the materials obtained from the Bedouin, have reunited documents belonging to four archives from the period of the Second Revolt.

The Archive of Babatha Daughter of Simeon

This very substantial archive of thirty-five documents composed in Jewish Aramaic, Greek, and Nabatean Aramaic has shed great light on Jewish legal practices in the years leading up to the Second Revolt. The earliest document is dated to 93/94 C.E.; the latest, 132 C.E., the eve of the outbreak of the revolt. Included among the documents are Babatha's marriage contract or *ketubba* (P. Yadin 10), a well-preserved Aramaic bequest to her of property by her father (P. Yadin 7), records of loan and lease, records of sale of wine and dates, and a number of papyri involving litigation about the rights of her son, legally an orphan at the death of her husband. Babatha lived primarily in Mahoza, a village in the territory of Arabia. She was married twice, the second time to a man named Judah Khthousion, who already had a wife. The Greek texts evidence her recourse to Gentile courts, contrary to (later) rabbinic dictates. She apparently once swore by the *tychē* or "genius" of the emperor — and so it is debated whether and to what extent she represents a typical Jewess of her time.

The Archive of Eleazar Son of Samuel

Eleazar was a well-to-do farmer in ʿEin Gedi. His archive comprises six papyri written in Hebrew and Aramaic (P. Yadin 44-47) and mostly concerns the lease and sublease of property. These contracts show that Bar Kokhba had taken over erstwhile imperial properties and was now leasing them to the Jews more or less as the emperor had done before the revolt.

The Archive of Salome Komaise, Daughter of Levi

Salome, like Babatha, was an inhabitant of Mahoza who fled to ʿEin Gedi at the outbreak of the Second Revolt. The two women may have been relatives, since they lived near each other in that village, had mutual friends, both ended up in the Cave of Letters, and apparently perished together. The archive consists of one Jewish Aramaic document (XḤev/Se 12) and six Greek ones (XḤev/Se 60-65), but at least one Nabatean papyrus (P. Yadin 2) also probably should be assigned here, and possibly also one or more of a half-dozen still unpublished Nabatean documents that seem to derive from the Cave of Letters. The archive begins in 125 C.E. and ends in 131 C.E. Included are deeds of sale and gift, land declarations, a marriage contract, and a tax receipt.

The Archive of Jonathan, the Son of Bayan

Jonathan was one of the military commanders at Ein Gedi, and his archive, perhaps brought to the cave by a female relative, consists entirely of letters (P. Yadin 49-63). They are composed in Hebrew, Jewish Aramaic, and Greek and were sent by Bar Kokhba's lieutenants to direct affairs in the important village. The letters probably date from the last year of the revolt, but none are actually dated by their writers, so this must remain inference. They largely concern matters of military supply and discipline, but also reveal Bar Kokhba as an observant Jew concerned to keep the major festivals even during wartime, and giving commands about tithing and religious practice.

BIBLIOGRAPHY

P. BENOIT, J. T. MILIK, AND R. DE VAUX 1961, *Les grottes de Murabbaʿat,* DJD 2, Oxford: Clarendon. • J. H. CHARLES-

WORTH ET AL. 2000, *Miscellaneous Texts from the Judaean Desert,* DJD 38, Oxford: Clarendon. • H. COTTON AND A. YARDENI 1997, *Aramaic, Hebrew and Greek Documentary Texts from Naḥal Ḥever and Other Sites,* DJD 27, Oxford: Clarendon. • D. GROPP ET AL. 2001, *Wadi Daliyeh II: The Samaria Papyri from Wadi Daliyeh and Qumran Cave 4 Miscellanea Part 2,* DJD 28, Oxford: Clarendon. • M. LEITH 1997, *Wadi Daliyeh I: The Wadi Daliyeh Seal Impressions,* DJD 24, Oxford: Clarendon. • N. LEWIS 1989, *The Documents from the Bar Kokhba Period in the Cave of Letters: The Greek Papyri,* Jerusalem: Israel Exploration Society, Hebrew University of Jerusalem, and Shrine of the Book. • E. NETZER 2004, "The Rebels' Archives at Masada," *IEJ* 54: 218-29. • O. PEDERSÉN 1998, *Archives and Libraries in the Ancient Near East 1500-300 B.C.*, Bethesda, Md.: CDL Press. • S. PFANN 2007, "Reassessing the Judean Desert Caves: Libraries, Archives, Genizas, and Hiding Places," *Bulletin of the Anglo-Israel Archaeological Society* 25: 47-70. • B. PORTEN 1968, *Archives from Elephantine,* Berkeley: University of California Press. • S. TALMON 1999, "Hebrew Fragments from Masada," *Masada VI: The Yigael Yadin Excavations 1963-1965, Final Reports,* ed. S. Talmon and Y. Yadin, Jerusalem: Israel Exploration Society. • V. TCHERIKOVER AND A. FUKS 1957, *Corpus Papyrorum Judaicarum I,* Cambridge: Harvard University Press. • E. TOV 1990, *The Greek Minor Prophets Scroll from Naḥal Ḥever (8ḤevXIIgr),* Oxford: Clarendon • E. TOV ET AL. 2002, *The Texts from the Judaean Desert: Indices,* DJD 39, Oxford: Clarendon. Y. YADIN ET AL. 2002, *The Documents from the Bar Kokhba Period in the Cave of Letters: Hebrew, Aramaic and Nabatean-Aramaic Papyri,* Jerusalem: Israel Exploration Society, Hebrew University of Jerusalem, Shrine of the Book.

See also: Babatha Archive; Dead Sea Scrolls; Elephantine; Masada; Murabbaʿat, Wadi; Naḥal Ḥever; Papyri

MICHAEL O. WISE

Arch of Titus

The Arch of Titus is a monument in Rome commemorating the sack of Jerusalem in 70 C.E. It is situated at the east entrance to the Roman Forum, on the Via Sacra, south of the temple of Amor and Roma, close to the Colosseum. The arch was probably commissioned around 81 C.E. by the emperor Domitian (ruled 81-96) soon after the death of his brother and predecessor, the emperor Titus (ruled 79-81), who as general had led the Roman troops that destroyed the Holy City and Temple, effectively ending the First Jewish Revolt against Rome.

The arch is 15.4 m. high, 13.5 m. wide, and 4.75 m. thick. It was originally constructed entirely in Pantelic marble, with four semi-columns on each side. Above the main cornice on the east side is a central tablet bearing the original dedicatory inscription in square capital letters:

SENATVS
POPVLVSQVE • ROMANVS
DIVO • TITO • DIVI • VESPASIANI • F[ILIO]
VESPASIANO • AVGVSTO

The Senate
and people of Rome
to the divine Titus Vespasianus Augustus, s[on] of
the divine Vespasianus.

The soffit or underside ceiling of the axial archway is coffered with a relief of the apotheosis of Titus, flying to heaven on an eagle. Two panel reliefs lining the passageway commemorate the joint triumph celebrated in Rome by Titus and his father Vespasian in the summer of 71. The south panel depicts Roman soldiers bearing spoils taken from the Jerusalem Temple, including the seven-branched lampstand (Hebr. *menorah;* Gr. *lychnia*), the showbread table, and two trumpets. They carry on poles three tablets or placards that would have explained the spoils to the crowds witnessing the original procession (the arch's placards are uninscribed). The north panel depicts Titus in triumphal procession; he is riding a quadriga (four-horse chariot) led by the goddess Roma and is crowned with Victoria, the goddess of victory, flying above him; attending him are lictors and other figures.

The relief of the spoils presented in the artistic reconstruction of Pietro Sante Bartoli from a book by Giovanni Pietro Bellori in 1690 is clearer than the panel's present appearance. Because the showbread table now lacks all but a tiny trace of the two "front" legs shown by Bartoli, there is debate about the table's original shape and the perspective from which the sculptor wanted to present it. Bartoli assumed a rectangular table presented in a frontal "false perspective." Pfanner (1983) assumes a three-quarters view focusing on one corner, with two sides visible. Yarden (1991) argues that the tabletop was hexagonal or octagonal. If this is accepted, the table would have formed a matched set with the arch menorah and its similarly hexagonal or octagonal base, qualifying the pair as among "the most wonderful works of art, universally renowned" (Josephus, *J.W.* 5.216).

The specimens of the table and menorah depicted on the Arch of Titus could indeed be faithful representations of items captured (*J.W.* 7.148) or recovered from the Temple. However, they were not the only specimens. A Temple priest handed over to the Romans "two lampstands similar to those deposited in the sanctuary, along with tables" (*J.W.* 6.388). This multiplicity of lampstands and tables agrees with *m. Ḥag.* 3:8, "For all the utensils that were in the Temple, they had a second and a third set." The set portrayed on the Arch of Titus was probably made under the direction of Herod. This could account for the unusual polygonal table top and the animal images on the base of the menorah (eagles, a dragon, and sea monsters). Other specimens may have originated in the Hasmonean period (cf. 1 Macc. 4:49 with 1:21; Josephus, *Ant.* 12.318).

Josephus accurately reports what would later be portrayed on the Arch of Titus: "a golden table, many talents in weight, and a lampstand, likewise made of gold," plus a copy of the Jewish law, not depicted on the arch (*J.W.* 7.148-152). After the triumph, these and other Temple artifacts were deposited in Vespasian's Temple of Peace, where they were on public display (*J.W.* 7.161).

Arch of Titus, relief of the spoils of the Jerusalem (Second) Temple

However, Titus's triumph does not represent the first time such objects were seen by the Romans. Pompey entered the Temple in 63 B.C.E. (cf. Tacitus, *Historiae* 5.9) and saw "the golden table and the sacred lampstand," though he refrained from touching them (Josephus, *Ant.* 14.72; cf. *J.W.* 1.152). The showbread table and menorah soon became Jewish national symbols, as on coins issued by Mattathias Antigonus in 39 B.C.E. This tradition continues today: Titus's menorah appears on the State of Israel's coat of arms.

BIBLIOGRAPHY

S. FINE 2005, *Art and Judaism in the Greco-Roman World: Toward a New Jewish Archeology,* Cambridge: Cambridge University Press, 78, 146-63. • M. PFANNER 1983, *Der Titusbogen,* Mainz: Zabern. • L. YARDEN 1991, *The Spoils of Jerusalem on the Arch of Titus: A Re-Investigation,* Stockholm: Svenska Institutet i Rom. DANIEL P. BAILEY

Aristeas, Letter of

The Letter of Aristeas is a pseudonymous Greek writing that purports to be a communication from a courtier of the Ptolemaic king Ptolemy II Philadelphus (285-247 B.C.E.) named Aristeas to his brother Philocrates. Aristeas tells of a deputation in which he participated to go from Alexandria to Jerusalem to fetch manuscripts of the Jewish Law (almost certainly the Pentateuch) and seventy-two Jewish scholars to translate them into Greek. In fact, the book is not what it pretends to be. In the first place, the title traditionally ascribed to the work is inaccurate. It is not a letter, and in §1 the author calls his work a "narrative" *(diēgēsis).* In the second place, the book's author was almost certainly not a Gentile and not a courtier of Ptolemy II, but an Alexandrian Jew living a considerable time after the supposed events that he narrates.

Contents

Although the translation of the Pentateuch frames the book, much more happens than a narration of that story. After a brief introduction establishing his identity and his role in the deputation, the narrator provides background about his mission. He claims that he was present when Ptolemy II charged his librarian, Demetrius of Phalerum, with collecting "all the books in the world." Demetrius reports to the king that he has not acquired the "laws of the Jews," since they needed to be translated. The king authorizes such a translation. At this moment, "Aristeas" takes the opportunity to lobby the king for the release of Jews who had been enslaved in Egypt. He appeals to the king's generosity and good graces by arguing that as long as Jews remain slaves in Egypt the project will have no rationale and that, since even Egyptians worship the same God as the Jews, only by different names, such a release would serve as a pious thank offering to God. To this emancipation the king assents.

Next comes a detailed account in the form of an official report by Demetrius about the plans for translation. The books of the Jews are written in Hebrew and have been rather carelessly copied at that. Demetrius argues that Ptolemy, by granting royal patronage to the project, will bring the books "to perfection." A deputation should go to Eleazar, the high priest of the Jews, to request six men from each Jewish tribe to go to Alexandria to translate the law. Again the king assents. He writes a letter to that effect to Eleazar and sends elaborate gifts for the Jewish Temple, which are given an elaborate description. "Aristeas" then embarks on the journey to Jerusalem, and he offers a fantastical description of Jerusalem and its environs, the Temple and the priests, and their temple service.

Eleazar selects outstanding men to be translators, and before they accompany the deputation back to Egypt, "Aristeas" asks the high priest about the Jewish law, especially matters of idolatry, food, drink, and clean and unclean animals. Eleazar responds with an allegorical exposition of the law that has a moral bent to it. So, for example, he notes that the birds that Jews eat are "clean" because they are tame and gentle. Moses has forbidden the unclean birds because they oppress others and acquire their food by injustice. These qualities remind the Jews of what God expects of their moral behavior.

When the translators return to Alexandria, the king prepares a series of banquets for the Jewish scholars at which he asks them questions about the nature of kingship. Their replies to the king's questions establish their exquisite intellects, and the king notes that they surpass even his own philosophers in their intelligence.

After wining and dining the translators, Demetrius sets them up on the island of Pharos, where they translate the Jewish law, the entire task taking seventy-two days, which, "Aristeas" remarks, happens "by some design." Afterward, Demetrius assembles the Jewish community before whom the translation "was read aloud to all." The Jews unanimously approve the translation and put a curse on anyone who would make any changes. Subsequently the king hears the translation and marvels at "the mind of the lawgiver." The book ends with the translators' departure back to Jerusalem after accepting more gifts from the king, and followed by a short epilogue.

Date and Provenance

Although *Aristeas* offers a story about the translation of the Septuagint, it certainly postdates the translation, which most scholars situate in the early to mid-third century B.C.E., by a significant amount of time. In the broadest terms, *Aristeas* must have been written after the reign of Ptolemy II (285-247 B.C.E.), a major character in the book, and before Josephus (late first century B.C.E.), who paraphrases the story in *Ant.* 12.12-118. A number of critical historical errors, such as making Demetrius of Phalerum Ptolemy II's librarian when he was active in the court of Ptolemy I Soter (and apparently was banished at the accession of Ptolemy II), rule out a date close to the reign of Philadelphus. Most scholars prefer a date somewhere in the middle to the latter part of the second century B.C.E., primarily because of a possible relationship to Aristobulus (usually dated in the middle of the second century B.C.E.) and because the work shows familiarity with Ptolemaic bureaucracy and court protocol of the period, particularly in the king's decree freeing the Jewish slaves (§§22–25), which shows remarkable similarity to a Ptolemaic papyrus concerning slaves (P. Rainer 24,552/C. Ord. Ptol. 21-22) that dates from the late 260s B.C.E. Due to this familiarity with Ptolemaic practices and its emphasis on Alexandrian Judaism, scholars almost unanimously place the work in Alexandria.

Purpose and Major Ideas

Scholars continue to disagree on the purpose of *Aristeas.* Whereas the legend of the translation of the Septuagint frames the work and is one of its important foci, it actually takes up very few of the 322 paragraphs that comprise the work. Nonetheless, this momentous accomplishment holds great significance for the author. Although scholars have worked hard to identify some historical kernel of this story, little to none of the legend reflects the translation's beginnings. Rather than an accurate account of the translation's inception, *Aristeas* propounds a myth of origins for the Septuagint, developed well after the execution of the translation, that provides the foundation for considering it as the sacred scriptures of the Greek-speaking, Alexandrian Jewish community. If we examine how *Aristeas* characterizes the Septuagint in the light of the translations themselves, the story in *Aristeas* is contradicted at every point. So, for example, *Aristeas* portrays the Septuagint as the highly philosophical and literary product of exemplary scholars who produced a work capable of standing on its own and worthy of awe and admiration. Yet, the Septuagint's textual-linguistic makeup suggests something very different. It is neither philosophical nor literary, and the close linguistic relationship between the Septuagint and its source texts suggests dependence of the one on the other. In short, the legend in *Aristeas* belongs to the later history of the use of the translation, its reception history, and not to the Septuagint's origins or stage of production. That the *Aristeas* legend remains deeply embedded in contemporary scholarly work on the Septuagint and in reconstructions of its origins demonstrates how compelling a story it is.

The author's use of Hellenistic genres and forms suggest that he had a good Greek education and a familiarity with Greek literature. So, for example, we can detect in the book the use of Greek historiography, the Hellenistic travelogue, *ekphrasis* (the rhetorical technique of describing a spectacular sight), and an interest in ethnography. Along with such familiarity, many aspects of the book highlight the commonalities between Greek and Jewish culture. Most notable and famous is §16, where "Aristeas" tells King Ptolemy that the Jews "revere God, the overseer and creator of all things, whom all also, even we, worship, O King, using different names, Zeus and Dis." Even though this paragraph along with others emphasizes the harmony that exists between Judaism and Egyptian Hellenistic society, the author does not want to collapse the two. Jews remain distinctive in the face of all this harmony. Whereas all people worship the same God under different names, our author is keen to note that this God is the *Jewish* God, not some generic deity. Particularly pointed is Eleazar's allegorical explanation of the Jewish law (§§128-71) in which he ridicules Gentile idolatry in the manner that we see in other Second Temple Jewish works, calling Egyptians "vain people" for worshiping animals. Moses gave the Jews their law precisely to keep them separate from the surrounding nations, having "fenced us around with broken palisades and with iron walls so that we might not intermingle with any other nations" (§139). Observance of the food laws keeps Jews separate in two ways: literally, in the practice of eating certain foods and not others, and allegorically, as reminders of the Jews' higher moral responsibility. So Jews only eat certain "tame" birds and not "wild and carnivorous ones" in order to remind them that they should live justly and not oppress others. *Aristeas* continues the theme of Jewish distinctiveness and indeed superiority in the series of banquets or symposia given in honor of the Jewish translators (§§187–300), during which the king interrogates each of the translators on the subject of ideal kingship. They perceptively answer all of his questions, in each case noting the Jewish God's role in the king's successful rule. At several points in the section (§§200–201, 235, 296), the author notes how even the king's Greek philosophers acknowledge the superiority of their Jewish colleagues.

In this respect, then, *Aristeas* tries to walk a rather thin line. On the one hand, the author wants to argue for the harmonious relationship between Jewish and Hellenistic Egyptian culture, a goal supported by Ptolemy's patronage of the translation and his gifts to the Jerusalem Temple combined with the Jews' loyalty to the king. On the other, he maintains the importance of Jewish separation and the superiority of Jewish values. Throughout his allegorical presentation of the Jewish law, the author assumes that Jews actually enact these laws in their daily lives. Indeed, the allegorical intent of the law lacks force and meaning without it. Whereas some scholars have seen in *Aristeas* a universalist tractate that does not effectively separate the Jews from their Egyptian neighbors, it seems more accurate to say that the author understood Judaism to have both universalist aspects, which it shares with the Hellenistic world in general, and particularist characteristics, which Moses enshrined in the Jewish law, which are incumbent on all Jews, and which prevent the assimilation or identification of Jewish culture with that of Hellenistic Egypt.

BIBLIOGRAPHY

M. HADAS 1951, *Aristeas to Philocrates (Letter of Aristeas)*, New York: Harper & Brothers. • E. GRUEN 1998, *Heritage and Hellenism: The Reinvention of Jewish Tradition*, Berkeley: University of California Press, 202-22. • S. HONIGMAN 2003, *The Septuagint and Homeric Scholarship in Alexandria*, London: Routledge. • H. G. MEECHAM 1932, *The Oldest Version of the Bible*, London: Holborn. • H. G. MEECHAM 1935, *The Letter of Aristeas*, Manchester: Manchester University Press. • A. PELLETIER 1962, *Lettre d'Aristée à Philocrate*, Paris: Cerf. • V. TCHERIKOVER 1958, "The Ideology of the Letter of Aristeas," *HTR* 51: 59-85. • B. G. WRIGHT 2006A, "The *Letter of Aristeas* and the Reception History of the Septuagint," *BIOSCS* 39: 47-67. • B. G. WRIGHT 2006B, "Translation as Scripture: The Septuagint in *Aristeas* and Philo," in *Septuagint Research: Issues and Challenges in the Study of the Greek Jewish Scriptures*, ed. W. Kraus and R. G. Wooden, Atlanta: Society of Biblical Literature, 47-61.

See also: Septuagint BENJAMIN G. WRIGHT III

Aristobulus

Aristobulus was an Alexandrian Jew who wrote philosophical interpretations of works in Greek about the Jewish lawgiver Moses during the first half of the second century B.C.E. While there has been disagreement among scholars regarding his identity, provenance, and time, his Jewishness and his *floruit* during the reign of Ptolemy Philometor VI (181-145) are now well settled.

Direct information on Aristobulus' life and work has not survived; we are dependent on quotations and testimonies. The earliest reference to Aristobulus is found in 2 Macc. 1:10, which is the introduction to a purported letter sent from Judah Maccabee and leaders in Jerusalem to the "Jews of Alexandria and to "Aristobulus, of the family of anointed priests, teacher of King Ptolemy" (ca. 164 B.C.E.). The significance of such identifications and honorifics is debated, as is the genuineness of the letter, but at the very least Aristobulus is to be considered a historical figure of that period. Clement of Alexandria, the Christian convert and teacher of the late second century B.C.E., identifies the Aristobulus mentioned in 2 Maccabees with the author of Jewish philosophical works, noting that Aristobulus wrote hefty tomes which show that the Peripatetic philosophy was dependent on the Law of Moses and the Prophets (*Stromata* 5.14.97).

Twice Clement cites passages of Aristobulus explicitly, and in several other places has clearly used his work. The best source, though, is Eusebius, the Christian apologetic historian of the third century, whose *Praeparatio Evangelica* provides four passages. One fragment regarding the lunar and solar positions during Passover was cited by Anatolius, the mid-third century bishop of Laodicea, and is now preserved in a quotation in Eusebius' *Ecclesiastical History* (7.32).

Though Aristobulus is called a Peripatetic in ancient testimony, the fragments of his work reveal a much more eclectic author who was influenced by other currents, including Stoic, Pythagorean, and Cynic. No title has been preserved for his work, but the fragments show that his project was to exegete and explain Mosaic texts, especially Genesis, Exodus, and Deuteronomy, as philosophical teachings that were in harmony with what he considered the best of Greek philosophy and literature. He even taught that "it is clear that Plato followed the tradition of the law that we (Jews) use . . . just as Pythagoras, having borrowed many of the things in our traditions, found room for them in his own doctrinal system." Aristobulus supported the plausibility of his claim by explaining that Jews — long before their translation of sacred texts into Greek in Ptolemaic times (cf. *Letter of Aristeas*) and even before their rule by the Persians — had "translated the matters concerning the exodus from Egypt . . ." along with the entire law.

Greeks such as Plato would therefore have had access to the work of Moses (*Praep. Evang.* 9.6; 13.12; Holladay 1995: 152-61). Aristobulus is the earliest known author to propound this notion of Greek philosophy depending on Jewish law, an idea that had a long history in Jewish authors (Philo, *Mos.* 2.2-3; Josephus, *Ag. Ap.* 2.168) and later Christian writers.

Other fragments give insight into Aristobulus' philosophy and his methods of reading it from his Mosaic texts. He presents God as a perfect, majestic, whole, unseen, all-sovereign, and transcendent power. He claims that "a proper conception of God" guides his exegesis. In harmony with the interpretive methods of Stoics, both metaphorical and allegorical, he stresses that anthropomorphic and other expressions in Jewish law must be read for higher philosophical meanings, so that God's hands, feet, face, and walking are "signifiers for the divine power." God must not be thought of in a "mythical, popular way of thinking. For what our lawgiver Moses wishes to say, he does so at many levels, using words that appear to have other referents (I mean, to things that can be seen); yet in doing so he actually speaks about natural [i.e., unseen] conditions and structures of a higher order," which can only be understood by those of higher intellects, such as Plato (*Praep. Evang.* 8.10; Holladay 1995: 136-37). Similarly, in another fragment, the Sabbath is a reminder of the "sevenfold *logos* . . . through which we have knowledge of things both human and divine" (*Praep. Evang.* 13.12; Holladay 1995: 185).

In presenting his interpretations, Aristobulus is eager to quote Greek authors to support his understandings and to show the consonance of Greek genius with Mosaic writings, and the originality of the latter. Orpheus, Aratus, Hesiod, Homer, Linus, and others are cited, sometimes in spurious or forged passages, though it is difficult to determine by whom. That he presents his explanations as an imagined dialogue with King Ptolemy as reader (*Praep. Evang.* 10.1; 13.11-12) shows how he envisioned Jewish learning relating to his Alexandrian surroundings. Like Jewish authors who followed him, Aristobulus understood Judaism as a proper philosophical school within the context of Hellenistic culture (*Praep. Evang.* 13.12).

With only fragments to go on, it is difficult to determine the intended readership and specific purposes of Aristobulus. While later Jewish authors, such as Philo and Josephus, do not cite Aristobulus, there is little doubt that he represents a crucial and influential Hellenistic Jewish view concerning the antiquity and importance of Jewish culture and its consonance with Greek philosophy. He is important for understanding the beginnings of allegorical interpretations of sacred Jewish literature, in a chain leading to Philo and eventually to early Christian interpreters, and even for the development of specific ideas within those traditions, such as the significance of the *logos.*

BIBLIOGRAPHY

J. M. G. BARCLAY 1996, *Jews in the Mediterranean Diaspora,* Edinburgh: Clark, 150-58. • J. J. COLLINS 2000, *Between Athens and Jerusalem,* 2d ed., Grand Rapids: Eerdmans, 186-90. • A. YARBRO COLLINS 1985, "Aristobulus," in *OTP* 2:831-42. • E. GRUEN 1998, *Heritage and Hellenism,* Berkeley: University of California, 246-53. • C. R. HOLLADAY 1995, *Fragments from Hellenistic Jewish Authors,* vol. 3, Chico, Calif.: Scholars Press. • N. WALTER 1964, *Der Thoraausleger Aristobulos,* Berlin: Akademie Verlag.

JAMES E. BOWLEY

Armenian

The Armenian literary tradition commenced in the fifth century C.E. with the invention of the alphabet by St. Mesrop Maštocʿ, traditionally dated to 404. The first work translated into Armenian was the Bible, and the fifth century C.E., particularly its first part, is reckoned to be the golden age of Armenian literature. By the end of that century, the Armenians had not only created a very substantial literary corpus in the Armenian language but had also translated a large number of Greek and Syriac religious works. In the late fifth century and for some time thereafter, in addition to translations into "ordinary" ancient Armenian, a Hellenizing style of translation from Greek developed, which strove to stay very close to Greek linguistic usage. It even calqued Greek word formations and syntactic constructions. A number of very significant Greek works, mainly of philosophical theology and the like, were translated into Hellenizing Armenian.

Early Jewish Works Preserved in Armenian

With the possible exception of a single talmudic passage (see below), no early Jewish works seem to have been translated directly into Armenian from Hebrew or Aramaic. The works enumerated in the following paragraphs were all translated from Greek or, in rarer instances, from Syriac. Moreover, Armenian translations of Jewish works were most probably made from Christian Greek copies and not Jewish Greek ones.

Although the Old Testament was the first Jewish work translated into Armenian, the exact extent of the ancient Armenian Old Testament canon is unknown. Yet it surely incorporated books such as Wisdom of Solomon, Sirach, Baruch, Judith, and Tobit, at least two books of Maccabees, and other "apocrypha" that were not included in the Hebrew canon. In what follows, the Armenian Old Testament is taken to contain those works usually found in Greek and Latin Bibles, since the scholarly problems of such "additional" works resemble those of the canonical books.

The other ancient Jewish compositions translated into Armenian may be divided into the following chief categories: (a) writings of Philo of Alexandria and some other Jewish Hellenistic works that came to be associated with the Armenian Philonic corpus; (b) works belonging to the category of the Pseudepigrapha, which are closely associated with the Armenian Old Testament and which occur exclusively or predominantly in Armenian Old Testament manuscripts; (c) other Pseudepigrapha that are not usually found in Armenian Old Testament manuscripts; (d) fragments of works that are attributed to "the Jewish books" or "the Jewish writings," including the above-mentioned talmudic fragment; and (e) a few other varied writings. The following discussion will encompass such works as were most likely translated into Armenian down to the end of the fifteenth century.

Philo

Several of Philo's treatises were translated from Greek into Hellenizing Armenian. Of particular interest are those works that survived only in Armenian and whose Greek text is lost. These are the following: (1) *Quaestiones in Genesin;* (2) *Quaestiones in Exodum;* (3) *De Providentia I and II;* and (4) *De Animalibus.* The *Quaestiones* and *De Animalibus* have been translated into English (the *De Providentia* is forthcoming).

De Jona and de Sampsone

The *De Jona* is a Jewish Hellenistic treatise, homiletic in character, about the prophet Jonah. A good edition has been published, and an unpublished English translation and introduction written by the late Hans Lewy exist in the archives of the Israel Academy of Sciences and Humanities. Lewy characterizes the work as a Jewish Hellenistic sermon, perhaps of the second century C.E., and as such it is potentially extremely important. The *De Sampsone* has not appeared in a critical edition but may be found in Aucher's edition of 1826. A German translation is now available (Siegert 1992).

Known Apocrypha and Pseudepigrapha

All the writings included in the Apocrypha exist in Armenian as part of the biblical corpus of the Old Testament. They have been published in various editions and are printed in Armenian Bibles, except for those issued by Protestant organizations. In the still standard printing of the Armenian Bible (Zohrabean 1805), based on the Latin Canon, the following works are included: 1 Esdras, Judith, Tobit, 1-3 Maccabees, Wisdom of Solomon, and Baruch. In an appendix are to be found Sirach (two versions; two more exist as well), *4 Ezra* (*3 Ezra* in Armenian), and the Prayer of Manasseh. In the extensive Canon List of Mxitʿar of Ayrivankʿ (fourteenth century), some additional works occur in the Old Testament. Intriguingly, not all these occur in full in the Bible manuscript copied by him: *3 Paralipomena* (in his Bible, a short text), 4 Maccabees, *Josephus Who Is Caiaphas the High Priest* (perhaps Josephus Flavius, but no Armenian of Josephus is known), *The Vision of Enoch* (an Armenian apocryphon), *Testaments of the Twelve Patriarchs, Joseph and Aseneth,* and *Deaths* [i.e., *Lives*] *of the Prophets.* In addition to all the above, Armenian liturgical Psalters contain the Canticles.

The textual worth of known works seems to be substantial, not differing in many cases from that of the Armenian witness to the Greek Old Testament. A critical edition of *4 Ezra* exists; it was translated into Armenian together with the biblical corpus and witnesses to a reworked Greek text. The *Testaments of Levi* and *Joseph* have been issued in critical editions, and a full edition of *Testaments of the Twelve Patriarchs* is underway. *Joseph and Aseneth* has been intensively studied by Burchard, and a critical edition is currently in preparation. An edition of Maccabees exists, and editions of some of the *Vitae Prophetarum* have been published. Further study of these significant apocryphal and pseudepigraphical works will doubtless contribute to their textual basis in Greek. For example, the Armenian ninth-century *Epitome of Testaments of the Twelve Patriarchs,* which reflects a developed text, is witness to a textual stage prior to the extant Greek manuscripts.

In the major collection of extrabiblical Armenian apocrypha (Yovsēpʿiancʿ 1896), the following Jewish writings may be noted in addition to those mentioned above: *Apocalypse of Moses* (Greek *Life of Adam and Eve*), *Questions of Ezra, Paralipomena Ieremiou* (in three recensions). There also exists another, independent form of the Adam Book, the *Penitence of Adam,* which has been published separately. Three versions of parts of the *Testament of Adam* are also extant in Armenian.

Previously Unknown Works

A list of names of the wives of the patriarchs, which originates in *Jubilees,* has been published. As in many Christian traditions, the story of the translation of the Septuagint had considerable circulation, ultimately deriving from *Aristeas,* but immediately from Epiphanius's *De Mensuris et Ponderibus.* In addition, extensive texts of the *Onomastica Sacra* are preserved in Armenian, which ultimately go back to Jewish sources. Lexicological texts relating to the Bible and Philo were also assembled. *The Signs of the Judgment,* also known as *Fifteen Signs before Doomsday,* exists in Armenian, Latin, and a medieval Hebrew translation made from the Latin. The Armenian version attributes it to "books of the Jews," while in Latin it is usually attributed to Jerome, famed for his knowledge of Hebrew. The body of the text has nothing notably Christian in it. A corpus of Armenian scholia on Philo and various texts associated with Sirach also exist.

The story of Ahikar is first witnessed in an Aramaic papyrus from Oxyrhynchus dated to the fifth century B.C.E. Ahikar plays a role in the book of Tobit, and his story is widespread in a number of Oriental Christian languages, including Armenian. The Armenian text has been critically edited. An unpublished text in the Matenadaran, ms. no. M5148 (1617-1618), is entitled "A Jewish Tradition concerning Mercy" (compare M0783). A canon list giving Hebrew names of the biblical books has been published.

B. Baba Batra 14b–15a

A baraitha from the Babylonian Talmud, *Baba Batra* 14b–15a, occurs in Armenian. It has been proposed that this was the result of oral transmission between Jews and Armenians. In the *Catalogue of Manuscripts* of the Matenadaran, ms. no. 3144 is entitled "Talmud" but is in fact a collection of Jewish legal material translated into Armenian.

BIBLIOGRAPHY

General

M. E. STONE 1982A, "Jewish Apocryphal Literature in the Armenian Church," *Le Muséon* 95: 285-309. • M. E. STONE 1996, "The Armenian Apocryphal Literature: Translation and Creation," in *Il Caucaso: Cerniera fra Culture dal Mediterraneo alla Persia (Secoli IV-XI)*, Spoleto: Presso la Sede del Centro, 611-46.

Hellenizing School, Philo, and Pseudo-Philo

H. LEWY 1936, *The Pseudo-Philonic De Jona, Part 1*, London: Christophers. • R. MARCUS 1953, *Philo Supplement I: Questions and Answers on Genesis*, LCL, Cambridge: Harvard University Press. • R. MARCUS 1984, *Philo, Supplement II: Questions and Answers on Exodus*, LCL, Cambridge, Mass.: Harvard University Press. • J. PARAMELLE 1984, *Philon d'Alexandrie: Questions sur la Genèse II 1-7*, Genève: Cramer. • F. SIEGERT 1988, *Philon von Alexandrien, über die Gottesbezeichnung "wohltätig verzehrendes Feuer" (De Deo)*, Tübingen: Mohr-Siebeck. • F. SIEGERT 1992, *Drei hellenistisch-jüdischen Predigten: Ps.-Philon, "Über Jona," "Über Jona" (Fragment), "Über Samson," II, Kommentar nebst Beobachtungen zur hellenistischen Vorgeschichte der Bibelhermeneutik*, Tübingen: Mohr-Siebeck. • A. TERIAN 1981, *Philonis Alexandrini De Animalibus: The Armenian Text with an Introduction, Translation, and Commentary*, Chico, Calif.: Scholars Press • A. TERIAN 1984, "A Philonic Fragment on the Decad," in *Nourished with Peace: Studies in Hellenistic Judaism in Memory of Samuel Sandmel*, ed. F. E. Greenspahn, E. Hilgert, and B. L. Mack, Chico, Calif.: Scholars Press, 173-82. • A. TERIAN FORTHCOMING, *Philonis Alexandrini De Providentia I-II*. • C. ZUCKERMANN, REV. M. E. STONE 1995, *Repertory of Published Armenian Translations of Classical Texts*, Jerusalem: Institute of African and Asian Studies (with appendix on Philo by Abraham Terian, with exhaustive bibliography).

Armenian Biblical and Apocryphal Writings

S. AJAMIAN 1992, *Catalogue of Armenian Bible Manuscripts*, Lisbon: C. Gulbenkian Foundation (in Armenian). • H. M. AMALYAN 1996, *The Books of Macccabees: Critical Text*, Yerevan: Academy of Sciences. • C. BURCHARD 1983, "Zur armenischen Übersetzung von Joseph und Aseneth," *Revue des Etudes Armeniennes* 17: 207-40. • C. BURCHARD 1996, "Neues von Joseph und Aseneth auf Armenisch," in idem, *Gesammelte Studien zu Joseph und Aseneth*, Leiden: Brill, 139-59. • F. C. CONYBEARE, J. R. HARRIS, ET AL. 1913, *The Story of Ahikar from the Aramaic, Syriac, Arabic, Armenian, Ethiopic, Old Turkish, Greek and Slavonic Versions*, Cambridge: Cambridge University Press. • J. ISSAVERDENS 1901, *The Uncanonical Writings of the Old Testament Found in the Armenian MSS. of the Library of St. Lazarus*, Venice: Mechitarist Press. • L. LIPSCOMB 1978, "A Tradition from the Book of Jubilees in Armenian," *JJS* 29: 149-63. • A. A. MARDIROSIAN 1969, *The Story and Counsels of Xikar the Wise*, Erevan: Academy (in Armenian). • M. E. STONE 1969, *The Testament of Levi: A First Study of the Armenian Manuscripts of the Testaments of the Twelve Patriarchs in the Convent of St. James, Jerusalem*, Jerusalem: St. James Press. • M. E. STONE 1973, "Some Observations on the Armenian Version of the Paralipomena of Jeremiah," *CBQ* 35: 47-59. • M. E. STONE 1975, *The Armenian Version of the Testament of Joseph*, Missoula: Scholars Press. • M. E. STONE 1976, "Armenian Canon Lists III: The Lists of Mechitar of Ayrivank' (c. 1285 C.E.)," *HTR* 69: 289-300. • M. E. STONE 1979, *The Armenian Version of 4 Ezra*, Missoula, Mont.: Scholars Press. • M. E. STONE 1981A, *The Penitence of Adam*, Leuven: Peeters. • M. E. STONE 1981B, *Signs of the Judgment, Onomastica Sacra and The Generations from Adam*, Chico, Calif.: Scholars Press. • M. E. STONE 1982B, *Armenian Apocrypha Relating to the Patriarchs and Prophets*, Jerusalem: Israel Academy of Sciences and Humanities, 129-57. • M. E. STONE 1986-1987, "The Epitome of the Testaments of the Twelve Patriarchs," *Revue des Etudes Armeniennes* 20: 69-107. • M. E. STONE 1995, "A New Edition and Translation of the *Questions of Ezra*," in *Solving Riddles and Untying Knots: Biblical, Epigraphic, and Semitic Studies in Honor of Jonas C. Greenfield*, ed. Z. Zevit, S. Gittin, and M. Sokoloff, Winona Lake, Ind.: Eisenbrauns, 293-316. • M. E. STONE (IN PREPARATION), *Critical Edition of the Armenian Version of the Testaments of the Twelve Patriarchs*. • M. E. STONE AND R. R. ERVINE 2000, *The Armenian Texts of Epiphanius of Salamis' De Mensuris et Ponderibus*, Leuven: Peeters. • S. YOVSĒP'IANC' 1896, *Uncanonical Books of the Old Testament*, Venice: Mechitarist Press (in Armenian). • J. ZOHRABEAN 1805, *The Scriptures of the Old and New Testaments*, Venice: Mechitarist Fathers.

MICHAEL E. STONE

Art

Jewish art in the Second Temple period was a creative endeavor characterized by a mixture of native traditions and pagan influences. Conspicuously noticeable is the almost complete lack of figurative or representational motifs. This aniconism stems from the reluctance of religiously observant Jews to violate the biblical prohibition of graven images (Exod. 20:4; Deut. 4:16; 27:15). However, whereas official and public art was strictly aniconic, the private homes of the wealthy Jewish nobility did sometimes use ornamentation with figurative motifs, usually birds. Only with the decline of Greco-Roman paganism during the third century C.E. did Jewish artistic attitudes undergo a noticeable change. An increasing openness to Greco-Roman aesthetic influences revealed itself in the use of pagan motifs, figures, and animals in Jewish synagogal and funerary art (Hachlili 1988: 65-83).

Architectural Ornamentation

The repertoire of motifs and ornamentation in Jewish art derived from the tradition of Roman art, especially its provincial and eastern tributaries. Among the stylistic elements Jewish artists borrowed were "endless" and "all-over" patterning, deep carving to accentuate the interplay of light and shade, symmetrical stylization, and *horror vacui* — the ornamental filling of all available space. The decoration of buildings, palaces, houses, and bathhouses in the Second Temple period involved the use of architectural embellishment, wall paintings, stucco-plaster moldings, and ornamental floor pavements.

Stonework

Decorative stonework featured in the architecture of buildings and tombs. Architectural members such as fragments of capitals, lintels, and friezes were found along the west and south retaining walls of the Jerusalem Temple. They probably came from the pilasters of the upper courses of the walls and from the royal stoa. The tunnels of the Hulda Gates on the Temple Mount were built of stone domes more than five meters in diameter. They were carved with geometric and floral motifs (fig. 1) that were mounted on columns and had walls built of ashlar stones. An alternative to brick, ashlar stones are large rectangular blocks of masonry sculpted with square edges and even faces; their external surface is typically smooth or polished and sometimes decorated with small grooves. Parts of stone columns, capitals, and bases were found in the Upper City of Jerusalem; among the remains were a Corinthian capital made of hard local stone bearing lily scrolls, a huge base, and a finely executed Ionic capital from monumental columns. These elements indicate craftsmanship of a high standard. Architectural decorations carved in stone column bases and capitals were also found at Masada (Foerster 1995: 80-139), and Corinthian capitals carved out of local stone and painted in gold were found at both Masada and Cypros (Netzer 2001: fig. 93). Stonework was especially characteristic of funerary art. Tomb facades were decoratively carved, and stone sarcophagi and ossuaries in particular exhibit a vast ensemble of local decorative stonework. A new type of ornamentation, produced by a special technique of stone carving *(Kerbschnitt)* using compass, ruler, and chisel, involved deep carvings and design patterns such as rosettes.

Figure 1. Photograph and artistic rendering of decorated stone dome of the Huldah Gates, Jerusalem

Wall Paintings

Wall paintings adorned many of the palaces, mansions, and houses of the Jewish aristocracy. Wall paintings like those found in the palace at Masada were made using the fresco technique (Foerster 1995: 13-25). The lower terrace of Masada's northern palace had a marbled pattern. Fragments of a frescoed wall were also found in the debris of the upper terrace, and in the bathhouse, frescoes covered the *tepidarium* (warm bath), the *apodyterium* (entry and dressing room), and the ceiling. Multicolored frescoed walls also decorated the bathhouse and other rooms of the palace-fortress at Herodium. Fragments of colored imitation-marble frescoes were found here and in the Hasmonean palace at Jericho. The walls of the third Herodian palace at Jericho were covered with marbled patterns and various other designs. Walls covered with frescoes in red and yellow were found in the Cypros fortress hall and bathhouse, and in the debris of the peristyle structure in the Alexandrium fortress.

The frescoes in Jerusalem houses included designs of plants and other motifs. A high artistic standard typical of Hellenistic painting, and reminiscent of early Pompeian wall paintings, is evident in the fashioning of garlands, pomegranates, apples, and leaves (Avigad 1983: 149-50, figs. 103-6; 168-74). Other houses in the Upper City of Jerusalem contained fragments of fresco with imitation marble patterns. The so-called House of Caiaphas on Mount Zion was adorned with elaborate frescoes decorated with portrayals of birds — a unique appearance in early Jewish art. The orchestra walls of the theater at Caesarea were decorated with fresco of imitation marble patterning. A wall painting has also been found in the monumental tomb of the Goliath family in Jericho (Hachlili 1985). The tomb has a unique painting depicted on three walls of the upper room, even though Jewish tombs did not usually have wall paintings. The main theme consists of vine branches bearing leaves and grapes, with birds perched between the branches. Some other motifs such as a wreath and ashlar stones are depicted on the wall opposite the entrance.

Stucco Moldings

Stucco moldings have been found among the remains of several Herodian palaces and buildings. They usually decorate ceilings and the upper parts of walls, and often cover columns made of local stone in order to make them appear fluted. The original styles and the standard of execution point to local workmanship, even though the ornamentation generally followed Roman examples. Bases and column drums, capitals, and ceilings covered with stucco were also found at the palaces, halls, and bathhouses atop Masada (Foerster 1995: 44-79). Stucco fragments with various profiles such as egg-and-dart decoration and tongue moldings were uncovered at Herodium. Stucco molded panels decorating painted walls were found in the third palace at Jericho. Fragments of molded stucco were also discovered in the fortresses at Alexandrium, Cypros, and Machaerus, and at the Hilkiya palace (Netzer 2001: figs. 65, 92, 116, 143). Some of the houses in the Upper City of Jerusalem were ornamented with stucco (Avigad 1983: 99-103, figs. 87-91). The large reception hall of one mansion was ornamented with white stucco imitating ashlar stones. Molded plaster fragments bearing the egg-and-dart motif were found in the debris of the hall and probably belonged to the ceiling.

Floor Pavements

Two types of floor pavements were used in Second Temple period buildings: mosaic pavements and floors paved in *opus sectile* style, in which figural patterns were composed in shapes cut to fit the component parts of the design.

Mosaics Mosaics decorated the floors of Herodian palaces and private homes of the Jerusalem nobility. At Masada a simple mosaic of black hexagons covered the floor of the upper terrace in the northern palace and the floor of the bathhouse court in the western palace. The western palace had two other polychrome mosaics. The first one had a geometric border and a central rendition of popular vegetation motifs including grapes, pomegranates, vine leaves, and fig leaves set within a frame of stylized olive branches. The center was rendered as a circle containing a number of intersecting circles (fig. 2). The second mosaic was located in the bathhouse corridor and portrayed a circle consisting of radial segments within a square. Mosaic pavements decorated several other palaces as well (Netzer 2001: figs. 99, 145-47, 160). A crudely fashioned and simple mosaic floor with squares and triangles was found in one of the rooms of Jericho palace III. Simple black-and-white mosaic floors were uncovered in the bathhouse at the Herodium palace, and several mosaic pavements decorated the bathhouse at Lower Herodium. A mosaic carpet with a design imitative of *opus sectile* floors was excavated at Caesarea. At Alexandrium, Cypros, and Machaerus, simple geometric mosaic floors were discovered in a peristyle or columned hall and in the bathhouses. Houses in the Upper City of Jerusalem revealed some ornamented and plain mosaic pavements, several of which were used in bathrooms (Avigad 1983: 144-46, figs. 150-51, 160-65). The central motif of these floors was usually a six-petal rosette (fig. 3). Only three mosaic floors have survived in living rooms. One has a rosette within a square frame. The corners bear a geometric pattern similar to the gamma motif. Another, partially preserved mosaic floor bears a central carpet of intertwined meanders framed by wave, guilloche, and crow-step patterns. One bath complex in a Jerusalem house had a mosaic with a wave border motif enclosing a circle with a multicolored and multipetaled rosette. In the corners were palmettes and a spindle bottle.

Opus Sectile Pavements Colored stone tiles decorated floors in some of the Herodian palaces. Pavements made using this technique rarely survived, their remains consisting of only a few tiles found in the debris of the structures. Usually only the bedding survived, containing the impression of the tiles that formed the design, the patterns of which may be reconstructed from the surviving impressions. The Masada bathhouse was paved with an *opus sectile* floor, probably replacing an earlier mosaic pavement (Foerster 1995: 158-61). *Opus sectile* pavements survived at the destroyed center of the *triclinium* at Jericho; it had designs of octagons and squares in the central carpet, surrounded by simple designs. At Cypros, fragments of an *opus sectile* floor were found in the bathhouse *caldarium*. A floor with traces of *opus sectile* tiles was found in a room of one of the houses located in the Upper City of Jerusalem; it depicts a design of interlocking circles made of black squares and red triangles.

Figure 2. Mosaic floors at Masada

Figure 3. Mosaic floors in houses of the Upper City, Jerusalem

Stone Objects and Vessels

Excavations at Jerusalem and other sites have yielded hand-carved stone objects such as cups with handles, square bowls, and vessels with multiple compartments. Most of the stone vessels were made of soft limestone and were either carved by hand or made on a lathe. They probably served as measuring cups for dry and liquid ingredients. The popularity of stone vessels can be explained by the halakic ruling known from later (rabbinic) sources that stone vessels do not transmit ritual impurity (*m. Kelim* 10:1; *m. Parah* 3:2).

Two types of stone tables were found in some of the houses excavated in the Upper City of Jerusalem (Avigad 1983: 167-74, figs. 185-86, 188-92, 194-95). The first type is a table with a rectangular top and a single, central leg carved in the form of a column, with the edges of the tabletop generally bearing floral or geometric carved motifs (fig. 4). One edge is usually plain, suggesting that the table was meant to stand against the wall. The second type is a smaller and lower round table that stood on three legs and probably ended in animal feet. Hellenistic and Roman paintings depicting such tables show that the rectangular ones were used to hold drinking vessels, while the round ones were used for meals.

Stone carving became a popular Jewish craft in Herodian times. The highly skilled carving represents an instantly recognizable style that developed from local artistic traditions. It utilized the locally available stone and created a new type of ornamentation. The existence of Jewish stonemasons is indicated by the appearance of stonemasons' marks and Hebrew letters found on column drums at Masada. Further evidence for the exis-

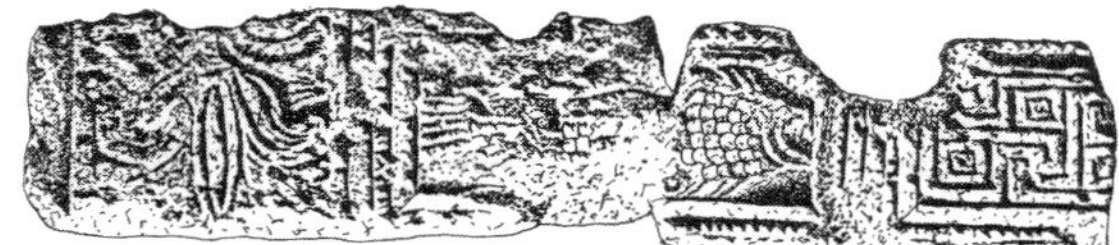

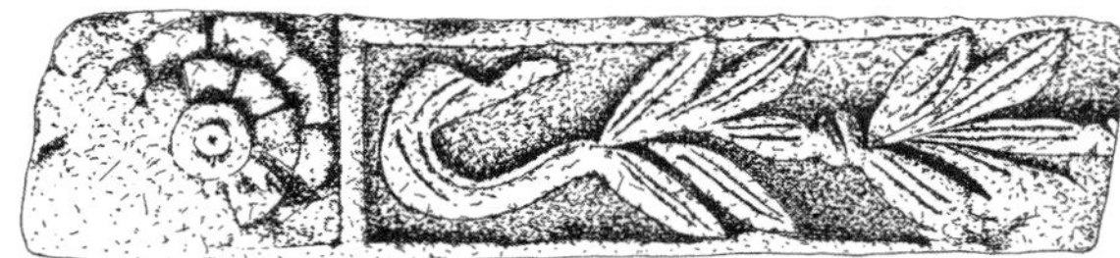

Figure 4. Artistic renderings of stone tabletops from houses in the Upper City, Jerusalem

tence of Jewish artists may be gathered from the choice of designs found on artifacts and monuments.

The Repertoire of Motifs

The range of themes and motifs in Jewish art of the Second Temple period fall into the following categories: symbolic motifs of the Temple vessels (the menorah and the showbread table), architectural patterns, geometric figures, plant motifs, bird and fish motifs, and motifs on Jewish coins.

The Menorah and Showbread Table

The two Temple vessels — the menorah and showbread table — were the most significant designs appearing in this period. They occur, for example, on the Arch of Titus in Rome and on both sides of a coin minted by King Mattathias Antigonus. A graffito of the menorah and showbread table was found incised on a plaster fragment from Jerusalem (fig. 5). Engraved menorahs were rendered on a sundial in Jerusalem, on graffiti on the wall of the corridor of Jason's Tomb, and on two ossuaries (Hachlili 2001: 42-50). The depiction of Temple vessels on the Arch of Titus was meant to reflect the Roman victory over Judea in 70 C.E., whereas the other incised depictions of the menorah represented spontaneous attempts by people who probably had seen the Temple menorah and wished to draw it from memory.

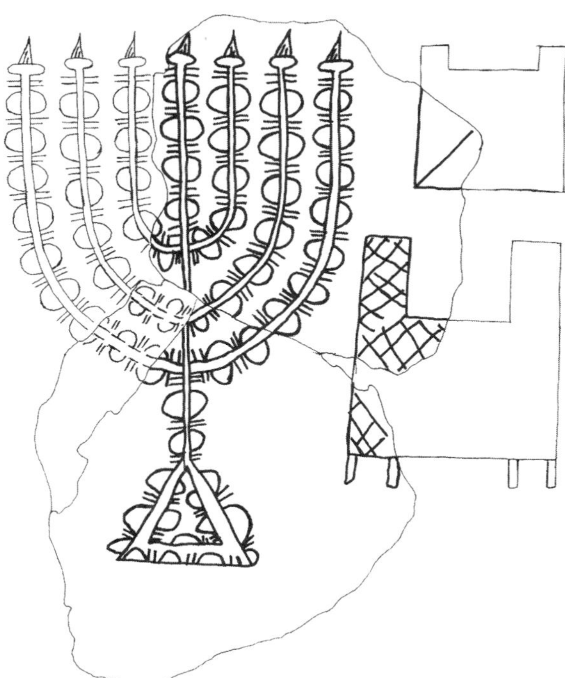

Figure 5. Drawing of menorah and showbread table incised on a plaster fragment from the Upper City, Jerusalem

Architectural Patterns

Architectural patterns rendered in fresco and stucco also decorated funerary art. A frequent design was the ashlar stone pattern; a good example was found in the large reception hall of a mansion in the Upper City of Jerusalem. The same motif was depicted in funerary art in the wall painting of the Goliath family tomb at Jericho and on ossuaries. Architectural decorative patterns such as walls covered by imitation marble have been found in fresco in the Herodian palaces at Masada and in Jerusalem houses. Ossuaries were decorated with metope patterns. Metopes are receding panels shaped like a circle, square, or rectangle; they are either plain or carved with sculpted reliefs. In several instances the motif of a *nefesh,* a tomb monument, was rendered on wall decoration and ossuaries (Hachlili 1981).

Geometric Figures

The most popular geometric figure was the rosette (Avi-Yonah 1981: 97-111). Developed out of a traditional geometric motif, it was executed with the aid of a compass (figs. 2, 3). It was used to ornament a wide range of objects, including architectural elements, stone tables, sundials (Avigad 1983: figs. 116, 185), and mosaic pavements. In funerary art, the rosette filled the spaces in Doric friezes on tomb facades. It also adorned sarcophagi and ossuaries. Other geometric motifs include meanders, waves, guilloches, lozenges, and hexagons. They appear in mosaics either as border designs or in the center of the pavement, and also feature in fresco and stucco. Geometric patterns appear in funerary art and usually consist of circles and intersecting lines. On ossuaries, the zigzag motif frequently appears as a frame.

Plant Motifs

Floral and vegetation motifs were considered by early Jewish artists as suitable for aniconic expression, for filling spaces, and for repetitive patterns. Plant motifs were either adopted from earlier Oriental designs or were imitations of local flora. Their form and composition were sometimes stylized into abstract or geometric patterns. They were used in architectural and funerary ornamentation. Depictions of acanthus leaves, lilies, flowers, wreaths, garlands, and branches are found on tomb façades, sarcophagi, and ossuaries. Vine branches, leaves, and grapes were especially popular motifs for decorating architectural elements. They were even more popular in funerary art and appear in the wall painting of the Goliath family tomb in Jericho (Hachlili 1985), on tomb façades in Jerusalem, on the Tomb of the Grapes, on a Nazirite sarcophagus, and on some ossuaries. Olive leaves decorated a stone table and pottery bowls from Jerusalem and Herodium.

Faunal and Other Motifs

Faunal motifs were rarely used in the Second Temple period. However, several birds appear among the vine branches in the wall painting of the Goliath family tomb in Jericho. In Jerusalem they appear on a palace fresco and were found incised on the handle of a stone vessel. A stucco fragment with an animal motif was found in a private building near the Temple Mount. Other motifs commonly used were the cornucopia and pomegranate; they appear on Herodian coins and ornamented a stone tabletop from Jerusalem.

Emblems on Coins

Emblems depicted on early Jewish coins were chosen to convey national, political, or religious meanings. Mattathias Antigonus (40-37 B.C.E.), the last Hasmonean king, minted his coins during a difficult time when he was usurped by Herod. His coins depict the Temple vessels (the menorah and the showbread table). By using them he evidently hoped to affirm his status as the legitimate king and high priest. Herod, who came from a non-Jewish Idumean family, was appointed king of Judea by Rome in 40 B.C.E., and in order to substantiate his right to reign he issued coins. The first group of coins struck in Samaria in 40-37 B.C.E. was minted to rival those of Antigonus and deliberately depicted designs imitative of the Roman Republican coins of 44-40 B.C.E. Among the Roman-inspired designs Herod adopted were the *caduceus* (winged staff with two snakes wrapped around it), the ceremonial cap of an *augur* (Roman priest who specialized in divination), and the *aphlaston* (fan-like ornament at the stern of ancient galleys). In this way Herod hoped to legitimate his claim to be the king duly appointed by the Romans. A second group of coins, struck in Jerusalem after Herod had become the sole *de facto* king in 37 B.C.E., depicts designs relating to the Jerusalem Temple (Meshorer 1982: 2:8-30). The later Herodian kings (Herod, Agrippa I, and Agrippa II) were likewise appointed and backed by Rome; like Herod, they also used designs on their coins that imitated Roman issues, although the emblems did not necessarily convey the same connotations. Motifs depicted on the coins minted by Jews during the First Jewish Revolt (66-70 C.E.) and the Bar Kokhba Revolt (132-135 C.E.) have religious and national significance. Among them are the façade of the Temple, Temple vessels, and the four species used during the Feast of Tabernacles (the lulav, ethrog, willow, and myrtle).

BIBLIOGRAPHY

N. AVIGAD 1983, *Discovering Jerusalem,* Jerusalem: Shikmona and Israel Exploration Society. • M. AVI-YONAH 1981, *Art in Ancient Palestine: Selected Studies,* Jerusalem: Magness. • S. FINE 2005, *Art and Judaism in the Greco-Roman Period: Toward a New Jewish Archaeology,* Cambridge: Cambridge University Press. • G. FOERSTER 1995, *Masada V: Art and Architecture,* Jerusalem: Israel Exploration Society and Hebrew University of Jerusalem. • R. HACHLILI 1981, "The *Nefesh:* The Jericho Column Pyramid," *PEQ* 113: 33-38. • R. HACHLILI 1985, "A Jewish Funerary Wall Painting of the First Century AD," *PEQ* 117: 112-27. • R. HACHLILI 1988, *Ancient Jewish Art and Archaeology in the Land of Israel,* Leiden: Brill. • R. HACHLILI 2001, *The Menorah, The Ancient Seven-armed Candelabrum: Origin, Form and Significance,* Leiden: Brill. • Y. MAGEN 2002, *The Stone Vessel Industry in the Second Temple Period: Excavations at Hizma and the Jerusalem Temple Mount,* Jerusalem: Israel Exploration Society. • Y. MESHORER 1982, *Ancient Jewish Coinage,* 2 vols., New York: Amphora Books. • Y. MESHORER 2001, *A Treasury of Jewish Coins: From the Persian Period to Bar Kokhba,* Jerusalem: Yad Ben-Zvi. • E. NETZER 2001, *The Palaces of the Hasmoneans and Herod the Great,* Jerusalem: Yad Ben-Zvi and Israel Exploration Society. • E. NETZER 2001-2004, *The Hasmonean and Herodian Palaces at Jericho: Final Report of the 1973-1987 Excavations,* 2 vols., Jerusalem: Israel Exploration Society. • L. Y. RAHMANI 1994, *Catalogue of Jewish Ossuaries in the Collections of the State of Israel,* Jerusalem: Israel Antiquities Authority.

See also: Architecture; Coins; Mosaics; Stone Vessels

RACHEL HACHLILI

Artapanus

Artapanus was a mid-second-century-B.C.E. Jewish historian who probably lived in Alexandria. (Jacobson 2006 is exceptional in denying that there is any good reason to think he was Jewish, but even he admits that he may have been Jewish.) Our knowledge of him is dependent on quotations by other authors. In his *Praeparatio Evangelica,* the fourth-century Christian bishop and historian Eusebius quotes three passages by Artapanus from a compilation made by the first-century-B.C.E. scholar Alexander Polyhistor of Rome, whose work is also nonextant except in quotation. Alexander refers to Artapanus's work by two different titles, *The Judaica* and *On the Jews.* Both labels likely refer to the same writing. The three excerpts are the only known fragments of Artapanus, though he was probably used by Josephus, who does not name him (Freudenthal 1894: 173).

The three quotations in Eusebius are all narratives about Jewish patriarchs. The first and shortest fragment (*Praep. Evang.* 9.18.1) gives an unusual etymology of "Jews" as deriving from the term "Hermiouth" and relates it to Abraham. It then goes on to state that Abraham came with his household to Egypt, remained there for twenty years, and taught the king astrology. Artapanus is our earliest representative of the popular tradition that Abraham was an astrologer.

The second fragment (*Praep. Evang.* 9.23.1-4), approximately thirty lines, presents a coherent summary of the story of Joseph, using Genesis 37, 39–47. According to Artapanus, Joseph was wiser than his brothers, who were jealous of him and plotted against him. He sought safety in Egypt with the help of Arab neighbors. In Egypt he found favor with the king and became the finance minister, reforming the nation's weak and unjust agricultural system into a prosperous enterprise. Joseph is also credited with inventing the Egyptian measuring system. For these reasons he was beloved by the Egyptians, and his family members moved from Syria to Egypt to be with him.

The third fragment (Eusebius, *Praep. Evang.* 9.27.1-37) is over 200 lines and tells an entertaining story of Moses, lauding him for bestowing on humanity many useful inventions including ships, machinery, weapons, and philosophy. Adopted by the barren queen and raised in the palace, Moses founded the Egyptian system of thirty-six *nomes* and assigned each its own god, priests, and writings. The priests were so impressed by his ability to interpret sacred writings that they called him Hermes, the Greek god identified with the Egyptian Thoth, deity of writing, science, and judgment. Artapanus says that Moses was called Musaeus by the Greeks, making him the teacher of the greatest Greek poet and musician, Orpheus. Moses also became a hero to the masses and a powerful military leader who managed to turn the Ethiopians into friends and persuaded them to adopt circumcision. Moses was also an impressive magician and miracle worker whom the jealous Egyptian king Chenephres sought to kill. Moses escaped to Midian and there married a priest's daughter. An encounter with a blazing fire from the ground and a divine voice encouraged him to invade Egypt. This invasion landed him in prison, but at night all the prison doors flew open and the guards either died or fell asleep. Moses used his powers and the power of the name of his god to perform miracles and unleash plagues. Again the king became jealous and began to mistreat all the Jews. Moses managed to lead the Jews out of Egypt and through the Red Sea, in which the pursuing Egyptian army was destroyed.

Artapanus's portrait of Moses differs from the typical Hellenistic depiction of him as a great lawgiver (cf. Hecataeus of Abdera, Eupolemus, Aristobulus, Philo, and Josephus). In the smaller fragments on Abraham and Joseph, Artapanus presents these heroes in unique and colorful ways as well.

Artapanus clearly used Jewish sources (e.g., a Greek translation of Genesis and Exodus), but he was also versed in Egyptian and Greek lore. His principal motivations in writing were not historical. Scholars have typically highlighted apologetic elements in his work, but Gruen has recently emphasized the inventive and entertaining qualities of his writing (Gruen 1998: 160). He was a talented and witty writer, knowledgeable of Jewish texts and traditions, and conversant with Egyptian and Greek cultures. His approach to Jewish texts and traditions allowed for liberal reinterpretation and creative interweaving with other sources.

BIBLIOGRAPHY

J. J. COLLINS 2000, *Between Athens and Jerusalem: Jewish Identity in the Hellenistic Diaspora,* 2d ed., Grand Rapids: Eerdmans, 37-46. • J. FREUDENTHAL 1874, *Alexander Polyhistor,* Breslau: Druck, 143-74, 215-18. • J. G. GAGER 1972, *Moses in Greco-Roman Paganism,* Nashville: Abingdon. • E. GRUEN 1998, *Heritage and Hellenism,* Berkeley: University of California. • C. R. HOLLADAY 1983, *Fragments from Hellenistic Jewish Authors,* Chico, Calif.: Scholars Press, 1: 189-243. • H. JACOBSON 2006, "Artapanus Judaeus," *JJS* 57: 210-21. • H. M. ZELLENTIN 2008, "The End of Jewish Egypt: Artapanus and the Second Exodus," in *Antiquity in Antiquity,* ed. G. Gardner and K. L. Osterloh, Tübingen: Mohr-Siebeck, 27-73.

JAMES E. BOWLEY

Asael/Azazel → Fallen Angels

Ascent to Heaven

Ascent to heaven is a widespread motif in numerous Near Eastern, Greco-Roman, Jewish, and Christian texts. Its counterpart in works reflecting an older cosmology is descent to the underworld. It is related to a variety of other material such as myths of dying and rising gods, visions of the divine throne room, the apotheosis of heroes, the immortality of the soul, dreams of flying, and voyages to mythic realms. The purpose of the ascent varies from work to work. Some depict it as an invasion of the heavenly realm in which human beings strive for immortality; others present it as a divine reward granted to exceptional human beings; still others employ it to anticipate the postmortem fate of the soul or of the righteous. In early Judaism, otherworldly journeys function mainly as vehicles of divine revelation; they validate the authority of their visionary heroes and underwrite the theological and moral message of their authors.

Ancient Near Eastern and Greco-Roman Background

In religions of the Near East, heaven was thought to be the abode of the gods and normally off limits to mortals, whose proper station is on earth. Against this conceptual background, Mesopotamian myths associated with Adapa and Etana report their failed attempts to ascend to heaven in order to attain eternal life.

In texts composed before the first century C.E., the abode of all the dead is usually located in the underworld. So in Homer's *Odyssey* the eponymous hero descends to Hades to receive instruction, witness punishments, and hear prophecies of his own fate. Similarly, the protagonist of Virgil's *Aeneid,* a work modeled on the *Odyssey,* goes down to the underworld in the company of the Sibyl and sees the souls of his progeny, the palace of Hades, and the fields of Elysium.

The ascent motif could also be adapted in the service of philosophy. In his *Proem* Parmenides (early fifth century B.C.E.) describes his being accompanied by the daughters of the sun on a chariot ride to heaven, where he consulted with a goddess who told him that he must learn "both the round, calm heart of truth and the untrustworthy opinions of mortals."

Otherworldly journeys were more frequently employed to reflect on the fate of the dead and their just deserts. For example, the Myth of Er in book 10 of Plato's *Republic* (fourth century B.C.E.) recounts how a man by that name died in battle but revived ten days later to tell of his journey in the afterlife, where he saw the celestial spheres, viewed the rewards and punishments of the dead, and witnessed the reincarnation of souls. In the Dream of Scipio, part of Cicero's treatise *On the Republic* (first century B.C.E.), the hero ascends to the stars and learns about the rewards awaiting the dutiful soldier in the afterlife. By the Common Era, the otherworldly journey was virtually a subgenre and had become so popular in Greco-Roman literature that it was parodied by the satirist Lucian in his works *Icaromenippus, Nekyomanteia,* and *Kataplous* (second century C.E.)

Hebrew Bible

The Hebrew Bible contains no full-blown account of an ascent to heaven. This lack reflects the ancient Israelite belief that heaven is not for mortals but for God and other divine beings. Yet some extraordinary heroes of Israelite lore were thought to have been taken there. This is the case with Enoch, the antediluvian patriarch in the seventh generation from Adam who "walked with God [or "divine beings": *'ĕlōhîm*] and then was not, for God took him" (Gen. 5:22, 24). Genesis does not specify where Enoch was taken and presumes that he did not return to earth, but early Jewish apocalypses written in his name have him going to heaven and coming back to earth to report what he saw there. Early Jewish tradition interpreted Moses' ascent of Mt. Sinai as only the first stop on a journey to heaven, and some sources took Deuteronomy's statement that no one knows the place of Moses' burial to mean that he was taken to heaven at the end of his life. Then there is the famous story of Elijah being caught up to heaven in a whirlwind aboard a horse-drawn chariot of fire (2 Kings 2:1-12); neither the journey nor its destination is described, only the prophet's departure.

The story of the Tower of Babel in Genesis 11, in which the builders aspire to establish "a city and a tower with its top in the heavens," was interpreted in later Jewish and Christian tradition as an aborted ascent to heaven, undertaken out of scientific curiosity, a desire to war against God, or a resolve to escape divine punishment in the event of another deluge (e.g., *Jub.* 10:19; *Sib. Or.* 3.100; *3 Bar.* 3:7-8; Philo, *QG* 2.82; *Confusione Linguarum* 111–14; Josephus, *Ant.* 1.109-21).

Early Jewish Apocalypses

In Second Temple literature, ascents to heaven are found chiefly in apocalypses in which a pseudonymous visionary (usually a hero of Israelite lore) goes on an otherworldly journey (often in the company of a guiding angel) in order to be taught the secrets of the cosmos or the eschatological destiny of humankind. By the Hellenistic period, the idea that good and bad people have different fates awaiting them in the afterlife had gained ascendancy, and the realms of the dead were relocated from the underworld to heavenly regions.

Book of the Watchers

The oldest Jewish ascent text is found in the *Book of the Watchers* (*1 Enoch* 1–36; late third century B.C.E.), where Enoch is caught up to heaven and sees the Great Glory enthroned (chaps. 14–16). The sights that Enoch sees in heaven rely on the throne visions of Ezekiel (chaps. 1–2, 8, 10). Heaven is a temple, angels are priests, and the visionary assumes angelic status by taking on the role of a priest. Enoch is given a sentence of divine judgment to convey to the rebellious Watchers. In the latter part of the book, he is taken by seven archangels on a guided tour of remote regions of the earth, where he sees the prison house of disobedient angels, the resting place of the dead, the storehouses of the elements, and the mountain of God and tree of life (chaps. 17–36). Behind the myth of the Watchers lies a veiled critique of the Jerusalem priesthood in the Hellenistic period.

Aramaic Levi and Testament of Levi

The essential features of ascent in the *Book of the Watchers* were taken up in several later texts, in which visionaries attain angelic status through priestly investiture. Such is the case in the fragmentary *Aramaic Levi Document* (third century B.C.E.), which describes one or more visions of the patriarch ascending to heaven. A fuller version of Levi's ascent appears in the Greek *Testament of Levi* (chaps. 2, 5, 8), a Christian work of the second century C.E. based on earlier Jewish sources including *Aramaic Levi.* Much of this material probably originated in response to the perceived corruption of the priesthood in the Hellenistic period (cf. *Jubilees* 30 and 32). Whereas the *Book of the Watchers* knows only one heaven, the *Testament of Levi* has seven. At an earlier stage of the text's development, the heavens numbered three, but that number was expanded to seven, which became the most common number by the turn of the era (*T. Levi* 2:7-12; 3:4-10). The number "seven" seems to derive not from the seven planetary spheres of Hellenistic cosmology but from the symbolic properties associated with the number in earlier Babylonian science and magic.

Similitudes of Enoch

The *Similitudes of Enoch* (*1 Enoch* 37–71), from the first century C.E., describes a heavenly journey in which the seer witnesses cosmological phenomena and is told of the eschatological punishment in store for the wicked and the vindication awaiting the righteous. In several respects Enoch's journey in the *Similitudes* is a continuation of the one in the *Book of the Watchers,* but here his tour culminates in a vision of a heavenly figure called the Chosen One, Messiah, and Son of Man, enthroned before the Lord of Spirits in the heavenly temple. At the end of the work, Enoch's body and spirit are transformed, and he is told, "You are the Son of Man who was born to righteousness" (71:14).

2 Enoch

The two most elaborate heavenly ascents are found in *2 Enoch* and *3 Baruch,* apocalypses from the late first or early second century C.E. that depict round-trip tours through a numbered series of heavens, each with distinctive contents. The tour in *2 Enoch* combines and rearranges some elements of *1 Enoch* 14 and 17–36, but its detailed reporting on the contents of the seven heavens is largely unique. Cosmological elements dominate the description of the first, fourth, and sixth heavens, whereas eschatological rewards and punishments receive attention in the second, third, and fifth. The third heaven contains the Garden of Eden and the abode of the righteous. In the seventh heaven, Enoch enters the heavenly throne room and is transformed to assume the status of an angel-like priest. He records his revelations in 360 books and is told the secrets of creation by God. The purpose of Enoch's revelations is primarily hortatory, and their ethical content is universal rather than distinctively Jewish.

3 Baruch

Similar to *2 Enoch* in content and purpose — though much shorter — is *3 Baruch.* This work opens with the seer mourning the destruction of Jerusalem. An angel appears and takes Baruch on a guided tour of five heavens. Along the way he sees the planners and builders of the Tower of Babel; a dragon devouring the bodies of the wicked in Hades; the sun chariot, phoenix, and moon; and a lake around which the souls of the righteous gather as birds to sing hymns. In the fifth heaven, Michael presides over the presentation of human prayers and good deeds, which he offers before God in a higher heaven (presumably the seventh). Baruch and his angel abruptly withdraw. The aborted ascent denies the visionary the sight of God in the celestial temple in a way that seems to underscore the inscrutability of the Deity. Accordingly, Baruch does not assume angelic status and is not invested with any priesthood. As in *2 Enoch,* personal eschatology and speculative cosmology combine to affirm God's control over the universe and to encourage right living. It is difficult to decide whether *3 Baruch* originated in Hellenistic Judaism or was composed in Christian circles.

Apocalypse of Abraham

The *Apocalypse of Abraham* is unique among early Jewish apocalypses for combining a review and periodization of history with a heavenly ascent. Preserved only in late Slavonic manuscripts, the work addresses the problem of evil in the world, the interplay of predestination and free will, and the suffering of Israel at the hands of the nations. It was written after the destruction of Jerusalem and the Temple in 70 C.E. and provides one of the earliest examples of merkavah mysticism. The first part of the work tells about Abraham's renunciation of idolatry (chaps. 1–8). The account of the covenant between the pieces in Genesis 15 then provides the occasion and framework for the ascent (chaps. 9–32). Abraham is guided by the angel Yahoel, who helps him overcome the opposition of the fallen angel-priest Azazel. He is taken directly to the highest heaven on the wing of a pigeon, one of the birds left from the sacrifice, to see the divine throne and worship God with a song that Yahoel has taught him. He looks down on the seventh, sixth, and fifth heavens, which are full of different classes of angels but empty of any gods. He sees the stars, the earth, and the place of torment under the earth; and witnesses the events of history, which climax in the destruction of the Temple, the advent of a false and true messiah, and a revelation concerning the punishment of the wicked and the reward of the righteous.

Dead Sea Scrolls

The covenanters of Qumran valued and copied earlier apocalypses like the books later collected in *1 Enoch* (except for the *Similitudes*). Yet no full-scale apocalypses — and hence no ascents to heaven — are preserved among their own sectarian compositions. Various Dead Sea Scrolls, however, employ ascent motifs. The *Songs of the Sabbath Sacrifice,* for instance, describes the worship of angels in the heavenly temple. Though not a sectarian composition, the work was prized because it supported the community's belief that its own worship took place in communion with the liturgy of angels.

The most interesting work in this regard is the so-called *Self-Glorification Hymn* (4Q471b; other recensions in 4Q427 frg. 7; 4Q491 frg. 11; and 1QH 26–27). This fragmentary text does not describe an ascent but evidently presupposes one. Speaking in the first person, an unidentified figure claims to be "seated . . . in heaven" and "reckoned with gods" and to have an "abode . . . in the holy congregation." He boasts of the incomparability of his glory and the irresistibility of his teaching. The implied speaker who recounts his apotheosis is certainly a human figure and perhaps the Teacher of Righteousness or the eschatological high priest.

Philo and Josephus

Philo of Alexandria developed earlier material concerning the ascents of Enoch, Moses, and Elijah, on the understanding that all three of these heroes entered heaven without seeing death. In one passage, he interprets LXX Gen. 5:24, "And he was not found, for God had translated him," to mean that Enoch was transported *(metatithēmi)* to the divine realm (*QG* 1.86). In another, he says that Enoch "changed his abode and journeyed as an emigrant from the mortal life to the immortal" (*Mutatione Nominum* 38). For Moses, Philo draws on conflicting traditions: in *QG* 1.86 (cf. *Sacrificiis* 8–10) he says that the lawgiver was taken to heaven without experiencing death and burial (contra Deut. 34:5), yet in *Mos.* 2.291 he affirms the opposite. Evidently, the exegetical stimulus for the belief that Moses did not die but was translated to heaven was provided by LXX Deut. 34:6, which says that "no one knew his burial place."

In several passages, Philo also speaks of the ascent of the soul, adapting the popular notion of the soul as a winged bird. Most strikingly, he spiritualizes the notion of heavenly ascent by giving an account of his own journey there in *Spec. Leg.* 3.1-2. In terms similar to those he used to describe the ascent of the mind (*De Opificio Mundi* 70), he tells how he "seemed to be borne aloft into the heights with a soul possessed by some God-sent inspiration, whirling around with the sun and the moon and the whole heaven and cosmos." His ascent enabled him to peer into the laws of Moses and reveal their contents to the multitudes (*Spec. Leg.* 3.6). Indeed, the people of Israel are the nation that ascends to God, in contrast to the invasion of divinity perpetrated by the emperor Caligula.

Like Philo, Josephus understands the fates of Enoch, Moses, and Elijah as heavenly ascents. Enoch "returned to the divinity" (*anechōrēse pros ton theon, Ant.* 1.85), and Elijah "disappeared *(aphanisthē)* from among men" (*Ant.* 9.28). Both "became invisible" *(gegonasin aphaneis),* and no one knows of their death." As for Moses, "he has written of himself in the sacred books that he died, for fear that any might say that by reason of his surpassing virtue he had gone back to the divinity" (*Ant.* 4.326). This statement implies that Moses did in fact ascend to heaven without dying; it was only his humility that kept him from writing as much at the end of Deuteronomy.

New Testament

Several passages in the New Testament speak of Christ's exaltation, but only the author of Luke-Acts actually describes Jesus' ascent to heaven. The dual accounts in Luke 24:50-53 and Acts 1:9-11 differ in a few details. In the former, the point of departure is Bethany, while in the latter it is evidently the Mt. of Olives overlooking Jerusalem. Further, in Acts "two men in white robes" (angels) appear and tell the disciples that Jesus will return in the same manner. The differences add literary variety to Luke's two-volume work.

As a reflex of its high Christology, the Gospel of John has Jesus tell Nicodemus, "No one has ascended to heaven except the one who descended from heaven — the Son of Man" (John 3:14). The statement has an unmistakably polemical edge and is probably intended to counter beliefs in the ascension of Moses and other worthies such as Enoch, Elijah, and Isaiah.

The book of Revelation briefly mentions but does not describe John the seer's ascent to heaven "in the spirit" (Rev. 4:1-2). Later in the book (11:3-14) the faithful testimony of God's people during the period of tribulation before the end is symbolized by the career of "two witnesses." Like Jesus, the ultimate faithful witness *(martys),* they have a prophetic career of mighty deeds and die in Jerusalem. Also like him, they rise from the dead and go to heaven in a cloud (11:12).

The longest account of heavenly ascent in the New Testament — and, apart from Philo, the only autobiographical account from antiquity — comes from Paul. While defending himself against the charges of rival apostles, he recounts how he was "caught up to the third heaven — whether in the body or out of the body, I do not know; God knows. . . . such a person . . . was caught up into Paradise and heard things that cannot be put into words *(arrhēta rhēmata),* which no one is permitted to speak" (2 Cor. 12:2-4). Paul's account depicts a one-stage journey in a three-heaven cosmology, with Paradise located in the third heaven. Some scholars have discerned here a merkavah vision of the sort reported in later Jewish texts.

Later Jewish and Christian Texts

The motif of heavenly ascent gained popularity in early Christianity. From the second century C.E. onward, the otherworldly journey was the most prominent type of apocalypse. Notable examples include the *Ascension of Isaiah,* the *Apocalypse of Peter,* and the *Apocalypse of Paul.* Some of the Coptic Gnostic texts in the Nag Hammadi Library contain ascent passages, as does the tractate *Poimandres* in the Corpus Hermeticum and the so-called *Mithras Liturgy* in the Greek Magical Papyri. The genre had an enormous influence in Western Christendom and reached its apex in Dante's *Divine Comedy.*

The theme also features in rabbinic texts that describe contemplation of the merkavah or throne chariot of God, and in the later Hekhalot literature, a corpus of mystical, magical, and liturgical material whose label derives from the celestial palaces or temples *(hêkālôt,* sg. *hêkāl)* in which God dwells and through which the visionary ascends. Important representatives are *Sepher Hekhalot* (also known as *3 Enoch*) and *Hekhalot Rabbati.* Apocalypses and other texts of the Second Temple period no doubt influenced these developed forms of Jewish mysticism, but the evidence is insufficient to indicate an unbroken tradition of speculation or praxis. A key difference between the ascent apocalypses and the Hekhalot texts is that in the former the visionary's journey is instigated by God and is usually undertaken without opposition or danger (*Apocalypse of Abraham* is the notable exception). In the latter corpus, the initiative comes from the adept. One even finds instructions on how to ascend, and the mystic typically encounters angelic hostility along the way.

BIBLIOGRAPHY

P. ALEXANDER 2007, *The Mystical Texts: Songs of the Sabbath Sacrifice and Related Texts,* London: Continuum. • L. CARLSSON 2006, *Round Trips to Heaven: Otherworldly Travelers in Early Judaism and Christianity,* Lund: Lund University; Stockholm: Almqvist & Wiksell. • J. J. COLLINS 2003, "Journeys to the World Beyond in Ancient Judaism," in *Apocalyptic and Eschatological Heritage: The Middle East and Celtic Realms,* ed. M. McNamara, Dublin: Four Courts, 20-36. • M. DEAN OTTING 1984, *Heavenly Journeys: A Study of the Motif in Hellenistic Jewish Literature,* Frankfurt: Lang. • M. HIMMELFARB 1993, *Ascent to Heaven in Jewish and Christian Apocalypses,* Oxford: Oxford University Press. • A. F. SEGAL 1980, "Heavenly Ascent in Hellenistic Judaism, Early Christianity and Their Environment," *ANRW* II.23.2: 1333-94. • J. D. TABOR 1986, *Things Unutterable: Paul's Ascent to Paradise in Its Greco-Roman, Judaic, and Early Christian Contexts,* Lanham, Md.: University Press of America. • A. YARBRO COLLINS 1996, "The Seven Heavens in Jewish and Christian Apocalypses," in eadem, *Cosmology and Eschatology in Jewish and Christian Apocalypticism,* Leiden: Brill.

See also: Apocalypse; Cosmology; Death and Afterlife; Heaven; Hekhalot Literature; Mysticism

DANIEL C. HARLOW

Asceticism

Asceticism (from Gr. *askēsis,* "discipline, exercise, training") is the practice of self-denial in areas such as sex, food, and drink. The reigning assumption of scholars in the mid-twentieth century was that asceticism in the West arose among Christians in the fourth century, while Judaism was essentially world-affirming. Any ascetic tendencies that appeared, such as those at Qumran, were minor or aberrant. It is true that Jewish tradition in general has downplayed a radical asceticism that would separate practitioners from the life of the household. Compared to the Christian asceticism of the fourth century and after, there is little in the Hebrew Bible, for instance, that would qualify. Numerous cases of an *ad hoc* or preparatory asceticism can be noted in which a person abstains from food or sex before making an earnest petition to God. Many of these continue into the postexilic and Hellenistic periods; one may note especially fasting in regard to grief and mourning (Zech. 7:3; 8:19; *4 Ezra* 10:4, 25-49), petitions to God in times of crisis (1 Macc. 3:47), and the reception of revelation (*4 Ezra* 5:13; 6:31).

The Matrix of Asceticism

In the rabbinic texts there are some isolated examples of celibacy and fasting, but they are few and far between. Fast days are discussed (*m. Taʿan.* 1:4–3:8), but most of these references constitute a continuation of biblical traditions and not the introduction of new practices. To be sure, some nuances have been traced. The rabbis in Palestine, falling under the influence of Western philosophy, favored ascetic practices over and above that practiced by the Babylonian rabbis. Each group was thus somewhat assimilated to the practices of its environment (Satlow 2003; Diamond 2004; Fraade 1986; Biale 1993; Boyarin 1993). The daily discipline of the rabbis was very similar in principle to that of the Stoics, and not to the extreme practices of fourth-century Christians.

Because of this absence of full-blown asceticism in Judaism, Ephraim Urbach (1988) assumed that Christian asceticism resulted from a disciplined application of Platonic dualism and a devaluation of the body. But this explanation is called into question when we note that in Greece as well there was little continuous asceticism, only the same sort of preparatory practices before solemn rituals — *ad hoc* asceticism — that we find in the Hebrew Bible. The matrix of asceticism was more complex and may have involved Judaism more than was previously believed. Just before the turn of the Common Era, new developments can be charted that place Jewish discourse on asceticism in a multicultural, colonial context. A number of new groups arose that emphasized ascetic practices: Neopythagoreans and Cynics among the Greeks, Essenes, and Therapeutae/Therapeutrides among Jews. Surprisingly, even the supreme realist Josephus notes in his autobiography that for three years he had been a disciple to a hermit-sage named Bannus (*Life* 11), without a hint that this would be viewed as a bizarre anomaly for a religious Jew. Philo, in condemning such renunciation, implies that he also knew of Jews who did so (*On Flight and Finding* 33–35). Further, first-century Christian texts, while sometimes mined for evidence that Jesus' followers were not ascetic, demonstrate instead that ascetic practices were either engaged in or debated in a number of communities (e.g., Matt. 6:16-18; Luke 18:12; *Did.* 8:1).

Defining Asceticism

In addition to more detailed discussions of varied Jewish practices, there has also been a dramatic rethinking of the very definition of asceticism. The extreme practices of Christian ascetics and comparative studies of religious ascetics around the world gave rise to a definition of asceticism as a continuous, extended, and extreme privation that separated one from family life. Michel Foucault (1986), followed by Geoffrey Harpham (1987) analyzed Western antiquity and focused instead on ascetic disciplines in everyday life. Asceticism as previously understood is only a more pronounced manifestation of the discipline of perfection practiced by anyone leading an intentionally moral life, whether Christian, Greek, Roman, Egyptian, or Jewish. This broadening of the definition of asceticism would appear at first to equalize all cultures, but Foucault also emphasized the quantitative distinction found in the early Christian developments and the new discourses of the self in Roman society. In this Roman/Christian context, the "technologies of the self" produced a "decentering of the self," that is, a focus on the depravity of the self as if viewed from the outside.

Asceticism in Early Judaism

Recent approaches have also discerned the discourse of the decentered self in early Jewish texts. Carol Newsom's analysis of the Qumran *Hodayot* or *Thanksgiving Psalms* stresses the correspondence between radical practices of the community and the psychological correlative of the discourse of the decentered self. She refers to this extreme confession of depravity as the "masochistic sublime" (Newsom 2004: 220). This is a new development in Jewish psalmody; even the penitential psalms of the Hebrew Bible acknowledge sin without emphasizing depravity. While the centered self of the Hebrew Bible can engage in *penitence,* the decentered self of Qumran must search out a new *discipline* to address the depravity.

Even earlier in Judaism we find evidence of a discourse of the decentered self, although it is not clear what practices or disciplines may have accompanied it. Between about 200 B.C.E. and 100 C.E. there appeared a number of Jewish novelistic texts that on the surface fully engage the activities of the everyday life of the wealthy: Greek additions to Daniel (Susanna, Bel and the Dragon, Prayer of Azariah, and the Song of the Three Jews), Esther (especially with the additions in its Greek versions), Judith, Tobit, and *Joseph and Aseneth.* (Omitted here are texts whose Jewish origin is disputed: *Testaments of the Twelve Patriarchs* and *Testament of Job. Joseph and Aseneth* is included, although its provenance and date are also contested.) Many of these texts focus on a female protagonist who comes to a central moment of moral decision, and in three of these she pauses to engage in a rending examination of her sinful self (Wills 2006). In LXX Esther, Judith, and *Joseph and Aseneth,* the female protagonist enters into a penitential process, condemns her beauty, takes off her rich garments, puts on the apparel of mourning, prays, and only afterward rebeautifies herself to reenter the world. The woman thus becomes the focalizing subject who engages the issues of self, depravity, and redemption through knowledge of depravity (which in principle requires discipline).

These observations force a rethinking of the cultural evolution of asceticism. What may have appeared as a gap, even a chasm, between the purely *ad hoc* asceticism of the Hebrew Bible and the continuous discipline of some later Jewish and Christian groups may be filled in. The penitential theology found in Ezra 9, Nehemiah 9, and Daniel 9 is associated with fasts, and preparatory fasts are featured in Esth. 4:16 and Jdt. 4:13; 8:6. Even an expiatory role for fasts may be expressed in *Pss. Sol.* 3:8. Theological exploration of the decentered self increased at the same time that new ascetic practices were being explored. Other crosscultural conclusions have been forthcoming. In rabbinic texts asceticism was sometimes said to be a substitute or compensation for sacrifice (*b. Berakot* 17a), but this should also be seen in a broader context: there is a negative correlation between sacrifice and asceticism throughout the ancient West. Three groups that opposed sacrifice, Neopythagoreans, Cynics, and Christians, also developed ascetic practices. Further, Jewish groups that opposed the Temple cult, such as the Dead Sea sect, instituted a celibate organization of their community. Even the *mišmārôt* and *maʿămādôt* fasts were intended to compensate for being at a distance from the Temple (Satlow 2003; Diamond 2004). Asceticism was taken up as an unmediated communion with God outside of the public cults of sacrifice.

The motive force of asceticism may not be so much "Greek" as colonial. The Jewish decentered self may have arisen as a form of colonial alienation, an extension of penitential theology. At any rate, the rabbis would step back from the extreme view of depravity with the doctrine of the good and evil *yeṣers* or inclinations. Through God's action, the human being would not require a special discipline outside the household in order to correct for sin.

BIBLIOGRAPHY

D. BIALE 1993, *Eros and the Jews: From Biblical Israel to Contemporary America*, New York: Basic. • D. BOYARIN 1993, *Carnal Israel: Reading Sex in Talmudic Culture*, Berkeley: University of California Press. • E. DIAMOND 2004, *Holy Men and Hunger Artists: Fasting and Asceticism in Rabbinic Culture*, Oxford: Oxford University Press. • M. FOUCAULT 1986, *The History of Sexuality*, vol. 3, *The Care of the Self*, New York: Pantheon. • S. FRAADE 1986, "Ascetic Aspects of Ancient Judaism," in *Jewish Spirituality: From the Bible through the Middle Ages*, ed. A. Green, New York: Crossroad, 253-88. • G. G. HARPHAM 1987, *The Ascetic Imperative in Culture and Criticism*, Chicago: University of Chicago Press. • C. NEWSOM 2005, *The Self as Symbolic Space: Constructing Identity and Community at Qumran*, Leiden: Brill. • M. L. SATLOW 2003, "'And on the Earth You Shall Sleep': *Talmud Torah* and Rabbinic Asceticism," *JR* 83: 204-25. • E. E. URBACH 1988, "Ascesis and Suffering in Talmudic and Midrashic Sources," in idem, *The World of the Sages: Collected Studies*, Jerusalem: Magnes, 437-58 (in Hebrew). • L. M. WILLS 2006, "Ascetic Theology before Asceticism? Jewish Narratives and the Decentering of the Self," *JAAR* 74: 902-25.

See also: Celibacy; Essenes; Fasting; Therapeutae

LAWRENCE M. WILLS

Asia Minor

Jewish Communities in Asia Minor

Josephus informs us that sometime between 210 and 205 B.C.E. Antiochus III transferred 2,000 Jewish families from Mesopotamia and Babylonia to Lydia and Phrygia as military settlers (*Ant.* 12.147-53). They were allowed to use their own laws, which probably gave these new Jewish communities an opportunity to become well established. 1 Maccabees 15:16-23 may indicate that by 139-138 B.C.E. Jews lived in Asia Minor in the kingdom, cities, and areas listed in that passage. A decree of the city of Pergamum written between 139 and 95 B.C.E. gives evidence for a Jewish community in the city (*Ant.* 14.247-55). Shortly after 88 B.C.E. Mithridates seized a huge amount of money on Cos, deposited there by Asian Jews; this suggests that the Jewish communities in Asia had by this time accumulated very significant financial resources (*Ant.* 14.110-14). Cicero writes that in 62 B.C.E. the Roman governor Flaccus seized the Jewish Temple tax from Apamea, Adramyttium, Laodicea, and Pergamum (*Pro Flacco* 28.66-69); in some cases the amounts were very considerable. Josephus and Philo also preserve some generally authentic documents, written by emperors, Roman administrators, or the cities themselves and to be dated from 49 B.C.E. to 2/3 C.E., which show that there were Jewish communities in the cities of Ephesus, Halicarnassus, Laodicea, Miletus, Sardis, and Tralles (Josephus, *Ant.* 14.185-267; 16.160-78; Philo, *Legatio ad Gaium* 245; 281–82; 315; cf. *Ant.* 16.27-61).

The New Testament provides information about Jewish communities in Pisidian Antioch, Iconium,

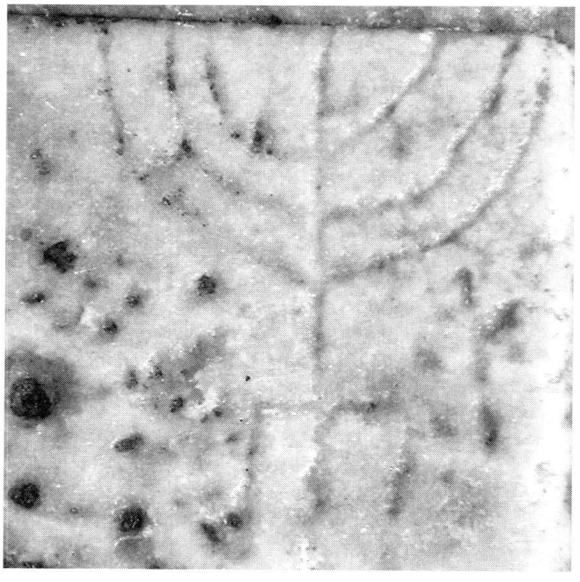

View of a menorah carved on one of the marble steps of the Libary of Celsus in Ephesus. This seven-branched lampstand is a rare archaeological indication of a Jewish presence in Ephesis, a major city in Asia Minor.
(www.HolyLandPhotos.org)

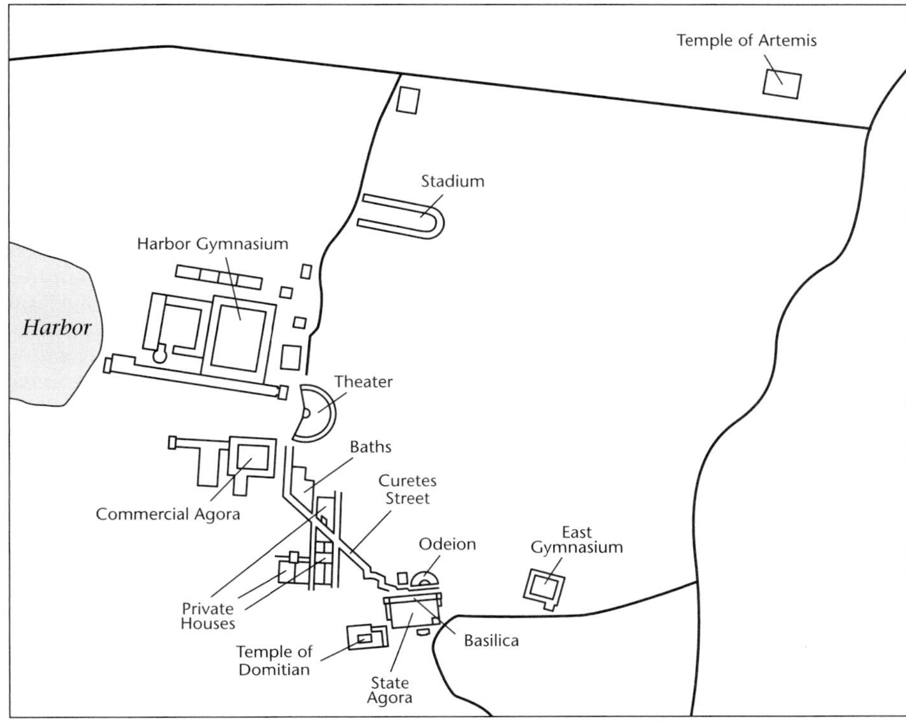

EPHESUS IN THE FIRST CENTURY C.E.

Ephesus, Smyrna, Philadelphia, and perhaps Lystra (Acts 13–14; 16:1-5; 18:19–19:41; Rev 2:9; 3:9). Acts 2:9-10 and 6:9-15 indicate that Jews lived in Cappadocia, Pontus, Asia, Phrygia, Pamphylia, and Cilicia. We can infer the existence of Jewish communities in the vicinity of Philadelphia and Magnesia, and Maeander and their influence on local Christians from the writings of Ignatius (*Phld.* 6:1-2; 8:2; *Magn.* 8:1; 9:1-2; 10:1-3). Passages in the *Martyrdom of Polycarp* and the *Martyrdom of Pionius* probably give evidence for the Jewish community in Smyrna in the second and third centuries C.E.

Synagogues have been discovered in Sardis and Priene, and inscriptions often provide us with evidence for communities about which the literary sources are silent. We have particularly significant inscriptional evidence from Acmonia, Apamea, Aphrodisias, Corycus, Hierapolis, and Sardis. All the known Jewish inscriptions from Asia Minor (numbering 258) are now given in the excellent volume edited by W. Ameling, *Inscriptiones Judaicae Orientis,* vol. 2, *Kleinasien,* published in 2004. P. Van der Horst (1990: 166-67) estimates that about one million Jews lived in Asia Minor in the first century C.E.; this number may be compared with the general estimate of the total Jewish population of the Diaspora at this time of five to six million.

Synagogue Buildings in Sardis and Priene

Sardis

In 1962 the largest synagogue building extant from antiquity was discovered in Sardis. It was an integral part of the bath-gymnasium complex that occupied a central position on a major thoroughfare in the city. The building was begun in the late second century C.E. and originally served as a Roman civil basilica. Probably around 270 C.E. (although the date continues to be debated), it was remodeled and became a synagogue, although we do not know exactly when or how the Jewish community acquired this notable building. Further remodeling was done by the Jewish community in the mid to late fourth century C.E. An atrium-like forecourt, colonnaded on all four sides and with a central fountain, led into the main hall, which was 59 m. × 18 m. and could accommodate over 1,000 people. The hall contained a shrine for the Torah and another probably for a menorah, a large apse lined with semicircular benches, and a large marble table flanked by Lydian stone lions in reuse. Elaborate mosaics covered the floor, and the walls were decorated with marble revetments. The community continued to use the synagogue until the destruction of the city in 616 C.E., which testifies to the enduring vitality of this Jewish community.

The style of the synagogue was determined by the building's previous history, by local architectural idioms, and by the local community. In many ways, the synagogue building as a whole was acculturated to the wider environment in Sardis to a significant degree. It contained over eighty inscriptions, which mainly concern donations and date from the fourth century C.E. and later; some are in Hebrew, but the vast majority are in Greek. These inscriptions and the building itself reveal a large, prosperous, and influential Jewish community that had considerable social status and was active in civic and political affairs. The community seems to have been integrated into the economic, social, and political life of Sardis to an unusual degree. Yet the strength of the Jewish identity of this community is also clear from the building itself. Although they were closely related to their wider society, Rajak (2001: 461) points out that such relations had their limits, and "[c]lose observation allows us still to detect expressions of separation" from the wider society. We can also note that Melito, the bishop of Sardis in the latter part of the second century C.E., was strongly polemical toward Israel in his *Peri Pascha*. This work may be seen in part as a reaction to the Jewish community in the city, although this is debated.

Priene

The only other synagogue discovered in Asia Minor is a remodeled house at Priene, probably to be dated to the third century C.E. A small forecourt led into the main room, which was 10 m. × 14 m. The main features in the otherwise plain room were a bench and a Torah niche in the Jerusalem-facing wall. Two reliefs with depictions of menorahs were found on the floor of the main room. The contrast between this building and the Sardis synagogue is striking. The two buildings show the diversity of Judaism in Asia Minor and also indicate that the local history of the community and the local context had a formative influence on Jewish communities.

Facets of Jewish Identity

Factors that enabled Diaspora Jewish communities to retain their identity include ethnicity, the ongoing life of the local Jewish community, links with Jerusalem and other Diaspora communities, the Torah, and key Jewish practices and beliefs such as worship of the one God of Israel, dietary laws, circumcision, and Sabbath observance (Barclay 1996: 399-444). Although our evidence is limited, we can suggest that many of these key facets of Jewish identity were important for the communities in Asia Minor.

Communal Life

The importance of local Jewish communities in Asia Minor for the preservation of Jewish identity is clear, for example, from the fact that communities petitioned the Roman authorities for the right to assemble and to govern their own communal life (*Ant.* 14.213-16). Synagogue buildings, festivals (e.g., *Ant.* 14.256-58), and Sabbath gatherings also played a part in fostering community life.

Links with Jerusalem

Links were maintained by Jews in Asia Minor with Jerusalem. Communities in Asia Minor seem to have faithfully paid the annual Temple tax to Jerusalem (e.g., Cicero, *Pro Flacco* 28.66-69), which shows the significance of the Temple and its worship and of Jerusalem to these communities (see also *Ant.* 16.167-68; 14.241-42; cf. Acts 2:9-11).

Torah and Temple Piety

The Torah was clearly vital for Jewish identity in Asia Minor. The importance of the Torah and the Temple is shown by the opposition of Jews from Asia and Cilicia (as well as elsewhere) to Stephen when they thought he was attacking the Temple and the unalterable nature of the Law (Acts 6:9-15). Jews in Asia Minor almost certainly opposed Paul (Acts 13:45, 50; 14:2-5, 19) because he did not require Gentile converts to come under the Torah (cf. Gal. 5:11; 6:12), a fact that shows the significance of the Torah for the Jews who opposed him (cf. Acts 21:27-29). A number of Jewish epitaphs contain grave curses that often draw on or allude to passages in the Septuagint, which suggests that the Scriptures functioned as an authority and guide for these communities. In both the Sardis and Priene synagogues, provision for the Law was a highly significant feature.

Other Practices and Beliefs

We have evidence that key Jewish practices and beliefs were important for the identity of the Jewish communities in Asia Minor. Worship of the one God of Israel was a feature of these communities (*Ant.* 12.126). Further, there is no clear evidence that these Jewish communities were syncretistic, as has sometimes been suggested (Trebilco 1991: 127-44). The importance of the Sabbath (*Ant.* 14.259-61), food laws (*Ant.* 14.225-27), and of following their "ancestral tradition" (*Ant.* 14.262-64) is shown by Jews in Asia Minor seeking permission from the Roman authorities with regard to these matters (*Ant.* 14.223-27).

Clear evidence for the retention of Jewish identity by these communities begins in the first century B.C.E. and continues through to the fourth century C.E. and later. Thus, these communities clearly understood themselves as Jewish. There is no clear evidence that Jewish communities in Asia Minor knew or followed rabbinic teaching, which in any case was not the "normative" form of Judaism in the Second Temple period.

Other Facets of Jewish Life

Women Leaders in Jewish Communities

Some inscriptions tell us about women leaders of Jewish communities. In the second or third century C.E., a woman named Rufina was *archisynagōgos* or "ruler of the synagogue" in Smyrna, and in the fourth century C.E. a certain Theopempte held the same office in Myndos. The title *archisynagōgis(s)a* is also found in an inscription from a town in Cappadocia (see *IJO*, vol. 2, no. 255). In Aphrodisias a person named Jael, who was probably a woman, held the title of *prostatēs*, indicating she was either "president" or "patron" of a group. Reynolds and Tannenbaum (1987), who originally published the inscription which mentions Jael, dated it to the early third century C.E.; however, Ameling (2004: 78-82) and Chaniotis (2000: 213-18) have recently argued for a date in the fourth or fifth century, while Gilbert (2004: 169-84) has advocated a fourth-century date. In Sebastopolis (in Bithynia/Pontus) an inscription from the fourth century tells us that a woman named Sara was a female elder (*presbytis;* see *IJO*, vol. 2, no. 161), and another inscription of the same date concerns one Lampetis, who is an *archōn* or "ruler" (*IJO*, vol. 2, no. 160). At Phocaea in Ionia in the third century C.E., a certain Tation built a synagogue for the community and was given a golden crown and the privilege of sitting in the seat of honor. We also know of nineteen women who made other donations to synagogues, either by themselves or jointly with their husbands.

Although the exact role women fulfilled when they held titles continues to be debated, a case can be made

ASIA MINOR

that women had a significant degree of involvement in leadership and patronage in some of the Jewish communities in Asia Minor (Trebilco 1991: 104-13). One reason for this was probably the prominence of women as benefactors and leaders in social and political life in Asia Minor in general. Thus, the Jewish communities were probably influenced by their environment in their openness to the involvement of women in the synagogue.

God-fearers

An inscription from Aphrodisias mentioned in the preceding section lists, along with a number of Jews (as is evident from many of their names), fifty-four Gentiles who are called *theosebis* [*sic*] (see Reynolds and Tannenbaum 1987). They seem to come into the category of "God-fearers," that is, Gentiles who could be formally associated with the Jewish community, were involved in at least some facets of synagogue life, and adopted some Jewish practices without becoming proselytes. Other inscriptions from Asia Minor indicating a strong probability that *theosebēs* designates a God-fearer come from Tralles, Sardis, and Miletus. God-fearers are most likely in view in Acts 13:16, 26, 50 and 14:1, although Luke uses different terms (see also *Ant.* 14.110). The existence of God-fearers points to the attraction of Gentiles to Judaism in Asia Minor and the openness of Jews to the involvement of Gentiles in their communities.

Jewish Communities in the Greek Cities

We have no clear evidence that Jews in Asia Minor possessed citizenship as a body in any Greek city. Josephus's statements suggesting that they did have citizenship (e.g., Josephus, *Ant.* 12.119; 12.125-26; 16.160; *Ag. Ap.* 2.37-39) are all historically dubious or ambiguous. Clearly, however, some individuals did obtain citizenship in their cities (e.g., Paul in Acts 21:39; see Trebilco 1991: 172). Some Jews in Asia Minor were also Roman citizens, "sufficiently many to make it worthwhile to issue special directives about them" (Barclay 1996: 271; see *Ant.* 14.10.13-19 §§228–40). Jews in Asia Minor, as elsewhere, generally organized themselves into communities, although the constitutional position of these communities varied from place to place and over time. The position of the Jewish community within any city probably depended on local factors such as when, how, and for what purpose it became established in that particular locality. The actual form of communal life probably varied from place to place, as is shown by the variety of terms used to express the notion of community, including the terms "the Jews," "the people," *synodos* ("assembly"), *katoikia* ("household"), *ethnos* ("people, nation") and *synagōgē* ("[place of] assembly, synagogue").

Periodic Hostility

Some Jewish communities in Asia Minor experienced periodic hostility from the cities in which they lived from 49 B.C.E. to 2 C.E., concerning matters such as synagogue assembly, the Temple tax, and observing the Sabbath (Josephus, *Ant.* 12.125-28; 14.185-267; 16.27-61, 160-78; Philo, *Legatio ad Gaium* 315; cf. Gruen 2002: 84-104). Such hostility was probably caused by the export of the Temple tax to Jerusalem at times when cities in Asia were experiencing severe economic problems, the lack of tolerance on the part of the cities toward communities that were distinctive and did not worship pagan gods, and the difficulties caused by significant Jewish groups that (for example) refused to attend court or do business on the Sabbath, thus creating awkward situations for the cities concerned.

Positive Relations

However, we have no evidence for hostility after 2 C.E., and positive evidence for good relations (see below) begins in the mid-first century C.E. and continues through to the end of the third century C.E. and beyond. Further, Jewish communities in Asia Minor did not support the Jews of Palestine in the war of 66-70 C.E., nor in the Bar Kokhba Revolt of 132-135 C.E.; and the Diaspora uprisings of 116-117 C.E. did not occur, as far as we know, in Asia Minor. Thus from early in the first century C.E., Jewish communities in Asia Minor seem to have lived peaceably and generally interacted positively with their wider communities, which was one factor that enabled them to flourish.

Active Civic Involvement

Some Jews and some Jewish communities took an active part in city life, into which they were integrated and socially assimilated to quite some degree. With regard to the first century B.C.E., Barclay (1996: 276-77) suggests: "The controversies which arose in these Asian cities reflect the significant integration of such Jews into civic life." We also know of Jews from the third century C.E. onward who held significant offices, such as the controller of the market, or city councilor in Acmonia, Aphrodisias, Corycos, Ephesus, Hypaepa, Sardis, and Side (e.g., *IJO*, vol. 2, nos. 32, 172, 220). Further, both the prominent position of the Sardis synagogue and the content of its inscriptions suggest that relations between the city of Sardis and the Jews were harmonious and that the community was a respected element in the city. There is also evidence of Jews being "good residents" who participated in the civic and cultural life of their cities, for example, by having the privilege of reserved seats in the Miletus theater or being involved in the Iasos and Hypaepa gymnasiums.

Jewish Influence in Apamea and Acmonia

A unique series of coins minted in Apamea from the end of the second century C.E. portrays Noah, his wife, and the ark. The coins suggest that the city of Apamea accepted the Jewish flood story as its own; the Jewish community seems to have been influential and respected in the city and able to convince the city of the validity of its own traditions. Important non-Jews also acted as patrons of, or were involved in or influenced by, Jewish communities. Thus, in Acmonia in the mid-first century C.E., the Gentile Julia Severa, who belonged to a nexus of leading families, built a synagogue for the Jewish community. According to Acts, some Jewish communities were able to stir up opposition to Christian preaching among Gentiles, including some in high places, which suggests that the Jewish communities concerned had influential contacts in their city (Acts 13:50; 14:2, 5, 19). Thus in Asia Minor Jewish communities were not isolated, insular groups but rather interacted regularly with Gentiles and were influential and respected in their cities, where they were very much at home and made a significant social contribution. Yet the evidence suggests that the Jewish communities generally did not abandon an active attention to Jewish tradition or compromise their Jewish identity.

Conclusions

The vitality of many of the Jewish communities in Asia Minor is clear from the evidence. The Sardis community, with its impressive synagogue, is perhaps the most revealing in this respect. And yet some communities, such as the community at Priene, were undoubtedly small. This underlines the diversity of these communities. Yet rather than forming introverted groups, these communities were at home in their local cities and interacted with the wider society. Some communities were influential and respected in their cities, and some attracted "God-fearers"; many were influenced by their environment and by local practices. Yet in many cases there is strong evidence for the retention of Jewish identity. It was as *Jewish* communities that they were a part of the life of their cities.

BIBLIOGRAPHY

W. AMELING 1996, "Die jüdischen Gemeinde im antiken Kleinasien," in *Jüdische Gemeinden und Organisationsformen von der Antike bis zur Gegenwart,* ed. R. Jütte and A. P. Kustermann, Vienna: Böhlau, 29-55. • W. AMELING, ED. 2004, *Inscriptiones Judaicae Orientis,* vol. 2, *Kleinasien,* Tübingen: Mohr-Siebeck. • J. M. G. BARCLAY 1996, *Jews in the Mediterranean Diaspora from Alexander to Trajan (323 BCE–117 CE),* Edinburgh: Clark, 259-81 • M. P. BONZ 1990, "The Jewish Community of Ancient Sardis: A Reassessment of its Rise to Prominence," *HSCP* 93: 343-59. • M. P. BONZ 1993, "Differing Approaches to Religious Benefaction: The Late Third-Century Acquisition of the Sardis Synagogue," *HTR* 86: 139-54. • M. P. BONZ 1994, "The Jewish Donor Inscriptions From Aphrodisias: Are They Both Third-Century, and Who Are the Theosebeis?" *HSCP* 96: 281-99. • M. P. BONZ 1999, "The Jewish Community of Ancient Sardis: Deconstruction and Reconstruction," in *Evolution of the Synagogue: Problems and Progress,* ed. H. C. Kee and L. H. Cohick, Harrisburg, Penn.: Trinity Press International, 106-22. • H. BOTERMANN 1990, "Die Synagogue von Sardes: Eine Synagogue aus dem 4. Jahrhundert?" *ZNW* 81: 103-21. • H. BOTERMANN 1993, "Griechisch-jüdische Epigraphik: Zur Datierung der Aphrodisias-Inschriften," *Zeitschrift für Papyrologie und Epigraphik* 98: 184-94. • A. CHANIOTIS 2002, "The Jews of Aphrodisias: New Evidence and Old Problems," *SCI* 22: 209-42. • F. M. CROSS 2002, "The Hebrew Inscriptions from Sardis," *HTR* 95: 3-19. • S. FINE, ED. 1996, *Sacred Realm: The Emergence of the Synagogue in the Ancient World,* New York: Oxford University Press. • E. L. GIBSON 2005, "Jews in the Inscriptions of Smyrna," *JJS* 56: 66-79. • G. GILBERT 2004, "Jews in Imperial Administration and Its Significance for Dating the Jewish Donor Inscription from Aphrodisias," *JSJ* 35: 169-84. • M. GOODMAN, ED. 1998, *Jews in a Graeco-Roman World,* Oxford: Clarendon. • E. S. GRUEN 2002, *Diaspora: Jews amidst Greeks and Romans,* Cambridge: Harvard University Press. • R. HACHLILI 1998, *Ancient Jewish Art and Archaeology in the Diaspora,* Leiden: Brill. • J. W. VAN HENTEN AND P. W. VAN DER HORST, EDS. 1994, *Studies in Early Jewish Epigraphy,* Leiden: Brill. • J. W. VAN HENTEN WITH A. BIJ DE VAATE 1996, "Jewish or Non-Jewish? Some Remarks on the Identification of Jewish Inscriptions from Asia Minor," *Bibliotheca Orientalis* 53: 16-28. • P. W. VAN DER HORST 1990, *Essays on the Jewish World of Early Christianity,* Freiburg: Universitätsverlag; Göttingen: Vandenhoeck & Ruprecht. • J. H. KROLL 2001, "The Greek Inscriptions of the Sardis Synagogue," *HTR* 94: 5-127 • I. LEVINSKAYA 1996, *The Book of Acts in Its Diaspora Setting,* Grand Rapids: Eerdmans. • E. MIRANDA 1999, "La comunità giudaica di Hierapolis di Frigia," *Epigraphica Anatolica* 31: 109-56. • B. OLSSON AND M. ZETTERHOLM, EDS. 2003, *The Ancient Synagogue from Its Origins until 200 C.E.,* Stockholm: Almqvist & Wiksell. • J. A. OVERMAN AND R. S. MACLENNAN, EDS. 1992, *Diaspora Jews and Judaism: Essays in Honor of, and in Dialogue with, A. Thomas Kraabel,* Atlanta: Scholars Press. • M. PUCCI BEN ZEEV 1998, *Jewish Rights in the Roman World: The Greek and Roman Documents Quoted by Josephus Flavius,* Tübingen: Mohr-Siebeck. • T. RAJAK 2001, *The Jewish Dialogue with Greece and Rome: Studies in Cultural and Social Interaction,* Leiden: Brill. • J. REYNOLDS AND R. TANNENBAUM 1987, *Jews and Godfearers at Aphrodisias: Greek Inscriptions with Commentary,* Cambridge: Cambridge Philological Society. • E. SCHÜRER 1973-87, *The History of the Jewish People in the Age of Jesus Christ,* 3 vols., rev. and ed. G. Vermes et al., Edinburgh: Clark. • P. R. Trebilco 1991, *Jewish Communities in Asia Minor,* Cambridge: Cambridge University Press. • B. WANDER 1998, *Gottesfürchtige und Sympathisanten: Studien zum heidnischen Umfeld von Diasporasynagogen,* Tübingen: Mohr-Siebeck. • M. H. WILLIAMS 1998, *The Jews among the Greeks and Romans: A Diaspora Sourcebook,* London: Duckworth.

See also: Antioch (Pisidian); Aphrodisias; God-fearers; Sardis PAUL TREBILCO

Assimilation, Acculturation, Accommodation

The terms *assimilation, acculturation,* and *accommodation* are used by sociologists and anthropologists with a range of meanings and a variety of nuance. They refer to the effects of contact and interaction between two or more distinct culture-bearing groups, but in some cases they are used more or less interchangeably, in others they have quite specific, but not standard, meanings. The term *assimilation* often carries a negative nuance, especially within anthropology, where it has implicitly signaled the dilution or loss of a pure or original culture; the others often bear a melancholic tone by association. In the case of early Judaism, scholars since the nineteenth century have generally adopted the Maccabean rhetoric of a fundamental antithesis be-

ASSIMILATION, ACCULTURATION, ACCOMMODATION

tween Judaism and Hellenism, so that any degree and almost any kind of Hellenization is taken to represent a deviation from authentic (or orthodox) Judaism. To gain a more accurate perspective on the cultural processes at work in the homeland or the Diaspora, one must either jettison these terms altogether (see Gruen 1998) or redefine them, in line with contemporary anthropological models. To follow this second route would be to recognize that (1) cultural change is continuous (no culture is static); (2) the effects of cultural contact are often bilateral, not simply unilateral (depending on the power relations between the two cultural entities); (3) cultural interaction can result in positive and creative cultural development; and (4) ethnic groups can remain relatively stable so long as they maintain some boundaries, even if there is considerable social and cultural contact across those boundaries, and even if the cultural "stuff" on each side of the boundary is largely identical. This last point, associated especially with the work of F. Barth (1969), suggests that there might be many cultural expressions of Judaism (Hellenistic, Egyptian, Roman, etc.) without threat to the integrity of the Jewish people, so long as certain agreed boundaries were maintained.

The analysis of cultural contact and its influences is bound to be complex and multi-dimensional. There are different kinds of contact, different spheres in which it operates, different degrees of engagement, and different levels of significance accorded to particular practices or beliefs. In the Hellenistic era it apparently mattered a thousand times more if a Jewish man was Hellenized in his genitals than if he was Hellenized in his speech: we need to be able to explain why. The *Letter of Aristeas* appears to us deeply Hellenized in its genre, moral norms, and philosophical values, yet it celebrates the preservation by Jews of "impenetrable fences and iron walls" (139). One way to resolve this apparent paradox is to distinguish between *assimilation* (forms of material or social convergence) and *acculturation* (the sharing of symbols, norms, and values). As the above examples indicate, it is possible to be deeply acculturated while maintaining key restrictions in certain aspects of social or material practice. We may reserve for a third category, *accommodation,* a rather different form of analysis; here the question is how agents employ the fruits of cultural interaction, to integrate the two cultures or, ironically, to defend and even extend the differentials between them (Barclay 1996: 82-102). Thus we may give further and distinct meanings to our three terms as follows:

Assimilation

If we deliberately limit the scope of this term to the material/physical and social/political dimensions of cultural practice, we may include under this heading the variety of ways in which Jews in our period adopted the artistic and architectural styles of other cultures, and were apparently little different from others in clothes or physical appearance, except in one very significant particular: the preservation of male circumcision. The significance of this trait in the choice of sexual partners, and thus in preserving the genealogical basis of Jewish ethnicity, is obvious (see Josephus, *Ant.* 1.192). In the social and political spheres, we find Jews playing prominent political roles in Hellenistic courts and in the corridors of Roman power (e.g., the Herodians, Dositheos in Alexandria, Tiberius Julius Alexander), acquiring citizen rites in Alexandria and elsewhere (or, on occasion, Roman citizenship), serving in numerous military roles alongside non-Jews, working as traders, farmhands, and artisans in the Egyptian countryside, negotiating with non-Jewish patrons and sympathizers, serving as slaves in Gentile homes, attending and participating in theaters and athletic competitions, and intermarrying with non-Jews (for Palestinian Judaism, see Hengel 1974; for the Diaspora, see Barclay 1996 and Collins 2000). Sociologically what matters in such contacts is their depth and breadth — the range of networks they entail and their wider influence on customs and habits. Where this influence touched issues of symbolic significance within the Jewish community (e.g., diet or Sabbath observance, regarded as distinctive ancestral customs), such assimilation took on particular importance; and for obvious reasons exogamy entailed a degree of assimilation strongly criticized in many of our early Jewish sources.

Acculturation

If we restrict this to less tangible aspects of cultural engagement (forms of communication, values, and norms), we may assess under this heading the ways in which Jewish self-expression and values were influenced by the cultures they experienced. In the Hellenistic era the adoption of Greek is an obvious example (and the Septuagint translation its necessary outcome). The extant Jewish literature in Greek also adopts many rhetorical and literary forms from its Mediterranean environment, such as the tragedy (*Exagōgē* by Ezekiel), the collection of maxims (the *Sentences* of Pseudo-Phocylides), the novel (*Joseph and Aseneth),* allegorical exegesis (Philo), and the large-scale history (Josephus). Within such literature we find Jews absorbing moral and philosophical norms, and even elements of Egyptian folklore (Artapanus).

The dimension we loosely characterize as religious is, in fact, an amalgam of social practices, artistic traditions, and philosophical beliefs. The Jewish tradition was particularly sensitive to the use of physical representations of the divine (with some ambiguities in definition), and generally averse to the Greek tradition of mythology; but Greek religious philosophy (especially Platonic and Stoic) was readily adopted by thinkers such as Aristobulus and Philo. Social practices include the linguistic (e.g., the use of religious formulas, or adoption of religious nomenclature), the artifactual (e.g., amulets, grave inscriptions, incantation bowls), and the ritual (sacrifices and prayers). Where Jews consistently adopted what were considered Greek rites, they were generally considered to have strayed too far from their "ancestral constitution" (e.g., Antiochus at Antioch, Josephus, *J.W.* 7.46-53); but there appears to have been some range of opinion and practice in other respects, with varying understandings of what constituted idolatry.

Accommodation

The question here is the ways in which the products of cultural confluence are put to use, the social and political agendas pursued by those in the "contact zone." Some Jewish literature in Greek seems designed primarily to build bridges of understanding between cultures (e.g., *Letter of Aristeas*); some, deeply influenced by Hellenistic *paideia,* takes a far more antagonistic stance, using Greek tools to lambast "Greeks" (e.g., 4 Maccabees). Most contains a complex and variable mixture of both strategies, remaining distinctively Jewish in its placement of the Jewish people as superior in antiquity, virtue, or access to philosophical truth. In this respect, such literature often reflects the ambiguity identified by postcolonial theory in the phenomenon of *hybridity,* where the adoption and adaptation of elements in the dominant culture can result in a subtle subversion of its universal claims. In any case, Jews often discovered means within other cultures with which to defend, develop, and bolster their own ethnic interests.

The political settlements encouraged by both Hellenistic and Roman rulers generally favored polyethnic pluralism rather than cultural or ethnic fusion, and in these circumstances it was normally possible for Jews to retain their ethnic institutions and the customs they considered most essential for their survival as an ethnic group. Endued with sufficient flexibility to adapt elements of the cultures they inhabited, the Jewish tradition also preserved sufficient self-regulating mechanisms (community leaders, with the common touchstone of the Torah) to enable a selective screening of the "ingested" material. Critically, Jews generally maintained key boundary markers, such as dietary restrictions, male circumcision, and an exclusive and aniconic religious practice, which gave a distinct character to the Jewish family and enabled the wider Jewish community to set limits to Jewish assimilation, and to make demanding requirements of those who wished to enter the community via proselytism.

BIBLIOGRAPHY

J. M. G. BARCLAY 1996, *Jews in the Mediterranean Diaspora from Alexander to Trajan (323 BCE–117 CE),* Edinburgh: Clark • F. BARTH, ED. 1969, *Social Groups and Boundaries: The Social Organisation of Cultural Difference,* London: Allen and Unwin • J. J. COLLINS 2000, *Between Athens and Jerusalem: Jewish Identity in the Hellenistic Diaspora,* 2d ed., Grand Rapids: Eerdmans • L. H. FELDMAN 1993, *Jew and Gentile in the Ancient World: Attitudes and Interactions from Alexander to Justinian,* Princeton: Princeton University Press • E. S. GRUEN 1998, *Heritage and Hellenism: The Reinvention of Jewish Tradition,* Berkeley: University of California Press • E. S. GRUEN 2002, *Diaspora: Jews amidst Greeks and Romans,* Cambridge: Harvard University Press. • M. HENGEL 1974, *Judaism and Hellenism: Studies in Their Encounter in Palestine during the Early Hellenistic Period,* London: SCM.

See also: Gentiles, Jewish Attitudes toward; Greek Philosophy; Greek Religion; Hellenism, Hellenization

JOHN M. G. BARCLAY

Associations

Associations are groups of individuals that voluntarily unite around a common interest and organize themselves into more or less permanent form by means of a formal, legally binding contract defining members' obligations to each other and to the society. In the Greco-Roman world, the size, purpose, organization, social status, and terms for voluntary associations and their members varied tremendously. Nevertheless certain features recur frequently enough to warrant mention: (1) obligation to associational by-laws or *nomoi;* (2) "democratic" authority; (3) scrutiny of initiates; (4) scrutiny of new officers and their duties; (5) dues and special fees; (6) meetings and banquets; (7) veneration of patrons or founders.

Associations in Early Judaism

Such features appear not only in the *nomoi* of Greco-Roman professional guilds, cultic groups, and other associations, but also in those of early Jewish societies. Arguably the strongest parallels between early Jewish and Greco-Roman associations come in the rule scrolls of the covenanters at Qumran (1QS; 1QSa; CD), which contain regulations on initiation, liturgy, meetings and communal meals, penal codes, and mention officers entrusted with specific tasks (see Weinfeld 1986). The tractate *Demai* in the Mishnah and Tosefta contains allusive descriptions of an association of "comrades" (*ḥăbērîm,* sg. *ḥābēr*) dedicated to strict observation of food purity laws. The *ḥăbērîm,* commonly regarded as a Pharisaic movement, also regulated initiation and possibly recognized a hierarchy of rank. Further evidence for Jewish associations appears in the descriptions of the Essenes and Therapeutae in Philo and Josephus, as well as in the literary and epigraphical evidence for Jewish synagogues in cities throughout the Mediterranean world. Comparative studies of Jewish and Greco-Roman associational activity reveal that Jewish communities in Palestine and the Diaspora fully participated in the general flourishing of associations in the Greco-Roman era.

Flourishing of Associations in the Greco-Roman era

While a few voluntary associations may be identified in the fifth century B.C.E. and earlier, the vast majority of evidence for their activity comes in the Greco-Roman era. Many scholars believe that the abundance of evidence from this period is not accidental but points to an unprecedented flourishing of voluntary associations throughout the Mediterranean world during the Greek and Roman imperial eras. The causes of this flourishing are not well understood, and for quite some time the theory prevailed that associations formed to compensate for the loss of traditional civic structures. Alongside this decline comes the idea that imperial authorities were, as a rule, hostile to the formation of vol-

ASSOCIATIONS

untary associations, and that they tolerated only those that were so well established that they could not be forced out of existence, such as cultic societies, or those that contributed directly to the welfare of the state. This highly negative view may be explained by the bias of the literary evidence, which treats associational activity almost exclusively when discussing problems, such as immoral behavior in second-century-B.C.E. Roman Dionysiac societies, riots at Rome by Jews under Claudius, riots during games at Pompeii during Nero's reign, or political subterfuge from Democratic Athens to the late Roman Republic and early Principate.

Inscriptional and papyrological evidence from the associations themselves suggests a much different story. Throughout the inscriptions we find evidence for cooperative and sometimes quite long-term relationships between associations and imperial authorities and their representatives. Frequently associational inscriptions celebrate the patronage of an imperial benefactor or other prominent citizen, and extend honorary membership to the patron. Even emperors who appear to have had the harshest attitudes toward associations in the literary texts, such as Trajan, receive such honors (*Inschriften von Ephesos* 3329). Associational inscriptions are distributed relatively evenly in time and space throughout the Greco-Roman Mediterranean (although Asia Minor is especially rich in inscriptions, and of course Egypt in papyri). This distribution gives the impression that associations were in fact an established and accepted social phenomenon. The nature of the evidence (expensive public inscriptions) and their contents, which repeatedly commemorate positive relations between the imperial regime and associations, suggest that the flourishing of associations and the spread of empires indeed went hand in hand. Contrary to the former view, however, it appears that associational flourishing resulted not from a decline in civic structures and morale, but from a new infusion of public interest and resources into private life.

Legal Status of Associations

The most important law on associations, according to the Roman jurist Gaius (*Digest of Justinian* 47.22.4), was composed by the Athenian reformer Solon. Solon's law suggests a positive state attitude toward associations; it assumes that they exist just as legitimately as short-term business contracts and extends legal protection to the terms of statutes, as long as associational activity does not violate state laws.

When associational activity became problematic, the state responded by withdrawing its guarantee that the statutes would be enforced, and by prohibiting members engaging in the contracts by which associations were formed. For example, when Roman Dionysiac societies became problematic, the Senate prohibited meetings, celebration of rites, election of officers, maintenance of a common fund, and the mutual obligations and contracts by which members forged a common identity (*Inscriptiones Latinae Selectae* 18). Similarly, Claudius punished restive Jewish associations in Rome by prohibiting their assemblies (Dio Cassius 60.6.6). It is important to note that where we find evidence of Roman suppression of associational activity it is local, limited in duration, and usually aimed at a specific group or set of groups. At no time do we find general laws prohibiting associations forming; rather, from time to time the authorities targeted specific associations that were causing or contributing to public disorder, or in some cases were thought to be potential threats.

Classifying Associations

It is notoriously difficult to formulate a typology that neatly accommodates ancient voluntary associations. Classification on the basis of purpose has a long history, and for good reason; some associations articulate their interests and purpose so clearly that they may be relatively easily categorized as "professional," "cultic," "ethnic," "mutual aid," "scholastic," "recreational," or "political." Numerous associations formed among merchants, such as salt sellers, stone carvers, and dyers of cloth. Another common type is the "mutual-aid society," which seems to have enabled relatively poor members to pool their resources in order to ensure that each could obtain support in hard times and, at life's end, a proper burial (e.g., *Inscriptiones Latinae Selectae* 7216). Ethnic groups formed societies throughout the cities; we find associations of merchants from Citium and Egypt in Athens, and in Jerusalem associations of Jews formed on the basis of their native cities: Cyrene, Alexandria, Cilicia, and Libya (Acts 6:9). Philosophical schools are perhaps the easiest to identify.

But the divisions between the types of groups rapidly breaks down when we take full account of the role that cult and political interest played in the formation of numerous associations. No association appears to have lacked a religious identity; merchants, "mutual-aid" and recreational societies, and philosophical schools commonly honored one god or group of gods as patron deities and structured activities to include their worship. Similarly, associations of all kinds appear to have cultivated political relations and interests; in the early second century C.E. the emperor Trajan denied a group's request to form a firefighters association because, he predicted, all such groups eventually devolve into politically disruptive parties. As we know from Cicero's descriptions of Roman politics, as well as from graffiti in Pompeii, associations of various types supported political candidates, sometimes violently. Another problem arises when we attempt to distinguish "recreational" societies from the others: all groups formed at least in part so that members could cultivate relationships with peers. Further, one of the commonest features of associational life is the banquet with wine, without which it seems unlikely that an association could attract members at all.

Other typologies have been proposed. Harland based his analysis upon five "webs of social connections" out of which associations arise: household, ethnicity, neighborhood, occupation, and cult. While this typology is similar to that based on purpose, it emphasizes the local character of associations and the social interactions out of which they typically developed (Harland 2003). Another typology takes into account the radical difference between associations that assimilated the ideology of the state, and those that resisted it. *Assimilative civic ideology* provides the foundation for claiming a place within civic institutions. It is found among numerous cultic groups, ethnic associations, "mutual aid societies," and professional guilds. On the other hand, *alternative civic ideologies* enabled participants to imagine themselves as citizens of a commonwealth superior to that which presently held power. The alternative, superior commonwealth generally coincided with the association (e.g., Stoic, Cynic, and Epicurean philosophical schools; Pauline *ekklēsiai;* and the covenanters at Qumran who wrote the Dead Sea Scrolls).

BIBLIOGRAPHY

R. ASCOUGH 2003, *Paul's Macedonian Associations: The Social Context of Philippians and 1 Thessalonians,* Tübingen: Mohr-Siebeck. • A. BAUMGARTEN 1998, "Graeco-Roman Voluntary Associations and Ancient Jewish Sects," in *Jews in a Graeco-Roman World,* ed. M. Goodman, Oxford: Clarendon, 93-111, 261-64. • N. BELAYCHE AND S. MIMOUNI, EDS. 2003, *Les communautés religieuses dans le monde gréco-romain: essais de definition,* Paris: Brepols. • Y. M. GILLIHAN 2007, *Civic Ideology among the Covenanters of the Dead Sea Scrolls and Other Greco-Roman Voluntary Associations,* Dissertation, University of Chicago. • P. HARLAND 2003, *Associations, Synagogues, and Congregations: Claiming a Place in Ancient Mediterranean Society,* Minneapolis: Fortress. • J. KLOPPENBORG AND S. WILSON, EDS. 1996, *Voluntary Associations in the Graeco-Roman World,* London: Routledge. • M. WEINFELD 1986, *The Organizational Pattern and the Penal Code of the Qumran Sect: A Comparison with Guilds and Religious Associations of the Hellenistic-Roman Period,* Fribourg: Editions Universitaires; Göttingen: Vandenhoeck & Ruprecht.

See also: Essenes; Sectarianism; Synagogues; Therapeutae YONDER MOYNIHAN GILLIHAN

Astronomy and Astrology

In antiquity the terms "astronomy" and "astrology" were used interchangeably. Ancient scholars were aware of the distinction between the two concepts implied by these words nowadays: one whereby we understand the movements of the sun, moon, and planets in relation to each other and to the earth; the other whereby we determine the influences that these configurations in relation to the zodiac exert on earth and human beings (Ptolemy of Alexandria, *Tetrabiblos* 1.1.1). Yet both lines of inquiry were often intimately related.

Both astronomy and astrology progressed tremendously from the Persian period onward. Mathematical models were developed to predict the recurrence of astronomical phenomena, and the zodiac was introduced as a schematic division of the ecliptic into twelve sections of 30° each. The signs of the zodiac enabled a more exact means of reference for computing and recording planetary positions. This knowledge was transmitted to Greece and to Greek-speaking Egypt before and during the Hellenistic period where it further developed.

Jewish interest in astronomy and astrology surfaces in the Hellenistic and Roman periods in Enochic literature and the Dead Sea Scrolls. The interest in astronomy was primarily for calendrical purposes. The relevance of astrological geography behind the animal imagery in Daniel 8 is debated, while the dating of the *Treatise of Shem* to the Second Temple period is uncertain. References to Abraham as astrological teacher and to astrological books by him indicate that an astrological work attributed to Abraham circulated in antiquity. The only evidence, however, for Jewish astrological literature comes from the Dead Sea Scrolls.

The earliest Jewish astronomical work is the *Astronomical Book* (*1 Enoch* 72–82). Composed in Aramaic in the third century B.C.E. or even earlier, the most complete text is extant in Ethiopic translation. Four Aramaic copies (4Q208-211), containing only the *Astronomical Book,* have turned up at Qumran. The oldest fragments date to the late third or early second century B.C.E. (4Q208).

The *Astronomical Book* purports to be a revelation by the angel Uriel to Enoch about the motion of the heavenly luminaries. *1 Enoch* 72 has the sun rising through six gates in the east and setting through six gates in the west, thus describing the declination of the sun's rising and setting points on the horizon during twelve months. The gates have nothing to do with zodiacal signs but refer to amplitudes of ca. 10° on the horizon. In addition, chap. 72 records the annual variation in the length of daytime and nighttime. This variation is measured on a scale of eighteen, reflecting an M:m ratio of 2:1, which results in a simple linear zigzag function rooted in Babylonian astronomy. Originally counting a 360-day year, the *Astronomical Book* subsequently developed the tradition of a 364-day year. After the year was divided into twelve months of thirty days each, an extra day was added between the seasons, at the end of months three, six, nine, and twelve. Leaders of stars who guard the correct course of the sun at the equinoxes and solstices rule these four extra days (*1 Enoch* 75:1-3; 82:4-8).

1 Enoch 73 has a fragmentary description of a linear scheme for the illumination of the moon's surface for the first two days of a lunar month, counting with both sevenths and fourteenths. *1 Enoch* 74:1-9 deals with the moon's illumination for the first fifteen days, but mainly describes the moon's course through the six gates, which it completes in one month. *1 Enoch* 78 and 79 constitute alternative attempts to align the moon's illumination with the solar course through the six gates. The so-called synchronistic calendar in the Aramaic fragments from Qumran (4Q208-209) contains a longer and more detailed description of most of the above elements. When the moon waxes it receives light every day over 1/14 of its surface, and when it wanes it loses light every day over 1/14 of its surface. However, Drawnel recently proposed that the Aramaic fragments mainly deal with the duration of lunar visibility during the night and day, similar to tablet 14 of the Babylonian as-

ASTRONOMY AND ASTROLOGY

trological series *Enuma Anu Enlil.* Increase and decrease of the illumination of the moon's surface are only marginal in the Aramaic text.

The Ethiopic *Astronomical Book* holds no concrete data for the stars, but 4Q211 shows that mathematical figures were used to measure some form of stellar phenomenon. The planets are not treated. Until now we lack Second Temple Jewish sources that mention or describe the planets by name (but see 4Q552-553 for a possible reference in an astrological sense). This lack of planetary data may be due to theological reasons (fear of idolatry) or simply a lack of skills to compute their movement.

The astronomy in the *Astronomical Book* reaches back to older Mesopotamian examples from the first half of the first millennium B.C.E. *(Enuma Anu Enlil, MUL.APIN)* and does not reflect contemporary Mesopotamian and Greek mathematical astronomy. Some Qumran calendar texts (4Q320, 4Q321, and 4Q321a) may have been influenced by later Babylonian lunar tradition, but this still represents nonmathematical astronomy. In Jewish tradition the *Astronomical Book* influenced other texts, such as the lunar phases in steps of 1/14 of the moon's illumination in 4Q317 and 4Q503. Together with other texts that consider lunar phases (4Q319, 4Q320-321a), this shows that antilunar polemics (*Jub.* 6:36) were not significant in Jewish calendrical discourse.

Whereas the *Astronomical Book* and related texts represent nonobservational, schematic astronomy, a stone disc from Qumran has been interpreted in various ways as an astronomical measuring device. Perhaps this object signifies the practice of observational astronomy, but its identification as well as how it worked is debated.

Two important areas of ancient astrology, general and individual, are both represented in the Dead Sea Scrolls. The Aramaic text 4Q318 covers mundane astrology dealing with peoples, provinces, and the palace, while 4Q186 points to personal astrology by referring to a person's horoscope. 4Q318 was copied around the turn of the era. The text consists of two parts: a *selenodromion* and a *brontologion.* The selenodromion describes the synodic movement of the moon through the zodiac during twelve months of thirty days each, counting a 360-day year. The schematic pattern of the lunar course, assuming a daily lunar velocity of 13;35,10°, is 2-2-3; 2-2-3; 2-2-3; 2-2-3; 2. After twenty-eight days the moon has traversed all twelve zodiacal signs and returns on the last two days to the sign in which it began. Thus, each new month the moon begins in another sign. Curiously, the cycle begins with the sign Taurus, not with Aries, but this has not been satisfactorily explained yet. The brontologion has predictions for when it thunders, presumably at the moment when the moon is in one of the signs. This sort of text appears both in Babylonian and Greco-Roman astrological traditions. It is possible that the Aramaic manuscripts 4Q552-553 also indicate general astrological interests. Spirits that appear as four trees and rule over certain geographical areas (Babylon and Persia are mentioned) may represent the four planets (Jupiter, Mars, Saturn, and Venus) connected with the four cardinal directions.

Unlike ancient horoscopes available in Babylonian, Greek, and Latin, there are no actual Jewish horoscopes in Hebrew or Aramaic extant from the Second Temple period. There are literary references to horoscopes in the Dead Sea Scrolls, to be sure. The Aramaic text 4Q534 refers to the horoscope *(molad)* of the elect of God. In *Instruction* the reader is encouraged to learn or examine people's horoscopes (4Q415 11 11; 4Q416 2 iii 9 [= 4Q418 9 + 8]; 4Q416 2 iii 20 [= 4Q418 10a, b 3]; 4Q417 2 i 11 [= 4Q416 2 i 6]; 4Q418 202 1). In *Instruction* and *Mysteries* the phrase *bet moledim* refers to people's horoscopes (4Q299 1 4; 3a ii–b 13; 5 5; 4Q415 2 ii 9). These general references do not go into any technical astrological details, and the manuscripts are too fragmentary to understand the original context.

Knowledge concerning celestial matters was controversial. Continuing older traditions (Deut. 4:19; 17:3; 18:10; Isa. 47:13; Jer. 10:2; Job 31:26-27), some Jewish sources rejected the interest in astronomy and astrology. Ben Sira's remark not to investigate things too difficult or hidden (Sir. 3:21-22) was possibly directed against contemporary celestial speculations (see also Philo, *On Dreams* 1.52-54; *Migration* 184). The Enochic *Book of the Watchers* (8:3) and *Jubilees* (8:3) trace astrological learning back to fallen angels. This is perhaps why the Enochic *Astronomical Book* ignores the astrologically important zodiacal signs. *Jubilees* 12:16-18 has Abraham observing the stars before leaving Ur and his astrological interests behind. Philo of Alexandria explained Abraham's emigration allegorically as a rejection of astrology (*Abraham* 68–84; *Migration* 176–87; cf. also *Heir* 96–99; Josephus, *Ant.* 1.155-57). Yet Jewish writers could also take pride in claiming that astrological learning originated with Enoch or Abraham, the latter instructing the Phoenicians and Egyptians about it (Artapanus in Eusebius, *Praep. Evang.* 9.18.1; Pseudo-Eupolemus in Eusebius, *Praep. Evang.* 9.17.2-9 [cf. also 9.18.2]; Josephus, *Ant.* 1.167-68; Josephus is somewhat ambivalent in his appreciation of astrology; see also *Ant.* 1.106). There simply was no ancient Jewish monolithic stance on astronomy and astrology.

BIBLIOGRAPHY

M. ALBANI 1994, *Astronomie und Schöpfungsglaube: Untersuchungen zum astronomischen Henochbuch,* Neukirchen-Vluyn: Neukirchener Verlag. • J. BEN-DOV 2008, *Head of All Years: Astronomy and Calendars at Qumran in Their Ancient Context,* Leiden: Brill. • H. DRAWNEL 2007, "Moon Computation in the *Aramaic Astronomical Book,*" *RevQ* 23: 3-41. • R. LEICHT 2006, *Untersuchungen zur Geschichte des astrologischen Literatur der Juden,* Tübingen: Mohr-Siebeck. • M. POPOVIĆ 2007, *Reading the Human Body: Physiognomics and Astrology in the Dead Sea Scrolls and Hellenistic–Early Roman Period Judaism,* Leiden: Brill.

See also: Horoscopes MLADEN POPOVIĆ

Athletics

Greek and Roman Practices

Greek athletics usually implied sports practiced in competitions for prizes. Classical forms are attested by the sixth century B.C.E. Competitions occurred during funerals for the elite and Pan-Hellenic games at Olympia, Delphi, Isthmia, and Nemea. These included chariot races, horseback races, footraces with and without armor, wrestling, and boxing. Other events were the *pankration* (which combined grappling and striking) and the *pentathlon* (which included a footrace, wrestling, discus throwing, javelin throwing, and the long jump). Prizes included crowns, trophies, and eventually cash.

Many factors contributed to the vitality of Greek athletics. Athletics was useful for military training, recreation, and entertainment. Athletic games celebrated many of the same ideals expressed in contests between musicians, poets, and playwrights. These included "excellence" (*aretē*, which embraced physical and intellectual virtue). Ancient medical treatises recommended the benefits of physical exercise. Patronage of athletics by kings and aristocrats redistributed wealth to lower classes in exchange for prestige and power. All of these factors contributed to the later adoption of Greek athletics by Jews.

In the Hellenistic period cities in the Near East began instituting athletic games on the Greek model. Typically these occurred during religious festivals at intervals of one to five years. Women appeared in games with increasing frequency as spectators, but opportunities for athletic training and competition by females were limited. In contrast, male citizens of all ages exercised regularly in the gymnasium found in any *polis* (a city with a Hellenistic constitution and a democratic assembly). Teenage males called ephebes (Gr. *ephēboi*) also passed through the ephebate (Gr. *ephēbeia*), a youth organization that consisted of formal training in athletics and other skills in the gymnasium.

By the Roman period, elite patronage of athletics had produced a massive infrastructure of buildings and industry. Cities enticed famous professional athletes from other regions through offers of citizenship and financial rewards. Increased ease of travel fostered guilds of roving athletes and a lively trade in beasts for Roman hunting shows.

The Romans introduced gladiatorial combats, which involved the use of weapons. In contrast to Greek contests between free citizens, Roman citizens of both genders traditionally appeared only as spectators in gladiatorial events. Most gladiators were male slaves. Daring free persons usually became gladiators only to escape poverty or win glory. Probably some Jews became gladiators for similar reasons (as later in *b. Giṭṭin* 46b–47a). Combats between professional gladiators were separate from combats between condemned criminals or defeated enemies, which were public executions. Typical examples include the Jews sent to the arena by Titus in 70 C.E. and the spectacles reportedly celebrated in Cyrenaica by victorious Jewish rebels in 116 C.E. (Josephus, *J.W.* 6.418; 7.23-24, 37-40, 96; Dio Cassius 68.32).

In addition to gymnasia, athletics required stadiums (for footraces and other events) and a Greek hippodrome or Roman circus (for horseback and chariot racing). Roman recreational practices promoted the building of public baths adjacent to gymnasia. These often included swimming pools and areas for ball playing. Roman spectacles usually were held in amphitheaters, which contained oval or elliptical arenas. Jewish elites occasionally were invited into the seating reserved for Roman upper classes (Josephus, *Ant.* 14.210).

Jewish Patronage and Participation

Comparison with other Near Eastern cultures suggests that Israelite and Jewish sports before the Hellenistic period included board games, footraces, wrestling, hunting, javelin throwing, and archery (e.g., Josephus, *Ag. Ap.* 1.200-204). The scarcity of evidence for these activities testifies to the contrast with the greater institutionalization found in Greek athletics. Indigenous traditions still helped Jews to adopt Greek athletics after the conquest of Alexander the Great.

One early Jewish patron of Greek athletics was the high priest Jason, who persuaded the Seleucid king Antiochus IV to allow him to establish a gymnasium in Jerusalem ca. 175 B.C.E. (1 Macc. 1:11-15; 2 Macc. 4:7-15). Many Jews welcomed this satellite campus for citizenship in Antioch. Later policies of Antiochus incited the Maccabean revolt, but the Hasmoneans who led the revolt did not destroy Jason's gymnasium. Probably it continued to be used for military and athletic training until 70 C.E. Hasmonean recreational tastes are indicated by the two swimming pools that John Hyrcanus I built at his palace in Jericho ca. 125-115 B.C.E. The twin pools may have been for different genders. Larger pools were added by Alexander Jannaeus. Herod the Great joined these together and built pools for his palaces in other cities. Roman models suggest that some structures in the palaces in Jericho may have been used as exercise yards (*palaestrae;* Varro, *De Re Rustica* 2.2).

Herod's gifts to Gentile cities included gymnasia, endowments for gymnasiarchies, and funding for the Olympic games (Josephus, *J.W.* 1.422-27; *Ant.* 16.147-49; *SEG* 45:1131; possibly *IJO* 1, Ach74). He built athletic complexes in Jerusalem, Caesarea, Jericho, Sebaste, and other cities in Palestine (*Ant.* 15.268, 341; 17.161; etc.). These often combined in one structure the functions of hippodrome, amphitheater, and stadium. Herod also established games in honor of Augustus at Jerusalem and Caesarea (*J.W.* 1.415; *Ant.* 15.268; 16.136-41). Herod's descendants continued his practices on a less ambitious scale. For example, the stadium at Tiberias and hippodrome at Tarichaeae probably were funded by Antipas (*J.W.* 2.599, 618; *Life* 92, 132). Consistent with his Roman upbringing, Agrippa I built an amphitheater in Berytus and celebrated its dedication with combats between 1,400 criminals (*Ant.* 19.335-37).

Patronage of athletics sometimes generated accusations of idolatry and other charges against these Jewish rulers (2 Macc. 4:17-20; Josephus, *Ant.* 15.267-91; 19.343-47; probably 19.332-34). These criticisms seem to have been aroused more often by games honoring imperial dynasties and deities than by buildings for athletics in Jewish cities. Probably these buildings were decorated with more restraint in this period than athletic complexes in Gentile cities, which were embellished with statues and altars for deities and rulers (contrast *Ant.* 15.272-79). Religious obstacles encountered by Jewish athletes in the Diaspora are exemplified by inscriptions mentioning Jewish youths enrolled in the ephebate, which registered their devotion to Hermes, Herakles, and other deities (*IJO* 1, Ach53; *IJO* 2:22, 47; *CJZC* 41; explicitly, *CJZC* 6, 7). Polytheistic practice was ubiquitous in Gentile cities, however, so accommodation was endemic to Diaspora life.

Athletics did present special challenges. Trainers and administrators of athletic institutions were often unsympathetic to Jewish purity laws (cf. Josephus, *Ant.* 12.120). Some Jews found athletic nudity offensive (*Jub.* 3:30-31; 1QS 7:14-16). Biblical traditions inspired dim views of the homosexuality, pederasty, and promiscuity associated with gymnasia and games. However, possible evidence for Jewish ephebe lovers suggests that none of these challenges was insuperable (*CJZC* 41).

Variety in the accommodations made by Jewish athletes is most evident for circumcision, which in a Greek athletic context posed the risk of ridicule and ostracism (*CPJ* 3.519; Philo, *In Flaccum* 36–40; cf. *Spec. Leg.* 1.1-3). Some Jews probably continued the native practice of wearing a loincloth or jockstrap (Thucydides 1.6). Others surgically reversed their circumcision (1 Macc. 1:15; 1 Cor. 7:18; *T. Moses* 8:1-3). Parents often precluded this by leaving their sons uncircumcised or performing an incomplete circumcision (*Jub.* 15:33-34). If enough of the foreskin remained in the latter case, a possible camouflage was to tie it up as some Greeks did, using a cord known as a *kynodesmē*. In Rome the use of a penis sheath provided an accepted alternative (Martial, *Epigrams* 7.82). Some circumcised Jews simply exercised nude (*CPJ* 3:519).

Jewish athletes unashamedly boasted of the prizes that they won in games held during Gentile religious festivals (*IJO* 2:189). Although many athletes in the games in Caesarea, Jerusalem, the Decapolis, and elsewhere in Palestine were professionals from other regions, proximity to Jewish communities suggests that Jews participated as athletes, staff, and spectators. Athletic skills were especially valued in households of Jewish elites (Josephus, *J.W.* 1.429-30; *Ant.* 16.313-14). Even someone as pious as Philo profited from a gymnasium education and enjoyed watching games in Alexandria (Philo, *Spec. Leg.* 2.229-30; *Prov.* 2.44-46, 58; *De Cherubim* 80–81; *De Agricultura* 111–21; *Quod Omnis Probus Liber Sit* 26, 110–13). Philo's fellow Jews disrupted civic games in Alexandria in 41 C.E. (*CPJ* 2:153). This disorder epitomized broader civic conflicts, but its setting probably testifies to disputes about Jewish athletes. Athletics shaped the symbolism, illustrations, and worldviews expressed by Jewish authors (Philo; 4 Macc. 17:11-16; Wis. 4:1-2; 1 Cor. 9:24-27; Heb. 12:1-4). Jews opposed to athletics probably represented only a minority in most Jewish communities during the Hellenistic and early Roman periods.

BIBLIOGRAPHY

R. DORAN 1990, "Jason's Gymnasium," in *Of Scribes and Scrolls*, ed. H. W. Attridge et al., Lanham, Md.: University Press of America, 99-109. • R. DORAN 2001, "The High Cost of a Good Education," in *Hellenism in the Land of Israel*, ed. J. J. Collins and G. E. Sterling, Notre Dame: University of Notre Dame Press, 94-115. • H. HARRIS 1976, *Greek Athletics and the Jews*, Cardiff: University of Wales Press. • A. KERKESLAGER 1997, "Maintaining Jewish Identity in the Greek Gymnasium," *JSJ* 28: 16-33. • M. LÄMMER 1982, "Griechische Agone und römische Spiele unter der Regierung des jüdischen Königs Agrippa I," *Kölner Beitrage zur Sportwissenschaft* 10-11: 199-237. • A. MAHONEY 2001, *Roman Sports and Spectacles*, Newburyport, Mass.: Focus. • S. MILLER 2004, *Ancient Greek Athletics*, New Haven: Yale University Press. • E. NETZER ET AL. 2001-2002, *Hasmonean and Herodian Palaces at Jericho*, 3 vols., Jerusalem: Israel Exploration Society. • Z. WEISS 1999, "The Jews and the Roman Games in Palestine," in *The Roman and Byzantine Near East*, vol. 2, *Some Recent Archaeological Research*, ed. J. Humphrey, Portsmouth, R.I.: Journal of Roman Archaeology, 23-49.

See also: Assimilation, Acculturation, Accommodation; Entertainment Structures; Gymnasium

ALLEN KERKESLAGER

Atonement

Atonement has become a heavily freighted theological concept in Jewish and Christian circles. Even in the Second Temple period it had several levels of meaning. The key verb is *kipper*, which can signify ritual purification, interpersonal reconciliation, ransoming, redeeming, or appeasing. In the Torah, it refers to the ritual cleansing of Temple furnishings and a corollary cleansing result for humans. The verb *kipper* is usually followed by a preposition, *bĕʿad* or *ʿal*, occasionally by the direct object marker *ʾet*. The priest performs *kipper* "for himself," "for you" (Lev. 16:6, 30), or "for the sanctuary" (Lev. 16:16). It is to cleanse the altar and the Holy Place (16:19-20), but the end result is "to cleanse you; from all your sins you shall be clean before the LORD" (16:30). The atonement process is not just an impersonal cleansing of the sanctuary; the priest is also "making atonement for himself and for the people" (Lev. 16:24). In Leviticus 4–5, the priest accomplishes *kipper* for a person who brings a sin offering or a guilt offering, and the person is then "forgiven" *(nislaḥ)* by God (4:26, 31; 5:13, 16; etc.).

Kipper also occurs in nonritual contexts, which helps to illuminate its range of meanings. *Kipper* can mean "forgive" (Ps. 79:9), with a decision to withhold punishment (Ps. 78:38). The aversion of punishment is clearly evident in a number of nonritual passages involving *kipper* (Gen. 32:20 [MT 32:21]; 2 Sam. 21:3-6).

Kōpher is a noun that is cognate with *kipper*. A *kōpher* is a payment or substitution that legally delivers someone from a penalty or punishment. It appeases the offended party or averts wrath; it can substitute for a sacrifice (Exod. 21:30; 30:16; Sklar 2005: 71-78). *Kōpher* can signify a bribe (1 Sam. 12:3; Prov. 6:35).

Practitioners and interpreters often spoke of sacrifice as a gift to God, but the *kōpher* concept reveals the element of self-interest even in a "gift." Several Hebrew prophets reacted strongly against the idea that God could be propitiated by gifts. They argued that God wants obedience, justice, and mercy *more than,* or *instead of,* sacrifice (1 Sam. 15:22; Hos. 6:6; Amos 5:22-25; Mic. 6:6-8).

The *kpr* root seems to have two primary meanings, "to purify" and "to ransom." It may be that the two meanings are related, that purification entails a ransoming of those who caused the impurity, while ransom implies purgation, since sin causes impurity (Sklar 2005: 147-50).

The Purification Offering and Yom Kippur

The main sacrifice used for purification was the *ḥaṭṭāʾt* offering, formerly translated as "sin offering" but now commonly called the "purification offering." Different places in the sanctuary required cleansing depending upon the nature of the sin or impurity, and upon who committed it. The most serious sin penetrated the Holy of Holies where (according to the Pentateuch) the Ark of the Covenant sat.

The cleansing blood could be daubed, sprinkled, tossed, or poured on the horns of the outer altar, on the inner (incense) altar, to the veil, or in the Holy of Holies. The latter occurred only on the year's most important day, Yom Kippur, the Day of Atonement, a very solemn occasion. On this day — and only on this day — the high priest entered the Holy of Holies and sprinkled the blood of the purification offerings directly onto the *kapporet,* the golden lid of the Ark of the Covenant (Lev. 16:14-15; Milgrom 1991: 38-43, 77). Older Bibles call the *kapporet* the "mercy seat," drawing upon Luther's translation. In Second Temple times, when there was no longer an ark or a *kapporet,* the priest is said to sprinkle the blood on the stone where the ark had once stood (*m. Yoma* 5). From biblical times to the present, Yom Kippur has been an occasion for fasting, repentance, and confession of sin.

The Scapegoat

Kipper occurs over a dozen times in Leviticus 16, in connection with the scapegoat as well as with sacrifice. The priest brings two identical and pure goats forward, and chooses one (by lot) to be the scapegoat, the other to be a purification offering (16:10). He lays his hands on the scapegoat's head and confesses over it "all the iniquities of the people of Israel, and all their transgressions, all their sins, putting them on the head of the goat, and sending it away into the wilderness" (16:21). The scapegoat does not deal with the highly symbolic concept of impurity, but with sin directly; it carries away the sins into the desert. The scapegoat is not an offering at all; it is a sin-porter — a quite primitive religious idea (Janowski 1982: 210-13).

Atonement in the Dead Sea Scrolls

The community of Jews at Qumran regarded the Temple cult in Jerusalem as corrupt, but they did not reject the cult in principle; indeed, they expected it to be reestablished in the future (1QM 2:5; 11QT 25:10–27:10). Still, since they were separated from the Temple cult in Jerusalem, they found other ways of obtaining atonement. The community itself was regarded as "an acceptable sacrifice for the land through . . . prayer, becoming . . . a sweet savor" (1QS 9:4-5). Sin is be atoned for "through an upright and humble attitude" (1QS 3:8). But this is possible only for members of the Qumran community. The outsider cannot be cleansed: "Unclean, unclean shall he be" (1QS 3:5).

The sect itself is a "temple for Israel . . . to atone for the land" (1QS 8:5-6). God purifies "all the eternally holy," and allows them to "make atonement for those who repent of sin" (4Q400 frg. 1 lines 15-16). Even the community's practice of internal discipline and punishment was seen as having an atoning function (1QS 5:6-7; 8:10, etc.).

There is eschatological atonement as well. 11QMelchizedek not only gives Melchizedek the role of leading the sons of light against the evil armies, but also, on "the Day of Atonement . . . he shall atone for all the sons of light" (12:7-8). This makes Melchizedek a heavenly and priestly savior, which finds parallel in another fragment, 4Q541, where an eschatological priest will "make atonement for all those of his generation." This concept also occurs in chap. 18 of the *Testament of Levi,* an early Christian work whose origins in early Judaism are disputed.

Spiritualization of the Sacrificial Idea

The Hebrew concepts were carried over into another language and into Diaspora communities when the Hebrew Bible was translated into Greek. As part of this process, Diaspora Jews came up with metaphorical concepts of atonement, which were appropriated in early Christianity.

The meaning of atonement had become a locus of debate even in biblical times, as certain prophets and psalmists focused on motives, becoming impatient with ritual. They developed a discourse where prayer or sincerity achieved what sacrifice was thought to accomplish: "The sacrifice acceptable to God is a broken spirit. . . . Let my prayer be counted as . . . an evening sacrifice" (Pss. 51:17; 141:2).

Second Temple authors utilize cultic language metaphorically. A Maccabean martyr's blood is called a "purification" (Gr. *katharsion*), a "ransom" *(antipsychon),* a "propitiatory" *(hilastērion)* death (4 Macc. 6:29; 17:21-22). In the New Testament, Christ is the new *hilastērion* (the LXX term for the *kapporet;* Rom 3:25); he is sent as an offering for sin (*peri hamartias,* Rom. 8:3).

There are varying spiritualizing strategies. The *Testament of Levi* speaks of a holy of holies "in the uppermost heaven . . . the archangels, who serve and offer propitiatory sacrifices . . . present to the Lord a pleasing odor, a rational and bloodless oblation" (3:4-6). What is

ATONEMENT

offered constitutes a propitiation, although by means better than the bloody cult.

Spiritualizing rhetoric expresses both continuity and change. Something other than the literal cult accomplishes what sacrifice was thought to do, yet the cultic pattern persists. Philo of Alexandria writes of "propitiating the Father of the universe with holy prayers" (*Mos.* 2.24).

The author of *Psalms of Solomon* reveres the Temple (1:8; 2:3; 8:12) but does not mention atonement with respect to it. Atonement comes through humility and confession (3:8; 9:6). On the other hand, Sirach says that right behavior achieves atonement, but he also supports the literal cult: "Those who honor their father atone for sins. . . . To forsake unrighteousness is an atonement. Do not appear before the Lord empty-handed. . . . The sacrifice of the righteous is acceptable" (3:3; 35:5-6, 9). In Sirach, at any rate, metaphorical statements about atonement imply nothing negative about the material cult.

Bibliography

P. Garnet 1977, *Salvation and Atonement in the Qumran Scrolls,* Tübingen: Mohr-Siebeck. • B. Janowski 1982, *Sühne als Heilsgeschehen: Studien zur Sühnetheologie der Priesterschrift und zur Wurzel KPR im Alten Orient und im Alten Testament,* Düsseldorf: Neukirchener Verlag. • J. Klawans 2006, *Purity, Sacrifice and the Temple,* New York: Oxford. • J. Milgrom 1991, *Leviticus 1–16,* Garden City, N.Y.: Doubleday. • J. Sklar 2005, *Sin, Impurity, Sacrifice, Atonement: The Priestly Conceptions,* Sheffield: Sheffield Phoenix. • D. Stökl Ben Ezra 2003, *The Impact of Yom Kippur on Early Christianity: The Day of Atonement from Second Temple Judaism to the Fifth Century,* Tübingen: Mohr-Siebeck.

See also: Sacrifices and Offerings; Sin

Stephen Finlan and Daniel P. Bailey

Atonement, Day of → Festivals and Holy Days

B

Babatha Archive

Babatha was a Jewish woman of early second-century-C.E. Provincia Arabia whose papers were found in the Judean Desert. The "archive" of these papers comprises some thirty-five legal documents written on papyrus variously in Greek, Nabatean, and Aramaic. They range in date from 93/94 to 132 C.E. and comprise the largest group of interrelated documents of this sort to have been found in the Judean Desert. The documents, whose designations in the Tov-Pfann list of texts from the Judean Desert are 5/6Ḥev 1-35, are generally known as P. Yadin (less commonly P. Babatha) or as the Babatha Archive. The documents record private transactions and the fulfillment (or demands for the fulfillment) of the rights and obligations created by those transactions. All of these relate in one way or another to Babatha and present an unusual opportunity to reconstruct some of the events in the life of a Jewish person of the second century C.E. whose relationship to religion and law was not that of a professional.

Discovery and Publication

The papyri were found in March 1961 in the course of the second season of the archaeological expedition led by Yigael Yadin, in the Cave of Letters at Naḥal Ḥever, about 5 km. southwest of ʿEin Gedi. The cave was so named for a cache of letters of Simeon Bar Kokhba that had been found in the course of the previous expedition in 1960. It apparently served as the hideaway from the Romans for people from ʿEin Gedi, including a commander in Bar Kokhba's forces. Hidden in a crevice was a pouch containing the carefully wrapped documents of the Babatha Archive. The archaeological context requires that it was placed there after November 134 C.E.

Detailed descriptions of the documents in the Babatha archive were published by Yadin in 1962 and most extensively in 1971 — as the "home-front" chapter in the emotionally nationalist account of the finds relating to the Bar Kokhba Revolt — but only three Greek documents (15, 27, and 28) were published promptly. The texts in their entirety were published only after Yadin's death, the Greek by Lewis 1989 (5, 11-35), and the Nabatean and Aramaic documents (1–4, 6–10) in Yadin et al. 2002.

Details of Babatha's Life

Babatha's name is derived from the Aramaic word for pupil of the eye, indicating someone especially precious. Her father was Simon son of Menaḥem, her mother Miriam daughter of Joseph son of Menashe (7.3, 24). Babatha is regularly identified as a Maozene, that is, of Maoza, the port in the district of Zoara at the southern end of the Dead Sea, in the Roman province of Arabia. Her family lived in Maoza at least since 99 C.E., when her father bought a palm grove there (3). By 120 C.E. she may have been married (7.24-25 provides for a widow's residence for Babatha, if necessary), to Jesus son of Joseph Zaboudos, also of Maoza. If the skeletons of the eight women aged fifteen to thirty found in the cave include that of Babatha, then she would have been aged sixteen or even younger at the time of her marriage.

By the first half of 124 C.E. she had a son, Jesus, still quite young since he was still a minor eight years later, and her husband was dead. The city council of Petra, the metropolis of the region — presumably acting by delegation from the provincial governor, in whose jurisdiction this matter would have been — assigned the orphan two guardians, one Jewish, one Nabatean (12). These invested the boy's capital and returned to Babatha an allowance for his support at the rate of one-half percent per month, half the usual interest rate. In 124 and 125 C.E., in an attempt to "fight city hall," Babatha petitioned the Roman provincial governor about this low rate and offered to triple that return if the boy's property were entrusted to her and secured by her own property (13-15). She apparently did not receive relief from the governor, for in 132 the guardians were still giving the allowance at the original rate (27), and her pouch contained three blank copies of the Roman judicial formula used to sue guardians for malfeasance (28-30). Ironically, had the case been governed by Jewish law, which of course the Petra city council could not be expected to apply, Babatha herself would likely have been awarded the guardianship. The procedure she

BABATHA ARCHIVE

proposed does appear as an accepted practice in Roman juristic sources, but only about a century later. The experience would not endear the Roman judicial administration to Babatha.

In 127 C.E. Babatha declared, for a provincial census, her ownership of four palm groves in Maoza, listing yields and taxes of each (16). Though we are not told directly how these groves came into her possession, at least one appears to have belonged to her father and was presumably given to Babatha as a gift before he gave his remaining property to his wife (3, 7).

By February 128 C.E. (17), and possibly as early as October 125 (14, 15), Babatha was remarried, to Judah son of Eleazar Kthousion son of Judah. His official residence was in ʿEin Gedi, where his family lived and he owned a home, but he lived in Maoza, where he also owned property. Judah was previously married to Miriam daughter of Beianos of ʿEin Gedi, perhaps the sister of the Bar Kokhba commander mentioned above. Contrary to the view of several modern scholars that Judah's marriages were polygamous, nothing in the documents indicates that he was still married to Miriam when he married Babatha. The Aramaic document recording Judah and Babatha's marriage (10) matches the traditional *ketubba,* as it would have been at that time. In February 128 Babatha deposited with her husband 300 denarii, probably a loan without a fixed term (17).

In April of that year Judah gave his daughter from his previous marriage, Shelamzion, in marriage to Judah Cimber son of Ananias son of Somalos, of ʿEin Gedi (18). Eleven days later he gave her his house in ʿEin Gedi as a gift, half to take effect after his death (19). Two years later Judah, Babatha's husband, was already dead when representatives of the orphans of his deceased brother Jesus conceded to Shelamzion rights to that house (20). That Shelamzion's documents were found among the papers of her stepmother Babatha would be consistent with Shelamzion being a minor and may indicate a notable measure of trust between the two women.

Babatha, now twice widowed by the age of twenty-five or younger, took possession of at least three groves owned by Judah in satisfaction of obligations under their marriage contract or loan. In September 130 she disposed of the produce of these groves by selling the crop before the harvest (21-22). This is explicitly permitted a widow in Jewish law, and just as explicitly forbidden in Roman law. An escape clause allowed the buyer, in case title was challenged, to rescind the deal and take a cash payment for the labor of date-picking instead. There is reason to think that just that happened. Once again Babatha was frustrated in her financial dealings because of the failure of Roman authorities to apply Jewish law even though she was Jewish and not a Roman citizen.

Two months later she was summoned to the court of the Roman provincial governor in Petra by the guardians of Judah's nephews to answer their claim to presumably these same groves (23). A plausible reconstruction of these events would be that the estate of Eleazar Khthousion, the father of Judah, Babatha's second husband, was never completely divided between Judah and

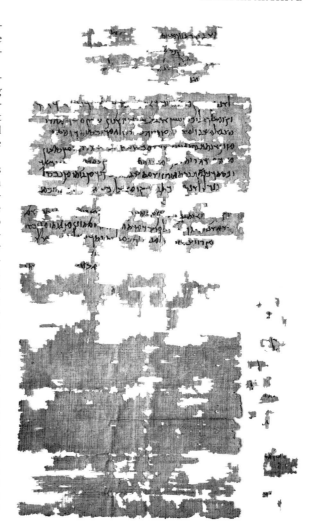

Marriage contract *(ketubba)* from the Babatha Archive
(Photo © The Israel Museum, Jerusalem)

his brother Jesus in their lifetimes, but held more or less in common, and that after their deaths representatives of the orphans of each came to a settlement in June 130. The orphans of Jesus relinquished rights to the house in ʿEin Gedi (20); Shelamzion the daughter of Judah relinquished rights to groves in Maoza, in a document which would naturally not be present in this archive. The question remained whether priority should have been given to the claims of Babatha or to those of Jesus' orphans. At the same time Babatha was embroiled in a suit with Miriam, Judah's first wife, over household goods of their late husband (26). The outcome of theses litigations is not known.

Significance

The documentation of these conflicts at law has led some scholars (e.g., Goodman 1991) to speak of Babatha's "enthusiasm for litigious confrontation." It should be noted, however, that in the latter two of the three suits recorded in the archive, it was not Babatha but her opponents who initiated the litigation. The facts of the payments to her son as she presents them certainly raise the suspicion of corruption on the part of the council-appointed guardians. A picture, then, of a very young widow of whom various parties tried to take unfair advantage is equally plausible.

That Babatha herself was Jewish need not be doubted, even though her name is unprecedented. All her known relatives, including her parents, bear characteristically Jewish names; her son is called "Jesus, a Jew" in an official document (12). She and her papers ended up in a cave with extreme Jewish nationalists. Nonetheless, the relation of Babatha and her society to the Judaism known from rabbinic literature has been the subject of controversy. Some scholars have stressed the absence of explicit reference to rabbis and rabbinic law, as well as the presence of some apparent violations of Jewish law. Others have found on the contrary considerable Jewish law, most notably in Babatha's marriage contract (10) and in the sale of dates (21-22), which are best read best in light of rabbinic literature. Since Babatha herself, though evidently a woman of means, was illiterate, apparently both in Greek and in Hebrew/Aramaic, all these features of her documents reflect less her own commitments than those of her society and are better treated in a general discussion of other contracts from the Judean Desert.

BIBLIOGRAPHY

Texts

N. LEWIS ET AL., EDS. 1989, *The Documents from the Bar Kokhba Period in the Cave of Letters: Greek Papyri*, Jerusalem: Israel Exploration Society. • Y. YADIN, J. C. GREENFIELD, A. YARDENI, AND B. LEVINE, EDS. 2002, *The Documents from the Bar Kokhba Period in the Cave of Letter: Hebrew, Aramaic and Nabataean-Aramaic Papyri*, Jerusalem: Israel Exploration Society.

Important reviews

G. W. BOWERSOCK 1991, "The Babatha Papyri, Masada, and Rome," *JRA* 4: 336-44. • M. GOODMAN 1991, "Babatha's Story," *Journal of Roman Studies* 81: 169-75. • B. ISAAC 1992, "The Babatha Archive: A Review Article," *IEJ* 42: 62-65. • H. I. NEWMAN 2004, "Old and New in the Documentary Papyri from the Bar Kochba Period," *SCI* 23: 239-54.

Studies

T. J. CHIUSI 2005, "Babatha vs. the Guardians of Her Son: A Struggle for Guardianship — Legal and Practical Aspects of P. Yadin 12-15, 27," in *Law in the Documents of the Judaean Desert*, ed. R. Katzoff and D. Schaps, Leiden: Brill, 105-32. • H. COTTON 1993, "The Guardianship of Jesus Son of Babatha: Roman and Local Law in the Province of Arabia," *Journal of Roman Studies* 83: 94-108. • H. M. COTTON 1998, "The Law of Succession in the Documents from the Judaean Desert Again," *SCI* 17: 115-23. • M. A. FRIEDMAN 1996, "Babatha's 'Ketubba': Some Preliminary Observations," *IEJ* 46: 55-76. • A. E. HANSON 2005, "The Widow Babatha and the Poor Orphan Boy," in *Law in the Documents of the Judaean Desert*, ed. R. Katzoff and D. Schaps, Leiden: Brill, 85-104. • R. KATZOFF 1995, "Polygamy in P. Yadin?" *Zeitschrift für Papyrologie und Epigraphik* 109: 128-32. • R. KATZOFF 2008, "*P. Yadin* 21 and Rabbinic Law on Widows' Rights," *JQR*. • J. G. OUDSHOORN 2007, *The Relationship between Roman and Local Law in the Babatha and Salome Komaise Archives*, Leiden: Brill. • Y. YADIN 1962, "Expedition D — The Cave of Letters," *IEJ* 12: 227-57. • Y. YADIN 1971, *Bar-Kokhba: The Rediscovery of the Legendary Hero of the Second Jewish Revolt against Rome*, New York: Random House.

See also: Contracts from the Judean Desert

RANON KATZOFF

Babel, Tower of

The biblical story of the Tower of Babel and resulting confusion of tongues in the Plain of Shinar (Gen. 11:1-9) presents the exegete with no shortage of challenges. Early Jewish interpreters responded creatively to these difficulties, often filling in details left unstated in the text of Genesis.

Why Was God So Upset?

The biblical account begins by noting the unity of humanity, exemplified by its common language. Commentators generally assumed this to be Hebrew (cf. *Jub.* 12:25-26; *Tg. Neof.* and *Tg. Ps.-J.* Gen. 11:1). Little is said, however, about what warranted God's divisive response to the decision to build the Tower. *Jubilees* (10:19) and the *Sibylline Oracles* (3.99-100) assume that it was built through a wanton desire to enter heaven. Philo (*QG* 2.82) and *3 Baruch* (3:7-8) add that it was constructed with the intent to wage war on God. *Targum Neofiti* (Gen. 11:4) punctuates this notion by claiming that a sword-wielding idol was to be placed on top of the Tower (cf. *Gen. Rab.* 38). Josephus (*Ant.* 1.109-21), in contrast, claims that the project was undertaken to avoid divine judgment in the event of another deluge. According to him, the Tower was built in rebellion against God's prudent command to spread out and colonize. For all of these sources, the true act of impiety lay in the arrogant impetus behind building the Tower, and not the act of building itself.

Who Built the Tower?

The Bible does not specify who built the Tower. However, due to links between the Tower of Babel narrative and Gen. 10:6-10 (e.g., the mention of Shinar), a number of early interpreters associated the Tower with Nimrod, grandson of Ham. Jewish views of this "mighty hunter" were uniformly negative (but cf. Syriac sources for a positive view) and frequently attributed the inspiration to build the Tower to him. Josephus (*Ant.* 1.113-15) places blame for the project squarely with Nimrod, who advised the people to disobey God and incited revolt. Philo (*QG* 2.82; *Gigantibus* 15) holds a similar opinion. Pseudo-Philo (*Biblical Antiquities* 6) names Nimrod as the most diabolical of three leaders overseeing the unseemly venture. In the LXX (Gen.

10:8-9) Nimrod is portrayed as a giant, perhaps leading to Pseudo-Eupolemus's assertion (in Eusebius, *Praep. Evang.* 9.17.2-3) that giants built the Tower.

Where Does the Story Belong?

As situated in the Bible, Gen. 11:1-9 is surrounded by genealogical sections containing the temporal phrase "after the flood." As a result, the passage is somewhat difficult to relate to its surrounding narrative. It is not surprising, therefore, that later opinions regarding its chronological placement varied, often contrasting with the biblical arrangement. Josephus places the story before Noah's death, between the flood story (Genesis 6–9) and his updated "Table of Nations" (Genesis 10). Here he follows the order earlier employed by the third sibyl (*Sib. Or.* 3.97-109). The *War Scroll* (1QM 10:14-15) implies this same arrangement in a list of God's mighty deeds, "of the confusion of tongues, of the separation of nations, of the dwelling of the clans, of the inheritance of the lands." *Jubilees* (10:18-26), however, etymologically links the events to Ragew, son of Peleg, necessitating a different chronology. According to this interpretation, Noah had already died and the earth had been divided yet remained largely uninhabited. The author of *Jubilees* gives a detailed description, including the Tower's height and the duration of its construction (10:21). Pseudo-Philo (*Biblical Antiquities* 6–7) mingles the story with themes from Daniel 3 and places it yet later, assigning Abram a central role as protagonist. A similar tradition may be present in 4Q464 (col. 1 frg. 3).

What Happened to the Tower?

God's statement, "let us go down and confuse their language" (Gen. 11:7), clearly made some interpreters uneasy due to its use of the plural "us" and its apparent anthropomorphism. In response, traditions arose that distanced these activities from God himself. The third *Sibylline Oracle* (3.101-3) suggests that God was speaking to the winds, often equated with his potencies elsewhere. *Jubilees* (10:22-24) portrays God speaking to the angels and descending along with them. Philo (*Confusione* 168–74) also considers "us" to refer to God's heavenly powers, which act on the earth through angels. Similarly, *Targum Pseudo-Jonathan* pictures God speaking to "the seventy angels who stand before him" (cf. *3 Enoch* 30:2). The number seventy (or seventy-two) commonly represented the sum of earthly nations in antiquity.

Although the Bible does not relate what ultimately happened to the Tower following the confusion of tongues, several sources provide a fitting conclusion. The *Sibylline Oracles* (3.101-3; 11.10-13), *Jubilees* (10:26), and Josephus (*Ant.* 1.118, quoting the sibyl) all recount that God sent a great wind to destroy the Tower, thus ending the bold attempt to reach heaven (also see *Midrash Tanḥuma, Noah* 18).

A Future Reversal

Some described the coming messianic age as a reversal of the confusion of languages at Babel. These likely took their cue from Zeph. 3:9-10, which states that God will give his scattered people "clear speech" in the coming restoration. This connection appears to be explicit in the fragmentary 4Q464 (col. 1 frg. 3). Other texts containing this theme are the *Testament of Judah* (25:3) and the book of Acts (2:1-11).

Philo *(De Confusione Linguarum)* devotes an entire allegorical treatise to Gen. 11:1-9. After exhorting those exegetes interested in the "literal" sense of Scripture to rebuff rash comparisons of the story with two popular Greco-Roman myths, Philo quickly turns to his characteristic allegorical method. The latter deals with general, moralistic principles gleaned from the narrative. The Tower and dispersion of peoples are also mentioned, with very little surrounding context, in 4Q243 (10) and 4Q244 (9, 13).

BIBLIOGRAPHY

E. ESHEL AND M. E. STONE 1995, "4Q464: 4QExposition on the Patriarchs," in DJD XIX, ed. J. VanderKam, J. Fitzmyer, et al., Oxford: Clarendon, 219-21. • S. INOWLOCKI 2006, "Josephus' Rewriting of the Babel Narrative (Gen 11:1-9)," *JSJ* 37:2, 169-91. • J. L. KUGEL 1998, *Traditions of the Bible*, Cambridge, Mass.: Harvard University Press, 227-42. • C. WESTERMANN 1984, *Genesis 1–11*, Minneapolis: Augsburg, 531-57.

DANIEL A. MACHIELA

Babylonian Culture

Though part of Hellenistic culture, Jewish civilization in Second Temple times was in many ways oriented toward the older cultural center of ancient Mesopotamia. The region's cuneiform culture, which enjoyed three millennia of vast literary and scientific achievements, had been in considerable decline by the mid-first millennium B.C.E., with a drastic deterioration in the use of the Akkadian language and cuneiform script. Yet the achievements of this culture shaped much of later Western culture. This influence is evident first and foremost in the area of Babylonian astral science, which was dominant in Roman Egypt by means of texts translated into Greek and Demotic. The transmission of Mesopotamian knowledge westward occurred either by direct contact with native Babylonian scholars (e.g., in the teachings of Berossos) or by the mediation of texts in Aramaic, the informal *lingua franca* of the ancient Near East in the first millennium B.C.E. Jewish literati held a special place in this cultural process, owing to the establishment of a Jewish community in Babylon already in the sixth to fifth centuries B.C.E., and to the mobility of individuals and media between Babylonia, Judea, and other Jewish centers. The late Babylonian contribution to early Judaism may be discerned in a variety of areas, including calendars and festivals, science and divination, hermeneutical techniques, Seleucid political history, literary genres and traditions, and apocalyptic thought.

Calendars and Festivals

Although it is hardly clear which calendar or calendars were used by Israelites in preexilic times, it is com-

BABYLONIAN CULTURE

monly accepted that the Babylonian Exile forged some of the central concepts of the postexilic Judean calendar. This process lasted for several centuries and was not limited to the time of the Exile. From the beginning of the Babylonian domination in Judea, biblical sources attest that the Jewish year began in the spring, as in the Babylonian calendar. Later on, the standard Babylonian month names (in their Aramaic form) were adopted by Jews. These month names are attested in the late books of the Hebrew Bible down to the present-day rabbinic calendar. Rabbinic sources reflect the use of a luni-solar calendar regulated by observation, a procedure that resembles those of ancient Mesopotamian scholars of the early first millennium B.C.E., before the Babylonian calendar itself began to be regulated by fixed-year cycles. In contrast, early Jewish apocalyptic texts like *1 Enoch* and *Jubilees,* as well as the Dead Sea Scrolls, use a 364-day calendar, which is directly dependent upon the Babylonian ideal year, used for astronomical calculations in a variety of Mesopotamian sources.

The rituals and symbolic significance attached to the Jewish New Year's Day, Rosh Hashanah, celebrated in the autumn at the beginning of the month Tishri, were fashioned to a great extent by the prominent Babylonian feast of the autumn New Year *(akitu, zagmukkû).* That festival marked the renewal of the kingship of the great Babylonian god Marduk, taking place in his temple in Babylon. It was the time when the gods convened to determine the fate of the king and the country for the coming year. Various rituals of purification and atonement were performed in the temple throughout the feast, which lasted for eleven days. This set of beliefs and practices reveals close similarities with the liturgy for Rosh Hashanah, as described in the Mishnah and related sources. In contrast, preexilic sources give little attention to the New Year.

Science and Divination

The transmission of Babylonian science to the West is attested mainly in texts from Roman Egypt, as well as in some earlier, marginal evidence relating to such figures as Berossos and Hipparchus. In addition, Aramaic sources of late antiquity and medieval times, some of them written on Mesopotamian soil, attest to the continuation of Babylonian medicine, divination, and magic in these periods. But the direct evidence for the circulation of Babylonian science in pre-Roman times appears exclusively in Jewish sources. Thus, the Enochic *Astronomical Book* (*1 Enoch* 72–82) reflects the astronomical concepts of the cuneiform compendium Mul.Apin, and the calendrical scrolls from Qumran (4Q320, 4Q321) make use of a slightly more advanced Babylonian tool for the measurement of lunar motion. The Qumran scrolls 4Q561 and 4Q186 contain manuals of physiognomy similar to Mesopotamian prototypes. The astrological scroll 4Q318 contains two astrological lists with close parallels in Mesopotamian literature, although they are also attested in later Greek sources. The scientific vocabulary in the Scrolls can be placed on a continuum between ancient Mesopotamian and late antique Aramaic texts. Finally, there are signs of a shift to the use of sexagesimal weights and measures in early Jewish sources (mainly the *Aramaic Levi Document* and possibly also the *New Jerusalem* texts), a method which reflects quite clearly the Mesopotamian scribal curriculum.

Hermeneutical Techniques

Early Jewish literature is to a great extent a hermeneutical project, utilizing the authority of Scripture to substantiate its formulation and renewal of religious concepts. Although the impulse for this exegetical undertaking is no doubt inner-Jewish, some of it may be traced to foreign exegetical activity. While it is common to connect this activity with the exegesis performed in the Hellenistic schools of Alexandria, the hermeneutical techniques of Assyrian and Babylonian scribes seem to be an important source of influence. In these schools one finds an extensive exegetical literature, the base texts being old myths, ancient scientific treatises, and central rituals of Mesopotamian religion. The commentators employ a variety of techniques, including an atomized, word-by-word exegesis reminiscent of *derash* or plain-sense interpretation and a numerical technique that resembles later Jewish numerical speculation.

Seleucid Political History

Only meager data are available for the political history of the Seleucid kingdoms. Information supplementing the books of the Maccabees and Josephus comes from the Babylonian astronomical diaries. These were daily records kept in Babylonia that, in addition to compiling astronomical data, kept track of political and economic developments. Some important facts relating to Antiochus IV's campaigns, for example, may be culled from this rich collection.

Literary Genres and Traditions

Jewish sources from Qumran mention several prominent Mesopotamian figures who are otherwise hardly known outside cuneiform literature. The Aramaic *Book of Giants* (later adopted by the Manichean sect in translations to Persian languages) mentions Gilgamesh and the monster Humbaba from the renowned *Gilgamesh Epic.* The so-called *Prayer of Nabonidus* (4Q242) preserves a Jewish tradition about the Babylonian king and his cure from his illness by a Jewish diviner, which led to the king's belief in the God of Israel. This story may have served as the background for Daniel 4, where the protagonist is the Babylonian king Nebuchadnezzar. The Qumran Scrolls, too, include examples of court tales with a Mesopotamian background, such as 4Q550, which is somewhat similar to *Ahiqar* and Tobit but also to the biblical book of Esther.

Apocalyptic Thought

Jewish apocalypticism, which formed in Judea in the third to second centuries B.C.E., owes some of its constituent ideas to Mesopotamian prototypes. Apart from the scientific ideas of the *Astronomical Book,* the very image of the primordial sage and seer Enoch depends upon Mesopotamian culture heroes like Enmeduranki,

Adapa, and Gilgamesh. The notion of primordial knowledge was readily adopted in the Hellenistic period, as part of the effort to trace the origins of culture to hoary antiquity. Further, apocalyptic predictions in the book of Daniel are close in formulation to the famous group of Mesopotamian prophecies, and resemble the predictions contained in the apodosis of Mesopotamian omens. This fact has important implications for understanding the relation between prophecy and apocalypticism.

BIBLIOGRAPHY
J. BEN-DOV 2008A, *Head of All Years: Astronomy and Calendars at Qumran in their Ancient Context,* Leiden: Brill. • J. BEN-DOV 2008B, "Reflections on New Year Feasts in Babylonia and Israel," *Shnaton* 19: 251-69 (in Hebrew). • H. DRAWNEL 2007, "Moon Computation in the *Aramaic Astronomical Book,*" *RQ* 23: 3-41. • M. J. GELLER 1995, "The Influence of Ancient Mesopotamia on Hellenistic Judaism," in *Civilizations of the Ancient Near East,* vol. 1, ed. J. M. Sasson, New York: Prentice Hall, 43-54. • D. GERA AND W. HOROWITZ 1997, "Antiochus IV in Life and Death: Evidence from the Babylonian Astronomical Diaries," *JAOS* 117: 240-45. • A. LEMAIRE 2010, "Nabonide et Gilgamesh: L'Araméen en Mésopotamie et à Qoumrân," in *The Aramaic Texts from Qumran,* ed. K. Berthelot and D. Stökl Ben-Ezra, Leiden: Brill. • S. J. LIEBERMAN 1987, "A Mesopotamian Background for the So-called *Aggadic* 'Measures' of Biblical Hermeneutics?" *HUCA* 58: 157-225. M. POPOVIĆ 2007, *Reading the Human Body: Physiognomics and Astrology in the Dead Sea Scrolls and Hellenistic-Early Roman Period Judaism,* Leiden: Brill. • J. C. VANDERKAM 1984, *Enoch and the Growth of an Apocalyptic Tradition,* Washington D.C.: Catholic Biblical Association of America. • J. C. VANDERKAM 2002, *From Revelation to Canon: Studies in the Hebrew Bible and Second Temple Literature,* Leiden: Brill, 241-75.

See also: Astronomy and Astrology; Calendars; Enoch

JONATHAN BEN-DOV

Babylonians

The Neo-Babylonian Empire

Babylonia had a long history. During the second millennium and first half of the first millennium B.C.E., it alternated with Assyria as one of the two main powers in Mesopotamia. Yet it is the short-lived Neo-Babylonian Empire — lasting less than a century — that we think of as characteristic of Babylonia. The Neo-Babylonian period and the sixth century B.C.E. marked a low point in the history of Judah, but this was also an extremely important period in history. For much of the time between 1100 and 600 B.C.E., Babylonia was a vassal state within the Neo-Assyrian Empire. The city of Babylon and its surrounding territory were always important, and the governor of Babylonia was often a member of the Assyrian royal family. Yet through these centuries Babylon frequently rebelled against its overlords, the instigator sometimes being a relative of the Assyrian ruler who had been made governor. One long-term rebel was the Babylonian Marduk-apla-iddina or Marduk-baladin II,

Neo-Babylonian Empire

625-605	Nabopolassar of Babylon
612	Medes and Babylonians conquer Nineveh; end of Assyrian Empire
609	King Josiah of Judah dies at Battle of Megiddo
605	Nebuchadnezzer defeats Egyptians at Battle of Carchemesh
605-562	Nebuchadnezzar creates New Babylonian Empire
601-598	King Jehoiakim of Judah rebels against Babylon
598/597	Siege of Jerusalem; King Jehoiachin of Judah exiled to Babylon
587/586	King Zedekiah of Judah rebels against Babylon; Nebuchadnezzer conquers Judah; Jerusalem falls; leading Judeans deported
586-538	Judean Exile in Babylon
562-560	Amel-Marduk
560-556	Neriglissar
556-539	Nabonidus
539	Conquest of Babylon by Cyrus of Persia

who was a thorn in the side of the Assyrians for many years (the Merodach-baladin of 2 Kings 20:12) and even briefly seized the Babylonian throne (705-703 B.C.E.).

Nabopolasser

With the weakening and contraction of the Assyrian Empire in the latter part of the seventh century B.C.E., Babylonia was able to challenge its subordination to Assyria. The king of Babylon was Nabopolasser the Chaldean. From his succession in 625 B.C.E., he worked successfully to gain Babylon's independence; then from about 615 B.C.E. he allied with the Medes, leading to the joint conquest of Nineveh in 612 B.C.E. that brought the end of the Assyrian Empire. A remnant of the Assyrian nation continued in the west, on the Euphrates, for another few years, propped up by the Egyptians. Pharaoh Necho II was on his way to support the Assyrians at Carchemesh when King Josiah of Judah met him at Megiddo in 609 B.C.E. and died in mysterious circumstances (2 Kings 23:29-30). In 605 B.C.E., when the crown prince Nebuchadnezzar was campaigning in place of his aged father, he defeated the Egyptians at the battle of Carchemesh (Jer. 46:2). Shortly afterward he received word of his father's death, marched with a small bodyguard straight across the desert to Babylon, and took the throne.

Nebuchadnezzar

Nebuchadnezzar was a remarkable individual, ruling for half the life of the Neo-Babylonian Empire. His name (Akk. *Nabû-kudurri-uṣur,* "Nabû, protect my offspring") is correctly represented in a few biblical passages as Nebuchadrezzar (e.g., Jer. 21:2; 50:17; Ezek. 26:7), but is generally given as Nebuchadnezzar (the conventional, if inaccurate, form is followed here). He continued to campaign in the west but engaged in a major battle with the Egyptians in 601 B.C.E. that caused great destruction on both sides. At this point, Jehoiakim rebelled (2 Kings 24:1). Although this rebellion is not explained in the biblical text, both the reason for it and the timing make sense in the light of Nebuchadnezzar's standoff with Egypt. It took several years for Nebuchadnezzar to recover, but he was bound to go against Judah. While recuperating his military strength, he instigated raiding parties against the rebellious vassals in the west, including Jehoiakim of Judah. But then in late 598 B.C.E. he marched against Jerusalem with a full army. By the time he arrived in early 597 B.C.E., Jehoiakim had died and Jehoiachin had succeeded him (2 Kings 24:8-17), and it was Jehoiachin who was taken captive to Babylon.

We know much about the first part of Nebuchadnezzar's reign because of the detailed information in the *Babylonian Chronicles*. Unfortunately, they cease in 594 B.C.E., and much of the rest of his reign is shrouded in obscurity. All we have are a few building inscriptions. This means that we have only the biblical text for the siege and fall of Jerusalem in 587/586 B.C.E. but, considering the accuracy of the text through the final years of the seventh and early years of the sixth century, we can have confidence in the basic accuracy of the information. As for other events mentioned in the Bible but in no other source, it may well be that Nebuchadnezzar besieged Tyre. Ezekiel 26:7 states that Nebuchadnezzar would come against Tyre and destroy it; however, Ezekiel's original prophecy seems to be corrected later on in Ezek. 29:17-20. This latter passage states that Nebuchadnezzar, having failed to take Tyre, will be given Egypt as a consolation prize. This suggests a genuine prophecy, reflecting Nebuchadnezzar's actual siege of Tyre, which then failed and required a further "revelation" to sort out the erroneous prediction.

On the other hand, there is no evidence for a forty-year period of desolation for Egypt, as predicted (Ezek. 29:8-16; 30:20-26). 2 Chronicles seems to be dependent on 2 Kings, and few of the additional passages are proved to have reliable information. The one specifically relating to Nebuchadnezzar is Jehoiakim's Babylonian captivity, and this goes contrary not only to 2 Kings but also the *Babylonian Chronicles*. As for Daniel, the writer seems to know of Nebuchadnezzar only through the biblical text. The siege of Jerusalem in Jehoiakim's third year (Dan. 1:1-2) is based on a partial misunderstanding of 2 Chronicles. The other stories in Daniel about Nebuchadnezzar seem at least in part based on legends rising out of the reign of Nabonidus (see below). The book of Judith ostensibly describes an invasion of Judah by Nebuchadnezzar. The book is a work of fiction with many errors about the historical situation during the Neo-Babylonian period. However, some scholars have suggested that Judith reflects some knowledge of Nebuchadnezzar III and IV, pretenders to the Babylonian throne in the early Persian period, during the reign of Darius I.

Nebuchadnezzar's Successors

Nebuchadnezzar was succeeded by his son Amel-Marduk (562-560 B.C.E.). The short reign of Nebuchadnezzar's son has long been known because of the reference to Evil-Merodach in 2 Kings 25:27-30. According to Berossus, he was executed by Neriglissar, his brother-in-law, who became the next king of Babylon (560-556 B.C.E.). We know little about Neriglissar except that he seems to have ruled in a period of instability. His son Labashi-marduk ruled only a few months (or even weeks) before he was overthrown in a coup and displaced by Nabonidus (556-539 B.C.E.). Nabonidus claimed, perhaps truthfully, to have no designs on the throne but to have been put there by others. In any case, he restored stability and then reigned for almost twenty years, with his son Belshazzar standing in for a number of years (Beaulieu 1989). The reason for Belshazzar's regency is that Nabonidus spent about a decade in Tema in the west, where he supported the cult of the moon god Sin. The exact reason for this is not known, though it has been speculated that this had something to do with trade or was in some other way a rational political decision. Nevertheless, this caused the powerful Marduk priesthood to become hostile, and Nabonidus was subsequently denigrated in the Babylonian tradition. He had returned to Babylon by the time of the attack by Cyrus's army in 539 B.C.E. Although he fled, he was captured but, instead of being executed, he was allowed to live out his life (contra Xenophon, *Cyropaedia* 7.5.30).

Neo-Babylonian History in the Book of Daniel

Finally, we should consider Neo-Babylonian history in the book of Daniel. Although Nabonidus is not mentioned by name in the biblical text, he is likely to lie behind some of the stories in Daniel about Nebuchadnezzar. Belshazzar is said to be the son of Nebuchadnezzar when he was actually the son of Nabonidus. The arrogant, hybristic, and "insane" Nebuchadnezzar in Daniel 4 reminds one of Nabonidus as described in the *Verse Account of Nabonidus* (*ANET* 312-15). Of special interest is Daniel's story about Belshazzar, who had been largely forgotten in the Greek and Latin tradition. Yet this does not mean that the information about Belshazzar is reliable; on the contrary, most of the Daniel narrative is legendary. Belshazzar was never king of Babylonia (the Babylonian sources never refer to him as king and make it clear that the new year festival was not celebrated, since it could only be done with the king present), and the events described in Daniel 5 about the final days of Babylon do not match the known historical situation (Grabbe 1988). The *Babylonian Chronicles* resume in the last days of Nabonidus and give valuable information about the fall of Babylon to Cyrus. Belshazzar is not mentioned in the final days of Babylon and may even have died by this time. As for "Darius the Mede," there was no such individual. He is a fictional character, cobbled together from bits and pieces of tradition, either by the author of Daniel or by one of his sources.

BIBLIOGRAPHY
R. ALBERTZ 2003, *Israel in Exile: The History and Literature of the Sixth Century B.C.E.*, Atlanta: Society of Biblical Literature. • P.-A. BEAULIEU 1989, *The Reign of Nabonidus, King of Babylon 556-539 B.C.*, New Haven: Yale University Press. • J. J. COLLINS 1993, *Daniel: A Commentary on the Book of Daniel.* Minneapolis: Fortress, 29-33. • R. P. DOUGHERTY 1929, *Nabonidus and Belshazzar: A Study of the Closing Events of the Neo-Babylonian Empire*, New Haven: Yale University Press. • L. L. GRABBE 1988, "Another Look at the *Gestalt* of 'Darius the Mede,'" *CBQ* 50: 198-213. • A. K. GRAYSON 1975, *Assyrian and Babylonian Chronicles*, Locust Valley, N.Y.: Augustin. • O. LIPSCHITS 2005, *The Rise and Fall of Jerusalem: Judah under Babylonian Rule*, Winona Lake, Ind.: Eisenbrauns.

See also: Nebuchadnezzer LESTER L. GRABBE

Babylonian Talmud

Overview

The Babylonian Talmud (Hebrew for "study") is the compendium of teachings that emerged from the Jewish rabbis of Babylonia (present-day Iraq). A parallel Talmud, called the Palestinian or Jerusalem Talmud (Yerushalmi in Hebrew), emerged from the rabbis of Roman Palestine. The Babylonian Talmud gained ascendancy over the Palestinian Talmud, garnering more cultural prestige and legal authority.

Each Talmud is composed of two elements, the Mishnah and the Gemara. The Mishnah is the corpus of law taught by the Tannaim (Aramaic for "repeaters"), the earliest generations of rabbis in Palestine, and edited by Rabbi Judah the Patriarch at the beginning of the third century C.E. The Gemara (Aramaic for "teaching tradition," used conventionally to refer to the Talmud) functions as a commentary on and expansion of the Mishnah and is organized according to the same structure (order, tractate, chapter). The core of the Babylonian Gemara was generated by the Amoraim (Aramaic for "interpreters"), the generations of rabbis in Palestine and Babylonia who succeeded the Tannaim. The amoraic teachings were in turn shaped and expanded upon by anonymous editors who are largely responsible for the characteristic features of the Babylonian Talmud as we know it today, which consists of a variety of literary genres (legal dicta, legal argumentation, Bible commentary, aphorisms, narratives, folklore, medical advice, astrology, etc.) and an almost dizzying panoply of themes and concerns. The Babylonian Talmud (known in Hebrew as the Bavli) became one of the most important collections in the Jewish canon besides the Hebrew Bible. Traditional Jews consider God's word to consist of two complementary components, the "written law" represented by the Hebrew Bible and the "oral law" represented by the Talmud and other rabbinic works.

Date

Each of the literary layers of the Talmud has its own set of chronological questions. The earliest rabbinic material within the Talmud is the tannaitic stratum, which consists of mishnayot and "baraitot," tannaitic teachings not canonized within the Mishnah. Some scholars think that some of this material dates back to the Second Temple period, but most would date the majority of this material to the second century C.E. or later. The latest material in the Talmud is likely the anonymous editorial material. Scholars debate whether this material was produced during the amoraic period, afterwards in the late fifth and early sixth centuries C.E., or even later. An important but problematic source of information regarding the dating of the Talmud is the *Epistle of Sherira Gaon* (Sherira, 966-1065 C.E.), the earliest written history of the Talmud. According to Sherira's account, a group of rabbis in the sixth century C.E. called the Savoraim added the final flourishes to the Talmud, clarifying ambiguous statements and inserting some teachings of their own. Some modern scholars contend, however, that the savoraic contribution was more substantial. The Talmud was considered a closed collection by the Geonim, the heads of the rabbinic academies from the end of the sixth century until the tenth century C.E., though the Talmud was still not linguistically fixed even then.

Composition History

The rabbinic material in the Talmud was composed by many generations of rabbis. The Tannaim lived primarily in second-century-C.E. Palestine, first in Judea and then later in the Galilee. These rabbis produced Hebrew-language traditions, mostly oral, that were transmitted within the world of the Tannaim but probably had little impact on the wider Jewish world. The later rabbis, the Amoraim, were a more diverse and influential group than their predecessors. The Babylonian Amoraim, who lasted until the close of the fifth century C.E., had their centers of learning in the towns of Nehardea, Mehoza, Sura, and Pumbedita. The framework of learning for the Amoraim was probably informal disciple circles (contra the previously held assumption, based on geonic accounts, that there were established academies in Babylonia in this era). Talmudic literature attests to a good deal of exchange between the rabbinic communities of Palestine and Babylonia; within the Babylonian Talmud can be found teachings from both Palestinian and Babylonian Amoraim. According to recent analysis, the Babylonian Amoraim were a more tightly circumscribed group than the Palestinian Amoraim. Reconstructing the rabbinic generations of both Tannaim and Amoraim is difficult, since different rabbis seem to have had the same name, and Talmud manuscripts display a great deal of variation with respect to rabbinic names. The only information known about the editors of the Talmud (called by some scholars the Stammaim, the "anonymous ones") has to be intuited from the dialectical and narrative literary materials they generated. The major source for the Savoraim is Sherira Gaon, who reconstructs the following chronology: the Savoraim began their reign almost immediately after the Amoraim ceased, reigned for fifty years, and then, after a fifty-year gap, were followed by the Geonim. The identities of the Amoraim and then later the Geonim are clearest, but the identities of the rabbis in between may never be precisely known.

Languages

The rabbinic languages of the Talmud are Hebrew and Aramaic. The tannaitic and earlier amoraic teachings are composed primarily in mishnaic (or rabbinic) Hebrew. Scholars have debated the degree to which the dialects of mishnaic Hebrew were a spoken language. The later amoraic and anonymous literary materials within the Talmud are composed primarily in Eastern Aramaic. Rabbinic Hebrew and Aramaic contain many loanwords from Greek and Persian.

Literary Features

Although the Babylonian Talmud is organized as a commentary on the Mishnah, it covers only thirty-seven of the Mishnah's sixty-three tractates. The missing commentary may have been lost, but more likely it never existed; the legal subjects lacking commentary did not have great relevance for the Babylonian Jewish community. The principles that implicitly drive the Gemara's commentary on the Mishnah are: (1) *harmonization:* the Gemara is concerned to show a minimum of disagreement among Tannaim; (2) *economy of language:* the Gemara supposes that the Tannaim formulated their texts without any superfluities; (3) *biblical support:* the Gemara seeks out a biblical basis for the mostly apodictic tannaitic traditions. The Gemara frequently emends tannaitic texts, reinterprets them, or narrows their scope according to these principles.

The Talmud is composed of various literary units: the tannaitic teachings (mishnah, baraita), the amoraic teachings (memra), and the pericopae into which both of these are knit, called the sugya (from Aram. *segi,* "to go"). Individual sugyot frequently repeat material from other sugyot and presuppose knowledge of them. Sources are usually clearly marked by the talmudic redactors: biblical verses, mishnayot, baraitot, and memrot are each introduced as such with characteristic technical terminology. Nevertheless, it can sometimes be difficult to determine where a quoted text ends and the anonymous redactor begins.

The Talmud is often said to be comprised of two literary genres, halakah and haggadah. Halakah, literally, "walking," comprises legal materials, while haggadah, "telling," includes all other materials such as stories, aphorisms, and homily. While halakah has traditionally been privileged, recent scholars have argued that the two genres are closely linked within the Talmud, such that frequently the halakah is meant to shed light on the haggadah and vice versa. The Talmud is best known for its legal dialectic, called in Aramaic *šaqla ve-tarya* ("give and take"). The legal dialectic is mostly anonymous, its style is dialogical and heavily rhetorical, and its concepts are complex and abstract.

Persian Cultural Context

The rabbinic community behind the Babylonian Talmud lived in Sassanid-ruled Persia, where the state religion was Zoroastrianism. The significance of the Zoroastrian cultural context for the Babylonian Talmud has recently been emphasized. Earlier scholars had looked at Persian loanwords and elements of Persian religion in the Bavli, and current scholars have compared Persian and talmudic legal dicta, narrative motifs, and marital practices. Scholars are also beginning to examine the significance of Eastern Roman provincial culture for the Bavli. A major source of evidence for Babylonian Jewish religious culture consists of Jewish incantation bowls and amulets found in the area, which provide a material counterpoint to the talmudic literary texts.

Relationship to Palestinian Talmud

The Babylonian Talmud's many parallels with the Palestinian Talmud raise the question: Did the redactors of the Babylonian Talmud already possess the Palestinian Talmud as it looks today, did they have some precursor to it, or did they have only discrete traditions? Recent work has argued that some Babylonian Talmud redactors had some Palestinian Talmud tractates in their full form, but this has not been proven for the Talmuds as a whole. Scholars have long explained legal divergences between the two Talmuds as a product of sociohistorical differences between the Babylonian and Palestinian communities. Recent work has argued that these halakic differences are due at least as frequently to ambiguities and textual issues in the tannaitic texts that both rabbinic communities were interpreting.

Textual History

The rabbis categorized their teachings as "oral Torah," privileging an oral mode of instruction, but Talmud scholars debate the extent to which its transmission was in fact oral. The Talmud itself describes both oral and written processes, and analysis of the Talmud's style supports the hypothesis that it was transmitted in some combination of oral and written modes. There is clear evidence for written copies of the Talmud by the middle of the eighth century, though the oldest extant manuscripts may date only to the tenth century. The Munich manuscript, originating in Paris in 1342, is the only complete manuscript of the Talmud. There are about twenty other lengthy Talmud manuscripts scattered around the libraries of Europe, the United States, and Russia, with the largest concentration in the Vatican. There are also many fragments from the Cairo genizah, only some of which have been published and analyzed. Many Talmud texts were lost over the centuries due to censorship and burning by the church. The edition of the Talmud used most widely today is the Vilna Shas (Shas being an acronym for the "six orders"), published by the Romm family printers in 1854. In this edition, the text of the Talmud appears in the center, the commentary of Rashi (Solomon ben Isaac, France, d. 1105) appears on the inside of the page, and the commentary of the Tosafot ("the supplements," Rashi's followers in Germany and France during the twelfth through fourteenth centuries) appears on the outside. A standard citation includes the name of the tractate, the folio number, and the folio side (a or b). Critical editions have been published for some tractates but not for the entire Talmud.

Talmud Scholarship

Traditional Talmud commentary exists in a variety of genres — commentaries, novellae, codes, responsa. Authorship is conventionally categorized according to three successive groups of commentators — Geonim (sixth to tenth centuries), Rishonim (eleventh to sixteenth centuries), and Aharonim (from the sixteenth century on). Many of these commentators worked in Europe, the Middle East, and North Africa, and a cultural divide is conventionally made between those in Christian Europe, called "Ashkenaz," and those in Muslim Europe, the Middle East, and North Africa, called "Sefarad."

Academic scholarship of the Talmud has its origins largely in the nineteenth-century German movement of the *Wissenschaft des Judentums.* Those scholars, who pioneered a historical-critical approach to rabbinic literature, authored foundational dictionaries, grammars, manuscript catalogs, and critical editions. Twentieth-century scholars continued in this vein, with the geographical centers moving from Europe to the United States and Israel. Scholars undertook synthetic histories of the talmudic period (G. Alon, I. Gafni), surveyed rabbinic theology and ethics (S. Schechter, E. Urbach), advanced Talmud text criticism (J. Epstein, S. Lieberman, E. Rosenthal, D. Halivni, S. Friedman), and attempted to reconstruct the redactional history of the Talmud (A. Weiss, H. Klein, J. Kaplan). The major innovations of the twentieth century lay in the fields of source criticism and cultural history. In the arena of source criticism, a new awareness was brought to the changes wrought by later editors to earlier traditions. A radical skepticism regarding access to early traditions was introduced by the prolific Jacob Neusner, who also questioned the historical accuracy of the Talmud's narratives, which began to be viewed as rhetorical shapers of culture and bearers of ideology rather than as mimetic reflections of reality.

Most recently, Talmud scholars have developed a variety of interdisciplinary approaches that include literary theory, critical legal studies, new historicism, gender studies, and postcolonial theory. Developing areas of interest include: the ideological assumptions and aspirations of talmudic dialectic; the construction of gender, the construction of the Gentile, and the construction of rabbinic authority within talmudic texts; the relationship of talmudic culture to other varieties of Judaism and other religious cultures in the same period; the interplay between historical and hermeneutical factors; the interplay between law and narrative; the Sassanian and Eastern Roman provincial context of talmudic culture; the role of the redactors vis-à-vis talmudic haggadah.

The Babylonian Talmud in Jewish Culture

The Babylonian Talmud became an authoritative text in the geonic period, but it did not go unchallenged. The Palestinian Talmud still held sway in some areas, the Karaites rejected the very notion of authoritative rabbinic tradition, and the Talmud was probably never accessible to the wide range of Jews. In early modern Europe, Jews influenced by the Enlightenment and, desiring to assimilate to Christian culture, attacked the Talmud as an emblem of Jewish parochialism. Jewish Orthodoxy developed as a response to new reforming movements and reasserted the complete and unchanging authority of the Talmud. Jews today engage in Talmud study in yeshivas in the United States, Israel, and elsewhere. Liberal Jews have also turned to Talmud study in something of a Talmud revival. In recent years, with the ordination of women rabbis in Reform and Conservative Judaism, the emergence of women religious leaders in Orthodoxy, as well as women academic scholars of Talmud, women have begun to take a prominent role in the study and teaching of Talmud.

BIBLIOGRAPHY

English Translations

I. EPSTEIN, ED. 1978, *Babylonian Talmud,* London: Soncino. • H. GOLDWURM AND N. SCHERMAN, EDS. 1990-2005, *Talmud Bavli: The Gemara: The Classic Vilna Edition,* Schottenstein Edition, Artscroll, Brooklyn: Mesorah.

CD-Roms

Soncino Classics Collection 1996, Chicago: Davka; Brooklyn: Judaica Press. • *Bar Ilan's Judaic Library (The Responsa Project)* 2006, Monsey, N.Y.: Torah Educational Software.

Studies

B. BOKSER 1990, "Talmudic Studies," in *The State of Jewish Studies,* ed. S. Cohen and E. Greenstein, New York: Jewish Theological Seminary. • D. BOYARIN 1993, *Carnal Israel: Reading Sex in Talmudic Culture,* Berkeley: University of California Press. • Y. ELMAN 2004, "Acculturation to Elite Persian Norms and Modes of Thought in the Babylonian Jewish Community of Late Antiquity," in *Neti'ot leDavid,* ed. Y. Elman et al., Jerusalem: Orhot, 31-56. • A. GOLDBERG 1987, "The Babylonian Talmud," in *The Literature of the Sages,* vol. 1, ed. S. Safrai, Philadelphia: Fortress, 323-45. • I. GAFNI 1990, *The Jews of Babylonia in the Talmudic Period,* Jerusalem: Zalman Shazar Center. • D. GOODBLATT 1981, "The Babylonian Talmud," in *The Study of Ancient Judaism,* vol. 2, ed. J. Neusner, New York: Ktav, 120-99. • L. JACOBS 1984, *The Talmudic Argument,* New York: Cambridge University Press. • R. KALMIN 1994, *Sages, Stories, Authors, and Editors in Rabbinic Babylonia,* Atlanta: Scholars Press. • D. KRAEMER 1990, *The Mind of the Talmud: An Intellectual History of the Bavli,* New York: Oxford University Press. • J. L. RUBENSTEIN 1999, *Talmudic Stories: Narrative Art, Composition, and Culture,* Baltimore: Johns Hopkins University Press. • J. L. RUBINSTEIN 2003, *The Culture of the Babylonian Talmud,* Baltimore: Johns Hopkins University Press. • G. STEMBERGER 1996, *Introduction to the Talmud and Midrash,* trans. M. Bockmuehl, Minneapolis: Fortress.

See also: Palestinian Talmud

BETH A. BERKOWITZ

Bandits → Resistance Movements

Baptism → Washing, Ritual

Barki Nafshi (4Q434-438)

The title *Barki Nafshi* (Hebrew for "Bless, O My Soul") refers to a Hebrew poetic text — a hymn or prayer of praise and thanksgiving — discovered in Cave 4 at Qumran and preserved in five collections of fragments (4Q434-438 = *Barkhi Nafshi*[a-e]) edited by Weinfeld and Seely (1999). The five collections of fragments are by different scribal hands that contain parallel and overlapping passages, a situation indicating that they were originally five copies of a larger text. While the fragmentary nature of the text makes it impossible to know its original length, several large fragments preserve about sixty relatively complete lines from which the general content of the poem can be described.

The name *Barki Nafshi* was chosen because the hymn begins with the phrase "Bless, O my soul, the Lord" *(barki nafšî ʾet-ʾădônāi)* — likely a deliberate imitation of the opening lines of Psalms 103 and 104, which also begin with this phrase. There is a medieval *Barki Nafshi* prayer in Judaism, but it does not appear to be related to the Qumran hymn. The scripts of the fragments can be dated between the Hasmonean and Herodian periods (150 B.C.E.-70 C.E.); however, there is no internal evidence for a more precise dating of the text. Since the constellation of vocabulary and theology is consistent with that known in sectarian texts at Qumran (especially the *Thanksgiving Hymns*), the editors hypothesize that the poem is of sectarian origin. However, because there is no distinctive sectarian vocabulary in *Barki Nafshi,* others argue that the hymn originated outside of the community and later was imported into Qumran, where it was accepted because its contents were consistent with the community's world view (Brooke 2000).

Barki Nafshi is a hymn or prayer in which the poet expresses praise and thanksgiving to the Lord for delivering and redeeming his people and for bestowing his grace on them. The poet blesses the Lord for delivering "the soul of the poor" and the helpless. He praises the Lord because "in the abundance of his mercy" he delivered them from their enemies, "he made darkness light before them," and "his angel encamped around them (4Q434 1 i 1-12). The poet continues praising the Lord for giving "knowledge to the wise," for writing the law in the poet's heart, and for making his "mouth like a sharp sword," to utter holy words (4Q437 1 1-7). Finally, the poet thanks the Lord for deliverance from the Gentiles and for rescuing his soul from the underworld (4Q437 2 i 10-12). As with much of the poetry from Qumran, the poet has created *Barki Nafshi* as a rich biblical mosaic — crafting his prayer using multiple lines, phrases and vocabulary taken from the Hebrew Bible — especially Isaiah, Jeremiah, and the Psalms.

A central and unifying theme of *Barki Nafshi* is God implanting in the poet and in his people a series of pious qualities (Seely 2000). For example, the Lord opens their eyes to see his ways and their ears to hear his teachings; he circumcises the foreskins of their hearts (4Q434 1 i 3-4); "he set their feet to the way" (4Q434 1 i 4). The poet praises God because "my heart you have commanded and my inmost parts you have taught well, lest your statutes be forgotten" (4Q436 1 i 5); "my foot you have strengthened" (4Q436 1 i 8); "the spirit of holiness you have set in my heart" (4Q436 1 ii 1); and "the stiff neck you have cast from me" (4Q436 1 ii 2).

Scholarly studies have begun to investigate *Barki Nafshi* in the context of Second Temple Judaism. Weinfeld (1992) has argued, from a series of parallel phrases, that 4Q434 contains an early form of the rabbinic prayer "Grace after Meals for Mourners." Seely (1996) has explored the prominent *Barki Nafshi* image of the "circumcised heart" as it relates to the Hebrew Bible, the New Testament, and the sectarian texts from Qumran.

Brooke (2000) postulates that *Barki Nafshi,* although of nonsectarian origin, was used by the Qumran community in the same way as other sectarian texts that describe certain physical features as distinctive hallmarks of those admitted to the community (*Community Rule, War Rule,* 4Q186, 4Q561, and 4Q534). Brooke argues that the Qumran community interpreted the scriptural metaphors for piety in *Barki Nafshi* involving the eyes, ears, lips, neck, hands, and feet, and the condition of the heart and spirit, as physiognomical information that could help determine a person's spiritual status, leading to either inclusion or exclusion from the community. Brooke compares these physiognomic texts with a contemporary Jewish text that includes a detailed description of the physical appearance of Aseneth in the process of her conversion to Judaism (*Jos. & Asen.* 16:16; 18:7-11).

Most recently Smith (2006) has identified the transplanting of pious qualities and God's granting his people a "pure heart" and a "spirit of holiness" in *Barki Nafshi* as part of the eschatological transformation promised by Deuteronomy (30:6), Jeremiah (32:39-40), and Ezekiel (11:19; 36:26) (cf. *Jubilees* and the Qumran sectarian texts *Community Rule* and *Thanksgiving Hymns*). Smith argues that the "spirit of holiness" may serve as a point of departure for understanding some of the occurrences of the term "Holy Spirit" in the New Testament.

BIBLIOGRAPHY

G. BROOKE 2000, "Body Parts in *Barkhi Nafshi* and the Qualifications for Membership of the Worshipping Community," in *Sapiential, Liturgical, and Poetical Texts from Qumran,* ed. D. Falk, F. García Martínez, and E. Schuller, Leiden: Brill, 79-94. • D. SEELY 1996, "The 'Circumcised Heart' in 4Q434 *Barkhi Nafshi,*" *RevQ* 17: 527-35. • D. SEELY 2000, "Implanting Pious Qualities as a Theme in the *Barki Nafshi* Hymns," in *The Dead Sea Scrolls Fifty Years after Their Discovery,* ed. L. H. Schiffman, E. Tov, and J. C. VanderKam, Jerusalem: Israel Exploration Society, 322-31. • B. D. SMITH 2006, "'Spirit of Holiness' as Eschatological Principle of Obedi-

BAR KOKHBA CAVES

ence," in *Christian Beginnings and the Dead Sea Scrolls,* ed. J. J. Collins and C. A. Evans, Grand Rapids: Baker, 75-99. • M. WEINFELD 1992, "Grace after Meals in Qumran, *JBL* 111: 427-40. • M. WEINFELD AND D. SEELY 1999, *"Barkhi Nafshi,"* in *Qumran Cave 4.XX: Poetic and Liturgical Texts, Part 2,* ed. E. G. Chazon et al., DJD 29, Oxford: Clarendon, 255-334.

DAVID ROLPH SEELY

Bar Kokhba Caves

The caves used by Jewish fighters during the Bar Kokhba Revolt (132-135 C.E.) can be divided into two groups: hiding complexes and refuge caves. The hiding complexes were hewn out of rock artificially under residential buildings. They are found mainly in the Judean Shephelah and also in the Hebron and Beth-El Mountains. The refuge caves are found mainly in the Judean Desert, in the cliffs overlooking the Dead Sea and the Jordan Valley. The refuge caves are all natural, and the artifacts found in them make it evident that they served as places of refuge at the end of the revolt.

The Hiding Complexes

The hiding complexes were carved in soft limestone, which is common in the Shephelah. Rock-cut systems of this sort have been discovered in more then 125 settlements in Judea. These complexes were mentioned by Dio Cassius (*Roman History* 69.12), who reported:

> The Jews purposely made of poor quality such weapons as they were called upon to furnish, in order that the Romans might reject them and that they themselves might thus have the use of them; but when he [Hadrian] went further away they openly revolted. To be sure, they did not dare engage with the Romans in the open field, but they occupied the advantageous positions in the country and strengthened them with mines and walls, in order that they might have places of refuge whenever they should be hard pressed, and might meet together unobserved underground; and they pierced these subterranean passages from above at intervals to let in air and light.

No archaeological finds support Dio's description of Jewish manufacture of defective weapons; on the contrary, the weapons excavated at rebel sites are identical to Roman ones. His remarks concerning the tunnels, hideaways, subterranean passageways, and shafts have, however, received confirmation with the discovery of hundreds of hiding complexes, particularly in the Judean Shephelah.

Most of the hiding places are concentrated between the area of Naḥal Shiloh (in the Benjamin Mountains) in the north, and Naḥal Shiqma (northeast of Beer-sheba) in the south. They were carved as networks of underground burrows, which are so narrow and low that one must crawl in order to pass through them. They are winding, sometimes featuring ninety-degree turns or changes in level by means of vertical shafts. Along some of the burrows are mechanisms for blocking them from inside. The purpose of the sharp turns, changes in level, and blocking features was to hamper the enemy from entering and to increase the enemy's vulnerability.

The hiding complexes can be divided into family complexes, public complexes, and escape routes. Their standard features suggest that they were made as a planned element of the strategy that the Jews used against the Roman army. Some small hiding systems had been installed in the early first century C.E. and were used during the First Jewish Revolt. The hiding-complex phenomenon seems to have reached its peak of sophistication and geographical range between the revolts and during the Bar Kokhba War.

The Refuge Caves

After the fall of Bethar at the end of the Bar Kokhba Revolt, in the summer and autumn of 135 C.E., Jewish refugees, mainly military commanders, administrators, and their families, fled to natural caves outside Judean villages. Most of these caves are in the Judean Desert. They are large caves or clusters of medium-sized caves, considerably distanced from civilization. Its seems that Jerome had them in mind when he wrote: "And the citizens of Judea came to such distress that they, together with their wives, their children, their gold and their silver, in which they trusted, remained in underground tunnels and deepest caves" (*Commentary on Isaiah* 2.15).

To date, thirty-five refuge caves from the end of the revolt, located on the steep cliffs along wadis in the Judean Desert, have been discovered. They are located between Wadi ed-Daliyeh in the north and Wadi Seiyal (Naḥal Ṣe'elim) in the south. Documents and scrolls were found in nine of these caves. The documents found in Wadi Murabbaʿat shed light on the situation in Herodium before and during the revolt. Although the documents found in a cave west of Jericho are fragmentary and do not supply much information, the documents found in the other seven caves (i.e., Cave of Letters, Cave of Horror, Cave of the Pool, Cave of Treasure, Har Yishai Cave, the Caves of Naḥal Arugot, and the Caves of Naḥal Ṣe'elim) all shed light on the situation in the village of ʿEin Gedi before and during the revolt. At the end of the revolt, the population in ʿEin Gedi was divided into native farmers and people who had fled to this village from the eastern shore of the Dead Sea. The documents found in the Cave of Letters are among the most important ever discovered in the Judean Desert. They shed light on the history of ʿEin Gedi as well as on the Jews who dwelled in the Roman province of Arabia.

Approximately half of the refuge caves were found by the Roman forces, who sometimes built siege camps above them, slowly starving the insurgents to death. Their desperation may be at issue in a legend found in *Lam. Rab.* 1:45,

> Those Jews who were hidden in the caves devoured the flesh of their slain brethren. Every day one of them ventured forth and brought the corpses to them, which they ate. One day they said, "Let one of

us go, and if he finds anything let him bring it and we shall have to eat." On going out he found the slain body of his father, which he took and buried, and marked the spot. He returned and reported that he had found nothing. Thereupon a second individual was sent to find food. He uncovered the body hidden by the first and brought it to the camp. Upon discovering that he had eaten from his father's corpse, the son exclaimed: "Woe to me! I have eaten the flesh of my father!"

Skeletons were found in five refuge caves, indicating that they were used by families, including young children (some who were only three years old when they were taken to the caves). The remains of vegetal foods found in the refuge caves (beans, pulses, vegetables, fruit) suggest that the Jews stayed there for a few weeks in the months of August and September of 135 C.E. Some of the siege warfare above the caves evidently lasted until the beginning of 136 C.E.

BIBLIOGRAPHY

H. ESHEL AND D. AMIT 1998, *Refuge Caves of the Bar Kokhba Revolt,* Tel Aviv: Israel Exploration Society (in Hebrew). • A. KLONER AND Y. TEPPER 1987, *The Hiding Complexes in the Judean Shephelah,* Tel Aviv: Israel Exploration Society (in Hebrew). • A. KLONER AND B. ZISSU 2003, "Hiding Complexes in Judaea: An Archaeological and Geographical Update on the Area of the Bar Kokhba Revolt," in *The Bar Kokhba War Reconsidered,* ed. P. Schäfer, Tübingen: Mohr-Siebeck, 181-216. • Y. YADIN 1971, *Bar-Kokhba: The Rediscovery of the Legendary Hero of the Second Jewish Revolt against Rome,* London: Weidenfeld and Nicolson. HANAN ESHEL†

Bar Kokhba Letters

The Bar Kokhba letters constitute a remnant of what must once have been a considerable correspondence among Simeon bar Kosiba, or "Bar Kokhba" as he was known by Christian sources, and his lieutenants and other military personnel during the years of the Bar Kokhba Revolt (132-136[?] C.E.). Unearthed in modern times in caves of the Judean Desert, the number of these letters is approximately twenty-six; exiguous fragments of other possible letters make the precise number uncertain. Of this total, twenty-five were missives sent by Bar Kosiba or his scribes and lieutenants to subordinates. Only one letter addressed to the Jewish leader from a subordinate has survived. It was never sent, presumably because of exigencies involved with the collapse of the revolt, and so ended up being cached along with other materials belonging to the intended messenger.

The letters are written in three languages, Aramaic, Hebrew, and Greek, and have considerable significance as evidence for Jewish language and literacy during the period. All were discovered in caves west of the Dead Sea between 1950 and 1965, although not all were discovered *in situ* by archaeologists. About half came onto the antiquities market thanks to Bedouin cave explorers who were seeking to profit from illicit foraging in caverns of the Judean Desert.

Sometimes included under the rubric of "Bar Kokhba Letters" are a considerable number of legal documents of the most varied sorts: IOUs, marriage contracts, tax receipts, contracts for the sale of homes and crops, census declarations, etc. These documents derive from the same and neighboring caves and provide crucial archaeological and historical context for the interpretation of the letters themselves.

Discovery

Written materials from caves in the Wadi Murabbaʿat began to be offered on the antiquities market by the Bedouin in late 1951. This offering alerted archaeologists that a new discovery had been made, and eventuated in the mounting of an archaeological expedition to explore the region. Between 21 January and 21 March of 1952 five caves in the Wadi yielded evidence of habitation and written materials from the late Second Temple period and beyond, and it was determined that the Bedouin offerings had originated in these same caves. Along with significant biblical manuscripts, autograph documents written in Hebrew, Aramaic, Greek, and Arabic were discovered, spanning the years from the first century B.C.E. to the tenth century C.E. By far the most important were those from Cave 2, documents originally dated by scholars to the time of the Bar Kokhba Revolt (although it is now known or suspected that approximately a dozen of the contracts and fiscal documents actually date from the time of the First Revolt, 66-73 C.E.). Among the materials deriving from Cave 2 were seven well-preserved letters, known today as Mur 42-48, along with the poorly preserved Mur 49-52, also possibly letters.

At about the same time, Bedouin had discovered and now offered for sale additional documentary and literary texts related to the Bar Kokhba Revolt. The find spot for these materials was a mystery; in the 1950s it came to be believed that they had derived from one or more caves in the Naḥal Ṣeʾelim. Accordingly, Israeli archaeologists explored that area between 24 January and 2 February 1960, but the documentary finds were sparse in the extreme. Today it is known that almost all of the putative Naḥal Ṣeʾelim finds actually originated in caves along the Naḥal Ḥever, and that the Bedouin pursued a policy of deception on the point to obfuscate their illegal activities there. These materials are designated so as to allow for the uncertainty of their derivation, using the rubric "XḤev/Se." Among them is XḤev/Se 30, the only letter intended for Simeon bar Kosiba. In fact it, too, probably originated in the caves of Naḥal Ḥever.

Archaeologists intent on further exploration of the Judean Caves proving to be so generous in their gifts to modern scholarship explored Naḥal Ḥever during a two-week campaign in 1960, and again in the spring of 1961. Here the discoveries were nothing short of spectacular. One of these caves, designated the "Cave of Letters," yielded three separate collections of documents to the explorers. One was a group of legal materials be-

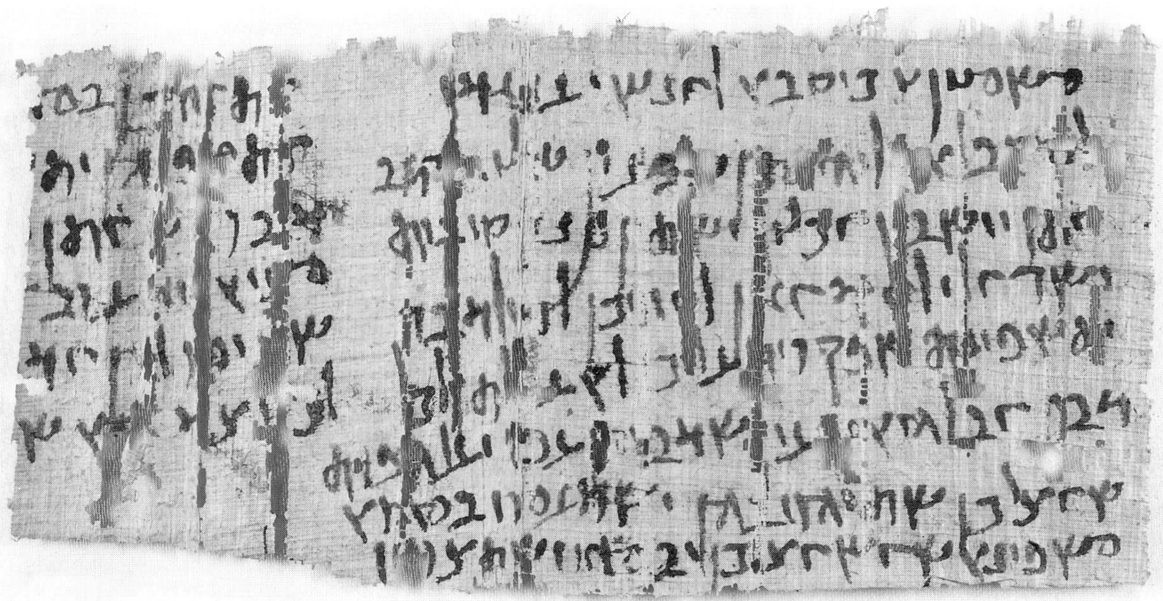

Hebrew letter of Ben Kosiba (Bar Kokhba) dispatched to ʿEin Gedi, reprimanding Masabala and Yehonatan for "living well, eating and drinking off the property of the House of Israel, and [caring] nothing about your brethren" *(Photo Clara Amit, Courtesy Israel Antiquities Authority)*

longing in antiquity to Babatha daughter of Simeon. These thirty-six documents were composed in Aramaic of two basic types, Judean and Nabatean, but also and principally in Greek. A second archive retrieved from the Cave of Letters was that of Eliezer bar Samuel; this packet of five contracts had slipped out from an elegant leather purse in which it had originally been secreted, and was found exposed between the rocks. It is possible that XḤev/Se 30 once belonged among the materials of this archive, for it was labeled on the outside, "Eliezer, for Simeon." One cannot be certain of the point, since Eliezer was a common Jewish name of the period, but in any event the letter almost certainly derives from the Cave of Letters and thus Eliezer bar Samuel's group of refugees. The third collection of documents from this cave comprised fifteen letters sent to the two military commanders jointly appointed over nearby ʿEin Gedi by Simeon bar Kosiba. Most of these letters addressed both men, Jonathan bar Bayan and Masabala bar Simeon, but four concern only Jonathan. Accordingly, he is believed to have been the owner of the archive.

All of the documentary papyri discovered by archaeologists in the Cave of Letters are today denominated as the Yadin Papyri (P. Yadin), after the famous Israeli archaeologist and politician who led the expeditions there. P. Yadin 49-63 comprise the letters.

It should be noted that a fourth archive from the Cave of Letters, once belonging to a young woman, Salome Komaise, had already been removed by the Bedouin before the scholars arrived. It was split up and sold at different times to scholars, with the claimed provenance of Naḥal Ṣe'elim. These seven papyri are not letters, but fiscal documents and contracts of different types. They are designated XḤev/Se 12, 60-65.

Contents

On the whole the Bar Kokhba correspondence deals with quotidian matters of military supply, discipline, and instructions regarding named individuals. Accordingly, the letters offer but little insight into the larger specifics of the revolt and the course of events. Since no surviving ancient historian described the revolt with anything approaching the thoroughness of Josephus as he wrote of the First Revolt, this absence of the big picture from the letters is the more regrettable. Perhaps the most informative of the letters for broader historical understanding is the one letter that was addressed to Simeon bar Kosiba, XḤev/Se 30. Although it is damaged and lacunose, a possible reading and translation of the Hebrew is as follows:

> To Simeon ben Kosiba, prince of Israel, from Simeon ben Mattanyah: Greetings, beloved father. Be informed that the Gentiles who were with ben [. . .] have assembled to me, though some of them are in the town. [. . . Also], "brothers" (i.e., Jewish fighters) from h[ere] have been struck, but we were not among them. Fa[rewell].
>
> Simeon ben Mattanah (different hand)

Two points are especially noteworthy here. First, Simeon ben Mattanyah (Mattanah is a hypocoristic following a well-known pattern) addresses his leader as "beloved father." This language is obviously atypical military address, in the ancient world or the modern.

One notes that the soldiers were "brothers," so the styling of Bar Kosiba as "father" is perhaps consistent, but the suspicion arises nevertheless that the relationship between author and addressee is "charismatic" in the sense made famous by Weber. This almost worshipful submission is, of course, not reflected in any of the letters sent by Bar Kosiba or his high officers to subordinates.

The significance of the charismatic element is that it has been a matter of controversy among historians of the revolt whether or not Bar Kosiba was really considered a "messiah," as his appellation "Son of the Star" (the meaning of Aram. "bar Kokhba") seems to imply. The language of XḤev/Se 30 can be read as supporting the idea that he was, indeed, so conceived by some Jewish followers.

The second point is perhaps more mundane but equally significant for historical understanding. The Gentiles referenced by the letter are clearly not the Roman opposition, but rather seem to be allies of the Jewish commander and his troops. Formerly they were mustered with another commander, whose name is partially lost; now, perhaps after that commander's death in battle, many of them have rallied to Simeon ben Mattanyah. Ancient sources do suggest that non-Jews joined in the revolt and thereby imply that it may have spread beyond the borders of the Jewish polity. The two ideas are related: Gentile support and the extent of the conflict. Many scholars have distrusted the ancient claims, and arguments continue about the geographic dimensions of the war against Rome. XḤev/Se 30 shows that non-Jews did join and therefore supports the view, now in the ascendancy in scholarship, that the war was far more threatening to Rome than a putative minor conflict confined to southern Judea might have been.

Formal Characteristics

The formulary of the Bar Kokhba letters is distinctly different from that of earlier Hebrew and Aramaic letters, so far as evidence allows comparison. In making this statement it is important to acknowledge at the outset that surviving evidence is far from abundant, and that known caches are sometimes separated from each other by large spans of time. Thus extant epigraphic Hebrew letters prior to the time of the Bar Kokhba Revolt are almost all to be dated between the years 630 and 587 B.C.E. Caution in drawing conclusions is therefore in order. Still, what may be said is that in comparison to the earlier epigraphic letters, the epistolographic formulas of the Bar Kokhba letters show marked change. Further, the nature of the change is in the direction of conformity to practices of the contemporary Greco-Roman world.

This conformity is most notable in the matter of opening and closing salutations. A typical contemporary Greek opening would be "X bids joy to Y"; Latin would be "X bids well-being to Y." Thus these formulas begin by identifying the sender and then the recipient, followed by a characteristic verb or verb + noun to convey good wishes. This is precisely what one finds in the Bar Kokhba letters, although they are mostly written in Hebrew and Aramaic, not Greek. A typical example would be P. Yadin 56: *Simeon bar Kosiba to Jonathan bar Bayan and to Masabala and to bar Hita: Peace (shelam), my brothers!*

Regarding closing salutations the situation is similar. Greek and Latin letters of the time end by wishing the recipient well, often using a single standard verb. This is what the Bar Kokhba letters do as well, ordinarily concluding with Hebr. *shalom* or the Aramaic equivalent. Frequently Greek and Latin letters would be authenticated at the end by the sender's actual signature (the rest of the letter having been composed by a scribe). This practice, too, is common in the Bar Kokhba correspondence, but it never happens in the earlier Hebrew letters that have survived.

Scholars of Greek and Latin epistolography often speak of typical types of letters, that is, letters that follow certain conventions in order to accomplish typical purposes, such as recommendation, invitation, exhortation, condolence, and consolation. To some degree one finds such formulaic approaches within the Bar Kokhba letters, too. Thus, for example, P. Yadin 63, a fragmentary letter in Aramaic, includes the phrase, "I have sent the letter to you by the hand of Simeon bar Ishmael." This phrase is typical of formulaic expressions found in Greco-Roman letters that are intended to vouch for, and sometimes to recommend for further service, the bearer of the letter.

Perhaps it goes without saying, but the Greek letters P. Yadin 52 and 57 follow Hellenistic practices entirely.

Language

Letters in the ancient world were generally conceived as a kind of substitute for personal presence. Accordingly, they tended to be composed in less formal language, in style registers closer to the conversation for which they were a stand-in. The Latin of Cicero's letters, for example, is markedly different from that of his speeches — much closer to ordinary speech, hence being known as *sermo cotidianus.* So too the Bar Kokhba correspondence is written in Hebrew and Aramaic that is less formal than that of the coeval legal materials, and differs notably from contemporary literary registers or dialects of both languages as known, for example, from the Dead Sea Scrolls. The Hebrew of the Dead Sea Scrolls largely represents more or less (often less) successful attempts at writing Biblical Hebrew; the Aramaic dialect of the Scrolls derives from earlier Official Aramaic and therefore to a large degree evidences the international morphology, syntax and lexicon of that earlier *lingua franca.* In contrast, the language of the Hebrew letters is akin to that of the Mishnah, though with more evident Aramaic influence than the Mishnah's transmission has retained. In the same way the Aramaic of the Bar Kokhba correspondence is the closest thing to spoken ancient Judean Aramaic that we have. Still, the Hebrew letters in particular occasionally manifest the scribe's acquaintance with Biblical Hebrew and so, for example, may use words with their biblical rather than their mishnaic meanings where these differ.

BIBLIOGRAPHY
P. BENOIT, J. T. MILIK, AND R. DE VAUX, EDS. 1961, *Les Grottes de Murabbaʿat,* DJD 2, Oxford: Clarendon. • J. H. CHARLESWORTH ET AL., EDS. 2000, *Miscellaneous Texts from the Judean Desert,* DJD 38, Oxford: Clarendon. • H. COTTON AND A. YARDENI, EDS. 1997, *Aramaic, Hebrew and Greek Documentary Texts from Nahal Hever and Other Sites,* DJD 27, Oxford: Clarendon. • H. ESHEL 2002, "Documents of the First Jewish Revolt from the Judean Desert," in *The First Jewish Revolt: Archaeology, History and Ideology,* ed. A. M. Berlin and J. A. Overman, London: Routledge, 157-63. • E. KUTSCHER 1977A, "The Hebrew and Aramaic Letters of Bar Koseba and His Contemporaries. Part I: The Aramaic Letters," in *Eduard Yechezkel Kutscher, Hebrew and Aramaic Studies,* ed. Z. Ben-Hayyim, A. Dotan, and G. Sarfatti, Jerusalem: Magnes, 36-53 (in Hebrew). • E. KUTSCHER 1977B, "The Hebrew and Aramaic Letters of Bar Koseba and His Contemporaries. Part II: The Hebrew Letters," in *Eduard Yechezkel Kutscher, Hebrew and Aramaic Studies,* ed. Z. Ben-Hayyim, A. Dotan, and G. Sarfatti, Jerusalem: Magnes, 54-70 (in Hebrew). • N. LEWIS 1989, *The Documents from the Bar Kokhba Period in the Cave of Letters: Greek Papyri,* Jerusalem: Israel Exploration Society. • Y. YADIN 1961, "Expedition D," *IEJ* 11: 36-52. • Y. YADIN 1962, "Expedition D — The Cave of the Letters," *IEJ* 12: 227-57. • Y. YADIN 1971, *Bar-Kokhba: The Rediscovery of the Legendary Hero of the Second Jewish Revolt against Rome,* London: Weidenfeld and Nelson. • Y. YADIN, J. C. GREENFIELD, A. YARDENI, AND B. LEVINE, EDS. 2002, *The Documents from the Bar Kokhba Period in the Cave of Letters: Hebrew, Aramaic and Nabataean-Aramaic Papyri,* Jerusalem: Israel Exploration Society.

MICHAEL O. WISE

Bar Kokhba Revolt

The fourth decade of the second century C.E. saw the outbreak of the final Jewish uprising against Roman rule in Palestine. Named the Bar Kokhba Revolt for its leader, its details remain shrouded in mystery. With no historical treatise to provide a systematic account of the revolt, and no lost work (Roman or Jewish) known to have described it, any scholarly attempt to reconstruct its course inevitably confronts the stumbling block of reliance on sources representing varying objectives, reliability, and dates, leaving many seminal issues unresolved. Still debated are the revolt's direct causes, the geographical extent of Bar Kokhba's regime, and whether it included Jerusalem, and the magnitude of the Roman reaction. Furthermore, the available literary, epigraphic, numismatic, and archaeological evidence reveals nothing of the revolt's military engagements.

So terse is the one extant historical account of the revolt — found in the abridged version of the third-century historian Cassius Dio's *Roman History* — that it fails to even name the rebel leader. Archaeological finds from 1952 to the present, mainly papyrological, fill the gaps somewhat; they by no means create, however, a coherent account of events in Palestine during the three-year revolt. What emerges is a partial picture of Bar Kokhba's leadership style and administration, the borders of his state, Jewish observance under wartime conditions, and the strong Roman reaction.

Cause of the Revolt

The sparse historical evidence focuses inconclusively on the foundation of the pagan city of Aelia Capitolina on the ruins of Jerusalem as the cause of the revolt (Cassius Dio, *Roman History* 69.12.1-2), or on Hadrian's ban on circumcision (*Historia Augusta, Vita Hadriani* 14.2). Although scholars are divided over the weight and historicity of these factors, the prevailing consensus ascribes a role to both.

Clouding the determination of cause is the church father Eusebius's dating of the establishment of Aelia Capitolina to 136 (*Hist. Eccl.* 4.6), thus making it an outcome of the revolt. Proof for an earlier founding of Aelia Capitolina comes, however, from coins minted there prior to this date, found in hoards concealed in the Judean Desert in 135 C.E. These hoards, which contain both Bar Kokhba and Aelia Capitolina coins, lend corroboration to Dio's account of Aelia Capitolina's founding in 130 during Hadrian's visit to that city.

The Leader of the Revolt

The discovery of documents in the Judean Desert in 1952 reconciled the ambiguity regarding the name of the revolt's leader left by its sparse documentation. Although earlier some scholars had maintained that Bar Kokhba (Hebrew for "son of the star") was his real name and that the appellation Bar Koziba (Hebrew for "son of disappointment") was a slur reflecting bitterness after the revolt, the Judean Desert documents categorically established that this leader's original name and title was Simeon ben Kosiba, Nasi Yisrael. Bar Kokhba was a soubriquet bestowed by his supporters, based on a messianic interpretation of Num. 24:17 ("A star [*kokhab*] will arise from Jacob") that later rabbinic tradition ascribed to Rabbi Akiba (*y. Taʿan.* 4:8, 68d).

Seventeen letters discovered in the Judean Desert that were dispatched from Simeon Ben Kosiba's headquarters not only disclosed his name but also shed light on his personality. The Ben Kosiba of the letters emerges as a demanding leader, a stickler for detail who constantly rebuked his subordinates for failing to fulfill their assignments scrupulously. Despite the infusion of information these letters provide, they leave many areas tantalizingly inaccessible; for example, because they are undated, they cannot be assigned to a specific point in the revolt — neither to its beginning, when Ben Kosiba was at the pinnacle of his strength, nor to its end, when his position was disastrous.

Ben Kosiba's undisputed position as the uprising's leader is backed by numismatic finds. Most rebel coins bear the name *Simeon;* the name of an unidentified individual, *Eleazar the Priest,* is inscribed on an additional group of coins. Three possible identifications have been proffered for the latter: Eleazar of Modi'in (ha-Moda'i), Eleazar ben Azariah, or Eleazar ben Harsom. But it is possible that Eleazar the Priest is otherwise unknown (i.e., not mentioned in the rabbinic literature). In any event, the presence of a priestly figure in the insurgent leadership suggests plans to capture Jerusalem and restore the Temple cult, aspirations not fulfilled.

Bar Kokhba's Administrative System

Judean Desert documents also provide a glimpse of Bar Kokhba's administrative system. Bar Kokhba appointed military commanders and civilian administrators, appointing them from the local population in the areas under his control. All told we know of seven commanders. One Yeshua ben Galgola, whose family lived in the village of Bet Bassi, near Herodium, was appointed commander of Herodium. Three individuals — Yonatan ben Ba'ayan, Masbala ben Simeon, and Eleazar ben Hitah — jointly commanded the ʿEin Gedi region. Fifteen letters from Yonatan ben Ba'ayan's personal archive show Ben Kosiba taking a close interest in administrative affairs and maintaining frequent contact with his commanders. Additional letters disclose the names of other commanders: Yehudah ben Manasseh, who served in Kiryat Arabaya, and a senior commander named Elisha, whom ʿEin Gedi's commanders had to obey. Another commander, Simeon ben Mahanim, reported to Ben Kosiba a military defeat in which "brethren were devoured." This letter's uncertain provenance makes it difficult to know which region Simeon ben Mahanim controlled.

In addition, Judean Desert documents reveal the existence of *parnasim* (district administrators) appointed by Bar Kokhba to oversee civilian matters. Regrettably, the scant information found in these documents discloses little more than their names and their involvement in land leasing and matters like weights-supervision. The documents also reflect changes in personnel: during year one of the revolt, Yehohanan ben Yeshua and Horon ben Yishmael served as ʿEin Gedi's *parnasim*, but during year three Yonatan ben Mahanim held this post. At Bet Mashiko, probably situated near Herodium, two *parnasim* were appointed, as a letter sent to Herodium commander Yeshua ben Galgola concerning the illegal confiscation of a cow divulges. Their failure to appeal to Herodium's civilian administrator is surprising. Finally, from an inscription on lead weights we learn of a *parnas* named Simeon Dasoi who served in the Shephelah.

The Course of the Revolt

Beginning and Geographic Extent

As best as can be determined, the revolt began in summer 132. The exact month in which "Year One" of the Bar Kokhba regime began is, however, a matter of debate. Life in Judea appears to have continued as usual during the revolt's first summer. This was not the case, though, for regions outside Judea, where Jews felt the effects of the revolt. Soon after its initial outbreak, Jews from the villages of Mehoza and Luhit in the Roman province of Arabia (Transjordan) left their homes. Sometime after August 132, two women, Babatha daughter of Simeon and Salome Komaise, fled from Mehoza, near Zoar, to ʿEin Gedi. When the revolt failed they left ʿEin Gedi and hid in a cave in Naḥal Ḥever, taking their documents with them.

Like many aspects of the Bar Kokhba regime, even its geographical extent remains uncertain, though it seems that Judea proper, but not Jerusalem, was under insurgent rule. Thirteen economic documents and twenty-three letters discovered in the Judean Desert show Ben Kosiba in control of the Herodium and ʿEin Gedi regions until 135, when the people to whom these documents belonged fled.

Coins and their geographical distribution make a crucial contribution to the discussion, even though most of these coins were unearthed during illegal excavations and their place of origin cannot be established. Rather than mint new coins, the Bar Kokhba regime reused Roman ones, and their blatant erasure of the imperial image and superimposition of Bar Kokhba's name certainly served propaganda purposes. Obviously, these over-struck coins were valid tender only in areas controlled by Bar Kokhba. Based on the discovery of hoards of imperial coins hidden by the Jewish insurgents (all predating 132), no doubt concealed against the eventuality of the revolt's failure or their departure from the region, we can posit a virtual state of economic isolation from neighboring regions.

Significantly, to date no Bar Kokhba coins have been discovered either in the well-excavated Galilee or in the much less-studied Transjordan area. Although this seems to exclude the Galilee from Bar Kokhba's state, it remains possible that local Jewish guerrilla forces saw military engagement there, and that Bar Kokhba's army operated beyond the borders of Judea — in Samaria, the Jezreel Valley, Transjordan, and perhaps even the Galilee.

"Galileans" are mentioned in a letter discovered in Wadi Murabbaʿat, in which Ben Kosiba threatens to clap Yeshua ben Galgola and his men in fetters if injury befalls the Galileans in his region. The identity of these Galileans has provoked scholarly debate. Some scholars think that Galilean means Christian; others identify them as Jews from Galilee who joined Bar Kokhba voluntarily or were otherwise forced to flee from the Galilee to Judea, taking refuge in the Herodium region. Given the absence of Bar Kokhba coins in the Galilee, which seems indicative of the revolt's failure to spread to this region, the latter explanation seems more likely. The Roman historian Dio comments, "Soon, however, all Judea had been stirred up, and the Jews everywhere were showing signs of disturbance, gathering together, and giving evidence of great hostility to the Romans, partly by secret and partly by overt acts." His remark may refer to Jews being forced to leave other areas, including the Province of Arabia and perhaps the Galilee, to seek refuge in regions under Bar Kokhba's command.

The Status of Jerusalem

Another frequently debated issue — whether Bar Kokhba captured Jerusalem — also hinges largely on numismatic evidence. The debate revolves around the question of the significance of Bar Kokhba tetradrachms that portray the Temple — leading some scholars to assert that Bar Kokhba captured Jerusalem

BAR KOKHBA REVOLT

and renewed the sacrificial cult — and whether the legend "For the Freedom of Jerusalem" on some coins pre- or postdates the anticipated conquest of Jerusalem. Others argue that, since these coins were expressly designed to encourage the insurgents, particularly in the third year when the Jewish military situation had deteriorated, they have no bearing on the issue.

Of the fifteen thousand coins unearthed in archaeological excavations in Jerusalem, only three coins overstruck by the insurgents have been discovered. This definitively proves that Ben Kosiba never captured Jerusalem. It remained under Roman control for the entire length of the war. Apparently, Roman soldiers took these three coins, along with a Bar Kokhba coin found in Caesarea, and one found in Hungary (in a Roman soldier's grave), as souvenirs. It seems likely that the minting of Roman Aelia Capitolina coins induced the counter-manufacture of Bar Kokhba coins inscribed with the words "For the Freedom of Jerusalem." This slogan perhaps served propaganda aims in the Jewish struggle to prevent Jerusalem from becoming a pagan city.

Together, the geographical distribution of both the coins and the hiding complexes suggests that, with the exception of Jerusalem, which remained in Roman hands throughout the war, Ben Kosiba controlled all of Judea, from the northern Negev to southern Samaria, during the revolt's initial period (132-33).

Collapse of the Revolt

Just as it is beyond our ability to reconstruct the insurgents' early successes in gaining control of Judea, it is difficult to trace when and how the Romans turned the tide in 134/35. The latest extant document known to have been written during the Bar Kokhba Revolt, a receipt waiving a post-divorce payment, is dated "On the twentieth of Sivan [June] Year [135] of the freedom of Israel in the name of Simeon Ben Kosibah," and the latest real estate transactions are dated a month earlier.

Undated letters found in the Judean Desert shed light on aspects of the collapse of Bar Kokhba's state but do not pinpoint when the collapse began. Letters from the administrators of Bet Mashiko to Yeshua ben Galgola noting Gentile proximity and citing this as their reason for not coming in person provide no clues as to when the Romans neared Herodium. A fragmentary Hebrew letter referring to people who perished by the sword and containing the expression "until the end" may be a report on a battle waged by Ben Kosiba's men. In a third fragmentary letter, ʿEin Gedi administrator Yonatan ben Mahanim requests the dispatching of a functionary "to bury the dead."

Ben Kosiba's letters dispatched to ʿEin Gedi also convey a sense of his dire straits at the war's end. In one letter, he reprimands Masbalah and Yonatan for "living well, eating and drinking off the property of the house of Israel, and [caring] nothing about your brethren." In others Bar Kokhba promises to punish those who disobey him, and even threatens to burn the houses occupied by refugees from Tekoa who had refused to join his cause. Also possibly indicative of the severity of Ben Kosiba's plight are two letters, obviously written before the Festival of Tabernacles, which discuss bringing the Four Species necessary for the celebration of the festival to Bar Kokhba's camp. In one of these letters, written in Aramaic, Ben Kosiba writes that he is providing two donkeys to transport the Four Species. On this basis, Yadin concluded that Bar Kokhba was experiencing difficulties, since provision of transport for the Four Species was required for them to reach his encampment.

The Ritual Observance of Bar Kokhba and His Supporters

In addition to the two letters about the Four Species necessary to observe Tabernacles, letters, economic documents, and other finds from caves in the Judean Desert show Ben Kosiba and the insurgents strictly observing Jewish law. Two letters relate to Sabbath observance: one requests that an officer be sent to Ben Kosiba before the Sabbath; another asks the Herodium commander for accommodations for his men over the Sabbath. Economic documents discovered in Wadi Murabbaʿat appear to indicate that the insurgents observed the sabbatical year, and artifacts found in the Cave of Letters reveal that, in accord with Jewish law (*m. ʿAbod. Zar.* 4:5), the insurgents defaced the pagan deities on bronze utensils taken as booty from Roman military units.

The Economic Situation

Three documents from the end of the Bar Kokhba Revolt illumine the economic reversal suffered in Bar Kokhba's state as the war came to a close: an escalating currency value was accompanied by a drastic decline in real estate value. In a deed penned on leather in Kislev of "Year Two (December 134) of the redemption of Israel by Simeon ben Kosiba the Nasi of Israel," Yehosef ben Hananyah borrowed one tetradrachm from the soldier Yehudah ben Yehudah. The borrower promised to repay the tetradrachm immediately upon request. The fact that this transaction was recorded on leather and signed by three witnesses clearly illustrates the enormous value of a tetradrachm at that time. A second document, written in the month of Adar in "Year Three of the liberation of Israel," relates to the purchase of a house in the village of Baarou by Hadad ben Yehudah from Eleazar ben Eleazar for only two tetradrachms. Even on the assumption that this house was in run-down condition, or very small, this document seems to indicate a drastic situation in Baarou in Winter 135. A document written in Iyyar (May) during Year Three reflects a similar situation. Overall, these documents may suggest that, in the economic conditions prevailing near the revolt's end, cash was favored over real estate holdings.

The Military Outcome

The war's last significant military engagement apparently took place at Bethar, Ben Kosiba's capital. The Roman siege complex consisted of five military camps and a four-kilometer dike. Rabbinic literature notes the large number of Jewish fighters killed trying to breach the dike. On the basis of the mishnaic dating of the Roman conquest of Bethar to the Ninth of Av (*m. Ta'an.* 4:6), we can posit that the city fell in summer 135.

Subjugating Judea was by no means an easy task. The precise nature of the Roman response — its magnitude, and the identification and number of participating legions and auxiliary units — is still open to debate. The list of the Roman forces that participated in suppressing the Bar Kokhba Revolt, compiled on the basis of epigraphic sources (tombstone and commemorative inscriptions, milestones, and diplomas), assists in a tentative estimate of their magnitude. The second-century Roman army was divided into legions comprised of heavy infantry, supposed to number 6,000 soldiers, and auxiliary forces — cavalry and archers — numbering either 480 or 850 soldiers. Participants from some eleven or twelve legions, plus soldiers from over thirty auxiliary units, some brought from Britain, took part in the fighting. In the case of legions mentioned in inscriptions, we cannot always determine whether the entire legion or only some specific units participated. Nevertheless, there is evidence that seven legions — II (Traiana), III (Cyrenaica), III (Gallica), VI (Ferrata), X (Fretensis), XII (Fulminata), XXII (Deiotariana) — participated in their entirety, and another four or five were at least partially represented.

The Roman Perception of and Response to the Revolt

W. Eck's convincing demonstration of the Roman perception of the uprising as a real threat essentially presents what he sees as the extraordinary measures the Romans took to suppress the revolt — the large number of troops and experienced generals they brought in — and their celebration of the final victory by awarding the highest military honors and erecting a triumphal arch. The Roman military force dispatched to quash the rebellion apparently numbered over 50,000 Roman soldiers. The size of Bar Kokhba's force remains entirely conjectural. Although certainly smaller than the Roman forces, given the magnitude of their antagonists' response, it must have numbered in the tens of thousands. Nor can we arrive at a realistic estimate of Roman losses during the war, although both Dio and the famous orator Fronto (a contemporary of Marcus Aurelius) note the large number of Roman casualties incurred in clashes with Jews. Fronto even went so far as to compare the number of casualties suffered in Judea with Roman losses in Britain.

Difficulty inheres even in the reconstruction of the precise succession in the Roman chain of command. When the revolt commenced, Q. Tineius Rufus was governing Judea, having been appointed to this post in 130 after previously serving as consul in Rome in 127. Following his service in Judea, he disappears from the scene without a trace. However, Dio omits any reference to Rufus, relating only that Hadrian appointed the former governor of Britain, Sextus Julius Severus, commander of the Roman forces in Palestine during the revolt. Indeed, epigraphic evidence shows that Severus was appointed governor of Judea and then of Syria. Yet surprisingly, Severus is mentioned neither in rabbinic sources nor by the church fathers. Rabbinic sources attribute the ban on circumcision and Rabbi Akiba's execution to Rufus; we can thus perhaps postulate a pre-Severan dating for both. The church fathers — Eusebius, for example (*Hist. Eccl.* 4.6), who notes that Rufus killed countless Jews and expropriated their lands — make no reference to Severus.

Because no historical source mentions both Rufus and Severus, placing the events connected to these two personages within a historical context is problematic. The proposed reconstruction of the turnover in the Roman leadership places Rufus in command of the Roman forces in Palestine when the revolt began and, if Eusebius's information is accurate, even enjoying some military success during the war's initial stages. It may be that Rufus died during the war, either in battle or of natural causes. For his part, upon first learning of the revolt in Winter 132 while in Athens, Hadrian evidently assumed command of the Roman forces in Palestine sometime during 133. Before departing Palestine for Rome in May 134, Hadrian sent to Britain for Julius Severus. Since an inscription from Britain shows his successor governing Britain in 135, we can date Severus's arrival in Palestine to late 134 or early 135.

The Aftermath of the Revolt

The Roman sense of having won a great victory emerges from Hadrian's second acclamation as imperator sometime after 135, following the revolt's suppression. According to Dio, Hadrian's best commanders accompanied Julius Severus to Judea. For their achievements in Judea, Severus and two others — Certus Publicus Marcellus, the governor of Syria, and T. Haterius Nepos, governor of the Province of Arabia — received the highest imperial Roman military honor: *ornamenta triumphalia.* The remains of a ten-meter triumphal arch dedicated to Hadrian following his second acclamation as imperator, discovered twelve km. south of Beth-shean (Scythopolis) near the Sixth Legion's camp at Tel Shalem, further corroborate the importance the Romans ascribed to their victory. Presumably, this arch's construction, built by Senate proclamation, dates to after the suppression of the Bar Kokhba Revolt. Unusual because its construction dates to a time when the Senate no longer dedicated triumphal arches in the provinces, and because of its monumental 40-cm.-high lettering, in all likelihood, it was erected in an open field south of Beth-shean to commemorate an important Hadrianic victory in the Bar Kokhba War. For Eck, the granting of the highest military honors and the building of a triumphal arch not only indicate the perceived seriousness of the revolt in Roman eyes but also that the fighting spread far beyond the borders of Judea, as far as the Province of Arabia and Syria.

Although Dio's figure of 985 as the number of villages destroyed during the war seems hyperbolic, without exception all Judean villages excavated appear to have been razed following the Bar Kokhba Revolt. This supports the distinct impression of almost total regional destruction following the war. Historical sources note the vast numbers of captives sold into slavery in Palestine and shipped abroad.

The Judean Jewish community never recovered from the Bar Kokhba War. In its wake Jews no longer formed the majority in Palestine, and the Jewish center moved to the Galilee. Subjected to a series of religious edicts designed to uproot nationalistic elements of Judaism, these remained in effect until Hadrian's death in 138. An additional, more lasting punitive measure taken by the Romans involved expunging Judea from the provincial name, changing it from *Provincia Judaea* to *Provincia Syria Palestina*. Although such name changes were not unheard of, never before or afterward was a nation's name expunged as the result of rebellion.

After the appalling failure of the Bar Kokhba Revolt, the Jews made no further attempts to achieve national independence. Within decades, the honorific *naśi*, which had been bestowed on Bar Kokhba as a military title, acquired a religious meaning. The next notable individual to be dubbed thus was Rabbi Judah ha-Nasi, the editor of the Mishnah. This shift encapsulates the decisive impact of the Bar Kokhba Revolt on Jewish history.

BIBLIOGRAPHY

S. APPLEBAUM 1976, *Prolegomena to the Study of the Second Jewish Revolt (A.D. 132-135)*, Oxford: Clarendon. • P. BENOIT, J. T. MILIK, AND R. DE VAUX, EDS. 1961, *Les Grottes de Murabba'ât*, DJD 2, Oxford: Clarendon. • H. ESHEL 2002, "Documents of the First Jewish Revolt from the Judean Desert," in *The First Jewish Revolt: Archaeology, History and Ideology*, ed. A. M. Berlin and J. A. Overman, London: Routledge, 157-63. • W. ECK 1999, "The Bar Kokhba Revolt: The Roman Point of View," *Journal of Roman Studies* 89: 76-89. • N. LEWIS 1989, *The Documents from the Bar Kokhba Period in the Cave of Letters: Greek Papyri*, Jerusalem: Israel Exploration Society. • L. MILDENBERG 1984, *The Coinage of the Bar Kokhba War*, Aarau: Sauerlinder. • P. SCHÄFER 1981, *Der Bar Kokhba Aufstand*, Tübingen: Mohr-Siebeck. • P. SCHÄFER, ED. 2003, *The Bar Kokhba War Reconsidered*, Tübingen: Mohr-Siebeck. • Y. YADIN 1971, *Bar-Kokhba: The Rediscovery of the Legendary Hero of the Second Jewish Revolt against Rome*, London: Weidenfeld and Nicolson. • Y. YADIN, J. C. GREENFIELD, A. YARDENI, AND B. LEVINE, EDS. 2002, *The Documents from the Bar Kokhba Period in the Cave of Letters: Hebrew, Aramaic and Nabataean-Aramaic Papyri*, Jerusalem: Israel Exploration Society.

HANAN ESHEL†

Baruch, First Book of

The book of Baruch is a composite work of three poetic sections concerning Israel's sinfulness (1:15–3:8), wisdom and the Torah (3:9–4:4), and the consolation of Jerusalem (4:5–5:9), all set within a narrative framework (1:1-14). The work is sometimes called 1 Baruch to distinguish it from the apocalypses known as *2 Baruch* (Syriac) and *3 Baruch* (Greek), as well as *4 Baruch* (also called the *Paraleipomena of Jeremiah*).

Central Themes and Message

What gives some unity to this collection is the interpretation of ancient Israel's history developed in Deuteronomy 28–33, 1–2 Samuel and 1–2 Kings, and Jeremiah 26–33. The major themes in that interpretation are sin, exile, repentance, and return/restoration. The basic theological message of the book of Baruch is that although Israel has brought upon itself the exile to Babylon by its sins (especially idolatry), if it repents, God will make good on his promises and bring about its return and restoration as his people once more.

Pseudonymous Authorship

The implied author is Baruch the son of Neriah, who served as scribe and secretary to Jeremiah (Jer. 36:27-32; 45:1-5). He is supposedly among the exiles in Babylon, though there is no evidence that Baruch was ever in Babylon. The work is generally regarded as pseudonymous, in large part because it uses biblical texts (Daniel 9, Job 28, Isaiah 40–66) that were composed after Baruch's death. The ascription of these poems to Baruch is best explained on the grounds that since Jeremiah prophesied about Jerusalem's destruction and the exile to Babylon, it was fitting that Baruch should offer further reflections on the Exile and the hope of Israel's return and restoration.

Language, Date, Location

The Greek text of Baruch appears in major Septuagint manuscripts, and provided the basis for the ancient versions (Latin, Syriac, Ethiopic, etc.). There is a consensus that the first part (1:1–3:8) was composed in Hebrew and translated into Greek. The other two main parts (3:9–4:4 and 4:5–5:9) may also have been originally written in Hebrew. There is no certainty about the work's place and date of composition. But most scholars locate it in Palestine between 200 and 50 B.C.E.

Genre

Although the work is clearly a composite, the various poems that make up the book of Baruch all rely on biblical texts for much of their wording and content. This kind of work is sometimes called "rewritten Bible." It can also be described in terms of intertextuality in that the author creates links with and new combinations out of existing biblical texts. The approach is sometimes also called the "anthological style" by which a writer produces a new work by gathering phrases from other books and joining them in new contexts.

Contents

The narrative setting (1:1-14) places Baruch among the Jewish exiles in Babylon, reading his book to Jeconiah the king of Judah and the exiled community. They decide to take up a collection for those Jews left in Jerusalem and to send back a replacement set of temple vessels. The assumption is that some kind of temple cult has continued despite the Temple's capture. They also instruct the people in Jerusalem to pray for King Nebuchadnezzar and for the exiles in Babylon, and to read aloud from the scroll that contains the present book of Baruch. The idea is that this scroll will explain why Israel went into exile (sin), what it must do now (repent, and obey the Torah), and what it can hope for (return and restoration).

The confession of sinfulness (1:15–3:8), which relies heavily on Daniel 9 and Jeremiah, may well itself be a composite. Its first part (1:15–2:10) contrasts God's justice and Israel's shame (1:15-18), traces Israel's disobedience throughout its history (1:19–2:5), and again contrasts God's justice and Israel's shame (2:6-10). Then in 2:11-35 it appeals to God's kindness and compassion to restore Israel to its land, and in 3:1-8 it urges God to remember that his name and power are at stake during Israel's present humiliation.

The wisdom poem (3:9–4:4) is based on Job 28, which is a poetic reflection on how hard it is for humans to find genuine wisdom. It is arranged in a concentric structure: A — wisdom and the Torah (3:9-14); B — the elusive character of wisdom (3:15-23); C — the greatness of "the house of God" (3:24-28); B′ — the elusive character of wisdom (3:29-37); and A′ — wisdom and the Torah (4:1-4). As in Sirach 24:23, wisdom is identified as "the book of the commandments of God, the law that endures forever" (4:1). The poem declares Israel "happy" because "we know what is pleasing to God" (4:4) through its possession and observance of the Torah.

Drawing extensively on Isaiah 40–66, the poem of consolation (4:5–5:9), which may also be a composite, begins by blaming the Exile on Israel's fall into idolatry, and presents two scenes in which Jerusalem is personified as a grieving mother. In the first scene (4:9-16) she reflects on the reason for her children's exile, and in the second scene (4:17-29) she looks forward to her children's eventual homecoming. Finally in 4:30–5:9 the narrator exhorts Jerusalem to prepare for their return and to look eastward where "God will lead Israel with joy in the light of his glory, with the mercy and righteousness that come from him" (5:9).

Significance

The work's reliance on the Deuteronomistic interpretation of ancient Israel's history in terms of sin, exile, repentance, and return/restoration, while thoroughly biblical, raises many historical and theological questions. The identification of wisdom and the Torah (4:1) as well as the personification of Jerusalem as a grieving mother in 4:9-29 are among the book's most striking features. Christian readers have found in 3:37 ("she [Wisdom] appeared on earth and lived with humankind") an anticipation of John 1:14 ("the Word became flesh and lived among us").

Bibliography

D. G. Burke 1982, *The Poetry of Baruch: A Reconstruction and Analysis of the Original Hebrew Text of Baruch 3:9–5:9*, Chico, Calif.: Scholars Press. • D. A. deSilva 2002, *Introducing the Apocrypha*, Grand Rapids: Baker, 198-213. • D. J. Harrington 1999, *Invitation to the Apocrypha*, Grand Rapids: Eerdmans, 92-102. • C. A. Moore 1977, *Daniel, Esther and Jeremiah: The Additions*, Garden City, N.Y.: Doubleday, 255-316. • E. Tov 1975, *The Book of Baruch, Also Called I Baruch (Greek and Hebrew)*, Missoula, Mont.: Scholars Press. • J. E. Wright 2003, *Baruch ben Neriah: From Biblical Scribe to Apocalyptic Seer*, Columbia, S.C.: University of South Carolina Press.

Daniel J. Harrington, S.J.

Baruch, Second Book of

The Syriac *Apocalypse of Baruch*, or *2 Baruch*, so titled to distinguish it from the apocryphal book of Baruch, is a pseudepigraphic apocalypse that purports to be written by Baruch, secretary to the prophet Jeremiah. In it Baruch provides a first-person account of the Babylonian destruction of Jerusalem and of the end-time revelations he received in the days thereafter. *2 Baruch* was composed in Israel in the wake of the First Jewish Revolt and responds to the fall of the Temple in the year 70 C.E. The recent trauma, tangible in almost every line, prompts Baruch to raise profound questions about the reasons for the calamity, the morality and justice of God, and the imminent end of history.

Content and Structure

2 Baruch consists of three parts. It begins with a narrative prologue (chaps. 1–9), which functions to introduce the fictitious setting of the book. On the day before the Babylonian destruction of the Jerusalem Temple in 587 B.C.E., God orders Baruch to leave the city. Baruch refuses and is then forced to witness the burning of the Temple. The middle part (chaps. 10–77) consists of a long disputation between Baruch and God following the sacking of Jerusalem in which the seer inquires about the reasons for the debacle and the future fate of Israel. The book ends (chaps. 78–87) with an epistle sent to the exiles in Assyria in which Baruch admonishes them not to lose heart and to observe the Torah of Moses.

This three-part division is suggested by the different genres employed in each respective section (first-person narrative, revelatory dialogue, epistle) as well as by certain narrative markers. It is less clear, however, how to divide further the substantial middle part of the book. Most interpreters have taken their lead from *4 Ezra*, a contemporary apocalypse closely related to *2 Baruch*. Since *4 Ezra* is structured in seven visions, according to this argument, *2 Baruch* also ought to have seven parts. But the compositions of the two texts are rather different. *2 Baruch* begins with a narrative and ends with an epistle, neither of which has a parallel in *4 Ezra*. Three times in the text Baruch addresses the people of Jerusalem to comfort them and to alleviate their anxiety (chaps. 31–34; 44–47; 77), which also has no parallel in *4 Ezra*. Baruch has two allegorical visions (chaps. 36–43; 53–76; some interpreters find a third vision in 27:1–30:5), whereas Ezra has seven. The obvious linguistic and thematic parallels between *4 Ezra* and *2 Baruch* notwithstanding, *2 Baruch* does not have a sevenfold structure. Instead, *2 Baruch* consists of a few set elements — Baruch's prayers, the continuous dialogue between the seer and God, Baruch's allegorical visions and their interpretations, and Baruch's public addresses — that are frequently repeated, yet without giving the text a rigid composition, let alone a symmetrical structure like that in *4 Ezra*.

The middle section of the apocalypse can be divided as follows. Chapters 13–20: revelatory dialogue between God and Baruch about God's judgment and the world to come; chap. 21: Baruch's prayer inquiring about the end time; chaps. 22–30: revelatory dialogue (continued) about the messiah and the resurrection of the dead; chaps. 31–34: Baruch's first public address; chap. 35: Baruch's prayer (lament) over the cessation of the sacrifices; chaps. 36–43: Baruch's allegorical vision of the forest; chaps. 44–47: Baruch's second public address; chap. 48: Baruch's prayer (petition) for God's protection; chaps. 48–52: revelatory dialogue (continued) about the resurrection and the promise for the righteous; chaps. 53–76: Baruch's vision of the cloud; chap. 77: Baruch's third public address.

Text, Original Language, and Date

No Jewish manuscripts of *2 Baruch* have survived, nor are there any quotations of or references to it in rabbinic literature. *2 Baruch* owes its survival to the fact that it was translated and preserved in Christian circles. The text is attested in a single Syriac manuscript, the famous Ambrosian Codex (ms. B. 21 [7aI in the Leiden Peshiṭta edition], fols. 257a-265b), the oldest complete Old Testament Peshiṭta manuscript, which dates from the sixth or seventh century. A few short sections are also included in Jacobite lectionaries (Dedering 1973). Throughout *2 Baruch*'s history of transmission, the epistle (chaps. 78–87) was separated from the apocalypse and transmitted independently. It survives in thirty-six manuscripts. The Ambrosian manuscript thus includes two recensions of the epistle, the independent form and the epistle in chaps. 78–87 (the text of the epistle is not included in the 1973 Leiden Peshiṭta edition of *2 Baruch*). Recently an Arabic version of *2 Baruch* has been published that presents a free, secondary rendering of the Syriac text (Leemhuis 1986).

The original language of *2 Baruch* is not known. The Syriac is a daughter translation of a Greek version, of which only a few lines survive among the Oxyrhynchus Papyri. In his seminal commentary on *2 Baruch,* Pierre Bogaert argued in favor of Greek as the original language (Bogaert 1969). It is much more likely, however, that the Greek is a translation from a Hebrew text that is no longer extant. A Hebrew original is suggested by the numerous parallels between *2 Baruch* and cognate writings, most obviously *4 Ezra,* which was originally written in Hebrew, and by the fact that in places the Syriac becomes intelligible only when we assume a translation from Hebrew.

2 Baruch was composed after the fall of Jerusalem in 70 C.E., which is referred to in 32:2-4, and before the Bar Kokhba Revolt of 132-135 C.E., which is not mentioned, presumably because it had not yet occurred. The setting of much of the book on the ruins of the Jerusalem temple, as well as the great pain over the destruction, suggests that not much time had elapsed between the burning of the city and the composition of the book. Beyond this there is nothing in *2 Baruch* that allows us to determine its date of origin with any certainty. Much has been made of the date in 1:1 and the passage in 28:1-2, but these are symbolic rather than referential and should not be interpreted literally.

The Place of *2 Baruch* in Early Judaism

2 Baruch is a "historical" apocalypse. There is no heavenly ascent or otherworldly journey, and the author does not engage in any extensive cosmological speculations. Instead, *2 Baruch* is entirely preoccupied with recent historical events and their implications for the life of the Jewish community.

The period following the devastation of Jerusalem in 70 C.E. was a complex time of social uncertainty and religious reorientation. The Mishnah describes the sages as the successors of the men of the "Great Synagogue" and, ultimately, of Moses who received the Torah at Mt. Sinai (*m. 'Abot* 1:1) — a powerful claim to authority. It is unlikely, however, that the history of post-70 C.E. Judaism was as linear as the mishnaic depiction of the sages wants us to believe. Second Temple Judaism consisted of many different groups, and there is no reason to assume that all Jewish groups suddenly ceased to exist or readily merged into what was to become rabbinic Judaism. The acceptance of rabbinic authority among Jews in Israel after the year 70 C.E. was gradual and most likely not far advanced by the time of the composition of *2 Baruch* (Goodman 2000). In the history of early Jewish thought, then, the half century between the destruction of Jerusalem in 70 C.E. and the Bar Kokhba Revolt was a unique period of transition, framed by the biblical era, which had come to an abrupt end with the Roman destruction of Jerusalem, and rabbinic Judaism, which was still in its formative stage and had not yet gained hegemony.

2 Baruch is very much a product of its time and, indeed, stands at the crossroad of various intersecting intellectual trajectories. Like few other pseudepigrapha, *2 Baruch* is an amalgam of diverse traditions. First, there is the influence of the Jewish Bible. *2 Baruch* is firmly rooted in the biblical tradition, as the book's fictitious setting in sixth-century Jerusalem and the choice of the author's pseudonym make clear. The narrative prologue, with its retelling of the tragic events of 587 B.C.E., is an example of "rewritten Bible," and the author often speaks in the biblical idiom.

Second, *2 Baruch* is the last in a series of early Jewish apocalypses of the historical type, which were no longer composed after the second century C.E. until the Middle Ages. The author is well familiar with and often fuses separate eschatologies, such as the expectation of a new Jerusalem (chaps. 4; 32; 59:4-11), the resurrection of the dead (chaps. 30; 49–51), and the appearance of the anointed one (chaps. 29–30; 39–40; 71–73).

Third, *2 Baruch* has many parallels with rabbinic literature, particularly with *Pesiqta Rabbati.* These include haggadic motifs, such as the fate of the Temple implements (chap. 6; 80:2) or the list of King Manasseh's wicked deeds (chap. 64:1-10), as well as theological views regarding Israel's sins as the prime reason for

Jerusalem's destruction and the centrality of observing the Mosaic Torah (chaps. 17–18; 32; 44; 48; 84).

Fourth, in places *2 Baruch* shows significant overlap with some New Testament writings, especially with the Pauline epistles. *2 Baruch* has much to contribute to the study of the formation of first-century Christianities.

Throughout its modern history of reading, which began with A. M. Ceriani's publication of the Syriac text in 1871, *2 Baruch* has often suffered from scholarly attempts to identify it with one or another of these traditions at the expense of the others, and without proper recognition of how they blend in this text. *2 Baruch* is a composite text, not in the sense of having multiple independent sources strung together by a clumsy redactor, as R. Kabisch and R. H. Charles argued a century ago, but in the sense of being an inclusive text whose aim is to integrate diverse strands of Jewish thought that were traditionally kept separate. The apocalyptic expectation of an imminent end, for example, is here combined with the view found in the book of Deuteronomy that keeping the Torah ensures a long and prosperous life.

The Significance of *2 Baruch*

It has become customary among scholars to assert that apocalyptic groups defined themselves in opposition to mainstream forms of religion. Apocalyptic conventicles were supposedly alienated and developed their own utopian systems of belief. While this is true in some cases, not all apocalyptic groups fit the pattern. There is nothing withdrawn or sectarian about *2 Baruch*. Instead, the author of *2 Baruch* develops a theological vision of Judaism that is both creative and viable. *2 Baruch* agrees with the rabbis in placing the observance of the Mosaic Torah at the center of its exhortations. However, it differs in its claim that the will of God cannot be discerned from the study of Torah alone but ultimately is known only through revelation. It also differs in its belief that the full restoration of Israel will come about only through divine intervention.

The significance of *2 Baruch* lies not merely in the fact that it presents a lost form of Judaism — an early Jewish apocalypse written by the "historical losers." Rather, the study of *2 Baruch* leads us to appreciate the complexity of the processes that led to the redefinition of Judaism following the first Jewish revolt.

Bibliography

P.-M. BOGAERT 1969, *L'Apocalypse Syriaque de Baruch*, Paris: Cerf. • R. H. CHARLES 1896, *The Apocalypse of Baruch*, London: Black. • S. DEDERING, ED. 1973, "Apocalypse of Baruch," in *The Old Testament in Syriac*, Leiden: Brill. • M. GOODMAN 2000, "The Rebuilding of Judea," in *The Cambridge Ancient History*, vol. 11, Cambridge: Cambridge University Press, 664-78. • A. F. J. KLIJN 1983, "2 (Syriac Apocalypse of) Baruch," in *OTP* 1:615-52. • F. LEEMHUIS ET AL. 1986, *The Arabic Text of the Apocalypse of Baruch*, Leiden: Brill. • F. J. MURPHY 1985, *The Structure and Meaning of Second Baruch*, Atlanta: Scholars Press. • R. NIR 2003, *The Destruction of Jerusalem and the Idea of Redemption in the Syriac Apocalypse of Baruch*, Atlanta: Society of Biblical Literature. • G. B. SAYLER 1984, *Have the Promises Failed? A Literary Analysis of 2 Baruch*, Chico, Calif.: Scholars Press. • B. VIOLET 1924, *Die Apokalypsen des Esra und des Baruch in deutscher Gestalt*, Leipzig: Hinrichs. • J. E. WRIGHT 2003, *Baruch ben Neriah: From Biblical Scribe to Apocalyptic Seer*, Columbia, S.C.: University of South Carolina Press.

MATTHIAS HENZE

Baruch, Third Book of

The Greek *Apocalypse of Baruch* or *3 Baruch* is a pseudepigraphic apocalypse of uncertain provenance that describes an otherworldly journey undertaken by Baruch the son of Neriah, the scribe of Jeremiah known from biblical tradition (Jeremiah 32, 36, 43, 45). It is called *3 Baruch* to distinguish it from the apocryphal book of Baruch, the Syriac apocalypse or *2 Baruch*, and *4 Baruch* (also called the *Paraleipomena of Jeremiah*).

Contents

Narrated in the first person by the visionary hero, the work opens with Baruch mourning the Babylonian destruction of Jerusalem, a setting typological for the aftermath of the Roman destruction of Jerusalem and the Second Temple in 70 C.E. An angel appears, urges Baruch to cease his lamentation, and invites him to witness the "mysteries of God." The angel then conducts Baruch on a guided tour of five heavens. In the first two heavens (chaps. 2–3) Baruch sees the builders and planners of the "tower of strife against God" undergoing punishment by having assumed hybrid animal forms. In the third heaven (chaps. 4–9) he gets a brief glimpse of Hades and encounters a dragon devouring the bodies of the wicked. He asks to be shown "the tree that caused Adam to stray" and is told about how "the vine of Samael" condemned Adam, stripping him of "the glory of God," and troubled Noah after the flood. Evidently still in the third heaven, Baruch proceeds to view the sun chariot and its entourage of angels, as well as the amazing phoenix, which protects the earth's inhabitants from the harmful rays of the sun, and the moon with her angelic retinue. When Baruch is taken to the fourth heaven (chap. 10), he beholds a multitude of birds around a celestial lake, where the souls of the righteous gather in choirs to hymn praises to God. From here he journeys to the fifth heaven (chaps. 11–16), where he watches the archangel Michael preside over a heavenly liturgy. Three groups of angels approach: the first group bears baskets filled with flowers, which are the virtues of the righteous; the second group carries baskets only partly filled; the third group comes empty handed, blackened in appearance and lamenting their assignment to wicked people (chaps. 12–13). Michael takes the flowers in a large bowl as he ascends to the presence of God, presumably in a higher, though unnumbered, heaven. When he returns, he brings oil as a reward for the righteous but a stern reprimand for sinners. At the end of the work (chaps. 15–17), Baruch and his angel withdraw abruptly from the fifth heaven. The seer returns to his former place, offers praise to God, and invites his audience to do likewise.

BARUCH, THIRD BOOK OF

The Two Manuscript Traditions

3 Baruch survives in Slavonic and Greek. Although there are critical editions of each (Greek: Picard 1967; Slavonic: Gaylord 1983a), at present there is no edition that takes both versions into account. The Slavonic tradition is represented by about a dozen late manuscripts of various origins (Bulgarian, Serbian, Croatian, Russian), ranging in date from the thirteenth to the early eighteenth century. They appear to derive ultimately from a single, very literal Slavic translation from the Greek dating to the Byzantine period. Greek uncial errors suggest that a division into two Greek families — the one represented by the extant Greek manuscripts; the other, by the Slavic tradition — occurred no later than the ninth or tenth century. The Slavonic may be superior to the extant Greek in at least the following areas: the introduction (1:1-2); the explicit New Testament citations or general Christian terminology in 4:15; 5:3; 15:4; and 16:2; the story of the planting of the garden by angels in the Slavonic at 4:7; and the structure and content of chap. 4. There are also several places in chaps. 10–16 where the Slavonic may preserve the better wording.

The Greek tradition of *3 Baruch* is not nearly so amply attested, being represented by only two very late manuscripts of the fifteenth to sixteenth centuries. The two manuscripts are nearly identical, sharing the same grammatical errors and orthographic peculiarities. Either one is a copy of the other, or else they both derive from the same parent manuscript. For all of their differences, though, the Slavonic and Greek traditions represent essentially the same text.

Issues in Interpretation

Literary Integrity

3 Baruch ends rather abruptly with the seer having ascended only as far as the fifth heaven and never having been granted a vision of God, despite repeated promises from his angel that he would see "the glory of God." This and other features in the text raise the possibility that the present ending is incomplete. Origen of Alexandria mentions a book of Baruch with seven heavens (*De Principiis* 2.3.6). The Slavonic, moreover, has a longer account in which Baruch is told that he will witness the glory of God, the resting place of the righteous, and the torment of the wicked. Only the latter is briefly described. If they are later additions, the distinctly Christian elements in both the Greek (13:4; 15:4; perhaps also 12:6; 13:2; 15:2; 16:2, 3) and Slavonic (13:4; 15:3; 16:2) may also point to an incomplete ending.

None of these features, however, is sufficient to deny the literary integrity of the work. Origen was almost certainly referring to a different, now lost Baruch work. The Slavonic ending itself looks truncated and may represent no more original a construction than the Greek. The Christian elements do not appear to have displaced any material, and Michael's ascent to a higher heaven may simply mean that the work presupposes a fuller cosmology, probably of seven heavens. That the visionary never visits the highest heaven and is never granted a throne-room theophany may represent a deliberate reversal of expectations raised earlier in the narrative (6:12; 7:2; 11:2). The present ending of the Greek may also be read as a fitting climax prepared for earlier in the narrative in such episodes as the arrested ascent of the tower figures in chap. 2, and Baruch's fearful response to the glory of the sun and phoenix in chap. 7. Baruch's journey would then be an aborted ascent; his being denied a vision of God in the celestial temple would underscore both the inscrutability of God and, perhaps, the dispensability of the Jerusalem Temple.

Jewish or Christian Composition?

Most interpreters have treated the present Greek version as fairly representative of the original work and situated it in the Hellenistic Jewish Diaspora of the late first or early second century (e.g., Picard 1970; Fischer 1978: 71-84; Harlow 1996: 77-108). Egypt is widely thought to be the place of composition. In its present forms, though, *3 Baruch* is a Christian document; it survives in Christian manuscripts and contains explicitly Christian elements in both the Greek and Slavonic traditions. The Christian elements, which are different in each version, are likely additions. But this does not necessarily indicate a Jewish original, since a Christian work need not have distinctively Christian contents if they are not called for by the subject matter. There is virtually nothing in *3 Baruch* that could not have been written by a Christian. Chapter 1, which depicts Baruch mourning the loss of the Temple, might be taken to represent a distinctly Jewish concern, but since it depicts Baruch in a rather conventional setting and posture, it may not be a reliable indicator of the concerns of the work's author or readership. The original authorship of the work must therefore remain an open question.

Purpose

If *3 Baruch* originated in Diaspora Judaism, it may have been intended to respond to the destruction of the Second Temple, by discouraging excessive mourning over its demise and by affirming that prayer and good deeds substitute for the sacrifices offered in a now defunct temple cult. If it originated in Christian circles, the apocalypse would have functioned to enjoin good works with the promise of eternal rewards. Regardless of its provenance, the present form of *3 Baruch* conveys a clear hortatory message. Its combination of individual eschatology, speculative cosmology, and universal ethics affirms God's sovereign control over the cosmos and encourages right living. This parenetic purpose would be fitting in a work of Hellenistic Judaism, with its tendency to emphasize ethical monotheism and to downplay the ethnic and exclusivist aspects of Jewish faith. Yet it would also make sense in a Christian work.

Bibliography

Critical Editions

H. Gaylord 1983a, "The Slavonic Version of III Baruch," Dissertation, Hebrew University of Jerusalem. • M. R. James 1897, "The Apocalypse of Baruch," in *Apocrypha Anecdota*, vol. 2, Cambridge: Cambridge University Press, li-lxxi. • J. C. Picard 1967, *Apocalypsis Baruchi Graece*, Leiden: Brill.

Studies

L. CARLSSON 2004, *Round Trips to Heaven: Otherworldly Travelers in Early Judaism and Christianity,* Lund: Lund University, 275-355. • M. DEAN-OTTING 1984, *Heavenly Journeys: A Study of the Motif in Hellenistic Jewish Literature,* Frankfurt: Peter Lang, 98-174. • U. FISCHER 1978, *Eschatologie und Jenseitserwartung im hellenistischen Diasporajudentum,* Berlin: de Gruyter, 71-84. • H. GAYLORD 1983B, "3 (Greek Apocalypse of) Baruch: A New Translation and Introduction," in *OTP* 1: 653-79. • D. C. HARLOW 1996, *The Greek Apocalypse of Baruch (3 Baruch) in Hellenistic Judaism and Early Christianity,* Leiden: Brill. • D. C. HARLOW 2001, "The Christianization of Early Jewish Pseudepigrapha: The Case of 3 Baruch," *JSJ* 32: 416-44. • M. R. JAMES 1915, "Notes on Apocrypha," *JTS* 16: 403-13. • J. C. PICARD, 1970, "Observations sur l'Apocalypse grecque de Baruch I: Cadre historique fictif et efficacité symbolique," *Semitica* 20: 77-103. • J. C. PICARD 1999, *Le continent apocryphe: Essai sur les littératures apocryphes juive et chrétienne,* Turnhout: Brepols, 55-161. • E. TURDEANU 1969, "L'Apocalypse de Baruch en Slave," *Revue des études slaves* 48: 23-48; rpt. *Apocryphes slaves et roumains de l'Ancien Testament,* Leiden: Brill, 1981, 364-91. • J. E. WRIGHT 2003, *Baruch ben Neriah: From Biblical Scribe to Apocalyptic Seer,* Columbia, S.C.: University of South Carolina Press.

DANIEL C. HARLOW

Baruch, Fourth Book of

4 Baruch is a modern designation for a pseudepigraphic work that describes the events surrounding the Babylonian destruction of Jerusalem and the Temple in 587 B.C.E. In Greek manuscripts the work is titled *Paraleipomena Jeremiou* or "Things Omitted from Jeremiah," and in Ethiopic manuscripts *The Rest of the Words of Baruch.* It is affiliated with other pseudepigraphical works attributed to Jeremiah and Baruch. The label *4 Baruch* is meant to distinguish it from the book of Baruch in the Old Testament Apocrypha (1 Baruch), 2 (Syriac) *Apocalypse of Baruch,* and 3 (Greek) *Apocalypse of Baruch.*

The Story

In *4 Baruch,* Jeremiah, the prophet of the fall of Jerusalem, is a priest who intercedes for the people (1:1–3:9), accompanies them into the Babylonian exile (3:11; 4:5), teaches them the Law (chap. 7), and finally leads them back to the Holy City (chap. 8). His companion Baruch (cf. Jeremiah 32, 36, 43, 45) is left behind, lamenting the destroyed city of Jerusalem (chap. 4). Baruch eventually sends the news to Jeremiah in Babylon that the Exile has come to an end (chaps. 6–7). In chap. 3 the figure of Abimelech the Ethiopian (cf. Jeremiah 38–39) enters the story. Before the destruction of Jerusalem and the deportation of the people, Jeremiah sends him to a vineyard to collect figs for the sick (3:9-16). There Abimelech sleeps for sixty-six years, and when he awakes he does not recognize the city (chap. 5). In his disorientation he meets an old man who explains to him what happened. The miraculous protection of the sleeping Abimelech and the preservation of the figs over the sixty-six years function as a symbol for the exiled: the (terrible) dream has passed, the Exile is over, and the return is imminent. Meanwhile, Jeremiah teaches the people the Law and thus prepares for their return. Finally, *4 Baruch* 8 tells the story of the return to Jerusalem as a controversy over the problem of mixed marriages, which leads to the foundation of Samaria. Chapter 9 concludes with a sacrifice and prayer of Jeremiah and narrates two different versions of his death, one of them overtly Christian.

Sources and Traditions

Besides the biblical book of Jeremiah, an important literary source is *2 Baruch,* which in its literary frame also addresses the events of 70 C.E. by using as a foil the biblical traditions concerning the events of 587 B.C.E. Similarities between *4 Baruch* and other writings such as *Pesiqta Rabbati* and the *Apocryphon of Jeremiah* cannot be explained by positing direct literary dependence or the existence of a cycle of legends (Riaud 1994) but rather by recognizing common ideas and shared traditions.

Into the plot taken from *2 Baruch,* the author of *4 Baruch* weaves the story of Abimelech's sleep. The promise of Jer. 39:16-18 provides the basis for the story of Abimelech's protection. The writer elaborates this promise of protection with the motif of a long sleep, derived from a tradition concerning Honi the Circle Drawer (*y. Taʿan.* 3:9, cf. a later version in *b. Taʿanit* 23a). The basic inspiration for the creation of such a story is the idea of the Exile passing like a dream found in Psalm 126. The motif of the figs, which is crucial for the story's twofold perspective, stems from Jeremiah 24.

4 Baruch 6–7 rearranges the motif of *2 Baruch* of Baruch sending a letter to exile by an eagle. Relying on the biblical traditions of Ezra 9–10 and Neh. 13:23-31, *4 Baruch* 8 raises the problem of mixed marriages at the time of the return and narrates the founding of Samaria (cf. 2 Kings 17:24-41) by those disobedient to Jeremiah. Nevertheless, the author maintains a positive attitude toward the Samaritans, which has parallels in rabbinic traditions of his time (cf. *y. Giṭ.* 1:4; *y. Ber.* 7:1). Despite their disobedience, the Samaritans still belong to Israel and thus the promise of a heavenly Jerusalem is also valid for them (*4 Bar.* 8:9).

Finally, the festival of sacrifices and the prayer of Jeremiah (*4 Baruch* 9) take up Isaiah 6 and the tradition of the Day of Atonement (Leviticus 16). While the description of the sacrifice recalls Ezra 3:4 and Neh. 8:13-18, the prayer of the prophet summarizes the message of *4 Baruch* and replaces the actual sacrifice. The idea of replacing sacrifices by prayer concurs again with rabbinic ideas (e.g., *b. Sukkah* 55b; *y. Yoma* 8:7). The author ends his story by noting the prophet's natural death, whereas the Christian redactor depicts Jeremiah as a Christian (see below).

Literary Genre

From a form-critical perspective, *4 Baruch* is not an apocalypse, as the close relation to *2 Baruch* might suggest. Yet it does critique apocalyptic expectations of the time. In a haggadic style, the book retells a chapter of Israel's history and includes theological interpretations for the purpose of instruction.

Original language

4 Baruch has often been claimed to be a Greek translation of a Hebrew (or Aramaic) original. Yet the references to the Jewish Bible in *4 Baruch* indicate that the Jewish author wrote originally in Greek (Schaller 1998). Hebraisms and Aramaisms cannot be regarded as strong criteria for the determination of the original language. Furthermore, the author orients the work toward Greek-speaking Diaspora Jews, which makes it necessary and probable that he wrote in their language. The distinctive Greek style of the work points to an author whose mother tongue was perhaps Hebrew or Aramaic, but who was familiar with the Greek tradition of the Jewish Scriptures.

Dating

Because it is dependent on *2 Baruch,* the end of the first century C.E. is the *terminus ad quem* for *4 Baruch.* The relationship between the Christian redaction and the *Ascension of Isaiah* suggests a date no later than the middle of the second century C.E. Harris (1899) based a precise dating on the number sixty-six (*4 Bar.* 5:1, 30; 6:5; 7:24). Adding sixty-six to the year of the destruction of Jerusalem (70 C.E.), he suggested the year 136 C.E., just after the Jews lost Jerusalem to the Romans in 135 C.E. Others have dated the work before the outbreak of the Bar Kokhba Revolt, around 130 C.E. (Riaud 1994 dates it to 118-130 C.E.). *4 Baruch* deals with the destruction of Jerusalem in 70 C.E., reflects the end of exile, is skeptical of messianic hopes for a restoration of the real Temple, and mirrors rabbinic discourse of the early second century (cf. Yoḥanan ben Zakkai and Rabbi Akiba in *ʾAbot R. Nat.* B 31; *y. Taʿan.* 4:5). Therefore, the most likely date is between 130 and 135 C.E., during the debate over Bar Kokhba and the fate of Jerusalem.

Theological ideas

Recognizing the historical setting of *4 Baruch* sheds further light on the book's intention. By emphasizing God's Law as the way to salvation, hope in the resurrection of the dead, and the expectation of a heavenly Jerusalem, the author addresses pressing issues of his time. A turning point in the fate of the Jewish people can only be expected from God (*4 Bar.* 6:13-22; 8:1-2), who will finally gather his people in the heavenly Jerusalem. The focus on God's Law and keeping his commandments — explained and proclaimed by the prophet — will lead them not only back to the earthly, but to the heavenly city (*4 Bar.* 5:34; Wolff 1991). This double orientation fits well into the period of the years before and during the Bar Kokhba Revolt, as the writer warns against a one-sided hope of political and cultic restoration. This view also correlates with the way in which the Temple motifs are finally drawn out. Sacrifice is certainly mentioned (9:1-2), but neither the temple vessels, about which Jeremiah was initially very concerned (chap. 3), nor the keys to the Temple (chap. 4) are ever returned. Accordingly, Jeremiah's sacrifice in 9:3-5 consists primarily of the intercessory prayer of a righteous man. Hence the theology found in *4 Baruch* seems close to that of Ben Zakkai and his successors. Given his broad awareness of Scripture, one may locate the author either in the school of Ben Zakkai or in circles around it. He probably wrote in Palestine, perhaps in Jerusalem. The work's critical stance toward apocalypticism (*2 Baruch*) reflects an effort to overcome the resignation and unrealistic expectations in apocalyptic thought (e.g., *4 Bar.* 4:9-10) in favor of hope for individual eschatological salvation.

The Christian Redaction

In *4 Bar.* 9:10-32, a Christian ending has been added to the Jewish writing. The Christian addition changes the story of Jeremiah's natural death into a martyrdom similar to the fate of Jeremiah in the *Life of Jeremiah* and of Isaiah in the *Ascension of Isaiah.* Linguistic features suggest the work of a Christian editor in the ambit of Johannine apocalyptic Christianity. Besides the Christian ending of the story, several passages earlier in the book, or even the book as a whole, have been considered the product of Christian composition (Harris 1889). This, however, cannot be established, because every other passage in question represents distinctively Jewish ideas. Similarly, evidence of Gnostic (or Christian Gnostic) influence (Philonenko 1996) cannot be found in *4 Baruch.*

The perspective on the Jewish people in the Christian conclusion indicates that this part was composed shortly after the Jewish original. Although in *4 Bar.* 9:10-32 the people stone Jeremiah to death and thus are more negatively portrayed than in 1:1–9:9, the Christian redaction is a constructive development of *4 Baruch's* line of thought after the catastrophe of 135 C.E. Its perspective is not necessarily anti-Jewish but rather an attempt to develop a positive view of Jewish history in the light of the failed rebellion. A missionary element can also be detected: the Jewish people should learn from their past and listen to the message of *4 Baruch,* which in the view of the Christian redactor ultimately points to the coming of Christ. The deployment of Jeremiah as a Christian witness to the messiah strengthens this position, for Jeremiah is already depicted as prophet of eschatological salvation earlier in the work (esp. *4 Bar.* 8:9). In the light of the failed (and thus false) messiah Bar Kokhba, this Christian redaction of a Jewish writing may have been particularly effective, at least within Christian groups.

Bibliography

G. DELLING 1967, *Jüdische Lehre und Frömmigkeit in den Paralipomena Jeremiae,* Berlin: Töpelmann. • J. R. HARRIS 1889, *The Rest of the Words of Baruch: A Christian Apocalypse of the Year 136 A.D.: The Text Revised with an Introduction.* London: Clay. • J. HERZER 2005, *Fourth Baruch (Paraleipomena Jeremiou): Translated with an Introduction and Commentary,* Atlanta: Scholars Press; Leiden: Brill. • M. PHILONENKO 1996, "Simples observations sur les Paralipomènes de Jérémie," *Revue d'histoire et de philosophie religieuses* 76: 157-177. • J. RIAUD 1994, *Les Paralipomènes du Prophète Jérémie: Présentation, texte original, traduction et commentaire,* Angers: Association Saint-Yves. • B. SCHALLER 1998, "Paralipomena Jeremiou," *JSHRZ* I.8: 659-777. • B. SCHALLER 2000, "Paralipomena Jeremiou: Annotated Bibliography in Historical Order," *JSP* 22: 91-118. • C. WOLFF 1991, "Irdisches und himmlisches Jerusalem — Die Heilshoffnung in den Paralipomena Jeremiae," *ZNW* 8: 147-58.

JENS HERZER

Baths

The Roman public bathhouse was an impressive architectural complex. It featured both hot and cold water installations as well as a wide range of other services — a sauna and massage parlors, swimming pools, open courts for recreation and sports, gardens, meeting rooms, food and oil stands, and at times even libraries and brothels. In ancient times, maintaining a regular supply of water required effort and resources. Throughout the Mediterranean world, people accumulated rain in cisterns, dug wells, and drew on natural springs and rivers, but water was generally used sparingly for essential practices like drinking. Washing and keeping clean were neither a top priority nor a frequent undertaking. Therefore, in the centuries before Roman arrival, it would have been unimaginable that practically everyone in the known world would attend a public bath on nearly a daily basis and immerse one's body in warm water. And yet, by the second century C.E., the Roman bathhouse could be seen throughout the empire, in cities, towns, and even small villages.

In addition to bathing, the bathhouse embodied many cultural facets of the Roman realm. Its space was suffused with sculpture and mosaics, representing local and imperial power as well as the mythological ethos of the time. Magic and medicine were frequently carried out there (e.g., *Papyri Graecae Magicae,* 2d ed., 2.50; 36.69-77; 127.3-4), along with an array of hedonistic experiences that cherished the human body — from athletics to nudity, from sex to the anointment of oils and perfumes (e.g., Ovid, *Ars Amatoria* 3.638-640; *CIL* 4.10677-78). As it catered to people from all walks of life, the bathhouse became a social arena, a unique environment where social hierarchy was both determined and blurred, where the governing class and the elite blended with the lower strata of society, including the poor, women, and slaves. The emergence of the Roman bath would significantly transform daily habits and would foster far-reaching cultural consequences; ultimately, it became a vital entity that encapsulated *romanitas,* the Roman experience of life.

History

The forerunner of the Roman public bathhouse may be seen in the bathing facilities of the Greeks, mainly those incorporated into the gymnasium. But in that institution washing the body was a secondary undertaking, inferior to athletic and intellectual activities, and limited to the privileged few who attended it. Early Greek public baths were known in the Hellenistic period, but on a much smaller scale and with limited attendance compared to the later Roman facilities. The Roman baths emerged almost concurrently in Asia Minor and southern Italy in the second century B.C.E., were built throughout the empire by the end of the first century B.C.E., and reached their peak in the first few centuries of the Common Era.

Roman engineers and architects refined and disseminated various technological advances over the centuries, including the development of cement as a cohesive substance and the growing employment of the arch. These resulted in a crucial, and easy-to-build, system for water transportation — the aqueduct (from Lat. *aqua,* "water," + *ducere,* "to lead, bring forward"). Large and small, implemented in multiple variations, the aqueducts facilitated the growing popularity of the baths by providing an abundant water supply to cities, towns, and military camps. By the second century C.E. thousands of bathhouses dotted the Mediterranean world; by the end of the fourth century C.E., the city of Rome alone had over 800 baths (856 is the number cited in the *Curiosum Urbis Regionum XIV* and the *Notitia Regionum Urbis XIV* [ed. Jordan, p. 573]; but cf. Fagan 1999: 357). Using taxes and contributions of the upper class, municipal authorities erected them for public use, usually free of charge. Other privately owned baths charged the masses entrance fees; groups and associations built semipublic baths and limited their access to members; the military added their own, as did the rich who wished to bathe in the private confines of their villas and mansions. Attending the baths, usually in the late hours of the afternoon before dinner, became a standard part of everyday life.

Architecture and Function

A typical bathhouse may have included a changing variety of facilities (see below), but ultimately it consisted of water and heat. Warming the water became easy with another technological innovation, ingenious in its simplicity — the hypocaust system (from Gr. *hypokauston,* "heating from underneath"). Builders would suspend the bathhouse floor (thus named *suspensura*) on numerous small pillars *(pilae)* made of layered tiles. A furnace in a side chamber *(praefurnium)* channeled hot air into the void under the raised floors, heating them — and the water above — before flowing outside through vertical canals at the sides of the room (see Vitruvius, *De Architectura* 5.10). This hot chamber (known as the *caldarium*) usually included a communal pool *(alveus),* a basin *(labrum)* for cold water, and at times benches around the walls. In addition to the heated nucleus, two other rooms offered water at varying temperatures — the *frigidarium,* a valuated room with cold water pools (known as *piscinae*), and the *tepidarium,* a mediating room between the cold and the warm. Other standard bathhouse rooms include the changing room *(apodyterium),* which provided niches and shelves for the storage of clothing, a sauna for both dry and wet sweat (*laconicum* and *sudatorium,* respectively), and a latrine.

BATHS

Outside the main building an open court *(palaestra)* — often surrounded by porticos — accommodated sports and exercise and frequently included an open-air swimming pool *(natatio)*.

These basic components of the baths were designed in numerous shapes and sizes. Some offered a circular plan where one walked in a specific direction from room to room, others were more linear in their contours, and many others maintained their own unique look. The huge, imperial baths of Rome (usually called *thermae*) could house thousands of attendants at once; the large urban facilities all over the empire (normally called *balaneia*) could host hundreds of bathers, and numerous others were smaller. Over time, bathing routines evolved, and people typically attended the bathhouse during the afternoon, before dinner. The standard procedure was as follows: after working out in the *palaestra*, they would alternate between hot and cold baths, attend the sauna, and if they had the means, end (or begin) by applying oil and then scraping it off with a strigil.

The hypocaust system showing the *suspensura* (the little columns that supported the floor) in the *caldarium* (steam room) of the large bathhouse at Masada. The furnace was located on the other side of the semi-circular opening in the wall. *(Jodi Magness)*

Jews in the Baths

Some modern scholars tend to characterize the relationship between Jews and the baths as hostile, as if many avoided this institution and renounced its pagan connotations. In fact, the opposite is true. As far as our sources tell us, Jews — just like their fellow residents of the Roman Mediterranean — were quite enthusiastic about the benefits of the baths. In one of many such examples, a rabbinic statement equates the biblical description of the "luxuries of common people" (Eccl. 2:8) with the contemporary bathhouse (*Eccl. Rab.* 2:8).

The dissemination of the Roman baths in the East did not occur until the first century C.E. But already in the Hellenistic period, archaeological data indicates that wealthy Jews were quick to incorporate Roman-style bathing into their dwellings, as can be seen in the Hasmonean palaces in Jericho, or the estate in south Judea called "the palace of Hilkiyah." In the early Roman period, written documentation records the existence of bathhouses in Herod's fortified palaces at Jerusalem (Josephus, *J.W.* 5.168, 241). Similarly, archaeological excavations add evidence for baths in Herod's strongholds at Jericho, Cypros (on the hilltop west of Jericho), Herodium, Masada, and Machaerus. The excavations in ʿEin Zur at Ramat ha-Nadiv, northeast of Caesarea, have uncovered a semipublic bathhouse on a large Jewish estate, dating to before the destruction of the Second Temple.

But in Palestine during the late Second Temple period, even regular Jewish towns seem to have had baths. One of the assassination attempts against Herod took place while the king was entering the inner rooms of a public bath at Isana, a Jewish village some 20 km. north of Jerusalem (Josephus, *J.W.* 1.340-41; *Ant.* 14.462-64). Remnants of another bath were unearthed in the village of Artas, not far from "Solomon's pools," south of Jerusalem. From the era subsequent to the destruction of the Second Temple, bathhouses were found in Jewish towns such as ʿEin Gedi (although scholars have misidentified this as a military bath) on the shores of the Dead Sea, and in Rama in the Upper Galilee. From the end of the second century and on, bathhouses became a fixture in every city and town of Roman Palestine.

From the same period, numerous halakic passages in the Mishnah and the Tosefta refer to the bathhouse in the most neutral terms, testifying to the flawless integration of this institution into Jewish life. In later periods, the bathhouse appears in countless anecdotes, short stories, and sayings throughout talmudic literature. Jews knew to associate the bathhouse with the Romans (*b. Šabbat* 33b), had a clear view of its architectural structure (*t. Ber.* 2:20; *t. B. Bat.* 3:33) and heating system (*y. Yom-tov* 60c), and were infatuated, like everyone else, with the effortless opportunity to immerse one's body in warm water (*Lam. Rab.* 3:18 [based on Geniza fragment TS C6.62]; *b. Šabbat* 25b). They were also well versed in the folklore of the bath and in the magical traditions that evolved around it (*Sefer ha-Razim* 3.16-31 [ed. Margalioth, p. 93]). The rabbis formulated a special prayer for entering the baths, meant to guard Jews from its various hazards — everything from slipping to getting scorched, from an unwanted erection to being injured by a collapsing hypocaust (*y. Berakot* 14b).

Some Jews may have had reservations about the nudity and licentious atmosphere that pervaded the place (*t. Ber.* 2:14, 20-21; *y. Ḥal.* 58c; Epiphanius, *Adversus Haereses* 30.7.5-6 [ed. Holl, p. 342]), just as others — including the Romans themselves (chief among them more than a few emperors) — voiced similar disdain. Some bathhouses around the empire maintained at least some segregation between the sexes (although admittedly most did not), so those who wished could have avoided seeing the opposite sex undressed. The same holds true for the statuary that adorned many bathhouses. Noncultic statues were permissible to many Jews (*m. ʿAbod. Zar.* 3:1), and in any case, bathhouses lacking three-dimensional ornamentation were not unheard of (e.g., Sidonius, *Epistulae* 2.2.4-7).

BIBLIOGRAPHY
Y. Z. ELIAV 2000, "The Roman Bath as a Jewish Institution: Another Look at the Encounter between Judaism and the Greco-Roman Culture," *JSJ* 31: 416-54. • G. G. FAGAN 1999, *Bathing in Public in the Roman World,* Ann Arbor: University of Michigan Press. • R. GINOUVÈS 1962, *Balaneutikè: Recherches sur le bain dans l'antiquité grecque,* Paris: Boccard. • M. JACOBS 1998, "Römische Thermenkultur im Spiegel des Talmud Yerushalmi," in *The Talmud Yerushalmi and Graeco-Roman Culture,* ed. P. Schäfer, Tübingen: Mohr-Siebeck, 219-311. • I. NIELSEN 1990, *Thermae et Balnea: The Architecture and Cultural History of Roman Public Baths,* 2 vols., Aarhus: Aarhus University Press. • R. REICH 1988, "The Hot-Bath House *(balneum),* the Miqweh and the Jewish Community in the Second Temple Period," *JJS* 39: 102-7. • F. YEGÜL 1992, *Baths and Bathing in Classical Antiquity,* New York: Architecture History Foundation; Cambridge: MIT Press.

See also: Aqueducts; Gymnasium; Miqva'ot

YARON Z. ELIAV

Baths, Ritual → Miqva'ot

Beatitudes (4QBeatitudes)

4QBeatitudes or 4Q525 is a wisdom text from Qumran that was published in 1998. It was probably written in the second century B.C.E. There is no unambiguous evidence that 4Q525 was composed by members of the Dead Sea sect.

A beatitude is a literary form that begins with the Hebrew word *'ašrê* (Gr. *makarios*), which means "happy" or "blessed." Beatitudes praise an ideal type of person who should be emulated. In the Bible and early Jewish literature, beatitudes are relatively common, but they generally occur alone or in pairs (e.g., Ps. 1:1; Sir. 25:8-9). 4Q525 includes a rare example of a sequence of beatitudes in Hebrew. The key section is 4Q525 2 ii + 3 1-6:

> [Happy is he who speaks truth] with a pure heart and does not slander with his tongue. Happy are those who cling to her statutes and do not cling to the ways of iniquity. Hap[py] are those who rejoice in her and do not burst out upon the ways of folly. Happy are those who seek her with pure hands and do not search for her with a deceitful heart. Happy is the man who has obtained wisdom, follows the Torah of the Most High, sets his heart toward her ways, controls himself with her disciplines and takes pleasure alw[ays] in her chastisements; who does not forsake her in the affliction of [his] trouble[s], does not abandon her in the time of anguish, does not forget her [in the days of] dread and who does not reject [her] with the humility of his soul.

This passage exhibits a literary structure with four beatitudes, each with an *'ašrê* statement, followed by another that describes something that the happy man does not do. The final beatitude is longer than the other four, producing a 4 + 1 format. The Sermon on the Mount has a series of eight structurally similar beatitudes (Matt. 5:3-10) followed by one that is much longer in Matt. 5:11. Since 4Q525 2 ii + 3 begins with the second half of a beatitude, it is reasonable to presume that there were additional beatitudes on column i of fragment 2, which has not survived.

4Q525 1 is considered the beginning of the composition. This poorly preserved text, like Prov. 1:1-7, encourages one "[to acqui]re wisdom and disci[pline], to understand." Line 1 of 4Q525 1 mentions "the wisdom that Go[d] gave to him." The antecedent of "him" is not clear, but the passage presents wisdom as something given by God. 4Q525 2 ii + 3 3-4 states that the happy man is one who seeks wisdom and the Torah. This reflects the view that the eudemonistic goal of Proverbs of living a moral and fulfilling life can be achieved by following the Torah. Ben Sira has a similar attitude.

4QBeatitudes consistently uses feminine language. One should seek "her statutes" and "rejoice in her" (4Q525 2 ii + 3 2). Fragment 5 of 4Q525 proclaims that those who fear God "keep her paths" and those who love God "humble themselves in her" (lines 9 and 13). In Hebrew both "wisdom" and "Torah" are feminine words. The issue is not to decide to which of these terms the text refers, but to understand that 4Q525 reveres the Torah as a major source of wisdom. Proverbs envisions wisdom as a woman who calls out to people to acquire learning (e.g., Prov. 8:17). There is no explicit description of wisdom personified as a woman in 4QBeatitudes. 4Q525 24 ii may be a poem uttered by Dame Wisdom, but not enough of the text has survived to state this conclusively. In this fragment a female speaker urges people to heed her words.

4QBeatitudes is written for students in training who are themselves to become teachers. 4Q525 14 ii envisions the death of an ideal addressee: "all who know you will walk together in your teaching . . . together they will mourn, and on your paths they will remember you" (lines 15-16). This passage also urges one to "answer correctly among princes" (line 25). This implies that the intended audience will speak before nobles or other powerful people. The emphasis on Torah would provide training in reading and writing that would be suitable for a scribe. Like Ben Sira, 4QBeatitudes may be the product of a retainer class. 4Q525 is a wisdom text that encourages one to live in a way that is characterized by study, ethics, and Torah piety.

BIBLIOGRAPHY
G. J. BROOKE 2005, "The Wisdom of Matthew's Beatitudes (4QBeat and Mt. 5:3-12)," in idem, *The Dead Sea Scrolls and the New Testament,* Minneapolis: Fortress, 217-34. • J. H. CHARLESWORTH 2000, "The Qumran Beatitudes (4Q525) and the New Testament (Mt 5:3-11, Lk 6:20-26)," *RHPR* 80: 13-35. • M. J. GOFF 2006, *Discerning Wisdom: The Sapiential Literature of the Dead Sea Scrolls,* Leiden: Brill, 198-229. É. PUECH 1998, *Qumrân Grotte 4.XVIII: Textes Hébreux (4Q521-4Q528, 4Q576-4Q579),* Oxford: Clarendon, 115-78.

MATTHEW GOFF

Behemoth

Behemoth (Hebr. *Behēmôt,* lit. "great beast") is a primordial beast and symbol of chaos that appears in the Hebrew Bible only at Job 40:15-24. In Second Temple literature he appears in a more developed form paired with Leviathan (*4 Ezra* 6:49-52, *2 Bar.* 29:4, and *1 Enoch* 60:7-10, 24ab). Though each text has individual peculiarities, all agree that God primordially separated the monsters (created on the fifth day) and by force placed Leviathan in the sea and Behemoth on dry land (specifically, a mountain in a mythical desert region; Whitney 2006: 54-55). The pair is also specifically preserved to be food for the righteous at the end of time. Though none of the three passages concerned with creation specifies how the transformation to food will take place, later rabbinic traditions concerning the defeat and preparation of the monsters for the eschatological feast point to an oral tradition where the final banquet is preceded by some form of combat involving the creatures, either with God's angelic army or between themselves (Whitney 2006: 127-52).

The only reference to Behemoth alone in Second Temple literature comes in a passage from the *Lives of the Prophets,* a work usually identified as Jewish and usually dated to the first century C.E. In the work's treatment of the prophet Daniel, Behemoth is depicted as confronting Nebuchadnezzar: "Behemoth used to come upon him, and he would forget that he had been a man." The text of the passage is problematic, though the comment that "in Jewish tradition Behemoth is a primeval monster, not a demon" (Hare 1983: 390 note f) confuses the issue at best. One attempt at making sense of the verse translates it as follows: "Then the mind of a dumb animal would (again) take possession of him" (Torrey 1946: 39). This translation presumes that the Hebrew text underlying the Greek originally read *lēb behēmôt,* "heart of dumb beasts." If this is correct, then Behemoth as such is not mentioned in the passage.

The development of the monstrous figure must have continued throughout the period, however, since a powerful image of Behemoth as a land monster corresponding to the aquatic Leviathan emerges clearly in rabbinic literature. One set of traditions places Behemoth on the hills from which flows the Jordan River (depicted as the "world river"), which ends in the deep, in the realm of Leviathan. The earthly monster and the aquatic monster thus encompass the life-giving waters within the world (Whitney 2006: 98-114).

The combat-banquet tradition noted above is dramatically amplified in rabbinic literature, which draws on imagery of the Roman-Byzantine hunt *(kynēgesia).* One midrashic text *(Midrash Alphabetot),* unfortunately imperfectly preserved, depicts God as slaughtering Behemoth, after it is captured through an angelic hunt, in the presence of the righteous for use at the banquet. The Roman-Byzantine hunt itself later became associated with a "wild beast contest" in which creatures battled against one another. Hence within the tradition a dramatic battle between Leviathan and Behemoth arose, in which the creatures kill each other before being prepared as food for the eschatological banquet (Schirmann 1971).

Bibliography

D. R. A. Hare 1983, "The Lives of the Prophets," in *OTP,* 1: 379-411 • J. Schirmann 1971, "The Battle between Behemoth and Leviathan according to an Ancient Hebrew Piyyut," *Proceedings of the Israel Academy of Sciences and Humanities* 4: 327-69. • C. C. Torrey 1946, *The Lives of the Prophets: Greek Text and Translation,* Philadelphia, Society of Biblical Literature. • M. K. Wakeman 1973, *God's Battle with the Monster: A Study in Biblical Imagery.* Leiden: Brill. • K. W. Whitney Jr. 2006, *Two Strange Beasts: Leviathan and Behemoth in Second Temple and Early Rabbinic Judaism,* Winona Lake, Ind.: Eisenbrauns.

See also: Leviathan K. William Whitney Jr.

Belial

Hebrew Bible

The noun Belial (Hebr. *bĕliyyaʿal*) occurs twenty-seven times in the Hebrew Bible. Although its etymology and precise meaning are matters of debate, the word typically denotes wicked behavior of some sort. The word appears frequently in the expressions "son/sons of belial" or "man/men of belial" (e.g., Deut. 13:14 [Eng. 13:13]; Judg. 19:22; 1 Sam. 2:12; 1 Sam. 25:25; Prov. 16:27), expressions which refer to evildoers of various kinds. In 1 Sam. 1:16, an emotionally distraught Hannah explains to Eli, who had mistaken her extreme anguish for drunkenness, that she is not in fact a "daughter of belial" as Eli suspects. In a handful of passages, *bĕliyyaʿal* also appears in conjunction with death and Sheol. For instance, the psalmist relates, "The cords of death encompassed me; the torrents of belial assailed me; the cords of Sheol entangled me" (18:5-6 [Eng. 18:4-5]; cf. 2 Sam. 22:5-6).

Early Jewish Literature

In the Jewish writings of the Second Temple period, *bĕliyyaʿal* continued to be used as a common noun, associated with wickedness and/or death as it had been in the earlier Hebrew literature (e.g., 4Q425 frgs. 1-3 line 7). But the word also began to be used in a new way, as the proper name of the superhuman nemesis of the righteous, Belial.

Belial in the Dead Sea Scrolls

Belial seems to have been the Dead Sea sect's name for the leading superhuman opponent of the righteous. The literature left by the sect describes Belial as an evil individual who, for the time being, exercises authority over humanity and even over some belonging to Israel. A recurring designation for the present eschatological age in the Dead Sea Scrolls is the "dominion of Belial" (1QS 1:18, 23-24; 2:19; 1QM 14:9-10; 4Q177 col. iii line 8; 4Q491 i 6). In this age, Belial wields authority over humankind and Israel through the agency of "his spirits" (CD 12:2; 1QM 14:8-10; 4Q271 frg. 5 col. i line 18). According to the *Rule of the Community,* the dominion of Belial is a period during which Israel is tested and sin runs rampant (1QS 1:17-18, 24).

In the *Damascus Document,* Belial has three nets with which he traps Israel. These are fornication, wealth, and defilement of the Temple (CD 4:12-19). But Belial's opposition to Israel is not restricted to these three nets. Belial also, for example, attempted to mislead Israel at the time of the exodus. The Egyptian magicians' ability to replicate the signs that Moses performed is credited to the scheming of Belial (CD 5:17-19). Belial, however, is not exclusively antagonistic to the will of the Deity. In the eschatological period, Belial will be the agent of God's punishment against evildoers (CD 8:2; 19:14). It is reasonable to assume that Belial is the name for the Satan figure in the *Damascus Document.* The teaching of this work concerning Belial resembles especially closely the teaching of the book of *Jubilees* regarding the Prince of Mastema/ Satan (cf. 4QpsJub[a] [= 4Q225] 2 ii 13-14, which may speak of the Prince of Mastema and Belial as two distinct beings).

The *War Scroll* (1QM) describes the final war which will be fought between the "sons of light" and the "sons of darkness." In this text, Michael is the angelic patron of the "sons of light," and Belial is the corresponding superhuman patron of the "sons of darkness," a group alternately referred to as "the army of Belial" (1QM 1:1, 13) and "the lot of Belial" (1QM 1:5; 4:2). Although the teaching of the *War Scroll* has been appropriately labeled "dualistic," it is important to qualify this label by recognizing that its dualism is limited. True to the monotheistic tradition that produced it, the *War Scroll* teaches that the God of Israel is ultimately sovereign over both good and evil. One passage declares explicitly that God created Belial as an angel of hostility (1QM 13:11). But the "sons of light," aided by God and an army angels, are guaranteed victory (1QM 12:8).

The word *bĕliyyaʿal* occurs in numerous other texts from the Dead Sea Scrolls. That this word could be understood either as a proper name or as a generic noun denoting wickedness or death makes it difficult to interpret some of the passages in which it occurs. The word appears prominently in several of the *Hodayot* (1QH[a]). Although *bĕliyyaʿal* in this collection of thanksgiving hymns is typically taken to be the proper name Belial, many of its occurrences would make at least as much sense interpreted as a generic noun (e.g., 1QH[a] 10:16, 22; 11:29, 32; 12:13; 13:26).

Belial in Other Early Jewish Writings

Another work whose use of *bĕliyyaʿal* is ambiguous is the book of *Jubilees* (second century B.C.E.). *Jubilees* 15:33 refers to certain "sons of belial/Belial" among Israel who do not circumcise their children. And in *Jub.* 1:20 Moses prays that God will not allow a "spirit of belial/Belial" to rule over Israel and cause them to sin. Instead, Moses asks God to create for them a "spirit of holiness" (*Jub.* 1:22). If *bĕliyyaʿal* in these passages is a proper name, then *Jubilees* contains the earliest such use of the word. It seems more likely, however, that the author of *Jubilees* intended by *bĕliyyaʿal* nothing more than "wickedness," as in the Hebrew Bible.

Sibylline Oracles 3.63-74 uses the name Beliar (the Greek form of Belial) for an eschatological human opponent. This Antichrist-like figure will perform great signs and mislead many people. In the end, however, he and those he deceives will be subject to God's judgment. Beliar also appears as a proper name for the Satan figure in early Christian literature. The name appears once in the New Testament. In 2 Cor. 6:14-15, a passage reminiscent of the *War Scroll,* the question is asked, "What fellowship is there between light and darkness? What agreement does Christ have with Beliar?" Beliar occupies a particularly important place in the theology of the *Testaments of the Twelve Patriarchs.* In this work, Beliar leads humankind to commit acts of violence and sexual immorality (e.g., *T. Reub.* 4:8, 11; *T. Dan* 1:7; *T. Benj.* 6:1; 7:1).

BIBLIOGRAPHY

J. J. COLLINS 1998, *The Apocalyptic Imagination: An Introduction to Jewish Apocalyptic Literature,* 2d ed., Grand Rapids: Eerdmans. • J. DUHAIME 1995, *War Scroll,* in *The Dead Sea Scrolls,* vol. 2, ed. J. H. Charlesworth, Tübingen: Mohr-Siebeck. • H. HUPPENBAUER 1959, "Belial in den Qumrantexten," *TZ* 15: 81-89. • H. KOSMALA 1965, "The Three Nets of Belial," *ASTI* 4: 91-113. • P. VON DER OSTEN-SACKEN 1969, *Gott und Belial,* Göttingen: Vandenhoeck & Ruprecht. • M. SEGAL 2007, *The Book of Jubilees: Rewritten Bible, Redaction, Ideology and Theology,* Leiden: Brill. • A. STEUDEL 2000, "God and Belial," in *The Dead Sea Scrolls: Fifty Years after Their Discovery,* ed. L. H. Schiffman et al., Jerusalem: Israel Exploration Society, 332-40.

See also: Satan and Related Figures

RYAN E. STOKES

Ben Sira, Book of

The book of Ben Sira is known by three names: (1) the Wisdom of Jesus Ben Sira (Hebr. *ben sîrāʾ*), the name by which the book is generally known, particularly in Hebrew; (2) Sirach (Gr. *Sirach*), usually referring to the Greek translation of the Hebrew made by the grandson of the author; and (3) Ecclesiasticus, the Latin version of the book included in the Vulgate. Ben Sira is part of the so-called Apocrypha and is usually included with those Jewish works in the category of "wisdom."

Original Language and Date

The book was composed in Hebrew in Jerusalem by a Jewish sage, who gives his name as Jesus son of Eleazar son of Sira (50:27), sometime between ca. 195 and 180 B.C.E. These dates can be established in relation to other contemporary figures whose dates are relatively secure. In the first instance, Ben Sira, in chap. 50, praises the Jewish high priest Simon II (219-196 B.C.E.), under whose tenure he lived and after whose death he probably wrote. In the second, Ben Sira shows no awareness of the tragic events that transpired under the

Seleucid ruler Antiochus IV (175-64 B.C.E.), which led to the Hasmonean Revolt. The Greek translation, the primary language of the book's transmission, was made by Ben Sira's grandson, who says in his prologue that he came to Egypt "in the thirty-eighth year of King Euergetes" (most likely Ptolemy VII Physcon Euergetes), about 132 B.C.E. There he translated the book, probably completing it sometime around the death of Ptolemy in 117 B.C.E., "for those living abroad if they wish to become learned, preparing their character to live by the law." Moving backward from grandson to grandfather would situate the book in the general period of 195-180 B.C.E.

Textual Transmission

The Wisdom of Ben Sira has gone through a very complicated history of transmission. Both the Hebrew and the Greek circulated in two separate forms. The original Hebrew text of Ben Sira (HTI) underwent a process of augmentation with additional proverbs that resulted in a second Hebrew recension (HTII). The grandson made his original translation (GI) from his grandfather's Hebrew, although by his time the Hebrew had apparently already suffered some in transmission. A second Greek recension (GII) was translated from the second Hebrew tradition. One additional complication attends the Greek tradition. Every Greek manuscript of Ben Sira contains a textual dislocation in which 30:25–33:13a and 33:13b–36:16a have been reversed in order. The great biblical scholar Jerome did not translate the Latin version included in the Vulgate, since he did not consider Ben Sira a "canonical book." The Vulgate, then, represents the Old Latin translation of the book, made perhaps as early as the second century C.E. Among the extant languages in which the book survives, which include Armenian and Coptic, the Old Latin and the Syriac constitute perhaps the important witnesses after the Greek and Hebrew texts, since the Old Latin depends on the expanded GII and the Syriac was translated on the basis of HTI and HTII, while also showing some influence from the Greek.

State of the Hebrew Text

Even though ultimately it was not included in the canon of the Hebrew Bible, Ben Sira enjoyed ongoing popularity, as evidenced by numerous rabbinic citations of proverbs in Ben Sira's name, only some of which came from the book as we know it. These quotations provide evidence for the ongoing process of the book's expansion. Gradually, however, the Hebrew text fell into obscurity. It seems to have survived into the Middle Ages in Qaraite communities on the margins of rabbinic Judaism, perhaps entering Qaraite hands as part of a find of Hebrew manuscripts in the area of the Dead Sea sometime around 800 C.E.

Until the late nineteenth century, Greek and Latin were the two primary languages in which Ben Sira was known. In 1896, however, Solomon Schechter of Cambridge University came into possession of a large quantity of manuscript fragments from the Cairo Geniza. Among them Schechter perceptively identified a number of pieces of Ben Sira. Since then scholars have isolated fragments of six separate Hebrew manuscripts from the Geniza, designated A through F. (For the most recent listing of all the passages extant in the Cairo Geniza manuscripts, see Skehan and Di Lella 1987: 52-53). In addition to the Geniza manuscripts, parts of Ben Sira in Hebrew were discovered at Qumran and Masada. Two small fragments of 6:14-15, 20-31 came to light among the Qumran Cave 2 finds (2Q18). Although not extensive, they do demonstrate that, even in an early period, the Hebrew of Ben Sira was written in stichometric (poetic) lines. Ben Sira 51 was included in the Cave 11 *Psalms Scroll* (11QPsalms[a] or 11Q5) along with several other nonbiblical compositions. The text is fragmentary and preserves verses 13-19, 30, and it differs dramatically from the Geniza version of chap. 51. Finally, during his Masada excavations, Yigael Yadin discovered the most extensive Judean Desert remains of Ben Sira. The Masada scroll (Mas1h) preserves 39:27–44:17 in whole or in part. This manuscript is the earliest copy of the book to survive, and its text is quite close to that of the Geniza manuscripts.

Ben Sira the Wise Scribe

Ben Sira was a scribe/sage who lived at a crucial moment in Jewish history. He almost certainly witnessed the changeover of authority over Judea from Ptolemaic to Seleucid hands around 200 B.C.E. As a scribe he was steeped in the traditions of ancient Israel, including both its wisdom traditions and those materials that would later be gathered together into its Scriptures. In Sir. 38:24–39:11, Ben Sira describes in capsule form the sage's occupation. He specifically contrasts the scribe/sage with farmers and artisans. Unlike other occupations, that of the scribe/sage requires "leisure time," since "only one who has little business can become wise," which he does by studying "the law of the Most High," by seeking out "the wisdom of all the ancients," and by being concerned "with prophecies." Through study and prayer, God gives the scribe/sage "a spirit of understanding," and he "will pour forth words of wisdom of his own." The result is praise and a good memory among the people. While Ben Sira's description suggests that he was fairly high on the social ladder — he was certainly no artisan or merchant — he was not positioned at the top. Other places in the book describe people like Ben Sira as dependent on the priestly and aristocratic classes for their economic well-being and social status, hence the designation "retainer" that is sometimes used to locate Ben Sira and those like him in their social world.

Contents

The book is more complex than the label "wisdom" sometimes might suggest. Ben Sira certainly contains numerous proverbs of practical import, most of which are intended to help his students navigate the nexus of occupational, social, and family networks that they will encounter. Among other matters, the sage gives advice on how to act at a banquet given by a rich person, how to watch over daughters, how to raise sons, how to manage one's money. Elsewhere, however, Ben Sira also shows a great deal of interest in existential matters. He ruminates on topics that we now relegate to science, such as the makeup of the cosmos (see the doctrine of the syzygies in 42:24), and in that light he tries to understand the place of human beings in the universe (e.g., 18:8-14). Chapters 44–50 form the most structured section of the book. In them Ben Sira glorifies a series of heroes from Israel's past, which culminates in his paean to the high priest Simon II.

Most of Ben Sira's proverbs are written in poetic bicola, with several often put together to form poems on a single topic (e.g., 6:5-17 on friendship). Although the book has no clearly observable overall structure, several broad themes run throughout it. Most prominent is the focus on fear of the Lord and the acquisition of wisdom. Ben Sira represents wisdom as a woman wooing the student, who single-mindedly should pursue her. In chap. 24, Lady Wisdom praises herself and narrates her mission from God to dwell in Israel and to minister in the Temple (24:10). This same cosmic wisdom, Ben Sira claims, is embodied in the Torah, "the law that Moses commanded us" (24:23). Thus, the scribe/sage who fears the Lord, through prayer and study, will reach his ultimate goal, finding wisdom. In chap. 51, which concludes the book, Ben Sira narrates his own pursuit of wisdom as a youth in an autobiographical poem in which he portrays his search with rather erotic overtones.

BIBLIOGRAPHY

R. A. ARGALL 1995, *1 Enoch and Sirach,* Atlanta: Scholars Press. • M. BAILLET 1962, "Ecclésiastique," in *Les 'Petites Grottes' de Qumrân,* ed. M. Baillet, J. T. Milik, and R. de Vaux, DJD 3, Oxford: Oxford University Press, 75-77. • P. C. BEENTJES 1997, *The Book of Ben Sira in Modern Research,* Berlin: de Gruyter. • P. C. BEENTJES 2003. *The Book of Ben Sira in Hebrew.* Leiden: Brill. • C. V. CAMP 1991, "Understanding a Patriarchy: Women in Second-Century Jerusalem through the Eyes of Ben Sira," in *"Women Like This": New Perspectives on Jewish Women in the Greco-Roman World,* ed. A.-J. Levine, Atlanta: Scholars Press, 1-39. • J. J. COLLINS 1997, *Jewish Wisdom in the Hellenistic Age,* Louisville: Westminster John Knox, 23-111. • J. HASPECKER 1967, *Gottesfurcht bei Jesus Sirach,* Rome: Pontifical Biblical Institute. • B. L. MACK 1985, *Wisdom and the Hebrew Epic: Ben Sira's Hymn in Praise of the Fathers,* Chicago: University of Chicago Press. • P. W. SKEHAN AND A. A. DI LELLA 1987, *The Wisdom of Ben Sira,* Garden City, N.Y.: Doubleday. • B. G. WRIGHT 1989, *No Small Difference: Sirach's Relationship to Its Hebrew Parent Text,* Atlanta: Scholars Press. • Y. YADIN 1965, *The Ben Sira Scroll from Masada,* Jerusalem: Israel Exploration Society. • Y. YADIN 1999, *The Ben Sira Scroll from Masada,* in *Masada VI: Yigael Yadin Excavations 1963-1965,* Jerusalem: Israel Exploration Society, 151-252. • J. ZIEGLER, ED. 1965, *Sapientia Iesu filii Sirach,* Göttingen: Vandenhoeck & Ruprecht.

BENJAMIN G. WRIGHT III

Berakhot (4Q286-290)

4QBerakhot has been preserved in five manuscripts (4Q286-290), dated paleographically between approximately 1 and 50 C.E. The text consists of a series of liturgical blessings and curses and a series of ordinances designated for an annual covenantal ceremony of the Qumran community. The ceremonial function of the text is characterized by opening rubrics such as "[F]urther they shall bless the God" (4Q286 frg. 7 col. i line 8), and by closing rubrics such as "the council of the community, all of them will say together: Amen. Amen" (4Q286 7 ii 1 = 4Q287 6:1). The curses are opened by rubrics such as "and they will speak up, saying 'Cursed be [B]elial . . . ,'" and closed by the liturgical response "Amen. Amen" (4Q286 7 ii 2, 5 = 4Q287 6:2, 4). This liturgical system (cf. Deuteronomy 27 and 1QS 1:16–2:18), together with the clause "year after year in order" (4Q287 4:1) and an ordinance referring to the muster of the members of the community (4Q286 17ab), indicates its annual covenantal ceremony.

The content of this ceremony consists of a fragmented communal confession (4Q286 1 i 7-8 and possibly frg. 9); a series of blessings addressed to God (4Q286 1 ii–7 i and 4Q287 1-5); a series of curses on Belial and his lot (4Q286 7 ii = 4Q287 6, and 4Q287 7-10); a series of ordinances (4Q286 20ab = 4Q288 1); a liturgy for expelling the willful sinner from the community (4Q289); and the conclusion of the ceremony (4Q290).

The covenantal ceremonies of the *Community Rule* (1QS) and that of 4QBerakhot express the dualistic ideology of the Qumran sect. However, the *Community Rule* represents this ideology only with a sectarian ceremony, of which the blessed ones are the men of the lot of God (the members of the community) and the cursed ones are the men of the lot of Belial (the community's opponents). 4QBerakhot represents this ideology by an ideal symbolic ceremony of the entire universe, of which the blessed one is God and the cursed ones are Belial and his lot. God is blessed by the holy angels and by the entire heavenly and earthly creation, including the members of the community. Belial and his lot are cursed in the preserved texts by the members of the community. Biblical phrases pertaining to the divine throne chariot and short descriptions of the earthly Temple are used for describing the heavenly throne and the angelic hosts (cf. the *Songs of the Sabbath Sacrifice*), and other biblical phrases are used for describing the entire creation.

The blessings God receives from the entire universe are described in a graduated order, from the heavenly to the earthly realms. These encompass the angels in the holy heavenly realm (4Q286 1 ii 1-4; 2:1-5; 4Q287 2ab), the angels with authority over the meteorological elements (4Q286 3), the creatures of the earthly realm (4Q286 5:1-8; 4Q287 3), and those of the seas, the rivers, and the deep (4Q286 5:9-11). However, the blessings God receives from his elect ones, the members of the community, are mentioned separately with those who have eternal knowledge to praise and bless God, the council of the angels of purification (4Q286 7 i; cf. 1QH^a

11[3]:21-23; 19[11]:9-14; frg. 10:7-8; 1QS 11:7b-8a). A graduated order of God's blessing is found in Psalm 148, *1 Enoch* 61:10-12, Prayer of Azariah 31-67, and other contexts. However, in 4QBerakhot this order is not just a catalogue of worshipers; rather, the author develops the list of worshipers with short, lively descriptions. The antithesis between the realm of God and the realm of Belial is the antithesis between holiness and abomination. The members of the Qumran community, who bless God and commit themselves to observe His ordinances, consider themselves as belonging to the holy realm of God, the Creator of the universe (cf. 1QM 10:11-14), whereas Belial and his lot represent the forces of impurity and hostility, as well as destruction and death (cf. a similar antithesis in 1QM 13:2-6). 4QBerakhot reflects a more developed form of the dualistic ideology than the covenantal ceremony in the Qumran *Community Rule,* but there is no information in the Scrolls concerning its particular usage by the community.

Bibliography

J. T. Milik 1972, "*Milkî-sedeq* et *Milkî-reša'* dans les anciens écrits juifs et chrétiens," *JJS* 23: 95-144. • B. Nitzan 1994, "4QBerakhot (4Q286-290): A Covenantal Ceremony in the Light of Related Texts," *RevQ* 16: 487-506. • B. Nitzan 1998, "Berakhot," in *Qumran Cave 4 VI, Poetical and Liturgical Text, Part 1,* DJD 11, ed. E. Eshel et al., Oxford: Clarendon, 1-74. • B. Nitzan 2000, "The Benedictions from Qumran for the Annual Covenantal Ceremony," in *The Dead Sea Scrolls: Fifty Years after Their Discovery 1947-1997,* ed. L. H. Schiffman et al., Jerusalem: Israel Exploration Society, 263-71.

Bilhah Nitzan

Berossus

Berossus was a Babylonian priest of Bel (Marduk) and author who flourished in the early third century B.C.E. Writing in Greek, he was the first native Babylonian to present Hellenistic readers an account of Babylonian tradition and history. His work, known as the *Babyloniaka* ("Babylonian Matters"), runs from creation to Alexander the Great. Berossus presented his work to the Seleucid monarch Antiochus I (281-262 B.C.E.), in whose court he may have served. It consisted of three books: book 1 on creation and the land of Mesopotamia, book 2 on Mesopotamian royal history from before the great flood down to the Babylonian king Nabunasir (747-734 B.C.E.), and book 3 on royal history down to Alexander the Great.

Unfortunately, the *Babyloniaka* is preserved only fragmentarily in citations of various authors, including the late first-century-C.E. Jewish historian Josephus, the fourth-century-C.E. Christian historian Eusebius, and the Byzantine chronicler George Syncellus. Berossus' work was apparently hard to obtain even in antiquity, and most authors cited him through an abridgement made by Alexander Polyhistor (first century B.C.E.), whose work likewise no longer survives except in quotation. This complex tradition of quotation via quotation created a confusing textual history of citations, so modern scholars are not always confident of the origin of passages credited to Berossus.

Like his contemporary the Egyptian priest and scholar Manetho, Berossus wrote from the standpoint of a conquered native culture for a Greek readership. He can thus be compared to Josephus, who in some respects saw Berossus's work as a model for his own. Berossus wrote to correct and inform Greek readers whose knowledge of Mesopotamian traditions was dependent on Greek historians whom he considered inaccurate. Josephus (*Ag. Ap.* 1.142), who frequently censures Greek authors, states that Berossus wrote to correct authors such as Ctesias, who were misinformed about Babylonian history.

Berossus is of interest because he gives unparalleled evidence of the content and state of ancient Mesopotamian traditions in the Hellenistic age. Scholars have recognized his faithful use of Akkadian texts, including versions of the *Enuma Elish,* the *Epic of Gilgamesh,* and royal king lists. The first book of the *Babyloniaka* opens with a typically Greek autobiography, followed by a brief description of Babylonian geography and of the state of humanity when humans lived as animals "without laws." At this point Berossus narrates the divine revelation to humans via the messenger Oannes, who told of Bel's creation of the world and humans, and of the ways of civilization and government. Book 2 chronicles the reigns of kings during the 432,000 years prior to the flood, the flood itself and its survivor Xisouthros, the reestablishment of the divine revelations for civilization, and the kings down to the Babylonian Nabunasir (747 B.C.E.). Book 3 takes the king list through the last Babylonians and Persians and down to the Greeks, spending significant time on the reigns of Sennacherib (705-681 B.C.E.) and Nebuchadnezzar II (605-562 B.C.E.).

Berossus is mentioned by a few Hellenistic and Roman writers (e.g., Pliny and Seneca) but was hardly influential, perhaps because his Greek was poor and he made little effort to explain his traditions to Greek minds. However, Josephus and Eusebius considered him of immense value. In his work *On the Antiquity of the Jews,* more commonly known as *Against Apion,* Josephus uses Berossus as an important witness against Greco-Roman authors who denied the antiquity and honor of the Jewish past. Josephus argues that from ancient times Egyptian and Babylonian priests like Berossus had kept accurate written records. He then cites numerous authors, including Berossus, who mention persons or events from Jewish history. Josephus finds in Berossus corroboration for the flood, Noah's descendants, Nebuchadnezzar's conquest of Jerusalem, and Cyrus's liberation of the Jews (*Ag. Ap.* 1.128-53). Elsewhere Josephus cites Berossus as a supporting witness to Jewish traditions about ancient worthies who lived for hundreds of years (*Ant.* 1.107). In addition, Josephus asserts that Berossus knew of Abraham, though not by name, and was aware that the patriarch was expert in astrology and lived ten generations after the flood (*Ant.* 1.158). If this disputed citation is ac-

BIBLICAL ANTIQUITIES (PSEUDO-PHILO)

cepted, then Berossus is the earliest known non-Jewish historian to mention Abraham.

BIBLIOGRAPHY

S. M. BURNSTEIN 1978, *The Babylonica of Berossus*, Malibu: Undena Publications. • F. JACOBY 1958, *Die Fragmente der griechischen Historiker*, vol. 3, part C, 364-95. • A. KUHRT 1987, "Berossus' *Babyloniaka* and Seleucid Rule in Babylonia," in *Hellenism in the East*, ed. A Kuhrt and S. Sherwin-White, 32-56. • M. STERN 1976, *Greek and Latin Authors on Jews and Judaism*, vol. 1, Jerusalem: Israel Academy of Sciences and Humanities, 55-65. • V. P. VERBRUGGHE AND J. M. WICKERSHAM 1996, *Berossus and Manetho, Introduced and Translated: Native Traditions in Ancient Mesopotamia and Egypt*, Ann Arbor: University of Michigan Press.

JAMES E. BOWLEY

Biblical Antiquities (Pseudo-Philo)

The *Biblical Antiquities* of Pseudo-Philo is a retelling of the biblical story from Adam to Saul's death. Although it was transmitted in the name of Philo, it is clearly not the work of the Alexandrian philosopher. The traditional Latin title *Liber Antiquitatum Biblicarum* ("Book of Biblical Antiquities") is not original to the book. It first appears in the sixteenth century, when it may have been so called because of its general similarity to the *Jewish Antiquities* of Josephus. The work survives in eighteen complete manuscripts and three fragmentary ones, all in Latin and originating in Germany and Austria. The manuscripts date to between the eleventh and the sixteenth centuries. The book ends abruptly with the dying Saul sending word to David that David's enemy, Saul, is about to expire. The abrupt ending has led to the hypothesis that the end of the manuscript is lost, but an attempt has been made to make sense of the ending as it stands, on analogy with the abrupt ending of Mark's gospel (Murphy 1991). There may also be material missing between 36:4 and 37:2, as well as between 37:5 and 38:1. Harrington produced a critical text, which he translated into English (Harrington 1985), and which appears in a French translation (Perrot and Bogaert 1976). Jacobson (1996) prints Harrington's Latin text, but his translation is not a simple translation of that text. Rather, in numerous cases he tries to get behind the Latin and putative Greek to what was most likely to be the original Hebrew and translates that. His commentary makes a detailed case for each of these reconstructions.

Language and Geographical Provenance

Harrington (1970) has shown that the *Biblical Antiquities* was originally written in Hebrew, and that a Greek translation stands between the original Hebrew and the surviving Latin. Parts of the *Biblical Antiquities* appear in Hebrew in the much later work *Chronicles of Jerahmeel*, but they do not represent the original Hebrew. Rather, they are a translation from the Latin. Since the original language was Hebrew and Pseudo-Philo follows a Palestinian text type (Harrington 1971), it is likely that the work was composed in Palestine. Similarity with *4 Ezra* and *2 Baruch*, works thought to originate in Palestine, also indicate a Palestinian origin.

Authorship

The fact that the *Biblical Antiquities* was passed down with a Latin translation of Philo's works might suggest that the work is by that Jewish philosopher, active in Alexandria during the first century C.E. However, the work is clearly not by Philo, nor does it claim to be. It does not employ his allegorical approach to Israel's sacred texts; nor do the author's interests match those of Philo. Furthermore, the author wrote in Hebrew, probably in Palestine. So Philonic authorship is out of the question, and the author is unknown. We know only that he was well educated and had extensive knowledge not only of the Bible but also of the exegetical traditions of his day. He was no mere collector of such traditions, since he wove them into a coherent narrative with its own character, themes, outlook, and tone.

Date

Scholars generally agree that the work dates from the first century. As first noted by M. R. James (1917), the *Biblical Antiquities* bears some resemblance in content and language to *4 Ezra* and *2 Baruch*, works written in the late first or early second century C.E. in response to the destruction of the Second Temple. Disagreement centers on whether it was composed before or after the destruction of Jerusalem by the Romans in 70 C.E. There is no clear reference to that event, but some, including Jacobson, read 19:7 as an indirect reference to it. That verse dates the fall of the First Temple to the seventeenth day of the fourth month (Tammuz), the same day on which Moses smashed the tablets of the Law on Sinai. Mishnah *Taʿan.* 4:6 and other rabbinic texts also date the smashing of the tablets to the seventeenth of Tammuz. The Bible says nothing about that day with respect to the fall of the First Temple, but instead focuses on the ninth of that month (e.g., Jer. 39:2; 52:6). Since both Pseudo-Philo and some rabbinic texts date certain events relevant to the First or Second Temple on the seventeenth, while the Bible does not connect the date to the fall of the First Temple, Cohn (1898) argued for taking 19:7 as a reference to the fall of the Second Temple. Jacobson restates and elaborates Cohn's arguments, adducing a number of features of the text that he feels support a date after 70. Bogaert (Perrot and Bogaert 1976) argues against this. He and others find the lack of a clear awareness of the fall of the Second Temple a persuasive argument. Further, there is no indication in the book that the sacrifices have ceased in the author's time. Both sides of the argument bring to bear other arguments regarding date, but to date no decisive arguments have been produced that allow great confidence when choosing between a date before or after the destruction of the Second Temple.

Genre

The genre of Pseudo-Philo is "rewritten Bible" (Fisk 2001). It is not a continuous commentary on the biblical text, as is found in midrash, and it tends to exhibit greater freedom with respect to the sacred text than is found in the Aramaic paraphrases of the Bible called targums. At times, Pseudo-Philo sticks close to the biblical narrative, but it adds, subtracts, and rewrites material with great liberty. Pseudo-Philo often brings in elements from other biblical passages to enhance some aspect of the passage he is rewriting. The closest parallels to the *Biblical Antiquities* are *Jubilees*, the *Jewish Antiquities* of Josephus, and the *Genesis Apocryphon* from the Qumran library. Another possible parallel is 1 and 2 Chronicles. It has been suggested that Pseudo-Philo was written to complement that book, since Pseudo-Philo covers the period from Adam to the death of Saul and the beginning of David's career, while the Chronicler's narrative begins with a brief chapter on Saul and then goes on to an extended treatment of David. Both works also manifest a predilection for genealogies. However, the themes and specific treatment of the sacred narrative differ greatly between Pseudo-Philo and the books of Chronicles. The genre of rewritten Bible fell out of favor after around 100 C.E., perhaps because of a movement toward a fixed biblical text, easily distinguishable from commentary on it, as in midrash, or paraphrase of it, as in the targums.

Major Themes

Divine Faithfulness

A number of themes run through the book, giving it a coherence and unity that would be lacking were it simply a collection of exegetical traditions. The most prominent theme is God's faithfulness to Israel. God continues to maintain a covenant relationship with Israel despite the repeated failures of the people and of some leaders. This theme is accompanied by a pessimistic picture of the people of Israel and indeed of all humans.

Divine Judgment

Given the prevalence of human sin and failure, it is not surprising to find many instances of punishment in the *Biblical Antiquities*. This gives the author many opportunities to demonstrate that the punishment, which comes from God, fits the crime. Pseudo-Philo finds a fairly strict retributive scheme in Israel's history. Where such a scheme is not present or is not sufficiently prominent in his biblical sources, the author rewrites the narrative to make it central.

Leadership

Leadership is a key concern of Pseudo-Philo. Good leadership consists of ascertaining and doing God's will. This is well illustrated by Abraham, who, refusing a chance to escape his enemies in the incident of the tower of Babel, relies on God instead and is rescued. Pseudo-Philo enhances the role of Israel's only female judge, Deborah. Israel's elders prove unreliable leaders when on their own they produce a proposal to refrain from intercourse so that their seed will not serve Egyptian idols. This emphasis on the will of God is also reflected in the theme that any plots conceived by Israel's enemies will inevitably fail if God plans otherwise. Language of planning and plotting is frequent in the book, and it serves to draw a marked distinction between God and humans.

Divine Providence

Pseudo-Philo emphasizes God's active role in Israel's history. It does so by reproducing places in the biblical text where God intervenes directly, as well as by introducing God into the text where he was not explicitly present originally. The author often uses direct address by God or even soliloquy so that the reader knows precisely what God's intentions are. Thus, dramatic irony is a feature of the narrative.

Idolatry

Concern about idolatry is evident in Pseudo-Philo. It is the sin that receives the most attention in the book. The Gentiles are idolatrous, and Israel risks contamination from their practices. Intermarriage is frowned upon by this author. Many other sins can be traced in one way or another to the failure to worship God and only God. This is most evident in chap. 25, when Kenaz forces transgressors to reveal their sins before being executed.

Protology and Eschatology

Pseudo-Philo does not retell Genesis 3, but he does assume the Garden of Eden story (13:8-9) and implies that humankind will regain what they lost if they turn from sin. The fullest description of the eschaton is placed on God's lips; it is located after the story of the flood (3:9-10) in order to emphasize the idea of moral causality. Every sin will be punished in this world and the next. The present age will pass away, and there will be a universal resurrection at which God will recompense both good and evil deeds. The earth's sterility will come to an end, and "there will be another earth and another heaven, an everlasting dwelling place." The book shows no interest in messianism.

Importance

No effort to assign the *Biblical Antiquities* to a known individual or group within first-century Judaism has won general assent. The work is best seen as a product of mainstream Jewish biblical interpretation in Palestine of the first century. It furnishes a valuable witness to how Israel's sacred traditions were read and adapted in such an environment. In some cases, Pseudo-Philo is the earliest witness we have for a given tradition. In other cases, he may well be original. Pseudo-Philo furnishes an excellent example of the kind of theology and adaptation of the biblical text to later circumstances that would be characteristic of nonsectarian Jewish thought around the turn of the eras.

BIBLIOGRAPHY

L. COHN 1898, "An Apocryphal Work Ascribed to Philo of Alexandria," *JQR* 10: 277-332. • BRUCE N. FISK 2001, *Do You Not Remember? Scripture, Story and Exegesis in the Rewritten Bible of Pseudo-Philo*, Sheffield: Sheffield Academic Press. • D. J. HARRINGTON 1970, "The Original Language of Pseudo-Philo's *Liber Antiquitatum Biblicarum*," *HTR* 63:503-14. • D. J.

HARRINGTON 1971, "The Biblical Text of Pseudo-Philo's *Liber Antiquitatum Biblicarum*," *CBQ* 33: 1-17. • D. J. HARRINGTON 1974, *The Hebrew Fragments of Pseudo-Philo's Liber Antiquitatum Biblicarum Preserved in the Chronicles of Jerahmeel*, Cambridge, Mass.: Society of Biblical Literature. • D. J. HARRINGTON 1985, "Pseudo-Philo," in *OTP* 2: 297-377. • D. J. HARRINGTON AND J. CAZEAUX 1976, *Pseudo-Philon: Les antiquités bibliques, 1: Introduction et texte critiques; traduction*, Paris: Cerf. • H. JACOBSON 1996, *A Commentary on Pseudo-Philo's* Liber Antiquitatum Biblicarum *with Latin Text and English Translation*, 2 vols., Leiden: Brill. • M. R. JAMES 1917, *The Biblical Antiquities of Philo*. • F. J. MURPHY 1991, *Pseudo-Philo: Rewriting the Bible*, New York: Oxford University Press. • G. W. NICKELSBURG 2005, *Jewish Literature between the Bible and the Mishnah*, rev. ed. Minneapolis: Fortress, 265-70. • C. PERROT AND P.-M. BOGAERT 1976, *Pseudo-Philon: Les antiquités bibliques, 2: Commentaire et index*, Paris: Cerf. FREDERICK J. MURPHY

Bickerman, Elias

Elias Bickerman (1897-1981) was born in Kishinev but grew up in St. Petersburg, where he studied with M. Rostovtzeff. After the victory of the Communists, he and his family left Russia, arriving in Berlin in 1922, where his teachers were E. Norden and U. Wilcken. He completed his doctorate in 1926 and his Habilitation in 1930, and he taught as a Privat-Dozent at the Institut für Altertumskunde. After the Nazis came to power, he moved to Paris in 1933 and then to the United States in 1942, both times with the help of grants from the Rockefeller Foundation. After ten difficult years in the USA, he was appointed Professor of Ancient History at Columbia University in 1952, where he remained until retirement in 1967. He died in Israel on August 31, 1981, and was buried in Jerusalem.

Bickerman saw himself primarily as a historian of the Greco-Roman world, and his numerous publications of the highest quality on classical antiquity justify that self-perception. Nevertheless, Bickerman devoted a significant part of his scholarly output to the Jews of antiquity. In the opinion of Arnaldo Momigliano (1908-1987), Bickerman was the most outstanding scholar of their generation, of classical antiquity in general, and of the Jews in the ancient world in particular.

In the earliest phase of his career as a historian of the Jews, Bickerman turned to documents concerning the Jews in Greek and Latin, which he studied in the context of the ancient world as a whole. His articles proving the authenticity and spelling out the significance of documents granting privileges to the Jews, such as "The Seleucid Charter for Jerusalem," are models of argument based on careful comparison with bureaucratic practice and formulas, as known from inscriptions and papyri. His revolutionary thesis on the origins of the persecutions of Antiochus IV, attributing the initiative to extreme Hellenizing Jews, as presented in *Der Gott der Makkabäer* (1937), was based on rejecting previous theories as inconsistent with ancient imperial policies, and with what is known of events in surrounding areas of ancient Judea at the time. According to Bickerman, Antiochus's actions made sense only when understood as having been inspired by the extreme Hellenizing Jewish leadership of Jerusalem. Bickerman's conclusions on this point were received with some skepticism, and several alternatives were proposed by other scholars.

After coming to the USA, perhaps as a consequence of his close friendship with key faculty and financial support from the Jewish Theological Seminary of America, Bickerman turned to writing about ancient Jewish sources preserved in Hebrew and Aramaic, languages he hardly knew. In articles such as "The Chain of the Pharisaic Tradition," "The Maxim of Antigonus of Socho," and "The Civic Prayer for Jerusalem," and in his book *Four Strange Books of the Bible* (1967), Bickerman took advantage of his familiarity with the world of antiquity to attempt a better explanation of aspects of the Jewish experience in the Greco-Roman world. In the last years of his life, Bickerman gathered his *opera minora* on Jewish and Christian topics; this material is now being reissued, with articles originally in French and German translated into English.

Bickerman's *magnum opus* as a historian of the Jews, *The Jews in the Greek Age* (1988), was published posthumously. This book surveyed the history of the Jews from the arrival of Alexander in the East until the Seleucid conquest. Originally prepared as a massive multivolume work with copious footnotes, and completed in 1963, it was rewritten in the months before Bickerman's death in reduced format, with text only and the notes dropped. Nevertheless, this book is a fully engaged piece of scholarship. One of the criticisms of Bickerman's thesis of the origins of the persecutions of Antiochus IV was that Hellenism in Jerusalem was not nearly so far advanced as needed to support Bickerman's conclusion. In response, Bickerman now traced the history of the interaction of Jews and Greeks, conceding that the significant Hellenization of the Jews took place only when that became the policy of the victorious Hasmoneans, but still arguing for enough contact with Greeks and transformation of the Jews until Seleucid rule to allow his hypothesis concerning the role of the ancient extreme Hellenizers to stand. To bolster these conclusions, Bickerman now focused on cultural history, including the literary works produced during that era, such as *Jubilees*, Ben Sira, and the translation of the Torah into Greek. He sought to put his finger on aspects of permanence and innovation in the era before Antiochus IV.

Bickerman's ultimate goal was expressed in the epigraph of the book, found in a draft version of the work preserved in the Bickerman archive at the Jewish Theological Seminary, in which he quoted a bit incorrectly Augustine, *Sermo* 362, 7: *"architectus aedificat per machinas transituras domum manentem"* (*PL* 39:1615 reads *mansuram*). For Bickerman, the divine architect had employed transient materials, the historical experience of the Jews in the ancient world, to create an eternal building — the complex integration of Jewish and Greek culture, with all its profound consequences for the Western world.

Bickerman saw himself as an objective historian, with no contemporary agenda, working hard to make himself a contemporary of the Jews in antiquity. That much of Bickerman's work has endured would seem to validate that self-perception. Yet Bickerman was also a historian committed to creating a usable past for the Jews, in which the extreme Hellenizing reformers were Jews who had gotten the relationship between the larger cultural world and Judaism "wrong," while those who had helped build the everlasting creation erected by the Jews in the Greek age, including the Maccabees and later rabbis, showed the right way to negotiate the interaction of the Jewish and Greek worlds.

BIBLIOGRAPHY

A. I. BAUMGARTEN 2007, "Elias Bickerman on the Hellenizing Reformers: A Case Study of an Unconvincing Case," *JQR* 97: 149-79. • A. I. BAUMGARTEN 2010, *Elias Bickerman as a Historian of the Jews,* Tübingen: Mohr-Siebeck. • E. J. BICKERMAN 1937, *Der Gott der Makkabäer,* Berlin: Schocken. • E. J. BICKERMAN 1967, *Four Strange Books of the Bible,* New York: Schocken. • E. J. BICKERMAN 1988, *The Jews in the Greek Age,* Cambridge: Harvard University Press. • E. J. BICKERMAN 2007, *Studies in Jewish and Christian History: A New Edition in English Including the God of the Maccabees,* ed. A. Tropper, Leiden: Brill.

ALBERT I. BAUMGARTEN

Birth, Miraculous

A miraculous birth is one in which a divine being plays a part, either by actually siring a child or by overcoming some obstacle that prevents a normal birth; alternately, supernatural events may accompany an otherwise ordinary birth.

Hebrew Bible

In the Hebrew Bible, miraculous birth stories follow a pattern in which YHWH opens barren women's wombs, enabling them to bear to their husbands sons: Isaac, Jacob, Joseph, Samuel, and Samson. Typically annunciations reveal the birth, name, and/or future role of the child. God intervenes in their births because these figures have roles in the divine plan. The story of the women who bore giants to the sons of God in Genesis 6, an episode connected to the evil that prompted the flood, is the exception to this pattern.

Early Jewish Literature

Retellings and Expansions of Biblical Birth Stories

Second Temple Jewish texts retell the biblical birth stories. They reinforce the biblical purposes and also highlight various concerns of the authors. For example, the changes that the book of *Jubilees* makes emphasize the author's interests in calendrical and priestly matters; the text turns Isaac's weaning-day feast into the first observance of the Feast of Booths and makes Isaac the ancestor of a kingdom of priests. Pseudo-Philo's *Biblical Antiquities* shows special interest in women, providing a name for Samson's mother and focusing on the maternal roles of her and Hannah. Philo *(De Abrahamo)* and Josephus *(Jewish Antiquities)* note the biblical figures' virtue, and sometimes link the virtue of the offspring with their extraordinary physical beauty.

These texts expand the biblical accounts, filling in gaps or elaborating with new scenes. The expansions generally evidence an idealizing tendency in their portrayals of biblical figures. *Jubilees* and Josephus change or omit Abraham laughing at God's announcement in Genesis 17 that Sarah will bear Isaac, and Philo similarly exonerates Sarah's laughter in Genesis 18. *Jubilees* downplays Jacob's negative feelings toward Leah. *Jubilees* and Philo mitigate the animosity of Sarah, Rachel, and Hannah toward their rivals (Hagar, Leah, and Peninnah), and Pseudo-Philo makes Hannah appear more sympathetic by making Peninnah even crueler than in the biblical text. However, Josephus, who tends to devalue women, emphasizes the rivalry between Rachel and Leah; he omits Peninnah's taunting altogether and presents Hannah as irrationally desperate for children. Josephus' Manoah is jealous of the handsome angel that brings the news of Samson's impending conception to his wife, and Pseudo-Philo has Manoah and wife argue daily over which of them is the infertile one.

The Watchers

1 Enoch 6–11 retells at length the only biblical account of divine siring. The Watchers, as *1 Enoch* calls them, are presented as fallen angels who first lower themselves to mate with women and then teach human beings various evils, such as magic, weaponry, and the arts of seduction. *1 Enoch* also depicts the offspring of these divine-human marriages as evil: they are giants who devour all the food on earth, then resort to cannibalizing the humans who are unable to keep them fed.

In addition to retelling the biblical miraculous birth stories, Second Temple literature assigns miraculous elements to the otherwise ordinary births of other figures, such as Moses. Philo *(De Vita Mosis)* and Josephus *(Jewish Antiquities)* describe at length the extraordinary beauty and precocious abilities of Moses, as does the later rabbinic *Midrash Exodus.* Josephus and Pseudo-Philo add annunciations about Moses' future role to their accounts of his birth.

Noah, Cain, and Melchizedek

Second Temple texts sensationalize to an even greater extent the births of Noah, Cain, and Melchizedek. *1 Enoch* 106–107 describes newborn Noah as snow white and rose red, with hair like white wool, emanating light from his eyes and praising God from the midwife's hands. Lamech takes one look and seeks assurance (the annunciation element) from his grandfather Enoch, who at that time lives with the angels, that the child is his and not the son of a divine being. The fragmentary Aramaic *Genesis Apocryphon* found at Qumran also relates Noah's birth; it lacks the description of infant Noah but expands upon Lamech's suspicion that a Watcher impregnated his wife. The *Life of Adam and Eve* says that newborn Cain ran and fetched a reed for Eve immediately after birth, and refers to him as *lucidus,* shining. Since the text earlier says Satan took on angelic brightness to deceive Eve, and later rabbinic texts claim that Satan had sex with her, this is perhaps suggestive of Satan being Cain's father. In *2 Enoch* 71–72, Melchizedek's mother is postmenopausal, barren, and not having sex with her husband when she becomes pregnant. When her suspicious husband wrongly accuses her, she protests her innocence and ignorance and falls down dead. Melchizedek emerges from her corpse; he is the size of a three-year-old, is wearing priestly garments, and immediately praises God. An annunciation later reveals his future priestly role.

Hellenistic Influences

The stranger aspects of these stories may be due to the influence of Hellenism, since anomalies commonly occur in significant Greek figures' birth narratives. While Noah's wool-like hair is reminiscent of the Ancient of Days in Daniel 7, white skin and rosy cheeks are common descriptors of beautiful women in Greek literature, which also associates great beauty with divine siring. Light imagery or a shining face often indicates association with divinity in both Jewish and Greek literature, as in Exodus 24, *Joseph and Aseneth* 6, and *Iliad* 18. Divinely sired mythical Greek heroes, like Heracles, exhibit uncommon abilities at an early age. Miracles accompany the births of superior historical Greeks about whom there are rumors of divine siring, such as Alexander the Great (Plutarch, *Lives*). Yet even when the Second Temple texts include elements that, in Greek stories, would indicate divine siring, the Jewish stories support the negative assessment in biblical literature of divine-human sexual mixing by denying it (Noah) or presenting it as evil (the Watchers). Rather, with the exception of Cain, the oddities indicate the same thing that YHWH's intervention in human births did in the Hebrew Bible: these are individuals who are to play positive roles in the divine plan.

New Testament

The New Testament infancy narratives adopt the basic miraculous birth story pattern found in the Hebrew Bible: impediment to conception, prebirth prophetic annunciation, divine intervention, and role in God's plan.

John the Baptist

The biblical pattern is obvious in Luke's account of John the Baptist's birth, where John's elderly, barren parents and the angelic annunciation to Zechariah about the birth, name, and future of their son evoke especially the birth stories of Isaac and Samson. Unlike Abraham and Sarah, whose doubt was neither rebuked nor punished, when Zechariah expresses disbelief, Gabriel strikes him deaf and dumb. After the birth, Elizabeth, who was not present for Gabriel's annunciation, and Zechariah, who must be asked his opinion through signs, independently insist on the name John. At this point Zechariah's affliction is removed, and all present marvel at what these miracles indicate about the boy's future.

Jesus

The accounts of Jesus' birth in Luke 1–2 and Matthew 1–2 utilize the biblical pattern. The obstacle to Mary's pregnancy is not barrenness but her virginity, as Luke indicates by Mary's question to Gabriel, and Matthew by stating explicitly that she had not been with Joseph. Both gospels attribute her pregnancy to the Holy Spirit. Later Christian theology expanded the virginal conception into virgin birth, and eventually to claims of Mary's perpetual virginity. The New Testament narratives also associate miraculous events with Jesus' birth: the appearance of a star that leads foreign dignitaries to him (Matt. 2:1-12), and a choir of angels singing of his cosmic significance (Luke 1:8-14).

Greco-Roman Theioi Andres

The presence of such elements may have been mediated through the miracle-containing Hellenistic Jewish birth stories, but it is likely that at least some, if not most, of the authors' intended audiences would have recognized Jesus' birth as indicating the arrival of a *theios anēr*. The "divine men" of Greco-Roman antiquity were individuals who exhibited a divine presence in their extraordinary virtue and/or supernatural conception, were benefactors to humanity, and were sometimes immortalized at the end of their lives.

In Christianity's first hundred years, this category included not only mythical figures like Heracles, Perseus, and Asclepius, but also such historical personages as Alexander, Augustus, and Apollonius of Tyana. Prophecies of their births might herald a challenge to an existing ruler, leading to attempts to thwart the conception or kill the infant; alternately, one or both parents would have prebirth dream-visions indicating the child's future greatness. It is not difficult to understand Joseph's dream-visions and Herod's massacre in Matthew 1–2 in this light. Similarly, Luke 2:11-14 calls Jesus a "savior" (a title found only here in the Synoptics) whose birth brings peace, which can be seen as a challenge to the rule of Augustus, widely known as a savior who brought peace to the Roman Empire. The Gentile Christians of the communities of Matthew and Luke would surely have been reminded of such *theioi andres*. In the second century of Christianity, as Docetism developed and Christianity became more independent from Judaism, expansions of Jesus' birth story elaborated on the cosmic miracles, becoming less similar to the Hebrew Bible-type miraculous births and more about the birth of a divine child.

Bibliography

O. Betz 1958, "Geistliche Schönheit," in *Die Leibhaftigkeit des Wortes*, ed. O. Michel and U. Mann, Hamburg: Furche, 71-86. • R. E. Brown 1993, *The Birth of the Messiah*, rev. ed., New York: Doubleday. • G. W. E. Nickelsburg 1998, "Patriarchs Who Worry about Their Wives: A Haggadic Tendency in the Genesis Apocryphon," in *Biblical Perspectives: Early Use and Interpretation of the Bible in Light of the Dead Sea Scrolls*, ed. M. E. Stone and E. G. Chazon, Leiden: Brill, 137-58. • C. Talbert 1975, "The Concept of Immortals in Mediterranean Antiquity," *JBL* 94: 419-36. • J. VanderKam 1992, "The

Birth of Noah," in *Intertestamental Essays in Honor of Józef Tadeusz Milik,* ed. Z. J. Kapera, Krakow: Enigma Press, 213-31.
BEVERLY A. BOW

Blasphemy

In the Hebrew Bible, there is no specific term that means "to blapheme" (Bock 1998: 30). Leviticus 24:10-23 became a classic text for the later understanding of "blasphemy." In the context of a fight, a man "expressly mentioned *(nqb)* the Name and he cursed *(qll)* and they brought him to Moses" (Milgrom 2001: 2107-8). The context suggests that the man cursed the other man in the name of Yahweh by calling upon Yahweh to bring some evil upon him. The judgment is that the man should be stoned. The principle is given in v. 16, "the one who expressly mentions the name of Yahweh shall be put to death."

The verb *blasphēmein* is used in the LXX but not as a technical term. A text that later became normative for "blasphemy" is Exod. 22:27 LXX (MT 22:28). It reads *theous ou kakologēseis kai archontas tou laou sou ou kakōs ereis* ("You shall not speak ill of gods, and you shall not revile rulers of your people"). The translator apparently took *'ĕlōhîm* (God) as a plural and made the "ruler" plural also for consistency of style. Philo probably alludes to this passage in his remark that Moses forbade proselytes to revile *(blasphēmein)* the gods whom others acknowledge lest they utter profane words against the God of Israel (*Spec. Leg.* 1.53).

Philo often uses the verb in a nontechnical sense. He apparently did not have a special verb that he used exclusively for offenses against God. He did, however, use the word group *blasphēmein* in a special way when discussing such offenses. In *Legat.* 45.367, he uses it for language that compromises the affirmation that only the God of Israel is divine. In *Somn.* 2.130-32, he uses it for speech that claims greater authority and power for a human being than he has a right to claim.

Like Philo, Josephus also used the word group *blasphēmein* for ordinary abusive speech among human beings. He also used the verb in a quasi-technical way, seeming to define "blasphemy" as pronouncing the divine name. This is apparent from his paraphrase of one of the classic biblical texts. In the LXX, Lev. 24:16 reads, *onomazōn de to onoma kyriou thanatō thanatousthō* ("but if he utters the name of the Lord [in his curse], let him die"). In *Ant.* 4.202, Josephus cites it as follows, "Let him that blasphemes God *(blasphēmēsas theon)* be stoned, then hung for a day, and buried ignominiously and in obscurity."

Pharisees and Sadducees apparently agreed that the blasphemer should be put to death but may have disagreed on the definition of blasphemy, the Sadducees defining it more broadly (like Philo), and the Pharisees more narrowly (like Josephus) (Bauckham 1999: 223). According to *m. Sanh.* 7:5, "The blasphemer is not culpable unless he pronounces the Name itself" (Yarbro Collins 2004: 381, 400). It may be that the rabbis of the Mishnah are the successors of the Pharisees in this regard.

The Gospels also use the word group *blasphēmein* in a variety of ways. For example, in Mark 7:22 and 15:29 the verb is used for ordinary abusive speech directed against human beings (Yarbro Collins 2004: 396). It is used in a quasi-technical religious sense in Mark 2:7 and 14:64 (Yarbro Collins 2004: 381, 398).

BIBLIOGRAPHY
R. BAUCKHAM 1999, "For What Offense Was James Put to Death?" in *James the Just and Christian Origins,* ed. B. Chilton and C. A. Evans, Leiden: Brill, 199-232. • M. BERNSTEIN 1983, "Ki Qelalat Elohim Taluy (Deut. 21:23): A Study in Early Jewish Exegesis," *JQR* 74.1: 21-45. • D. L. BOCK 1998, *Blasphemy and Exaltation in Judaism and the Final Examination of Jesus: A Philological-Historical Study of the Key Jewish Themes Impacting Mark 14:61-64,* Tübingen: Mohr-Siebeck. • J. MILGROM 2001, *Leviticus 23–27,* New York: Doubleday. • S. M. PAUL 1985, "A Case Study of 'Neglected' Blasphemy," *JNES* 42: 291-94. • A. YARBRO COLLINS 2004, "The Charge of Blasphemy in Mark 14.64," *JSNT* 26: 379-401.
ADELA YARBRO COLLINS

Boethusians

The Boethusians *(baytôsîn/baytûsîn)* were an early Jewish group who evidently emerged in the Herodian period and who appear only in rabbinic literature, where they are closely related to, and often interchangeable with, the Sadducees. They feature in halakic controversies with the Pharisees and early rabbis. The name occurs only once in the Mishnah but several times in the Tosefta; it is spelled in different ways, and its origin is debated.

Halakic Disagreements with Pharisees and Early Rabbis

The Boethusians opposed harvesting the Omer grain offering on the day after the first day of the Passover festival, since it might fall on the Sabbath. They interpreted "the morrow of the Sabbath" as Sunday, thus preventing the violation of the Sabbath by harvesting the Omer (*m. Menaḥ.* 10:3; *t. Menaḥ.* 10:23). The Boethusians opposed the practice of striking the willow branches on Hoshana Rabba, when it falls on the Sabbath. They even put rocks on the willow branches in the Temple in order to prevent striking them on the Sabbath (*t. Sukk.* 3:1; *b. Sukk.* 43b). It is possible that they did acknowledge this practice, but in contrast to the Pharisees, they emphasized the priority of the observance of the Sabbath. The Boethusians required physical punishment for the individual who injured his fellow's body, literally interpreting the scriptural command of an "an eye for an eye, a tooth for a tooth." The Pharisees, on the other hand, deduced that this verse alludes to monetary compensation equal to the physical injury (Scholion to *Megillat Taʿanit,* Oxford manuscript, 10th of Tammuz). One Boethusian also argued that one should not write on the leather made from the skin of a nonkosher animal (*b. Šabb.* 108b).

In several other instances, the view that the rabbis

attributed to the Boethusians is ascribed to the Sadducees elsewhere in the rabbinic corpus. The Boethusians disagreed with the Pharisees or rabbis regarding the date of Pentecost (*t. Roš Haš.* 1:15; *b. Menaḥ.* 65b). They rejected the pharisaic ruling of *ʿerub hazerot* (literally "sharing of courtyards," a procedure of transforming the courtyard or alley into common property which allows its use on the Sabbath), and refrained from moving vessels from the house to the courtyard or vice versa (*b. ʿErub.* 68b). The Boethusians held that on the Day of Atonement the high priest should burn incense in the *hekhal* before he enters the *debir* (the Holy of Holies). The Pharisees, on the other hand, insisted that the high priest should first enter the *debir* and then burn incense there (*t. Yom.* 1:8; *y. Yom.* 1:5, 39a). The Boethusians also rejected lay cultic rituals such as the pharisaic practice of pouring water on the altar in the *śimḥat bêt ha-šôʾēbâ* ceremony (literally "the joyous [procession] to the house of drawing water") on Sukkot. Rabbinic sources even mention a case where a Boethusian priest poured water on his feet instead of on the altar and was pelted by the laity with citrons (*t. Sukk.* 3:16; a somewhat similar incident is attributed to Alexander Jannaeus in *Ant.* 13.372). They may have objected to it as a nonscriptural ritual, and perhaps also because in the course of the ritual lay people entered the priestly court when they encircled the altar.

While the Boethusians argued that the daily sacrifices should be financed by individuals (perhaps the serving priests), the Pharisees insisted that the entire Jewish population should sponsor them and determined the half-shekel payment in which every Jew had an equal share in financing the sacrificial cult (Scholion to *Megillat Taʿanit,* beginning of Oxford manuscript). The Pharisees argued that the cereal offering (probably the one accompanying the *shelamim* sacrifice/peace offering) should be offered on the altar. The Boethusians responded that this cereal offering should be given to the priests, who eat it as holy food, just as they eat other cereal offerings (Scholion to *Megillat Taʿanit,* Oxford manuscript, 27th of Marheshvan).

There are several conceptual differences between the Boethusians and the Pharisees or early rabbis. The Boethusians were more committed to the literal sense of Scripture, rejecting nonscriptural categories, definitions, and values which were followed or invented by the Pharisees. In terms of religious and social tendencies, the Boethusians presented a strictness regarding prohibitions, taboos, and penalties and stressed the centrality of the priesthood or the high priest. In a sense, they seemed to hold a rather different concept of holiness which was more sensitive to desecration than the rabbinic concept.

Attempts at Identification with Other Jewish Groups

Sadducees

Many scholars have tried to identify the Boethusians with other sects or parties mentioned in Josephus' writings and the New Testament. The traditional view (e.g., Le Moyne and Stern) identified them with the Sadducees, since in many cases in rabbinic literature the Boethusians are interchangeable with the Sadducees. Herr maintained that although the Boethusians were quite similar to the Sadducees, they were nonetheless an independent party, smaller than the Sadducees.

Essenes

Recently, Sussman revived the view already held by Azariah de Rossi in the sixteenth century and later adopted by Grintz and Lieberman, according to which the Boethusians should be identified with the Essenes (and allegedly identical with the Qumran sect). This view is based on the assumption that the name of the *baytôsîn,* which in some manuscripts of the Tosefta reads *bêt sîn,* is a corruption of *bet issiyîm,* "house of Essenes."

Identifying the Boethusians with the Essenes, however, involves three difficulties. First, the Boethusians are described in rabbinic literature as high priests who head the Temple service (*t. Yoma* 1:8; *t. Sukk.* 3:16) and struggled with the Pharisees or early rabbis trying to impose their own system on the people as a whole. In various ceremonies, such as the water libation and the harvesting of the Omer, the Pharisees tried to publicly demonstrate that the law should follow their rule and "to deny the view of the Boethusians." In the case of the striking of the willow branches on the Sabbath, the Boethusians even attempted to impose their system in the Temple (*t. Sukk.* 3:1). The Essenes, on the other hand, were a dissenting sect with no leadership position, their attitude to the Temple was somewhat hostile (*Ant.* 18.19), and they certainly did not direct the ritual or serve as high priests. Second, according to *ʾAbot de Rabbi Nathan* (version A, chap. 5; version B, chap. 10), the school named for Boethus used silver and gold vessels and denied the doctrine of the world to come. The Essenes, in contrast, lived simple, modest lives and believed in the immortality of the soul (*J.W.* 2.124-51, 154-58; *Ant.* 18.18). Third, the philological identification of Bet (Es)sin with the Essenes was refuted by Schremer. Nowhere in rabbinic literature are groups or sects referred to as Bet [= house] + proper noun with the latter in the plural, but only in the singular (e.g., Bet Hillel, Bet Shammai), so that the correct reading would seem to be Baytôsîm = Boethusians.

Herodians

Several scholars also maintained that the Herodians of the New Testaments (Mark 3:6; 8:15; 12:13; Matt. 22:16) should be identified with the Boethusians (e.g., Hoehner 1972). Since in the gospels the Herodians are interchangeable with the Sadducees or high priests, this is quite possible, and also supports the close relationship between the Boethusians and the Sadducees.

High Priests of the House of Boethus

In fact, the Boethusians should be identified with the high priests of the house of Boethus, nominated by Herod, his successors, and Roman governors. These high priests not only served Roman political interests but also defended Jewish religious rights. Together with the houses of Hanan, Kathros, and Phiabi, which should probably be identified as Sadducean, the high priests of the house of Boethus were part of the Sadducean priestly aristocracy. Since the house of Boethus was the most dominant among these high-priestly families, it may have given its name to a whole party which was part of the Sadducean movement. Hence for the rabbis, the Boethusians could have simply been synonymous with the Sadducees. The halakic differences between the Boethusians and the Sadducees may have been minor, and it is possible that the rabbis did not differentiate between them at all.

Bibliography

Y. M. Grintz 1953, "The Members of the Yaḥad, Essenes, Beit (Es)sin," *Sinai* 32: 11-43 (in Hebrew). • M. D. Herr 1981, "Who Were the Boethusians?" in *Proceedings of the Seventh World Congress of Jewish Studies: Studies in Talmud, Halacha and Midrash*, Jerusalem: World Union of Jewish Studies, 1: 1-20 (in Hebrew). • H. W. Hoehner 1972, *Herod Antipas*, Cambridge: Cambridge University Press, 335-42. • S. Lieberman 1972, *Tosefta ki-Feshutah*, Jerusalem: Jewish Theological Seminary, 4: 870; 5: 1358 (in Hebrew). • J. Le Moyne 1972, *Les Sadducéens*, Paris: Gabalda. • E. Regev 1988, "The Sectarian Controversies about the Cereal Offerings," *DSD* 5.1: 33-56. • E. Regev 2005a, *The Sadducees and Their Halakhah: Religion and Society in the Second Temple Period*, Jerusalem: Yad Izhak Ben-Zvi (in Hebrew). • E. Regev 2005b, "Were the Priests All the Same? Qumranic Halakhah in Comparison with Sadducean Halakhah," *DSD* 12.2: 158-88. • E. Regev 2006, "The Sadducees, the Pharisees and the Sacred: Meaning and Ideology in the Halakhic Controversies between the Sadducees and the Pharisees, *Review of Rabbinic Judaism* 9: 126-40. • A. Schremer 1997, "The Name of the Boethusians: A Reconsideration of Suggested Explanations and Another One," *JJS* 48: 289-99.

Eyal Regev

Booths, Festival of → Festivals and Holy Days

Bousset, Wilhelm

Wilhelm Bousset (1865-1920) made notable contributions to the study of early Judaism and Christianity in the form of influential monographs on the Antichrist (1895, Eng. trans. 1896), apocalypticism (1903a), Second Temple Judaism (1892 and 1903b), Gnosticism (1907), and Christology (1913, Eng. trans. 1970), in addition to numerous articles and reviews of well over 100 books. He was one of the most influential scholars of the *Religionsgeschichtliche*, or "history of religions" school, a group of German academics who advocated the integration of the study of extracanonical texts and "Oriental" religions into biblical studies. After studying under Adolf von Harnack at Leipzig, Bousset moved on to Göttingen and eventually became an associate professor there in 1896.

Bousset's impact on the study of early Judaism has come to be regarded as less than salutary. His literary corpus is the *locus classicus* for the concept of *Spätjudentum*, or "late Judaism," the notion that Judaism in the time of Jesus had lost all the liveliness of the prophetic age and had been reduced to crass legalism and empty ritual, which was the antithesis of the authentic religiosity represented by Jesus and the early Christians. The title of Bousset's 1892 work on Judaism encapsulates this viewpoint: *Jesu Predigt in ihrem Gegensatz zum Judentum* ("Jesus' Preaching in Contrast to Judaism"). In his more well-known book on Judaism, *Die Religion des Judentums im neutestamentlichen Zeitalter* ("The Religion of Judaism in the New Testament Era"), Bousset was more willing to see late Judaism as the soil necessary to produce the "creative miracle" of the Christian gospel (1903b). In this work, Bousset set out to describe Judaism from the Maccabean era until the time of the Jewish revolt under Hadrian (roughly 160 B.C.E. to 135 C.E.). He culled his description chiefly from the Pseudepigrapha, and within that corpus he relied largely on apocalyptic literature. The resulting picture was of a religion with a distant, unapproachable deity and a belief system that was tainted by Iranian influences (such as dualism) and limited by "national" instead of "universal" concerns. The "person of Jesus" and the gospel brought about a "denationalization" of Judaism, and subsequent Judaism need not have existed at all.

These claims provoked a strong response from German Jewish scholars. The most pointed reply came from the rabbi Felix Perles (1903). Perles critiqued Bousset for allowing his work to be guided by the Gospels' polemical statements against the Jews. He also charged Bousset with mishandling Hebrew sources and neglecting rabbinic materials. Perles and other critics argued that halakic and haggadic writings were necessary in any fair depiction of ancient Judaism. Bousset addressed his critics in a rebuttal arguing that rabbinic material was outside the time period that interested him (1903c). On the whole, however, Bousset's actual engagement with his detractors' arguments was minimal in comparison to his repetitive assertions and polemics (see Moore 1921). In many ways this discussion of early Judaism was part of a larger debate about the continuing relevance of Christianity and modern Judaism among contemporary German intellectuals, which accounts for the ferocity of the debate (see Wiese 2005).

The second edition of *Die Religion des Judentums* appeared in 1906, and while it rearranged some material and had a few additions, the bulk of the content and the overall tone were the same as the first edition. A decade later, more substantive changes in Bousset's view of Judaism became evident. While he still insisted on the objective superiority of Christianity to Judaism, he was critical of his own earlier work and began to stress instead the continuities between early Judaism and early Christianity (Bousset 1915).

Although Bousset's works on Judaism were never translated into English, his opinions about Jews and Judaism were disseminated to an English readership through the hasty translations of his popular handbooks for Christians on such topics as the "essence" of religion (1903d, Eng. trans. 1907) and Protestant belief

(1908, Eng. trans. 1909). In these works, Bousset placed Judaism into his larger developmental framework of "religion" as a cultural phenomenon. Protestant Christianity was the pinnacle of human religious achievement, and Judaism, along with other religions, appeared as a foil. Christianity was universal; Judaism was national. Christianity represented the best in ethics and morality, while the Judaism of the Pharisees was preoccupied with "trifles" and "ensnared in outward observances."

Bousset died of a heart attack in 1920, but the influence of his early ideas continued to be felt throughout the twentieth century. The fourth edition of *Die Religion des Judentums* appeared in 1966. His depiction of Judaism was one of the main targets of E. P. Sanders's polemic in *Paul and Palestinian Judaism* (1977), but in spite of Sanders's work, some Christian scholars still cling to various aspects of Bousset's Judaism.

BIBLIOGRAPHY

W. BAIRD 2002, *History of New Testament Research,* Minneapolis: Fortress, 2: 243-47. • W. BOUSSET 1892, *Jesu Predigt in ihrem Gegensatz zum Judentum: Ein religionsgeschichtlicher Vergleich,* Göttingen: Vandenhoeck & Ruprecht. • W. BOUSSET 1895, *Der Antichrist in der Überlieferung des Judentums, des Neuen Testaments und der alten Kirche,* Göttingen: Vandenhoeck & Ruprecht; Eng. trans. 1896 by A. H. Keane as *The Antichrist Legend,* London: Hutchinson. • W. BOUSSET 1903A, *Die jüdische Apokalyptik, ihre Religionsgeschichtliche Herkunft und ihre Bedeutung für das Neue Testament,* Berlin: Reuther & Reichard. • W. BOUSSET 1903B, *Die Religion des Judentums in neutestamentlichen Zeitalter,* Berlin: Reuther und Reichard. • W. BOUSSET 1903C, *Volksfrömmigkeit und Schriftgelehrtentum: Antwort auf Herrn Perles' Kritik meiner "Religion des Judentums im N.T. Zeitalter,"* Berlin: Reuther & Reichard. • W. BOUSSET 1903D, *Das Wesen der Religion,* Halle: Gebauer-Schwetschke; Eng. trans. 1907 by F. B. Low as *What Is Religion?* London: Unwin. • W. BOUSSET 1907, *Hauptprobleme der Gnosis,* Göttingen: Vandenhoeck & Ruprecht. • W. BOUSSET 1908, *Unser Gottesglaube,* Tübingen: Mohr-Siebeck; Eng. trans. 1909 by F. B. Low as *The Faith of a Modern Protestant,* New York: Scribner's. • W. BOUSSET 1913, *Kyrios Christos,* Göttingen: Vandenhoeck & Ruprecht; Eng. trans. 1970 by J. E. Steely, Nashville: Abingdon. • W. BOUSSET 1915, "Literatur und Religion des Spätjudentums und des rabbinischen Judentums," *Theologische Rundschau* 18: 23-37, 41-58, 115-31, 269-92. • G. F. MOORE 1921, "Christian Writers on Judaism," *HTR* 14: 197-254. • F. PERLES 1903, *Bousset's* Religion des Judentums im neutestamentlichen Zeitalter: *Kritisch untersucht,* Berlin: Peiser. • E. P. SANDERS 1977, *Paul and Palestinian Judaism,* Philadelphia: Fortress. • A. F. VERHEULE 1973, *Wilhelm Bousset: Leben und Werk,* Amsterdam: Van Bottenburg. • C. WIESE 2005, *Challenging Colonial Discourse: Jewish Studies and Protestant Theology in Wilhelmine Germany,* trans. B. Harshav and C. Wiese, Leiden: Brill.

BRENT NONGBRI

Burial Practices

Jewish burial customs in the Second Temple period are known from finds at the two main excavated cemeteries of Jerusalem and Jericho, which were located outside the city limits.

Forms and Features of Early Jewish Burial

The burial places consist of rock-hewn loculi tombs, which are the most common form of tomb in the Second Temple period. The tombs contain a square burial chamber, often with a pit dug into its floor to enable a person to stand upright. One to three arched loculi are hewn into three walls, the entrance wall excepted, and the loculi are sealed with blocking stones or by mud brick and small stones (fig. 1). In some Jerusalem tombs another type of burial is found, the arcosolia, which is a bench-like aperture with an arched ceiling hewn into the length of the wall, which probably is a later type of burial. A few tombs also have a courtyard, which apparently served for community meetings probably as the "mourning place" in the Goliath tomb in Jericho. Sometimes a *miqveh* (ritual bath) is attached to the courtyard.

The Jericho cemetery evidence proves that the loculi tombs were designed first to accommodate pri-

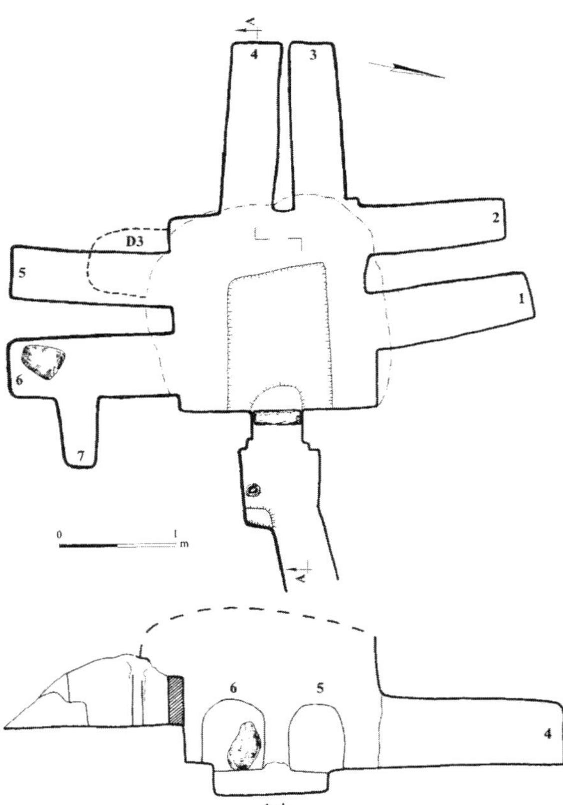

Figure 1. Plan of rock-hewn loculi tombs of the Second Temple Period

mary burial in wooden coffins. The same tomb plan continued to be used for ossuary burials. The orientation of the burials in the coffins has no special significance, as the bodies were placed in all directions; so were the bones in ossuaries. Grave goods were found in both wooden coffins and ossuary tombs. Personal possessions were mostly found with women and children in their wooden coffins, and objects of daily life were regularly placed in the tomb itself.

The Jerusalem and Jericho cemeteries reflect differences between social classes, evident in the monumental tombs in the Kidron Valley in Jerusalem and burial of families in loculi tombs of various sizes and quality. In Jericho the Goliath family tomb with its wall painting and two rooms indicates that it was the tomb of a prominent family.

Another form of Jewish burial was found at the Qumran and ʿEin el-Ghuweir cemeteries. Almost all tombs are oriented in a north-south axis, as seen on the surface at the Qumran cemetery. This was usually also the orientation of the body in the grave. The grave is hewn in the ground, with a pile of stones placed on top, as found at both Qumran and ʿEin el-Ghuweir (fig. 2). A similar form of burial was discovered in a group of tombs at Beth Zafafa in Jerusalem (Zissu 1998). The sole form of these burials is an individual interment in the shaft or rarely in a wooden coffin. It is clear that the individual burials at Qumran and ʿEin el-Ghuweir are not family tombs, since they inter only a single body, have no inscription, and no commemoration whatsoever. These cemeteries possibly served a Jewish Second Temple sect, the Essenes.

Primary and Secondary Burial

The excavations in the extended Jerusalem necropolis and the Jericho cemetery reveal that in the first century C.E. a marked change occurred: secondary burial of the bones, placed either in individual limestone ossuaries or in communal burials in loculi, replaced primary burial in wooden coffins or in loculi (Hachlili 2005: 4-10; Hachlili and Killebrew 1999: 166-75). In Jerusalem, primary burials in wooden coffins did not survive, owing to poor preservation of organic material. Burial in wooden coffins was also practiced in ʿEin Gedi (Hadas 1994) and in the cemetery of the Qumran sect. In secondary burials, the ossuaries

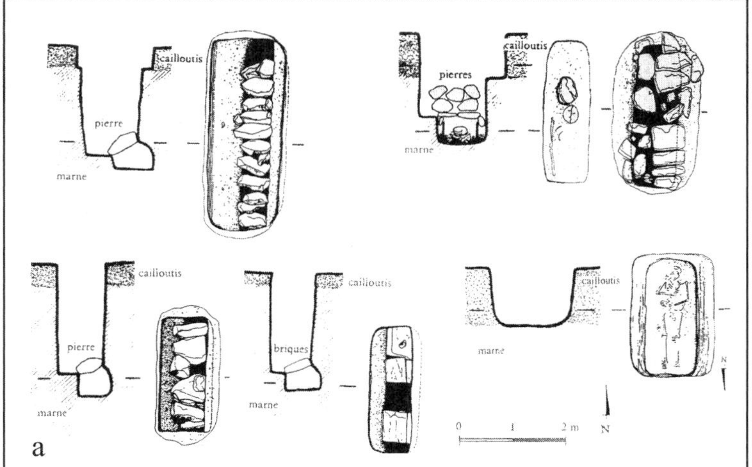

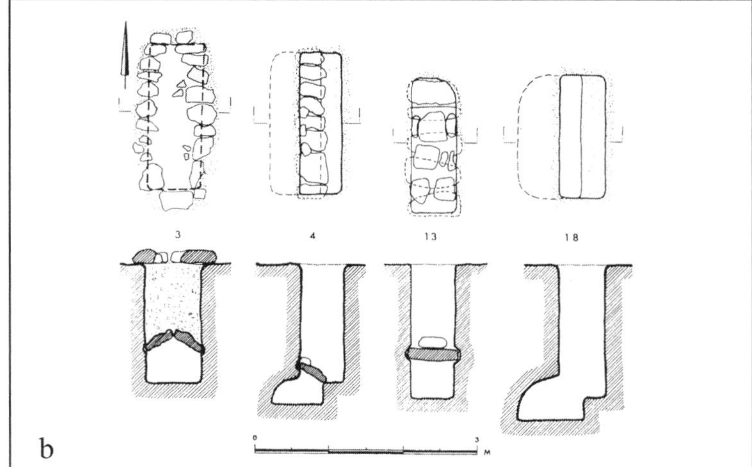

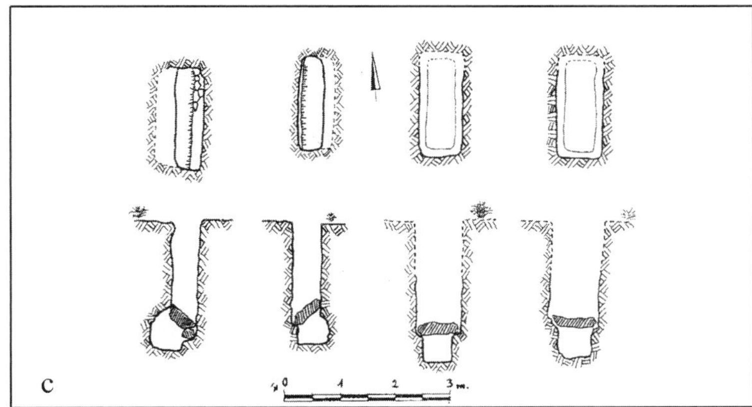

Figure 2. Plan of tombs at Qumran, ʿEin el-Ghuweir, and Jerusalem

Figure 3. Four decorated ossuaries used for secondary burial of skeletal remains

were sometimes decorated and inscriptions were incised or written on the front, back, or sides, mentioning the deceased's name and family relations (fig. 3).

No theory has so far been able to account for this drastic change in burial customs; unfortunately, all sources dealing with the secondary burial of bones in ossuaries only describe the custom without mentioning the reasons for its sudden appearance (Hachlili 2005: 447-79). It is most extraordinary that in the Second Temple period burial customs, which are usually among the most conservative practices in a society, underwent rapid changes. Still, these customs were short-lived and show little affinity with either the earlier Israelite customs or the later Jewish rituals of late antiquity, which contain only traces of these Second Temple period customs.

Individuals and Families

Burial practices of the late Second Temple period reflect the importance that Jews attached to the individual and the family. This regard is reflected in the plan of the loculi tomb, which provided for individual burial of coffins or ossuaries in separate loculi, while at the same time allowing a family to be buried together in the same tomb. It seems that members of the entire population and not just the upper classes were given individual burials. This practice is probably related to the increasing importance bestowed on the individual in contemporary Hellenistic society, and to the Jewish belief in individual resurrection of the body. This belief is reflected in sources dating as early as the second century B.C.E. (Rahmani 1994: 53-61).

Funerary Art

The ornamentation of tombs in the Second Temple period was a rich and varied art. It consisted of decorated tomb façades, sarcophagi, and ossuaries, as well as wall paintings and graffiti (Hachlili 2005: 127-162). Monumental tombs in Jerusalem exhibit a composite style, an amalgamation of stylistic features influenced by Hellenistic-Roman architecture and by Oriental elements (fig. 4).

Ossuary Ornamentation

Most the ossuaries found in Jerusalem are undecorated, whereas in Jericho most are decorated. The assembly of motifs decorating ossuaries is quite varied and consists of architectural, geometric, and plant motifs. These motifs are similar to those appearing in other arts of the Second Temple period. Stone ossuary workshops and artists probably had a repertoire, presumably in the form of a pattern book, to which reference could be repeatedly made. The ornamentation is carved into the soft stone of the ossuaries with the aid of tools such as a ruler and compass. Few ossuaries are painted. The commonest type of ossuary ornamentation is a scheme consisting of a frame of zigzag lines, incised or chip-carved, within two straight lines. This

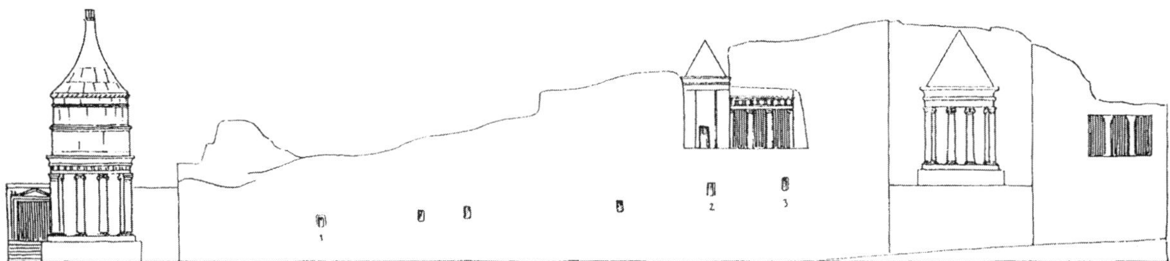

Figure 4. Drawing of monumental tombs in the Kidron Valley, Jerusalem

frame is usually divided into two and sometimes more metopes (spaces) that are filled generally with six-petaled rosettes (fig. 3). Rahmani's contention (1994: 25-28) that the repertoire of motifs decorating the ossuaries is inspired by the tomb's surroundings seems to be the most acceptable. It was part of a general ensemble of decorative patterns used in Second Temple period art, several of which are found solely in funerary art.

Sarcophagi Decoration

The ornamentation of the few sarcophagi found in tombs in Jerusalem differs from that of ossuaries in both design and execution, although the motifs are similar, consisting of plants, rosettes, vine branches, bunches of grapes, and acanthus leaves. The sarcophagi are usually depicted in high relief, are skillfully executed, and their design is richer and more elaborate. The richer and beautifully reliefed sarcophagi were probably much more expensive so that only wealthy families would have been able to afford them.

Wall Paintings

A wall painting was discovered in the monumental Goliath family tomb in the Jericho necropolis. The painting is enclosed by a red frame on three walls of the tomb. The vine motif is the subject of paintings on both north and south walls. Several birds perch on the vines (fig. 5). The Jericho tomb painting was most likely executed at the same time as the tomb itself was hewn, evidently for the benefit of the tomb's visitors and to indicate the family's prominent position.

Drawings and Graffiti

Several drawings and graffiti in charcoal of three ships and a recumbent stag appear on the northern and southern walls of the porch of Jason's tomb in Jerusalem. On the eastern wall of the porch graffiti of five menorahs are scratched. A charcoal drawing of a *nefesh,* a column pyramid, was discovered on a tomb wall in the Jericho cemetery. Funerary art motifs are typical of local Jewish art of the Second Temple period.

Figure 5. Drawing of the "Goliath family" tomb at Jericho

BIBLIOGRAPHY

N. AVIGAD 1950-51, "The Rock-carved Facades of the Jerusalem Necropolis," *IEJ* 1: 96-109. • N. AVIGAD 1954, *Ancient Monuments in the Kidron Valley,* Jerusalem: Bialik Institute (in Hebrew). • P. BAR-ADON 1977, "Another Settlement of the Judean Desert Sect at ʿAin el-Ghuweir on the Dead Sea," *BASOR* 227: 1-25. • R. DE VAUX 1973, *Archaeology and the Dead Sea Scrolls,* London: British Academy, Oxford University Press. • H. ESHEL ET AL. 2002, "New Data on the Cemetery East of Khirbet of Qumran," *DSD* 9: 135-65. • R. HACHLILI 2000, "The Qumran Cemetery: A Reconsideration," in *The Dead Sea Scrolls: Fifty Years after Their Discovery,* ed. L. H. Schiffman et al., Jerusalem: Israel Exploration Society and Shrine of the Book Israel Museum, 661-72. • R. HACHLILI 2005, *Jewish Funerary Customs, Practices and Rites in the Second Temple Period,* Leiden: Brill. • R. HACHLILI AND A. KILLEBREW 1983, "Jewish Funerary Customs during the Second Temple Period in

Light of the Excavations at the Jericho Necropolis," *PEQ* 115: 109-39. • R. HACHLILI AND A. KILLEBREW 1999, *Jericho: The Jewish Cemetery of the Second Temple Period,* Jerusalem: Israel Antiquities Authority. • G. HADAS 1994, "Nine Tombs of the Second Temple Period at ʿEn Gedi," *ʿAtiqot* 24 (in Hebrew; Eng. abstract, pp. 1*-8*). • J.-B. HUMBERT AND A. CHAMBON, 1994, *Fouilles de Khirbet Qumran et de Aïn Feshkha,* Fribourg: Academic Press. • A. KLONER AND B. ZISSU 2003, *The Necropolis of Jerusalem in the Second Temple Period,* Jerusalem: Yad Ben-Zvi and Israel Exploration Society (in Hebrew). • L. Y. RAHMANI 1994, *Catalogue of Jewish Ossuaries in the Collections of the State of Israel,* Jerusalem: Israel Antiquity Authority and Israel Academy of Sciences and Humanities. • B. ZISSU 1998, "'Qumran Type' Graves in Jerusalem: Archaeological Evidence of an Essene Community?" *DSD* 5: 158-71.

See also: Ossuaries

RACHEL HACHLILI

C

Caesarea Maritima

Caesarea Maritima (Gr. *Paralios Kaisareia*) was a major port city on the Mediterranean coast of Israel, about halfway between the modern cities of Tel Aviv and Haifa. It was built on the remains of a Sidonian colony called Strato's Tower, dating from the Persian period. The town was of minor importance during its 300-year history, and when Herod rebuilt the site, he renamed it in honor of the Roman emperor Augustus. Because Herod clearly intended the city to play a major role in his kingdom, he made enormous investments of time and money in building this cosmopolitan center. Built over a twelve-year period (22-10/9 B.C.E.), Caesarea's completion was celebrated with lavish dedicatory festivities (*Ant.* 16.136-41). The city enabled Herod to achieve many of his goals: to make his kingdom an integral part of the Roman world; to demonstrate his loyalty to the emperor and goodwill toward his pagan subjects; to enhance the commercial vitality, economic life, and security of his realm; and to enlarge his fame as a builder and benefactor.

Caesarea bore two distinct features from its inception. First, it was clearly intended to be a Roman and pagan city. A temple to Roma and Augustus was built on an elevated podium facing the harbor (*Ant.* 15.339), and some decades later, as the well-known Pilate inscription attests, a temple to the emperor Tiberius was also erected in the city. In addition, Herod constructed a theater and amphitheater-hippodrome there, and these facilities played an important role in Caesarea's quadrennial games organized by the king, which included musical, athletic, gladiatorial, and horse-racing events (*Ant.* 16.137-38).

A second feature of the city was the commercial-

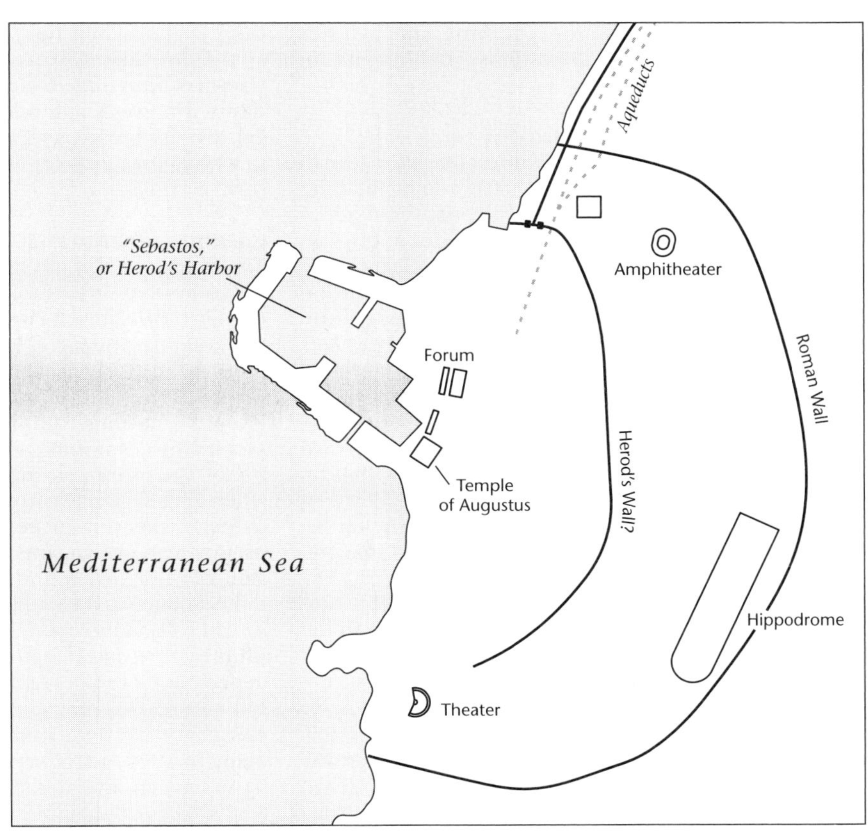

Caesarea Maritima

The amphitheater-hippodrome built by Herod the Great at Caesarea Maritima *(www.HolyLandPhotos.org)*

economic importance of its elaborate and impressive harbor facilities. These included a broad promenade, storerooms, lodgings for sailors and travelers, as well as several colossal statues atop columns and a tower named Drusion (probably a lighthouse) flanking its entrance (*J.W.* 1.411-14).

The Jewish Community in Caesarea

Although unattested, there was undoubtedly a Jewish community in the city from the outset, and by the mid-first century C.E. it appears to have constituted about half the city's population. By the late thirties of the first century, a Christian community with a significant number of *sebomenoi* was established there. The centurion Cornelius brought the apostle Peter to Caesarea to initiate those assembled into the church. According to Acts 10, this event was a major turning point in the development of the nascent church.

Caesarea achieved unequivocal prominence in 6 C.E., when it became the capital of the newly formed province of Judea, and thereafter it competed with Jerusalem in importance for sixty years (6-66 C.E.). With the destruction of Jerusalem, Caesarea became the undisputed metropolis of the province and retained this preeminence for centuries to come.

A major Jewish-pagan confrontation, possibly simmering beneath the surface for decades, erupted in the city during the late fifties (*J.W.* 2.266-70; *Ant.* 20.173-78) over the issue of *isopoliteia,* whereby the Jews demanded to be accorded equal status in the city's *polis.* According to Josephus, the Jews initiated the struggle, claiming that the city was theirs since its founder was Jewish. The Greeks, for their part, argued that Herod had intended Caesarea to be a pagan city, citing as proof the prominence accorded its statues, temples, and Hellenistic ambience.

The struggle at first involved only verbal arguments and mutual recriminations, but eventually led to open violence in the city's streets. Yet, although victory belonged to the Jews, the Roman procurator soon committed his troops to the fray. In the ensuing battle many Jews were killed while others were captured and their homes plundered. The dispute was then referred to Rome where, after several years, the emperor Nero ruled against the Jews. Hostilities continued, including an attempted desecration of the local synagogue; and when the Greeks gained the upper hand, the Jews fled the city. All this occurred on the eve of the outbreak of the revolt against Rome in 66 C.E. (*J.W.* 2.266-70, 284-92; *Ant.* 20.173-78, 182-84, 362).

During the revolt, the city served as the military headquarters of the Roman army. It is from here that campaigns were launched, and the city provided winter quarters for two of the three legions then fighting. At the successful conclusion of hostilities, Titus incarcerated many captives in Caesarean prisons. He celebrated his brother's birthday with great splendor there, holding elaborate games with wild beasts as well as gladiatorial contests in which, Josephus reports, some 2,500 prisoners died (*J.W.* 7.37-38).

Caesarea after the First Revolt

The diminution, if not disappearance, of the local Jewish community after 66 C.E. rendered Caesarea an even more typically pagan city. Vespasian raised Caesarea to the rank of a Roman colony, the first city to be so honored by the Flavian emperor. Its official name was *Colonia Prima Flavia Augusta Caesarensis,* and it was given exemptions from the *tributum capitis* and *tributum soli* by Vespasian and Titus, respectively. As the status of Caesarea was furthered enhanced by the title "metropolis," the territory under its control now came to include southern Palestine and the southern regions of Provincia Arabia, and undoubtedly led to the expansion of the *officium* and garrison in the city. Caesarea thereby solidified its status as the most prominent city in the province, which included Samaria, Judea, Idumea, the coastal region, and parts of the Galilee. Evidence points to the fact that the city enjoyed a limited, but nevertheless active, cultural and religious life. Numerous renovations and additions to the theater were made in subsequent centuries — the *odeum* was built by Vespasian, the aqueduct was enlarged by Hadrian, who also built a temple *(Hadrianeum),* a bath was constructed by Antoninus Pius, a hippodrome was erected in the eastern part of the city, and a *Mithraeum* was located near the port — all of which enhanced the physical comfort as well as cultural, religious, and social life of the local population.

Caesarea in the Third and Fourth Centuries

By the third century, Caesarea had become a truly cosmopolitan city. The Jewish, Christian, and Samaritan communities lived alongside the pagan one, while none of them appears to have enjoyed a numerical majority. Pagan life in Caesarea continued to flourish despite the emergence of other large communities. The municipal mint issued an impressive series of city coins representing traditional pagan deities (e.g., Zeus, Apollo, Dionysios, Athena), as well as Serapis and the local goddess Tyche. Alongside the religious life, athletic contests and games continued to be held in the city, including the traditional quadrennial games inaugurated by Herod. The local Pythian Games, established by Septimius Severus in Caesarea, were reputedly among the most famous in the eastern Mediterranean in the third century.

A school of rhetorical, legal, and literary studies was also located in the city. Although most of our information in this regard derives from the fourth century, it may well have existed as early as the third, and it continued to function until the sixth century.

The Jewish community of Caesarea also included a rabbinic component. A number of leading sages resided there, Rabbi Hoshaya in the first part of the third century, Rabbi Yosi bar Ḥanina a generation later, and Rabbi Abbahu around the turn of the fourth century. Caesarea's academy ranked alongside those of Tiberias and Sepphoris but was tailored to meet the needs of the local community. In a well-known account from the Babylonian Talmud (*b. ʿAbodah Zarah* 4a), Rabbi Abbahu explained that he was more adept at conducting polemics with local Christian interlocutors than his Babylonian counterpart since, he believed, this was required of Caesarean sages.

The Jewish community absorbed a significant degree of Greek culture. This is attested by the existence of at least one local synagogue wherein the Jews gathering for worship were not able to recite even the most basic of prayers (the *Shemaʿ*) in Hebrew, saying it instead in Greek (*y. Soṭah* 7, 21b). Similarly, some Caesarean rabbis, especially Rabbi Abbahu, demonstrated an extensive knowledge of Greek. As part of the cosmopolitan scene, such knowledge was a desideratum, given the Jewish community's frequent contacts not only with Christians but with *minim* (heretics) as well.

Many Samaritans settled in and around Caesarea in the third and fourth centuries, and some apparently served in the municipal government. There appears to have been a great deal of hostility between these Samaritans and the Caesarean sages, as noted in a number of rabbinic sources. Indeed, it was Rabbi Abbahu who, having accused certain Samaritan officials of idolatry, finally prevailed in issuing a ban on their food. Later on, another sage issued a ruling indicating that Samaritans were to be regarded no differently than Gentiles. In the wake of a series of unsuccessful rebellions in the late fifth and sixth centuries, the local Samaritan community was seriously affected, resulting in their dwindling numbers and fading resilience toward the end of Late Antiquity.

Eusebius first takes note of the Caesarean church in connection with the Quartodeciman controversy toward the end of the second century C.E. (*Hist. Eccl.* 5.23). The Caesarean bishop Theophilus is mentioned as having initiated and organized a local synod to deal with this issue together with Narcissus of Jerusalem. The relationship between these two bishoprics during the second and third centuries is not clear. Each had a claim to leadership, Caesarea as the larger and more influential community located in the provincial capital, Jerusalem as the mother church of Christianity that retained an esteemed place in ecclesiastical circles. Nevertheless, Caesarea was acknowledged as the most important see in Palestine during these centuries, in large part owing to a number of outstanding leaders who resided in that community.

Caesarea's prominence in the mid-third century was primarily due to the presence there of Origen, one of the foremost church fathers of his day. Consulted by emperors, honored by bishops, and sought out by pagan and Christian alike, he was unsurpassed in his contribution to Christian thought and in his service to the local community. Having visited Caesarea a number of times, Origen moved to the city ca. 253 C.E. During the two decades of his residence there, Christian and pagan students flocked to the city from all over the Roman East to study with him (Eusebius, *Hist. Eccl.* 6.19).

Caesarea maintained its reputation as a center of Christian learning even after Origen's death. Pamphilus succeeded Origen as head of the school, his major achievement being the organization of a large library containing the works of Origen and other writers (*Hist. Eccl.* 6.32).

Eusebius became the city's bishop around 315 and held this position until his death ca. 339. His political activism played a major role at the Council of Nicea, where he defended Caesarea's preeminence in face of the Jerusalem church and hosted a council regarding the Arian controversy. In addition to the regular duties of a bishop, Eusebius's literary pursuits consumed much of his time. His works spanned a wide range of genres — history, apologetics, geography, exegesis, panegyrics, homiletics, and theology.

The history of Caesarea after the fourth century is shrouded in mystery because we have virtually no literary sources from this era. The pagan community gradually disappeared, and the Samaritans, as noted, were severely reduced in numbers and status as a result of their insurrections. Rabbinic sources reflecting some degree of historical reality (e.g., the Jerusalem Talmud) cease to exist toward the end of the fourth century, and nothing further is known of the local Jewish community other than scattered archaeological finds, including remains of one synagogue. The Christian community indeed flourished, with the most poignant indication being the erection of a church on the mound facing the harbor, which replaced the pagan temple built by Herod. By the fifth century, Jerusalem had surpassed

Caesarea in the church hierarchy and now became recognized as one of the five Patriarchates, together with Rome, Constantinople, Alexandria, and Antioch.

Whatever the fate of its various communities, Caesarea reached its apogee as a political center at the beginning of the fourth century, when it functioned as the capital of an expansive province. In the course of the fourth and fifth centuries, however, Palestine was subdivided on several occasions, and while Caesarea continued to function as a capital, the area under its control, *Palaestina Prima,* shrank considerably.

Caesarea's Significance

In reviewing the history of Caesarea during these centuries, perhaps the most salient feature of the city was its cosmopolitan character. From the very beginning, the city was meant to form a bridge between Judea and the rest of the Roman world — geographically, politically, culturally, and religiously. The earliest and clearest expression of this role is to be found in the city's impressive port facilities built by Herod. As a commercial emporium, Caesarea connected Judea with the Mediterranean world more than any other city in his kingdom. In subsequent centuries, the local Jewish and Christian communities likewise exhibited this cosmopolitan dimension, maintaining distinctive cultural ties with the larger Roman world. Rabbi Abbahu on the Jewish side, and Origen and Eusebius on the Christian, are stellar examples of this proclivity. Thus, Herod's dream of building a city that would bridge the two worlds, the Judean and Roman, continued to find expression in later communities, albeit in ways far different from what the king had originally envisioned.

BIBLIOGRAPHY

T. L. DONALDSON, ED. 2000, *Religious Rivalries and the Struggle for Success in Caesarea Maritima,* Waterloo, Ont.: Wilfrid Laurier University Press. • G. DOWNEY 1975, "Caesarea and the Christian Church," in *The Joint Expedition to Caesarea Maritima,* vol. 1, *Studies in the History of Caesarea Maritima,* ed. C. T. Fritsch, Missoula, Mont.: Scholars Press. • A. FROVA 1966, *Scavi di Caesarea Maritima,* Rome: Bretschneider. • K. G. HOLUM 1982, "Caesarea and the Samaritans," in *City, Town and Countryside in the Early Byzantine Era,* ed. R. L. Hohlfelder, New York: Columbia University Press, 65-73. • K. G. HOLUM ET AL., EDS. 1988, *King Herod's Dream: Caesarea on the Sea,* New York: Norton and Company. • K. HOLUM ET AL. 1993, "Caesarea," in *New Encyclopedia of Archaeological Excavations in the Holy Land,* vol. 1, ed. E. Stern, Jerusalem: Israel Exploration Society, 270-91. • L. M. HOPFE 1990, "Caesarea Palaestinae as a Religious Center," in *ANRW* II.18.4, 2380-2411. • N. DE LANGE 1976, *Origen and the Jews: Studies in Jewish-Christian Relations in Third-Century Palestine,* Cambridge: Cambridge University Press. • L. I. LEVINE 1974, "The Jewish-Greek Conflict in First-Century Caesarea," *JJS* 25: 381-97. • L. I. LEVINE 1975A, *Roman Caesarea: An Archaeological-Topographical Study,* Qedem 2, Jerusalem: Hebrew University. • L. I. LEVINE 1975B, *Caesarea under Roman Rule,* Leiden: Brill. • A. RABAN AND K. G. HOLUM, EDS. 1996, *Caesarea Maritima: A Retrospective after Two Millennia,* Leiden: Brill. • J. RINGEL 1975, *Césarée de Palestine: Étude historique et archéologique,* Paris: Ophrys. • R. L. VANN, ED. 1992, *Caesarea Papers: Straton's Tower, Herod's Harbour, and Roman and Byzantine Caesarea,* Ann Arbor, Mich.: Journal of Roman Archaeology.

LEE I. LEVINE

Cain and Abel

Hebrew Bible

Genesis 4:1-16 tells the story of Cain, the first son of Adam and Eve, including his birth and that of his brother Abel; their respective occupations as a farmer and a shepherd; the offerings they brought from the revenues of their work, and how Abel's sacrifice was noticed, but that of Cain ignored; Cain's angry reaction and the reprimand he received on this account from God; how Cain killed his brother Abel in the field and received divine punishment, mitigated because of Cain's supplication; and how he migrated to the land of Nod. The story is continued with a brief list of Cain's descendants (4:17-22), culminating in the figure of Lamech, who proclaims that Cain is avenged seven times, but Lamech himself seventy-seven times.

The story in the Hebrew Bible is very compact, giving the impression of a string of discrete anecdotes. Moreover, the text may have suffered during its transmission, as a comparison with the Septuagint's text suggests.

Jubilees

In *Jubilees* 4, the material from Genesis 4 is transformed into a unified story. The rejection of Cain's sacrifice is turned into the reason why Cain killed Abel. Furthermore, the author of *Jubilees* has omitted several details, presumably in order to smooth the story out; the most remarkable of these is the omission of the sevenfold revenge and of the figure of Lamech. Finally, and most importantly, he has supplemented the story with various pieces of tradition: the name of Cain and Abel's sister Ewan (*Jub.* 4:1; she also became Cain's wife, *Jub.* 4:9; this is firmly denied by Philo, *On the Posterity of Cain* 34; the provenance of Cain's wife Themech is not mentioned in Ps.-Philo, *Bib. Ant.* 2:2); and the cause of Cain's death: his stone house collapsed upon him, fulfilling the heavenly commandment that a murderer should be killed with the material with which he had slain his victim (*Jub.* 4:31-32; cf. the *Book of the Covenant*).

Philo of Alexandria

The figure of Cain was of considerable interest to Philo of Alexandria, who devoted the second half of his treatise *On the Cherubim* to him, as well as *On the Sacrifices of Cain and Abel, The Worse Attacks the Better,* and the first half of *On the Posterity of Cain.* In his *Questions and Answers on Genesis* 58–79, Philo exposes many of the difficulties of the story, for example, "How did Cain know that his sacrifice was rejected?" (*QG* 63); "Why does the omniscient God ask Cain where his brother is?" (*QG* 68; cf. *Det.* 57); "How can Cain fear to be killed by people, if the only other people in the world are his parents?" (74). As often, Philo handles such difficulties by transposing the figures of the narrative into representatives of certain ideas and values and their interrelationships (Najman 2003).

The name Cain, meaning "possession" (*Cher.* 52), stands for the misapprehension under which the human mind labors when it thinks that it possesses anything, whereas God is the only owner of everything (*Cher.* 57–66; 124; cf. *Sacr.* 2). In contrast, "Abel" represents the mental virtue of giving all credit to God. "Cain" and "Abel," therefore, represent the inimical principles of "self-love" versus "love of God" (*Sacr.* 3; *Det.* 32; *Post.* 21). Both are innate to the human mind, which distinguishes humans from the angels and the irrational beings.

The story of Cain and Abel illustrates this when it says that Cain sacrificed "after a while," and not the firstfruits of his crop (*Sacr.* 52); virtuous deeds, however, tolerate no delay (*Sacr.* 53), and the one who performs them always strives for perfection, to thank and honor God (*Sacr.* 65, 74). When Cain slew Abel, he slew himself, for virtue cannot be killed by self-love, as appears from the fact that afterward Abel cried out, and the dead cannot cry out (*Det.* 47–48). This scene, then, illustrates that a man who murders the incorruptible that is within him, kills himself (*Det.* 49) and accomplishes nothing (*Det.* 70).

Philo admits that he does not understand the literal sense of Gen. 4:15 (about the sevenfold vengeance), but he takes it as a reference to the seven irrational parts of the soul (*Det.* 167). That Genesis fails to report Cain's death means for Philo that foolishness is immortal (*Det.* 178; *Conf.* 122; *Fuga* 60–61, 64).

Josephus

In his rendering of the story of Cain and Abel in *Ant.* 1.52-67, Josephus contrasts the brothers as eager for profit and virtue, respectively (*Ant.* 1.52). When God preferred Abel's offering to that of Cain, because he is honored more by nature's gifts than by artificial products (*Ant.* 1.54), Cain killed his brother out of jealousy and hid his corpse (*Ant.* 1.55; cf. Gr. *Life and Adam and Eve* 40). God cursed him and his progeny to the seventh generation (Josephus' solution for the sevenfold vengeance, *Ant.* 1.58) but saved him from being killed by wild animals (*Ant.* 1.59; cf. the problem as formulated by Philo, *QG* 74, cited above). In his land of exile, Cain, together with his wife (who is not mentioned before, although Josephus had mentioned that Adam and Eve also have daughters; *Ant.* 1.52), developed a life of lust, crime, and exuberance, and thus ended the simple way of life (*Ant.* 1.60-61). He thus inaugurated the life of depravity that eventually led to the flood (*Ant.* 1.66; cf. 72, 76; and Wis. 10:4).

Allusions

In other early Jewish writings, Cain and Abel are mentioned in passing on a few occasions. The cry of Abel's blood is interpreted as his spirit forever taking Cain's posterity to the heavenly court until it is finally wiped from the face of the earth (*1 Enoch* 22:7; cf. Heb. 11:4; 12:24; Hilhorst 2003). Elsewhere, allusion is made to Cain and Abel as the prototypes of sinners and righteous ones (Wis. 10:3; *4 Macc.* 18:11) or to Cain alone as the first fratricide (*Bib. Ant.* 16:2; 59:4). The blood of Abel is mentioned as a powerful image of the innocent victims of violent death (Gr. *Life of Adam and Eve* 1–3; cf. 2 Macc. 8:3; Heb. 12:24; *m. Sanh.* 4:6).

BIBLIOGRAPHY

T. HILHORST 2003, "Abel's Speaking in Hebrews 11.4 and 12.24," in *Eve's Children: The Biblical Stories Retold and Interpreted in Jewish and Christian Traditions,* ed. G. P. Luttikhuizen, Leiden: Brill, 119-27. • J. L. KUGEL 1998, *Traditions of the Bible,* Cambridge, Mass.: Harvard University Press, 146-69. • H. NAJMAN 2003, "Cain and Abel as Character Traits: A Study in the Allegorical Typology of Philo of Alexandria," in *Eve's Children,* ed. G. P. Luttikhuizen, 107-18. • J. T. A. G. M. VAN RUITEN 2000, *Primaeval History Interpreted: The Rewriting of Genesis 1–11 in the Book of Jubilees,* Leiden: Brill, 113-79.

JOHANNES TROMP

Calendars

Hebrew Bible

The fact that the Hebrew Bible is seldom explicit about calendar practices engendered many calendrical conflicts in early Judaism. It is not entirely clear whether the Bible attests to one or more calendrical systems. Several elements of biblical calendars that affected the practice in later times will be discussed here.

Biblical sources use two main sets of month names. While many texts name the months using ordinal numbers, beginning from the Spring New Year, late biblical books use the Babylonian month names, beginning with Tishri in the autumn. The former practice appears mainly in priestly sources and Ezekiel. Both practices continued into later Jewish literature. Ordinal month names are used in the 364-day calendar tradition and occasionally in the Apocrypha (e.g., 1 Macc. 4:52; 9:3), while a great majority of all other texts, especially rabbinic literature, retained the Babylonian names of the months.

From Gen. 1:14 we learn that both moon and sun were used for time reckoning without preference for either of them. Ps. 104:19 was interpreted as evidence for the exclusive use of the moon in calendar reckoning, although its meaning is not entirely clear (cf. Ibn-Ezra). The calendar practice in use throughout the ancient Near East, including the Levant, was lunisolar. Given the lack of more conclusive information, we may assume that this was the prevalent practice in ancient Israel, too. In the religious rhetoric of the Bible, the calendar was not considered a factor that distinguished Israelite identity from that of the Gentiles, so it is hard to posit a unique Israelite calendar in the biblical period.

This situation is a major difficulty for the hypothesis of A. Jaubert, who suggested that priestly texts in the Pentateuch attest to the use of a unique Israelite 364-

day year. Accordingly it has been claimed that the 364-day year was the official temple calendar already in the early Second Temple period (VanderKam 2000: 81-104). Jaubert's view, though attractive, has been widely criticized and is now generally rejected. The dates in the Genesis flood story have also been taken as evidence for the existence of a 364-day year, but the text in Genesis (MT and versions) is not clear enough to support this claim.

The first annual harvest festival is timed in Lev. 23:15 as "the day after the Sabbath" but with no specific date. This problem sparked a ferocious debate in postbiblical times, possibly also within biblical literature. The date of the Festival of Weeks, celebrated seven weeks after the earlier festival, depends on the same debate: whether the weeks had to be full — counted from Sunday to Sabbath — or whether they could be "nominal" weeks regardless of the starting day. It is clear that the division of time into units of seven, as in the counting of weeks in the harvest festivals, is an ancient principle of Israelite time reckoning. This principle was augmented in Second Temple literature by additional seven-based counts: of days, weeks, years, and jubilees.

The Lunisolar Calendar in Early Judaism

General

The first explicit reference for a lunar time reckoning is Sir. 43:7 (cf. 50:8 and versions). This verse elaborates on Ps. 104:19, but in contrast to the latter it seems to relate to contemporary calendar conflicts. A lunisolar calendar is reflected also in the writings of Josephus and Philo, and most extensively in rabbinic sources. Rabbinic literature contains abundant information on calendar regulation, but it is generally later than the Second Temple period. Given the popularity of the lunisolar calendar in the non-Jewish environment, as well as the continuity from Ben Sira to the Mishnah, it is hard to assume that this calendar was introduced in Judah only under Antiochus IV (*pace* VanderKam 2000: 105-27).

Calendars became a debated topic around the time of the Maccabean revolt, in the mid-second century B.C.E. This debate, reflected in contemporary literature like *Jubilees,* is connected with the appearance of the 364-day calendar tradition. Calendar practice became a crucial aspect of defining sectarian identity, and Jewish identity in general. Not only the nature of the year but also other calendrical topics came under debate, such as the dates for the annual festivals and the time of the New Year.

Relation to Non-Jewish Calendars

It is not entirely clear when Jews began to promote a normative Jewish calendar (Stern 2001). Under the Persian Empire, Jews in Egypt and Babylonia followed the imperial lunisolar calendar, not only for civil needs but also for ritual ones. A crucial part in the change must have been played by Egyptian Jewry in Ptolemaic times, which could not follow the Egyptian civil calendar for its ritual needs and had to create its own calendar reckoning instead. Under Seleucid rule, Jews seem to have used the state calendar, which was practically identical with the lunisolar Babylonian system. This possibility gains support from the similarity of rabbinic calendrical methods with Babylonian practices for observing the new moon. The conflict with foreign calendars gained much attention with the inauguration of the Julian calendar, which caused considerable problems in early rabbinic literature. Several rabbis even considered the proper length of the year to be 365 days (*m. ʿArak.* 9:3, *b. ʿArak.* 31:2). However, mishnaic calendrical treatises completely ignore the Julian year. Accordingly, the Judean public and at least some Diaspora communities at the beginning of the second century C.E. relied on the lunisolar count rather than on the civil Julian calendar.

Observation vs. Calculation

From the early fifth century B.C.E. on, a nineteen-year intercalation cycle was used in Mesopotamia to regulate the lunisolar calendar. In contrast, early rabbinic texts take pains to base the calendar regulation on actual sightings of the moon. According to tractate *Roš Haššana* the sanctification of the new moon could not gain efficacy without an actual human report, despite the fact that R. Gamliel was aware of certain astronomical notions (*m. Roš Haš.* 2:6; *t. Roš Haš.* 1:17). Calendrical conditions were thus never predictable, and Diaspora Jews had to act according to the information supplied by the central Palestinian court. Thus, numerous rabbinic statements stress that calendar regulation is a human prerogative rather than a divinely ordained perpetual order (*m. Roš Haš.* 2:9; *Midrash Exodus* 15). Intercalation was similarly enacted ad hoc. In early rabbinic sources, intercalation was determined every year according to the ripeness of cereal crops and fruit (*t. Sanh.* 2:2, 12). Only secondarily was it necessitated by the need to coordinate the beginning of the lunar year with the date of the *tequfah* or equinox.

However, early rabbinic literature attests also to several nonobservational aspects of the calendar. For example, *m. ʿArak.* 2:2 and *t. ʿArak.* 1:7, 11 give numerical rules for the use of full (thirty-day) months; a statement in *b. Roš Haš.* 19:2 may indicate that the month of Elul was never full (but the meaning is not entirely clear); intercalation was avoided in the *Shemitah* (Sabbatical year) even if astronomical reality demanded it (*t. Sanh.* 2:9). Future research must therefore ascertain whether the mishnaic stance against a calculated calendar reflects reality or ideology.

Calendrical Authority

According to the Mishnah, in Second Temple times the Palestinian court assumed a prominent role in calendrical decisions, especially in the Syrian and Babylonian Diaspora. Various media were used to publicize the court's decisions, such as a chain of fire signals lit from Jerusalem to Babylonia and Syria at new moon, and special messengers who were employed for this purpose by the court (*m. Roš Haš.* 1–2). However, the extent to which Diaspora communities obeyed the Palestinian rabbinic court after 70 C.E. and into talmudic times is not quite clear.

The Mishnah accords prominence to the head of the Judean court. Most traditions on this issue are centered on the personalities of R. Gamliel the elder and his Yavnean descendant bearing the same name (e.g., *m. ʿEd.* 7:7; *b. Sanhedrin* 11b). The *locus classicus* for this authority is *m. Roš Haš.* 2:8-9, where R. Gamliel imposes his calendrical decisions on opposing rabbis. S. Talmon (1989: 186-99) pointed to the similarity between this story and the calendrical conflict described in *Pesher Habakkuk* (1QpHab 11:2-8). However, this mishnaic notion should be reconsidered, especially with regard to pre-70 times, since it should be expected that the authority would lie with the Hasmonean ruler or the high priest rather than with the head of a court; such a priestly authority is indeed mentioned in *m. Roš Haš.* 1:7 (cf. *t. Roš Haš.* 2:9).

The 364-day Year

General

The 364-day year is a schematic year, whose essential characteristic is the ideal numerical relations it incorporates. It was this characteristic, rather than its proximity to the solar year, that was dominant in the creation and use of the 364-day year. Thus it should not be designated a solar year. The year is divided into four quarters of ninety-one days. These quarters in turn are divided into months, with thirty days in each of the first two months, and thirty-one days in the last month of every quarter. The year is neatly divided into weeks: fifty-two weeks per year and thirteen per quarter. The number 364 thus incorporates the typological numbers 4, 7, and 13. The 364-day year also easily fits into longer cycles of years — 3, 6, 49, and 294 years — whose structure presents attractive numerical combinations.

The fact that the year is structured on the number seven was crucial for its acceptance in Judah, possibly also for the first introduction of the number 364 into early Jewish literature in the *Astronomical Book* of *1 Enoch* 72–82. The year always begins on the fourth day of the week, so festivals always occur on the same day. Accordingly, no festival ever occurs on the Sabbath. To avoid offering festival sacrifices on the Sabbath was a typical sectarian statute at Qumran (CD 11:17-18) that was easily accomplished under the framework of the 364-day year.

Although the 364-day calendar tradition is reflected in various sources and historical periods, it may be regarded as a stable calendrical tradition (*contra* Glessmer 1999). The only possible exception for this rule is the book of *Jubilees* (see below). Although the 364-day calendar tradition took into account other calendrical systems — notably the lunar count in Qumranic texts — the 364-day year was the exclusive marker for cultic time in the circles that practiced it.

The origin of the 364-day calendar, however, remains obscure. Its earliest use, in the Enochic *Astronomical Book,* reveals close relations to Babylonian astronomical compositions from the seventh century B.C.E. (Ben-Dov 2008A). Later Babylonian methods appear in the lunar tables from Qumran. Given additional indicators of Babylonian influence in the Enochic tradition, it seems that the speculative wisdom of early Jewish apocalypticism borrowed the 364-day year together with many other ideas from the ancient Mesopotamian scientific milieu.

The 364-day year fails to match the length of the actual solar year, which is around 365.25 days. Unless a mechanism of intercalation is applied to it, the 364-day year lags behind the agricultural year after a short period, and the gap grows with time. This weakness created problems for the Qumran community's belief that the seasons are a heavenly sign. Many attempts were therefore made to construct an intercalation mechanism. However, the literature of the Qumran *yaḥad* repeatedly defines the 364-day year as a divinely ordained system reflecting the true order of the world, and it is hard to see how a different length of the year could ever have been maintained. In addition, any added period of time would ruin the intricate *mišmārôt* cycle (priestly term of service in the Temple). Further, Qumran calendrical texts show no signs of intercalation. It is possible that the *mišmārôt* as an ideal year was never intercalated (Beckwith 1996). The existence of a regular method for intercalation would have been unacceptable, because such a method would admit the inadequacy of the 364-day year. However, it cannot be ruled out that the calendar was regulated on an ad hoc basis when the gap with the true solar year became exceedingly great.

History

The earliest explicit evidence for the 364-day calendar tradition in early Jewish literature is the Enochic *Astronomical Book* (*1 Enoch* 72–82), which dates to the third century B.C.E. The *Astronomical Book* gives models for the annual orbit of the sun and the moon in space and time within the framework of a 364-day year. Those models were originally designed for an ideal astronomical 360-day year. The 364-day year represents an improvement, created by adding to it four additional (or "epagomenal") days, in which the sun reaches its cardinal points (*1 Enoch* 75:1-2; 82:4b-8). The *Astronomical Book* uses the 364-day year exclusively as a scientific concept, with no recourse to Sabbaths, festivals, and priests. The 364-day year is a schematic year, designed to account for the orbits of all the heavenly luminaries. The models of the *Astronomical Book* do not exceed the limits of one schematic year (*1 Enoch* 74:10-16 in its present form is a late addition).

The lunar models of the *Astronomical Book* were a cause for debate around the mid-second century B.C.E. Whereas the *Astronomical Book* and 4Q317 give much attention to lunar models, as do later *mišmārôt* texts from Qumran, lunar models are strongly opposed in the book of *Jubilees. Jubilees* 6:35-37 expresses a harsh antilunar tendency, which is exceptional in the 364-day calendar tradition. The antilunar statement in *Jubilees* 6 probably refers not only to the lunisolar calendar, but also to other calendars that contained lunar elements, including the synchronistic tables of the *Astronomical Book.* Since difficulties arise from the lunar models in the *Astronomical Book, Jubilees* rejects any value given to lunar theory in calendrical reckoning. A solution for this conflict is reflected in treatises like 4Q317, where the triennial cycle is fully structured and the lunar models of the *Astronomical Book* are refashioned to overcome previous difficulties. With this rejoinder to the criticism leveled by *Jubilees,* the moon continued to be included in subsequent compositions of the 364-day calendar tradition. Apart from its antilunar tendency, *Jubilees* is unique in that it never mentions the days of the week and the lengths of months, which are important aspects of the 364-day calendar tradition. These and other differences mark *Jubilees* as exceptional in the tradition.

Jubilees makes use of religious-halakic aspects of the 364-day year rather than astronomical aspects. The festival calendar of the *Temple Scroll* uses the 364-day year in a similar way. This composition emphasizes the heptadic (sevenfold) traits of the year when prescribing counts of seven weeks for each of its new harvest festivals. Although it does not explicitly mention the number 364, its similarity to *Jubilees* together with the continuity of the special harvest festivals in later Qumran calendars tie the *Temple Scroll* closely to the 364-day calendar tradition.

Foundational documents of the Qumran community, such as the *Damascus Document,* the *Community Rule,* and several pesharim, make recurrent mention of the calendar as a religious principle, but they do not yield specific calendrical details. A calendrical list is added at the beginning of 4Q394, a copy of MMT. The 364-day calendar tradition reaches its peak with the calendrical corpus from Qumran (see below), after which it is no longer mentioned in Jewish literature. A late occurrence of the 364-day year comes in 11QPs[a] col. 27, which was copied in the first century C.E. but was probably composed earlier. Calendar conflicts reoccur often in later rabbinic literature, and a great number of them are probably related to the sectarian 364-day calendar tradition.

Calendrical Scrolls from Qumran

The calendrical scrolls from Qumran underscore the relation of the 364-day year to Jewish ritual by recording the dates of the festivals, beginnings of months, and Sabbaths for every year. They also add a priestly element to the calendar in the form of *mišmārôt,* the priestly courses serving in the Temple. A six-year cycle was devised in order to divide the terms of office in the Temple between the twenty-four priestly families (6 years × 52 weeks = 24 *mišmārôt* × 13 weeks of service).

A group of *mišmārôt* documents (4Q320, 4Q321, and 4Q321a) continues the line of the *Astronomical Book* and 4Q317 when synchronizing the 364-day year with the lunar cycle. This synchronism serves a scientific purpose: the three lunar phenomena recorded in the scrolls are a basic set of astronomical data used elsewhere in the ancient Near East. These lunar data do not attest to the observance of a lunar calendar at Qumran since they had no relevance for the cult. Nor do they mark the full moon as the beginning of the lunar months, as was commonly claimed in the past (see Ben-Dov, 2008A).

Most calendrical documents cover a time span of either a single 364-day year or a six-year cycle. Certain sectarian authors sought to synchronize the six-year cycle with the *Shemitah* cycle of seven years, which was popular in apocalyptic literature. The two cycles are fully integrated in the list of *'ôtôt* ("signs") in 4Q319, where a superstructure of six jubilees (= 294 years) is built in order to incorporate all the various periods of time that have a place in the 364-day calendar tradition.

Bibliography

R. T. Beckwith 1996, *Calendar and Chronology, Jewish and Christian,* Leiden: Brill. • J. Ben-Dov 2008a, *Head of All Years: Astronomy and Calendars at Qumran in Their Ancient Context,* Leiden: Brill. • J. Ben-Dov 2008b, "Reflections on New Year Feasts in Babylonia and Israel," *Shnaton* 19: 251-269 (in Hebrew). • U. Glessmer 1999, "Calendars in the Qumran Scrolls," in *The Dead Sea Scrolls after Fifty Years,* vol. 2, ed. P. W. Flint and J. C. VanderKam, Leiden: Brill, 213-78. • M. D. Herr 1976, "The Calendar," in *The Jewish People in the First Century,* vol. 2, ed. S. Safrai and M. Stern, Assen: Van Gorcum; Philadelphia: Fortress, 834-64. • S. Stern 2001, *Calendar and Community: A History of the Jewish Calendar, 2nd Century BCE–10th Century CE,* Oxford: Oxford University Press. • S. Talmon 1989, *The World of Qumran from Within,* Jerusalem: Magnes; Leiden: Brill. • J. C. VanderKam 1998, *Calendars in the Dead Sea Scrolls: Measuring Time,* London: Routledge. • J. C. VanderKam 2000, *From Revelation to Canon: Studies in the Hebrew Bible and Second Temple Literature,* Leiden: Brill.

See also: Mishmarot; 'Otot — Jonathan Ben-Dov

Canon, Canonization

The Term "Canon"

The term "canon" is derived from the Greek word *kanōn,* which is itself related to Hebr. *qāneh,* meaning a "reed," which could be used as a measuring stick. In early Christianity, the word was used for "the rule of faith," beginning in the second century C.E. It came to be used for a fixed collection of sacred books only in the fourth century C.E. The term is anachronistic in the context of Second Temple Judaism, but it is commonly used with reference to any fixed corpus of authoritative writings. The problem is that it is often difficult to know just when the various corpora of authoritative writings in ancient Judaism became fixed.

The Traditional View and Its Revision

The traditional Jewish view ascribes the fixing of the canon, and its division into three sections, to Ezra and the "men of the Great Assembly." This view has been discredited for some time. In the late nineteenth century a new consensus emerged. On this view, the Torah was canonized in the time of Ezra, and the Prophets were complete by the time of Ben Sira. (Consequently, the book of Daniel is not included among the Prophets in the Hebrew Bible). The Writings were believed to have been closed at the Council of Jamnia (Yavneh) about 90 C.E. The larger canon of the Christian church was thought to have been the canon of Alexandrian, or more broadly Diaspora, Judaism. All aspects of this consensus have been undermined. There was no distinctive Alexandrian canon. Neither did the deliberations of the sages at Jamnia constitute a council, or issue binding decrees in the manner of later church councils. They rather had the character of an academy or school. Moreover, it is now clear that the Torah had not reached its final form in the time of Ezra.

The Open-Ended Nature of the Canon

The idea of a normative book, by which right religious practice can be judged, appears already in the reform of King Josiah of Judah in the late seventh century B.C.E. Josiah invoked "the book of the law," which had allegedly been found in the Temple, as the warrant for his reforms. This law corresponded to some form of the book of Deuteronomy, but not the whole book as we now know it. After the Babylonian Exile, Ezra is said to have received Persian authorization to impose the law of his God, and to have forced people to divorce their foreign wives on that basis. The books of Ezra and Nehemiah, however, make no mention of the Day of Atonement, although Nehemiah 8 describes the observances of the seventh month, including the Feast of Sukkot. It is apparent, then, that the Law of Moses had not reached its final form in the time of Ezra, even though there was a normative religious law in written form.

The book of Ben Sira is often taken as a landmark in the development of the canon. Ben Sira himself says that all wisdom is "the book of the covenant of the Most High God, the law that Moses commanded us" (Sir. 24:23). His "Praise of the Fathers" in chaps. 44–49 refers to most of the leading figures known to us from the biblical corpus, with some notable exceptions (Ruth, Esther, Daniel, but also Ezra). Nonetheless, he does not regard either the Law of Moses or the other Scriptures as *exclusive* sources of wisdom. The wise man not only devotes himself to the study of the law of the Most High, but also seeks out the wisdom of all the ancients and is concerned with proverbs and parables as well as prophecies (Sir. 38:34–39:1). Of course the later church fathers, who undoubtedly had canonical Scriptures, did not consider them to be the *exclusive* source of wisdom either. Ben Sira's ecumenical pursuit of wisdom does not negate the high status he gives the Torah. But he does not seem to have a closed canon.

His grandson, who translated the book into Greek about 117 B.C.E., wrote in a preface that his grandfather, who "had devoted himself especially to the reading of the Law and Prophets and other books of our ancestors, and had acquired considerable proficiency in them, was himself also led to write something pertaining to instruction and wisdom." He further refers to "the Law and the Prophets and the others that followed them" and to "the Law and the Prophets and the rest of the books." These statements have often been taken as the earliest references to a tripartite canon. It seems clear, however, that the "other books" are open-ended. Ben Sira seems to have entertained the hope that his own book might be numbered among them. Moreover, it is not necessarily clear what is included in the Prophets. Ben Sira knew all the prophets of the Hebrew Bible and refers to the Twelve as such. It is not apparent, however, that he makes any distinction between the prophetic books and Nehemiah. In the New Testament period, David was often regarded as a prophet and the Psalms as prophecy (e.g., Acts 2:30). The Law and the Prophets were established categories of authoritative writings by the time of Ben Sira, but we cannot be sure just how these corpora were defined.

According to 2 Macc. 2:14-15, Nehemiah founded a library and collected the books about the kings and prophets, the writings of David, and letters of kings about votive offerings. In the same way, Judas Maccabaeus also collected all the books that had been lost on account of the war against the Seleucids. It has sometimes been suggested that Judas established the canon of Scripture at this time (second century B.C.E.), but there is no indication that Judas distinguished between canonical and noncanonical books, or that he classified the collected writings in any way.

The Situation Reflected in the Dead Sea Scrolls

The discovery of the Dead Sea Scrolls has complicated rather than simplified our understanding of the development of the canon. There is no doubt that the Torah of Moses was accorded fundamental importance. According to the "Well Midrash" on Num. 21:18 in the *Damascus Document,* "the Well is the Law, and those who dug it were the converts of Israel. . . ." The Staff is "the Interpreter of the Law." When the *Community Rule* instructs the sectarians to prepare in the wilderness the way of the Lord, it specifies that "this is the study of the Law which He commanded by the hand of Moses." In fact, it is now clear that the *raison d'être* of the sect was grounded in its distinctive interpretation of the Law of Moses. Halakah, the exegesis of revealed Law, first becomes a major issue in Jewish life in the late second or early first century B.C.E. The fundamental revelation of the Law was supplemented by "all that has been revealed from age to age" and by what "the Prophets have revealed by his holy spirit" (1QS 8). The authoritative status of the Prophets and Psalms is confirmed by the fact that they are subject to a special form of interpretation in the Pesharim, where the words of the prophets are applied to the experience of the community in the end of days. The pesher mode of interpretation could also be applied to prophetic passages in the Torah (4Q252, *Pesher Genesis*). Daniel is interpreted in pesher-like style in the *Florilegium* and in the *Melchizedek Scroll.* Apart from Psalms and Daniel, none of the books now found in the Writings is interpreted in this way.

The most explicit comment on the authoritative writings of the day is found in the halakic document 4QMMT. This document is addressed to a religious leader of Israel, most probably a high priest, and it sets out the reasons why the community had separated itself from the majority of the people. It appeals to the leader to consider the validity of the sectarian interpretation of Scripture: "We have [written] to you so that you may study (carefully) the book of Moses and the books of the

Prophets and (the writings of) David [and the events of] ages past" (composite text C 10-11; DJD edition). This text is admittedly reconstructed, but the appeal to Moses and the Prophets seems clear. The point is that blessings or curses will follow, depending on how the Law is observed. This text has often been taken as evidence for a tripartite canon. The reference to "ages past" (literally, "generation and generation") has even been taken as a reference to Chronicles, the last book of the Hebrew Bible. But the text cannot support this interpretation. The "events of ages past," if this reconstruction is correct, is only a general reference to the history of Israel and Judah. The text is highly important, nonetheless, since it shows that that the sect shared a basic corpus of scriptures with other Jews, including the leaders in Jerusalem. That corpus consisted of the Torah, Prophets, and Psalms. While David is mentioned separately, he was often regarded as a prophet, and the book of Psalms as prophecy.

Most witnesses through the New Testament period refer to a bipartite collection of authoritative writings, the Law and the Prophets (Matt. 5:17; 7:12; 11:13; 16:16; 22:40; Luke 16:29-31; Acts 13:15; 24:14; 28:23; Rom. 3:21). Luke 24:44 is exceptional in the New Testament in referring to "the Law of Moses, the Prophets, and the Psalms." A similar view of Scripture is implied in Philo's account of the Therapeutae (*De Vita Contemplativa* 25). In each house they had a consecrated room into which they took nothing but "laws and oracles delivered through the mouth of the prophets, and psalms and anything else which fosters and perfects knowledge and piety." This passage, too, has often been taken as evidence of a tripartite canon, but the last category is clearly open-ended.

The Scrolls complicate the story of the emerging canon in another way. Books circulated in different textual forms. Examples include a text of Exodus that corresponds to the Samaritan recension except that it lacks the distinctively Samaritan mention of Mt. Gerizim at Exod. 20:17, and a text of Jeremiah that agrees with the short recension found in the LXX. The most controversial example is provided by the *Psalms Scroll* from Qumran Cave 11, which contains most of the last third of the Psalter in an unconventional arrangement. It also includes a poem identical with 2 Sam. 23:1-7 ("The Last Words of David") and several apocryphal psalms. There is also a prose catalogue of David's compositions, placed neither at the beginning nor at the end. There has been debate as to whether this scroll should be regarded as a "biblical" manuscript. Some scholars have argued that it was a collection for liturgical use. It is difficult to see, however, why a catalogue of David's works should be included in a liturgical collection. Whatever use was made of this scroll, no distinction was made at Qumran between canonical and apocryphal compositions. There is no reason to regard this scroll as less authoritative than others that conform to the later Hebrew Bible. The authority of a book was not restricted to a particular textual form.

Moreover, several parabiblical books were closely related to what we know as the biblical text. In some cases, it is difficult to decide whether a composition is a variant form of a "biblical" book or a different but related work. The text known as 4QReworked Pentateuch (4Q158, 364-367) has been described as a running text of the entire Pentateuch interlaced with exegetical comments. It resembles the Samaritan Pentateuch at many points. There is no formal indication that would distinguish this text from a "biblical" manuscript. Other texts, such as the *Temple Scroll* and *Jubilees,* are less closely related to our biblical text, but there is reason to believe that they too were regarded as authoritative formulations of the Law of Moses, at least by the sectarians who preserved the Scrolls. A number of other texts that were later regarded as apocryphal appear to have been authoritative at least in sectarian circles. These include most of *1 Enoch,* which like *Jubilees* was later canonical in the Ethiopian Church, the *Psalms of Joshua,* which is cited in the *Testimonia* (4Q175) and an apocryphon of Levi, which is cited in the *Damascus Document.* In all then, the Scrolls suggest that the Law, the Prophets, and the Psalms were regarded as normative, but at least some of these books existed in more than one textual form.

Evidence of the First Century C.E.

The delimitation of a fixed number of biblical books is first attested at the end of the first century C.E. In his tract *Against Apion,* written in the last decade of the century, Josephus makes the claim that the records of the Jewish people are more reliable than those of the Greeks:

> We do not possess myriads of inconsistent books, conflicting with each other. Our books, those which are justly accredited, are but two and twenty, and contain the record of all time. Of these, five are the books of Moses, comprising the laws and the traditional history from the birth of man down to the death of the lawgiver. . . . From the death of Moses until Artaxerxes, who succeeded Xerxes as king of Persia, the prophets subsequent to Moses wrote the history of the events of their own times in thirteen books. The remaining four books contain hymns to God and precepts for the conduct of human life. (*Ag. Ap.* 1.37-41)

Josephus evidently classified what we would call the historical books with the Prophets.

In the roughly contemporary book of *4 Ezra,* we are told that the Law had been burned when Jerusalem was destroyed, but it was revealed anew to Ezra. He was told to "make public the twenty-four books that you wrote first and let the worthy and the unworthy read them; but keep the seventy that were written last, in order to give them to the wise among your people" (*4 Ezra* 14:45-47).

It is generally assumed that *4 Ezra*'s twenty-four books are the same as Josephus's twenty-two, but counted differently. Judges-Ruth and Jeremiah-Lamentations were sometimes counted each as one book, for a total of twenty-two, while twenty-four is the standard number in talmudic sources. Josephus paraphrases Esther and Daniel in his *Antiquities.* He also tells the story of Darius's guards, which is found only in the apocryphal book of 1 Esdras, but this may be an issue of text rather than canon.

Josephus and *4 Ezra* were contemporary with the sages at Jamnia, but the delimitation of the books was not the result of a conciliar decree. It may well be that it reflected the tradition of the Pharisees, already before 70 C.E. After 70, we still read of rabbinic disputes about Song of Songs and Qoheleth (*m. Yad.* 3:5). But other books, such as *1 Enoch* and *Jubilees,* which had been regarded as authoritative by some Jews, were henceforth excluded. By restricting the number of "properly accredited books," the sages provided a common frame of reference for their debates and reduced the risk of sectarian division.

BIBLIOGRAPHY

J. J. COLLINS 1997, "Before the Canon: Scriptures in Second Temple Judaism," in idem, *Seers, Sibyls and Sages in Hellenistic-Roman Judaism,* Leiden: Brill, 3-21. • A. LANGE 2004, "From Literature to Scripture: The Unity and Plurality of the Hebrew Scriptures in Light of the Qumran Library," in *One Scripture or Many? Canon from Biblical, Theological and Philosophical Perspectives,* ed. C. Helmer and C. Landmesser, Oxford: Oxford University Press, 51-107. • L. M. MCDONALD AND J. A. SANDERS, EDS. 2002, *The Canon Debate,* Peabody, Mass. Hendrickson. • E. ULRICH 2003, "The Non-attestation of a Tripartite Canon in 4QMMT," *CBQ* 65: 202-14. • J. C. VANDERKAM 2000, "Revealed Literature in the Second Temple Period," in idem, *From Revelation to Canon: Studies in the Hebrew Bible and Second Temple Literature,* Leiden: Brill, 1-30.

JOHN J. COLLINS

Catacombs

Catacombs are underground cemeteries consisting of an extensive network of subterranean galleries and burial chambers. They have been preserved in many parts of the Roman world but occur most commonly on the outskirts of Rome, where some sixty of them have been preserved, and in other parts of Italy, most notably in Naples and on Sicily. In Rome inhumation in catacombs first got underway in the course of the second century C.E., but it became the predominant mode of burial only in the fourth century C.E. when significant portions of the population began to convert to Christianity. From the fifth century C.E. onward burial in Roman catacombs declined steadily, to be replaced with burials above ground, usually in or around churches.

In the Near East, by contrast, catacombs never made much of an appearance. There the family tomb had always been paramount, and this continued to be the case well throughout antiquity and beyond. In addition to poorly preserved evidence of an early Christian catacomb in Homs in Syria, and isolated early Christian evidence from Alexandria in Egypt, the single most important collection of catacombs is a series of Jewish subterranean burial complexes that have been discovered in Beth She'arim, near Haifa. The catacombs of Beth She'arim were used for burial from the second through the mid-fourth century C.E. After that, burial may have continued, but if it did, this happened on a much smaller scale than had been the case previously.

Evidence for Early Jewish Catacombs

Differing from the smaller family tombs *(hypogea)* that preceded them, the catacombs of Rome have traditionally been regarded as a typically Christian invention; they were seen as cemeteries financed by the church specifically for the burial of the poor. While recent research has questioned large-scale church involvement, radiocarbon dating of evidence from the Jewish catacombs of Rome now also raises the possibility that burial in catacombs may have been a Jewish rather than a Christian invention. No fewer than four Jewish catacombs have been discovered in Rome, three of which have been preserved to this day. Even though these Jewish catacombs were used continuously until the early fifth century C.E., burial in one of them — the so-called Villa Torlonia catacomb — may have begun as early as the late first century C.E.

Rome's pagan population does not seem to have practiced burial in catacombs on a large scale. Pagan materials occur here and there in the early Christian catacombs of Rome, but their presence either resulted from the incorporation of previously existing pagan *hypogea,* or can be shown to have resulted from the fact that conversion to Christianity was a drawn-out process. In the Jewish catacombs of Rome, only Jews were laid to rest.

The Catacombs of Rome

Research in the catacombs of Rome has traditionally focused on the inscriptions and on the artwork from the catacombs, with special emphasis on their theological meaning and ideological import. As a result, little is known about the demography of those buried there. This is especially lamentable because these subterranean cemeteries did not merely serve the rich and famous. Rather, they functioned as communal cemeteries, containing a representative cross-section of the population at large (with an estimated total of up to one million graves).

The catacombs of Rome house the largest coherent body of late-antique wall painting that has survived from antiquity. Without it, it would be impossible to reconstruct the genesis of early Christian art in its relation to Jewish and pagan contemporary artistic practices. Current studies of these pictorial materials have largely abandoned the earlier hypothesis of a Jewish origin of early Christian art. Rather, early Christian and Jewish art are seen as on a par, that is, as originating from and operating within a matrix that was generally late antique. While artistic remains from the Jewish catacombs of Rome show a clear predilection for symbolic themes, including Judaism's symbol par excellence, the menorah or seven-branched candelabrum, early Christian art prefers biblical themes taken from the Hebrew Bible and the New Testament. Scenes taken from the former predominate until the late third century C.E. In the fourth century, they were replaced by themes taken from the latter.

The inscriptions from the catacombs of Rome are a particularly precious source of information concerning the commemorative, linguistic, onomastic, and religious practices of those memorialized in them. The epitaphs from the Jewish catacombs of Rome date mostly to the third and fourth centuries C.E. They follow contemporary non-Jewish epigraphic practices to a surprisingly large extent: just as the language that one encounters in them is typically late antique (*koine* Greek and vulgar Latin respectively, with hardly any evidence for Hebrew and Aramaic), so the names follow typically Roman onomastic practices. It is only in content (and in their decoration with Jewish symbols) that these inscriptions differ from contemporary epigraphic materials: again and again, they stress the importance of the community service of the deceased (e.g., *archisynagōgos, presbyter*).

The Catacombs of Beth She'arim

The Jewish catacombs discovered in Beth She'arim are exceptional in that in the Land of Israel — in the Jerusalem area as well as in Galilee — the predominant form of burial always was the family *hypogeum*. Excavations have revealed a massive underground necropolis consisting of at least thirty underground complexes that contained the well-preserved remains of some 200 sarcophagi along with numerous funerary inscriptions and decorations in relief. These finds indicate that after the Bar Kokhba Revolt (132-135 C.E.) primary inhumation replaced the practice of secondary burial in ossuaries almost entirely. The discoveries at Beth She'arim have revolutionized our understanding of ancient Jewish art in that they document that even in the land of Israel itself the Jews of antiquity did not eschew figurative art. These discoveries have also fundamentally altered our views on how Jews in the Roman period responded to and made use of the cultural trappings of Greco-Roman civilization. Thus, even in the Jewish heartland — at a site where the Sanhedrin is known to have operated for some time and the redactor of the Mishnah, Jehudah ha-Nasi, is supposed to have been buried — inscriptions in Greek were not uncommon. And not just any Greek: some inscriptions even contain poems in Homeric hexametric verse, with references to such un-Jewish notions as Hades and Moira.

Even so, the evidence found at Beth She'arim should not be considered as indicative of a population that was on its way to merging entirely with Greco-Roman civilization. Next to Greek inscriptions, significant numbers of inscriptions in Hebrew, Aramaic, and Palmyrene also survive. The title "rabbi" occurs more than once in these inscriptions. The inscriptions finally also indicate that a surprisingly large number of the deceased that were buried here did not originate from the surrounding area, but hailed from all over the ancient Near East. All this evidence goes to show that Beth She'arim was very much a Jewish necropolis; it was here that prominent Jews rested, in the conviction that it was in the Holy Land specifically that the resurrection of the dead would one day take place.

Some of the Beth She'arim catacombs are similar to their Jewish counterparts in Rome in that its builders tried to accommodate as many burials as possible. Others, however, being considerably more monumental in both external and internal appearance, seem to have had a slightly different function; inscriptions confirm that the people that were laid to rest there must primarily have been individuals that were well-to-do. Even though, therefore, the catacombs of Beth She'arim are formally not dissimilar from their Jewish counterparts in Rome, they differ from them in their supraregional function. Thus, the catacombs of Beth She'arim confirm what has been observed previously: in Rome burial in catacombs was common and always a community affair; in the Near East burial in catacombs was exceptional and reserved for the happy few.

BIBLIOGRAPHY

N. AVIGAD 1976, *Beth She'arim: Report on the Excavations during 1953–1958*, New Brunswick: Rutgers University Press. • S. J. D. COHEN 1984, "Epigraphical Rabbis," *JQR* 72: 1-17. • R. HACHLILI 1988, *Ancient Jewish Art and Archaeology in the Land of Israel*, Leiden: Brill. • R. HACHLILI 1998, *Ancient Jewish Art and Archaeology in the Diaspora*, Leiden: Brill. • B. MAZAR AND N. AVIGAD 1973, *Beth She'arim I: Report on the Excavations during 1936-1940*, New Brunswick: Rutgers University Press. • D. NOY 1995, *Jewish Inscriptions of Western Europe*, vol. 2, *The City of Rome*, Cambridge: Cambridge University Press. • L. V. RUTGERS 1995, *The Jews in Late Ancient Rome*, Leiden: Brill. • L. V. RUTGERS 2000, *Subterranean Rome*, Leuven: Peeters. • L. V. RUTGERS ET AL. 2005, "Christian Catacombs of Rome Inspired by Jewish Archetypes," *Nature* 436: 339. P. PERGOLA 1997, *Le catacombe romane*, Rome: La nuova Italia scientifica. • T. RAJAK 1998, "The Rabbinic Dead and the Diaspora Dead at Beth She'arim," in *The Talmud Yerushalmi and Graeco-Roman Culture*, ed. P. Schaefer, Tübingen: Mohr-Siebeck, 1: 349-66. • M. SCHWABE AND B. LIFSHITZ 1974, *Beth She'arim II: The Greek Inscriptions*, New Brunswick: Rutgers University Press. • N. ZIMMERMANN 2002, *Werkstatgruppen römischer Katakombenmalerei*, Münster: Aschendorff. • E. REBILLARD 2003, *Réligion et sepulture*, Paris: Éditions de l'École des hautes études en sciences sociales. • N. V. FIOCCHI ET AL. 2006, *The Christian Catacombs of Rome*, Regensburg: Schnell and Steiner.

See also: Burial Practices LEONARD V. RUTGERS

Catenae (4Q177, 4Q182)

4QCatena consists of two fragmentary Hebrew manuscripts from Qumran, labeled 4QCatena A (4Q177) and 4QCatena B (4Q182). 4QCatena A includes thirty-four fragments, twenty of which have been reconstructed into five columns, each originally with sixteen lines of text (listed as cols. 8–12 by Annette Steudel, though more commonly as 1–5, as below). The manuscript has been dated to the early or late Herodian period (Strugnell 1970 and Steudel 1994, respectively). The composition itself probably comes from the second half of the first century B.C.E.

4QCatena A is characterized by a series of quotations from the Psalms, along with further quotations from various named prophetic books and Deuteronomy. This led the original editor (Allegro 1968) to designate the work a *catena* (Latin for "chain"). Quotations from the Psalms are introduced with the words "he said," referring to David, and those from other Scriptures by a phrase such as "it is written about them in the book of [name] the prophet." According to Steudel's generally accepted reconstruction of the fragments, the Psalms are not cited in any order known from various Qumran psalters.

Between the scriptural quotations are interpretive comments, so the genre of the work is best understood as thematic pesher or commentary, similar in form to 4QFlorilegium and 4QMelchizedek. In this regard, the term *pesher* is used twice in the fragments, but only when introducing the interpretation of Psalms (2:9; 3:6). Scriptural citations occur in forms that are sometimes close to the MT, at other times similar to the LXX. The work is clearly a product of Qumran sectarians, as indicated by the use of the terms "sons of light" (e.g., 2:7), "seekers of smooth things" (2:12), "interpreter of the law" (2:5), "council of the community" (3:5), and "men of Belial" (e.g., 2:4). The frequent use of the phrase "the last days" confirms that the work deals with eschatological matters.

The manuscript is too fragmentary to be precise about its meaning. Column 1 begins in mid-sentence, so the beginning of the composition is lost. Yet a number of its themes can still be identified. There are references to the opponents of the author's community — including the "seekers of smooth things" (2:12) — who rebel against the Torah (3:14) and make the "sons of light" stumble (2:7). For the community, therefore, it is a time of testing and refining during the dominion of Belial (3:8), for the sake of their purification (2:10; 1:3). Ultimately, however, the community will be forgiven (3:10) and vindicated (4:11-16) and their opponents destroyed (4:8-9, 16). All this transpires in accordance with what is written on heavenly tablets (3:12), a deterministic perspective familiar from other sectarian documents (cf. 1QS 3:15-16). With copious citations from the Psalms and Prophets, the composition explains how the events and experiences of the author's community represent the fulfillment of the Scriptures in the last days.

4QCatena B (4Q182) consists of two small fragments, one with five partial lines, the other with parts of three. The manuscript was dated by Strugnell to the early or mid-Herodian period (30 B.C.E.–30 C.E.). 4Q182 was associated with 4Q177 because it, too, mentions "the last days" (frg. 1 line 1; frg. 2 line 1) and because it uses the same formulaic introduction for a scriptural citation: "[as it is wr]itten concerning them in the book of Jerem[iah]" (frg. 1 line 4). Thematically, it also relates to 4Q177, since it seems to envision condemnation for the author's enemies. Thus, Jer. 5:7a ("Why should I forgive you?") is cited after the mention of those "who will stiffen their necks" and who "threw off restraint defiantly to profane," probably references to opponents of the sect. The manuscript is too fragmentary to say more than this.

Steudel has argued that 4Q Catena A (4Q177) and 4QFlorilegium (4Q174) (perhaps along with 4Q178, 4Q182, and 4Q183) are manuscript copies of the same composition, which she entitled "4QMidrash on Eschatology." Her view is based on several similarities between the two manuscripts: both quote the Psalms heavily and perhaps in order — 4QFlorilegium citing Psalms 1–5 and 4QCatena A citing Psalms 5–6, 11–17; both use the same formulaic words for introducing Scripture; both use characteristic sectarian vocabulary; and both interpret the Scriptures to lay out an eschatological scenario. Response to Steudel's thesis has been mixed. Certainly the two manuscripts reflect similar works, but in the absence of any textual overlap between them, it remains difficult to conclude that they are the same composition.

BIBLIOGRAPHY

J. M. ALLEGRO WITH A. A. ANDERSON 1968, "Catena (A)" and "Catena (B)," in *Qumran Cave IV, I (4Q158–4Q186)*, DJD 5, Oxford: Oxford University Press, 67-74, 80-81. • J. G. CAMPBELL 2004, *The Exegetical Texts*, London: Clark. • J. MILGROM WITH L. NOVAKOVIC 2002, "Catena A (4Q177 = 4QCat[a])" and "Catena B (4Q182 = 4QCat[b])," in *The Dead Sea Scrolls*, vol. 6B, *Pesharim, Other Commentaries, and Related Documents*, ed. J. H. Charlesworth, Tübingen: Mohr-Siebeck; Louisville: Westminster John Knox. • A. STEUDEL 1994, *Der Midrasch zur Eschatologie (4QMidrEschat[a,b])*, Leiden: Brill. • J. STRUGNELL 1970, "Notes en marge du volume V des 'Discoveries in the Judaean Desert of Jordan,'" *RQ* 7: 236-48, 256.

KENNETH E. POMYKALA

Celibacy

Celibacy is the practice of abstaining from sex and marriage for ideological reasons. Because celibacy is a central theme in Christian tradition, the question of its possible roots in Second Temple Judaism has been a perennial subject of interest among students of ancient Christianity. Noting the rabbinic stress on marriage, sexual activity, and procreation, scholars frequently construct a sharp difference between Christianity and Judaism with respect to celibacy. The former is said to have promulgated celibacy, while the latter is said to have entirely rejected it.

A Range of Perspectives

That rabbinic Judaism does not approve of celibacy is beyond any doubt. Numerous classical rabbinic texts testify that marriage, sexual activity, and procreation were highly valued by the rabbis, both for social and religious reasons. At the same time, one can find not even a single rabbinic text in praise of celibacy. Even the alleged celibate Rabbi Shimon ben Azzai, who was criticized by his fellows for not having fulfilled the duty of procreation, never challenged the rabbinic view; on the contrary, he affirmed it in principle (*t. Yebam.* 8:7). Hence, the pro-marital stance of rabbinic Judaism stands beyond any doubt.

However, recent scholarship has warned against

imposing rabbinic ideals on earlier forms of Judaism in the Second Temple period. Even if we were to accept the attribution of a pro-marital stance in the earliest rabbinic documents (*m. Giṭ.* 4:5) to the schools of Hillel and Shammai (and there is no decisive reason to doubt it), and consequently to trace back this attitude to the early first century C.E., this would not change the fact that Second Temple Judaism was diverse. That classical rabbinic texts lay much emphasis on the duty of procreation and on the positive value of marriage must therefore not be taken simplistically to indicate that all types of Second Temple Judaism shared these views. Following this line of thought, various scholars have asserted that there were many radical groups within Judaism during the Second Temple period who highly valued celibacy (e.g., Brown 1988: 39).

Celibacy in the Second Temple Period

There is, indeed, some evidence for the existence of deliberate abstinence from marriage among some Jews in the Second Temple period. Most notable in this respect are the Essenes. According to Philo, "No Essene ever takes a wife" (*Hypoth.* 11.14). A similar impression is given in Pliny the Elder's description of the Essenes, whom he regards as "remarkable beyond all the other tribes in the whole world, as it has no women and has renounced all sexual desire" (*Naturalis Historia* 5.73). These statements, however, seem to be an exaggeration. Josephus, who knows of a group of Essenes who "disdain" marriage (*J.W.* 2.120), is careful to tell us elsewhere, "There is yet another order of the Essenes which, while at one with the rest in its way of life, differs from them in its views on marriage. They think that those who decline to marry cut off the chief function of life, the propagation of the species, and, what is more, that if all were to adopt the same view, mankind would very quickly die out" (*J.W.* 2.160).

It has been suggested that a passage in the *Damascus Document* (CD 6:11–7:6) implicitly refers to a group of sectarians who did not marry and did not beget children. This interpretation rests on the manner in which the immediately following passage is introduced: "And if they dwell in camps according to the order of the land and take wives and beget children. . . ." The conditional phrase "and if" seems to imply that the former passage refers to a group of sectarians who did not take wives and beget children (Qimron 1992: 289-90). This interpretation of the text is plausible, yet an explicit reference to celibacy is not to be found there, nor in any other passage in the Dead Sea Scrolls (Baumgarten 2000). On the contrary, marriage, women, and children are frequently mentioned in the Scrolls (e.g., *Rule of the Congregation* [1Q28a] 1:11; *Temple Scroll* [11Q19] 57:17-19), and various rules pertaining to marriage are to be found even in the *Damascus Document* itself (e.g., CD 4:20–5:11; 4Q270 7 i 12-13). The picture emerging from the Dead Sea Scrolls, as well as from Josephus' testimony, therefore indicates that, even among those sectarian groups that practiced celibacy, it was a marginal phenomenon.

Celibacy as Ideologically Motivated

What characterizes celibacy, and differentiates it from postponed marriage, on the one hand, and from abstention from second marriage in old age, on the other, is an *ideological* rejection of marriage and sexuality, which stems from a view of marriage as an obstacle to religious perfection. Since a man's age at his first marriage was relatively high among Jews of the Second Temple period (Schremer 1996), the fact that some young people stayed unmarried does not necessarily indicate that they were celibate. What is required in order to establish such a designation is to show that these young people were motivated by an explicit ideological renunciation of sexuality. Yet, even among those Jewish sectarians of the Second Temple era who are said to have been celibate, we know virtually nothing of their motivations or their attitudes to their brethren who did not refrain from marriage.

Louis Ginzberg (1976: 31) suggested that the reason underlying the sexual renunciation of those sectarians hinted at by the *Damascus Document* was their view of their habitat as the city of the Temple, in which, according to their halakah, sexual relations were prohibited (CD 12:1-2; 11QT[a] 45:7-12). This suggestion was later developed by Qimron (1992) and adopted by Baumgarten (2000). It does not imply, however, a rejection of sexuality and marriage as such, only a restriction on their practice in a particular place.

Likewise, Philo's reasoning for the Essenes' abstinence from marriage is not religious or ideological but rather practical: "They eschew marriage because they clearly discern it to be the sole or the principal danger to the maintenance of the communal life. . . . For he who is either fast bound in the love lures of his wife or under the stress of nature makes his children his first care ceases to be the same to others and unconsciously has become a different man and has passed from freedom into slavery" (*Hypoth.* 11.14-17). This stance is similar to the one expressed by the apostle Paul, who approved of marriage but preferred celibacy because it allowed one to attend to the "affairs of the Lord" without interference or anxiety, as the end of the age approached (1 Cor. 7:25-35). Such a line of reasoning is also not very far from the preference expressed by the third-century Palestinian rabbi, Yoḥanan ben Nafha, who ruled that a student of Torah should first devote himself to the study of Torah and only later marry, since it is impossible for one to be dedicated to the Torah while having a burden on his neck (*b. Qiddušin* 29b). Just as one should not suggest, based on Rabbi Yoḥanan's statement, that rabbinic Judaism promulgated celibacy (in fact Rabbi Yoḥanan himself is known to have married and had children [*b. Berakot* 5b; *b. Qiddušin* 71b; *y. Giṭ.* 7:6]), so too one should be cautious in applying the term "celibacy" to the lifestyle of unmarried Essenes, or that of any other group of Jews alleged to have deliberately refrained from marriage.

BIBLIOGRAPHY

J. M. BAUMGARTEN 2000, "Celibacy," in *Encyclopedia of the Dead Sea Scrolls*, ed. L. H. Schiffman and J. C. VanderKam, Ox-

CHARLES, ROBERT HENRY

ford: Oxford University Press, 1:122-25. • P. BROWN 1988, *The Body and Society: Men, Women, and Sexual Renunciation in Early Christianity,* New York: Columbia University Press. • L. GINZBERG 1976, *An Unknown Jewish Sect,* New York: Jewish Theological Seminary of America. • E. QIMRON 1992, "Celibacy in the Dead Sea Scrolls and the Two Kinds of Sectarians," in *The Madrid Qumran Congress,* vol. 1, ed. J. T. Barrera and L. V. Montaner, Leiden: Brill, 287-94. • A. SCHREMER 1996, "Men's Age at Marriage in Jewish Palestine of the Hellenistic and Roman Periods," *Zion* 61: 45-66 (in Hebrew). • A. SCHREMER 2003, *Male and Female He Created Them: Jewish Marriage in the Late Second Temple, Mishnaic and Talmudic Periods,* Jerusalem: Zalman Shazar Center (in Hebrew).

See also: Family; Marriage and Divorce; Sexuality

ADIEL SCHREMER

Charles, Robert Henry

R. H. Charles (1855-1931) was the foremost interpreter of the Old Testament Pseudepigrapha, and especially its apocalyptic literature, in the decades surrounding the turn of the twentieth century. Born in Cookstown, Northern Ireland, he was educated at Belfast Academy and Trinity College in Dublin. Ordained as a priest in the Anglican Church, he served parishes in London from 1883 to 1889. When ill health forced his retirement, he spent a year in Germany, where he took up the study of Jewish religion in the Greco-Roman period. When he returned to England, he spent most of his scholarly career at Oxford University. Throughout that career he maintained an association with the Anglican Church, in which he was appointed an archdeacon and a canon of Westminster.

Charles was a scholar with a rare and broad combination of intellectual talents and interests: classical and Semitic linguistic skills, a mastery of the newly emerging corpus of ancient Jewish apocalypses, theological interests, historical and literary inclinations, and a critical judgment expressed with candor and fairness. He is perhaps best known as the editor of the two-volume *Apocrypha and Pseudepigrapha of the Old Testament* (1912), a tool that served three generations of biblical students and scholars. However, his prodigious personal scholarly oeuvre was also highly influential among his contemporaries and foundational in the history of the study of Judaism. It included critical editions of the texts of *Jubilees* (Ethiopic and Latin, 1895), *1 Enoch* (Ethiopic, Greek, and Latin, 1906), and the *Testaments of the Twelve Patriarchs* (Greek and Armenian, 1908); translations with extended introductions and brief but packed commentary on *1 Enoch* (1893), *2 Baruch* (1896), the *Assumption of Moses* (1897), the *Ascension of Isaiah* (1900), *Jubilees* (1902), and the *Testaments of the Twelve Patriarchs* (1908); *1 Enoch* in a new edition (1912); a commentary on *2 Enoch* (1896); a translation of the Cairo *Damascus Document* (1912); a monograph on *Eschatology: The Doctrine of a Future Life in Israel, Judaism and Christianity* (1899, 1913); a volume on *Religious Development between the Old and New Testaments* (1914); and exhaustive commentaries on the canonical books of Revelation (2 vols., 1920) and Daniel (1929).

What is striking about Charles's studies of the apocalyptic literature, however, is the manner in which his rational Western mind, with its desire for consistency and its aversion to symbolic narrative, sometimes hindered his understanding of the literature he treasured so highly and was otherwise so well equipped to interpret (Manson 1949; Barr 1975). Thus, in order to explain contradictions that he perceived in the eschatology of the apocalypses, he sometimes appealed to the source-critical methods that were in vogue in Germany, where he had begun his study of the literature; and to tidy up difficulties that he found in the text, he emended it or excised lines from it. More problematic was his critique, expressed with "deep regret," that the "one-sided," "legalistic" rabbinic Judaism that "came into being after the Fall of Jerusalem" had lost interest in the apocalyptic theology that was "the true child of Prophecy." Also regrettable was his perception that the Judaism of his own time had become "to a great extent a barren faith, and lost its leadership in the spiritual things of the world" (Charles 1912: vi).

These exceptions notwithstanding, Charles's work is still to be appreciated as a benchmark in humanistic scholarship. Although his editions of *Jubilees, 1 Enoch,* and the *Testaments of the Twelve Patriarchs* are outdated due to the discovery of new manuscripts and new evaluations of the textual evidence, they played a crucial role in the history of scholarship for more than fifty years. And although they, too, are outdated by new data and methods, his translations of the texts are still valuable as philologically sound renderings of the ancient texts, and his commentaries need to be consulted by specialists working on these ancient works.

BIBLIOGRAPHY

J. BARR 1975, "Jewish Apocalyptic in Recent Scholarly Study," *BJRL* 58: 9-35. • R. H. CHARLES 1893, *The Book of Enoch,* Oxford: Clarendon. • R. H. CHARLES 1895, *The Ethiopic Version of the Hebrew Book of Jubilees,* Oxford: Clarendon. • R. H. CHARLES 1896, *The Apocalypse of Baruch,* London: Black. • R. H. CHARLES AND W. R. MORFILL 1896, *The Book of the Secrets of Enoch,* Oxford: Clarendon. • R. H. CHARLES 1897, *The Assumption of Moses,* London: Black. • R. H. CHARLES 1899, *A Critical History of the Doctrine of a Future Life,* London: Black. • R. H. CHARLES 1900, *The Ascension of Isaiah,* London: Black. • R. H. CHARLES 1902, *The Book of Jubilees or the Little Genesis,* London: Black. • R. H. CHARLES 1906, *The Ethiopic Version of Book of Enoch,* Oxford: Clarendon. • R. H. CHARLES 1908, *The Greek Versions of the Testaments of the Twelve Patriarchs,* Oxford: Clarendon. • R. H. CHARLES 1912, *The Book of Enoch or 1 Enoch: Translated from the Editor's Ethiopic Text,* Oxford: Clarendon. • R. H. CHARLES 1913, *Eschatology: The Doctrine of a Future Life in Israel, Judaism and Christianity,* London: Black (rpt. New York: Schocken, 1963 with an introduction by G. W. Buchanan). • R. H. CHARLES, ED. 1913, *The Apocrypha and Pseudepigrapha of the Old Testament,* 2 vols., Oxford: Clarendon. • R. H. CHARLES 1920, *A Critical and Exegetical Commentary on the Revelation of St. John,* 2 vols., Edinburgh:

Clark. • R. H. CHARLES 1929, *A Critical and Exegetical Commentary on the Book of Daniel,* Oxford: Clarendon. • T. W. MANSON 1949, "Charles, Robert Henry," in *The Dictionary of National Biography,* 1931-1940, ed. L. G. Wickham Legg, Oxford: Oxford University Press, 169-70.

GEORGE W. E. NICKELSBURG

Chronicles, Books of 1–2

Considered a single book in the Hebrew Bible, Chronicles is a literary product of the Second Temple period. In the Jewish canon, it is the last book in the third division of the Tanak. In the LXX, it is placed between Kingdoms and Ezra-Nehemiah, a position that is adopted in English versions of the Old Testament. The work begins with genealogies extending from Adam to the postexilic period (1 Chronicles 1–9) and continues with a history of the United Monarchy (1 Chronicles 10–2 Chronicles 9) and the Kingdom of Judah (2 Chronicles 10–36). Most of the narrative deals with the reigns of David (1 Chronicles 11–29) and Solomon (2 Chronicles 1–9).

Date

The current consensus dates the book in the late Persian or early Hellenistic eras, often during the fourth century B.C.E. While some scholars contend that allusions to Hellenistic thought, events, and literary conventions may be observed in Chronicles, there is nothing that requires a date into the third century, excluding the complicated Davidic genealogy of 1 Chron. 3:17-24. In this corrupt text, the versions preserved disagree on the number of generations that follow Zerubbabel. The MT contains six generations, while the LXX continues to eleven. Presuming that the book was composed near the time its latest genealogy ends, scholars argue for dates ranging from the late fifth to the early third century.

Apart from these verses, often considered part of a late redactional layer, the earliest possible date is reflected by the anachronistic reference to a Persian coin, the *daric,* in 1 Chron. 29:7. This coin was first minted by King Darius I of Persia around 515 B.C.E. The latest possible date is often regarded as sometime prior to the work of Eupolemus, a Hellenistic Jewish writer active in the second century B.C.E., who cites the Greek translation of Chronicles, titled *Paraleipomena* ("Things Omitted"). Since enough time must be allowed for the Hebrew text of Chronicles to be composed, to be taken to Egypt, to be translated into Greek, and then to be used authoritatively by this author, the mid to late third century as the latest time for its composition seems reasonable.

Authorship

The wide range of dates parallels suggestions for authorship. Rabbinic tradition names Ezra (with some final work by Nehemiah), although the book's anonymous author has been termed "the Chronicler" by modern scholars since the mid-nineteenth century. The book's interest in the Temple in Jerusalem and its personnel points strongly to someone invested in its operations, whether as a priest, Levite, or even levitical singer.

Until the last four decades, Chronicles was assumed to be part of a larger work known as the "Chronicler's History," which included Chronicles and Ezra-Nehemiah. These books, it was thought, were edited as a unified collection. The character of 1 Esdras, a Greek work in the Apocrypha that contains 2 Chronicles 35–36, Ezra 1–10, Neh. 8:1-13a, and some additional material, has been used to support this view. However, 1 Esdras indicates only that these books were read and interpreted together at a later time. The diverse content found in Chronicles and Ezra-Nehemiah on numerous theological and ideological issues suggests that the works originated in distinct circles. Thus, almost all recent scholars of both books have chosen to address Chronicles and Ezra-Nehemiah separately.

Genre

The ambiguity over date and authorship continues in the determination of genre. The literary form of Chronicles is unique in the ancient world. This is largely a result of the spectrum of subgenres it contains, which include lists, linear and segmented genealogies, speeches, prophetic oracles, a letter, legislation regarding cultic organization and practice, source citations, poetry, and narrative. Chronicles is variously classified as history, midrash, exegesis, "rewritten Bible," and theology.

Themes

Chronicles emphasizes a host of themes: Temple and cult; "seeking YHWH" and religious observance; immediate retribution; an expanded definition of "Israel"; and Davidic kingship.

Temple and Cult

The Temple and its services dominate the Chronicler's portrayal of Israelite history from Adam to Cyrus, especially in contrast to the apparent source in the parallel account of Samuel–Kings. In Chronicles, the righteous kings consistently advocate on behalf of the Temple and reform its procedures. David himself institutes the organizational structure of its personnel, which Solomon implements. However, all of this innovation is done in continuity with the Mosaic Torah, another repeated emphasis. Thus, Chronicles allows for changes to be made in the present and future without jeopardizing claims to fidelity to the past.

Seeking YHWH

While the Temple is the center for religious practice, the Chronicler's notion of piety and religious observance is conveyed by the phrase "seeking YHWH." This multivalent term expresses exemplary belief and action through both ritual participation at the Temple and the personal "condition of the heart" of the worshiper. In such contexts, the Chronicler makes references to "joy," humility, prayer, music, and generous voluntary giving.

Immediate Retribution

Chronicles promotes the idea that righteous belief and practice will be rewarded immediately. Almost always, rewards will occur within the individual's lifetime. Thus, one generation's sin neither impinges on the next generation's ability to be righteous nor inflicts them with punishment, as is the case in the book of Kings.

All Israel

Using the characteristic phrase "all Israel," the Chronicler extends the definition of those regarded as belonging to the righteous community. In contrast to the more exclusive stances of the Pentateuch and Ezra-Nehemiah, Chronicles does not reject intermarriage but instead welcomes foreigners who align themselves with the people of YHWH; this is clear especially in the explicit inclusion of foreigners in the genealogies of 1 Chronicles 1–9. In contrast to Kings, Chronicles invites Northerners to participate in the community and its religious observances (2 Chron. 11:13-17; 15:8-12; 30:1-22). The Chronicler even holds out hope for the possible restoration of those tribes deported by Assyria centuries earlier (2 Chron. 30:6-9). Thus, "all Israel" includes not only those who returned from the Babylonian Exile, but all those who associate themselves with the people and worship of YHWH.

Davidic Kingship

As the leaders of "all Israel," the Davidic kings play an important role. The Davidic throne is equated with the kingdom of YHWH (1 Chron. 10:14; 17:1-15; 28:5; 29:23), and its two first rulers are presented in an almost idealized manner. The foibles, sins, and intrigues of David and Solomon recounted in Samuel and Kings are omitted. However, David is not perfect, just polished (see 1 Chron. 15:13; 21:1, 3, 8; 22:8; 28:3). In contrast, Solomon does no wrong.

This positive presentation of the Davidic monarchy has resulted in many scholars arguing for a "messianic" or "royal" eschatology in Chronicles that awaits the dynasty's future restoration. Others have seen a "replacement" of the Davidides by either the Temple or the Persians, among many options. While the Chronicler may allow for the restoration of the Davidic dynasty, nothing in Chronicles requires it. The details are unclear; nevertheless, the articulation of hope for a better reality in the future does seem to underlie much of the Chronicler's construction of the past.

Reception and Interpretation in the Second Temple Period

The influence of Chronicles during the Second Temple Period was marginal, but it can be assessed in a number of ways. Although the narrative of Samuel–Kings was often preferred by later writings, many did make use of the unique content of Chronicles. Of particular importance are the following: (1) 1 Esdras includes a rewritten form of the end of 2 Chronicles. (2) Sirach 47:8-10 notes that David established the singers and musicians in the Temple liturgy, which reflects the Chronicler's account or at least a similar tradition. (3) The *Prayer of Manasseh* reports the details of his repentance as glossed only in 2 Chron. 33:12-13. (4) Several texts, such as the *Testament of Moses* and the *Lives of the Prophets,* contain miscellaneous information about Israelite kings and prophets known only from the Chronicler's narrative. (5) Pseudo-Philo's *Biblical Antiquities* seems to parallel the content and sequence of 1 Chronicles 1–10.

A few texts, such as *2 Baruch* and *Martyrdom of Isaiah,* reject or are in tension with the Chronicler's unique material. Yet two early Jewish historians, Josephus and Eupolemus, made explicit and extensive use of the Chronicler's unique content as a source for their histories. Chronicles is present among the Dead Sea Scrolls in only one small fragment (4Q118). Its influence may be seen in 4Q522, which alludes to David's preparations for building the Temple. Also, it is probable that the content of Chronicles lies behind some of the details of the Temple outlined in the *Temple Scroll* (11Q19-20) and the *New Jerusalem* fragments (2Q24; 4Q554-555; 5Q15; 11Q18). The New Testament contains little explicit reference to Chronicles. The most significant is the convoluted reference to the death of Zechariah in Matt. 23:35. The verse suggests a Hebrew canon that ends with Chronicles (see 2 Chron. 24:20-22), although the name of Zechariah's father is incorrect.

BIBLIOGRAPHY

E. BEN ZVI 1988, "The Authority of 1–2 Chronicles in the Late Second Temple Period," *JSP* 3: 59-88. • M. GRAHAM, K. HOGLUND, AND S. MCKENZIE, EDS. 1997, *The Chronicler as Historian,* Sheffield: Sheffield Academic. • M. GRAHAM AND S. MCKENZIE, EDS. 1999, *The Chronicler as Author,* Sheffield: Sheffield Academic. • M. GRAHAM, S. MCKENZIE, AND G. KNOPPERS, EDS. 2003, *The Chronicler as Theologian,* London: T&T Clark. • S. JAPHET 1993, *I & II Chronicles,* Louisville: Westminster John Knox. • I. KALIMI 2005, *An Ancient Israelite Historian: Studies in the Chronicler, His Time, Place and Writing,* Assen: Van Gorcum. • I. KALIMI 1998, "History of Interpretation: The Book of Chronicles in Jewish Tradition from Daniel to Spinoza," *RB* 105: 5-41. • R. KLEIN 2006, *1 Chronicles,* Minneapolis: Fortress. • G. KNOPPERS 2004, *I Chronicles 1–9,* New York: Doubleday. • G. KNOPPERS 2004A, *1 Chronicles 10-29,* New York: Doubleday. • S. SCHWEITZER 2007, *Reading Utopia in Chronicles,* London: T&T Clark. • H. WILLIAMSON 1977, *Israel in the Books of Chronicles,* Cambridge: Cambridge University Press.

STEVEN J. SCHWEITZER

Chronography

Chronography refers to the formulation of a system for dating events and measuring time. Early Jewish authors employed no uniform set of conventions in their attempts at reckoning time or dividing history into epochs. The "era of creation" becomes normative only in later Jewish sources (Finegan 1998: 108). The idiosyncratic calendar of the *Book of Jubilees,* a work composed in Hebrew in the late second century B.C.E., also reckons time from the creation of the universe. *Jubilees* groups years, each consisting of 364 days, into cycles of forty-nine years, which are further divided into cycles of seven "weeks" of years. *Jubilees'* dating of the universal flood in the seventh year of the fifth week of the twenty-seventh jubilee (*Jub.* 5:31) would equal year 1309 from creation ([26 × 49] + [7 × 5] = 1309).

Variety of Dating Systems

Jewish authors targeting a broader audience generally preferred more recognizable dating systems. When 1 Maccabees dates the beginning of the reign of Antiochus IV Epiphanes in "the one hundred and thirty-seventh year of the kingdom of the Greeks" (1:10), the author, as he does elsewhere, counts years according to the Seleucid era, a civic era widely used and understood in the Greek-speaking East (Bickerman 1980: 71-72). 1 Macc. 13:41-42 states that starting in the third year of the high priesthood of Simon the Hasmonean, the era from the first year of Simon began to be used in contracts drawn up in Judea. But this new practice failed to stem continued Jewish use of the older and more established Seleucid era, which in Jewish sources was also known as the "era of contracts" (Finegan 1998: 104).

Olympiad dating, favored by historians and chroniclers, was another widely used chronological instrument adopted by Jewish historians. First introduced in the third century B.C.E., it numbered four-year Olympiad cycles sequentially from the first dated Olympic Games (= 776 B.C.E.) and assigned a number to each year of the cycle. Although the Olympic Games began in mid-summer, Olympiad years were often adjusted to conform to the beginning of other calendar years (Bickerman 1980: 76).

Josephus adheres to the same practice in the *Antiquities.* In this work, he sometimes numbers years according to the Seleucid and Olympiad eras, and months and days according to the Macedonian and Jewish calendars. Thus, the date of the desecration of the Temple by Antiochus Epiphanes (= December 25, 167 B.C.E.) is given as the 155th year of the Seleucid era and "the twenty-fifth day of the month, which by us is called Chisleu and by the Macedonians Apellaios, in the 153rd Olympiad" (*Ant.* 12.248).

Biblical Chronology

Establishing a chronology of biblical history depended on the version of the Bible being used. The differences between the versions could be considerable, especially for the twenty or twenty-one generations from Adam to Abraham. The age of these patriarchs when they fathered a successor is almost uniformly 100 years higher in the Septuagint than in the traditional Hebrew version. The Septuagint also includes a postdiluvian patriarch (Kenan) lacking in the Hebrew (Gen. 10:24). Since the measurement of time was determined genealogically, the disparity between the two versions increased over each generation, reaching a total of almost 1400 years.

This discrepancy is reflected in the sources. Demetrius "the chronographer," a Hellenistic Jewish writer of the late third century B.C.E., adheres quite closely to the chronology of the Septuagint. The biblical chronology of Josephus' *Antiquities* appears to have been influenced by both traditions (Wacholder 1976: 108). This is also true of *Jubilees.* While generally following the chronology found in the Hebrew Bible, the preserved text of *Jubilees* also includes the postdiluvian Kenan (*Jub.* 8:2). For places in which biblical chronology was lacking, these same authors did not hesitate to contribute their own improvements. Demetrius, who knows a chronologically "corrected" text of the Septuagint, provides the year and month of the births of each of the twelve sons of Jacob (Wacholder 1976: 110-11). Included among the many elaborations of biblical chronology found in the book of *Jubilees* is a very detailed chronology of events from the creation of Adam to the expulsion from Paradise (*Jub.* 3:1-35).

Motivations

Apocalyptic Speculation

Jewish authors found various reasons for pursuing the study of chronology. The author of *Jubilees* treats the subject as a divinely inspired science. The prologue to that work describes its "history of the division of the days of the law and of the testimony, of the events of the years, of their jubilees throughout all the years of the world" as a revelation to Moses on Mt. Sinai. Befitting the providential mind that revealed this chronology, the divisions of time in *Jubilees* are symmetrical, all of them multiples of the number seven. Schematic chronology is also integral to some of the better-known apocalyptic surveys of history. One well-known example is Daniel's apocalypse of seventy weeks (9:24-27). Revealed to Daniel through the angel Gabriel, it preordains for the people and the Holy City "seventy weeks of years" (= 490 years), which are then segmented into periods of seven and sixty-two weeks, followed by one final week. Divisions of history similar to Daniel's found in other sources of the Second Temple period suggest that it was a formulation deeply embedded in Jewish apocalyptic speculation (Adler 1996: 208-12).

Exegetical Problem-Solving

For Demetrius, the first known Greek-speaking Jewish writer of the Hellenistic period to engage in serious exploration of the subject, chronography was a more scholastic exercise, concerned chiefly with resolving problems in the biblical text. A question that especially interested him and many chronographers afterward had to do with a passage in Exodus assigning 430 years to the Israelite sojourn in Egypt (Exod. 12:40-41). This number substantially exceeded the total that could be arrived at by adding up the individual generations. Demetrius' own solution was based on the Septuagint text of Exodus, which understood the 430 years to represent the length of the Israelite sojourn in both Egypt *and* Canaan. Expanding on this reading, Demetrius arrived at a chronology that divided the 430 years into two segments of exactly the same length: 215 years in Canaan and 215 years in Egypt (Wacholder 1976: 110-11).

Apologetics

Among Hellenistic Jewish writers after Demetrius, chronology was often pressed into the service of apologetics. Proving the antiquity and hence cultural superiority of the peoples on whose behalf they wrote was a favorite pursuit of many ethnic historians in the Hellenistic world. "Each nation," writes Josephus in *Against Apion* (2.152), "endeavors to trace its own institutions back to the remotest date, in order to create the impression that, far from imitating others, it has been the one to set its neighbors an example of orderly life under law." Jewish apologists and historians joined in the contest. Josephus, for example, boasts of the fact that Jewish history encompassed over 5,000 years of continuous history (*Ant.* 1.13) and that the Exodus preceded the Trojan War by nearly 1,000 years (*Ag. Ap.* 1.104).

To establish the superior antiquity of the Jews meant, however, that historians could no longer concentrate their attention, as Demetrius had done, strictly on biblical chronology. It required comparison and correlation with the records of other peoples. Moses, a figure familiar to non-Jewish readers and celebrated in Hellenistic Jewish sources as both a lawgiver and culture hero, was the focus of much of this research into comparative chronology. According to Eusebius of Caesarea (Helm 1984: 7.16-17), the Jewish historian Justus of Tiberias, a contemporary of Josephus, was one of many earlier writers who proved that Moses lived during the reign of Inachus, the first Argive king and a figure reputed to be of the very remote past. Josephus himself calls Moses the "most ancient of all legislators in the records of the whole world," and reminds his readers that even Moses' detractors had to acknowledge his antiquity. In comparison with Moses, Josephus writes, the great lawgivers of the Greeks were "born but yesterday" (*Ag. Ap.* 2.154).

Jewish Chronography in Christianity

The exploration of chronology in early Christianity owes a great debt to its Jewish heritage. The dating of Moses in the reign of Inachus was a standard article of Christian apologetic in the second and third centuries C.E. Christian apocalyptic chronology in many cases simply elaborated upon older Jewish formulations. In its original context, Daniel's vision of seventy weeks culminated with Antiochus Epiphanes' sacrilege against the Jerusalem Temple. But both Jewish and later Christian commentators repeatedly reinterpreted and adapted the passage to explain new crises (Adler 1996: 217-38). The division of the ages of the world into six 1,000-year periods, already attested in Christian sources of the second century, was itself an idea probably arising out of Jewish apocalyptic speculation of the Second Temple period.

BIBLIOGRAPHY

W. ADLER 1996, "The Apocalyptic Survey of History Adapted by Christians: Daniel's Prophecy of 70 Weeks," in *The Jewish Apocalyptic Heritage in Early Christianity,* ed. J. C. VanderKam and W. Adler, Assen: Van Gorcum; Minneapolis: Fortress, 199-236. • E. BICKERMAN 1980, *Chronology of the Ancient World,* 2d ed., Cornell: Cornell University Press. • J. FINEGAN 1998, *Handbook of Biblical Chronology,* rev. ed., Peabody, Mass.: Hendrickson. • L. I. GRABBE, "Chronography in Hellenistic Jewish Historiography," *SBLSP* 17: 43-68. • R. HELM, ED. 1984, *Die Chronik des Hieronymus,* 3rd ed., GCS, *Eusebius Werke,* vol. 7, Berlin: Akademie Verlag. • B. Z. WACHOLDER 1976, "Biblical Chronology in the Hellenistic World Chronicles," in *Essays on Jewish Chronology and Chronography,* ed. B. Z. Wacholder, New York: Ktav, 106-36.

WILLIAM ADLER

Circumcision

Circumcision (literally, "cutting around") is the excision of the foreskin or prepuce on the end of the penis to uncover the glans or corona. While its origins are unknown, circumcision is, and has long been, practiced in disparate cultures throughout the world. The oldest evidence of the rite in the Near East dates to the third millennium B.C.E. This article reviews ancient Jewish circumcision traditions from their roots in the Hebrew Bible to early Christian and tannaitic writings.

Hebrew Bible

Circumcision texts can be delimited by appearances of *mwl,* "circumcise," and *ʿārāl,* "foreskin." Circumcision and foreskin imagery can be either literal, referring to the penis, or metaphorical, in association with diverse body parts (heart, lips, ears) and fruit trees.

Circumcision, first mandated to Abraham, is identified as the "sign of the covenant" between God and Israel (Gen. 17:9-14), that is, the sign of Israel's commitment to observing God's dictates. The covenant implications also inhere in numerous circumcision texts. Circumcision is required for participation in the Paschal offering (Exod. 12:43-49), because Passover is the covenant commemoration par excellence. Every Israelite male is circumcised by Joshua at Gilgal upon entry into Canaan (Josh. 5:2-9), signifying the realization of the covenantal promise of land (Gen. 17:8; Exod. 6:4). A "foreskinned heart" is a metaphor for rejection of God's covenant, while circumcision indicates a recommitment to the covenant and a restoration of divine favor (Lev. 26:41; Deut. 10:16; 30:6; Jer. 4:4; 9:25). Similarly, the expression "foreskinned ear" indicates an inability to hear God's commands (Jer. 6:10), and the phrase "foreskinned lips" (Exod. 6:12, 30) is used of Moses' demur that he is unequipped to tell Pharaoh to let the Israelites go.

Circumcision must be carried out on the eighth day of a boy's life (Gen. 17:12; 21:4; Lev. 12:3), that day constituting the onset of ritual, or sacral, viability. (For eighth-day regulations regarding sacrificial animals, priestly ordination, and altar consecration, see Exod. 22:30; Lev. 8:33–9:24; 22:26-27; Ezek. 43:18-27). The penalty for failure to circumcise is *kareth,* "cutting off," of the offenders from their people (Gen. 17:14). *Kareth* is a divine withdrawal of the covenant promises; it can entail premature death, extirpation, loss of family or land, or a harried afterlife (cf. Ezek. 28:10; 31:18; 32:19-32, which threaten a lower place in Sheol for those who die uncircumcised). The cryptic "bridegroom of blood" pericope in Exod. 4:24-26, where Moses is attacked by God and the danger is forestalled when Zipporah performs a circumcision (upon whom is uncertain), suggests an apotropaic valence for the rite.

Israelites are to circumcise their male slaves (Gen. 17:12-13), and any resident alien *(gēr)* who elects to partake of the Passover must also be circumcised (Exod. 12:43-49). Circumcision of foreigners, however, does not afford them entry into the Israelite community, nor does it grant them a stake in the covenantal relationship with God. Many peoples practice circumcision (Jer. 9:25-26), with Abraham's circumcision of Ishmael (Gen. 17:23-27) serving as an etiology. The Philistines are labeled *hā-ʿărēlîm,* "the foreskinned people" (e.g., Judg. 14:3; 15:18; 1 Sam. 14:6; 17:26; 31:4; 2 Sam. 1:20; 1 Chron. 10:4), while *ʿārēl* can also denote foreignness more generally (Isa. 52:1; Ezek. 44:7, 9). In Genesis 34, Jacob's sons Simeon and Levi, avenging the rape of their sister Dinah, massacre the Shechemites by convincing them to undergo circumcision and then attacking them during their recuperation.

Leviticus 19:23-25 brands fruit from a tree's initial three years as "foreskinned," and forbids its consumption. In the fourth year, the mature fruit must be dedicated to God, and in the fifth, it may be used at the discretion of its human owners.

The Septuagint

In the Septuagint and other ancient Greek versions, the Greek terms *peritomē* ("circumcise") and *akrobystia,* ("foreskin") are, in most cases, utilized to translate the Hebrew terms *mwl* and *ʿārēl,* the exceptions being the circumcision metaphors. For example, LXX substitutes "inarticulate" for "foreskinned lips" (Exod. 6:12, 30), and "hard heart" for "foreskinned heart" (Deut. 10:16; Jer. 4:4). A pattern of rendering "foreskin" as "impurity" and "circumcision" as "purification" is also in evidence (LXX Lev. 19:23; Deut. 30:6; Josh. 5:4; Symmachus Exod. 6:12, 30; Jer. 4:4). (Note that Philo's exegesis of Lev. 19:23-25 in *De Plantatione* 93–139 and *De Virtutibus* 155–60 is based upon the LXX.) The LXX features a few noteworthy modifications and expansions. In Exod. 4:24-26, it is the circumcision *blood* that averts the death of Moses, and according to Josh. 21:40 and 24:31, the stone knives used for the circumcision at Gilgal were saved and buried with Joshua. Esther's prayer (Addition C) includes a declaration that she "loathes the bed of the uncircumcised," and in Esth. 8:17 converts to Judaism are circumcised (cf. also Jdt. 14:10; Josephus, *Ant.* 11.285).

The Targums

The Aramaic targums employ *gzr,* "cut," when translating Hebr. *mwl,* thereby producing an interesting semantic phenomenon. Since the formulaic biblical phrase for covenant making is *krt bryt,* "*cut* a covenant" (*gzr* in Aramaic), covenant symbolism becomes intrinsic to most targumic circumcision passages. As in the Greek versions, the targums recast many of the circumcision metaphors. Harmonizing with Exod. 4:10, the Aramaic versions rewrite Moses' foreskinned lips (Exod. 6:12, 30) as a speech defect, rendering the phrase as "heavy of speech" *(Onqelos* and *Pseudo-Jonathan),* "halting" *(Neofiti),* and "stuttering" (Syriac). Similarly, the foreskinned ear (Jer. 6:10) is read as "dull." In Lev. 19:23, all the targums substitute "rejected" for "foreskinned," in line with the disposition, rather than the symbolism, of the premature fruit (cf. Josephus, *Ant.* 4.226-27). The various references to "foreskinned heart" are rendered by the targums with "stubborn" (*Tg. Ps.-J.* Lev. 26:41; *Tg. Onq.* and *Tg. Ps.-J.* Deut. 10:16; *Tg. Onq.* and *Tg. Ps.-J.* Deut. 30:6), "foolish" (*Tg. Onq.* Lev. 26:41; *Tg. Neof.* Deut. 10:16), and "wicked" (*Tg. Neof.* Lev. 26:41; *Tg. Jer.* 4:4; *Tg. Ezek.* 44:7-9). The targums also evince a homology between circumcision and sacrificial blood. Aramaic renditions of Exod. 4:24-26 declare that the circumcision blood atones for Moses' guilt, and glosses in *Tg. Ps.-J.* Exod. 12:13 and *Tg. Ezek.* 16:6 aver that Israel is redeemed by the blood of circumcision and the Paschal offering.

1 Maccabees

1 Maccabees is the earliest Jewish work where the term "covenant" is treated as synonymous with "circumcision," a usage that becomes widespread in subsequent Jewish traditions. One of the catalysts for Mattathias' uprising is Antiochus IV's outlawing of circumcision (1 Macc. 1:48, 60-63; cf. 2 Macc. 6:10; 4 Macc. 4:25; Josephus, *Ant.* 12:253-56; *J.W.* 1:34). The harshest polemic in 1 Maccabees is directed at Jewish apostates, who are emblematized by their rejection of circumcision (1 Macc. 1:13-15; cf. Josephus, *Ant.* 12.241). After gaining power, the Hasmoneans forcibly circumcise Jews, along with neighboring peoples such as the Idumeans and Itureans, whom they subjugate and convert to Judaism (1 Macc. 2:46; cf. Josephus, *Ant.* 12.278; 13.257-58, 318-19).

Pseudepigrapha and Dead Sea Scrolls

In its opening historiographic peroration, the book of *Jubilees* employs the metaphor of a circumcised heart to signal the restoration of Israel to God's favor after a period of apostasy and alienation (*Jub.* 1:22-24). Later, the circumcision legislation in Genesis (*Jub.* 15:11-14) is followed by an addendum stressing the magnitude of the rite; the angels were created circumcised, and Jews who observe the command stand in their holy company. Those who spurn the covenantal rite, or perform incomplete circumcisions, are characterized as "sons of destruction" and "sons of Beliar" who will incur irrevocable divine punishment (*Jub.* 15:22-34).

Several Qumran texts accentuate the necessity of circumcision. CD 16:6, which cites *Jubilees,* states that Abraham "circumcised himself on the day of his knowledge," perhaps referring to an angelic revelation received by the patriarch. The *Hodayot* (1QH^a 14:20, and parallels) speak of God's holy path upon which "the uncircumcised, defiled, and depraved may not pass," and a fragmentary work (4Q458 frg. 2 col. ii line 4) al-

CIRCUMCISION

ludes to the "swallowing up" of the uncircumcised in the end time. The scrolls feature several distinctive iterations of the circumcision metaphors. Those joining the community must have their *yēṣer,* "inclination," circumcised (1QS 5:5) and are warned against hating with a foreskinned heart (1QS 5:26). Liturgies acknowledge God for saving his people by circumcising their hearts (*Barki Nafshi,* 4Q434 1 i 4) and petition God to "circumcise our hearts" to uphold the covenant (*Dibrei Hame'orot,* 4Q504 frg. 4 line 11; cf. *Havineinu, b. Berakot* 29a). Deceitful people are typified by their foreskinned lips (1QH[a] 10:18), and the community's arch opponent, the Wicked Priest, is characterized by his foreskinned heart (1QpHab 11:13). On the other hand, supplicants humbly confess to foreskinned ears or lips (1QH[a] 21:5; 10:7), the latter constituting a potential identification of the author, perhaps the Teacher of Righteousness himself, with Moses.

Pseudo-Philo portrays Moses as having been born circumcised (*Bib. Ant.* 9:13-15), a condition also applied in rabbinic lore to a host of biblical figures (e.g., *'Abot de Rabbi Nathan* A 2; *Midr. Ps.* 9:7). *2 Baruch* retells Josiah's reform (2 Kings 23:1-27; 2 Chron. 34:29-33) with a Greco-Roman sensibility, noting that the king ensured the circumcision of every Israelite (2 Bar. 66:5). The *Testament of Moses* (8:1-3) alludes to the persecution of Jews, who are singled out by their circumcision, even those who attempted to erase their distinctive mark through epispasm (cf. 1 Cor. 7:18; Celsus, *De Medicina* 7.25.1-2). The circumcision subterfuge in Genesis 34 was problematic for many ancient Jewish tradents, who either inveighed against it (*T. Levi* 6) or omitted it altogether (*Jubilees* 30; Josephus, *Ant.* 1.337-42; Theodotus, frg. 5, in Eusebius, *Praep. Evang.* 9.22.8-9).

Hellenistic Jewish Writers

Philo of Alexandria upholds the importance of circumcision, asserting that it both cleanses ritually and protects penile and reproductive health (*Spec. Leg.* 1.1-11; *QG* 3.46-52, 61-62). Typically, Philo also allegorizes the rite, explaining that excision of superfluous phallic tissue represents the purging of heart and soul from excessive desire and sinful inclinations (ibid.), but he also cautions that a symbolic understanding of circumcision is not exclusive of its literal practice (*De Migratione Abrahami* 92).

Josephus principally replicates his sources when dealing with circumcision. He promises an extensive discourse on the practice (*Ant.* 1.192), likely to be taken up in his unwritten (or lost) work *Customs and Origins.* Though Josephus reports, without judgment, the Hasmoneans' forcible circumcision of Gentiles, he objects unequivocally to such coercion in his own day (*Life* 113). His account of the conversion of the royal house of Adiabene (*Ant.* 20.17-96) broaches what was undoubtedly a live debate about the extent to which circumcision was necessary for proselytes, resolving the question in favor of the rite's centrality (see also *Ant.* 20.139).

Conversely, *Joseph and Aseneth* envisions conversion without circumcision. Several Hellenistic authors discuss circumcision in light of Egyptian or Ethiopian practice, perhaps to legitimate the Jewish rite for a Gentile, or more assimilated Jewish, audience (e.g., Josephus, *Ag. Ap.* 2.140-143; 1.668-171, citing Herodotus, *Historiae* 2.104; Artapanus, frg. 3, in Eusebius, *Praep. Evang.* 9.27.10)

New Testament and Early Christianity

The trend in the New Testament is to declare circumcision irrelevant, without condemning its practice by Jewish members of the Jesus movement. Jesus and John's circumcisions are reported in the Lukan infancy narrative (Luke 1:59; 2:21), but the Apostolic Council in Jerusalem determines that Gentile converts and members of the community need not be circumcised (Acts 15:1-11; 21:25). A circumcision ideology is fully voiced in the Pauline writings. Circumcision of the flesh is superfluous and obviated by circumcision of the heart, brought about through faith in Jesus, which is sufficiently redemptive in and of itself (Rom. 2:25–5:5; 1 Cor. 7:17-20; Gal. 5:1-15; 6:11-18; Eph. 2:11-12; Philippians 3; cf. also *Odes Sol.* 11:2 for a poetic image of circumcision by the Holy Spirit). In this respect, circumcision is equated with baptism (Col. 2:6-19). Justin Martyr (*Dialogue with Trypho* 18–19, 24, 27–29, 92, 113–14) and the *Epistle of Barnabas* (9; 10:12) reaffirm the Pauline outlook while adding a harsh anti-Jewish polemic. *Barnabas* asserts that the circumcision imperative is evil and false (9:3-4), and Justin interprets circumcision as a sign of the Jews' rejection of and by God, and of their deserved suffering under Roman rule (*Dialogue with Trypho* 16; 19).

Tannaitic Literature

Circumcision regulations are widely diffused in rabbinic literature, the most important and extensive unit being *m. Šabb.* 18:3–19:6, where key elements of the circumcision process are laid out. Timing is emphasized: an infant may not be circumcised before the eighth day or after the twelfth (cf. *m. 'Arak* 2:2), and circumcision overrides the prohibition of Sabbath labor (cf. *m. Šabb.* 9:3). Circumcision may be postponed, however, even indefinitely, in cases of grave health risks (cf. *m. Neg.* 7:5).

Three components comprise the core of the circumcision ritual; *mîlâ* (cutting), *pĕrî'â* (peeling back the foreskin to expose the corona), and *mĕṣîṣâ* (blood drawing). The *pĕrî'â* requirements are quite stringent to prevent the appearance of uncircumcision and to deter reversal through epispasm (cf. *m. Yebam.* 8:1; *Mekilta R. Shimon b. Yohai, Bo* 12:45). Anyone may perform a circumcision save a deaf person, a minor, or one who is mentally defective (*m. Meg.* 2:4), and circumcision is one of thirty-six commands whose transgression warrants the *kareth* penalty (*m. Ker.* 1:1). Circumcision, along with immersion and sacrifice, is required for all male proselytes (*Sifre Numbers* 108), and timely circumcision is crucial for a convert's Passover observance (*m. Pesaḥ.* 3:7; 5:3; 8:8 [= *m. 'Ed.* 5:2]).

Several haggadic passages provide an ideological framework for the practice of circumcision. King David enters the bathhouse naked and celebrates his circumcision as a mark of the covenant, even absent his fringes and phylacteries (*Sifre Deuteronomy* 36). Levi is praised as the only tribe that practiced circumcision during the desert wandering (*Sifre Numbers* 67). *Mekilta Bo* 5 highlights the redemptive power of circumcision (and Paschal) blood (cf. *Tg. Ezek.* 16:6; *Tg. Ps.-J.* 12:13), while *m. ʾAbot* 3:11 declares that anyone who "abrogates the covenant of Abraham" has no share in the world to come. An encomium to the rite (*m. Ned.* 3:11) features a string of statements, each beginning with the phrase "Great is circumcision," culminating with the acclamation "Great is circumcision because if not for it, the Holy One Blessed Be He would not have created the world."

Synthesis

In the Hebrew Bible, circumcision, both literal and metaphorical, is of great consequence as the mark of the covenant. Its ramifications, however, are internal, bearing solely upon the relationship between Israel and God. In the postbiblical era, circumcision also became an external dynamic, as a defining sign of Jewish identity and a communal boundary marker, in part because the practice was abhorred in Greco-Roman society at large (for Greco-Roman derogation of circumcision, see Horace, *Satirae* 1.9.68-74; Petronius, *Satyrica* 68.8; 102.14; Martial, *Epigrams* 7.30, 55, 82; 11.94; Juvenal, *Satirae* 14.99; Strabo, *Geography* 16.2.37; Tacitus, *Historiae* 5.2; Suetonius, *Domitian* 12.2). Early Jewish literature manifests a more robust effort at regulating circumcision, and a wider range of meanings are ascribed to the ritual. Circumcision also begins to function as a boundary marker between early Judaism and emergent Christianity. Christian tradents deemed circumcision as at best extraneous, while Jews held ever faster to the practice.

BIBLIOGRAPHY

R. ABUSCH 2003, "Circumcision and Castration under Roman Law in the Early Empire," in *Covenant of Circumcision: New Perspectives on an Ancient Jewish Rite,* ed. E. W. Mark, Hanover, N.H.: Brandeis University Press, 75-86. • D. BERNAT 2008, *Sign of the Covenant: Circumcision in the Priestly Traditions,* Atlanta: Society of Biblical Literature. • S. J. D. COHEN 2005, *Why Aren't Jewish Women Circumcised: Gender and Covenant in Judaism,* Berkeley: University of California Press. • J. J. COLLINS 1985, "A Symbol of Otherness: Circumcision and Salvation in the First Century," in *"To See Ourselves as Others See Us": Christians, Jews, and "Others" in Late Antiquity,* ed. J. Neusner and E. Frerichs, Chico, Calif.: Scholars Press, 163-86. • D. FLUSSER AND S. SAFRAI 1980, "Who Sanctified the Beloved in the Womb?" *Immanuel* 11: 46-55. • R. G. HALL 1988, "Epispasm and the Dating of Ancient Jewish Writings," *JSP* 2: 71-86. • R. D. HECHT 1984, "The Exegetical Contexts of Philo's Interpretation of Circumcision," in *Nourished with Peace: Studies in Hellenistic Judaism in Memory of Samuel Sandmel,* ed. F. Greenspahn, E. Hilgert, and B. Mack, Chico, Calif.: Scholars Press, 51-79. • L. HOFFMAN 1996, *Covenant of Blood: Circumcision and Gender in Rabbinic Judaism,* Chicago: University of Chicago Press. • R. LE DEAUT 1982, "Le thème de la circoncision du coeur (Deut XXX 6, Jer IV 4) dans les versions anciennes (LXX et Targum) et à Qumran," in *Congress Volume Vienna 1980,* ed. J. A. Emerton, Leiden: Brill, 178-205. • S. C. MIMOUNI 2007, *La circoncision dans le monde Judéen aux époques Grecque et Romaine: Histoire d'un conflit interne au judaïsme,* Paris/Louvain: Peeters. • J. M. SASSON 1966, "Circumcision in the Ancient Near East," *JBL* 85: 473-76. • D. R. SEELY 1996, "The 'Circumcised Heart' in *4Q434 Barki Nafshi,*" *RQ* 17: 527-35. • G. VERMES 1958, "Baptism and Jewish Exegesis: New Light from Ancient Sources," *NTS* 4: 308-19.

See also: Adiabene

DAVID A. BERNAT

Cisterns and Reservoirs

Cisterns and reservoirs are facilities for collecting and storing water. Cisterns were cut out of rock or dug in the earth and surfaced with stone or plaster pavement and walls to prevent seepage. They were constructed mainly for private use, and their capacity frequently reached a few dozen cubic meters. Reservoirs were much larger installations built for public use and were capable of holding hundreds of cubic meters of water. They typically measured 10-20 m. long, 8-12 m. wide, and 5-8 m. deep, but many exceeded these dimensions. Most were rectangular in shape with either a flat or arched roof.

Rainwater is the primary source of water in Israel. The springs concentrated in the Jordan Valley and in the hilly regions of the country provided the inhabitants of those areas with flowing water year-round, but a majority of the population received only the rainwater that fell exclusively, and in limited amounts, during the winter, which lasts only four-five months; and with extreme changes between the north, which is relatively rich in precipitation (up to 1,000 mm. multiyear average) and the parched south (less than 100 mm. multiyear average). In order to exist under such conditions and meet their needs, people learned to collect and store the rainwater when it fell.

A decisive phase in the development of water collection and long-term storage abilities began with the use of plaster (made mainly of lime) to seal the reservoirs and prevent the seepage of water from them. Lime production by burning limestone at high temperatures originated in the preceramic Neolithic age (ca. 7000 B.C.E.), but its use in cisterns and reservoirs began only in the Canaanite period. Some place this as far back as the Early Canaanite period (ca. 2500 B.C.E.), while others date this to the Late Canaanite period, or even to the beginning of the Israelite period (ca. 1200 B.C.E.). As technological and engineering knowledge advanced, especially in the Hellenistic and Roman periods, water storage installations became increasingly complex and sophisticated.

We know of a diverse range of water storage facilities from antiquity, some characteristic of the entire land of Israel, while others were typical of a specific region. No essential changes occurred in their architectural form in the different periods, and their dating is generally based on the architectural complex in which they are incorporated, on inscriptions and other dated finds, and also on distinctions between the types of waterproof plaster, which in many instances provide a

CISTERNS AND RESERVOIRS

chronological indicator. In terms of their size and purpose, these installations may be divided into the following main categories: cisterns, public roofed reservoirs, and open pools.

Cisterns

Cisterns are the most common water storage installations throughout Israel. Most are round and bell-shaped. Because their pavement and walls were coated with waterproof plaster to prevent water loss, the cistern served as a metaphor for the Torah scholar who forgets nothing of what he has learned: "a plastered cistern that loses not a drop" (*m. 'Abot* 2:8).

Thousands of ancient cisterns exist, and many are still in use. They are located in towns, smaller settlements, and open, undeveloped areas, where they were used by herders, farmers, and travelers. In the towns and farmhouses, drainage systems were carefully built to provide drainage for roofs and paved courtyards. Archaeological evidence in private and public buildings shows the fine craftsmanship invested in these drainage systems. Cisterns were also located in low-lying areas to collect runoff water from higher elevations. Conduits cut in the slopes brought the runoff water to a shallow sinking basin where silt, stones, and dirt carried by the water could sink, the clean water then entering the cistern itself through the openings beside the entrenchment. Only the conduits and upper opening of the cistern were visible aboveground. This opening was marked by a large stone in which a hole was cut, to which a stone stopper or a wooden or iron door was often attached. This stone was the "entrenchment" *(huliyah)* of the cistern, the narrow opening through which water was drawn with a rope and bucket. Rainwater, however, did not fill the cistern through this opening but flowed into it through conduits that brought water from afar. This was the realistic basis for the popular aphorism "A handful cannot satisfy a lion, nor can a pit be filled up from its entrenchment" (*b. Berakot* 3b).

Public Roofed Reservoirs

From the Hellenistic period to the late medieval period, large reservoirs for public use were built in cities, fortresses, military encampments, agricultural estates, and the like. The flat or arched roof of these reservoirs was entirely cut in bedrock or built, mostly of a system of arches that supported stone slabs. A thick plaster coating on the sides and pavement sealed the reservoir and prevented seepage.

Series of such reservoirs were built on the steep bedrock slopes at the top of the fortresses constructed during the Second Temple period by the Hasmonean rulers and by Herod, mainly in desert areas such as Masada overlooking the Dead Sea, Cypros above Jericho, and Alexandrion in the northern Jordan Valley. They were also installed at strategic points along the central mountain line, as at Horvat Kefira, west of Jerusalem. These installations, which were among the prominent characteristic features of the fortresses, enabled them to withstand even prolonged siege.

One or more aqueducts brought water to the reservoirs, by gravitational force, from a distance of hundreds or even thousands of meters. The water source was usually rainwater collected from the slopes of neighboring hills, or from floods in nearby streambeds. In the latter case, a dam would be built in the streambed, at a location higher than the level of the reservoir, to trap a portion of the floodwater and divert it to the conduit that would direct it to the reservoir. A sinking basin to collect dirt would be built close to where the water entered the closed reservoir, within which the water would be drawn through openings in its roof or at the top of one of its sides. More sophisticated installations contained a system of secondary trenches or ceramic (or, in rare instances, lead) pipes that distributed the reservoir's water to consumers for various purposes: for drinking and washing in homes, for bathing in public bathhouses, and for fountains and nympheon structures in Roman cities. In the Byzantine and Crusader eras, reservoirs supplied water for the irrigation of vegetables and fruit trees at estates and monasteries. The public reservoirs usually had a capacity of hundreds of cubic meters.

Open Pools

Along with closed reservoirs, which were generally located within settlements, tremendous open pools were often built or dug to receive excess rainwater after the system of conduits had completely filled the domestic cisterns and the closed public reservoirs. This is clearly exemplified in Jerusalem, a mountainous city built on a number of hills; huge pools filled with excess rainwater were built in the valleys between the hills. These include the Sultan's Pool, the Sheep Pool (Bethesda), the Pool of Israel, and the Pool of Siloam (which was supplied by both rain and springwater). Some of these structures had their beginnings in the Iron Age (the First Temple period) and remain in use to the present. In these pools, the pool wall in the lower part of the valley streambed was very thick and built of large stones, to serve as a dam stopping the floodwaters from flowing downstream, and to enable their collection, in quantities reaching thousands or even tens of thousands of cubic meters. Waterproof plaster prevented seepage from these open pools. Their exposure to the sun resulted in considerable evaporation over time and promoted the development of algae, water plants, and even animals within the water. The quality of the water in the open pools was therefore inferior to that in the other types of reservoirs, but their water usually supplied all the needs filled by the closed reservoirs. In sophisticated waterworks, such as those of Second Temple period Jericho and Jerusalem, which were based on springs and a system of aqueducts, open pools were built both in the heart of the water system (Solomon's Pool in Jerusalem) and at the place where the aqueduct reached its destination (Hezekiah's Pool in the Upper City of Jerusalem, Birket Musa in the Hasmonean and Herodian palaces in the Jericho Valley).

Open pools of much more modest capacity (of only dozens of cubic meters) were commonly used in agricultural irrigation systems fed by springs or wells and were active the year round. In these systems, they regulated the water and distributed it to different plots in the daily operation of the irrigation system.

BIBLIOGRAPHY
D. AMIT, J. PATRICH, AND Y. HIRSCHFELD, EDS. 2002, *The Aqueducts of Israel,* Portsmouth, R.I.: Journal of Roman Archaeology. • M. BROSHI 2001, *Bread, Wine, Walls and Scrolls,* London: Continuum. • A. T. HODGE 1992, *Roman Aqueducts & Water Supply,* London: Duckworth. • R. RUBIN 1988, "Water Conservation Methods in Israel's Negev Desert in Late Antiquity," *Journal of Historical Geography* 14: 229-44.

See also: Aqueducts DAVID AMIT

Civic Rights of Jews → Rights of Jews in the Roman World

Cleodemus Malchus

Cleodemus, also called Malchus, was a second-century-B.C.E. Hellenistic author of whom information is sparse and none of it direct. Knowledge of Cleodemus depends on one quotation in Josephus' *Jewish Antiquities* (1.240-41). Josephus did not read Cleodemus directly but found him in the well-known compilation made by Cornelius Alexander Polyhistor of Rome, who lived in the mid-first century B.C.E. Alexander actually refers to him as "Cleodemus, the prophet, also called Malchus." Eusebius, the Christian apologetic historian of the third century, also cites Cleodemus but does so by quoting the Josephus passage (*Praep. Evang.* 9.20.2-4).

Cleodemus has been variously identified by scholars as Jewish, Samaritan, or pagan, either Phoenician or Syrian. The name "Malchus" is clearly Semitic, deriving from *m-l-k,* "king," but one cannot say with certainly whether Cleodemus was Jewish, Samaritan, or of some other Semitic ethnicity. While it is *prima facie* likely that the fragment was authored by a Jew or Samaritan, an author from a different Semitic background is also possible since parallels in content can be found. Unfortunately, there is no record of the title of Cleodemus' work, though perhaps the best suggestion is that this fragment was found in Alexander Polyhistor's work on Libya, which may suggest that Cleodemus' book was also concerning Libya or a related topic.

Cleodemus is significant as an example of a popular Hellenistic mode of literature about the past that synthesized Eastern traditions (e.g., North African, Mesopotamian, Levantian, and Persian) with Greek traditions. More specifically, Cleodemus combines Jewish traditions regarding Abraham stemming from Genesis with Greek ethnographic, founder, and hero stories. Josephus calls upon Alexander Polyhistor's citation of Cleodemus as testimony to the veracity of his own statements regarding Abraham's progeny as colony founders (*Ant.* 1.238-39).

According to Gen. 25:1-6 Abraham married a certain Keturah after his wife Sarah died. Listed are their six sons, seven grandsons, and three great-grandsons. Cleodemus mentions three of them by name, Iapheras, Sures, and Iaphras, and gives important information regarding their subsequent history. The city of Ephra, which may refer to Carthage or some now unknown African city, was named after Iaphers; Sures is the eponymous ancestor of Assyria; and the entire continent of Africa took its name from Iaphras. "Africa" for most Latin authors was equivalent to the Greek "Libya" and referred to the parts of the continent not considered Egypt. Thus, Abraham's children were presented as the eponymous ancestors of a city and of nations, in both Asia and Africa. In terms of ethnographic relations, such claims are qualitatively no different than those of the earlier Israelite authors who linked well-known peoples and nations to Israelite ancestors (e.g., Gen. 10:1-32; 25:1-6).

Cleodemus proceeds to give an etiological explanation for the significance of Iapheras and Iaphras that involves them in a legend of the famous Heracles and makes Abraham an ancestor to some of the children of Heracles. Heracles, son of Zeus and Alcmene, was a popular hero even among non-Greeks, and he was often identified with foreign deities. The myth of Heracles defeating the Libyan giant Antaeus is known from many authors (e.g., Pindar, Euripides, Apollodorus, and Plutarch). Antaeus, son of Posidon, was the not-so-hospitable ruler of Libya who killed strangers by forcing them to wrestle. Heracles took the bait but defeated and killed the ill-tempered ruler. According to Cleodemus, Abraham's sons were accomplices in this famous heroic deed. What is more, Abraham's granddaughter marries Heracles and the bloodline of the Greek hero is mixed with that of the Jewish patriarch. The progeny of the two is a people of North Africa known as the Sophakes.

Having such a small scrap of his overall work, one cannot be confident of the genre of Cleodemus' writing. Numerous authors before and after Cleodemus link a variety of foreign peoples and individuals to stories of Heracles; it was a widespread historiographic and mythological convention (cf. Plutarch, *Sertorius* 9.4-5). It is also likely that Cleodemus drew on Greek sources before him for his Greco-African narrative. Regardless of original intentions (of Cleodemus or the author of Genesis), such claims were sometimes taken as serious history, as Josephus' argument makes clear. Similarly, according to a putative Spartan letter cited in 1 Macc. 12:21, the "Spartans and the Jews are brethren and are of the family of Abraham."

Cleodemus' claims should not be overstated; his fragment is not a fulsome aggrandizement of Jews that credits Abraham with being the great ancestor of the Greeks or other important cultures (e.g., Egypt, Rome, Persia, and Babylon). He interweaves Jewish and non-Jewish traditions that connect Jewish, Greek, African, and Asian "histories" and peoples. Historical, literary, cultural, and even religious weavings were one way that Jewish authors negotiated their own traditions in their Hellenistic environment. Cleodemus' work also represents popular assumptions about etymology as he explains the origin of some current people names and

CLOTHING AND DRESS

shows the common Hellenistic belief in the antiquity of Eastern peoples.

BIBLIOGRAPHY

R. DORAN 1985, "Cleodemus Malchus," in *OTP* 2:883-87. • E. GRUEN 1998, *Heritage and Hellenism,* Berkeley: University of California Press, 151-53. • C. R. HOLLADAY 1983, *Fragments from Hellenistic Jewish Authors,* vol. 1, Chico, Calif.: Scholars Press, 245-59. • F. JACOBY 1958, *Die Fragmente der griechischen Historiker,* Leiden: Brill, 3C: 686-87. • E. SCHÜRER 1986, *The History of the Jewish People in the Age of Jesus Christ,* vol. 3.1, rev. and ed. G. Vermes et al., Edinburgh: Clark, 526-28.

See also: Greek Authors on Jews and Judaism

JAMES E. BOWLEY

Clothing and Dress

There are two main sources for knowledge of how Jews dressed in the Second Temple period: material evidence and textual evidence. The material evidence itself is of two types: artistic representations (e.g., coins, sculptures, mosaics) and actual articles of clothing recovered from archaeological excavations (e.g., at Qumran, ʿEin Gedi, Masada, and the Cave of Letters). The textual evidence also comes in two forms: incidental mention in literary works (e.g., *Testament* of *Job, Joseph and Aseneth,* the Gospels) and halakic rulings recorded in later rabbinic literature. With a few notable exceptions, the articles of clothing that Jews wore in the Persian, Hellenistic, and early Roman periods, in both the land of Israel and the Diaspora, resembled to a large extent the styles of dress typical of non-Jews.

Functions of clothing

In addition to providing protection from the elements, clothing served as an identification of Jewish nationality, status (e.g., social, economic, and marital), and task engagement (e.g., worship, occupation). Items of clothing could also provide apotropaic protection (the power to ward off evil or bad luck). The provisions in rabbinic literature reflect a desire to prevent the adoption of non-Jewish clothing, curb extravagance, ensure ritual cleanliness, and, particularly for women, ensure their chastity. Scholars differ on the extent to which the rabbinic rulings on clothing were actually observed by all classes and in all locations; the rulings, for example, may have been followed more strictly among the rabbinic families and in larger cities, but less so among peasants and in small, agricultural villages. Particular distinctions in dress required by religion were the prohibition against mixing two different fibers in a single garment *(shaatnez)* and, for men, the wearing of *tzitzit* (tassels) and leaving their hair and beard long.

Children's Garments

A mother snugly wrapped her baby in cloth or blankets (swaddling) to help the baby acquire straight limbs and posture. A toddler was dressed in a tunic (a rectangular cloth with neck and arm holes). To ward off evil, mothers tied an amulet bag at the corner(s) of the child's tunic. A child's tunic found in the Cave of Letters had at each of its four corners small amulet bags, filled variously with a large salt crystal, seeds, some rat dung, and unidentified materials.

Men's Garments

While the minimum proper dress in public for a man consisted of a white cloak with *tzitzit* and tunic *(haluq),* normal dress included a belt, an undertunic, shoes, and, for married men, a hat. Additional male garments could include a second cloak, trousers, breeches, a girdle for the loins, money belt, neck scarf, felt cap, an apron, shoes, and slippers/socks.

The tying of *tzitzit,* made by twining blue or purple *(tekkelet)* wool thread at the corners of a cloak, was a distinctly Jewish custom and a reminder of the covenant between God and the Israelites (Num. 15:37-41). A current theory is that the dye came from the ink sacs of the Murex mollusk. The rectangular fringed cloak *(tallit)* had selvages longer than the borders. Scholars, rabbis, and elite men wore tallits more finely woven and larger than those of common men. Scholars' tallits were so large that the purple stripes (sg. *ʿimrah*) of their tunics were hidden.

The construction of the Jewish tunic *(haluq)* is disputed. A number of scholars state that, unlike the

Bronze mirrors with wooden mirror cases from the Cave of Letters in Naḥal Ḥever *(Israel Exploration Society)*

Wool tunics with colored stripes *(clavi)* from the Cave of Letters in Naḥal Ḥever *(Israel Exploration Society)*

Greco-Roman tunic (made by sewing two rectangular pieces of cloth together at the shoulders and sides), the Jewish tunic was made of a single piece of cloth. Yet the tunics found in the Cave of Letters were woven in two pieces like the Greco-Roman tunic. Rabbinic literature declared a tunic completed, for purposes of ritual cleanliness, when its neck hole was formed, a final stage that could occur only when two pieces of cloth were joined together (*t. Kelim* 5:1). Other rulings indicate that the tunic was made of two pieces of cloth (*y. Šabb.* 15a; *m. Neg.* 11:9). Such construction enabled its wearer to replace only that side of the tunic that had become ritually unclean, rather than discarding a whole tunic made of a single piece of cloth. The front and backs of tunics could be decorated with purple stripes that ran vertically down from each shoulder, front and back; these stripes presumably were borrowed from Roman tunics.

The Cave of Letters produced wool mantles with inwoven reddish-brown or blackish bands; these bands were either gamma-shaped or notched. Colored clothing was gendered: while *Sifre Deuteronomy* (115b) proscribes a woman from wearing a man's white garments and a man from wearing colored garments, there is evidence that men did wear dyed clothing (*b. Mo'ed Qaṭan* 23a). Some mantles had small checkerboard boxes generally interpreted as weavers' marks.

A distinctly Jewish custom was the wearing of *tefillin* or phylacteries, small boxes containing scriptures written on parchment strips and tied to the left upper arm (if right-handed) or right upper arm (if left-handed) and to the forehead. Observance of this custom varied according to social status, time, and place. It was obligatory in rabbinic times, but ignored in some places in the Diaspora.

Occupational clothing mentioned in rabbinic literature includes leather hunting gloves, and, for workmen, leather sleeves and chest protectors. For strenuous work, a man might strip down to his loincloth, as did Peter when fishing (John 21:7).

Footwear for both sexes included laced shoes and leather sandals. As they were Roman military footwear, hobnailed shoes were forbidden.

Priestly Garments

When in the Temple, priests wore garments and turbans made of very fine linen. The high priest wore garments that signified his role as an intermediary between God and Israel. Over his linen tunic, he wore a sleeveless woolen blue robe decorated with linen pomegranates. Its fringe was composed of small golden bells alternating with tassels of blue, purple, and scarlet wool threads (the only exception to *shaatnez*). The all-linen chest garment (ephod), decorated with blue, purple, scarlet, and gold linen threads, hung from his shoulders by two shoulder straps, each with an onyx stone engraved with the names of six of the tribes of Israel. The urim and thummin (sacred lots made of jewel or stone and used to discern the divine will) were attached to the ephod. The all-linen breastplate, placed over the ephod, was similarly made, but had twelve precious stones, each engraved with a tribal name, arranged in three rows. On his head he wore a turban decorated with a triple golden crown (Josephus, *Ant.* 3.7.6) and a gold plate that hung from a blue thread and was engraved with the phrase "Holy to the LORD." Levite priests kept hair and beards trimmed.

Women's Garments

In general, women wore a long tunic belted under their breasts, and again around their waists, in such a way as to produce a deep over-fold of material hanging to hip level. Rabbinic literature assumes that, ideally, maidens generally were secluded in their homes and, if ever outside of the house, veiled their heads with a mantle. A bride's uncovered head, however, proclaimed her virginity. Prior to the destruction of the Temple, a bride wore an elaborate crown constructed of salt and brimstone, with entwined myrtle, roses, and gold thread. She wore a richly decorated gown and much jewelry.

A husband was required to provide his wife annually clothing to the value of fifty *zuzin* (silver *denarii*) each year; on each of the three feasts, he had also to provide her with a cap, a belt, and shoes. The married woman's dressing of her head could include plaited

Cosmetic items from dwellings of Jewish rebels at Masada, including a wooden comb (lower right), a bronze mirror case (upper right), and bronze eye-shadow sticks (lower left)

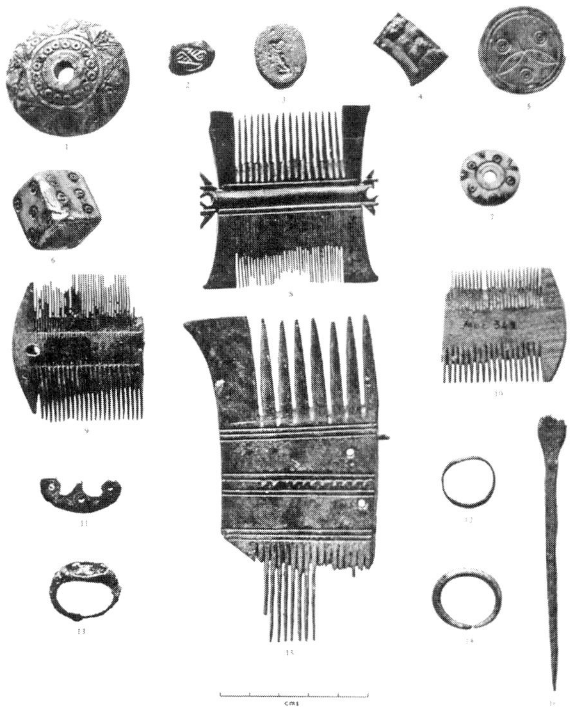

A spindle whorl (upper left), wooden combs (center), and an iron cosmetic spoon (lower right) from the caves in Wadi Murabbaʿat

hair and the wearing of two kerchiefs, a forehead band, hairnet, and ribbons that hung down to her chin. She was required to veil her head when praying and when going out of the home; appearing with uncovered head in public was grounds for divorce, and an adulteress was punished by having her veil torn off. Some women also veiled their heads within the house as a matter of morality and religious duty. Richer women might wear wigs, and some women wore phylacteries. Cosmetics included eye shadow, rouge, and perfume.

Mourning Garments

Both men and women covered their heads and concealed their faces. They also poured dust on their heads and tore their garments or exchanged them for rough sackcloth or black clothing. Men might shave the front of their hair, and women cut their hair.

Jewelry

Until the fourth century C.E., Jewish custom frowned on the wearing of jewelry. Rabbinic literature ruled that a woman might not wear in public head bangles, nose-rings, rings with no seals, and tiaras with the picture of Jerusalem. Other items of feminine jewelry included gold earrings, necklaces, bracelets, and anklets. The extent to which Hellenistic jewelry styles influenced Jewish styles is unclear, but in the Roman period, glass beads and cameo stones became more common, as did the Roman style of setting semi-precious stones and pearls in gold. Men wore signet rings as a sign of their identity and authority.

Non-Jewish Clothing

Though the rabbis forbade the wearing of the Roman togas, the use of transliterated Greek and Latin clothing words in rabbinic literature indicates that the wearing of Greco-Roman clothing was common. Rabbinic literature mentions Dalmatian garments, Cilician shaggy goat's hair cloaks, and cloaks made in Brundisium (Italy).

BIBLIOGRAPHY

L. ARCHER 1990, *Her Price Is beyond Rubies: The Jewish Woman in Graeco-Roman Palestine,* Sheffield: JSOT Press. • C. BAKER 2004, "Imagined Households," in *Religion and Society in Roman Palestine: Old Questions, New Approaches,* ed. D. Edwards, New York: Routledge, 113-28. • D. EDWARDS 1992, "Dress and Ornamentation," in *ABD,* vol. 2, New York: Doubleday, 232-38. • T. ILAN 1996, *Jewish Women in Greco-Roman Palestine,* Peabody, Mass.: Hendrickson. • L. ROUSSIN 1994, "Costume in Roman Palestine: Archaeological Remains and the Evidence from the Mishnah," in *The World of Roman Costume,* ed. J. Sebesta and L. Bonfante, Madison: University of Wisconsin Press, 182-90.

See also: Jewelry JUDITH LYNN SEBESTA

Coins

Since they were introduced some 2,600 years ago, coins have become an integral part of daily life, reflecting in their own way some of humanity's deepest aspirations. From generation to generation, kings, rulers, cities, and states have issued countless numbers of coins, which offer a wealth of insight into the actions of individuals and societies. Although diminutive in size, coins are significant historical documents. Their symbols and inscriptions make it possible to trace the unwritten history of states and cities and to verify obscure accounts from other sources. Most important, because coins constitute direct physical evidence of a period, they have a certain advantage over information from literary sources — especially since ancient historians often copied their material from other writers, and most did not actually witness the events they wrote about. Deciphering the language of coins — their vocabulary of symbols and abbreviated inscriptions — uncovers a treasure trove of information about the societies that minted them.

Coins of the Persian Period

The earliest phase of the monetary phenomenon in Palestine (late sixth to early fifth centuries B.C.E.) is witnessed by the presence of Greek Archaic silver coins and later Athenian issues. The silver coinages of Philistia (southern Palestine), those of Ashdod, Ashkelon, and Gaza, date to the mid-fifth and fourth centuries B.C.E. and represent the next meaningful phase in the monetary development of Palestine: the transition into a coined economy. These three coastal cities of Philistia were prosperous under the Achaemenid rule, benefiting from a semi-autonomous status, as is evident from their municipal issues.

During the late Persian period (fourth century B.C.E.), silver issues of several denominations were struck at Samaria, and numerous minute silver coins were issued in Jerusalem, bearing the Paleo-Hebrew legend YHD. Apparently this latter expression had a twofold meaning and indicates the name of the city Jerusalem as the capital *(bîrtā')* of Judah the province *(mĕdintā')*. This assumption is based on the fact that, at the time of the minting of these coins and during the previous centuries, YHD was the name of Jerusalem. 2 Chronicles 2:26, 28 mentions that Amaziah king of Judah was buried with his fathers in the city of Judah (769 B.C.E.). There is no doubt that the "city of Judah" is Jerusalem, the burial place of Judean kings. On the other hand, *Yehud* was the current name of the province Judah during the fifth and fourth centuries B.C.E. Some of the YHD issues used as prototypes the Athenian tetradrachm, which was the international currency of the fifth and forth centuries B.C.E.

In addition, we find local motifs such as the lily flower (fleur-de-lis). This white flower, the *lilium candidum*, was a symbol of purity and was regarded as the choicest among flowers. In the words of the prophet Hosea, "I will be like the dew for Israel; he shall blossom like the lily" (Hos. 14:6). The lily is also referred to allegorically in the Song of Songs (Cant. 2:1) and was a favorite simile later in Hebrew poetry. This flower was also an important source of perfume, which was certainly used for sacred purposes and constituted one of the main kinds of spices used in ancient times. Though not found in profusion in Israel today, we may assume that it was once common in all parts of the country. The motif of the lily is apparently derived from the design that graced the capitals of the two main pillars which stood in front of the Temple — Jachin and Boaz. The lily became a popular motif in Jewish art of the Second Temple period and appears in other coins struck in Jerusalem during the second and first centuries B.C.E. under Antiochus VII, John Hyrcanus I, and Alexander Jannaeus.

Ptolemaic Coins of Judah

Jerusalem was virtually the only mint of the Ptolemaic kingdom to strike silver fractions, while the Lagid kings were promoting the use of bronze coinage with a similar range of values. The principal motifs appearing on these coins — the portrait of the Ptolemaic ruler and the eagle — used as prototypes the most characteristic designs appearing on Ptolemaic coinage. Regular precious metal production ceased at the other Syro-Phoenician mints in the sixth year of Ptolemy III. Accordingly, 241/40 B.C.E. may be the date at which the Jerusalem mint finally closed.

Hasmonean Coins

After a long hiatus in which Jewish coins were not struck, the Jerusalem mint began to function, this time under Hasmonean rule. From then on, the minting of Jewish coins continued without interruption during almost two centuries under the rule of the Hasmonean and Herodian kings. Hasmonean coins are distinguished by their long and interesting inscriptions in the Paleo-Hebrew script, as well as in Aramaic and Greek. They also form the largest group of Jewish coins depicting motifs connected mainly with fertility.

Bronze prutah of Mattathias Antigonus (40-37 B.C.E.). Obverse: The Temple menorah surrounded by Greek legend, "The King Anti[gonus]." Reverse: The showbread table with Paleo-Hebrew legend, "Mattityah high priest." *(Israel Museum inventory nos. 3650, 14232)*

On the coins of John Hyrcanus I and Alexander Jannaeus (ca. 128-76 B.C.E.), the lily appears again. Other coins bear the designs of an anchor, a star and diadem, a palm branch, and a helmet. Most of these motifs were barrowed from the repertoire of Seleucid coin designs but appear here in a Jewish fashion. However, the most prominent symbol of Hasmonean coins is undoubtedly the double cornucopia with a pomegranate between them and an inscription within a wreath on the reverse of the coin.

Mattathias Antigonus (40-37 B.C.E.), the last Hasmonean ruler, struck large and impressive bronze coins, apparently as a challenge to Herod the Great, who was appointed king of Judea by the Romans in 40 B.C.E. In 37 B.C.E., Herod conquered Jerusalem and Hasmonean rule came to an end.

Herodian Issues

In general, coins have universally borne symbols, identifying the despot, dynast, elected official, or appointed body. Different designs have been employed to express their claim to rule, the most common one being the ruler's portrait. However, coins intended for Jewish populations were generally different in that the second commandment forbade the use of graven images. Consequently, on many Jewish coins a variety of other symbols such as wreaths, diadems, royal canopies, helmets, and scepters were used. However, on several Herodian coins there are portraits of the Jewish kings and their children.

For 130 years, the Herodian dynasty maintained its rule over large portions of the ancient land of Israel. Herod was an ambitious king who attempted to attract the attention and admiration of his masters, the Romans. To this end he invested vast amounts of money in projects such as the Temple in Jerusalem, the palace of Masada, and the harbor at Caesarea. Herod used only generalized symbols on his coins such as an anchor, a helmet, or a palm branch.

When Herod died in 4 B.C.E., he left his kingdom to his three sons. Herod Archelaus became the ethnarch of Judah, Herod Antipas the tetrarch of the Galilee, and Herod Philip the tetrarch of the Golan, Batanea, and Trachonitis.

Herod Archelaus' coins, minted in Jerusalem from 4 B.C.E. to 6 C.E., usually bear maritime symbols since the important harbor of Caesarea was in his domain. The coins of Herod Antipas (4 B.C.E. to 39 C.E.) were minted in Tiberias, which he founded in 19 C.E. in honor of the emperor Tiberius. Antipas' coins depict palm branches, palm trees, and clusters of dates, all symbols of the region over which he presided. Herod Philip (4 B.C.E. to 34 C.E.) minted his coins at Caesarea Paneas (Philippi). The pagan nature of his coins reflects the large non-Jewish population under his jurisdiction. The issues he minted with his own portrait are the earliest known coins bearing the portrait of a Jewish ruler.

Agrippa I (37 to 44 C.E.), the grandson of Herod, was appointed king of Judah by the emperor Gaius Caligula. Jewish symbols such as three ears of barley appear on his coins, which were struck in Jerusalem in 42 C.E. However, Agrippa's most famous coins are those with his portrait and that of his son Agrippa II, and an issue with the inscription "coin of King Agrippa" in Greek.

Coins of the First Jewish Revolt

The coins issued during the First Jewish War against Rome are the most famous among ancient Jewish coinage, but they were correctly identified only a few decades ago (mainly as a result of archaeological excavation and the discovery of hoards). During the five years of the war (66-70 C.E.), an abundance of impressive silver shekels and half shekels were struck depicting the omer cup and the legend "Shekel of Israel" in Paleo-Hebrew on the obverse, and a stem with three pomegranates and the legend "Jerusalem the Holy" on the reverse. The shekels are dated according to the years of the war (from one to five). During the second, third, and fourth years of the war, the mint of Jerusalem produced bronze coins as well.

Shekel from year one of the First Jewish Revolt. The Hebrew shekel depicts a chalice on the obverse and a branch with three pomegranates encircled by a border of dots on the reverse. Minted in Jerusalem 66 C.E. *(Israel Museum, inventory no. 1475)*

The Siloam Hoard of Tyrian and Jewish shekels from the First Jewish Revolt (66–70 C.E.) originally held approximately 40 coins, of which only 12 remain. These coins provided one of the first clues for the correct dating of Jewish shekels from the First Revolt. *(Israel Museum)*

Bar Kokhba Coinage

In the late summer of 132 C.E. the Jews in Judea began a long and bitter war against the Roman Empire. They were led by Shimʿon ben Kosiba, who became popularly known as Bar Kokhba or "Son of Star." The man called himself "Shimʿon Prince of Israel" and usurped the imperial prerogative of coinage. Only in the late autumn of 135 C.E. did his rule finally come to an end. In their over three years of independence, the rebels created a Jewish state. For the economy of this state they needed money.

The Bar Kokhba Revolt Hoard (135 C.E.), a sampling of coins in circulation during the period. The hoard includes Roman and Bar Kokhba coins that were themselves struck over Roman originals. *(Israel Museum)*

Roman silver and bronze coins were available in quantity, and the rebels could have used these without further ado. But this would have answered neither the spirit nor the goals of Shimʿon and his men. The rebels undoubtedly understood that widely circulating coins offered the best means of propaganda in their time. For that reason, they created their own coinage, silver tetradrachms (four drachms), drachms or denarii, and three bronze denominations, simply and quickly by overstriking the Roman imperial and provincial coins with Jewish motifs and Paleo-Hebrew legends devoted to Jerusalem and the famous Temple. This act not only symbolized the desired sovereignty of the Jewish people but also their opposition and partial victory over their Roman oppressors by defacing in the process the original Roman coins.

BIBLIOGRAPHY
H. GITLER AND C. LORBER 2006, "A New Chronology for the Ptolemaic Yehud Coinage," *American Journal of Numismatics* 18: 1-41. • H. GITLER AND O. TAL 2006, *The Coinage of Philistia of the Fifth and Fourth Centuries BC: A Study of the Earliest Coins of Palestine,* Milan: Ennerre. • Y. MESHORER 1982, *Ancient Jewish Coinage,* 2 vols., New York: Amphora Books. • Y. MESHORER 2001, *A Treasury of Jewish Coins: From the Persian Period to Bar Kokhba,* New York: Amphora Books. • Y. MESHORER, AND S. QEDAR 1999, *Samarian Coinage,* Jerusalem: Israel Numismatic Society. HAIM GITLER

Common Judaism → Sanders, Ed Parish

Contracts from the Judean Desert

About sixty-five documents from the Judean Desert are contracts and other business papers that represent some seventy-five transactions. Approximately twenty of the contracts are for the sale of real estate, whether fields or houses. Sixteen, if those of P. Murabbaʿat 24 are counted separately, are leases of real estate. Eleven are contracts of deposit, loan, or acknowledgment of debt; nine are contracts of marriage or dowry. There are also scattered documents recording the purchase of crops, receipt of gifts, sale of movables, concession of rights, and proceedings of divorce. Nearly all the texts are written on papyrus, as nonliterary documents in antiquity generally were.

Locations of the Finds

Most of the contracts were found in caves at Wadi Murabbaʿat and Naḥal Ḥever, the same caves that yielded letters of Shimʿon Bar Kokhba, the leader of the Second Jewish Revolt against Rome. At least some and perhaps all of those formerly ascribed to Naḥal Ṣe'elim probably came from Naḥal Ḥever. In nearly all the documents, one or both contracting parties are Jewish. In a few cases, the documents relate to property subsequently owned by Jews. All but two or three (P. Mur 18 [55/56 C.E.], P. Yadin 36 [59-69 C.E.], and P. Mur 114 [possibly 171 C.E.]) are dated explicitly or by paleography to the years 70-135 C.E., that is, from the end of the First Revolt to the end of the Bar Kokhba Revolt, mostly toward the end of the period. The documents were presumably brought to the caves by Jews who left their homes during the critical parts of the latter revolt, and either died in the caves or, if they succeeded in escaping, left the documents behind.

Languages Represented

About half of the documents (counting P. Mur 24 as one) are written in Aramaic, the traditional language in the region for legal transactions. About a quarter are in Greek, the language of civil administration in the eastern provinces of the Roman Empire. Nine are in Hebrew, all from the years 133-135 C.E., and represent 60 percent of the contracts from those years (76 percent, if the eleven contracts of P. Mur 24 are counted separately). This statistic reflects the nationalist revival of Hebrew associated with the Bar Kokhba Revolt. Six contracts are in Nabatean and were written in the region of Arabia, all but one when that region was still an independent kingdom. The proportion of documents written in Greek is substantially higher for those written in the Province of Arabia than for those written in Judea. What governed the choice of language between Aramaic and Greek is not clear. The determining factor was evidently not the main language of the parties involved; in nearly half of the Greek documents, the subscriptions of the parties are written in Aramaic.

Contracts Written in Duplicate

About half the contracts were drawn up in duplicate, with the scribe writing the text twice on the same sheet of papyrus, one copy above the other. The lower copy was usually written first. The upper copy was then folded in narrow horizontal strips from the top down, tied with string looped and knotted at several points, and in at least one case (P. Mur 29) sealed. Witnesses affixed their signatures on the back of the sheet, one next to each of the ties, perpendicular to the direction of the writing of the text on the front. The bottom copy was similarly folded in horizontal strips from the bottom up, but was neither tied nor sealed. The advantage of this elaborate procedure was that the inner sealed copy could provide authentication of the text if challenged.

This practice of writing a contract in duplicate is familiar from Greek documents found in Egypt dating mainly from the third century B.C.E. By the end of that century, the practice fell into decline in Egypt, and by the first century B.C.E. it had disappeared almost entirely. Where Greek double documents have appeared elsewhere, as in Dura Europos, the inner copy is abbreviated in varying degrees. In contracts found in the Judean Desert, however, the inner text is generally a complete, unabridged copy of the outer text, even when registry in a public archive is anticipated, as in P. Yadin 19. It is now accepted that the double document form did not originate with the Greeks but rather was adopted by them from their eastern, Semitic neighbors, for which cuneiform precedents have been adduced. The full use of this form by Jews even in Greek-language contracts may therefore be taken as an expression of their Jewish and Semitic heritage, rather than of Hellenization. This is likely the form of the sale document mentioned in Jer. 32:11, 14 and is apparently the *geṭ mĕkūšar* discussed in *m. B. Bat.* 10:1 and the associated pericopes in each Talmud.

Signatures and Subscriptions

The contracts are generally signed by witnesses, in varying numbers, mostly three, five, or seven, exceptionally two or six. In addition, the contracts are generally signed by at least one of the parties. Talmudic literature refers to this practice, even though the halakha insists that only the signatures of the witnesses are legally determinative. In talmudic literature it seems that such subscriptions by the parties took the form of a simple statement such as "I, so-and-so, wrote this [the signature]." Subscriptions in Greek contracts from Egypt contain summaries of the transactions. In contracts from the Judean desert, the style of the subscription matches the language of the main body of the document. In documents whose main language is Aramaic, the subscription is invariably of the short, talmudic form. In documents whose main language is Greek, the subscription is in the form of a summary, regardless of whether the subscription itself is written in Greek or, as is often the case, in Aramaic.

Formal and Stylistic Features

Of the Greek documents sufficiently preserved for a determination, most are couched in the form of a *homologia,* a declaration by one (or less commonly by both) of the parties acknowledging that a binding transaction took place or that an obligation was undertaken. Thus the main body of the text begins with a form of the verb *homologeō,* "acknowledge." Most of these are couched in subjective style, that is, the verb "acknowledge" is in the first person, and references to the parties are thereafter in the first and second persons. A small number (P. Mur 115, P. Yadin 17, and perhaps P. Yadin 37) are couched in objective style, with the verb for "acknowledge" and all subsequent references to the parties in the third person, in *oratio obliqua.* Three Greek documents are not homologies but rather assert directly in objective style that a transaction occurred. Two of these, P. Yadin 18 and P. Ḥever 69, are marriage documents; the third, P. Yadin 19, is a gift given on the occasion of the marriage in P. Yadin 18. A fourth document, P. Yadin 37 = P. Ḥever 65, also a marriage contract, may well be of this form.

The Hebrew and Aramaic documents are evenly divided in this respect. Those couched as a *homologia* have the verb for "say" in the third person and continue in the first and second persons of *oratio directa.* The others are in either objective, subjective, or mixed style. Two declarations of indebtedness, P. Mur. 18 in Aramaic and P. Ḥever 49 in Hebrew (see Broshi and Qimron 1994), present an enigma because of anomalies at the beginning or end. These documents are best taken as straight homologies, closely modeled on the Greek, despite the odd placement of the parties' signatures at the end (Katzoff in Gulak 1994). Some scholars, though, take the introductory verb "acknowledge" as a passive whose subject is the name of the creditor, despite the problematic syntax thus created and the absence of Greek or Aramaic models.

Several documents end with a phrase to the effect that, having been asked, one or both of the parties to the transaction acknowledged that the transaction was done correctly (P. Yadin 17, 18, 20, 21, 22, 37). This is a declaration that the Roman *stipulatio* had taken place and would have the effect in Roman law of turning the obligation into a unilateral, *stricti iuris* one. It is doubtful whether a proper exchange of question and answer of the Roman *stipulatio* really took place in any of these cases, but it is significant for the extent of Romanization in the region that the scribes took the trouble to write the phrase into the written contracts, nearly a century before this was done in Egypt and in Dura Europos.

On the whole, the contents and usage of the contracts in Hebrew and Aramaic are what may be expected on the basis of rabbinic literature. P. Yadin 10, Babatha's *ketubba* or marriage contract (Friedman 1996), and the sale documents (Schiffman 2005) are the most striking in this respect. Similarly, the contracts written in Greek follow the conventions of Greek documents known from Egypt. Even the Greek documents display elements drawn from the Jewish tradition in otherwise inexplicable divergences from usual Greek practice (contra Wasserstein 1989 and Cotton 1998).

Bibliography

Inventory of the Documents

H. M. Cotton, W. E. H. Cockle, and F. G. B. Millar 1995, "The Papyrology of the Roman Near East: A Survey," *Journal of Roman Studies* 85: 214-35.

Texts

P. Benoit, J. T. Milik, and R. de Vaux, eds. 1961, *Les Grottes de Murabbaʿât,* DJD 2, Oxford: Clarendon. • H. M. Cotton and A. Yardeni, eds. 1997, *Aramaic, Hebrew and Greek Documentary Texts from Naḥal Ḥever and Other Sites with an Appendix Containing Alleged Qumran Texts (The Seiyal Collection II),* DJD 27, Oxford: Clarendon. • N. Lewis, ed. 1989, *The Documents from the Bar Kokhba Period in the Cave of Letters: Greek Papyri,* Jerusalem: Israel Exploration Society. • Y. Yadin and J. C. Greenfield, eds. 1989, *Aramaic and Nabatean Signatures and Subscriptions,* Jerusalem: Israel Exploration Society. • Y. Yadin, J. C. Greenfield, A. Yardeni, and B. Levine, eds. 2002, *The Documents from the Bar Kokhba Period in the Cave of Letters: Hebrew, Aramaic and Nabatean-Aramaic Papyri,* Jerusalem: Israel Exploration Society.

Studies

M. Broshi and E. Qimron 1986, "A House Sale Deed from Kefar Baru from the Time of Bar Kokhba," *IEJ* 36: 201-14. • M. Broshi and E. Qimron 1994, "A Hebrew I.O.U. Note from the Second Year of the Bar Kokhba Revolt," *JJS* 45: 286-94. • H. M. Cotton 1998, "The Rabbis and the Documents," in *Jews in a Graeco-Roman World,* ed. M. Goodman, Oxford:

Oxford University Press, 167-79. • M. A. FRIEDMAN 1996, "Babatha's 'Ketubba': Some Preliminary Observations," *IEJ* 46: 55-76. • A. GULAK 1994, *Legal Documents in the Talmud in Light of Greek Papyri and Greek and Roman Law,* ed. and suppl. R. Katzoff, Jerusalem: Magnes. • R. KATZOFF 1987, "Part II: Legal Commentary," in N. Lewis, R. Katzoff, and J. Greenfield, "Papyrus Yadin 18," *IEJ* 37: 229-50 at 236-47. • R. KATZOFF 1991, "Papyrus Yadin 18 Again: A Rejoinder," *JQR* 82: 171-76. • R. KATZOFF 1994, "An Interpretation of P. Yadin 19: A Jewish Gift after Death," *Proceedings of the 20th International Congress of Papyrologists, 23-29 August, 1992,* ed. A. Bülow-Jacobsen, Copenhagen: Museum Tusculanum Press, 562-65. • R. KATZOFF 2007, "P. Yadin 21 and Rabbinic Law on Widows' Rights," *JQR* 97: 545-75. • M. R. LEHMANN 1963, "Studies in the Murabbaʿat and Naḥal Ḥever Documents," *RevQ* 4: 53-81. • Z. SAFRAI 2005, "Halakhic Observance in the Judean Desert Documents," in *Law in the Documents of the Judaean Desert,* ed. R. Katzoff and D. Schaps, Leiden: Brill, 205-36. • L. H. SCHIFFMAN 2005, "Reflections on the Deeds of Sale from the Judaean Desert in Light of Rabbinic Literature," in *Law in the Documents of the Judaean Desert,* ed. R. Katzoff and D. Schaps, Leiden: Brill, 85-203. • A. WASSERSTEIN 1989, "A Marriage Contract from the Province of Arabia Nova: Notes on Papyrus Yadin 18," *JQR* 80: 93-130. • R. YARON 1960, "The Murabbaʿat Documents," *JJS* 11: 57-171.

See also: Babatha; Bar Kokhba Letters; Ḥever, Naḥal; Murabbaʿat, Wadi; Papyri RANON KATZOFF

Conversion and Proselytism

A range of literary and epigraphic sources attest to a widespread phenomenon of attraction to and participation in Judaism among Gentiles in antiquity. These sources have often been interpreted as evidence for a concerted effort among ancient Jews of winning converts through proselytization among the Gentiles. An accurate account of the evidence requires a terminological distinction between conversion and proselytism and an assessment of how these categories may best be applied to describe the phenomena in question.

Degrees of Commitment

Conversion to Judaism in the ancient world is often broadly defined as a Gentile's adoption of any number of characteristically Jewish ritual practices or beliefs. For instance, a Gentile might be identified as a convert merely for having recognized the God of the Jews as one among many, or alternatively, for having rejected polytheism in favor of the monotheism typically identified with Judaism. On a more mundane level, a Gentile likewise might be counted as a Jewish convert for having simply extended favors or benefits to Jewish acquaintances. Commitments of this sort did not require one's absolute dedication to Judaism and concomitant rejection of his or her prior religious or cultural orientation (Cohen 1999: 140-56).

Modern scholars often describe the Gentiles who made such commitments as informal converts to Judaism, referring to them semi-technically as Jewish sympathizers or as God-fearers. However, there is little evidence that ancient Jews considered these Gentiles to have been anything more than friends. The modern scholarly construction of informal conversion presupposes xenophobic Jewish legal standards that prohibited social contact with Gentiles who had not converted to Judaism in some undefined capacity. In fact, Jewish law made no distinction between those Gentiles who were favorably disposed to Jews and those who were not.

Formal Conversion

In contrast, Jewish law did maintain a well-defined legal category for those Gentiles who undertook formal conversion to Judaism. A formal convert ideally was to be extended the legal status of the resident alien (Hebr. *gēr*), a term which the LXX typically renders as *prosēlytos* ("one who has arrived at"; cf. *apostatēs,* "one standing apart from"). Unlike the so-called informal converts, a proselyte was to assume the normative legal status of one who was Jewish by birth (cf. Lev. 18:26; 19:33-34; Num. 15:14-16).

Proselytes were expected to integrate themselves into their local Jewish communities, as well as to commit to complete observance of the traditional Jewish law and cult. The book of Judith succinctly expresses what was expected of a male proselyte in reference to the conversion of Achior the Ammonite, who reportedly "believed firmly in God, and was circumcised, and joined the house of Israel" (Jdt. 14:10). Complete observance of the Law demanded circumcision as a prerequisite for formal conversion to Judaism for men (see, e.g., Josephus, *Ant.* 20.38-48; cf. Collins 1985). For example, the book of Esther's unique reference to the Gentiles who "became Jews" (Esth. 8:17; Hebr. *mityāhădîm*) is rendered in the LXX as "were circumcised" *(perietemonto).* Male circumcision was also required of the Arabs who were compelled to join the Jewish nation upon being subjugated by the Hasmonean kings (Josephus, *Ant.* 13.257-58, 319; Strabo, *Geography* 16.2.34). The fact that circumcision was a prerequisite for formal conversion to Judaism motivated many early Christian authors to deter their readers from likewise adopting the ritual as a prerequisite for conversion to Christianity (e.g., Acts 15:1-5; Gal 2:1-21; Ignatius, *Phld.* 6:1).

Female Proselytes

Although female proselytes were held to the same standards of practice as their male counterparts, they lacked a symbolic ritual of conversion equivalent to male circumcision (although cf. Cohen 2005: 59-61). Initially, the only visible expression of conversion for a woman was her marriage to a Jewish man. The pseudepigraphic book *Joseph and Aseneth* depicts the Egyptian proselyte Aseneth as having undertaken an elaborate penitential process which included her demonstrative rejection of her native religion (*Jos. & Asen.* 10:10-13) in anticipation of her marriage to the Israelite scion Joseph. Although Aseneth's conversion is finalized by her consumption of a magical honeycomb (*Jos. & Asen.* 16:15-16), this esoteric rite is otherwise unattested and should not be considered a normative element of the conversion process for women. Perhaps seeking to rectify the lack of a definitive ritual for women, certain early rabbis tried to institute the penitential rite of immersion as an integral feature of the process of conversion for women and men alike (Cohen 1999: 218-25).

Proselyte Terminology

Ancient Jewish texts provide ample evidence of the occurrence of proselytism under the legal rubric of the *ger* during the Hellenistic and early Roman periods. For instance, Philo's elaboration of Exod. 22:20, an early reference to laws of the *gēr,* includes praise for proselytes who had joined the Jewish community (*Spec Leg.* 1.51-53). However, usage of the term outside of its scriptural context was relatively infrequent. Philo generally preferred to use the term *epēlys* ("alien") in reference to formal converts (e.g., *Praem.* 152; *Virt.* 102–104, 182, 219), while Josephus employed no uniform title for the various Jewish converts and sympathizers whom he discussed throughout his writings (see, e.g., *Ag. Ap.* 2.123-24, 209-10, 261, 282-86; *J.W.* 7.45; *Ant.* 14.110; 18.82; 20.195). Nonetheless, it is clear that Josephus associated the scriptural category of the *ger* with formal conversion to Judaism, as he alluded to the normative status of the scriptural law in effectuating the conversion of the royal house of Adiabene (*Ant.* 20.17-48, 75). The early rabbis likewise used the legal rubric of the *ger* as the basis for their legislation on formal conversion to Judaism.

The sporadic use of the proselyte terminology among Jewish writers seems to indicate that its technical implications were largely unknown among Gentiles. Indeed, Gentile authors who referred both to formal and to informal conversion to Judaism appear to have been unfamiliar with the term (cf., e.g., Horace, *Satirae* 1.4.142-43; Tacitus, *Historiae* 5.5; Juvenal, *Satirae* 14.96-106; Epictetus, in Arrian, *Epicteti Dissertationes* 2.19-20). Among literary sources, the proselyte terminology appears with regularity only in the New Testament book of Acts, where it used in apposition to other "Jews" or "Hebrews" who aligned themselves with the Christian mission (Acts 2:10-11; 6:5; 13:43). Although these references seem to make the dubious claim that proselytes were more inclined to join the Christian mission than other Jews, they also seem to make a genuine appeal to the mechanics of ancient Jewish proselytism. Also of interest in this respect is the Gospel of Matthew's unparalleled use of the term *prosēlytos* in what appears to be a reference to a Jewish initiate to the sect of the Pharisees (Matt. 23:15).

Although seldom used during the period under consideration, the term *prosēlytos* appears regularly in Jewish funerary inscriptions recovered throughout the Roman Empire. The epigraphic record thus clearly indicates that conversion to Judaism continued to occur long after the initiation of the Christian mission to the Gentiles.

A Jewish Mission to the Gentiles?

In light of the aforementioned evidence for widespread Gentile attraction to Judaism prior to the emergence of Christianity, there has been some debate over whether the impetus for Christian proselytizing was predicated upon an earlier Jewish mission to the Gentiles. Those who endorse this theory further intimate that the success of Jewish proselytizing in the Second Temple period provided the groundswell of receptivity to monotheism upon which the success of the Christian mission was based. In addition to the direct evidence for Jewish proselytism, this argument presupposes that the ancient Jewish apologetic literature directed toward Gentile audiences effectively served as missionary propaganda (Feldman 1993: 288-341). However, the literary sources offer little insight into the motivations behind those Gentiles who were attracted to Judaism in antiquity. Moreover, while they certainly aimed to win friends and supporters, no ancient Jewish authors expressed intentions to attract converts through their work. The few ancient witnesses that may be construed as allusions to Jewish proselytism are consistently hostile toward Judaism and present no substantive evidence of concerted missionary activity. Therefore, the argument in favor of active Jewish proselytizing among the Gentiles is highly conjectural (Goodman 1994: 60-90).

Motivations for Conversion

Even without the benefit of an active mission to the Gentiles, the demographic proliferation of Jews in the ancient world may reasonably be associated with the frequency of self-motivated conversion to Judaism. Many Gentiles aligned themselves with Judaism or undertook formal conversion in order to gain any of the many social advantages that came with one's alignment with a Jewish community. This casual attitude likely reflects a social reality in which people were motivated to convert to Judaism for reasons other than personal piety. Wealthy Gentiles may have aligned themselves with local Jewish communities in the interest of euergetism, while impoverished ones may have done so in the interest of benefiting from such efforts. Slaves were often compelled to convert in order to participate in their Jewish owners' household activities. Young men and women were compelled to convert in order to marry Jewish spouses (Feldman 2003). Superstitious individuals may have been attracted to certain aspects of Jewish religious culture (Liebeschuetz 2001). Conversions of this sort, motivated by practical rather than ideological purposes, are not discouraged in the ancient sources and need not have been predicated upon active Jewish missionary activity.

Bibliography

S. J. D. Cohen 1999, *The Beginnings of Jewishness,* Berkeley: University of California Press. • S. J. D. Cohen 2005, *Why Aren't Jewish Women Circumcised?* Berkeley: University of California Press. • J. J. Collins 1985, "A Symbol of Otherness: Circumcision and Salvation in the First Century," in *To See Ourselves as Others See Us,* ed. J. Neusner and E. S. Frerichs, Chico: Scholars Press, 163-86. • T. L. Donaldson 2008, *Judaism and the Gentiles: Jewish Patterns of Universalism to 135 CE.* Waco, Tex.: Baylor University Press. • L. H.

Feldman 1993, *Jew and Gentile in the Ancient World*, Princeton: Princeton University Press. • L. H. FELDMAN 2003, "Conversion to Judaism in Classical Antiquity," *HUCA* 74: 115-56. • M. GOODMAN 1994, *Mission and Conversion*, Oxford: Clarendon. • W. LIEBESCHUETZ 2001, "The Influence of Judaism among Non-Jews in the Imperial Period," *JJS* 52: 235-52. • S. MCKNIGHT 1991, *Light among the Gentiles: Jewish Missionary Activity in the Second Temple Period*, Minneapolis: Fortress.

See also: Circumcision; God-fearers

JOSHUA EZRA BURNS

Copper Scroll (3Q15)

The *Copper Scroll* (3Q315) is one of the most sensational, if elusive, texts found among the Dead Sea Scrolls. Inscribed on rolled-up metal sheets, the scroll was discovered in 1952 in a cave about 2 km. north of Qumran, but it could not be analyzed because its oxidized condition made it too brittle to open. In 1955-1957, Henry Wright Baker of Manchester University, with involvement from John Allegro, managed to reveal the scroll's contents by cutting it into pieces, and transcriptions, translations, and photos of its Hebrew text were soon published. These were hardly definitive, but subsequent restoration and computer and x-ray imaging have yielded improved readings, reinvigorating the study of this intriguing text, if not solving the puzzles that it poses.

The scroll records a list of sixty or so treasures hidden in various locales (cisterns, tunnels, pools, etc.), each of its sections identifying a hiding place, instructing the text's reader to dig a certain distance there, and ending with a brief description of the treasure itself, sometimes accompanied by mysterious Greek letters yet to be decoded. All the hiding places seem to be in the land of Israel — most in the Judean wilderness in the vicinity of Jericho and Qumran, it seems, but a few farther afield in places like Mt. Gerizim. Scholars differ in how they interpret the scroll's measurements but agree that the treasure was immense, by one reckoning totaling 200 tons of gold and silver.

The extant portion of the scroll does not contain information about why or when it was composed, so scholars can only conjecture about such matters. The script in which the scroll is written, an engraved variant of a Herodian period script, places it in the period between 25-135 C.E., but scholars vary widely in how they date its paleography within this period, placing the scroll's composition at various points between the First Jewish Revolt (66-70 C.E.) and the Bar Kokhba Revolt (132-135 C.E.). The proximity of Cave 3 to Qumran makes it tempting to link the scroll to the sect presumed to have lived at the latter site, but nothing in the language or subject matter of the scroll itself, or among the texts and artifacts found near the scroll in Cave 3, clinches that association.

Just as mysterious as the scroll itself are the hidden objects that it records, an immense treasure that includes hoards of gold and silver, jars, cups, and other

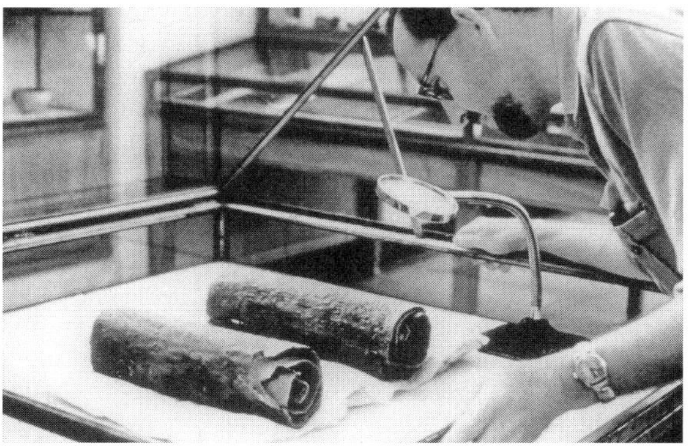

John Marco Allegro examining the unopened rolls of the Copper Scroll *(Estate of John Allegro)*

vessels, sacred garments, and scrolls, including, it seems, another copy of the *Copper Scroll* itself (col. 12 lines 10-13). Where did these objects come from and why were they hidden? The most popular theory is that the treasure came from the Second Temple itself and was hidden during the First Jewish Revolt to protect it from the Romans. Consistent with this hypothesis is the apparently religious nature of many of the treasures — cult vessels, tithes, sacred garments — but one cannot rule out competing explanations. One view holds that the scroll records the whereabouts of offerings on their way to the Temple when it was destroyed in 70 C.E.; another speculates that its treasure was collected by the Qumran sect as it waited for the Jerusalem Temple to be displaced by the eschatological Temple.

What connects all these hypotheses is the assumption that the treasure recorded in the scroll really existed, an assumption that not all scholars accept. Sometime in the Hellenistic period, a legend developed that the ark and other fabled cult objects from Solomon's Temple had been hidden underground at the time of its destruction (cf. 2 Macc. 2:4-8). A number of scholars, most notably J. T. Milik, who published the official version of the scroll in the Discoveries in the Judaean Desert series, argued for the scroll as a reflection of this legend, a view supported by the seemingly implausible amount of treasure, and by an intriguing medieval parallel, a text known as *Masseket Kelim* that recorded a long list of cultic vessels from Solomon's Temple allegedly hidden at the time of its destruction, and that even makes reference to a "copper scroll."

Few scholars today accept these arguments, finding nothing myth-like about the scroll's dry and precise itemization, or implausible about the treasure when compared with the assets of other large temples in antiquity. On the other hand, Hellenistic Greek lore, especially a story recounted by Pausanias about the hiding of a metal scroll, shows that artifacts similar to the *Copper Scroll* could have mythological associations in the Greco-Roman period (Pausanias, *Description of Greece* 4.20.4; 4.26.8). Ultimately, there is no way to tell from the text itself whether its treasure really existed or, if so, why it was hidden. Attempts to find it have led nowhere, but the scroll's resistance to demystification has only intensified its power to fascinate both scholars and the public.

BIBLIOGRAPHY

M. BAILLET, J. T. MILIK, AND R. DE VAUX, EDS. 1962, *Les 'petites grottes' de Qumran,* DJD 3, Oxford: Clarendon, 200-302. • P. K. MCCARTER 1994. "The Copper Scroll Treasure as an Accumulation of Religious Offerings," in *Methods of Investigation of the Dead Sea Scrolls and the Khirbet Qumran Site,* ed. M. O. Wise et al., New York: New York Academy of Sciences, 133-48. • G. J. BROOKE AND P. R. DAVIES, EDS., 2002, *Copper Scroll Studies,* Sheffield: Sheffield Academic Press. • J. K. LEFKOVITZ 1997, *The Copper Scroll — 3Q15: A Reevaluation: A New Reading, Translation and Commentary,* Leiden: Brill. • A. WOLTERS 1996, *The Copper Scroll: Overview, Text and Translation,* Sheffield: Sheffield Academic Press.

STEVEN WEITZMAN

Cosmology

Humans have always been in awe of the teeming cosmos overhead and have sought to comprehend it. Our images of the cosmos reveal almost as much about our perceptions of ourselves and our place in that cosmos as about the cosmos itself. These images are inspired by questions about the core issues of human experience, and the answers proffered focus on the origin and nature of the physical cosmos and the place of individuals and groups within it. While the basic meaning of the term "cosmos" (Gr. *kosmos*) is "order," fifth-century Greek philosophers used it as a technical term for the "ordered" universe. Thus, the term "cosmology" (Gr. *kosmologia,* from *kosmos* + *logia,* speech/discourse [about]), refers to the systematic analysis of the ordered universe in an effort to understand and perhaps influence its operations in ways that benefit humans. Cosmology also reveals a society's understanding of itself as an entity within the cosmos.

Cosmology in the Ancient Near East

Ancient Near Eastern peoples developed myths that explained the origins of the cosmos and their place in it. Most all peoples of the ancient Near East imagined the cosmos as a three-tiered structure: netherworld, earthly realm, and heavenly world. Each society had more than one cosmology to explain the cosmos. The classic Mesopotamian cosmology is found in the Babylonian creation epic, the *Enuma Elish.* It explains how the god Marduk created the cosmos and why he is the chief god in the Babylonian pantheon. After defeating the goddess Tiamat and her cosmic allies, Marduk used the carcasses of the vanquished gods to create the cosmos and appointed humans the task of serving the gods. This myth also identifies the netherworld as a watery place named after the god of that realm, Apsu. The *Enuma Elish,* therefore, explains how and why the cosmos is structured as it is; accounts for the appearance and movements of the celestial bodies; and explains humans' role within the cosmos.

Cosmology in Ancient Greece and Rome

Greek cosmology in the Homeric Age (ca. 1200-700 B.C.E.) paralleled the tripartite ancient Near Eastern cosmological models with a flat earth encircled by water and resting on pillars, situated between the heavenly and netherworldly regions (Homer, *Iliad* 14.246; 18.607; 21.194; *Odyssey* 10.467–12.6; 24.1; Hesiod, *Works and Days* 168–75). Pythagoras (ca. 575-500 B.C.E.) and his successors, the Pythagoreans, created cosmologies based more on physics. Anaxagoras (ca. 500-428 B.C.E.) theorized that the planets circled the earth, each in its own orbit. Plato followed this model (cf. *Republic* 10 and *Timaeus* 38), but Aristotle transformed it from a theoretical model into an actual physical mechanism with a total of fifty-five nestled spheres encircling the earth *(On the Heavens).* This "geocentric cosmology" is commonly referred to as the "Ptolemaic model," after its classic exposition by Claudius Ptolemy of Alexandria (ca. 100-170 C.E.; cf. Cicero, *Republic* 6.9-26; *De Natura Deorum* 2.20.52-53; *De Divinatione* 2.43.91). Some philosophers further imagined that as one descends from the outermost heavenly regions, the regions become increasingly disorderly and corrupt. Thus, while earth was where imperfection, impurity, and disorder reigned, the heavenly realm was perfect, pure, and entirely orderly. Again, these Greco-Roman cosmologies reveal both scientific traditions and society's cultural values. These images gave definition to and a rational interpretation of the space separating the divine and human realms.

Cosmology in the Hebrew Bible

The Hebrew Bible could not have been clearer about cosmology from the outset: "In the beginning God created the heavens and the earth" (Gen. 1:1). The Priestly creation account in Genesis 1 was written in the exilic or postexilic eras. Its authors knew ancient Near Eastern creation myths such as the *Enuma Elish* that involved a cosmic battle, and this account appears to draw on some of these motifs, including the use of the evocative term *tĕhôm,* "deep" (cf. the sea goddess Tiamat in the *Enuma Elish*). Nonetheless, Genesis 1 recasts these old motifs of struggle between gods within a strictly monotheistic ideology wherein God alone is the actor who transforms chaos into structured holiness (cf. Gen. 2:3; Exod. 20:11; Isa. 45:12; Pss. 8:4; 33:6; 146:6; Prov. 3:19; Neh. 9:6). At the end of Genesis 1 God, humans, and nature are at peace and in their appropriate places, and the Creator deems this structured holiness as "very good" (Gen. 1:31). Genesis 1, therefore, presents what the biblical editors suggest is the divine pattern for the cosmos and for civilization: God outside of creation, everything located and functioning in its appropriate place, and all following a holy pattern of work and rest.

The biblical phrase for cosmos is "[the] heaven[s] and [the] earth." By citing the two ends of the cosmic spectrum, this phrase refers to heaven, earth, and all that is in, on, between, and around (above and below) them. The ancient Israelites, like their ancient Near Eastern neighbors, imagined the universe as a tripartite structure: heaven/sky above, earth in the middle, and netherworld or Sheol below. The Hebrew word *šāmayim* can be translated into English as either "heaven" (realm of the gods) or "sky" (atmosphere or celestial realm). While this term has analogs in other Semitic languages, its exact origin is unclear. One creative suggestion is that it may be related to the Akkadian phrase *ša-mê*, "place of water." When the ancient Israelites looked skyward, they imagined that they were looking at the bluish "floor" of heaven, and this floor was composed of water (Gen. 1:6-8; 7:11; cf. Jer. 10:13; 51:16; Ps. 148:4) or, according to some passages, stone (Exod. 24:9-10; Ezek 1:26, 10:1).

The Hebrew suffix *-ayim* on the term *šāmayim* typically signifies things that occur naturally in pairs, but in this case the form is plural, leading some scholars to suspect that ancient Israel had a notion of multiple heavens. But this plural form more likely expresses the sky's vastness from horizon to horizon (cf. Deut. 4:32; 30:4; Isa. 13:5; 40:12; 55:9; Jer. 31:37; 49:36; Ps. 103:11; Neh. 1:9). Likewise, the phrases "heaven of heaven" and "heaven and the heaven of heaven" do not necessarily refer to a multiple-heaven cosmology. Rather, these phrases follow the Hebrew syntactic construction for expressing a superlative — "the vast heavens/sky." The term "firmament" *(rāqîaʿ)* denotes the atmosphere in which the celestial bodies move, and can also be used as a synonym for "heaven/sky" (Gen. 1:6-8; 14-17, 20; Ps. 19:2).

Although biblical tradition prefers a monotheistic cosmology, some ancient Israelites and Judahites imagined their god YHWH presiding over a council of divine beings (cf. Deut. 32:8; Ps. 82:1; Job 1:6). Such an image reveals aspects of the intellectual heritage Israel and Judah shared with their neighbors. In this regard the phrase "hosts of heaven" *(ṣĕbâʾôt šāmayim)* designates this assembly of heavenly beings and/or celestial bodies (cf. Deut. 4:19; 17:3; 1 Kings 22:19; 2 Kings 17:16; 21:3, 5; 23:4-5; Isa. 34:4; 45:12; Jer. 8:2; 19:13; 33:22; Zeph. 1:5; Neh. 9:6). Numerous nameless heavenly beings or "messengers" appear in the Hebrew Bible (e.g., Gen. 6:2, 4; 21:17; Exod. 15:11; Deut. 32:8; Judg. 13:3; Zech. 1:9-14; Pss. 29:1; 35:5-6; 89:7; Job 1:6; 2:1; 38:7). In the Second Temple period these beings eventually individuate and receive personal names (Michael, Gabriel, etc.) and titles (archangel, commander, etc.). This evolving speculation on heavenly beings and realms was due not simply to outside influences but to developments that had been going on for some time. The gods who at an earlier stage of Israelite religion were superior or equal to Yahweh were first made his peers, then subordinate gods, and finally "angels" created to serve him.

Apart from the apparent reference to the Pleiades *(kĕsîl)* and the constellation Orion *(kîmâ)* in Job 9:9; 38:31-33 and Amos 5:8, the Hebrew Bible contains no strictly astronomical texts. Several passages betray, however, Israelite and Judahite familiarity with astronomy and astrology, if only in a negative manner (Deut. 4:19; 2 Kings 23:5; Isa. 47:13). Alongside these texts, archaeological evidence such as the geographical orientation of temples relative to the eastern horizon indicates that these people practiced astronomical observation and worship. Some Israelites and Judahites imagined that the celestial bodies were divine beings (cf. Exod. 20:4; Deut. 4:19; 17:3; 2 Kings 17:16; 21:3-5; 23:5; Isa. 47:13; Jer. 8:2; 19:13; 44:17-19; Ezek. 8:14, 16; Amos 5:26; Zeph. 1:5; Job 31:26-28). The people worshiped the celestial objects because their livelihood depended on nature for survival, and because the objects are related to nature's daily and seasonal changes. For strict Yahwists, however, the celestial bodies were not gods at all but merely objects created by Yahweh and under his control. Since these strict Yahwists were the final editors of the Hebrew Bible, their ideas on cosmology dominate the narrative. Nonetheless, it is certain that the people of Israel and Judah, along with their neighbors, paid close attention to the teeming cosmos above their heads.

Cosmology in Early Judaism

The conquest of the Near East by Alexander and the subsequent Hellenization of the region had a transformative impact on emerging Jewish culture. The latest book in the Hebrew Bible, the book of Daniel, dates to the second century B.C.E. and exhibits Hellenistic cosmological features. Notable in this regard is Dan. 12:2-3, which presents an entirely new way of conceptualizing humanity's relationship with the cosmos in the afterlife. Rather than remain in the realm of the dead (Sheol), the righteous will rise and ascend to heaven. This ascent accords with Hellenistic cosmological models that identify the farthest heavenly realm as the realm of purity to which the righteous soul wishes to ascend. Thus, Greek images of the righteous soul longing to return to its cosmic place of origin in the ethereal realm of purity have influenced this example of early Jewish cosmology and religion.

In the first century C.E., the Jewish philosopher Philo of Alexandria articulated Jewish tradition in terms of Greco-Roman philosophy. Throughout his writings he exhibits a thorough understanding of the major Greco-Roman cosmological models and philosophical schools. "Ptolemaic cosmology" guides much of his reinterpretation of ancient Jewish creation traditions (cf. *Heres* 207–14, 221–24; *De Cherubim* 21–25). He imagined that the uncreated God, the "Maker," who was completely outside of creation, created the cosmos and all its constituent elements (*Heres* 134, 140) by divine will or the divine *Logos* (*Opificio Mundi* 23–24; *Leg. Alleg.* 3.96) and according to a preexisting divine plan (*Opificio Mundi* 16–20, 25, 29; cf. Exod. 25:9, 40). He also noted that the soul longs to return to its place of origin in the ethereal realm of purity and permanence (cf. *QG* 4.74; *Heres* 275–78; *Leg. Alleg.* 1.105-8). Thus, in many respects Philo represents a Jewish version of Middle Platonic cosmology.

Not every version of early Jewish cosmology adopted Greek models, however. Fragments and multiple copies of the third-century-B.C.E. *Astronomical Book* Enoch (*1 Enoch* 72–82) were found among the Dead Sea Scrolls and indicate that the Qumran sectarians used this text well into the first century C.E. This quasi-scientific text explains the orderly functioning of the cosmos, and its cosmology follows ancient Near Eastern patterns: the celestial bodies do not encircle the earth but enter and exit the sky through gates on the horizons. The text suggests that the traditional cosmology found in the Hebrew Bible continued to serve the religious and social values of some early Jewish communities. Some Jews, then, were either unaware of or unwilling to adopt Greco-Roman cosmologies and their concomitant religious values.

Cosmology in Early Christianity

The early Christian communities were heirs of both biblical tradition and Greco-Roman culture. Thus early Christian texts naturally reflect Greco-Roman cosmology. John 1:1-18, the prologue to the Gospel of John, is a Hellenistic reinterpretation of the creation story in Genesis 1 and intends to demonstrate Jesus' divinity by equating him with the powerful and creative word, the Logos (Gr. *logos*) of God. The Fourth Gospel asserts that the preincarnate, divine Son was present at creation and was God's mediator or agent in creation. Johannine cosmology, therefore, expresses a Christian community's understanding of the cosmos and of God's relationship to it.

Second Corinthians 12 recounts Paul's ascent to the third heaven. Heavenly ascents became a popular motif during the Greco-Roman eras. Such ascents appear in Jewish texts (e.g., *1 Enoch* 1–36; 2 *Enoch; Testament of Levi; Apocalypse of Abraham; 3 Baruch*) and Christian writings (e.g., *Apocalypse of Paul; Ascension of Isaiah; Apocalypse of Esdras*). They typically involve a schema of multiple heavens, thereby demonstrating their adoption of Greco-Roman cosmology. Moreover, these texts also depend on cosmological images that locate the divine realm in the farthest region of the cosmos, the only place where absolute purity, perfection, and permanence reign. The ascent texts reflect the authors' perception of their place within and access to the cosmos both during life and in the afterlife.

The book of Revelation ends with the dissolution and revivification of the cosmos. The monsters of chaos that hearken back to the *tannînîm* in Genesis 1 and the biblical Leviathan and Behemoth (cf. Isa 27:1; Ps. 74:12-14; Job 40:15) are finally vanquished (Revelation 12–13, 21). Order — cosmos — is restored. The story ends when a new heaven and new earth appear (21:1), all things are made new (21:5), and the author proclaims, "Now at last God dwells with humankind" (21:3). The book of Revelation suggests that the cosmological quest has returned humanity to an Edenic beginning.

Among other cosmologies in late antiquity were those associated with various groups that early church fathers and modern scholars have labeled Gnosticism. Although there is no single Gnostic cosmology, in general Gnostic cosmologies are based on Greco-Roman astronomy and maintain a strict material and ethical dualism. The deity resides in the highest realm, well outside the physical universe, which is corrupt and deteriorating. The physical universe was created not by the supreme deity, but by a lower, ignorant, and arrogant demiurge who is also subject to the inferior qualities of the physical universe. This creator god or demiurge is an inferior being, and its creation is likewise horribly compromised: "The world came about through a mistake" (*Gos. Phil.* 2.3.75). It is only by attaining knowledge (Gr. *gnōsis*) of the mysteries of the cosmos and how to escape its corrupt nature that humans can transcend this decaying realm and find a place in the realm of perfection, purity, and permanence. Thus, Gnostic soteriology is intimately tied to its cosmology, for only correct cosmic knowledge leads to deliverance from this world and its limitations.

BIBLIOGRAPHY

J. J. COLLINS 2004, "Cosmology: Time and History," in *Religions of the Ancient World: A Guide,* ed. S. Iles Johnson, Cambridge: Belknap/Harvard University Press, 59-70. • R. J. CLIFFORD 1994, *Creation Accounts in the Near East and in the Bible,* Washington, D.C.: Catholic Biblical Association. • M. HIMMELFARB 1993, *Ascent to Heaven in Jewish and Christian Apocalypses,* Oxford: Oxford University Press. • W. HOROWITZ 1998, *Mesopotamian Cosmic Geography,* Winona Lake, Ind.: Eisenbrauns. • C. HOUTMAN 1993, *Der Himmel im Alten Testament,* Leiden: Brill. • K. RUDOLPH 1987, *Gnosis: The Nature and History of Gnosticism,* San Francisco: Harper & Row. • J. E. WRIGHT 2000, *The Early History of Heaven,* Oxford: Oxford University Press. • A. YARBRO COLLINS 1996, *Cosmology and Eschatology in Jewish and Christian Apocalypticism,* Leiden: Brill.

See also: Angels; Ascent to Heaven; Astronomy and Astrology; Death and Afterlife; Geography, Mythic

J. EDWARD WRIGHT

Court Tales

In the broadest sense, a court tale may be defined as a narrative that takes place at the court of a high-status person (most often a king, but also a governor, chieftain, or other high official) and centers on the relationship of the person of high status with his/her subordinates, that is, courtiers. In this broad sense, court narratives are found in the folklore of nearly all cultures throughout history. In the context of early Jewish literature, a "court tale" refers specifically to a narrative set in the court of a foreign king, involving a wise and righteous Jewish courtier as the hero who emerges triumphant from a web of palace intrigue. The narrative pattern can be traced as far back as the complex of narratives surrounding the figure of Joseph at the court of Pharaoh in Genesis 37–50, but became particularly popular with the rise of tales set in a postexilic (Persian or Hellenistic) Diaspora setting. The Jewish court tales *par excellence* are Daniel and Esther, which followed closely the biblical narratives surrounding Joseph, and the (non-Jewish, but popular with Jewish readers) *Tale of Ahiqar.*

Other Jewish narratives also reflect the near ubiquitous influence of the foreign king/court over Jewish life in the Diaspora; in this category might be counted the *Letter of Aristeas,* 3 Maccabees, some parts of 2 Maccabees, Judith, Tobit, and the narratives centered around the figure of Alexander the Great at Jerusalem in Josephus' *Antiquities*. However, these texts are not typically defined as court tales or discussed in the scholarly literature under that heading. The chapter "Kings and Jews" in Erich Gruen's *Heritage and Hellenism* (1998) is a good example of a study which looks at the broad range of narratives involving the adventures of Jews at court, without restricting itself to the genre of the court tale as such. The remainder of this article will restrict itself to discussing the Jewish court tale as more narrowly defined.

The analysis of the "literary type" or "form" of the court tale is fairly well developed in scholarship. The seminal article for modern discussions is Humphreys 1973. In it he argued that although in their present form Esther and Daniel each have their own unique literary orientation (Esther as an etiology for the Feast of Purim, Daniel as an apocalypse) and can be interpreted (in his view) as highly "exclusive and nationalistic" in their attitude toward Gentiles, both preserve the outlines of an earlier narrative form, the court tale, in which the main focus was on the success of the courtier at the court of the foreign king, and the advantages that the Jewish community could garner from the success of the courtier. In other words, Humphreys argued, the narrative pattern of the court tale was originally oriented toward creating a positive model for Jewish life in the Diaspora.

In addition to close analysis of the narratives of Esther and Daniel, Humphreys identified four elements in the postexilic cultural matrix which contributed to the development of the court tale in Jewish literature: (1) Jeremiah's letter to the exiles of the first deportation, encouraging them to focus on the positive aspects of their new life in a foreign land (Jer. 29:4-7); (2) the figure of Nehemiah, a Jewish courtier in the service of Artaxerxes I, who successfully used his position at court to promote the resettlement of the Jews in the land, the rebuilding of Jerusalem, and the rebuilding of the Temple; (3) the tales of Joseph at the court of Pharaoh in Genesis 37–50; and (4) the Aramaic version of the *Tale of Ahiqar* discovered at the Jewish military colony at Elephantine in Egypt, suggesting that the tale was popular with Jewish readers in the Diaspora even though Ahiqar was not Jewish. The latter two (the Joseph narrative, and the *Tale of Ahiqar*) have often been analyzed by subsequent scholars as full-fledged court tales in their own right.

Humphreys distinguishes in his analysis between two different types of court tales: (1) the "court conflict," in which a dangerous rivalry among courtiers threatens the life of a Jewish hero, but the rivalry is inevitably resolved with the Jewish courtier emerging triumphant, enjoying the full protection of the king's favor; and (2) the less confrontational "court contest," in which a Jewish courtier competes with other courtiers to solve a problem and is able to succeed where all others have failed.

This distinction between "court conflict" and "court contest" was more fully developed in an analysis of Daniel 1–6 offered by Collins 1975. According to this typological division, Daniel chapters 2, 4, and 5 can be understood as "court contests," while the story of Esther and Daniel 3 and 6 should be interpreted as "court conflicts." In the category of court conflicts, the narrative of Esther revolves (at least in part) around the rivalry between Mordecai and Haman and the ultimate discomfiture of Haman. In Daniel 3, Daniel's three companions (Daniel himself appears nowhere in the story) are slandered by rivals at court and tested in the fiery furnace, emerging unharmed by the providence of God. In Daniel 6, Daniel himself is caught in a trap set by jealous rival courtiers, and emerges alive and triumphant from the lion's den. In the category of the "court contest," in Daniel 2, Daniel is able to intuit the king's dream and interpret the meaning of the statue where all the other courtiers have failed, garnering rewards and praise — even though his interpretation of the dream predicts the ultimate collapse of all earthly kingdoms. In Daniel 4, Daniel is again able to interpret Nebuchadnezzar's dream predicting his future descent into and return from madness, leading Nebuchadnezzar ultimately to repent and acknowledge the power of the Most High. In Daniel 5, Daniel alone is able to interpret the riddle of the handwriting on the wall (too late to save Belshazzar, whose reign as the last of the Babylonians is already doomed).

The definition of the Jewish court tale established by Humphreys and Collins, with its further division into the subcategories of the "court contest" and "court conflict," has come to be widespread in the literature, but is subject to moderate critique by Niditch and Doran (1997), who complain, with some justice, that Humphreys simply "lists a loose collection of . . . shared motifs in no particular order." (The identification of the Jewish novel as a genre suffers from a somewhat similar approach.) Niditch and Doran argue that a strict form-critical study should isolate not only individual motifs but also the way in which they are ordered or patterned. As an example of the stricter type of approach they advocate, they provide a close analysis of one particular pattern, the one identified by folklore scholars Aarne and Thompson as Type 922 under the heading of "Clever Acts and Words." In this pattern, represented in Jewish (or quasi-Jewish) literature by Daniel 2, Genesis 41, and *Ahiqar* 5–7:

(1) A person of lower status . . . IS CALLED BEFORE a person of higher status . . . TO ANSWER difficult questions or solve a problem requiring insight. . . .
(2) The person of high status POSES the problem which no one seems capable of solving.
(3) The person of lower status . . . DOES SOLVE the problem.
(4) The person of lower status IS REWARDED for answering. . . .

This more narrowly defined analysis is salutary in that it emphasizes the importance of identifying a full narrative pattern, as opposed to a potpourri of motifs. However, it is inherently limited in its ability to be generalized to a broader variety of narratives. Wills 1990 rightly insists on taking a broader approach, while praising Niditch and Doran as a successful example of the structuralist folklore approach applied to one narrow subset of Jewish court tales.

The most extensive study of Jewish court tales to date is Wills 1990. Wills thoroughly explores and critiques the various methodological approaches that have been taken to the court tale and advocates a fairly broad and flexible genre designation, that of the Jewish "wisdom court legend." Like Humphreys, Wills seeks to "understand Daniel 1–6 and Esther and Daniel in the context of their genre" (Wills 1990: 193), but he also provides an important background chapter on court legends in Near Eastern literature. Among a variety of possible nonbiblical Near Eastern parallels, he examines, in addition to the *Tale of Ahiqar,* legends surrounding the Persian Zoroaster at the court of King Hystaspes (problematic, due to the very late date of the sources in which they are preserved); Egyptian wisdom literature, particularly *Onkhsheshonq;* Ionian and Lydian legends drawn upon by Herodotus in his *Histories;* and the *Life of Aesop.* Among preexilic biblical parallels he considers not only the Joseph narrative (Genesis 37–50), but also several shorter narrative fragments, including Nathan's parable rebuking King David (2 Sam. 12:1-14), the wise woman of Tekoa (2 Sam. 14:1-17), and an anonymous prophet's chastisement of King Ahab (1 Kings 20:39-43). Although it does not allow for in-depth analysis of any one of these parallels, the attempt to place Jewish court legends within a much broader Near Eastern literary context is a particularly valuable contribution of Wills's study.

The bulk of Wills's study is devoted to a detailed text-critical analysis of the traditions underlying the present forms of Daniel and Esther, in an attempt to isolate the characteristic elements of the "wisdom court legend" shared by both texts, as distinct from the later literary stages of development followed by Daniel and Esther in both their Greek and Hebrew forms. While scholars may differ on particular points of text-critical analysis or about issues raised by Daniel and Esther in their present form, Wills's study remains the most comprehensive and in many ways the definitive study for the genre of the Jewish court tale. It has been less successful in attempting to reassert and expand upon the link between the court tale and wisdom literature (biblical and Near Eastern), a link made earlier by Talmon (1963) and von Rad (1966), but one which has not enjoyed great favor in more recent scholarship.

BIBLIOGRAPHY

J. J. COLLINS 1975, "The Court-Tales in Daniel and the Development of Apocalyptic," *JBL* 94: 218-34. • E. GRUEN 1998, *Heritage and Hellenism: The Reinvention of Jewish Tradition,* Berkeley: University of California Press, 189-245. • W. L. HUMPHREYS 1973, "A Life-Style for Diaspora: A Study of the Tales of Esther and Daniel," *JBL* 92: 211-23. • S. NIDITCH AND R. DORAN 1977, "The Success Story of the Wise Courtier: A Formal Approach," *JBL* 96: 179-93. • S. TALMON 1963, "Wisdom in the Book of Esther," *VT* 13: 419-55. • G. VON RAD 1966, "The Joseph Narrative and Ancient Wisdom," in idem, *The Problem of the Pentateuch and Other Essays,* New York: McGraw-Hill, 292-300. • L. M. WILLS 1990, *The Jew in the Court of the Foreign King: Ancient Jewish Court Legends,* Minneapolis: Fortress. • L. M. WILLS 1995, *The Jewish Novel in the Ancient World,* Ithaca: Cornell University Press, 41-50, 93-98.

See also: Daniel, Book of; Esther, Book of; Novels

SARA RAUP JOHNSON

Covenant

A covenant (Hebr. *bĕrît;* Gr. *diathēkē*) is a solemn pact or agreement between two or more parties. The Hebrew Bible refers to covenants made by God with the patriarchs, the people of Israel, and with King David: the Noachic, the Abrahamic, the Sinaitic, the Deuteronomic, and the Davidic. These covenants serve to define and regulate the relationship between God and his people, however broadly or narrowly the latter are defined in each case. The whole subject of covenant is complicated by the fact that the Bible refers to a multiplicity of overlapping covenants, which sometimes creates tension or crossover between the covenants in the various biblical texts. There is considerable variety and tension in the way the biblical tradition treats the individual covenants themselves. Such complications are further compounded when Jewish literature of the Second Temple period takes up the biblical traditions about the covenants and applies them in novel ways according to the new historical circumstances.

Hebrew Bible

The Noachic Covenant

The first occurrence of "covenant" in the Bible, Gen. 6:18, contains the promise that God will establish his covenant with Noah. The flood ends after "God remembered Noah" (Gen. 8:1), just as he later delivered Israel from bondage in Egypt and brought the people through the Sea of Reeds after he had "remembered his covenant with Abraham and Isaac and Jacob" (Exod. 2:23-25). The similarity between the two events goes even further: in both cases, God established a covenant after the deliverance. Thus, God made a covenant with Noah after the flood (Gen. 9:1-17), just as he did with Israel after the exodus from Egypt (on which see further below). Indeed, based apparently on the similarity between the two covenants, the ancient covenant with Noah and his descendants after the flood will be recapitulated in the postexilic period (Isaiah 54). Here, then, is an example of the kind of crossover between the covenants that we find in biblical texts, as well as the reverberations that these interactions have in the subsequent tradition.

However, there are also major differences between the Noachic and the Sinaitic covenants. Whereas the Noachic covenant is an "everlasting covenant between God and all living creatures" (Gen. 9:16), the Sinaitic covenant was made only with Israel and was not called "eternal." In several respects, the Noahic covenant is more like the Abrahamic covenant, insofar as both are characterized as "eternal" (for the Abrahamic covenant as "eternal," cf. Gen. 17:7, 13, 19), and both are established with a "sign" that commemorates the covenant in perpetuity (i.e., the rainbow [Gen. 9:12, 13, 17] and circumcision [Gen. 17:9-14], respectively).

The Abrahamic Covenant

The calling of Abram in Gen. 12:1-3 does not refer to a "covenant," but the sudden and unexpected promises to Abram in this text — great nation, great name, blessing — echo throughout Genesis (cf. 26:2-5; 46:2-4) and the rest of the Torah, including passages that do explicitly refer to "covenant."

In Genesis 15, the Yahwistic (J) version of the covenant with Abraham, YHWH unilaterally promises Abram an heir and a land, concluded by a ceremony in which YHWH (symbolized by the "smoking fire pot" and "flaming torch") passes between the pieces of the divided sacrificial animals (v. 17), an act that the narrator summarizes in the statement, "On that day YHWH made a covenant with Abram" (v. 18).

In Genesis 17, the Priestly (P) version of the covenant with Abraham, God reveals himself to Abram as El Shaddai and promises to establish his covenant between himself and Abram, in order to make the latter the father of a multitude of nations (vv. 1-4). The changes of name from Abram to Abraham and from Sarai to Sarah occur at this point, emphasizing the centrality of this couple in the establishment of the promised new people. As an "everlasting covenant" (vv. 7, 13, 19), the Abrahamic covenant emphasizes progeny, the transference of the covenant through the generations of Abraham's descendants. It is no coincidence that the "sign" of the covenant should be incised in the male organ of reproduction (vv. 13-14). Since circumcision is thus seen as a *sine qua non* of the covenantal relationship between God and his people, subsequent Judaism made it essential as well.

The Sinai Covenant

According to Exod 2:23-25, divine remembrance of the Abrahamic covenant immediately sets the plan for the deliverance of Israel from Egypt in motion, as the same God who appeared to the patriarchs as El Shaddai and established a covenant with them now appears to Moses as YHWH, who has remembered his covenant (6:2-5; cf. Lev 26:42, referring to future acts of divine redemption after national apostasy).

The twofold covenant formula, which occurs frequently in the Hebrew Bible with minor variations in the exact wording, reflects the marriage and adoption formulas, implying that the covenantal relationship between God and Israel mirrors the strong bond of matrimony or the parent-child relationship. Indeed, since YHWH's relationship to Israel is similar to that between a husband and wife, violating the second commandment by committing idolatry provokes God to a jealousy similar to that of a husband against his adulterous wife (20:4-6; cf. Hosea 1–3; Isa. 54:5-7; Ezekiel 16).

The ultimate goal of the exodus is not merely to deliver Israel from bondage in Egypt, but to bring them into this bilateral, covenantal relationship with God, "that I might dwell among them" (29:45-46), which means, quite concretely, that God will travel with them in the portable sanctuary (the Tabernacle), and that they will live in his presence. Thus, having been delivered from bondage in Egypt, the people eventually come to Sinai, where they enter into covenantal relationship with YHWH (19:3-5).

The covenant at Sinai in Exodus 19–24 represents the momentous revelation to the entire people of Israel that actually establishes the relationship between God and Israel and regulates every aspect of the people's way of life, especially with respect to a holy place (the Tabernacle and ultimately the permanent Temple [cf. Exod 15:17]) and holy time (the Sabbath, "a covenant for all time" [31:16]). Although Exodus presents the Sinaitic covenant as being in continuity with the earlier Abrahamic covenant (Genesis 15 and 17), the Sinaitic covenant goes beyond the Abrahamic by imposing specific, detailed obligations on Israel that make the covenantal relationship between God and Israel contingent upon the people's consistent obedience to the Law. There is, then, a tension between the two covenants — conditional and unconditional — that one can trace all the way to the letters of Paul (cf. Gal. 3:15-18).

The terms of the covenant are laid out in the Decalogue (20:2-14) and the "Book of the Covenant" (20:19–23:33). The first commandments that God proclaimed to the Israelites were the Decalogue (20:2-14), which included laws governing relationships both between humankind and God and between one human being and another. Three of the laws ordained here between humankind and God became defining characteristics of subsequent Judaism (in addition to circumcision, the sign of the Abrahamic covenant): that is, the prohibition against worshiping other gods (v. 3); the prohibition against idolatry (vv. 4-6); and the requirement to keep the Sabbath (vv. 6-11). In both Judaism and Christianity, a distinction was seen between the Decalogue, given by God directly to the people, and other laws given indirectly through Moses.

Violation and Renewal of the Covenant

Even before the ink is dry on the contract, so to speak, Israel breaks the covenant while still at Sinai. In Exod. 31:18–34:35, the golden calf incident represents a fundamental breach of the previously ratified covenant stipulations. The destruction of the tablets by Moses upon his return to the Israelite camp symbolizs the annulment of the covenant (Exod 32:19), whereupon God refuses to go in the midst of the people (33:3). Nevertheless, according to Exodus 34, God restored the broken covenant through reiterating and strengthening the stipulations of the previous covenant. Although the covenant with Israel is hardly mentioned at all outside the Torah, the prophetic tradition does have a similar concept of the "new" (or, perhaps better, "renewed") covenant in the aftermath of national apostasy, although there the restoration of Israel involves not merely a reinforcement of the previous covenant, but rather divine intervention to enable the people's obedience from the heart (Jer. 31:31-34; Ezek. 11:19-20; 36:26-27).

Deuteronomy

Poised on the plains of Moab, ready to enter the promised land, the Israelites receive a "reiteration" of the covenant that had been given at Horeb/Sinai a generation earlier. However, the text astonishingly emphasizes that the Sinatic covenant was actually made with this new generation: "YHWH our God made a covenant with us at Horeb. It was not with our fathers that YHWH made this covenant, but with us, the living, every one of us who is here today" (Deut. 5:2-3; cf. 4:10-14; 11:2-7; 27:9; 29:1-8, 24; but cf. 28:69). Nevertheless, what follows in the text is not an exact copy of the earlier Decalogue and Book of the Covenant in Exodus, but rather a legal corpus that is more loosely patterned after its precursor, replete with additions and modifications.

Early Judaism

Jewish writings of the Second Temple period continue to use a leapfrog method similar to that employed in Deuteronomy, ignoring or severely compressing God's covenantal dealings with the intervening generations. They also present new formulations of the covenant as though they were the original revelation to Moses on Sinai (e.g., *Jubilees*), as they seek both to harmonize the Scriptures and to actualize the covenant in new historical situations.

Covenant in the Septuagint

Because of several translational issues, the Septuagint presents a special case with respect to Jewish covenantal traditions in the Second Temple period. The Septuagint's default translation of Hebr. *bĕrît* ("covenant") by *diathēkē* ("last will, testament") is a calque, that is, a word whose semantic range has been adjusted in common usage to incorporate a component of meaning derived from a counterpart in another language. In this case, the component of meaning that carries over is that God himself sets the terms of a written and binding arrangement. In other respects, the choice of *diathēkē* as a translation value for the Hebrew term is less than successful because it can also convey unintended connotations. Insofar as subsequent Jewish and Christian writings adopted this Septuagintal usage, the potential for misunderstanding persists.

Another issue is whether the individual stipulations of the covenant were faithfully rendered in the Greek translation. It has been argued, for example, that some of the covenant stipulations were modified in the Greek translation to conform to currently prevailing practices in Ptolemaic Egypt when the translation of the Torah was made.

Covenant during the Maccabean Crisis

The historic covenant with Israel became a flash point during the Maccabean crisis. Speaking of Antiochus IV Epiphanes, Dan. 11:30 states: "He will return and rage against the holy covenant. He will act and turn and attend to those who abandon the holy covenant." Here it should be noted that one "covenant" is replaced by another, for referring evidently to the same events, Dan. 9:27 states that Antiochus "will make a firm covenant with the multitude [i.e., the Hellenizing Jews (cf. 1 Macc. 1:11)] for one week." In response to this situation, Mattathias reportedly vowed: "Even if all the nations that live under the rule of the king obey him . . . yet I and my sons and my brothers will live by the covenant of our fathers" (1 Macc. 2:19-22; cf. 1:63). It was during the persecution under Antiochus IV that the Prayer of Azariah was written. Formally, this prayer belongs to a group of Second Temple prayers that exhibit a strongly Deuteronomistic perspective and contain several basic elements, including the fact that God keeps covenant and that the people have not (e.g., Psalm 106; Ezra 9:6-15; Neh. 9:4-37; Dan. 9:4-19; Bar. 1:15–3:8; and the *Words of the Heavenly Luminaries* from Qumran [4QDibHam[a]]).

The Covenant at Qumran

The Qumran community, as well as the wider Essene movement to which it belonged, has been described as "the community of the renewed covenant," because the foundation documents that the group itself produced (esp. 1QS, 1QSa, CD, 1QpHab, 1QM) frequently refer to the "covenant" and/or the "(re)new(ed) covenant." The Qumran covenanters had a sectarian notion of the covenant, insofar as they considered themselves the only one group within Israel to be keeping it. The history of Israel was for them no longer an adequate grounding for the obligation to keep the covenant, and they therefore claimed to possess a higher revelation. The strong dualism and determinism of the sectarian texts, especially in the "Treatise on the Two Spirits" in 1QS 3–4, effectively redefined the terms of membership in the covenant people: the spirit of truth has been appointed by God only for the predestined sons of light. The "Treatise on the Two Spirits" may be an addition to 1QS, but its dualism informs the covenant renewal ceremony in cols. 1–3.

It is instructive in this regard also to consider the older apocalypses that were foundational to the group, that is, writings that were found in multiple copies at Qumran and obviously influenced the community's own compositions (e.g., CD 16:1-4 juxtaposes the Law of Moses and the *Book of Jubilees*). The Qumran community preserved the older apocalypses of *1 Enoch*, *Jubilees*, and Daniel. In the Enochic tradition, the unchanging laws of nature contrasted with human disobedience to the laws meant for people, whereas the Law of Moses given at Sinai is missing from this tradition. In contrast, both Daniel and *Jubilees* have stories about keeping the Law of Moses and apocalyptic visions, with Daniel having more on apocalyptic visions and *Jubilees* more on keeping the Law of Moses. In comparison to these tendencies, the Dead Sea Scrolls exhibit the same combination of *both* Mosaic Law *and* apocalypse as in Daniel and *Jubilees*, with the proportions of each more like those of *Jubilees* (i.e., more on the Law of Moses and less on apocalypse). Nevertheless, the Enochic tradition was also very influential at Qumran.

The Covenant in Jubilees

Jubilees is indeed crucial in this discussion, because it forms an important exegetical bridge between the

Enochic tradition, which it in part incorporates, and the Qumran scrolls. Yet the actual relationship of the Sinaitic covenant to the true purpose of the book should not be obscured by its opening setting on Mt. Sinai. Superficially, *Jubilees* is a reworking of Genesis 1 to Exodus 24, and, as shown by the beginning and the end of the book, the setting of the book is portrayed as the actual revelation given to Moses on Mt. Sinai. Thus, *Jubilees* opens (*Jub.* 1:1-4) with the Lord summoning Moses to ascend the mountain to meet with him, referring to Moses' stay on the mountain (Exod. 24:18; cf. 34:28) that took place the day after the covenantal ceremonies described in Exodus 19–24. The book also ends with a direct reference to the revelation to Moses on Mt. Sinai (*Jub.* 50:2: "On Mt. Sinai I [*sc.* the Angel of the Presence] told you about the Sabbaths of the land and the years of jubilees in the Sabbaths of the years").

Scattered throughout *Jubilees* are also several reminders that the contents of this book are addressed to Moses (on Mt. Sinai). Obviously, therefore, the author(s) of *Jubilees* wanted the revelation and covenant at Sinai to be understood in light of the whole biblical history that preceded it (Genesis 1 through Exodus 24). *Jubilees* is not so much a covenantal book as an apocalypse within a covenantal setting that inherently lends it authority, and in so doing somewhat relativizes the Sinaitic covenant by asserting, for example, that the election of Israel goes back not to the exodus from Egypt or to the making of the covenant at Sinai, but to the very beginning of creation (*Jub.* 2:19-22). Moreover, many of the laws that were given to Israel on Sinai according to the biblical record actually date back to earlier periods (e.g., the Festival of Weeks was instituted not at Sinai [Exod. 23:16; 34:22], but when Noah disembarked from the ark [*Jub.* 6:17-19]).

BIBLIOGRAPHY

R. J. BAUTCH 2008, *Covenant by Kingship: Articulating the Mosaic Covenant in the Second Temple Period,* Edinburgh: Clark. • D. CARSON ET AL., EDS., 2001, 2004, *Justification and Variegated Nomism,* 2 vols., Grand Rapids: Baker Academic. • E. CHRISTIANSEN 1995, *The Covenant in Judaism and Paul: A Study in Ritual Boundaries as Identity Markers,* Leiden: Brill. • M. ELLIOTT 2000, *The Survivors of Israel: A Reconsideration of the Theology of Pre-Christian Judaism,* Grand Rapids: Eerdmans. • B. HALPERN-AMARU 1994, *Rewriting the Bible: Land and Covenant in Post-Biblical Jewish Literature,* Valley Forge, Penn.: Trinity Press International. • H. NAJMAN 2003, *Seconding Sinai: The Development of Mosaic Discourse in Second Temple Judaism,* Leiden: Brill. • S. PORTER AND J. DE ROO, EDS. 2003, *The Concept of the Covenant in the Second Temple Period,* Leiden: Brill. • E. P. SANDERS 1977, *Paul and Palestinian Judaism,* London: SMC. • L. SCHIFFMAN 2004, "The Concept of Covenant in the Qumran Scrolls and Rabbinic Literature," in *The Idea of Biblical Interpretation: Essays in Honor of James L. Kugel,* ed. H. Najman and J. Newman, Leiden: Brill, 257-78. • A. M. SCHWEMER 1996, "Zum Verhältnis von Diatheke und Nomos in den Schriften der jüdischen Diaspora Ägyptens in hellenistisch-römischer Zeit," in *Bund und Tora: Zur theologischen Begriffsgeschichte in alttestamentlicher, frühjüdischer und urchristlicher Tradition,* ed. F. Avemarie and H. Lichtenberger, Tübingen: Mohr-Siebeck, 67-109.

See also: Covenantal Nomism; Election

JAMES M. SCOTT

Covenantal Nomism

The phrase "covenantal nomism" refers to two central facets of early Jewish belief, the covenant and Torah observance, and to the relationship between them. The phrase has become part of the currency of early Jewish and New Testament studies as a result of E. P. Sanders's groundbreaking *Paul and Palestinian Judaism* (1977), the classic exposition of covenantal nomism. Sanders's principal aim was to dismantle old constructions of Judaism as legalistic and to replace them with a portrait of Jewish religion that was rooted in divine grace and election. Sanders's particular targets were Protestant NT scholars such as Paul Billerbeck and Rudolf Bultmann; his aim was to bring to the fore the emphases of more neglected scholars such as G. F. Moore.

Characteristics of "Covenantal Nomism"

This centrality of God's grace and mercy is expressed in the "covenantal" half of the phrase. Jewish religion cannot be characterized as legalistic, Sanders argued, because of God's gratuity, clearly to be seen in his choice of Israel and in his promises of blessing. God grants mercy to Israel *before* he institutes the commandments. "Getting in" is purely the result of God's activity; it is not a consequence of human effort. There are reasons given in rabbinic literature for God's choice of Israel, but these function merely to emphasize that God is reasonable and not capricious. The default position is that "all Israelites have a share in the world to come" (*m. Sanh.* 10:1). Obedience to the covenant is not impossible, and allowance is made for transgressions through the processes of the sacrificial system. Only high-handed sin that renounces the covenant can place people outside of God's mercy. Most Israelites carry out the obedience requisite for "staying in" the covenant.

So "nomism" is very much the secondary element in the phrase, which is not to say that it is insignificant. Torah observance, for Sanders, does not lead to a status that is not already possessed by the Israelite. Its function is to *maintain* the position in the covenant that God has already granted. Nomism, then, is not the means to salvation. Deeds are certainly not, on this scheme, weighed so that salvation and condemnation are awarded on the basis of works. It is the covenant, with its components of divine election and promise, which guarantees the salvation of all Israelites, with the exception of a small minority of egregious apostates.

Sanders expounds this pattern of religion principally from tannaitic Judaism. Perhaps the classic statement of covenantal nomism for Sanders comes from Rabbi Joshua b. Karha: "Why does the section *Hear, O Israel* precede *And it shall come to pass if ye shall hearken [diligently to my commandments]?* So that a man may

COVENANTAL NOMISM

first take upon him the yoke of the kingdom of heaven and afterward take upon him the yoke of the commandments" (*m. Ber.* 2:2). Similarly, in a comment on the Decalogue, God says in the *Mekilta:* "Now, just as you have accepted my reign, you must also accept my decrees" (*Mekilta* Baḥodesh 6 on Exod. 20:3-6). Tannaitic Judaism, on Sanders's account, emphasizes the priority of grace over the commandments.

The replacement of a deeds-based judgment by a merciful judgment also meant that Sanders could undermine the old picture of Judaism as a religion of anxiety, in which each individual Jew would nervously await his or her works being weighed in the balance. Given God's promises and his provision for atonement, the disposition of rabbinic religion was not fear but "the joy of the Torah." Moreover, the old picture of God as a distant figure, who in the Hellenistic period was supposedly thought to be more and more removed from the world, was in fact alien to the rabbis, who regarded God's forgiveness and presence as immediately available to Jewish experience.

The Dead Sea Scrolls for Sanders shared many of the same features. God has made a covenant with his people, a covenant that may be referred to either as a new covenant, or as an ancient covenant whose hidden elements have come to light only in the recent history of the Qumran community. This covenant is almost synonymous with salvation. The prominence of grace in the Scrolls is evident in particular in the Qumran *Community Rule* (1QS 3–4), with its stress on predestination. God's election of the community is accompanied by the revelation that brings saving knowledge. The commandments that the sectarians are obliged to obey should be seen in this light: they are granted by divine revelation. Obedience is, again, the consequence of being in the covenant and the requirement for remaining therein. Transgression is serious for the community, but again there is ample provision for it. Only a small minority of sins are punishable by expulsion from the community. The great majority of transgressions can be dealt with by smaller scale penances in the case of sins against the community, and there are other means specified such as fasting and "prayer rightly offered" (1QS 9:4-5).

All this is within the wider framework of the grace of God, whose mercy is evident particularly in the emphatic confessions of sin that characterize the Qumran *Hodayot:* "In my troubles you comfort me; I delight in forgiveness; I regret my former transgression. And I know that there is hope because of your kindness, and trust because of the abundance of your strength" (1QH 17:13-14). Again, the prayer of confession at the end of 1QS reinforces this picture: "As for me, if I stumble, the mercies of God shall be my eternal salvation. If I stagger because of the sin of the flesh, my justification shall be by the righteousness of God that endures for ever" (1QS 11:11-12). To a large extent, the question of reward and punishment at the final judgment does not arise, since salvation is enjoyed in the community's present existence.

Much the same pattern is seen by Sanders in the Apocrypha and Pseudepigrapha. Ben Sira, for example, despite its many differences from rabbinic thought, shares with the rabbis a system whereby commandments should be obeyed, but transgression can be forgiven as a result of repentance. Again, in *Jubilees* election and the covenant are prominent, and although the author enjoins rigorous obedience, the sacrificial system is probably assumed to be effective, and unwitting sins are atoned for by prayer. In the *Psalms of Solomon,* the righteousness of God punishes the wicked for their sins. As Sanders emphasizes elsewhere, however, requital for deeds is not a symmetrical process: punishment is on the basis of deeds, but salvation is on the basis of God's mercy. Only *4 Ezra* breaks with the covenantal-nomist pattern; for the author of that work, the disaster of the destruction of the Temple evidently means that the system has collapsed. *4 Ezra* is the exception that proves the rule: it *is* characterized by legalistic perfectionism.

In sum, then, covenantal nomism refers to a pattern of religion with two key emphases: "getting in" by God's gracious election (covenantal) and "staying in" through Torah observance (nomism). God also provides for transgression through the sacrificial system, and since final salvation is ultimately the result of his election rather than the obedience of Israelites, it is attributed to God's mercy and is by no means a consequence of perfection or a preponderance of good deeds over bad.

Responses to Sanders

Sanders's *Paul and Palestinian Judaism* has been one of the most influential books in Jewish studies in recent times and as such has generated a large body of literature in response. Initial reactions were largely positive, particularly among New Testament scholars, and one consequence was a reevaluation of significant aspects of Pauline theology, especially justification (the "new perspective on Paul"). Many have endorsed Sanders's conclusions about particular works or corpora such as the *Psalms of Solomon* (Winninge 1995) and the Dead Sea Scrolls (Abegg 1999). Other works have been strongly critical of Sanders. Seifrid's assessment of the *Psalms of Solomon,* for example, is rather different from that of Winninge. Martin McNamara has questioned whether "covenantal nomism" is a fitting designation of any early Jewish literature, on the grounds that "nomism" presumes a response of obedience that is too fixed and inflexible.

There has also been a significant body of work that has aimed to sift through the positive and negative aspects of Sanders's work. Friedrich Avemarie's reevaluation of the rabbinic evidence has welcomed Sanders's emphasis on grace and election in tannaitic and later literature, but it also shows up some of the shortcomings of *Paul and Palestinian Judaism.* He makes the point that while older literature may have presented a one-sided picture of Judaism in which grace is swallowed up by legalism, Sanders actually reacts in the opposite direction and presents a similarly one-sided picture that gives election and the covenant an all-encompassing place that it does not really have in the ancient literature, where in fact there is also important evidence for deeds being determinative of final salvation (e.g., *y. Qiddushin* 61d; *b. Sanhedrin* 81a; *m. 'Abot* 3:15; *t. Sanh.* 13:3; *t. Qidd.* 1:14). In rabbinic literature, divine grace and human deeds are not seen in competition with one another, but are rather two parallel aspects of rabbinic "soteriology."

Other work has similarly reevaluated the literature from before the rabbinic period. Again, the importance of election is paramount, but as in the later literature, divine grace does not mean that human righteousness cannot be seen as crucial, the way to final salvation. In *Psalms of Solomon,* "the one who does righteousness stores up life for himself with the Lord" (*Pss. Sol.* 9:5; cf. 14:2-3), and yet later in the same *Psalm,* the author can write, "You have chosen the seed of Abraham above all the nations, and have set your name upon us, O Lord, and you will never cast us off" (*Pss. Sol.* 9:9). Similarly, in Qumran the importance of divine predestination is indisputable, and yet there is also a stress on the role of obedience in final vindication: "Consider all these things . . . so that you may rejoice at the end of time. . . . And this will be reckoned to you as righteousness, since you will be doing what is righteous and good in his eyes . . ." (4QMMT C 26-32). The two themes of saving election *and* eschatological life through obedience can stand side by side.

Some scholars have extended Sanders's conclusions about covenantal nomism to argue that it was also the structure of early Christian, and even Pauline, thought. Sanders resisted this conclusion himself, because of the participationist dimensions of Paul's theology. However, because he argues that Paul retained the basic scheme of "getting in by grace, staying in by works," others, although probably a minority, regard Paul as also a covenantal nomist.

Evaluation and Legacy

Since the publication of *Paul and Palestinian Judaism,* there has been a fair degree of discussion, some quite heated, over the validity of the covenantal nomism hypothesis. This discussion has consisted of large numbers of scholars accepting the challenge for the first time of interpreting Jewish texts firsthand. In Jewish studies and in New Testament scholarship most recently, however, the debate has been somewhat becalmed. Some of the points made by Sanders in response to the excesses of nineteenth- and twentieth-century Christian scholarship on Judaism have been widely accepted. The stronger elements of Sanders's position — the need to interpret Jewish texts on their own terms, and the importance of election and grace in Judaism — have been absorbed. On the other hand, some of Sanders's own one-sided tendencies have been treated with more caution. It is impossible, however, to talk in simple terms of a single reception of Sanders: different scholarly communities (particularly in New Testament scholarship) continue to appropriate the covenantal nomism theory differently. For some, it can be a fairly flexible category that can absorb more than the two minimal poles implied in the name. For others, its failure to do justice to the diversity of early Judaism, its static character, and its de-emphasis of obedience as a criterion for eschatological salvation are serious defects.

Bibliography

M. G. Abegg 1999, "4QMMT C 27, 31 and 'Works Righteousness,'" *DSD* 6: 139-47. • P. S. Alexander, 1986, Review of Sanders, *Jesus and Judaism, JJS* 37: 103-6. • F. Avemarie 1996, *Tora und Leben: Untersuchungen zur Heilsbedeutung der Tora in der frühen rabbinischen Literatur,* Tübingen: Mohr-Siebeck. • F. Avemarie 1999, "Erwählung und Vergeltung: Zur optionalen Struktur rabbinischer Soteriologie," *NTS* 45: 108-26. • D. A. Carson, P. T. O'Brien, M. A. Seifrid, eds. 2001-2004, *Justification and Variegated Nomism,* 2 vols., Tübingen: Mohr-Siebeck. • J. D. G. Dunn 2006, *The New Perspective on Paul,* Tübingen: Mohr-Siebeck. • M. A. Elliott 2000, *The Survivors of Israel: A Reconsideration of the Theology of Pre-Christian Judaism,* Grand Rapids: Eerdmans. • S. J. Gathercole 2002, *Where Is Boasting? Early Jewish Soteriology and Paul's Response in Romans 1–5,* Grand Rapids: Eerdmans. • T. Laato 1995, *Paul and Judaism: An Anthropological Approach,* Atlanta: Scholars Press. • G. F. Moore 1927-1930, *Judaism in the First Centuries of the Christian Era: The Age of the Tannaim,* 3 vols., Cambridge, Mass.: Harvard University Press. • E. P. Sanders 1977, *Paul and Palestinian Judaism,* Philadelphia: Fortress. • E. P. Sanders 1985, *Jesus and Judaism,* Philadelphia: Fortress. • M. A. Seifrid 1992, *Justification by Faith: The Origin and Development of a Central Pauline Theme,* Leiden: Brill. • M. Winninge 1995, *Sinners and the Righteous: A Comparative Study of the Psalms of Solomon and Paul's Letters,* Stockholm: Almqvist & Wiksell. • K. Yinger 1999, *Paul, Judaism and Judgement according to Deeds,* Cambridge: Cambridge University Press.

See also: Covenant; Election; Grace; Judgment; Moore, George Foote; Sanders, Ed Parish

Simon J. Gathercole

Creation

The Jewish belief that the world and humanity were created by God is based on the creation narratives in Genesis 1–2 and other passages in the Hebrew Scriptures (e.g., Psalm 104; Job 38:7), passages that have analogies with other creation myths in ancient Near Eastern texts. The basic belief was expanded and interpreted considerably in later retellings in early Jewish literature. The creation of heaven and earth can be differentiated from related narratives, such as the story of Adam, Eve, and the Serpent in Genesis 3.

Genesis 1–2

Genesis 1 and 2 offer two creation stories, one in 1:1–2:4a, attributed to the Priestly source of the Pentateuch and dated to the sixth or fifth century B.C.E., and one in 2:4b–3:24, attributed to the J source, dated to the tenth or ninth century. According to Gen. 1:1–2:4a, the world was created in six days by God speaking everything into existence. On day one, God created light; on day two, the firmament and the separation of waters; on day three, the earth, sea, and vegetation; on day four, the heavenly luminaries; on day five, sea creatures and birds; and on day six, land animals and humans. On day seven, the Creator rested. Whether Genesis 1 advocates *creatio ex nihilo* depends on whether one translates the initial clause of v. 1 "When God began creating" or "In the beginning God created" and whether the chaos in v. 2 is presumed to have existed before creation or to have resulted from it. P emphasizes much more than J that humanity is God's central creature, made in God's image (Gen. 1:26). The account in Genesis 2 has no specific time span but implies that God's creative activity lasted a single day. The precreation scenario is also different than in Genesis 1 (a desert oasis irrigated by underground springs instead of dark, watery chaos), as is the order and method of creation. The Creator is depicted acting in more anthropomorphic terms — forming, breathing, planting, fashioning. Instead of making an indeterminate number of males and females at the climax of creation, YHWH forms one male, plants a garden, makes land animals and birds, and then fashions one woman from the man.

The ancient Near Eastern texts most closely related to the biblical narratives are the Babylonian creation myth *Enuma Elish,* and the Canaanite mythic cycle from Ugarit. In both cases there is a conflict between a god (Marduk, Baal) and a sea monster or between a dragon and the sea that results in the creation of heaven and earth. The Garden of Eden story in Genesis 2–3 may be located in the Persian Gulf (as the Sumerians thought) or in Armenia. The word "Eden" may be derived from Akk. *edinu,* "steppe or plain." The tree of knowledge and the tree of life mentioned in the Eden story may partly go back to the magic plant in the Mesopotamian *Gilgamesh Epic.*

Most of the creation texts in the Hebrew Bible date from the exilic and postexilic periods: Genesis 1 (P), Deutero- and Trito-Isaiah, Ezekiel, Malachi, and Psalms. The Septuagint translates *bārā'* seventeen times by *ktizein* and fifteen times by *poiein;* in other cases, it employs a whole range of other verbs.

Creation is more widely interpreted in the period of early Judaism, as is witnessed in numerous passages from the Apocrypha, Pseudepigrapha, Philo, and Josephus, where elements of the biblical narratives are retold and reinterpreted.

Apocrypha

Among the Apocrypha, we find interpretations of the creation story in Judith, Sirach, Wisdom of Solomon, 2 and 4 Maccabees, and in some of the additions to the book of Daniel.

In Jdt. 9:5 the author describes God as the one who has "designed" things both present and future and who "intended" to do so. This reveals a view of history as part of creation, and of God having a prior plan for creation, a clear example of wisdom thinking. Another verse speaks of God more liturgically (Jdt. 9:12, "creator of the waters, king of all your creation"; Jdt. 13:18, "blessed be the Lord God, who created the heavens and the earth"). All creatures must serve God, as they were made by God's word and spirit, which formed them (Jdt. 16:14).

The Wisdom of Solomon speaks of God having "made all things by his word" (9:1). It depicts creation as "out of formless matter" (11:17) and praises God for not only creating but also sustaining all things (11:21-25). A final verse speaks of the possibility of knowing God through creation (13:1).

Isolated passages in the Apocrypha point to the heavens and the earth and to humankind as God's work ("not out of things that existed," 2 Macc. 7:28), and others speak of God as the creator of light (Bar. 3:33) or mention other aspects of God's creation (e.g., LXX Dan. 4:37; Bel and the Dragon 5; and Esth. 4:17c; 3 Macc. 2:3; 4 Macc. 11:5). But it is the author of Sirach who elaborates most on the topic. In addition to a passage that speaks of God having left humanity in the power of its own inclination (Sir. 15:14), and one that differentiates between the various ordered divisions of the divine work of creation and their obedient character (Sir. 16:26-30), there is also a full creation poem in Sir. 42:15–43:33. It is a panegyric to God's creation, including the sun, moon, stars, rainbow, and nature's marvels.

Pseudepigrapha

One brief passage in the *Letter of Aristeas* says that the freeing of Jewish captives in Egypt (at the time the Septuagint was written) was a liberation "for the human race, being the creation of God" (17). Two quite different passages argue that it is more desirable to honor God's creation as a whole than objects from creation (136 and 139).

In the *Psalms of Solomon* we find creation used as an expression for both the beginning and the history of the world: "[Solomon] considered the judgments of God since the creation of heaven and earth; I proved God right in his judgments from eternity" (*Ps. Sol.* 8:7). Another verse states that God created the stars in order to fix time from day to day and that they never deviate from their appointed course (*Ps. Sol.* 18:10).

Creation passages can also be found in *Jubilees,* though it is more concerned with Genesis 6 (e.g., *Jub.* 5:12 on the mating of angels with humans in Gen. 6:1-4). Furthermore, one finds isolated affirmations of God's creation "by his word" (*Jub.* 12; 12:4), and a prayer of Rebecca to "the Most High God who created heaven and earth" (*Jub.* 25:11).

In the *Book of the Watchers* (*1 Enoch* 1–36) Enoch sees "the storerooms of all the winds and how with them [the Creator] has embroidered all creation as well as the foundations of the earth" (18:1). The Lord of Glory has performed these blessed miracles in order to manifest them to his angels, to the winds, "and to the people so that they might praise the effect of all his creation" (36:4). The stars and the four seasons have been appointed "the leaders of the chiefs of the thousands" (75:1), but above all stands the "Lord of all the creation of the world" (82:7) and "the Lord of all creation of heaven" (84:2), who has created all, rules all, and knows, sees, and hears all (84:3).

Other passages in *1 Enoch* praise specific elements of the created order, including the unwavering luminaries that appear in their respective seasons, and the unchanging fixedness of all God's work on earth, including summer, winter, water, clouds, and dew (2:1-3); everything functions as God has ordered it (5:1-3). The orderliness of creation is invoked to criticize the waywardness of humanity. God the Creator also knew before the world's creation everything that would happen from generation to generation (39:11). A small wisdom poem on creation is found in the *Similitudes of Enoch:* heaven was suspended before the creation of the world; earth is founded upon the water; the sea rests on a foundation of sand; sun, moon, and stars move according to a fixed course, as do all the other elements of creation (69:16-25; cf. 101:6-8; and 83:3, 11 from the point of view of Enoch's vision).

Little is added to this by the author of *2 Enoch,* except the underlining of a few theological nuances, such as the insistence that God created everything from nothing and that not even the angels know about the secret plan of creation (24:2-5). God "created mankind . . . in a facsimile of his own face. Small and great the Lord created" (44:1). One day, the creation will come to an end and make way for a new and eternal age (65:7).

According to the *Sibylline Oracles* 3, God created "by a word" not only heaven and the sea, the untiring sun, full moon, and shining stars, but also "strong Mother Tethys," springs and rivers, imperishable fire, days, nights, wild beasts, serpents, and birds, as well as Adam "of four letters, the first-formed man, fulfilling by his name east and west and south and north" (*Sib. Or.* 3.24-26). Book 4 focuses on nature, praising God as the Creator of night, day, sun, stars, moon, fish-filled sea, land, rivers and perennial springs, "things created for life, showers which engender the fruit of the soil, and trees, both vine and olive" (*Sib. Or.* 4.13-17).

In *4 Ezra* the focus falls on the creation of Adam: "he was the workmanship of your hands, and you breathed into him the breath of life, and he was made alive in your presence" (3:4-5), with the sole purpose of identifying human sin as the cause of evil in the world (3:21; 4:30). This sin would influence every person until creation's renewal at the end of time (7:75), which, according to *2 Baruch,* would be preceded by a time of trial (*2 Bar.* 32:6; cf. 30:3). Everything was known to God and was planned before it was created (*4 Ezra* 6:1-6, 8-10; cf. *2 Bar.* 14:17), including the age to come, when there will be no evil, deceit, corruption, or death, but when human hearts will convert to a different spirit, and there will be faithfulness and truth (*4 Ezra* 6:26-28; cf. 11:46). This will occur after a seven-day return to primeval silence (*4 Ezra* 7:30) and the temporary messianic kingdom, from which only a few will be saved while many perish (*4 Ezra* 7:45-61; cf. 8:53). For this reason Ezra begs God to have mercy on creation (*4 Ezra* 8:8, 45, 47). The book of *2 Baruch* adds further nuance to these issues in *4 Ezra,* such as God's having created the earth and fixed the firmament "by the word and fastened the height of heaven by the spirit, the one who in the beginning of the world called that which did not yet exist and they obeyed you" (*2 Bar.* 21:4-5; cf. Baruch's prayer in chap. 48; 56:4).

In the *Testament of Moses,* creation is used as a fixed point to calculate events, such as the date of the exodus "twenty five hundred years after the creation of the world" (1:2). God created the world for the sake of his people but "did not make its purpose known openly from the beginning so that the nations might be found guilty, indeed that they might abjectly declare themselves guilty by their own (mistaken) discussions (of creation's purpose)" (1:12-13). Moses is to deposit this writing and the books that God will entrust to him "in the place which (God) has chosen from the beginning of the creation of the world" (1:17). As in *4 Ezra* and *2 Baruch,* God's kingdom will appear at the end of time and be manifest "throughout his whole creation" (10:1).

In the *Testament of Abraham,* Abraham takes a heavenly journey and sees examples of sins committed in early biblical times until it is said that he should "go round all the creation which I made, because his heart is not moved for sinners, but my heart is" (12:12-13 [B]). It is obvious from this passage that by "creation" the world and its history are meant. Creation is also used as background for a panegyric to Abraham himself, the "friend of God" — "In all the creation that God created, there is not to be found one like you. For even God himself has searched and has not found such a one on the entire earth" (*T. Abr.* [B] 13:10-11).

The *Testaments of the Twelve Patriarchs* contain several creation passages. In the *Testament of Reuben,* Reuben mentions seven spirits of deceit established against humankind as well "the other seven spirits . . . given to man at creation so that by them every human deed (is done)" (*T. Reub.* 2:3). The passage has in view human senses and faculties, the spirits of life, sight, hearing, smell, speech, taste, and procreation, which is "the last in the creation" (2:9). In the *Testament of Levi,* Levi speaks of a final judgment of the "sons of men" and mentions several catastrophic signs of the end, among which is that all creation will be distraught (*T. Levi* 4:1). In the *Testament of Naphtali,* Naphtali refers to three dimensions of the creation of a human body: "for all the creation of the Most High was according to height, measure, and standard," and compares the Creator with a potter and the body with a vessel (*T. Naph.* 2:3). This passage can clearly be classified among the wisdom sayings on creation. A final sapiential passage speaks of the other "products" of God's "workmanship" through which one can "discern the Lord who made all things" (*T. Naph.* 3:4).

Philo of Alexandria

Philo's most systematic interpretation of the Genesis creation narratives is found in his treatise *De Opificio Mundi (On the Creation of the World).* After a summary of Genesis 1–3, Philo offers the necessary background for understanding the laws of Moses. The work has an important eschatological and ethical dimension, as the glorious times of old (the period of Adam and Eve in Paradise before their expulsion) will return once the right religious and moral conditions have been met.

Philo also uses the creation story to discuss philosophical questions about the origin of the world in dialogue with Epicurean, Platonic, and Stoic ideas, ideas which for him all originate from Moses. Among these issues are that God exists and is good, that the world has a beginning, that all creatures coexist in a hierarchical order, that behind the visible world there is an intelligible world, and that the world is like a city and its inhabitants are its citizens. For Philo, God did not create the world *ex nihilo* but actively shaped preexistent, passive matter (cf. the Wisdom of Solomon).

Philo recognizes that the two accounts of humanity's creation in Genesis are different. Instead of trying to harmonize them, he asserts that the account in Genesis 1 describes the creation of ideal, incorporeal man, while the second depicts the earthly type as a copy of the ideal (*Opif.* 69–71, 134–35).

Josephus

For Josephus there is only one creator of the universe (*Ant.* 1.155), who is also addressed in a prayer for a meal as the creator of all substance (*Ant.* 1.272) and is blessed by David as "the father and parent of the universe, and the author of human and divine things" (*Ant.* 7.380). In other passages God is called the creator of the Jewish nation (*J.W.* 3.354; 5.377), who has endowed the souls of the Jews with such a temper that they despise death (*J.W.* 3.356), although the Creator is against such an impiety as suicide (*J.W.* 3.369; 3.379).

New Testament

The three main Greek words for "creation" found in the New Testament are *ktizō* ("to create"); *ktisma* ("creature"); and *ktisis* ("creation"). Behind the use of these expressions we find three central theological concepts: God as creator of the world, the corruption of creation, and hope for a new creation.

God as Creator of the World

Many New Testament passages speak about the creation of the world as the beginning of everything. Numerous other passages refer to further aspects of this central concept. In all of this, however, the purpose of almost all New Testament authors' speaking of God's creation of the world seems to be twofold. First, the frequent mention of the creation as the beginning of the world is used to show that there was nothing prior to the world's existence, thereby highlighting God's creative power, sovereignty, and authority. Creation by the Word refers to everything that has been created (cf. Rom. 4:17; 2 Cor. 4:6; Eph. 3:9; Col. 1:16; Rev. 10:6). Hence the author of Revelation concludes that every creature will worship God because he is the creator of everything (Rev. 4:8-11). Second, the relationship between Creator and creature is put in the correct light: every creature has been created and willed by God, and every creature is therefore subject to God (Rom. 11:36). This includes even the Son, who besides being subject to the Father embodies the goal of all history, namely, that in the end God will be all in all (1 Cor. 15:28). Revelation 4–5 affirms the same essential truths in apocalyptic language. By depicting the glory of God's throne it reveals that God is creator and that all creation, as it unfolds in every single event in history, is subject to him and his plan for the cosmos.

The Old Creation

The New Testament also speaks of the human race's failure to reflect its original, created glory. Several passages speak of this failure, its cause, its consequences, and its eschatological solution. These and other aspects are found or hinted at in a variety of passages, but they are especially prominent in the Epistles and in the book of Revelation. The whole of Romans 1–11 touches on the subject in one way or another (e.g., Rom. 1:19-20, "Ever since the creation of the world his eternal power and divine nature, invisible though they are, have been understood and seen through the things he has made"; 8:19-20, "the creation waits with eager longing for the revealing of the children of God; for the creation was subjected to futility, not of its own will but by the will of the one who subjected it, in hope"). Most New Testament passages that invoke creation and new creation imply that the history of the world and of humanity falls into three main epochs: (1) the ideal period from the creation of the world until the transgression of Adam; (2) the period since Adam's disobedience, that is, the present epoch; and (3) the eschatological future, in which the glory of old will be restored. However, instead of speaking of creation as "fallen," as later Christian writers would, the New Testament speaks of a creation that has been corrupted. The notion of creation's being corrupted by Adam's primordial sin was not typical of Second Temple Judaism but developed only at the turn of the eras, in the theology of Paul and his slightly later contemporaries, the authors of *4 Ezra, 2 Baruch,* and in the early Adam and Eve literature. Aspects of creation's corruption include vanity, temporality, temptation, and death itself, all under the dominion of the god of this world, Satan. In this respect, Paul speaks of the world not as creation *(ktisis)* but cosmos *(kosmos)* and of humankind not as creature *(ktisma)* but flesh *(sarx).* Across the NT corpus, from the Gospels, to the Epistles, to Revelation, the world and the human race are the site of a cosmic conflict between Satan and God in Christ.

The New Creation

An important aspect of New Testament theology is the belief that humanity and the rest of the created order have their eschatological destiny in a "new heaven and new earth" (Rev. 21:1) or a "new creation" (2 Cor. 5:16). We find this not-always-clearly-formulated concept almost exclusively in the Pauline and non-Pauline epistles. The best-known text is found in Romans 8:

> For the creation waits with eager longing for the revealing of the children of God; for the creation was subjected to futility, not of its own will but by the will of the one who subjected it, in hope that the creation itself will be set free from its bondage to decay and will obtain the freedom of the glory of the children of God. (Rom. 8:18-22)

Similar passages are found elsewhere. The hope for a

new creation has its corollary in anthropology and ethics. In the end the new creation in Christ will restore God's glory in man, as it was meant to be from the very beginning of creation. The state of humanity as a fleshly being can only be overcome by his future state as a spiritual *(pneumatikos)* one. This change from flesh to Spirit, from an old to a new humanity, is presently being effected in the life of believers by the Spirit, preparing them for the new creation in Christ *(kainē ktisis en Christō),* which will be an embodied existence on an earth that is renewed and no longer subject to decay or death.

Rabbinic Literature

Rabbinic reflections about the creation are found in a variety of mishnaic, talmudic, and midrashic texts. The date of these passages ranges from the second century C.E. to late antiquity. They reflect various thoughts on the creation without representing a systematic theology. Esoteric speculation about the *Maʿaśeh Bereshit,* the "work of creation" in Genesis 1–3, and about the *Maʿaśeh Merkavah* or "work of the chariot" in Ezekiel 1–2, goes back to the same period (*m. Ḥag.* 2:1). The rabbis of the tannaitic period clearly had an interest in cosmogony but strived to free it from Gnostic and heretical speculation. They were interested in questions such as whether the heavens were created before the earth or at the same time, what existed before the creation (e.g., wisdom, the name of the messiah), what the role of the angels was, and on which day of the year the world was made.

BIBLIOGRAPHY

R. J. CLIFFORD 1994, *Creation Accounts in the Ancient Near East and in the Bible,* Washington, D.C.: Catholic Biblical Association of America. • R. J. CLIFFORD AND J. J. COLLINS, EDS. 1992, *Creation in the Biblical Tradition,* Washington, D.C.: Catholic Biblical Association of America. • J. FRISHMAN AND L. VAN ROMPAY, EDS. 1997, *The Book of Genesis in Jewish and Oriental Christian Interpretation,* Louvain: Peeters. • J. L. KUGEL 1998, *Traditions of the Bible: A Guide to the Bible As It Was at the Start of the Common Era,* Cambridge: Harvard University Press, 43-91. • K. KÖNIG AND E. ZENGER 2000, *To Begin With, God Created: Biblical Theologies of Creation,* Collegeville, Minn.: Liturgical Press. • G. P. LUTTIKHUIZEN, ED. 1999, *Paradise Interpreted: Representations of Biblical Paradise in Judaism and Christianity,* Leiden: Brill. • G. P. LUTTIKHUIZEN, ED. 2000, *The Creation of Man and Woman: Interpretation of the Biblical Narratives in Jewish and Christian Traditions,* Leiden: Brill. • J. VAN RUITEN 2000, *Primaeval History Interpreted: The Rewriting of Genesis 1–11 in the Book of Jubilees,* Leiden: Brill. • D. T. RUNIA 2001, *Philo of Alexandria: On the Creation of the Cosmos according to Moses: Introduction, Translation and Commentary,* Leiden: Brill. • T. H. TOBIN 1983, *The Creation of Man: Philo and the History of Interpretation,* Washington, D.C.: Catholic Biblical Association of America.

See also: Adam and Eve; Garden of Eden — Paradise

GERBERN S. OEGEMA

Crucifixion

Historical Aspects

Crucifixion seems to have been introduced by the Persians, to judge from sources such as Esth. 7:9-10, Ezra 6:11, and Herodotus (e.g., 1.128.2). By the fourth century B.C.E., the Greek world had become familiar with it; Alexander, the Diadochi, the Ptolemies, and the Seleucids all employed the method. Antiochus III, whose Seleucid empire began to rule the Jews directly in 203 B.C.E., famously crucified several enemies. His successor, Antiochus IV Epiphanes, imposed the penalty on Jewish loyalists during the early stages of the Maccabean Revolt, according to Josephus (*Ant.* 12.256).

For the Romans crucifixion was a form of *supplicium,* the severest kind of legal penalty. According to the jurist Julius Paulus in the *Sententiae,* it could be imposed upon Romans for the crimes of desertion to the enemy, the betrayal of state secrets, inciting to rebellion, murder, casting of horoscopes to discover the future health of rulers, magic, and certain kinds of falsification of wills. As a rule the Romans inflicted this type of punishment only on members of the lower classes and noncitizens. The elite would suffer death by less painful and less shameful means (the infliction of pain and shame being as much the point as execution when crucifixion was used). During the period of Roman rule over the Jews, crucifixion is known to have been employed on a number of occasions; Josephus relates that in the wake of the First Revolt, Titus crucified Jewish prisoners and once, near Tekoa, Josephus discovered among the crucified three of his own relatives (*Vita* 420). On the whole, however, ancient literature is spare in its descriptions of this practice, perhaps because, as Martin Hengel has suggested, even its mention was offensive to the aesthetic sensibilities of litterateurs.

Literary Aspects

Still, Jewish literature in the period of Early Judaism does refer to the practice. When the book of Esther was translated from Hebrew into Greek in 77 B.C.E. (assuming the colophon refers to Ptolemy XII), the translator understood Haman's execution as a crucifixion and so rendered the broad Hebrew term *tālāh,* which can mean various kinds of hanging, by the Greek *stauroō,* which is unambiguously "crucify." One may reasonably suppose that the translator understood the Hebrew of Esther in terms of usage current in his own day, and so conclude that the verb *tālāh* was now the customary Hebrew locution to express the idea of crucifixion. This point is of importance for the understanding of two apparent references to the practice in the Dead Sea Scrolls.

The first reference occurs in the primary copy of the *Temple Scroll* (11Q19 54:6-9). This portion is a rewriting of Deut. 21:22-23, which requires that a guilty person be executed, then hung on a tree — the object of the hanging being exposure, not execution. The *Temple Scroll* says instead:

> If a man is a traitor against his people and gives them up to a foreign nation, so doing evil to his people, you

> are to hang *(tālāh)* him on a tree until dead. On the testimony of two or three witnesses he will be put to death, and they themselves shall hang him on a tree. If a man is convicted of a capital offense and flees to the nations, cursing his people and the children of Israel, you are to hang him, too, upon a tree until dead.

Notable here is that the writer has reversed the order of Deuteronomy's clauses, so requiring the hanging to occur while the criminal is alive: crucifixion. Also important to note is the two crimes for which the penalty of crucifixion is to apply, betrayal of state secrets and desertion to the enemy. These are among the crimes for which Roman jurisprudence specified the application of this form of *supplicium*, suggesting that the author of the *Temple Scroll* (or his source here) was familiar with aspects of contemporary Roman law.

The second reference to crucifixion is to be found in the *Pesher Nahum* (4Q169 frg. 3-4 col. i lines 6-9). Commenting on Nahum 2:12-13, the author writes:

> "[He fills] his cave [with prey], his den with game." This refers to the Lion of Wrath [. . . ven]geance against the Seekers of Smooth Things, because he used to hang men alive, [as it was done] in Israel of old. For to anyone hanging alive on the tree [the verse ap]plies: "Behold, I am against [you, says the Lord of Hosts]."

Prior to the discovery and analysis of the *Temple Scroll*, it had been usual to argue that *Pesher Nahum* opposed crucifixion and hence to restore the critical lacuna above differently: "alive [which was never done] in Israel of old." Yigael Yadin, the editor of the *Temple Scroll*, proposed the restoration adopted here, and it has since become the majority view.

Scholars generally agree that the crucifixions described by *Pesher Nahum* are those narrated by Josephus in his description of the reign of Alexander Jannaeus (103-76 B.C.E.). Engaged in a civil war against a coalition that included the Pharisees, Jannaeus was able to quash the revolt after years of warfare, and turned next to the punishment of the revolt's leaders. He crucified some 800 men, probably in 88 B.C.E. (*Ant.* 13.380). The Pharisees had invited the Seleucid king, Demetrius III Eucerus, to ally with them and invade Judea. This was, of course, treason, and they died for it by the penalty required for that crime according to the *Temple Scroll* and Roman law. The author of *Pesher Nahum* evidently approved.

Bibliography

J. M. Allegro 1968, *Qumran Cave 4, I (4Q158-186)*, DJD 5, Oxford: Clarendon. • J. Baumgarten 1972, "Does TLH in the Temple Scroll Refer to Crucifixion?" *JBL* 91: 472-81. • M. Hengel 1977, *Crucifixion in the Ancient World and the Folly of the Message of the Cross*, trans. J. Bowden, Philadelphia: Fortress. • Y. Yadin 1971, "Pesher Nahum (4QpNahum) Reconsidered," *IEJ* 21: 1-12. • Y. Yadin 1983, *The Temple Scroll*, 3 vols. and supplementary plates, Jerusalem: Israel Exploration Society/Hebrew University of Jerusalem/Shrine of the Book.

Michael O. Wise

Cyprus

Origins of the Jewish Community

The origins of Jewish communities on Cyprus parallel the origins of Judaism. By the Early Bronze Age, Cyprus was exporting copper, pine, and opium. Trade promoted immigration from Syria-Palestine before the Israelites formed an ethnic identity. Semitic immigrants mixed with natives and successive immigrations of Minoans and Myceneans. Many settlements were abandoned by ca. 1050 B.C.E. During the next two centuries, Greek immigrants contributed to a hybrid Cypriot culture that spoke Greek. Cyprus or its Greek element might be the "Alashya" of Bronze Age texts and the "Elishah" of later biblical texts (Gen. 10:4; Ezek. 27:7; 1 Chron. 1:7).

During the ninth-seventh centuries B.C.E., the Phoenician city of Tyre established colonies on Cyprus with temples to Astarte and Baal-Melqart. Israel and Judah developed connections with Cyprus partly through relations with Tyre. This may explain links between Tyre and "Kittim" in Isa. 23:1, 12; Ezek. 27:6. The term derives from the Phoenician colony of Kition (Josephus *Ant.* 9.283-87). Kittim thus might indicate Cyprus or its Phoenician population (as also Num. 24:24; Jer. 2:10). However, Kittim may refer to other islands or coastlands dominated by Greeks (Gen. 10:4; 1 Chron. 1:7; 1 Macc. 1:1; Josephus, *Ant.* 1.128; even Romans, Dan. 11:30; 1QpHab; 1QM). The same ambiguity appears in the use of Kittim for mercenaries allied with Judah in ostraca from Arad (seventh-sixth centuries B.C.E.).

Jews are not easily distinguished from other Semitic inhabitants of Cyprus. Jews in Kition in the late Persian period used Phoenician and shared a cemetery with Phoenicians (*IJO* 3, Cyp6-8). In one example the father of the deceased bore a Yahwistic name (ʿAzaryahu; *IJO* 3, Cyp7). The deceased's own name celebrated his birth as a gift from Astarte (Muttun'ashtart). This preserves a polytheism typical of earlier Israelites. The son's powerful role as "chief of the scribes" confirms his integration into Kition's Phoenician community.

Jews in the Hellenistic and Roman Periods

Some sources often cited as evidence for Jews on Cyprus merely testify to political dynamics between Cyprus and Palestine (1 Macc. 15:23; 2 Macc. 12:2). Others only indicate that Jews were familiar with Cyprus (Josephus, *Ant.* 20.51; *Sib. Or.* 3.457-58; 4.128-29, 143-44; 5.450-54). Yet it is safe to accept Philo's claim that Cyprus had a large Jewish population in the first century (*Legatio ad Gaium* 238).

The resources that attracted earlier Israelites brought fresh infusions of Jewish sailors, merchants, and refugees from economic distress. Other Jews probably came as mercenaries of the Ptolemies or enslaved prisoners of war (Josephus, *Ant.* 13.284-87, 324-51). As typical in such cases, many probably intermarried with natives. Most Jews became invisible in epigraphic records because they adopted Greek names. An inscription from Kourion may mention "Onias" (second-first century B.C.E.; *IJO* 3, Cyp5). This might have memorialized a Jewish benefactor on Cyprus or some relationship with a Jewish priest in Egypt or Palestine. An inscription from Amathus might refer to a Jewish civic official (second century B.C.E.; *IJO* 3, App27). Jewish coins from Palestine found at sites on Cyprus provide a fuller picture. These currently number around 200 and date from late second century B.C.E. to late first century C.E.

Augustus gave Herod the Great the profits from half the Cypriot copper mines (Josephus, *Ant.* 16.128). He also entrusted Herod with managing the other half. This does not imply any role for Jews outside Herod's circle (so also for *Ant.* 17.335-36). No connection to Herod's mining should be assumed in *IGRR* 3.938 (where Mitford rejects the reading "Herod"). One can only speculate about whether mining interests encouraged the marriage of Herod's granddaughter Alexandra to a Cypriot elite named Timios (*Ant.* 18.131). It is not even certain that Timios was Jewish. Josephus's reference to a Cypriot Jew named Atomos in the court of Felix still might confirm that some Jews were among the island's elites (*Ant.* 20.142).

Cypriot metallurgy was associated with medicine and magic. However, the role of Jewish magic on Cyprus is exaggerated. Josephus alludes to magic in his story of Atomos. But he could mean that Atomos merely "pretended" to be a magician. This story probably informed Acts 13:6-12, whose author probably knew the works of Josephus. Acts inspired later Christian legends of Jewish magic. Pliny does not localize Jewish magic in *Naturalis Historia* 30.11. He just distinguishes its antiquity from Cypriot magic. A Jewish month name in a Flavian horoscope from Tremithus probably indicates Jewish authorship (*IJO* 3, App24). But Jewish words in third-century curse tablets from Amathus are just syncretism routine in magic (*Kourion* 127-42).

Legends of apostolic origins for Cypriot Christianity are not credible. Acts identifies Cyprus with Barnabas and pre-Pauline missionaries (4:36-37; 11:19-20; possibly 21:16). This sets the stage for visits by Barnabas and Paul (13:4-13; 15:39-40). No hint of this appears in Paul's letters. Probably unknown Jewish Christians did reach Cyprus in Paul's time. But their communities could not have survived the revolt of 116-117 C.E. Even Gentile Christians would have been lynched as Jewish sympathizers. Christianity was reintroduced by Gentile missionaries after the revolt.

Analogies with other regions indicate that the Jewish revolt in 66-70 C.E. polarized Jews and Gentiles on Cyprus. Coins of the revolt found on Cyprus suggest that an influx of Jewish rebels and refugees added to the tension. After 70, the Jewish tax decisively classified Cypriot Jews with foreign enemies of Rome.

Revolt and Return

The large size of the Cypriot Jewish community is confirmed by initial Jewish successes in the revolt of 116-117. The relative synchronism of rebellions in diverse regions suggests an overall strategy orchestrated by communication between these regions. Cypriot Jews probably played a key role by disrupting shipments of grain and Roman troops. Such a strategy explains the need for naval forces to suppress the revolt (Eusebius, *Hist Eccl.* 4.2). It also complements the activity of Jews in the Nile delta (Appian, *Liber Arabicus* F19). The strategic importance of Cyprus is further indicated by preservation of the name of its rebel commander (Artemion; Dio 68.32.2).

Dio says Jews slaughtered 240,000 people on Cyprus (68.32.2). Eusebius claims Jews destroyed Salamis and eradicated its Gentiles (*Chronicon,* Trajan 19). These are probably exaggerations. But one should not underestimate the destruction. As in Egypt and Cyrenaica, local Roman garrisons may have been weakened by Trajan's diversion of troops to his Parthian campaign. This unwittingly would have aided the Jewish uprising. Suppressing the revolt required Roman troops from outside of Cyprus (Eusebius, *Hist. Eccl.* 4.2; *ILS* 9491; *AE* 1953.171). Archaeological and epigraphic evidence for subsequent construction and Hadrianic benefactions probably indicates recovery efforts (Salamis, *IGRR* 3.989; *Opusc. Arch.* 6 [1950] 89 [48]; *Salamis* 92, 92a, 93, 94; possibly *Salamis* 13; Lapethos, *IGRR* 3.934; Kourion, *SEG* 25.1095; *Kourion* 85, 104; Carpasia, *SEG* 20.319).

Dio implies that all Cypriot Jews were annihilated (68.32.3). This need not be doubted. It probably reflects an order by Trajan. It is also a logical consequence of terror aroused by Jewish victories. Most Jews could be identified through records for the Jewish tax. Escape was limited by the sea. None who remained could have survived. Similar considerations confirm Dio's claim that Jews were not welcome for generations (as in Egypt; *CPJ* 2.450).

Immigration, not survival of the revolt, explains the reemergence of Judaism on Cyprus. A dedication to "the highest god" from Limassol dating second-third century was erected by "Sambon" (*SEG* 41.1475). Claims of Jewish influence on this cult must be rejected. "Highest" was widely used for Greek deities. Nevertheless, Jews probably used variants of "Sambon" attested from the second-third century in Amathus and Limassol (*SEG* 26.1467; 29.1573; 38.1530; 41.1425, 1475; probably *BCH* 3 [1879] 174 [47]). Undated examples in Amathus probably come from this period (*Athena* 22 [1910] 141 [4]). Probably this is also true of the "Martha" and the "Demetria daughter of Sambon" in Amathus (Murray, *Excavations in Cyprus,* 96 [29, 63]). Immigration probably introduced the rabbinic movement (*IJO* 3, Cyp1). Jews certainly were on Cyprus in the third to seventh centuries (*IJO* 3, Cyp1-4).

Bibliography

D. Campbell 2005, "Possible Inscriptional Attestation to Sergius Paul[l]us," *JTS* 56: 1-29. • A. Destrooper-Georgiades 2006, "Jewish Coins Found in Cyprus," *Israel Numismatic Research* 1:37-49. • F. Dobbs-Allsopp et al. 2005, *Hebrew Inscriptions,* New Haven: Yale University Press. • H. Hauben 2005, "Herod the Great and the Copper Mines of Cyprus," *Ancient Society* 35: 175-95. • M. Heltzer 1989, "Epigraphic Evidence concerning a Jewish Settlement in Kition in the Achaemenid Period," *Aula Orientalis* 7:189-206. • V. Kara-

GEORGHIS AND C. VERMEULE 1964-66, *Sculptures from Salamis,* 2 vols., Nicosia: Department of Antiquities. • T. PHILLIPS 2006, "The Genre of Acts," *Currents in Biblical Research* 4:365-396. • M. PUCCI BEN ZEEV 2005, *Diaspora Judaism in Turmoil, 116/117 CE*, Leuven: Peeters.

ALLEN KERKESLAGER

Cyrenaica

Cyrenaica is the eastern coastal region of modern-day Libya in North Africa. It was settled by Greeks in the seventh century B.C.E., and its major cities, Cyrene, Berenice, Arsinoë, Ptolemais, and Apollonia, formed a Pentapolis (Pliny, *Historia Naturalis* 5.31). During most of the Hellenistic age, Cyrenaica was under Ptolemaic control. It came under Roman rule in 96 B.C.E. A significant Jewish community in Cyrenaica, Cyrene in particular, dates from at least the Hellenistic period (Strabo, cited in Josephus, *Ant.* 16.7.2).

Political relationships in Palestine suggest that Israelites may have sailed with the Phoenicians who colonized Carthage in the ninth-eighth centuries B.C.E. Sea routes to Carthage make it likely that Phoenicians established settlements in Cyrenaica at that time, but most traces of these settlements disappeared as Greeks colonized Derna and other sites in the early seventh century B.C.E. During the sixth century B.C.E., Greek colonists pushed Berber pastoralists out of parts of the highlands and coastal plain.

A Paleo-Hebrew seal reportedly from Cyrene suggests that the growing prosperity may have attracted immigrants from Judah (*CJZC* 28). Since Jewish mercenaries served with the Persian armies in Egypt, Jews also may have been among the Persian troops who marched from Egypt into Cyrenaica to destroy Barka in ca. 514 B.C.E. (Herodotus, *Historia* 4.165-67, 200-205; cf. 3.13, 91). Yet the Hebrew Bible's vague comments about distant Greek colonies suggest minimal familiarity with Cyrenaica. Its allusions to Libya refer primarily to indigenous Africans who were known in Palestine through their role in Egyptian politics (Gen. 10:6, 13; Jer. 46:9; Ezek. 27:10; 30:5; 38:5; Nah. 3:9; 1 Chron. 1:8, 11; 2 Chron. 12:3; 16:8; Dan. 11:43).

Jews in Cyrenaica in the Hellenistic Period

Jews were probably among the military colonists and veterans that the Ptolemies settled in Cyrenaica in the third and second centuries B.C.E. (Josephus, *Ag. Ap.* 2.44; possibly *CJZC* 40). The Ptolemies also may have installed Jewish elites in bureaucratic posts in Cyrenaica to reward or preserve their loyalty during wars with the Seleucids and internal dynastic struggles. A Jewish aristocrat with a name popular in the region was Jason of Cyrene, who wrote a five-volume history of the Maccabean Revolt shortly after it occurred (2 Macc. 2:19-32). Jason probably had visited Jerusalem, but he could have written in Cyrene or Alexandria if he had sources from Palestine.

Jason's Hellenistic education suggests that some Jews obtained citizenship in the region's Hellenistic cities. Most Jewish military colonists held a lower status. This put them at a disadvantage during the disorder created by Ptolemaic civil wars in the late second century B.C.E. Nothing should be inferred about Jews in Cyrenaica from 1 Macc. 15:23, where Rome directs Cyrene to support Jews in Palestine (15:19).

Jews in Cyrenaica in the Early Roman Period

Jews lost all remnants of royal patronage when Rome inherited the region's royal lands from Ptolemy Apion in 96 B.C.E. Military colonists working as tenants on these lands were placed at the mercy of tax farmers *(publicani).* This is just one possible source of ethnic conflict in Cyrene reportedly suppressed by the Roman general Lucullus in 87/86 B.C.E. (Josephus, *Ant.* 14.114-19). Cyrenaica became a Roman province in 75/74 B.C.E. Yet Jews in some cities continued to enjoy some of the privileges of the organizational structure *(politeuma)* of a Ptolemaic military colony until well into the reign of Augustus (Berenice, *CJZC* 70, 71; probably Cyrene, Josephus, *Ant.* 14.114-19).

Most evidence for Jews in Cyrenaica dates from 31 B.C.E. to 117 C.E., a period that saw a fresh influx of Jews, many from Palestine (*CJZC* 74). The Augustan reorganization of the province encouraged Jewish immigration partly by expanding protections on Jewish practices to include Cyrenaica (Josephus *Ant.* 16.160-61, 169-70). Some Jews may have come as refugees or enslaved captives from revolts in Palestine in 40-37 B.C.E., 6 C.E., and 66-70 C.E. Movement from Cyrenaica to Palestine is also attested (Josephus, *J.W.* 6.114; *CJZC* 29b, 35; Mark 15:21).

Most Jews adopted Greek names. Patrons of Jewish communities included Roman citizens, at least one of whom was probably Jewish (*CJZC* 70; less likely, 71). Latin names may indicate that other Jews acquired Roman citizenship (*CJZC* 12, 72, App. 13c). Female slaves may be indicated by Jewish names in Roman family tombs (*CJZC* 31d, 43c; proximity of tombs to 31-33 might indicate that others inside are Jews). Roman reliance on the desert and local militias to protect the cities from bandits may have eased Jewish access to Greek citizenship, because some obtained military training in the gymnasium (*CJZC* 6-7, 41). Some exercised prestigious responsibilities (auditor [*nomophylax*], *CJZC* 8; ambassador, *CJZC* 36). Jews in Berenice who called their meeting place an "amphitheater" reveal their social preferences for things Greek (*CJZC* 71). Others in the same city remodeled a "synagogue" in 55/56 C.E. (*CJZC* 72).

Cyrenaica during the Jewish Revolts

By the time of the Jewish revolt of 66-73 C.E., the population of Cyrenaica was demonstrably Romanized. This cultural development irritated tensions that may have been ignited when 2,000 Roman troops were sent from Cyrenaica to help suppress the revolt in Palestine in 66 (Josephus, *J.W.* 2.494). Hostilities were further aroused by Jewish refugees and rebels who fled to Cyrenaica, a flight attested by a Jewish coin from "Year 2" of the revolt that was found in Cyrene (*CJZC* 27). After the fall of the Jerusalem Temple, Sicarii led by Jonathan the weaver reportedly inspired 2,000 of the region's Jews to embark on what was probably an apocalyptic reenactment of the exodus designed to retake Jerusalem (Josephus, *J.W.* 7.437-53; *Vita* 424–25). This attempt was crushed by the Roman governor Catullus, who slaughtered "most" of Cyrene's Jewish elite, whom Josephus numbers at 3,000 (perhaps including Ishmael in *J.W.* 6.114).

Josephus says that their confiscated properties became the emperor's possession, a transfer that supplied funds to maintain troop loyalty and complemented Vespasian's resumption of public land surveys, which provided revenue to stabilize the economy. Land registration and the Jewish tax helped Greek elites identify and seize plots cultivated by Jewish tenant farmers, who had lost influential advocates with the execution of the Jewish aristocracy.

Other Jews arrived from the Jerusalem area after 70. Their presence is indicated by tombs of the late first and early second centuries that include improvised ossuaries (*CJZC* 60; Rowe's tombs N 2-5, 401). Ossuary production flourished with the Jerusalem Temple stone industry. One approach to continuing the practice in Cyrenaica was to imitate the niches cut into tomb walls to hold Roman funerary busts. Jews in Teucheira and Cyrene cut rectangular niches into tomb walls and later sealed the open side with stone slabs. These ossuary niches were similar in size to ossuaries from Palestine. Another approach was to break off the top of locally made amphorae so that bones could be placed inside. At least one of the Jewish tombs at Teucheira had a menorah inscribed on its façade to memorialize the Temple.

The humiliation of the Jewish tax and frustrating limits on agricultural opportunities forged Jews in Cyrenaica into unprecedented unity. This fact may explain why the Diaspora Jewish uprisings of 116-117 began or quickly erupted in Cyrenaica. Roman garrisons in Cyrenaica may have been unwittingly weakened by transfers to Parthia. Jewish success is probably attested in Berenice by a hoard of 1,800 coins that its Gentile owner failed to retrieve (*CJZC* 75). Destruction was widespread, but Cyrene probably fared worse than coastal cities. Its defenses were weakened by its inland location, which required walls on all sides that thinly distributed its military resources. Much of the city was burned. Structures damaged or destroyed include the Augusteum, agora, basilica, gymnasium, baths, civic archive, theater, and numerous temples (to Apollo, Artemis, the Dioscuri, Hecate, Isis, Zeus, and others; *CJZC* 17-23; *SEG* 48.2057 [28.1566]; *AE* 1946.0177; 1974.0673, 0678). Jewish control of Cyrene is suggested by the long time required for destroying the massive temple of Zeus, damage to roads that isolated Cyrene from Apollonia and Balagrae, and a large menorah cut into the road to Balagrae (*CJZC* 24-25, 30 bis; *AE* 1919.0090).

In the wake of this devastation, Jews left behind after their forces marched to Egypt were doomed to speedy execution. On arriving in Egypt, the invaders were joined by reinforcements. Jews boasted initial victories outside of Alexandria and in the Delta region, but few if any could have survived the war's end.

The depopulation of Cyrenaica presented a security risk (Dio 68.32.1-3). Trajan settled 3,000 veterans there while the revolt still raged elsewhere (*SEG* 17.584; possibly *CJZC* 40[b]; *SEG* 52.1843). Further resettlement and rebuilding under Hadrian was needed to restore the region's prosperity.

Such an environment discouraged Jewish immigration. An inscription from the end of the second century is probably Christian rather than Jewish (*CJZC* 37). Even Gentile Christianity was not firmly reestablished until the mid-third century (Eusebius *Hist. Eccl.* 7.26). Jews may have farmed in Marmarika at the end of the second century (*CJZC* 77). They are not well attested in Cyrenaica until the fourth century (*SEG* 37.1702 [31.1578b]; Procopius, *De Aedificiis* 6.2.21-23; Synesius, *Epistolae* 5–6).

Bibliography

S. Applebaum 1979, *Jews and Greeks in Ancient Cyrene,* Leiden: Brill. • G. Barker, J. Lloyd, and J. Reynolds, 1985, *Cyrenaica in Antiquity,* Oxford: British Archaeological Reports. • M. Bowsky 1987, "M. Tittius Sex. F. Aem. and the Jews of Berenice," *American Journal of Philology* 108: 495-510. • J.-J. Callot 1999, *Recherches sur les cultes en Cyrénaïque durant le haut-empire Romain,* Paris: Boccard. • M. Pucci Ben Zeev 2005, *Diaspora Judaism in Turmoil, 116/117 CE,* Leuven: Peeters. • J. Thorn 2005, *The Necropolis of Cyrene,* Rome: Bretschneider. • S. Walker 2002, "Hadrian and the Renewal of Cyrene," *Libyan Studies* 33:45-56. • G. Wright 1963, "Excavations at Tocra Incorporating Archaeological Evidence of a Community of the Diaspora," *PEQ* 95: 22-64.

See also: Diaspora Uprisings

Allen Kerkeslager

Cyrene → Cyrenaica

Cyrus the Great

The grandson of Cyrus I and son of Cambyses I, Cyrus the Great or Cyrus II founded the Achaemenid dynasty that ruled over the Persian Empire. In addition to minor references and fragments, the main sources for information on the life and activities of Cyrus include the *Histories* of Herodotus (1.46-216), the Cyrus Cylinder, the *Nabonidus Chronicle,* the Behistun Inscription, and the embellished account in the *Cyropaedia* by Xenophon. Cyrus succeeded his father as ruler in 559 B.C.E. and began expanding Persian rule over Media, Lydia, Parthia, India, and Babylonia. Cyrus conquered Babylon in 539 B.C.E. without much difficulty. According to the Cyrus Cylinder, the actions undertaken by Cyrus reflect his support for the chief Babylonian deity Marduk. The Cyrus Cylinder also proclaims that some groups who had been forcibly relocated from other regions into Babylonian territory would be allowed to return to their homelands, that sanctuaries were restored, and that images were returned.

This permission granted to diverse peoples finds an echo in the biblical traditions concerning Cyrus. The

The Cyrus Cylinder, written in Akkadian cuneiform script, celebrating the Persian king's peaceful entry into and benevolent rule over Babylon under the divine patronage of the god Marduk (539–530 B.C.E.) *(British Museum)*

first is found in Second Isaiah (Isa. 44:24–45:13). Other passages and allusions within Second Isaiah (chaps. 40–55) have been suggested by scholars (see Fried 2002: 390-91). However, Cyrus is named explicitly only in this text. He is the anointed *(māšîaḥ)* of YHWH who will be instrumental in the process of Israel's restoration. The call for the exiles to return to the land is proclaimed in response to what God is perceived to be doing through the historical events surrounding the activities of Cyrus.

This exaltation of Cyrus is also found in the two virtually parallel accounts in Ezra 1:1-4 and 2 Chron. 36:22-23. This Edict of Cyrus presents a Yahwistic version of the Cyrus Cylinder, and without the language of anointing from Second Isaiah. In both texts, Cyrus allows the exiled Israelites to return to the land and to rebuild YHWH's Temple, in fulfillment of the prophet Jeremiah's prediction of the end of Israel's exile. In Ezra 1:5-11, Cyrus is also said to have returned the various temple vessels plundered by the Babylonians to Sheshbazzar the prince of Judah. Thus, in both books Cyrus is directly responsible for the deliverance of the people of Israel from exile and for the impetus to rebuild the Temple.

Appeal is made to the Edict of Cyrus in other contexts in the book of Ezra (3:7; 4:3; 5:13-17; 6:1-5; 6:14). In the first instance, the actions undertaken to begin rebuilding the Temple at the time of Zerubbabel are stated to be in accordance with Cyrus' proclamation. The subsequent three references all concern resistance to the efforts to rebuild the Temple. The Edict of Cyrus is invoked as the determining factor in allowing the project to resume at the time of King Darius I. The final verse parallels the command of God with the decrees made by Persian rulers that resulted in the completion of the Temple. Thus, the authority of Cyrus and his legacy in the biblical traditions are exceptionally high.

According to some scholars, this laudatory view of Cyrus indicates a replacement of the Davidic dynasty by the Persian kings in Second Isaiah and in Chronicles (Fried 2002; Braun 2003: 160-64). If so, this could imply an acceptance of the current political *status quo* in contrast to the desire for independence under a "messianic" Davidic king who would liberate Israel from foreign rule.

One additional set of references to King Cyrus appears in the Hebrew Bible. The activity of the prophet Daniel is portrayed as extending from the time of Nebuchadnezzar around 605 B.C.E. until at least the third year of Cyrus around 535 B.C.E. (Dan. 1:21; 6:28; 10:1). In addition, the narrative account of Belshazzar's feast and his subsequent demise records his death, but Cyrus is not named (5:30). Daniel's literary setting reflects the Babylonian and early Persian periods, and these references to Cyrus maintain that historical context despite the apparent Maccabean era reflected in chaps. 7–12, and most obviously transparent in 10:1–11:39.

Finally, in the context of his retelling the book of Daniel, Josephus mentions Cyrus as the one who conquered Babylon and allowed the people of Israel to return to the land (*Ant.* 10.231-32; 247-48; 11.1-20). Josephus also claims that Cyrus did this in response to reading the prophecies about him in the book of Isaiah (*Ant.* 11.5-7). This parallels Josephus' claim that Alexander the Great was aware of the statements in the book of Daniel that relate to his impending victory over the Persians (*Ant.* 11.329-39).

Bibliography

J. Berquist 1995, *Judaism in Persia's Shadow,* Minneapolis: Fortress, 23-44. • R. Braun 2003, "Cyrus in Second and Third Isaiah, Chronicles, Ezra and Nehemiah," in *The Chronicler as*

Theologian, ed. M. Graham, S. McKenzie, and G. Knoppers, London: Clark, 146-64. • P. BRIANT 2002, *From Cyrus to Alexander,* Winona Lake, Ind.: Eisenbrauns, 13-50. • L. FRIED 2002, "Cyrus the Messiah? The Historical Background to Isaiah 45:1," *HTR* 95: 373-93. • A. KUHRT 1983, "The Cyrus Cylinder and Achaemenid Royal Policy," *JSOT* 25: 83-98. • E. YAMAUCHI 1996, *Persia and the Bible,* Grand Rapids: Baker, 65-93.

STEVEN J. SCHWEITZER

D

Daliyeh, Wadi ed-

The Wadi ed-Daliyeh, situated halfway between Jericho and Samaria, is a deep canyon with steep, cave-riddled cliffs. Its significance for early Judaism lies in the finds associated with one particular cave, the Mugharat Abu-Shinjeh (Cave of the Father of the Dagger). In 1962 scholarly attention was drawn to the cave when members of the Ta'amireh tribe (the same tribe who had discovered the Dead Sea Scrolls) brought a cache of papyrus fragments to the Jerusalem antiquities market. Discrete inquiries and detective work enabled scholars to identify the Mugharat Abu-Shinjeh as the source of the Bedouins' treasure. This included not only fragments of papyrus documents (now known as the Samaria Papyri) but also masses of jewelry and coins from the mid-fourth century B.C.E. Salvage excavations at the looted cave led by Paul Lapp and sponsored by the American School of Oriental Research in Jerusalem took place in January 1963 and February 1964.

Material evidence from the cave falls into three categories: (1) finds purchased on the antiquities market in 1962, including the papyrus fragments now known as the Samaria Papyri (Gropp 2001), and the Wadi ed-Daliyeh seal impressions (Leith 1997), now in the collection of the Rockefeller Museum, Jerusalem; (2) other artifacts believed to originate with the 1962 offering by the Ta'amireh, primarily coins (identified in catalogues as belonging to the "Nablus Hoard" or the "Samaria Hoard") and jewelry that made their way via the international antiquities trade into the collections of museums, numismatic societies, and private owners; and (3) discoveries made during the ASOR excavations.

The excavation confirmed the find spot and thus established the historical context of the Samaria Papyri, their clay sealings (bullae), and the coins. Still in the cave were the ransacked skeletal remains of at least thirty-one men and sixteen women along with more papyrus fragments, traces of food and clothing, pottery, reed matting, and a few additional clay bullae. Achaemenid date formulas on the Samaria Papyri, all of them legal documents drawn up in the city of Samaria, established their chronological horizon between about 375 and 335 B.C.E., just prior to the conquest of Syria-Palestine by Alexander the Great in 332 B.C.E.. Similarly, the Phoenician and Samarian coins all date to the third quarter of the fourth century, the latest a Tyrian issue of 334. These data, along with the other archaeological evidence and Curtius Rufus's report (*Historiae Alexandri Magni* IV, 8.34.9-11), suggested to the excavators that the cave had served as the last refuge for perhaps as many as 100 elite Samarians and their families who had fled the city in 331 after an abortive rebellion against Alexander's prefect. There they appear to have been caught and killed in retaliation, probably by asphyxiation from a fire set outside the mouth of the cave.

While current scholarly consensus locates the "Samaritan schism" in the Hellenistic or even the Roman period and recognizes that Samarians and Judeans shared the same Hebrew Pentateuch throughout the Persian period (Cross 1998), biblical scholars have proved strangely reluctant to include Samaria more than superficially in their assessments of postexilic Yahwism. This article's use of the term "Samarian" represents a lexical gesture acknowledging that in the early postexilic period both Judea and Samaria, not to mention the Elephantine community, variously communicated, competed, and cooperated as keepers of the Yahwistic flame (Cross 1998). Considered as a whole and in the light of other biblical and archaeological evidence, the Wadi ed-Daliyeh finds present a surprisingly multifaceted perspective on the religious, cultural, political, and economic landscape of Samaria in the elusive Persian period.

Samaria Papyri

On the one hand, the Wadi ed-Daliyeh material demonstrates that as a province of successive foreign powers, Samaria had absorbed its share of foreign cultural influences. On the other hand, the data also point to continuity with and preservation of earlier Israelite traditions in Samaria despite the Assyrian conquest and deportations 400 years earlier. For example, Samarians in the fourth century B.C.E. wrote their contracts in the Imperial Aramaic language and script of the Persian chancellery and used formularies that reflect cross-fertilization between neo-Babylonian and Aramaic legal traditions. However, unlike the late fifth-century Elephantine Papyri, the Samaria Papyri contain few if any Persianisms even though geographically and politically the province of Samaria was closer than Upper Egypt to Persian power centers in Asia Minor and Mesopotamia (Gropp 2001).

The majority of the eighteen more or less legible fragments come from slave sales. Other fragments appear to record pledges of a slave in exchange for a loan, the sale of a house and of living quarters, a slave manumission, a vineyard offered in pledge, and perhaps a judicial settlement by oath. All the documents are private, drawn up in the "city of Samaria," and clearly considered important by the fleeing refugees. The names of the buyers, sellers, and even the slaves (notably always with a patronymic) are predominantly Yahwistic or Hebrew, although the odd Aramaic, Phoenician, Edomite, Akkadian, or Persian name does appear. One document records the purchase of a male and female slave by a woman with a Hebrew name.

The single most famous object from Wadi ed-Daliyeh is the clay seal impression, inscribed in paleo-Hebrew, "Yeshayahu, son of Sanballat, Governor of Samaria," probably the great-grandson of the Samarian governor of the same name who so irked Nehemiah, his counterpart in Judah. On the basis of this sealing and references in the Elephantine Papyri, it appears not only that the Sanballat family ruled a stable Samaria for the last century of the Persian period but also, in view of their names — Yeshayahu, Shelemiah, Delaiah, Hananiah — that, at the very least, early Israel's national deity continued to demand the public homage of Samaria's leadership.

The reference in one papyrus to the sale of a *niškātā'* has fueled conjecture that the city of Samaria had at least one temple, perhaps dedicated to Yahweh; the Hebrew cognate, *liškāh,* is used in Neh. 13:7, 8 to refer to a chamber in Jerusalem's "house of God" (Eshel 1996). The absence of archaeological evidence in Samaria for such a temple hardly rules it out; the only evidence for a temple to Yahweh in Jerusalem during the Persian period is also exclusively textual. Furthermore, archaeological evidence for Samarian cult activity on Mt. Gerizim in the fourth century remains inconclusive (*pace* Stern and Magen 2000).

Seal Impressions

Dozens of impressions among the Wadi ed-Daliyeh bullae come from Greek-style finger rings decorated with classical Greek motifs. They attest to the Samarian elite's participation in the steadily expanding Greek *oikoumenē* of the western Persian Empire. Classical Greek designs outnumbered Persian Court-style or traditional Near Eastern animal motifs by a factor of two to one. At the same time, the two impressions from seals inscribed in paleo-Hebrew — at least one, if not both, of which belonged to a fourth-century Samarian governor — indicate the survival of the aniconic seal style of Iron-Age Israel and Judah. Furthermore, even as Samarians expressed their preference for Greek style seals, their avoidance of Persian or Mesopotamian cultic ritual scenes of the sort that appear on seals from Phoenician cities may attest to Samarian religious sensitivity.

Coins

Coins minted in Samaria (Meshorer and Qedar 1999) as in Judea occur mostly in small denominations meant for local use. Many Samarian coin images derive from Phoenician, Athenian, and Cilician prototypes. They display a much more eclectic array of designs than the bullae and a far greater proportion of Persian style images than any other Syro-Palestinian mint. Some thirty-five types are inscribed with the names of officials. Among cities of Syria Palestine, Samaria alone appears to have been important enough to be minting coins stamped with the name of the satrap, Mazaeus. As on Judean coins, the script types of the Samarian coins fluctuate, with names written in Aramaic or paleo-Hebrew or what can look like a combination of script types. The name of one Samarian governor appears in Aramaic on one coin and in paleo-Hebrew on another. The coins thus suggest a transitional stage between Hebrew and Aramaic.

Four or five different coin types read "Jeroboam," linking Samaria to the ancient Israelite royal tradition. And close parallels between at least five coin designs and late ninth-century motifs from Kuntillet Ajrud, where "Yahweh of Samaria" is linked with the name, Asherah, are further indications of continuity from the Iron Age into the Persian period at Samaria. One particularly intriguing Samarian coin appears to represent a goddess in a temple whose courtyard contains a sacred tree, an image strikingly reminiscent of Prov. 3:18 and 9:1-5.

In sum, the finds from the Wadi ed-Daliyeh suggest that the biblical picture of an exclusive postexilic Yahwism centered on Judah and Jerusalem must be recognized as a reflex of ideologies originating in specific Judean circles. Any attempt to understand Yahwism in the Persian period without consideration of Samaria as a locus of religious influence cannot lay claim to comprehensiveness.

Bibliography

F. M. Cross 1971, "Papyri of the Fourth Century B.C. from Daliyeh," in *New Directions in Biblical Archaeology,* ed. D. N. Freedman and J. N. Greenfield, Garden City, N.Y.: Doubleday, 45-69. • F. M. Cross 1998, "Samaria and Jerusalem in the Era of the Restoration," in idem, *From Epic to Canon: History and Literature in Ancient Israel,* Baltimore: Johns Hopkins University Press, 173-202. • H. Eshel 1996, "Wadi ed-Daliyeh Papyrus 14 and the Samaritan Temple," *Zion* 61: 125-36 (in Hebrew). • D. M. Gropp 2001, *Wadi Daliyeh II and Qumran Miscellanea, Part 2: The Samaria Papyri from Wadi Daliyeh,* DJD 28, Oxford: Clarendon, 1-117. • M. J. W. Leith 1997, *Wadi Daliyeh I, The Wadi Daliyeh Seal Impressions,* DJD 24, Oxford: Clarendon. • M. J. W. Leith 2000, "Seals and Coins in Persian Period Samaria," in *The Dead Sea Scrolls Fifty Years after Their Discovery,* ed. L. Schiffman et al., Jerusalem: Israel Exploration Society, 691-707. • Y. Meshorer and S. Qedar 1999, *Samarian Coinage,* Jerusalem: Israel Numismatic Society. • E. Stern and Y. Magen 2000, "The First

Samaritan Temple on Mt. Gerizim, New Archaeological Evidence," *Qadmoniot* 119-24. MARY JOAN WINN LEITH

Damascus

History

At the end of the thirteenth century B.C.E., Semitic tribes known as Arameans migrated into the northern and central parts of Syria; by the end of the eleventh century B.C.E., they had formed several tribal kingdoms. The southernmost, Aram-Zobah, included Damascus and constituted a serious threat to the newly founded kingdom of Israel under David. In connection with the war against Ammon (2 Samuel 10), David faced the army of the Arameans, which had been hired by Ammon, and defeated the Arameans and their king Hadadezer. Later on, David took revenge on the king because of his intervention in the Ammonite war and attacked Aramean territory. The Israelite king won a decisive victory, put garrisons in Damascus, and ruled the area as a province for some time (2 Sam. 8:3-8). During the reign of Solomon (ca. 960-922 B.C.E.), however, the Aramean states regained their supremacy and hostilities between the two kingdoms continued to erupt.

The subsequent period was dominated by the increasing threat from the Assyrian Empire. While the Hittite states in northern Syria submitted to Assyrian supremacy, the Assyrian invasion of the southern parts was effectively aggravated by the formation of successful alliances by the Arameans kingdoms of Damascus and Hamath, among others, sometimes supported also by Israel. These temporary alliances did not stop occasional reciprocal Aramean or Israelite attempts to expand their territory. In general, Damascus was surprisingly efficient in warding off the Assyrian endeavor to control the region until 732 B.C.E., when Tiglath-pileser III succeeded in capturing the city and deporting its population to Assyria.

Very little is known about Damascus during the Assyrian, Babylonian, and Persian periods. The city retained its position as the chief city of Syria and benefited from the flourishing trade in the area. During a period when the Assyrian Empire was beginning to disintegrate at the end of the seventh century B.C.E., Damascus became part of Egypt. It remained so until Nebuchadnezzar II brought Syria into the Babylonian Empire at the beginning of the sixth century B.C.E. Eventually, the city became part of the newly founded fifth satrapy of the Persian Empire.

With Alexander's conquest of the region following the battle at Issus in 333 B.C.E., a new era for Damascus commenced, at least initially, although not a desirable one. After Alexander's death in 323 B.C.E., his vast empire was divided among his leading generals. In the following struggle for power, Antigonus (Antigonus I Monophthalmus) was able to subdue large parts of Alexander's empire, but he was eventually defeated at Ipsus in 301 B.C.E. through an alliance formed by Seleucus (after 305 B.C.E., Seleucus I Nicator), Cassander, and Lysimachus. The southern parts of Syria, including Damascus, were assigned to Ptolemy I Soter of Egypt, who had supported the alliance but not actively participated in the fighting. In the subsequent period, the recurrent conflicts between the Seleucids and the Ptolemies over the region ultimately facilitated the Roman conquest of the area in the mid-first century B.C.E.

The Ptolemaic rulers seem to have been more interested in the coastland and the fertile inland than in Damascus. No attempts were made to develop Greek institutions in the city or to implant a Greek population. It was important only as a military outpost. During Ptolemaic rule, Damascus remained a Semitic city administered from the central government in Alexandria. For a short period, after the second Syrian war in 253 B.C.E., Damascus came under Seleucid rule but was retaken by Seleucus II in the third Syrian war (245-241 B.C.E.). Only after the victory of Antiochus III over Ptolemy V in the fifth Syrian war (202-200 B.C.E.) did Damascus become part of the Seleucid kingdom.

During the Seleucid era, probably under the rule of Antiochus III (223-287 B.C.E.) and Antiochus IV Epiphanes (175-163 B.C.E.), attempts were made to turn Damascus into a Greek city. But the sources even for this period are very limited. As the Seleucid kingdom disintegrated and was beginning to lose its power over the southern parts of the region, political disorder increased, and Damascus was lost to the Nabatean king Aretas III in 87 B.C.E. In 72 B.C.E., however, the Armenian king Tigranes II, who seized Syria in 83 B.C.E., brought his army as far as Damascus. The intervention of the Romans in 64 B.C.E. would eventually bring stability to the southern parts of Syria, but only after Octavian had defeated the alliance between Anthony and Cleopatra at Actium in 31 B.C.E.

Damascus benefited enormously from the Roman assumption of power, and its economic and political importance increased to an unparalleled level. It was the largest self-governing city in the southern part of the Roman province of Syria. A Roman prefect was probably stationed in the city, although there is no evidence of any major military presence in the area, apart from a locally raised auxiliary unit. This is an important indication of increased political stability in the region. The Syrian legions were stationed in the northern parts, especially around Antioch, which remained the capital of the province. During the first century C.E., the extensive building projects that had been initiated earlier by Julius Caesar in the northern parts of the region, especially in Antioch, now spread to distant parts of the province. A new civic quarter was added, and Herod contributed a theater and a gymnasium as a way of expressing his gratitude toward Augustus. The culmination of the Roman monumentalization process in Damascus was, however, the enlargement of the original Greek Zeus-Hadad temple area, which was turned into a massive temple to Jupiter, outclassing any other Roman building project in Syria.

The Jews of Damascus

We are able to gain only glimpses of the Jewish community in Damascus. It is probable that the Jewish presence dates back to the Persian period, and during the Hellenistic period it is more than likely that a Jewish community existed in the city, but this can only be inferred from Josephus' general statement that Jews were especially numerous in Syria (*J.W.* 7.43). One reason for this, Josephus states, was the proximity to the Jewish homeland, which certainly makes it likely that Jews migrated to Damascus, especially after the Seleucid assumption of power in 200 B.C.E., when the city had a certain upswing. Antioch, however, remained a more attractive choice.

Josephus mentions the Jewish community in Damascus in connection with the outbreak of the Jewish War in 66 B.C.E. Reports of disturbances come from many places, predominately from cities in the proximity of Judea (*J.W.* 2.458-60). Josephus claims that the Jewish population in Damascus was rounded up, probably in Herod's theater, and slaughtered (*J.W.* 2.559-61; 7.368; cf. *Life* 26–27). The figures given by Josephus (10,000 or 18,000 men, women, and children) may be an exaggeration, but they indicate the existence of a large Jewish community in the city. Josephus' narrative contains another interesting detail: the non-Jewish men did not trust their wives when planning the extermination of the Jews of Damascus, since many of the women were deeply attached to Judaism (*J.W.* 2.560). This suggests that the situation in Damascus was similar to that of other Syrian cities: the Jewish community probably enjoyed certain privileges and was relatively well integrated into the community. In times of political turmoil, however, attraction could easily turn into hostility.

The existence of a Jewish community in Antioch during the first century C.E. is also confirmed by Luke (Acts 9:22), who states that Paul, after having been called to be the apostle to the non-Jewish world on the road to Damascus, tried to convince the Jews who lived in the city that Jesus was the messiah of Israel. Luke's story also confirms the existence of synagogues in the city. Before his calling, Luke writes that Paul was given a letter from the high priest in Jerusalem to the synagogues in Damascus, stating that any adherent to the Jesus movement should be brought to Jerusalem (Acts 9:1-2). The historicity of the passage has been called into question, since many scholars find it unlikely that the authority of the high priest could be extended to a city outside of Jewish territory. If it reflects a historical situation, as suggested by Binder (1999), it may indicate the existence of a legal Jewish entity, such as a *politeuma,* known from other locations, Alexandria in particular, and probably also Antioch. Thus, while the sources do not reveal much about the Jewish community in Damascus, there is evidence that it did not differ substantially from those in other Syrian cities.

BIBLIOGRAPHY

J. M. G. BARCLAY 1996, *Jews in the Mediterranean Diaspora: From Alexander to Trajan (323 BCE–117 CE),* Edinburgh: Clark, 242-58 • D. D. BINDER 1999, *Into the Temple Courts: The Place of the Synagogue in the Second Temple Period,* Atlanta: Society of Biblical Literature. • R. BURNS 2005, *Damascus: A History,* London: Routledge. • K. BUTCHER 2003, *Roman Syria and the Near East,* London: British Museum Press. • L. I. LEVINE 2000, *The Ancient Synagogue: The First Thousand Years,* New Haven: Yale University Press. • F. MILLAR 1993, *The Roman Near East, 31 BC–337 CE,* Cambridge: Harvard University Press.

See also: Antioch (Syrian); Syria

MAGNUS ZETTERHOLM

Damascus Document

The *Damascus Document,* also known as the *Zadokite Fragments,* is an early Jewish work containing laws and exhortations. It is preserved in two medieval manuscripts from Cairo as well as ten fragmentary ancient manuscripts from Qumran.

Medieval Manuscripts from Cairo

Two medieval copies of this early Jewish work were found in the *genizah* (storeroom) of the Ben Ezra synagogue in Cairo in 1896. Manuscript A (CD 1–16) comprises sixteen pages and dates from the tenth century C.E. Manuscript B dates from the twelfth century C.E. and contains two pages (CD 19 and 20) that partly overlap with manuscript A. The contents of the document are customarily divided into the Admonition (CD 1–8; 19–20) and the Laws (CD 9–16). However, on the basis of the order of the material in two of the ancient manuscripts from Qumran ($4QD^a$ and $4QD^e$), the correct ordering of the pages containing the Laws is now known to have been CD 15–16 followed by CD 9–14. The customary pages numbers are nevertheless maintained. The medieval manuscripts were first published in 1910 by the Cambridge Talmud scholar Solomon Schechter under the title *Fragments of a Zadokite Work* on the basis of a number of favorable references to "the sons of Zadok" (cf., e.g., CD 3:20b–4:4a). The title *Damascus Document* was chosen because of a series of references to "the land of Damascus" and "Damascus" in the Admonition (cf., e.g., CD 6:5.19; 7:15.19; 8:21; 19:34; 20:12). The abbreviation CD stands for Cairo Damascus.

Fragmentary Manuscripts from Qumran

Just over half a century after the discoveries in Cairo, ten ancient copies dating from the first century B.C.E. to the first half of the first century C.E. were found among the Dead Sea Scrolls in Qumran Caves 4, 5, and 6 ($4QD^{a-h}$; 5QD; 6QD). The fragments from Caves 5 and 6 contain very little text. The eight fragmentary manuscripts from Cave 4 include both material overlapping with CD, with only minor variants and a significant amount of additional text relating to the Admonition and especially the Laws. It is probable that the shorter text attested by the Cairo *genizah* manuscripts emerged through accidental loss, although a process of deliberate omission cannot be ruled out.

Content and Main Areas of Scholarly Research

The Cave 4 manuscripts preserve additional text comprising both the beginning and end of the composition.

The opening lines are preserved in 4QD[a] 1 a-b 1:1-5a, although, regrettably, the very opening words did not survive. The document opens with an admonition to the sons of light to keep away from the wrong paths until the time judgment has been completed. The composition closes, as attested by 4QD[a] 11 and 4QD[e] 7, with a description of a ceremony at which insubordinate members are expelled as well as a reference to a communal assembly in the third month that includes a ritual cursing of those who have transgressed the law.

Community Origins and Early History

The presence of several accounts of the origins and early history of a Jewish reform movement in the Admonition of the document has generated much scholarly interest. Ever since the discovery of the Dead Sea Scrolls copies, scholars have attempted to arrive at a picture of the emergence and early history of the community behind the Qumran library on the basis of these accounts and a number of veiled references to the community's past in other texts, especially the pesharim. The Admonition places the community's inception 390 years after the destruction of Jerusalem, but the number is symbolic (cf. Ezek. 4:5). The emergence of the movement is followed soon after by the arrival of a "teacher of righteousness" who provides guidance to the new movement (CD 1). The final pages of the Admonition (CD 19–20) speak of the teacher's death. CD 6 refers to two related figures: an "interpreter of the law," who is sometimes identified with the teacher, as well as the expectation of "one who will teach righteousness at the end of days." The text further asserts that the members of the reform movement that emerged 390 years after the Exile have their roots in the remnant that pleased God after the destruction of Jerusalem by Nebuchadnezzar in the sixth century B.C.E. and the subsequent deportation of an important element of the Judean population to Babylonia. These claims have led to a debate among scholars as to whether these claims to exilic roots should be taken literally as pointing to a movement that began in the eastern Diaspora (esp. Murphy-O'Connor 1974) or whether these claims are best taken as theological statements (e.g., Knibb 1987).

Closely tied in with this debate is the interpretation of a number of allusive phrases and terms in the document that can be interpreted in a variety of ways. Pride of place is held by the phrase "the penitents/returnees/captivity/captives (all four translations of Hebr. *šby* are possible and have been endorsed by scholars) of Israel who departed from the land of Judah to sojourn in the land of Damascus" (CD 6:5//4QD[b] 2:11; see also CD 4:2-3; 8:16// CD 19:29; 4QD[a] 5 i 15). Murphy-O'Connor and others take these statements as referring to a physical return of exiles from the Babylonian captivity ("Damascus") to Palestine in the second century B.C.E. Knibb and others, on the other hand, prefer to interpret this phrase as speaking of a reform movement that is marked off from the rest of Israel by their penitence, a term based on the Hebrew root *šûb,* which can mean both "return" or "repent." The setting of the movement's location in "the land of Damascus" is based on the reference to "Damascus" in Amos 5:27, which is cited and interpreted in CD 7:14-15. "Damascus" has been interpreted as God's chosen place for the community's location, as a cipher for Babylon, or literally as Damascus in Syria.

The allusive language of the so-called historical passages in the Admonition have a strong foundation in Scripture (see Campbell 1995), and it is therefore very difficult to derive reliable historical data from them. The authors behind these texts were steeped in the Scriptures to the extent that they saw their own emergence and fate directly interlinked with their interpretation of the Scriptures and their place in the history of God's dealings with his people. Shemaryahu Talmon speaks of a "conceptual implantation in the biblical world" (Talmon 1989: 24). This characteristic feature makes it well nigh impossible for modern scholars to distinguish the historical from the theological in these accounts, and it may well be that our desire to distinguish the two is alien to the text. Most recently Grossman (2002) has approached these issues under the heading "New Historiography" and emphasized the partiality of any reconstructions and the important role played by ideological forces in the processes of writing and reading the "historical" sections of the text.

Law

The legal part of the document comprises expositions of Jewish legal interpretation ranging from grounds for disqualifying priests, agricultural laws, skin disease and flux, and a wife suspected of adultery, to the Sabbath. The legal part of the document also contains prescriptions for the organization of a family-based community that dwelled in camps presided over by an overseer. In this category of material fall the admission process (CD 15:5–16:6//4QD), the stipulations for the organization and leadership of the camps by an overseer (CD 12:22–14:18//4QD), and the penal code (CD 14:18-22//4QD). Both the discovery of a significant amount of additional legal material in the Qumran manuscripts of the *Damascus Document* and the publication of other important legal texts from Qumran (esp. the *Temple Scroll* and 4QMMT) have led to a fuller appreciation of the centrality of legal interpretation in the Dead Sea Scrolls and the communities responsible for them.

Women

Most recently scholars have begun to investigate the role of women in the *Damascus Document,* and here the Cave 4 manuscripts have provided important new evidence (see Wassen 2005).

Source and Redaction Criticism

Largely because of the varied nature of the contents of the document, scholars have attempted to make a case for the composite nature of the Admonition and the Laws by suggesting ways in which the text may have grown. Thus, for instance, a case has been made in favor of distinguishing an original core of the Admonition that goes back to a parent movement and was subsequently supplemented by the Qumran community (so

Davies 1983). For the Laws, it has been suggested that a stratum of halakah stands apart from blocks of communal legislation by virtue of its national orientation (so Hempel 1998).

Relationship to Other Texts

The *Damascus Document* shows signs of close links to a number of other texts from Qumran. 4QMiscellaneous Rules (4Q265), for instance, covers a number of themes also treated in the *Damascus Document* such as the Sabbath and a penal code. The *Damascus Document* also overlaps both thematically and sporadically word for word with parts of the *Community Rule.* The complex relationship of these two key documents is central to scholarly endeavors to depict the communities reflected in the Dead Sea Scrolls. The legal section of the *Damascus Document* covers a number of halakic areas dealt with in other legal works from Qumran (esp. 4QMMT and 4QOrdinances[a]) such as gleanings, the ritual requirements for the red cow ceremony, and the ritual impurity of people and objects through contact with Gentiles.

Messianism

The *Damascus Document* contains a number of references to messianic figures, a feature that has attracted a fair amount of interest. A notable characteristic of these expected future figures is that they at times share their titles with figures otherwise referred to in the past tense. This is the case with the past "teacher of righteousness" (CD 1) and "the one who will teach righteousness at the end of days" (CD 6). The ambiguous phrase "the messiah of Aaron and Israel" occurs at CD 19:10-11; 12:23–13:1; 14:9//4QD (see also CD 19:35–20:1 for a related expression). This phrase has been taken to refer either to a single messiah or to two messiahs. Other than referring to an expectation of these figures, the document has very little to say about their role in the eschatological scenario.

In sum, the *Damascus Document* is one of the most important nonbiblical documents to have been found at Qumran. It covers a wide range of legal issues that were of importance to Jews in the late Second Temple period. It also provides invaluable descriptions of the origins and early history of a second-century-B.C.E. Jewish reform movement, even though those origins are frequently phrased in veiled language and ideologically charged terms. The description of the organization of a community in camps is unique among the DSS, in spite of a number of intriguing connections to other texts, especially the *Community Rule.*

BIBLIOGRAPHY

J. M. BAUMGARTEN 1996, *Qumran Cave 4.XIII: The Damascus Document (4Q266-273),* DJD 18, Oxford, Clarendon. • J. M. BAUMGARTEN AND D. R. SCHWARTZ 1995, "The Damascus Document," in *The Dead Sea Scrolls: Hebrew, Aramaic, and Greek Texts with English Translations,* vol. 2, *Damascus Document, War Scroll and Related Documents,* ed. J. H. Charlesworth, Louisville: Westminster John Knox, 4-79. • J. G. CAMPBELL 1995, *The Use of Scripture in the Damascus Document 1–8, 19–20,* Berlin: de Gruyter. • P. R. DAVIES 1983, *The Damascus Covenant: An Interpretation of the "Damascus Document,"* Sheffield: Sheffield Academic Press. • M. L. GROSSMAN 2002, *Reading for History in the Damascus Document: A Methodological Study,* Leiden, Brill. • C. HEMPEL 1998, *The Laws of the Damascus Document: Source, Traditions and Redaction,* Leiden: Brill. • C. HEMPEL 2000, *The Damascus Texts,* Sheffield: Sheffield Academic Press. • S. HULTGREN 2007, *From the Damascus Covenant to the Covenant of the Community,* Leiden: Brill, 141-232. • M. A. KNIBB 1987, "Exile in the Damascus Document," *JSOT* 25: 99-117. • J. MURPHY-O'CONNOR 1974, "The Essenes and Their History," *RB* 81: 215-44. • S. TALMON 1989, "Between the Bible and the Mishna," in idem, *The World of Qumran from Within: Collected Studies,* Jerusalem: Magnes, 11-52. • B. Z. WACHOLDER 2006, *The New Damascus Document: The Midrash on the Eschatological Torah of the Dead Sea Scrolls: Reconstruction, Translation and Commentary,* Leiden: Brill. • C. WASSEN 2005, *Women in the Damascus Document,* Atlanta: Society of Biblical Literature.

CHARLOTTE HEMPEL

Daniel, Additions to

The Additions to Daniel consist of three extended passages that are included in the ancient Greek versions of the biblical book of Daniel but are not found in the Masoretic Text (MT): the tale of Susanna, the stories of Bel and the Snake, and the Prayer of Azariah and the Song (or Hymn) of the Three. The Additions are translations from lost Semitic originals.

There are two ancient Greek versions of the book of Daniel. The Old Greek (OG) version proved to be so unsatisfactory that it was utterly superseded by the version of Theodotion (θ′) and survives only in a few venues containing its Hexaplaric recension and, in its most accurate witness, the pre-Hexaplaric Papyrus 967. (The Hexapla was a compilation of different ancient texts of the Hebrew Bible in six parallel columns, made by Origen of Alexandria.) The OG of Daniel was produced in Egypt around 100 B.C.E.; based on its use in the New Testament, θ′ Daniel (or proto-θ′ Daniel, as some hold) was completed no more than a century later. The text of OG Daniel diverges most from that of θ′ Daniel at chaps. 4–6, which suggests that it employed a variant Aramaic *Vorlage* at this point. Tellingly, the greatest degree of discrepancy between the Greek versions and MT Daniel occurs at chaps. 3–6, that is, the collection of independently circulating Aramaic court tales around which the rest of the book later accreted. Otherwise, the Semitic *Vorlage* of both Greek versions was much like the text of MT Daniel, the antiquity of which is confirmed by manuscript copies of Daniel among the Dead Sea Scrolls. However, the Greek Additions appear in different forms in OG and θ′ Daniel, particularly with respect to the story of Susanna.

The Prayer of Azariah and the Song of the Three

The Prayer of Azariah and the Song of the Three appear in the Greek versions following what in the MT is Dan. 3:23. The scene is the fiery furnace, wherein Azariah,

Hananiah, and Mishael have been cast for refusing to worship the statue erected by King Nebuchadnezzar. The Prayer (LXX 3:26-45) is a traditional communal piece, shoehorned into its present position in the text by the addition of an introduction (3:24-25) and a brief prose narrative (3:46-50). It is a penitential type of prayer, common in early Judaism, involving a confession of sins, a reminder of the covenantal promises, and a plea for divine assistance. Its Deuteronomic perspective is reflected in MT Daniel, but only in the similarly penitential prayer in chap. 9, where it is rejected, although it stands behind the theology of history in 4Q243-244.

The Song of the Three (3:51-90), in whose rhythmic praises of God some authorities distinguish a separate ode and psalm, was also originally an independent text. Several clues hint that both the prayer and the song were composed in Hebrew (cf. the Hebrew forms of the names of the three young men), although the possibility of Aramaic cannot be discounted. The intervening prose narrative, whose Greek versions almost completely agree, might be the original prelude to the song, a fragment from the proto-MT collection of court tales inadvertently omitted during the formation of MT Daniel, or a free composition created to bridge prayer and song and to explain how the fire miraculously failed to injure the three.

Susanna

The two other additions occupy different positions in the Greek versions: OG Daniel concludes with Susanna and Bel and the Snake (Papyrus 967 reverses the order, concluding with Susanna), while θ′ Daniel begins with Susanna and concludes with Bel and the Snake. The story of Susanna, which may be classified as a folktale, romance, or wisdom tale, is simple, entertaining, and powerful. Susanna, faithful to Jewish law despite living in exile, is framed by two elders after she rejects their adulterous advances. The community condemns her, but the young Daniel cross-examines the elders separately, establishes the truth, and prevents the shedding of innocent blood. Daniel's presence in the story is anomalous, however. Although his insight is sparked by supernatural intervention, the story is not set in a royal court and does not involve a divine mystery, and its message turns on neither Daniel's faithfulness nor a conflict with Gentile authorities. These elements stand in tension with the court tales of MT Daniel, suggesting that Susanna was composed before the final redaction of the book in 164 B.C.E. Linguistic evidence suggests a Hebrew *Vorlage* of OG Susanna and thus a Palestinian provenance. It was perhaps part of the cycle of Daniel texts that circulated in the decades before the Maccabean Revolt, and might be as old as the fourth century B.C.E.

Bel and the Snake

Bel and the Snake offers variations of a similar story with an identical message. In the first tale, Daniel demonstrates that a statue of Bel is naught but a lifeless idol by proving it is the priests and their families who actually consume the food and drink offered to it. In the second, Daniel kills a snake worshiped by the Babylonians, for which, in a scene recalling MT Daniel 6, he is cast into the lions' den. An angel carries the prophet Habakkuk to Babylon to drop food for Daniel, who thus survives his ordeal. As with the case of Susanna, the characteristic elements of the court tales of Daniel are either missing in Bel and the Snake or not as pronounced. Aramaic (OG) and Hebrew (θ′) versions of the stories possibly existed contemporaneously. This evidence, plus the correspondence with Daniel 6 and the fact that Daniel is a priest (OG; cf. MT Daniel 1), tentatively implies a date before the final redaction and widespread circulation of the book. A Palestinian provenance seems likely.

Influence

Although 1 Macc. 2:59-60 cites Daniel and the Three, Josephus does not mention the Greek Additions. They are not especially prominent in postbiblical Jewish writings. In later Christianity, however, Susanna was an immensely popular figure.

BIBLIOGRAPHY

D. W. CLANTON 2006, *The Good, the Bold, and the Beautiful: The Story of Susanna and Its Renaissance Interpretations,* London: T&T Clark. • J. J. COLLINS, 1993, *Daniel,* Minneapolis: Fortress. • K. KOCH 1987, *Deuterokanonische Zusätze zum Danielbuch,* Neukirchen-Vluyn: Neukirchener Verlag. • C. A. MOORE 1977, *Daniel, Esther, and Jeremiah: The Additions,* Garden City, N.Y.: Doubleday. • M. J. STEUSSI 1993, *Gardens in Babylon: Narrative and Faith in the Greek Legends of Daniel,* Atlanta: Scholars Press.

LORENZO DITOMMASO

Daniel, Book of

The book of Daniel is written in two languages, Hebrew (1:1–2:4a; 8:1–12:13) and Aramaic (2:4b–7:28), and is composed of two distinct types of literature: court tales (chaps. 1–6), which are narrated almost exclusively in the third person, and mediated revelations (chaps. 7–12), which are recounted in the first person. These revelations make the book the only full-blown example of the genre apocalypse in the Hebrew Bible. Eight fragmentary manuscript copies of Daniel were discovered among the Dead Sea Scrolls; the earliest, 4QDan^c (4Q114), dates from the end of the second century B.C.E. The text of these copies confirms the antiquity of the MT form of the book in its sequence of languages and order of material, as well as, in the main, its consonantal framework. The ancient Greek form of Daniel, however, which is extant in two versions, significantly diverges from the MT in certain chapters, and also contains a considerable amount of additional material. The relationship among the forms and versions of the book remains incompletely understood.

Although the precise details of its composition history are shrouded, the theory of the fundamental unity of MT Daniel cannot be maintained in view of the manifold signs of editorial activity evident in its present form. Questions of the date, provenance, and purposes of the book are inseparable from the issues surrounding its composition and redaction.

The Aramaic Court Tales

Origin

The oldest section of Daniel is the core collection of four Aramaic tales that currently constitute chaps. 3–6: the Fiery Furnace, Nebuchadnezzar's Madness, the Writing on the Wall, and the Lions' Den. The existence of the Greek Additions and the discovery of the Aramaic fragments among the Dead Sea Scrolls suggest that the collection (and MT Daniel as a whole) emerged amidst a multiplicity of compositions, not all of which were selected for inclusion. The distant background of the tales is obscure. A judicial figure named *Dnil* appears in the Aqhat legend from Ugarit, while Ezekiel cites a *Danel* who is righteous (14:14, 20) and wise (28:3). Yet, if the *Prayer of Nabonidus* (4Q242) is any indication, some tales were adapted from Neo-Babylonian originals (note the recurrence of Daniel's Chaldean name, *Belteshazzar,* at 1:7; 2:26; etc.) or from Jewish narratives where Daniel was not initially featured, such as the tale of the Fiery Furnace. Whatever the origin of its constituents, the collection circulated independently in a version antecedent to MT Daniel 3–6, the existence of which might account for the high degree of divergence between the MT and the Greek versions of these chapters. It is unclear whether the story of Nebuchadnezzar's Dream in chap. 2, whose four-kingdom schema was adapted from a very old tradition, was part of the core collection or a later addition. Chapter 1, possibly translated from an Aramaic original, is an editorial prefix explaining Daniel's presence in Babylon. It once served to contextualize the stories of chaps. 2–6 but now functions as the introduction to the entire book.

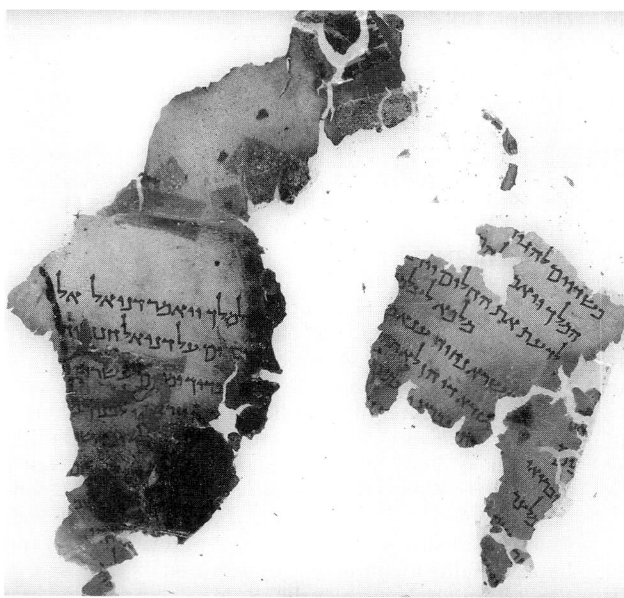

Fragments of the A manuscript of Daniel found in Cave 1 near Qumran (1QDan[a]) *(Photograph by Bruce and Kenneth Zuckerman and Marilyn Lundberg, West Semitic Research. Courtesy Syriac Orthodox Church of Antioch, Archdiocese of the Eastern United States)*

Diaspora Setting and Function

The venue of the tales in the royal court, their comparatively benign portraits of foreign monarchs, and their firm assumption that with God's help pious Jews can prosper in an alien land, denote a Diaspora setting of relative Gentile tolerance. The historical review of chap. 2 terminates with an allusion to dynastic intermarriages between the Ptolemies and Seleucids and does not refer to the hated Antiochus IV. A setting in the Eastern Diaspora in the second half of the third century B.C.E. most convincingly accounts for the aggregate of these data. The chief purpose of the tales, which was realized through the figure of Daniel the pious man and wise courtier, and which the final redaction of the book accommodated, was to provide a model by which the apparently contrary themes of faithfulness to Jewish law and success in a Gentile milieu were brought into harmony. In this respect the court tales have their closest analogues in other Diaspora literature of the period, notably Esther.

The Apocalyptic Visions

Date and Composition

The four revelations comprising the second half of Daniel are a response to the national-religious crisis precipitated by the policies of the Seleucid king, Antiochus IV. The unfulfilled prophecy that Antiochus would perish in the final battle (11:40-45) fixes the *terminus ante quem* of the revelation, and thus the final redaction of MT Daniel, at 164 B.C.E., shortly before his actual death in Persia, and also before the rededication of the Temple, which the book does not mention. It is unlikely that the four revelations were produced simultaneously or were affixed *en bloc* to the court tales, since each is designed in part to update its predecessors. The vision in chap. 7, which continues the Aramaic of chap. 6, reinterprets the disclosure of the four kingdoms presented earlier in chap. 2. The next three revelations are written in Hebrew, perhaps due to heightened nationalist sentiments. The vision of chap. 8, which like chap. 7 is richly textured through an abundant use of mythological imagery, is almost completely devoted to an elucidation of political and military events after Alexander the Great. Chapter 9 is not a vision, but a radical, angelic reinterpretation of Jeremiah's prophecy of seventy years of exile (Jer. 25:11-12; 29:10). It frames a long prayer (9:4b-19) whose originally independent form might be preserved in one of the Dead Sea copies, 4QDan[e] (4Q116). The final revelation in chaps. 10–12 is conveyed through angelic discourse. Distinguished by the detail of its portrayal of contemporary events and the limpidity of its eschatological expectations, it includes what many authorities identify as the sole reference in the Hebrew Bible to the anticipation of individual resurrection (12:2, but cf. Isa. 26:14-19).

The formation of the revelations and their association with Daniel are intrinsically linked to the development of apocalyptic historiography in early Judaism. The concept of mystery *(rāz),* which is central to the book, represents, perhaps hypostatically, certain profound and eternal verities whose worldly manifestations are expressed as (or through) what might be called fields of knowledge. These verities were not obvious to the casual or imperceptive observer or, alternately, could be apprehended only by those possessing extraordinary personal qualities or who had benefited from special instruction. The mantic ability of Daniel to reveal mysteries in the form of dreams (chaps. 2 and 4) or cryptic writing (chap. 5) freighted a specifically historiographic function: Daniel was able to explain the meaning of the past and foretell the future. In the court tales, this function was subordinate to the chief purpose outlined above. In the revelations of Daniel 7–12, however, it became their *raison d'être.* The intolerable strain of the events of Antiochus's reign forged a new theology of history wherein any resolution of the present state of affairs could not be imagined to occur within the pale of history.

Theology of History

This new theology deliberately rejected the old Deuteronomic theology of history (cf. Daniel 9), which concentrated on the observable historical consequences of the covenantal relationship between God and Israel. In the new theology, present-day tribulations were not contingent on Israel's recent actions, but instead represented elements of a sweeping divine plan for humanity. The plan, though, was hidden; the product of a transcendent reality, its pattern and goal could not be deduced through human insight alone. Accordingly, even gifted wise men like Daniel had to rely on angelic mediation to interpret their visions. The attribution of these visions to Daniel, a proven herald of historical forecasts, authenticated their message and established a self-validating historiography that, by encompassing both memory and revelation, permitted not only the *ex eventu* explanation of past history and current events but, most crucially, the predicative disclosure of eschatological hopes. The message of the revelations, supported by this internally rational and consistent historiography, is that despite the terrible severity of these tribulations, God still controls history (cf. Isa. 41:1-10) and has not abandoned his people.

Function

The message in turn supports the purpose, consolation, by the disclosure that the tribulations will swiftly cease (each revelation contains a prediction of their duration: 7:25; 8:14; 9:25-27; and 12:7, with eleventh-hour updates at 12:11-12), and reassurance, through the guarantee that the oppressors will be overthrown and righteousness rewarded. The correlation of this purpose with the faithfulness of Daniel in the court tales is patent if imperfect, suggesting that the redactor of the final form of the book envisioned a two-tier philosophy of corporate predestination and personal free will whose parameters were not completely described.

Setting

The provenance of the revelations is difficult to establish but was different from that of the court tales. Based principally on reconstructions of the social circles responsible for Daniel and the New Testament book of Revelation, apocalypses were long thought to be products of marginal, oppressed communities. Yet the events of Antiochus IV's reign were intensely polarizing, and at various stages coalitions of widely diverse groups might have joined and fragmented under the banner of resistance (cf. the insincere joiners of 11:34). The wise ones, or *maśkîlîm,* are singled out (11:33; 12:3), although their probable quietism would appear to exclude their association with the militant *ḥăsîdîm/asidaioi* described in 1 and 2 Maccabees. The function of the *maśkîlîm* was to instruct the common people (11:33), presumably regarding the aforementioned mysteries disclosed by Daniel, where eternal life is promised to the righteous (12:2-3). The book does not emphasize priests or their concerns (cf. the Greek addition of Bel and the Dragon, where Daniel is a priest), while its correspondence with the writings of the Dead Sea sectarians, although noteworthy on several levels, is most appropriately understood as part of a general apocalyptic tradition whose elements to a significant degree were shaped by MT Daniel itself. There is a definite scribal tenor to the book, evident not only in the mantic persona of Daniel the dream-interpreter and vision-recipient, but also in the emphasis on the *maśkîlîm* and their interpretative and didactic functions. The composition of the revelations and the final redaction of the book almost certainly occurred in Palestine, perhaps at or near Jerusalem.

Influence in Judaism and Christianity

The book of Daniel exerted a tremendous influence on subsequent Jewish and Christian thought. Despite the late date of its final redaction, many groups rapidly accepted the book as authoritative. 1 Maccabees 2:59-60 refers to the stories of Daniel 3 and 6. 4QFlorilegium offers a form of Dan. 12:10 as a proof text (4Q174 1-3 ii 3-4[sup]), ascribing the passage to "Daniel the Prophet" (on the title, cf. Josephus, *Ant.* 10.249, 266-67; Matt. 24:15), while 11QMelchizedek refers to "the Messiah of the Spirit, of whom Daniel spoke" (11Q13 2:18, referring perhaps to Dan. 9:24-26). Other Jewish texts of the period quote Daniel frequently, employ Danielic language, or utilize themes and images that, while perhaps antecedent to Daniel, reached their characteristic form in the book.

In the New Testament, the Synoptic Gospels cite or allude to Daniel copiously, while Revelation, although never quoting Daniel directly, employs several of its motifs. The influence of Daniel on early Jewish and Christian writings is particularly notable regarding the figure of the Son of Man (cf. Dan. 7:13), the idea of the eschatological adversary, and, more broadly, the concepts of the periodization of history and the succession of kingdoms. Daniel also substantially affected the development of apocalyptic literature, establishing a pattern for historical apocalypses that was more or less copied by all subsequent examples, while the revelatory details of the book have proven to be an inexhaustible fount of data for its literalist interpreters over the past two millennia. Perhaps most significantly, the development of apocalyptic historiography, whose eschatological themes have demonstrated a remarkable persistence and whose functions have dovetailed with various nationalistic purposes, has had profound ramifications for ancient, medieval, and even modern communities.

BIBLIOGRAPHY

J. J. COLLINS 1993, *Daniel*, Minneapolis: Fortress. • J. J. COLLINS AND P. W. FLINT, EDS. 2001, *The Book of Daniel: Composition and Reception*, 2 vols., Leiden: Brill. • J. E. GOLDINGAY 1987, *Daniel*, Dallas: Word. • L. F. HARTMAN AND A. A. DILELLA 1978, *The Book of Daniel*, Garden City, N.Y.: Doubleday. • K. KOCH 1980, *Das Buch Daniel*, Darmstadt: Wissenschaftliche Buchgesellschaft. • K. KOCH 2005, *Daniel: Kapitel 1,1–4,34*, Neukirchen-Vluyn: Neukirchener Verlag. • A. LACOCQUE 1976, *Le Livre de Daniel*, Neuchatel: Delachaux. • J. H. C. LEBRAM 1984, *Das Buch Daniel*, Zürich: Theologischer Verlag.

See also: Daniel, Additions to; Daniel, Pseudo-Texts LORENZO DITOMMASO

Daniel, Pseudo-Texts

The term *Pseudo-Daniel* refers to four Aramaic texts (4Q242, 4Q243-244, 4Q245, and 4Q246) that mention Daniel or are closely connected with themes or figures characteristic to the biblical book of Daniel. Each text is known only from fragments of manuscript copies discovered in Qumran Cave 4, although none is a product of the Qumran community.

Prayer of Nabonidus (4Q242)

The *Prayer of Nabonidus* describes how King Nabonidus of Babylon fell ill and spent seven years in Teiman. The king's illness, caused by his idolatry, was relieved only after he accepted the advice of an unnamed Jewish diviner to proclaim his praise of the one true God. Although the *Prayer* does not refer to Daniel, and the offense of idolatry is more reminiscent of Daniel 3 and 5, the account of the king's illness exhibits important parallels with the story of Nebuchadnezzar's madness that survives in different forms in the MT and LXX versions of Daniel 4. There are similarities, too, with the account of Nabonidus' exile in Teima in Arabia that is preserved in Babylonian chronicles and inscriptions. The *Prayer of Nabonidus* possibly represents the earliest extant Jewish form of the Babylonian account, whose distinctive additions include a Jewish protagonist and the motif of divine punishment. As such, it might date from the third century B.C.E., before the first gathering of the court tales that appear in redacted form as MT Daniel 2–6. 4Q242 itself was copied in the second quarter of the first century B.C.E.

Pseudo-Daniel[a-b] (4Q243-244)

4QPseudo-Daniel[a-b] consists of forty identifiable fragments of one manuscript copy (4Q243) and fourteen more of a second (4Q244). Both copies date from the first half of the first century C.E. A likely reconstruction of the order of the fragments begins with a description of Daniel at the court of King Belshazzar, which is followed by an apocalyptic review of history that extends from the primeval period through the Hellenistic era, culminating in the eschatological age. It is unclear whether the revelation is imparted through a vision or by some kind of written record (4Q243 frg. 6). While 4Q243-244 shares with the biblical Daniel the characteristic genres of court tale and *vaticinium ex eventu*, there are significant differences. Unlike the book of Daniel, where tales and revelations constitute distinct literary units, in 4Q243-244 both genres appear together in one narrative. Its revelation is related in the third person instead of the first, and its details are not couched in the cryptic, allusive language typical of apocalyptic literature. Most significantly, the theology of history of 4Q243-244 is resolutely Deuteronomic. Its review of history, which encompasses the preexilic period, structures past events in order to illustrate the historical consequences of the covenantal relationship between God and Israel. In contrast, the reviews of Daniel 2, 5, and 7–12 focus on foreign kings and international affairs after the Babylonian exile, and are framed by a highly schematized historiography, which while affirming God's ultimate control of history downplays divine reciprocity and thus consciously rejects the Deuteronomic perspective. This is apparent in chap. 9, where the Deuteronomic theology of the prayer is shown to rest on a mistaken understanding of history. In its form and theology, 4Q243-244 stands between the court tales and the revelatory visions of the book of Daniel. As such, it may have been composed in the first decades of the second century B.C.E.

Pseudo-Daniel[c] (4Q245)

The four fragments of 4Q245 (4QPseudo-Daniel[c]), once considered part of 4Q243-244, are the remains of a discrete document copied in the early part of the first century C.E. Its major extant portion resembles 4Q243-244 in that it mentions Daniel and a book or another type of writing, but it also preserves lists of priests and kings. The priestly list recalls a similar rotation in MT 1 Chron. 5:27-41, except that the roster of 4Q245 embraces Abiathar, priest of Shiloh, and extends into the Hellenistic period to include the Hasmoneans Jonathan and Simon. Not enough of the text survives to offer anything other than speculation as to the context of the lists of 4Q245 or the significance of their components. The name of Simon provides the *terminus post quem* of the composition of the text: the last third of the second century B.C.E., during the reign of John Hyrcanus.

4QApocalypse ar (4Q246)
4QApocalypse ar consists of a single fragment from the last decades of the first century B.C.E. that preserves one column of text and portions of another. It is also frequently referred to as the *Aramaic Son of God Text* because it refers to the appearance, within the framework of an apocalyptic review of history, of a figure who will be called "the son of God" *(brh dy ʾl)* and named "the son of the Most High" (*br ʿlywn)* (4Q246 col. ii line 1). Scholars have proposed various candidates for this figure, including the Antichrist, the Jewish people collectively, an angelic captain such as Michael, a nonmessianic royal character or, more likely, a Davidic/royal messianic type. Another explanation is that the figure is the last monarch of the final earthly kingdom, perhaps none other than the despised Antiochus IV Epiphanes. Much depends on whether 4Q246 ii 4, where the attention of the text shifts to the kingdom of heaven, marks the transition from a present state of oppression to an anticipated state of relief, along the lines of Daniel 2 or 7. In its phraseology (e.g., 4Q246 ii 5 par. Dan. 7:27), themes, and general tenor, 4Q246 echoes the historical reviews and eschatological expectations of Daniel. Accordingly, the text might be approximately contemporary to the final redaction of MT Daniel in 164 B.C.E. An identification of the figure of the Son of God with Antiochus would also assume such a date. 4Q246 has attracted much attention in recent New Testament scholarship, in light of its striking verbal parallels to the annunciation scene in Luke 1:30-35. If the messianic interpretation of the fragment is correct, this would mean that at the turn of the era "Son of God" was a Jewish title for the messiah and not one that Christians could have adapted only from Greco-Roman paganism.

Related Texts
In addition to the four Pseudo-Daniel texts, several other fragmentary writings display points of contact with the biblical Daniel but are too poorly preserved to allow for definite conclusions. 4Q551 (4QDaniel Susanna? ar) involves an unnamed judicial figure in a court setting, and so appears to be related to the story of Susanna, which is extant only in the ancient Greek versions of Daniel. Like the *Prayer of Nabonidus,* 4Q551 could represent an Aramaic tale that in a later incarnation found its way into one stream of the biblical Daniel tradition. 4QFour Kingdoms, extant in two manuscripts (4Q552-553) of early first-century-C.E. vintage, contains an (angelic?) interpretation of a vision or dream of four trees that, despite superficial similarities, preserves a different version of the sequential, four-kingdom schema of Daniel 2 and 7. A few words among the small fragments of the Aramaic 4Q489 (pap4QApocalypse ar) also appear in Daniel, but nothing substantive can be asserted. Other writings, such as 4QHistorical Text A (4Q248), which is written in Hebrew, may have in their historical details a correspondence with the events described in Daniel 11. Longer, better-preserved texts such as the *War Scroll* and the Aramaic *New Jerusalem* text also share a basic eschatological horizon and specific correlations with the revelatory chapters of Daniel.

Significance
The principal importance of the Pseudo-Daniel texts is the light they shed on the composition history of Daniel. Although the evolutionary theory of the biblical book long antedates the discovery of these texts, and while many of their details remain obscure, their existence greatly augments our knowledge of the cycle of Aramaic Daniel material that circulated throughout the third and second centuries B.C.E. and from which, at least in part, the book of Daniel was formed.

The enduring appeal of the figure of Daniel and the legitimacy awarded to literature attributed to his name ensured the ongoing production of Daniel apocrypha in postbiblical Judaism and Christianity. His story, for example, was retold and augmented many times, often to bridge apparent gaps in the biblical record or to resolve its notorious chronological inconsistencies. Prognostic texts attributed to the prophet were composed to address a variety of topics, including dream interpretation (e.g., the *Somniale Danielis*). The most important Daniel apocrypha, though, were the pseudonymous apocalypses and apocalyptic oracles that appeared from the late fourth century C.E. onward. Restricted in their provenance to the lands of the Eastern Mediterranean and Middle East, these texts number at least two dozen and have come down to us in multiple languages. Especially popular among Byzantine Christians, who regarded them as forecasts of divine deliverance from recurrent Muslim invasions, they were also assimilated and produced by Jewish and Muslim communities of the era.

BIBLIOGRAPHY

Texts

J. J. COLLINS 1996, "4Q Prayer of Nabonidus ar" (83-93); J. J. COLLINS AND P. W. FLINT 1996, "Pseudo-Daniel" (95-164); and É. PUECH 1996, "4Q*Apocryphe de Daniel* ar" (165-84), in *Qumran Cave 4.XVII: Parabiblical Texts, Part 3,* DJD 22, Oxford: Clarendon.

Studies

L. DITOMMASO 2005A, "4Q*Pseudo-Daniel*$^{a-b}$ (4Q243-4Q244) and the Book of Daniel," *DSD* 12:101-33. • L. DITOMMASO 2005B, *The Book of Daniel and the Apocryphal Daniel Literature,* Leiden: Brill. • P. W. FLINT 2001, "The Daniel Tradition at Qumran," in *The Book of Daniel: Composition and Reception,* 2 vols., ed. J. J. Collins and P. W. Flint, Leiden: Brill, 2: 329-67. • F. GARCÍA MARTÍNEZ 1992, "4QPseudo Daniel Aramaic and the Pseudo-Danielic Literature," in idem, *Qumran and Apocalyptic,* Leiden: Brill: 137-61.

See also: Daniel, Additions to; Daniel, Book of

LORENZO DITOMMASO

David

David is already a many-sided figure in the Hebrew Bible, where he is presented as king, dynastic head, warrior, musician, godly man, and more. In the literature of early Judaism, these depictions were developed and augmented with even more images.

Progenitor of the Messiah

The image of David as progenitor of the messiah is rooted in biblical texts such as 2 Sam. 7:11-16; Psalm 89; Isa. 11:1-10; and Jer. 33:14-26, where it is affirmed that a Davidic descendant will rule over Israel in perpetuity. In the absence of an actual monarchy, these texts could be interpreted in terms of an eschatological king or messiah. The first unambiguous reference to David as progenitor of the messiah comes in *Psalms of Solomon* 17, where God is asked to raise up a "son of David." Likewise, four texts from Qumran (4QpGen[a], 4QFlor, 4QpIsa[a], 4Q285) articulate expectations for a messiah called the Branch of David. Finally, in *4 Ezra* 12, a cosmic eschatological redeemer who ushers in the age to come is said to arise from the posterity of David. While lightly attested in early Jewish texts, this image of David is frequent in both early Christianity and rabbinic Judaism.

Victorious Warrior

David as a victorious warrior is already strongly represented in the books of Samuel: he slays Goliath (1 Sam. 17:48-49), has spectacular success against the Philistines (1 Sam. 21:11), captures Jerusalem, and subdues Moab, Aram, and Edom among others (cf. 2 Sam. 22:35-46; cf. Ps. 89:22-23). In the Second Temple period, Chronicles (ca. 400 B.C.E.) recounts many of the battle accounts in Samuel. Ben Sira, too, highlights David's military prowess, citing his killing of Goliath and his victory over enemies on every side (Sir. 47:3-7). According to 1 Macc. 4:30-35, when outnumbered by Seleucid forces, Judas Maccabee prayed for victory to the God "who crushed the attack of the mighty warrior by the hand of your servant David." For Eupolemus, beyond David's successful campaigns against foes mentioned in Samuel, David waged war against the Phoenicians, Itureans, Nabateans, and Nabadeans. In the *War Scroll* from Qumran, a victory hymn celebrates how God delivered Goliath into the hands of David because he trusted in God's powerful name (1QM 11:2). This same emphasis is reflected in Josephus' characterization of David (cf. *Ant.* 6.196). In Pseudo-Philo, David's victory over Goliath is accomplished with the help of the angel "Zervihel, the angel in charge of might and warfare" (*Bib. Ant.* 61:5).

Ideal Ruler and King

In the Hebrew Bible David is portrayed as an ideal king. He replaces Saul because God wants a king who is a man after his own heart (1 Sam. 13:14; cf. Ps. 78:70-72) and serves as the standard of faithful kingship in the Deuteronomistic History (cf. 2 Kings 16:2-3; 22:2). Chronicles enhances the ideal character of David's rule: he does not struggle to attain the throne, and the rebellions against him by Absalom and Sheba are omitted. Ben Sira explains that God exalted David's power forever and gave him a covenant of kingship and a glorious throne (47:11), and David is numbered, alongside Hezekiah and Josiah, with the good kings of Judah (49:4). First Maccabees notes that David inherited the throne of a kingdom because of his loyalty (1 Macc. 2:57), while the *Words of the Luminaries*, a penitential prayer from Qumran, calls David a "shepherd prince" (4Q504 1–2 iv 6-8). 4QMMT explicitly holds up David as a model king (4Q398 14–17 ii 25-26). Acts 13:22 explains that God made David king because he was a man dear to God's heart who would do God's pleasure. Josephus also sees David as an ideal king, describing his qualifications for his Roman readers in terms of David's virtues (*Ant.* 6.160).

Psalmist

The image of David as psalmist was widespread during the Second Temple period. In Scripture David is portrayed as a musician who enters Saul's service (1 Sam. 16:14-23) and as one who sings two songs, a lament over Saul and Jonathan (2 Sam. 1:17-27) and a hymn of praise for deliverance (2 Sam. 22:1-51), though he is not explicitly designated as the composer of either. Amos 6:5 refers to those "who sing idle songs to the sound of the harp and like David improvise on instruments of music." In the Second Temple era, however, David is characterized as both musician and psalmist. Chronicles states that David not only organized the music for the Temple cult by building instruments, assigning musicians, and appointing songs for various occasions (cf. 1 Chron. 15:16-24; 16:4-42), but also composed liturgical songs or psalms (2 Chron. 29:30). 4QPs[a] contains superscriptions that relate a psalm to some event in David's life, presuming Davidic authorship of the psalm. 4QMMT assumes David as the psalmist when it exhorts its readers to "understand the Books of Moses and the Books of the Prophets and David . . ." (4Q398 14–17 i 10-11). Likewise, 2 Maccabees (ca. 100 B.C.E.) declares that David is the author of psalms, referring to "books about the kings and prophets, and the writings of David . . ." (2 Macc. 2:13). A prose passage at the conclusion of a Qumran *Psalms Scroll* attributes to David 3,600 psalms, along with numerous other songs, for a total of 4,005 (11QPs[a] 27:4-10). Philo calls David "a sacred poet" (*Plantatione* 29) and "God's psalmist" (*Confutatione* 149), while *4 Maccabees* refers to a man who "sang the songs of the psalmist David" (*4 Macc.* 18:15). New Testament texts also refer to David as author of the psalms (e.g., Mark 12:36; Acts 1:16; 2:34; 4:25; Rom. 4:6; 11:9; Heb. 4:7), and according to Pseudo-Philo, when David was anointed king by Samuel, he sang a psalm (*Ant. Bib.* 59:4). Josephus, too, states that David "composed songs and hymns to God" (*Ant.* 7.305). Overall, David's reputation as psalmist was an expanding one: while the Masoretic Psalter attributes seventy-three psalms to David, the LXX assigns him eighty-six, the Peshiṭta even more, and some rabbinic texts all of them.

Prophet

Though David is never called a prophet in biblical texts before 400 C.E., a few texts hold potential for such a characterization. The last words of David (2 Samuel 23) are introduced as an oracle of David (v. 1), and David says, "The spirit of the LORD speaks through me, his word is upon my tongue" (v. 2). In the Second Temple period, Chronicles associates David with prophecy even more closely, since Temple singing is understood as prophecy (1 Chron. 25:1) and David is said to have composed materials for Temple singing (2 Chron. 29:30; cf. also 2 Chron. 8:14, where David is called "the man of God," a designation reserved in Chronicles for prophets). Nehemiah 12:24 also connects David's prophetic status with cultic praise and psalmody.

At Qumran, David was perceived as a prophet. This is implied by the pesharim, which interpret only the prophetic books and Psalms, suggesting that the Psalms — including Davidic psalms — were construed as words of prophets. Further, the *Psalms Scroll* attributes 4,005 songs to David: "All these he uttered through prophecy given him from before the Most High" (11QPs[a] 27:11). Several New Testament texts speak of David as a prophet, such as Acts 2:30, "Since he (David) was a prophet, he knew that God had sworn with an oath to him that he would put one of his descendants on the throne." Philo attributes prophetic status to the authors of the psalms (cf. *Heres* 290), some of which he attributes to David; and Josephus explains that at the dedication of the Temple, Solomon told the people that "they saw the fulfillment of these things in accordance with David's prophecies" (*Ant.* 8.109-10).

Founder of the Jerusalem Cult

According to the books of Samuel, David's association with cultic matters was limited: he brings the Ark of the Covenant to Jerusalem (2 Samuel 6); he wants to build a temple for God (2 Sam. 7:1-7); he erects an altar on the threshing floor of Araunah (2 Sam. 24:18-25); and his sons are described as priests (2 Sam. 8:18). By contrast, in Chronicles David is devoted to cultic matters: he prepares for the building of the Temple, presents its design, and organizes cultic personnel, liturgy, and activities (1 Chron. 22:1; 25:1; 28:19). Likewise, in Ezra-Nehemiah cultic personnel, liturgy, and conduct are handled according to the directions of David (cf. also 1 Esdras). Ben Sira praises David for placing singers before the altar, giving beauty to the festivals, and arranging their times throughout the year (Sir. 47:9-10). For his part, Josephus repeats from Chronicles how David prepared to build the Temple and organized the cult, although he greatly abbreviates the Chronicler's account (*Ant.* 7.363-67; 375-79). Thus, the image of David as founder of the cult is a tradition that becomes dominant in Chronicles and closely related literature but is rarely attested thereafter.

Man of Piety and Righteousness

The books of Samuel already depict David as a man of great godliness though one marked by incidences of moral failure. Early Jewish texts tend to highlight his godliness and to minimize his failures. Chronicles sanitizes David's image: there is no adultery with Bathsheba and no murder of Uriah. David's one moral failure mentioned in Chronicles — taking a census — is used by the author to present David as the model penitent. Ben Sira says David loved his maker and that God took away his sin (47:8, 11). 1 Maccabees 2:57 and 4QMMT (4Q398 14–17 ii 25-26) refer to David's piety, the latter text specifically mentioning that he was pardoned. The *Damascus Document* excuses David's polygamy, adding that David's deeds were praised, except for the murder of Uriah (CD 5:5). The Qumran *War Scroll* states that Goliath was delivered into David's hand because David trusted in God rather than weapons (1QM 11:2). The Qumran *Psalms Scroll* offers the highest praise, saying that David was "perfect in all his ways before God and men" (11QPs[a] 27:3). Philo explains that David found "his gladness in God alone" (*De Plantatione* 39). The author of the Epistle to the Hebrews lists David among the heroes of faith (Heb. 11:32), and 4 Macc. 3:1-18 presents him as an example of how reason can overcome the desires. According to Pseudo-Philo, David did not know why Saul hated him because he was just and had no wickedness (*Bib. Ant.* 62:5). Josephus says of David, "He was a most excellent man and possessed of every virtue . . . never once did he do wrong, except in the matter of Uriah's wife" (*Ant.* 7.390-91; cf. also *Ant.* 7.153). As if this were not praise enough, the *Apocalypse of Zephaniah* numbers David, along with Enoch, Elijah, Abraham, Isaac, and Jacob, among the righteous whose souls did not pass through Hades but ascended directly to God.

Exorcist

The seedbed for the image of David as exorcist was the description of him playing the lyre to relieve Saul from the evil spirit that tormented him (1 Sam. 16:23). Consequently, in 11QPs[a] 27:9-10 David is said to have composed four songs "to be sung over the possessed," one of which may be preserved in an apocryphal psalm attributed to David (11QapocPs v 4) designed to drive out a demon that attacks in the night. Josephus explains that David was recruited to Saul's court as one "with the power to charm away spirits and to play upon the harp . . . and chant his songs" (*Ant.* 6.166). Lastly, Pseudo-Philo also tells the story of David playing songs to drive away the evil spirit from Saul (*Bib. Ant.* 60:1-3), exhorting the demon not to be troublesome.

BIBLIOGRAPHY

L. H. FELDMAN 1989, "Josephus' Portrait of David," *HUCA* 60: 129-74. • J. L. KUGEL 1990, "David the Prophet," in *Poetry and Prophecy: The Beginnings of a Literary Tradition,* ed. J. L. Kugel, Ithaca, N.Y.: Cornell University Press, 45-55. • K. E. POMYKALA 2004, "Images of David in Early Judaism," in *Of Scribes and Sages: Early Jewish Interpretation and Transmission of Scripture,* vol. 1, ed. C. A. Evans, London: Clark, 33-46. • E. M. MENN 2003, "Sweet Singer of Israel: David and the Psalms in Early Judaism," in *Psalms in Community: Jewish and Christian Textual, Liturgical, and Artistic Traditions,* ed. H. W. Attridge and M. E. Fassler. Atlanta: Society of Biblical Literature, 61-74. • Y. MIURA 2007, *David in Luke-Acts: His Portrayal in the Light of Early Judaism,* Tübingen: Mohr-Siebeck.

KENNETH E. POMYKALA

David Apocryphon

The *David Apocryphon* from Qumran (4Q22) is a fragmentary manuscript consisting of two columns, each with four lines of Hebrew text. Maurice Baillet (1962) dated the manuscript to the first century C.E. ("rather late Herodian"). He suspected that the text related to the story of David and Goliath and therefore named it *David Apocryphon?*, but he indicated his uncertainty by adding a question mark to the title.

The work is now recognized as a piece of a larger composition that mentions several biblical figures, including Joseph, Moses, Og, and Zimri. This is clear because col. i of 2Q22 overlaps with 4Q373 frgs. 1+2, which in turn overlap with 4Q372 (frg. 19), a manuscript further sharing text with 4Q371. Therefore, 4Q371-373 and 2Q22 seem to represent parts or versions of the same composition in which narrative material provides a setting for autobiographical psalms by biblical figures. (As a consequence, 4Q371-373, originally labeled *Apocryphon of Joseph*$^{a-c}$, has been renamed 4QNarrative and Poetic Composition^{a-c} in the DJD series. 2Q22 has retained its original title.)

The composition probably dates from the second century B.C.E., since it presumes the presence of the Samaritan temple on Mt. Gerizim, which was destroyed by John Hyrcanus in ca. 112/111 B.C.E. 4Q371-373 was copied during the Hasmonean and early Herodian periods, so 2Q22 represents a late Herodian version of a composition that had been copied for more than a century and a half. The composition does not appear to be sectarian in character.

When 2Q22 col. i (text underlined) is supplemented by 4Q373 frgs. 1 + 2 and 4Q372 frg. 19, the passage reads as follows:

2. all his servants with Og [
3. cubits and a half his height and two [cubits his width . . .] a spear like a cedar [
4. a shield like a tower. The one who is swift of fo[ot
5. the ones who were distant seven stades. He did not stand [
6. and I did not do it again, but <u>yhwh our God</u> shattered him; <u>with the edge of</u> [the sword . . .
7. I made <u>deadly slings with bows and not</u> [
8. For [w]<u>ar to capture fortified cities and to terrify</u> [
9. [ ] <u>and now</u> [

Since the passage includes first-person narration, it appears to be part of an autobiographical psalm, though the speaker is not identified. Baillet thought the passage referred to David's battle with Goliath, especially because of the reference to "slings." Shemaryahu Talmon, however, suggested that the text concerned Moses' defeat of Og, the king of Bashan, who is mentioned in line 2. More recently, Eileen Schuller has supported Baillet's initial proposal. Specifically, Goliath is the only figure in the Bible whose dimensions are described in half-cubits, as is the figure in line 2. Goliath was a giant, which fits the description of the figure in lines 2 and 3, and Og, also characterized as a giant in later Jewish tradition, is probably invoked by way of comparison. Moreover, there was widespread interest in the David-Goliath story during the Second Temple period (cf. Sir. 47:4-6; 1 Macc. 4:30; 1QM 9:1-2; 11Ps^{a} 28:13-14; Ps.-Philo, *Bib. Ant.* 61:1-9). Another piece of the larger composition — 4Q372 frg. 2 — has affinities with 2Q22. It contains the phrases "mountain of Bashan" and "his head with a dea[dly] stone," the latter almost certainly a reference to the death of Goliath.

In sum, 2Q22 is likely a portion of an autobiographical psalm in which David celebrates and praises God for his victory over Goliath, perhaps as a model for how God gives victory to his people over seemingly more powerful foreign enemies — a theme that would have resonated with many Jews in the Hasmonean and Herodian periods. Column ii is very general in character, mentioning God's kindness toward Israel, his words or paths, and his deliverance of "them" to judgment. Its text does not overlap with any part of 4Q371-373, but it is nevertheless consistent with the hymnic style and theme of divine praise found elsewhere in the larger composition.

BIBLIOGRAPHY

M. BAILLET, J. T. MILIK, AND R. DE VAUX, EDS. 1962, *Les 'Petites Grottes' de Qumrân,* DJD 3, Oxford: Clarendon, 81-82. • E. SCHULLER AND M. BERNSTEIN 2001, "4Q71-373," in *Qumran Cave 4. XXVIII: Miscellanea, Part 2,* DJD 28, Oxford: Clarendon, 151-204. • E. SCHULLER 1992, "A Preliminary Study of 4Q373 and Some Related (?) Fragments," in *The Madrid Qumran Congress,* vol. 2, ed. J. T. Barrera and L. V. Montaner, Leiden: Brill, 515-30. • S. TALMON 1989, *The World of Qumran from Within: Collected Studies,* Jerusalem: Magnes; Leiden: Brill, 244-72, esp. 262-64.

KENNETH E. POMYKALA

Dead, Abode of → Death and Afterlife

Dead Sea Scrolls

The Dead Sea Scrolls are the fragmentary remains of a library found in caves near Qumran, a site off the northwest shore of the Dead Sea. The texts belonged to a Jewish sectarian group usually identified as the Essenes. Inscribed mostly on goat skin and some papyrus, the texts include fragments of nearly every book of the Hebrew Bible and a host of other texts that have long been assigned to three categories: previously known Jewish apocrypha and pseudepigrapha; previously unknown Jewish apocrypha and pseudepigrapha; and works authored by the members of the community, sectarian texts. The scrolls are written in Hebrew, Aramaic, and Greek.

Discovery and Publication

Bedouin searching the caves of the Judean Desert (presumably for antiquities of some cash value) discovered Cave 1 in 1947. There they found seven carefully wrapped scrolls stored in clay jars. Among the well-preserved scrolls from Cave 1 are two nearly complete manuscripts of the book of Isaiah and a copy of the *Community Rule,* the group's charter document. Cave 11, the last cave to be discovered, was opened in 1956 and also yielded a small number of well-preserved scrolls, including a large *Psalms Scroll* and a copy of the

Original entrance to Cave 4, first discovered by the Bedouin in 1954

Temple Scroll. These were the only caves to yield substantially complete manuscripts. The most significant yield, however, came from Cave 4, discovered by the Bedouin in 1952. Through purchases from Bedouin dealers and an official excavation of the site, the Cave 4 manuscripts were reunited in the Rockefeller Museum in east Jerusalem, and it soon became apparent that the cave had housed something akin to a community library, in a collection of what was then estimated to be nearly 600 manuscripts. Although these scrolls were highly fragmentary thanks to a number of incursions into the caves over the centuries (e.g., at the time of the Roman destruction of the site during the war between Rome and the Jews [ca. 68 C.E.]; by the Bedouin in 1952), the basic work of reassembling the scattered remains was largely finished before 1960, when the original team of scholars left Jerusalem for their regular academic posts.

Further discoveries of scrolls have been insignificant compared to the yields of Caves 1, 4, and 11. Cave 3 provided the famous *Copper Scroll,* which contained detailed instructions for locating a treasure in the Judean Desert (never found); there is, however, a growing consensus that the manuscript is unrelated to the rest of the Dead Sea Scrolls; it may have been a map for locating the Temple treasure, hidden in the desert during the first war between Rome and the Jews [66-70 C.E.]). Since the Oslo Accords of 1993 promised land in the desert to a new Palestinian state, explorations of additional caves have been undertaken in the hope of finding further deposits; the results, though, have been underwhelming and it seems likely that we have, at around 900 manuscripts, the sum of the library of Qumran recoverable two millennia after its creators and keepers passed from the scene.

Even though the vast majority of the scrolls had been discovered before 1956 and the basic transcriptions of virtually all of them had been made before 1960, the path to complete publication of the texts was long and tortured. Because of too small an editorial team and a degree of scholarly compulsion to do more with the texts than merely transcribe and translate them for others to assess, there was a considerable delay. A watershed moment along the way toward expediting their publication came in 1990 with the reorganization of the editorial team to increase its numbers and religious diversity (to include Jewish scholars in particular). Under the leadership of Emanuel Tov (Hebrew University) assisted by Eugene Ulrich (University of Notre Dame), and Émile Puech (École Biblique, Jerusalem/CNRS, Paris), among others, the process of producing transcriptions and translations with notes and commentary moved along quickly. No substantial scrolls remain unpublished in one form or another, and the vast majority are now available in the official publication series, Discoveries in the Judaean Desert (Oxford University Press).

Questions of Authorship, Date and Provenance

Several hypotheses regarding the authorship, date, and provenance of the scrolls have been offered over the years, but the dominant theory remains that the library at Qumran belonged to a group of Essenes.

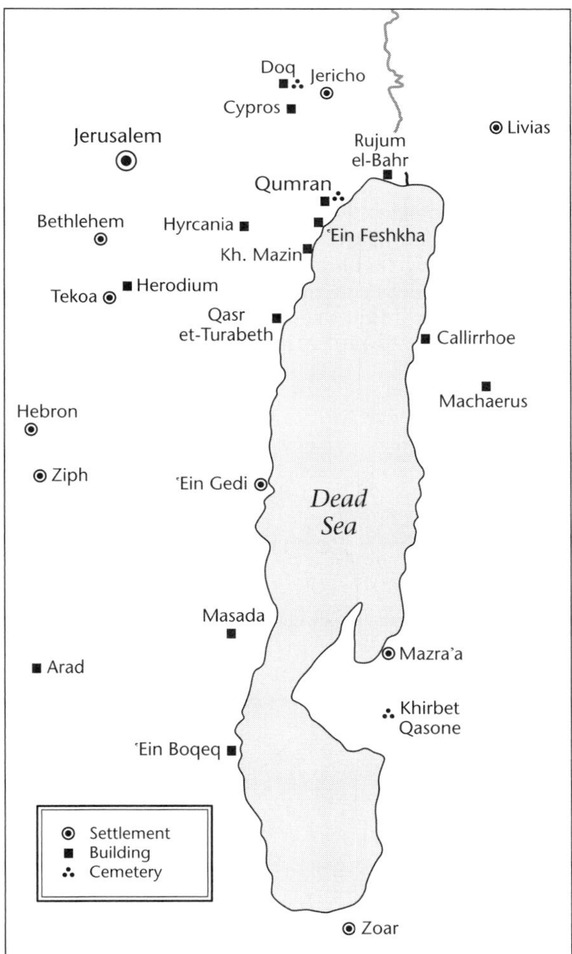

THE DEAD SEA REGION

The Essene Hypothesis

The association of the Qumran site with the group described by Josephus and Philo as the Essenes is secured by Pliny's observation that the Essenes were located on the western edge of the Dead Sea (Josephus, *J.W.* 2.119-61; *Ant.* 13.171-73; 18.18-22; Philo, *Every Good Man Is Free* 75-91; *Hypothetica;* Pliny, *Natural History* 5.73). The correlation between the texts from Qumran and most (though not all) aspects of the Essenes' theology (e.g., predestination; afterlife) and practice (e.g., communalism; initiation rites and procedures) described by Philo and Josephus settles for many the community's identity. Some inconsistencies remain between the scrolls and the Greek writers' descriptions, but they are generally explained as the result of the classical writers' particular biases and/or gaps in knowledge (see, e.g., Cross 1995). Two variations on the Essene hypothesis deserve mention. The Groningen Hypothesis (García Martínez 1988) views the Qumran group as a post–Maccabean Revolt breakaway sect from the pre-Maccabean Essenes, and Gabriele Boccaccini (1998) argues that the people of the scrolls were offspring of a more ancient "Enochic Judaism" that also sowed the seeds of the groups centered on John the Baptist and Jesus.

The Sadducean Hypothesis

The observation that some legal positions articulated in the scrolls closely parallel those ascribed to the Sadducees by rabbinic literature (e.g., 4QMMT B 55-58 and *m. Yad.* 4:7 on streams of liquid) has prompted other scholars to associate the Dead Sea Scrolls with a Sadducean group (Baumgarten 1980; Schiffman 1995). However, some key theological differences between the scrolls and Sadducean views (e.g., predestination; angelology) suggest that the common ground is only in a shared tendency toward stringent legal interpretations.

Overview of Khirbet Qumran and surrounding area *(Phoenix Data Systems / Neal and Joel Bierling)*

Other Hypotheses

Other minority views suggest that the scrolls were the possessions of a previously unknown Jewish group (Talmon 1994); they were deposited in the desert for safekeeping during the war with Rome by a consortium of Jewish libraries in Jerusalem (and the Qumran site was unrelated to the scrolls (Golb 1995); or they were the product of a failed form of Christianity (R. Eisenman). These approaches have not garnered significant followings.

Contents of the Scrolls

The most common way to classify and describe the scrolls in the past was to distinguish among biblical texts, previously known and previously unknown pseudepigrapha and apocrypha, and so-called sectarian texts, works we assume from their distinctive vocabulary and ideology to have been written by members of the community. This approach fails, though, inasmuch as the latter category of texts is not always as certain as we might like, the Jewish Bible was not yet completely formed as such, and some of the previously unknown pseudepigrapha could just as easily be sectarian compositions. The alternative approach followed here is to address as a group the scrolls categorized *today* as biblical, and treat the remaining scrolls according to very broad genre categories without particular regard for whether they were authored by the community or not.

Biblical Scrolls and Apocrypha

More than 220 of the scrolls preserve parts of the present Hebrew Bible and the Christian "Old Testament Apocrypha." At thirty-six manuscripts, the Psalms are the best represented. Deuteronomy comes in second at thirty scrolls, followed by Genesis (24), Isaiah (22) Exodus (18), Leviticus (17), Numbers (11), and the Minor Prophets (10). The remaining books of the Hebrew Scriptures vary in count between eight (Daniel) and zero (Nehemiah; Esther). Apocrypha found at Qumran include Tobit (four Aramaic manuscripts and one Hebrew manuscript), Psalms 154–55, Ben Sira, and Letter of Jeremiah. Apart from a handful of texts in Aramaic and Greek, the biblical scrolls are in Hebrew; some are written in a paleo-Hebrew script.

In addition to providing the oldest textual witnesses to virtually all of the books of the Hebrew Bible, the biblical scrolls also reveal that textual diversity was the norm as late as the turn of the eras. Several models explain this textual pluralism: a theory of local texts that assigns specific texts Egyptian, Babylonian, and Palestinian provenances (Cross 1995); a theory of complete textual variety owing to creative practices among authors and copyists (Talmon 1975); a theory of textual variety that allows for five different text types (Tov 2002); and a theory of successive literary editions (Ulrich 1999).

Legal Texts

At the center of the Qumran sect's interests was the elaboration of the laws of the Hebrew Scriptures and related legal traditions to construct their distinctive halakic profile, one marked both by extraordinary stringency and breadth. *Some Works of the Law,* 4QMMT (4Q394-399) especially shows the stringency, and the *Temple Scroll* (4Q524; 11Q19-20) exemplifies the breadth. 4QMMT, mainly a collection of legal rulings, offers consistently more rigorous legal rulings than those supported by a competing party referred to by the author; for example, impurity communicates more readily, and sacrificial boundaries require greater respect. The focus on elaborating laws relating to sacrifice and festival observances in the *Temple Scroll* expresses the community's interest in broadening the law. Among the many other halakic texts the *Purification Rules* (4Q274, 4Q276-278) exemplify the blend of these two impulses.

Rules

In the category of rule books are community charters, documents detailing regulations for the group's life together at Qumran and elsewhere. The *Damascus Document* is the latter sort of text (CD; 4Q266-273; 5Q12; 6Q15), offering guidance on marriage, family life, and social encounters with non-Essenes alongside regulations for community-specific structures. By contrast, although the *Community Rule* (1QS; 4Q255-264; 4Q319; 5Q11) addresses broad matters such as the community's worldview in the "Treatise on the Two Spirits" (1QS 3:13–4:26) and the liturgies for annual covenantal ceremonies (1QS 1:16–2:18), its chief focus is on establishing patterns of conduct for community members (e.g., community structure, 1QS 5:8–6:23; penal code, 8:16–9:2). A third rule text captures another dimension of the Essenes' thought, their intense eschatological interests: the *War Rule* (1QM; 4Q491-497) establishes the guidelines for conducting the final battle between the Sons of Light (members of the community) and the Sons of Darkness (everyone else) that will presage God's intervention to bring history to a close.

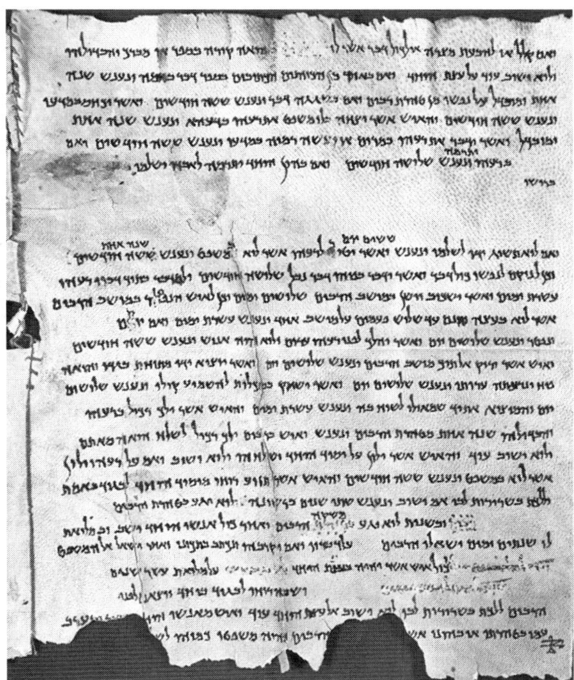

1QS Rule of the Community Scroll. This document contains rules and regulations for the community at Qumran. *(John Trever)*

Scriptural Interpretation

Because applying the emerging Hebrew Scriptures to their own circumstances was of as much interest to the community as halakic reasoning, many scrolls fall into the broad category of biblical interpretation. Some of these texts may have been composed by community members, but many were probably adopted by the group. These include rearranged portions of Torah (*Reworked Pentateuch,* 4Q364-367; 4Q368?); rewritten and expanded episodes and sections from the Hebrew Scriptures (e.g., *Aramaic Levi Document,* 4Q213-214; *Pseudo-Jubilees,* 4Q225-227; *Apocryphon of Joshua,* 4Q123; 4Q378-379 [episodes]; *Jubilees,* 4Q216-224 and others; *1 Enoch,* 4Q201-212 and others; *Genesis Apocryphon,* 1Q20 [whole sections]); accounts associated with scriptural figures (e.g., Moses, 1Q22; 2Q21; 4Q375-376; 4Q385a; Noah, 1Q19[bis]; 4Q534; Jeremiah, 4Q383-384; 4Q385b); and so-called "continuous" and "thematic" commentaries on Hebrew Scriptures (e.g., *Pesher to Hosea,* 4Q166-167; *Pesher to Habakkuk,* 1QpHab; *Pesher to Psalms,* 1Q16; 4Q171; 4Q173 [continuous]; *Florilegium,* 4Q174; *Catena A,* 4Q177; *Melchizedek,* 11Q13 [thematic]). The latter category encompasses the *pesher,* the community's trademark interpretive mode which quotes passages of scriptural text and explains its meaning *(pešer)* as relating to contemporary circumstances.

Calendars, Liturgies, Prayers, Blessings, and Hymns

To order its religious life the community also composed and/or preserved texts for public and private ritual. Calendars scheduled festivals and the phases of the moon, crucial aspects of establishing the festal date book (e.g., *Calendrical Documents,* 4Q322-324; 4Q327; *Phases of the Moon,* 4Q317); synchronized priestly courses with other temporal measures (e.g., *'Otot,* 4Q319; 4Q322-324); and correlated lunar and solar reckonings of time (e.g., *Calendrical Document,* 4Q320). Liturgies provided orders of service for general and specific events (e.g., 4Q409; 4Q502). Prayer texts and blessings addressed various kinds of speech to God and between members of the community (e.g., *Daily Prayers,* 4Q503; *Words of the Heavenly Luminaries,* 4Q504-506; *Songs of Sabbath Sacrifice,* 4Q400-407; 11Q17; *Festival Prayers,* 1Q34-34[bis]; 4Q507-509; *Berakhot,* 4Q286-290). And hymns preserve songs that the community sang in various ritual contexts (*Hymns,* 3Q6; 6Q18; 8Q5; *Sapiential Hymn,* 4Q411; *Eschatological Hymn,* 4Q457b; *Self-Glorification Hymn,* 4Q471b).

A work that can be counted among the hymns, but that deserves its own category is *Hodayot,* a collection of poetic hymns or psalms for the leader of the community and/or members of the community to sing (1QH; 1Q35; 4Q427-432). These are significant not only for their possible association with the community leader referred to as the "Teacher of Righteousness," but also for their clear expression of the community's theological anthropology.

Wisdom Texts

The major representative of sapiential literature in the Dead Sea Scrolls is *Instruction* (1Q26; 4Q415-418a; 4Q418c; 4Q423), a work by a sage that addresses money and family management, social relations, and the like. Its uniqueness lies in its claim that those who truly understand mundane reality have access to the "mystery of the way things are/will be" and will therefore grasp (and presumably act in accord with) God's plan for history. Other texts in this category include *Wiles of the Wicked Woman* (4Q184; 4Q220-241) and *Beatitudes* (4Q525).

Eschatological Texts

Unsurprisingly, many of the scrolls have eschatological content (e.g., "Treatise on the Two Spirits" [1QS 3:13–4:26] presumes a certain eschatological vision). Oddly enough, though, only a handful can be classified as eschatological at the level of genre: the *New Jerusalem Text* (1Q32; 2Q24; 4Q554; 4Q554a-4Q555; 5Q15; 11Q18) and the *Messianic Apocalypse* (4Q521) especially fit in this category. The *War Rule* also belongs on this short list.

The foregoing survey of the DSS demonstrates the breadth of their concern and, correspondingly, the intellectual and religious complexity of their creators and curators. While it was tempting soon after their initial discovery to characterize the group as an apocalyptic and messianic Jewish sect, and more recently as a community of halakic rigorists, a survey of the collection as a whole indicates the need to resist such limiting categorizations. Rather, we must explore the full range of ideas articulated in the library as a clue to the worldview(s) of the people who preserved, copied, and composed them.

Bibliography

J. Baumgarten 1980, "The Pharisaic-Sadducean Controversies about Purity and the Qumran Texts," *JJS* 3: 157-70. • G. Boccaccini 1998, *Beyond the Essene Hypothesis: The Parting of the Ways between Qumran and Enochic Judaism,* Grand Rapids: Eerdmans. • J. J. Collins 2009, *Beyond the Qumran Community,* Grand Rapids: Eerdmans. • F. M. Cross 1995, *The Ancient Library of Qumran,* rev. ed., Minneapolis: Fortress. • P. W. Flint and J. C. VanderKam, eds. 1999, *The Dead Sea Scrolls after Fifty Years,* 2 vols., Leiden: Brill. • F. García Martínez 1988, *Qumran Origins and Early History: A Groningen Hypothesis, Folia Orientalia* 25: 113-36. • F. García Martínez 1996, *The Dead Sea Scrolls Translated,* 2d ed., Leiden: Brill; Grand Rapids: Eerdmans. • N. Golb 1995, *Who Wrote the Dead Sea Scrolls? The Search for the Secret of Qumran,* New York: Scribner. • L. H. Schiffman 1995, *Reclaiming the Dead Sea Scrolls,* New York: Doubleday. • L. H. Schiffman and J. C. VanderKam, eds. 2000, *Encyclopedia of the Dead Scrolls,* 2 vols., Oxford: Oxford University Press. • H. Stegemann 1998, *The Library of Qumran,* Grand Rapids: Eerdmans. • S. Talmon 1975, "The Textual Study of the Bible — A New Outlook," in *Qumran and the History of the Biblical Text,* ed. F. M. Cross and S. Talmon, Cambridge: Harvard University Press, 321-400. • S. Talmon 1994, "The Community of the Renewed Covenant: Between Judaism and Christianity," in *The Community of the Renewed Covenant: The Notre Dame Symposium on the Dead Sea Scrolls,* ed. E. Ulrich and J. VanderKam, Notre Dame: University of Notre Dame Press, 3-24. • E. Tov 2002, "The Biblical Texts from the Judean Desert — An Overview and Analysis of All the Published Texts," in *The Bible as Book: The Hebrew Bible and the Judean Desert Discoveries,* ed. E. Herbert and E. Tov, London: British Library, 139-66. • E. C. Ulrich 1999, *The Dead Seas Scrolls and the Origins of the Bible,* Grand Rapids: Eerdmans. • J. C. VanderKam and P. W. Flint 2002, *The Meaning of the Dead Sea Scrolls: Their Significance for Understanding the Bible, Judaism, Jesus, and Christianity,* San Francisco: HarperSanFrancisco. • G. Vermes 1997, *The Complete Dead Sea Scrolls in English,* London: Penguin.

See also: Essenes; Qumran

Robert A. Kugler

Death and Afterlife

The Hebrew Bible

For most of the biblical period, the afterlife was conceived as the dreary existence of shades in Sheol, the dark and gloomy underworld. This was the Hebrew counterpart of the Greek Hades. It is often referred to as "the Pit." There the dead cannot even praise the Lord. While the prospect of Sheol gives rise to a certain amount of angst in the Psalms, it is generally accepted with equanimity in the Hebrew Bible. "Whether life is for ten years or a hundred or a thousand, there are no questions asked in Hades," wrote Ben Sira in the early second century B.C.E. Qoheleth is exceptional insofar as the prospect of death threatens to undermine the meaningfulness of life, which is perceived as mere "vanity" and chasing after wind. When Qoheleth, who should also be dated to the Hellenistic period, close to the time of Ben Sira, asked, "Who knows whether the human spirit goes upward and the spirit of animals goes downward to the earth?" (Qoh. 3:21), he was most probably challenging the emerging belief in a more meaningful life after death.

In the Hebrew Bible, there are only a few hints at the possibility of a beatific afterlife. Enoch and Elijah were taken up to heaven, but their cases were exceptional. A few Psalms express the hope for exceptional deliverance: "But God will ransom my soul from the power of Sheol, for he will receive me," says Ps. 49:15, although the same psalm says that "mortals cannot abide in their pomp; they are like the animals that perish" (compare Pss. 16:9-10; 73:23-26).

In the early postexilic period, the language of resurrection is used metaphorically for the restoration of the nation, most famously in Ezekiel's vision of the valley full of dry bones (Ezekiel 37). Isaiah 26:19 (part of the so-called "Apocalypse of Isaiah," Isaiah 24–27), which says: "your dead shall live, their corpses shall arise," should also be understood in terms of national restoration (although some scholars take it as a reference to individual resurrection).

The first unambiguous reference individual resurrection in the Hebrew Bible is found in Dan. 12:1-3: "Many of those who sleep in the land of dust shall awake, some to everlasting life, and some to shame and everlasting contempt. The wise shall shine like the brightness of the sky, and those who lead many to righteousness like the stars forever and ever." In Daniel, resurrection is not universal but applies to the very good and the very bad. The reward of the wise *(maśkîlîm)* is that they become like the stars. This formulation may be influenced by the notion of astral immortality (whereby souls of the dead become stars), which was current in Greece as early as the fifth century B.C.E. In Semitic tradition, however, the stars were the heavenly host, and to shine like the stars means to become companions to the hosts of heaven, that is, the angels. This is clear in the *Epistle of Enoch,* an apocalyptic writing roughly contemporary with Daniel (*1 Enoch* 104:1-6).

The idea of resurrection at the end of history was attested in Zoroastrianism before it appears in ancient Judaism. It is likely that Jewish apocalypticism was influenced by Zoroastrian models in some cases, although specific instances are difficult to prove. The manner in which resurrection is imagined in the earliest apocalypses, however, does not seem especially similar to Zoroastrianism.

The Early Apocalyptic Literature

Some sections of *1 Enoch,* which express the hope for a differentiated afterlife, are older than Daniel. *1 Enoch* 22, in the *Book of the Watchers,* contains a description of the chambers where the spirits of the dead are kept, separated into categories, to await the final judgment. *1 Enoch* 27 describes the place where that judgment will take place. The motif of the waiting chambers is exceptional, however.

It is not apparent that resurrection in Daniel, or in the *Epistle of Enoch,* entails a body of flesh and blood. Rather, the *nepeš,* which has some bodily qualities, is taken up to heaven. Also, the *Book of Jubilees* says of the righteous that "their bodies will rest in the earth, and their spirits will have much joy" (*Jub.* 23:31). The later *Similitudes of Enoch* also envisions angelic transformation. Physical resurrection is attested in 2 Maccabees 7, where the martyrs hope to get their bodies back in the resurrection, and also in the Pseudo-Ezekiel text from Qumran (4Q385, 386), but it is by no means the standard Jewish belief. The more typical hope concerns what Paul, in 1 Corinthians 15, would call a "spiritual body."

The Dead Sea Scrolls and the Essenes

The sectarian texts found at Qumran express a clear belief in reward and punishment after death, but they do not express this in terms of resurrection. Rather, the fate of the wicked and righteous seems to follow without interruption. Remarkably, the Dead Sea Scrolls have very little to say about death. In the *Hodayot,* the hymnist typically claims to be already rescued from the "Pit" and exalted to join the fellowship of the host of heaven (e.g., 1QH[a] 11:19-23; 1QH[a] 19:10-14). This accords well with the statement of Josephus that the Essenes believed that bodies were corruptible but souls immortal (*J.W.* 2.154). According to Josephus, the Essenes believed that the wicked would be condemned to a gloomy recess with incessant punishments, and this too is paralleled in the Dead Sea Scrolls. There is no Hebrew parallel, however, for the Isles of the Blessed, to which the righteous would allegedly go, in Essene belief. The church father Hippolytus attributes a belief in bodily resurrection to the Essenes, but his account is confused. Nonetheless, some scholars accept his testimony and claim to find support for it in the Scrolls (so especially Puech 1993). There is no doubt that the people who wrote the Scrolls were familiar with belief in resurrection, since they had copies of Daniel, and the belief is also attested in some nonsectarian texts found at Qumran (4Q521, the *Messianic Apocalypse,* and 4Qpseudo-Ezekiel). Nonetheless, this does not seem to be the dominant expectation of the afterlife in the Scrolls.

Hellenistic Judaism

In the Hellenistic Diaspora, many Jews accepted the Platonic conception of the immortality of the soul. This belief is expressed especially in the Wisdom of Solomon and in the writings of Philo. It should be noted, however, that belief in bodily resurrection is also found in writings from the Diaspora, notably 2 Maccabees and the *Fourth Sibylline Oracle* (from the late first century C.E.). Pseudo-Phocylides, in a very complex and difficult passage, seems to endorse both the hope of resurrection and the immortality of the soul (Collins 2005).

Pharisees and Sadducees

There does not appear to have been any orthodoxy in Judaism on the subject of life after death around the turn of the era. The Pharisees believed in resurrection. The Sadducees did not. Some Hellenistic Jewish writings also lack any attestation of belief in an afterlife (*Sibylline Oracles* 3 and 5). Belief in afterlife appears only sporadically in Jewish epitaphs from this period (van der Horst 1991). Some epitaphs from Leontopolis in Egypt express "good and hopeful expectation," and one says that the soul of the deceased has gone to the holy ones. There is little consistency on the subject, however.

Early Christianity

Belief in resurrection was of central importance for the rise of Christianity. According to Paul, if Christ was not raised from the dead, his proclamation would be in vain (1 Corinthians 15). Paul, however, did not conceive of the resurrection as an isolated miracle. Rather, it was the firstfruits of the general resurrection, which could not be far away. Paul believed that some of his listeners would not die, but would be taken up to meet the Lord in the air (1 Thess. 4:17). Paul conceived of resurrection in terms of a spiritual body, and conspicuously fails to mention an empty tomb. In the Gospels, in contrast, the empty tomb becomes the primary symbol of the resurrection.

Later Judaism

The apocalyptic writings of the late first century C.E. provide a synthesis of various strands of eschatological expectation. The general resurrection, as a public event, is of major importance in *4 Ezra* and *2 Baruch.* But these apocalypses retain the idea that the risen righteous become like the angels. According to *2 Bar.* 51:12, the splendor of the righteous will exceed even the splendor of the angels. In the Gospels, too, we read that those risen from the dead will not marry or be given in marriage, but are like the angels in heaven (Mark 12:25). Some of the later Jewish apocalypses *(3 Baruch, 2 Enoch, Testament of Abraham),* however, speak of the judgment of the dead without speaking of resurrection.

Belief in afterlife is not as prominent in rabbinic Judaism as it is in Christianity. Nonetheless, G. F. Moore could write that "the primary eschatological doctrine of Judaism is the resurrection, the revivification of the dead" (Moore 1927: 2:379). Heretics have no share in the world to come. Moreover, anyone who denied the resurrection could have no share in the world to come: "The following are those who have no portion in the World to Come: Whosoever says that the revivification of the dead is not from the Torah; or the Torah is not from Heaven" (*m. Sanh.* 10:1).

BIBLIOGRAPHY

J. R. ASHER 2000, *Polarity and Change in 1 Corinthians 15,* Tübingen: Mohr-Siebeck. • A. J. AVERY-PECK AND J. NEUSNER EDS. 2000, *Judaism in Late Antiquity. Part 4. Death, Life-After-Death, Resurrection and the World-to-Come in the Judaisms of Antiquity,* Leiden: Brill. • J. J. COLLINS 2005, "Life after Death in Pseudo-Phocylides," in idem, *Jewish Cult and Hellenistic Culture,* Leiden: Brill, 128-42. • P. W. VAN DER HORST 1991, *Ancient Jewish Epitaphs,* Kampen: Kok Pharos. • M. LABAHN AND M. LANG, ED. 2007, *Lebendige Hoffnung — Ewiger Tod?! Jenseitsvorstellungen im Hellenismus, Judentum und Christentum,* Leipzig: Evangelische Verlagsanstalt. • D. B. MARTIN 1995, *The Corinthian Body,* New Haven: Yale University Press. • G. F. MOORE 1927, *Judaism in the First Centuries of the Christian Era,* New York: Schocken. • G. W. E. NICKELSBURG 2006, *Resurrection, Immortality, and Eternal Life in Intertestamental Judaism and Early Christianity,* expanded ed., Cambridge: Harvard University Press. • P. PERKINS 1984, *Resurrection: New Testament Witness and Contemporary Reflection,* Garden City: Doubleday. • É. PUECH 1993, *La croyance des Esséniens en la vie future: Immortalité, resurrection, vie éternelle? Histoire d'un croyance dans le judaïsme ancien,* 2 vols., Paris: Gabalda. • A. F. SEGAL 2004, *Life after Death: The History of the Afterlife in Western Religion,* New York: Doubleday. • N. T. WRIGHT 2003, *The Resurrection of the Son of God,* Minneapolis: Fortress.

See also: Resurrection JOHN J. COLLINS

Decalogue

The Decalogue (a term from the Greek phrase for "ten words"), otherwise known as the Ten Commandments, consists of a series of commands given by God to Moses at Mt. Sinai. The Decalogue has been said to be the essence of the Jewish legal tradition in antiquity. Ancient sources support this view. However, the rabbinic tradition does not celebrate the Decalogue over the other laws.

In addition to the two different versions in the Pentateuch (Exod. 20:1-17; Deut. 5:6-21) and the so-called Yahwist Decalogue in Exodus 34, there are also different versions in the Septuagint and the Samaritan Pentateuch. Lists of commandments that overlap partially with the Decalogue are found in Lev. 19:1-18 and Deut. 27:15-26. Reworkings are found in the prophetic writings (Amos, Hosea, and Jeremiah) and in the Psalms (e.g., Psalms 50 and 81). Reworkings and citations of the Pentateuch are also present in writings found at Qumran (e.g., Tefillin and 1QS), Philo of Alexandria, Josephus, the Nash Papyrus, as well as in the Pauline corpus and the Gospels of Matthew and Mark (e.g., Mark 12:28-31).

There is an ongoing debate concerning the "original" version of the Decalogue. It seems clear that there were a growing number of traditions that developed, incorporated, and recast the Decalogue, in ways that were similar to Pentateuchal rewritings of Genesis or of the narrative portions of Exodus. The ordering of the commandments varied. More significant variations occur in the ways the commandments are interpreted in the various Second Temple communities. The Decalogue was a fluid text that changed repeatedly through transmission and interpretation.

The Decalogue functions in two different ways in early Judaism. It is incorporated into Jewish liturgies (e.g., in the DSS and the Nash Papyrus) and can also provide a legal framework for the details of Jewish law (e.g., in Philo of Alexandria's essay *On the Decalogue*).

Decalogue as Early Jewish Liturgy

Repetition and liturgical performance of the Decalogue may have served as a symbolic way of returning to Sinai. The Sinaitic theophany was not a one-time event but one that was repeated throughout the history of Israel. So the Decalogue was received at the beginning of Israelite history as a covenant between God and Israel, and communal performance could be understood as a renewal of the covenant. In many Second Temple writings (e.g., 2 Chron. 15:8-15; 2 Macc. 12:31-32; Josephus' *Jewish War;* the book of Acts; *Jubilees;* the Qumran *Commu-*

nity Rule; and Philo's *On the Contemplative Life*), Shavuot (the Feast of Weeks) is understood as a repetition of Sinaitic revelation that included the divine utterance of the Decalogue. To this day, Jewish communities stand when the Decalogue is read in a liturgical setting.

The Nash Papyrus is another witness to the liturgical use of the Decalogue. It consists of four fragments, acquired in 1903 in Egypt by W. L. Nash and first described by Stanley A. Cook. It was then the earliest Hebrew copy of parts of the biblical texts. The Nash Papyrus preserved the Shema and the Decalogue, with its own distinctive readings of the Decalogue. These readings are closer to the variants in Philo and many of the LXX manuscripts and in some cases show affinity to the Decalogue in Matthew. The current scholarly consensus is that the Nash Papyrus is a second-century-B.C.E. liturgical text (though some scholars had originally wanted to date it later to the first or second century C.E.). That the Decalogue was preserved in this liturgical text further suggests that it was part of the Jewish liturgical tradition already in the Second Temple period. It was performed by the community along with the Shema. Rabbinic traditions provide corroborating support as well.

The text of the Decalogue is included in the Tefillin found at Qumran, unlike rabbinic Tefillin. It seems very plausible that in late Second Temple times, the Decalogue was generally included in Tefillin but was later excluded due to the polemical charge, cited in both Talmuds (*y. Berakot* 3c; *b. Berakot* 12a), that some regarded the Decalogue as the *only* law given at Sinai. This inclusion of the Decalogue in the Qumran Tefillin further supports the claim that the Decalogue had a liturgical function in early Judaism.

Decalogue as Legal Framework

Recently Bilhah Nitzan has argued that 1QS 5:1–9:11 and its Cave 4 parallels reflect "the basic pattern of a set of ten principles (Decalogue) that was elaborated and adapted for practical implementation according to its order." This is not a repetition or a reordering of the Decalogue but a catalogue of ten legal principles that reflects a deliberate attempt on the part of the community to construct a community "Decalogue."

Philo of Alexandria composed an entire essay entitled *On the Decalogue.* In it he explains each of the ten utterances or oracles in legal, moral, and philosophical terms. But the purpose of the essay is to introduce his essays *On the Special Laws.* According to Philo, the ten utterances are actually ten heads or categories of law, under which all the details of the laws may be arranged. On this account, although the Decalogue is itself privileged as being the very words of the divinity with all of the extraordinary detail of revelation, it is not said to be more important than the special laws. However, Philo spends a great deal of time explaining how each of the ten utterances has universal and philosophical significance for the world as a whole. This is part of his broader project to show how the Law of Moses is compatible with (at times he even suggests synonymous with) the universal law of nature.

According to Philo, the Decalogue is divided into two parts. The first five commandments concern relations between human beings and the Divine, and the second five concern those among humans. However, he also claims that even the second five have an effect not only on the body but also on the soul.

The fourth commandment is to keep the holy seventh day, the Sabbath. Philo claims that this is a day that should be devoted to philosophical contemplation and that no work at all can be done on this day. Philo focuses on the reason that one keeps the Sabbath day: God observed it, so human beings must follow God in all ways. For Philo the Sabbath day is of universal, not particular significance.

The fifth commandment belongs to both the first part and the second part. According to Philo, those who are disrespectful to their immediate and visible parents cannot possibly be respectful to their invisible Father and Creator, God. Moreover, Philo argues, procreation is like creation. If you reject your natural obligation to your parents, how could you respect the obligation you have to God?

Philo claims that the Decalogue was proclaimed by God, whereas the special laws were proclaimed by Moses, whom he calls the most perfect prophet. But for Philo the special laws are not on a lower level but written with divine inspiration and present a clear and detailed account of what is already intended in the divine ten utterances. Before concluding, Philo reminds his readers that the details are already implicit in the ten heads or categories (i.e., the Decalogue). The example he cites is Passover, which for him is already implied in the fourth commandment about observing the holy Sabbath day.

BIBLIOGRAPHY

D. C. ALLISON, JR. 1994, "Mark 12:28-31 and the Decalogue," in *The Gospels and the Scriptures of Israel,* ed. C. A. Evans and W. R. Stegner, Sheffield: Sheffield Academic Press, 270-78. • Y. AMIR 1990, "The Decalogue according to Philo," in *The Ten Commandments in History and Tradition,* ed. B.-Z. Segal, Jerusalem: Magnes, 121-60. • G. J. BROOKE 2003, "Deuteronomy 5–6 in the Phylacteries from Qumran," in *Emanuel: Studies in the Hebrew Bible, the Septuagint, and the Dead Sea Scrolls in Honor of Emanuel Tov,* ed. S. M. Paul, Leiden: Brill, 57-70. • D. FLUSSER 1990, "The Ten Commandments and the New Testament," in *The Ten Commandments in History and Tradition,* ed. B.-Z. Segal, Jerusalem: Magnes, 219-46. • R. A. FREUND 1998, "The Decalogue in Early Judaism and Christianity," in *The Function of Scripture in Early Judaism and Christian Tradition,* ed. C. A. Evans and J. A. Sanders, Sheffield: Sheffield Academic Press, 124-41. • R. H. FULLER 2006, "The Decalogue in the New Testament," *Interpretation* 43: 243-55. • I. HIMBAZA 2002, "Le Décalogue de Papyrus Nash, Philon, 4Qphyl G, 8Qphyl 3 ET 4Qmez A," *RevQ* 20: 411-28. • I. HIMBAZA 2004, *Le Décalogue et l'histoire du texte,* Fribourg: Academic Press. • B. NITZAN FORTHCOMING, "The Decalogue Pattern in the Qumran Rule of the Community," in *Qumran Cave 1 Revisited,* ed. D. K. Falk et al., Leiden: Brill. • E. URBACH 1990, "The Role of the Ten Commandments in Jewish Worship," in *The Ten Commandments in History and*

Tradition, ed. B.-Z. Segal, Jerusalem: Magnes, 161-90. • M. WEINFELD 1990, "The Uniqueness of the Decalogue and Its Place in Jewish Tradition," in *The Ten Commandments in History and Tradition,* ed. B.-Z. Segal, Jerusalem: Magnes, 1-44.

HINDY NAJMAN

Decapolis

The term "Decapolis" (Greek for "ten cities") refers to a group of cities during the Roman period located east of Galilee and Samaria, across the Jordan River. The term occurs several times in ancient sources; it is mentioned not only by historians such as Josephus, but also in the New Testament and in inscriptions from the early centuries of the Common Era. In his work *Naturalis Historia,* Pliny the Elder (ca. 23-79 C.E.) lists the cities as Damascus, Philadelphia, Raphana, Scythopolis (the only city west of the Jordan River), Gadara, Hippos, Dion, Pella, Gerasa, and Canatha. Other sources, however, associate as many as eighteen or nineteen cities with the region.

An Area, Not a League

The ancient sources never apply the term "league" *(symmachia)* to the Decapolis; the designation is regional and not political, the reference always being to the Decapolis *area (Regio Decapolitana).* The Greek city-states *(poleis)* zealously guarded their independence, but whenever any external danger threatened, they would establish a military alliance by uniting themselves into a league. One of the better-known examples was the Delian league, established in 478 B.C.E. under the leadership of Athens. Leagues were also founded at times on a common ethnic or cultic basis. The representatives of cities in the league would meet once a year at a commonly shared cultic center to decide on matters of mutual concern. The cities of the Decapolis, by contrast, did not have a formal political or military affiliation. What they did have was territorial proximity, a shared urban autonomy as *poleis,* economic and commercial relations, cultural affinities, and shared religious concerns.

Cultural Features

The Decapolis area included cities that saw themselves as *poleis* in all respects. The group of cities created a territorial continuity that stretched from Raphana in the north to Philadelphia in the south and from Beth-Shean (Scythopolis) in the west to Canatha in the east. Most of the cities were founded during the Seleucid period (second century B.C.E.), but Pella and Philadelphia were apparently founded by the Ptolemies (third century B.C.E.).

Demography

Very little is known about the demography of the cities in the Decapolis. The names appearing on the numerous inscriptions found in the region tell us nothing about the ethnic mix of the inhabitants, because both the Nabateans and the Jews tended to adopt Greek names. Most of the population was probably of Semitic origin, and among them were probably the descendants of Nabateans who had ruled the region to the east of the Decapolis and had close ties with it. As *poleis,* the cities were governed by elected municipal councils and did everything to demonstrate that they were actually city-states.

Public Buildings

Public buildings were erected for the residents and funded by them, which is further proof of the cities' status as *poleis.* The construction of various buildings — mainly temples, theaters, and bathhouses but also decorative buildings such as *nymphaea* (fountain houses) and *tetrakionia* (monuments at street intersections) — was intended not only to provide for the welfare of the residents but to function as a source of pride for the city, by demonstrating its wealth and achievements.

Urban Planning

The cities in the Decapolis region did not resemble each other in their urban plans. Each city proposed its own particular planning solutions, but with regard to the choice of public buildings and their style of decoration, there was a surprising similarity among them. In all of them there were colonnaded streets that were impressive thoroughfares leading from one city compound to another.

View of Scythopolis (Beth Shean), a principal city of the Decapolis and the only one located west of the Jordan River. Foreground: remains of the Roman city; background: the ancient Tel *(Phoenix Data Systems / Neal and Joel Bierling)*

Architecture

Prominent among the entertainment structures was the theater. Each city in the Decapolis had at least one. In Gerasa there were three, and in Philadelphia and Gadara there were two. In Gadara and Beth-Shean there were also circuses. The many bathhouses and the select number of decorative structures inspired by Roman architecture, with triumphal arches and *tetrapyla* (quadrifonic arches), indicate the degree of Roman penetration and influence, which is also shown in the temples typical for that region. The architectonic decorations were also an expression of the rich and fascinating merging together of Hellenistic and Roman sources of inspiration. The architecture in the Decapolis was therefore of an eclectic and baroque character, deriving its inspiration from both East and West alongside the local taste. There was a conspicuous tendency in these cities for monumentalization. The location of the temples and sanctuaries, along with the impressive thoroughfares and decorative buildings, created an attractive city panorama that gave evidence of wealth and power.

The region of the Decapolis offers a typical example of the attraction and charm of classical culture. The Jewish, Nabatean, and Syro-Phoenician East was influenced by the trends, ideas, and lifestyles that the Greeks and Macedonians brought with them, though this was not merely a matter of imitation and the acceptance of ready-made models. The architects and artists who worked in the Decapolis region showed creativity and inventive abilities that deserve appreciation. The spatial planning solutions, as expressed in Gerasa, Gadara, or Philadelphia, confirm this. The impressive public buildings, with their decorative façades facing the colonnaded streets, indicate a rich and fascinating city panorama. The *Pax Romana* and open borders generated an economic prosperity that allowed the cities to direct their resources to construction, to demonstrate their wealth and power, and to compete with each other in magnificent temples and public buildings.

History of the Region

The most ancient and reliable historical source on the Decapolis is Pliny the Elder, who describes the *Regio Decapolitana* as being near Judea, in the direction of Syria. He emphasizes that not everyone identifies the same number of cities with the region. An additional list of the cities appears in Josephus (*Ant.* 14.76). Ptolemy includes several other cities besides those already listed, including Heliopolis, Saana, Ina, Abila of Lysanias, Captilolias, Adra, Gadora, and Samoulis (*Geographica* 5.1.422). The Decapolis is also mentioned three times in the New Testament (Matt. 4:25; Mark 5:20; 7:31), though without individual cities being named.

Founding

The concept of the Decapolis is associated in the minds of historians with the new order that Pompey installed along the eastern shores of the Mediterranean after the fall of the Seleucid Empire in 63 B.C.E. and the liberation of the cities from Hasmonean rule. The cities of the Decapolis had much in common. Most of them were founded during the Hellenistic period under Seleucid rule, and they were given the encouragement and support of the Seleucid monarchs, who saw them as a counterweight to the kingdoms that lay to the west (the Kingdom of Judea) and to the east (the Nabatean Kingdom). Most of the population in the cities was Hellenized, and the citizens saw themselves as citizens of a *polis* in every respect.

Herodian and Early Roman Periods

The arrival of Pompey marked the end of the short-lived Hasmonean hegemony over the cities of the Decapolis and their freedom as independent *poleis.* Like the Seleucids, the Romans favored the independence of these cities and wished to promote them as a counterweight to the Judean and Nabatean kingdoms. Several of the cities minted coins with inscriptions such as *autonomos* ("independent"), *eleutheros* ("free"), *asylos* ("sovereign"), and *hieros* ("sacred"). From the days of Pompey the cities were part of *Provincia Syria.* Yet the Roman authorities did not hesitate to transfer Hippos (Sussita) and Gadara to the area ruled by Herod. Understandably this was not at all pleasant for the residents of those cities, and in the year 20 B.C.E. the residents of Gadara requested to be released from Herod's rule and become once again a part of *Provincia Syria.*

Inclusion in Provincia Arabia

After the dissolution of the Nabatean Kingdom by Trajan in 106 C.E., the Decapolis region was included in *Provincia Arabia,* a new province that more or less extended over the former kingdom of the Nabateans. From then onward, the residents of the Decapolis were subject to the governor of the new province, who was stationed in Bosra. All in all, the Decapolis exemplifies a phenomenon typical of the Greek and Roman world, that of adjacent cities being grouped together, formed into a residential area of a uniform character, and given a general name to refer to them all.

Jews and Judaism

The region of the Decapolis had been part of the Davidic kingdom (2 Sam. 8:5-15; Josephus, *Ant.* 7.104), a circumstance that doubtless fueled Jewish claims on the area in the Hasmonean period. In the second and first centuries B.C.E., Jews and Nabateans had rival designs on the region, as Seleucid hegemony weakened. When the Hasmonean king John Hyrcanus conquered several cities in the Decapolis, he forced its inhabitants to adopt Jewish customs (Josephus, *J.W.* 1.104; *Ant.* 13.393-97). Alexander Jannaeus died while trying to capture the fortress of Ragaba in the region of Gerasa (*Ant.* 13.398). In 64 B.C.E., shortly before Pompey's arrival, the cities of Gadara, Dium, Pella, and Scythopolis fell under Jewish control. Jewish claims on the region came to an end with Pompey's intervention in 64-63 B.C.E.

Although the demography of the cities is difficult to establish, there were evidently several Jewish communities in the Decapolis by the first century C.E. When the First Jewish Revolt broke out in 66 C.E., Jews attacked several cities in the Decapolis. The Jews of Scythopolis were massacred after being forced by their Gentile neighbors to defend the city against the onslaught of the Jews fighting in the revolt (*J.W.* 2.446-77; 7.364). The same fate met Jews living in Hippos and Gadara. According to Eusebius, Jewish Christians from Jerusalem fled to Pella before the city fell in 70 C.E. (*Hist. Eccl.* 3.5.5; cf. Epiphanius, *Adversus Haereses* 29.7.7-8).

Bibliography

M. AVI-YONAH 1966, *The Holy Land from the Persian to the Arab Conquest*, Grand Rapids: Baker. • G. BOWERSOCK 1983, *Roman Arabia*, Cambridge, Mass.: Harvard University Press. • K. BUTCHER 2003, *Roman Syria and the Near East*, London: British Museum. • A. HOFFMANN 2002, "Topographie und Stadtgeschichte von Gadara/Umm Qais," in *Gadara-Gerasa und die Dekapolis*, ed. A. Hoffmann and S. Kerner, Mainz: Philipp von Zabern, 98-124. • A. H. M. JONES 1971, *The Cities of the Eastern Roman Provinces*, 2d ed., Oxford: Oxford University Press. • C. H. KRAELING 1938, *Gerasa, City of the Decapolis*, New Haven: Yale University Press. • F. MILLAR 1993, *The Roman Near East 31 BC–AD 337*, Cambridge, Mass.: Harvard University Press. • A. NORTHEDGE, ED., 1992, *Studies on Roman and Islamic Amman*, Oxford: British Academy. • A. SEGAL 1997, *From Function to Monument: Urban Landscapes of Roman Palestine, Syria and Provincia Arabia*, Oxford: Oxbow. • A. SEGAL ET AL. 2004, *Hippos-Sussita: Fifth Season of Excavations and Summary of All Five Seasons (2000-2004)*, Haifa: Haifa University Press. • A. SPIJKERMAN 1978, *The Coins of the Decapolis and Provincia Arabia*, ed. M. Piccirillo, Jerusalem: Franciscan Printing Press. • Y. TSAFRIR AND G. FOERSTER 1997, "Urbanism at Scythopolis/Beth Shean in the Fourth to Seventh Centuries," *Dumbarton Oaks Papers* 51: 85-146. • F. ZAYADINE, ED., 1986, *Jerash Archaeological Project 1981-1983*, Amman: Department of Antiquities.

ARTHUR SEGAL

Demetrius the Chronographer

Demetrius, often dubbed the Chronographer by modern interpreters, was a Hellenistic Jewish author of the third century B.C.E. who attempted to deal with literary and historical problems raised in the text of Genesis and Exodus. As with many Jewish authors of the Hellenistic age, Demetrius' writings survive only in a handful of citations, most of them found in the *Praeparatio Evangelica* of Eusebius of Caesarea (fourth century C.E.). Of these, the longest by far is a synopsis of biblical history from Jacob to Moses (*Praep. Evang.* 9.21.1-19 = frg. 2, Holladay 1983). The remaining excerpts deal with a problem in the genealogies of Moses and Zipporah (9.29.1-3 = frg. 3, Holladay 1983), a brief notice of events described in Exod. 15:22-27 (9.29.15 = frg. 4, Holladay 1983), and an explanation of how the Israelites managed to acquire arms during the exodus (9.29.16 = frg. 5, Holladay 1983). An unattributed fragment treating the sacrifice of Isaac is also believed to originate with Demetrius (9.19.14 = frg. 1, Holladay 1983).

In his *Stromata* (1.21.141.1-2 = frg. 6, Holladay 1983), Clement of Alexandria (second century C.E.) cites another passage from a work of Demetrius entitled *On the Kings in Judea*. Hardly an apt description of the contents of the other five citations, it raises the possibility that material surviving from Demetrius originated from more than one work. In the same excerpt, a chronological notice about the date of the Assyrian captivity allows us to fix the time of his writing. Since ancient chronographers commonly dated events by counting up the years to the author's own time, Demetrius' calculation of 573 years from the Assyrian captivity up to the reign of Ptolemy IV implies that he was contemporary with the reign of this Ptolemaic king (ca. 222-205 B.C.E.).

The modern description of Demetrius as a "chronographer" arises from the author's attention to chronological problems in the biblical narrative. The best example of this is his detailed chronology of Israelite history from Jacob to Moses, in the course of which he supplies dates lacking in the biblical text. The author's interest in chronology does not necessarily mean, however, that the work from which this excerpt originated took the form of a chronicle. The subjects Demetrius addresses extend well beyond the realm of chronology. Frequently, he prefaces his discussion of them by posing a question. "Someone asks," he writes in one place, "how the Israelites obtained weapons, seeing that they had departed from Egypt unarmed." This is also the way he frames his account of Joseph's reception of his family in Egypt. "There is a problem," he writes here, "as to why Joseph gave Benjamin a fivefold portion at the meal even though he would not be able to consume so much meat" (cf. Gen. 43:34). Freudenthal (1875: 44-46; see also Hanson 1985: 845) is probably correct in tracing Demetrius' question and answer format to an ancient literary exercise popularized by the Greek Sophists and well attested in Alexandrian literary scholarship. Practitioners of this method would analyze a well-known work by posing and resolving real or perceived problems in the text. Philo's own appropriation of the method shows that Alexandrian Jewish writers found it a helpful way to explore problems in the biblical text. If Demetrius represents an early example of the same technique, it would illustrate how a specialized field like biblical chronography developed from a branch of literary criticism.

What Demetrius calls the "sacred book" is the Greek translation of Jewish scriptures that came to be known as the Septuagint. His knowledge of relatively technical problems in the Septuagint version of Genesis and Exodus suggests that even as early as the reign of Ptolemy IV, the Greek text was the object of in-depth study. Readings from the Septuagint known to Demetrius may also shed light on its textual history (Freudenthal 1875: 50-51). One example is Demetrius' chronology from Adam up to the flood. In some of the witnesses to the Septuagint text of Gen. 5:25, Methuselah is said to have been 187 years at the time when he fathered Lamech. This reading is probably a scribal correction of 167 years: by lengthening the time from Adam to the flood from 2,242 years to 2,262 years, the additional twenty years ensured that Methuselah was already dead at the time of the catastrophe. Since Demetrius' own chronology presupposes the longer chronology, it would appear that this correction occurred at a very early date.

While explanations and expansions of the biblical narrative similar to Demetrius' appear later in Josephus and some rabbinic sources (Freudenthal 1875: 46, 67-68), it is difficult to establish clear lines of dependence. Eusebius' own knowledge of Demetrius was indirect, based on excerpts previously compiled by Alexander Polyhistor, a Greek scholar of the first century B.C.E. Alexander was not always a painstaking excerptor, and it remains unclear whether Demetrius himself or a later editor is to blame for the sometimes glaring numerical discrepancies in the surviving material (see Freudenthal 1875: 52-62; Bickerman 1980: 355-58).

BIBLIOGRAPHY

E. BICKERMAN 1980, "The Jewish Historian Demetrius," in idem, *Studies in Jewish and Christian History*, vol. 2, Leiden: Brill, 347-58. • J. FREUDENTHAL 1875, *Alexander Polyhistor und die von ihm erhaltenen Reste jüdischer und samaritanischer Geschichtswerke*, Breslau: Skutsch. • J. S. HANSON 1985, "Demetrius the Chronographer," in *OTP* 2: 843-54. • C. HOLLADAY 1983, *Fragments from Hellenistic Jewish Authors*, vol. 1, *Historians*, Chico: Scholars Press, 51-91.

WILLIAM ADLER

Demons and Exorcism

Belief in demons or evil spirits was widespread among Jews in the Second Temple period, and in certain circles was a central feature of their worldview. Exorcism, the practice of expelling demons from people through adjuration and ritual techniques, is also widely attested. The relevant evidence survives in *materia magica* (magical books, incantations, amulets, curse tablets), and in literary compositions. Most of the former material dates after the Second Temple period.

Origins and Categories of Demons

In the Hebrew Bible there are only a handful of references to demons (*šēdîm*, Deut. 32:17; Ps. 106: 37; *śĕʿîrîm*, "hairy demons, satyrs," in Lev. 17:7; 2 Chron. 11:15; Isa. 13:21; 34:14), and their origin is never the subject of speculation. The most notable mention comes in 1 Sam. 16:23 (cf. 18:10), which tells how an "evil spirit" *(rûaḥ rāʿāh)* from YHWH tormented Saul but would depart whenever the young courtier David played the harp.

In Second Temple literature there are two main explanations regarding the origin of evil spirits and demons: according to one, evil spirits are described as the offspring of the fallen angels or Watchers and the "daughters of the men" (cf. Gen. 6:1-4); according to the other, God created the evil spirits in the primeval era. The earliest known Second Temple source for the origin of demons is the Enoch literature, in particular the *Book of the Watchers* (*1 Enoch* 1–36, late third century B.C.E.), itself based on a combination of distinct traditions concerning the fallen angels Šemihazah and Asael. According to *1 Enoch* 10:15, evil spirits are the offspring of the Watchers. This core tradition underwent further development, for example in *1 Enoch* 15, where the offspring of the forbidden union between the Watchers and human women are the giants. At this point, the traditions regarding the origins of the evil spirits diverge: either the giants themselves are the evil spirits, or the evil spirits emerge from the corpses of the giants. The evil spirits are also mentioned in Enoch's first mythic journey (*1 Enoch* 19), where it says that they led human beings astray by changing their form and tempted them to sacrifice to demons.

The notion that God created evil spirits during the six days of creation is less widespread and has as its major witness the dualistic worldview of the Qumran sect, as represented mainly in the *Community Rule* (1QS), the *War Scroll* (1QM), and 4QBerakhot (4Q286-287). According to these texts, the world is divided between the sons of light and the sons of darkness. Each side has angelic forces that participate in the cosmic battle. The good angels are led by the angel of light, Michael, whereas the evil angelic forces are led by Belial. A related passage attributing the creation of evil spirits to God is found in Pseudo-Philo, *Biblical Antiquities* 60, which mentions the psalm recited by David while exorcising the evil spirit from Saul.

The demonology of the Second Temple period seems to envisage a clear distinction between angels and demons. A demon is a noncorporeal being, neither human nor angelic, that causes harm and mischief to humans in a variety of ways. The DSS use mainly general titles, such as "spirits of the angels of destruction," "spirits of the bastards," and "demons." In the sectarian texts from Qumran, two evil spirits have proper names: Belial and Mastema. These figures make their first appearance in *Jubilees* and show up later in other Jewish sources. Although their origin is never explicitly related, in character and earthly doings they resemble the evil spirits described in the Watchers myth insofar as they lead human beings astray. At times, the descriptions of Belial and Mastema are parallel and even interchangeable.

Apotropaic Texts

The term "apotropaism" refers to the practice of using techniques such as charms and spells to ward off demonic influence. Prayers and hymns that address God and ask his protection from evil spirits fall under this category as well. This type of prayer, already known from the First Temple period, became more common in the Second Temple period. The oldest Jewish prayer known to have apotropaic use is the priestly blessing found in Leviticus 19 and Numbers 6. It also appears in ninth- and eighth-century-B.C.E. inscriptions, such as the inscription found at Kuntillet ʿAjrud, as well as the silver amulets found in Ketef Hinom in Jerusalem, which quote an abbreviated version of Numbers 6.

The author of the Qumran *Community Rule* used these priestly blessings. In 1QS 2 we find an adapted and enlarged version of the priestly blessing. The opposite of this blessing is found in a curse recited by the Levites during the same ceremony, against "the people of Belial's lot." Psalm 91, viewed by rabbinic traditions as "anti-demonic song," is also an early apotropaic hymn. In 11Q11 this psalm was adapted in order to be used as an apotropaic prayer.

At Qumran other nonsectarian apotropaic prayers can be found. Such is the case with the prayers of Noah (*Jub.* 6:1-7) and Abram (*Jub.* 12:19-20), which share the element of a request for divine protection from evil spirits who lead people astray. In the *Aramaic Levi Document,* Levi says, "And let not any *satan* have power over me, to make me stray from your path" (3:4-9). The same request is found in *Plea for Deliverance* (11QPs[a] col. 19). Finally, in Psalm 155:11-13 (11QPs[a] 24) the author requests of God, "Purify me, O Lord, from (the) evil scourge, [and] let it not turn again upon me. Dry up its roots from me, and let its le[av]es not flourish within me" (vv. 11-13).

Three sectarian scrolls from Qumran contain apotropaic hymns (1QH[a] frg. 4, 4Q444, 4Q510-511, and 6Q8). The summary of David's compositions in 11QPs[a] — where David is said to have composed "songs for making music over the stricken" — may indicate that 4Q510-511 contains two sets of four hymns, presumably recited by the members of the sect during the four days of *Piguim* (i.e., on the four corners of the 364-day calendar). Those days were probably not part of the months, and were therefore considered dangerous.

Incantation Texts

Three texts found at Qumran can be grouped together as incantation texts. They were probably not composed within the Qumran sect but brought from elsewhere. The first is 4Q560, which includes quotations from a magical book. Its first column mentions two groups of male and female demons, a well-known phenomenon found in amulets and magic bowls. Its second fragment seems to consist of various incantations, of which only the beginning has survived: "I adjure you, O spirit." The second text is 11Q11, which includes a collection of incantations to be uttered "in the name of God." The third incantation of this sort is the poorly preserved 8Q5, which reads, "By your mighty name, I exorcise and ad[jure. . . ." The texts share the following elements: (1) The demons and the spirits are addressed directly in the second person singular or plural and are interrogated about their identity, with a reminder given to the demon of its origin. (2) The adjurations use the verb "adjure," a formula very common in later incantation texts of the Byzantine period. (3) Some incantations are pronounced in the name of God (often using the Tetragrammaton) and include threats directed against the demon, the most popular of which is to seal them in the abyss with iron chains. Some of these elements can be found in the mostly later Greek and Aramaic magical papyri.

The incantations and the apotropaic hymns and prayers have some shared elements, but the differences between them are more significant. The incantations in general, and 11Q11 in particular, are directly addressed to the demon, who sometimes has a particular name, while in other cases only general names such as "the demon" are found. The apotropaic prayers, on the other hand, use nonvocative titles such as "the demon," "Lilith," and "the howlers." The formal terminology used in the apotropaic prayers also differs from that of the incantation texts. While in the latter the most common phrase is "I adjure," this statement is absent from the apotropaic prayers, which use a variety of different verbs. Another terminological difference relates to the name of God. In the early incantation texts found at Qumran, the Tetragrammaton is frequently used, whereas the later incantations found on amulets and magical papyri from the later Roman period onward substitute epithets of God and descriptions of his miraculous deeds. Further, in the incantations, the exorcist tries to stop the harm done by the evil forces "from now on, and forever." The apotropaic prayers, by contrast, have the wording "not for all the eternal time, but at the age of their dominion," phrases that limit the time of the destruction effected by the spirits but do not envision a definite end to them.

Narrative Depictions of Exorcism

The oldest narrative description of exorcism in Second Temple literature comes in the book of Tobit, an early Jewish novella that may date as early as the fourth or third century B.C.E. In this work the angel Raphael teaches Tobias, the son of Tobit, how to ward off the demon Asmodeus by burning the liver and gall of a fish. The jealous demon had been killing a succession of husbands of Sarah (Tobias's cousin and betrothed) on their wedding nights.

In the *Genesis Apocryphon,* an expansive rewriting of Genesis composed in Aramaic and dating perhaps to the third or second century B.C.E., Abram lays his hand on the head of Pharaoh and prays that an evil spirit depart from his house. The demon had been sent by God to afflict Pharaoh's household as punishment for his taking Sarai into his harem (1QapGen 20:28-29).

In his *Jewish Antiquities* (first century C.E.) the Jewish historian Flavius Josephus presents an expansive rewriting of 1 Kings' account of King Solomon in which he says:

> God granted him knowledge of the art used against demons for the benefit of healing people. He also composed incantations by which illnesses are relieved and left behind forms of exorcisms by which those possessed by demons drive them out, never to return. (*Ant.* 8.45)

In the following lines, the historian tells how in the presence of Vespasian an exorcist named Eleazar cured people of demonic possession. His technique was to put under the nose of the possessed a ring with a root prescribed by Solomon under its seal, drawing the demon out through the person's nose while invoking Solomon's name and reciting incantations the king had composed. To prove the efficacy of his technique, Eleazar would command the demon to upset a nearby cup or basin of water.

Solomon's reputation as an exorcist and magician is reflected already in the Wisdom of Solomon, an apocryphal writing from the first century B.C.E. included in the Septuagint. It attributes to Solomon knowledge concerning the "power of spirits" as well as "the varieties of plants and virtues of roots" (5:20). These traditions and others reached their fullest development in the *Testament of Solomon,* a Christian work of the third century C.E. that includes earlier Jewish material.

The most extensive narrative material concerning demons and exorcism in the Second Temple period is provided by the Synoptic Gospels and Acts. The Gospel of Mark highlights exorcism as a major aspect of Jesus' healing career in the Galilee. Jesus' first miracle is the expulsion of an unclean spirit from a man in a Capernaum synagogue (Mark 1:21-28 pars. Matt. 7:28-29; Luke 4:33-37). The spirit calls out, "What have you to do with us, Jesus of Nazareth? Have you come to destroy us? I know who you are, the Holy One of God." Jesus rebukes the spirit, commands it to be silent, whereupon it convulses the man, cries out, and leaves. In a later, summary passage the Markan narrator observes that Jesus "would not permit the demons to speak, because they knew him" (1:34). The most elaborate account in the Gospels is the exorcism of a demon named "Legion" from a man in a graveyard in the city of Gerasa in Transjordan (Mark 5:1-20 pars. Matt. 8:28-34; Luke 8:26-39).

References to Jewish exorcists besides Jesus are found in Mark 9:38-39 (par. Luke 9:49-50) and in Acts 19:13-16. The Acts passage tells how in Ephesus Paul was able to cause evil spirits to depart from the afflicted even at a distance, by the application of handkerchiefs and aprons that had touched his body. It also recounts an episode of failed exorcism undertaken by some itinerant Jewish exorcists, identified as seven sons of a high priest named Sceva. On one occasion when they tried to invoke the name of Jesus, the evil spirit responded, "Jesus I know, and Paul I know, but who are you?" The possessed man then jumped on the exorcists and beat them so that they fled naked.

BIBLIOGRAPHY

P. S. ALEXANDER 1999, "The Demonology of the Dead Sea Scrolls," in *The Dead Sea Scrolls after Fifty Years,* vol. 2, ed. P. Flint and J. VanderKam, Leiden: Brill, 331-53. • G. BOHAK 2008, *Ancient Jewish Magic: A History,* Cambridge: Cambridge University Press, 70-142. • D. DULING 1983, "Testament of Solomon," in *OTP* 1:935-87. • E. ESHEL 2003, "Apotropaic Prayers in Second Temple Period," in *Liturgical Perspectives: Prayer and Poetry in Light of the Dead Sea Scrolls,* ed. E. G. Chazon, Leiden: Brill, 69-88. • A. LANGE, H. LICHTENBERGER, AND K. F. D. RÖMHELD, EDS. 2003, *Die Dämonen: Die Dämonologie der israelitisch-jüdischen und frühchristlichen Literatur im Kontext ihrer Umwelt,* Tübingen: Mohr-Siebeck. • M. KISTER 1997, "Demons, Theology and Abraham's Covenant (CD 16:4-6 and Related Texts)," in *The Dead Sea Scrolls at Fifty,* ed. R. A. Kugler and E. M. Schuller, Atlanta: Scholars Press, 167-84. • D. L. PENNEY AND M. O. WISE 1994, "By the Power of Beelzebub: An Aramaic Incantation Formula from Qumran (4Q560)," *JBL* 113: 627-50. • E. SORENSEN 2002, "Possession and Exorcism in Ancient Israel and Early Judaism," in idem, *Possession and Exorcism in the New Testament and Early Christianity,* Tübingen: Mohr-Siebeck, 47-74. • P. A. TORIJANO 2002, *Solomon the Esoteric King: From King to Magus, Development of a Tradition,* Leiden: Brill. • G. W. TWELFTREE 1993, *Jesus the Exorcist,* Tübingen: Mohr-Siebeck. • A. T. WRIGHT 2005, *The Origin of Evil Spirits,* Tübingen: Mohr-Siebeck.

See also: Amulets; Divination and Magic; Magic Bowls and Incantations

ESTHER ESHEL AND DANIEL C. HARLOW

Determinism

The word "determinism" was coined by late eighteenth-century German philosophy. It refers to the philosophical notion that everything that happens in time and space is fixed or determined by a necessary chain of causation. A divine principle or God is what determines everything to happen in a fixed order. Ideally, God's sovereignty is understood to be absolute. In the words of Augustine: "The will of God is the necessity of things" (*De Genesi ad Litteram* 6.15.26). Closely related to the issue of determinism is the theological notion of predestination. This entails the idea that God is actively involved in predetermining the course of events in relation to the destiny of individual human beings in terms of their salvation or damnation. The difficulty with this notion of divine election to salvation or damnation of individuals arises in relation to human free will and the possibility or impossibility for people to ascertain their fate by their own volition. These issues have a long and complex theological and philosophical history. One should not force ancient Jewish sources into a systematic framework guided by later formulations and conceptualizations.

The concept denoted by the word "determinism" is much older than eighteenth-century German philosophy, going back to antiquity. Its classic and most systematic formulation is found in Stoic philosophy where the notion of *heimarmenē* ("that which is allotted" or "fate") is central. Fate is the everlasting cause of things; it is why past things happened, why present things are now happening, and why future things will be (Cicero, *De Divinatione* 1.126). Fate is not a mechanical necessity, but a rational principle and an organizing power within the universe, effecting God's plan. A doctrine of divine providence has therefore a prominent place in Stoic thinking. The cosmos is administered by mind and providence (Diogenes Laertius 7.138). The universe was understood as a determined whole of cosmic sympathy. The determined order of the cosmos justified the practice of divination, most clearly in the form of astrology. Nevertheless, the Stoics also envisioned the possibility of human free will and responsibility. By distinguishing between different types of fate (simple and conjoined) human actions could indeed influence the course of events in a deterministic universe.

Ben Sira acknowledges human free will. Recalling Deut. 30:15-20, he stresses human volition to make the right choice and live according to God's Law. God created human beings and left them in the power of their will (15:11-20). However, Ben Sira also emphasizes determinism and divine providence. Before everything was created, it was known to God (Sir. 23:20). God considers that which is to come (42:18-19) and he can see from eternity to eternity (39:20). God has divided people antithetically, differentiating their ways (11:16; 33:11-15). Good things were created for the good and both good and bad things for sinners (16:16; 39:25). This does not entail individual predestination, but it does strengthen the notion of a predetermined order in Ben Sira's thinking. Ben Sira possibly interacts with Stoic ideas, but also has biblical antecedents in Job, Qohelet, and Proverbs. Stoic influence is clearer in the Wisdom of Solomon, where the issues of determinism and divine providence surface (Wis. 6:7; 14:3; 17:2).

Like Ben Sira, Philo recognizes both human volition and divine providence and determinism. Philo can emphasize human free will, by which human beings often make the wrong choice (*De Confusione Linguarum* 178-179). Arguing against astral fatalism (*De Providentia* 1.77-88), Philo upholds that every person is a free moral agent and therefore responsible for the choices he makes. At the same time, Philo stresses divine providence, saying that "providence is the cause of all in all." Philo does not explain the relation between free will and providence. But he could also regard human beings only as instruments through which God acts (Barclay 2006).

Josephus uses the notion of *heimarmenē* to distinguish between the Pharisees, Sadducees, and Essenes when he presents these Jewish groups to his Roman readers (*J.W.* 2.162-66; *Ant.* 13.171-73; 18.13, 18). The Essenes are presented as having a completely deterministic outlook, leaving all things to God and declaring "that Fate is mistress of all things, and that nothing befalls men unless it be in accordance with her decree." The Sadducees are described as emphasizing human volition and denying that our actions are determined, while the Pharisees are portrayed as the middle position; some events being predetermined, others not. Scholars have seen the Pharisaic position reflected in the later rabbinic dictum "All is foreseen and choice is granted" (*m. 'Abot* 3:15). Scholars have argued that Josephus' description of the Essene position on fate is in correspondence with what is found in the Dead Sea Scrolls.

The Dead Sea Scrolls, more specifically the sectarian texts, contain the most forceful expression of deterministic thinking in ancient Judaism. God is presented as the ontological basis of everything and everyone. Everything happens in accordance with God's plan. Before human beings come into being, their deeds are fixed (1QS 3:15-18; 1QH 9:7-9, 19-20; 4Q402 4 12-15 + MasŠirŠabb 1 1-6). Because God has determined everything, everything unfolds according to a divine plan and divine foreknowledge. An important element of the divine plan is the predestined destruction of those who rebel against the proper way and who abhor the decrees. The predestination of the individual is strongly expressed (1QS 11:10-11, 17-18; CD 2:2-10; 1QH 7:15-28). This leaves the impression that human beings are without any real influence on their destiny. God has established their destiny before he created them. Human salvation and damnation depend upon God's will. Yet, there also seems to be room for human agency in determining the course of events. Scholars have stressed the voluntary nature of the Qumran community. Individuals could choose to turn away from the paths of wickedness and to walk in the right and perfect way according to God's will. And even community members could stray, hindered by Belial and his spirits who undertook attempts to divert the elect from the perfect path. Sectarian writings demonstrate that the group was preoccupied with disciplining members. Various magical texts illustrate the concern with averting outside evil. Here, mention must be made of 4Q186, a physiognomic-astrological text often adduced as evidence of an absolute determinism in the Dead Sea Scrolls. This understanding of 4Q186 is too fatalistic and not in agreement with many aspects of ancient astrology. Knowledge of the cosmic relations and circumstances leaves room for human agency to do something about things that are seemingly destined to be.

Regarding the Qumran community, scholars have stressed either a strict determinism or free will, or they have seen a delicate balance between predestination and free will in line with the Pharisaic position ascribed by Josephus, or they have explained the different notions from an evolutionary perspective. The available evidence does not indicate that the authors of the scrolls tried to solve the determinism/free will paradox, or that an attempt was made to harmonize these two issues.

Both sectarian and nonsectarian texts point to the idea of a preexistent order of history and creation inscribed on heavenly tablets and revealed to those worthy to have knowledge of it (Lange 1995). History unfolds according to God's will (e.g., 1QpHab 7:5-14; 1QS 1:14-15; 4Q180 1 1-10). The ordering of history into successive periods, often expressed by reference to heavenly tablets, is a deterministic notion attested in various ancient Jewish texts (Job 1:26-29; Daniel 2; 7; *1 Enoch* 85–90; 91:12-17; 93:1-10; 1QH 9:23-25).

Finally, an interesting feature of ancient Jewish deterministic thought is the reference to a predetermined number of souls to be saved in *4 Ezra* (4:36; 5:41; 7:47, 51, 59-61; 8:1-3; 9:15, 21; 10:57; cf. *2 Bar.* 30:2; *Apoc. Ab.* 29:17). This does not concern the predestined individual, but the total number of those to be saved. Human free will, to act contrary to God's will, is emphasized in *4 Ezra* (7:19-24, 72; 8:56; cf. *1 Enoch* 98:4), although a predetermined view of fixed times is also expressed (e.g., 4:27, 33-34, 37; 5:49; 6:5-6; 13:58). The tension between determinism and free will remains unresolved.

BIBLIOGRAPHY

J. M. G. BARCLAY 2006, "'By the Grace of God I Am What I Am': Grace and Agency in Philo and Paul," in *Divine and*

Human Agency in Paul and His Cultural Environment, ed. J. M. G. Barclay and S. J. Gathercole, London: Clark, 140-57. • R. BERGMEIER 1980, *Glaube als Gabe nach Johannes: Religions- und theologiegeschichtliche Studien zum prädestinationischen Dualismus im vierten Evangelium*, Stuttgart: Kohlhammer. • M. BOCKMUEHL 2001, "1QS and Salvation at Qumran," in *Justification and Variegated Nomism*, vol. 1, *The Complexities of Second Temple Judaism*, ed. D. A. Carson et al., Tübingen: Mohr-Siebeck; Grand Rapids: Baker Academic, 381-414. • J. DUHAIME 2000, "Determinism," in *Encyclopedia of the Dead Sea Scrolls*, ed. L. H. Schiffman and J. C. VanderKam, New York: Oxford University Press, 194-98. • P. FRICK 1999, *Divine Providence in Philo of Alexandria*, Tübingen: Mohr-Siebeck. • A. LANGE 1995, *Weisheit und Prädestination: Weisheitliche Urordnung und Prädestination in den Textfunden von Qumran*, Leiden: Brill. • G. MAIER 1971, *Mensch und freier Wille nach den jüdischen Religionsparteien zwischen Ben Sira und Paulus*, Tübingen: Mohr-Siebeck. • C. MARTONE 2000, "Qumran and Stoicism: An Analysis of Some Common Traits," in *The Dead Sea Scrolls Fifty Years after Their Discovery, 1947-1997*, ed. L. H. Schiffman, E. Tov, and J. C. VanderKam, Jerusalem: Israel Exploration Society, 617-22. • J. SELLARS 2006, *Stoicism*, Chesham: Acumen. • U. WICKE-REUTER 2000, *Göttliche Providenz und menschliche Verantwortung bei Ben Sira und in der Frühen Stoa*, Berlin: de Gruyter. MLADEN POPOVIĆ

Deuteronomistic History

The term "Deuteronomistic (or Deuteronomic) History" is the name coined for the original, unified work theorized to incorporate the books of Deuteronomy through Kings in the Hebrew Bible, that is, Deuteronomy plus the Former Prophets (Joshua, Judges, 1-2 Samuel, 1-2 Kings). The book of Ruth, which English Bibles, following the Septuagint, place between Judges and 1 Samuel, falls in the third section of the Hebrew canon known as the Writings *(Kĕtûvîm)*.

Martin Noth

The hypothesis of the Deuteronomistic History (DtrH) was initiated in 1943 by Martin Noth's work *Überlieferungsgeschichtliche Studien* (2d ed. 1991). In contrast to previous scholarship, which treated the Former Prophets either as independent books strung together by Deuteronomistic editing or as an extension of the Pentateuch, Noth proposed that Deuteronomy through Kings represented an original unit by a single author. Noth's primary evidence for common authorship was a series of passages throughout these books — typically in the form of speeches delivered by major characters at key junctures — that shared a common writing style and vocabulary and served to structure the entire work (Josh. 1:11-15; 12; 23; Judg. 2:11-22; 1 Sam. 12:1-25; 1 Kings 8:12-51; 2 Kings 17:7-18, 22-23). In addition, Noth pointed to a common chronology and a common theological outlook shared by these books as further evidence.

Noth dated the DtrH to the Babylonian Exile, shortly after 562 B.C.E., the date of the last event recorded in 2 Kings (25:27-30). He identified its place of composition as Mizpah, which served as the administrative capital of the former kingdom of Judah following the destruction of Jerusalem (2 Kings 25:22-26). The author of this work, whom Noth dubbed the Deuteronomistic Historian or Dtr for short, was a single individual who worked as both an author and an editor. In Noth's reconstruction, Dtr gathered traditions about Israel and Judah, both oral and written, to which he had access following their demise as independent kingdoms. He selected from these traditions and combined them into a unified whole by means of various techniques of linking and harmonization. Dtr's purpose in writing, Noth believed, was to explain why Israel and Judah had come to ruin, "eine Ätiologie des Nuls," in Noth's words. Such ruin had been forecast in the book of Deuteronomy as the inevitable result of sin. Indeed, Deuteronomy in an early form was a formative source for Dtr. He placed the Deuteronomic laws at the head of his work as the criteria for the evaluation of Israel's history. Above all, the doctrine that prosperity and disaster were the inevitable results of righteousness and sin, respectively, served as the template for Dtr's unfolding of Israel's history. Hence Noth's designation of the work as the *Deuteronomistic* History.

Subsequent Developments

Purpose

Noth's view that Deuteronomy plus the Former Prophets were originally a single work received broad, though not universal, acceptance for most of the remainder of the twentieth century. Within the basic contours of the theory, however, some scholars suggested adjustments that proved to be prescient of larger issues. Gerhard Von Rad and Hans Walter Wolff each questioned Noth's conclusion that Dtr's purpose was entirely negative. Shortly after Noth, Von Rad noted the importance of the promise to David in the DtrH, suggesting that it functioned to explain the postponement of God's judgment against Judah. He further suggested that the final episode in 2 Kings, detailing Jehoiachin's release from prison, might hint that God could begin to restore his people with this remaining heir to the Davidic throne. Somewhat later, Wolff (1961) also found hope in the opportunity for repentance, which he perceived as a recurring theme throughout the DtrH.

Composition

In the 1970s two competing theories about the composition of the DtrH emerged that greatly influenced further research. These were adumbrated by an older study of Alfred Jepsen that was actually written prior to Noth's but published subsequently due to the war (Jepsen 1956). While Jepsen's analysis seconded Noth's theory in reference to the use of traditional sources and the date of the final form of Kings, his reconstruction of a complex redactional process underlying that final product differed from Noth's understanding of Dtr as the compiler and author/editor of the work. To be sure, Noth had found both older sources behind and secondary additions to the DtrH, but he had denied the existence of any systematic redaction before or after Dtr. Jepsen's redactional model was an alternative to Noth's that would be favored by many subsequent scholars.

The two redactional models that gained currency beginning in the 1970s were based on proposals by Rudolf Smend and Frank Cross. Smend found evidence of redactional activity in a handful of texts in Joshua and Judges, where he believed that Dtr's basic work, which he called DtrG (for *Grundschrift*), had been revised by a writer with an interest in law ("DtrN" for Nomistic). This basic insight was developed by Smend's students, Walter Dietrich and Timo Veijola, who argued for an intermediate, prophetic redaction (DtrP) in the books of Samuel and Kings. This "layer model" of the so-called Smend or Göttingen school has become dominant in Europe. It has also become increasingly complex, as adherents have proposed additional Dtr redactors in different books as well as distinct hands within a given Dtr layer (e.g., $DtrN^1$, $DtrN^2$, $DtrN^3$), to the point that it is not uncommon for as many as a dozen distinct layers to be perceived within a given passage of, say, two or three dozen verses.

Cross began by noting the validity of certain arguments for a preexilic edition of the book of Kings that had been voiced by scholars before Noth. He then traced two contrasting themes that he found running throughout Kings. These were the sin of Jeroboam, which climaxes with the fall of Samaria (2 Kings 17), and the faithfulness of David, which reaches its climax with Josiah. On the basis of these two themes, Cross suggested that the initial edition of the DtrH, or Dtr^1, had been written during Josiah's reign to support his reform and that it had ended suddenly, or been left unfinished, when Josiah was unexpectedly killed in battle (2 Kings 23:29). This initial edition was revised by an exilic editor (Dtr^2) who added the current ending (2 Kings 23:25b–25:30) and a series of glosses that presupposed the Exile in some way. This "block model" has been particularly influential in North America. Its proponents have developed it in various ways, arguing for more extensive Dtr^2 influence or positing pre-Dtr^1 editions, such as a collection of northern prophetic stories or a Hezekian Dtr (Campbell and O'Brien 2000; Halpern and Vanderhooft 1991; Weippert 1972).

Status Quo

It is probably fair to say that the majority of scholars today would endorse some variation of one of the two redactional models. There have been a few attempts to combine the two by proposing exilic (and Persian) redaction(s) of preexilic, independent blocks of material (Lohfink 1981; Römer 1996). However, there are those who have retained Noth's view of a single exilic author/editor, adducing further arguments in its favor. One of these latter is John Van Seters, whose study of ancient history writing as a genre concluded that Greek works provide the best analogues to the DtrH (Van Seters 1983). Thus, he contended, Dtr should be regarded as an author, like Herodotus, who exercised creativity in his organization of source materials as well as in filling the gaps between them. Van Seters' work has generated intense debate about the meanings of history and historiography as applied to biblical literature.

A trend that is nascent at present is a return full circle to pre-Noth scholarship by denying the existence of the DtrH as an original unit. Thus far, advocates of this return are limited in number, though distinguished in prominence (Auld 1999; Knauf 1996; Rösel 2000; Westermann 1994; Würthwein 1994). Their argumentation is primarily a critique of the tradition following Noth rather than a comprehensive alternative. The theory of an original DtrH remains dominant, though the widespread disagreement about the specifics of its authorship, date, and purpose may contribute to a decline in the consensus.

Reception and Interpretation

The influence of the DtrH on subsequent interpretation of the Bible can hardly be overstated. As the only independent history of Israel extant from antiquity, it has shaped all further understanding of Israelite history in Judaism and Christianity. It was the principal source on ancient Israel for later Jewish historians, such as the author of 1-2 Chronicles and Josephus (Feldman 1999). Its interpretation of Israel's history was accepted by the New Testament writers, early church fathers, and mishnaic rabbis. The essence of this interpretation is that the demise of the people of Israel came about as their just deserts for centuries of unfaithfulness to the Law promulgated through Moses as the covenant with God and the constitution for the nation. The continuing theological impact of the DtrH is evident not only in its perspective on reward and punishment but also in doctrines such as the promise to David of an enduring house and the election of Jerusalem as the exclusive site of legitimate worship.

Bibliography

A. G. Auld 1999, "The Deuteronomists and the Former Prophets, or What Makes the Former Prophets Deuteronomistic?" in *Those Elusive Deuteronomists: The Phenomenon of Pan-Deuteronomism,* ed. L. S. Schearing and S. L. McKenzie, Sheffield: Sheffield Academic Press, 116-26. • A. F. Campbell and M. A. O'Brien 2000, *Unfolding the Deuteronomistic History: Origins, Upgrades, Present Text,* Minneapolis: Fortress. • F. M. Cross 1973, *Canaanite Myth and Hebrew Epic: Essays in the History of the Religion of Israel,* Cambridge: Harvard University Press, 274-89. • W. Dietrich 1972, *Prophetie und Geschichte. Eine redaktionsgeschichtliche Untersuchung zum deuteronomistischen Geschichtswerk,* Göttingen: Vandenhoeck & Ruprecht. • L. H. Feldman 1999, *Josephus's Interpretation of the Bible,* Los Angeles: University of California Press. • B. Halpern and D. S. Vanderhooft 1991, "The Editions of Kings in the 7th-6th Centuries B.C.E.," *HUCA* 62: 304-16. • A. Jepsen 1956, *Die Quellen des Königsbuches,* 2d ed., Halle: Max Niemeyer. • E. A. Knauf 1996, "Does 'Deuteronomistic Historiography' (DH) Exist?" in *Israel Constructs Its History: Deuteronomistic Historiography in Recent Research,* ed. A. de Pury, T. Römer, and J.-D. Macchi, Sheffield: Sheffield Academic Press, 388-98. • N. Lohfink 1981, "Kerygmata des Deuteronomistischen Geschichtswerks," in *Die Botschaft und die Boten: Festschrift für Hans Walter Wolff zum 70. Geburtstag,* ed. J. Jeremiah and L. Perlitt, Neukirchen-Vluyn: Neukirchener Verlag, 87-100. • R. D. NELSON 1981, *The Double Redaction of the Deuteronomistic History,* Sheffield: JSOT. • N. NOTH 1991, *The Deuteronomistic History,* 2d ed., Sheffield: JSOT. • G. VON RAD 1966, "The Deuteronomic Theology of History in I and II Kings," in *The Problem of the Hexateuch and Other Essays,* trans. E. W. T. Dicken, New York: McGraw-Hill, 205-21. • T. RÖMER 2007, *The So-Called Deuteronomistic History,* London: Clark. • T. RÖMER AND A. DE PURY 1996, "Deuteronomistic Historiography (DH): History of Research and Debated Issues," in *Israel Constructs Its History: Deuteronomistic Historiography in Recent Research,* ed. A. de Pury, T. Römer, and J.-D. Macchi, Sheffield: Sheffield Academic Press, 24-141. • H. N. RÖSEL 2000, "Does a Comprehensive 'Leitmotiv' Exist in the Deuteronomistic History?" in *The Future of the Deuteronomistic History,* ed. T. Römer, Leuven: Peeters, 195-211. • R. SMEND 1971, "Das Gesetz und die Völker: Ein Beitrag zur deuteronomistischen Redaktionsgeschichte," in *Probleme biblischer Theologie: Gerhard von Rad zum 70. Geburtstag,* ed. H. W. Wolff, Munich: Kaiser, 494-509. • J. VAN SETERS 1983, *In Search of History: Historiography in the Ancient World and the Origins of Biblical History,* New Haven: Yale University Press. • T. VEIJOLA 1975, *Das ewige Dynastie: David und die Entstehung seiner Dynastie nach der deuteronomistischen Darstellung,* Helsinki: Suomalainen Tiedeakatemia. • T. VEIJOLA 1977, *Das Königtum in der Beurteilung der deuteronomistischen Historiographie,* Helsinki: Suomalainen Tiedeakatemia. • H. WEIPPERT 1972, "Die 'deuteronomistischen' Beurteilung des Könige von Israel und Juda und das Problem der Redaktion der Königsbücher," *Bib* 53: 301-39. • C. WESTERMANN 1994, *Die Geschichtsbücher des Alten Testaments: Gab es ein deuteronomistisches Geschichtswerk?,* Gütersloh: Kaiser. • H. W. WOLFF 1961, "Das Kerygma des deuteronomischen Geschichtswerk," *ZAW* 73: 171-86. • E. WÜRTHWEIN 1994, "Erwägungen zum sog. Deuteronomistischen Geschichtswerk. Eine Skizze," in idem, *Studien zum Deuteronomistischen Geschichtswerk,* Berlin: de Gruyter, 1-11.

STEVEN L. MCKENZIE

Devil → Satan and Related Figures

Diadochoi

Diadochoi is an ancient Greek word meaning "successors." Ancient historians use it regularly when they refer to the inheritance or sharing of military or political power. Modern historians have, on the other hand, reserved the use of the term for Alexander the Great's generals who inherited his empire upon his death, becoming initially his successors only *de facto,* but later also *de jure.* The initial history of the Diadochi can be followed through three main stages: (1) the definition of their roles at Alexander's death; (2) the reassessment of their roles two years later; and (3) their self-declaration as kings.

Division of Rule at Alexander's Death

Alexander the Great died in June of 323 B.C.E. in Babylon without a direct heir, when his wife Roxane, daughter of the Persian governor of the easternmost province of Bactria, was in her last months of pregnancy. The need to provide the empire with a guide prompted Alexander's Macedonian generals to assemble in Babylon a few days after the king's death. Among heated discussions and sharp disagreements, often resulting in armed confrontations between the infantry and the cavalry, the generals eventually agreed to preserve the empire in its present extension and to recognize Alexander's Argead family as the ruling dynasty. Philip Arrhideus, Alexander's mentally unstable half-brother and the only member of the Argead family on the field, was put on the throne by the infantry, on the condition imposed by the cavalry that he would share the throne with Alexander's soon-to-be-born child. Perdikkas, Alexander's highest-ranking cavalry general, to whom the king had given his personal ring seal before his death, became the supervisor of the whole empire. He confirmed Antipater, to whom Alexander the Great had granted special powers prior to his departure from Greece in 334 B.C.E., while Crateros became the protector of Arrhideos' kingdom. Pedikkas then allotted the empire's western provinces to the other Macedonian generals, leaving the easternmost provinces to the governors previously appointed by Alexander, mainly local Persian aristocrats. The sources list twelve generals to whom Perdikkas assigned as many western territories. That Crateros became the protector of Arrhideos and the governor of Macedon concurrently meant in practice that the royal family had to abandon Babylon to be headquartered back in the Macedonian fatherland. The agreement at Babylon, despite the apparent positive settlement, was inherently vitiated by, on the one side, the lack of full control of some provinces of the empire, and on the other by the lack of consultation with other generals to whom Alexander had previously assigned to some territories and who therefore could not be present at Babylon.

Such a scenario resulted in an explosive situation producing several decades of internecine wars. The first significant contflict occurred in 322 B.C.E. when Ptolemy Lagos, governor of Egypt, kidnapped in Damascus the royal hearse with Alexander's embalmed body, which Perdikkas was taking from Babylon to Macedon for burial. Ptolemy took it to Egypt and used it to build his personal power there, probably under the claim that Alexander had to be buried in Siwah, the Egyptian oasis from whose oracle he had learned in 331 B.C.E. that the Egyptian god Ammon was his father. Perdikkas led an unsuccessful military expedition to Egypt to recover Alexander's corpse, which was fatal for him. The death of the empire's supervisor required a reassessment among the generals, which took place at Triparadeisos at the foot of the Antilebanon Mountains.

The Settlement at Triparadeisos

Several factors made the scenario of Triparadeisos in 321 B.C.E. more decisive than the one of Babylon. The

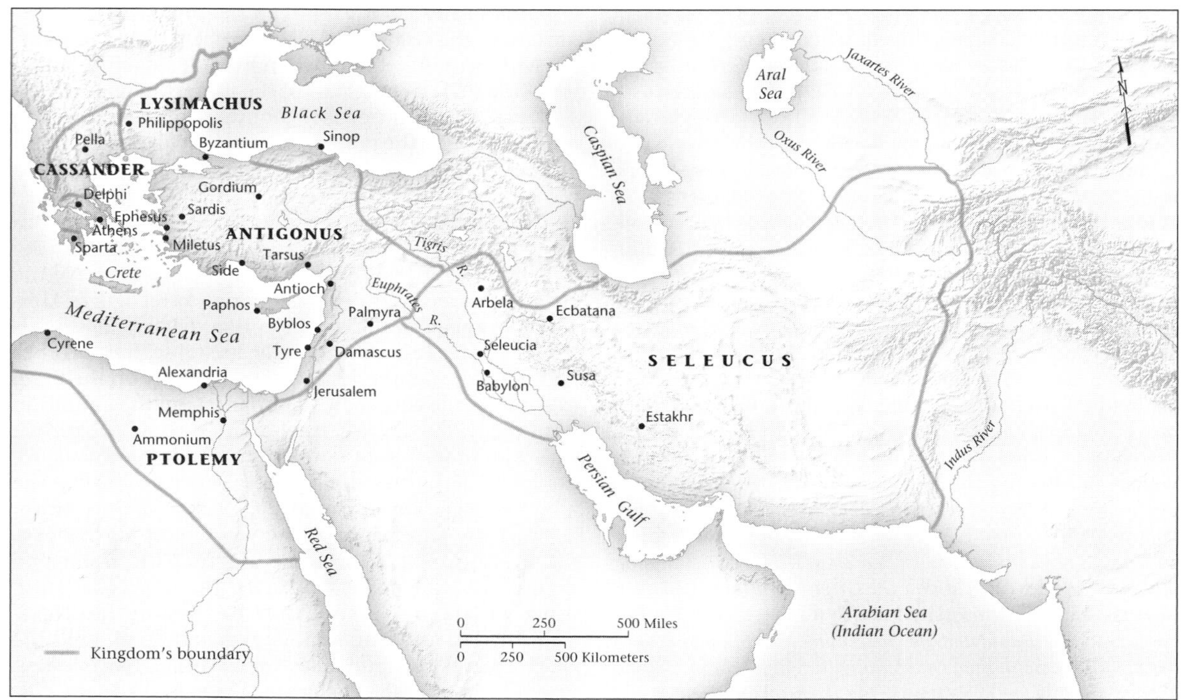

The Near East under the Diadochoi

birth of Alexander's child, named Alexander IV, reinforced the Argead dynastic position; now there was indeed a direct heir to the throne. The relative closer geographical proximity of Triparadeisos to Macedon with respect to Babylon also caused the Argead family, especially in the person of Alexander the Great's mother Olympia, now grandmother of his child, to be able to submit their claim directly to the assembly in the interest of the young Alexander IV. In addition, the generals had now established their areas of influence, which they tried either to maintain or to expand through diplomatic or military means. The agreement of Triparadeisos confirmed the centrality of Alexander's dynastic line in the person of Alexander IV, but still in association with Philip Arrhideos. The young age of the one and the mental instability of the other also recommended the appointment of a guardian in the person of Antipater, the highest-ranking general at this moment.

Antipater gave all the Eastern provinces with the exception of three to Macedonian generals, overturning Alexander's and Perdikkas' policy, and allotted Babylon to Seleucus. Of the western provinces, the only outstanding change concerned Cappadocia and Paphlagonia, whose governor, Eumenes, was removed from the political map. Cassander was now head of the cavalry, and Antigonus head of the army with the task of protecting the kings and fighting against Eumenes. The centralized commands of the cavalry to Cassander and of the army to Antigonus reinforced the recognition of the role of the Argead family. However, at Antipater's return to Macedon with the royal court, Olympia left for Epirus in disapproval of the confirmation of Philip Arrhideos.

Wars to Establish Individual Kingdoms

Antipater's death in 319 B.C.E. caused the fragile balance among the imperial powers to tilt toward the formation of individual kingdoms. His son Cassander, in an effort to reinforce his role as Antipater's legitimate descendant and governor of Greece against his father's appointed Polyperchon, appropriated the entire Argead family, including the kings. For the next decade major wars occurred among Antigonus, Eumenes, Cassander, Ptolemy, and Seleucus, all of which could be ascribed to the implementation of the Triparadeisos settlement, but some of which took place because of individual resistance to, or different interpretation of, that same implementation. In the next agreement of 314 B.C.E. only Cassander, Lysimachus, Ptolemy, and Antigonus divided among themselves the responsibilities and the territories of the empire, claiming to operate on behalf of Alexander IV, now the sole king and living Argead, after Olympia had Philip Arrhideos killed and Cassander had Olympia assassinated. Seleucus, whom Antigonus had prevented from reaching his allotted province of Babylon since Triparadeisos, was not included in the agreement. Only after Antigonus' death in 311 B.C.E. at the Battle of Issos would Seleucus be able to recover his extensive Mesopotamian and Iranian territories, to which he added Mediterranean Syria. By 310 B.C.E. Cassander had Roxane and Alexander IV killed. The empire had now no king; Polyperchon's attempt to put Alexander's illegitimate son Heracles on to the throne in 309 B.C.E. was ineffective.

The diadochoi declared themselves kings of their respective territories only in 305 B.C.E., apparently after they all were acclaimed kings by their subjects in the aftermath of major military victories. Antigonus' death in 311 B.C.E. and Cassander's death some years later allowed fundamental changes. Demetrius, Antigonus' son, could set foot in Greece through the conquest of Athens, eventually including Macedon, and start the Antigonid dynasty, which would rule continental Greece until the Roman conquest in 168 B.C.E. Until his death in 281 B.C.E. at the battle of Curupedios, Lysimachus was king of a territory encompassing Thrace and some of the Anatolian provinces. Seleucus founded the Seleucid dynasty, which would rule a territory initially extending from Syria to the Indus River and to which he annexed Anatolia at Lysimachus' death. Eventually Seleucus' empire was reduced to Syria, which the Romans conquered in 63 B.C.E. Ptolemy became king of Egypt and of the nearby coastal Libya; the Ptolemaic dynasty ruled Egypt until Octavian imposed Roman rule there in 31 B.C.E.

Relations with the Jews

From the early period of the Hellenistic kingdoms, there is little information about the relationship between the diadochoi and the Jews, even though Mesopotamia and especially Judea were territorially at the center of most of their disputes. In this period of major political uncertainty, the situation in Judea seems not to have differed from what the Jews had experienced under the Persian Empire and Alexander. A mutual agreement between the central authority — whoever this may have been — and the appointed local governor on the one side, and the Temple hierarchy on the other, guaranteed the respect of the Jewish ancestral customs. A major disruption occurred, however, in 312/311 B.C.E., when Ptolemy Lagos deported people from Judea and Samaria in the wake of his campaign in Coele-Syria against Demetrios, son of Antigonus, for control of the region.

BIBLIOGRAPHY

P. GREEN 1990, *Alexander to Actium: The Historical Evolution of the Hellenistic Age,* Berkeley: University of California Press. • E. S. GRUEN, 1985, "The Coronation of the Diadochoi," in *The Craft of the Ancient Historian,* ed. J. W. Eadie and J. Ober, Lanham, Md.: University Press of America, 253-71. • R. A. BILLOWS 1990, *Antigonos the One-Eyed and the Creation of the Hellenistic State,* Berkeley: University of California Press. • J. D. GRAINGER 1990, *Seleukos Nikator: Constructing a Hellenistic Kingdom,* London: Routledge.

SANDRA GAMBETTI

Diaspora Revolt → Diaspora Uprisings

Diaspora Uprisings (116-117 C.E.)

Toward the end of Trajan's reign violent Jewish uprisings broke out more or less at the same time in several places in the Mediterranean world. Concerning their possible causes, one may recall the general ferment prevailing among Diaspora Jews after the destruction of the Temple in 70 C.E., when they had to pay the demeaning tax of the *Fiscus Judaicus* imposed on all Jews of the Roman Empire. The causes of these uprisings certainly included local factors as well. In Egypt, for example, social, economical, political, and ideological competition and rivalry between the Jews and their Greek neighbors are attested since the third century B.C.E., and twice earlier in Trajan's days — in 112 and in the summer of 115 — armed attacks had been perpetrated by Greeks against Jews (*CPJ* 2:157, 158, 435), the last of which may definitely be considered a direct cause of the Jewish disorders.

Events in Libya, Egypt, and Cyprus

Eusebius' statement that the uprisings broke out in the eighteenth year of Trajan's reign (*Hist. Eccl.* 4.2.1), 115 C.E., is problematic in view of the fact that in Egypt, in October 115 the Greek responsible for an armed attack against the Jews had not yet been punished, as we learn from *CPJ* 2:435. Moreover, the ostraca found in the Jewish quarter of Apollinopolis Magna (Edfu) show that the receipts for the payment of various taxes paid by the Jews abruptly stopped at the end of May 116. The Jewish uprising in Egypt, therefore, seems to have started later than May 116.

From extant papyri we learn that on June 19 the *stratēgos* Apollonios, who was personally involved in the conflict, had requested the purchase of new arms (P. Gissenses 47), and at the beginning of September Apollonios' wife Aline was deeply concerned for his safety (*CPJ* 2:436). It therefore appears that the Jewish uprising in Egypt started between May and August 116. As for the date given by Eusebius, it may derive from a misunderstanding of one of his sources, perhaps to be identified with the work of the historian Appian.

The events of the revolts are described mainly by Dio and Eusebius. In Libya, the Jews attacked their Greek and Roman neighbors, led by Andreas, according to Dio, or by Lukuas, according to Eusebius — either two different persons or one person with two names, a common practice at the time. To Lukuas, Eusebius ascribes the title "king," a fact that has led scholars to assume that the uprising had a messianic background. The evidence, however, is scanty.

The epigraphical material attests attacks directed by the Jews against temples, statues of gods, and centers of Greek civic life. In the city of Cyrene, in the sanctuary of Apollo, "the baths with the porticoes, ballcourts and other neighboring buildings . . . were destroyed and burnt down in the Jewish revolt" (*CJZC* 23). The temple of Hecate, too, was "des[troyed] and [burnt down in] the Jewish revolt" (*CJZC* 21), and vast destruction is attested also in the Caesareum (*CJZC* 17, 18, 19) and in the temple of Zeus (*CJZC* 22).

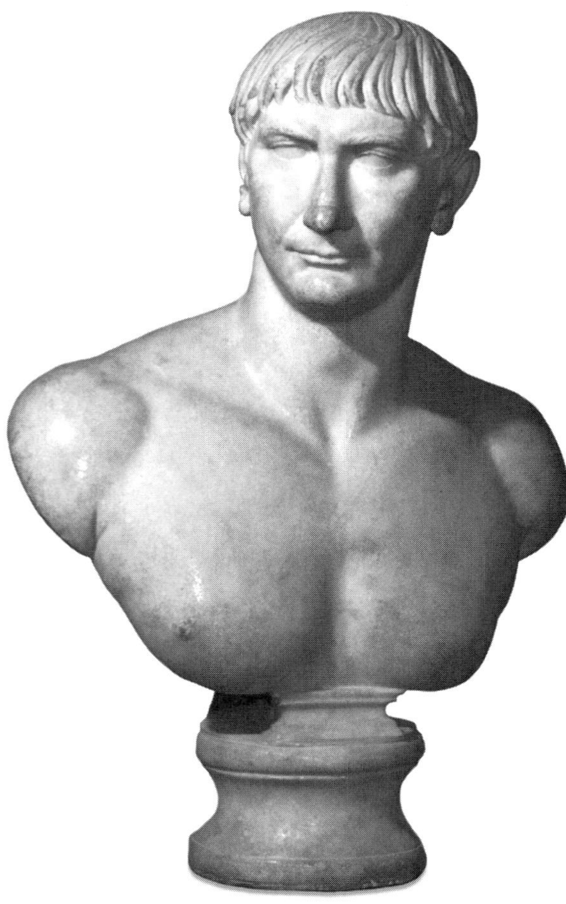

Bust of the Roman emperor Trajan (ruled 98–117 C.E.), near the end of whose reign several violent Jewish uprisings occurred in Egypt and other places in the Mediterranean world *(British Museum)*

Possibly fearing that Roman military forces might arrive from the sea, the Jews tried to destroy the road connection between Cyrene and its port, Apollonia, as attested by a milestone, while a representation of a seven-branched candelabrum, deeply incised in the rock surface of a stretch of road northwest of Balagre, suggests interference with the route between Cyrene and her neighbors to the west. Dio attributes shockingly violent and cruel behavior to the Jews (Dio 68.32.1-3), in line with the well-established literary tradition concerning the description of revolts by "barbarians" against the Roman establishment.

As for the events in Cyprus, epigraphical evidence is almost absent and only the name of the leader, a certain Artemion, survives in the account of Dio (68.32.2). Here, too, we get an impression of great destruction. Dio states that in Cyprus "two hundred and forty thousand perished" (68.32.2), and Orosius writes that "all the Greek inhabitants of Salamis were killed" (7.12.8).

More details are available concerning the events transpiring in Egypt, where, according to Eusebius, the local Jews acted in cooperation with those of Libya (*Hist. Eccl.* 4.2.3). Papyri found in Egypt attest that the uprising covered large sections of the country: the Athribite district, the vicinity of Memphis (*CPJ* 2:438-39) — a strategic center known for its anti-Semitism — the Fayum (*CPJ* 2:449), Oxyrhynchus (*CPJ* 2:445, 447, 450), and the Herakleopolite nome (*CPJ* 2:445). Further south, effects of fighting are recorded for the Kynopolite (*CPJ* 2:445), the Hermopolite (*CPJ* 2:436, 438, 442, 443, 446), the Lycopolite, and the Apollinopolite districts (*CPJ* 2:444, 436). Appian, who happened to be in Egypt at the time of the uprising, writes that the Jews seized the waterways (*Roman History,* frg. 19) and destroyed the shrine of Nemesis near Alexandria "for the exigencies of the war" (*Bella Civilia* 2.90).

Jewish victories at the first stage (see, e.g., *CPJ* 2:438) may be explained by the fact that a small number of Roman military forces was probably available on the scene, while most forces had been sent to the East where Trajan was fighting against the Parthians. The Greeks fought back, led by their *stratēgoi* — the most well known is Apollonios — and helped both by the Egyptian peasants and the Romans. The Roman prefect himself, Rutilius Lupus, may have personally participated in the engagements. From the account of Dio we may infer that only in the late spring of 117 did Trajan take serious measures to repress Jewish disorders decisively and send to Egypt one of his best generals, Marcius Turbo, with land and sea forces including cavalry, as Eusebius writes. Turbo "waged war vigorously against them in many battles for a considerable time and killed many thousands of Jews, not only those of Cyrene but also those of Egypt" (*Hist. Eccl.* 4.2.3-4). One of these battles may be that which led to a victory over the Jews in the vicinity of Memphis (cf. *CPJ* 2:439).

We hear about the military forces active in the repression of the Jewish rebellion from the papyri. The *legio XXII Deiotariana* and the *legio III Cyrenaica* fought against the Jews. We have the very names of a number of Roman legionaries belonging to these legions who were killed in combat. The *cohors I Augusta praetoria Lusitanorum equitata,* too, is attested in Egypt as having suffered heavy losses in Egypt during the early summer of 117. We also learn about a plan for the mobilization of impressive military forces: the fleets from Misenum and Ravenna, the *legio III Cyrenaica,* and additional auxiliary units such as the *cohors I Flavia Cilicum equitata.*

Military actions took place in Libya as well, where, during the war against the Jews, the Roman *praefectus castrorum* mentioned by Artemidoros Daldianus (*Oneirocriticon* 4.24) was killed. As for Cyprus, Trajan sent there another of his generals, Caius Valerius Rufus, tribune of the Seventh Legion *Claudia Pia Fidelis Praetoria,* with a detachment of soldiers on a military expedition.

The harsh character of the Roman repression in Egypt is attested by Appian, who states that in his day Trajan "exterminated" the Jewish race in Egypt (*Bella Civilia* 2.90), and by the Jerusalem Talmud, which emphasizes the destruction of the Great Synagogue of Alex-

DIASPORA UPRISINGS (116-117 C.E.)

andria, one of the glories of Egyptian Jewry (*y. Sukk.* 5.5, 55b).

The uprising was surely crushed before the autumn of 117 (see *CPJ* 2:443) and possibly by the summer. At Oxyrhynchus, the victory over the Jews was commemorated by a festival that was still observed some eighty years later (*CPJ* 2:450).

Consequences

In Egypt, agriculture suffered (*CPJ* 2:444), slave labor and textiles were apparently in short supply (*CPJ* 2:442), and signs of an economic crisis have been identified in unstable prices and in a shortage of basic essentials such as bread (P. Oxyrhynchus 1454; P. Gissenses 79). Damage to buildings, temples, and roads is attested by inscriptions, especially at Cyrene, and according to Eusebius' *Chronicon* the cities of Salamis and Alexandria were completely destroyed. Later sources such as Orosius go so far as to state that had Hadrian not later collected settlers from elsewhere and sent them to Libya to found colonies, the land would have remained completely depopulated (Orosius, *Historia adversus Paganos* 7.12.6). The actual extent of the destruction, however, is difficult to ascertain.

The Jews in Egypt, Libya, and Cyprus almost disappear from the sources after 117 C.E. In Egypt, the land that had belonged to the Jews was confiscated by the Roman government (*CPJ* 2:445, 448; P. Berolensis inv. 7440; P. Berolensis inv. 8143), and a consequence of the revolt may have been the abolition of the activities of the Jewish court at Alexandria (*t. Pe'ah* 4:6; *t. Ketub.* 3:1).

The Revolt in Mesopotamia

After relating the events of the uprisings in the other countries, Eusebius tells us that in Mesopotamia Trajan ordered Lusius Quietus, another famous general of his, to fight harshly against the Jews (*Chronicon,* ed. Helm, p. 196; *Hist. Eccl.* 4.2.5). Dio does not speak about the Jews but mentions a rebellion against Roman rule in Mesopotamia about May 116, repressed by the same general, Lusius Quietus (68.30.1-2). One may therefore assume that the revolt of the Jews mentioned by Eusebius may be identified with one episode of the revolt reported by Dio, especially since Dio, too, establishes a connection between Lusius Quietus and the Jews, observing that "among others who subdued the Jews was Lusius, who was sent by Trajan" (68.32.3).

In Mesopotamia, therefore, differently from what happened in the other countries, the Jews seem to have taken up arms together with other local population groups in order to prevent the Roman occupation when it could still be avoided. This comes as no surprise, in view of the relatively good position enjoyed by the Jews in the Parthian Empire as compared to that of their brethren living under Roman government.

What Happened in Judea?

Dio and Eusebius, the main sources for the Jewish revolts, fail to mention a revolt in Judea, but both of them report that after his military operations against the Jews in Mesopotamia, Quietus was elected consul and appointed governor of Judea by Trajan (Dio 68.32.5; Eusebius, *Hist. Eccl.* 4.2.5). We have no details concerning exactly what happened in Judea, but a "war of Kitos" that occurred between the Great War (66-70 C.E.) and that of Bar Kokhba (132-135 C.E.) is mentioned in two rabbinic sources (*Seder ʿOlam Rabbah* 30 and *m. Soṭah* 9:14) and is apparently referred to in the different versions of the story of Lulianus and Pappus.

Some sort of military operation taking place in Judea in Trajan's reign is attested also by a Roman epitaph found in Sardinia, which mentions an *expeditio Judaeae* among the wars fought by Trajan. Active in this campaign, perhaps, was the *vexillatio* of the *legio III Cyrenaica* attested in Jerusalem later than February 116 C.E.

The events that took place in Judea in 117, obscure as they are in their details, nevertheless seem to have been serious enough to be responsible for the change of the status of the province of Judea from praetorian to consular, with the addition of a second legion, the *legio II Traiana,* at some point before 120 B.C.E. It may therefore have been no accident that Lusius Quietus had been elected consul before being sent to Judea.

The change of the status of Judea was to remain a permanent one. After Lusius Quietus, all the known governors sent to Judea were of consular rank. Clearly, the events in Judea had been significant enough to justify the change in its status. One may therefore assume that Dio and Eusebius do not mention the events of Judea simply because they did not reach proportions similar to those reached by the uprisings in the other countries.

Conclusion

The uprisings in Egypt, Cyprus, and Libya ended in total disaster; in Mesopotamia, too, the rebellion in which the Jews had a part was harshly repressed. However, there is no doubt that the simultaneity of the uprisings in the different countries was meaningful in that it compelled Trajan to remove from the Parthian front military forces led by his best generals. At the same time, the resistance in Mesopotamia was not yet quelled, as the unsuccessful siege of Hatra, taking place prior to June 117, demonstrates. All this coincided with Trajan's sickness and death, thus proving decisive in preventing the annexation of Mesopotamia. Scholars may be correct in suggesting that Hadrian's withdrawal from the East was necessitated not so much by the situation but rather by his policy of rejecting imperial expansion, in deliberate contrast with Trajan. In any case, and in spite of the triumph celebrated during the funerals of Trajan, the Parthian war had failed: the Jews of Babylon succeeded in remaining out of the Roman Empire.

Bibliography

Sources

G. Lüderitz 1983, *Corpus jüdischer Zeugnisse aus der Cyrenaika,* Wiesbaden: Reichert. • V. Tcherikover and A. Fuks, ed. 1960, *Corpus Papyrorum Judaicorum,* vol. 2, Cambridge, Mass.: Harvard University Press.

Studies

T. D. BARNES 1989, "Trajan and the Jews," *JJS* 40: 145-62. • A. FUKS 1953, "The Jewish Revolt in Egypt (AD 115-117) in the Light of the Papyri," *Aegyptus* 33: 13-58. • A. FUKS 1984, "Aspects of the Revolt in AD 115-117," in idem, *Social Conflict in Ancient Greece,* Jerusalem: Magnes; Leiden: Brill, 322-56. • M. HENGEL 1983, "Messianische Hoffnung und politischer 'Radikalismus' in der jüdisch-hellenistischen Diaspora," in *Apocalypticism in the Mediterranean World and the Near East,* ed. D. Hellholm, Tübingen: Mohr-Siebeck, 653-84. • W. HORBURY 1996, "The Beginnings of the Jewish Revolt under Trajan," in *Geschichte-Tradition-Reflexion: Festschrift für Martin Hengel zum 70. Geburtstag,* vol. 1, ed. P. Schäfer, Tübingen: Mohr-Siebeck, 283-304. • J. MÉLÈZE MODRZEJEWSKI 1989, "*Ioudaioi apheremenoi:* La fin de la communauté juive d'Egypte (115-117 de n.é)," in *Symposion 1985: Vorträge zur griechischen und hellenistischen Rechtsgeschichte (Ringberg, 24-26 Juli 1985),* Köln: Böhlau, 337-61. • M. PUCCI 1981, *La rivolta ebraica al tempo di Traiano,* Pisa: Giardini. • M. PUCCI BEN ZEEV 2005, *Diaspora Judaism in Turmoil, 116/117 CE: Ancient Sources and Modern Insights,* Louvain: Peeters.

MIRIAM PUCCI BEN ZEEV

Diet in Palestine

For the last five millennia, from the early Bronze Age on, the diet of people in the Mediterranean world has hardly changed. A real change in Palestine took place only in the twentieth century with a mass Jewish immigration and influx of imported food stuffs caused by population growth, changing tastes, and cheaper transportation. Along with archaeological finds and literary sources, this practically unaltered diet allows us to draw parallels from modern to ancient Palestinian society. Until recently it was customary to speak about the basic triad of bread, wine, and oil. It is more accurate to make the triad a quartet by adding to it legumes, a very important category of vital nutritional value.

Bread

Bread was, and still is, the most important item in the food basket of Mediterranean societies. The word "bread" is synonymous in Hebrew and in many other languages with food in general. In ancient societies, bread constituted around half of a person's caloric intake. In today's world, grain supplies only 20 percent of the caloric intake. Wheat is superior to almost all kinds of grain (e.g., maize, rice) in its nutritional value. Besides starch (60-80 percent), it contains components for building protein (8-14 percent). The caloric value of cereal, fairly similar in all types, is very high. In a kilogram of unground wheat there are more calories than in the same amount of beef (3,320 in wheat vs. 2,970 in beef).

Bread was made either from wheat flour or barley. Barley is the inferior of the two due to its low gluten content (gluten is a nitrogenous, gluey substance in grain that makes dough rise), its poor taste, and its being difficult to digest. Barley is grown mostly in semi-arid areas where wheat does not grow well, and is less sensitive than wheat to soil salinity. (This is why it is the main crop in southern Mesopotamia.)

Cottage milling is a slow and difficult process. In an hour of hard labor using a handmill, no more than 0.8 kg. of flour is produced from 1 kg. of wheat. Because the daily per capita consumption of wheat was about 0.5 kg., a homemaker needed to do some three hours of milling in order to provide for a family of five or six. The work was done during the last hours of night, so that with daybreak the housewife could prepare the dough and make the bread before the grown-up members of the family left for work. This bread must have been very similar to the pita bread produced today.

Legumes

Legumes were second in importance to bread, being high in nutritional value. They contain considerable amounts of protein components but require cereal proteins to complement them for optimum value. Legumes are eaten both fresh and as dried seeds. Leguminous dried seeds, like cereal seeds, can be stored for a long time — an important feature in a premodern economy. The most important legumes were lentils, beans, peas, chickpeas, and lupines.

Fruit

In the Roman period some thirty different kinds of fruit trees flourished in Palestine. In the biblical period there were far fewer, since many kinds of trees of the rosaceous family need grafting, a practice that was introduced quite late. The most important appear as five of the seven "species" (Deut. 8:8): vine, olive, fig, date, and pomegranate. (Grapes, wine, and olives are discussed below.)

The fig tree is one of the country's most characteristic features. Its needs are minimal, and it can grow in almost all soils. It can be eaten fresh but it is primarily consumed dry. Its significance is evidenced by the fact that by the talmudic period there were no fewer than thirty-six verbs concerning its cultivation.

Dates

Although the date palm is not mentioned specifically as one of the seven species, talmudic sages equated the date with the "honey" mentioned among them. This tree requires a hot climate and plenty of water. Because it can withstand high salinity, it was grown almost exclusively in the Jordan Valley and near the Dead Sea. Its very high sugar content makes it a very desirable fruit and lends it a long shelf life. From the early Iron Age onward, date wine replaced the traditional barley beer. The discovery of five vats (four in the Jericho royal estate and one near Qumran) testify that date wine was produced in Palestine in the Hellenistic and early Roman periods, but it may have been produced already in biblical times.

Vine and Wine

Grapes were the chief fruit in biblical times. They can be eaten fresh or dried and preserved for a relatively long time to be consumed as raisins. However, it seems that a great deal of the product, if not most of it, was turned into wine. Hundreds of winepresses all over the country, from the limestone hills of the Galilee to the loose sands of the Negev, testify to the ubiquitous production of wine.

It is a safe estimate that, on average, an adult man consumed around 700 grams daily, which contributed about one-quarter of his caloric intake and about one-third of the required intake of iron. But wine was imbibed not mainly as a beverage to accompany meals but as a help to make life bearable or even merry — "wine to gladden the heart of man" (Ps. 104:15).

Olive Oil

Olive oil is high in calories (9,000 per kg.) but practically devoid of vitamins and protein. It has a pleasant taste and can be stored for a long time. Easy to grow and with minimal demands, olive groves were cultivated all over the country. The olive tree's greatest drawback is the unpredictability of its yield. Even today, with advanced agronomical methods, there is a very marked difference in the yields of consecutive years, which can reach a factor of 4:1. Some of the olives were preserved, most likely pickled in brine and aromatic herbs, to be eaten; others, perhaps most, were pressed for oil.

Meat

The consumption of meat in Palestine was relatively high in the Iron Age, when the region was underpopulated and underdeveloped, and a lot of land was available for pasture. With time, though, more and more land was cultivated so that pastureland became scarce. By the Roman period, meat was beyond the reach of most people, who consumed it only on holidays, feast days, and festive occasions like weddings. Sacrifices were also occasions for eating meat.

The non-Jewish population of Palestine enjoyed nonkosher meat: pig and boar, camel, horse, and donkey. It is noteworthy that no pig bones have been unearthed in archaeological digs in the Israelite central mountains from the very beginning of Iron Age I onward.

Fish

Before the twentieth century, the only people who ate fresh fish in Palestine were those who lived along the Mediterranean coast or around the Sea of Galilee. Consumption inland must have been minimal. (Archaeological excavations have recently unearthed fish bones in Jerusalem and Lachish.) Only preserved fish (brined, dried, or smoked) was edible after being transported. Both the Mediterranean and the Sea of Galilee are quite poor sources of fish and could not have supplied more than a couple of kilograms per capita annually.

Milk and Honey

The land of Israel is described as "a land flowing with milk and honey," an expression that appears some twenty times in the Hebrew Bible (e.g., Exod. 3:8, 17; 13:5; 33:3). They are the only two foods that are "natural," that is, they do not require cultivation. The only food common to all human beings is milk. In some parts of the world, people continue consuming milk after being weaned (e.g., the Middle East, Europe, North America), while in some parts (e.g., China, West Africa) they do not. The main source for dairy products for Jews was cows and small cattle (sheep and goats), mostly the latter, which give milk only for a brief period. Thus, the surpluses had to be conserved by making butter and hard cheese.

Vegetables

Palestine in the Roman period, as talmudic literature attests, enjoyed at least thirty kinds of vegetables, both cultivated and wild. Almost all green leaves that taste good and are not poisonous are suitable for salad. Of the leafy vegetables, cabbage was probably the most popular. Onions and garlic were also very much in demand. Even the poorest of the poor could supplement their diet at no cost with wild plants full of vitamins, especially ascorbic acid (vitamin C).

BIBLIOGRAPHY

M. BROSHI 2001, *Bread, Wine, Walls and Scrolls,* Sheffield: Sheffield Academic Press, 121-43, 144-72. • M. BROSHI 2007, "Date Beer and Date Wine in Antiquity," *PEQ* 139: 55-59. • G. DALMAN 1928-1942, *Arbeit und Sitte in Palestina,* 7 vols., Gütersloh: Bertelsmann (rpt. 1964). • K. F. KIPPLE AND K. C. OMELAS, EDS. 2000, *The Cambridge World History of Food,* Cambridge: Cambridge University Press. • I. LOEW 1924-1934, *Die Flora der Juden,* 4 vols., Vienna: Löwit (rpt. Hildesheim: Holms, 1967). • N. MACDONALD 2008, *What Did the Ancient Israelites Eat? Diet in Biblical Times,* Grand Rapids: Eerdmans. • D. ZOHARY AND M. HOPF 2000, *Domestication of Plants in the Old World,* 3d ed., Oxford and New York: Oxford University Press. • M. ZOHARY 1982, *Plants of the Bible,* Cambridge: Cambridge University Press.

MAGEN BROSHI

Dietary Laws → Meals; Purity and Impurity

Divination and Magic

Divination is the attempt to foretell the future through the generation and interpretation of signs and portents. It is a common feature of all human cultures and in Jewish tradition is attested already in the Hebrew Bible. The Scriptures condemn a wide range of diviners and divinatory techniques (esp. in Deut. 18:9-14), are familiar with the magical techniques used by other peoples (e.g., Ezek. 21:26-27), and even recognize their general efficacy (as in 1 Sam. 28:7-20, where the female medium *(baʿălat ʾôb)* at Endor successfully summons Samuel's ghost and has it accurately foretell the future). Some passages describe Israelites who used different methods of divination (e.g., Gen. 24:10-14); others promise that the prophets will provide the Israelites with excellent substitutes for the Gentiles' diviners (Deut. 18:14-22) and approve of some divinatory technologies (esp. the Urim and Thummim, whose exact nature remains unknown).

Magic, the attempt to change reality through specialized ritual techniques, is also a cross-cultural phenomenon and is equally well attested in the Hebrew Bible. The Bible condemns and forbids various magical practices (esp. in Deut. 18:9-14), but it also repeatedly acknowledges their efficacy (as when it reports the great wonders performed by Pharaoh's sorcerers in Exodus 7–8) and describes a range of magical procedures, such as the elaborate manner by which Joshua crosses the Jordan and destroys the walls of Jericho (Joshua 3–4 and 6, respectively), or the ordeal enjoined for the conviction of a woman suspected of adultery (Num. 5:11-31). It also gives several glowing reports of charismatic "men of God" who performed wondrous deeds (as in the many miracles wrought by Elijah and Elisha) and even beat powerful magicians at their own game (as Moses and Aaron repeatedly do in Pharaoh's court).

Given the strong presence of magic and divination within the Jewish Scriptures, it is hardly surprising that in later periods, too, divination and magic were generally condemned, but widely practiced, throughout Jewish society. Many of the magical technologies common in the Hellenistic and Roman Near East — such as the wearing of amulets, the use of exorcisms, the practice of numerous specialized forms of divination (astrology, physiognomy, and so on) — were simply not covered by the biblical legislation, and thus could not easily be forbidden, as long as they did not verge on idolatry or other prohibited activities.

Jewish Discourse on Divination and Magic

In Jewish discourse on magic in the Second Temple period, there is a whole spectrum of negative attitudes, from the surprisingly brief comment of Josephus that the use of *pharmaka* (a word that refers to poisons, potions, and magical activities) is forbidden by the Jewish Torah (*Ant.* 4.279), through the detailed list of all the forbidden magical and divinatory technologies taught by the fallen angels to the daughters of men (*1 Enoch* 7:1; 8:3), to the insistence that Jews simply do not practice any magic or divination (*Sib. Or.* 3.218-30). Yet the book of *Jubilees* claims that many antidemonic remedies were taught to Noah by the angels, at God's behest, and that Noah wrote them all in a special book (*Jub.* 10:10-14). Josephus, moreover, gives a glowing description of a Jewish exorcist in action (*Ant.* 8.45-49), and the Dead Sea Scrolls reflect frequent use of exorcism and divination.

In the extensive discussions of magic and divination in rabbinic literature, one finds the expected prohibitions (e.g., *m. Sanh.* 7:4, 11) and condemnations (as well as the frequent association of magic with women), but also an emerging category of licit magic, such as various types of beneficial medical magic (e.g., *b. Šabbat* 67a), or the magical technologies used by some rabbis to create animate creatures (*b. Sanhedrin* 65b and 67b). There are also attempts to distinguish between divination which is forbidden and that which is not (e.g., *b. Ḥullin* 95b). Sometimes the rabbis even insist that a certain divinatory practice is permitted but does not really work (*b. Sanhedrin* 101a), and in some cases — especially where astrology is at issue — they admit that the practice generally works but insist that the Jews, or at least some Jews, are immune to such influences. This ambivalent attitude reflects in part the popularity of magic and divination in wide segments of Jewish society, and the rabbis' conviction that much of it was indeed effective. But it also helped legitimize many types of magical and divinatory practices, and paved the way for the flourishing of Jewish magic in the Middle Ages, even at the heart of the religious establishment.

The Second Temple Period

When turning to the actual magical and divinatory practices known to and utilized by Jews in the Second Temple period, one must face the problem that, except in those cases where techniques are transmitted in written form, or involve the act of writing as part of the praxis itself, there is little archaeological evidence testifying to their use. And even the evidence we do have is very limited in terms of what it can teach us. Amulets, for example, seem to have been widely used by Jews throughout antiquity, but when we find in an ancient tomb a small statuette of a "pagan" divinity, or the pierced tooth of a dog or a wolf, it is often impossible to prove that the users of such amulets were indeed Jews. Even when the Jewish origins of a certain find are not in dispute — such as the T-shirt with apotropaic "knots" found in the Cave of Letters, and definitely worn by one of the Jewish children who fled there with their families during the Bar Kokhba Revolt — the find itself is not very helpful in reconstructing the magical rituals used by its producers and users. So it is only the production of written magical texts, and especially those that happen to have been written on more durable writing surfaces (metals, gems, clay, and so on, as against papyrus and vellum, which are destroyed by humidity, worms, and microorganisms), or to have ended up in very dry areas (such as the Judean Desert or the parts of Egypt not flooded by the Nile), that enables us to study some of the technologies used by Jews at the time. This also means that our knowledge of this field is in a constant state of flux, since new sources are being discovered all the time.

Divination

In the realm of divination, the Dead Sea Scrolls provide interesting glimpses into the Qumranites' familiarity with, and likely use of, different astrological techniques (such as the brontologion of 4Q318). Jewish interest in astrology is well attested in other sources, too. The Dead Sea Scrolls also demonstrate the use of physiognomical divination, which apparently enabled the sect's members (and especially its supervisors) to judge from each member's appearance how many shares of "light" and "darkness" he possessed (as in 4Q186 and 4Q561).

Unfortunately, while the Jewish use of many other techniques of divination in the Second Temple period is extremely likely — one may think, for example, of divination for personal needs (whether a sick person will live, whom a certain person will marry, and so on) and for community affairs (whether there will be enough rain in the coming year, whether war will break out, and so on) — our evidence regarding such matters is only haphazard. For instance, some traditions found in rabbinic literature insist that from the direction of the smoke of the Temple sacrifices on the last day of the festival of Tabernacles one could divine the yield of the coming agricultural season, thus knowing who would become rich and who poor (*b. B. Batra* 147a; *b. Yoma* 21b; similar claims in *Lev. Rab.* 20:4). This example offers a tantalizing hint at the possible involvement of the Jerusalem Temple and its many priests in divination. The rabbis also recount a story of the wonder-working Ḥanina ben Dosa, who could tell from the fluency of the prayer in his own mouth whether a certain patient would live or die (*m. Ber.* 5:5) — a sure sign that the holy men of the Second Temple period were providing the population extensive services in the realm of magic and divination, as we shall note at greater length below.

Magic

Moving from divination to magic, we may note the supreme importance of exorcism as the best-attested Jewish magical practice of the time. This may be due in part to the fact that, although the actual exorcism necessitated no writing (as it would in some later phases of Jewish magic), it often did include much verbal activity. These verbal components sometimes were transmitted in written forms, especially in hymns and adjurations to be recited over the demon-afflicted person or to ward off a perceived demonic attack. There is an interesting array of such exorcistic texts, some of which are embedded in literary works that do not otherwise say much about magic (e.g., Noah's exorcistic prayer in *Jub.* 10:3-6, and especially David's exorcism of Saul with a hymn, fully quoted in Pseudo-Philo, *Biblical Antiquities* 60), while others have been preserved among the Dead Sea Scrolls (e.g., 4Q510-511, 11Q11, and 4Q560), or among the papyri from Egypt (e.g., the exorcistic Greek-Jewish text published in Benoit 1951, or the Jewish exorcism embedded in *PGM* 4:3007-86). The importance of exorcisms in Jewish culture at the time, and the proliferation and use of different exorcistic techniques, are well attested in other sources, too — from the descriptions of the expulsion of Asmodeus in the book of Tobit, through the New Testament's recurrent descriptions of Jesus, Paul, and other Jewish exorcists in action, to references by non-Jewish writers to Jewish exorcists and their reputation as healers (e.g., Lucian, *Tragoedopodagra* 171–73; cf. also his *Philopseudes* 16).

Although exorcism may be the only Jewish magical practice of the Second Temple period that we can reconstruct with some detail, it certainly was not the only magical technology known to, or utilized by, Jews at the time. In the writings of Josephus, for example, we find ample evidence for the use of aggressive and erotic magic in Herod's court (see, e.g., *J.W.* 1.583 and *Ant.* 17.62-63). The Jewish use of such technologies is corroborated by stray finds from Delos (see the two inscribed curses in *CIJ* 1:725 = *IJO*, vol. 1, Ach 70 and Ach 71), by some remarks and traditions found in rabbinic literature (such as the insinuations regarding the priestly uses of aggressive magic in *t. Menaḥ.* 13:21), and by stories of holy men who were asked to use their great powers to curse wayward individuals or communities (e.g., compare the requests made of Ḥoni the Circle Drawer in Josephus, *Ant.* 14.22-24, with the request made of Jesus in Luke 9:51-56, or with Paul's actions in Acts 13:9-11).

Unfortunately, a full picture of Second Temple period Jewish magic cannot be reconstructed from such meager evidence, and it is quite possible that the presence of the Jerusalem Temple and its priests on the one hand, and of a whole range of Jewish holy men on the other, assured a steady supply of magical services for all the needs of the Jewish population, and thus inhibited the growth of a full-blown professional Jewish magical technology.

Late Antiquity

For the period from the third or fourth century C.E. up to the Muslim conquest, our evidence is far more extensive. On the one hand, we have the rabbinic literature, which displays much interest in magic and divination, and a surprising willingness — especially pronounced in the Babylonian Talmud — to provide its readers with much technical information in matters of medicinal magic, the handling of demons, astrology, and even aggressive magic. On the other hand, we have an extensive, and constantly growing, corpus of textual and archaeological evidence pertaining to Jewish magical activity in Aramaic, Hebrew, and Greek — a sure sign of the growing "scribalization" of the Jewish magical tradition.

Thus, while Temple-related magical services were no longer available after 70 C.E., and while exorcisms and holy men seem to have gone out of favor in the Jewish society of late antiquity — perhaps because they became closely associated with the Christian movement — we have a lot of evidence for the rise of professional Jewish magicians, that is, of men (and women?) who owned written manuals of magical instructions, and who produced written, and often quite elaborate, magical objects for their paying clients. The identity of these magicians may have varied; some were professional physicians, others may have belonged to the rabbinic class, and some may have been more mystically oriented. But there is no need to think of a closed social group of Jewish magical practitioners. Rather, we may imagine a loose network of ritual experts whose expertise was transmitted in written form and included the production of written magical objects — some of which are accessible to us even today.

These Jewish magicians, moreover, were often in touch with their non-Jewish colleagues, as may be judged both from the proliferation of Jewish elements (and especially the powerful names of the Jewish god and his many angels) in "pagan" magical texts in Greek, and from the appearance in Jewish magical texts in Hebrew and Aramaic of magical techniques, practices, signs, and symbols whose origins lie in the Greco-Egyptian magical tradition.

DIVINATION AND MAGIC

Types of Evidence

The large corpus of textual and archaeological evidence for ancient Jewish magic may be divided broadly into three categories. First, there are the "finished products," often prepared for named individuals, which include magic bowls (found only in Babylonia); amulets inscribed on thin sheets of gold, silver, bronze, and lead; engraved magical gems; and aggressive spells inscribed on potsherds or on thin sheets of metal. These tend to be relatively short texts, but their late-antique origins are certain, as is, in most cases, their identification as Jewish (i.e., produced by Jewish practitioners, though not necessarily for Jewish clients). Unfortunately, most divinatory technologies do not call for the production of such "finished products," which is why our knowledge of late-antique Jewish divination is more limited than that of late-antique Jewish magic.

Second, there are magical recipes strung together in endless series without any internal logic and structure, a fact due to their being mere conglomerates of individual prescriptions, gathered together over the magician's entire career. Unfortunately, such collections were written on papyrus and vellum, and thus perished long ago (except for a few fragments of Aramaic magical papyri found in Egypt). Yet, since they kept on being transmitted in later periods, many distant copies have been found in the Cairo Genizah.

Third, there are "literary" books of magic, such as *Sepher ha-Razim,* the *Sword of Moses,* the *Havdala de-Rabbi Akiba,* and many similar works that are characterized by a more unified literary structure, within which the magical recipes are then embedded. This category also includes the many divinatory technologies transmitted in lists, tables, or technical manuals, such as physiognomical judgments based on the minute analysis of different parts of a person's body; twitch-divination texts that predict a person's future from the involuntary twitches of different muscles; lists of good and bad days *(hēmerologia)* or hours *(hōrologia);* divination from thunders, earthquakes, and rain patterns; and many types of astrological prognostications. Such texts have not reached us in their late-antique forms, but they are amply attested in the Cairo Genizah and in numerous non-Genizah manuscripts. In some cases, they display clear signs of their late-antique origins, including the use of Palestinian (or Babylonian) Jewish Aramaic, the proliferation of Greek (or Persian and even Akkadian) loanwords, and their extensive borrowing of Egyptian and Greek (or Babylonian and Mandaic) magical and divinatory technologies.

Range of Techniques

Turning from the texts' layout and structure to their actual contents, we may note the proliferation of a wide range of magical and divinatory technologies, to be used for any number of human needs. Reading the titles that precede many magical recipes and explain their aims, we find recipes to heal the sick, to induce love or hate between individuals, to harm one's opponents, to release people harmed by aggressive magic, to "jump the path" by traveling at great speed from point A to point B, and so on. We also find — in addition to the above-mentioned manuals of divination based on the observation of different natural phenomena — a long range of recipes and techniques intended to foretell the future, by adjuring an angel to reveal the future, by requesting a dream in which the answer to a specific question would be disclosed, or by producing a sign indicating whether a certain event would happen or not.

To achieve their many aims, Jewish magicians used a wide array of techniques, including the adjuration of angels and demons (though not of God himself, who was mostly seen as superior to the forces of magic, but as tacitly approving of their use). They also performed elaborate rituals (including sacrifices, especially of fowl), employing exotic or everyday materials (from the mucus of a black ox or the heart of a lion cub to seven ordinary pebbles or a hollow wooden cane) as well as special signs and "abracadabra" words.

Perhaps the most characteristic feature of ancient Jewish magic is its recurrent use of verbal and scribal elements, that is, the oral recitation and writing down of long prayers and adjurations. These elements include extensive lists of demons and diseases, and of the names of God and his angels; powerful biblical verses (such as Exod. 15:26; Num. 6:24-26; Psalm 91; and Zech. 3:2); and numerous references to such important biblical and parabiblical precedents as God's destruction of Sodom and Gomorrah, the rod of Moses and its many miracles, Solomon's rule over the demons, and the rescue of Abraham and of Daniel's three friends from fiery furnaces. It is these elements — coupled with the Jewish magicians' apparent desire to avoid appealing to the "pagan" gods (in spite of the occasional invocation of Helios, who clearly enjoyed a special status in some parts of late-antique Jewish society) or to Jesus — that give ancient Jewish magic its uniquely "Jewish" flavor.

Present and Future Research

Though neglected by earlier scholars, who preferred to think of Jews and Judaism as free of "superstition" and magic, Jewish magic and divination have become legitimate objects of concerted scholarly study only in the last generation. This area of research may therefore be characterized as a very young field, and one that is constantly evolving. Perhaps more important, the last generation has seen an exponential rise in the quantity and quality of evidence at our disposal, an explosive growth that does not seem to have reached its peak just yet. So, for example, the mere expression of scholarly interest in ancient Jewish amulets has resulted in dozens of additional amulets being excavated (by archaeologists, and unfortunately also by robbers) all over the eastern Mediterranean, and in many more such finds being "rediscovered" in museum basements all over the world. The growing interest in the magical texts from the Cairo Genizah already bore many important fruits, but many more still lay in store. The current turmoil in Iraq has led to the flooding of the antiquities markets with hundreds, and perhaps even thousands, of new Aramaic (as well as Mandaic and Syriac) magic bowls. And the systematic study of the hundreds of Jewish magical manuscripts from the Middle Ages and the modern period, some of which are hundreds of pages long, is bound to shed much more light on the Jewish magical texts and practices of late antiquity. Thus, while the above survey reflects our current knowledge of ancient Jewish magic, that knowledge is bound to be transformed by a wave of new sources, new approaches, and new studies.

BIBLIOGRAPHY

P. S. ALEXANDER 1986, "Incantations and Books of Magic," in E. Schürer, *The History of the Jewish People in the Age of Jesus Christ,* rev. and ed. G. Vermes, F. Millar and M. Goodman, vol. 3.1, Edinburgh: Clark, 342-79. • P. S. ALEXANDER 1996, "Physiognomy, Initiation, and Rank in the Qumran Community," in *Geschichte-Tradition-Reflexion: Festschrift für Martin Hengel zum 70. Geburtstag,* 3 vols., ed. H. Cancik, H. Lichtenberger, and P. Schäfer, Tübingen: Mohr-Siebeck, 1:385-94. • P. S. ALEXANDER 1997, "'Wrestling against Wickedness in High Places': Magic in the Worldview of the Qumran Community," in *The Scrolls and the Scriptures: Qumran Fifty Years After,* ed. S. E. Porter and C. A. Evans, Sheffield: Sheffield Academic Press, 318-37. • P. S. ALEXANDER 1999, "Jewish Elements in Gnosticism and Magic, c. CE 70–c. CE 270," in *The Cambridge History of Judaism,* vol. 3, *The Early Roman Period,* ed. W. Horbury et al., Cambridge: Cambridge University Press, 1052-78. • P. BENOIT 1951, "Fragments d'une prière contre les esprits impurs?," *RB* 58: 549-65. • L. BLAU 1898, *Das altjüdische Zauberwesen,* Strasbourg: Trubner (2d ed., Berlin: Lamm, 1914). • G. BOHAK 1996, "Traditions of Magic in Late Antiquity," Exhibition Catalogue, University of Michigan, February 1996 (also available on-line at http://www.lib.umich.edu/pap/magic). • G. BOHAK 2004, "Jewish Myth in Pagan Magic in Antiquity," in *Myths in Judaism: History, Thought, Literature,* ed. I. Gruenwald and M. Idel, Jerusalem: Zalman Shazar Center, 97-122 (in Hebrew). • G. BOHAK 2007, *Ancient Jewish Magic,* Cambridge: Cambridge University Press. • J. GOLDIN 1976, "The Magic of Magic and Superstition," in *Aspects of Religious Propaganda in Judaism and Early Christianity,* ed. E. Schüssler Fiorenza, Notre Dame: University of Notre Dame Press, 115-47. • Y. HARARI 1998, "Early Jewish Magic: Methodological and Phenomenological Studies," Dissertation, Hebrew University of Jerusalem (in Hebrew). Y. HARARI 2006, "The Sages and the Occult," in *The Literature of the Sages,* Second Part, ed. S. Safrai et al., Assen: Van Gorcum; Minneapolis: Fortress, 21-64. • R. LEICHT 2006, *Astrologumena Judaica: Untersuchungen zur Geschichte der Astrologischen Literatur der Juden,* Tübingen: Mohr-Siebeck. • R. LESSES 1998, *Ritual Practices to Gain Power: Angels, Incantations, and Revelation in Early Jewish Mysticism,* Harrisburg, Penn.: Trinity. • J. NAVEH AND S. SHAKED 1993, *Magic Spells and Formulae: Aramaic Incantations of Late Antiquity,* Jerusalem: Magnes. • J. NAVEH AND S. SHAKED 1998, *Amulets and Magic Bowls: Aramaic Incantations of Late Antiquity,* 3d ed., Jerusalem: Magnes. • P. SCHÄFER AND S. SHAKED 1994-, *Magische Texte aus der Kairoer Geniza,* Tübingen: Mohr-Siebeck (vol. 4 forthcoming). • L. H. SCHIFFMAN AND M. D. SWARTZ 1992, *Hebrew and Aramaic Incantation Texts from the Cairo Genizah: Selected Texts from Taylor-Schechter Box K1,* Sheffield: Sheffield Academic Press. • M. D. SWARTZ 2001, "The Dead Sea Scrolls and Later Jewish Magic and Mysticism," *DSD* 8: 182-93. • M. D. SWARTZ 2006, "Jewish Magic in Late Antiquity," in *The Cambridge History of Judaism,* vol. 4, *The Late Roman-Rabbinic Period,* ed. S. T. Katz, Cambridge: Cambridge University Press, 699-720. • J. TRACHTENBERG 1939, *Jewish Magic and Superstition: A Study in Folk Religion,* New York: Behrman's Jewish Book House (rpt. Philadelphia: University of Pennsylvania Press, 2004).

See also: Amulets; Astronomy and Astrology; Demons and Exorcism; Magic Bowls and Incantations; Solomon, Testament of GIDEON BOHAK

Domestic Dwellings in Roman Palestine

The growing interest in domestic architecture of the Roman and Byzantine periods in Palestine is inspired by similar studies devoted to dwellings of the Bronze and Iron Ages. The impetus for reconstructing both monumental and domestic structures for these earlier periods was often the desire to understand more fully and accurately the physical milieu of the biblical events. S. Krauss (1910) made the earliest attempt to re-create the material setting of the Roman period from talmudic texts, devoting several volumes to the topic of daily life. More than half a century later, H. K. Beebe (1968; 1975) undertook a similar study, the results of which were still only thinly supported by field discoveries. The only comprehensive study of domestic architecture in Roman-Byzantine Palestine to date was conducted by Y. Hirschfeld (1995), who integrated both archaeological finds and written evidence from contemporary literature, primarily rabbinic. Finally, and most recently, J. L. Reed (2000; 2001) and J. D. Crossan, in their quest for the historical Jesus, conducted a more limited chronological and geographical investigation by taking an interdisciplinary approach, combining both literary and archaeological sources to re-create daily life in first-century Galilee.

Sources

Most of our knowledge about domestic architecture in Roman Palestine derives from archaeological surveys and excavations of relatively well-preserved dwellings. In addition to the material evidence, rabbinic literature provides detailed information about most aspects of daily life and society in Palestine at this time, particularly domestic structures and features of the household (Hirschfeld 1995: 18-19). In most cases, however, one must take into consideration the chronological and regional limitations of this data.

Domestic structures are frequently exposed as a result of excavations that have as their primary goal the uncovering of civic centers or monumental structures, such as those at Sepphoris (Hoglund and Meyers 1996; Meyers 2008; Weiss 2008). Only rarely are dwellings one of the predetermined primary foci of an archaeological investigation. Among the major sites where considerable efforts and means have been devoted to the exploration of domestic life are Capernaum (Corbo 1977; 1982), ʿEin Gedi (Hirschfeld 2007), Gamla (Syon and Yavor 2005; Berlin 2006: 133–56), Jerusalem (Avigad

DOMESTIC DWELLINGS IN ROMAN PALESTINE

1980; Geva 2000: vol. 1; vol. 3, esp. 1-78), Mampsis (Negev 1988), Meiron (Meyers, Strange, and Meyers 1981: 23-77), Qatzrin (Killebrew and Fine 1991; Killebrew and Maʿoz), and Susiya (Hirschfeld 2008).

Architectural Characteristics

Most dwellings consisted of square or rectangular rooms forming a single building or partially attached buildings with perpendicular walls. One or several courtyards were almost always a typical feature of such dwellings throughout the Mediterranean region. Inconsistencies regarding the location of the courtyard in relation to the rest of the structure are dependent upon the available terrain and its topography. In a flat environment, courtyards tended to occupy central locations, whereas in hilly or terraced settings the courtyard was usually placed in a marginal location.

The roof was a hub of daily activities and was therefore completely flat. The New Testament describes a house with a tiled roof (Luke 5:19), but no remains of any such roof tiles have been found in association with private dwellings. Literary sources indicate that the roofs were surrounded by a parapet (*m. B. Bat.* 4:1).

Rabbinic sources distinguish between a dwelling's lower level *(bayit)* and upper level *(ʿălîyāh)* (*m. B. Meṣ.* 10:1; *m. B. Bat.* 2:2; *m. Ned.* 7:4). Many Roman and Byzantine houses surveyed in ancient Palestine have evidence of such an upper story. Sometimes the remains of an *exedra,* or balcony, have been found. The upper levels, both the roofs and second-story living quarters, could be accessed either by ladder or by stone staircases supported by stone vaults or a retaining wall. Arches were only rarely used above ground before the Byzantine era. The existing archaeological record indicates that doorways generally consisted of rectangular openings, most less than one meter wide. Unlike the roughly trimmed stones of the overall structure, the stones of the thresholds and doorposts were usually distinguished by a more even dressing. Interior passageways seem to have been simple, while main entrances usually contained sockets for the insertion of doorposts (Hirschfeld 1995: 249-55).

Windows in the exterior walls of the first floor were rare. In most cases, they were probably located on the upper level to ensure the privacy and security of the inhabitants. This location also allowed for circulating air and light. Most houses excavated in the Galilee and Golan have interior walls with windows, a feature also known in the Hauran and Bashan regions. They are usually located in the rooms immediately adjacent to the courtyard, thereby allowing air and light to enter the rear rooms. Most multileveled structures had recesses, or niches, set in their interior walls that were used primarily as wall cupboards to store clothes, dishes, and other utensils.

Most surfaces of walls and ceilings, and sometimes floors, were covered with a smooth plaster coating. In addition to the technical advantages of its low cost, and quick and easy use during construction, plaster was considered aesthetically desirable in this period. Well-smoothened plaster walls were sometimes used as a base for fresco and stucco decorations. From the second century B.C.E. onward, the fresco was used to embellish the walls of lavish houses and palaces in Palestine. Generally speaking, the literary sources conflict with the archaeological evidence, which testifies to the widespread use of wall decorations.

The flooring of both the first and second stories, even more than the wall finishings, reflect the socioeconomic status of a dwelling's tenants. In simple houses, the floor was laid primarily with compacted earth or, where built on natural rock, leveled with earth or clay. In upper-class dwellings, the floors were made of hewn or polished stone, as was the case in the Jerusalem Temple (*m. Tamid* 1:1; *m. Mid.* 1:8). Some floors were paved with mosaics or *opus sectile* (inlaid designs of larger, cut stones). Because wall paintings can be an indicator of room type, the paving method in dwellings can also help to determine the character or function of a specific room. According to *t. Kelim, B. Meṣiʿa* 11:10, rugs and mats were fastened to the floor with nails, apparently as a protection against the rough and cold floors.

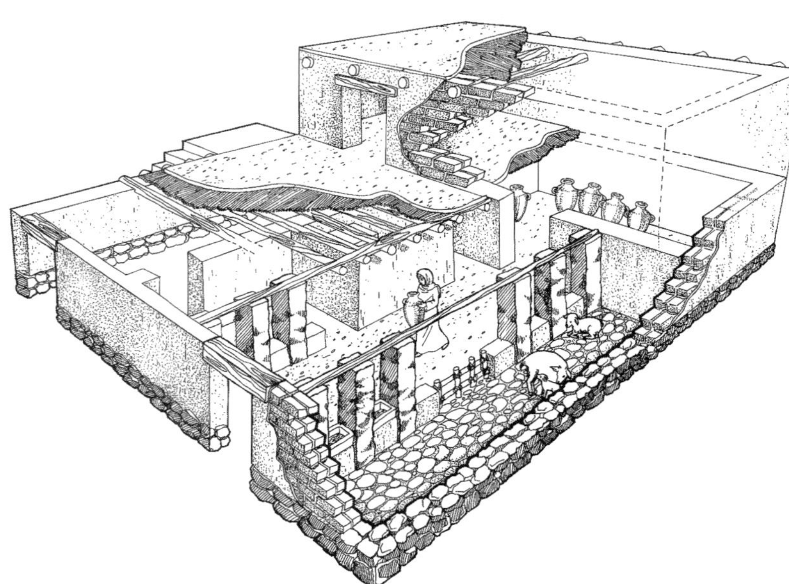

Artist's rendering of a modest domestic dwelling *(Giselle S. Hasel)*

In contrast to the widespread use of engraved stones in public buildings, especially in the Roman period, their appearance in domestic structures is confined to a few lintels, capitals, and architraves. Disregarding the chronological factor, the quality and quantity of decorative elements in domestic structures were determined not only by the socioeconomic standing of the owner, but also by the level of his exposure to Greco-Roman culture.

Unlike the construction of monumental architecture, which frequently used imported materials and non-local construction techniques and styles, domestic architecture was usually executed with local materials and building techniques. The clear preference for stone as a building material in Palestine is due primarily to its abundance. While in the biblical period stone was used mostly for the foundations of brick structures, from the Hellenistic period onward houses built entirely of stone became increasingly common (Hirschfeld 1995: 218). As in the Hauran, the majority of houses and other structures excavated in the eastern Galilee and Golan were built of the local basalt. Talmudic evidence informs us that certain types of wood (e.g., sycamore and cedar) were used in domestic construction in Palestine (*b. Baba Meṣiʿa* 117b).

The problem of attributing one specific function to a particular architectural space has been recognized in the context of the Roman villa (Wallace-Hadrill 1988) and is often applicable to the Palestinian dwelling. The texts attest not only that various tenants or families shared domestic spaces but that multiple activities were performed in one and the same location. Rabbinic literature describes two interior rooms, the *traklin* and the *kiton,* both of which served multiple functions. The *traklin,* deriving from the Latin word *triclinium,* was the largest and most important room in the house. In private dwellings, it was where families dined together and held special celebrations (*m. ʿErub.* 6:6; *t. Kelim, B. Meṣiʿa* 5:3). The texts also suggest that this room could be shared by the joint tenants of a household (*m. B. Bat.* 1:6). Unlike the *triclinium* of the Roman villa, the *traklin* was not used exclusively for dining and representational purposes but also for other daily domestic activities such as cooking, baking, and washing. The other room mentioned in rabbinic literature is the *kiton,* derived from the Greek *koiton,* meaning "bedroom" (Krauss 1910: 528-29) and is usually located adjacent to the *traklin.* The courtyard and the roof, both of which served similar purposes, were used as frequently as interior rooms. According to rabbinic sources, roofs were used for eating, praying, keeping animals, fruit, and vegetables, and drying olives (*m. Ḥul.* 3:1; *m. Tohor.* 9:6; *m. Makš.* 6:1-2; *b. Pesaḥim* 85b–86a). Courtyards provided space for wells, drinking troughs, structures for animals, and bathhouses, as well as for activities such as cooking, grinding wheat, washing clothes, and eating (Krauss 1910). Other rabbinic references indicate that the courtyard, like the *traklin,* was generally shared by the tenants of two dwelling units (*t. ʿErub.* 7:9). *Miqvaʾot* (ritual baths) were used by Jews for ritual bathing. Bathtubs or even complete bathhouses have been found only in the more luxurious dwellings. Given the limited number of latrines uncovered in archaeological excavations, most people must have used chamber pots or relieved themselves in the open. Furniture, such as beds and cupboards, were often used as dividers (*t. Pesaḥ.* 1:3; *y. Pesaḥ.* 1:27b; *y. Baba Batra* 6, 15c). Alternatively, wooden boards or plastered jars served as partitions (*m. ʾOhol.* 6:2). The archaeological remains, of course, attest only to the more permanent solutions, such as solid or fenestrated stone walls.

Bibliography

N. Avigad 1980, *Discovering Jerusalem,* Jerusalem: Shikmona and Israel Exploration Society. • H. K. Beebe 1968, "Ancient Palestinian Dwellings," *BA* 31: 38-58. • H. K. Beebe 1975, "Domestic Architecture and the New Testament," *BA* 38: 89-104. • A. M. Berlin 2006, *Gamla I: The Pottery of the Second Temple Period,* Jerusalem: Israel Antiquities Authority. • V. Corbo 1977, "Sotto la sinagoga di Cafarnao un'Insula della Città," *Liber Annuus* 27: 156-72. • V. Corbo 1982, "Ripreso a Cafarnao: Lo Scavo della Città," *Liber Annuus* 32: 427-46. • J. D. Crossan and J. L. Reed 2000, *Excavating Jesus: Beneath the Stones, Behind the Texts,* San Francisco: Harper. • H. Geva, ed. 2000, *Jewish Quarter Excavations in the Old City of Jerusalem Conducted by Nahman Avigad, 1969-1982,* 3 vols., Jerusalem: Israel Exploration Society. • Y. Hirschfeld 1995, *The Palestinian Dwelling in the Roman-Byzantine Period,* Jerusalem: Franciscan Printing Press. • Y. Hirschfeld 2007, *En Gedi Excavations, Part II: Final Report (1996–2002),* Jerusalem: Israel Exploration Society and Institute of Archaeology, Hebrew University of Jerusalem. • Y. Hirschfeld 2008, "A Jewish Dwelling at Horvat Susiya," in *From Antioch to Alexandria: Recent Studies on Domestic Architecture,* ed. K. Galor and T. Waliszewski, Warsaw: Warsaw University Press. • K. Hoglund and E. Meyers 1996, "The Residential Quarter on the Western Summit," in *Sepphoris in Galilee: Crosscurrents of Culture,* ed. R. Nagy et al., Winona Lake, Ind.: Eisenbrauns, 39-43. • A. Killebrew and S. Fine 1991, "Qatzrin: Reconstructing Village Life in Talmudic Times," *BAR* 17: 44-56. • A. Killebrew and Z. Maʿoz 1988, "Ancient Qasrin: Synagogue and Village," *BA* 51: 5-19. • S. Krauss 1910, *Talmudische Archäologie,* vol. 1, Leipzig: Fock. • E. Meyers 2008, "The Problems of Gendered Space in Syro-Palestinian Domestic Architecture: The Case of Roman-Period Galilee," in *From Antioch to Alexandria: Recent Studies on Domestic Architecture,* ed. K. Galor and T. Waliszewski, Warsaw: Warsaw University Press. • E. Meyers, J. Strange, and C. Meyers 1981, *Excavations at Ancient Meiron, Upper Galilee, Israel 1971-72, 1974-75, 1977,* Cambridge, Mass.: American Schools of Oriental Research. • A. Negev 1988, *The Architecture of Mampsis, Final Report I: The Middle and Late Nabatean Periods,* Qedem 26, Jerusalem: Institute of Archaeology, Hebrew University of Jerusalem. • J. L. Reed 2000, *Archaeology and the Galilean Jesus: A Reexamination of the Evidence,* Harrisburg, Penn.: Trinity. • J. L. Reed 2001, "Galilean Archaeology and the Historical Jesus," in *Jesus Then and Now: Images of Jesus in History and Christology,* ed. M. W. Meyer and C. Hughes, Harrisburg, Penn.: Trinity, 113-29. • D. Syon and Z. Yavor 2005, "Gamla 1997-2000," *ʿAtiqot* 50: 46-52. • A. Wallace-Hadrill 1988, "The Social Structure of the Roman House," *Papers of the British School at Rome* 56: 43-97. • Z. Weiss 2008, "Private Architecture in the Public Sphere: Urban Dwellings in Roman and Byzantine Sepphoris," in *From Antioch to Alexandria: Recent*

Studies on Domestic Architecture, ed. K. Galor and T. Waliszewski, Warsaw: Warsaw University Press.

KATHARINA GALOR

Dream and Vision Reports

Ancient Mediterranean and Near Eastern peoples maintained that dreams and visions constituted genuine communications with the divine realm. In both literature and cult, dream and vision reports reflect cross-cultural patterns that remained standardized for millennia (Oppenheim 1956; Noegel 2007). Early Jewish dream and vision reports share these traditional patterns, but are more numerous and often more intricate than visionary reports in other cultures, including preexilic texts of the Bible. Hundreds of dream and vision reports appear in the Apocrypha, Pseudepigrapha, Dead Sea Scrolls, Josephus, Philo, and New Testament, exhibiting complex forms and content related to specifically Jewish concerns, such as the validity of the covenantal promises, the fate of Israel in relation to the nations, access to the God of Israel, and the proper functioning of the Temple cult. Through the literary convention of pseudepigraphy, early Jewish authors present dreams and visions as authoritative prophecy, although later rabbinic sources diminish the status of dreams to only "one-sixtieth part of prophecy" (*b. Berakot* 57b; cf. *'Abot de Rabbi Nathan* 30b–31a).

Sources

Dream and vision reports appear in early Jewish literature in a variety of literary genres, including apocalypses *(1 Enoch; 2 Baruch; 4 Ezra; Apocalypse of Abraham; 2 Enoch; Testament of Levi*), midrashic rewritings of biblical narrative (e.g., Pseudo-Philo's *Biblical Antiquities; Jubilees; Life of Adam and Eve;* Additions to Esther; *Testament of Job;* Ezekiel the Tragedian), testaments (e.g., *Testament of Naphtali; Testament of Joseph*), histories (e.g., 2 Maccabees; Josephus' *Antiquities of the Jews* and *Jewish War*), novellas (*Joseph and Aseneth*), the autobiographical *Life* of Josephus, and various genres represented in the New Testament, including gospel (Matthew; Mark), historical novel (Acts), epistle (2 Corinthians), and apocalypse (Revelation). Several writings in the Qumran scrolls also show a pronounced interest in dreams and visions (e.g., 11QJob Targum; 1QGenesis Apocryphon; 4QBook of Giants; 4QElect of God; 4QAramaic Levi; 4QVision of Amram; 4QPrayer of Nabonidus; *Songs of the Sabbath Sacrifice*). The occurrence of dreams and visions in every early Jewish text that either is or contains an apocalypse is noteworthy, suggesting that these forms of revelation are crucial to the outlook of apocalypticism if not also to the genre apocalypse (Collins 1979: 6; Rowland 1982: 9-22, 58-61, 70-72, 214-47; Flannery-Dailey 2004: 270-78; Stone 1980: 27-35, 42-46; Otzen 1984: 204-12).

Vocabulary

Extant forms of early Jewish texts, which are preserved in a variety of languages (Hebrew, Aramaic, Greek, Syriac, Ethiopic, Slavonic, Latin), use the nouns we translate "dream" and "vision" interchangeably. The vocabulary stresses the action of *seeing* a dream or vision. While some visionary episodes are clearly related to the experience of nightly dreaming, with emphasis laid on the acts of being asleep at night and later awakening (e.g., *1 Enoch* 13:8-10; 83:3-6), overall the variety of formulations ("dreams," "visions," or "dream-visions") suggests a spectrum of hypnagogic events in which an altered state of perception facilitates an encounter with a divine being and/or the receipt of divine revelation. Thus, it is often difficult or impossible to distinguish visionary episodes from epiphanies.

Types

Early Jewish dream and vision reports follow certain literary types that are well established in the ancient Near East and Mediterranean sources, including: (a) *the message dream or vision,* in which a divine figure appears, stands, and relates a clear message, (b) *the auditory message dream,* in which a divine voice speaks with a clear message although no bodily form is visible, (c) *the symbolic dream or vision,* in which the divine message is coded in symbols needing interpretation by an authoritative interpreter, often an angel, (d) *the waking dream,* in which revelation is given to a sleeping dreamer but continues when the dreamer awakens, and (e) *visionary journeys,* in which the soul of a dreamer or visionary tours hitherto unreachable spheres (Oppenheim 1956: 186-206; cf. Flannery-Dailey 2004: 119-29, 170-200). To these may be added (f) *epiphanies,* or apparitions of heavenly beings (e.g., Dan. 10:4–12:13; *2 Bar.* 6:4–7:1; 2 Macc. 3:25-34, 5:2-3; cf. 2 Kings 6:17, 20). All of these types of dreams and visions were believed to be divinely sent; although Jews of antiquity undoubtedly did have mundane dreams relating to personal concerns, they are lacking in early Jewish literature, though well attested in rabbinic sources (e.g., *b. Berakot* 55a-57b).

Characteristic Functions

More than previous authors, early Jewish authors explore the erasure of temporal, spatial, and physiological constraints afforded by the visionary motif, lending new emphases to traditional functions of dreams and visions, namely, the conferral of extraordinary knowledge, divine favor (or punishment), and healing.

Revealed Knowledge

The transcendent knowledge revealed in dreams and visions pertains to events on a temporal spectrum extending from the precreation and primordial periods (e.g., *2 Baruch* 56) to the age to come (particularly in the apocalypses). Without spatial and physiological restraints, seers take visionary journeys through the cosmos, learning cosmological secrets and witnessing events in remote regions of heaven and earth as a mark of divine favor (e.g., *1 Enoch* 13–36; *Testament of Levi* 2–5; *Apocalypse of Abraham*).

Visionary knowledge also includes revelations of heavenly scripture (e.g., 4QApocryphon of Jacob; *T. Naph.* 5:8; *1 Enoch* 81:1; 103:2; 106:19), divinely facili-

DREAM AND VISION REPORTS

tated interpretations of familiar Scripture (e.g., Josephus, *J.W.* 3.351-54; cf. Daniel 9), and written records of the visionary experience, often as part of the dream or vision report itself (e.g., 4QVision of Amram; *Jub.* 1:5, 27; 32:26; Dan. 7:1; *4 Ezra* 14:37-48; *1 Enoch* 14:1; 82:1; *2 Enoch* 23:4-6). Like written texts, symbolic dreams and visions require interpretation by an authoritative reader, usually the Lord or an angel, although sometimes human scribes function in this role (4QBook of Giants; Dan. 1:17; 7:16-27; *2 Enoch* 23:1-3; *Ladder of Jacob* 2:22–7:35). Typically, a single definitive interpretation of the symbolism denotes a fixed future, in contrast to the polyvalence of rabbinic dream interpretation (*b. Berakot* 10b, 55b; see Alvstad 2005).

Divine Favor

Recipients of divinely sent dreams and visions are almost always male (cf. *Bib. Ant.* 9:10; *Jub.* 35:6; Josephus, *J.W.* 2.114-16; *Ant.* 17.349-53; *Ag. Ap.* 1.106-7; Matt. 27:19). God makes covenants with the patriarchs in several early Jewish dreams (*Jubilees* 14, 27, 32; 4QApocryphon of Jacob; 1QGenesis Apocryphon) reflecting similar biblical traditions (Gen. 15:12-21; 28:10-22). Other pseudepigraphic Israelite heroes are promised special destinies (e.g., Moses in the *Exagōgē* of Ezekiel the Tragedian 74–89; *2 Bar.* 76:2-4; *2 Enoch* 1:8), and Israel is often promised an ultimate triumph. A few privileged patriarchs, such as Levi (*T. Levi* 8:2-17), Enoch (*2 Enoch* 22:8-11), and Moses (*1 Enoch* 89:36), are transformed into angelic beings in dream or vision reports (cf. Dan. 12:3; *1 Enoch* 108:11-15). Divine favor also takes the form of dream warnings meant to protect (e.g., 1QGenesis Apocryphon; cf. Matthew 2), or help prepare for a family member's death or absence (e.g., *Jub.* 35:6; *T. Abraham* 7; *2 Enoch* 1:9). Some dreams or visions grant priestly investiture (*2 Enoch* 22; 69–70; *T. Levi* 8; 4QAramaic Levi; *Jubilees* 32), kingship (Josephus, *Ant.* 6.38), or other promotions (Josephus, *Life* 208–9). Conversely, they also warn of the removal of offices (Josephus, *Ant.* 5.348-52; Pseudo-Philo, *Biblical Antiquities* 53; cf. 4QVision of Samuel), or decree other forms of divine punishment (e.g., 4QBook of Giants; *1 Enoch* 15, 83–84).

Healing

In Hellenistic dream cults, dreams were incubated primarily in the hopes of healing physical and mental distress (LiDonnici 1995). By contrast, in early Jewish dream and vision reports, healings of physical illness rarely occur, except perhaps in the transformed motif of the angel who touches and heals a dreamer or visionary overcome by the visionary experience itself (e.g., Dan. 8:17-19; 10:16-19; *4 Ezra* 5:15; 10:29-31; cf. *Apoc. Abr.* 10:2-5). The healing of mental distress is, however, prominent; and many seers who commence visionary episodes in anguish end by expressing joy. Whereas in the Hellenistic examples mental suffering usually pertains to individual complaints, the early Jewish laments and prayers leading to visionary experiences address the collective plight of the Jewish people (e.g., *2 Baruch* 3–6; 35–37; *4 Ezra* 3–5; 9–12).

Characteristic Features

Setting and Contents

Many early Jewish dreams and visions presuppose that heaven is a *hekhal,* or palace-temple, from which the God of Israel rules on a throne, or merkavah, while surrounded by a host of angels performing typically royal and cultic activities (Himmelfarb 1993). Familiar characters include God's glory on the divine throne, angelic priests, angelic scribes acting as record keepers, angelic heralds, and angelic dream interpreters (a priestly function in antiquity). The rituals associated with dream and vision reports are also familiar from cultic contexts, including purification, lament, prayer, sacrifice, and resting in a sacred area. These actions are sometimes incubatory, triggering a visionary episode (e.g., *2 Bar.* 35:1–36:1; *4 Ezra* 9:24-37), and some accounts portray mass incubation (Ps.-Philo, *Bib. Ant.* 23:2-3; *2 Enoch* 69:3-5; Josephus, *Ant.* 11.326-28; cf. 2 Chron. 1:2-7).

Angels

In comparison with biblical accounts, angelology in early Jewish literature in general is well developed, with the appearance of personal names, definite personalities, and new roles for angels in the visionary traditions, including scribes, priests, revealers, warriors, healers, tour guides for cosmic journeys, and interpreters for the content of symbolic visions (for the latter see, e.g., Dan. 7:16-28; *2 Bar.* 55:3; cf. Zech. 1:14; 2:1-17).

Visionary Journeys

Ezekiel's visionary journeys (Ezekiel 8–11), together with the dream journeys of Enoch that they inform (*1 Enoch* 13:7–36:4), are immensely influential elaborations of earlier, simpler examples from cognate traditions (e.g., *Vision of the Netherworld; Story of Sinuhe*). The motif of heavenly ascent in a dream or vision appears in several early Jewish visionary texts (*1 Enoch* 1–36; *T. Levi* 2–5), sometimes in ways that blur distinctions between visions, epiphanies, and soul journeys (e.g., *2 Enoch; Apocalypse of Zephaniah; Apocalypse of Abraham; 3 Baruch;* cf. 2 Cor. 12:1-3; *Gospel of Mary;* Hekhalot texts). Gaining access to the divine throne or heavenly *hekhal* is also an important motif in dream and vision reports that lack a clear notion of ascent (e.g., *4 Ezra* 10; Daniel 7; Ezekiel the Tragedian, *Exagōgē* 68–89).

Death

As in ancient Near Eastern and Mediterranean traditions, early Jewish texts often intertwine death with dreams and visions. For example, deceased figures appear as dream messengers (Josephus, *Ant.* 17.349-53; 2 Macc. 15:12-16); dreamers foresee death (e.g., *Jub.* 35:6; *T. Abr.* 7:1-7); Enoch views the abode of the dead (*1 Enoch* 22:1-14); and the ascent of the soul at death is once presented as a dream journey (*T. Abr.* [Recension B] 14:7). Visionary episodes predicting existence after death reflect the variety of conceptions present in early Judaism, whether reward and punishment for the soul after death (*1 Enoch* 22), astral immortality (*1 Enoch*

108), a return to Eden (*1 Enoch* 25), a collective resurrection and judgment in the postmessianic age (*4 Ezra* 7:32, 78-101), or a special destiny without death for rare individuals (e.g., *4 Ezra* 14:9; *2 Bar.* 76:1-2).

Bibliography

E. ALVSTAD 2005, "Oneirocritics and Midrash: On Reading Dreams and Scripture," in *From Bible to Midrash: Portrayals and Interpretative Practices,* ed. H. Trautner-Kromann, Lund: Arcus, 123-48. • J. J. COLLINS, ED. 1979, *Apocalypse: The Morphology of a Genre, Semeia* 14, Missoula, Mont.: Scholars Press. • F. FLANNERY-DAILEY 2004, *Dreamers, Scribes, and Priests: Jewish Dreams in the Hellenistic and Roman Eras,* Leiden: Brill. • R. GNUSE 1996, *Dreams and Dream Reports in the Writings of Josephus: A Traditio-Historical Analysis,* Leiden: Brill. • J. S. HANSON 1980, "Dreams and Visions in the Graeco-Roman World and Early Christianity," in *ANRW Principat* 23.2, Berlin: de Gruyter, 1395-1427. • G. HASAN-ROKEM 1999, "Communication with the Dead in Jewish Dream Culture," in *Dream Cultures: Explorations in the Comparative History of Dreaming,* ed. D. Shulman and G. Stroumsa, New York: Oxford University Press, 213-32. • M. HIMMELFARB 1993, *Ascent to Heaven in Jewish and Christian Apocalypses,* New York: Oxford University Press. • N. LEWIS 1976, *The Interpretation of Dreams and Portents in Antiquity,* Toronto: Hackert. • L. LIDONNICI 1995, *The Epidaurian Miracle Inscriptions: Text, Translation and Commentary,* Atlanta: Scholars Press. • P. C. MILLER 1994, *Dreams in Late Antiquity,* Princeton: Princeton University Press. • B. NÄF 2004, *Traum und Traumdeutung im Altertum,* Darmstadt: Wissenschaftliche Buchgesellscaft. • S. B. NOEGEL 2007, *Nocturnal Ciphers: The Allusive Language of Dreams in the Ancient Near East,* New Haven, Conn.: American Oriental Society. • A. L. OPPENHEIM 1956, *The Interpretation of Dreams in the Ancient Near East: With a Translation of an Assyrian Dream-Book,* Philadelphia: American Philosophical Society. • B. OTZEN 1984, "Heavenly Visions in Early Judaism," in *In the Shelter of Elyon: Essays on Ancient Palestinian Life and Literature in Honor of G. W. Ahlström,* ed. W. B. Barrick and J. R. Spencer, Sheffield: JSOT, 199-215. • M. E. STONE 1980, *Scriptures, Sects and Visions: A Profile of Judaism from Ezra to the Jewish Revolt,* Philadelphia: Fortress. • C. ROWLAND 1982, *The Open Heaven: A Study of Apocalyptic in Judaism and Early Christianity,* London: SPCK. • S. ZEITLIN 1975, "Dreams and Their Interpretation from the Biblical Period to the Tannaitic Time: An Historical Study," *JQR* 66: 1-18.

FRANCES FLANNERY

Dreams, Book of (1 Enoch 83–90)

The *Book of Dreams* is the fourth booklet in *1 Enoch* and takes up eight chapters (83–90). Chapters 83–84 comprise the first dream vision, and chaps. 85–90 the so-called *Animal Apocalypse.* These two visions are complementary. Both occur in the house of Mahalalel, Enoch's grandfather, but they come at different times and differ in content. The first takes place when Enoch is learning to write, the second before he gets married. The first dream deals with the imminence of the first great "end," that is, the great flood. The *Animal Apocalypse,* on the other hand, goes beyond the flood and narrates the coming of a second end, the eschaton. The idea of someone's interceding for humankind (chaps. 83–84) and for Israel (chaps. 85–90) also connects the two dreams. In the first dream, Enoch is concerned for the earth or for humankind; in the second, there is a concern for the people of Israel.

The First Dream Vision (Chaps. 83–84)

Since it is not possible to make a link with any historical event or person, the first dream vision's precise date of composition is unknown. The dream can be divided into two sections, a vision proper and a prayer. In the vision, Enoch sees a cataclysm that symbolizes the coming of the Great Flood. Heaven is thrown to the earth, and mountains and trees fall. Enoch's reaction of fear may be compared to his lamentations during the suffering of the sheep in the *Animal Apocalypse.* His grandfather wakes him and asks him why he is crying. Enoch then narrates the details of the vision to his grandfather, who recommends that he pray so that "a remnant" may be saved. In 83:11 Enoch obtains a confirmation that his prayer has been heard in the fact that the sun, moon, stars, and earth are in harmony.

The first dream reflects several traditions found in other early Enochic works. Allusion to the *Astronomical Book* is made in 83:11 and to the *Book of the Watchers* in 84:4. The theme of Enoch as intercessor (83:8, 10; 84) is also found in the *Book of the Watchers* (13:4-7) and the *Animal Apocalypse* (89:57; 90:3). Patrick Tiller thinks that the first dream gives legitimacy to the heirs of the Enochic tradition, a community that considered itself a righteous remnant: "the righteous and true fleshes rise up as a seed-bearing plant forever" (Tiller 1993: 99).

The Animal Apocalypse (Chaps. 85–90)

The *Animal Apocalypse* seems to have existed independently before being incorporated into *1 Enoch.* It is usually dated to 165 or 164 B.C.E. on the basis of an allusion to Judas Maccabaeus. The vision is presented in the form of an allegory of the history of humankind and of Israel in which most of the characters are animals of the sort one would find in a fable. Angels are represented by human beings, Israel is symbolized by sheep, and God is called the Lord of the sheep.

The narrative may be summarized as follows: A bull and a heifer (Adam and Eve) come out of the earth. Two little bulls, one black and one red (Cain and Abel), go with them. The little black bull kills the red one. Stars (angels) fall down and unite with heifers (women) causing the birth of camels, elephants, and wild asses (the giants). The latter provoke great chaos by eating all living beings. Seven white men (angels) come down to earth. Three of them lift Enoch up from the earth onto a high tower (celestial temple), while the four others put the stars in chains. A flood follows. Thanks to a boat, the life of the white bull and his little ones (Noah and family) is spared. The three bulls (sons of Noah) beget various kinds of animals, among which is born a white bull (Abraham) that begets a wild ass (Ishmael) and a white bull (Isaac), which in turn brings forth a black wild boar (Esau) and a white sheep (Jacob) with twelve sheep (the patriarchs). One of the sheep (Joseph) is handed over to asses (Midianites), who in turn hand it over to wolves (Egyptians). The story continues with allusions to Moses, Aaron, the exodus, and deliverance at the sea; the encampment at Sinai and Moses' going up the mountain; the golden calf episode and death and apotheosis of Moses; the crossing of the Jordan and entry into Canaan; the careers of Samuel, Saul, David, and his "house"; Solomon and the building of the Temple (described as a "tower"); and the career of the prophets, including Elijah's ascent to heaven. The period of the divided monarchy in Israel is characterized by the sheep going astray. Wild animals are introduced to punish the sheep and destroy their house. The Lord of the sheep hands them over to seventy shepherds (angelic patrons or guardians), who transgress the instructions given to them and inflict suffering on the sheep. When the reign of the shepherds is over, the Lord of the sheep intervenes to help the sheep that have opened their eyes (the author's group). A final battle ensues between the sheep, led by a ram (usually understood as Judas Maccabaeus), and the other animals. Along with the still blinded sheep (apostate Israelites), the shepherds and the fallen stars are condemned and punished. The sheep's house is destroyed and rebuilt — evidently an allusion to the restoration of Jerusalem but without the Temple. All the righteous animals gather in the new house. Finally, a new white bull appears and all the animals are transformed into bulls.

The similarity between the *Animal Apocalypse* and Daniel 9 has been underlined by scholars. Both texts interpret Jeremiah's seventy years (Jeremiah 25) to represent seventy weeks of years (70 × 7 = 490 years), and both seem to have been written during the Maccabean crisis. Many scholars think that the *Animal Apocalypse* depicts Israel taking up the sword. Most interpreters identify the ram with a great horn in 90:9 as Judas Maccabaeus and conclude that *Animal Apocalypse* is militant in character. This conclusion, however, requires careful study (Assefa 2007). The *Animal Apocalypse* has also been compared to the *Apocalypse of Weeks* since both works engage in a periodization of history. The *Animal Apocalypse,* however, focuses mainly on the latter stages of history and on the seventy shepherds.

Some scholars think that the *Animal Apocalypse* diminishes the importance of Moses — Enoch gains in prestige since he is the recipient of the revelation. We should ask, though, whether the work permits a clear comparison between Enoch and Moses. The former is a spectator, whereas the latter is an actor, with Enoch observing the actions of Moses from a celestial temple. Moses plays a key role in the history of Israel, and he becomes a "man," which symbolically implies that he achieves angelic status. Strikingly, though, while Moses and Sinai figure in the story, nothing is said about the making of the covenant or the giving of the Torah.

BIBLIOGRAPHY

D. ASSEFA 2007, *L'apocalypse des animaux (1 En 85–90): Une propagande militaire?* Leiden: Brill. • G. BOCCACCINI, ED. 2005, *Enoch and Qumran Origins: New Light on a Forgotten Connection,* Grand Rapids: Eerdmans, 17-72. D. DIMANT 1982A, "History according to the Vision of the Animals (Ethiopic Enoch 85–90)," in *Jerusalem Studies in Jewish Thought* 1, 2: 18-37 (in Hebrew). • D. DIMANT 1982B, "Jerusalem and the Temple in the *Animal Apocalypse*" (*Ethiopic Enoch* 85–90) in the Light of the Ideology of the Dead Sea Sect," *Shenaton* 5-6: 177-93 (in Hebrew). • P. A. TILLER 1993, *A Commentary on the Animal Apocalypse of 1 Enoch,* Atlanta: Scholars Press. • P. A. TILLER 1997, "The 'Eternal Planting' in the Dead Sea Scrolls," *DSD* 4: 312-35. • J. C. VANDERKAM 2004, "Open and Closed Eyes in the *Animal Apocalypse* (*1 Enoch* 85–90)," in *The Idea of Biblical Interpretation,* ed. H. Najman and J. Newman, Leiden: Brill, 279-92.

DANIEL ASSEFA

Dualism

Definitions

The term *dualism* was used first by Thomas Hyde in his *Historia Religionis Veterum Persarum* (Oxford 1700) to describe the religion of ancient Iran. Against a continuing dilution of the term which included dualities, polarities, or pairs of opposites, Ugo Bianchi has introduced a strict definition of dualism as a worldview of two irreducible principles the opposition of which is fundamental for the existence of the world and humankind. Bianchi distinguishes *radical* and *moderate* (two or one principles), *dialectical* and *eschatological* (eternal dualism or one limited in time), *pro-* and *anti-cosmic* dualism (the world seen as neutral or negative). In Judaism, however, these distinctions are too broad: the world is never seen as negative; any reign of evil is always regarded as limited in time, and any concept of a radical dualism of two powers does not exist since it would undermine the dominance of the Creator. Thus in the Hebrew Bible one sometimes meets with the emphasis that God is the author of good and evil, light and darkness (Isa. 45:7).

Other, more detailed criteria have been used for dualism by scholars working on early Jewish and Christian materials. These have been collected by Jörg Frey (1997: 282-85) in ten categories: *metaphysical* (two equal cosmic powers as the cause of the world), *cosmic* (the world and humanity divided into two opposing but not necessarily coeternal or causal forces), *spatial* (division into heaven and earth, above and below, etc.), *eschatological* or *temporal* (two separate aeons or ages), *ethical* (humankind divided into good against evil), *soteriological* (division not on account of deeds but of faith and obedience versus unbelief and disobedience), *theological* or *prophetic* (God and humanity, Creator and creation), *physical* (matter against spirit), anthropological (the separate principles of body and soul), and *psychological* (the internal division between good and evil intentions). Some of these categories can be used at the same time, and some do not apply in the Jewish context: either they do not exist (e.g., the metaphysical dualism of Zoroastrianism), or they apply to all Jewish texts (e.g., theological dualism). The category of a *soteriological* dualism applies more to Christian texts, such as the Gospel of John, where faith in Christ becomes a defining principle against "the world" understood as the realm of human ignorance and unbelief.

Hebrew Bible

Genuine dualism does not exist in the older, preexilic texts of the Hebrew Bible. In the wisdom traditions, occasionally certain dualistic motifs occur. The later traditions, particularly the apocalyptic ones (e.g., Daniel 7–12) affirm the superiority of the creator God but hold that the state of the present world is caused and determined by a tension of two opposing forces. This dualism culminates in the sectarian separation of the Qumran community from the rest of the Jewish world. A very different kind of dualism can be found in the philosophical view on mind and matter in Hellenistic Judaism.

Wisdom Literature

There is no genuine spatial dualism in Jewish wisdom texts. Most texts assume a world divided into three parts: heaven, world, and underworld (e.g., Prov. 8:22-31; Job 17:13; 26:6; 31:2). Occasionally, however, a certain contrast between heaven as the place of God's presence (Sir. 1:8) and earth as the area of human life (e.g., Qoh. 1:13; 3:1; 11:2) is developed (e.g., Ps. 119:89-90; Psalm 73).

More important for the wisdom texts is the ethical division between the righteous and the wicked on the basis of religious and moral behavior (e.g., Proverbs 10–15; Psalm 1). The righteous are rewarded and the wicked punished (Wisdom 1–5; 16–19). Ben Sira expands this view into the more fundamental contrast of two opposed groups (Sir. 42:23-26), particularly God's people and the other nations (Sir. 36:1-19), according to the idea of creation as structured in contrasting pairs (Sir. 33:9-10).

None of the biblical wisdom texts develops the spatial and ethical duality into a genuine dualism of conflicting powers. This changes with the introduction of apocalyptic ideas and cosmic dualism into wisdom texts, as in some of the wisdom texts found in Qumran (e.g., 4QSapiential Work A, and the *Book of Mysteries* [1Q27 frg. 1 col. i lines 3-4]).

Apocalyptic Literature

In apocalyptic literature the world is consistently described in contrasts and conflicts. There is the temporal dualism between this age and the one to come (Daniel 7; *4 Ezra* 5:1-13; 6:7-10; 7:50, 112) but also the spatial dualism between the heavens as the place of God and his powers, on the one hand, and the earth as the site of the conflict between God and his opponents, on the other (Dan. 4:34; 10:10-21; *1 Enoch* 14). On the human level this leads to an ethical dualism, the idea that humankind is divided into the righteous and the wicked (Dan. 12:10; *1 Enoch* 1:1; 93:2-4; 98:9-16; *4 Ezra* 8:47, 59). At times one group is associated with light and the other with darkness (e.g., *1 Enoch* 108:11-14). When human beings are seen as caught in a cosmic battle between the forces of good and evil, light and darkness (1QM), a cosmic dualism is introduced. In nonsectarian Jewish apocalyptic texts, the righteous are usually identified with the descendants of Abraham (*Jub.* 24:29) and the wicked with the Gentile nations (*Jub.* 23:24; 24:28; 1QM 1:6; 18:2-3).

The myths about the fall of the angels have influenced the formation of apocalyptic concepts of cosmic dualism. The rebellion of the sons of God (e.g., the Day Star and Son of Dawn in Isaiah 14) is applied to Antiochus IV and the spiritual powers in their battle against Michael in Daniel 8–12. The myth of the heavenly revolt is related to that of the angels' refusal to worship the image of God in Adam, for which they are thrown down on earth (e.g., *Life of Adam and Eve*). Another, more important myth is that of the fall of the sons of God and their union with human women (Gen. 6:1-4), which is presented in detail in the *Book of the Watchers* (*1 Enoch* 1–36) and in *Jubilees*. The Watchers lust after human women; under their leaders Shemihazah and Azael (*1 Enoch* 6; 8) — or, as in *Jubilees*, Mastema or Belial (*Jub.* 1:20; 15:33) — they teach humanity all kinds of reprehensible knowledge that leads to violence and deceit. The women give birth to evil giants, whose violence threatens to destroy life on earth (*1 Enoch* 6–8; *Jub.* 4:15.22; 5:1-19; 7:21-33). The Watchers are bound by God and his angels. In *1 Enoch* the flood kills their offspring, the giants (*1 Enoch* 9–11), but their evil spirits survive and continue to plague mankind (*1 Enoch* 12–16). In *Jubilees* the giants are not killed by the flood (*Jub.* 10:1-5; 5:8-9). In both texts evil is a created phenomenon — even Mastema, their leader, can be conquered by God (*Jub.* 48:15) — but it is a superhuman reality nonetheless. The present situation of humankind is explained through a cosmic dualism between God and his angels on the one side and these fallen spirits on the other (*Jub.* 10:1-15; 11:5).

The Dead Sea Scrolls

Dualism becomes particularly important in a sectarian worldview. Consequently, among the Qumran documents many and diverse dualistic texts were found, not all of them written by the community or *yaḥad*.

Some wisdom texts from Cave 4 there develop the ethical dualism of the later wisdom tradition into a cosmic dualism: 4QWiles of the Wicked Woman (4Q184); 4QSapiential Work A; the *Book of Mysteries* (1Q27 ii 2–ii 10, 4Q299, 4Q300; 4Q413). A sizeable number of fragmentary copies of Enochic texts and *Jubilees* were found in Qumran. Their cosmic dualism has also influenced other texts; for example, the Aramaic materials associated with Levi, Qahat, and Amram, which regard human beings as influenced by evil spirits (cf. *1 Enoch* 40:7); and the pseudo-Moses text 4Q390, which is based on *Jubilees*. A number of poetic texts aim to hold the evil spirits at bay; thus the apotropaic incantation poems of 11QapPs[a] address the conflict between the holy people and their enemies, particularly the evil spirits (cf. *1 Enoch* 10:4-7). And the *Songs of the Maskil* in 4Q510 and 4Q511 serve exorcistic purposes in binding the evil spirits though the prayer of the sage. Other texts serve the purpose of identifying the "sons of darkness" by means of their physiognomy and the position of the stars at birth or at conception (4Q186 = 4QCryptic and 4Q561). Probably none of these texts originated in the *yaḥad* or had a sectarian outlook. But because many of them were found in several copies in Qumran, they appear to have been relevant to the community.

The *War Scroll* from Qumran (esp. 1QM 1, 13, 15–19) presents an apocalyptic scenario that combines temporal, spatial, and ethical but mainly cosmic dualism in the description of the final war between God and the sons of light on one side and Belial and his lot, the sons of darkness, on the other. 1QM is based on material from outside the community, from the Maccabean wars, which has been adapted by the Qumran *yaḥad.* No longer referring to Israel and its conflict with the nations, the dualism is transferred to the *yaḥad* in opposition to the rest of the world.

Another dualistic text is the "Teaching on the Two Spirits" (1QS 3:13–4:26), which combines apocalyptic and wisdom thought. God is described as the creator of everything. Humankind is divided into two groups, the sons of light, governed by the spirit of truth, and the sons of darkness, ruled by the spirit of deceit. Each group is characterized by their ethical behavior. At the time of God's intervention through his cleansing spirit, each will receive reward or punishment. Until then the spirit of deceit attempts to cause the sons of light to stumble. The instruction combines cosmic, ethical, and eschatological dualism in an ultimate conflict between two powers with a psychological dualism of an internal struggle inside the human heart. Some scholars regard this sort of dualism as influenced by Zoroastrian teaching (*Yasna* 30, 45; the *Yasna* contains the sacred liturgical texts of the *Avesta* [Zoroastrian scriptures], which include the *Gathas,* the sacred hymns of Zarathushtra). Others regard it as a development of Jewish wisdom traditions (cf. Duhaime 2000: 219; Collins 1997: 41-47). It is found already in the Aramaic *Visions of Amram* (Kobelski), and is taken up in several sectarian texts. Thus the *Damascus Document* refers to the teaching on the two spirits (1QS 4:22-26) as well as the Enochic Watchers (CD 2:2-13; 4:12–6:11). Further possible quotations of 1QS 4:26 could be 1QH^{a} 8:11-12 (= Sukenik 14:11-12) and 4Q181 1 ii 5. However, the complex dualism of the "Teaching on the Two Spirits" is not taken over completely but only the idea of the divine election and the conflict between the community and the outside world, emphasizing the cosmic element and ignoring the psychological one. This could indicate that the instruction originated outside the community, although it received a prominent place as the conclusion to the covenant liturgy right at the beginning of the *Community Rule* (1QS).

The covenant liturgy in 1QS 1:1–3:12 is a genuine piece of sectarian dualism, originating from inside the Qumran *yaḥad.* During the ceremony, the members swear an oath of allegiance to the community. The ceremony evokes an ethical and cosmic dualism by liturgically dividing the community from "all the men of the lot of Belial" through a series of blessings and curses. This liturgy corresponds in large parts to the blessings and curses in 4QBerakhot (4Q280, 4Q286, and 4Q287).

Parts of the *Hodayot* call up an ethical dualism between the righteous, who are aware of their failings and who repent, and the wicked, who do not adhere to God's laws (1QH^{a} 11:20-37 = 3:19:36 Sukenik; 12:6–13: 6 = 4:5–5:4 Sukenik and col. 7 = col. 15 Sukenik). A similar cosmic and ethical dualism, related to the community's history, can be found in some of the pesharim and related texts (1QpHab 4:17b–5:12a; 4QpPs 37 2:1–4:18; 4Q180).

The cosmic dualism of the rebellion of the angels appears in 11QMelchizedek, where the two angelic beings Melchizedek and Belial are contrasted. There is no ethical dualism, but the reigns of Belial and Melchizedek are seen as separate in time. A similar eschatological dualism is expressed in the *Midrash on Eschatology* (4Q174 and 4Q177).

A fundamental feature of the dualism at Qumran is the division of humankind into two different "lots," that of God and that of his opponent (variously called Belial, Melchiresha', and Mastema). A cosmic and eschatological dualism is dominant, while the ethical aspect shows itself mainly in the obedience to the community rules. Perhaps the community's dualism can also be observed in other aspects of their sectarian life. Thus their use of the solar calendar may be related to their calling themselves the sons of light (Dimant 1998: 60-69). On the whole, the various dualistic texts serve to define the *yaḥad*'s sectarian way of life against the background of and in opposition to its surroundings — Jewish and Gentile.

Philosophical Dualism

There is one passage in Philo that refers to a tradition similar to the "Teaching on the Two Spirits": in his *Questions on Exodus* 12:23c he explains the dualism of the two powers inside the human soul, one for salvation and the other for perdition (*QE* 1.23). However, he immediately emphasizes the psychological contrast of two different inclinations, whose conflict influences the moral behavior of the individual. Unlike the Dead Sea Scrolls, Philo emphasizes the psychological dualism in order to integrate this unfamiliar tradition into his philosophical concept.

More congenial to Philo's thought is the dualism of matter and spirit (*Opificio Mundi* 16–36) as well as the anthropological dualism of mind and body or, in Philo's terms, sense and perception (*Leg.* 1.1; *Heres* 63–85), which derives from Platonic and generally Hellenistic philosophical thought.

Bibliography

J. H. Charlesworth 1990, "A Critical Comparison of the Dualism in 1QS 3:13–4:26 and the 'Dualism' Contained in the Gospel of John," in *John and the Dead Sea Scrolls,* ed. J. H. Charlesworth, New York: Crossroad, 76-106. • J. J. Collins 1997, *Apocalypticism in the Dead Sea Scrolls,* London: Routledge. • D. Dimant 1998, "Dualism at Qumran: New Perspectives," in *Caves of Enlightenment: Proceedings of the American Schools of Oriental Research Dead Sea Scrolls Jubilee Sympo-*

sium (1947-1997), ed. J. H. Charlesworth, North Richland Hills, Tex.: Bibal, 55-73. • J. DUHAIME 2000, "Dualism," in *Encyclopedia of the Dead Sea Scrolls,* vol. 1, ed. L. H. Schiffman and J. C. VanderKam, Oxford: Oxford University Press, 215-20. • J. FREY 1997, "Different Patterns of Dualistic Thought in the Qumran Library: Reflections on Their Background and History," in *Legal Texts and Legal Issues: Proceedings of the Second Meeting of the International Organization for Qumran Studies Cambridge 1995,* ed. M. Bernstein et al., Leiden: Brill, 275-335. • J. G. GAMMIE 1974, "Spatial and Ethical Dualism in Jewish Wisdom and Apocalyptic Literature," *JBL* 93: 356-85. • P. J. KOBELSKI 1981, *Melchizedek and Melchiresha',* Washington, D.C.: Catholic Biblical Association. A. F. SEGAL 1987, "Dualism in Judaism, Christianity, and Gnosticism," in idem, *The Other Judaisms of Late Antiquity,* Atlanta: Scholars Press, 1-40. • S. SHAKED 1994, *Dualism in Transformation: Varieties of Religion in Sasanian Iran,* London: School of Oriental and African Studies, University of London. • L. T. STUCKENBRUCK 2004, "The Origins of Evil in Jewish Apocalyptic Tradition: The Interpretation of Genesis 6:1-4 in the Second and Third Centuries B.C.E.," in *The Fall of the Angels,* ed. C. Auffarth and L. Stuckenbruck, Leiden: Brill, 87-118. • G. WIDENGREN, A. HULTGÅRD, AND M. PHILONENKO 1995, *Apocalyptique iranienne et dualisme qoumrânienne,* Paris: Maisonneuve.

See also: Apocalypticism; Eschatology; Persian Religion; Satan and Related Figures

JUTTA LEONHARDT-BALZER

E

Ecclesiastes → Qohelet

Economics in Palestine

For the inhabitants of the Greco-Roman world, the word *oikonomia* referred to the management of one's household or "estate" *(oikos)*. If we define *economy* in modern terms as the production, management, distribution, and consumption of goods and services, we would be speaking about a segment of human activity that the ancients did not separate from the social and political aspects of the culture. One result of this unitary vision of society is that extant sources contain very scant and fragmentary information on the economics of Greco-Roman communities. Consequently, the study of ancient economy has remained intractable and controversial.

The Economics of Roman Palestine

The study of the economy of Jewish Palestine in the Second Temple period is rendered even more complicated by the fact that scholars have tended to focus synchronically on first-century "issues," especially factors that might explain the revolt of 66-70 C.E. and the rise of early Christianity. The dearth of literary evidence for the early Roman period has forced studies on the economy of ancient Palestine to concentrate on the later, post-70 Roman period. These studies rely heavily on evidence drawn from rabbinic literature. The relevance of such evidence is, however, controversial even for the later Roman period; it is more so for the earlier period. It is doubtful that archaeology can completely answer the many vital and disputed questions raised by the study of ancient economies. However, the greater integration of archaeological discoveries, analyzed in their own terms, can enable historians not just to interpret or confirm extant literary evidence, but especially to formulate hypotheses.

An Agrarian Economy

It is widely acknowledged that the economy of Palestine in the Second Temple period, like the economies of the surrounding regions, was based on agriculture and was mostly subsistent; most producers worked on the land and consumed most of what they produced. As in the study of the economy of the larger Greco-Roman world, what is disputed is the extent of "surplus" produced over and above the subsistent needs of the peasant family, how that surplus was produced and circulated, and who benefited from the production and circulation.

Many recent studies on the economy of Palestine are influenced by works in economic anthropology and social scientific studies of peasant societies. They are dominated by the "primitivist" model of the ancient economy developed especially by Moses Finley. According to this approach, Jewish society comprised a vast majority of peasant producers and a small minority of elite city dwellers. Peasants survived on the barest minimum. There was little left over after the small surplus they produced had been taken from them by the elite as taxes, rents, and tithes. The elite were the ruling class of Palestine: government officials, military personnel, priests and other temple functionaries, and intellectuals. These and their subordinate "retainers" either were not directly involved in agricultural production or did not produce enough for their needs. They derived their livelihood and wealth from the labors of peasants, on the bases of status-driven legal claims, without any exchange of return values in goods and services. Thus, urbanization in Palestine is typically viewed in negative terms, since cities were centers of consumption, rather than centers of manufacture and trade, with a parasitic relationship to the countryside.

Fitting scant extant information into this model often entails trimming the foot to fit the shoe. Moreover, the model itself has long been criticized, particularly its concept of the "consumer city" and the neglect of the role of trade and manufacture in the ancient economy. Historians of the economy of ancient Palestine should now be cognizant that Finley's model is an ideal type. It does not in itself constitute historical evidence and certainly cannot substitute for economic history. Among historians of the ancient economy, further methodological debate and especially regionally focused inquiries and case studies have led to significant modifications of the primitivist model. Such studies are largely lacking for Second Temple Palestine.

The fact that agriculture was the basis of economic life in Second Temple Palestine is widely testified to by extant sources. Land and agricultural produce were the objects of direct taxation in the Hellenistic period (Josephus, *Ant.* 13.49), under the Herods (*Ant.* 15.303, 365) and the Romans (*Ant.* 14.202-3, 205-6; 18.274). Agricultural production was mostly subsistent; growers' first priority was to meet the consumption needs of their families. Thus, production and exchange of surpluses were mostly dictated not by "market" demands, but rather by the need to procure the vital items that one neither grew nor produced for oneself: shelter, clothing, tools, salt, spices, and other items. Taxes, religious offerings, rents, and gifts were also media for the flow of agricultural surplus. It is worth noting, first, that it is wrong to establish the "market" as the sole medium and measure of the distribution and exchange of goods in the ancient economy. Temple and other religious offerings, for instance, though generative of trade, were exchange that produced other, nonmarket values. Second, it has been argued that in Palestine, as in the rest of the Greco-Roman world, the exigencies of taxation led to an increase in production.

The archaeological and literary data do not exist for Second Temple Palestine that would permit scholars confidently to estimate its population. Estimates vary widely from one million to well over two million. Population growth and other demographic changes in the territory over time cannot be assessed. The absence of demographic figures means particularly that no reliable economic relationship can be established between the territory's population (and its needs in material goods and services) and the resources of the territory. Thus, for example, discussions about overpopulation, demographic pressures, and the shortage of arable land at certain times during our period are necessarily speculative. Despite some evidence from archaeological surveys, debates about the sizes of family plots are also conjectural.

Since agrarian economic structure is determined by availability and possession of land and labor, the problem of the structure of land ownership in Second Temple Palestine has been central to the discussion of its economy. It has been postulated that Palestine followed the trend noted especially in Italy toward an increasing concentration of land into large estates controlled by a few city-dwelling landowners. This trend accelerated in Palestine in the first century C.E. because of the following factors: (1) the appropriation of land by the Herods as royal estates; (2) the apportioning of large tracts of land (appropriated from Jewish peasants) by Herod and his sons to their supporters and family members; (3) the foundation of military colonies especially by Herod; (4) the forfeiture of land by wealthy landowners on account of peasant indebtedness induced by crushing taxation, high rents, and crop failure; (5) and the confiscation of land for new foundations.

It is usually assumed not only that private estates swallowed up most of the fertile land but that up to a half or two-thirds of the land was Herod's private property. The result was peasant landlessness, tenancy, hired day labor, and banditry. Unfortunately, the inference that large estates were the dominant mode of agricultural settlement in Palestine is driven by theory. There is simply no evidence to support such conclusions. Whereas extant sources do indicate a relation between the inability to pay taxes and banditry (e.g., *Ant.* 18.274), the overall negative impact of taxation in the early Roman period on peasants has been grossly exaggerated. There are no known Roman landowners in Herod's kingdom, no *ager publicus,* and no traces of Roman-style estates in Jewish Palestine.

However, both literary sources and archaeological remains show that royal and private estates existed in Palestine from the Persian to the end of the early Roman periods. Nehemiah is credited with socioeconomic reforms that prevented "the nobles and the officials" from accumulating land foreclosed from impoverished and indebted inhabitants of Palestine (Neh. 5:1-13). The Hasmoneans owned landed property, partly inherited from their Hellenistic predecessors and partly acquired from freshly conquered territories. In the Herodian period estates were in the forms of royal lands, gift lands, and private estates. Herod owned the palm and balsam groves in ʿEin Gedi and Jericho (*Ant.* 9.7; 14.54; 15.93-96, 106-7, 132, 217; *J.W.* 1.138, 361-62, 397; 4.467-69; Pliny, *Naturalis Historia* 5.73; 12.111-23; Strabo, *Geographica* 16.2.41). He inherited these estates from the kings who preceded him (Pliny, *Naturalis Historia* 12.111). He also founded a palm grove and agricultural settlement at Phasaelis (*Ant.* 16.145; 18.31; *J.W.* 1.418; 2.167). Later, his son Archelaus developed the settlement Archelaïs (*Ant.* 17.340). Herod's most prominent land grants were to his veterans in Samaria/Sebaste (*Ant.* 15.296; *J.W.* 1.403), Gaba (*Ant.* 15.294; *J.W.* 3.36), and Heshbon (*Ant.* 15.294). After Octavian expanded his kingdom in 30 and 23 B.C.E., he settled 3,000 Idumeans in Trachonitis (*Ant.* 16.285, 292) and founded a colony for Babylonian and other Jews in Batanea (*Ant.* 17.23-31). Herod certainly owned land elsewhere, especially in the territories added to his kingdom by Octavian.

Herod gave land to members of his family (*Ant.* 17.147). One needs to distinguish between the transfer of tax revenues (Antipater [*Ant.* 16.250; see 17.96]; Pherora [*Ant.* 15.362; *J.W.* 1.483]; Salome [*Ant.* 17.321; *J.W.* 2.98]) and grants of estates (Salome [Phasaelis, *Ant.* 17.321; *J.W.* 2.98]; later, Berenice [*Life* 118–19]). Throughout his reign he gave land to his political supporters, despoiling the old Hasmonean aristocracy and his opponents in favor of a new aristocracy (*Ant.* 15.5-7; 17.305, 307; *J.W.* 1.293). These estates were not all in Jewish territory. Ptolemy had property in Samaria (*Ant.* 17.289; *J.W.* 2.69); Costobar's was in Idumea (*Ant.* 15.264); and Crispus, an official under Agrippa I, had an estate in Transjordania (*Life* 33).

There is no evidence that Herod and his scions changed the land ownership structure in Jewish Palestine, beyond the property and the acquisition practices they inherited, or that under them the consolidation of

ECONOMICS IN PALESTINE

estates was increased. No evidence exists that they acquired property by dispossessing freeholding Jewish peasants, converting them into tenants. Antipas was the first of the Herods to establish *poleis* in Jewish territory: Sepphoris, Tiberias, and Livias. Tiberias, the new foundation among them, was located in an abandoned, though fertile, burial ground (*Ant.* 18.27; 36-38; *J.W.* 2.168; cf. 3.516-21)). The city's conscripted inhabitants, including freed slaves, received land grants. No estates have been found in Galilee; Antipas' deposition was not due to unrest or complaints against him.

The appearance of rich landowners in the New Testament, particularly the Gospels, has been taken to reflect the preponderance of large estates in Herodian Palestine (Luke 12:16-21; 15:11-32; 16:1-8, 19; 20:9-16// Mark 12:1-9//Matt. 20:1-16; 21:33-41). Even if these passages described conditions in Palestine, they do not enable us to estimate the ownership pattern, especially given that the material also contains descriptions of individuals with small holdings, worked by the family and/or a single slave (Luke 17:7-9; 13:6-9; 14:17-19; Matt. 21:28-31; 13:45-46). Jesus' disciples are reported to have left their property, including fields, to follow him (Matt. 19:29//Mark 10:29-30), and early Christians sold their landholdings (Acts 4:34, 36-37; 5:1-11).

Although archaeological excavations have uncovered some estates dating from the Persian to the early Roman periods, much attention needs to be given to the dating of the data, since it appears that the number of estates in Jewish Palestine increased drastically in the later, Byzantine period. For the earlier periods, it is safe to say that, despite the presence of royal and private estates, the majority of land was independently held by small landowners.

Family holdings were worked by members of the family with the help of slave labor. Larger units employed the labor of tenant farmers, slaves, and occasional free hired laborers. Larger agricultural units had distinct advantages over smaller family holdings. The size of the holding and availability of resources allowed for better strategic planning and long-term development of the land. Profit could be maximized by cultivating different crops, and some holdings could specialize in certain crops, for example, olives or grapes. The ability to adopt new technologies would facilitate better and greater exploitation of the land, leading to increased yield and profit. Archelaus is known to have diverted half the water supply of a village for the irrigation of his estate, Archelaïs, which was afterward famed for the number of palms and the quality of dates (*Ant.* 17.340; 18.31; Pliny, *Naturalis Historia* 13.44). The estates in Jericho and ʿEin Gedi were served with aqueducts, dams, efficient drainage, constructed bridges, and roads.

Larger agricultural establishments would have provided the basis for an economy of scale. Their overall impact would have been limited, however, by the nature of available labor and technology. In any event, the lack of quantitative data and analysis on how much land actually belonged to estates renders the discussion of the economic significance of land ownership structure grossly inadequate.

Trade and Manufacture

Trade is one of the principal ways in which consumers have access to the goods that they do not grow or produce. Greater trade assumes and leads to a greater specialization of labor, in both agricultural and nonagricultural productions. Justification for discounting the significance of trade and nonagricultural production in the economy of Second Temple Palestine is found in Josephus' (*Ag. Ap.* 1.60) assertion that, Palestine not being a maritime nation, since its cities were built far from the sea, the Jews were not attracted by commerce with the outside world. They devoted themselves to cultivating their productive country. Hence, the Jewish economy is often thought to have been closed and self-sufficient, with very little exporting or importing. The scale of internal trade was small. There were no commercial centers (except Jerusalem), only temporary or seasonal local markets, meeting on Mondays and Thursdays. Rural communities were served by the traveling salesmen.

Interregional and foreign trade and nonagricultural production appear to have been more extensive than Josephus' apologetic statement allows. Palestine was fertile and productive (*J.W.* 3.42-44; 49–50; 516–21). In general, sufficient grain could have been produced to avoid the need for importation. However, since grain was imported during emergency and famine (*Ant.* 14.299-316; 20.51-52; 101), it may also have been imported at other times. Archaeological excavations have uncovered pottery from outside the territory. Palestine produced no metals, apart from copper. It imported the metal needed for agricultural, construction, and military purposes. Although clothing was most likely produced from local wool and flax, Jews must have imported fine linen. They probably participated in the silk trade. Spices that flowed from the east though Idumea to Gaza were in great demand for the Temple cult.

With Pompey's conquest in 63 B.C.E. the Jewish state lost the coastal cities and was indeed landlocked (*Ant.* 14.76; *J.W.* 1.156). In 47 B.C.E. Julius Caesar returned the seaport city of Joppa to the Jews (*Ant.* 14.205, 207-8). Caesar judged the commercial traffic through Joppa, and the resulting *portoria,* significant enough to merit a special tribute imposed on the Jews for its "land, the harbor and export" (*Ant.* 14.206). Earlier, Simon the Hasmonean's capture of the city was celebrated as the crown of all his honors (1 Macc. 14:5). His kingdom's involvement with external trade was important for Herod. He increased his control over the coastal overland trade route by rebuilding Antipatris (*Ant.* 16.142-43; *J.W.* 1.417; 4.443) as well as the seaport at Anthedon (Agrippias [*Ant.* 13.357; *J.W.* 1.87, 416]). According to Josephus (*Ant.* 15.333-34), Herod built Caesarea and its harbor as a remedy for the insufficiencies of the seaport at Joppa. Caesarea was the largest and the most sophisticated harbor in the Mediterranean. It remained for centuries the principal seaport entry into Palestine and Syria, controlling the patterns of trade in the region. Jews participated in the commercial activities of the city and harbor (*J.W.* 2.266-70, 287).

Studies of the distribution of common pottery have

pointed to the presence of regional trade in Palestine. The production of clay pottery was an important and widespread industry in Palestine. Such pottery comprised the utensils of everyday life. It attracted ritual impurities, was otherwise easily breakable, and could not be repaired if damaged. The distribution of clay pottery may not establish either the quantity or quality of trade generally.

The Gospels suggest that wealthy aristocrats invested in business ventures through their slaves (Matt. 25:14-30//Luke 19:12-26). There is inscriptional evidence of regional and local trade from the Hellenistic to early Roman periods. Sales attracted taxes. Herod reportedly imposed taxes upon public purchases and sales, possibly in the markets of Palestine (*Ant.* 17.205; *J.W.* 2.4). In 37 C.E. the governor of Syria, Vitellius, remitted to the inhabitants of Jerusalem the taxes that had been imposed upon the sale of agricultural produce (*Ant.* 18.90).

Balsam and dates were two of Palestine's main exports to the Greco-Roman world, and both came to symbolize the region (Pliny, *Naturalis Historia* 12.111; Tacitus, *Historiae* 5.6). In the Roman Empire, Balsam, which Josephus (*J.W.* 4.469) calls "the most precious of all the local plants," grew only in the Jordan Valley. Myrrh was also exported. Olive oil was considered a "blessing of mankind" and, with grain and wine, it was an absolute necessity for life in the Greco-Roman world. Traditional peasant diet derived up to a third of its calorie content from olive oil. It was the premier fuel for lighting and formed the base for other products: soaps, medications, skin ointments, perfume, and cosmetics. The oil was produced, marketed, and consumed in very large quantities. Apart from the production of oil, olives could be salted, pickled, rolled, or boiled for eating.

Olive oil's centrality to life in Jewish Palestine was noted from ancient times (Deut. 11:14; 2 Kings 18:32; Isa. 1:6; Eccl. 9:7-8). Josephus observes that the hills of Galilee were a special home to the olive (*J.W.* 2.592; 3.516), though the plant had adapted to other parts of Palestine. In the Hellenistic and early Roman periods, a custom developed that the Jews of Palestine and the Diaspora could not use foreign, that is, Grecian oil (*Ant.* 12.119-20; *J.W.* 2.591; *Life* 74). This requirement that Jews use "pure oil" (oil bought from other Jews) made it possible for John Gischala, during the revolt of 66 C.E., to make enormous profits by exporting oil from Galilee to the Jews of Caesarea Philippi (*J.W.* 2.591-92; *Life* 74–76). Gischala's commercial venture illustrates the fact that there was a demand and mechanism not only for regional, but also for long-distance trade in large volumes of quality oil from Palestine. Archaeological excavations have uncovered many oil presses that were used by estates, collectivities, and individual farm units for the production of oil.

Wine also would have been traded, at least locally. As elsewhere in the Roman Empire, the cultivation of olive trees and the production of oil would have been conducive to some specialized economy of scale. Trade in oil (and wine) supported other, nonagricultural productions and services, such as the production of amphorae and transportation.

These productions and services were also assumed by the fishing industry. Fish was an important component of the diet in Palestine, as in the rest of the ancient world, and was consumed in large quantities. In Palestine fish came from the Mediterranean, the Jordan River, and the Lake of Tiberias. The fishing industry flourished in the early Roman period. Several of the disciples of Jesus were fishermen. Fishermen constituted a significant segment of the population of Tiberias during the revolt of 66 C.E. (*Life* 36, 66, 134), and Josephus could, apparently, put together a fleet of 230 fishing boats from Tarichaea for his mock attack on Tiberias (*J.W.* 2.635-37). Some of the fish were salted and sold in local and regional markets.

Salt was not only a spice but also a mineral, dietary necessity, and large amounts were sold and consumed. It was expensive and probably attracted a tax under the Seleucids (*Ant.* 13.49). Salt was produced in the mountains of the Dead Sea area. During our period, the Dead Sea itself was known in the ancient world for asphalt (bitumen), used in the preparation of medicines and for embalming (Pliny, *Naturalis Historia* 5.72; 7.65; 28.80).

In spite of all the factors pointing to the presence of trade and other nonagricultural economic activities in Palestine, the absence in our sources of qualitative and quantitative information make it impossible to evaluate the extent and significance of these activities. In any event, one must not lose sight of the fact that grain production by Jewish peasants could not account for the relative prosperity of Palestine in the Herodian period. Herod conducted his imperial politics and domestic agenda with an eye on their economic benefits, particularly opening his kingdom to trade. Locally, the numerous building projects initiated by Herod, his sons after him, and others created employment for stone workers in the quarries, stone smoothers and polishers, skilled masons, plasterers, carpenters and other artisans, transportation workers, and other laborers. The Gospel tradition is unanimous in stating that Jesus, like his father, was a carpenter.

Foremost among the building programs in Palestine were the projects on the Temple Mount. The Jewish state in the Hellenistic and early Roman periods was a Temple state. Herod's Temple was a vast and complex economic enterprise. At its construction and for more than eighty years afterward work in the Temple provided employment for thousands of artisans, builders, tradesmen, and craftsmen (*Ant.* 15.390; 20.219-22; *J.W.* 5.36). The Temple's sacrificial demands stimulated livestock farming: cattle, sheep, and doves. There were provisions in the Temple complex for commercial activities. The most significant economic value of the Herodian Temple was in instituting and promoting mass pilgrimage of Diaspora Jews to Jerusalem. The economy received a continuous injection of large sums of money collected abroad, in the forms of Temple tax and votive gifts, and transported to the Temple by pilgrims (*Ant.* 14.112-13; 16.28, 162-65; 17.26; 18.312-13; *J.W.* 5.201-5; Philo, *Legatio ad Gaium* 156–57). These funds flowed into the general economy of the region through the purchase of sacrificial victims and other needs for the Temple, the provision of employment for the thousands who worked to maintain and beautify the complex, and the buying power of Temple officials. Pilgrims spent money in Jerusalem and the surrounding territory on transportation, food, lodging, souvenirs, personal needs, and whatever they required for sacrifices and worship. Pliny (*Naturalis Historia* 5.70) writes that Jerusalem was in the first century "by far the most famous city of the East and not of Judea only." The wealth of the city, and of the region, was due largely to the sanctity of its Temple.

BIBLIOGRAPHY

D. FIENSY 1991, *The Social History of Palestine in the Herodian Period: The Land Is Mine,* Lewiston, N.Y.: Edwin Mellen. • M. FINLEY 1973, *The Ancient Economy,* Berkeley: University of California Press. • M. FINLEY 1977, "The Ancient City: From Fustel de Coulanges to Max Weber and Beyond," *Comparative Studies in Society and Ancient History* 19: 305-27. • M. FREDERIKSEN 1975, "Theory, Evidence and the Ancient Economy," *Journal of Roman Studies* 65: 164-71. • S. FREYNE 1995, "Herodian Economics in Galilee: Searching for a Suitable Model," in *Modelling Early Christianity: Social Scientific Studies of the New Testament in Its Context,* ed. P. Esler, New York: Routledge, 23-46. • P. GARNSEY, K. HOPKINS AND C. WHITTAKER, EDS. 1983, *Trade in the Ancient Economy,* Berkeley: University of California Press. • M. GOODMAN 1990, "Kosher Olive Oil in Antiquity," in *A Tribute to Geza Vermes: Essays on Jewish and Christian Literature and History,* ed. P. Davies and R. White, Sheffield: Sheffield Academic Press, 227-45. • M. GOODMAN 1999, "The Pilgrimage Economy of Jerusalem in the Second Temple Period," in *Jerusalem: Its Sanctity and Centrality to Judaism, Christianity, and Islam,* ed. L. Levine, New York: Continuum, 69-76. • G. HAMEL 1990, *Poverty and Charity in Roman Palestine: First Three Centuries C.E.,* Berkeley: University of California Press. • P. HARLAND 2002, "The Economy of First-Century Palestine: State of the Scholarly Discussion," in *Handbook of Early Christianity: Social Science Approaches,* ed. A. Blasi, J. Duhaime, and P.-A. Turcotte, Walnut Creek, Calif.: Alta Mira, 511-27. • J. MANNING AND I. MORRIS, EDS. 2005, *The Ancient Economy: Evidence and Models,* Stanford, Calif.: Stanford University Press. • D. OAKMAN 1986, *Jesus and the Economic Questions of His Day,* Lewiston, N.Y.: Edwin Mellen. • H. PARKINS AND C. SMITH, EDS. 1998, *Trade, Traders and the Ancient City,* New York: Routledge. • J. PASTOR 1997, *Land and Economy in Ancient Palestine.* London: Routledge. • P. RICHARDSON 1996, *Herod: King of the Jews and Friend of the Romans,* Columbia: University of South Carolina Press. • Z. SAFRAI 1994, *The Economy of Roman Palestine,* London: Routledge. • E. P. SANDERS 1992, *Judaism: Practice and Belief, 63 BCE–66 CE,* London: SCM Press. • F. UDOH 2005, *To Caesar What Is Caesar's: Tribute, Taxes, and Imperial Administration in Early Roman Palestine (63 B.C.E.–70 C.E.),* Providence, R.I.: Brown University Press.

See also: Agriculture; Temple Tax; Tithing; Tribute and Taxes

FABIAN E. UDOH

Education

It is a paradox that although many writings in the Hebrew Bible and in Second Temple literature are the products of school activity, there is very little discussion of schools in the texts themselves. Relevant sources from the Second Temple period provide only indirect and incidental evidence of Jewish education. Most of the direct evidence for school education comes from later, rabbinic sources.

History

Evidence for education in the land of Israel predates the Persian period. For example, there are writing exercises from Kuntillat Ajrud in the Sinai that date to the preexilic period. In the wisdom books of the Hebrew Bible, mother and father are the primary educators of children (Prov. 1:8). Immediately after a basic declaration of faith and ethics (Deut. 6:4-5), the book of Deuteronomy describes a family educational program: "Keep these words in your heart. Teach them diligently to your children and talk about them" (Deut. 6:6-7). Deuteronomy also commands historical inquiry and remembrance (Deut. 32:7; cf. Ps. 78:4). According to Ezra 7:25, the Persian king Artaxerxes issued a royal decree commissioning Ezra to appoint officials to teach Judeans the Law of their God. Even if this decree is not historical, it represents an ideal developed in a crucial scene in which Ezra reads the Law of Moses before all the people — men, women, and older children. He stands on a wooden platform, and the Hebrew text is translated (into Aramaic) and interpreted (Neh. 8:1-12). These few verses witness to the beginning of synagogue worship, targum, and midrash. Women and children are notably included in the public assembly, even though women would not normally be students in Jewish schools.

Sources

Hellenistic Period

For the early Hellenistic period, there are four significant witnesses to Jewish education.

1. Greek gymnasia, the bearers of Greek civic culture, were introduced into Jerusalem by some high-priestly families in the second century B.C.E. (1 Macc. 1:1-15; see Doran 2001; Doran 2002).

2. The Maccabean traditionalists reacted to this move by developing schools of their own. We get a sense of an old scribal school or academy from Ben Sira, especially in his description of the life of the scribe (Sir. 38:24-34; 39:1-1). The scribe has leisure to study; he studies the Torah above all but also the wisdom of the ancient world including Babylon, Egypt, and Greece; he studies Israelite prophecy, aphorisms, and parables; he travels to learn more; he rises early to pray, combines study and prayer, acknowledging his need for divine guidance; he preaches, teaches, lectures in the community, and serves as an advisor in the government; he is thus not at the top of the social ladder but has an honored place.

3. The library discovered in the caves near Qumran provides evidence of an alternate priestly group alien-

ated from the Temple establishment. They lived by a set of strict community rules, combining study with prayer and copying all the books of the Hebrew Bible except Esther, along with other works that we could call Apocrypha and Pseudepigrapha. The members of this group were thus both conservative traditionalists and remarkably creative masters of the biblical tradition. Their rule of life mandated round-the-clock study of Torah (1QS 6:6-8), or at least a regular evening study period for a third of the night, with time to ask questions.

4. The Wisdom of Solomon, an Alexandrian work written in Greek, provides a good example of early Hellenistic Judaism. It shows how Jews of the Diaspora could master much of Greek philosophy (middle Platonism and Stoicism, in particular) while still retaining the Deuteronomic polemic against idolatry as well as the Exodus traditions.

Roman Period

From the Roman period, important witnesses to Jewish education include Philo, Josephus, and early rabbinic writings, especially *Pirqê 'Abot.* Philo is the outstanding representative of the great synagogue at Alexandria and its adjoined school. The Septuagint is his Bible, and he comments in depth on the Pentateuch. His culture includes a wide range of Greek philosophy. He illustrates the synthesis of two cultures achieved by Hellenistic allegorical exegesis of the Bible. He presents the synagogue as a school of virtue and of nature; for him, the Torah is natural law. It is also the true and highest culture *(paideia).* Children are taught the written law and the unwritten customs or oral law (*Life of Moses* 1.215-16; *Embassy to Gaius* 115; 210; *On Planting* 144; *On the Preliminary Studies,* passim).

Josephus (*Ag. Ap.* 1.60; 2.170-78; 204; *Ant.* 4.209-11; 20.264) represents the traditions of Aramaic-speaking Palestinian Judaism of the first century C.E., but in Greek dress. Thus he speaks of the major Judean parties as though they were philosophical schools analogous to the four Athenian schools. Like Philo, he emphasizes the role of Torah in teaching the four cardinal virtues. He states that the education of children and the observance of both the written laws and the oral tradition are the highest priorities. He argues that the Mosaic legislation is superior to various Greek polities because it combines both theoretical and practical training. He enjoins sobriety and affirms that regular Sabbath study makes ignorance of the Law inexcusable. He adds to earlier legislation that slaves should be present at the reading of the Law. He asserts that for Jews true wisdom consists in an exact knowledge of the Law and the capacity to interpret it well, rather than in rhetorical training or mastery of many languages. In this respect, Josephus is a direct witness to an idea found in later, rabbinic literature.

The Mishnah tractate *Pirqê 'Abot,* which was written ca. 220 C.E., contains both earlier sayings and later additions and glosses. It is the only mishnaic tractate to be included in the Jewish prayer book *(Siddur).* Its teaching was developed in the talmudic tractate *'Abot de Rabbi Nathan,* both of whose recensions (A and B, but especially B) emphasize study. *Pirqê 'Abot* solidifies into a fixed ideology Torah study as the central value of rabbinic Judaism. Study is the goal of Jewish life and the highest joy. The opening paragraph (1:1) traces the rabbinic chain of tradition back to Moses and Sinai. Sinai here serves as a reverent circumlocution for God so that the tradition is theologically anchored. At the same time, the tradition is secured through successors: Joshua, the elders, the prophets, the scribes, and the rabbis. (Notably, priests are not mentioned.) There follows a command to raise up many disciples — an educational goal — and to make a fence around the Torah. The most probable meaning of this fence is that the rabbis are to formulate laws supplementary to those in Scripture, to act as a safeguard and protection for those chief laws.

Primary Education

According to a late addition in *Pirqê 'Abot* (5:21), boys began reading and memorizing Leviticus at age five, moving on to the Mishnah at age ten and then the Talmud at fifteen. This is an idealized program. Aqiba did not begin to study until he was in his late forties; Eliezer ben Hyrcanus began at twenty-one (*'Abot de Rabbi Nathan* [A] 6; [B] 12–13).

Jewish primary schools developed later than did secondary schools. There is relatively little evidence for their presence before the first century C.E. (*y. Ketub.* 8:11 [32c]), though the elementary school exercises from Kuntillat Ajrud noted above should not be forgotten. Their late development may owe to the biblical injunction that children be taught at home. In a Hebrew primary school *(bêt sēper* or *bêt sôpēr),* boys from ages six to ten were taught by a scribe *(sôpēr).* Discipline was usually strict. The boys studied a curriculum that resembled that of Hellenistic reading schools, though with Hebrew replacing Greek and Latin and the Torah substituting for Homer and the classics. They began with the alphabet, learning to recite it backward and forward (*b. Šabbat* 31), and then moved on to reading and memorizing biblical texts, reciting parts of the liturgy, and (in regions where Aramaic was spoken) translating into Aramaic (targum).

Secondary Education

The existence of a Jewish secondary school *(bêt midraš)* is attested as early as the second century B.C.E. (Sir. 51:23). The Jewish school was the equivalent of the Greek gymnasium, with students living in intimacy with their master and learning both theory and practice. Boys aged ten to thirteen years began studying the oral Torah, both midrash (commenting on a continuous text) and Mishnah (studying texts arranged topically). Paul probably is referring to the oral Torah in Gal. 1:14. A Diaspora Jew from Tarsus whom the book of Acts (22:3) describes studying in Jerusalem under Gamaliel, he says that he "advanced in Judaism beyond many of my own age, so extremely zealous was I for the traditions of my fathers."

Evidently, Greek was not taught in Jewish secondary schools, but students who needed it for their future careers could go to a Greek school to learn it. After mastering the oral law, Jewish teenagers could go on to study biblical exegesis at a more advanced level. This was the preferred route for those who wanted training to become a scribe, teacher, judge, or synagogue official. Under the tutelage of a rabbi-scholar, boys in their mid and late teens could also pursue other subjects such as astronomy, mathematics, and mystical or philosophical studies. A student's course of studies was concluded by a laying on of hands *(semiha)* and the awarding of a diploma signed by the rabbi. This rite was not an ordination but an attestation that the student had become a master of Jewish learning.

Vocational Training and Informal Education

Boys above age thirteen who did not continue their studies received vocational training, either from their fathers (*t. Qidd.* 1:11) or by being apprenticed to a master craftsman. There were also opportunities for informal study outside of schools. On Sabbaths and during festivals, the synagogue became the setting for the public reading of the targums to the Torah and Prophets, followed by a sermon. Reading in the synagogue was done by members of the congregation who were invited to do so (cf. Luke 4:16-30). For Jewish males, Torah study was expected to be lifelong.

Settings and Structures

Until the Temple was destroyed, the buildings in which Jewish education in the land of Israel took place were the porticoes of the Temple and then, alongside and after the Temple, schoolrooms within or next to houses of prayer and assembly (cf. Sir. 51:23); or, for children, a room *(heder)*. The Theodotus inscription attests that from the first century C.E. onward, synagogues became buildings devoted to Jewish education and worship. Their primary function was the study and teaching of Torah, besides having a secondary function as a guest house or inn.

After 70 C.E., the rabbinical academy in Israel relocated for a time to Jamnia (Yavneh). It absorbed the judicial function of the law courts (Sanhedrin) and the legislative function, in a manner analogous to a church synod. Schools were financed by local communities. The ideal was that one should not accept direct payment for teaching Torah, so a series of indirect subventions was devised. For example, a teacher (who usually had a trade as well) could open up his stall to sell his wares an hour before other traders on market day, and he could be compensated for not working at a lucrative craft. There were also tithes for sages of priestly descent and, later, tax exemptions or taxes for the *naśi*.

BIBLIOGRAPHY

M. ABERBACH 1982, *Jewish Education in the Period of the Mishnah and Talmud,* Jerusalem: Reuven (in Hebrew). • J. BLENKINSOPP 1995, "The Sage," in idem, *Sage, Priest, and Prophet: Religious and Intellectual Leadership in Ancient Israel,* Louisville: Westminster John Knox, 9-65. • D. M. CARR 2005, *Writing on the Tablet of the Heart: Origins of Scripture and Literature,* New York: Oxford University Press. • J. L. CRENSHAW 1998, *Education in Ancient Israel: Across the Deadening Silence,* New York: Anchor. • R. DORAN 2001, "The High Cost of a Good Education," in *Hellenism in the Land of Israel,* ed. J. J. Collins and G. E. Sterling, Notre Dame: University of Notre Dame Press, 94-115. • R. DORAN 2002, "Jewish Education in the Seleucid Period," in *Second Temple Studies,* vol. 3, *Studies in Politics, Class, and Material Culture,* ed. P. R. Davies and J. M. Halligan, London: Sheffield Academic Press, 116-32. • N. H. DRAZIN 1940, *History of Jewish Education from 515 B.C.E. to 200 C.E.*, Baltimore: Johns Hopkins University Press. • E. EBNER 1956, *Elementary Education in Ancient Israel during the Tannaitic Period (10–220 C.E.),* New York: Bloch. • B. EGO AND H. MERKEL, EDS. 2005, *Religioses Lernen in der biblischen, frühjudischen und frühchristlichen Überlieferung,* Tübingen: Mohr-Siebeck. • B. LANG 1979, "Schule und Unterricht im alten Israel," in *La sagesse de l'Ancien Testament,* ed. M. Gilbert, Leuven: Peeters. • A. LEMAIRE 1981, *Les écoles et la formation de la Bible dans l'ancien Israël,* Göttingen: Vandenhoeck & Ruprecht. • A. MENDELSON 1982, *Secular Education in Philo of Alexandria,* Cincinnati: Hebrew Union College Press. • S. SAFRAI 1971, *Jewish Society through the Ages,* ed. H. H. Ben Sasson and S. Ettinger, New York: Schocken • S. SAFRAI 1976, "Education and the Study of Torah," in *The Jewish People in the First Century,* vol. 2, ed. S. Safrai and M. Stern, Assen: Van Gorcum; Philadelphia: Fortress, 945-70. • M. SCHWABE 1949, "On Jewish and Graeco-Roman Elementary Schools in the Days of the Mishnah and Talmud," *Tarbiz* 21: 112-23 (in Hebrew). • B. T. VIVIANO 1978, *Study as Worship: Aboth and the New Testament,* Leiden: Brill.

See also: Gymnasium BENEDICT T. VIVIANO

Egypt

The first evidence of a Jewish presence in Egypt in the Second Temple period concerns a military settlement at Elephantine on the border between Egypt and Nubia, which existed until at least the end of the fifth century B.C.E. Jews living in Egypt are also mentioned by Jeremiah (44:1; 46:14). However, it was only with Alexander the Great's conquest of Egypt in 332 B.C.E. that immigration of Jews and other groups from around the Mediterranean began on a large scale, encouraged particularly by Ptolemy I (305-282 B.C.E.).

The Ptolemaic Period

Evidence for Jewish Settlement

Some Aramaic and Greek epitaphs from the early Ptolemaic period confirm the presence of Jews at Alexandria. Josephus claims in different places that Alexander (*J.W.* 2.487; *Ag. Ap.* 2.35) or Ptolemy I (*Ant.* 12.8) gave the Jews equal status with the Greeks at Alexandria, but this is an attempt to use history to support the Jewish cause in the later intercommunal troubles in the city. Alexandria's population consisted of a Greek elite, various other ethnic groups who were encouraged to settle there, and a native Egyptian element with no rights in the city. According to Philo (*In Flaccum* 55), the Jews, who became by far the most important of the non-Greek ethnic groups, lived throughout the city but mainly concentrated in two of the five "quarters." Josephus (*J.W.* 2.488)

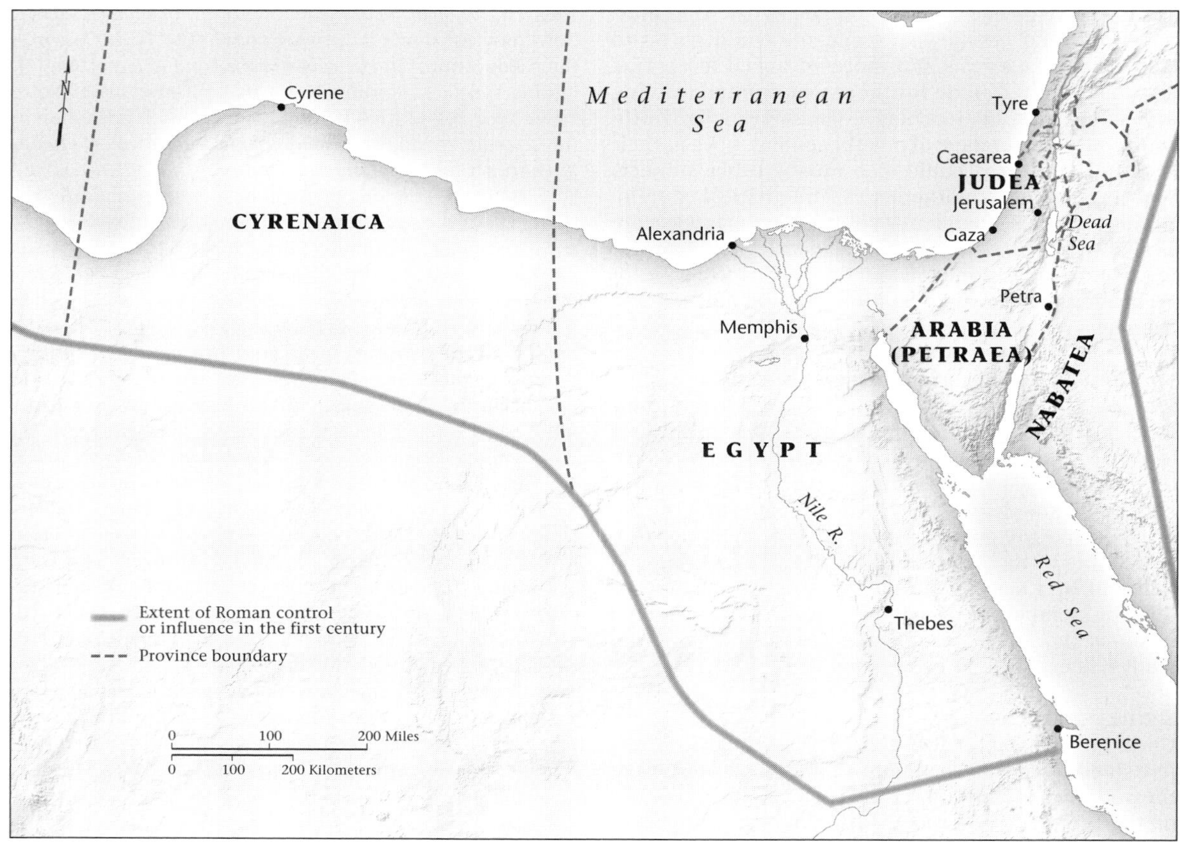

EGYPT IN THE EARLY ROMAN PERIOD

states that the Ptolemies allocated them an area of the city for their exclusive use, but this view may have been influenced by later developments. Some Jews came as soldiers in the Ptolemaic army, from which native Egyptians were excluded, and some of these were given the status of cleruchs, military settlers with substantial plots of land in the countryside. There is also evidence from papyri of Jews in a variety of civilian occupations.

Relations of Egyptian Jews with Judea

Judea was under the control of the Ptolemies for most of the period until 198 B.C.E., which must have facilitated emigration to Egypt. There is some evidence of interaction between the Egyptian Jews and Jerusalem. 1 Maccabees 15:16-21, supposedly a letter from Rome to "King Ptolemy," tells him to hand over to "Simon the High Priest" any Jewish "traitors" who have fled to Egypt. 2 Maccabees begins with "letters to the Jews in Egypt," dated to the second half of the second century B.C.E., encouraging the Egyptian Jews to celebrate the purification of the Temple by the Maccabees.

Relations of Egyptian Jews with Non-Jews

There is also evidence of local hostility to the Jews. Manetho, an Egyptian priest and courtier of Ptolemy II (282-246 B.C.E.), attacked them in writings which are known, possibly in a later, edited form, from their refutation by Josephus (*Ag. Ap.* 1.73). Manetho seems to have recorded Egyptian versions of the biblical stories of Joseph and Moses, identifying the Hyksos (so-called "shepherd-kings" who ruled Egypt in the seventeenth to sixteenth centuries B.C.E.) as Judeans and making Moses a renegade Egyptian priest who led an exodus of lepers. These ideas were still current in the first century C.E.

A very different view of relations between Jews and non-Jews in Egypt is found in the *Letter of Aristeas*. This is a work of Jewish authorship by someone who seems to have had inside knowledge of the Ptolemaic court (Aristeas is not the name of the real author but of a Gentile courtier to whom the writing is attributed). It aims to portray happy coexistence and mutual respect between Ptolemaic rulers and Jewish subjects. Its date is very uncertain; the second century B.C.E. is generally accepted, and the last part of the century may be the most likely. Its subject is the creation of the Septuagint, the Greek version of Jewish Scripture. This translation probably happened not on the initiative of Ptolemy II, as the *Letter* claims, but in response to the needs of Alexandrian Jews who required texts in Greek, the main language of Alexandria, rather than in Hebrew. The most likely date of the translation of the Torah is the mid-third century B.C.E., with Greek versions of the other books added later. An annual festival to celebrate the translation was still held on the island of Pharos in the first century C.E. (Philo, *Mos.* 2.41).

Jewish Self-Organization

Some towns outside Alexandria had Jewish districts or streets, and at least in Herakleopolis the Jews seem to have been organized as a self-governing *politeuma.* A number of Greek inscriptions from the Nile Delta area show the existence of Jewish prayer houses *(proseuchai),* and also show their communities' loyalty to their Ptolemaic rulers; the inscriptions are dedications "on behalf of" the monarchs (not "to" them), and they avoid the divine titulature of calling the king a god which is normally found in Egyptian inscriptions. They cover most of the Ptolemaic period: the earliest is from Schedia (reign of Ptolemy III, 246-221 B.C.E.) and the latest from Gabbary, Alexandria, probably to be dated to 37 B.C.E.; there are also examples from Athribis, Nitriai, and Xenephyris. At Athribis, the principal dedicator had the title "chief of police" *(epistatēs tōn phylakitōn).* There is also a synagogue inscription from Arsinoe-Crocodilopolis in the Fayûm area further south, dated to the reign of Ptolemy III, and papyri show that there were two synagogues there in the Roman period. There was a synagogue at Alexandrou Nesos in the Fayûm in 217 B.C.E. One synagogue had a plaque recording that Ptolemy VIII (145-116 B.C.E.) had declared it "inviolate" *(asylos).*

Jews and non-Jews must have shared local facilities in most places, and there is ample evidence for interaction. At the temple of Pan at El-Kanaïs on the road from Apollinopolis Magna (Edfu) to Berenice on the Red Sea, there was a custom of inscribing thanksgivings to the god on the rock face. Two men who specifically describe themselves as Jews did this, giving their thanks to an unnamed god *(theos)* rather than to Pan, and a man named Lazarus recorded that he had come for the third time.

3 Maccabees

The work known as 3 Maccabees (although it has nothing to do with the Maccabees) is set in the time of Ptolemy IV (225-205 B.C.E.) and shows an attempt by that king to massacre (by trampling with elephants) the Egyptian Jews who refused to convert to the worship of Dionysus. The story seems to be fantasy (though Mélèze-Modrzejewski 1995: 149-52 makes a case for some historicity), probably written in the Roman period since it appears to mention the poll tax, which was only instituted then. However, there are some accurate Ptolemaic details, including a courtier named Dositheus son of Drimylus, of Jewish origin, whose name is also found in papyri (*CPJ* 127) as royal secretary *(hypomnematographos)* in ca. 240-224 B.C.E. and as a priest of Alexander and the Ptolemies in 223-222 B.C.E. Josephus (*Ag. Ap.* 2.53-55) tells a similar story of a Ptolemy trying to massacre Jews, but set in the reign of Ptolemy VIII (145-116 B.C.E.), and says that an annual festival was held by the Alexandrian Jews to celebrate their unexpected and miraculous delivery from this danger.

The Temple at Leontopolis

Ptolemy VI (180-145 B.C.E.) permitted the foundation of a breakaway Jewish temple by Onias IV, the son of the high priest Onias III who left Jerusalem after his father's deposition in ca. 174 B.C.E. and the subsequent troubles (Josephus, *Ant.* 12.387; *J.W.* 7.423 attributes it to Onias III himself, but this must be a mistake). The new temple was linked to a military colony referred to as "the land of Onias," and was built on an abandoned pagan site at Leontopolis on the eastern edge of the Nile Delta. Its existence was justified by reference to Isa. 19:18-19, which prophesies that there will be "an altar to the LORD in the midst of the land of Egypt, and a pillar to the LORD at its border." The settlement was strategically important to the Ptolemies as a defense against the Seleucids who now controlled Judea, and could have formed a useful starting point for a Ptolemaic attempt to recapture Judea. Josephus (*Ag. Ap.* 2.48) says with obvious exaggeration that Onias and another Jew, Dositheus, were generals of the whole Ptolemaic army. There are a few references to the temple at Leontopolis in rabbinic literature, but none at all in Alexandrian Jewish writings, and it seems that it was a focus only for the Jews who settled around it and not for all Egyptian Jews. Excavations in the late nineteenth century produced little evidence for the temple, but many Greek epitaphs were found for people with distinctively Jewish names; a number of these are dated to the reign of Augustus (30 B.C.E.–14 C.E.). The temple continued to function until Vespasian ordered its closure and spoliation in 74 C.E. for fear of its becoming a stronghold for surviving rebels.

Jewish Involvement in Ptolemaic Politics

The Jews of Onias' settlement and those of Alexandria became involved in Ptolemaic dynastic politics, which descended increasingly into factional fighting and civil war. They supported Cleopatra II, widow of Ptolemy VI (who died in 145 B.C.E.), against Ptolemy VIII; this is the context of Josephus' account of the attempted massacre referred to above. Onias IV, or more probably his sons Chelkias and Ananias, supported Cleopatra III against her son Ptolemy IX (joint reign 116-107 B.C.E.), and Ananias persuaded her not to try to conquer Judea (Josephus, *Ag. Ap.* 2.48-53; *Ant.* 13.287 quoting Strabo, *Ant.* 13.349, 354). A late source mentions Alexandrian violence against the Jews under Ptolemy X (107-88 B.C.E.) (Jordanes, *Romana* 81, probably based on Jerome).

The restoration by Roman forces of Ptolemy XII in 55 B.C.E. seems to have had Jewish support both from Judea and from a Jewish military unit guarding the border at Pelusium at the eastern end of the Delta (Josephus, *J.W.* 1.175; *Ant.* 14.98-99). Julius Caesar also received help from the land of Onias when he was trapped at Alexandria in 48-47 B.C.E.; Antipater (the father of Herod the Great) persuaded the Jews there to allow the relieving force through (Josephus, *J.W.* 1.187-92;

Ant. 14.127-32). Cleopatra VII, the last of the Ptolemaic rulers, was on bad terms with Herod, who survived as a Roman client king through the protection of Mark Antony, and this may be why she was also hostile to the Jews of Alexandria, refusing them food rations during a famine (Josephus, *Ag. Ap.* 2.60).

Egyptian Jewish Literature

Jewish literature in Greek flourished in Ptolemaic Egypt. Numerous works have survived only in fragments, usually preserved by Christian writers. Many of them show the influence of the Septuagint. Demetrius (probably in the late third century B.C.E.) wrote a history based on biblical stories about Jacob and Moses, with clarified chronology. Artapanus wrote on Abraham, Joseph, and Moses, to whom he attributed the beginning of the annual flooding of the Nile. Ezekiel wrote a Greek tragedy based on the Exodus story. Aristobulus, who seems to have dedicated his work to Ptolemy VI, wrote philosophical texts which identified Moses as the founder of philosophy. *Joseph and Aseneth* is a Greek novel with the theme of Aseneth's conversion to Judaism. *Sibylline Oracles* 3 contains "prophecies" put into the mouth of a Jewish Sibyl. The Wisdom of Solomon probably comes from late Ptolemaic Egypt, although different opinions have been expressed about both date and provenance; it shows much Greek cultural influence, but Barclay (1996:184) argues that its main theme is antagonism between Jews and non-Jews. The *Testament of Job* is thought by many to come from early Roman Egypt, probably in the context of the difficulties experienced by the Alexandrian Jews.

The Roman Period

The Civic Status of Alexandrian Jews

It is likely that the Roman takeover of Egypt in 30 B.C.E. was welcomed by the Jewish population. According to Josephus (*Ag. Ap.* 2.37, 61) Augustus erected a stele at Alexandria confirming the rights that Alexander and the Ptolemies had given to the Jews. These rights are not specified but presumably included religious freedom and some degree of self-government. There has been debate about whether the Jews of Alexandria were organized as an autonomous *politeuma* as other ethnic groups of originally military settlers were, and it has been argued (Honigman 2003) that they were, but that the literary sources other than the *Letter of Aristeas* do not mention it because they prefer to represent the Jewish population as having equal rights with the Alexandrians rather than a special and separate status. Philo (*In Flaccum* 43) claims that there were a million Jews in Egypt in the early Roman period, living in Alexandria and throughout the rest of Egypt (the *chōra*), but this is clearly an exaggeration. Méléze-Modrzejewski (1995: 74) suggests that Jews numbered roughly 300,000 or 4 percent of the total population.

The situation of the Jews of Alexandria under Roman rule was somewhat anomalous. They had their own council of elders *(gērousia),* which Augustus instituted, probably in 10-12 C.E., in place of an individual leader called the *genarch* (Philo, *In Flaccum* 74; Josephus, *Ant.* 14.117, refers to the *ethnarch*). The city itself had no council *(boulē),* an exceptional position for a Greek city and one which became a major grievance against Rome. Alexandrian citizenship was largely confined to those of purely Greek descent, but some Jewish families, including Philo's, apparently acquired it without giving up their Jewish identity. Philo criticized people who abandoned Jewish observance to help their social advancement, and also those whose allegorical interpretation of Jewish law was used as a justification for not keeping Jewish customs; assimilation was evidently a controversial issue. When Augustus instituted the poll tax *(laographia)* in Egypt, the question of citizenship became crucial, since Alexandrian citizens did not have to pay it. The Jewish population was subject to it, like the Egyptians, and the Jews' lower status was symbolized when Germanicus excluded them from a corn distribution to citizens in 19 C.E. (Josephus, *Ag. Ap.* 2.63-64).

Thus the Jews of Alexandria resented having to pay the poll tax and being classed with the Egyptians, while the Alexandrian citizens resented the privileges that the Jewish community had in the city. It has been argued that the Alexandrian Greeks used the Jews as scapegoats for their hostility to the Romans (van der Horst 2002), but also that there was no perceived identification of Roman and Jewish interests (Alston 2002). Philo's tendency to blame the setbacks of the Jews on "Egyptians" rather than Greeks is clearly a rhetorical strategy, since he and others like him regarded themselves as entitled to membership of the Alexandrian Greek elite.

The First Anti-Jewish Pogrom

In 38 C.E. communal tensions at Alexandria came to a head with what was effectively the first recorded pogrom, vividly if selectively described by Philo, an eyewitness, in his work *In Flaccum* (translation and commentary in van der Horst 2003). A visit to Alexandria by Agrippa I, who was on his way from Rome to take up his role as client king in part of Herod the Great's old kingdom, sparked the trouble. His acclamation by the Jews must have been felt as an affront by the Alexandrians, whose grievances were aggravated by what they perceived as favoritism toward the Jews. The Roman governor of Egypt, A. Avillius Flaccus, wished to ingratiate himself with the new emperor Caligula and probably with the leaders of the Alexandrians, and may have felt his position undermined by Agrippa I. He encouraged the Alexandrians as they looted houses, desecrated synagogues by setting up busts of the emperor in them, and murdered Jews. The Jews who previously lived throughout the city were ghettoized in the Delta quarter. A large group was forced to eat pork in the theater. Flaccus declared them aliens within the city, which removed the rights they previously enjoyed. There was also a military search of Jewish houses looking for concealed weapons.

Philo does not make it very clear how the violence ended, but Flaccus was replaced as governor and arrested, probably for unconnected reasons. The Jews used Agrippa I to send an appeal to the emperor Caligula, but they also sent their own delegation to Rome to report their grievances. This was led by Philo himself, who has left a vivid account (*Legatio ad Gaium;* text and commentary in Smallwood 1970). The opposing delegation that the Alexandrians sent at the same time was led by Apion, whose anti-Jewish writings were later given a literary response by Josephus in his *Contra Apionem* (text and commentary in Barclay 2007).

The Literary Legacy of Philo of Alexandria

The huge literary output of Philo, writing in Greek at Alexandria in the early Roman period, had plenty of precedent. His works have survived in their own right, but their transmission was eventually by Christian rather than Jewish scribes. Philo was at home in the literary worlds of both Jewish theology and Greek philosophy. He had a gymnasium-based Greek education and seems to have attended civic events, although it has been argued that he was of Jewish priestly ancestry. He was a member of a very wealthy and influential family which probably acquired Roman citizenship from Augustus, and his view of Rome is normally positive. His brother Alexander held the post of *alabarch* (controller of customs) and was manager of the Egyptian property of Antonia (mother of the future emperor Claudius); he was so wealthy that he was able to have the nine gates of Herod's Temple overlaid with plates of silver and gold. Alexander's son Tiberius Julius Alexander (see below) held very high rank in Roman imperial administration, and another son, Marcus Julius Alexander, married Berenice the daughter of Agrippa I.

Most of Philo's writings are on theology and the interpretation of the Scriptures, but some provide information on the world in which he lived. One of his treatises *(De Vita Contemplativa)* describes a small community which he calls the Therapeutae; their name probably indicates "servants of God" rather than "healers." It is not clear whether Philo's description is based on personal experience, but it is now generally accepted as being reasonably factual. They lived a monastic lifestyle near Lake Mareotis just outside Alexandria, studying Scripture. The community included both men and women ("mostly aged virgins"), who were partially segregated when common meetings were held on the Sabbath but joined in ecstatic singing together; members normally lived in individual huts. Recent work suggests that the Therapeutae came from the Alexandrian Jewish elite and deliberately located themselves near the city (Taylor 2003). Similarities have been noted between the Therapeutae and the Essenes, a group of which Philo also had some knowledge.

The Claudian Embassy and Edict

When Caligula was assassinated in 41 C.E., some Alexandrian Jews took the opportunity to carry out reprisal attacks (Josephus, *Ant.* 19.278-79). New delegations were sent from Alexandria by both sides, and Claudius apparently had to deal with both old and new Jewish delegations separately. Barclay (1996: 57) suggests that Philo's group represented wealthy and placatory Jews while the second delegation was more militant. Claudius' decision has been preserved on papyrus (*CPJ* 153). He confirmed the Jews' right to practice their religion, but otherwise told them not to ask for more than they already had "in a city not their own," presumably rejecting any claim to Alexandrian citizenship, and making it impossible for anyone to retain Jewish identity while joining the Alexandrian elite. There has been much debate about whether the Alexandrian Jews hoped to achieve citizenship for all or were concerned only about their rights of self-government and not full citizenship. The issues are set out very clearly by Barclay (1996: 60-71). The leaders of the Greek delegation, Isidorus and Lampon, are depicted in a very hostile manner by Philo, who calls Isidorus a revolutionary *(stasiarchēs),* but an alternative view of them as Alexandrian patriots can be found in some texts that depict the embassy to Claudius from the Greek point of view (Musurillo 1954). In the *Acta Isidori,* Isidorus is depicted as calling Agrippa I "a three-obol Jew" and Claudius "the cast-off son of the Jewess Salome."

Egyptian Jewish Reactions to the First Revolt

During the Jewish War of 66-70 C.E., the Egyptian Jews appear to have been divided in their attitude. Communal violence at Alexandria in 66 led to violent suppression by the governor, Philo's nephew Tiberius Julius Alexander (who had been governor of Judea in 46-48). After three Jews were burned alive, the Jews attacked the Alexandrian citizens assembled in the amphitheater and two legions were used to suppress them. Josephus (*J.W.* 2.489-98) claims, no doubt with exaggeration, that 50,000 Jews were killed. There is no evidence of direct support from Egypt for the rebels in Judea. According to Josephus (*Ant.* 12.121-24), after the defeat of the rebels, Titus refused to strip the Alexandrian Jews of their remaining rights. Defeated rebels who fled to Egypt from Judea tried to foment revolt in Alexandria, but they were denounced by the *gērousia* and 600 were handed over to the Roman authorities (Josephus, *J.W.* 7.409-20).

The Jewish Tax

The Jewish tax imposed by Vespasian after the fall of Jerusalem meant that for the first time all Jews throughout Egypt (and everywhere else in the Roman Empire) had to be registered. The workings of the tax are well documented in Egypt because of the survival of a large number of ostraca from Apollinopolis Magna recording individual payments. It was a heavy burden as it was payable by all Jews aged three to sixty-two.

Delegations to Trajan

Jews and Greeks from Alexandria sent further delegations to Rome in the time of Trajan. This time the event is recorded only from the Greek point of view (*CPJ* 157). The fragmentary papyrus records the audience in an imaginative form with a bust of Serapis breaking into a sweat, and the issues at stake are not clear. Hermaiscus refers to "impious Jews" *(anosioi Ioudaioi),* a term also used in the context of the subsequent revolt. The emperor is depicted as being influenced by Jewish advisers, precisely the opposite of what Philo said about Caligula.

The Diaspora Revolt under Trajan

In 115-117 C.E., there was a major Jewish revolt in some of Rome's eastern provinces. Its details are unclear because of the very limited source material, and there has been much debate about the events and their causes. Papyri show that the revolt in Egypt probably began in mid-115 (*CPJ* 435), before Trajan's forces suffered a setback in Mesopotamia in mid-116, but at a time when the military presence in Egypt was depleted by his Parthian campaign. It is not clear if the conflict spread from Egypt to Cyrenaica or vice versa (the sources are contradictory), but Jews from Cyrenaica entered Egypt to join in, and the Cyrenaican leader Lukuas appears to have presented himself as a messianic figure.

Communal tension at Alexandria seems to have led to a full-scale civil war in the city in which both the Serapeum and the Great Synagogue were destroyed. A rabbinic source (*y. Sukkah* 5.1) attributes the destruction to "the evil Trajan"; the existence of the Great Synagogue, a building of such size that the congregation could not all hear the speakers, is, however, never mentioned by Philo. Roman intervention at this point appears to have been intended to protect the Jews after they were defeated. However, the revolt spread throughout Egypt in mid-116. One legion was defeated, and the rebels destroyed pagan temples. Appian (frg. 19) gives a firsthand account of escaping from the Jews across the Nile Delta, and *CPJ* 437 records a woman's prayer to Hermes that the Jews would not "roast" her son. A special force commanded by Q. Marcius Turbo was needed to suppress the revolt, fighting along with Egyptian villagers, and the Jews were defeated at Memphis in early 117. Much Jewish property was confiscated, and there is little evidence for Jews in the Egyptian *chōra* during the next century. "Jewish streets" at Oxyrhynchus and Hermopolis no longer had Jewish inhabitants. At Oxyrhynchus, the defeat of the revolt was still celebrated annually over eighty years later (*CPJ* 450).

BIBLIOGRAPHY

R. ALSTON 2002, *The City in Roman and Byzantine Egypt,* London: Routledge. • J. M. G. BARCLAY 1996, *Jews in the Mediterranean Diaspora,* Berkeley: University of California Press. • J. M. G. BARCLAY 2007, *Flavius Josephus: Against Apion,* Leiden: Brill. • P. M. FRASER 1972, *Ptolemaic Alexandria,* 3 vols., Oxford: Clarendon. • S. GAMBETTI 2009, *The Alexandrian Riots of 38 CE and the Persecution of the Jews,* Leiden: Brill. • S. HONIGMAN 2003, "Politeumata and Ethnicity in Ptolemaic Egypt," *Ancient Society* 33: 61-102. • W. HORBURY AND D. NOY 1993, *Jewish Inscriptions of Graeco-Roman Egypt,* Cambridge: Cambridge University Press. • A. KASHER 1985, *The Jews in Hellenistic and Roman Egypt: The Struggle for Equal Rights,* Tübingen: Mohr-Siebeck. • N. LEWIS 1983, *Life in Egypt under Roman Rule,* Oxford: Oxford University Press. • J. MÉLÈZE-MODRZEJEWSKI 1995, *The Jews of Egypt from Rameses II to Emperor Hadrian,* Edinburgh: Clark. • H. MUSURILLO 1954, *Acts of the Pagan Martyrs,* vol. 1, Oxford: Clarendon. • E. M. SMALLWOOD 1970, *Philo: Legatio ad Gaium,* 2d ed., Leiden: Brill. • J. E. TAYLOR 2003, *Jewish Women Philosophers of First-Century Alexandria: Philo's Therapeutae Reconsidered,* Oxford: Oxford University Press. • V. TCHERIKOVER, A. FUKS, AND M. STERN, EDS. 1957-64, *Corpus Papyrorum Judaicarum,* 3 vols., Cambridge: Harvard University Press. • V. TCHERIKOVER 1959, *Hellenistic Civilization and the Jews,* Philadelphia: Jewish Publication Society. • P. W. VAN DER HORST 2002, "The First Pogrom: Alexandria 38 CE," *European Review* 10: 469-84. • P. W. VAN DER HORST 2003, *Philo's Flaccus: The First Pogrom,* Leiden: Brill.

See also: Alexandria; Diaspora Uprisings (116-117 C.E.); Elephantine, Elephantine Papyri; Oniads; Ptolemies; Therapeutae DAVID NOY

ʿEin Feshkha

ʿEin Feshkha (Hebr. *Einot Zukim*) is located by brackish springs on the shore of the Dead Sea, 3 km. south of Qumran. The site was excavated by Roland de Vaux in 1958 and by Yizhar Hirschfeld in 2001.

The main building consists of an open courtyard surrounded by rooms, which was entered through two doorways on the east side. De Vaux suggested that the rooms on the north and south sides of the courtyard were storerooms. One of these rooms yielded a cylindrical stone weight inscribed with the letters LEB. A staircase on the southeast side of the building provided access to a roof terrace above the rooms on the northern and southern sides of the courtyard as well as to a second story of rooms on the western side. De Vaux suggested that these rooms served as residential quarters or offices.

Fragments of stone vessels were recovered in several rooms, including a large vase (71 cm. high) with an incised Hebrew inscription. Carefully cut square and triangular tiles made of gray and white stone were found in various loci, with the largest concentration coming from the open area to the north of the main building. De Vaux hypothesized that the tiles had been brought to the site and stored there for a planned construction that was never carried out, and he noted that the tiles were too few in number to pave a floor. De Vaux distinguished two main occupation phases at ʿEin Feshkha. According to him, Period I at ʿEin Feshkha was contemporary with Period Ib at Qumran (ca. 100-31 B.C.E.). However, Jodi Magness has suggested that Period I at ʿEin Feshkha dates to the reign of Herod the Great and postdates the earthquake of 31 B.C.E. Period II at ʿEin Feshkha appears be contemporary with Period II at Qumran, ending at the time of the First Jewish Revolt against the Romans. At the end of the first century or early in the second century, the rooms along the northern side of the courtyard were reoccupied, perhaps by Jewish rebels at the time of the Bar Kokhba Revolt. There was limited reoccupation of the southwest enclosure during the Byzantine period.

The area to the southwest of the main building was enclosed by walls measuring over forty meters on each side. A row of stone piers running parallel to the north wall supported an open porch or shed that could have provided temporary shelter for people or animals, or, as de Vaux suggested, might have been used as a drying shed for reeds or dates. In the Byzantine period (fifth to sixth centuries), a square room at the east end of the porch was rebuilt. This limited Byzantine reoccupation is probably associated with monastic activity.

Like the area to the southwest, the area to the north of the main building was enclosed by walls. The western half of the area seems to have been empty, but the eastern half contained a system of basins and water channels. The water apparently came from a freshwater spring at a higher level to the west that has now dried up. From its point of origin, the water was brought through the north wall of the enclosure via a sluice gate. Channels carried the water into a series of industrial basins and tanks to the southeast. Large stones carved roughly in the form of cylinders were used in the industrial activities conducted in this area.

De Vaux suggested that this industrial area was a tannery for the curing of animal hides. However, an analysis of deposits taken from the installations failed to turn up any traces of tannin or animal hairs. Therefore, Frederick Zeuner suggested that the pools were used to raise fish. However, de Vaux noted that the small size of the basins would have limited the number of fish that could be raised, while the presence of plaster on the basin walls would have inhibited the growth of algae and other plants on which fish feed. More recently, Robert Donceel and Mireille Belis have each suggested that the basins were used for the dyeing of textiles (using madder or indigo plants). Finally, based on similarities with installations at Herodian Jericho, Ehud Netzer has suggested that date wine was produced at ʿEin Feshkha.

Bibliography

K. Galor, J.-B. Humbert, and J. Zangenberg, eds. 2006, *Qumran: The Site of the Dead Sea Scrolls: Archaeological Interpretations and Debates,* Brill: Leiden. • Y. Hirschfeld 2004a, "Excavations at ʿEin Feshkha, 2001: Final Report," *IEJ* 54: 37-74. • Y. Hirschfeld 2004b, *Qumran in Context: Reassessing the Archaeological Evidence,* Peabody, Mass.: Hendrickson. • J.-B. Humbert and A. Chambon, eds. 1994, *Fouilles de Khirbet Qumrân et de Aïn Feshkha I: Album de Photographies, Repertoire du Fonds Photographique, Synthese des Notes de Chantier du P. Roland de Vaux OP,* Fribourg: Editions Universitaires. • J.-B. Humbert and A. Chambon, eds. 2003, *Excavations of Khirbet Qumran and Ain Feshka: Synthesis of Roland de Vaux's Notes,* trans. S. J. Pfann, Fribourg: Academic Press (Eng. trans., with corrections, of the 1994 French volume). • J.-B. Humbert and J. Gunneweg, eds. 2003, *Khirbet Qumran et ʿAin Feshkha II: Studies of Anthropology, Physics and Chemistry,* Fribourg: Academic Press. • J. Magness 2002, *The Archaeology of Qumran and the Dead Sea Scrolls,* Grand Rapids: Eerdmans. • R. de Vaux 1973, *Archaeology and the Dead Sea Scrolls,* Oxford: British Academy.

Jodi Magness

ʿEin Gedi

The oasis of ʿEin Gedi is situated between the eastern edge of the Judean Desert and the western shore of the Dead Sea. It is famous for its excellent palm tree plantations and spice gardens, and is irrigated by freshwater springs, which are the best in the region. In this remote place, far from the main roads, a Jewish village existed for a long period of time.

The contradiction between the large area of cultivated land in the oasis in the past and the small flow of the springs today is attributed by many scholars to climate changes. The prosperity of the oasis in the early Roman and the Byzantine periods evidently owed to an increased precipitation that amplified the spring's flow. The increase allowed the extension of the cultivated land of the oasis.

The settled farmers of ʿEin Gedi made their living from artificial irrigation agriculture. The combination of arid weather and perennial springs enabled them to grow palm trees and cash crops including spices, as described by ancient historians such as Josephus and Pliny. The water was supplied by water systems that flooded the fields on the terraces. After soaking the field area, the water was allowed to continue on to lower terraces. The time set for irrigation of every plot, by the hour and day in the week, was dictated by the water rights assigned to every plot, as mentioned in Judean Desert documents. There was also a system for water control, which regulated the functioning of the irrigation systems.

Three main crops were grown at ʿEin Gedi: palm trees, barley, and balsam. The leading crop of the region was, and still is, the palm tree. The best date species were even exported abroad (as is done today), and Jews were not allowed to sell some excellent species to Gentiles, as they might have been sacrificed to their gods (*m. ʿAbod. Zar.* 1:5).

Life at ʿEin Gedi was connected to the cultivation of palm trees: "No part of the palm tree is wasted: the dates are for eating; the *lulav* branches are for waving in praise on Sukkot; the dry thatch is for roofing; the fibers are for ropes; the leaves are for sieves; and the trunk is for house beams" (*Midr. Bamidbar Rab.* 3:1). Even the rest of it was used as fuel for the ovens, and indeed ash was seen during the archaeological survey and excavations in the agricultural terraces.

The first permanent building in the ʿEin Gedi oasis was built during the Chalcolithic period, when a shrine was erected near the ʿEin Gedi spring. After a long gap, Jews established a settlement in the seventh century B.C.E. Thereafter a Jewish village existed with a history of growth, ruin, and rebuilding until the middle of the sixth century C.E.

During the Second Temple Period, the village of ʿEin Gedi had houses that were exposed and adjacent to each other. Typical soft lime stone vessels and many Judean coins as well as a few Hellenistic and Nabatean coins have been found, along with local pottery and only one imported jar. Those who died there were buried enshrouded in cloth and placed within wooden coffins inside their family tombs. According to the latest coins found, the village was destroyed not earlier than 67/68 C.E. The village was rebuilt a few years later but in a different place, on the site where the Byzantine synagogue was eventually established. Few huts were built in the remotest part of the oasis. These huts were poorly constructed, without permanent roofs, and were used temporarily at the height of the harvest season. Some scholars regard it as an Essene village.

It is not clear when ʿEin Gedi became the property of the governing ruler of the region, whether during the Persian period or perhaps at the beginning of the Iron Age. Documents from the Judean Desert dating to the second century C.E. mention ʿEin Gedi as a village of the Roman Imperator. Thereafter it passed to Bar Kokhba, who included ʿEin Gedi among the properties of his state, Beit Israel.

Information concerning ʿEin Gedi diminishes in later periods. In the fourth century C.E., Eusebius described it as large village of Jews. The village synagogue of the sixth century C.E. has a decorated mosaic floor with inscriptions. One inscription forbids the members of the village to reveal the secret of the village — a secret that remains until today. Some say that the secret was connected with the balsam production, others that it may have been part of ancient prayers. A fire destroyed both the synagogue and the village in the sixth century, which ended a continuous period of Jewish settlement that was renewed only in the twentieth century, after the establishment of the State of Israel.

BIBLIOGRAPHY

E. STERN AND Y. HIRSCHFELD, EDS. 2007, *Excavations at En-Gedi: Final Report,* 2 vols., Jerusalem: Israel Exploration Society. • D. USSISHKIN 1980, "The Ghassulian Shrine at En-Gedi," *Tel Aviv* 7: 1-44. • G. HADAS 1994, "Nine Tombs of the Second Temple Period at ʿEn Gedi," *ʿAtiqot* 24: 1*-8* (Hebr. with Eng. abstract). • G. HADAS 2004, "Beer Barrels from Tel Goren, Ein Gedi," *RB* 11: 409-18. • G. HADAS 2005, "Excavations at the Village of ʿEn Gedi: 1993-1995," *ʿAtiqot* 49: 136-37 (summary). • G. HADAS, N. LIFSCHITZ, AND G. BONANI 2005, "Two Ancient Wooden Anchors from Ein Gedi, on the Dead Sea, Israel," *The International Journal of Nautical Archaeology* 34: 307-15. • G. HADAS FORTHCOMING, *The Archaeological Survey of ʿEn Gedi,* Jerusalem: Israel Antiquities Authority.

GIDEON HADAS

Elders

The Hebrew word for "elder" (*zāqēn;* OG *presbys* or *presbyteros*) derives from "beard" *(zāqān).* The plural "elders" occurs almost 200 times in biblical literature. In ancient Israel the elders functioned in leadership roles at the tribal and village levels. We hear of "elders of the city" (Deut. 21:3; 22:15, 17; Judg. 8:16; Ruth 4:2; 1 Sam. 16:4; Jdt. 6:16; 10:6; 13:12), "elders of the tribe(s)" (Deut. 5:23; 29:10; Josh. 24:1), "elders of Israel" (Exod. 3:16, 18; 12:21; 24:1; Lev. 9:1; Num. 11:16; Deut. 27:1; 1 Macc. 11:23; along with "heads of the tribes"; cf. Deut. 29:10; 1 Kings 8:1; 2 Chron. 5:2), "elders of the people" (Exod. 4:29; 19:7; Num. 11:16; Jer. 19:1), "elders of the congregation" (Lev. 4:15; Judg. 21:16), "elders of the land" (1 Kings 20:7; Jer. 26:17; Prov. 31:23), and "elders of the Jews" (Ezra 5:5, 9; 6:7-18, 14). Similar language is used in reference to non-Israelite peoples (cf. Gen 50:7, "all the elders of the land of Egypt"; Num. 22:4, "elders of Midian"; 22:7, "elders of Moab").

The quasi-judicial role of the tribal and village elders is also attested in biblical literature. We see this in the close association of elders with "judges" (Deut. 21:2; Josh. 8:33; 23:2; 24:1; Ezra 10:14; 1 Esdr. 9:13) or elders in the context of the village gate or gates, where decisions regarding criminal or civil matters will be settled (Deut. 21:19; 22:15; 25:7; Ruth 4:11; Prov. 31:23; Job 29:7; Jdt. 10:6; 13:12). The fate of the lazy, disobedient son is to be heard at the village gate (Deut. 21:18-21), while the fate of Ruth the Moabite is settled by the elders at the gate of Bethlehem (Ruth 4:1-12).

A few passages speak of "seventy elders" of Israel (Exod. 24:1, 9; Num. 11:16, 24-25; Ezek. 8:11), which may have given rise to the seventy-member Council, or Sanhedrin (Matt. 5:22; Mark 13:9; 14:55; 15:1; Acts 4:15; Philo, *De Ebrietate* 165; *In Flaccum* 74, "our council of elders, which our savior and benefactor Augustus elected to manage the affairs of the Jewish nation"; Josephus, *Ant.* 14.167-80; *m. Sanh.* 1:6, "the greater Sanhedrin was made up of one and seventy").

Biblical literature also speaks of "elders of the priests" *(ziqnē hakkohănîm),* who apparently have greater authority (2 Kings 19:2; Isa. 37:2; Jer. 19:1; cf. 11QTemple[a] 15:18; 16:2; 11QTemple[b] 1:23, 25), which may be the equivalent of the "princes of the priests" in Ezra 8:29.

In the New Testament Gospels and Acts "chief priests" *(archiereis)* and "elders" *(presbyteroi)* frequently appear together (e.g., Mark 8:31; 11:27; 14:43; Acts 4:23; 23:14; 25:15; cf. Matt. 21:23; 26:3; Luke 22:66, "elders of the people"), especially in the Temple precincts, and may approximate the social and political function of the elders and "princes of the priests" in earlier times. These elders not only opposed Jesus, but also the apostles and the early church (Acts 4:5, 8; 6:12; 22:5; 23:14; 24:1; 25:15).

Following the Jewish social model, the early Christian church also recognized or appointed elders (Acts 11:30; 14:23; 15:2, 4, 6, 22, 23; 16:4; 20:17-18). Just as in the Gospels we hear of "chief priests and elders," so in the book of Acts we hear of "apostles and elders" (Acts 15:2, 4, 6, 22, 23; 16:4). In some of the New Testament epistles reference is made to "elders" as leaders in Christian churches and communities (1 Tim. 5:17, 19; Titus 1:5; Jas. 5:14; 1 Pet. 5:1, 5; 2 John 1; 3 John 1; cf. 1 Tim. 4:14, "council of elders," *presbytērion*). The book of Revelation several times refers to twenty-four elders who prostrate themselves and worship before the throne of God (Rev. 4:10; 5:5, 6, 8, 11, 14; 7:11, 13; 11:16; 14:3; 19:4). Although it is far from certain, these twenty-four elders may represent the twelve tribes of Israel and the twelve apostles, perhaps pointing to the full complement of God's people.

The early function of elder continues beyond the

apostolic period. Clement admonishes the Corinthians to respect their leaders and to honor their elders (*1 Clem.* 21:6). Similarly, the author of *2 Clement* urges his readers to heed the authority of their elders (*2 Clem.* 17:3, 5). The *Shepherd of Hermas* speaks of the "elders who preside over the Church" (8:3). In the extant fragments of his work Papias speaks of the elders as those who had heard the very words of the apostles (frgs. 3 and 14): "And if by chance someone who had been a follower of the elders should come my way, I inquired about the words of the elders — what Andrew or Peter said, or Philip, or Thomas or James, or John or Matthew or any other of the Lord's disciples, and whatever Aristion and the elder John, the Lord's disciples, were saying. For I did not think that information from books would profit me as much as information from a living and abiding voice" (frg. 3).

Bibliography

A. F. J. Klijn 1959, "Scribes, Pharisees, High Priests, and Elders in the New Testament," *NovT* 3: 259-67. • T. M. Willis 2001, *The Elders of the City: A Study of the Elders-Laws in Deuteronomy,* Atlanta: Society of Biblical Literature. • T. M. Willis 1991, "Yahweh's Elders (Isa 24,23): Senior Officials of the Divine Court," *ZAW* 103: 375-85.

See also: Sanhedrin Craig A. Evans

Election

God's choice of Israel dominates the Hebrew Bible and Second Temple Jewish literature. It is rooted in the election of Abraham, Isaac, and Jacob; the heirs of Jacob are then the patriarchs of the twelve tribes. Israel in the Old Testament is God's "treasured possession," chosen "out of all the peoples who are on the face of the earth" (Deut. 7:6), and this election is a sovereign act of God that is not a result of any special characteristics of Israel (Deut. 7:7; cf. 9:4-5). Concomitant with Israel's election is the gift of the land, the institution of the covenant and Torah, and the promise of blessing in response to the commandments (although the curses of the covenant would attend disobedience). The intention of the election of Abraham and the nation of Israel was apparently the blessing of all the nations (Gen. 12:3; cf. Deut. 4:6). The ultimate purpose of God's election of Israel is his own glory (Isa. 49:3; Jer. 13:11).

By and large, this picture of election as a unilateral act purely of divine choice also dominates the postbiblical literature; there is of course the requirement of obedient commitment to YHWH in response to this election, but the election itself is solely a divine choice. However, a minority report survives as well: the motif of God's offer of the covenant and commandments to all the nations, an offer which Israel alone accepted. This is spelled out in *Sifre Deuteronomy* §343: God went first to the Edomites, who would not accept the Torah because of the commandment not to murder; he then went to the Ammonites and Moabites, who objected to the commandment not to commit adultery, and so on. God finally offered the Law to Israel: "So Israel accepted the Torah, with all of its explanations and details, as well as the seven commandments that the children of Noah had not been able to observe and had cast off" (trans. Hammer). This tradition is also found in *b. ʿAbodah Zarah* 2b, but it is uncertain how early it is.

A second minority report comes in connection with the merits of the patriarchs. This theme is well known as a feature of tannaitic Judaism and beyond, but it can probably also be found earlier. In *T. Reub.* 15:1-4, the author describes the destruction of the Temple and the Exile, an exile of such devastating proportions that "except on account of Abraham, Isaac and Jacob, our fathers, not a single one of our descendants would be left on earth" (cf. *T. Asher* 7:7). Some scholars see the motif in Ps.-Philo, *Bib. Ant.* 35:3b: "but he (God) will have mercy as no one else has mercy on the nation of Israel, yet not on your account, but on account of those who have fallen asleep." In some other works, David fulfills a similar function to the patriarchs. The reference to the *ḥasdei David* in Isa. 55:3 is taken by some early interpreters to refer to the promises made *to* David (e.g., LXX Isaiah; Acts 13:34), but by others as meaning the pious deeds of David (perhaps as early as 4QMMT C 25-26). E. P. Sanders (1977) explains the motifs of Israel's consent and the merits of the patriarchs as guarding against the idea that God's election is arbitrary rather than as viewing acceptance and obedience as playing a real role in election. At the other extreme, VanLandingham (2006) has argued that the election of Israel is envisaged as the reward for her good deeds throughout Jewish literature, though this is very much a marginal view.

Themes in the Apocrypha and Pseudepigrapha

The phrase "the elect" is prominent in *1 Enoch* as a designation of the righteous (e.g., *1 Enoch* 1:1, 8, etc.), and in the *Similitudes* this occurs alongside "the Elect One" as a title for the messiah (e.g., *1 Enoch* 61:5). In *Jubilees,* God's election of Israel is expressed in the language of his separating, sanctifying, and blessing a people for himself (*Jub.* 2:19); they are the chosen seed of Jacob, God's firstborn son (2:20). The language of Israel as God's chosen and beloved is prominent in *Psalms of Solomon* (esp. *Psalms of Solomon* 7, 11, and 18). This election is unchangeable: "For you have chosen the seed of Abraham above all the nations, and have set your name upon us, O Lord; and you will never cast us off" (9:9). In the *Testament of Moses,* God created the world on behalf of Israel (*T. Mos.* 1:12). This is a development upon biblical thought, but much of the rest of the work reproduces biblical ideas of election: God remembers Israel because of the covenant he made with the patriarchs (4:5), and Israel will be redeemed at the end, being lifted up on an eagle (10:8). Election also results in eschatological salvation for the nation in Ps.-Philo (*Bib. Ant.* 23:13). Israel's destruction is unimaginable: "It will sooner happen that this age will be ended forever or the world will sink into the immeasurable deep or the heart of the abyss will touch the stars than that the race of the sons of Israel will be ended" (*Bib. Ant.* 9:3). Even after the destruction of the Temple and life under foreign rule, Israel is loved by God (*2 Bar.* 5:1) and called beloved on account of his own name (*2 Bar.* 21:21).

One of the most popular images for expressing election is that of the book of life. This starts already in the Hebrew Bible (Exod. 32:32-33; Ps. 69:28; Mal. 3:16), although some passages do not distinguish between the book as a list of the *righteous* and as a list simply of the *living*. Election is probably in view, for example, in *Jos. & As.* 15:2-6, in which an angel visits Aseneth to reassure her: "Take courage, Aseneth. Behold, your name was written in the book of life, and it will never be erased" (15:4). There is variation in early Jewish literature, however, as to whether this book of life is a list of the predestined elect as here, or is written subsequent to righteous deeds (e.g., *Apoc. Zeph.* 3:7; *b. Roš Haššana* 16b). In the New Testament, the motif is most prominent in the book of Revelation (e.g., Rev. 21:27, "the Lamb's book of life").

The Qumran Literature

In the Dead Sea Scrolls, the election of the nation of ethnic Israel is very much overshadowed by the predestination of the "sons of light," that is, the *yaḥad* or sectarian association known from the Scrolls. The passage often called the "Treatise on the Two Spirits" in 1QS 3–4 (sometimes regarded as a presectarian work later inserted into 1QS) describes how the sons of light and the sons of darkness both come from their respective sources but inevitably carry out everything that God has ordained for them. A number of scholars harmonize 1QS with the physiognomic texts, in which all people are granted nine portions of spirits; the righteous have a preponderance of good, the unrighteous a majority of evil (4Q186; cf. 4Q561). The *Thanksgiving Hymns (Hodayot)* also emphasize predestination, with the emphasis on God's revelation of knowledge to the unworthy recipient of election. The Qumran sectarians expected that in the end of days Israel would be restored under their leadership (1QSa). The function of election language in the DSS is by and large to emphasize God's awesome sovereignty over against human contingency, and to reinforce the belief in the ultimate vindication of the sons of light.

The New Testament

John the Baptist's preaching questions in a different manner the elect status of Israelites who do not obey God. He addresses a group of Pharisees and Sadducees as a brood of vipers, and says: "And do not presume to say to yourselves, 'We have Abraham as our father,' for I tell you, God is able to raise up from these stones children for Abraham" (Matt. 3:9//Luke 3:8).

Jesus and the authors of the New Testament continued in this direction. The rejection of Jesus as messiah by the majority of his Jewish contemporaries, and the acceptance of the gospel by a disproportionate number of Gentiles led to a new articulation of election. Much New Testament scholarship has pointed to possible questionings of Israel's ongoing significance in Matt. 21:43 ("the kingdom of God will be taken away from you and given to a people producing its fruits") and John 8, in which Jesus denies that the Jews who had believed in him are children of God and of Abraham, and calls the devil their father (John 8:39-42, 44). In parallel with this, the disciples of Jesus are called "the elect" (e.g., Mark 13:20, 22, 27). As in *1 Enoch,* Jesus' messiahship is expressed in his being chosen by God; the language used is of Jesus being the "beloved Son" in whom God is pleased (Mark 1:11//Matt. 3:17//Luke 3:22). One of the distinctive features of Jesus' status in the Gospels, however, is that he is also the *subject* of election: "All things have been handed over to me by my Father. And no one knows the Son except the Father, and no one knows the Father except the Son and *those to whom the Son chooses to reveal him*" (Matt. 11:27// Luke 10:22).

The apostle Paul has a complex attitude to his Jewish contemporaries. In Galatians he uses the phrase "the Israel of God" in a way that suggests the inclusion of Gentile Christians (Gal. 6:16). An even more radical statement can be found in Romans 2, where Paul states that circumcision does not make a Jew; only circumcision of the heart by the Holy Spirit does so (Rom. 2:29). Indeed, the Jew who disobeys Torah has effectively become uncircumcised (2:25). On the other hand, he continues to affirm the privileges of Israel: circumcision and the oracles of God (3:1-2), as well as the covenants, adoption, glory, the Law, the cult, the promises, the patriarchs, and even the messiah (9:3-5). He also anticipates the salvation at the eschaton of a great body of Israelites alongside the Gentiles (11:25-27). Though this is a very controversial passage, Paul goes on to reaffirm the unchangeable nature of Israel's election: "for the gifts and call of God are irrevocable" (11:29). Israel may be hostile to the gospel, but election means that she is still beloved of God because of the patriarchs (11:28).

Paul's language (if not the ideas behind it) was picked up in the second century by several Christian authors who talked in terms of a strong supersessionism: the Gentile church had effectively replaced Israel in God's purposes (*Epistle of Barnabas;* Justin Martyr). Another direction in which Pauline language is taken is the self-designation of the so-called Valentinian Gnostics as the *pneumatikoi* (cf. 1 Cor. 2:13, 15; 3:1); Theodotus, for example, talks of "the spiritual seed, that is, the elect" (Clement, *Excerpta ex Theodoto* 1). The most influential of Paul's passages, however, have probably been Rom. 8:29-30 and Eph. 1:3-10, which talk of God's predestination of the elect "before the foundation of the world" so that they will be "conformed to the image of his Son" Jesus Christ. As with the election of Israel (Isa. 49:3; Jer. 13:11; *2 Bar.* 21:21), God chose the church for his glory (Eph. 1:4-6).

Early Rabbinic Literature

Election features extensively in rabbinic literature. The idea testifies to God's love for his people (e.g., *b. Berakot* 11b–12a). They are the nation on whom he has set his name: "I am God for all those who come into the world, nevertheless I have conferred my name particularly on my people Israel" (*Mekilta, Kaspa* 4 on Exod. 23:17).

Election results in the privilege of Torah, which then provides the opportunity for righteousness (*m. Mak.* 3:16).

The most extensively discussed passage on election from tannaitic literature has been *m. Sanh.* 10:1: "All Israelites have a share in the world to come." In fact, this statement is absent from some important witnesses and is probably secondary. However, there are still a number of passages that assume that the soteriological divide is between Israel and the nations (e.g., *Mekilta, Nezikin* 10 on Exod. 21:30). The relation between election and the soteriological value of deeds is not worked out in a systematic way, however. The "old perspective" on Judaism, according to which rabbinic theology was caricatured as being based on a weighing of deeds in the balance, has rightly been criticized by E. P. Sanders (1977), who stresses the central importance of election and gratuity in the self-understanding of tannaitic Judaism. On the other hand, Sanders replaced this one-sided picture with a construction that merely reversed the relationship. He relativized the importance of deeds by taking election as the central fact into which the strong statements in rabbinic Judaism about judgment according to deeds needed to be fitted. More recently, scholars such as F. Avemarie (1999) have rejected a systematizing approach to the evidence and recognized that the rabbis could at different times adopt an election-based approach or an obedience-based approach. Each could be absolutized in a particular instance without reference to the other.

BIBLIOGRAPHY

F. AVEMARIE 1999, "Erwählung und Vergeltung: Zur optionalen Struktur rabbinischer Soteriologie," *NTS* 45: 108-26. • M. A. ELLIOTT 2000, *The Survivors of Israel: A Reconsideration of the Theology of Pre-Christian Judaism,* Grand Rapids: Eerdmans. • T. ESKOLA 1998, *Theodicy and Predestination in Pauline Soteriology,* Tübingen: Mohr-Siebeck. • B. W. HELFGOTT 1954, *The Doctrine of Election in Tannaitic Literature,* New York: King's Crown Press. • J. S. KAMINSKY 2007, *Yet I Loved Jacob: Reclaiming the Biblical Concept of Election,* Nashville: Abingdon. • A. LANGE 1995A, *Weisheit und Prädestination: Weisheitliche Urordnung und Prädestination in den Textfunden von Qumran,* Leiden: Brill. • A. LANGE 1995B, "Wisdom and Predestination in the Dead Sea Scrolls," *DSD* 2: 340-54. • E. MERRILL 1975, *Qumran and Predestination: A Theological Study of the Thanksgiving Hymns,* Leiden: Brill. • E. P. SANDERS 1997, *Paul and Palestinian Judaism,* Philadelphia: Fortress. • C. VANLANDINGHAM 2006, *Judgment and Justification in Early Judaism and the Apostle Paul,* Peabody, Mass.: Hendrickson.

See also: Covenant; Covenantal Nomism; Judgment; Sanders, Ed Parish

SIMON J. GATHERCOLE

Elect of God (4Q534-536)

In 1964 Jean Starcky published the first part of a fragmentary Aramaic composition that describes a figure called the "elect of God" and his miraculous birth. Strarcky interpreted the text to speak of a messianic figure. In an article published a year later (1965), Joseph Fitzmyer rejected the messianic interpretation and identified the "elect of God" (4Q534 frg. 1 i 10) with Noah, the main hero of the biblical flood story whose quasi-miraculous birth is described in the last chapters of *Ethiopic Enoch* (*1 Enoch* 106–7) and in the first columns of the *Genesis Apocryphon* (1QapGen). Émile Puech, editor of the text in the DJD series (2001: 117-70), followed this interpretive thread as well and called the text 4QNaissance de Noe. One should, however, be cautioned that the Aramaic text does not mention Noah even once. The main narrator remains anonymous, and the identity of the elect of God is nowhere explicitly stated.

The manuscript survives in three fragments: 4Q534 (4QNaissance de Noe[a]), 4Q535 (4QNaissance de Noe[b]), and 4Q536 (4QNaissance de Noe[c]). The fragments are written in a round, semiformal Herodian script and so are dated by Puech to the last thirty years of the first century B.C.E. Since the text does not contain vocabulary characteristic of the Qumran sect, Puech thinks it may have been composed before 152 B.C.E.

The following outline of the content must remain hypothetical:

1. Description of the birth of the boy (4Q535 frg. 3; 4Q536 frg. 1)
2. Physiognomic description of the marks on his body (4Q534 frg. 1 col. i lines 1-3a)
3. Education and wisdom of the elect of God (4Q534 1 i 3b–15)
   a. His learning of the three books (lines 3b-5)
   b. Knowledge received from wise visionaries (line 6)
   c. Counsel and prudence characterize his actions (line 7)
   d. Knowledge of all the mysteries of humanity and of all living things (line 8)
   e. Accomplishment of his calculations due to his being the elect of God (lines 9-15)
4. Remarks about his birth and physiognomy (4Q534 1 ii + 2 19)
5. Future devastation by water (?) (4Q534 1 ii + 2 12–20)
6. Revelation of the mysteries, teaching of the Elect (?), and human wisdom (4Q536 2 ii and 3)
7. Blessing for the wise, woes for the foolish (4Q536 2 ii 7–12a + 4Q534 frg. 7 1-6)
8. Conclusion (4Q536 2 ii 12b–13)

The description of the boy at birth has led to the text's being given a horoscopic interpretation in line with Mesopotamian divination and Greco-Roman astrological treatises (Starcky 1964: 64-65). Mention of calculations also suggests an astrologic context (Puech 2001: 140-41). Fitzmyer (1965: 370) rejects the astrological interpretation because the text does not mention stars or the Zodiac.

Another possible line of interpretation focuses on the text's sapiential elements. The three books that the boy learns were hypothetically identified by Grelot

(1975) as the Enochic *Book of the Watchers, Book of Dreams,* and *Astronomical Book.* Grelot's identification assumes Fitzmyer's interpretation of the elect of God as Noah. The didactic elements are reminiscent of Aramaic didactic literature *(Aramaic Levi Document, Admonitions [Testament] of Qahat, Visions of Amram, Astronomical Book).* These compositions establish a pattern of transmitting knowledge from one generation of priestly apprentices to the other. The sons of Levi, Qahat, and Amram are presented as disciples, and the sapiential character of these writings is strongly accentuated. The *Aramaic Levi Document* adopted some Babylonian practices of scribal education and applied it to the education of priestly apprentices (Drawnel 2004).

If the identification of the elect of God with Noah is correct, then his learning of the three presumably Enochic books would constitute a key link in the transmission of Enochic knowledge from prediluvian times to the postdiluvian patriarchs. In the *Aramaic Levi Document* (v. 57) Abraham learns prescriptions about blood in the writing of the book of Noah; both Enoch and Levi learn about calculation; and while Levi uses this metro-arithmetical knowledge for sacrificial purposes, Enoch learns calculation from the angel Uriel for astronomical purposes. Enochic astronomy was influenced by Babylonian tradition, in which astronomical calculations served astrological previsions (Rochberg 2004). Thus the *Elect of God* composition should be treated as a sapiential text with apocalyptic overtones and probable astrological influence.

BIBLIOGRAPHY

H. DRAWNEL 2004, *An Aramaic Wisdom Text from Qumran: A New Interpretation of the Levi Document,* Leiden: Brill. • H. DRAWNEL 2006, "Priestly Education in the *Aramaic Levi Document (Visions of Levi)* and *Aramaic Astronomical Book* (4Q208–211)," *RevQ* 22/4: 547-74. • J. A. FITZMYER 1965, "The Aramaic 'Elect of God' Text from Qumran Cave IV," *CBQ* 27: 348-72. • P. Grelot 1975, "Hénoch et ses Écritures," *RB* 82: 481-500. • É. PUECH, 2001, *Qumran Grotte 4. XXII: Textes Araméens, première partie, 4Q529-549,* DJD 31, Oxford: Clarendon. • F. ROCHBERG 2004, *The Heavenly Writing: Divination, Horoscopy, and Astronomy in Mesopotamian Culture,* Cambridge: Cambridge University Press. • J. STARCKY 1964, "Un texte messianique araméen de la grotte 4 de Qumran," in *École des Langues Orientales Anciennes de l'Institut Catholique de Paris: Mémorial du Cinquantenaire 1914-1964,* Paris: Bloud & Gay, 51-66. HENRYK DRAWNEL

Elephantine, Elephantine Papyri

Elephantine (Aram. *Yeb;* Egyp. *'Abu or Yebu;* Gr. *Ieb*) is the name of an island in the Nile River facing the modern Egyptian city of Aswan (ancient Syene). The island of Elephantine is located south of the first cataract at 24° 05′ N 32° 53′ E. Its size is ca. 0.75 miles long from north to south, and about 0.25 mile wide at its widest. The island presents evidence of local occupation since predynastic times, and a step pyramid dating back to the Old Kingdom still stands. It was the site of a Jewish colony composed mainly of soldiers and their families. In the nineteenth and twentieth centuries, archaeologists discovered a large number of Aramaic documents from the Persian period (late sixth to fourth century B.C.E.).

Origins, Organization, and Composition of the Jewish Colony

B. Porten (1968) considered three different periods when Jews from the land of Israel might have settled in Elephantine: (1) the period from the Syro-Ephraimite War until the siege of Jerusalem, 735-701 B.C.E.; (2) the period when King Manasseh of Judah (ruled ca. 697-642 B.C.E.) supported Egypt; and (3) the period between the accession of King Jehoiakin, 609 B.C.E., and the flight to Egypt led by Johanan b. Kareah. More recently (2003) he provided additional support for the theory that sees the establishment of the Jewish garrison with a temple at Elephantine ca. 650 B.C.E. as very similar to the establishment of the Jewish garrison with a temple in the land of Onias, where disaffected priests with prophetic support entered into service of the king and built a temple like the one in Jerusalem.

The building of a temple in Elephantine could have been an attempt to provide an alternative place of worship as a reaction to Manasseh's "paganization" of the Jerusalem Temple, as Porten suggests, or to cover the religious needs of the Jewish community already there. On the other hand, K. van der Toorn (1992) sees the origin of the Jewish settlement in seventh-century Israel and traces the origin of the Arameans to North Syria.

The Aramean and Jewish soldiers settled at Elephantine and Syene provided the Persian administration military support in Egypt's southern border. They were settled with their families and organized by *(ḥaylā)* "garrison," *(degel)* "detachment," and *(mea')* "century." In the Persian period the term "detachment" was used in Egypt to designate both Egyptians and Jewish military units (*TAD* A4.5:1). The garrison *TAD* B2.9:5; B8.10:6 was divided into detachments and subdivided into centuries *TAD* A5.5:7; B4.4:8; B4.3:11; B4.4:6; B4.4:10; C3.15:19-20, 31, 54). The "century" unit was also used in Israel for both military and civil service (see Exod. 18:21; Num. 31:48; 2 Kings 11:14, 19). In Elephantine parties of contracts were identified by their ethnic identities (Jewish, Aramean, etc.) and detachment. The ethnic term served the administrative function of identifying one's position in the Elephantine bureaucracy. The terms "Jewish" and "Aramean" seem to reflect an organizational scheme imposed with the purpose of providing an administrative structure. "Aramean" would be an ethnic-administrative term used by the Persian administration, while "Judean" would be an ethnic-communitarian term.

The Aramaic Papyri

The corpus of Aramaic papyri from Egypt comprises thirty-five letters dated between the late sixth century and the early fourth century. Twenty-eight are associated with Elephantine-Syene (*TAD* A2.1-4; A3.1-10; 4.1-

ELEPHANTINE, ELEPHANTINE PAPYRI

10; 5.2, 5; 6.1, 20), one comes from el-Hibe (*TAD* A3.11), three from Luxor (*TAD* A2.5-7), one from Saqqara (*TAD* A5.1), and two from unknown provenance (*TAD* A5.3, 4). The letters can be categorized as (1) *personal or family letters* (*TAD* A2.1-7; 3:1-11) dealing with personal matters, private business, or family concerns; (2) *communal letters* coming from the Jedaniah b. Gemariah archive (*TAD* A4.1-10) and concerned with religious matters related to the observance of the Passover and the turmoil that led to the destruction of Elephantine's temple and the subsequent request for the permission to rebuilt it; (3) *official letters,* comprising five fragments (*TAD* A5.1-5) and the correspondence of the satrap Arsames (*TAD* A6.3-16). Within this corpus it is possible to trace at least thirty formulaic expressions with various degrees of similarity with Demotic, Late Egyptian, and Akkadian epistolary formulas.

Legal Traditions

The Elephantine corpus includes forty-three contracts and several fragments dated during the fifth century B.C.E. The mention of Babylonians, Caspians, Khwarezmians, Bactrians, Medes, Magians, Persians, Arameans, and Egyptians as parties or witnesses within the legal documents of the Jewish community suggests that the business law which governed the transactions of the Jewish soldiers was not different from that which governed the transactions of the rest of the ethnic groups represented in Elephantine-Syene. Two of the scribes, Nabutukulti b. Nabuzeribni (*TAD* B2.11) and Raukhshana b. Nergal(u)shezib (*TAD* B3.9), have non-Hebrew-Aramaic names and patronymics, and another two, Attarshuri b. Nabuzeribni (*TAD* B2.3 and B2.4) and Bunni b. Mannuki (B3.2), have a non-Hebrew-Aramaic element in their names. The progressive assimilation that we find in the onomasticon of Elephantine-Syene points to the cultural compatibility of the various groups.

Designations of the Parties Involved

The documents tend to reflect the personal status of each party in relation to the others. In letters among equals, the term "to my brother" is used (*TAD* A3.6:1, 5), while someone would address his superior as his "lord" or "lady" and describe himself as his "slave" or "servant" (*TAD* A4.7:1; A4.2:1, 17; A3.7:1). This is also valid for family relationships, where a father is addressed as "my lord" and the sender describes himself as "his servant." The expression "citizens of Elephantine" might refer only to the leadership, landowners, or heads of families. The expression is used in the Bible in that sense (Josh. 24:11; Judg. 9:6; 20:5; 1 Sam. 23:11). All the slaves mentioned in the Elephantine documents had Egyptian names. Slavery was not necessarily a permanent status in Elephantine and, perhaps, serfdom or servitude would be a better word to describe it. Ta(p)met, the servant mentioned in the document of wifehood *TAD* B3.3:7, was probably born free when she married Ananiah b. Azariah and seems to have become a free person later on (*TAD* B3.5; B3.6). Servants bore a brand in their right hands with the name of their master, as stated in *TAD* B2.11:4-5: "PN, a slave (. . .) branded on his right hand (with) a brand reading (in) Aramaic like this (belonging) to Mibtaḥiah." Contemporary Demotic texts attest to the practice of self-sales where the person sells himself as servant for a limited period. Slaves in Elephantine were considered as any other movable property and, as such, would be seized as security in cases of unpaid debts (*TAD* B3.1:10; *TAD* B3.13:11).

Sale Documents

The complete documents of sales (*TAD* B3.4; B3.12) are composed *ex latere alienatoris* following a standard formulary that includes the date, parties, and abstract of the transaction, description of the performance (in sales, the amount of the payment), a declaration of satisfaction by the seller with the price received, a description of the property, a formula of transfer, the declaration of rights of the buyer (investiture), a quitclaim by the seller, a general warranty against suits by third parties, the name of the scribe, a dictation clause, the name of the witnesses, and an endorsement. The endorsement of the document of sale makes clear that the conveyance is precisely that by stating "Document of a house which PN sold (to PN)" (*TAD* B3.4:25; *TAD* B3.12:35).

Bequests and Inheritance

There are no wills or testaments in the Elephantine corpus. Inheritance was regulated by custom law and provisions in wifehood documents and bequests (*TAD* B2.3; B3.5; B3.10). Hereditary property is conveyed, including the formula "and your sons after you" (*TAD* B2.3:9 passim) in the investiture clause after the rights of the *alienator* are stated. The formula "and your sons after you," however, does not specifically limit the right of the *alienator* to transfer property (for such limitations see B2.4:6-8). Only one document deals with a division of inheritance (*TAD* B2.11) in which the brothers Maḥseiah and Jedaniah, sons of Nathan, divide between themselves two Egyptian slaves formerly property of their mother Mibtaḥiah. The fact that the whole Mibtaḥiah archive ended up in the hands of Jedaniah suggests that he was the firstborn and had preferential hereditary rights. In addition, the formula "and your sons after you" seems to imply that sons and not daughters were the primary inheritors. It can be assumed that daughters had a right to inheritance in case the property holder died without sons (cf. Num. 27:8); as they appear as possible claimants in the covenant of nonclaim formula (*TAD* B2.2:32-34), it seems that in case there were sons, daughters received property by bequests during the life of the father. Those bequests could take effect immediately, and in this case they used the formula "in my lifetime and at my death" (*TAD* B2.3:3), or after the death of the father, when they used the formula "at my death" (*TAD* B3.10:18). In the case of the death of a husband without children the wife received "control" over the property, while in the case of the death of the wife the husband received full proprietary rights and "inherited" the wife's property (*TAD* B2.6:21).

ELEPHANTINE, ELEPHANTINE PAPYRI

The rights of widows without children are usually established in the marriage contracts. For example, *TAD* B3.8, a marriage contract between Ananiah b. Haggai (husband) and Zaccur b. Meshullam (father-in-law) concerning Jehoishma (wife/daughter), stipulates that if Haggai dies without children then the rights of Jehoishma are limited to the usufruct of his property as long as she does not remarry (*TAD* B3.8:33). If Jehoishma dies, however, all of her property would become her husband's.

Loans and Deposit

The papyri attest to the loan of small sums of money (*TAD* B3.1; *TAD* B4.2, four shekels each) and grain (*TAD* B3.13). The documents begin with the statement "you have given me a loan." The interest rate for money loans was as high as 60 percent per year. When the loan was considered repaid, the lender would transfer the deed attesting to the loan to the borrower. In some cases, when loans of grain were not repaid the borrower would threaten to convert the loan into a money loan, a type of loan that could accrue interest as opposed to the grain loan (*TAD* B3.12). When loans were not repaid in a timely manner, the lender would take a pledge from the borrower (*TAD* B3.1; *TAD* B3.13). The loan documents usually list the objects that could be taken as a pledge by the lender if such a situation arose (*TAD* B3.13). See also *TAD* B3.13:2-4; *TAD* B3.1:3; *TAD* B4.2:1. Debts arising from previous transactions were declared by the statement "You have upon me" (*TAD* B4.5.2; B4.6:3) followed by the amount owed. Goods left in deposit are mentioned in *TAD* B2.9, where they were cause for litigation.

Marriage and Divorce

The Elephantine corpus includes three complete marriage contracts (*TAD* B3.3; B2.6 and B3.8) and a few fragments (*TAD* B6.4; B6.3; B6.1; and B6.2). The documents are drawn between the bridegroom and the head of the family of the bride, or, in the case of the handmaiden Tamet, her master. The main purpose is to regulate the pecuniary rights resulting from the union. The documents record the request of the bridegroom to the guardian to receive the bride as his wife, the *verba solemna* "she is my wife and I am her husband from this day and forever," the payment of a *mōhar* by the bridegroom to the bride's guardian which became part of the bride's dowry, the description of the dowry that consisted of cash, clothes, utensils, and various goods, stipulations in case of divorce, and regulation of some marital duties like not taking another spouse (*TAD* B3.8:33-34) or the denial of conjugal rights (*TAD* B3.8:37).

All the marriage contracts include divorce clauses that allow both spouses to end the marriage. The spouse who wants to initiate the divorce "stands up in the congregation" and declares "I hate" the other spouse (*TAD* B2.6:23, 27; B3.3:7, 9; B3.8:21, 24). The party who initiates the divorce is liable to pay a penalty called "money of hatred" (*TAD* B2.6:23; B3.3:8, 9, 22, 25). In case it is the wife who initiates the divorce, she would loose the *mōhar*, but in any case she is entitled to keep the property that she brought with her at the time of the agreement. After the divorce, the woman is free to return to her father's home or to go wherever she pleases (*TAD* B2.6:25, 29; B3.8:26, 28). Tamet, being Zaccur's handmaiden, did not enjoy that right (*TAD* B3.3).

The Courts

The "chief" and the "troop commander" or "troop commander of Syene" had jurisdiction over legal and military matters. A body alternately labeled "judges" (*TAD* B5.1:3; *TAD* B2.2:6), "judges of the king" (*TAD* B5.1:3), "judges of the province," and "judges, overseers, and hearers" (*TAD* A4.5:8-10) was present in judicial decisions, and the documents refer to them as the judicial body to which complaints and suits are addressed. The "assembly" mentioned in the marriage contracts as the body to which a declaration of divorce should be addressed does not seem to have had any decisive judicial function but to serve as a means of making the dissolution of the marriage public, thereby preventing any future charge or suspicion of adultery. Moreover, the lack of any evidence of an autonomous Jewish court suggests that the disputes arising out of Aramaic and out of Egyptian Demotic contracts were adjudicated by the same forum.

Religion

A temple to YHWH had been erected in Elephantine before the arrival of Cambyses in Egypt (525 B.C.E.). There regular meal offerings (cf. Exod. 29:40; Num. 28:1), incense offerings (cf. Exod. 30:1ff; 34ff), and burnt offerings (cf. Exod. 29:38-42) were made (*TAD* A4.7:21-22). Mention is also made of prayers and sacrifices of wellbeing (*TAD* A4.7:26-27). The temple was destroyed in the summer of 410 B.C.E. by priests of the Egyptian god Khnub and by Vidranga, the military commander (cf. *TAD* A4.5; A4.7). The mourning for the destruction of the temple (*TAD* A4.7:20-21) included wearing sackcloth and fasting (cf. Exod. 34:28; Dan. 10:3), sexual abstinence (cf. Lam. 5:3), and abstinence from drinking and anointing (cf. 2 Sam. 12:20; 14:2; Dan. 10:3). Just as the Jewish community had their temple to YHWH on the island, the Arameans had temples on the mainland devoted to the Semitic deities Bethel and the Queen of Heaven (*TAD* A2.1:1), Banit (*TAD* A2.2:1; 2.4:1), and Nabu (*TAD* A2.3:1). A list of temple contributions (*TAD* C3.15) shows that the funds were distributed among YHWH and two Aramean deities, Eshem-Bethel and Anath-Bethel. The Sabbath day is mentioned in several ostraca (*TAD* D7.10:5; 12:9; 16:2; 28:4; 35:7; 48:5; D19.7:1), but none of them suggests that it was considered a day of rest or implies any religious practice associated with it. The letter *TAD* A4.1 (419/18 B.C.E.), addressed to the Jewish troop, contains instructions for the celebration of the Passover including eating unleavened bread and abstaining from work on the first and last day of the seven days' celebration.

Bibliography

A. E. Cowley 1923, *Aramaic Papyri of the Fifth Century B.C.*, Oxford: Clarendon. • P.-E. Dion 2002, "La religion des papyrus d'Eléphantine: un reflect du Juda d'avant l'exil," in *Kein Land für sich Allein: Studien zum Kulturkontakt in Kanaan, Israel/Palästina und Ebirnâri für Manfred Weippert zum 65. Geburtstag,* ed. U. Hübner and E. Axel, Freibourg: Universitätsverlag; Göttingen: Vandenhoeck & Ruprecht, 243-54. • E. G. H. KRAELING 1953, *The Brooklyn Museum Aramaic Papyri: New Documents of the Fifth Century* B.C. *from the Jewish Colony at Elephantine,* New Haven: Yale University Press. • B. PORTEN 1968, *Archives from Elephantine: The Life of an Ancient Jewish Military Colony,* Berkeley: University of California Press. • B. PORTEN 1996, *The Elephantine Papyri in English: Three Millennia of Cross-Cultural Continuity and Change,* Leiden: Brill. • B. PORTEN 2003, "Settlement of the Jews at Elephantine and the Arameans at Syene," in *Judah and Judeans in the Neo-Babylonian Period,* ed. O. Lipschits and J. Blenkinsopp, Winona Lake, Ind.: Eisenbrauns, 451-66. • B. PORTEN AND A. YARDENI 1986-1999, *Textbook of Aramaic Documents from Ancient Egypt,* 4 vols., Jerusalem: Academon. • S. G. ROSENBERG 2004, "The Jewish Temple at Elephantine," *Near Eastern Archaeology* 67: 4-13. • K. VAN DER TOORN 1992, "Anat-Yahu, Some Other Deities, and the Jews of Elephantine," *Numen* 39: 80-101. • R. YARON 1961, *Introduction to the Law of the Aramaic Papyri,* Oxford: Clarendon.

ALEJANDRO F. BOTTA

Elijah

Hebrew Bible

The career of Elijah, the ninth-century-B.C.E. prophet and miracle worker, is narrated in the books of Kings (1 Kings 17–19; 21:17-29; 2 Kings 1:1–2:12). He is depicted as a faithful defender of Yahwism, sent to challenge the syncretism promoted by the royal household. A distinctive feature of Elijah's ministry is that, according to 2 Kings 2:11, Elijah did not die but was taken up into heaven by a whirlwind, in a chariot of fire. However, no mention is made in Kings of Elijah's future return; indeed, the passing of his spirit to Elisha may exclude this idea.

The first reference to an expectation of Elijah's return appears at the end of Malachi (Mal. 3:23-24 = RSV 4:5-6), where the prophecy is recorded that Elijah is to be sent before the day of the Lord with the task of reconciliation: "Behold, I will send you Elijah the prophet before the great and terrible day of the LORD comes. And he will turn the hearts of fathers to their children and the hearts of children to their fathers, lest I come and smite the land with a curse." In the Septuagint version of Mal. 3:23-24, the translators insert "the Tishbite" to make the connection with the Kings narrative clear (cf. 1 Kings 17:1). This addition simply makes explicit an implicit feature of the MT, where the use of the definite article ("Elijah *the* prophet") suggests that he is readily identifiable. The Malachi reference to Elijah as harbinger of the day of the Lord therefore represents this figure as the prophet who escaped death, ascended to heaven, and will subsequently return.

Early Jewish Tradition

Elijah's Eschatological Functions

Outside the Hebrew Bible, Elijah became a popular figure appealed to in a variety of texts of differing dates and provenances. A recurring theme in many of these documents is speculation about the prophet's return. Thus Ben Sira ends his encomium of Elijah (Sir. 48:1-11) by referring to the prophet's second coming, echoing the language of Malachi. However, in addition to bringing reconciliation between parents and children, Elijah is now expected to "restore the tribes of Jacob."

Expectation of Elijah's return can also be found in Qumran material, with 4Q558 preserving an Aramaic citation of Mal. 3:23a. 4Q382 includes a paraphrase of the Elijah cycle, with the longest surviving fragment summarizing Elijah's impending departure (2 Kings 2:3-4). Unfortunately, the evidence is too sparse to provide any clear picture of Elijah's place in the eschatology of the Qumran sect.

Zeal for the Law

The importance of Elijah is indicated in 1 Macc. 2:58, where Mattathias includes the prophet in his list of ancestors whose deeds should be remembered: "Elijah because of his great zeal for the law was taken up into heaven." The zeal attributed to Elijah is a feature that led many interpreters to connect him with Phinehas (Numbers 25). Pseudo-Philo's *Biblical Antiquities* 48:1 clearly portrays Phinehas as Elijah, who will be brought forth to suffer death when God remembers the world. Similarly, *Targum Pseudo-Jonathan* on Exod. 6:18 states, "Phinehas is Elijah the high priest who is to be sent to the exiles of Israel at the end of days." Both these sources demonstrate the continuing expectation of Phinehas-Elijah's return at the end of days.

Elijah and Enoch

Phinehas is not the only figure with whom Elijah came to be associated. Josephus connects the prophet with Enoch. Following his tendency to rationalize miracles, Josephus downplays the event of Elijah's translation to heaven; nevertheless he states, "Now about that time Elijah disappeared from among men, and to this day no one knows his end. . . . However, concerning Elijah and Enoch, who lived before the Flood, it is written in the sacred books that they became invisible, and no one knows of their death." This concludes Josephus' detailed summary of Elijah's career in his *Jewish Antiquities* (*Ant.* 8.316-62; 9.18-28); notably he does not include an encomium, in contrast to his presentation of many other biblical heroes. He also omits references to Elijah's zeal, probably for political reasons, given his apologetic agenda.

The association of Elijah with Enoch is also reflected in Philo's *Questions on Genesis* 1.86, where his translation to heaven is likened to Enoch's disappearance in Gen. 5:24 (cf. *4 Ezra* 6:26). Although the association of Elijah with Enoch can be found in Jewish sources from the Second Temple period, no mention is made of their future martyrdom, a feature that emerges in later tradition (see, e.g., the Coptic *Apocalypse of Elijah*).

Elijah as Forerunner of the Messiah?

The New Testament presents an array of Elijah traditions, naming the prophet twenty-nine times (of which twenty-seven references are found in the Gospels). Sometimes Elijah's activities are appealed to as a paradigm for Jesus' ministry (e.g., Luke 4:25-26), but more frequently the named references emphasize Elijah's "coming" or "appearance" (e.g., Mark 9:13, "Elijah has come"; Matt. 11:14, "he is Elijah who is to come"; Luke 9:8, "some said that Elijah had appeared").

The Synoptic Gospels all record that Elijah appeared alongside Moses and Jesus at the Transfiguration (Mark 9:4 pars.). This provokes discussion among the disciples about the return of Elijah: "Why do the scribes say that first Elijah must come?" (Mark 9:11). This reference to the scribes' expectation that Elijah "comes first" has widely been interpreted as evidence for the Jewish belief that the prophet would be the forerunner of the messiah upon his return (see Allison 1984), but this is by no means universally accepted and could refer to his role as forerunner of the day of the Lord (so Faierstein 1981; Fitzmyer 1985; Miller 2007).

Jesus responds to the disciples' perplexity by affirming that Elijah does come first to restore all things, and furthermore, "Elijah has come, and they did to him whatever they pleased, as it is written of him" (Mark 9:12-13). Matthew provides clarification with his addition, "Then the disciples understood that he was speaking to them about John the Baptist" (Matt. 17:13). As in Malachi and Sirach, Elijah is assigned the task of restoration.

John the Baptist as the Returned Elijah?

Matthew's identification of John the Baptist as Elijah returned in Matt. 17:13 comes as no surprise: he has already made the connection explicit in Matt. 11:14 ("If you are willing to accept it, he is Elijah who is to come"). Following Mark, Matthew depicts John wearing clothing that resembled Elijah's (Matt. 3:4) and appearing at the Jordan, where Elijah was taken up into heaven (2 Kings 2:6). This identification of John the Baptist as the returned Elijah contrasts with John's explicit rejection of any such identification in the Fourth Gospel (John 1:21). Moreover, in some circles *Jesus* was regarded as Elijah returned (Mark 6:15; 8:28 par.). The Gospels therefore point to a range of Elijah traditions, associating the return of Elijah with both John the Baptist and Jesus. They also raise significant questions about how an individual could be identified as Elijah returned (see Joynes 2005). The four evangelists adopt different positions in their presentation of these traditions.

Elijah as Arbiter and Judge

Roughly contemporaneous with the Gospels, *Lives of the Prophets* 21 provides further discussion of Elijah. It includes a long summary of the miracles Elijah performed, following the biblical account, but in addition it supplies details about the prophet's birth. In this context, Elijah's father receives reassurance: "Do not be afraid, for his dwelling will be light and his word judgment, and he will judge Israel." The priestly connection attributed to Elijah ("of Aaron's tribe") is particularly noteworthy. It is ironic that Elijah should be included in a document aimed at venerating prophets' graves, in view of the mystery surrounding his end as acknowledged by the author ("finally he was taken up in a chariot of fire").

The Mishnah demonstrates that Elijah came to be regarded as a future arbiter and judge. Disputes that could not be resolved were to be left "until Elijah comes" (*m. Šeqal.* 2:5; *m. B. Meṣiʿa* 1:8; 2:8; 3:4-5). Through Elijah the resurrection of the dead is also expected to occur (*m. Soṭa* 9:15). *Mishnah ʿEduyyot* 8:7 reveals that the Malachi prophecy of Elijah as reconciler and peacemaker continued to be influential.

In the Second Temple period, then, Elijah was regarded as a hero of the past. His zeal for the Torah is a feature lauded by some and downplayed by others. However, most attention is given to his miraculous translation to heaven and speculation about his subsequent return. Clearly, the expectation of Elijah's return was not an isolated idea found only in Malachi but one that gained broader acceptance. Despite the prominence given to Elijah in Christianity, the prophet remained (and still remains) an important figure in Judaism.

BIBLIOGRAPHY

D. ALLISON 1984, "Elijah Must Come First," *JBL* 103: 256-58. • R. BAUCKHAM 1976, "The Martyrdom of Enoch and Elijah: Jewish or Christian?" *JBL* 95: 447-58. • M. M. FAIERSTEIN 1981, "Why Do the Scribes Say That Elijah Must Come First?" *JBL* 100: 75-86. • L. H. FELDMAN 1994, "Josephus' Portrait of Elijah," *JSOT* 8: 61-86. • J. A. FITZMYER 1985, "More about Elijah Coming First," *JBL* 104: 295-96. • C. E. JOYNES 2005, "The Returned Elijah? John the Baptist's Angelic Identity in the Gospel of Mark," *SJT* 58: 455-67. • D. M. MILLER 2007, "The Messenger, the Lord, and the Coming Judgement in the Reception History of Malachi," *NTS* 53: 1-16. • M. ÖHLER 1997, *Elia im Neuen Testament: Untersuchungen zur Bedeutung des alttestamentlichen Propheten im Neuen Testament,* Berlin: de Gruyter. • M. ÖHLER 1999, "The Expectation of Elijah and the Presence of the Kingdom of God," *JBL* 118: 461-76. • J. C. POIRIER 2003, "The Endtime Return of Elijah and Moses at Qumran," *DSD* 10: 221-42. • J. A. T. ROBINSON 1958, "Elijah, John and Jesus: An Essay in Detection," *NTS* 4: 263-81.

See also: Elisha; John the Baptist

CHRISTINE E. JOYNES

Elisha

Hebrew Bible

The story of Elisha appears in 1 Kings 19:16, 19-21 and 2 Kings 2–13. He is remembered as a miracle-working prophet who was called by Elijah and became his successor, receiving the latter's mantle and a double portion of his spirit (1 Kings 19:16; 2 Kings 2:9-13). 2 Kings makes the prophetic deeds of the two prophets resemble each other. Both part the Jordan (2 Kings 2:8, 14), raise the dead (1 Kings 17:17-24; 2 Kings 4:8-37), multiply food miraculously (1 Kings 17:8-16; 2 Kings 4:42-44), and are, immediately before death, addressed with "Father, father! The chariots of Israel and its horsemen!" (2 Kings 2:12; 13:14).

Later Tradition

In subsequent tradition Elisha is always in the shadow of Elijah and garners much less attention. The Hebrew Bible fails to speak of him outside of Kings (contrast Mal. 4:5, which envisages the return of Elijah). Likewise, Philo nowhere refers to Elisha. It is symptomatic that, although the New Testament names Elijah over thirty times, it names Elisha only once (Luke 4:27 — although the accounts of Jesus calling disciples in Mark 1:16-20 par.; 2:13-14 par.; and Matt. 8:18-22 = Luke 9:57-62 as well as the story of his feeding 5,000 in Mark 6:30-44 par. are modeled upon 1 Kings 19:19-21 and 2 Kings 4:42-44, respectively).

Elisha also goes unnamed in most of the Apocrypha and Pseudepigrapha, although CD A 8.20 mentions him in passing, and 4Q481A may contain fragments of a lost Elisha apocryphon (the extant scraps seem to paraphrase and supplement 2 Kings 2:14-16). Sirach 48:12-14, however, offers a brief retrospective of his life and work. The Hebrew reads: "When Elijah was concealed in the whirlwind, Elisha was filled with his spirit. He did twice as many signs [as Elijah] [cf. 2 Kings 2:9] and miracles with every utterance of his mouth. During his many days he feared no one, and no one could intimidate his spirit. No deed was beyond his ability, and in death his body prophesied." The last assertion, so oddly expressed, seems to be a reference to 2 Kings 13:20-21, where contact with Elisha's bones causes a dead man to return to life.

Lives of the Prophets

The *Lives of the Prophets* includes a longer summary of Elisha's career. After the conclusion of the *Life of the Prophet Elijah,* which mentions that Elisha crossed the Jordan with Elijah (chap. 14), the book's next section is entitled the *Life of the Prophet Elisha,* and it is wholly dedicated to Elijah's successor. It largely summarizes miracle stories from 2 Kings, mostly in their canonical order — Elisha divided the Jordan (2 Kings 2:13-14), purified foul water (2:19-22), summoned bears to maul children (2:23-24), multiplied oil for a widow (4:1-7), raised the dead (4:8-37), rendered poisoned food edible (4:38-41), made an axe head float (6:1-7), cured a leper (5:1-27), and blinded an army (6:8-23); and after death, his bones brought a dead man to life (13:20-21). The *Life of the Prophet Elisha* departs significantly from 2 Kings only in its narration of the prophet's birth and death. Concerning the latter, it informs us that Elisha died in Samaria, which 2 Kings does not say and indeed seemingly excludes. Concerning the former, the *Life of the Prophet Elisha* 1–2 passes on the tale, without scriptural foundation, that, when Elijah was born in Gilgal, the golden calf (cf. 2 Kings 10:29; 17:16) bellowed so loudly that it was heard in Jerusalem, and the (high?) priest, in response, declared through the Urim that a prophet who would destroy idols had just arrived in Israel.

Josephus

A thorough treatment of Elisha appears in Josephus, *Ant.* 8.352-54; 9.27-183. This consistently sympathetic rewriting of portions of Kings, which characterizes Elisha's actions as "glorious" (9.46, 182), presents the prophet as having been just, humane, merciful, and hospitable (9.50, 58, 59, 182; cf. *J.W.* 4.462). In order to craft this exemplary portrait, Josephus omits several biblical stories in which Elisha acts rashly or harshly (e.g., 1 Kings 19:17, 21; 2 Kings 5:27). Josephus likewise, in accord with his general habit of downplaying or rationalizing biblical miracles, drops a number of astounding wonders reported in 2 Kings (4:38-41; 4:42-44; 5:1-19, 20-27; 6:1-7).

Josephus discreetly ignores 2 Kings 2:23-25, where Elisha, in response to the taunting of children, calls forth bears which maul forty-two boys. It seems likely enough that Josephus found the story morally distasteful, as did some of the rabbis later on (e.g., *b. Soṭah* 47a). Moreover, *T. Abr.* 10:6-7, 12-14 has God rebuke Abraham when he, acting like Elisha, commands beasts to come out of a thicket to devour certain sinners, and Ps.-Clem. *Hom.* 16:20 similarly rejects Elisha's act of vengeance. Origen felt moved to allegorize the folk tale (*Homily on Ezekiel* 4.7). Obviously discomfort with the Elisha of 2 Kings 2:23-25 was not uncommon.

BIBLIOGRAPHY

L. H. FELDMAN 1998, *Studies in Josephus' Rewritten Bible,* Leiden: Brill, 334-51.

DALE C. ALLISON JR.

Enoch

Enoch is the seventh antediluvian patriarch, son of Jared and father of Methuselah. The terse account of Enoch's life in Gen. 5:21-24 attests to several important features of his story. It says that the patriarch lived only 365 years, a life span unusually short in comparison with that of other members of the Sethite genealogy. He also walked with *ha-'ĕlōhîm,* which can be interpreted either as a sign of his piety toward God or his association with angels. Finally, he was taken by God, which may implicitly refer to his ascension and installation in heaven.

While the Genesis account gives only scant and enigmatic details, in the earliest Enochic writings gathered in the collection known as *1 (Ethiopic) Apocalypse of Enoch* or simply *1 Enoch,* the seventh antediluvian patriarch has a set of highly developed roles: sage, diviner, scribe, expert in secrets, and priest. Such elaborations represent the result of a substantial and lengthy conceptual development, the impressive scope and antiquity of which has been reaffirmed by the discovery of the Qumran Enochic materials.

Mesopotamian Background

In view of the complexity of the patriarch's profile already present in the earliest Enochic writings, scholars believe that some Mesopotamian influences, especially traditions about the seventh antediluvian king Enmeduranki, contributed to the evolution of Enoch. Enmeduranki (Enmeduranna) was the king of Sippar, the city of the sun-god Šamaš. In the Sumerian King List, he occupies the seventh place, which in the Genesis genealogy belongs to Enoch. A cuneiform tablet from Nineveh describes Enmeduranki as a translated figure who entered the divine assembly and received the heavenly tablets. In one of the earliest Enochic booklets, the *Book of the Watchers* (*1 Enoch* 36), Enoch is depicted in several roles that show striking similarities to those of Enmeduranki. Just like his Mesopotamian counterpart, Enoch is skilled in the art of divination; he is able to receive and interpret mantic dreams. Like Enmeduranki, he travels to the divine throne and becomes initiated into the heavenly secrets by celestial beings. He then brings this celestial knowledge back to earth and, similar to Enmeduranki, shares it with the people and with his son. Enoch's life span of 365 years reflects the number of days in the solar year and may also constitute a link with Enmeduranki, who was the priest of the solar deity Šamaš. Enoch's access to the divine throne in the celestial temple, the prototype of the Jerusalem Temple, establishes him as a heavenly priest like Enmeduranki and secures the sacerdotal significance of his revelation.

Mediatorial Functions

Enoch is often depicted in Second Temple and later literature as a mediator of revelations that often were in polemical opposition to the official ideology. This mediatorial function profoundly shaped the cluster of the traditional roles that Enochic lore ascribed to its hero. Enoch's role as a mediator of divine revelation may be implicitly reflected even in his name. While several etymologies for it have been proposed, many scholars suggest that it may be related to the Hebrew root *ḥnk,* in the sense "to train up," "to dedicate," or "to initiate."

The patriarch's mediatorial functions loom large in Enochic lore. He is depicted not only dispatching knowledge from the celestial to the terrestrial realm but also conveying messages received in the lower realms to God and other celestial beings. This two-way communication involves specific media of knowledge represented by the heavenly tablets and by Enoch's petitions and testimonies written on behalf of fallen creatures. His functions as mediator are not confined to a particular realm or a particular petitioner, since his clients include a range of divine, angelic, human, and composite creatures.

In the *Book of the Watchers,* Enoch mediates on behalf of rebellious beings that include the fallen Watchers and the Giants. In *2 Enoch* the elders of the earth ask him for intercession. In the *Genesis Apocryphon* Enoch's son Methuselah consults him to obtain special knowledge about the extraordinary birth of Lamech's son Noah. Enoch's mediating activities also are not limited by specific chronological boundaries. He mediates in the generation of the flood, but he is also expected to be a mediator and a witness of divine judgment at the end of days. *2 Enoch* 36:3 stresses the enduring scope of the patriarch's mediating activities when it mentions the Lord's invitation to Enoch to become his celestial scribe and witness of the divine judgment forever.

Revealer of Esoteric Lore

Enochic materials emphasize that the knowledge transmitted by their hero is not an ordinary revelation but an ultimate wisdom of perennial value. This eternal quality of the revelation is stressed in the Cairo Genizah manuscript of Sir. 44:16, which identifies Enoch as "the sign of knowledge for all generations." The patriarch's prowess in the uttermost heavenly secrets is deeply woven into the fabric of Enochic myth and is set against the expertise in celestial knowledge that the fallen Watchers once possessed. Already in the Enoch *Astronomical Book* (*1 Enoch* 72–82), the possession and revelation of cosmological and astronomical secrets becomes a major function of the elevated Enoch. The origin of this role in Enochic tradition can be traced to *1 Enoch* 72:1, 74:2, and 80:1, which depict the patriarch as a recipient of angelic revelations, including the celestial knowledge of astronomical, meteorological, and calendrical lore. He remains in this capacity in the majority of the materials associated with the early Enochic circle. In the *Book of the Similitudes* (*1 Enoch* 37–71) Enoch is portrayed as the one who "saw all secrets of heaven" (41:1). *Jubilees* 4:17 also attests to this peculiar role. Later merkabah mysticism also underscores the role of Enoch as the "knower of secrets"; thus according to *3 Enoch* 11:2, Enoch-Metatron is able to behold "deep secrets and wonderful mysteries."

Scribal Functions

Enoch's role as an expert in the secrets of heaven and earth cannot be separated from his scribal functions, which are documented already in the *Book of the Watchers* and the *Astronomical Book.* In *1 Enoch* 12:4 and 15:11 Enoch is defined by the honorific "scribe of righteousness." In *1 Enoch* 74:2, Enoch writes down the instructions of his *angelus interpres* Uriel regarding the secrets of the heavenly bodies and their movements. In *1 Enoch* 81:6, Uriel advises the patriarch to record the knowledge he has received in the celestial realm so that he can share it with his children during his upcoming visitation of the earth. Qumran fragments of the *Book of Giants* (4Q203 frg. 8 line 4 and 4Q530 frg. 2 line 14) label Enoch as a distinguished scribe or "the scribe set apart." In *Jub.* 4:17 he is credited with learning the art of writing, instruction, and wisdom and with writing down in a book the signs of the sky. In Merkabah tradition, Enoch-Metatron is depicted as a scribe who has a throne in the heavenly realm; according to *b. Ḥagigah* 15a, the privilege of sitting beside God was accorded solely to Metatron because he had been commissioned by God to sit and write down the merits of Israel.

Other Roles

Late Second Temple Enochic materials, including the *Book of the Similitudes* and *2 Enoch,* try to enhance Enoch's profile by transferring to him many additional elevated characteristics and titles. In the *Similitudes* Enoch is identified with several biblical figures including Deutero-Isaiah's "servant of the LORD" and Daniel's "one like a son of man," in an attempt to underline his crucial role in the eschatological judgment. *2 Enoch* further develops the elevated profile, anticipating his prominent role as the supreme angel Metatron in rabbinic and Hekhalot literature. Some early Christian materials (e.g., Heb. 11:5-6; Jude 14; *Barn.* 4:16) reaffirm the distinguished role of Enoch and the esteemed status of Enochic lore.

BIBLIOGRAPHY

G. BOCCACCINI, ED. 2005, *Enoch and Qumran Origins: New Light on a Forgotten Connection,* Grand Rapids: Eerdmans. • G. BOCCACCINI, ED. 2007, *Enoch and the Messiah Son of Man: Revisiting the Book of Parables,* Grand Rapids: Eerdmans. • G. BOCCACCINI AND J. J. COLLINS, ED. 2007, *The Early Enoch Literature,* Leiden: Brill. • R. H. CHARLES 1912, *The Book of Enoch,* Oxford: Oxford University Press. • P. GRELOT 1958, "La légende d'Hénoch dans les apocryphes et dans la Bible: Origine et signification," *RSR* 46: 5-26, 181-210. • H. KVANVIG 1988, *Roots of Apocalyptic: The Mesopotamian Background of the Enoch Figure and of the Son of Man,* Neukirchen-Vluyn: Neukirchener Verlag. • J. T. MILIK 1976, *The Books of Enoch: Aramaic Fragments of Qumrân Cave 4,* Oxford: Clarendon. • G. W. E. NICKELSBURG 2001, *1 Enoch 1: A Commentary on the Book of 1 Enoch, Chapters 1–36; 81–108,* Minneapolis: Fortress. • A. ORLOV 2005, *The Enoch-Metatron Tradition,* Tübingen: Mohr-Siebeck. • J. C. VANDERKAM 1984, *Enoch and the Growth of an Apocalyptic Tradition,* Washington, D.C.: Catholic Biblical Association of America. • J. C. VANDERKAM 1995, *Enoch: A Man for All Generations,* Columbia: University of South Carolina Press.

See also: Metatron; Son of Man

ANDREI A. ORLOV

Enoch, Astronomical Book of (1 Enoch 72–82)

The fourth section in *1 Enoch,* chaps. 72–82, calls itself "The Book about the Motion of the Heavenly Luminaries"; in scholarly usage it is often named the *Book of the Luminaries* or the *Astronomical Book.* It contains revelations from the angel Uriel, whom God appointed as the leader of all the celestial lights, to the patriarch Enoch, who transmitted this astronomical wisdom to his posterity.

Contents

In the revelations Uriel discloses information about the movement of the sun, moon, and stars through six gates located on the eastern and six corresponding ones on the western horizon and relates their movements to the annual calendars. The angel tells Enoch that the sun remains for thirty days in each of the six gates (arcs of the horizon) in its two annual passages through them, with an extra day at the end of each season (the equinoxes and solstices); the result is a solar year lasting 364 days (chap. 72). The writer criticizes those who do not include the extra four days in their reckoning of the year and who thus follow a schematic calendar of 360 days (75:1-3; 82:4-8) — a system well known from cuneiform sources. The stars define the same 364-day calendar, while the moon measures a shorter year of 354 days (74:12-17). Beginning at 75:4, the text takes up other openings in the sky, including twelve gates through which the winds blow (three in each of the cardinal directions); the writer also lists the kinds of weather associated with the different winds (chap. 76). In chap. 77 one reads about the four quarters of the earth and seven prominent mountains, rivers, and islands on it. With chap. 78 the text returns to astronomical topics, especially the moon. The message of the booklet seemingly comes to an end in chap. 79: in v. 1 Enoch tells his son: "I have shown you everything, and the law of all the stars is completed" (see also v. 6: "This is the appearance and the likeness of each luminary that Uriel, the great angel who is their leader, showed me"). Yet, chap. 80:2-8 follows with a revelation about the deterioration of the natural world, including the luminaries, that will occur in the days of the sinners. *1 Enoch* 81:1–82:3 narrate how the angels returned Enoch to his home for one year so that he could pass along the wisdom he received from Uriel to his son Methuselah and his other offspring. Then from 82:4 until the end of the booklet (82:20) astronomical topics are again under consideration. It is clear that some material was lost after 82:20 because the reader is led to believe in 82:13 that a description of the four seasons will follow but only the first two are depicted in the last verses (vv. 15-20).

Textual History

There is relatively early testimony to the existence of an astronomical work associated with Enoch. Pseudo-Eupolemus, often thought to have written in the early second century B.C.E., mentions Enoch as the one who discovered astrology and may say he transmitted the information to Methuselah, although he does not credit him with authoring a book. The *Book of Jubilees* (mid-second century B.C.E.) does refer to an astronomical composition by the seventh patriarch (4:16-25), and the presence of Aramaic copies of such a work in Qumran Cave 4 has offered confirmatory evidence of its early date.

Aramaic

J. T. Milik identified four fragmentary copies of an *Astronomical Book of Enoch* from Qumran Cave 4 (4QEnastr[a-d] [4Q208-211]). While they have made an invaluable contribution to knowledge about the book, comparing the text of these copies with the Ethiopic versions of *1 Enoch* 72–82 has uncovered a set of problems in the transmission of the booklet. As Milik himself noted, the first copy, 4Q208, which he dated by paleographical criteria to the late third or early second century B.C.E., contains the remains of a lengthy synchronistic calendar (one correlating the moon and sun) that survives only in very abbreviated summaries in the Ethiopic (e.g., 73:1–74:9). None of the surviving Aramaic fragments connects Enoch with this calendar. There is reason for thinking, however, that the synchronistic calendar belongs to an Enochic writing, because 4Q209 (from the Herodian period) contains both remnants of that calendar and sections that overlap with *1 Enoch* 76–79, 82. 4Q210 (mid-first century B.C.E.) also preserves textual overlaps with chaps. 76–79, but 4Q211 (between 50 and 1 B.C.E.) again has no correspondence with the Ethiopic version of *1 Enoch* 72–82. Milik hypothesized that it contains the lost ending of the astronomical work, one that mentioned the seasons (the word *Winter* figures in it) omitted from the conclusion of the Ethiopic version of chap. 82 and gave the results of observations about the stars. There is some doubt whether it does align so closely with the end of chap. 82; if it followed the end of the text of Ethiopic chap. 82, it did so at some remove, because there is no clear evidence that a section about Autumn precedes the reference to Winter. Also, the way in which the Aramaic text speaks about Winter does not correspond with the formulaic presentation of the first two seasons in 82:15-20. Milik thought that the Aramaic form of the *Astronomical Book* was so long that it alone filled a scroll, so that it was not copied on the same scroll with other Enochic texts.

Greek

There is indirect evidence that an Enochic astronomical work existed in Greek, presumably translated from an Aramaic base text. However, there are to date no secure identifications of any such copies. Milik believed he had found fragments of a Greek version among the Oxyrhynchus Papyri (P. Oxy. XVII 2069 frgs. 3 and possibly 4-5), but their small size and battered condition preclude certainty. Only for frg. 3^{v} (77:7–78:1?) can a plausible case be made.

Ethiopic

From Greek the work was translated into Ethiopic, the only language in which it survives as a complete literary entity. The survival of the work in Ethiopic resulted from its being a component in *1 Enoch* — a collection of Enochic writings that achieved canonical status in the Abyssinian church. A large number of copies of *1 Enoch* written in the classical form of Ethiopic (Geʿez) are now available for study (about fifty dating from before the twentieth century [see Nickelsburg 2001: 17]).

Sources

Scholars have expressed different theories regarding the sources from which the writer derived his astronomical information. A. Dillmann (1853) and R. H. Charles (1912) thought he collected statements scattered throughout the Hebrew Bible, but that can hardly be the explanation for all of the information. Charles also believed the writer knew about some Greek calendar systems but held a low opinion of his scientific abilities. More recently, several experts (especially Albani 1994 and Ben-Dov 2008) have uncovered a whole series of close parallels between the Enochic astronomy and the traditional astronomy found in cuneiform texts such as MUL.APIN (an astronomical compendium) and *Enuma Anu Enlil* (a celestial omen series). Examples of parallels are the 360-day year that underlies some calculations in *1 Enoch* 72–82 (e.g., 74:11) but is opposed in other passages (75:1-3; 82:4-7); 2:1 as the extreme ratio of light and darkness at the solstices; and an association between astronomical and geographical phenomena. These and other similarities raise the possibility that the person who wrote the Aramaic *Astronomical Book of Enoch* lived in the eastern Diaspora.

Date of Composition

The date when the Enochic astronomical work was composed is unknown, but one can narrow the possibilities. One important factor in the contemporary debates about the date of the original book is Milik's claim that 4Q208 was copied in the late third or early second century B.C.E. His verdict has not gone unchallenged, but the manuscript is probably from the second century B.C.E., as accelerator mass spectrometry (AMS) testing has shown. Furthermore, there is a second-century-B.C.E. reference to an Enochic book about astronomy in *Jub.* 4:17, 18, 21. It is not unlikely that the Aramaic *Astronomical Book* is the oldest composition attributed to Enoch, dating from the perhaps the third century B.C.E.

Literary Issues

Early in the history of scholarship on the Ethiopic version, some (e.g., A. Dillmann 1853) regarded almost all of *1 Enoch* (less the *Book of Parables,* chaps. 37–71) as a single composition from the pen of one author, with chaps. 72–82 being a part of that unity (he thought 82:9-20 was an addition from a Noah source); but most students of the text have spotted evidence for more than one hand at work in it, although they have not always agreed about which passages were added and which are original. Some scholars have identified as additions those sections that do not treat astronomical subjects (e.g., chaps. 76–77 [e.g., Beer 1900]) on the grounds that they would not be expected in such a work — a view now known to be false on the basis of parallels in Mesopotamian astronomical texts. Experts have also noticed that the booklet seems to end several times (75:3-7; 79:1, 6; 82:1-8) and have proposed that chap. 82 belongs before chap. 79. There is textual support for one change in order in the latter part of the booklet: 4QEnastr^{b} 26 has text that corresponds with the Ethiopic in this order: 79:3-5 + 78:17–79:2. Chapters 80:2–82:3 manifest other problems leading to questions about authorial unity. *1 Enoch* 80:2-8 conflicts with key themes elsewhere in the booklet (e.g., righteousness is not related to correct calendar calculation as in chaps. 72–79, 82; the unchangeable character of the luminaries before the new creation [72:1] is contradicted), and 81:1–82:3 presupposes that Enoch has been in the company of seven angels (81:5; a variant reading is *three*) whereas elsewhere in chaps. 72–82 he is with Uriel alone.

O. Neugebauer (1985) claimed that most of chaps. 72–82 preserves two parallel versions of an Enochic astronomical work: each of the two included sections about the sun, moon, and stars.

72–76 (74 may not belong)
77:1–79:1

The lunar sections are very similar and both have geographic sections attached to them.

The remaining material consists of fragments drawn from other versions (79:2–80:1; 82:4-20), while 80:2–82:3 is an extraneous unit.

J. Ben-Dov (2008) accepts Neugebauer's thesis but nuances it slightly:

Sun	72	78:1-5
Moon Type I	73	78:6-9, 10-14, 17
Moon Type II	74:1-9, 17	78:15-16; 79:3-5
Stars	75:1-3, 8-9	82:4-8, 9-12
Winds/Weather	75:4-7; 76	77; 82:13-20 (4Q211 1 ii-iii)

A major flaw in these explanations is that there is really only one solar section (chap. 72) that furnishes all of the basic information (e.g., about the gates) presupposed in the other sections. Hence, one could say that there is a solar unit (chap. 72) followed by two parallel sections dealing with the moon, stars, and geographical topics. Parts of both of those two parallel sections are attested in 4QEnastr[b-c].

There is solid reason to believe that the Ethiopic version is an abbreviated form of a much longer Enochic astronomical book. The Aramaic evidence suggests as much, but there are other Ethiopic texts (not copies of *1 Enoch* 72–82) that contain detailed information related to the synchronistic calendar and that are attributed to Enoch (e.g., Ethiopic ms. 64 of the Bibliothéque Nationale, which contains the detailed information underlying but not fully reproduced in 74:1-9). It may be that for its literary location in *1 Enoch,* only a summary of the lengthy astronomical sections was prepared, while the more detailed and complicated astronomical information was removed from it and placed in tables that experts could consult but were not needed or appropriate in a scriptural work.

Influence

The astronomy revealed to Enoch and incorporated in one way or another in the Aramaic *Astronomical Book* and in the Ethiopic version had a modest impact on Jewish, Christian, and Ethiopian astronomy. The Enochic system was significant for the calendrists known from the Dead Sea Scrolls. In those texts (especially 4Q317-30) the Enochic solar and lunar calendars are employed. A few early Christian writers mention an astronomical book of Enoch (Anatolius of Laodicea and Origen, both in the third century). In Ethiopia, Enoch's astronomy was one of the major sources of calendaric knowledge along with data from Alexandrian astronomy in the Christian era.

BIBLIOGRAPHY

M. ALBANI 1994, *Astronomie und Schöpfungsglaube: Untersuchungen zum astronomischen Henochbuch,* Neukirchen-Vluyn: Neukirchener Verlag. • G. BEER 1900, "Das Buch Henoch," in *Die Apokryphen und Pseudepigraphen des Alten Testaments,* vol. 2, ed. E. Kautzsch, Tübingen: Mohr, 217-310. • J. BEN-DOV 2008, *Head of All Years: Astronomy and Calendars at Qumran in Their Ancient Context,* Leiden: Brill. • R. H. CHARLES 1912, *The Book of Enoch or 1 Enoch,* Oxford: Clarendon. • A. DILLMANN 1853, *Das Buch Henoch,* Leipzig: Vogel. • J. T. MILIK 1976, *The Books of Enoch: Aramaic Fragments of Qumrân Cave 4,* Oxford: Clarendon. • O. NEUGEBAUER 1985, "The 'Astronomical' Chapters (72-82)," in M. Black, *The Book of Enoch or I Enoch,* Leiden: Brill, 387-419. • G. W. E. NICKELSBURG 2001, *1 Enoch 1: A Commentary on the Book of 1 Enoch, Chapters 1–36; 81–108,* Minneapolis: Fortress. • G. W. E. NICKELSBURG AND J. C. VANDERKAM 2004, *Enoch: A New Translation,* Minneapolis: Fortress. • D. OLSON 2004, *Enoch: A New Translation,* North Richland Hills, Tex.: BIBAL. • E. J. C. TIGCHELAAR AND F. GARCÍA MARTÍNEZ 2000, "4QAstronomical Enoch[a-b]," in *Qumran Cave 4. XXVI: Cryptic Texts and Miscellanea, Part 1,* DJD 36, Oxford: Clarendon, 95-172. • J. C. VANDERKAM 1984, *Enoch and the Growth of an Apocalyptic Tradition,* Washington, D.C.: Catholic Biblical Association.

JAMES C. VANDERKAM

Enoch, Epistle of (1 Enoch 91–108)

In roughly chronological order, the literary units in *1 Enoch* 91–108 are as follows: (1) *Apocalypse of Weeks* (93:1-10; 91:11-17); (2) *Epistle of Enoch* (92:1-5; 93:11-105:2); (3) *Exhortation* (91:1-10, 18-19); (4) *Birth of Noah* (106:1–107:3); (5) *Eschatological Admonition* (108:1-15). Except for the *Eschatological Admonition,* which was composed during the late first century C.E., the other works originated during the second century B.C.E. Aramaic manuscripts from the Dead Sea Scrolls (4Q204, 4Q212) show that, soon after their composition, they were beginning to be organized around a series of revelatory disclosures by Enoch to his son Methuselah (91:1-2; 92:1; 106:1, 7–107:3). This testamentary form was part of a trend that was also occurring in other Enochic writings from the period, such as the *Book of Dreams* (83:1), *Animal Apocalypse* (85:1-3), and insertions into *Astronomical Book* (81:5-6; 82:1). The *Eschatological Admonition,* which also presents itself as revelation mediated to Methuselah by Enoch, was probably composed as an addition to the existing corpus.

Apocalypse of Weeks (93:1-10; 91:11-17)

Together with the much longer *Animal Apocalypse,* the *Apocalypse of Weeks* is structured around a review of the history of the world from the perspective of an Enochic community. This history, which spans from an initial time of "righteousness" until a period of "many weeks without number," is periodized into a scheme of ten "weeks." The awareness in the text that these periods could be further subdivided — for example, into seven parts each (93:3, 91:15) — highlights how much details in *Apocalypse of Weeks* result from a highly selective pro-

ENOCH, EPISTLE OF (1 ENOCH 91–108)

cess. In the history, the seventh week is pivotal: it is the time of the writer, who refers to a community of "chosen ones . . . to whom will be given sevenfold wisdom and knowledge." The first seven weeks cover crucial events in the writer's and his community's past: birth of Enoch (1); the rise of evil, the Great Flood, Noah, law for sinners (2); choice of Abraham as a "plant of righteousness" (3); the giving of the Mosaic Torah (4); building of the First Temple (5); time of apostasy, Elijah, burning of the Temple, exile (6); rise of a wicked generation, election of chosen ones "from the eternal plant of righteousness" (7). The final three weeks are concerned with the writer's and the Enoch community's future during which, in stages, the wicked will be punished and the righteous will be rewarded: punishment of sinners by the righteous, building of the (heavenly) Temple (8); destruction of the works of the wicked, all humanity "will look to the path of uprightness" (9); and eternal judgment (10). The "seventh part" of the tenth week provides the climax to the history, when the "first heaven" is replaced by a "new heaven."

The *Apocalypse of Weeks* is already embedded within the *Epistle of Enoch* in 4Q212, which may be dated to the mid-first century B.C.E. However, the absence of any allusion to the Maccabean Revolt or persecution by Antiochus IV Epiphanes (beginning 167 B.C.E.) suggests that the mention of the "wicked generation" in week seven refers more generally to those Jews who were participating in the Hellenizing reforms introduced in Jerusalem after Antiochus came to power (175-170 B.C.E.).

Epistle of Enoch **(92:1-5; 93:11–105:2)**

This work gave the early Enoch tradition new form and content. In its present form, the composition is not actually an "epistle"; however, at 100:6 the Greek text refers to "the words of this epistle" and appends the title "Epistle of Enoch" after its text, which concludes at 107:3. The *Epistle* opens with words that reflect a testamentary instruction (92:1, Aramaic text), followed by several further passages that comprise the introduction: a declaration about eschatological reward and punishment (92:2-5), contemplation on the immeasurable wisdom of God in creation (93:11-14), and a principled description of the paths of righteousness and wrongdoing (94:1-5).

The heart of the *Epistle* (94:6–104:8) consists of three parts. First, in a lengthy section, the writer pronounces six woe-oracles against "sinners" and intersperses them with other forms of denunciation along with words of comfort for the pious. The sinners are presented as Jews who have their own (false) teachings (98:9–99:2), engage in idolatrous activities, and belong to an elite class accused of economic oppression and enslavement of the righteous. On the other hand, the writer presents the pious as unjustly disadvantaged economically, without social influence, and as the legitimate heirs of Enochic teaching. Second, the woe oracles are followed by an account of how creation functions as a divine agent to reinforce the helplessness of sinners (100:10–102:3). Third, the writer engages in a fictive discourse that combats the view of dead sinners that there is no advantage in either earthly existence or in Sheol for the righteous, whose postmortem state seems no different than their own (102:4–104:8).

The *Epistle* concludes (104:9–105:2) by returning to themes found in the opening passages of the work (esp. 92:1-5 and 94:1-5). In 104:10-11 the writer complains against those who have misrepresented Enochic tradition and, according to the Greek text to 104:11, "write in their own names." At the very end of the work, the text anticipates a time when Enochic wisdom will be disseminated to "the children of the earth."

Throughout the *Epistle* the writer adopts a prophetic tone. More than in any other part of *1 Enoch,* he addresses the wicked and the righteous directly. In focusing alternatively on eschatological punishment and reward, he does more than merely predict the eventual implementation of divine justice; the text implies the author's belief that his denunciations play a formal (and crucial) role in bringing the anticipated judgment about. He understands himself as a prophet who supports the cause of a helpless pious community who have no voice of their own. As in *Apocalypse of Weeks,* the absence of any allusions to events leading up to and during the Maccabean Revolt or their aftermath suggests a date of composition to the first third of the second century B.C.E.

Exhortation **(91:1-10, 18-19)**

This short piece is introduced by the most elaborate testamentary scene in *1 Enoch* 91–108, as Enoch not only summons Methuselah but also his brothers for instruction. The passage picks up a number of themes found elsewhere in *1 Enoch,* especially the *Epistle* (92:1-5; 94:1-5) and the additions to *Astronomical Book* in 81:1–82:3. The instruction of this section encourages readers to "love" righteousness and reject wrongdoing (91:3-4, 18-19). This exhortation frames a two-stage prediction of the future from the vantage point of the fictive Enoch: the first stage is the Great (Noachic) Flood, which follows an increase in wrongdoing and is a definitive manifestation of divine punishment; the second stage, concerned with the eschatological future, is modeled on the first, except more intense: all wickedness and idolatrous activity will be destroyed, and the righteous will be rewarded when they rise from their "sleep."

Since the *Exhortation* assumes the existence of other Enochic materials (92:1-5; 94:1-5; 81:1–82:3), it may be dated to sometime from the middle to the second half of the second century B.C.E.

Birth of Noah **(106:1–107:3)**

This work follows the *Epistle,* and already had this position by the end of the first century B.C.E. (4Q204). Enoch is made to recount the story of the miraculous birth of Noah, who emerges from his mother's womb with angelic features and able to praise God. The work, however, is ultimately concerned with the etymological significance of Noah's name, which is taken to mean (a) having "rest" (106:18 Greek, from LXX Gen. 5:29), (b) "relief" (107:3; Gen. 5:29), and (c) "to be left as a remnant" (106:16). The story of Noah and the flood is taken as a type of eschatological judgment and salvation (106:13-17; 106:19–107:1). The date of the work in its present form may be assigned to sometime between the writing of *Exhortation,* on which it depends (see 91:5-9), and the date of its appearance in the Enoch corpus in 4Q204.

Eschatological Admonition (108:1-15)

This appendix to the Enochic corpus is found only in Ethiopic manuscripts. As a revelation given by Enoch to Methuselah, it is addressed to a writer's pious contemporaries who "keep the law in the last days" (108:1) while living in poverty and undergoing persecution. The vision of the punishment of the wicked in the text (108:4-7, 14-15) reassures the pious that the sins of the wicked will not go unpunished while they will be rewarded for their faithfulness (108:11-14). The thematic affinity between this chapter and Jewish and Christian literature from the late first century C.E. suggests a date to this time.

BIBLIOGRAPHY

G. BOCCACCINI, ED. 2005, *Enoch and Qumran Origins: New Light on a Forgotten Connection,* Grand Rapids: Eerdmans, 185-246. • G. W. E. NICKELSBURG 2001, *1 Enoch 1,* Minneapolis: Fortress. • L. T. STUCKENBRUCK 2007, *1 Enoch 91–108,* Berlin: de Gruyter. • J. C. VANDERKAM 1984, *Enoch and the Growth of Apocalyptic Tradition,* Washington, D.C.: Catholic Biblical Association.

LOREN T. STUCKENBRUCK

Enoch, Ethiopic Apocalypse of (1 Enoch)

The Ethiopic *Apocalypse of Enoch* or *1 Enoch* is a compilation of five originally independent works attributed to the seventh man from Adam (Gen. 5:18-24). The five Enoch works are the *Book of the Watchers* (chaps. 1–36), the *Book of Parables* or *Similitudes* (chaps. 37–71), the *Astronomical Book* or *Book of the Luminaries* (chaps. 82–92), the *Book of Dreams* (chaps. 83–90), and the so-called *Epistle of Enoch* (chaps. 91–108). The earliest books are the *Book of the Watchers* and the *Astronomical Book,* which date to the third century B.C.E. The latest book is the *Similitudes,* which dates to the first century B.C.E. or C.E. All parts of *1 Enoch* were originally composed in Aramaic and then translated into Greek and other languages. The full collection survives only in an Ethiopic version represented by no fewer than ninety manuscripts, the oldest of which are from the fifteenth century. *1 Enoch* was translated into Ethiopic together with other biblical texts between the fourth and sixth centuries. Aramaic fragments of all parts of the compilation except for the *Similitudes* were discovered in Qumran Cave 4. Aramaic fragments of a related Enochic work, the *Book of Giants,* were also discovered there, and J. T. Milik proposed that this work originally stood in place of the *Similitudes* to form an Enochic "Pentateuch," but this is not widely accepted.

While *1 Enoch* became canonical in the Ethiopian church, it was lost to the Western world for many centuries. Some excerpts were preserved in Greek in the *Chronography* of George Sycellus. In 1773 the Ethiopic was discovered by the Scottish explorer James Bruce, who was searching for the sources of the Nile. He brought back three manuscripts. Parts of these were published in Latin in 1800. The full text was published in English in 1821 by Richard Laurence of Oxford (later archbishop of Cashel in Ireland). Laurence also published the first Ethiopic text of *1 Enoch* in 1838. These publications contributed greatly to the recognition of a genre of apocalyptic literature in ancient Judaism.

The various component parts of *1 Enoch* are discussed separately in this volume.

BIBLIOGRAPHY

R. H. CHARLES 1912, *The Book of Enoch or 1 Enoch,* Oxford: Clarendon. • M. A. KNIBB 1978, *The Ethiopic Book of Enoch: A New Edition in the Light of the Aramaic Dead Sea Fragments,* 2 vols., Oxford: Clarendon. • R. LAURENCE 1821, *The Book of Enoch, an apocryphal production, supposed to have been lost for ages; but discovered at the close of the last century in Abyssinia; now first translated from an Ethiopic Ms. in the Bodleian Library,* Oxford: Parker. • J. T. MILIK 1976, *The Books of Enoch,* Oxford: Clarendon. • G. W. E. NICKELSBURG 2001, *1 Enoch 1,* Minneapolis: Fortress. • G. W. E. NICKELSBURG AND J. C. VANDERKAM 2004, *1 Enoch: A New Translation,* Minneapolis: Fortress.

See also: Watchers, Book of the (1 Enoch 1–36); Enoch, Similitudes of (1 Enoch 37–71); Enoch, Astronomical Book of (1 Enoch 72–82); Dreams, Book of (1 Enoch 83–90); Enoch, Epistle of (1 Enoch 91–108)

JOHN J. COLLINS

Enoch, Similitudes of (1 Enoch 37–71)

The *Book of Parables* or *Similitudes of Enoch* (*1 Enoch* 37–71; for the title, see 68:1) forms the second, and latest, of the five sections or booklets that together make up the Ethiopic *Book of Enoch (1 Enoch).* It has attracted considerable attention both because of its importance within the corpus of Enochic writings and because of the evidence it provides of the way in which the Son of Man traditions of Daniel 7 were interpreted in Judaism.

Composition and Content

The *Book of Parables* contains a variety of material and apparently acquired its present form over a period of time, but it has, at least on the surface, a clear structure and literary form. It is divided up, apart from an introduction (chap. 37) and a conclusion (chaps. 70–71), into three individual "parables" (38:1-44; 45:1–57:3; 58:1–69:29), and the whole work is held together as the report of an otherworldly journey. The text describes how clouds and a storm wind carry Enoch up into heaven (39:3; cf. 52:1), where he sees not only cosmological phenomena (e.g., 41:3-8, the secrets of the lightning, the thunder, the winds, and so on), but also the divine throne room in which the Chosen One/the Son of Man is enthroned before the Lord of Spirits (e.g., 46:1-8; 61:8).

Enoch's Otherworldly Journey

As an account of an otherworldly journey, the *Parables* represent in effect a continuation of the account of the otherworldly journey that forms the second part of the *Book of the Watchers* (*1 Enoch* 1–36). The latter describes how Enoch ascended to the throne room of God, where he received a message of judgment to deliver to the Watchers (*1 Enoch* 14:8–16:4), and how immediately thereafter he was led by the angels on a journey around the cosmos (*1 Enoch* 17–36). The journey described in the *Parables* represents in some respects a continuation of this earlier journey, and this connection is indicated in the text itself by the fact that the *Parables* are headed "The second vision which he saw" (37:1), which recalls the earlier vision that Enoch had seen (1:2), and by the use of the term "parable" to describe the contents of this section (37:5; 38:1; 45:1; 58:1). The use of this term in the *Parables* seems to have been based on its occurrence at the beginning of the *Book of the Watchers* in 1:2, although a wider background for its use does exist in the occurrence of the term in the Balaam narrative (e.g., Num. 23:7, 18) and in prophetic texts (e.g., Ezek. 17:2; 20:49; Mic. 2:4) to refer to a figurative discourse. The authors of the *Parables* seem to have drawn their inspiration from the other sections of *1 Enoch*, and particularly from the *Book of the Watchers*, on which they modeled their own work.

Vision Reports

Some of the most typical material in the *Parables*, like that in chaps. 17–36, consists of reports of what Enoch had seen that are introduced by the phrases "And there I saw" or "And there my eyes saw," and in some cases these vision reports have been expanded in a stereotyped way by a question from Enoch and an answer from an angel. In chap. 46, for example, Enoch's vision of one who had a head of days and of another with him whose face had the appearance of a man (v. 1) is followed by a question to one of the angels accompanying him concerning the Son of Man and the Head of Days (v. 2), and by a lengthy explanation from the angel of the significance of the vision (vv. 3-8). Vision reports of this kind are used in eight passages (40:1-10; 43:1-4; 46:1-8; 52:1-9; 53:1-7; 54:1-6 + 55:3-4; 56:1-4; 61:1-5) that are concerned with the central themes of the *Book of Parables*: the glory of the Lord of Spirits, the judgment of the Son of Man, the punishment of the kings and the mighty and the Watchers, the salvation of the righteous, and cosmic phenomena.

Enthronement and Judgment

In addition to the vision reports, two other groups of passages in the *Book of Parables* should be mentioned. First, there is a series of descriptive statements concerning the enthronement of the Son of Man and the events connected with the judgment (e.g., 48:2-7, 8-10; 50:1-5; 63:1-12). These have been loosely attached to the material in visionary form, often simply by the introductory formula "(And) in those days," familiar from the prophetic literature. Secondly, there is a group of passages that are concerned with the story of Noah and that may have been taken from a preexistent *Book of Noah* (54:7–55:2; 60:1-25; 65:1–67:3). The story of the judgment that occurred in the time of Noah functions in *1 Enoch* as a paradigm of the judgment that will occur at the end of the age, and that is probably why the material concerning Noah was included. But since the Noah passages in the *Parables* do not fit naturally into their context, it is not clear whether they are original or whether they were added at a secondary stage. Similar doubts have been raised about other passages, for example, 42:1-3 and 56:5–57:3a.

The Righteous

The *Parables* reflect the viewpoint of a group who call themselves "the righteous" and have suffered ill-treatment and persecution at the hands of their opponents (53:7; 62:11); it appears, from the reference to the cry of the blood of the righteous for vengeance (47:1-2; cf. 48:7), that some had even been put to death. The enemies of the righteous are sometimes referred to simply as "the sinners," but there are also frequent references to a group described as "the kings of the earth and the strong who possess the dry ground" (48:8) or "the kings and the mighty" (62:1; 63:1), or by some similar phrase. It appears that the *Parables* stem from a dissident group that were being oppressed by the ruling powers and their supporters, and one of the main aims of the work is to assure the righteous that they will ultimately enjoy salvation. The dead will rise (51:1; 62:15), judgment will take place (see, e.g., 46:3-8; 47:3-4; 48:8-10; 62:1-2), heaven and earth will be transformed (45:4-5), the righteous will enjoy eternal life on a restored earth with the Chosen One/Son of Man (45:4-6; 51:4-5; 58:2-6; 62:13-16), and the sinners will be punished (see, e.g., 38:3-5; 41:2; 45:2; 53:2; 69:27-29) and will be burnt in Gehenna (48:9; 54:2; 63:10). Sometimes, for example in 54:1-6 and particularly in 67:4-13, the punishment of the kings and the mighty is linked to that of the Watchers, the angels who, according to the tradition preserved in the *Book of the Watchers*, were responsible for the introduction of sin into the world. The use of the story of the Watchers in the *Book of Parables* provides further evidence of the way in which the authors were influenced by the *Book of the Watchers*.

Chosen One, Son of Man, Messiah

A central element in what is said about the judgment in the *Parables* concerns the role played by the individual called "the Chosen One" (45:3, and frequently), "the Son of Man" (46:2, and frequently), "the Messiah" (48:10; 52:4), and "the Righteous and Chosen One" (53:6). A whole series of passages describes, from slightly different viewpoints, the enthronement of the Chosen One/Son of Man before the Lord of Spirits, and his role, on behalf of the Lord of Sprits, as judge of the sinners and savior of the righteous (see, e.g., 48:2-7; 49:2-4; 51:3; 61:8; 62:1-3; 69:27). In the elaboration of this theme, the authors drew on a wide range of scriptural traditions, particularly the Son of Man vision (Dan. 7:9-10, 13-14; cf. *1 Enoch* 46:1), passages in Isaiah concerning the ideal future ruler (Isa 9:7; 11:1-9; cf.

1 Enoch 46:3; 49), the Servant Songs (Isa. 49:1-7; 52:13–53:12; cf. *1 Enoch* 48; 62–63), the passage in Proverbs concerning the preexistent figure of wisdom (Prov. 8:23-26; cf. *1 Enoch* 48:2-3), and a whole range of other prophetic passages referring to future judgment and salvation. The Chosen One/Son of Man is presented as a preexistent, exalted heavenly being and as such may be compared with the messianic figures who appear in other documents of the period, notably the messiah in 2 Esdras [*4 Ezra*] 11–13, Melchizedek in 11QMelchizedek (11Q13), and the son of God figure in 4QAramaic Apocalypse (4Q246).

It comes as something of a surprise that, whereas throughout *1 Enoch* 38–69 Enoch is clearly distinguished from the Son of Man — whom he sees and describes — in *1 Enoch* 70–71 Enoch is himself identified as the Son of Man (see 71:14). However, it is likely that chaps. 70–71 were added at a secondary stage to the *Book of Parables* and represent a reinterpretation of the Son of Man tradition.

Cosmic Phenomena

The account of what Enoch sees in the course of his heavenly journey includes descriptions both of the divine throne room and of cosmic phenomena (e.g., 41:3-8; 43:1-4; 59:1-3), and the presence of the latter seems at first sight somewhat strange. Similar descriptions do form part of the account of Enoch's journey around the cosmos in the *Book of the Watchers* (see 17:1–18:5; 33–36), and the function of material of this kind may in part be to present Enoch as one who had knowledge of everything, as one who really had visited the heavenly regions.

Date and Provenance

It is difficult to date the *Parables* precisely because the few historical allusions that have been proposed (e.g., the supposed allusion in 56:5-8 to the Parthian intervention in Jerusalem in 40 B.C.E.) provide very uncertain evidence. But it is likely that "the kings and the mighty" represent the Roman authorities, and a good case has been made for the view that the *Parables* date from around the turn of the era. As an alternative view, it has been suggested, by the present writer, that the *Parables* date from around the end of the first century C.E. and were intended as a response to the fall of Jerusalem in 70 C.E. It is in any case likely that the *Parables* come from Jerusalem or the surrounding area.

Language and Transmission

The *Parables* have survived only in Classical Ethiopic (Ge'ez). It is very likely that they were composed in Aramaic (or, conceivably, in Hebrew) and subsequently translated into Greek, exactly as in the case of the other sections of *1 Enoch*, but no trace of either the Aramaic original or the Greek translation of the *Parables* has been found. It is, however, clear that the Ethiopic translation of the *Parables*, like that of *1 Enoch* as a whole, was made from a Greek text. We have no knowledge of the circumstances in which the *Parables* were translated into Greek, but it is a reasonable assumption that it was at the Greek stage that the *Parables* were incorporated as the second item in the corpus of Enochic writings to form the fivefold *Book of Enoch* now known from the Ethiopic version, and that this whole process was completed by the early decades of the second century at the latest. In contrast, there are good grounds for thinking that the Greek text of *1 Enoch* was translated into Ge'ez in the fifth or sixth century as part of the translation of the Scriptures into Ethiopic. It should, however, be pointed out that the oldest surviving manuscripts of the Ethiopic version of *1 Enoch* date from no earlier than the fifteenth century.

Bibliography

G. Boccaccini, ed. 2007, *Enoch and the Messiah Son of Man: Revisiting the Book of Parables*, Grand Rapids: Eerdmans. • J. J. Collins 1998, *The Apocalyptic Imagination*, 2d ed., Grand Rapids: Eerdmans, 177-93. • M. A. Knibb 1978, *The Ethiopic Book of Enoch: A New Edition in the Light of the Aramaic Dead Sea Fragments*, 2 vols., Oxford: Clarendon Press. • M. A. Knibb 1985, "The Parables of Enoch," in *Outside the Old Testament*, ed. M. de Jonge, Cambridge: Cambridge University Press, 43-55. • M. A. Knibb 1995, "Messianism in the Pseudepigrapha in the Light of the Scrolls," *DSD* 2: 165-84. • M. A. Knibb 2007a, "The Structure and Composition of the Book of Parables," in *Enoch and the Messiah Son of Man*, ed. G. Boccaccini, Grand Rapids: Eerdmans, 48-64. • M. A. Knibb 2007b, "The Book of Enoch or Books of Enoch? The Textual Evidence for 1 Enoch," in *The Early Enoch Literature*, ed. G. Boccaccini and J. J. Collins, Leiden: Brill, 21-40. • G. W. E. Nickelsburg 2005, *Jewish Literature between the Bible and the Mishnah: A Historical and Literary Introduction*, 2d ed., Minneapolis: Fortress, 248-56. • G. W. E. Nickelsburg 2006, *Resurrection, Immortality, and Eternal Life in Intertestamental Judaism and Early Christianity*, rev. ed., Cambridge, Mass.: Harvard University Press, 94-111, 284-88. • J. C. VanderKam 1992, "Righteous One, Messiah, Chosen One, and Son of Man in 1 Enoch 37–71," in *The Messiah: Developments in Earliest Judaism and Christianity*, ed. J. H. Charlesworth, Minneapolis: Fortress, 169-91.

Michael A. Knibb

Enoch, Slavonic Apocalypse of (2 Enoch)

2 Enoch is an early Jewish pseudepigraphon preserved principally in the Slavonic language but also in a few recently discovered Coptic fragments. The central theme of the text is the ascent of the seventh antediluvian patriarch Enoch through the heavens, his luminous metamorphosis near the throne of glory, and his initiation into the heavenly mysteries.

Contents

The book, which combines the features of an apocalypse and a testament, can be divided into three parts. The first part (chaps. 1–38) describes Enoch's heavenly journey, which culminates in his encounter with the Deity, who reveals to the seer the secrets of creation. After the encounter Enoch returns to earth to instruct his children in the celestial knowledge he received from

God and the angels. The second part (chaps. 39–67) begins with Enoch's testamentary admonitions to his sons during his short visit to earth and ends with the second ascension of the patriarch. The third part of the book (chaps. 68–73) describes the priestly functions of Enoch's family, the miraculous birth of Melchizedek, and the flood.

Slavonic Manuscripts and Recensions

2 Enoch has survived in more than twenty Slavonic manuscripts and fragments dated from the fourteenth to eighteenth centuries C.E. These Slavonic materials did not circulate independently but were included in collections that often rearranged, abbreviated, or expanded them. Typically, Jewish pseudepigraphical texts were transmitted in Slavic milieux as part of larger historiographical, ethical, and liturgical codices and compendia, in which ideologically marginal and mainstream materials were mixed with each other. Only a small number of the manuscripts, namely, A (0:1–72:10), U (0:1–72:10), B (0:1–72:10), and R (0:1–73:9), give a full account of the story leading up to the flood. Manuscript J (0:1–71:4) goes to chap. 71. Manuscripts P (0:1–68:7), N (0:1–67:3), V (1:1–67:3), and B^2 (1:1–67:3) contain only the first two parts of the book and end with Enoch's second ascension. Manuscript L (0:1–33:8) goes to chap. 33. The rest of the manuscripts give only fragments of the different parts of the book: P^2 (28:1–32:2), Tr (67:1; 70–72), Syn (71; 72), Rum (71:1–73:1), G (65:1-4; 65:6-8), Chr (fragments from chaps. 11–58), Chr^2 (11:1–15:3), K (71:1–72:10), and I (70:22–72:9). A large group of the manuscripts (MPr, TSS 253, TSS 489, TSS 682) are copies of the compilation of rearranged materials from chaps. 40–65 of *2 Enoch* from a judicial codex known as *The Just Balance (Merilo Pravednoe).*

Scholarly consensus holds that *2 Enoch* exists in longer and shorter recensions, although some scholars have proposed the existence of three or even four recensions (Andersen 1983). The longer and shorter recensions of *2 Enoch* differ not only in length but also in the character of the text, and both of them preserve original material. Manuscripts R, J, and P represent the longer recension. Manuscripts U, A, B, V, N, B^2, and L represent the manuscripts of the shorter recension. Manuscripts P^2, Tr, Syn, Rum, MPr, TSS 253, TSS 489, TSS 682, G, Chr, Chr^2, I, and K represent fragments of the longer or shorter recensions. Although several stemmas of the relationships between the manuscripts have been proposed, they must be regarded as provisional until critical editions of the major manuscripts become available (Andersen 1983).

Recently Discovered Coptic Fragments

During his work preparing Coptic manuscripts for publication, Joost Hagen, a doctoral student at Leiden University, recently came across transcriptions and photographs of some Coptic fragments of *2 Enoch.* The forgotten fragments derive from a find made in 1972 during excavations by the British Egypt Exploration Society at Qasr Ibrim, one of the capital cities of Nubia during its Christian phase, which extended from the fifth to fifteenth centuries. Since at this writing (April 2009) Hagen is the only scholar to have examined the materials, any statements about them must be very tentative for now.

According to Hagen, there are four fragments, which are evidently remnants of four consecutive leaves of a parchment codex. The fourth fragment is rather small and not yet placed with certainty; no photograph of it is yet available, only the transcription of its text made by one of the excavators. For the other three fragments, both this transcription and two sets of photographs are available. The present location of the fragments themselves is unknown, but they may be in one of the museums or storage facilities of the Egyptian Antiquities Organization.

Hagen reports that the Coptic fragments contain chaps. 36–42 of *2 Enoch.* He takes them to represent a text of the short recension, since they lack chap. 38 and some other parts of the long recension, and since the material in chap. 39 precedes that in chap. 37. The text also contains the material at the end of chap. 36 that is present only in the oldest Slavonic manuscript of the work, U (15th century), and in the closely related manuscript A (16th century).

In Hagen's opinion the Coptic manuscript of *2 Enoch* likely belonged to a church library before the year 1172, or even before 956, two important dates in the history of Qasr Ibrim. Hagen's initial paleographic study has led him to suggest a tentative date for the fragments in the eighth, ninth, or perhaps tenth century. A date in this range would mean that the Coptic fragments are a century or more older than the translation of *2 Enoch* into Slavonic (11th to 12th century), and several hundred years older than the earliest Slavonic witness (14th century).

Original Language

Most scholars believe that the Slavonic version was translated from Greek, since the text has material that makes sense only in the Greek language. For example, in chap. 30 there is a tradition that derives Adam's name from the Greek designations of the four corners of the earth. Semitisms in the text, such as *Ophanim* and *Raqia Arabot,* point to the possibility of a Semitic *Vorlage* behind the Greek version. Nevertheless, some scholars warn that the Semitisms might be "due to the cultivation of a biblical style in the Greek original" (Andersen 1983). The possibility of direct translation from Hebrew into Slavonic has also been suggested (Mescherskij 1965). Yet this suggestion has met strong criticism from experts who "find it thoroughly unlikely that translations from Hebrew into any sort of written Slavic were made in any region of Slavdom before the middle of the fifteenth century" (Lunt and Taube 1988). The possibility that *2 Enoch* was composed in Greek and that it originated in Egypt may be strengthened by the reported discovery of Coptic fragments of the work, since most early Coptic texts were translated from a Greek original.

Date

The date of *2 Enoch* can be deduced solely from internal evidence. Most arguments for an early dating have been based on the work's portrait of the Jerusalem Temple and its ongoing practices and customs. In this respect, scholars have attempted to find hints that might indicate that the Temple was still standing when the original text was composed. These discussions are not new, since already in his first systematic exploration of the text published in 1896, R. H. Charles used references to Temple practices to argue for an early date for the apocalypse, which he placed in the first century before the destruction of the Second Temple in 70 C.E. (Charles and Morfill 1896). Charles and scholars after him also noted that *2 Enoch* gives no indication that the destruction of the Temple had already occurred by the time of the book's composition; nowhere does the text express feelings of sadness or mourning about the loss of the Holy Place.

Affirmations of the value of animal sacrifice and Enoch's halakic instructions found in chap. 59 appear to be fashioned not in a preservationist, mishnaic mode but rather as if they reflected sacrificial practices that still existed when the author was writing. There is also an intensive and consistent effort on the part of the author to legitimize the central place of worship, which in reference to the place Ahuzan — a cryptic name for the Temple Mount in Jerusalem — is explicitly connected with the Jerusalem Temple. Scholars have also noted indications of the ongoing practice of pilgrimage to the central place of worship. These indications could be expected in a text written in the Diaspora. Thus in his instructions to his children, Enoch repeatedly encourages them to bring gifts before the face of God for the remission of sins, a practice which appears to recall well-known sacrificial customs widespread in the Second Temple period (Böttrich 1992). Further, the Slavonic apocalypse contains a direct command to visit the Temple three times a day, an injunction that would be difficult to fulfill if the sanctuary had been already destroyed.

Jewish or Christian Authorship

Although several hypotheses about Christian authorship of the book have been put forward, none of them has withstood scholarly scrutiny. Besides the early hypothesis of a Bogomil provenance (Maunder 1918), the most consistent effort to establish the Christian provenance of the work was offered by the French Slavist André Vaillant (Vaillant 1952). His position was later supported by J. T. Milik, who argued that the apocalypse was written by a Byzantine monk in the ninth century C.E. (Milik 1976). Both Vaillant's and Milik's positions have been widely rejected. The vast majority of scholars maintain a Jewish provenance for the original work.

Geographical Provenance

Since the pioneering work of R. H. Charles, an Alexandrian provenance for *2 Enoch* has dominated scholarly discussion. Charles proposed that the apocalypse was written by a Hellenized Jew in Alexandria. The text appears to attest to some themes that were distinctive of the Alexandrian environment. One such cluster of motifs deals with traditions concerning Adam. Thus in *2 Enoch* 30:13 the Lord tells Enoch that he created Adam out of the seven "components" and assigned to Adam a name from four of the components: from East — (A), from West — (D), from North — (A), and from South — (M). Earlier testimony to this anagram of Adam's name can be found in the third book of the *Sibylline Oracles,* a composition probably written in Egypt around 160-50 B.C.E. Another reference comes in the writings of the Hermetic author Zosimos of Panopolis, who lived in Alexandria in the late third or early fourth century C.E. (Böttrich 1995). Other Adamic motifs found in *2 Enoch,* such as the tradition about Adam's role as governor of the earth, also seem to point to Alexandria since they exhibit similarities with traditions found in Philo (*De Opificio Mundi* 88; 148).

The description of phoenixes and chalkydras, mythical creatures that Enoch encounters during his celestial tour, might also point to Egypt. Charles noted this imagery, and Van den Broek's study of phoenix traditions confirms Charles's hypothesis that *2 Enoch* reflects the Egyptian syncretism of Roman times (Van den Broek 1972).

Theology

The theological universe of *2 Enoch* is deeply rooted in the Enochic tradition of Jewish apocalypticism in the Second Temple period. Yet the text attempts to reshape these traditions by adding a new mystical dimension. The figure of Enoch portrayed in the various sections of *2 Enoch* appears to be more elaborate than that in the early Second Temple tractates of *1 Enoch.* For the first time, *2 Enoch* seeks to depict Enoch not simply as a human taken to heaven and transformed into an angel, but as a celestial being exalted above the angelic world (Orlov 2005). In this attempt, one may find the origins of another, very different image of Enoch that was developed much later in rabbinic Merkavah and Hekhalot mysticism: the image of the supreme angel Metatron, "the Prince of the Presence." The titles of the patriarch found in the Slavonic apocalypse are different from those attested in the early Enoch literature. They bear a close resemblance to the titles given Metatron in some Hekhalot sources (Odeberg 1928). These developments demonstrate that *2 Enoch* represents a bridge between the early Enoch traditions and the later mystical rabbinic and Hekhalot ones.

BIBLIOGRAPHY

F. ANDERSEN 1983, "2 (Slavonic Apocalypse of) Enoch," in *OTP* 91-221. • C. BÖTTRICH 1992, *Weltweisheit, Menschheitsethik, Urkult: Studien zum slavischen Henochbuch,* Tübingen: Mohr-Siebeck. • C. BÖTTRICH 1995, *Adam als Mikrokosmos: Eine Untersuchung zum Slavischen Henochbuch,* Frankfurt am Main: Peter Lang. • R. H. CHARLES AND W. R. MORFILL 1896, *The Book of the Secrets of Enoch,* Oxford: Clarendon Press. • H. G. LUNT AND M. TAUBE 1988, "Early East Slavic Translations from Hebrew," *Russian Linguistics* 12: 147-87. • A. S. D. MAUNDER 1918, "The Date and Place of Writing of the *Slavonic Book of Enoch*," *The Observatory* 41: 309-16. • N. MESHCHERSKIJ 1965, "K voprosu ob istochnikah slavjanskoj knigi Enoha," *Kratkie soobshchenija Instituta narodov Azii* 86: 72-78. • J. T. MILIK 1976, *The Books of Enoch: Aramaic Fragments of Qumran Cave 4,* Oxford: Clarendon. • H. ODEBERG 1928, *3 Enoch or the Hebrew Book of Enoch,* Cambridge: Cambridge University Press. • A. ORLOV 2005, *The Enoch-Metatron Tradition,* Tübingen: Mohr-Siebeck. • M. SOKOLOV 1910, "Materialy i zametki po starinnoj slavjanskoj literature. Vypusk tretij, VII. Slavjanskaja Kniga Enoha Pravednogo. Teksty, latinskij perevod i izsledovanie. Posmertnyj trud avtora prigotovil k izdaniju M. Speranskij," *Chtenija v Obshchestve Istorii i Drevnostej Rossijskih* 4: 1-167. • A. VAILLANT 1952, *Le livre des secrets d'Hénoch: Texte slave et traduction française,* Paris: l'Institut d'études slaves. • R. VAN DEN BROEK 1972, *The Myth of the Phoenix according to Classical and Early Christian Traditions,* Leiden: Brill.

ANDREI A. ORLOV

Enosh

In the Bible, Enosh (Hebr. *'ĕnôš*) is the son of Seth and the grandson of Adam. Apart from his presence in genealogical lists detailing the progression of the descendants of Seth (Gen. 5:6-11; 1 Chron. 1:1), the only narrative elaboration devoted to him is the syntactically difficult redactional comment in Gen. 4:26: "And to Seth also was born a son, and he named him Enosh. Then was begun invocation with the Name YHWH." The proper noun *'ĕnôš* signifies "humankind," a designation that mirrors the meaning of the name of his grandfather Adam. It is likely, given the rich history of speculative thought surrounding the figure of Seth, that some circles interpreted the posited father-son relationship of Seth and Enosh as emphasizing Seth's status as the (true) ancestor of humankind, a status that Adam forfeited when he transgressed the command of God.

Great ambiguity surrounds the figure of Enosh on account of the multiple ways of understanding the latter half of Gen. 4:26 ("then was begun invocation with the Name YHWH"). Christian and so-called Gnostic groups tend to give the clause a positive valence, the former seeing Enosh as one who cultivated and established the proper liturgical service of the one god, and the latter (where attested) tending to view Enosh as a righteous successor to Seth who perpetuated his father's legacy of righteousness and guarded and transmitted his forebears' writings and teachings. It is in fact as a conduit, rather than producer, of written works that Enosh achieves what fleeting fame he enjoys among such groups; it is largely thanks to him that the written testimonia associated with Adam and Seth were preserved. Few writings are ascribed to his hand, and even those are arguably due to scholastic conflation or confusion with more renowned figures; thus the reference to two inscribed stelae erected by Enosh in the Armenian historian Moses Khorenatsʿi is likely based on Josephus' (*Ant.* 1.69-71) description of a similar action performed by the collective descendants of Seth. Similarly, when the thirteenth-century Syriac *Book of the Bee* avers that Enosh "was the first to author books on the courses of the stars and zodiacal signs," it is likely that Enosh has been confused here with the more illustrious figures of Enoch or Seth, both of whom are famous in parabiblical sources for their astronomical discoveries. The so-called *Prayer of Enosh* (4Q369) allegedly recovered among the Dead Sea Scrolls has been conclusively shown to be a chimera (Kugel 1998).

It is within Mandeism, a Mesopotamian "Gnostic" movement, that Enosh attains true individuality as an author and revelatory messenger. Living on earth in his material identity as son of Seth, he fortuitously escapes drowning in a flood brought on by demonic adversaries by being transported to heaven by an emissary of the principal Mandean deity. There he is installed as a heavenly entity known as the "great Anōsh." Portions of the Mandean scriptures are attributed to him; for example, the eleventh book of the *Right Ginzā* is introduced as "the mystery and book of the great Anōsh, son of the great Shitil (i.e., Seth), son of the great Adam." He also functions in certain narrative sources as a divine emissary warning humans of imminent catastrophes.

In contrast to the ways in which the character of Enosh developed in Christian writings and works traditionally labeled Gnostic, classical Jewish tradition normally ascribes a negative connotation to the phraseology of Gen. 4:26b by reading it as an etiology for false religion: "then was begun the naming [of material objects] with the Name YHWH." In other words, Enosh and/or his generation marked the first appearance in the world of idolatry (*b. Šabbat* 118b; *Tg. Ps.-J.* Gen. 4:26). Representative of this thread is the brief haggadic tale found in the medieval *Midrash Bereshit Rabbati* (ed. Albeck, p. 41):

> What did the people of his (Enosh's) generation do? They arose and piled together all the silver, gold, pearls, and precious stones that were in the world and made a large pedestal. They then erected an idol on it, and they worshipped it and made offerings to it. They also directed harsh words toward Heaven, as Scripture says: "Then they said to God, 'Leave us alone!'" (Job 21:14).

Due to the depravity associated with Enosh and his generation, his name is sometimes parsed as *anūsh* ("weak, diseased"), and a number of rabbinic sources speak of a mini-deluge that engulfed "one-third of the world" in his time (e.g., *Sifre Deuteronomy* §43). Here one might compare the similar linkage of a flood with Enosh in the Mandean tradition, as mentioned above. It seems possible that these specific traditions about the appearance of corruption on earth in the third generation (Adam-Seth-Enosh) are the remnants of a primitive narrative cycle about the early history of humanity which lacked the motifs of angelic sin, disobedience in the Garden, and primal murder that characterize some or all of the other extant stories.

BIBLIOGRAPHY

S. D. FRAADE 1984, *Enosh and His Generation: Pre-Israelite Hero and History in Postbiblical Interpretation,* Chico, Calif.:

ENTERTAINMENT STRUCTURES

Scholars Press. • L. GINZBERG 1925, *The Legends of the Jews,* Philadelphia: Jewish Publication Society of America, 5: 151-52. • J. KUGEL 1998, "4Q369 'Prayer of Enosh' and Ancient Biblical Interpretation," *DSD* 5: 119-48. • J. C. REEVES 1996, *Heralds of That Good Realm: Syro-Mesopotamian Gnosis and Jewish Traditions,* Leiden: Brill.

JOHN C. REEVES

Entertainment Structures

In the Hellenistic and Roman periods, games in the style of the Greek "Crown Games" of Olympia, Delphi, Nemea, and Isthmia gained popularity. Competing for status and prestige, more and more cities throughout the East established similar quadrennial or biennial games, erecting entertainment structures to serve as their venues. The traditional Greek games consisted of theatrical shows, musical events, athletic contests *(gymnika),* and horse and chariot races *(hyppika).* The Romans added spectacles, which included gladiatorial combats *(munera),* animal hunts *(venationes),* and wild-beast fighting. Shows, or games (*ludi* in the Latin), organized on behalf of city councils, were also held on the occasion of annual feasts, religious ceremonies, the visit of dignitaries, and other special events. Four distinct entertainment structures were known in the Greco-Roman world: the theater, the stadium, and the hippodrome were born in Greece, while the amphitheater originated in Rome. The Roman circus is equivalent to the Greek hippodrome, though there are some differences.

Greek and Roman Structures

The Greek theater had a circular orchestra with a stage tent or house *(skēnē)* at its edge. It was a simple structure with no elevated stage in front. The tiers of seats *(cavea)* were retained against a hillside and encompassed more than a semicircle of the orchestra. Passages *(parodoi)* separated the *cavea* and the *skēnē.* With the evolution of Greek drama, the stage house became more and more elaborate. The Greek stadium was either rectangular or U-shaped, had an arena of around 200 m. long surrounded by earth embankments, and served for athletic competitions *(gymnika).* The Greek hippodrome, with an arena 500-600 m. long, was used for horse and chariot races *(hyppika).* The spectators either stood or sat on earth embankments that surrounded the arena.

The earliest Roman theaters were casual wooden structures. Stage houses could be monumental, including columns and marble revetments, wall mosaics, and paintings, but these too were temporary structures that were dismantled at the end of festivals. In the Roman theater the orchestra shrank to a semicircle. It was encompassed by a semicircular auditorium that was sometimes built on a plain, retained by a substructure of vaulted passages *(vomitoria)* that led to the seats. On the other side of the orchestra there was an elevated stage *(pulpitum)* with a decorated façade *(proscaenium).* The *skēnē* behind became more and more elaborate, with a high façade *(scaene frons)* decorated by colonnaded recesses *(exedrae).* The auditorium and the stage building were bonded together.

The Roman circus evolved independently of the Greek hippodrome. Roman chariot races were organized in a different manner, the stalls *(carceres)* were differently laid, and in the arena there were particular installations: the central barrier along the arena was composed of a series of elongated shallow reflection pools *(euripus)* decorated with statues, and an obelisk in between. The turning points on both ends *(meta prima* and *meta secunda)* were marked by huge stone cones. The seats were retained by two parallel walls, or on parallel vaults with a slanting roof, set perpendicular to the area (or radial, under the curved end, the *sphendonē*). The Circus Maximus in Rome (with an arena of 580 m. × 80 m.) set the pattern for other circuses. Roman stadia, common in the provinces of Asia Minor, Syria, and Palestina, were elaborate U-shaped masonry structures. Unlike the Greek stadia, they had stone seats retained on a substructure of vaults.

The oval amphitheater, for the staging of spectacles, was a distinct Roman invention. Convicted criminals were delivered to the wild beasts in these shows. It was first built of wood, being erected for the occasion in the forum, or in the field near graveyards.

In the East the stadium and the theater were used for the staging of various spectacles. Accordingly, Greek and Latin authors of the late Hellenistic period were not precise in their use of terms. The term *theater* is very widely applied; literally, it means "a place for viewing something," so it can be employed for any building with spectator accommodation. Philo uses it for a stadium, as do later authors. Likewise, the term *amphitheater* was used indifferently by authors and in inscriptions to designate a stadium, or a much larger hippodrome/circus, rather than an oval Roman *amphitheatrum,* which was known in the first century B.C.E. as *spectaculum.* Similarly, Josephus speaks about a hippodrome or an amphitheater at Jerusalem (*Ant.* 15.268; *J.W.* 2.44) and Jericho (*Ant.* 17.174-78, 193-94; *J.W.* 1.659-66), but he was actually referring to a small hippodrome or stadium where not only *gymnika* but also *hyppika* were held. Hence the term "hippo-stadium" has been coined by modern scholars to designate such multipurpose structures.

Structures of the Hellenistic Period

Prior to Herod there were very few entertainment structures in the Hellenistic Near East; some are known only from the literary sources. The most famous was the hippodrome of Alexandria, the *Lageion,* built by Ptolemy I Lagus (367-283 B.C.E.). Horse and chariot races were held there, as well as contests and shows. According to 3 Maccabees, under Ptolemy IV Philopator the Jews of Alexandria who refused to worship Dionysus were herded into the hippodrome, to be trampled to death by 500 elephants that had been intoxicated by wine and incense. But the beasts turned instead against the king's troops (3 Macc. 5:36–6:21). A hippodrome also existed outside the city wall of Damascus in the early first century B.C.E. (*Ant.* 13.389). Since no remains are known, it

ENTERTAINMENT STRUCTURES

may have been a casual course, set against a natural slope on the occasion of a specific contest. An arena for chariot racing on the Greek style probably existed at Daphne from at least the late third century B.C.E., but not in Antioch proper. The first formally constructed hippodrome there was donated to the city in 67 B.C.E.

A U-shaped stadium measuring around 30 × 230 m. was uncovered in 1954 in Marathus (Amrit) in Phoenicia, where Alexander the Great spent four days while his army conquered Damascus. It has been dated by its excavators to the fourth-third century B.C.E., thus preceding by about three centuries any other built stadium in the region. Otherwise, there are no remains of any Hellenistic stadiums in the Levant. Likewise, Hellenistic theaters are not known in the Near East prior to Herod.

Structures of the Herodian Period

Wooden Theaters

In *Jerusalem* there was a casual wooden structure decorated with trophies and armor held on wooden armature, which looked like human images and sparked a great protest. Since it was made of wood, the theater disappeared without leaving any trace other than in the writings of Josephus (*Ant.* 15.268-81).

In *Jericho* the evidence for a wooden theater is clearer. Here the theater was a component of the multipurpose entertainment structure, a hippo-stadium. The seats must have been of wood, since no stone remains of seats have been found, only a concave embankment of earth that served as a *theatron.* The *cavea* was retained by a semicircular wall, seventy meters in diameter. It could have seated around 3,000 spectators. An Ionic colonnade, plastered to imitate marble, adorned the top of the *cavea.* The stage building was set on the rear part of a platform, elevated about a meter above the arena, which measured 25 × 80 m., and extended across the entire width of the *cavea.*

Stone Theaters

Caesarea had a stone theater (*Ant.* 15.341). It was inaugurated in 10 B.C.E. as one of the venues for the consecration feast of the city. The theater faced west, toward the sea. Distinctive remains of the Herodian structure have been found at a depth of 0.7–2.3 m. under the better-preserved Severan phase. Its external diameter was 90-100 m., and it accommodated 3,000 to 4,000 spectators. A compromise between the old Hellenistic tradition and the new Roman standards is reflected in the auditorium, which is partially retained against the hillock and partially built; in the orchestra, which was extended beyond a semicircle; in the layout of the stairways; and in the shape of the *scaene frons.* Both the semicircular shape of the auditorium and the very existence of a stage are Roman features.

Sebaste had a theater that according to its excavators was built in the Severan period (190-225 C.E.). Its layout of five or seven wedges of seats *(cunei)* and its six stairways follow the Hellenistic pattern, and the orchestra is more than half a circle. The auditorium was built against the slope of the acropolis, in a Hellenistic manner. This theater may have had an earlier phase, and it may be that the Herodian building projects at Sebaste also included a theater and not just a stadium, as in Jerusalem and Jericho.

Sepphoris had a theater with a diameter of seventy-four meters that was built against the hill and facing north. Its precise date is debated by archaeologists, but it seems to have been built by Herod Antipas. It had twenty-four rows of seats in two tiers, for around 3,000 spectators. In the late first or early second century, it was expanded with the addition of an upper tier of seats with eleven more rows to accommodate an extra 2,000 people.

Stadia, Amphitheaters, and Hippodromes

Herodian stadia have been found in *Sebaste, Jericho, Caesarea,* and *Tiberias.* The simpler racecourse of Herodium should be also included in this group. All are built of stone. Only two are referred to as stadia by Josephus: Caesarea (*J.W.* 2.172; *Ant.* 18.57) and Tiberias (*J.W.* 2.618; *Life* 92; 331; cf. *y. ʿErub.* 5:1, 22b). Those at Caesarea and Jericho are referred to by him as *amphitheatron* or *hippodromon,* but the remains indicate that they were multipurpose hippo-stadia. The amphitheater/hippodrome of Jerusalem, built in 28 B.C.E., was the oldest of these edifices. It left no extant remains, and even its location is a matter of debate. Like the theater, it seems to have been a wooden structure. Only its podium, on which the wooden seats were set, may have been a stone embankment. The hippodrome of Tarichea may have resembled the stadium in Tiberias. According to Josephus 100,000 people assembled there in protest against him in 66/67 C.E. The number seems to be exaggerated. The extant structures are of two main types: rectangular (Sebaste and Herodium), and U-shaped or amphitheatrical with a *sphendonē* on one end (Jericho, Caesarea, and Tiberias).

In *Sebaste,* construction of a stadium began in 27 B.C.E. The rectangular arena (194.5 m. × 58.5 m.) was surrounded on all four sides by porticos with no seats. No starting gates for horse races have been found, but the exceptional width in comparison to regular stadia for athletics suggests that horse and chariot races could have been held there. The back walls were covered by frescos in colorful panels. Scratches incised on these panels depict crude figures engaged in boxing or wrestling.

At *Herodium,* the racecourse measured 25 × 350 m and was retained by two parallel walls. It was located on a long terrace below the lower palace and had no seats. The course was too narrow for chariot races, but horse races could have taken place there.

Jericho had a *hippodromon* or *amphitheatron* that, according to Josephus, was the setting for notable Jews being arrested at Herod's command (*Ant.* 17.174-78, 193-94; *J.W.* 659-66). The remains indicate that it was a composite, multipurpose structure comprised of a wide stadium, a theater, and a palaestra. The term *hippodromon* indicates that equestrian races took place there, even though starting gates and turning posts have not been found. They must have been of wood. The structure itself was built of mud bricks. The arena mea-

View of the turning end of the hippodrome used for chariot races at Caesarea Maritima *(www.HolyLandPhotos.org)*

sured 315 × 83 m. (or just 310 × 73 m. if it had porticos). The northern side of the arena was occupied by the wooden theater described above. It served as the *sphendonē* of the stadium. The palaestra, to its north, was built on top of an artificial platform (ca. 92 × ca. 70 m.) elevated ten to twelve m. above its immediate surroundings, with a central courtyard. The southern face of this platform retained the *sphendonē.* This elevated palaestra, public or royal in character, served to receive, house, and entertain important guests, but it may have also have functioned as a gymnasium with a central *palaestra* (cf. Vitruvius, *De Architectura* 5.11) under the auspices of the king.

In *Caesarea,* the *amphitheatron* or "great stadium" had stone rather than wooden seats, and not just on the *sphendonē* side, but on the two long sides as well. The *cavea,* holding twelve rows with a total seating capacity of 10,000, enclosed an arena measuring 301 × 50.5 m. on the east, south, and west. The seats were retained by two parallel walls. The starting gates *(carceres)* enclosed the arena on the north. Here three phases can be discerned. Phase I, with three sub-phases, dates to the Herodian period, with five stalls on each side of a central gate. The podium wall, retaining the seats, was plastered and decorated by frescos. At the southern end of the arena, about twenty-five meters north of the southern entrance, are remains of the turning post, the *meta prima.* There was no stone barrier. The starting gates of the Herodian phase were set parallel to each other and to the longitudinal axis of the arena. This arrangement indicates that the chariots started their course in parallel lanes, as at Olympia. The destination of the chariots was the far turning post, the *meta prima.* Races according to the Roman style, in radial lanes, were introduced to Caesarea only early in the second century C.E. when, in phase II, the layout of the stalls became radial rather than parallel.

In *Tiberias,* a "stadium" appears only at the beginning of the First Jewish Revolt, when Josephus served as commander in Galilee (*J.W.* 2.617-19; 3.539; *Life* 91–92, 96, 331). It was constructed by Herod Antipas to accommodate celebrations in honor of the emperor Tiberius, in the dedication feast of the city shortly before 19/20 C.E. Only the podium of the *sphendonē* and short sections of the lateral walls have been uncovered. It was built on the seashore, with the *sphendonē* on its southern side. The length is still unknown, but the width of the arena measured about 58 m.

Jewish Participation in Greco-Roman Entertainment Culture

In the Hellenistic and Roman periods, the Jews became strongly exposed to new cultural values and practices — including athletics, which were performed in the nude. These and other public events became an efficient means of assimilation and acculturation to the wider Greco-Roman culture and threatened the old values. But this does not necessarily mean that in embracing these forms of popular culture Jews abandoned their ancestral laws and customs. The Jews of Asia and Syria, including Antioch, refrained from using oil made by Gentiles and were granted by Seleucus I Nicator (312-281 B.C.E.) the right to get from the gymnasiarch a sum of money equal to the value of the oil allotted to Gentiles in the gymnasium. This right prevailed down to the time of Josephus (*Ant.* 12.120).

The introduction of a gymnasium and an ephebate (a youth organization for education in a gymnasium) in Jerusalem by the high priest Jason in 175 B.C.E. aroused great enthusiasm for Hellenism and led to the spread of non-Jewish customs. Young priests left their duties and headed to the racecourse. When the quadrennial festival was held at Tyre, Jason sent three official delegates (1 Macc. 1:14-15; 2 Macc. 4:7-20; Josephus, *Ant.* 12.241). But these moves also met with bold opposition, which finally led to the Maccabean Revolt.

A more vigorous move toward acculturation on a grander scale began with Herod a century and a half later. In 28 B.C.E. he established quadrennial games in Jerusalem, in honor of Augustus. The venues were a theater and an amphitheater. This enterprise was successful but encountered resistance (*Ant.* 15.268-91). Yet multitudes were overwhelmed by the shows and were willing to suspend their cultural scruples in order to enjoy the new amenities. Later Herod constructed entertainment facilities in Samaria (27 B.C.E.) and Caesarea. At the inauguration of Caesarea in 10 B.C.E., he instituted quadrennial Isactian Games to commemorate the momentous victory of Octavian (Augustus) at Actium (*Ant.*

16.137-41; *J.W.* 1.21). Augustus and Julia sent equipment and utensils for these games, which attracted large crowds, and Herod offered prizes not only to the victors but also to those who won second and third place.

The construction of entertainment facilities on such a large scale was a novelty. Herod had theaters built in Jerusalem, Jericho (so *Ant.* 17.161 in some manuscripts), Caesarea, Sidon, and Damascus; and amphitheaters or hippodromes (actually multipurpose hippo-stadia) in Jerusalem, Jericho, and Caesarea. Gymnasia were constructed only outside his realm, in Tripolis, Damascus, and Ptolemais, and in Cos he set a yearly endowment for the gymnasiarch (*J.W.* 1.422-23). His son, Herod Antipas, built a stadium in Tiberias, a theater in Sepphoris, and a hippodrome in Tarichea. The first arena designated for gladiatorial combats was donated to Berytus by Herod's grandson Agrippa I. Two armies, each of 700 warriors (condemned criminals according to Josephus), were fighting there when it was inaugurated. Agrippa also donated a theater to Berytus (*Ant.* 19.335-37).

In time, more and more Jews attended the shows, especially in the Diaspora. The philosophical and historical writings of Philo of Alexandria are rich with similes, allegories, and episodes reflecting his and his fellow Jews' acquaintance with events in the theater and in the arena. Very vivid is his description of the attitude of the mob in the hippodrome of Alexandria, jumping into the arena from their seats, and being crushed by the wheels of the chariots and the hooves of the horses (*De Providentia* 58). The writings of the apostle Paul reflect a similar acquaintance, and both he and Philo were observant Jews. Envoys sent to Rome or other cities attended shows. Among the privileges by Julius Caesar to Hyrcanus II and his sons when in Rome was permission to sit with the members of the senatorial order as spectators at the contests of gladiators and wild beasts (*Ant.* 14.210). A stele from the time of Augustus was erected by the Jewish community of Berenice in Cyrenaica; it honored a Roman benefactor and was placed in a most conspicuous place in the *amphitheatron.*

Herod must have attended many games and shows in his travels in the cities of the Mediterranean and on his three visits to Rome. In 17 B.C.E. (*Ant.* 16.6) he attended the Centennial Games *(ludi saeculares)* in Rome, which coincided with the tenth anniversary of the Principate. In June of 12 B.C.E., as a reward for his munificence in providing funds for the Olympic Games, Herod was named perpetual president *(agōnothetēs)* of the games (*Ant.* 16.149; *J.W.* 1.426-27). In this capacity he was able to learn in detail the way Olympic Games were organized and to meet the foremost Greek athletes and artists of the time. On this and other occasions, he saw and no doubt learned much about the organization of Greek and Roman games, while examining closely the structures in which they were held.

After the Herodians, the next wave of construction of entertainment structures in the Roman provinces of Palestina and Arabia came under the Flavians (69-96 C.E.) and continued mainly under Hadrian (117-138 C.E.) and Septimius Severus (193-211 C.E.). In the second and third century, each city boasted one or two theaters. Some also had a stadium, and the largest among them (Caesarea, Bosra, Tyre, Berytus, Laodicea, Antioch, and Alexandria) also had a full-fledged Roman circus. Some cities (Caesarea, Bostra, Eleutheropolis) had an oval amphitheater. This urban reality of the Roman Empire was known to the rabbinic sages and is reflected in several passages in rabbinic literature that refer to *theatra, stadion,* and *kynegion.* Attending shows became quite normal for Jews, though it was not encouraged by the rabbis.

BIBLIOGRAPHY

R. A. BATEY 2006, "Did Antipas Build the Sepphoris Theatre?" in *Jesus and Archaeology,* ed. J. H. Charlesworth, Grand Rapids: Eerdmans, 111-19. • H. A. HARRIS 1976, *Greek Athletics and the Jews,* Cardiff: University of Wales Press. • J. H. HUMPHREY 1986, *Roman Circuses: Arenas for Chariot Racing,* Berkeley: University of California Press. • J. H. HUMPHREY 1996, "'Amphitheatrical' Hippo-Stadia," in *Caesarea Maritima: A Retrospective after Two Millennia,* ed. A. Raban and K. G. Holum, Leiden: Brill, 121-29. • M. LÄMMER 1974, "Die Kaiserspiele von Caesarea im Dienste der Politik des Königs Herodes," *Kölner Beiträge zur Sportwissenschaft* 3: 95-164. • M. LÄMMER 1981, "The Attitude of King Agrippa I towards Greek Contests and Roman Games," in *Physical Education and Sports in the Jewish History and Culture,* ed. U. Simri, Netanya: Wingate Institute, 7-17. • A. LICHTENBERGER 2006, "Jesus and the Theater in Jerusalem," in *Jesus and Archaeology,"* ed. J. H. Charlesworth, Grand Rapids: Eerdmans, 283-99. • A. MAHONEY 2001, *Roman Sports and Spectacles,* Newburyport, Mass.: Focus. • J. PATRICH 2002A, "Herod's Hippodrome/Stadium at Caesarea and the Games Conducted Therein," in *What Has Athens to Do with Jerusalem: Essays in Honor of Gideon Foerster,* ed. L. V. Rutgers, Leuven: Peeters, 29-38. • J. PATRICH 2002B, "Herod's Theater in Jerusalem — A New Proposal," *IEJ* 52: 231-39. • Y. PORATH 1996, "Herod's 'Amphitheater' at Caesarea," *Qadmoniot* 29: 93-99 (in Hebrew). • Y. PORATH 2000, "The Wall Paintings on the Podium of Herod's Amphitheatron at Caesarea," *Michmanim* 14: 42-48 and color plate 7 (in Hebrew with Eng. summary on pp. 17*-18*). • D. R. ROLLER 1998, *The Building Program of Herod the Great,* Berkeley and Los Angeles: University of California Press. • D. R. SCHWARTZ 1992, "Caesarea and Its 'Isactium': Epigraphy, Numismatics, and Herodian Chronology," in idem, *Studies in the Jewish Background of Christianity,* Tübingen: Mohr-Siebeck, 167-81. • A. SEGAL 1995, *Theatres in Roman Palestine and Provincia Arabia,* Leiden: Brill. • Z. WEISS 1996, "The Jews and the Games in Roman Caesarea," in *Caesarea Maritima: A Retrospective after Two Millennia,* ed. A. Raban and K. G. Holum, Leiden: Brill, 443-53.

See also: Athletics; Gymnasium; Theaters

JOSEPH PATRICH

Eschatology

Eschatology means "talk about the end." The term has its origin in theological discourse about the "last things" (resurrection and judgment of the dead, and ensuing reward and punishment).

In the biblical corpus, the prophets predicted the "end," or destruction, of Israel (e.g., Amos 8:2; Ezek. 7:2). This was sometimes associated with "the day of the LORD" (e.g., Amos 5:18; Isa. 2:12; 13:9-13; Zeph. 1:7; 2:14; cf. Mal. 3:2). This would be a day of judgment on Israel and/or the nations, but it would not entail the end of history. In the postexilic period, we find the idea of a general judgment on all the nations, not just on the immediate enemies of Israel (e.g., Ezekiel 39; Joel 3). We also find in the Bible the concept of "the end of days" (*ʾaḥărît hayyāmîm).* This phrase originally meant "in the course of time," or "in future days." A cognate expression in this sense is found in Akkadian. The phrase appears in Gen. 49:2 (blessing of Jacob) and Num. 24:24 (Balaam's oracle). Both passages contain old prophetic texts, which originally referred to the unspecified future, but were interpreted in the postexilic period to refer to the final period of history. Usually, *ʾaḥărît hayyāmîm* has positive connotations for Israel (Isaiah 2; Micah 4; Dan. 2:28). Much of the eschatological expectation of Second Temple Judaism is *restorative;* it is concerned with the restoration of Israel to an idealized form of its former state. The restored state would be led by a messiah, that is to say, a legitimate king from the Davidic line, who would restore the monarchy and be the fulfillment of the promise to David in 2 Samuel 7 (e.g., Isaiah 11; Jeremiah 23; 33).

Postexilic prophecy increasingly predicts more far-reaching, definitive changes. The so-called "Apocalypse of Isaiah" (Isaiah 24–27) says that God will swallow up Death forever, and slay the Dragon that is in the sea. This mythological language suggests the removal of the most fundamental causes of human distress. Isaiah 65 speaks of the creation of a new heaven and a new earth, in which people will live longer lives; anyone who dies aged 100 will be considered a mere youth. Isaiah 11:1-9, which may be postexilic, describes the transformation of nature in the messianic age, so that the wolf will lie down with the lamb. It is generally assumed, however, that these passages are poetic, and not to be taken literally. Ezekiel 37 uses the language of resurrection as a metaphor for the restoration of Israel. Isaiah 26:19 is sometimes thought to refer to individual resurrection, but this too should probably be understood metaphorically.

Apocalyptic Eschatology

A significant new development is attested in the apocalyptic literature of the early second century B.C.E. The book of Daniel, written about 164 B.C.E., describes a vision in which beasts rise from the sea but are subjected to divine judgment and destroyed. The beasts represent kingdoms, but they also represent the forces of chaos depicted in ancient Near Eastern mythology. They are contrasted with a human-like figure, "one like a son of man," who comes on the clouds of heaven and receives a definitive "kingdom" on behalf of "the people of the holy ones." This figure is most plausibly identified with the archangel Michael, who appears as the "prince of Israel" in chaps. 10–12. (Despite the kingdom imagery, Daniel does not speak of a messianic king from the line of David. Messianic expectation is also lacking in the earliest apocalypses of Enoch.) The triumph of Michael is preceded by a period of exceptional distress.

This vision was a response to the persecution of Judeans by Antiochus Epiphanes in 168-164 B.C.E., and assured the faithful that the suffering could be endured because the end was at hand. Daniel is exceptional among ancient apocalyptic writings in attempting to predict the time until the end. Such predictions are notoriously subject to reinterpretation. In Daniel 9, Jeremiah's prophecy that Jerusalem would lie desolate for seventy years is explained as referring to seventy *weeks of years,* or 490 years. Daniel's prediction of the time of the end was interpreted in similar ways and was the subject of eschatological speculation down to the Middle Ages.

But Daniel not only spoke about a kingdom, or the time until the end, but also of the resurrection and judgment of individuals (Dan. 12:1-3). Daniel does not anticipate that all will be raised, but only the very good and the very bad: "Many of those who sleep in the land of dust shall awake, some to everlasting life, and some to shame and everlasting contempt." The wise leaders *(maśkîlîm),* who are the heroes in time of persecution, are raised up to shine like the stars. The roughly contemporary *Epistle of Enoch* also promises the righteous that they "will shine like the luminaries of heaven . . . and the portals of heaven will be opened for you" (*1 Enoch* 104:2) and that they "will be companions of the host of heaven." Stars often symbolize angels or heavenly beings in ancient Near Eastern literature. The righteous are promised a heavenly immortality. It is possible that the astral imagery was suggested by contemporary Greek ideas of astral immortality. Daniel is the only book in the Hebrew Bible where belief in the resurrection of individuals from the dead is clearly expressed. This belief supplements the more traditional hope for an eschatological Jewish kingdom and was especially relevant in the time of persecution.

Belief in resurrection or immortality is also expressed in other ways in the early Enoch literature. In the *Book of the Watchers,* Enoch sees the abodes of the dead, where the wicked and righteous are segregated in anticipation of the final judgment (*1 Enoch* 22). The *Animal Apocalypse* (*1 Enoch* 85–90) ends with a scene of resurrection and judgment. According to the *Apocalypse of Weeks* (*1 Enoch* 93; 91:11-17), the world will be written down for destruction in the ninth week, and the first heaven will pass away and a new heaven will appear in the tenth week. In the apocalypses of the early second century B.C.E., this is as close as we come to the idea of an end of the world. (In contrast, this idea is well attested in the first century C.E.) The book of *Jubilees,* which is closely related to the Enoch literature, says that the bodies of the righteous will rest in the earth but their spirits will have much joy, apparently a form of afterlife that will not require bodily resurrection (chap. 23). None of the early (second century B.C.E.) apocalypses speaks clearly of a resurrection of a body of flesh and blood. This is also true of the *Similitudes of Enoch* (*1 Enoch* 37–71) from the early first century C.E. There the righteous dead are said to live with the angels, but there is no mention of earthly resurrection. The rulers of the earth will be subject to a final judgment over which the Son of Man will preside. The Son of Man is a figure in one of Enoch's visions, obviously modeled on Daniel 7. In the *Similitudes* he is called "messiah," among other things, but he is not said to be a descendant of David. Rather he is a heavenly figure, more exalted in status than the archangels.

Not all strands of early Judaism accepted the idea of beatific afterlife or of judgment after death. Ben Sira, roughly contemporary with the early Enoch apocalypses, flatly rejects such ideas, as does Qoheleth. The Pharisees allegedly affirmed resurrection, but the Sadducees denied it (Acts 23:6-8). In the Greek-speaking Diaspora, many Jews (but by no means all) subscribed to the Platonic idea of the immortality of the soul.

Eschatology in the Dead Sea Scrolls

The expression *'aḥărît hayyāmîm* ("end of days") occurs more than thirty times in the Dead Sea Scrolls. The Scrolls attest to a revival of messianic expectation and speak of multiple messiahs, primarily the messiah of Israel (presumably the Davidic messiah) and the priestly messiah of Aaron. There is also occasional mention of an eschatological prophet, who will herald the coming of the end-time. The *'aḥărît hayyāmîm* is the period when the messiahs will come (1QSa) and so is at least partly future, but it has already begun. 4QMMT declares, "This is the end of days." It is a time of testing, but it is also a time of incipient salvation. In many of the eschatological writings of this period, including Daniel, the period before the end is one of especially acute distress. According to the Qumran *War Rule*, there will be a great eschatological battle between the sons of light, aided by Michael and his angels, and the sons of darkness, including the Kittim (probably the Romans), aided by Belial. The *Damascus Document* says that in those days "Belial is loose against Israel" (CD 4:12-13). A hymn in the *Hodayot* alludes to the destruction of the world by fire (1QH^a col. 11), but it is not clear whether this was a matter of belief or only a poetic metaphor. A number of texts in the Scrolls (the *Temple Scroll*, the *New Jerusalem* text, 1QSa) anticipate an era when the Torah, as interpreted by the sectarians, will be properly observed. Typically, the priests will hold the highest authority in that situation. According to 1QSa, even when the messiah of Israel comes he will still defer to the authority of the priests. This expectation is restorative, although the state to be restored conforms to a sectarian ideal.

Several texts, including the Qumran *Community Rule*, make clear that the sectarians expected eternal life. Whether they also expected resurrection is controversial. The *Hodayot* speak of life "on the height" in the company of the angels and imply that the sectarians had already achieved this in their present life. (This is sometimes called "realized eschatology.") Consequently, there is very little discussion of death in the Scrolls. A few hymns use the language of resurrection, but it is not clear whether this is metaphorical. The idea of resurrection was certainly known at Qumran, from Enoch and Daniel, and it is explicit in 4Q521 (a text that begins, "Heaven and earth will obey his messiah"), as one of the works of the Lord in the end-time, and in 4Qpseudo-Ezekiel (4Q386), but it is not clear whether any of these texts were composed within the sect. The Qumran sectarians do not appear to have used the language of resurrection by preference when speaking of their hope for immortality. Josephus suggests that the Essenes believed in immortality but not in resurrection. Hippolytus claims that they affirmed resurrection, but his account of the Essenes is confused.

Greek-speaking Judaism

In Jewish literature from the Greek-speaking Diaspora, belief in afterlife often takes the form of immortality of the soul, under the influence of Platonic philosophy (Philo, Wisdom of Solomon, 4 Maccabees). National restoration plays little role in these texts, with a notable exception in Philo's treatise *De Praemiis et Poenis*. The earliest attestations of the resurrection of a body of flesh and blood are also in Greek: 2 Maccabees 7, where the martyrs hope to get back the limbs cut off by their torturers, and *Sib. Or.* 4.181-82, which speaks of bones (cf. Ezekiel 37). Pseudo-Phocylides affirms both bodily resurrection and the immortality of the soul, and says that the righteous dead become "gods." Josephus also expresses belief in both resurrection (in the form of metempsychosis) and the immortality of the soul.

The *Sibylline Oracles*, which were compiled over several hundred years, present varied eschatological beliefs. The oldest oracles, in *Sibylline Oracle* 3, expect a restoration of Jewish fortunes in the reign of the seventh king of Egypt from the line of the Greeks. Typically, the time before the rise of this king is a time of grave distress. It is likely that the sibyl expected deliverance to come from a quite specific king, Ptolemy VI Philometor of Egypt, whose patronage of Jews is well known, or his son, Ptolemy Neos Philopator. The expectation was not fulfilled. The fifth book, which was composed in Egypt and dates from the early second century C.E., describes both an eschatological adversary (an "antichrist" figure) modeled on Nero, who was for a time expected to return from the East, and also a savior king, who was expected to come from heaven and restore Jerusalem. This oracle ends with a bleak vision of cosmic destruction. Neither *Sib. Or.* 3 nor *Sib. Or.* 5 expresses a belief in resurrection or personal immortality. Both *Sib. Or.* 4 and *Sib. Or.* 1–2, which date from the first century C.E., divide the course of history into numbered periods and end with resurrection and judgment. These oracles also predict the destruction of the world by fire, as a counterpart to its earlier destruction by water in the time of the flood. These oracles represent a different strand of sibylline tradition and come not from Egypt but from Syria or Asia Minor.

The Later Apocalypses

Apocalypses written in the late first century C.E. combine different eschatological traditions. On the one hand, there is the expectation of the restoration of Israel in an earthly, messianic kingdom. On the other, there is the apocalyptic expectation of the end of this world and the resurrection and judgment of the dead. In *4 Ezra* 7, the messiah reigns on earth for four hundred years. Then he dies, and creation returns to primeval silence for seven days. Then the new creation, resurrection, and judgment follow. There is a similar scenario in *2 Baruch,* and also in the book of Revelation, where the interim reign is 1,000 years. In *4 Ezra* 11–12, the messiah son of David berates the Romans for their crimes. He also appears in chapter 13, riding on a cloud, in the manner of the "one like a son of man" in Daniel 7. He is at once the restorer of Israel and the transcendent, heavenly judge.

Other apocalypses from this period that originated in the Diaspora *(3 Baruch, 2 Enoch)* abandon the theme of national restoration, focusing instead on visions of multiple heavens that include the abodes of the blessed and the damned. This expectation of heavenly afterlife was widespread in the eastern Mediterranean world in late antiquity. The expectation of an end of history, however, followed by a public resurrection of the dead, was distinctively Jewish, although it is also found in Persian tradition. The dating of the Persian traditions is problematic, and consequently there is no consensus as to whether they influenced the development of these ideas in Judaism.

BIBLIOGRAPHY

J. J. COLLINS 1997, *Apocalypticism in the Dead Sea Scrolls,* London: Routledge. • J. J. COLLINS 1998, *The Apocalyptic Imagination,* 2d ed., Grand Rapids: Eerdmans. • J. J. COLLINS, ED. 1998, *The Encyclopedia of Apocalypticism,* vol. 1, *The Origins of Apocalypticism in Judaism and Christianity,* New York: Continuum. • G. W. E. NICKELSBURG 2006, *Resurrection, Immortality, and Eternal Life in Intertestamental Judaism,* 2d ed., Cambridge: Harvard University Press. • É. PUECH 1993, *La croyance des Esséniens en la vie future: Immortalité, résurrection, vie éternelle?,* 2 vols., Paris: Gabalda.

See also: Apocalypse; Apocalypticism; Death and Afterlife JOHN J. COLLINS

Esdras, First Book of

The book of 1 Esdras is an early Jewish work that relates the story of the exile of the people of Judah to Babylon and their subsequent return to the homeland in the sixth century B.C.E. In the standard version of the LXX, 1 Esdras is called Esdras A, separating it from the texts of Ezra and Nehemiah, which comprise Esdras B. In the Latin Vulgate, beginning in the time of Jerome, 1 Esdras is called 3 Esdras, following 1 Esdras (Ezra) and 2 Esdras (Nehemiah). 1 Esdras is also referred to as the "Greek Ezra" in order to distinguish it from other versions. The book is classified among the Apocrypha in Catholic and Protestant traditions and considered deuterocanonical in the Russian and Eastern Orthodox churches.

Theme

The book is concerned with the condition of Judah from the time of King Josiah in the late seventh century B.C.E. until the return of the exiles in the mid-sixth century B.C.E. The focus of the book falls on the rebuilding of the Temple and its institutions and on the people who helped restore worship there. This theme begins with Josiah's Passover celebration in 1:1-22 and continues through the rest of the book. The book culminates with Ezra's Torah reading (9:44-55). Thus, the text focuses on the faithful leaders — Zerubbabel, Sheshbazzar, and Ezra — who restore proper worship in Jerusalem.

Contents

The content of 1 Esdras parallels the material in 2 Chron. 35:1–36:23, sections of Ezra 1–11, and Neh. 7:73–8:12. In many cases, it overlaps in form and content. In other cases, there is original material that does not appear in other sources. The overlap of 1 Esdras with 2 Chronicles, Ezra, and Nehemiah appears as follows:

1 Esdras	**Parallel material**
1:1-55	2 Chron. 35:1–36:21
2:1-15	Ezra 1:1-11
2:16-30	Ezra 4:7-24
3:1–5:6	no parallel material
5:7-46	Ezra 2:1-70
5:47-73	Ezra 3:1–4:5
6:1–7:15	Ezra 4:24–6:22
8:1–9:55	Ezra 7:1–10:44 and Neh. 7:73–8:12

The parallel material shows that only a small portion of 2 Chronicles and Nehemiah appears in the text, but most of Ezra overlaps. Yet the Story of the Three Youths (Contest of the Bodyguards) in 3:1–4:63, which has no parallel in the canonical material, represents an independent tradition. This independent story fits into the category of court tales, a genre of wisdom literature also found in the books of Ahiqar, Judith, Daniel, and Esther.

Composition

The date of composition is much later than the material reflected in the text, which is set from the time of Josiah's reforms (621 B.C.E.) to the period of Ezra's reforms (mid-fifth century B.C.E.). The oldest version of 1 Esdras is in Greek and probably dates to the second century B.C.E. Although an exact date of composition is unclear, Flavius Josephus employed 1 Esdras when compiling books 10 and 11 of his *Jewish Antiquities* in the late first century C.E., thus indicating a date of composition no later than the mid-first century C.E.

There are three main positions concerning the composition of the book. The first position holds that the text is a fragment of a larger work that lost both the beginning and the end. Scholars who support this position hold that this fragment is important because it represents the oldest translation of Chronicles, Ezra, and Nehemiah (Thackeray 1909: 13). The second position maintains that 1 Esdras is a compilation of texts that uses parts of Chronicles, Ezra, and Nehemiah (Williamson 1977: 12-36). Further, some scholars argue that the parent text, stylistically and linguistically similar to Daniel and Esther, was written originally in Hebrew and

Aramaic. A third position posits that the book may represent an independent tradition relying heavily on the material in Ezra but also containing both additions and conflations (Knoppers 2004: 56-58). This independent tradition may reflect a debate in early Judaism on the position of the characters of Ezra and Nehemiah in rebuilding Jerusalem.

Outline

The End of the Monarchy in Judah (1:1-33)

The text opens abruptly with the reforms of Josiah in 621 B.C.E., thus focusing on the Temple in Jerusalem and cultic life during the time of Passover. Josiah then arranges the priests, Levites, and other Temple personnel, thereby instituting proper Temple practice in Jerusalem. By beginning the text with this event, the story centers around the theme of proper Temple practices, an emphasis that continues through the rest of the book. The importance of Josiah's reforms is emphasized in 1:19, which says, "None of the kings of Israel had kept such a Passover as was kept by Josiah and the priests and Levites and the people of Judah and all of Israel who were living in Jerusalem."

The story then turns to the death of Josiah, who was killed not for his own sins but for the sins of the people. 1 Esdras interprets Josiah's death at the hands of Pharaoh Neco as divine judgment on Judah. Josiah himself is not portrayed in a negative light but rather as a great leader who followed the Law of YHWH.

From Josiah's death in 609 B.C.E. to the end of the kingdom of Judah in 587 B.C.E., each subsequent king does not uphold the Law, and so the Lord punishes Judah by bringing Nebuchadnezzar, king of Babylon. Not only are the kings corrupt, but also the Temple personnel, who are condemned to exile, but only for seventy years, following the prophetic prediction in Jeremiah (Jer. 25:11-12; 29:10).

The Beginning of the Return from Exile (2:1-30)

In year one of Cyrus, king of Persia (539 B.C.E.), the first return of the exiles from Babylon occurs. The decree of Cyrus allows for the return of the exiles, whose spirits are kindled with the priests and Levites to return home. The Temple vessels are given to Sheshbazzar, the leader of the returnees. The local population in Judah appears to be less than pleased by this return and writes to the king of Persia to complain, which halts the rebuilding in Jerusalem. 1 Esdras places Artaxerxes as the successor of Cyrus, who died in 530 B.C.E., a chronological problem because Artaxerxes reigned from 465 to 424 B.C.E.

The Contest of the Bodyguards (3:1–4:63)

Set in the court of Darius, king of Persia, the narrative tells the story of a feast that Darius holds for his officials at which three young men who are the bodyguards of the king suggest a contest for the king and his nobles to judge. To win the game, the young men must give the best answer to the riddle of what the strongest thing anywhere is. Their answers are written down and placed under the pillow of the king. The young men's responses are wine, the king, women, and truth. They are then called to defend their positions. The winner is the third youth, Zerubbabel, who argues that women and truth are the strongest of all. Zerubbabel's winning request is that he be allowed to return to Jerusalem and rebuild the Temple and city walls. The king grants Zerubbabel's request, and he prepares to leave. The story concludes with a list of returnees who accompanied Zerubbabel.

Return from Exile and Rebuilding the Temple (5:1–7:15)

A second return takes place in the second year of the reign of Darius (520 B.C.E.) headed by Zerubbabel and the priest Jeshua, along with several other families (5:7-46). Upon their arrival in Jerusalem, the returnees begin to restore sacrifice (5:47-53), marked by the Feast of Booths. The Temple foundation is laid, and the neighbors want to help with the building project. Their help is refused and so they oppose the construction, questioning who gave the authority to undertake the project. After inquiry is made, a royal scroll is found in the archives at Ecbatana; the scroll contains the decree of King Cyrus to rebuild the Temple in Jerusalem. King Darius then allows the rebuilding to take place and also orders the local officials to give support to the sacrifices. Finally, the Temple is complete and the people celebrate Passover, which harkens back to Josiah's Passover mentioned in chap. 1.

Ezra's Reforms (8:1–9:55)

The last wave of returnees comes with Ezra, the priest-scribe, in the seventh year of Artaxerxes. With his return from Babylon, he brings the Temple vessels to Jerusalem. He then begins his mission to purge the people who have married non-Jewish women (8:68-96). The book ends with Ezra reading from the Torah at the east gate of the Temple. Thus, the importance of the Temple and proper worship is made clear at the beginning and end of the book.

BIBLIOGRAPHY

R. J. COGGINS AND M. KNIBB 1979, *The First and Second Books of Esdras,* Cambridge: Cambridge University Press. • S. JELLICOE 1968, *The Septuagint and Modern Study,* Oxford, Oxford University Press. • G. N. KNOPPERS 2004, *I Chronicles 1–9,* New York: Doubleday. • J. M. MYERS 1974, *I and II Esdras,* Garden City, N.Y.: Doubleday. • Z. TALSHIR 1999, *1 Esdras: From Origin to Translation,* Atlanta: Society of Biblical Literature. • H. THACKERAY 1909, *A Grammar of the Old Testament in Greek according to the Septuagint,* Cambridge: Cambridge University Press. • H. M. G. WILLIAMSON 1977, *Israel in the Book of Chronicles,* Cambridge: Cambridge University Press.

DEIRDRE N. FULTON

Esotericism → Mysticism

Essenes

The Essenes were a Jewish religious group of the late Second Temple period, one of the three "parties" *(hairēseis)* mentioned by Josephus. Unlike the Pharisees and Sadducees, they are mentioned neither in the New Testament nor in rabbinic literature. According to most scholars, they are identified with or related to the group behind the Qumran library. If this is correct, the "sectarian" Dead Sea Scrolls from Qumran were written by the Essenes, who are otherwise mentioned only by Greek and Latin authors.

For the name "Essenes," numerous explanations have been suggested. Philo associates it with Gr. *hosiotēs,* "holiness." Modern scholars have proposed various derivations: (a) Aram. *ʾsyyʾ,* "healers" (with reference to Philo's Therapeutae); (b) Hebr. *ʿśh,* "to do" (as "doers of the law"); (c) a local name *Essa;* or even (d) the priests of the Ephesian Artemis named *essēnas.* The best explanation derives the name from (e) the Aram. *ḥsyʾ* (plural *ḥsyn* or *hsyyʾ*), "the pious (ones)," which suggests a connection with the *ḥăsîdîm (hasidaioi)* of the Maccabean era (1 Macc. 2:42). This is supported by the use of *ḥsyh* for "the pious" in the (pre-Qumran) *Aramaic Levi Document* (4Q213a frg. 3–4 line 6) and the mention of a place called *meṣad ḥasîdîm,* "fortress of the pious," in a letter from Wadi Murabbaʿat (Mur 45 6), written in 134/135 C.E.

Greco-Roman Sources

Several Greek and Latin authors mention the Essenes (Gr. *Essaioi* or *Essēnois;* Lat. *Esseni*). The main sources, in chronological order, are Philo, *Quod Omnis Probus Liber Sit* 75–91, *Hypothetica [Apologia pro Iudaeis]* (in Eusebius, *Praep. Evang.* 8.11.1-18), and *Vita Contemplativa* (featuring a group called the Therapeutae); Pliny the Elder, *Natural History* 5.73; and Flavius Josephus, *J.W.* 1.78-80; 2.111-13; 2.119-61; 2.566-68; 3.9-12; 5.142-45; *Ant.* 13.171-72; 15.371-79; 18.18-22; and *Life* 10–12. According to some scholars (Smith 1958; Puech 1993: 2:710-12), Hippolytus (*Refutatio* 9.18.2–9.28.2) gives information independent of Josephus, as do Solinus (*Memorabilia* 35.10-11), in a passage with more details than Pliny, and the pagan orator Dio of Prus, in a speech reported by Synesios of Cyrene (*Dio* 3.2; cf. Stern 1974-1980: 2:118-19; VanderKam and Flint 2002: 241-42).

The classical sources differ in their character, genre, and numerous details. This calls for a critical evaluation of their respective tendencies, possible sources, and historical reliability.

Pliny visited Judea in spring 70 C.E. together with Titus but probably never came down to the Dead Sea. In his description of that region in his *Natural History* he inserts an ethnographic note about a unique "tribe" *(gens)* living off the west bank of the Dead Sea, between Jericho and ʿEin Gedi, without money and without women but only in the company of palm trees, keeping their number only by the stream of people joining them in repentance for their past life. Pliny may have drawn on a source reporting curiosities in an exaggerated style. His location of the group has led scholars to link the texts from the caves and the ruins nearby with the Essenes.

In two accounts, Philo depicts the Essenes as a remarkable example of Jewish virtue and real freedom. He describes them as a voluntary association of Palestinian Jews, comprised exclusively of mature men dedicated to holiness, practicing a community of goods, and living in small villages, not in towns, and without slaves. They work hard in agriculture and crafts, but do not produce weapons or practice commerce. They sanctify the seventh day, keep constant purity, reject women and marriage, but zealously study ethics and pursue the love of others. Having no firsthand knowledge, Philo presumably drew on sources that he interpreted according to his own philosophical ideals. As a counterpart to the Essenes, who led an "active life," Philo also describes a group called Therapeutae, who lived a more "contemplative life" near the Mareotic Lake in the vicinity of Alexandria. The Therapeutae may have been an Egyptian offshoot of the Essenes.

The works of Josephus provide the most detailed references. Notwithstanding the serious doubts about his claim that he was initiated to all Jewish parties in his youth (*Vita* 11), he must be credited some firsthand knowledge. Josephus mentions an Essene named John as commander (*J.W.* 2.567; 3.11) and notes the Essenes' endurance during the Jewish War (*J.W.* 2.151-52). But like his sources, Josephus represents only an external perspective.

Josephus' earliest chronological reference to the Essenes comes in his account of Jonathan (161-143/2 B.C.E.). In *Ant.* 13.171-72 (cf. 18.11) and *J.W.* 2.119, 162-66, Josephus introduces the three "parties" *(hairēseis)* that evidently emerged at that time. They are described by use of a pattern comparing them with the Greek schools of Stoics, Epicureans, and Pythagoreans, and are distinguished by their attitudes toward the ideas of fate and immortality. Obviously, this is a Hellenistic rendering of Palestinian Jewish debates on human responsibility and the resurrection. Josephus probably took the pattern from a source, and he contrasts the three main Jewish groups with a group he calls the "fourth philosophy." The latter group is said to be responsible for the revolt and for the final defeat of the Jews, whereas the other Jewish groups, chiefly the Essenes, are depicted as a peaceful and honorable people. A second type of reference comes in anecdotes on the individual Essenes Judas, Simon, and Menahem, who uttered political prophecies, Judas foretelling the death of Antigonus, Simon the end of Aristobulus, and Menahem the kingship of Herod, who later favored the Essenes for this reason.

Two reports in Josephus (*J.W.* 2.119-61 and *Ant.* 18.18-22) provide more detailed information on Essene customs and teachings. Like Philo, Josephus depicts the Essenes as an ideal association of virtuous, peaceful, and pious Jews, unparalleled among the Greeks and barbarians (*Ant.* 18.20). The Essenes send offerings to the Temple, but perform their own sacrifices in a different kind of purity (*Ant.* 18.19). They regard oil as a defilement, immerse daily in cold water, and eat a communal meal in strict purity. Zealously they study the works of the ancients. Josephus also describes their admission procedures, including times of probation, their purifying baths, and their solemn vows "to hate the wicked and to fight alongside the just" (*J.W.* 2.139), "to love truth and pursue liars," and to "reveal nothing to outsiders" (*J.W.* 2.141). Josephus also mentions the expulsion of members who commit faults and gives other details of their daily life, such as their covering of their excrement (*J.W.* 2.148-49).

There are numerous discrepancies among the main external sources. Philo calls the group *Essaioi,* Pliny refers to them (in Latin) as *Esseni,* and Josephus uses both *Essaioi* and *Essēnoi,* possibly because he found both forms of the name in his sources. Whereas Philo and Josephus describe the Essenes as an association of Jews, Pliny mentions only a "tribe" without pointing to its Jewishness. According to Pliny, the Essenes live by the Dead Sea, whereas Philo and Josephus locate them throughout Judea, Philo only in villages, not in towns.

The differences between the accounts on aspects such as celibacy and marriage, pacifism and resistance, political prophecy and quiet, rural life may be due partly to the authors' respective apologetic and idealizing interests; others may be due to their use of sources or to their referring to different subgroups or different periods of the movement. All the accounts provide more information on customs and curiosities and less on beliefs and doctrines, perhaps because the Essenes kept their teachings secret from outsiders (*J.W.* 2.142; cf. 1QS 4:5-6; 9:16-17; 10:24-25). Furthermore, doctrinal matters (e.g., regarding fate and immortality) are described in Hellenistic terms that are hardly appropriate for a Palestinian Jewish group. Particularities of scriptural interpretation, eschatological expectations, and matters of calendar or purity are not mentioned. Thus any reconstruction of Essene customs and beliefs solely from the classical sources must be regarded as incomplete. A comprehensive view can be gained only if the primary sources, the texts of the Qumran library, are critically included. They can also help to determine the historical value of the Greek and Roman accounts.

The Qumran Texts

Long before the Qumran finds, L. Ginzberg had suggested that the so-called *Damascus Document* (CD) from the Cairo Geniza was an Essene text. Immediately after the first Qumran discoveries, E. L. Sukenik and others established the Essene hypothesis, inspired by Pliny's localization of the Essenes near the Dead Sea and supported by an impressive list of parallels between Philo and Josephus on the one hand and the Qumran texts on the other, on matters such as the group's admissions process, hierarchical structure, community of goods, communal meals, purification rites, Sabbath observance, and religious beliefs such as determinism, afterlife, and angels (Beall 1988). At the same time, the ruins of Qumran were interpreted as an Essene settlement (or even "monastery") by R. de Vaux. This was the predominant view until the 1980s. Since then, the relation between the Scrolls and the Essenes has frequently been questioned, due to a growing awareness of the variety within the Qumran library on the publication of previously unknown documents in the 1990s. The original interpretation of the ruins has also been questioned by alternative proposals that have described the site variously as a military fortress, a country villa, a commercial entrepôt, or a farm complex. But in most of these alternate explanations, the origin of the library is left unexplained or the links between the caves and the settlement are either ignored or dismissed.

In view of these debates, the Essene hypothesis deserves several modifications. Although scholars still debate the criteria for determining which Scrolls are "sectarian" (i.e., not just copied but composed by the Qumran group), it is at least clear that most of the texts in the Qumran library were not composed by the community itself. Therefore, only the community writings (esp. 1QS, 1QSa, CD and 4QD, 1QH, the pesharim, and 4QMMT) can serve for the comparison with the classical sources and for reconstructing Essene beliefs. Further discrepancies among the Qumran rule scrolls may point to different subgroups or stages of development in the history of the community. Moreover, these rules were not written for the inhabitants of Qumran, since the settlement was established only around 100 B.C.E., but for other Essene groups. This is also in accordance with the numbers given by Josephus and Philo (4,000 Essenes; 6,000 Pharisees), which are ideal but at least show that the Essenes were not an irrelevant "sect" and certainly not confined to the inhabitants of the site of Qumran, which was used only for particular purposes (Scripture study, possibly scrolls production, but also agriculture and other activities).

With these modifications, the identification of the community behind the Qumran library with the Essenes remains the most plausible. Most decisive are two rather marginal elements from the list of parallels: the mention of the Essene avoidance of oil as a source of defilement (*J.W.* 2.123) coincides with the halakic view that oil transmits ritual impurity (4QMMT frg. B lines 55-58; 4Q513 frg. 13 line 4; CD 12:15-17), and the prohibition of spitting (*J.W.* 2.147) has an analogy in the penal code of the *Community Rule* (1QS 7:13). A fragmentary text given the title *Rebukes of the Overseer* (4Q477) confirms that the penal code was practiced, and an ostracon from Qumran (if the suggested reading is correct) seems to document the practice of the community of goods in accordance with the rule scrolls.

Doctrines and Customs

The most decisive focus in the Qumran literature is Scripture and a particular form of inspired scriptural interpretation. The Essenes believed that their leader, the Teacher of Righteousness, had revealed to them the true and definitive interpretation of the Torah. 4QMMT explains the separation from others by reference to halakic disputes, and the pesharim interpret the words of the Hebrew prophets in relation to the present history of the group, on the conviction that they were living in the end of days. Their main obligation is to study the

Torah and the prophets (1QS 8:14), in order to live according to God's will. In this respect, the Essenes regarded themselves not as a sect or faction but as the legitimate remnant (CD 1:4), the true Israel at the end of the age (1QSa 1:1). They understood repenting and joining the group as entering God's covenant (1QS 1:16). Their conservatism is obvious in their adherence to the older, 364-day calendar (cf. *1 Enoch* 72–82, *Jubilees,* 4QMMT), as well as in numerous details of their halakah (cf. 4QMMT). They still considered the Jerusalem Temple as God's dwelling place (CD 1:3), but it had been defiled, and so they anticipated the eschatological erection of a new, pure temple (cf. 11QT). For this reason they refrained from the invalid offerings and festivals celebrated (in their view) at the wrong time, but they evidently still visited the Temple for prayer and teaching or to bring donations (*J.W.* 1.78-80; 2.111-13; *Ant.* 18.19). Whether they sacrificed elsewhere remains unclear, but they clearly regarded themselves as a new, living temple (4QMidrEschat 3:6; 1QS 8:5; 9:6) that worshiped in communion with the angels (1QS 11:7-8; 1QSa 2:3-9; 4QŠirŠabb) and that offered their spiritual sacrifices of obedience and prayer.

The Essenes' worldview consists of a strict determinism (cf. 1QS 3:15) and an elaborate dualism as expressed, for example, in the curses against outsiders in their covenant liturgy (1QS 2:5-18) and in their expectation of an eschatological war between light and darkness that would bring about the final defeat of Belial and his "lot" (1QM). The understanding of the afterlife remains unclear in the Qumran texts, but the number of copies of Daniel in their library and perhaps also the burial customs at Qumran may suggest an expectation of life beyond the grave. Among the various messianic images, the most distinctive one is the expectation of two messiahs, a royal "messiah of Israel" and a priestly "messiah of Aaron" (1QS 11:11), based on Zech. 4:14, in accordance with their assertion of priestly superiority and their call for separation between the royal and priestly offices.

Whereas the Greco-Roman sources render Essene doctrines only partially, they give fuller and more reliable information regarding customs and lifestyle. Philo and Josephus note the hierarchical structure of the group and the obedience to the overseers (*J.W.* 2.135; cf. 1QS 5:2-3; 6:11-13), although the Scrolls are much more precise regarding the leadership of Zadokite priests. There is also general agreement on a multiyear admission process (*J.W.* 2.137-38; 1QS 6:14-23), which is unique in ancient Judaism. Most prominent in all accounts is the mention of communal property (cf. 1QS 1:11), although it remains unclear whether some individual property was tolerated (1QS 6:18-20). Common funds were required, for example, for the common meals and other communal obligations (CD 14:12-14). The immersions mentioned by Josephus (*J.W.* 2.129) are also described in more detail in the Scrolls. In contrast with general Jewish purity rules, the Essene baths were restricted to members, who were allowed access only after a year of introductory studies and could be excluded temporarily or permanently in case of transgressions. Differing from other Jews, the Essenes also immersed before their common meals, which they ate in rigid purity.

The most difficult point to decide is the question of marriage. Contrary to Philo and Pliny (who had no firsthand knowledge), Josephus concedes the existence of married Essenes. This also coheres with 1QSa and CD, where we find mention of women and children in the community (1QSa 1:4; 7:6-7). In the *Damascus Document,* remarriage seems to be prohibited (CD 4:20–5:2), and marriage is reduced to the function of regulating sexual activities (CD 5:6-11). The regulations in the *Community Rule,* however, do not mention wives. Probably there was a subgroup of unmarried members (1QS 8:10-11; 9:5-6), but, contrary to Philo and Pliny, not all Essenes were unmarried.

History

Together, the account in CD 1:5-11, the pesharim, and the excavations from Qumran can be used to reconstruct the group's history. Some scholars have tried to understand the Qumran community as a continuation of groups returning from Babylon (J. Murphy-O'Connor), of earlier Palestinian apocalyptic movements (F. García Martínez), or of the Enochic tradition (Boccaccini 1998). But CD 1:5-11, the halakic debate in 4QMMT, Josephus' first mention of the Essenes in the time of Jonathan (*Ant.* 13.171), and the derivation of their name from the Hasidim (1 Macc. 2:42; 7:13-14) all suggest that the decisive process of group formation took place during and after the Maccabean crisis. The most important figures are the so-called Teacher of Righteousness and his opponent, the Wicked Priest. There have been numerous attempts to identify both figures, especially the Wicked Priest, which has been taken as a sobriquet for the Hasmonean Jonathan (so H. Stegemann) or his brother Simon (so F. M. Cross), or as a title that could be applied to a succession of high priests (the Groningen Hypothesis).

According to Stegemann (1992: 153-61), the Teacher of Righteousness was a Zadokite high priest, probably the person who served after the death of Alcimus (159 B.C.E.) and before Jonathan usurped the office in 152 B.C.E. His name is kept in silence in the pro-Hasmonean 1 Maccabees, but the consequence Josephus draws from this — that there were seven years without any high priest (*Ant.* 20.237) — is totally impossible. Although he was expelled from office, this Zadokite was still considered by his supporters to be the legitimate high priest. Jonathan, on the other hand, was no Zadokite and lacked the requisite high-priestly purity because of his having fought in wars. Moreover, being dependent on the Seleucids, he probably had adopted their calendar. The cult in the Jerusalem Temple was therefore regarded by many Jews as illegitimate, impure, and invalid. The Wicked Priest even tried to kill his rival, the Teacher of Righteousness, but failed (1QpHab 9:2-8; 4Q171 col. iv lines 7-9). The Teacher of Righteousness had gone into exile and joined a group, possibly called the New Covenant, in the land of Damascus (CD 7:18-20), where he formed a new union of different groups that opposed Jonathan's claim to the high priesthood. In contrast to some of its precursor groups, this union (cf. the term *ha-yaḥad* in the Qumran texts) was now dominated by priestly (Zadokite) elements, and so there are good reasons to confine the use of the word "Essene" to this unified group, not use it for the various precursor groups.

Thus, the Essene movement resulted from a schism caused by the usurpation of the high priesthood by Jonathan in 152 B.C.E. The priests who stayed in the Temple and the Hasmonean dynasty were later established as the "Sadducees." Another schism, this one within the Essenes, is referred to in the Qumran texts. The mention of the "man of the lie" and "seekers of smooth things" (people with a less rigid interpretation of Torah and purity) points to a group that turned back to the Temple and its calendar and probably gained influence as Pharisees.

For the later period, there are only few hints. The Qumran settlement was established around 100 B.C.E. (Magness 2002), but Essenes still lived all over Judea and beyond. Probably forty years after the Teacher's death (about 110 B.C.E.), the Essenes expected the end, but it did not come (1QpHab 7:6-14). In the *Nahum Pesher,* Alexander Jannaeus, who persecuted the Pharisees (*Ant.* 13.380-83; *J.W.* 1.96-98), is called the "lion of wrath" (4QpNah 1:5-7), but the *King Jonathan Text* (4Q448) openly applauds him. This shows that the Essenes were not implacably hostile toward the Hasmoneans but reacted flexibly to political developments. Their influence may have grown under Herod the Great (*J.W.* 15.378), but earlier views that they abandoned Qumran (after an earthquake in 31 B.C.E.) and moved to an Essene Quarter in Jerusalem must be dismissed in view of the archaeological evidence that the site was not abandoned for a long period (Magness 2002: 68). In 68 C.E., Qumran was destroyed by the Romans. Possibly some Essenes joined the revolt, considering it the final eschatological battle (cf. 1QM), whereas others died for their convictions without active resistance (*J.W.* 2.152-53). The war was probably the end of the group, although individuals may have survived and transmitted some ideas to the rabbinic tradition. The notion that the Essenes had a major influence on emerging Christianity, either by direct links between an Essene Quarter and the early Jesus movement or by Essenes joining the messianic Jesus movement after 70 C.E., is highly improbable.

BIBLIOGRAPHY

Sources

A. ADAM AND C. BURCHARD 1972, *Antike Berichte über die Essener,* 2d ed., Berlin: de Gruyter. • M. STERN 1974-1980, *Greek and Latin Authors on Jews and Judaism,* 3 vols., Jerusalem: Israel Academy. • G. VERMES AND M. GOODMAN 1989, *The Essenes according to the Classical Sources,* Sheffield: JSOT.

Studies

T. S. BEALL 1988, *Josephus' Description of the Essenes Illustrated by the Dead Sea Scrolls,* Cambridge: Cambridge University Press. • R. BERGMEIER 1993, *Die Essener-Berichte des Flavius Josephus.* Kampen: Kok Pharos. • G. BOCCACCINI 1998, *Beyond the Essene Hypothesis,* Grand Rapids: Eerdmans. • P. R. CALLAWAY 1988, *The History of the Qumran Community,* Sheffield: JSOT. • L. CANSDALE 1997, *Qumran and the Essenes,* Tübingen: Mohr-Siebeck. • J. J. COLLINS 1992, "Essenes," in *ABD,* ed. D. N. Freedman, New York: Doubleday, 2:619-26. • J. J. COLLINS 2009, *Beyond the Qumran Community,* Grand Rapids: Eerdmans. • J. FREY 2003, "Zur historischen Auswertung der antiken Essenerberichte," in *Qumran kontrovers: Beiträge zu den Textfunden vom Toten Meer,* ed. J. Frey and H. Stegemann, Paderborn: Bonifatius, 23-56. • S. MASON 2000, "What Josephus Says about Essenes in his Judean War," in *Text and Artifact in the Religions of Mediterranean Antiquity: Essays in Honour of Peter Richardson,* ed. Stephen G. Wilson and Michel Desjardins, Waterloo, Ont.: Wilfred Laurier University Press, 434-67. • S. MASON 2007, "Essenes and Lurking Spartans in Josephus' *Judean War:* From Story to History," in *Making History: Josephus and Historical Method,* ed. Z. Rodgers. Leiden: Brill, 219-61. • J. MAGNESS 2002, *The Archaeology of Qumran and The Dead Sea Scrolls,* Grand Rapids: Eerdmans. • É. PUECH 1993, *La croyance des Esséniens en la vie future: Immortalité, résurrection, vie éternelle?,* 2 vols., Paris: Gabalda. • M. SMITH 1958, "The Description of the Essenes in Josephus and the Philosophoumena," *HUCA* 29: 273-313. • E. SCHÜRER 1979, *The History of the Jewish People in the Age of Jesus Christ,* rev. and ed. G. Vermes and F. Millar, Edinburgh: Clark, 2:555-97. • H. STEGEMANN 1992, "The Qumran Essenes: Local Members of the Main Jewish Union in Late Second Temple Times," in *The Madrid Qumran Congress,* ed. J. Trebolle Barrera and L. Vegas Montaner, Leiden: Brill, 1:83-166. • H. STEGEMANN 1998, *The Library of Qumran: On the Essenes, Qumran, John the Baptist, and Jesus,* Grand Rapids: Eerdmans; Leiden: Brill. • J. C. VANDERKAM 1999, "Identity and History of the Community," in *The Dead Sea Scrolls after Fifty Years: A Comprehensive Assessment,* ed. P. W. Flint and J. C. VanderKam, Leiden: Brill, 2:487-533. • J. VANDERKAM AND P. FLINT 2002, *The Meaning of the Dead Sea Scrolls,* San Francisco: HarperSanFrancisco. • G. VERMES AND M. GOODMAN 1989, *The Essenes according to the Classical Sources,* Sheffield: Sheffield Academic Press. • S. WAGNER 1960, *Die Essener in der wissenschaftlichen Diskussion vom Ausgang des 18. bis zum Beginn des 20. Jahrhunderts,* Berlin: de Gruyter.

See also: Dead Sea Scrolls; Qumran JÖRG FREY

Esther, Book of

The book of Esther tells how the Jews in the Persian Empire were delivered from the threat of extermination and consequently initiated a commemorative festival, Purim. The book, known in Hebrew as *Ha-megillah,* "the Scroll," is read in the synagogue on Purim. Purim falls on the 14th of Adar, in accordance with Esth. 9:17, 20-23. In certain cities (particularly Jerusalem) the holiday is celebrated on the 15th of Adar, in accordance with Esth. 9:19. The holiday is celebrated as a carnival with costumes, boisterous noise, and drinking.

Story and Structure

The narrative has three main parts and proceeds in several distinct units of events in a particular time and place. These can be called "Acts."

Part 1. Setting the Stage

Act I (1:1-22): Queen Vashti is deposed for refusing King Xerxes' command to appear at the men's banquet, and a decree is issued requiring all women to obey their husbands.

Act II (2:1-23): Esther, a Jewish girl being raised by her cousin Mordecai, is chosen to replace Vashti as queen. At this time, Mordecai exposes a plot to assassinate the king.

Part 2. Haman's Scheme and Its Defeat

Act III (3:1-15): A new vizier, Haman, from the tribe of Agag, is infuriated by Mordecai's refusal to bow down to him. Haman slanders the Jewish people to the king (without identifying them) and receives permission to issue a decree allowing them to be exterminated. By the casting of lots, called *purim,* the 13th of Adar is determined to be the day of proscription. The decree goes forth to all the empire.

Act IV (4:1-17): When the decree is issued, Mordecai contacts Esther in the palace and tells her to go to the king to plead for the Jews' lives. Esther accepts the charge, but proceeds according to her own plan.

Act V (5:1-8): At the risk of her life, Esther goes to the throne room, and the king allows her to approach. She invites him and Haman to a banquet, at which time she invites them to a second banquet.

Act VI (5:9–6:14): Haman goes home bloated with pride. But that night, the king is reminded that Mordecai once saved his life. He commands that Mordecai receive public honors, during which he is to be escorted by none other than Haman. Haman is humiliated.

Act VII (7:1-10): At the second banquet, Esther denounces Haman. He falls at Esther's feet to beg for his life. When the king sees this, he assumes that Haman is trying to rape the queen, and he orders Haman to be executed.

Act VIII (8:1-8): According to the book's premise, Persian decrees cannot be annulled. Not knowing how to deal with this, the king grants Mordecai and Esther the authority to act against Haman's decree.

Act IX (8:9-17): Mordecai responds by issuing a counter-decree allowing the Jews to defend themselves.

Act X (9:1-19): On the day decreed, the 13th of Adar, the Jews gather and defend themselves successfully against their assailants. The Jews spontaneously celebrate the respite from fighting on the 14th of Adar. In Susa, the fighting continues on the 14th of Adar, followed by a celebration on the 15th of Adar.

Part 3. The Establishment of Purim and Its Aftermath

Act XI (9:20-32): At Mordecai's suggestion, the Jews formally obligate themselves and future generations to celebrate these days as an annual festival, and Esther confirms their decision.

Act XII (10:1-3): Epilogue. Mordecai continues to serve the king as vizier, to his own honor and the king's profit.

Historicity

The story takes place between the third and twelfth years of the reign of Ahasuerus, king of Persia. Ahasuerus is known to the West by his Greek name, Xerxes, that is to say, Xerxes I the Great, who reigned from 485 to 465 B.C.E. The book has traditionally been dated to that period, and the author was assumed to be Mordecai himself, who, it is said, "wrote these things down" (9:20). A record of the events is also said to be found in "the book of the chronicles of the kings of Media and Persia" (10:3).

However, the book contains features that argue against its historicity and, at the same time, against a Persian-period dating. The book contradicts what we know of Persian history from sources close to that time, particularly the Greek historian Herodotus, who traveled to the East in the mid-fifth century B.C.E. The queen of Persia had to come from one of seven noble families, and Xerxes' queen during this period was actually Amestris. When Esther is supposed to have been chosen queen, in the seventh year of Xerxes' reign according to 2:16, Xerxes was away fighting in Greece. It is, moreover, hardly conceivable that Mordecai, who was exiled from Jerusalem in 597 B.C.E. (2:6), would be alive and active in the twelfth year of Xerxes' reign (473 B.C.E.) and, according to 10:3, well beyond. It is implausible that the historical Xerxes, who was well in control of his empire, would have allowed anarchy and civil war or that such massive battles would go without trace in the historical record. To be sure, there are local touches that lend verisimilitude to the story, such as the Persian names and office titles, but such things would be known to later times and other places. Some scholars have proposed that the story has a "historical core," but no event in the Persian period on which the story could be based is known.

In sum, the story of Esther is a legend told from a distance, from a time when the reign of Xerxes was remembered imprecisely and with much exaggeration. The book was probably written in the Hellenistic period, most likely in the third century B.C.E. The validity of the story lies not in its historical accuracy but in its representation of a *type* of event that has occurred in Jewish history.

Genre

The genre or classification of Esther may be defined in several ways. It purports to be a *historical narrative* reporting actual events. A presumption of historicity would be necessary to justify the establishment of the holiday of Purim. The book is a *historical novella* insofar as it relates a purportedly historical event as a dramatic story, one that resembles the Greek novellas, popular in Hellenistic times, in several ways. It is a *festival etiology,* because it explains the origin of a religious practice, the celebration of Purim. It is also a *festival reading,* meant to be read publicly to renew the people's memory of the event.

Message

The practical message of the book is that Purim is to be celebrated as a perpetual holiday. But the story itself carries a further teaching, namely that Jews of the Diaspora have the resources to save themselves from disaster. Even in an empire that is not inherently inimical, the Jews are likely to face murderous schemes and have to defend themselves with courage and cleverness. Lacking a king and army, Jewish leaders, or Jews who find themselves forced to lead, must use their wits, courage, personal connections, and courtly dexterity to protect their fellow Jews. The Jewish people must respond to the call of the Jewish leaders with courage and, if necessary, the force of arms. Then, in dialogue with those leaders, the Jews may take upon themselves new religious practices and obligations.

Where is God in all this? The strangest thing about the book of Esther is that he is not mentioned. The Jews do not pray to God for salvation; he does not step in to give them victory; they do not sing his praises afterward. Some have taken this silence to reflect a secular nationalism. Others, including all early interpreters and most modern ones, believe that God is simply assumed to be present and active. Traditionally "another place" (NJPS, "another quarter") in 4:14 is thought to allude to God. Another possibility is that the silence contributes to a deliberate indeterminacy; it conveys the message that Jews should not lose faith and courage even in a crisis in which God's activity is itself unclear.

Transmission and Interpretation

No copies or fragments of the book of Esther were found among the Dead Sea Scrolls at Qumran. It is unclear whether this is due to the accidents of preservation or to a rejection of the book, for theological or calendrical reasons, by the sectarians who lived there. A few texts (e.g., 4Q550[a-f]; *Temple Scroll* 64:9) contain reminiscences of the book of Esther and suggest that it was indeed known to them and used by them.

There appear to have been disputes about the canonical status of Esther as late as the third century C.E. According to a later report in the Talmud (*b. Megillah* 7a; *b. Sanhedrin* 100a), some rabbis doubted that it was written in the Holy Spirit and that it "defiles the hands," usually understood as a paradoxical expression for divine inspiration. But the book was being treated as sacred scripture well before that time, and the disputes were probably academic, not practical.

The earliest interpretation of the book of Esther is to be found in the Greek translation, the Septuagint. The most important feature of this translation is the explicit introduction of God into the events. Josephus' account in *Ant.* 11.6 (93 C.E.) is another reshaping of the tale in Greek; it places special emphasis on the role of Law.

The earliest Hebrew interpretation of Esther is an extensive midrashic discussion in the tractate *Megillah* (10a–17a) in the Babylonian Talmud. There are also two Aramaic targums to Esther. Both are interpretive, but of the two, Targum II is the more periphrastic and expansive and draws extensively on midrash.

BIBLIOGRAPHY

A. BERLIN 2001, *Esther,* Philadelphia: Jewish Publication Society. • F. W. BUSH 1996, *Ruth, Esther,* Dallas: Word Books. • D. J. A. CLINES 1984, *The Esther Scroll,* Sheffield: Sheffield Academic Press. • M. V. FOX 1999, *Character and Ideology in the Book of Esther,* Grand Rapids: Eerdmans. • J. D. LEVENSON 1997, *Esther,* Louisville: Westminster John Knox. • E. SEGAL 1994, *The Babylonian Esther Midrash: A Critical Commentary,* Atlanta: Scholars Press. • B. D. WALFISH 1993, *Esther in Medieval Garb: Jewish Interpretation of the Book of Esther in the Middle Ages,* Albany: SUNY Press.

See also: Esther, Greek Version of; Tales of the Persian Court (4Q550) MICHAEL V. FOX

Esther, Greek Version of

The ancient Greek translation of the book of Esther in the Septuagint (LXX) includes six supplemental passages, called Additions A–F, as well some expansions and changes elsewhere. The Additions address the issues of Esther's dietary practices in the palace, her sexual relations with the Persian king, the absence of prayers in the crisis, and, above all, the absence of the mention of God in the Hebrew version of the book. God is often mentioned in the Additions and in a few other verses in the LXX of Esther, namely 2:20, 4:8, and 6:13. These changes result in a book quite different in character from the Masoretic Text (MT) of Esther. They adjust the book to the beliefs and expectations of a later Jewish audience.

The Additions are imbedded in various places in the story. They are integral parts of the Greek version and should ideally be read in a complete translation of the LXX. Nevertheless, they also make sense when read in their proper places in a translation of the MT.

The Additions were probably composed in Ptolemaic Egypt between the late second century B.C.E. and the middle of the first century C.E. They are not by a single author. Additions B and E (decree and counter-decree) have the same author. Additions C and D are really a single unit, reporting Mordecai's and Esther's prayers and Esther's approach to the king. Addition F is a later interpretation of Addition A.

Though the Additions are Jewish in origin, they were preserved only in Christian manuscript traditions. Jews ceased to use the LXX in the early centuries C.E., whereas it had authoritative status among Christians for many centuries and is still sacred Scripture for Eastern Christians. The Additions have some parallels in the midrashim (see tractate *Megillah* in the Babylonian Talmud), in the Aramaic translation Targum Esther I (*Targum Rishon*) and especially in the periphrastic and expansionistic Targum Esther II *(Targum Sheni).*

Addition A

The Septuagint Esther begins with a dream in which Mordecai sees a colossal struggle between two dragons. As they come forward, "all the nations" prepare to fight against the Jews, who are called the "righteous nation." It is a day of affliction and tumult, and the Jews are in danger. They cry out to God, and he sends hope — a "tiny spring," which becomes a river of salvation. Whereas in the MT the Jews are not attacked by all the nations but only by certain "enemies," in the LXX the world is divided into the Jews and their enemies. The fact that Mordecai foresees the course of events in a dream shows them to be predetermined. Addition A continues with a version of Mordecai's exposure of the assassination plot which differs from the MT's 2:21-23. (The Septuagint still has the equivalent of MT 2:21-23.)

Addition B

Addition B, which replaces the material in MT 3:13-14, is an expansive form of the royal edict to destroy the Jews. In pompous prose, the king proclaims that his motive in ordering the mass murder is to ensure the peace of the realm. He repeats Haman's allegations that the Jews, alone of all nations, are hostile to the peace and laws of the realm, and he decrees their extermination.

Addition C

In the MT, prayers for salvation are not recounted, but are only alluded to — in Mordecai's mourning (4:1) and in the fast that Esther declares (4:16). Prayer is the expected response to crisis, and Addition C supplies the lack with material following MT 4:14. The prayers also deal with issues that, as early exegesis shows, troubled Jewish readers. In his prayer, Mordecai explains that it was not out of pride that he refused to bow to Haman (C vv. 1-11). In her prayer, Esther insists that she takes no pleasure in her luxurious state or her marriage to the foreigner (C vv. 12-30). These things have been imposed on her. Moreover, she has avoided forbidden food and wine. Both beseech God to save the Jews.

Addition D

Addition D follows C v. 30. Esther enters the throne room in splendid attire, supported by two maidservants. When she sees the awesome king, she faints in agitation. Whereas in the MT (4:16–5:1) Esther simply summons her courage and enters the throne room, in Addition D she is nervous, frail, and stereotypically feminine as she approaches the king and flatters him to win his favor. The king is an awe-inspiring but kindly husband.

Addition E

In Addition E, which follows 8:12, the king writes a second letter to his subjects. He excuses his earlier decision on the grounds that he had been deceived by Haman, and he publicly voids "Haman's" decree (which was actually his own). In philosophical tones he moralizes about how excess honor can corrupt some men — namely, Haman — and praises the Jews for following the just laws of the living God. The king also commands his subjects to allow the Jews to obey their own customs. Addition E presents a far more flattering view of Gentile royalty than does the Hebrew book. It is noteworthy that in 9:16 the Septuagint reduces the scope of the slaughter by changing the MT's 75,000 enemies killed outside Susa to 15,000.

Addition F

In retrospect, Mordecai decodes the symbolism of the dream reported in Addition A (follows 10:3). The two dragons are Haman and Mordecai. The small spring is Esther. A new element is that God made two lots, one for Israel and one for the nations, and these lots fell on the day in which God vindicated his people. Addition F is a later interpretation of both Addition A and the motif of "lots" in 9:26.

The Additions, along with the smaller changes, show the ongoing engagement of Jews in the interpretation of the book of Esther. They also illustrate how the Bible can be shaped, in part, by the addition of later interpretative expansions and rewritings.

There is another ancient Greek version of Esther, known as the Alpha-Text. It is known from only five medieval manuscripts but goes back much farther. It is significantly different from both the MT and the Septuagint. According to one view, the Alpha-Text is a revision of the Septuagint. According to another, it is based on a different, perhaps earlier, Hebrew form of the Esther story. The Septuagintal Additions were later inserted into the original Alpha-Text.

BIBLIOGRAPHY

A. BERLIN 2001, *Esther,* Philadelphia: Jewish Publication Society. • F. W. BUSH 1996, *Ruth, Esther,* Dallas: Word Books. • D. J. A. CLINES 1984, *The Esther Scroll,* Sheffield: Sheffield Academic Press. • M. V. FOX 1999, *Character and Ideology in the Book of Esther,* Grand Rapids: Eerdmans. • K. H. JOBES 1996, *The Alpha-text of Esther: Its Character and Relationship to the Masoretic Text,* Atlanta: Scholars Press. • J. D. LEVENSON 1997, *Esther,* Louisville: Westminster John Knox. • C. A. MOORE 1977, *Daniel, Esther, and Jeremiah: The Additions,* Garden City, N.Y.: Doubleday. • K. DE TROYER 2000, *The End of the Alpha Text of the Book of Esther: Translation and Narrative Technique in MT 8:1-17, LXX 8:1-17, and AT 7:14-41,* Atlanta: SBL.

MICHAEL V. FOX

Esther, Proto- → Tales of the Persian Court

Ethics

The term "ethics" refers to the moral principles and values that govern the conduct of an individual and/or a group. It also embraces the virtues to be cultivated and the vices to be avoided, as well as the good and bad actions that flow from them.

In early Jewish writings, ethical teachings are generally set in the religious context of the Torah, and are shaped largely by the Decalogue (Exod. 20:1-17; Deut. 5:6-21) and related texts such as the Holiness Code (Leviticus 18–20) and Deuteronomy 12–26. Early Jewish writers drew most of their principles and values from the Hebrew Scriptures, and placed them in broader sapiential, eschatological, or philosophical contexts.

Palestinian Jews were concerned mainly to link their ethical teachings to biblical traditions about creation and Israel's past (Sirach) and/or to place them in an eschatological context (*1 Enoch,* Qumran texts). Diaspora Jewish authors like Philo were especially eager to show the correspondence of the Torah with right reason and nature. Since nearly all early Jewish writings are concerned with practice, almost every text has ethical implications. The works treated here are among those that are most relevant for understanding ethics in early Judaism.

Palestinian Judaism

Ben Sira

The most extensive and comprehensive source for ethics in Palestinian Judaism is the book of Sirach. Written in Hebrew ca. 180 B.C.E. and translated into Greek by the author's grandson in Egypt ca. 117 B.C.E., the Wisdom of Jesus Ben Sira is the product of the author's many years of teaching in his wisdom school in Jerusalem. While his work is a wisdom book like Proverbs and Ecclesiastes, Ben Sira was more concerned than they were to integrate ancient Near Eastern sapiential traditions and the moral teachings of the Hebrew Bible. One of the most important passages in his book comes after the long and elegant self-presentation of Wisdom finding her home on Mt. Zion at the Jerusalem Temple (24:1-22). As a commentary on the poem, Ben Sira immediately notes: "All this is the book of the covenant of the Most High God, the law that Moses commanded us" (24:23). In other words, Ben Sira identifies wisdom with the Torah, and suggests that real wisdom is to be found in the Law of Moses.

The two great theological themes in Sirach are the search for wisdom and the fear of the Lord. The book is punctuated by poems about seeking wisdom (1:1-10; 4:11-19; 6:18-37; etc.) that provide at least one of its structural principles. Near its end are a hymn in praise of God's works in creation (42:15–43:33) and a long reflection on the great heroes of Israel's history (44:1–50:24). But the bulk of the book is devoted to Ben Sira's instructions on various ethical topics.

In the ethical sections Ben Sira is the instructor, and his principal audience seems to have been elite young men preparing for careers as sages and public figures. His work is formation *(Bildung)* literature. While using the standard sapiential literary forms (maxims, admonitions, beatitudes, etc.), Ben Sira in many cases develops a topic or idea in paragraph form, and often gives reasons for the wisdom of his statements. The ethical topics treated in Sirach include friendship, happiness, honor and shame, manners, money, domestic relationships (wives and husbands, parents and children, masters and slaves), social relations, social justice, and caution in speech.

In some cases Ben Sira merely provides an extended commentary on biblical teachings. For example, his treatment of the duties of adult children with regard to their parents in 3:1-16 is an extended reflection on the Decalogue's commandment to honor one's parents (Exod. 20:12; Deut. 5:16). By contrast, in the following passage (3:17-29) his praise of humility and warning against intellectual pride (Greek philosophy?), while theological in orientation, rely on what might pass for basic human wisdom and are presented in general sapiential terms.

Ben Sira is generally silent about matters pertaining to eschatology. He was skeptical about life after death and about a last judgment with rewards and punishments. For him, the proper reward for a life lived wisely and righteously was a "good name," that is, a reputation that would live on for generations to come.

Epistle of Enoch

The strand of Palestinian Judaism represented by *1 Enoch* and some key texts found at Qumran insist on placing ethics in the context of eschatological rewards and punishments. The part of *1 Enoch* known as the *Epistle of Enoch* (chaps. 91–107) purports to be Enoch's farewell discourse or testament to his children. In it he repeatedly encourages them to love righteousness and to walk in it. He contrasts what should be their behavior with that of the wicked. His many comments on the way of the wicked take the form of a series of "woes" or maledictions pronounced especially upon the wealthy and powerful who were oppressing the righteous in Israel. For example, in *1 Enoch* 94:6 the patriarch warns: "Woe to those who build oppression and injustice, who lay foundations for deceit. They shall soon be demolished; and they shall have no peace."

The woes bear witness to the social and economic tensions in Palestinian Judaism in the second century B.C.E., and especially the resentment smoldering among those who sought to walk in righteousness. Enoch's advice to the righteous is that they should look forward to the divine judgment in which the righteous will be at last vindicated and rewarded with eternal happiness, and the wicked oppressors confronted with divine justice and punished. The exhortation ends with an assurance that the deeds of the righteous are inscribed on the heavenly tablets that will guide the proceedings at the last judgment.

Qumran Community Rule

The Qumran *Rule of the Community* (1QS), as the title indicates, contains many rules and regulations governing the life of a specific Jewish religious community (most often identified as Essenes) and its members. However, the instruction about the "two spirits" (1QS 3:13–4:25) provides a comprehensive theological and ethical framework that embraces all humankind and allows community members to find their place in that framework.

The instruction promotes a theological and ethical vision aptly described as "modified apocalyptic dualism." In line with a Jewish worldview, it insists on the absolute sovereignty of the God of Israel ("the God of knowledge") and the role of humankind within creation. It regards the present age as ruled by two great spirits: the Prince of Light, and the Angel of Darkness. It locates all humans as living under the influence of one of these two spirits. The children of light, led by the Prince of Light, do the deeds of light, whereas the children of darkness, led by the Angel of Darkness, do the deeds of darkness. The spirit that predominates in each person determines the side on which each one belongs. The cosmic struggle will continue until the divine "visitation," when the Angel of Darkness and his followers will be completely defeated and destroyed, and the Prince of Light and his followers will be vindicated and rewarded with eternal blessing. The dualism of the instruction is "modified" in the sense that God's sovereignty at the beginning and the end of human history is acknowledged. And it is "apocalyptic" in the sense that the eschatological "visitation" puts a decisive end to the struggle within human history.

This instruction on the two spirits is also noteworthy for its lists of virtues and vices, a feature found in various Greco-Roman ethical works and in the New Testament. These lists purport to provide catalogues of "the signs identifying their works during their lifetimes," that is, the typical attitudes and behaviors that characterize the children of light and the children of darkness. Those who belong to the children of light manifest "a spirit of humility, patience, abundant charity, unending goodness, understanding and intelligence," and so forth. Those who belong to the children of darkness are marked by "greed, and slackness in the search for righteousness, wickedness and lies, haughtiness and pride, falseness and deceit, cruelty and abundant evil," and so on. For members of the early Jewish community addressed in the instruction, these lists present the virtues to be cultivated and the vices to be avoided as they await in hope and prepare for the divine visitation.

4QInstruction

Though probably not a "sectarian" work (i.e., a work composed by and expressly for the Qumran community), the composition known as 4QInstruction (formerly designated *Sapiential Work A*) was present at Qumran in six or more copies, and seems to have influenced the language and thought of sectarian works such as the *Hodayot* and *Rule of the Community.* In this substantial work, a senior sage addresses someone who seeks greater understanding. In scope and size it is comparable to the book of Sirach. However, from the start (4Q416 1), it places its "ethical" advice in the context of both creation and the last judgment. It views the present age as a preparation for the divine visitation and eternal life with God.

Moreover, whereas those addressed by Ben Sira seem to have been among the social and cultural elite, those addressed in 4QInstruction seem to be economically poor and are often reminded of their low social status (with the caveat that real status comes from living wisely and righteously). The ethical advice imparted in its admonitions concerns social relations, a proper lifestyle, money matters, and domestic relationships. The instructor often bolsters his advice with biblical quotations and allusions, and offers frequent reminders about the eschatological context in which his instructions appear.

Philo

The most extensive and comprehensive presentation of early Jewish ethics from the Diaspora appears in the writings of Philo of Alexandria (ca. 20 B.C.E.–50 C.E.). Philo used the Ten Commandments as the framework for systematizing and explaining core Jewish beliefs about God and human conduct. He sought to provide his fellow Jews with rational foundations for their traditional religious and ethical practices, and to rebut the claims of non-Jews that Jews were foolish and even perverse in their thinking and way of life.

In his treatise *On the Decalogue,* Philo first explains why the Ten Commandments were issued in the wilderness, why there are ten, and why they are expressed in the second-person singular form. Then he insists on dividing the Ten Commandments into two sets of five. The first five pertain to God and parents (who are like God) and concern God's monarchical rule, idolatry, swearing, Sabbath observance, and honoring parents. The second set of five contains prohibitions against adultery, murder (note the order!), theft, false witness, and covetousness or lust.

In treating each commandment, Philo shows how it is to be understood and why it accords with right reason and nature. While Philo's major source is the Greek Bible, he strengthens his case by appealing also to reason, human experience, and even pagan philosophy (as when he treats the tenth commandment with the help of the Stoic concept of the four passions; see 142–53). He regards the Ten Commandments as summaries of all the laws scattered throughout the Pentateuch, and in his four books *On the Special Laws* he shows how they fit under those headings. He concludes *On the Decalogue* by noting that no penalties are attached to the Ten Commandments, and he explains that God did so in order that humans might choose "the best" not out of fear but rather by taking "the good sense of reason for their counselor" (177).

Philo's treatise *On the Virtues* consists of four sections devoted to courage or "manliness," humaneness or kindness, repentance, and nobility. He contends that true courage flows from wisdom and knowledge, that the Mosaic Law is extraordinary for its humane character, that repentance makes possible a "second chance" in many areas of life, and that nobility is more a matter of personal character and action than having famous ancestors or descendants.

The longest and most convincing part of the treatise (51–174) is Philo's attempt to show how humane the Mosaic Law is. After describing "humaneness" *(philanthrōpia)* as the twin of "piety" *(eusebeia),* Philo points to Moses' choice of a successor in Joshua (rather than a family member) and offers as proofs of Moses' humaneness as a lawgiver various laws pertaining to his fellow Israelites, proselytes, settlers, enemies in wartime, beasts of burden, slaves, irrational animals, and plants, respectively. He concludes that God gave these statutes to Israel in order to "set them out of the reach of arrogance and pride" (161). A major reason for Philo's writing this and other treatises on the Mosaic Law was to answer the charges of "clever libelers" who accused Jews of misanthropy and claimed that their laws enjoined "unsociable and unfriendly practices"

(141). On the contrary, Philo replies that the Jewish law excels all others in its humaneness.

Among the extracts of Philo's writings preserved by Eusebius in *Praeparatio Evangelica* is a short piece described as "the constitution" *(politeia)* of the Jewish nation." Extracted from the work known as the *Hypothetica,* the passage emphasizes the scope and strictness of the Mosaic Law in comparison with Gentile law codes. It claims that in the Mosaic Law "everything is clear and simple," and gives examples pertaining to sexual abuse, family life, property, and the humane treatment of animals.

When discussing matters of detail, Philo lays down as a general principle a version of the "golden rule": "What a man would hate to suffer he must not do himself to others" (7.6). Among the examples of the strictness of the Jewish law, Philo treats human reproduction and its prevention: "He must not make abortive the generative power of men by gelding nor that of women by sterilizing drugs and other devices" (7.7). The second part of the "constitution" (7.10-20) is a defense of observing the Sabbath day and the sabbatical year in terms of the natural values of physical rest and ecological concern. Despite Eusebius' description, the passage is not so much a constitution as an epitome of laws that illustrate the breadth of the Mosaic Law and its superiority in the order of reason.

Josephus

Similar in content, purpose, and tone to Philo's "constitution" is the summary of the Jewish law offered by Josephus (ca. 37–100 C.E.) in *Ag. Ap.* 2.190-219. The work as a whole is a response to criticisms and slanders made by non-Jews, with Josephus arguing for the antiquity and superiority of Judaism. Toward the end of his work, Josephus contends that there is no "more saintly government" than what is presented in the Law of Moses.

After emphasizing the foundational Jewish beliefs in one God and one temple, Josephus describes the strict sexual ethics of Judaism: monogamy as the rule, sexual relations for procreation only, sodomy as punishable by death, no abortion or infanticide, and so on. Then he discusses the importance given to educating children in the Jewish tradition, the simplicity of Jewish funeral rites, the duty of honoring parents, the need for showing absolute integrity in business and social dealings, and the humane treatment of all those in need (including animals). Josephus concludes by taking pride in the very severe penalties imposed by the Mosaic Law for various offenses, and he invokes life after death as a source of consolation for those Jews who may suffer death because of their fidelity to the Jewish law. He states that for such persons "God has granted a renewed existence and in the revolution of the ages the gift of a better life" (2.218).

Pseudo-Phocylides

The *Sentences of Pseudo-Phocylides* is a 230-line poem written in Ionic Greek hexameters. While purporting to be the work of a Greek poet of the sixth century B.C.E., it is in fact a Jewish composition from the late first century B.C.E. or early first century C.E., most likely at Alexandria. Its Jewish character is clear from its insistence on monotheism (54) and resurrection (103-4). It is a compendium of biblical ethics presented in nonbiblical garb. It was written to show Jews and Gentiles alike the convergence between Jewish and Greek ethical teachings. It deals with virtues such as justice, mercy, honesty, self-control, moderation, industry, and chastity. It warns against love of money, envy, presumption, boasting, and all kinds of wickedness. It gives special attention to marriage (175–206) and family life (207–27). It recommends marriage as a way to immortality ("lest you die nameless") and as in accord with nature. It encourages chastity within marriage and warns against the many temptations associated with sexuality. In particular, it prohibits abortion and infanticide (184–85).

Testaments of the Twelve Patriarchs

There is general agreement that the *Testaments of the Twelve Patriarchs* as we now have it was composed in Greek, displays a certain conceptual unity while preserving earlier traditions, and contains many passages that portray Jesus Christ as the fulfillment of Jewish hopes. The scholarly debate concerns the nature of the work. Is it an early Jewish composition with some Christian scribal interpolations? Or is it a Christian composition that integrates some early Jewish source materials? Although earlier scholarship assumed its basic Jewish character, it has more recently come to be viewed as a Christian work from the second century C.E. that used Jewish sources. In either case, it contains some features of the dualistic ethical framework found in the Qumran *Rule of the Community* 3–4: two spirits, two ways, and two impulses in tension within the person.

The *Testaments of the Twelve Patriarchs* presents farewell discourses by each of Jacob's sons. In each case the patriarch, knowing that he is about to die, summons his sons, recounts incidents from his earlier life, and draws moral lessons about certain vices to be avoided and/or virtues to be pursued. The vices include fornication (Reuben, Simeon); envy and jealousy (Simeon); priestly arrogance (Levi); drunkenness, fornication, and love of money (Judah); falsehood and anger (Dan); and hate (Gad). The virtues include courage (Judah); simplicity (Issachar); mercy and compassion (Zebulun); natural goodness (Naphtali); single-mindedness (Asher); chastity (Joseph); and focus on the good (Benjamin).

BIBLIOGRAPHY

K. BERGER 1972, *Die Gesetzauslegung Jesu,* Neukirchen-Vluyn: Neukirchener Verlag. • J. J. COLLINS 1997, *Jewish Wisdom in the Hellenistic Age,* Louisville: Westminster John Knox. • J. J. COLLINS 2000, *Between Athens and Jerusalem,* 2d ed., Grand Rapids: Eerdmans, 155-85. • L. H. FELDMAN AND J. R. LEVISON, EDS. 1996, *Josephus'* Contra Apionem, Leiden: Brill. • D. J. HARRINGTON 1996, *Wisdom Texts from Qumran,* London and New York: Routledge. • D. J. HARRINGTON 2005, *Jesus Ben Sira of Jerusalem,* Collegeville, Minn.: Liturgical Press. • R. A. KUGLER 2001, *The Testaments of the Twelve Patriarchs,* Sheffield: Sheffield Academic Press. • K. W. NIE-

BUHR 1987, *Gesetz und Paränese: Katechismusartige Weisungsreihen in der frühjüdischen Literatur,* Tübingen: Mohr-Siebeck. • K. SCHENK 2005, *A Brief Guide to Philo,* Louisville: Westminster John Knox. • P. W. VAN DER HORST 1978, *The Sentences of Pseudo-Phocylides,* Leiden: Brill.

DANIEL J. HARRINGTON, S.J.

Ethiopic

Ethiopic is a Semitic language formally spoken in Ethiopia and still used in the liturgy of the Christian church in Ethiopia. The language has two principal dialects: North Ethiopic and South Ethiopic. The oldest northern dialect is Geʾez, which is regarded as Classic Ethiopic. Among early Jewish writings preserved in Ethiopic are not only books eventually canonized as part of the Jewish Bible and Christian Old Testament but several writings associated with the Apocrypha and Pseudepigrapha. Ethiopian tradition, however, does not make the same distinction between "canonical" and "deuterocanonical" that Western canons make. For that reason, early Jewish literature from the Second Temple preserved in Ethiopic cannot be discussed apart from the Ethiopic version of the Scriptures.

Jewish Pseudepigrapha Preserved in Ethiopic

Some Ethiopic biblical manuscripts provide very important textual witnesses to early Jewish pseudepigrapha. Most notable in this respect are the *Book of Enoch* or *1 Enoch* (which survives in full only in Ethiopic), the *Book of Jubilees,* the *Ascension of Isaiah,* and the *Paraleipomena of Jeremiah (Rest of the Words of Baruch* or *4 Baruch*). The Ethiopic versions of *1 Enoch* and *Jubilees* especially have attracted renewed attention in light of the discovery of Aramaic fragments of *Enoch* and Hebrew fragments of *Jubilees* among the Dead Sea Scrolls. Other pseudepigraphic works were translated into Ethiopic from Arabic in the fourteenth and fifteenth centuries; these include such works as the *Testament of Abraham* and the Ethiopic *Book of Baruch* or *5 Baruch.* Most of these works still await full critical editions or new editions. For *1 Enoch,* see Knibb 1978; for *Jubilees,* VanderKam 1989; for *Ascension of Isaiah,* Bettiolo et al. 1995; for *Paraleipomena of Jeremiah,* Dilmann 1950; for *5 Baruch,* Halévy 1902; for the Christian version of the *Testament of Abraham,* Aešcoly 1951: 66-75; for the Falasha version of *Testament of Abraham,* Conti Rossini 1922 and Aešcoly 1951: 49-65; for the *Lives of the Prophets* [Ezekiel and Daniel], Knibb 1980).

The Ethiopic Biblical Canons

The Bible was translated rather literally from the Greek Septuagint into Geʿez between the fourth and sixth centuries C.E. The text was revised in accordance with Syriac-based Arabic texts in the fourteenth century. In the fifteenth or sixteenth century, the Ethiopic version seems to have undergone a further revision to bring it into conformity with the Hebrew (cf. Knibb 1999; Ullendorff 1968). The Old Testament has had a strong influence on Ethiopian Christianity. This is visible in the liturgy, oral poetry, literature, traditional teaching, and daily life of Ethiopian Christians.

According to the Ethiopian Orthodox Church, the sacred Scriptures consist of eighty-one books. The Amharic Bible published in 1961 contains the following books: Genesis, Exodus, Leviticus, Numbers, Deuteronomy, Joshua, Judges, 1 and 2 Samuel, 1 and 2 Kings, 1 and 2 Chronicles, *Jubilees, Enoch,* Ezra, Nehemiah, 1 Ezra Apocalypse (Ezra Sutu'el), 1 Ezra, Tobit, Judith, Esther, Ethiopic 1 Maccabees, Ethiopic 2-3 Maccabees (totally different from the books of the Septuagint), Job, Psalms, Messale (Proverbs 1–24) and Tägsas (Proverbs 25–31), Wisdom, Qohelet, Song of Songs, Sirach, Isaiah, Jeremiah, Baruch, Lamentations, Ezekiel, Daniel, Hosea, Amos, Micah, Joel, Obadiah, Jonah, Nahum, Habakkuk, Zephaniah, Haggai, Zechariah, and Malachi.

A second edition of the Amharic Bible (1988) adds the Prayer of Manasseh, the *Rest of Jeremiah (4 Baruch),* and Baruch. The book of Daniel is divided into several sections: Susanna, the Song of the Three Youths in the Furnace, and the Rest of Daniel. The *Ascension of Isaiah* is not included in either edition. A new edition of the Bible by the Ethiopian Orthodox Church is in process, and there seem to be no major changes in the inclusion of the books listed above.

These two lists reflect a "narrow" Ethiopian biblical canon and a "broader" one, with the categories of narrow and broad applying to the New Testament. In both forms the total numbers eighty-one. The narrow one includes fifty-four books in the Old Testament and twenty-seven in the New Testament. The broad one has forty-six books in the Old Testament and thirty-five in the New Testament (Cowley 1974: 319-20). The broader canon of the Ethiopic New Testament has eight additional books: four sections of the *Synodos* (a collection of material attributed to the apostles and early church councils); two parts of the Ethiopic *Book of the Covenant;* the Ethiopic *Clement;* and the Ethiopic *Didascalia.* This canon is unique in that no other contemporary church has more than twenty-seven books in the distinctively Christian part of its Bible. The *Beta Israel* or *Falashas* of Ethiopia, whose Jewish origins are still being debated among scholars (Ullendorff 1968: 16-17; Rodinson 1964; Amakeletch 1997), do not accept the New Testament but have the same text of the Old Testament as Ethiopian Christians.

The question of the Ethiopian biblical canon is complicated and far from being settled. The concept of "canon" itself is loose; there is still no official and definitive declaration on that matter from the Ethiopian Orthodox Church. Neither the canonical list in the *Synodos* nor the one in the *Fetha Negest* (*The Law of Kings,* a book of law in use since the sixteenth century) has eighty-one books. The *Book of Enoch* and the *Book of Jubilees* are, for instance, missing from both lists. The commentary of the *Fetha Negest* tries to justify this omission. According to Beckwith (1985: 494-95) and Brandt (2000: 81-82), the *Synodos* and the *Fetha Negest* derive from late Egyptian sources and therefore do not give an accurate image of the Ethiopic canon that existed immediately after the adoption of Christianity. The study of the Ethiopian biblical texts requires critical editions of the whole Geʿez Bible, but this has only been partially accomplished (cf. Knibb 1999: 113-16).

Function of the Texts in Ethiopian Christianity

Among the most quoted books of the Hebrew Bible, the Psalms enjoy a prominent place; they are recited during funeral services. Next is the book of Exodus, which gives prominence to the Tent of Meeting, the Tabernacle, the figure of Moses, and the crossing of the Red Sea. Among the prophets, Isaiah takes a leading role; it is read regularly during Lent. The Song of Songs is also frequently used liturgically; sections are read or sung during the liturgical celebrations of marriage, on Holy Saturday, during funeral services, and on the Saturdays of the liturgical season called *Zamana Tsege* (Flower), which extends from *Maskaram* 26 (October 6) to *Hedar* 5 (November 14).

Biblical texts are integral to the Solemn Vespers, Lauds, and other parts of the divine office. In the *Gebra Hemamat,* the liturgy for Holy Week, long portions from the Bible are read although nothing is taken for these liturgies from the *Book of Enoch* or the *Book of Jubilees.* Enoch is nevertheless quoted in the Book of Saints *(Synaxary),* where his ascension is celebrated on 27 *Ter* (February 4). In the same month, Elijah's ascension is commemorated, together with the deaths of Abel, Noah, and Micah. Moses, Isaiah, Jonah, Job, Judith, Tobit, and Susanna are celebrated in *Meskerem* (September 11 to October 10), the first month in the Ethiopian calendar. The *Degua,* the liturgical book of Ethiopia, makes constant reference to biblical figures of the Old Testament. In a section reserved for Elijah, his intercession is invoked together with Enoch's (cf. *Zemene Astemehero*). During the Eucharistic celebration, however, readings are taken from the New Testament only.

The *Book of Jubilees* (*Jub.* 3:9-13) should be mentioned together with Lev. 12:2-7 with regard to the time for the purifying of a woman who gives birth; it varies according to the sex of the child: a boy is baptized forty days after his birth, a girl after eighty days (cf. *Jub.* 3:9). Male children are circumcised on the eighth day after birth. The Sabbath is observed mainly in northern Ethiopia, where the religious movement founded by Saint Ewostatewos (fourteenth century) strongly advocated its keeping. In the book called *Teʾezaza Sanbat (The Order of Sabbath),* a book cherished by the *Beta Israel,* the Sabbath is deemed very important and praised with personification. The text is influenced by the *Book of Jubilees.* The *Tabot,* basically the equivalent of an altar, is strongly linked with the Ark of the Covenant and the tablets of the Law given at Sinai.

Such features have often led to the question of Jewish influence on Ethiopian Christianity, its origin and its nature being still a matter of debate (cf. Ullendorff 1968; Hammerschmidt 1965). Some look for an influence that existed prior to the introduction of Christianity in the fourth century. Other scholars, however, think that the "Jewish elements" are proper not only to the Ethiopian Church but to most ancient churches (Pedersen 1999: 203-216).

The impact of the Bible and early Jewish literature in Ethiopia is not limited to liturgy but extends to other areas as well. The Psalms, for instance, play a significant role in the formation of the faithful. Knowing how to read them in Geʿez is part of traditional education, and a prize is given to young boys who demonstrate that stage of competence.

Interpretation of the Texts

The traditional Ethiopian interpretation of biblical and other religious literature, called *Andemta,* is in "fundamental conti-

Page of a fifteenth-century-C.E. Ethiopian Bible with the text of 1 Enoch in Geʾez book script. The complete 1 Enoch is known only in the Ethiopic version. *(The Schøyen Collection, MS 1748)*

nuity with earlier commentaries" that flourished in ancient Christianity (Cowley 1974: 375). The commentaries interpret various biblical passages in the light of others. The name *Andemta* ("Another says . . .") implies a diversity of interpretation and a search for the deeper meaning of given texts.

Figures like Abel, Enoch, Noah, and Abraham are often foils of Jesus or Mary. Many verses that refer to the "son of man" in the Enochic *Book of Parables* (*1 Enoch* 37–71) are understood as references to Christ. Similarly, the last part of the *Animal Apocalypse* (*1 Enoch* 85–90) is read as an allegory of the church, the apostles, and Christ. In the Enochic *Apocalypse of Weeks*, the eighth week is taken to refer to the coming of Christ. The promise of God to rebuild his sanctuary in *Jub.* 1:17 is interpreted in polyvalent terms as a reference to the Tent of Meeting, the Temple, Mary, and the church. The miraculous figs that remained fresh after sixty-six years in the *Paraleipomena of Jeremiah* 5–7 are compared to Christ's redemption.

Not all interpretations are christological, though. In the Songs of Songs, for instance, the breasts mentioned in 4:2 and 7:2 are associated with the two tablets of the Ten Commandments. The sentence "as a lily among brambles, so is my love among maidens" (2:2) is connected with the house of Israel located in the midst of Moab and Ammon. In the phrase "with great delight I sat in his shadow" (2:3), the shade is linked with the tent of Abraham (Genesis 18).

The nature of Old Testament citations and allusions in Ethiopic literature requires thorough study. It can be merely apologetic as in the *Book of Mysteries* and the *Book of Light* (both written in the fifteenth century), wherein the *Book of Jubilees* is mentioned in support of celebrating the Sabbath with a dignity equal to that given to Sunday. In the *Book of Mystery* there is even a reference to the angels of holiness and the angels of the presence who rest on the Sabbath (cf. *Jub.* 2:17-19). The *Book of Enoch* is extensively quoted in the *Book of the Nativity (Mesehafa Milad)*, a polemical work, effectively arguing that the coming of Christ was announced by Enoch. The *Kebre Negest (Glory of the Kings)* puts forth what may be called "rewritten scripture" as well as proofs and didactic verses (Ullendorff 1968: 77-78). The *Qene*, poems or hymns created by Ethiopian-learned chanters, often for liturgical services, draw heavily on symbols from the Old Testament and early Jewish literature for their metaphors.

Besides explicit quotations from biblical and early Jewish texts, the broader influence of biblical texts and biblical genres on Ethiopic literature deserves mention. This influence extends not only to content but also to form. The influence of the *Book of Enoch* and *Fourth Ezra* on the style of saints' lives, for example, is noteworthy. Further studies are needed for a better understanding of this phenomenon.

BIBLIOGRAPHY

A. Z. AEŠCOLY 1951, *Recueil de textes falachas*, Paris: Institut d'Ethnologie. • T. AMAKELETCH 1997, "About the Identity of the Beta Israel," in *Ethiopia in Broader Perspective: Papers of the XIIIth International Conference of Ethiopian Studies, Kyoto: 12-17 December*, Kyoto: Shokado Booksellers, 3:195-210. • R. BECKWITH 1985, "The Canon in the Early Ethiopian Church," in idem, *The Old Testament Canon of the New Testament Church*, London: SPCK, 478-505. • P. BETTIOLO ET AL. 1995, *Ascensio Isaiae: Textus*, Turnhout: Brepols. • P. BRANDT 2000, "Geflecht aus 81 Büchern: Zur Variantenreichen Gestalt des äthiopischen Biblekanons," *Aethiopica* 3: 79-115. • R. COWLEY 1974, "The Biblical Canon of the Ethiopian Orthodox Church Today," *Ostkirchliche Studien* 23: 318-323. • A.-M. DENIS 2000, *Introduction à la littérature religieuse judéo-hellénistique*, 2 vols., Turnhout: Brepols. • A. DILMANN 1950, *Chrestomathia Aethiopica edita et glossario explanata*, 2d ed., Addenda et corrigenda adiecit E. Littmann, Berlin: Akademie-Verlag, 1-15. • G. HAILE 1988, "The Forty-Nine-Hour Sabbath of the Ethiopian Church," *JSS* 23: 233-54. • J. HALÉVY 1902, *Te'ezâza Sanbat (Commandements du Sabbat), accompagné de six autres écrits pseudo-épigraphiques*, Paris: Leroux. • E. HAMMERSCHMIDT 1965, "Jewish Elements in the Cult of the Ethiopian Church," *Journal of Ethiopian Studies* 3: 1-12. • D. KESSLER 1996, *The Falashas: A Short History of the Ethiopian Jews*, 3d ed., London: Routledge. • M. A. KNIBB 1978, *The Ethiopic Book of Enoch: A Critical Edition in Light of the Aramaic Dead Sea Fragments*, 2 vols., Oxford: Clarendon. • M. A. KNIBB 1980, "The Ethiopic Version of the Lives of the Prophets: Ezekiel and Daniel," *Bulletin of the School of Oriental and African Studies, University of London* 43: 197-206 and plates I-III. • M. A. KNIBB 1999, *Translating the Bible: The Ethiopic Version of the Old Testament*, Oxford: Oxford University Press. • K. S. PEDERSEN 1999, "Is the Church of Ethiopia a Judaic Church?" *Warszawskie Studia Teologiczne* 12: 203-16. • M. RODINSON 1964, "Sur la Question des influences Juives en Ethiopie," *JSS* 9: 11-19. • C. CONTI ROSSINI 1922, "Nuovi appunti sui giudei d'Abissinia," in *Rendiconti of the R. Accademia Nazionale dei Lincei*, 5th series, vol. 31, Rome: Tipografia della R. Accademia dei Lincei, 221-40. • E. ULLENDORFF 1968, *Ethiopia and the Bible*, Oxford: Oxford University Press. • J. C. VANDERKAM 1989, *The Book of Jubilees: A Critical Text*, 2 vols., Leuven: Peeters. • K. WENDT 1964, "Der Kampf um den Kanon heiliger Schriften in der äthiopischen Kirche der Reformen des XV Jahrhunderts," *JSS* 9: 107-13. • DIBE KULU ZWEDE 1994, *Eighty-One Sacred Books and Sources-Canons*, Addis Abeba: Commercial Printing Press, 286-90.

DANIEL ASSEFA

Eupolemus

Writer and Work

Six passages are ascribed to a writer named Eupolemus. Five of the passages are cited by Eusebius of Caesarea quoting the work of the mid-first-century-B.C.E. writer, Alexander Polyhistor. Alternate versions of two of these passages are found in Clement of Alexandria, who also preserved a passage not found in Eusebius. Many scholars maintain that one of the passages should be attributed to an unknown "Pseudo-Eupolemus."

Although Josephus (*Ag. Ap.* 1.218) listed him among Greek historians, most scholars have concluded, based on the content of the passages, that he was a Jewish author. Because the passage found only in Clement gives a date from the mid-second century B.C.E., and because of the unusualness of the name, most scholars identify him with the Eupolemus, son of John of the priestly family of Hakkoz, sent by Judas Maccabaeus on a diplomatic mission to Rome (1 Macc. 8:17; see also 2 Macc. 4:11).

Clement states that the title of the work was *On the Kings in Judea*, while Eusebius holds that the title was *On the Prophecy of/about Elijah*. Since Elijah nowhere is mentioned in the passages, most scholars prefer the title as found in Clement.

Contents

The first passage, ascribed by Alexander Polyhistor to Eupolemus but assigned by most scholars to Pseudo-Eupolemus, describes Abraham as the teacher of astronomy to the Phoenicians and then to the Egyptians. The second depicts Moses as the first wise man and the inventor of the alphabet, which was then handed on from the Jews to the Phoenicians and then to the Greeks. The sixth passage, which provides a chronology from Adam to 158/157 B.C.E., dates the exodus under Moses to 2738 B.C.E. The third passage, after a brief summary of events from Moses to David, contains a lengthy description of the building of the Temple and includes correspondence between Solomon and King Vaphres of Egypt and King Hiram of Tyre, both of whom are addressed by Solomon as if they were subordinate to him. The short next passage emphasizes Solomon's wealth and the peacefulness of his reign. The fifth passage describes how the prophet Jeremiah criticized the idol worship of the Jews and how the king threatened to burn him alive. At this, Jeremiah prophesied the coming captivity in Babylon and its fulfillment under Nebuchadnezzar.

Character

Given that the passages have come to us filtered through the lens of Alexander Polyhistor, one has to be cautious in assessing the work of Eupolemus. The work was originally written in Greek. The long passage on the construction of the Temple evidences knowledge of the LXX as well as the Hebrew text, and it suggests some knowledge of Greek writers, notably Ctesias and possibly Herodotus. Eupolemus appears to prefer the version of biblical history found in Chronicles over that found in Kings, but not exclusively. Eupolemus, however, has not regurgitated the biblical text but has provided his own telling of biblical history. Biblical figures are bearers of culture, and the Temple becomes larger and more glorious than the biblical description. David's conquests are larger, and the nations conquered reflect nations at the time of Eupolemus' writing. Like other Hellenistic historians, he includes documents, written in the style of Hellenistic letters. Because the largest part of the preserved work deals with the construction of the Temple, it is tempting to see this as reflecting the life experience of Eupolemus, who had seen the Temple violated by Antiochus IV and purified by Judas Maccabaeus.

Significance

There were many rewritings of sacred literature in the Second Temple period, but Eupolemus wrote in Greek and emphasized the national superiority of the Jews. Moses invented the alphabet and also was the first to write down laws; in so doing, he was the first to bring culture and civilization, since laws bring societies into existence. The kingdom of David and Solomon is vast, and Solomon's riches exceeding. Egypt and Phoenicia are subordinate to him, and his temple is magnificent in its proportions. Here Eupolemus vaunts the prestige of the Jews and stresses that they are not an insignificant nation. Within this encomium, however, is also the theme that the king must listen to the prophet, or the kingdom will perish. This last sentiment corresponds to the call for a trustworthy prophet in 1 Macc. 4:47 and 14:41. Finally, if his work was intended to be heard by Jews, then it presupposes an audience capable of understanding Greek, perhaps preferring Greek to Hebrew.

BIBLIOGRAPHY

F. FALLON 1985, "Eupolemus," in *OTP* 2: 861-72. • C. R. HOLLADAY 1983, *Fragments from Hellenistic Jewish Authors*, vol. 1, *Historians*, Chico: Scholars Press, 93-156. • G. E. STERLING 1992, *Historiography and Self-definition: Josephos, Luke-Acts and Apologetic Historiography*, Leiden: Brill, 207-222. • B. Z. WACHOLDER 1974, *Eupolemus: A Study of Judaeo-Greek Literature*, Cincinnati: Hebrew Union College, Jewish Institute of Religion. • N. WALTER 1976, "Eupolemus," in *JSHRZ* 1.2; 93-108.

ROBERT DORAN

Eupolemus, Pseudo-

In his section on the life of Abraham in his *Preparation for the Gospel*, Eusebius of Caesarea quotes two passages from Alexander Polyhistor of the first century B.C.E., one of which Alexander attributes to Eupolemus (the Jewish historian of the second century B.C.E.), the other to anonymous works. Scholars usually combine these two passages and attribute them to an unknown writer designated Pseudo-Eupolemus.

The Passages

The first quickly recapitulates Genesis 10–11, but without the distinction between the descendants of Shem, Ham, and Japheth. Abraham is described as the discoverer of astronomy. Abraham's travels are then recounted, first to Phoenicia, where he teaches their king astronomy, and where his prowess as a warrior is shown as in Genesis 14. The author then combines the two accounts of Abraham's wife given to Pharaoh as his sister (Genesis 12 and 20) and emphasizes, as in the *Genesis Apocryphon*, that Pharaoh did not have intercourse with Sarah. While in Egypt, Abraham taught the Egyptian priests in Heliopolis astronomy. Abraham traced the original discovery of astronomy back to Enoch, as in *1 Enoch* 41, 43–44, and 72–82. At the end is a genealogy of the nations.

The second passage starts in Babylon, where Abraham is said to be descended from giants whom the gods destroyed because of their wickedness. One giant, Belus, escaped the gods, founded Babylon, and built a tower. Abraham was instructed in astronomy, then went to Phoenicia where he taught it, and then on to Egypt. The first section of this passage is so unlike what is found in the second that some assign only the mention of Abraham's travels to Pseudo-Eupolemus.

The Combination of the Passages

Although Polyhistor attributed the two passages to different authors, scholars have combined them. In both, the building of the tower was traced back to giants; Belus figured prominently in both; Abraham was descended from these giants; Phoenicia was the name designating Canaan; Abraham taught astronomy to the Phoenicians and then to the Egyptians. These arguments are not compelling. Giants are said to have built Babylon in the LXX (Gen. 10:8-10). The order of the events narrated is quite different. In the first fragment, the giants who escaped the flood built the tower which *God* overthrew and were dispersed; in the second, the giants were destroyed by *the gods* for some undisclosed wickedness and, after that, the tower was built and was not the cause of any divine chastisement. The mention of Belus in the first fragment occurs in a primeval genealogy that interrupts the flow of Abraham's statement about how Enoch invented astronomy and passed it on through his son Methuselah. It may not be an integral part of the passage but an insertion by Polyhistor. Canaan is called Phoenicia in the LXX (Exod. 16:35; Josh. 5:1). The first fragment does not state explicitly, as the second fragment does, that Abraham was descended from the giants, but connects him with Enoch. The correspondences do not prove the same author, but use of the same tradition.

The First Passage

This passage is not attributed by most scholars to Eupolemus for two reasons. First, biblical figures are linked to characters from Babylonian and Greek mythology; for example, Enoch is the same as Atlas. However, as noted above, this genealogical snippet does not appear to be integral to the passage but probably stems from Polyhistor. Second, in this fragment, the temple Argarizin is interpreted as "Mount of the Most High." How could a Jew do this for the temple of the Samaritans? Josephus (*J.W.* 1.63) likewise designates Shechem as Argarizin, and LXX Gen. 14:18 calls Melchizedek "priest of the Most High God." Hostility between Jews and Samaritans became more pronounced after the destruction of the temple in Shechem by John Hyrcanus in 108 B.C.E. The debate about the existence of Pseudo-Eupolemus thus continues.

Significance

Scholars who attribute both of these passages to a Pseudo-Eupolemus emphasize the universalistic tendencies of the author. He is at pains to connect the Jewish Scriptures with world history. The designation of Gerizin as temple of the Most High evidences his Samaritan bias, while placing Babylonia as the origin of knowledge may reveal a pro-Seleucid strain. Those who see the primeval genealogy in the first passage as an insertion into a fragment from the work of Eupolemus and the second passage as a compilation of Alexander Polyhistor see evidence of the same reworking of the biblical narrative as one finds in other passages attributed to Eupolemus.

BIBLIOGRAPHY

R. DORAN 1985, "Pseudo-Eupolemus," in *OTP* 2:873-79. • J. FREUDENTHAL 1875, *Alexander Polyhistor und die von ihm erhaltenen Reste jüdaischer und samaritanischer Geschichtswerke,* Breslau: H. Skutsch. • C. R. HOLLADAY 1983, *Fragments from Hellenistic Jewish Authors,* vol. 1, *Historians,* Chico: Scholars Press, 157-87. • G. E. STERLING 1992, *Historiography and Self-definition: Josephos, Luke-Acts and Apologetic Historiography,* Leiden: Brill, 187-206. • N. WALTER 1965, "Zu Pseudo-Eupolemus," *Klio* 43-45: 282-90. • N. WALTER 1976, "Pseudo-Eupolemus," in *JSHRZ* 1.2: 137-43.

ROBERT DORAN

Evil

The origins and problem of evil were topics in which Jewish theologians of the Second Temple period took a great deal of interest. The literature they left behind reveals the variety of ways in which these religious thinkers tried to come to terms with one of religion's most vexing problems. Although the authors of this literature agreed that all creation was subject to the God of Israel, there was considerable disagreement as to just how things under this God's control went awry. Was it God or humanity itself that was responsible for the human moral predicament? Another matter of some discussion was the work of evil spirits and other superhuman beings, who although subject to God were permitted to participate in humanity's degradation. Often, in order to comprehend their present situation, these theologians would look to the earliest events in human history as recorded in the book of Genesis for illumination.

Fallen Angels and Evil Spirits

The Watcher Myth

In Gen. 6:1-4, one reads the story of a time when certain "sons of God" intermingled sexually with the "daughters of man." This brief and enigmatic account proved to be fertile ground for the reflection of early Jewish communities who saw in this story a paradigm for understanding their own time. An expansion of this story is found in several writings from the Second Temple period, the primary example of which is the *Book of the Watchers* (*1 Enoch* 1–36; for this interpretive tradition, see also *Jub.* 5:1-11; CD 2:17-21; Jude 6). In this retelling of the Genesis account, the sons of God are angelic beings called "watchers." These watchers transgress the proper boundaries between human and divine by entering into sexual relationships with human women and begetting by them a mixed race of giants. Their giant offspring also sin, committing egregious acts of violence against humanity. For their misdeeds, God has the watchers bound until the time of judgment and sends a great deluge to wipe the giants from the face of the earth. Only the righteous Noah and his family survive. The lamentable situation created by the watchers and the ensuing judgment are intended to prefigure the eschatological period in which evil would be vanquished and the righteous would be saved.

Forbidden Angelic Revelation

Unfortunately for humanity, the watchers' activity on earth included more than sexual misconduct. The watchers also taught humans how to practice the illicit arts of sorcery and divination (*1 Enoch* 7:1; 8:3; 9:8). The culpability of humans in the sin that led to the flood receives special emphasis in a later redactional stratum of the *Book of the Watchers.* In this stratum, a watcher by the name of Asael teaches humans the craft of metalwork for the purposes of manufacturing implements of war and jewelry. Asael also shows humans how to produce cosmetics (8:1-2). In doing these things, humans become guilty of the same two sins for which the watchers and their giant offspring are condemned, sexual immorality and violence. While it is not uncommon for scholars to speak of the watcher myth as found in the *Book of Watchers* as an explanation for *the* origin of evil, this is probably somewhat of an overstatement. The primary function of the myth as it appears in the early Jewish literature is paradigmatic, not etiological. Just as the watchers and giants sinned and were punished, so sinners would rise in the final period only to fall in God's judgment. The story, nonetheless, does contain some etiological components by which certain illicit practices of the present are explained as stemming from the revelation of sinful angels to humans in the antediluvian period. The *Book of Jubilees* likewise attributes the origin of divinatory practices to the teaching of the watchers. The contribution of *Jubilees* to this etiology is an explanation how the antediluvian teaching came into postdiluvian hands. According to this work, Noah's great-grandson Kainan discovered a stone on which was engraved the teaching of the watchers. Kainan kept his discovery a secret from Noah, who would have most certainly disapproved (8:1-4).

Evil Spirits and Satan

In the Hebrew Bible, "evil spirits" and "satans" did not take pleasure in leading humans into rebellion against God. These figures were in God's service and functioned as agents of divine punishment against those who had already offended the deity. This punishment might be accomplished, however, by leading a human to commit some error of disastrous consequence (e.g., Judg. 9:23-24; 1 Chron. 21:1), a tactic which no doubt contributed to later elaborations of these figures' deluding activity. In addition to an etiology of illicit arts, the *Book of the Watchers* contains an account of the origin of evil spirits. *1 Enoch* 15:8–16:1 relates that the fleshly, mortal half of the watchers' mixed children would perish. The spiritual, immortal half of these beings, however, would live on as evil spirits, creating all sorts of physical ills for humans. An alternate form of this etiology appears in *1 Enoch* 19:1, where in addition to physically assaulting humans, the evil spirits are said to lead humans to worship false gods.

In the *Book of Jubilees,* these evil spirits make several appearances. The spirits in this book subject humans to physical illness, lead them to commit idolatry, and cause humans to commit acts of violence against one another (*Jub.* 10:1-14; 11:4-6). *Jubilees* also teaches that these troubling spirits are subordinate to an individual called (the Prince of) Mastema. Mastema is identified as the satan (or, perhaps, Satan), who is responsible for punishing transgressors (*Jub.* 10:1-14). But it is clear that Mastema exceeds his role as an agent of divine punishment, and takes on a more general adversarial role against humans and Israel (e.g., *Jub.* 11:5; 19:28; 48:2, 9, 12-18). In *Jub.* 1:20, another name for the arch-adversary is given, Belial. Although "belial/Belial" may be a common noun, as it is in the Hebrew Bible (e.g., Deut. 13:14; cf. *Jub.* 15:33), it is usually taken in *Jub.* 1:20 as the name of the chief opponent of Israel, who accuses them and leads them into all kinds of sins. Belial also holds a prominent position as the chief opponent of good in several of the Dead Sea Scrolls (on which see below).

Adam, Eve, and the Fall of Humanity

Given the central role that the disobedience of Adam and Eve reported in Genesis 3 plays in early Christian explanations of the human moral condition (e.g., Rom. 5:12-21), it is striking how little attention this passage receives in pre-Christian Jewish discussions of evil. Sirach contains a passing reference to Eve's act and its implications for later generations. In the midst of a series of warnings about the perils of having an evil wife, Ben Sira remarks, "From a woman sin had its beginning, and because of her we all die" (Sir. 25:24). Given the context of this statement in Sirach and the fact that this comment is in tension with other sayings of Ben Sira (e.g., Sir. 17:1-12), one should probably not make too much of the place of Eve's transgression in the theology of Ben Sira. Nevertheless, this statement does attest to the existence of an attribution of human sin to the disobedience of Eve in pre-Christian Judaism.

Near the end of the first century C.E., *4 Ezra* claims that Adam's sin was the result of his having an "evil heart." Adam's descendants, it would seem, have inherited this "evil root," and as a result they sin (*4 Ezra* 3:21-22). In 7:118, Ezra exclaims, "O Adam, what have you done? For though it was you who sinned, the fall was not yours alone, but ours also who are your descendants," explicitly blaming humanity's moral predicament on Adam's transgression. The early second-century C.E. *2 Baruch,* however, warns against blaming Adam for the sins of subsequent generations: "Adam is, therefore, not the cause, except only for himself, but each of us has become our own Adam" (*2 Bar.* 54:19). For the author of *2 Baruch,* a propensity for sin is not inherited; all individuals are responsible for their own behavior.

Human vs. Divine Responsibility

A fairly lengthy discussion of the relationship between divine sovereignty and human choice is found in Sir. 15:11-20. This section of Ben Sira's wisdom opens with the admonition, "Do not say, 'It was the Lord's doing that I fell away'; for he does not do what he hates" (Sir. 15:11). Ben Sira proceeds to explain, "It was he [God] who created humankind in the beginning, and he left them in the power of their own inclination" (Sir. 15:14). For Ben Sira, the individual has a choice to make between right and wrong, and this choice is subject only to the person's "inclination." This verse would seem to indicate that a person's "inclination," a translation of Hebr. *yēṣer,* is neutral. At the very least, the *yēṣer* is conceived of as something internal to the person, and the person's will, according to Ben Sira, is not subject to external, divine manipulation for evil (Collins 1997: 34). Similar defenses of God from involvement in human sin appear in *1 Enoch* 98:4-5 and Jas. 1:13-15. But in the case of Ben Sira, the teaching is complicated by the fact that another passage, Sir. 33:7-14, stands in some tension with it. This passage attributes the fate of all creation to the design of the deity. Even humans like clay are formed according to the divine potter's will, whether for blessing or curse. Although it is difficult to find a statement in the early Jewish literature explicitly blaming God for human sin, the teaching to which passages like Sirach 15 responds may have been something like that found in the *Damascus Document:* "But those whom he [God] hated he caused to stray" (CD 2:13).

The Dualism of the Dead Sea Scrolls

Within the parameters of monotheism shared by their fellow Jews, in which God was considered to be supreme over all, the authors of several of the Dead Sea Scrolls held to a kind of dualism in which humans are believed to be under the influence of two types of superhuman beings, one good and the other evil. The "Treatise on the Two Spirits," found in cols. 3-4 of some copies of the *Rule of the Community,* is exemplary in this regard. This text teaches that God has placed in humankind two spirits, "the spirits of truth and of deceit," which determine, respectively, humanity's good and evil deeds. This text says that a figure called the "Prince of Lights" has dominion over the righteous and that the "Angel of Darkness" is in charge of the wicked. These opposing angelic leaders appear in a number of other texts from the Dead Sea Scrolls. The leader of the righteous is identified in some of these passages as the angel Michael (e.g., 1QM 17:6-7), and the Angel of Darkness elsewhere goes by the name of Belial or Melchiresha' (e.g., 1QS 2:5; 4Q287 frg. 7 col. ii; 4Q544 frg. 2). Another text found near Qumran (4Q186) teaches an anthropology in which individuals consist of nine parts. Each part is allotted either to the house of light or conversely to the house of darkness, and the person's character, presumably, is determined by his ratio of light to darkness. This text even goes so far as to provide criteria for determining a person's ratio based on his physical features. The dualism of the Dead Sea Scrolls is often compared to the dualism of Persian Zoroastrianism.

Bibliography

G. Boccaccini 1998, *Beyond the Essene Hypothesis: The Parting of the Ways between Qumran and Enochic Judaism,* Grand Rapids: Eerdmans. • J. J. Collins 1997, *Apocalypticism in the Dead Sea Scrolls,* London: Routledge, 30-51. • J. J. Collins 2004, "Before the Fall: The Earliest Interpretations of Adam and Eve," in *The Idea of Biblical Interpretation: Essays in Honor of James L. Kugel,* ed. H. Najman and J. H. Newman, Leiden: Brill, 293-308. • J. Duhaime 2000, "Dualism," in *Encyclopedia of the Dead Sea Scrolls,* ed. L. H. Schiffman and J. C. VanderKam, Oxford: Oxford University Press, 215-20. • F. García-Martínez 1998, "Apocalypticism in the Dead Sea Scrolls," in *The Encyclopedia of Apocalypticism,* ed. B. McGinn, J. J. Collins, and S. J. Stein, New York: Continuum, 1:162-92. • M. Philonenko 1995, "Mythe et histoire qoumrânienne des deux Esprits: Ses origins iraniennes et ses prolongements dans le judaïsme essénien et le christianisme antique," in *Apocalyptique Iranienne et Dualisme Qoumrânien,* ed. G. Widengren, M. Philonenko, and A. Hultgård, Paris: Maisonneuve, 163-211. • P. Sacchi 1990, *Jewish Apocalyptic and Its History,* trans. W. J. Short, Sheffield: Sheffield Academic Press, 72-87. • M. E. Stone 1990, *Fourth Ezra: A Commentary on the Fourth Book of Ezra,* Minneapolis: Fortress, 64-65. • L. T. Stuckenbruck 2004, "The Origins of Evil in Jewish Apocalyptic Tradition: The Interpretation of Genesis 6:1-4 in the Second and Third Centuries b.c.e.," in *The Fall of the Angels,* ed. C. Auffarth and L. T. Stuckenbruck, Leiden: Brill, 86-118.

See also: Adam and Eve; Determinism; Dualism; Fallen Angels; Satan and Related Figures

Ryan E. Stokes

Exile

Exile generally refers to the geographical displacement of a person or community from a homeland. In early Jewish history, exile most often refers to the Babylonian conquest and the deportation of the people of Judah to Babylon in 586 b.c.e. By the late Second Temple period, however, exile had taken on broader theological connotations of displacement, both literal and metaphorical, in the Jewish experience. Indeed, even some Jews in Palestine understood themselves to be living in exile, thus translating the concept from the geographical to the metaphorical and/or eschatological realm.

"Exile" versus "Diaspora"

"Exile" (Hebr. *gālût*) for Jews frequently connotes a sense of powerlessness and divine judgment. A related term, "Diaspora" (Gr. *diaspora*), also describes the experience of Jews living outside of Palestine, which by the late Second Temple period numbered more than those inside. Some find the label "Diaspora" to be a positive, or at least neutral, description of the voluntary emigration of Jewish communities, while the term "exile" connotes the forced deportation of Jews. Yet neither term is wholly positive or negative; indeed, their semantic ranges overlap in that they occasionally occur together (Tob. 3:4; *Pss. Sol.* 17:17-18; 4Q216 ii 14-15; *Gen. Rab.* 73:5). Some Diaspora Jews viewed their condition to be the result of the curse of exile, while others understood their experience to be more positive and permanent (Scott 1997). Both Josephus and Philo, themselves Diaspora Jews, were somewhat ambiguous about their state (Feldman 1997); although quite settled in Alexandria, Philo envisions an eventual ingathering of the Jews abroad (*Praem.* 29.165), whereas Josephus proudly notes that Jews are spread throughout the world (*J.W.* 6.442; 7.43; *Ant.* 14.114) and foresees no end to the Exile.

Exile in the Hebrew Bible

In the Hebrew Bible, exile appears as a historical and national experience. The northern tribes of Israel were exiled by the Assyrians in 722 B.C.E. (2 Kings 17), and the Babylonians later deported prominent Judean populations in 598/7 and 587/6 B.C.E. (2 Kings 25). The latter is remembered most poignantly and is usually thought to have ended in 538 B.C.E. with Cyrus' decree (Ezra 6:3-5). In Deuteronomic theology, this deportation was interpreted as punishment for breaking God's covenant (e.g., Deut. 4:23-28) and could be remedied by a return to the land if Israel repented (Deut. 4:29-31).

The biblical prophets also assess the Exile in terms of the conditionality of God's covenant; it was for them the result of divine judgment (e.g., Isa. 5:13; 44:9-20; Amos 5:26-27) and a test of Israel's faithfulness (Ezek. 20:5-26), through which a faithful remnant would emerge (Jer. 23:3; Hag. 1:12; Zech. 8:6). Some prophets warned that exile would come with disobedience, yet they also offered hope to faithful Israel in the form of a return, thus developing a nascent "theology of exile." Finally, the book of Daniel was also influential on later writers, as it grapples with exile in an eschatological context, where Babylon becomes a symbol for metaphorical exile found also in later apocalyptic texts.

Exile in Second Temple Literature

The Apocrypha and Pseudepigrapha mention exile in three primary contexts: (1) as part of a review of Israel's history; (2) as the focus of a theological reflection on God's covenant and its conditionality; and (3) within an eschatological context alongside other apocalyptic themes. Nevertheless, many texts incorporate some or all of these three fluid categories.

A number of texts recall the Babylonian Exile as part of their review of history (e.g., *T. Moses* 3–4; *Sib. Or.* 3.265-94; *Pss. Sol.* 9:1-2; *1 Enoch* 89:66-72; *Jub.* 1:13-18). Other texts reflect more systematically about the theological conditions for and ramifications of Israel in exile, usually by considering the Babylonian Exile to be the paradigmatic test of covenantal theology. Thus, some authors reevaluate this event with an eye toward understanding their current political and religious instability (e.g., 1 Esdras; *2 Baruch; 4 Baruch;* Epistle of Jeremiah). *4 Ezra,* set in exile, concludes that God delivered Jerusalem to her enemies because of transgression (3:27), and *2 Baruch* confirms that Judah's sin led to her downfall (1:4-5). Usually Israel's sin is only vaguely described, although idolatry and apostasy are mentioned (*T. Moses* 3–4; *Sib. Or.* 3; *Jub.* 1:7-18; cf. 4QMMT[c] 18b-20, 21b-22; *m. 'Abot* 5:9; *b. Šabbat* 33a).

Although less prominent, the fate of the ten northern tribes of Israel is also a source of speculation. For instance, the book of Tobit recounts the story of a Galilean Israelite exiled to Nineveh. Elsewhere it is also thought that the "lost tribes" resided in a remote land east of the Euphrates (e.g., *Ant.* 8.271). Josephus, among others, also hints that their deportation was the result of sin (*Ant.* 8.271; *2 Bar.* 1:4-5), although *4 Ezra* concludes that they removed themselves to a remote land to devote themselves to the Law and that these tribes would be gathered back to the land at the end time (*4 Ezra* 13:12-13, 39-50; cf. *Sib. Or.* 2.168-76; *T. Jos.* 19:1-7; *T. Naphtali* 6; *T. Moses* 2–4; *Ant.* 11.133; *m. Sanh.* 10:3).

Exile and Apocalypticism

The notion of exile is also thematized within the context of apocalyptic literature. Fueled by political instability and the failure to regain an independent Israel under a Davidic ruler, many began to think Jews were living in a continual state of exile, one that could be remedied only by the coming of the messianic age. Only a few eschatological texts mention exile as a limited event. Of the few that mention a return (cf. *T. Jud.* 24:5; *T. Dan* 9:9), the *Testament of Moses* describes both the Judeans and the lost ten tribes as exiles ("slaves") for only seventy-seven years (3:10-14; cf. Jer. 25:11-12). The *Third Sibylline Oracle* also delimits Israel's exilic condition, mentioning that the Temple will be desolate for seven decades but will be restored "as it was before" (*Sib. Or.* 3.280-82; 3.294). More frequently, writers interpreted their current epoch to be one that began with the Babylonian Exile and continued until the end times (*1-3 Enoch,* Baruch, *2 Baruch, 4 Ezra,* and *Testaments of the Twelve Patriarchs*), often neglecting to mention any historical return from the Babylonian captivity (*1 Enoch* 91:11-17; 93:1-10; cf. *T. Levi* 10; 14–15; *T. Gad* 8:2). Here the implication is that Israel continues to live in exile until the final judgment (Knibb 1976: 259; cf. protracted exile in *1 Enoch* 85–90). The book of *Jubilees* mentions a glorious ingathering from the nations, when God will again inhabit the sanctuary and Israel will abide by the covenant, most likely in a future age (VanderKam 1997: 104).

Exile in the Dead Sea Scrolls

At least some members of the Dead Sea sect also saw themselves as living in a continual state of exile until the time when God judged the nations (1QM 1:2-3). For them, exile was a symbol of alienation from the powers that were in Jerusalem, and true restoration would come only with the messianic age.

Exile appears in the Scrolls in two primary ways. First, it is mentioned as a historical event marking the sect's origins. The *Damascus Document* (CD) traces the beginning of the group to "the time of wrath, 390 years after he [God] had given them into the hand of Nebuchadnezzar. . . . [God] caused a plant root to spring from Israel and Aaron" (1:5-7; cf. *Jub.* 1.16; *1 Enoch* 93:10; Ezek. 4:5). Here, as elsewhere, the authors skip over any historical "return" from exile; rather, they telescope the founding of their group as the next notable event. In

4Q390, however, the first ones to go up from the land of captivity in order to build the Temple are said to be an exception to the general pattern of lawlessness.

Second, exilic imagery is used to describe the experience of sect members. The Wicked Priest pursues the Teacher of Righteousness to "his place of exile" (1QpHab 11:4-8), possibly Qumran, where he is driven like "a bird from its nest" (4Q177 frg. 1 lines 8-9). Elsewhere, the covenanters describe their sojourn as living in exile "beyond Damascus," whether the reference is to be taken literally or symbolically (cf. Amos 5:37; 1QM 1:2-3). Theologically, exile serves as a medium through which sect members could cast their own contemporary displacement, one destined to endure until the eschaton.

Some, including the rabbis, found redeeming or expiatory qualities to exile itself (*m. Berakot* 56a; *m. 'Abot* 4:14), as it allowed Jews to become a "light to the nations" (*b. Pesaḥim* 87b). However, most regarded it as a conditional state to be overcome. Theological reevaluations of exile therefore offered Jews hope for political and/or religious restoration in the Second Temple period, sometimes even to a better state than before (*2 Bar.* 85:4-5). Conceptually speaking, then, whether it was geographical or metaphorical, exile served to reinforce a unifying self-consciousness among Jews who no longer shared a common language, culture, or geography and ultimately was a condition that could be mitigated, by an ingathering of the exiles and/or the coming of the messianic age.

BIBLIOGRAPHY

M. ABEGG 1997, "Exile and the Dead Sea Scrolls," in *Exile*, ed. J. M. Scott, Leiden: Brill, 111-25. • L. H. FELDMAN 1997, "The Concept of Exile in Josephus," in *Exile*, ed. J. M. Scott, Leiden: Brill, 145-72. • I. GAFNI 1997, *Land, Center and Diaspora*, Sheffield: Sheffield Academic Press. • D. GOWAN 1977, "The Exile in Jewish Apocalyptic," in *Scripture in History and Theology*, ed. A. Merrill and T. Overholt, Pittsburgh: Pickwick, 205-23. • M. A. KNIBB 1976, "The Exile in the Literature of the Intertestamental Period," *Heythrop Journal* 17: 253-72. • M. A. KNIBB 1983, "Exile in the Damascus Document," *JSOT* 25: 99-117. • G. PORTON 1997, "The Idea of Exile in Early Rabbinic Midrash," in *Exile*, ed. J. M. Scott, Leiden: Brill, 249-64. • D. SMITH-CHRISTOPHER 2002, *A Biblical Theology of Exile*, Minneapolis: Fortress. • J. M. SCOTT, ED. 1997, *Exile: Old Testament, Jewish and Christian Perspectives*, Leiden: Brill. • J. VANDERKAM 1997, "Exile in Jewish Apocalyptic Literature," in *Exile*, ed. J. M. Scott, Leiden: Brill, 89-109.

See also: Restoration ALISON SCHOFIELD

Exodus, the

By the Hellenistic period, the Israelite exodus from Egypt was long established as the foundational story of Jewish origins, but it was not the only story of Jewish origins that circulated in the Hellenistic world.

Greco-Roman Accounts

Hecataeus of Abdera

Hecataeus of Abdera, who wrote at the court of Ptolemy I (ca. 300 B.C.E.), claimed that Judea was settled by people who had been expelled from Egypt as foreigners in a time of pestilence (Diodorus, book 40). He says that their leader was Moses and that he founded Jerusalem. He goes on to give a quite positive account of Mosaic legislation but adds that "as a result of their own expulsion from Egypt, he [Moses] introduced a somewhat unsocial and intolerant mode of life." It is unlikely that Hecataeus had read the book of Exodus. He probably had some Jewish informants, but he mainly relied on Egyptian priests. His account of Jewish origins depends on Egyptian traditions about the expulsion of the Hyksos, people from Syria who had ruled Egypt for a time in the middle of the second millennium B.C.E.

Manetho

A related account was circulated by the Egyptian writer Manetho, around the same time. Manetho claimed that Jerusalem was built by the Hyksos, after they had been expelled from Egypt. (This part of his account is accepted by Josephus, *Ag. Ap.* 1.228-52.) But he also recounts that a king named Amenophis tried to purge the country of lepers and sent some 80,000 of them to work in stone quarries. These later rebelled under a leader named Osarseph, who made laws hostile to Egyptian religion and summoned the Shepherds (Hyksos) from Jerusalem to help him. The king took the sacred animals and fled to Ethiopia. In his absence, the people from Jerusalem ravaged the land. Osarseph changed his name to Moses. Eventually the king returned and drove them out. Manetho, like Hecataeus, seems to have had no direct knowledge of the biblical story of the exodus. His account was largely based on traditions about the Hyksos, enhanced by some traditions relating to the "monotheistic" reforms of Akhenaten, when some priests were sent to the stone quarries.

Early Jewish Jewish Accounts

Artapanus

These pagan accounts elicited a very colorful rejoinder from the Jewish writer Artapanus, who wrote in Egypt in the late third or second century B.C.E. His account agrees with the biblical story in several details. Moses is introduced as a Jewish child, adopted into the family of an Egyptian ruler. He kills an Egyptian in self-defense, and flees to Arabia, where he marries the daughter of Raguel. He witnesses the burning bush and hears a divine voice. He returns to Egypt, performs signs for the king, and afflicts the Egyptians with plagues. He notes that the Jews despoiled the Egyptians and crossed the Red Sea. From verbal echoes, and the name Ragouelos, it is apparent that Artapanus knew the story in its Septuagintal form. He embellishes the story, however, with many details that have no biblical basis. Thus Moses is identified with Mousaeus, and as the teacher of Orpheus. He is credited with various inventions for the benefit of the Egyptians, including the cult of animals, especially the Apis bull. His successes arouse the envy of the king, who sends him on a campaign against Ethiopia with a makeshift army. He succeeds there and even teaches the Ethiopians circumcision. Because of the continued plotting of the king, however, he flees to Arabia. This is the occasion for the killing of the Egyptian, and the encounter with Raguel. At first he restrains Raguel from invading Egypt, but eventually he is told by a divine voice to go and rescue the Jews. From this point on, the narrative follows the biblical account, but there are still embellishments; for example, the Egyptians dedicate the rod to Isis because of the wonders wrought by Moses with his rod.

This free adaptation of the exodus story must be seen as an exercise in the "competitive historiography" that flourished in the Hellenistic age, in which writers from different peoples attributed mighty exploits to their ancestors. For Artapanus, it was a source of ethnic pride that Moses had invented the animal cults, which were greatly revered by the Egyptians even if they were anathema to biblical law. It is possible that the story is deliberately humorous, as Erich Gruen has argued, but it also had an apologetic character, insofar as it refuted the derogatory account of Manetho and depicted Moses in glorious terms.

Ezekiel the Tragedian

Another colorful adaptation of the exodus story by a Hellenistic Jewish writer is found in the fragments of Ezekiel the tragedian, who wrote somewhere between the late third and early first century B.C.E. Ezekiel cast the story in the form of a Greek tragedy. He follows the biblical story closely, but with some significant departures. In his treatment of the Passover, he does not mention the requirement of circumcision. Moses is said to have had a dream in which he was enthroned on Mt. Sinai, on a throne vacated by a "man" who is usually thought to be God. While the vision is interpreted to mean that Moses will be a judge and leader, it presupposes midrashic traditions based on Exod. 7:2 ("I have made you a god to pharaoh"). Moses is also depicted as god and king in Philo (*Mos.* 1.1, 158). Another major departure from the biblical text is a description of a phoenix, evidently prompted by the reference to palm trees (Gr. *phoinikēs*) at Elim (LXX Exod. 15:27). The significance of the phoenix is not explained, but the bird was associated with the renewal of life in ancient Egypt.

Wisdom of Solomon

Another major treatment of the exodus story in Hellenistic Judaism is found in the Wisdom of Solomon 11–19 (early first century C.E.). The book does not mention Jews or Egyptians by name, but treats the story typologically, as referring to "a holy people" and their adversaries. The latter were punished for animal worship and idolatry, but God showed mercy by giving them opportunity to repent. The holy people, in contrast, were nurtured in the wilderness. The miracle of the exodus is described as a refashioning of creation and is explained by a musical analogy: "for the elements changed places with one another, as on a harp the notes vary the nature of the rhythm, while each note remains the same" (19:18).

Josephus

Josephus devotes a considerable part of his treatise *Against Apion* to refuting hostile accounts of Jewish origins by pagan writers. His own account is found in *Ant.* 2.217-349. He boasts, "I have recounted each detail here just as I found it in the sacred books," but while he reproduces the biblical story, he also adds some embellishments, notably a story of a campaign led by Moses against Ethiopia (2.238-53), culminating in Moses' marriage to an Ethiopian princess (cf. the reference to Moses' "Cushite" wife in Num. 12:1). As in Artapanus, Moses flees to Arabia because of the envy of the king, but no mention is made of killing an Egyptian. The credibility of the parting of the sea is supported by an anecdote about a similar incident in the campaign of Alexander the Great, at the Pamphylian Sea (2.348).

Jubilees

The most noteworthy retelling of the exodus in a Semitic language source in this period is found in the book of *Jubilees,* chaps. 47–50, which is part of a story supposedly told to Moses by the angel of the presence. A noteworthy feature of this account is the role of Mastema, leader of the demons, who helped the Egyptian sorcerers and persuaded the Egyptians to pursue the Israelites. Yet it was also the powers of Mastema that were let loose to kill all the firstborn in the land of Egypt (49:2). The account in *Jubilees* dwells at length on the proper observance of the Passover. It concludes with a discourse on the laws of the Sabbath in chap. 50.

A New Exodus

Another noteworthy feature of the interpretation of the exodus in this period is the typological use, which takes the exodus as the paradigm of a new beginning. This usage was already found in Second Isaiah (Isaiah 40–55), which depicted the return from the Babylonian Exile as a new exodus. The community described in the Dead Sea Scrolls was supposed to go into the wilderness to prepare the way of the Lord (1QS 8). A similar exodus typology is associated with John the Baptist in the New Testament (Matt. 3:3; Mark 1:2-3; Luke 3:4).

BIBLIOGRAPHY

S. L. BERRIN 2005, "Anti-semitism, Assimilation, and Ancient Jewish Apologia: The Story of the Exodus in the Writings of Josephus Flavius," *Journal of the Australian Association for Jewish Studies* 11: 20-34. • S. CHEON 1997, *The Exodus Story in the Wisdom of Solomon: A Study in Biblical Interpretation,* Sheffield: Sheffield Academic Press. • J. J. COLLINS 2005, "Reinventing Exodus: Exegesis and Legend in Hellenistic Egypt," in idem, *Jewish Cult and Hellenistic Culture,* Leiden: Brill, 44-57. • P. ENNS 1997, *Exodus Retold: Ancient Exegesis of the Departure from Egypt in Wis 10:15-21 and 19:1-9,* Atlanta: Scholars Press. • E. S. GRUEN 1998, "The Use and Abuse of the Exodus Story," in idem, *Heritage and Hellenism,* Berkeley, Calif.: University of California Press, 41-72. • J. L. KUGEL 1998, *Traditions of the Bible,* Cambridge, Mass.: Harvard University Press, 543-612.

JOHN J. COLLINS

Ezekiel, Book of

The book of Ezekiel is largely the product of the sixth-century-B.C.E. prophet, described in the superscription of the book (Ezek. 1:1-3) as a priest taken into exile during the first Babylonian deportation (597 B.C.E.). Ezekiel writes for the Babylonian community, offering its members a powerful theological explanation for their exile. He asserts that God has not abandoned the exilic community, but rather dwells *with* them and has preserved them from the *real* judgment that he is about to execute on a defiled Jerusalem. The city's destruction, however, will also be its purging, after which the righteous exiles will return and reestablish it and its temple.

Ezekiel's best-known visions include the dry bones vision (37:1-11), the vision of the new temple and its environs (chaps. 40–48), and the two so-called throne chariot visions, theophanies that occupy several chapters of the book (1:4-28; 8:1–11:24). Ezekiel's visions are extremely elaborate, often involving a heavenly guide. The book's oracles and allegories also are striking and structurally complex. One memorable allegory important to Jewish groups in the Second Temple period is the allegory of the eagle and the vine (chap. 17). Important oracles include the oracle against the shepherds of Israel (chap. 34) and the apocalyptic oracle of Gog and Magog (chaps. 38–39).

Ezekiel at Qumran

Although only six partial manuscripts of Ezekiel have been found at Qumran, few biblical prophets interested the Qumran community more. Given some of Ezekiel's theological and historical concerns, it is not surprising that the community at Qumran found the book intriguing. Like Ezekiel's community in Babylon, they saw themselves as a preserved remnant in exile and awaited the destruction of Jerusalem and its Temple. As God had left the Jerusalem Temple of Ezekiel's time (Ezekiel 11), so he had left the Second Temple — if he had ever dwelt in it at all (CD 1:3-4; 7:14-15). Thus an important and unique element in the theology of Ezekiel (that God can and will leave Jerusalem to join those in exile) is mirrored in the self-perception of the Qumran community.

Given these affinities, it should not be surprising that the Dead Sea Scrolls contain some twenty-seven allusions to material in twenty-three chapters of Ezekiel. In addition to the quantity of literary connections, the Qumran literature seems remarkably sensitive to the message and context of Ezekiel in its deployment of allusions to the book.

Uses of Ezekiel in material from the Judean Desert tend to fall into several different categories (Manning 2004). At the simplest level, the Qumran community applied certain terminology in Ezekiel to itself and its enemies. It used the epithets "those who sigh and groan" (Ezek. 9:4; CD 19:7-13) and "righteous exiles" (Ezek. 11:5, 20:3-5, etc.; CD 1:3-4, 1QM 1:2-3) to refer to itself; the epithet "the sons of Zadok" to refer to its priests (Ezek. 44:15; *Damascus Rule* 3:20); and the phrase "builders of the wall" to refer to its enemies (Ezek. 13:9-16; 22:17-26; CD 4:17-18; 19:30-35; 20:3-4; 4Q424 1:1, 4-5). Other Ezekielian literary motifs alluded to at Qumran include the "heart of flesh" (Ezek. 36:22-27; *Hodayot* 14:10; 21:10-13) and agricultural imagery associated with the vine allegory of Ezekiel 31.

On a more sophisticated level, the Qumran community seems to have understood some of Ezekiel's oracles more holistically as prophecy. The *War Scroll* interprets Ezekiel's Gog oracle as future prediction and speaks of a cosmic enemy of the community that will be destroyed by God in a cosmic battle yet to be fought (1QM 11:15-16). The *Damascus Document* and *New Jerusalem* allude to Ezekiel's vision of a restored temple, city, and priesthood (Ezekiel 40–48), also reading it as unfulfilled prophecy. However, where Ezekiel's vision emphasizes the restored *temple,* the Qumran material tends to emphasize either a restored and renewed *priesthood (Damascus Document)* or a restored *city (New Jerusalem).*

Pseudo-Ezekiel or the Ezekiel Apocryphon

References by Josephus to a "second book" of Ezekiel, quotations of patristic writers, and the discovery of fragmentary manuscripts at Qumran have persuaded scholars that one or more apocryphal texts attributed to Ezekiel existed in antiquity. The Qumran fragments derive from a pseudo-prophetic reworking of the biblical book. The text contained rewritten, quoted, or expanded oracular and visionary material. Important themes include the resurrection of the dead and the vision of the divine throne chariot. Because of the paucity of the evidence, the contents, provenance, and purpose of the apocryphon reflected in the Greek quotations are still very much under discussion. One fragment contains a parable about a blind man and a lame man that has no basis in the book of Ezekiel.

Merkavah Traditions

The theophanic visions of Ezekiel (chaps. 1–3, 8–10) became the touchstone for what came to be called the merkavah (throne-chariot) tradition in early and later Jewish mystical literature and theology. Although this tradition developed much more fully after 300 C.E., interest in Ezekiel's visions begins much earlier, perhaps even with the earliest (and now unknown) editors of the biblical book. These early editors made the decision to identify the "living creatures" (Ezek. 1:5) with cherubim (Ezek. 10:20) and thus allowed the earliest readers to ignore the Babylonian context of the biblical book and to substitute instead a setting within the heavenly throne room (Halperin 1988). Moving the location of the vision to the heavenly throne room allowed linkages to other theophanic visions (Isaiah, Zechariah, Elijah, and the Sinai theophany). Already at Qumran it seems that the original vision of Ezekiel, designed to reassure the Babylonian exiles of God's presence among them *apart from the Temple,* had taken on an expanded significance. The *Songs of the Sabbath Sacrifice,* with its emphasis on an "inner room," presumes a cultic context absent in Ezekiel's original vision (Newsom 1985). The attention of the community is directed to a temple, specifically the heavenly temple. Later, the Hekhalot literature would describe the way in which one could mystically "ascend" to that heavenly temple.

Ezekiel in Other Second Temple Literature

While allusions to the book of Ezekiel are much less frequent in other Second Temple literature — just eleven outside the New Testament (Manning 2004) — two particular texts of Ezekiel were evidently quite popular. Ezekiel's vision of the divine throne chariot (chaps. 1–3, 8–10) was appropriated at least five times. Ben Sira's reference to the throne vision notes simply that Ezekiel "saw the vision of glory, which he showed him on the chariot of the cherubim." Further references to the divine throne vision appear in the *Testament of Levi* (5:1) and *1 Enoch* (14:8-25, 71:1-2). In both cases, the visionary describes the heavenly temple and the divine throne in language remarkably reminiscent of Ezekiel.

The dry bones vision of Ezekiel 37 is referred to only twice in Second Temple literature outside the Dead Sea Scrolls, both times as a support for the idea of a final resurrection. In 4 Maccabees, the author tells the reader that Eleazar enabled his sons to persevere through persecution by teaching them about the resurrection using the teachings of Moses, Solomon, and Ezekiel (4 Macc. 18:17). The vision of the resurrected bones is also cited for a similar purpose in the *Lives of the Prophets* (3:12), a work that may have originated in early Judaism but that might have been composed in Christian circles in the Byzantine era.

New Testament

Although several Pauline texts contain minor allusions to Ezekiel, most New Testament allusions come from the Gospel of John and the book of Revelation. The most important of these is found in John 10:1-33, where the Fourth Evangelist places in Jesus' mouth an extended metaphor of himself as the good shepherd. The passage contains enough similarities to Ezekiel 34 (a critique of the "shepherds of Israel") to indicate that the New Testament text may be drawn from Ezekiel (Manning 2004). For the Fourth Gospel, the messianic elements of Ezekiel 34 find their fulfillment in Jesus, the Davidic shepherd (Ezek. 34:23) and the divine son (Ezek. 34:15).

Revelation's use of Ezekiel consists mainly in a redeployment of the most powerful images and literary ideas of that book. These include the dry bones vision (Ezek. 37:1-11; Rev. 11:11), the throne chariot vision (Ezekiel 1–3; Rev. 4:1-11), economic hardship during the exile and the destruction of Jerusalem (Ezek. 4:16; Rev. 6:6), the battle with Gog and Magog (Ezekiel 38–39; Rev. 20:8), the consumption of a sweet-tasting scroll that turns sour in the stomach (Ezek. 2:8–3:3; Rev. 10:9-11), and the measurement of the Temple (Ezekiel 40–48; Rev. 11:1).

BIBLIOGRAPHY

D. DIMANT 2000, "Pseudo-Ezekiel," in *Qumran Cave 4 XXI. Parabiblical Texts, Part 4: Pseudo-Prophetic Texts,* DJD 30, Oxford: Clarendon, 7-88. • D. J. HALPERIN 1988, *Faces of the Chariot: Early Jewish Responses to Ezekiel's Vision,* Tübingen: Mohr-Siebeck. • H. J. DE JONGE AND J. TROMP, EDS. 2007, *The Book of Ezekiel and Its Influence,* London: Ashgate. • J. LUST 1986, "Ezekiel Manuscripts from Qumran: Preliminary Edition of 4QEz a and b," in *Ezekiel and His Book: Textual and Literary Criticism and Their Interrelation,* ed. J. Lust, Leuven: Leuven University Press. • G. T. MANNING JR., 2004, *Echoes of a Prophet: The Use of Ezekiel in the Gospel of John and in the Literature of the Second Temple Period,* Sheffield: Sheffield Academic Press. • J. R. MUELLER 1994, *Five Fragments of the Apocryphon of Ezekiel: A Critical Study,* Sheffield: JSOT. • C. NEWSOM 1985, *Songs of the Sabbath Sacrifice: A Critical Edition,* Atlanta: Scholars Press. • M. E. STONE, B. G. WRIGHT, AND D. SATRAN, EDS. 2000, *The Apocryphal Ezekiel,* Atlanta: Scholars Press. • W. ZIMMERLI 1979-1983, *Ezekiel,* 2 vols., Philadelphia: Fortress.

D. NATHAN PHINNEY

Ezekiel the Tragedian

Ezekiel is the only Jewish playwright from antiquity known to us. He probably lived in Alexandria in the middle of the second century B.C.E. Fragments from only one play, the *Exagōgē,* have been preserved, although according to Clement of Alexandria (*Stromateis* 1.23.155) he wrote more than one drama. The title *Exagōgē* is derived from the Greek verb *exagein,* "to lead out," a verb used for the exodus from Egypt in Exod. 16:3 LXX. It is written in iambic trimeters, the meter traditionally used for plays in Greek antiquity. In a variety of ways, Ezekiel is indebted to his great Greek predecessors (Aeschylus, Sophocles, and Euripides; [see Jacobson 1983]). Only some 269 verses have been preserved in the form of quotations by later authors (Alexander Polyhistor, Clement of Alexandria, Eusebius of Caesarea, and Eustathius of Antioch [Holladay 1989]).

Significance

The remains of this play are important in more than one respect. First, almost all of the extensive Greek dramatic literature of the Hellenistic period has been lost, and the *Exagōgē* is the only play of which considerable portions are still extant. For that reason, it is a most valuable source for the study of postclassical drama, showing, for instance, that the unity of time and place that had been maintained by and large in classical drama had now been almost completely dropped (Snell 1971; Vogt 1983). Second, it is the earliest Jewish play known to us and the only one preserved from antiquity. As such, the drama is a fascinating specimen of what could be achieved when a Hellenized Jew molded biblical material into Greek dramatic forms. Third, although the author primarily followed the LXX version of the book of Exodus, his deviations from it represent an interesting witness to early Jewish haggadah (Jacobson 1983). Finally, Ezekiel is also the author of one of the earliest passages containing the idea of an originally human but now divine vice-regent or plenipotentiary of God, a concept that was to play a more important role in later Jewish and Christian texts (Van der Horst 1983; Ruffatto 2006).

Contents

As far as it is possible to reconstruct the play, the outline is as follows. In the first scene (vv. 1-65), Moses summarizes in a long monologue the events recorded in Exodus 1–2. This is followed by the encounter with Raguel's daughters (with several postbiblical elements, e.g., that Zipporah is identical to the Ethiopian wife of Moses in Num. 12:1; compare vv. 60-62 with *Targum Neofiti* 1 to Num. 12:1).

The second scene (vv. 66-89) contains, besides a short dialogue between Zipporah and a certain Chum, another nonbiblical scene, namely a report by Moses about a strange dream or vision he had in which he saw God enthroned on the summit of Mt. Sinai. God beckons Moses to come to the throne, hands over his regalia (scepter and crown) to him, descends from the throne, and orders Moses to sit upon it, whereupon a host of heavenly beings prostrate before him. It seems that all power in heaven and earth has been put into the hands of Moses (cf. Matt. 28:18). Afterward, Moses' father-in-law Raguel explains the dream as predicting Moses' future as a great leader and prophet.

This scene has become the focus of a heated scholarly debate. Does it reflect an early form of merkavah (throne) mysticism? Does it portray a divinized Moses who rules the universe in God's stead (but what, then, about Raguel's interpretation)? Is it a polemic against traditions about Enoch-Metatron's exaltation to divine status? Or does it reflect rivalry with traditions about the angelic veneration of Adam? Does the scene mean no more than that Moses acts on earth with God's authority (i.e., the Torah is God-given)?

In view of other clear indications of rivalry between traditions about Enoch and Moses, it would seem that Enochic literature and the *Exagōgē* present competing paradigms and that Ezekiel has attributed to Moses what had elsewhere been claimed for Enoch and has elevated Moses' status over that of his rival. But no consensus has been reached on the interpretation of this intriguing scene (see Jacobson 1983; Van der Horst 1983; Holladay 1989; Lanfranchi 2006; Ruffatto 2006; Bunta [forthcoming]).

The third scene (vv. 90-174) describes how God commands Moses from the burning bush to lead his people out of Egypt (Exodus 3) and how he removes Moses' doubts by performing the miracles with the rod and the leprous hand (Exodus 4). Subsequently, in a long monologue, God enumerates the ten plagues that he will bring upon Egypt (Exodus 7–11; these plagues could, of course, not be enacted on stage) and gives the rules for the institution of Passover (Exod. 12:1-20). In a fourth scene (vv. 175-92), Moses repeats these rules before the elders of the people (Exod. 12:21-28), with the significant omission of the obligatory circumcision of all participants (as a concession to Ezekiel's pagan audience?).

In the fifth scene (vv. 193-242), an Egyptian messenger gives a lively eyewitness account of the complete destruction of the Egyptian army in the Red Sea (Exodus 14, again with significant haggadic additions), which is evidently inspired by Aeschylus' *Persians*, where the crushing defeat of the Persian army is reported to the Persian queen, another well-known device for realizing dramatic scenes which were impossible to stage. In the sixth scene (vv. 243-69), scouts report to Moses that they have found a paradisiacal place for the encampment (Elim; see Exod. 15:27) and describe at length a marvelous bird of gigantic size that they have seen there. Undoubtedly this bird is the mythical phoenix, whose appearance is usually a symbol of the inauguration of a new era in history (or salvation history; see Jacobson 1983: 157-64).

There must have been more acts in the play than the scenes enumerated here, especially in view of the great time gap between vv. 192 and 193 (scenes 4 and 5), but we do not know how many. Even so, the *Exagōgē*'s synthesis of biblical story, postbiblical haggadah, and Greek literary form makes it one of the most fascinating products of Hellenistic Judaism.

BIBLIOGRAPHY

S. N. BUNTA 2005, "Moses, Adam, and the Glory of the Lord in Ezekiel the Tragedian," Dissertation, Marquette University. • C. R. HOLLADAY 1989, *Fragments from Hellenistic-Jewish Authors*, vol. 2, *Poets*, Atlanta: Scholars Press, 301-529. • P. W. VAN DER HORST 1983, "Moses' Throne Vision in Ezekiel the Dramatist," *JJS* 34: 21-29. • P. W. VAN DER HORST 1984, "Some Notes on the *Exagoge* of Ezekiel," *Mnemosyne* 37: 354-75. • H. JACOBSON 1983, *The Exagoge of Ezekiel*, Cambridge: Cambridge University Press. • P. LANFRANCHI 2006, *L'Exagoge d'Ezéchiel le tragique: Introduction, texte, traduction et commentaire*, Leiden: Brill. • A. ORLOV 2007, "Moses' Heavenly Counterpart in the Book of Jubilees and the Exagoge of Ezekiel the Tragedian," *Bib* 88: 153-73. • R. G. ROBERTSON 1985, "Ezekiel the Tragedian," in *OTP* 2:803-19. • K. J. RUFFATTO 2006, "Polemics with Enochic Traditions in the *Exagoge* of Ezekiel the Tragedian," *JSP* 15: 195-210. • B. SNELL 1971, "Ezechiels Moses-Drama," in idem, *Szenen aus griechischen Dramen*, Berlin: de Gruyter, 170-93. • E. VOGT 1983, *Tragiker Ezechiel*, JSHRZ 4.3, Gütersloh: Gütersloher Verlagshaus. PIETER W. VAN DER HORST

Ezra, Book of

The book of Ezra is our main source in the Bible that addresses the years immediately following the conquest of Babylon by the Persian Empire under Cyrus until the years of Artaxerxes I (roughly 539-425 B.C.E.), although some scholars date Ezra's visit to Jerusalem to the reign of Artaxerxes II, around 398 B.C.E. Together, the books of Ezra and Nehemiah deal with successive returns of groups of Judeans who were deported from Palestine (or, more likely, some of the next generation) by the Babylonians under King Nebuchadnezzar.

Ezra and Nehemiah as a Unified Project

Following some ancient sources (*b. Baba Batra* 14b–15a; Eusebius, *Hist. Eccl.* 4.26.14), modern biblical scholars typically regard the books of Ezra and Nehemiah as parts of a single work. There is a strong link between the events of the two books, even though the pre-

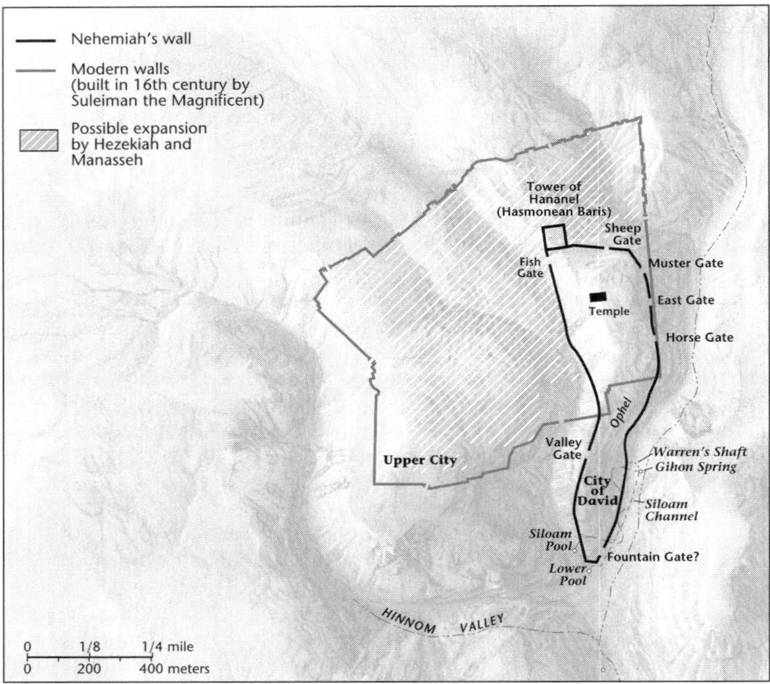

Jerusalem in the Postexilic Period

cise sequence of those events remains controversial (e.g., Who came first, Ezra or Nehemiah?). There are also texts that appear in both books, most notably the list of persons in the community in Ezra 2 and repeated almost verbatim in Nehemiah 7. These short books combine different types of writing, including putative quotations of royal correspondence, lengthy prayers, descriptions of selected events and political intrigue, and, in the case of Nehemiah, material often referred to as "memoirs." Finally, the Greek books of Esdras (A and B) contain similar material, but also include other stories of characters from this time period (e.g., Zerubbabel). The combined evidence suggests that all these textual traditions had been subject to considerable rewriting and editing for centuries before stabilizing into the forms we now have (Pakkala 2004).

Three basic units of text are normally distinguished for analysis of Ezra and Nehemiah. These are (1) Ezra 1–6, the correspondence surrounding the earlier returns of former exiles in the years immediately following Cyrus' conquest of Babylon and the accession of Darius 1 (ca. 539-515 B.C.E.); (2) the so-called Ezra Memoir, which consists of Ezra 7–10 and Ezra's prayer in Nehemiah 8; and (3) the Nehemiah Memoir, comprised of Neh. 1:1–7:4 and 11:1–13:31.

The Ezra Memoir

For most of the twentieth century, the Ezra Memoir was considered a fairly reliable history, if not an actual eyewitness account, of the events surrounding the journey of Ezra to Jerusalem in 458 B.C.E. (or 398). In this material, Ezra (described as a Zadokite priest and scribe) is commissioned to return to Jerusalem to bring financial donations for the construction of the Temple, to deliver certain "vessels" for use in worship, and to give a message to the "treasurers" of the province that they must provide funds and release the Temple (and all Temple personnel) from all normal tax and tribute requirements. A good deal of debate centers on the final part of this commission as given in Ezra 7:25-26, which appears to commission Ezra to teach and even impose the "laws of your God." This final portion backs up Ezra's authority with severe threats of death, banishment, or confiscation of property (similar to the threats that often concluded ancient treaty formulations). It is also likely that the descriptions and prayer in Neh. 8:1-8 and especially Neh. 9:6-38 (accepting the Greek textual witness to the presence of Ezra in Neh. 9:6) relate to the carrying out of these religious reforms. This material may have been moved from its original location between chap. 8 and chap. 9 of Ezra and thus originally preceded the identification of the mixed marriage problem, and Ezra's anguished prayer in response.

Ezra 9–10 deals with the issue of mixed marriages between recent returnees and descendants of the earlier returnees who came back to Judea before Ezra's journey (presumably the groups briefly discussed in Ezra 1–6 and referred to as the "sons of the exile" in Ezra 6:16, 19; 8:35; and 10:7). Ezra's solution is to stir his supporters toward a mass, public divorce of foreign wives. This mixed-marriage crisis has been the center of a great deal of debate regarding the book of Ezra — not only the reasons for it, but also whether Ezra exceeded his authorization in forcing such an action. It is widely noted that Ezra's definition of acceptable marriage partners is defined in even more narrow ethnic terms than the Mosaic expectations regarding mixed marriages known from Exodus and Deuteronomy. Thus, it is often suggested that Ezra's sudden disappearance, and the precipitous sudden ending of the book, may reflect Persian annoyance that he exceeded his mandate and actually stirred up more instability in the region with his extremist views (Smith-Christopher 1994; Janzen 2002).

Social and Political Context

Scholarly attention has recently turned to the social and political context of the historical missions of Ezra and Nehemiah in the Persian Empire. The influential thesis of Hoglund (1992) argued that the missions of Ezra and especially Nehemiah were both part of Persian imperial interests in shoring up their western front, as they faced both Egyptian and Greek rebellions and resistance in the mid-fifth century B.C.E. Lipshits (2006), however, has recently followed Briant (2002) in seriously questioning the significance of Judah for Persian military interests; more important to the Persians was the strategic coastal region, where archaeological evidence of Persian garrisons is more plentiful. Furthermore, Lipshits argues that there is little archaeological evidence of a significant population in Jerusalem itself; he estimates that the total population of the city during the Persian period was only about 1,500 residents — much lower than previous estimates. More attention may have shifted to Jerusalem with the arrival and work of Nehemiah as governor, 141 years after the devastation of Jerusalem by the Babylonians in 586 B.C.E.

Such observations are forcing a reassessment of the significance of the work of Ezra, which is being increasingly viewed as entirely religious in character and motivation and perhaps of concern only to a relatively small number of people from the Diaspora communities and to portions of the local population in Judah, which would have consisted of rural village settlements with no major urban area. How much Ezra's mission was a matter of Persian interest and of local Judean religious concern, then, turns on two debated issues: the ostensibly "official" correspondence in the book of Ezra, and the nature of the imperial "law" apparently authorizing Ezra to travel to Jerusalem.

The Persian Correspondence

Throughout most of the twentieth century, there was a general consensus that at least some of the Persian correspondence quoted in Ezra 1–6 was based on genuine material. While debate continued about the form of the edict of Cyrus in Ezra 1:2-4 (especially its religious affirmations of "the God of Heaven," "God of Israel," etc.), more confidence was expressed about those letters noted in Ezra 5:6–6:12. This debate continues to simmer, however. Grabbe, for instance, expresses very little confidence in the historical reliability of virtually any of the Persian correspondence, after examining such issues as the presence of Persian loanwords, the literary styles of epistle writing, and the arguably Jewish religious language that would not be expected in authentic Persian correspondence. He allows for the possibility that the letter of Tattenai (5:7-17) might be close to an original document but is cautious even about this example.

Persian Interest in Jewish Law

A second area of debate has been the issue of Persian authorization of the laws enacted by Ezra. Did Ezra have official Persian support to enact Jewish religious law? Was the Pentateuch, our present "Law of Moses," at least partially a product of Persian interest in maintaining religious stability in Judea, and therefore in imposing religious and social law through the priestly envoy Ezra? The issue was raised in 1984 by Peter Frei and Klaus Koch, based on a variety of contemporaneous texts and inscriptions (from Egypt, Asia Minor, and Palestine) that reveal a common Persian policy of taking interest in the religious and overtly political traditions of local populations and cultures under their jurisdiction. Responses from scholars whose concerns focus mainly on Ezra and Nehemiah, however, raise serious objections; they point not only to the occasionally negative attitudes toward the Persians noted in biblical texts (Ezra's prayer in Neh. 9:36-37; cf. Watts 2001) but also to the paucity of evidence that Ezra's "law codes" bore a close resemblance to the legal material now in the books of Exodus, Leviticus, and Deuteronomy.

Few doubt the importance of coming to terms with the historical and textual problems of the books of Ezra and Nehemiah, but their importance has generated controversy on virtually every point of discussion.

BIBLIOGRAPHY

R. ALBERTZ 2003, *Israel in Exile: The History and Literature of the Sixth Century B.C.E.*, Atlanta: The Society of Biblical Literature. • J. BLENKINSOPP 1988, *Ezra-Nehemiah: A Commentary,* London: SCM. • P. BRIANT 2002, *From Cyrus to Alexander: A History of the Persian Empire,* Winona Lake, Ind.: Eisenbrauns. • T. ESKENAZI 1988, *In an Age of Prose: A Literary Approach to Ezra-Nehemiah,* Atlanta: Scholars Press. • L. GRABBE 1998, *Ezra-Nehemiah,* London: Routledge. • L. GRABBE 2001, "The Law of Moses in the Ezra Tradition: More Virtual than Real?" in *Persia and Torah: The Theory of Imperial Authorization of the Pentateuch,* ed. J. Watts, Atlanta: Society of Biblical Literature, 91-114. • K. HOGLUND 1992, *Achaemenid Imperial Administration in Syria-Palestine and the Missions of Ezra and Nehemiah,* Atlanta: Scholars Press. • D. JANZEN 2002, *Witch-hunts, Purity and Social Boundaries: The Expulsion of the Foreign Women in Ezra 9–10,* Sheffield: Sheffield Academic Press. • S. JAPHET 1968, "The Supposed Common Authorship of Chronicles and Ezra-Nehemiah Investigated Anew," *VT* 18: 330-71. • O. LIPSHITS AND M. OEMING, EDS. 2006, *Judah and the Judeans in the Persian Period,* Winona Lake, Ind.: Eisenbrauns. • J. PAKKALA 2004, *Ezra the Scribe: The Development of Ezra 7–10 and Nehemiah 8,* Berlin: de Gruyter. • D. SMITH-CHRISTOPHER 1994, "The Mixed Marriage Crisis in Ezra 9–10 and Nehemiah 13," in *Second Temple Studies,* ed. T. Eskenazi and K. Richards, Sheffield: Sheffield Academic Press: 243-65. • J. WATTS, ED. 2001, *Persia and Torah: The Theory of Imperial Authorization of the Pentateuch,* Atlanta: Society of Biblical Literature. • H. G. M. WILLIAMSON 1985, *Ezra, Nehemiah,* Waco, Tex.: Word.

See also: Nehemiah, Book of

DANIEL L. SMITH-CHRISTOPHER

Ezra, Fourth Book of

Fourth Ezra is an early Jewish apocalypse comprising chaps. 3–14 of 2 Esdras in the Apocrypha. Chapters 1–2 and 15–16 of 2 Esdras are independent Christian apocalypses (known as *5 Ezra* and *6 Ezra,* respectively) that were appended to the Latin version of *4 Ezra,* which was included in an appendix to the Vulgate. It is very likely that the original language of *4 Ezra* was Hebrew (or possibly Aramaic), but none of the original text survives. There were two independent Greek translations, from one of which the Latin and Syriac versions derive, while the second Greek translation is reflected in the Ethiopic and Armenian versions, two independent Arabic versions, a partial Georgian version, and a fragment in Coptic.

Pseudepigraphic Setting and Date

Fourth Ezra is set in the Babylonian Exile, thirty years after the destruction of Jerusalem, an anachronistic setting for the biblical Ezra, who lived more than a century later. Perhaps in acknowledgment of the chronological problem, the visionary identifies himself as "Salathiel [i.e., Shealtiel, the son of Jehoiachin, according to 1 Chron. 3:17], who am also called Ezra" (3:1). Nevertheless, the protagonist and putative author of the book is clearly meant to be the biblical Ezra, since in the epilogue (chap. 14) he takes on the role of restorer and promulgator of the Torah. The pseudepigraphic setting loosely parallels the circumstances of the author, who probably wrote in Palestine near the end of the first century C.E., in response to the destruction of the Second Temple by the Romans. The clearest indication of the date of composition is that the Eagle Vision (chaps. 11–12) apparently predicts the onset of the messianic age during the reign of Domitian (81–96 C.E.), but the interpretation of that vision shows some signs of "updating," so it is possible that the book was completed somewhat later. Fourth Ezra had been translated into Greek by 190 C.E., since Clement of Alexandria quotes from it in his *Stromateis*.

Structure

Although in the heyday of source criticism a majority of scholars (e.g., R. Kabisch, G. H. Box, and W. O. E. Oesterley) viewed *4 Ezra* as a composite of several short apocalypses, Hermann Gunkel was convinced of its "creative unity" and psychological depth. The inconsistencies that others ascribed to different sources, Gunkel attributed to conflicts in the mind of a single author who was deeply troubled by the calamity that had befallen Jerusalem. Most current scholarship follows Gunkel in regarding *4 Ezra* as a carefully structured composition that depicts the transformation of its protagonist from a despairing skeptic to a believer in the imminent redemption of Israel.

The book is divided into seven episodes, traditionally referred to as visions. The first three episodes (3:1–9:25), however, contain little visual imagery and are more aptly called dialogues. Each dialogue begins with a lament by Ezra, followed by a dispute between Ezra and the angel Uriel. Each of the first two dialogues concludes with a predictive passage in which Ezra takes a more docile stance in relation to Uriel, while the longer third dialogue alternates between dispute and prediction.

The fourth episode (9:26–10:59) is pivotal in that it begins with a lament like the first three, but the dialogue that follows is between Ezra and a mourning woman. The woman echoes the despairing tone of Ezra in the dialogues, while Ezra "consoles" her in the stern manner of Uriel. When in the midst of their conversation, the woman is suddenly transformed into a city before his eyes, Ezra is terrified and cries out for Uriel, who then reappears in the role of *angelus interpres* and explains that the woman is Zion; Ezra has been shown a vision of the New Jerusalem.

The fifth and sixth episodes (chaps. 11–13) are described as dream visions and are loosely based on Daniel 7. Upon waking from each dream, Ezra prays to the Most High for an interpretation and receives one from an unnamed speaker (probably Uriel, but perhaps the Most High). In the final episode (chap. 14), sometimes called the epilogue, the angelic intermediary has disappeared and Ezra receives instructions directly from God. He is inspired to dictate twenty-four books representing the Hebrew Scriptures, which had supposedly been destroyed by the Babylonians, along with seventy esoteric books.

The Dialogues

The most original part of *4 Ezra* is the series of three dialogues in which Ezra raises troubling questions of theodicy and refuses to let them drop, despite Uriel's attempts to divert his attention to the eschatological future. Uriel fails to answer to Ezra's satisfaction two interrelated questions raised in Ezra's first lament: why did God create humankind with an inclination to evil; and given that Israel has kept God's commandments better than any other nation, why has God abandoned them to their enemies? In the first two dialogues, Uriel refuses to answer Ezra's questions directly on the grounds that "the way of the Most High" is beyond human comprehension (4:11; 5:35). Indirectly, however, Uriel addresses the question of Israel's calamity by revealing that the present world will soon come to an end and that the righteous will be rewarded and the guilty punished in the final judgment. As for the problem of the inclination to evil, Uriel acknowledges that "a grain of evil seed was sown in Adam's heart from the beginning" (4:30), but he insists that "the law of God" is an effective antidote to it: God has told human beings "what they should do to live, and what they should observe to avoid punishment" (7:20-21).

Uriel's answers are unsatisfactory to Ezra for two reasons. First, Uriel rejects Ezra's assumption that Israel has kept the commandments better than other nations; the vast majority have been unfaithful to the covenant (7:22-24, 129-31). Second, Uriel freely admits that only a very few individuals will be saved in the final judgment (7:60-61; 8:3), those who "withstood danger every hour so that they might keep the law of the Lawgiver perfectly" (7:89). Because Ezra believes that the inclination to evil is universal and more powerful than the Torah (3:22), he shifts his focus in the third dialogue to the fate of sinful humankind, eloquently appealing to God to show mercy toward his creation (8:4-36). Uriel, however, insists that divine compassion and mercy will have no role in the final judgment (7:33, 115). At the end of the third dialogue, Ezra remains unconvinced that divine justice requires that only a few will be saved.

The Visions

The fourth episode is remarkable from a structural perspective, in that Ezra's dialogue with the mourning woman prior to her transformation into a city is actually part of the first vision, in that her words point to the history of Zion, according to Uriel's interpretation. The first of the three visions reveals very little about the eschatological events, however; at most it implies that Jerusalem will not be rebuilt by human hands, but rather replaced by an "established city" of divine origin (10:27; cf. 10:44, 54; 13:36).

The second vision is explicitly derived from Daniel 7: the eagle with twelve wings and three heads that represents the Roman Empire is identified as "the fourth kingdom which appeared in a vision to your brother Daniel" (12:11). The plot of the eagle vision differs from Daniel 7, however, in that a lion, who is subsequently identified as the messiah (12:31-32), appears to pronounce judgment on the eagle (11:36-46). The third vision also focuses on the role of the messiah in the eschatological events, but here the messiah is represented by a figure that resembles the "one like a son of man" in Daniel 7:13 (13:3, 25-26). Consistent with the previous vision, the messiah's primary role is to judge and destroy the nations by means of the Torah, which is symbolized by fire in the vision (13:38; cf. 13:10-11).

Although the mention of the Torah in the interpretation of the third vision recalls Uriel's emphasis on the Torah as the instrument of judgment in the dialogues (cf. 7:37), in general the eschatology of the visions is much more nationally oriented than that of the dialogues, which focus on the judgment of individuals. Instead of just a few righteous individuals, the Messiah in the third vision gathers to himself a "multitude" consisting of the dispersed tribes as well as those who remained in the Holy Land (13:12-13, 39-50).

The Epilogue

The final episode (chap.14) embellishes Ezra's historical role as promulgator of the Torah by portraying him as a second Moses, restoring the supposedly lost Torah (here understood to include all of the Hebrew Scriptures) by means of divinely inspired dictation to five scribes. In addition to the twenty-four books of Scripture, which are to be made public, Ezra dictates seventy esoteric books, which are reserved for the wise (14:45-46). Given that Ezra was earlier told to write down the things that had been revealed to him and to teach them only to the wise (12:37-38), the seventy books are generally assumed to contain eschatological secrets. The epilogue also contains a speech by Ezra to the people, defending God's justice in exiling them for failing to keep the commandments, but also promising, "if you, then, will rule over your minds and discipline your hearts, you shall be kept alive, and after death you shall obtain mercy" (14:34). This shows that while Ezra has accepted Uriel's message that it is possible to overcome the evil inclination, he has not given up his own belief in divine mercy.

Open Questions of Interpretation

Although most current scholarship agrees on the unity of *4 Ezra,* there are various ways of understanding the relationship of the dialogues to the visions and epilogue. One approach, taken by Egon Brandenburger and Wolfgang Harnisch, reads the dialogues as a reflection of theological debates in the author's time. Both of these scholars identify the author's views with those of Uriel in the dialogues, but Brandenburger reads the visions as confirming the "apocalyptic wisdom" theology of Uriel, while Harnisch regards the two visions based on Daniel 7 as secondary.

Michael Stone and other followers of Gunkel's psychological approach focus more on the transformation of Ezra in the course of the book than on the radical theological claims of Uriel. Stone in particular views Ezra's transformation as a "conversion" that begins on an intellectual level in the dialogues and is completed by the profound religious experience portrayed in the visions. Bruce W. Longenecker attempts to synthesize the insights of the psychological approach with a careful analysis of Uriel's theology, but he follows Brandenburger in interpreting the visions as confirming Uriel's arguments in the dialogues.

The visions address Ezra's legitimate concern with the fate of Israel, which is rooted in Deuteronomic theology. Although the visions do not directly contradict the dialogues, they focus much more on the salvation of a remnant of Israel and the destruction of their enemies, which presents a problem for any interpretation that identifies the author's perspective with Uriel's individualistic eschatology in the dialogues. Given that the author abandoned both the dialogue form and Uriel as a distinct character in the second half of the book, it seems likely that he sympathized with Ezra's anguished questioning and intended the dialogues to be inconclusive. If so, the structure of the book holds the key to its interpretation: the shift from dialogue to vision form represents the author's conviction that the questions of theodicy he raises through Ezra in the dialogues cannot adequately be addressed through rational discourse, but only through the religious symbolism of the visions.

BIBLIOGRAPHY

G. H. BOX 1912, *The Ezra-Apocalypse,* London: Pitman. • E. BRANDENBURGER 1981, *Die Verborgenheit Gottes im Weltgeschehen: Das literarische und theologische Problem des 4. Esrabuches,* Zürich: Theologischer Verlag. • J. J. COLLINS 1998, *The Apocalyptic Imagination: An Introduction to Jewish Apocalyptic Literature,* 2d ed., Grand Rapids: Eerdmans, 195-212. • H. GUNKEL 1900, "Das vierte Buch Esra," in *Die Apokryphen und Pseudepigraphen des alten Testaments,* 2 vols., ed. E. Kautzsch, Tübingen: Mohr, 2: 331-401. • W. HARNISCH 1969, *Verhängnis und Verheißung der Geschichte: Untersuchungen zum Zeit- und Geschichtsverständnis im. 4. Buch Esra und in der syr. Baruchapokalypse,* Göttingen: Vandenhoeck & Ruprecht. • K. M. HOGAN 2008, *Theologies in Conflict in 4 Ezra: Wisdom Debate and Apocalyptic Solution,* Leiden: Brill. • R. KABISCH 1889, *Das vierte Buch Esra auf seine Quellen untersucht,* Göttingen: Vandenhoeck & Ruprecht. • B. W. LONGENECKER 1995, *Second Esdras*, Sheffield: Sheffield Academic Press. • W. O. E. OESTERLEY 1933, *2 Esdras (The Ezra Apocalypse)*, London: Methuen. • M. E. STONE 1990, *Fourth Ezra: A Commentary on the Book of Fourth Ezra*, Minneapolis: Fortress. • A. L. THOMPSON 1977, *Responsibility for Evil in the Theodicy of 4 Ezra*, Missoula, Mont.: Scholars Press. • B. VIOLET 1910, *Die Esra-Apokalypse 1: Die Überlieferung*, Leipzig: Hinrichs. • T. W. WILLET 1989, *Eschatology in the Theodicies of 2 Baruch and 4 Ezra*, Sheffield: JSOT Press.

KARINA MARTIN HOGAN

F

Faith/Faithfulness

Hebrew Bible

The concept of "faith/faithfulness" in early Judaism is largely an extension of its meaning in the Hebrew Bible or Old Testament, where the meanings of the Hebrew term *'ĕmûnâ* and the Greek word *pistis* are often equivalent to "trust," "trustworthiness," or "fidelity." The faithful are those who are obedient to God (Deut. 32:20). God acts in faithfulness, that is, trustworthiness (LXX Ps. 32:4), and the righteous live by God's faithfulness (LXX Hab. 2:4; cf. MT Hab. 2:4). Along with Hab. 2:4, Gen. 15:6 is echoed throughout early Jewish literature, "Abraham trusted in God, and it was reckoned to him as righteousness." Abraham is considered righteous because he trusted God to fulfill his promise. Faith in the Old Testament, then, is essentially trust in God, the one who is faithful (Deut. 7:9).

Dead Sea Scrolls

In the Qumran literature, the *Pesher on Habakkuk* interprets Hab. 2:4, "the righteous one lives by faith," to mean faithfulness to the Teacher of Righteousness, the community's founder, and this faithfulness is also coupled with observing the Law (1QpHab 8:1-3). As in the Old Testament, God is described as faithful (1QS 1:19; 11Q5 20:20). However, not only is God faithful, but the covenant of God is faithful to save those who walk in it (CD 14:2), and God's people are to be faithful to him (1QS 8:1-4; 10:25; cf. CD 1:3; 20:23). In 1QM 13:2-3, all who serve God are also those who know him in faith.

Apocrypha and Pseudepigrapha

Among the books traditionally identified as Apocrypha, the Wisdom of Jesus Ben Sira makes the most references to faith/faithfulness. Ben Sira understands faith/faithfulness in close connection with obedience, and it is also God's faithfulness that demands faith of the righteous. Wisdom is created in the faithful while they are in the womb, and the fear of the Lord is the beginning of that wisdom (1:14). Yet Ben Sira also states that wisdom is gained by keeping the commands (1:25-26). Faith in God is paralleled with ordering one's way aright (2:6), and trust in God is based on God's faithfulness (2:10-12) and is described as obedience to his ways (2:15-16). Toward the end of Ben Sira, Abraham (44:20; see also *Jub.* 24:11), Moses (45:4), and Samuel (46:15) are presented as examples of this faithful obedience, and with regard to Abraham, this faithfulness is specifically related to his keeping of the Law.

In the Wisdom of Solomon, faith can be both a realization or knowledge of who God is (12:17) and trust in God. The verb *pisteuō* is used in parallel with the verb *peithō*, "to trust" (16:24, 26; cf. 3:9) and *homologeō*, "to acknowledge" (18:13). The righteous are those who do not distrust God (1:2); they also trust in God's oaths (18:6; cf. 12:21). The wicked, on the other hand, do not trust God (10:7), and this is further indicated by the inclusion of "unfaithfulness" in a list of sins (14:25).

4 Maccabees closely connects faith with remaining faithful in the face of persecution. Eleazer is lauded as an example for his faith in God and God's laws rather than those of man (7:19, 21). Likewise, the mother of the seven sons trusts that God is faithful and exhorts her sons who are tortured and killed to have the same faith as Abraham, Daniel, and others (16:16-23). Faith in 4 Maccabees involves confidence that God's laws are right and that they must be obeyed over the laws of humans (16:24-25; cf. 8:5-7).

In the *Similitudes of Enoch* (*1 Enoch* 37–71), the faithful are the righteous who depend on the name of the Lord of Spirits, who is himself faithful (63:8), but the unfaithful are the kings of the earth who deny the Lord of Spirits (*1 Enoch* 46:7-8). Obedience and faith are closely connected in *2 Baruch.* Good things come to those who believe (*2 Bar.* 42:2), and those who are spotless are those who subject themselves to God and his law in faith (54:5; cf. 54:21; 59:2; see also *4 Ezra* 9:7-8).

Josephus and Philo

Most references to *pistis* in the writings of Josephus carry the meaning of "trust." Faith can indicate a pledge or oath (*Ant.* 16.390; 18.328), and the verb *pisteuō* can mean to entrust someone or something to another person (*Ant.* 9.212). When Josephus speaks of faith in a religious context, it can refer to the faithfulness of God

(*Ant.* 17.179) and to the content of faith (*Ant.* 18.14). He also speaks of faith as belief in God (*Ant.* 4.5) and knowledge of God (*Ant.* 6.263).

Philo shows similarity with the Old Testament use of faith/faithfulness as trust or trustworthiness. The virtue of faithfulness can apply to a person (*Joseph* 258; *Moses* 2, 177), to God (*Sacrifices* 93), or to a person's trust or confidence in God (*Migration* 43–44). In contrast to most of the Jewish works mentioned above, Philo also equates faith with the content of belief (*Decalogue* 15) and with intellectual acknowledgment of a fact or idea (*Virtues* 216). For Philo, faith is "the queen of virtues" (*Abraham* 270) and leads to the good things in life, such as happiness and success (*Abraham* 266–69; *Alleg. Interp.* 3.164).

New Testament

Although the Gospel of John never uses the noun *pistis,* the verb *pisteuō* is used frequently in the sense of "to believe" in Jesus (John 3:16; 9:35). Somewhat like Philo, Johannine belief thus includes an intellectual acceptance (belief) that Jesus is Messiah and Son of God (20:31; also 11:27; cf. 16:27).

For Paul, the Old Testament emphasis on faithful obedience to the Torah as a means of attaining righteousness has been replaced by faith in Jesus (Rom. 3:21-31; Gal. 2:15-20). In some passages, "faith" in Jesus is equivalent to "belief" in Jesus (although some scholars translate the expression *pistis Iēsou Christou* in Rom. 3:22 and Gal. 2:16 as "faithfulness of Jesus"). To have faith can also mean to accept the proclamation about the crucified and risen Jesus (Rom. 10:9-14), and to confess the Lordship of Jesus involves "the obedience of faith" or commitment (Rom. 1:5; 16:26). While Paul appeals to the example of Abraham like many Jewish writers before him, for him God's righteousness is given through faith in Jesus and not through "works of the Law," that is, the requirements of the Torah such as circumcision, dietary restrictions, and Sabbath observance (Rom. 4:1-13; Gal. 3:2-9).

The author of Hebrews defines faith as "the assurance of things hoped for, the conviction of things not seen" (11:1). The list of the faithful in chap. 11 suggests that the author has an OT understanding of faith as trust, obedience, and faithful endurance; however, faith also includes believing that God exists (11:6).

Early Rabbinic Literature

Faith in rabbinic literature bears closer resemblance to biblical usage than to other examples in early Judaism. Joseph is spoken of as trustworthy because he dealt with his brothers in good faith (*Gen. Rab.* 100:9). Faith in God means confidence or trust in God (e.g., *Gen. Rab.* 32:6; *Mekilta de Rabbi Ishmael, Beshallah* 7 on Exod. 14:31).

Bibliography

D. B. Garlington 1991, *The 'Obedience of Faith': A Pauline Phrase in Historical Context,* Tübingen: Mohr-Siebeck. • W. Grundmann 1968, "The Teacher of Righteousness of Qumran and the Question of Justification by Faith in the Theology of the Apostle Paul," in *Paul and Qumran,* ed. J. Murphy-O'Connor, London: Chapman. • R. B. Hays 1983, *The Faith of Jesus Christ: An Investigation of the Narrative Substructure of Galatians 3:1–4:11,* Atlanta: Scholars Press; rpt. Grand Rapids: Eerdmans, 2002. • C. A. Keller 1970, "Glaube in der Weisheit Salomo," in *Wort–Gebot–Glaube,* ed. J. J. Stamm et al., Zürich: Zwingli. • D. R. Lindsay 1993, *Josephus and Faith,* Leiden: Brill. • D. Lührmann 1973, "Pistis im Judentum," *ZNW* 64: 19-38.

Benjamin E. Reynolds

Fallen Angels

Are angels capable of sin, and have they ever rebelled against God's rule? In the Hebrew Bible, there are only hints of such possibilities (e.g., Gen. 6:1-4; Isa. 14:12). With the intensification of Jewish interest in angels and demons during the Second Temple period, however, there emerged a rich body of traditions concerning fallen angels. These traditions formed part of Jewish reflection on the events leading up to the flood (cf. Genesis 6–8). Accordingly, discussions of fallen angels paralleled and informed the early history of interpretation of Gen. 6:1-4 — an infamously terse passage that describes how "sons of God" *(bĕnê 'ĕlōhîm)* came to earth, took wives from the "daughters of men," and sired *Nephilim* and/or Giants.

Fallen Angels in the *Book of the Watchers*

The *Book of the Watchers* in *1 Enoch* (1–36) preserves our earliest explicit discussion of fallen angels (ca. third century B.C.E.). The account of their descent is here part of a discourse attributed to Enoch (cf. Gen. 5:18-24) and is introduced with a paraphrase of Gen. 6:1-2 (*1 Enoch* 6:1-2). The "sons of God" are identified as members of a class of angels called Watchers (*'îrîn;* cf. Dan. 4:17).

The *Book of the Watchers* describes their activities in detail (chaps. 6–16), even listing their names (6:7). It states that 200 Watchers came down to earth during the lifetime of Enoch's father Jared (cf. Gen. 5:18), because they saw women and wished to have wives and children (6:2). They descended onto Mt. Hermon, where their leader Shemihazah made them swear an oath (6:3-7). Thereafter, they defiled themselves with human women (7:1). The products of this union were Giants, who devoured animals, people, and each other (7:3-5). In addition, the fallen angels revealed heavenly secrets and taught corrupting knowledge. Asael taught people how to work metal, make weapons and jewelry, and produce cosmetics (8:1). Other Watchers taught spell-binding, root-cutting, and celestial divination (7:1; 8:2-3). By their sexual and pedagogical misdeeds, they caused sin and suffering to spread throughout the earth (9:8-9; 10:8).

Whereas Gen. 6:1-4 describes the actions of the "sons of God," the *Book of the Watchers* also explains the consequences. Although the fallen angels ask Enoch to intercede on their behalf (13:4-6), this human sage is commissioned to rebuke them (13:1-3; 15:1-7).

By God's command, they are then bound by archangels, to await eschatological judgment (10:4-6, 11). Until then, humankind must suffer as a result of their transgressions: not only do people still practice the skills taught by these wayward Watchers, but the spirits of their sons are the demons who torment men and women (15:8-9).

Between the second century B.C.E. and first century C.E., this account was influential, shaping the understanding of antediluvian history and the exegesis of Gen. 6:1-4 among Palestinian and Diaspora Jews (Reed 2005). The influence of the *Book of the Watchers* may even be seen in some New Testament writings (Jude 6; 1 Pet. 3:18-20; 2 Pet. 2:9-10; cf. 1 Cor. 11:2-7). Early references to the fallen angels exhibit three main concerns: (1) their role in the origins of evil, (2) the relationship of their sins to the sins of humans, and (3) the significance of their punishment for understanding divine justice.

Fallen Angels and the Origins of Evil

Beginning in the second century B.C.E., we find efforts to assert human responsibility for sin and to downplay the fallen angels' culpability for the origins of evil. This is achieved, in part, through the suppression or minimization of traditions about their corrupting teachings.

In the *Animal Apocalypse* (*1 Enoch* 86–89), angels are represented by stars. One star falls first, followed by others, who transform into "bulls" (i.e., men) that mingle with "cows" (i.e., women), thus causing earthly chaos. Born of this intermingling are destructive offspring. Heavenly angels then intervene and imprison their fallen brethren. Although the *Animal Apocalypse* closely follows the order of events in the *Book of the Watchers* (esp. *1 Enoch* 6–11), it makes no mention of their teachings or their demonic sons. Here, their negative influence on human history ends with their imprisonment.

The *Book of Jubilees* may also draw on the *Book of the Watchers,* even as it diminishes the role of the fallen angels in the origins and spread of sin (VanderKam 1999). It is only after narratives about Adam, Eve, and Cain that fallen angels are even mentioned. *Jubilees,* moreover, removes the possibility of rebellion in heaven. Here, the Watchers are sent to earth on a divine mission to teach humankind (4:15; 5:6), and they succumb to sexual desire only after a long sojourn on earth. Likewise, *Jubilees* limits their pedagogical sins to the transmission of divinatory skills (8:3-4). As in the *Book of the Watchers,* the spirits of the sons of the fallen angels are identified with demons (10:5). According to *Jubilees,* however, God imprisoned most of the demons soon after the flood, and He allowed some to roam the earth only because of the wickedness of humankind (10:7-9). The aftereffects of angelic descent are thus minimized, while human responsibility and divine order are affirmed.

The same pattern is found in sources from the first century B.C.E. and first century C.E. Early Jewish and Christian sources stress the sexual sins of the fallen angels, omit reference to their teachings, and downplay their role in the origins of evil (Reed 2005). Far from suggesting that fallen angels are responsible for human sin and suffering, some even assert the opposite. In *2 Baruch,* for instance, humankind is held culpable for the fall of the angels (56:9-16). The *Testament of Reuben* blames women in particular (5:4-6). The sole exception to this pattern is the enigmatic *Similitudes of Enoch* (*1 Enoch* 37–71), which retains the image of the fallen angels found in the *Book of the Watchers.*

Fallen Angels as Paradigmatic for Human Sin and Punishment

Already in the *Book of the Watchers, Animal Apocalypse,* and *Jubilees,* fallen angels seem to be likened to wayward humans. The coupling of angels and women in the *Book of the Watchers* may function as a veiled critique of improper priestly marriages (Suter 1979; Nickelsburg 1981). In the *Animal Apocalypse* and *Jubilees,* this paradigmatic act of defilement is paralleled with the defilement caused by Jewish intermarriage with Gentiles (Reed 2005).

Elsewhere, the story of the fallen angels becomes a cautionary tale about sexual desire. Fallen angels are a common feature in early lists of paradigmatic sinners. Ben Sira and the *Testament of Naphtali* pair them with the Sodomites (Sir. 16:7-9; *T. Naph.* 3:4-5; so too Jude 6-7; 2 Pet. 2:4-6). The *Damascus Document* and *Testament of Reuben* present them as examples of those who fall prey to lust (CD [A] 2:7-19; *T. Reuben* 5). Their sins and punishment are held up as a warning: the power of sexual desire is so great that even angels can succumb, but no creature escapes divine justice. Perhaps as a result of their paradigmatic function, early sources often pay special attention to their punishment (*1 Enoch* 10; 90:21-24; 91:15; *Jub.* 5:3-11; cf. 4Q180; *Sib. Or.* 1.90-103), and their otherworldly prisons are a site for visits by holy men (*1 Enoch* 18:12–19:3; *2 Enoch* 18:1-2; 1 Pet. 3:18-20).

From the Flood to the Beginning of Time

Early Jewish traditions about the fallen angels and their demonic sons developed alongside nascent traditions about Satan. For the latter, precedents are found in *Jubilees'* treatment of Mastema and in the many references in Qumran literature to Mastema and Belial (Davidson 1992). These demonic leaders are often likened to the Satan *(ha-śāṭān)* of the Hebrew Bible, who operates within the divine justice system and who tests humankind at God's behest (e.g., Job 1–2).

Increasingly, however, traditions about the *śāṭān* absorbed elements of traditions about the Watchers — including ideas about the origins of evil in heavenly rebellion. Sources from the first century C.E. and following describe the fall of Satan and his hosts (e.g., Luke 10:18; *Vita Adam et Evae* 12–17). This fall is placed at the beginning of time, associated with the sin of pride, and elaborated with reference to Isa. 14:12 and Ezekiel 28.

By the end of the second century C.E., rabbinic Jews seem to have rejected both the *Book of the Watchers* and the interpretation of the "sons of God" of Gen. 6:1-4 as angels. In the fourth and fifth centuries, many Christians did the same, and they reinterpreted earlier references to the fallen angels (e.g., 2 Pet. 2:9-10) in terms of Satan and his hosts. Nevertheless, speculation about the Watchers continued in some circles, as suggested by the resurgence of interest in these figures among Jews and Christians in the Middle Ages.

BIBLIOGRAPHY

C. AUFFARTH AND L. T. STUCKENBRUCK, EDS. 2004, *The Fall of the Angels,* Leiden: Brill. • J. J. COLLINS 2008, "The Sons of God and the Daughters of Men," in *Sacred Marriages: The Divine-Human Sexual Metaphor from Sumer to Early Christianity,* ed. Martti Nissinen and Risto Uro, Winona Lake, Ind.: Eisenbrauns, 259-74. M. DAVIDSON 1992, *Angels at Qumran,* Sheffield: Sheffield Academic Press. • G. W. E. NICKELSBURG 1981, "Enoch, Levi, and Peter: The Recipients of Revelation in Upper Galilee," *JBL* 100: 575-600. • A. Y. REED 2005, *Fallen Angels and the History of Judaism and Christianity: The Reception of Enochic Literature,* Cambridge: Cambridge University Press, 2005. • D. SUTER 1979, "Fallen Angel, Fallen Priest: The Problem of Family Purity in 1 Enoch 6-16," *HUCA* 50: 115-35. • J. C. VANDERKAM 1999, "The Angel Story in the Book of Jubilees," in *Pseudepigraphic Perspectives,* ed. E. Chazon and M. E. Stone, Leiden: Brill, 151-70. • A. T. WRIGHT 2005, *The Origin of Evil Spirits,* Tübingen: Mohr-Siebeck.

See also: Angels; Evil; Satan and Related Figures; Sons of God ANNETTE YOSHIKO REED

Family

Because of the central role of the family in society, most early Jewish literature touches on marriage, and some authors repeatedly discuss family behavior (especially Josephus, Philo, Sirach, and Pseudo-Phocylides). However, these writers do not didactically address all facets of marriage (e.g., betrothal, age at marriage, marriage certificates), so they must be supplemented by rabbinic sources. Although rabbinic literature was penned after the Second Temple period, the conservative nature of rabbinic thought permits cautious use of the more primitive rabbinic dictums, particularly when correlated with earlier sources. Additionally, extant Jewish marriage certificates from the Second Temple age have been found at Elephantine and, from a slightly later period, in the Judean desert.

Since all sources probably originate from masculine literate individuals, we should acknowledge our limited ability to represent the full range of ancient views. Furthermore, Second Temple Judaism encompassed diverse communities and eras, so we must allow for variations in practice, even if there remains substantial unity in early Jewish views of marriage and family.

Extent and Leadership of Family

The family unit for most Second Temple individuals extended beyond the nuclear family. People remained in substantial contact with their parents and siblings, at times living in the same house or compound. The father usually acted as the head of the family, and carried the formal responsibilities for family decisions and finances, including negotiating marriages for his children. A married woman ceased to be under the authority of her father, and instead found herself under the authority of her husband and his family (see below). When a father died, his family responsibilities typically fell on the oldest adult son. This is not to say that other family members were powerless, but they influenced family decisions more indirectly. In such a society, a woman or child could be at severe economic and social disadvantage (especially widows and orphans, who lacked living members in their extended family). However, there is occasional evidence of Jewish women with independent financial means, and also of women who negotiated their own marriages.

Entrance into Marriage

The concept of a duty to marry is widely found in the sources from this period (e.g., Pseudo-Phocylides 175–76). Nonetheless, some ancient Jewish sects promoted celibacy (especially the Essenes and Therapeutae) and thus apparently usurped the family as the central social unit. Others admired these celibates for their religious rigor (Philo, *On the Contemplative Life* 18-20). However, even the Essenes recognized the need for some sectarians to marry for the sake of procreation, a fact that complicates identification of possible Essene archaeological sites (cf. Josephus, *J.W.* 2.120-21, 160-61).

The typical age of marriage in early Judaism is difficult to determine with certainty since the evidence is either occasional (in historical sources and inscriptions) or later than the Second Temple (in rabbinic teaching). The rabbis commonly expected a male to marry around his late teens or early twenties (*b. Qiddušin* 30a; *m. 'Abot* 5:21; cf. 1QSa 1:9-11), after having studied the Torah (*b. Qiddušin* 29b, although with the dissent of Rab Judah). Daughters would likely be married shortly after puberty (on which see *m. Nid.* 5:6-8; and corroborated by some epigraphic sources; contrast *b. Niddah* 45a).

Marriages were probably most often arranged. The approval of the father, or eldest male sibling, of the future bride was paramount (Tob. 7:11-14; Josephus, *Ag. Ap.* 2.200; *m. Ketub.* 4:4), although the bride's wishes likely exercised some influence (cf. Pseudo-Phocylides 204; *m. Yebam.* 13:1-2). In one case, where a man was marrying a slave, he conducted the transaction with the slave's owner (certificate K2 from Elephantine). However, marrying a slave woman or a prostitute met with disapproval in Josephus (*Ant.* 4.244-45).

Jewish people were often expected to marry fellow Jews, expanding on biblical precedent (Philo, *Spec. Leg.* 3.29; *Jub.* 30:7-17; cf. Tacitus, *Historiae* 5.5.2). However, sometimes Gentile proselytes to Judaism were seen as acceptable marriage partners (esp. *Joseph and Aseneth;* and cf. *m. Qidd.* 4:1, 7). Marriage of Jewish tribal cousins was considered by some to be an honorable duty (Tob. 4:12-13; Jdt. 8:2; and repeatedly in *Jubilees*), although it was also widely recognized that the Torah provided clear limits on incestuous marriages (e.g., Lev. 18:6-17; Pseudo-Phocylides 179–83; Josephus, *Ant.* 3.274; extended in CD 5:7-11; 11QTemple 66:12-17). Levitical law limited whom priests and high priests could marry (Lev. 21:7, 13-15), and these limitations were still remembered and even extended in early Judaism (Josephus *Ant.* 3.276-77). Polygamy was discouraged by many Jewish authors (e.g., Philo, *Spec. Leg.* 2.135-39; CD 4:20-22). Nonetheless, there is evidence of the continued existence of polygamy, especially among Herodian royalty (Josephus, *Ant.* 14.300; *J.W.* 1.477, 562).

Many sources indicate that a betrothal was expected prior to marriage. This betrothal involved a promise of marriage and included more legal obligations than present-day Western forms of engagement. In Jewish law the betrothed couple could be treated in some respects as if they were already married. This is most noticeable in the Deuteronomic edict, which is continued in Second Temple teaching, that sexual acts with another's betrothed were considered adultery (Deut. 22:23-29; Josephus, *Ant.* 4.251-52). The breaking of a betrothal apparently necessitated a "writ of divorce" just like the cessation of a marriage (*m. Giṭ.* 6:2; *m. Qidd.* 1:1; cf. Matt. 1:19). The initiation of betrothal could entail a ceremony (Josephus, *J.W.* 1.559; *m. Pesaḥ.* 3:7). Betrothal itself might last for many months or longer, allowing time to prepare for married life and to arrange the necessary monies (*m. Ketub.* 5:2).

Monetary and Legal Aspects of Marriage

Marriage, beyond a formal commitment, also involved an exchange of monies. The woman typically entered marriage bearing a dowry consisting of coins or valuable objects. Such a dowry could be substantial for a wealthy woman (Pseudo-Phocylides 199–200; cf. Josephus, *Ant.* 16.228). Poor women could have their dowries underwritten (Philo, *On Flight and Finding* 29) or exempted by prior agreement (*m. Ketub.* 6:5). The dowry formally belonged to the husband, but could revert back to the woman's control upon death of her husband or upon divorce (see Elephantine documents K2 and K7). Often the extant dowry lists (from Elephantine and the Greek texts from the Judean Desert) include items actually utilized by the wife herself (such as her own cooking pots or clothing).

The monetary responsibilities of the groom varied during the several hundred years of the Second Temple era. Marriage contracts from Elephantine in Egypt indicate that, in order to enter into marriage, a husband had to make a substantial *mōhar* payment to his future wife's father (or to her male guardian). This appears consistent with biblical precedent (e.g., Gen. 34:12; Exod. 22:15-16 [= 22:16-17 Eng.]). At least one extant marriage contract implies that this could form an addition to the woman's dowry (P. Yadin 18; cf. Elephantine document C15). However, by the time of the Mishnah (ca. 200 C.E.) the rabbis assumed that the future husband must merely make the *ketubbah* (a promissory device due the woman or her children upon his death or upon divorce). The rabbis established the minimum *ketubbah* amount as 200 denarii for a virgin and 100 denarii for a woman who had been previously married (*m. Ketub.* 1:2; 5:1). An important rabbinic tradition indicates that Simeon ben Shetach (first-century B.C.E.) ordained the change from a *mōhar* premarital payment to the father to the promissory *ketubbah* system (*t. Ketub.* 12:1; *y. Ketub.* 8.32b-c; *b. Ketubbah* 82b). The rabbis attribute this change either to making it easier for the husband to enter into marriage (since he might otherwise not have sufficient funds to pay her guardian before marriage) or to this making it harder to divorce (since divorce obligated the husband to pay a substantial amount to his former wife). The accuracy of the Simeon tradition has been challenged (Satlow 2001), although others have sought to defend its plausibility (Chapman 2003). In any case, it is clear that the monetary responsibilities of the husband were in transition in this period, as evidenced further by extant marriage certificates.

Marriage certificates, signed by all parties, provided proof of marriage and stated the legal/monetary obligations upon the husband and wife (cf. Tob. 7:14; *m. Ketub.* 4:7-12). Such a certificate was called a *ketubbah* (the same term also designates the monetary payment involved). Several Jewish certificates have been discovered at Elephantine (from fifth-century-B.C.E. Egypt) and in the Judean Desert (mostly from the second century C.E.). These were legal documents, focusing on money and responsibilities rather than on marital affections. They listed the dates and parties involved, stated obligations (should a spouse die or should there be a divorce), and often closed with signatures and witnesses.

There are distinctive elements among three categories of extant marriage certificates (some variations occur within each category). In the Elephantine documents the bridegroom typically speaks in the first person, addresses his wife's father (or other male guardian), stipulates a *mōhar* payment to the guardian, and lists the dowry items his wife brings into the marriage. In the later Aramaic documents from the Judean Desert, the husband directly addresses his wife, discusses the promissory *ketubbah* payment, declares that their marriage is "according to the law of Moses," and states stipulations strongly reminiscent of mishnaic rules (*m. Ketub.* 4:7-12). Finally, the Greek contracts from the Judean Desert follow a more Hellenized form: bearing the names of civic rulers for dating purposes, being written in the third person, and discussing principally the dowry without mentioning any *ketubbah* payment. Thus, the Greek documents evidence the incorporation of Hellenistic marriage law, while the Aramaic documents reflect a change from the earlier *mōhar* payment (at Elephantine) to the later *ketubbah* promise (a change cohering with rabbinic teaching).

Not everyone engaged a scribe to write a marriage certificate. The rabbis permitted three ways to enter into betrothal: by certificate, by exchange of money, or by the sexual act (*m. Qidd.* 1:1). Although they clearly preferred the certificate, the rabbis also developed a series of rules for marriages should a proper certificate be lacking (cf. *m. Ketub.* 4:7-12).

A few marriage ceremonies are mentioned in the sources. These involved several days of feasting; most sources imply seven days (e.g., *Jos. & Asen.* 21:5-8). Rabbinic literature also discusses the wife's ritual bath and her procession to her husband's house. One important ceremonial event involved the verification of the wife's virginity, since her lack of virginity could result in a severe penalty (Deut. 22:13-21; 11QTemple 65:7-15; Josephus. *Ant.* 4.246-48).

Duties in Marriage

Rabbinic sources list typical patriarchal marital roles for husbands and wives (e.g., *m. Ketub.* 5:5-9). The husband provided financially for the family, and led and cared for his wife and children. The wife provided clothing and food for the family, engaged in sexual intercourse with her husband, and birthed and nursed children. The authority of the husband over his wife is also asserted in many sources (e.g., Josephus, *Ag. Ap.* 2.201; 4Q416 2 iv 2-10), particularly his right to annul her vows (e.g., CD 16:10-12; Philo, *Spec. Leg.* 2.24). Women, especially virgin daughters, might be cloistered in the house to prevent their interaction with other men (e.g., Pseudo-Phocylides 215–17; cf. 2 Macc. 3:19). Nonetheless, one cannot assume that these patriarchal roles represented the actual practices of all, since some authors caustically remarked about situations when these roles were disregarded (cf. Pseudo-Phocylides 199–200; Sir. 33:19). Moreover, husbands could also be instructed to love and care for their wives (Pseudo-Phocylides 193–97).

If the wife's duties remained unfulfilled, the husband could divorce her, although the Pharisees and others debated the circumstances permitting such a divorce (*m. Giṭ.* 9:10; cf. Josephus, *Ant.* 4.253; Sir. 25:16-26; Matt. 19:3-9). Modern scholars debate whether the wife in that era could divorce her husband. According to the Mishnah, a wife under some circumstances could ask that her betrothal be dissolved (*m. Yebam.* 13:1). Remarriage was common in this period, whether due to divorce or to the early death of a spouse (e.g., from childbirth).

The Torah specified penalties for adultery, and Second Temple sources also insisted that sexual relations were permissible only between a husband and wife (e.g., Exod. 20:14; Pseudo-Phocylides 3; Josephus, *Ant.* 3.274; cf. Wis. 3:16-19). The legal consequences of infidelity, however, could be less stringent on men.

Family Obligations

Many Second Temple authors mandated procreation, and some wrote that children provided the only legitimate rationale for marriage (Josephus, *Ag. Ap.* 2.199; cf. Philo, *Spec. Leg.* 3.36; Pseudo-Phocylides 175–76). The first-century-C.E. schools of Hillel and Shammai debated the number of children required; two appears to be the minimum (*m. Yebam.* 6:6). Epigraphical evidence points to a high rate of childhood mortality, and some modern scholars suggest that less than half reached adulthood.

Nonetheless, methods of birth control were known among the rabbis (e.g., *b. Yebamot* 34b; 12b), even if they usually spoke against such practices. Due to the scarcity of relevant sources, it is difficult to estimate the frequency of use of birth control. Certainly the sources consistently reject abortion and infanticide (e.g., Philo, *Hypoth.* 7.7; Josephus, *Ag. Ap.* 2.202; *Sib. Or.* 3.765-66), despite the frequent occurrence of these acts in Gentile society.

The literature repeatedly asserts that children, in keeping with the biblical mandate, must honor their parents (Exod. 20:12; Philo, *Spec. Leg.* 2.224-41; Pseudo-Phocylides 8; Josephus, *Ag. Ap.* 2.206; 4Q416 2 iii 15-19). Ben Sira even states that obedience to one's parents earns merit in the heavenly economy (Sir. 3:1-16).

Parents were to instruct and discipline their children. Corporal discipline is assumed in some sources (e.g., Sir. 30:1-13); however, there are also cautions against harshness (Pseudo-Phocylides 207). The biblical mandate in the Shema to instruct the child (Deut. 6:7) prompted the religious education of children (Josephus, *Ag. Ap.* 2.204; Philo, *Spec. Leg.* 4.141), and formal teachers could be employed to this end (Philo, *Embassy* 115). It is likely that formal Jewish education was in transition during this period. The Qumran sect and later rabbinic orders clearly required some religious schooling (1QSa 1:6-16; *m. 'Abot* 5:21). However, significant Jewish debate surrounded the second-century-B.C.E. attempt to bring Hellenistic education to Jerusalem via the gymnasium (1 Macc. 1:14; 2 Macc. 4:12).

Upon the death of the mother, the extant marriage certificates often required the father to continue to provide for their children (lest he remarry and be tempted to treat his earlier household more contemptuously). Otherwise, it was assumed, in light of biblical law, that the inheritance of the father should go primarily to his sons, although daughters need not be excluded, especially if they remained unmarried (Philo, *Spec. Leg.* 2.124-39).

Hellenistic and Roman society considered household slaves part of the family system. Similarly, Jewish family codes could discuss slavery (Pseudo-Phocylides 223–27). Slaves were to submit to their masters, and masters were to treat slaves without undue harshness (Sir. 7:21; 33:30-31), although chains and torture could be employed (Sir. 33:24-28). Some Jewish groups, such as the Essenes, appear to have rejected personal ownership of slaves (Philo, *Hypoth.* 11.4), while others thought Jews could own only Gentile slaves (Philo, *Spec. Leg.* 2.123).

BIBLIOGRAPHY

P. BALLA 2005, *The Child-Parent Relationship in the New Testament and Its Environment,* Peabody, Mass.: Hendrickson. • D. W. CHAPMAN 2003, "Marriage and Family in Second Temple Judaism," in *Marriage and Family in the Biblical World,* ed. K. M. Campbell, Downers Grove, Ill.: InterVarsity, 183-239. • J. J. COLLINS 1997, "Marriage, Divorce, and Family in Second Temple Judaism," in *Families in Ancient Israel,* ed. L. G. Perdue et al., Louisville: Westminster John Knox, 104-62. • S. SAFRAI 1976, "Home and Family," in *The Jewish People in the First Century,* ed. S. Safrai and M. Stern, vol. 2, Philadelphia: Fortress, 2: 728-92. • M. L. SATLOW 2001, *Jewish Marriage in Antiquity,* Princeton: Princeton University Press.

See also: Marriage and Divorce

DAVID W. CHAPMAN

Family Religion

The family constituted the key social and economic unit within Second Temple Jewish society. It was only natural that the family also played a crucial role in shaping the religious practices and traditions of Second Temple Judaism. During this period religious identity was shaped by an intricate interplay of commonly followed religious traditions, adherence to specific interpretations of the Torah, cultural practices, and family traditions.

When studying family religion, one has to distinguish between the idealistic descriptions in literary texts and the actual religious life of Second Temple Jewish households. The evidence for the latter is limited. Still, there are reasons to believe that religious practices within families were influenced by multiple cultural identities prevailing in the Jewish society of the time. Thus in the third century B.C.E. Hecataeus of Abdera noted that contemporaneous Jewish families followed both native (legislated by Moses) and foreign practices on such key occasions as marriage and the burial of the dead (Diodorus Siculus, *Bibliotheca Historica* 40.3.8).

At the same time, the avoidance of pictorial representations in private houses as well as the abundance of ritual baths *(miqva'ot)* indicates that the population of Second Temple Judea followed the laws of the Torah. The exact combination of foreign and native religious observances was probably often determined by the customs of individual households. So according to Tob. 1:8, Tobit followed practices "in accordance with the command prescribed in the Law of Moses and the instructions enjoined by Deborah the mother of Hananiel our grandfather."

Families and Second Temple Sects

Families provided key building blocks within Second Temple religious movements commonly known as "sects." The covenant renewal ceremony of the Ezra-Nehemiah movement (Nehemiah 8–10) presupposes that families and their heads constituted the basis of the movement. They also played an important role in the formulation of the movement's religious ideology.

A similar picture emerges from the sectarian documents discovered at Qumran. Such texts as the *Damascus Document,* 4QMMT, and the *Rule of the Congregation* presuppose that households of means constituted key units within the structure of the sectarian movement. Halakic regulations detailed by the *Damascus Document* envision that the individual family functioned as a religiously significant space within which the pure life of the congregation was carried out. As a result, the daily life of a household formed the main object of halakic regulations. According to the *Rule of the Congregation,* one's advancement within (a utopian?) sectarian structure was directly related to his position within the patriarchal household.

On the whole, there are significant parallels between these documents and the descriptions of the Ezra-Nehemiah movement. In both cases families seem to have played a crucial role in the social and religious organization of the movements. The religious life of families was meticulously regulated precisely because it was deemed crucial for larger religious projects advanced by the sects. The portrayals of families and their religious life become idealistic constructs within a "holiness discourse" that seeks to establish a perfect religious community.

The situation, however, changes once we turn to the *Community Rule,* another key collection of regulations produced by the Dead Sea sectarians. In this document the family is all but invisible. Instead, the focus shifts to a community of like-minded adult (male?) individuals who have made a conscious decision to adhere to a particular interpretation of the Torah. Instead of regulating the relationships within the family, the *Community Rule* regulates the relations among individual members of the community and between an individual member and the community as a whole. Family life no longer constitutes an important part of the sectarian holiness discourse. Instead the association of like-minded adult individuals becomes the embodiment of sanctity and religious knowledge, whereas the family is relegated to the position of religious neutrality at best and hindrance at worst.

Both association-type and family-centered religious discourse coexisted within the Dead Sea movement and in Second Temple Judaism as a whole. The coexistence was not always an easy one, as the growing appeal of asceticism among the association-type movements seems to indicate. In other cases, however, families managed to maintain their status as religiously significant units alongside association-like study circles of religious masters and their disciples. Such apparently was the case in Pharisaic and rabbinic Judaism.

Families and Rabbis

The actual role of family practices in early rabbinic Judaism is not always easy to establish, since most of our written evidence comes from heavily edited texts produced within rabbinic study circles. Yet it seems that family practices played an important role in shaping early rabbinic halakah. It is possible that such central religious rituals of rabbinic Judaism as the celebration of Passover evolved from the family practices of early rabbis that were later canonized in classic rabbinic texts. In antiquity ways to celebrate the Seder varied considerably from one household to another, depending, among other things, on a household's social and cultural background (Passover Haggadah; *t. Pisha* 10:12; *m. Pesaḥ.* 7:2; *t. Beṣah* 2:15). Occasionally, halakic practices of a respected rabbinic household could constitute role models of piety emulated by other people. Most of the relevant traditions in early rabbinic texts are associated with the name of Rabban Gamaliel (second century C.E.) and his household (*m. Beṣah* 2:6-7; *m. Šabb.* 1:9; *t. Beṣah* 2:12-14, 16). R. Gamaliel's practices had mostly to do with specific ways of behaving on the Sabbath and during festivals.

Other family members, and not just its head, occasionally serve as authoritative transmitters of halakah in rabbinic sources. Several rabbinic texts refer to family slaves, maidservants, and daughters of the head of the family as valid transmitters of halakic practices (*m. Sukk.* 2:1; *t. Kelim B. Qam.* 4:17; *t. Kelim B. Meṣiʿa* 1:6). Their knowledge would come not as a result of formal training but simply by virtue of daily exposure to a lifestyle conducted in accordance with certain rules of pious behavior. The family as a whole embodied halakic traditions even though its head, by virtue of his status as *paterfamilias,* served as the most natural mouthpiece for such practices.

There is scant archaeological evidence for early rabbinic families, most of it coming from tomb inscriptions commemorating rabbis in the necropolis of Beth Shearim. It is possible that actual rabbinic families were significantly less uniform in their religious and cultural identity than rabbinic texts would like us to believe. The presence of marble and stone sarcophagi richly adorned with Greco-Roman mythological motifs right next to much more moderate rabbinic burials may reflect a variety of cultural commitments within actual rabbinic households. To what degree the complexity of multiple cultural identities might have influenced halakic observances within rabbinic families remains a matter of conjecture. Yet, even some mishnaic texts recognize that a family's exposure to Greco-Roman cultural conventions entailed changes in halakic practices and observances within such a family (*t. Soṭah* 15:8; *t. ʿAbod. Zar.* 3:4-5). In nonrabbinic families the degree of cultural and religious syncretism could be even higher, judging from Hebrew and Aramaic magical prayers to Helios contained in the late-antique work *Sefer ha-Razim.*

Early rabbinic texts composed within rabbinic study circles, such as the Mishnah, the Tosefta, and early midrashim, both affirm and attempt to control the religious functions of the Jewish household. The family remains the main social and economic unit within the rabbinic vision of Jewish society. It also constitutes the space within which Jews fulfill most of Torah's commandments. As such the family takes center stage in rabbinic Judaism's holiness project. Rabbinic texts draw distinctions between religious obligations of different family members, emphasizing the religious role of *paterfamilias* (*m. Qidd.* 1:7-8; *t. Qidd.* 1:10-11; *m. Ber.* 3:3). In this respect, rabbinic regulations come remarkably close to both pagan and early Christian "household codes." At the same time, the rabbis deny any legislative validity to household practices. Individual families and their halakic traditions are granted no power to serve as role models for the rest of "Israel" if they come into conflict with halakic regulations produced by rabbinic study circles. The Mishnah and the Tosefta repeatedly distinguish between "the practices of one's fathers" (or "one's father's household") and those of "Israel" (*m. Nid.* 4:2 and Rabban Gamaliel's traditions discussed above). The latter are determined exclusively by halakah produced within study circles. When family practices do not agree with those of "Israel," they are either rejected or categorized as private piety not binding on the rest of the society. On the whole, rabbinic discourse produced within study circles accepts the religious validity of the family space but also seeks to exercise thorough control of familial religious practices.

BIBLIOGRAPHY

J. J. COLLINS 1997, "Marriage, Divorce, and Family in Second Temple Judaism," in L. G. Perdue et al., *Families in Ancient Israel,* Louisville: Westminster John Knox, 104-62. • C. FONROBERT 2001, "When Women Walk in the Ways of Their Fathers: On Gendering the Rabbinic Claim for Authority," *Journal of the History of Sexuality* 10: 398-415. • M. SATLOW 2001, *Jewish Marriage in Antiquity,* Princeton: Princeton University Press. • A. SIVERTSEV 2005, *Households, Sects, and the Origins of Rabbinic Judaism,* Leiden: Brill.

ALEXEI SIVERTSEV

Fasting

Fasting is the practice of abstaining from eating and drinking for a preset period of time. It is an ancient and universal religious phenomenon, attested long before the Second Temple period. In addition to the fixed fast on the Day of Atonement, fasts were undertaken in biblical times in order to ask God for victory in battle and for relief in times of drought, famine, or pestilence. Fasts also functioned as public and private expressions of mourning as well as acts of repentance.

Fasting in the Second Temple Period

Individual and public fasts are mentioned in a number of early Jewish sources. Evidently, the early Second Temple period saw an intensification of the practice of fasting among Jews, as exemplified by the three-day fast in Esther (4:16), and the fasts referred to in the books of Ezra (8:21-23; 9:5–10:6), Nehemiah (1:4; 9:1), and Daniel (9:3; 10:2-3). A culture of multiple fasts perhaps constitutes the backdrop for *Megillat Taʿanit,* a late Second Temple Pharisaic work listing days on which it is forbidden to fast. The Roman historian Tacitus (*Histories* 5.4.3) also testifies to frequent fasts among the Jews (cf. Josephus, *Ag. Ap.* 2.282; Matt. 9:14).

Further attestation to a heightened practice of fasting among Jews during this period is perhaps reflected in references in Gentile works to the Jewish practice of fasting on the Sabbath. The closing of the period saw an identifiable increase in the tendency toward fasting and asceticism in the wake of the national disaster engendered by the destruction of the Second Temple (*t. Soṭah* 15:11-12; Urbach 1988). Nonetheless, during the late Second Temple period and afterward, some circles expressed reservations regarding the practice of fasting (Matt. 9:14-15; Mark 2:18-20; Luke 5:33-35; *b. Taʿanit* 11a).

Public Fast Days

The detailed description of public fast days in *m. Taʿanit* (1:4–3:8), which designates the circumstances dictating the declaration of public fasts, preserves some Second Temple traditions (2:5; 3:6). In the Mishnah, the most prominent reason prompting this step was lack of rain (as in the biblical precedent; see Jer. 14:1-12). Other prevailing grounds for public fasts are also mentioned in earlier sources, such as the two wartime fasts in 1 Macc. 3:17 (cf. Josephus, *Ant.* 12.290) and 3:47, where the accompanying ceremony is described in detail. This motive appears in other sources as well (e.g., 2 Macc. 13:12; Jdt. 4:13; Josephus, *Life* 290). National mourning in the wake of a disaster constituted an additional reason for public fasts (1 Bar. 1:5; *2 Bar.* 5:7, 9:2; *4 Ezra* 10:4, 25-49; Elephantine [Cowley 30:15; 31:14]; Josephus, *Ant.* 5.36-37, 166). Apart from mass participation, the public nature of these fasts inhered in expressions of mourning (wearing ashes and sackcloth; tearing clothes), display of desecrated ritual objects, recitation of prayers, sermons by leading personalities, or the reading of selections from sacred books.

Individual Fasts

More evidence for individual, as opposed to public, fasts comes from the Second Temple period. Prompting such fasts were personal or public mourning (e.g., *4 Ezra* 5:20; 10:4); repentance (e.g., *Jos. & Asen.* 13:9; *Pss. Sol.* 3:8; *T. Sim.* 3:5; *T. Mos.* 9:6-7); self-control and prevention of sin (*T. Jos.* 3:4; 4:8; 10:1-2); preparation for an apocalyptic revelation (*2 Bar.* 20:5-6; 43:3; *4 Ezra* 5:13-20; 6:31-35); ascetic piety (Luke 2:37; 18:12; Mark 2:18); and combinations of the above (e.g., Jdt. 8:6; *2 Bar.* 12:5; *4 Ezra* 5:20). Some personal fasts involved only partial abstinence from food and drink (such as meat and wine; see *T. Reub.* 1:10; *T. Jud.* 15:4; cf. *m. Taʿan.* 4:7) and not a total fast.

Fast Days in the Dead Sea Scrolls

Given the Qumran sect's ascetic nature, we might expect abundant attestation to the phenomenon of fasting in its literature. Accordingly, some have suggested that the sectarian calendar had a fixed fast day in commemoration of the sect's rescue from starvation during Herod's reign through fasting (Flusser 1987). However, there is no evidence in the Dead Sea Scrolls for the existence of any fast days, private or public, except for the Day of Atonement (Hacham 2001). This lack can perhaps be attributed to the fact that the Qumran community replaced the physical aspects of repentance that fasting entails with other, more spiritual means just as they had replaced sacrifice with prayer. Note, however, that Philo (*De Vita Contemplativa* 34–35) ascribes various practices involving abstinence from food as characteristic of the Therapeutae.

The Sabbath: A Fast Day?

In contrast to Second Temple sources (Jdt. 8:6; *Jub.* 50:12) and rabbinic sources forbidding fasting on the Sabbath, several Greek and Roman authors (Strabo, Pompeius Trogus, Suetonius' quotation of Augustus' letter, Petronius, and Martial) explicitly testify to the Sabbath as a fast day for Jews. Many scholars attribute this to confusion on the part of the Gentile authors, who mistakenly concluded from the Jewish practice of not lighting fires or cooking on the Sabbath that Jews abstained from eating. Others (Gilat 1982) have taken the opposite position and argued that certain Jewish circles engaged in fasting and daylong study on the Sabbath; because non-Jewish authors were familiar only with these circles, they remained unaware of any other type of Sabbath observance.

Four Commemorative Fast Days

After the destruction of the First Temple, four fixed fast days were established to commemorate the fall of the kingdom of Judah (Zech. 8:19): in the fourth, fifth, seventh, and tenth months. The building of the Second Temple provoked the question of whether these fast days should continue to be observed (Zech. 7:3). There is no clear evidence that these fasts were in fact observed during the Second Temple period. According to Josephus, Jerusalem was twice conquered on the same day of the third month (*Ant.* 14.66, 487). It is difficult to know whether he is referring to the Day of Atonement or to one of the four fast days. Some suggest that he is referring to *ad hoc* fasts (Rosenthal 1967). It appears, however, that they were not fast days at all; evidently, Josephus' tendency to emphasize Jewish religious zeal in wartime led him to take mistaken information from his non-Jewish sources.

Scholarly discussion of commemorative fast days during the Second Temple period has centered mainly on the Ninth of Ab, which commemorates the actual destruction of the Temple. Relying on *m. Roš Haš.* 1:3, some have argued that Jews fasted on the Ninth of Ab even during the Second Temple period, for its last hundred years at least (Epstein 2003). Others take the opposite position, claiming that Jews did not (Alon 1980).

No references to the other commemorative fasts have survived in the sources. After the destruction of the Temple, Jews definitely observed the fast of the Ninth of Ab and probably of the Seventeenth of Tammuz as well (*m. Taʿan.* 4:6), but there is no evidence for the observance of the other two commemorative fasts during the tannaitic period.

The Meanings and Motivations of Fasting

Fasts carry a variety of underlying meanings. Intrinsic to fasting is a self-abnegation that manifests the sorry state of the persons fasting. Together with prayer, fasting serves as a means of convincing God to answer requests and to effect release from difficulty (*y. Taʿanit* 65a). The self-injury inherent in fasting also concretizes its accompanying harsh degradation and the necessity for altered behavior and repentance (Sir. 34:31). Fasting can also be seen as a substitute for sacrifice or as facilitating its acceptance (Jer. 14:12; *m. Taʿan.* 4:3; *b. Berakot* 17a; Urbach 1988: 442-45); as an expression of austere piety that purifies the individual and brings him closer to God (Philo, *Mos.* 2.23-24); or as a vehicle enabling the individual to experience apocalyptic visions and revelations of celestial secrets. These aims of fasting exhibit not only continuity with biblical tradition but also Hellenistic influence.

Bibliography

G. Alon 1980, *The Jews in Their Land in the Talmudic Age (70-640 C.E.)*, Jerusalem: Magnes, 265-66. • H. A. Brongers

1977, "Fasting in Israel in Biblical and Post-Biblical Times," *OTS* 20: 1-21. • J. N. EPSTEIN 2003, *Introduction to the Mishnaic Text,* 3d ed., Jerusalem: Magnes, 2: 1012-14 (in Hebrew). • D. FLUSSER 1987, "Qumran and the Famine during the Reign of Herod," *Israel Museum Journal* 6: 7-16. • Y. D. GILAT 1982, "On Fasting on the Sabbath," *Tarbiz* 52:1-15 (in Hebrew). • N. HACHAM 2001, "Communal Fasts in the Judean Desert Scrolls," in *Historical Perspectives: From the Hasmoneans to Bar Kokhba in Light of the Dead Sea Scrolls,* ed. D. Goodlatt, A. Pinnick, and D. R. Schwartz, Leiden: Brill, 127-45. • D. LEVINE 2001, *Communal Fasts and Rabbinic Sermons: Theory and Practice in the Talmudic Period,* Israel: Hakibbutz Hameuchad (in Hebrew). • J. ROSENTHAL 1967, "The Four Commemorative Fast Days," in *The Seventy-fifth Anniversary Volume of the Jewish Quarterly Review,* 446-59. • E. E. URBACH 1988, "Ascesis and Suffering in Talmudic and Midrashic Sources," in *The World of the Sages: Collected Studies,* Jerusalem: Magnes, 437-58 (in Hebrew).

See also: Asceticism NOAH HACHAM

Festivals and Holy Days

The cycle of appointed times in the sacred calendar of the Torah includes New Moon feasts, three pilgrimage festivals (Passover/Unleavened Bread, Weeks, and Booths), a festival of trumpet blasts, and the Day of Atonement (Leviticus 23; Numbers 28–29). During the Second Temple period, the Temple celebration of these was lavish. The pilgrimage festivals especially were occasions of great joy, drawing large crowds even from throughout the Diaspora (e.g., Josephus, *J.W.* 6.422-26; Philo, *Spec. Leg.* 1.69-70; Acts 2:5-11), with money from a second tithe to spend in Jerusalem. They provided the only occasions for assembly of all Israel and thus nurtured a sense of identity and common values (see Philo, *Spec. Leg.* 1.12). They also provided a focus for national aspirations and opportunities to discuss issues and make resolutions affecting Jewish communities. These included occasions for complaints and appeals to the governor (Josephus, *J.W.* 2.280; *Ant.* 18.90-95, 120-23; cf. 2 Macc. 11:27-33), and anger frequently flared into violent protest. Because of the large crowds, during the early Roman period troops were on high alert (Matt. 26:5; *Ant.* 20.107), and occasional confrontations cost thousands of lives (*J.W.* 2.10-13; 2.224-27; 6.420-21; *Ant.* 17.213-18; 20.106-12).

There is less evidence about how the festivals were observed in communities at a distance from Jerusalem (Galilee, Diaspora) by those unable to make pilgrimage, but there are hints of festive meals and assemblies (e.g., *Ant.* 14.213-16, 241-42, 257-61), which probably included Torah readings, prayer, and singing or reciting Psalms. After the destruction of the Temple, however, a major transformation was necessary for the continued observance of the festivals without sacrifice at all. Popular elements that had been tangential to the sacrificial cult became more central, and the sacrifices were spiritualized and replaced by formalized prayer and reflection on laws. Besides the Torah festivals, numerous additional festivals and fasts originated during the Second Temple period to commemorate significant events for the community or nation, but few of these continued after the destruction of the Temple.

Passover (Pesaḥ) and the Festival of Unleavened Bread (Maṣot)

The observances of Passover and the Festival of Unleavened Bread may have ancient roots in separate agrarian spring fertility rites, and in offerings of the firstlings of livestock and firstfruits of grain. In the Hebrew Scriptures, however, they are presented as joint festivals with significance both as historical rites for the Israelites related to their flight from Egypt, and as perennial commemoration of the exodus to be observed throughout subsequent generations (see Exodus 12–13; 23:15; 34:18; Lev. 23:4-8; Num. 9:1-15; 28:16-25; 33:3; Deut. 16:1-8; Josh. 5:10-12; 2 Kings 23:21-23; Ezek. 45:21-25; 2 Chron. 8:12-14; 30:1-27; 35:1-19; Ezra 6:19-22).

The story is told most fully in Exodus 12. On the night of their flight from Egypt, the head of each Israelite household was to slaughter a lamb and smear its blood around the door of their home. This was to protect the family from the plague of death. Each family roasted its lamb whole and ate the meat during the night with unleavened bread and bitter herbs, in haste and dressed for travel.

The scriptural instructions for perennial observance represent different stages of development, from a localized family ritual (Exodus 12–13) to a national pilgrimage holiday centralized at Jerusalem (Deut. 16:1-8; 2 Kings 23:21-23; 2 Chron. 30:1-27; Ezra 6:19-22). It is the latter state of affairs that mostly determined the character of Passover throughout the Second Temple period. The main details, which closely follow biblical instructions, are as follows. All adult males are obligated — on pain of exclusion — to make pilgrimage to Jerusalem unless prevented by impurity from contact with a corpse or by travel (those so prevented are allowed to delay observance until the 14th of the following month). Toward sunset on the 14th of Nisan (literally "between the evenings"), the head of each household brings a yearling unblemished animal (the *Pesaḥ;* usually a lamb or kid) to the Temple and slaughters it there. Each family grouping cooks and eats their sacrificial animal that night, taking care not to break any bones, accompanied with unleavened bread and bitter herbs, burning any remains by morning. That entire week — Nisan 15-21 — is observed joyfully as a festival, marked by avoidance of food with leaven and making special offerings by fire in addition to the regular burnt offerings. The first and the last days are solemn assemblies on which the people are to rest from work. Priests and Levites offer prayers and sing hymns to God accompanied by music. Increasingly, Passover *(Pesaḥ)* and the Festival of Unleavened Bread *(Hag ha-Maṣot)* are treated as a unit, with one or the other term referring to both together.

The extrabiblical sources from the Second Temple period mostly describe practices in Jerusalem and largely agree on the outline described above, but they also reflect various developments and distinct emphases. Some features first attested in various of these sources became common practices in the Second Temple period, including scouring the house to remove yeast (Passover Papyrus from Elephantine; 1 Cor. 5:6-8); arrival in Jerusalem a week early to complete purification before Passover (*J.W.* 6.290; John 12:1; *Megillat Ta'anit);* alms for the poor (John 13:29; *m. Pesaḥ.* 10:1); the drinking of wine during the Passover meal (*Jub.* 49:6; Mark 14:23); and prayers and singing in the family Passover celebration (*Jub.* 49:6, Wis. 18:9; *David's Compositions* [11Q5 27:7-8]; Philo, *Spec. Leg.* 2.148; Mark 14:26; e.g., the Hallel Psalms [Psalms 113–118] and the Song of the Sea [Exod. 15:1-21]).

Fragments of some prayers for Passover survive among the Dead Sea Scrolls. The collection of *Daily Prayers* (4Q503 frgs. 1-3) seems to include prayers for Passover and the first day of Unleavened Bread, including allusions to protection from the plague, redemption, and pilgrimage festivals appointed as times of joy. A prayer for Passover in the collection of *Festival Prayers* (4Q505 frgs. 125 + 127) refers to the night of the Passover meal as the "night of vigil," an allusion to Exod. 12:42, along with references to protection from the plague, deliverance, and God's miracles on their behalf. Other unidentified prayers that allude to the Exodus story might also be for Passover (e.g., 1Q34 frg. 3 i// 4Q508 1).

Certain practices in the biblical instructions come to be discontinued, such as the smearing of blood around the doorframe, and eating the Passover meal in travel dress.

There are a number of matters in which the sources reflect debates and/or changes during the Second Temple period. *Jubilees* (49) and the *Temple Scroll* (11QT[a] 17:6-16) agree that the obligation to make pilgrimage pertains to males twenty and older, that is, as a national census (cf. Num. 1:2-3), and that the Passover meal was restricted to the Temple courts (cf. Deut. 16:7). Sources from the first century C.E. show that women and children often came on pilgrimage — perhaps supporting the picture in the Mishnah that the requirement for pilgrimage was extended to the age of thirteen — and that the Passover meal was eaten in private homes within Jerusalem (see *Ant.* 11.109; Luke 2:41; Philo, *Spec. Leg.* 2.148; *m. Pesaḥ.* 8:1). If on these points *Jubilees* and the *Temple Scroll* reflect actual practice rather than exegesis in the second century B.C.E., this indicates a partial shift in the character of Passover from national to family celebration and temple to home; that is, movement toward the earlier character of Passover. Similarly, in the early postexilic community, the rites of slaughtering the Paschal offerings originally carried out by the people had been taken over by the priests (2 Chron. 30:17-18; Ezra 6:19-22), but Philo (*Mos.* 2.224; *Spec. Leg.* 2.245) explicitly attests that in the first century, the people themselves slaughtered their own Paschal offering — acting as priests — confirming the depiction of the Mishnah (*Pesaḥ.* 5:6). It is likely that these changes are at least in part related to political changes following the end of the Hasmonean dynasty, and the vast increase in the numbers of pilgrims encouraged under Herod's expansion of the Temple.

The time for slaughtering the Paschal victim is ambiguous in the Torah: "between the two evenings" in Exod. 12:6 and "in the evening toward sunset" in Deut. 16:6. Various sources show concern to define this time more precisely; part of the concern was to clarify whether the Paschal offering should precede *(Temple Scroll, Jubilees)* or follow (Josephus, Mishnah) the daily burnt offering, which was also to be offered "between the two evenings" (Num. 28:4).

Some of the sources represent distinctive interpretations of Passover. As part of its tendency to associate each of the feasts with a patriarch, *Jubilees* connects the Passover with the story of the binding of Isaac: as Isaac is preserved against the scheme of Mastema (Satan) to destroy him (*Jub.* 18:18-19), so the blood of the Paschal offering protects the Israelites from the destroyer Mastema (cf. Heb. 11:28). The motif of the dedication of the firstborn also serves as a link. *Jubilees* suggests that the ritual of the Paschal offering has an ongoing apotropaic effect: if the ritual is carried out correctly and not a bone is broken, no bone of Israel will be broken and the people will not suffer plague in the coming year (*Jub.* 49:13-15).

Philo uniquely explains the name of Passover as "the Crossing Feast" and is primarily concerned to give expositions on the allegorical meanings of Passover and the Festival of Unleavened Bread as a purification of the soul and a reminder of the creation of the world.

Early Christian literature makes Passover the major backdrop for a theological understanding of the passion of Christ. Although the Last Supper was probably not a Passover meal, the Synoptic Gospels present it as one, with elements of the meal as signs of future redemption through Jesus. The Gospel of John more realistically places the meal before Passover and presents Jesus as the Paschal sacrifice (also 1 Cor. 5:6-8; Melito of Sardis).

Jews who did not make pilgrimage — especially those in the Diaspora — would observe the Festival of Unleavened Bread in their communities, as is well illustrated by the Passover Papyrus. This letter to the Jewish garrison in Elephantine Egypt in 419 B.C.E. authorizing observance of the festival mentions rest on the first and last days, avoiding food with leaven (including beer), and removing leaven from the house. Whether or not such Jews also carried out the Passover offering and/or meal in communities away from Jerusalem, however, is less clear, but it seems that the general practice was to restrict this to Jerusalem, as implied by Deuteronomy 16. The Samaritans are the only certain exception, offering Passover sacrifices on Mt. Gerizim, but there were probably others as well. Passover offerings were probably made at the Elephantine temple until its destruction in 411 B.C.E. (the Passover Papyrus mentions observing the Passover on the 14th and encourages them to be ritually pure, and an ostracon dating to ca. 500 B.C.E. instructs, "when you make the Passover . . ."), and similarly at the temple of Onias in Leontopolis (170 B.C.E.–73 C.E.; *J.W.* 7.423-36; *Ant.* 13.62-73; cf. *m. Menaḥ.* 13:10).

Some have suggested that the curious burials of animal bones at Qumran might be from Passover meals, although this is far from certain. It is unlikely, however, that there was a widespread practice of local Passover slaughter. If there had been such a precedent, it should have continued and even spread after the destruction of the Temple, but this did not happen.

What is clear is that Passover was dramatically transformed after the destruction of the Temple in 70 C.E. The rabbinic answer to the loss of the Temple was to resurrect the idea of the Passover meal as a local home ritual as in Exodus 12, but not the practice of local sacrifice (which would be strange if it was already an established precedent). The rabbis championed the view that the Passover meal should be continued without a Passover offering, replaced by a ritual of story, a symbolic meal, and prayer known as the *Seder Haggadah.* Basic elements of rehearsing the story of Israel's deliverance from Egypt and offering prayers and songs of praise may already have been part of the private Passover meal in homes before 70 C.E. (cf. Mark 14), but the *seder* as a detailed ritual was the rabbinic response to the Temple's destruction, shaped by this new historical reality as well as exegesis of Scripture, and influenced by symposia customs in Greco-Roman culture. The *seder* ritual is first described in the Mishnah (*Pesaḥim* 10), edited around 200 C.E., but strong allusions to it in the tract *On Pascha* by Melito of Sardis shows that it must have been well established much earlier. The earliest form is as follows. (1) The first cup of wine is poured, and the father recites a blessing over the wine and the blessing for the day (there was debate between the schools of Shammai and Hillel over the order of these blessings). (2) The food is brought: unleavened bread, lettuce, and a fruit and nut puree called *Haroseth.* In Jerusalem in the days of the Temple, the meal focused on the meat of the *Pesaḥ* sacrifice, but in the *seder* the food is symbolic and eaten in symbolic amounts, with the focus on an exposition. (3) The second cup of wine is poured; a son asks questions about the special food of this meal; the father answers by expounding the passage "A wandering Aramean was my father . . ." (Deut. 26:5-7). (4) The third cup is poured; the father recites grace after meals. (5) The fourth cup is poured; the father recites the *Hallel* and the blessing over song. To set this meal apart, revelry (the original meaning of *afikomen*) is expressly forbidden after the meal. According to the Mishnah (*m. Meg.* 3:5), the synagogue Torah reading for Passover was from Leviticus 23.

Festival of Weeks (Shavuot), Pentecost, or Firstfruits (Bikkurim)

In the Torah (see Exod. 23:16; 34:22; Lev. 23:15-21; Num. 28:26-31; Deut. 16:9-12), the Festival of Firstfruits/Harvest (Exod. 23:16; Num. 28:26) marks the last stage of the grain harvest with the offering of firstfruits of wheat. It has no fixed date in Torah but is to be observed seven weeks after the offering of the first ripe sheaf of barley (Deut. 16:9; cf. Lev. 23:15-16), and so it is also referred to as the "Festival of Weeks" (*Shavuʿot;* Exod. 34:22; Num. 28:26; Deut. 16:10). Greek-speaking Jews commonly referred to it as "Pentecost" because of this fifty-day period (e.g., 2 Macc. 12:32; Philo, *Spec. Leg.* 2.176; Josephus, *Ant.* 3.252; Acts 2:1; 20:16; 1 Cor. 16:8).

The distinctive offering consists of two loaves of leavened bread made from the new wheat of the harvest, elevated before God as a firstfruits offering. This is accompanied by various animal sacrifices according to Lev. 23:16-20 and Num. 28:26-31, although there are minor discrepancies between the two lists. It is to be a sacred day of rest. Weeks is the least emphasized of the pilgrimage feasts in the Bible (ignored in Ezekiel 45), and the only one with no fixed date and no commemoration associated with it.

During the Second Temple period, the ambiguities surrounding this festival were addressed in various ways, and by the second century B.C.E., Weeks was the most important of the festivals for certain pious communities (represented by *Jubilees,* the *Temple Scroll,* and the sectarian texts from Qumran). There were three main developments.

First, the date on which the Festival of Weeks should be observed was the subject of considerable debate among different Jewish groups. Leviticus 23 gives no date to the Waving of the Sheaf, from which Weeks is to be calculated, but mentions it immediately after the description of Passover and indicates that it takes place on "the day after the Sabbath" (Lev. 23:11, 15). According to Josh. 5:10-12, the Israelites first ate produce of the land of Canaan on the day after Passover. The Pharisees equated the "day after the Sabbath" with the second day of Passover (Nisan 16), the first being a day of rest. This was the dominant view and determined the practice; it is attested in the Septuagint and Targums (Lev. 23:9), Philo (*Spec. Leg.* 2.162), Josephus (*Ant.* 3.250), and the Mishnah (cf. *m. Menaḥ.* 10:2-3). Weeks, observed fifty days later, would fall in the early part of the third month (the 6th to 8th), but without a fixed date since the months could have 29 or 30 days. Against this, other groups (especially those with priestly interests) insisted that the "day after the Sabbath" must refer to an actual Sabbath, not a festival day. The Sadducees argued that the Waving of the Sheaf should be on the Sunday falling within the Passover week (cf. *m. Ḥag.* 2:4; also Samaritans and Karaites). Weeks would then occur somewhere between the 6th and 14th of the third month. In the calendar used by *Jubilees* (see 44:1-4; cf. 15:1; 29:1-8), the *Temple Scroll* (18:10-15), and at Qumran (e.g., 4Q320 4 iii), the Waving of the Sheaf took place on the Sunday *after* the Passover week. Since in this calendar, every date always occurred on the same day of the week, and Nisan 15 fell on a Wednesday, the Waving of the Sheaf fell on Nisan 26, and the Festival of Weeks, always on the 15th of the 3rd month, always a Sunday.

Second, the festival came to be associated with the revelation of Torah on Mt. Sinai and the covenant between God and Israel. How soon this became a widely accepted motif is not known. For the author of *Jubilees* in the second century B.C.E., the Festival of Weeks is the most important festival. It is not only a commemoration of covenants, but renewing the covenant by oaths every year is a central part of its observance (*Jub.* 6:17-22; also *Jub.* 6:1, 10-11; 15:1; 22:1-5; 29:7-8; 44:1-4). The festival was kept in heaven and first observed on earth by Noah in his covenant with God (Genesis 9), then by Abraham (Genesis 17), Isaac, and Jacob, and then Moses at Mt. Sinai (Exod. 19:1). The sectarian communities seen in the Qumran texts apparently celebrated their annual covenant ceremony at this festival, although this must be inferred from disparate data (see 1QS 1:18-2:25; 4Q266 11 16-18//4Q270 7 ii 11-12). The *Temple Scroll* makes no reference to Weeks as a commemoration of covenant.

Philo notes that it is also the "chief feast" of the Therapeutae, a Jewish group in Egypt similar to the Essenes, and describes how they observe it with a symposium-style banquet dedicated to exposition of scripture, singing hymns, and prayer (*Contempl. Vita* 8.65). He does not mention an association with covenants.

In early Christianity, this festival came to be associated with the pouring out of the Holy Spirit (Acts 2:1-11), with overtones of new covenant and revelation.

No hint of a commemorative or theological meaning appears in any other source from the Second Temple period, however. In Philo and Josephus, as well as Tobit (2:1), 2 Maccabees (12:32), and Pseudo-Philo (13:5), Weeks retains its character solely as an agricultural festival of firstfruits. This may suggest that it was first among somewhat disenfranchised groups that expanded meanings for Weeks were nurtured. In the Mishnah, too, Weeks is a purely agricultural festival, and there is reflection of its loss of status after the destruction of the Temple: it does not merit a separate tractate like other festivals (but cf. *m. Bikkurim*), and there is debate whether it no longer has the stature of the pilgrimage festivals (cf. *m. Mo'ed Qat.* 3:6). It is commonly referred to as Atzeret, a term used in the Torah for the solemn assembly at the end of Passover and Sukkot; for the Mishnah, Weeks is effectively an appendix to Passover. Only later is attested the rabbinic view associating the Festival of Weeks with the revelation of Torah to Moses on Mt. Sinai. It is called the "Festival of the Giving of the Torah." This motif is also reflected in the synagogue Torah readings: whereas in the Mishnah, the Torah portion for Weeks is Deut. 16:9-12 (*m. Meg.* 3:5), the Talmud also mentions Exodus 19 (*b. Megillah* 31a).

The third development concerns the clarification of various details of halakah related to the festival. Whatever the origin of the discrepancy between the lists of animal sacrifices in Lev. 23:18-19 and Num. 28:27-31, in the Second Temple period these were taken as cumulative offerings (e.g., a total of fourteen lambs), as indicated in the *Temple Scroll* (cf. details of the other firstfruits festivals: 11QT[a] 19:16; 20:2; 22:3); Josephus (*Ant.* 3.253), and the Mishnah (*m. Menaḥ.* 4:2-3; here as two different sets of offerings). The *Temple Scroll* clarifies that the elevated loaves must be wheat and must be made from new grain (11QT[a] 18:14-15), in line with the general view. Instead of two loaves of bread, however, the *Temple Scroll* uniquely indicates that there should be twelve, one for each tribe, as similarly with the other firstfruits offerings. It also uniquely indicates an additional separate offering of "new bread made of fresh ripe ears" (11QT[a] 19:6-7), apparently applying Lev. 2:14 to all firstfruits offerings, in contrast to rabbis who applied it only to the offering of the barley sheaf (*m. Menah.* 10:4). These two different bread offerings may be implied by the comment in *Jubilees* (6:21) that this festival is double, both Weeks and Firstfruits. Most prominently, though, the *Temple Scroll* uses the Festival of Weeks as a model for a sequence of four firstfruits festivals, all separated by fifty days, and with analogous offerings: barley, wheat, wine, and oil. Another matter was whether the new wheat could be eaten before the firstfruits offering. According to the Mishnah, this was allowed (*m. Menaḥ.* 10:3), but a fragmentary Qumran text (*Halakhah A,* 4Q251 frg. 5) makes clear the view that until the offering of the firstfruits of wheat — the elevation of the loaves — it is forbidden to eat of the new wheat, and that this principle applied to all of the first-fruits offerings mentioned in the *Temple Scroll.*

Fragments of prayers for the festival survive at Qumran, in a collection of *Festival Prayers* that were probably used but not composed there. One refers to the festival as the Day of Firstfruits (4Q509 frgs. 131-132 ii) and mentions freewill offerings. Another possible prayer for Weeks (1Q34 3 ii; = 4Q509 97+98 i) refers to renewal of covenant and revelation of Law on Mt. Sinai, motifs connected with the festival in *Jubilees* and Qumran.

Booths or Tabernacles (Sukkot)

The greatest of the agricultural festivals comes in the autumn, between the end of the harvest and the beginning of sowing, "the festival of ingathering at the end/turn of the year" (Exod. 23:16; 34:22). It has a liminal character from its agricultural context that endures throughout its subsequent transformations: both joyous celebration of the completion of the fruit harvest, and ritual appeal for the autumn rains so critical for successful sowing and fertility in the coming year (cf. Deut. 11:4; Jer. 5:24). As the major pilgrimage festival, it could be referred to as "the festival of the LORD" (Lev. 23:39; Hos. 9:5; cf. Judg. 21:19; *Jub.* 16:28) or "the festival" (*ḥag;* 1 Kings 8:2; Ezek. 45:25).

The Torah prescriptions (Lev. 23:34-36, 39-43; Num. 29:12-38; Deut. 16:13-15) reflect different stages of development, but ultimately Tabernacles was transformed into a national festival at the centralized Temple in Jerusalem lasting seven days, beginning with a sacred day of rest on the fifteenth of the seventh month, and followed by an additional sacred rest day (*Shemini Atzeret* = "eighth day assembly"). The elaborate Temple ritual calls for vast numbers of animal sacrifices each day (Num. 29:12-38). Torah prescribes only two other rituals. First, as a commemoration of God's provision for the Israelites on the journey from Egypt to Canaan, the people are to live in booths — no longer the huts of those who stayed in the fields during harvest, but ritualized reminders of the wilderness journey (Lev. 23:42-43). This is such a prominent feature that "Festival of

Booths" (Sukkot) became the most common name (e.g., Lev. 23:34; Deut. 16:13; 31:10; Zech. 14:18; 1 Macc. 10:21; 2 Macc. 1:9; *Jub.* 16:21; Qumran calendrical texts; Philo; Josephus; John 7:2). Second, Lev. 23:40 prescribes, "On the first day you shall take the fruit of majestic trees, branches of palm trees, boughs of leafy trees, and willows of the brook; and you shall rejoice before the LORD your God for seven days" (NRSV). Although it is not explicit what was to be done with the branches, it probably refers to a procession by the people as a fertility rite.

Throughout the Second Temple period, Sukkot retained the basic features of the descriptions in Torah, and is the Temple festival *par excellence.* Numerous sources attest large crowds of pilgrims and great pageantry, with music and song by Temple singers, joyous processions, and popular rituals. Major developments include the attraction of various popular rituals to the Temple, and the clarification and definition of Torah prescriptions with regard to the branches and booths. In the restoration of the festival after the return from exile, Ezra 3:1-4 and Neh. 8:13-18 emphasize that the prescriptions of Torah were followed with regard to sacrifices, branches and booths, but there is no mention of procession. Rather, Lev. 23:40 is understood to list generic examples of leafy branches to be used for building the booths mentioned in Lev. 23:42; "the fruit of majestic trees" is understood as a general reference to branches of various kinds, and so Neh. 8:16 paraphrases the list as "leaves of olive, pine, myrtle, palm, and (other) leafy trees." The *Temple Scroll* (11QT[a] 42:10-17) reflects a similar interpretation: there is no mention of fruit or a procession. Moreover, it specifies that the booths must be built "each year on the festival," apparently understanding Lev. 23:40 to prescribe the gathering of building materials on the first day of the festival.

From the second century B.C.E. on, sources regularly emphasize a procession around the altar with festal bouquets as a central ritual at the Temple, and it is clear that they regard this to be what Lev. 23:40 prescribes (*Jub.* 16:30-31; 2 Macc. 10:6-8; Josephus, *Ant.* 13.372-73; Plutarch, *Quaestionum Convivialum* 4.6.2; *m. Sukkah* 4:5; perhaps 4Q409 1 i 11 and 4Q502 frg. 99 2). The Mishnah (*m. Sukkah* 3) identifies the vegetation of Lev. 23:40 with four specific species to be carried: a citron *(etrog),* and a bouquet *(lulav)* of palm, willow, and myrtle branches. This appears as early as Pseudo-Philo (63 B.C.E.–70 C.E.), and also in Josephus (*Ant.* 3.245) and the targums to Lev. 23:40. Coins of the First Revolt (dating 69-70 C.E.) depict the *lulav* and *etrog* — possibly reflecting their prominence at the preeminent national festival. During the second revolt (132-135 C.E.), a letter from Bar Kokhba shows great efforts to acquire the four species in large quantities for his troops to celebrate the festival (5/6Ḥev. Ep. 15; cf. 3), and coins minted by the revolutionaries depicting the *lulav* and *etrog* opposite the Temple façade show the close association of the procession with Temple ritual.

People sang psalms during the procession with branches (2 Macc. 10:6-8; 4Q409 frg. 1 i 11; possibly 4Q502 frg. 99 2), as was common with pilgrimage processions in general. The Mishnah (*m. Sukkah* 4:5) indicates that during the procession, the people would recite the Hallel Psalms (Psalms 113–118) and shake the *lulav* at the beginning and end of Psalm 118, and at the cry for God's help in v. 25, "Save us *(hošîʿâna),* O LORD, . . . grant prosperity." Such a practice is probably the setting for the palm branch procession with hosannas in John 12:12-19 (although there placed near Passover). More generally, music and psalms of praise by the Temple singers (2 Chron. 5:3, 11-14; 2 Macc. 1:30; 10:6-7) as well as communal thanksgiving (*Jub.* 16:31; 32:7; Philo, *Spec. Leg.* 2.204, 209; Josephus, *Ant.* 11.154-57) and supplication (2 Chron. 6:1-42; Nehemiah 9; Philo, *Spec. Leg.* 2.209; Josephus, *Ant.* 13.304) are well attested at Sukkot throughout the Second Temple period. Besides Psalm 118, whose motifs made it especially suitable for the festival, Psalm 81 was explicitly associated with Sukkot (see v. 4), and in the second century B.C.E. a heading was added to the Greek translation of Psalm 29 (LXX Psalm 28) to indicate that it is "for the holiday of Sukkot." *David's Compositions* (11Q5 27:7-8) mentions thirty songs of David for new moons and festivals, apparently assuming one for each of the eight days of Sukkot. Supplications included public confession of sin (cf. 1 Kings 8; Nehemiah 9) and petition for the welfare of the community, especially rain, good crops, and return of the dispersed. Prayer for rain at Sukkot is implicit in Zech. 14:16-19 and Ps.-Philo, *Bib. Ant.* 13:7, and explicit in *Tg. Ps.-J.* to Lev. 23:36, "you shall hold an assembly to pray to God for rain." 2 Macc. 1:23-29 reflects the type of prayer for the welfare of the community at Sukkot (cf. 1:9, 18), and the collection of *Festival Prayers* at Qumran preserves fragments of prayers for Sukkot (probably 4Q509 frgs. 8; 10 i; 12 i + 13; 10 ii + 11). The latter is similar in both style and content to litanies called *hošānôt* used in the later synagogue liturgy for Sukkot and shows that these are based on forms of prayer from Temple times.

The Mishnah describes several other popular rituals at the Temple that are not attested in earlier sources: a water libation poured out at the altar, the lighting of large lamps in the Temple courtyard at the end of the first day, and a joyous celebration with flute playing. John's Gospel (7:37-39; 8:12-20) may allude to these as the background for Jesus' sayings about water and light.

It seems that there was some resistance to the incursion of such popular rituals into the domain of the priests, since rabbinic literature alludes to debates between Pharisees and Sadducees (e.g., *m. Sukkah* 4:9; *t. Sukkah* 3:1). Resistance is perhaps implied also by the interpretations of Nehemiah 8 and the *Temple Scroll* discussed earlier.

The *Temple Scroll* focuses exclusively on official Temple rites: the sacrifices of Numbers 29 (11QT[a] 27:10–29:1), clarifying that the goat for the sin offering must be accompanied by cereal and drink offerings; and the construction of booths, but only mentioning booths for elders and tribal leaders on the roof of the Temple (11QT[a] 42:10-17; 44:6-16). There is no mention of procession with branches; in its view, the branches are for the booths, which must be constructed anew each year. At least in what survives, it seems to ignore all popular ritual at the feast.

Jubilees, characteristically, presents Abraham as the first to observe Sukkot, celebrating the birth of Isaac (*Jub.* 16:15-31). According to the "testimony of the heavenly tablets," it is a seven-day festival with daily sacrifices and incense, living in booths, seven processions around the altar each day with a bouquet of branches and fruit and wearing wreaths on the head, and offering praise and thanks to God every morning. The wearing of wreaths and sevenfold circuit of the altar are not mentioned elsewhere. *Jubilees* also associates Sukkot with Jacob's dream at Bethel, the selection of Levi to the priesthood, the establishment of the Temple at Jerusalem, and the institution of second tithe (*Jubilees* 32; cf. 31:3). Jacob is the first to observe the eighth day, which he calls the "Addition" (32:27).

It is unclear how Sukkot may have been observed by the sectarian communities represented among the Dead Sea Scrolls, which likely did not partake in Temple pilgrimage due to calendar differences. Judging from its mention in the calendrical texts, they did keep it. The observance probably included the following practices associated with Sukkot in various liturgical texts found at Qumran, although these are not all sectarian texts: praise, procession with branches, singing Psalms, and petitionary prayers (4Q409 frg. 1 i 11; 4Q502 frg. 99; 11QPs[a], *David's Compositions, Festival Prayers*). It is safe to assume they also built and dwelt in temporary booths, but it is unlikely they offered sacrifices outside the Temple.

Philo (*Flaccus* 116–24) gives a similar picture for the observance of Sukkot in Diaspora communities. He indicates that in Alexandria around the turn of the era it was the custom to erect booths and to gather at meeting houses for communal prayers and songs of praise. There is no mention of a procession with branches, which could suggest that while the Temple stood this was regarded as a Temple ritual. Philo himself emphasizes a spiritual significance to the festival falling at the autumn equinox, illustrating the duty to thank God as the source of all good things.

Zechariah's depiction (14:16-19) of universal pilgrimage to Jerusalem to celebrate Sukkot is the basis of a motif associating Sukkot with eschatological redemption reflected in Revelation and the Gospel of John (John 7:37-39; 8:12-20). Zechariah 14 was one of the prophetic readings for the festival (*b. Megillah* 31a).

Sukkot survived the destruction of the Temple as a major festival celebrated in local communities. It focused on the building and dwelling in booths, and the procession with the four species — incorporated into the synagogue — accompanied by psalms and prayers. Memory of the sacrifices endures in the synagogue Torah readings (cf. *m. Meg.* 3:5). The Mishnah takes pains to demonstrate that the synagogue observance is rooted in the Torah instructions about the Temple ritual *(m. Sukkah).* A papyrus dating to the second century C.E. (*CPJ* 452a) mentioning expenses associated with keeping the "vigil of the Festival of Sukkot" hints at lavish celebration.

Day of Atonement (Yom Kippur)

According to the biblical instructions (Leviticus 16; 23:26-32; Num. 29:7-11; cf. Exod. 30:10), the tenth day of the seventh month was set aside to purify the sanctuary and the people. In the Temple ritual, the priest would offer special sacrifices and confess the people's sins over a goat sent into the wilderness. The obligation on the people was to observe this day as a "most holy day," a Sabbath of complete rest, and to practice self-affliction (from evening of the ninth day to the evening of the tenth). Emphasis on the priestly ritual is reflected in the biblical term "Day of the Atonements" (*Yôm ha-Kippurîm;* Lev. 23:27; 25:9). In the Second Temple period, the part of the people increased greatly in importance. The fasting of the people became so prominent a feature that the day was often called "the Fast," especially by Greek-speaking Jews (e.g., Philo). Beyond anything explicit in the biblical laws, remorse, confession, and penitential prayers by the people came to be central features, and these were emphasized as effecting atonement of sin (see *Jub.* 5:17-18; 34:18-19; 4Q508 frg. 2 2-3; 4Q509 frg. 16 3; Ps.-Philo, *Bib. Ant.* 13:6; Philo, *Spec. Leg.* 2.196; *Legatio ad Gaium* 306). This shift from the Temple to the home and community was especially prominent in the Diaspora, the sectarian communities glimpsed in Qumran scrolls, and more widely after the destruction of the Temple in 70 C.E.

For the priestly ritual as carried out in the Second Temple, the main source is the Mishnah (edited ca. 200 C.E.), which preserves some authentic traditions from the time of the Temple not mentioned in the Torah but backed up by other sources from the Second Temple period (esp. Philo, *Temple Scroll,* and *Epistle of Barnabas*). The Mishnah must be used with care since it also contains idealized retrojections based on analogy with later synagogue practice. The basic features of the Temple ritual are as follows. In preparation, the high priest was quarantined for the preceding week and underwent instruction and ritual purification. The Temple rituals of the day fell into three main parts, accompanied by vestment changes for the high priest. In the first part, the high priest bathed and put on the normal golden festal garments to offer the morning daily whole-offering of a lamb. For the second part, which consisted of rituals particular to the Day of Atonement involving entry into the Holy of Holies, the high priest bathed again and donned special white linen garments (cf. Philo, *Somn.* 1.216-17). There were two sets of activities: purging the most holy items of the Temple of impurity resulting from sins of the people, and removing the sins — the source of impurity — far from the sanctuary and the people. For the former ritual, the high priest slaughtered a bull for himself and his family and a goat for the people. In each case, the blood was drained into a bowl. The high priest entered the Holy of Holies with a pan of burning incense, which he placed on the rock where the Ark of the Covenant used to rest, and said a short intercessory prayer before exiting (Philo, *Legatio ad Gaium* 306; *m. Yoma* 5:1). He then brought in the blood of the bull, and then of the goat, sprinkling some of each on the place of the ark, and then also on the outside of the curtain and on the altar. For the latter ritual of removing sins, a live goat was used. The fate of the pair of goats was chosen by lot, with red wool tied to the neck of the one to be slaughtered and to the head of the one to carry the sins of the people. Laying his hands on the one goat, the high priest confessed over it the sins of the nation. The scapegoat, thus bearing the sins of the nation, was abused and driven to the wilderness, where it was pushed to its death in a ravine (Philo, *De Plantatione* 61; *m. Yoma* 6:6; cf. *1 Enoch* 10:4-8). It seems likely that the high priest recited some supplications for the people at the conclusion of the sacrificial service, but the readings mentioned in the Mishnah are probably a retrojection from the synagogue.

Having completed the actions particular to the Day of Atonement, the high priest bathed and changed once more into the normal festal garments for the third set of rituals, the customary festival burnt offerings, followed by the daily evening whole offering.

Already in the late Second Temple period, the people played a very active part in the Day of Atonement, not only for those who could be spectators of the Temple rituals (Sirach 50), but in Jewish communities throughout the world, so that the day became one of the most renowned of Jewish holy days (Philo, *Mos.* 2.23-24). The rituals of the people focused on two activities: fasting and prayer (*Jub.* 5:17-18; 34:18-19; *Festival Prayers;* 11Q5 27:2-11 [*David's Compositions*]; *Ps. Sol.* 3:8; Philo, *Spec. Leg.* 193-203; *Mos.* 2.23-24, *Legatio ad Gaium* 306; Delos Inscription; Ps.-Philo, *Bib. Ant.* 13:6). The self-affliction prescribed in Torah was practiced as a daylong fast, when observants abstained from food and drink and engaged in various other acts of self-denial (e.g., refraining from washing, anointing with oil, wearing sandals, and sexual activity; *m. Yoma* 8:1). Without precedent in Torah, the day was devoted to services of communal confession, penitential prayer, and praise to God so lengthy that Philo could describe them as occupying the entire day (see esp. Philo, *Spec. Leg.* 2.196). It is this emphasis on the prayer of the people that came to be central to the synagogue liturgy, so that from ancient times the liturgy of the Day of Atonement was famously lengthy. Together, these activities of the people were seen as effective in atoning for sin. Some prayers for the Day of Atonement are preserved in a scroll of *Festival Prayers* from Qumran (e.g., 1Q34 1 + 2; 4Q509 frgs. 5-6 ii, 7; 4Q508 frgs. 2, 22 + 23), which probably reflect a more general Jewish practice. These show similar motifs to those in the later synagogue liturgy such as repentance, God's knowledge of all things, appeal to God's mercy, and rehearsal of Torah instructions.

Torah readings in the synagogue almost certainly included the prescriptions for the Day of Atonement (Leviticus 16; 23:27-32; Num. 29:7-11), which the Mishnah projects into the priestly ritual in the Temple (*m. Yoma* 7:1). These readings would serve as a liturgical reenactment of the Temple ritual, especially after the destruction of the Temple, but it is unclear how early the tradition of a full poetic reenactment *(Seder ʿAbodah)* began. What texts served as the Haftarah readings is also unclear, although Jonah and Isa. 57:15–58:14 are early candidates (*b. Megilla* 31a).

Despite being a solemn fast, the Day of Atonement also was widely regarded as a festival to be celebrated with joy (e.g., Philo, *Spec. Leg.* 1.186-87; *Tg. Neof.* Lev. 23:26-32; 11Q5 27:2-11 [*David's Compositions*]). The Mishnah (e.g., *m. Yoma* 7:4; *m. Taʿan.* 4:8), as well as pagan and Christian sources, refers to festivities at the end of the Day of Atonement including feasting and dancing. Some pious groups apparently objected to festivities on the day as a desecration of the solemn fast that should focus on mourning for sin (*Jub.* 34:19; CD 6:18-19; *Festival Prayers* [4Q509 16 iv 2-4]). The matter seems to have been one of the points of dispute that alienated the movement associated with the Teacher of Righteousness from both the Temple priesthood and the Pharisees, in addition to their sharp difference over calendar, according to which the fast fell on a different day of the year (1QpHab 11:4-8; 1QH[a] 12:5-12; CD 6:18-19).

The Day of Atonement was the subject of considerable theological reflection. In apocalyptic and mystical traditions, the entrance of the high priest into the Holy of Holies became a model for ascent to the heavenly throne (e.g., *1 Enoch* 14:8-25; *T. Levi* 3:4-5; *Songs of the Sabbath Sacrifice*). The scapegoat "for Azazel" was appropriated as a model for the eschatological casting into the abyss of the chief demon Asael (*1 Enoch* 10:4-8; *Book of Giants;* 4Q180, 4Q181; *Apocalypse of Abraham*). In the sectarian Qumran Scrolls, the current "time of affliction" is a prolonged eschatological Day of Atonement to which the community submits as atoning suffering (e.g., 4Q171 frg. 1-10 ii 8-11). 11QMelchizedek presents the Day of Atonement as the model of eschatological judgment and salvation. The Day of Atonement as a day of judgment and destiny continued as a central image in rabbinic Judaism. In early Christianity, the apocalyptic motifs had strong currency, but everything is subsumed in Christ. Christ is the high priest who enters the heavenly holy of holies (Hebrews); both goats are a type of Christ, who is an atoning sacrifice (Rom. 3:25) and the abused bearer of sins (*Epistle of Barnabas,* Tertullian).

Feast of Trumpets

In the Torah, the first of the seventh month is unique among the New Moons in having status as one of the fixed times *(moʿadîm),* a sacred occasion *(miqrāʾ qodeš),* and a day of rest *(Šabbaton)* on which menial labor was proscribed (Lev. 23:23-25; Num. 29:1-6). It is described as a "memorial proclaimed by (horn) blasts," and a "day of (horn) blasts." The rituals consist of the blowing of a ram's horn and the offering of additional sacrifices beyond those of the New Moon.

When the day is named in sources of the Second Temple period, it is called the Day of Memorial (Qumran calendrical texts; 4Q409 1 i 5) or the Feast of Trumpets (Philo, *Spec. Leg.* 1.186; Ps.-Philo, *Bib. Ant.* 13:6). In contrast to its later function as a solemn fast preparing for the Day of Atonement, up to the Mishnah it is regarded as a festival to be celebrated with joy and feasting. Ezra assembled the people to read the Torah on this occasion (Neh. 8:9-12), urging them to rejoice and not grieve. The *Temple Scroll* (11QT[a] 25:9) adds to the Torah instructions the requirement to rejoice. Rejoicing is a dominant motif of a prayer for this festival found at Qumran (*Festival Prayers* 4Q509 frg. 3 8 [// 1Q34 frg. 2 + 1 4]): "[Bless]ed be the Lord who has caused [us] to rejoice. . . ." Philo emphasizes thanksgiving for Torah and peace (*Spec. Leg.* 2.188-92).

The *Temple Scroll* combines the Torah instructions (11QT[a] 25:2-10) and treats the first of the seventh month as a model for a similar festival on the first of Nisan (11QT[a] 14:9-18; also *Jub.* 7:2-6; 1QapGen 13:14). In the 364-day solar calendar, it is one of four special days dividing the seasons (along with the first of the first, fourth, and tenth months; *1 Enoch* 75:1; 82:11). *Jubilees* (6:22-29) states that Noah ordained these as Days of Memorial related to events during the flood. The *Community Rule* from Qumran refers to these as "heads of the years" (1QS 10:6).

A liturgical text from Qumran mentions the Day of Memorial as a time appointed for praising God with horn blasts (4Q409 1 i 5; cf. 1QS 10:6). Philo also associates thanksgiving with the horn blasts. This probably refers to praise of the people rather than the Temple singers (cf. 1 Chron. 23:31). Additionally, the Qumran *Festival Prayers* preserves a communal petition for the day (4Q509 frgs. 1 + 2, 3; //1Q34 frgs. 2 + 1). Although it is fragmentary, it shows the motifs of prayer for peace, the gathering of exiles, God's mercies, and rain, and praises God who gives joy.

After the destruction of the Temple, there were three main developments. First, the liturgical status of the New Year *(Roš Haššana)* became predominantly a time of judgment at the beginning of the year (*m. Roš Haš.* 1:1-2). Second, by the middle of the second century, the New Year was tied to the Day of Atonement (*t. Roš Haš.* 1:13), and increasingly took on the character of a fast initiating a season of repentance. Third, this is reflected above all in the development of the synagogue liturgy, where New Year acquires lengthy penitential prayers and cries for help *(sĕlîhôt)* that are also used on fast days (cf. *t. Ber.* 1:6). By the time of R. Aqiba (early second century C.E.), there was an effort to define special blessings with biblical passages added to the *Amidah* that focus on God as king, judge, and redeemer (*m. Roš Haš.* 4:5). The major motifs show some continuity with the earlier evidence: the horn blasts *(shofar)* associated with the giving of Torah on Mt. Sinai and the gathering of exiles, judgment, and God as merciful and making peace.

New Moons

The observation of the new moon was a central feature of the Israelite calendar, marked by feasts and sacrifices (1 Samuel 20; cf. 2 Kings 4:23). As defined in the Torah, the New Moon was announced by the blowing of trumpets as a "memorial" (Num. 10:10; cf. Ps. 81:3), and its sacrifices were in addition to those of the Sabbath and festivals (Num. 28:11-15). Although it is not expressly defined as a rest day, apparently no business was to be transacted (Amos 8:5). Throughout the Second Temple period, the New Moon was classed with Sabbaths and festivals (e.g., 1 Macc. 10:34; *Jub.* 1:14; 6:34, 38), and observed with additional Temple sacrifices (2 Chron. 2:4; 8:13; 31:3; Ezra 3:5; Neh. 10:33; 11QT[a] 14:1-8; 25:7; Philo, *Spec. Leg.* 1.177; Josephus, *Ant.* 3.238) accompanied by songs of praise (1 Chron. 23:30-31; 11QPs[a] 27:7-8). Away from Jerusalem and in the Diaspora it also seems to have been kept as a feast day for which mourning is inappropriate (Jdt. 8:6; Gal. 4:10; Col. 2:16).

Those who followed the 364-day solar calendar also regarded the beginning of the month as an appointed time along with Sabbaths and festivals (*Jub.* 1:14; 2:9; 6:34, 38; 1QS 10:3-5; 1QM 2:4; 4QpHos[a] 2:15-17), but apparently the first of the solar month rather than the new moon, which they regarded as wayward (*Jub.* 2:9; 1QS 10:3-5). Nevertheless, the calendrical texts from Qumran show that they might still meticulously tracked observance of the new moon and full moon (e.g., 4Q321). According to the *Community Rule,* the first of the month is a time appointed for praise in the community (1QS 10:3-5).

After the destruction of the Temple, the new moon gradually lost its status as a solemn feast day, but was marked in the synagogue with Torah reading (Num. 28:11-15; *m. Meg.* 3:6) and special blessings. For the Mishnah, details about the observation of the new moon are most important *(m. Roš Haš.).*

Feasts of the Second Temple Period

Numerous minor festivals originated during the Second Temple period to commemorate significant events for the community or nation, usually an averted disaster. These would be observed by feasting, songs and prayers of thanksgiving, and a ban on fasting and mourning, but no restrictions on work. For example, 2 Macc. 15:35-36 mentions a commemoration of Judas Maccabaeus' defeat of the Seleucid general Nicanor celebrated on the thirteenth day of the twelfth month. Simon Maccabaeus decreed an annual festival to commemorate his capture of the Jerusalem citadel in 141 B.C.E. (1 Macc. 13:49-52). In Alexandria, Jews celebrated festivals to commemorate the translation of the Torah into Greek (Philo, *Mos.* 2.41-42), and a miraculous deliverance from persecution (according to Josephus [*Ag. Ap.* 2.55], under Ptolemy VII Physcon in the second century B.C.E.; according to 3 Maccabees [6:30-36; 7:15, 19-20], under Ptolemy IV Philopator in the third century B.C.E.). A work compiled around 66 C.E., *Megillat Taʿanit,* lists such extra-Torah minor festivals on which Jews are not to fast. Such occasions might be alluded to as "days of rejoicing" in Judith (8:6). Only two of these commemorative festivals continued to be observed after the destruction of the Temple: Hanukkah and Purim.

Purim

Purim is a minor feast on the 14th and 15th of Adar (the twelfth month; usually falls in March) to commemorate the deliverance of Jews in Persia from persecution. The book of Esther gives a legendary account of the origins: a beautiful Jewess named Esther becomes Queen to the Persian king Ahasueras (Xerxes), and encouraged by her uncle Mordecai she uses her position to foil a plot by an official named Haman to destroy the Jews. Esther 9:20-32 mentions festal letters sent by Mordecai and Esther to all Jews throughout Persia to establish the observance of the festival with joyful feasting and almsgiving. It explains the name *Purim* ("lots") as a reference to the fate of destruction Haman had sought for the Jews, which was returned on his own head. It was established throughout the Jewish world by the second century B.C.E., as attested by a reference to "Mordecai's Day" on the 14th of Adar at the end of 2 Maccabees (15:36), and a note added to the end of the LXX version of Esther about a letter sent from Jerusalem to Egypt endorsing the feast. It was not universally accepted; the pious Jews associated with *Jubilees*, the *Temple Scroll*, and the sectarian texts from Qumran evidently did not observe it. In the first century C.E., the *Megillat Taʿanit* lists Adar 14 and 15 as feast days on which fasting is prohibited, and Josephus (*Ant.* 11.292-95) recounts the establishment of the feast. The Mishnah *(m. Megilla)* is the earliest source to mention the festive reading of the scroll of Esther, which became its central feature, and the Torah portion (Exod. 17:8-16) about Amalek, Haman's ancestor (Esth. 3:1). In general, the festival was more readily accepted than the status of Esther as Scripture, which was debated into the third and fourth centuries C.E.

Hanukkah

The Festival of Dedication (*Hanukkah* in Hebrew) commemorates the restoration of the Temple and dedication of the altar by Judas Maccabaeus in 164 B.C.E. It is celebrated for eight days, beginning on the anniversary of the defilement of the altar under Antiochus IV Epiphanes in 167 B.C.E., the 25th day of Kislev (see 1 Macc. 1:59), the ninth month (it usually falls in December).

The ancient sources agree on these points, and that it was observed in the Temple with feasting, abundant sacrifices, rejoicing, songs of praise, and music (1 Macc. 4:36-59; 2 Macc. 1:10-2:18; Josephus, *Ant.* 12.316-26; cf. *Megillat Taʿanit*), but they offer different models and rationales. Implicitly summoning the precedents of Solomon (1 Kings 8) and Hezekiah (2 Chronicles 29), 1 Maccabees (4:36-59; late second B.C.E.) presents Hanukkah as an eight-day celebration of "the dedication of the altar," which Judas timed to coincide with the anniversary of its defilement. 2 Maccabees (before 125 B.C.E.), on the other hand, refers to the "purification of the Temple" as modeled on the Festival of Booths, and thus adds mention of a procession with branches (2 Macc. 1:1–2:18; 10:1-8; cf. 1 Kings 8:65-66; 2 Chron. 7:8-10). Two letters at the beginning of 2 Maccabees try to persuade Jews in Egypt to keep this new festival. The second letter (2 Macc. 1:10–2:18) introduces a founding legend about a miraculous fire that lit the altar at the consecration of the Second Temple by Nehemiah (contrast Ezra 6:13-22), on the pattern of fire from heaven at the dedication of the altar by Moses (Lev. 9:23-24) and Solomon (2 Chron. 7:1). The letter assumes fire as a prominent feature of the festival ("celebrate the festival of booths and of fire," 2 Macc. 1:18), for which this legend gives a strained explanation.

Josephus (*Ant.* 12.316-26) also implies a prominent ritual involving fire when he states that it is called the "Festival of Lights," but he offers a completely different explanation for it: it commemorates the unexpected appearance (taken as a pun on "light") of the right to worship. The lighting of lamps on the festival is mentioned in the Mishnah (*m. B. Qam.* 6:6), and the procedure — lighting one lamp the first day and adding one more each day — was debated in the first century (*b. Šabbat* 21b). As a reflection of the murky origin of the ritual, rabbinic literature cites two further legends to explain it. According to one (*b. Šabbat* 21b), the Maccabees found a small jar with one day's worth of oil for the Temple lamps, but miraculously it kept the lamps lit for eight days. According to the other (*Pesiq. Rab.* 2:5), when the Maccabees entered the Temple they found eight iron spears on which they lit lamps.

After the destruction of the Temple, the observance of Hanukkah was carried on primarily in the home with the lighting of lamps, and in the synagogue with Torah reading about the dedication offerings in Numbers 7, a special prayer of thanksgiving ("For the Miracles") inserted into the *Amidah,* and recitation of Hallel Psalms. Thus, it continues the three main features of the Maccabean reconsecration of the Temple recalled in the "For the Miracles" prayer: relighting of the Temple lamps, restoration of the sacrifice, and renewal of praise.

As a Maccabean festival, Hanukkah was not universally accepted. It does not appear in festival lists among the Dead Sea Scrolls. The Gospel of John (10:22), on the other hand, depicts Jesus in the Temple for the festival.

Additional Festivals in the Temple Scroll

The festal calendar represented in the *Temple Scroll* at Qumran must date no later than the early second century B.C.E. It is based on a 364-day solar calendar so that the festivals always fall on the same day of the week, and it includes several Temple festivals that may be more idealizations than reality. One of its most prominent features is an extension of the principle of Weeks to create a series of four firstfruits festivals at fifty-day intervals, counting inclusively so that each falls on a Sunday. It fixes the waving of the sheaf as the firstfruits of barley to the Sunday following the Passover week (1/26), so that the Festival of Weeks as the firstfruits of wheat (11QT^a 18:10–19:9) seven weeks later also has a fixed date (3/15). It adds two further firstfruits festivals with fixed dates on the analogy of the Festival of Weeks and with similar offerings prescribed in great detail: a Festival of New Wine (5/3; 11QT^a 19:11–21:10) and a Festival of Oil (6/22; 11QT^a 21:12-23). In both cases, they "atone" for the wine and oil to release the year's produce for consumption. Moreover, the tithes of each produce must be consumed within the respective year of its firstfruits offering (11QT^a 43:3-17). The Festival of Oil is also mentioned in the calendrical texts from Qumran (4Q394 frg. 1-2 col. v lines 4-7; 4Q324d frg. 6 line 3) and in a list of festivals added to Leviticus 23 in the *Reworked Pentateuch* (4Q365 frg. 23 line 9).

The *Temple Scroll* also gives details for a six-day Festival of Wood Offering, following the Feast of Oil, probably near the end of the sixth month (11QT^a 23–25; cf. 11:13; 43:3-4). It details sacrifices to be brought by two tribes each day, beginning with Levi and Judah (see *Reworked Pentateuch* 4Q365 frg. 23 lines 9-12). Josephus (*J.W.* 2.425) indicates the existence of a single "Festival of Wood Offering" in the first century C.E., apparently in the fifth month. The offering was defunct after the destruction of the Temple, and the Mishnah shows no knowledge of a festival, assuming that offerings of wood had been brought at nine different times throughout the year (*m. Ta'an.* 4:4-5).

On the model of the Day of Memorial on the first of the seventh month (Lev. 23:23-25; Num. 29:1-6), the *Temple Scroll* (11QT^a 14:9-18) also presents the first day of the first month (Nisan) as a parallel festival. This is also attested in *Jubilees* (7:2-6) and the *Genesis Apocryphon* (1QapGen 13:14).

Uniquely, the *Temple Scroll* makes of the procedures for Moses to consecrate Aaron and his sons as priests (Exodus 29; Leviticus 8–9) an annual celebration of the Days of Ordination (11QT^a 15:3–17:5). Beginning on the first day of the first month, there are seven days of consecration with two bulls, a ram, and a basket of bread offered each day, with the newly consecrated priests beginning service on the eighth day. This mostly follows the scriptural precedent, but with several innovations, notably elder priests taking the place of Moses, and two bulls instead of one.

Fasts

Public fasts were frequently called on occasions of great need for the community, especially failure of the autumn rains *(m. Ta'anit),* but annual public fasts were kept to a minimum in Judaism. The only annual public fast instituted in the Torah was the Day of Atonement. In the wake of the Babylonian Exile, four commemorative fasts were added to mourn disasters associated with the conquest and destruction in the fourth, fifth, seventh, and tenth months (Zech. 7:3-5; 8:19); respectively, they are the breaching of the walls of Jerusalem (Jer. 52:6-7), the destruction of the Temple (2 Kings 25:8-9; Jer. 52:12-13), the assassination of Gedaliah (2 Kings 25:25; Jer. 41:1-2), and the beginning of the siege of Jerusalem (2 Kings 25:1; Jer. 52:4). It is not clear whether these were observed throughout the Second Temple period, but after 70 C.E., two of these became commemorations also of events related to the destruction of the Second Temple (*m. Ta'an.* 4:6): the fourth-month fast mourning the cessation of sacrifice, observed on the seventeenth of Tammuz, and the fifth-month fast mourning the burning of the Second Temple (*J.W.* 6.248-250), observed on the ninth of Ab. The latter also became a commemoration of Bar Kokhba's defeat in the second century.

BIBLIOGRAPHY

J. M. BAUMGARTEN 1999, "Yom Kippur in the Qumran Scrolls and Second Temple Sources," *DSD* 6, 2: 184-91. • B. M. BOKSER 1984, *The Origins of the Seder: The Passover Rite and Early Rabbinic Judaism,* Berkeley: University of California Press. • J. MILGROM 2001, *Leviticus 23–27,* New York: Doubleday. • A. M. RABELLO 2000, "L'observance des fêtes juives dan l'Empire romain," *ANRW* II/21.2: 1288-1312. • J. L. RUBENSTEIN 1995, *The History of Sukkot in the Second Temple and Rabbinic Periods,* Atlanta: Scholars Press. • S. SAFRAI 1976, "Religion in Everyday Life," in *The Jewish People in the First Century,* ed. S. Safrai and M. Stern, Philadelphia: Fortress, 793-833. • E. P. SANDERS 1992, *Judaism: Practice and Belief 63 BCE–66 CE,* Philadelphia: Trinity Press International, 125-45. • J. B.-Z. SEGAL 1963, *The Hebrew Passover from the Earliest Times to A.D. 70,* Oxford: Oxford University Press. • D. STÖKL BEN EZRA 2003, *The Impact of Yom Kippur on Early Christianity: The Day of Atonement from the Second Temple to the Fifth Century,* Tübingen: Mohr-Siebeck. • J. TABORY 2006, "Jewish Festivals in Late Antiquity," *CHJ* 4: 556-72. • H. ULFGARD 1998, *The Story of Sukkot: The Setting, Shaping, and Sequel of the Biblical Feast of Tabernacles,* Tübingen: Mohr Siebeck. • J. C. VANDERKAM 1998, *Calendars in the Dead Sea Scrolls: Measuring Time,* London: Routledge.

DANIEL K. FALK

Firstfruits, Festival of → Festivals and Holy Days

First Jewish Revolt → Revolt, First Jewish

Flood

Both biblical and Near Eastern tradition knew of a universal flood that destroyed humanity. In the biblical account (Genesis 6–9), the flood is a catastrophic act of divine judgment precipitated by earthly corruption and wickedness. Early Jewish exegetes interpreted this story in a number of ways, often with specific questions and concerns in mind.

Reasons for the Flood

The Bible leaves much unsaid in describing what brought about the flood (Gen. 6:1-4, 5-8, 11-13). Desiring a more comprehensive explanation, some interpreters imported their own understandings of what constituted wickedness when discussing the event. All sources attribute the flood to the activities of one or more of the following parties: (1) wayward "sons of God" (cf. Gen. 6:1-2), most commonly interpreted as angelic beings called Watchers; (2) corrupt humans (cf. Gen. 6:5-6, 11-12); (3) a combination of the two, which may include the offspring of intercourse between the first two categories: the Giants (or Nephilim; cf. Gen. 6:3).

The Watchers are depicted as ultimately responsible for the flood in *1 Enoch* (5–11; 54; 65–67; 83–84; 86–89; 106–7), *Jubilees* (4:22; 5:6-20; 7:20-25), and the *Testament of Naphtali* (3:5), although humans, animals, and the Giants quickly join in their corrupt ways. Despite the Watchers' contributing role in the flood, this specific judgment is reserved for humans and animals alone, with the Watchers being bound and reserved for later judgment (cf. Jude 7), and the Giants forced to kill each other in a great, divinely induced battle. In 3 Maccabees (2:4) the Giants are also destroyed in the flood. Other sources, such as 4Q370, the *Testament of Reuben* (5:6), and Josephus (*Ant.* 1.72-79), may acknowledge the sinful angels and/or Giants but place more emphasis on humankind's role in bringing the flood. 4Q370 does this parenetically, exhorting contemporary listeners to right conduct. Josephus urges a similar response by casting human sin in terms of current Hellenistic ideas of vice.

Like Josephus, Philo of Alexandria (*QG* 1.99; 2.13, 28) employs Hellenistic standards of morality when speaking of the flood's cause. However, he betrays little or no awareness of the Watcher and Giant traditions assumed by most other Jewish sources of the period; instead, he attributes the flood primarily to human deficiency. Hence, for Philo the flood occurs because people have turned away from virtue to vice, largely through ingratitude for God's gifts.

Chronology of the Flood

The precision and significance of the dates associated with the flood were another area of interest for those reading Genesis. This concern was fed by inconsistencies within the biblical account and perhaps by discrepancies between variant editions of its text as well (e.g., in the MT, LXX, and SP). *Jubilees* (4:33–6:38) presents a harmonized and logical rendition of the flood, avoiding the doublets and irregularities of the biblical account. Its chronology is elaborated in order to support the author's advocacy of the solar calendar, even to the point of associating flood events with the four, requisite intercalary days (6:23-27). A similar impetus lies behind the exegetical reworking of 4Q252 (1:1–2:7), which fits the flood chronology neatly into a single, 364-day solar year. Chronological awareness is also reflected in the *Sibylline Oracles* (1:280), Josephus (*Ant.* 1.80-82, 89-92), and Philo (*QG* 2.17, 47), although they represent various opinions regarding the duration of the flood. Philo alone employs an elaborate dual-calendar system.

Some exegetes drew a connection between flood-related events and the celebration of later Israelite festivals. Although in Genesis this link is not explicit, the association of such festivals with a primordial patriarch like Noah clearly enhanced their antiquity and authority. The most explicit text in this regard is *Jubilees*, although Josephus (*Ant.* 1.80-82) and Philo are also aware of the issue.

Opportunity for Repentance

A tradition closely related to chronology claims that God afforded corrupt humanity ample time to repent before sending the flood. Variations of this theme are found in the *Sibylline Oracles* (1.125-95), Philo (*QG* 1.91; 2.13), *Targums Neofiti* and *Pseudo-Jonathan* (Gen. 6:3), and 1 Peter (3:20). The tradition continued to flourish in later rabbinic and Christian interpretation (e.g., *1 Clem.* 7:5-6; *Sepher ha-Yashar* 5:11; *Midrash Tanḥuma, Noah* 5).

Prefigurement of Eschatological Judgment

An influential contribution of early Jewish exegesis was its strong typological link between the flood and the eschatological judgment. In time this caused each event to be understood in light of the other, the former being enacted through water and the latter by fire. The *Sibylline Oracles* (1.195-270; 2.196-213; 3.618, 760-61; 4.171-78) divide history into two epochs, the first coming to an end by water (i.e., the flood) and the second by fire. In Josephus (*Ant.* 1.70-71) and the Latin *Life of Adam and Eve* (49) the same twofold destruction necessitates the erection of two pillars inscribed with primordial knowledge. These traditions may reflect Greco-Roman ideas of the "Great Year," in which world history was broken into two declining ages, each culminating in great destruction. Explicit connections between the flood and final judgment also appear in the Gospel of Matthew (24:37-39) and 2 Peter (3:5-7), the latter stating that the present heavens and earth are "reserved for fire" (cf. Zeph. 3:8). An eschatological destruction by fire is also mentioned in *1 Enoch* (90; 108) and 1QHodayot[a] (3:29-33). Later rabbinic portrayals of a flood of boiling water (e.g., *Lev. Rab.* 7:6) may reflect a collation of the above traditions.

The Landing of the Ark

Although the Bible specifies "the mountains of Ararat" (Gen. 8:4) as the spot where the ark alighted, readers throughout history have sought more specific locations. The Second Temple period was no exception, with a number of views being advanced. The *Genesis Apocryphon* (12:13), *Jubilees* (5:28), and 4Q244 (frg. 8) locate the ark on Mt. Lubar, the *Sibylline Oracles* (1.261-74) in Phrygia, and Josephus (*Ant.* 1.92) in Armenia. Some reported that the remains were still visible as a witness to the flood.

BIBLIOGRAPHY

J. J. COLLINS 1974, *The Sibylline Oracles of Egyptian Judaism,* Missoula, Mont.: Scholars Press, 101-4. • F. GARCÍA MARTÍNEZ 1998, "Interpretations of the Flood in the Dead Sea Scrolls," in *Interpretations of the Flood,* ed. F. García Martínez and G. P. Luttikhuizen, Leiden: Brill, 86-108. • J. L. KUGEL 1998, *Traditions of the Bible,* Cambridge, Mass.: Harvard University Press, 171-226. • J. VAN RUITEN 1998, "The Interpretation of the Flood Story in the Book of Jubilees," in *Interpretations of the Flood,* ed. F. García Martínez and G. P. Luttikhuizen, Leiden: Brill, 66-85. • C. WESTERMANN 1984, *Genesis 1–11,* Minneapolis: Augsburg, 363-458.

See also: Noah DANIEL A. MACHIELA

Florilegium (4Q174)

The document 4Q174 was eventually named *Florilegium,* "anthology," by J. M. Allegro, its principal editor. The generic name has been widely adopted, though from early on many, including Allegro himself, have also referred to the composition as some kind of eschatological midrash, not least because the word "midrash" occurs in a nontechnical sense in the introduction of the pesher on the Psalms. Altogether, twenty-six fragments have been assigned to this manuscript, and most of them have been reconstructed by A. Steudel into a convincing order of six columns on three sheets of leather. The manuscript is in Herodian script from the end of the first century B.C.E. or the beginning of the first century C.E.

The group of large fragments was first published in 1958. In two columns of writing (now Steudel's cols. 3 and 4) there is the end of a thematic commentary on 2 Sam. 7:10-14 and the start of a pesher on the Psalms. The composition as a whole is thus made up of exegetical works of more than one type, though the significance of that has yet to be fully discerned. After a citation from the principal passage being interpreted, the exegesis has a formulaic introduction, a leading statement, and then supporting scriptural quotations. The interpretation of 2 Sam. 7:10-11 is supported by Exod. 15:17-18 and 2 Sam. 7:11b; of 2 Sam. 7:13-14 by Amos 9:11; of Ps. 1:1 by Isa. 8:11 and Ezek. 37:23; of Ps. 2:1-2 by Dan. 12:10 and 11:32. These supporting quotations are not presented arbitrarily but are linked to one another and the principal citation through catchword association.

The interpreter enjoys working with the double meaning of "house" in Nathan's oracle. The house is interpreted first in relation to the Temple. Three sanctuaries are mentioned: the sanctuary that was laid waste because of Israel's sin, the future sanctuary that God will establish for himself (cf. 11QT^{a} 29:9-10), and the *miqdāš 'ādām,* "human sanctuary," or "sanctuary of Adam." There is little in the sectarian compositions from Qumran on the significance of the restoration of Adam, though the *Damascus Document* (CD 3:20) does refer to his glory. It is thus quite likely that the author of the exegesis was aware of the ambiguity of his phrasing, suggesting that the interim eschatological sanctuary was made up of the members of the community whose very existence was an anticipation of the restoration of the glory of Adam. In that sanctuary there are offerings; close analysis of the writing seems to favor the playful reading "works of thanksgiving *(twdh),*" though a strong minority of scholars still prefers to read the more prosaic "works of the Law *(twrh).*"

The principal fragments of 4Q174 have often been cited in discussions of sectarian messianic views. In the interpretation of the second kind of house of 2 Sam. 7:13-14 the "son" of Nathan's oracle is identified as the "shoot of David" (Jer. 23:5; 33:15; cf. 4Q252 5, 3; 4Q285 7, 3-4; 11Q14 1 i 11); he is to be accompanied by the "interpreter of the Law" (cf. CD 6:7; 7:18), variously identified by scholars as either the eschatological Priest-messiah or as the Prophet, perhaps even the Teacher of Righteousness *redivivus.* Whatever the case, 4Q174 seems to reflect the diarchic messianism of several other sectarian compositions. Psalm 2:7 is not cited explicitly, but the interpretation seems to understand the reference to "son" there as signifying the community as the "elect [pl.] of Israel"; in this way, the kingship of the royal messiah is democratized. The messianic content of 4Q174 can be compared with several passages in the New Testament: notably, in Heb. 1:5, Ps. 2:7 and 2 Sam. 7:14 are combined in a catalogue of scriptural texts used to show that the son was not an angel.

Fragments 6-10 seem to contain a thematic commentary on the blessings of Moses in Deut. 33:8-11 (Levi; cf. 4Q174); 33:12 (Benjamin); and 33:20-21 (Gad). Steudel places this in "canonical" order, before the interpretation of the oracle of Nathan and the pesher on the Psalms. Another fragment cites Isa. 65:22-23, apparently in a supporting role. Overall the work is very close in structure, form, and content to 4Q177, 4Q178, 4Q182, and 4Q183.

BIBLIOGRAPHY

G. J. BROOKE 1985, *Exegesis at Qumran: 4QFlorilegium in Its Jewish Context,* Sheffield: JSOT Press; rpt. Atlanta: Society of Biblical Literature, 2006. • G. J. BROOKE 2005, "Thematic Commentaries on Prophetic Scriptures," in *Biblical Interpretation at Qumran,* ed. M. Henze, Grand Rapids: Eerdmans, 143-49. • J. MILGROM 2002, "Florilegium: A Midrash on 2 Samuel and Psalms 1–2 (4Q174 = 4QFlor)," in *The Dead Sea Scrolls: Hebrew, Aramaic, and Greek Texts with English Translations,* vol. 6B, *Pesharim, Other Commentaries, and Related Documents,* ed. J. H. Charlesworth, Tübingen: Mohr-Siebeck; Louisville: Westminster John Knox, 248-63. • A. STEUDEL 1994, *Der Midrasch zur Eschatologie aus der Qumrangemeinde (4QMidrEschat$^{a.b}$),* Leiden: Brill.

GEORGE J. BROOKE

Food → Diet in Palestine

Fortresses and Palaces

A series of fortifications were built in the Dead Sea region of Judea by members of the Hasmonean and Herodian dynasties. The region along the Jordan Valley and the Dead Sea, which is predominantly mountainous, provides several isolated mountaintops and hilltops on which first the Hasmoneans and then Herod built a string of fortified palaces. These fortresses, which contained both stout defenses and palaces, served a variety of functions including controlling traffic arteries, securing the kingdom's border against neighboring nations, storing royal valuables, detaining important political enemies, and, perhaps most importantly, providing safe havens of refuge in times of turmoil. There is even evidence that members of the royal family (usually those who had fallen afoul of the ruling monarch) were buried at some of these fortresses, in particular Hyrcania. Additionally, each fortress possessed a sophisticated system of water collection, in which run-off flowing down adjacent hills and mountains was diverted into hewn cisterns at the foot of the fortresses. Running from north to south, this network of fortresses included Alexandrion, Doq/Dagon, Cypros, Hyrcania, Herodium, Machaerus, and Masada. (This article also discusses the Antonia fortress in

FORTRESSES AND PALACES

Jerusalem and Herod's palace in that city. For palaces at ʿAraq el-Emir and Jericho, see the articles on those sites and the article on Architecture.)

Alexandrion

The fortress of Alexandrion (modern Qarn el-Sartabeh) is located at the peak of a mountain on an eastern spur of the Samarian hills in the northern part of the Jericho Valley. Alexandrion first appears in the written record as one of the three fortresses Salome Alexandra refused to entrust to her son Judah Aristobulus II because all of her most valuable possessions were held there (Josephus, *Ant.* 13.417). Later, during the civil war between Aristobulus and his brother John Hyrcanus II, Aristobulus retreated to the fortress until he was ordered to surrender by Pompey (Josephus, *J.W.* 1.133-37; *Ant.* 14.48-53). During the campaign of Aulus Gabinius (57 B.C.E.), Alexander, son of Aristobulus, occupied Alexandrion and resisted the Roman siege until Gabinius finally offered amnesty in exchange for his surrender. After Alexander surrendered the fort, Gabinius destroyed it (*J.W.* 1.160-70; *Ant.* 14.82-91). The destruction could not have been total because only twenty years later, while engaged in his war with Antigonus, Herod sent his younger brother Pheroras to fortify Alexandrion (*J.W.* 1.308; *Ant.* 14.419).

At Alexandrion, excavators found two strata, one on top of the other. The archaeological remains, along with the evidence from Josephus, suggest that the Hasmoneans built a fortress at the site, but that later Herod significantly refurbished and expanded it. It is likely that Alexandrion's primary function changed during the course of Herod's reign. In the early years, when his hold on power was less secure, the fortress aspect of the site would have been more important. As his control solidified, the primary function would have shifted more to that of a palatial residence and storehouse for royal treasure.

Doq/Dagon

Located to the west of and about 300 m. above modern-day Jericho, Doq/Dagon was the site of the betrayal and murder of Simon Maccabee and two of his sons in 134 B.C.E. by his son-in-law Ptolemy, son of Abubos. Ptolemy, the *stratēgos* of Jericho, invited his father-in-law to a banquet, and when Simon and his sons became intoxicated, Ptolemy ordered his men to seize their weapons and murder them (1 Macc. 16:11-17; *Ant.* 13.228). Simon's surviving son, John Hyrcanus I, sought revenge and besieged his brother-in-law in the fortress. However, Ptolemy forced him to withdraw from the siege by threatening to kill Hyrcanus' mother, whom Ptolemy had captured, by throwing her from the walls of the fortress (*Ant.* 13.230-34).

Archaeological remains at Dagon include Ionic capitals, monumental walls, cisterns, and other architectural elements scattered around the site. These remains suggest the existence of a palatial building at the fortress. Dagon, like the other desert fortresses, had an extensive water system with one aqueduct and nine cisterns. However, the water system seems to date to the Hasmonean period, in contrast to the other fortresses, whose water systems were constructed during the Herodian period.

Cypros

Situated upon a conical hilltop overlooking Jericho, Cypros provides an excellent view of the plain of Jericho below. Archaeologists have uncovered both Hasmonean and Herodian remains at this site. Among the Hasmonean remains, most of which were uncovered on the summit of the hill, are cisterns, a ritual bath, and fragments of capitals. These remains suggest the existence of a palace on the site during the Hasmonean period. Although far from certain, this site may have been one of the Hasmonean fortresses (either Threx or Taurus) that was destroyed by Pompey in 63 B.C.E. Ehud Netzer, among others, argues for such a connection (Netzer 2006).

While the Hasmonean-era fortress may have been impressive, it was clearly much smaller than the rebuilt fortress constructed during the reign of Herod. Josephus states that Herod built the fortress and named it in honor of his mother, Cypros (*J.W.* 1.417; *Ant.* 16.143). Herodian Cypros was divided into two parts, one on the mountaintop and the other about thirty m. below it. Excavators found two bathhouses, one on each level, and lavish architectural decorations in both Upper and Lower Cypros, including mosaic and *opus sectile* floors, colorful frescoes, painted Corinthian capitals, and well-executed stucco work. These decorations testify to the wealth and luxury of the site. Cypros also had a complex water system that seems to have been built originally under the Hasmoneans but expanded significantly by Herod.

Hyrcania

The fortress of Hyrcania sits on the western edge of the Hyrcania Valley, on an elongated hilltop 248 m. above sea level and about 200 m. above the valley. Hyrcania first appears in Josephus as one of the three fortresses where Salome Alexandra kept her most treasured possessions (*Ant.* 13.417). Alexander Jannaeus probably built the fortress and named it after his father John Hyrcanus. Alexander, son of Aristobulus, refortified the fortress, but Aulus Gabinius destroyed it in 57 B.C.E. (*J.W.* 1.161, 167). The fortress was rebuilt, and Mattathias Antigonus' sister barricaded herself in the fortress after Antigonus' defeat in 37 B.C.E. On the eve of the Battle of Actium, Herod finally captured the fortress and expelled Antigonus' sister (*J.W.* 1.364). Herod entertained Agrippa at Hyrcania, but the fort seems to have been used primarily as a place of detention and execution for political prisoners such as Herod's son Antipater.

Little remains of Hyrcania, and the fortress has never been properly excavated. Nevertheless, surveys of the site have found a rectangular structure located on a leveled area of the hilltop. This structure contains a central courtyard with rooms built around it on the north, east, and west. Hasmonean and Herodian masonry have been found at the site, suggesting that it was in use during both periods. Southeast of the fortress is a small graveyard, which was partly surrounded by a wall. Ceramic finds date these to the Herodian period, and it is tempting to connect them with the executions reported by Josephus (*Ant.* 15.366), although this remains unclear.

Herodium

The mount of Herodium (today's Jebel Fureidis) has the form of a truncated cone and resembles a volcanic crater. For Herod, the site's location only 12 km. from Jerusalem and its pleasant climate made it an ideal place for a fortified palace complex. It also had a personal significance for Herod, for on a single day in 40 B.C.E. he had fled to the site from Jerusalem to escape the forces of Mattathias Antigonus, the last Hasmonean ruler, and his allies the Parthians; prevailed over Antigonus in a battle there; and then witnessed the traumatic accidental death of his mother. It was probably to commemorate these events and to perpetuate his memory that Herod named the site after himself, used it as his main summer palace, and chose it as his burial place.

Greater Herodium consists of a fortified palace on the hill (Upper Herodium) and a complex of buildings at its foot (Lower Herodium). The remains of the palace-fortress on Upper Herodium are partly concealed within the mountain. The building is surrounded by a cylindrical casing of two parallel walls 3.4 m. apart, with an outer diameter of 63 m. Four towers protruded from it. Three of them were semicircular, but the eastern tower was round and rose several stories to a height of 25 m. above the central courtyard. It contained elaborate chambers and a small mansion on the roof that probably did double duty as a watch and signaling post. The royal mansion's eastern wing consisted of a large colonnaded courtyard, its western end of residential quarters. At the southern end was a Roman-style dining room or *triclinium* (ca. 15 × 10 m.), and at the northern end were five rooms comprising a Roman-style bathhouse.

Lower Herodium had an extensive pool complex at its center. The pool, which measured 69 × 45 m. and was

Herodium, mountain palace-fortress of Herod the Great *(Hanan Isachar)*

3 m. deep, served both as a reservoir and a recreation facility for swimming and boating. The largest building at Lower Herodium was a rectangular palace built on an elevated platform. To the north of this palace was a lengthy elevated course or terrace 350 m. long and 30 m. wide. At the course's western end was a monumental building measuring 15 × 14 m.

On the northern side of the course and east of the monumental building was a colonnade 3 m. wide and 40 m. long. Opposite it, on the eastern side of the course, stood a rectangular building with a large, stepped pool *(miqveh)*. The former presence of another monumental building nearby is indicated by a group of large ashlar stones found in secondary use among the remains of a Byzantine church.

Josephus says that Herod was buried at Herodium, and he gives a lengthy account of the king's funeral procession (*J.W.* 1.667-69) but no description of his tomb. Until recently scholars debated whether Herod would have built the tomb on the summit of Herodium, inside the mountain, or at its base. Several features had suggested to Netzer that Lower Herodium was the location of Herod's tomb compound: its elevated terrace, which was too narrow for a hippodrome and too long for a stadium but ideal for a funeral procession; its monumental building's unusual position (partially cut into the rocky slope and at the end of a long, open course); the proximity of a large *miqveh* (a rare feature in Herod's other building projects); and the large group of ashlars, suggestive of a missing tomb monument (Netzer 1981; 2006: 196-99). But in April 2007 Netzer and his team made a dramatic discovery: evi-

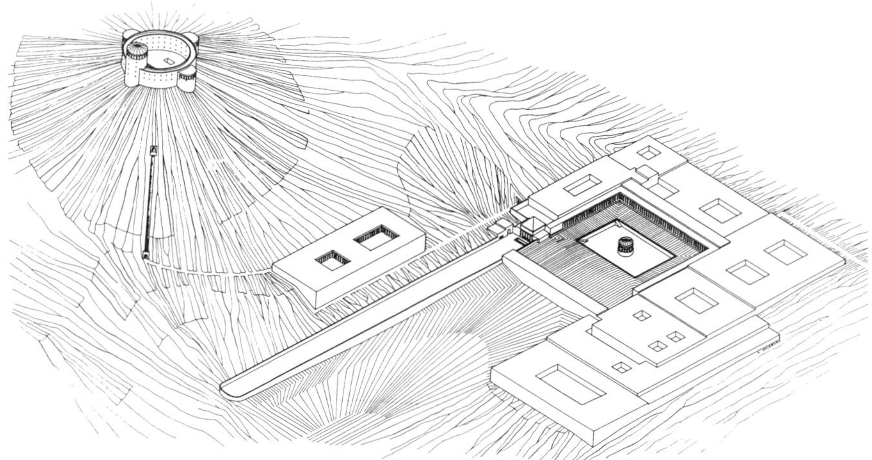

View of Greater Herodium from the northeast *(Ehud Netzer)*

dence of Herod's mausoleum and sarcophagus on the mount's northeastern slope at the end of a monumental staircase. The team exposed a 9-m. wall of expertly cut limestone blocks, as well as three massive blocks of white limestone of the type known as "meleche." The quality of the stone, the expert masonry, and the degree of decoration suggested that this had to be Herod's tomb. The mausoleum is thought to have stood 24 m. high, and to have had a podium, a cube-shaped first story, a cylindrical second story, and a high-peaked, conical roof similar to the one atop the Absalom tomb in the Kidron Valley. Netzer's team also found hundreds of ornately decorated, red limestone fragments, one of them bearing an intricately carved rosette common in funerary art. These fragments had made up the sarcophagus, whose reassembly indicates that it was some 2.5 m. long. Hammer marks on the fragments indicate that it was deliberately destroyed, probably by Jewish rebels during the First Revolt (66-70 C.E.).

Machaerus

Machaerus sits on the summit of a mountain in the highlands of Moab, overlooking the Dead Sea and the Judean Desert. It likely was constructed as a border fortress along the frontier between Judea and the Nabatean kingdom. It seems to have been built by Alexander Jannaeus (103-76 B.C.E.), and it was one of the three fortresses at which Salome Alexandra kept her royal treasure (*Ant.* 13.417). During the Hasmonean civil war, partisans of Aristobulus seized the fortress, and Gabinius destroyed it in 57 B.C.E. (*J.W.* 1.168). During the reign of Herod Antipas, John the Baptist was imprisoned and executed here (*Ant.* 18.116-19).

Excavators have found mostly Herodian-era remains. However, below the Herodian stratum, they also found the upper parts of the walls of the Hasmonean fortress, which mostly include the fortifications surrounding the summit and three rectangular towers. A stepped pool was also found, which resembled Hasmonean pools found at other desert fortresses. Unlike the other desert fortresses, Machaerus likely received few royal visits, and thus it is not surprising that the fortress is significantly smaller than others and has fewer palatial features.

Jerusalem

The Antonia fortress was probably the first building erected by Herod in Jerusalem. Named after Mark Antony, it was built on the site of an older fort erected by John Hyrcanus I named "Baris." Josephus gives a detailed description of it in *J.W.* 238-46. It was quite lavishly appointed, with cloisters, baths, and spacious courtyards. Archaeologists disagree over the exact dimensions of the structure, but it may have been as large as 150 × 90 m. Its foundation was partially cut out of the rock and had sloping sides. Ehud Netzer believes that its upper structure resembled the round building at Herodium. It had four towers, one at each corner, rising 5 m. above the central structure. Three of the towers were ca. 20 m. high, but the southeastern one reached to ca. 35 m. and offered a commanding view of the Temple Mount, overlooking the precinct's northwest corner.

Herod's main residence in Jerusalem was a fortress-palace situated along the western side of the Upper City. Once again, Josephus offers a lengthy description (*J.W.* 5.176-81). Though the historian does not give the palace's dimensions, some think that it measured ca. 300 × 100 m. The palace was completely enclosed by a wall interspersed at equal distances with towers. It contained immense banquet halls and enough bedrooms to accommodate hundreds of guests. The rooms were surfaced with a variety of stones, and their ceilings had immense beams. The palace also had numerous circular cloisters leading into one another, with different sorts of columns in each, as wells as courtyards, linked to one another with corridors, that boasted groves of trees, canals, and ponds.

The palace was integrated with the city's fortifications on the west, and north of the palace were three great multistoried towers constructed of large stone blocks (*J.W.* 5.163-75). The towers were built on a solid, elevated platform, ca. 20 × 18 m. in area, whose maximum height was 19 m. Herod named the towers for friends and relatives: Phasael (ca. 45 m.) after his brother, Hippicus (ca. 40 m.) after a friend, and Mariamne (ca. 27 m.) after one of his wives. The Phasael tower was as tall as a modern 15-story building. All three of them had royal chambers within.

Herod the Great's main palace in Jerusalem, with the three multistoried towers and the Antonia Fortress in the background *(www.HolyLandPhotos.com)*

FORTRESSES AND PALACES

Masada

Undoubtedly the most impressive of the desert fortresses, and perhaps the most impressive Herodian palace, Masada was constructed on a rock promontory high above the Dead Sea Valley. This promontory is separated from the cliffs on both sides and was thus easily defensible. Josephus states that Jonathan, the Hasmonean high priest, was the first to build at Masada (*J.W.* 7.285). Most scholars think that this Jonathan was Alexander Jannaeus (103-76 B.C.E.) and not Jonathan, son of Mattathias (161-143/2 B.C.E.). Before becoming king, Herod visited Masada twice. In 42 B.C.E. and at the behest of John Hyrcanus II, he expelled a group of rebels who had seized some of the desert fortresses (*J.W.* 1.237-38; *Ant.* 14.296). A few years later, in ca. 39/38 B.C.E., he rescued members of his family who were being besieged by the Hasmonean Mattathias Antigonus (*J.W.* 1.293-295; *Ant.* 14.397). Despite the literary evidence, archaeologists have not uncovered any conclusive evidence of Hasmonean occupation at Masada.

Masada contains two large palaces and a few other smaller palatial buildings. According to Ehud Netzer, these edifices were constructed in three phases: ca. 35 B.C.E., ca. 25 B.C.E., and ca. 15 B.C.E. The so-called western palace and the smaller palatial buildings nearby seem to have been begun during the first phase, although the western palace was expanded during the second and third phases as well. These early palaces were characterized by central peristyle courtyards surrounded on all sides by rooms. This general layout is so similar to the typical floor plan of a Hasmonean palace that Netzer and others originally believed these palaces were actually Hasmonean constructions (Netzer 2006).

The most impressive construction at Masada, however, is the northern palace. Constructed on three terraces jutting out from the rock, this palace was a technological and architectural marvel, providing breathtaking views from the north, east, and west. The upper terrace, which contains the residential quarters but also functioned as a reception area, is crowned on its northern edge with a semicircular courtyard, bordered by a double colonnade. The inner part of this courtyard may have contained a formal garden. On the middle terrace, Herod constructed a rounded *tholos*-type reception hall. The lower terrace consisted of a square hall surrounded by colonnades. A small bathhouse was constructed just below this terrace. A much larger bathhouse stood adjacent to the upper terrace. A strong casemate wall surrounds the fortress with towers placed along its perimeter. In addition, Herod's builders constructed an elaborate water storage system, including twelve huge cisterns in the northwest cliff and additional cisterns on the hilltop.

At the beginning of the Great Revolt (66-70 B.C.E.), Masada was defended by a Roman garrison. This garrison was attacked and overpowered by the Sicarii, a small revolutionary group led by Eleazar ben Jair. After the destruction of the Temple in 70 B.C.E., additional Sicarii, who had fled Jerusalem, joined their compatriots at the fortress. In 72 B.C.E., the Roman governor of Judea, Lucius Flavius Silva, besieged Masada. After several failed attempts to breach the wall, he ordered the construction of a circumvallation wall and then a rampart against the western face of the plateau. In the spring of 73, the Romans finally breached the walls, but when they entered the fortress, they discovered that the

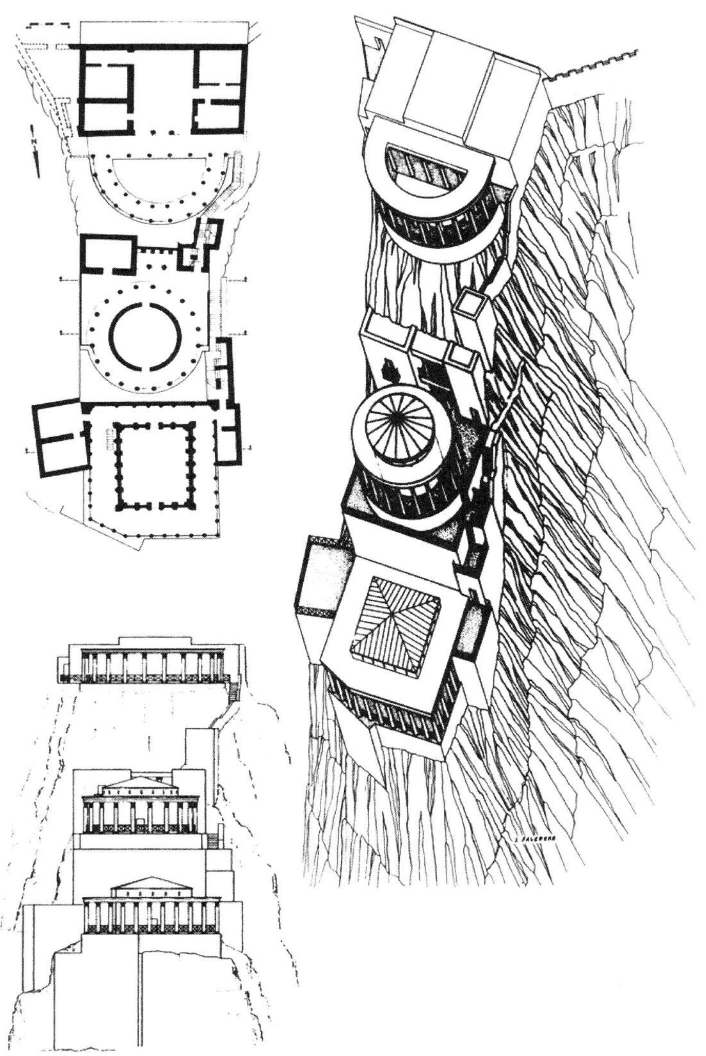

Reconstructed plan, elevation from the north, and isometric view of the northern palace at Masada *(Ehud Netzer)*

defenders had committed mass suicide rather than be captured and enslaved (*J.W.* 7.275-406).

Skeletal remains were discovered in the lower terrace of the northern palace and in a small cave a few meters below the wall in the southern cliff. In addition, small ostraca, written in the same hand, and each containing one name, were found beside the inner gates of the entrance to the storerooms. These may be the lots mentioned by Josephus that the Sicarii used to determine the order of their suicide. Among the group was one with the name "ben Jair" on it, and it may have referred to the Sicarii commander, Eleazar ben Jair.

BIBLIOGRAPHY

D. AMIT, J. PATRICH, AND Y. HIRSCHFELD, EDS. 2002, *The Aqueducts of Israel,* Portsmouth, R.I.: Journal of Roman Archaeology. • S. JAPP 2000, *Die Baupolitik Herodes des Grossen: Die Bedeutung der Architektur für die Herrschaftslegitimation eines Römischen Klientelkönigs,* Rahden: Leidorf. • A. LICHTENBERGER 1999, *Die Baupolitik Herodes des Grossen,* Wiesbaden: Harrassowitz. • E. NETZER 1981, *Greater Herodium,* Jerusalem: Hebrew University of Jerusalem. • E. NETZER, ED. 2006, *The Architecture of Herod, the Great Builder,* Tübingen: Mohr-Siebeck. • P. RICHARDSON 2004, *Building Jewish in the Roman East,* Waco, Tex.: Baylor University Press. • D. W. ROLLER 1998, *The Building Program of Herod the Great,* Berkeley: University of California Press, 1998. • Y. YADIN 1966, *Masada: Herod's Fortress and the Zealot's Last Stand,* New York: Random House.

See also: ʿAraq el-Emir; Architecture; Jericho; Masada

ADAM MARSHAK AND DANIEL C. HARLOW

Fourth Philosophy → Resistance Movements

Funerary Customs → Burial Practices

G

Gabriel, Vision of

The Vision of Gabriel is a Hebrew text written in ink on a slab of limestone, which is thought to have been found on the eastern side of the Dead Sea. (The exact provenance is uncertain.) The lower part of the stone is brown, suggesting that it was covered by earth, and so it is thought to have been a monument or memorial. The script has been dated to the turn of the era by Ada Yardeni. There are some eighty-seven lines of text, but many are extremely fragmentary. One passage is addressed to "my servant David," who is told to ask of Ephraim that he place a sign. He is assured that "in three days you will know," for "the evil has been broken by righteousness." There is also reference to a "wicked shoot" (using the word *ṣmḥ*, which often has messianic connotations). David is also told that an angel is supporting him. The speaker then quotes Hag. 2:6: "in a little while I will shake the heavens and the earth." Later, there is an enigmatic reference to three shepherds. An even more enigmatic statement at line 67 reads "proclaim to him about the blood. This is their chariot." For much of the composition, the speaker seems to be God, but line 77 reads, "Who am I? I am Gabriel."

It is apparent that the text is some kind of apocalyptic vision, promising imminent deliverance for Jerusalem, and entailing a role for a Davidic messiah. Israel Knohl has proposed a far-reaching interpretation. He dates the text around the turn of the era, in the context of upheavals after the death of Herod. He regards Ephraim as a messianic figure (the messiah son of Joseph), the earliest reference to this figure. At line 67, he takes the reference to a chariot to mean that certain people were to be taken up to heaven. At line 80, the editors read "for three days" (the preposition is *l*), followed by the letter *ḥ*. Knohl reads the word *ḥ'yh*, "live" (with an *'aleph* as second letter before the *yod*), and takes this as a reference to resurrection after three days. He makes the admittedly conjectural suggestion that the figure who was to be resurrected was one Simon, a leader of the revolt after Herod's death. In view of the fragmentary state of the text, such suggestions must be viewed with great caution. The text has been published only very recently, and no consensus as to its interpretation has yet emerged.

BIBLIOGRAPHY

A. YARDENI AND B. ELITZUR 2007, "Document: A First-Century BCE Prophetic Text Written on a Stone: First Publication," *Cathedra* 123: 155-66 (in Hebrew). • I. KNOHL 2008, "'By Three Days, Live': Messiahs, Resurrection, and Ascent to Heaven in *Hazon Gabriel*," *JR* 88: 147-58. • I. KNOHL 2009, *Messiahs and Resurrections in Gabriel Revelation*, London: Continuum.

JOHN J. COLLINS

Galilee

Hellenistic and Early Roman Periods

The designation Galilee, meaning "the circle," applied to the whole northern region of the land of Israel, is derived in all probability from the experience of the early Israelites inhabiting the interior highlands and surrounded by Canaanite city-states. The Galilean tribes were Zebulun, Naphtali, and Asher, with the tribe of Dan migrating north later. The various accounts of the different tribes and their characteristics (Genesis 49; Deuteronomy 33; Judges 5), though dated to the period of the Judges, may well reflect later situations where the issue of ethnic identity came under threat from various sources. Certainly the north bore the brunt of the Assyrian onslaught of the eighth century B.C.E. with Tiglath-pileser III's invasion, resulting in the destruction and possibly the depopulation of many centers in upper and lower Galilee (2 Kings 15, 29; Isa. 8:23). However, unlike the case of Samaria some ten years later (2 Kings 17, 23), there is no mention of a foreign, non-Israelite population being introduced to Galilee at that time.

Galilee next appears in the historical record in the mid-second century B.C.E. when an independent Jewish state emerged under the successors of the Maccabees, the Hasmoneans. They initiated campaigns of expansion, which eventually led to the establishment of a kingdom that territorially was as extensive as that of David and Solomon in the ninth century. For the first time in almost a millennium, therefore, Galilee and Judea were under the same native rule, with Jerusalem again the political as well as the religious capital. At the same time, the name *Ioudaios* began to be used not just for the inhabitants of Judea but for all who embraced the Jewish temple ideology by worshiping in Jerusalem. By the mid-first century B.C.E., however, Rome was emerging as master of the eastern Mediterranean, and the Hasmoneans had been replaced by the Herodians, an Idumean dynasty entrusted by Rome to maintain its interests in the region as client kings. Galilee, with Sepphoris as the administrative center for the region, was recognized as a Jewish territory, together with Judea proper and Perea beyond the Jordan. They were, however, soon incorporated into the kingdom of Herod the Great and were expected to make their contribution to honoring his Roman patron, Augustus.

The long reign of Herod as king of the Jews (40-4 B.C.E.) made a deep impact on every aspect of both Galilean and Judean society. On his death Augustus refused to appoint any of Herod's sons as his successor, assigning instead different regions to each: Galilee and Perea to Antipas; Judea to Archelaus; and Batanea, Trachonitis, and Auranitis in northern Transjordan to Philip. Galilee was once again, therefore, administratively separate from Judea, something that is reflected in Matthew's gospel, in explaining how Jesus, though born in Judea, came to live in the north: "His father Joseph, hearing that Archelaus ruled in Judea in the place of Herod, his father, took the child and his mother to Galilee and came to live at Nazareth" (Matt. 2:23).

Antipas aspired to but was never given the title king, only that of tetrarch. He ruled in Galilee and Perea until 39 C.E., when he too was deposed and his territory was handed over to his nephew Agrippa I. Despite this lesser status, he continued with the style and policy of his father in ensuring that Roman concerns were taken care of in his territories. John the Baptist suffered at his hands, probably not for the reason in the Gospels (Mark 6:13-30), but for that given by Josephus, namely, that John's popularity and espousal of justice for the poor gave cause for concern that an uprising might occur (*Ant.* 18.116-19). This would have been deemed a serious failure in imperial eyes, since client kings were tolerated only if they could be seen to ensure stability and loyalty to Rome and its values. Antipas also continued his father's tradition of honoring the Roman overlords through monumental buildings in Galilee. According to Josephus, Sepphoris was made "the ornament of all Galilee" and named *Autokratoris,* probably alluding to Augustus as sole ruler (*Ant.* 18.27). In 19 C.E. he founded a new city, Tiberias, on the lakefront, honoring Augustus' successor as emperor.

The subsequent history of Galilee has to do with its gradual incorporation into the system of direct Roman rule in Palestine and the east generally. Two periods of Herodian rule were interspersed with the incorporation of the region into the procuratorial province of Judea. Agrippa I (41-44 C.E.) ruled a territory including Galilee that was as large as that of his grandfather, Herod the Great. His son, Agrippa II, was given a section of eastern lower Galilee by Nero, either in 57 or 64 C.E. After the First Revolt against Rome in 66-70 C.E., Agrippa seems to have been trusted because of his opposition to the revolt. Unfortunately, our literary sources are largely silent with regard to possible administrative changes in Galilee. The stationing of one Roman legion (the tenth *Fretensis*) in Jerusalem was deemed adequate, suggesting that Galilee could easily be controlled by the existing structures, provincial and municipal. Somewhat later (possibly as early 117 C.E.) a second legion (the sixth *Ferrata*) was placed in the Jezreel Plain, and cities that had been loyal to Rome, such as Sepphoris, had their status and roles extended, as exemplified in the change of name to Diocaesarea. The Bar Kokhba Revolt (132-35 C.E.) seems to have bypassed Galilee, and there is no evidence of aggressive Roman intervention in the region, unlike Judea. Rather, the process of more intense Romanization is evident in various other respects such as art and architecture, epigraphy, and the development of the road system. This suggests that the Jewish leadership had learned to accommodate itself to Roman rule and that the imperial authorities were content to negotiate with the local elites, as elsewhere throughout the empire.

Opinions vary as to the extent to which Jewish life was restored in Galilee after 135 C.E. As Jews were expelled from the south, many settled in Galilee, where the number of Jewish settlements seems to have increased considerably. The archaeological evidence has been variously interpreted, to indicate a thriving and relatively prosperous Jewish life up to the mid-fourth century C.E., or a virtual capitulation to Roman culture by the majority of the inhabitants.

Religious and Cultural Affiliations

Just who were the Galileans? One can distinguish three broad lines of response in the contemporary discussion. One proposal, by the German scholar Albrecht Alt, maintains that the Galileans of the later sources are direct descendants of the old Israelite population, who had remained undisturbed in the first wave of Assyrian conquest of the north, and who had maintained their essential Yahwistic beliefs. The inhabitants of Galilee freely and naturally joined the *ethnos tōn Ioudaiōn* when the opportunity arose after the Hasmonean expansion to the north. More recently, Richard Horsley has also espoused the notion of the old Israelite population remaining undisturbed in Galilee, but he sees the situation in Hasmonean times quite differently. Over the centuries the Galileans had developed their own customs and practices that made them quite different from the Judeans, despite their sharing the same Yahwistic beliefs based on the Pentateuch. Thus the Hasmonean expansion represented not a liberation but an imposition on the Galileans of the laws of the Judeans.

The very opposite view is held by scholars who accept the phrase "Galilee of the nations" (Isa. 8:23; 1 Macc. 5:15) as an accurate description of the population of the region and its cultural affiliations, especially from the Hellenistic period onward. This view reached its most virulent expression with the claim that Galilee was pagan *(heidnisch)* and that Jesus was therefore in all probability not a Jew. Not everybody who accepts the notion of pagan influences in Galilee goes quite that far. Instead, Galileans are seen as having been more exposed to Hellenistic culture generally, so that they espoused a more open form of Judaism, influenced as they were by the ethos of the surrounding cities. More recently this emphasis on Greco-Roman culture in Galilee has taken the form of the claim of Cynic influences on the population there. Since the Cynics were an urban phenomenon, proponents of a Cynic presence there speak also of an urbanized Galilee, but there is little support for such claims in the available evidence.

A third position, the one that best corresponds to the archaeological evidence, speaks of the Judaization of Galilee from the south by the Hasmoneans. Again, there are variations to this account. Some scholars have accepted Josephus' version (*Ant.* 13.319), according to which the Hasmonean Aristobulus I had in 104 B.C.E. forcibly circumcised the Itureans, a seminomadic Arab people who had infiltrated into upper Galilee. Such a background, if accepted, would have made the Galilean Jews, as recent converts, suspect in the eyes of their southern co-religionists, thus explaining some later disparaging remarks by the rabbis about the Galilean lack of piety. Others, on the basis of the material culture, believe that Galilee was settled from the south in the wake of the Hasmonean conquests. This would explain their loyalty to Jerusalem and its worship documented in the literary sources, since they would have been of Judean stock originally and were sent to Galilee because of their support for the Hasmoneans.

The case for a pagan Galilee is poorly supported by the literary evidence and receives no support whatsoever from the archaeological explorations. Nor is there any real evidence of a lasting Iturean presence in the region either. There are also several problems with the idea of Galilean Israelites, not least the likelihood of a largely peasant population maintaining a separate Yahwistic identity over the centuries in the absence of a communal cultic center. Thus, the theory of the Judaization of Galilee from the south would appear to be the most likely hypothesis in our present state of knowledge. Surveys have shown a marked increase of new foundations from the Hasmonean period onward and at the same time the destruction of older sites, like Har Mispe Yamim, which had a pagan cult center. Excavations at sites such as Sepphoris, Jotapata, Gamla, and Meiron, as well as lesser sites, have uncovered such instruments of the distinctive Jewish way of life as ritual baths, stone jars, and natively produced ceramic household ware, all indicators of a concern with ritual purity emanating from Jerusalem and its temple and an avoidance of the cultural ethos of the encircling pagan cities.

Social Stratification

Most recent social historians of Roman Palestine adopt Gerhard Lenski's model of agrarian empires as their working hypothesis. This envisages a pyramidal view of society in which most of the power, prestige, and privilege resides at the top among the narrow band of ruling elite and native aristocracy, if and when these are to be distinguished. Beneath these are the retainer classes who help to maintain the status quo on behalf of the elites, thereby gaining for themselves some measure of relative prestige. A further layer down are the peasants, that is, the free landowners who are the mainstay of the society but who cannot themselves aspire to going higher on the social scale. Instead, for one reason or another they are in constant danger of being demoted to the landless poor and destitute, either due to increased taxation, a bad harvest, or simple aggrandizement of property by the ruling elites. Such a model certainly fits well in general terms with what we know of Roman Galilee, once certain adjustments are made to this ideal picture to account for local circumstances.

While Antipas was never given the title "king" but simply that of "tetrarch," there is no doubt that within Galilee itself he and his court represented the ruling elite. Augustus had decreed that he could have a personal income of 200 talents from the territories of Galilee and Perea, and presumably he could also introduce special levies for building and other projects, especially when these were intended to honor the imperial household (*Ant.* 17.18). Not only did Antipas and his immediate family benefit from these concessions, but a new class seems to have emerged around him, called in the Gospels the Herodians, presumably as a replacement for the older, native Hasmonean aristocracy who had disappeared after Herod the Great's takeover.

The retainer class included "the grandees [*megistanes*], military officers, [*chiliarchoi*], and leading men [*prōtoi*] of Galilee" (Mark 6:21; cf. *Ant.* 18.251-52 for the *chiliarchoi; Ant.* 18.122, 261-309 for the *prōtoi*). The *chiliarchoi* suggest that Antipas had a permanent army, however small, as distinct from the militia that he might call up for a particular engagement. The *prōtoi tēs Galilaias* are clearly influential Jews, concerned at least ostensibly with religious affairs but also with the maintenance of law and order, and the payment of tribute to Rome. The *megistanes* seem to be local lords on whom the ruler could normally rely for active support in times of crisis, rather than court officers or administrative officers. Other functionaries also appear in the literature. Mention of the *archēai* in Sepphoris immediately suggests keepers of official records and scribes of various kinds. We can also assume a whole network of lesser officials within the highly bureaucratic structures that had been put in place from the early Hellenistic period by the Ptolemies, and that would have simply been inherited by successive regimes thereafter. These officials would have included market managers *(agoranomoi),* tax collectors *(telōnai),* estate mangers *(oikonomoi),* judges *(kritai),* and prison officers *(hypēretai/ praktōres),* all of whom are alluded to in the Gospels. The tax collectors appear to be ubiquitous, an indication perhaps of the demands that were being made on people, not just to meet the tribute due to Antipas himself, but also various other levies and tolls. The payment at least of the *tributum soli* or land tax was in kind, as indicated by the mention of imperial granaries in Upper Galilee at the outbreak of the First Revolt. Presumably there were others throughout the region also (*Life*

71.119). In addition, there was the *tributum capitis* or personal tax, which was a regular feature of the Roman tax system, and the collection of this would have imposed another layer of bureaucratic retainers on the Galilean social structure.

Beneath the retainers comes the peasantry. These may include owners of small, family-sized holdings (10-15 hectares) or tenants who engaged in subsistence farming while paying a rent, usually in kind, to an absentee landowner. Ideally, all Jews were intended to participate in the land, and the whole structure of tithing and agricultural offerings for the Temple was built on that assumption. However, imperial domination had seen the emergence of large estates in Palestine, as elsewhere, and this inevitably put pressure on the traditional landowning system, as can be seen by the land reform of Nehemiah already in the Persian period (Neh. 5:1-11). While the Hasmoneans subscribed to the Israelite ideal of "every man under his own vine" (1 Macc. 14:10), there is plenty of evidence that they too continued the policy of large estates in the conquered territories, as did the Herodians also. This pressure on the system meant that more and more people were driven off the land and reduced to penury.

Economic Systems

The pertinent question concerning the Galilean economy is the extent to which the benefits of its agricultural products accrued to the peasants themselves or were creamed off by the ruling elite in taxes and other exactions. If the Galilean land-ownership pattern represented a combination of large estates and family-run holdings, then it would seem that some degree of commercial independence should be granted to the Galilean peasants. However, the refurbishment of Sepphoris and the building of Tiberias must have marked a turning point in the Galilean economy. Their construction coincided with Jesus' public ministry and provides the most immediate backdrop to his particular emphasis on the blessedness of the destitute and the call for trust in God's provident care for all. The new Herodian class had to be accommodated with adequate allotments in order to maintain a luxurious lifestyle (cf. Matt. 11:19), and inevitably this meant pressure on the peasants. Debt was followed by appropriation of property, with slavery or brigandage as the only alternative ways of life.

Yet this picture has to be balanced by the evidence from later sources, which shows that a Jewish peasant class did survive the crisis of the two revolts. We find the rabbinic sources replete with references to markets, village traders, and laws concerning buying and selling. This cannot be dismissed as mere idealization of later generations but is rather a continuation of patterns we can already discern in such first-century sources as the Gospels and Josephus' writings. However, the dividing line between subsistence and penury was a thin one, as the threatened strike by the Galilean peasants that occurred in the reign of the emperor Gaius Caligula (39 C.E.) demonstrates. In protest at the proposed erection of the emperor's statue in the Jerusalem Temple, they decided not to till the land, and significantly some members of the Herodian family were dismayed, fearing that there would not be sufficient resources to pay the annual tribute, thus leading to social anarchy (*Ant.* 8.273-74).

Josephus mentions that John of Gischala used Tyrian money in his transactions with his fellow Jews from Syria. This piece of information is in line with archaeological evidence from various sites, where Tyrian coinage seems to dominate the numismatic finds at locations not just in Upper Galilee, such as Meiron, Gischala, and Khirbet Shema, but even at Gamla and Jotapata, both Lower Galilean strongholds of Jewish nationalism in the First Revolt. This suggests trading links with the important Phoenician port, despite the cultural differences between the city of Tyre and its Jewish hinterland, which could often boil over into open hostility (*J.W.* 4.05). Most surprising is the fact that the Tyrian half-shekel was deemed to be "the coin of the sanctuary" which all male Jews were obliged to pay for the upkeep of the Jerusalem Temple. The usual reason given is that the Tyrian money had retained a constant value in terms of its silver content for over a century and a half (126 B.C.E.–56 C.E.), whereas other currencies in the region had been debased. It may also be due to the fact that Tyrian money was in far greater supply than any other currency, native or foreign. The Tyrian mint was recognized by Rome as the most important one in the region, and the Herodians were not allowed to produce silver coins. Thus, we cannot infer from the quantity of coins alone that Galilean commercial relations were concentrated on that one Phoenician city.

The Galilean economy was motivated by values and attitudes that were directly opposed to those of the Jewish religious worldview which both the Galilean peasants and their Jerusalem religious leaders espoused, at least in theory. In order to maintain their elite lifestyle, the Herodians creamed off the wealth of the land for their own benefit, without giving anything back in return. The Jewish ideal, on the other hand, espoused an inclusive community in which all shared in the blessings of the land and its fruits. It was during the long reign of Antipas that this conflict became apparent for the Galilean peasants in the changing ethos represented by Sepphoris and Tiberias. These two centers and their upkeep drained the countryside of its resources, natural and human, thereby causing resentment and opposition. This opposition comes into clear light during the First Revolt, when both cities were attacked by Galileans who sought to vent their resentment on the aristocratic inhabitants and their opulent lifestyles (*Life* 66.301, 373-80). However, this feeling of distance, even resentment, can be detected some forty years earlier during the ministry of Jesus to the villages of Galilee. Neither Sepphoris nor Tiberias is mentioned in the Gospels, but the lifestyle of those dwelling "in the houses of kings" is viewed critically when contrasted with the values of John the Baptist and Jesus.

Galilee and the Two Revolts

Galilee's participation in the First Revolt shows that even a predominantly Jewish region had many internal tensions, as native "strong men" like John of Gischala and

Justus of Tiberias resented and resisted the imposition by the Jerusalem revolutionary council in 66 C.E. of the Judean priestly figure, Josephus, as governor of the province. Even more striking was Sepphoris' refusal to engage in the revolt, something that benefited it subsequently in the postrevolt setting. Nor is there evidence that Galilee was involved in the Bar Kokhba Revolt of 132-35 C.E. Ironically — and contrary to some modern claims about its revolutionary character — Galilee became the home of the rabbinic movement. This was to ensure the survival of Jewish religious identity by providing the setting for the literary output represented by the Mishnah and, later, the Palestinian Talmud. This literary achievement, together with the architectural remains of the synagogues from the late Roman period, shows how alive the memory of the Temple and its rituals remained, despite the destruction of Jerusalem and its subsequent transformation into a pagan city, Aelia Capitolina.

Synagogue at Gamla in the southern Golan, built at the time of Alexander Jannaeus (first century B.C.E.) and destroyed by Vespasian and Titus (67 C.E.) Benches line the unpaved hall on all four sides. *(Phoenix Data Systems / Neal and Joel Bierling)*

BIBLIOGRAPHY

M. AVIAM 2004, *Jews, Pagans and Christians in the Galilee,* Rochester: University of Rochester Press. • M. A. CHANCEY 2002, *The Myth of a Gentile Galilee,* Cambridge: Cambridge University Press. • M. A. CHANCEY 2005, *Greco-Roman Culture and the Galilee of Jesus,* Cambridge: Cambridge University Press. • D. EDWARDS AND T. MCCOLLOUGH, EDS. 1997, *Archaeology and the Galilee: Texts and Contexts in Greco-Roman and Byzantine Periods,* Atlanta: Scholars Press. • S. FREYNE 1980, *Galilee from Alexander the Great to Hadrian: A Study of Second Temple Judaism,* Wilmington, Del.: Glazier (rpt. Edinburgh: Clark, 1998). • S. FREYNE 1988, *Galilee, Jesus and the Gospels: Literary Approaches and Historical Investigations,* Dublin: Gill; Minneapolis: Augsburg-Fortress. • S. FREYNE 2000, *Galilee and Gospel: Collected Essays* Tübingen: Mohr-Siebeck. • K. C. HANSON AND D. OAKMAN 1998, *Palestine in the Time of Jesus: Social Structures and Social Conflicts,* Minneapolis: Fortress. • R. HORSLEY 1995, *Galilee: History, Politics, People,* Valley Forge, Penn.: Trinity Press International. • M. H. JENSEN 2006, *Herod Antipas in Galilee,* Tübingen: Mohr-Siebeck. • L. LEVINE, ED. 1992, *The Galilee in Late Antiquity,* New York: Jewish Theological Seminary of America. • E. M. MEYERS 1999, *Galilee through the Centuries: Confluence of Cultures,* Winona Lake, Ind.: Eisenbrauns. • J. REED 2000, *Archaeology and the Galilean Jesus,* Harrisburg, Penn.: Trinity Press International.

See also: Gamla; Iturea; Jotapata; Romanization; Sepphoris; Tiberias

SEAN FREYNE

Gamla

Gamla (also spelled Gamala) was a Jewish village located in the southern Golan Heights that was the location of a major siege during the First Jewish Revolt against the Romans (*J.W.* 4.1-83). The city was formerly identified with the site of Tel ed-Dra', located on the present Israel-Syria border, based on the similarity between the name Gamla and the nearby village of Jamleh. Because Josephus wrote that the Sea of Galilee and Tarichaeae were visible from Gamla (*J.W.* 4.2), Y. Gal proposed in 1968 that the ruin known as es-Salam (or es-Sanam) was a more fitting locale. Excavations of this site conducted under the direction of the late Shmarya Gutmann (1976-1989), and later renewed by his successors (1997-2000), have uncovered extensive remains of a Second Temple town that was besieged by Roman forces during the First Jewish Revolt. This evidence has led the majority of scholars to accept the identification of es-Salam with Gamla.

Gamla is perhaps the best-preserved town to have been besieged during the First Jewish Revolt. It is situated on an isolated hill that resembles a reclining camel, which led early settlers to call it Gamla (Aramaic for "camel"). Gamla is naturally fortified by steep ravines on all but its eastern side. A narrow saddle connecting the town with the plateau above provides the only point of entry. Excavations have uncovered remains of an Early Bronze I-II Age (ca. 3200-2500 B.C.E.) settlement, whose precise size and dimensions have yet to be determined. Gamla remained unoccupied until approximately 150 B.C.E. when a new town was constructed atop the Bronze Age ruins. The Jewish character of this Hasmonean town is evident by the discovery of numerous *mikva'ot* (ritual baths), stone vessels, and a building widely held to be a synagogue. Over 2,000 basalt ballista stones, 1,600 iron arrowheads, 100 catapult bolts, and other weapons, as well as pieces of Roman armor, testify to the ferocity of the Roman siege that took place there. Archaeological and numismatic evidence indicate that Gamla was destroyed and abandoned in the second half of the first century C.E.

Nothing is known about Gamla's early history. According to Josephus, it was controlled for a time by a tyrant named Demetrius. He was removed by Alexander Jannaeus in about 83-80 B.C.E. (*J.W.* 1.105; *Ant.* 13.394), after which the town came under Jewish sovereignty. Gamla underwent a period of expansion during the reign of Herod the Great. When the First Jewish Revolt began, Gamla's residents initially remained loyal to Rome (*Life* 46, 59–61), but they soon joined the revolt. The town came under the jurisdiction of Josephus, who constructed its defenses (*J.W.* 2.572-76). Before the arrival of the Romans, Gamla was weakened by internal fighting and a seven-month siege by the forces of King Agrippa II (*J.W.* 4.10; *Life* 59–61, 114, 179–87). In 67 C.E. the Roman general Vespasian and his son Titus besieged the town for an additional thirty days (*J.W.* 4.11-83). According to Josephus' account, the Romans killed 4,000 of Gamla's inhabitants, many of whom were refugees from other towns. An additional 5,000 people plunged to their deaths from Gamla's crest (*J.W.* 4.79-80).

The site of Gamla covers an area of approximately 100 dunams (25 acres). Archaeological excavations have uncovered evidence of a prosperous neighborhood comprised of elaborate homes with frescoes and stuccoed walls, two olive presses (with attached *miqva'ot*), flower mills, and a synagogue. Some of the structures were roofed with basalt slabs. A spacious three-level mansion that cuts into the town's hillside built of smooth ashlar masonry has been partially uncovered. Excavations have also revealed a portion of a large first-century-C.E. building made of extremely large ashlars with wide aisles that has tentatively been identified as a basilica. Gamla's synagogue is a large, rectangular structure (25.5 × 17 m.) that contains three rows of benches around its four walls, with a large *miqveh* at its entrance. The small room attached to the synagogue may have been a study room. Numismatic and ceramic evidence suggests that the synagogue was built in the first century B.C.E., making it possibly the oldest known synagogue discovered in Israel. Weaponry from the Roman siege has been found in the majority of Gamla's buildings. A pile of ballista stones discovered 300 m. outside Gamla's wall was likely the location of a Roman ballista emplacement. Seven unique coins from the First Jewish Revolt have been found bearing the legend "For the redemption of Jerusalem the H(oly)." These coins were minted at Gamla as propaganda during the revolt and are similar to those produced in Jerusalem at the same time. A few scholars have challenged the accuracy of Josephus' account of Gamla's siege, suggesting that perhaps the mass death he records never occurred. An international team of experts is preparing the final reports of the Gutmann excavations.

BIBLIOGRAPHY

K. ATKINSON 2006, "Noble Deaths at Gamla and Masada?: A Critical Assessment of Josephus's Accounts of Jewish Resistance in Light of Archaeological Discoveries," in *Making History: Josephus and Historical Method,* ed. Z. Rogers, Leiden: Brill, 349-71. • B. BAR-KOCHVA 1976, "Gamla in Gaulanitis," *Zeitschrift des deutschen Palästina-Vereins* 92: 54-71. • A. BERLIN 2006, *Gamla I: The Pottery of the Second Temple Period,* Jerusalem: Israel Antiquities Authority. • S. GUTMAN 1993, "Gamla," in *Encyclopedia of Archaeological Excavations in the Holy Land,* ed. E. Stern et al., Jerusalem: Israel Exploration Society, 2: 459-63. • Z. U. MA'OZ 1981, "The Synagogue of Gamla and the Typology of Second-Temple Synagogues," in *Ancient Synagogues Revealed,* ed. L. I. Levine, Jerusalem: Israel Exploration Society, 35-41. • D. SYON, 1992-1993, "The Coins from Gamala: Interim Report," *Israel Numismatic Journal* 12: 34-55. • D. SYON 2002, "Gamla: City of Refuge," in *The First Jewish Revolt: Archaeology, History, and Ideology,* ed. A. M. Berlin and J. A. Overman, London: Routledge, 134-53. • D. SYON AND Z. YAVOR 2005, "Gamla 1997-2000," *'Atiqot* 50: 1-35.

KENNETH ATKINSON

Garden of Eden — Paradise

In early Judaism, the term "Paradise" or "Garden of Eden" occurs in various senses. It is present in shorter or longer retellings of the story of Genesis 2–3, where Eden is an earthly region, whether it was created before the creation of the world or on the third or sixth day of creation. In some texts, the garden remains on earth as an abode of God and the righteous after Adam and Eve have left. In other texts, it also occurs as a place in (the third) heaven, sometimes as an eschatological reward for the righteous in the beyond.

1 Enoch

The *Book of the Watchers* (*1 Enoch* 1–36) already existed at the beginning of the second century B.C.E. It seems to be an independent witness to the tradition used by the author of Genesis 2–3. At the end of his second journey, Enoch arrives at the Paradise of righteousness located in the very east of the world (*1 Enoch* 32:3), corresponding more or less to the Garden of Eden. He sees there many kinds of large, beautiful, sweet-smelling trees. Adam and Eve ate from the tree of knowledge and learned knowledge (32:6). The Tree of Life is described in *1 Enoch* 24–25 as located in the middle of seven mountains somewhere in the northwest, sometimes identified with a second Paradise. Its fruit will be for life, its fragrance will be in the bones of the elect, and the righteous will live a long life.

The Paradise of righteousness is also mentioned in the *Astronomical Book of Enoch* (*1 Enoch* 72–82), which was written in the second century B.C.E. It is part of a description of the three concentric parts of the world; Paradise seems to be located at the outer part (*1 Enoch* 77:3). The *Book of Parables* (*1 Enoch* 37–71), from the first century C.E. or slightly earlier, refers to the "garden of the righteous ones" (60:23), and the "garden of life" where the first fathers, the chosen, and the righteous dwell (61:12). This garden is located in the northwest (70:3-4) and is identified with the place where Enoch was taken up (60:6; cf. *Jub.* 4:23).

The Book of Jubilees

The book of *Jubilees,* written in the middle of the second century B.C.E., contains a rewriting and interpretation of Genesis 2–3 (*Jub.* 3:1-31). The events that happen in the Garden of Eden in the second week of creation are presented as a chronological continuation of the creation of the world which took place during the first week. The Garden of Eden itself is created on the third day of creation (2:7). Both Adam and Eve are created outside the Garden of Eden, and *Jubilees* delays the entrance of Adam and Eve into the garden by forty-eighty days in relation to the halakah concerning women giving birth. Because Eden is interpreted as a sanctuary, Temple laws are applied to the garden. Therefore Adam and Eve could not have sexual relations in the Garden of Eden. Adam is acting as a priest when he burns incense at the gate of the garden (3:27). Like the priests, Adam, too, is explicitly bidden to cover his nakedness. There is no reference to the Tree of Life. Therefore it is not necessary to mention the cherubim and the flaming sword guarding the way to this Tree of Life (Gen. 3:24). Finally, the expulsion scene in *Jubilees* is quite considerably toned down, in line with the tendency to minimize the negative side of Eden as much as possible. Paradise remains even after Adam and Eve have left the garden. The location is on earth. It is said that the floodwaters did not come onto any of its land (*Jub.* 4:24). When Noah divides the earth among his sons (*Jub.* 8:10–9:15), it is made clear that the Garden of Eden is the most eastern part of the territory of Shem (8:16; cf. 8:21). It is the "holy of holies" and one of the residences of the Lord on earth, alongside Zion and Mt. Sinai (8:19). These three holy places face one another, and are located at the axes of the world. In 4:26, the mountain of the east is also mentioned as the abode of God on earth. After Enoch was taken from human society, he was led into the Garden of Eden, where he wrote down the judgment and condemnation of the world (4:23).

Texts from Qumran

The story of the Garden of Eden (Genesis 2–3) is scarcely represented in the biblical manuscripts preserved, and seems not to have had a strong influence in the nonbiblical compositions found in the different caves of Qumran. No rewritings of the Eden narrative have been preserved, and only a few texts refer in passing to the Garden of Eden or the Tree of Knowledge (cf. 4Q303; 4Q305 col. ii; 4Q422, col. i; 4Q423 frg. 2 1-4; 4Q504 frg. 8). It appears that Genesis 2–3 was used most to expound on the relationship between male and female, and to express humanity's God-given authority over the earth. Several texts state that God gave knowledge and insight to Adam. No concern with the location and present or future function of Eden can be found. In 4Q265 the Garden of Eden is used as the basis for a halakic rule. The author of this text is using the story of Eden in the rewritten form found in *Jubilees*, and the main points are the same.

Sibylline Oracles

The first two books of the *Sibylline Oracles* contain Jewish oracles with a Christian redaction. The original Jewish oracles can probably be dated to about the turn of the era. The text of *Sib. Or.* 1.5-64 retells the story of the creation freely, although the general structure of the passage follows Genesis 1–3 quite closely. The first part (1.5-21) is concerned with the creation of the world until the creation of man. The second part (1.22-37) forms a parallel to Genesis 2. It describes the creation of man and woman in three stages: the making of the male in the image of God (1.22-23), the placing of the man in the garden (1.24-25), and the creation of the woman to satisfy the loneliness of the man (1.26-37). The creation and description of the garden are reduced to the words "an ambrosial garden" (1.25) and "the luxuriant plantation of the garden" (1.26). The third part (1.38-64) is concerned with the story of temptation and transgression and runs parallel with Genesis 3. The prohibition to eat from the tree forms the direct introduction to this part of the story (1.38-39). Although Eve is the one who persuades Adam to eat from the fruit of the tree (1.42-45), it is the serpent who is seen as the primary responsible being (1.39-41). He is in fact the only one who is cursed (1.59-64), whereas the curse on Adam and Eve is lightened very greatly because it is connected with the blessing of God (1.50-58).

2 Enoch

2 Enoch was written probably in the first century C.E., originally possibly in Greek, but has been passed down only in the Slavonic language. On the one hand, Paradise is the garden that according to Gen. 2:8 God planted on earth as a residence for Adam and Eve (30:1; 31:2, 6; 70:25; 71:28), enclosed with armed guards, angels aflame with fire on the third day of creation (30:1). The rewriting of Genesis 2–3 is integrated into the description of the sixth day of creation, when Adam and Eve were created and placed in the garden. On this very day they were also driven away (30:8–32:1). On the other hand, Paradise is a place in the beyond, sometimes specified as the third heaven (8:1–9:1; 42:3; 65:10; 66:8; 71:28; 72:1, 5, 9). It is then the abode of the just (9; 42:3; 65:10), and the place to which Melchizedek is transported (71:28; 72:1, 5, 9). The text speaks about the creation of the garden in the east (31:1), whereas Enoch ascended to the east into the Paradise of Eden, which is open as far as the third heaven (42:3). This is based on the depiction that the earthly garden of Eden is in direct connection with the heavenly Paradise. In *2 Enoch* 8:1–9:1, Enoch is sitting in the third heaven, and he is looking down at Paradise (8:1). A tree is rooted in the earthly garden and reaches up to the third heaven, where it covers the heavenly Paradise. The exit that leads to earth is probably the root of the tree in the Garden of Eden (8:4). The earthly Paradise is described as inconceivably pleasant. Trees are in full bloom, and their fruits are ripe and sweet-smelling (8:1-2). The geography of the rivers is somewhat different from that of the biblical text of Genesis. The four rivers come from two sources, two streams. In *2 Enoch*, the rivers seem to have already divided before they enter Paradise, and from there, when they leave Paradise and descend to the earth, they are divided again into 40 rivers. In the end they evaporate, and apparently return to Paradise in the form of rain, or perhaps mist (8:5-6).

The Greek Life of Adam and Eve

The *Life of Adam and Eve* is a Jewish or a Christian work, possibly from the second century C.E. It is preserved in several languages, including probably the original Greek. The reworking of Genesis 3 in the Greek version is a retelling of the story told in the form of two flashbacks, one by Adam (chaps. 7–8) and one, in a much more detailed way, by Eve (chaps. 15–30), both delivered at Adam's deathbed. Eve describes the situation in Paradise (chap. 15) and how Satan seduced the serpent (chap. 16), the serpent Eve (chaps. 17–19), and Eve her husband Adam (chap. 21). God returns to Paradise to judge Adam sitting in a chariot drawn by cherubim, while the archangel sounds the trumpet (chaps. 22–23). Thereupon, Adam, Eve and the serpent are condemned for their actions (chaps. 24–26). When the angels eject Adam and Eve from Paradise, Adam asks in vain to stay a little while in Paradise in order to beg God for mercy (chap. 27) and to be allowed to eat from the Tree of Life (chap. 28). However, he is allowed to take fragrances (crocus, nard, reed, cinnamon) from Paradise, so that after he has left he will be able to make an offering to God (chap. 29). Adam is taken into the Paradise in the third heaven, and he is buried together with his son Abel.

Josephus

In his *Jewish Antiquities* 1.35-51, Josephus rewrites the story of Genesis 2–3 to make the story intelligible to his Greek audience, although he did not refrain from telling of the formation of Eve from Adam's rib (*Ant.* 1.35) or the order to abstain from the Tree of Life (1.37). Josephus changes the order of biblical events by placing the creation of the first woman almost immediately after the creation of the first man (1.35), but still before the planting of the garden in the east (1.37). Josephus does not identify the location of the garden in Eden. He probably has no information about the precise location of Eden (1.37-38). The garden is watered by one river surrounding the entire earth. The conception of a stream, the Okeanos, flowing around the earth, is found among the Greeks from an early period (cf. Herodotus 2.23). Eve is made fully responsible for the fall, since both Adam and Eve were commanded by God not to eat of the tree (*Ant.* 1.40). In line with his misogynic tendencies, Josephus stresses that Adam's listening to the voice of his wife was folly (1.49). He has developed a picture of the original bliss of mankind, following a tradition found in Hesiod, that men lived without sorrow of heart, remote and free from toil and grief (1.46). The notion of food springing up spontaneously is mentioned several times (1.46, 49, 54). In Josephus, it is God and not Adam who gives names to the animals (1.35). Josephus has omitted the biblical statement that God made coats of skin for Adam and Eve. He has likewise left out the reference to the cherubim that God placed at the entrance to the garden.

4 Ezra

The term "Paradise" (Garden of Eden) seems to occur in various senses in *4 Ezra,* a work from the late first century C.E. In 3:4-7, the garden occurs in a short retelling of the story of Genesis 2–3. Adam was put into this garden, which God had planted with his right hand. When Adam transgressed the commandment, God appointed death for him and for his descendants (3:7). We have here the oldest attestation of the idea that Paradise was created before the creation of the world (3:6; cf. 6:2). The other use of the term is in the context of eschatological reward for the righteous (7:123; 8:52). In 7:36, Paradise is the place of delight and located opposite Gehenna. Perhaps 4:7-8 also reflects a view of an existing Paradise in heaven. Little information is offered about the nature of this Paradise. Certain elements of Genesis 2 are connected with the heavenly Paradise, for example, the incorruptible fruit (7:123) and the Tree of Life (8:52).

Pseudo-Philo

Pseudo-Philo's *Biblical Antiquities,* a Jewish work probably written in the first half of the second century C.E., contains a short reference to the events in Paradise shown in a revelation to Moses (*Bib. Ant.* 13:8). God says that Adam could have remained there had he not sinned. God recalls that Adam transgressed since he was persuaded by his wife, who was deceived by the serpent, with the result that death was decreed for all. A passing reference to Adam in Paradise may be found in 26:6: "He created Adam as the first created one and showed him everything so that when Adam sinned thereby, then he might refuse all these things." During the establishment of the covenant on Mt. Sinai, Paradise gave off "the scent of its fruit, and the cedars of Lebanon were shaken from their roots" (32:8).

Other Texts

A few other texts refer to the Garden of Eden or to Paradise. As an earthly place, it occurs in the *Apocalypse of Abraham,* where the Garden of Eden is shown to Abraham in a vision: "the Garden of Eden and its fruits, and the source and the river flowing from it, and its trees and their flowering, making fruits, and I saw men doing justice in it, their food and their rest" (*Apoc. Abr.* 21:6), and in *3 Baruch,* where an angel tells Baruch that the floodwaters entered Paradise and killed every flower, but removed the sprig of the vine completely and brought it outside (*3 Bar.* 4:10). Both as an earthly and heavenly location, it appears in *2 Bar.* 4:3-6, where it is said that the New Jerusalem and Paradise were shown to Adam but removed from him when he sinned. The similarity between the tabernacle and Paradise is preserved by God. Other texts locate Paradise in heaven as an eschatological dwelling place for the righteous. In the *Testament of Abraham* (recension A), Michael brings Abraham toward the east, to the first gate of heaven, where he sees "the gate of the righteous, which leads to life, and those who enter through it come into paradise" (*T. Abr.* 11:10). In the *Testament of Levi* (18:10) it is said that God "shall open the gates of paradise; he shall remove the sword that has threatened since Adam, and he will grant to the saints to eat of the tree of life" (18:10-11). In the *Testament of Dan* the saints refresh themselves in Eden (5:12).

BIBLIOGRAPHY
J. L. KUGEL 1998, *Traditions of the Bible: A Guide to the Bible As It Was at the Start of the Common Era,* Cambridge: Harvard University Press, 93-144. • G. P. LUTTIKHUIZEN, ED. 1999, *Paradise Interpreted: Representations of Biblical Paradise in Judaism and Christianity,* Leiden: Brill. • G. P. LUTTIKHUIZEN, ED. 2000, *The Creation of Man and Woman: Interpretation of the Biblical Narratives in Jewish and Christian Traditions,* Leiden: Brill. • J. VAN RUITEN 2000, *Primaeval History Interpreted: The Rewriting of Genesis 1–11 in the Book of Jubilees,* Leiden: Brill.
JACQUES VAN RUITEN

Gematria

Gematria is a numerological technique that consists of calculating the numerical value of a word or a phrase by adding up the values of all its letters, often in order to find or demonstrate the supposed relations between different words and concepts by proving the equivalence of their gematria values.

The use of letters to designate numerals (e.g., in Hebrew *ʾālep* = 1, *bêt* = 2 . . . *yōd* = 10, *kap* = 20 . . . *qôp* = 100, *rêš* = 200, etc.) seems to have been a Greek invention, and the calculation of the numerical value of whole words, though attested already in ancient Mesopotamia, was borrowed by the Jews from the Greek world. In Greek, the technique was mostly known as *isopsephos* (literally, "of equal numerical value") and was used, for example, by the opponents of a certain Damagoras to prove that "Damagoras" = "a pest" *(loimos)* (*Greek Anthology* 11.334) and by professional dream interpreters to prove that when a sick person dreams of an old lady the dream foretells his death, since "old lady" *(graus)* = 704 = "burial" *(hēekphora)* (Artemidorus, *Oneirocriticon* 4.24).

Another Greek term, *geōmetrikos arithmos* (literally, "geometric number"), was used in a numerological sense in some neo-Pythagorean and neo-Platonic circles in the Hellenistic and Roman periods, and this may have been the source of the Jewish name for this technique, *gemaṭria.* Moreover, the exegetical uses of such techniques were well known to Greek and Oriental grammarians, as may be seen, for example, from Apion's claim that the *Iliad* began with the word "wrath" *(mēnin)* because the first two letters of that word equal 48, the number of books in the *Iliad* and the *Odyssey* combined (Seneca, *Epistles* 88.40).

That the Jews borrowed this technique from the Greek world may also explain why its first attested appearances in Jewish sources are in the NT book of Revelation and in *3 Baruch,* two works written by Greek-speaking Jews, and why in both texts gematrias are used to calculate the numerical values, according to the Hebrew alphabet, of Greek (and Latin) names and words. Thus the most famous example — the "number of the beast" in Rev. 13:18, calculated as 666 — seems to be based on the gematria sum of the letters making up the Hebrew spelling of the name of Nero(n) Caesar, the Roman emperor: *nûn* (50) + *rêš* (200) + *waw* (6) + *nûn* (50) + *qôp* (100) + *samek* (60) + *rêš* (200) = 666. In another Judeo-Greek text, the *Fifth Sibylline Oracle* (lines 12-51), we find a list of Roman emperors identified by the gematria value of the first letters of their names; this too is a well-known technique in the writing of Greek oracles (see Lucian, *Alexander* 11 and *Sib. Or.* 1.137-46).

While the earliest Jewish uses of this technique may have been limited to Greek-speaking Jews, it soon was adopted by their Hebrew- and Aramaic-speaking brethren, and is explicitly mentioned, and used, by rabbis of the second century C.E. (but note the claim in *b. Sukkah* 28a concerning Yoḥanan ben Zakkai's knowledge of gematria, which would push it back to the first century C.E.). The rabbis even recognized gematria as one of the thirty-two "measures" (exegetical techniques) by which the Torah may be expounded, thus granting this technique a canonical status within the Jewish exegetical tradition. And yet, the use of this technique in rabbinic literature is rather limited; in the realm of halakah, it was sometimes used to prop up well-known rulings that had no explicit biblical support (see, e.g., *b. Nazir* 5a); in the realm of haggadah, it was used mainly as a colorful embellishment to rabbinic sermons (e.g., *b. Niddah* 38b), or to counter the christological demonstrations of early Christian exegesis. In the best-known example, the Christian *Epistle of Barnabas* 9:8 insists that the reference in Gen. 14:14 to Abraham's 318 armed men, a number written in Greek as *TIH,* in fact points to the cross and to the first two letters of the name of Jesus, whereas the rabbis claim that 318 is the gematria value of "Eliezer," thus proving that the verse in fact referred only to Abraham's faithful servant (*b. Nedarim* 32a; *Gen. Rab.* 42:2 [Theodor-Albeck, p. 416]).

In later rabbinic literature, and especially in the writings of medieval and later Kabbalah, gematria became much more prominent, and many new types of gematrias were developed (e.g., using the numerical value of each letter by adding up the value of the letters used to spell it out, so that *yōd,* for example, equals *yōd* [10] + *wāw* [6] + *dālet* [4] = 20). The proliferation of many different types of gematria calculations enabled the adept to discover many new relations and equivalences between otherwise unrelated words and phrases, thus increasing its utility for its users, but also exposing it to severe attacks from its many critics (such as Rabbi Leo Modena, *Ari Nohem,* chap. 10). In the modern Jewish world, such gematrias remain widely popular in some Jewish circles, as a playful pastime, as a major exegetical tool, or as a means with which to dazzle the ignorant.

BIBLIOGRAPHY
G. BOHAK 1990, "Greek-Hebrew Gematrias in *3 Baruch* and Revelation," *JSP* 7: 119-21. • F. DORNSEIFF 1925, *Das Alphabet in Mystik und Magie,* 2d ed., Leipzig: Teubner, 91-118. • G. SCHOLEM 1971, "Gematria," *EncJud* 7: 369-74 (rpt. in idem, *Kabbalah,* Jerusalem: Keter, 1974, 337-43). • S. SAMBURSKY 1978, "On the Origin and Significance of the Term *Gematria,*" *JJS* 29: 35-38. • S. J. LIEBERMAN 1987, "A Mesopotamian Background for the So-Called *Aggadic* 'Measures' of Biblical Hermeneutics?" *HUCA* 58: 157-225.
GIDEON BOHAK

Genealogies

Genealogies (Heb. *tôlĕdôt*) are records, either oral or written, of a person or persons from a single ancestor or ancestors. The Hebrew Bible contains two major sections of genealogies: one in Genesis, consisting of the foundation genealogies; the other in the postexilic books of Chronicles, Ezra, and Nehemiah, presenting the genealogical material in Genesis as well as new genealogical lists. Genealogies also appear in the New Testament, in the Gospels of Matthew and Luke. These types of records have been found throughout Mesopotamia and Egypt as well as ancient Greece and Rome.

Categories of Genealogies

Genealogies fall into two broad categories, both in written and oral form. The first type is referred to as a segmented genealogy, also called horizontal or lateral genealogy, where two or more lines of descent come from a single ancestor (e.g., 1 Chron. 1:5-27). This type of genealogy allows for members from one lineage to be linked to a common ancestor. Segmented genealogies can function as a way to highlight relationships, both social and political, between people, clans, towns, regions, and other places (Knoppers 2004: 247).

The second type of genealogy is called a linear or vertical genealogy. This type concentrates on a single line from one ancestor to his descendants, with a clear vertical line tying the names together (e.g., Ezra 7:1-5). Unlike segmented genealogies, linear genealogies provide only a limited amount of information, such as the right of inheritance, power, status, or position of an individual. In a few cases, these types of genealogical structures are not mutually exclusive but work together, as in 1 Chron. 5:27–6:65 (6:1-80). Genealogies are listed in either a descending line, from parent to child, or an ascending line from child to parent.

Genealogies in the Hebrew Bible

In postexilic Israel, genealogies played an important role in fostering a social organization based on kinship groups. All together, they serve several purposes:

To Show the Relationship between Israel and Its Neighbors

The assertion of common ancestry was intended to highlight the differences between Israel and its neighbors. This purpose is reflected in the genealogical material in Genesis and also in 1 Chron. 1:5-27, which lists the descendants of Noah — Shem, Ham, and Japheth. In this case, Noah's sons also represent regions or lands. Thus, this genealogy has a dual purpose: to list the children of Noah and to provide a list of his children in order to outline the emergence of different people groups. In 1 Chron. 2:1, Israel finally appears in the biblical text as a person as well as the father of a people group, after the surrounding nations have already been established.

To Legitimize a Hierarchy or Status

The importance of one's ancestry helped shape social status and ultimately identity. Examples of genealogies to legitimize positions are found in 1 Chron. 5:27-41; 9:11-16; Ezra 7:1-5; and Neh. 11:11-19. This type of list seems to have been of great importance only when the family line was connected to cultic roles, such as the priestly or levitical lines (Johnson 1988: 79).

To Assert the Purity of a Group of People

In Ezra and Nehemiah a genealogy is commonly employed in order to legitimize one group over another. Ezra and Nehemiah provide several different lists, with the clear goal of recording the priests and Levites who were considered appropriate to participate in cultic life. There are also examples of genealogies that delegitimize people from their place in the community. Both Ezra and Nehemiah use genealogies to "demote" a priest from his position. In Ezra 2:61-63, the descendants of the priestly line of Habaiah, Hakkoz, and Barzillai "looked for their entries in the genealogical records, but they were not found there, and so they were excluded from the priesthood as unclean" (see also Neh. 7:63-65). They were then told to consult the Urim and Thummim, or to have their case reviewed before they could resume their duties. In the Hebrew Bible, the books of Ezra and Nehemiah are the most concerned with the use of genealogies to show true ancestry (Johnson 1988: 43). This interest became all the more important in the Second Temple period.

To Distinguish Historical Periods of Time

An effort to distinguish historical epochs is found in 1 Chron. 5:27-41 (6:1-15), where the priestly line is split into the priests from the period of the exodus to the time of the building of the Temple by Solomon, and from Solomon to the Exile. Such a splitting serves as a way to base a genealogy on historical events and thus place it into a specific context. It is difficult, however, to use this type of genealogy for reconstruction purposes, since textual traditions often reflect discrepancies and since this type of list is a symbolic contrivance.

Genealogies in Early Judaism

In early Judaism great importance was placed on ancestry and pure genealogical lines, especially concerning the priesthood. The books of Ezra, Nehemiah, and 1 Esdras reflect a concern for ritual purity that continues through the Second Temple period. This is evident in the writings of Josephus, who highlights the importance of ancestry, particularly for the priestly class. In defense of his historical methodology and the records he draws upon, Josephus emphasizes the significance of proper record-keeping, specifically concerning the priestly genealogies:

> Not only did our ancestors in the first instance set over this business men of the highest character, devoted to the service of God, but they took precautions to ensure that the priests' lineage should be kept unadulterated and pure. A member of the priestly order must, to beget a family, marry a woman of his own race, without regard to her wealth

> or other distinctions; but he must investigate her pedigree, obtaining the genealogy from the archives and producing a number of witnesses. And this practice of ours is not confined to the home country of Judea, but wherever there is a Jewish colony, there too a strict account is kept by the priest of their marriage. (*Ag. Ap.* 1.7)

Thus, according to Josephus, genealogies of the priestly families were kept in all major Jewish centers, including Jerusalem and in certain Diaspora communities, such as Egypt and Babylon, in order to facilitate proper marriages. Later rabbinic traditions also reflect the value assigned to a "pure" genealogy for priestly families. The presence of the mother in genealogies became increasingly prominent in Second Temple Judaism and is reflected in the New Testament, specifically in the genealogy of Jesus in Matt. 1:1-17.

Genealogies in the New Testament

In contrast to the Hebrew Bible, the New Testament rarely has genealogies. The two most complete genealogies, in Matt. 1:1-17 and Luke 3:23-38, deal with the ancestry of Jesus.

Matthew 1:1-17 provides a genealogy (Gr. *genealogica*) that lists Jesus' ancestors from Abraham to Joseph. This linear genealogy includes four women in the line of descent — Tamar, Rahab, Ruth, and Bathsheba, the wife of Uriah the Hittite. All four of these women were non-Israelites, and all of them had questionable sexual histories. Together these features prepare for the inclusion of Gentiles in the people of God and for the unusual circumstances of Mary's virginal conception. Matthew's genealogy is also notable for dividing history into three distinct periods, characterized by fourteen generations each. This is clearly stated in v. 17, which asserts, "So all the generations from Abraham to David are fourteen generations and from David to the deportation to Babylon, fourteen generations, and from the deportation to Babylon to the messiah fourteen generations." To arrive at the number *fourteen,* Matthew had to omit several generations of figures named in 1 Chronicles.

Luke 3:23-38 employs a linear genealogical record, but in reverse order, beginning with Jesus and ending with Adam, the "son of God." The genealogy starts by giving Jesus' age at the beginning of his ministry. Luke lists more names between Jesus and Abraham than Matthew does, and from Jesus to David most of Luke's names differ from those in Matthew's list. In contrast to Matthew's list, Luke's record does not trace Jesus' line through kings, contains no women, and has eleven series of seven names each, for a total of seventy-seven names. The genealogy in Luke is closely tied with Jesus' baptism, an event narrated earlier in the chapter, in order to secure Jesus' status as Israel's prophet-messiah and son of God.

BIBLIOGRAPHY

R. E. BROWN 1973, *The Birth of the Messiah,* Garden City, N.Y.: Doubleday. • C. T. DAVIS 1973, "The Fulfillment of Creation: A Study of Matthew's Genealogy," *JAAR* 41: 520-35. • M. D. JOHNSON 1988, *The Purpose of Biblical Genealogies,* 2d. ed., Oxford: Oxford University Press. • G. N. KNOPPERS 2004, *I Chronicles 1–9,* New York: Doubleday. • G. RENDSBURG 1990, "The Internal Consistency and Historical Reliability of the Biblical Genealogies," *VT* 40: 185-206. • J. SASSON 1978, "A Genealogical 'Convention' in Biblical Chronography?" *ZAW* 90: 171-85. • H. G. M. WILLIAMSON 1977, *Israel in the Book of Chronicles,* Cambridge: Cambridge University Press. • R. R. WILSON 1977, *Genealogy and History in the Biblical World,* New Haven: Yale University Press.

DEIRDRE N. FULTON

Genesis and Exodus, Commentary on (4Q422)

Among the fragmentary works from Qumran Cave 4 is a document (4Q422) that reworks passages from Genesis and Exodus. The principal fragments of this poorly preserved manuscript share several features which justify their association: the same scribal hand (typologically Hasmonean; late second or early first century B.C.E.), similar shapes indicating that they were preserved lying on top of one another, similar coloration and translucence, indications of two layers of writing (frgs. 2, 3, 4, 8, 10d and 10e), and above average line length (ca. 85 letter spaces). Fragment 4 has the same shape as the upper part of frg. 10a, and one of its very partially preserved words is discernible more readily on the back of frg. 10a; poorly legible letters on frg. 1 are similarly discernible on the back of frg. 2. The similar features and the way the turns of the manuscript can be reconstructed on the basis of the preservation of writing on the back of some fragments has given the editors confidence to suggest what the first three columns of the manuscript might have looked like.

The remains of the first three columns of this *Commentary on Genesis and Exodus* are a selected reworking of the early parts of Genesis and Exodus. There was no attempt to offer a rewritten form of all of Genesis; the first two columns present material summarily from Genesis 1–9. In the first column there is a paraphrase of the two accounts of creation; a couple of lines represent the end of Genesis 1, and then, after mention of God's Holy Spirit, there is a series of allusions to a summary of the narrative of Adam and Eve in the Garden of Eden and their disobedience. It is as if the two creation accounts have been woven together and harmonized. Several other compositions from Qumran's Cave 4 have very similar concerns in summarizing Genesis 1–3, especially *Meditation on Creation A*[a] (4Q303). In 4Q422 the disobedience of Adam and Eve in the first instance leads swiftly to comments on the evil inclination of Gen. 6:5 and thence to the judgment displayed in the flood, just as Pharaoh's hardness of heart leads swiftly to the plagues.

The third column mentions the midwives of Exod. 1:15-21, the throwing of the sons of the Israelites into the Nile, the sending of Moses and his vision of God in the burning bush, and the mission of Moses and Aaron at Pharaoh's court; then come the descriptions of the plagues in more detail.

One wonders why the exposition's compiler jumped from the immediate aftermath of the flood narrative to the description of the events leading up to the Exodus. One possibility is that both the flood and the plagues can be understood as destructive judgmental reversals of creation that lead to the salvation of new creations, first of humankind, second of Israel. In 4Q422 col. 2 the story of the flood is followed directly by a paraphrase of creation motifs in Genesis 9 that are a reiteration of Genesis 1. This theological parallelism of destruction and new creation might be most evident in 4Q422 col. 3, line 7, where the hardening of Pharaoh's heart is done so that Israel would know it "for eternal generations." The same purpose is assigned the covenantal rainbow in Gen. 9:12 (4Q422 col. 2, lines 10-11): it is for "eternal generations."

For the plagues 4Q422 follows the order of Exodus for the first five; for the last three the order is that of Ps. 105:32-36 (hail, locusts, death of firstborn). The language of the description is often closest to the phrasing of Psalm 78. The descriptions are poetically presented as in Psalms 78 and 105. The proximity of much of the language and form of this section to the Psalms and to some other liturgical texts (cf. 4Q392; 4Q501) makes it possible that the rewritten form of Exodus was dependent in some way on its use in a cultic context such as Passover.

There are a further twenty small fragments assigned to the manuscript that have not as yet been put in suitable places in the composition; indeed, some may belong to other compositions.

BIBLIOGRAPHY

T. ELGVIN 1994, "The Genesis Section of 4Q422 (4QparaGen-Exod)," *DSD* 1: 180-96. • T. ELGVIN AND E. TOV 1994, "422: 4QParaphrase of Genesis and Exodus," in H. Attridge et al., *Qumran Cave 4.VIII: Parabiblical Texts, Part 1,* DJD 13, Oxford: Clarendon Press, 417-41. • T. ELGVIN AND E. TOV 2005, "4Q422 (4QParaphrase of Gen and Exod)," in *Parabiblical Texts,* ed. D. W. Parry and E. Tov, Leiden: Brill, 570-77. • D. PETERS 2006, "Noah in the Dead Sea Scrolls," Dissertation, University of Manchester. • E. TOV 1994, "The Exodus Section of 4Q422," *DSD* 1: 197-209. • E. TOV 1995, "A Paraphrase of Exodus: 4Q422," in *Solving Riddles and Untying Knots: Biblical, Epigraphic, and Semitic Studies in Honor of Jonas C. Greenfield,* ed. Z. Zevit, S. Gitin, and M. Sokoloff, Winona Lake, Ind.: Eisenbrauns, 351-63.

GEORGE J. BROOKE

Genesis Apocryphon

The *Genesis Apocryphon* (1Q20 or 1QapGen) is one of the first seven scrolls discovered in Cave 1 at Qumran, and the final one to be unrolled. The scroll, opened in 1956, contains the remains of twenty-two columns but was originally longer. The sheet to the right of col. 22 was clearly cut away in antiquity, its text breaking off in the middle of a sentence. It is now generally accepted that some fragments survived from at least one column before col. 1, which has been labeled col. 0. The work is an Aramaic composition that rewrites Gen. 5:18–15:5 — with additions, omissions, and expansions to the narratives. It covers the material from Enoch to Abram's vision of the stars. The work is generally dated to the second or first century B.C.E., but an earlier date in the third century B.C.E. should not be ruled out.

Narrative Technique

The author of 1QapGen rewrites and rearranges the material found in Genesis in order to tell the story more smoothly, and to embed answers to unasked questions within its narrative. In the approach taken by the author or his sources, the nature of the rewriting is uneven, with much more extrabiblical material, and much less actual biblical interpretation, being furnished in the earlier portions of the stories of Enoch and Noah than in the final four columns devoted to the story of Abram. The central character in each section narrates in the first person, a storytelling technique that contributes to the vividness of the narrative. Only in the last segment of 1QapGen, beginning with the material parallel to Genesis 14, does the narration move to third person. Another stylistic hallmark of 1QapGen is its employment of biblical idiom in its composition, but not necessarily in the contexts where the idiom occurs in the Bible. At times the use of biblical language indicates a harmonization or rearrangement of material to resolve exegetical or interpretive difficulties.

It is generally agreed that the Aramaic texts found at Qumran were not composed by the Qumran sect, so 1QapGen might belong to the common Jewish literature of the Second Temple era. When describing Noah's celebration of the production of wine from his new vineyard in the fifth year, rather than the fourth (col. 12), 1QapGen coincides with sectarian, rather than later rabbinic practice. On the other hand, the reference to endogamy in Noah's choosing his children's spouses (col. 6) may point to general Second Temple, and not necessarily sectarian, practice.

The Enoch Cycle

The surviving text of 1QapGen can be divided into three cycles: the Enoch cycle, the Noah cycle and the Abram cycle. This division is supported by the physical marker of blank lines left between the cycles, that is, in col. 5 line 28, at the end of the Enoch cycle, and in col. 18 line 23, at the end of the Noah cycle. Since the beginning and end of the scroll have not been preserved, it might have originally included additional cycles. From the extant text, we can see a well-written story, with smoothly connected individual components that employ shared themes and terminology. Thus, each cycle does not seem to be an independent composition taken from written sources and just introduced to the 1QapGen. This, in turn, does not exclude the possibility of its use of earlier sources, which is probably the case in the Enoch cycle, where clear connection with 1 Enoch is found. It would seem that this literary technique could be termed a "chain of traditions." The way the story is told, Enoch, like Noah, struggles with a sinful generation, here of the Fallen Angels and their sinful offspring. Enoch seems to be singled out as the only righ-

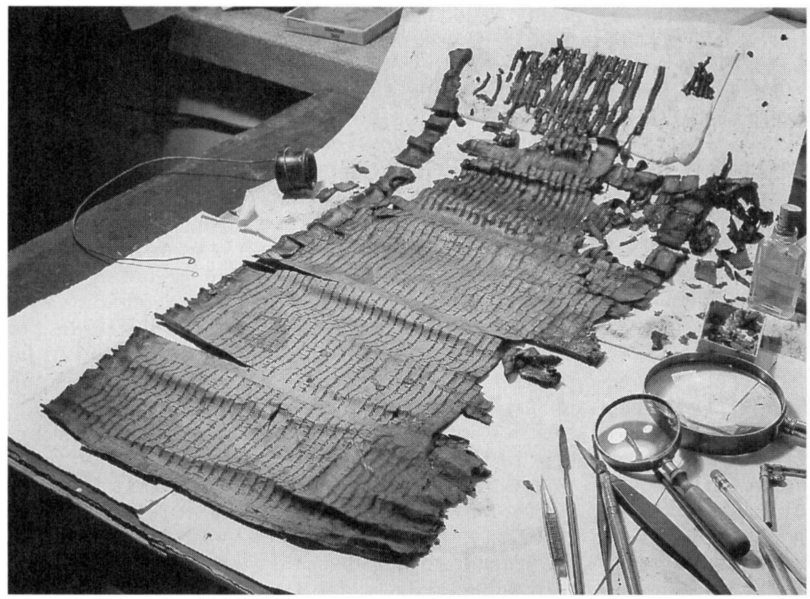

The Aramaic Genesis Apocryphon (1Q20 or 1QapGen) found in Cave 1 near Qumran *(Israel Museum)*

teous person, as Abram will later be singled out with respect to Sodom, serving as the mediator between the sinners and God, bringing their appeal to heaven. Like Abram, Enoch too has immediate communication with God, having various visions regarding the future of humanity, to be compared with Genesis 15. By the same token, Noah is described in terms similar to Abram, being the ultimate righteous individual who has visions regarding the future of humanity. Furthermore, not only does the author use parallels between the main three characters, but within these cycles one also finds secondary characters, which serve transitional functions. Each of these is used as a link connecting the former and later main figures, thus creating even closer connections between the cycles. Thus one might characterize the figure of Lamech as a secondary figure who serves as the link between Enoch and Noah, by appealing to Enoch in regard to Noah's miraculous birth. The end of the Noah cycle and the beginning of the Abraham cycle have not survived, but based on the Noah story, we might tentatively expect parts of cols. 17-18 to be devoted to the figure of Shem as a "secondary character."

As for the Enoch cycle, one might suspect that col. 0 was preceded by additional passages devoted to the story of the Fallen Angels, which together with the surviving reference to this myth might be added to other such compositions found in the Qumran library. It is worth noting in this context that references to the Watchers are found on numerous occasions in the surviving parts of this composition — not only in the Enoch cycle, especially in col. 0-1, but also in the words of Lamech (2:1, 16) and probably in the words of Enoch referring to "the days of Jared my father" (3:3), and in his answer to Methuselah (5:3-4). The Watchers also appear in Noah's vision (6:19-20). The Enoch cycle appears to be closely related to *1 Enoch* and *Jubilees.* Their genetic relationships need to be studied further.

The Noah Cycle

The Noah cycle begins with the title "A [cop]y of the words of Noah" (5:29). While some detailed descriptions included in this part expand upon a very short biblical base, such as Noah's righteousness mentioned in Gen. 6:9, other elements have no parallel at all, not only in Genesis, but also in other parallel accounts, such as *1 Enoch* and *Jubilees.* Another significant difference is that Noah is described only in a positive way, as an observer of the Law. Thus, the biblical description of Noah being drunk and shamed is reinterpreted in cols. 12–15 in an opposite manner, where Noah is described as having a set of symbolic dream visions.

In contrast to its biblical source, one outstanding feature of Noah's biography in 1QapGen is the large number of divine communications to Noah, including dreams. Some of these are nonsymbolic dreams, which contain immediately comprehensible divine instructions. In cols. 6–7, this type of dream is associated with the antediluvian period, mainly the fall of the Watchers, while the second type, the symbolic dream visions, is covered in cols. 13–15. In the first antediluvian vision (6:11-12), God appears to Noah, and he "is shown and informed about the conduct of the sons of heaven" (6:11), a mystery he then hides and doesn't tell anyone. Next, Noah is visited by "[an em]issary of the Great Holy One" (6:15) who seems to explain to him the Watchers' behavior and its result in the bloodshed of the Nefilim. Thus, this vision and Noah's communication with God which follows, seems to explain to him the reasons why God decided to destroy the world as a result of the Fallen Angels' deeds. What is left of this vision is nonsymbolic in nature. It might have been followed by another heavenly communication, maybe including building instructions (see 7:19-20). The second set of symbolic dream visions in cols. 13–14 is poorly preserved, including at least three separate dreams. In composing this dream sequence, the author of 1QapGen did not follow one specific biblical source; rather, he drew the various images found in these visions from different biblical visions belonging to this genre. The first dream refers both to an object made of gold, silver, stone, and pottery as well as iron, from which everyone is breaking off pieces, and to trees: "chopping every tree and taking it for themselves" (13:8). This dream bears striking parallels to Nebuchadnezzar's dreams of the statue made of iron and clay in Daniel 2, and of the great tree in Daniel 4. The second dream vision concerns a large olive tree, which is being destroyed by the "[four] winds of heaven" (13:16). This reference to the "[four] winds of heaven" is related to Belshazzar's dream of the four beasts in Daniel 7. The third, and most significant, is the cedar tree dream. It combines both the element of symbolic use of the cedar for persons, and prediction of future events. The details of the dream itself have not been preserved; it can, however, be reconstructed from its partially preserved interpretation. In this dream Noah sees a large cedar tree, with three branches. The interpretation of the dream identifies the different parts of the tree. Thus Noah is the cedar, and the three shoots are Noah's three sons. Shem can be identified as the first scion, described as "coming forth from the cedar and having grown to a height" (14:10). The further characterization of Shem as "the first scion reaching to the stump of the cedar" (14:11), which is interpreted in this son's name-midrash, introduces the metaphor of an upright planting. The cedar dream vision of 1QapGen also contains predictive elements. It foretells the future of Ham and Japheth, according to which they will depart from their father, moving "left," that is north, and "right," to the south. This probably refers to Japheth going to Europe, and Ham to Africa, as implemented in the division of the world described in cols. 16–17. After a blank space in the text we find yet another development involving prediction in the cedar image. Using the image of "some of their boughs entering into the midst of the first one" (14:17), 1QapGen foresees acts of aggression to be conducted by the descendants of Ham and Japheth against Shem. This part of the vision probably refers to the period when Canaan inhabited the southern part of Syria. *Jubilees* 10:28-34 describes how Canaan violently seized "the land of Lebanon as far as the river of Egypt." Originally assigned to Shem, because Ham takes this land, he is cursed by his father and brothers. Furthermore, according to *Jubilees,* Madai, one of Japheth's sons, negotiated with Shem's sons Elam, Asshur, and Arpachshad to be allowed to settle within the patrimony of Shem (*Jub.* 10:35). No reference to the conflict or negotiations between the brothers has been preserved in the columns of 1QapGen treating the division of the world among Noah's descendants. Finally, the last part of the Noah cycle is the division of the land. Two columns at least — cols. 16 and 17 and perhaps some of the almost unpreserved col. 18 — are devoted to the division of the earth among Noah's sons. Accordingly, the author of the Noah story gives considerable weight to this topic.

The division of the world among Noah's sons and grandsons is described in 1QapGen (cols. 16–17), *Jubilees* (8–9), and Josephus (*Ant.* 1.122-47). A comparison of these sources reflects both reliance on Genesis 10 and a shared cartographical basis for their construction of the world, namely, an updated version of the ancient, sixth-century-B.C.E. Ionian world map, based on Dicaearchus' (ca. 326-296 B.C.E.) division of the world by a median running through the Pillars of Hercules, the Taurus Mountains, and the Himalayas. Of these texts, it seems that 1QapGen is the oldest surviving Second Temple period text mapping the inhabited world. Both *Jubilees* and 1QapGen provide detailed descriptions of each son's allotment, with many parallels including shared terminology, mainly land-related terms taken from Joshua 15. Nevertheless, there are significant differences between 1QapGen and *Jubilees,* some of which enable us to draw conclusions with regard to the interrelationship of these texts. The most crucial difference lies in the actual lots given to each son and in the prominence *Jubilees* ascribes to Jerusalem. According to *Jubilees,* Shem received all of Asia Minor, together with Syria, Phoenicia, and Palestine, whereas, according to 1QapGen, the region of Asia Minor belonged to Japheth. In that respect, 1QapGen accords with the map of Shem's lot according to Josephus (*Ant.* 1.122). Moreover, the surviving text of 1QapGen documents no concept of Jerusalem's superiority. In Lud's allotment, 1QapGen mentions "the Sea of the East" (17:10). The "Sea of the East" can be identified as the "Mauq Sea" in *Jubilees,* the present-day Sea of Azov. This reference to the Sea of the East reflects the orientation from Greece, with Delphi at the center. Thus, as opposed to *Jubilees,* which converts the Ionian map to a Jewish perspective, placing Jerusalem at the center of the world, 1QapGen retains the focus of the original Ionian map. Only someone using Greece as a reference point could refer to the Sea of Azov as the "Sea of the East." Some scholars suggest that the author of *Jubilees* utilized and adapted 1QapGen to his needs, or that both authors used a common source. It seems that 1QapGen is the older source and the original Ionian map can still be traced in it. This text was later used by the author of *Jubilees,* and he converted it to fit his Jewish perspective, awarding Shem the major portion and function — as he received all of Asia Minor, together with Syria, Phoenicia, and Palestine — and placing Jerusalem at the center of the world.

The Abram Cycle

The transition from the Noah portion to the Abram cycle apparently occurred in col. 18:25. The portion of 1QapGen devoted to the early adventures of Abram (cols. 19-22) is far better preserved than the segment dealing with the earlier material in Genesis, and it also differs from it in its handling of the biblical material, adhering much more closely to the biblical story-line. As we have seen in the Noah cycle, the author shows knowledge of the land of Israel's geography. Thus, based on the account of Gen. 13:14, the author of 1QapGen adds the command to go up "to Ramat-Hazor" (21:8). Ramat Hazor is the mountain identified with Baal Hazor (2 Sam. 13:23), which is about 8 km. northeast of Bethel. This is the highest place in Samaria, from which one can see Transjordan, the Mediterranean Sea, and the hills in the south.

Columns 19–20 give an elaborate retelling of the sojourn of Abram and Sarai in Egypt. The visit of Abram and Sarai to Egypt is expanded at a number of points, but the story retains its fundamental shape. In the biblical account we do not hear how the Egyptian officials came to meet Abram and Sarai, but it does mention their fascination with Sarai's beauty (Gen. 12:14-15), and they give gifts to Abram because of Sarai (12:16). This story raises a few exegetical questions, mainly concerning Abram's behavior, but also Sarai's exceptional beauty, taking into consideration her advanced age (she was already sixty-five when they first came to Canaan). Thus, according to 1QapGen, on the way to Egypt Abram had a symbolic dream. In his dream Abram saw a cedar, which people were trying to cut down, and a palm tree, which was left alone. But the palm tree cried out, saying: "'Do not cut down the tree, for we are both sprung from one stock.' So the cedar was spared by the protection of the palm tree" (19:16). This dream warns of impending danger to Sarai when they enter Egypt and thus serves as a justification for Abram's subsequent deceptive behavior. The result of this dream was a delay of their descent to Egypt for five years. Before descending to Egypt, they are said to live in Hebron, which was built only two years earlier (19:9). By adding that chronology, the text makes use of Num. 13:22: "Now Hebron was built seven years before Zoan in Egypt." The same tradition is found in *Jub.* 13:12: "Now Tanis in Egypt was built at that time — seven years after Hebron," and echoed in Josephus (*Ant.* 1.170). During that period we hear of Abram's wisdom; when the Egyptian nobles came to Abram, "[. . . They as]ked erudition and wisdom and truth for themselves," and Abram said, "So I read before them the book of the words of Enoch" (19:24-25). It is then that the nobles probably realized Sarai's special appearance. Basing themselves on Gen 12:15, ancient sources (e.g., Philo, *De Abrahamo* 91–98) as well as medieval commentators referred to the beauty of Sarai. But the most remarkable description is found in 1QapGen (20:2-8), which presents a poetic description of her beauty modeled on the style of the Song of Songs (as well as the ideal women described in Prov. 31:10-31), as reported by the nobles of Pharaoh. In it they describe her beauty and her wisdom, as well as her domestic skill. The poem concludes: "Above all women her beauty is greatest; her beauty is far above them all. Together with all this beauty there is much wisdom in her, and whatever she does with her hands is perfect" (20:6-8). Sarai is then taken from Abram "by force" (20:11), thus "I Abram wept bitterly in the night — I and Lot. . . . That night I prayed and entreated and asked for mercy" (20:11-12), which is then followed by Abram's prayer.

Sarai's stay with Pharaoh is specified as two years in length, and Pharaoh's afflictions are said to be due to an evil spirit, which smote him and his household. Only after Abram lays hands upon him and prays for him is Pharaoh relieved of divine punishment (20:16-29). It was only then, after Sarai was returned to Abram, that Pharaoh gave both Abram and Sarai many gifts, together with Hagar, and they all, together with Lot and his Egyptian wife, went up from Egypt (20:29-34). In the changed sequence, Abram's gifts are no longer problematic.

Abram then returns to Canaan, views the entire land, and traverses it. With the beginning of the equivalent of Genesis 14 (1QapGen 21:23), the narrative shifts from Abram speaking in the first person to a third-person narrator telling the story of the war of the kings. This portion of 1QapGen is closer to the biblical text of Genesis than any other, and there are points at which it resembles an Aramaic Targum of Genesis. With the progress of the story into Genesis 15 at the bottom of col. 22, the third-person narration continues. The text of 1QapGen breaks off in the middle of its rendition of Gen. 15:4.

BIBLIOGRAPHY

N. AVIGAD AND Y. YADIN 1956, *A Genesis Apocryphon: A Scroll from the Wilderness of Judaea*, Jerusalem: Magnes Press and Shrine of the Book. • E. ESHEL 2007, "The *Imago Mundi* of 1QapGen," in *Heavenly Tablets: Interpretation, Identity and Tradition in Ancient Judaism*, ed. L. LiDonnici and A. Lieber, Leiden: Brill, 111-31. • D. K. FALK 2007, *The Parabiblical Texts*, London: Clark, 26-106. • J. A. FITZMYER 2004, *1QapGen of Qumran Cave I: A Commentary*, 3d ed., Rome: Biblical Institute Press. • J. C. GREENFIELD AND E. QIMRON 1992, "1QapGen Col. XII," *Abr-Nahrain Supplement* 3: 70-77. • D. A. MACHIELA 2009, *The Genesis Apocryphon (1Q20): A Reevaluation of Its Interpretative Character with a New Text Edition*, Leiden: Brill. • M. E. MORGENSTERN, E. QIMRON, AND D. SIVAN 1995, "The Hitherto Unpublished Columns of 1QapGen," *Abr-Nahrain* 33: 30-54.

ESTHER ESHEL

Genesis Commentaries (4Q252-254)

Among the manuscripts from the Qumran caves, there are several exegetical works that are based on Genesis, such as the copies of the *Reworked Pentateuch* (4Q158, 4Q364-365), several copies of the book of *Jubilees*, the *Genesis Apocryphon*, the *Patriarchal Narrative* (4Q464), and the *Commentary on Genesis and Exodus* (4Q422). Four manuscripts have been associated together as *Commentaries on Genesis*. Though they share some minor features, there is not much overlap between them, so they should be construed as four different exegetical works rather than as four copies of the same work. As such they illustrate further the widespread interest in Genesis in the late Second Temple period.

Commentary on Genesis A (4Q252)

The most extensive of these Genesis commentaries, *Commentary on Genesis A* (4Q252; last half of first century B.C.E.), is preserved on a single piece of parchment that contained six columns. The extant portions of 4Q252 contain, in the order of Genesis itself, interpretations of the flood narrative, the curse of Canaan, the entry of Abram into the land, the covenant of the pieces, the destruction of Sodom and Gomorrah, the binding of Isaac, the blessing of Isaac, the defeat of the Amalekites, and the blessings of Jacob. Other topics might also have been covered, but it is unlikely that there was any discussion of topics before Noah and the flood. The composition is striking because it is made up of several different kinds of exegesis and so seems to have been compiled of extracts from other exegetical works. The best-preserved section presents a rewritten form of Genesis 6–8 in which the focus is on various chronological and calendrical details: the flood lasts exactly 364 days, and the various dates in the year are identified distinctively both as days of the month and days of the week. The destruction of Sodom and Gomorrah is retold with halakic reference to the Deuteronomic laws of war that would put those cities under the sacrificial ban. The blessings of Jacob are interpreted in the manner of the sectarian pesharim, perhaps because, like some prophecies, they were considered to be still unfulfilled; only in this final section is there explicit sectarian vocabulary ("men of the community").

No single theme, however, connects all the various sections of exegesis in *Commentary on Genesis A,* but there is a collection of overlapping concerns. Several items seem interested in the exposition of the plain meaning of the text, especially in matters of chronology. Some items seem to be concerned with the inheritance and right occupation of the land, some with election and rejection, some with blessings and curses. Some items can be linked through their concern with sexual misdemeanors. The absence of Joseph from the extant fragments might be significant.

Commentary on Genesis B (4Q253)

The first of the three fragments of the *Commentary on Genesis B* (4Q253; last half of first century B.C.E.) mentions in turn Israel, the ark, and a statute made known to Noah; perhaps there is some similarity between this and *Jubilees* 6, where the children of Israel are also mentioned in association with the covenant that Noah makes before God. The other two fragments contain respectively cultic terminology that can be suitably linked to Jacob and mention of Belial, the common sectarian designation for Satan.

Commentary on Genesis C (4Q254)

Seventeen fragments are assigned to *Commentary on Genesis C* (4Q254; last quarter of first century B.C.E.). Not unlike 4Q252, though there is virtually no overlap in phrasing, their content includes a description of the ark, the curse of Canaan, mention of Hagar, the sacrifice of Isaac, some possible allusions to the Joseph cycle and Joseph as interpreter, and the blessings of Jacob. Of note is the phrase "two sons of oil" (Zech. 4:14), probably used in the messianic interpretation of Gen. 49:8-12. The common sectarian self-designation "the men of the community" occurs in fragment 4 (cf. 1QS 5:1).

Commentary on Genesis D (4Q254a)

The three small fragments assigned to *Commentary on Genesis D* (4Q254a; turn of the era) all concern Noah and the flood, especially the measurements of the ark, the date of disembarkation, and what the raven makes known to the latter generations.

BIBLIOGRAPHY

M. J. BERNSTEIN 1994A, "4Q252: From Re-Written Bible to Biblical Commentary," *JJS* 45: 1-27. • M. J. BERNSTEIN 1994B, "4Q252: Method and Context, Genre and Sources," *JQR* 85: 61-79. • G. J. BROOKE 1994A, "The Genre of 4Q252: From Poetry to Pesher," *DSD* 1: 160-79. • G. J. BROOKE 1994B, "The Thematic Content of 4Q252," *JQR* 85: 33-59. • G. J. BROOKE 1996, "Commentaries on Genesis," in G. J. Brooke et al., *Qumran Cave 4.XVII: Parabiblical Texts Part 3,* DJD 22, Oxford: Clarendon, 185-212, 217-36. • J. SAUKKONEN 2005, *The Story behind the Text: Scriptural Interpretation in 4Q252,* Helsinki: University of Helsinki Press. • J. TRAFTON 2002, "Commentary on Genesis A (4Q252 = 4QCommGen A = 4QPBless)," in *The Dead Sea Scrolls: Hebrew, Aramaic, and Greek Texts with English Translations,* vol. 6B, *Pesharim, Other Commentaries, and Related Documents,* ed. J. H. Charlesworth, Tübingen: Mohr-Siebeck; Louisville: Westminster John Knox, 203-19.

GEORGE J. BROOKE

Gentile Attitudes toward Jews and Judaism

In trying to assess how non-Jews in the ancient world viewed Jews and Judaism, three factors must always be kept in mind. First, there was a great difference between the learned and detached discussions of some intellectuals — such as Plutarch's discussion of whether the Jewish God really is Dionysus (*Quaestiones Convivialum* 4.6) or Tacitus' survey of the different accounts of the Jews' exodus from Egypt (*Historiae* 5.2-4) — and the less sophisticated reactions of the average man on the street. Moreover, while the former have been preserved in the literary heritage of classical antiquity, the views of the common people on the one hand, and of kings and emperors on the other, are much harder to reconstruct. Second, the term "Gentiles" is a Jewish (and, from the first century C.E., also a Christian) term applied collectively to all non-Jews (and, by Christians, to non-Christian non-Jews), and Gentiles themselves applied other divisions to the human race, based on class (free men vs. slaves and rulers vs. subjects), gender (males and females) or ethnicity (Romans, Greeks, Egyptians, Persians, Jews, and so on). Thus the very search for some unified "Gentile" view of Jews and Judaism threatens to distort our view of the issue. Third, we must always recall that the people of antiquity had only a limited notion of "race" in the modern sense of the word, and although they insisted that some people (such as black Africans, or white-skinned Germans) were somatically different from members of other groups, Jews rarely figured in any such discussions. So if Jews were different from other people, this difference was due not to their innate physical appearance and mental capabilities but to their culture, and especially their religious beliefs and practices. Moreover, this difference was only relative, since other ethnic groups (such as Egyptians and Persians) also differed greatly from the rest of humanity, particularly when it came to matters of religion, law, and native customs.

Jews Attaining High-Ranking Positions

Since such differences were seen as a matter of ancestral heritage and personal choice, those Jews who chose to "overcome" these differences by adopting all the trappings of the ruling culture (what some ancient Jews

GENTILE ATTITUDES TOWARD JEWS AND JUDAISM

called "apostates" from the Jewish way of life) could easily be accepted into their host society. Thus, in the late third century B.C.E. we hear of Dositheus son of Drimylus, a courtier in the Ptolemaic court whose career is also attested by some Greek and Demotic papyri and who was a Jew who had abandoned his ancestral laws and beliefs (3 Macc. 1:3). In the first century C.E., we hear of Tiberius Julius Alexander, the nephew of the Jewish philosopher and exegete Philo and the son of Alexander (see below), who abandoned the Jewish way of life (Josephus, *Ant.* 20.100) and became first a governor of Judea and then the prefect of Egypt, an important position in the Roman imperial administration. We also hear of a certain Halityrus, a Jewish mime-actor who was a favorite of the emperor Nero (Josephus, *Life* 16).

Even those Jews who remained loyal to their ancestral laws could be promoted to high-ranking positions, or make their mark on the non-Jewish societies in which they lived. In the mid-second century B.C.E., the Jewish refugees from the turbulent events in Palestine were warmly accepted by the Ptolemies, with their commanders earning high positions in the Ptolemaic army. In Roman Judea, the rise to power of Herod and his descendants (some of whom clung to the Jewish way of life more persistently than others) provides an example of the Roman preference to have the distant regions of their empire ruled by local dynasts, as long as their loyalty to Rome was not in doubt. And in Roman Alexandria there was Philo's brother, Alexander, who was a high-ranking Jewish official in the Roman administration, and who was steadfast in his Jewish piety but apparently failed to convince his son to follow suit (Josephus, *Ant.* 20.100). It must be stressed, however, that such Jews seem to have been a rarity in the ancient world, certainly when compared with the prominence of Jewish artists, scientists, and even politicians in pre-Nazi Germany or in the contemporary United States. Given the preferences and biases of ancient Jewish culture, Jews had little to contribute in the realms of plastic art, music, grammar, rhetoric, and philosophy, and those fields of cultural activity in which Jews did excel — such as the interpretation of their religious texts and the composition of new ones — were of very little interest to the "pagan" world around them.

Negative Views and Reactions

Leaving the Jewish and "pagan" elites aside, and turning to humbler folk, we note two contrary patterns, typical of the Greek and Roman views of all the Oriental peoples: on the one hand, we see a mockery of the Jews' peculiar practices, and sometimes even a great deal of animosity directed toward them; on the other hand, we see some attraction to their peculiar beliefs and practices, including even conversion to Judaism. Turning to the negative views and reactions first, we may note the proliferation, first among Egypto-Greek writers and then among Greek and Roman writers, of hostile versions of the story of the Jews' exodus from Egypt, including, for example, the claim that they worshiped a statue of an ass, honoring the animal which had showed them the way in the wilderness. Also noteworthy are the recurrent — and mostly negative — references to Jewish circumcision, to the Jewish dietary laws (and especially the abstention from pork), and to the Sabbath, which was seen by many non-Jewish observers as a sign of the Jews' inherent laziness. Such claims formed a part of a wider discourse on Orientals as degenerate, effeminate, and superstitious; but the existence of a large Jewish diaspora, and the refusal of many Jews to assimilate into their host societies, probably exacerbated the stereotypes associated with them. That Jews were well aware of such Gentile attitudes is made clear by Philo's description of how the emperor Caligula made fun of the Jewish envoys who came to plead with him by deliberately reciting God's Ineffable Name and mocking their abstention from pork (*Legatio ad Gaium* 353, 361-62), Josephus' recurrent attempts to combat such stereotypes (most notably in his *Against Apion*), and Rabbi Abbahu's description of the anti-Jewish mimes of fourth-century Caesarea (*Lamentations Rabbah,* Petiḥta 17 and Parasha 3.14).

Anti-Jewish sentiments could also erupt in more sinister forms, be it the famous anti-Jewish riot in Alexandria in 38 C.E., described at great length, and with much horror, by Philo (*In Flaccum* 55–72; *Legatio* 120–31), or the civic celebration in late-second-century Oxyrhynchus of the (Roman) destruction of the Jewish communities of Egypt in 115-117 C.E. (*CPJ* 2:450). And while physical violence may have been quite rare, objections to Jewish residence in Greek towns, and to the granting of special privileges to enable them to live according to their own ancestral customs, seem to have been more common (see, e.g., the documents adduced by Josephus, *Ant.* 14.185-267, or the anti-Jewish remarks in the so-called *Acts of the Alexandrian Martyrs*), and in some of the cities of Palestine the very nature of the town — "Jewish" or "Syrian" — was in dispute, as may be seen from the events in Caesarea in the period leading to the Great Revolt (Josephus, *Ant.* 20.173-78, 182-84).

Positive Views and Interactions

Yet "pogroms" and "Jew-baiting" were only one side of the coin; on its other side was admiration for the Jewish way of life and even an acceptance of all, or some, of its tenets. This too is part of a wider discourse on "Oriental wisdom," but while admiration for and participation in Oriental philosophies and religions were quite common throughout the Greco-Roman world, the Jews' uniqueness as an ethno-religious community meant that non-Jews could become Jews by a ritual of formal conversion. Although the scope of the latter phenomenon is extremely hard to assess, individual cases are easy to come by, from descriptions in Jewish works of fiction (Jdt. 14:10) and nonfiction (such as the conversion of the royal house of Adiabene, described by Josephus in *Ant.* 20.17-96), to epigraphic remains of actual converts (e.g., epitaphs which identify the deceased person as a proselyte).

While conversion to Judaism may have been quite rare — especially since not all Jews were equally open to the acceptance of such newcomers — the number of non-Jews who displayed an appreciation of, and perhaps even a taste for, some of the Jewish customs seems to have been much larger. The Jewish God could easily be worshiped by non-Jews, some of whom simply added Iao, Sabaoth, Adonai, and so on to their pantheon of potent gods (as may be seen, e.g., in the Greek magical papyri, amuletic gems, and aggressive curse tablets). The Jewish synagogues served, especially on the Sabbath, as Jewish centers of prayer and study, but they also attracted large numbers of non-Jews (and, in late-antiquity, a large number of Christians), some of whom even observed some of the Jewish commandments. Moreover, in some cases non-Jews married Jewish spouses (e.g., Josephus, *Ant.* 18.345) and even gave their children some sense of their Jewish origins (see, e.g., Acts 16:1).

Distinctive Factors Influencing Gentile Attitudes

While both condemnation and admiration of the Jews, as of other Oriental nations, are well attested in all periods of ancient history, three factors seem to have made a great difference in "Gentile" attitudes toward Jews. One factor was the Jews' political fortunes, and especially their frequent and bloody revolts — first, the successful revolt under the Hasmoneans, and the Hasmonean territorial expansion at the expense of the "pagan" cities of Palestine, and then the great disasters of 70 and 135 C.E., which enervated the Jews' closest neighbors, flooded the markets with Jewish slaves, and increased the Jews' reputation for religious fanaticism.

Another factor was the Jews' own insistence on ethnic and religious self-separation, and their relative success in establishing a code of behavior that assured their ethnic survival even in diasporic conditions. Thus, whereas most Oriental immigrants to Greek cities were expected to assimilate into their host society and "disappear" within a few generations, many Diaspora Jews insisted on staying away from the local temples, marrying only within the fold, and sometimes even eating only or mostly with other Jews, all of which contributed much to their image as haughty and aloof.

Finally, a third factor, and the one that proved the most decisive for later periods of Jewish history, was the rise of Christianity, which began as a Jewish sect persecuted by the Roman authorities and by some Jews but soon turned to the "Gentiles" with its message of monotheism and salvation and eventually conquered the Roman Empire from within. This process brought the Jews' ancient culture a much greater degree of visibility (as may be seen from the detailed readings of the Greek Bible by the likes of Celsus in the late second century C.E. or Julian in the fourth), but eventually, with the triumph of Christianity in the early fourth century C.E., it also turned the Jews into a singular minority. Whereas in pre-Christian society they were one Oriental nation out of many, and certainly not the most populous, exotic, or culturally important one, in the post-Christian world they were left as the sole group that refused to accept the new dispensation. Coupled with the anti-Jewish bias inherent in some passages of the Christian Scriptures, this process spelled the birth of medieval Christian anti-Semitism, which made use of some of the older anti-Jewish stereotypes, but added to them many new accusations of its own, including that of deicide.

BIBLIOGRAPHY

G. BOHAK 2003, "The Ibis and the Jewish Question: Ancient 'Anti-Semitism' in Historical Perspective," in *Jews and Gentiles in the Holy Land in the Days of the Second Temple, the Mishnah, and the Talmud,* ed. M. Mor et al., Jerusalem: Ben Zvi, 27-43. • J. J. COLLINS 2005, "Anti-Semitism in Antiquity?: The Case of Alexandria," in *Ancient Judaism in Its Hellenistic Context,* ed. C. Bakhos, Leiden: Brill, 9-29. • N. DE LANGE 1991, "The Origins of Anti-Semitism: Ancient Evidence and Modern Interpretations," in *Anti-Semitism in Times of Crisis,* ed. S. L. Gilman and S. T. Katz, New York: New York University Press, 21-37. • L. H. FELDMAN 1993, *Jew and Gentile in the Ancient World: Attitudes and Interactions from Alexander to Justinian,* Princeton: Princeton University Press. • J. G. GAGER 1985, *The Origins of Anti-Semitism: Attitudes toward Judaism in Pagan and Christian Antiquity,* New York and Oxford: Oxford University Press. • B. ISAAC 2004, *The Invention of Racism in Classical Antiquity,* Princeton: Princeton University Press. • M. STERN 1976-84, *Greek and Latin Authors on Jews and Judaism,* 3 vols., Jerusalem: Israel Academy of Sciences and Humanities. • P. SCHÄFER 1997, *Judeophobia: Attitudes toward the Jews in the Ancient World,* Cambridge: Harvard University Press. • J. N. SEVENSTER 1977, *The Roots of Pagan Anti-Semitism in the Ancient World,* Leiden: Brill. • Z. YAVETZ 1993, "Judeophobia in Classical Antiquity: A Different Approach," *JJS* 44: 3-22.

See also: Greek Authors on Jews and Judaism; Latin Authors on Jews and Judaism GIDEON BOHAK

Gentiles, Jewish Attitudes toward

Jewish attitudes toward Gentiles start with an understanding that Jews are set apart from Gentiles and that this separation is of divine origin. God selected Israel to be a treasured possession and holy nation. In return Israel is commanded to worship God, and God alone, and not to follow the practices of Gentiles. Gentiles often take on the role of the consummate "other." The rabbis carry this understanding to a hyperbolic extreme in suggesting that any Gentile who renounces idolatry could be credited with having fulfilled the entire Torah (*b. Ḥullin* 5a) and could be called a Jew (*b. Megillah* 13a). Much of the discussion about Gentiles, therefore, serves the purpose of defining proper Jewish practice and Jewish identity. Jewish attitudes toward Gentiles center around six issues: (1) Jewish involvement with Gentile religious practices; (2) Gentile religious practices in general; (3) interactions between Jews and Gentiles; (4) the presence of Gentiles in the land of Israel; (5) Gentiles and purity; and (6) the status of Gentiles in a future time of judgment.

Jewish Involvement in Gentile Religious Practices

Although actual practice may have differed, biblical texts demand that the people of Israel demonstrate exclusive fealty to God (Exod. 20:3). The worship of Gen-

GENTILES, JEWISH ATTITUDES TOWARD

tile deities is treated as a serious violation of the covenant. The consequences for such actions are dire, including expulsion from the land. This attitude continues throughout the Second Temple period, although Jews could also acknowledge that the God they worshiped was the same as a god worshiped by Gentiles, although by different names. Philo, reasoning like a Stoic philosopher, presumes that Gentiles with proper understanding acknowledge the supreme Father of gods and Maker of the whole universe (*Spec. Leg.* 2.165). The refusal to acknowledge Gentile deities was not absolute. Jews occasionally invoked the name of a Gentile deity, participated in the activities of a pagan sanctuary, or displayed images with unmistakable pagan associations. These occurrences, however, are in the minority and the nature of the religious conviction remains unclear. The rabbis expanded the prohibition against Jewish association with Gentile religious practices. Not only the practice itself, but even the appearance of participation or support was forbidden, thus strengthening the boundary between Jews and Gentile religious practices. A Jew should not make use of Gentile wine, on the assumption that it played a part in pagan rituals, or bend down to pick up an object dropped in front of an idol, fearing that such an act could be construed as an act of worship.

Gentile Religious Practice in General

Jewish attitudes toward Gentile religious practices themselves vary widely. Within their own lands Gentiles are permitted, even expected, to worship their own gods (Deut. 4:19), although some traditions, many from the exilic period and later, deride Gentiles for their worship of idols in any location (Isaiah 44). The latter attitude becomes more pronounced under the growing understanding of the God of Israel as the one, true God (Isa. 45:5). From this perspective, Gentile worship became increasingly understood not merely as foreign but false. In the Second Temple period this attitude often expressed itself in claims that Gentiles worship false gods and bring their offerings in vain to lifeless idols. These views not only mocked Gentile worship as foolish, but connected false beliefs with perverse acts, including murder, theft, licentiousness, infanticide, and cannibalism. Texts such as Wisdom of Solomon and *Sibylline Oracles* display particularly harsh condemnations of Gentiles, their religious practices, and the resulting immoral behaviors. Most rabbinic perspectives consider idolatry as the quintessential Gentile behavior that separates Gentiles from Jews. Gentiles display ignorance of God, are prone to violent and licentious behavior, and pose a physical danger to Jews. While Gentiles as a group were often the target of suspicion and ridicule, individual Gentiles could be recognized as righteous and worthy of respect.

A contrasting attitude of tolerance toward Gentile worship can also be found in Jewish literature of this period. The Septuagint takes Exod. 22:27, which in Hebrew presents an injunction against blasphemy, to read, "Do not speak ill of gods," translating the Hebrew *'ĕlōhîm* ("gods") in the plural, thereby proscribing criticism against Gentile gods. The attitude is repeated by Philo (*Spec. Leg.* 1.53; *Mos.* 2.205) and Josephus, who acknowledges that it is permissible for Gentiles to worship their gods (*Ant.* 4.207; *Ag. Ap.* 2.237). According to several Jewish texts many aspects of Gentile culture are not only admirable but even the product of Jewish invention. Artapanus, for instance, credits Moses with being the teacher of Orpheus, the legendary founder of music. Such beliefs fostered a confident attitude; living among Gentiles posed no problems, as long as one remained identified as a Jew. The rabbis too counseled against overt hostility to pagan shrines (*Sipre Deuteronomy* 61), and could also accept that Gentiles living in their own lands do not really worship idols but are complying with their ancestral traditions (*b. Ḥullin* 13b). Statues of deities could be accepted as merely decorative, and Jewish craft workers were permitted to sell goods benefiting pagan shrines.

Interactions between Jews and Gentiles

When engaging Gentiles apart from their religious practices, Jews often displayed attitudes of tolerance and respect. Pentateuchal traditions and prophetic pronouncements command Israel to treat such persons with respect, in part because Israelites themselves once lived as strangers (Exod. 22:20), and require that laws apply both to Israelites and Gentiles living in the land, including the provision of material support (Num. 15:15-16). Some exceptions applied. Gentiles were forbidden to eat the Passover offering (Exod. 12:43), and Israelites were permitted to loan money with interest to Gentiles but not to other Israelites (Deut. 23:20-21). As Jews increasingly lived alongside Gentiles, they retained distinctive practices, such as observance of the Sabbath, and institutions, such as the synagogue, and often expressed concern that intimate contacts with Gentiles might compromise Jewish identity or draw a Jew into immoral behavior. Such attitudes, however, rarely prevented Jews from mixing with Gentiles in daily life. Jews were educated in the gymnasium, attended performances in theaters, relaxed in bathhouses, engaged in business transactions with Gentiles, and worked in shops alongside them.

One major exception was marriage. The Bible prohibits marriages between Israelites and specific ethnic groups, largely out of fear that such unions would cause Israelites to abandon the covenant with God (Exod. 34:16). By the early Second Temple period, some Jews, such as Ezra (Ezra 9–10), advocated a universal prohibition against marriage with Gentiles. Many Jews followed his lead; any exogamous relation could be perceived as a threat to living in accordance with Jewish traditions or to an individual's or the community's purity. The literature of the period regularly promotes the practice of endogamy (Tob. 4:12; *Jub.* 30:7-17; *T. Levi* 9:10; Philo, *Spec. Leg.* 3.29). In *Joseph and Aseneth,* Joseph refuses to contemplate any relation with the Gentile Aseneth. Only after her conversion does Joseph acknowledge Aseneth's beauty and consent to marriage. Other practices of *amixia* (separation from non-Jews), such as refusal to eat with Gentiles (*Jub.* 22:16; 3 Macc.

3:3-7), stemmed mainly from a desire to insure that Jewish laws were observed rather than any specific attitude about Gentiles.

Rabbis often repeated the basic claim that Israel is not to mix with Gentiles (*Exod. Rab.* 31:1). Their discussions, however, reflect an attitude that not only permits but expects that Jews will engage Gentiles in close personal, professional, financial, and social relations, such as working land owned by or conducting business transactions with a Gentile. Rabbis assumed that interactions with Gentiles were necessary and normal, and they regulated interactions between Jews and Gentiles in order to facilitate proper conduct and prevent situations that might engage a Jew in prohibited practices. Rabbis also acknowledged the need to work with Gentiles in social and philanthropic causes and offer assistance to both Jew and Gentile, although their disposition was often motivated by a desire to develop harmonious living conditions rather than a genuine respect for Gentiles.

Jews by and large held a positive attitude toward Gentiles who wished to join the Jewish people as converts, although Jews rarely if at all sought them out through missionary activity. Jews also welcomed Gentiles who engaged Judaism and Jewish communities through less formal relationships. Often designated as God-fearers, such persons might participate in synagogue or festival activities and were honored for their contributions to the Jewish community. The rabbis describe how Gentiles who adhered to certain norms of behavior (e.g., refraining from murder and theft) could enjoy their own separate but equally valid covenant with God as "children of Noah" (*t. ʿAbod. Zar.* 8:4).

Gentile Presence in the Land of Israel

Biblical traditions require that only the god of Israel may be worshiped in the land of Israel. The worship of foreign deities, by Jews or Gentiles, is prohibited. The reforms of King Josiah in the seventh century B.C.E. sought to enforce this policy. In the Second Temple period, new encounters between Gentiles and Jews in the land of Israel caused attitudes to expand in different directions. The Maccabean Revolt erupted in part from differing Jewish attitudes toward the propriety of Gentile cultural and religious practices and institutions. While some Jews embraced these changes, supporters of the revolt sought to forestall what they considered the introduction of foreign religious practices in Judea and the effacement of any meaningful Jewish distinction from Gentiles. In the aftermath, the Hasmoneans aimed to preserve a land devoid of Gentile religious presence by dismantling pagan shrines (*Ant.* 12.344), and requiring the conversion of Gentiles who, through conquest, had now become residents in their kingdom. During this time, Gentile participation at the Temple, the holiest site in the land, became increasingly controversial. Whereas Gentiles were initially welcomed to participate in the Temple's activities (Num. 15:14-16), voices of dissent could be heard condemning their presence as profaning the sanctuary (Ezek. 44:5-9; 4QFlorilegium; Josephus, *J.W.* 2.409-17). By the end of the Second Temple period, Gentiles were restricted to a small section on the southern edge of the Temple Mount (Josephus, *J.W.* 5.194).

Gentiles and Ritual Purity

Biblical texts exclude Gentiles from the regulations of ritual purity, except corpse impurity. A Gentile corpse can convey impurity (Numbers 19; 31), and Gentiles can contract impurity from corpses (Num. 19:10) and eating animal carcasses (Lev. 17:15-16). In the Second Temple period, the book of Ezra and scattered opinions preserved in later Jewish literature apply the category of ritual impurity to Gentiles in novel ways, making Gentiles more generally susceptible to and transmitters of both ritual and moral impurity. The rhetoric of impurity employed in most Second Temple literature, however, tends to focus on the moral impurity of Gentiles and the idols they worship (*Jub.* 22:17-22), thus providing Jews with familiar language with which to condemn Gentile religious ideas and practices and the immorality that resulted from them.

The rabbis devote extensive attention to the topic of purity. Their discussions of Gentiles and impurity, while relatively rare, for the most part follow the positions set forth in biblical texts. At several points, however, the rabbis apply certain laws of ritual purity to Gentiles. Gentiles defile in a way similar to that of a *zāb/zābāh* (person suffering from a genital discharge) (*t. Zab.* 2:1), and idols and their associated objects can convey ritual impurity on analogy with a menstruant or a dead creeping thing (*m. Šabb.* 9:1; *m. ʿAbod. Zar.* 3:6; *t. Zab.* 5:7). Early rabbinic sources do not explain why the rabbis came to this understanding. In all likelihood, these attitudes developed as a strategy to prevent contacts with Gentiles and their religious objects that might have compromised a Jew's religious identity.

Gentiles and the Future Judgment

The status of Gentiles in a future time of judgment receives little attention in Jewish texts. Biblical texts mostly envision a time when Gentiles will come to acknowledge the God of Israel and present themselves at the Temple in Jerusalem (Isa. 56:6-7; 66:23; Micah 4; Zechariah 14). The attitude persists throughout the Second Temple period (Tob. 14:6; Sirach 36; *T. Levi* 14:4; *Ps. Sol.* 17:34). As Jews developed more grandiose eschatological scenarios, the status of Gentiles becomes more of an issue. On the one hand, *Jubilees* expresses the idea that salvation belongs only to the Jews, whereas the *Testament of Abraham* emphasizes that ethical behavior rather than covenantal affiliation establishes the basis for divine judgment. Rabbis, like previous generations of Jews, imagine a future in which Gentiles would come to worship God. The differing attitudes on the future disposition of Gentiles can be seen in the interpretations of the phrase, "The wicked shall depart to Sheol, all the nations that forget God" (Ps. 9:17). Rabbi Eliezer reportedly argued that no Gentile would inherit the world to come, while Rabbi Joshua, emphasizing the phrase "who ignore God," concluded that there are righteous Gentiles and that they will inherit the world to come (*m. Sanh.* 10:2).

BIBLIOGRAPHY

T. L. DONALDSON 2008, *Judaism and the Gentiles: Jewish Patterns of Universalism (to 135 CE)*, Waco, Tex.: Baylor University Press. • R. GOLDENBERG 1998, *The Nations That Know Thee Not: Ancient Jewish Attitudes toward Other Religions*, New York: New York University Press, 1998. • M. GOODMAN 1994, *Mission and Conversion: Proselytizing in the Religious History of the Roman Empire*, Oxford: Oxford University Press. • C. HAYES 2002, *Gentile Impurities and Jewish Identities*, Oxford: Oxford University Press. • J. KLAWANS 1995, "Notions of Gentile Impurity in Ancient Judaism," *AJS Review* 20: 285-312. • D. NOVAK 1983, *The Image of the Non-Jew in Judaism*, New York: Edwin Mellen. • G. PORTON 1988, *Goyim: Gentiles and Israelites in Mishnah-Tosefta*, Atlanta: Scholars Press. • G. N. STANTON AND G. STROUMSA, EDS. 1998, *Tolerance and Intolerance in Early Judaism and Christianity*, Cambridge: Cambridge University Press. • S. STERN 1994, *Jewish Identity in Early Rabbinic Writings*, Leiden: Brill.

See also: Pagan Religions GARY GILBERT

Geography, Mythic

Mythic geography may be defined as particular sites, topography, regions, or realms that have a legendary quality to them and are in some manner ordinarily inaccessible to humankind. The expression itself may be artificial or anachronistic with regard to an ancient audience who might not have understood such sites to be "mythical" in either the ancient or contemporary sense of the word; in fact, such sites might be said to reflect or inform the worldview and mental map of an ancient audience. Still there were certain locales represented as extraordinary, remote, and unreachable in the Greco-Roman world to all but a few, sites which play a role especially in the journeys of heroes and seers to the ends of the earth or to heavenly realms or in descriptions of the afterlife. It is not surprising, then, that descriptions of mythic geography are often associated with visionary experiences relayed in texts.

Geography was understood from the Hellenistic period onward to refer to descriptions of the earth, written or drawn, but could also encompass representations of the universe. Cosmology is further relevant to a discussion of mythic geography since sites once placed, per a Near Eastern view of a tripartite cosmos, in the chthonic realm (netherworld) or on earth were relocated to the heavens in the wake of astronomical speculation in the Greco-Roman world. Thus, the realm of the dead and postmortem paradises later come to be situated in multiple heavens (e.g., *3 Bar.* 4:3). Examination of mythic geography also demonstrates the interplay of various cultures and peoples as imagery and language unique to one tradition is often adopted and adapted, as is apparent in the Jewish (and Christian) use of the Greco-Roman notion of Hades (e.g., Tob. 13:2; Josephus, *Ant.* 18.14; Matt. 11:23; *Sib. Or.* 2.228). Mythic geography includes sites associated with the netherworld and postmortem places of punishment, certain phenomena associated with nature and the cosmos (one might think of descriptions as "pseudo-scientific"), and places associated with divinity and paradises.

The Realm of the Dead and Postmortem Places of Punishment

Mesopotamian, Levantine, and thus also Israelite tradition associated the chthonic realm with a netherworld or pit (e.g., Jonah 2:3-7; Pss. 30:4; 88:4-5). Sheol, understood by some as a shadowy abode of the dead to which one descends (e.g., Isa. 38:10; 18; Ps. 6:6; Job 7:9), also had an association with the grave and is a term well attested within the Hebrew Bible. While references to Sheol are found in texts of the Hellenistic period (e.g., Qoh. 9:10), the infernal realm is described variously within Jewish traditions of the Greco-Roman world. Such diversity is apparent in the third-century-B.C.E. *Book of the Watchers*, which depicts the realm of the dead as a mountain to the west (*1 Enoch* 22:1-13) reminiscent of Egyptian representations of the infernal realm. Within the mountain are hollow compartments that house the souls of the dead until the Day of Judgment (*1 Enoch* 22:1-2; cf. also *4 Ezra* 7:95). The realm of the dead, sometimes called Hades in early Jewish literature (see above) and perhaps understood as well as a temporary place for the deceased, may be indicated also by references to infernal rivers comparable to the Pyriphlegethon, Styx, Cocytus, and Acheron (*Sib. Or.* 4.185; *Apoc. Paul* §22; cf. *1 Enoch* 17:5-6; Homer, *Odyssey* 10.508-15; 11.15-59; Plato, *Phaedrus* 112E-113C).

Especially prominent are places associated with postmortem punishment in the literature of this period. Tartarus, a subterranean prison or abyss where the titans of Greek mythology were punished (e.g., Homer, *Iliad* 8.13-16; Hesiod, *Theogony* 713–48; Plato, *Phaedrus* 113E–114A), likewise appears in early Judaism (2 Pet. 2:4; *Sib. Or.* 1.101) as a place of imprisonment especially in association with celestial beings, like the host of heaven (LXX Prov. 30:16 or *1 Enoch* 20:2 [Gr^{Pan}; Eth BM 485; Berl, Tana 9]; cf. Isa. 24:21-22). Near Eastern traditions which also posited penal sites for celestial beings (e.g., *Enuma Elish* 5:1-10) may have influenced some Jewish authors to locate such places to the East or at the eastern horizon; in *1 Enoch* 18:13-16 (par. *1 Enoch* 21:3-6) and the Hebrew *Apocalypse of Elijah* disobedient stars are confined or punished in the east (cf. also *T. Abr.* Rec. A 11:1, where the easternmost region of the ethereal realm serves as the site of judgment for souls). It is also the case that places of punishment or imprisonment were traditionally juxtaposed with a mythic mountain of God (e.g., Isa. 14:15) and therefore were frequently presented as found at the lowest depths (*1 Enoch* 10:11-13; 21:7-10; 90:24).

Places of punishment in Second Temple literature are also situated in wastelands devoid of life (*1 Enoch* 10:4; 18:12 [par. 21:1]; 108:3), recalling the ancient Near Eastern trope of the dangers of the uninhabited realm (cf. Isa 13:20-22). Gehenna (a transliteration of the Hebrew for the Valley of Hinnom) is situated in Jerusalem, but it is distanced from its ancient audience in a temporal sense. The Valley of Hinnom (Gehenna), used previously for immolation of children and worship of

Molech and Baal (Jer. 7:31; 19:4-5; 32:35; 2 Chron. 28:3; 33:6), comes to be understood in early Judaism as a place of fiery punishment or as the place of judgment for apostates in the end times (e.g., *1 Enoch* 27:1-3; 90:26; Mark 9:43, 45, 47; *2 Bar.* 59:11; *Sib. Or.* 1.103; 2.292; *Ascen. Isa.* 4:1).

The Ends of the Earth

The ends of the earth were also understood as terrain which could feature unusual or exotic inhabitants or could be host to other numinous sites. Following the three-story universe of Mesopotamian cosmology and ancient Israelite tradition, some early Jewish literature presents the earth essentially as a flat disc encircled by a body of water (cf. *1 Enoch* 17:6), much like Okeanos (cf., e.g., Strabo, *Geography* 1.18) or the Babylonian river *marratu* (as featured in the Babylonian Mappa Mundi). At the ends of the earth, one might encounter extraordinary natural phenomena (rivers which feed into the abyss [*1 Enoch* 17:8]; magnificent fauna and trees [*1 Enoch* 28–32] or animals [*1 Enoch* 33:1]), mountains of precious jewels (*1 Enoch* 18:6-8 par. 24:2-3; cf. Ezek. 28:13-14), storehouses for stars and elements such as wind (*1 Enoch* 17:3; 18:1), the cornerstone of the earth (*1 Enoch* 18:2), or pillars that would hold up the vault of heaven (*1 Enoch* 18:3). These sorts of phenomena are mentioned also in wisdom literature (e.g., Job 26; 28; 38), which underscores that the wonders are in the purview of God alone. At the ends of the earth, one might also encounter an exceptional individual like Enoch who no longer dwells among humankind (*1 Enoch* 106-7). Unusual individuals at or beyond the edges of the earth and wonders along the earthly perimeter recall Gilgamesh's journey to Utnapishtim (*Epic of Gilgamesh* 9) or the fantastical stories told by Greek ethnographers of peripheral geography (cf. Pindar, *Pythian Odes* 10.29-48; Herodotus, *History* 4.32-36; Pseudo-Callisthenes, *Iskandarnama*). Overall, such features found at the ends of the earth were understood as largely inaccessible to humankind (cf. *1 Enoch* 19:3) and seemed to signal proximity to the realm of the dead, a type of paradise or spheres restricted to divinity. For example, Okeanos, the river which separated the inhabited world from the infernal realm, comes to serve explicitly as a site of judgment (*T. Abr.* Rec. B 8).

Places Associated with Divinity and Paradises

Mythic geography also embraces certain realms associated with the spheres of holiness, sites of theophany, and paradises (such as Eden). Mountains were often seen as home to divinities (Zaphon or Olympus) and as conduits between heaven and earth. Sinai and Zion function within the Hebrew Scriptures and in Jewish literature of the Greco-Roman period as places uniquely associated with the God of Israel. Sinai, notable because of its association with the exodus and the giving of the Torah (Exodus 19–24), and the South in general (Deut. 33:2; Judg. 5:4) retain significance in early Judaism; Sinai (*1 Enoch* 1:4; *Jub.* 8:19; Ezekiel the Tragedian 68–82), a mountain to the South (perhaps to be understood as Sinai; cf. *1 Enoch* 18:6, 8 [par. *1 Enoch* 25:3]; *Apocalypse of Zephaniah* 3) and the region of the South (*1 Enoch* 77:1) continue to serve as theophanic sites or to be known as sacred space in the Hellenistic and early Roman periods. While Zion, the Temple Mount, and Jerusalem occupy the very center of the world in some early Jewish texts (*1 Enoch* 26:1; *Jub.* 4:26; 8:19), they too take on mythic features as they are imbued with eschatological import; with the return of God, for example, the elect are to gather in Jerusalem where they will enjoy long lives as a result of a veritable tree of life replanted in the vicinity of the Temple (*1 Enoch* 25:5-6). Additional mountains figure prominently in some Second Temple traditions. Mount Hermon, in the northern part of Israel, for example, acts as a conduit between heaven and earth by which celestial beings descend and humans ascend (*1 Enoch* 6:6; 13:7–16:4; Greek *T. Levi* 6:1). Moreover, there are unnamed mountains that reach to the heavens or are distinguished by their incredible height (*1 Enoch* 17:2; 77:4), recalling Canaanite and biblical Zaphon, the mountain in the northernmost reaches.

Paradise as associated with Eden or as a realm of the dead for the blessed also figures into the mythic landscape of early Jewish literature. Eden, the idyllic garden of Adam and Eve (cf. Genesis 2–3) or the Garden of God (cf. Ezek. 28:13-14), is presented as removed from humankind in some manner (*1 Enoch* 32). In the case of *1 Enoch* 32, Eden is renamed the Paradise of righteousness (or of truth), though it is transparently related to the garden of Genesis 2–3 in this later context through allusions to the primogenitors and to a tree of wisdom (cf. *1 Enoch* 77:3, which situates Paradise on earth). Eden or Paradise came to be associated with the Temple Mount (and Holy of Holies; *1 Enoch* 25:5-6; *Jub.* 8:19), much as paradisiacal imagery is applied to the Temple and Jerusalem in certain biblical texts (e.g., Ezek. 47:1-12). At the same time, Paradise is presented as a resting place for the righteous or elect, sometimes at the ends of the earth (Greek *Apoc. Ezra* 5:21) and beyond Okeanos (Josephus, *J.W.* 2.154-58), but in later tradition it is transposed to a heavenly locale (*1 Enoch* 70:1-2). Interestingly, the various mythic sites and realms were not collapsed into one or two locations. Instead, works such as *Jubilees* (*Jub.* 4:26) and the Enochic corpus make clear that various sacred sites captured the religious imagination of Jews in the Hellenistic and early Roman periods and contributed to a worldview informed by many liminal places.

BIBLIOGRAPHY

P. S. ALEXANDER 1992, "Early Jewish Geography," in *ABD*, ed. D. N. Freedman, New York: Doubleday, 2: 977-88. • R. BAUCKHAM 1998, *The Fate of the Dead*, Leiden: Brill, 9-96. • K. COBLENTZ BAUTCH 2003, *A Study of the Geography of 1 Enoch 17–19: "No One Has Seen What I Have Seen,"* Leiden: Brill. • W. HOROWITZ 1998, *Mesopotamian Cosmic Geography*, Winona Lake, Ind.: Eisenbrauns, 20-42, 96-106, 268-362. • J. ROMM 1994, *The Edges of the Earth in Ancient Thought*, Princeton: Princeton University Press, 45-81.

See also: Ascent to Heaven; Death and Afterlife

KELLEY COBLENTZ BAUTCH

Gerizim, Mount

At 881 m. (2,890 ft.) high, Mt. Gerizim (*har gĕrizîm* in Hebrew; Jebel eṭ-Ṭūr in Arabic) is located southwest of ancient Shechem, modern Tell Balāṭa, near Nablus (ancient Neapolis) in Palestine. Its religious importance goes back to pre-Israelite times, as is shown by finds from the Middle Bronze Age IIC (1650-1450 B.C.E.) at Khirbet et-Tanānir on the northeast lower slope and by the discovery of some limestone capitals, possibly from a (pagan) temple of the seventh century B.C.E.

In the Bible, Mt. Gerizim is connected with the blessings that were to be pronounced on it (Deut. 11:29; 27:12; cf. also Josh. 8:33), whereas curses were to be uttered on neighboring Mt. Ebal (Jebel Islāmiye in Arabic). The statement in Deut. 11:30, "As you know, they [Mt. Gerizim and Mt. Ebal] are beyond the Jordan, some distance to the west, in the land of the Canaanites who live in the Arabah, opposite Gilgal, beside the oak of Moreh," gave rise to a dispute about the location of the two mountains in patristic and rabbinic writings. The sixth-century-C.E. Madaba map recorded two locations for Mt. Gerizim, one by Jericho, the other by Neapolis (modern Nablus). In the *Copper Scroll,* discovered in a cave near the Dead Sea in 1952, Mt. Gerizim is listed as one of the places where treasures, probably from the Temple in Jerusalem, were hidden (3Q15 12:4).

According to Josephus (*Ant.* 11.321-24), the Samaritans built a temple on the mountain with the permission of Alexander the Great. Recent archaeological excavations, however, make it likely that the temple was built already in the Persian period. It became the religious focus of the Samaritans and eventually the only sanctuary recognized by them. Rebuilt and enlarged in the Hellenistic period (ca. 200 B.C.E.), it was surrounded by a large walled city of approximately 10,000 inhabitants.

Two inscriptions from the Greek island of Delos dating to ca. 160 B.C.E. testify that the local Samaritans sent offerings to "hallowed Mt. Gerizim." The temple is mentioned in 2 Macc. 6:2. In 112-111 B.C.E. the Hasmonean priest-king John Hyrcanus (134-104 B.C.E.) destroyed the temple and the city; neither was ever rebuilt, and eventually the memory of the temple was lost to the Samaritan tradition. In the second century C.E. a Roman temple was erected, probably by Emperor Antoninus Pius (138-61 C.E.), on the northern, lower peak called Tell er-Rās. The temple, together with the long staircase leading up to it, is depicted on city coins of Neapolis from the mid-second to the mid-third century C.E. and mentioned in later Samaritan chronicles; it was in existence until the fourth century.

To punish the Samaritans for their revolt in 484 C.E., Emperor Zeno (474-491) built a fortified church on the summit of Mt. Gerizim and dedicated it to Mary the Mother of God (Theotokos). After further clashes between Christians and Samaritans, Emperor Justinian I (527-565) added another wall. The church was destroyed in the eighth or ninth century. Remains of both the church and the wall are still visible today.

For the Samaritans, Mt. Gerizim has remained the focus of religious life until today. They locate on it major biblical events, from the creation of the world to Isaac's near-sacrifice and Joshua's erection of the twelve stones taken from the river Jordan. Three times a year, on the Feast of Unleavened Bread (Maṣṣot), the Feast of Weeks (Shavuʿot), and the Feast of Booths (Sukkot), they make a pilgrimage to the top of the mountain, and at Passover they slaughter, roast, and eat sheep as prescribed in Exodus 12.

In the Samaritan version of the Pentateuch, the biblical phrase "the place which YHWH your God *will* choose" was changed in all twenty-one occurrences in the book of Deuteronomy to "the place which YHWH your God *has chosen*" in order to emphasize that Mt. Gerizim, not Jerusalem, was the location of the sanctuary chosen by God from the beginning. The Samaritan tenth commandment consists of a compilation of verses from Exodus and Deuteronomy that underline the sacredness of Mt. Gerizim. The midrashic composition entitled *Tibåt (or Memar) Mårqe,* attributed to the third-fourth-century-C.E. Samaritan scholar and poet Marqe, enumerates thirteen honorary titles for the mountain taken from Genesis, Exodus, and Deuteronomy.

BIBLIOGRAPHY

Y. MAGEN 1993, "Gerizim, Mount," in *New Encyclopedia of Archaeological Excavations in the Holy Land,* ed. E. Stern, Jerusalem: Israel Exploration Society and Carta; New York: Simon & Schuster, 2: 484-92. • Y. MAGEN 2007, "The Dating of the First Phase of the Samaritan Temple on Mount Gerizim in Light of the Archaeological Evidence," in *Judah and the Judeans in the Fourth Century B.C.E.*, ed., O. Lipschits, G. N. Knoppers, and R. Albertz, eds., Winona Lake, Ind.: Eisenbrauns, 157-211. • Y. MAGEN, H. MISGAV, AND L. TSFANIA 2004, *Mount Gerizim Excavations,* vol. 1, *The Aramaic, Hebrew and Samaritan Inscriptions,* Jerusalem: Israel Antiquities Authority. • E. STERN AND Y. MAGEN 2002, "Archaeological Evidence for the First Stage of the Samaritan Temple on Mount Gerizim," *IEJ* 52: 49-57. • Y. TSAFRIR, L. DI SEGNI, AND J. GREEN 1994, *Tabula Imperii Romani: Iudaea-Palaestina, Eretz Israel in the Hellenistic, Roman and Byzantine Periods,* Jerusalem: Israel Academy of Sciences and Humanities, 133-

View looking west at Mt. Gerizim (on the left, south) and Mt. Ebal (on the right, north) *(www.HolyLandPhotos.org)*

34. • L. M. WHITE 1987, "The Delos Synagogue Revisited: Recent Fieldwork in the Graeco-Roman Diaspora," *HTR* 80: 133-60. • L. M. WHITE 1992, *The Social Origins of Christian Architecture,* Valley Forge, Pa.: Trinity Press International, 2: 40-342.

See also: Samaria; Samaria-Sebaste; Samaritan Pentateuch; Samaritanism REINHARD PUMMER

Giants

In biblical tradition, the giants are a legendary race of creatures of enormous size and prodigious strength. The Hebrew word usually translated "giants" is *gibbōrîm,* which literally means "strong ones." It is glossed in Gen. 6:4 as "the famous heroes of antiquity" *(ʾăšer mēʿôlām ʾanšê haššēm).*

The label "giants" is typically applied in proto-ethnographic literature to those persons or peoples who are biologically, chronologically, and/or spatially distant from contemporary cultural norms. Giants are thus freaks or monsters who do not fit within the accepted parameters that govern society. There can even be some question as to whether they should be categorized as human.

In the ancient popular imagination, those responsible for the construction of monumental stone works of the distant past (e.g., the infamous Tower of Babel) must have been superhuman in size, strength, and physical prowess. Hence Pseudo-Eupolemus (second century B.C.E.) can confidently label them giants and even include Abraham among their number. The relatively lengthy life spans ascribed to the early generations of humanity by the biblical writers undoubtedly facilitated this impression.

In biblical and early Jewish literature, beings termed giants prowl two textual landscapes: (1) They are associated with certain pre-Israelite ethnic groups who inhabited areas near the territory assigned by God to the people of Israel; as such, they pose a dangerous threat to the security of prominent cultural heroes or the nascent nation. (2) They are also situated within the antediluvian period of human history and are assigned the principal blame for provoking a universal deluge during the generation of Noah.

The prosopography of these giants is a confusing mixture of local traditions. One Hebrew lexeme closely associated with the twinned trope of giant and aboriginal inhabitant is the term *ʿănaq* (also *ha-ʿanaq*). This term is applied to a legendary character whose offspring (*bĕnê ʿAnaq* or *ʿAnāqîm;* in English Bibles: "sons of Anak," "Anakites," or "Anakim") are encountered by Israel during the course of their wilderness wanderings. The people were reportedly reluctant to enter the promised land due to the presence there of the "Nephilim, descendants of the Anakites, who were numbered among the Nephilim" (Num. 13:33). That these were deemed giants emerges from the immediate narrative context, the versional renderings of the proper noun *Nĕfīlîm,* and the testimony of Qur'ān 5:20-26 wherein v. 22 explicitly terms the promised land's inhabitants "giants" *(jabbārin).* Use of the rare noun *Nĕfīlîm* in the pentateuchal passage was purposely intended to connect Anak and his progeny with the primeval story involving the doings of angels, human women, Nephilim, and the "giants" now alluded to in Gen 6:1-4.

Legends surrounding the ancient sacred site of Kiriath-arba (Hebron) identify Anak as the "child of Arba" (Josh. 15:13; 21:11), Arba as "the greatest of the Anakim (Josh. 14:15), and Sheshai, Ahiman, and Talmai as the monstrous offspring of Anak and/or Arba (see Num. 13:22; Josh. 11:21-22; 15:13-14; cf. Josephus, *Ant.* 5.125, who notes that the local residents continue to show tourists the bones of these giants).

In Deut. 2:10-11, the Anakim are linked with the Rephaim, a term with linguistic and thematic connections to the ancient Canaanite royal funerary cult. Moreover, the book of *Jubilees* flatly states that the Rephaim were giants (*Jub.* 29:9). Biblical ethnology places the Rephaim and their associated clans of the Emim (Deut. 2:10-11) and the Zamzummim (Deut. 2:20-21) in the lowland regions of the south on both sides of the Jordan and around the Dead Sea, as well as the central and northern Transjordan. These groups suffered decimation over time thanks to the destructive effects of pillage and conquest (Gen. 14:1-11; Deut. 2:4–3:17).

A popular legend credits Moses and the Israelites with the slaying of "the only one left of the Rephaim" (Deut. 3:11; Josh. 12:4; 13:12), a figure named Og, the king of Bashan. The Deuteronomist draws attention to this king's iron bed, which was displayed in Rabbat-Ammon; this may be a reference to the impressive size and weight of his sarcophagus. Og's narrative role as a survivor from the Rephaim bears two distinct senses. Some traditions identify Og's group with those Rephaim whom Amrafel and his allies killed in Ashterot-karnaim (Gen. 14:5); Og is then the refugee who reported the news of this debacle to Abram at Mamre (Gen. 14:13).

Continuing this patriarchal association, *Tg. Yer.* Deut. 3:2 relates that Og subsequently ridiculed Abraham and Sarah for their inability to produce children: hence God extended Og's life for many years so that he could ultimately be slain by their descendants. Other traditions (e.g., *Tg. Ps.-J.* Deut. 3:11) effect an equation between Og's Rephaim and the giants of antediluvian lore, and explain that Og was the sole survivor of the giants who perished in the waters of the flood during the time of Noah.

Another closely related narrative complex embedded in Muslim lore names ʿUj (= Og) as the son of ʿAnāq, who is there identified as the twin sister of Seth and the wife of Cain. According to this legend, ʿAnāq was the first female child born to Adam and Eve after their expulsion from Eden, and she became the first human to engage in sexual sins.

The overlap of the giant motif with the realm of sexuality and the notion of forbidden unions (cf. *Jub.* 20:5) leads conveniently to the other prominent textual locus for giants in early Jewish literature, namely, the fractured myth now present in Gen. 6:1-4 whose fuller lineaments are visible in ancient sources like *1 Enoch* and *Jubilees.* Therein giants are held to be the monstrous offspring of miscegenate unions between human women and a rogue group of divine beings (the *bĕnê ha-'ĕlōhîm* or "sons of god"). Although the biblical account remains silent about the consequences of these sexual encounters for the antediluvian social order — instead inviting the hearer/reader to view these giants as the ancestors of the autochthonous giants of the conquest traditions (Gen. 6:4) — other sources are unanimous in their assessment of ensuing events: the giants provoke so much mayhem and murder that God is forced to intervene in the form of a universal deluge.

Sources diverge with regard to their fate. Some envision a watery demise (perhaps Gen. 7:19-20 and Job 26:5; *1 Enoch* 9:6; 4Q370 line 6 end; CD 2:19-21; *Tg. Ps.-J.* Deut. 2:11; 3:11; Ephrem Syrus, *Carmina Nisibena* 1.4.4-5). Others describe how the giants killed each other in internecine combat prior to the onset of the flood (*Jub.* 5:7-9; *1 Enoch* 10:9; 14:6; 88:2). Second Temple literature also hints at a much richer narrative development which the biblical texts suppress: both *Jubilees* (7:21-22) and *1 Enoch* (86:4; 88:2; 7:2 in the Greek version of Syncellus) allude to the existence of at least three different classes of giants. Multiple copies of an Aramaic composition containing stories about the giants were recovered among the Dead Sea Scrolls. And medieval Jewish and Muslim tales about the antediluvian era preserve analogous legends, some of which are rooted in Second Temple sources.

BIBLIOGRAPHY

M. GRÜNBAUM 1893, *Neue Beiträge zur semitischen Sagenkunde,* Leiden: Brill. • J. C. REEVES 1993, "Utnapishtim in the Book of Giants?" *JBL* 112: 110-15. • W. STEPHENS 1984, "De Historia Gigantum: Theological Anthropology before Rabelais," *Traditio* 40: 43-89. • W. STEPHENS 1989, *Giants in Those Days: Folklore, Ancient History, and Nationalism,* Lincoln: University of Nebraska Press. • L. T. STUCKENBRUCK, 1997, *The Book of Giants from Qumran: Texts, Translation, and Commentary,* Tübingen: Mohr-Siebeck.

JOHN C. REEVES

Giants, Book of

The *Book of Giants* is available in fragments that come down to us through Manichaean sources in several languages (Middle Persian, Uygur, Sogdian, Coptic, Latin, Parthian) and through nine, perhaps ten, Dead Sea manuscripts in Aramaic (1Q23, 1Q24?, 2Q26, 4Q203, 4Q206a, 4Q530, 4Q531, 4Q532, 4Q533, 6Q8). The evidence demonstrates an affinity between this work and the *Book of the Watchers* (*1 Enoch* 1–36), on the one hand, and the biblical book of Daniel (chap. 7), on the other. Since a vision of divine judgment in the *Book of Giants* is less developed than its counterpart in Daniel (7:9-14), its composition may predate the final composition of Daniel and so be assigned to the first third of the second century B.C.E.

Genre

Scholars have debated whether or not the *Book of Giants* was integrated into a collection of Enochic works among the Dead Sea Scrolls. This depends partly on whether or not 4Q203 and 4Q204 (which contains the Enochic *Book of the Watchers, Animal Apocalypse, Epistle of Enoch,* and *Birth of Noah*), copied by the same scribe, formed part of the same manuscript. If it was being treated as part of an Enochic corpus, the *Book of Giants* is not, unlike the compositions of *1 Enoch,* a pseudepigraphon told as a first-person account in the name of the patriarch.

Instead, it is a mythical legend of anonymous authorship that recasts the tradition of the fallen angels as found in the *Book of the Watchers* by focusing on the giants' point of view. The giants, also called "nephilim" in the work (cf. Gen. 6:4), are the offspring of the rebellious angels and "the daughters of men." Together with their angelic progenitors, they are largely blamed for the deterioration of conditions on earth during the time before the great flood. Thus the story line in *Book of Giants* emphasizes how the giants come to learn that they will be held to account and punished for their violent oppression of humanity.

Story Line

There has been some debate on how the narrative of the book was structured. The reconstructed story line is based on several criteria: (a) the physical relationships between the Dead Sea Scrolls fragments themselves, first within the manuscripts themselves and then in a few overlaps between the different manuscripts; (b) structural clues provided in the content of the text; (c) overlaps and comparison with the later Manichaean materials; and (d) similar or analogous story lines in other early Jewish literature (e.g., *Book of the Watchers, Jubilees,* and other Dead Sea texts).

The sequence of events in the *Book of Giants* may have been as follows (bracketed parts, for which there is no manuscript evidence, are inferred):

(a) an account about the angels' fall and siring of giants through human women (4Q531 1);
(b) the giants' violent activities on earth against nature and humans (1Q23 9 + 14 + 15; 4Q206a i + 4Q533 4; 4Q531 2-3; 4Q532 2);
(c) a report about these events is brought to Enoch's attention (4Q206 2)
(d) Enoch petitions God about the situation (4Q203 9-10; 4Q531 4; 4Q531 17);
(e) conversations among the giants about their deeds (4Q203 1);
(f) a first pair of dreams given to the giants (2Q26; 6Q8 2);
(g) [a first journey to Enoch by the giant Mahaway (cf. 4Q531 14?), with a first tablet read;]
(h) disagreement between the giants 'Ohyah and Hahyah about the meaning of the dreams (6Q8 1);
(i) admission of the fallen angels' powerlessness (4Q531 22);
(j) 'Ohyah and the giant Gilgamesh (?) interpret their

dreams pessimistically and optimistically (4Q531 22);

(k) [initial punishment of the angel Azazel (cf. 4Q203 7a];

(l) the giants anticipate their judgment (4Q203 13);

(m) an initial punishment of the giants (4Q203 7b i) and intramural fighting among the giants (cf. 4Q531 7);

(n) reading of the second tablet (4Q203 8; 4Q530 1; cf. 4Q203 7b ii);

(o) Gilgamesh and some giants remain hopeful (4Q530 2 ii + 6 + 7 i + 8-11 + 12.1-3);

(p) second pair of dreams given to 'Ohyah and Hahyah (4Q530 2 ii + 6 + 7 i + 8-11 + 12.4-20);

(q) Mahaway's second journey to Enoch (4Q530 2 ii + 6 + 7 i + 8-11 + 12.20-24 and 4Q530 7 ii 3-10);

(r) Enoch's interpretation of the second pair of dreams (4Q530 7 ii 10-11); and

(s) prophecy (Enoch's?) of final bliss (1Q23 1 + 6 + 22).

After this, there would have been just enough space (based on a reconstruction of 4Q530) to have included a brief narrative about events of the great flood portended in the dreams (Noah and his sons' deliverance, and the giants' punishment).

Special Features of the Book

The *Book of Giants* recounts and elaborates on the myth of the fallen angels that is found in or alluded to in a number of other Second Temple texts: *1 Enoch* 6–11, 12–16; *1 Enoch* 85–88; *Jubilees* 5–10; *1 Enoch* 106–7; *Genesis Apocryphon* 2–5; *Pseudo-Eupolemus* (in Eusebius, *Praep. Evang.* 9.17.1-9; 9.18.2); CD 2; 4Q180-181; 4Q370; 11Q11; 4Q510-511 par. 4Q444; Sir. 16:7; Wis. 14:6; 3 Macc. 2:4; Philo, *De Gigantibus; 3 Bar.* 4:10. The very fragmentary evidence of *Book of Giants,* when compared with these other texts, allows for the identification of several distinguishable features. These characteristics are as follows: first, and most obviously, the story of the antediluvian fall of the angels is only here told from the perspective of the giants themselves, who serve as protagonists in the narrative. The giants' activities are not only recounted, but they themselves also become the recipients of revelation that they will be punished for their malevolent deeds. The effect of the story is to reinforce the view that demonic evil is aware of its ultimate demise in a world that is under divine rule.

Second, in extant Second Temple literature, it is only in the *Book of Giants* that the giants are actually given proper names. The names, as far as they are preserved, are 'Aḥiram, 'Adk, Mahaway (who functions as a mediary between the giants and Enoch), 'Ohyah and Hahyah (brothers and offspring of the fallen angel Shemiḥazah), Ḥobabis(h), and Gilgames(h). These proper names indicate how much of the narrative centers on an account of antediluvian evil and its punishment from the giants' point of view. Significantly, at least two of the names, Ḥobabis(h) and Gilgames(h), have their background in the famous *Gilgamesh Epic,* where their equivalents — Humbaba (Neo-Assyrian; Huwawa in the Old Babylonian tradition) and Gilgamesh — engage in a fierce battle as the latter and his companion Enkidu try to gain entrance to the Cedar Forest.

Third, more explicitly than in the *Book of Watchers* (*1 Enoch* 10), the great flood plays a crucial role in the *Book of Giants* as a decisive act of judgment against the giants. The flood exemplifies the unbridgeable gap between humans (Noah and his sons) who escape the flood and the giants who are unable to escape punishment. The event is thus placed in service of drawing a categorical line of distinction between human nature and the giants. Perhaps to a greater degree than any other document from the Second Temple period, the *Book of Giants* may be regarded as a response to traditions that were casually treating Noah, and even Abraham, as giants (so the *Pseudo-Eupolemus* fragments cited by Eusebius). Humanity, as created by God, is the object of God's redemptive activity in the world, and not giants who are illegitimate mixtures between realms that should be kept apart (similarly, see the assertions in *Birth of Noah* in *1 Enoch* 106:1–107:3 and *Genesis Apocryphon* cols. 2–5 that Noah was not sired by the fallen angels).

Bibliography

E. Cook 1996, "The Book of Giants. 4Q203, 1Q23, 2Q26, 4Q530-532, 6Q8," in *The Dead Sea Scrolls: A New Translation,* ed. M. Wise, M. Abegg, and E. Cook, San Francisco: Harper, 246-50. • W. B. Henning 1943-1946, "The Book of Giants," *BSOAS* 11: 52-74. • J. T. Milik 1976, *The Books of Enoch: Aramaic Fragments from Qumrân Cave 4,* Oxford: Clarendon. • É. Puech 1999, "Les fragments 1 & 3 du Livre de Géants de la Grotte 6 (6Q8 1-3)," *RevQ* 74: 227-38. • É. Puech 2001, "4Q530; 4Q531; 4Q532; 4Q533 [and 4Q206a 1-2]," in *Qumran Grotte 4.XXII: Textes araméens, première partie: 4Q529-549,* DJD 31, Oxford: Clarendon, 1-115. • J. C. Reeves 1992, *Jewish Lore in Manichaean Cosmology: Studies in the Book of Giants Tradition,* Cincinnati: Hebrew Union College. • J. C. Reeves 1993, "Utnapishtim in the Book of Giants?" *JBL* 112: 110-15. • O. Skjaervø 1995, "Iranian Epic and the Manichean *Book of Giants:* Irano-Manichaica III," *Acta Orientalia Academiae Scientiarum Hungaricae* 48: 187-223. • L. T. Stuckenbruck 1997, *The Book of Giants from Qumran,* Tübingen: Mohr-Siebeck. • L. T. Stuckenbruck 2000, "4Q203, 1Q23-24; 2Q26; 6Q8," in *Qumran Cave 4.XXVI: Cryptic Texts,* DJD 36, Oxford: Clarendon, 8-94. • L. T. Stuckenbruck 2003, "Giant Mythology and Demonology: From the Ancient Near East to the Dead Sea Scrolls," in *Die Dämonen/Demons,* ed. A. Lange et al., Tübingen: Mohr-Siebeck, 318-38. • W. Sundermann 1984, "Ein weiteres Fragment aus Manis Gigantenbuch," in *Orientalia J. Duchesne-Guillemin emerito oblata,* Leiden: Brill, 491-505. • J. Wilkens 2000, "Neue Fragmente aus Manis Gigantenbuch," *Zeitschrift der Deutschen Morgenländischen Gesellschaft* 150: 133-76.

Loren T. Stuckenbruck

Gnosticism

The term "Gnosticism" was coined in the eighteenth century to describe an ill-defined and broadly diffuse set of ancient religious phenomena associated with knowledge (Gr. *gnōsis*) as the path toward salvation. In modern scholarship, Gnosticism is usually understood as a kind of philosophical and religious revolt staged by a disaffected intellectual elite who protested against the dominant cultural and social structures of late antiquity. The dualistic and antiworldly outlook of Gnosticism received expression in a myth depicting humanity's enslavement to the powers governing the physical cosmos. In the various formulations of this myth, the human spirit is trapped in a fleshly body and imprisoned in a material realm governed by a hostile lower god. Escape from this realm depends upon the experience of gnosis into one's true origin, nature, and destiny, so as to enable the enlightened to return home to the transcendent spiritual realm with the true God in the highest heaven.

Gnosticism and Judaism

The commonly posited nexus between Gnosticism and Judaism has been addressed in two lines of inquiry: (1) whether some movements in early Judaism contributed to or even originated religious currents in late antiquity labeled Gnostic by early church fathers and modern scholars; and (2) whether certain texts and interpretive traditions in the Hekhalot, Maʿaseh Bereshit, and Maʿaseh Merkavah literature constitute a parallel brand of Jewish gnosis.

There has been a pronounced trend over the past decade to question the cogency of the very label Gnosticism and to deny it meaningfulness as a heuristic category in the study of ancient religions (e.g., Williams 1996; King 2003). In this trend, the prevalent classification of various religious movements as species of Gnosticism is accused of presuming an identity of orientation, expression, and purpose among these movements and of masking their important differences. Such a lumping together encourages scholars to work within flawed paradigms that posit dubious historical relationships. This approach is typified when Gnosticism is considered a distinct type of religiosity that can be situated alongside other reified categories of religious or cultural identity such as Judaism, Christianity, and Hellenism.

Over the past two centuries the genealogy of Gnosticism has been traced backward to a variety of older non-Western worldviews (Indian, Iranian, and Babylonian roots have each had their advocates), certain Greek philosophical currents, imagined renegade Jewish thinkers, influential Christian heretics, and varying combinations of two or more of these ideational strands. Since the discovery and publication of the Nag Hammadi Codices, it has been common to emphasize the indebtedness of Gnosticism to Judaism and to argue that Gnosticism reacted to or even grew out of Jewish teachings (e.g., Grant 1966; Wilson 1974; Rudolph 1983; Pearson 1984). The Gnostic literature excerpted by heresiologists or recovered in manuscripts has been seen to exhibit a number of features which point to Judaism's constitutive role. These include:

- the use of early Jewish literary genres like the pseudepigraphic apocalypse or testament;
- the narrative prominence of biblical characters like Adam, Eve, Cain, and Seth;
- the occasional quotation of or reference to Jewish biblical texts (e.g., Gen. 1:26; Exod. 20:5; Isa. 46:9);
- the presence of wordplays suggestive of a Semitic linguistic background (e.g., *Testimony of Truth* 46:28–47:4; *Hypostasis of the Archons* 89:11–90:12, where the occurrences of the proper name "Eve," the noun "serpent," and the verb "instruct" can reflect a dependence upon a series of puns in Aramaic);
- the presence of unusual terminology that may indicate knowledge of or reliance upon exegetical traditions known from Jewish midrashic literature (e.g., "abortions" [Hebr. *nĕfālîm*] as a reading of the term Nephilim found in Hebrew versions of Gen. 6:4);
- the clear echoes of the story of the angelic Watchers known from early Jewish texts like those compiled in *1 Enoch;*
- the employment of a demonology featuring biblical or postbiblical names or epithets like Sabaoth, Samael, or Sakla(s), as well as the proliferation of faux-Semitic designations such as Yaldabaoth, Barbelo, and Eleleth; and
- the likely derivation of the female figure of Sophia from a wisdom theology in which her name is usually explained as the Greek rendering of an allegedly hypostatized Hebrew *ḥokmâ.*

While the cumulative weight of these oft-cited features may seem impressive at first glance, a closer assessment reveals a number of problems with a strictly Jewish provenance for these aspects of Gnostic literature. First, the features are not unique to Jewish and Gnostic literatures. Christian writers, too, employed the apocalyptic and the testamentary genres and composed pseudepigrapha as well; indeed, these types of literary works were rife among a variety of ancient religious traditions (nativist, hermetic, Zoroastrian, Manichean, etc.). Characters like Adam or Noah and passages like those from the books of Exodus or Isaiah also appear in Christian writings, as do written versions of numerous stories and traditions like those attested in *1 Enoch.* Knowledge of the legend of the Watchers or fallen angels was widespread among all the biblically affiliated religious communities in late antiquity; its literary promulgation, creative adaptation, and learned exposition need not be limited to the activities of disaffected Jewish scribes or teachers. Similarly one cannot restrict the manipulation of Semitic linguistic features to the Jews alone; various dialects of Aramaic, for example, were spoken and written by nativist and Christian communities over a broad swathe of territory stretching from central Asia to the shores of the Mediterranean. Some of these communities (e.g., Mandeism) likely possessed and transmitted scriptural and exegetical traditions analogous to those branded as Gnostic by ancient heresiologists and modern scholars. So, too, Semitic-sounding names, whether authentic or fake, are not confined to Jewish texts; they swarm throughout the multilingual corpus of magical amulets, charms, and grimoires produced by a number of ethnic and religious groups in late antiquity, serving no doubt to impart a hint of Oriental mystery to their recipes and adjurations. Finally, any literate Grecophone for whom texts like Proverbs, Ben Sira, or the Wisdom of Solomon enjoyed some level of cultural authority (note that all three are contained in most early Christian canons) could construct a divine female entity named Sophia thanks to the easily accessible Old Greek collections of biblical works.

Second, many scholars who advocate a Jewish matrix for Gnosticism falsely presume a geographic and diachronic uniformity of discourse and practice for Judaism in the eastern Roman Empire. While the presence of a few "aberrant" strands (e.g., Essenes; Philo; the *minim*) is acknowledged and often privileged as a possible font for Gnosticism, by and large Second Temple Judaism is assumed to be essentially equivalent to rabbinic Judaism. Even though no one expresses the equation quite so blatantly, the underlying assumption is plainly at work in most of the proffered reconstructions. Similarly, the vast sea of literature generated by rabbinic sages and their scholastic heirs over the course of several centuries in a variety of locales and cultural contexts is treated as if it were an atemporal verbal continuum whose components were always accessible and perennially meaningful at every place and point in time. This anachronistic approach often results in the accumulation of assemblages of textual citations that disregard the very real differences in provenance and cultural context reflected in such compilations as *Genesis Rabbah*, the Babylonian Talmud, *Midrash ha-Gadol*, and the Zohar, in authors like Philo, or in the tradents of *Sefer Yetzira* and *Targum Pseudo-Jonathan*. The massing of undifferentiated piles of alleged evidence reflects a superficial use of concordances and indices and a fundamental misunderstanding of the complexities of ancient Judaism.

Nevertheless, when one carefully attends to the cultural contexts of the literary and material evidence, it is undeniable that there are some homologies between certain forms of Jewish religious expression and material conventionally associated with Gnosticism. In this sense Gershom Scholem was correct to speak of a type of Jewish gnosis in the Hekhalot and other mystical texts that intriguingly resembles aspects of traditions evidenced in the Nag Hammadi texts and patristic citations (Scholem 1965). Although Scholem and others have sought to situate the earliest expressions of this type of religiosity in the late tannaitic and early amoraic periods — thus rendering them contemporary with the *floruit* of Gnosticism as conventionally defined — no manuscript evidence has emerged that would confirm such an early dating for the Hekhalot corpus.

Even so, within indisputably early Jewish material there are affinities with certain motifs and themes found in so-called Gnostic literature. For example, a number of passages in early Jewish sources clearly model or at least presuppose a binitarian or even ditheistic divine realm, some of whose aspects recur in medieval mystical literature (Segal 1977). Moreover, in some passages of the Dead Sea Scrolls (e.g., 1QS 3–4) there is a fundamental bifurcation of the physical realm into warring camps associated with the categories of light and darkness, or good and evil, each of which is under the control of an angelic being or "prince" *(śar)*. Knowledge and illumination are associated with the adherents of light, while foolishness and wickedness pervade the servants of darkness, whose ultimate destiny is death and perdition. Like the textual remains of "Gnosticism," the Dead Sea Scrolls also have passages that focus on the formation of the cosmos and primordial times. Some of these passages mirror the content of Genesis and its interpretive traditions, but a number do not. It is these latter narrative formulations that arguably preserve (rather than rewrite) portions of the ancestral epic lore out of which fixed biblical canons eventually crystallized.

Recognition of a common discursive heritage in all biblically affiliated religious groups suggests an alternative explanation for the affinities among their different expressions, including those associated with Judaism and Gnosticism. Instead of envisioning "Gnosticism" emerging out of or in response to "Judaism," it is better to think of several local and national narrative discourses being received, manipulated, and even freshly minted by the ethnic and ideological claimants to Israelite culture throughout the Hellenistic and early Roman periods. As the material evidence increasingly attests, some of these statements and pronouncements move in directions that hostile observers and modern scholars brand as Gnostic. Others, though, follow trajectories that eventually lead to the application of labels like Samaritan, Rabbanite, and so on. Still others reject, blend, and refine various combinations of the welter of interpretive streams as they converse and interact with one another. The core value that unites all of these disparate expressions of social identity is an exegetical fixation upon Israel's cultural memory, creatively transformed in novel and unexpected ways.

BIBLIOGRAPHY

R. M. GRANT 1966, *Gnosticism and Early Christianity*, 2d ed., New York: Columbia University Press. • I. GRUENWALD 1988, *From Apocalypticism to Gnosticism: Studies in Apocalypticism, Merkavah Mysticism, and Gnosticism*, Frankfurt: Lang. • K. L. KING 2003, *What Is Gnosticism?* Cambridge, Mass.: Harvard University Press. • B. A. PEARSON 1984, "Jewish Sources in Gnostic Literature," in *Jewish Writings of the Second Temple Period*, ed. M. E. Stone, Assen: Van Gorcum; Philadelphia: Fortress, 443-81. • B. A. PEARSON 1986, "The Problem of 'Jewish Gnostic' Literature," in *Nag Hammadi, Gnosticism, and Early Christianity*, ed. C. W. Hedrick and R. Hodgson Jr., Peabody, Mass.: Hendrickson, 15-35. • J. C. REEVES 1996, *Heralds of That Good Realm: Syro-Mesopotamian Gnosis and Jewish Traditions*, Leiden: Brill. • K. RUDOLPH 1983, *Gnosis: The Nature and History of Gnosticism*, trans. R. M. Wilson, San Francisco: Harper & Row. • G. G. SCHOLEM 1965, *Jewish Gnosticism, Merkabah Mysticism, and Talmudic Tradition*, 2d ed., New York: Jewish Theological Seminary of America. • A. F. SEGAL 1977, *Two Powers in Heaven: Early Rabbinic Reports about*

Christianity and Gnosticism, Leiden: Brill. • M. A. WILLIAMS 1996, *Rethinking "Gnosticism": An Argument for Dismantling a Dubious Category,* Princeton: Princeton University Press. • R. McL. WILSON 1974, "Jewish Gnosis and Gnostic Origins: A Survey," *HUCA* 45: 177-89.

See also: Hekhalot Literature; Mysticism

JOHN C. REEVES

God-fearers

A number of ancient witnesses attest to the existence of Gentiles who adhered to certain characteristically Jewish practices and beliefs without undertaking formal conversion to Judaism. In contrast to proselytes, or Gentiles who did formally convert to Judaism, these individuals had no defined status in the Jewish legal tradition and thus occupied no fixed position within ancient Jewish society. These Gentiles were often described in terms that appear to reflect a common commitment to fear the God of the Jews (cf. Deut. 10:20). Many modern scholars have therefore classified these individuals as God-fearers. Although it is often assumed that the so-called God-fearers were semiproselytes, which is to say informal converts to Judaism, the diverse evidence of the phenomenon in question resists such a uniform definition.

The Book of Acts

The point of origin for most discussions of the God-fearers is the New Testament book of Acts. The book's author uses the Greek terms *phoboumenos* (Acts 10:2, 22, 35; 13:16, 26) and *sebomenos* (Acts 13:43, 50; 16:14; 17:4, 17, 18:7), often with the object *ton theon* (Greek for "[the] God"), in reference to Gentiles who "fear" or "revere" the God of the Jews. The book locates these sympathetic Gentiles in proximity to the Jewish communities which Peter and Paul visited in the first century C.E. However, the book's narrative misrepresents the roles that these friendly Gentiles played within ancient Jewish society. Underlying the author's depiction of the God-fearers is a presumption that they shared a common attraction to Judaism that somehow fell short of formal conversion. The book therefore presents Christianity as a means for these semiproselytes to achieve soteriological equality with the Jews without having to assume the halakic burdens incurred by converting to Judaism. However, the book of Acts only refers to God-fearers when contrasting them to those Jews who rejected the apostolic mission. As Gentiles who were already favorably disposed toward certain aspects of the Judaism, the God-fearers in Acts invariably embrace Christianity. By deploying them merely as a supply of potential Christian converts, the author of Acts adduces the God-fearers only in order to validate the Christian mission to the Gentiles (Kraabel 1981). As a result, the author's apologetic agenda yields a distorted image of the God-fearers as a defined class of semiproselytes without offering any insight onto why these Gentiles might have been attracted to Judaism in the first place.

Nevertheless, the book's implication of the God-fearers as a prominent presence in the Jewish communities of the Diaspora seems to reflect a credible aspect of the phenomenon of proselytism. The God-fearers in Acts evince an intermediate stage of concerted interest in Judaism which was likely an obligatory stage of the process of formal conversion.

Other Literary Sources

Although the phenomenon in question is attested in a range of ancient literary sources, the God-fearer typology occasionally appears outside the New Testament. Referring to Aseneth's impending conversion to Judaism, the pseudepigraphic *Testament of Joseph* counts the Egyptian princess among the *sebomenoi ton theon,* or "those who revere God" (*T. Jos.* 4:6). Josephus employs the term *sebomenoi* in reference to Gentiles who contributed to the Temple treasury (*Ant.* 14.110) as well as the related term *theosebēs,* or "one who reveres God," in reference to Nero's wife Poppaea Sabina (*Ant.* 20.195). The Roman satirist Juvenal uses the Latin term *metuens,* or "one who reveres," in reference to a Gentile who observed the Jewish Sabbath (*Sat.* 14.96). Justin Martyr, perhaps alluding to God-fearers, contrasts the *phoboumenoi ton theon,* Gentiles who allegedly followed certain Jewish laws, with Gentile Christians who neglected these laws (*Dialogus cum Tryphone* 10.3-4, 24.3). Later rabbinic texts refer to friendly Gentiles as *yîrê šāmayim* ("those who fear heaven"), juxtaposing this designation with the standard terms for Jews and proselytes (e.g., *Mekhilta* 18). The substitution of the denominative "heaven" for "God" should be attributed to the lack of an idiomatic Hebrew equivalent to the Greek term *theos,* which the rabbis would not have considered a violation of the third commandment. Although the rabbis were favorably disposed toward these individuals, they afforded them no special status for practical purposes, in contrast to proselytes, who were classified under the biblical law of the "alien" (Hebr. *gēr;* cf. Feldman 1993: 342-82).

Although they all apply variations of the terminology employed in Acts, these literary witnesses do not indicate that the God-fearer typology connoted a common standard of commitment to Judaism. For example, while indicating that many Gentiles venerated the God of the Jews, they do not indicate that these Gentiles had concomitantly rejected all other deities and cults in favor of Judaism. Since this commitment was a prerequisite for formal conversion, it seems unfeasible to assume that these God-fearers were classified as such according to a fixed typology of semiproselytes. Therefore, the God-fearers should not be categorically distinguished from the many other Gentiles who were favorably inclined toward Judaism. Nevertheless, these sources both corroborate and advance our knowledge of the social phenomenon underlying the use of the God-fearer typology in the book of Acts.

Epigraphic Evidence

Amicable social interaction between Jews and Gentiles continued long after the first century. Although the literary sources generally portray God-fearers as Gentiles who participated in aspects of Jewish practice or belief, a range of later epigraphic evidence culled from sites throughout the Mediterranean seem to apply the God-fearer typology to Gentiles who simply maintained good social relations with their Jewish neighbors. Perhaps not coincidentally, many of the inscriptions featuring the God-fearer typology derive from Asia Minor, the primary setting of the God-fearers in the book of Acts. A number of inscriptions seem to indicate that Jewish leaders conferred the honorific title *theosebēs* upon Gentiles affiliated with their local communal institutions (cf. Wander 1998: 87-137). For instance, a second-century inscription from the theater of Miletus (*CIJ* 748 = *IJO* ii.37) records the "place of the Jews and God-fearers," probably indicating that a section of the seats had been jointly sponsored by members of the local Jewish community and their Gentile associates, although the text may also be read to refer to "the Jews who are God-fearers" (cf. Mitchell 1999: 118 n. 113).

Other such inscriptions have been found among the remains of ancient synagogues in Philadelphia, Sardis, and Tralles. A pair of late-fourth-century inscriptions discovered in Aphrodisias (*IJO* ii.14) commemorates the dedication of a public food bank on behalf of the local Jewish community (Chaniotis 2002). The inscriptions record the contributions of a number of Jews along with three Jewish proselytes and no fewer than fifty-four individuals clearly labeled as *theosebeis*. The dramatic disproportion of God-fearers to proselytes makes it unlikely that the former uniformly intended to formally convert to Judaism. The so-called God-fearers of Aphrodisias seem to have achieved their status within the local Jewish community by contributing to the establishment of a food bank for the needy (Reynolds and Tannenbaum 1987: 26-28). While offering no insight into why these Gentiles decided to contribute to a Jewish charitable institution, the Aphrodisias inscriptions offer explicit demonstration of how the God-fearer typology functioned in relation to the more immediately identifiable social categories of Jew and proselyte.

Explaining the Typology

In light of the overriding ambiguity of references to the God-fearers, it remains unclear how or why the God-fearer typology entered the parlance of ancient Judaism. Perhaps the most inviting explanation involves the prevalence of a pagan cult that lent itself to syncretistic interpretation with the Jewish cult. Worship of a deity called *theos hypsistos* ("the most high god") took root throughout the Mediterranean in the second century B.C.E. and remained popular through antiquity. Inscriptions referring to the cult of *theos hypsistos* regularly employ variants of the term *theosebēs* in reference to its adherents, directly paralleling the terminology which Jews seem to have applied to amicable Gentiles. Although the cult of *theos hypsistos* entailed its own unique set of rituals, its basically monotheistic premise likely provided a common theological idiom which could be shared by Jews and their Gentile neighbors. Some devotees of *theos hypsistos* might have identified the God of the Jews with their own patron deity, while some Jews might have likewise acknowledged *theos hypsistos* as an equivalent of their own God. These monotheistic Gentiles likely found favorable company in the Greek-speaking synagogues of the Jewish Diaspora. Because the cult of *theos hypsistos* was popular in many areas of Jewish settlement, particularly Asia Minor, it is possible that the Jewish God-fearer typology was derived from the very terms which these monotheistic Gentiles used to express their own cultic affiliations (Mitchell 1999: 115-21).

BIBLIOGRAPHY

A. CHANIOTIS 2002, "The Jews of Aphrodisias: New Evidence and Old Problems," *SCI* 21: 209-42. • T. L. DONALDSON 2008, *Judaism and the Gentiles: Jewish Patterns of Universalism to 135 CE*, Waco, Tex.: Baylor University Press. • L. H. FELDMAN 1993, *Jew and Gentile in the Ancient World*, Princeton: Princeton University Press. • A. T. KRAABEL 1981, "The Disappearance of the 'God-Fearers,'" *Numen* 28: 113-26. • S. MITCHELL 1999, "The Cult of Theos Hypsistos between Pagans, Jews, and Christians," in *Pagan Monotheism in Late Antiquity*, ed. P. Athanassiadi and M. Frede, Oxford: Oxford University Press, 81-148. • J. REYNOLDS AND R. TANNENBAUM 1987, *Jews and God-fearers at Aphrodisias: Greek Inscriptions with Commentary*, Cambridge: Cambridge Philological Society. • B. WANDER 1998, *Gottesfürchtige und Sympathisanten*, Tübingen: Mohr-Siebeck.

See also: Aphrodisias; Conversion and Proselytism

JOSHUA EZRA BURNS

Goodenough, Erwin Ramsdell

E. R. Goodenough (1893-1965) was educated at Hamilton College, Drew Theological Seminary, Garrett Biblical Institute, and Harvard University. After receiving a D.Phil. degree from Oxford in 1923 at the age of thirty, he spent his entire professional academic career at Yale University, beginning as an instructor in 1923 and culminating as the John A. Hoober Professor of Religion from 1959 to 1962 and Professor Emeritus from 1962 until his death in 1965. He served as the president of the Society of Biblical Literature in 1951.

Goodenough was a scholar of great promise at an early age — and of vast erudition later in life. His work on the textual and material sources of early Judaism was both widely admired and roundly criticized by his contemporaries. Since his death, his contribution to scholarship has been similarly assessed: in some areas his research displays an unparalleled scope and mastery of the ancient sources, but in others his conclusions seem to overreach the limits of those sources. Nevertheless, his work remains useful and challenging even if many of his views about the early religious history of Judaism have not been embraced.

Goodenough was a proponent and practitioner of *Religionswissenschaft*, which in his words "proposes precisely in the realm of the religious to move from empirical data to hypothesis, and from hypothesis back to data, and to correct hypothesis by data, as nearly as possible in scientific fashion." But he was also aware that such a method could not itself claim absolute rational truths, since even science "offers no royal road to knowledge, but an unblazed trail into the wilderness, where, if we travel with understanding, we travel with awareness of its vastness, but move from tree to tree" (Goodenough 1959: 3, 17).

It is this methodology that underlies his most famous and important contribution, the massive thirteen-volume *Jewish Symbols of the Greco-Roman World* (1953-1968), a work he published over the course of fifteen years with little or no help from other researchers. In these tomes Goodenough offered a comprehensive catalogue of ancient Jewish *realia* and attempted to synthesize the material remains into a revised picture of ancient Jewish religious life, one that is not well represented in Second Temple and rabbinic textual sources. His broad conclusions were an extension of his earlier work on Philo of Alexandria (*By Light, Light,* 1935) into the realm of Jewish religious artifacts. Goodenough was convinced that Judaism had, in the context of Greco-Roman culture, become in essence a kind of mystery religion — both in Palestine and in the Diaspora — whose symbolic values and sacramental practices were encoded in Jewish art and architecture of the era. This Jewish mystical religion, judging by the archaeological record, would have comprised the substantial majority of religious Jews; rabbinic Judaism, therefore, would then have been representative of an anti-iconic movement that would have been decisively in the minority.

The widespread resistance to Goodenough's theories was based primarily upon a rejection of his central claim that religious symbols — such as the fish or the rosette or the cup — had constant "values," and that the meaning of Jewish symbols thus had direct correspondence to, say, Dionysian counterparts. Indeed, the fact that the precise contours of such a mystical and sacramental paganism could not be posited with any certainty rendered moot any sustained comparison with Jewish symbols (and called into question whether such symbols were inherently symbolic of anything). Goodenough took the rejection of his work to derive not from his own flawed argumentation but from scholarly and religious prejudice in favor of a more traditional view of ancient Judaism.

In effect, what Goodenough offered was a completely revised picture of mainstream Jewish religious attitudes during Greco-Roman times. But the ambitiousness of the *Symbols* project was not matched by its impact on the study of ancient Judaism. Though it provided new and ready access to a rich trove of ancient archaeological material, it did not revolutionize modern historiography of Judaism as Goodenough must have hoped. He wrote in the final volume of *Jewish Symbols,* "Scholars have repeatedly said to me, 'At least you will always be remembered and used for your collection of material.' . . . I have not spent thirty years as a mere collector: I was trying to make a point."

In any case, despite the lack of enthusiasm for his sweeping revision of ancient Jewish religion, his work — beyond the collections themselves — did open the door to a new way of thinking about the literary and material remains of ancient Judaism. As Morton Smith noted, "Rabbinic literature would never have led us to expect the decorations of Dura [Europos] or Beth Shearim or the Roman catacombs. Therefore it seems likely that the varieties of Judaism which produced these various expressions often differed greatly from those represented in rabbinic literature. One of the major results of Goodenough's work has been to produce general recognition of this fact" (Smith 1967: 64).

Goodenough's papers are housed at Yale University Library in the Manuscripts and Archives Department. They consist of his writings, lectures, notes, and personal papers, much of which pertains to his seminal *Jewish Symbols.*

BIBLIOGRAPHY

E. FRERICHS AND J. NEUSNER, EDS. 1986, *Goodenough on the History and Religion of Judaism,* Atlanta: Scholars Press. • J. GOLDSTEIN 1990, *Semites, Iranians, Greeks and Romans: Studies in Their Interactions,* Atlanta: Scholars Press, 57-66 • E. R. GOODENOUGH 1935, *By Light, Light: The Mystical Gospel of Hellenistic Judaism,* New Haven: Yale University Press. • E. R. GOODENOUGH, 1953-68, *Jewish Symbols in the Greco-Roman Period,* 13 vols., New York: Pantheon. • E. R. GOODENOUGH 1959, "Religionswissenschaft," *Numen* 6: 77-95. • G. LEASE 1972, "Jewish Mystery Cults Since Goodenough," *ANRW* 20.2: 858-80. • J. PETUCHOWSKI 1981, "Judaism as 'Mystery' — The Hidden Agenda?" *HUCA* 52: 141-52. • M. SMITH 1967, "Goodenough's Jewish Symbols in Retrospect," *JBL* 86: 53-68.

See also: Mystery Religion, Judaism as

SAMUEL THOMAS

Grace

The study of grace in early Jewish theology is easily distorted by inappropriate expectations or confessional biases. Our extant Jewish literature is diverse, written in a range of genres and for very varied purposes; to distil from each text a theology of grace may be to make unrealistic demands of sometimes highly rhetorical and unsystematic material. Sanders's identification of a "pattern of religion" in Palestinian Jewish texts (1977) entails a similar problem. Sanders finds within nearly all these texts a common pattern of "covenantal nomism": one "gets in" by God's electing grace, and "stays in" by obedience to the Law. The pattern here is not only hugely generalized (thus tending to flatten out the contours of each text), but is also excessively abstract: any "thick" description of Judaism would wish to include in its analysis the specific historical conditions of these texts, and the social and practical (not just literary) expressions of the Jewish religion. Thus repeated efforts to prove or disprove Sanders's thesis are less helpful than reconsideration of each text (or text group) with a view to its specific emphases and particular context.

Also to be resisted are the implicit (Christian) theological biases, which measure the Jewish material by reference to some ideal type of grace. This ideal generally puts a premium on the "priority" of grace, namely that God's action is unconditioned by human work or worth. Hence the attraction of covenantal nomism, and the consensus that this is a better form of religion than "works righteousness," where human activity "earns" divine favor: even Sanders, while rebutting Protestant caricatures of Palestinian Judaism, speaks of a "healthy relationship" in covenantal nomism between gift and demand (1977: 427). Sometimes also operative is an ideal of "pure" grace, in which divine and human agency are considered mutually exclusive forces and gift is regarded as properly gracious only when it is not returned; thus any element of reciprocity or any demand for human obedience as a condition of salvation is seen as compromising God's unilateral and unconditional grace. To read the Jewish material properly, interpreters have to rid themselves of such ideals and need to be alert to varied treatments of the theme of God's mercy/grace, with differing emphases and diverse connections to other theological motifs. Here there is space for no more than a few samples of that diversity.

Wisdom of Solomon

The Wisdom of Solomon reflects the pressures experienced by Egyptian Jews in the late Ptolemaic/early Roman era, and discusses divine action in the world in terms of God's treatment of the "righteous" and the "ungodly." By contrasting the plagues with the wilderness miracles, the author develops a rich analysis of divine judgment and divine mercy (thematized most explicitly in Wis. 11:21–12:27). God's mercy is universal (he loves all that he has made), and he graciously allows time for sinners to repent, but eventually his judgment must fall on the wicked; since his people are less wicked, and since they have received his promises, they are merely chastened, not utterly destroyed. Divine grace here operates within a matrix of demand, sin, repentance, and justice, its universal application modified by the distinction between God's "children" and "the ungodly."

Philo of Alexandria

Philo found hidden meaning in the Scriptures through allegorical interpretation, influenced by contemporary (early Roman) Alexandrian philosophy. For him the prime manifestation of divine grace is the creation itself, which God gifted to itself, not from need but because his nature is beneficent (*Quod Deus Sit Immutabilis* 107–9). The proper human response is gratitude that God is the cause of all good (not directly of evil or judgment), including even human virtue, though Philo also stresses human effort and will. The acme of salvation is the ascent of the soul to the contemplation of God, and here Philo insists that God draws the soul up to himself, without human aid (*De Praemiis et Poenis* 36–46). Thus his discussion of grace pays little if any attention to covenant but is situated within the universal frame of Creator and creation, and focuses not on eschatological judgment but on the relation between divine and human agency within the ordinary struggle for virtue and in the extraordinary possibility of divine illumination.

Dead Sea Scrolls

The sectarian literature among the Dead Sea Scrolls reflects the experience of a community which has broken away from the mainstream of Jewish society, a pure community rescued from the corrupt mass of sinful Jews (and still more sinful Gentiles). A strong note of predestinarianism puts a heavy accent on the divine will: "to those whom he has selected he has given [wisdom and knowledge] as an everlasting possession" (1QS 11:7). In the eloquent hymns of the community God's mercy, kindness, and goodness are repeatedly praised for the rescue of each individual from sin and error (1QH 6–20) and for their operation in the history of Israel (4Q504). God's grace is here operational not only in the equipping of the elect with the Holy Spirit and with knowledge, but also in repeatedly forgiving their sins and overriding their deep-seated depravity.

Paul

The maverick Jew, Paul, also reflected deeply on divine grace, but in an equally distinctive way. For him, the supreme act of grace took place in God's gift of his Son, Jesus, whose death and resurrection broke the power of sin and enabled the advent of "newness of life" (Rom. 5:12–6:11). Paul's own experience, turning from persecution of the church to be its chief apostle to the Gentiles, made a particular imprint on his theology. He attributes his "call" to the grace of God that operated outside the parameters of the Torah (Gal. 1:13-16), and the call he now communicates to Gentiles, across the ethnic boundary, he interprets as a radical instantiation of the covenantal grace that chose Abraham and the patriarchs (Romans 9–11). This sometimes occasions a sharp antithesis between grace and human "work" (Rom. 4:1-6; 11:1-6), though the labor of life "in Christ" is also presented as a kind of energism — the agency of the Spirit operating in and through the human will and work (Phil. 2:12-13).

4 Ezra

In the aftermath of the Judean War (66-70 C.E.), *4 Ezra* wrestles with traditional notions of God's covenantal mercy; history has apparently refuted the notion of God's favor to Israel. Through dialogue with Uriel and a series of visions the author stresses the mystery of God's ways, but also the necessity for just punishment of the wicked, if not in the present at least at the end of this age. A dramatic appeal to God's grace and mercy, traditionally accorded even to sinful Israel (Exod. 34:6-7), is here rebutted; God will save only the righteous remnant of Israel, those who have faithfully kept the law (*4 Ezra* 7:132–8:3). Such an extreme emphasis on the need for observance of the Law is required not by some theological break with covenantal nomism but by history itself, that is, God's apparent judgment on the majority of Israel in the debacle of the war.

Rabbinic Literature

Rabbinic literature offers a complex variety of statements concerning divine justice and divine mercy, not easily systematized since their purpose is usually homiletic and prompted by particular biblical texts. If they generally assume a covenantal relationship between Israel and God, the stress is very often on the necessity to keep the Law in order to inherit life — naturally so in literature whose chief purpose is to interpret and apply that Law. Rabbinic statements on reward, worth, and merit dispel any notion of caprice on the part of God; that God graciously forgives the repentant is never in doubt. Programmatic statements on judgment by divine goodness and by the "majority of deeds" (*m. ʾAbot* 3:15) seem designed to revel in the paradox that God's demands are as serious as his mercy is assured.

All these texts draw from a biblical pool that issues both strenuous demands for obedience and comforting promises of divine mercy. They vary not only in their emphasis on divine grace (sometimes foregrounded, sometimes assumed or even downplayed), and not only in the balances they do (or do not) strike between grace and justice, and between divine grace and human agency. They also vary in their location of divine grace: in creation, in the election of Israel, in the choice of a remnant, in personal crises, in the cross and resurrection of Jesus, in moral and spiritual empowerment, in the forgiveness of sins, or in the final judgment. The topic is never "grace" in the abstract, but grace in one or more of these spheres of divine action, while the weight of emphasis and the web of associations are deeply influenced by the social and historical context.

BIBLIOGRAPHY

F. AVEMARIE 1996, *Tora und Leben: Untersuchungen zur Heilsbedeutung der Tora in der frühen rabbinischen Literatur,* Tübingen: Mohr-Siebeck • J. M. G. BARCLAY AND S. J. GATHERCOLE, EDS. 2006, *Divine and Human Agency in Paul and His Cultural Environment,* London: Clark • D. A. CARSON, P. T. O'BRIEN AND M. A. SEIFRID, EDS. 2001, *Justification and Variegated Nomism,* vol. 1, *The Complexities of Second Temple Judaism,* Tübingen: Mohr-Siebeck • E. P. SANDERS 1977, *Paul and Palestinian Judaism,* London: SCM.

See also: Covenantal Nomism

JOHN M. G. BARCLAY

Greece and the Aegean

Jewish Communities in Greece and the Aegean

The earliest evidence for the presence of Jews in Greece and the Aegean is an inscription from the sanctuary of Amphiaraus at Oropus in Attica that is dated to the late fourth or early third century B.C.E. The inscription records the manumission of Moschus "(son of) Moschion, a Jew" and his subsequent dedication of the stele bearing the inscription to Amphiaraus and Hygeia (*IJO,* vol. 1, Ach 45). A number of epitaphs from Athens dated to the fourth or third century B.C.E. have been considered Jewish by some scholars (Urdahl 1968: 45-49) due to the occurrence of Semitic names. This, however, does not seem likely (*IJO,* vol. 1, 144-45). Inscriptions also testify to the presence of Jews and Jewish communities of the second-third century C.E. in Thessaloniki, Macedonia, Platea, Achea, Arcadia, and Taenarum, and of the Peloponnesus in the first century. By far the most abundant epigraphic evidence for the period covered by this article comes from Larissa, Thessaly, Athens and Delphi, Achea, and Delos. Inscriptions honoring Herod the Great were found in Athens (*IJO,* vol. 1, Ach 38-39) and Delos (found on Syros, *IJO,* vol. 1, Ach 74).

Synagogues have been found on the island of Delos and at Stobi, Macedonia. The purpose of the building designated as a "synagogue" on Delos is still disputed, but it seems that from the beginning of the first century B.C.E. it may have served as a meeting place of a Jewish association. Stobi presents important information about Jewish communal life in one of the great administrative and, later, ecclesiastical centers of the Roman province of Macedonia.

Jewish communities in Greece and the Aegean are mentioned in the literary sources. However, this information is somewhat meager compared to the epigraphic and archaeological evidence. According to Tacitus, the Jews acquired their ethnicity from the mountains of Ida, which he locates in Crete (*Histories* 5.2.1). A *scholion* on Aristophanes, *Acharnenses* 156, suggests that the Thracian tribe Odomantes were Jews, probably because they practiced circumcision (*GLAJJ,* vol. 3, p. 60). This evidence is no doubt legendary. According to 1 Macc. 15:23, Delos and Gortyn (Crete) received a letter from Rome about the Jews in 140 B.C.E., which may indicate a Jewish presence in these places. However, the statements in 1 Macc. 12:6-18, 12:20-23, and 14:20-23 (cf. Josephus, *Ant.* 12.225-27) that claim kinship between the Jews and the Spartans through Abraham cannot be taken as a proof for the presence of Jews in Hellenistic Sparta. The notion of a correspondence between Onias I and the Spartan king Areus I seems to be a piece of Jewish propaganda, an attempt by the Jews "to assimilate Greeks into their own traditions rather than subordinate themselves to Hellenism" (Gruen 1996: 264).

Important historical information about the presence of Jews and Jewish communities in Greece and the Aegean is provided by Philo and Josephus. According to Philo, in the first century C.E. there were Jewish colonies in the regions of Europe, Macedonia, Boeotia, Aetolia, Attica, and the Peloponnesus. He also lists communities in Argos and Corinth and on the islands of Eubea and Crete (*Legatio* 281–82). Josephus lists two decrees from around 49 B.C.E. issued by the Roman consul L. Cornelius Lentulus and by Julius Caesar, which reaffirmed the exemption of the Jews of Delos from military service and recognized their right to live according to their customs (*Ant.* 14.213-16; 231-32). The second decree is addressed to the people of Paros, which may suggest that there was a Jewish community on the island. During the Great Revolt of 66 C.E. Vespasian sent 6,000 Jewish captives from Magdala to work as slaves on the construction of the Isthmian Canal near Corinth (*J.W.* 3.540). Josephus also provides evidence about the Jews of Crete. He married a Jewish woman from a leading Jewish family of Crete, presumably at Rome in the 70s C.E. (*Vita* 427). The impostor Alexander, who claimed to be Herod's son, received financial help from Cretan Jews (*J.W.* 2.101-3; *Ant.* 17.324-38).

According to the New Testament, Jews from Crete were present in Jerusalem for Pentecost and Paul visited Jewish communities in Philippi, Thessaloniki, Berea, Athens, and Corinth. There were synagogues in Berea, Thessaloniki, Athens, and Corinth (Acts 2:10; 16:12-39; 17:1-15, 17; 18:4-8).

All the currently known Jewish inscriptions from Greece, the Balkans, and the Aegean are now edited by D. Noy, A. Panayotov, and H. Bloedhorn, *Inscriptiones Judaicae Orientis,* vol. 1, *Eastern Europe,* published in 2004. The volume also deals extensively with the archaeological and literary evidence about the presence of Jews and Jewish communities in the region.

Synagogue Buildings in Delos and Stobi

Delos

The building of the synagogue of Delos was discovered in 1912-1913 by Andre Plassart. He identified the building as a synagogue solely on the basis of the dedications to *Theos Hypsistos* and *Hypsistos* found *in situ* during the excavations (Plassart 1914: 526-30; *IJO,* vol. 1, 211-19). Philippe Bruneau conducted a second excavation of the site in 1962 and in 2000-2003. Monika Trümper conducted a new survey of the building. The building is situated on the eastern seashore of Delos, a short distance from the harbor of Ghournia. It is located in what appears to be a residential quarter, close to the stadium and the gymnasium. This is a rectangular building (15.5 × 28.15 m.) with a façade oriented toward the east. Originally, it consisted of one large hall measuring 16.90 × 14.40 m. on the interior, with three entrances from the east. An additional room divided into several chambers (ca. 9.5–10.2 × 15.055 m.) was attached to the main hall on the south. The northwest chamber of this room had access to a vaulted water cistern, which extends under the floor of the main hall. The building had a roofed portico including a row of columns that run parallel to the façade. Bruneau, followed by White and Binder, dates the original construction of the building to the second century B.C.E. (*IJO,* vol. 1, 214). Sometime after the disastrous raids of Mithridates VI (120-63 B.C.E.) in 88 B.C.E., the building underwent a major renovation (Bruneau 1982: 496-97). The renovation involved partition of the main hall into two almost identical large rooms (A = 7.85 × 14.90 m.; B = 8.22 × 14.90 m.). The partition wall had three doorways allowing direct communication between rooms A and B. Both rooms were equipped with marble benches. Room A has benches on its north and west walls and a carved marble *thronos* on the west wall. There were also benches on the west and south walls of room B and at the northwestern corner of the roofed portico. The arrangement of the benches suggests that they were placed after the reconstruction of the building.

It has been suggested that the *thronos* was similar to the so-called seat of Moses referred to in Matt. 23:2 and reserved for the leaders of the Jewish community (Kraabel 1984: 491-94; Binder 1999: 306). However, the *thronos* is almost identical to the *proedros* chairs reserved for the presidents found in the Greek theaters and gymnasiums and was probably brought from the nearby gymnasium together with other *spolia* used in the renovation after the Mithridatic raids (*IJO,* vol. 1, 215). A small niche (18 × 25 cm.) on the wall north of the *thronos* was considered a receptacle for Torah scrolls by some scholars (White 1987: 148). However, the addition of Torah niches is normally a later feature of synagogue architecture, so this was probably used as a lamp niche (Trümper 2004: 538). The building existed at least until the end of the second century or the beginning of the third century C.E. and was later used by lime burners whose kiln is still visible in the center of room A. In her recent study of the building, Trümper distinguishes four phases of construction, two predating 88 B.C.E. and two dating from 88 B.C.E. to the second century C.E. This, however, does not contradict the general construction history of the building suggested by Bruneau.

The building was conceived as a public edifice and not as a private house as suggested by White (White 1987: 151-52). It was originally built as a monumental hall with a large, integrated water reservoir accessed from the south. The building was accessed through a courtyard and three entrances from the east. The reconstruction of the building after 88 B.C.E. preserved its public character (Trümper 2004: 557-69).

The identification of the building as a synagogue is based solely on the epigraphic evidence discovered during Plassart's excavations. Following Bruneau, he described the building as the synagogue of "orthodox" Jews and identified a second Jewish residence near the stadium of Delos (Bruneau 1982: 499-504). This suggestion, however, has not proven convincing. Five votive inscriptions dedicated to *Theos Hypsistos* and *Hypsistos* inscribed on white marble altar-shaped bases, some of them closely resembling the altar incense burners popular on Delos, were found in rooms A and B of the building (Trümper 2004: 585-86). The inscriptions are dated to the first century B.C.E. and second century C.E. (*IJO,* vol. 1, Ach 60-64). Plassart thinks that *Theos Hypsistos* refers to the God of Israel. However, these inscriptions do not differ in content and form from the other known dedications to *Theos Hypsistos, Zeus Hypsistos,* and *Hypsistos;* they refer to healing through miraculous divine intervention (*IJO,* vol. 1, Ach 62) and most probably to a successful manumission (*IJO,* vol. 1, Ach 64). As Mitchell puts it, "We should not neglect the point that the sanctuary is also a Greek one, containing dedications set up by persons with Greek names for Theos Hypsistos" (Mitchell 1999: 98). However, the occurrence of *Theos Hypsistos* in two Jewish epitaphs from Rheneia, the burial island of Delos (*IJO,* vol. 1, Ach 70-71), which date to the second or first century B.C.E., indicates that *Theos Hypsistos* was an accepted description of the God of Israel among the Jews on Delos.

The use of *proseuchē* with the meaning of a prayer or vow, found by Plassart in a votive inscription from the alleged second Jewish residence on Delos near the

GREECE AND THE AEGEAN

stadium, also suggests Jewish influence (*IJO,* vol. 1, Ach 65). This, together with the literary evidence of Delian Jewry, may suggest that the building housed the meetings of a Jewish community on Delos. However, the life and practices of this community are difficult to discern. We know from Josephus that the local Jews were allowed to contribute money to common meals and to follow their ancestral customs (*Ant.* 14.213-16; 231-32). The epitaphs of Rheneia refer to the Day of Atonement (*IJO,* vol. 1, Ach 70-71). Trümper suggests that the bases were used as altars for incense offerings during the synagogue service (Trümper 2004: 585-86).

It is not impossible that the building housed a Jewish association that borrowed from or assimilated to pagan practice, as is suggested by the form of the dedications to *Theos Hypsistos.* Following the discovery 92.5 m. to the north of the building of two Samaritan honorific inscriptions dated to the third or second century B.C.E., Kraabel suggested that it was possibly a Samaritan synagogue (Kraabel 1984: 333; *IJO,* vol. 1, Ach 66-67). The stelae were found lying next to a wall of a building that has not been excavated, and their connection to the alleged synagogue is not clear. Whether the building should be described as the synagogue of the Jewish community of Delos or not remains open until further excavations of the site and the surrounding area are conducted.

Stobi

The existence of a synagogue in Stobi has been known since 1931 when the donation inscription of Claudius Tiberius Polycharmus was found. According to the inscription, dated to the second-third century CE, Polycharmus donated the ground floor of his house, including a *triclinium* (dining room) and *tetrastoon* (study room), to the local Jewish community (*IJO,* vol. 1, Mac 1). In 1970 the first building of the synagogue was discovered during the joint Yugoslav-American excavations of the ancient city. The problem with the identification of the building was that Polycharmus' inscription was found inscribed on a column in the courtyard of a three-aisle basilica in the central area of the city, which the original excavators thought to be a synagogue (*IJO,* vol. 1, 57-58). In 1946 Kitzinger suggested that the basilica was a Christian structure and that the column belonged to an earlier edifice on the same site. The latter view proved accurate when the excavations, conducted under the direction of James Wiseman and Djordje Mano-Zissi, revealed that there are two buildings, one immediately above the other, below the level of the basilica (designated the Central Basilica). The older edifice (designated Synagogue I) was identified as the synagogue of Polycharmus and was dated to the late second or early third century C.E. The later building was designated Synagogue II and was dated to the late third or early fourth century C.E.

The precise architectural plan of Synagogue I and the earlier buildings cannot be determined because of the complicated stratification of the site. According to Poehlman, the inscription of Polycharmus suggests that the building he donated was "a two-storied house that had a colonnaded courtyard, dining room, and probably rooms large enough (separately or combined) to house an assembly on the bottom floor. Upstairs there were living quarters. Of course the roof was tiled. All this basically gives us a picture of a middle or upper middle class house, possibly a villa, in a rather typical Mediterranean style" (Poehlman 1981: 238). None of these rooms has been identified with confidence. Polycharmus' house (Synagogue I) was probably built over an earlier edifice dated to the early first century B.C.E.

The remains of the synagogue itself are indicated only by a few parts of walls, which were reused in Synagogue II (Poehlman 1981: 239; *IJO,* vol. 1, 58-59). A small courtyard (3.7 × 6 m.) with an oven and paved with flagstones was discovered below the mosaic floor of Synagogue II in the center of the nave of the Central Basilica. Poehlman concludes that the excavated building of Synagogue I was originally a domestic structure with a small inner courtyard with service rooms to the south (Poehlman 1981: 242-43). Also found during the excavations were a number of plaster fragments with *dipinti* mentioning Polycharmus and another inscription, painted on a marble plaque, honoring his benefaction (*IJO,* vol. 1, 59). On the basis of this evidence, the building was identified as the one donated by Polycharmus to the Jewish community of Stobi. However, the additional rooms mentioned in the inscription — the *triclinium* and *tetrastoon* — have not been located. According to Wiseman the earthquake that severely damaged the theater at Stobi and several other public buildings in the late third century may also have caused the destruction of Synagogue I (Wiseman 1986: 41).

Soon after the destruction of Polycharmus' synagogue, another building was constructed on the same site. Synagogue II was a long rectangular structure with one large hall measuring 13.3 × 7.6 m. and two smaller rooms attached from the south. The main hall was accessed from the west through a forecourt paved with mosaic. The walls of the main hall were decorated with frescoes, its windows and doors adorned with decorative stucco mouldings bearing floral motifs, and the entire floor paved with mosaic. The mosaic floor is made of separate patches of mosaic with a geometric design, which suggests several stages in its construction. A small stepped platform standing against the east wall of the main hall was probably used as a *bema.* The discovery of three menorah graffiti scratched on the plaster coating of one of the service rooms confirmed that the building was a synagogue (*IJO,* vol. 1, 61). An inscription witnessing the repair of the mosaic floor of Synagogue II in the fourth or fifth century C.E. was discovered in 1977. At the beginning of the fifth century, Synagogue II was supplanted by the construction of the Central Basilica.

Information about the Jewish community of Stobi is provided by the inscription of Claudius Tiberius Polycharmus. Polycharmus was a Roman citizen and an active donor to the Jewish community in Stobi. He was presented with the honorific title of *patēr synagōgēs* ("father of the community") after donating the ground floor of his house to serve as a meeting place of the community. His donation refers to domestically organized worship: the congregation gathered in one or two rooms of his house, while he was still living in another part of the building. The importance of the Torah for the everyday life of the community is stressed by the fact that Polycharmus explicitly noted in his inscription that he had lived his "whole life according to [the prescriptions of] Judaism" (lines 6-9). The significance of the Law for the Jews of Stobi is also confirmed by the description of their gathering place as a "holy place" *(hagios topos)* by Polycharmus. The sanctity of the synagogue is confirmed by another votive referring to the "Holy God" *(hagios theos)* found during the excavations of Synagogue I (*IJO*, vol. 1, Mac 5). The community may have had some connections to the office of the Patriarch in Palestine or at least was aware of the existence of this institution as suggested by the dedication of Polycharmus (line 27).

By the end of the third century C.E., the Jewish community was integrated into the economic and social life of Stobi. This is suggested by the fact that a new synagogue building was erected almost immediately after the destruction of Polycharmus' house. The rise of Stobi as an ecclesiastical center in the fourth and fifth centuries may have caused the decline of the Jewish community in the town, which led to the appropriation of its property and destruction of the synagogue.

Jewish Identity and Communal Life

There is little to suggest the extent and exact organization of Jewish communal life in Greece and the Aegean. However, a number of the sources suggest that some Jews and whole communities maintained their identity and followed the prescriptions of the Law, observing key Jewish festivals like the Day of Atonement, keeping the Sabbath, and practicing circumcision. However, certain Jews were assimilated to pagan practices, as evidenced by two manumissions from Oropus and Delphi dated to the fourth-third centuries and second-first centuries B.C.E., respectively (*IJO*, vol. 1, Ach 44-45). The first inscription is the only evidence for a Jew undergoing incubation in a pagan temple (the Amphiareion at Oropus). The second inscription is a standard manumission from Delphi, but it provides a rare example of a Jew manumitting a slave in a pagan temple. It is, however, possible that in both cases the pagan sanctuary was used because of the greater security it gave to the manumission.

Marble relief from Corinth bearing three menorot (menorahs), the seven-branched candelabra of Jewish tradition *(www.HolyLandPhotos.org)*

The cult of *Theos Hypsistos* was popular in Greece and the Aegean and may have influenced some Jews or even whole communities. Such influence may be suggested for Delos, although in this case influence in the opposite direction, of Judaism on the cult of *Hypsistos*, is also possible. Paul's exorcism of the slave girl in Philippi probably took place at a sanctuary of *Theos Hypsistos* (Mitchell 1999: 110, 115-16). Judaism probably influenced some pagan cults as suggested by a votive inscription from Assenovgrad in Thrace, dated to the second century C.E., which attributes the epithet *eulogētos* to the deity named in the votive. This suggests a cult heavily influenced by Judaism (*IJO*, vol. 1, Thr 5).

Jewish communities flourished in the main administrative centers of Greece, the Balkans, and the Aegean rim — at Thessaloniki, Stobi, Athens, Corinth, Argos, Delos, and Crete. Some of them made their way to the region as slaves, as evidenced by Josephus (*J.W.* 3.540), by two manumissions from Delphi, and, possibly, by a funerary inscription from Athens (*IJO*, vol. 1, Ach 26; Ach 43-44). The inscriptions are dated to the second century B.C.E. and the first century C.E.; they state the ethnicity of the slaves ("a Jew by race" at Delphi) or the place of their origin (Jerusalem, Athens). It is possible that the slaves mentioned in these inscriptions were captives from the campaigns of Antiochus IV (175-163 B.C.E.) in Judea (Delphi) or the sack of Jerusalem in 70 C.E. (Athens). One of the slaves manumitted in Delphi bore the personal name Ioudaios, a common practice among slaves and ex-slaves, while in the other inscription the daughters of the manumitted slave Antigona bore the theophoric names Dorothea and Theodora. The names used by Jews in the region varied from place to place. Some of them were common Jewish names like Ananias (Athens, second century B.C.E.; *IJO*, vol. 1, Ach 33) and Benjamin (Athens, second-third century C.E.; *IJO*, vol. 1, Ach 27), while others preferred phonetic substitutes like Symeon (*IJO*, vol. 1, Ach 33) or chose names because of their meaning, like Justus ("righteous"), as evidenced in Taenarum (*IJO*, vol. 1, Ach 55). Some Jews even had double names like Claudius Tiberius Polycharmus from Stobi, who was also called Achyrios ("chaff-man"; Williams 2007: 316). However, the majority bore Greek or Latin pagan names.

The center of Jewish communal life in several cities in the Balkans and the Aegean was the synagogue. According to the book of Acts, there were synagogues in Berea, Thessalonica, Athens, and Corinth (Acts 2:10; 16:12-39; 17:1-15, 17; 18:4-8). The synagogues were used for gathering as a community, reading the Torah, and celebrating the Sabbath and the annual Jewish festivals. The institution and the building of the synagogue were considered holy by the Jews of Stobi (*IJO*, vol. 1, Mac 1, line 11). The importance of these factors for the preservation of the Jewish identity of these communities is suggested by the evidence of Josephus that the Jews of

Delos, and probably of Paros, petitioned and were granted by the Roman authorities the right "to live in accordance with their customs and to contribute money to common meals and sacred rites" (*Ant.* 14.213-15).

The Torah was also an important feature in Jewish life of the Diaspora. The text of two epitaphs from Rheneia, the burial island of Delos, dated to the second-first century B.C.E., includes many allusions to the LXX. The epitaphs also provide the first epigraphic evidence for the observance of the Day of Atonement in the Jewish Diaspora (*IJO*, vol. 1, Ach 70-71). The reading of the Torah and the celebration of the Sabbath were common in the first century in the Jewish communities of Thessalonica, Berea, and Corinth (Acts 17:1-2, 10-11; 18:4). This was also the case in Stobi, in the late second century C.E., where observing the prescriptions of the Jewish Law was an important feature in the life of the Jewish community.

The position of the Jewish communities in the cities of their residence is difficult to discern. It most probably depended on the local social, economic, and political environment. The communities are described with different terms in the epigraphic and literary sources: "the Jews" (Thessalonica, Berea, Athens), "the people" (Larissa, Thessaly), and *synagōgē* (Stobi). This again may have been influenced by local factors. However, there is virtually no information about their organization; the only evidence we have is that Crispus held the office of *archisynagōgos* ("head of the synagogue") at Corinth (Acts 18:8). Some communities, like the one in Stobi, conferred the honorary title of *patēr synagōgēs* ("father of the community") on prominent donors.

Little is known about the occupation of Jews in the Greek cities of Greece and the Aegean. Paul stayed with a Jewish family of tentmakers in Corinth (Acts 18:3). An epitaph from Athens dated to the second or third century C.E. refers to the office of *proscholos* held by a Jew called Benjamin (*IJO*, vol. 1, Ach 27). The common translation of the term as "assistant schoolmaster" prompted the suggestion that there was a school for Jewish children in Athens. However, the deceased could have been a doorkeeper for a pagan grammarian in Athens (Levinskaya 1996: 161-62).

Individual Jews possessed citizenship; an example is Claudius Tiberius Polycharmus, the benefactor of the Jews at Stobi, who was a Roman citizen. However, there is no information concerning what type of citizenship, if any, was held by members of other Jewish communities in the region.

Some communities were well established in the social and economic life of their cities, and by the first century C.E. they attracted a number of Gentiles to Judaism. The synagogues in Thessalonica, Athens, and Corinth were frequented by Gentiles who attached themselves to the Jewish community by attending the synagogue service, following certain Jewish practices, or celebrating Jewish festivals. They are described with the terms *sebomenoi ton theon* ("servants of God," also known as "God-fearers"; Acts 17:4, 17; 18:7). There was also a Jewish place of prayer in the open air along the river Gangites near Philippi that was frequented by God-fearers (Acts 16:13-14; cf. Koukouli-Chrysantaki 1998: 21-22). Diaspora communities in the region maintained good relations and communication. According to Acts, envoys of the Jewish community of Thessalonica were sent to the community in Berea to incite opposition to Paul's preaching (Acts 17:13).

The Jewish communities in Greece and the Aegean were not affected by the revolt of 66-70 C.E., the Bar Kokhba War of 132-135 C.E., or the Diaspora Revolt of 115-117 C.E. There is no evidence that individual Jews or communities from the area participated in these events. Sporadic hostility toward certain communities, such as the suspension of the right of the Jewish communities of Delos and Paros to follow their customs, as indicated by the edict of Julius Caesar of 49 B.C.E., probably owed to local circumstances. A peaceful atmosphere secured the prosperity of the Jewish communities in the region until the fifth century C.E. Jews enjoyed privileges like exemption from military service and were allowed to conduct their communal life according to the prescriptions of their ancestral religion. Some of the Jewish communities were well established in the main administrative and political centers of the region and, although influenced by the local practices, they managed successfully to preserve their Jewish identity.

Bibliography

P. Bruneau 1982, "Les 'Israelites de Délos' et la juiverie délienne," *BCH* 106: 465-504. • P. Bruneau 1988, "Juifs et Samaritains a Délos" in *L'art juif au Moyen Âge,* ed. M. Mentré, Paris: Berg International, 91-93. • E. Gruen 1996, "The Purported Jewish-Spartan Affiliation," in *Transitions to Empire: Essays in Greco-Roman History in Honor of E. Badian,* ed. R. W. Wallace and E. M. Harris, Norman and London: University of Oklahoma Press, 254-69. • E. Habas-Rubin 2001, "The Dedication of Polycharmos from Stobi: Problems of Dating and Interpretation," *JQR* 92: 41-78. • M. Hengel 1966, "Die Synagogeninscrift von Stobi," *ZNW* 57: 145-83. • T. Ilan 2006, "The New Jewish Inscriptions from Hierapolis and the Question of Jewish Diaspora Cemeteries," *SCI* 25: 71-86. • C. Koukouli-Chrysantaki 1998, "Colonia Iulia Augusta Philippensis," in *Philippi at the Time of Paul and after His Death,* ed. C. Bakirtzis and H. Koester, Harrisburg, Penn.: Trinity Press International, 5-35. • A. T. Kraabel 1984, "New Evidence of the Samaritan Diaspora Has Been Found on Delos," *BA* 47, 44-46. • L. Levine 1999, "The Hellenistic-Roman Diaspora 70-235 CE: The Archaeological Evidence," in *The Cambridge History of Judaism,* vol. 3, *The Early Roman Period,* ed. W. Horbury, W. D. Davies, and J. Sturdy, Cambridge: Cambridge University Press, 991-1024. • I. Levinskaya 1996, *The Book of Acts in Its Diaspora Setting,* Grand Rapids: Eerdmans. • I. Levinskaya 1996, "Was There a Jewish School in Athens?" *Hyperboreus* 2: 198-201. • B. D. Mazur 1935, *Studies on Jewry in Greece,* vol. 1, Athens: Hestia. • S. Mitchell 1999, "The Cult of *Theos Hypsistos* between Pagans, Jews, and Christians," in *Pagan Monotheism in Late Antiquity,* ed. P. Athanassiadi and M. Frede, Oxford: Oxford University Press, 81-146. • D. Noy, A. Panayotov, and H. Bloedhorn, eds. 2004, *Inscriptiones Judaicae Orientis,* vol. 1, *Eastern Europe,* Tübingen: Mohr-Siebeck. • A. OVADIAH 1998, "Ancient Jewish Communities in Macedonia and Thrace," in *Hellenic and Jewish Arts: Interaction, Tradition and Renewal,* ed. A. Ovadiah, Tel Aviv: Ramot, 185-98. • W. POEHLMAN 1981, "The Polycharmos Inscription and Synagogue I at Stobi," in *Studies in the Antiquities of Stobi,* vol. 3, ed. J. Wiseman and B. Aleksova, Titov Veles: Macedonian Review Editions; Princeton: Princeton University Press. • N. P. STAVROULAKIS AND T. J. DE VINNEY 1992, *Jewish Sites and Synagogues of Greece,* Athens: Talos. • M. TRÜMPER 2004, "The Oldest Original Synagogue Building in the Diaspora: The Delos Synagogue Reconsidered," *Hesperia* 73: 513-98. • L. URDAHL 1968, "The Jews of Attica," *Symbolae Osloensis* 43: 39-56. • P. W. VAN DER HORST 1988, "The Jews of Ancient Crete," *JJS* 39: 183-200. • P. W. VAN DER HORST 1990, "The Samaritan Diaspora in Antiquity," in idem, *Essays on the Jewish World of Early Christianity,* Freiburg: Universitätsverlag; Göttingen: Vandenhoeck & Ruprecht, 136-47. • L. M. WHITE 1987, "The Delos Synagogue Revisited: Recent Fieldwork in the Graeco-Roman Diaspora," *HTR* 80: 133-60. • M. H. WILLIAMS 2007, "The Use of Alternative Names by Diaspora Jews in Graeco-Roman Antiquity," *JSJ* 38: 307-27. • J. WISEMAN 1986, "Archaeology and History at Stobi, Macedonia," in *Rome and the Provinces: Studies in the Transformation of Art and Architecture in the Mediterranean World,* ed. C. B. McClendon, New Haven: Yale University Press, 37-50, 75-83.

ALEXANDER PANAYOTOV

Greek

Jewish Use of Greek

From the start of the Hellenistic era (the final quarter of the fourth century B.C.E.), Jews began to use Greek. That process most probably began in the then rapidly growing Diaspora in the eastern part of the Mediterranean (not in the Babylonian Diaspora, however, where Jews continued to speak Aramaic), but in the long run it also took place in the Jewish homeland of Palestine. The same applies to the Samaritans. Even if there is reason to disbelieve the story of Aristotle's meeting with a highly educated Jewish philosopher (a man "with a Greek soul") in the thirties of the fourth century B.C.E. (Clearchus *apud* Josephus, *Ag. Ap.* 1.176-81), the story indicates that by 300 B.C.E. Greeks already could imagine the phenomenon of a deeply Hellenized Jew. And one does not have to wait long before the first Jewish books written in Greek begin to circulate.

Literary Evidence

The oldest Jewish document in the Greek language is the Septuagint (LXX) translation of the Torah, the Greek Pentateuch, which came into being in the Jewish community of Alexandria, most probably because such a translation was needed for use in the synagogue, where the original Hebrew was no longer understood by the second or third generation of Alexandrian Jews (Schürer 1986: 3.1:474-93). In the following three centuries the other parts of the Hebrew Bible were also translated into Greek, not necessarily in Alexandria; some parts were probably translated in Jerusalem.

This translation gave rise to a host of Jewish literature in Greek, mainly inspired by the Bible. Jews engaged in historiography (Demetrius and Eupolemus) and wrote novels (Artapanus), dramas (Ezekiel), epic poetry (Philo and Theodotus), didactic poetry (Pseudo-Phocylides), and in other genres, all of them with biblical themes (Denis-Haelewyck 2000). Only very few of these writings have been preserved in a complete form (e.g., Pseudo-Phocylides); most of them are either lost or have been preserved only in the form of quotations by later authors (usually church fathers). Most regrettably, all of the work of the man called "the Jewish Homer," Sosates, is lost.

The great exceptions to fragmentary preservation are the works of two first-century-C.E. scholars, the philosopher Philo and the historian Josephus, whose works have been preserved almost *in toto* (again in Christian circles). We also have a few remnants of a Judeo-Greek treatise on alchemy by Maria Alchemista, the only known female Jewish writer from antiquity. When not writing in classical Greek, these authors used standard Koine. In spite of occasional Hebraisms or Septuagintalisms, the idea that there was a special type of "Jewish Greek" is a fiction (Horsley 1989).

Epigraphic Evidence

Literature is the main but not the only source for our knowledge of the use of Greek by Jews, for there is also epigraphic evidence (van der Horst 2001). Some 3,500 Jewish inscriptions have been found so far, and their number is growing steadily through new archaeological finds. The Greek ones form some 75 percent of the total of these inscriptions. In the Diaspora the percentage of Greek inscriptions was about 85 percent (the rest being in Latin and Hebrew), but even in the land of Israel it was around 60-65 percent of 1,800 inscriptions (the rest being in Hebrew and Aramaic), although the latter number may have to be revised somewhat in the future, after the material in the database of the *Corpus Inscriptionum Iudaeae et Palestinae* project in Israel becomes available.

What do these numbers imply? It would be overly hasty to conclude that 76 percent of all Jews in the Hellenistic and Roman periods spoke Greek as their first language, because there is the problem of how representative these inscriptions are. There are some factors that may distort the nature of the evidence. To begin with the number of inscriptions as compared to the number of Jews in our period, we have the epitaphs or honorary inscriptions of only an extremely tiny minority. If we take the almost one thousand years between Alexander and Muhammad to comprise about thirty-three generations (thirty years for one generation), and if we take a generation to average one million Jews (in Palestine only), then we have around 1,800 inscriptions for thirty-three million Jews: that is to say, one inscription for every 18,500 Jews. Even if the average number of Jews per generation were reduced further, we would not even reach 0.025 percent. From a statistical point of view, this is a hopeless situation, for what can we say about the 99.975 percent of Jews whose tombstones or honorary inscriptions have not been preserved, if they even had any? Is it possible that the Greek inscriptions belong only to a very tiny upper class of less than 1 percent of Jews, whereas the vast majority of the people would never phrase their inscriptions in Greek?

This is a very improbable suggestion for the following reasons. Many Jews were definitely too poor to erect tombstones inscribed with epitaphs, but that does not necessarily imply that the inscribed stones we do have all derive from the upper classes. There is ample indication that the epitaphs in Greek represent a wide spectrum of the population. There is a great difference between a metrical epitaph in Homeric hexameters engraved upon luxurious and expensive sarcophagi, on the one hand, and poorly scratched names on potsherds or on wall plaster marking the graves of the deceased, on the other (we have many of the latter sort). The former is a manifestation of wealth and status; the latter is usually the contrary. To be sure, the desire to emulate Greco-Roman mores was far more pronounced among the upper than the lower social strata (Levine 1998: 24), but there are numerous very simple and poorly executed tombstones with inscriptions in poor Greek that undeniably stem from these lower strata of Jewish society. The persons who had their tombstones in Beth She'arim inscribed with Greek epitaphs include not only rabbis and public officers but also merchants and craftsmen. The very poverty and vulgarity of the language of these inscriptions shows that it was spoken by the people and not written by learned men only (Lieberman 1965: 30).

As for the many synagogue inscriptions in Greek from the land of Israel, there can be little doubt that most of them were meant to be read by the regular visitors to these buildings, that is, the common people who were members of the local community and were supposed to be able to make sense of them.

Papyri and Other Evidence

The epigraphic material should not be considered in isolation. Papyri (Cotton, Cockle and Millar 1995; Porter 1997), the legends of coins, and the literary sources (Hengel 1974: 88-102) also suggest strongly that many Jews in Judea and the Galilee were able to speak or understand Greek, even if they did not belong to the upper classes.

There is, for instance, the much debated and very significant Greek papyrus letter by Soumaios from the Bar Kokhba archive (one of the three that are in Greek, Papyrus Yadin 52; see Fitzmyer 1979: 36). This letter almost certainly implies that the author (perhaps Bar Kokhba himself or one of his fellow soldiers) was not able to write Hebrew or Aramaic and for that reason wrote in Greek. Of the thirty or so documents in this archive, the vast majority (90 percent) were purposefully written in Hebrew and Aramaic, which is quite understandable in a religiously motivated and nationalist revolt. But there are three documents in Greek. And there can be little doubt that this was due to the fact that, for many Palestinian Jews, Greek, the *lingua franca* of the Near East in the Roman period, had become the language of daily life, even for the followers of the Jewish leader of the Second Revolt, who used the archaic Hebrew script on his coins. This letter demonstrates that the use of Greek did not apply to the cultural elite only, for the letter was written in a sloppy hand and bristles with spelling errors. Moreover, the writer of the letter expected his Jewish addressees to be able to read it, besides the other ones addressed to them in Hebrew and Aramaic.

Similar observations could be made, *mutatis mutandis,* on the Murabba'at papyri and the documents from the Babatha archive, the majority of which are in Greek (Lewis 1989). In this connection it is telling that of the 609 papyri from the Roman Near East in general found outside Egypt — the *vast* majority of which are from Roman and Byzantine Palestine — some 325 are in Greek. That is almost 55 percent. The important observation in rabbinic literature to the effect that in Caesarea Maritima (and certainly elsewhere) synagogue services were conducted in Greek (*y. Soṭah* 8:1, 21b) leads to the same conclusion, which in turn is confirmed by the famous Justinian *Novella* 146 (of the year 553 C.E.). Telling, too, are the finds of Greek documents in Qumran, Masada, and other sites in the Judean Desert (VanderKam 2001), and the thousands of Greek loanwords in rabbinic literature.

Location and Chronology

Another factor that may distort our picture is that a majority of the inscriptions were found in urban centers, not in the countryside, so that the figures we have may yield averages that do not accurately reflect either cities or countryside, although they certainly do reflect cities more accurately than the countryside.

A further distinction that has to be made is chronological. There is little doubt that the process of Hellenization was, in general, a progressive one. The degree of Hellenization was clearly of a different order in the first to fourth centuries C.E. than in the third to first centuries B.C.E. (Levine 1998: 26). Even though the production of Jewish literature in Greek decreased after 70 C.E., the proportion of Greek inscriptions as compared to Hebrew and Aramaic ones increases (except in Jerusalem, where there is a drop-off of epitaphs in general after 70 C.E.). It would seem that what once was limited to certain circles or strata of society gradually permeated other societal areas as well. For most, or at least many, of the Jews in Palestine, Greek probably remained a second language, certainly outside the urban areas. In the Mediterranean Diaspora, however, Greek was the native language of almost all Jews (except for a very limited number in the West, who had adopted Latin).

Bibliography

H. M. Cotton, W. E. H. Cockle, and F. G. B. Millar 1995, "The Papyrology of the Roman Near East: A Survey," *Journal of Roman Studies* 85: 214-35. • A. M. Denis and J. C. Haelewyck, eds. 2000, *Introduction à la littérature religieuse judéo-hellénistique,* 2 vols., Turnhout: Brepols. • L. H. Feldman 2006, "How Much Hellenism in the Land of Israel?" in idem, *Judaism and Hellenism Reconsidered,* Leiden: Brill, 71-102. • J. A. FITZMYER 1979, "The Languages of Palestine in the First Century A.D.," in idem, *A Wandering Aramean: Collected Aramaic Essays,* Missoula, Mont.: Scholars Press, 29-56. • M. HENGEL 1974, *Judaism and Hellenism: Studies in Their Encounter in Palestine during the Early Hellenistic Period,* Philadelphia: Fortress. • G. H. R. HORSLEY 1989, "The Fiction of 'Jewish Greek,'" in idem, *New Documents Illustrating Early Christianity,* vol. 5, Sydney: Macquarie University, 5-40. • P. W. VAN DER HORST 2001, "Greek in Jewish Palestine in the Light of Jewish Epigraphy," in *Hellenism in the Land of Israel,* ed. J. J. Collins and G. E. Sterling, Notre Dame: University of Notre Dame Press, 154-74, reprinted in idem, *Japheth in the Tents of Shem: Studies on Jewish Hellenism in Antiquity,* Leuven: Peeters, 2002, 9-26. • L. I. LEVINE 1998, *Judaism and Hellenism in Antiquity,* Seattle: University of Washington Press. • N. LEWIS 1989, *The Documents from the Bar Kokhba Period in the Cave of Letters: Greek Papyri,* Jerusalem: Israel Exploration Society. • S. LIEBERMAN 1965, *Greek in Jewish Palestine: Studies in the Life and Manners of Jewish Palestine in the II-IV Centuries C.E.,* New York: Feldheim. • G. MUSSIES 1976, "Greek in Palestine and the Diaspora," in *The Jewish People in the First Century,* vol. 2, ed. S. Safrai and M. Stern, Assen: Van Gorcum; Philadelphia: Fortress, 1040-64. • S. E. PORTER 1997, "The Greek Papyri of the Judaean Desert and the World of the Roman East," in *The Scrolls and the Scriptures: Qumran Fifty Years After,* ed. S. E. Porter and C. A. Evans, Sheffield: Sheffield Academic Press, 293-316. • E. SCHÜRER 1986-87, *The History of the Jewish People in the Age of Jesus Christ,* rev. ed. G. Vermes et al., vol. 3, parts 1 and 2, Edinburgh: Clark, 3.1:470-704; 3.2:705-890. • J. C. VANDERKAM 2001, "Greek at Qumran," in *Hellenism in the Land of Israel,* ed. J. J. Collins and G. E. Sterling, Notre Dame: University of Notre Dame Press, 177-83.

PIETER W. VAN DER HORST

Greek Authors on Jews and Judaism

Antiquity has left us a substantial body of Greek literature about Judea and the Judean people, including some important works written by prominent Jewish authors, such as the historian Josephus and the philosopher Philo of Alexandria, as well as a number of other individual Greek texts composed by various Jewish authors (Collins 2000). The present entry, however, is limited to material written in Greek by *non-Judean* authors before the emperor Hadrian's establishment of Aelia Capitolina on the site of Jerusalem in 135 C.E. The material covered here is the rich Greek ethnographic tradition that treated Judeans as one among many nations *(ethnē),* such as Egyptians, Scythians, Thracians, or Romans. The works of these authors present a wealth of perceptions about Judea and the Judeans or Jews *(Ioudaioi),* although not even once in this literary corpus do we find the term now commonly translated as "Judaism" — *Ioudaismos.* Menahem Stern has provided an exhaustive collection of all these Greek primary sources along with English translations in *Greek and Latin Authors on Jews and Judaism* (1974-1984). A number of Stern's entries are simply brief notes about the geography of Judea or reports of the existence of works now unfortunately lost to us, such as the *Judean History (Ioudaikē Historia)* in six books by Teucer of Cyzicus, a little-known writer of the first century B.C.E. mentioned in the Suda (Stern no. 54). The present article concentrates on the material from Greek authors that provides somewhat more sustained descriptions of Jews and their practices.

Characteristics of the Sources

A word must be said at the outset about the nature of the sources. Most of the relevant material survives only as excerpts or summaries (the line between these two is sometimes indistinct) in the works of later Jewish and Christian writers who had their own reasons for choosing to employ their selections. A very large proportion of these fragments are preserved in the works of Josephus, especially his highly polemical tract *Against Apion* (see Barclay 2007). In this text, likely written around 100 C.E., Josephus is at pains to establish the antiquity of the Judean nation and to portray Judeans as exemplars of Roman virtues (Goodman 1994). He proceeds by citing authors who attest to the early existence of the Judean people and then rebutting authors (largely Greek writers from Egypt) that he thinks slander Judeans. Josephus essentially construes Greek writers as either wholly pro-Judean or wholly anti-Judean, and this method of presentation persists in some modern scholarship (e.g., Feldman 1993). There have, however, been recent efforts to move beyond Josephus' dichotomy (Gruen 1998). In addition to Josephus, the other major source for fragmentary Greek opinions about Judeans is the *Preparation for the Gospel (Praeparatio Evangelica)* of the Christian author Eusebius of Caesarea, who was active under the reign of Constantine in the early fourth century. Along with citing the authors Josephus collects in *Against Apion,* Eusebius, in order to establish the antiquity of the Christian *ethnos,* also provides selections of other Greek authors who wrote about Jews. Thus, while we have evidence of the *existence* in antiquity of extended ethnographic treatises entirely dedicated to describing Judeans, most of what actually survives is highly edited, second- or third-hand accounts deployed in specific polemical contexts, sometimes centuries after the authors whose opinions are related.

The Early Hellenistic Period

In the course of *Against Apion,* Josephus writes that one Clearchus of Soli (ca. 300 B.C.E.) narrates a story in which his teacher, Aristotle, had met a Jew. Aristotle is duly impressed and finds the Jew to be "Greek in both language and soul" in spite of the fact that Judeans are "descended from the Indian philosophers" (*Ag. Ap.* 1.180 = Stern no. 15). Porphyry, the philosopher of the third century C.E., records that another of Aristotle's students, Theophrastus (372-287 B.C.E.), mentions "the Syrians, among whom are the Jews" in the context of a discussion of sacrifice, reports that they were "philosophers by race," and seems to say that they practiced human sacrifice ("they were the first to institute sacrifices

GREEK AUTHORS ON JEWS AND JUDAISM

both of other living beings and of themselves") in the context of a discussion on the different sacrificial practices of various nations (Porphyry, *On Abstinence* 2.26 = Stern no. 4). Josephus also claims that Theophrastus had sufficient knowledge of Jews to know the Hebrew term *korban* (*Ag. Ap.* 1.167 = Stern no. 5). These would appear to be the earliest instances of Greek authors taking note of the Jewish people.

Hecataeus of Abdera

The material ascribed to Hecataeus of Abdera (ca. 360-290 B.C.E.) presents some special difficulties. During the reign of Ptolemy I, Hecataeus visited Egypt and composed a work on the region, the *Aegyptica.* This book seems to have had an excursus on the Judeans, and it later served as a source for the *Bibliotheca Historica* of the historian Diodorus Siculus in the middle of the first century B.C.E. Much of what Diodorus has to say about Jews, however, exists only in the form of a paraphrase by the ninth-century patriarch of Constantinople, Photius. The manuscripts of Photius attribute this material to Hecataeus of Miletus (ca. 500 B.C.E.), but scholars universally regard this point as a mistake on Photius' part and believe that the material in Photius' summary of Diodorus is based on the excursus on the Judeans from the *Aegyptiaca* of Hecataeus of Abdera.

The excerpt relates that "in ancient times," a plague roused native Egyptians to expel foreigners *(xenoi).* Among those expelled were a group who formed a "colony" *(apoikia)* in the "utterly uninhabited" region of Judea and were led by Moses, a man "outstanding both for his wisdom and his courage." Moses founded Jerusalem, set up the Temple there along with the priesthood, and established the laws and civic institutions. While the young men of the Judeans were manly, steadfast, and able to endure hardships, the way of life that Moses instituted was "misanthropic and hostile to foreigners" *(apanthrōpos kai misoxenos).* The conclusion of the excerpt notes that the traditional way of life of the Judeans was disturbed under the rule of the Persians and the Macedonians (Photius, *Bibliotheca* 244.380 = Stern no. 11).

In spite of the complicated history of the excerpt (Photius summarizing Diodorus summarizing Hecataeus), scholars are in agreement that this material on Judeans accurately reflects the opinions of Hecataeus. The material fits well into usual generic conventions of the Greek ethnographic tradition — describing the founder of a people and his establishment of their laws and institutions as well as passing judgment on various customs of the people.

This fragment from Diodorus, however, constitutes only a portion of the writings about Judeans circulating under the name of Hecataeus. Josephus attributes to Hecataeus a work entitled *On the Judeans (Peri Ioudaiōn)* and quotes extensively from it in *Against Apion* (*Ag. Ap.* 1.183-205; 2.43 = Stern nos. 12-13). According to Josephus, Hecataeus lavishly praised Judeans' fidelity to their laws as well as the size of their population and the beauty of their region. Yet doubts about the authenticity of this work arose already in antiquity and continue today. In fact, some scholars now regard this material as the work of a Judean author (dubbed Pseudo-Hecataeus), who likely wrote in the first century B.C.E. Others contend that *On the Judeans* is an authentic product of Hecataeus edited by a Judean author, while still others maintain that it is entirely the work of the actual Hecataeus (see Bar-Kochva 1996, who concludes that "the passages attributed to Hecataeus of Abdera in *Against Apion* cannot be accepted as authentic," p. 249). In any case, the lack of certainty should encourage caution in using Josephus' excerpts from *On the Judeans* as an example of Greek opinions about Judeans.

The Middle and Late Hellenistic Period

As Greek influence in the East continued to spread, Judeans continued to be of interest to Greek ethnographers, and it is in the second century B.C.E. that we first begin to see some of the descriptions of Judeans that would become common in the Roman era. Mnaseas of Patara, upon whom Josephus says Apion relied for his description of Jews worshiping a "golden head of a pack-ass," likely wrote in the early second century B.C.E. (*Ag. Ap.* 2.112-14 = Stern no. 28). A visitor to Alexandria during the middle of the second century, Agatharchides of Cnidus, briefly mentions Jews. According to Josephus, Agatharchides describes them as having a "custom of abstaining from work every seventh day; on those occasions, they neither bear arms nor take any agricultural operations in hand, nor engage in any other form of public service, but pray with outstretched hands in the temples until the evening" (*Ag. Ap.* 1.209 = Stern no. 30a). Josephus also notes that Agatharchides refers to Jewish practices as "superstition" *(desidaimonia),* a term that would become popular over the next three centuries (*Ant.* 12.5-6 = Stern no. 30b).

This was also a time period when non-Jews began to show an interest in the figure of Solomon. Josephus mentions two writers of this period, Menander of Ephesus and Dius, who briefly refer to Solomon in connection with Phoenician history. They describe Solomon as the king or ruler of Jerusalem and find him noteworthy because he issued "problems" *(problēmata)* or "riddles" *(ainigmata)* that a Phoenician was able to solve (*Ag. Ap.* 1.112-20 = Stern nos. 35 and 36). By the beginning of the first century B.C.E., Judeans begin to turn up in the poetry of Greek authors, as attested by two lines of a poem of Meleager of Gadara that seem to describe a Judean: "If love for a Sabbath-keeper *(sabbatikos pothos)* grips you, it is no surprise; Eros burns hot even on cold Sabbaths *(sabbasi)*" (*Greek Anthology* 5.160 = Stern no. 43). Along with Sabbath observance, the perception that Jews disliked association with other peoples also became a common trope in this time. Josephus claims that Apollonius Molon (one of Cicero's teachers in Rhodes) described Jews as "atheists and misanthropes *(atheous kai misanthrōpous)*" (*Ag. Ap.* 2.148 = Stern no. 49). Apollonius further says that Jews "do not welcome people with other preconceived opinions about god" and that they show "no desire to associ-

GREEK AUTHORS ON JEWS AND JUDAISM

ate with those who have chosen to adopt a different way of life" (*Ag. Ap.* 2.258 = Stern no. 50). Eusebius also preserves some of Apollonius' statements about Jews in the form of a garbled account of Jewish origins that appears to rely on stories about the patriarchs in Genesis (*Praep. Evang.* 9.19.1-3 = Stern no. 46).

Josephus' treatment of Apollonius may also provide a clue to Josephus' *modus operandi* for assessing Greek authors in *Against Apion.* While Apollonius is one of the authors that Josephus depicts as staunchly anti-Jewish, there is nothing in the material preserved in Eusebius that is explicitly anti-Jewish, and Josephus himself states that Apollonius "has not grouped his accusations together, but scattered them here and there over his work" (*Ag. Ap.* 2.148 = Stern no. 49). If this is Josephus' usual practice, we should be even more cautious in relying upon his judgments about Greek writers in *Against Apion.*

The Early Roman Period

Around the time of the conquest of Jerusalem by Pompey the Great in 63 B.C.E., there appears to have been a surge in the production of literature about Judea and Judeans. In addition to the *Judean History* of Teucer of Cyzicus, Eusebius informs us that Alexander Polyhistor also composed a work entitled *Peri Ioudaiōn,* or *On the Judeans* (*Praep. Evang.* 9.17-39 = Stern no. 51a). It is difficult to discern the exact contents of Alexander's *On the Judeans,* but it is clear that he relied on a number of Jewish and non-Jewish authors in composing the work. In the excerpt from Eusebius, Alexander refers to and even preserves portions of writings about Judeans from several authors, including Eupolemus, Artapanus, Ezekiel the Tragedian, Timochares, and Apollonius Molon. Clement of Alexandria says that Alexander's *On the Judeans* also contained "letters of Solomon *(tinas epistolas solomōnos)*" (*Stromata* I, 21.130.3 = Stern no. 51b).

Of the authors preserved in Alexander Polyhistor, Artapanus deserves special attention. Although scholars since the nineteenth century almost universally have identified Artapanus as Jewish, it is at least possible that he was not (Jacobsen 2006). Since no ancient author gives any indication that Artapanus was a Jew, this determination must be made on the basis of the contents of the fragments of Artapanus that Alexander Polyhistor (by way of Eusebius) preserves. Attributed to Artapanus are two works (or, perhaps more likely, one work given two different names): the *Judean History* and *On the Judeans* (Eusebius, *Praep. Evang.* 9.18-27). These works contain stories that are clearly based on tales from the Pentateuch but include such embellishments as the claim that Moses established Egyptian cultic rites, including the worship of cats and dogs (*Praep. Evang.* 9.27). Whether or not such claims could be made by a Jew depends on the flexibility of one's notions of Jewish identity. It is at least worth noting, though, that neither the titles of the works attributed to Artapanus nor the apparent contents of these works seem out of place in the non-Jewish Greek ethnographic tradition.

Diodorus of Siculus preserves material about Judeans from sources other than Hecataeus. He claims that Judeans inherited the custom of circumcising male children from the Egyptians (Diodorus, *Bibliotheca Historica* 1.28.1-3 = Stern no. 55) and connects Moyses and his laws to a god called Iao (*Bibliotheca Historica* 1.94.2 = Stern no. 58), a name by which the Judean god would frequently be invoked in Greek magical spells throughout antiquity. In another portion of the *Bibliotheca* that survives only in the work of Photius, Diodorus gives a second account of the origin of the Judean nation that diverges somewhat from the story attributed to Hecataeus. In a digression from his description of the sack of Jerusalem by Antiochus IV, Diodorus mentions that the ancestors of the Judeans were driven from Egypt because they had a skin disease. The Judeans then took up residence in Jerusalem and its environs and "made their hatred of people *(to misos to pros tous anthrōpous)* into a tradition" and "introduced outlandish laws: not to break bread with any other race, nor to show them any goodwill at all" (Photius, *Bibliotheca* 244.379 = Stern no. 63).

This same passage of Diodorus also recounts Antiochus IV's discovery of "a marble statue of a bearded man with a scroll seated on an ass" in the Temple in Jerusalem. Antiochus thought this figure was Moses, "the founder of Jerusalem and the organizer of the nation" *(ho ktisas ta Hierosolyma kai systēsamenos to ethnos).* Diodorus also seems to have been aware of the more recent history of the Judeans. He tells a story of a delegation of Judeans that met Pompey to complain about Hasmonean usurpation of both the priesthood and kingship of the Judeans, claiming that "it was by means of a horde of mercenaries, and by outrages and countless impious murders that they had established themselves as kings" (Diodorus, *Bibliotheca Historica,* 40.2, summarized in the writings of the tenth-century scholar, Constantinus Porphyrogenitus, *De Sententiis* 404.20 = Stern no. 64).

A similar description of the Hasmoneans as local thugs appears in the writings of Strabo of Amaseia, who composed works of history and geography in the age of Augustus. The historical *Hypomnēmata* survives only in a few stray fragments, mostly contained in Josephus' *Antiquities* (books 13-15). The *Geographica,* however, has reached us in nearly complete form and preserves a number of interesting perceptions of Judeans. While describing the region of Syria, Strabo turns to the history of the Judean people (*Geographica* 16.2.34-36 = Stern no. 115). He notes that the ancestors of the Judeans are Egyptians and relates that an Egyptian priest named Moses led away "thoughtful men" to Judea by advocating the worship of a single deity that "encompasses us all and encompasses land and sea — the thing which we call heaven, or universe, or the nature of all that exists." Strabo writes that while some of Moses' successors were "good and pious," at a later point "superstitious men were appointed to the priesthood." From these men "arose the bands of robbers; for some revolted and harassed the country, both their own country and that of their neighbors, whereas others, cooperating with the rulers, seized the property of others

GREEK AUTHORS ON JEWS AND JUDAISM

and subdued much of Syria and Phoenicia." After interspersing various geographic observations about Judea and its surroundings, Strabo returns to narrating Pompey's overthrow of the Hasmoneans and the quick rise to power of Herod the Great.

In the course of this historical account, Strabo also mentions what he regards as typical Jewish customs. In this passage, he points out that it was the Jews' superstition that led to some of their characteristic practices, such as "abstinence from flesh, from which it is their custom to abstain even today, and circumcisions and excisions." By the latter term, "excisions" *(ektomai),* Strabo seems to mean some manner of female genital mutilation, as other passing references make clear. When he discusses a people called the Creophagi, he notes that "the males have their sexual glands mutilated *(koloboi tas balanous)*" and "the women are excised in the Judean way *(Ioudaïkōs ektetmēmenai)*" (*Geographica* 16.4.9 = Stern no. 118). This seems to be the only ancient reference to such a practice among Jews.

One of the great misfortunes in the transmission of ancient manuscripts to the present day is the nearly total loss of the writings of Nicolaus of Damascus. Nicolaus was a member of the entourage of Herod the Great around 15 B.C.E. and a prolific writer and scholar, producing a massive work of history in 144 books. According to Josephus, he also may have written a book dedicated solely to Judeans. Josephus says that in the fourth book of his *Histories,* Nicolaus writes about one "Abrames" who came from the "land of the Chaldees" and reigned in Damascus. "But, not long after, he left this country also with his people for the land then called Canaan but now Judea, where he settled, he and his numerous descendants, whose history I shall recount in another book" (*Ant.* 1.159-60 = Stern no. 83). It is unknown whether the book was ever written. A firsthand account of a non-Jewish writer who served in the court of Herod the Great would have provided an ideal supplement and counterbalance to the material that Josephus presents in *Against Apion.*

Apion himself belongs to the group of Greek authors writing about Jews in roughly this time period. He was a grammarian active in Alexandria in the first half of the first century C.E. Josephus informs us that Apion was the delegate of the Greek Alexandrians in an embassy to Emperor Gaius concerning a dispute that broke out between Greeks and Jews in Alexandria (*Ant.* 18.257). Like several ethnographers already mentioned, Apion composed a history of Egypt that seems to have contained some extensive references to Jewish history, and Josephus presents some of this material in *Against Apion.* Clement of Alexandria, a Christian author of the second century C.E., attributes to Apion a separate book, *Against the Judeans* (*Stromata* 1.21.101 = Stern no. 163b), but scholars for the most part regard this as a mistaken reference to the third and/or fourth book of Apion's history of Egypt.

Most of what survives of Apion's work is embedded in Josephus' polemic in *Against Apion,* and Josephus' indignation with Apion as a slanderer of Jews is everywhere apparent. Yet, if Josephus can be taken as reliable on the matter, Apion's writings about Judeans contained some variety in contents. Some of the fragments Josephus relates are basically objective observations. For example, Apion writes that Jews "are not masters of an empire, but rather slaves, first of one nation, then of another, and that calamity has more than once befallen [Jerusalem]" (*Ag. Ap.* 2.125 = Stern no. 174). Other fragments of Apion's work read like stock ethnic libels, as when Josephus records that Apion "denounces us for sacrificing domestic animals and for not eating pork, and he derides the practice of circumcision" (*Ag. Ap.* 2.137 = Stern no. 176). Still other sections relate to specific historical circumstances such as the question of Jewish rights in Alexandria. According to Josephus, Apion asks, "Why, then, if [Jews] are citizens, do they not worship the same gods as the Alexandrians?" (*Ag. Ap.* 2.65-73 = Stern no. 169). Only a relatively small portion of the fragments Josephus preserves are the kind of unbelievable allegations worthy of Josephus' rebuke. These include the accusation that Jews celebrate an annual festival in which they "kidnap a Greek foreigner, fatten him up for a year, and then convey him to a wood, where they slay him, sacrifice his body with their customary ritual, partake of his flesh, and, while immolating the Greek, swear an oath of hostility to the Greeks" (*Ag. Ap.* 2.94-96 = Stern no. 171). In all, there appears to be little in Apion's writings about Jews that does not match the usual content of the Greek ethnographic tradition.

By the second half of the first century C.E., it is Latin writers rather than Greek writers that provide the bulk of the surviving commentary on Jews and Judaism. The next Greek author to mention Jews in any detail is the Stoic teacher Epictetus. His lectures, which were either recorded or summarized by his pupil Arrian, are thought to have taken place in Nicopolis in Greece in the first quarter of the first century C.E. In these lectures, Epictetus twice contrasts Jewish dietary habits to those of Syrians, Egyptians, and Romans (*Dissertations* 1.11.12-13 and 1.22.4 = Stern nos. 252 and 253). Epictetus' other statement about Jews is especially interesting:

> Why, then, do you call yourself a Stoic, why do you deceive the multitude, why do you act the part of a Judean, when you are a Greek? Do you not know how each person is called a Judean, a Syrian, or an Egyptian? And when we see someone vacillating, we are accustomed to say, "He is not a Judean; he is just pretending." But when he takes up the state of mind of one who has been baptized and made a choice, then he is a Judean in both reality and name. So also we are falsely baptized, Judeans in word, but in deed something else, not in harmony with reason, far from applying the principles we profess, yet priding ourselves for being people who know them. (*Dissertations* 2.9.19-21 = Stern no. 254)

Here again Epictetus labels Judeans as one of several ethnic groups with unique practices, but he also seems to characterize them as a kind of philosophical school comparable to the Stoics. The portion of the passage referring to baptism may well be early evidence for the practice of baptism as an initiation rite among Judeans. Yet Epictetus may be referring to people whom some modern scholars might describe as Christians.

One final author from the early second century merits our attention, Plutarch of Chaeronea (ca. 50-120 C.E.). Jews play minor roles in some of Plutarch's biographical sketches of famous figures, the *Lives*. More extended treatments of Jews occur in his so-called moral writings. In his discussion of worship practices that are excessive or wrongheaded *(desidaimonia)*, Plutarch includes in his list "Sabbath keeping *(sabbatismos)*" (*On Superstition* 8 = Stern no. 255). Among the examples of dinnertime conversations recorded in Plutarch's *Quaestionum Convivialum* (*Table Talk*) are two discussions relating specifically to Jews (*Table Talk* 4.4.4–4.6.2 = Stern no. 258). The first question is whether Jews abstain from pork out of reverence for or aversion to pigs. One participant argues that Jews consider the pig sacred because "it was the first to cut the soil with its projecting snout, thus producing a furrow and teaching man the function of a ploughshare." The counterargument is that Jews do not eat pigs because they fear contracting a skin disease from them. The second question, "Who is the god of the Jews?" *(tis ho gar Ioudaiois theos)*, leads to an extended discussion of the affinities between Jewish worship and the worship of Dionysus. An Athenian adherent of Dionysus dominates the conversation by pointing out parallels between several Jewish customs (the Feast of Tabernacles, Sabbath practices, musical Levites, and the garments of the high priest) and Dionysiac practices.

Conclusion and Postscript

On the whole, the Greek authors surveyed here show an interest in Judeans that is consonant with interest shown to other ethnic groups in antiquity. Some of the descriptive elements surveyed here may be no more than rhetorical tropes (such as tales of exotic peoples who practice human sacrifice), and we should certainly expect that descriptions of Judeans and opinions about them would vary widely in different time periods and in different regions in the Greek and Roman worlds. For example, many non-Jews living in Alexandria in the early Roman era seem to have been especially hostile to Jews (Collins 2005). In spite of the impression of a widespread and deep animosity toward Judeans left by some of Josephus' comments in *Against Apion*, it seems that in the eyes of historians and ethnographers writing in Greek, the Jews were simply another ethnic group with some curious characteristic practices, some worthy of praise, others worthy of censure.

Finally, it would be remiss to conclude without briefly discussing Greek literature about Jews written by Christians, if for no other reason than that Christians were responsible for the selection and preservation of nearly all the references to Judeans in Greek literature that we possess. Even the extant manuscripts of Josephus come down to us through Christian scribes. Also, it is in the works of Christian writers that *Ioudaismos* becomes a much more commonly used term. While the word *Ioudaismos* is first found in writers who claim a Jewish heritage (2 Macc. 2:21; 8:1; 14:38; 4 Macc. 4:26; Gal. 1:13-14), it comes into more regular use among Christian authors writing in Greek starting in the second century. A good example is Ignatius, a bishop of Antioch active in the early second century who uses the term *Ioudaismos* on two occasions, each time in direct contrast to the term *Christianismos* (*Magn.* 10:3 and *Phld.* 6:1). Later Christian authors invoke *Ioudaioi* and *Ioudaismos* in order to make them a precursor to (and negative foil for) the newly emerging Christian movement (Boyarin 2001; Mason 2007). This Christian set of interests in Jews came to dominate later portrayals of them written in Greek.

BIBLIOGRAPHY

J. M. G. BARCLAY 2007, *Flavius Josephus: Against Apion*, Leiden: Brill. • B. BAR-KOCHVA 1996, *Pseudo-Hecataeus, 'On the Jews': Legitimizing the Jewish Diaspora*, Berkeley: University of California Press. • D. BOYARIN 2001, "Justin Martyr Invents Judaism," *Church History* 70: 427-61. • J. J. COLLINS 2000, *Between Athens and Jerusalem*, 2d ed., Grand Rapids: Eerdmans. • J. J. COLLINS 2005, "Anti-Semitism in Antiquity? The Case of Alexandria," in *Ancient Judaism in Its Hellenistic Context*, ed. C. Bakhos, Leiden: Brill. • L. H. FELDMAN 1993, *Jew and Gentile in the Ancient World*, Princeton: Princeton University Press. • M. GOODMAN 1994, "Josephus as Roman Citizen," in *Josephus and the History of the Greco-Roman Period*, ed. F. Parente and J. Sievers, Leiden: Brill. • E. S. GRUEN 1998, "The Use and Abuse of the Exodus Story," *Jewish History* 12: 93-122. • H. JACOBSEN 2006, "Artapanus Judaeus," *JJS* 57: 210-21. • S. MASON 2007, "Jews, Judeans, Judaizing, Judaism: Problems of Categorization in Ancient History," *JSJ* 38: 457-512. • M. STERN 1974-84, *Greek and Latin Authors on Jews and Judaism*, 3 vols., Jerusalem: Israel Academy of Sciences and Humanities.

See also: Latin Authors on Jews and Judaism

BRENT NONGBRI

Greek Philosophy

Early Jewish Uses of Greek Philosophy

Early Greek references to the Jews included the notion that they were a race of philosophers or descendants of the philosophers of India (Stern 1974: 1:10, 46, 50). Moreover, the Greek inclination to idealize Eastern wisdom led to the assertion that Pythagoras had introduced many points of Jewish law into his philosophy (Stern 1976: 1:95). A reflection of this Greek tendency is found in various Hellenistic Jewish writings and culminates in Philo's statements that pagan lawgivers borrowed from Moses, and that Heraclitus and Zeno also derived some of their teachings from the great Jewish prophet (*Spec. Leg.* 4.61; *QG* 4.152; *Leg. Alleg.* 1.108; *Prob.* 57). The reality, of course, was quite the reverse. It was the Greek philosophical tradition that had inseminated the Jewish mind in an encounter that took place largely in the Diaspora, since the sages of the land of Israel were essentially indifferent to philosophical speculation, though in a general way even they were not completely untouched by it.

The initial penetration of Greek philosophical thought would appear to have occurred in the writings of the Jewish wisdom tradition, for the wisdom schools had international connections and their members were frequently recruited for foreign service. We thus begin the assessment of our theme with the biblical text of Qohelet, and continues with the extracanonical Wisdom of Ben Sira, Wisdom of Solomon, and 4 Maccabees.

Qohelet

The first glimmer of Jewish contact with the philosophical genius of the Hellenic mind appears to involve an interaction that is largely contextual and reflects a broad level of Greek conceptuality and mood rather than specific schools of thought or technical doctrines. Qohelet's highly introspective reporting, which constantly draws attention to his personal reactions to various situations in an apparent effort to persuade by empathy (2:2, 17; 7:26), has no close parallels in other wisdom literature and is clearly reminiscent of Socratic dialogue. Indeed, Socrates' relentless probing, which in Plato's early dialogues invariably ends in utter perplexity and puzzlement, is closely analogous to Qohelet's endless questioning and his firm conviction that the true nature of the divine plan for humanity constitutes an impenetrable mystery (3:11; 7:23-24; 8:17). For Qohelet the sage's task is not only to give counsel but to rouse people from their certainties. Von Loewenclau (1986) compares Qoh. 12:11, "the sayings of the wise are like goads" with Plato's *Apology* 30e, where Socrates describes himself as one who attaches himself to the city "as a gadfly to a horse that is sluggish on account of its size and needs to be aroused by stinging." Significantly, Qohelet describes his activity not as teaching but as "studying and probing" (1:13; 7:25). Socrates similarly says, "I was never anyone's teacher" (*Apology* 33a), and "I know that I do not know" (*Apology* 21d). Von Loewenclau also draws an interesting parallel between the complaint that Socrates "keeps repeating the same thing" (*Gorgias* 490e) and the fact that Qohelet's mind is similarly fixed on one basic theme, *hebel* ("meaninglessness"), a word that recurs no fewer than thirty times, in addition to the recurrence of other keywords to which he is addicted, such as *miqrê* ("fate"), *ʿāmāl* ("toil), and *yitrôn* ("profit"). Levy (1912) and Amir (1964-65) have noted the resemblance between the recurrent *hebel* judgment of Qohelet and the aphorism attributed to the Cynic Monimus of Syracuse (fourth century B.C.E.) declaring all human supposition to be illusion (*typhos*, literally "smoke"; Diogenes Laertius 6.83).

Hengel (1974: 115-28) cites a series of Greek texts that reflect popular Greek philosophy and provide close parallels to Qohelet. The latter's obsession, for example, with the incalculability of death, which renders us like animals trapped in a snare (9:12), is paralleled in a Greek epitaph from the third century B.C.E. (the most likely date of Qohelet): "Truly the gods take no account of mortals; no, like animals we are pulled hither and thither by chance, in life as in death" (cf. Qoh. 3:19).

Fox (1989: 47) correctly remarks that "underlying Qohelet's *hebel* judgments is an assumption that the system should be rational . . . that actions should invariably produce appropriate consequences." This demand for rationality constitutes the heart of the mainstream tradition in Greek philosophy. It is this fundamental drive for rationality that prevents Qohelet from ignoring the ineluctable absurdity that characterizes the human enterprise as a whole and thus sharply distinguishes his approach from that of the rest of the Jewish wisdom tradition.

The Wisdom of Ben Sira

In an age when Hellenistic wisdom dominated the civilized world, Ben Sira did his best to broaden the bounds of the Mosaic Law so that it would encompass universal wisdom. As Collins (1997) has remarked, his so-called nationalization of wisdom constituted in reality the universalization of the Torah. It is especially, however, in his confrontation with the existence of evil that he moves beyond the earlier wisdom tradition and is actively engaged in adapting Stoic arguments for the formulation of his main solution to this problem. In Sir. 33:7-14, he seeks to reconcile the unity of creation with a divine plan that consistently discriminates between pairs of opposites: good and evil, life and death, the sinner and the godly: "See now all the works of the Most High: they come in pairs, the one the opposite of the other" (33:15). This evidently implies that the universe consists of a harmony of opposites in accordance with a mysterious divine design.

The Stoics set forth a similar doctrine. Like Sirach they taught that this is the best possible world, and that notwithstanding apparent imperfections, Nature so organized each part that harmony is present in the whole (Cicero, *De Natura Deorum* 2.58; Epictetus, *Diatribes* 1.12.16). As for the evil of natural disasters, "it has a rationale peculiar to itself . . . and is not without usefulness in relation to the whole, for without it there could be no good" (Chrysippus in Plutarch, *Moralia* 1065b). Ben Sira's attitude is similar: "No cause then to say, 'What is the purpose of this?' Everything is chosen to satisfy a need" (39:21). The very elements that are good for the god-fearing turn to evil for sinners (39:28-31). The more recalcitrant problem, however, was that of moral evil, and here again both Sirach and the Stoics employ the same approach. Logic requires the existence of both good and evil. In his treatise *On Providence* Chrysippus argued that there could not be an idea of justice if there were no acts of injustice (Aulus Gellius, *Noctes Atticae* 7.1.2-4).

Wisdom of Solomon

In the Wisdom of Solomon, the Hellenistic Jewish wisdom tradition so palpably verges on the philosophical that we can readily identify this book's Middle Platonist affinities and its considerable use of Greek philosophical terminology. The centrality of its Platonic teaching of the immortality of the soul represents a new emphasis in Jewish tradition. Even more significant, however, is the fact that Plato's doctrine of the adverse influence of body on soul (*Phaedrus* 66b; *Respublica* 611c) and the superior state of soul over its bodily form (*Symposium* 208e) is faithfully echoed in Wis. 4:1, where it is said that it is better to be childless, provided one is virtuous, and in 9:15, where, in a verse replete with Platonic phraseology, the author speaks of "a perishable body weighing down the soul and a tent of clay encumbering a mind full of cares" (cf. Plato, *Phaedrus* 81c; 247b).

In sketching his own spiritual odyssey, the author confesses to a passion for Lady Wisdom that had gripped him from early youth and had led him to cast his lot with her forever. This unbridled love for wisdom is vividly reflected in his magnificent fivefold description of her, in which she is conceived as an eternal emanation of God's power and glory (7:25-26, 29-30), a Neopythagorean notion that even the more philosophically ambitious Philo was reluctant to express explicitly. As for the creation of the world, he adopts the Platonic notion that it was created "out of formless matter" (11:17), a view not inconsonant with that of the rabbis.

In Wis. 7:22-24 the author describes Wisdom by a series of twenty-one epithets (such as intelligent, subtle, agile, unsullied, unhindered), borrowed largely from Greek philosophy, especially that of the Stoa. Posidonius, for example, had defined God as "intelligent breath pervading the whole of substance," and Stoics had defined the soul as a "subtle, self-moving body" (*Stoicorum Veterum Fragmenta* [*SVF*] 2.780). What characterizes the Stoic *pneuma* ("breath") above all, however, is that it pervades and permeates all things (*SVF* 2.780). In a fine ode to Wisdom's saving power in history (10:1-21), the author assimilates the old covenantal salvation history with its miraculous divine irruptions to the immanent divine ordering of human events as mediated by the continuous activity of Wisdom. As the Divine Mind immanent within the universe and guiding and controlling all its dynamic operations, Wisdom represents the entire range of human knowledge (7:17-21).

4 Maccabees

In 4 Maccabees, which was probably written in the first century C.E., we have an overtly philosophical discourse on the theme of the mastery of devout reason over the emotions, illustrated by a panegyric of the martyrs (Eleazar, the seven brethren, and their mother), which the author binds to the discourse (the first three chapters) by repeated reference to his main thesis. The essential component in the book's argument is that the Torah is consistent with the world order. In the confrontation between Antiochus IV and Eleazar, the king claims that the Jewish ban on eating pork shows that Judaism is not in accord with nature (5:8-9). In his response, Eleazar, identified both as a philosopher and an expert in the Law (5:4), argues that the Torah in fact inculcates in its followers the virtues of temperance, courage, justice, and piety (5:22-25). His reasoning is couched in the idiom of natural-law theory: "For believing that the Law has been established from God, we know that the Creator of the world, in laying down the Law, feels for us in accordance with [our] nature and commands us to eat whatever is well suited to our soul" (5:25-26, my translation). The same language, which coincides with Philo's firm conviction that the Mosaic Law is the truest reflection of the Logos (*Opificio Mundi* 3), had also been used by Pseudo-Aristeas (143, 161), when he insisted that the Torah's strange food laws were legislated "with a view to truth and as a token of right reason." The thrust of Eleazar's statement is that *nomos* and *physis*, deriving as they do from one Creator, cannot be mutually antagonistic. The Law is perfectly rational, and the term *logismos* ("reasoning"), as Redditt (1983) has noted, occurs characteristically seventy-three times, for the most part in the context of the author's recurring theme that human reason is sovereign over the emotions.

Gutman (1958) and Hadas (1953) think that Eleazar's position is modeled on that of Socrates in Plato's *Gorgias*, where, in answer to Callicles' objection that the tyrant can subject his victim to torture, Socrates insists that any injustice is worse and more shameful for the man who does it than for the one who suffers it (580e). Moreover, at the final judgment, says Socrates, the soul will be subjected to the ultimate scrutiny of justice. The author of 4 Maccabees similarly justifies the fate of the martyrs by emphasizing the immortality of the soul and its future vindication. Although there are clear echoes of Stoic teaching in the book, this may simply indicate that the author's philosophical orientation is that of the highly stoicized Middle Platonism of the age. Wolfson (1948: 2:270) argued that the author of 4 Maccabees opposed the Stoic ideal of the extirpation of the passions rather than mere control over them. Renehan (1972) has correctly pointed out, however, that the Platonizing Middle Stoic Posidonius had also maintained that the passions cannot be eradicated. But the Middle Platonists generally followed the Middle Stoa in this matter, so once again the author's orientation points in the direction of Middle Platonism. This is further strengthened by the author's injection into his discussion of the triumph of the brothers' reason over the passions the topic of fraternal affection, which formed another emotional obstacle for the "athletes of virtue" to overcome. As pointed out by Klauck (1990) and deSilva (2006: 210-17), much of what one finds in 4 Maccabees on this topic can also be found in Plutarch's treatise *De Fraterno Amore* (*Moralia* 478–90).

Aristobulus

Aristobulus (second century B.C.E.) inaugurates an interpretative approach to Scripture that dimly prefigures that of Philo. Like the latter, he aims to establish that the Torah's teaching is in accord with philosophical truth. To this end he takes great pains to interpret anthropomorphic descriptions of God allegorically. He thus maintains that the biblical expression "hand of God" signifies the divine power, the "standing of God" (Gen. 28:13; Exod. 17:6) refers to the immutability of God's creation, and the "voice of God" to the establishment of things, for as Moses continually says in his description of creation, "And God spoke, and it came to pass." As for God's resting on the seventh day, this does not signify the end of his work but only that "after he had finished ordering all things, he so orders them for all time" (cf. Philo, *Leg. Alleg.* 1.6), and the "work of the six days" refers to the establishment of the course of time and the hierarchical structure of the universe (frgs. 2, 4, and 5 in Yarbro Collins 1985: 837-42).

Philo of Alexandria

Although fully acquainted with the Greek philosophical texts at first hand, Philo is not to be regarded as an original philosopher, nor did he claim that distinction himself. He saw his task more modestly as that of the great reconciler who would bridge two disparate traditions that were both close to his heart. Although there is still no consensus, it is likely that the apparent eclecticism of his thought is in fact representative of Middle Platonism, a philosophical tradition marked by Stoicizing and Pythagorizing tendencies, including a strong dose of number symbolism.

Since Philo's mystical theology bars a direct approach to God's essence, it must be sought through the oblique traces disclosed by its noetic aspect, the Divine Mind or Logos. Philo delineates the dynamics of the Logos' activity by defining its two constitutive polar principles, Goodness or the Creative Power, and Sovereignty or the Ruling Power, which are clearly reminiscent of the principles of Unlimit and Limit in Plato's *Philebus* (23c-31a) and reappear in Plotinus' two logical moments in the emergence of Intellect, where we find unlimited Intelligible Matter proceeding from the One and then turning back to its source for definition (*Enneades* 2.4.5; 5.4.2).

Although the human soul, as a fragment of the Logos, might be thought to have a natural claim on immortality, the latter can be forfeited if the soul is not properly assimilated to its divine source. From Philo's Platonist perspective, the body is a corpse entombing the soul, which at its death returns to its own proper life (*Legum Allegoriae* 107–8; cf. Plato, *Respublica* 585b). Alternatively, its sojourn in the body may be taken to be a period of exile (*QG* 3.10), a theme undoubtedly familiar to Philo from Middle Platonic exegesis of Homer's *Odyssey*, according to which Odysseus' arduous homeward journey symbolizes the soul's labors in its attempt to return to its original home (Plutarch, *Moralia* 745-46). The Abraham of Philo is a mystical philosopher who, after having mastered the general studies (symbolized by Hagar), at which stage all he could produce was Ishmael or sophistry, has abandoned the realm of sense (symbolized by his parting with Lot) for the intelligible world and, despite his initial flirtation with Chaldean (i.e., Stoic) pantheism, has attained to the highest vision of Deity, resulting in his transformation into a perfect embodiment of natural law (Sandmel 1956).

Philo's ethical theory is thoroughly grounded in Stoic teaching and is fully encapsulated in their common ideal of *philanthrōpia*, humanity or benevolence. All human beings are kinsmen and brothers inasmuch as they share the gift of rationality (*De Decalogo* 41). Like the Stoic Panaetius, Philo emphasizes the positive aspect of justice as an active beneficence. In the second part of his treatise *De Virtutibus*, devoted to *philanthrōpia* (51-74), Philo points out that it has *eusebeia* ("piety") as its sister and twin, for the love of God involves the love of humanity (*De Decalogo* 134). Benevolence also requires a benign attitude toward slaves, and Philo's position on this matter is essentially in line with that of the Stoa (*SVF* 3.349-66). His attitude toward war is also very similar to that of the Stoa. The injunctions concerning war in Deut. 20:10 he conveniently limits to war against those who revolt from an alliance, in the conviction, as Colson has remarked, that "the Law could never have intended to sanction wars of conquest."

BIBLIOGRAPHY

Y. AMIR 1964-65, "On the Question of the Relationship between Qohelet and Greek Wisdom," *Bet Miqra* 22: 36-38 (in Hebrew). • J. J. COLLINS 1997, *Jewish Wisdom in the Hellenistic Age*, Louisville: Westminster John Knox. • J. J. COLLINS 2000, *Between Athens and Jerusalem*, 2d ed., Grand Rapids: Eerdmans, 186-209. • D. DESILVA 2006, *4 Maccabees*, Leiden: Brill. • M. FOX 1989, *Qohelet and His Contradictions*, Decatur, Ga.: Almond Press. • Y. GUTMAN 1958, *The Beginnings of Jewish Hellenistic Literature*, vol. 1, Jerusalem: Bialik Institute, 186-220 (in Hebrew). • M. HADAS 1953, *The Third and Fourth Books of Maccabees*, New York: Harper, 115-18. • M. HENGEL 1974, *Judaism and Hellenism*, vol. 1, Philadelphia: Fortress, 115-30. • H.-J. KLAUCK 1990, "Brotherly Love in Plutarch and in 4 Maccabees," in *Greeks, Romans, Christians*, ed. D. Balch, Minneapolis: Fortress, 144-56. • L. LEVY 1912, *Das Buch Qohelet*, Leipzig: Hinrichs. • I. VON LOEWENCLAU 1986, "Kohelet und Sokrates," *ZAW* 98: 327-38. • P. REDDITT 1983, "The Conception of Nomos in Fourth Maccabees," *CBQ* 45: 249-70. • R. RENEHAN 1972, "The Greek Philosophical Background of Fourth Maccabees," *Rheinisches Museum für Philologie* 115: 223-38. • S. SANDMEL 1956, *Philo's Place in Judaism*, Cincinnati: Hebrew Union College, 96-211. • M. STERN 1974, *Greek and Latin Authors on Jews and Judaism*, 3 vols., Jerusalem: Israel Academy of Sciences and Humanities. • D. WINSTON 1979, *Wisdom of Solomon*, Garden City, N.Y.: Doubleday. • D. WINSTON 2001, *The Ancestral Philosophy: Hellenistic Philosophy in Second Temple Judaism: Essays of David Winston*, ed. G. Sterling, Providence: Brown Judaic Studies, 11-32. • H. WOLFSON 1948, *Philo*, 2 vols., Cambridge, Mass.: Harvard University Press. • A. YARBRO COLLINS 1985, "Aristobulus," in *OTP* 2.831-42.

DAVID WINSTON

Greek Religions

The Jewish Encounter with Greek Religions

During the Second Temple period, and particularly after the conquest of the Near East by Alexander the Great at the end of the fourth century, Jews in Palestine and the Diaspora came into increasing contact with Greek religion in various forms. In the environs of historic Israel, local deities were identified with Greek figures in a complex process of cultural syncretism. Thus at Tyre, Melqart was identified with the Greek hero who became a god, Herakles. Further east, at Palmyra, Herakles was identified with the Mesopotamian underworld deity, Nergal. Temples to other deities identified with Greek

The temple of Olympian Zeus in Athens, with the Acropolis in the background
(Nicholas Wolterstorff)

names are found in the cities of the Decapolis, at Gerasa, for example, to Zeus and Artemis. Beth-Shean/ Scythopolis claimed to be founded by Dionysus and to contain the tomb of his nurse, Nysa. Epigraphical evidence indicates that Zeus was also worshiped in the city, perhaps in tandem with Dionysus, a connection made also in the Hellenistic reform at Jerusalem. North of the Sea of Galilee, at a site called Panion in the third century B.C.E., later Paneas, was located a cave and a spring dedicated to the god Pan, perhaps a Greek identification of a local Baal. Herod the Great would later build a temple to Augustus at the site (Josephus, *Ant.* 15.360-64; *J.W.* 1.404-6). In the old Philistine cities along the coast, religion flourished in Greek forms. Apollo was worshiped at Ashkelon, and one tradition reports that the grandfather of Herod the Great was, as a child, a servant in Apollo's temple (Eusebius, *Hist. Eccl.* 1.6.2-3). Herod also dramatically affected the life of the coast with the creation of Caesarea Maritima, which later became the provincial capital. The city housed a mixed population of Jews and Gentiles, whose religious practices were respected. These included a Mithraeum, or sanctuary to the Greco-Persian deity Mithras, whose cult was popular in the imperial period.

The surge of Hellenistic culture in the third century B.C.E. did not leave untouched the traditional heartland of Israelite civilization in the highlands of Judea and Samaria. Some factions, including the ruling classes of Samaria and some elements of the Jerusalem priesthood, assimilated native religious traditions to the new ecumenical forms and interpreted local practices in broadly acceptable terms. The Samaritans requested that their temple on Mt. Gerizim be renamed in honor of Zeus, the chief deity of the Greek pantheon, with the title "Friend of Strangers," perhaps a play on the place name *gēr* (2 Macc. 6:2; Josephus, *Ant.* 11.257-64).

In Jerusalem, similar impulses emerged, but with different results. The high priest Jason inaugurated a gymnasium (2 Macc. 4:9-17), which may have involved some veneration of the traditional patrons of the gymnasium, such as Herakles. Direct evidence for such practice is lacking, but Jason is reported to have sent funds for sacrifices to Herakles at Tyre (2 Macc. 4:18-20). Others, faithful to the Israelite tradition of worshipping Yahweh alone, staunchly resisted, leading to the Maccabean Revolt and the response by Antiochus IV Epiphanes. The Greek king supported the assimilationist faction by attempting to impose Greek religious forms on Jerusalem and its Temple, including naming it for Olympian Zeus (2 Macc. 6:2), perhaps a translation of Baal ha-shamayim, introducing forbidden sacrifices (1 Macc. 1:41-50; 2 Macc. 6:5) and Dionysiac processions (2 Macc. 6:7). The Syrian general Nicanor later (2 Macc. 14:33) threatened to destroy the Temple and replace it with a sanctuary to Dionysus. (Some Greeks seem to have thought that the God of the Jews was a variant of Dionysus. See Plutarch, *Quaestionum Convivialum* [Table Talk 4.4.4–4.6.2].) Such actions introducing Greek cultic elements were viewed by the traditionalist resistance as a "desolating abomination" (Dan. 9:27). The ultimate success of the Maccabean Revolt ensured that whatever other accommodations with the wider culture might be tolerated, elements of Greek cult would be excluded from Jerusalem. Continued vigilance against such intrusions is evident in the Roman period in the protests against Pilate's attempt to introduce legionary standards into Jerusalem (Josephus, *J.W.* 2.169-74; *Ant.* 18.55-57) and the resistance to the attempt by the emperor Gaius to establish his statue in Jerusalem (Josephus, *J.W.* 2.184-203; *Ant.* 18.240-308; Philo, *Legatio ad Gaium*).

The Use of Greek Religion in Early Jewish Literature

The fragmentary literary remains of Jewish authors from the early Hellenistic period display some openness to assimilation with Greek religious traditions. Theodotus, particularly interested in Samaria, identified the eponymous founder of the city, Shechem, as the son of Hermes, understood no doubt to be a deified human being (in Eusebius, *Praep. Evan.* 9.22.1). Cleodemus Malchus gave an account of Israelite history in which Herakles married a granddaughter of Abraham (Josephus, *Ant.* 1.241). Mythical figures, duly rationalized, could thus be used to link local traditions to the broader culture, without any religious commitment.

Some Jewish authors of the Hellenistic and early Roman periods composed works imitating Greek genres and occasionally using Greek mythical figures. The

Sibylline Oracles make reference to the gods Kronos and Zeus (*Sib. Or.* 11.133-41) and to the Titans known from Hesiod's *Theogony* (*Sib. Or.* 1.307-23; 3.110-55), interpreting the tales in a rationalistic (or "Euhemerist") way as stories of human beings. The *Oracles* also use epithets well known from association with Zeus ("lightning giver") or Poseidon ("earth shaker") in alluding to the God of Israel (*Sib. Or.* 2.16). The *Oracles* can also simply dismiss Greek deities, such as Rhea, Kronos, and Zeus, as "lifeless demons, likenesses of dead corpses" (*Sib. Or.* 8.45-47).

The curt dismissal of Greek deities finds parallels in other literature that defines Jewish identity as one that excludes any participation in the worship of alien deities. This critical stance, continuing the prophetic critique of idolatry (e.g., Isa. 44:9-20; Jer. 10:1-16), finds eloquent expression in the Wisdom of Solomon, from the late Hellenistic or early Roman period in Egypt, which ridicules the making of idols (Wisdom 13) or prayer to them (Wisdom 14), and offers a psychological explanation of the origins of the practice of worshiping them (Wisdom 15).

While the Wisdom of Solomon draws a clear boundary line against any improper cult, it significantly adopts from the tradition of Greek philosophy a conceptual tool with important religious dimensions. Its hymnic praise of Wisdom (Wis. 7:22–8:1) uses language most at home in Stoic notions of the *pneuma*. The Stoics identified that rational force, which pervades and holds all things together, as Zeus. The Wisdom of Solomon does not follow that precedent and does not thereby reduce God to an immanent principle of cosmic order. Yet it does, in effect, affirm that God's presence in the world can be understood in Stoic terms.

The strategy of the Wisdom of Solomon is replicated on a grander scale in the work of the philosopher and exegete Philo. He too defines clear boundaries within which Jewish monotheism is to be lived out. Yet he also employs conceptual tools from Greek philosophical traditions. The most important of these is the Platonic postulate of a world of ideas that gives coherence and meaning to the world of experience. Philo's notion of the Logos or Word of God combines an understanding of the realm of forms or ideas, now understood to be concepts in the mind of God, with the Stoic notion of the immanent rational force field. Philo is careful not to use the religious labels for these metaphysical principles that contemporary Greek philosophers might have deployed. Yet, like the Wisdom of Solomon, Philo uses Greek religious philosophy to explain his own Jewish monotheism.

BIBLIOGRAPHY

J. J. COLLINS AND G. E. STERLING, EDS. 2001, *Hellenism in the Land of Israel*, Notre Dame: University of Notre Dame Press. • L. H. FELDMAN 2006, *Judaism and Hellenism Reconsidered*, Leiden: Brill. • M. HENGEL 1974, *Judaism and Hellenism: Studies in Their Encounter in Palestine during the Early Hellenistic Period*, trans. J. Bowden, Philadelphia: Fortress. • A. TRIPOLITIS 2002, *Religions of the Hellenistic Age*, Grand Rapids: Eerdmans. • J. ZANGENBERG, H. W. ATTRIDGE, AND D. B. MARTIN, EDS. 2007, *Religion, Ethnicity and Identity in Ancient Galilee: A Region in Transition*, Tübingen: Mohr-Siebeck.

See also: Greek Philosophy; Hellenism, Hellenization

HAROLD W. ATTRIDGE

Gymnasium

History

The gymnasium was a signature institution of Greek civic, athletic, and intellectual culture. Greek athletic contests occurred during funerals and festivals as early as the Bronze Age. However, the origins of the gymnasium probably date to the seventh-sixth centuries B.C.E., when power in Greek cities shifted from kings to heavily armed citizens known as hoplites. Some events in Greek athletic contests bore little resemblance to techniques used in hoplite warfare. Nevertheless, hoplites seem to have institutionalized athletic training to foster military skills and consolidate democratic rivalry to royal courts. Motivation also came from recreational habits and the emerging ideal of "excellence" *(aretē)*, which embraced physical and intellectual prowess. Another factor was the regularization of Pan-Hellenic games, which rewarded consistent training.

Some of the earliest gymnasia emerged in groves associated with cult centers in Athens. Probably by ca. 500 B.C.E. these included the Academy, the Lykeion, and the Cynosarges. In the next two centuries these acquired reputations for education and philosophy. Other Greek cities experienced similar developments, partly under Athenian influence. By the early Hellenistic period, gymnasia around the Mediterranean demonstrated enough consistency to function as social clubs for the Hellenistic elite and selected non-Greek subjects. Birth or civic award remained the basis for citizenship in a *polis* (a city with a Hellenistic constitution and democratic assembly). But in most cases teenage male citizens known as ephebes (Gr. *ephēboi*) passed through the ephebate (Gr. *ephēbeia*), an institution that offered formal training in athletics and other skills in the gymnasium) prior to entering the citizen assembly. This consisted of two or more years of gymnasium training in military skills, athletics, politics, civic religion, and intellectual disciplines. This rite of passage transformed gymnasium education into a marker of Hellenistic civic identity and a prerequisite for social advancement.

After the Roman conquest, gymnasium education became even more desirable because Hellenistic elites often were favored with awards of Roman citizenship and lucrative posts in provincial bureaucracies. At the same time, citizenship in each polis was regulated more carefully because the Romans used social class to determine tax rates and legal privileges. These opposing dynamics often generated civic conflicts, in some cases involving Jews.

Architecture and Operation

A gymnasium was an architectural complex rather than a single building. Its most consistent feature was a *palaestra.* This was a roofed colonnade (peristyle) around an open square or rectangular courtyard of earth or sand that could be used for wrestling and other exercises. The inner sides of excavated courtyards often are 25-40 m., but sizes vary widely (e.g., 14 × 14 m. at Delphi; 57 × 86 m. at Cyrene). Rooms with paved floors adjoined one or more of the outer sides of the colonnade. These usually included a lecture hall with benches for seating (an *exedra*), which was often identified as a clubroom (*ephebeum* in Latin; *ephēbeion* in Greek); a dressing room *(apodytērion);* a room for bathing *(loutron);* and a storeroom for olive oil and equipment used by athletes. Other rooms sometimes were built for boxing, ball playing, additional lecture halls, a library, a shrine, and functions unique to local traditions. A complete gymnasium usually had one or more tracks for running, often including a covered colonnaded track *(xystos)* and a parallel open-air track *(paradromos).* Tracks were a *stadion* in length, with standards varying in a range of 164 to 210 m. Gymnasia were decorated with altars and statues of Hermes, Herakles, and local deities; inscriptions and statues honoring rulers, patrons, and athletes; student graffiti; trees, mosaics, paintings, and gifts. In the Roman period, gymnasia often were furnished with elaborate bath complexes and swimming pools. In some cases a gymnasium was used for functions otherwise associated with the Roman forum, such as tribunals and assemblies (Josephus, *J.W.* 2.344).

A gymnasium was frequented by lecturers, athletic trainers, maintenance staff, and male citizens of all ages. Education was privately arranged and occurred in any setting where teachers could operate, not just the gymnasium. Only ephebic training was unique to the gymnasium. This was administered by elected civic magistrates, of whom the chief usually was called *gymnasiarch.* The gymnasiarch also managed the gymnasium's athletic games, oil supply, and other affairs. This carried considerable expense, prestige, and power. Gymnasiarchs thus might have been involved in the disputes over monetary compensation granted to Jewish citizens of Antioch who did not want to use Gentile oil (Josephus, *Ant.* 12.120; cf. *J.W.* 2.123; *Life* 74). But the role of gymnasiarchs in the attacks on the Jews of Alexandria in 38 C.E. has been greatly exaggerated.

Jews in the Gymnasium

The ideals of the gymnasium appealed to many Jews. An especially powerful attraction was the political and economic benefits of citizenship in a Greek *polis.* This motivated the high priest Jason to construct a gymnasium in Jerusalem early in the reign of the Seleucid king Antiochus IV (1 Macc. 1:11-15; 2 Macc. 4:7-15). Antiochus offered citizenship in Antioch to Jews who passed through the ephebate. This was a strategy to neutralize political parties in Jerusalem that sided with the Ptolemies in Egypt. Propaganda for the Hasmonean leaders of the

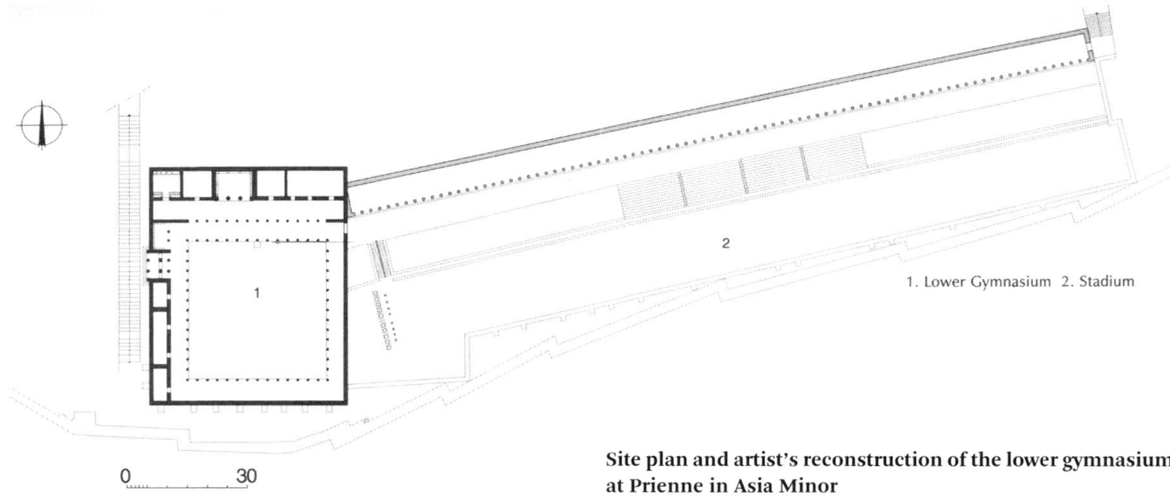

Site plan and artist's reconstruction of the lower gymnasium at Prienne in Asia Minor

Maccabean Revolt accused Jason's allies of apostasy. But the cause of the Maccabean Revolt was the subsequent policies of Antiochus, not Jason's reforms. The role of the priestly aristocracy in Jason's gymnasium and analogies with contemporary gymnasia suggest that lectures and other activities in this gymnasium may even have promoted indigenous Jewish traditions. This does not diminish the potential for conflicts over varying degrees of athletic nudity and foreign religious elements. But such conflicts did not reach crisis proportions until after the gymnasium began to be used by Gentile troops garrisoned in Jerusalem by Antiochus.

The Hasmoneans maintained a standing army, constructed swimming pools at their palaces in Jericho, and engaged in other practices suggesting a lively interest in athletics. They even built a palace in Jerusalem next to Jason's gymnasium, which probably continued to operate until 70 C.E. This is suggested by references in Josephus to a structure called the *xystos* (*J.W.* 2.344; 6.376-77; *Ant.* 20.189-92; cf. Pausanias 6.23.1; Justin, *Dialogue with Trypho* 1, 9).

Patronage of athletics by Herod and his descendants suggests that other gymnasia could be found in Palestine. Herod's gifts included gymnasia or in some cases endowments of gymnasiarchies to cities outside his kingdom, including nearby Tripolis, Damascus, and Ptolemais (Josephus, *J.W.* 1.422-23; *SEG* 45:1131; possibly *IJO*, vol. 1, Ach 74). He may have done the same within his kingdom, because he established hippodrome-stadiums and games in both Caesarea and Jerusalem. A gymnasium also must have been present in each city organized on the model of a polis by Herod and his descendants, including Sebaste, Tiberias, Bethsaida, Caesarea Philippi, and others. Excavations at Jericho have uncovered a multipurpose theater-hippodrome-gymnasium complex. This suggests that gymnasia in the small cities of Palestine did not always follow typical patterns and therefore may escape identification in the interpretation of archaeological remains.

Diaspora Jews participated as citizens in the gymnasium of Antioch (Josephus, *Ant.* 12.119-20). They appear in ephebic lists and graffiti in Asia Minor, Cyrenaica, and in a later period Greece (*IJO*, vol. 1, Ach 53; *IJO*, 2:22, 47; *CJZC* 6, 7, 41). Vivid testimony to gymnasium training appears in the family history and writings of Philo of Alexandria (*Spec. Leg.* 2.229-30; *Prov.* 2.44-46; *De Mutatione Nominum* 80–88; *De Congressu* 6–80). Some Jews may have shared in the polytheism of the gymnasium, including ephebate rituals for Hermes and Herakles (*CJZC* 6, 7), but many found ways to accommodate such rituals to monotheism. Ethnic conflicts sometimes erupted because Jewish distinctives made Jews easy targets for efforts to restrict access to civic privileges (*CPJ* 2:151, 153). Most obstacles to civic privileges were not unique to Jews, however, until the eruption of the Jewish revolt in Palestine in 66 C.E. provided a pretext. The injustices that followed partly explain why Jews violently destroyed the gymnasium and civic buildings in Cyrene at the beginning of the revolt of 116-117 C.E. But Jewish ephebes appear in other regions after this point (*IJO*, vol. 1, Ach 53; *IJO*, 2:47). Integration of Jews into their environment is also implied in the renovation of the gymnasium at Sardis in the late third century C.E. One section became a synagogue while the rest retained its civic functions.

Ironically, athletic nudity and social interaction in the gymnasium promoted the visibility of circumcision and other markers of Jewish identity that attracted much less attention before the Hellenistic period (*CPJ* 3:519; Martial, *Epigrams* 7.82; cf. Philo, *In Flaccum* 34–40). This helped fuel programmatic responses by Jewish reformers, the apostle Paul, the emperor Hadrian, and others. The impact of the gymnasium on the history of Judaism is often underappreciated.

Bibliography

J. Delorme 1960, *Gymnasion: Étude sur les monuments consacrés à l'éducation en Grèce (des origines à l'Empire romain)*, Paris: Boccard. • R. Doran 1990, "Jason's Gymnasium," in *Of Scribes and Scrolls*, ed. H. W. Attridge et al., Lanham, Md.: University Press of America, 99-109. • R. Doran 2001, "The High Cost of a Good Education," in *Hellenism in the Land of Israel*, ed. J. J. Collins and G. E. Sterling, Notre Dame: University of Notre Dame Press, 94-115. • R. Doran 2002, "Jewish Education in the Seleucid Period," *Second Temple Studies*, vol. 3, *Studies in Politics, Class, and Material Culture*, ed. P. R. Davies and J. M. Halligan, London: Sheffield Academic Press, 116-32. • P. Gauthier and M. B. Hatzopoulos 1993, *La loi gymnasiarchique de Beroia*, Athens: Centre de Recherches de l'Antiquité Grecque et Romain; Paris: Boccard. • A. Kerkeslager 2005, "The Absence of Dionysios, Lampo, and Isidoros from the Violence in Alexandria in 38 C.E.," *SPhA* 17: 49-94.

See also: Assimilation, Acculturation, Accommodation; Athletics

Allen Kerkeslager

H

Hanukkah → Festivals and Holy Days

Hasideans

The Hasideans were a group of Jews who participated in the Maccabean Revolt in the second century B.C.E. The term "Hasideans" is an English transliteration of Gr. *Asidaioi,* which is a transliteration of Hebr. *ḥăsîdîm* ("Hasidim," meaning "pious ones") or of its Aramaic form *ḥasîdayyā'*. The Greek term receives mention in 1 Macc. 2:42 and 7:13 and in 2 Macc. 14:6. The manuscript evidence for the first reference has been questioned (Schwartz 1994). Estimates of their significance range from Martin Hengel, who considers them the forerunners of the Essenes, the Pharisees, and the authors of apocalyptic literature such as the book of Daniel (Hengel 1974) to Philip Davies, who questions whether there was even a formal group that bore that title (Davies 1977). The former viewpoint continues to hold sway in continental scholarship (Mittmann-Richert 2000: 23, 51). A careful analysis of the relevant passages is the necessary basis for any claims made about this group.

In 1 Macc. 2:42 the Hasideans are referred to as a *synagōgē* ("company") of mighty men (or warriors) who willingly offered themselves for the Law. They joined the priest Mattathias and his allies in resisting the forces of the Seleucid king Antiochus IV, even when attacked on the Sabbath. Many scholars identify the Hasideans with those Jews who sought righteousness and justice and retreated to the desert for refuge, as described in 1 Macc. 2:29-38. The literary basis for such a connection, though, is not evident. The claim being made is rather that the Hasideans aligned themselves with the broader insurrection.

In 1 Macc. 7:12-18 the Hasideans are portrayed as a leading group in Israel. Here they are described as a "company of scribes" who were "first among the Israelites." In this passage, however, their political significance is discounted. While Judah Maccabee and his brothers reject the "peaceable but treacherous words" of Alcimus and Bacchides, the Hasideans appear before Alcimus and Bacchides to ask for just terms. The pro-Hasmonean author of 1 Maccabees portrays the Hasideans as naive since they trusted Alcimus, a priest of the line of Aaron, even though he had been appointed by the Seleucid ruler Demetrius. Earlier in the chapter, Alcimus is portrayed as the leader of the lawless and impious in Israel. As a result of their naive trust, Alcimus is able to seize and kill sixty of the Hasideans. The author of 1 Maccabees describes this event utilizing Ps. 79:2b-3, a lament for the pious and for Jerusalem. Modern historians have used this text as evidence of the religious piety of the Hasideans. The argument is that they were susceptible to the persuasion of Aaron because they sought religious goals rather than the political ends of the Maccabees. In this view, they thought that Alcimus would uphold the rights of the pious to observe the Jewish religion, which was their sole interest. Historians who interpret the evidence in this manner often find the origins of the Essenes, Pharisees, and apocalypticists in the Hasideans.

2 Maccabees 14:6-10 places the charges against Judah Maccabee in the mouth of Alcimus and identifies Judah as the leader of the Hasideans. Under his leadership they are guilty of continuing to foment strife and rebellion throughout Israel. One of the main aims of 2 Maccabees is to portray the heroic nature and role of Judah Maccabee, and the Hasideans serve to support that aim.

The Hasideans probably were a particular group, since 1 and 2 Maccabees transliterate the Hebrew term *Ḥăsîdîm* as a proper name *(Asidaioi)* rather than translate it into Greek as a substantival adjective (*hosioi,* "pious ones"). Even so, the three references to the Hasideans leave us with very limited clues concerning their actual nature and contributions. It seems unlikely that they were simply pacifists who briefly deviated from their basic ideology in support of Mattathias or that they were the religious wing of the revolution that broke ranks with the Hasmoneans when their religious objectives were accomplished. The evidence suggests rather that they were members of the developing scribal circles in Palestinian Judaism.

There is no reason to understand passages such as Ps. 149:1 ("assembly of the pious") and other uses of the word *ḥasîd* throughout the Psalms as references to the Hasideans. The same is true of the appearances of the term *hosioi* (the Greek translation of *ḥăsîdîm*) in the *Psalms of Solomon* (cf. "synagogue of the pious" in *Ps. Sol.* 17:16).

The Dead Sea Scrolls often use the term *ḥăsîdîm* but not to designate a particular group. The appearances of the term in 4QMessianic Apocalypse (4Q521 2 + 4 ii 5, 7) and 11QApocryphal Psalms (18:10; 19:7; 22:3, 6) do not point to a distinct group in the history of the Qumran community but are common adjectives designating piety, as in the biblical Psalms. The phrase *'îš ḥăsîdîm* is employed with reference to David in 4QMMT (4Q398 14-17 ii, 1), where it means "man of pious deeds."

The Hebrew term *ḥăsîdîm* appears in early rabbinic literature. It is used as an adjective to describe certain figures such as Honi the Circle Drawer and Hillel the Elder. The miracle worker Ḥanina ben Dosa is sometimes designated a *ḥasîd* by modern scholars, but he is not referred to as such in tannaitic literature. However, since he is described in ways similar to the "early Hasidim" in rabbinic literature, the designation is not without basis.

A potential historical connection between the *ḥăsîdîm* of rabbinic literature and the Hasideans of 1 and 2 Maccabees has been sought in references to the "first" or "early" Hasidim *(ḥăsîdîm hārîšonîm)* in *m. Ber.* 5:1; *t. B. Qam.* 2:6; *b. Niddah* 38ab; *b. Nedarim* 10a; and *b. Menaḥot* 40b–41a. However, the term *ḥăsîdîm* in these passages designates those of exemplary behavior or exceptional piety rather than authoritative persons with defined opinions in halakic disputes, let alone members of a religious movement in the second century B.C.E. Even if the *ḥăsîdîm* mentioned in rabbinic literature were identified as a concrete historical movement, there would still be no basis to associate them with the Hasideans described in 1 and 2 Maccabees.

BIBLIOGRAPHY

D. BERMAN 1979, "Hasidim in Rabbinic Traditions," *SBLSP* 2 (1979): 15-33. • P. R. DAVIES 1977, "Hasidim in the Maccabean Period," *JJS* 28: 127-40. • M. HENGEL 1974, *Judaism and Hellenism: Studies in Their Encounter in Palestine during the Early Hellenistic Period,* trans. J. Bowden, 2 vols., Philadelphia: Fortress. • J. KAMPEN 1988, *The Hasideans and the Origin of Pharisaism: A Study in 1 and 2 Maccabees,* Atlanta: Scholars Press. • U. MITTMANN-RICHERT 2000, *Historische und legendarische Erzählungen,* JSHRZ VI,1, Gütersloh: Gütersloher Verlagshaus. • D. R. SCHWARTZ 1994, "Hasidim in I Maccabees 2:42," *SCI* 13: 7-18. • J. SIEVERS 1990, *The Hasmoneans and Their Supporters: From Mattathias to the Death of John Hyrcanus I,* Atlanta: Scholars Press.

JOHN KAMPEN

Hasmoneans

The Hasmoneans were a Jewish dynasty that was instrumental in liberating Judea from Seleucid rule, beginning around 167 B.C.E. For several generations they served as high priests, governors, and rulers, until Roman intervention in 63 B.C.E. curtailed their role and Herod the Great ousted the last Hasmonean king, Mattathias Antigonus (37 B.C.E.). The origin of the family's name is obscure but is most plausibly related to an otherwise unknown eponymous ancestor by the name of *Ḥašmônay* (*m. Mid.* 1:6 and elsewhere in rabbinic literature; *Asamōnaios* in Josephus, *J.W.* 1.36; cf. *Ant.* 12.265 and passim). Sometimes the term is restricted to John Hyrcanus I and his descendants, while here as in Josephus and in rabbinic literature it is used in reference to the preceding generations as well.

Family Background

The Hasmoneans had their home base in Modein, northwest of Jerusalem, where Simon is said to have built a grandiose family tomb (1 Macc. 13:25-30; cf. 2:70; 9:19; Josephus, *J.W.* 1.36). The family claimed to belong to the priestly course of Joarib (1 Macc. 2:1; 14:29; cf. 1 Chron. 24:7), but its Aaronite descent may not have been beyond doubt (see Schofield and VanderKam 2005). Between 152 and 35 B.C.E., nine Hasmoneans served as high priests in Jerusalem. While Judas Maccabaeus and his father Mattathias before him apparently held only informal leadership positions, the Hasmonean high priests held civil and sometimes military offices as well. They were gradually recognized as governors or local rulers by different Seleucid kings. A certain independence was proclaimed about 142 B.C.E. by Simon (1 Macc. 13:41-42; *J.W.* 1.53), but autonomy was not complete until the last decade of the second century. Beginning with John Hyrcanus I, the Hasmoneans issued their own coinage, generally bronze coins of small denomination (Meshorer 2001; Ostermann 2005). By the end of the second century, they were able to claim the title of king, which they held until the Roman intervention in 63 B.C.E. After that, Hyrcanus II was allowed to continue to hold the office of high priest and ethnarch ("ruler over a people"). The renewed royal claim of Mattathias Antigonus (40-37 B.C.E.) was short-lived and gave way to the rule of King Herod the Great, who under political pressure from Queen Cleopatra and Mark Antony named one last Hasmonean, Jonathan Aristobulus III, high priest for about one year (35 B.C.E.).

The popularity of the Hasmoneans obviously changed over the years. Judas was considered a hero by people with very different views (cf. 1 Macc. 3:1-9; 9:20-22; 2 Macc. 15:7-17; *1 Enoch* 90:9-16). His successors gradually gathered wider support, but their high priesthood did not remain uncontested. Opposition to some of them is expressed in different sources (1QpHab 8:8-13 and passim; 1 Macc. 10:61; 11:21, 25-26; *J.W.* 1.48; *Ant.* 13.291, 372-73; *b. Qidd.* 66a). Yet the most severe blow to the Hasmoneans' position seems to have come through the internecine strife between the two sons of Shelamzion Alexandra, Hyrcanus II and Aristobulus II, which precipitated Roman intervention. According to Josephus, who sometimes prided himself on being descended from the Hasmoneans (*Ant.* 16.187; *Life* 1–4), even the last high priest from this family, Jonathan Aristobulus III, enjoyed great popularity, in part be-

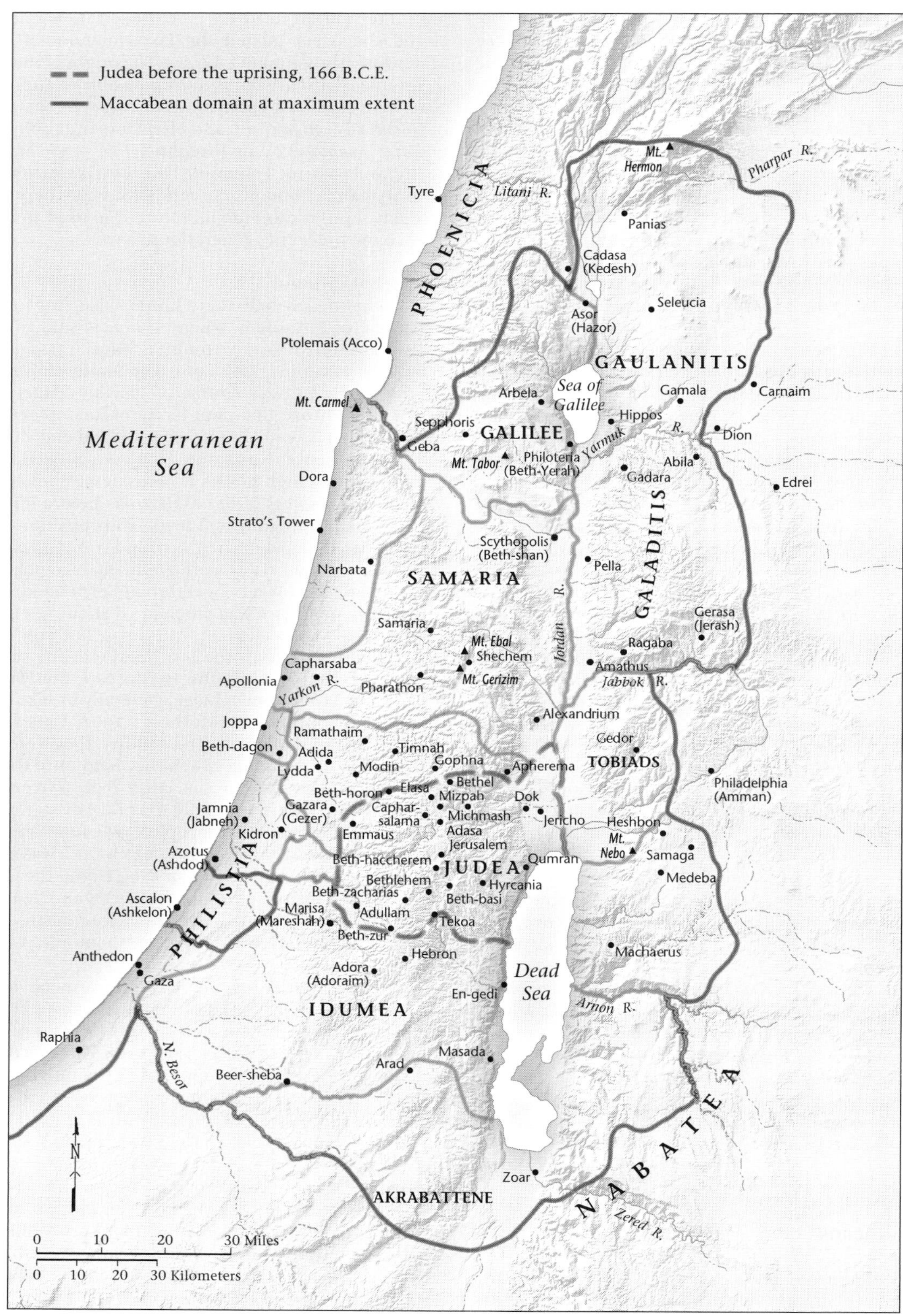

PALESTINE UNDER THE HASMONEANS

cause of his ancestry (*Ant.* 15.52-57). The quest for dynastic legitimacy seems to have played a role in Herod's marriage to Mariamne (*J.W.* 1.240-41), the granddaughter of Hyrcanus II and Aristobulus II, and in the marriage of Herod's son Antipater to a daughter of King Mattathias Antigonus (*Ant.* 17.92). Herod did not rest until he had eliminated all male descendants of the Hasmoneans (*Ant.* 15.266). Even after his death (4 B.C.E.), the Hasmonean house remained so popular that someone impersonating a son of Mariamne at least briefly attracted widespread support among Diaspora Jews (*J.W.* 2.101-10; *Ant.* 17.324-38).

The Beginnings of Revolt

Mattathias

Mattathias (died ca. 166 B.C.E.) is said to have refused to offer a pagan sacrifice in Modein and thereby to have initiated a revolt against the decree of Antiochus IV Epiphanes that forbade under threat of death the observance of Jewish Law (1 Macc. 2:1-28; cf. Josephus, *J.W.* 1.36-37). He is compared to Phinehas (cf. Num. 25:1-15) in his zeal for Torah observance. The account of his actions in 1 Macc. 2:1-70, however, seems to be greatly influenced by later dynastic concerns, including the legitimacy of the Hasmonean high priesthood (Sievers 1990: 29-37).

Judas Maccabaeus

Judas is listed as the third of five sons of Mattathias (1 Macc. 2:4). His surname may be related to the Hebrew/Aramaic root *mqb* (perhaps "hammer-like"). It gave the title to books about him and his brothers (1-2 Maccabees; the books of 3-4 Maccabees have no direct relation to Judas or his family). "Maccabees" is sometimes used as a quasi-synonym of "Hasmoneans" but elsewhere refers to other persecuted Jews of this period. Judas became the leader of a growing popular revolt against the Seleucid authorities and their Judean supporters. After initial victories, he was able to have the defiled Temple of Jerusalem purified and rededicated (1 Macc. 4:36-59; 2 Macc. 10:1-8; Josephus, *Ant.* 12.316-25; *Megillat Taʿanit,* 25 Kislev). This event was and still is remembered in the Jewish feast of Hanukkah ("dedication"; *b. Šabbat* 21b; cf. John 10:22). Despite this success and the revocation of Antiochus IV's decree, the revolt continued. Judas seems to have sought support from Rome through a formal alliance (1 Maccabees 8; 2 Macc. 4:11) that was renewed by several of his successors. He was killed in battle in early 161 or 160 B.C.E. (1 Macc. 9:5-18; *J.W.* 1.47; *Ant.* 12.422-30) after being abandoned by many of his earlier followers.

Hasmonean High Priests and Rulers

Jonathan

Following Judas' death, his brother Jonathan took over as leader of the rebellion (1 Macc. 9:28–12:48; *J.W.* 1.48-49; *Ant.* 13.5-192). After years of relative obscurity, he was courted by several contenders for the Seleucid throne and accepted the high priesthood from King Alexander Balas (152 B.C.E.; 1 Macc. 10:15-21). While maintaining a strong military force, Jonathan achieved more by diplomacy than by warfare, cooperating with Alexander Balas and fostering alliances with Rome and allegedly even with Sparta (1 Macc. 12:1-23). Opposition to him came from different quarters. He may be the figure called "the Wicked Priest" in some Dead Sea Scrolls (1QpHab 8:8-13 and passim; VanderKam 2004: 265-70). Jonathan was killed by order of the Seleucid pretender Tryphon after being captured through a ruse (143/2 B.C.E.; 1 Macc. 12:48–13:23; *J.W.* 1.49; *Ant.* 13.191-209).

Simon

The last surviving brother, Simon, took over a leadership position immediately after Jonathan's capture. He, too, became high priest, although the details of his appointment remain obscure. Only in his third year was he confirmed in office by a popular assembly (1 Macc. 14:27-49; Sievers 1990: 119-27; van Henten 2001). In the meantime he had conquered Gazara (Gezer) and the Akra ("citadel"), a fortified quarter of Jerusalem that had remained in the hands of opponents of the Hasmoneans for over twenty-five years (1 Macc. 1:33-38; 13:49-52). Like all his brothers, he died a violent death: early in 134 B.C.E. he was killed by his own son-in-law, who sought in vain to gain power over Judea (1 Macc. 16:11-16; *J.W.* 1.54; *Ant.* 13.228).

John Hyrcanus I

John Hyrcanus (134-104 B.C.E.) succeeded his father Simon as high priest. The Seleucids, however, still maintained their claim of sovereignty and taxation over Judea. Antiochus VII Sidetes attacked Jerusalem soon after Hyrcanus' accession. After a protracted siege, Hyrcanus was able to achieve a compromise that included payment of tribute and military support for Antiochus' eastern campaign but left Jerusalem without a Seleucid garrison (*J.W.* 1.61; *Ant.* 13.236-53; Diodorus Siculus 34-35.1.1-5; Pseudo-Plutarch, *Apophthegms of Kings and Great Commanders,* p. 184 E-F). Apparently only during his last years did Hyrcanus conquer additional territory for Judea in Idumea to the south and in Samaria and Lower Galilee to the north (*J.W.* 1.62-66). The destruction of the buildings on Mt. Gerizim, including the Samaritan temple precinct, has recently been confirmed by archaeological excavations. The numismatic evidence there and at other sites points to a conquest by Hyrcanus in 111 B.C.E. or shortly thereafter. Toward the end of his life, Hyrcanus had to deal with inner-Judean opposition. Whether this meant a change of his allegiance from the Pharisees to the Sadducees, as Josephus reports (*Ant.* 13.288-99), cannot be confirmed.

Judas Aristobulus I

Judas Aristobulus I (104-103 B.C.E.) became high priest after his father's death. According to Josephus, he was the first Hasmonean to assume the title of king (*J.W.* 1.70; *Ant.* 13.301; 20.240-41; but contrast Strabo, *Geography* 16.2.40). Power struggles within his family allegedly induced Aristobulus to put his mother and his brother Antigonus to death. He himself fell ill and died shortly thereafter.

Alexander Jannaeus

Alexander Jannaeus (103-76 B.C.E.) took over the high priesthood and kingship after his brother Aristobulus I. He made additional conquests, leading the Hasmonean kingdom to its largest extension (including much of Galilee and Transjordan, and the coastal region from the Carmel mountain range to the south of Gaza). Internal opposition to his rule was strong, especially during his later years. This led to bloody civil war, with the temporary intervention of one of the last Seleucid kings, Demetrius III, in 88 B.C.E., and the public execution of many of Jannaeus' enemies. According to Josephus, Jannaeus had 800 of them crucified and their wives and children slain before their eyes (*J.W.* 1.97; *Ant.* 13.380). These events are also remembered in 4QpNah frgs. 3-4 col. i lines 2-8, where the name of Demetrius is partially preserved and Jannaeus is called "the Lion of Wrath." Another text from Qumran (4Q448) has been interpreted as a prayer for the welfare of Jannaeus, but this interpretation is disputed (VanderKam 2004: 335-36; Xeravits 2007: 213-17).

Shelamzion Alexandra

Shelamzion Alexandra (76-67 B.C.E.) is probably to be distinguished from Salina/Salome Alexandra, the wife of Aristobulus I (Ilan 2006: 50-58). She succeeded her husband Alexander Jannaeus after his death. Her name is given only as Alexandra by Josephus, but her true Hebrew name, Shelamzion, is now attested at Qumran (4Q331 1 ii 7; 4Q332 frg. 2 line 4; Ilan 2006: 61-63). Such female succession was nearly unprecedented in the history of Judea but was probably influenced by the practice in neighboring Ptolemaic Egypt, where it had become quite common. The queen appointed the elder of her two sons, Hyrcanus II, high priest and associated herself with the Pharisees, who had been among the internal enemies persecuted by her husband. She allowed them to take action against her husband's supporters. She was able to maintain external peace, relying on a largely mercenary army. Rabbinic literature generally views her in a favorable light. Josephus, whose work is here partly based on Herod's court historian Nicolaus of Damascus, gives contradictory evaluations of her reign (*Ant.* 13.430-32).

Aristobulus II

Aristobulus II, the younger of the two sons of Queen Shelamzion, supplanted his brother Hyrcanus II, who was already high priest and designated to become king. Hyrcanus, however, was induced by Antipater, the father of King Herod the Great, to seek reinstatement. With assistance from the Arab king Aretas, they defeated Aristobulus II and besieged his remaining supporters in Jerusalem. The siege was lifted by the threat of Roman intervention. When later both Hasmoneans asked the Roman leader Pompey, then in Damascus, for his support, a third Judean delegation accused both of them of trying to enslave their people and petitioned that neither of them be king (*Ant.* 14.41-45; Diodorus Siculus 40.2). When Aristobulus did not obey Roman orders and the fights between the brothers continued, Pompey advanced against Jerusalem and conquered it after a three-month siege in the summer of 63 B.C.E. He now assigned the high priesthood again to Hyrcanus II, while Aristobulus was sent to Rome as a prisoner. After escaping and being recaptured, Aristobulus was sent by Julius Caesar to fight against Pompey but was poisoned by partisans of Pompey before he could go into action (49 B.C.E.; *J.W.* 1.183-84; *Ant.* 14.123-24).

Hyrcanus II

Hyrcanus II served as high priest during the reign of his mother, assumed royal power upon her death, was ousted almost immediately by his brother, and was reinstated as high priest and ethnarch by Pompey in 63 B.C.E. He is said to have been lacking initiative and to have been entirely under the influence of Antipater, the father of Herod the Great. Yet Hyrcanus' active involvement in support of Julius Caesar and his allies is evidenced in Roman documents (*Ant.* 14.190-212) and in the historians Asinius Pollio, Hypsicrates, and Strabo (*Ant.* 14.138-39). He was confirmed in office by Caesar in 47 B.C.E. but was ousted by his nephew Mattathias Antigonus in 40 B.C.E. The latter not only had him put into Parthian custody but also mutilated his ears in order to disqualify him from high-priestly service (cf. Lev. 21:17-21). After being freed by the Parthians, he returned to Jerusalem ca. 36 B.C.E. He was killed by Herod in 30 B.C.E. because his very existence was seen as a challenge to Herod's claim to royalty (*J.W.* 1.433-34; *Ant.* 15.164-82).

Mattathias Antigonus

Antigonus, who briefly served as the last Hasmonean ruler in 40-37 B.C.E., was brought to power by the Parthians. On his coins (Meshorer 2001: 218-20, pl. 42-43), his titles are given as "high priest" (in Hebrew) and "king" (in Greek). He was besieged in Jerusalem by Herod, who conquered the city through brutal Roman intervention. Antigonus was taken into Roman custody and beheaded in Antioch, apparently out of fear that his continued popularity might be dangerous to Herod's rule and thus might undermine Roman control (*J.W.* 1.347-57; *Ant.* 14.470–15.10).

Jonathan Aristobulus III

Aristobulus III was briefly made high priest in 35 B.C.E. Within one year of his appointment, he was drowned in a pool at the Hasmonean palace in Jericho, allegedly by order of Herod (*J.W.* 1.437; *Ant.* 15.53-56; Netzer 2001).

Other Hasmoneans

Among the Hasmoneans who did not reach official leadership positions, the best known are those who became part of Herod's court, in particular his wife Mariamne (*J.W.* 1.241, 262, 432-44; *Ant.* 15.23-239) and her mother, Alexandra (*Ant.* 15.23-251). Herod's sons by Mariamne, Alexander and Aristobulus, also prided themselves on their Hasmonean ancestry. All four of them were killed by order of Herod because they too were perceived as a threat to his own dynastic aspirations. The prominence given by Josephus, especially in

Hasmonean Leaders
Mattathias (died ca. 166 B.C.E.)
Judas Maccabaeus (167-161/160)
Jonathan (153-143, first to hold the title of high priest)
Simon (142-134, high priest and ethnarch by popular acclamation)
John Hyrcanus I (134-104)
Judas Aristobulus I (104-103, first to hold the title of king)
Alexander Jannaeus (103-76)
Shelamzion Alexandra (76-67, appointed son Hyrcanus II high priest)
Hyrcanus II (67-66, 63-40)
Aristobulus II (66-63)
Hyrcanus II (63-40, restored as high priest but demoted to ethnarch)
Mattathias Antigonus (40-37 B.C.E.)
Jonathan Aristobulus III (35 B.C.E., only as high priest)

the *Antiquities,* to the above-mentioned and other Hasmonean women is due in part to the biases of his main source for the period, Nicolaus of Damascus. Yet it is clear that several Hasmonean women in addition to Shelamzion Alexandra became active in areas that had been largely dominated by males.

Legacy
For over a century, the Hasmonean family played a central role in the life of Judea and of Judaism. It was the tenacity of the martyrs and the courage of Judas Maccabee and his companions that saved monotheism for Judaism and thus for humanity. The development of distinct Jewish groups in the late Second Temple period occurred partly in response to some of the later Hasmoneans. Thus the influence of the Hasmoneans reaches well beyond their own time.

BIBLIOGRAPHY
H. ESHEL 2008, *The Dead Sea Scrolls and the Hasmonean State,* Grand Rapids: Eerdmans. • J. W. VAN HENTEN 2001, "The Honorary Decree for Simon the Maccabee (1 Macc 14:25-49) in Its Hellenistic Context," in *Hellenism in the Land of Israel,* ed. J. J. Collins and G. E. Sterling, Notre Dame: University of Notre Dame Press, 116-45. • T. ILAN 2006, *Silencing the Queen: The Literary Histories of Shelamzion and Other Jewish Women,* Tübingen: Mohr-Siebeck. • Y. MESHORER 2001, *A Treasury of Jewish Coins: From the Persian Period to Bar Kokhba,* Jerusalem: Yad Ben-Zvi; Nyack, N.Y.: Amphora Books. • E. NETZER 2001, *The Palaces of the Hasmoneans and Herod the Great,* Jerusalem: Yad Ben-Zvi. • E. NODET 2005, *La crise maccabéenne: Historiographie juive et traditions bibliques,* Paris: Cerf. • S. OSTERMANN 2005, *Die Münzen der Hasmonäere,* Fribourg: Universitätsverlag; Göttingen: Vandenhoeck & Ruprecht. • U. RAPPAPORT 2004, *The First Book of Maccabees: Introduction, Hebrew Translation, and Commentary,* Jerusalem: Yad Ben-Zvi. • A. SCHOFIELD AND J. C. VANDERKAM 2005, "Were the Hasmoneans Zadokites?" *JBL* 124: 73-87. • D. R. SCHWARTZ 2008, *2 Maccabees,* Berlin: de Gruyter. • J. SIEVERS 1990, *The Hasmoneans and Their Supporters: From Mattathias to the Death of John Hyrcanus I,* Atlanta: Scholars Press. • M. STERN 1995, *Hasmonaean Judaea in the Hellenistic World,* ed. D. R. Schwartz, Jerusalem: Zalman Shazar Center (in Hebrew). • J. C. VANDERKAM 2004, *From Joshua to Caiaphas: High Priests after the Exile,* Minneapolis: Fortress. • G. G. XERAVITS 2007, "From the Forefathers to the 'Angry Lion': Qumran and the Hasmonaeans," in *The Books of the Maccabees: History, Theology, Ideology,* ed. G. G. Xeravits and J. Zsengellér, Leiden: Brill.

See also: High Priests; Judas Maccabaeus; Maccabean Revolt; Seleucids JOSEPH SIEVERS

Healing

In both biblical tradition and early Judaism, the concept of health *(šālôm* from Hebrew root *šlm)* includes physical, emotional, social, and spiritual well-being. The term for healing comes from a different Hebrew root, *rp'*, which assumes some rupture that must be remedied by a return to well-being. Like *šālôm, rp'* has connotations that extend beyond the bodily sense. Both terms reflect a deep cultural association between bodily health and other forms of well-being.

Hebrew Bible
Before the Second Temple Period, one major understanding of healing characterized Israelite culture: since God sent illnesses primarily for one's sins, the acceptable remedies were repentance and prayer. Regarding health professionals, early biblical texts depict prophets as the appropriate and effective mediators of healing; early references to physicians are consistently negative (Avalos 1995). Leviticus prescribes a limited role for the Temple priests, who are to ascertain whether healing has occurred, especially for skin diseases, but the priests do not appear to have played a significant role in the actual healing of the person while he or she was sick. Apotropaic prayers, however, may have been included in Temple liturgies and in personal practice.

Second Temple Literature

Debate over the Role of Physicians
Second Temple literature shows a growing debate about the role of physicians. Early Jewish belief maintained the traditional view that God was responsible for all healing. Thus reconciling this claim with the role of a human practitioner of a craft posed some difficulty. Perhaps the best-known positive statement about the physician comes from Ben Sira:

> Honor physicians for their services, for the Lord created them;
> for their gift of healing comes from the Most High,
> and they are rewarded by the king. . . .
> The Lord created medicines out of the earth,
> and the sensible will not despise them. . . .

> By them [medicinal plants] the physician heals
> and takes away pain;
> the pharmacist makes a mixture from them.
> (Sir. 38:1-2, 4, 7 [NRSV])

The author appears to be correcting a negative view of physicians that saw them as competitors with God; instead, he treats their skills as a type of mediation between God and human beings. Further, the text specifically includes herbalists as acceptable consultants who use God's creation to benefit humankind. After this passage, the text recommends prayer and repentance from sins as essential constituents of healing. In short, Ben Sira has incorporated physicians and herbalists into the older view that all healing comes from God.

Similarly, Philo treats medical knowledge as part of the wisdom available to human beings. His work shows detailed reference to the Hippocratic corpus, without advocating particular Greek theories of disease and healing (Hogan 1992). The book of *Jubilees* reaches a similar conclusion with a different justification. There, angels instruct Noah and his sons in the use of medicines for healing (10:10-13; see below). This new, positive view of physicians is well established by the talmudic period. There is, for example, the statement: "The sages in the school of R. Ishmael taught: 'He shall cause him to be healed' (Exod. 21:19). From this verse we infer that permission has been given [by Heaven] to the physician to heal" (*b. Berakot* 60a). This position becomes the dominant one in rabbinic Judaism.

Several bodies of Second Temple literature maintain the traditional view that God heals, and thus leave little or no room for health professionals. Qumran literature maintains and amplifies the traditional view, such that there is nothing for a physician to do. In 1QS, the good spirits provide health and the evil spirits send diseases; thus the proper remedy for a bodily sickness would be exorcism. Several psalms or psalm-like prayers have apotropaic content, apparently on the assumption that the best remedy for sickness is to remain healthy (e.g., 11QapPs[a], 11Q5, and 11Q6). Although more dualistic than earlier Israelite literature, the Qumran texts maintain the traditional practices for seeking remedies for sickness: repentance and prayer. The healings in the *Testaments of the Twelve Patriarchs* are similar, as are those in the Gospels. The latter do not explicitly prohibit consulting doctors, but Mark's passing reference in the pericope about the woman with the hemorrhage suggests that one is better off without them: "She had endured much under many physicians, and had spent all that she had; and she was no better, but rather grew worse" (Mark 5:26). The same is true of Tobit's repeated attempts to treat his incipient blindness: "I went to physicians to be healed, but the more they treated me with ointments the more my vision was obscured by the white films, until I became completely blind" (Tob. 2:10).

These sources do not view consultation of doctors as inherently irreligious or disloyal to God, but neither do they consider such an approach best for one's health. Disparate as they may be in other ways, DSS, the *Testaments,* the Gospels, and Tobit share a fairly traditional view of how healing occurs and what sort of intermediation is appropriate.

Atypical in its extreme negativity about medical knowledge, *1 Enoch* proposes a rather diabolical view. In the *Book of the Watchers,* pharmacological knowledge appears on the list of items the Watchers improperly disclosed to human beings: "And they taught them magical medicine, incantations, the cutting of roots, and taught them about plants" (*1 Enoch* 7:1b; cf. 8:3).

The association of medical practices with non-Israelite cults occurs in earlier literature. Deuteronomy (18:9-14) bans a number of religious practices, the performers of which may also have had a medical role (Avalos 1995). Unlike the earlier literature, the Enochic *Book of the Watchers* provides an etiological myth that explains how human beings came by such knowledge, and why these practices compete with God's power and providence. Indeed, once the Watchers are bound, God provides a legitimate medical intermediary: the archangel Raphael.

The Archangel Raphael

Raphael is not named in the Tanak. Indeed, he comes into his own in Second Temple literature, as the angel in charge of healing. Even so, the significance of his medical power varies in different texts. In the *Book of the Watchers,* Raphael seems to replace the illegitimate medical practices taught by the Watchers (*1 Enoch* 10:7). Thus he compensates for the withdrawal of improperly disclosed medical knowledge. However, his central role in the book of Tobit defies the neat categories of *1 Enoch.* As noted above, Tobit's consultation with physicians worsened his condition; he then prays for death. Raphael is sent to heal both Tobit's blindness and Sarah's affliction by the demon. Since Sarah cannot fulfill her proper social role as a wife, she is, in effect, disabled by the demon. The author treats both conditions as falling within the jurisdiction of the healing angel. Yet Raphael does little directly, instead instructing Tobias in the use of fish parts to perform an exorcism and a healing. The use of prayer at the exorcism and of blessing at the healing gives divine power the ultimately efficacious role. At the same time, the book of Tobit creates a positive role for both heavenly intermediaries and for medicinal use of substances. If the book stops short of endorsing the medical professional, it nevertheless shows through the figure of Raphael how such a profession might function in a religiously appropriate way. Finally, although the book of *Jubilees* does not name Raphael, the angel of the presence who speaks to Moses throughout the work explains healing thus:

> And he [God] told one of us to teach Noah all of their healing because he knew they would not walk uprightly and would not strive righteously. . . . And the healing of all their illnesses together with their seductions we told Noah so that he might heal by means of herbs of the earth. And Noah wrote everything in a book just as we taught him according to ever kind of healing. (*Jub.* 10:10-13; trans. Wintermute)

In short, *1 Enoch,* Tobit, and *Jubilees* all prescribe a medical function to angelic intermediaries.

In contrast to earlier literature, then, Second Temple literature reveals a debate about intermediate figures in healing. Physicians and herbalists seem to have gained some religious legitimacy that they did not have in the preexilic period, but neither was their acceptance universal. Avalos (1995) suggests that the decline of prophecy left a gap into which new medical practitioners could emerge. Further, the prominence of healing angels can be seen in general terms as a case of the period's prolific angelology. Like human practitioners, however, Raphael and others are depicted as mediating figures — heavenly counterparts to the human physicians, whose gifts come from God.

BIBLIOGRAPHY

H. AVALOS 1995, *Illness and Health Care in the Ancient Near East: The Role of the Temple in Greece, Mesopotamia, and Israel,* Atlanta: Scholars Press. • L. P. HOGAN 1992, *Healing in the Second Temple Period,* Göttingen: Vandenhoeck & Ruprecht. • A. KLEINMAN 1980, *Patients and Healers in the Context of Culture: Explorations of the Borderland between Anthropology, Medicine and Psychiatry,* Berkeley: University of California Press. • J. PREUSS 1978, *Biblical and Talmudic Medicine,* trans. F. Rosner, New York: Sanhedrin. • F. ROSNER 2000, *Encyclopedia of Medicine in the Bible and the Talmud,* Jerusalem: Jason Aronson. • K. SEYBOLD AND ULRICH B. MUELLER 1981, *Sickness and Healing,* trans. D. W. Stott, Nashville: Abingdon. • J. WILKINSON 1998, *The Bible and Healing: A Medical and Theological Commentary,* Grand Rapids: Eerdmans.

See also: Demons and Exorcism; Divination and Magic; Medicine and Hygiene; Sickness and Disease

REBECCA RAPHAEL

Heaven

In ancient literature the term "heaven" can be used in an astronomical sense, referring to the "sky," or in a religious sense, referring to the divine realm outside the physical cosmos. This dual usage appears in the lexica of virtually every Near Eastern or Mediterranean language: Akk. *šamu,* Hebr. *šāmayim,* Aram. *šāmâ',* Gr. *ouranos,* and Lat. *caelum.* The reason is that ancient people imagined that the gods resided somewhere in the mysterious realm "up there."

The Ancient Near East

The people of the ancient Near East sought to know as much as possible about the celestial realm where gods resided. Their scholars carefully observed, calculated, and interpreted the movements of the celestial bodies, thinking that they were the physical manifestations of the gods and that their movements or appearance might foreshadow events on earth. Their images of a god's celestial abode were inspired by what they knew of monumental structures such as temples and royal palaces, because these buildings represented the grandest of built structures. They imagined a god's earthly temple as the miniature of its celestial counterpoint. Moreover, since the king's palace was the most elaborate residence these people could imagine, they used its floor plan, images, and protocols to depict the divine realm (Wright 2000: 26-51).

The ancient Mesopotamians for the most part did not imagine human beings "going to heaven." Some myths suggest that super mortals might be granted entrance into heaven by the gods, but that was granted to very few indeed (e.g., Enmeduranki and Utuabzu; cf. *Myth of Adapa and Etana*). The ancient Egyptians, on the other hand, developed elaborate beliefs about heavenly afterlife, and these evolved through time. In the third millennium B.C.E. it was thought that only the divine Pharaoh could ascend to heaven after death *(Pyramid Texts).* During the second millennium this heavenly afterlife appears to have been available to the royal family and other notables *(Coffin Texts).* Finally, during the first millennium heavenly afterlife was thoroughly democratized and made available to commoners *(Book of the Dead).*

The Hebrew Bible

Ancient Israelite cosmology imagined the cosmos as a tripartite structure with heaven above, earth in the middle, and the netherworld below. The Hebrew word *šāmayim* can be translated as either "heaven" or "sky." What appears to be a dual ending (i.e., *-ayim*) is actually plural. Some have understood this form, as well as the phrases "heaven of heaven(s)," and "heaven and the heaven of heaven(s)," to imply that the ancient Israelites had a notion of multiple heavens. Rather, these phrases are better understood as Hebrew superlative phrases, and they are best rendered as "vast heaven" or "the farthest reaches of the sky."

The Hebrew Bible begins with an unambiguous cosmological assertion: "In the beginning God created the cosmos," literally "heaven and earth" (Gen. 1:1). Apart from standard terms for "create" or "make," the Hebrew Bible uses other terms to describe how God created the celestial realm, and these reflect Israelite images of this realm. One such image is that of a cosmic canopy. This image appears in the use of the verb *nāṭāh* ("stretch out" or "spread") to describe how God "stretched heaven out" as a canopy or tent over the earth (2 Sam. 22:10; Isa. 40:22; 42:5; 44:24; 45:12; 51:13; Jer. 10:12; 51:15; Zech. 12:1; Ps. 104:2; Job 9:8; cf. Gen. 12:8; 26:25). Another image of the material composition of perhaps the floor of the heavenly realm involves a solid substance. The term *rāqîaʿ,* "firmament," is based on the root *(rqʿ)* and means "stamp out" or "forge." This term suggests that some imagined the *rāqîaʿ* as a firm substance that constituted the vault or dome of the sky. It must be remembered, however, that the ancient Israelites held these and other images together as parts of a large complex of ideas about the heavenly realms. The various depictions of "heaven" in the Hebrew Bible indicate that there never was one universal image but several (Houtman 1993: 282-317).

The Hebrew Bible also reveals some details about how ancient Israelites imagined their relationship to the heavenly realm. The biblical editors' general picture suggests that heaven had no place for humans and was reserved exclusively for God and perhaps other divine beings: "Heaven is Yahweh's heaven, but the earth he has given to humans. The dead do not praise Yahweh, nor do all those who go down to silence" (Ps. 115:16-17). This psalm suggests that the dead descended into the netherworld (Sheol) and did not ascend into "Yahweh's heaven." Even the holy prophet Samuel did not "go to heaven"; he died and descended into the netherworld (1 Samuel 28). Some passages even suggest that the very thought of ascending to heaven is evidence of wickedness, not piety (Isa. 14:9-10; Ezek. 28:2, 6; cf. Prov. 30:4). There were, however, two possible exceptions to this rule: Enoch (Gen. 5:21-24) and Elijah (2 Kings 2:1-18). In both cases there are ambiguities regarding the ultimate fate of these two notables, and some later Jewish and Christian traditions locate them on earth, often at the mystical ends of the earth (Wright 2004).

The latest books of the Hebrew Bible, composed in the postexilic period, reflect a shift in beliefs about humans ascending to heaven. These late texts (Eccl. 3:21; Dan. 12:1-3; cf. Psalms 16, 49, 73) indicate the emergence of a belief in a heavenly afterlife for the righteous. These texts were composed when Jews lived under Persian and Greek rule, and Jewish speculations about the afterlife were being increasingly influenced by "foreign" beliefs. As Jews interacted with the Greek cosmologies, they reimagined the cosmos and their place in it. Most telling in this respect is Dan. 12:1-3: "Many of those who sleep in the dust of the earth shall awake, some to eternal life, and some to shame and eternal contempt. But the wise shall shine like the brightness of the sky, and those who lead many to righteousness, like the stars forever and ever." This second-century-B.C.E. text's image of a heavenly afterlife for the righteous differs radically from images elsewhere in the Hebrew Bible and represents a reinterpretation of humanity's relationship with the cosmos. While earlier texts imagined that all would descend into the realm of the dead (Sheol) at death, Daniel 12 maintains that the righteous will not only rise from the dead but ascend to heaven. (So also the roughly contemporary *Epistle of Enoch.*) While the theme of the heavenly ascent of the soul became common in Greek and Roman environments, it appears in Jewish texts here for the first time.

The Greco-Roman World

Ancient Greek scholars explored heaven (Gr. *ouranos;* plural *ouranoi*) in terms of both science and philosophy. Most early Greeks had a tripartite cosmology (heaven, earth, under world) that paralleled the ancient Near Eastern model in many respects. Similarly, early Greek images of humans' relationship to the heavenly realm were much like those in the Near East: humans could not ascend to the heavenly realm either during life or in the afterlife. Heaven was the realm of the gods, and it was only notable heroes and super mortals who could escape the netherworld to live at the paradisiacal ends of the earth, the Elysian Fields.

This began to change, however, during the Classical and Hellenistic eras when Greek scholars developed new observational techniques and mathematical calculations, which led to new models of the cosmos. These models imagined the cosmos as a set of nestled, concentric spheres each containing a planet, moon, or star orbiting the earth, which itself stood motionless at the center of the cosmos, the Ptolemaic cosmology. These cosmological speculations also led to innovations in philosophy. Greeks viewed the outermost reaches of the cosmos as the unchanging realm of perfection and purity, and after the fifth century B.C.E. Greeks imagined that after death the soul was released from the physical body and sought to ascend to this realm. Souls were purified as they ascended, and when they arrived at the highest heaven, they were perfect, returning to what was thought to be the soul's original state (Bousset 1901). Moreover, the boundary between human and divine became much more malleable, and tales of notables' ascent to heaven to join the gods become abundant in Greco-Roman literature (e.g., Plato's *Myth of Er; Cicero's Dream of Scipio;* Apollonius of Tyana).

Early Judaism

Early Jewish images of heaven emerged from a vast complex of images found either in the Hebrew Bible or forged from encounters with Greco-Roman philosophy and cosmology (Bietenhard 1951). Daniel 12:1-3 is the earliest Jewish text to use Hellenistic images, but it was not alone. As in the Greek world, many early Jewish texts exhibit interest in astronomy (e.g., *Testament of Shem;* Philo). While some texts seem to utilize the tripartite cosmology of the Hebrew Bible (*1 Enoch;* several Dead Sea Scrolls), many use a multiple-heaven cosmology (e.g., *Apocalypse of Abraham, 3 Baruch, Testament of Levi,* Philo, *Apocalypse of Zephaniah*). Jewish texts also began using narratives of heavenly ascent either during life or at death, narratives that became popular during the Greco-Roman era (e.g., *1 Enoch* 39; Wis. 3:1-9; cf. Himmelfarb 1993; Nickelsburg 2006). For example, a portion of the *Book of the Watchers* (*1 Enoch* 1–36, third or second century B.C.E.) recounts Enoch's ascent to heaven (chaps. 14–16). Enoch sees God's heavenly temple as well as the regions where wicked beings are punished and the righteous rewarded. Eventually, Enoch returns to earth and recounts his travels for the benefit of his contemporaries. *Fourth Ezra,* a Jewish text of the first century C.E., contains a debate between Ezra and the angel Uriel on theodicy. During the debate Ezra learns that after death a person's soul wishes to ascend to the divine realm but must be judged first (*4 Ezra* 7:32, 75-101). If the person lived a righteous life, then his or her soul ascends safely to heaven, but if not, then it suffers punishment (*4 Ezra* 7:32, 80, 95; cf. 4:35). One purpose of these ascent tales describing postmortem punishment and reward is to inculcate religious values. The reader learns that to qualify for admission into heaven and to avoid punishment, one must live a righteous life as defined by that text and its community.

Early Christianity

The early Christian community was originally a sect within Judaism, and so its texts reflect images of heaven already attested in Judaism. The statements attributed to Jesus in the canonical Gospels mostly imagine heaven in the traditional single heaven model. He is reported to have said that people are rewarded in heaven for righteous behavior on earth (Matt. 5:12; 6:20), and that heaven is a mansion with many rooms (John 14:2). Throughout the Gospel of John, and in accord with its "high Christology," Jesus, again following a Greco-Roman model, is depicted as the incarnation of a heavenly being who came to earth and returned to heaven after his crucifixion. Early Christians likewise believed that after his resurrection Jesus ascended to heaven, whence they awaited his return (Acts 1:9-11; cf. Mark 16:19).

Paul's epistles use Greco-Roman cosmology and describe heaven as a place for the righteous. In 2 Cor. 12:1-4 he recounts his ascent to heaven (Tabor 1986); he reports that he ascended to the "third heaven," where he learned secrets that he was either unauthorized or unable to recount (2 Cor. 12:2, 4). Elsewhere in the same letter, he envisions believers going to be with Christ in heaven immediately upon their death, in a kind of intermediate state between their death and their resurrection at the return of Christ (2 Cor. 5:6-8). Paul told his followers in Thessalonica that all Christians, the living and the dead, would be raised from the dead via a transformation and ascend to meet Jesus "in the air" at his return (1 Thess. 4:13-18; cf. 1 Cor. 15:51-52). After meeting Jesus in the air, though, they will presumably accompany him to earth, where he will establish God's kingdom in a transformed creation "set free from its bondage to decay" (Rom. 8:21).

Gnostic Christian texts, following Greco-Roman cosmology and Gnostic soteriology, state that the region beyond the physical realm is characterized by purity, perfection, and permanence. The physical cosmos, on the other hand, is corrupt and perishing. Those who wish to escape the confines of the physical realm must acquire the Gnostic special cosmological knowledge that will prepare their souls for a postmortem ascent to the Divine.

Other early Christian texts also speculate on the punishments and rewards awaiting individuals as they seek to ascend to heaven after death (Himmelfarb 1993; Russell 1997). The *Apocalypse of Paul* details the excruciating punishments inflicted on the wicked and the lavish rewards awaiting the righteous. The *Ascension of Isaiah* presents each higher heaven as successively more glorious than the others, and the highest heaven as the ultimate destiny of the righteous. Such beliefs provide motivation to endure suffering and to live the kind of life that will warrant admission into heaven. Knowledge of the heavenly realm, therefore, is used to persuade people to adopt or remain loyal to certain beliefs and ethical systems.

BIBLIOGRAPHY

H. BIETENHARD 1951, *Die himmlische Welt im Urchristentum und Spätjudentum,* Tübingen: Mohr-Siebeck. • W. BOUSSET 1901, "Die Himmelsreise der Seele," *Archiv für Religionswissenschaft* 4: 136-69, 229-73. • M. HIMMELFARB 1993, *Ascent to Heaven in Jewish and Christian Apocalypses,* Oxford: Oxford University Press. • C. HOUTMAN 1993, *Der Himmel im Alten Testament,* Leiden: Brill. • C. MCDANNELL AND B. LANG 1988, *Heaven: A History,* New Haven: Yale University Press. • G. W. E. NICKELSBURG 2006, *Resurrection, Immortality, and Eternal Life in Intertestamental Judaism and Early Christianity,* expanded ed., Cambridge: Harvard University Press. • J. B. RUSSELL 1997, *A History of Heaven: The Singing Silence,* Princeton: Princeton University Press. • J. D. TABOR 1986, *Things Unutterable: Paul's Ascent to Paradise in Its Greco-Roman, Judaic, and Early Christian Contexts,* Lanham, Md.: University Press of America. • J. E. WRIGHT 2000, *The Early History of Heaven,* New York: Oxford. • J. E. WRIGHT 2004, "Whither Elijah? The Ascension of Elijah in Biblical and Pseudepigraphic Traditions," in *Things Revealed: Studies in Early Jewish and Christian Literature in Honor of Michael E. Stone,* ed. E. Chazon et al., Leiden: Brill, 123-38. • C. ZALESKI AND P. ZALESKI, EDS. 2000, *The Book of Heaven: An Anthology of Writings from Ancient to Modern Times,* Oxford: Oxford University Press.

See also: Ascent to Heaven; Cosmology; Death and Afterlife; Garden of Eden — Paradise; Geography, Mythic

J. EDWARD WRIGHT

Hebrew

Hebrew is a Canaanite dialect belonging to the Northwest Semitic family of languages. It was spoken among the population of ancient Israel in the region of Palestine; as a result, most of the texts canonized in the Hebrew Bible were written in Hebrew. As a biblical language, Hebrew enjoyed the status of both a sacred and a classical tongue and was emulated by later texts. From the Persian period (539-332 B.C.E.) until the destruction of the Temple (70 C.E.), Hebrew gradually lost its literary position and changed to such a degree that the written language reflected a quite different language system than its biblical ancestor. One can speak about three periods: (1) Classical Hebrew, (2) Middle Hebrew, and (3) Late Hebrew. Traditionally, these phases of the language are related to the major texts written in each of the respective periods: (1) Biblical Hebrew (subdivided into Classical Hebrew and Late Biblical Hebrew), (2) Ben Sira and Qumran Hebrew, and (3) Mishnaic Hebrew.

However, this classification reflects only the written language. There is good evidence that the later manifestations of the language reflect to some degree a different, earlier dialect (since they have certain grammatical forms that reflect an earlier stage of the language). In addition, there are good reasons to believe that, to some degree, the later form of Hebrew was already spoken colloquially at the time of the composition of the Bible, since it is occasionally found in direct quotations even in early biblical texts.

From the time of the Assyrian period, speakers of Hebrew were exposed to other non-Canaanite Semitic languages, especially Akkadian and Aramaic. With the Persian period, Indo-European languages began to impact Hebrew: first Persian, and later, after the conquests of Alexander the Great (333-323 B.C.E.), Greek, and, with the expansion of the Roman Empire, Latin. This linguistic contact had its influence first and foremost on the lexicon, but to some degree on the grammar as well.

Our sources for the language of this period consist of two types. The first is nonliterary material: papyri, epigraphic texts written on pottery shards, and inscriptions embedded in mosaics and stones. The second is literary texts that originated in the relevant period, but of which we have manuscript evidence only from later periods.

Hebrew as a Written Language

Hellenistic Period (332-165 B.C.E.)

Among the most important Hebrew texts from the Hellenistic period are some of the latest books of the Bible. Chapters 2–7 of the book of Daniel were written in Aramaic during these years. Chapter 1 is in Hebrew, but scholars posit that this chapter was written as an introduction to the Aramaic section and was perhaps composed originally in Aramaic. For other late biblical books, such as Joel, Ecclesiastes, and the last chapters of Zechariah, there is controversy about whether they should be dated to the Hellenistic period or to an earlier period.

Although the Septuagint is a Greek compilation, it still serves as a witness to the Hebrew of this period. Among the biblical books that are found only in the Septuagint and not in the Masoretic text, there exists evidence that some of them were probably first written in Hebrew. For example, certain idioms in the Greek of the book of Judith resemble Hebrew idioms. Similarly, the book of Tobit was written either in Hebrew or in Aramaic, and translated shortly after to the other. Our best example of a Hebrew original for a Septuagintal text is the book of Ben Sira. The prologue to this book, a later addition made by Ben Sira's grandson, indicates that the text was written first in Hebrew in Jerusalem during the first quarter of the second century B.C.E. Subsequently, the text was translated into Greek by the grandson. Although the composition did not survive in Hebrew in its entirety, about 68 percent of the book is preserved in Hebrew fragments found among the Dead Sea Scrolls and at Masada. Other Hebrew fragments were found in medieval manuscripts in the Cairo Geniza, and several lines are quoted in the Talmud. Overall, the language of Ben Sira is archaic; it attempts to imitate the biblical language both grammatically and lexically. However, occasional deviations from the biblical language reveal its similarities to Mishnaic Hebrew and Aramaic.

The Hebrew inscriptions from this period are principally biblical quotations from the Samaritan community, including an excerpt from the Decalogue.

Hasmonean Period (165-63 B.C.E.)

Hebrew was at least one of the official languages of the Hasmonean dynasty, if not the only one in some periods, as can be deduced from Hebrew coins found from the period of Hyrcanus I (135-104 B.C.E.), Aristobulus I (104-103 B.C.E.), and Alexander Jannaeus (103-76 B.C.E.).

As for biblical texts, it is clear from historical allusions in Daniel 8–12 that the second, Hebrew part of the book of Daniel is from the Hasmonean period. The contemporary chronicle, 1 Maccabees, was written in Hebrew (as some of the idioms indicate). Like Judith, however, it survives only in its Greek translation in the Septuagint.

Outside of the biblical canon, other major Hebrew literary texts from this period are found in the collection of the Dead Sea Scrolls, which contain significant sectarian and nonsectarian texts. The fragments of *Miqṣat Maʿaśê ha-Torah* (4QMMT), with its sectarian halakah, were copied from a text originating from this period. It is similarly accepted that the book of *Jubilees* was written in Hebrew in the middle of the second century B.C.E. In addition, many scholars date the *Temple Scroll* to the Hasmonean period, but it should be noted that others think that the original text was written even before the founding of the Qumran community. Given the Qumran sectarians' anti-Hasmonean stance, the prayer in Hebrew for King Jonathan, the Hebrew name of Alexander Jannaeus, is an unexpected find among the Scrolls.

Roman Period through the First Revolt (63 B.C.E.–73 C.E.)

The capture of Jerusalem by Pompey in 63 B.C.E. marks the beginning of the Roman period in Jewish history, the end of Jewish self-governance in Palestine, and the introduction of another Indo-European language, Latin.

Many of the hundreds of scrolls found in the caves near Qumran and those found at Masada date to this period, the period in which the occupation of both sites ended. The scrolls that date to this time consist of biblical texts and commentaries on them (the pesharim); texts later deemed apocryphal, sectarian texts such as the *Rule of the Community* and the *Damascus Document,* hymns, and the nonliterary text of the *Copper Scroll.* The vast majority of the texts from Qumran are in Hebrew, with a minority written in Aramaic and Greek. The Hebrew texts indicate a shift from Classical Hebrew to the later stage of Hebrew. Most of the texts are written in a style that seeks to imitate biblical texts. Despite this imitation, however, many features of the later stages can still be identified, especially in terms of the lexicon but also in terms of the grammar. Some of the scrolls attest a significantly different style that can be characterized as Proto-Mishnaic Hebrew, most notably among them the *Copper Scroll.*

The literary texts show some grammatical innovations that are not found either in the earlier period or later (e.g., the forms of the pronominal suffixes). It is well accepted among scholars that these are not a reflection of a different dialect ("Qumran" Hebrew), but merely an overimitation of the biblical style.

Another group of texts dating to the time of the Second Temple, or at least to the years immediately following its destruction, are chapters or even entire tractates in the Mishnah. Tractates *Tamid* and *Middot* and certain chapters of *Yoma* describe the Temple in the present tense and preserve some older features of the Hebrew language.

A few Hebrew inscriptions, mostly funerary inscriptions, have been found around Jerusalem and come from the last decades of the Second Temple period. They consist mostly of names and are surrounded by inscriptions in Aramaic and Greek. Many epigraphic texts from inhabitants of Masada from 66 to 73 C.E. have been discovered as well. Containing lists and short instructions in Hebrew and Aramaic, they attest to the everyday uses of the language. The Hebrew texts are mostly (but not exclusively) concerned with the observance of purity laws and other Temple practices. Lastly, Hebrew coins from the time of the First Revolt have been discovered as well.

Roman Period through the Second Revolt (74-135 C.E.)

Many quotations from some of the major rabbinic figures from period between the revolts, the Tannaim, can be found in the Mishnah, Tosefta, and the legal Midrashim. This literature was probably first handed on orally and only later transmitted in written form. Thus, although the earliest manuscripts of this literature are only from the Middle Ages, they do attest to the language of this period. This large corpus is written in Mishnaic Hebrew, a linguistic system significantly different from biblical Hebrew. Mishnaic Hebrew was influenced to some extent by Aramaic, but at the same time it includes features that cannot be explained by contact with Aramaic and therefore must be considered products of internal development. From a linguistic point of view, this development could have occurred only in a spoken language. In addition, some believe the earliest manifestations of the Jewish poetry known as the *Piyyut* also stem from this period.

Most of the epigraphic evidence from this period comes from the years of the Second Revolt led by Bar Kokhba (132-135 C.E.). This corpus includes letters, legal documents, coins, and other objects bearing testimony to daily uses of the language. The language of these documents is Mishnaic Hebrew. However, it reflects a different dialect than the one found in the rabbinic literature.

Hebrew as a Spoken Language

It is difficult to decipher from written texts alone the relationships and interactions of spoken languages. This task is made more challenging because we have evidence only from certain regions. However, examination of texts in different languages that did originate from the same location, together with some linguistic considerations, offers at least a partial picture.

Jews in Palestine during the Hellenistic period were clearly bilingual and perhaps even trilingual. While it is clear that some of the Diaspora communities no longer knew Hebrew (as the need for translations suggests) or even used it for liturgical purposes, still it is certain that in Palestine Hebrew was a living language. Beyond this understanding, however, it is hard to suggest any sociological or geographical criteria according to which Hebrew was used. Some have suggested that it was the "high language" spoken by the Temple clergy, whereas others have proposed that it was used mostly in rural areas. Some have suggested that the nationalist frame of mind surrounding both revolts promoted the use of Hebrew. There are indeed more letters and legal documents in Hebrew from the Bar Kokhba period, and there is some linguistic evidence that this was intentional. On the other hand, there are Aramaic letters from the same circles. It is now generally agreed that these types of broad hypotheses are too simplistic.

The texts from this period (Josephus, New Testament, and rabbinic literature) indicate that there were Jewish communities in which Greek was dominant and others in which Aramaic or Hebrew was more central. From a linguistic point of view, there were probably mutual influences between Hebrew and Aramaic. Nevertheless, both languages show developments that occur typologically only in spoken languages. In addition, there are texts in Aramaic that seem to indicate a Hebrew-speaking writer and vice versa.

Another historical question concerns the shift from Biblical Hebrew to Mishnaic Hebrew. This process was clearly gradual, but it is unclear why after the First Revolt more and more texts were written in the mishnaic dialect, a dialect that earlier was mainly used colloquially. Different theories have been suggested for this shift. It has been proposed that it had to do with the nationalism of the period, or with socioeconomic changes in the ruling class. However, two other considerations should be taken into account. First, the nature of the texts from this period should be remembered. Epigraphic texts cannot be considered alongside literary texts since the two groups represent different genres and probably registers. Similarly, rabbinic texts transmitted orally should not be given the same linguistic considerations as texts transmitted in written form. Second, in such a discussion we should bear in mind all of the linguistic developments in the entire region. A similar development happened at the same time in the Aramaic language throughout the region. We see a shift from Middle Aramaic to Late Aramaic that was characterized by the use of local dialects for literary purposes as well.

BIBLIOGRAPHY

J. BARR 1989, "Hebrew, Aramaic and Greek in the Hellenistic Period," in *The Cambridge History of Judaism,* vol. 2, ed. W. D. Davies and L. Finkelstein, Cambridge: Cambridge University Press, 79-114. • J. NAVEH 1992, *On Sherd and Papyrus: Aramaic and Hebrew Inscriptions from the Second Temple, Mishnaic Hebrew and Talmudic periods,* Jerusalem: Magnes. • A. SÁENZ-BADILLOS 1993, *History of the Hebrew Language,* Cambridge: Cambridge University Press. • S. SCHWARTZ 1995, "Language, Power and Identity in Ancient Palestine," *Past and Present* 148: 3-47.

ELITZUR AVRAHAM BAR-ASHER

Hebrews, Epistle to the

The New Testament Epistle to the Hebrews is an early Christian homily characterized by its distinctive presentation of Jesus as the eternal, heavenly high priest in order to encourage the recipients to persevere in their commitment to Christ.

Authorship

Though Hebrews often is classified alongside the Catholic (or General) Epistles and Revelation in modern discussion, historically this has not been the case. Instead, the book ultimately owes its inclusion in the New Testament canon to the insistence in the ancient Eastern churches — and ultimately a compromise consensus with the West — that Paul was its author, and as such the book circulated in the manuscript tradition in the Pauline corpus. Difficulties with this identification were long recognized, however, and throughout the centuries numerous alternate proposals for authorship have been offered (especially figures in the Pauline orbit, including Barnabas, Apollos, Silas/Silvanus, even Aquila and Priscilla).

The theory of Pauline authorship is easily dismissed for several reasons, including literary style, theological emphases, and especially the author's claim in 2:3 to have been evangelized by an earlier generation of believers (even if read broadly, this is extremely difficult to reconcile with Paul's insistence in Galatians 1–2 that no human taught him the gospel). Most modern scholars are reluctant to speculate on the personal identity of the author and instead focus on his characteristics. The author's use of the Greek language generally is regarded as the most refined in the New Testament, and he utilizes numerous sophisticated rhetorical techniques (including *synkrisis* [comparing and contrasting]; see below). Alongside this he displays much facility with Jewish exegetical methods and traditions. The author is steeped in the Septuagint yet also draws positively from Greco-Roman mythological and philosophical traditions. Taken together, these characteristics point to a Jewish-Christian author whose background was in the Greek-speaking Diaspora. The book normally is considered an epistle, though it lacks marks of such in its opening section; increasingly scholars note its homiletic nature.

Destination and Date

Though in the early church the book was understood as written to Jewish Christians in Jerusalem, scholars today normally assume a Roman destination; the phrase "those from Italy send greetings" (13:24) most naturally implies an author and associates writing back to their home congregation. Most scholars today date Hebrews broadly to ca. 60-100 C.E., with the upper range determined by use of the book in *1 Clement*. Other scholars attempt to date Hebrews much more precisely in the 60s, especially in the context of Nero's persecutions. Attempts to date the book in light of the author's silence about the destruction of the Jewish Temple in 70 C.E. falter because Hebrews' sacrificial discussions consistently address the Tabernacle — admittedly sometimes with confusion about its physical arrangement (9:4) — rather than the Temple. Also, his language implying a continuing sacrificial system does not assist in dating, because both rabbinic and patristic writers used similar language for centuries. The author seems to know the Jewish sacrificial system chiefly through exegesis, not firsthand experience.

Audience and Situation

The author's emphasis on exegesis of texts from the Jewish Scriptures (especially the Pentateuch and Psalms), his frequent use of exemplars (both positive and negative) drawn from these narratives, and his extended comparison of Jesus' activities with aspects of the Jewish sacrificial system typically have been cited by interpreters as evidence that the Jewish identity of the recipients is a key to interpretation of the book. As such, English-language scholarship on Hebrews long was dominated by theories that the author was warning the Jewish-Christian recipients not to renounce Christianity and return to their ancestral faith or else was exhorting them finally to make a full break from the synagogue.

Most recent major studies, however, avoid these sorts of conclusions. While a few scholars have argued (unpersuasively) that elements in the text demand instead a Gentile readership, ultimately the ethnicity of the recipients is not a determinative factor for interpretation of the book. Rather, the author's comments concern the recipients' fidelity to Christ; the problem addressed is cessation of faith and obedience, not attraction to alternative teachings. The author repeatedly warns against or chides the readers for laxity in their commitment to their confession (2:1-4; 3:7–4:13; 5:11–6:8; 10:26-39; 12:18-29), and he notes the failure of some to assemble together (10:25). Persecution seems to be a factor in their wavering (10:32-34), though the author notes that no blood has been shed among the recipients (12:4). No restoration is possible for those who abandon their faith (6:4-8), though the author confidently notes that his addressees have not yet met this dire fate (6:9-12).

Message

As noted above, the author often cites characters from the Hebrew Scriptures as instructive examples for the readers. Negatively, the recipients are warned not to imitate the unfaithful Israelites of the exodus generation who died in the wilderness and fell short of God's "rest" because of their unbelief (3:7–4:13); the journey motif of this passage is prominent in the book, and only persons who endure to the very end may truly be considered faithful. Positively, the recipients are to persevere in faithful obedience to God, confident of a reality not yet seen, following the examples of Abraham, Moses, and numerous other figures from the past (including some from texts later included among the Apocrypha and Pseudepigrapha; 11:1–12:2); clearly the author understands the faithful persons of Judaism and the Jesus movement in continuity as one people of God. Thus while some interpreters have understood Hebrews' argumentation as anti-Jewish, the opposite is the case. Similarly, the author's use of *synkrisis* demands that he praise Jesus by comparing him with figures from the Hebrew Scriptures (angels, Moses, Melchizedek, the levitical priests, etc.) whom he also highly esteemed. Because the author writes chiefly to encourage continuing Christian faith, the status of contemporary non-Christian Jews is not an issue in Hebrews, much less a point of polemic (even in 8:13 and 13:9-10).

Inspiration for the faithfulness demanded by the author is to be found in Jesus, the divine Son who was appointed by God as heavenly high priest. Jesus displayed solidarity with humanity in his incarnation (2:5-18). He was prepared for his priestly service by experiencing the human plight, yet he did so without sin; as high priest he was fully sympathetic with humanity and offered himself as the ultimate, final sacrifice (4:14–5:10). Like that of Melchizedek, his was a priesthood outside of and superior to Israel's levitical system (7:1-10). Jesus' priesthood surpassed that of the Levites in numerous ways, including the finality of his sacrifice and his service in the heavenly tabernacle (rather than an earthy, physical sanctuary); as such he is mediator of the new covenant prophesied in Jer. 31:31-34 (7:11–10:39). Now exalted and seated beside God, he has prepared the way for his people into God's presence (6:19-20) and has made atonement for them (1:3; 8:11-12).

Jewish Background and Character

Hebrews' explicit presentation of Jesus as high priest is distinctive in the New Testament, and numerous scholars have sought to identify influences on this author's thought. Ernst Käsemann famously proposed (and later renounced) the view that the conceptual background of Hebrews is to be found in Gnosticism. Though this position occasionally still is defended, most interpreters have instead argued that the author is strongly indebted to some stream of Jewish tradition. In the mid-twentieth century Ceslas Spicq provided the classic articulation of the view that the author of Hebrews was deeply influenced by Philo of Alexandria. Spicq, who identified the author as a former student of Philo, particularly emphasized the relationship between Philo's discussion of the Logos and Hebrews' presentation of Jesus as priest.

Though scholars continue to debate the relationship between the thought of Hebrews and of Philo, especially whether the author of Hebrews shares Philo's Platonic cosmology, the discovery of the Dead Sea Scrolls did much to dampen enthusiasm for Spicq's fuller thesis and refocused scholarly investigations of the Jewish background of Hebrews on this emerging corpus. Early claims that the Qumran expectation doctrine of the "messiah of Aaron" influenced the presentation of Jesus as a messianic priest in Hebrews were largely abandoned in the 1960s, but more significant have been comparisons of the portraits of Melchizedek in the Qumran texts (especially 11Q13) and in Hebrews. Though certainly these presentations are not identical, in both traditions Melchizedek is a priestly, heavenly figure associated with the Day of Atonement. The author of Hebrews also reflects Melchizedek traditions found in other Second Temple Jewish literature (e.g., the popular etymologies in Heb. 7:2 for the name Melchizedek and his position as king of Salem were also used by Josephus and Philo).

Another similarity between the Qumran texts and Hebrews can be found in their use of Scripture. In Heb. 1:5-14, the author cites a catena of biblical quotations to explain the superiority of the Son over the angels in a manner similar to the Qumran *testimonia* or excerpted texts. More significantly, the author of Hebrews utilizes the exegetical method of midrash, or interpreting one text in light of another, which also is the preferred approach of the author of 11Q13. In Heb. 3:7–4:13, Ps. 95:7-11 is interpreted in light of Gen. 2:2 to explain the nature of God's rest, but Hebrews' most ambitious use of this method involves Ps. 110, by which Jesus' status as priest is explained. By citing Ps. 2:7 and Ps. 110:1 at the beginning and end of the catena of Heb. 1:5-14, the author subtly connects these psalms and establishes that the exalted, divine Son is addressed by God in both texts. This allows him to assert in 5:5-6 that Jesus, the Son addressed in Ps. 2:7, is also the person granted an eternal priesthood by divine oath in Ps. 110:4. Citation of this latter verse introduces Melchizedek into the argument, and in Heb. 7:1-10 the author further explains how Jesus' priesthood is like Melchizedek's. After noting in 7:3 that both are eternal figures without (levitical) genealogies, the author playfully incorporates Gen. 14:18-20 into his midrash of Ps. 110:4 to prove Melchizedek's superiority over the levitical priesthood. The ultimate purpose, though, is to explain that Jesus also is superior to the levitical priests, and the implications of this are developed in 7:11–10:39.

Numerous other aspects of Hebrews reveal the author's indebtedness to various streams of early Judaism, but a few examples must suffice. Language used for the personified Wisdom figure is reapplied to the Son (cf. Wis. 7:26 and Heb. 1:3). The author assumes exegetical traditions common in Second Temple Judaism, such as the beauty of the infant Moses (11:23) and the role of angels in the delivery of the Law to Moses at Sinai (2:2). Likewise, Hebrews' conception of a heavenly sanctuary and divine throne room is familiar from descriptions of God's dwelling in various Second Temple Jewish texts, as is his assertion that his era was that of the "last days" (1:2). And Hebrews' concern to validate Jesus' priestly status is reminiscent of efforts — also using midrash — in *Jubilees* and the *Aramaic Levi Document* (later also in *Testament of Levi*) to explain God's selection of Levi as priest. The author can approach Scripture in ways reminiscent of the Qumran *testimonia* or excerpted texts (1:5-14), or he can practice midrash by interpreting one text in light of another (3:7–4:13; 5:5-6; 7:1-10).

Bibliography

H. W. Attridge 1989, *Hebrews,* Philadelphia: Fortress. • E. Käsemann 1984, *The Wandering People of God,* trans. R. A. Harrisville and I. Sundberg, Minneapolis: Augsburg. • L. T.

JOHNSON 2006, *Hebrews: A Commentary,* Louisville: Westminster John Knox. • C. KOESTER 2001, *Hebrews,* New York: Doubleday. • W. LANE 1991, *Hebrews,* 2 vols., Dallas: Word. • B. LINDARS 1991, *The Theology of the Letter to the Hebrews,* Cambridge: Cambridge University Press. • E. F. MASON 2008, *'You Are a Priest Forever': Second Temple Jewish Messianism and the Christology of the Epistle to the Hebrews,* Leiden: Brill. • C. SPICQ 1952-1953, *L'Epître aux Hébreux,* 2 vols., Paris: Gabalda.

See also: Melchizedek; Melchizedek Scroll (11Q13)

ERIC F. MASON

Hecataeus, Pseudo-

An authentic passage of Hecataeus of Abdera (ca. 300 B.C.E.) on the Jews is preserved in the fortieth book of the history of Diodorus. The provenance of other passages attributed to him, however, is disputed. Clement of Alexandria refers to a work of Hecataeus, *On Abraham and the Egyptians* (*Stromateis* 5.223), and cites from it verses attributed to Sophocles in praise of monotheism. This work is also mentioned by Josephus (*Ant.* 1.159), but it is universally regarded as spurious. Little can be said about it. The *Letter of Aristeas* 31 quotes Hecataeus as saying that the books of Scripture are holy. Again, little can be said about this. The admiring tone invites suspicion, although Doran (1985) accepts it as authentic. The main controversy, however, centers on passages attributed to Hecataeus by Josephus (*Ag. Ap.* 1.183-205; 2.43).

The long passage in *Against Apion* 1 is allegedly derived from a book of Hecataeus, *On the Jews.* It claims that a chief priest named Ezechias led a group of Jews who migrated voluntarily to Egypt under Ptolemy I. There is no other record of such a migration, and Ptolemy I is known to have treated Judeans harshly. No high priest named Hezekiah is known from written sources. There are, however, coins with the legend "Hezekiah the Governor," from the last years of the Persian Empire, or just "Hezekiah," from the time after the conquest of Alexander. Whether this man was a priest we do not know, but the office of the high priest was distinct from that of the governor. We do not know whether he migrated to Egypt.

Pseudo-Hecataeus praises the Jews for their fidelity to their laws and claims that they withstood torture by Persian rulers. There is no other evidence of religious persecution of Jews by the Persians. This passage may reflect experiences of the Maccabean era. Again, the passage attributed to Hecataeus claims that Jews razed temples and altars constructed by foreigners, and says that they deserve praise for this. There is no evidence for such conduct before the Maccabean era, and it is implausible that Hecataeus should find such conduct praiseworthy.

Myriads of Jews allegedly migrated to Phoenicia as well as Egypt in the wake of Alexander's conquest. This claim, again, cannot be verified. The passage goes on to say that there were many fortresses of the Jews, but only one fortified city, Jerusalem. Jews obviously had no fortresses under their control in the Persian era; they acquired them only when the Hasmoneans came to power. The size of Judea is greatly exaggerated and roughly corresponds to its extent under John Hyrcanus, nearly 200 years later. The size of Jerusalem is likewise inflated (50 stadia in circumference, whereas historically it was only 12 stadia in the time of Hecataeus). The number of inhabitants is even more inflated at 120,000, whereas it would have been less than 10,000 at the time. The Temple is located, inaccurately, in the center of the city.

This long passage concludes by recounting an incident involving a Jewish archer named Mosollamus who killed a bird while a seer was trying to prognosticate on the basis of its motions, thereby showing that it could not anticipate the future. The authentic Hecataeus, however, is respectful of omens and is unlikely to have praised a Jew for mocking them.

Finally, the passage in *Ag. Ap.* 2.42-43 claims that Alexander annexed the land of Samaria to Judea, free of tribute. This claim is not supported by any other source and seems implausible in light of the relative size and importance of Samaria and Judea.

In short, practically everything in the passages attributed to Hecataeus by Josephus is problematic. Some details (e.g., persecution and torture) seem to reflect the Maccabean period; others (e.g., the multiplicity of fortresses), the rule of the Hasmoneans. Bar Kochva (1996) argues that Pseudo-Hecataeus depends on the *Letter of Aristeas.* A date around 100 B.C.E., some two centuries after Hecataeus of Abdera, seems likely.

The work *On the Jews,* attributed to Hecataeus, then, belongs to the corpus of pseudepigraphic works supposedly written by Gentile authors, such as the *Sibylline Oracles,* the sayings of Pseudo-Phocylides, and the pseudo-Orphic verses. These writings reflect, whether directly or indirectly, on the glory of Judaism and its teachings. Such promotion is an exercise in apologetics, even if it was intended primarily for Jewish readers.

BIBLIOGRAPHY

B. BAR-KOCHVA 1996, *Pseudo-Hecataeus on the Jews: Legitimizing the Jewish Diaspora,* Berkeley: University of California Press. • R. DORAN 1985, "Pseudo-Hecataeus," in *OTP* 2: 905-19. • C. R. HOLLADAY 1983, *Fragments from Hellenistic Jewish Authors,* vol. 1, *Historians,* Chico, Calif.: Scholars Press, 277-335. • M. STERN 1976, *Greek and Latin Authors on Jews and Judaism,* vol. 1, Jerusalem: The Israel Academy of Sciences and Humanities, 35-44. • N. WALTER 1976, "Pseudo-Hekataios I und II," in *JSHRZ* 1.2: 144-60.

JOHN J. COLLINS

Hecataeus of Abdera

Hecataeus was a Greek philosopher, grammarian, and ethnographer who lived in the fourth century B.C.E. A prolific writer, he wrote, among other works, one entitled *On the Hyperboreans* and another one known as the *Aigyptiaca* (on Egyptian history, geography, and culture). Probably in the latter, Hecataeus also wrote an excursus on the Jews, their origins, customs, and political organization. Now lost, the *Aigyptiaca* has been partly transmitted by Diodorus. But the section on the Jews (Diodorus 40.3.1-8) is known only through a summary made by the Byzantine patriarch Photius. However, on the whole the text we possess may be considered approximately faithful to Hecataeus, even if not his *ipsissima verba.*

Hecataeus' description of the Jews represents one of the earliest passages dealing with Jews in Greek literature. They are depicted as foreigners who were expelled from Egypt because of a plague that afflicted the Egyptian population, which had been corrupted by alien rites. Under the leadership of Moses, a brave and wise man, most of the immigrants settled in Judea, at that time an uninhabited land, whereas the "most outstanding and active" among the foreigners, led by Danaus and Cadmus, eventually populated Greece. Moses founded cities, had the Jerusalem Temple built, divided the people into twelve tribes, and established political and religious institutions, as well as rituals connected to a monotheistic and aniconic cult. The Jews are also described as a people who never had a king and who were ruled by priests, a remark which makes sense in the context of the Persian period. Hecataeus' account contains numerous mistakes but also accurate pieces of information. Although he did not have access to biblical texts, he certainly had some Jewish source.

Some details in Hecataeus' description, such as the military training of youth, the division of the land in equal lots, the interdiction to sell one's individual plot, and the concern about scarcity of manpower *(oligandria),* show that Hecataeus tends to describe the Jews in a Spartan light. Indeed, Greek patterns of thought pervade the whole excursus, rendering the entire text fundamentally Greek in outlook.

One sentence in Hecataeus' account that has received much attention is also to be understood in this perspective. The text states that Jews have laws which distinguish them from other peoples, and that, because of their expulsion from Egypt, they have chosen "a kind of misanthropic and inhospitable way of life." In other words, the Jews are implicitly compared to a well-known character of Greek comedies, the misanthrope, generally a person who had suffered at the hands of men and therefore avoided their company. In Greek literature, however, the word "misanthropic" characterizes individuals, not peoples. The peculiar use of this word in connection with the Jews reveals Hecataeus' surprise at the Jewish way of life. However, his description is not hostile and may even be considered globally positive. This may explain why a work, *On the Jews,* was ascribed to him — wrongly — by some Jewish sources.

Although many scholars have argued that Hecataeus' account of the origins of the Jews depends on Egyptian traditions such as those known through the work of the Egyptian priest Manetho, this part of his text is also best understood in the context of Greek ethnography. Diodorus' description of Egypt (in book 1), which is said to be inspired to a large extent by Hecataeus, does not contain any allusion to the Egyptian stories about lepers expelled from Egypt. Moreover, Hecataeus' account in Diodorus 40.3 does not mention the expulsion of sick or impure people. It is the Egyptians themselves who are afflicted with a plague, not the foreigners who dwell among them. Actually, Hecataeus' description of the expulsion of Jews and Greeks who founded colonies is deeply influenced by Herodotus' *Histories,* by Greek stereotypes about Egyptian hostility toward foreigners, and by Greek discussions about a possible Egyptian origin of Danaus and Cadmus. Hecataeus' interest in the Jews was limited, and his perspective, like that of other Greek ethnographers, "hellenocentric."

BIBLIOGRAPHY

K. BERTHELOT 2003, *Philanthrōpia judaica: Le débat autour de la "misanthropie" des lois juives dans l'Antiquité,* Leiden: Brill, 80-94, 101-6. • W. JAEGER 1938, "Greeks and Jews," *Journal of Religion* 18: 127-43. • D. MENDELS 1983, "Hecataeus of Abdera and a Jewish *Patrios Politeia* of the Persian Period (Diodorus Siculus 40.3)," *ZAW* 95: 96-110. • W. SPOERRI 1988, "Hekataios von Abdera," *Reallexikon für Antike und Christentum* 14: 275-310. • M. STERN 1998, *Greek and Latin Authors on Jews and Judaism,* 5th ed., Jerusalem: Israel Academy of Sciences and Humanities, 1:20-35. • E. WILL AND C. ORRIEUX 1986, *Ioudaïsmos-Hellénismos: Essai sur le judaïsme judéen à l'Epoque hellenistique,* Nancy: Presses Universitaires de Nancy, 83-93.

See also: Hecataeus, Pseudo-

KATELL BERTHELOT

Hekhalot Literature

The writings that make up the Hekhalot corpus represent the earliest freestanding collections of Jewish mystical, magical, and liturgical traditions. This diverse body of materials resists easy geographic and chronological classification. Written primarily in Hebrew and Aramaic, Hekhalot literature developed very gradually in the major centers of Jewish learning — Byzantine Palestine and Sassanian Persia. While the corpus does contain some literary traditions from the "classic" rabbinic period (ca. 200–600 C.E.), it seems to have emerged as a distinct class of texts only toward the end of late antiquity, likely between 600 and 900 C.E. (Boustan 2006). Moreover, Hekhalot literature never reached a closed or definitive form, but continued to be adapted by Jewish scribes throughout the Middle Ages and into the early modern period (ca. 900–1500 C.E.).

The term "Hekhalot" comes from the Hebrew word for the celestial palaces or temples *(hêkālôt,* pl. of *hêkāl)* within which God is said in this literature to reside and through which the visionary ascends toward him and his angelic host. The form of religious praxis and experience described in Hekhalot literature is often also referred to as "Merkabah mysticism" because it draws on and develops long-standing speculative and ecstatic traditions concerning the prophet Ezekiel's vision of the divine chariot-throne (the merkavah of Ezekiel 1, 10).

The Variety of Interests and Genres

It must be stressed, however, that the majority of the Hekhalot corpus does not in fact address the theme of the visionary ascent. At least as prominent within many Hekhalot compositions are prescriptions for adjurational techniques designed to gain the assistance of various angelic intermediaries for often quite practical aims. The Hekhalot corpus also encompasses a wide and eclectic range of other literary genres, most importantly: exhaustive catalogues of the limbs of God's gigantic body (the *Shiur Qomah*); cosmological speculation; physiognomic and astrological material; and vast numbers of poetic compositions detailing the liturgies performed by the angels in heaven and by Israel on earth. Heterogeneity in both literary form and religious sensibility is a constitutive feature of virtually all Hekhalot compositions.

The nature of the relationship between the two principal axes of the corpus — narratives in which a human actor ascends to heaven, and adjurational material designed to bring angelic beings down to earth — remains a subject of great debate among scholars. The groundbreaking writings of Gershom Scholem on Hekhalot literature accord temporal and thematic priority to the ascent narratives (Scholem 1954; Scholem 1965). For Scholem, these heavenly journeys directly continue the form of ecstatic mysticism already attested in earlier Jewish (and Christian) apocalyptic writings, such as *1 Enoch* 14, Daniel 7, and Paul's second letter to the Corinthians 12:1-4. By contrast, Scholem viewed the incorporation of "magico-ritual" elements into the corpus as a belated development that marked the degeneration of its original "mystical" impulse. More recently, however, scholarship has emphasized the degree to which ritual practices pervade every aspect of Hekhalot literature — and are inseparable from its larger religious program. Indeed, in both heavenly ascent and angelic adjuration, movement between the earthly and heavenly realms is achieved primarily through the meticulous performance of ritual speech and action.

Pseudonymous Attribution

As in much late antique rabbinic literature, the authorial voice of Hekhalot literature is anonymous and collective. Hekhalot texts employ figures from the legendary rabbinic past as their primary protagonists and spokesmen — most commonly, R. Ishmael, R. Akiva, and R. Neunya ben ha-Qanah (second century C.E.). These rabbinic authorities not only serve as the main characters in the narrative portions of this literature; Hekhalot texts directly attribute to these rabbis their instructional content as well. This framework of pseudonymous attribution both constitutes the primary organizational structure of Hekhalot texts and serves as their central authorizing strategy by anchoring them in the increasingly hegemonic rabbinic tradition.

Delimiting the Corpus

Scholars have yet to reach a consensus concerning precisely which criteria mark a text as a Hekhalot composition or how best to delimit the corpus. Numerous texts, such as the late-antique magical handbook *Sefer ha-Razim* or the posttalmudic martyrology *The Story of the Ten Martyrs,* share certain narrative, formal, or thematic affinities with Hekhalot literature, while differing from it in other important respects. No generalizations are possible; research should be conducted on a case-by-case basis to determine how specific compositions fit within the general discursive matrix of Hekhalot literature. The following compositions, however, are generally considered to belong to Hekhalot literature proper: *3 (Hebrew) Enoch* or *Sefer Hekhalot; Hekhalot Rabbati* ("The Greater [Book of Celestial] Palaces"); *Hekhalot Zutarti* ("The Lesser [Book of Celestial] Palaces"); *Maʿaseh Merkavah* ("The Working of the Chariot"); *Merkavah Rabbah* ("The Great [Book of] the Chariot"). All of these compositions can be most easily consulted in Schäfer's *Synopse zur Hekhalot-Literatur,* a synoptic edition of seven medieval manuscripts that contain the Hekhalot corpus in a variety of textual forms and configurations (Schäfer 1981).

Embedded within or appended to the major building blocks of the corpus are a number of generically distinct texts. Most significant are a series of relatively autonomous adjurational complexes known as the *Sar ha-Torah* ("Prince of the Torah") texts, which promise the practitioner assistance in acquiring and retaining knowledge of Torah. Similarly, the *Shiur Qomah* ("The Measure of the Height [of the Divine Body]") forms a distinct class of texts that are incorporated in a variety of ways into larger Hekhalot compositions.

In addition, more than twenty fragments of Hekhalot texts have been retrieved from the Cairo Genizah (Schäfer 1984). Most of these fragments reflect versions of material found in the medieval manuscripts, though a few represent previously unknown Hekhalot compositions. Significant differences exist between the materials contained in the Genizah fragments and those that crystallized in the European manuscript tradition; this disparity between the "Oriental" and "European" branches of the literary tradition strongly suggests that Hekhalot literature existed in a variety of forms and was transmitted along multiple regional trajectories.

Composition and Redaction

The compositional and redactional processes that produced both the individual Hekhalot compositions and the corpus as a whole were enormously complex. The Hekhalot manuscript tradition is characterized by extreme fluidity. It has, therefore, not proved possible to reconstruct either a fixed *Urtext* or a finally redacted form for most of the major Hekhalot compositions — and, in all likelihood, such stable beginning and end points of the transmission process never existed. Peter Schäfer has made the compelling case that Hekhalot literature cannot simply be divided into stable "books" or "works," but represents a relatively open-ended set of both longer and shorter textual units that remained in flux as they were transmitted and actively refashioned by medieval scribes and scholars (Schäfer 1988).

Sociocultural Contexts

The heterogeneity, fluidity, and pseudonymity of Hekhalot texts have created formidable obstacles for studying the sociocultural context(s) out of which this literature emerged. Scholem — and others in his wake — situated Hekhalot literature squarely within the main currents of rabbinic Judaism, even tracing its origins back to the second-century circles of R. Akiva himself. Others have mounted precisely the opposite argument, finding in this literature the voices of non- or anti-rabbinic Jews. Most significantly, David Halperin has argued that Hekhalot literature was produced by the Jewish "masses" (*ʿammei hā-ʾāretz*) who, finding themselves dispossessed by the emergent rabbinic dispensation, longed to acquire mastery of the Torah through more immediate "magical" means than through many years of study (Halperin 1988).

In the only thorough sociological analysis of Hekhalot literature published to date, Michael Swartz argues that the promises of textual mastery and perfect memory in the *Sar ha-Torah* texts in particular reflect the aspirations of the "secondary elites" who served late-antique Jewish communities as minor ritual functionaries (Swartz 1996). These relatively low-status scribes were profoundly influenced by the scholastic culture of the rabbis, while at the same time being excluded from (full) access to rabbinic institutions of learning. Their position at the margins of the rabbinic movement would thus account for the palpable tension within Hekhalot literature between the rabbinic values it embraces and its very nonrabbinic emphasis on the revelatory power of ritual-liturgical practice. In this view, the creators of Hekhalot literature deployed rabbinic figures and discourses with the aim of appropriating rabbinic authority for themselves.

Whatever its precise social background, Hekhalot literature advocates a religious ideology that seems to be at odds with the conception of power and authority articulated in classic rabbinic literature. A number of scholars have argued that Hekhalot literature transmits "priestly" traditions that have their roots in the Second Temple period, prior to the emergence of the rabbinic movement. We have seen above that the centrality of the motif of heavenly ascent within the Hekhalot corpus and Second Temple apocalyptic literature has led some to view both groups of sources as literary expressions of a common tradition of ecstatic mysticism. More recently, Rachel Elior and others have suggested that the imaginative depictions of the heavenly cult that fill Hekhalot literature reflect the religious orientation of actual priestly groups that (may have) played an influential role within the synagogue communities of late-antique Palestine (Elior 2004).

Relation to Second Temple Literature

Hekhalot literature provides important evidence for the historical continuity and change in early Judaism and early Christianity. For example, Hekhalot literature shares clear thematic and generic affinities with a wide variety of texts found at Qumran, especially among liturgical, ritual, divinatory, demonological, and physiognomic sources (Swartz 2001). Scholars, however, disagree sharply about the historical significance of these similarities. For example, it has been argued that the Hekhalot hymns build upon the type of liturgical traditions found in the Qumran *Songs of the Sabbath Sacrifice,* with their distinctive "numinous" style and exegetical elaboration of Ezekiel's throne-vision. At the same time, the apparent absence of a *direct* literary relationship between these texts, as well as important differences in their ritual-liturgical settings, caution against drawing facile conclusions concerning sociohistorical or even phenomenological continuities between them. The use of categories such as "mysticism" and "magic" should not be allowed to overshadow analysis of concrete formal and thematic similarities *and* differences across the various corpora. Still, the task of situating Hekhalot literature within the larger landscape of early Judaism is only in its infancy.

Bibliography

R. S. Boustan 2006, "The Emergence of Pseudonymous Attribution in Hekhalot Literature: Empirical Evidence from the Jewish 'Magical' Corpora," *JSQ* 13: 1-21. • J. R. Davila 2001, *Descenders in the Chariot: The People behind the Hekhalot Literature,* Leiden: Brill. • R. Elior 2004, "*Hekhalot* and *Merkavah* Literature: Its Relation to the Temple, the Heavenly Temple, and the 'Diminished Temple,'" in *Continuity and Renewal: Jews and Judaism in Byzantine-Christian Palestine,* ed. L. I. Levine, Jerusalem: Yad Ben-Zvi, 107-42 (in Hebrew). • I. Gruenwald 1980, *Apocalyptic and Merkavah Mysticism,* Leiden: Brill. • D. J. Halperin 1988, *The Faces of the Chariot: Early Jewish Reponses to Ezekiel's Vision,* Tübingen: Mohr-Siebeck. • M. Himmelfarb 1988, "Heavenly Ascent and the Relationship of the Apocalypses and the Hekhalot Literature," *HUCA* 59: 73-100. • P. Schäfer 1988, *Hekhalot-Studien,* Tübingen: Mohr-Siebeck. • P. Schäfer 1981, *Synopse zur Hekhalot-Literatur,* Tübingen: Mohr-Siebeck. • P. Schäfer 1984, *Geniza-Fragmente zur Hekhalot-Literatur,* Tübingen: Mohr-Siebeck. • P. Schäfer 2009, *The Origins of Jewish Mysticism,* Tübingen: Mohr-Siebeck. • G. G. Scholem 1954, *Major Trends in Jewish Mysticism,* New York: Schocken, 40-79. G. G. Scholem 1965, *Jewish Gnosticism, Merkabah Mysticism, and Talmudic Tradition,* New York: Jewish Theological Seminary of America. • M. D. Swartz 1996, *Scholastic Magic: Ritual and Revelation in Early Jewish Mysticism,* Princeton: Princeton University Press. M. D. Swartz 2001, "The Dead Sea Scrolls and Later Jewish Magic and Mysticism," *DSD* 8: 182-93.

See also: Mysticism

Raʿanan S. Boustan

Heliopolis

The city of Heliopolis in Egypt was an important cultic and religious center in Pharaonic times (its Egyptian name, *Iunu,* reemerging in the Hebrew Bible as *ʾÔn*), but it was in a state of decline in the last millennium B.C.E. Herodotus, who visited it in the fifth century B.C.E., observes that the Heliopolitans "are said to be the most learned of all Egyptians," but he has little to say about the site or its temples (Herodotus 2.3, 59, 63).

By the time it was visited by Strabo in 24 B.C.E., Heliopolis was mostly a deserted set of ruins, but it still retained some of its ancient prestige, and the occasional visitor was proudly shown the exact place where Plato and Eudoxus had studied under their Egyptian teachers (Strabo, *Geography* 17.1.27-29). In a similar fashion, Solon (Plutarch, *Solon* 26), Pythagoras (in Plutarch, *De Iside et Osiride* 10), Alexander the Great (Athenagoras, *Legatio pro Christianis* 28), and other notable Greek figures were said to have benefited much from the wisdom of the town's famous priests, and so too Moses, who was said to have been such a priest himself (Manetho, quoted in Josephus, *Ag. Ap.* 1.237-50).

In the Hebrew Bible, Heliopolis is mentioned in several different contexts. In the Joseph stories of Genesis 39–50, Joseph marries Aseneth, the daughter of the priest of On, and begets Manasseh and Ephraim (Gen. 41:45, 50; 46:20). Jeremiah foretells the coming destruction of the Egyptian temples and the pillars of Bet Shemesh (i.e., the "House of the Sun," Heliopolis; Jer. 43:13), and Ezekiel foretells the destruction of different Egyptian cities, including On (Ezek. 30:17; on the spelling *'Āwen,* see below). But the most important reference to Heliopolis in the Hebrew Bible is in Isa. 19:18-19, where the prophet foretells that "On that day there shall be five cities in the land of Egypt speaking the language of Canaan and swearing to the LORD of Hosts; one of them shall be called the City of the Sun. On that day there shall be an altar to the LORD in the land of Egypt, and a pillar for the LORD by its frontier."

Several centuries after this prophecy was uttered, an attempt was made to fulfill its promise when Onias IV fled Jerusalem and established several military colonies in the Heliopolite nome (= district), and built a Jewish temple there. Both acts were supported by Ptolemy VI Philometor (ruled 180-145 B.C.E.), who saw in the foreign settlers in Heliopolis an excellent buffer against invasions from the northeast and a reliable force in case of native Egyptian insurrections. He was not disappointed, for the Jewish settlers remained loyal to the Ptolemies throughout the second century B.C.E. The native Egyptians may have been less pleased with this arrangement, and with the Jewish presence in an ancient Egyptian cultic center, and their resentment seems to surface in an *ex eventu* Greek prophecy (*CPJ* 3:520) foretelling how the Jews would one day inhabit "the Land of the Sun" and cause much trouble there.

While the Oniad presence in the Heliopolite nome is attested by literary and archeological evidence — for example, both Strabo (quoted by Josephus, *Ant.* 13.287) and a Jewish metrical inscription (*CIJ* 2:1530 = *JIGRE* 38) refer to the region as "the Land of Onias" — the exact location of the temple remains unknown. Josephus (*Ant.* 13.65-71) cites two letters which claim that it was built in a place called "Leontopolis" in the Heliopolite nome, but such a place is not otherwise attested. Moreover, in spite of the claims of Flinders Petrie to have found the remains of Onias' temple at Tell-el-Yahoudieh, it seems clear that the temple — which was destroyed by the Romans in 73 or 74 C.E. — has yet to be identified. Unfortunately, the fact that much of the old Heliopolite nome is now buried under Cairo's neighborhoods of Matariyah and ʿAin Shams makes the systematic excavation of the Oniad settlements and their temple virtually impossible.

The temple of Onias did leave some traces in the literary records of ancient Jews, including the different versions of Isa. 19:18 that have reached us. Thus, whereas 1QIsa[a] preserves the likely original reading when it refers to the city which will be built in Egypt as *ʿîr ha-ḥeres,* "the City of the Sun," the LXX reading of this verse calls the city *Asedek* (apparently a Greek transliteration of the Hebrew word *ha-ṣedeq,* "righteousness" or "justice"), and the MT at this point reads *ʿîr ha-heres,* "the City of Destruction." This unusual textual variety clearly reflects the different views of the texts' readers and users concerning the legitimacy of the Jewish temple in Heliopolis, with the Septuagint representing the agenda of some of the temple's supporters and the MT being refashioned by its critics (the same is true for Ezek. 30:17, where the name On [*'wn*] is vocalized as *'āwen,* "evil," instead of *'ôn,* in a way reminiscent of the derogatory name given to the shrine of Bethel in Hos. 4:15; 5:8; 10:5, 8). Less polemical is *Tg. Ps.-J.* Isa. 19:18, which merely "updates" Isaiah's prophecy by referring to the Jewish altar in "the city of Heliopolis, which will be destroyed."

A passage in the *Sibylline Oracles* (5.493-511) speaks of a Jewish temple that would one day be built in Egypt, and how it would later be destroyed — a description that seems to have been influenced by the fate of Onias' temple. And it has been suggested that the Jewish novel *Joseph and Aseneth,* which tells the story of Joseph's marriage with Aseneth, in biblical Heliopolis, and includes a quasi-apocalyptic scene with a symbolic revelation mediated by a great angel, was written by the Jews of Greco-Roman Heliopolis in veiled support of their own presence there.

Yet the temple of Onias may have been of little significance for the Jews of Alexandria, especially once the Roman conquest of Palestine (63 B.C.E.) and Egypt (30 B.C.E.) united Alexandria and Jerusalem under a single empire, and a century of *pax Romana* gave the Jews of Egypt easier access to the Jerusalem Temple. In subsequent Jewish history, Heliopolis and the Jewish temple there were only a faint, and confused, memory (see, e.g., *m. Menaḥ.* 13:10 and *b. Menaḥot* 109b–110a).

BIBLIOGRAPHY

G. BOHAK 1996, *Joseph and Aseneth and the Jewish Temple in Heliopolis,* Atlanta: Scholars Press. • L. CAPPONI 2007, *Il tempio di Leontopoli in Egitto: Identità politica e religiosa dei Giudei di Onia (c. 150 a.C–73 d.C.),* Pisa: ETS. • W. M. FLINDERS PETRIE 1915, *Heliopolis, Kafr Ammar and Shurafa,* London: School of Archaeology and Bernard Quaritch. • J. FREY 1999, "Temple and Rival Temple: The Cases of Elephantine, Mt. Gerizim, and Leontopolis," in *Gemeinde ohne Tempel/Community without Temple: Zur Substituierung und Transformation des Jerusalemer Tempels und seines Kultes im Alten Testament, antiken Judentum und frühen Christentum,* ed. B. Ego, A. Lange and P. Pilhofer, Tübingen: Mohr-Siebeck, 171-203. • F. L. GRIFFITH 1890, *The Antiquities of*

Tell el Yahoudieh, London: Egypt Exploration Fund. • E. S. GRUEN 1997, "The Origins and Objectives of Onias' Temple," *SCI* 16: 47-70. • R. HAYWARD 1982, "The Jewish Temple at Leontopolis: A Reconsideration," *JJS* 33: 429-43. • J. MÉLÈZE MODRZEJEWSKI 1995, *The Jews of Egypt: From Rameses II to Emperor Hadrian,* trans. R. Cornman, Edinburgh: Clark. • E. NAVILLE 1890, *The Mound of the Jews and the City of Onias,* London: Egypt Exploration Fund (in the same volume as F. L. Griffith above). • S. QUIRKE 2001, *The Cult of Ra: Sun-Worship in Ancient Egypt,* London: Thames & Hudson. • P. SCHÄFER 1998, "'From Jerusalem the Great to Alexandria the Small': The Relationship between Palestine and Egypt in the Graeco-Roman World," in *The Talmud Yerushalmi and Graeco-Roman Culture,* vol. 1, ed. P. Schäfer, Tübingen: Mohr-Siebeck, 129-140. • D. R. SCHWARTZ 1997, "The Jews of Egypt between Onias' Temple and the Jerusalem Temple and Heaven," *Zion* 62: 5-22 (in Hebrew). • J. E. TAYLOR 1998, "A Second Temple in Egypt: The Evidence for the Zadokite Temple of Onias," *JSJ* 29: 297-321. • A. WASSERSTEIN 1993, "Notes on the Temple of Onias at Leontopolis," *ICS* 18: 119-29.

See also: Oniads GIDEON BOHAK

Hellenism, Hellenization

"Hebraism" and "Hellenism"

The dichotomy of Judaism and Hellenism has a long history. Perhaps its most famous formulation came in Matthew Arnold's *Culture and Anarchy,* published in 1869, which denoted the contending positions as "Hebraism" and "Hellenism." The terms served as handy metaphors for a range of polarities: Jew and Greek, monotheism and polytheism, religion and reason, faith and skepticism, tradition and innovation. Arnold was not the first. Heinrich Heine, a generation earlier, had drawn a comparable contrast between Jews and Greeks, between those who seek joyless religion and those who take pleasure in life, even asserting that all peoples fall into one category or the other. But Arnold's articulation became the classic one. In his view "Hebraism," a stand-in for contemporary Puritanism, evoked a rigid focus on moral conduct, a spiritual straitjacket that underscored sin and conscience, whereas "Hellenism" represented critical thinking, rationality, and a striving after beauty. The dualism goes back at least as far as the third century C.E. when the African churchman Tertullian famously asked, "What has Athens to do with Jerusalem?"

A Clash of Cultures?

Did this conceptualization derive from a clash of cultures in antiquity? Did the infiltration of Hellenism signal an adulteration of Jewish faith and principles? So it appeared to the author of 2 Maccabees, composed probably in the late second or early first century B.C.E. He looked back to the pivotal contest three quarters of a century earlier featured by the Maccabean rebellion against the oppression of the Hellenic king Antiochus IV. The author of that work is the first to use the terms "Hellenism" and "Judaism" and suggests (on the face of it) that they represent contending forces. The idea that these concepts represent rival ways of life stems in large part from this key text. Yet a fundamental paradox plagues the reconstruction. 2 Maccabees was itself composed in Greek by an author steeped in Hellenic historiography. His frame of reference was Greek, and his judgments were couched in terminology and values that reflect Hellenic thinking. He may deplore from a distance the introduction of a gymnasium into Jerusalem, the collaboration of the priests, and the trappings of a Greek city. But the very fact that such developments occurred without controversy at the time reflects a Jewish openness to Hellenic institutions and indicates a much more ambiguous and complex relationship.

The conquests of Alexander the Great had made the Greek presence in the Near East far more conspicuous than ever before, putting Jews under the sway of Greek rulers in the homeland and setting them amidst a Greek culture in the cities of the Diaspora. But Alexander and his successors had not come east to impose Hellenism on the "barbarian." Intercultural exchange rather than an imperialist installation of the dominant culture marked the Hellenistic period in the Near East. Antiochus IV was a brief aberration, hardly a representative example — and even he had largely political motives, no commitment to a spread of Hellenism. Jews, in general, did not confront the necessity of either conforming or resisting.

Defining "Hellenism" and "Hellenization"

And what was "Hellenism" anyway? The coming of the Greeks produced an intricate mix of peoples and traditions. The "Hellenic" culture with which Jews came into contact was no unalloyed strain (if ever such a strain existed). It rested on a Greek amalgam with a Phoenician substratum on the Mediterranean coast, with Egyptian elements in Alexandria, with Mesopotamian institutions in Babylon, and a bewildering combination of peoples in Asia Minor. In Palestine itself the Greek ingredient mingled with indigenous communities in Galilee, in Idumea, and even in Jerusalem.

In what sense, then, did Jews become "Hellenized"? They spoke, read, and composed in Greek in cities all over the Mediterranean, and gained familiarity with Greek artifacts, practices, and modes of understanding even in Palestine. But no reason exists to equate this with a contamination of Judaism or the undermining of adherence to tradition.

The Hellenism of the Hasmoneans

Even the classic instance of Maccabean mobilization against the brutal decrees of Antiochus IV Epiphanes did not amount to a clash of cultures. Jews fought against the policies of the king, not against "Hellenism." Judas Maccabaeus himself conducted most of his campaigns against peoples of Palestine who had been there long before the advent of the Greeks, reliving biblical battles with Canaanites, Ammonites, Edomites, and Philistines. Greeks as such were not his targets. And the Jewish captain proved perfectly willing to engage in negotiations with officers and ministers of the Seleucid king. He could proudly celebrate the rededication of the Temple without claiming it as a triumph over the forces of Hellenism.

Judas' successors, the line of Hasmonean dynasts, went further. They entered regularly into diplomatic dealings with Greek kings, adopted Greek names, donned garb and paraded emblems redolent with Hellenic significance, erected monuments, displayed stelae and minted coinage inspired by Greek models, hired mercenaries, and even took on royal titulature. Jonathan, brother and successor of Judas, for instance, received the salutation of "friend of the king," obtained purple robes and gold vessels, even confirmation as high priest, at the hands of Seleucid monarchs. His brother Simon, in turn, also enjoyed the endorsement of the Seleucid crown and a variety of privileges guaranteed by those who contended for that crown. Jews set up a bronze inscription (itself in imitation of Greek practice) to commemorate the deeds of Simon and his brothers on behalf of the Jewish people — but also a reminder that his position was assured by the favor of the Greek monarchy. Simon, moreover, raised an impressive tomb to the honor of his family consisting of seven pyramids, trophies of armor, and sculpted ships, a striking amalgam of Greek and Near Eastern elements that exemplified the Hellenistic character of the Hasmonean house. In the next generation John Hyrcanus became the first Jewish ruler to issue coins, a practice adopted by those who followed him. The issues notably employed symbols long familiar in the Hellenistic world, including even the anchor, emblematic of the Seleucid dynasty. At the same time they avoided placing any portraits of humans or animals on the coins. A comparable nod to both Greek and Jewish tradition can be found in the names of the Hasmoneans sported on the bronze currency: Greek names on one side, Hebrew on the other.

The point here is not that the Hasmoneans were appealing to two separate constituencies. Bronze coins (essentially small change) would not have circulated much outside the Jewish communities. Rather, they advertised the fact that a Jewish nation could embrace Hellenic conventions without compromising its integrity and could operate comfortably within the context of a Hellenic world. One of the Hasmoneans, Aristobulus, felt free to style himself as "philhellene." Yet our Jewish sources charge none of the successors of Judas with betraying the legacy of the Maccabean rebellion. Embrace of a range of Hellenic customs and institutions was perfectly compatible with maintaining adherence to the traditions of the forefathers.

In short, even the dynasty of the Maccabees, normally taken as quintessential representatives of a Jewish struggle against "Hellenism," plainly saw their accomplishment in a very different light. The developments in second- and first-century-B.C.E. Palestine did not constitute a process of Hellenization in which Jews were passive recipients or indeed active aggrandizers of Greek culture. Increasing Jewish exposure to and adaptation of Hellenic practices was largely an unconscious, uncalculated, indeed unnoticed, phenomenon that interfered little, if at all, with the ancestral precepts of the faith. Hellenization, insofar as the term carries any meaning (it is a purely modern construct), represents an enrichment of Judaism, not a thrust in a cultural war.

Hellenism and the Jewish Heritage

The Jews of the Diaspora, of course, dwelled in cities suffused with Greek language, society, and culture. For them "Hellenism" would have been no meaningful concept at all. Many of them had been part and parcel of Greek communities for several generations, an integral part of their being. Greek was their language almost everywhere in the Mediterranean world outside of Palestine (and to no small degree even there). One may note that even the Jewish communities in Rome were still Greek-speaking in late antiquity.

Yet Diaspora Jews held to the convictions of their ancestors, maintained an unbroken connection to their past, and possessed a clear sense of their own identity. The absorption of Greek culture and the retention of their ancient heritage were perfectly compatible concepts. The former simply became a means to express the latter.

The translation of the Hebrew Bible into Greek, probably in third-century-B.C.E. Alexandria, exemplifies that blend. Jews who had lost command of the ancient tongue considered it a prime objective to render the sacred Scriptures intelligible in their own language. The new version acquired the sanctity of the old, not a replacement but an exact replica (so, at least, it was portrayed). The expression of the Jews' deepest beliefs and fundamental lore in the language of the Diaspora signals the embrace of Hellenism for the advance of Judaism.

The availability of the Septuagint proved to be a spur for the flourishing of a Jewish literature in Greek, moving in the tracks of long-established Hellenic paradigms. Jewish writers, especially in Alexandria, composed epic and tragedy, wrote history, produced philosophy, and indulged in imaginative fiction. Yet they fixed their focus consistently upon refashioning their own heritage. And, while working within the categories of Greek literature and learning, they reversed the Hellenic framework and claimed it for themselves.

Numerous examples can be cited. Surviving fragments of the Jewish epic poets Theodotus and Philo deal with subjects like the tale of Dinah in Genesis 34 and the eminence of the Hebrew patriarchs. The historian Demetrius sought to clear up chronological puzzles and to apply critical method to ostensible inconsistencies in the biblical tradition. Ezekiel composed a Greek tragedy on the topic of the exodus. And the fictional narrative, *Joseph and Aseneth,* possessed clear affinities with Greek romances, but drew inspiration for its tale from the Pentateuch (though going well beyond it).

Even more striking, Jewish intellectuals reconceived Hellenic achievements as due to Hebraic precedents. Aristobulus, a Jew of wide philosophic and literary interests, writing probably in Alexandria in the mid-

THE JEWISH DIASPORA

second century B.C.E., produced an extended commentary on the Torah. In his conception, Moses' law code became the inspiration for Hellenic philosophical and poetic traditions. Among other things, Aristobulus alleged that Pythagoras borrowed much from the books of Moses and that Plato was a devoted reader of the Scriptures, poring over every detail and faithfully following their prescriptions. And he made a still more grandiose claim. Aristobulus found common ground among all thinkers in the importance of maintaining reverence toward God, a principle enshrined in the Bible and thus providing the central foundation for Greek philosophy.

That line persisted in Jewish writings. The great philosopher Philo of Alexandria in the first century C.E. carried on the theme. He traced the impact of Jewish learning back to the pre-Socratic thinker Heraclitus and saw its effect in the verses of Hesiod, the teachings of Socrates, and the Stoic doctrines of Zeno. The Jewish historian Josephus also adopts the posture that the cream of Greek thinkers, Pythagoras, Anaxagoras, Plato, and the Stoics, share kindred views about the nature of God — and they can all be traced back to Moses. Josephus further picks up the parallel between Moses and Greek lawgivers. He notes with some verve that Moses well preceded his counterparts, Lycurgus, Solon, Zaleucus, and the rest, who have to take a back seat to their Hebrew predecessor and could never quite match his standards.

The Jews have the better of it in this conceptualizing. But the terms of the comparison itself constitute the central point. This is no mere competition or one-upmanship. Reciprocity rather than rivalry takes precedence. "Hellenism" did not inject an alien element into Jewish self-perception but provided modes of thinking and expression that could enhance that self-perception. The idea of "Hellenization" misconceives the complicated interconnections of the Second Temple period. Judaism and Hellenism were overlapping, not clashing, cultures.

BIBLIOGRAPHY

J. K. AITKEN 2004, "Review Essay on Hengel, *Judaism and Hellenism*," *JBL* 123: 331-41. • J. J. COLLINS AND G. E. STERLING, EDS. 2001, *Hellenism in the Land of Israel.* Notre Dame, Ind.: University of Notre Dame. • J. J. COLLINS 2005, "Cult and Culture: The Limits of Hellenization in Judea," in idem, *Jewish Cult and Hellenistic Culture,* Leiden: Brill, 21-43. • E. S. GRUEN 1998, *Heritage and Hellenism: The Reinvention of Jewish Tradition,* Berkeley: University of California Press. • M. HENGEL 1974, *Judaism and Hellenism: Studies in their Encounter in Palestine during the Early Hellenistic Period,* 2 vols., Philadelphia: Fortress. • L. I. LEVINE 1998, *Judaism and Hellenism in Antiquity,* Seattle: University of Washington Press. • A. MOMIGLIANO 1994, "Jews and Greeks," in idem, *Essays on Ancient and Modern Judaism,* Chicago: University of Chicago Press, 10-28. • T. RAJAK 2001, "The Hasmoneans and the Uses of Hellenism," in eadem, *The Jewish Dialogue with Greece and Rome: Studies in Cultural and Social Interaction,* Leiden: Brill, 61-80. • Y. SHAVIT 1997, *Athens in Jerusalem: Classical Antiquity and*

Hellenism in the Making of the Modern Secular Jew, London: Littman Library of Jewish Civilization.

See also: Romanization ERICH S. GRUEN

Hengel, Martin

Martin Hengel (1926-2009) was a German Protestant theologian and scholar of the New Testament and early Judaism. Raised in a Swabian pietistic family, he studied theology in Tübingen and Heidelberg (1947-1951) before serving as *Repetent* (tutor) in the famous Tübingen *Stift* (1954-1955) and assistant of Otto Michel (1955-1957). He also worked as the sales manager (1953-1954) and then director (1957-1964) of his family's textile company. Hengel was professor of New Testament in Erlangen (1968-1972) and then, until his retirement, professor of New Testament and early Judaism and director of the *Institut für antikes Judentum und hellenistische Religionsgeschichte* in Tübingen (1972-1992). In addition to serving as editor of several important scholarly series, Hengel trained numerous scholars and inspired a variety of international scholarly exchange programs. He held honorary doctorates from Uppsala, St. Andrews, Durham, Strasbourg, Cambridge, and Dublin, and was a member of several academies.

In 1959 Hengel finished his Tübingen dissertation on the Zealots, a pioneering work of social history, long before such became fashionable in the late 60s. In his magisterial habilitation thesis on Judaism and Hellenism (1967), Hengel demonstrated the encounter of Palestinian Judaism with Hellenistic culture from Alexander to the Hasmoneans. With this work, he contributed to overcoming the rigid alternative, posed by the History-of-Religions school and adopted by Rudolf Bultmann, between Palestinian and Hellenistic Judaism at the turn of the eras. His work was a massive study of the early Hellenization of Judaism in the land of Israel, even before the Hellenistic reform that led to the Maccabean Revolt. He then drew out the consequences of those insights for the religio-historical interpretation of early Christianity in numerous subsequent studies (e.g., on the Jewish, as opposed to pagan origins of Christology and the basically Jewish character of Paul's thought).

As a New Testament scholar, Hengel reacted against the influence of Bultmann and his followers, who privileged syncretistic and Gnostic materials as the crucial background of early Christianity and often neglected early Judaism and proper historical work. Hengel argued instead for a thoroughgoing Jewish influence in early Christianity and the need for an in-depth knowledge of early Jewish materials. In New Testament scholarship he called for attention to the widest possible range of sources "from Ezra to Origen": Jewish, Greco-Roman, and Patristic materials, including the texts from Qumran and Nag Hammadi, as well as papyri, inscriptions, and archaeology. He advocated the predominant role of philological and historical methods in exegesis over against all ideological approaches.

Hengel's work has had a major influence on contemporary study of early Judaism, even if his historical syntheses have been subject to refinement and criticism. For instance, his portrait of the Hasidim and their ideology at the time of the Maccabean Revolt has been questioned in light of the paucity of evidence for this group, and his emphasis on the unity of the Jewish resistance against Rome has been criticized. Debate also continues over the extent and nature of Hellenization in the land of Israel. Despite the attempts to critique and refine Hengel's views, however, there is no doubting his imposing erudition, his lasting contributions, and his reputation as one of the most important modern interpreters of early Judaism.

BIBLIOGRAPHY

J. K. AITKEN 2004, "Review Essay on Hengel, *Judaism and Hellenism,*" *JBL* 123: 331-41. • H. CANCIK, H. LICHTENBERGER AND P. SCHÄFER, EDS., 1996, *Geschichte–Tradition–Reflexion: Festschrift für Martin Hengel zum 70. Geburtstag,* 3 vols., Tübingen: Mohr-Siebeck. • J. J. COLLINS 1989, "Judaism as *Praeparatio Evangelica* in the Work of Martin Hengel," *RSR* 15: 226-28. • L. H. FELDMAN 1977, "Hengel's *Judaism and Hellenism* in Retrospect," *JBL* 96: 371-82. • L. H. FELDMAN 2006, "How Much Hellenism in the Land of Israel?" in idem, *Judaism and Hellenism Reconsidered,* Leiden: Brill, 71-102. • M. HENGEL 1974, *Judaism and Hellenism,* 2 vols., London: SCM (Eng. trans. of *Judentum und Hellenismus,* 2d ed., Tübingen: Mohr-Siebeck, 1973). • M. HENGEL 1976, *The Son of God: The Origins of Christology and the History of Jewish-Hellenistic Religion,* London: SCM. • M. HENGEL 1977, *Crucifixion,* London: SCM; Philadelphia: Fortress. • M. HENGEL 1980, *Jews, Greeks and Barbarians,* London: SCM (Eng. trans. of *Juden, Griechen und Barbaren,* Stuttgart: Katholisches Bibelwerk, 1976). • M. HENGEL 1981, *The Atonement,* London: SCM. • M. HENGEL AND H. LICHTENBERGER 1981, "Die Hellenisierung des antiken Judentums als Praeparatio Evangelica," *Humanistische Bildung* 4: 1-30. • M. HENGEL 1989A, *The Zealots,* Edinburgh: Clark (Eng. trans. of *Die Zeloten,* Leiden: Brill, 1961; 2d ed. 1976). • M. HENGEL WITH C. MARKSCHIES 1989B, *The 'Hellenization' of Judaea in the First Century after Christ,* London: SCM. • M. HENGEL WITH R. DEINES 1991, *The Pre-Christian Paul,* London: SCM. • M. HENGEL 1993, "A Gentile in the Wilderness: My Encounter with Jews and Judaism," in *Overcoming Fear between Jews and Christians,* ed. J. H. Charlesworth, New York: Interfaith Institute, 7-83. • M. HENGEL 1995, *Studies in Early Christology,* Edinburgh: Clark, 1995. • M. HENGEL 1996, *Judaica et Hellenistica: Kleine Schriften I,* Tübingen: Mohr-Siebeck. • M. HENGEL 1999, *Judaica, Hellenistica et Christiana: Kleine Schriften II,* Tübingen: Mohr-Siebeck. • M. HENGEL 2001, "Judaism and Hellenism Revisited," in *Hellenism in the Land of Israel,* ed. J. J. Collins and G. E. Sterling, Notre Dame: University of Notre Dame Press, 6-37. • M. HENGEL 2002A, *The Septuagint as Christian Scripture,* Edinburgh: Clark. • M. HENGEL 2002B, *Paulus und Jakobus: Kleine Schriften III,* Tübingen: Mohr-Siebeck. • M. HENGEL WITH A. M. SCHWEMER 2007, *Jesus und das Judentum: Geschichte des Frühen Christentums I,* Tübingen: Mohr-Siebeck. • F. MILLAR 1978, "The Background of the Maccabean Revolution: Reflections on Martin Hengel's *Judaism and Hellenism,*" *JJS* 29: 1-21.

JÖRG FREY

Herakleopolis Papyri

The Herakleopolis Papyri, also known as the Jewish Politeuma Papyri (P. Polit. Iud.), date from 144/3 to 133/2 B.C.E. and provide a uniquely detailed snapshot of daily life for Egyptian Jews living under Ptolemaic rule. They were recovered from mummy cartonnage discovered at the site of ancient Herakleopolis in the Fayûm region of Egypt. Written in Greek, the papyri include citizen petitions to the officials (archons, politarchs, and elders) of a Jewish *politeuma*, that is, a self-governing community of resident aliens (*P.Polit.Iud.* 1–16) and correspondence between officials in the region (17–20). The petitions address disputes regarding personal honor (1–2), marriage arrangements and dowries (3–5), the law of persons (6–7), and business transactions (8–12). The letters between officials concern a release of prisoners, the fallout from a disturbance in Peempasbytis, and summonses to appear before judges. Although the petitions end the debate over whether the Jews of Ptolemaic Egypt were permitted to organize themselves as a *politeuma* (they were), the legal reasoning reflected in them indicates that the petitioners did not embrace fully the concomitant right to govern their corporate life according to Jewish law. The few explicit uses of Torah are subsumed under hybrid Greco-Egyptian legal norms.

Until the papyri were published in 2001 by Cowey and Maresch, some doubt remained as to whether the Jews of Ptolemaic Egypt had the right to form *politeumata*. Indeed, the uses of the term *politeuma* in association with Jews known prior to publication of the papyri were ambiguous in their meaning (*Letter of Aristeas* 310; *CIG* 5361-5362 [two inscriptions of the first century B.C.E. from Berenice in Cyrenaica]; for discussion of the texts, see Lüderitz 1994: 204-21). The papyri settle this issue once and for all. The phrase "the *politeuma* of the *Ioudaioi*" in *P.Polit.Iud.* 8.5; 20.8-9, a *politeuma* member's explicit self-identification as a *Ioudaios* ("Jew/Judean"; 2.2, 4), and the wealth of theophoric names (e.g., Dorotheos [7.2, 26, 29, 38; 8.13, 38] and Theodotos [6.2, 41; 8.6, 37; 13.2; 17.2-3]) leave no doubt as to the ethnicity of the *politeuma* members.

The petitions also provide significant new evidence that military settlers who shared the same ethnicity formed the core of Ptolemaic-era *politeumata* (see Honigman 2003: 64-67). *P.Polit.Iud.* 1 concerns a dispute in the wharf area of Herakleopolis, the location of the fortress where soldiers were garrisoned. The powers exercised by the leaders of the *politeuma* closely match those of the garrison commander *(phrourarch)*, now known from the *Phrourarch Dioskyrides Papyri* (Cowey and Maresch 2003; see esp. *P.Phrur.Diosk.* 1, concerning a domestic disturbance involving a *Ioudaios*).

Some have assumed that if the Jews did have the privilege to form *politeumata*, they would have exercised the right to govern themselves by their ancestral laws and thus distinguish themselves from their non-Jewish neighbors (Kasher 1985). Although the petitions from Herakleopolis generally do not support that view, they do show that the petitioners were nonetheless aware of and willing to call upon Jewish law whenever it served their legal interests.

Evidence of the petitioners' overwhelming reliance on non-Jewish normative systems abounds. For example, the disputes regarding marriage arrangements and dowries reflect Greek and Egyptian practices and omit the biblical *mōhar* or "bride price" (*P.Polit.Iud.* 3–5; cf. Gen. 34:12; Exod. 22:16; 1 Sam. 18:25). A petition requesting the return of an orphan to her proper guardian depends on Greek common law (*P.Polit.Iud.* 7; see Kugler forthcoming). Loans are made at the standard Ptolemaic business interest rate of 24 percent (*P.Polit.Iud.* 8; cf. Exod. 22:24; Lev. 25:35-38; Deut. 23:20-21). A Jew eschews his own ethnic label for that of a *Persēs tēs Epigonēs* ("Persian of the Succession/Younger Generation"), a fictive identity taken by poor credit risks to qualify for a loan in the early second century B.C.E. (*P.Polit.Iud.* 8; on this use of the otherwise mysterious ethnic title, see Ruprecht 1985: 19; and *P.Dion.* 30.3-4). And according to Greek custom a woman is represented by a *kyrios* (6).

At the same time, close analysis of the legal reasoning in the papyri uncovers evidence that the petitioners also appealed to the Torah when it could strengthen their legal arguments. For example, a guardian seeking the return of his ward under Greek common law cites his keeping of the levitical law concerning care for one's destitute kin (Lev. 25:35-38) as evidence of his suitability as a guardian (*BGU* IV 1070 [218 C.E.]; *P.Harris* I 68 [225 C.E.]; *P.Teb.* II 326 [266-267 C.E.]; *SB* V 7558 [173 C.E.]; for a discussion of *P.Polit.Iud.* 7, see Kugler). Likewise, a petitioner contesting the giving of his fiancé by her father to another man courted the woman according to Egyptian norms and made a premarital pact with her father typical of Greek practice. Yet the same petitioner invoked Num. 30:3 to remind the father of the binding nature of his promise to give his daughter to him, and he cited Deut. 24:1 to argue that the father had not issued the "customary writ of separation" necessary to free a woman for betrothal to another man.

It seems likely that further examination of the papyri will multiply such instances of the petitioners' strategic use of ancestral Jewish law to supplement a chiefly Greco-Egyptian normative system. The implications of this discovery for understanding Jewish ethnicity and identity in Hellenistic Egypt remain to be teased out and are likely to be important.

BIBLIOGRAPHY

E. BICKERMAN 1956, "Two Legal Interpretations of the Septuagint," *Revue internationale des droits de l'antiquité* 3: 81-104. • J. M. S. COWEY AND K. MARESCH, EDS. 2001, *Urkunden des Politeuma der Juden von Herakleopolis (144/3-133/2 v. Chr.) (P.Polit.Iud.): Papyri aus Sammlungen von Heidelberg, Köln, München und Wien,* Wiesbaden: Westdeutscher Verlag. • J. M. S. COWEY, K. MARESCH, AND C. BARNES, EDS. 2003, *Das Archiv des Phrurarchen Dioskurides (154–145 v. Chr.?) (P.Phrur.Diosk.): Papyri aus Sammlungen von Heidelberg, Köln, München und Wien,* Paderborn: Ferdinand Schöningh. • S. HONIGMAN 2003, "*Politeumata* and Ethnicity in Ptolemaic and Roman Egypt," *Ancient Society* 33: 61-

102. • A. KASHER 1985, *The Jews in Hellenistic and Roman Egypt,* Leiden: Brill. • R. KUGLER FORTHCOMING, "Dorotheos Petitions for the Return of Philippa (*P.Polit.Iud.* 7): A Case Study in the Jews and Their Law in Ptolemaic Egypt," in *Proceedings of the XXVth International Congress of Papyrology,* Ann Arbor: University of Michigan Press. • G. LÜDERITZ 1994, "What Is the *Politeuma?*" in *Studies in Early Jewish Epigraphy,* ed. J. W. van Henten and P. W. van der Horst, Leiden: Brill, 183-225. • H. J. RUPPRECHT 1985, *Untersuchungen zum Darlehen im Recht der graeco-aegyptischen Papyri der Ptolemäerzeit,* Munich: Beck.

ROBERT A. KUGLER

Hermon, Mount

At 2,814 m. (9,230 ft.), Mt. Hermon (Hebr. *ḥermôn*) is the highest and southernmost part of the Anti-Lebanon mountain range, located at the northern boundary of the land of Israel. Meaning "sacred" or "set apart," its name defines both the character of the region and the role of the mountain in myth and literature.

Religious Associations

Hermon was traditionally regarded as the place of the assembly of the gods. More specifically, it was the residence of Baʿal Hermon (cf. Judg. 3:3; 1 Chron. 5:23), the Lord of Oaths. A dedicatory inscription made to this "greatest and most holy of gods" and directed at those taking oaths was found in one of the open-air temples at the mountain's summit. The numinous quality of the mountain's vistas made it a magnet for temples and cult sites. More than thirty such have been identified throughout the region, a number of them dating to the Hellenistic or early Roman period (Dar 1993). During this time, Baʿal Hermon became increasingly identified with Baʿal Shamin, the Lord of Heaven, who was himself emerging as the focus of a pagan celestial monotheism in Syria and Phoenicia, a development reflected in the iconography of some of the temples in the Hermon region. Mt. Hermon was evidently also regarded as a place of visions and revelations. It is the site of Enoch's incubation oracle in *1 Enoch* 13, and of Peter's confession of Jesus as the Messiah at Caesarea Philippi in Matthew 16.

The Story of the Watchers (*1 Enoch* 6–16)

In biblical tradition, Hermon functions as a boundary marker for the northern extension of the land of Israel. It is included in the sacred geography of the Psalms (Ps. 42:7; 89:13), possibly as the result of the transfer of levitical traditions south to Jerusalem following the Assyrian destruction of northern sanctuaries like Dan in the eighth century B.C.E. In the Second Temple period, however, Hermon took on a new role in sacred geography. In the story of the fall of the Watchers in *1 Enoch* 6–16, it is the location of the Watchers' oath as they descend to earth to seek human wives. The narrative thus draws both upon the role of Hermon as a sacred place where the gods assemble, oaths are taken, and visions are received, and upon its meteorological significance as the place of the descent of the dew, rain, and snow. The Watchers who descend upon the mountain represent celestial and meteorological powers. One of them is named Hermoni, a reflection of Baʿal Hermon. They take an oath to secure human wives, and the divine-earthly union issues in the birth of violent giants and the corruption of the earth.

The story of the oath revolves around a pun on the name "Hermon," while a second pun emerges in the verb *yarad,* "to descend," tying the narrative to the "days of Jared," the father of Enoch. Some, however, have speculated that the original intent of the pun referred to the "days of the *Yarid,*" a regional pagan festival mentioned both in Lucian and the Talmud (so Clermont-Ganneau 1903; E. Lipinski 1971). *Yarad* also suggests the Jordan River. The geographical references to Hermon and Dan, coupled with some of the cultural features of the Enoch narrative (including a celestial monotheism), are sufficiently precise to suggest knowledge of the sanctuary at Dan and the Hermon region on the part of the author of *1 Enoch* 6–16.

Scholars are at odds over whether the story of the fall of the Watchers in *1 Enoch* is an expansion of the story of the sons of God and the daughters of humanity in Gen. 6:1-4, or whether the biblical version is a condensation of an older tradition that recrudesced in the Enochic literature. Given that the material specific to the Hermon region is to be found in apparent additions to the Genesis story, it seems more likely that the Enochic version amplifies Genesis through traditions encountered in the north and originating in Tyre. In his discussion of Tyre, Philo of Byblos describes four giants representing four mountains, including Hermon, who beget exceptional children through encounters with women (*Phoenician History* 156–57). Kedesh, an outpost of Tyre in Upper Galilee, may be the source of such material.

The Iturean Incursion

Another scholarly dispute relates to the ethnic character of the Itureans and the date of their incursion into the Hermon region. Some treat the Itureans as Arabic in origin and date their move into Mt. Hermon to the third century (Dar 1993), while others associate them ethnically with Phoenicia and date their incursion to the second century (Maʿoz 1997). The dispute affects the reconstruction of Jewish-Iturean relations in the period, including the claim by Josephus that the Itureans were forcibly converted to Judaism.

BIBLIOGRAPHY

C. S. CLERMONT-GANNEAU 1903, "Le Mont Hermon et son dieu d'après une inscription inédite," *Recueil D'Archéologie Orientale* 5: 346-66. • S. DAR 1993, *Settlements and Cult Sites on Mount Hermon, Israel,* Oxford: Tempvs Reparatvm. • E. LIPINSKI 1971, "El's Abode: Mythological Traditions Related to Mount Hermon," *Orientalis Lovaniensia Periodica* 2: 13-69. • Z. U. MAʿOZ 1997, "Review of Dar, S., *Settlements and Cult Sites on Mount Hermon, Israel,*" *IEJ* 47: 279-83. • G. W. E. NICKELSBURG 2001, *1 Enoch,* vol. 1, Minneapolis: Fortress, 238-47. • D. W. SUTER 2003, "Why Galilee? Galilean Regionalism in the Interpretation of *1 Enoch* 6–16," *Henoch* 25: 167-212.

DAVID W. SUTER

Herod the Great

Herod (ca. 74-4 B.C.E.) was an Idumean noble who usurped the throne of Judea from the Hasmoneans and reigned as King of Judea from 37 until 4 B.C.E. He skillfully negotiated the complex world of Greco-Roman Judea and brought his kingdom to its greatest economic success and political importance.

The Young Courtier

Herod was the second son of Antipater the Idumean and Cypros, a Nabatean princess. He had three brothers, Phasael, Joseph, and Pheroras, and a sister named Salome. He grew up as a member of a powerful family of nobles in the court of the Hasmonean John Hyrcanus II. Herod's grandfather, Antipas, had served as *stratēgos* of Idumea under Alexander Jannaeus (Josephus, *Ant.* 14.10). His father, Antipater, likely succeeded Antipas as *stratēgos* but quickly rose to the pinnacle of power in the Hasmonean court and eventually became *epitropos* (procurator) of Judea (*J.W.* 1.199; *Ant.* 14.143). In 47 B.C.E., Antipater appointed his sons Phasael and Herod *stratēgeoi* of Jerusalem and Galilee respectively. According to Josephus, each governed quite effectively. Herod, in particular, had tremendous success in suppressing a group of bandits who were ravaging the districts on the Syrian frontier that bordered Galilee (*J.W.* 1.204-5; *Ant.* 14.158-60). Through his success, Herod earned the favor and goodwill of the Romans, and his achievements brought him to the attention of the proconsul of Syria, Sextus Julius Caesar, who later appointed him *stratēgos* of Coele-Syria and Samaria (*J.W.* 1.205; *Ant.* 14.160).

In 43 B.C.E., shortly after the assassination of Julius Caesar, Antipater was poisoned (*J.W.* 1.225-26; *Ant.* 14.280-84). Herod and his brother Phasael assumed their father's position and became Hyrcanus' most important officials. In 42 B.C.E., Marc Antony appointed them tetrarchs of Galilee and Judea (*J.W.* 1.244; *Ant.* 14.326). When the Parthians and their ally, the Hasmonean Mattathias Antigonus, invaded Judea in 40 B.C.E., Phasael and Hyrcanus were captured, and Phasael committed suicide rather than become a hostage. Herod, who was unaware of his brother's fate, decided to flee Jerusalem with his wife, mother, mother-in-law, and other family members. After installing his family at Masada, he fled to Rome to secure its support against the Parthians and Antigonus. With the support of Antony and Octavian, the Senate proclaimed Herod King of Judea and promised him military aid in his war against Antigonus (*J.W.* 1.282-85; *Ant.* 14.381-89). Herod's war was part of the larger Parthian campaign planned by Antony. Having secured military support, Herod returned to Judea, where he faced stiff resistance. Three years passed before he was able to defeat Antigonus and capture Jerusalem. In 37 B.C.E., he entered the capital as King of Judea (*J.W.* 1.349-57; *Ant.* 14.476-91).

The King of Judea

Upon ascending to the throne, Herod immediately faced the issue of legitimacy. In his attempt to solidify his regime, he turned to the most recent source of authority, the Hasmoneans. Through architecture, coin issues, and dynastic maneuvering, he linked himself with this dynastic family and asserted his own independence by adapting their imagery to suit his own needs. Although Herod ultimately turned to other means of legitimization, this early attempt at creating and maintaining legitimacy was a significant political strategy. It reflected his conscious realization that while force of arms might have taken Jerusalem and Judea, he needed legitimacy to govern it.

Herod's other major concern in the early years of his rule was Cleopatra. By the mid-30s B.C.E., she had become extremely powerful and influential with Antony. Once she had secured her control over Egypt, Cleopatra attempted to re-create the Ptolemaic Empire of her ancestors. This empire included Judea and Syria, and Herod presented a serious obstacle to achieving this goal. Undeterred, Cleopatra used her influence with Antony to seize territory from Herod and other neighboring dynasts. In the Donation of Alexandria (34 B.C.E.), Antony ceded her control of the Plain of Jericho and all of the territory of Syria south of the Eleutherus River except Tyre and Sidon. In an attempt to minimize potential conflict while still retaining possession of the land, Herod acquiesced to the loss of formal control over the territory but agreed to lease it from Cleopatra for a large sum of money. In this way, he could receive the income from this fertile region and yet remain on good terms with the Egyptian queen.

Despite Cleopatra's ambitions, Herod held onto his kingdom. Moreover, he was able to rule in relative security until 30 B.C.E., when Antony and Cleopatra were defeated at the Battle of Actium, which was fought off the western coast of Greece. Herod immediately recognized the need to switch loyalties, so he hastened to Rhodes to persuade the victorious Octavian that he could serve the new regime as a loyal client king. Octavian confirmed Herod's position and enlarged his kingdom (*J.W.* 1.386-97; *Ant.* 15.187-201). For the next twenty-six years, Herod provided a reliable ally on the eastern border, kept the peace, and promoted Romanization in Judea. In response, Octavian, later known as Augustus, awarded Herod territories such as Trachonitis, Batanea, and Auranitis in 24/23 B.C.E. and Ulatha and Paneas in 20 B.C.E. He also gave Herod control of the copper mines on Cyprus and half of their revenue. By the end of his reign, Herod ruled over a kingdom that rivaled all previous Jewish monarchies in size, wealth, and importance within the Mediterranean world.

Although he enjoyed great success in foreign policy, Herod's ability to control his own family and his court was less successful. In his quest to secure his throne, he ruthlessly executed anyone perceived as a threat to his regime: his brother-in-law Aristobulus, his grandfather-in-law John Hyrcanus II, his wife the Hasmonean princess Mariamne, and his mother-in-law Alexandra. He also executed three of his sons and heirs, Alexander and Aristobulus, the sons of Mariamne (7 B.C.E.), and Antipater the son of his first wife Doris (4 B.C.E.). While such political murders may have been necessary, they un-

Extent of Herod's kingdom
Herodian fortress city
Decapolis city (time of Herod)
Other city
ABILENE
Abila
ITUREA
Abana R.
Sidon
Damascus
SYRIA
Mt. Hermon
Leontes R.
Pharpar R.
Tyre
Caesarea Philippi
PHOENICIA
GAULANITIS
L. Huleh
Hazor
TRACHONITIS
Raphana
J. Jarmuk
GALILEE
TETRARCHY OF PHILIP
Ptolemais (Acco)
Chorazin
Bethsaida
Capernaum
Sea of Galilee
Gennesaret
Gergesa
Mt. Carmel
Cana
Magdala
Hippos
BATANEA
Kishon R.
Sepphoris
Tiberias
Yarmuk R.
Mediterranean Sea
Nazareth
Mt. Tabor
AURANITIS
Abila
Dor
Gadara
Nain
Megiddo
Caesarea (Strato's Tower)
Scythopolis
Pella
R.
Dion
SAMARIA
DECAPOLIS
Sebaste (Samaria)
Salim?
Amathus
Gerasa
Mt. Ebal
Mt. Gerizim
Sychar
Jordan
Jabbok R.
Me Jarkon
Joppa
Antipatris (Aphek)
Alexandrium
PEREA
Philadelphia (Amman)
(SEMI-INDEPENDENT MUNICIPALITY)
Jericho
Mt. Olivet
Cyprus
Esbus (Heshbon)
Azotus (Ashdod)
Jamnia
Emmaus
Bethany
Jerusalem
Medeba
Bethany beyond Jordan
Bethlehem
Hyrcania
Ashkelon
JUDEA
Herodium
Machaerus
Hebron
Gaza
Adora
Dead Sea
Arnon R.
Raphia
IDUMEA
Masada
Besor Br.
Beer-sheba
Arad
Malatha
NABATEA
N
0 10 20 30 Miles
0 10 20 30 Kilometers
Zered Br.

THE KINGDOM OF HEROD THE GREAT

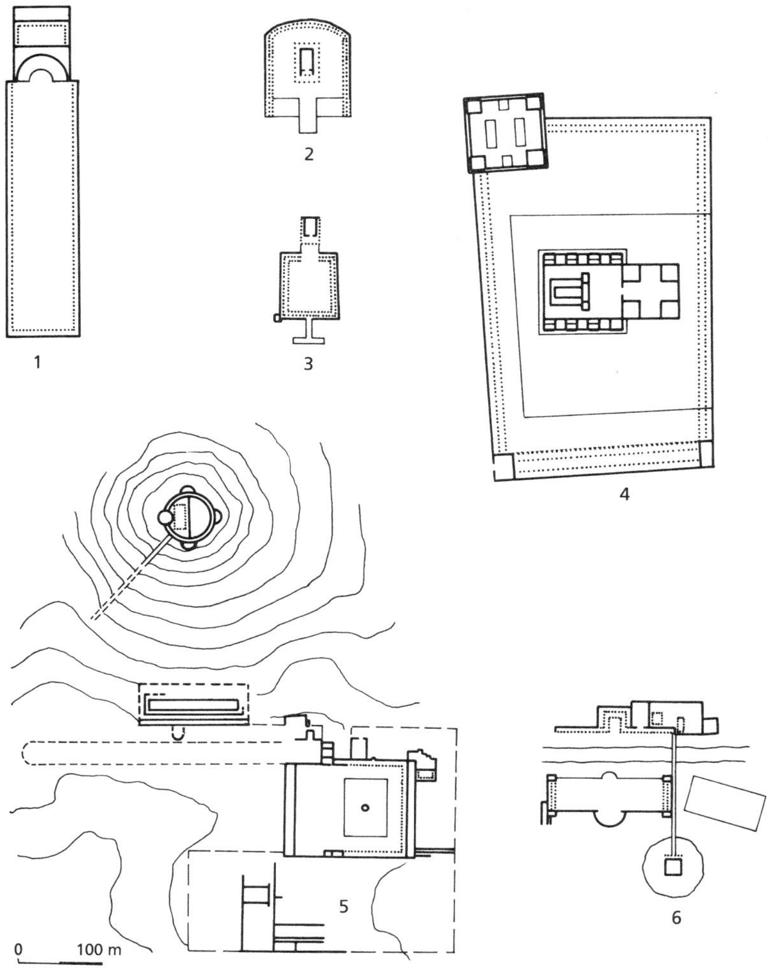

Architectural complexes built by Herod (on one scale). 1. Jericho's hippodrome; 2. Caesarea's temple; 3. Sebaste's temple; 4. Jerusalem's Temple Mount; 5. Herodium; 6. Jericho's Third Palace *(Ehud Netzer)*

doubtedly led to a climate of fear and suspicion among the Herodian courtiers. When Herod died in 4 B.C.E., a series of disturbances and riots broke out all over the kingdom. Such turmoil suggests that many in his kingdom did not approve of his rule. Nevertheless, while not the most popular monarch, he managed to achieve enough support from those with political agency to rule without significant disturbance for over thirty years and to pass on his kingdom to his chosen successors.

Client of the Romans

One of the critical areas in which Herod achieved exceptional results was in the realm of client kingship. After the defeat of the Antigonid king Perseus at the Battle of Pydna in 146 B.C.E., Rome became the dominant power in the Mediterranean. As its sphere of influence increased, it made a series of alliances and friendships with less powerful kingdoms and cities. These relationships, which were based on reciprocal obligation and political friendship, became a sort of clientage between Rome, as the patron, and the semi-independent monarchies, as the clients. Herod thrived in this relationship. Throughout his reign, Herod consistently proved his value to a succession of Roman leaders. He provided a stable and friendly ally, assisted in Roman defense policy in the East, honored his successive patrons, and facilitated the cultural assimilation and Romanization of his kingdom. By fulfilling these obligations, Herod ensured the support and friendship of Rome's leaders and the Senate. This support was crucial to Herod's success as it solidified his regime and deterred potential enemies both foreign and domestic.

The Benefactor and Patron

Herod was also a prolific benefactor and patron of Greco-Roman cities throughout the eastern Mediterranean. Josephus recounts a litany of benefactions offered to numerous cities. For example, Herod provided gymnasia for Tripolis, Damascus, and Ptolemais, as well as marketplaces for Berytus and Tyre. He also constructed theaters for Sidon and Damascus, provided money for the rebuilding of the temple of Pythian Apollo at Rhodes, and endowed the Olympic Games (*J.W.* 1.422-28; *Ant.* 16.146-49). Two inscriptions found on the Acropolis in Athens testify to his benefactions to that city. Herod had multiple motives for his generosity. On the one hand, he wished to appear to be a typical Hellenistic king, and royal *euergetism* was the norm for such monarchs. By bestowing gifts and patronage on cities, Herod enhanced his own reputation with other dynasts and neighbors. He also strengthened ties of loyalty and friendship between Judea and other kingdoms and cities in the eastern Mediterranean. Finally, Herod may also have been seeking to improve the status of the local Jewish communities. Benevolence from a Jewish king could only improve the locals' opinions of the Jews in their midst.

The Builder

Herod was also a prolific builder, and his building program is perhaps his most well-known achievement. He commissioned the construction of an impressive array of structures and urban projects including desert fortresses, palaces, cities, and, of course, the reconstruction and enlargement of the Jerusalem Temple. His

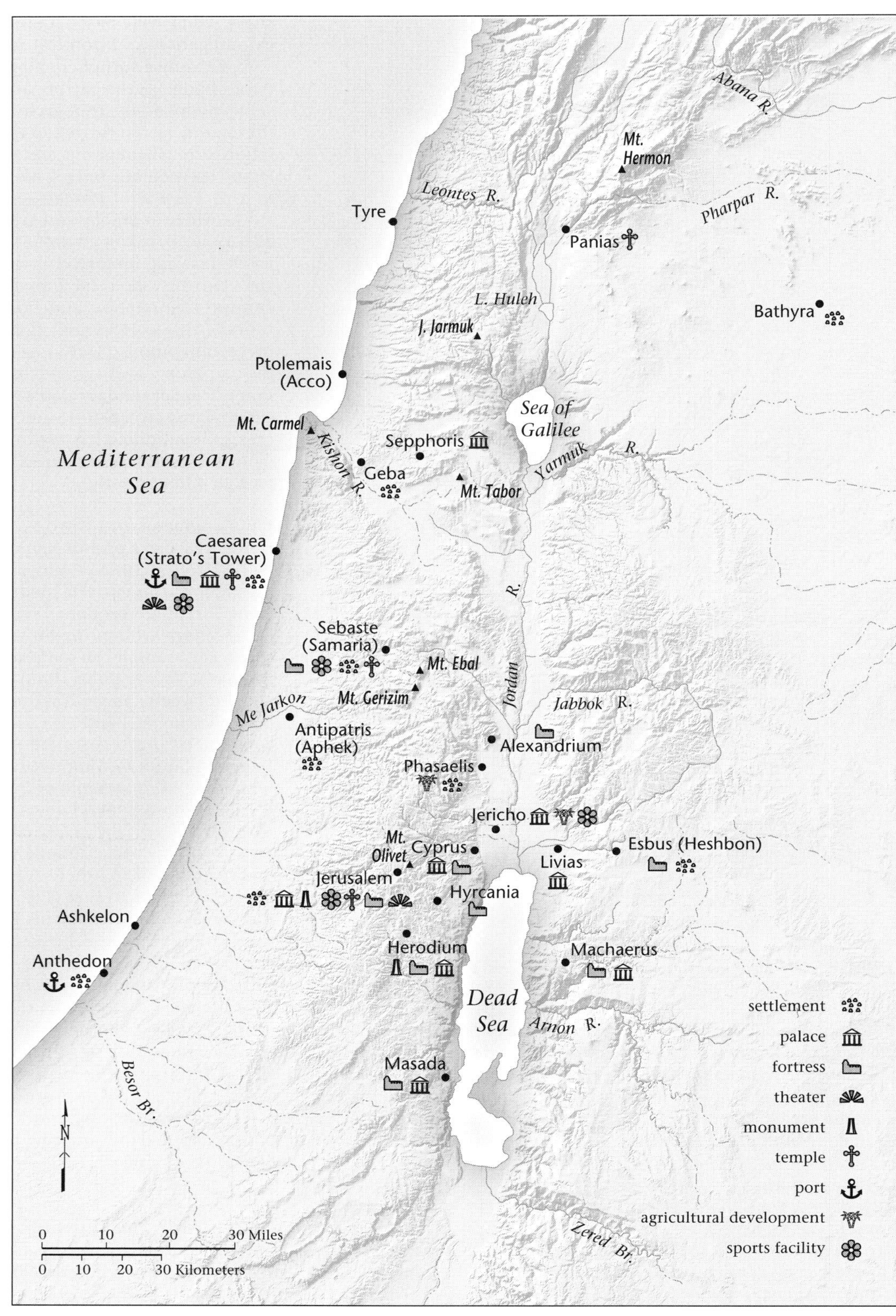

Abana R.
Mt. Hermon
Leontes R.
Pharpar R.
Tyre
Panias
L. Huleh
Bathyra
J. Jarmuk
Ptolemais (Acco)
Sea of Galilee
Mt. Carmel
Kishon R.
Sepphoris
Mediterranean Sea
Geba
Yarmuk R.
Mt. Tabor
Caesarea (Strato's Tower)
Jordan R.
Sebaste (Samaria)
Mt. Ebal
Mt. Gerizim
Me Jarkon
Jabbok R.
Antipatris (Aphek)
Alexandrium
Phasaelis
Jericho
Mt. Olivet
Cyprus
Esbus (Heshbon)
Livias
Jerusalem
Hyrcania
Ashkelon
Herodium
Machaerus
Anthedon
Dead Sea
Arnon R.
Masada
Besor Br.
Zered Br.
N
0 10 20 30 Miles
0 10 20 30 Kilometers
settlement
palace
fortress
theater
monument
temple
port
agricultural development
sports facility

Herod the Great's Building Projects

View of Jerusalem looking east-southeast, showing Herod's palace in the foreground and the stadium and theater in the background *(www.HolyLandPhotos.org)*

desert fortresses, which stretched along the Jordan Valley and Dead Sea regions, were built upon several isolated mountain and hilltops. Many of the fortresses, which were actually fortified palaces, were originally Hasmonean constructions, but Herod expanded and enlarged them. They served a variety of functions including controlling traffic arteries, securing the kingdom's border against neighboring nations, and providing safe havens of refuge in times of turmoil.

During the course of his reign, Herod also constructed or rebuilt several towns and cities. The most impressive of these are Sebaste and Caesarea Maritima, his two cities dedicated to Augustus. Caesarea was Herod's urban masterpiece. The city, which became his new capital, took twelve years to complete (completed ca. 10/9 B.C.E.) and included magnificently decorated civic, financial, and residential buildings as well as an architecturally stunning palace that jutted out into the sea atop a conspicuous promontory. Caesarea also possessed a completely artificial harbor, which Herod named *Sebastos* in honor of Augustus. When Sebastos was finished, it became the largest artificial port on the Mediterranean coast. In addition, Herod constructed a large temple to Augustus and Rome in the center of the city. This edifice contained gigantic statues of Augustus and Rome, rivaling, according to Josephus, the Olympian statue of Zeus and the Hera at Argos (*J.W.* 1.408-14; *Ant.* 15.331-41). Herod also rebuilt the Gazan city of Anthedon and renamed it Agrippium in honor of Marcus Agrippa (*J.W.* 1.416).

The reconstruction and renovation of the Jerusalem Temple was the centerpiece of Herod's building program (*J.W.* 1.401; *Ant.* 15.380-425). As Josephus recounts, Herod wanted to rebuild and expand the Temple because he knew that this would be the most notable of his accomplishments and the one that would earn him eternal fame (*Ant.* 15.380). Further, as Herod himself emphasized in his speech before the people, the rebuilding would be a tremendous and conspicuous act of piety (*Ant.* 15.382-87). This project, which began around 20 B.C.E., was gargantuan in scale. The expansion of the Temple's esplanade involved the construction of massive retaining walls and the removal of huge chunks of earth. When completed, the *temenos,* at about 144,000 square meters, was the largest sanctuary site in the ancient world. The sanctuary itself also received significant renovations. In addition, Herod constructed lavish porticos and a reception hall, the *Stoa Basileia,* whose columns had a diameter that was, according to Josephus, the spread of three men's arms (*Ant.* 15.413).

The rebuilding was a major success. It employed tens of thousands of laborers, and since work on the Temple was not fully completed until 64 C.E., it provided lifetime employment for thousands of workers and even their descendants. Furthermore, Herod accomplished this project at the most important and conspicuous site in his entire kingdom. No other initiative during his reign accumulated more prestige and fame for him among his Jewish subjects than his work on the Temple Mount. It solidified his position as a Jewish king, elevated the status of the Temple Mount in the Roman Empire, and transformed it into the largest sanctuary site in the ancient world. It also embellished the Temple to such a degree that the rabbis would state emphatically, "He who has not seen the Temple of Herod has never seen a beautiful building" (*b. Baba Batra* 4a).

Herod and the Diaspora

As King of Judea, Herod also became an active patron of Diaspora Jews. In 14 B.C.E., while in Asia visiting Marcus Agrippa, Herod assisted the Ionian Jews in their petition to achieve self-rule *(isonomia)* and confirm their citizenship (*Ant.* 16.27-65). He may also have acted as a patron for the Jews of Cyrene, who requested that Augustus intercede on their behalf and uphold their *isonomia* (*Ant.* 16.160-73). In addition, Herod sought to include the Diaspora in the cultic life of the Temple. He accomplished this by promoting and supporting increased pilgrimage to Jerusalem. By the end of Herod's reign, Judea and its capital had become a major pilgrimage site for Jews all over the Mediterranean as well

Herod the Great (ca. 74–4 B.C.E.)

ca. 74	Born
48	Hyrcanus II and Antipater (Herod's father) assist Caesar against Ptolemy XIII
47	Caesar confirms Hyrcanus as high priest and ethnarch; appoints Antipater procurator of Judea and Herod governor of Galilee; Herod summoned before Sanhedrin
44	Julius Caesar murdered; Cassius takes Syria; Herod collects tribute for Cassius
43	Herod made governor of Coele-Syria by Cassius; Antipater murdered by Nabatean king Malichus; Herod kills Malichus in reprisal
42	Cassius and Brutus killed at Battle of Philippi; Herod expels Antigonus from Judea
41	Herod defends himself before Marc Antony; Herod and brother Phasael made tetrarchs
40	Parthians defeat Hyrcanus and Phasael, install Antigonus as king; Antigonus mutilates Hyrcanus; Phasael dies; Herod escapes Judea, appeals to Antony in Rome, and is declared king of the Jews
39	Besieges Antigonus' forces in Jerusalem with support of Roman ally Silo
38	Captures bandits of Arbela, subdues Galilee, assists Antony's forces against the Parthians; avenges murder of brother Joseph in Jericho
37	Besieges Jerusalem with Roman ally Sosius; marries Mariamne I; captures Jerusalem; Antigonus executed
35	Appoints brother-in-law Aristobulus III high priest; has him murdered
34	Cleopatra given part of Herod's territory and visits Judea
32	Goes to war against Nabateans
31	Switches allegiance to Octavian (the future Augustus) after the latter defeats Antony at the Battle of Actium
30	Hyrcanus II executed; Octavian confirms Herod's rule and extends his domain
29-28	Has Mariamne and her mother Alexandra executed
27	Begins rebuilding of Samaria, renamed Sebaste in honor of Augustus
25	Has brother-in-law Costabarus executed; founds quadrennial games in Jerusalem
24-22	Imports grain from Egypt to relieve drought and famine in Judea; waives one third of taxes; builds palace in Jerusalem and fortress at Herodium; marries Mariamne II; given control of Trachonitis, Batanaea, and Auranitis by Augustus; begins rebuilding of Strato's Tower and renames it Caesarea
20	Begins refurbishment and expansion of Jerusalem Temple
14	Joins Marcus Agrippa in Asia; defends Jewish rights; waives a quarter of taxes in Judea; son Antipater II arrives at court
12	Accuses sons Alexander and Aristobulus before Augustus; financially supports the Olympic Games
10/9	Celebrates rebuilding of Caesarea; goes to war with Nabateans
8/7	Has sons Alexander and Aristobulus executed; deals harshly with Pharisees
6?	Antipater goes to Rome; Herod's first will
5	Antipater returns to Judea, is tried, and is imprisoned; Herod's second will
4	Herod punishes Judas, Matthias, and their disciples over golden eagle incident; has Antipater executed; issues final will; dies

as those living as far away as Babylon. Herod's extensive building program in Jerusalem completely changed the city. Most importantly, perhaps, his enlargement and refurbishment of the Temple Mount enabled the holy site to function as a first-rate pilgrimage site that could accommodate a large number of religious visitors.

Herod and Judaism

Herod's relationship with his Jewish subjects was complex. In the past, many scholars have accused him of being anti-Jewish at worst and ambivalent at best. However, a close analysis of the evidence indicates that Herod saw himself as a Jewish king. Certainly he accommodated his personal beliefs to political necessity. This strategy might not have made him the most observant Jew, but it hardly means that he was hostile toward Judaism.

Indeed, there are several indications that Herod was, for the most part, an observant Jew. Perhaps the most famous is the quip of Augustus, which Macrobius recorded in his *Saturnalia,* that he "would rather be Herod's pig than his son" (2.4.1). Such a joke would only make sense if the Judean king actually did keep kosher and thus refrained from eating pork.

Herod's almost total avoidance of figurative art in his coins and private residences also illustrates his personal piety (Meshorer 2001). For a king as supposedly hostile to Judaism as Herod, it is altogether striking that no offensive images, and certainly no figural representations, appear on his coins aside from one coin that has an eagle on the reverse. The appearance of this eagle, however, is not as offensive as might initially appear, especially when one considers that the Tyrian shekel, the only coin accepted as legal tender within the Temple itself, had the head of Herakles-Melqart on the obverse and an eagle on the reverse. If Jews could pay the Temple tax and purchase sacrificial animals only with a coin that had *two* figural images on it and not complain about it, then it is reasonable to assume that they would not have found a Herodian coin with an eagle any more offensive. Herod's hesitation to place images on his coins is even more noteworthy when we consider that his son Philip placed likenesses of the heads of Augustus, Livia, and Tiberius as well as his own image on his coins. His grandson Agrippa I (who was even king of Judea) also put his own image, that of his son, Agrippa II, and that of his wife Cypros on his coins. Further, even in Herod's most private palaces, sites far away from a potentially hostile crowd, archaeologists have uncovered few examples of figurative representations. Instead, these palaces were decorated with mostly geometric patterns along with a few depictions of designs prominent in Jewish art such as olive branches, pomegranates, fig leaves and vines (Netzer 2007).

It is certainly true that Herod had his religious conflicts with certain segments of the Judean population. The most famous example is the eagle incident in which a group of religious Jews tore down the golden eagle Herod had placed above one of the Temple's gates. When Herod became seriously ill, and a rumor began to circulate that he had died, two teachers, Judah ben Sephoraeus and Mattathias ben Margalus, exhorted their students to help them cut down the eagle and destroy it because it violated the second commandment. These two teachers, along with a group of students, climbed upon the gate, knocked the eagle to the ground, and cut it up with axes (*J.W.* 1.649-51; *Ant.* 17.151-56). They were immediately caught, and ultimately Herod sentenced the teachers and their accomplices to death by burning (*J.W.* 1.652-55; *Ant.* 17.156-60, 167).

This would seem to be a clear case of Herod violating Jewish law. However, scholars such as Peter Richardson have argued that the rules against graven images were more lenient than one might think. For example, a passage in the Mishnah argues that images not treated as gods were not prohibited (*m. ʿAbod. Zar.* 3:4). Further, most scholars date the erection of the eagle to the period between 18 and 15 B.C.E. If true, the eagle would have been perched above the Temple gate for more than ten years before the teachers and their students destroyed it. In that time, tens of thousands of Jews would have walked through the gate and under the eagle without complaint and without considering the Temple defiled or polluted. Only a small group of religious Jews objected enough to act, and then only when they believed Herod was dead. Their attack may therefore be seen not as a religious objection but as an assault on a symbol of Herod's regime, which they vigorously opposed. Even the First Temple and possibly the Second contained religious images within the precinct, specifically the cherubim who stood on either side of the Ark of the Covenant. In the end, some of Herod's subjects certainly objected to the eagle and its location above a gate of the Temple. However, it seems that the majority of Jews were either not offended or not offended enough to act.

Although Herod may not have been the most pious of Jews, he definitely saw himself as Jewish, and his religious conflicts seem to have been limited in scope and more a matter of interpretation than outright refusal to uphold, and hostility toward, Jewish law.

BIBLIOGRAPHY

J. AVIRAM, G. FOERSTER, AND E. NETZER, EDS. 1989-1995, *Masada: The Yigael Yadin Excavations 1963-1965, Final Reports,* 5 vols., Jerusalem: Israel Exploration Society. • D. C. BRAUND 1984, *Rome and the Friendly King,* London: Helm. • M. GRANT 1971, *Herod the Great,* New York: American Heritage Press. • N. KOKKINOS 1998, *The Herodian Dynasty: Origins, Roles in Society and Eclipse,* Sheffield: Sheffield Academic Press. • A. LICHTENBERGER 1999, *Die Baupolitik Herodes des Grossen,* Wiesbaden: Harrassowitz. • A. K. MARSHAK 2008, "Herod the Great and the Power of Image: Political Self-Presentation in the Herodian Dynasty," Dissertation, Yale University. • Y. MESHORER 2001, *A Treasury of Jewish Coins: From the Persian Period to Bar Kokhba,* Jerusalem: Yad Ben-Zvi; Nyack, N.Y.: Amphora Books. • E. NETZER 2006, *The Architecture of Herod, the Great Builder,* Tübingen: Mohr-Siebeck. • P. RICHARDSON 1996, *Herod: King of the Jews and Friend of the Romans,* Columbia: University of South Carolina Press. • P. RICHARDSON 2004, *Building Jewish in the Roman East,* Waco, Tex.: Baylor University Press. • D. W. ROLLER 1998, *The Building Program of Herod the Great,* Berkeley: University of California Press. • A. SCHALIT 1969, *König Herodes: Der Mann und Sein Werk,* Berlin: de Gruyter.

See also: Caesarea Maritima; Fortresses and Palaces; Herodian Dynasty; Masada; Romanization; Samaria-Sebaste ADAM MARSHAK

Herodian Dynasty

Herod the Great and the dynasty he founded were also known as the Antipatrids. They were a family of Idumean nobles who ultimately became the ruling dynasty of Judea and its surrounding territories until the end of the first century C.E. Its most famous members are Herod the Great, Archelaus, Herod Antipas, Herod Philip, Herod Agrippa I, and Herod Agrippa II.

Origins

The Herodian Dynasty actually began with Herod the Great's grandfather, Antipas, and thus it might be more accurate to refer to the family as the Antipatrids. This Antipas was the *stratēgos* of Idumea under Alexander Jannaeus around the beginning of the first century B.C.E. (Josephus, *Ant.* 14.10). The Antipatrids were Idumean nobles, but it is unclear exactly where they came from. Some scholars have speculated that the Antipatrids were from the city of Ascalon (Kokkinos 1998). However, these conclusions rest on rather weak and hypothetical evidence. Nevertheless, the Antipatrids were a powerful Idumean family with strong political connections and influence. As the Hasmoneans extended their control over Idumea, Antipatrid support and loyalty would have been a huge asset.

It is likely that Antipas' son, Antipater, succeeded him as *stratēgos* of Idumea. Antipater, who had four sons — Phasael, Joseph, Pheroras, and, most importantly, Herod — quickly became the real power behind the throne. He was especially skilled at winning and exploiting friendships with local rulers such as the Nabatean king Aretas III. During the civil war between

John Hyrcanus II and Judah Aristobulus II, Antipas persuaded Aretas to shelter Hyrcanus and to assist him in reconquering Judea (Josephus, *J.W.* 1.123-27; *Ant.* 14.14-21). When Pompey intervened in the civil war, Antipater secured his friendship and support. Antipater realigned his political loyalties and those of his family when he realized that Julius Caesar had supplanted Pompey as the preeminent Roman. In 48 B.C.E., with Caesar in trouble in Alexandria, Antipater came to his aid. He persuaded the Arab chieftains and the various dynasts in Syria to support Caesar as well. He also recruited the Jews of Egypt to Caesar's cause, and led an army of 3,000 Judean soldiers into Egypt to assist the besieged Roman general. In recognition of his support, Caesar bestowed Roman citizenship on Antipater and his family (*J.W.* 1.187-94; *Ant.* 14.127-39).

Antipater was now clearly the preeminent man at court. However, he still had powerful enemies. In 43 B.C.E., shortly after the assassination of Julius Caesar, Antipater himself was poisoned (*J.W.* 1.225-26; *Ant.* 14.280-84). Herod and his brother Phasael assumed their father's position and became the preeminent men in the Judean court. In 42 B.C.E., Marc Antony appointed them tetrarchs of Galilee and Judea respectively (*J.W.* 1.244; *Ant.* 14.326). When the Parthians and their ally, the Hasmonean Mattathias Antigonus, invaded Judea in 40 B.C.E., Phasael and Herod were in charge of Jerusalem's defenses. Phasael accompanied Hyrcanus on an embassy to the Parthian general's camp, and both of them were arrested and imprisoned. Rather than be used as a hostage, Phasael committed suicide by dashing his head against a rock. Herod fled to Rome to secure its support against the Parthians and Antigonus. With the backing of the Triumvirs, the Roman Senate proclaimed Herod King of Judea and promised him military aid in his war against Antigonus (*J.W.* 1.282-85; *Ant.* 14.381-89). Three years passed before he was able to defeat Antigonus and capture Jerusalem. In 37 B.C.E., he entered Jerusalem as King of Judea (*J.W.* 1.349-57; *Ant.* 14.476-91).

Herod, King of Judea

In Herod's early reign, one of his major concerns was establishing and maintaining his own legitimacy. Since he was an Idumean with an Arab mother, his lineage was somewhat suspect. Further, he was a commoner who had risen to power through Roman support, and, as such, he had no real royal connections. His other major concern in the early years of his rule was Cleopatra. By the mid-30s B.C.E., she had become extremely powerful and was looking to reclaim the Ptolemaic Empire of old. This empire included Judea and Syria, and Herod was a serious obstacle. In the Donation of Alexandria (34 B.C.E.), Antony ceded her control of the Plain of Jericho and all of the territory of Syria south of the Eleutherus River except Tyre and Sidon. Rather than oppose her openly, Herod chose instead to minimize his conflicts with her and acquiesced to the loss of formal control over the territory. However, in order to retain use and control of the lost territory, he agreed to lease the Plain of Jericho from Cleopatra.

Despite Cleopatra's ambitions, Herod kept his kingdom and was able to rule in relative security until 30 B.C.E., when Antony and Cleopatra were defeated at the Battle of Actium, which was fought off the coast of Acarnania, Greece. Herod immediately recognized the need to switch loyalties, and in this vein he hastened to Rhodes to persuade the victorious Octavian that he could fit well into the new regime as a loyal and friendly client king. Octavian confirmed Herod's position and enlarged his kingdom (*J.W.* 1.386-97; *Ant.* 15.187-201). For the next twenty-six years, Herod provided a stable and friendly ally on the eastern border, kept the peace and promoted Romanization in Judea. In response, Octavian, who after 27 B.C.E. was known as Augustus, awarded Herod additional territories such as Trachonitis, Batanea, and Auranitis in 24/23 B.C.E. and Ulatha and Paneas in 20 B.C.E. He also gave Herod control of the copper mines on Cyprus and half of their revenue. By the end of his reign, Herod ruled over a kingdom that rivaled all previous Jewish monarchies in size, wealth, and importance within the Mediterranean world.

Herod also had an elaborate building program. He commissioned the construction of an impressive array of buildings and urban projects including desert fortresses, palaces, cities, and, of course, the reconstruction and enlargement of the Jerusalem Temple. His construction projects used the latest architectural technologies and the most innovative designs. His renovation and enhancement of the Jerusalem Temple is perhaps his most famous project, and he transformed it into the largest sanctuary site in the ancient world. Among his other building projects were sites designed to highlight his close relationship with Rome. For example, he constructed the Antonia, a fortress next to the Temple Mount and named for Marc Antony. He also built three temples to Augustus and Rome, two cities in honor of Augustus, Sebaste, and Caesarea Maritima, and a city, Agrippium, in honor of Marcus Agrippa.

Despite his numerous political and economic successes, Herod's reign was also marked by a series of domestic difficulties. His relationship with his Jewish subjects was strained throughout his reign because of his dubious background as well as his somewhat ambiguous attitude toward Judaism. In addition, internal dissension among his own family caused Herod numerous disturbances. His efficient and ruthless purge of the remaining Hasmonean royalty included his grandfather-in-law Hyrcanus, his mother-in-law, his brother-in-law, and even his wife, Mariamne. He also executed three of his sons and heirs: Alexander and Aristobulus, the sons of Mariamne (7 B.C.E.), and Antipater, the son of his Idumean wife, Doris (4 B.C.E.). A series of riots and disturbances broke out after his death in 4 B.C.E., and such social disorder suggests that a significant portion of the population did not support his regime. Nevertheless, he seems to have achieved enough legitimacy and authority to reign without significant disturbance for over thirty years and to pass on his kingdom to his chosen successors.

Herod's Successors

Although Herod had made a will indicating his preference for succession and division of his kingdom, Augustus was free to enact it as he deemed best. Rival sons of the dead king flocked to Rome in order to plead their case. Additionally, a delegation of Judean nobles traveled to Rome to ask Augustus to annex the kingdom to the province of Syria. In the end, Augustus chose to honor Herod's will, and he divided the kingdom between three of Herod's sons, Archelaus, Herod Antipas and Herod Philip. Archelaus received the heartland of the kingdom, Judea, Samaria and Idumea, but only the title of ethnarch instead of king. Galilee and the Perea went to Herod Antipas, who received the title of tetrarch, and Herod Philip, who also became a tetrarch, received Batanea, Trachonitis, Auranitis, and other nearby territories. (*J.W.* 1.14-15, 20-38, 80-100; *Ant.* 17.219-49, 299-320).

Archelaus

Archelaus' reign was an unmitigated disaster. His cruelty and oppressive measures enraged his subjects, and in 6 C.E., Augustus banished Archelaus to Vienne in Gaul. Judea then became a province governed by a procurator (*J.W.* 1.39-79, 111-17; *Ant.* 17.250-98, 339-55).

Herod Philip

Herod Philip, on the other hand, ruled in relative peace, and little is known of his reign. Jews were a minority in his kingdom, and most of the inhabitants were of Syrian or Arab descent. During his reign, he rebuilt the city of Paneas and renamed it Caesarea Philippi in honor of himself and Augustus. He also expanded and embellished Bethsaida, renaming it Julias, in honor of Augustus' daughter Julia (*J.W.* 1.168; *Ant.* 18.28). When Philip died childless in 34 C.E., the emperor Tiberius attached his realm to the province of Syria (*Ant.* 18.106-8).

Herod Antipas

Herod Antipas ruled for more than forty years, longer than either of his brothers, and was a valuable ally and client king throughout his reign. He rebuilt Sepphoris in Galilee and Betharamphtha in the Perea, renaming them Autocratoris and Livias respectively (*J.W.* 1.168; *Ant.* 18.27). His most impressive urban project, however, was the construction of his new capital city Tiberias in honor of the emperor Tiberius. Coin evidence suggests the city was dedicated in the twenty-fourth year of Antipas' reign (19/20 C.E.). Since the city was constructed atop a graveyard, pious Jews initially refused to live there. Eventually, though, the city became a center of Jewish learning and study (*J.W.* 1.168; *Ant.* 18.36-38).

As with his father, Antipas' personal life was less successful. His first marriage was to a Nabatean princess, Phasaelis, the eldest daughter of Aretas IV. Later, he became enamored with his niece, Herodias, who had also been married to two of Antipas' half-brothers, Herod Philip and Herod, son of Mariamne, the daughter of Simon Boethus (Kokkinos 1998). While marriage to one's niece or one's ex-sister-in-law was permitted, marriage to a woman who was both was rather unusual. Indeed, besides angering Aretas, Antipas' divorce of Phasaelis and marriage to Herodias provoked the criticism of John the Baptist, whom Antipas arrested and later executed (Mark 6:14-29; Matt. 14:1-12; Luke 3:19-20; *Ant.* 18.116-19). War broke out between Aretas and Antipas, and Antipas was soundly defeated. His subjects attributed this defeat to his execution of John (*Ant.* 18.113-16).

Herod Agrippa I

In 37 C.E., upon the ascension of Gaius Caligula, Antipas' nephew Herod Agrippa I, who was also Herodias' brother, was appointed king in the territory of Herod Philip. Herodias, believing that her husband also should receive the royal title, urged him to go to Rome and petition the new emperor. However, Herod Agrippa, who disliked and distrusted his uncle, sent his freedman, Fortunatus, to Rome with letters accusing Antipas of treason. Persuaded by these letters, Gaius deposed Antipas and exiled him to Lugdunum in Gaul (present-day Lyon). Because of her status as Agrippa's sister, Gaius was willing to permit Herodias to retain her property and not go into exile with her husband. Nevertheless, she voluntarily chose to share Antipas' fate (*J.W.* 1.181-83; *Ant.* 18.237-54).

Herod Agrippa I, who was named after Herod's Roman friend Marcus Agrippa, was Herod's grandson. When his father and uncle were executed in 7 B.C.E., he was sent to Rome to be educated alongside the imperial family. Among his companions in his youth was the future emperor Claudius, the son of Antonia and Drusus (*Ant.* 18.165). Herod Agrippa also seems to have been good friends with Drusus the Younger, the son of the emperor Tiberius (*Ant.* 18.143).

After Drusus' death in 23 B.C.E., Agrippa was forced to leave Rome, because his presence there reminded Tiberius of his dead son. Herod Agrippa spent the next few years in the East, but ultimately returned to Rome seeking imperial favor again. Through the intervention of Antonia, who had been a good friend of Agrippa's mother, Agrippa secured a potentially lucrative and influential position as companion to the emperor's grandson, Tiberius Gemellus. Agrippa, however, decided that Gaius Caligula was the better individual to court, and he spent lavish amounts of money entertaining the young Roman prince (*J.W.* 12.178-79; *Ant.* 18.166-67).

During his friendship with Caligula, Agrippa encouraged the young prince's ambition, and this resulted in his imprisonment by Tiberius (*J.W.* 2.179-80; *Ant.* 18.168-204). When Tiberius died, Caligula succeeded him. One of his first official acts was to free Agrippa, present him with a golden chain as a symbol of his prior incarceration, and bestow upon him the title of king over the territory that his uncle Philip had governed (*J.W.* 2.181; *Ant.* 18.237). When he was *en route* to take over his kingdom, he paid a visit to Alexandria, which became the occasion for anti-Jewish riots by the Alexandrians, who mocked the Jewish king in the theater.

After the banishment of Antipas in 39 C.E., Caligula enlarged Agrippa's kingdom by annexing Galilee and the Perea (*Ant.* 18.252). Shortly before the assassination of Caligula, Agrippa returned to Rome, and after Caligula's murder, Agrippa was a crucial advisor to Claudius and helped to secure his accession as emperor (*J.W.* 2.204-13; *Ant.* 18.236-67). As a reward for his services, Claudius made Agrippa king over the territory once ruled by his grandfather, Herod the Great. Claudius also appointed Agrippa's brother Herod, ruler of Chalcis in Lebanon (*J.W.* 2.215-17; *Ant.* 18.274-77).

Herod Agrippa returned to Judea and seemed to govern it with a large degree of popular support. The rabbinic corpus as well as Josephus testifies to Agrippa's enthusiasm and zeal for Judaism. After Passover in 44 C.E., Agrippa traveled to Caesarea to attend the games being held there in honor of Claudius. According to Josephus, in the midst of the festival, Agrippa saw an owl perched over his head. During his imprisonment by Tiberius he had seen a similar omen, which had been interpreted as portending his speedy release. However, he had been warned that if he should see the same sight again, he would die within five days. Agrippa immediately fell ill with violent pains, and he died five days later (*Ant.* 19.343-52). A slightly different version of this story appears in Acts, where Agrippa is criticized for killing James, the brother of John and arresting Peter (Acts 12).

Herod Agrippa II

At the time of Agrippa's death, his heir and namesake, Herod Agrippa II, was only a young man, about 17. Because of his youth, Claudius returned Judea to the rule of a Roman procurator (*J.W.* 2.220; *Ant.* 18.362-63).

Herod Agrippa II lived at the court of Claudius, and upon the death of his uncle, Herod of Chalcis, in 48 C.E. he inherited the oversight of the Temple. In 48/49, Claudius bestowed upon him the tetrarchy of Chalcis (*J.W.* 2.223; *Ant.* 20.104), but Agrippa II then exchanged this tetrarchy for an enlarged version of his grand-uncle Philip's tetrarchy in 53 (*J.W.* 1.247; *Ant.* 20.138). Under Nero, Agrippa received a portion of Galilee, including the cities of Tiberias and Tarichea and a portion of Perea (*Ant.* 20.159). According to the book of Acts, Paul of Tarsus pleaded his case before Agrippa and his sister Berenice in ca. 59 C.E. (Acts 25:13–26:32).

Agrippa and Berenice owed their positions and status to the Romans, and they put this loyalty to Rome first. When disturbances broke out in Jerusalem in 66 C.E., Agrippa and Berenice at first tried to defuse the situation by appealing for calm. However, their efforts ultimately failed, and they were expelled from the city (*J.W.* 2.309-14, 334-35, 343-406). When Vespasian's son Titus began his campaign to capture Jerusalem in 70 C.E., Agrippa provided an army to support him (Tacitus, *Historiae* 5.1). After the revolt was crushed, Vespasian rewarded Agrippa and Berenice for their loyalty as well as their support for his seizure of the imperial throne (Tacitus, *Hist.* 2.81; *J.W.* 4.498-500). Furthermore, during the war Berenice had begun a liaison with Titus. In 75 C.E. he summoned her to Rome to live with him in the palace, and she hoped to become his wife. However, public opinion opposed such a union, and Titus was forced to forsake Berenice when he became emperor in 79 C.E. (Dio Cassius, *Historiae* 66.15.4; 66.18.1; Suetonius, *Titus* 7.1). Agrippa also went to Rome and while there supplied Josephus with information for his books (*Vita* 364-66). Agrippa died childless in Rome at the end of the first century C.E.

Other Herodians

Beginning in Herod's reign and continuing into the first century C.E., the Herodian family played a central role in the administration of Judea. For example, a certain Antipas, who was a descendant of Herod's brother Phasael, was in charge of the public treasury when the Jewish Revolt broke out (*J.W.* 4.140). Other leading Herodians at this time were Costobarus and Saul, the grandsons of Herod's sister Salome. At the outbreak of the revolt, the Jewish provisional government sent them along with Antipas to Herod Agrippa II to request his help (*J.W.* 2.418, 421).

As the first century C.E. progressed, the Herodian family expanded further into the Near East and beyond, eventually occupying royal thrones outside of Judea. The Herodians placed two family members on the throne of Armenia, Tigranes V, the grandson of Herod the Great, and Tigranes VI, the nephew of Tigranes V. Additionally, Tigranes VI's son, Alexander, became King of Cilicia. Explicit evidence of the family begins to disappear at the end of the first century C.E., but traces of them survive into the middle of the second century C.E. The Herodians may even have placed a family member in the Senate. Some have argued that Gaius Julius Alexander Berenicianus, who was consul in 117 C.E. and proconsul of Asia in 132, was the great-great-great grandson of Herod the Great (Kokkinos 1998). If true, it would mean that this Idumean family, who began as local nobility, had finally reached the pinnacle of provincial success by attaining senatorial and consular status.

Bibliography

D. C. Braund 1984, *Rome and the Friendly King,* London: Helm; New York: St. Martin's. • K. C. Hanson 1989, "The Herodians and Mediterranean Kinship," *Biblical Theology Bulletin,* 19: 75-84, 142-51. • H. Hoehner 1972, *Herod Antipas,* Cambridge: Cambridge University Press. • M. Hørning Jensen 2006, *Herod Antipas in Galilee: Literary and Archaeological Sources on the Reign of Herod Antipas and Its Socio-economic Impact on Galilee,* Tübingen: Mohr-Siebeck. • A. H. M. Jones 1967, *The Herods of Judea,* 2d ed., Oxford: Clarendon. • A. Kasher 1988, *Jews, Idumaeans and Ancient Arabs: Relations of the Jews in Eretz-Israel with Nations of the Frontier and the Desert during the Hellenistic and Roman Era (332 BCE–70 CE),* Tübingen: Mohr-Siebeck. • N. Kokkinos 1998, *The Herodian Dynasty: Origins, Roles in Society and Eclipse,* Sheffield: Sheffield Academic Press. • P. Richardson 1996, *Herod: King of the Jews and Friend of the Romans,* Columbia: University of South Carolina Press. • A. Schalit 1969, *König Herodes: Der Mann und Sein Werk,* Berlin: de Gruyter. • D. R. Schwartz 1990, *Agrippa I: The Last King of Judaea,* Tübingen: Mohr-Siebeck. • M. Stern 1974, "The Reign of Herod and the Herodian Dynasty," in *The Jewish*

People in the First Century, vol. 1, ed. S. Safrai and M. Stern, Assen: Van Gorcum; Philadelphia: Fortress, 216-307.

See also: Herod the Great ADAM MARSHAK

Ḥever, Naḥal

Naḥal Ḥever, one of the deepest canyons in the Judean Desert, drains into the Dead Sea about seven km. (four miles) south of ʿEin Gedi. The caves in Naḥal Ḥever were first explored by Yohanan Aharoni in 1953 and 1955 and then in 1960-1961. The northern cave (Cave of Letters) was excavated then by Yigael Yadin, and the southern cave (the Cave of Horror) by Aharoni. In 1991 an additional Bar Kokhba refuge cave was discovered in the west portion of Naḥal Ḥever (Cave of the Tetradrachm).

The most important finds in Naḥal Ḥever were discovered during Yadin's expedition in the Cave of Letters, the largest cave on the northern bank of Naḥal Ḥever. Approximately 150 m. (450 ft.) long, it has two openings and contains three halls. In 1960 a burial chamber containing the skeletons of nineteen people was found in the cave, as well as a hoard of nineteen bronze artifacts used for ritual worship, a fragment from a scroll of the book of Psalms (both found in hall A), and fifteen letters that were sent from Bar Kokhba's headquarters and reached one of the three commanders of ʿEin Gedi, a man named Jonathan son of Baianos (found in hall C, the inner portion of the cave). One letter is written on a wooden slat, the rest on papyri. Nine letters are written in Aramaic, four are in Hebrew, and two in Greek.

In 1961 more hoards were found in the inner part of the cave, including the archive of a woman named Babatha, the daughter of Simeon. Her archive contains thirty-five documents and was found together with a small archive of six documents belonging to a farmer from ʿEin Gedi named Eliezer, son of Samuel. All of Eliezer's documents bear a date from the Bar Kokhba era. Also in the 1961 season, a fragment of a scroll from the book of Numbers and a fragment of a Nabatean document were found near one of the openings of the cave.

In addition to discovering these archives, Yadin also found a marriage contract of a woman named Salome Komaïse, daughter of Levi. This document was dropped by the Bedouin in the tunnel that connects hall B with the inner part of the cave. Seven documents that belong to the archive of Salome Komaïse are part of the so-called Wadi Seiyal collection. This is a group of documents that were found in the Judean Desert by Bedouin and brought in 1952 and 1953 to the Rockefeller Museum in East Jerusalem. On the basis of this document we may conclude that the Salome Komaïse archive, like the other three archives from the Cave of Letters, was hidden in the inner hall of the cave.

The documents found in the Cave of Letters are essential for the study of the Bar Kokhba Revolt. Of the seventeen letters known to have been sent from Bar Kokhba's headquarters, fifteen were found in the Cave of Letters. We know of thirteen documents dated according to the era of Bar Kokhba, and six of them are from the Cave of Letters. Thanks to these archaeological finds, Babatha is the only person who lived in the land of Israel at that time whose biography we can reconstruct. From the documents found in the Cave of Letters we can also learn about some interesting differences between the archives that belonged to males and those that belonged to females in the early Roman period. And the archives of Babatha and Salome Komaïse in particular yield information about the Jewish population that lived on the eastern shore of the Dead Sea before the Bar Kokhba Revolt.

The letters of Jonathan son of Baianos tell us a little about the personality of Simeon Bar Kokhba. Two letters (one in Aramaic and one in Greek) deal with bringing to the Bar Kokhba camp the four kinds of plants used on the Feast of Tabernacles (Sukkot). One of the Greek letters reveals the exact pronunciation of the name of Revolt's leader, Bar Kosiba. From the letters we learn who the three commanders of ʿEin Gedi were. One of the letters identifies the commander of Qiryat ʿArabayyah, and two letters describe the people of Tekoa as shirkers. From the archive of Eliezer son of Samuel we learn about the agriculture of ʿEin Gedi and about the administrators of ʿEin Gedi during the Bar Kokhba Revolt.

Interestingly, the documents from the Cave of Letters also show that there was a correlation between the rank of the commanders of the Bar Kokhba Revolt and the distances they fled. Its seems that some of the refugees who fled to the Cave of Letters were able to leave the cave alive, in contrast to the Cave of Horror, which is situated on the southern bank of Naḥal Ḥever, where more than forty skeletons were discovered. Some fragments of scrolls were found in the Cave of Horror (the Greek Minor Prophets and a prayer). Two economic documents were probably found by the Bedouin in the Cave of the Tetradrachm.

BIBLIOGRAPHY

N. LEWIS 1989, *The Documents from the Bar Kokhba Period in the Cave of Letters: Greek Papyri,* Jerusalem: Israel Exploration Society. • Y. YADIN 1963, *The Finds from the Bar Kokhba Period in the Cave of Letters,* Jerusalem: Israel Exploration Society 1963. • Y. YADIN, J. C. GREENFIELD, A. YARDENI, AND B. LEVINE, EDS. 2002, *The Documents from the Bar Kokhba Period in the Cave of Letters: Hebrew, Aramaic and Nabataean-Aramaic Papyri,* Jerusalem: Israel Exploration Society.

See also: Babatha Archives; Bar Kokhba Caves; Bar Kokhba Letters; Bar Kokhba Revolt; Papyri

HANAN ESHEL†

High Priests

The high priest was the leading cultic official throughout the Second Temple period, and some high priests were also the chief governmental leaders of the Judean nation.

Terms

A frequent designation for the high priest in Hebrew sources is *hakkōhēn haggādôl* (Hag. 1:12, 14; 2:2, 4;

Zech. 3:1, 8; 6:11; Neh. 3:1, 20; 13:28; cf. Num. 35:25, 28 [twice]; Josh. 20:6). The title appears to derive from the expression attested in Lev. 21:10: "The priest who is exalted above his fellows *(hakkōhēn haggādôl mē'ḥāw).*" In Greek the title can be translated literally *(ho hiereus ho megas)* or as *archiereus,* although this term can also be used for high-ranking priests who were not serving as high priests. Other Hebrew forms of the title for the highest-ranking priest are *hakkōhēn hārō'š* (2 Chron. 31:10; Ezra 7:5) and *kōhēn hārō'š* (2 Kings 25:18 = Jer. 52:24; 2 Chron. 19:11; 24:11; 26:20; 31:10 [all referring to priests of the First Temple]). In Aramaic the title is *kahănā' rabbā'* (e.g., *TAD* A4.7 = *CAP* 30 line 18).

List of the High Priests

From the age of the First Temple, when presumably there were high priests (some are called *hakkōhēn haggādôl:* Jehoiada [2 Kings 12:11]; Hilkiah [2 Kings 22:4, 8; 23:4; 2 Chron. 34:9]), no complete list of the men who held the office has been preserved. 2 Kings 25:18 (= Jer. 52:24) mentions "the chief priest *(kōhēn hārō'š)* Seraiah" as one of those whom Nebuzaradan brought to King Nebuchadnezzar, who had them executed (25:19-21). According to the genealogy in 1 Chronicles 6, Seraiah was the father of Jehozadak who went into exile (6:15-16). This Jehozadak is listed as the father of Joshua/Jeshua, the first high priest of the Second Temple. In this fashion, the historians establish a family continuity between the last high priest of the First Temple and the first high priest of the Second Temple.

Without so designating them, the Hebrew Bible provides a genealogical list of the first six high priests of the Second Temple (Neh. 11:10-11; cf. v. 22); Josephus reproduces the list and continues it until the end of the period — fifty-one names in all (he mentions them in his narratives, and he also gives a separate list of the high priests in the First and Second Temples, *Ant.* 20.224-51). There are confirmations of some names in these lists from other sources.

Joshua
Joiakim
Eliashib (Nehemiah's contemporary)
Joiada
Johanan (mentioned in a papyrus from Elephantine, dated 407 B.C.E. [*TAD* A4.7 = *AP* 30])
Jaddua (contemporary of Alexander the Great)
Onias I (1 Macc. 12:20-23?)
Simon I (Sirach 50?)
Eleazar (the *Letter of Aristeas* identifies him as the high priest when the Torah was translated into Greek)
Manasseh
Onias II
Simon II
Onias III (?-175 B.C.E.) (2 Maccabees)
Jason (175-72) (2 Maccabees)
Menelaus (172-62) (2 Maccabees)
[Onias IV, a son of Onias III who may have served as high priest briefly]
Alcimus (162-60/59) (1-2 Maccabees)
Jonathan (152-42) (first Hasmonean high priest, civil and military leader; 1-2 Maccabees)
Simon [III] (142-34) (1-2 Maccabees)
John Hyrcanus (134-104) (1 Maccabees)
Aristobulus I (104-103)
Alexander Jannaeus (103-76)
Hyrcanus II (76-67, 63-40)
Aristobulus II (67-63)
Antigonus (40-37) (last Hasmonean high priest and king)
Ananel (37-35, 35-30?) (the first of Herod's appointees as high priest)
Aristobulus III (35) (the last Hasmonean high priest)
Jesus son of Phiabi (30-24/22)
Simon son of Boethus (24/22-25)
Mattathias son of Theophilus (5-4)
Joazar son of Boethus (4 B.C.E.?-6 C.E.)
Eleazar son of Boethus (4 B.C.E.)
Jesus son of Seë (4 B.C.E.-?)
Ananus son of Seth/Sethi (6-15 C.E.) (the Annas of the New Testament [Luke 3:2; John 18:13, 24; Acts 4:6])
Ishmael son of Phiabi (15-16?)
Eleazar son of Ananus (16-17?)
Simon son of Camith (17-18)
Joseph Caiaphas (18-36/37) (high priest when Jesus was arrested [Matt. 26:3, 57; Luke 3:2; John 11:49; 18:13-14, 24, 28; Acts 4:6])
Jonathan son of Ananus (36 or 37)
Theophilus son of Ananus (37-41)
Simon Cantheras son of Boethus (41-42)
Matthias son of Ananus (42-43?)
Elionaeus son of Cantheras (43?-45)
Joseph son of Camei (45-48)
Ananias son of Nedebaeus (48-59) (the high priest involved in the trial of Paul [Acts 23:2; 24:1])
Ishmael son of Phiabi (59-61)
Joseph son of Simon (61-62)
Ananus son of Ananus (62) (the high priest who had James executed)
Jesus son of Demnaeus (62-63?)
Jesus son of Gamaliel (63-64)
Matthias son of Theophilus (64-66?)
Phannias son of Samuel (68?)

With the destruction of the Temple in 70 C.E., there was no longer a need for a high priest.

It has been suggested that the Qumran Teacher of Righteousness was the high priest or acting high priest in the seven-year gap between Alcimus and Jonathan (159-152 B.C.E.), but there is no decisive evidence in favor of this hypothesis. Jonathan is often identified as the Wicked Priest of the Qumran texts; it is at least clear that the title *Wicked Priest (hakkôhēn hārāšā')* is a wordplay on *hakkôhēn hārô'š.*

Roles and Duties

No extensive description of high-priestly duties has survived. Leviticus 21:10-15, the passage that supplies the descriptive phrase from which the high-priestly title *hakkōhēn haggādôl* derives, names requirements for the high priest beyond those that apply to all priests; the fact that he has received the anointing oil on his head is mentioned twice in this section (vv. 10, 12). The special rules are:

1. He is not to dishevel his hair or tear his vestments (for his vestments, see Exod. 28:1-39).
2. He is not to go where there is a corpse, even of one of his nearest relatives.
3. He is not to leave the sanctuary "and thus profane the sanctuary of his God." This rule may relate to the previous one: that is, he was not to depart from the sanctuary for the sake of mourning or burial. There is no evidence the high priests felt obligated to remain in the Temple complex; some of them, for example the Hasmoneans, traveled extensively.
4. He is to marry only a virgin from his own kin so as not to profane his offspring. Since the office was supposed to be hereditary (Lev. 16:32; Num. 20:22-29; Neh. 12:10-11; 11QT[a] 15:15-16), the purity of the line was of paramount importance.

Leviticus 16 also underscores the central role that Aaron, the first of the chief priests, played on the Day of Atonement, including entering the Holy of Holies several times, a practice that continued in Second Temple times (Josephus, *J.W.* 5.236-37).

The special clothing of the high priest, described in detail in Exod. 28:1-39; 39:1-31, is mentioned several times in Second Temple literature (e.g., Zech. 3:4-5; Sir. 50:5-11; Wis. 18:24; *J.W.* 5.230-37; *Ant.* 3.159-78; see also *m. Yoma* 3:7; 7:3-5). Those garments, rich in theological associations, aroused strong emotions in crowds at the Temple so that for a time Roman officials kept them under their control between the festivals when the high priest wore them (*J.W.* 5; *Ant.* 15.403-9; 18.94-95; 20.6, 11-14).

For the Second Temple period, there are a few references in the Hebrew Bible to the work performed by a high priest. Joshua was involved in the process of building the altar and the Second Temple (Ezra 3:2, 8-9; 4:3; 5:2). Zechariah 3 contains a prophecy about his responsibility for and duties in the Temple courts, while 4:14 appears to include him as one of the two anointed ones; 6:9-15 speak of a crown for him and good relations between him and the Branch (Zerubbabel). Eliashib took part in rebuilding the wall of Jerusalem (Neh. 3:2). Major roles of the high priests in other sources are:

Cultic

The high priests are rarely described as actually offering sacrifices, but several episodes, such as the one when Alexander Jannaeus was pelted with fruit as he was officiating at the altar during a celebration of the Festival of Booths (*J.W.* 1.88-89; *Ant.* 13.372-74), document the fact that they did carry out this quintessential priestly function. Sirach 50 furnishes a detailed account of an offering made by the high priest Simon (probably Simon I) and the splendid vestments that he wore while doing so. Josephus reports that the young Hasmonean high priest Aristobulus III made such a favorable impression on the crowd as he offered sacrifice at the Festival of Booths that Herod determined to murder him because of his popularity (*Ant.* 15.50-56).

Civil/Military

There are a few instances in the pre-Hasmonean era when a high priest is said to have engaged in diplomacy or other acts suggesting he was the head of state, but the sources are difficult to verify and perhaps idealistic. Judith 4:6, 8, 14; 15:8 seem to attribute such a role to Joiakim; Johanan was asked to engage in diplomacy in *TAD* A4.7 = *AP* 30; Jaddua is said to have had an alliance with King Darius III, apparently with military implications (*Ant.* 11.317-19); Onias I (?) may have led his people into an alliance of friendship with the Spartans (1 Macc. 12:20-23; *Ant.* 12.226-27); Eleazar corresponded with Ptolemy II, according to the *Letter of Aristeas;* and Onias II paid a sort of tribute to the Ptolemaic king (*Ant.* 12.156-72). There definitely were times in the Persian and early Hellenistic periods when a governor served (e.g., Zerubbabel when Joshua was high priest, or Nehemiah when Eliashib was high priest) and when, therefore, the high priest would not have been the political leader. With the advent of the Hasmonean high priesthood, the person holding that office also became the top civil authority and military commander in Judea. Beginning with Aristobulus I (possibly with Alexander Jannaeus), these leaders advanced a stage farther by adopting the title of king and were able to keep it until the Roman conquest in 63 B.C.E. (although Hyrcanus II is occasionally referred to as king after 63 B.C.E. [e.g., *J.W.* 1.201-3; *Ant.* 15.15] and Antigonus reclaimed the title during his short reign [40-37 B.C.E.]). When Herod appointed high priests, they seem to have lost much of their political power, while they remained important leaders in other respects and exercised weighty influence, in some cases even after leaving office (e.g., Ananias [*Ant.* 20.205-13]; Ananus son of Ananus [*J.W.* 2.562-63, 648-51; 4.151-325]).

Judicial

There are several accounts of high priests presiding over judicial bodies (e.g., a sanhedrin) and engaged in trials. A famous incident occurred when Hyrcanus II presided over the trial of Herod (*J.W.* 1.210-15; *Ant.* 14.168-84); others are Caiaphas' involvement in the interrogation and condemnation of Jesus (Matt. 26:3, 57; John 18:13-14, 24, 28), Ananias' role in the case against Paul (Acts 23:2; 24:1), and Ananus son of Ananus' part in the death of James (*Ant.* 20.199-203).

An Ideal High Priest and Eschatological Hopes

A series of Second Temple texts focuses attention on Levi, the eponymous ancestor of Aaron and thus of the high priests. The earliest reference is in Mal. 2:4-7, but other works go much farther than Malachi. The *Aramaic Levi Document* exalts Levi as the recipient of divine revelation and appointee to the priesthood; he demonstrated his mettle in avenging the abuse of his sister Dinah at Shechem. *Jubilees* 30–32 offers similar expansions on the sparse and negative data about Levi in Genesis. Later still, the Greek *Testament of Levi* continues in this vein of honoring Levi. Among the Qumran texts are a *Testament of Qahat* (4Q542) and the *Visions of Amram* (4Q543-548), texts centering on more immediate ancestors of Aaron.

Some of the Dead Sea Scrolls express the belief that in the last days there will be two messianic leaders, one a descendant of David and the other a priest. The Qumran *Community Rule* predicts that a prophet and the messiahs of Aaron and Israel will arise at the end of the age (1QS 9:9-11); the *Damascus Document* contains four references to the messiah (singular) of Aaron and Israel (CD 12:23–13:1; 14:18-19; 19:10-11; 19:33–20:1), phrasing that may entail two messiahs. The priestly messiah appears at the eschatological meal described in 1QSa 2:11-22, although it seems he is not labeled "messiah" in the passage. The priestly messiah also appears to be the leader called "the interpreter of the Law" (4QFlorilegium [4Q174] 1:10-13; CD 7:18-19). The *War Scroll* anticipates that the chief priest *(kōhēn hārō'š)* will carry out sacerdotal functions in the final conflict (1QM 10:2; 13:1-6; 15:4; 16:13; 18:5; 19:1). In a related but different way, the New Testament Epistle to the Hebrews presents Jesus as an eternal priest of the heavenly sanctuary, modeled on the order of Melchizedek (e.g., Hebrews 7). Melchizedek, a priest, is presented as a heavenly judge in 11QMelchizedek (11Q13) but his priestly role is not emphasized.

BIBLIOGRAPHY

M. BRUTTI 2006, *The Development of the High Priesthood during the Pre-Hasmonean Period: History, Ideology, Theology*, Leiden: Brill. • R. HORSLEY 1986, "High Priests and the Politics of Roman Palestine: A Contextual Analysis of the Evidence in Josephus," *JSJ* 17: 23-55. • A. HUNT 2006, *Missing Priests: The Zadokites in Tradition and History*, New York: T&T Clark. • J. JEREMIAS 1969, *Jerusalem in the Time of Jesus: An Investigation into Economic and Social Conditions during the New Testament Period*, Philadelphia: Fortress. • D. W. ROOK 2000, *Zadok's Heirs: The Role and Development of the High Priesthood in Ancient Israel*, Oxford: Oxford University Press. • J. SCHAPER 2000, *Priester und Leviten im achämenidischen Juda: Studien zur Kult- und Sozialgeschichte Israels in persischer Zeit*, Tübingen: Mohr-Siebeck. • A. SCHOFIELD AND J. VANDERKAM 2005, "Were the Hasmoneans Zadokites?" *JBL* 124: 73-87. • B. SCOLNIC 1999, *Chronology and Papponomy: A List of Judean High Priests of the Persian Period*, Atlanta: Scholars Press. • J. C. VANDERKAM 2004, *From Joshua to Caiaphas: High Priests after the Exile*, Minneapolis: Fortress.

JAMES C. VANDERKAM

Hillel

Hillel was the most prominent named scholar of the Second Temple period. The title of honor *ha-Zāqēn*, "the Elder," is often appended to his name. Hillel arrived in the land of Israel from Babylonia during the second half of the first century B.C.E. and became a disciple of the sages Shemaiah and Avtalyon. (His name, attested already in biblical times [Judg. 13:12, 15], appears vocalized in early manuscripts as *Hellel*, reflecting contemporary pronunciation.) The precise dates of his birth and death are unknown, but it is assumed that he lived several decades into the first century C.E. He and his colleague Shammai are listed as the last of the "Pairs" of scholars *(Zûgôt)*, and he is considered the forefather of the aristocratic line of patriarchs including Gamaliel I and II and Judah the Patriarch; tradition connects him on his mother's side to King David.

While undoubtedly a historical figure who left a significant mark on subsequent Jewish religious culture and law (although he is known only from rabbinic sources), Hillel became associated with much anecdotal material emphasizing especially his patience and personal piety but also his dedication to the study of Torah. His legal decisions are reported in areas covering the entire range of Jewish oral law: priestly and levitical gifts (tithes, *ḥallah*), purities, civil and matrimonial law, sacrificial law, and ritual. His sensitivity to social issues is evident in several decrees associated with his name. The *prozbul* that he enacted allowed lenders to receive payments from their debtors even after the sabbatical year, effectively annulling the biblical law of cancellation of debts during that year, and thereby insuring the continued practice of extending loans and credit to those in need (*m. Šeb.* 10:3). A second decree concerned the sale of houses in walled cities which, according to biblical law (Lev. 25:29-30), may be reacquired ("redeemed") by the seller only within a year. When it became the practice of the buyers of such houses to prevent the redemption by going into hiding at the end of twelve months, Hillel decreed that the previous owner (the seller) might unilaterally deposit the proceeds of the sale in the temple treasury and repossess the house (*m. ʿArak.* 9:4). Another legal decision concerned the dubious status of children born in Alexandria to mothers who had previously been officially engaged to one man but had married another: whereas other sages were of the opinion that these children should be considered illegitimate (the mothers never being properly divorced from their previous fiancés who, as was the custom, had written out documents of engagement), Hillel, basing himself on a close reading of the document of engagement, decreed these engagements to be void, thus insuring the children's legitimate status (*t. Ketub.* 4:9).

These legal decisions portray a leader of strong authority who was capable of providing creative legal solutions to redress situations of potential social inequity. Hillel's leadership and legal authority, as well as his respect for the people as significant partners in the legal process, are attested in other legal decisions, such as his proof for the permissibility of offering the Paschal sacrifice on a Sabbath, which is bolstered by an appeal to tradition and to popular custom (*t. Pesaḥ.* 4:13); as a result he was appointed *naśîʾ* (president of the legal council). In this context he is described as having applied exegetical rules (canons) in expounding scriptural law (*t. Sanh.* 7:11; cf. *y. Pesaḥ.* 6:1, *b. Pesaḥim* 66a); this is considered by some scholars as evidence of his role in the propagation of legal exegesis of Scripture *(midrash)*, although others view it as a projection onto the historical

Hillel of techniques typical in later tradition (Schwartz 1997).

Many later tales describe Hillel as a sage of wide knowledge and almost infinite patience, coupled with a love and acceptance of every man and an uncanny ability to appease and teach even those who at first were hostile to him and his teachings. Thus, to one who claimed to believe only in the written Torah, he taught the inadequacy of relying on the written text without the authority of the oral Torah; and to a potential proselyte who had demanded to be taught the entire Torah "while standing on one leg," he epitomized all religious teaching of the Torah through the dictum of the Golden Rule, "that which is hateful to you do not do unto others," adding, significantly, "all the rest (of the Torah's laws) are specifications (of this principle); go now and study (them)" (*ʾAbot de Rabbi Nathan* A 16; *b. Šabbat* 31a). In these tales his character is contrasted with that of his colleague Shammai, who is portrayed as strict and unbending as Hillel is flexible and patient. While some of Shammai's rulings reflect a strict and inclusive interpretation of the Law, of the three or four recorded disputes between Hillel and Shammai it is difficult to distinguish between stricter or more lenient attitudes. With regard to their disciples, however, the situation is different: the "House of Hillel" *(Bêt Hillel)* is often noted for leniency in its rulings as opposed to the greater stringency of the "House of Shammai" *(Bêt Shammai).*

The anecdotes regarding Hillel, while not necessarily historical, nonetheless provide a true, if idealized, portrayal of the type of legal authority of Second Temple Judaism described elsewhere as Pharisaic, with authoritative knowledge of the ancient oral traditions, beloved of the populace, active in the Temple, and combating the opposing claims of those who would denigrate the importance of the oral or written Torah. Hillel's character as a popular teacher is also evident in his many epigrammatic sayings, some in Aramaic, which have become bywords of Jewish culture: "Be a disciple of Aaron: love peace and pursue it, love all creatures and draw them close to the Torah" (*m. ʾAbot* 1:12); "If I am not for myself, who will be for me? If I am only for myself, what am I? If not now, when?" (*m. ʾAbot* 1:14). A deep appreciation of Hillel's character and work as exemplifying Second Temple ideals of ethical living, piety and the teaching of Torah is accurately reflected in his eulogy: "Behold a modest man, behold a pious man, disciple of Ezra" (*t. Soṭah* 13:3).

BIBLIOGRAPHY

I. BEN-SHALOM 1992, "Hillel the Elder: His Character and Work in Historical Context," in *Leaders and Leadership in Jewish and World History,* ed. I. Malkin and Z. Tzahor, Jerusalem: Shazar Center, 103-32 (in Hebrew). • I. BEN-SHALOM 1993, *The School of Shammai and the Zealots' Struggle against Rome,* Jerusalem: Yad Izhak Ben-Zvi, 69-109 (in Hebrew). • D. FLUSSER 1997, "Hillel and Jesus: Two Ways of Self-Awareness," in *Hillel and Jesus: Comparative Studies of Two Major Religious Leaders,* ed. J. H. Charlesworth and L. L. Johns, Minneapolis: Fortress, 71-107. • L. GINZBERG 1955, "The Significance of the Halachah for Jewish History," in idem, *On Jewish Law and Lore,* Philadelphia: Jewish Publication Society, 75-124. • N. N. GLATZER 1956, *Hillel the Elder,* Jerusalem: Schocken. • J. NEUSNER 1971, *The Rabbinic Traditions about the Pharisees before 70,* Leiden: Brill, 1:212-340, 3:255-72. • C. SAFRAI 1997, "Sayings and Legends in the Hillel Tradition," in *Hillel and Jesus,* ed. J. H. Charlesworth and L. L. Johns, Minneapolis: Fortress, 306-20. • E. SCHÜRER 1979, *The History of the Jewish People in the Age of Jesus Christ,* rev. and ed. G. Vermes, F. Millar, and M. Black, Edinburgh: Clark, 2:363-67. • D. R. SCHWARTZ 1997, "Hillel and Scripture: From Authority to Exegesis," in *Hillel and Jesus,* ed. J. H. Charlesworth and L. L. Johns, Minneapolis: Fortress, 335-62. • S. ZEITLIN 1964, "Hillel and the Hermeneutic Rules," *JQR* 54: 161-73.

See also: Shammai

PAUL MANDEL

Historiography

Preservation

Early Jewish Hellenistic historiography should be viewed against the background of historiography in the Classical, Hellenistic, and Near Eastern worlds. Hellenistic historiography was in the process of forming a "canon" of historical works in Greek and Latin. It will suffice to mention a line of historians starting from Ephoros through Timaeus, the Hellenistic Alexander historians, Hieronymus of Cardia, Duris of Samos, Phylarchus, Polybius, and Poseidonius of Apamea. Of those the work of only one (Polybius) has survived (though not in its entirety), the others being known from fragments found in the later historians who used them. Several factors contributed to this outcome. Some books were lost because they were not favorably received by later generations; some were cannibalized to such an extent that the originals were lost; others achieved canonicity and caused their own sources to disappear. Epitomes may have led to the loss of the full originals, and there were probably other factors as well.

Even less of Near Eastern historiography of the Hellenistic period has survived. No historical work remains intact; there are only fragments and summaries preserved in Greek historiography. "Nationalistic" histories such as the *Indica* of Megasthenes, the *Babyloniaca* of Berossus, the *Aegyptiaca* of Hecataeus of Abdera and of Manetho, and the *Lybica* of Dionysius Scytobrachion — all survive only in fragmentary form in later writers. This genre of ethnic or nationalistic history writing developed in the Hellenistic East and has survived mainly in Western compositions, such as the *Bibliotheke* of Diodorus Siculus. It tended to be mythological in approach and did not tackle the recent past or the actual present.

Judaic historical literature in the Hellenistic period, say, between 300 and 50 B.C.E., is quite sparse. The last historical books to be included in the canon of the Hebrew Bible belong mostly to the Persian period. They are written in Hebrew (some chapters are in Aramaic), and they include the books of Ezra-Nehemiah, Esther, Chronicles, and parts of Daniel. The work known as 1 Esdras in the Septuagint and 3 Esdras in the Vulgate is, for the most part, a Greek translation of material paralleled in 2 Chron. 35:1–36:21, Ezra, and Neh. 7:72–8:13. These are typical biblical historical writings in the style of the earlier books of Samuel and Kings. The book of Esther, whose additions stem from the Hellenistic period, and, in a way, Daniel, whose later chapters also belong to the Hellenistic era, may be considered historical novellas and not real histories.

After the books of Ezra-Nehemiah, which relate the history of the Jews during a short stretch of the Persian era, there is no linear Jewish history until the second century B.C.E. This amounts to a period of more than 200 years without any written history. Daniel 11 has some allusions to recent history of the Hellenistic period, but it cannot be regarded as a historical account.

After this long hiatus, the two books of Maccabees are the only works to offer a narrative of the recent history of the Jews. (Josippon's survey cannot be considered real history.) There are two possible explanations for this chronological caesura in the writing of history: either there were accounts that disappeared, or the Jews felt no need to write history as such and the Maccabean books were an exception. The second possibility is the more likely, since we have no evidence for the existence of history writings during this time span. After Maccabees, no significant Jewish history exists until the modern era. The exception is Josephus, but he wrote in line with pagan Hellenistic authors. It seems probable that the writing of the two books of Maccabees was a result of the dramatic national revival of the second century B.C.E.

Considering the extant and reported wealth of contemporaneous historical writing in the Greek West and the Hellenistic East, the Jews left very little record of their own recent history. And when what does survive is examined, it becomes clear that genuinely historical material is extremely meager. This conclusion is applicable both to the Jews in the land of Israel and to those in the Hellenistic Diaspora. It is perhaps not coincidental that in the first century B.C.E. it was not the Jews who wrote their history, but a non-Jew, Nicolaus of Damascus, whose work was so extensively drawn upon by Josephus and others that his books have disappeared.

Genres

During the second and first centuries B.C.E., there were different sorts of writings current in Judaism that contained historical material. (1) Books offering linear histories of recent events. Here we can place only 1 and 2 Maccabees (and a few allusive passages in 3 and 4 Maccabees). But these were not annalistic like the works of Polybius (second century B.C.E. in Greek) and Livy (late first century B.C.E. to early first century C.E. in Latin). That is, they did not leave abundant informative accounts of events in sequence. First and Second Maccabees have enormous gaps in information even in what they do narrate, and they leave out whole spans of time and even greater blocks of information. Nevertheless, if these two books had been lost to posterity, we would have only Josephus' partial account in the *Antiquities* for this crucial period in Jewish history. And yet Josephus used mainly 1 Maccabees. (2) Writings that refer to the distant Jewish past and try to reshape it for political, theological, and social reasons. These were written in the genre of so-called creative historiography that can be found also in the literary output of the surrounding Hellenistic world. (3) Works of historical fiction such as Esther (and its additions), Susanna, Judith, and 3 and 4 Maccabees. (4) Eschatological compositions in which present history is used to demonstrate the active intervention of God in events and to predict the future.

Linear Historiography

It is remarkable that only two Jewish historical books of the Hellenistic age, 1 and 2 Maccabees, were preserved, and that only through the Septuagint, by the church. While it is commonly claimed that 1 Maccabees was written originally in Hebrew, 2 Maccabees was certainly written in Greek. First Maccabees intends to offer a "full" account of the history it describes. Second Maccabees is an epitome of five original volumes, written by Jason of Cyrene. First Maccabees covers a longer period, from the beginning of the Maccabean uprising to the mid-second century B.C.E. — about forty years. For its part, 2 Maccabees concentrates on Judas Maccabaeus and the years leading to his rule. First Maccabees was probably written after the middle of the second century B.C.E. in Palestine; 2 Maccabees some decades later, in Egypt (the epitome was probably written in Egypt, though Jason wrote in Cyrene).

The two books differ in mode of composition. First Maccabees imitates the historical books of the Bible in some respects, whereas 2 Maccabees is written in the mode of tragic or "pathetic" historiography and stands with Polybius as Hellenistic historiography in Greek. In its present form, 1 Maccabees should be viewed as a Hellenistic creation since it was translated into Greek, and we do not know what happened to the Hebrew version (mentioned by the church father Jerome).

These two isolated instances of Jewish historiography between the Chronicler and Josephus (400-500 years) share some significant features. To begin with, all their sources have completely disappeared. This loss is in accord with the "rule" that sources used in writings that become central and sometimes even canonical simply disappear in the course of time. (An analogy in early Christian literature is the lost Q document adapted by the Gospels of Matthew and Luke.) Many of the sources were probably oral, as a comment in 1 Macc. 9:22 suggests: "The rest of the acts of Judah, his battles, the exploits which he performed, and his greatness are not written down; for they were very many."

The sources used by the two books were of varying nature, ranging from official documents (of the Seleucids, for instance), sometimes cited verbatim (their authenticity is endlessly debated by scholars), to memories that can be defined as oral tradition, to imaginative literary works. Both of these features render 1 and 2 Maccabees problematic when compared to the classical histories of Thucydides, Xenophon, or Polybius. Thus 1 Maccabees preserves documents such as the correspondence with Sparta (1 Macc. 12:1-23) and the letter of Demetrius I to the Jews (1 Macc. 10:25-45), and 2 Maccabees includes the letters to the Jews from Lysias (11:16-21) and from the Roman legates (11:34-38), among others. But both books abound in stories that have little if any historical value. For instance, in 1 Macc. 6:8-13 Antiochus Epiphanes acknowledges that his fatal illness is God's judgment on him for his war against the Jews (cf. 2 Maccabees 9). The famous stories about martyrdom in 2 Maccabees 6–7 may have a historical kernel, but most of the narrative contains the literary embellishment of the author or his source (perhaps expressing an "Ur martyrdom" text which is also evident in 4 Maccabees 5–18). The same can be said about the story of Heliodorus in the Temple (2 Macc. 3:8-40), a story which resembles the one told about Ptolemy IV in 3 Maccabees 1–2. In both books a variety of other imaginative elements are interwoven in the narrative and obscure the historical truth.

The attempt made by the authors of 1 and 2 Maccabees to write a linear historical narrative was not always successful. Sometimes we have breaks of two or more years in the account (e.g., 1 Macc. 1:28-29), and in episodes that the authors do narrate usually only a fragmentary picture is presented (e.g., 2 Maccabees 8 does not state the time and place of action, and does not give realistic numbers).

Further, both 1 and 2 Maccabees are extremely opinionated concerning ethical and social matters, and this jeopardizes the narrative and its truthfulness, since at times the authors express their views as if they were factual details. For instance, 1 Macc. 2:29-41 goes out of its way to present two examples of behavior that Jews could adopt against the enemy on the Sabbath (2 Maccabees tackles this as well in 8:25-28). Second Maccabees 8:16-20 is another example of a general statement of a truth rather than a factual account.

Also typical of both Maccabean books is that historical events are usually made to revolve around individuals (Judas, his father, and his brothers in 1 Maccabees; Judas in 2 Maccabees). This narrative focus limits the density of information that a historical writing can provide. Instead of offering a comprehensive account, the deeds of a hero in certain circumstances dominate (compare Plutarch's *Lives* or the Gospels). A related problem in perspective is that the Judeo-centricity and anti-Hellenistic stance taken by 1 and 2 Maccabees result in a lack of serious engagement with the wider world. And in both books the narratives are weighed down with theological bias. In 2 Maccabees in particular the theological interpretation of events usually hampers the objective narration of history (e.g., 2 Macc. 6:12-17 is devoted to the author's theory of sin and punishment).

Many attempts have been made to demonstrate a literary relationship between 1 and 2 Maccabees. Since 2 Maccabees is later than 1 Maccabees, certain episodes in the former might rely on the earlier text. However, a careful comparison between the few relevant episodes that probably overlap shows that 2 Maccabees may have adapted sources that 1 Maccabees also drew on but narrates them in a completely different manner. For instance, the return of Judas from Gilead is recounted in 1 Macc. 5:45-54 and somewhat differently in 2 Macc. 12:27-31. Here and there the two works drew on the same sources but reworked them in separate ways. The so-called Edict of Restrictions against the Jews issued by Antiochus IV is presented very differently in the two works. 2 Maccabees does not speak of it as emphatically as 1 Maccabees does (1 Macc. 1:41-53; 2 Macc. 6:1-11). Josephus, in his account of this period, probably used 1 Maccabees but in a slightly different version than the one we have today.

The two books of Maccabees have very little in common with their counterparts in the Hellenistic West in terms of methods and quality of historical narrative (even though Jason of Cyrene and/or his epitomator probably knew Polybius). The main aim of Jews in writing history was to convey moral, political, and religious positions, whereas in the West the main aim was to write down events that "happened" and to offer a comprehensive historical account as far as the sources permitted.

Creative Historiography

Under the rubric "creative" historiography belong books that imitated and embellished the biblical narrative, such as the Aramaic *Genesis Apocryphon,* the book of *Jubilees,* and the *Biblical Antiquities* of Pseudo-Philo. Works of this sort rewrite biblical historical narratives without consideration for accuracy. They also alter the roles of biblical heroes and mix time spans. For instance, in *Jubilees* the relationship of Esau and Isaac is presented differently than in the book of Genesis. Both of them get different roles and personalities, and the Jewish festivals are already being celebrated by the patriarchs. The extensive alterations reflect a desire to illustrate a moral and political lesson by changing the past. In the production of this genre of history writing, alternative versions of biblical history were invented during the Hellenistic period.

Jews produced a number of works in the tradition of Hellenistic historiography. Sadly, these survive only in fragments excerpted in later compilers, chiefly the first-century-B.C.E. grammarian L. Cornelius Alexander of Miletus, nicknamed "Polyhistor," who composed a now lost treatise *On the Jews.* Even his fragments have not come down to us directly but via quotations in Josephus and in the church fathers Clement of Alexandria (second century C.E.) and Eusebius of Caesarea (third-fourth century C.E.). The most notable Hellenistic Jewish historians in this category are Demetrius the Chronographer (third century B.C.E.), Eupolemus (mid-second century B.C.E.), Pseudo-Eupolemus (the mistaken attribution of an anonymous Samaritan of the second century B.C.E.), and Artapanus (third or second century B.C.E.).

All of these works pretend to tackle the "real" history of the past, but in effect remain in the realm of imagination. None of them narrates history of the recent past or present. This is not only a Jewish phenomenon but can be found as well in the non-Jewish historical literature of the Hellenistic Near East, in writers such as Manetho, Hecataeus of Abdera, Berossus, and others. Eupolemus' *On the Kings of Judea* may serve as an example. In it he fabricates a correspondence between a Pharaoh called Vaphres (not identified, and probably an invention of the author) and David and his son Solomon concerning the building of the Temple in Jerusalem. The correspondence does not appear in the Hebrew Bible and was probably invented to prove an urgent political and theological point. Thus history is used in a fabricated form for instruction and for gaining legitimacy for contemporary doings. In a similar vein, Artapanus, who wrote a composition titled *On the Jews,* makes Moses the teacher of Orpheus, the inventor of Egyptian technology and the hieroglyphs, as well as the initiator of the division of Egypt into thirty-six *nomes* and the appointment of the local gods to be worshiped. Artapanus writes a "competitive" history in order to illustrate the cultural and political contributions of the Jews to Egypt in the distant past.

Historical Novellas

Several works from the early Hellenistic period are monographs with narratives set in various historical periods and with varying degrees of historical verisimilitude but embellished with fictional features. Here we can place the books of Tobit, Judith, the Greek Esther, Susanna and Bel and the Dragon, 3 and 4 Maccabees, *Joseph and Aseneth,* and two narrative cycles incorporated by Josephus into his *Jewish Antiquities:* the Tale of the Tobiads and the Royal House of Adiabene. They share some features with historical narrative but are better classified as novellas. They are the literary successors of the biblical books of Ruth, Daniel, and Esther and have several features in common with them, such as the presentation of a central Jewish hero or heroine who saves the nation at a crucial juncture or shows great courage (e.g., Daniel, Esther, Judith, Eleazar the priest in 3 Maccabees, Eleazar in 4 Maccabees). They also have many supernatural features (e.g., 3 Macc. 6:16-21; cf. 2 Macc. 3:22-27). Elements of the narrative setting are sometimes historically realistic. For instance, the court of Ahasuerus in Esther is depicted like a typical Eastern court, and the one of Ptolemy IV in 3 Maccabees as a typical Ptolemaic one. The arena in 3 Maccabees in which elephants are put in order to trample the Jews is a typical public space in a Hellenistic town. The martyrdom of the seven brothers in 4 Maccabees 8–18 (cf. 2 Maccabees 6–7) is not a realistic scene in itself, but the fact of martyrdom was real.

Apocalyptic Historiography

Eschatological rewritings of history, often under the guise of *ex eventu* prophecy but sometimes in figurative schematizations, are found in several "historical" apocalypses such as the Enochic *Apocalypse of Weeks* (*1 Enoch* 93) and *Animal Apocalypse* (*1 Enoch* 83–91), Daniel 7–12, and *Jubilees,* and in the pesher commentaries from Qumran. The pesharim, for example, use politics and recent historical events to show that Scripture has already predicted all that would happen in history. In other words, God directs the course of history and conveyed bits of it through his prophets hundreds of years earlier. For instance, in its interpretation of Nah. 2:12b, *Pesher Nahum* says, "[And no one to disturb. Its interpretation concerns Deme]trius, king of Greece, who sought to enter Jerusalem on the advice of the Seekers-after-smooth-things" (frg. 3–4 col. i line 2). This hermeneutical approach, if not the precise exegetical form, was picked up by the Gospel of Matthew and by several of the church fathers. Eusebius in his *Praeparatio Evangelica* and his *Demonstratio Evangelica* shows that Scripture has anticipated the coming of Jesus and its consequences.

Were it not for the church in the first centuries of the Common Era, most of the works mentioned above would have been lost, since the rabbis considered most of them "external books." Two main reasons can be given for the lack of Jewish history writing during a stretch of 400 years. First, in the First Temple period and at the beginning of the Second, Jews could attend to God's words about the course and correct interpretation of history by attending to the oracles of the classical Hebrew prophets — Isaiah, Jeremiah, Haggai, Zechariah, and Malachi, among others. History was still being written at that time. But prophecy in its classical form eventually ceased, and, according to 1 Maccabees, matters would not change until a "prophet would arise" (4:46). This popular attitude probably had repercussions on the writing of history. The strong link between prophecy and the writing of history could not exist when prophecy was lacking. The pesharim from Qumran and the apocalyptic literature reflect the only attempts to interpret God's words and deeds in history, but they did so in only a limited manner and not with full-blown historiography.

A second reason for the long break in the Jewish writing of history may be sought in the later view of the rabbis that God, not human beings, is responsible for history. That this notion may have earlier roots is suggested by 2 Macc. 8:4, where God is called on to "remember." The history of the Jews was embodied in memory. The "memory of the whole" — as we hear in a very old prayer, the Mussaf for Rosh Hashanah, in the so-called *Zichronot* — is the domain of God, so the human being should not try to compete with the Almighty by writing history. This is perhaps why historiography became a nonissue throughout Jewish history until the rejection of Orthodoxy in the modern era.

Josephus

With Josephus Flavius in the first century C.E., the Jews suddenly acquired a true historian writing in Greek. In his work, we are in the domain of a genre of history writing that can be considered Western — Greek, not Jewish — and that resembles the work of historians like Dionysius of Halicarnassus. What are Josephus' links to Jewish historiography of the early Hellenistic period? To begin with, he made use of some earlier writings, probably 1 Maccabees rather than 2 Maccabees. And in certain of his books, especially the *Jewish Antiquities,* he naturally adopted literary features of biblical historiography but presented them in a typical Hellenistic garb. Unlike modern historians, when relying on earlier material (even if rather legendary, as in his use of the *Letter of Aristeas* and 3 Maccabees), he did so with no critical detachment. Yet he knew Jewish history very well, had a regard for earlier narratives, and took them seriously.

BIBLIOGRAPHY

H. W. ATTRIDGE 1984, "Historiography," in *Jewish Writings of the Second Temple Period*, ed. M. E. Stone, Assen: Van Gorcum; Philadelphia: Fortress. • J. J. COLLINS 2000, *Between Athens and Jerusalem: Jewish Identity in the Hellenistic Diaspora*, 2d ed., Grand Rapids: Eerdmans. • R. DORAN 1981, *Temple Propaganda: The Purpose and Character of 2 Maccabees*, Washington, D.C.: Catholic Biblical Association of America. • H. ESHEL 2008, *The Dead Sea Scrolls and the Hasmonean State*, Grand Rapids: Eerdmans. • R. G. HALL 1991, *Revealed Histories: Techniques for Ancient Jewish and Christian Historiography*, Sheffield: Sheffield Academic Press. • C. R. HOLLADAY 1983, *Fragments from Hellenistic Jewish Authors*, vol. 1, *Historians*, Chico, Calif.: Scholars Press. • S. INOWLOCKI 2006, *Eusebius and the Jewish Authors: His Citation Technique in an Apologetic Context*, Leiden: Brill. • S. R. JOHNSON 2004, *Historical Fictions and Hellenistic Jewish Identity: Third Maccabees in Its Cultural Context*, Berkeley: University of California Press. • D. MENDELS 1987, *The Land of Israel as a Political Concept in Hasmonean Literature*, Tübingen: Mohr-Siebeck. • D. MENDELS 1998, *Identity, Religion and Historiography: Studies in Hellenistic History*, Sheffield: Sheffield Academic Press. • D. MENDELS 2004, *Memory in Jewish, Pagan and Christian Societies of the Graeco-Roman World*, London: Clark. • D. MENDELS 2007, "Living with Fragments of the Past, and Why Did the Rabbis Avoid Writing History?" in *Antiquity in Antiquity*, ed. P. Schäfer, Tübingen: Mohr-Siebeck. • D. Mendels 2008, "How Was Antiquity Treated in Societies with a Hellenistic Heritage? And Why Did the Rabbis Avoid Writing History?" in *Antiquity in Antiquity: Jewish and Christian Pasts in the Graeco-Roman World*, ed. G. Gardner and K. Osterloh, Tübingen, Mohr-Siebeck, 1-20. • U. RAPPAPORT 2004, *The First Book of Maccabees: Introduction, Hebrew Translation, and Commentary*, Jerusalem: Yad Ben-Zvi (in Hebrew). • D. R. SCHWARTZ 2008, *2 Maccabees*, Berlin: de Gruyter. • J. SIEVERS 2001, *Synopsis of the Greek Sources for the Hasmonean Period*, Rome: Editrice Pontificio Istituto Biblico. • G. E. STERLING 1992, *Historiography and Self-Definition: Josephos, Luke-Acts, and Apologetic Historiography*, Leiden: Brill. • L. M. WILLS 2002, *Ancient Jewish Novels: An Anthology*, Oxford: Oxford University Press.

See also: Alexander Polyhistor; Apologetic Literature; Artapanus; Chronography; Eupolemus; Josephus

DORON MENDELS

Hodayot (1QH and Related Texts)

The *Thanksgiving Psalms* (*Hodayot* in Hebrew) is a collection of approximately thirty poems that give thanks to God. Seven copies of the collection were found in the caves near Qumran, and this relatively large number indicates its importance. These psalms reflect the distinctive vocabulary and religious ideas that marked the type of Judaism found in other primary works of the Qumran community such as the *Rule of the Community* and the *War Scroll*. Although there are still many unanswered questions about the composition and use of these poems, they are an important resource for understanding the piety and religious devotion of those who composed and recited them.

The Manuscripts

The largest and most complete copy is the scroll found by the Bedouin in Cave 1 near Qumran, and purchased by Eliezer Sukenik of the Hebrew University of Jerusalem in November 1947 ($1QH^a$). This is a very large scroll with forty-one or forty-two lines per page; the size, care in preparation, and beautiful calligraphy indicate that this was an important scroll that had some status in the community. It was copied in the last quarter of the first century B.C.E. by two scribes. In 1955 Sukenik published photographs and a transcription of all the pieces of this very damaged scroll. Later, H. Stegemann and E. Puech (working independently) reconstructed how the columns and fragmentary pieces had originally fit together. They were able to show that the original scroll was 4.5 m. in length and twenty-eight columns long, and they recovered the original order of the psalms.

In Cave 1, archaeologists found two more small pieces that were very similar both in handwriting and in content. These were published in 1955 by J. T. Milik, who first suggested that that they were part of Sukenik's manuscript. But it was soon recognized that the shapes of these fragments were very different than anything preserved from $1QH^a$ and that the text actually overlapped with material in Sukenik's manuscript. This means that these two small fragments must be from a second copy ($1QH^b$).

From the fragments founds in Cave 4, six more manuscripts were identified that contained text that overlapped with $1QH^a$ (4Q427-432). Five were written on animal skins ($4QH^{a-e}$) and one ($4QpapH^f$) on papyrus. These manuscripts were assigned to John Strugnell, who did the initial identification and analysis; they were published by Eileen Schuller in 1999. The amount of material that is preserved in these badly damaged copies is limited, but there are some places where a Cave 4 fragment preserves words and phrases, even partial psalms, that are not found in $1QH^a$. The earliest manuscript, $4QH^b$, was copied about 100-75 B.C.E. and preserves the same psalms in the same order as in $1QH^a$. $4QH^a$ was copied closer to the end of the first century B.C.E., and preserves a different order. One manuscript, $4QH^c$, is very small (only twelve lines in narrow columns) and must have contained only a part of the collection, probably the group of psalms associated especially with the Teacher (see below); the same is perhaps the case with $4QpapH^f$. Much more study of all the manuscripts will be required to explain the origin, growth, and interrelationship of these differing collections.

HODAYOT (1QH AND RELATED TEXTS)

Content and Composition

There are approximately thirty psalms in the collection (the exact number is not certain because the text is so fragmentary and often the transitions between the end of one psalm and the beginning of the next are missing). These poems are modeled on the biblical Psalms, especially the "individual psalms of thanksgiving," but there is considerable diversity in both form and content, rather than a strict imitation of the biblical form. As is typical in sectarian literature, the divine name (the tetragrammaton) is never used.

All these psalms start with a fixed introductory formula, either "I thank you, O Lord" or "Blessed are you, Lord"; the latter formula also often introduces a sub-section within a long poem. The psalmist immediately states his reason for offering thanks by recounting what God has done for him: for example, "because you have placed my soul in the bundle of the living" (1QH^a 10:22); "because you have redeemed my soul from the pit" (1QH^a 11:20); "for you have illumined my face by your covenant" (1QH^a 12:6); "because you have dealt wondrously with dust and mightily with a creature of clay" (1QH^a 19:6). Other reasons frequently cited for giving thanks are that God has granted the psalmist knowledge of marvelous mysteries (e.g., 1QH^a 12:28-29) and brought him into the community (the *yaḥad*), giving him fellowship with the elect on earth and with the angels in heaven (e.g., 1QH^a 11:23-24). As in the biblical Psalms, the psalmist recounts at length the trials and sufferings that have been inflicted upon him and how he has been delivered by God's gracious help; betrayal, persecution, and exile as the result of the perfidiousness of his enemies are more common motifs than complaints of physical illness.

The main body of each psalm can be quite varied in form and content. Sometimes there is an extended and elaborate development of a specific image or motif, for example, a tree planted in a garden (1QH^a 16:5-27), a fortified city (1QH^a 14:28-32), or a woman in labor (1QH^a 11:8-14). In a few psalms, there are extended descriptions of the eschatological future, with particular emphasis on the destruction of Belial and all the spirits of wickedness (1QH^a 11:26-37). One long poem toward the end of 1QH^a (23:1–25:33) reflects on the fallen angels and the introduction of sin into the world. Many psalms treat major theological themes, especially creation, the two ways, and divine determination of all that happens. There is no standard concluding formula; in the biblical psalms of thanksgiving there was often mention in the concluding section of offering sacrifice and fulfilling vows in the Temple, but this element is not found in any of these texts.

These psalms seem very "biblical-like" because they make extensive use of biblical phraseology and images. Hundreds of allusions have been identified, most of them from the Psalms, Isaiah, and Deuteronomy. Only rarely is there a direct quotation of as much as a whole line; instead, the biblical words and phrases are reworked and reconfigured in an anthological style.

Authorship and Unity

When he first read these psalms, Sukenik assumed that the entire collection was a unified work, "a collection of songs expressing the views and feelings of one of the members of the sect." He suggested that this author could have been the Teacher of Righteousness himself since certain passages describe how God had given the psalmist a special revelation that he is to share with the members of his community (e.g., "through me, you have enlightened the face of the Many," 1QH^a 12:28). References to how the psalmist was persecuted and expelled (e.g., "they have banished me from my land like a bird from the nest," 1QH^a 12:9-10) could be referring to the suffering and exile of the Teacher at the hands of the Wicked Priest, as described in other works such as *Pesher Habakkuk*.

More detailed study, however, has shown that this is not a unitary work. In the 1960s a number of scholars proposed that the collection should be subdivided into two major categories on the basis of content, vocabulary, and style. In the first group of psalms, the so-called "Hymns of the Teacher," the person who speaks has an exalted position and often makes the claim to function as a mediator of revelation to others; the betrayal, persecution, and sufferings of the speaker are recounted in lengthy detail; certain words and phrases are repeated frequently in these psalms, while other lexical items never appear. At least eight psalms of this type (some commentators would add a few more) are grouped together in cols. 10-17, that is, in the middle of the reconstructed 1QH^a scroll, and it is these same psalms that are found in 4QH^c and 4QH^f. They have often been read autobiographically as a source of information about the personal religious experience of the Teacher of Righteousness as well as the early formative years of the community; a minority of scholars have emphasized, however, that much of this language is very formulaic and taken from the biblical psalter, and could be applied more generally to any member of the community.

In the second category of psalms, the so-called "Hymns of the Community," the "I" seems to be the corporate voice of the community. The reasons for giving thanks are more generic, and there is less claim of personal privilege or position. The author claims that he already enjoys a fellowship with the angels and other blessings (joy, the gift of the Holy Spirit) that are typically associated with eschatological salvation, though there is a strong sense of a divine intervention that is still to come, especially in terms of judgment. Even in his present life within the *yaḥad,* God has purified the psalmist "so that he can take a place with the host of the holy ones and can enter into communion with the congregation of the sons of heaven" (1QH^a 11:23). A distinctive trope in these psalms is the extended reflection, often expressed in the form of a series of rhetorical questions, about the sinful condition and misery of humankind: "What is one born of a woman in the midst of all your awesome works? He is a construction of dust and kneaded with water; his foundation is sinful guilt and ignominious shame and a source of uncleanness; a spirit of perversity rules over him" (1QH^a 5:31-33). But these same psalms are confident in divine grace, mercy, and righteousness as the basis for salvation, and so the psalmist confesses, "I know that righteousness is yours, and in your mercy . . ." (1QH[a] 19:20-21).

Purpose and Use

We know very little with certainty about how these psalms were actually used at Qumran. There are no specific headings or concrete directions for usage on a certain day, month, week, or year like those in other prayer collections. The length of many of the compositions, the absence of set formulas and congregational responses, and the complexity of both the poetic style and the development of ideas have suggested to many scholars that they were intended primarily for personal private meditation and/or instruction.

But at least some of these psalms may have been used liturgically in the worship life of the community. There are certain rubric-type headings that indicate that in 1QH[a] the collection was divided into five sections, like the five books of the Psalter. Themes such as the weakness and sinfulness of the human condition and the doxological confession of divine graciousness would be especially appropriate on occasions such as the liturgy for entrance into and renewal of the covenant (1QS 1:18–2:18); perhaps secondarily, these psalms came to be used as part of the daily "entering the covenant of God" (1QS 10:10). There are certain themes in common with the morning blessings in later rabbinic prayer (e.g., knowledge; creation) but the links are general rather than specific. It is tempting to wonder whether these psalms might have been used when the Many gathered to "watch together for a third of each night of the year . . . to bless together" (1QS 6:8).

Given how little we know about the actual shape and content of liturgical life and practice at Qumran, it may simply not be possible to resolve the question of personal versus communal use with any certainty. A more fruitful avenue of inquiry is that explored recently by Carol Newson, who concentrates not on reconstructing their *Sitz-im-Leben* but rather asks how they functioned rhetorically in the ongoing life of the community. The repeated use of this poetry, with its rich imagery, emotive power, and distinctive worldview, must have been an important factor in shaping the self-identity and self-understanding of the members of the community.

BIBLIOGRAPHY

Editions

J. T. MILIK 1955, *Discoveries in the Judaean Desert I,* Oxford: Clarendon, 135-37. • E. SCHULLER 1999, "4Q427–432," in *Qumran Cave 4.II: Poetical and Liturgical Texts, Part 2,* DJD 29, Oxford: Clarendon, 69-232. • E. SUKENIK 1955, *The Dead Sea Scrolls of Hebrew University,* Jerusalem: Magnes.

Reconstruction

E. PUECH 1988, "Quelques aspects de la restauration du Rouleau des Hymnes (1QH)," *JJS* 39: 38-55. • H. STEGEMANN 2000, "The Material Reconstruction of 1QHodayot," in *The Dead Sea Scrolls: Fifty Years after Their Discovery 1947-1997,* ed. L. H. Schiffman, E. Tov, and J. C. VanderKam, Jerusalem: Israel Exploration Society and Shrine of the Book, Israel Museum, 272-84.

Bibliography

E. SCHULLER AND L. DITOMMASO 1997, "A Bibliography of the Hodayot 1968-1996," *DSD* 4: 55-101.

Studies

S. HOLM-NIELSEN 1960, *Hodayot: Psalms from Qumran,* Aarhus: Universitetsforlaget. • J. HUGHES 2006, *Scriptural Allusions and Exegesis in the Hodayot,* Leiden: Brill. • C. NEWSOM 2004, *The Self as Symbolic Space: Constructing Identity and Community at Qumran,* Leiden: Brill, 191-346.

See also: Hymns, Prayers, and Psalms; Psalms, Apocryphal; Psalms, Book of EILEEN SCHULLER

Holiness

Holiness (Heb. *qōdeš, qĕdûšāh*) is a supernatural force that can be defined loosely as "divine energy." At its core, holiness is another way of saying "God." The Dead Sea Scrolls use the terms *Qôdeš, Ha-Qôdeš* ("the Holy One"), and *Qôdeš Qôdāšîm* ("Holy of Holies") as synonyms for God (1QS 10:4; 1QSb 4:28; CD 6:1; 20:22), and the favorite rabbinic title for God is "the Holy One, Blessed Be He." God's essence alone is holy (1 Sam. 2:2); other persons and items can partake of holiness only by extension and divine designation. Holy persons, animals, places, objects, and times, because they belong to God and his sphere of activity, reflect but do not inherently possess or generate holiness.

The Hebrew verb *qdš* means "to separate, consecrate, set apart" (Qal). In other verb forms, it means "to show oneself holy or be treated as holy" *(Niph'al);* "to impose separation" on something or someone else *(Pi'el);* "to be made holy, consecrated, or dedicated" *(Pu'al);* "to set apart" for God as a gift *(Hiph'il);* and "to sanctify" oneself from impurity *(Hithpa'el).* The word *hieros* is the most frequent Greek term for "sacred" and marks out items which are owned by or associated with the gods. The central element in the word is "outside the realm of the ordinary," usually referring to supernatural power. Whereas for Greeks and Romans, natural elements and human beings, both living and dead, were often considered gods, Israel's God remains distinct from his creation.

Hebrew Bible

The holiness of God is composed of two major facets. On the one hand, the Holy One is the omnipotent "Other" whose mighty energy is represented by fire (Exod. 3:5; 19:12-23). His holiness is distinct, perfect, and sovereign. The psalmist exhorts the earth to tremble before the Holy One, who is always victorious (Pss. 96:9; 98:1). Israel is warned not to approach God's holiness directly; rather, it is mediated by the cult. Punishments for sacrilege are severe, including death (Exod. 33:20; Num. 4:20; 18:3; Judg. 13:22; 1 Kings 19:13). On the other hand, holiness is absolutely moral and undeniably good. Indeed, the Greek philosophers refer to "the Good" as the divine principle, but the Jewish god is a being concerned with the welfare of his people.

According to Jewish Scripture, all Israel is considered holy by divine election (Exod. 19:6; Deut. 7:4-6), but she must maintain her status by imitating God's holiness. The levitical command, "Be holy because I [God] am holy," first appears in the context of ritually pure food laws (Lev. 11:44). Israel maintains separation from pagans by distinctive rituals, for example, circumcision, Sabbath observance, food, and purity. The second instance of the call to holiness (Lev. 19:2) precedes a list of primarily ethical obligations, from respecting one's parents (19:3) and loving one's neighbor (19:18) to paying employee wages on time (19:13). Thus, Israel is exhorted to withdraw from what is morally evil and to emulate the divine holiness through a life of ethical goodness. Holiness is not mere separation *from* the world but a separation or dedication to perform the divine will *in* the world.

In the priestly system purity is necessary for the activation of holiness (Exod. 22:30 [Eng. 22:31]). Impurity of any kind, ritual or moral, can impinge on God's realm and bring destruction on the community. God's house and his agents, the priests, as well as all gifts brought to him, whether food offerings or animal sacrifices, are holy. Some items are *qôdeš qodāšîm,* "most holy": God's inner sanctuary, the high priest, and certain sacrificial offerings. As in other ancient cultures, sacred personnel and items in Israel are privileged and restricted from common usage. They must be physically perfect for use in the sanctuary.

Second Temple Judaism

In the era of the Second Temple, holiness intensified in Jewish circles. In particular, there was a tendency to extend the holiness of the Temple outward to include all of Jerusalem (cf. Isa. 52:1; Joel 4:17). Josephus reports that Antiochus III upheld Jerusalem's claim to purity even in nonfestival periods by forbidding impure animals or their hides from being brought into the city (*Ant.* 12.145-46).

This expansion of holiness in early Judaism is most obvious in the Dead Sea Scrolls. Personnel labeled *qôdeš qodāšîm* include all priests, not just the high priest (4Q397 55:6-8; 1QS 8:5-6; 9:2-8; cf. 4Q400 1:19). In the *Temple Scroll, qôdeš* applies to the entire city of the sanctuary and is enforced by severe purity regulations (11Q19 35:8-9; 45:7-12; 47:4; cf. "Jerusalem is the camp of holiness," 4Q394 3:10-13; CD 12:1-2). The Qumran community referred to itself as a "temple of men" (4Q174) set apart for Torah study in the desert (CD 20:2-7; 1QS 9:20). The group's holiness was supported by stringent purity laws. Physically impaired persons were considered a hindrance to the presence of the holy angels within the community (CD 15:15-16; 1QM 7:3-5; 4Q394 3:19-20; 4:1-4; cf. 11Q19 45:12-14).

Rabbinic Literature

While the rabbis analyzed the cultic aspect of holiness in detail (cf. *m. Qodašim*), they focused even more on the ethical goodness of holiness, especially as it relates to Israel. Favorite terms for expressing the beneficent divine presence in Israel are *Šekinah,* "Dwelling"; *Ruaḥ ha-Qōdeš,* "Holy Spirit"; and *Šem ha-Qōdeš,* "Holy Name." At the same time, Israel must maintain her status by observing the Torah: "Be holy, for as long as you fulfill my commandments you are sanctified, but if you neglect them you become profaned" (*Num. Rab.* 17:6). In particular, sexual immorality is antonymic to holiness (*Sifra* 93b; *Num. Rab.* 9:7).

The rabbis formulated the concept of *qiddush ha-Šem,* "hallowing the Name." A Jew can cause God's name to be sanctified, or acknowledged as holy, by doing deeds of mercy, like the maligned Sarah who still nursed the children of pagan women (*Gen. Rab.* 53:9; *Pirqe de Rabbi Eliezer* 146b). By imitating God's goodness, Israel actualizes his holiness in the world (cf. *Lev. Rab.* 24:4). The ultimate act of *qiddush ha-Šem* is to lay down one's life rather than succumb to idolatry (*b. Berakot* 61b).

Early Christianity

Christianity inherited the concept of holiness from Israelite and Second Temple Jewish tradition but reinterpreted it light of Jesus Christ. According to the New Testament, Jesus shares the inherent holiness of God, of which separation, power, and sinlessness are key elements (Heb. 7:26; cf. Rom. 1:3-4). Believers derive their holy status from their relationship with Christ (1 Cor. 1:30). As people of God, they are both holy by election and responsible for moral conduct (e.g., 2 Cor. 7:1; Eph. 5:27). The component of ritual purity in holiness gradually disappeared in Christianity.

BIBLIOGRAPHY

H. K. HARRINGTON 2001, *Holiness: Rabbinic Judaism in the Graeco-Roman World,* London: Routledge. • J. MILGROM 1991-2000, *Leviticus,* 3 vols., New York: Doubleday. • J. NAUDE 1999, "Holiness in the Dead Sea Scrolls," in *The Dead Sea Scrolls after Fifty Years: A Comprehensive Assessment,* ed. P. W. Flint and J. C. VanderKam, vol. 2, Leiden: Brill, 171-99.

HANNAH K. HARRINGTON

Homily

Although the New Testament provides evidence for preaching in synagogues after the weekly reading of the Torah and the Prophets (Luke 4:16-21; Acts 13:15), no homilies from the Second Temple period have survived in their original form. Yet, for well over a century scholars have speculated that certain Greek texts were based on or had incorporated Jewish homilies. These suggestions have been problematic, because we have no clear knowledge of the nature of synagogue homily from this period, and the arguments tend to be circular.

Textual Sources

Nevertheless, a number of monographs and essays have detected a synagogal-homiletical source behind a wide variety of Greek texts. These texts include passages in works that are now included among the Apocrypha and Pseudepigrapha (Susanna, 4 Maccabees, Epistle of Jeremiah, Tobit, Wisdom of Solomon, and parts of the *Testaments of the Twelve Patriarchs*) as well as sections of Josephus' and especially of Philo's writings. Various noncanonical Christian writings (e.g., *1 Clement, 2 Clement, Didache, Epistle of Barnabas,* and *Shepherd of Hermas*) have also been judged to be modeled, in whole or in part, on synagogue homilies. But it has been especially the New Testament that has invited the scrutiny of scholars. The speeches in Acts, especially Paul's sermon in chapter 13 and Stephen's speech in chapter 7; some of Jesus' sermons in the Gospels, particularly John 6:31-58, Luke 4:17-22, and Matthew 5–7; Hebrews, in whole or in part; James; and other smaller units (e.g., Romans 4; 1 Cor. 2:6-8; 10:1-14; Gal. 3:6-29) are thought to have originated as or been modeled on synagogue homilies.

Features Indicating Homiletic Origin

Homily and Diatribe

One of the most detailed treatments of the early Jewish homily was H. Thyen's monograph of 1955. Thyen surveyed a wide range of texts and believed he was able to discover the Jewish homilies or homiletical features underlying them. He maintained that the following features pointed toward a homiletical origin: use of first person plural in addressing the reader (audience), *Haustafeln* and vice lists, parenesis, rhetorical techniques such as anaphora, explanation of individual verses from the Septuagint "in homiletical fashion," invitations to prayer or praise of God, and especially the employment of diatribe (a dialogical style of argument that relies on the address of an imaginary opponent, the anticipation of possible objections, and the refutation of false conclusions). Thyen's work demonstrated the important connection between Jewish synagogue preaching (especially in the Diaspora) and early Christian teaching.

Logos Paraklēseōs

Others working on the genre of early (Second Temple) Jewish homily have sought to identify sermons from the synagogues by appealing to a common pattern. One of the suggested sermon types is the *logos paraklēseōs* or "word of exhortation" (cf. Acts 13:15; Heb. 13:22). Although several scholars have posited that this type of homily was common in the first century C.E. and that it influenced the New Testament, there is no firm agreement on the structure of these orations. L. Wills (1984) suggested the following structure: (1) a list of *exempla* — either scripture quotations or examples from the past or present (e.g. Acts 13:16-37); (2) a conclusion based on the *exempla* (e.g., Acts 13:38-39); and (3) an exhortation (e.g., Acts 13:40-41).

Inclusio Pattern

P. Borgen (1965) maintains that two works of Philo (*De Mutationes Nominum* 253-63; *Leg.* 3.162-68) and John 6:31-58 exhibit a pattern of arrangement that may have been common for the Jewish synagogues in the first century C.E.: (1) The opening and closing parts of the homily correspond to each other and paraphrase the scripture quotation. (2) In addition to the main quotation, there is at least one subordinate quotation from the Hebrew Scriptures. (3) Words from the scripture text are paraphrased or quoted in the homily. Each part of the text is then expounded in sequence.

Rabbinic Genres

Still other scholars have proposed that rabbinic types of homily so common in the midrashim of the second through sixth centuries C.E. *(Tanḥuma, Pisiqta de Rav Kahana,* and *Pisiqta Rabbati)* were already being used in the synagogues in the late Second Temple period. The most discussed of these genres is the proem (Hebr. *petiḥah*). The proem was tied to the weekly Torah reading by means of an artistic and creative connection with another scripture text, usually from the Writings *(ketuvîm).* The second text opened the proem, and the speaker then wove his "string of pearls" before quoting the Torah text at the end of the homily. J. W. Bowker (1967) asserted that Acts 13:17-41 was a "proem type" of sermon based on Deut. 4:25-46 and 1 Sam. 13:14. It does not have all the features of a true classical proem but witnesses to a time when the proem form was not entirely fixed. G. Gelardini (2005) suggests that Heb. 1:1–4:4 was originally a proem based on the Torah reading (Exod. 31:18–32:35) for the ninth day of the month of Av, the day of fasting and repentance.

A second rabbinic genre was the *yelammedenu* ("let [our rabbi] teach us") form. This form was less structured than the proem and was based on questions from the congregation about the Torah reading. Bowker proposes that Acts 15:14-21 and Romans 4 are early examples of this homiletic form (Bowker 1967). A. Finkel (1964) offers Mark 2:23-28, 3:1-6, and 10:1-15 as examples. Other scholars have been less confident that there are any examples in the Second Temple period of the *yelammedenu* form.

Influences on Synagogal Homilies

Some interpreters have concluded that the homiletical forms of the synagogue of the Second Temple period were a Jewish innovation, independent of classical-rhetorical influences. H. W. Attridge (1990), for example, insists that the "word of exhortation" genre was invented in Diaspora synagogues to help Jewish attendants understand the weekly scripture text. But others see the sermon types that would become standard in the talmudic period as already existing — though less fixed in form — by the first century C.E. The proem and *yelammedenu* types of homilies of a later period can still serve to interpret Greek texts of the late Second Temple Period, according to this view. If this is right, then the Palestinian, rabbinic homiletic tradition exerted the strongest influence on Jewish preaching even in the Diaspora. Still others look for influences from Greek culture. It has already been mentioned that Thyen believed that Greek diatribe was one of the most important distinguishing features of the preaching of the Hellenistic Jewish synagogues (Thyen 1955). C. C. Black (1988) has argued that the genre *logos paraklēseōs* is really only a slight variant of the classical-rhetorical outline and that it therefore developed under Greek influence. Accordingly, he offers the following outline of Paul's sermon in Acts based on Greco-Roman rhetorical conventions:

Acts 13:16b	*exordium*
Acts 13:17-25	*narratio*
Acts 13:26	*propositio*
Acts 13:27-37	*probatio*
Acts 13:38-41	epilogue

Criticisms

Critics of this approach (see especially Donfried 1974) have been hesitant to follow Thyen's results. In particular they charge that he (and those following his lead) failed adequately to define the homily genre and that he was uncritically dependent on R. Bultmann's treatment of the Cynic-Stoic diatribe. Others criticize alternate approaches, questioning whether rabbinic materials from the second to sixth centuries may be used to analyze first-century texts. J. Heinemann (1971) especially has doubted that the proem form was in use in the first century.

Assessment

There is still work to do to establish the structure and characteristics of the Jewish homily in the Second Temple period. The difficulty remains that we have no certain criteria with which to judge the hypothetical homilies. Thus, in the eyes of different interpreters a text such as the sermon of Acts 13 may be considered alternately an example of *logos paraklēseōs,* of proem, or of Greek rhetoric. Yet certain trends have emerged. First, most scholars think that at least some of the sermons and speeches of Acts were based on synagogal models, and most agree that Hebrews was originally a synagogue homily. Second, most interpreters seem inclined to use the rabbinic materials in spite of their late date. These materials offer the only certain examples of Jewish homily with which to compare the Greek texts from the Second Temple period.

BIBLIOGRAPHY

H. W. ATTRIDGE 1990, "Paraenesis in a Homily *(logos paraklēseōs):* The Possible Location of, and Socialization in the 'Epistle to the Hebrews,'" *Semeia* 50: 211-26. • C. C. BLACK 1988, "The Rhetorical Form of the Hellenistic Jewish and Early Christian Sermon: A Response to Lawrence Wills," *HTR* 81: 1-18. • P. BORGEN 1965, *Bread from Heaven,* Leiden: Brill. • J. W. BOWKER 1967, "Speeches in Acts: A Study in Proem and Yelammedenu Form," *NTS* 14: 96-111. • W. CARR 1977, "The Rulers of This Age: 1 Corinthians 1.6-8," *NTS* 23: 20-35. • K. P. DONFRIED 1974, *The Setting of Second Clement in Early Christianity,* Leiden: Brill. • A. FINKEL 1964, *The Pharisees and the Teacher of Nazareth,* Leiden: Brill. • G. GELARDINI 2005, "Hebrews: An Ancient Synagogue Homily for *Tisha Be-Av,*" in *Hebrews: Contemporary Methods, New Insights,* ed. G. Gelardini, Leiden: Brill, 107-27. • J. HEINEMANN 1971, "The Proem in the Aggadic Midrashim," in *Studies in Aggadah and Folk-Literature,* ed. J. Heinemann and D. Noy, *Scripta Hierosolymitana* 22, Jerusalem: Magnes, 100-122. • M. SMITH 1951, *Tannaitic Parallels to the Gospels,* Philadelphia: Society of Biblical Literature. • W. R. STEGNER 1988, "The Ancient Jewish Synagogue Homily," in *Greco-Roman Literature and the New Testament,* ed. D. E. Aune, Atlanta: Scholars Press, 51-67. • J. SWETNAM 1969, "On the Literary Genre of the 'Epistle' to the Hebrews," *NovT* 11: 261-69. • H. THYEN 1955, *Der Stil der Jüdisch-Hellenistischen Homilie,* Göttingen: Vandenhoeck & Ruprecht. • L. WILLS 1984, "The Form of the Sermon in Hellenistic Judaism and Early Christianity," *HTR* 77: 277-99.

DAVID A. FIENSY

Horoscopes

Modern scholars have (mis) identified two texts from Qumran as horoscopes: the Hebrew manuscript 4Q186 and the Aramaic manuscript 4Q561 (another text, 4Q534, was only initially referred to as horoscopic in nature). Intriguingly, 4Q186 is written in reverse order from left to right and in different scripts (square, paleo-Hebrew, Greek, and cryptic). Both copies date between 50 B.C.E. and 20 C.E.

The remains of these texts do not contain the actual horoscopes of particular individuals. 4Q186 is concerned with personal astrology, referring to the horoscope *(molad)* under which someone was born (4Q186 1 ii 8-9). But it does not have the usual features of ancient horoscopes, such as the date of birth or references to the zodiacal position of the sun, moon, or any of the five planets known in antiquity (Mercury, Venus, Mars, Jupiter, and Saturn). Rather, 4Q186 represents a catalogue of physiognomic and astrological content. 4Q561 is a purely physiognomic list and has no astrological references at all. It gives the physical descriptions from head to toe of different types of people, with some hints of predictions.

Many scholars regard 4Q186 as an astrological text that deals with the influence of the stars on the human body and spirit. The human spirit *(ruaḥ)* is divided on a nine-point scale between the "house of light" and the "house of darkness," which scholars interpret in light of the "Treatise on the Two Spirits" in the *Rule of the Community* (1QS 3:13–4:26). Measuring the amount of light and darkness in people, 4Q186 would be another example of the dualistic worldview of the Qumran community.

Schmidt argues that 4Q186 makes predictions about people's physiognomies and divisions between light and darkness on the basis of their date of conception, not of birth. Schmidt uses the subdivision of the zodiac into thirty-six decans (three for each sign), assumes half of them are diurnal (in the "house of light") and half nocturnal (in the "house of darkness"), and presupposes a nine-month duration of pregnancy. 4Q186 indicates the date of conception by the particular decan rising above the eastern horizon at that time, "foot of *Taurus*" being the first decan of that sign (4Q186 1 ii 9). This allows one to designate nine variable decans as diurnal or nocturnal during pregnancy, explaining the division between light and darkness in 4Q186.

Albani (1999) rightly argues that the words "foot of *Taurus*" presuppose another partition of the zodiacal sign, indicating the point where the sign is divided into parts above (the "house of light") and below the horizon (the "house of darkness"). The ascendant (in Greek *horoskopos*) is that specific part of the sign rising above the eastern horizon at the moment of birth. This is what is referred to by "foot of *Taurus*" (4Q186 1 ii 8-9). Using an ancient astrological list (Rhetorius-Teucer) in which *Taurus* is divided into nine parts and reading *rewaḥ* ("space") instead of *ruaḥ*, Albani suggests that the sign *Taurus* has a space of six parts in the house of light, which have already risen above the horizon, and of three parts in the house of darkness, which are still below the horizon (4Q186 1 ii 7-8).

The division of the zodiacal sign in 4Q186 has a complex astrological background, combining and distorting the concepts of *dodecatemoria* (the division of the signs into twelve parts of 2;30° each) and of *melothesia* (the idea that planets or signs control a specific part of the human body). However, what is divided is not the sign, but its spirit. The reading *rewaḥ* is unlikely. The division between the "house of light" and the "house of darkness" is astrologically the result of the ascendant's position vis-à-vis the eastern horizon, but in 4Q186 this is understood in terms of the zodiacal spirit being divided between light and darkness, which determines its nature. 4Q186 maps out the connections between people of different types of physiognomy that, as a consequence of their moment of birth, accompany them. Structured according to physiognomic descriptions, 4Q186 reverses the relation between astrology and physiognomics. From a person's physiognomy an observer may gather astrological knowledge. According to 4Q186, the human body reveals the zodiacal sign that ascended at the moment of birth and the division of the zodiacal spirit between light and darkness.

BIBLIOGRAPHY

M. ALBANI 1999, "Horoscopes in the Qumran Scrolls," in *The Dead Sea Scrolls after Fifty Years: A Comprehensive Assessment*, vol. 2, ed. P. W. Flint and J. C. VanderKam, Leiden: Brill, 279-330. • P. S. ALEXANDER 1996, "Physiognomy, Initiation, and Rank in the Qumran Community," *Geschichte–Tradition–Reflexion*, vol. 1, ed. H. Cancik et al., vol. 1, Tübingen: Mohr-Siebeck, 385-94. • M. POPOVIĆ 2007, *Reading the Human Body: Physiognomics and Astrology in the Dead Sea Scrolls and Hellenistic-Early Roman Period Judaism*, Leiden: Brill. • F. SCHMIDT 1997, "Astrologie juive ancienne: Essai d'interprétation de *4QCryptique* (4Q186)," *RevQ* 18: 125-41.

MLADEN POPOVIĆ

Hymns, Prayers, and Psalms

Various developments in the scholarly understanding of late Second Temple hymns, prayers, and psalms have taken place in the last several decades. These advances owe in part to the discovery and study of the Qumran texts, which sparked a renewed interest in the literature of early Judaism. Study of the texts that fall broadly into this category offers insight into the complex process of scripturalization that developed during this period. These deeply human expressions of joy or despair directed *to* God were transformed into sacred Scripture fundamentally understood to be *from* God (Kugel 1986). Part of this process involved cloaking the new composition within an authoritative guise by using classic biblical phraseology and traditional interpretive motifs (Newman 1999). For example, Neh. 9:6-31 makes strong use of biblical imagery, specifically Deuteronomic language and motifs interspersed with Priestly elements, in its rehearsal of salvation history in vv. 5-31, concluding with a petition that appeals to God's graciousness and mercy in vv. 32-37. Similarly, the prayer in Jdt. 9:2-14 makes use of biblical language and motifs from Exodus 15 and Genesis 34.

Hymns, prayers, and psalms from the Second Temple period make extensive and varied use of scriptural allusions and may also employ exegetical maneuvers similar to those found in biblical texts. The intentional use and redeployment of Scripture is not a sign of the lack of creativity of these ancient authors but a feature of a complex process that functions to authorize these compositions by associating them with the authority of older texts (Najman 2003). The authors freely drew upon a number of compositional techniques. These include quoting or alluding to distinct biblical passages, modeling new compositions on one or more biblical passages, creating a chain of quotations in the style of a *florilegium*, assembling a pastiche of biblical quotations and allusions into a new composition, and freely composing new compositions based on traditional biblical motifs or images.

Formal Categorization and Literary Styles

In classifying this body of literature, problems arise when formal categories and literary styles are derived from biblical exemplars. Postbiblical hymns, prayers, and psalms have often been described in light of preexisting literary categories formulated from classical Hebrew models, resulting in characterizations that cast later writings as imitations of varying degrees or as mixed forms. Scholarly descriptions of postbiblical compositions as "hybrid" forms are unsatisfying and sometimes reflect a modern lack of familiarity with ancient compositional techniques. The limitations of using categories based on classical biblical exemplars are especially apparent in the case of the hymns, prayers, and psalms discovered at Qumran, many of which had not been previously known. Indeed, categories exert powerful influence over how texts are understood, yet in the case of hymns, prayers, and psalms the categories themselves are shifting and are not consistently defined in the scholarly literature.

In a similar fashion, the literary styles of postbiblical poetical and liturgical writings have often been assessed on expectations formed from classical biblical Hebrew poetry rather than from comparisons with contemporaneous writings. This has resulted in unhelpful characterizations of Second Temple writings, which often freely used biblical images and language, as imitations of varying degrees of success. One example of this comes from the book of Sirach, which when compared with the literary style found in the classical Hebrew book of Proverbs was found to be deficient in one way or another. These expectations also colored how the first generation of Scrolls scholars viewed these newly discovered writings. Early assessments of the poetic style of the *Hodayot* reflect a bias toward classical biblical forms and style, so much so that the Qumran style was described early on as "very poor poetry characterized by irregular meter, rather weak use of parallelism, frequent and monotonous repetition of words, and the apparent absence of any firm principle of construction" (Thiering 1963). These scholarly perceptions rightly appear outdated to readers today. Such an approach fails to do justice to the particular aspects of poetry of this time, particularly in light of the developments taking place in the current scholarly understanding of the processes of scripturalization and canonization in the Second Temple period.

A number of questions remain about the relationship between hymns, prayers, and psalms during the late Second Temple period to other writings of that time. Their appearance throughout Jewish apocalypses, the prominence of wisdom motifs within them (e.g., 1QH; Bar. 3:9–4:4), and their precise role in the liturgy and worship of the late Second Temple period have yet to be fully studied.

Drawing Distinctions between Hymns, Prayers, and Psalms

The traditional scholarly conceptualization of categories based on classical Hebrew types typically distinguishes between the manner of performance of these types, identifying "hymns" as sung poetic compositions that praise God, "psalms" as poetic liturgical compositions, and "prayers" as recited prose compositions.

Of the three categories prayer is perhaps used most loosely to refer inclusively to any communication between humanity and God. There are many ways scholars have attempted to restrict the broad understanding of prayer as any communication between humanity and God. The first of these attempts limits this category to prose compositions and not poetry (into which would fall "hymns" and "psalms"). Even so, some scholars have even expanded the idea of prayer to include every type of poetry used in the worship of God. This standard approach of distinguishing literature on the basis of prosaic or poetic characteristics may wrongly presume that the distinction between prose and poetry in the ancient world strictly followed such literary conventions at all (Kugel 1981). The category of prayer has also been restricted to petition and not praise. Such a range in meaning of the idea of prayer may have also been understood in the ancient world. Plato evidently viewed prayer primarily as petition (*Politics* 290d), while both Philo and Origen presumed prayer to include both petition and praise (Philo, *Spec. Leg.* 1.224 and *De Plantatione* 135; Origen, *On Prayer* 14.2). Furthermore, it is possible to distinguish between various understandings of petition and praise, depending upon their different purposes. Yet another attempt to delimit prayer texts may specify that they include only the second-person address to God, while "hymns" or "psalms" may be composed in either third-person or second-person address to God. These issues are further complicated by the question of whether or not a prayer composition actually functioned as a means of communicating with God, as it is possible that its composition may have been for a literary purpose.

Prayer includes the following distinct elements: a sender, a message, and a purpose. This purpose may be to seek results or to maintain relationships. The sender may be an individual or a community, and the message may be one of praise, thanksgiving, lament, petition, or contrition. One challenge to the study of prayer in early Judaism is that prior to the discovery of the Dead Sea Scrolls, relatively few written prayer texts survived in any significant degree prior to the ninth-century Jewish copies of the *Siddur.* From what can be pieced together from the prayer texts at Qumran, the community of the Dead Sea Scrolls had a rich prayer life that included morning and evening prayers as well as daily and Sabbath prayers. Examples of collections of these prayers are *The Daily Prayers* (4Q503), *Words of the Luminaries* (4Q504), and the *Songs of Sabbath Sacrifice* (4Q400-407, 11Q17). Among the interesting themes that appear in these early prayer texts is that of praying with or like the angels (4Q503) and prayer as a sacrificial offering apart from the Temple cult (1QS 9:4-5) (Schuller 2000). How much of this can be extended to early Christian and contemporary Jewish practice is not clear at this time, although some have argued in favor of seeing at least some of the Qumran prayer texts as presectarian in origin (4Q504).

Strictly literary studies of prayer literature from this time period may be enriched by social-scientific approaches that examine these texts from a cross-cultural perspective with a focus on the phenomenon of communication (Malina 1980). Malina's definition of prayer is as follows: "a socially meaningful act of communication, bearing directly upon persons perceived as somehow supporting, maintaining, and controlling the order of existence of the one praying, and performed with the purpose of getting results from or in the interaction of communication" (Malina 1980: 215). The five elements of prayer according to this model include (1) the sender (either an individual or a group); (2) the message (petition, adoration, contrition, or thanksgiving); (3) the medium of the prayer (verbal and nonverbal forms of communication of many types); (4) the recipient (God); and (5) the purpose or the results that are sought (Malina 1980).

One area of growing interest in recent scholarship is the proliferation of confessional and penitential prayer during the Second Temple period (Werline 1998; cf. Bautch 2003). The biblical penitential psalms category (Psalms 6, 32, 38, 51, 102, 130, and 143) was traditionally classified as part of the broader group of lament psalms by Gunkel (1933). Yet, with the exception of Psalm 51, not all of these were thought by him to exhibit strong penitential content. Instead, this category was a remnant of medieval theological readings of them. Scholarship on this type of literature was reconceptualized with the work of Westermann and his theological discussion of the influence of Deuteronomic theology upon the form of the lament (Westermann 1981). Pure lament and complaint against God becomes impermissible in light of the growing Deuteronomic emphasis on the guilt of Judah's disobedience. Recent scholarly understandings of penitential prayer have tended to move away from a strictly form-critical approach in favor of a traditio-historical perspective that takes into account the impact of these theological and ideological influences from the Second Temple period.

Penitential prayers are characterized by the following elements: confession of sins, acknowledging that God's judgment is just, rehearsal of God's mercy in history; and a concluding appeal to God for mercy in the current context (see Ezra 9:6-15, Neh. 1:5-11 and 9:6-37, and Dan. 9:4-19; Pr. Azar. 1:3-22; *Words of the Luminaries* frg. 1-2 lines 5-7; *Communal Confession* [4Q393]). More importantly, current scholars recognize how a wide range of social settings, including contemporary experiences like the Holocaust, and a variety of literary contexts, as well as performance, all contribute to the shaping of modern understandings of genre (Nasuti 1999).

Hymns and Psalms

Both hymns and psalms are sung poetic compositions and so will be discussed together. These texts may be embedded in other literature and also found in collections (Psalter, *Psalms of Solomon,* Hellenistic Synagogal Prayers, *Odes of Solomon,* 1QH). Hymns proper are specified as poetic compositions sung in praise of God. In classic literary studies of these texts, hymns may be understood as a specific type of the larger category of psalms. While psalms are also loosely discussed in the scholarly literature, perhaps the best place to begin is with the classic understandings of these terms. Hermann Gunkel (1933), in his classic formulation of form-critical categories for the biblical psalms, identified seven types: hymns of praise, laments (including psalms of trust and thanksgiving psalms), royal psalms, wisdom psalms, liturgical psalms, and historical psalms. Gunkel's form-critical work presumed that these literary types originated in a cultic context, and this operative assumption continued in the work of Sigmund Mowinckel, who examined the biblical forms from the perspective of the wider ancient Near Eastern literary context (Mowinckel 1962).

The presumed relationship between the Temple cult and literary form is far less certain in the current scholarly study of the hymns, prayers, and psalms dated from the time of Alexander's conquest through the Bar Kokhba Revolt (ca. 321 B.C.E.–135 C.E.). While older scholarship may have confidently situated this type of literature within a specific context of worship, the automatic relationship between prayer literature and the cult is less frequently assumed today. If the role of the biblical psalms in the Temple worship is unclear, it is all the more unclear what liturgical function nonbiblical psalms and hymns might have enjoyed outside of a Temple context. It may be said, however, that broad statements suggesting that the rise of prayer literature during the late Second Temple period was a sign that prayer was replacing Temple sacrifice are inadequate in accounting for all of the varied developments taking place during this time. The relationship between prayer literature and the sacrificial cult is far more nuanced and complex than has been previously thought (Falk 2000), and far too broad a topic to treat adequately here. Clearly the scholarly understanding of the poetic and liturgical compositions during this period is complicated by the many unanswered historical questions about the nature of the composition of these writings and the experience of these texts within the cult.

Literary Contexts

Apocrypha and Pseudepigrapha

Hymns, prayers, and psalms are well represented in the apocryphal and pseudepigraphal literature. Because they are discrete anonymous compositions that make use of stereotypical language, and are easily moved from one literary context to another, questions concerning their provenance and authorship are difficult to answer. This mobility may also complicate the identification of which literary context is primary and which is secondary. Some examples of these "floating" compositions that have multiple literary contexts include the prayer found in both Baruch 5 and the *Psalms of Solomon* 11. Another example of this phenomenon is the apocryphal Psalm 151 A/B, known only in Greek, Latin, and Syriac manuscripts, which may be included in the Qumran scroll 11QPs^{a}, although the particular form found at Qumran has significant variations. Independent hymns, prayers, and psalms originally composed for and embedded in narrative contexts may have found their way into liturgical use. At the same time, those compositions that may have begun as liturgical writings may have been absorbed into different literary contexts at later times. A significant number of penitential prayers and confessions are found embedded in narrative contexts (e.g., Ezra 9:6-15; Neh. 9:6-37; Dan. 9:4-19; Jdt. 9:2-14; Tob. 3:2-6, 11-15; Add. Esth. 13:9-17; 14:3-19; Bar. 1:15–3:8; 2 *Bar.* 48:2-24; 54:1-22; 1 Macc. 3:50-53; 4:30-33; 3 Macc. 2:2-20; 6:2-15; *Jub.* 10:3-6; *Joseph and Aseneth* 12–13; *Prayer of Manasseh;* Josephus, *Ant.* 4.3.2; 2.16.1). While it is difficult to determine with certainty if these hymns, prayers, and psalms were primarily liturgical or literary, compositions embedded in literary contexts often fit well the plot and progression of the larger narrative context (Chesnutt and Newman 1997).

Dead Sea Scrolls

A wide-ranging collection of hymns, prayers, and psalms constitutes a significant portion of the total number of manuscripts catalogued from the Qumran discovery. Approximately 200 nonbiblical psalms and prayer texts, including many not previously known to scholars, have been counted. Even so, there was little indication during the first twenty-five years of Scrolls scholarship that hymns, prayers, and psalms would constitute such a significant proportion of the literature from Qumran, and even now much work in analyzing these finds remains to be done (Schuller 1994: 156).

While no complete copy of the Psalter was found at Qumran, the book was well represented among the biblical books, numbering 39 copies and including manuscripts found in Qumran Caves 1, 2, 3, 5, 6, 8, and 11, Naḥal Ḥever, and Masada. Many of the nonbiblical hymns, prayers, and psalms identified at Qumran appear in various literary contexts. In addition to collections *(Songs of Sabbath Sacrifice* and *Hodayot),* they appear embedded in various types of works such as the rule texts (1QS 10) and in a number of pseudepigraphic writings (prayers of Abraham in 1QapGen, of Levi in 4QTLevi ar[b], and of Joseph in 4Q372, and prayers in copies of Tobit and *Jubilees*) (Chazon and Bernstein 1997).

According to Schuller, there are many reasons why this body of literature has been among the slowest of the Qumran texts to be explored to a full degree even sixty years after their discovery (Schuller 2004: 412-15). The primary challenge of working with this type of literature was the poor condition of the texts themselves. Much of the early work on these texts sought to prepare an *editio princeps* and demanded specialized skills. Reconstructions of texts were based on a careful study of the material aspects of fragments since there was no literary exemplar. For various reasons peculiar to this scroll, a revised critical edition of the large collection of compositions known as the *Hodayot* from Cave 1 appeared only in 2009. This particular collection of writings unknown to scholars prior to 1947, has been classified at different times as hymns and as psalms. It was not until much later that scholars began systematically studying these compositions from a literary and theological perspective. Even today, sixty years after their discovery, there remains much work to be done with this literature from Qumran.

One challenge to studying this type of literature from Qumran is the classification of writings into sectarian or nonsectarian and liturgical or nonliturgical. While it was commonly assumed in the early generation of scholarship on the Scrolls that anything nonbiblical was automatically deemed sectarian, today the discussion of sectarian classification continues with far more nuance. Scholars are increasingly reluctant to assign a sectarian designation to texts since it is possible for a text to be authored by one community and used later by another. It is also conceivable for sectarian authors to have composed nonpolemical writings. Problems with classification continue with the discussion of the liturgical or nonliturgical status of some of the compositions from Qumran, although here the presence of explicit marks of liturgical usage may make some easier than others to identify. These signs may include the use of the first-person plural and internal reference to a particular liturgical occasion. Liturgical use may also be indicated by the presence of formulaic elements such as "and they shall answer and they shall say," as may be seen in the case of 4Q503, 4Q266, and 4Q286. The thirteen *Songs of the Sabbath Sacrifice* have been situated by most scholars within the liturgical cycle of one quarter of a full year. Other texts that have been argued to be a presectarian liturgical composition are *4QDibHam,* the collection of daily prayers (4Q503), and festival prayers (4Q507-9; 1Q34) (Chazon 1992).

Early Christian Literature

Many hymns, prayers, and psalms found in early Christian literature bear a strong resemblance to Jewish forms, exhibiting literary features such as parallelism and extended descriptions commonly found in Hebrew poetical and liturgical writings (e.g., the *Magnificat* [Luke 1:46-55], the *Benedictus* [Luke 1:68-79], and the *Nunc Dimittis* [Luke 2:29-32]). Fragments of longer hymnic compositions appear in the Pauline corpus (Eph. 5:14; 1 Tim. 3:16 and 6:15-16; 2 Tim. 2:11-13; Titus 3:4-7; Phil. 2:6-11) and in the book of Revelation (1:4-8; 4:8, 11; 5:9-10, 12; 11:15, 17-18; 15:3-4; 22:17). These hymnic fragments may include liturgical or doctrinal emphases.

Syriac literature provides a particularly rich source of information about hymns, prayers, and psalms in early Christianity. Early collections of Christian poetical literature that may have had a liturgical background include the *Odes of Solomon,* which are dated to approximately the second century C.E. in Syria. These writings have survived in Greek and Syriac, with a few compositions having been absorbed into the Greek *Pistis Sophia,* an early Gnostic work (Brock 1979). Both these and the hymns written by Ephrem the Syrian (d. 373) are notable for their rich imagery and use of Scripture. Both doctrinal and liturgical emphases are obvious in Ephrem's hymns, and their exegetical maneuvers were long noted as being like those found in Jewish interpretative writings. An example of early Christian prayer texts is found in the *Acts of Thomas,* which was written in Syriac but later translated into Greek. This text contains a number of prayers of interest for the study of the development of Christian baptismal liturgy as they provide evidence for the practice of anointing baptism. Much remains to be done in the study of how the hymns, prayers, and psalms in early Christian writings may be related to the developments observed in early Jewish literature.

BIBLIOGRAPHY

R. J. BAUTCH 2003, *Developments in Genre between Post-Exilic Penitential Prayers and the Psalms of Communal Lament,* Atlanta: Scholars Press. • S. P. BROCK 1979, *The Holy Spirit in the Syrian Baptismal Tradition,* Poona: Anita Printers. • E. G. CHAZON 1992, "Is *Divrei ha-me'orot* a Sectarian Prayer?" in *The Dead Sea Scrolls: Forty Years of Research,* ed. D. Dimant and U. Rappaport, Leiden: Brill, 3-17. • E. G. CHAZON AND M. J. BERNSTEIN 1997, "An Introduction to Prayer at Qumran," in *Prayer from Alexander to Constantine,* ed. M. Kiley et al., New York: Routledge, 9-13. • R. D. CHESNUTT AND J. NEWMAN 1997, "Prayers in the Apocrypha and Pseudepigrapha," in *Prayer from Alexander to Constantine,* ed. M. Kiley et al., New York: Routledge, 38-42. • D. FALK 2000, "Qumran Prayer Texts and the Temple," in *Sapiential, Liturgical and Poetical Texts from Qumran,* ed. D. K. Falk,

F. García Martínez, and E. M. Schuller, Leiden: Brill. • H. GUNKEL 1933, *Einleitung in die Psalmen: Die Gattungen der religiösen Lyrik Israels,* Göttingen: Vandenhoeck & Ruprecht. • J. L. KUGEL 1981, *The Idea of Biblical Poetry,* Baltimore: Johns Hopkins University Press. • B. J. MALINA 1980, "What is Prayer?" *TBT* 18: 214-20. • S. MOWINCKEL 1962, *The Psalms in Israel's Worship,* New York: Abingdon; rpt. Grand Rapids: Eerdmans, 2004. • H. NAJMAN 2003, *Seconding Sinai: The Development of Mosaic Discourse in Second Temple Judaism,* Leiden: Brill. • H. P. NASUTI 1999, *Defining the Sacred Songs: Genre, Tradition, and the Post-Critical Interpretation of the Psalms,* Sheffield: Sheffield Academic Press. • J. H. NEWMAN 1999, *Praying by the Book: The Scripturalization of Prayer in Second Temple Judaism,* Atlanta: Scholars Press. • J. H. NEYREY 2007, *Give God the Glory: Ancient Prayer and Worship in Cultural Perspective,* Grand Rapids: Eerdmans. • E. M. SCHULLER 1994, "Prayer, Hymnic, and Liturgical Texts," in *The Community of the Renewed Covenant: The Notre Dame Symposium on the Dead Sea Scrolls,* ed. E. Ulrich and J. VanderKam, Notre Dame: University of Notre Dame Press, 153-71. • E. M. SCHULLER 2000, "Petitionary Prayer and the Religion of Qumran," in *Religion in the Dead Sea Scrolls,* ed. J. J. Collins and R. A. Kugler, Grand Rapids: Eerdmans, 29-45. • E. M. SCHULLER 2004, "Prayer at Qumran," in *Prayer from Tobit to Qumran,* ed. R. Egger-Wenzel and J. Corley, Berlin: de Gruyter, 411-28. • E. M. SCHULLER 2006, "Prayers and Psalms from the Pre-Maccabean Period," *DSD* 13: 306-18. • H. STEGEMANN WITH E. SCHULLER 2009, *Qumran Cave 1.III: 1QHodayot^{a}, with Incorporation of 1QHodayot^{b} and 4QHodayot$^{a\text{-}f}$,* DJD 40, Oxford: Clarendon. • B. THIERING 1963, "The Poetic Forms of the Hodayot," *JSS* 8: 189-209. • C. WESTERMANN 1981, *Praise and Lament in the Psalms,* trans. K. R. Crim and R. N. Soulen, Atlanta: John Knox. • R. A. WERLINE 1998, *Penitential Prayer in Second Temple Judaism: The Development of a Religious Institution,* Atlanta: Scholars Press.

ANGELA KIM HARKINS

I

Idols and Images

The Mosaic Law forbids Jews to venerate gods other than Yahweh the God of Israel and stipulates that Yahweh jealously guards his claim to exclusivity. Unrelated to this stance in origin, but easily connected with it, is the aniconic character of the cult of Yahweh in the Jerusalem Temple, at least in the Persian and later periods. In the Hellenistic and Roman periods, the philosophical implications of this matter were discovered and developed.

No Other Gods

The prohibition of making images of living beings to prostrate oneself before them (e.g., Exod. 20:4-5, 23; 34:17; Lev. 19:4; 26:1; Deut. 4:15-19; 5:8) was originally directed against the cult of other divine beings than the main deity of Judah in the Temple of Jerusalem. The prohibition was expanded to include the setting up of images in Jerusalem of any living being, regardless of whether they were actively venerated or not; the simple risk of images attracting admiration from their beholders (thus detracting from the total devotion due to the God of Israel) was sufficient reason to interdict all images in Jerusalem.

In the first century C.E. Jewish sensitivities about images desecrating the Holy City by their presence seem to have reached a high point. Josephus has several accounts of Jewish resistance, sometimes violent, against the introduction of Roman iconic symbols into the city, including a golden eagle erected by Herod over the great gate of the Temple (*J.W.* 1.650); standards with the image of Caesar, introduced by Pilate (*J.W.* 2.169; *Ant.* 18.55; Philo, *Leg.* 299–305, refers to the same episode, but in his report the objects in question were gilded shields attached to the façade of Herod's palace in Jerusalem), and a statue of Emperor Gaius (Josephus, *J.W.* 2.95; *Ant.* 28.261; cf. *Vita* 2.73, 75; Philo, *Leg.* 184–89).

Yet Josephus seems unbothered by images on several other occasions, as in his description of the large carved animals adorning Hyrcanus' palace in Transjordan (*Ant.* 12.230) and the rich decoration of Herod's palace in Jerusalem (*J.W.* 5.181). There is reason to assume, then, that a rigorous stance against images in Jerusalem was not always the general rule. It may be that the Roman imperial cult was felt to be a particularly offensive form of idolatry; or it may perhaps be that first-century-C.E. resistance against Roman rule in general fueled Judean fervor in this respect (for both Josephus' ambivalence toward images, and the waves of iconoclasm in first-century Palestine, even outside Jerusalem, see Vogel 1999). The latter possibility would form an analogy with the Maccabean era, when Antiochus IV Epiphanes' cultic reforms (which probably included the erection of an idol in the Temple; see Dan. 9:27; 11:31; 12:11; 1 Macc. 1:54; cf. 1:43) were used by the Hasmoneans to incite popular resistance against Seleucid rule (cf. Gruen 1998; Fine 2005).

Aniconic Cult and Monotheism

The historical reason why there was no image of God in the Jerusalem Temple is unknown; if there ever was one (as has been argued), it may have been stolen by the Babylonians when they conquered Jerusalem. In any case, the cultic regulations preserved in the Mosaic laws assume that there was none, and evidence from non-Jewish sources confirms this. When the Roman general Pompey entered the Holy of Holies in the Jerusalem Temple, he was amazed to find it empty.

When asked for the reason why the Jerusalem cult was aniconic, Jewish authors in the Hellenistic and Roman periods are often seen to identify their God with the supreme divine being of Hellenistic philosophy, the divinity that transcends all, and therefore cannot be described or depicted with the limited means available to creatures (see, e.g., *Sib. Or.* 3.11-14). Indeed, Greek visitors to Jerusalem were impressed by the aniconic cult of the Jews, because they, too, believed that it reflected monotheism (or pantheism; see, e.g., Strabo, *Geography* 16.2.36; Cassius Dio, *Roman History* 37.15.2; for further references, see Stern 1974: 306); monotheism as a philosophical principle was highly valued in Hellenistic intellectual circles.

Other anti-Jewish pagan authors mocked their aniconism and cast suspicion on Jewish monotheism as an expression of scorn for other gods (e.g., Tacitus, *History* 5.5.4-5), or atheism. The mockery, however, was gladly reciprocated: Jewish literature knows numerous instances of authors who ridicule the pagan habit of making images of the gods and venerating them (e.g., Bel and the Dragon; Epistle of Jeremiah; *Joseph and Aseneth* 13; *Jubilees* 11; 12; 20; 22; *Letter of Aristeas* 134-38; Wisdom of Solomon 13–15; Philo, *De Decalogo* 66; Josephus, *Ag. Ap.* 2.252; *Apocalypse of Abraham*). The ridicule of idolatry was also very much in vogue among pagan philosophers. Therefore, it seems that the Jewish authors mentioned were following a more general trend, although many of the literary motifs used by the Jewish authors are already known in the Hebrew Bible (Tromp 1995).

Jewish Hostility toward Idols outside Judea

Outside Judea images representing various deities were everywhere and impossible to ignore. Jews outside Judea who wished to take a principled aniconic and monotheistic stance were bound to be faced with various problems.

First, rejecting the cults of the cities in which they lived would block them from full integration into society. For people to be regarded as full members of society, it was required that they participate in the rituals and festivities connected with the local deities. This is most clearly illustrated by the famous passage from Apion's writings, quoted by Josephus, where it is scornfully asked why Jews, if they want to be Alexandrians, do not respect the Alexandrian gods (*Ag. Ap.* 2.6).

Second, the rejection of sacrifices to local gods as idolatrous denied Jews access to the main supply of meat, since the right to slaughter animals was usually reserved for temples, where meat was offered to the gods before it was sold to the public (Berthiaume 1982). Since all meat on sale was regarded as sacrificial meat, many Jews considered its consumption illicit. A decree of Julius Caesar preserved by Josephus (*Ant.* 14.215-16) permits the Jews of Parium to enjoy their own *thiasoi.* This term normally applies to sacrificial meals; it seems that in this case, the Jewish community of Parium received permission to have their own communal meals, and use animals slaughtered by themselves or according to their own rites. That this explicit permission was apparently needed illustrates that the Jewish rejection of idolatry could cause them practical problems in daily life.

Third, a rigorous attitude toward images could even restrict Jews' moving about in public space: the cities where they lived were full of images of deities, and even looking at these while passing by could be construed as a form of reverence toward them (Blidstein 1974). The avoidance of images in public space does not seem to have been discussed before the rabbinic age.

Adaptability

Although many Jews were prepared to bear the full burden of their rejection of images, even outside Jerusalem and Judea, there is evidence that others were willing to make concessions. For instance, Josephus, who firmly disapproved of setting up idols in Jerusalem, also relates that Herod took part in sacrifices to the Roman gods when he thought this appropriate. Josephus himself shows no sign of disapproval while narrating this event (*Ant.* 14.388). Most of all, however, the very fact that there were Jews who were fully integrated into Greek societies suggests that they must have been willing to compromise, even on the matter of offering sacrifice to local deities (Rajak 2001).

As a final point, it should be noted that images in Jewish houses (see, e.g., 2 Macc. 2:29) and even synagogues (e.g., the spectacular frescoes in the third-century-C.E. synagogue of Dura-Europos; see Kraeling 1956) bear witness to an attitude that did not mistake every image for an idol. This is particularly clear in the archaeological record for the second century C.E. onward (Fine 2005).

BIBLIOGRAPHY

S. BARTON, ED. 2007, *Idolatry: False Worship in the Bible, Early Judaism and Christianity,* London: Clark/Continuum. • G. BERTHIAUME 1982, *Les rôles du mágeiros: Etude sur la boucherie, la cuisine et le sacrifice dans la Grèce ancienn,* Leiden: Brill. • G. J. BLIDSTEIN 1974, "R. Yohanan, Idolatry, and Public Privilege," *JSJ* 5: 154-61. • S. FINE 2005, *Art and Judaism in the Greco-Roman World: Toward a New Jewish Archaeology,* Cambridge: Cambridge University Press. • E. S. GRUEN 1998, *Heritage and Hellenism: The Reinvention of Jewish Tradition,* Berkeley: University of California Press, 1-40. • C. H. KRAELING 1956, *The Synagogue: The Excavations at Dura-Europos, Final Report VIII, Part 1,* New Haven: Yale University Press. • T. RAJAK 2001, "Jews and Christians as Groups in a Pagan World," in eadem, *The Jewish Dialogue with Greece and Rome: Studies in Cultural and Social Interaction,* Leiden: Brill, 355-72 • M. STERN 1974, *Greek and Latin Authors on Jews and Judaism,* vol. 1, Jerusalem: Israel Academy of Sciences and Humanities. • J. TROMP 1995, "The Critique of Idolatry in the Context of Jewish Monotheism," in *Aspects of Religious Contact and Conflict in the Ancient World,* ed. P. W. van der Horst, Utrecht: Faculteit der Godgeleerdheid, 105-20. • M. VOGEL 1999, "Vita 64-69, das Bilderverbot und die Galiläapolitik des Josephus," *JSJ* 30: 65-79.

See also: Pagan Religions JOHANNES TROMP

Idumea

During the Second Temple period, Idumea was the name of a territory that encompassed the region roughly between the southern Judean hill country and the northern part of the Negev Desert. The most important cities in Idumea were Adora, Betabris, Hebron, and Marisa. Idumea was strategically important because whoever ruled it controlled major east-west trade routes between the Mediterranean coast and the Transjordan as well as north-south trade routes from Eilat to the rest of the Levant.

Early History

The name Idumea (*Idymaia* in Greek) derives from "Edom," which denotes a Semitic-speaking nomadic tribal group that lived in the region south of the Dead Sea in what is now Israel and Jordan. According to Genesis, Jacob's son, Esau, was the ancestor of the Edomites (Gen. 25:28-34; 36:1-43). The Edomites' original territory extended from the Sinai Peninsula as far as Kadesh Barnea and southward to the seaport of Eilat. Moab bordered Edomite territory on the north. As the biblical story suggests, the Edomites, while not Israelites, nonetheless shared many cultural norms with the Israelites, including male circumcision (Jer. 9:26-26).

By the end of the seventh and beginning of the sixth century B.C.E., pressure from Arab tribes (later known as Nabateans) on their southeastern flank forced the Edomites to expand into the Negev, which brought them into open conflict with the Kingdom of Judah (Arad Ostracon 24). Migration into the Negev likely was gradual but probably accelerated after the destruction of the kingdom of Judah by Nebuchadnezzar in 587 B.C.E. In particular, Edomite invaders seem to have used Judah's conquest and the ensuing power vacuum to gain control of the regions in which they had previously entered. Such a move could not have occurred without the consent and even cooperation of the Babylonian kingdom. Because of this exploitation, Edom henceforth becomes a symbol of evil in Jewish memory, as illustrated in the biblical book of Obadiah.

According to the *Chronicle of Nabonidus*, the Persian king defeated and conquered the Edomites in 553 B.C.E., but even this conquest did not stop Edomite migration into southern Judea and the Dead Sea region. Around the middle of the fifth century B.C.E., Idumea fell under the control of the Arab Geshem, King of Qedar, who seems to have been allied with, but independent from, the Persians (Neh. 2:9; 6:1-6; cf. Herodotus, *Historiae* 3.88). This Arab kingdom remained independent from Persia until the end of their empire when it was included in the satrapy of Syria-Phoenicia (Diodorus Siculus 19.98.1).

While literary sources state that during the Persian period the area south of Beth-Zur was politically controlled by the Arab kingdom, archaeological evidence indicates that the population was quite mixed, including Arabs, Sidonians, and Nabateans, and probably Judeans. The appearance of people with Arabic, Idumean, and Aramaic names also supports this conclusion. Still, the Idumean element seems to have been prominent and even dominant in the southern Judean part of the region, the area between Beth-Zur and Beer-sheba. In the area south of Beer-sheba, Arab culture seems to have been preeminent (Kasher 1988).

Hellenistic and Hasmonean Eras

During the Hellenistic period, the region fell under the sway of various Diadochi, including the Ptolemies and Seleucids. By 311 B.C.E., Idumea was organized as an *eparchy* (Diodorus Siculus 19.95.2), although a governor *(stratēgos)* is not mentioned in the sources until the Seleucid period (2 Macc. 12:32). During the Roman period, Idumea was apparently a *toparchy*, as evidenced by Josephus and Strabo (*J.W.* 3.55; Strabo, *Geog.* 16.2.2, 34).

In 165 B.C.E., after revolting against Seleucid control, Judah Maccabee and his followers attacked Gorgias, the *stratēgos* of Idumea, defeated him, and followed him across the border of Judea into Idumea (1 Macc. 4:15; 2 Macc. 10:15, 17; 12:32; Josephus, *Ant.* 12.308). In the ensuing battle, King Antiochus IV's viceroy, Lysias, attacked the Maccabees from Idumea but was eventually defeated by Judah and his forces at Beth-Zur. Judah fortified Beth-Zur against attacks from Idumea (1 Macc. 4:61) and then resumed his attacks on Idumea, achieving great success in these campaigns (1 Macc. 5:3; *Ant.* 12.328). He sacked and looted Hebron (1 Macc. 5:65; *Ant.* 12.353) as well as Marisa and Ashdod (*Ant.* 12.353). Undismayed by these setbacks, Lysias again attacked Judah's army from Idumea (1 Macc. 6:31, 50; *Ant.* 12.367). Later, during the hegemony of Judah's brother Jonathan, the Seleucid general and future king Tryphon used Idumea as a base from which to launch a campaign against Jerusalem (1 Macc. 13:20; *Ant.* 13.207-9). Seleucid control of Idumea continued until the reign of John Hyrcanus I, the son and successor of Judah's brother Simon.

Almost as soon as Hyrcanus took control of Judea, the Seleucid monarch, Antiochus VII Sidetes, invaded Judea and besieged Jerusalem. Hyrcanus retained his throne only after paying a huge indemnity and offering hostages. Hyrcanus also agreed to accompany Sidetes on his Parthian campaign. However, Sidetes died in 129 B.C.E. while on campaign, and Hyrcanus exploited the ensuing power vacuum by expanding his territory. One of his first targets was Idumea, which Josephus states he conquered in the same year, although evidence from coins and tomb inscriptions indicates that the conquest may not have taken place until 111/110 B.C.E. According to Josephus, Hyrcanus forcibly "converted" the native population (*J.W.* 1.63; *Ant.* 13.257). The actual situation was probably more complicated. U. Rappaport and A. Kasher have theorized that those who refused to adopt Jewish customs were driven into exile, particularly Egypt, although this is far from certain. Recently, other scholars have argued that the "conversion" was more of a political accommodation to Judean rule than a cultural transformation.

Nevertheless, for those who stayed, life probably went on as normal, the major difference being that the Idumeans were now subject to the dynasty in Jerusalem. The Hasmoneans seem to have ruled Idumea through local elites who enjoyed the status of "friendship" with the Judean rulers. The most prominent family to arise out of Idumea was the Antipatrids (anachronistically known as the Herodians). The first known member of the family, Antipas (father of Antipater and grandfather of Herod), served as governor *(stratēgos)* of Idumea during the reign of Alexander Jannaeus. Antipater, the father of Herod, succeeded his father in the post and became the most powerful official in the court of John Hyrcanus II. Together with the Nabatean king Aretas III, Antipater supported Hyrcanus II in his civil war with his brother Aristobulus II.

During this civil war, both sides appealed to Pompey, who in 63 B.C.E. intervened in the conflict, conquering and reorganizing the Hasmonean kingdom, and freeing numerous Greek cities from Hasmonean control. Idumea seems to have remained under the control of John Hyrcanus II, although Pompey placed Hyrcanus' kingdom under the purview of the governor of Syria (*J.W.* 1.156-57; *Ant.* 14.74-76). A weakened Hyrcanus continued to rule, but increasingly relied on Antipater and his two sons. Antipater's increasing power led to sharp conflicts with rival courtiers including a certain Malichus, who ultimately poisoned Antipater. While Malichus' origins seem to be Nabatean, there may have been other Idumeans in the court of Hyrcanus as well.

Herodian Period

After the death of Antipater, his sons, Phasael and Herod, became the most powerful men in Hyrcanus' court, serving as *stratēgoi* and tetrarchs of Judea and Galilee, respectively. In 40 B.C.E., the Parthians invaded Judea, took Phasael and Hyrcanus captive, and drove Herod from the city. Unsurprisingly given his family background, Herod fled to Idumea and ordered his troops to hide themselves within the region, a move which suggests that a number of them had local connections (*J.W.* 1.263-68; *Ant.* 14.353, 361-64). When Herod returned from Rome after being appointed King of the Judeans by the Senate, he found many supporters and volunteers for his army in Idumea (*J.W.* 1.302; *Ant.* 15.411). It is likely that many of these individuals were clients of his family. Some may have joined out of ethnic loyalty, while others no doubt saw an opportunity for personal advancement.

Once Herod secured the throne of Judea, he began installing his supporters in positions of power. He appointed an Idumean, Costobarus, as *stratēgos* of Idumea and Gaza. Herod also married his sister Salome to Costobarus (*J.W.* 1.486; *Ant.* 15.252-57). Costobarus later proved disloyal, plotting with Cleopatra to detach Idumea from Herod's realm and rule it himself. Besides being a simple desire for power, Costobarus' plot seems to have had some quasi-nationalist elements. Josephus states that the *stratēgos,* who possessed a theophoric name, honoring Qos, the ancestral god of the Idumeans, and whose ancestors had been priests of this same god, did not agree with the Judaization of Idumea and longed for a return to ancestral customs. Unfortunately for him, in 28/27 B.C.E. his plot was discovered and he was executed (*Ant.* 15.252-57). Ironically, Herod, whose Idumean lineage was derided by the Hasmonean Mattathias Antigonus, was not Idumean enough for Costobarus.

From a military standpoint, Idumea was an important reservoir from which Herod could draw support, and he clearly used this resource as evidenced by the 3,000 Idumeans he settled in the unstable Trachonitis region. Like the Babylonian colony at Bathyra, the Idumeans were expected to patrol the region, guard caravans, and maintain peace (*Ant.* 16.292). During the Trachonitide Revolt of 10/9 B.C.E., the Idumean colony was attacked and despoiled.

During his reign, Herod was responsible for the construction of two massive enclosures at Hebron and Mamre, two sites closely associated with the patriarch Abraham. Scholars disagree about whether Herod was trying to promote native Idumean cult traditions or conversely attempting to suppress Idumean religious traditions in favor of Judean ones. Herod may have been simultaneously appealing to both groups, Jews and Idumeans, and depicting himself as a pious king through his veneration of sites central to the common ancestor Abraham.

Widespread disturbances and revolts broke out after Herod's death in 4 B.C.E. Josephus narrates one episode in which the Idumean military colonists helped repress the revolt of a certain Simon in Perea (*J.W.* 2.53). According to Augustus' settlement of Herod's will, Idumea fell under the jurisdiction of Archelaus, Herod's son and the ethnarch of Judea (*J.W.* 2.93-98; *Ant.* 17.319). When Archelaus was removed from power in 6 C.E., Idumea, along with the rest of his kingdom, became a Roman province (*J.W.* 2.113, 117; *Ant.* 17.342-55). It was part of Herod Agrippa's kingdom from 41 C.E. until his death in 44. After Agrippa' death, Idumea was governed by the procurator of Judea as one of the toparchies of Judea (*J.W.* 3.55).

The Great Revolt

When revolution broke out in Judea in 66 C.E., the revolutionary government in Jerusalem immediately appointed commanders over the various toparchies, including the joint commanders of Idumea, Joshua b. Sapphas and Eleazar b. Ananias (*J.W.* 2.566). During the internal power struggles of 68 and 69 C.E., factional leaders sought Idumean support, and this support was pivotal to determining who controlled the city. Other warlords such as Simon bar Gioras exploited the chaos and attacked Idumea itself, plundering it and forcing a significant percentage of the population of the region to flee to Jerusalem (*J.W.* 4.511-37, 556). In the final siege of Jerusalem, the Idumeans, who allied with various factions, played a central role in the failed defense of the city.

Idumea seems to have suffered tremendously during the Great Revolt. Vespasian permitted his army to decimate the population, ravage the land, and then occupy it (*J.W.* 4.447-48). After the destruction of Jerusalem in 70 C.E., Idumea was absorbed into the province of Judea. Following the revolt, there are no contemporary accounts of the region, and it ceases to have any known history independent of Judea.

Bibiography

M. Gihon 1967, "Idumea and the Herodian Limes," *IEJ* 17: 27-42. • B. Isaac 1984, "Bandits in Judaea and Arabia," *Harvard Studies in Classical Philology* 88: 171-203. • A. Kasher 1988, *Jews, Idumaeans and Ancient Arabs: Relations of the Jews in Eretz-Israel with Nations of the Frontier and the Desert during the Hellenistic and Roman Era (332 BCE–70 CE),* Tübingen: Mohr-Siebeck. • N. Kokkinos 1998, *The Herodian Dynasty: Origins, Roles in Society and Eclipse,* Sheffield, Eng.: Sheffield Academic Press. • E. D. Oren and U. Rappaport 1984, "The Necropolis of Maresha-Beth Govrin," *IEJ* 34: 114-

53. • S. QEDAR 1992-1993, "The Coins of Marisa: A New Mint," *Israel Numismatic Journal* 12: 27-33.

ADAM MARSHAK

Immersion → Washing, Ritual

Imperial Cult, Jews and the

In the Hellenistic and early Roman periods, worship of a ruler was neither a uniform practice nor a clearly defined concept. According to Plutarch, the earliest known example of bestowing divine honors in the Greek world appears to have been to Lysander, by the people of Samos during the Peloponnesian War (Plutarch, *Lysander* 18.3). It was during the rule of Alexander the Great that a ruler cult became a widespread practice. The successors of Alexander accepted and even actively promoted the ruler cult in the context of their own court: Antiochus I declared his deceased father Seleucus I a deity in 280 B.C.E., while the Ptolemies had founded a ruler cult center at Alexandria by 284 B.C.E. As to how individual cities articulated the ruler cult, there was no one universal or mandated manner. Some honored rulers by constructing temples and/or altars, others with festivals, statues placed in existing temples, and even priesthoods dedicated to the veneration of the ruler. At its core, the ruler cult provided a mechanism by which subjects could acknowledge the authority and power of the ruler and by which the ruling power could voice its claim to such power.

The Eastern Extension of the Cult

Although the imperial cult is primarily discussed within a Roman context, it is important to note that the whole concept was foreign to the Roman way of thinking. Only as Roman influence extended eastward did the ruler cult enter into the Roman political and religious landscape. One of the earliest examples of a Roman having a cult established in his honor is T. Quinctius Flaminius, by the inhabitants of Chalcis in 191 B.C.E. (Plutarch, *Flaminius* 16.3-4). It was not until the time of Julius Caesar that the ruler cult entered the mainstream of Roman thinking. Although there remains much debate about whether it was during his lifetime or immediately after his death, Julius Caesar was the first Roman ruler to be recognized as a deity. The decision of the Senate in 42 B.C.E. to formally declare Caesar *Divus Julius* marked a point of no return. It set in place the basic precedent for the treatment of all subsequent rulers: the expectation that emperors would be deified by the Senate after their death (Appian, *Bella Civilia* 2.148). The founding of the Roman Empire by Augustus opened the way for the spread of what is best described as emperor worship (Gradel 2002). Depending on the geographical location and particular group involved, emperor worship took a large variety of forms. It was quick to develop, particularly in the eastern parts of the empire, in cities such as Pergamum and Ephesus in 29 B.C.E. and in Mytilene in ca. 25 B.C.E. Most emperors were content to accept the role of *divi filius*, as first adopted by Augustus, and although accepting of any emperor worship offered by provincials, they were careful not to require that they be worshiped as living deities. Two important exceptions to this principle in the early Roman period were Caligula and Domitian. Their assertion of deity during their lifetime indicates the limitations of emperor worship from a Roman perspective: whereas other Julio-Claudian and Flavian emperors were declared to be deities by the Senate, Caligula and Domitian were not accorded such divine status.

The Jewish Reaction

There are allusions to the ruler cult in Jewish writings that indicate an aversion to, and rejection of, the practice from the Hellenistic period onward. Much of the critique is broad in its scope and of a derogatory nature, depicting the use of images to venerate rulers as a form of idolatry. This critique was based upon the Jewish adherence to monotheism and to aniconic forms of worship (Wis. 14:17-21; *Sib. Or.* 3.545-49; *Letter of Aristeas* 135; Philo, *Legatio ad Gaium* 118; Josephus, *Ag. Ap.* 2.190-92). There are also several examples of individual figures alluded to as failing to acknowledge their status as humans in writings intended primarily for a Jewish audience (e.g., Pompey in *Pss. Sol.* 2:28-29; Antiochus IV in 2 Macc. 9:8-12). Other than Philo's account of his role in the delegation to Caligula, Josephus is the source for most of our information about Jewish interaction with emperor worship in the early Roman period. Both authors were very critical of the practice. At the same time, they struggled with a sense of embarrassment that Jews could not employ this increasingly popular vehicle for expressing loyalty to the emperor (Philo, *Legatio* 353–57; *In Flaccum* 48–52; Josephus, *Ag. Ap.* 2.65-67, 73; *Ant.* 4.137-38; 12.125-26). An important factor in considering the significance of the material in Josephus and Philo is that they were, for the most part, addressing unusual circumstances, namely, life under the two Roman emperors who promoted themselves as living deities (Philo under Caligula, Josephus under Domitian).

Criticism of emperor worship is also evident within the early Christian movement. This is particularly evident in chaps. 13 and 17 of the book of Revelation, in John's description of the beast from the sea and the beast from the land, the latter of which promotes worship of the first beast and its "image." Given the likely provenance of Revelation in Asia Minor, a province where there were many examples of the imperial cult being in operation, it is understandable that the topic was a vital issue. The allusions to emperor worship are intertwined with suggestions of physical torment for the faithful, or at least the prospect thereof (Rev. 13:7; 17:6). Whether Revelation is responding to actual experiences of localized persecution because of nonparticipation or envisions it as a future prospect remains debated (see Thompson 1990; Friesen 2001 and 2005).

Although there is no example of Jews participating in the worship of a Roman emperor, there is evidence that they found ways by which honor and veneration could be expressed. Shields and various dedications were displayed in synagogues at Alexandria (Philo, *Legatio ad Gaium* 133). In the Jewish homeland Herod instituted the daily offering of sacrifices for the well-being of Rome and the emperor in the Jerusalem Temple (Josephus, *Ant.* 2.197; *Ag. Ap.* 2.77; Philo, *Legatio* 157, 317). Herod went even further with his decision to construct three substantial temples dedicated to Rome and the emperor at Caesarea Maritima, Sebaste, and in the vicinity of Banias. These temples helped ensure a tangible physical expression of Jewish loyalty to the Roman ruler that rivaled any similar structures found in the surrounding regions of the empire.

There are several occasions when the ruler cult was used by non-Jews and by Jews as the vehicle for furthering their own interests. There were two significant conflicts caused by the ruler imposing a version of the ruler cult upon the Jews in their homeland: Antiochus IV Epiphanes (1 Macc. 1:41-51; 2 Macc. 6.1-2) and Caligula (Josephus, *J.W.* 2.184-203; *Ant.* 18.261-309; Philo, *Legatio* 186–88). On both occasions the ruler cult was used as a response to an existing problem: actions by Jews thought to warrant punishment. Antiochus IV believed the Jews had initiated a rebellion against his rule, while Caligula was responding to news that Jews had removed statues of him placed in their synagogue by local residents (*Legatio* 203). The actions of Antiochus IV and Gaius, however, were short-lived. Antiochus IV's punishment was instrumental in precipitating the Maccabean Revolt, which eventually saw the rise of Hasmonean rule, while Gaius' order that his statue be erected in the Jerusalem Temple was met by a massive protest, and the incident was finally resolved by the murder of the emperor in Rome. Although Josephus does not describe any examples of trouble caused by Domitian's assertion of divine status, he defended the fact that Jews did not participate in such activity in his works written during that reign (*Ag. Ap.* 2.73-78). The central component of the defense was mention of the sacrifices previously offered at the Jerusalem Temple on behalf of the well-being of the emperor and Rome. That those sacrifices had ceased some fifteen years earlier in 70 C.E., when the Temple was destroyed, made nonparticipation by Jews difficult to defend.

Anti-Jewish Exploitations of the Cult

At a community level, Josephus and Philo include a number of examples of non-Jews employing the ruler cult as a way of challenging the position of Jews. At Alexandria, Jamnia, and Dora non-Jewish residents placed images of the emperor in synagogues (Philo, *Legatio* 132–34 [Alexandria]; 200-202 [Jamnia]; Josephus, *Ant.* 19.300-311 [Dora]). The Jewish responses to these actions varied: at Alexandria, appeals were made to the local Roman authority to intervene but without success; at Jamnia the Jews removed the images; and at Dora the request that the Roman authority intervene was successful; the images were removed and a warning issued that such attempts to intimidate the Jews not be repeated. The events in Jerusalem in 66 C.E. at the start of the war against Rome show that the symbolic importance of the ruler cult was recognized by Jews. The decision to cease offering the daily sacrifice on behalf of Rome and the emperor marked the beginning of the war, asserting independence from Roman control (*Ant.* 2.409).

The role played by the ruler cult in relations between Jews and their Roman overlords was a balancing act. For the most part, Jewish nonparticipation in such activity was just one further example of their "strange" ways, as suggested by the remarks of Tacitus (*Historiae* 5.5.4). Because it was a popular channel for subjects to express their loyalty to Rome, nonparticipation meant it could easily become a weapon used against Jews, but the fact that the standard Roman attitude did not view emperor worship as a requirement should not be underestimated in determining how the ruler cult impacted relations between Jews and Rome.

BIBLIOGRAPHY

M. BERNETT 2007, *Der Kaiserkult in Judäa unter den Herodiern und Römern,* Tübingen: Mohr-Siebeck. • P. BILDE 1978, "The Roman Emperor Gaius (Caligula)'s Attempt to Erect His Statue in the Temple of Jerusalem," *Studia Theologica* 32: 67-93. • L. CERFAUX AND J. TONDRIAU 1957, *Le culte des souverains dans la civilisation gréco-romaine,* Tournai: Desclée. • S. J. FRIESEN 1993, *Twice Neokoros: Ephesus, Asia and the Cult of the Flavian Imperial Family,* Leiden: Brill. • S. J. FRIESEN 2001, *Imperial Cults and the Apocalypse of John: Reading Revelation in the Ruins,* Oxford: Oxford University Press. • S. J. FRIESEN 2005, "Satan's Throne, Imperial Cults and Social Settings of Revelation," *JSNT* 27: 351-73. • I. GRADEL 2002, *Emperor Worship and Roman Religion,* Oxford: Clarendon Press • J. S. MCLAREN 2005, "Jews and the Imperial Cult: From Augustus to Domitian," *JSNT* 27: 257-78. • S. R. F. PRICE 1983, *Rituals and Power: The Roman Imperial Cult in Asia Minor,* Cambridge: Cambridge University Press • A. SMALL, ED. 1996, *Subject and Ruler: The Cult of the Ruling Power in Classical Antiquity,* Ann Arbor: University of Michigan Press. • J. E. TAYLOR 2006, "Pontius Pilate and the Imperial Cult in Roman Judaea," *NTS* 52: 555-82. • L. L. THOMPSON 1990, *The Book of Revelation: Apocalypse and Empire,* Oxford University Press.

See also: Roman Emperors JAMES S. MCLAREN

Inscriptions

Through Jewish literature from antiquity we come into contact primarily with the literate and learned circles of Jewish society, and so we come to know the ideas and ideals of the upper class. The voice of the common man and woman is hardly heard in those pages. It is precisely in introducing us to the common Jewish people, their thoughts and speech and action, their fears and hopes, their griefs and joys, that inscriptions make one of their most valuable contributions to our knowledge of the world of ancient Judaism. In this sense inscriptions are highly valuable testimonies to Jewish living (Kant 1987).

Criteria for Discerning the "Jewishness" of Inscriptions

How does one know that an ancient inscription on stone, marble, or clay is Jewish? That is a much more complicated question than was formerly thought. It is often very hard, if not impossible, to tell whether an inscription is Jewish, Christian, or pagan (Kraemer 1991). The onomastic criterion, used very often, is very unreliable because, especially in later antiquity, Christians began more and more to use biblical and Jewish names; and even among pagan Greeks and Romans one can observe that "Jewish" names such as Sambathion gained in popularity. In fact there are hardly any names which can be said to have been used exclusively by Jews (Kraemer 1986: 191). Nor is the presence of Jewish symbols alongside the text, such as a menorah or a *lulav,* always necessarily an indicator of Jewishness, since it is well known that sometimes (Judaizing) Christians and pagans used them as well, just as Jews in turn sometimes used Christian symbols (Figueras 1983: 22-23). Jewish "technical terms" are indicative of Jewishness *only* if they are exclusively Jewish (e.g., Sabbath), which is not the case, for example, with the term *synagōgē* (which can mean any meeting or assembly) and with several other "Jewish" technical terms. An origin in what are known to have been places of exclusively Jewish nature is also a somewhat doubtful criterion since exclusively Jewish places are very rare, especially in the Diaspora, except for the Jewish catacombs in Rome (Leon 1960; Rutgers 2000). But even there it is not improbable that, after these burial places ceased to be used by Jews, some pagans or Christians deposited the bodies of their deceased there.

A rigorous application of criteria would, therefore, require us to regard an inscription as Jewish only when a number of factors reinforce one another. For example, Jewish burial place plus Jewish symbols and epithets (e.g., *philentolos,* "lover of the commandments"), or biblical names plus Jewish technical terms and functions (e.g., *archisynagōgos,* "head of the synagogue") together would indicate a Jewish provenance. On the one hand, such a methodological strictness runs the risk of excluding valuable material the Jewishness of which is not manifest. On the other hand, methodological slackness in this matter runs the risk of including non-Jewish material that may blur the picture. It is better, for the sake of clarity, to stay on the strict side, without being overly rigorous. That is to say, applying two or three criteria together is far preferable to applying only one, the more so since in late antiquity Judaism, Christianity, and paganism were not always mutually exclusive categories (van der Horst 1991: 16-18).

The Abba inscription, on the wall of a tomb found north of the Old City of Jerusalem, is written in Aramaic using Paleo-Hebrew script. It describes the occupant of the tomb as "Abba, son of the priest Eleaz(ar), son of Aaron the high (priest)." *(Courtesy Israel Antiquities Authority)*

Number, Type, Languages, and Features

From the period between Alexander the Great and Muhammad some 3,500 Jewish inscriptions are extant, the vast majority of them epitaphs (van der Horst 2006: 86). They are an important but still neglected source for the study of Jewish life and thought in late antiquity. Though there are some 1,000 Jewish inscriptions in Hebrew, Aramaic, and Latin, these amount to less than 30 percent of the total number. The heavy preponderance of Greek is an impressive testimony to the influence of Hellenistic culture on the Jews in this period, not only in the Diaspora but also in the land of Israel, where a great number of Jewish Greek inscriptions have been found (van der Horst 2002). Even rabbis and their families in the famous rabbinic center of Beth Sheʿarim in the Galilee phrased most of their tomb inscriptions in Greek (Mazar et al. 1973-1976). Some of the Beth Sheʿarim inscriptions are even in the form of Greek hexametric poems with Homeric phraseology and diction. It was only from the sixth century C.E. onward that Greek was gradually replaced by Hebrew in epigraphs.

The forms, formulas, and motifs in the inscriptions all testify to the influence of Greek epigraphic habits. That is only to be expected since there was hardly a strong Israelite tradition of composing inscriptions. It was the Greeks who had elevated epigraphy (both funerary and honorary inscriptions) to a form of art. In Jewish epitaphs we find Greek forms like hexametric and iambic poems; Greek literary motifs like death as marriage to the god of the netherworld; Greek mythological figures such as Hades, Charon, Lethe, and others; all kinds of concepts and formulas of pagan origin (although probably filled with a new sense in some cases, e.g., Moira, originally the goddess of Fate); the Greek notion of astral immortality; and Greek epigraphical conventions like the dialogue of the deceased with the passer-by, threats or even curses aimed at potential tomb robbers (van der Horst 1991: 40-60). Furthermore, in nonfunerary material, we find typically Greek honorary and dedicatory inscriptions (from synagogues), declarations of manumission of slaves, and so forth (Lifshitz 1967; Gibson 1999).

Geographical Spread

The geographical spread of these inscriptions reveals even better than the literary sources that Jews were indeed living all over the ancient world, from Morocco and Spain in the west to Iraq in the east, from the Black Sea in the north to the southern border of Egypt (literary sources testifying to that spread are, e.g., Philo, *In Flaccum* 46; *Legatio ad Gaium* 214; Josephus, *J.W.* 2.398; 7.43; Seneca *apud* Augustine, *Civitas Dei* 6.11; Acts 2:9-11; 15:21). This is especially true for the Roman period, from which the majority of the inscriptions date, although from places such as Leontopolis in Egypt (with its rival Jewish temple) or the Greek island of Delos there is plenty of epigraphical evidence for a strongly Hellenized Jewry from as early as the second century B.C.E. onward. Especially notable is a very unusual epitaph with a prayer for vengeance on Yom Kippur found on two second-century-B.C.E. tombstones from Rheneia, a little island near Delos, with its many allusions to the LXX version of the Pentateuch (see *IJO*, vol. 1, Ach 70 and 71 = Noy et al. 2004: 235-42).

The Theodotus inscription, marking the dedication of a synagogue in Jerusalem in the early first century C.E. (*CIJ* 2.1400, Greek uncials on limestone, 75 cm. × 41 cm.) *(Courtesy Israel Antiquities Authority)*

Jewish Social and Religious Involvement

From many of the inscriptions it is apparent that Jews were often fully integrated into the surrounding society. Some inscriptions, for instance, indicate that Jews were members of the local city council or held other important public offices (e.g., in Sardis see *IJO*, vol. 2, nos. 53-145 = Ameling 2004: 209-97). It seems, however, that it was especially in western Asia Minor that Jews reached these high positions; for the city of Rome and other major cultural centers, there is only sparse evidence, although the Jews probably nowhere lived in splendid isolation, as far as we can judge (Kant 1987). It should be added, however, that functions in the religious community are mentioned much more often than secular professions and occupations, which is an important indication that the synagogue community played a major role in the life of many late-antique Jews (van der Horst 1991: 85-101). Most frequent are the titles "father of the synagogue" *(patēr synagōgēs)*, "leader of the synagogue" *(archisynagōgēs)*, and "scribe/secretary" *(grammateus)*.

Often inscriptions are our only sources that provide information about the titles of synagogue officials in the Diaspora. Moreover, they reveal that in several Diaspora synagogues women had positions of leadership (Brooten 1982; van der Horst 1991: 102-13), which is another indication that it was not until the early Middle Ages that the rabbis began to dominate Diaspora communities. On the whole, the inscriptions reveal surprisingly little influence of rabbinic ideas (Cohen 1981), even though laudatory epithets such as "loving the Torah," "loving the commandments," "loving the synagogue," and the frequent mention of synagogue functions leave us in no doubt about the religious commitment of many Jews.

Death and the Afterlife

The average age at death (mentioned in more than 600 epitaphs) turns out to be around twenty-eight years. Although it is very hard to determine how representative this is, it may be said that most probably the Jews shared with pagans both the fate of a short life expectancy — in the Roman Empire as a whole, it was somewhere between twenty and thirty years on average — and the fate of a high infant and child mortality, probably not half of those born reaching adulthood (van der Horst 1991: 73-84).

Even though one would expect in such a situation clear expressions of hope for some sort of afterlife, most of the epitaphs yield very little information concerning the ideas of either the survivors or the deceased about life after death. Only a handful of inscriptions testifies to a variety of forms of belief in afterlife (the traditional conception of the gloomy netherworld, immortality of the soul, becoming a star, and so forth), and only a few inscriptions that explicitly confess a belief in the resurrection of the body (Park 2000). This need not imply that it is only the authors of these few epitaphs who believed in the afterlife — in early Christian epitaphs this belief finds expression relatively rarely as well — but it cannot be said on the basis of this evidence that Jews widely believed in life after death or resurrection. (It must be added that it is unclear what is implied by epitaphs that exhort the deceased to keep courage [Park 2000: 47-63].)

What does find expression often is grief about the

untimely death of the beloved one(s), much as in pagan epitaphs. Frequently one finds laments over the loss of young persons who had died without having had the chance of marrying or begetting children, which was felt to be a particularly cruel form of unfinished life (van der Horst 1991: 40-60). Contrary to the practice of the early Christians, who frequently referred to or quoted passages from the Bible in their funerary inscriptions, Jews were more reserved in this respect. Over against the wide repertoire of biblical texts in Christian inscriptions (Felle 2006), Jews seem to have restricted themselves almost entirely to two biblical passages, Prov. 10:7 ("the memory of the righteous one is a blessing") and 1 Sam. 25:29 ("may his/her life be bound in the bundle of the living"), which are quoted rather freely in both the LXX version and in that of Aquila (van der Horst 1991: 37-39).

BIBLIOGRAPHY

W. AMELING 2004, *Inscriptiones Judaicae Orientis,* vol. 2, *Kleinasien,* Tübingen: Mohr-Siebeck. • B. J. BROOTEN 1982, *Women Leaders in the Ancient Synagogue,* Chico, Calif.: Scholars Press. • S. J. D. COHEN 1981, "Epigraphical Rabbis," *JQR* 72: 1-17. • A. E. FELLE 2006, *Biblia epigraphica: La sacra scrittura nella documentazione epigrafica dell'* orbis christianus antiquus *(III-VIII secolo),* Bari: Edipuglia. • P. FIGUERAS 1983, *Decorated Jewish Ossuaries,* Leiden: Brill. • J.-B. FREY 1936-1952, *Corpus Inscriptionum Judaicarum: Recueil des inscriptions juives qui vont du IIIe siècle avant Jésus-Christ au VIIe siècle de notre ére,* 2 vols., Rome: Pontificio istituto di archeologia Cristiana (vol. 1 was reprinted with a prolegomenon containing many *addenda* by B. Lifshitz in 1975, New York: Ktav). • E. L. GIBSON 1999, *The Jewish Manumission Inscriptions of the Bosporus Kingdom,* Tübingen: Mohr-Siebeck. • J. W. VAN HENTEN AND P. W. VAN DER HORST, EDS. 1994, *Studies in Early Jewish Epigraphy,* Leiden: Brill. • W. HORBURY AND D. NOY 1992, *Jewish Inscriptions of Graeco-Roman Egypt,* Cambridge: Cambridge University Press. • P. W. VAN DER HORST 1991, *Ancient Jewish Epitaphs: An Introductory Survey of a Millennium of Jewish Funerary Epigraphy (300 BCE–700 CE),* Kampen: Kok Pharos. • P. W. VAN DER HORST 2002, "Greek in Jewish Palestine in the Light of Jewish Epigraphy," in idem, *Japheth in the Tents of Shem: Studies on Jewish Hellenism in Antiquity,* Leuven: Peeters. • P. W. VAN DER HORST 2006, "Inscriptiones Judaicae Orientis: A Review Article," in idem, *Jews and Christians in Their Graeco-Roman Context: Selected Essays on Early Judaism, Samaritanism, Hellenism, and Christianity,* Tübingen: Mohr-Siebeck, 71-86. • L. H. KANT 1987, "Jewish Inscriptions in Greek and Latin," *ANRW* II.20.2, Berlin: de Gruyter, 671-713. • R. S. KRAEMER 1986, "Hellenistic Jewish Women: The Epigraphical Evidence," in *SBL 1986 Seminar Papers,* Atlanta: Scholars Press, 183-200. • R. S. KRAEMER 1991, "Jewish Tuna and Christian Fish: Identifying Religious Affiliation in Epigraphic Sources," *HTR* 84: 141-62. • H. J. LEON 1960, *The Jews of Ancient Rome* (updated ed. by C. A. Osiek, Peabody, Mass.: Hendrickson, 1995). • B. LIFSHITZ 1967, *Donateurs et fondateurs dans les synagogues juives,* Paris: Gabalda. • G. LÜDERITZ AND J. M. REYNOLDS 1983, *Corpus jüdischer Zeugnisse aus der Cyrenaika,* Wiesbaden: Reichert. • B. MAZAR, M. SCHWABE, B. LIFSHITZ, AND N. AVIGAD 1973-1976, *Beth She'arim I-III,* 3 vols., Jerusalem: Massada. • D. NOY 1993, *Jewish Inscriptions of Western Europe,* vol. 1, *Italy (Excluding the City of Rome), Spain and Gaul,* Cambridge: Cambridge University Press. • D. NOY 1995, *Jewish Inscriptions of Western Europe,* vol. 2, *The City of Rome,* Cambridge: Cambridge University Press. • D. NOY AND H. BLOEDHORN 2004, *Inscriptiones Judaicae Orientis,* vol. 3, *Syria and Cyprus,* Tübingen: Mohr-Siebeck. • D. NOY, A. PANAYOTOV, AND H. BLOEDHORN 2004, *Inscriptiones Judaicae Orientis,* vol. 1, *Eastern Europe,* Tübingen: Mohr-Siebeck. • J. S. PARK 2000, *Conceptions of Afterlife in Jewish Inscriptions with Special Reference to Pauline Literature,* Tübingen: Mohr-Siebeck. • L. Y. RACHMANI 1994, *A Catalogue of Jewish Ossuaries in the Collections of the State of Israel,* Jerusalem: Israel Academy of Sciences and Humanities. • L. V. RUTGERS 2000, *Subterranean Rome,* Leuven: Peeters.

See also: Burial Practices; Catacombs; Greek; Papyri; Synagogues

PIETER W. VAN DER HORST

Instruction (4QInstruction)

4QInstruction is the largest wisdom text of the Dead Sea Scrolls. Portions of six manuscripts of the work have survived (1Q26; 4Q415-18, 4Q423), and the numerous fragments associated with 4Q418 may include remnants of at least one other copy of 4QInstruction. The text is also known as "Sapiential Work A" and "Musar le-Mevin" (Instruction for a Maven). The composition was probably written in the second century B.C.E.

4QInstruction is a self-consciously pedagogical document. The author constantly addresses a student, who is referred to as a *mēbîn,* or "understanding one." He is to develop a love of learning: "Increase in understanding greatly, and from all of your teachers get ever more instruction" (4Q418 81 17). The *mēbîn* is often addressed in the singular, but the composition is designed for a group of students *(mĕbînîm)* (4Q418 123 ii 4; 4Q418 221 3).

Many of the teachings in 4QInstruction are in continuity with the traditional wisdom of Proverbs, which contains ethical advice and practical instruction regarding ordinary spheres of life. 4QInstruction urges the *mēbîn* to practice filial piety (4Q416 2 iii 15-19). The text teaches moderation with regard to food (4Q416 2 ii 18-20). The prompt payment of debts is a major preoccupation of 4QInstruction, and this is also the case in Proverbs (e.g., 4Q416 2 ii 4-6; Prov. 17:18).

The *mēbîn* is repeatedly urged to contemplate the *rāz nihyeh,* an enigmatic phrase that can be translated "the mystery that is to be." The *rāz nihyeh* represents an appeal to supernatural revelation. The *mēbîn* can learn about various topics through reflection upon this heavenly disclosure, such as the knowledge of good and evil and the fates of people after death (4Q417 1 i 6-8; 4Q417 2 i 10-12). The *rāz nihyeh* is associated with a tripartite division of time (past, present, and future) (4Q418 123 ii 3-4), and 4Q417 1 i 8-9 claims that God fashioned the world by means of this mystery (compare Prov. 3:19). The mystery that is to be represents the full extent of God's dominion over history and creation, manifested as a deterministic plan that orchestrates events which is presented as a revealed truth to the addressee.

The *rāz nihyeh* signifies a departure from older wisdom. In Proverbs the world has a divinely sanctioned order, but it can be perceived through empirical observation. In 4QInstruction the world requires supernatural revelation to be fully understood. This form of epistemology is more like that of the apocalypses than traditional wisdom. An apocalypse is a genre of literature that flourished in the late Second Temple period, characterized by the disclosure of revelation to the elect, the theme of eschatological judgment, and a concern for the angelic world. These features are prominent in 4QInstruction, which can be understood as having an apocalyptic worldview. The *mēbîn* belongs to an elect community. He is taught that he has been separated from "the spirit of flesh" and that he is among the "lot of angels" (4Q418 81 1-5). 4Q416 1, which is widely considered to be the beginning of the composition, proclaims God's final judgment, in which "the spirit of flesh" will be destroyed (4Q416 1 12; cf. 4Q418 69 ii). By contrast, "all the sons of his truth will be accepted with favor" (4Q416 1 10). This apparently refers to the elect addressees. "The spirit of flesh" designates those who do not possess elect status. The addressee is also likened to Adam. 4QInstruction claims that the *mēbîn* has been given possession of the Garden of Eden, which he is to tend and nurture (4Q423 1). This is probably a metaphor for his elect status and his acquisition of wisdom, which requires devotion and study.

While 4QInstruction makes several extraordinary assertions about the *mēbîn*, other aspects of his life are surprisingly ordinary. Several texts assume that the addressee is a farmer (e.g., 4Q423 3; 4Q418 103 ii), and 4QInstruction repeatedly uses the refrain, "You are poor." 4Q417 2 i 17-20 gives advice for someone who does not have enough food. The prominence of advice regarding indebtedness accords with a low social station. The addressees found meaning and dignity, despite the difficult realities they faced, by considering themselves among the elect with special access to heavenly revelation.

BIBLIOGRAPHY

M. J. GOFF 2003, *The Worldly and Heavenly Wisdom of 4QInstruction,* Leiden: Brill. • M. J. GOFF 2005, "Discerning Trajectories: 4QInstruction and the Sapiential Background of the Sayings Source Q," *JBL* 124/4: 657-73. • J. STRUGNELL AND D. J. HARRINGTON 1999, *Qumran Cave 4.XXIV: Sapiential Texts, Part 2. 4QInstruction (Mûsār lĕ Mēvîn),* DJD 34, Oxford: Clarendon. • E. J. C. TIGCHELAAR 2001, *To Increase Learning for the Understanding Ones: Reading and Reconstructing the Fragmentary Early Jewish Sapiential Text 4QInstruction,* Leiden: Brill. • B. G. WOLD 2005, *Women, Men and Angels: The Qumran Wisdom Document 'Musar le Mevin' and Its Allusions to Genesis Creation Traditions,* Tübingen: Mohr-Siebeck.

MATTHEW GOFF

Intermarriage

Intermarriage between Jews and Gentiles was a matter of grave concern to many of those writing in the Hellenistic and Roman periods. Though the Pentateuch in fact contains no blanket prohibition on intermarriage, many Jewish texts from the Second Temple period and later draw upon and reformulate various biblical laws and narratives in their condemnations of this practice.

Intermarriage in the Hebrew Bible

Deuteronomy 7:1-6 forbade the Israelites from intermarrying with seven groups: the Hittites, Girgashites, Amorites, Canaanites, Perizzites, Hivites, and Jebusites. The rationale given is that spouses from these groups would turn away the Israelites from worshiping Yahweh to serve other gods (cf. Exod. 34:11-16; Numbers 25). Deuteronomy 23 contains what also might be a partial prohibition on intermarriage; vv. 3-8 state that no Ammonite or Moabite may be admitted to "the assembly of Yahweh, even to the tenth generation," and that Edomites and Egyptians may not be admitted until the third generation. While it is more likely that the phrase "admit to the assembly of Yahweh" originally denoted participation in the Yahwistic cult rather than intermarriage, the law is ambiguous and would later be interpreted as referring to intermarriage (see below). Despite these passages, one also finds in preexilic biblical materials many examples of intermarriage between Israelites and non-Israelites, and texts such as Deuteronomy 21 even explicitly allow for intermarriage in certain cases.

The situation changes markedly in the postexilic books of Ezra and Nehemiah. Ezra 9 provides a very strong statement against intermarriage of any kind, stating that many of the Israelites, including priests and Levites, had been intermarrying with "the Canaanites, the Hittites, the Perizzites, the Jebusites, the Ammonites, the Moabites, the Egyptians, and the Amorites." Thus, "the holy seed has mixed itself with the peoples of the land." In this way, the text collapses the list of peoples in Deuteronomy 7 with that in Deuteronomy 23, and provides a very different rationale for prohibiting intermarriage than does either of those passages: one rooted not only in the sinful *behavior* of foreign groups, but also — and perhaps more importantly — in the holy nature of the Israelite people itself. Any intermingling of Israelite "seed" with that of Gentiles constitutes a desecration *(maʿal)* of the holiness of that seed (Ezra 9:2, 4; 10:2, 6, 10; Neh. 13:27). To make its framing of a general prohibition on intermarriage even stronger, Ezra 9 also draws upon Lev. 19:19 and Deut. 22:9-11, which prohibit the mixing of unlike species or substances. The viewpoint found in Nehemiah is similar to that of Ezra: it, too, characterizes intermarriage as a desecration and states that it defiles the priesthood (13:27-29). In addition, Neh. 13:1-3 explicitly interprets the injunction in Deuteronomy 23 against Ammonites and Moabites entering the assembly of Yahweh as a ban on intermarriage, and utilizes that text to justify the expulsion of foreigners (cf. Neh.

9:1-2; 10:28-31.) Dating from the same period as Ezra-Nehemiah is the book of Malachi, which criticizes intermarriage as well (Mal. 2:10-12).

Also assigned by many scholars to the Persian period, though its dating remains contentious, is the book of Ruth. The book advocates a more inclusive view of foreigners (cf. Isa. 56:1-8), even going so far as to present Ruth, a Moabite woman, as the great-grandmother of King David (Ruth 4:17-22). Some scholars propose that the book was written, at least in part, to counter the stance reflected in Ezra-Nehemiah.

Intermarriage in Second Temple Sources

Many Jewish texts of the Hellenistic and Roman periods share Ezra-Nehemiah's opposition to intermarriage, though they formulate this stance in different ways. The text most closely aligned with the viewpoint of Ezra-Nehemiah is perhaps that of *Jubilees.* A work dating to the second century B.C.E., *Jubilees* declares that Israel was separated from the rest of the nations as a people holy to God already at the time of creation, and seems to characterize Israel as being quasi-angelic in nature (*Jub.* 2:17-24; Kugel 1996: 25-27). It is therefore unsurprising that the text sees intermarriage as wholly inappropriate and offensive. In *Jubilees* 22, Abraham enjoins Jacob to separate himself from Gentiles, "because their deeds are defiled, and all of their ways are contaminated and despicable and abominable" (*Jub.* 22:16). *Jub.* 30:7-17 places an explicit prohibition on intermarriage in the midst of its retelling of the rape of Dinah story (Genesis 34), calling marriages to Gentiles a "defilement" and "contemptible" and equating them with the prostitution condemned by Lev. 21:9. *Jub.* 30:10 also equates giving one's child to a Gentile in marriage with giving one's seed to Molech, an act prohibited in Lev. 18:21 and 20:1-5, and originally signifying child sacrifice, not intermarriage (cf. *Tg. Ps.-J.* Lev. 18:21; *Peshiṭta* Lev. 18:21). For other statements in the book criticizing intermarriage, see *Jub.* 20:4; 22:20; 25:1-3; and 27:10.

Sharing *Jubilees'* contempt for intermarriage is the Greek version of the book of Esther, which has the heroine state that she despises "the bed of the uncircumcised and of any alien" (addition C, 14:15). The *Testament of Levi* is similarly negative, listing among the evils of the Israelites marriage with Gentile women (14:6) and placing an exhortation not to marry Gentiles in the mouth of Jacob (9:10). However, unlike *Jubilees, T. Levi* does not utilize its retelling of the Dinah episode as an opportunity to condemn intermarriage. Also, the *Biblical Antiquities* of Pseudo-Philo describes sexual relations with foreign women as a sin against God (*Bib. Ant.* 18:13; cf. 43:5).

Other texts of the period also critique intermarriage, but in less harsh terms. For example, Philo explains the law prohibiting intermarriage, which he sees as Mosaic, by stating that such marriages might lead one's children to become impious (*Spec. Leg.* 3.29; he likely has Deut. 7:1-6 in mind here). Josephus similarly interprets the prohibition as deriving from Mosaic Law and sees the same reasoning behind it (*Ant.* 8.187-88). Notably, the latter's retelling of the controversy over intermarriage in Ezra lacks the holy seed rhetoric so prominent in that book (*Ant.* 11.139-53; cf. 4.134-55). In the book of Tobit, the title character counsels his son not to marry foreigners (4:12-13; cf. *T. Job* 45:4), but it does so as part of a larger theme of encouraging endogamy proper (i.e., marriage within one's own kinship group; see Tobit 1:9; 3:17; 4:12-13; 6:11-12; 7:10-11; cf. *Aramaic Levi* 6:4; 12; *Spec. Leg.* 1.126; Jdt. 8:2). Although *Joseph and Aseneth* deems it inappropriate for a Jewish man to have sexual relations with or marry a Gentile woman (8:5-6), this text also clearly allows for the conversion of Gentiles to Judaism (cf. Theodotus), something inconceivable for *Jubilees,* not only because it was written in the second century B.C.E. when the process of conversion was still in its infancy (Cohen 1999: 109-39), but also because of its belief in the genealogical, quasi-angelic holiness of Israel.

A document containing ambiguous, but noteworthy statements concerning intermarriage is the text from Qumran called *Miqṣat Maʿaśê ha-Torah,* or 4QMMT. Though this text is fragmentary, it does seem to follow Nehemiah and other texts in interpreting Deut. 23:3 as a ban on intermarriage (A frg. 8 col. iii; C col. i; D frg. 5; cf. 4QFlorilegium, which instead takes the verse to refer to foreigners entering the Temple). Similarly, the text refers to Lev. 19:19 in another, much disputed passage condemning intermarriage (C col. iv; D frgs. 6-13, lines 12-14). Due to the fragmentary nature of the text, it is unclear whether 4QMMT speaks of marriage between Israelites and Gentiles (Hayes 2002: 82-91; Sharp 1997) or between priests and nonpriests, which would signify that its authors saw Lev. 21:13-15, which requires the high priest to marry only a woman of priestly stock, as applying to all men of the priestly line (Himmelfarb 1999).

Intermarriage in Rabbinic Texts

Rabbinic sources differ in their framing of intermarriage. On the whole, both the holy seed ideology of Ezra and the interpretation of Lev. 18:21 and 20:1-5 as referring to intermarriage are rejected (*m. Meg.* 4:9; *b. Megillah* 25a; cf. *y. Meg.* 4:10; 75:3; Werman 1997: 17-19; Cohen 1999: 254; Hayes 2002). Intermarriage between Jews and Gentile converts to Judaism is generally unproblematic to the rabbis, though rabbinic law did place certain disabilities on converts (Hayes 2002; Cohen 1999). Marriage to unconverted Gentiles was prohibited, however. Most rabbinic texts state or imply that a fear of idolatry and immorality is what underlies this. In addition, some rabbinic sources attribute ritual impurity to Gentiles, probably as a disincentive to intermarriage (Hayes 2002).

Social Realities

Whether or not intermarriage between Jews and Gentiles was in fact a common practice demographically in the ancient world is almost impossible to ascertain. Although the number of texts that decry intermarriage is numerous, neither 1-2 Maccabees nor Ben Sira makes any reference to the phenomenon (Himmelfarb 1999), and various social factors, such as a preference for kin-based endogamy (*Ant.* 12.186-89; 16.194; 17.18, 19; 18.136, 137; 19.277) on the part of both Jews and Greeks (Satlow 2001: 143), imply that intermarriage would have been relatively uncommon. It is possible, then, that polemics against intermarriage may have served as rhetorical shorthand for denunciation of assimilation of all kinds.

BIBLIOGRAPHY

S. J. D. COHEN 1999, *The Beginnings of Jewishness: Boundaries, Varieties, Uncertainties,* Berkeley: University of California Press. • C. E. HAYES 2002, *Gentile Impurities and Jewish Identities: Intermarriage and Conversion from the Bible to the Talmud,* New York: Oxford. • M. HIMMELFARB 1999, "Levi, Phinehas, and the Problem of Intermarriage at the Time of the Maccabean Revolt," *JSQ* 6: 1-24. • J. KUGEL 1996, "The Holiness of Israel and the Land in Second Temple Times," in *Texts, Temples, and Traditions: A Tribute to Menahem Haran,* ed. M. V. Fox et al., Winona Lake, Ind.: Eisenbrauns, 21-32. • M. L. SATLOW 2001, *Jewish Marriage in Antiquity,* Princeton: Princeton University Press. • C. J. SHARP 1997, "Phinehan Zeal and Rhetorical Strategy in 4QMMT," *RevQ* 70: 207-22. • C. WERMAN 1997, "*Jubilees* 30: Building a Paradigm for the Ban on Intermarriage," *HTR* 90: 1-22.

See also: Family; Gentiles, Jewish Attitudes toward; Marriage and Divorce

TRACY M. LEMOS

Ioudaios

Greek *Ioudaios* (fem. *Ioudaia;* pl. *Ioudaioi*) and Lat. *Iudaeus* (fem. *Iudaea.* pl. *Iudaei*) ultimately derive from Hebr. *Yehudi,* which means in the first instance "a member of the tribe of Judah." This meaning seems to have disappeared from common usage by the Hellenistic period. As Josephus explains (*Ant.* 11.173), "From the time they went up from Babylon they were called by this name *(Ioudaioi)* after the tribe of Judah." In the period of interest to us, the word *Ioudaios* has two main meanings: (1) a Judean (a function of birth and/or geography); (2) a Jew (a function of religion or culture). In addition, in some passages of Josephus the word (in the plural) seems to mean (3) citizens or allies of the Judean state (a function of politics). Before ca. 100 B.C.E. *Ioudaios* always and only meant "Judean" in sense 1, a usage that remains common even in Roman times (esp. Josephus). *Ioudaios* in sense 2 is first attested in 2 Maccabees.

Ioudaios as Judean

First and foremost, a *Ioudaios* is a Judean, that is, a member of the Judean people or nation (*ethnos* in Greek, or a similar term) living in the ethnic homeland of Judea (*Ioudaia* in Greek). The historian Polybius (quoted by Josephus, *Ant.* 12.135-36) defines the *ethnos* of the Judeans as "those who dwell around the temple that is called 'Hierosolyma.'" Numerous Seleucid documents preserved by 1 Maccabees are addressed to the *ethnos* of the *Ioudaioi,* that is, "the nation of the Judeans." The Romans, too, saw the Judeans as an *ethnos.* Josephus regularly uses *Ioudaios/oi* to mean "Judean," so much so that the Josephan phrase *Ioudaios to genos* always means "Judean by birth," not "Jewish by birth."

As an ethnic-geographic term, *Ioudaios* is parallel to terms like Egyptian, Cappadocian, Thracian, and Phrygian, which are both ethnic and geographic. In certain contexts, of course, the ethnic meaning may have primacy over the geographic, while in other contexts the geographic meaning may have primacy over the ethnic, but both meanings are present. As an ethnic-geographic term, *Ioudaios* is best translated "Judean." The onomastic link between people and land is explained by Josephus (*Ant.* 11.173, a continuation of the passage cited just above), "As this tribe [the tribe of Judah] was the first to come to those parts, both the people themselves and the country have taken their name from it." Almost four hundred years before Josephus, Clearchus of Soli, a disciple of Aristotle (ca. 300 B.C.E.), had made a similar point: "The Judeans take their name from their place, for the place that they inhabit is named Judea" (quoted by Josephus, *Ag. Ap.* 1.179). As an ethnic-geographic term "Judean" is more ambiguous than Phrygian, Egyptian, Lydian, and the like because Judea is the name of both a country (the entire land of Israel) and a district (in contrast with the other districts Idumea, Galilee, Perea, and Samaria). Thus, the category "Judean" sometimes includes Idumean, Galilean, Perean, and Samarian, and sometimes excludes them (a good example: *J.W.* 2.43).

Many Judeans, of course, lived outside of Judea. For them the geographical component of the name *Ioudaios* was much attenuated and the ethnic meaning came to the fore. Throughout antiquity Jews of the Diaspora were members of local associations or corporations. At first these associations were defined ethnically; that is, membership will have been open primarily or exclusively to people who themselves, or whose ancestors, had been members of the ethnic-geographic polity of Judea. Until the time of Augustus, and perhaps even after, the Alexandrian Jewish community was led by a "head of the nation" *(ethnarch* or *genarch).* The emperor Claudius addresses "the Judeans in Alexandria," even referring to them explicitly as a "nation." Many scholars have argued that some or all of the Jews of Alexandria constituted an ethnic corporation. Several inscriptions mention "the ethnic corporation *(politeuma)* of the Judeans in Berenike." In several places in the Greek Diaspora the Jews called their local community *laos,* "the people," which seems to be an ethnic self-designation; more commonly they call themselves *hoi Ioudaioi,* "the Judeans," of a specific place.

The ethnic reference of "Judean" was so strong that both the Judeans themselves and the Greeks and Romans had a sense that all Judeans everywhere somehow belonged to a single group. Strabo (quoted by Josephus, *Ant.* 14.115) remarks that the Judeans "have made their way already into every city, and it is not easy to find any place in the habitable world which has not received this nation and in which it has not made its power felt." In a letter attributed by Aristeas to Ptolemy Philadelphus, the king expresses his wish to bestow benefactions on "all the Judeans in the civilized world and their descendants." A letter attributed by Josephus (*Ant.* 19.288) to the emperor Claudius includes a reference to "the Judeans throughout the empire under the Romans." In these passages "the Judeans" constitute an "ethnic" category, not a political or administrative one, since no empire-wide political structure embracing all Judeans ever existed in either the Hellenistic or early Roman empires.

Ioudaios as Jew

As a religious or cultural label, a *Ioudaios* is someone who believes (or is supposed to believe) certain distinctive tenets and who follows (or is supposed to follow) certain distinctive practices; in other words, a *Ioudaios* is a Jew, someone who worships the God whose temple is in Jerusalem (after 70 C.E.: whose temple had been in Jerusalem). The earliest examples of this usage are in 2 Maccabees. In 2 Macc. 6:6, as a result of the persecution "People could neither keep the Sabbath, nor observe the festivals of their ancestors, nor so much as confess themselves to be Jews"; in 2 Macc. 9:17, the arch-villain Antiochus IV Epiphanes, afflicted by God with severe torments and hoping for divine mercy, pledges to grant the Jews various benefactions, even going so far as "to become a Jew" *(Ioudaion esesthai).* Another good example of this usage is in Josephus' description of the conversion of the royal house of Adiabene (*Ant.* 20.38-39). The prince realizes that "to be truly a *Ioudaios*" is impossible without circumcision, but his mother warns him that his subjects will not tolerate rule by a king who is a *Ioudaios.* In this passage, which speaks about conversion to Judaism, the ethnic-geographic meaning of *Ioudaios* is entirely absent, and only a religious meaning is intended. Gentiles cannot change the ethnos of their birth, but they can change their religion. An Adiabenian prince cannot become a Judean, but he, like Antiochus Epiphanes before him, can become a Jew.

Ioudaios as Citizen or Ally of the Judean State

Ioudaios can also be a political designation. A number of passages in Josephus suggest that the Hasmonean state was constituted as a league of *Ioudaioi* (Judeans) with several neighboring peoples, notably the Idumeans. Josephus reports that after the conquest of Idumea by Hyrcanus the Idumeans "have continued to be Judeans" (*Ant.* 13.257-58). Ethnically, of course, the Idumeans are not Judeans, but by joining the Judeans they have become known as Judeans and become Judeans. The Idumeans and the Judeans merged in an alliance, and, since the Judeans were the dominant partner in this alliance, the allies too became known as Judeans, just as all members of the Achean League were known (in some contexts) as Acheans, and all the nations of Italy were known (in some contexts) as Romans, and so forth.

Translating *Ioudaios*

All occurrences of the term *Ioudaios* before the middle or end of the second century B.C.E. should be translated not by "Jew," a religious term, but by "Judean," an ethnic-geographical term. In the second half of the second century B.C.E., the term *Ioudaios* for the first time is applied even to people who are not ethnic or geographical Judeans but who either have come to believe in the God of the Judeans (i.e., they have become "Jews") or have joined the Judean state as allies or citizens (i.e., they have become "Judeans" in a political sense). Behind this semantic shift lies a significant development in the history of Judaism, namely, the ability of outsiders to enter the Judean polity, either through religious/cultural conversion or through political enfranchisement.

BIBLIOGRAPHY
S. J. D. COHEN 1999, *The Beginnings of Jewishness,* Berkeley: University of California Press, 69-106. • J. H. ELLIOTT 2007, "Jesus the Israelite Was neither a 'Jew' nor a 'Christian': On Correcting Misleading Nomenclature," in *Journal for the Study of the Historical Jesus* 5: 119-54. • G. A. P. HARVEY 1996, *The True Israel: Uses of the Names Jew, Hebrew and Israel in Ancient Jewish and Early Christian Literature,* Leiden: Brill. • M. LOWE 1976, "Who Were the *Ioudaioi?" NovT* 18: 101-30. • S. MASON 2007, "Jews, Judaeans, Judaizing, Judaism: Problems of Categorization in Ancient History," *JJS* 38:457-512. • P. J. TOMSON 1986, "The Names Israel and Jew in Ancient Judaism," *Bijdragen: Tijdschrift voor filosofie en theologie* 47: 120-40.

SHAYE J. D. COHEN

Isaac

Hebrew Bible

The Israelite patriarch Isaac was the son of Abraham and Sarah. In both wives and wells, the canonical Isaac largely replicates his father's life, contributing little beyond a genealogical bridge between Israel's forefather Abraham and its namesake Jacob. The few details unique to Isaac's life manifest questionable qualities such as his passivity (Genesis 22), overriding hunger (Gen. 25:28; 27:4-33), and blind ignorance (Gen. 27:1, 21-27). This biblical portrait makes the depictions of Isaac in early Judaism all the more remarkable. Indeed, this period produces no one, monolithic interpretation of Isaac, but rather a kaleidoscope of images refracting Scripture's portrait through the lenses of contemporary experiences and context. The resulting configurations of Isaac embody key aspects of each author's vision of faithfulness.

Early Jewish Literature

Jubilees

The book of *Jubilees* shows a keen awareness of Isaac's perceived shortcomings and endeavors to rewrite events commensurate with the author's sensibilities (VanderKam 2001). Isaac's lie about Rebekah being his sister is omitted, as is his dubious reason for favoring Esau (a taste for wild game). Isaac's mistaken preference is later corrected in *Jub.* 35:13-17, where Isaac is said to realize Esau's depravity in the face of Jacob's overwhelming righteousness, and the impropriety of

Isaac's blessing is explained away as a heavenly turn of affairs to distract Isaac's mind (*Jub.* 26:18). More problematic is Isaac's oath of peace sworn to the Philistine leaders, which potentially could have been understood as obligatory to Isaac's descendants, thereby rendering later Israelite attacks on the Philistines as violations of this patriarchal oath. Here *Jubilees* alters the biblical scene, depicting Isaac as swearing under compulsion; the author then places in Isaac's mouth an eternal curse of complete destruction upon the Philistines (*Jub.* 24:25-33). This antagonism toward Gentiles is consistent with the outlook of *Jubilees,* and the addition of Isaac's prophetic (!) blessing of Levi (*Jub.* 31:11-17), coming close on the heals of Levi's zealous annihilation of the men of Shechem for their defilement of the twelve-year-old Dinah (*Jubilees* 30; cf. Genesis 34), confirms the transformation of Isaac into a patriarch upholding hostile boundaries separating Jews from Gentiles.

Isaac's birth and legacy are also areas of interpretive augmentation in *Jubilees.* The angels not only reveal that Sarah will conceive (cf. Gen. 18:10-14), but also that his name Isaac was ordained and written in the (preexistent?) heavenly tablets (*Jub.* 16:3-4). Isaac is also lauded as the solitary one through whom kings of nations will come (*Jub.* 15:16; cf. Gen. 17:16, which designates Sarai), a "righteous planting for all generations" (*Jub.* 16:26; cf. *Jub.* 21:24; *1 Enoch* 10:16; 93:5, 10) from whom a "holy seed . . . not counted among the nations" would emerge. Though still overshadowed by Abraham, Jacob, and even Rebekah (whose portraits are all elevated in *Jubilees;* cf. Endres 1987), when compared to his canonical *Urbild,* the reinterpreted Isaac of *Jubilees* is nonetheless a figure of improved stature and importance.

Philo

In Philo, the figure of Isaac achieves singular mythic proportion, overshadowing all but Moses (Goodenough 1935). Rooted in his philosophical and symbolic interpretation of Scripture, Philo upholds Isaac as representing perfection (*Mut.* 88), possessing the gifts of God in full (*Congr.* 38); he is entirely free of passions (*Det.* 46; cf. *Sacr.* 110), set on the eager pursuit of the divine (*Cher.* 8). In short, Isaac is the foremost member of the race of immortal and most perfect beings (*Sacr.* 7), the paradigm of joyful faith (*Praem.* 31–35), and the vision of self-taught wisdom (*Det.* 29–31) who nourishes others through his teaching (*Migr.* 140) and cheers peace-loving souls (*Mut.* 131). Noting that Isaac alone of the three archpatriarchs does not have his name changed, Philo (reconfiguring Plutarch's tripartite educational theory) deduces that Isaac is "self-taught" by nature and perfect in virtue (*Mut.* 88; *Sobr.* 8), not requiring the improvements that Abraham (representing "learning") and Jacob (representing "practice") needed, as symbolized by their name changes (*Mut.* 12, 88; cf. *Somniis* 167-68; *Vita* 1.76). Isaac's superiority is likewise symbolically confirmed to Philo by his strict monogamy, for whereas Abraham and Jacob each had several legitimate partners who represented the need for a variety of studies to complete their acquisition of virtue, Isaac's full reception of God's perfect gifts had no need of "concubine" arts but wished only for the "wife" of perseverance (i.e., Rebekah) so that God's mercies would remain everlasting (*Congr.* 34–38).

The fact that Isaac alone is commanded to remain in the land (Gen. 26:2) elevates the "proper citizen" and "native inhabitant" Isaac (*Mut.* 147; *Somn.* 160), who abides in the abundant land of virtue and wisdom, above the sojourner Abraham and practicer Jacob (*Migr.* 27-29; cf. *Det.* 46; *Somn.* 1.160-62, 66-67; *Fug.* 67; *Sobr.* 13; *Ebr.* 20). In all these respects Isaac is the pinnacle of piety in Philonic thought, the foremost of the patriarchs (who for Philo are themselves "laws incarnate and vocal," the archetypes upon which the written laws of Moses are based [*Abrahamo* 1–6]).

Isaac's excellence in Philo even exceeds the bounds of mere humanity (*Mut.* 130–32). Regarding Isaac's birth, Philo takes the biblical promise that God will "visit" Sarah (Gen. 18:10-14) quite literally, asserting that God — and not Abraham — is Isaac's true father. (*Cher.* 45; cf. *Det.* 60; *Somn.* 173). Similarly, Philo interprets Sarah's proclamation that "The LORD has caused me laughter" (Gen 21:6) to mean that the Lord has begotten Isaac, since the name "Isaac" means "laughter" (*Mut.* 137; cf. *Det.* 124). This notion that Isaac is the embodiment of laughter and joy (*Abr.* 201; *Leg.* 3.86-87; *Mut.* 157; *QG* 3.53; *QG* 4.17) also paves the way for Philo's belief in Isaac's preexistence (asserted of Jacob in *The Prayer of Joseph*). Rather than interpreting Sarah's laughter negatively, Philo finds it indicative of Isaac's preexistence, for she could not have laughed if Laughter (i.e., Isaac) had not already been made and excellently endowed (*Mut.* 157–66; cf. *Leg.* 3.85-87).

Josephus

For Josephus, Isaac embodies Jewish heroism, classically defined in terms of noble birth, filial piety, and virtue (Feldman 1998). Isaac's favorable lineage is noted at his near sacrifice (*Ant.* 1.229-32), as is his reverence for his father and ancestors (*Ant.* 1.222, 232). Josephus' Isaac also exhibits all the cardinal virtues. His wisdom is emphasized in Josephus' rewriting of the well conflict with Abimelech (Gen. 26:17-33), which lauds the achievement of security via judicious deliberation (*Ant.* 1.261) rather than struggle (Gen. 26.21). Isaac's bravery is exalted at his near sacrifice (*Ant* 1.232), augmented by the fact that in the *Antiquities* Isaac is a twenty-five-year-old adult, and though capable of physically resisting Abraham, Isaac nonetheless rushes unbound to the altar for slaughter (*Ant.* 1.232). Josephus omits all references to Isaac's intemperate love of game (*Ant.* 1.258, 267-70), instead proclaiming Isaac's self-control in response to Esau's exogamy (*Ant.* 1.266) and his return from the hunt to receive the blessing already given to Jacob (*Ant.* 1.274). Isaac's virtuous embodiment of justice is both stated (1.232) and imputed via depictions of his gratefulness (*Ant.* 1.264) and sympathy (*Ant.* 1.275); tellingly, Josephus omits Isaac's deceitful characterization of Rebekah as his sister (Gen. 26.7-9), thereby preserving his image of truthfulness. Finally, Isaac's piety dominates his self-sacrifice, characterized by Josephus as his priestly "zeal for worship" (*Ant.* 1.222), his building of the altar (*Ant.* 1.227, contra Gen. 22:9), and his acceptance of God's command as his ground for existence (*Ant.* 1.232).

Josephus' classical cast of Isaac nonetheless betrays a substructure of Jewish militancy. Lest Isaac's self-control with Abimelech be taken as a sign of weakness, Josephus implies that Isaac held a "secret enmity" against Abimelech, giving rise to the Philistine king's fear that Isaac would avenge himself for his injuries (1.263). Similarly, despite downplaying the land promises to Abraham overall, Josephus characterizes the reward for the near sacrifice as a great dominion *(megalēn hēgemonian),* asserting that Abraham's offspring will subdue Canaan by force of arms (*hoplois; Ant.* 1.234-35; cf. 1.185; 1.191). While Josephus omits Isaac's blessing of Jacob that states "Let nations bow down to you" (Gen. 27.29), he substitutes a prayer from Isaac that Jacob will be a delight to friends, but a terror to his foes (*Ant.* 1.273). All of these examples likely reflect indwelled interpretative dimensions known to Josephus the warrior-priest, repackaged to commend Jewish fortitude in Roman dress to imperial Rome, its newest "friend."

Other Texts

There are also scattered glimpses of a final area of interpretive speculation: Isaac's posthumous fate. Josephus has Abraham declare that in his sacrificial death Isaac is being sent to God the Father (*Ant.* 2.30; cf. Pseudo-Philo, *Bib. Ant.* 32:3-4; *T. Abr.* [A] 20:14) to be near to God and intercede for Abraham (*Ant.* 1.230). 4 Maccabees 13:17 makes a similar claim that the exalted martyrs will be received in heaven by Abraham, Isaac, and Jacob, and 4 Macc. 17:18 confirms that the divine throne room is envisioned (cf. 9:8). 4 Maccabees 7:19 additionally asserts that the patriarchs currently live to God, a point that Mark 12:26-27 (and pars.) uses to provide pentateuchal support for the resurrection (cf. Heb. 11:17-19). Though beliefs regarding Isaac's sacrificial death and subsequent resurrection, attested in later haggadic tradition (Spiegel 1969), have yet to be securely dated to the Second Temple time period, the essential components for such an interpretation are largely in place. Overall, these interpretive developments represent a thorough transformation of the biblical Isaac from beginning to end — including even a posthumous "beginning-again."

BIBLIOGRAPHY

J. ENDRES 1987, *Biblical Interpretation in the Book of Jubilees,* Washington, D.C.: Catholic Biblical Association of America. • L. FELDMAN 1998, *Josephus's Interpretation of the Bible,* Berkeley: University of California Press, 290-303. • E. R. GOODENOUGH 1935, *By Light, Light: The Mystic Gospel of Hellenistic Judaism,* New Haven: Yale University Press, 153-66. • J. L. KUGEL 1998, *Traditions of the Bible: A Guide to the Bible as It Was at the Start of the Common Era,* Cambridge: Harvard University Press, 301-26. • S. SPIEGEL 1969, *The Last Trial,* New York: Schocken. • J. C. VANDERKAM 2001, *The Book of Jubilees,* Sheffield: Sheffield Academic Press, 111-12.

See also: Aqedah JASON J. RIPLEY

Isaiah, Ascension of

The *Ascension of Isaiah* is an early Christian apocalypse that describes the persecution and death of Isaiah, the reign of Beliar, and the descent and ascent of the Beloved. The *Ascension* is treasured in the Ethiopian Church and remembered in the Greek, Latin, and Slavonic Churches.

Contents

The *Ascension of Isaiah* divides naturally into two parts. In the "Martyrdom of Isaiah" (chaps. 1–5), Manasseh, king of Judah, persecutes the prophets and saws Isaiah in two. In the "Vision of Isaiah" (chaps. 6–11), Isaiah travels through the heavens to see the Beloved descending incognito to earth and Sheol and then reascending in glory to sit at God's right hand.

Hezekiah bequeaths godly prophecy to Manasseh, but Manasseh prefers Beliar to God. The false prophet Belchira discovers Isaiah in frugal retirement and accuses Isaiah of contravening Moses by claiming to see God. Inspired by Beliar, Manasseh seizes Isaiah. The narrator explains Beliar's ire: Isaiah had disclosed the descent and ascent of the Beloved, the church pursuing vainglory, the persecution of the apostolic prophets, the descent of Beliar to reign, and the coming of the Lord to reprove the disordered universe. Isaiah, having sent other prophets to safety, speaks by the Holy Spirit until he is sawed in two.

The *Ascension of Isaiah* then reverts to the happier days of Hezekiah. After opening a heavenly door for a worshiping prophetic school, Isaiah falls in a trance and ascends heavenward. In the firmament, Isaiah sees envious angels fighting, but in each of the seven heavens he finds angels praising the descending heavenly glory. In the sixth and seventh heavens, Isaiah worships the Beloved and the Angel of the Spirit before raising his eyes to an unendurable glimpse of God's Great Glory. He then hears the Father of the Lord summon the Beloved to descend incognito, disturbing neither heaven's worship nor firmament's strife. On earth born of Mary and crucified, the Beloved descends to Sheol. Rising in glory he sends out the twelve and ascends, commanding worship from Satan and his hosts and then from each level of heaven. When he takes his seat at the right hand of the Great Glory, the Angel of the Spirit and all the righteous also take their thrones and worship. Isaiah returns, reports the vision, and, in conclusion, invites the reader to share in heavenly glory: "But as for you, be in the Holy Spirit that you may receive your robes, and the thrones and crowns of glory, which are placed in the seventh heaven" (*Ascen. Isa.* 11:40; Knibb 1985, 176).

Versions and Recensions

Although the *Ascension of Isaiah* originally appeared in Greek, it exists only in an Ethiopic version. Enough of the Greek survives to show that the Ethiopic translation is accurate, astute, appreciative — and more elegant than the original! Smaller fragments exist in Latin and two dialects of Coptic.

"The Vision of Isaiah" (chaps. 6–11), exists also in a second, shorter recension in Latin and Slavonic. The second recension has revised the story to address a later audience. A few manuscripts further abridge the Slavonic version.

A Greek rearrangement and summary of the *Ascension of Isaiah,* known as the Greek Legend, exists in two manuscripts of the eleventh and twelfth centuries. Its author has created a "saint's life" of Isaiah: it summarizes the "Vision of Isaiah" in temporal sequence and ends with the death of Isaiah.

Therefore, the Ethiopic *Ascension of Isaiah* is the best witness to the primitive work; the Coptic, Greek, and Latin fragments of the first recension are valuable for recovering the text. The second recension, though a step removed from the earlier work, when used carefully, can help establish readings of the primitive "Vision of Isaiah," and the Greek Legend, though even further from the *Ascension of Isaiah,* can sometimes confirm conjectures about the original Greek.

Date and Place of Origin

Earlier analyses dismembered the *Ascension of Isaiah* into a series of sources: a Jewish martyrdom source, a Christian apocalypse, and perhaps a Jewish ascent source. Little remained to date the completed *Ascension of Isaiah.* Recent consensus understands the *Ascension* as a unity. An early Christian prophet wrote the *Ascension of Isaiah* to win a hearing from those captivated by earthly glory and blind to the healing beauties of heavenly glory. The "Martyrdom of Isaiah" (chaps. 1–5) is not a Jewish martyrdom source but the first half of the completed work. It prepares readers to heed a prophetic school that practices heavenly ascent. The "Vision of Isaiah" (chaps. 6–11) reveals the divine glory and the descent of the Beloved to bring it to earth. Vindication of the descent and ascent of the Beloved, of prophetic ascent to see God, and of the summons from earthly vainglory to life-giving heavenly glory structures the entire work. Evidence formerly applied only to the "Martyrdom source" now helps date the *Ascension of Isaiah.*

4 Baruch quotes *Ascen. Isa.* 3:17, alludes distinctly to *Ascen. Isa.* 3:7-10, and knows the death of Isaiah and his vision of the Son's descent (*4 Bar.* 9:19-22). Jeremiah's trance (*4 Bar.* 9:7-14) may reflect Isaiah's (*Ascen. Isa.* 6:10-12, 17). *4 Baruch* is usually dated no later than the middle of the second century. The *Gospel of Peter* 10 (39–40), also from the middle of the second century, depicts the resurrection in terms reminiscent of *Ascen. Isa.* 3:16-17. Evils in the church (*Ascen. Isa.* 3:21-31) resemble those in 1 and 2 Timothy, 2 Peter, and *1 Clement.* The setting within a prophetic school that both honed prophetic practice and wrote the visions of the prophets has strong contacts with the epistles of Ignatius, the Gospel and Epistles of John, Revelation, and the *Odes of Solomon.* The *Ascension of Isaiah* (4:2-3) knows Nero as archetypal demonic ruler and probably alludes to the death of Peter (if we follow the singular reading of the Greek) or perhaps to the deaths of Peter and Paul (if we follow the plural Ethiopic). Taken together, these data suggest an early second- or late first-century date for the completed *Ascension of Isaiah.*

Affiliations and Significance

The *Ascension of Isaiah* venerates Jesus of Nazareth. Yet the categories it uses to understand the Beloved and his descent in human form are Jewish. Like the Son of Man in the *Similitudes of Enoch,* Israel in the *Prayer of Joseph,* and Melchizedek in 11QMelchizdek, the Beloved is the highest heavenly power before God. Like Metatron in *3 Enoch,* Melchizedek in 11QMelchizedek, and Yahoel in the *Apocalypse of Abraham,* the Beloved bears the divine name (*Ascen. Isa.* 9:5). Like Israel descending to become Jacob in the *Prayer of Joseph,* the Beloved descends to become Jesus. In the *Similitudes,* Enoch ascends to become the Son of Man (*1 Enoch* 70:1–71:17) on God's throne (*1 Enoch* 51:8; 55:4); in the *Ascension of Isaiah,* the Beloved ascends to a throne at God's right hand (*Ascen. Isa.* 11:22-33). As the Son of Man receives worship (*1 Enoch* 40:5; 48:4-10; 52:9), so too does the Beloved (*Ascen. Isa.* 9:27-32; 10:19; 11:22-33). In *2 Enoch,* Enoch, having become one of the highest angels (*2 Enoch* 22:9-10), descends on behalf of human beings and then reascends to his high office (*2 Enoch* 36–38; 67). The *Ascension of Isaiah* is as Jewish as it is Christian, and probably as Gnostic as either. Since it was likely written before Judaism, Christianity, and Gnosticism become mutually exclusive, the *Ascension of Isaiah* belongs as naturally in histories of merkavah mysticism or Gnosticism as in histories of christological or trinitarian doctrine.

The *Ascension of Isaiah* has a distinctive soteriology. Seven theophanic angels manifest the glory of God appropriate for each heaven. The first five heavens worship the divine glory through five theophanic throne angels. Inhabitants of the sixth and seventh heavens see and worship the Angel of the Holy Spirit and the Beloved, but only in the seventh heaven do the righteous dead, the Angel of the Holy Spirit, and the Beloved see and worship the Great Glory directly. Theophany by theophany the glory of God descends heaven by heaven, provoking the praise that streams back up to the Great Glory. The heavens are nourished by a respiration of divine glory. However, angels of the firmament, distracted by their own glory, have severed firmament, air, earth, and Sheol from the respiration of glory. The Beloved descends to manifest the divine glory in Sheol, earth, air, firmament, and in each heaven, restoring the downward and upward flow of divine glory, to reconnect perceptive wills with the beatific vision. Perhaps a glory soteriology may surface elsewhere (see John 1:14; 2:11; 5:41-44; 7:18; 12:39-43; 1 Cor. 2:7-16; 2 Cor. 3:12–4:7; Rom. 1:23; 3:23; 5:2; 8:18-23; 9:23; Col. 1:18-20, 25-27; Heb. 2:6-10; Ignatius, *Eph.* 19:1–20:1), but nowhere else so clearly.

The *Ascension of Isaiah* stands at an important historical juncture. It presents the earliest surviving picture of relations among Father, Son, and Spirit. It offers one of the clearest windows on early Christian prophetic conflict resembling that in Revelation, John, Ignatius, *Odes of Solomon*, and perhaps the *Didache*. It preserves otherwise missing links between earlier Jewish apocalyptic writings and later merkavah ascent texts and between ancient Jewish wisdom and hymnody and later Gnostic systems. Historically and doctrinally significant as well as beautiful to one whose Gestalt can shift to see, the *Ascension of Isaiah* invites further study.

BIBLIOGRAPHY

A. ACERBI 1989, *L'Ascensione di Isaia: Cristologia e profetismo in Siria nei primi decenni del II secolo*, Milan: Università Cattolica del Sacro Cuore. • R. BAUCKHAM 1998, "The Ascension of Isaiah: Genre, Unity and Date," in idem, *The Fate of the Dead: Studies in Jewish and Christian Apocalypses*, 363-90. • P. BETTIOLO ET AL. 1995, *Ascensio Isaie*, Turnhout: Brepols. • P. C. BORI 1980, "L'estasi del profeta: *Ascensio Isaiae* 6 e l'antico profetismo cristiano," *Cristianesimo nella Storia* 1: 367-89. • R. H. CHARLES 1900, *The Ascension of Isaiah*, London: Black. • R. G. HALL 1990, "The Ascension of Isaiah: Community Situation, Date, and Place in Early Christianity," *JBL* 109: 289-306. • R. G. HALL 1994, "Isaiah's Ascent to See the Beloved: An Ancient Jewish Source for the Ascension of Isaiah?" *JBL* 113: 463-84. • R. G. HALL 2004, "Disjunction of Heavenly and Earthly Times in the Ascension of Isaiah," *JSJ* 35: 17-36. • D. D. HANNAH 1999, "The Ascension of Isaiah and Docetic Christology," *VC* 53: 165-96. • D. D. HANNAH 1999, "Isaiah's Vision in the Ascension of Isaiah and in the Early Church," *JTS* 50: 80-101. • M. A. KNIBB 1985, "Ascension of Isaiah: A New Translation and Introduction," in *OTP* 2:143-76. • J. KNIGHT 1995, *The Ascension of Isaiah*, Sheffield: Sheffield Academic Press. • J. KNIGHT 1996, *Disciples of the Beloved One: The Christology, Social Setting and Theological Context of the Ascension of Isaiah*, Sheffield: Sheffield Academic Press. • E. NORELLI 1994, *L'Ascensione di Isaia: Studi su un apocrifo al crocevia dei cristianesimi*, Bologna: Edizioni Dehoniane Bologna. • E. NORELLI 1995, *Ascensio Isaiae: Commentarius*, Turnhout: Brepols. • M. PESCE, ED. 1983, *Isaia, il diletto e la chiesa: Visione ed esegesi profetica cristiano-primitiva nell'Ascensione di Isaia*, Brescia: Paideia. • M. PESCE 1984, *Il "Martirio de Isaia" non esiste: L'Ascension di Isaia e le tradizioni guidaiche sull'uccisione del profeta*, Bologna: Edizioni Dehoniane Bologna. • L. T. STUCKENBRUCK 1999, "The Ascension of Isaiah: Monotheism and Christology," in *Monotheism and the Worship of Jesus*, ed. J. Davila et al., Leiden: Brill, 70-89. • L. T. STUCKENBRUCK 2004, "The Holy Spirit and the Ascension of Isaiah," in *The Holy Spirit and Christian Origins: Essays in Honor of James D. G. Dunn*, ed. G. N. Stanton et al., Grand Rapids: Eerdmans, 308-20.

ROBERT G. HALL

Isaiah, Book of

Isaiah is the first book of the Hebrew latter prophets. Two issues come to the fore when considering Isaiah in early Judaism: the extent to which the book is a product of the Second Temple period (for our purposes, 321 B.C.E.–135 C.E.) and the book's reception and use in that period.

The Book and Its Formation

Modern scholars divide the book into two sections. Isaiah 1–39 is associated with Isaiah son of Amos ("First Isaiah"), who lived in Jerusalem in the eighth century B.C.E. Isaiah 40–66 is associated with the era of Babylon's downfall and Persia's rise, starting in the 530s B.C.E. Scholars further subdivide these two sections. Most regard chaps. 24–27 (the "Isaianic Apocalypse") as a Persian- or Hellenistic-era addition to First Isaiah, and chaps. 34–35 as stemming from the same author(s) as the second section. In recent decades many have argued that large sections of chaps. 1–39 were composed in the Persian (537-336 B.C.E.) and Hellenistic eras (after 336). Many passages in chaps. 1–39 are said to include an eighth-century base text, additions from later in the preexilic period, and supplements from the exilic, Persian, and Hellenistic eras; others consist entirely of later material without any eighth-century or even preexilic base. Similarly, the second section is also subdivided. Most scholars regard Isaiah 40–55 or 40–53 as the product of a prophet who lived in Babylon on the eve of its fall to the Persians. For want of another name, scholars call this prophet Deutero-Isaiah or Second Isaiah. Isaiah 56–66 (or 54–66) is attributed either to a single prophet ("Trito-Isaiah" or "Third Isaiah") who lived in the land of Israel in the Persian era, or to a series of prophets and disciples or scribes in the Persian and Hellenistic eras. Some scholars accept the division of the text into multiple layers but argue that the final form of the book achieves a significant degree of unity, in large part due to editorial work of scribes who produced the latest layers even as they revised earlier ones.

The attempts to break the two main blocks of material into manifold subdivisions have not been successful. They often take integrated poems that make excellent sense as they stand and divide them into a series of nearly unreadable fragments. Linguistic evidence for these attempts cannot be proffered. Readings that contextualize the bulk of each section in the eighth and sixth centuries make more sense than attempts to contextualize motley splinters in the seventh through fourth. In all likelihood, chaps. 13–14 were reworked by scribes in the sixth century or later, and chaps. 24–27 were added in the postexilic era. There is no reason to doubt that the rest of chaps. 1–33 were written in the eighth century. Chapters 36–39 contain narratives about Isaiah, the product of authors who cannot be dated with confidence. Chapters 40–66 and 34–35 were composed by a prophet in the Babylonian Exile and in the early restoration period in the land of Israel after Cyrus allowed Judean exiles to emigrate to their ancestral homeland. Alternatively, these chapters may contain the work of an exilic prophet and disciples who lived in the land of Israel a generation later. In either case, these chapters form a unity with a consistent literary style, theology, and attitude toward earlier tradition. Some scholars have attempted to identify within these chapters several layers of thinking concerning eschatology, some allegedly earlier and closer to classical prophecy, some later and closer to apocalyptic literature. These attempts are based on far-fetched readings, and they arbitrarily import later ideas into the crucial passages.

Attitudes toward the Davidic Monarchy

Of particular significance to the study of early Judaism are the varying attitudes toward Davidic monarchy in the book. First Isaiah is one of the most enthusiastic monarchists in Scripture, while Second Isaiah rejects the idea of a human king. Following the covenant of grant (Psalm 89; 2 Samuel 7), First Isaiah trusts an eternal royal line descended from David. He never condemns the institution of monarchy, even when frustrated by a particular king. He reacts with horror to the prospect of the monarch being replaced with someone from another family (chaps. 7–8). His hopes for the future are bound up with David's family; the era of universal peace he predicts will be ushered in by an ideal prophet-king (2:1-4; chaps. 9 and 11). Chapters 40–66 and 34–35, however, evince no loyalty to the Davidic monarchy. Even though the royal family still existed in this prophet's day, Second Isaiah does not hope for the renewal of its rule. Whenever Second Isaiah borrows phrasing from older royal texts, whether from First Isaiah or Psalms, this prophet of restoration pointedly omits any reference to the king and applies whatever motif was associated with him to the entire nation Israel.

The tension within the book on the question of kingship foreshadows a significant debate in early Judaism. For most of the Persian and the early Hellenistic periods, we find no indications that Jews hoped for the renewal of Davidic monarchy. But at some point during the Hellenistic period, this hope blossomed, leading to the various forms of messianism so well known from late Second Temple Judaism, from early Christianity, and from rabbinic texts.

Reception and Use

Isaiah crystallized into one basic text type at an early period. Our textual witnesses (MT, LXX, DSS) all represent the same basic text type, whereas Jeremiah and Esther, for example, are extant in two types of significantly different lengths and order of passages. Thus Isaiah's evolution ceased before the translation of LXX. Ben Sira (early second century B.C.E.) knew a book that included both major sections; he refers to Isaiah as author of material clearly identifiable as coming from chaps. 36–39 and 40 (Sir. 48:20-25).

Nineteen manuscripts of Isaiah have been found in the caves near Qumran, most of them extremely fragmentary; one text, however, known as 1QIsa[a], contains almost the entire book in excellent condition. Most of the Qumran fragments closely resemble the MT, but 1QIsa[a] differs from the MT in interesting ways even though it belongs to the same basic text type. Kutscher demonstrates that this manuscript's language has been updated. The MT is written in classical biblical Hebrew with almost no elements of late biblical Hebrew of the Hellenistic and Roman periods, but 1QIsa[a] is full of those elements. Its spelling, for example, very frequently includes vowel letters, an orthographic feature that became more common in late biblical Hebrew and very common thereafter. Obscure words that fell out of Hebrew in the Hellenistic and Roman periods were later often replaced with words known to us from the DSS or rabbinic texts. Thus a comparison of the MT and 1QIsa[a] plays a crucial role in the study of the Hebrew language's development.

Isaiah proved to be one of the most popular books in early Judaism (Hannah 2005; Blenkinsopp 2006). Fragments of no fewer than six commentaries (pesharim) were found at Qumran. There is an Aramaic Targum of Isaiah. The popularity of the book is due to several factors that made the scroll fertile ground for messianic predictions: fervent loyalty to the Davidic monarchy in the first part of the book; prophecies of comfort and salvation in the second part; descriptions of a suffering figure surprisingly vindicated in the second part (esp. chap. 53); and prophecies of universal peace and recognition of the one God throughout the book. Isaiah is quoted more than any other prophetic book in both the New Testament and rabbinic literature. In the synagogue liturgy that crystallized in the Middle Ages, more prophetic lectionaries were taken from Isaiah than from any other book. This is not simply due to its length. In Ashkenazic practice nineteen lectionaries are from Isaiah, and even though the books of Kings and Jeremiah are longer than Isaiah, they contribute only sixteen and nine, respectively.

BIBLIOGRAPHY

K. BALTZER 2001, *Deutero-Isaiah: A Commentary on Isaiah 40–55*, trans. M. Kohl, Minneapolis: Augsburg Fortress. • J. BLENKINSOPP 2000, *Isaiah 1–39: A New Translation with Introduction and Commentary*, New York: Doubleday. • J. BLENKINSOPP 2002, *Isaiah 40–55: A New Translation with Introduction and Commentary*, New York: Doubleday. • J. BLENKINSOPP 2003, *Isaiah 56–66: A New Translation with Introduction and Commentary*, New York: Doubleday. • J. BLENKINSOPP 2006, *Opening the Sealed Book: Interpretations of the Book of Isaiah in Late Antiquity*, Grand Rapids: Eerdmans. • C. C. BROYLES AND C. A. EVANS, EDS. 1997, *Writing and Reading the Scroll of Isaiah: Studies of an Interpretative Tradition*, 2 vols. Leiden: Brill. • B. CHILDS 2001, *Isaiah: A Commentary*, Louisville: Westminster John Knox. • D. D. HANNAH 2005, "Isaiah within Judaism of the Second Temple Period," in *Isaiah in the New Testament*, ed. S. Moyise and M. J. J. Menken, London: Clark, 7-33. • R. MELUGIN AND M. SWEENEY, EDS. 1996, *New Visions of Isaiah*, Sheffield: Sheffield Academic Press. • C. SEITZ 1991, *Zion's Final Destiny: The Development of the Book of Isaiah*, Minneapolis: Fortress. • B. SOMMER 1998, *A Prophet Reads Scripture: Allusion in Isaiah 40–66*, Stanford: Stanford University Press. • M. SWEENEY 1996, *Isaiah 1–39*, Grand Rapids: Eerdmans. • C. WESTERMANN 1969, *Isaiah 40–66*, Philadelphia: Westminster. • H. M. G. WILLIAMSON 1994, *The Book Called Isaiah: Deutero-Isaiah's Role in Composition and Redaction*, Oxford: Clarendon.

See also: Isaiah Scrolls BENJAMIN D. SOMMER

Isaiah Scrolls

The discovery of twenty-two copies of Isaiah in the Judean Desert represents one of the most significant archaeological finds of the twentieth century. These texts, discovered between the years 1947 and 1952, have enhanced our understanding of the textual history of the Bible, and translators have utilized them for modern translations of the Bible.

The Qumran caves, located near the northwestern area of the Dead Sea, yielded twenty-one copies of the book of Isaiah — two from Cave 1, eighteen from Cave 4, and one from Cave 5. An additional copy of Isaiah (making a total of twenty-two copies) was discovered south of Qumran in a cave at Wadi Murabbaʿat. All twenty-two copies of Isaiah are written in Hebrew. Most of these scrolls are severely damaged and fragmented, owing to long-term exposure to the elements.

Altogether, the Isaiah scrolls represent about 10 percent of all biblical scrolls discovered at Qumran. This statistic alone indicates that Isaiah held a prominent place in the Qumran community, but other indications also reveal Isaiah's significance. Isaiah's book is treated as an authoritative work by the Qumran covenanters; in their sectarian writings, they cite, paraphrase, and allude to Isaiah more than any other prophet. These Isaiah quotations and allusions are located in legal, eschatological, and poetic contexts of the sectarian writings and reveal ideological and theological positions of the Qumran community. In addition to the twenty-two Isaiah scrolls themselves and the sectarian writings that include quotes and allusions to Isaiah, the Qumran discoveries included six Isaiah pesharim (commentaries).

The Isaiah scrolls present a view of what biblical manuscripts looked like at the end of the Second Temple era, before the stabilization of the Hebrew text after the first century C.E. Unlike the Masoretic Text (MT), with its consonantal and vocalization framework and system of notes, accents, and versification, the Isaiah scrolls feature handwritten manuscripts without vocalization or accents. Additionally, the scrolls contain interlinear or marginal corrections, scribal marks and notations, a different paragraphing system, and special morphological and orthographic features.

1QIsaiah[a]

1QIsaiah[a], or the Great Isaiah Scroll, is perhaps the best-known biblical scroll found at Qumran. It was one of the initial scrolls found in Qumran Cave 1 in 1947. It was wrapped in a linen cloth and stored in a clay jar. It consists of seventeen pieces of sheepskin sewn together into a single scroll and shows signs of being well used before it was stored away. The scroll comprises fifty-four columns of text that vary in width and average about twenty-nine lines of text per column. Measuring almost twenty-four feet in length and about ten inches in height, 1QIsaiah[a] is the longest of the Qumran biblical scrolls. Its paragraphing system and intratextual divisions are elaborate and unlike those of MT. Through paleographic analysis of the Hebrew script, scholars date the scroll to about 125 B.C.E. 1QIsaiah[a] represents a significant find because it includes all sixty-six chapters of Isaiah, except for minor lacunae, enabling scholars to conduct a complete study of this text. In contrast, the other Isaiah texts from Qumran, as fragmented and incomplete manuscripts, may slightly distort understandings of Isaiah's textual history.

The scroll has a number of scribal interventions, where the copyist or a subsequent scribe corrected readings or entered notations between the lines and in the margins. In addition, 1QIsaiah[a] has approximately 1,400 variant readings when compared to the MT, most of them minor (see below). Many of these variants deal with orthography, or spelling, and taken as a whole 1QIsaiah[a] displays a fuller orthography than the MT, meaning the scroll has more consonants in certain words. Some of the scroll's textual variants result from accidental errors that occurred during the transmission of the text by one or more generations of copyists. These include haplography, dittography, graphic similarity,

Column 6 of the Great Isaiah Scroll (1QIsa[a]) found in Cave 1 near Qumran *(John C. Trever)*

misdivision of words, interchange of letters, transposition of texts, and so forth. These errors are more or less typical among biblical scrolls and manuscripts from the last two centuries before the Common Era, and perhaps earlier, although a paucity of textual examples from earlier periods prevents a thorough investigation.

The scribe(s) who copied the Isaiah scroll from a master copy *(Vorlage)* had a free or liberal approach to the text, characterized by exegetical or editorial pluses, morphological smoothing and updating, harmonizations, phonetic variants, and modernizations of terms. There is also evidence that a well-intended scribe simplified the text for an audience that no longer understood classical Hebrew forms. His editorial tendencies resulted in a popularization of certain terms, some from Aramaic that reflected the language of Palestine in his time period. It is because of these modernizations that some scholars have concluded that 1QIsaiah[a] was a nonofficial, popular, or vulgar text.

Notwithstanding 1QIsaiah[a]'s variant readings, it shares many textual affinities with the proto-Masoretic text. The scroll also has more than two dozen readings where it agrees with the Septuagint (LXX) versus the MT. Of all the Qumran Isaiah scrolls, 1QIsaiah[a] displays more textual agreements with the LXX, but this may be due to the fact that both 1QIsaiah[a] and LXX date to approximately the same period and both demonstrate a free rendering, in some of their readings, of their *Vorlagen.*

1QIsaiah[b]

1QIsaiah[b] is the second largest of the Isaiah scrolls, although it is fragmented and missing a number of chapters and verses, especially from the first half of the book. This scroll was written in the Herodian bookhand and dates to the turn of the era. 1QIsaiah[b]'s readings correspond closely to those of the MT — more so than any of the other Qumran scrolls. And yet this scroll deviates from the MT with about 200 minor variants; half of them are deviations of orthography, and the other half deal with function rather than content words (e.g., the conjunction *wāw,* the definite article, missing letters, and different prepositions or pronouns).

4QIsaiah[a-r]

in 1952, Qumran Cave 4 yielded eighteen copies of Isaiah. All eighteen are written in either Hasmonean or Herodian scripts and date between the years 175 B.C.E. and 50 C.E. All Cave 4 Isaiah scrolls are written on leather except for 4QIsaiah[p], which is inscribed on papyrus. Compared to 1QIsaiah[a-b], 4QIsaiah[a-r] are quite fragmented and have many gaps in the text. 4QIsaiah[b] and 4QIsaiah[c] are the best preserved of the Cave 4 Isaiah texts; 4QIsaiah[b] contains remnants of thirty-six chapters, and 4QIsaiah[c] has parts of twenty-four. Fewer fragments survive from 4QIsaiah[a,d,e,f], and only between one and eight fragments survive from 4QIsaiah[g-r].

The readings of 4QIsaiah[a-r] reflect the consonantal text of the MT, meaning their character is proto-Masoretic, although some 4QIsaiah manuscripts are too fragmented to make a precise judgment. At the same time, these scrolls exhibit minor textual variants that are not regularly aligned with a particular Hebrew or Greek text. Of all of the 4QIsaiah manuscripts, 4QIsaiah[e,f] exhibit the most differences from the MT and are textually situated somewhere between 1QIsaiah[a] and 1QIsaiah[b]. The orthography is mixed in the 4QIsaiah texts, at times fuller than the MT but often less full. 4QIsaiah manuscripts have a different paragraphing system and different textual divisions than the MT. 4QIsaiah[c] exhibits a few unique traits, because its scribe consistently wrote the Tetragrammaton and other names of God in Paleo-Hebrew script.

5QIsaiah and MurIsaiah

Beyond the Isaiah scrolls from Caves 1 and 4, two other copies of Isaiah were discovered in the Judean Desert, one at Qumran Cave 5 and the other at Wadi Murabbaʿat, located south of Qumran. 5QIsaiah, consisting of two small fragments and dating to the Herodian period, includes words from Isa. 40:16–19. MurIsaiah dates to approximately the time of the First Jewish Revolt (66-73/74 C.E.) and comprises words from Isa. 1:4-14.

Significance of the Isaiah Scrolls

The Isaiah scrolls are significant finds, not only because they predate by approximately 1,000 years the medieval copies of the MT, but because they help to fill gaps of knowledge with regard to scribal conventions and styles, orthography, textual variants, and other aspects of a biblical scroll from the late Second Temple era.

Scribal Conventions

The scribes' stylistic methods and conventions, including paragraphing and text divisions, marginal and interlinear notations, and paleographic features, reveal the textual character of the Isaiah scrolls. Taken as a whole, these conventions disclose the nature of the scribal school that produced them. 1QIsaiah[a], in particular, presents a singular example of an ancient scroll that contains manifold scribal interventions.

Orthography

The scrolls' assortment of orthographic features have revealed much regarding spelling practices at the turn of the era, especially with regard to full versus defective spelling and the usage of certain Hebrew consonants (especially *wāw, yōd,* and *hē*).

New Readings

The Isaiah scrolls provide new readings that apparently have been unknown to the world for approximately two millennia. Bible translation committees have incorporated a number of these new readings into modern translations. For instance, *Tanakh: The Holy Scriptures,* published by the Jewish Publication Society, occasionally utilizes variant readings from 1QIsaiah[a] in its English translation or refers to them in footnotes. One such example occurs in Isa. 21:8, where the MT reads *lion (ʾryh);* 1QIsaiah[a] reads *the watcher (rʾh),* a word that better fits the context of the passage, "and the watcher cried, 'My lord, I stand continually upon the watchtower all day, and I am stationed at my post all night.'" Because *lion* and *the watcher* in the Hebrew language are graphically similar, a copyist likely made a simple error when he copied this word onto his new scroll.

Another example noted in *Tanakh* is located in Isa. 33:8, where the MT reads *cities (ʿrym)* versus 1QIsaiah[a]'s *pact (ʿdym),* again an example of graphic similarity. The reading of 1QIsaiah[a] corresponds well with the parallelism, "A covenant has been renounced, a pact rejected." Isaiah 14:4 sets forth a third example, one accepted by a number of modern translations, including *Tanakh,* the New International Version, and the New English Bible. In this verse 1QIsaiah[a] reads *mrhbh,* meaning "oppression." This fits the parallel structure, "How is oppression ended! How is the taskmaster vanished." *Tanakh* notes at the bottom of the page, "The traditional reading [of MT] *madhebah* is of unknown meaning."

The Isaiah scrolls are important texts for both academic and popular audiences because they provide many insights into the scribal and orthographic conventions that existed at the turn of the era. They also enable a fuller understanding of the textual history of the Bible, at least for the book of Isaiah.

BIBLIOGRAPHY

C. C. BROYLES AND C. A. EVANS, EDS. 1997, *Writing and Reading the Scroll of Isaiah,* 2 vols., Leiden: Brill. • E. Y. KUTSCHER 1974, *The Language and Linguistic Background of the Isaiah Scroll (1QIsa[a]),* Leiden: Brill. • D. W. PARRY AND E. QIMRON 1998, *A New Edition of the Great Isaiah Scroll (1QIsa[a]),* Leiden: Brill. • E. QIMRON 1979, *The Language and Linguistic Background of the Isaiah Scroll by E. Y. Kutscher: Indices and Corrections,* Leiden: Brill. • E. ULRICH ET AL. 1997, *Qumran Cave 4.10: The Prophets,* DJD 15, Oxford: Clarendon. • E. ULRICH AND P. W. FLINT 2010, *Qumran Cave 1.II: The Isaiah Scrolls: Part 1 and 2,* DJD 32, Oxford: Clarendon.

DONALD W. PARRY

Ishmael ben Elisha

Rabbinic literature provides little secure biographical information concerning the tanna Rabbi Ishmael son of Elisha (flourished first third of the second century C.E.). Rabbinic texts almost always refer to this figure simply as Rabbi Ishmael, without his patronymic. Virtually nothing is known about his education, though a later Babylonian tradition asserts that he was the disciple of Rabbi Neḥunya ben ha-Qanah (*b. Šebiʿit* 26a). Rabbinic sources present Rabbi Ishmael as advocating a hermeneutical approach to Scripture that was diametrically opposed to the more context-free exegetical wordplay championed by Rabbi Aqiba. This stance is reflected in his dictum that "the Torah speaks in the language of human beings" (*Sifre Numbers* §112 [Horovitz 121]). Rabbi Ishmael is thus likewise associated with a canonical set of thirteen hermeneutical principles *(middôt)* by which he is said to have interpreted Scripture (*Midr. ha-Gadol* Exod. 21:1; *Midr. ha-Gadol* Lev. 1:2).

In addition to these traditions, a number of rabbinic narratives present him as the scion of a high-priestly family (*b. Ketubbot* 105b; *b. Giṭṭin* 58a; *b. Ḥullin* 49a). A statement attributed to Rabbi Ishmael in the Tosefta (*t. Ḥal.* 1:10) even suggests that his father may have served as high priest when the Jerusalem Temple still stood. These biographical details would have robust afterlife in later rabbinic and postrabbinic sources, in which Rabbi Ishmael emerges as one of the central heroes of rabbinic and postrabbinic martyrology and the early Jewish "mystical" traditions of the Hekhalot literature (Boustan 2005: 51-148).

Scholars, however, diverge fundamentally in their assessments of the historical value of these testimonies. In his comprehensive study of Rabbi Ishmael traditions, Gary Porton raises doubts about each aspect of Rabbi Ishmael's biography, concluding that the traditions regarding both his consistent hermeneutical philosophy and his priestly status are creations of later rabbinic writers (Porton 1976-1982: 4:160-214). By contrast, Marc Hirshman has argued that Rabbi Ishmael was not only himself from a priestly family, but was also heir to Second Temple priestly traditions that came to form a coherent "universalistic" current within early rabbinic thought advocating the dissemination of the Torah among the Gentiles (Hirshman 1999, 2000).

Whether or not the narratives concerning Rabbi Ishmael and the statements attributed to him in rabbinic sources can be used to reconstruct the biography of a historical individual, the figure of Rabbi Ishmael has left a powerful mark on the formal organization of early rabbinic literature, especially the tannaitic (or halakic) midrashim. More than a century ago, David Tsvi Hoffmann demonstrated that these early midrashic compilations could be divided into two distinct groups on both formal and hermeneutical grounds, assigning one group to the "school of Rabbi Akiba" and the other to the "school of Rabbi Ishmael" (Kahana 2006: 4-5). Some scholars have periodically questioned whether these midrashic collections did in fact originate in two separate branches of the rabbinic movement and have instead suggested that they reflect the tendency among later amoraic redactors to harmonize content and attribution (Harris 1995: 51-72). Nonetheless, the formal categorization proposed by Hoffmann remains the consensus among most scholars, even if the complexities of the redactional process as well as various inconsistencies in the evidence caution against overly facile generalization about the teachings and activities of Rabbi Ishmael and his peers in the earliest generations of the rabbinic movement (Kahana 2006: 17-39).

Azzan Yadin has helpfully suggested that scholars uncouple the issues of literary form and historical origins; despite persistent uncertainties regarding the dating and identities of the redactors of these early midrashic compilations, they have still left us with two groups of texts that exhibit distinct sets of exegetical terminology and distinct inventories of named sages (Yadin 2004). Moreover, Yadin argues that the legal hermeneutics characteristic of the "Rabbi Ishmael" compendia, which treat Scripture itself as the sole legitimate source of law and seek to marginalize extra-scriptural traditions, have strong affinities with earlier priestly exegetical practices, as reflected in halakic texts from Qumran such as 4QMMT. This reconstruction remains to be further tested and refined. Still, Yadin's work not only suggests that the early rabbinic movement and its exegetical practices were more variegated than heretofore assumed, but also raises the possibility of discursive continuities between Second Temple and rabbinic Judaism, without relying on the strict historicity of rabbinic biographical traditions like those concerning Rabbi Ishmael.

BIBLIOGRAPHY

R. S. BOUSTAN 2005, *From Martyr to Mystic: Rabbinic Martyrology and the Making of Merkavah Mysticism,* Tübingen: Mohr-Siebeck. • J. HARRIS 1995, *How Do We Know This: Midrash and the Fragmentation of Modern Judaism,* Albany: SUNY Press. • M. HIRSHMAN 1999, *Torah for the Entire World,* Tel Aviv: Hakibbutz Hameuchad (in Hebrew). • M. HIRSHMAN 2000, "Rabbinic Universalism in the Second and Third Centuries," *HTR* 93: 101-15. • M. I. KAHANA 2006, "The Halakhic Midrashim," in *The Literature of the Sages: Second Part,* ed. S. Safrai et al., Assen: Van Gorcum; Minneapolis: Fortress, 31-105. • GARY G. PORTON 1976-1982, *The Traditions of Rabbi Ishmael,* 4 vols., Leiden: Brill. • A. YADIN 2004, *Scripture as Logos: Rabbi Ishmael and the Origins of Midrash,* Philadelphia: University of Pennsylvania Press.

RA'ANAN BOUSTAN

Iturea

Iturea is a region of the Beqaʿ Valley in southern Lebanon that emerged on the stage of Jewish history in the late Hellenistic period. A power vacuum emerged in the Near East with the breakup of the Seleucid kingdom, before Rome had entered the arena. The Itureans began to establish a principality in the Beqaʿ Valley with Chalcis as the capital (Strabo, *Geographica* 16.2.10, 18, 20; cf. Josephus, *Ant.* 14.126; *J.W.* 1.185 and an inscription from the first century C.E. that links their citadel [*castellum*] with Lebanon).

Political and Military History

Three rulers of Iturea are known both from literary and numismatic evidence, mainly because of their involvement with Roman expansion in the East. Ptolemy the son of Mennaeus ruled Iturea from ca. 80 to 40 B.C.E., with the titles *ethnarchus* and *archiereus* on his coins. He was involved in expanding the territory, threatening even Damascus, on the eve of Pompey's arrival in the East in the mid-first century B.C.E. Pompey restricted Ptolemy's advances and destroyed some of his fortresses, imposing a heavy war indemnity of 1,000 talents, according to Strabo (*Ant.* 14.39; cf. 13.392, 418). Still Ptolemy continued his engagement in international politics, supporting the ousted Hasmonean Aristobulus II and later his son Antigonus in the civil war with Herod the Great that resulted in the Parthian invasion of Palestine (*Ant.* 14.123-26).

Ptolemy's son Lysanias took over the ethnarchy on his father's death in ca. 40 B.C.E. and is given the title "king" on some coins. However, he ran afoul of Antony and Cleopatra, had to cede part at least of his territory to Cleopatra, and later was executed on the pretext of being involved in bringing about the incursion of Parthians into Palestine (*Ant.* 14.330-32; 15.92). The last known member of what in all probability was a dynasty is Zenodorus, whose territories in Batanea, Trachonitis, and Auranitis were transferred to Herod the Great by Augustus in 24/3 B.C.E., ostensibly because of his failure to root out the brigands. A few years later, on Zenodorus' death in 20 B.C.E., the territories of Banias and Ulatha (Huleh), south of Hermon (*Ant.* 15.342-53, 359-60), were also bequeathed to Herod by Augustus.

This evidence strongly suggests that Iturea was of considerable importance to the larger Roman policies in the region. Presumably this had to do with their strategic geographical location in the hinterland of Damascus, providing a bridge between the Mediterranean coast and the interior. Client kingdoms in both Judea and Nabatea in the south served Rome well in this regard, but the Itureans had leanings toward the Parthians and paid the price for this decision. The repeated mention of brigandage in the pro-Roman sources must be judged against this background.

The division of these territories in the first century C.E. suggests that Rome first adopted a policy of divide and conquer, before ultimately incorporating the whole region into the provincial system. Four seemingly separate subregions are mentioned in relation to various interventions and concessions to later Herodians. In addition to Batanea, Trachonitis, and Auranitis, mentioned earlier, Banias and Ulatha also passed to Herod on the death of Zenodorus — at least suggesting different administrative districts. Furthermore, the original territory of the Itureans seems to have been divided also in the Roman period (cf. Luke 3:1).

The Iturean People

There is virtual unanimity among modern scholars that the Itureans were an Arabian tribe, who only in the late Hellenistic period became sedentary. Prior to that, we are to think of them as seminomads who wandered around steppe lands on the borders of the Arabian Desert and later practiced brigandage on the trading caravans from the East. But there are inherent improbabilities with the profile of a seminomadic tribe coming into possession of a fertile territory such as the Beqaʿ Valley and undergoing Hellenization, at least as far as nomenclature is concerned, in a relatively short space of time. The name Ptolemy points to the immediate post-Alexander era when the Ptolemies, not the Seleucids, were in control of this contested region of Coele-Syria.

The earliest appearance of the Greek name *Itouraioi* is the LXX translation of 1 Chron. 5:19. Here it is used to render Hebr. *yĕṭur,* whereas earlier the same name is merely transliterated from Hebrew to Greek lettering (Gen. 25:15; 1 Chron. 1:31). This linking of the Itureans with the sons of Ishmael has further influenced their identification with the Arabs, even though biblical genealogies are notoriously unreliable in terms of historical reconstruction. In the second century B.C.E., Eupolemus lists *Ituraioi* among the peoples conquered by David. The Itureans were certainly established as a recognizable ethnic entity by the mid-second century B.C.E., and probably earlier. Appian and Pliny the Elder describe them as Syrians, whereas Strabo and Dio connect them with Arab(ian)s. The main question is whether the Beqaʿ Valley was their original location from whence they expanded southward and eastward to the Hauran and to Galilee, or whether they had actually originated in the Arabian peninsula and migrated north as seminomads. The former seems the more plausible scenario.

Religion and Renown

One finds a great variety of religio-cultural expression in different regions where the Itureans are presumed to have lived. In the "home" territory of the Beqaʿ, for example, the great shrine of Baalbek/Heliopolis has yielded very little of its pre-Hellenistic past. It would be reasonable to infer from other parallels that sun worship had existed there previously, and that the later temple to Jupiter was an *interpretatio Graeca* of an older Baal Shamem, with particular reference to sun worship. Smaller cult sites in the same region, such as those at Niha or Hosn Niha, give a better sense of how Greek forms can blend with older, "Semitic" features in terms of names and dress. In contrast, other shrines such as those found in Har Senaim, just four km. from Banias, and which the excavator, Shimon Dar, describes as "Iturean," show few signs of Hellenistic influence, though some Greek dedicatory inscriptions were found. These shrines consist of standing stelae located within an open-air enclosure, one of which has a rock as a central feature, thus suggesting a much older type of aniconic worship, even though a relief of Helios with seven rays emanating from the head has been engraved on an altar.

One feature of earlier Iturean life hinted at in the literary sources, which seems to have survived into later times, is their skill and bravery as fighters. We find many inscriptions and diplomata or military honors referring to Iturean cohorts throughout the various Roman provinces, east and west. In particular, their skill as archers seems to have been recognized.

Relationship with Judeans

The Iturean relationship with the Judeans is highly illuminating. According to Josephus, Aristobulus I made war on the Itureans and acquired a good part of their territory for Judea and compelled the inhabitants, if they wished to remain in their country, "to be circumcised and to live in accordance with the laws of the Judeans" (*Ant.* 13.318). Josephus supports this account with reference to Strabo's citation of the Greco-Alexandrine writer Timagenes. But in fact Timagenes does not speak of Aristobulus making war on the Itureans, but rather of him making friends with them. The subsequent befriending by Ptolemy son of Mennaeus of the Hasmonean successors Aristobulus II and his son Antigonus in the struggle against Herod makes Josephus' account questionable. One can easily envisage a scenario of friendship, based on common interests by these two peoples, even if Aristobulus I had indeed attempted to incorporate Iturea into his kingdom. If indeed an engagement took place between Aristobulus and the Itureans, it was much more likely to have been in their territory than in Galilee, despite the persistence of modern scholarship, following Schürer, in speaking of Itureans having occupied most, if not all of Galilee, and in some instances supposing that Galilean Jews were forcibly circumcised Itureans. In this instance at least, it was the Judeans, and not the Itureans, who were more likely to have been the aggressors.

BIBLIOGRAPHY

S. DAR 1993, *Settlements and Cult Sites on Mount Hermon, Israel: Iturean Culture in the Hellenistic and Roman Periods,* Oxford: Tempus Reparatum. • S. FREYNE 2001, "Galileans, Phoenicians and Itureans: A Study of Regional Contrasts in the Hellenistic Age," in *Hellenism in the Land of Israel,* ed. J. J. Collins and G. E. Sterling, Notre Dame: Notre Dame University Press, 184-217. • E. MYERS 2007, "The Itureans: Challenging Misconceptions and Evaluating the Primary Sources," Dissertation, University of Toronto. • F. MILLAR 1994, *The Roman Near East, 31 BC–AD 337,* Cambridge: Harvard University Press. • E. SCHÜRER 1973, *The History of the Jewish People in the Age of Jesus Christ,* vol. 1, rev. and ed. G. Vermes et al., Edinburgh: Clark, 561-73.

SEAN FREYNE

J

Jacob

Hebrew Bible

Jacob is the younger twin son of Isaac and Rebekah. In the biblical accounts of the patriarchs, he gets the most coverage. The Bible presents both negative and positive aspects of Jacob's life, such as his deceiving his father and blessing his children. His life is presented as a struggle with human beings and God (Gen. 32:28), beginning from the womb with Esau from whom he took the birthright (through purchase) and blessing (by deceit). As a result, he was forced to flee to his uncle Laban's from Esau's wrath. On the way, he had a dream at Bethel and saw a ladder joining earth to heaven (Gen. 28:12, 17-19). After struggling under Laban's employment, he left with two wives and their maidservants, through whom he became the father of twelve sons from whom were descended the tribes of Israel. Jacob's testament (Genesis 48–50), in which he blesses his sons, alludes to the future of the tribes.

Early Jewish Writings

Early Jewish authors and writings such as Philo, Josephus, *Jubilees,* the *Ladder of Jacob,* the *Prayer of Jacob,* and the *Testament of Jacob* tend to enhance the biblical portrait of Jacob and his family, portraying them in a more favorable light. Perhaps this tendency is due to embarrassment, particularly with the negative accounts in the early life of the eponymous ancestor of the people of Israel.

In retellings of Jacob's relations with Esau, Jacob is portrayed as a virtuous scholar (*Jub.* 35:12-13; 19:13-14; cf. *Tg. Onq.* Gen. 25:27; *Tg. Neof.* Gen. 25:27) and practitioner of wisdom (Philo, *On Flight and Finding* 52), while Esau is a violent and wicked warrior (Obad. 1:10), the father of the Edomites and Amalekites who persecute Israel. According to *Jubilees,* Jacob killed Esau with the sword (chaps. 37–38). Esau was also seen to typify Rome, the oppressor of the Jewish people (*4 Ezra* 6:8-10; *Ladd. Jac.* 5:8-11; cf. *Gen. Rab.* 65:19; *Midr. ha-Gadol* 25:26. In contrast with other early Jewish writings, Josephus, mostly through omitting from his *Antiquities of the Jews* passages in Genesis thought to denigrate Esau, attempted to avoid antagonizing the Romans.

According to some sources, Jacob received the blessing from Isaac because it was God's will, even though his attire was deceiving, and he told the truth in so doing (*Jub.* 26:12-19; Philo, *QG* 4.196).

The Ladder of Jacob (first century C.E.) recounts the story of Jacob fleeing to Laban and his dream about the ladder in more detail than does the biblical account. The ladder has twelve steps with two faces or busts of kings on each rung. Jacob prays to God for the dream to be interpreted. The archangel Sariel comes to Jacob, interprets the dream, and changes his name to Israel. According to Sariel, the ladder refers to this age, and the twelve steps with the busts are the periods of this age with the godless Gentile rulers who will inflict, exile, and enslave Jacob's descendants in the future (1:1-6; 5:1-9, 16).

According to *Jubilees* (second century B.C.E.), Laban was following a heavenly ordinance in giving his oldest daughter Leah to Jacob, and Jacob, assuming it was Rachel, discovered the deed after it was too late to complain (28:6). According to Josephus, Laban wanted to marry off his unattractive first daughter to Jacob, who was deceived by darkness and wine (*Ant.* 1.301).

Jacob's wrestling with God in Genesis 32 was a wrestling with an angel (Hos. 12:4-5 [Eng. 12:3-4]), and he was renamed Israel, which means, according to Josephus, "one who has contended with or stood up to an angel of God" (*Ant.* 1.333). Other accounts interpret the name Israel as "being strong with [the help] of God" (Gen. 32:29 LXX) or as a "victor with God" (Wis. 10:12). Alternatively, Philo, perhaps understanding Israel as *ʾîš rāʾâ ʾēl,* etymologizes the name as "a man who sees God" (*Dreams* 1.171, *Flight* 208; cf. Gen 32:30). The *Prayer of Joseph* (first or early second century C.E.) develops the story of Jacob's wrestling by depicting Jacob as the incarnation of the angel Israel (again etymologized as "a man who sees God"), the firstborn of every living thing, archangel, chief captain of the sons of God, and first minister of God; he confronts his rival in the angel Uriel.

Jacob's response to the rape of his daughter Dinah

and the subsequent slaughter of the Shechemites by his sons Simeon and Levi (Genesis 34) is enhanced in several early Jewish writings. These texts justify and even give divine sanction for the sons' action, reflecting strong disapproval of the defiling of an Israelite virgin and intermarriage between the children of Israel and the Canaanites (*Jub.* 30:3-6, 11-14; *T. Levi* 6:8–7:1, Josephus, *Ant.* 1.337-38, cf. Deut 7:3-6). Later Jacob did curse the anger of Simeon and Levi (Gen. 49:5-7).

Jacob's favoritism toward his younger son Joseph was justified because of Joseph's wisdom (Philo, *On the Life of Joseph* 4), physical beauty, and intelligent mind (Josephus, *Ant.* 2.9), and because he resembled Jacob in all things (*T. Jos.* 18:4). Joseph was able to resist the seductive advances of Potipher's wife because he kept the face of his father before his eyes and remembered his father's commandments (*Jos. & Asen.* 7:4-5).

In Jacob's testament to his sons, he foretells the future of Israel and transfers the double portion normally given to the firstborn Reuben to Joseph's sons (*Jub.* 45:14), due to Joseph's virtue and Reuben's sin with Bilhah (33:3-5). Jacob offers prayers (Josephus, *Ant.* 2.194; *T. Reu.* 1:7; *T. Jud.* 19:2) and exhorts against fornication (*Jub.* 39:6). The motif of Jacob praying is taken up in *The Prayer of Jacob* (first or second century C.E.), which contains the patriarch's request for wisdom, a heart filled with good things, and immortality (17–19).

Jacob is mentioned in various Dead Sea Scrolls, including the *Apocryphon of Jacob* (4Q537), the *Temple Scroll* (29:10), and the *Apocryphon of Joseph* (4Q372 3 i 9), texts that associate the Temple and priesthood with God's covenant with Jacob at Bethel. 4QReworked Pentateuch (4Q158 7-9) expands Gen. 32:29 by giving the content of God's blessing on Jacob at Penuel: Jacob will be fertile, blessed with knowledge and intelligence, and delivered from all violence. The *Commentary on Genesis* A (4Q252 4:5-7) contains a pesher on Jacob's blessing of Reuben in Gen. 49:3-4. Jacob reproves his son because he lay with Bilhah.

New Testament and Rabbinic Judaism

In the New Testament, Paul cites Jacob as an example of God's sovereignty in electing believing Gentiles (Rom. 9:10-13, quoting Mal. 1:2, "Jacob I loved, but Esau I hated"). The Fourth Gospel makes Christ as the Son of Man the focus of Jacob's dream at Bethel, in effect depicting Christ as Jacob's ladder (John 1:50-51). It also depicts Jesus speaking with the woman of Samaria at "Jacob's well" in Sychar, a Samaritan village near ancient Shechem (John 4).

Rabbinic writings justify Jacob gaining the birthright and blessing but disapprove of his marriage to two sisters (*b. Pesaḥim* 119b), his treatment of Leah, and his favoritism toward Joseph (*b. Šabbat* 10b; *b. Megillah* 16b; *Gen. Rab.* 84:8).

Bibliography

L. H. Feldman 1988-89, "Josephus' Portrait of Jacob," *JQR* 79: 101-51. • R. Good 2000, "Jacob," in *Encyclopedia of the Dead Sea Scrolls*, ed. L. H. Schiffman and J. C. VanderKam, Oxford: Oxford University Press, 1: 395-96. • J. L. Kugel 1997, *Traditions of the Bible: A Guide to the Bible as It Was at the Start of the Common Era*, Cambridge: Harvard University Press, 351-401. • J. L. Kugel 2006, *The Ladder of Jacob: Ancient Interpretations of the Biblical Story of Jacob and His Children*, Princeton: Princeton University Press.

See also: Joseph, Prayer of Roger Good

James, Epistle of

The "James" (or "Jacob") to whom this New Testament letter "to the twelve tribes in the Diaspora" is attributed is identified only as a "slave of God and of the Lord Jesus Christ" (1:1). Though a common name in antiquity, it is generally agreed that the James referred to here is the one identified by Paul as Jesus' brother and a key leader, with the apostles Peter and John, of the earliest Christ group in Jerusalem — a community which consisted primarily if not entirely of Jews (Gal. 1:18–2:13; cf. Acts 15; 21:17-26). If this ascription, as some hold, is genuine, then the Letter of James would present crucial evidence for this early Jewish group. However, even if the letter is a pseudonymous work of the late first or early second century, as others argue, the text nonetheless seems to reflect a group for whom devotion to Jesus did not mean being something other than Jewish.

Martin Luther complained that this letter "has nothing of the nature of the gospel about it," citing its lack of any apparent interest in either the death and resurrection of Jesus or the Holy Spirit, on the one hand, and its strong emphasis on the Law on the other (Jackson-McCabe 2001: 2-3). The absence of such typically Christian features, particularly coupled with the presence of characteristically Jewish ones, led several scholars in the late nineteenth and early twentieth centuries to argue that James's two lone explicit references to Jesus (1:1; 2:1) were in fact later additions to an originally non-Christian Jewish text (e.g., Spitta 1896). This argument, however, failed to convince many since the letter is in other respects quite similar to other New Testament literature. Specifically, its general ethos and even a number of its specific teachings are strongly reminiscent of Jesus as he appears in the Synoptic Gospels, while its notion that Lev. 19:18 can serve as a summary of the Law and its grappling with the question of the role of "faith" and "works" in being "saved" or "justified" recall the letters of Paul (Jas. 2:8-11, 14-26; cf., e.g., Gal. 2:15–3:14; 5:14). That James is in fact a product of the early Jesus movement is an uncontested consensus in contemporary scholarship.

With respect to the issue of this letter's significance for early Judaism, then, the key question is less whether James is Jewish or Christian than the role of, and relation between, the various Jewish and Christian features within the world of the text. To what extent is the religious system reflected in James comparable to the systems of other early Christian works and to those of early Jewish works?

Traditionally, critical scholarship on James has answered this question by positing *behind* the text of James — that is, in the assumptions of its author and audience — something akin to "the gospel" whose absence was felt by Luther. Allusions to this "gospel" are regularly found in the references to the *logos* with or by which God "gave us birth" (1:18), and which has "the power to save your souls" (1:21). The more typically Jewish elements in the text are then taken to be subordinate to this core Christian gospel; more or less like the Hellenistic ideas contained in the text, they represent traditional concepts or notions that have been appropriated from Judaism but reinterpreted in "Christianizing" — or what generally amounts to "universalizing" — ways. Thus the text's emphasis on "the law of freedom" is often interpreted not with reference to the Torah *per se,* but as an indication that the text "conceived [of] Christianity as a law, including and fulfilling the old one" (Ropes 1916: 178). Put another way, James's "law of freedom" is simply "the norm of Christian piety," "a new Christian law" that does not include particularly Jewish customs regarding circumcision, diet, and cult (e.g., Dibelius 1988: 116). Similarly, the letter's address to "the twelve tribes in the Diaspora" is frequently interpreted as having no ethnic significance whatsoever. It is rather "Christendom on earth" (Dibelius 1988: 66), "the Christian church conceived as the true Israel" (Ropes 1916: 118). At most, it may refer specifically to the Jewish believers within the Christian church (Hort 1909: xxii-xxiii).

A basic point of debate for those who approach the text in this way is whether the preponderance of Jewish traditions appropriated in the text is such that it implies that the author and audience were themselves ethnically (even if not religiously) Jewish (so Ropes 1916: 39-43, 47-48), or whether one may simply be encountering the sort of Gentile arrogation of Jewish tradition that one finds in 1 Peter and in other early Christian literature (so Dibelius 1988: 24). This issue is sometimes intertwined with the question of the authenticity of the letter as a composition of James of Jerusalem.

The traditional approach to the question has been complicated by broader trends in scholarship since World War II. Cognizant of the great diversity within both early Judaism and early Christianity, and increasingly reticent regarding essentialist approaches to the religious phenomena of antiquity, scholars are now more prone to see the traditionally distinct categories of "Judaism" and "Christianity" as not infrequently overlapping in the actual religious groups of the first centuries of the Common Era. In this context, a number of James's interpreters have been more inclined to see the Jewish dimensions of the text as integral to its religious system rather than traditions that have been "adopted" by a separate, Christian system. Recent decades have thus seen a number of studies attempting to clarify anew the religious thought of James, particularly in light of Second Temple Judaism. A number of authors have come to argue that James represents a "wisdom theology" reminiscent of early Jewish wisdom literature, while others emphasize its points of contact with Jewish apocalypticism (see Konradt 1999).

The difference this has made is evident, among other things, in the ways that James's "law of freedom" has been interpreted in more recent scholarship on the letter. In contrast to the traditional view, it is now frequently argued that this law is in fact the scriptural Torah, however precisely interpreted. The question for those who interpret it this way, then, is what to make of James's equation of the Torah with *logos* in 1:21-25. For some, it means that one should not draw a "hard-and-fast distinction" between Gospel and Torah in James (Johnson 1995: 205, 215); the two are complementary, not contradictory ideals in this work (Hartin 2003: 105-8). Others have made the case that James's *logos* should not be interpreted with reference to "the gospel" at all. It has been argued, for example, that the equation of "implanted *logos*" and "perfect law of freedom" is better understood in light of works like 4 Maccabees, the *Apostolic Constitutions,* and the writings of Philo, which present the Torah as a written expression of the "natural law" identified by the Stoics as human reason *(logos)* (Jackson-McCabe 2001). In either case, the text's devotion to Jesus is not understood to be in any way incompatible with its emphasis on keeping, as James puts it, "the whole law" (2:10).

The letter's address to "the twelve tribes in the Diaspora" has likewise been subject to a different line of interpretation in this new scholarly climate. Specifically, it has become increasingly recognized that this phrase was not merely a synonym for "Israel" but had a very specific and potent association with Jewish national restoration, independence, and (especially Davidic) messianism at the time of the Roman subjugation of Judah around the turn of the Common Era (Hartin 2003: 53-55; Johnson 1995: 169-72; Jackson-McCabe 2003). In works like the *Psalms of Solomon* and the Dead Sea Scrolls, for example, one sees sectarian Jewish groups of this period identifying themselves closely with a future restoration of Israel along the lines of the idealized kingdom of David: a twelve-tribe people once again, unified under a messianic king. The use of this highly charged designation in James, a work that clearly hopes for the imminent Parousia of its own messiah, is now taken to suggest that it, too, was produced within an analogous Jewish sect. Indeed, particularly when coupled with its lack of interest in the traditional themes associated by Luther with "the gospel," James's understanding of Jesus may have as much or more in common with early Jewish messianism than with the christologies of other New Testament and early Christian works (Jackson-McCabe 2003).

As interpreted in recent scholarship, the Letter of James is a work that challenges our normally dichotomous use of the categories "Christian" and "Judaism." While clearly exhibiting Christ veneration, the work represents no less an example of early Judaism for that. Indeed, one might now say that the Letter of James is Jewish precisely because of, not in spite of, its veneration of Jesus.

BIBLIOGRAPHY

M. DIBELIUS 1988, *James,* 11th ed., Philadelphia: Fortress. • P. HARTIN 2003, *James,* Collegeville, Minn.: Liturgical Press. • F. J. A. HORT 1909, *The Epistle of St. James,* London:

Macmillan. • M. JACKSON-MCCABE 2001, *Logos and Law in the Letter of James,* Leiden: Brill. • M. JACKSON-MCCABE 2003, "The Messiah Jesus in the Mythic World of James," *JBL* 122: 701-30. • L. T. JOHNSON 1995, *The Letter of James,* New York: Doubleday. • M. KONRADT 1999, "Theologie in der 'strohernen Epistel,'" *VF* 44: 54-78. • J. H. ROPES 1916, *The Epistle of St. James,* Edinburgh: Clark. • F. SPITTA 1896, *Der Brief des Jakobus,* Göttingen: Vandenhoeck & Ruprecht.

MATT JACKSON-MCCABE

Jamnia → Yavneh

Jeremiah, Letter of

The Letter of Jeremiah is an early Jewish polemic against the worship of pagan gods, with particular attention to statues and other material representations of the deities ("idols"). This "letter" takes the form of advice written by the prophet Jeremiah to Jews who were about to be exiled to Babylon (see Jeremiah 29). Much of its content and many of its phrases are taken from Jer. 10:1-15. Similar denigrations of idols are found in Second Isaiah (40:18-20; 41:6-6; 44:9-20; 46:1-7), the Psalms (115:4-8; 135:15-18), and Deuteronomy (4:27-28). These and related themes are developed in other early Jewish writings such as Bel and the Dragon, Wisdom 13–15, *Apocalypse of Abraham,* Paul's Letter to the Romans (1:18-32), and the rabbinic tractates on *ʿAbodah Zarah* ("foreign worship").

The primary text of the work is in Greek, though a Hebrew original is likely. In some manuscripts in the Greek Septuagint tradition, the work appears as a separate composition between Lamentations and Ezekiel, while in the Latin and related traditions it is chapter 6 in the book of Baruch. A small fragment of the Greek version was found in Qumran Cave 7 (7QLXXEpJer), and has been dated to the first century B.C.E.

The work could have been composed at any time between the sixth and second century B.C.E. The several references to Babylonian religious practices (see vv. 4, 11, 30-32, 41, 43) might suggest a relatively early date for the Hebrew original, though how much firsthand knowledge the author had of pagan cults is debated. Beyond the obvious links to Jer. 10:1-15 and 29, the ascription to the prophet Jeremiah is dubious, and the work is generally regarded as pseudonymous. It could have been written in either the Diaspora or the land of Israel. Its literary form is more that of a polemical sermon than a letter. It is best viewed as a passionate homily, designed to persuade other Jews to avoid idolatry when they are outside the land of Israel. Its content would fit not only the situation of the exilic generation but also that of Diaspora (and even Palestinian) Jews throughout the Second Temple period.

Adopting the persona of Jeremiah, the author explains that Jews were being taken to Babylon "because of the sins you have committed before God" (v. 2). He warns them that while in exile they will be exposed to "gods made of silver and gold and wood" (v. 4), and reminds them that must say in their heart, "It is you, O Lord, whom we must worship" (v. 6).

Having set the scene in vv. 1-7, "Jeremiah" presents ten short warnings against idolatry, and concludes each unit in good rhetorical style with a comment that the since the idols are not really gods but only human creations, there is no reason to worship them. He offers reflections about the idols' helplessness (vv. 8-16), uselessness (vv. 17-23), lifelessness (vv. 24-29), powerlessness (vv. 30-40a), foolishness and shamefulness (vv. 40b-44), and so on. The repetition of the criticisms has the rhetorical effect of highlighting the seriousness of the situation and the need for Jews to stay away from idol worship. Each unit ends with a refrain to the effect that "they are not gods; so do not fear them" (v. 16; see vv. 23, 29, 65, 69) or "Why then must anyone think that they are gods, or call them gods?" (v. 40; see vv. 44, 52, 56, 64). Drawing on Jer. 10:5, the final unit compares the idols to "a scarecrow in a cucumber bed, which guards nothing" (v. 70). The writer's parting advice is this: "Better, therefore, is someone upright who has no idols; such a person will be far above reproach" (v. 73).

The fundamental criticism against the idols is that they cannot do what the God of Israel does (vv. 34-38, 66-69). The author never entertains the thought that the statues and images may have been regarded as representations of the various deities, not actual objects of worship. The author's main concern is keeping other Jews from foreign cults, not writing a treatise on comparative religion. The work is remarkable for its absolutist defense of Jewish monotheism. For this author, the God of Israel is the only God.

The author also criticizes pagan priests who show no compunction about stealing from the offerings made to their gods (see Bel and the Dragon) and consorting with prostitutes. Moreover, he warns that idolatry leads to immorality and contends that the best course of action for Jews in the Diaspora is to stay away from idols entirely (see 1 John 5:21).

BIBLIOGRAPHY

D. A. DESILVA 2002, *Introducing the Apocrypha,* Grand Rapids: Baker, 214-21. • D. J. HARRINGTON 1999, *Invitation to the Apocrypha,* Grand Rapids: Eerdmans, 103-8. • C. A. MOORE 1977, *Daniel, Esther and Jeremiah: The Additions,* Garden City, N.Y.: Doubleday, 317-58.

DANIEL J. HARRINGTON, S.J.

Jeremiah and Lamentations

The books of Jeremiah and Lamentations reflect sixth-century Judah's experience of geopolitical upheaval and military subjugation that culminated in the Babylonian sack of Jerusalem in 587 B.C.E. Jeremiah wrestles with issues of ideology and international politics during the years of Babylonian aggression against Judah and in the early years of the Diaspora. Some editorial additions may show awareness of the rise of Persian hegemony (e.g., Jer. 51:11, 28), but most of the Jeremiah traditions likely received their final form prior to the

JEREMIAH AND LAMENTATIONS

Persian period. Lamentations represents the siege and fall of Jerusalem with a vivid pathos that suggests to some interpreters that those events lay in the recent past. Arguments for the diction of Lamentations as Late Biblical Hebrew predating the latest books in the canon (Qohelet and Daniel) support the probability that Lamentations was composed in the exilic period.

Jeremiah

Composition

The book of Jeremiah represents the prophesying of a Benjaminite from a priestly family in Anathoth from the thirteenth year of the reign of Josiah of Judah (627 B.C.E.) until shortly after 587 B.C.E. This literarily complex work contains poetic oracles, laments, biographical stories about Jeremiah, symbolic sign-acts, hortatory addresses, and oracles against foreign nations. Semantic and stylistic considerations have led some to argue that complexes of material in chaps. 27–29 and 30–31 had their own transmission histories. The book underwent editing in two distinct text traditions, as can be seen in the LXX of Jeremiah, which is roughly one eighth shorter than the MT and presents numerous variant readings, omissions, and reorganizations of minor and major blocks of text. Jeremiah is one of the texts of the Hebrew Bible whose textual status was most fluid in the early period of its reception. The striking recensional and text-critical differences between the Old Greek and Masoretic traditions of Jeremiah are due to a host of complicated reasons that include thoroughgoing editorial expansions in the MT tradition and haplography and other scribal errors in the *Vorlage* of the Old Greek text-type. The divergent text traditions witness to the important role of Jewish scribes, not merely as copyists but as "authors," in the preservation and elaboration of scriptural traditions for particular historical communities.

Poetic oracles of judgment against Judah and Jerusalem in the first half of Jeremiah are considered by many to have come from the historical prophet, although scholars continue to debate the viability of methodological assumptions underlying any search for an older core of prophecies traceable to the historical Jeremiah. The oracles of judgment have been supplemented by laments that express the suffering of the prophet (11:18–12:6, 15:10-21, 17:14-18, 18:18-23, 20:7-13, and 20:14-18), the so-called "Book of Consolation" in chaps. 30–31, oracles against foreign nations (chaps. 46–51), and extensive prose additions composed by traditionists with close ties to Deuteronomistic ideology.

Theological Themes in Political Context

The commissioning of Jeremiah in 1:4-10 asserts the power of the prophetic word to enact divine judgment and catalyze restoration, and the rest of the book unfolds along this dual trajectory. Some readers see a muted hope finally displacing the rhetoric of judgment in the final form of the book, but others argue that the two viewpoints are never reconciled with each other and that the tension between them is constitutive of the Jeremianic witness. Early Jeremiah traditions excoriate Judah for idolatry and trusting in political alliances; later prose sections emphasize that the people of Judah have historically refused to heed the prophets. The pressures of Babylonian colonization exacerbated internecine strife among groups in Judah, in the Babylonian Diaspora, and in Egypt after the fall of Jerusalem (chaps. 24 and 42–44). Incisive prophetic critique of the monarchy (here, Jehoiakim and Zedekiah) and Temple officials provides evidence for the high valuation of dissent in ancient Jewish cultural politics. In the Jeremiah prose, a struggle for political authority can be discerned between those promoting an accommodationist posture ("submit to Babylon and live") and others who counseled resistance. In later centuries, that same tension would continue to enliven Jewish politics, dividing pragmatists from idealists who advocated nonassimilation. The latter group, broadly construed, would include the traditionists responsible for writing Ezra-Nehemiah, the Hasmoneans, and the Zealots.

Reception

Jeremiah traditions were taken up by Deutero-Isaiah (Isaiah 40–55), who reverses Jeremianic oracles of doom and rearticulates words of hope drawn from Jeremiah 30–31. The figures of Jeremiah and his scribe Baruch generated significant interest in the Second Temple period. Two Hellenistic-era documents, the book of Baruch and the Letter of Jeremiah, explore issues of powerlessness and shame afflicting Jews in the Diaspora, suggesting that in steadfast observance of Torah and rejection of idolatry God's people would find new hope. Among the fragments of Jeremiah found in the Dead Sea Scrolls, 4QJer^{b} represents the shorter text tradition seen in the LXX and thus is of particular significance for text-critical work on Jeremiah. Another text, 4Q384-5^{b}, presents fragments of an apocryphal story of Jeremiah in Egypt.

Lamentations

Composition

The book of Lamentations is theological protest literature bewailing the trauma that befell Judah when the Babylonians destroyed Jerusalem. The genre of lament over a fallen city was well known in the ancient Near East, and a number of extrabiblical exemplars predate Lamentations, including the Mesopotamian "Lament for the Destruction of Ur," datable to about the twentieth century B.C.E. Of the five artistically composed poems that make up Lamentations, the first four are organized according to an alphabetical acrostic (with minor variations), and the fifth chapter contains twenty-two lines, reflecting the number of letters of the Hebrew alphabet. The sophisticated poetic parallelism, artistic use of enjambment, and employment of the pathos-enhancing *qinah* meter in Lamentations testify further to the artistry with which this book was constructed.

Theological Themes in Political Context

Lamentations presents the horrors of siege in stark imagery to evoke the sympathy of the audience. The discourse of Lamentations is performed through the dramatic personification of Jerusalem as Daughter Zion, an ironizing of the traditional image of God as shepherd at the heart of the book (Lam. 3:1-18), and the use of diverse speaking voices in the book, a rhetorical gesture that insists on the value of multiple perspectives on suffering. Lamentations expresses grief and anger at the disproportionate brutality of Zion's punishment, hopes for God's mercy in the midst of despair, and underlines the tenacity of the Judean survivors.

Reception

Deutero-Isaiah drew on Lamentations, reversing its images of violation and affirming hope for postexilic Judah and Jerusalem. The Septuagint adds a superscription that Lamentations was authored by Jeremiah, a tradition perhaps rooted in 2 Chron. 35:25 and taken up in many ancient writings, including the Vulgate, the targum to Lamentations, and the Babylonian Talmud. The suggestion of Jeremianic authorship, while improbable, demonstrates readerly discernment of resonances between the two books regarding historical context and the anguished timbre of the authorial voices. Four fragments of Lamentations were discovered among the Dead Sea Scrolls; nonbiblical Qumran texts that allude to Lamentations include a lament over Zion (4Q179) that quotes Lam. 1:1. *Lamentations Rabbah* explores themes that include the destruction of the Temple as the consequence of Israel's idolatry, the efficacy of divine punishment to induce Israel's repentance, the defense of Israel by biblical tradition personified as Abraham, Isaac, Jacob, Moses, and Rachel, and the conflicting dynamics of Jewish life under Roman rule culminating in the Bar Kokhba Revolt of 132-35 C.E. Lamentations was used historically to commemorate the destruction of the First Temple, and it has functioned as a liturgical response to disasters befalling Jews in subsequent generations, including the razing of the Second Temple in 70 C.E. and a variety of catastrophes into the modern period. Lamentations is read in synagogues on the fast day of Tisha b'Av.

BIBLIOGRAPHY

A. BERLIN 2002, *Lamentations,* Louisville: Westminster John Knox. • A. COOPER 2001, "The Message of Lamentations," *JANES* 28:1-18. • A. R. P. DIAMOND, K. O'CONNOR, AND L. STULMAN, EDS. 1999, *Troubling Jeremiah,* Sheffield: Sheffield Academic. • D. DIMANT 1994, "An Apocryphon of Jeremiah from Cave 4 (4Q385b = 4Q385 16)," in *New Qumran Texts and Studies,* ed. G. J. Brooke, Leiden: Brill, 11-30. • F. W. DOBBS-ALLSOPP 2002, *Lamentations,* Louisville: Westminster John Knox. • W. L. HOLLADAY 1986-1989, *Jeremiah,* 2 vols., Philadelphia: Fortress. • T. LINAFELT 2000, *Surviving Lamentations: Catastrophe, Lament, and Protest in the Afterlife of a Biblical Book,* Chicago: University of Chicago Press. • W. MCKANE 1986-1996, *A Critical and Exegetical Commentary on Jeremiah,* 2 vols., Edinburgh: Clark. • M. SMITH 1995, "Apocryphon of Jeremiah," in *Qumran Cave 4, XIV. Parabiblical Texts Part 2,* DJD 19, ed. M. Broshi et al., Oxford: Clarendon, 137-52. • L. STULMAN 1998, *Order amid Chaos: Jeremiah as Symbolic Tapestry,* Sheffield: Sheffield Academic. • E. TOV 1985, "The Literary History of the Book of Jeremiah in the Light of Its Textual History," in *Empirical Models for Biblical Criticism,* ed. J. Tigay, Philadelphia: University of Pennsylvania Press, 211-37.

CAROLYN J. SHARP

Jericho

South of modern Jericho, near the ancient road that descended from Jerusalem along Wadi Qelt, stands the site known as Tulul Abu el-ʿAlayiq. According to scholars, this was the location of Jericho during the Second Temple period. By the middle of the second century B.C.E., Jericho had gained strategic importance both economically and militarily, serving as an agricultural center, a crossroad, and a winter resort for Jerusalem's nobility. A significant Jewish population is attested in this period by the survey and excavation of a nearby cemetery.

Jericho was also a site for political intrigue in the Hasmonean and Herodian eras. Simon Maccabee and two of his sons were murdered at a banquet there in 134 B.C.E. by his son-in-law, Ptolemy son of Abubos, the *stratēgos* of Jericho (1 Macc. 16:11-17; *Ant.* 13.228). Simon's surviving son, John Hyrcanus, avenged his father's death and laid siege to the fortress where the murders occurred. According to Josephus, in 35 B.C.E. Herod arranged for the murder of the high priest Aristobulus III by drowning (*Ant.* 15.50-58). And just before his death in 4 B.C.E., Herod had members of the Jewish nobility imprisoned in the Hippodrome at Jericho, ordering that they be executed as soon as he died (*Ant.* 18.177-79). On his death, however, the order was not carried out.

History of Excavation

Jericho was first excavated in 1868 by Charles Warren, followed by excavations between 1907 and 1913 under Ernst Sellin and Carl Watzinger. Excavations were renewed in 1950 by James Kelso and Dimitri Baramki and in 1951 by James Pritchard. However, the most extensive and significant research of the site was carried out by Ehud Netzer, beginning in 1973, under the auspices of the Hebrew University of Jerusalem. It was Netzer who exposed the palatial complex south of the Second Temple–period city, used by the Hasmoneans, and afterward by Herod and his sons, as their winter residence.

A large agricultural estate, the "Royal Estate," was discovered north of the palatial complex. It was surrounded by a wall and contained a number of agricultural installations. According to Josephus, date palms and balsam plants were grown here, the latter producing oil that was among the costliest substances in antiquity (*J.W.* 4.468-70; cf. Strabo, *Geography* 16.241; Pliny, *Natural History* 6.14).

Water was supplied to both the agriculture estate and the palaces by means of an aqueduct built by the Hasmoneans, which carried water to the site from three springs in Wadi Qelt. During the reign of Alexander Jannaeus (103-76 B.C.E.), an additional aqueduct was constructed, bringing water to the site from springs in the Na'aran Valley. Netzer exposed the intersection of the two aqueducts, which reflect sophisticated planning.

The Hasmonean and Herodian Palaces

It was the warm winter weather, the abundance of water, and the proximity to Jerusalem that led the Hasmoneans to establish their winter palaces at the site. The chain of desert fortresses to the west added a strong sense of security. The remains of six impressive palaces were discovered, containing numerous gardens and water pools.

The First Winter Palace

The first palace was constructed by John Hyrcanus (134-104 B.C.E.) south of the Royal Estate. The square-shaped structure surrounded a central courtyard (18 × 25 m.), and contained both service and residential rooms. It apparently had two stories and between forty and fifty rooms. The southern wing was the palace's ceremonial wing. Several of the rooms in the northern wing featured stucco decorations apparently intended to mimic marble slabs. A ritual bath *(miqveh),* one of the earliest found to date in Israel, was found in this wing. The *miqveh* comprised two deep pools, one of them stepped, and each measuring 2.2 × 4 m. and 2.5 m. deep. Preserved in their entirety were the pools' inlets and outlets, as well as the lead pipe that connected the two pools. Two recreational pools (the "twin swimming pools") were built to the west of the palace.

The Fortified Palace

Adjacent to the swimming pools and superimposing the first palace, Alexander Jannaeus built a fortified palace enclosed by a wall atop a glacis and surrounded by a moat. Built of mud bricks, the palace was almost entirely destroyed and its layout cannot be ascertained.

The Twin Palaces

The third Hasmonean palace, dubbed by the excavators "the twin palaces," was apparently constructed by Alexandra Salome (76-67 B.C.E.). It features two nearly identical wings that faced each other, measuring 22.5 × 22.5 m. Each wing contained a central courtyard surrounded by four wings, as well as a triclinium (Roman-style dining room) that was located south of the courtyard and was open from every direction. Also found in each wing was a staircase, indicating the presence of a second story, and the remains of a bathhouse, ritual baths, and rooms decorated in colored frescos.

Herod's First Palace

The first of Herod's palaces at Jericho, located south of Wadi Qelt, was constructed ca. 35 B.C.E. The rectangular-shaped structure was built of mud bricks and measured 46 × 87 m. The main entrance was through a large room that, in turn, led into a central peristyle courtyard. From the courtyard one could enter most of the palace itself. A triclinium measuring 12.5 × 18 m. was found west of the courtyard, and was surrounded

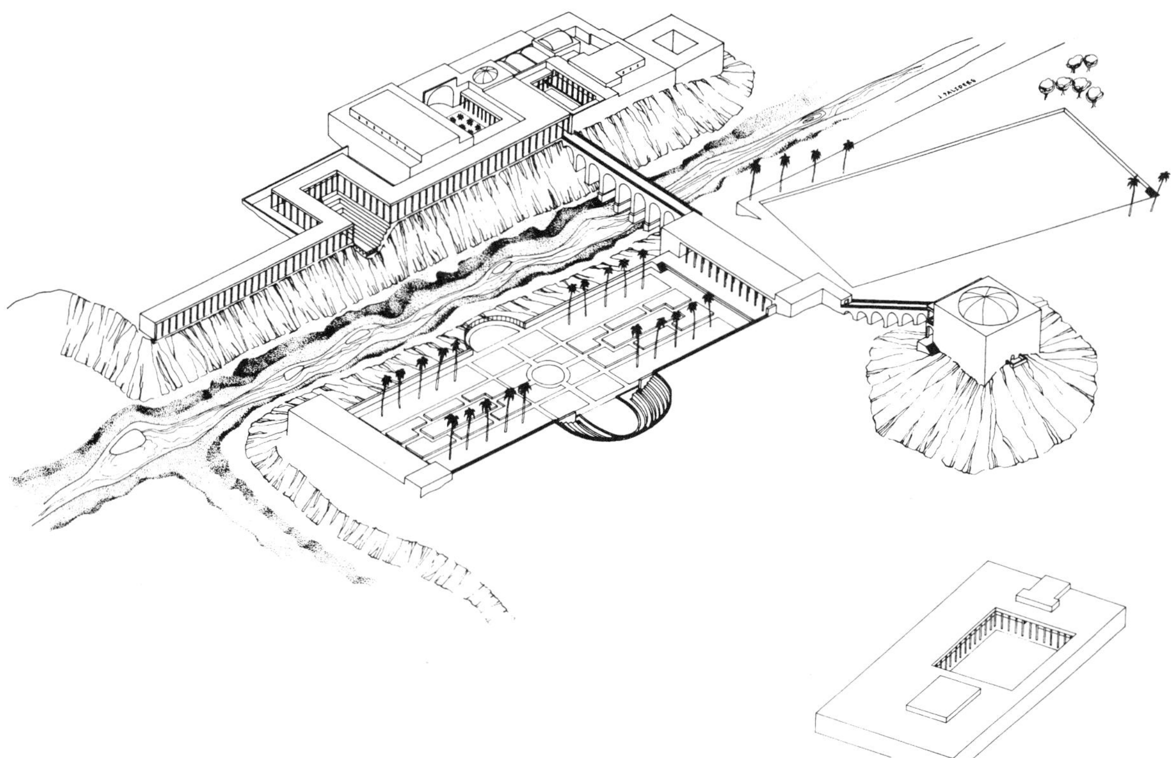

Isometric view from the southwest of Herod's first and third palaces at Jericho *(Ehud Netzer)*

by rows of columns on three sides. Two bathing installations were found. The first, west of the entrance room, was a Roman-style bathhouse with six rooms, paved in black and white mosaics featuring geometric designs. Netzer believes that this was the earliest of all of Herod's bathhouses, and it reflects the direct influence of Roman culture and architecture in his kingdom. The second, east of the entrance room, was a *miqveh*. It included a stepped immersion pool and another pool *(otzar)*.

Little of the palace's decorations have survived. Apart from the bathhouse mosaics, also found were a few columns, capitals, and entablature fragments.

Herod's Second Palace

As opposed to Herod's first palace, which faced inward, his second palace was open to the surrounding view. It was divided into two wings. The northern wing, 33 × 58 m., surrounded a central peristyle courtyard. Interestingly, the level of the courtyard garden was 80-90 cm. higher than that of the colonnade floors. The southern end of the wing contained a large room decorated with frescos and may have served as a triclinium. On either side were apparently entrance and dwelling rooms. South of these rooms was a veranda open to the dramatic view. Herod combined the "twin swimming pools" to create a single pool measuring 18 × 32 m.

The palace's relatively small bathhouse was built southwest of the pool, and comprised the dressing room *(apodyterium)*, cold room *(frigidarium)* with a stepped immersion pool, warm room *(tepidarium)*, and hot room *(caldarium)* in which the hypocaust pillars were entirely preserved. Only a few of the hot-air pipes *(tubuli)* were preserved *in situ*. Very little has survived of the bathhouse mosaic floors and the frescos that adorned its walls.

Herod's Third Palace

Herod's third, finely planned palace comprised four wings: the central and largest was dubbed "the northern wing" and was spread out north of the wadi, whereas the remaining wings were situated to its south. The southern wings contained a sunken garden, a large pool, and a huge artificial mound. The northern wing contained halls, reception rooms, two peristyle courtyards, and a Roman-style bathhouse. An adjacent structure to the east may have served as servants' quarters. All but one of the northern wing's rooms were decorated with frescos.

The peristyle courtyard, 14.4 × 20.5 m., was surrounded by colonnades on either three or four sides. The colonnade columns were painted red or black, and featured Corinthian columns. The lower part of the columns was smooth, while their upper part was covered with grooved plaster. The columns were found collapsed in the courtyard, evidence of the earthquake that destroyed much of the palace during the first century C.E. North of the courtyard was the entrance to the five-roomed bathhouse, including a caldarium heated by a hypocaust, a *frigidarium* containing a stepped pool, and a circular room (8 m. in diameter) that appears to have been the *sudatorium* (sweat room).

The western courtyard was surrounded by a row of columns on three sides. Its fourth side was flanked by an exedra (7 m. in diameter) built of Roman concrete and roofed by a half-dome. The courtyard columns featured Ionic capitals and were also found collapsed, indicative of the above-mentioned earthquake. Numerous fresco fragments displaying floral motifs were found in the courtyard, apparently originating in the courtyard walls. A garden, 9.3 × 12.7 m., was in the center of the courtyard, containing seven rows of clay flowerpots.

One of the most impressive finds from this wing is a huge reception room, 19 × 29 m., located in its western side. To date, this is the largest Roman-period room found in Israel. It was paved almost entirely with colorful stone tiles laid in *opus sectile* (large, specially cut) fashion.

The sunken garden of the southern wings was situated within a rectangular-shaped structure measuring 40 × 145 m. Its southern façade was built into the hillside, and featured a large stepped niche in its center containing numerous flowerpots. East of the garden was a huge pool, 42 × 90 m., the largest at the site.

The artificial mound found south of the sunken garden was created by building a frame of high walls to create hollow cells, which were subsequently filled with earth and stones. Earth was then heaped outside the frame. A staircase ascended to the lone circular reception hall (15 m. in diameter) at the top, whose walls were adorned with colorful frescos. Visitors to the hall were greeted with a wonderful view of the Jordan Valley. Herod's third palace remained in use by members of his family until the First Jewish Revolt against Rome (66-70 C.E.).

BIBLIOGRAPHY

G. GARBRECHET AND E. NETZER 1991, "Die Wasserversorgung des geschichtlichen Jericho und seiner königlichen Anlagen (Gut, Winter paläste)," *Leichtweiss-Institut Fur Wasserbau der Technischen Universität Braunschweig, Mitteilungen* 115: 1-37. • G. L. KELSO AND D. C. BARAMKI 1955, *Excavations at New Testament Jericho and Khirbet En-Nitla*, New Haven: American Schools of Oriental Research. • E. NETZER 1999, *The Palaces of the Hasmoneans and Herod the Great*, Mainz: Philipp von Zabern. • E. NETZER 2001, *Hasmonean and Herodian Palaces at Jericho, Final Reports of the 1973-1987 Excavations*, vol. 1, *Stratigraphy and Architecture*, Jerusalem: Israel Exploration Society. • E. NETZER AND R. LAUREYS-CHACHY 2004, *Hasmonean and Herodian Palaces at Jericho, Final Reports of the 1973-1987 Excavations*, vol. 2, *Stratigraphy and Architecture*, Jerusalem: Israel Exploration Society. • E. NETZER 2006, *The Architecture of Herod, The Great Builder*, Tübingen: Mohr-Siebeck. • J. B. PRITCHARD 1958, *The Excavation at Herodian Jericho, 1951*, New Haven: American Schools of Oriental Research.

OREN GUTFELD

Jerusalem

Jerusalem was the capital of Judea in the Hellenistic and Roman eras, and the spiritual center of Judaism in the Second Temple period. The city experienced dramatic growth in the Second Temple period (538 B.C.E.–70 C.E.), achieving unprecedented political, religious, and spiritual prominence. This process peaked during the Herodian era (37 B.C.E.–70 C.E.), when the city gained international recognition as "by far the most famous of the cities of the East" (Pliny the Elder, *Natural History* 5.70).

Jerusalem's enhanced stature resulted from various factors. As capital of the Hasmonean and Herodian realms, its urban life underwent profound changes. Equally significant was the emergence of a large Jewish population, numbering in the millions in both Judea and the Diaspora, who looked to Jerusalem as their sacred center. Moreover, the city's political and physical dimensions went hand in hand with its spiritual growth. Coincidentally, these dimensions all peaked simultaneously in the first century C.E., on the eve of the city's destruction in the revolt against Rome.

Information concerning the history and character of Jerusalem in the Second Temple period is far from uniform. The sources available for the Persian period (538-332 B.C.E.) are sparse; only some half-dozen biblical books (Ezra, Nehemiah, Chronicles, Haggai, Zechariah, Malachi, and perhaps Nahum and Joel) can be dated to this era. Archaeological finds are virtually nil. Documentation for the early Hellenistic era (332-175 B.C.E.) shares much the same fate. However, beginning with the second century (175-141 B.C.E.), and especially with the rise of the Hasmonean dynasty (141-63 B.C.E.), we are witness to a greater abundance of primary sources, including the second half of Daniel, 1 and 2 Maccabees, a series of apocryphal and pseudepigraphic books (e.g., *Jubilees*, parts of *1 Enoch*, the *Testaments of the Twelve Patriarchs*, and Judith), Josephus, the Dead Sea Scrolls, some pagan writings, and far more archaeological finds than known before.

However, we are infinitely better informed about the history of the city during the next 130 years, from Pompey's conquest in 63 B.C.E. to the destruction in 70 C.E., primarily because of Josephus' very detailed accounts in his *Jewish War* and *Antiquities*. These are supplemented by the New Testament Gospels and Acts, early rabbinic traditions, several apocryphal books (e.g., *Psalms of Solomon*, parts of the *Testament of Moses*), the writings of the Jewish philosopher Philo of Alexandria, and a number of Roman writers. Moreover, Herod's monumental building projects are well reflected in the city's archaeological remains, especially those uncovered since 1967, which have had an enormous impact on our understanding of the public sphere (the vicinity of the Temple Mount) and the private domain (the residential quarters in the Upper City excavations). In light of this greater availability of information, our discussion of Jerusalem in the Herodian and early Roman eras will be far more detailed than that of the earlier periods.

The Persian Period

Very little is known about Jerusalem at this time. Jews began returning to the city from Babylonia following Cyrus' proclamation of 538 B.C.E. encouraging and actively supporting such a move, much as he did with respect to other peoples in his realm. The narrative in Ezra 1–6 focuses primarily on the building of the altar and Temple, which, it is claimed, was often disrupted by local and foreign elements, including Persian officials. Jerusalem as a city comes much more into play in the fifth century B.C.E., with the arrival of Nehemiah, a Jew in the service of the royal court in Persia. Devoting much of his time to local affairs, he first set out to restore the city wall. Nehemiah's description of the city confirms that it was considerably smaller than at the time of its destruction some 150 years earlier.

While the construction work in Jerusalem in all likelihood was welcomed by the local inhabitants, it was bitterly opposed by outside elements who, nevertheless, were deeply involved in the city's affairs: Sanballat, governor of Samaria; Tobias the Ammonite, a Jewish landowner east of the Jordan River; and Geshem the Arab, apparently from the southern regions of Judah or Transjordan (Neh. 3:33–4:17; 6:1-19). The first two had close ties with the inhabitants of Jerusalem, especially the aristocratic and priestly circles (Neh. 6:17-19).

The socioeconomic hardships that had befallen many of the city's inhabitants likewise engaged Nehemiah's attention. Economic crises (perhaps now exacerbated by the burden of rebuilding the city's wall) led to polarization, with members of the priesthood, affluent families, and local officials aligning themselves on one side, and farmers, small landowners, and Nehemiah on the other (Neh. 5:2-5). Nehemiah saw to it that fields and vineyards were returned to their original owners and that burdensome debts were canceled. He forced this arrangement on creditors at a public meeting, not unexpectedly winning for himself the gratitude and loyalty of the populace. Nehemiah further eased the people's burden by forgoing his food allowance and personally contributed to the wall's construction by having his own servants help with the labor (Neh. 5:14-18).

Nehemiah's activities bear a striking resemblance to those of the populist leaders in the Greek cities of the sixth and fifth centuries B.C.E. These leaders based their rule on the broad support of the lower and middle classes by fortifying and strengthening cities, instituting major social and economic reforms (such as the cancellation of debts and the return of land), standing firm in the face of external foes, and initiating cultic reforms. These forceful leaders, or tyrants, often cultivated specific groups within their society and used these alliances to pursue other objectives on their political agenda. Nehemiah, for his part, granted many rights to the Levites, who then became his most ardent supporters (Neh. 8:11; 9:4, 5; 10:1-29, 38-40; 12:27-30; 13:10-13, 29-31).

Ezra and Nehemiah's work was epitomized by a series of public meetings held near the city's Water Gate in the month of Tishri (September-October), 444 B.C.E. There the people vowed to "to follow the Torah of God given through Moses, the servant of God, and to observe carefully all the commandments of the LORD our Lord, His rules and laws" (Neh. 10:30). Despite the enthusiasm ostensibly generated by the convocation ceremony reported in Nehemiah 8–10, it seems that matters soon reverted to the *status quo ante.* Nehemiah went back to Persia after twelve years of activity in Jerusalem, only to return soon after to find a situation that was completely different from the one he had left behind. Intermarriage was again rampant, Tobias the Ammonite was reensconced in a room of the Temple, tithes were not being given to the Levites, Temple-related commandments were being ignored, and both Jews and foreigners (Tyrians) were violating the Sabbath. Nehemiah set out to rectify these matters (Neh. 13:4-31), but the degree of his success is unknown owing to the termination of his memoirs at this point.

The Hellenistic Era

Following Alexander's conquest of the East, Jerusalem found itself under Ptolemaic (ca. 320-198 B.C.E.) and then Seleucid (198-141 B.C.E.) rule. We have almost no information regarding the former era. Ptolemy I gained control of the city on four occasions (320, 312, 302, and 301 B.C.E.), but the accounts about how this was done and the responses of Jerusalem's inhabitants are at odds with each other. The high priest and *gērousia* (council of elders) headed the local government at this time, enabling the city to retain a distinctly traditional ambience.

Nevertheless, Jerusalem's integration into the Hellenistic world was indeed in evidence. Alongside stamped jar handles featuring a pentagram with the name "Jerusalem" in paleo-Hebrew script, about 1,000 stamped jar handles from the island of Rhodes have also been found. These amphorae probably contained imported wine, as was the case in many other cities at the time. Given the large number of handles discovered, there can be little doubt that such imports were primarily intended for Jerusalem's inhabitants, and not for the small Ptolemaic military garrison residing in the city. If ordinary Jerusalemites used this wine, we cannot assume that this was in violation of any Jewish norm prohibiting the consumption of Gentile wine. It is far more likely that these later rabbinic laws had not yet been formulated and thus there were no religious constraints regarding the use of Gentile wine at the time.

A further indication of such economic ties with the outside world is documented in the Zenon Papyri, named after an official who was sent on a mission to Palestine in 259 B.C.E. to report on Ptolemaic economic interests in the country. Jerusalem appears on several lists, indicating that Zenon and his entourage had occasion to visit the city. Josephus also informs us of the Tobiad family's involvement in international affairs. Having borrowed money from friends in Samaria, Joseph, a member of this family, obtained tax-collecting rights from the Egyptian authorities for all of Coele-Syria, including Judea, Phoenicia, Syria, and parts of Transjordan. Other attestations of international contacts are more problematic historically, such as diplomatic ties with Sparta under the high priest Onias I (1 Macc. 12:20-23; *Ant.* 12.4, 10, 225-27), and the dispatching of seventy-two learned men from Jerusalem to Alexandria to undertake the translation of the Bible at the request of Ptolemy II (*Letter of Aristeas* 32).

Following the Seleucid conquest, Antiochus III issued an edict guaranteeing Jerusalem and its leadership certain rights and privileges, in essence ratifying the status quo: "And all the members of the nation shall have a form of government in accordance with the laws of their country, and the senate, the priests, the scribes of the Temple and the Temple-singers shall be relieved from the poll-tax and the crown-tax and the salt-tax which they pay" (*Ant.* 12.142). It is in this light that the reforms introduced by the high priest less than twenty-five years later become even more intriguing.

The report in 2 Macc. 4:7-17 describes the process by which a priest named Jason bought the high priesthood from King Antiochus IV Epiphanes and proceeded to convert Jerusalem into a Greek *polis,* replete with a *gymnasium* and *ephebium* for the training of Greek citizens. Scholarly opinion has been divided over the extent and nature of Jason's reforms and the degree of Hellenization he was introducing. The issue has two related components, one social and the other cultural: (1) Were the Hellenizers a numerically small coterie within the population representing but a thin aristocratic veneer of the city's population? (2) Was the transformation of Jerusalem into a *polis* a relatively isolated act, or did it represent the culmination of a long process of acculturation that now finally found expression in these public areas of city life as well? Regretfully, our sources for the earlier period are too sparse to allow for anything more than educated guesses.

Jason's success in gaining control of the city opened a political Pandora's box. A few years later, another priest, Menelaus, followed suit and likewise bought the high priesthood from the king. This led to a rivalry between the two priests culminating in violent urban upheavals. After quashing this violence, Antiochus IV pillaged the city, confiscated the Temple's sacred objects, and built a fortress there (the Akra, which continued to exist for some twenty-seven years, down to 141 B.C.E.). A year or so later, in December 167, the king initiated an unprecedented religious persecution, the precise reasons for which remain unclear. However, three years later, both the city and Temple were reconquered by Judah Maccabee and his forces; the menorah was rekindled and traditional worship reinstated.

Hasmonean Jerusalem

With the establishment of Hasmonean hegemony in 141 B.C.E., Jerusalem entered a new stage in its history as the capital of an independent state. Replacing the district of Yehud of the Persian and early Hellenistic periods, the Hasmonean realm expanded by leaps and bounds, encompassing an area roughly the size of David's and Solomon's kingdoms, and becoming a significant regional power by the beginning of the first century B.C.E. The important events in Jerusalem, together with the development of the city at this time, were inextricably intertwined with the Hasmonean leadership. The cultural creativity and religious ferment that became part and parcel of Jerusalem society were in large measure a reflection of the dynamic leadership wielded by this dynasty. The Hasmoneans were instrumental in providing the economic means for Jerusalem's growth and constituted the decisive factor in shaping the city's social, religious, and cultural agendas no less than its political and geographical ones.

The dynamic growth of the city was undoubtedly a response to the traumatic events that had taken place in previous decades. Since it had been subjected to Greek rule for almost two centuries, and with the memory of the religious persecution still fresh in its mind, it is quite likely that the population's sense of relief and salvation on the one hand, coupled with the pride and self-confidence of having achieved independence on the other, released enormous energies that fueled growth and creativity. However, without the firm and vigorous political leadership that the Hasmoneans provided, and the territorial expansion that resulted from their vigorous foreign policy, it is doubtful whether these energies would have been fully harnessed to produce such a wide range of institutional and literary expressions (e.g., 1 and 2 Maccabees). More than ever before, the power to shape city life was concentrated in the hands of one particular family that was able to dictate public policy almost at will. Thus, to a great extent, Jerusalem came to reflect the Hasmonean agenda and its priorities.

The city developed rapidly in a westerly direction in the latter half of the second century B.C.E., more than quadrupling its area to some 150 acres. By the first century B.C.E., even this greatly expanded area became insufficient for its burgeoning population, necessitating the construction of a second wall to the north that would incorporate an additional 60 to 70 acres. It may be assumed that Jerusalem's population also increased dramatically under the Hasmoneans. Applying the generally accepted estimate of population density (i.e., perhaps as many as 160 persons per acre), a city the size of Hasmonean Jerusalem would have had a population of about 25,000. Such a significant increase undoubtedly included a wide variety of people, affording a distinct urban ambience. As a political capital, Jerusalem attracted officials and officeholders; as a regional military power, it now incorporated officers and soldiers associated with the Hasmonean armies; as a reinvigorated religious center (see below), it became a magnet for Jews everywhere to visit and for members of the newly crystallized religious sects to reside. As the largest city in Judea, Jerusalem undoubtedly attracted many who came to the city from outlying rural areas in search of economic, social, and political opportunities. Merchants and artisans alike were an integral part of the city's socioeconomic fabric, but, once again, the paucity of sources for this period does not allow for elaboration. To this inventory of residents one can add the poorer classes of laborers and even slaves.

Jerusalem appears to have remained an overwhelmingly Jewish city throughout this era. The Hasmoneans' exclusively monotheistic bent, coupled with an intolerance of pagan worship, probably made the city rather inhospitable to non-Jews. Places of worship for pagan cults and temples to deities were nonexistent in the city. The increased emphasis on the centrality of the Temple and related practices would certainly have added to pagan discomfort.

Only two buildings are specifically noted with regard to the Hasmonean Jerusalem. One is the Hasmonean palace that, according to 1 Macc. 13:52, replaced the Seleucid Akra. The other is the Baris, a fortress-palace built north of the Temple. The landscape of Second Temple Jerusalem also included a necropolis located outside the city's walls. Although the remains found therein date to the Herodian period, many of these burial caves were undoubtedly used in this earlier period. The tombs of Jason and Bnei Hezir are clearly Hasmonean enterprises. That of the priestly Hezir family is located in the Qidron Valley just east of the city, while that of Jason (also probably of priestly lineage) is located to the west, in today's Rehavia neighborhood. Both tombs were built in typically Hellenistic fashion. Finally, the Temple merited much attention and restoration by various Hasmonean rulers, although the precise nature of their activity is unknown.

The priestly class was the leading group in Jerusalem at this time. Not only did priests bear primary responsibility for the Temple, but by all indications many hailed from Jerusalem's social, economic, and political elite. Hasmonean Jerusalem served as the breeding ground for the emergence of identifiable religious sects. The Sadducees, by virtue of their being priests and involved in Temple affairs, were clearly based in Jerusalem, as were the Pharisees. A number of their traditions indicate that most functioned in Jerusalem, and thus it is reasonable to assume that the city was the primary arena of sectarian activity. The ongoing struggle between the Pharisees and Sadducees throughout this period would seem to indicate that each group was well represented in the city. Although the Essenes' center was located in Qumran, the sect also had a foothold in Jerusalem. The city was very much in their consciousness since it was because of their opposition to the Temple's new leadership, that is, the Hasmoneans, that the sect coalesced, with many fleeing to the desert.

Religious sectarianism was an unusual occurrence in ancient Judaism. Historical circumstances of the mid-second century seem to have been conducive for spawning such groups. As a time of transition and upheaval following the trauma of Antiochus' persecutions and the desecration of the Temple, the emergence of the new Hasmonean society was undoubtedly viewed by many with exhilaration and pride, by others with disdain and profound disillusionment. Some may have been either alienated or stimulated by a variety of circumstances: the effects of urbanization; the awareness of Hellenistic influences that were now making ever-greater inroads; the Hasmonean usurpation of the high priesthood and the resulting problematic religious priorities; overly ambitious military activity; the increasingly centralized authority achieved by the Hasmonean synthesis of political and religious roles; or a combination of some or all of the above. Since there were significant differences among the sects, it is likely that the different factors listed above (and perhaps others as well) played varying roles in the formation of each.

A striking feature of Hasmonean Jerusalem was the simultaneous presence of ever-growing manifestations of Hellenism alongside the development of increasingly strident expressions of a particularistic Judaism. The former is evident not only in the archaeological finds, but in almost every literary source from this era — the first two books of the Maccabees, Judith, *Jubilees,* the Additions to Esther, and even the Qumran Scrolls. The latter dimension is apparent in the greater centrality of the Temple and related observances, the emphasis on ritual purity, the emergence of a unique aniconic art, the appearance and spread of *miqva'ot* (ritual baths), a rigorous policy against the local pagan population, and the implementation of a newly conceived policy of conversion. What is of interest is that these two dimensions were often not mutually exclusive; both could be found in the same group, and even at the same time among different people.

Herodian Jerusalem

By all accounts, Herod was the dominant figure in the history of Jerusalem in the early Roman period, not only in his own reign but for several generations thereafter as well. The king's unswerving loyalty to Rome won him a large measure of autonomy, and Judea's political integration into the imperial system was paralleled by a significantly increased adoption of Greek and Roman cultural models and styles. The ruling classes in Jerusalem now came to include new components, while most of the previous circle of leadership, specifically the Hasmoneans and their supporters, was removed from power, if not physically eliminated.

Herod's insecurities explain not only the presence of Roman soldiers in Jerusalem during his first years of power, but also the decision to erect major defensive installations in the city (*Ant.* 15.247-48). One such project involved the rebuilding of the palace-fortress north of the Temple Mount that Herod named "Antonia," after Marc Antony. The building served as the king's residence for some ten years, after which it assumed a military function. A second project, probably carried out at this time, was the construction of three massive towers in the western part of Jerusalem, the Upper City, that were to thwart an attack on one of the city's most vulnerable quarters.

Jerusalem benefited greatly from Herod's largesse. In addition to Antonia and the three towers, Herod initiated a series of projects that completely changed the face of the city. The Upper City to the west — the location of Herod's sumptuous palace, the refurbished Hasmonean palace and nearby *xystus* (perhaps a *gymnasium*), in all probability a theater, an agora, and homes of the city's wealthy residents, including the domicile of the high priest — was a prime beneficiary. Elsewhere in Jerusalem a hippodrome was constructed (an amphitheater was built somewhere outside the city's walls), in addition to a *bouleutērion* (council building), monumental tombs, streets, markets, shops, an expanded aqueduct, and reservoir systems.

When the opportunity presented itself, Herod responded with generosity to the plight of his people. The years 25-24 B.C.E. witnessed a severe drought that affected Judea and much of Syria, and was accompanied by illness and plague. Herod sold his personal belongings in order to buy grain in Egypt for distribution to the needy — first to his own subjects and then beyond, to those living outside his realm, in Syria. He also had food prepared for the elderly and infirm, and those incapable of caring for themselves, while providing clothing for the indigent. Josephus emphasizes, apparently quite tendentiously, the degree to which Herod's actions had a favorable impact on his subjects, transforming hostility and suspicion into gratitude and respect (*Ant.* 15.299-316).

Several years later (ca. 20 C.E.), the king remitted from his own coffers a third of the city's outstanding taxes to further assuage the feelings of a popula-

View of Jerusalem looking north, showing the four towers of the Antonia Fortress on the right (east) *(www.HolyLandPhotos.org)*

tion that objected to some of his actions (*Ant.* 15.365), and once again, in the year 13 C.E., upon his return from Asia Minor, he canceled a quarter of the tax burden (*Ant.* 16.64). However, Herod's crowning achievement toward his Jewish subjects was the rebuilding of the Jerusalem Temple and Temple Mount. This project lasted for years, serving as a source of employment for thousands, although it was also accompanied by the imposition of heavy taxes and forced labor (*Ant.* 15.380-425).

Herodian rule engendered a marked increase in the scope of outside influences on the life of the city. Archaeological remains have brought to light architectural patterns and artistic motifs attesting to a widespread adoption and adaptation of models and styles originating in the wider Hellenistic world. Moreover, Herod sent his sons to Rome not only for an education, but also to give them the opportunity to become familiarized with Roman mores and to cultivate personal relationships (*J.W.* 1.435, 445; *Ant.* 15.342; and elsewhere). Hellenism likewise finds expression in the names of a number of Jerusalem's residents, such as Cleopatra, one of Herod's wives and mother of Herod and Philip (*Ant.* 17.21), and Theophilus son of the high priest Ananus (*Ant.* 19.297).

There can be little question that the upper classes of the city's population were appreciably Hellenized. Their elaborate homes in the Upper City, impressive funerary monuments, and widespread use of Greek (including Greek names) all point in this direction. Some 37 percent of the inscriptions found in Herodian Jerusalem — mostly funerary — are in (or include) Greek. The presence of a series of major entertainment institutions in the city offered the populace exposure to cultural and athletic performances enjoyed in leading urban centers throughout the empire.

On an official level, a number of Jerusalem institutions reflected a typical Roman provincial setting. The presence of a *polis*-type government, with a *boulē*/*bouleutērion* and sanhedrin (a ruler's personal cabinet or council), lent the city a Hellenistic ambience that existed side by side with the Temple and priesthood. The physical and functional prominence of the Temple Mount's basilica, not to speak of its *temenos* (sacred area), constituted yet another link with typical Hellenistic-Roman institutions of other cities. To these we may add the other public buildings noted above that were patterned after Hellenistic models and likewise lent a cosmopolitan air to Jerusalem.

The use of Hellenistic and Roman funerary customs was widespread among the city's entire population, and not just the wealthy. Ranging from the more elaborate and ostentatious monuments to the very simply hewn cave, these tombs represent a wide spectrum of the city's population. The same holds true with respect to the contents of these tombs and the ornateness of their ossuaries and sarcophagi. Finally, because the overwhelming majority of Second Temple inscriptions come from funerary settings, the epigraphic evidence may well be reflective of the society as a whole. The two spoken languages of the period, Aramaic and Greek, are predominant, while Hebrew and Latin were less common.

These Greco-Roman influences stemmed largely from the fact that Jerusalem was now an inextricable part of the Roman Empire and that Herod actively encouraged and facilitated such acculturation. However, another important component of this phenomenon was Diaspora Jewry. Jewish communities throughout the Roman world, immersed in Greco-Roman culture, kept in close touch with Jerusalem. Frequent visits to the city by Diaspora Jews for the festivals, not to speak of the existence of many Diaspora communities residing in the city on a permanent basis, significantly contributed to its exposure to and absorption of outside influences.

However, just as there was a marked influence of Hellenism on Jerusalem, there were also many instances in which such influences were ignored, radically altered, or entirely rejected because they were either unsuitable or offensive to Jewish religious sensibilities. These mixed attitudes are clearly evident in Second Temple Jerusalem: the hippodrome seems to have been located not far from the Temple, and most homes of wealthy priests

View of Jerusalem just north of the Herodian palace complex showing in the background the Temple and, on the far left, two towers of the Antonia Fortress *(www.HolyLandPhotos.org)*

and others contained Hellenistic-Roman decorations alongside ritual baths and aniconic art; even Herod himself was careful to avoid placing figural representations in his palaces and public buildings (within Jewish Judea), and he demanded circumcision before allowing female members of his family to marry non-Jews. Thus, even more than under Hasmonean rule, Jerusalem now occupied a most unusual position within the province of Judea. On the one hand, it was the most Jewish of all its cities and, on the other, it was the most Hellenized. Jerusalem's Janus-type posture made it unique in Jewish society in particular and throughout the larger Roman world in general.

Direct Roman Rule: The Early Years (6-41 C.E.)

Following the introduction of direct Roman rule over Judea in 6 C.E., and with Caesarea as its newly designated political capital, Jerusalem's status was bound to change. Nevertheless, it continued to function as the focal city for the Jewish population and appears to have maintained its status as the de facto capital of Jewish Judea. Given the extensive autonomy enjoyed by the country's Jews, it was only natural that they would continue to regard Jerusalem as their center for religious, juridical, social, and even, in some cases, political matters. The leadership, which functioned on a countrywide scale and included the high priests, the Jerusalem aristocracy, and the sects, continued to reside in the city.

The period of direct Roman rule preceding the destruction of the Second Temple included two distinct time frames (6-41 and 44-66 C.E.) separated by the brief reign of Agrippa I (41-44 C.E.). Much of the first period appears to have been generally uneventful and calm. In summing up the situation in the province during the reign of Emperor Tiberius (14-37 C.E.), Tacitus wrote: "Under Tiberius all was quiet" (*Histories* 5.9.2); indeed, Josephus reports very little about events of this time, mentioning only several minor incidents in the city at the outset of the period. It would appear that the overwhelming majority of Jerusalem's citizens were willing to give direct Roman rule a chance. Those in leadership positions, such as the priestly and aristocratic circles, were committed to maintaining a cooperative relationship with Rome.

However, a major turn in the relations between the Jews and the Roman administration occurred under Pontius Pilate, procurator of Judea from 26-36/37 C.E., as a result of a series of incidents that took place in Jerusalem:

By introducing Roman military standards bearing images of the emperor into the city, Pilate flouted the prohibition against the use of figural images. The Jews vigorously protested and immediately sent a delegation to Caesarea to plead with Pilate to remove the offensive standards. When the Roman governor realized the extent of their opposition (some Jews reputedly evinced a willingness to die rather than see their laws and city violated), he ordered that the standards be removed from the city (*J.W.* 2.169-77).

Somewhat later, Pilate appropriated Temple funds for the construction of an aqueduct. The impropriety of such an action is not clear, as the use of sacred funds for municipal purposes, including the construction of an aqueduct, is implicitly sanctioned in *m. Šeqal.* 4:2 (although this rabbinic tradition may reflect a more liberal interpretation of how such funds might be dispensed than what was, in fact, operative in first-century Jerusalem under priestly rule). The Jerusalem population protested against this act not only by petitioning but also by shouting insults and abuses at the procurator. In retaliation, Pilate's soldiers then attacked the crowd, killing and wounding many (*Ant.* 18.55-62).

A third incident in Jerusalem, this time reported by Philo, involved the offense taken by the Jews to the placing of gilded shields bearing inscriptions inside Herod's palace. Once again, it is difficult to understand why gilded shields or the use of dedicatory inscriptions would have been offensive. Indeed, Philo himself reports that a main synagogue in Alexandria contained such shields honoring the emperor (*Legatio ad Gaium* 20, 133). Perhaps by this time Pilate had so exacerbated his relations with Jerusalem's populace that any action by him, however benign, would have been interpreted as an effrontery. However, the Jews' response in this case was markedly different. Taking advantage of the presence in the city of a number of members of the Herodian family, a delegation that also included the local aristocracy requested Pilate to remove these shields. When he refused, the Jews appealed to the emperor, who acceded to their request (Philo, *Legatio* 299–305).

The New Testament has also preserved a number of references attesting to heightened tension in the city at this time. Luke states that Pilate mingled the blood of the Galileans with that of their sacrifices — from which we may infer that these people were executed while on pilgrimage to Jerusalem (Luke 13:1).

Furthermore, the New Testament accounts of Jesus being sentenced to death together with two others may be an indication of Pilate's political apprehensions as well as the atmosphere of hostility and tension that may have pervaded certain constituencies gathered in Jerusalem for the festival seasons. These holiday gatherings, especially on Passover, commemorating the deliverance from Egypt and perhaps harboring thoughts of redemption, may have inspired in some an air of messianic expectation that a miraculous supernatural event was about to unfold. Thus, the Gospels' portrayal of Jesus' experience in the city may provide additional evidence for the prevailing tensions with the Romans under Pilate.

One further incident soon after was Emperor Caligula's announcement in 40 C.E. that he intended to erect his statue in the Jerusalem Temple. How the local Jerusalem populace reacted to this is unknown, and the plan was soon scrapped following the emperor's death.

Jerusalem under Agrippa I (41-44 C.E.)

Following Caligula's death in 41 C.E., Roman policy toward Judea once again shifted. His successor, Claudius, sought to placate Jewish sensibilities by appointing his

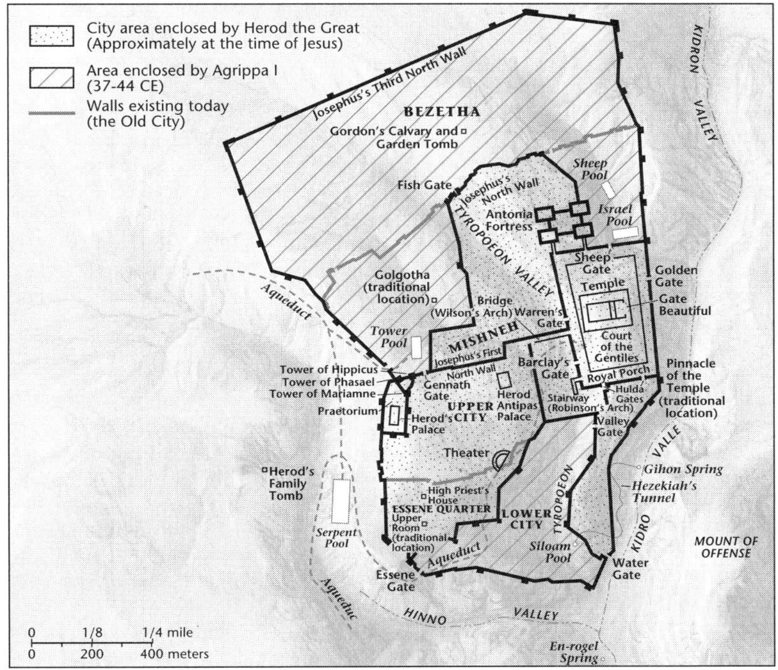

JERUSALEM IN THE FIRST CENTURY C.E.

friend Agrippa I, grandson of Herod, as king. Josephus and later rabbinic literature are generally quite positive regarding Agrippa's rule. The former, for instance, notes Agrippa's punctiliousness with regard to purification laws and sacrifices (*Ant.* 19.328-31).

In another vein, Agrippa adopted a harsh policy vis-à-vis the Jerusalem church or, more precisely, toward some of its leaders. According to Acts 12:1-19, Agrippa (referred to here as King Herod) executed James, brother of John, and imprisoned Peter, who later miraculously escaped. Despite the narrative's heavy literary and theological overlay (the use of the name Herod, a Herodian persecutor, the Passover setting, Peter's miraculous escape, Agrippa's subsequent death), it is entirely possible that Agrippa adopted a characteristically priestly-Sadducean policy of hostility toward the local church. The "approval of the Jews" for his actions noted in Acts may, in fact, refer primarily to that of contemporary priestly circles.

Two initiatives undertaken by Agrippa impacted directly on the Jerusalem populace. The first was his personal remittance of taxes on houses (*Ant.* 19.299), which apparently relieved people of a major tax burden. The second was his decision to build a third wall for Jerusalem. Josephus notes that the wall was to be erected north of the city and would have constituted a formidable barrier. The Roman reaction was sharp; perhaps fearful of a future revolt, the Romans assumed that such an undertaking would render the city impregnable (*Ant.* 19.326-27). It is hard to fathom how Agrippa, who had spent almost his entire life in Rome before becoming king, would ever have entertained the thought of revolt, nor is it clear why the Romans would have been suspicious of a possible insurrection.

Procuratorial Rule (44-66 C.E.): On the Brink of Chaos

Josephus has a great deal to say about the events of the two decades leading up to the revolt, because the overriding goal in his *Jewish War* (further expanded in *Antiquities*) was to describe the tensions and conflicts that led to the revolt and destruction of Jerusalem. Nevertheless, these accounts are selective and tendentious. Josephus himself was a contemporary of these events who played a significant role in them and had definite opinions regarding the causes and responsibility for the eventual calamity.

Josephus reports that matters now went from bad to worse during this twenty-two-year period. Between territorial disputes with pagan neighbors, tensions with the Samaritans, friction vis-à-vis various Roman procurators and soldiers, and mounting internal turmoil (brigandage, messianic pretenders, socioeconomic strains, urban violence, and extreme political agitators who resorted to assassination tactics), the situation deteriorated to the point where turmoil and instability had become endemic in Judea, and particularly in Jerusalem.

The collapse of law and order in the 50s and 60s presented many Jews with an opportunity not only for self-aggrandizement but for settling political and religious accounts. Thus, in the hiatus following Festus' death and before Albinus assumed his position in 62 C.E., the high priest Ananus, an avowed Sadducee, convened a meeting of a sanhedrin to try James, brother of Jesus. The sentence was presumably carried out, evoking the protest of some Jerusalemites who proceeded to inform Albinus that such an act was illegal because the governor had not authorized it. Ananus was subsequently deposed by Agrippa II, who had charge over such matters.

The crisis during these years was greatly exacerbated by the absence of a strong leadership in the city. The high priesthood, for one, was thrown into disarray by the frequent changes in leadership wrought by Agrippa. These turnovers were clearly destabilizing, as was the fact that no other group or individual was able or willing to fill the gap, neither the Herodians, the Jerusalem aristocracy, the Pharisees, nor even the Roman provincial government itself. In the end, this may have been the single most decisive factor in the unraveling of the social and political fabric of Jerusalem and consequently that of the entire Judean society.

Jerusalem's Urban Configuration

Jerusalem had reached an unprecedented size, both physically and demographically, by the mid-first century C.E. In the previous century and a half, the city had tripled in size, reflecting in no small measure its enhanced stature as the religious center of the Jews, whose numbers and geographical dispersion were unparalleled in antiquity. As a result of these factors plus the monumental Herodian buildings and others erected thereafter, the city became internationally renowned. Pliny the Elder, as noted, writing in the mid-first century C.E., describes Jerusalem as "by far the most famous of the cities in the East" (*Natural History* 5.70), and Tacitus refers to it as the capital of the Jews with "a Temple possessing enormous riches" (*Histories* 5.8.1).

The rapid growth of the city's population continued at least into the fifth decade of the first century C.E., when Agrippa I found it necessary to initiate the construction of a third wall. Because such construction was thwarted by the Roman government, this wall was completed only twenty-five years later by rebels at the outbreak of the Jewish revolt against Rome (*J.W.* 5.155).

Population estimates for Jerusalem in the first century C.E. range between 25,000 and 225,000. A very common method of assessing a city's population is by multiplying the estimated population density per acre by the area of the city. Thus, since by the end of the Second Temple period Jerusalem encompassed some 450 acres, and assuming approximately 160 persons per acre, we might then conclude that the city numbered approximately 70,000 to 75,000 permanent residents. However, given the fact that the city's area included a large tract of land (about half the overall total) that only recently had been included within the city — an area that, by Josephus' own admission, was less densely settled — we should probably lower our estimate somewhat, and assume a figure between 60,000 and 70,000. J. Wilkinson studied the water supply system of the city and also concluded that there were about 75,000 inhabitants.

Jerusalem, then, would have been a sizeable city for its time, although not in the same demographic league as Rome, Alexandria, Antioch, or even Carthage, Apamea, Pergamum, and Ephesus. With a population of at least 60,000, Jerusalem qualified as a large metropolis in the second rank of provincial cities. However, if we also take into consideration that three times a year, on the Jewish festivals, the city's population grew substantially, perhaps doubling or trebling itself for days and weeks (if not longer), we should imagine that the city was occupied by a far more numerous and diverse population than any fixed number of permanent residents would indicate.

With regard to the city's social configuration, we are confronted by an intriguing picture of hierarchy and diversity, definitiveness and fluidity, commonality and divisiveness. Unquestionably, the Temple set the tone for the city in many ways — politically, socially, economically, and religiously. The high priests were in many respects the city's leaders, and the Temple's needs determined much of the city's economy. The Temple defined the city's character religiously as well; the Jewish Sabbath and holidays set its rhythm, and Temple-related customs regulated much of its religious behavior.

Yet, even within Jerusalem's hierarchical ambience, the city's inhabitants found much room to maneuver, adapt, refine, and create independent social and religious arrangements. Part of this was due to the fact that some features of Jerusalem's cultural and religious profile were fashioned by a nonpriestly agenda outside the Temple. Herod had reshaped the city, an urban aristocracy played a vital role, the various sects followed their own dictates, Greco-Roman culture had its impact in myriad ways, and Diaspora Jewry was active in many aspects of city life.

Thus, given the composite nature of this society, the Temple's influence and the image of religious uniformity must be carefully gauged. The religious arena fluctuated between a state of stability and ferment ever since Hasmonean times. As a result, some people were driven to new and, at times, radical social, political, and religious agendas, others to a more conservative posture.

Even with this diversity, the Jerusalem religious establishment continued to wield an enormous degree of religious authority, not only in the city itself but throughout Judea and the Diaspora. That many literary sources attack the Temple and its leadership should not automatically dictate our assessment of the first-century Jerusalem's religious scene. Whether it be the contemporary Qumran Scrolls, the later New Testament material, or the even later rabbinic literature, these sources — which are all tendentious — criticize the Temple, its cult, and its leadership, and invariably offer a religious alternative to the Temple establishment.

One has only to look beyond the overt polemics of several competing religious elites to realize that a large majority of the people held very different perspectives of the Temple and priesthood. For instance, while some New Testament traditions reflect varying degrees of hostility toward Jerusalem's institutions, many bear witness to the generally acknowledged power and authority of Jerusalem's religious leaders and the Temple by Judean (including Galilean) and Diaspora Jews alike. According to Acts 9:1-2, the Jerusalem high priest presumably held a position of authority and respect among the Jews of Damascus, since Paul asked him for letters (of introduction?) that would enable him to undertake the persecution of Christians in that city. Similarly, when Paul reached Rome the leaders of the Jewish community there were hesitant to talk with him at first, having received no letter of introduction from Judea (Acts 28:17-22). The Jews' allegiance to the Temple, as expressed in their mass pilgrimages and donations of vast amounts of money, is in itself enough to confirm the preeminence of this institution in first-century Jewish life.

By the mid-first century C.E., on the eve of its destruction, Jerusalem reached the peak of its physical growth and religious status. Over the six hundred years of the Second Temple period, the city had outgrown its original modest site on the eastern ridge, expanding first westward and then northward; it had increased fifteen-fold, having at first occupied an area of some 30 acres and eventually encompassing approximately 450 acres. Numbering approximately 5,000 at the beginning of this era, Jerusalem's population had now reached a total of 60,000 to 70,000 permanent residents. Once serving as the center of a small, isolated district on the western fringes of the Persian Empire, Jerusalem had become the metropolis of an expanded Judea, an area stretching from the Galilee to the northern Negev, and from the Mediterranean to Transjordan. Jerusalem had also assumed the role of spiritual center for some four to eight million Jews (including God-fearers) living in the Roman Empire, a number that may have comprised close to 10 percent of the empire's total population.

Ironically, Jerusalem was destroyed at its zenith. At the height of its influence and prestige, first-century Jerusalem became enveloped in turmoil, gradually descending into anarchy that resulted in a direct armed conflict with the greatest military power of this era.

Josephus says of Titus when visiting the city after 70 (and here, perhaps, interjecting his own thoughts as well): "On his way he visited Jerusalem, and contrasting the sorry scene of desolation before his eyes with the former splendor of the city, and calling to mind the grandeur of its ruined buildings and their pristine beauty, he commiserated its destruction" (*J.W.* 7.112).

In concluding the first edition of his *Jewish War*, to which a seventh book was later added, Josephus himself raises a profound issue in the face of the painful historical reality of Jerusalem in ruins. His thoughts are laden with far-reaching theological and social notions: "How is it that neither its antiquity, nor its ample wealth, nor its people spread over the whole habitable world, nor yet the great glory of its religious rites, could do anything to avert its ruin? Thus ended the siege of Jerusalem" (*J.W.* 6.442).

BIBLIOGRAPHY

N. AVIGAD 1983, *Discovering Jerusalem*, Jerusalem: Shikmona and Israel Exploration Society. • A. BAUMGARTEN 1997, *The Flourishing of Jewish Sects in the Maccabean Era: An Interpretation*, Leiden: Brill. • M. BROSHI 1975, "La population de l'ancienne Jérusalem," *RB* 82: 5-14. • T. A. BUSINK 1970, *Der Tempel von Jerusalem von Salomon bis Herodes: Einer archäologisch-historische Studie unter Berücksichtigung des westsemitischen Tempelbaus*, 2 vols., Leiden: Brill. • H. GEVA, ED. 1987, *Ancient Jerusalem Revealed*, Jerusalem: Israel Exploration Society. • M. GOODMAN 1987, *The Ruling Class of Judaea: The Origins of the Jewish Revolt against Rome AD 66–70*, Cambridge: Cambridge University Press. • J. JEREMIAS 1969, *Jerusalem in the Time of Jesus: An Investigation into Economic and Social Conditions during the New Testament Period*, Philadelphia: Fortress. • L. I. LEVINE 1998, *Judaism and Hellenism in Antiquity: Conflict or Confluence?* Seattle: University of Washington Press. • L. I. LEVINE 2002, *Jerusalem: Portrait of the City in the Second Temple Period (538 BCE–70 CE)*, Philadelphia: Jewish Publication Society. • P. RICHARDSON 1996, *Herod: King of the Jews and Friend of the Romans*, Columbia: University of South Carolina Press. • E. P. SANDERS 1992, *Judaism: Practice and Belief 63 BCE–66 CE*, London: SCM. • J. WILKINSON 1974, "Ancient Jerusalem: Its Water Supply and Population," *PEQ* 106: 33-51. • Y. YADIN 1975, *Jerusalem Revealed: Archaeology in the Holy City, 1968–1974*, trans. R. Grafman, Jerusalem: Israel Exploration Society.

LEE I. LEVINE

Jerusalem, New

The New Jerusalem is the idealized or ideal Jerusalem of the future, the anticipation of which appears throughout the literature of early Judaism and Christianity, most notably in the biblical prophets and in the New Testament book of Revelation. The city is not normally named, important exceptions being "The LORD Is There" in Ezek. 48:35 and "the new Jerusalem" in Rev. 3:12 (cf. 21:2), the latter more an appellation than a proper title. In many cases a new Temple may be assumed where only a new Jerusalem is explicitly anticipated, although some writings, such as Ezekiel or the *New Jerusalem* text, describe both city and Temple, while others, such as the *Temple Scroll* and the *Apocalypse of Weeks*, focus on the Temple. In the *Animal Apocalypse*, the "house" that is to come was probably envisioned to function as both city and Temple. In the new city of Revelation, the Temple is unnecessary, since its function is assumed by God and the Lamb (21:22). In every occurrence, the New Jerusalem is built, rebuilt, appears, descends, or is otherwise manifested through divine agency.

Foundational Ideas

The theme of the New Jerusalem is rooted in several motifs, including (a) the belief in the centrality of Jerusalem as the holy city of God and the royal city of David (e.g., 1 Kings 8:44; 11:32, 26; 14:21; 2 Kings 21:7), the eternal site of temple and throne, never to be conquered (Psalms 46, 48, etc.); (b) ideas of restoration and renewal in ancient mythology, specifically the hope for a new creation (Isa. 65:17; 66:22; *1 Enoch* 91:14, 16) and/or the reconstitution of the terrestrial paradise, either renewed (*1 Enoch* 45:3-5) or utopian (Ps. 102:25-27); and (c) the *omphalos* ("navel") tradition, which in its formulations may encompass the notions of an ideal or heavenly city as the *axis mundi*, the cosmic mountain, or Jerusalem/Zion as the navel of the world (Ezek. 5:5; 38:12; *1 Enoch* 26:1; *Jub.* 8:12, 19). Near Eastern and classical perspectives on planned urban design likely influenced the descriptions of the New Jerusalem that exhibit regular architectural features or an orthogonal city pattern.

Associated Motifs

Expectations recurrently connected with the city and temple in the end time include elements of the classic reversal-of-fortune motif: (a) the ingathering of Israel (e.g., Isa. 27:12-13; 45:13; 49:19-20; Joel 3:2; Zeph. 3:19-20; Zech. 8:7-8; Tob. 13:10-14; *Pss. Sol.* 11:2-6; 17:26), accommodating the prospect of the return of the exiles

(Sir. 36:13, 16; Tob. 14:5) or the reenfranchisement of the dispossessed (Ezek. 47:13–48:29); (b) the humbling of the oppressor nations (e.g., Isa. 2:2-3 par Mic. 4:1; *Apostrophe to Zion* at 11Q5 col. xxii lines 11-12; *Ps. Sol.* 17:30-31; *T. Dan* 5:12-13), occasionally as a result of a great war (Ezekiel 38–39; Joel 3:9-12), and their acknowledgment of the sovereignty of God (Tob. 13:11; *Sib. Or.* 3.710-23); and, above all, (c) the magnificence, wealth, and strength of the future city and the security of its inhabitants.

The image of a strong, prosperous, and peaceful city is evoked by such elements as (a) its splendid brilliance (Isa. 60:2-3; Bar. 5:1; *Sib. Or.* 5.420-28; *4 Ezra* 10:25, 50, 55), constructed, as it sometimes is, from marble and adorned with precious stones and fine gold (Isa. 49:18; 54:11-17; Tob. 13:16-17; 2Q24 frg. 3 line 2; 4Q554 frg. 2 col. ii line 15; Rev. 21:11-21); (b) the presence of rivers, a spring, or another ample source of fresh water (Ezek. 47:1-12; Zech. 14:8; 4Q554 frg. 4 lines 1-2; Rev. 22:1), a symbol of life-giving fertility and a sign of the presence of God; (c) the city's defensive structures, such as impregnable walls and massive towers; (d) its open gates (Rev 21:25), which signify peace, and through which commerce and trade pass freely; and (e) its lively plazas, where the young play and the old meet to talk and relax without worry (e.g., Zech. 8:4-5).

Idealized (Restored) vs. Ideal (Utopian)

The theme of the New Jerusalem appears in many different forms, which permits the imposition of multiple, overlapping classifications. A general distinction, however, may be made between the expectation of a restored Jerusalem and that of a utopian Jerusalem. The distinction hinges on the quality of the description of the city and its contexts. The idea of the restored Jerusalem envisions a future renewal of the city to its most pristine state (e.g., Isa. 33:17-24; 60:1-22; 62:1-12; 65:17-25; Jeremiah 30–33; Tobit 13). Such descriptions, based on a combination of yearning and reality, often portray the rosy picture in its fullest detail, including ample references to the social and economic bases of the city's prosperity, such as irrigated fields, bountiful crops, and the steady presence of trade via caravan and ship (Isa. 60:9-17; Amos 9:14-15; Zeph. 3:20; Zech. 1:17, 2:8). In this representation, the refreshed future city will not be larger than the present one, and even if it must be raised up partly from ruins or otherwise made whole again (Isa. 44:24-28; 49:17; 52:9; 54:14; 61:4; Tob. 13:16; 4Q462 frg. 1 line 14; the *Apostrophe to Zion*), it is the Jerusalem that in its irregular perimeter and familiar landmarks (esp. Jer. 31:38-40) will be instantly recognizable to its population (*4 Baruch* 5). The *Animal Apocalypse* recalls an even more distant past, revivifying the idea of the desert camp in its conception of the New Jerusalem (*1 Enoch* 90:28-36).

The ideal Jerusalem, on the other hand, represents a utopian city which in its physical dimensions, architectural details, and static sociopolitical setting is far more divorced from the Jerusalem of history. Its characteristic form is the monumental New Jerusalem, the illustrations of which include Ezekiel 40–48 (esp. 48:16, 30-35), the *New Jerusalem* text (esp. 4Q554 + 4Q554a par. 5Q15), the *Reworked Pentateuch* (4Q365a), *Sib. Or.* 5.420-33, and Rev. 21:2–22:5, with the monumental New Temple the subject of the *Temple Scroll.* The principal characteristics of this subtype are its square or rectangular perimeters, regular design features, and tremendous size. The most excessive example, the New Jerusalem of Revelation, circumscribes an area 12,000 stadia square (21:16), or approximately nine times the size of France. The measurements of the city, its walls, and its intramural structures are frequently described in blueprint-like detail, an antecedent of which is the belief that the plans of Jerusalem are inscribed on God's palms (Isa. 49:16). The New Jerusalem of the *Animal Apocalypse,* although restored rather than utopian, is probably monumental, inasmuch as it is large, broad, and full of inhabitants (*1 Enoch* 90:36).

Terrestrial vs. Heavenly

Another distinction may be made between the anticipation of an earthly Jerusalem and that of heavenly Jerusalem. The majority of the references to the New Jerusalem describe a terrestrial city, a state suggested in many cases by supplementary details. For instance, Tobit 13 speaks of the rebuilding of the city (13:10, 16) and includes a curse on those who would seek to reduce its walls, demolish its towers, and set fire to its houses (13:12). Several examples, however, are indisputably heavenly: *2 Enoch* (55:2), the *Apocalypse of Elijah* (1:10), Galatians (4:26-27), the Epistle to the Hebrews (12:22; 13:14), and, most famously, Revelation (21:2–22:5), where the New Jerusalem descends from heaven (21:2). It is certainly possible that the New Jerusalem of the *Animal Apocalypse,* which the Lord of the sheep brings to earth, originates in heaven (*1 Enoch* 90:28). The New Jerusalem of *4 Ezra* 7:26 (cf. 8:52; 10:27-59; 13:36), unseen and then seen, is likely a heavenly, preexistent city, to be manifested on earth at the appointed time. In *2 Bar.* 4:1-6 the city is definitely heavenly (and preexistent), but other passages (*2 Bar.* 32:1-5 and 68:5-7) describe a terrestrial city.

The tremendous influence of the heavenly, ideal city of Revelation 21–22 occasionally has colored how scholars have understood the theme of the New Jerusalem. For instance, it can obscure the fact that these categories are not automatically overlapping: the monumental ideal cities of Ezekiel and the *New Jerusalem* text found at Qumran, for instance, are terrestrial structures, not heavenly. Moreover, the book's late date and terminal position in the New Testament (and thus in Christian Bibles) can create the somewhat distorted impression, reinforced by the other clear examples of the type, which are equally late in date, that its gigantic heavenly city stands at the end of a single, neat developmental trajectory that originated in the modest prophetic expectations for a renewed, earthly Jerusalem. Yet ideal, monumental illustrations of the theme appear in early texts like Ezekiel, while instances of restored and earthly cities alike persist in later ones like Tobit.

Relation to Apocalyptic Eschatology

Ideal and heavenly types are encountered more in the later literature, suggesting that the conception of the New Jerusalem gradually underwent a general historical development. The likely catalyst was the rise of apocalypticism in early Judaism, although it must be stressed that the New Jerusalem is neither a component of the ideology nor integrally associated with the genre apocalypse. One of the principal causes of the creation of an apocalyptic historiography was the emergent belief that the normal processes of history, inasmuch as they were understood to operate within established historiographies such as that embedded in the Deuteronomic tradition, could no longer theologically explain present-day circumstances or encompass the expectation for their reversal and a restoration of fortune. Instead, such expectations were increasingly believed to require God's unique and decisive action at the conclusion of history.

The utopian New Jerusalem therefore represents the form of the theme unfettered by the limitations of the historically possible and reflects in its architectural perfection the fundamentally static nature of its eschatological setting. At the same time, a different stream of apocalypticism came to encompass the idea of a transcendental spatial reality attainable through otherworldly journeys. The heavenly Jerusalem, then, represents the ideal form of the theme carried to its logical extreme. With the addition of the ultimate atemporal element of preexistence, the expectation of a physical New Jerusalem completely escaped the restrictions of time and space. What remained was its dislocation from the physical, where the New Jerusalem is understood allegorically or metaphorically. Philo of Alexandria writes about an invisible city of God, whose location is the soul (*Somn.* 2.37-38), while the fourth *Sibylline Oracle* speaks of the immaterial temple of God (*Sib. Or.* 4.6-11; cf. Heb. 8:1-5; 9:11-12), but for the most part this secondary development of the theme postdates the Second Temple era.

In short, by the late Second Temple period, the theme of the New Jerusalem had become a relatively common, though not necessarily characteristic, element of apocalyptic eschatology. In the main, it was in its utopian, heavenly, and sometimes preexistent form that the theme was bequeathed to Judaism and Christianity of the late antique and early medieval periods.

BIBLIOGRAPHY

G. BISSOLI 1994, *Il tempio nella letteratura giudaica e neotestamentaria: Studio sulla corrispondenza fra tempio celeste e tempio terrestre,* Jerusalem: Franciscan. • O. BÖCHER 1983, "Die heilige Stadt in Völkerkrieg," in idem, *Kirche in Zeit und Endzeit: Aufsätze zur Offenbarung des Johannes,* Neukirchen-Vluyn: Neukirchener Verlag, 113-32. • L. DITOMMASO 2005, *The Dead Sea New Jerusalem Text: Contents and Contexts,* Tübingen: Mohr-Siebeck. • W. MÜLLER 1961, *Die heilige Stadt: Roma quadrata, himmlisches Jerusalem und die Mythe vom Weltnabel,* Stuttgart: Kohlhammer. • U. SIM 1996, *Das himmlische Jerusalem in Apk 21,2–22,5 im Kontext biblisch-jüdischer Tradition und antiken Städtebaus,* Trier: Wissenschaftlicher Verlag. • P. SÖLLNER 1998, *Jerusalem, die hochgebaute Stadt: Eschatologisches und himmlisches Jerusalem im Frühjudentum und im frühen Christentum,* Tübingen: Franke.

See also: Ascent to Heaven; Heaven; New Jerusalem Text

LORENZO DITOMMASO

Jerusalem Talmud → Palestinian Talmud

Jesus Movement

The Name

The label "the Jesus Movement" is often used to denote the disciples of Jesus of Nazareth who continued as an identifiable group (or groups) in the years following Jesus' death. The phrase is not very satisfactory, since the word "movement" carries overtones that may not be appropriate. Indeed, it is not easy to find an adequate term to describe the beginnings of Christianity. Perhaps the best designation for the beginnings of the Jesus movement would be a Jewish messianic sect, or messianic renewal movement within Second Temple Judaism.

The title "Christianity" itself did not emerge until early in the second century (Ignatius, *Magn.* 10:1-3; *Rom.* 3:3; *Phil.* 6:1; *Mart. Pol.* 10:1) and would carry unavoidably anachronistic overtones. The term "Christians" may already have been coined by the late 30s C.E. (Acts 11:26) but seems to have been initiated and initially used only by hostile authorities (Acts 26:28; 1 Pet. 4:16; Tacitus, *Annals* 15.44.2; Pliny, *Epistles* 10.96) and to have been accepted by those described by it with some unwillingness. According to the Acts of the Apostles, the two descriptive terms which seem to have served both participants and onlookers most effectively were "the Way" (Acts 9:2; 19:9, 23; 22:4; 24:14, 22) and "sect" or "the sect of the Nazarenes" (Acts 24:5, 14; 28:22).

A striking feature of this early usage is the implied understanding that the movement thus referred to was part of the spectrum of Second Temple Judaism. The Qumran covenanters similarly thought of themselves as "the Way" (1QS 9:17-18, 21; 10:21; CD 1:13; 2:6), and "sect" (Gr. *hairesis*) is a term used both by Josephus and by the author of Acts in reference to other groups or factions within Second Temple Judaism — notably Pharisees, Sadducees, and Essenes (Josephus, *J.W.* 2.119-66; *Ant.* 18.11-25; Acts 5:17; 15:5; 26:5). When we add other self-referential terms used by Paul and others, such as "saints" (e.g., Acts 9:13, 32, 41; Rom. 1:7; 1 Cor. 1:2; Phil. 1:1) or the "elect" (Rom. 8:33; Col. 3:12), it becomes still clearer that the members of the new movement(s) thought of themselves as in direct continuity with and part of the religion of Israel, that is, what we now refer to as Second Temple Judaism. The fact that such terms continued to be used even when the new movement began to recruit heavily from non-Jewish circles is a reminder of how central and fundamental this aspect of Christian identity was to its first leaders. This strongly

JESUS MOVEMENT

suggests that the naming of the new movement's members as "Christians" was understood on all sides not as defining members of a new religion but as designating those referred to as followers or supporters of Christ (Lat. *Christiani*) analogously to the partisans of Herod, Herodians *(Herodiani),* and supporters of Caesar *(Caesariani).* It is also probable that in the large cities fringing the Mediterranean, the earliest (Christian) house- or apartment-churches were tolerated by the Roman authorities (who were always suspicious of the potential subversiveness of clubs and associations) because they were seen as offshoots of the Jewish communities in these cities, whose rights of assembly had been safeguarded by statute since the time of Julius Caesar.

One Center or Many?

The Acts of the Apostles narrates the beginnings of the Jesus movement as centered on Jerusalem, from Pentecost following the Passover during which Jesus was crucified (Acts 2). However, the first three New Testament Gospels' accounts of Jesus' own mission (primarily in the Galilee) have prompted the question whether there was a continuing influence of Jesus' mission in Galilee *independent* of Jerusalem. Acts itself provides several hints that there might have been other centers — particularly 9:31 ("the church throughout Judea, Galilee, and Samaria") and 18:24–19:7 (disciples who knew only the baptism of John). In recent years this suspicion that Acts does not tell the whole story has been compounded with the view that the so-called Q material, sayings of Jesus common to the Gospels of Matthew and Luke that appear to come from a common written (?) source (designated Q, from the German word for "source," *Quelle*), itself constitutes evidence of a Galilean community that revered Jesus primarily as a teacher and made little of his death and resurrection.

This understanding of Q, however, builds too much on sand. The focus and sequence of Acts is entirely credible: (1) The leadership of the new movement in Jerusalem was evidently made up primarily of the most prominent Galilean disciples of Jesus and members of Jesus' family (Acts 1:13-14; Gal. 2:9). That they should regard Jerusalem as the obvious focal point for what they expected to happen would naturally lead them to center themselves in Jerusalem. (2) Saul, the converted persecutor of the new movement, that is, Paul the apostle, had strained relationships with the Jerusalem church for most of his career as apostle to the Gentiles (e.g., Gal. 2:6, 11-16), but at no time does he even hint that there might be other centers for the beginnings of the movement to rival Jerusalem. (3) The Q material does not carry with it as a necessary corollary that we envisage a "Q community"; nor should it be assumed that the Q material was the only tradition about Jesus known to such a community or that the community's distinctive concerns and beliefs can be directly read from the Q material as exclusive of other emphases. (4) The apparent lack of interest in the Jesus tradition in the letters of the New Testament need not imply that the material in the Gospels and the gospel preached by Paul and the other early evangelists ran on two (or more) quite unrelated tracks. The oral traditions about Jesus (which were to become the written Gospels) were certainly circulating widely within the churches of the first generation; how could those converted to become "Christ-ians" not be concerned to know about whom they were following (Jesus Christ)? As Dio Chrysostom observed: "Whoever really follows anyone surely knows what the person was like, and by imitating his acts and his words he tries as best he can to make himself like him" (*Orationes* 55.4). No doubt such traditions about Jesus' mission and teaching formed a sounding board again and again set resonating by the particular teachings of the early church founders and teachers. The Letter of James is a good example of a stream of teaching that drew both on traditional Jewish wisdom and on the more recent wisdom of Jesus of Nazareth.

That said, however, it is evident that the Q material (or Q-type material) circulated widely beyond the New Testament Gospels, to reemerge most notably in the developed forms of the *Gospel of Thomas.* Whether these streams or strands should be regarded as also part of "the Jesus movement" is much disputed. Most probably they are to be seen as streams flowing (along with Jewish wisdom, and Christian belief in a redeemer figure) into the great melting pot of late first- and early second-century religiosity in the Mediterranean world, a melting pot from which diverse combinations and permutations, notably the Gnostic sects, emerged during and after that period.

Distinctive Features Reflected in Paul and Acts

Two distinctive features of the Jesus movement are strongly marked not only in Acts but in the other earliest (particularly Pauline) writings of the New Testament. The first is the beliefs about Jesus, which seem to have characterized the new movement from the first.

- *Jesus had been raised from the dead.* Few if any can doubt that the chief participants of the new movement saw or had visions of Jesus after his death, which they understood, surprisingly and uniquely, as witnessing Jesus resurrected by God (the traditions of 1 Cor. 15:5-7 go back to Paul's conversion, about two years after Jesus' execution). This claim, that the event expected for the end of time (the resurrection of the dead) had already begun (Rom. 1:4; 1 Cor. 15:20, 23), gave the new movement its distinctive eschatological character.
- This resurrection following Jesus' crucifixion meant that *the assertion of Jesus as messiah, the basis for his being handed over to the Roman authorities* (Mark 15:1-2; etc.), *had to be redefined in terms of suffering* (Acts 3:18; 17:3). Isaiah 53, interpreted as a messianic text, was prominent in this redefinition (Acts 8:32-35; Rom. 4:25; 1 Pet. 2:21-24). This emphasis came quickly to characterize his followers — "Christ-ians," followers of Christ — so that when the term *Christiani* (a Latinism) was coined by the Roman authorities it contained no threaten-

ing political overtones, "Christ" soon functioning simply as a proper name.

- *The resurrected Jesus had been exalted to God's right hand in heaven and given to share his Lordship.* Here the influence of Ps. 110:1 was crucial (e.g., Acts 2:34-35; Rom. 8:34; 1 Cor. 15:25; 1 Pet. 3:22) and soon resulted in astonishing assertions of Jesus' heavenly status (esp. 1 Cor. 8:6; Phil. 3:10-11), including the authority to bestow God's Spirit (Acts 2:33).
- *Henceforth his disciples took their authority from him, acting "in his name"* (Acts 3–4). The sense of Jesus' authorization and continuing presence among them must lie in large part behind his followers taking up once again John the Baptist's practice of immersing those ready to make commitments to this Lord Jesus (though Jesus himself had not baptized; 1 Cor. 1:12-15), and helps explain both the shared experience to which Paul refers as being "in Christ" and the importance of the shared meal (1 Cor. 10:16).
- *The imminent coming (parousia) or return of Jesus from heaven was also keenly expected* (Acts 3:19-21; 1 Cor. 16:22; 1 Thess. 1:10).

The second distinctive feature was *the equally eschatological conviction that the Spirit promised for the last days had been poured out upon them.* This again is not simply the claim of Acts (Acts 2:16-21) but is implicit, for example, in Paul's understanding of the gift of the Spirit as the firstfruits of the resurrection of the whole person (Rom. 8:23), and of Christian experience as experience of the new covenant, characterized by the life-giving Spirit (2 Cor. 3:3-6). Charismatic vitality and excess were undoubted features of the new movement. Pentecost and Easter together most clearly characterize and define earliest Christianity.

The extent to which all this resulted in a degree of divorce from traditional emphases in Second Temple Judaism is disputed. Beyond the two distinctives just outlined, the original Jerusalem congregations of the new sect do not seem to have created substantive controversy. They continued to attend the Temple "at the hour of prayer" (Acts 3:1), to attract priests (6:7) and Pharisees (15:5), and are also described as "many thousands" and "all zealous for the law" (21:20). Belief in a crucified messiah who had been resurrected from the dead was certainly an oddity, but neither crucifixion nor belief in resurrection as such was un-Jewish. Many Judeans had been crucified by Alexander Jannaeus (Josephus, *J.W.* 1.97; 4QpNah 1:7-8) and during the final siege of Jerusalem in 70 C.E. (*J.W.* 5.450-51); none of them were renounced as apostates in consequence.

However, there quickly arose another faction within the earliest movement, the "Hellenists" of Acts 6:1, with Stephen as their chief spokesman. He seems to have revived the teaching of Jesus on the Temple that had led to Jesus' arrest (Mark 14:55-58, etc.) and to have developed a still stronger critique of Israel's dependence on the Temple as the dwelling place for God (Acts 6:14; 7:48-50). As a result he was lynched (Acts 7:54-60), and his fellow Hellenists (Greek-speaking Jews from the Diaspora) were driven out from Jerusalem (8:1, 4; 11:19). The unexpected corollary was that, as they went, they took the message about Jesus with them and won many adherents, both in Samaria and on the Palestinian and Syrian coast right up to Antioch, the capital of the Roman East (Acts 8; 11:19-21).

In this unexpected expansion, the same spiritual vitality spilling over among non-Jewish hearers of the early Christian preaching resulted in the new sect opening the door to non-Jews (Acts 10:1–11:18; Gal. 2:6-9). The congregations that resulted were characteristically charismatic in character (Acts 13:1; 1 Corinthians 12–14), in some contrast with the Judean assemblies, which gathered around elders, somewhat on the synagogue model (Acts 11:30; 15:2-6, 22-23; 16:4; 21:18; James 5:14).

Here it should be recalled that missionary compulsion was not at all characteristic of Second Temple Judaism. "Judaism," after all, was an ethnic religion, the religion of the Jews/Judeans. However, the Jesus movement quickly became distinctive within Second Temple Judaism precisely by developing such a strong evangelistic thrust directed toward Gentiles (e.g., Acts 11:20-21; Rom. 1:5; Gal. 2:7-9). At the same time, it should also be noted that Paul, the chief "apostle to the Gentiles" (Rom. 11:13), saw his mission very much in terms of carrying out *Israel's* prophetic commission to be a light to the Gentiles (Gal. 1:15-16, echoing Isa. 49:1-6). In making this last claim, Paul challenged the perception that his Jewish detractors had of his role: he would never have agreed that he was an "apostate" from Israel; on the contrary, he was God's instrument in fulfilling the third strand of the promise to Abraham, a blessing to the nations (Gal. 3:8-9). In any attempt to redefine embryonic Christianity as (a form of) eschatological, messianic Judaism, Paul, even in his role as "apostle to the Gentiles," should not be excluded.

Other Strands

The focus upon Paul, which the Acts of the Apostles and Paul's own letters make almost unavoidable, should not marginalize the other strands attested not least within the New Testament.

James

James, the brother of Jesus, appears to have emerged as leader of the Jesus people in Jerusalem (Gal. 2:9; Acts 15:13-21; 21:17-25). The implication of Gal. 2:12 and Acts 15 is that he exercised a conservative or traditionalist influence which was determinative in Jerusalem and in the churches which followed the Jerusalem church's lead. But he is also remembered as agreeing with Paul that Gentile believers need not be circumcised (Gal. 2:6-9), as presenting a positive theology and model for Jewish and Gentile believers to engage in fellowship together (Acts 15:16-17, 19-20), and as writing to a wide swathe of similarly conservative believers in Messiah Jesus across the Diaspora (Jas. 1:1).

James is also remembered with great respect in subsequent Jewish-Christian tradition (as in Ps.-Clem.

Recogn. 1.43, 72). And although that strand of the Jesus movement eventually came to be regarded as "heretical" Jewish Christianity, it was in significant continuity with the Jerusalem Christianity of James, so that James can be properly regarded as one of the principal architects of the Jesus movement. Here we should recall the various indications in rabbinic sources of continuing contact between Jews and Christians (e.g., rabbinic rulings on the *sifrei minim [t. Yad.* 2:13; *t. Šabb.* 13(14):5], which probably at least included Christian writings or Christian Torah scrolls in particular), and the persistence of "Nazarenes" as the name for Syrian Christians, adopted also by the Persians, the Armenians, and later the Arabs. The Christian father Jerome attests what he regarded as "a sect among the Jews" or "Nazaraei," who "wish to be both Jews and Christians" (*Epistles* 112.13). These groups are all most naturally associated with the James-end of the spectrum of the Jesus movement. Also worth pondering is the reappearance in the late twentieth century of a similar but different kind of Jewish Christianity, the so-called Messianic Jews or Jews for Jesus, who raise questions today for both Jews and Christians that are similar to those raised by "Jewish Christianity" in the early centuries.

Peter

Peter is described in the tradition of Matthew's Gospel as the rock (Gr. *petra*) on which Christ would build his church (Matt. 16:18). And the preservation of his Aramaic nickname, Cephas (*kepha',* "rock") in passages such as Gal. 1:18 and 2:9 gives the tradition a good foundation. This significance must stretch beyond the division of missionary labor agreed upon in Jerusalem between Peter and Paul — Peter for Jews, Paul for Gentiles (Gal. 2:7-9). At least we can affirm a Petrine missionary responsibility among Jewish communities, reaching first to the Judean coast (Acts 9:32–10:48), and including Antioch (Gal. 2:11-12). But wider travel is indicated in 1 Cor. 9:5, is hinted at in the support Cephas/Peter had among (probably) Jewish believers in Corinth (1 Cor. 1:12; 3:22), and is attested also in the traditions of his being executed in Rome (Eusebius, *Hist. Eccl.* 2.25.8; cf. 1 Pet. 5:13 and Irenaeus, *Adversus Haereses* 3.1.2). More striking is his prominence and the esteem with which he is regarded in Matthew's Gospel (usually located in Upper Galilee or Lower Syria), and by his links with Pontus, Galatia, Cappadocia, Asia, and Bithynia in the letter attributed to him (1 Pet. 1:1). He probably was something of a bridge-man between James and Paul, and though the James-end of the spectrum seems to have fallen off, or become somewhat detached, Peter evidently assured a degree of continuity between Jesus and mainline Christianity that Paul could never have been able to achieve on his own.

The Gospel of John

With the fourth Christian (canonical) gospel, John, the picture becomes somewhat different. For those familiar with the Gospels of Matthew, Mark, and Luke, the Gospel of John reads strangely, full of lengthy dialogues rather than aphorisms, and with the focus of Jesus' message on Jesus himself (as the Son sent by the Father) rather than on the kingdom of God. Most strikingly, it evinces a level of reflection on divine revelation that fully shared with current Jewish reflection on divine Wisdom (and Philo's reflection on the Logos). The explicit claim that Jesus incarnated the self-revelation of God (in Wisdom/Logos), and did so in a way that superseded the equivalent revelation in Torah (John 1:14-18), was bound to put still more strain on the new sect's standing within post-70 Judaism. It is not surprising, then, that we hear of strong objections to the self-claims of Jesus as infringing upon the unity of God (John 5:18; 10:33). The presentation of Jesus' significance that we find in the Fourth Gospel provoked objections that we do not hear in relation to Paul. Nor is it surprising to hear of Jesus' followers being expelled from synagogues (John 9:22; 12:42; 16:2); a clear parting of the ways had evidently happened between ongoing Judaism and the strand of the Jesus movement represented by John. Where all this happened is far from clear (in Christian tradition John ended up in Ephesus), but Syria is as good a guess as any.

The Epistle to the Hebrews

An equivalent rupture seems to be indicated by the letter to the Hebrews. This work (more a homily than a letter) was probably written with a view to converts who hankered after the substantiality of the Temple cult (probably after the Temple's destruction). But it meets the challenge by completely ignoring any hope for the Temple's restoration and by disowning the whole priestly cult of Jerusalem as passé, a prefigurative shadow now wholly superseded by what Jesus accomplished in his death and resurrection. In thus establishing the new covenant, Jesus made the first covenant obsolete and abolished its regulations (Hebrews 8–10). Here is certainly anticipated the supersessionism that became such a dominant strand in later Christianity's attitude to rabbinic Judaism (Barnabas, Melito, and beyond).

A similar confrontationist attitude is indicated by such passages as Rev. 2:9 (which refers to "the slander of those who say that they are Jews and are not, but are a synagogue of Satan") and passages in the letters of Ignatius of Antioch (e.g., *Magn.* 10:3 and *Phil.* 6:1, where "Christianity" is defined precisely in contrast to "Judaism").

Ongoing Relations with Judaism

Yet this confrontationist trend, which came to dominate relations between Christianity and rabbinic Judaism, has to be qualified by two other considerations. One is that rabbinic Judaism itself was only part of the spectrum of Judaism in the post–70 C.E. era. After the two revolts against Rome (in 66-70/73 and 132-135), Christianity and Judaism were both heirs of Second Temple Judaism, both "Rebecca's children," and any *exclusive* claim to that heritage by either is historically unwarranted. Further, we should recall that much of Second Temple Jewish literature (the LXX, the Pseudepigrapha, and the works of Philo and Josephus) has come down to us only through its preservation in Christian circles. Also to be recalled are the thoroughly Jewish character of Christian documents like the *Didascalia* (where Jews are referred to as "brothers") and the degree to which documents like the *Testaments of the Twelve Patriarchs* and the *Apostolic Constitutions* simply reworked or incorporated Jewish material. The overlap between Christianity and the broader spectrum of Second Temple Judaism continued as an integral facet of Christianity's character and heritage.

The other caveat is that the tendency of Christianity to define itself over against and by antithesis to Judaism seems to have been a deliberate policy of the Christian leadership in their early attempt to give Christianity a sharper outline and clearer identity, over against Judaism and the Gnostic sects in particular. But there is also clear evidence that Christian laity had to be repeatedly warned against and urged not to attend the synagogue on the Sabbath or to observe the Jewish festivals (Origen, *Homily on Leviticus* 5.8; *Selecta on Exodus* 12.46; Chrysostom, *Homilies against the Jews* 1; Council of Antioch). Likewise, the rabbis seem to have made similar attempts to prevent or limit contact between those under their sway and *minim,* who almost certainly included Jews who revered Jesus as Messiah (*t. Ḥul.* 2:20-21). However much the leaders, on both sides, pushed for a clear "parting of the ways," there were many, probably on both sides, who continued to think of the relationship between Christianity and Judaism in symbiotic terms.

BIBLIOGRAPHY

R. BAUCKHAM, ED. 1995, *The Book of Acts in Its Palestinian Setting,* Grand Rapids: Eerdmans. • D. BOYARIN 2004, *Border Lines: The Partition of Judaeo-Christianity,* Philadelphia: University of Pennsylvania Press. • T. L. DONALDSON 1997, *Paul and the Gentiles: Remapping the Apostle's Convictional World,* Minneapolis: Fortress. • J. D. G. DUNN 2006, *The Partings of the Ways between Christianity and Judaism and Their Significance for the Character of Christianity,* 2d ed., London: SCM. • J. D. G. DUNN 2008, *Christianity in the Making,* vol. 2, *Beginning from Jerusalem,* Grand Rapids: Eerdmans. • M. GOODMAN 2007, *Judaism in the Roman World: Collected Essays,* Leiden: Brill. • M. HENGEL AND A. M. SCHWEMER 1997, *Paul between Damascus and Antioch,* London: SCM. • G. JOSSA 2006, *Jews or Christians? The Followers of Jesus in Search of Their Own Identity,* Tübingen: Mohr-Siebeck. • J. LIEU 2004, *Christian Identity in the Jewish and Graeco-Roman World,* Oxford: Oxford University Press. • A. F. SEGAL 1986, *Rebecca's Children: Judaism and Christianity in the Roman World,* Cambridge, Mass.: Harvard University Press. • A. J. M. WEDDERBURN 2004, *A History of the First Christians,* London: Clark. • L. M. WHITE 2004, *From Jesus to Christianity,* San Francisco: HarperSanFrancisco.

See also: Jewish Christianity; Luke-Acts; Parting of the Ways; Paul JAMES D. G. DUNN

Jesus of Nazareth

Jesus was an eschatological prophet and the founder of what became the Christian movement. In his lifetime he was called "Jesus son of Joseph" (Luke 4:22; John 1:45; 6:42), "Jesus of Nazareth" (Acts 10:38), or "Jesus the Nazarene" (Mark 1:24; Luke 24:19 [some translations do not distinguish "the Nazarene" from "of Nazareth"]). "Christ" is a title, the English form of Gr. *christos,* "anointed" (which translates Hebr. *māšîaḥ,* "messiah"). Acts 2:36 and other passages show knowledge that "the Christ" was properly a title, but in many New Testament books, including Paul's letters, the name and title are used together as Jesus' name: "Jesus Christ" or "Christ Jesus" (e.g., Rom. 1:1; 3:24). Paul sometimes simply used "Christ" as Jesus' name (e.g., Rom. 5:6).

Life

Jesus was a Galilean whose home was Nazareth, a village near Sepphoris, one of the two major cities of Galilee. He was born shortly before the death of Herod the Great (Matthew 2; Luke 1:5), which was in 4 B.C.E. The year of Jesus' death is uncertain, probably sometime between 29 and 33.

Jesus' parents were Joseph and Mary, but according to Matthew and Luke, Joseph was only his legal father. They report that Mary was a virgin when Jesus was conceived (Matt. 1:18; cf. Luke 1:35). Joseph is said to have been a "carpenter," a craftsman who worked with his hands (Matt. 13:55); according to Mark 6:3, Jesus also was a carpenter.

Luke reports that as a child Jesus had precocious learning (Luke 2:41-52), but there is no other evidence about his childhood or early development. As a young adult, he went to be baptized by a prophet, John the Baptist, and shortly thereafter began a career as an itinerant preacher and healer (Mark 1:2-15). During this short career of less than one year he attracted considerable attention. When he went to Jerusalem to observe Passover ca. 30 C.E. (between 29 and 33), he was arrested, tried, and executed. Convinced that he still lived and had appeared to them, his disciples began to convert others to belief in him; these efforts eventually led to a new religion, Christianity.

Sources

The only substantial sources for the life and message of Jesus are the New Testament Gospels, Matthew, Mark, Luke, and John. Reliable (but meager) evidence is found in the letters of Paul. There are many sayings attributed to Jesus and stories told about him in noncanonical literature, especially the apocryphal Gospels, and occasionally a reinvestigation of this material leads to the proposal that some of it is "authentic." Although possible in principle, and although a few authentic traditions probably have been preserved outside the Christian canon, it is unlikely that noncanonical sources can contribute substantially to understanding the historical Jesus. A few references to Jesus occur in Roman sources, but these are dependent on early Christianity and do not provide independent evidence. A reference to Jesus in Josephus (*Ant.* 18.63-64) has been heavily revised by Christian scribes, and the original statement cannot be recovered.

The Gospels attributed to Matthew, Mark, and

Luke agree so closely that it is possible to study them together in a synopsis (arranged in parallel columns). John is remarkably different, and can be reconciled with the Synoptics only in very general ways. One may, however, distinguish John's discourse material from the narrative outline and evaluate them separately. In the Synoptic Gospels (Matthew, Mark, Luke), Jesus teaches in short aphorisms and parables, using similes and similar figures of speech, many drawn from agricultural and village life. The principal subject is the kingdom of God; he seldom refers to himself. When asked for a "sign" to prove his authority, he refuses (Mark 8:11-12). In John, however, Jesus teaches in long metaphorical discourses, in which he himself is the main subject. His miracles are described as "signs" that support the self-descriptions in the discourses and prove who he is. Faced with the choice between John and the Synoptics, scholars have almost unanimously chosen the Synoptic Gospels as giving the substance and manner of Jesus' teaching.

John's narrative outline is also different from the Synoptics, but here the choice is less clear. In the Synoptics, it appears that Jesus' ministry lasted less than one year, since they mention Passover only once during Jesus' adulthood, the occasion of his last, fatal trip to Jerusalem. John, however, cites three Passovers, and thus a ministry of more than two years. John narrates several trips to Jerusalem during Jesus' ministry. Either narrative outline is possible. A ministry of more than two years, however, leaves more questions unanswered than does a ministry of a few months. Jesus and his disciples were itinerant; they traveled around Galilee and its immediate environs, and Jesus taught and healed in various towns and villages, as well as in the countryside and by the shore of the Sea of Galilee. None of the Gospels explains how they lived (though Luke 8:1-3 mentions some female supporters), but the omission is more glaring in John.

This discussion makes clear how little we really know about the life of Jesus. The Gospels provide the information that the authors regarded as necessary in the Christian communities in which they worked. The mundane details of Jesus' life — where he slept, how he ate, where he took refuge in bad weather — are barely mentioned. From the perspective of a modern historian, the sources are deficient in other ways as well. The characters on the whole are "flat": emotions, motives, and personalities are seldom mentioned. Jesus is sometimes angry and sometimes compassionate (Mark 3:5; 6:34), but one can say little more. Because of his letters, we know more about Paul the man than about Jesus the man.

This deficiency is understandable when one considers the history of the material in the Synoptic Gospels. They consist of brief, self-contained passages called "pericopes," which the Synoptic authors arranged in different contexts as they saw fit, frequently according to similarity of subject matter. The heart of each passage has been stripped of the elements that surrounded it in real life, and the central unit applied to various situations by different users, including the authors of the Gospels.

Moreover, not all the sayings and deeds in the Gospels are reports of things that Jesus actually said and did. The early Christians believed that Jesus was alive in heaven, and they spoke to him in prayer. He sometimes answered (2 Cor. 12:7-10; cf. 1 Cor. 2:13). The early Christians did not distinguish between "the historical Jesus" and "the heavenly Lord" as firmly as most modern people do, and some sayings heard in prayer almost certainly came into the Gospels as sayings uttered by Jesus in his lifetime.

This means that we no longer have the original immediate context of Jesus' sayings and deeds, and we are somewhat uncertain as to which passages in the Gospels go back to the historical Jesus. Without context, we cannot reconstruct the original meaning of the individual passages with certainty. Jesus said, "Love your enemies" (Matt. 5:44). We do not know the original circumstances in which he said this, and so we do not know whom he had in mind. This robs us of precision in interpreting individual passages.

Public Career

We can, however, find the overall context and the general history of Jesus' ministry, and this provides certainty to the thrust of his teaching as a whole. Jesus' public career began when he was baptized by John the Baptist, an eschatological prophet who proclaimed that the Day of Judgment was at hand. Jesus seems to have accepted this. Subsequently Jesus gathered twelve disciples, representing the twelve tribes of Israel, proclaimed the arrival of the kingdom of God, predicted the destruction of the Temple and its rebuilding "without hands," and shared a final meal with his disciples in which he said that he would drink wine again with them in the kingdom of God. After Jesus' death, his disciples formed a small community which expected him to return and bring in the kingdom. This group spread, and its members continued to expect Jesus to return in the near future, inaugurating a kingdom in which the world would be transformed.

This outline of Jesus' career shows that he was an eschatological prophet, much like John the Baptist and a few other first-century Jewish prophets such as Theudas. Like John, Jesus believed in the coming judgment, but the thrust of his mission was more toward inclusion than condemnation.

Teaching

The Kingdom of God

Jesus proclaimed the eschatological kingdom of God. "Eschatological" in this sense has to do with "last things" rather than "the end of the world." Ancient Jewish eschatologists actually thought of God's definitive intervention in the world, which would transform the world and its inhabitants, not destroy them. Jews believed that God had previously intervened in history (e.g., the exodus from Egypt, the conquest of Canaan), and hoped that he would do so again, but in an even more decisive manner. There would be peace and tranquility in society and nature (cf. Isa. 2:2-4), and the world would be governed in accordance with the will of God.

Jesus shared this overall view. In particular, he thought that the original twelve tribes of Israel would be reassembled (Matt. 19:28; cf. the call of twelve disciples), that the order of society would be reversed, so that the meek and lowly would have plenty (Matt. 5:5), that sinners and reprobates would somehow be included (Mark 2:17; Matt. 11:19), and that he and his disciples would hold the chief positions (Mark 10:29-31, 35-40; Matt. 19:28-29).

In Jesus' view, the kingdom of God existed in heaven, and individuals would enter it on death (e.g., Mark 9:47). God's power was in some respects omnipresent, and Jesus may have seen "the kingdom" in the sense of God's presence as especially evident in his own words and deeds. But Jesus was an eschatologist: in the future, the kingdom would *come to earth* in its full power and glory, at which time God's will would be done "on earth as it is in heaven" (Matt. 6:10). Jesus died before this expectation was fulfilled, and this, coupled with the resurrection appearances, led his followers to expect his return in the near future, bringing in the kingdom and ruling in God's stead (1 Thess. 4:13-18; vv. 15-17 modify a saying of the historical Jesus about the coming Son of Man found in Matt. 24:27-28; 16:27-28; cf. 1 Cor. 15:23-28). The fact that the early Christian movement expected the kingdom to arrive in the very near future is one of the strongest indications that this had been Jesus' own expectation during his lifetime. Early in his career, Paul thought that he and most other Christians would be alive when the kingdom arrived (1 Thessalonians 4), but later he entertained the possibility of his own prior death (Phil. 1:20-26). One can see the diminishing expectation in the Gospels (compare Mark 9:1 and John 21:21-23), an expectation that Jesus' followers had to modify as the decades passed.

Preparation and Discipleship

Jesus called some people to follow him and to give up everything in order to do so (Mark 1:16-20). He expected others to give their possessions to the poor, even though they did not join his itinerant ministry (Mark 10:17-31). He counseled all to fix their attention on the kingdom, not on material possessions (Matt. 6:19-21, 25-34; Luke 12:13-21). Their reward would be great in the kingdom.

The Poor and Sinners

The themes of reversal and inclusion require fuller presentation. The poor, the meek, the lowly, and sinners loom large in the Synoptic Gospels. Jesus came especially to *call* them, but he seems also to have *favored* them. In the coming kingdom, the last would be first (Mark 10:31). Those who held the chief positions in the present world would be demoted (Luke 14:7-11). Those who gave up everything and followed him would receive "a hundredfold" (Mark 10:30). Sinners, typified by the tax collectors, would be included in the kingdom (Matt. 21:31). Their inclusion probably rests in part on Jesus' sympathy for those who were in his own social and economic class and below it. Jesus and his disciples were not themselves from the very bottom of society; his father worked with his hands, but he was not destitute. Some of Jesus' disciples were from families who owned their own fishing boats and had houses (Mark 1:19, 29). They were not rich, but they also were not day laborers, beggars, or homeless. Jesus' sympathy, however, went out to those in the latter categories. His message had a social dimension in two respects: he thought that in the kingdom there would still be social relationships, and he thought that the disadvantaged in the present world would be in some sense advantaged in the new age (Matt. 5:3-11; Luke 6:20-23). The promise of houses and lands in Matt. 19:29-30; Mark 10:29-30 may be metaphorical, but Jesus also may have envisaged a future society in which property would still count, though it would be redistributed.

Jesus' call of sinners, according to Luke, meant that he called them to repentance (Luke 5:32; but cf. Matt. 9:13; Mark 2:17). It is probable that Jesus' message was more radical than merely that transgressors should repent. He called them, rather, to accept him and his message, and promised inclusion in the kingdom if they did so. This doubtless included moral reformation — followers of Jesus would not continue to cheat and defraud — but he probably meant that they did not have to conform precisely to the standards of righteous Jewish society, which would require repayment of money or goods, an additional fine, and presentation of a guilt offering (Lev. 6:1-7). Accepting him and being like him and his disciples was what God required.

Self-Conception

Jesus attached enormous weight to his own mission and person. Scholarly preoccupation with titles obscures the issue. He sometimes called himself "Son of Man," and indirectly accepted "Messiah" (or "Christ") and "Son of God" (Matt. 16:16; Mark 14:61-62; but cf. the par. Mark 8:29 = Luke 9:20; Matt. 26:63-64 = Luke 22:67-70), but he did not make an issue of titles. He called people to follow him, not to give him some appellation. Jesus thought that he was God's last emissary, that he and his disciples would rule in the coming kingdom, and that people who accepted him would be included in it.

Jewish Law

Numerous passages in the Gospels concern the Jewish Law. According to one set, especially prominent in the Sermon on the Mount (Matthew 5–7), Jesus called his followers to extremely strict observance of the Torah (5:17-48). According to the second set, he was deficient in strict observance and transgressed current opinions about some aspects of the Law, especially the Sabbath (e.g., Mark 3:1-3). It is at least conceivable that both positions were true, that he was strict about marriage and divorce (Matt. 5:31-32; Mark 10:2-12) but lax about the Sabbath. The issue of Jesus' stance toward the Law is highly technical. In general, the legal disputes in the Gospels fall well within the parameters of legal disputes in first-century Judaism. Some people opposed minor cures on the Sabbath, but others permitted them. The

JESUS OF NAZARETH

Sadducees regarded the Pharisees as too lax in observance of the Sabbath. Some Jews washed their hands before eating (Mark 7:5), but others did not. There were many disagreements about purity, and the two main parties within Pharisaism (the Shammaites and Hillelites) disagreed over menstrual impurity, a much more serious matter than hand washing.

One statement in particular does oppose Jewish Law as universally understood. All Jews agreed on a long list of prohibited foods, including pork and shellfish (cf. Leviticus 11; Deuteronomy 14), which set them apart from other people. According to Mark 7:19, Jesus "declared all foods clean," which directly opposed the Law of God as given to Moses. However, this is not in the parallel passage in Matthew 15, and Peter seems to have learned it first after Jesus' death, by means of a heavenly revelation (Acts 10:9-16). Jesus did not, then, directly oppose any aspect of the sacred Law.

He probably did, however, have legal disputes, in which he defended himself by quoting scriptural precedent, which would mean that he had not set himself against the Law (e.g., Mark 2:23-28). However, Jesus was *autonomous;* he made his own rules with regard to how to observe the Law, and he decided how to defend himself when criticized. Ordinarily legal debates were between competing camps or schools. Jesus was by no means the only person in ancient Judaism who struck out on his own, acting in accord with his own perception of God's will, and so he was not uniquely troubling in this respect, but such behavior might nevertheless be suspicious.

Ethics

Jesus demanded complete devotion to God, putting it far ahead of devotion to self and even to family (Mark 3:31-35; Matt. 10:35-37). People should be willing to give up everything in order to obtain what was most precious (Matt. 13:44-46). Observance of the Law should be not only external but internal: hatred and lust, as well as murder and adultery, are wrong (Matt. 5:21-26, 27-30).

Miracles

Besides being a prophet and teacher, Jesus was also a healer and miracle worker. In the first century, healers and miracle workers were fairly well known, and were not considered superhuman beings. Jesus granted that others could also perform miracles, such as exorcisms, even if they did not follow him (Matt. 12:27; Mark 9:38-41; 6:7). Thus the significance of this very important aspect of his life is frequently misunderstood. In Jesus' own context, it was granted that various people could heal and perform nature miracles, such as causing rain. The question was by what power or spirit they did so. Some of Jesus' opponents accused him of casting out demons by the prince of demons (Mark 3:19b-22; Matt. 12:24; Luke 11:18); he replied that he did so by the Spirit of God (Matt. 12:28; Luke 11:20).

Controversy

The Crowds

Jesus' reputation as healer had one very important historical consequence: he attracted crowds. This is the main theme of the early chapters of Mark (e.g., 1:28, 45; 2:2). Crowds meant that more people would hear his message, which was an advantage, but there were disadvantages. People who came hoping for cures often had only a selfish interest. Moreover, crowds were politically dangerous. One reason Herod Antipas executed John the Baptist was that he attracted such large crowds that Antipas feared an uprising (Josephus, *Ant.* 18.116-19).

Jesus' message was not necessarily socially dangerous. The promise of future reversal might make some people uneasy, since it could be preliminary to social revolution, and Jesus' promise to sinners might irritate the scrupulous, but without crowds these aspects of his message would not matter much. He did not strike at the heart of the Jewish religion as such: he did not deny the election of Abraham and the requirement of circumcision; he did not denounce Moses and the Law. Nevertheless, because Jesus was autonomous and therefore unpredictable, some people regarded him with hostility and suspicion.

The Scribes and Pharisees

The scribes and Pharisees were two largely distinct groups, though presumably some scribes were Pharisees. A scribe was someone who had legal knowledge and who drew up legal documents; every village had at least one scribe. Pharisees were members of a party who believed in resurrection and in following legal traditions that were ascribed not to the Bible but to the fathers or elders of their own party. They were also well-known legal experts; thus the partial overlap of scribes and Pharisees. It appears from subsequent rabbinic traditions, however, that most Pharisees were small landowners and tradesmen, not professional scribes.

In Mark's view, Jesus' main disputants in Galilee were scribes; according to Matthew they were Pharisees. One may accept this apparently conflicting evidence as at least generally accurate: people knowledgeable about Jewish law and tradition would have scrutinized Jesus carefully, and they doubtless sometimes challenged his behavior and teaching (e.g., Mark 2:6, 16; 3:22; Matt. 9:11; 12:2). According to Matt. 12:14 and Mark 3:6, the Pharisees (Mark adds "with the Herodians") planned to destroy Jesus. If this plot was actually hatched, however, it seems that nothing came of it, since the Pharisees did not play a significant role in the events that led to Jesus' death. Only one passage in Matthew, none in Mark and Luke, gives them any role at all (Matt. 27:62).

Put another way, some people in Galilee may have distrusted Jesus, but he was never charged formally with disregard of the Law, and opposition in Galilee did not lead to his death.

Jesus' Last Week

Around the year 30 Jesus and his disciples went to Jerusalem from Galilee to observe Passover. He presumably went a week early, as did perhaps as many as 200,000 or 300,000 other Jews, in order to be purified of corpse impurity (Num. 9:10-12; 19:1-22). The Gospels do not mention purification, but they do place Jesus in the vicinity of the Temple in the days preceding Passover. Jesus entered Jerusalem on a donkey, perhaps himself intending to recall Zech. 9:9 (Matt. 21:4-5). This touched off a demonstration by his followers, who hailed him as either "Son of David" (Matt. 21:9) or "the one who comes in the name of the Lord" (Mark 11:9). Jerusalem at Passover was dangerous; it was well known to both the high priest (Caiaphas), who governed the city, and the Roman prefect (Pilate), to whom the high priest was responsible and who would intervene in case of trouble, that the festivals were likely times of uprisings. The prefect, who ordinarily lived in Caesarea, came to Jerusalem during the festivals with his troops, who patrolled the roofs of the Temple porticoes. A large demonstration would probably have led to Jesus' immediate arrest. From the fact that he lived for several more days, we may infer that the crowd was relatively small.

Jesus spent some time teaching and debating (Mark 12), and told his disciples that the Temple would be destroyed (13:1-2). On one of these days of purification prior to the Passover sacrifice and meal, he performed his most dramatic symbolic action. He entered the part of the Temple precincts where worshipers exchanged their coins to pay the annual Temple tax of two drachmas and also bought pigeons to sacrifice. Jesus turned over some of the tables (Mark 11:15-19), an action that led "the chief priests and the scribes" (Luke adds, "and the principal men of the people") to plan to have him executed (Mark 11:18; Luke 19:47; cf. Mark 14:1-2 par.).

The disciples found a room for the Passover meal, and one of them bought an animal and sacrificed it in the Temple (Mark 14:12-16). At the meal, Jesus blessed the bread and wine, designating the bread "my body" and the wine "the blood of the covenant" or "the new covenant in my blood" (Mark 14:22-25; the variant is in Luke 22:20; 1 Cor. 11:25).

After supper, Jesus took his disciples to the Mount of Olives to pray. While there, Judas led armed men, sent by the chief priests, who arrested him (Mark 14:43-52). Jesus was taken to the high priest, who had gathered some of his councilors (called collectively "the Sanhedrin"). He was first accused of threatening to destroy the Temple, but this charge was not upheld. The high priest asked him if he were "the Christ, the Son of God." According to Mark, he said "yes" and then predicted the arrival of the Son of Man. According to Matthew, he said, "You say so, *but* I tell you that you will see the Son of Man," apparently implying a negative answer to the question. According to Luke, he was more ambiguous: "If I tell you, you will not believe" and "You say that I am" (Mark 14:61-62; Matt. 26:63-64; Luke 22:67-70).

Whatever the charge, the high priest had evidently already decided that Jesus had to die, and he cried "blasphemy" and rent his garments, a dramatic sign of mourning that the Bible prohibits the high priest from making (Lev. 21:10). The council agreed that Jesus should be sent to Pilate with the recommendation to execute him.

It is doubtful that titles were actually the issue. As Mark (followed by Matthew and generally by Luke) presents the scene, the first attempt was to have Jesus executed for threatening the Temple. That did not work, and so Caiaphas employed a ruse and simply declared whatever Jesus said (about which we must remain uncertain) to be blasphemy.

Pilate did not care about the fine points of Jewish law. To him, Jesus was a potential troublemaker, and he ordered his execution. Matthew, Luke, and John give Pilate a rather good character and show him as troubled over the decision, but yielding to Jewish insistence (Matt. 27:11-26; Luke 23:1-25; John 18:28-40). This reflects the fact that the early church had to make its way in the Roman Empire and did not wish its leader to be thought of as truly guilty in Roman eyes. Pilate is known from other evidence to have been callous, cruel, and given to wanton executions (Philo, *Leg.* 38.302). He was finally dismissed from office for executing a group of Samaritans (Josephus, *Ant.* 18.85-89). Probably he sent Jesus to his death without anguishing over the decision very much.

Jesus was crucified as would-be "king of the Jews" (Mark 15:26 par.). On the cross, he was taunted as the one who would destroy the Temple (Mark 15:29). These two charges explain the decision to execute him. His own thinking was almost certainly that God would destroy the Temple as part of the new kingdom, perhaps rebuilding it himself (Mark 14:58; cf. 11QT 29:8-10). Caiaphas and his advisors probably understood Jesus well enough: they knew that he was a prophet and that his small band could not damage the Temple seriously. But Jesus had made a minor assault on the Temple, and predicted its destruction. These were inflammatory acts in a city that, at festival time, was prone to uprisings. The high priest, under Roman rule, had the responsibility to keep the peace, and he and his advisors acted accordingly (cf. John 11:50).

Jesus' preaching of "the kingdom of God" was also potentially inflammatory. The phrase could have various meanings, but it certainly did not mean that Rome would continue to govern Judea. Many people resented Roman rule, and Rome was quick to dispatch people who became too vocal. Pilate did not think that Jesus and his followers constituted a military threat. Had he thought so, he would have had the disciples executed, either at the time or later, when they returned to Jerusalem to take up their new mission.

Thus no one thought that Jesus could actually destroy the Temple or that he could create a serious revolt in favor of a new kingdom. Nevertheless, inflammatory speech was dangerous, Jesus had a following, the city was packed with pilgrims who were celebrating the exodus from Egypt and Israel's liberation from foreign bondage, and Jesus had committed a small act of violence in the sacred precincts. He was executed for being what he was: an eschatological prophet.

Jesus thought the kingdom was at hand and that he and his disciples would soon feast in it. It is possible that even to the end he expected divine intervention (cf. Mark 15:34).

The Resurrection

What happened next changed history in a way quite different from what Jesus seems to have anticipated. He appeared to some of his followers after his death. The details are uncertain, since our sources disagree on the people who saw him and the places of his appearances. According to Matthew, an angel showed Mary Magdalene and "the other Mary" the empty tomb, and told them to tell the disciples to go to Galilee. While still in Jerusalem, they saw Jesus, who told them the same thing. Jesus appeared just once more, to the disciples in Galilee. Matthew's account is basically implied in Mark (Mark 14:28; 16:7), though Mark lacks a resurrection story, ending with the empty tomb. According to Luke, however, the disciples never left Jerusalem and environs. The women (Mary Magdalene, Joanna, Mary the mother of James, and "the other women") found the empty tomb. "Two men in dazzling clothes" told them that Jesus had been raised. Later, Jesus appeared to two followers on the road to Emmaus, then to Peter, then the disciples. John (including chap. 21, usually thought to be an appendix) combines appearances in Galilee and Jerusalem. Acts, though written by the same author, has a more extended series of appearances than Luke, but like Luke places all the appearances in or near Jerusalem. Paul's long list of people to whom Jesus appeared does not agree very closely with the other accounts.

Faced with such evidence, we can hardly say "what really happened." Two points are important: (1) The sources wish to describe the resurrected Jesus as neither a resuscitated corpse, a badly wounded man staggering around, nor as a ghost. According to Luke, the first two disciples to see Jesus walked with him for several hours without recognizing him (Luke 24:13-32). He could also disappear and reappear at will (Luke 24:31, 36). According to Paul, the bodies of Christian believers will be transformed to be like the Lord's, and the resurrection body will not be "flesh and blood" (1 Cor. 15:42-53). Although substantially transformed, Jesus was not a ghost. Luke says this explicitly (Luke 24:37-39), and Paul insists on "body," choosing the term "spiritual body" rather than "spirit" or "ghost" (both Gr. *pneuma*). The authors, in other words, were trying to explain something for which they did not have a precise vocabulary.

(2) It is difficult to accuse our sources, or the first believers, of deliberate fraud. A plot to foster belief in the resurrection would probably have resulted in a more consistent story. We seem, instead, to have competition: "I saw him"; "So did I"; "The woman saw him first"; "No, I did; they didn't see him at all." Some of the witnesses of the resurrection would give their lives for their belief, which makes fraud unlikely.

The uncertainties are substantial, and, given the accounts in our sources, certainty is unobtainable. We may say of the disciples' experiences of the resurrection approximately what the sources allow us to say of the life and message of Jesus: we have fairly good general knowledge, though many details are uncertain or open to question.

BIBLIOGRAPHY

D. ALLISON 1998, *Jesus of Nazareth: Millenarian Prophet*, Minneapolis: Fortress. • M. BORG 1987, *Jesus: A New Vision*, San Francisco: Harper & Row. • J. D. CROSSAN 1991, *The Historical Jesus: The Life of a Mediterranean Jewish Peasant*, San Francisco: HarperCollins. • J. D. G. DUNN 2003, *Jesus Remembered*, Grand Rapids: Eerdmans. • B. D. EHRMAN 1999, *Jesus: Apocalyptic Prophet of the New Millennium*, Oxford: Oxford University Press. • P. FREDRIKSEN 1999, *Jesus of Nazareth, King of the Jews*, New York: Knopf. • M. HENGEL WITH A. M. SCHWEMER 2007, *Jesus und das Judentum*, Tübingen: Mohr-Siebeck. • J. P. MEIER 1991-2009, *A Marginal Jew: Rethinking the Historical Jesus*, 4 vols., New Haven: Yale University Press. • E. P. SANDERS 1985, *Jesus and Judaism*, Philadelphia, Fortress. • E. P. SANDERS 1990, *Jewish Law from Jesus to the Mishnah*, Philadelphia: Fortress. • E. P. SANDERS 1993, *The Historical Figure of Jesus*, London: Penguin. • G. THEISSEN AND A. MERZ 1996, *The Historical Jesus: A Comprehensive Guide*, Minneapolis: Fortress. • G. VERMES 1973, *Jesus the Jew*, Philadelphia: Fortress. • G. VERMES 1993, *The Religion of Jesus the Jew*, Minneapolis: Fortress. • N. T. WRIGHT 1996, *Jesus and the Victory of God*, Minneapolis: Fortress.

See also: Jesus Movement E. P. SANDERS

Jewelry

As a means of personal adornment, jewelry was an expression of the innate desire of both women and men to beautify themselves, an aesthetic conception which has been shaped by times and the dictates of religious and social attitudes and perceptions as well as of fashion. The Hellenistic and Roman periods can be considered one of the most creative and innovative periods in jewelry production, yet this is not reflected in areas of Jewish settlement. There are references to the wearing of jewelry in the Hebrew Bible and in the Mishnah and Talmuds, but these often convey what the rabbinic authorities wished to see and not what was actually seen.

There are two reasons for the apparent paucity of finds from Jewish domestic and funerary contexts. First, Jews were not involved in prosperous long-distance trade, the pecuniary base for gold. Second, the majority of Jews did not follow a Greco-Roman lifestyle and even despised luxuries such as jewelry.

Finds from controlled archaeological excavations (Jerusalem, Jericho, Qumran, ʿEin Gedi, the Judean Desert caves, and hiding places in the Shephelah) include simple jewels and toilet articles, seldom of gold and silver but mainly of bronze, iron, and copper alloy; gemstones for finger rings; necklaces of beads made from semiprecious stones and glass; and dress ornaments like fibulae (ornamental clasps and brooches), mirrors, and boxes.

Grave Offerings and Coins

In the late Second Temple period, Jews adopted the pagan custom of placing grave offerings and even coins (Charon's fee) in tombs; personal gifts were generally restricted to women and children. The intention was not for use in the afterlife but to arouse the grief of the mourners. Jewelry is rarely found in tombs (Vitto 2000: 91-92), and even more unusual is their decoration with pagan motifs (Sussman 1992: fig. 15 for a gemstone with a bust of Apollo). Yet, there is sufficient evidence for the prohibition of graven images being observed in the religious and public domain, but not strictly adhered to in private life (Hershkovitz 2003). Only a small number of items can be securely dated to the period prior to the destruction of Jerusalem in 70 C.E. or attributed to Jews hiding during the Second Jewish Revolt in 132-135 C.E. L. Y. Rahmani (1980) has convincingly shown that some late Second Temple period tombs in the Jerusalem area, originally used by Jews, were reused by foreigners, probably Roman legionaries, in the late second or early third century, and that this phenomenon is a result of the legalization of marriages between noncommissioned officers and local women from the reign of Septimius Severus (193-211 C.E.) onward.

Amulets and Pendants

A ceramic mold for jewelry from the City of David excavations, dated to a time before the first half of the first century C.E., is evidence for the existence of local artisans. The items to be manufactured included an earring and three pendants. The semicircular earring consists of two concentric rows of ten granules each and a small disk for attaching a semiprecious stone (no. 1), a common late Hellenistic and early Roman form probably of Syrian origin. The three pendants are a rectangular one, either a thymiaterion (incense burner) or an altar (no. 2); a bud (no. 3); and a ball (no. 4). They belong to the popular class of small amulets worn as pendants. A necklace consisting of a chain of links and beads with five amulets suspended from a ring (a key, an amphora, a basket, a lamp, and a pomegranate) from Jerusalem is attributed to the Severan period, even though the stylized naturalism points to a late Hellenistic date (Ridder 1920). A small silver pendant from the Jewish hiding caves carries a female head with the facial details deliberately disfigured, probably for ideological reasons (Kloner and Tepper 1987: 355).

Earrings and Nose Rings

A Hellenistic burial cave in the Shephelah contained a gold earring in the shape of a ram's head and a bossed gold disc with a Gorgon head, attached to the clothing of the deceased. The style is Greco-Persian and the burial is to be attributed to Greek settlers of the early Hellenistic period, definitely not to local Idumean or Jewish inhabitants (Kloner, Regev, and Rappaport 1992). In the Roman period simple gold earrings, single or in pairs (fig. 1), were retrieved from several burial caves around Jerusalem (Aceldama, Dominus Flevit); some were made of thin strips of sheet-gold; others were hoop- and boat-shaped and decorated with a tiny bunch of grapes, a pearl, or bezel-set stone.

The treasure trove from Beth Guvrin-Eleutheropolis is well dated by Hadrianic coins and was hidden during the Second Jewish Revolt, most likely by Jewish inhabitants, even though Vespasian had stationed Roman units in Idumea after the First Revolt. The locally manufactured assemblage is influenced by Italo-Roman goldsmiths (Pfeiler 1970: 61-64). In the late second and third century the tradition is continued in the finds from several tombs of the Roman garrison in Jerusalem and from the pagan population of western Galilee and southern Phoenicia (Abu-ʿUqsa 2002).

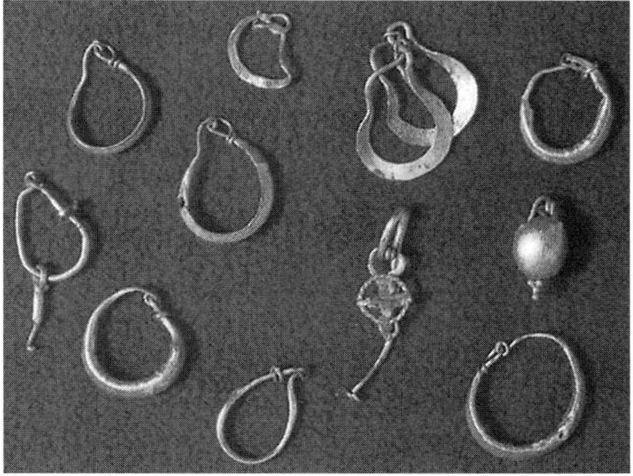

Figure 1. Gold earrings of the Roman period found in burial caves around Jerusalem *(Renate Rosenthal-Heginbottom)*

Mainly second-century burials in a Galilean cemetery are evidence for the custom of burying women and children with gold earrings and nose rings as well with coins in their mouth (Mazar 1994). The nose ring *(nesem)* is mentioned among the jewels a woman was allowed to wear on the Sabbath (*m. Šabb.* 6:1). Their use is confirmed by their location within the skull of female burials in the Nabatean necropolis of Mampsis in the Negev.

Gemstones for Rings

Gemstones set in gold and bronze finger rings are rare in Jewish domestic and funerary contexts. A carnelian intaglio with the zodiac sign of the scorpion (fig. 2) came to light in the Burnt House of the Jewish Quarter excavations in the destruction layer of 70 C.E. Another gem of brown glass paste with the goddess Fortuna/

Figure 2. A carnelian intaglio with the zodiac sign of the scorpion from the Burnt House in Jerusalem *(Renate Rosenthal-Heginbottom)*

Figure 3. Carnelian and glass beads for a necklace, from a tomb at ʿEin Gedi *(Renate Rosenthal-Heginbottom)*

Demeter was found in a building of the first centuries B.C.E. and C.E. There are other gemstones with mythological subjects, as well as animals and floral subjects from Jerusalem, Masada, and Gamla, some of which belonged to Gentiles or Roman soldiers.

Beads for Necklaces

In three burials at ʿEin Gedi, more than 200 beads, mostly of glass but some of carnelian and agate (fig. 3), are evidence for the widespread use of necklaces (Hadas 1994).

Accessories

Three items are not jewelry in a strict sense: dress accessories like bronze fibulae (ornamental claps or brooches), hand mirrors, and boxes. A noninscribed fibula of the Aucissa type from the Jewish Quarter excavations is dated to the reign of Herod the Great. About a dozen fibulae, mostly without the name, were found as grave goods (at Jerusalem and Mishmar Ha-ʿEmeq) or settlement waste (at Dor, Gamla, Samaria, Jerusalem, Masada, and Horvat Dafita — a Nabatean fort on the incense route from Petra to Gaza); some of them can be attributed to Jewish inhabitants. Particularly in the first century C.E., but also later, these fibulae were common all over the Roman world. They were worn by girls and women in matching pairs on the shoulders, holding an "overtunic" that was pinned to the bodice over the breast by a brooch.

Mirrors and Jewelry Boxes

Small lead mirrors with a convex glass pane were common in the Roman provinces of Europe. At Masada a fragment of the circular metal frame from the western palace in the phase dating to 20-4 B.C.E. indicates their use by Jewish women. Bronze mirrors and the locks of wooden jewelry boxes together with earrings, silver bracelets, bronze finger rings, glass beads, and bronze links of a necklace have been unearthed in burials of the first-second century C.E. in the north (Edelstein 2002a). In most cases the ethnicity of the tomb's occupants remains an intriguing question.

BIBLIOGRAPHY

H. ABU-ʿUqsa 2002, "Two Burial Caves at Hurfeish," in *Eretz Zafon: Studies in Galilean Archaeology*, ed. Z. Gal, Jerusalem: Israel Antiquities Authority, 134-39. • G. EDELSTEIN 2002A, "A Section of the Hellenistic-Roman Cemetery at Berit Ahim," *ʿAtiqot* 43: 75*-98*, 257-58. • G. EDELSTEIN 2002B, "Two Burial Caves from the Roman Period near Tel Qedesh," 99*-105, 259 (in Hebr.). • G. HADAS 1994, "Nine Tombs of the Second Temple Period at ʿEn Gedi," *ʿAtiqot* 24:1-8 (in Hebr. with Eng. summary). • M. HERSHKOVITZ 2003, "Gemstones," in *Jewish Quarter Excavations in the Old City of Jerusalem Conducted by Nahum Avigad, 1969-1982*, vol. 2, *The Finds from Areas A, W and X-2: Final Report*, ed. H. Geva, Jerusalem: Israel Exploration Society, 296-301. • A. KLONER AND Y. TEPPER 1987, *The Hiding Complexes in the Judean Shephelah*, Tel Aviv (in Hebr.). • A. KLONER, D. REGEV, AND U. RAPPAPORT 1992, "A Hellenistic Burial Cave in the Judean Shephelah," *ʿAtiqot* 21: 27*-50* (in Hebr.). • E. MAZAR 1994, "A Burial Ground of the Roman Period at Gesher Haziv," *ʿAtiqot* 25: 77-93. • B. PFEILER 1970, *Römischer Goldschmuck des ersten und zweiten Jahrhunderts n.Chr. nach datierten Funden*, Mainz: Zabern. • L. Y. RAHMANI 1980, "A Jewish Rock-Cut Tomb on Mount Scopus," *ʿAtiqot* 14: 49-64. • A. DE RIDDER 1920, "Parure de Jérusalem," *Syria* 1: 99-107. • R. ROSENTHAL-HEGINBOTTOM 1992, "Two Jewelry Molds," in *Excavations in the City of David 1978-1985 Directed by Yigal Shiloh*, vol. 3, *Stratigraphical, Environmental, and Other Reports*, Qedem 33, ed. A. De Groot and D. T. Ariel, Jerusalem: Institute of Archaeology, Hebrew University, 275-78. • R. ROSENTHAL-HEGINBOTTOM 2005, "Lead Mirrors," *Michmanin* 19: 35*-41*. • V. SUSSMAN 1992, "A Burial Cave on Mount Scopus," *ʿAtiqot* 21: 89-96. • F. VITTO 2000, "Burial Caves from the Second Temple Period in Jerusalem (Mount Scopus, Givʿat Hamivtar, Neveh Yaʿaqov)," *ʿAtiqot* 40: 65-121.

RENATE ROSENTHAL-HEGINBOTTOM

Jewish Christianity

The term "Jewish Christianity" is a modern invention. In its broadest sense, it denotes figures, texts, and groups that combine elements of Judaism and Christianity in ways that differ from the combinations now called "Christian." Scholars thus define the term differently, depending on their assessment of the nature of Christianity's origins in Second Temple Judaism and on their opinions about the scope and significance of its connections to post-Christian forms of Judaism. Most often, the term describes religious form(s) cultivated (1) by people of Jewish ethnicity who hold a belief in Jesus as a significant figure in salvation history and/or (2) by people of any ethnicity who combine devotion to Christ with observance of precepts of the Torah (esp. circumcision and dietary laws). In recent decades, the value of the term has become a topic of lively scholarly debate.

"Jewish Christianity" and Christian Origins

Jesus and his apostles were all Jews. From one perspective, all of the earliest Christians were thus "Jewish Christians." Already within the New Testament, however, we find references to debates over whether

Gentiles need to be circumcised and follow Jewish dietary laws to be saved through Christ. Unnamed figures are credited with the view that Gentile converts must be circumcised (Gal. 2:12; Acts 15:1-5). In addition, Paul associates the apostle James with the maintenance of ritual purity through separation from Gentiles, particularly at meals (Gal. 2:11-14; cf. Acts 10:28; Col. 2:21). By contrast, Paul — the self-styled "apostle to the Gentiles" (Rom. 11:13; Gal. 2:2) — proclaims that Torah observance is not incumbent on Gentiles (e.g., Romans 1–9; Galatians 1–3; 5:2-6). In Acts, Peter seems initially to assume that the precepts of the Torah apply to all members of the Jesus movement. Due to visions from God (Acts 10:10–16, 28) as well as his own deliberations (Acts 15:6-21), he becomes convinced that circumcision is unnecessary for Gentile converts and that Jesus' followers need only avoid fornication, blood, improperly slaughtered meat, and food offered to idols (esp. Acts 10:10-16; 15:20; cf. 1 Cor. 10:27-29; *t. ʿAbod. Zar.* 8:4).

Soon after the inception of critical research on the New Testament, such references came to form the basis for scholarly theories about an early conflict between "Jewish Christianity" and "Gentile Christianity." Ferdinand Christian Baur (1792-1860) popularized this view. Building on previous research, Baur proposed that the issue of Torah observance remained divisive in the primitive church. Questioning the historicity of Acts' account, he interpreted its harmonious picture of the apostolic age as an attempt to gloss over the conflicts described by Paul (esp. Gal. 2:11). In his view, the primitive church was split into two factions. "Jewish Christianity" was the form of Christianity that was promoted by James, Peter, and the Jerusalem church. "Gentile Christianity" consisted largely of Paul's challenge to this form of Christianity.

In nineteenth- and twentieth-century scholarship, Baur's dichotomous model was deemed too simplistic to describe the geographical, cultural, and doctrinal diversity of first-century Christianity. Nevertheless, his articulation of Jewish Christianity remains influential. New Testament scholars have sought traces of Jewish Christianity in texts and traditions associated with James and Peter (Myllykoski 2006). The term and its variants (esp. "Christian Judaism") have also been prominent in research on New Testament texts with particularly close ties to first-century Judaism, such as the Gospel of Matthew and book of Revelation (Saldarini 1994; Jackson-McCabe 2006).

These approaches, however, have not been without their critics. Some dismiss the term "Jewish Christianity" as irrelevant or misleading when applied to the first century C.E., due to the Jewish cultural matrix of all forms of Christianity at this time. Raymond Brown, for instance, has suggested that there were multiple forms of first-century Christianity, each of which was "Jewish" in its own ways (e.g., eschatology, exegesis, messianism, ritual practice; Brown 1983).

Postapostolic "Jewish Christianity"

Were there any heirs to the first-century believers, mentioned by Paul and Luke, who viewed Torah observance as necessary for salvation through Christ? Traditionally, scholarly answers to these questions followed the framework laid out by two fourth-century Christian authors, namely, Eusebius and Epiphanius. Eusebius describes the Jerusalem church as founded by James and led by bishops of Jewish ethnicity (*Hist. Eccl.* 4.5.1-4). He stresses, however, that members of the Jerusalem congregation fled to Pella prior to the destruction of Jerusalem in 70 C.E. (*Hist. Eccl.* 3.5.3). He further suggests that the line of Jewish bishops ended with the failure of the Bar Kokhba Revolt in 135 C.E., when Jerusalem became a Roman city (*Hist. Eccl.* 4.6.1-4). When he mentions other Christians who were Jewish in ethnicity or ritual practice, he confines them to the rubric of the Ebionite "heresy" (*Hist. Eccl.* 3.27; 5.8.10; 6.17).

Eusebius' description of the Ebionites builds on earlier references to this group by Irenaeus (e.g., *Against Heresies* 3.15; 3.21.1; 4.33.4; 5.1.3) and Origen (e.g., *On First Principles* 4.3.8; *Homily on Genesis* 3.5; *Against Celsus* 2.1; 5.65; *Homily on Matthew* 11.12). Ebionites are described as Jewish converts to Christianity who favored the Gospel of Matthew, rejected Paul, and observed precepts of the Torah; some are said to have viewed Jesus as solely human. Whereas Eusebius synthesizes earlier heresiological traditions, Epiphanius adds to the traditional account, describing their practices of ritual purity and vegetarianism (*Panarion* 30.2.3-6; 30.15.3) as well as their use of writings about James and Peter similar to material now found in the Pseudo-Clementine *Homilies* and *Recognitions* (30.15-16). Epiphanius is also the first author to mention the Nazoreans. He notes that Nazoreans are Jewish in ethnicity, differing from other Jews only in their belief in Christ (28.7.5); accordingly, they read both the Old Testament and Gospel of Matthew in Hebrew (29.7.4; 29.9.4).

Scholars continue to debate whether the Ebionites and/or Nazoreans evolved from the Jerusalem church of James and Peter (cf. *Pan.* 29.7.7-8; 30.2.7-9). Nevertheless, the heresiological characterization of these groups has been generally accepted. Whether or not Jewish Christianity is seen to be an ancient and distinctive variety of Christianity, its postapostolic expressions have thus been dismissed as marginal, at best, and deviant, at worst. Accordingly, the fate of Jewish Christianity is often described as a process of rapid decline from an initial period of glory in the apostolic age to a denigrated status on the periphery of the (predominantly Gentile) church of later centuries. It is assumed that Jewish Christianity was relegated to irrelevance by Christianity's "parting of the ways" with Judaism.

Concurrent with recent challenges to traditional views of this parting of the ways, however, fresh efforts have been made to look beyond the biases in the secondhand accounts of patristic authors like Eusebius and Epiphanius, and attention has been drawn to other evidence for Jewish-Christian forms of belief and practice. In the Old Testament Pseudepigrapha and New Testament Apocrypha, for instance, it may be possible to glimpse hints of some of the different ways that early Christians negotiated their relationships to Jews and

Judaism. Many of the approaches differ from those found in patristic literature; by our modern standards, some seem Jewish-Christian. It has been suggested, for instance, that a mutually exclusive understanding of Jewish and Christian identities does not suffice to describe the views of ritual purity, religious identity, and the eschatological fate of Israel in texts such as the *Didache, Testaments of the Twelve Patriarchs, Ascension of Isaiah, Apocalypse of Peter,* and *5* and *6 Ezra* (e.g., Bauckham 1998; Frankfurter 2003). The survival of Jewish-Christian forms of worship in late-antique Palestine may be attested by references in the classical rabbinic literature as well as by patristic quotations from "Jewish" gospels circulating in the area. The flourishing of multiple varieties of Jewish Christianity in late antique Syria is similarly suggested by evidence of the *Didascalia Apostolorum* and Pseudo-Clementine literature (Fonrobert 2001; Reed 2006).

Such evidence may help to shed a broader perspective on patristic references to Jewish Christianity. Writing in the second century, Justin Martyr refers to Jewish converts to Christianity who keep the Torah; he accepts this approach to Christ-devotion, provided that "Jewish Christians" do not promote Torah observance among Gentiles (*Dialogue with Trypho the Jew* 46–47). Later patristic authors are less sympathetic. Nevertheless, it may be significant that most references to Jewish-Christian sects and gospels date from the period of the Christianization of Palestine. Concurrent with the intensification of interest in Jewish Christians in the fourth and fifth centuries, we also find fervent condemnations of Christians who adopt Jewish practices (e.g., Chrysostom, *Homilies against the Judaizers* 3.4). Taken together, such references may attest the attraction of Torah observance for a variety of late antique Christians, both Jewish and non-Jewish, particularly in Syria and Palestine.

Usefulness of the Category

In recent years, scholars have increasingly stressed the ritual and doctrinal diversity of both Second Temple Judaism and early Christianity, and the category of Jewish Christianity has come under fire: "Jewish" according to whom? "Christian" where and for whom? The problems with positing a single "orthodox" Christianity in the first four centuries C.E. are matched by the fluid and contested nature of the definition of "Jew." Although traditional scholarship tended to characterize post-70 Judaism as wholly rabbinic, new studies have suggested that the establishment of rabbinic hegemony was a gradual process. Particularly in light of fresh insights into the diversity of post-70 Judaism, some scholars have pointed to the problems with making any global assumptions about the proclivities that purportedly come with Jewish ethnicity (Fonrobert 2001).

If it is no longer feasible to speak of a single "Christianity" in interaction with a single "Judaism," how can one speak of a single "Jewish Christianity" in the border space between them? One solution is to jettison the term "Jewish Christianity" (Taylor 1990). Another solution is to limit its use to the specific Jewish Christianity of a specific text or group (Klijn 1974) and/or to allow for a variety of "Jewish Christianities" (Visotzky 1989). Others have suggested that the term "Jewish Christianity" may retain some heuristic value, precisely because of its power to unsettle modern assumptions about the mutual exclusivity of Jewish and Christian identities (Jackson-McCabe 2007).

Since the eighteenth century, research on Jewish Christianity has enriched our understanding of Christianity's complex relationship to Judaism, drawing our attention to texts, groups, and figures that exhibit more and different "Jewish" features than we now associate with Christianity. Studies in this area have also helped us to map the diversity of early Christianity and Judaism and to explore the continued interchange between them. In the process, they have also recovered the lost voices of certain ancient Christians who — in contrast to the supersessionism propounded by many patristic authors — chose to embrace Christianity's Jewish heritage in their own beliefs and practices.

BIBLIOGRAPHY

R. BAUCKHAM 1998, "Jews and Jewish Christians in the Land of Israel at the Time of the Bar Kochba War, with Special Reference to the Apocalypse of Peter," in *Tolerance and Intolerance in Early Judaism and Christianity,* ed. G. Stanton and G. Stroumsa, Cambridge: Cambridge University Press, 228-38. • R. E. BROWN 1983, "Not Jewish-Christianity and Gentile Christianity but Types of Jewish/Gentile Christianity," *CBQ* 45: 74-79. • J. CARLETON PAGET 1999, "Jewish-Christianity," in *The Cambridge History of Judaism,* vol. 3, *The Early Roman Period,* ed. W. Horbury et al., Cambridge: Cambridge University Press, 733–42. • C. E. FONROBERT 2001, "The Didascalia Apostolorum: A Mishnah for the Disciples of Jesus," *JECS* 9: 483-509. • D. FRANKFURTER 2003, "Beyond 'Jewish Christianity': Continuing Religious Sub-Cultures of the Second and Third Centuries and Their Documents," in *The Ways that Never Parted: Jews and Christians in Late Antiquity and the Early Middle Ages,* ed. A. H. Becker and A. Y. Reed, Tübingen: Mohr-Siebeck, 131-44. • M. JACKSON-MCCABE, ED. 2007, *Jewish Christianities Reconsidered,* Minneapolis: Fortress. • A. F. J. KLIJN 1974, "The Study of Jewish-Christianity," *NTS* 20: 419-31. • A. F. J. KLIJN AND G. J. REININK 1973, *Patristic Evidence for Jewish-Christian Sects,* Leiden: Brill. • M. MYLLYKOSKI 2006, "James the Just in History and Tradition: Perspectives of Past and Present Scholarship (Part I)," *CBR* 5: 73-122. • A. Y. REED 2006, "Rabbis, Jewish Christians and Other Late Antique Jews: Reflections on the Fate of Judaism(s) after 70 C.E.," in *The Changing Face of Judaism, Christianity and Other Greco-Roman Religions in Antiquity,* ed. I. Henderson and G. Oegema, Gütersloh: Gütersloher Verlagshaus, 323-48. • A. J. SALDARINI 1994, *Matthew's Christian-Jewish Community,* Chicago: University of Chicago Press. • O. SKARSAUNE AND R. HVALVIK, EDS. 2007, *Jewish Believers in Jesus: The Early Centuries,* Peabody, Mass.: Hendrickson. • J. E. TAYLOR 1990, "The Phenomenon of Early Jewish-Christianity: Reality or Scholarly Invention?" *VC* 44: 313-34. • B. L. VISOTZKY 1989, "Prolegomenon to the Study of Jewish-Christianities in Rabbinic Literature," *AJS Review* 14: 47-70.

See also: Jesus Movement; Parting of the Ways

ANNETTE YOSHIKO REED

Job, Book of

The book of Job appears in the Hebrew Bible among the Writings *(Kĕtûvîm)* and in the Christian canon as one of the poetical books of the Old Testament. Scholars group Job with the wisdom writings, along with Proverbs, Ecclesiastes, and, in the Apocrypha, Sirach and Wisdom of Solomon. Unlike these books, however, Job is neither a collection of wise sayings nor an instruction by a wisdom teacher. Rather, it is a traditional story about a righteous man who is tested by terrible suffering in order to determine the motives for his righteousness. This story, however, has been amplified by means of a highly sophisticated cycle of poetic speeches in which various characters in the story examine and debate the issues raised by Job's situation. Many of its themes and concerns, however, are similar to those that preoccupy other wisdom books.

Structure, Composition, and Date

The book of Job is composed by means of the juxtaposition of several different genres and literary styles. Job 1–2 and 42:7-17 contain the traditional tale of Job the pious. Scholars debate whether the tale is a straightforward rendering of an old oral tale (probably originating in Edom or North Arabia, the likely site of Job's homeland, Uz; Job 1:1) or a sophisticated literary imitation of such a tale. The poetic dialogue between Job and the friends who come to comfort him (chaps. 3–31) is an example of an ancient Near Eastern wisdom dialogue in which conventional and skeptical views about the reasons for suffering, the rationality of the world, and the nature of the gods are set over against one another in a sophisticated display of learned poetry. Contained within the dialogue is a poem on the elusiveness of wisdom (chap. 28), a skeptical counterpart to wisdom poems found in Proverbs 8, Sirach 24, and Bar. 3:9–4:4, which describe how wisdom is accessible to humankind in general or to Israel in particular (cf., however, *1 Enoch* 42). The long set of speeches by Elihu (chaps. 32–37) are generally thought to be a later addition to the book by a reader dissatisfied with the friends' (and perhaps God's) answers to Job. The divine speeches from the whirlwind and Job's brief replies (38:1–42:6) are unparalleled in genre but employ many well-known ancient Near Eastern mythic motifs. Although the book of Job gives little internal clue to the date of its composition, several linguistic, poetic, and traditio-historical features suggest that a date in the fifth or fourth centuries B.C.E. is most likely.

Theological and Religious Issues

Each major section of the book focuses on different issues raised by the presence of suffering in the world. The prose tale sets up the test of Job by God and the Accuser in an attempt to explore the question of whether human piety ("fear of God") is motivated primarily by an expectation of divine blessing. The wisdom dialogue between Job and his friends explores the issue of the proper response to suffering and whether suffering can be rationally comprehended as part of a moral universe. The friends argue that the proper response to suffering is a stance of hopeful waiting, combined with prayer, and repentance for any conscious or unconscious offense committed against God. They argue for the reality of a moral order and ultimately come to believe that Job must be suffering deservedly. Elihu's speeches, although they provide some distinctive nuances (e.g., an interest in the psychology of repentance), remain within the same paradigm. Job's insistence on his righteous innocence or at least the disproportion between any guilt and his suffering leads him to frame the issues in legal terms as unjust treatment by God and to envision a resolution based on a trial with God. The divine speeches, composed by the poet to be deliberately elusive, expose the inadequacy of a legal framework for comprehending suffering in the world. Through images that feature both the reliable structures of creation and the presence of chaotic forces, they contest the limited anthropocentric perspectives of both Job and his friends. The regulated balance of order and disorder in the world cannot simply be equated with a moral order.

Ancient Near Eastern Parallels

The discovery and translation of Mesopotamian texts in the late nineteenth century brought to light a number of texts that resemble the poetic portions of Job. Several texts feature a pious sufferer who has been mysteriously struck by acute suffering and who has been restored to well-being by his god (e.g., *I Will Praise the Lord of Wisdom, The Sumerian Job,* and *Dialogue between a Man and His God*). In none of these texts, however, does the sufferer insist on his innocence and utter bitter, blasphemous words, as Job does. In religious orientation they resemble more closely Israelite thanksgiving psalms. The text that bears the closest generic resemblance to Job is the *Babylonian Theodicy,* a poetic wisdom dialogue composed ca. 1,000 B.C.E. but popular into the second century B.C.E. As in Job 3–31, a skeptical and embittered sufferer complains to his friend, who attempts to console him by articulating the conventional explanations and justifications for suffering. Polite but barbed introductions, evocative of those of Job and his friends, introduce the alternating speeches. In contrast to the book of Job, however, the dialogue ends inconclusively and without any response from the gods themselves. The Egyptian *Dispute of a Man with His Ba* and *The Complaints of Kha-Kheper-Re-Seneb* are perhaps also related to the genre of the wisdom dialogue.

In addition to its parallels with literary characters and genres the book of Job reflects knowledge of ancient Near Eastern mythological traditions, present in particular in the divine speeches. Most prominent are repeated references to the cosmogonic struggles between the creator God and the forces of chaos, imaged as the Sea, Rahab, or Leviathan (Job 3:8; 7:12; 10:13; 26:12; 38:8-11; 41:1-34). Various features of cosmic geography in chap. 38 (e.g., the doors of the sea, the springs of the sea, the gates of death, the dwelling places of light and darkness, and the storehouses of snow and hail) also have parallels in Ugaritic and

Mesopotamian mythic and epic traditions. It is also possible that the descriptions of the legendary monsters Behemoth and Leviathan in chaps. 40–41 use motifs from the Egyptian mythic traditions concerning Horus and Seth.

Job and Second Temple Judaism

The mythic motifs in Job are for the most part elements of a common Near Eastern religious culture. The specific literary parallels between Job and Mesopotamian texts, however, suggest more direct cultural influence, which might have been facilitated by the Jewish Diaspora in Mesopotamia resulting from the Babylonian Exile and its aftermath. Other Second Temple texts, such as those of Daniel 1–6 and *1 Enoch,* also reflect knowledge of Mesopotamian culture and traditions.

Whether or not the intellectual boldness in the speeches of Job and God grow out of the religious and cultural disruptions of the Babylonian Exile and postexilic period is debated. Skeptical elements are present in Mesopotamian and Egyptian literatures even in second-millennium texts. But the strong elements of moral and religious skepticism both in Job and in Qohelet (Ecclesiastes), also a text of the Second Temple period, may indicate a new radicalism in the Israelite wisdom tradition as it developed in Judaism in the Persian and Hellenistic periods.

Although the book of Job has no direct relation to the apocalyptic literature that also developed during this time, it shares with apocalypses a fascination with the elusive knowledge of the cosmos that humans can perceive but not grasp. Indeed, the knowledge granted to Enoch in his earthly and heavenly journeys (*1 Enoch* 17–36) might almost be a claim that what God said Job and other humans could not know was in fact revealed to Enoch. The problem of evil was also a topic of concern to apocalyptic literature, but the evolving role of the Adversary (Hebr. *ha-śāṭān*) shows how differently Job and the apocalyptic tradition tend to frame the issue. Whereas in Job the Adversary is something of a provocateur in the heavenly court, his task is to find and expose evil and disloyalty in humans (cf. the similar portrait of the Adversary in the late sixth-century text of Zechariah 3). In the dualism of apocalyptic traditions this figure is increasingly cast as a malicious opponent of God who attacks and brings evil upon the righteous. The term *satan* comes to be used as a proper name (e.g., *Jub.* 23:29; *T. Moses* 10:1) rather than as the term for an office or function in the heavenly court.

Texts and Traditions of Job in Second Temple Judaism

Four fragmentary texts of Job were found at Qumran, two of which (2Q15 and 4Q99) confirm that the Elihu speeches were part of the composition by the second century B.C.E. One text (4Q101) is written in paleo-Hebrew script. Since otherwise this script is generally used for books of the Pentateuch, the paleo-Hebrew may indicate belief in the Mosaic authorship of Job, a tradition known also in rabbinic sources. In addition, an Aramaic translation of Job is attested (4Q157; 11Q10), apparently containing a shorter ending than the canonical Job.

The Septuagint translation of Job is approximately 15-20 percent shorter than the Hebrew text of Job. Whether it is a translation of an alternative Hebrew edition of Job or was abridged in translation is uncertain. The Septuagint Job includes a number of additions to the legend of Job, developing the role of Job's wife in chap. 2 and providing additional information about Job's homeland and ancestors at the end of the book.

The *Testament of Job,* a Greek text probably composed in Alexandria in the first century B.C.E., has Job retell his story to his children at the end of his life in a version that features the virtue of endurance (cf. Jas. 5:11). The work enhances both the roles of Job's wife and his three daughters, whose share in Job's inheritance is interpreted as sashes that allow them to understand the language of the angels. In general the *Testament of Job* reflects the religious perspectives of Hellenistic Judaism.

BIBLIOGRAPHY

S. E. BALLENTINE 2006, *Job,* Macon, Ga.: Smyth & Helwys. • D. J. A. CLINES 1989, *Job 1–20,* Dallas: Word. • K. DELL 1991, *The Book of Job as Skeptical Literature,* Berlin: de Gruyter. • N. HABEL 1985, *The Book of Job,* Philadelphia: Westminster. • C. A. NEWSOM 2003, *The Book of Job: A Contest of Moral Imaginations,* New York: Oxford University Press. • S. J. VICCHIO 2006, *The Image of the Biblical Job, A History,* vol. 1, *Job in the Ancient World,* Eugene, Ore.: Wipf and Stock.

CAROL A. NEWSOM

Job, Testament of

The *Testament of Job* is a retelling of the story of Job, framed as his deathbed speech to his children. In basic structure, it conforms to the testamentary genre (Collins 1974). Consistent with the association of biblical heroes with specific virtues in other testaments, Job is here celebrated as a paragon of patient endurance. Whereas most testaments feature lengthy ethical exhortations, however, the *Testament of Job* consists almost wholly of narrative. Its account of Job's experiences follows the book of Job and stands in a close relationship to the LXX version. It also addresses many of the same concerns found in the LXX additions to Job (2:9a-d; 42:17a-e), including Job's lineage, postmortem fate, and the plight of his wife. Departures from the MT and LXX Job include its explanation of the reasons for Job's suffering and its emphasis on his knowledge of heavenly realities. Although its precise date and authorship are uncertain, the majority of scholars situate the formation of the text among Jews in Egypt in the first century B.C.E. or first century C.E.

Characters

The *Testament of Job* dramatically develops the biographies and personalities of characters from the book of Job. Its characterization of Job recalls the prose framework of the biblical book (Job 1–2; 42:7-17): Job is lauded as a righteous man who bears suffering with unwavering faith. Whereas the poetic portions of the book of Job (Job 3:1–42:6) depict Job as challenging God, doubting divine justice, and denying resurrection, the *Testament of Job* assures the reader that Job remained steadfast in his trust in the promised reward of the righteous (cf. LXX Job 42:17a). The most striking departure from biblical images of Job concerns his wisdom: whereas the biblical Job is unaware of the true reasons for his suffering and incapable of understanding the secrets of the cosmos and Creator, the Job of the *Testament of Job* infers the error of idolatry, knowingly brings suffering upon himself, sees through demonic deception, and glimpses heavenly realities.

Whereas MT Job contains no hint of Job's place in the history of Israel, the *Testament of Job* connects him with the line of Abraham by genealogy and marriage. Consistent with Hellenistic Jewish traditions about Job (e.g., LXX Job 42:17b-e; Aristeas *apud* Eusebius, *Praep. Evang.* 9.25.1-4), it identifies him with Jobab, a descendant of Esau in the Edomite king list of Gen. 36:31-39. Here Jobab/Job is also a king, albeit of Egypt (28:29) rather than Edom (cf. Gen. 36:33). The *Testament of Job* further suggests that Job married Dinah after the death of his first wife (1:6; cf. Ps.-Philo, *Bib. Ant.* 8:7-8; *Gen. Rab.* 57:4). In addition, elements of Job's biography may be modeled on biblical and early Jewish traditions about Abraham: both are converts who infer the truth of monotheism, receive a name change from God, battle idol worship, and endure a series of trials (Jacobs 1970).

The *Testament of Job* richly develops the character of Satan (Kee 1974; Kirkegaard 2004). In the book of Job, Satan is a prosecutor in the heavenly court who tests Job with God's authority and sanction. Similarly, the *Testament of Job* describes Satan as asking God's permission for all actions against Job. Its demonology, however, goes well beyond the biblical book. Satan's role is here interpreted in terms of the early Jewish understanding of demons as the objects of false worship (cf. LXX Ps. 95:5; *1 Enoch* 19:1). To this demonic deception, all but Job are blind. In the first half of the *Testament of Job,* Satan tries to undermine Job by disguises and trickery. In the second half, the focus shifts to Job's human adversaries, and Satan acts through Elihu.

The *Testament of Job* also provides further details about Job's family. Most celebrated is its concern for female characters (e.g., van der Horst in van der Horst and Knibb 1989; Kugler and Rohrbaugh 2004). Although Job's wife is mentioned only in passing in MT Job (2:9; cf. LXX), the *Testament of Job* gives her a name, a story, and a song. Here called Sitidos, she is one of two women in the story who fall prey to demonic deception, together with the unnamed maidservant who opens the door when Satan visits in the guise of a beggar. This association of women and ignorance stands in contrast with the characterization of Job's daughters by his second wife, Dinah. At the end of the book, they receive a spiritual inheritance that empowers them to transcend earthly concerns and to participate in heavenly realities.

Contents

Like other texts of the testamentary genre, the *Testament of Job* begins with a third-person narrative preamble (1:2-4): aged and ill, Job calls his children to him to hear his words. The body of the *Testament of Job* purports to record his firsthand account of the events described in the book of Job. This account unfolds in two parts: his struggle against Satan (chaps. 2–27; cf. Job 1:1-3:1) and his debates with his friends and Elihu (chaps. 28–44; cf. Job 3:2–37:24).

As in the book of Job, Satan is responsible for Job's loss of property, progeny, and health. Here, however, Job knowingly angers Satan. Their struggle begins when Job has doubts about the idolatrous temple near his home (2:2-4). An angel appears to him (chaps. 3–4), and Job learns that the temple is "the place of Satan, by whom men are deceived" (3:6). When Job asks the angel for permission to destroy it, the angel warns him that Satan will respond with wrath (4:3-6). Job is assured, however, that Satan cannot rob him of his life or soul; if he endures the attacks, his riches will be doubled, and he will be resurrected after death (4:6-9). In full awareness of the suffering to come, Job demolishes Satan's temple (5:1-3).

Satan first appears as a beggar at his door (chaps. 6–7). Despite his legendary generosity (chaps. 9–15), Job refuses to give him anything but a burnt loaf. Unable to gain power over Job by taking food from his hands, Satan ascends to heaven to ask God for permission to destroy his possessions (chap. 8). He annihilates Job's livestock, causing his subjects to rise up against him (chap. 16). Disguised as the king of Persia, Satan then tries to foment open revolt (17:1-4). The only thing stopping the people is fear of retribution from Job's children, so Satan causes a house to collapse upon them (17:5–18:3; cf. Job 1:19). Job laments their deaths but remains resolute (chap. 19; cf. Job 1:21). Satan thus asks God for permission to afflict Job's body (20:1-3). Appearing as a whirlwind (cf. Job 38:1), he overturns Job's throne and strikes him with plague (20:4-9; cf. Job 2:7-8).

Job's endurance is contrasted with Sitidos' response to the loss of their children and status (chaps. 21–26). As Job sits on a dung heap for decades (cf. Job 2:8), the former noblewoman is reduced to servitude. When the people refuse to give him bread, she gives him part of her own portion and even turns to begging. Satan takes advantage of her by disguising himself as a bread seller. He asks for the hair off her head in exchange for bread. By this humiliation, Sitidos is broken: she laments, blames Job for the loss of her children and status, and entreats him to speak against God (cf. Job 2:9). Her humiliation, however, becomes the catalyst for Job's triumph (chaps. 26–27). Although he chastises his wife for not distinguishing truth from deception, he also rebukes Satan for attacking him through trickery. Satan is shamed and admits defeat, prompting Job to proclaim the preeminence of the virtue of endurance.

The second part of the story concerns the visit of Job's three friends and Elihu. When Eliphaz laments Job's loss of wealth, he answers by proclaiming the greater riches that await him in heaven (chaps. 31–34). When Bildad doubts his sanity, Job praises God's power (35:1–38:5). When Zophar offers physicians, Job stresses that all healing comes from God (38:6-8). Sitidos begs the kings for help in obtaining a proper burial for her children, but Job forbids it, assuring her of their place in heaven; having obtained some measure of consolation, she dies (chaps. 39–40). Lastly, Elihu comes and speaks against Job in demonic inspiration (chap. 41).

As in the book of Job, these dialogues culminate with God's appearance in a whirlwind (chaps. 42–44). Whereas the biblical theophany expresses the unbridgeable gap between divine and human knowledge (Job 38–41), the version in the *Testament of Job* occasions the exposure of Elihu's evil and the vindication of Job. Job's friends recognize their error in doubting Job and offer atoning sacrifices. Where the book of Job recounts the restitution of his earthly wealth (Job 42:10-15), the *Testament of Job* stresses the riches he has won in heaven.

The final chapters (chaps. 45–53) begin with a brief ethical exhortation, followed by a third-person description of the division of Job's inheritance. His estate is divided among his sons, causing complaint among his daughters. They, however, then receive "an inheritance better than [their] seven brothers" (46:4): multicolored cords that have the power to heal and protect, enabling them to transcend earthly concerns and to sing in the language of angels. A first-person comment attributed to Job's brother Nereus (51:1-4) describes how their hymns were recorded in writing. The text ends with the death of Job and the deliverance of his soul in a chariot to heaven.

Date, Authorship, and Provenance

The earliest manuscript evidence for the *Testament of Job* is a fragmentary fifth-century Coptic papyrus (Papyrus Cologne 3221; Römer and Thissen in van der Horst and Knibb 1989). In addition, four medieval manuscripts survive in Greek, and three in Slavonic. In light of its close relationship to LXX Job, most scholars now hold that it was originally composed in Greek. An Egyptian provenance is suggested by its depiction of Job as the king of Egypt (28:29) and by the early evidence for its circulation in Coptic. While some have sought to isolate different sources or strata within the text (Spittler 1983; van der Horst in van der Horst and Knibb 1989), others have emphasized the literary coherence of its present form (Collins 1974; Schaller in van der Horst and Knibb 1989).

For clues about its authorship, scholars have often turned to its unusual depiction of Job's daughters. Some point to the Therapeutae, an ascetic group described by Philo of Alexandria as including both men and women in worship (Philonenko 1958), and/or to the New Prophecy, an early Christian movement in which female prophets were prominent (Spittler 1983). Parallels from the Dead Sea Scrolls and Hekhalot literature, however, complicate attempts to associate the text within any single known group (Kee 1974; van der Horst in van der Horst and Knibb 1989).

The work's dependence on LXX Job allows for a *terminus a quo* of 150 B.C.E., the approximate date of the OG translation of Job. The Coptic fragment establishes the *terminus ad quem* firmly in the fifth century C.E., and a possible allusion by Tertullian (*De Patientia* 14.5) may attest the circulation of some form of the text already in the third century (cf. Jas. 5:11; *1 Clem.* 26:3). Although the evidence does not permit a precise dating, most scholars now accept the hypothesis of its Egyptian Jewish origins; they thus date the text, in whole or part, prior to the revolt of 116-117 C.E. (See, however, Davila 2005:195-99, who concludes that "although composition by a Jew, or for that matter a God-fearer, cannot be ruled out, if we start from the manuscript evidence and move backward only as needed, no positive evidence compels us to move beyond a Greek work written in Christian, perhaps Egyptian, circles by the early fifth century C.E.")

If the work is Jewish, its concern for the loss of wealth and status may reflect the situation of Egyptian Jews under Roman rule (Kugler and Rohrbaugh 2004), and its emphasis on endurance may reflect their precarious situation in the first century C.E. (Collins 1974). Whatever its precise origins, its ascetic and martyrological themes probably account for its transmission by Egyptian Christians.

BIBLIOGRAPHY

J. J. COLLINS 1974, "Structure and Meaning in the Testament of Job," *SBLSP* 1: 35-52. • J. R. DAVILA 2005, *The Provenance of the Pseudepigrapha*, 195-99, Leiden: Brill. • I. JACOBS 1970, "Literary Motifs in the Testament of Job," *JJS* 21: 1-10. • H. C. KEE 1974, "Satan, Magic, and Salvation in the Testament of Job," *SBLSP* 1: 53-76. • R. A. KRAFT 1974, *The Testament of Job according to the SV Text*, Missoula, Mont.: Scholars Press. • B. A. KIRKEGAARD 2004, "Satan in the Testament of Job: A Literary Analysis," in *Of Scribes and Sages: Early Jewish Interpretation and Transmission of Scripture*, vol. 2, ed. C. A. Evans, New York: Clark, 4-19. • R. A. KUGLER AND R. L. ROHRBAUGH 2004, "On Women and Honor in the Testament of Job," *JSP* 14: 43-62 • M. PHILONENKO 1958, "Le Testament de Job et la Thérapeutes," *Semitica* 8:41-53. • R. P. SPITTLER 1983, "The Testament of Job," in *OTP* 1:829-68 • P. W. VAN DER HORST AND M. A. KNIBB, EDS. 1989, *Studies on the Testament of Job*, Cambridge: Cambridge University Press.

ANNETTE YOSHIKO REED

Job Targum (4Q157, 11Q10)

In the Judean Desert, remnants of two manuscripts of an Aramaic translation or targum of the biblical book of Job have been found. 4Q157 (4QtgJob), copied in the first half of the first century C.E., consists of only two fragments, the largest preserving parts of Job 3:5-9 and 4:16–5:4. 11Q10 (11QtgJob) was copied by an inexperienced scribe, in an irregular and idiosyncratic late-Herodian script and with scribal errors. It preserves the damaged inner part of the scroll and many fragments, representing sections of the last thirty-nine columns of the scroll. Its contents range from Job 17:4 to 42:12. It is plausible that 4Q157 and 11Q10 are copies of the same translation.

Rabbinic literature (e.g., *b. Šabbat* 115a) refers to the existence of an Aramaic translation of Job in first-century-C.E. Palestine and reports that Gamliel the Elder determined that it should be stored away. The Qumran *Job Targum* is not related to the medieval Jewish targum of Job; indeed, it has few, if any, of the features typical of the later rabbinic targumic tradition, so it should be classified as a translation rather than as a precursor of the rabbinic targums. Further, the *Job Targum* does not seem to have influenced the Peshiṭta version of Job, and there is no evidence that it is the "Syriac book" referred to in the LXX addition to Job 42:17.

Most differences between the *Job Targum* and the Hebrew text of Job may be explained by the translation techniques of the translator, but occasionally there are indications that the translator used a text that differed from the Masoretic Text (e.g., in Job 35:11; 42:9). The translation lacks stichs and hemistichs that are found in the Hebrew text (21:23; 33:27a; 34:25b; 37:17b; 39:24), but sometimes it reflects a longer text than the MT (after 31:29 and 33:24). Correspondences with the LXX against the MT, as in the text following 33:24, indicate that the Hebrew text of Job was not yet fixed in the second century B.C.E. The suggestion made in the edition of 11Q10 by Van der Ploeg and van der Woude (1971) that the end of MT Job (42:12-17) was missing in the translation has been falsified by the subsequent identification of fragments preserving part of Job 42:12.

The date and provenance of the *Job Targum* are disputed. Scholars initially placed the text linguistically between biblical Aramaic and the Aramaic of the *Genesis Apocryphon,* with dates varying from the third to the first century B.C.E. A Palestinian provenance is not certain, and Muraoka (1974) suggested on linguistic grounds an origin in the East. Presently scholars are more cautious with regard to basing a date on a limited number of linguistic features. There is no evidence for a sectarian provenance of the translation, or even of the manuscript 11Q10. Unlike MT Job 42:11, 11Q10 does not mention Job's sisters eating with him, which may or may not reflect a celibate tendency.

The interests of the translator are manifest in his modifications of the source text (taken to be similar to the MT). Thus, the translation underscores the sovereignty of God as creator and explicitly adds the concept of wisdom to creation passages by using "wisdom" for other cognitive terms (Job 38:4; 39:26; 42:2), perhaps influenced by other wisdom literature. The *Job Targum* seems more concerned with the judgment of the unjust than the MT is (e.g., in the translation in 37:14, "when there is a case of law-breaking on it"). Job is depicted as a righteous sufferer upon whom knowledge has been bestowed, as opposed to Elihu. Thus, in the translation Job has "knowledge" and Elihu only "words" (compare Job 21:3; 32:10, 17 in the MT and 11Q10). It may not be coincidence that MT Job 42:3, which states that Job did not understand, is not found in 11Q10, which has after 42:2 a rendering of 40:5. In Job 42:6 the Aramaic translation does not state that Job *repented* in dust and ashes, but that he *became* dust and ashes, perhaps in order to remove the suggestion that Job was guilty. The evidence for the specific interests of the translator is cumulative, though, since each case may also be explained differently. Noteworthy is the innovative concept that 11Q10 shares with LXX Job 42:9 against the MT, that God forgave the sins of the friends because of Job's intercession.

BIBLIOGRAPHY

F. GARCÍA MARTÍNEZ, E. J. C. TIGCHELAAR, AND A. S. VAN DER WOUDE 1997, *Qumran Cave 11.II: 11Q2-18, 11Q20-31,* DJD 23, Oxford: Clarendon, 79-180. • T. MURAOKA 1974, "The Aramaic of the Old Targum of Job from Qumran Cave XI," *JJS* 25: 425-43. • M. SOKOLOFF 1974, *The Targum to Job from Qumran Cave XI,* Ramat-Gan: Bar-Ilan University. • D. SHEPHERD 2004, *Targum and Translation: A Reconsideration of the Qumran Aramaic Version of Job,* Assen: Van Gorcum. • J. P. M. VAN DER PLOEG AND A. S. VAN DER WOUDE 1971, *Le Targum de Job de la Grotte XI de Qumrân,* Leiden: Brill.

EIBERT TIGCHELAAR

John, Gospel of

The Jewishness of the Fourth Gospel

The Fourth Gospel's portrayal of Jews and Judaism is a highly complex and controversial issue, due both to the ambiguities of the text and to the Gospel's role in the history of Christian anti-Judaism and anti-Semitism. On the one hand, the Gospel situates its narrative and theology firmly within a Jewish milieu that reflects both the tensions within first-century Judaism and the overall context of Roman domination. Although the term "Jew" is applied only once to Jesus (4:9) and never directly to the disciples, it is obvious that Jesus, his disciples, and his detractors were Jewish, as were the crowds who listened to his teachings, witnessed his miracles, and decided either to follow him or to doubt him. The Gospel presumes the Jewish monotheistic belief in the one God, creator of heaven and earth, and in a messiah or redeemer who will usher in the messianic age, and acknowledges the major markers of Jewish identity such as Torah, Temple, Sabbath, and the pilgrimage festivals. Furthermore, the Gospel draws on prevalent Jewish themes and tradition (e.g., wisdom motifs), imagery (e.g., light/darkness; bread from heaven), and modes of argumentation (e.g., proof-texting).

The Term *Hoi Ioudaioi*

The ambiguities are raised by the Gospel's depictions of Jews and its attempts to articulate how and why its view of ultimate reality, in which Jesus is the one who mediates the relationship between humankind and the divine, is superior to a Judaism in which Jesus does not play this same role. The term *hoi Ioudaioi* itself is problematic. Some scholars have argued that this term refers specifically to Judeans, that is, residents of Judea, while others argue that *hoi Ioudaioi* already had a more general meaning that is adequately represented by the

English phrase "the Jews" in that it included ethnic, geographic, political, and religious dimensions and extended geographically to include all those in Palestine or the Diaspora for whom the Torah was sacred scripture, who held to a monotheistic belief system centered on the God of Israel and affiliated themselves with Jerusalem and Judea on religious, political, and ethnic grounds. That the Gospel was likely written in Asia Minor, that is, far from Judea, may lend support to the latter view.

Of the 196 New Testament occurrences of *hoi Ioudaioi,* 70 occur in the Fourth Gospel. Only 4:22, in which Jesus proclaims that "salvation is from the Jews," is unambiguously positive. A number of the occurrences are entirely neutral and descriptive. In this category are included the references to Jewish festivals (2:13; 5:1; 6:4; 7:2; 11:55), Jewish practices (2:6; 19:40), and to the Jews as a social, political, or ethnic group (3:1; 18:20, 33; 19:19-21). In John 4, the term functions to distinguish Jews from another group, namely, the Samaritans (John 4:9). Another group of passages portray the Jews as wavering between belief in Jesus and nonbelief. In some passages the choice is ultimately for nonbelief (2:18-20; 6:41-52; 10:19, 24); elsewhere the crowds are divided (7:11-15, 35); occasionally their choice is unequivocally for Jesus (11:36, 45; 12:9; 13:44). The rest are negative, including passages that portray Jews as unequivocally unbelieving and/or as actively seeking to harm or kill him.

The Narrative Role of the "Jews"

Within the narrative, the Jews play a crucial role as Jesus' principal adversaries. John claims that the Jews were preoccupied by a desire to kill Jesus (7:1), and that their venom extended to Jesus' followers, whom they expelled from the synagogue (9:22; 12:42; 16:2) and threatened with death (16:2). The Jews persecute Jesus for healing on the Sabbath (5:16), and for calling God his own Father, "thereby making himself equal to God" (5:18). They attempt to stone him (8:59 and 10:31) and, after the resurrection of Lazarus, their leaders plot Jesus' death. John assigns the Jewish leaders the primary role in inciting Pilate to pronounce the death sentence. In response to Pilate's offer to release Jesus, the chief priests and police shout, "Crucify him! Crucify him!" (19:15).

Within the Gospel's rhetoric, "the Jews" (like "the world") symbolize those who do not believe; they live in darkness, and will face God's wrath, hatred, and eternal condemnation. They are frequently contrasted to believers, who are associated with light, salvation, love, and eternal life (cf. John 8:12; 3:18; 7:7; 8:52). The Jews' absolute rejection of Jesus excludes them from his promise of salvation (12:37). The Jews may believe that they enjoy an exclusive covenantal relationship with God based on their Abrahamic ancestry and their firm commitment to monotheism (8:39, 41). According to the Gospel of John, however, God has now redrawn the rules so that relationship with God can be experienced only through Jesus his Son. It is not God who has fathered the Jews, but the Devil (8:44).

Is the Fourth Gospel Anti-Jewish?

The negative roles of the Jews in the Gospel's narrative and rhetoric raise a difficult question: Is the Gospel of John anti-Jewish? That is, does it intend to promote or encourage negative attitudes toward Jews as a racial, ethnic, or religious group? On one level, the answer is easy, for the Gospel is clearly concerned not with these three categories of identity, but only with the question of belief or disbelief in Jesus. Jews who believe in Jesus, such as the disciples, are "good"; it is nonbelief, regardless of identity, that is "bad."

This response, however, does not go deep enough. Obviously ethnicity and race are not factors; faith alone determines whether one is on the negative or positive side of the ledger. But religion is another matter. While John's understanding of a Jesus-centered faith system is built upon a Jewish foundation, Judaism apart from faith in Jesus is consistently portrayed as inferior. It is no longer a valid or viable path to covenantal relationship with God because Jesus, and only Jesus, is "the way, and the truth, and the life" (14:6). In 2:13-22, for example, Jesus takes ownership of the Temple, which he claims is "his Father's house," and in John 6 the people gather around Jesus at the time of the Passover instead of making pilgrimage to Jerusalem, as Jewish law encouraged. The notion that Jesus has inaugurated a new way of relating to God that replaces earlier paths is made explicit in Jesus' exchange with the Samaritan woman, in which he declares that "the hour is coming when you will worship the Father neither on this mountain [Gerizim] nor in Jerusalem [the Temple], . . . [but] the true worshipers will worship the Father in spirit and truth" (4:21-23), that is, in belief that Jesus is God's only Son.

Synagogue Expulsion in the Fourth Gospel

One way that interpreters have tried to account for the Gospel's harsh sayings about the Jews is to look to the broader historical context within which the Gospel was written, and specifically the relationship between the community within which and for which many scholars believe the Gospel was written — "the Johannine community" — and the Jews among whom they lived — "the synagogue." The paucity of information makes it extremely difficult to construct this context, but many interpreters find a clue in John 9:22, 12:42, and 16:2, which refer to the expulsion from the synagogue of those Jews who confess Jesus to be the Messiah. Given that expulsion from the synagogue was unlikely to have occurred in Jesus' lifetime, many scholars, following Martyn (2003) and Brown (1979), argue that these passages refer to an expulsion of Jewish-Christians from the synagogue toward the end of the first century. In John 9:22 the parents of the man born blind are afraid to respond to questioning about how their son's sight was restored "because they were afraid of the Jews; for the Jews had already agreed that anyone who confessed Jesus to be the Messiah would be put out of the synagogue." This passage suggests to Martyn and Brown that the expulsion was the consequence of a formal agreement or decision reached by an authoritative Jewish group. If so, the Gospel's negative comments about the Jews can be viewed, and perhaps excused, as a natural response to Jewish expulsion and persecution.

Problems with the Expulsion Theory

Despite its popularity, this theory is problematic on many levels. In the first place, it may strike one as being motivated more by the desire to deflect the charge that the Fourth Gospel may be anti-Jewish than by strictly historical considerations. Further, from a historical perspective, the theological diversity within early Judaism, and the fact that at least one eminent rabbi, Akiba, would apparently refer to another man, Simon Bar Kosiba, as the messiah (ca. 132-35 C.E.), cast doubt on the theory that the Jewish authorities would expel Jewish-Christians from the synagogue for considering a man to be the messiah.

The Birkat Ha-minîm

Another historical issue pertains to the mechanism that would have been used to expel Jews from the synagogue on account of their beliefs. Some have argued that the specific instrument through which this exclusion was accomplished was the addition of a "blessing" (in fact, a curse) on heretics — *birkat ha-minîm* — to the *ʿAmidah,* the central prayer of the Jewish liturgy. By recruiting suspected Christians as prayer leaders, the community leaders could observe whether and how they recited this benediction. Failure to do so would be seen as a sign of their allegiance to Jesus as the Christ and would result in their exclusion from the synagogue and, in effect, from the Jewish community as such. This theory was compelling until it was shown that the *birkat ha-minîm* could not have been used as a tool to expel Christians from the community, since there is no evidence that it existed in the first century in a form that would have applied to believers in Christ (Kimelman 1981). Furthermore, it is highly unlikely that there existed a central Jewish institution that would have had the authority at this time to promulgate decrees affecting the broader Jewish community.

Methodological Issues

Methodological considerations also cast doubt on the expulsion theory. The expulsion theory is based on the assumption that the Gospel tells two stories simultaneously: the story of Jesus, set in Palestine in the 30s of the first century, and the story of the Johannine community, set in Asia Minor about sixty years later. But the expulsion theory is based upon a two-level reading not of the Gospel as a whole, but only of selected passages, namely, the three passages that explicitly mention expulsion from the synagogue. If the two-level reading strategy is expanded beyond these three passages, a very different view of the Johannine group and its relationship to the Jewish community emerges. A two-level reading of John 11, for example, in which Jews come to comfort Mary and Martha of Bethany — widely known to be believers in Jesus — for the death of their brother Lazarus, would imply that Jews did not dissociate themselves from Jewish-Christians, as one would have expected had a ban or expulsion order been in place.

A Gradual, Deepening Divide

More likely than a specific ban is a gradually deepening divide between the Jewish believers in Jesus for whom the Gospel was primarily written, and the Jews who did not share their belief. This divide could have been caused in part by demography, with the possible absorption of Samaritan and Gentile believers into the Johannine community, and by the natural tendency of Johannine believers to define themselves over against the Jewish community with which they shared so much but which did not adhere to their belief that Jesus was the Messiah and the Son of God (20:30-31).

BIBLIOGRAPHY

R. E. BROWN 1979, *The Community of the Beloved Disciple,* New York: Paulist Press. • S. J. D. COHEN 1999, *The Beginnings of Jewishness: Boundaries, Varieties, Uncertainties,* Berkeley: University of California Press. • R. A. CULPEPPER 1983, *Anatomy of the Fourth Gospel: A Study in Literary Design,* Philadelphia: Fortress. • R. KIMELMAN 1981, "*Birkat Ha-Minim* and the Lack of Evidence for an Anti-Christian Jewish Prayer in Late Antiquity," in *Jewish and Christian Self-Definition,* vol. 2, ed. E. P. Sanders et al., Philadelphia: Fortress, 226-44, 391-403. • J. L. MARTYN 2003, *History and Theology in the Fourth Gospel,* 3d ed., Louisville: Westminster John Knox. • A. REINHARTZ 2001A, *Befriending the Beloved Disciple: A Jewish Reading of the Gospel of John,* New York: Continuum. • A. REINHARTZ 2001B, "'Jews' and Jews in the Fourth Gospel," in *Anti-Judaism and the Fourth Gospel,* ed. R. Bieringer et al., Assen: Van Gorcum; Louisville: Westminster John Knox, 341-56.

ADELE REINHARTZ

John the Baptist

John the Immerser or John the Baptist (*ho baptistēs* in, e.g., Mark 8:28; Josephus, *Ant.* 18.117; *ho baptizōn* in Mark 1:4; 6:14, 24) was a charismatic Jewish teacher active from "the fifteenth year of the emperor Tiberius" (Luke 3:1-3), that is, from 19 August 28 C.E. He was imprisoned in the fortress of Machaerus (*Ant.* 18:119) just before Jesus of Nazareth began his own mission (Luke 3:19-20; cf. Mark 6:17; Matt. 11:2; 14:3; a different chronology is provided in John 3:22–4:3) and was beheaded by Herod Antipas prior to Jesus' execution, which took place earlier than 37 C.E., when the Roman prefect of Judea, Pontius Pilate, was recalled.

John's birth was the subject of a nativity story that in its extant form is interwoven with a more miraculous narrative regarding the conception of Jesus (Luke 1:3-80). In this story Zechariah, a priest of the Abijah division, is chosen to burn incense in the Temple and encounters the angel Gabriel, who announces John's conception. Because Zechariah doubts this (he and his wife are both old), he is struck dumb, a condition that is removed after Zechariah writes down his son's name at John's circumcision. John is identified as a relative of Jesus through his mother Mary (Luke 1:36). Much of the

JOHN THE BAPTIST

language and substance of the account is derived from the biblical narratives of the births of Samson and Samuel (LXX Judg. 13:2-25; 1 Kgdms. 1:1–2:11). The traditional site of John's birth is En Karim, where over time a cluster of sites associated with John have been venerated.

The teaching of John is sparsely recorded but was seen as a prophetic call to turn Israel back to righteousness before the end of the age (Luke 1:15-17). He challenged all Israel ("You brood of vipers!" Luke 3:7; cf. Matt. 3:7), declaring that people had to repent of sin in order to ensure inward and outward purity in preparation for the imminent end, when the Coming One would arrive, since at that time God would divide Israel between the righteous, who would be immersed in the Holy Spirit, and the sinful, who would be burned up in a sea of fire (Mark 1:8; Matt. 3:11-12; Luke 3:16-18). Repentance would be shown by "fruit," that is, works of righteousness and lovingkindness such as sharing possessions with the poor. In John's view it was not possible to rely on the inherited *zĕkût* (merit) of Abraham (Luke 3:7-14; cf. Matt. 3:7-10); righteousness was an individual matter that called for a public confession of sin immediately prior to immersion (Mark 1:5; Matt. 3:6).

John's baptism was in line with other Jewish immersions in being for the removal of ritual impurity. He performed it in the highly effective natural flow of the Jordan River (cf. *m. Miqw.* 1:1-8). His immersion was new in that he insisted that bodily ritual impurity could not be removed without prior purification of the heart through repentance and forgiveness of sins. While the Gospels are slightly ambiguous on this point, it is clarified by Josephus (*Ant.* 18.117):

> He was a good man who was exhorting the Jews to practice virtue and righteousness towards each other and to act with piety towards God, and (then) come together for immersion. Because then indeed the immersion would now appear acceptable to Him, since it was not about pleading forgiveness for certain sins they had done but for a purification of the body, now that the soul had been cleansed already by righteousness.

John's baptism was therefore called "an immersion of repentance for the forgiveness of sins" (Mark 1:4 and pars.).

John appealed to multitudes of people in Judean society, from Pharisees (Matt. 3:7; *Gospel of the Ebionites* in Epiphanius, *Panarion* 30.13.4) to the socially excluded such as tax collectors and women deemed immoral (Matt. 21:31-2). He had a group of disciples (e.g., Mark 2:18; 6:26; Matt. 11:2; Luke 7:18) and was referred to as a "teacher" (Luke 3:12) of "the way of righteousness" (Matt. 21:32; cf. Mark 12:14). In John 5:16-19 it is noted that the Judeans "rejoiced for a time in his light." Josephus comments that such was the immense popularity of John that the ruler responsible for his death, Herod Antipas, was believed to have been punished by God when his army was annihilated by the Nabatean king Aretas IV (ca. 37 C.E.; *Ant.* 18.116-19). A more skeptical attitude toward John may have prevailed in Galilee, where Jesus railed against "this generation" because it would accept neither John's nor his own message. There is also a comment that the Pharisees and lawyers (in Galilee?) were not immersed by John (Luke 7:29-35; Matt. 11:11, 16-19; *Gospel of Thomas* 46; cf. Matt. 23:25-26).

John is presented as working in Perea in the uncultivated "wilderness" region proximate to the Jordan, near a place called Bethabara or Bethany (John 1:28; 3:26; 10:40), which lay within the jurisdiction of Herod Antipas. He is also associated with Aenon near Salem (Tell Shalem; John 3:23) in the region of the Decapolis. Both sites were close to the Jordan and placed him conceptually in association with Joshua, who led Israel into the promised land after parting the Jordan (Josh. 3:14-17), and also Elijah, who likewise parted the river (2 Kings 2:8) and ascended into heaven nearby (1 Kings 2:9-11). According to the Synoptic Gospels, Jesus identified John as Elijah *redivivus* (Mark 9:9-13; Matt. 17:9-13; Luke 1:15-17), but there is a tradition that John denied that he was Elijah (John 1:21-27), and indeed some people said that Jesus was Elijah (Mark 8:28 and pars.). The appearance of John as described in the Gospels is designed to recall Elijah: he wears camel-hair cloth with a skin tied around his loins (Mark 1:6a and pars; cf. 2 Kings 1:8; 4 Kgdms. 1:8 [LXX]). However, camel hair was used for sackcloth, which was a common garment of prophets in general (Zech. 13:4; Isa. 20:2; Rev. 11:3); it was clearly rough clothing, as Jesus ironically indicated (Matt. 11:8; Luke 7:25), and was indicative of extreme piety.

John may have been a *nāzîr* (Num. 6:1-21) like Samson and Samuel (*m. Nazir* 9:5). This means he would have avoided corpses and wine (cf. Luke 1:5; 7:33-34; Matt. 11:18-19) and let his hair grow long.

Despite much scholarly speculation, no compelling evidence associates John with the Essenes (as described in Philo, *Quod Omnis Probus Liber Sit* 75–91; *Hypoth.* 11.1-18; Josephus, *J.W.* 2.119-61; *Ant.* 15.18-22; Pliny, *Natural History* 5.15.73). Indeed, there are a number of striking differences in the way John and the Essenes are described. John was an isolated individual in the wilderness, whereas the Essenes lived in communities in towns and villages. John's immersion in water was not connected with participation in an exclusive community. The sharing of food and clothing John advocated applied to all Israel (cf. Ezek. 18:5-9), not specifically to a chosen few. The Essenes ate meals of bread and wine, which are precisely the foods John did not eat, relying instead on what he found naturally, like the ascetic Bannos (Josephus, *Life* 11), particularly "locusts and wild honey" (Mark 1:6; Matt. 3:4). The Essenes wore white; John's camel-hair cloth would have been brown.

John was one of a number of charismatic, prophetic figures in first-century Judea. Shortly after John, a Samaritan prophet assembled a crowd near Mt. Gerizim to witness the uncovering of sacred vessels there (Josephus, *Ant.* 18.85-87). During the tenure of the Roman governor Fadus, a man named Theudas claimed he would part the Jordan (44-46 C.E.; *Ant.* 20.97-98; Acts 5:36). A leader known as "the Egyptian" brought a

JONATHAN THE KING TEXT (4Q448)

crowd from the wilderness to the Mount of Olives (*Ant.* 20.169-72; *J.W.* 2.261-63; Acts 21:38; cf. *J.W.* 2.258-60; *Ant.* 20.167-68). The Roman authorities, perceiving the revolutionary dimensions of their religious messages, swiftly destroyed the popular leaders and their movements. Likewise, Herod Antipas considered the huge popular support for John and his teaching dangerous for security (*Ant.* 18.118-19).

John exacerbated Antipas' fears by specifically criticizing him for divorcing the daughter of the Nabatean King Aretas IV in order to marry his living half-brother's wife Herodias, since, according to the priestly code, a man who marries his living brother's wife is impure (Lev. 18:16). John denounced him additionally for "all the evil things that Herod had done" (Luke 3:19-20). The story of Antipas' reluctance to kill John as given in Mark (Luke 6:17-29; Matt. 14:3-12) is highly indebted to motifs in the book of Esther and may reflect popular speculation.

In Christian tradition John is hailed as the precursor to Jesus as messiah, with Jesus' immersion by John in the Jordan and associated vision (Mark 1:9-11 and pars.) marking the beginning of his mission. Many scholars consider John's acclamation of Jesus as the messiah to be a construct of the early Jesus movement.

BIBLIOGRAPHY

C. MURPHY 2003, *John the Baptist, Prophet of Purity for a New Age,* Collegeville, Minn.: Liturgical Press. • C. R. KAZMIERSKI 1996, *John the Baptist: Prophet and Evangelist,* Collegeville, Minn.: Liturgical Press. • J. E. TAYLOR 1997, *The Immerser: John the Baptist within Second Temple Judaism,* Grand Rapids: Eerdmans. • R. L. WEBB 1991, *John the Baptizer and Prophet: A Socio-Historical Study,* Sheffield: JSOT Press.

See also: Prophecy and Prophets

JOAN E. TAYLOR

Jonathan the King Text (4Q448)

The Qumran document 4Q448 is notable for mentioning twice the name of King Jonathan (i.e., Alexander Jannaeus, who ruled 103-76 B.C.E.). It preserves fragments of three columns, an upper and two lower ones. Column A is a hymn in praise of God, while cols. B-C are a prayer for the welfare of King Jonathan. The last six lines of col. A include parts of Psalm 154, which is known from 11QPs[a] and from several Syriac manuscripts. The work is not a composition of the Qumran community, since several words and phrases in it are not characteristic of the sectarian scrolls from Qumran, and since Qumran authors did not normally mention Hasmonean rulers by name. The scroll was written by a supporter of the Hasmoneans and was evidently brought to Qumran by someone who joined the sect.

4Q448 and Psalm 154

A Hebrew version of Psalm 154 has been preserved in 11QPs[a]. Column A of 4Q448 preserves verses of the first and fifth units of this psalm (vv. 1, 3, 16-18, and 20). The redactor of Psalm 154 integrated the first part into the beginning of the psalm and the second part into its conclusion, taking the second and fourth units from a composition speaking about Lady Wisdom (vv. 5-8, 12-15), and adding the third unit, claiming that one who praises God is as favorable to Him as one who offers sacrifices (vv. 9-11). The Syriac title of Psalm 154 reads: "The Prayer of Hezekiah, when the Assyrians were surrounding him; and he asked God for deliverance from them." Based on this wording, line 5 of col. A may be reconstructed to read: "They were terrified of Senna[cherib and cried out]" (cf. 2 Chron. 32:20; Jonah 1:5; 4Q382). 2 Kings 19:4 mentions that Hezekiah asked Isaiah to "pray for the remnant that still survives," but no such prayer is documented in 2 Kings, which rather gives a prophecy delivered by Isaiah that Sennacherib would not conquer Jerusalem. Later, 2 Chron. 32:20 added a description of Hezekiah and Isaiah praying and crying to heaven for the salvation of Jerusalem. The proposed reconstruction suggests that the hymnic unit of 4Q448 was attributed to Hezekiah and Isaiah (cf. Sir. 48:17-21; Josephus, *Ant.* 10.12). The prayer for King Jonathan probably ended up on the same scroll alongside the prayer attributed to Hezekiah and Isaiah because of a typological link between Sennacherib's campaign in 701 B.C.E. and Ptolemy Lathyrus' invasion of Judea in 103 B.C.E.

The Prayer for the Welfare of King Jonathan

Column B of 4Q448 reads as follows: "Keep guard, O Holy One, over King Jonathan and over all the congregation of your people Israel who are in the four corners of heaven. Let them all be at peace, and upon your kingdom may your name be blessed." It not entirely clear to whose kingdom, God's or Jonathan's, the author is referring, and the ambiguity may be deliberate. In any case, the prayer seems implicitly to equate the Hasmonean kingdom with the kingdom of God.

At the end of line 4 in col. C, the text seems to shift from a plea to a thanksgiving prayer. God is praised for having placed his name upon Israel and for delivering King Jonathan on the "day of war." Then it follows that King Jonathan was assisted by God and achieved a military success on a day of war.

King Jonathan should be identified with Alexander Jannaeus. This identification is based on the fact that Jonathan son of Mattathias was a high priest but not a king. Besides Alexander Jannaeus, no other kings of the Second Temple period were named Jonathan. Josephus describes four battles in which Alexander Jannaeus was unexpectedly rescued. One of these battles may be intended in the phrase "day of war" of 4Q448. The first such battle occurred in 103/2 B.C.E., when Ptolemy Lathyrus failed to conquer Jerusalem.

Isaiah 10:24-34 describes the campaign of Sennacherib against Jerusalem. Commentating on these verses, the pesher preserved in 4QpIsa[a] (frg. 2-6 col. ii) interprets them as referring to Ptolemy Lathyrus' campaign against Alexander Jannaeus in 103-102 B.C.E. That the psalm copied in col. A of 4Q448 relates to Sennacherib's campaign suggests that the *Prayer for the Welfare of King Jonathan* was composed just after 103 B.C.E.

A minority view argues that the text is not a prayer *for* King Jonathan but should be translated "Rise up, O Lord, *against* King Jonathan, and as for all the congregation of your people Israel, . . . let them be at peace" (Main 1998). The dispute hinges on the meaning of the Hebrew preposition *ʿal.*

BIBLIOGRAPHY

E. ESHEL, H. ESHEL, AND A. YARDENI 1998, "448. 4QApocryphal Psalm and Prayer," in *Qumran Cave 4. VI: Poetical and Liturgical Texts,* vol. 1, ed. E. Eshel et al., DJD 11, Oxford: Clarendon, 403-25. • H. ESHEL 2008, "A Prayer for the Welfare of King Jonathan," in idem, *The Dead Sea Scrolls and the Hasmonean State,* Grand Rapids: Eerdmans, 101-15. • H. ESHEL AND E. ESHEL 2000, "4Q448, Psalm 154 (Syriac), Sirach 48:20 and 4QpIsa[a]," *JBL* 119: 645-59. • A. LEMAIRE 2000, "Attestation textuelle et critique littéraire: 4Q448 col. A et Psaulme 154," in *The Dead Sea Scrolls: Fifty Years after Their Discovery,* ed. L. H. Schiffman, E. Tov, and J. C. VanderKam, Jerusalem: Israel Exploration Society, 12-18. • E. MAIN 1998, "For King Jonathan or Against? The Use of the Bible in 4Q448," in *Biblical Perspectives: Early Use and Interpretation of the Bible in Light of the Dead Sea Scrolls,* ed. M. E. Stone and E. G. Chazon, Leiden: Brill, 113-15. • E. QIMRON 1992, "On the Blessing for King Jonathan," *Tarbiz* 61: 565-66 (in Hebrew).

ESTHER ESHEL

Joseph

The biblical figure of Joseph (Genesis 37–50) relates to important subjects of Second Temple Judaism, such as the relationship between the land of Israel and the Diaspora, the individual vis-à-vis the family, sexual ethics, and divine providence in "secular" history. Moreover, in the Genesis narrative Joseph is far from perfect, and his character raises questions concerning the nature of Scripture and its interpretation. Did early Jewish interpreters accept the human flaws of biblical heroes, or did they rather draw ideal images, assuming that the Bible presents nothing but ethical paradigms? Since every interpretative process involves both a close reading of Scripture and an application of the exegete's own ideas and cultural background, the changing image of Joseph in early Jewish sources throws light on how this story was read and updated in different contexts.

While Joseph became famous in later Jewish tradition for his encounter with Potiphar's wife, earlier interpreters took a wider interest in the novel-like narrative of his life, the longest in the Pentateuch. The evidence from Alexandrian Jewish exegetes dates to an early period and thus serves as a foil for interpretations in the land of Israel, many of which emerged later. On the whole, Alexandrian Jews were proud of their forefather, because he had attained such a powerful position in their land of residence. Accordingly, they appreciated especially his governing and personality.

Artapanus, writing probably toward the end of the third century B.C.E. somewhere in Hellenistic Egypt, provides a most lively and positive image of Joseph. In his paraphrase of Scripture, which is not based on direct quotations or a detailed analysis of the text, no mention is made of Joseph's provocative behavior toward his brothers or his colorful coat (Gen. 37:1-2). Nor is he depicted as a victim of his brothers' envy. Artapanus instead has him arrange his own departure for Egypt and arrive there as a wise and accomplished hero (Eusebius, *Praep. Evang.* 9.23.1). His career is crowned by every success: his administration made a lasting contribution to Egypt, he was loved by the Egyptians, and he married Aseneth, the daughter of the Heliopolitan priest (9.23.2-4). Joseph's encounter with Potiphar's wife is not even mentioned, probably because Artapanus wanted to see his hero completely integrated into Greco-Egyptian society and culture.

A similar line of interpretation is visible in the Wisdom of Solomon and *Joseph and Aseneth,* both Jewish documents from pre-Christian, Roman Egypt whose precise dates cannot be known. Both highlight Joseph's power, the author of the Wisdom of Solomon speaking of his receiving the "scepter of a kingdom" (Wis. 10:14), while in *Joseph and Aseneth* he is called the "powerful of God" who carries a "royal staff," and Pentephres is more than happy to be his host and to give his daughter in marriage to him (*Jos. & Asen.* 3:5; 4:7; 5:5). Moreover, in both writings the contrast between the Hebrews and the Egyptians is stressed, with the result that in *Joseph and Aseneth* the female protagonist converts to Judaism (*Jos. & Asen.* 10:1–13:15).

The Jewish philosopher and exegete Philo of Alexandria (ca. 20 B.C.E.–45 C.E.) provides the most complex picture of Joseph. He devotes a whole treatise to the figure *(De Iosepho)* and offers interpretations of key passages throughout his corpus. Many scholars have been struck by the fact that in his biography of Joseph Philo is very sympathetic to the hero, praising him as an ideal politician, while especially in *De Somniis* he criticizes him for adopting Egyptian vice. Some scholars acknowledge the discrepancy and resolve it by arguing for different contexts — a Jewish and Roman audience (Goodenough 1938), or by recognizing that Philo's positive valuation of Joseph as a literal-historical figure is complemented by his negative use of him as a symbol of Jewish assimilation to Egyptian culture (Niehoff 1992). Others have attempted to show that Philo's portraits of Joseph are coherent (Bassler 1985). In any case, Philo's presentation of Joseph shows a variety otherwise characteristic of rabbinic midrashim.

Philo highlights two aspects of Joseph's life: his outstanding talents in his youth, which inevitably stirred his brothers' envy but also prepared him for his future role as governor of Egypt (*On the Life of Joseph* 4–5), and his distance from the inferior Egyptian culture. Philo makes a special point of stressing the reasons why Joseph rejected Potiphar's wife. He has Joseph say to her, "We, the descendants of the Hebrews, live under special customs and laws" that require an unusual degree of austerity and self-discipline especially in sexual matters (*Joseph* 42). In the same spirit, Philo's Jacob is more than relieved to learn that despite his prolonged sojourn in Egypt his son Joseph has not assimilated to Egyptian ways (*Joseph* 254).

Looking at interpretations of Joseph in the land of Israel, it is immediately obvious that there is little if any interest in his administration of Egypt. This feature can easily be explained by reference to the historical and geographical context of these exegetes. Moreover, a radical shift is conspicuous: while early interpreters saw Joseph in a favorable light, amoraic teachers in the rabbinic midrash *Genesis Rabbah* depicted him in far more critical terms, suggesting that he had provoked his brothers and wished to have an affair with Potiphar's wife.

Important signposts in this development from a positive to a negative image are the book of *Jubilees* and Josephus. Both authors interpret Joseph favorably, taking his side in the conflict with his brothers. The book of *Jubilees* not only integrates the Joseph story into its special calendar, grounding the Day of Atonement in Jacob's mourning for Joseph, whom he thought dead (*Jub.* 34:18-19), but generally highlights the brothers' cruelty (42:25). Furthermore, Joseph's motives for refusing the overtures of Potiphar's wife are for the first time carefully analyzed: he did not surrender because he "remembered the Lord and the words that Jacob his father used to read from among the words of Abraham" (39:6).

Having been educated in Jerusalem but writing in Rome toward the end of the first century C.E., Josephus took a particular and highly personal interest in the figure of Joseph. Not only did they share the same name, but both claimed to have received prophetic dreams indicative of future events. Moreover, both Josephus and Joseph entertained a tense relationship with their brothers. Given these similarities, it is not surprising that Josephus presented his biblical namesake in the same apologetic manner as his own life story. He thus stressed Joseph's innocence and outstanding gifts (*Ant.* 2.9-10) as well as the visions, which inevitably stirred his brothers' envy and revenge (*Ant.* 2.11-22). In his account, the brothers go to Shechem in order to kill him (*Ant.* 2.18). Precisely the same features characterize Josephus' story of his own life: he was gifted with prophetic dreams (*J.W.* 3.392-402), but his brothers continued to envy and hate him, even planning several assaults on his person (*J.W.* 5.541-43; 3.400-406; *Vita* 302).

Genesis Rabbah, the first systematic rabbinic interpretation of the book of Genesis, was redacted probably around 400 C.E. in the land of Israel. It presents a completely new picture of Joseph. While some tannaitic exegetes, such as R. Judah and R. Nehemia, insisted that Joseph remained chaste in relation to Potiphar's wife, amoraic teachers began to suggest that he himself desired an affair and was only prevented either by physical shortcomings or a last-minute remembrance of his father. Similarly, rabbinic interpreters dwelt on Joseph's evil report on his brothers, suggesting that this had prompted God to test him by sending Potiphar's wife to tempt him. These new perspectives reflect both an intense belief in theodicy, which requires the interpreters to look for human guilt, and an increased focus on sexuality as a very real threat. Significantly, the latter is also shared by Christian sources and may point to a common background.

BIBLIOGRAPHY

J. BASSLER 1985, "Philo on Joseph: The Basic Coherence of *De Josepho* and *De Somniis* II," *JSJ* 16: 240-55. • E. R. GOODENOUGH 1938, *The Politics of Philo Judaeus: Theory and Practice,* New Haven: Yale University Press. • E. S. GRUEN 1998, *Heritage and Hellenism: The Reinvention of Jewish Tradition,* Berkeley: University of California Press, 73-109. • J. L. KUGEL 1990, *In Potiphar's House,* San Francisco: HarperSanFrancisco. • M. R. NIEHOFF 1992, *The Figure of Joseph in Post-Biblical Jewish Literature,* Leiden: Brill. • M. R. NIEHOFF 2005, "New Garments for Biblical Joseph," in *Biblical Interpretation: History, Context, Reality,* ed. C. Helmer, Atlanta: Scholars Press, 33-56.

MAREN NIEHOFF

Joseph, Apocryphon of (4Q371-373)

Renamed "4QNarrative and Poetic Composition[a-c]" in the official DJD edition, the scroll fragments 4Q371-373 are commonly and collectively known by their former name, the *Apocryphon of Joseph.* The ambiguity of the renaming reflects the continuing scholarly debate concerning genre, additional named characters, and the identity and function of the "Joseph" figure in the text.

To the three copies of the *Apocryphon,* comprised of ten fragments of 4Q371, twenty-six fragments of 4Q372 and two fragments of 4Q373 may be added two fragments of 2QApocryphon of David? (2Q22) and a possible fifth manuscript located in the PAM 43.680 photograph. Each scroll shares overlapping material with at least one of the other manuscripts. Likely composed while the Samaritan temple was still standing during the Hellenistic period, the *Apocryphon* continued to be copied from the early Hasmonean period though to the late Herodian period (100 B.C.E. to mid-first century C.E.).

The *Apocryphon of Joseph* is generically complex with diverse forms of narrative sometimes oddly juxtaposed with poetic sections that variously take the form of lament, hymnic praise, wisdom psalm, or narrative praise. Embedded in the narrative are first-person speeches or psalms by some of Israel's heroes. Although Joseph figures strongly in the larger fragments, references to David, Moses, Goliath or Og, Zimri, and the five kings of Midian also appear in the smaller portions.

Fragment 1 of 4Q372, "A Text about Joseph," is the longest fragment and overlaps considerably with 4Q371 frg. 1. The narrative portion (lines 1-15) preserves a "sin–exile–return" passage naming Levi, Judah, and Benjamin as returnees from exile and describing the fate of the descendants of Joseph, who was "cast into lands he did not know among a foreign nation." In place of (the true descendants of) Joseph who remained in exile, others — possibly the Samaritans — occupied the tribal allotment of Ephraim and Manasseh and built a "high place upon the high mountain." In lines 16-36, Joseph's lament embodies an anti-Samaritan polemic that calls on God to render judgment against an enemy who wrongfully occupies the land.

According to the scholarly consensus, "Joseph" was not meant to recall the idealized biblical figure but was rather a cipher for the northern tribes who traced their descent from Joseph and who were displaced in exile (e.g., Schuller and Bernstein 2001: 170). These "true" descendants of Joseph and their continuing exilic plight had significance for the author concerning the full restoration of Judah (Thiessen 2008). The *Apocryphon's* Joseph is only obliquely evoked, unlike other "Joseph" texts in the Qumran corpus — 4QGen[j] frg. 1 line 2 (4Q9; cf. Gen. 41:16), *Jubilees, Aramaic Levi Document*, 4QText Concerning Rachel and Joseph (4Q474), and the Aramaic 4QTJoseph ar (4Q539) — that clearly and variously expand or idealize the biblical Joseph as a wise sage, mediator between God and foreigner, obedient to God's law against adultery, or Rachel's most loved son.

Although it is unlikely that it was a sectarian composition, the text as preserved at Qumran continued to be copied and transmitted for well over a century, allowing for fresh, contemporizing interpretations to emerge as developing movements preserving the texts sought their distinctive self-identities. For example, the Qumran covenanters may have substituted their disaffection with the Jerusalem Temple and priesthood for the text's original polemic against Samaritans and their temple on Mt. Gerizim, transforming Joseph into an archetype for itself that epitomized the community's self-understanding as a people still in exile (Kugler 2006: 267-77).

BIBLIOGRAPHY

M. J. BERNSTEIN 2003, "Poetry and Prose in 4Q371-373: *Narrative and Poetic Composition[a,b,c]*," in *Liturgical Perspectives: Prayer and Poetry in Light of the Dead Sea Scrolls*, ed. E. G. Chazon, Leiden: Brill, 19-33. • R. A. KUGLER 2006, "Joseph at Qumrân (I): The Importance of 4Q372 Frg. 1 in Extending a Tradition," in *Studies in the Hebrew Bible, Qumran, and the Septuagint Presented to Eugene Ulrich*, ed. P. W. Flint, E. Tov, and J. C. VanderKam, Leiden: Brill, 261-78. • E. SCHULLER AND M. BERNSTEIN 2001, "4Q371-373," in *Qumran Cave 4.XXVIII: Miscellanea, Part 2*, DJD 28, Oxford: Clarendon Press, 151-204. • E. SCHULLER 1992, "The Psalm of 4Q372 1 within the Context of Second Temple Prayer," *CBQ* 54: 67-79. • E. J. TIGCHELAAR 2004, "On the Unidentified Fragments of *DJD XXXIII* and PAM 43.680: A New Manuscript of *4QNarrative and Poetic Composition*, and Fragments of *4Q13, 4Q269, 4Q525* and *4QSb*(?)," *RevQ* 21: 477-85. • M. THIESSEN 2008, "4Q372 1 and the Continuation of Joseph's Exile," *DSD* 15: 380-95.

DOROTHY M. PETERS

Joseph, Prayer of

The *Prayer of Joseph* is a largely lost work remarkable for its depiction of the Israelite patriarch Jacob as the incarnation of the angel Israel. Eleven hundred lines long according to the *Stichometry* of Nicephorus, it survives in only three Greek excerpts quoted in the writings of Origen of Alexandria. Fragment A is a nine-sentence quotation in Origen's *Commentary on John* (2:31 [25]). Fragment B is a single sentence from Origen cited in Gregory and Basil's compilation of Origeniana, the *Philocalia* (33.15); in Eusebius of Caesarea's *Preparation of the Gospel* (6.11.64); and in the Latin *Commentary on Genesis* by Procopius of Gaza (29). Fragment C, which paraphrases Fragment A and quotes Fragment B, also stems from the *Philocalia* (33.19).

Fragment A

Origen introduces the largest excerpt by noting that the *Prayer of Joseph* is "an apocryphon presently in use among the Hebrews." He cites it to support his view that John the Baptist was an angel (the *angelos* announced in Mal. 3:1) who assumed a human body in order to prepare the way for Jesus.

> I, Jacob, the one speaking to you, am also Israel, an angel of God and a ruling spirit. And Abraham and Isaac were created before *(proektsithēsan)* every work. And I, Jacob, the one called Jacob by human beings but whose name is Israel, am the one called by God "Israel," "a man seeing God," because I myself am the firstborn of every living thing given life by God. And when I was coming up from Syrian Mesopotamia, Uriel, the angel of God, came forth and said that I had descended to earth and tabernacled among men and that I had been called by the name of Jacob. And he envied me and fought with me and wrestled with me, saying that his name and the name that is before every angel had precedence over my name. I told him his name and his rank among the sons of God: "Are you not Uriel, the eighth after me? And am I not Israel, archangel of the power of the Lord and chief captain among the sons of God? Am I not Israel, the first minister in God's presence?" And I invoked the inextinguishable name of my God.

Genre

Jacob here is evidently speaking to Joseph and his sons, and the larger work was likely devoted, at least in part, to a retelling of Jacob's deathbed blessings on Joseph's sons in Genesis 48. The genre of the now lost work is beyond knowing with certainty. The title is anomalous, since the surviving fragments contain no prayer and do not mention Joseph. The work may have been a testament that included a lengthy prayer attributed to Joseph. The predictive element typical of testaments is hinted at in Fragment B, in which Jacob says, "For I have read in the tablets of heaven all that shall befall you and your sons."

Midrashic Character and Affiliations

Fragment A develops the story of Jacob's wrestling match with the mysterious "man" at the ford of the Jabbok in Gen. 32:24-31, where Jacob is given the name Israel. The fragment's identification of the "man" as an angel is an interpretation, familiar from targumic and midrashic sources, that takes its cue from Gen. 32:2 ("Jacob went on his way and the *angels* of God met him") and Hos. 12:4 ("He [Jacob] struggled with an *angel* and overcame"). Jacob's apparent ignorance of his heavenly nature until informed of it by Uriel is puzzling. Fragment C says that Jacob recognized his heavenly status "while doing service in the body, being reminded of it by the archangel Uriel." Whether this notion has its impulse somewhere in the text of Genesis is unclear. It does, however, have a loose analogy in Enoch's being informed that he is the heavenly Son of Man figure whom his guiding angel has been showing him in visions (*1 Enoch* 71:14).

The folk etymology of the name Israel as "a man seeing God," which is a play on the words *ʾîš rāʾâ ʾēl*, depends on Gen. 32:31, where Jacob calls the place of his wrestling Peniel and says, "For I have seen God face to face and yet lived." Jacob-Israel's claim to be "the firstborn of every living thing" ultimately rests on Exod. 4:22, where God calls the nation of Israel his "firstborn son" (cf. *Jub.* 19:29, where Abraham is given the same title). The notion that the patriarchs were formed before creation is known in midrashic sources (e.g., *Exod. Rab.* 19:7). The angel Uriel's envy of Jacob builds on the biblical tradition of Esau's conflict with his brother. A well-known midrash, in fact, identifies Jacob's assailant at the Jabbok with the patron angel of Esau (*Gen. Rab.* 77:3). The conflict between the two figures also resonates with the theme of angelic rivalry so prominent in merkavah traditions and later Hekhalot texts. The titles "archangel of the power of the Lord" and "chief captain among the sons of God" are epithets often given to the angel Michael, while the job description "first minister in God's presence" evokes merkavah traditions that personify the nation of Israel as an angel bearing the same name who leads the heavenly choir (Smith 1985: 702).

Date, Original Language, and Provenance

The citation in Origen's *Commentary on John* supplies a latest possible date of 231 C.E. for the *Prayer of Joseph*, which in turn points to the first century or very early second century as the time of composition. The original language and provenance of the work are uncertain. On the basis of affiliations with Aramaic materials, some scholars suggest an Aramaic original written by a Jew in the land of Israel. Yet Greek may just as well be the language of composition. Although Origen's assertion of the work's currency among Jews may be accurate, the author may have been a Christian, writing perhaps in Egypt, who drew on early Jewish midrashic and mystical traditions. In favor of this possibility is the fact that the term *proektsithēsan* ("precreated") in line 2 of fragment A and the phrase "imperishable name" in line 9 are rare terms known only from later Christian texts.

Complicating the issue of authorship and provenance is the fact that the *Prayer of Joseph* has affinities with such a wide range of Jewish and Christian sources, from Palestinian targumic and midrashic traditions to Jewish merkavah and Hekhalot materials to Christian texts in the New Testament, the Nag Hammadi Library, and the church fathers. The diverse spectrum of associations is most readily seen in the striking titles that the *Prayer of Joseph* confers on Jacob-Israel. Thus, the etymologizing of "Israel" as "a man seeing God" depends upon a Hebrew wordplay that is rarely made in Hebrew texts but common in Philo and the church fathers. Three other titles — "firstborn," "archangel," and "a man seeing God" — are conferred upon the *logos* by Philo in *De Confusione Linguarum* 146 and on the angel Israel in the Coptic Gnostic treatise *On the Origin of the World* (NHC II,5). The title "firstborn of every creature" is applied to Christ in the deutero-Pauline letter to the Colossians (1:15) and in the *Dialogue with Trypho* (125:3), where Justin Martyr explicitly identifies the preincarnate Christ as the angel Israel who wrestled with Jacob. With so broad an array of parallels, it is impossible to specify the original authorship and provenance of *Prayer of Joseph* with any confidence.

Purpose and Significance

If the work's provenance is difficult to identify, so too is its intended purpose. It has been variously labeled a Jewish-Christian work, a Gnostic text, an anti-Christian work, and even an anti-Jewish polemic. Citing several religio-historical parallels, J. Z. Smith has situated the work in a Hellenistic Jewish mystical setting and suggested that it had a ritual use. In this view, the patriarch Jacob's presumed ascent to heaven in order to assume his rightful heavenly station provided believers with a model that they could appropriate for their own attainment of salvation through mystical ascent. The suggestion is intriguing but, given the sparseness of the preserved text, it must remain tentative. Nevertheless, what survives of the *Prayer of Joseph* offers a tantalizing example of midrashic ingenuity putting exegetical traditions centered on Genesis 32 in service of speculative and mystical interests.

BIBLIOGRAPHY

A.-M. DENIS 1970, *Fragmenta pseudepigraphorum quae supersunt graeca*, Leiden: Brill, 61-62. • A.-M. DENIS ET AL. 2000, *Introduction à la littérature religieuse Judéo-Hellénistique*, vol. 1, *Pseudépigrapha de l'Ancien Testament*, Turnhout: Brepols, 331-43. • M. R. JAMES 1920, *The Lost Apocrypha of the Old Testament*, London: SPCK, 1-31. • J. L. KUGEL 1998, *Traditions of the Bible*, Cambridge, Mass.: Harvard University Press, 384-88, 397-99. • H. PRIEBATSCH 1937, *Die Josephgeschichte in der Weltliteratur*, Breslau: Priebatsch, 8-44. • P. SCHÄFER 1977, "The Rivalry between Angels and Men in the *Prayer of Joseph* and Rabbinic Literature," in *Proceedings of the Sixth World Congress of Jewish Studies*, vol. 3, ed. A. Shinan, Jerusalem: World Union of Jewish Studies, 511-15 (in Hebrew). • J. Z. SMITH 1968, "The Prayer of Joseph," in *Religions in Antiquity: Essays in Honor of Erwin Ramsdell Goodenough*, ed. J. Neusner, Leiden: Brill, 253-94; reprinted with an afterword in idem, *Map Is Not Territory: Studies in the History of Religions*, Leiden: Brill, 1978, 24-66. • J. Z. SMITH 1985, "Prayer of Joseph," in *OTP* 2:699-714.

DANIEL C. HARLOW

Joseph and Aseneth

Joseph and Aseneth is an early Jewish novel that expands upon the story of Joseph in Genesis 37–50. Composed in Greek, most likely in Hellenistic Egypt, the work can be divided into two parts (chaps. 1–21 and 22–29).

Contents

Chapters 1–21 recount the events that led up to the marriage of Joseph and Aseneth, the daughter of an Egyptian priest (according to Gen. 41:45); it portrays Aseneth's initial encounter with Joseph and her subsequent conversion to Judaism. Within this section, chaps. 9–18 narrate Aseneth shifting her allegiance to the "God Most High." She forsakes her Egyptian worship practices, and she repents, fasts, and prays to God Most High for seven days in isolation. At the end of this penitential period, a messenger of God visits her and promises that (1) her name will be inscribed in the book of life, (2) she will partake in the life-giving ways of following the God of Joseph, (3) she will become a city of refuge for all those devoted to God, and (4) she will marry Joseph. Aseneth's encounter with the angelic figure concludes with a miraculous scene in which she eats from an extraordinary honeycomb, and the angelic figure summons unusual bees to emerge from the comb's cells. After the angelic figure departs, Aseneth and Joseph meet again, embrace each other, and ultimately marry.

Chapters 22–29 present a threat to this marital union whereby Pharaoh's son takes advantage of the strained relations between the sons of Jacob to serve his own interests. In an effort to gain Aseneth as his wife, Pharaoh's son plans an ambush to kidnap Aseneth and to kill both Joseph and Pharaoh. He first tries to enlist the help of Levi and Simeon, but when that fails, he successfully recruits the sons of Bilhah and Zilpah by convincing them that Joseph intends to harm them in the future (which is false). Several unexpected events, however, thwart the covert operation. Pharaoh's son is not able to murder his father, Benjamin severely injures Pharaoh's son and single-handedly slays the Egyptian forces that had accompanied Pharaoh's son, and Levi and the other sons of Jacob destroy the remaining military forces and pursue the sons of Bilhah and Zilpah in order to kill them. Sensing their imminent defeat, Dan, Gad, Naphtali, and Asher decide to kill Aseneth, but God responds to Aseneth's prayers by reducing the men's swords to ashes. In fear of what they had witnessed, the men beg her for forgiveness and ask her to protect them from their brothers. Aseneth ensures their safety, and she convinces Levi and the other brothers to forgive the sons of Bilhah and Zilpah because men who worship God should not "repay evil for evil." In a change of heart, Levi also tries to save the life of Pharaoh's son, but eventually he dies. Soon afterward, Pharaoh also dies, and he leaves his crown for Joseph, who reigns forty-eight years in Egypt and then bequeaths the crown to a male relative of Pharaoh.

Genre

There are notable affinities between *Joseph and Aseneth* and a particular group of Greek novels (*Chaereas and Callirhoe* by Chariton, the *Ephesiaka* by Xenophon of Ephesus, *Leucippe and Clitophon* by Achilles Tatius, *Daphnis and Chloe* by Longus, and the *Aithiopika* by Heliodorus). These narratives share a similar plot in which two characters, a female and a male, fall in love, marry, and spend the rest of their lives in happiness after encountering a series of obstacles that prevent the success of their union. *Joseph and Aseneth* also utilizes literary themes and techniques similar to those that these novels employ; the heroine and the hero are portrayed as the best nobility has to offer, the narrative focuses on the characters' emotions in the unfolding of the plot, and the symmetrical relationship shared by the protagonists is used to advocate the social significance of marriage.

Joseph and Aseneth also reveals unique features when compared to the other Greek novels. Most obvious are (1) Aseneth's encounter with the angelic figure and the symbolic expression of her conversion to Judaism; and (2) the narrative's prescriptions for those who worship the God of Joseph: (a) polytheists must convert to the sole worship and allegiance to God Most High before marrying devotees of this god, and (b) anyone who reveres God Most High should not "repay evil for evil." These distinctions, however, have less to do with genre and more to do with perspective. The other ancient Greek novels are set within a polytheistic worldview, and their story lines do not defend affiliation to a particular cult. *Joseph and Aseneth* may presume a polytheistic setting, but it promotes a monotheistic worldview that requires a different sequence of events than that which other Greek novels present. Both protagonists must endorse this worldview, so Aseneth converts. Since Joseph's allegiance to God is well documented in Genesis 37–50, the work alludes to this characterization of Joseph and spends considerably more time developing the portrayal of Aseneth's devotion to God; accordingly, the focus on the male protagonist is less than what is found in the other Greek novels.

In addition, unlike the deities in other Greek novels, the sole deity in *Joseph and Aseneth* does not create obstacles for the protagonists; the causes for separation between the hero and the heroine are ascribed to other characters. Finally, the focus on the religious worship of Aseneth and Joseph and the instructional tone of this narrative relate to the social context of the initial audience; the work uses the Greek novel to construct the Jewish identity of its audience in Greco-Roman Egypt. All these modifications alter how the plot unfolds in comparison to the story line of other Greek novels, but they are not dependent on a different genre.

Second Temple Jewish Context

Joseph and Aseneth displays literary features and topics that echo what is found in other Jewish literature from the Second Temple period. The work is replete with imagery, phraseology, and characterizations from the Septuagint. It not only refers several times to the story of Joseph in Genesis, but it also incorporates several biblical texts (e.g., from Daniel, Ezekiel, Judges, Psalms, and Zechariah) in its formulation of Aseneth's devotion to God and in its presentation of her encounter with the angelic figure. Furthermore, it employs wisdom imagery in its portrayal of Aseneth's greatness (conveyed in the consumption of the honeycomb and the special status Aseneth is granted) and refers to other biblical texts in the presentation of the plot (e.g., Genesis 34 in chap. 23 and 1 Samuel 17 in chap. 27). It also expands upon the historical significance of Joseph in Egypt. In particular, it concludes with Joseph's long-term reign over Egypt, and this particular embellishment is shared by other Jewish texts from Hellenistic Egypt (e.g., Artapanus, Philo's *De Iosepho,* and Wisdom of Solomon).

Joseph and Aseneth also presents several points of contact between Hebrews and Egyptians and between members of Joseph's family that illustrate the challenge of constructing a Jewish identity in a culturally complex environment. Many Second Temple writers attempted to delineate a clear boundary for Jewish identity and to formulate a way for Jews to participate in a polytheistic society. *Joseph and Aseneth* contributes to this discussion by reflecting on the issues of intermarriage and the justification of retaliatory violence. It defines legitimate marriage only in terms of religious affiliation and practice, and by doing so, it is silent about the significance of heredity. In the second half of the narrative, members of Joseph's family shift their interpretation of when to refrain from retaliation, and the narrative promotes the forgiveness of even the most egregious acts (whether carried out by polytheists or by those who worship God Most High).

Textual Issues, Date, Provenance, and Authorship

Manuscripts, Original Language, and Transmission

As with other Old Testament Pseudepigrapha, text-critical issues produce several challenges for the dating, location, and authorship of the original composition. Currently, there are ninety-one manuscripts known to preserve all or a portion of this narrative; sixteen manuscripts are in Greek, and the rest represent versions in seven languages (Syriac, Latin, Armenian, Serbo-Slavonic, Modern Greek, Romanian, and traces of an Ethiopian version). Most scholars agree that *Joseph and Aseneth* was originally composed in Greek, but many disagree on which manuscripts best reflect the earliest form of the narrative.

The majority of scholars have depended upon the preliminary reconstruction by Christoph Burchard, but recently it has been argued that Marc Philonenko's reconstruction better represents the initial text (so Standhartinger 1995; Kraemer 1998). Both reconstructions, however, are problematic, and the transmission history of this narrative is much more complex than implied by the two reconstructions. When one compares the multiple witnesses, it becomes apparent that they exhibit both a uniform quality in the transmission of the work (i.e., they share in common the basic story line and much of the same imagery and phraseology) and a fluid quality in its transmission (e.g., some witnesses omit scenes and others embellish them). Nonetheless, one can reasonably reconstruct a detailed framework for the narrative that can serve as a reflection of the original composition.

Date and Provenance

The manuscripts date from the sixth to seventeenth centuries C.E., but most scholars agree that the archetype was produced earlier. Difficulties arise in proposing a more precise date because no other known literary sources from antiquity refer to the work, and the narrative itself does not provide any explicit references to the date of its composition. As a result, scholars place the origin of *Joseph and Aseneth* within a time period and social context that make best sense of the literary devices the work uses and the issues that it raises.

The extensive use of the Septuagint and narration of social tension in an Egyptian environment are the primary reasons why most scholars place the original composition in Hellenistic Egypt. Papyrological and epigraphical evidence confirm that a significant Jewish population existed in Egypt during this period, and several early Jewish writings are attributed to this region, especially to Alexandria (e.g., the works of Philo, *Letter of Aristeas,* and Wisdom of Solomon). *Joseph and Aseneth* is usually dated between 100 B.C.E. and 115 C.E. in order to provide a conservative estimate for the Greek translation of the biblical books that the work utilizes (at the earliest) and to account for the decimation of Jewish life in Egypt under Trajan's rule (at the latest).

The issues of date and provenance continue to be debated. Kraemer (1998) has argued for a much later date (third to fourth centuries C.E.) and a different location (e.g., Asia Minor or Syria), but her proposals have not gained widespread acceptance. Many of the reasons that she uses to place the work in late antiquity could also be used to place it in the Second Temple period (e.g., the significant role of the angelic figure and the royal representation of Joseph). Standhartinger (1995) agrees with the more commonly accepted date range, but she proposes that the work could have been written anywhere in the Greco-Roman Diaspora.

Jewish or Christian Composition

Equally consequential is the issue of original Jewish or Christian composition. Despite the current trend in Pseudepigrapha studies to give Christian authorship serious consideration, most recent scholarship continues to affirm that *Joseph and Aseneth* was written for a Jewish audience (Standhartinger 1995; Bohak 1996; Chesnutt 1995; Humphrey 2000; Burchard 2003). This position has been challenged by Kraemer (1998), who argues that it could be a Christian composition. Yet the fact that later Christian communities found this narrative appealing does not invalidate the more common opinion (see esp. Collins 2005).

BIBLIOGRAPHY

G. BOHAK 1996, *Joseph and Aseneth and the Jewish Temple in Heliopolis,* Atlanta: Scholars Press. • C. BURCHARD 1965, *Untersuchungen zu Joseph und Aseneth,* Tübingen Mohr-

Siebeck. • C. BURCHARD 1985, "Joseph and Aseneth," in *OTP* 2:177-247. • C. BURCHARD 1996, *Gesammelte Studien zu Joseph und Aseneth,* Leiden: Brill. • C. BURCHARD 2003, *Joseph und Aseneth,* Leiden: Brill. • R. D. CHESNUTT 1995, *From Death to Life: Conversion in Joseph and Aseneth,* Sheffield: Sheffield Academic Press. • J. J. COLLINS 2005, "*Joseph and Aseneth:* Jewish or Christian?" *JSP* 14: 97-112. • S. DOCHERTY 2004, "*Joseph and Aseneth:* Rewritten Bible or Narrative Expansion?" *JSJ* 35: 27-48. • C. HEZSER 1997, "'Joseph and Aseneth' in the Context of Ancient Greek Novels," *Frankfurter Judaistische Beiträge* 24: 1-40. • E. M. HUMPHREY 2000, *Joseph and Aseneth,* Sheffield: Sheffield Academic Press. • R. S. KRAEMER 1998, *When Aseneth Met Joseph: A Late Antique Tale of the Biblical Patriarch and His Egyptian Wife, Reconsidered,* New York: Oxford University Press. • M. PHILONENKO 1968, *Joseph et Aséneth: Introduction, texte critique, traduction et notes,* Leiden: Brill. • D. SÄNGER 1980, *Antikes Judentum und die Mysterien: Religionsgeschichtliche Untersuchungen zu Joseph und Aseneth,* Tübingen: Mohr-Siebeck. • A. STANDHARTINGER 1995, *Das Frauenbild im Judentum der hellenistischen Zeit: Ein Beitrag anhand von "Joseph und Aseneth,"* Leiden: Brill. • J. TROMP 1999, "On the Jewish Origin of Joseph and Aseneth," in *Recycling Biblical Figures,* ed. A. Brenner and J. W. van Henten, Leiden: Brill, 266-71.

PATRICIA AHEARNE-KROLL

Josephus

Josephus was a general during the First Jewish Revolt against Rome who later wrote historical, autobiographical, and apologetic works under the patronage of the Flavian emperors. His writings constitute the single most important source for Judaism in the early Roman period and, after the Bible, the most extensive ancient narrative of Jewish history.

Josephus was born Yoseph bar Mattityahu in Jerusalem in 37 C.E. Although his family did not belong to the small high-priestly circle, it must have enjoyed high standing in the city's hereditary aristocracy. Only so can we explain Josephus' Greek education, his dispatch to Rome on an embassy at the age of twenty-six (63-64 C.E.), his selection as regional commander of Galilee at the outbreak of war against Rome (late 66 C.E.), his land holdings in Jerusalem, and his network of high-level friendships in the city. After just four or five months of organizing Galilee's defenses against the 60,000-strong advancing Roman forces, by May of 67 C.E. he was driven back to the fortified hill at Jotapata (Yodefat). There he surrendered to Vespasian and his son Titus, after a siege of some weeks (July 1-2, 67). For most of the war he remained a captive, assisting the Romans with translation, interrogation, and negotiation, especially during the siege of Jerusalem under Titus' legions from May to September 70 C.E. After the city's fall, Josephus accompanied the victorious general, sailing back with him from Alexandria to Rome (71 C.E.) and observing the shared triumph of imperial father and son.

Before Vespasian's departure from Judea in 69 C.E., he reportedly freed Josephus from chains. At some point thereafter, Josephus received Roman citizenship and the traditional three-part name honoring his benefactors, "Titus Flavius Josephus." Although he uses only "Joseph(us)" in his writings, we know about the *nomen* "Flavius" from later writers, and it confirms the expected three-part citizen's name, derived from Titus Flavius Vespasianus (shared by Vespasian and Titus). Other benefactions from the imperial family, though not extravagant by contemporary standards, showed appropriate treatment of their dependent: at least initial accommodation in the family's private residence on Rome's Quirinal hill, some sort of maintenance money, and a parcel of land in Judea's coastal plains to replace the real estate in Jerusalem that had been spoiled by war and occupation.

As far as we know, Josephus lived the balance of his life in Rome. In the tradition of the retired statesman-soldier (though only 34), he began a literary career that would produce three substantial works in thirty books: the seven-volume *Jewish War* (mostly written by 79, completed by 81); the twenty-volume *Jewish Antiquities* with its appendix (*Life* of Josephus), completed in 93/94; and a sequel, the systematic treatment of Judean antiquity in two volumes known as *Against Apion.* Josephus may have died at any point from about 95/96 to the early second century C.E. A notice from the ninth-century Patriarch Photius puts the death of King Agrippa II, which Josephus mentions in his *Life,* at 100 C.E. Although the issue is still debated, most scholars think that this notice should not be given decisive weight, leaving Josephus free to have written his later works and to have died before 100 C.E. We have no way of determining his death date.

The *Vita*

The *Life of Josephus* provides a clear example of the difficulty of moving from story to history. In scholarship, this work has been thought to hold the key to Josephus' historical career for the following reason. At *Life* 40 and again in an excursus at 336-67, Josephus reports that his adversary Justus, a well-educated dignitary from Tiberias who later served on the staff of King Agrippa II, had written his own account of at least part of the war, in which Justus took issue with Josephus' *War,* especially as it concerned Josephus' behavior in Galilee. Scholars moved from that observation to the proposal that the entire *Life* must be a response to Justus, whose claims obviously stung Josephus. This appeared all the more likely because in *Life* Josephus often changes his story over against *War.* Now he claims, for example, that he was sent to Galilee with two others, to pacify the region, not as a sole general; his rival John of Gischala had much more understandable motives than *War* had allowed; and the delegation sent from Jerusalem to oust Josephus was much more important and well connected in Jerusalem than *War* had volunteered. Scholars concluded that if the entire *Life* responds to Justus, we are in a good position to figure out the historical truth: we not only have Josephus' preferred account *(War),* but we can reconstruct Justus' challenge by mirror-reading Josephus' responses. Thus, if Josephus claims to have rejected bribes and preserved every woman's honor (*Life* 80, 259), then Justus must have accused him on these accounts, and those charges provide a window into Josephus' historical career.

The fundamental problem with all this is that it ignores Josephus' own statements about his reasons for writing the *Life*. He introduces it at the end of the *Antiquities* as an autobiographical appendix, motivated by his desire to celebrate his credentials, including his ancestry, education, and events of his life; after that he will conclude his *Antiquities* (*Ant.* 20.262-67). Correspondingly, at the end of the *Life* (430) he declares that he will indeed now close the *Antiquities,* having surveyed the events of his life and offered material for assessing his character. The *Life* was clearly written as an autobiographical addendum to the magnum opus, to which it is joined in most surviving manuscripts, and it was understood by Eusebius to be part of the larger work (*Hist. Eccl.* 3.10.8-11). It did not need a separate motive.

The main reason for writing "lives" in antiquity was rhetorical, to demonstrate character with illustrative material. That is precisely what Josephus claims to be doing, and he follows the prescribed categories for such exercises, moving from illustrious ancestral pedigree (1–6) to prodigious education (7–12), to remarkable achievements in public life, featuring especially military exploits (13–412), to benefactions received from illustrious friends and bestowed on the less powerful. This is the material that constitutes his *Life;* he focuses on the five months between his appointment to Galilee and the beginning of the siege because that is the only period of his life from which he could illustrate his military-political achievements.

A standard technique in ancient rhetoric for exposing one's own good character was the polemical contrast with some convenient wretched person who behaved with despicable unworthiness. In the *Life* Josephus uses several such characters: Agrippa's commander Varus, his own priestly colleague, John of Gischala, the delegation sent from Jerusalem, and indeed Justus of Tiberias. But Justus is not targeted until near the end of the work, with a decisive turn to this new subject: "Having come this far in the narrative, I want to go through a few points against Justus, the very one who has written an *oeuvre* about these things" (336). It is difficult to see how Josephus' audiences could have understood him to be responding to Justus all along. He elsewhere demonstrates his ability to establish his targets at the outset of a work, when he devotes his work to combating them (*J.W.* 1.1-2; *Ag. Ap.* 1.1-5).

The *Life* thus appears to be Josephus' effort, in a rather hurried composition, to close his major work with an appendix "About the Author." His historical accounts have been an extension of his personal character and status, which he will now elaborate according to the accepted criteria.

If this approach to the *Life* is correct, the work does not (alas) offer us better historical traction than any other work. In fact, the text shows much the same relationship to the parallel stories in *War* 2–3 that *Antiquities* 13–20 shows in relation to *War* 1–2. In both cases Josephus exhibits an evident, sometimes breathtaking freedom in rewriting the story: rearranging the order of events, with sometimes different *dramatis personae* in different relationships to each other, and offering different moral evaluations. It is only more striking in *Life* because the subject is Josephus' own career. This freedom, although unsettling for historical work, accords with the prescriptions of rhetoric, particularly the mandate not to repeat the same things, and with his contemporary Plutarch's reuse of material in different ways (cf. also the Gospels, though by different authors). Josephus is unique only because we have such complete texts in which he retells the same events.

This new approach to *Life* tries to deal with his narrative as a whole, and this implies a concern also for the shape or structure. The structure of *Life* resembles that of his other works in that it reveals his taste for symmetrical or "periodic" (chiastic, concentric) design: matching opening and closing panels and then a movement toward and away from a central fulcrum, with paired "antiphonal" elements along the way. In the *Life* this is

Chronology of Josephus' Life

37	Born Yoseph bar Mattityahu in Jerusalem
53	Samples the three major Jewish sects: Pharisees, Sadducees, and Essenes; begins three years of discipleship with the desert ascetic Bannus
56	Returns to Jerusalem; joins the Pharisees in his public life
63/64	Leads delegation to court of Emperor Nero in order to secure the release of imprisoned Jewish priests; gains support of Poppaea Sabina, Nero's mistress
66	Chosen by revolutionary council to command Jewish forces in Galilee at the start of the First Jewish Revolt; opposed in Galilee by John of Gischala
67	Surrenders to Vespasian's forces at Jotapata (Yodefat) after escape from Roman siege; predicts that Vespasian will become emperor
67-69	Held in Roman custody
70	Acts as mediator in Roman camp during siege of Jerusalem
71	Resides in Rome under imperial patronage, with Roman citizenship and name Titus Flavius Josephus
ca. 73	Publishes Aramaic edition of the *Jewish War*
75-79/81	Publishes Greek edition of the *Jewish War*
93/94	Completes the *Jewish Antiquities* and his *Life*
post 93/94	Publishes *Against Apion* (a defense of Judaism)
post 95/96	Dies

particularly obvious because only the opening and closing sections have to do with Josephus' family life; they also both include a voyage to Rome, benefactions from the wife of a ruling emperor, and providential rescue (1-16, 414-29). As we have noted, the references to Justus and his rival account come near the beginning and near the end of the work (40, 336). At the one-quarter and three-quarter marks are two revolts from Josephus' leadership in Tiberias, stories that share strikingly similar features (85-103, 276-308). The delegation from Jerusalem straddles the middle section (189-332), and at the center of everything sits *Life*'s only dream revelation (208-9), furnishing divine confirmation of Josephus' mission. It marks itself as a fulcrum by the repetition of key terms in reverse order before (206-7) and after (210-12) the episode.

Observing such a structure takes nothing away from others that may operate in the narrative at the same time. Dramatic structure, in this case building to a climax in Josephus' final confrontation with the delegation (271-304), operates under its own logic. Concentric or ring composition is, however, a noteworthy aesthetic feature of Josephus' designs.

Josephus' Reception and Interpretation

In the ancient world members of the elite classes were educated to write in all genres, but always under the assumptions and principles of rhetoric (the art and science of convincing audiences). History was the statesman's genre par excellence: there he exercised his moral authority to expose the admirable and the execrable, to describe intractable problems and solutions, and to narrate catastrophes to be avoided in the future. Historians were valued not because of any independent verification of their accuracy, which was generally impossible, but because they were effective in conveying — by some combination of personal prestige, quality of writing, and moral appropriateness — a compelling account of human motives, foibles, and virtues.

In such a competitive context for the status of moral arbiter, it was natural that one author would typically win out and become "the authority" for his period. We know of several others who wrote histories overlapping with Josephus', two by name (Nicolaus of Damascus and Justus of Tiberias) and unnamed Greeks and Romans who treated the Judean war before him (cf. *J.W.* 1.1-8). But whereas all of those are lost to us (except in those places where Nicolaus' 144-volume history overlapped with Josephus' history), Josephus' thirty volumes have reached us intact. At some point he became the exclusive authority for Judean history and geography from King Herod to the end of the Judean-Roman war in 73 C.E. Photius apparently still had access to Justus' writings, but he favored Josephus against Justus, even parroting Josephus' dismissal of his rival, and Justus' works did not survive much longer. The die had been cast long before.

How did this happen? The initial boost provided by the regime's endorsement of Josephus' *War* seems to have brought him to the attention of Christian authors in the second and third centuries C.E., who cite him with increasing emphasis through Origen in the third century. The influential fourth-century bishop and court panegyrist Eusebius is crucial for Josephus' legacy, because of his extensive use of Josephus and because of his own subsequent importance as the "father of church history." Eusebius' exploitation of "the most distinguished of historians among the Hebrews" (*Hist. Eccl.* 1.5.3) reflects the general Christian perception of the time: here is an outsider who cannot be accused of Christian tendentiousness, who yet describes in lurid detail the fall of Jerusalem (predicted by Jesus, according to the Gospels, as divine punishment on the Jews for failing to accept Jesus), and who excoriates the failings of his own people in the process. Josephus' heartbreaking story of the starving aristocratic woman who cooked and ate her own infant child during the siege of Jerusalem (*J.W.* 6.200-214) was particularly useful to Eusebius and later Christian teachers, who wished to claim that the Jews, obviously capable of such depravity, had been justly punished by God and excluded from their heritage in salvation history. Josephus' incidental mention of Jesus of Nazareth (*Ant.* 18.63-64: the *testimonium flavianum*), which treats him respectfully — though our existing version has undergone at least a little doctoring in the manuscript tradition — led to its being cited even more than the story of Maria's cannibalism.

The problem was that Josephus himself had entirely different points to make about the fall of Jerusalem, and about Jesus and the countless other individuals he mentions — as a Thucydidean-Polybian sort of statesman lamenting political folly. Whereas a scholar such as Eusebius could exploit Josephus' lack of association with Christian belief for rhetorical traction, by interweaving large quotations with Christian claims as if the two were providentially compatible, other writers of the period felt that his factual material should be liberated from his "Jewish unbelief." So, later in Eusebius' century, the unknown author we call Pseudo-Hegesippus reworked the Greek *War* into Latin, inserting pieces from *Antiquities* but removing what seemed too Jewish (replaced by abundant Christian glosses), to produce an account of Jerusalem's fall that would be safe for Christian readers. Centuries later the opposite tack was taken by the Cambridge mathematician William Whiston, who in his celebrated 1737 translation of Josephus, still in wide circulation today, understood him to be an Ebionite Christian.

From late antiquity and the Middle Ages we have little or no evidence of Jewish interest in the writings of this famous priest. This can be explained by his surrender to the Romans under conditions that smacked of betrayal and cowardice; his writing in Greek and in isolation from the growing rabbinic literature based in postwar Judea, Galilee, and Mesopotamia; and his enthusiastic use by Christian apologists, albeit without his approval, against the Jews. The wide-ranging tenth-century chronicle known as *Yosippon* does nothing to alter this picture, for the name is a corruption based on a mistake; even if it does use material from Josephus along with many other sources, its readers were interested in the legends and not in Josephus. His legacy has remained one of suspicion in the Jewish world until the present, although this has begun to change in the past three decades under the combined force of dazzling archaeological finds, for which Josephus' narratives provide explanations, and a new effort to read his narratives on their own terms, free of assumptions about his life and morals.

The modern critical study of Josephus, from the mid-nineteenth century, was curiously parallel to Pseudo-Hegesippus in its concern to rescue Josephus' "factual material" from its narrative framework, though for different reasons. This time he was simply not considered a writer worth exploring. What mattered — as in most ancient texts for these early critics — were the sources he used, which should take us as close as we can get to what actually happened. Isolating and excising Josephus' sources appeared to be a straightforward exercise. First, the critic should remove the obvious overlay of self-aggrandizement and moral evaluation, the very things that Josephus wrote to provide. In any case, Josephus' moral universe was thought to consist of little more than the rhetoric of an opportunist and coward: the mouthpiece of Roman masters in *War,* who later gave up writing propaganda to dwell on his native traditions, but still did little more than stitch together the work of others and call it his own. Since a Judean priest could not have had a very deep knowledge of Greek literature and rhetoric, according to older assumptions, he could not have personally investigated, understood, or written most of what goes under his name. By assiduous alertness to repetitions, changes of vocabulary for the same object, doublets, apparent changes of outlook, and *hapax legomena,* one could hope to identify the "seams" of his editing work and reconstruct his sources for reuse on a more scientific basis.

New Approaches

The past quarter-century has witnessed a sea change in the scholarly use of Josephus. The most important catalyst for this change was the completion of the *Complete Concordance* in 1983, followed quickly by the development of electronic databases that include Josephus along with countless other ancient texts. These fundamental new resources disabled at a stroke all the guesswork and speculation about Josephus' tendencies and interests as an author, and about his use of sources; one now has to prove one's claims. At the same time, scholars influenced by what has been called "the linguistic turn" in all areas of the humanities — the insight that language is always constructed, never neutral, and that it is a significant problem to get beyond language to objective truth — now have the tools to explore Josephus' language. For the first time they can undertake sustained analysis of his diction, phrasing, and even incidental traits (particles, Atticizing forms, neologisms), also in comparison with his literary context. This close analysis has opened the door to considering long-neglected compositional features known from contemporary writing: rhetorical devices, paradox, polyphony, and irony.

This kind of study, which has energized the burgeoning field of "Josephus studies," has already demonstrated a general unity of language and thought across the Josephan corpus, and the surprising sophistication of those parts that have received intensive study. A negative consequence is that the old criteria for source criticism have been disqualified as rules of thumb: Josephus himself, it turns out, tends to vary language for the same object; to use A-B-A patterns, repetitions, and doublets; to change narrative voice or outlook for effect; and to use new word forms that happen to come into vogue from Plutarch onward — and so cannot be attributed to older sources. Since these traits are evident also in Josephus' autobiography, they must be deliberate and not a clumsy effort to sew together poorly understood sources. There is no doubt that Josephus used sources for most of what he wrote about, since he could not have known the events personally. Extracting sources from his finished work, however, may be as difficult as reconstituting the eggs from a baked cake. What we have now is his artful creation. It always remains possible that any particular oddity might be explicable as the vestige of a source, but our first obligation is to understand it as part of the composition; only if it does not seem to fit should we turn to sources (along with clumsiness, literary assistants, manuscript transcription errors, or later doctoring) as a possible explanation. Study of Josephus' language also undercuts assumptions about any radical differences of purpose from his earliest work to his latest: they show a substantial continuity of concern to articulate, defend, and even promote Judean law, custom, and character as contributions to human existence.

This new approach has direct implications in two other areas: the use of Josephus' works for historical study and our estimation of the historical man. As for history, it is no longer possible to imagine that some pieces of his narratives are simply neutral or factual, begging to be stripped out and presented in history books as facts. To remove elements from the story, in which words and phrases are chosen in relation to others, merely destroys their narrative meaning; it does not thereby produce facts. The logic of recent analysis drives us toward viewing Josephus' (and other ancient writers') historical narratives as artistic productions, not unlike historical films that we may watch today. In both cases the art undoubtedly derives from real events and lives, but we cannot simply move from the production to some underlying reality.

As for Josephus' life, it used to be that Josephus was understood first of all by presumed facts of his life story, especially his "betrayal" at Jotapata. He himself portrays his surrender at length and colorfully, with his miraculous survival of the murder-suicide pact he first agreed to, on the strength of his belief that he had a message from God. That story and much of his reported behavior before Jotapata have suggested to modern readers a distasteful duplicity and double-dealing with the people under his care. Scholars used to feel justified, on the basis of these facts, in dismissing his writings as opportunistic.

The new approach emphasizes, by contrast, that

we know nothing about Josephus' life apart from what he chose to include in his narratives. If we seek first to understand them, we quickly realize that the matrix of double-dealing and misleading the public, which he openly declares as his program (*Life* 17–22), was also part and parcel of elite political life in the Roman Empire: these were not democratic societies with an educated middle class and Enlightenment values. Josephus and his peers considered it their *duty* to mislead "the masses" as the situation demanded, appearing to support popular demands when necessary, seeking to terminate dangerous impulses when possible. Josephus must have portrayed his wily tricks and deceptions in the expectation of respect, not condemnation, from his audience. At any rate, since they are colorful literary creations, we cannot extract them from the narrative, judge them negatively by our ethical principles, and make them the basis for our views of the historical Josephus.

If we postpone our speculations about what may lie *beneath* Josephus' literary legacy, and turn our attention to exploring the surviving narratives in their literary and historical contexts, we begin to wonder at the impact they must have made on whatever audiences he was able to assemble in Rome. He first, in *War*, explained the tragedy of the recent war as a chain of small, typical situations and events that led to unintended consequences; in the process he tried consistently to redefine the standard postwar image of the Judean national character. About fifteen years later, in *Antiquities–Life*, he offered a detailed account of Judean history, culture, and law from creation to his own time, masterfully distilling a single story from the biblical narrative along the way. Again the focus is on the character of this people with such a rich and ancient heritage of noble laws. His final work (*Apion*) is a forceful and sometimes rollicking attack, apparently designed for the same amenable audiences, on writers who have disparaged the very aspects of the Judean character and constitution that his *Antiquities* had celebrated.

Notwithstanding both traditional Christian and scholarly (ab)use, it is becoming increasingly clear that we have in Josephus a major and energetic spokesman for Judean culture in the Roman period.

BIBLIOGRAPHY

P. BILDE 1988, *Flavius Josephus between Jerusalem and Rome: His Life, His Works and Their Importance,* Sheffield: JSOT Press. • S. J. D. COHEN 1979, *Josephus in Galilee and Rome: His Vita and Development as a Historian,* Leiden: Brill. • J. EDMONDSON, S. MASON, AND J. RIVES, EDS. 2005, *Flavius Josephus and Flavian Rome,* Oxford: Oxford University Press • L. H. FELDMAN AND G. HATA, EDS. 1987, *Josephus, Judaism, and Christianity,* Detroit: Wayne State University Press. • L. H. FELDMAN AND G. HATA, EDS. 1989, *Josephus, the Bible, and History,* Detroit: Wayne State University Press • M. HADAS-LEBEL 1993, *Flavius Josephus: Eyewitness to Rome's First-Century Conquest of Judea,* New York: Macmillan. • R. LAQUEUR 1920, *Der Jüdische Historiker Flavius Josephus: Ein Biographischer Versuch auf Neuer Quellenkritischer Grundlage,* Gießen: Münchow [English trans. C. Disler at pace.cns.yorku.ca]. • S. MASON, ED. 1998, *Understanding Josephus: Seven Perspectives,* Sheffield: Sheffield Academic Press. • S. MASON 2001, *Flavius Josephus: Translation and Commentary,* vol. 9, *Life of Josephus,* Leiden: Brill. • S. MASON 2003A, "Contradiction or Counterpoint? Josephus and Historical Method," *Review of Rabbinic Judaism* 6: 145-88. • S. MASON 2003B, *Josephus and the New Testament,* 2d ed., Peabody, Mass.: Hendrickson. • J. S. MCLAREN 1998, *Turbulent Times? Josephus and Scholarship on Judaea in the First Century,* Sheffield: Sheffield Academic Press • J. H. NEYREY, "Josephus' *Vita* and the Encomium: A Native Model of Personality," *JSJ* 25: 177-206. • F. PARENTE AND J. SIEVERS, EDS. 1994, *Josephus and the History of the Greco-Roman Period: Essays in Memory of Morton Smith,* Leiden: Brill. • T. RAJAK 2002, *Josephus: The Historian and His Society,* 2d ed., London: Duckworth. • Z. RODGERS, ED. 2007, *Making History: Josephus and Historical Method,* Leiden: Brill • J. SIEVERS AND G. LEMBI, EDS. 2005, *Josephus and Jewish History in Flavian Rome and Beyond,* Leiden: Brill. • H. ST. J. THACKERAY 1929, *Josephus: The Man and the Historian,* New York: Jewish Institute of Religion.

See also: Josephus, Against Apion; Historiography; Josephus, Jewish Antiquities; Josephus, Jewish War

STEVE MASON

Josephus, Against Apion

The treatise known as *Against Apion* is the last of Josephus' extant works, written as a sequel to his *Judean* (or *Jewish*) *Antiquities* and in place of his previously advertised treatise on *Customs and Reasons* (see *Ant.* 4.198; 20.268). The familiar title *Against Apion* represents only one quarter of its content; it is only in the first half of book 2 that Josephus responds to the Alexandrian scholar and politician, Apion. Josephus never gives a label to this work, and its range of topics led some early readers to call it *On the Antiquity of the Judeans* (Origen) or *Against the Greeks* (Porphyry), or to describe it in some composite expression of its themes (Jerome). It was written toward the end of Josephus' life, at the earliest in 95/96 C.E. (i.e., directly after the composition of *Antiquities* in 93 C.E.), but possibly later in the 90s or even the early 100s C.E.; since there are no unambiguous references in the text to contemporary circumstances, and because we do not know the date of Josephus' death, a more exact dating is impossible.

Contents

The work takes its starting point from a skeptical reception of *Antiquities,* as some reportedly doubted Josephus' claims for the extreme antiquity of the Judean nation (see *Ag. Ap.* 1.1-5). Josephus' first major task (1.6-218) is to prove this antiquity, primarily through the provision of "witnesses" to the existence (and achievements) of Judeans from non-Judean sources. An initial prolegomenon (1.6-56) discusses the methods and sources of historiography, in particular the deficiencies of the much heralded Greek historians, whose apparent ignorance of Judeans cast doubt on Judean claims to antiquity. Josephus turns the tables on such critics by

JOSEPHUS, AGAINST APION

undermining all trust in Greek historiography, and praising the accuracy of Judean records (notably their scriptures, 1.28-56). After a brief explanation of Greek ignorance of Judeans (1.60-68), he then marshals his main witnesses, Egyptian, Phoenician, Chaldean, and even Greek (1.69-218). The Egyptian evidence, drawn from Manetho (1.73-105), concerns the "Hyksos," whose violent rule of Egypt Josephus artificially takes to refer to Joseph and the Israelite sojourn in Egypt. Phoenician evidence (1.106-27), from Dios and Menander, concerns the legendary connection between Solomon and Hiram of Tyre. The chief Chaldean witness (1.128-60) is Berossus, whose account of Nebuchadnezzar made passing reference to "Syrian" captives transported to Babylon. Finally, seven authors are collected in a medley of Greek witnesses (1.161-214): Hermippus (on Pythagoras' interest in Judean customs), Theophrastus (on the Korban oath), Herodotus (on the "Syrian" use of circumcision), Cheorilus (on a race of warriors from the "Solyman hills"), Clearchus (on Aristotle's encounter with a philosophical Judean), Hecataeus (on Jerusalem and Judeans in the early Hellenistic era), and Agatharchides (on the capture of Jerusalem by Ptolemy I). In several cases, Josephus has to force the evidence to find some reference to Judeans, and the long quotations from "Hecataeus" probably derive not from the genuine Greek historian but from a Judean author writing under his name (Bar-Kochva 1996). Even the genuine material concerns Judeans of no great antiquity, and Josephus often changes the topic of discussion to Greek admiration of Judeans. Nonetheless, the accumulation of evidence encourages him to think he has proved to any reasonable person's satisfaction that Judean history stretches back, as he claims, to a period well before the Trojan War.

In the second part of the treatise (1.219–2.286), Josephus takes on a different task, the refutation of a large number of "slanders" that have been leveled at the Judean nation from a variety of sources. In the first place, he gathers and critiques three related "Egyptian" accounts of the expulsion from Egypt of a diseased/polluted people, variously connected with Judean origins. Josephus first cites and refutes Manetho's legend of a polluted mass of Egyptians, banished to Avaris, but aided by invading "Solymites" in their sacrilegious ravaging of Egypt (1.227-87); his extended critique (1.252-87) is a model of ancient literary criticism. He then compares and contrasts the parallel accounts in Chaeremon (1.288-303) and Lysimachus (1.304-20), pointing out inconsistencies or absurdities in (his abbreviated versions of) their stories.

Book 2 then raises the vitriolic tone of the treatise with an extended discussion of hostile comments made about Judeans by the Alexandrian scholar, Apion (2.1-144). Apion had made mischievous comments on Judean origins that Josephus briefly refutes (2.8-32), but he had also given an extended account of Judean history in Egypt from Alexander onward, painting the Judeans as a rebellious element in the population, hostile both to the Ptolemies and to the Romans. Josephus provides a lengthy riposte to this version of history (2.33-78), with particular focus on relations with Romans, since Apion, a prominent figure during and after the Alexandrian riots of 38 C.E., had clearly cast aspersions on the loyalty and legal/political claims of Alexandrian Jews. A third part of Josephus' response (2.79-114) answers Apion's slurs on Judean cult and culture — that Judeans worshipped in their temple the head of an ass; that they conducted an annual ritual slaughter of a Greek, with a cannibalistic feast and an oath of hostility against Greeks; that their miserable history showed their insignificance and religious impiety; and that their food laws and practice of circumcision proved their "barbarian" character. Josephus' rhetoric here rises to its greatest heights in counter-invective, climaxing in a passage gloating over Apion's miserable death (2.141-44). Throughout he makes great play on Apion's "Egyptian" ethnicity, exploiting Greek and Roman stereotypes about that supposedly unstable people with their absurd animal cults.

The refutation of slanders continues through the rest of book 2, but in a different mode (2.145-286, considered by some a separate and third part of the treatise). Starting from the attacks on Judean culture by Apollonius Molon, Josephus provides a positive description of Moses' legislation and the structure of his constitution (2.151-89), emphasizing the unity of word and action, and the superior understanding of the nature, rule, and providence of God ("theocracy") offered by Moses. He then gives a summary of select laws (2.190-218), focusing on the Temple, on sexual/family laws, and on friendliness to outsiders. Josephus next expands his emphasis on Judean endurance (2.219-35), by comparison with the famous resilience of the Spartans. In the final part of this section (2.236-86), he answers Apollonius' criticisms of Judean religious and social separatism; with an amusing assault on Greek mythology (heavily dependent on Greek philosophy), he defends Judean religious difference but finishes on a positive note by claiming that Moses has long been imitated by Greek philosophers, and that Judean customs continue to be copied by ordinary observers. A final peroration (2.287-96) sums up the work and claims that no greater constitution could be imagined or invented.

Genre

The genre of the treatise is primarily apologetic; even the first part, the proof of Judean antiquity, is presented within the larger frame of response to scurrilous libels and hostile doubts. The work constitutes, in fact, the only known example of ethnic "apology" from antiquity, and the first Judean text explicitly formulated in this originally legal genre (see Barclay 2007: xxx-xxxvi). In overall arrangement, and in many of its individual arguments, its rhetoric is highly skilled, enlivened by effective point-scoring, amusing character assassination, and clever manipulation of classical tropes. While there is evidence of some dependence on sources (e.g., in the overlap of materials in 2.145-286 with Pseudo-Phocylides and the Philonic tract *Hypothetica*), the bulk of the credit for this rhetorical performance must go to Josephus himself, by now sufficiently proficient in the Greco-Roman rhetorical tradition to use it for his own purposes.

Setting, Audience, and Purpose
The treatise was written in Rome in a context where highly diverse opinions about Judean culture were in circulation. Anti-Judean stereotypes flourished (witness those recycled and embellished by Tacitus a few years later), and in 95 C.E. Domitian staged political trials against individuals accused of "drifting into Judean ways" (Dio 67.14.1-2); but the hostility expressed in both cases was the flip side of the evident attraction of Judean culture to some Romans. The treatise declares itself to be addressed to sympathetic non-Judeans (1.1; 2.147, 296) and also implies, by its assumptions about readers' knowledge, values, and interest, an interested non-Judean audience, more likely to be identified with the label "Roman" than "Greek." The actual audience intended by Josephus is another matter, much harder to discern, but may have included both non-Judean sympathizers (hardly those genuinely hostile to Judeans) and educated (Romanized) Judeans in Rome. If it had this double intended audience, its purpose was also perhaps twofold: to instruct, encourage, and confirm Judeans that they stood on robust cultural ground, with a constitution better than any other, and to attract support and interest from actual or potential sympathizers among the non-Judean population (probably not to gain proselytes, though that purpose cannot be ruled out).

Impact and Significance
The treatise was of interest and value to early Christian apologists up to and including Eusebius, but became so marginal to the Josephan corpus that it barely survived; its thin textual tradition is incomplete in Greek, and a large lacuna (2.51-113) is filled only by the sixth-century Latin translation. In the modern era, however, the text has proven to be extremely significant, for a variety of reasons. Some of its citations (e.g., from Manetho and Berossus) are very precious evidence regarding ancient authors otherwise barely extant, of great interest to experts in Egyptian and Babylonian history. Moreover, Josephus' collection of material displaying hostility to Judeans has provided the richest and most diverse source for scholarly theories on ancient hostility to Judeans (sometimes inaccurately labeled "anti-Semitism"), even though Josephus often misrepresents its sources and motivations. More positively, this full-scale "apology" for Judean culture constitutes our most informative source on the concerns and techniques of Judean apologetics, and Josephus' skillful use of Greco-Roman cultural tropes is a fine example of Judean accommodation, susceptible in part to the sort of cultural analysis employed in postcolonial criticism. Particular attention has been focused on his presentation of the Judean constitution (2.145-286), whose semiphilosophical agenda bears many points of contact with Plato's *Laws*. Josephus appears to coin the potent term "theocracy" (2.165), and his particular collection of laws, with their continuing stress on the Temple and the priests (2.190-218), remains an intriguing product of the post-70 era. His selection of these laws, and his comment on their moral and cultural significance, remains one of the most impressive attempts to present Judean culture in terms understandable and attractive to those reared in the Greco-Roman tradition. Comparing Moses' constitution favorably with both the Athenian and the Spartan systems, Josephus indicates how Judean culture outclasses all its rivals, and why it attracts imitation by both philosophers and the ordinary "masses." Finally, the specifically Roman accents of this treatise, in its political stance and its adoption of Romanized values, suggests a partial trend toward the "Romanization" of Judean tradition, at least as envisaged by this articulate and culturally sensitive Roman citizen from Judea.

BIBLIOGRAPHY

J. M. G. BARCLAY 2007, *Flavius Josephus: Translation and Commentary,* vol. 10, *Against Apion,* Leiden: Brill. • B. BAR-KOCHVA 1996, *Pseudo-Hecataeus "On the Jews": Legitimizing the Jewish Diaspora,* Berkeley: University of California Press. • L. H. FELDMAN AND J. R. LEVISON, EDS. 1996, *Josephus' Contra Apionem: Studies in Its Character and Context,* Leiden: Brill. • C. GERBER 1997, *Ein Bild des Judentums für Nichtjuden von Flavius Josephus: Untersuchungen zu seiner Schrift Contra Apionem,* Leiden: Brill. • M. GOODMAN 1999, "Josephus' Treatise *Against Apion,*" in *Apologetics in the Roman Empire: Pagans, Jews and Christians,* ed. M. Edwards, M. Goodman, and S. Price, Oxford: Oxford University Press, 45-58. • E. S. GRUEN 2005, "Greeks and Jews: Mutual Misperceptions in Josephus' *Contra Apionem,*" in *Ancient Judaism in Its Hellenistic Context,* ed. C. Bakhos, Leiden: Brill, 31-51. • A. KASHER 1997, *Flavius Josephus: Against Apion,* Jerusalem: Zalman Shazar Center (in Hebrew). • D. LABOW 2005, *Flavius Josephus Contra Apionem Buch I,* Stuttgart: Kohlhammer. • P. SCHÄFER 1997, *Judeophobia: Attitudes towards the Jews in the Ancient World,* Cambridge: Harvard University Press • L. TROIANI 1977, *Commento storico al 'Contra Apione' di Giuseppe,* Pisa: Giardini.

JOHN M. G. BARCLAY

Josephus, Jewish Antiquities

The *Jewish Antiquities* (or *Judean Antiquities*) is a twenty-volume primer of Jewish history and culture written by the first-century historian Flavius Josephus. Books 1–11 offer a paraphrase and reworking of the Bible, from creation to the return from the Babylonian Exile. Books 12–20 survey Jewish history in the Persian, Hellenistic, and early Roman periods down to the eve of the First Jewish Revolt against Rome.

Occasion and Date
Although the *Antiquities* turned out to be Josephus' *magnum opus,* he may not have initially intended it as a separate work. He claims that he had planned to include ancient history already in the *Judean War* (*Ant.* 1.6-7), which he wrote in the 70s C.E. and completed before Titus died in September 81 (*Life* 363). In the course of preparing such a comprehensive history, however, he

JOSEPHUS, JEWISH ANTIQUITIES

realized that the older material was too copious and so crafted the *War* as a balanced monograph in its own right, with a matching beginning and end (*Ant.* 1.6-7). Presumably, this means that the first volume of prewar history, covering the Hasmoneans and Herod (*J.W.* 1), corresponded to the final volume on postwar events (*J.W.* 7). Reserving detailed treatment of the more distant past for a later study, alas, put him in the familiar writer's bind: the prospect of finishing the job was overwhelming. He credits a wealthier friend named Epaphroditus — a common name, not yet convincingly identified — with constant encouragement to complete the task (*Ant.* 1.8-9), something he achieved late in Domitian's reign (93/94 C.E.) at the age of 55 (*Ant.* 20.267).

Purpose

What exactly was Josephus' task in launching this separate major work? In speaking of his abandoned plan for a super-*War,* he relates that he had intended to discuss there "*who the Judeans were* from the beginning, what fortunes they had experienced, under what sort of lawgiver they were trained for piety and the exercise of the other virtues, and the number of the wars they had fought in the long ages past" before the recent conflict (*Ant.* 1.6; note the martial emphasis). This, then, is what he will narrate in the *Antiquities.* In casting about for a model of presenting Judean culture to foreigners, he seizes upon the high priest Eleazar, who had reportedly authorized the Greek translation of Scripture at the request of King Ptolemy II (cf. *Letter of Aristeas* 33). What Eleazar had given the king, in keeping with the Judean tradition of "not jealously hoarding beautiful things," was a Greek version of "our law and the framework of our constitution" (*Ant.* 1.10-11). Josephus brings all this together by declaring that his object now is to imitate Eleazar's magnanimity but also to go further: to render not only the laws but all the Judean sacred writings into Greek, thus presenting a history of "many strange undoings, fortunes of war, manly achievements of generals, and reversals of constitution" (*Ant.* 1.13; note again the military emphasis). He stresses the moral lesson to be learned from such an account: that those who follow these ancient prescriptions, which also embody the laws of nature, find success and happiness, whereas those who depart from them meet disaster (*Ant.* 1.14-50, 20).

This opening prospectus is striking for a number of reasons. First, it highlights the much overlooked connection between *Antiquities* and *War* in Josephus' conception. He begins *Antiquities* by recalling his reasons for writing *War* (*Ant.* 1.1-4) and assumes his audience's knowledge of the earlier work as he often refers to it for detailed information (*Ant.* 1.203; 13.173, 298; 18.11, 259). He thus offers *Antiquities* as a sort of prequel containing the earlier history. Most important is the connection of theme and tone between the two works. *War* had aimed at defending the Judean character from predictable calumnies following the catastrophe of 70 C.E. (*J.W.* 1.1-2, 6-8; *Ant.* 1.3-4). There Josephus foregrounded the Judean virtues — not given much exposure in other accounts — of manly courage, toughness, and contempt for death. Conspicuous in the above descriptions of *Antiquities* is the role of wars, generals, and manly deeds in the ancient Judean past. (The Greek and Latin words for "virtue" both meant, in the first instance, "manliness.") Just as *War* had sought to explore the Judeans' character from the recent conflict, so *Antiquities* will show "who they were *from the beginning.*"

This is where the language of "constitution" comes into play. Among Greek ethnographers, from at least a half-millennium before Josephus' time, it was a common assumption that the many peoples of the inhabited earth *(oikoumenē)* had different characters as a function of their diverse geographical and climactic situations, and that their various political constitutions, laws, and customs reflected those national characters. In some tension with this idea was the equally common view that constitutions were inherently unstable, constantly progressing and regressing in cycles, with monarchy degenerating to tyranny, democracy to mob rule, and aristocracy to oligarchy, so that each type yielded over time to another. Josephus sits on both sides of this fence, highlighting in the prologue *both* the superiority of the apparently unchanging Judean constitution *and* its many vicissitudes over time.

Intended Audience

A final noteworthy feature of *Antiquities'* prologue is its tone of outreach. In contrast to *War* and *Apion,* where he claims to feel compelled to counter the denouncers of his people, Josephus presents the *Antiquities* as a gift to a Greek-speaking audience that has demanded it (*Ant.* 1.5). This raises the question: Was he really writing for outsiders, or following the well-known apologist's tactic of "preaching to the converted" by appearing to address foreigners? If we lay aside his programmatic statements about writing for non-Jews (*Ant.* 1.5, 9; 20.262), which might have been easily added for rhetorical purposes, even in the most inconspicuous places the narrative sustains the impression that its expected audience was not Jewish. As in *War,* Josephus assumes that his audience knows Roman reference points but feels compelled to explain even the most basic elements of Judean culture, such as Sabbath, circumcision, and priesthood (*Ant.* 1.128-29; 3.317; 13.171, 297; 14.1-3, 186-87; 16.175; 17.254). He supports his account wherever possible with reference to non-Jewish evidence, makes frequent comparisons with Greek traditions, and feels it necessary to introduce the Judean laws or "constitution" with great care (*Ant.* 3.90-92, 222-86; 4.194-319). His consciousness of writing for outsiders is perhaps clearest when he concedes that he has had to rearrange the biblical text — in case any of his countrymen should happen to see this and complain (4.197).

But were there significant numbers of Gentiles in Rome so keen to learn of Judean culture that they would have remained alert through *Antiquities'* twenty volumes, let alone insisted that Josephus complete the work? As it happens, a surprisingly large proportion of the small amount of evidence we have concerning

Judean culture in the capital at Josephus' time reflects a certain fascination in some quarters with Judean ways. Tacitus speaks with disgust about those who are converted to these foreign customs, abandoning their native land, families, and ancestral rites to support Jerusalem (*Historiae* 5.5). Suetonius (*Domitian* 12.2) mentions as a noteworthy feature of Domitian's reign his ruthless collection of the tax payable by Jews after 70, even from those who either covered up their Jewish origins or secretly lived Jewish lives without confessing it (suggesting sympathizers or quiet converts). Cassius Dio claims that Domitian executed his cousin, a serving consul, along with many others for the "atheism" implicit in their adoption of Judean ways (67.14.2); he later reports that the emperor Nerva stopped hearing accusations against people who had taken up a Judean life (68.1.2). Finally, Epictetus and Juvenal independently seize upon conversion to Judean customs to illustrate some other moral point (Arrian, *Epicteti Dissertationes* 2.9.20; Juvenal 5.14.96-106); so the phenomenon must have been obvious enough. This concentrated evidence for committed interest from foreigners, in authors who say little else about Judeans, is confirmed by incidental remarks in Josephus concerning various Greek cities of the East (*J.W.* 2.463, 560). It may help to explain his decision to feature stories of conversion to Judean law and piety near the beginning and end of *Antiquities:* Abraham's adoption of monotheism and efforts to convert Egyptians (*Ant.* 1.154-68) matches the Adiabenian royal family's risky embrace of a Judean identity in the first century (*Ant.* 20.17-96).

Josephus presents *Antiquities,* then, as a primer in Judean law, history, and culture, brought over into Greek from the sacred records, for interested outsiders in Rome represented by Epaphroditus. The nature of his biblical paraphrase (books 1–11) has attracted the lion's share of technical research on *Antiquities.* On the one hand, his obvious adjustments to the Bible by way of omission, rearrangement, and sometimes major addition — for example, his much elaborated story of Joseph and Potiphar's wife or Moses' Ethiopian campaign — are usually attributed to novelistic or Hellenizing tendencies (though the latter invites the question, to what extent he actually thought in common Mediterranean categories, rather than consciously bending his material). On the other hand, his extensive reworking of source material has greatly complicated the assessment of his underlying biblical text. Did he follow the Hebrew text throughout, as he implies? (His proper nouns often differ in form from those used by the LXX.) Was his Hebrew text significantly different from our Masoretic text, and would this help to explain some of his divergences? Did he change his procedure from making an original translation at the beginning to exploiting existing Greek models, as he wearied of the project? If he used existing Greek texts, which ones did he have at his disposal? Was he influenced by Aramaic, targum-like paraphrases? To what extent did he, consciously or unconsciously, incorporate existing oral traditions into his retelling of the biblical story, and how much of the narrative is original with him? These issues remain debated.

With much more space available for the early history than *War* had afforded him, Josephus also takes the opportunity to expand, in *Antiquities* 13–17, what he had compressed into *War* 1. Books 18–20 include often quite different versions of episodes from the first half of *War* 2, supplemented by substantial new Roman and Mesopotamian material.

Although scholars have understandably been tempted to view *Antiquities'* postbiblical material as an afterthought, since the prologue envisions only a rewriting of the sacred texts, that possibility seems excluded by *Apion* 1.54. There, writing after the completion of *Antiquities,* Josephus continues to describe the work as nothing more than his Greek version of the Judean sacred writings. Evidently, that is what mattered most to him: the later material must have continued or illustrated themes from the trunk of the work.

Scholarship

As recently as 1988 a comprehensive survey of Josephus scholarship reported the near absence of studies on either the aims or structure of *Antiquities* as a whole. Indeed, *Antiquities* has provided the clearest case of the general scholarly neglect of Josephus' compositional interests, in favor of a preoccupation with his sources. Most early critics did not even ask about his authorial aims but dissected *Antiquities* into large composite sources (e.g., books 1–13 *en bloc*), which anonymous authors had allegedly prepared for other uses — probably in Alexandria — and they did the heavy lifting of which our author was thought incapable. Josephus, these scholars imagined in keeping with the assumptions of the day, found such material ready-made and stitched it into the work we now possess.

With the studies of Richard Laqueur and Henry St.-John Thackeray in the early twentieth century, this radical source criticism was replaced with a biographical proposal: that having written *War* in the service of Flavian propaganda, Josephus later repented of this betrayal and turned to explicating his nation's laws and culture in a defensive-apologetic vein. For this he needed new patrons to replace the imperial family: hence the appearance of Epaphroditus (though there is no reason why the Greek patron should not have been among Josephus' audience for *War*). More or less loosely connected with this influential theory of a reconversion to nationalism was a subsidiary proposal — dominant through the 1970s to early 1990s and still occasionally found — that Josephus wrote *Antiquities* to ingratiate himself with the budding rabbinic movement at Yavneh and reconfigured his political allegiances to do so, in particular promoting the Pharisees as rabbinic progenitors.

Every piece of evidence for this construction has been seriously challenged in recent years. Careful reading of *War* does not commend it as Roman propaganda; Josephus claims to be writing against such partisan works. Josephus himself stresses the unity of purpose between his two major works, showing no hint of embarrassment over *War. Antiquities* introduces the Pharisees very late in the piece (13.171) and treats them with general disdain. Josephus' understanding of legal practice *(halakah)* shows no consistent correlation with rabbinic prescriptions. Finally, scholarship on the early rabbinic movement increasingly stresses its isolation and limited influence before the end of the second or even third century. The field thus remains open for closer inquiry into the overall purposes of such a large work as *Antiquities.*

One problem in generating comprehensive interpretations arises from scholarly specialization. As academic interest focused intently on what lies beneath Josephus' narratives rather than on the finished works, those who treated the biblical paraphrase of *Antiquities* 1–11 were required to have skills in comparative scriptural interpretation, to be specialists in Hebrew and Aramaic, rabbinic literature, Dead Sea Scrolls, and "rewritten Bible." Excellent and finely grained studies of the biblical paraphrase therefore flourished, but quite independently of any concern for the *Antiquities* as a whole. On the other end, a Roman historian could publish an excellent translation and commentary of *Antiquities* 19, covering the death of Gaius Caligula and the accession of Claudius, but paying no attention to the narrative of which the story is a part (Wiseman 1991). This piecemeal approach seemed justified when the leading Josephus scholar of the early twentieth century declared *Antiquities* a "patchwork," artificially drawn out to twenty volumes, with whatever sources Josephus could find, in order to match the earlier *Roman Antiquities* by Dionysius of Halicarnassus (Thackeray 1929: 56-69).

But what would a real audience in the first century have made of the entire work? Would they have found it so disjointed? Would they have needed the skills of a biblical scholar with access to the Hebrew Bible, LXX, Dead Sea Scrolls, and other resources to understand the first half? Would they have reached book 12 and declared that the rest was not for them? Evidently not. Josephus takes pains to develop the themes announced in the prologue throughout the whole narrative, and he leaves clear structural markers along the way to make the narrative coherent and manageable.

Structure

As to structure, we have noted Josephus' evident care in designing *War,* as well as the thematic correspondence between books 1 and 20 of *Antiquities:* both are set in or near Mesopotamia and have to do with conversion. This correspondence is enhanced by Josephus' mention in the later story of Noah's ark, with the same language he had used to describe it in book 1 (20.24-26; 1.90-92). This suggests the same kind of symmetrical composition that his other works attest. *Antiquities'* unmistakable turning point, for example, comes precisely halfway through, at the end of book 10, with the fall of the First Temple and its implications for understanding divine providence *(pronoia)* — a marked theme of the work; book 20 ends on the eve of the Second Temple's destruction, referring the audience to *War* for the rest (20.258). Books 9–10 and 11–12 chart the path to the destruction of Solomon's Temple and its rebuilding afterward. Along the way, other matching panels command our attention: the elaboration of the peerless Judean constitution in books 3 and 4 corresponds to the Judean and Roman constitutional crises, caused by tyrannical monarchs and their succession woes, in books 17–19. The careers of King Saul (book 6) and King Herod (books 14–17) have striking similarities, as these outstanding representatives of manly virtue are undone by the fatal flaws of tyrants. The whole work thus reflects a coherent design. This design precludes the common but antecedently implausible assumption that Josephus made it up as he went along, filling the later volumes with a miscellaneous hodgepodge.

An Illustrative Theme: The Judean Constitution

The question of unity is decisively settled by the work's coherence of theme. Of the continuing themes from the prologue, one must suffice here as an illustration: that of the constitution, introduced above. In a later summary (*Apion* 2.287) Josephus reflects that he wrote the *Antiquities* in order to give a detailed account of the Judean laws and constitution. The prologue also establishes the theme as fundamental, and it remains prominent throughout. Thus at the end of book 20 he provides a summary of the constitutional changes, using the word *politeia* repeatedly (20.229, 251, 261): the nation began as an aristocracy, then was subject to monarchs (under judges and prophets), to kings, to priestly aristocrats again, to kings (later Hasmoneans and Herodians), and most recently to priestly aristocrats — including himself — after the removal of Archelaus in 6 C.E. Between the prologue and these concluding summaries, pointed asides keep the audience aware of the theme. It emerges that, although the form of government did change over time, its normative shape — so Moses and Samuel already insisted (*Ant.* 4.223; 6.36, 84) — was that of an aristocracy anchored in the hereditary priesthood (cf. 5.135; 6.267-68; 11.111; 14.91). The high priest offers effective leadership, with many advantages of a monarch but only as *primus inter pares.* This system obviates the two main pitfalls of kingship: the inevitable tendency to tyranny (cf. Herodotus 3.80) and the problem of hereditary succession; even if a king should personally avoid tyranny, children are often not like their parents (*Ant.* 6.33-34). Collegial aristocracy, by allowing the prominence of one leader but from within a group of families, affords the advantages of unified direction without either tyranny or succession woes.

With such rare and partial exceptions as David and Solomon, Josephus portrays kingship as a disastrous aberration whenever tried, leading as Samuel had warned to outrages against the law, tyrannical behavior — marked especially by the murder and plunder of the nobility — and the downfall of the state. Here, incidentally, is the important back-story of *War:* in the earlier work it was precisely individuals whom Josephus styled "tyrants" who revolted against the collegial priestly aristocracy and thus fomented the civil strife that led to Jerusalem's recent fall (*J.W.* 1.9-10). In both works it is the Hasmonean Aristobulus who transforms the government into a monarchy, with disastrous consequences for native rule (*J.W.* 1.70; *Ant.* 13.401). In *Antiquities* Josephus apparently devotes so much space in the later work to the world-famous King Herod (books 14–17) because his reign furnishes a case study in kingship: it was a crucible of tyranny, undermined by his perpetual anxiety about succession as he clung to absolute power in the present. Herod had constantly to rewrite his will and groom new successors from the offspring of his various wives, not least because he would tyrannically execute those who seemed eager to replace him. His many violations of the law led to his predictably gruesome death (17.164-92).

Josephus goes on to apply these same themes and language clusters to Roman rulers in the early decades of his life (*Antiquities* 18–19). Tiberius, who tyrannically sent more nobles to death, at his personal whim, than anyone else (*Ant.* 18.226), faced a bizarre succession crisis that produced the miscreant Gaius Caligula, who himself thrived on harassing the Senate and those of noble birth (19.2). His grisly end after a short tyranny, recounted in minute detail, illustrates the same divine retribution that had overtaken Herod. Most remarkably, Josephus gives full play to the senatorial discussion that followed Gaius' death concerning the need to restore aristocratic-senatorial liberty, and he as narrator joins the senators in painting *all* the rulers from Julius Caesar onward as tyrants (19.169-74). This is striking, unparalleled in Roman literature of the time, and opposed to the strategies taken by Seneca or Dio Chrysostom in advocating virtuous kingship as a model for the Roman emperor. It is a fascinating question how Josephus' clear challenge to Roman (as well as Judean) monarchy actually fared among a Roman audience at the time of Domitian's tyranny, only a couple of years before his assassination in 96 C.E.

This we cannot know; nor can we get beyond speculation about the relationship between such political themes and the interest of Josephus' Roman audiences in Judean culture. At any rate, the constitutional theme provides one rich vein of narrative unity in *Antiquities.* There are several others, such as interest in temple and cult, the historiographical and rhetorical interest in rounded portraiture and moral assessment, and the philosophical character of both Judean culture as a whole and its leading representatives (Abraham, Moses, Solomon, Daniel, and the philosophical schools). In the absence of an ancient category matching our "religion," this philosophical color both grounds the political analysis and facilitates the adoption of Judean ways. As Josephus remarks to his eager audience at the beginning of the *Antiquities* (1.25): "For those who truly want to explore the reasons for each thing [in the laws], the investigation would be rich and highly philosophical."

BIBLIOGRAPHY

H. W. ATTRIDGE 1976, *The Interpretation of Biblical History in the Antiquitates Judaicae of Flavius Josephus,* Missoula, Mont.: Scholars Press. • C. T. BEGG 1993, *Josephus' Account of the Early Divided Monarchy (AJ 8,212-420): Rewriting the Bible,* Leuven: Leuven University Press. • C. T. BEGG 2000, *Josephus' Story of the Later Monarchy,* Leuven: Leuven University Press. • C. T. BEGG 2005, *Flavius Josephus: Translation and Commentary,* vol. 4, *Judean Antiquities 5–7,* Leiden: Brill. • C. T. BEGG AND P. SPILSBURY 2005, *Flavius Josephus: Translation and Commentary,* vol. 5, *Judean Antiquities 8–10,* Leiden: Brill. • L. H. FELDMAN 1988, "Use, Authority, and Exegesis of Mikra in the Writings of Josephus," in *Mikra: Text, Translation, Reading, and Interpretation of the Hebrew Bible in Ancient Judaism and Early Christianity,* ed. M. J. Mulder and H. Sysling, Assen: van Gorcum, 455-518. • L. H. FELDMAN 1998A, *Studies in Josephus' Rewritten Bible,* Leiden: Brill. • L. H. FELDMAN 1998B, *Josephus's Interpretation of the Bible,* Berkeley: University of California Press. • L. H. FELDMAN 2000, *Flavius Josephus: Translation and Commentary,* vol. 3, *Judean Antiquities 1–4,* Leiden: Brill. • T. W. FRANXMAN 1979, *Genesis and the Jewish Antiquities of Flavius Josephus,* Rome: Biblical Institute Press. • R. LAQUEUR 1920, *Der Jüdische Historiker Flavius Josephus: Ein Biographischer Versuch auf Neuer Quellenkritischer Grundlage,* Gießen: Münchow [Eng. trans. C. Disler at pace.cns.yorku.ca]. • S. MASON 1991, *Flavius Josephus on the Pharisees: A Composition-Critical Study,* Leiden: Brill. • D. NAKMAN 2004, "The Halakhah in the Writings of Flavius Josephus," Ph.D. dissertation, Bar Ilan University [in Hebr.; Eng. summary at pace.cns.yorku.ca]. • E. NODET 1990, *Flavius Josèphe: Les Antiquités Juives,* Paris: Cerf. • S. SCHWARTZ 1990, *Josephus and Judaean Politics,* Leiden: Brill. • L. SEMENCHENKO 2002, "Hellenistic Motifs in the *Jewish Antiquities* of Flavius Josephus," Ph.D. dissertation, Russian Academy of Sciences, Moscow [in Russian; English summary at pace.cns.yorku.ca]. • M. SMITH 1956, "Palestinian Judaism in the First Century," in *Israel: Its Role in Civilization,* ed. M. Davis, New York: Harper & Brothers, 67-81. • P. SPILSBURY 1998, *The Image of the Jew in Flavius Josephus' Paraphrase of the Bible,* Tübingen: Mohr-Siebeck. • G. E. STERLING 1992, *Historiography and Self-Definition: Josephos, Luke-Acts, and Apologetic Historiography,* Leiden: Brill. • H. ST.-J. THACKERAY 1929, *Josephus: The Man and the Historian,* New York: Jewish Institute of Religion. • T. P. WISEMAN 1991, *Death of an Emperor: Flavius Josephus,* Exeter: University of Exeter Press.

STEVE MASON

Josephus, Jewish War

The first of the extant works written by the first-century historian Flavius Josephus, the *Jewish War* provides a vivid account of the conflict that resulted in the destruction of Jerusalem and its Temple in 70 C.E. The decision of Josephus to describe the work as the *Jewish War* (*J.W.* 1.1; *Ant.* 1.203; 18.11; 20.258; *Life* 412) has helped encourage the view that he was approaching the subject matter from a Roman perspective. Although the choice might indicate at least one possible target audience, a Roman readership, it most likely reflects the commonplace label being used at the time in Rome to describe the war, rather than the standpoint held by Josephus. It is clear that Josephus was not the first person, nor the last one, to write about the conflict (*J.W.* 1.1-2, 7-8; *Life* 336–38, 360). According to Josephus, there was an earlier version written in his native language, Aramaic, for

JOSEPHUS, JEWISH WAR

those Jews who lived to the east of the Roman Empire (*J.W.* 1.3, 6). The precise nature of the relationship between the original version and the extant Greek work is not possible to establish. Given the extent to which the *Antiquities* 1–10 "translation" offers a rewriting of the biblical narrative, there is good reason to view the Greek version as far more than a literal translation of the earlier work. As acknowledged by Josephus, the process of constructing the text in Greek required assistance (*Ag. Ap.* 1.50), a claim that appears to be confirmed by the fact that *Judean War* displays a greater sophistication and eloquence in style than any of the latter works.

Date

There is no external evidence indicating when the text was written. A number of internal markers point to a date during the reign of Titus for books 1-6 and suggest that book 7 was added during the reign of Domitian. The latest datable event is the reference to the Temple of Peace constructed by Vespasian (*J.W.* 7.158-62), which was dedicated in 75 C.E. In the context of asserting the accuracy of his version of events, Josephus claims he presented copies of the text to Titus and Vespasian (*Ag. Ap.* 1.50-51). If this claim is accurate, it is best understood as Josephus sending selected extracts of what was still a work in progress. Elsewhere, Josephus states that he sent material to Titus and Agrippa II in order to receive their letter of recommendation (*Life* 363–67). Titus has a much larger profile than Vespasian; he is singled out in the preface (*J.W.* 1.10) and then dominates the account of the siege of Jerusalem. Even more significant for determining the dating is the negative reference to C. Caecina Alienus (*J.W.* 4.634-44). Such a depiction was plausible only after 79 C.E., when Caecina was executed for allegedly plotting against Titus. The attempt to promote the prowess of Domitian (*J.W.* 7.85-88), along with the disparate nature of the subject matter, suggests that book 7 was added at some stage during Domitian's reign.

Contents

The arrangement of the work into seven books was the choice of Josephus (*J.W.* 1.30; *Ant.* 18.11; *Life* 412). He intended the work to rival other accounts, deliberately modeling it along classical lines (*J.W.* 1.1-2, 7-8). A detailed preface stakes his claim to be writing an authoritative account of the war, as a participant and eyewitness concerned to provide readers with the truth of what happened (*J.W.* 1.13-16, 22, 30). The background to the war is outlined in books 1-2. Josephus makes the assault on the Temple by Antiochus IV the starting point (*J.W.* 1.31-35). He then outlines the rise of the Hasmoneans and their subsequent rule (*J.W.* 1.36-170). The vast bulk of book 1 describes the life and career of Herod (*J.W.* 1.171-673). The first part of book 2 provides a brief account of the activities of Herod's sons and the two periods of direct Roman rule interspersed with the reigns of Agrippa I and Agrippa II (*J.W.* 2.1-276). The remainder of book 2 provides a detailed account of when and how the war began and the first moves by the main protagonists (*J.W.* 2.277-654). In book 3 Josephus describes the campaign of Vespasian in Galilee, with the assault on Jotapata, where Josephus surrendered, forming the main focus of the narrative (*J.W.* 3.141-408). There are four different areas of interest in book 4: the completion of the campaign in Galilee (*J.W.* 4.1-120), of which the capture of Gamla formed the key component (*J.W.* 4.2-83); the state of affairs in Jerusalem, with a particular emphasis being placed on fighting among the Jews (*J.W.* 4.121-409); the isolation of Jerusalem in preparation for the final assault (*J.W.* 4.410-90); and the fighting among the Romans that resulted in Vespasian becoming emperor and Titus being dispatched to lead the attack on Jerusalem (*J.W.* 4.491-663). The preparations for the siege and the detailed account of the actual assault on Jerusalem constitute books 5 and 6. The capture and destruction of the Temple dominate the narrative (*J.W.* 6.233-442). Book 7 is a rather eclectic collection of subject matter: the return of Titus to Rome and the subsequent triumph, which is described in detail (*J.W.* 7.1-157), interspersed with the description of several other revolts (*J.W.* 7.75-95); the aforementioned reference to the Temple of Peace; the capture of the remaining pockets of resistance (*J.W.* 7.163-408), of which the assault on Masada dominates (*J.W.* 7.252-406); and a brief account of the suppression of resistance in North Africa (*J.W.* 7.409-53). Josephus concludes his account with a short epilogue commending the work to his readers (*J.W.* 7.454-55).

Setting, Audience, and Purpose

The setting in which Josephus constructed the work is fundamental for any interpretation of what he wrote. Rome had been a city of much upheaval in its recent past. Romans had fought one another in the actual city in 69 C.E. in the battle for control after the death of Nero, with the symbolic temple of Jupiter destroyed in the process. The rebellion in Judea became an extremely important propaganda tool for the new Flavian ruler, Vespasian, to establish the credentials of his family to hold power, hence the triumph, the commemorative arch, coinage, and public buildings funded from the spoils. The decision of Titus and Domitian to continue to issue coinage celebrating the victory, and Domitian's construction of the now existing Arch of Titus, further reinforced the ongoing significance of the war. It is not surprising, therefore, that accounts of the conflict were in circulation and that Josephus, as a participant, decided to write his own version.

Josephus does not identify a target audience for his Greek version of the work. He asserts that the account was written in order to offer an accurate record of what took place (*J.W.* 1.6-8) and, in the context of explaining a long digression on the Roman army, that he wanted to discourage others from taking up arms against the Romans (*J.W.* 3.108-9). It is likely that Josephus saw his target audience as including Jews and interested Romans. Many Jews residing in Rome would have wanted to know more about what took place, especially given the public celebration and display of victory spoils from the war. At the same time, the numerous explanatory notes regarding Jewish customs and important historical figures, including Judas Maccabee, suggest an intended audience that was not familiar with the Jewish heritage. The submission of extracts to Agrippa II and to Vespasian and Titus suggests that Josephus wanted his work to be part of the public domain.

There has been a long-standing but misguided view that Josephus wrote his account as an instrument of Flavian propaganda. Crucial to this view are the exoneration of Titus for responsibility regarding the destruction of the Temple (*J.W.* 1.28; 6.236-66) and the numerous speeches of Titus pleading with the Jews to avoid allowing the Temple to become a battleground. It is important that these passages, along with the entire work, are read within the context of the contemporary literary and political environment. Criticism had to be veiled and expressed with due care since there was no freedom to voice opposition in an explicit manner. It is important to be open to reading Josephus' account of the war, and the role played by the Flavians, as one with nuance, in which irony was at play. Hence, although the inscription on the original Arch of Titus declared he was the first to capture Jerusalem (*CIL* 6.944), immediately after describing the destruction of the Temple in book 6, Josephus' reader was informed that the city had been captured on a number of previous occasions (*J.W.* 6.435-42). The work is a complex combination of a defense of the way Josephus and his associates behaved in the war and of the Jewish community at large as it sought to live under Roman rule in the postwar years.

Reception and Significance

Irrespective of who Josephus hoped would read and preserve his work, it was within a Christian setting that his account of the war received its most significant positive reception. Eusebius of Caesarea quoted large sections of the siege of Jerusalem as part of his claim that the destruction of city and its Temple were divine punishment (*Hist. Eccl.* 3.5.7; 3.7.1-9). Consequently, Josephus came to be regarded as an important source of the war. Assessment of what value should be placed on the text has been traditionally connected with discussion of the character of Josephus and the question of the way he used sources. The fact that Josephus, by his own admission, was a leader in the rebel forces (*J.W.* 2.569-71) who surrendered to the Romans (*J.W.* 3.383-408), and then offered advice and counsel to the rebels in Jerusalem that they should also surrender (*J.W.* 6.96-110), has often attracted strong criticism of his behavior. At the same time, Josephus has been criticized for relying heavily on the notes of Vespasian and Titus in constructing his account (*Life* 358; *Ag. Ap.* 1.56), and for uncritically drawing material directly from other sources (e.g., Nicolaus of Damascus).

There is no doubt that the text provides a rich resource of information on life in Judea in the first century C.E. and important aspects of Roman history, ranging from details of Roman military practice (*J.W.* 3.70-107) to the thorough description of the triumphal procession (*J.W.* 7.123-57). The various digressions, on topography and buildings, reflect an accurate knowledge of subject matter, and many of the archaeological excavations of locations described by Josephus have affirmed the general nature of his account. It is, however, important that material is not cited without due attention being paid to its context, within the text and within the political and literary context of Flavian Rome. Such elaborate elements as the speeches associated with major characters at key stages in the narrative indicate the extent to which the *Jewish War* is a crafted work (e.g., the speech of Agrippa II on the nature of Roman rule at the start of the war, *J.W.* 2.345-404). Most important, it must be remembered that the text was written after the event. The reconstruction of the situation in Judea before the war and of how the war unfolded was formed with the perspective of hindsight. It was written to explain how and why the disastrous events of 70 C.E. had taken place and what the future possibly entailed for the Jewish people. Josephus laid blame upon the Romans, depicting several governors as actively provoking the Jews to take up arms. He also interpreted what had happened as part of divine activity. God used the Romans as an instrument of punishment inflicted upon the Jews because of the actions of a rogue element within the community. Whatever claim to victory Rome asserted, Josephus assigned the control and direction of how events unfolded to the God of the Jews.

BIBLIOGRAPHY

S. J. D. COHEN 1982, "Masada: Literary Tradition, Archaeological Remains, and the Credibility of Josephus," *JJS* 33: 385-405. • G. HATA 1975-76, "Is the Greek Version of Josephus' *Jewish War* a Translation or a Rewriting of the First Version?" *JQR* N.S. 66: 89-108. • H. LINDER 1972, *Die Geschichtsauffassung des Flavius Josephus im Bellum Iudaicum*, Leiden: Brill. • S. MASON 2003, *Josephus and the New Testament*, 2d ed., Peabody, Mass.: Hendrickson. • S. MASON 2008, *Flavius Josephus: Translation and Commentary: Jewish War 1–4*, Leiden: Brill. • J. S. MCLAREN 1998, *Turbulent Times? Josephus and Scholarship on Judaea in the First Century CE*, Sheffield: Sheffield Academic Press. • J. S. MCLAREN 2005, "A Reluctant Provincial: Josephus and the Roman Empire in *Jewish War*," in *The Gospel of Matthew in Its Roman Imperial Context*, ed. J. Riches and D. C. Sim, London: T&T Clark, 34-48. • J. S. MCLAREN 2007, "Delving into the Dark Side: Josephus' Foresight as Hindsight," in *Making History: Josephus and Historical Method*, ed. Z. Rodgers, Leiden: Brill, 49-67. • F. PARENTE 2005, "The Impotence of Titus, or Flavius Josephus's *Bellum Judaicum* as an Example of 'Pathetic' Historiography," in *Josephus and History in Flavian Rome and Beyond*, ed. J. Sievers and G. Lembi, Leiden: Brill, 45-69. • J. J. PRICE 1992, *Jerusalem under Siege: The Collapse of the Jewish State, 66-70 CE*, Leiden: Brill. • J. J. PRICE 2005, "The Provincial Historian in Rome," in *Josephus and History in Flavian Rome and Beyond*, ed. J. Sievers and G. Lembi, Leiden: Brill, 101-18. • T. RAJAK 2002, *Josephus: The Historian and His Society*, 2d ed., London: Duckworth. • S. SCHWARTZ 1986, "The Composition and Publication of Josephus' 'Bellum Judaicum' Book 7," *HTR* 79: 373-86. • W. WEBER 1921, *Josephus und Vespasian: Untersuchungen zu dem jüdischen Krieg des Flavius Josephus*, Hildesheim: Olms. • Z. YAVETZ 1975, "Reflections on Titus and Josephus," *Greek, Roman and Byzantine Studies* 16: 411-32.

See also: Josephus; Jewish Antiquities

JAMES S. MCLAREN

Joshua, Apocryphon of

The *Apocryphon of Joshua* is an early Jewish work pertaining to Joshua, the successor of Moses. It is extant in various fragments among the Dead Sea Scrolls: 4Q378, 4Q379, 4Q522, 5Q9, and possibly in Mas 11 and 4Q123. It was initially called *Psalms of Joshua* because of 4Q379 frg. 22 ("When Joshua finished praying and offering psalms of praise . . .").

The contents of the *Apocryphon of Joshua* may be summarized as follows: (1) mourning for Moses (4Q379 frg. 14; cf. Deut. 34:8-12; Josh. 1:1-9); (2) transference of leadership from Moses to Joshua (4Q379 frgs. 3–4; cf. Deut. 34:9; Joshua 1); (3) crossing of the Jordan River (4Q378 frg. 12; cf. Joshua 3); (4) movement of the Ark of the Covenant (4Q522 frg. 8 col. ii; 4Q379 frg. 26; cf. Joshua 3–4); (5) curse on the rebuilder of Jericho (4Q379 frg. 22; cf. Josh. 6:26); (6) sin of Achan (4Q378 frg. 6; cf. Joshua 7); (7) blessings on or near Mt. Gerizim (4Q378 frgs. 15–17; cf. Josh. 8:30-35); (8) ruse of the Gibeonites (4Q522 frg. 9 col. ii; 4Q378 frg. 22; cf. Josh. 9:3-27); (9) standing still of the sun (4Q378 frg. 26, esp. line 5; cf. Josh 10:12-15); (10) summary of Joshua's victories (3Q379 frg. 3; cf. Josh 13); (11) lists of tribes and areas not conquered (4Q522 frg. 9 col. i; cf. Joshua 15–20); (12) mention of the levitical cities (4Q379 frg. 1; 4Q522 frg. 9 col. i; 4Q123?; cf. Joshua 21); (13) summary of the conquests (4Q378 frg. 11 [in Joshua's words]; Mas 11; cf. Josh. 21:43-45 [in God's words]); and (14) Joshua's final speech (4Q378 frg. 19 col. ii; 4Q379 frg. 17; Mas 11; cf. Joshua 23–24). The covenanters of Qumran may well have viewed the prayers and psalms in the *Apocryphon of Joshua* as actually uttered by the hero of the conquest.

In recent work Dimant has investigated three significant points of contact with other important traditions at Qumran (Dimant 2005). First, she considers the role of jubilee in the *Apocryphon of Joshua*. She calls attention to 4Q379 frg. 12, where the crossing of the Jordan River is described: "They crossed over on dry ground in the first month of the forty-first year of their exodus from the land of Egypt. This is the year for jubilees, at the beginning of their entrance into the land of Canaan" (lines 3-6). The link between entry into Canaan and the beginning of the sabbatical years is also made in the book of *Jubilees* (cf. *Jub.* 50:2). Dimant concludes that the *Apocryphon of Joshua* emanated from circles that valued the ideology of *Jubilees.*

Second, Dimant observes important points of contact between the *Apocryphon of Joshua* (esp. 4Q522 frg. 9 col. ii) and the *Temple Scroll* (esp. 11QT^a 56:13–59:21). 4Q522 provides a rationale for why Joshua was not able to erect the Tabernacle on Mt. Zion and underscores Joshua's fault by asserting that he did not consult the Urim and Thummim (4Q522 9 ii 10-11; cf. Num. 27:21). The book of Joshua says only that Israel did not consult God (Josh. 9:14). Dimant notes that the allusion to Num. 27:21 in this context coheres with 11QT^a 58:18-21, in connection with royal responsibilities. The *Apocryphon of Joshua* "apparently reworked the biblical story of Joshua from the perspective of the supremacy of the priesthood, a notion cherished by the Qumran sectaries and related circles" (Dimant 2005: 121).

Third, Dimant also calls attention to the "curse of Joshua" in 4Q379 22 ii 8-15, which contains a pesher on Josh. 6:26. She believes that a portion of this material has been quoted in 4QTestimonia (= 4Q175). The pesher of the *Apocryphon of Joshua* is similar to the pesher exegesis found in the sectarian scrolls.

These parallels suggest that the *Apocryphon of Joshua* stands between the sectarian scrolls from Qumran and the nonsectarian scrolls found there: it offers none of the distinctive terminology found in the sectarian scrolls, yet it presents ideas that were important to the sectaries of Qumran. This is so in the case of other texts, such as *Jubilees* and the *Temple Scroll,* which were not composed by the sectaries but hold to many compatible views.

BIBLIOGRAPHY

H. BURGMANN 1992, "Der 'Sitz im Leben' in den Josuafluch-Texten, in 4Q379 22 II und 4QTestimonia (Zusammenfassung)," in *Weitere Lösbare Qumranprobleme,* ed. Z. Kapera, Cracow: Enigma, 123-25. • D. DIMANT 2005, "Between Sectarian and Non-Sectarian: The Case of the Apocryphon of Joshua," in *Reworking the Bible: Apocryphal and Related Texts at Qumran,* ed. E. G. Chazon et al., Leiden: Brill, 105-34. • H. ESHEL 1991-1992, "The Historical Background of the Pesher Interpreting Joshua's Curse on the Builders of Jericho," *RevQ* 15: 409-20. • C. A. NEWSOM 1996, "4Q378 and 4Q379: An Apocryphon of Joshua," in *Qumranstudien,* ed. H.-J. Fabry et al., Göttingen: Vandenhoeck & Ruprecht, 35-85. • S. TALMON 1996, "Fragments of a Joshua Apocryphon–Masada 1039-211 (final photo 5254)," *JJS* 47: 128-39. • E. TOV 1998, "The Rewritten Book of Joshua as Found at Qumran and Masada," in *Biblical Perspectives: Early Use and Interpretation of the Bible in Light of the Dead Sea Scrolls,* ed., M. E. Stone and E. G. Chazon, Leiden: Brill, 233-56.

CRAIG A. EVANS

Joshua (Jeshua), the High Priest

Joshua (Jeshua) ben Jehozadak is historically speaking the first individual to bear the title "high priest" *(hakkōhēn haggādôl).* He appears in the books of Haggai, Zechariah, Ezra, and Nehemiah as one of the early returnees to Judah in the late sixth century B.C.E. after the Babylonian Exile, and is praised in Sir. 49:12 for his role alongside the Davidic governor Zerubbabel in rebuilding the Temple. Unlike his contemporary Zerubbabel, Joshua is not mentioned in the genealogies in Chronicles; however, his father Jehozadak appears in 1 Chron. 6:14-15 (Hebr. 5:40-41) as the son of Seraiah, whom 2 Kings 25:18 describes as "chief priest" *(kōhēn hārōš)* in the Jerusalem Temple at the time of Nebuchadnezzar's destruction of the Temple (587 B.C.E.). Seraiah was put to death (2 Kings 25:21), but Jehozadak is said to have been exiled (1 Chron. 6:15 [Hebr. 5:41]), and so if the Chronicler's information is correct, Joshua ben Jehozadak would have been the grandson of Jerusalem's last preexilic chief priest. As such, Joshua is often regarded as a member of the Zadokites, a group of priests associated with the Jerusalem Temple who during or soon after the Exile claimed the exclusive right to serve there (Ezek. 40:46), and who in light of 1 Chron. 6:1-15 (Hebr. 5:27-41) are traditionally associated specifically with the high priesthood.

Ben Sira's association of Joshua with rebuilding the Temple reflects the context in which Joshua appears in the books of Haggai, Zechariah, and Ezra. In the book of Haggai, Joshua "the high priest" and Zerubbabel the governor are addressed jointly by the prophet, who urges them to proceed with rebuilding the Temple (1:1, 12-15) and later encourages them and the people to keep on with the work (2:1-9). In Zechariah, Joshua "the high priest" appears in the so-called night vision (1:7–6:8), which scholars agree is related to the question of rebuilding the Temple, and he is also the subject of a prophetic symbolic act and oracle again related to Temple building (6:9-15). The book of Ezra, too, places Joshua (Jeshua) alongside Zerubbabel and associates them both with rebuilding the Temple (3:1-2, 8-13). Although there are chronological discrepancies between the Ezra and Haggai/Zechariah materials, leading to the question of whether the prophetic materials reflect the start of rebuilding work or its resumption after an earlier start and hiatus, the tradition that Joshua was one of those closely associated with rebuilding the Temple in the early postexilic period is clear.

Joshua's association with the Davidic governor Zerubbabel is often taken as an indicator of increased status for the postexilic high priest as compared with his preexilic counterparts, although caution should also be exercised so as not to read too much into what is really very little information. Certainly, both Haggai and Ezra show Joshua alongside Zerubbabel, but the main focus of the material where the two men appear together is Temple building, and it is only natural that the high priest would have a lively interest and involvement in such matters, since his very position depended on the existence of a temple in which to officiate. Indeed, the involvement of both Zerubbabel and Joshua in the context of Temple building is reminiscent of the relationship between monarch and chief priest in preexilic days, which would not in itself seem to indicate an increased status for the priest. The material in Zechariah is more suggestive. That Joshua's cultic responsibilities were an important aspect of his office is indicated by the vision in Zech. 3:1-9, where he is shown being symbolically cleansed and clothed anew for service, and is given oversight of the Temple. However, in addition to this, in 6:9-15 he is the subject of a prophetic sign (act) and oracle, whereby he is to be crowned (6:11), and an oracle is then delivered to him about the man called "the Branch," who will build the Temple and have royal honor (6:12-13). Commentators have assumed that the pericope in its present form reflects a significant increase in Joshua's status, perhaps after Zerubbabel's disappearance, but the links between this passage and Jeremiah 33 indicate that Zechariah 6 presents a picture of joint, harmonious rule between king and priest rather than the exaltation of priestly power (VanderKam 2004). A similar joint arrangement seems to be envisaged in Zech. 4:11-14, where a vision of two olive trees standing to the left and right of a golden lamp stand and supplying it with oil is generally understood to refer to Zerubbabel and Joshua as joint leaders. How long Joshua remained in office as high priest, or when he died, is unknown.

BIBLIOGRAPHY

B. HALPERN 1978, "The Ritual Background of Zechariah's Temple Song," *CBQ* 40:167-90. • P. REDDITT 1992, "Zerubbabel, Joshua, and the Night Visions of Zechariah," *CBQ* 54: 249-59. • D. ROOKE 2000, *Zadok's Heirs,* Oxford: Oxford University Press, 125-58, 197-201. • J. VANDERKAM 2004, *From Joshua to Caiaphas: High Priests after the Exile,* Minneapolis: Fortress, 1-42.

DEBORAH W. ROOKE

Jotapata

Jotapata was a village in Lower Galilee made famous by Josephus' account of the Roman siege there and his resulting capture during the First Jewish Revolt against Rome (*J.W.* 3.110-14, 141-288, 316-39, 340-408). It likely corresponds to the Yodefat mentioned in *m. ʿArak.* 9:6 as an ancient fortified site and in *Mišmārôt* 6 as the home of a priestly course. On the basis of Josephus' description of its location and topography (particularly his reference in *J.W.* 3.158-59 to steep slopes on all but its northern side), it has been identified with a site located approximately nine kilometers north of Sepphoris, midway between the Sea of Galilee and the Mediterranean Sea. Excavations in the 1990s revealed that it had been a thriving community prior to its destruction by the Romans. Left undisturbed for nearly 2,000 years, it is one of our best-preserved first-century-C.E. Galilean sites.

The settlement was founded in the late fourth or early third century B.C.E. when fortifications were constructed on the top of the hill. Coins minted by the coastal cities and the Seleucids suggest a predominantly western economic orientation. The site's numismatic profile shifted drastically, however, at the end of the second century B.C.E. At that point, the influx of Seleucid and Phoenician coins ceased and was replaced with the introduction of Hasmonean coinage from the south. This change probably reflects the incorporation of the region into the Hasmonean kingdom.

The community continued to expand until the revolt. Construction on the southern plateau may reflect an orthogonal design and thus a degree of civic planning. Houses were of various sizes and styles, some of them probably multistoried (Richardson 2004). One large elite residence was decorated with two frescoed walls and a frescoed floor. With their yellow and red panels, multicolored bands, and stripes, and their resemblance to marble, the frescoes are comparable to those in Herod the Great's palaces, Jerusalem mansions, and even the simpler designs at Pompeii. The presence of such decorations at a rural site is unusual. Architectural fragments such as column drums, a sizable doorjamb, and part of an architrave suggest the presence of a large, possibly public building. Most of the site's pottery consisted of Galilean wares, with almost no imported fine tableware. Other notable finds include an etched stone with images that have been interpreted as a crab and a tree-flanked mausoleum (Aviam 2004) and a Semitic ostracon, one of the few nonnumismatic inscriptions from first-century-C.E. Galilee (Adan-Bayewitz and Aviam 1997). Two *miqva'ot* (ritual baths) reflect a concern with Jewish ritual purity, as do the approximately 150 fragments of stones vessels that were found scattered across the site in both modest and sizable houses.

Two olive presses, three pottery kilns, and approximately 220 loom weights attest to a variety of economic activities and to a certain level of local self-sufficiency. Jotapata's vitality and growth in the first century C.E. undercuts theories that Galilee at that time was characterized by poverty and economic instability. Similarly, the Hasmonean coins (particularly those of Alexander Jannaeus) in its numismatic corpus (approximately 42 percent of the total coinage) and the sparse number of Herodian coins call into question suggestions that the first century C.E. ushered in the region's rapid monetarization.

Josephus describes Jotapata as the strongest of the Galilean communities he had fortified at the start of the revolt (*J.W.* 3.111; cf. *J.W.* 2.573; *Life* 188). He returned there from Tiberias in the late Spring of 67 C.E., shortly after the beginning of the Roman siege. To what extent he is responsible for strengthening its fortifications is unknowable, but it is clear that they had grown considerably since the village's Hellenistic foundation. Several walls, some of them of casemate construction, are securely dated to the time of the revolt. One was built over a pottery kiln, suggesting haste in construction; fill used to reinforce another wall included a ballista stone that had apparently been hurled into the town by Roman artillery.

Excavations recovered ample evidence of the seven-week battle: a siege ramp and earthworks on the northern slope; dozens of arrowheads, including some for use with catapults; numerous ballista stones made from local limestone; a rolling stone; possibly a Roman sword or dagger tip; and nails from Roman boots. Residences and cisterns across the site contained human bones, collaborating Josephus' depiction of a massacre, though not his impossible claim of 40,000 victims (*J.W.* 3.338). One cistern held the heaped remains of more than twenty people, including eight children. The settlement's destruction is securely dated by numismatic data to the revolt. Although a smaller village, Khirbet Shifat, sprang up at its base, Jotapata itself was never resettled.

As the Romans broke through the town's northern wall, Josephus sought refuge in a sizable pit (presumably a cistern) where he discovered forty other notable citizens in hiding. When these survivors were discovered three days later, Josephus' companions initially threatened to kill him if he attempted to surrender. He then suggested that the group commit suicide en masse, drawing lots to determine the order in which its members would kill each other. Whether by luck or ruse, Josephus' choice of lot left him one of the last two men alive, at which point they abandoned the plan. Climbing out, Josephus was taken to Vespasian, whom he flattered by predicting that both he and his son would be emperor. In doing so, Josephus secured not only his survival but also the favor of the Flavian family. History owes the ample information about early Judaism and the Roman world found in his books to his survival in a Jotapata cistern.

BIBLIOGRAPHY

D. ADAN-BAYEWITZ AND M. AVIAM 1997, "Iotapata, Josephus, and the Siege of 67: Preliminary Report on the 1992-1994 Seasons," *Journal of Roman Archaeology* 10: 131-165. • M. AVIAM 2004, "The Archaeology of the Battle at Yodefat," in idem, *Jews, Pagans and Christians in the Galilee,* Rochester: University of Rochester Press, 110-22. • W. S. GREEN 2001, "It Takes a Village: Preliminary Reflections on Yodefat in the History of Judaism," in *Religious Texts and Material Contexts,* ed. J. Neusner and J. F. Strange, Lanham, Md.: University Press of America, 141-49. • P. RICHARDSON 2004, *Building Jewish in the Roman East,* Waco, Tex.: Baylor University Press.

See also: Galilee; Gamla; Josephus; Revolt, First Jewish

MARK A. CHANCEY

Jubilees, Book of

Contents and Structure

The book of *Jubilees* presents a rewritten version of Genesis 1 through Exodus 19, including additions, omissions, changes, and rearrangement of the biblical text. The work consists of fifty chapters and generally follows the order of the biblical narrative. It is framed by an opening narrative that takes place at Mt. Sinai on the sixteenth day of the third month (1:1). According to both *Jubilees* and Qumran sectarian literature, this day is the morrow of the day of the covenant, on which God instructs an angel of the presence to dictate to Moses "from the beginning of the creation until the time when my temple is built among them throughout the ages of eternity." The angel follows God's command, proceeds to relate to Moses the stories of the Pentateuch until Sinai, and serves as the narrator throughout the entire composition.

While generally following the biblical order of events, *Jubilees* makes certain changes that are motivated by its particular chronological interests, in order to present a sequential story from creation until the entry of the people of Israel into the promised land. For example, the location of the sale of Joseph (34:10) is placed before the death of Isaac (36:18), in contrast to the biblical description according to which the sale of Joseph (Genesis 37) takes place after Isaac's death (Gen. 35:29).

The book can be divided by content into a number of major sections:

1. Chapter 1: introduction, narrative framework
2. Chapters 2–10: stories about Adam and Noah (primeval history)
3. Chapters 11–23:8: stories about Abraham
4. Chapter 23:9-32: apocalyptic appendix following Abraham's death
5. Chapters 24–45: stories about Jacob and his sons
6. Chapters 46–49: Slavery in Egypt and the Exodus
7. Chapter 50: Conclusion

While units 2-3 and 5-6 correspond to the stories in the Torah, sections 1, 4, and 7 are formally different from the structure of the Pentateuch and serve to frame the book, at the beginning, middle, and end. Sections 1 and 4 describe how Israel will "forget" the proper observance of the laws and will thus behave sinfully. Chapter 23 refers to inner-Jewish halakic tensions and even internecine warfare, between the "young" and the "old" in Israel, over the proper interpretation of the laws (23:19-20). Following punishment from God, Israel will eventually turn from its sinful ways and once again observe the laws and the covenant properly. This inner-Jewish halakic polemic perhaps offers a clue to the provenance of chap. 23, as originating in the "young" group whose proper understanding will eventually be confirmed (Kister 1986). While most of the stories in *Jubilees* correspond to the pentateuchal accounts in terms of their length, the later chapters are presented in a more abridged form. This is especially true of the Exodus narrative, which is condensed into chaps. 46–49, including the Passover laws in chap. 49.

Composition and Redaction

Most scholars posit that *Jubilees* is the work of a single author, but this assumption has been recently challenged, most extensively by Segal (2007), who proposes that the book is the result of redaction of earlier sources, including rewritten stories and other genres such as testamentary literature. The hand of the redactor can be found in the legal passages appended to the rewritten narratives, in passages with similar terminology to the legal passages (including chaps. 1; 2; 6; 23:9-32), and in the chronological framework. In its worldview, exegetical techniques, calendar, and halakah, the redactional layer is very close to the positions expressed in the sectarian scrolls from Qumran.

Date

Most scholars date *Jubilees* to the second century B.C.E., but they disagree over the precise period of composition and the cultural climate at that time. VanderKam (2001) dates the book to 161-140 B.C.E., with a preference for the years 161-152. In contrast, based on the absence of any mention of the decrees of Antiochus IV in 23:9-32, and on the polemical demand found elsewhere in the book to separate from the Gentiles, Nickelsburg (1984) suggests that the book was composed as a reaction to the Hellenistic reform in Jerusalem of 175 B.C.E. but before the decrees of 167 C.E. Kister (1986), on the other hand, suggests that the lack of mention of Antiochus' decrees in chap. 23 indicates that they had long passed and were no longer an issue; he therefore dates the book to sometime after 140 B.C.E.

Manuscripts and Versions

Jubilees was written in Hebrew, translated into Greek, and then from Greek into Geʿez (ancient Ethiopic) and Latin. Fifteen fragmentary Hebrew manuscripts have been preserved among the Dead Sea Scrolls; the oldest of them, 4Q216, is dated paleographically to about 125-100 B.C.E. This high number of copies indicates the special status of the book within the Qumran community. No direct Greek textual evidence is known today, although some quotations of the book have been preserved by church fathers. The entire book has been preserved in multiple manuscripts in its entirety only in Geʿez, while the Latin translation, partially preserved in one manuscript, contains approximately one-third of the original composition.

Notable Features

Jubilees presents itself as divine revelation, with God speaking directly to Moses in chap. 1 and an angel of the presence dictating the contents of the book to him from the tablets of heaven. The work is notable in a number of significant areas:

Laws before Sinai and Covenant

Throughout the book, various legal passages, based on the pentateuchal laws, have been juxtaposed to the pre-Sinaitic narratives. These laws are sometimes given as the result of a biblical character's actions (e.g., 16:20-31). In other instances, the pentateuchal law is described as already recorded on the heavenly tablets, and is either observed or not observed by the Israelite patriarch in the narrative. Thus in contrast to the Pentateuch, in *Jubilees* the laws were not first given at Sinai but rather at the time of creation, beginning with the presentation of the Sabbath laws to Israel (2:24-33). The specific laws presented were not selected for their own sake (although there is a preponderance of laws regarding the calendar and festivals) but as a function of the narratives themselves. For example, following the story of Reuben and Bilhah, *Jubilees* 33 presents a legal passage warning against intercourse with one's father's spouse and against sexual impropriety in general. Similarly, *Jubilees* 30 includes a polemical halakic passage against marriage with a foreigner, following the story of Shechem and Dinah. The retrojection of lawgiving to the pre-Sinaitic period is an outgrowth of God's election of and covenant with Israel from creation (chap. 2). According to the biblical conception, any covenant with God includes stipulations (e.g., Exod. 19:5-6), and thus from the moment Israel was chosen, there was a need for laws. The laws are recorded on the heavenly tablets, thus indicating their eternal nature.

The following is a list of the legal passages in *Jubilees:* (1) 2:24b-33; 50:6-13a: Sabbath; (2) 3:8-14: impurity of postpartum mother; (3) 3:30-31: covering of nakedness; (4) 4:5-6: murder; (5) 4:31-32: *lex talionis;* (6) 6:17-22: Festival of Weeks *(Šĕbūʿôt)* or Oaths *(Šābūʿôt);* (7) 6:23-38: calendar; (8) 7:1-6, 35-37: fourth-year fruits; (9) 13:25: first tithe; (10) 15:25-34: circumcision; (11) 16:20: Festival of Booths *(Sukkôt);* (12) 18:18: Festival of Unleavened Bread *(Maṣṣot);* (13) 21:5: sacrifices; (14) 28:6: marriage to an older sister; (15) chap. 30: marriage with a foreigner; (16) 32:9-15: second tithe; (17) 32:27-29: eighth day of Festival of Booths; (18) 33:9b-20: intercourse with father's wife; (19) 34:18-19: Day of Atonement; (20) 41:23-26: intercourse with daughter-in-law; (21) chap. 49: Passover.

Chronology and Calendar

All events from the beginning of creation until the entry into the land are dated according to a heptadic (sevenfold) system of jubilees (periods of forty-nine years) and weeks (periods of seven years). The book covers a "jubilee of jubilees" (fifty jubilees or 50 × 49 = 2,450 years) and culminates in Israel's liberation from slavery and the return to the promised land in the fiftieth jubilee (50:4). The periods used in the chronological framework are based upon the laws of Sabbath and jubilee years detailed in Leviticus 25. In the jubilee year, all slaves are liberated and return to their inherited land. *Jubilees* implements this law, which in its biblical context refers to the individual, on a national scale (VanderKam 2000). The bounding of the entire composition in a complete cycle of jubilees reflects an attempt to periodize history, a common practice in Second Temple texts. At the end of this period, when Israel returned to its land, a new period of history begins.

The same interest in periodization can be seen in the 364-day solar calendar promoted in the book (2:8-9; 6:32-38). The year is divided into four quarters of ninety-one days, each consisting of three months of thirty days, with an additional day at the end of the third month. Since the number 364 is divisible by seven, the calendar consists of exactly fifty-two weeks. Similarly, each ninety-one-day quarter consists of exactly thirteen weeks. This divisibility guarantees that the dates of the calendar remain consistent, always falling on the same day of the week. Each year (and each quarter within the year) opens on a Wednesday, the day on which the heavenly luminaries (especially the sun) were created. The same 364-day calendar was preserved in the Qumran Scrolls.

Angelology

Jubilees assigns an important role to heavenly beings in the administration of the world. The angels are divided into two camps, good and evil. Among the good angels, the angels of the presence and the angels of holiness are the "two great kinds" (2:18, according to the Geʿez translation). They were created on the first day of creation, together with angels of lower status, who are responsible for the forces of nature (2:2). The angels of the presence and angels of holiness assist God and his nation, Israel (18:9 [Abraham]; 48:11, 13, 15-16). The angels have observed the Sabbath laws with the Lord from the time of creation (2:17-21) and were created circumcised (15:27). The angels also have the responsibility of teaching humankind (3:15; 4:15) and serve as intermediaries between God and human beings (e.g., 3:1, 4-5, 12, 15; 4:6, 15; 5:6, 23; 8:10; 10:7, 10-13). In certain instances, an angel in *Jubilees* stands in place of God in the Pentateuch, most conspicuously in the narrative frame, in which the angel of the presence speaks to Moses at Sinai, dictating to him from the heavenly tablets. The general effect of the insertion of the angels into the stories is the distancing of God from the everyday events of the world, transforming him into a more transcendent deity.

Parallel to the good heavenly forces, there are also evil spiritual beings that operate in the world. The head of the evil forces is named either Belial (1:20; 15:33) or Mastema (10:1-13; 11:5, 11; 17:16–18:19; 19:26; 48; 49:2). Mastema's role in the Aqedah story (Genesis 22; *Jub.* 17:16–18:19) is identical to that of Satan in the narrative frame of Job, and *Jub.* 10:11 even refers to him as Satan. Evil spirits, the descendants of the Watchers (10:5), serve under Mastema's control in order to cause humanity to sin and bring about their punishment, possibly even death (7:27; 10:1-13). They are also responsible for the illnesses in the world (10:12-13). According to *Jub.* 10:1-13, God imprisoned the spirits in the place of judgment in response to Noah's prayer but released one-tenth of them at the request of Mastema. The evil forces are appointed over the nations, while God alone has responsibility for Israel (15:31-32).

Priestly Outlook

In the rewritten stories in *Jubilees,* the patriarchs behave like priests: Adam and Enoch offer incense (3:27; 4:25), and other forefathers (Adam, Noah, Abraham) bring sacrifices. When Jacob blesses his sons, Levi receives the preferred blessing (31:12-17), and in general he is elevated above his brothers in chaps. 30–32. Levi is the only one of Jacob's sons to inherit his father's and ancestors' books, "so that he could preserve them and renew them" (45:16). In addition, the laws of sacrifices and the cult are given special emphasis throughout the book (e.g., 7:30-32; 21:5-8). All Israelites are considered priests, apparently in light of the way the covenant is formulated in Exod. 19:6, which describes the entire people as "a kingdom of priests and a holy nation." This motif recurs a number of times in *Jubilees* and has also influenced a number of halakic positions taken in the book, specifically those regarding purity, impurity, and fornication (e.g., 20:4 [cf. Lev. 21:9]; 33:20). Based upon these considerations, it has been suggested that the author of this book was of priestly origins.

BIBLIOGRAPHY

R. H. CHARLES 1902, *The Book of Jubilees or the Little Genesis,* London: Adam and Charles Black. • G. L. DAVENPORT 1971, *The Eschatology of the Book of Jubilees,* Leiden: Brill. • J. C. ENDRES 1987, *Biblical Interpretation in the Book of Jubilees,* Washington, D.C.: Catholic Biblical Association. • M. KISTER 1986, "Concerning the History of the Essenes: A Study of the *Animal Apocalypse,* the *Book of Jubilees,* and the *Damascus Covenant,*" *Tarbiz* 56: 1-18 (in Hebrew). • J. KUGEL 2009, "On the Interpolations in the Book of Jubilees," *RevQ* 24: 215-72. • G. W. E. NICKELSBURG 1984, "The Bible Rewritten and Expanded," in *Jewish Writings of the Second Temple Period,* ed. M. E. Stone, Assen: Van Gorcum; Philadelphia: Fortress, 89-156. • M. SEGAL 2007, *The Book of Jubilees: Rewritten Bible, Redaction, Ideology and Theology,* Leiden: Brill. • J. VAN RUITEN 2000, *Primaeval History Interpreted: The Rewriting of Genesis 1–11 in the Book of Jubilees,* Leiden: Brill. • J. C. VANDERKAM 1977, *Textual and Historical Studies in the Book of Jubilees,* Missoula, Mont.: Scholars Press. • J. C. VANDERKAM 1989, *The Book of Jubilees: A Critical Text,* 2 vols., Leuven: Peeters. • J. C. VANDERKAM 2000, "Studies in the Chronology of the Book of Jubilees," in idem, *From Revelation to Canon,* Leiden: Brill, 522-44. • J. C. VANDERKAM 2001, *The Book of Jubilees,* Sheffield: Sheffield Academic Press. • J. C. VANDERKAM AND J. T. MILIK 1994, "Jubilees," in *Qumran Cave 4 VIII: Parabiblical Texts Part I,* DJD 13, Oxford: Clarendon, 1-140.

MICHAEL SEGAL

Judah

In the Hebrew Bible Judah is the fourth son of Jacob and Leah (Gen. 29:35), and the eponymous ancestor of the tribe of Judah. He plays a significant role in the Joseph story (Genesis 37–50), pleading with his brothers for Joseph's life and overseeing the activity of Benjamin in Egypt. His marriage to a Canaanite woman, the fate of his sons, and his sexual liaison with his daughter-in-law Tamar receive special attention (Genesis 38). In the Blessing of Jacob, Judah is described as a person of military prowess and the son from whom rulers would come (Gen. 49:8-12).

In the literature of early Judaism, 1 Chronicles lists Judah and his sons first in the genealogies of Jacob (1 Chron. 2:3–4:23), explaining that Reuben forfeited his leading place by defiling his father's bed and that Judah "became more prominent among his brothers and a ruler came from him," this last phrase referring to David (5:1-2; cf. 28:4). Brief mention of Judah occurs in Demetrius the Chronographer (ca. 250-200 B.C.E.), who gives dates for events in Judah's life (frgs. 2:3, 8, 27).

Judah receives more extensive treatment in *Jubilees* (late second century B.C.E.). Several nonbiblical stories highlight his military ability: he is blessed by Isaac (not Jacob) with might and to be a prince (*Jub.* 31:18-20); he assists Jacob in defeating a group of Amorite kings (34:1-9); and he plays a central role in subjugating Esau's sons, a tradition indicative of hostilities between Judah and Idumea in the author's own time (38:1-14). In his retelling of the incident with Tamar (41:1-28), the author of *Jubilees* rehabilitates Judah. Judah gives Tamar as a wife for his son Er from the daughters of Aram, not the Canaanites. Judah's failure to keep his promise to Tamar is now at the request of his Canaanite wife. And after his incestuous liaison with Tamar, he repents and is explicitly forgiven. *Jubilees* also recounts Judah's role in the Joseph story (42:1–44:10), though it omits the account of Judah convincing his brothers to spare Joseph's life by selling him to the Ishmaelites (34:10-11).

Praising the military might of Judas Maccabee, 1 Macc. 3:4 calls him "a lion in his deeds, like a lion's cub roaring for prey," probably an allusion to the blessing of Judas' namesake in Gen. 49:9. On the other hand, according to a nonbiblical story in *Joseph and Aseneth,* the sons of Leah, including Judah, annihilate the forces of their brothers, the sons of Bilhah and Zilpah, who were ambushing Aseneth, Joseph's Egyptian wife, but Levi and Simeon, not Judah, take the lead in the conflict. Among the Dead Sea Scrolls, 3QTJud? (3Q7), 4QTJud? (4Q484), and 4QTJud ar (4Q538) are apparently related to the later *Testament of Judah,* though Judah is not named in these fragments. In a Qumran sectarian document, his name does appear in the phrase "descendants of Judah," but in a fragmentary context (4Q177 iii 12). More substantially, another sectarian document, 4QCommentary on Genesis A (4Q252), quotes the Blessing of Judah — "A ruler shall not depart from the tribe of Judah" (Gen. 49:10) — as a basis for the expectation of a Davidic messiah.

Philo often refers to the meaning of Judah's name ("praise" or "thanks"; cf. Gen. 29:35). Thus, Judah symbolizes the man who makes confession of thankfulness, the highest virtue, so indicated by Leah ceasing to bear children after Judah (e.g., *Legat.* 1.80; 2.95-96; *Plantatione* 134–36; cf. Gen. 30:9); and because thankfulness takes a person out of himself — toward God — Judah is exempt from body and matter (*Leg.* 1.82). Further, Judah, who seeks the veiled Tamar, represents the lover of learning (*Congressu* 125–26); when he seeks to recover his pledges left with Tamar, he is one who seeks piety (*Fuga* 149–50); and the pledges by which he is identified symbolize God's work in the world (*Mutatione* 134–36). Twice Philo calls Judah a king (*Congressu* 125; *Somn.* 2.44). In the New Testament, Judah is listed in the genealogies of Jesus (Matt. 1:2; Luke 3:33), with Matthew specifically referring to Judah's sons through Tamar. The Epistle to the Hebrews notes that "our Lord" was descended from Judah, a nonpriestly tribe (7:14). And Rev. 5:5 calls Jesus "the lion of the tribe of Judah," echoing Judah's military prowess (Gen. 49:9).

Josephus, like Philo, draws attention to the meaning of Judah's name, "thanksgiving" (*Ant.* 1.304). He also embellishes Judah's piety in the Joseph story (though see *Ant.* 2.32-33). So Judah assures Jacob that he will take care of Benjamin on the trip to Egypt, but adds that "nothing could be done to him save what God might send" (*Ant.* 2.116-17). And he presents a long, impassioned plea to Joseph for mercy toward Benjamin and, going beyond the biblical account, offers to suffer any punishment — even death — in Benjamin's place (*Ant.* 2.139-59). Further, in Josephus' paraphrase of 1 Chron. 28:4 David says that Judah was appointed king (*Ant.* 7.372). Josephus, however, omits the story about Judah and Tamar. In contrast to Josephus, Pseudo-Philo says little about Judah: besides noting Judah's genealogical information (*Bib. Ant.* 8:6, 11), he explains that Tamar, wanting to avoid sexual relations with Gentiles, preferred intercourse with her father-in-law, who is left unnamed (9:5).

In the *Testament of Judah,* Judah recounts Jacob's

blessing that he will be king (1:6), and his might is on display through his victories over animals (chap. 2), Canaanite kings (chap. 3; cf. *Jub.* 34:1-9), and others (chaps. 4–7), especially the sons of Esau (chap. 9; cf. *Jub.* 38:1-4). He explains that because Tamar was a daughter of Aram, his Canaanite wife would not let his three sons impregnate her (chap. 10). Judah married a Canaanite only because of youthful impulses and the effects of strong drink that led to intercourse with her (chap. 11), as well as a large dowry of gold (13:4), but eventually he cursed her and she died in her wickedness (11:4-5). Moreover, he had intercourse with Tamar because he was drunk and she tricked him (chap. 12). In his exhortation to his sons, therefore, Judah warns against the beauty of women and promiscuity, the dangers of wine, and love of money (chaps. 13–26). Judah affirms that he repented of his sinful ways (15:4) and that God pardoned him because he acted in ignorance (19:3-4). Judah will be the forefather of a messiah from his line (24:1-6). Elsewhere in the *Testaments of the Twelve Patriarchs* Judah is identified as the one who received kingship (e.g., *T. Issachar* 5:7-8; *T. Simeon* 7:1-2) but usually alongside the declaration that Levi received the priesthood, to which the kingship was explicitly subordinated (*T. Jud.* 21:1-2).

BIBLIOGRAPHY

J. L. KUGEL 1998, *Traditions of the Bible,* Cambridge: Harvard University Press, 351-499. • E. M. MENN 1997, *Judah and Tamar (Genesis 38) in Ancient Jewish Exegesis,* Leiden: Brill.

KENNETH E. POMYKALA

Judaizing

The English verb "to judaize" derives from the Christian Lat. *judaizare,* which in turn derives from the Gr. *ioudaïzein,* "to judaize." The Greek verb, which is a compound of an ethnikon and the suffix *-izein,* belongs to the same family of verbs as *mēdizein,* "to Medize"; *kilikizein,* "to Cilicize"; and *hellēnizein,* "to Hellenize," a family of verbs with numerous exemplars in classical, non-Jewish, non-Christian Greek. These verbs typically have three basic meanings: (1) to give political support (a political meaning); (2) to adopt customs or manners (a cultural meaning); (3) to speak a language (a linguistic meaning). Thus, to illustrate, (1) "to Medize" *(mēdizein)* means to give political support to the Medes or Persians, that is, to side with the Medes (and "Medism," *mēdismos,* denotes political support for the Medes); (2) "to Cilicize" *(kilikizein)* denotes the adoption of the customs and manners of the Cilicians; and (3) "to Hellenize" *(hellēnizein)* means, in the first instance, to speak Greek, or to speak Greek correctly (and "Hellenism" means, in the first instance, pure Greek style).

The word *ioudaïzein* appears only five times in non-Christian Greek: once in a classical author (Plutarch, *Life of Cicero* 7.6) and four times in Jewish Greek (LXX Esth. 8:17; Paul, Gal. 2:14; Josephus, *J.W.* 2.454 and 562). The four non-Pauline passages can be satisfactorily construed with either the political meaning or the cultural, even though modern scholars almost always construe these passages with the cultural meaning. In the Plutarchean passage and the two Josephan passages, the political meaning seems preferable. *Ioudaïzein* seems never to mean "to speak Judean"; when Josephus wished to say "to speak Hebrew," he used the verb *hebraïzein* (*J.W.* 6.96).

Early Christian Usage

Paul's letter to the Galatians ("I said to Cephas before them all, 'If you, though a Jew, live like a Gentile and not like a Jew, how can you compel the Gentiles to judaize?'" [2:14]) is the only text in Jewish Greek to use the verb *ioudaïzein* unambiguously in its cultural sense. Here "to Judaize" clearly means "to live like a Jew." This passage was enormously influential; it bequeathed the word *ioudaïzein* and its cultural meaning to the Christian Greek of the following centuries. The word appears dozens of times, almost always meaning to adopt the customs and manners of the Jews. As in Gal. 2:14, the Jewish customs and manners that are meant are religious ones, observances that are prescribed by the Torah (circumcision, Sabbath and festivals, abstention from pork, etc.). Within this Pauline framework Christian writers invested the word with new meanings and new overtones. These new meanings are (more or less in chronological order from the second century to the fourth): to be a Jew or to become a Jew, to interpret the Old Testament "literally," or to deny the divinity of Christ.

To Be a Jew or to Become a Jew

This is a new usage of the word. In classical Greek *-izein* verbs mean not "to be" or "to become" but "to be like"; so, for example, *mēdizein* means not "to be a Mede" or "to become a Mede" but for a non-Mede "to behave like a Mede." Thus in classical Greek *ioudaïzein* could not mean either "to be a Jew" or "to become a Jew," but in Christian usage it does. This usage, which seems to occur first in Clement of Alexandria (ca. 150-125), reflects the Pauline equation of "the Law" with "Judaism." Adopting Jewish customs and manners was not merely to imitate the Jews, it was to become one of them. Observance of the Jewish laws was Judaism.

To Interpret the Old Testament "Literally"

For Origen (ca. 185-254) a Christian who observes the rituals of the "Old Testament" has been influenced (misled, Origen would say) by a literal reading of the text; Augustine would later expound the contrast between Christian spirituality and Jewish carnality, most evident in the Jewish "literal" reading of the commandments of the Torah. Jerome refers to *nostri iudaizantes,* "our Judaizers," Christians who apparently followed a literal reading of the biblical prophecies concerning the second coming and the end time.

To Deny the Divinity of Christ

Any Christology that was too "low," that is, that made the second person of the Trinity too inferior to the first, was attacked by its opponents as a "Judaizing" theology, and its proponents were dubbed "Judaizers." The reason for this is not so much that the Jews reject Jesus — after all, the Jews reject Jesus altogether, not merely Jesus' divinity — but that Judaism as a theological abstraction represents belief in a single undifferentiated God. Thus the Arian creed "there was a time when Christ was not" was deemed "Jewish." Not only Arius but Eunomius, Marcellus, and Sabellius were said to have "Judaized" through their denial of the preexistence and/or divinity of Christ. Sometimes they were even called "Jews."

In sum, when some ancient Christians describe other ancient Christians as "Judaizers" or call a Christian idea or practice "Judaizing," they are taking a position on a question of Christian theology; they are making a polemical statement against what, in their opinion, is *not* true Christianity. The valence of the word is invariably polemical and abusive. (Indeed, in classical Greek *-izein* verbs usually have an insulting or mocking tone.) Some modern scholars use these words when analyzing some forms of ancient Christianity, not fully appreciating that these terms are polemical, vague, and laden with enormous theological baggage. These terms are best avoided in modern discussions except, of course, in discussions of ancient texts that actually use these words. To call a Christian practice "Judaizing" is to label it and to polemicize against it, not to explain it.

Further, an ancient accusation of "Judaizing" does not necessarily imply contact with, or influence from, contemporary Jews or Judaism. Wherever *ioudaïzein* means to practice the rituals of the Hebrew Scriptures, or to interpret the Hebrew Scriptures literally, or to deny the divinity of Christ, the Judaism to which the verb is referring is in all likelihood just an abstraction of Christian theology, since for Christians Judaism represents the "literal" observance of the commandments of the Torah and an undifferentiated monotheism (as opposed to Christianity with its differentiated monotheism). In recent years many scholars have pointed to Christian "Judaizing" as evidence for the continued vitality and attractiveness of Judaism in late-antique society, but the argument is overstated. The Christian impulse to observe the "Jewish" laws of "the Old Testament" is generated by ideas and tensions that are internal to Christianity and does not necessarily spring from Jewish influence or a desire to imitate Jews.

BIBLIOGRAPHY

S. J. D. COHEN 1999, *The Beginnings of Jewishness,* Berkeley: University of California Press, 175-97. • L. H. FELDMAN 1993, *Jew and Gentile in the Ancient World,* Princeton: Princeton University Press. • M. MURRAY 2004, *Playing a Jewish Game: Gentile Christian Judaizing in the First and Second Centuries CE*, Waterloo, Ont.: Wilfred Laurier University Press. • M. SIMON 1986, *Verus Israel: A Study of the Relations between Christians and Jews in the Roman Empire AD 135–425,* Oxford: Oxford University Press for Littman Library, 1986). • M. TAYLOR 1995, *Anti-Judaism and Early Christian Identity,* Leiden: Brill.

See also: Adversus Judaeos Literature

SHAYE J. D. COHEN

Judas Maccabaeus

Judas, named Maccabaeus (Hebr. *makabi,* presumably from Hebr. *makebet,* "hammer"), was the leader of the Jewish rebels who disobeyed the decree of the Seleucid king Antiochus IV to abrogate the laws of the Jewish religion and the traditional cult at the Temple of Jerusalem. In 166 B.C.E. he became leader of the revolt after the death of his father Mattathias, who in the village of Modein (Modiin) had initiated the violent opposition to the religious persecution. Judas confronted Seleucid armies on the battlefield, was victorious in many engagements, and died in battle in 160 B.C.E.

Almost all we know about Judas comes from 1 Maccabees and 2 Maccabees. 1 Maccabees tells a bit about his family and recounts his military achievements (3:1–9:22). In the second half of 2 Maccabees (chaps. 8–15), Judas is the unquestioned hero. The two books depict Judas as a courageous military leader who defeated Seleucid armies and hostile neighbors.

Some of the sources used in the two books may have been witnesses who took part in Judas' battles and exploits. There may also have been an earlier life of Judas that was used by one or by both of them, as well as a combination of various sources adapted in each book according to its aims. Josephus' statement that Judas became high priest (*Ant.* 12.414, 419, 434) is unsubstantiated.

1 Maccabees is the principal source about Judas' family. Judas was the third among the five sons of Mattathias (1 Macc. 2:1-5), whose family belonged to the priestly order *(mishmār)* of Joarib. In the list of the twenty-four priestly families in 1 Chronicles 24, Joarib is first (24:7), but the list is probably not arranged in hierarchic order; the place of Joarib at its top is likely a later insertion intended to glorify the Hasmonean dynasty.

In Mattathias' deathbed testament, Simon is given precedence over Judas, but Judas is the one depicted there as "strong and brave from boyhood" (2:66). This characterization accords with the image of Judas in 1 Maccabees, but it does not do justice to other traits of his personality (see below).

In recording the battles of Judas, we follow the narrative of 1 Maccabees, whose author was a native Judean and was therefore more familiar with the Judean landscape and geography than was the author of 2 Maccabees. The first recorded battle of the Jewish rebels under the command of Judas was against a mixed force of local combatants and some Seleucid soldiers from Samaria. Judas ambushed them and as booty gained the sword of their commander, Apollonius (1 Macc. 3:10-12).

The second battle was against Seron, who was impelled to win prestige for himself after the unexpected defeat of Apollonius (1 Macc. 3:13-24). He entered Judea from the west, whereas Apollonius marched from the north, both of them striving to join forces with the army and the Hellenizers in Jerusalem. Seron's fate was similar to that of Apollonius.

These two defeats forced Lysias, who had been appointed viceroy and governor of the western part of the

Seleucid Empire when Antiochus IV went on an expedition to the East, to send a stronger army under more professional commanders to crush the revolt. This time Judas was confronted with a much more serious military challenge. In this battle his military ability was shown at its best: he took care to strengthen the morale of his men; he employed battlefield intelligence for planning his tactical maneuvers; he cunningly misled the enemy about his plans and tightened the discipline of his troops. The result of the Battle of Emmaus in 165 B.C.E. was a decisive victory of the rebels over a royal Seleucid army (1 Macc. 3:38–4:23).

The defeat of his commanders forced Lysias to confront the rebels himself. His army met Judas at Beth-Zur, at the southern border of Judea (1 Macc. 4:28-35). None of the armies won the day, and Lysias retreated to Antioch because of more urgent affairs (the death of Antiochus IV at the end of 164 B.C.E. and its consequences).

At the end of 164 B.C.E., Judas took advantage of this hiatus to enter Jerusalem, purify the Temple, and rededicate it. He also waged war to rescue Jews who lived outside of Judea and had been attacked by their Gentile neighbors. The chronological order of these battles is not clear, but they show the growing military power of Judas and the more daring exploits he was able to execute.

Judas also laid siege to the Akra but could not storm the citadel. The soldiers and the Hellenizers who were besieged there called on Lysias for help. Judas met him at Beth-Zechariah (1 Macc. 6:28-47). Lysias' army was more powerful than any of the former expeditions sent against the rebels and included war elephants. Judas was forced to end the siege on the Akra and was himself besieged in the Temple Mount. In spite of his dire situation, he succeeded in holding off Lysias, who was obliged to return to Antioch. Lysias had reservations about the religious persecution itself, and consequently he made a truce with the Jews and cancelled the decree that had set off the rebellion (formally it was cancelled by the boy king Antiochus V; see 2 Macc. 11:22-26).

The revocation of the persecution weakened the support Judas got from the population in Judea for the continuation of the revolt. He was victorious in some skirmishes against Nicanor, a commander sent by the new king, Demetrius I, to quell the revolt, but was finally killed in battle against Bacchides in 160 B.C.E. (2 Macc. 9:11-18).

Judas' achievements on the battlefield show his exceptional military talent as a tactician and strategist. He also showed outstanding leadership and political acumen by sending a mission to Rome to obtain a treaty (2 Maccabees 8). Our sources do not indicate whether he had acquired any military experience before the revolt, yet in view of his achievements it is a reasonable assumption that he had some military background. Judas' military and political activities had long-term results in Jewish history, and he became a paragon of national and religious liberation in both Jewish and Christian tradition.

BIBLIOGRAPHY

B. BAR-KOCHVA 1989, *Judas Maccabaeus: The Jewish Struggle against the Seleucids*, Cambridge: Cambridge University Press. • U. RAPPAPORT 2007, "Lysias — An Outstanding Seleucid Politician," in *Studies in Josephus and the Varieties of Ancient Judaism*, ed. S. Cohen and J. Schwartz, Leiden: Brill, 169-75.

See also: Hasmoneans; Maccabees, First Book of; Maccabees, Second Book of URIEL RAPPAPORT

Jude, Epistle of

The brief Epistle of Jude is one of two works in the New Testament presented as writings of a brother of Jesus (cf. Mark 6:3 par.; Eusebius, *Hist. Eccl.* 3.19-20). While by no means an uncommon Jewish name in antiquity, the Jude (or Judas) to whom this letter is attributed is identified further as the "brother of James" (v. 1) — an identification that makes sense only if the James in question is assumed to be immediately recognizable to the very general audience to whom the letter is addressed ("those who are called, who are beloved by God and kept safe by Jesus Christ"). As in the case of the Epistle of James, this is almost certainly James "the brother of the Lord" (Gal. 1:19), who was the most important among a number of relatives of Jesus who assumed leadership roles in the Christian movement after Jesus' death (1 Cor. 9:5; Eusebius, *Hist. Eccl.* 4.224; 3.19.1–3.20.7).

If, as some hold, the text is a genuine composition of this Jude, it would represent a valuable source of evidence for Jewish Christ devotion in first-century Palestine. Many modern scholars, however, suggest it is better understood as a later, pseudonymous work, not least because it seems to view the apostles as a past reality, not a present one (v. 17). In that case, its provenance is an open question.

The central concern of the letter is a manner of devotion to Christ about which little can be said other than that it was at odds with that espoused by the author. The authorial voice targets those whom it styles as "grumblers and malcontents" (v. 16), as "dreamers" who "reject authority" (v. 8) and create divisions in the group (v. 19). This combination may suggest that those targeted appealed to revelatory experiences, perhaps to counter the authority claimed for the author's own viewpoint. The fact that such people are said to "deny our only Master and Lord, Jesus Christ" (v. 4) and to "slander the glorious ones" — apparently a reference to angels — would seem to indicate that they were operating within a mythic frame of reference different from that assumed by the author. The significance of their supposed denial of Jesus should not be overestimated, however, since it is clear that they participated in the ritual life of the author's group (v. 12; cf. v. 4: "among you"). Perhaps, along with his characterization of them as "devoid of the Spirit" (v. 19), it reflects above all the author's sense that their rejection of his own viewpoint represents a rejection of Christ and disallows the possibility of their possession of a genuinely prophetic spirit.

It is similarly difficult to know what to make of the repeated charge that they "pervert the grace of our God" into a libertine immorality (vv. 4, 8, 16, 18), or that they are self-interested "flatterers" (v. 16) motivated by greed (v. 11). Such charges are stock features of an ancient invective typically hurled at rival teachers, and to which the apostle Paul, for example, was himself not immune (cf., e.g., Rom. 3:8; 1 Thess. 2:3-5).

Whatever the precise character of these rivals, the author aims to turn his readers against them. Fundamental to the letter's strategy in this respect is the identification of its own position as the original and apostolic one — "the faith that was once and for all entrusted to the saints" (v. 3) — and the portrayal of the rivals as interlopers who pervert it (vv. 4, 17-18), and indeed for less-than-noble reasons (vv. 10-11, 16).

Interestingly, however, the illegitimacy of the rivals (and, conversely, the legitimacy of the text's own position) is not established simply or even primarily by appeal to "the apostles of our Lord Jesus Christ" (v. 17) but to the Jewish Scriptures. The heart of the letter consists of a rapid-fire series of allusions to figures and events from those Scriptures, juxtaposed to the situation identified in the text in order to contextualize it and thus assign it meaning. The rivals are said (v. 11) to "go the way of Cain" (cf. Gen. 4:1-16); to "abandon themselves to Balaam's error" (cf. Numbers 22–25); to "perish in Korah's rebellion" (cf. Numbers 16). In this way they are framed as the latest manifestation of a long-standing type: people who knew God but went their own way and were ultimately punished for it. The text is particularly emphatic on this last point, offering a series of scriptural examples of God's punishment of such people: the "eternal fire" in response to the immorality of Sodom and Gomorrah (v. 7; cf. Gen. 18:16–19:29); the destruction of the Israelites "who did not believe" even after the Exodus (v. 5; cf. Num. 14:1-35; 26:64-65); and the chaining of the angels who did not keep their proper place to await final judgment (v. 6; cf. *1 Enoch* 6–21). The rivals' "slander" of "the glorious ones," further, is contrasted with the behavior of "the archangel Michael" who, according to a now-lost work apparently called the *Assumption of Moses,* refrained from slandering even the Devil when the two were engaged in a dispute (vv. 8-10). The text, finally, finds prophecy regarding the appearance of these rivals not only from the apostles (vv. 17-19), but already on the lips of "Enoch, in the seventh generation from Adam," in *1 Enoch* 1:9 (vv. 14-16).

Whether an authentic writing of Jude or, more likely, the work of a later author interested in claiming the authority of Jesus' brother for his own, this text is interesting not least for its use of works like *1 Enoch* and the *Assumption of Moses* as Scripture. If this caused consternation on the part of some of its later Christian readers, it apparently presented no problem for the author of 2 Peter, who incorporated substantial portions of Jude into his own composition.

BIBLIOGRAPHY

R. J. BAUCKHAM 1983, *Jude, 2 Peter,* Waco, Tex.: Word Books. • R. J. BAUCKHAM 1990, *Jude and the Relatives of Jesus in the Early Church,* Edinburgh: Clark. • A. GERDMAR 2001, *Rethinking the Judaism-Hellenism Dichotomy: A Historiographical Case Study of Second Peter and Jude,* Stockholm: Almqvist & Wiksell. • A. CHESTER AND R. P. MARTIN 1994, *The Theology of the Letters of James, Peter and Jude,* Cambridge: Cambridge University Press. • D. F. WATSON 1988, *Invention, Arrangement and Style: Rhetorical Criticism of Jude and 2 Peter,* Atlanta: Scholars Press.

MATT JACKSON-MCCABE

Judea

Geographic Extent

Judea or Judaea *(Ioudaia/Iudaea)* is a Hellenistic form for Hebr. *Eretz Yehudah* or "land of Judah," a region inhabited by a "Judean" *(Ioudaios)* or a "Jew" *(Yehudi).* There is no clear-cut geographic definition for the term "Judea." In the strict geographic sense, it relates to Jerusalem and the surrounding hills (the Hebron, Judean, Jerusalem, and Bethel mountains) and to the desert wilderness eastward to the Dead Sea, while in a broader sense it might be defined, following the Mishnah (*m. Šeb.* 9:2), as "Hill(s), Shephelah and Valley (= Coastal Plain)," including the mountains just mentioned, the hilly areas of the Shephelah to the west of Jerusalem, the Lod Basin, and the southern Coastal Plain from the Raphia region to Joppa (Jaffa).

The Mishnah (*m. Giṭ.* 7:7) marks Antipatris as the (northwestern) border of Judea, and rabbinic literature occasionally defines Judea as extending from this city southward to the unidentified settlement of Gevat (e.g., *b. Yebamot* 62b). Mishnah *Maʿaś. Š.* 5:2 seems to define Judea as the area included in all directions within a day's walking distance from Jerusalem: Eilat (= Mamre or Terebinthos [near Hebron]) from the south, Acraba(t) from the north, Lod from the west, and the Jordan River from the east.

Josephus sets the borders of Judea as the village of Anuathu Borcaeus (ten miles from Neapolis on the road to Jerusalem) in the north, the town of Orda (in the northern Negev) in the south, the Jordan River in the east, and Joppa in the west (Josephus, *J.W.* 3.51).

Both the geographic and administrative boundaries of Judea, as well as its demographic makeup, were often in flux, resulting in confusion. The same geographic and/or administrative terms might relate at times to either all of Judea or to part of it. For example, *Darom/Daroma,* literally meaning "south," could, during the Second Temple period and afterward, refer to Judea in the sense of "south" as opposed to "north" or the Galilee. However, this phrase could also relate to the southern Hebron Mountains or to Lod, all locations in Judea (Schwartz 1986: 33-41).

The original geographic connotation of Judah relates to the territory occupied by the tribe of Judah, essentially between Jerusalem and Hebron to the south, to the Dead Sea in the east, to the Shephelah in the west, and to the territories of Dan and Benjamin to north (Josh. 15:21-62). Josephus refers to this area as "Upper Idumea" (*Ant.* 5.81). Later Judah came to mean the "Kingdom of Judah," whose capital was Jerusalem —

The Judean Desert *(Phoenix Data Systems / Neal and Joel Bierling)*

the "Southern Kingdom" as opposed to the "Northern Kingdom" of Israel.

The Persian Period

During the period of the Restoration, Judah became the Persian province of *Yehud* (the Aramaic form of Judah/Yehudah), although it also might have still been known as Yehudah (Ezra 6:7) or even the province of the Judeans. The boundaries of this province were Bethel in the north, Beth Zur in the south, the Jordan River in the east, and the area of Emmaus-Modiin in the west (Ezra 2; Nehemiah 7), although the boundary line might have been further eastward (Lipschits 2005). These boundaries remained fixed until the establishment of the Hasmonean state under Jonathan, when they began to change in the wake of political developments, occasional Hasmonean success on the battlefield, and expanded Jewish settlement outside the borders of Persian-Hellenistic Judea.

The Hellenistic and Hasmonean Periods

The use of Judah/Judea as a geographic term and region continued into the Hellenistic period. Hecataeus of Abdera (ca. 300 B.C.E.) refers to "what is now called Judea *(Ioudaia)*" (*Aegyptiaca, apud* Diodorus Siculus, *Bibliotheca Historia* 40.3 [Stern 1974, 1:26 (#11)]); and Clearchus of Soli (c. 300 B.C.E.) states, "the district that they (= *Ioudaioi*) inhabit is known as *Ioudaia* (*De Somno, apud* Josephus *Ag. Ap.* 1.179 [Stern 1974, 1:49 (#15)]).

At first, "Judea" remained basically contiguous with some form of the "land of Judah," in contradistinction to other geographic (or administrative) regions of the land of Israel such as the Galilee or the Perea (*m. Šeb.* 9:2).

Jonathan received from opposing Seleucid kings the area of Accaron (Ekron) in the Coastal Plain, and the toparchies of Lod, Arimathea (Ramathaim), and Apharaema (Ephraim) were transferred from southern Samaria and became part of northern Judea (1 Macc. 10:30, 38, 89; 11:28, 34, 57). His brother Simon conquered Gazara (Gezer) and turned Joppa into a Jewish port, extending "Jewish Judea" to the sea (1 Macc. 12:43, 47-48; 14:4; 15:19).

John Hyrcanus extended the boundaries of "Jewish Judea" outside of Judea proper, conquering portions of the Perea and Samaria. He annexed Idumea to Judea, forcing the Idumeans to convert or leave; most seemed to have preferred the former and stayed (Josephus, *Ant.* 13.257-58). The coastal cities of Jamnia (Yavneh) and Azotus (Ashdod) were also conquered. Acraba in eastern Samaria, formerly on the border of Judea, was transferred to it (*Ant.* 13.337-38).

Most of the conquests of Aristobolus and Alexander Jannaeus were far removed from geographic Judea, except for the conquest of Gaza and its environs by Jannaeus (*Ant.* 13.357-64; *J.W.* 1.87).

Roman Period

Many of the areas technically far outside of Judea conquered by Jannaeus or by Herod became part of *Provincia Judaea* in 6 C.E., when the term "Judea-Judaea" took on a new administrative meaning with little connection to the geographic background of the phrase (cf. Luke 4:44; 23:5; Acts 10:37), or when it might refer to the entire land of Israel. The extensions of the boundaries of the Hasmonean state outside of Judea, even in its most extensive context, might explain why the residents of "Judea" preferred the term "*ethnos* of the Judeans" and why their kings preferred to be known as "King of the Judeans" (and not of Judah) (Goodblatt 1998).

The boundaries of *Provincia Judaea* were not permanently fixed. Its capital was Caesarea and not Jerusalem, and in 39 C.E. it also received the Galilee and Perea. At first it was ruled by a *Praefectus,* then by a *Procurator,* and finally by a *Legatus pro praetore,* terms reflecting changes in the status of the ruler and the Roman forces policing the province, from *auxilia* to legion. After the Bar-Kokhba War, the name of the province was changed to *Syria Palaestina.*

Division into Administrative Units

Judea in all of its administrative and geographic senses was divided into smaller administrative units, and these too tended to be in flux throughout the Second Temple period. While there is no agreement among scholars as to the exact composition of these units in the Persian period, it is likely that the province of Yehud was divided into the following subdistricts or *pelakhim:* Jerusalem, Cela (biblical Qeʿilah), Masepha (Mizpeh), Beth Ha-Kerem, Beth Zur, and Jericho, with Jerusalem as the capital. The term *pelakhim* appears in rabbinic literature in relation to going up on pilgrimage to Jerusalem to bring firstfruits (*t. Bik.* 2:8), but the administrative context of the phrase is not clear here.

The administrative makeup of Judea in the Hellenistic and Hasmonean periods is far from clear. The *pelekh* was now the toparchy, and new toparchies were undoubtedly created as the boundaries of Judea expanded, as in the case of the toparchies of Lod, Arimathea, and Apharaema, which became part of Judea during the time of Jonathan. Some scholars saw the twenty-four *mishmarot* mentioned in *m. Taʿan.* 4:2 as corresponding to the number of toparchies in Judea, but this is considered doubtful today.

More information is available from the Roman period, although much of it undoubtedly reflects earlier periods. Pliny tells us that "The rest of Judea is divided into ten toparchies in the following order: the district of Jericho, which has numerous palm-groves and springs of water, and those of Emmaus, Lydda, Joppa, Acraba, Gophna, Timna, Betholeptephe, Orine, where Jerusalem was formerly situated, by far the most famous city of the east and not of Judea only, and Herodium with the celebrated town of the same name" (*Natural History* 5.70). Pliny also mentions the coastal cities of Rapha, Gaza, Anthedon, the free town of Ascalon, Azotus, the two towns of Iamnea (Jamnia = the town of that name and port city), and the Phoenician city of Joppa (5.68). He does not include them as toparchies of Judea. He also describes the Dead Sea (5.72).

According to Josephus (*J.W.* 3.54-55), Judea was divided into eleven toparchies. The main differences between Pliny's and Josephus' lists are that Josephus adds Idumea and ʿEin Gedi to the lists of toparchies and refers to Jamnia and Joppa as toparchies only in an appendix to the list. Josephus uses Pelle for Betholeptephe and instead of Orine has Jerusalem. The latter discrepancies are of little import. Pelle was either a mistake or it was just an assimilated form of Betholeptephe, identified with Beit Nattif, and the use of Orine (Oreine), the hill country (surrounding Jerusalem), for Jerusalem has not upset scholars. However, both the discrepancies in the lists concerning what was included (Idumea and ʿEin Gedi) and the status of Jamnia and Joppa have elicited much scholarly reaction.

A number of solutions have been posited for the discrepancies in the lists. Pliny's lists might be dependent on an earlier source and reflect Herodian times, while Josephus describes the reality of the mid-first century C.E. Or perhaps the list in Josephus reflects the period right before the First Jewish Revolt and that of Pliny the period afterward. The major problem seems to be the status of Idumea, which traditionally was divided into two toparchies, a western one with Beth Govrin, near deserted Marisa, its central city; and an eastern one whose center was ʿEin Gedi. Many scholars today find it convenient just to combine the lists.

Much of this administrative framework of Judea continued to exist even after the First Jewish Revolt. Documents from the Judean Desert and its environs refer to local administrative centers in Herodium, Acraba, Gophna, and ʿEin Gedi. Ziph in the southern Mt. Hebron region may have become the regional capital of Idumea (Zissu 2001: 233-34).

Types of Settlement

There were various types of settlements in Judea. Josephus and the New Testament mention the city *(polis)* and the village *(kōmē).* In between, according to Josephus, was the town *(polixnion).* Talmudic literature mentions the pagan city *(kerakh),* the city *(ʿir),* and the village *(kefar).* In rabbinic literature, municipal status was determined by the existence and availability of certain religious services, and thus geographically the city might be more of a town. The capitals of the toparchies listed above, some far from being cities, as well as other central villages, might be defined as cities or towns in the rabbinic sense. The rabbinic village, lacking municipal services, was for the most part located in the rural sphere, in farming and agricultural regions.

One of the most common types of settlement in this area would have been the village and its satellite or offshoot settlements. Josephus, the New Testament, and the rabbis mention numerous villages in Judea. Archaeological research has also uncovered villages in Judea not mentioned in literary sources, such as Kiriat Sefer in the Modiin region or H. ʿEthri in the Shephelah. These villages were rather large; archaeologists have uncovered in them residential areas as well as public areas and buildings, and they were apparently Jewish for long periods. Landscape and settlement archaeology has also revealed the existence of other types of rural settlements in Judea, such as simple farmsteads (e.g., Pisgat Zeev, Jerusalem), fortified farmsteads (e.g., H. al-Sira, western Jerusalem mountains), manor houses (villas [Roman villa], e.g., Hilkiah's Palace [H. Murak], west of Hebron and Tel Goded near Beth Gubrin), and possible fortified manor houses, which may actually have been fortified villages. There might also have been agricultural settlements around fortified towers (e.g., Rujm Hamiri, southern Mt. Hebron region), but these may have also been fortified road stations (Zissu 2001: 249-70)

Agriculture

Much of Judea was fertile and suitable for agriculture, a feature that served as the basis for a good deal of its economy. Josephus, in his description of the land of Israel (*J.W.* 3.48-50) describes Judea (and Samaria) as composed of hills and plains with a light and fertile soil appropriate for agriculture. It has an abundance of trees, produces fruit from trees both wild and cultivated, has abundant rainfall and sweet running water, and produces ample grass, resulting in high milk production of the cows there. Both the Hasmoneans and the Herodians invested in agricultural development, enabling cultivation of semiarid regions bordering on the desert. The proof of the intensive agricultural activity in Judea, according to Josephus, is that it could support a large population.

The *Letter of Aristeas*, purportedly reflecting the Hellenistic age, states that "cultivation of every kind is carried on and an abundant harvest reaped" (*Aristeas* 108). While this was undoubtedly an exaggeration, much of Judea was fertile and many different crops were grown. Even if a crop was not predominant, it might have been important. Although not much wheat was cultivated there, for instance, some of what was grown was apparently of very high quality, such as that from Machmas northeast of Jerusalem, or from Zanoua in the Shephelah. Both were cited as the source of the finest flour for the Temple (*m. Menaḥ.* 8:1). In the more southern regions of Judea, barley, which requires less water than wheat, was cultivated. Beth Rima and Beth Laban in northern Judea (or southern Samaria) produced high quality wine for the Temple (*m. Menaḥ.* 8:6), and grapes and figs were common in other areas of Judea (Neh. 13:15). While olives grew in the hilly regions of Judea, this region was not particularly known for its olives or olive oil. Dates were grown in the warm valley of the Jericho region, and balsam was cultivated in the "balsam strip" from Jericho to ʿEin Gedi. There was sufficient grazing land in parts of the Shephelah for cattle and in the southern regions for sheep. The Jericho region was one of the most fertile in the land of Israel, with numerous types of luxuriant date palms, allowing the production of a high-quality date honey, not much inferior to that of bees, also produced there. It also had the "juicy" balsam mentioned above, cypress trees, and the myrobalanus. The area was so fertile as to be called "divine" (Josephus, *J.W.* 4.459-74).

BIBLIOGRAPHY

M. AVI-YONAH 1966, *The Holy Land, from the Persian to Arab Conquests 536 B.C. to A.D. 640: A Historical Geography*, Grand Rapids: Baker. • D. GOODBLATT 1998, "From Judeans to Israel: Names of Jewish States in Antiquity," *JSJ* 29: 1-36. • S. KLEIN 1939, *Eretz Yehudah*, Tel-Aviv: Dvir (in Hebrew). • O. LIPSCHITS 2005, *The Rise and Fall of Jerusalem: Judah under Babylonian Rule*, Winona Lake, Ind.: Eisenbrauns. • J. SCHWARTZ 1986, *Jewish Settlement in Judaea after the Bar-Kochba War until the Arab Conquest*, Jerusalem: Magnes. • J. SCHWARTZ 1991, *Lod (Lydda), Israel from its Origins through the Byzantine Period 5600 B.C.E.–640 C.E.* Oxford: Tempus Reparatum. • M. STERN 1974, *Greek and Latin Authors on Jews and Judaism*, vol. 1, *From Herodotus to Plutarch*, Jerusalem: Israel Academy of Sciences and Humanities. • B. ZISSU 2001, "Rural Settlement in the Judaean Hills and Foothills from the Late Second Temple Period to the Bar Kokhba Revolt," Doctoral dissertation, Hebrew University of Jerusalem.

JOSHUA J. SCHWARTZ

Judgment

Divine judgment is ubiquitous in the literature of early Judaism and forms a central concern in some documents. Earlier scholarship tended to maintain that following the Law while awaiting the judgment was the *summa* of Jewish devotion (e.g., Bousset 1926: 202). Recent research, however, has shown that great diversity characterizes conceptions of judgment in Second Temple literature. No systematic doctrine of judgment existed in early Judaism. Divine judgment is found wherever God, or a representative appointed by God, is involved in some judging activity. Most commonly, punitive actions against evildoers are prominent, but judgment is not restricted to negative or forensic matters, since ruling, deciding, and delivering also qualify as acts of divine judgment.

Hebrew Bible

The language and conceptions of divine judgment in early Jewish literature generally represent developments of the same found in the Hebrew Bible. The Hebrew term (usually *šāpat*) covers a wide range of activities, both human and divine. The English translation of the term as "judgment" is unfortunate, since it suggests only forensic concepts (deciding a legal case), usually negative (legal guilt or condemnation). *Šāpat*, however, can refer more broadly to various executive functions aimed at maintaining justice or *šālôm*. Thus, governing, ruling, restoring, delivering, and punishing are equally valid renderings in various places (e.g., Judg. 2:16; 3:10; Psalm 82).

As "judge of all the earth" God rescues Lot and punishes Sodom (Gen. 18:25), decides between the righteous and the wicked (1 Kings 8:32), rescues those who look to him (Lam. 3:58-59), executes punishment upon sinful Israelites (1 Sam. 3:13), and rules or establishes justice for the peoples (Isa. 51:5). This divine administration of justice takes place normally in localized earthly events in human history, but in some texts it occurs in the heavens (Ps. 82:1), has a future or eschatological setting (Joel 4:2, 12), or is universal (Eccl. 12:14). The phrase "the day of the LORD" makes its appearance especially in the prophets (e.g., Isa. 13:6, 9; Amos 5:18). Typically, God judges on the basis of Torah and the covenant with Israel (e.g., Deuteronomy 28–31); tensions arise, however, when a good or evil life does not result in the appropriate divine blessing or curse (e.g., Job; Ecclesiastes; Psalm 44).

Early Jewish Literature

Types of Judgment

Divine judgment takes a variety of forms in Second Temple literature. Not infrequently, it takes the form of a military engagement, crushing the opponents of God and bringing deliverance to God's people (e.g., *1 Enoch* 1:3-9; 1QM 1:4-5, 14-15; *T. Levi* 3:3). Increasingly, however, forensic judgment scenarios appear, as witnessed in the LXX translation of *šāpat* by the more forensically oriented Greek term *krinein*. Courtroom scenes, appearing already in the Hebrew Bible, occur repeatedly in early Jewish texts: God sits upon a judgment throne, examines evidence, hears witnesses, and passes sentence (e.g., *1 Enoch* 47:3; 90:20-26; *4 Ezra* 7:33; *2 Bar.* 83:1-3; Sir. 35:14-15; *Testament of Abraham* 13–15).

A variety of means are employed in arriving at this judicial sentence. Souls (or deeds) can be weighed in a scale (e.g., *1 Enoch* 61:8; *2 Enoch* 44:5; 52:15; *T. Abr.* 12:13-14; 13:10). Betraying possible Egyptian or Greek influence, some writings contain a list of individuals' good or evil deeds, or the names of the righteous or wicked (*Jub.* 30:19-23; *1 Enoch* 89:70; 98:8; CD 20:19-20; *2 Bar.* 24:1; *2 Enoch* 52:15). Thus, the judgment sentence is "according to deeds" (Ps.-Philo, *Bib. Ant.* 3:10; Sir. 16:12-14). Criteria for this sentence usually relate in some fashion to the Torah and covenant with Israel (e.g., *Bib. Ant.* 11:2; Tob. 3:5; *4 Ezra* 7:19-25). Rather than flawless obedience, one's heart and deeds must demonstrate adherence to and love of God's Torah. In contrast to the wicked, the righteous or elect are typically shown mercy in this judgment (*Pss. Sol.* 2:33-35). In the Dead Sea Scrolls, one's adherence to the Torah as expounded by the Teacher of Righteousness is crucial (1QpHab 8:1-3).

Strictly speaking, these court scenes do not *determine* the guilt or innocence of the accused, since the parties typically enter already with labels such as "sinners," "righteous," "elect," or "enemies." Such a forensic determination of a status heretofore unclear does not appear in early Jewish texts until the late first or early second century C.E. (Reiser 1997: 149; cf. *Testament of Abraham; b. Berakot* 28b). Instead, forensic judgment publicly reveals and confirms the status of groups and individuals.

Earthly or Heavenly Judgment

Divine judgment can still take place within human history and on earth, through illness, death, warfare, or catastrophe. However, descriptions of the place of judgment grow increasingly transcendent (e.g., *4 Ezra* 7). Suggested reasons include the loss of earthly hope among Jewish groups along with the influence of Hellenistic dualism and apocalypticism. Earlier attempts to tie this earthly/heavenly distinction to differences of apocalyptic versus rabbinic, or Palestinian versus Diaspora, perspectives have been largely abandoned. For most scholars these increasingly heavenly and transcendent scenes of judgment indicate belief in a supramundane, wholly discontinuous new age or reality. A minority of scholars, however, take the language of transcendence as metaphorical for a strictly this-worldly expectation: salvation is essentially conceived as *here*, as earthly, with no suggestion of anything like transcendence (Reiser 1997: 148).

Agents of Judgment

God is normally the judge (*1 Enoch* 47; *T. Mos.* 10:7). In numerous texts, however, other figures are listed as judging, though their authorization by the divine judge is nearly always assumed: angels generally (CD 2:5-6); the Watchers in *1 Enoch;* named angels (e.g., "Michael" in 1QM 17:7-8); messiah(s) (e.g., *Pss. Sol.* 17–18; *1 Enoch* 37–71; *4 Ezra* 12:31-35); Melchizedek (11QMelch; in this text, Melchizedek may be another name for Michael); Abel (*T. Abr.* 13:3); and the elect (1QpHab 5:4-5). In some cases, these other figures are agents of God's judgment who execute the penalty rather than pronounce the sentence (e.g., *1 Enoch* 54:6).

Individual or Collective Judgment

Judgment upon groups (nations, kingdoms) predominates in the Hebrew Bible, which often envisions the destruction of Israel's enemies. Such collective judgment is also envisioned in Second Temple literature, in both military and forensic scenes. However, an increasing interest in the postmortem judgment of individuals emerges, especially in apocalypses (e.g., *1 Enoch* 1–36; *3 Baruch; 2 Enoch; Testament of Abraham;* cf. Fischer 1978: 37-123). Yet the collective viewpoint is seldom absent, since the judged individuals are often members of groups: the wicked, the righteous, Gentiles, and Israel (e.g., *Apocalypse of Abraham*).

Objects of Judgment

The most common objects of judgment are those receiving punishment, such as wicked individuals, the enemies of God or of Israel, or even inhabitants of cosmic realms (e.g., Belial, apostate angels). Earlier scholarship asserted an exemption from such judgment for Israel and Israelites (cf. Wis. 15:2a, "For even if we sin we are yours"). However, it is increasingly recognized that punitive judgment not only divides Israel from the nations but can also fall upon Israel and her leaders (Wis. 6:4-8; *1 Enoch* 62–63) and can separate righteous from unrighteous individuals within Israel (Pr. Azar. 1:3-9; CD 8; 19). Judgment upon the righteous normally results in some form of reward, but this is less frequently mentioned than punishment of the unrighteous. In some texts this judgment is universal (e.g., *1 Enoch* 1; 81; *Jubilees* 5; *T. Benj.* 10:8-9) and can include the living as well as the dead (e.g., *1 Enoch* 51; *4 Ezra* 7:32-44).

Time of Judgment

The older view in preexilic Israelite religion that divine judgments are experienced in this life is still attested in early Jewish literature (e.g., Wisdom 12; Tob. 1:18; CD 1), though the emphasis shifts decidedly from the past or present to the future. The precise timing of such future judgment yields an almost bewildering variety, including at or near the moment of death (4 Macc. 17:12; 18:23), some unspecified time after death (*4 Ezra* 14:34-35), during an intermediate period between death and the eschaton, at some point near entry to the age to come, or following a messianic interim period (*4 Ezra* 7:26-44) and/or a general resurrection (*2 Bar.* 50:1-4). In numerous texts this last conception is referred to as the "great" or "eternal" judgment (e.g., *1 Enoch* 25:4; 91:9; *Jub.* 5:10). Most texts show little concern to harmonize such variations in timing. An exception is the *Testament of Abraham,* which envisions three separate judgment events: immediately after death, later judgment of nations, and universal judgment (chap. 13). In some texts the transition from one's status in this age to that in the next occurs without any explicit judgment scene, particularly in the case of righteous martyrs (4 Maccabees 14).

Purposes and Outcomes of Judgment

Both warnings of punishment and promises of reward are frequent in early Jewish texts. Even the warnings, however, generally serve a positive purpose for the hearers. Since outsiders would not normally be expected to hear these words, the threats of judgment upon them serve to strengthen Jewish listeners. Likewise, the warnings of potential negative judgment addressed to Jews can serve to lead such sinners in Israel to repent as well as to strengthen the obedient to stand firm in the face of suffering and temptation. Thus, divine judgment is of more interest as a motivational tool than as an object of doctrinal reflection per se.

The punishment of the wicked applies in some texts to the enemies of Israel, in others to sinners within Israel, and in others to humanity without such clear distinctions. The forms of such punishment vary widely, including everlasting imprisonment (*1 Enoch* 69:28), destruction by sword or fire (*Jub.* 9:15; 36:10; *T. Zeb.* 10:3), eternal torment (Jdt. 16:17), and annihilation (1QS 4:12-14; 5:13).

The reward of the righteous is likewise described in quite varied ways, including lasting memory among the living, (eternal) life, happiness, deliverance from oppression, enjoyment of earthly or heavenly goods, and immortality or resurrection. This last item, resurrection of the body, becomes increasingly important in postmortem judgment scenes (Nickelsburg 1972). In some texts human beings are raised for judgment, while in others resurrection is the result of the judgment.

New Testament and Rabbinic Literature

The Jewish character of the early Jesus movement is clearly seen in its large-scale continuity with Jewish views of divine judgment. Nevertheless, certain crucial differences also become apparent. The agents and recipients of judgment are largely the same, though the risen Jesus as Christ or Lord (or "Son of Man") now appears more centrally as judge alongside God, and the resurrection of the dead becomes more central (see esp. 1 Corinthians 15; Revelation 20). Most of the same means, outcomes, and scenes occur, including the relationship between judgment and human deeds (e.g., 1 Cor. 3:12-15; 2 Cor. 5:10; Rom. 2:12-16; 14:10-11; Matt. 25:31-46; Jas. 2:14-26). However, the standard is now more often expressed in terms of relationship to Christ than to the Jewish Torah (e.g., Rom. 2:16; but cf. Matt. 5:17-20). The major shift involves the inaugurated or "realized" eschatology of the New Testament, whereby divine judgment has in one sense already occurred (e.g., John 3:18, 36; 5:22, 24, 26), but in another sense is yet to come (e.g., 1 Thess. 4:6; 1 Cor. 3:12-15; Rom. 2:16; 14:10; Acts 24:25).

Rabbinic literature maintains belief in most of the conceptions of divine judgment uncovered thus far, including military judgment, reward and punishment in this life, resurrection and last judgment. Debate over the fate of Gentiles occurs more often. Since rabbinic sayings focus normally on behavior in this life, one does not often find speculation about divine judgment, except as that may have behavioral relevance. Older handbooks on rabbinic Judaism tended to give a false picture by assembling texts without regard to this underlying concern for present behavior. While rabbinic texts do place heightened emphasis on an individual's keeping of Torah commands, this is due to their concern for personal behavior rather than to a supposed legalistic view of obedience and judgment (*m. Sanh.* 10:1; *m. Qidd.* 4:14; *Sipre Numbers* 44). Human repentance is viewed as particularly effective in this literature to overcome judgment upon sins, and God is portrayed as leaning more toward mercy than strict justice (*b. Roš Haššana* 17).

BIBLIOGRAPHY

W. BOUSSET 1926, *Die Religion des Judentums im späthellenistischen Zeitalter,* 3d ed., Tübingen: Mohr. • U. FISCHER 1978, *Eschatologie und Jenseitserwartung im hellenistischen Diasporajudentum,* Berlin: de Gruyter. • K. MÜLLER 1994, "Gott als Richter und die Erscheinungsweisen seiner Gerichte in den Schriften des Frühjudentums," in *Weltgericht und Weltvollendung: Zukunftsbilder im Neuen Testament,* ed. H.-J. Klauck, Freiburg: Herder, 23-53. • G. W. E. NICKELSBURG 1972 (rev. ed. 2006), *Resurrection, Immortality, and Eternal Life in Intertestamental Judaism,* Cambridge: Harvard University Press. • M. REISER 1997, *Jesus and Judgment: The Eschatological Proclamation in Its Jewish Context,* trans. L. M. Maloney, Minneapolis: Fortress. • C. VANLANDINGHAM 2006, *Judgment and Justification in Early Judaism and the Apostle Paul,* Peabody, Mass.: Hendrickson. • P. VOLZ 1934, *Die Eschatologie der jüdischen Gemeinde im neutestamentlichen Zeitalter nach den Quellen der rabbinischen, apokalyptischen und apokryphen Literatur,* 2d ed., Tübingen: Mohr. • K. L. YINGER 1999, *Paul, Judaism, and Judgement according to Deeds,* Cambridge: Cambridge University Press.

KENT L. YINGER

Judith, Book of

The book of Judith is an early Jewish writing included among the books of the Apocrypha. It is an artfully crafted tale that functions as a didactic proof text for a theology of zealous activism rooted in faith in the God of Israel.

Contents

The protagonist, Judith, is a pious, beautiful widow who lives in Bethulia, a town on the main road to Jerusalem that is being besieged by the forces of an overwhelmingly powerful monarch. The water supply of Bethulia cut off, the town elders are prepared to surrender if divine intervention does not come within five days. Rejecting their passivity, reproaching them for doubting God's providential care, and putting a time limit on divine intervention, Judith prayerfully invokes the deeds of her ancestor Simeon (Genesis 34) and initiates her own plan of action. With only her female servant to accompany her, she goes to the camp of the enemy, using her beauty to seductively deceive the commanding general. In celebratory anticipation of having his pleasure with the beautiful Judith, the general drinks himself into a stupor, whereupon she kills him. Returning with his head to Bethulia, she arouses the Judeans to action, and they put the leaderless, frightened enemy to flight. With Jerusalem and the Temple secure, Judith and all Judea celebrate the victory God wrought "by the hand of a woman."

Structure

The book has a symmetrical, chiastic structure. The first half (chaps. 1–7) is a dramatic presentation of an extraordinarily powerful king who, distressed by affronts to his imperial authority, develops a plan of revenge and sends his chief general, Holofernes, on an extensive military campaign that comes to terrorize and threaten Jerusalem and the Temple. The second half (chaps. 8–16) focuses on the extraordinarily pious Judith, her distress when initial faith and courage succumb to doubt and fear, the plan of action she undertakes in response, the terror of the enemy forces at its successful execution, and Israel's victory. With the major characters as their spokespersons, contrasting theological perspectives dominate each part of the work. In the first half, the enemy monarch and Holofernes set forth the claim that power and military might convey universal sovereignty and divinity on its bearer (2:5-13; 6:2-4). Achior, the leader of Ammonite forces allied to them, indicates that a different principle governs the Israelites, whose strength rests in fidelity to their God; but he and his perspective are rebuked and quite literally cast off (5:1–6:13). In the second half, Judith rebukes those who lack faith in God (8:12-27) and asserts that the only true god is the God of Israel who protects His people Israel (9:7-14), a position that is subsequently echoed by the rescued Achior, who converts and joins the community of Israel (14:10).

Genre

With multiple references to known persons, places, and dates, the presentation has the appearance of a historical account. However, absurd combinations, blatant inaccuracies, and inner contradictions suggest from the outset that the author employs the historical style as a literary device for conflating characters, events, and dates that happened over centuries. Most striking of such conflations is the portrayal of the enemy and the timing of its threat to Jerusalem. The Assyrians are identified as the imperial enemy power, thereby suggesting a setting in the eighth century B.C.E. The powerful king of these Assyrians is Nebuchadnezzar (1:1), intimating the historical Babylonian king, Nebuchadnezzar II (605-562 B.C.E.), who besieged and destroyed Jerusalem in the eighteenth year of his reign, 587-586 B.C.E. (Jer. 32:1; 52:29). In the eighteenth year of his reign, Judith's Assyrian Nebuchadnezzar authorizes the campaign that endangers Jerusalem and the Temple (2:2). The commander of his forces, Holofernes, who, like his own aide, Bagoas, bears a historical Persian name, threatens the security of Jerusalem when the Judeans have just returned from exile (538 B.C.E.) and had consecrated "the sacred vessels and the altar and the temple after their profanation" (165 B.C.E.; 4:3)! The creative "historical" setting bespeaks the adoption of multiple scriptural motifs and the fusion of names and events from different eras all merged within a story line also evocative of the author's own time. For these reasons, modern scholars regard Judith as a work of historical fiction — an early Jewish novella or short story.

Date

The consensus of contemporary scholarship assigns the final redaction, if not the entire composition, of the book of Judith to the Maccabean-Hasmonean era. In support of such a dating are the thematic centrality of faithful religious zeal; the import of personal piety, prayer, and observance of the Law; and the focus on Jerusalem and the Temple. Particularly convincing are literary elements that indicate the influence of 1–2 Maccabees, such as the reference to reconsecration of profaned temple vessels in 4:3 (cf. 1 Macc. 4:36-35); the use of Rabshakeh's claims for his patron king, Sennacherib, in 2 Kings 18–19/Isaiah 36–27 (spoken by Holofernes in Jdt. 6:2-4; alluded to by Judah Maccabee in 1 Macc. 7:41-42); the display of the head of the slain enemy general (Holofernes in Jdt. 14:1, 11; Nicanor in 1 Macc. 7:47; 2 Macc. 15:35); and the account of pursuit and plunder of the enemy (Jdt. 15:1-8; 1 Macc. 7:43-47a). A more precise dating remains elusive, with some scholars favoring the 160s B.C.E. and others a date in the post–Maccabean-Hasmonean era.

Original Language

Nothing is known of the author, who presumably lived in Palestine. It is generally agreed that Judith was originally written in Hebrew, but no fragments of the work have been found at Qumran and no ancient Hebrew text has been preserved. Evidence for a Hebrew *Vorlage* rests primarily upon Hebraisms in the Greek translation extant in four Septuagint codices. That there also was an early Aramaic translation is evident from Jerome, who refers in the preface to his Vulgate translation to a "Chaldean" version that served as a control for eliminating "faulty variant readings" in older Latin texts. Nothing is known of Jerome's "Chaldean" source; it may have been a translation from the Hebrew or, more likely, from the Greek. Three medieval Hebrew manuscripts of Judith are extant; according to one scholar (Dubarle 1966), they reflect ancient Hebrew versions behind the Aramaic text used by Jerome; but the more dominant position views them as translations from the Latin. Also extant are Syriac, Coptic, and Ethiopic versions of Judith, all translations of the LXX.

Influence in Jewish and Christian Tradition

The book of Judith was not included in the Hebrew Bible. Its exclusion has been attributed, among other factors, to the late date of the book's composition and to its positive presentation of the conversion of Achior, which is problematic in its acceptance of an Ammonite convert (cf. Deut. 23:3) and in it omission of the rite of ritual immersion required by the rabbis.

There are no explicit references to Judith in Second Temple or early rabbinic literature. There is, however, sufficient literary evidence to suggest the influence of Judith on Pseudo-Philo's treatment of the narrative of Jael and Sisera (*Biblical Antiquities* 31). Less clear is the relationship between Judith and the Additions to Esther. Thematic elements in Addition D have led one scholar to posit that it may have been inspired by Judith at some point in their respective Hebrew stages (Moore 1985: 212-26).

The earliest evidence of rabbinic awareness of the story comes from the tenth or eleventh century. Adaptations of the legend are found in multiple Judith midrashim *(Ma'aseh Yehudit)* and liturgical poems *(piyyutim)*. Allusions to the story of Judith appear in the Talmud commentary of R. Samuel b. Meir (Rashbam) (1085-1184) and thereafter in that of R. Nissim ben Reuben Gerondi *(RaN)* (1310-1375?). In these sources, as well as in later illustrated manuscripts and Jewish ritual art, Judith is associated with the Maccabees and the celebration of the festival of Hanukkah.

The transmission of Judith in Christian circles is a more continuous one. With some Eastern church fathers demurring, the book of Judith entered the Catholic canon as a deuterocanonical work and attained the quasisacred status attributed to apocryphal books by the Protestants. The story and its heroine became prominent subjects in European music, literature, and art, where Judith is variously portrayed as a symbol for the church, as the personification of civic virtue, as a licentious, immoral woman, and most recently, by some feminist interpreters, as a failed example of female leadership.

While the questions of date and historicity have long occupied scholars, contemporary scholarship on Judith has also focused on literary aspects of the work. Particular attention has been directed to its compositional structure, its use of irony and humor, the nature and significance of its use of biblical allusions and motifs, and, from a feminist perspective, the portrayal of its heroine.

BIBLIOGRAPHY

T. CRAVEN 1983, *Artistry and Faith in the Book of Judith*, Chico, Calif.: Scholars Press. • A. M. DUBARLE 1966, *Judith: Formes et sens des diverses traditions*, Rome: Pontifical Biblical Institute, 1: 20-79. • J. GRINTZ 1986, *Sefer Yehudit*, rpt., Jerusalem: Bialik Institute (in Hebrew). • C. MOORE 1985, *Judith: A New Translation with Introduction and Commentary*, Garden City, N.Y.: Doubleday. • P. SKEHAN 1963, "The Hand of Judith," *CBQ* 25: 94-110. • M. STOCKER 1998, *Judith, Sexual Warrior: Women and Power in Western Culture*, New Haven and London: Yale University Press. • J. C. VANDERKAM, ED. 1992, *'No One Spoke Ill of Her': Essays on Judith*, Atlanta: Scholars Press.

BETSY HALPERN-AMARU

Julius Caesar, Gaius

Gaius Julius Caesar (100-44 B.C.E.) was a Roman statesman, general, and writer who flourished in the final years of the Roman Republic. Among the mourners who crowded around the funeral pyre of the murdered Caesar in 44 B.C.E., Jews were particularly conspicuous (Suetonius, *Divus Iulius* 84.5). That they should have been moved to demonstrate their grief so publicly is not surprising. With the dictator's death, Jews everywhere in the Roman world had lost the most powerful Roman patron they had ever had.

The Jews of Judea, in particular, had many reasons for feeling grateful to Caesar. During his brief rule over Rome (48-44 B.C.E.) he had largely removed the humiliations inflicted upon them, first, by Pompey the Great, Rome's conqueror of the East, and then by Aulus Gabinius, an early Roman governor of Syria. In the immediate aftermath of the Roman conquest of Judea in 63 B.C.E., Pompey had deliberately deprived the Jews of prestige and power. After reducing their country from an independent kingdom to an ethnarchy paying tribute to Rome, he had forbidden the ruler he had appointed for them, the high priest Hyrcanus II, to rebuild the walls of Jerusalem and had confiscated nearly all of their recent territorial conquests, most seriously Joppa, their only port on the Mediterranean. Gabinius had gone even further: following repeated outbreaks of unrest in Judea, he had dissolved the ethnarchy, created five councils in its place, and left Hyrcanus with only his high-priestly title and duties (55 B.C.E.). Caesar's victory over Pompey in the civil war of 49-48 B.C.E. had led to an almost total reversal of these measures. Not only did Caesar make Hyrcanus and his children hereditary ethnarchs of Judea, but he permitted the refortification of Jerusalem and returned to Jewish control Joppa and various other places confiscated by Pompey.

Diaspora Jews, especially those of Asia Minor, also had reason to be grateful to Caesar. The efforts of Pompey's supporters during the recent civil war to conscript them as soldiers and to billet troops upon them had posed a serious threat to their way of life. Not only did Caesar's victory end this threat; Diaspora Jews found their security and prestige enhanced by the positive measures he subsequently took on their behalf. These included authorizing Hyrcanus II to champion their interests and stipulating that demands should not be made of them that were incompatible with the observance of their ancestral customs.

Why was Caesar so supportive of the Jews? In some works of scholarship (e.g., Smallwood 1981) Caesar's enactments are regularly described as the Jews' Magna Carta, the intent of which was to establish Judaism as a permitted religion *(religio licita)* and thus to protect the Jews' religious liberty for all time. That view, however, no longer enjoys credence among scholars. Not only is the charter model now seen to be anachronistic, but the very concept of "permitted religion" has been shown to be invalid (Rajak 1984). Caesar's actions are easily explicable in traditional Roman terms; they were favors given for services rendered or expected. Thus the concessions granted to the Jews of Judea in 47 B.C.E. were simply Caesar's quid pro quo for the military help they had given him the previous year in Egypt. No less politically motivated were Caesar's enactments vis-à-vis the Diaspora; at the time of their promulgation (47 B.C.E.) resistance to his rule from Pompey's erstwhile supporters was building up in Rome's western provinces, so military action would have to be taken there soon. Therefore it would be of immense value to have as happy clients a significant element of the population of the Roman East (Gruen 2002). While the beneficiaries of these enactments hoped that they would remain in force indefinitely, there was no guarantee of that happening. Just as Caesar had, for reasons of political expediency, reversed the ad hoc measures taken by Pompey and Gabinius, so there was every chance that whoever followed him in power might do the same to his enactments. Although Caesar's adopted son and heir, the future emperor Augustus, did continue his policy toward the Jews for the most part, the Jews who circled Caesar's funeral-pyre in 44 B.C.E. were not to know that — hence the conspicuous outpouring of grief recorded by Suetonius.

BIBLIOGRAPHY

A. GOLDSWORTHY 2006, *Caesar: Life of a Colossus,* New Haven: Yale University Press. • E. S. GRUEN 2002, *Diaspora: Jews amidst Greeks and Romans,* Cambridge, Mass. and London, England: Harvard University Press. • M. PUCCI BEN-ZEEV 1998, *Jewish Rights in the Roman World: The Greek and Roman Documents Quoted by Josephus Flavius,* Tübingen: Mohr-Siebeck. • T. RAJAK 1984, "Was There a Roman Charter for the Jews?" *Journal of Roman Studies* 74: 107-23. • E. SCHÜRER 1973, *The History of the Jewish People in the Age of Jesus Christ,* vol. 1, rev. and ed. G. Vermes and F. Millar, Edinburgh: Clark, 270-75. • E. M. SMALLWOOD 1981, *The Jews under Roman Rule from Pompey to Diocletian,* Leiden: Brill, 36-43, 134-36.

MARGARET H. WILLIAMS

Justus of Tiberias

Justus of Tiberias was a Jewish political leader, author, and rival to the Jewish historian Josephus during the tumultuous late first century C.E. in Galilee. Unfortunately, information about his life is preserved only in the works of his political, military, and later writing adversary, Josephus, in his work *The Life.*

According to Josephus, Justus was the son of Pistus, a prominent leader of Tiberias, and was versed in Greek culture. He wrote and no doubt spoke fluent Greek. In the mid-60s he joined the revolt against Rome that was gaining strength in the Roman territory of Palestine (which included Judea and Samaria) and the areas of Galilee controlled by the client king Agrippa II, which included the city of Tiberias. Somewhat reluctantly, perhaps, Justus joined the revolution in 66, but before the region of Galilee was resubjugated by Roman force, Justus had fled to Agrippa II, who had unwaveringly supported Rome against the revolutionaries. However, the Roman general and later emperor (69-79) Vespasian sentenced Justus to be executed for his role. Agrippa II and his sister Bernice managed to have the sentence changed to a lengthy imprisonment (*Life* 341–43). After the revolt, Justus seems to have fallen in and out of favor with Agrippa, at times serving as his private secretary.

It is difficult to determine the role and attitude of Justus during the revolution. Josephus would have his readers believe that Justus was among those most responsible for fomenting rebellion against Rome, stirring up insurrection in Galilee, and leading attacks on Greek cities and villages of the Decapolis (*Life* 36, 340–44), all for the sake of gaining power for himself. Even after the war, Josephus accuses Justus of knavish trickery while in the service of Agrippa II (*Life* 36, 340–44, 355–60). But Josephus' judgments must be understood in light of his own role in the revolution and the rivalry between himself and Justus as postwar, pro-Roman historians. It seems unlikely that Justus was a committed and eager revolutionary, in light of his continued, if troubled, close relationship with Agrippa II, who faithfully stood by Roman rule.

Three titled works are attributed to Justus by ancient authors, though only two seem certain. Unfortunately his writings do not survive directly but only in a few quotations by later authors. The first is his *Jewish War,* which Josephus considered a direct rival to his own work on the war. In fact, Josephus' personal memoir of his wartime actions, *The Life,* is a polemic against Justus' account. Ironically, Josephus' *Life* is the only known work to preserve small segments of Justus' *Jewish War.* Justus apparently attacked Josephus for his role as Jewish general, blaming him for inciting the people of Tiberias against Rome and Agrippa II (*Life* 340). The extent of Justus' *Jewish War* is unknown, but it at least covered the revolt in Galilee and the Roman response led by Vespasian. Justus did not publish his work for more than twenty years after the events, waiting until the deaths of Vespasian, Titus, and Agrippa II (*Life* 359–60).

Another work of Justus, *Chronicle of the Jewish Kings,* is cited by three later authors, Julius Africanus (160-240 C.E.), a Christian historian and miscellany collector; Eusebius (260-340 C.E.), the Christian apologetic historian, and Diogenes Laertius, a third-century biographer of philosophers. *Chronicle of the Jewish Kings* seems to have been a general history of the Jews from Moses until the author's own time, the rule of Agrippa II. It was influential for some later Christian historians, such as the Byzantine historian George Syncellus in the ninth century. The third work, mentioned only by Jerome, was a biblical commentary, but there is no other attestation or hint of such a work.

Although little can be known about the actual life of Justus of Tiberias, and even less about his writings, it is clear that he stood in a long line of Hellenistic Jewish historians along with his contemporary Josephus, and before them Eupolemus, Pseudo-Eupolemus, Artapanus, Cleodemus Malchus, and others. These authors wrote for other Jews but also for interested non-Jews. Like the others, Justus was negotiating between his own

Jewish traditions and the culture of the larger Hellenized Roman Empire. Like Josephus, he was connected to persons of power, and in his life and writings he was forced to compromise and fuse local and personal Jewish interests, loyalties, and traditions with those of the Empire and Hellenistic culture.

BIBLIOGRAPHY

A. BARZANÒ 1987, "Giusto di Tiberiade," *ANRW* II.20.1: 337-58. • S. J. D. COHEN 1979, *Josephus in Galilee and Rome*, Leiden: Brill. • C. R. HOLLADAY 1983, *Fragments from Hellenistic Jewish Authors*, vol. 1, *Historians*, Chico, Calif.: Scholars Press, 371-89. • S. MASON 2001, *Flavius Josephus: Translation and Commentary*, vol. 9, *Life of Josephus*, Leiden: Brill. • T. RAJAK 1973, "Justus of Tiberias," *Classical Quarterly* 23: 345-68. • E. SCHÜRER 1986, *The History of the Jewish People in the Age of Jesus Christ*, vol. 1, rev. and ed. G. Vermes et al., Edinburgh: Clark, 34-37.

JAMES E. BOWLEY

Kashrut → Meals; Purity and Impurity

Kingdom of God

Jewish texts often use "kingdom" in a purely secular sense, to denote a territory or politically organized unit under monarchical rule (e.g., Gen. 10:10; Num. 32:33). Thus we read of the "kingdom of Israel" (1 Sam. 15:28; 24:20) or the "kingdom of Judah" (2 Chron. 11:17; cf. *T. Jud.* 17:3) or of the "kingdom" of this or that ruler (1 Kings 2:12; 1 Chron. 10:14). But when God is conceived of as being the true monarch of Israel (Num. 23:21; 1 Sam. 8:4-9; Josephus, *Ant.* 6.60), the expression "kingdom of Yahweh" also occurs (1 Chron. 28:5; 2 Chron. 13:8). "Kingdom of God," however, is rare before the turn of the era; the phrase and its synonym, "kingdom of heaven," become common only in Christian and rabbinic writings.

God's Kingship: Three Understandings

At some point in time, God's kingship was envisaged as extending beyond the chosen people and their land: Israel's God became the king of all of the world and indeed of all creation (Pss. 22:8; 47; 103:9; Dan. 4:32; *1 Enoch* 84:2). This conception, however, generated problems, for it was obvious that God's will is not consistently done by any government or individual, and so in what sense God is the ruler of all was unclear. The theological problem generated by the disparity between mundane reality and confession of God's universal kingship fostered at least three different ways of conceptualizing the divine kingdom.

Spiritual and Ethical Conceptions

Some spiritualized that kingdom, reinterpreting it either as God's sovereign power (Dan. 3:33; 2 Macc. 1:7; *Ps. Sol.* 17:3) or as the reality that manifests itself when individuals submit themselves to the divine government in the here and now. In this way "kingdom" lost its political and territorial meanings and became, as in much of rabbinic literature (e.g., *b. Berakot* 13b), a purely religious and ethical expression.

The Wisdom of Solomon illustrates the ethical conception of the divine kingdom. It says that, when wisdom guides individuals on the right path, she reveals to them "the kingdom of God" (Wis. 10:10). The antithesis of this statement appears in 6:3-4, which concerns unrighteous rulers. Although they have received their sovereignty from the Most High and have been summoned to be "servants of his kingdom," they have failed to rule rightly.

Philo likewise gives God's "kingdom" an ethical sense. According to him, the virtuous sage is the true king (*Somn.* 2.243-44), and whereas "other kingdoms" are established through wars and violence, "the kingdom of the sage comes by the gift of God, and the virtuous individual who receives it brings no harm to anyone, but the acquisition and enjoyment of good things to all his subjects, to whom he is the herald of peace and order" (*Abr.* 261; cf. *Sacr.* 49; *Migr.* 197; *Prob.* 125–26; also 4 Macc. 2:23; *T. Jud.* 15:2).

The Heavenly Realm

A second way of reconceptualizing the kingdom of God was to equate it with a transmundane realm, to think of God as now ruling perfectly in the heavens above. This transference of "kingdom" to the heavenly realm, analogous to the transference of "Jerusalem" to that realm (Gal. 4:26; *Par. Jer.* 5:35), appears in Wis. 6:17-20 and *T. Abr.* 7:7, both of which imagine the righteous entering the kingdom upon death (cf. *T. Isaac* 2:8). Other texts, however, teach that, through mystical ascent or revelatory texts, one can learn about or encounter the upper kingdom even now. The *Songs of the Sabbath Sacrifice,* for example, offer details of the angelic worship in the upper world, and in this book "kingdom" often means something close to what we call "heaven," as in 4Q405 23 ii 10-11: "These are the princes of those marvelously clothed for service, the princes of the kingdom, the kingdom of the holy ones of the King of holiness in all the heights of the sanctuaries of his glorious kingdom" (cf. 4Q400 1 ii 1-3; 2 4; 4Q403 1 ii 10). One may compare *3 Bar.* 11:2, where Michael the archangel has the keys to the "kingdom," that is, the highest heaven, where God's throne is (cf. also *T. Job* 33:9; 34:4).

God's Eschatological Rule and Realm

A third way of dealing with the disjunction between the affirmation of God's kingship and present realities was to emphasize that, however bad things seem now, God's kingdom will, after a final judgment, someday establish itself everywhere and for always (cf. Isa. 52:7; Obad. 21; Zech. 14:9). "Kingdom (of God)" thereby became shorthand for God's eschatological rule and realm, when earth will see the divine will done perfectly as it is now done perfectly in heaven (although the concept is often present without the word "kingdom" being used). Daniel employs "kingdom" this way in 2:44; 7:14, 18, 27. So too do several of the Dead Sea Scrolls — 4Q246 ("His kingdom will be an everlasting kingdom and all his ways in truth. He will judge the earth in truth and all will make peace. The sword will cease from the earth and all provinces will worship him"); 4Q521 ("He will glorify the pious on the throne of an eternal kingdom . . ."); 1QSb 4:25-26 ("May you attend upon the service in the temple of the kingdom and decree destiny in company with the angels of the Presence"; cf. perhaps 1QM 6:6).

The eschatological application of "kingdom" is not confined to Daniel and the Scrolls. *2 Baruch* says that God's anointed will sit down in "eternal peace" on "the throne of the kingdom" (73:1). The *Testament of Judah* prophesies that "the Shoot of David" will "illumine" the scepter of Judah's eschatological "kingdom" (4:4-5). The *Testament of Moses* promises that God's "kingdom" will "appear throughout his creation," and that this will coincide with the end of Satan (10:1). Here God's kingdom is implicitly set over against Satan's kingdom. When the one comes, the other goes. So God's kingdom has its rival or antithesis — an idea otherwise attested in *T. Dan* 6:2, 4; Matt. 12:26 = 12:18 (cf. *T. Sim.* 2:7; *T. Jud.* 19:4 and those New Testament texts in which Satan rules the world: Matt. 4:8; Luke 4:5; John 12:31; 14:30; 16:11).

Rabbinic literature also occasionally gives "kingdom" eschatological sense, as in the Kaddish prayer: "May he [God] establish his kingdom in your lifetime and in your days, and in the lifetime of the whole house of Israel, speedily and at a near time." The targum to the prophets supplies additional examples. In it the clause, "the kingdom of the Lord will be revealed," is characteristic: it refers to the theophany that will introduce the new world (e.g., *Tg. Isa.* 31:4; *Tg. Mic.* 4:7; *Tg. Zech.* 14:9).

Perhaps the most common themes associated with God's eschatological kingdom are its universality, its temporal nearness, and its everlasting nature (although a few texts, such as *4 Ezra, 2 Baruch,* and Revelation, envision a temporal messianic kingdom). The third *Sibylline Oracle,* like the New Testament (e.g., 1 Cor. 15:25; 2 Pet. 1:11; Luke 10:9), attests to each of these themes. *Sib. Or.* 3.46-48 reads: "But when Rome will also rule over Egypt . . . then the most great kingdom of the immortal king will become manifest over men." Here God's kingdom will rule over every human being: "over men" means "over all people." *Sib. Or.* 3.767 has this: "And then, indeed, he will raise up a kingdom for all ages." Here God's kingdom is without end and, as in 3:46-48, its imminence is implicit; the present situation will not long endure.

BIBLIOGRAPHY

G. R. BEASLEY-MURRAY 1986, *Jesus and the Kingdom of God,* Grand Rapids: Eerdmans. • J. BRIGHT 1953, *The Kingdom of God,* Nashville: Abingdon. • J. CARMIGNAC 1986, "Roi, royauté et royaume dans le liturgie angélique," *RevQ* 12: 177-86. • J. J. COLLINS 1997, "The Kingdom of God in the Apocrypha and Pseudepigrapha," in idem, *Seers, Sibyls, and Sages in Hellenistic Judaism,* Leiden: Brill, 99-114. • M. HENGEL AND A. M. SCHWEMER, ED. 1991, *Königsherrschaft Gottes und himmlischer Kult,* Tübingen: Mohr-Siebeck. • W. L. WILLIS, ED. 1987, *The Kingdom of God in 20th-Century Interpretation,* Peabody, Mass.: Hendrickson.

DALE C. ALLISON, JR.

Kingship

During the Second Temple period, the Jewish people were ruled by both foreign and native kings. Beginning in the late sixth century B.C.E., Judah came under the Persian monarchy. After 332 B.C.E., Alexander the Great and his successors — the Ptolemaic and Seleucid kings — reigned over Jews in Judah and throughout the Greek East and Mesopotamia. After the Maccabean Revolt (167-164 B.C.E.), the Hasmoneans reestablished native rule in Palestine, first as high priests and by 104 B.C.E. as kings. When the Hasmonean dynasty ended in 63 B.C.E., Jews throughout the Mediterranean world came under the reign of Rome, and for those in Palestine, from 40 B.C.E. onward, under the rule of the Jewish client king Herod the Great and his descendants. During this time, Jewish ideas about kingship were primarily influenced by traditions from the Hebrew Bible, though also by the institution of Hellenistic kingship. An understanding of kingship in early Judaism requires attention both to the historical institution of kingship and to the literary sources that expressed ideas about kingship.

Kingship in Ancient Israel and the Greco-Roman World

Native kings ruled in ancient Israel from ca. 1000 to 586 B.C.E., and so not surprisingly the Hebrew Bible contains a variety of traditions about Israelite kingship. The most widely attested tradition, however, is the royal ideology of the Davidic dynasty (cf. 2 Samuel 7; 1 Kings 2:1-4; Psalms 2; 72; 89; 110; 132; Isa. 9:1-7). According to this ideology, Davidic kings were appointed by God to rule Israel in perpetuity. They were to provide security from enemy nations and establish justice for their people; they would build and oversee the Jerusalem Temple and preside over a fertile and prosperous land. In short, as "God's son" the king would represent God's rule and mediate divine blessings to the people. The dynastic promise could be conceived as unconditional (2 Samuel 7) or dependent on the obedience of the king (Psalm 132); sometimes it was said to be secured by a covenant (Psalm 89; 2 Samuel 23).

Beyond this royal ideology, other ideas about kingship are present: Deut. 17:14-20 envisions a limited form of monarchy wherein the king's conduct is restricted and his rule to be guided by the Law; Gen. 49:8-

12 speaks of the scepter remaining with the tribe of Judah; Num. 24:17-19 refers to a future king arising out of Israel; and Isa. 32:1-8 uses language from the wisdom tradition to characterize an ideal king. Further, some scholars have argued for a tradition of popular, charismatic kingship, citing examples such as Abimelech, Saul, Jeroboam, and David during his rise to power. Important, too, is an antimonarchical tradition (Judg. 8:22-23; 9:1-15; 1 Sam. 8:1-22; 10:17-19), in which human kingship is understood as a rejection of God's kingship.

With the fall of Judah in 586 B.C.E., native Israelite kingship came to an end. In turn, exilic and postexilic biblical literature reflects new ideas about kingship, including hopes for the restoration of the monarchy (cf. Hag. 2:20-23; Jer. 33:14-26), transfer of the Davidic king's role to the people (Isa. 55:3-5), setting hopes of restoration on a foreign king, Cyrus (Isa. 45:1), and valuing Davidic kingship for establishing the Jerusalem Temple and cult (Chronicles). The actual governance of Judah, however, was in the hands of Jewish high priests, a theocratic system that would last through Persian, Hellenistic, and even Hasmonean hegemony.

In the Greek world, political philosophers became interested in kingship as a form of governance after 400 B.C.E. due to the breakdown of the democratically ruled city-state and for centuries thereafter produced numerous treatises setting forth their theories about the basis and character of kingship. Nonetheless, the actual institution of Hellenistic kingship was created by Alexander the Great and his successors. Though thoroughly Greek, these kings legitimated their rule over native peoples by claiming to be the heirs of ancient Near Eastern monarchs; thus, in Egypt the Ptolemies reigned as successors to the Pharaohs, a status seemingly accepted by the populace. Typical features of Hellenistic kingship also included a drive for territorial expansion, the use of mercenaries, multiple palaces, multiple wives, minting of coins, and putative genealogical links to ancient mythological figures. In addition, especially outside of Greece, Hellenistic kings were worshiped as deities.

Jewish Kingship in History

In the aftermath of their victory over Seleucid forces, the Maccabees established an independent priestly monarchy. In 152 B.C.E., Jonathan assumed the high-priestly office while maintaining civil authority. By 140 B.C.E., his brother Simon would be recognized as high priest, commander, and ethnarch of the Jews (1 Macc. 14:47), inaugurating the Hasmonean dynasty, which would last until the Roman general Pompey took control of Palestine in 63 B.C.E. Initially, however, the Hasmoneans avoided the title of king, perhaps because they wanted to distinguish themselves from the very Hellenistic rulers they had resisted. Yet, in 104 B.C.E. Aristobulus I took the title of king (Josephus, *Ant.* 13.301), as did his successors — Alexander Jannaeus, Aristobulus II, and Hyrcanus II.

Like all rulers, the Hasmonean priest-kings faced the question of legitimation, especially since they were not from the traditional high-priestly family of Zadokite priests or from the royal (Davidic) line. First Maccabees, a work containing Hasmonean ideology, claims that their rule was sanctioned by foreign states (1 Macc. 14:16-24), by the Judean people (14:25-49), and most importantly by God, who accomplished his purposes through them (5:61-62). Like heroes of old, especially Phinehas, they were rewarded by God for their faithfulness and mighty deeds (2:51-60). Even so, they encountered opposition from the Pharisees, some of whom opposed the merger of high-priestly and civil/royal offices (*Ant.* 13.291-95). Likewise, resistance to this arrangement helps explain why priestly and royal figures are kept separate in Qumran literature. Nonetheless, Hyrcanus II's intervention with Rome on behalf of Diaspora Jews indicates that he saw himself not only as King of Judea, but as King of the Jews (*Ant.* 14:223-24; cf. also *Ant.* 15.14-15)

The Hasmoneans assimilated some aspects of Hellenistic kingship: they used mercenaries, expanded their territory, engaged in diplomatic intrigue with foreign nations, adopted Greek names, claimed kinship with the Spartans, and named their dynasty after an early ancestor. Josephus even calls Aristobulus I *philhellene* (*Ant.* 13.318). On the other hand, unlike Hellenistic kings, the Hasmoneans were native rulers, had one wife, imprinted no images on their coins, and certainly were not worshiped as gods. Further Hellenization would await the next Jewish royal dynasty, the Herodian.

Herod the Great was appointed King of Judea by the Roman Senate in 40 B.C.E., a decision ratified by Octavian (Augustus) in 30 B.C.E. As a Roman client king Herod had near absolute power in the domestic sphere, though he could take no independent foreign policy or military action. His role included keeping order, collecting taxes, supporting Roman policy, and appointing the Jewish high priest. His mediation on behalf of Jews in Asia suggests that Herod, too, aspired to be King of the Jews, though in the end he and his successors failed to serve as symbols of Jewish national identity. Not only did the Herodians face continued doubts about their legitimacy from the populace, but the division of Herod's kingdom among his three sons (none of whom held the title "king," but see Matt. 14:9) further diminished any sense of national kingship. The brief reign of Herod Agrippa I as king over his grandfather's entire kingdom (41-44 C.E.) did little to change this perception. Indeed, Agrippa II, who ruled over only a portion of his father's realm, sided with Rome during the Jewish revolt in 66-70 C.E. As always, the first loyalty of the Herodians was to Rome.

Under the Herodians, Jewish kingship was virtually indistinguishable from Hellenistic kingship. Being of Idumean stock, Herod and his successors were perceived by many of their Jewish subjects as foreigners, more like the Macedonian kings who ruled over ancient Near Eastern kingdoms than the native Hasmoneans. The Herodians established Greek cities named for their Roman patrons and built multiple palaces. They used foreign troops in their armies, and Herod engaged in polygamy. They also sought to accommodate non-Jewish subjects by building pagan shrines for them. There was, however, no ruler cult, although Agrippa I was acclaimed as a god by Gentile supporters, an event that was interpreted as the cause of his death shortly thereafter (Josephus, *Ant.* 19.343-52; Acts 12:20-23). On the other hand, the Herodians did respect Jewish religious sensibilities — their coins and buildings did not display divine, human, or animal images (except for the Roman eagle Herod installed over the gate of the Temple), and Agrippa I, who was remembered as the most pious of Herodians, is said to have read Deut. 17:14-20, the Torah's statement on kingship (*m. Soṭah* 8:8).

Nonetheless, for many of their subjects, Herodian kings lacked legitimacy: they had been appointed by foreigners; their ancestry was not from a traditional royal line but an Idumean one that had only recently converted to Judaism; and Herod's attempt to legitimate his kingship by marrying the Hasmonean princess Mariamne was undermined by his brutal elimination of the rest of the Hasmonean royal family, including eventually Mariamne and her two sons. Opposition to Herodian kings was also fueled by their repressive tactics and Hellenizing ways.

In contrast to Herodian kingship, the tradition of Jewish popular kingship that emerged in this period was decidedly anti-Roman. Representatives of this form of kingship include Judas, son of Hezekias; Herod's slave Simon; and Athronges, who were active in the aftermath of King Herod's death (4 B.C.E.); the Sicarii leader Menahem and Simon bar Giora, figures during the First Jewish Revolt (66-70 C.E.); and Bar Kosiba, the leader of the Second Revolt (132-135 C.E.). Each claimed — or was acclaimed by his followers — to be the Jewish king. Indeed, Bar Kosiba's title — Bar Kokhba ("son of the star") — derives from the promise of a future king in Num. 24:17. These figures were charismatic leaders, apparently of humble origin, who marshaled popular support and peasant fighters against Roman and Herodian rule. Their movements appear similar to movements of popular kingship in ancient Israel, which were likewise led by charismatic leaders who with popular support fought for liberation from foreign domination.

Of course, some Jews rejected the institution of human kingship. When Hyrcanus II and Aristobulus II pleaded their cases for the Hasmonean crown before Pompey, some Jews not only opposed them but objected to the very idea of Jewish kingship. Josephus explains, "The nation was against them both and asked not to be ruled by a king, saying that it was the custom of their country to obey the priests of God," and that the two claimants "were seeking to change their form of government in order that they might become a nation of slaves" (*Ant.* 14.41). Forty years of Hasmonean kingship had not extinguished a preference for theocratic rule by high priests. After Herod's death, when his son Archelaus came before Augustus to seek the crown, a Jewish delegation asked "to be delivered from kingship and such forms of rule," preferring to be under the Roman governor of Syria (*Ant.* 17.314). Moreover, when Rome instituted direct rule of Judea in 6 C.E., Judas the Galilean, founder of the sect Josephus calls the Fourth Philosophy, led an armed revolt based on the view that "God alone is their leader and master" (*Ant.* 18.23). Josephus reports that there was wide support for the Fourth Philosophy (*Ant.* 18.9), an apparent revival of the Israelite antimonarchical tradition.

Jewish Literary Sources on Kingship

Ben Sira, a Jerusalem sage living in the late third or early second century B.C.E., addresses kingship in his book of wisdom. Of primary importance for him is that God is king (Sir. 1:8; 50:15); accordingly, it is God who establishes all earthly rulers (10:4). Further, the qualities most appropriate to human kings are those of the divine king — wisdom, mercy, and justice — and he warns that kings should not be overly exalted (10:5-18), a sentiment perhaps aimed at the ruler cults associated with the Ptolemaic and Seleucid kings. Ben Sira's view of kingship appears most influenced by Deuteronomic conceptions of kingship, though it is consistent with Greek ideas, which he may have known. In his "Praise of the Ancestors," Ben Sira offers a decidedly mixed evaluation of the kings of ancient Israel, concluding that because of their sin the kings of Judah came to an end (48:5), and further assigns the roles and symbols of kingship to priestly figures. This interpretation of Israelite kingship supported Ben Sira's ideal of theocratic rule by high priests.

Ezekiel the Tragedian (late third or early second century B.C.E.), in his play *The Exagōgē,* depicts Moses as a universal king (lines 68-89). Moses dreams that God asks him to take God's place on a great throne on the top of Mt. Sinai, along with God's crown and scepter. From the throne Moses can see the whole world, at which point the stars fall at his feet. Ezekiel was an author from the Egyptian Diaspora, and his view of Moses' universal kingship may have been a response to notions of universal kingship among the Ptolemies. Eupolemus, a mid-second-century-B.C.E. historian and ambassador to Rome for Judas Maccabee, wrote a work entitled *On the Kings of Judea.* Its surviving fragments present a glorious depiction of David and Solomon, especially the former's military conquests and the latter's Temple building. A work reminiscent of Chronicles, its positive portrayal of Israelite kingship may have served as nationalistic support for Maccabean rulers and their expansionist aims.

The *Letter of Aristeas* (ca. 130 B.C.E.), a work from the Egyptian Diaspora, tells the story of how the Hebrew Scriptures were translated into Greek. It includes a set of fictional banquet scenes in which the host, the Egyptian king Ptolemy II, questions seventy-two Jewish sages about the nature and practice of kingship. In every case, the sages recommend that the king act in accord with virtues such as justice, patience, benevolence, temperance, and impartiality, and that he avoid pride and tyranny, for a good king imitates God. And kings should recognize that "God rules all things" and "guides the actions of all of us" (195). There is little in the sage's conception of kingship that is distinctively

Jewish, except perhaps the sages' routine mention of God at the end of their advice. Instead, their conception parallels Hellenistic treatises of kingship, even on the point of the king imitating God. Here kingship is articulated in universalistic terms.

The most extensive treatment of kingship in early Judaism comes from a section of the *Temple Scroll* called the Law of the King (11QT 56:12–59:21). Typically dated to the last third of the second century B.C.E., the *Temple Scroll* appears to come from a group related but antecedent to the sectarians at Qumran. The Law of the King is an interpretation and elaboration of Deut. 17:14-20. Following this biblical text, it requires that the king be an Israelite chosen by God, a king who refrains from accumulating horses and wealth. The biblical prohibition against multiplying wives is strengthened, however, to require monogamy, no doubt in contrast to the practice of Hellenistic kings. Moreover, while Deut. 17:20 instructs the king to write out a copy of the Law for himself so that he may rule in accord with it, the Law of the King instructs the priests in charge of the Law to do this for the king. Obedience to God's Law would result in peace, prosperity, and long rule for the king and his descendants; disobedience will mean exile for his people and the end of his dynasty.

The duties of the king in the *Temple Scroll* consist of military and judicial affairs. He is to appoint an army and a royal guard, the latter to protect the king from foreign capture, a provision likely motivated by the capture and execution of Jonathan Maccabee by the Seleucid Trypho (ca. 142 B.C.E.). Yet, the king's war-making activities and share of the plunder are restricted, features distinguishing the conduct of the Jewish king from the territorial expansion policies of Hellenistic kings. The king's judicial activities are to be marked by righteous judgments and exercised in consultation with a council composed of leaders, priests, and Levites, whom the king may not treat haughtily or ignore. In this regard, the royal office is distinct from the office of high priest, resulting in a model of Jewish governance contrary to the Hasmonean merger of priestly and civil rule. Noteworthy, too, is the absence of ideas associated with Judean royal ideology, such as divine sonship, Davidic lineage, or unconditional rule; instead, the perspective is Deuteronomic. Altogether, the Jewish kingship envisioned in the *Temple Scroll* is carefully circumscribed and conditional. And while derived from the biblical text, it reflects a response to Hellenistic and Hasmonean rulers.

Texts that describe a royal messiah — an eschatological king — entail a concept of Jewish kingship. Hence, in the Dead Sea Scrolls, the legitimate king was expected to be of Davidic descent. He will be righteous and mighty, the latter quality being especially important for the king's primary task of defeating Israel's enemies and judging the nations. Nonetheless, the king will be subordinate to the authority of the priests. According to *Psalms of Solomon* 17 (ca. 50 B.C.E.), the ideal king will be a "son of David," possessing the qualities of power, righteousness, compassion, and especially wisdom. As a universal king, he will destroy the unrighteous and judge the nations. Appointed by God, he will serve as the representative of God's kingship, mediating divine blessings to the people. In contrast to the *Temple Scroll* and the Qumran sectarian writings, the *Psalms* have no priests in view. Jewish kingship is presented rather in terms of the Davidic royal ideology, particularly as articulated in Isa. 11:1-5. In the *Testaments of the Twelve Patriarchs,* kingship belongs to a descendant of Judah, who will bring salvation by destroying Israel's enemies. Kingship, however, is regularly presented alongside the priesthood from the tribe of Levi, to which it is explicitly subordinated (*T. Jud.* 21:1-2)

For Philo of Alexandria (first half of first century C.E.) reflection on kingship begins with the premise that "God is the first and sole king of the universe" (*De Posteritate Caini* 101). For the ideal in human kingship, Philo passes over Israelite kings such as David and Solomon, turning instead to Adam, Melchizedek, Abraham, and especially Moses. Moses was the true king because of his goodness, closeness to God, and desire to benefit his subjects (*Mos.* 1.148-62); he embodied the Hellenistic ideal of the king as the "living law" (162). Although Philo's model kings are Jewish, his understanding of kingship is thoroughly Hellenistic.

Josephus (end of the first century C.E.) can fairly be labeled antimonarchical. In his retelling of the law on kingship from Deut. 17:14-20, he begins, "Aristocracy, with the life that is lived under it, is indeed the best . . . for God suffices for your ruler" (*Ant.* 4.223). Moreover, when Israel seeks a king, Samuel opposes monarchy because of "his innate righteousness and his hatred of kings" (*Ant.* 6.36). While a few kings are presented positively, such as David and Solomon, the Davidic dynastic promise is muted and reference to its unconditional character is deleted. Then, after following the sins and failings of the Judean kings, Josephus reports the end of the dynasty (*Ant.* 10.143). His story of the downfall of the Hasmoneans begins with Aristobulus I's declaration of kingship (*Ant.* 13.300-301), and he never tires of detailing King Herod's corruption. Josephus has no place for Jewish kingship; his ideal government is a priestly aristocracy (*Ag. Ap.* 2.184-89). Josephus evidently differed from his promonarchical rival, Justus of Tiberias, who served as secretary to King Agrippa II and wrote a chronicle of the kings of the Jews, beginning with Moses and ending with Agrippa.

Finally, some Jewish works offer a perspective on foreign kingship, with views ranging from positive to very negative. Thus, *Sibylline Oracle* 3 (ca. 150 B.C.E.) looks for God to appoint a "king from the sun" (652-56), who will bring an end to war and inaugurate an age when God's people would be strong (191-94). This ideal king, however, will come from the Ptolemaic line. Likewise, Josephus applies a biblical text about a world ruler, interpreted by some to refer to a Jewish figure, to Vespasian, the Roman general and future emperor (*J.W.* 6.312-13). These positive views of foreign kingship recall Deutero-Isaiah's assessment of Cyrus as a divinely appointed king. Other views are less positive, but still accepting. In the court tales of Daniel 1–6, Persian kings are portrayed as misguided, though seemingly open to recognizing the sovereignty of the Jewish God. And while Philo vigorously opposed worship of Emperor Gaius Caligula, he was otherwise accepting of Roman kingship *(Legatio ad Gaium).* More darkly, the apocalyptic visions in Daniel 7–12 characterize foreign kings as representative of demonic powers, symbolized by beasts from the sea; they oppress God's people and will eventually be destroyed. Similarly, in *1 Enoch* 46:3-8, the Son of Man will destroy earthly kings, who did not glorify and obey God, the source of their kingship.

BIBLIOGRAPHY

J. DAY, ED. 1998, *King and Messiah in Israel and the Ancient Near East,* Sheffield: Sheffield University Press. • K. E. POMYKALA 1995, *The Davidic Dynasty Tradition in Early Judaism,* Atlanta: Scholars Press. • D. MENDELS 1997, *The Rise and Fall of Jewish Nationalism,* 2d ed., Grand Rapids: Eerdmans, 55-79, 209-42. • T. RAJAK ET AL., EDS. 2007, *Jewish Perspectives on Hellenistic Rulers,* Berkeley: University of California Press.

See also: Messianism KENNETH E. POMYKALA

Kittim → Pesharim

Kosher Food → Meals; Purity and Impurity

L

Land, Concept of

The concept of the land within the corpus of Second Temple literature is to a significant extent an interpretive response to the presentation of the land concept in the extant scriptural traditions. Believing in the ongoing relevance of Scripture, Second Temple writers engage its treatment of the land directly through rewriting narrative and indirectly through brief citation, allusion, and paraphrase. In these engagements conceptualizations are reworked, reformulated, and, at times, undermined in light of contemporary realities and concerns.

In the Torah, promise and possession of the land are the key signatures of covenantal history. The narratives of Israel's forbears open with the first patriarch sighting and sojourning in the land; possession of the land is the pivot in the triad of promises that comprises the patriarchal covenant; and divine assurances of return accompany every patriarchal departure from the land. The idea of the land is comparably crucial to the story of the nation. Recollection of the patriarchal promise of the land and anticipation of its future conquest frame the narrative of the redemption from Egypt; the Sinai covenant creates a direct link between God, the land, and the Law; and tenure of the land is conditional on fidelity to God's covenant. Consequently, living in the land becomes a primary gauge of the quality of Israel's relationship with God, for, in direct contrast to the patriarchal covenant with its assurance of eternal possession of the land, the Sinai formulation of the covenant threatens the possibility of exile expressed in the covenant curses. The tension between these two conceptions of land and covenant lays the foundation for an eschatology in which the punishment of dispossession is necessarily followed by future redemption and restoration to the land. Developed in the Latter Prophets, this historical eschatology makes the ingathering of exiles and restoration of the land to an idealized condition the cardinal features of an end time.

The Land Promise and the Patriarchal Covenant

In none of the Second Temple texts that rewrite Torah narrative is the promise of the land to the patriarchs given the centrality that it receives in the scriptural presentation. In a number of works the priority is shifted to a facet of the patriarchal covenant that is perceived as at risk in the contemporary world of the author. In the rewriting of Genesis undertaken in *Jubilees*, alterations to wording and context of the covenant-making narratives make the assurance of God's special relationship with the patriarchal progeny the definitive feature of the covenant. The *Testament of Moses* explicitly affirms the promise of the land to "the fathers," but its central motif involves God's oath to preserve Abraham's seed. The recollections of the patriarchal covenant scattered throughout Pseudo-Philo's rewriting of Joshua and Judges emphasize the promise of great numbers and peoplehood. Josephus, who transforms covenantal encounter into forecasts of future destiny and God's blessings into divine assistance, places references to the land promise in noncovenantal contexts and either deletes strong land-focused passages or reworks them to accentuate predictions of great population growth.

Works that include only a single allusion to the patriarchal covenant demonstrate a similar shift of focus. In the Prayer of Azariah (1:12-14) and the *Damascus Document* (1:5), the covenant is associated with the promise of numbers. God's special relationship with Abraham's descendants is stressed in 3 Macc. 6:3, *Pss. Sol.* 9:9, and *4 Ezra* 3:15, and in Judith 5, where the Gentile Achior, who had made no mention of a land promise in his earlier account of Israel's forbears, makes a point of God's activity within Israel's history.

Only in contexts that involve activation of God's mercy to affect return from exile are the patriarchs mentioned with specific reference to the promise of the land. An intercessory prayer for the return of the Babylonian exiles in the *Testament of Moses* appeals to God's promise of the land to the patriarchs (*T. Mos.* 3:9). Baruch recalls a divine assurance that once God returns the exiles to the land sworn to the patriarchs, He "will never again remove" them "from the land that I have given them" (Bar. 2:34-35). In more eschatological contexts, the dying Tobit testifies to a time when everyone will live "in safety forever in the land of Abraham, and it will be given over to them" (Tob. 14:7 Long Version);

and in *2 Baruch* the promise to the patriarchs assures that before the eschaton all those who had been dispersed would be returned (*2 Bar.* 78:7).

At play in these treatments is an interest in demonstrating that historical events — the Babylonian Exile, by now a vivid part of national memory, and in the case of *2 Baruch,* the events of 70 C.E. — did not invalidate God's promise that the patriarchal progeny would eternally possess the land (Gen. 13:15; 17:8). Some texts shield that promise from the vicissitudes of history by shifting its eternal aspect to another component of the covenant; eschatological treatments connect the eternality to a permanent end of all exile; and in several instances a point is made of the inalienable nature of Israel's right of ownership.

The Nature of the Land

Although the author of the book of *Jubilees* at one point has the land promise encompass "all the land that is beneath the sky" and eternal rule over "the entire earth" (*Jub.* 32:19; cf. Sir. 44:21), *Jubilees* is one of the few Second Temple texts that otherwise retains the territorial borders delineated in the patriarchal narratives of Genesis. The geography also appears in a tale that grounds the assurance of eternal possession of the land in the postdiluvian division of the world. In that tale, the land, with borders encompassing those in Genesis, is within the territory eternally allotted to Shem, who assigns it to his son Arpachshad, ancestor of Abraham (*Jub.* 8:12-17; 9:4). All of Noah's sons and grandsons take an oath foreswearing "until eternity" occupation of another's share (*Jub.* 9:14-15); but Ham's son Canaan violates the oath and settles together with his sons in the land belonging to the line of Shem. Consequently the territory came to bear his name (*Jub.* 10:29-34).

A claim of legitimate inheritance is made in other texts as well (e.g., 1 Macc. 15:33; Jdt. 4:16-21; Ps.-Philo, *Bib. Ant.* 39:9), but the metahistorical grounding in *Jubilees* establishes the broadest of claims. All the territory within the delineated borders is universally recognized as the eternal possession of the line of Arpachshad, that is, Abraham and his progeny. Regardless of who physically resides there, regardless of conquest or control, be it partial or full, temporary or permanent, and regardless of name, the land is the inalienable inheritance of Israel. Such claims eliminate the dissonance between patriarchal promise and historical experience, but the metahistorical conceptualization does not readily conform to scriptural notions that the land belongs to God (Lev. 25:23; cf. Josh. 22:19) or that it possesses special properties. Indeed, the closest *Jubilees* comes to ascribing such characteristics to the land is in an indication that Shem's allotment encompassed "the holy of holies . . . the residence of the Lord" (*Jub.* 8:18-21) and in a single reference to the lasting purity of the land in the end time (*Jub.* 50:5).

In other Second Temple works, the holiness associated with God's house and Jerusalem is expanded to include the entire land, and the phrase "holy land" employed in Zech. 2:16, appears in a wide range of texts (e.g., 2 Macc. 1:7; *Bib. Ant.* 19:10; Wis. 12:3; and *2 Bar.* 71:1; 84:8). The purity of the land, an extension of its holiness, is fully developed in the *Temple Scroll,* where the purity is exegetically derived from God's presence within the wilderness camp rather than from the biblical concept of the land belonging to God. Divine ownership or election of the land is explicitly stated in *4 Ezra* 5:24 and CD 1:7, and suggested in Wis. 12:3. Also evident, but generally undeveloped in Second Temple literature, is the biblical personification of the land (*2 Bar.* 71:1) and the attribution to it of metaphysical qualities (*Bib. Ant.* 7:4; 19:10).

The Land and the Law

In their treatments of past history, Second Temple writers affirm the biblical connection between loss of the land and violation of the Law, often expressing it in terms of the paradigm of sin, punishment (exile), repentance, and return (Deut. 4:28-30). When they turn to the postrestoration period, however, the Deuteronomic linkage becomes problematic. Not only does it permit the possibility of another exile (i.e., a cyclical pattern such as only Josephus entertains; cf. *Ant.* 4.314), but the reality of postexilic life in the land does not conform to the splendor of the restoration envisioned in Deuteronomy and the classical prophets. Some texts explicitly confront that dissonance and, to account for it, modify the paradigm. Others ignore the dissonance by treating the Second Temple era within a collapsed paradigm of ongoing sin and punishment that, significantly, does not include loss of the land. Another set of texts acknowledges the functioning of the sin/punishment paradigm in Israel's past but deliberately excludes contemporary events from its workings.

The first strategy is evident in Tobit, *Jubilees,* Baruch, and, to some extent, the *Testament of Moses,* each of which develops the notion of a flawed return. Tobit has the return generated by divine mercy rather than repentance and uses the inferiority of the rebuilt Temple as a symbol of the imperfect restoration (14:5 Long Version). In *Jubilees* repentance precedes the return from Babylonian Exile, but return to the land is no longer a culminating point. Only a more intense postexile repentance will restore Israel's special relationship with God, the focal point of the covenant throughout *Jubilees* (1:15). Baruch also requires greater repentance after the return (Bar. 2:8), because those in the land (those who were not exiled = those who returned from exile) are apt to repeat the sin of not faithfully serving the foreign kings (Nebuchadnezzar and Belshazzar = Antiochus IV and Antiochus V) God had set over them (Bar. 1:11-13). The notion of imperfect return is also suggested in the *Testament of Moses,* where even the possibility of repentance is rejected. Instead, an intercessory plea patterned on Moses' intercession at Sinai (Deut. 9:26-29 recollecting Exod. 32:13) ends the Babylonian Exile, with another cycle of sin and punishment coming thereafter (*T. Mos.* 4:5-6; 5-8)

Other biblical prototypes, comparably unrelated to the land, are used in works that view contemporary hardships through the lens of a collapsed paradigm of ongoing sin and punishment. Daniel 9 is the model for several apocalyptic treatments that portray the years after the return from the Babylonian Exile as an ongoing state of exile (*1 Enoch* 93:8-10 [the *Apocalypse of Weeks*]; *1 Enoch* 89:68-75; 90:1-8 [the *Animal Apocalypse*]; and *T. Levi* 17:10-11; cf. CD 1). 1 Maccabees employs motifs from the Torah narratives of the wilderness years and presents the Maccabean leaders as Moses/Phinehas-like characters opposing Zimri-like Hellenizers who had made forbidden covenants with the Gentiles (1 Macc. 1:40; 3:55-56; 5:44-45, 55-62). The author of 2 Maccabees portrays Antiochus' persecution as punishment for the sin of Hellenization and has the martyrs, citing Deut. 32:26, pray that God relent from his anger (2 Macc. 7:6). Suggesting a parallel between the postrestoration era and the early conquest years, Pseudo-Philo's rewriting of Joshua and Judges follows the model of Deut. 31:16-18 and attributes hardships and suffering to temporary abandonment by God (*Bib. Ant.* 13:10). The motif of God's hidden face is also employed in the *Damascus Document,* but there the hiding is not from Israel (as in Deut. 31:17-18; Ezek. 39:23) but rather "from the land" (CD 2:9). In other texts the punishment motif is combined with the notion that suffering is itself a reflection of God's presence and mercy, since it disciplines, cleanses, and encourages repentance (Tobit 13; 2 Macc. 6:12-16; *Pss. Sol.* 10:1-2; and, with a more universal perspective, Wis. 12:2).

A more radical position that totally disengages contemporary experience from both land and covenant appears in Judith 8 and *Testament of Moses* 9. Paralleling the suffering of her community with God's testing of the patriarchs, Judith explicitly rejects any connection between the siege being laid against her town and violation of the covenant (Jdt. 8:18-20, 25-27). In the *Testament of Moses* the disengagement is placed in the mouth of Taxo, who, confronting Israel's great suffering, proclaims, "Never did our fathers or their ancestors tempt God by transgressing His commandments" (*T. Mos.* 9:2-4).

Concern with threats to Jerusalem and desecration of the Temple is evident in treatments of postexilic history (e.g., Judith; 1, 2 Maccabees). Yet Second Temple writers generally do not imagine loss of the land, be it a punishment, a divine testing, or a mode of disciplining, as a contemporary possibility. There is a notion of contemporary voluntary exile in the *Psalms of Solomon* and in the Qumran texts. In the pseudepigraphic work, it is a flight from the evils wrought by Pompey in Jerusalem (*Pss. Sol.* 17:16-17); in the sectarian works, it is a purifying temporary return to the wilderness (in a reenacting of the biblical wilderness years; 1QS 8:12b-14; 9:18-20) or a voluntary escape from sinful pollution in the land of Judah (CD 4:3; 6:5).

The absence of a strong focus on the land in Second Temple accounts of contemporary history is not unrelated to the import assigned to the land concept in sacred literature. When land concepts cannot be adapted to fit an extended, often troubled, postexilic period of living in the land, writers do not challenge scriptural land theology outright. Instead, they employ alternative motifs and models to place their own era within the context of covenantal history.

Eschatology

In contrast to the treatment of contemporary history, many Second Temple texts incorporate a land concept in their visions of the end time. Frequently it is the ingathering of the northern tribes and all exiles. In Tob. 14:7 (Long Version) and *2 Bar.* 78:7 the ingathering is associated with promises to the patriarchs; in *4 Ezra* 13:40-48 it is a precondition for final judgment; and in *Pss. Sol.* 11:2-3 it is simply an aspect of the end time. Where ingathering of exiles is not central, conceptions of the eschaton feature other land-related motifs. The author of *Jubilees* envisions a time when a truly purified Israel "will live confidently in the entire land . . . and the land will be pure from that time until eternity" (*Jub.* 50:5). The *Testament of Moses* closes with an assurance that "it is not possible for the nations to drive [the Israelites] out or extinguish them completely. For God, who has foreseen all things in the world, will go forth . . ." (*T. Mos.* 12:12). In *Pseudo-Philo,* Moses is promised that after the final judgment he and his fathers will dwell in the "place of sanctification" that God had shown him on a heavenly tour (*Bib. Ant.* 19:13). Even Josephus, who includes no concept of covenanted land in his presentation of the scriptural narrative, envisions, albeit in Hellenistic terms, a future for the land as a motherland center for an overflowing population living in an eternal diaspora (*Ant.* 4.115-16).

BIBLIOGRAPHY

I. GAFNI 1997, *Land, Center and Dispersion: Jewish Constructs in Late Antiquity,* Sheffield: Sheffield Academic Press. • L. FELDMAN 1997, "The Concept of Exile in Josephus," in *Exile: Old Testament, Jewish, and Christian Conceptions,* ed. J. M. Scott, Leiden: Brill, 145-72. • B. HALPERN-AMARU 1994, *Rewriting the Bible: Land and Covenant in Post-Biblical Jewish Literature,* Valley Forge, Penn.: Trinity Press International. • B. HALPERN-AMARU 1997, "Exile and Return in *Jubilees,*" in *Exile: Old Testament, Jewish, and Christian Conceptions,* ed. J. M. Scott, Leiden: Brill, 127-44. • M. A. KNIBB 1983, "Exile in the Damascus Document," *JSOT* 25: 99-117.

BETSY HALPERN AMARU

Latin

Early Jewish Literature Preserved in Latin

There are numerous Old Testament pseudepigrapha preserved in Latin by the Catholic Church of western and central Europe. Biblical apocrypha aside, only a small number of them may reflect an originally Jewish document relatively intact, that is, without having been edited by successive copyists to accommodate specific Christian interests. Thus, the extant Latin fragments of the book of *Jubilees* are largely congruent with the Ethiopic version and the Qumran fragments; the Latin text of the *Assumption of Moses,* also fragmentarily preserved, shows no trace of having been revised in a Christian sense; and the Christianization of the Latin version of *4 Ezra* 3–14 is limited to the incidental addition of "Christ" to the phrase "my [i.e., God's] son" in 7:29 (there is no such addition in the Syriac or Armenian version). It is usually assumed that the Latin *Book of Biblical Antiquities* is also of Jewish origin, although its relatively late attestation should warn against taking this for granted.

No Jewish original may be suspected for most other Old Testament pseudepigrapha preserved in Latin. Even if the *Life of Adam and Eve,* for instance, could be proven to go back to a Jewish original (which is contested), the Latin form of this writing is so developed and so remote from its earliest traceable stages that it would be far-fetched to suppose a Jewish hand in its production. It does contain traditions that are absent from earlier stages but are nonetheless demonstrably Jewish in origin; but this fact does not justify the assumption that other traditions in it, for which no such demonstration can be made, are equally of Jewish origin.

The question of Jewish origin is related to that of the original language of composition. No Old Testament pseudepigrapha originally composed in Latin are thought to have been of Jewish origin. Latin pseudepigrapha that are considered to reflect Jewish originals are commonly thought to be translations from Greek — this is virtually certain for the *Assumption of Moses* and *4 Ezra,* and likely for many others. A Hebrew original for such writings is often supposed but difficult to prove; in the case of writings that are preserved only in translations from Greek, the supposition of a Hebrew original underlying the hypothetical Greek text is necessarily speculative (the presence of Hebrew fragments of the book of *Jubilees* among the Qumran scrolls is a fortunate exception).

Early Jewish Literature in the Latin Bible

The Latin Bible has preserved several Jewish writings that are absent from the Hebrew Bible but present in the Septuagint. In the case of these "apocryphal" writings, no distinction needs to be made between the OL translations and the Vulgate Bible, since Jerome did not produce fresh translations from the Greek for the Apocrypha, allegedly because he had no Hebrew originals for them to improve on the extant Greek texts. Most Vulgate codices and editions of the Bible include versions of writings known from the Septuagint, but not from the Hebrew Bible: *Judith, Tobit* (designated as *Tobias*), *First* and *Second Maccabees, Wisdom of Solomon, Wisdom of Jesus ben Sira, Baruch* (including the *Epistle of Jeremiah*), and the additions to Daniel and Esther (duly marked with *obeloi,* and grouped together at the end of the writing in the case of Esther).

To the Greek biblical book of *1 Esdras* corresponds the Latin *3 Ezra,* added to the current editions of the Vulgate in an appendix after the New Testament, together with the *Prayer of Manasseh, Psalm 151,* and *4 Ezra.* For the last writing, Syriac, Arabic, and Armenian, but no Greek evidence is extant; next to the Syriac, the Latin version is undoubtedly the most important witness to it. The Latin biblical tradition shows no trace of *3 Maccabees.* An extrabiblical recension of the *Passion of the Maccabean Martyrs* exists, depending on *4 Maccabees.*

Old Testament Pseudepigrapha in Latin

The texts of a considerable number of Latin pseudepigrapha are conveniently brought together in Denis 1993. The Christian church of western and central Europe transmitted Old Testament pseudepigrapha until the fifteenth century. It seems that the art of printing, which boomed after its invention, was a major factor in the termination of their transmission. Printing became a major vehicle of intellectual communication in the urban culture of humanists, and it rapidly rendered obsolete the monasteries' function of manually copying texts. At the same time, the new dominant culture of academic scholars, concentrating on biblical and classical literature, had but little interest for hagiographical and parabiblical literature. In this part of the world (as opposed to, e.g., Greece, eastern Europe, and Ethiopia), most Old Testament pseudepigrapha were lost and forgotten by the year 1600, at least in written form (a remarkable exception being the *Testaments of the Twelve Patriarchs;* see H. J. de Jonge 1975) though oral culture naturally continued. A number of them were afterward recovered with the greatest difficulty by scholars who had a specific interest in them, as they were thought to reflect the historical circumstances from which Christianity emerged. As a result, their original function as part of the living tradition of the church until the Middle Ages (and afterward, insofar as oral tradition is concerned) is frequently overlooked even today (Picard 1999; M. de Jonge 2003; Davila 2005).

Of the better-known pseudepigrapha, the Latin tradition largely ignores *Testament of Abraham, Apocalypse of Abraham, Ezekiel the Tragedian, Joseph and Aseneth, Psalms of Solomon, Paralipomena of Jeremiah, 2 Baruch, 3 Baruch, Testament of Job,* and *Sentences of Phocylides.* Of other pseudepigrapha, there exist only small fragments or quotations, as in the case of *1 Enoch* (apart from the quotations of this writing in New Testament scripture: *1 Enoch* 106:1-18 in an eighth-century anthology; and quotations by various early Christian authors; Denis 2000), or secondary attestations (e.g., the *Epistle of Aristeas,* as used by Josephus and preserved in the Latin translations of his work).

That no traces of many writings exist in the Latin tradition does not imply that these were never received in the European church. Even if they did not turn out to be very successful, some lost pseudepigrapha were once known in the West, as is testified, for instance, by the presence of quotations of such works as *2 Baruch* by Cyprianus; *3 Baruch* by Valerius (Denis 2000). Substantial fragments of the *Book of Jannes and Jambres* are known only in Coptic, but a fragment preserved in an ancient English *Life of St. Margaret* no doubt presupposes a Latin stage (Pietersma 1994).

Conversely, it may be noted that the Latin church did its part in producing Old Testament pseudepigrapha of its own. This ongoing tradition is illustrated by the *Vision of the Holy Ezra* and several books of Latin *Sibylline Oracles.* There is much research still to be done in the area of originally Latin pseudepigrapha of the Old Testament, as is evidenced by, for instance, the preliminary studies into the pseudepigraphical Daniel literature by DiTommaso 2005; or by the studies into the western European tradition concerning the *Life of Adam and Eve* by Pettorelli 1999, and Murdoch and Tasioulas 2002.

Writings such as these, as well as Latin recensions of writings, show that the transmission of Old Testament pseudepigrapha was ongoing. The question of their possible Jewish origin may have been of little concern to western European scribes. To them, the issue of whether such writings could be the vehicles of bona fide information about matters of faith and truth was probably much more important — indeed, to the Latin church a "genuinely Jewish" origin may not always have been a recommendation in this respect.

In summary, the Latin tradition shows a variegated picture of the Old Testament pseudepigrapha: many apocryphal writings are known both in Greek and Latin, but some works that are common in the Eastern churches are lacking in the Western tradition, whereas other writings that must at some stage have been familiar in the East are now preserved only in Latin. Moreover, a number of Greek pseudepigrapha for which no manuscript evidence in Latin exists must still have been known in the West, in light of quotations in Latin ecclesiastical authors.

This situation reminds us that there is no such thing as a "corpus" of Old Testament apocrypha and pseudepigrapha, but only separate writings that happened to be transmitted in Latin (or not) and that were expected to answer particular needs of the Christian church in this part of the world. Consequently, the question of why they were transmitted, and in whose interest, needs to be answered for each individual writing, not as part of a supposedly secondary or even tertiary "canon" of pseudepigrapha. This is underlined by the fact that many parabiblical writings have been transmitted in the context of biblical commentaries, or as parts of hagiographical collections, a fact suggesting that they had little inherent authority but may often have served as homiletical resources or, in the case of the Daniel prognostica, as "magical" books.

BIBLIOGRAPHY

J. R. DAVILA 2005, *The Provenance of the Pseudepigrapha: Jewish, Christian, or Other?* Leiden: Brill. • A.-M. DENIS 1993, *Concordance latine des pseudépigraphes d'Ancien Testament,* Turnhout: Brepols. • A.-M. DENIS AND J.-C. HAELEWYCK 2000, *Introduction à la littérature religieuse judéo-hellénistique,* Turnhout: Brepols. • L. DITOMMASO 2005, *The Book of Daniel and the Apocryphal Daniel Literature,* Leiden: Brill. • H. J. DE JONGE 1975, "Die Patriarchentestamente von Roger Bacon bis Richard Simon," in *Studies on the Testaments of the Twelve Patriarchs,* ed. M. de Jonge, Leiden: Brill, 3-42. • M. DE JONGE 2003, *Pseudepigrapha of the Old Testament as Part of Christian Literature,* Leiden: Brill. • B. MURDOCH AND J. A. TASIOULAS 2002, *The Apocryphal Lives of Adam and Eve,* Exeter: University of Exeter Press. • J. P. PETTORELLI 1999, "La Vie latine d'Adam et éve: analyse de la tradition manuscrite," *Apocrypha* 10: 195-296. • J.-C. Picard 1999, *Le continent apocryphe: Essai sur les littératures apocryphes juive et chrétienne,* Turnhout: Brepols. • A. PIETERSMA 1994, *The Apocryphon of Jannes and Jambres the Magicians,* Leiden: Brill.

JOHANNES TROMP

Latin Authors on Jews and Judaism

References to Jews and Judaism are to be found in a large number of works written by Latin authors from the time of the Roman conquest of Judea in 63 B.C.E., down to the reign of the emperor Hadrian (117-138 C.E.). During that period, Judaism is known to have attracted considerable interest among the non-Jewish inhabitants of Rome and her provinces, to the extent that some of them even underwent full conversion to it. Unfortunately, the views of sympathizers such as these are not to be found in surviving Latin literature. What dominates the record, written exclusively by, and mainly for, élite Roman males, is largely negative comments on the Jews and Judaism. In the eyes of Rome's élite, Rome's conquest of the Jews demonstrated the superiority of not only the Romans themselves but their gods and religious system *(religio)* too. Hence the contempt with which they regarded the Jews; Cicero, for instance, describes them as "a nation born for servitude" (*De Provinciis Consularibus* 5.10). Hence also the derogatory term *superstitio* regularly applied by Latin writers to Judaism.

Factors Affecting the Portrayal of Jews and Judaism

There are reasons other than Roman feelings of superiority for the sources' negativity. Literary genre, which dictated to an extraordinary extent not only what should be written but how it should be presented, plays a crucial role here. Most of the surviving references to Jews and Judaism in Latin literature occur in writings of a satiric nature, whether satire proper, a formal genre of poetry invented by the Romans, or satirically inclined works such as the scoptic (mocking) epigrams for which the Flavian poet Martial is famous. Although Roman satirical writing does sometimes employ gentle humor and refined language to make its point, more commonly it relies upon ridicule, invective, and gross obscenity. So it is hardly surprising that the portrayal of the Jews and Judaism in satire is generally offensive.

Satire is not the only genre to give rise to negativity about the Jews. The second most important type of Latin literary source material for Jews and Judaism is Roman ethnographic writing. In this area of literary endeavor, as in so many others, the Romans were largely content to absorb what the Greeks had produced rather than to engage in original research of their own. Since the overwhelming tenor of Greek ethnographical writing about Jews and Judaism, especially that emanating from Alexandria in Egypt, is hostile, inevitably the tone of Latin ethnography is largely hostile too. Note must be also taken of the conventions of Roman forensic oratory. A legitimate law court practice for undermining the credibility of an opponent's case was to engage in ethnic insults. Jews did not escape such ugly ethnic smearing.

Finally, the part played by political developments

in the negative representation of the Jews and their religion in Latin literature deserves brief consideration. In the Julio-Claudian period (14-68 C.E.) relations between Jews and Romans, which had been fairly cordial during the long reign of Augustus (27 B.C.E.–14 C.E.), steadily deteriorated. Under both the emperor Tiberius (14-37 C.E.) and the emperor Claudius (41-54 C.E.), Jews were expelled from Rome in large numbers. In the province of Judea itself, the Roman governors struggled increasingly hard to maintain law and order (Goodman 1987). The revolt that broke out there in 66 C.E. was one of the most serious with which Rome ever had to deal. From 70 C.E. onward, it suited the Flavians, who had suppressed that revolt and now succeeded the Julio-Claudians as Rome's ruling family, to make their victory over the Jews the centerpiece of their dynastic propaganda. It is small wonder, then, that in the course of the first century Roman comments on the Jews and Judaism take on an increasingly hostile tone. The revolts of Jews in several eastern provinces (e.g., newly acquired Mesopotamia) toward the end of the emperor Trajan's reign (98-117 C.E.) did nothing to soften the attitudes of Roman élites. It was those revolts that in large part contributed to Hadrian's decision early in his reign (117 C.E.) to abandon all of Trajan's Mesopotamian conquests.

Not every comment on the Jews and their religion in Latin literature is hostile. Varro, an antiquarian scholar writing during the late republic, commends the Jews for their imageless worship, which in his view resembled early Roman religious practice (*Res Divinae*, cited by Augustine, *City of God* 4.31). The antiquarian-minded imperial biographer Suetonius comments neutrally upon the Jews in several places, as in their mourning at the funeral pyre of the murdered Caesar in 44 B.C.E. (*Divus Iulius* 84.5). But these are rare exceptions. In general, the comments of Latin writers on the Jews and their religious practices are unremittingly negative. (A comprehensive collection of these comments can be found in Stern 1974-1984.)

Cicero

Cicero, the earliest Latin writer whose comments upon the Jews and Judaism survive — in a forensic speech delivered in Rome in 59 B.C.E. — inveighs against the local Jews for their rowdiness, cliquishness, and disorderly public behavior. He denounces Jews in general as an irredeemably alien people, hopelessly in thrall to a barbarous superstition *(barbara superstitio)*, their customs and beliefs utterly incompatible with those of the Romans (*Pro Flacco* 28.66-69). Cicero himself may not have believed a word of this; in *Pro Cluentio* 139 he explicitly warns people against assuming that his courtroom remarks represent his personal views. But even if his own views on the Jews must remain uncertain, his forensic purpose in *Pro Flacco* 28.66-69 is not in doubt. Among the accusers of his client L. Valerius Flaccus, a former governor of the province of Asia on trial for extortion, were the Jews of that province whose Temple tax money Flaccus had seized and impounded. By depicting Jews in such unflattering terms, Cicero aimed to prejudice the jury, entirely composed of élite Roman males, against them and hence to weaken the force of the Jewish charge against his client. Flaccus' acquittal (Marshall 1975) shows that in his immediate aim Cicero was successful. However, in the long term he proved effective, too; such was the impact of his words that Judaism as a barbarous superstition subsequently became a veritable leitmotif in Latin writing on the Jews.

The Poets Horace, Ovid, and Tibullus

Compared with Cicero's comments on the Jews, the stray remarks on Judaism and the Jews found in the poetry of the Augustan period are mild. Although Horace in some of his *Sermones* mocks the Jews for their clannishness, superstitiousness, and the bizarre customs of circumcision and Sabbath observance, his tone is decidedly gentle and his vocabulary relatively inoffensive. Mild ridicule rather than fierce denunciation is meted out to Judaizing Romans such as the Sabbath-observing Aristius Fuscus who appears in *Sermones* 1.9, and in *Sermones* 1.4 the Jewish pressure-group tactics which so irritated Cicero (*Pro Flacco* 28.66) are turned into a joke.

Ovid in two of his love manuals exploits the Sabbath ("the seventh-day festival of the Syrian Jew") for comic purposes: it's a good day for picking up girls and since the shops are closed you'll be spared having to buy presents for them (Ovid, *Ars Amatoria* 1.75-80 and 413-16; *Remedia Amoris* 217–20)! The brief allusion of Tibullus, another love poet, to the Sabbath as a day on which traveling is taboo, is mild in tone (Tibullus, *Carmina* 1.3.15-18). Mostly this lack of venom is a question of genre.

Horace's chosen instrument of satire in his *Sermones* (= Conversation Pieces), as he makes clear in his defense of his art in *Sermones* 1.4, is gentle humor rather than fierce invective; in love poetry of the kinds produced by Ovid and Tibullus ethnic vituperation is wholly out of place. But the general climate of opinion may have been a factor, too. Augustus was known to be well disposed toward the Jews, especially those of Rome (Philo, *Legatio ad Gaium* 155–58), and his recorded comments on the Jewish pork taboo and Sabbath practices, while revealing a wry sense of humor, display not a grain of malice (Macrobius, *Saturnalia* 2.4.11 = Stern no. 543; Suetonius, *Divus Augustus* 76.2; Williams 2004).

The Historians Livy and Pompeius Trogus

It was not only the poets of the Augustan era who included references to the Jews and Judaism in their works. The historian Livy is known to have written about them, probably in book 102 of his *History of Rome* in the context of Pompey's conquest of Judea. However, apart from one brief comment on the aniconic nature of the Jewish cult quoted in a later source (*Scholia in Lucanum* 2.593 = Stern no. 133), none of his Jewish material has survived.

More fortunate has been his provincial contemporary, Pompeius Trogus, substantial sections of whose universal history, curiously entitled *Historiae Philippicae* (Philippic Histories), have come down to us in an abbreviated version put together several centuries later by the otherwise unknown Justin. One of these sections, the part dealing with the reconquest of Judea in 135 B.C.E. by the Seleucid monarch Antiochus VII Sidetes, has as its preface a brief excursus on Jewish history and customs (Justin, *Historiae Philippicae* 36.1.9–3.9). Besides drawing upon Greek (and therefore hostile) sources, Trogus also made use, possibly indirectly, of Jewish materials such as the Bible. Hence he produced an unusually favorable version of early Jewish history. Joseph, for instance, is lauded for his comprehensive knowledge of things both human and divine and Moses is noted for his physical beauty. There is also an unusually generous interpretation of certain Jewish customs. Jewish self-segregation, for example, is not seen as misanthropy, the usual Greek explanation. Rather, it is attributed to Jewish consideration for Gentiles — having been expelled from Egypt because of their leprous state (here the hostile construction placed upon the exodus by the Greeks is allowed momentarily to intrude), the Jews set themselves apart because they did not wish to give any offense to their neighbors. What impact, if any, this historian from Narbonese Gaul (modern Provence) had upon Augustan Rome is impossible to determine. No contemporary writer mentions him; further, certain features of his work suggest that his target audience/readership was the élite of the western provinces. His Jewish excursus is important, however, because it contains information not preserved in any other source (e.g., Dasmascene traditions about early Jewish history) and because it reveals a refreshingly dispassionate attitude toward the Jews and their customs.

Valerius Maximus

The only surviving Latin writer from the early Julio-Claudian period to mention the Jews is Valerius Maximus, whose compilation of memorable deeds and sayings *(Facta et Dicta Memorabilia),* written under the emperor Tiberius (14-37 C.E.), includes beneath the rubric *De Superstitionibus (Concerning Superstitions)* a description of an otherwise unknown expulsion of the Jews from Rome in 139 B.C.E. (Stern nos. 147a and 147b). Although the details have become hopelessly scrambled in transmission (Lane 1979), this evidence is important for illustrating the continuing existence of the negative attitude of the Roman élite toward *barbarae superstitiones* first evidenced in Cicero's *Pro Flacco.*

Seneca, Persius, and Petronius

Toward the end of Nero's reign (60s C.E.), the tone of Latin writing becomes noticeably harsher. For the Stoic philosopher Seneca, as reported by Augustine (*City of God* 6.11), the Jews were "a most criminal race" *(gens sceleratissima)* who through their absurd custom of resting on the Sabbath forfeited, through sheer idleness, a whole seventh of their life. Equally ridiculous, in Seneca's view, was their lighting of lamps on the Sabbath "since the gods do not need light, neither do men take pleasure in soot" (*Epistulae Morales* 95.47). Comparably contemptible were those people who adopted Jewish customs — at least the Jews were "aware of the origin and meaning of their rites," but non-Jews "go through a ritual not knowing why they do so" (Seneca, *De Superstitione,* as cited by Augustine, *City of God* 6.11).

Seneca's fellow Stoic, the satirical poet Persius, was no less scornful of the Jews. For him, Jewish rituals on the day of Herod, by which he probably means the Sabbath, serve as a paradigm for the enslaving effects of superstition upon the one who aspires to reach the Stoic goal of mental freedom. Persius subjects those rituals (lamplighting, consumption of fish and wine, prayer) to merciless ridicule.

Petronius, too, lampoons Jewish customs. In a particularly vicious satirical passage usually attributed to him (Fragment 37 = Stern no. 195), the Jewish pork taboo, for instance, is wickedly caricatured as pig worship, and circumcision is so obscenely described that scholars usually leave his words untranslated out of embarrassment (e.g., Heseltine in LCL; an exception is Schäfer 1997: 77-78).

Despite their manifest hostility, these passages reveal an increasing knowledge on the part of élite Romans about the Jews and their practices. Had Sabbath rituals not been commonly known about, the references to them would have been largely meaningless to a Roman readership. This is particularly the case with Persius, whose language is allusive in the extreme. Beneath the scurrility of Petronius' treatment of Judaism in Fragment 37 a considerable knowledge of Jewish practices has been detected. Petronius is well aware, for instance, of the crucial importance of circumcision as an initiatory rite for Jewish males. He knows that it was not performed out of perversity, as Tacitus was later to contend (*Histories* 5.5.2), but constituted the most fundamental aspect of Jewishness for male Jews.

Pliny the Elder and Quintilian

After 70 C.E., the tone of Roman writings on the Jews becomes even nastier, a hardly unexpected development in a city where the Jews' recent defeat at the hands of the Flavians was constantly advertised through demeaning images on both coins and public monuments (Millar 2005). In a throwaway remark in his *Natural History,* Pliny the Elder, a well-known supporter of the new régime, refers to the Jews as a race renowned for its contempt for the divine powers (*gens contumelia numinum insignis; Naturalis Historia* 13.46 = Stern no. 214). In the eyes of Quintilian, master rhetorician and Flavian courtier, the influence of Moses, founder of the Jewish superstition *(primus Iudaicae superstitionis auctor)* and creator of a race deadly to others *(perniciosam ceteris gentem),* was wholly malign (*Institutio Oratoria* 3.7.21 = Stern no. 230).

Martial

More graphically and specifically hostile, however, are the epigrams of Martial, a Roman of Spanish extraction eager to make a career for himself in the imperial capital by flattering Vespasian's successors, the emperors Titus and Domitian. Martial's specialty was the scoptic epigram, a short and witty poem, common (but not universal) features of which were satirical treatment of the subject, vituperative language, and gross obscenity. Since most of his comments on the Jews come in poems of this kind (*Epigrammata* 7.30, 35, 55, 82 and 11.94), it is not surprising that their general tone is extremely offensive.

Common to all the poems just listed are jokes about the circumcised state of the Jews, for which an epithet of extreme coarseness, hitherto avoided by Latin writers on the Jews, is generally used: *verpus.* Not only does this word characterize the physical appearance of the circumcised male organ but it implies its indulgence in excessive and unnatural sexual practices. Circumcised males, however, were not the only Jews to become the butt of Martial's humor. In *Epigrammata* 4.4, a comic poem consisting of a list of bad smells addressed to the hypermalodorous Bassa, Jewesses are mocked for their stinking breath, the result of fasting on the Sabbath. In *Epigrammata* 12.57, another "list" poem in which Martial comically piles up the nuisances to be endured by the impoverished resident of Rome, we meet the Jewish urchin *a matre doctus rogare* (taught by his mother to beg). Disagreeable as most of Martial's Jewish references are, their influence on the subsequent portrayal of Jews in literature was considerable. In the following century, the satirist Juvenal developed the theme of Jewish beggary at Rome, and Tacitus incorporated into his historical work the idea of Jewish libidinousness, a slander, like Jewish smelliness, that was destined to enjoy a very long run in European writings of an anti-Semitic character.

Tacitus

Although Tacitus' *Histories,* the context in which his ethnographic excursus on the Jews (*Histories* 5.1-10) appears, was published in the early years of the second century C.E. under the emperor Trajan, Tacitus is essentially a product of Flavian Rome, the bulk of his public career having taken place under that dynasty. Despite having lived for several decades in the same city as the Jewish scholar and writer, Flavius Josephus, there is no sign in Tacitus' writings on the Jews that he had ever consulted any of Josephus' works on Jewish customs and history. In composing his ethnographical account, conventionally inserted in his narrative just before the final showdown between the Romans and their enemies (in this case the final stand of the Jews against Titus in Jerusalem in 70 C.E.), he made heavy use of Alexandrian Greek writers such as Lysimachus, notorious for their hostility to the Jews. Hence the extensive treatment Tacitus accords their version of the origin of the Jewish state: it resulted from the Jews' expulsion from Egypt on account of their diseased (leprous) state. (This version is given as much space as the other five accounts of Jewish origins put together!) Hence also the prominence accorded to two pet Greek literary themes, Jewish misanthropy and Jewish unsociability: "the Jews are extremely loyal towards one another and always ready to show compassion, but towards every other people they feel only hate and enmity. They sit apart at meals and they sleep apart" (*Histories* 5.5.1).

Tacitus exploited Roman sources as well, in order to construct an almost wholly negative picture of the Jews and their influence upon others. The fundamental incompatibility of Romans and Jews, first given expression in surviving Latin literature by Cicero (*Pro Flacco* 28.69), resurfaces here and is further developed. Tacitus alleges that Jewish aniconic monotheism automatically leads to the withholding of honor from the emperor (*Histories* 5.5.4). Also given a fresh airing and further developed is the charge, first seen in Seneca, that Jewish Sabbath observance was simply motivated by idleness. The Jews were so taken by the charms of indolence *(blandiente inertia),* Tacitus claims, that they gave over each seventh year (= the sabbatical year) to total inactivity (5.4.3). The influence of Martial's fantasy, that the Jews had a liking for excessive and unnatural sex, is also evident; Tacitus accuses them of being a race prone to lust *(proiectissima ad libidinem gens)* among whom nothing (of a sexual nature) is unlawful (*inter se nihil inlicitum;* 5.5.2). Judaism's attraction to Romans, a topic treated by Horace with amusement and by Seneca with only mild contempt, is portrayed by Tacitus as a threat to the very fabric of Roman society: "the earliest lesson they (Roman converts to Judaism) receive is to despise the gods, to disown their country, and to regard their parents, children, and brothers as of little account" (5.5.2).

How much of this Tacitus actually believed is impossible to know. What we see in the Jewish excursus is a master rhetorician at work, constructing in Latin of exquisite sophistication (Bloch 2002) a case against the enemies of Rome whose comprehensive defeat at the hands of Titus he is about to describe (5.2.1). In Tacitus' eyes, the Jewish rebels of 70 C.E. are representatives of an alien and perverse race who "regard as profane all that we [Romans] hold sacred and permit all that we abhor" (5.4.1) and whose customs are "base and abominable and owing their persistence to their depravity" (5.5.1). Thus he spares no effort to prove that the harsh treatment they are about to receive is fully merited.

Suetonius

After the sheer nastiness of Martial and Tacitus, it is a relief to turn to their contemporary, the biographer Suetonius. Although scurrility is a well-known feature of his *Lives of the Caesars,* composed in the first quarter of the second century C.E., his comments on the Jews and Judaism are remarkable for their unsensational and factual character. His description of the Jews' lamentations at the bier of the murdered Julius Caesar in 44 B.C.E. (*Divus Iulius* 84.5) has already been noted, as has his reference to Augustus' joke about Jewish Sabbath practices (*Divus Augustus* 76.2). The latter is a precious piece of evidence because it consists of a verbatim quotation from a letter written by that very emperor to his stepson Tiberius. Other allusions in Suetonius to the Jews are no less valuable. At *Divus Augustus* 93 he records how Rome's first emperor congratulated his adopted son and heir Gaius Caesar for not offering up prayers in the Temple at Jerusalem when he passed through Judea in 1 B.C.E. — a unique piece of information that reveals the limits of Augustus' toleration of Judaism. Although that emperor was prepared to respect Jewish religious susceptibilities, the involvement of élite Romans in Judaism was not to be countenanced, a position of which Suetonius himself clearly approved.

In the biographies of Augustus' successors, too, snippets of information occurring in no other Latin source are to be found. Tiberius' put-down of a Jewish scholar *(grammaticus)* from Rhodes by means of a pointed joke about the sabbatical year shows just how early knowledge of that particular Jewish custom had penetrated élite Roman circles (*Tiberius* 32.2; Williams 1994). Suetonius' reference to Claudius' expulsion of the Jews from Rome is unique in suggesting that infighting between Jews and Christians may have been the cause of that clampdown (*Divus Claudius* 25.4). Of special value are Suetonius' comments on Domitian's collection of the Jewish tax (*Domitianus* 12.2). Here the biographer provides an invaluable eyewitness account: as a young man he had seen a ninety-year-old man strip-searched in court to determine whether or not he had been circumcised — circumstantial evidence in Roman eyes for being Jewish and thus making a man liable to the Jewish tax.

Suetonius, unlike Tacitus, nowhere makes an overt judgment about Judaism and the Jews. However, his categorization of certain incidents reveals what his views were. Tiberius' expulsion of the Jews from Rome in 19 C.E., attested also by Tacitus, is classed among that emperor's "good acts"; he was taking action against disseminators of foreign (and therefore undesirable) religious rites (*Tiberius* 36). Claudius' expulsion of the capital's Jews, interestingly, is placed in a section on foreign affairs. This shows that Suetonius must have regarded them as an irremediably alien element in the population, even though a substantial part of Roman Jewry had become enfranchised already in Augustus' reign (Philo, *Legatio ad Gaium* 157–58).

Juvenal

Finally, we come to the satirist Juvenal, most of whose works were composed under the emperor Hadrian (117-38 C.E.), though the earliest may have been written toward the end of Trajan's reign. The strong influence exercised by the poet Martial upon Juvenal, a personal friend, is widely recognized by scholars. So it is not surprising that in Juvenal's handling of Jewish themes there are several echoes of the Flavian epigrammatist's work. Like Martial, Juvenal uses the loathsome epithet *verpus* to describe the Jews (*Satire* 14.104). Like him, he also uses Jewish street-types for satirical purposes; at *Satire* 3.10-18, the beggarly inhabitants of a squatter camp at the Porta Capena, derisively described as possessing no more than a basket (for scraps?) and some hay (for bedding?); at *Satire* 6.542-47, the palsied Jewish beggar-woman, who preys upon the superstitions of wealthy Roman matrons by telling fortunes "for the minutest of coins" *(aere minuto)*.

But there is more to Juvenal's writing on the Jews than the crude satirizing of Roman low-life. Despite the hostility with which he writes about Jews, Juvenal actually knows quite a lot about Judaism. Uniquely, for a Latin author, he knows the technical term for a Jewish assembly hall or prayer house (*proseucha; Satire* 3.296). Uniquely, among pagan authors, he knows about the removal of shoes by the Jews when on holy ground (*Satire* 6.159) and he distinguishes very precisely between God-fearers *(metuentes)*, on the one hand, and full converts, on the other. While the former do no more than observe the Sabbath, abstain from pork, and worship "the clouds and spirit of heaven," the latter's commitment to Judaism is marked by circumcision (*Satire* 14.96-106). Converts he describes in language that seems to echo Tacitus' outburst at *Histories* 5.5.2, suggesting that the latter's Jewish excursus must have been known to him.

Juvenal's personal views on the Jews and Judaism, as on other matters, are unknowable. His regular practice of using a *persona* (mask) as a vehicle for his satire makes it virtually impossible to know what he himself thought about anything. However, Juvenal, no less than the other authors surveyed here, was not operating in a vacuum. His poetry, like all the texts examined above, was intended for élite consumption and pleasure, whether through private reading or public performance. So even if his satires do not reflect precisely his own views, they certainly tell us what he thought would play well with his élite readership. From the generally negative tone of his remarks, it can safely be inferred that within the Roman élite of the Trajanic and Hadrianic periods there was no great liking or admiration for either the Jews or Judaism, to put it mildly. In part that was because the Jews were a subject people and therefore despised. But the main reason was Judaism itself, which had come to be perceived widely not only as a preposterous and mean set of socioreligious customs, *mos absurdus sordidusque,* as Tacitus had famously put it (*Histories* 5.5.5), but the very fount of the Jews' enduring rebelliousness toward Rome. Thus Hadrian attempted to suppress Judaism altogether by banning circumcision and turning Jerusalem into the pagan city of Aelia Capitolina. How Latin writers of the time reacted to the bloody consequences of that attempt, there is no means of knowing since after Juvenal, Latin writing on the Jews and Judaism virtually dries up for several centuries.

BIBLIOGRAPHY

J. M. G. BARCLAY 1996, *Jews in the Mediterranean Diaspora,* Edinburgh: Clark. • D. S. BARRETT 1984, "Martial, Jews and Circumcision," *Liverpool Classical Monthly* 9: 42-46. • R. S. BLOCH 2002, *Antike Vorstellungen vom Judentum: Der Judenexkurs des Tacitus im Rahmen der griechisch-römischen Ethnographie,* Stuttgart: Steiner. • L. H. FELDMAN 1993, *Jew and Gentile in the Ancient World,* Princeton: Princeton University Press. • M. GOODMAN 1987, *The Ruling Class of Judaea,* Cambridge: Cambridge University Press. • E. S. GRUEN 2002, *Diaspora: Jews amidst Greeks and Romans,* Cambridge: Harvard University Press. • E. N. LANE 1979, "Sabazius and the Jews in Valerius Maximus: A Re-examination," *Journal of Roman Studies* 69: 35-38. • A. J. MARSHALL 1975, "Flaccus and the Jews of Asia (Cicero *Pro Flacco* 28.67-9)," *Phoenix* 29: 139-54. • F. MILLAR 2005, "Last Year in Jerusalem: Monuments of

LATIN VERSIONS OF THE HEBREW BIBLE

the Jewish War in Rome," in *Flavius Josephus and Flavian Rome*, ed. J. Edmondson, S. Mason, and J. Rives, Oxford: Oxford University Press, 101-28. • P. SCHÄFER 1997, *Judeophobia: Attitudes toward the Jews in the Ancient World*, Cambridge: Harvard University Press. • M. STERN 1974-1984, *Greek and Latin Authors on Jews and Judaism*, 3 vols., Jerusalem: Israel Academy of Sciences and Humanities. • B. WARDY 1979, "Jewish Religion in Pagan Literature," *ANRW* II.19.1, 592-644. • M. H. WILLIAMS 1994, "Tiberius and the Disobliging Grammarian of Rhodes: Suetonius *Vita Tiberi* 32.2 Reconsidered," *Latomus* 54: 625-33. • M. H. WILLIAMS 2004, "Being a Jew in Rome: Sabbath Fasting as an Expression of Romano-Jewish Identity," in *Negotiating Diaspora: Jewish Strategies in the Roman Empire*, ed. J. M. G. Barclay, London: Clark, 8-18.

See also: Greek Authors on Jews and Judaism

MARGARET H. WILLIAMS

Latin Versions of the Hebrew Bible

Christian literature in Latin originated in the second century in North Africa. There is not enough information to indicate that biblical texts in Latin originated in Jewish communities, and there is no reference at all to the use of Latin in synagogue worship.

The Latin versions, the Old Latin and the Vulgate, contribute to knowledge of the oldest Greek text of the Hebrew Bible and even at times of Hebrew variants unknown in the rest of the manuscript tradition. They have also provided some of the most meaningful concepts of Western Christian theology, as well as many expressions and formulas in the Latin liturgy.

The Old Latin Version

Origin and language

The term "Old Latin" does not refer to a single and complete translation of the Bible into Latin but denotes all the translations prior to Jerome's Vulgate (end of the fourth century). Biblical texts in the Latin language had their origin in North African communities, which probably spoke Latin. At the end of the second century, Tertullian was using an already existing Latin version. Later, Cyprian of Carthage provides numerous biblical quotations, lengthy and faithfully transmitted, taken from a translation that agrees substantially with the text of later manuscripts. This translation is known as the "African" version not because it has certain linguistic idiosyncrasies requiring it to be located in Africa, but simply because this was the Latin translation circulating in Carthage before 250.

This ancient version was written in the vernacular of the people, as shown by the use of vulgar or late Latin terms, Greek loanwords, grammatical and syntactical deviations from classical Latin, and constructions introduced by *quod* or *quia*. Sometimes the Greek loanwords took on new connotations in Latin, and some Latin terms acquired new meaning owing to biblical influence.

History

The history of the OL is the history of a continuous revision of its text to adapt it to a Greek text that differed from the one used in the primitive version, as well as to changes in the tastes, style, and vocabulary of the developing Latin language. African vocabulary was replaced by European vocabulary. Toward the end of the fourth century, different recensions known as "European" were already circulating in Italy, Gaul, and Spain. Augustine complained in his time that there seemed to be as many versions as codices. However, the differences among these recensions should not create the impression that different original translations existed, since they all retain traces of the archetypal African text. All the factors mentioned (numerous text forms, textual corruption, careless language and style, and so forth) were determinative in making the need felt in the fourth century for completely revising the old version and making a new Latin version. From this century on, the Vulgate version of Jerome gradually replaced the old version. However, the manuscripts of the OL remained in circulation until the close of the eighth century.

Textual Filiation and Critical Value

The textual tradition represented by the Latin version is much richer and more varied than the Greek tradition. The OL translates a Greek text of the second century, earlier than the recension used by Origen. Its text has therefore considerable critical value.

In *Exodus*, the *Monacensis* codex of the OL knew a different version of chaps. 36-40, where the LXX lacks some sections of the MT, and in a few places also adds details.

In the historical books, particularly in *1-2 Samuel* as attested in the Qumran manuscripts from cave 4, the OL represents a proto-Lucianic Greek text, very close to the Original Greek version, which was based on a Hebrew text different from that of the Masoretic tradition (Ulrich 1980).

In *Jeremiah* the *Wirceburgensis* codex of the OL omits Jer. 39:1-2 of the MT, and Origen's Greek text marks them with an asterisk. This agreement shows that originally these verses did not appear in the text of the LXX, and neither did vv. 4-13. This is another example showing the importance of the OL as a witness to the oldest Septuagint and to a very old form of the Hebrew.

In *Ezekiel* the OL codex *Wirceburgensis* and Greek manuscript 967 are the only witnesses preserved that show that the order of chaps. 37–39 according to the MT is not original. The oldest text followed the sequence 38-39-37 and omitted 36:23c-28.

In *Daniel* papyrus 967 represents the more original form of the Greek text, showing the order of chaps. 1–4, 7–8, 5–6, and 9–12, followed by the stories of *Bel and the Dragon* and *Susanna*. This arrangement is found in the Latin writer Quodvultdeus.

In *Song of Songs* the OL presents the same verse order in chap. 5 as Greek Papyrus R 952 (5:12, 14b, 13, 14a, 15). In *Job* the OL quotations of the Latin Fathers attest a short text (as compared with MT) very close to the

Greek original. In the book of *Esther,* "The Greek model of the Old Latin (La-GrIII) represents the first Greek translation of the book, and the other two forms, the *L* text (GrII) and the LXX text (GrI), are later" (Haelewyck).

In the apocrypha the OL preserves the original order of the text of *Ecclesiasticus* (Ben Sira) against the whole Greek manuscript tradition, which has 33:13b–36:10 before 30:25–33:15a. In *Baruch* the OL transmits four textual forms, two of them dependent on the older Greek. *Judith* has been transmitted in three forms: those of "LXX," the "Lucianic" text, and ms. 58, followed by OL. The closer the variants are to the text of ms. 58, the higher the guarantee of originality. In *Tobit* the OL, although not free of corruptions and contaminations, contributes to the reconstruction of the text of the Sinaitic recension (G^{II}), the oldest of the three types of Greek texts. In *1 Maccabees* the OL text often departs from the known Greek manuscript tradition; in many cases it attests a lost Greek text, superior to the one we know. In *2 Maccabees* the OL and the Armenian version bear joint witness to a now lost short form of the Greek text. Most parts of the OL additions in the *Wisdom of Solomon* go back to the first Greek text.

Sources and Editions

Among the relatively few manuscripts of the OL that have been preserved, the oldest ones go back to the fifth century. The very conservatism of the liturgical tradition explains the fact that copies of the Psalter are the most numerous, and palimpsests and papyri are included among them. The quotations from the fathers are also an important source for the text of the OL. Particularly important are the quotations by Cyprian, Lucifer of Cagliari, Tyconius, Jerome, Augustine, and some florilegia such as the *Liber de Diuinis Scripturis* (or *Speculum,* a pseudo-Augustinian work). Still indispensable is the collection of quotations compiled by P. Sabatier in his work *Bibliorum sacrorum latinae versiones antiquae seu Vetus Italica* (1745-1749). The critical edition of *Genesis* (B. Fischer), *Isaiah* (R. Gryson), and *Sirach/Ecclesiasticus* (W. Thiele) has already appeared, and *Song of Songs* (E. Schulz-Flügel), *Ruth* (B. Gescher), *Esther* (J.-C. Haelewyck), *Tobit* (J.-M. Auwers) and *Judith* (P.-M. Bogaert) are being prepared.

The Vulgate

Origin and History

The name "Vulgate" was given from the sixteenth century to the translation made by Jerome toward the end of the fourth century. He seems to have had an adequate knowledge of Hebrew. He frequently consulted Jewish scholars, and he himself recommended doing so in cases of doubt. His work did not follow a systematic plan or a consistent method. A first version of the Psalter from the Greek text cannot be identical with the Roman Psalter used in Italy during the Middle Ages and in the Basilica of St. Peter in Rome until very recently (De Bruyne). A new recension made by Jerome from the Greek hexaplaric text resulted in the Gallican Psalter. This is the text used by the Sixto-Clementine Vulgate (1592). The text of *Job* and several fragments of *Song of Songs* and *Proverbs* correspond to this version, based on the hexaplaric text.

In 392 Jerome switched to working on the Hebrew text, guided by the principle of preference for "the true Hebrew" *(veritas hebraica),* not so much the actual Hebrew text but the versions made by the Jews Aquila, Symmachus, and Theodotion (C. Estin). Jerome began this new work with the Psalter called *iuxta Hebraeos* and continued it with the prophetic books, which included *Daniel* and the obelized supplements. Between 392 and 394 he translated *I-IV Reges, Job,* and *Ezra-Nehemiah;* in 394-496, the first and second books of *Chronicles;* in 398 *Proverbs, Qohelet,* and *Song of Songs;* and around 400, the Pentateuch. He completed the translation of the Hebrew Bible in 405 with the books of *Esther* and its obelized additions, *Joshua, Judges,* and *Ruth.*

From the deuterocanonical books, which did not form part of the *veritas hebraica,* Jerome translated *Tobit* and *Judith.* However, the church was neither willing nor able to do without these books, so the manuscript translation of the Vulgate included an OL translation of the remaining deuterocanonical books. As a result, not everything included in the Vulgate was translated by Jerome, and not all his translations became part of the Vulgate. It includes the translations by Jerome made from the Hebrew text (except for the Psalter), the version of *Tobit* and *Judith,* and his revision of the Psalter made from Origen's Hexapla, as well as old revisions of the OL for the remaining deuterocanonical books. The hexaplaric revisions made by Jerome do not form part of the Vulgate, except for the Psalter.

Augustine had reservations about the Vulgate because he thought that the Greek text of the church tradition should not be passed over in favor of the Hebrew text. During the eighth to ninth centuries, the Vulgate replaced the OL, although the latter refused to disappear. The contamination of both texts and the process of corruption of the Vulgate manuscripts led to the revisions by Cassiodorus (ca. 570) and Alcuin (730/735-804). Besides these recensions, there were different forms of the text of the Vulgate in Italy, France, Ireland, and Spain. In the Renaissance there was a reaction against the corrupt condition of the text of the Vulgate, which coincided with the start of a return to the original Greek text. The Council of Trent (1456) declared that the Vulgate was the authentic version of the Catholic Church, although this did not mean neglect of an obvious reference to the original Hebrew and Greek texts.

Text-critical Value

As shown by the frequent Septuagentalisms and Semitisms of his version, Jerome used the best Greek witnesses he could obtain and the form of the Hebrew text known at his time. This was already virtually identical to the medieval Masoretic Text, with very rare variants. Therefore, one of the interesting points of the *Vulgate* lies in the readings of Aquila and Symmachus that the Latin text allows to be traced.

The Old Testament has been critically edited by the Benedictines of San Girolamo in Rome: *Biblia Sacra iuxta Latinam vulgatam versionem iussu Pii PP. XI*, 17 vols., Città del Vaticano, 1926-1987. A complete edition with an abridged apparatus has been edited by R. Gryson et al., *Biblia Sacra iuxta Vulgatam Versionem*, Stuttgart, 1994.

BIBLIOGRAPHY

S. BERGER 1983, *Histoire de la Vulgate pendant les premiers siècles du moyen âge*, Paris: Hachette, rpt. Hildesheim: Olms, 1976. • A. V. BILLEN 1927, *The Old Latin Texts of the Heptateuch*, Cambridge: Cambridge University Press. • D. S. BLONDHEIM 1925, *Les parlers juifs judéo-romans et la* vetus Latina: *Étude sur les rapports entre les traductions bibliques en langue romane des juifs au moyen âge et les anciennes versions*, Paris: Champion. • P.-M. BOGAERT, 1964-, "Bulletin de la Bible Latine," *Revue Bénédictine, Supplements*. • P.-M. BOGAERT 1988, "La Bible latine des origines au moyen âge," *Revue théologique de Louvain* 19: 137-59, 276-314. • F. C. BURKITT 1896, *The Old Latin and the Itala*, Cambridge: Cambridge University Press. • D. DE BRUYNE 1930, "Le problème du psautier romain," *Revue Bénédictine* 42: 101-26. • B. FISCHER 1977, *Novae Concordantiae Bibliorum Sacrorum iuxta Vulgatam Versionem Critice Editam*, 5 vols., Stuttgart: Frommann. • R. GRYSON 1999, *Altlateinische Handschriften/Manuscrits Vieux Latins*, vol. 1, Mss 1-275, Freiburg: Herder. • R. GRYSON 2004, *Altlateinische Handschriften/Manuscrits Vieux Latins*, vol. 2, Mss 300-485, Freiburg: Herder. • F. STUMMER 1928, *Einführung in die lateinische Bibel*, Paderborn: Schöningh. • E. ULRICH 1980, "The Old Latin Translation of the LXX and the Hebrew Scrolls from Qumran," in *The Hebrew and Greek Texts of Samuel: 1980 Proceedings IOSCS*, ed. E. Tov, Jerusalem: Academon, 121-65.

JULIO C. TREBOLLE-BARRERA

Legal Texts

Legal issues are of prime concern in Second Temple literature. Many of the compositions from that period, mainly from the Dead Sea Scrolls, include extensive discussions of legal matters. Yet most of them are not legal texts per se but compositions that contain legal material. Such, for example, is 4QMMT, the halakic document known as *Some of the Works of the Law*. Though it has enriched our knowledge of law at Qumran greatly, it is not a compendium of law but a polemical document that deals with certain halakic issues.

Legal Texts from Qumran

The main intent of some Dead Sea Scrolls is no doubt to present matters of law, and so they may rightly be termed legal texts. A number of scrolls treat only one halakic topic; others constitute an anthology covering a wide range of different legal issues. Among the scrolls dedicated to only one subject are the group of scrolls 4Q274, 4Q276-278 (4QṬohorot[a,b,c]). Only a few, small fragments of 4QṬohorot B and C have survived, and all of them relate to one issue: the preparation of the purification water made from the ashes of the red heifer. Though we can never be sure of the original scope of any given scroll, it is most plausible that purification was the only subject of this group. The same can be said of 4QṬohara[a]. The three extant fragments of this scroll contain a fairly substantial amount of text. Fragment 1 deals with the procedure for sprinkling purifying water, and frgs. 2-3 relate to the susceptibility of fruits to impurity. Thus it seems that the entire scroll was devoted to various aspects of purity laws.

Two additional scrolls should also be mentioned here: 4Q264[a] (4QHalakah[b]), whose sole concern is Sabbath law, and 4Q249 *(Midrash Sefer Moshe)*, which is probably concerned with the laws of leprosy. *Midrash Sefer Moshe* is also unique in that its title has been written on the *verso* of the papyrus. Though the title may have been added at a later stage (a possibility supported by the fact that it is written in regular Hebrew letters and not in cryptic characters, as the composition itself is), it nevertheless testifies to the writer's understanding of its nature, namely, an exegesis of (a portion of) the Torah of Moses.

Genres

Legal texts from Qumran are written in two very distinctive genres. One is a rewriting of the Pentateuch and is best represented by the *Temple Scroll*. The other usually brings together a set of injunctions on the same legal topic; the unit opens with a heading, and the ordinances are phrased apodictically. A large portion of the legal material in the *Damascus Document* is written in this fashion and will be used in what follows to represent this genre.

The *Temple Scroll* is primarily a halakic work and as such a "legal text." To describe its approach to halakah is equivalent to describing its literary genre. Put briefly, its language is biblical in nature, and it may be assigned to the broad category of "rewritten Bible." Even the pericopes containing innovative content are worded in biblical form. A good example of the *Temple Scroll*'s technique comes in its presentation of the deuteronomic law permitting those living at a distance from the Temple to slaughter sheep and cattle for consumption (Deuteronomy 12). To the biblical injunction, the *Temple Scroll* introduces two changes, one halakic and the other linguistic (53:4-8). Halakically, it adds the obligation to cover the blood with dust, taken from Lev. 17:13, which relates to a captured bird or wild animal. The deuteronomic verse, on the other hand, speaks of consuming cattle. The *Temple Scroll*'s incorporation of the command in Leviticus into the deuteronomic law extends this obligation to cattle as well. This type of harmonizing exegesis, which applies details regarding one matter to a second similar one, attempts to resolve contradictions between different biblical commandments. What is noteworthy is that the biblical source is indistinguishable from the exegetical innovation, which is seamlessly incorporated into the biblical text. The exegesis is implicit, never explicit as in formal commentaries such as the pesharim.

The second change is linguistic in nature. A prominent feature of the scroll is its use of direct divine speech, often shifting from biblical third to divine first person, as in the conclusion of our passage: "And you shall do what is right and good in my sight, for I am the

LORD your God." This contrasts with the biblical "for you will be doing what is right in the eyes of the LORD." The intent of this characteristic shift is to convey the statements in question as the unmediated words of God: not Moses speaking in God's name as in Deuteronomy but a direct divine command issued at Sinai. In short, the *Temple Scroll* does not simply refer to the biblical text but presents itself as the Torah.

Similar to the *Temple Scroll* in its approach is the group of texts known as *Reworked Pentateuch* (4Q158, 4Q364-367). These documents are not primarily halakic but contain citations (or paraphrases) of different biblical pericopes, some of which happen to be halakic. What is of importance here is that these texts share the distinctive attributes of the *Temple Scroll* outlined above, namely, they are written in biblical language with no differentiation between innovation and pentateuchal text. In several places the text joins verses taken from various places in the Pentateuch to create a single harmonious unit, a trait shared by these texts and the *Temple Scroll.* The reworking consists also of nonbiblical additions, mainly exegetical in nature, which range from one to eight lines in length. At least one of these (4QRP[c] [4Q365] frg. 23) is a halakic addition found nowhere in the Pentateuch treating the Festivals of Wood and Fresh Oil. It is important to stress that these additions, exegeses, and harmonistic alterations are all formulated in biblical language and compose an organic text, linguistically indistinguishable from their pentateuchal base.

The second halakic genre represented at Qumran is best represented by the *Damascus Document* (CD). Within Qumran sectarian literature, CD is indisputably the work containing the largest organized corpus of laws. Unlike the *Temple Scroll,* which presents itself as "Torah," the *Damascus Document* makes a clear distinction between biblical source and halakic exegesis. CD uses topical rubrics to create large units, each containing a few rulings of the same subject. Each of the units opens with one of three headings: "concerning X" (e.g., "concerning purification by water," 10:10); a citation from a related biblical verse marked by "And as to that which he said" (e.g., "And as to that which he said, 'You shall not take vengeance nor keep a grudge against the sons of your people,'" 9:2); or a combination of the two: "Concerning X as to that which he said" (e.g., "Concerning oaths: as to that which he said, 'Let not your hand help you,'" 9:8). The laws themselves are mainly worded apodictically, without scriptural proof, and are stated as either positive commandments (e.g., "it means to abide by every binding oath in which a man promises to do anything from the Law," CD 16:7-8) or negative ones (e.g., "a man may not go about in the field to do his desired activity on the Sabbath," 10:20).

Even in those instances where the halakic unit opens with a citation, it does not necessarily follow that the laws in question were derived from the verse itself. Rather, the citation functions as a topical heading. It should be stressed that the writers provide no clues about the exegetical process whereby the halakic details are derived. Even if scholars can provisionally reconstruct the exegetical process, the intent of the halakah as stated is to establish its existence rather than to reveal to the reader how it was created. CD 16:6-9 provides as good example of this point: "As for that which he said, 'observe what comes out of your lips' (Deut. 23:24), it means to abide by every binding oath in which a man promises to do anything from the Law: he may not break it, even at the price of death. Any promise a man makes to depart from the Law he shall not keep, even at the price of death." This passage contains two injunctions: the first enjoins anyone who has taken a vow to observe a biblical commandment to keep his oath; the second treats the converse, forbidding an individual who has taken an oath to transgress a biblical commandment to fulfill this oath, requiring that he not deviate from the Torah. As the rubric testifies, these two laws are linked to the biblical injunction found in Deut. 23:24. It can even be conjectured that the *Damascus Document*'s double halakah is grounded in the duality of the verse: "you are to keep, and you are to do." In this case, "keep" means to avoid doing what is prohibited, while "do" means to implement what should be done. Nonetheless, this is a reconstruction; no explicit statement as such appears in the passage itself. Furthermore — and this is the crux of the matter — the writer nowhere indicates how he derived the severe and absolute nature of these obligations, to be adhered to even at the "price of death." It is also noteworthy that, in its original context, the biblical verse does not treat the fulfillment of commandments but the case of someone who has made a vow.

In several instances in the *Damascus Document,* the halakah stated is followed by a pentateuchal or prophetic verse, often prefaced by the formula "As it is written" or the like. The use of the word *kî* ("as") indicates that for the writer this verse serves as the source for the halakah in question, yet nowhere does the writer explain the halakah's derivation from the verse in question. Indeed, as a rule, the *Damascus Document* does not explain how the halakah was extracted from the biblical verses.

Genre and Authority

The two types of legal texts differ sharply in regard to the source for their authority. While the *Temple Scroll* and other rewritten Bible texts present themselves as the binding words of God, the *Damascus Document* and other texts written in the same genre recognize the Torah as the source of the Law and present themselves as authorized exegesis of the holy text. This is in accord with CD's concept of the two layers of the Torah, the revealed and the hidden, that is, the simple meaning evident on the surface of Scripture versus the hidden meaning that is revealed only to God's chosen people, the members of the *Yaḥad,* through his servant the Teacher of Righteousness.

It is instructive to compare the two Qumranic halakic genres with the two genres used in later rabbinic literature: the Mishnah and the (legal) midrash. The midrash, like the "rewritten Bible" compositions from Qumran, is arranged according to and closely follows the pentateuchal text. The Mishnah, on the other hand, is organized in topical fashion, a system that develops the approach reflected in the *Damascus Document.* Yet there is also an opposite aspect to the relations between these two literatures. It is the Mishnah that, similar to the *Temple Scroll,* presents itself as an authoritative text independent of any previous holy Scripture, while the midrash, by quoting and expounding the Torah, puts itself in the position of the commentator and not that of the legislator. In this respects the midrash is similar to the *Damascus Document* rather than to the *Temple Scroll.*

Form and Structure

Other scrolls that contain legal instructions exhibit varied combinations of literary forms. Some use the two genres described above alternately; others combine legal and narrative portions together, a mixture that makes it difficult, and sometimes impossible, to discover the rationale behind the structure of these compositions. In some cases scrolls are arranged according to a biblical passage, though the laws themselves are phrased in the abstract style typical of CD. 4Q251 (4QHalakah[a]) is one such example. Eight fragments of this scroll survive, and not one of them physically matches another. Several of its fragments present legal rulings apodictically, similar to the *Damascus Document;* others utilize the style of rewritten Bible. Fragment 11 is of the first genre. It contains a series of laws phrased apodictically that relate to two matters: the prohibition against consuming a newborn animal that is less than seven days old, and the prohibition against eating "an]imals that have died a natural death or a torn beast that did not live." The origin for this conjunction is undoubtedly Exod. 22:29-30, where these same prohibitions appear and in the same order. Furthermore, frgs. 9 and 10 relate to firstfruits and firstborn animals respectively, which happen to be the subject of the preceding verse (22:28).

The fact that the laws in these fragments are phrased in the abstract style of the *Damascus Document,* and not in the genre of rewritten Bible, makes their biblical arrangement even more significant. It appears that although the abstract style is usually used for a topical arrangement of laws, independent of their biblical origins, sometimes even in this genre the organizational pattern follows the biblical order. For example, careful analysis of all the fragments of 4Q251 reveals that it is based on the sequence of laws in the Covenant Code (Exod. 21:1–23:19), which the scroll interprets either in the form of rewritten Pentateuch or in apodictic language. Because the fragments cannot be matched physically, it is impossible to determine whether the scroll originally covered the entire sequence of the covenantal laws, or whether, like some other scrolls, it treated only a few of the subjects found therein, skipping over others. Similarly it is impossible to determine whether the halakic sections worded in the style of CD were created by the author of the scroll in their present context, or were perhaps cited by the redactor from other works at his disposal. In any event, 4Q251 is a carefully edited composition with a sequential exegesis of an entire biblical pericope.

4Q265 and 4Q159 combine halakic and nonhalakic sections. In the case of 4Q159, no satisfactory explanation has yet been given for its purpose or for its strange collection of legal ordinances and its inclusion of what appears to be a pesher on the biblical story regarding Moses' actions after the episode of the golden calf (Exod. 32:20; 33:7-8). The scroll's fragmentary state may render this conundrum irresolvable. As for 4Q265, at least a partial explanation can be offered. The scroll's seven identifiable fragments include an odd combination of communal rules, laws pertaining to Sabbath and Passover, a pesher, and a reworked Pentateuch-like section. Fragment 7 of the scroll consists of three parts: (1) some Sabbath laws; (2) a section mentioning the *Yaḥad;* and (3) a retelling of the Genesis story of the creation of Eve out of Adam's rib and their entrance into the Garden of Eden, to which some details from the laws pertaining to impurity after childbirth have been added. Part 3 is actually a short version of the material in *Jubilees* 3. Apparently all three sections of this fragment follow the sequence of *Jubilees.* Chapter 2 of that book is devoted to the Sabbath. According to *Jubilees,* after instructing the angels to keep the Sabbath, God told them that he had chosen one nation, the offspring of Jacob, to be his firstborn son and instructed his people to rest on the Sabbath to consecrate it and to bless the Creator for choosing them, "so that their deeds [= performing these commandments] will go up as a pleasing fragrance, which is acceptable before him always" (*Jub.* 2:22). Surprisingly, the phrases "pleasing fragrance" and "be acceptable" also appear in part 2 of 4Q265 frg. 7, in conjunction with two references to the council of the *Yaḥad,* just after the section that deals with Sabbath laws. As is well known, in the Qumran sect's theology, the *Yaḥad* is the "true" Israel that replaces the rest of the people of Israel as the "chosen" ones. Fragment 7 of 4Q265 is thus a reworked version of *Jubilees* 2–3; its sequence follows that of *Jubilees,* adjusting it to the *Yaḥad* ideology.

The above examples illustrate that several scrolls from Qumran are structurally based on earlier scriptural works, including not only the Pentateuch but also *Jubilees.*

Range of Subject Matter

Very much like the Torah, the halakic scrolls refer to all aspects of life, religious and civil. The *Damascus Document* contains side-by-side passages dealing with leprosy and bodily discharges, on the one hand, and laws about the goring ox and compensation to an injured slave, on the other hand. Though most of the legal subjects dealt with in the Dead Sea Scrolls are biblical in their origin, some are unique and have no explicit biblical precedent. The latter pertain to the community's life, institutions, and organizational patterns. In a number of places the scrolls explicitly indicate as much in the titles given to the sections dealing with these subjects (e.g., CD 10:4, "This is the rule for the judges of the community"; CD 12:22, "This is the rule for the gathering of the camps").

Nevertheless it is important to stress that there is

no reason to assume that the sectarians considered these laws as less authoritative than the biblical ones. On the contrary, the way in which CD and other compositions integrate these laws with the others suggests that there was no difference in status between them. Moreover, some of the typically sectarian laws are in fact the Qumranic version and implementation of the biblical law. Such, for example, are the laws of reproof that were central to the community's judicial system. Though unique in their details and sectarian in their nature, they are explicitly based on Lev. 19:16-18. In other cases, the link between the sectarian legislation and its biblical source is not as explicit but still exists. The sectarian regulations limiting the social and commercial contacts with nonmembers are probably based on the biblical injunction not to associate with the Gentiles, and the first ten offenses listed in the penal code of the *Community Rule* (1QS 6:24–7:25) are most likely based on Lev. 19:11-13. In any case, for the members of the *Yaḥad* all the rules and instructions were considered a representation of God's will; they did not differentiate between biblical and nonbiblical ordinances.

Some halakic topics are surprisingly missing from the Dead Sea Scrolls. The absence of a specific issue from the Scrolls may simply owe to the fact that not all the library of the Qumran sectarians survived. Still, in light of the variety and richness of the scrolls that have been found, we may consider them as fairly representative of the contents of the Qumran library and tentatively assume that issues missing from existing scrolls were not dealt with in lost scrolls. Theoretically two opposing reasons for the absence of certain topics present themselves: either the halakic issue in question was so obvious that it required no detailed regulations, or it was not practiced at Qumran. The former is probably the case with *tefillin* (phylacteries); although they are never mentioned in the scrolls, the remains of several were found at Qumran, making it clear that the members of the sect wore them. But should we assume the same concerning *tzitzit* (fringes), or conclude that wearing them was not practiced at Qumran, since doing so is mentioned nowhere in the Scrolls?

Two additional subjects should be pointed out that are not mentioned in the Scrolls. One is the prohibition against cooking a kid in its mother's milk. This prohibition is repeated three times in the Torah (Exod. 23:19; 34:24; Deut. 14:21) and is extended in rabbinic literature to include any mixing of meat with milk. The other issue includes all the regulations concerning the festivals. For example, the prohibition on consuming leavened bread during Passover, a very serious matter in the Torah, is totally missing in the Scrolls. Similarly, there is no reference in the Scrolls to the biblical requirement to reside in booths during the Festival of Booths (except in the *Temple Scroll* (42:12-17), in the context of the sacrificial cult). Nor is there any reference to the four species the Torah mandates to be used in celebrating the festival. Both these commandments receive extensive attention in later rabbinic literature.

Non-Qumranic Legal Texts

None of the other scrolls from the Judean Desert found outside the Qumran caves can be termed legal texts, though some of them contain valuable information on legal issues for the period extending from the first century B.C.E. to the second century C.E. So from the Babatha Archive we can learn about marriage and other financial agreements of her time, and from the letters of Bar Kokhba some information on religious practices can be gathered. The only non-Qumran legal composition from the Second Temple period is the *Scroll of Fasting (Megillat Taʿanit),* which has come down to us within the rabbinic tradition. *Megillat Taʿanit* is actually a list of thirty-six days on which there were significant victories and happy events in the history of the Jews during Hasmonean times. The historical background behind each of them remains unclear. The scroll forbids fasting on these days and in some cases also proscribes delivering memorial addresses for the dead.

Bibliography

J. M. Baumgarten 1996, *Qumran Cave 4.XIII: The Damascus Document (4Q266-273),* DJD 18, Oxford: Clarendon. • J. M. Baumgarten 1998, "Scripture and Law in 4Q265," in *Biblical Perspectives: Early Use and Interpretation of the Bible in Light of the Dead Sea Scrolls,* ed. M. E. Stone and E. G. Chazon, Leiden: Brill, 25-33. • J. M. Baumgarten et al. 1999, *Qumran Cave 4.XXV: Halakhic Texts,* DJD 35, Oxford: Clarendon. • J. M. Baumgarten 2000, "The Laws of the Damascus Document: Between Bible and Mishnah," in *The Damascus Document: A Centennial of Discovery,* ed. J. M. Baumgarten, E. G. Chazon, and A. Pinnick, Leiden: Brill, 17-26. • C. Hempel 2000, *The Damascus Texts,* Sheffield: Sheffield Academic Press. • V. Noam 2003, *Megillat Taʾanit,* Jerusalem, Yad Ben-Tsevi. • L. H. Schiffman 1994, *Reclaiming the Dead Sea Scrolls,* Philadelphia: Jewish Publication Society. • A. Shemesh 2005, "4Q251: *Midrash Mishpati,*" *DSD* 12: 280-302. • A. Shemesh 2008, "The Scriptural Background of the Penal Code in The Rule of the Community and Damascus Document," *DSD* 15: 191-224. • A. Shemesh and C. Werman 2003, "Halakhah at Qumran: Genre and Authority," *DSD* 10: 104-29.

See also: Damascus Document; Midrash, Midrashim; Ordinances; Reworked Pentateuch; Temple Scroll

Aharon Shemesh

Leontopolis → Heliopolis

Letters

A letter is a written communication sent by one person or group to another person or group. Typically, letters contain greetings, requests and instructions, and information. A letter may be considered "Jewish" if it is found in Jewish literary sources, or in the archaeological remains of a site of Jewish habitation. Letters may also contain distinctively Jewish language such as blessings in the name of God or references to distinctively Jewish cultural practices and festivals. But the distinc-

LETTERS

tion is not always straightforward, particularly in a mixed community like Elephantine. Early Jewish letters are found in two kinds of sources: literary and epigraphic. The literary letters are those preserved in larger narrative works, often in translation and sometimes only in excerpts. The epigraphic material, which has not passed through the hand of editors and copyists, is more valuable for analysis. (The New Testament letters are not included here.)

Literary Letters

Hebrew Bible

A handful of books in the Hebrew Bible contain references to letters, excerpts of letters, and occasionally the full text of a letter or edict with epistolary features. Samuel and Kings contain several references to letters, usually containing only an excerpt or précis of the content. Only in 2 Kings 19:10 is there an epistolary formula, "Thus shall you speak to Hezekiah, king of Judah," and an explicit reference to delivering the message orally and in writing. A few references to letters attributed to the period of the monarchy are found in 2 Chronicles (2:11-16 [MT vv. 10-15]; 30:1).

The Aramaic portions of Ezra contain five letters relating to the reconstruction of Jerusalem and the Temple, and the return of Jews from the exile in Babylon to the land of Judah (4:11b-16, 17-22; 5:7b-17; 6:2b-12; 7:12-26). Whatever their value as historical sources, these are remarkably similar in form and style to official Aramaic correspondence from Elephantine in Egypt. Even the memorandum in Ezra 6:2b-5 has a close parallel in *TAD* A 4.9. Other letters from the postexilic period are alluded to in Nehemiah and Esther.

Two biblical passages speak of "letters" from prophets, which are actually collections of prophetic oracles (Jer. 29:4-28; 2 Chron. 21:12-15). Similarly, one epigraphic letter (Lachish 3:19-20) refers to a letter written by "the prophet," whose content is epitomized in a single word: "Beware!"

Second Temple Literature

Several narrative works written in the Second Temple period include letters (see Alexander 1984; Taatz 1991; Klauck 2006: 229-89). Some of these may be authentic (e.g., some of those in 1 and 2 Maccabees), while others are (at least in the eyes of modern scholars) transparently fictional (those in 3 Maccabees, Eupolemus, Pseudo-Aristeas, Greek Esther, Daniel, Epistle of Jeremiah, *2 Baruch,* and *4 Baruch*). The genuineness of several others, however, is disputed (e.g., some of the letters in 1 and 2 Maccabees and in books 12–14 of Josephus' *Antiquities*); doubts about their authenticity are raised by features like anachronistic epistolary formulas and historical errors. In their present literary contexts, these letters serve a variety of narrative functions: to document past events, to support an author's apologetic aims, to impart a degree of verisimilitude to the work, or to add texture to the narrative.

The books of the Maccabees make extensive use of letters, especially epistolary edicts reminiscent of those found in Hellenistic historians. 1 Maccabees cites eleven letters, some sent by Jews, others set by Seleucid kings and by other rulers to the Jews. 2 Maccabees is prefaced by two letters from leaders in Jerusalem to Jews in the Diaspora about celebrating the festival of Hanukkah (2 Macc. 1:1-10; 1:10–2:18). It also includes three letters from Antiochus IV Epiphanes (9:19-27; 11:23-26, 27-33), one from his regent Lysias (11:17-21), and one from the Roman ambassadors Quintus Memmius and Titus Manius (11:34-38). 3 Maccabees has two letters ostensibly from Ptolemy IV Philopator (221-204 B.C.E.) to his generals (3 Macc. 3:12-29; 7:1-9).

A fragment from a work by the Jewish historian Eupolemus (in Eusebius, *Praep. Evang.* 9.31-34) has four letters supposedly exchanged by King Solomon, Hiram King of Tyre, and Pharaoh. The so-called *Letter of Aristeas* (which is not a letter) quotes a letter claiming to derive from Ptolemy II Philadelphus (285-246 B.C.E.) and addressed to the high priest Eliezer in Jerusalem, along with the latter's reply (*Epistle of Aristeas* 35–40; 41–46). The Greek version of the book of Esther includes two edicts of the Persian king Artaxerxes that have an epistolary framework (Addition B 1-7 [3:13a-g]; Addition E 1-24 [8:12a-x]). The book of Daniel cites a royal letter from Nebuchadnezzar in which he recounts for his subjects "the signs and wonders that the Most High has worked for me" (Dan. 4:1-37 [MT 3:31–4:33]) and a brief one from Darius the Mede in which he enjoins fear of the God of Daniel on all his subjects (Dan. 6:25-27 [MT 6:26-27]). Although it has an epistolary prescript identifying it as "a copy of a letter from Jeremiah sent to those who were to be taken to Babylon as exiles by the king of the Babylonia," the Letter of Jeremiah is actually a short homily against idol worship (inspired by Jeremiah 10 and 29). The apocryphal book of Baruch or 1 Baruch is titled in some manuscripts "The Epistle of Baruch," but the work is not in epistolary form.

Two writings placed in the category of Old Testament Pseudepigrapha and associated with the biblical figure Baruch, the secretary of the prophet Jeremiah, have letters embedded within their narratives. The final section of the Syriac Apocalypse of Baruch or *2 Baruch* presents the text of a letter that Baruch sent to "the nine and half tribes across the River Euphrates," encouraging them and admonishing them to observe the Torah (*2 Baruch* 78–87). The work known alternately as the *Paraleipomena Ieremiou* (Greek for "The Things Omitted from Jeremiah"), *The Rest of the Words of Baruch,* or *4 Baruch* contains a letter allegedly addressed by Baruch to Jeremiah and Jeremiah's reply (*4 Bar.* 6:17-23; 7:23-29). The so-called *Epistle of Enoch* (*1 Enoch* 91–108) is misnamed, since it does not have the form of a letter.

Finally, Philo's *Legatio ad Gaium* incorporates summaries of several letters, and Josephus lards his narratives with some thirty-seven letters. Thirteen of these derive from the Bible and other known works (e.g., *Letter of Aristeas;* 1 Maccabees); the others come from sources that are no longer extant.

Rabbinic Literature

A few letters and letter fragments attributed to tannaitic sages are found in rabbinic literature. Three Aramaic letters are attributed to Rabban Gamaliel (*y. Sanhedrin* 18d; *y. Maʿaśer Šeni* 56c; *t. Sanh.* 2:6). Two Hebrew letters supposedly sent by R. Shimon b. Gamaliel and R. Yoḥanan b. Zakkai are preserved in *Midrash Tannaim* to Deut. 26:23. A single letter supposedly from the Jews of Jerusalem to the Jews of Alexandria about Judah b. Tabbai (first century B.C.E.) becoming Nasi is preserved in *y. Ḥagigah* 77d (cf. *y. Sanhedrin* 23c; *b. Soṭah* 47a). The opening of a letter ostensibly from Judah ha-Nasi (died ca. 220 C.E.) to the emperor Antoninus is preserved in *Gen. Rab.* 77:5.

Epigraphic Letters

Murabbaʿat 17a

What may be the earliest fragment of a personal letter in Hebrew dates from the late eighth or early seventh century B.C.E. Barely legible, it is the erased first writing on a papyrus palimpsest from Wadi Murabbaʿat. It reads in its entirety: "[. . .]yahu says to you: I send greetings to your household. Pay no attention to [wh]at [. . . i]s telling you. [. . .]" (DJD 2.17a; Lindenberger 2003: no. 67b).

Meṣad Ḥashavyahu Ostracon

A unique Hebrew text in epistolary form was discovered near Yavneh-Yam in Israel. Dating from the second half of the eighth century, it is a judicial petition from a laborer to a person in authority, demanding redress from a certain Hoshayahu ben-Shobi, who, the petitioner alleges, unjustly confiscated his outer garment.

Arad Letters

Two important collections of Hebrew letters date from the late seventh and early sixth centuries, the period just before the Babylonian conquest. The earlier of these comes from Arad, a border fortress and food storage depot located between Beer-sheba and the Dead Sea. The letters — twenty-one or twenty-two ostraca, mostly fragmentary — are of two types: official military communication (reports on troop disposition, intelligence reports, etc.; e.g., Arad 24, 40), and orders concerning rations (e.g., Arad 1-3, 16-18). Several refer to security threats from nearby Edom. One fragment (Arad 88) appears to be the beginning of a proclamation from a new king, possibly Jehoahaz or Jehoiakim. The ration letters are requisitions for foodstuffs such as grain, bread, wine, vinegar, and olive oil. One alludes in passing to a man who has taken residence (asylum?) in the Temple (Arad 18:9-10). Several mention "Greeks," either mercenaries or middlemen in the service of the Judahite army.

Lachish Letters

A second collection dates from a few years later (ca. 589 B.C.E.), and comes from Tell ed-Duweir, generally identified as biblical Lachish, another fortress, situated between Ashkelon and Hebron. Of twenty-two inscribed ostraca, twelve can be identified as letters. There are unresolved questions concerning their interpretation. The texts appear to be copies or drafts of letters sent from Lachish by a certain Hoshayahu to an addressee named Yaush, probably in Jerusalem (Lindenberger 2003: 117; for alternative possibilities and bibliography, see Pardee 1982: 67-114). Hoshayahu was apparently an officer responsible for communications and intelligence, who sent and received reports to his superiors, often with trenchant political and military comments. One letter refers to transporting witnesses for a legal proceeding and to testing a signal fire, apparently part of an interregional communications system (Lachish 4). In another, the writer complains bitterly of statements made by persons in high places who are undermining troop morale (Lachish 6). These letters provide a vivid supplement to the biblical accounts of Judah's final days.

Elephantine Letters

Significant collections of Jewish epigraphic letters in Aramaic come from Egypt, primarily from the island of Elephantine near Aswan, where there was a colony of Jewish mercenary soldiers during the fifth century B.C.E. and earlier. Two groups of letters were found: ostraca dating from around 475 B.C.E., and papyri from over half a century later. Some fifty of the published ostraca are letters, many extremely fragmentary, and many more remain unpublished. They are mainly informal notes between friends and family members about everyday affairs: food, clothing, debts, and management of slaves. One mentions a garment donated to the local temple (*TAD* D7.18: 21). Another mentions a religious society called a *marzēaḥ* (13:3; *TAD* D7.29:3; cf. Amos 6:7; Jer. 16:5). Of the papyri, ten belong to a community archive. There are eight letters (one in two drafts) and a memorandum of a ninth communication, all dating to the last two decades of the fifth century. Most bear the name of the community leader Yedaniah as recipient or sender. One badly broken letter details the manner of celebrating the festival of Unleavened Bread (*TAD* A4.1). Several others speak of hostilities between Jews and Egyptians. The most dramatic event related is the destruction of the community's temple in a riot by Egyptian soldiers. This is narrated in great detail in a letter in which the community leaders petition the governor of Judah for permission to rebuild their house of worship (*TAD* A4.7–4.8). Other letters contain Jewish names and details of commercial ventures.

Qumran

There are no true letters from Qumran. The document known as *Some of the Works of the Law* (4QMMT) has been termed a "Halakhic Letter" but is more accurately described as a treatise with a few epistolary features.

Bar Kokhba Letters

The fourth major group of Jewish epigraphic letters dates to the time of Bar Kokhba's revolt against Rome (132-135 C.E.). These consist of five Hebrew letters (plus fragments) from Murabbaʿat and some thirteen letters from Naḥal Ḥever (eight in Aramaic, three in Hebrew and two in Greek, plus fragments). Most were written or dictated by the leader of the revolt, Shim'on ben Kosiba (bar Kosiba in Aramaic) to other commanders in the region. They deal with such day-to-day issues as casualties (Mur 45), supply lines, living conditions (Mur 44, 45, 5/6 Ḥev. 54, 58, 59), faltering morale, and shaky discipline among the troops (Mur 43, 44, 5/6 Ḥev. 54, 55). In one case a soldier is commended for selfless acts, burying the dead and (caring for?) the poor (Mur 46). In another, the addressees are censured for self-indulgence: "You sit, eat, and drink from the goods of the House of Israel, and care nothing for your brothers" (5/6 Ḥev. 49).

Greek Papyri

The papyri collected in *Corpus Papyrorum Judaicarum* (ed. Tcherikover and Fuks) contain a few examples of personal and business letters by Jewish correspondents (see Klauck 2006: 251-52).

Writing a Letter

Jeremiah 36, in which the prophet dictates a collection of oracles and instructs Baruch to deliver them aloud in the Temple, does not call this text a "letter." But the process, described in minute detail — dictation to a scribe, instructions for delivery, oral delivery by the scribe (twice in this case), deposit of the written letter in an archive, retrieval for subsequent reading aloud — is instructive. Aside from a few unique circumstances (e.g., the destruction of the letter during the final reading), this can be assumed to be what ordinarily happened in the writing and delivery of a letter. As for the mechanics, the epigraphic letters, whether ostraca or papyri, were generally written with a reed pen, using inks of different composition. Those from Egypt used a mixture of lampblack and gum arabic; the inks in some letters from Israel show a metallic content.

Abbreviations and Numerals

In the Hebrew and Aramaic epigraphic letters, a few abbreviations are found: the letter *šin (š)* for shekel and the letter *bêt (b)* for *bath,* a large liquid measure, in the Hebrew letters; the letter *'alep (')* for *ardab,* an Egyptian measure of capacity, in Aramaic letters; and the letters *lp* once for "thousand" *('elep).* Numbers are sometimes spelled out in words, but numeric symbols are also frequent. Different systems of numeric notation were used in the Egyptian Aramaic letters and in the Arad correspondence. The Arad collection also shows two specialized symbols representing the *ḥomer* and *leteḥ* (dry units of measure). Abbreviations are almost completely lacking in the biblical letters. In one (Ezra 7:12), we find the Aramaic word *gĕmîr* (literally, "finished") where introductory formulas would be expected. The sense appears to be *"et cetera,"* meaning, "Fill in the appropriate formulas here." There may be places in the epigraphic letters where introductory or blessing formulas are lacking, on the understanding that these would be added orally.

Written or Oral Communication?

It has sometimes been assumed (e.g., by Klauck 2006) that biblical references to "sending" or "sending word" refer to oral messages, and that written letters can be assumed only when this is made explicit by the use of such Hebrew words as "wrote" *(kātab),* "in writing" *(biktab),* or one of the Hebrew-Aramaic nouns for "letter" *(sēper, miktāb, 'igrâ).* This is not borne out by the epigraphic letters, in which the Hebrew-Aramaic verb "send" *(šlḥ)* or the phrase "send to say" is often used alone to refer to *written* communication (*TAD* A4.3:9; 4.7:29; *TAD* D7.9:5; 7.20:7; and Arad 24:18). In any case, the distinction in antiquity was not great. Ancient letters were intended to be read aloud to the recipient. The written text served as an *aide memoire* to a messenger and provided a permanent file copy for future reference.

Formal Features of Letters

The epigraphic letters vary greatly in style and formality, from short notes with few epistolary traits beyond naming the recipient and the Hebrew-Aramaic word for "greetings" *(šlm)* to formal letters following a typical pattern: Initial Address (prescript) — Initial Greeting (blessing) — Body — Concluding Formulas — Outside Address (see Lindenberger 2003: 7-10; Fitzmyer 1981; Pardee 1982).

Religious Observances Mentioned in Letters

A number of letters mention Jewish religious observances. An early fifth-century Elephantine merchant exhorts a correspondent to unload a shipment of vegetables quickly before the onset of the Sabbath (*TAD* D7.16, see also 7.10:5; 7.35:7). Another asks the recipient, "Let us know when you will be celebrating Passover," perhaps indicating that the festival did not yet have a fixed date (*TAD* D7.6:8-9). The so-called Passover Papyrus, from about half a century later, does not actually mention Passover in the surviving fragments, but gives detailed regulations for observing Unleavened Bread, some of which are at variance with biblical practice (TAD A4.1; see Lindenberger 2003: 61-62). The Bar Kokhba correspondence also refers to Sabbath observance (Mur 44, 50). One letter orders that "palm branches, citrons, myrtle branches, and willow boughs," the so-called four species for celebrating Sukkot, be provided for the soldiers (5/6 Ḥev. 57; see 52).

BIBLIOGRAPHY

Y. AHARONI 1981, *Arad Inscriptions,* Jerusalem: Israel Exploration Society. • P. S. ALEXANDER 1984, "Epistolary Literature," in *Jewish Writings of the Second Temple Period,* ed. M. E. Stone, Assen: Van Gorcum; Philadelphia: Fortress, 579-96. • J. A. FITZMYER 1981, "Aramaic Epistolography," *Semeia* 22: 25-56. • H.-J. KLAUCK 2006, *Ancient Letters and the New Testament,* Waco, Tex.: Baylor University Press. • J. M. LINDENBERGER 2000, "Letters," in *Encyclopedia of the Dead Sea Scrolls,* vol. 1, ed. L. H. Schiffman and J. C. VanderKam, Oxford: Oxford University Press, 480-85. • J. M. LINDENBERGER 2003, *Ancient Aramaic and Hebrew Letters,* 2d ed., Atlanta: Scholars Press. • D. PARDEE 1982, *Handbook of Ancient Hebrew Letters,* Chico, Calif.: Scholars Press. • B. PORTEN AND A. YARDENI 1986, *Textbook of Aramaic Documents from Ancient Egypt,* vol. 1, *Letters,* Winona Lake, Ind.: Eisenbrauns [abbrev. *TAD* A]. • B. PORTEN AND A. YARDENI 1999, *Textbook of Aramaic Documents from Ancient Egypt,* vol. 4, *Ostraca and Assorted Inscriptions,* Winona Lake, Ind.: Eisenbrauns [abbrev. *TAD* D]. • D. SCHWIDERSKI 2000, *Handbuch des nordwestsemitischen Briefformulars: Ein Beitrag zur Echtsheitsfrage der Aramaischen Briefe des Esrabuches,* Berlin: de Gruyter. • I. TAATZ 1991, *Frühjudische Briefe: Die paulinischen Briefe im Rahmen der offiziellen religiosen Briefe des Frühjudentums,* Göttingen: Vandenhoeck & Ruprecht.

See also: Bar Kokhba Letters; Elephantine, Elephantine Papyri; Ḥever, Naḥal; Murabbaʿat, Wadi; Papyri

JAMES M. LINDENBERGER

Levi

Israelite patriarch and third son of Jacob, Levi is best known as the eponymous ancestor of all Israelite-Jewish priests (Exod. 4:14; Numbers 3; Deut. 33:8-11; Mal. 2:4-7; 1 Chronicles 6). Yet the single event from Levi's life recorded in the Scriptures renders him an ambiguous figure: according to Genesis 34 he and his brother Simeon avenged the rape of their sister Dinah by tricking and slaughtering the Shechemites, an act that evoked their father Jacob' s dying condemnation in place of a blessing (Gen. 49:5-7). This ambiguous biblical portrait of Levi provided the resources for a "Levi tradition" in early Jewish literature.

The *Aramaic Levi Document* (third century B.C.E.) is the oldest surviving work in the tradition, and the first to put Levi's zeal at Shechem in service to his role as progenitor of the priesthood. *Aramaic Levi* includes a recollection of Genesis 34, Levi's prayer, his heavenly-visionary and earthly ordination, instructions on carrying out his priestly duties, his life history, and his wisdom speech. *Aramaic Levi* deploys Genesis 34 to prove Levi's zeal for Israel's purity, and it evokes Deut. 33:8-11, Mal. 2:4-7, and other biblical passages to depict Levi as an ideal priest, a righteous interpreter and teacher of the Law, and a man of wisdom.

Jubilees (second century B.C.E.) either drew directly on *Aramaic Levi* or shared with it the same or similar sources in telling Levi's story (*Jub.* 30; 32:1-15). It relates the Shechem episode, Levi's ordination to the priesthood by Jacob, the fulfillment of Jacob's tithe through Levi (cf. Gen 28:22), and the first Feast of Tabernacles. The story serves *Jubilees'* aims to establish laws and festivals in the ancestral period (32:6-15) and to sanitize the biblical account of the ancestors (Levi and Jacob in Genesis 34; Jacob in Gen. 28:22), while also exalting Levi as a zealous progenitor of a pure priesthood.

Because of their concern to respond to the Jerusalem priesthood's perceived corruption, the Qumran Essenes included in the Dead Sea Scrolls copies of *Aramaic Levi* and *Jubilees.* Levi, the purity-obsessed ideal priest, epitomized their hopes for the priestly office. The Essenes also possessed other texts that contributed to the Levi tradition by elevating Levi and his descendants to a privileged status. In several places Levi appears as a fourth member with the other patriarchs in the traditional three-part genealogy (Abraham, Isaac, Jacob, *and Levi;* 4Q225 2 ii 12); his descendants take elevated positions in the community's ideal temple (e.g., 11Q19 21 nearly equalizes the Levites with the priests in prerogatives); and the Levites play prominent roles in the community's yearly and eschatological liturgies (e.g., 1QS 1–2; 1QM 7–8).

The *Testaments of the Twelve Patriarchs,* although a Christian work of the second century C.E., depended on Jewish sources from the second century B.C.E., including *Aramaic Levi.* In the *Testaments,* other patriarchs exalt Levi as the progenitor of the priestly line and a teacher of wisdom and law (e.g., *T. Reu.* 6:5-8; *T. Iss.* 5:7) and a coauthor with Judah of Israel's messianic salvation (*T. Sim.* 7:1-2). The *Testament of Levi* redeploys traditions also found in *Aramaic Levi* to set Levi's testimony apart from that of the other patriarchs and to establish his close relationship with God. Here, too, he is the hero at Shechem, the progenitor of the pure priesthood, and an able teacher of wisdom and law; the new element is his sponsorship of a messianic line with soteriological significance.

Datable to the second century B.C.E., Theodotus' epic poem uses the Shechem incident to legitimate Judean claims against the Samaritans during the Hasmonean era (Eusebius, *Praep. Evang.* 9.22). Levi (and Simeon) are unapologetically depicted as doers of violence against Shechem in poetry replete with gruesome battle scenes reminiscent of Homer's *Iliad.*

Although its date and Jewish or Christian provenance are uncertain, *Joseph and Aseneth* is often assigned to the turn of the eras and is regarded by most scholars as an early Jewish work. Anomalously, it portrays Levi not as a priestly figure but a seer, prophet, and military hero. Aseneth favors him for his access to heavenly secrets (22:7-9), and when Pharaoh's son fails to recruit Levi and Simeon to help overthrow Joseph so that he can take Aseneth for his own and obtains the help of Dan and Gad instead (23:1–24:16), Levi prophetically reveals the plotters' intentions, and he and his brothers outmaneuver the attackers (27:1-6). Afterward Levi blesses Aseneth (28:15) and saves Pharaoh's son from Benjamin to return him to Pharaoh, who does obeisance before Levi (29:1-7).

Several first-century-C.E. authors echo the earlier themes in the Levi tradition. Philo associates Levi with the priesthood (*De Plantatione* 63–64; *De Fuga et Inventione* 73–74; 93); with vengeance-filled defense of purity (*De Migratione Abrahami* 224; *De Mutatione Nominum* 200); and with dignity, honor, and wisdom (*De Sacrificiis Abelis et Caini* 119; *De Somniis* 2.34). Josephus retells Genesis 34 to exonerate Jacob and blames bad relations with non-Israelites on Levi and Simeon's violent action (*Ant.* 1.339). Yet he sees the Levites' assignment to the priesthood as the consequence of their relief from "war and warfare" (*Ant.* 4.67). 4 Maccabees (2:19) regards Jacob's condemnation of Levi and Simeon's violence (Gen. 49:5-7) as evidence that it was contrary to reason.

BIBLIOGRAPHY

M. DE JONGE AND J. TROMP 1998, "Jacob's Son Levi in the Old Testament Pseudepigrapha and Related Literature," in

Biblical Figures outside the Bible, ed. M. E. Stone and T. A. Bergren, Harrisburg, Penn.: Trinity Press International, 203-36. • J. L. KUGEL 1993, "Levi's Elevation to the Priesthood in Second Temple Writings," *HTR* 86: 1-64. • R. A. KUGLER 1996, *From Patriarch to Priest: The Levi-Priestly Tradition from Aramaic Levi to Testament of Levi,* Atlanta: Scholars Press.

See also: Aramaic Levi Document

ROBERT A. KUGLER

Leviathan

Leviathan is a mythic sea monster and symbol of primordial chaos. It appears in the Hebrew Bible at Job 3:8; 40:25–41:26; Pss. 74:14; 104:24. In Second Temple literature (*4 Ezra* 6:49-52; *2 Bar.* 29:4; *1 Enoch* 60:7-10, 24ab), Leviathan emerges in a more developed form and is paired with Behemoth, a land creature. These texts agree that God primordially separated the monsters (created on the fifth day) and forced Leviathan into the sea and Behemoth onto dry land (Whitney 2006: 54-55). The pair is also preserved to be food for the righteous at the end of time. Though none of the three passages specifies how the transformation to food will take place, later rabbinic references rely on an oral tradition in which the final banquet is preceded by some form of combat involving the creatures, either with God's angelic army or between themselves (Whitney 2006: 127-52).

References to Leviathan alone appear in two other Second Temple works, the *Apocalypse of Abraham* and the *Ladder of Jacob.* In the former, Abraham's angelic guide Yahoel is appointed "to hold the Leviathans" since through him "is subjugated the attack and menace of every reptile" (*Apoc. Abr.* 10:10). The plurality here is a reflex of the same tradition to which *1 Enoch* 60:7-8 alludes, that Leviathan and Behemoth represent a primal pair of a single monstrous species. Here that same pair is described under the rubric of "the Leviathans." Why must they be held? Abraham says, "And I saw there the sea and its islands, and its cattle, and its fish, and Leviathan and his realm and his bed and his lairs, and the world which lay upon him, and his motions and the destruction he caused the world" (*Apoc. Abr.* 21:4). Leviathan lies at the very fountains of the deep. He provides the foundation upon which the world is built, a tradition reflected in later rabbinic cosmology (Whitney 2006: 114-27). Thus it is not surprising that the destruction of earthquakes is seen to stem from Leviathan's movements. Appropriately, the angel who bears the divine name (Yahoel) is appointed to exercise control of such monsters.

In the *Ladder of Jacob* Leviathan appears at the end of a list of eschatological signs. "And they will cry out, and the Lord will hear them; and he will pour out his anger on Leviathan the sea monster, and kill the heathen Falkon with the sword, for against the God of gods he will exalt himself" (*Lad. Jac.* 6:13; long recension 6:3). The strange name "Falkon" is a mistranscription of an original Hebrew epithet of Leviathan (*ʿăqallāṯôn)* begun in Greek and developed further in Old Church Slavonic, the language in which the *Ladder of Jacob* is now preserved (Whitney 2006: 88-90). Here, then, the increasing level of eschatological chaos culminates with the appearance of Leviathan, the ancient chaos monster, which God defeats in order to restore order to the creation.

The sea monster Leviathan thus appears in two forms in Second Temple literature. Drawing on biblical references, the texts depict him as an ancient chaos monster who symbolizes disorder in creation; God subdues the forces of chaos by defeating Leviathan primordially, presently, and eschatologically. The victory is confirmed as Leviathan and Behemoth are consumed by the righteous at a great feast at the end of time.

Rabbinic Jewish tradition elaborates on the monstrous nature of Leviathan, noting his tumultuous effect upon the sea (cf. Job 41:23). The combat-banquet tradition is dramatically amplified by drawing on imagery of the Roman-Byzantine hunt *(kynēgesia),* which later became associated, in the arena, with a "wild beast contest." Hence a dramatic battle between Leviathan and Behemoth arose in which the creatures kill each other before being prepared as food for the eschatological banquet (Schirmann 1971).

BIBLIOGRAPHY

J. DAY, 1985, *God's Conflict with the Dragon and the Sea,* Cambridge: Cambridge University Press. • H. G. LUNT 1983, "Ladder of Jacob," in *OTP,* 2: 401-11. • R. RUBINKIEWICZ 1983, "Apocalypse of Abraham," in *OTP* 1: 681-705. • J. SCHIRMANN 1971, "The Battle between Behemoth and Leviathan according to an Ancient Hebrew *Piyyut,*" *Proceedings of the Israel Academy of Sciences and Humanities,* 4: 327-69. • M. K. WAKEMAN 1973, *God's Battle with the Monster: A Study in Biblical Imagery,* Leiden: Brill. • K. W. WHITNEY, JR. 2006, *Two Strange Beasts: Leviathan and Behemoth in Second Temple and Early Rabbinic Judaism,* Winona Lake, Ind.: Eisenbrauns.

See also: Behemoth

K. WILLIAM WHITNEY, JR.

Levites

In postexilic biblical usage, the term Levites carries two rather different meanings. It refers both to the professional class of religious functionaries (who can be described as second-rank priests, as a *clerus minor*) at the postexilic Jerusalem Temple and to the individuals who are, in genealogies preserved in the Hebrew Bible (e.g., 1 Chron. 5:27–6:66), perceived to be the descendants of Levi, the son of Jacob and Leah (Gen. 35:23). Tradition has it that Levi was cursed by his father, which is the biblical explanation for the members of the "tribe" of Levi being dispersed and having no tribal territory of their own (Gen. 29:34; 34:25-31; 35:23; 49:5-7). If employed in the genealogical sense, the term "Levites" includes the first-rank priests of the Jerusalem Temple, the "Aaronides," because they, too, are seen to be ultimately descended, through Aaron, from Levi. Thus the whole of the postexilic Temple priesthood is traced back to Levi.

The two different uses of the designation Levites have led to much confusion, not least in scholarship. The postexilic genealogies are significant in this respect, and a comparison between 1 Chron. 23:6 and 1 Chron. 23:13-14 is especially instructive. Whereas it is true that Gershon, Kohath, Merari, and their descendants are all members of the tribe of Levi, it is also true that the genealogies differentiate, with regard to the Kohathites, between the sons of Amram, Aaron, and Moses. While the descendants of the former constitute the priesthood, the descendants of the latter are the "Levites" in the technical sense of the term. All of this is the result of an attempt to rewrite history by rewriting genealogies, an approach amply documented by anthropologists in societies the world over.

The historical, preexilic Levites were often given priestly and related functions in private sanctuaries (but possibly not in official, state temples), as is documented in texts like Judges 17–18. Because of their status as a landless tribe, they were protected by special rules and stipulations which were supposed to secure their upkeep (cf. Deut. 12:19; 14:27). The result of the cult centralization introduced by Josiah was the abolition of all sanctuaries bar the Jerusalem Temple, which deprived all priests of YHWH outside the Jerusalem Temple (i.e., the historical Levites and other priestly families, like the Abiatharides at Anathoth) of their livelihoods.

The only way for the Levites to continue to officiate — and thus to survive — was to enter the service of what was now the central and only sanctuary. In spite of efforts to give them equal status with the Jerusalem priests (cf. Deut. 18:1-8), whose ranks they were now forced to join, they ended up in (quasi-)priestly but second-rank positions. The roots for this relegation to second place go back to the time before the rededication of the Jerusalem Temple in 515 B.C.E.; Ezek. 44:6-16 promotes the concept of two classes of priestly personnel. The same concept informs passages such as Numbers 3–4 and 18. Both the Ezekiel and the Numbers passages are drawn from the same traditional material, as has been demonstrated by Gese. Ezekiel's view is yet stricter than that promoted by Numbers. In any case the differentiation between "priests" and "Levites" goes back to at least the late exilic period.

Throughout the whole of the Achaemenid period and beyond, the Levites (as a class of religious functionaries) lived in an uneasy relationship with their supposed "brothers" (cf. Deut. 18:1-8), the "Aaronides," and struggled to define their functions and identity over against both their effective superiors, the Aaronides, and the ranks of lower Temple clergy. Apart from their altar duties, which entailed some priestly functions but not the actual blood rite (cf. Ezek. 44:15), they seem to have fulfilled auxiliary functions (e.g., Ezek. 44:10-14).

Both Nehemiah and Ezra (the present author assumes that Ezra *succeeded* Nehemiah) had good reasons to use the Levites as allies against the recalcitrant priests (the Aaronides) of the postexilic Temple. Nehemiah 8 describes the Levites as the key figures in the proclamation of the Torah; they are depicted as interpreters and exegetes of the texts that are being read out.

There seems to have been a development in the "job description" of the Levites: whereas their duties were restricted to those of second-rank priests entrusted with the duties of auxiliaries when the Second Temple was dedicated, they took on other duties later. It is one of the most remarkable developments in the time after Ezra that Levites (used here to refer to the professional class), singers, and doorkeepers were amalgamated into one single class of cult personnel in the Jerusalem Temple. These changes are documented especially in Chronicles, where they are legitimized by a new construal of the genealogies of the "Levites" (here used in the genealogical sense) and the claim that the hierarchy in question was established in the time of David.

Does this change imply that the class of the Levites was "demoted" relative to that of the first-rank priests, or, rather, that the singers and doorkeepers had risen in status? Given the fact that Nehemiah and Ezra had both strengthened the position of the Levites over against the priests and had assigned new tasks to the Levites, the new arrangement looks very much like a significant strengthening of the Levites' position within the Temple hierarchy, a position that was further reinforced by amalgamating them with the singers and doorkeepers. The new class of Temple personnel thus formed a powerful counterbalance to that of the priests.

1 Chronicles 23–26 depicts an elaborate system of levitical and priestly orders of service. This system seems to reflect the actual hierarchy of the late Achaemenid period, when centuries of often conflicting developments in the forming of the Jerusalem Temple hierarchy resulted in some stability. The material situation of the Levites improved, too. Nehemiah had been the first to ensure regular provision for them, and the system he had introduced survived into the late Achaemenid period and beyond (cf. 2 Chron. 31:4-15). The cultic order that was established in the late Achaemenid period and that is reflected in 1 Chronicles 23–26 remained essentially the same until the demise of the Jerusalem Temple in 70 C.E.

In the Hellenistic period, the frictions between priests and Levites persisted, as Josephus indicates in *Ant.* 20.216. This is further proof that the reorganization of the priesthood(s) of Judah and Jerusalem, necessitated by the Josianic reform, had led to tensions which were never fully resolved, either in the Persian period or in the Hellenistic-Roman era. At the same time, the relative importance of the Levites was further strengthened because the role they had now assumed, namely, that of interpreters of the written Torah, became more and more important in Judean society. The key function of the cultic system, that is, the execution of bloody sacrifice, remained firmly in the hands of the first-rank priests, the Aaronides. Here was foreshadowed the later conflict between the Pharisees and the Sadducees. Indeed, that conflict may well be described as a transformation of the classic confrontation between the Levites and the Aaronides which had left its imprint on hundreds of years of the Jerusalem sanctuary's history.

Throughout the Hellenistic period the significance of cultic sacrifice declined, as becomes obvious from the fact that the Pharisees, whose activity was centered so exclusively on the interpretation of the written Law and its application to everyday life (without priestly help!), assumed such an important role in Judean society from the second century B.C.E. onward. Indeed, the work of the Levites in scriptural interpretation and religious instruction had laid the foundation for the concept of Scripture and tradition which informed Pharisaic piety. It was to be the centrally important concept of the Jewish *praxis pietatis* that survived the Jewish War and was at the root of the rabbinic regeneration of Judaism after 70 C.E.

BIBLIOGRAPHY

J. WELLHAUSEN 1905, *Prolegomena zur Geschichte Israels,* 5th ed., Berlin: Reimer. • H. VOGELSTEIN 1889, *Der Kampf zwischen Priestern und Leviten seit den Tagen Ezechiels: Eine historisch-kritische Untersuchung,* Stettin: Nagel. • A. H. J. GUNNEWEG 1965, *Leviten und Priester: Hauptlinien der Traditionsbildung und Geschichte des israelitisch-jüdischen Kultpersonals,* Göttingen: Vandenhoeck & Ruprecht. • H. GESE 1984, "Zur Geschichte der Kultsänger am zweiten Tempel," in idem, *Vom Sinai zum Zion: Alttestamentliche Beiträge zur biblischen Theologie,* 2d ed., Müncher: Kaiser, 147-58. • U. DAHMEN 1996, *Priester und Leviten im Deuteronomium: Literarkritische und redaktionsgeschichtliche Studien,* Bodenheim: Philo. • A. CODY 1969, *A History of Old Testament Priesthood,* Rome: Pontifical Biblical Institute. • J. SCHAPER 2000, *Priester und Leviten im achämenidischen Juda: Studien zur Kult- und Sozialgeschichte Israels in persischer Zeit,* Tübingen: Mohr-Siebeck.

JOACHIM SCHAPER

Leviticus Targum (4Q156)

The *Leviticus Targum* 4Q156 (4QtgLev) is one of only three apparent Aramaic translations of the Bible found at Qumran. The other two are both translations of the book of Job: 11Q10 (11QtgJob) and 4Q157 (4QtgJob).

The *Leviticus Targum* comprises portions of Lev. 16:12-15 and 16:18-21, those verses that provide an account of the ritual performed by the high priest on Yom Kippur, specifically, the presentation of the bull as a sin offering for himself and his household, the placing of the blood of a bull and goat upon the altar, and the preparation of the goat to be sent into the wilderness. The two fragments translate the Hebrew with little expansion of the text. The manuscript has been dated on paleographic grounds to the late second or early first centuries B.C.E. (Milik 1977).

The text of 4Q156 has been compared to the MT, *Targum Neofiti, Targum Onqelos, Targum Pseudo-Jonathan,* the *Samaritan Targum,* and the Syriac Peshiṭta, and while it does not correspond precisely to any of the other Aramaic targums, it emulates *Onqelos* in staying close to the Hebrew text. In spite of those literal tendencies, some interpretive elements may nevertheless be present.

The most interesting features of the *Targum,* some of which may point to an interpretive purpose, are:

1. The use of two vertical dots as section dividers, something like the *sop pasuq* used as a verse divider in later Masoretic texts. The vertical dots are found in lines 3, 6, and 7 of frg. 1, and lines 1, 5, and 6 of frg. 2. Three of the dividers correspond to verse divisions in the MT of Lev. 16:12, 14, and 20.
2. The use of the noun *ksy'*, "cover," to translate Hebr. *kprt* in 16:14. The precise meaning of the root *kpr* is not clear, and the various suggestions include "to cover," "to wipe away," "to smear over," and "to expiate" (see Fitzmyer 1978-1979). The LXX translates *kprt* most often as *hilastērion,* "means of expiation," and the Peshiṭta uses the root *hsy,* "to pity, spare." The Latin translates with *propitiatorium,* except for six times, when it employs *oraculum* (Fitzmyer 1978-1979). The fact that all of the other targums simply use the Aramaic cognate *kpwrt'* (*Onqelos* and *Pseudo-Jonathan*), or *kprth* (*Neofiti* and the *Samaritan Targum*) may mean that 4Q156, in using the term *ksy'*, is interpreting a nuance of the Hebrew rather than simply mirroring it. Stuckenbruck and Freedman (2002) suggest that the use of *ksy'* indicates that the translators of 4Q156, possibly a group from outside the Jerusalem priesthood, did not think the term *kprt* had a specific theological meaning. Beyer (1984) suggests that the use of *ksy'* points to a time earlier than the second century B.C.E. for the original translation.
3. The omission of a translation of Hebr. *pny* in 16:14 = col. 1, line 6 (other targums translate with *'py*). It is possible that this omission is correlated with the use of *ksy'* to translate *kprt,* in that it may involve a different visual concept of the *kprt.*
4. The addition of the word *byt* in front of *qdš'* (Hebr. *hqdš*) in 16:20.
5. The change in word order in Lev. 16:14, so that *whzh b'ṣb'w 'l pny hkkpprt qdmh wlpny hkkpprt yzh* ("and sprinkle [it] with his finger on the eastern front of the *kappôret,* and before the *kappôret* he shall sprinkle") in the MT becomes in 4QtgLev *wydh b'ṣb'th ']l ksy': wqdm ksy' lmdnḥ'* [*ydh* ("and sprinkle [it] with his finger up]on the cover, and before the cover toward the east he shall sprinkle"). This may reflect a different Hebrew *Vorlage* than that used by the MT, but it may be an attempt to solve an ambiguity in the Hebrew which makes it unclear whether it is the *kappôret* that is sprinkled with blood in both cases, or first the *kappôret,* then the floor between the *kappôret* and the entrance to the inner shrine containing the ark (Milgrom 1991).

It may be significant that 4QtgLev, despite its fragmentary nature, departs from the other targumic traditions and the Peshiṭta, and differs also from the proto-MT. Whether it thus reflects a different Hebrew *Vorlage,* or is reflecting an attempt to interpret the Hebrew, as is done by later targums, cannot be definitively deter-

LITERACY AND READING

mined on the basis of such limited data. Yet extant differences may well give an intriguing indication of interpretive purpose beyond translation.

BIBLIOGRAPHY

K. BEYER 1984, *Die aramäischen Texte vom Toten Meer,* Göttingen: Vandenhoeck & Ruprecht, 278-80. • J. A. FITZMYER 1978-1979, "The Targum of Leviticus from Cave 4," *Maarav* 1: 5-23. • J. MILGROM 1991, *Leviticus 1–16,* New York: Doubleday. • J. T. MILIK 1977, "Targum du Lévitique (4Q156)," in *Qumran Grotte 4, II, 4Q128-4Q157,* ed. R. de Vaux and J. T. Milik, DJD 6, Oxford: Clarendon, 86-89, pl. XXVIII. • L. T. STUCKENBRUCK 1995, "Bibliography on 4QTgLev (4Q156)," in *Qumran Questions,* ed. J. H. Charlesworth, Sheffield: Sheffield Academic Press. • L. T. STUCKENBRUCK AND D. N. FREEDMAN 2002, "The Fragments of a Targum to Leviticus in Qumran Cave 4 (4Q156): A Linguistic Comparison and Assessment," in *Targum and Scripture: Studies in Aramaic Translations and Interpretation in Memory of Ernest G. Clarke,* ed. Paul V. M. Flesher, Leiden: Brill, 79-95.

See also: Targum, Targumim

MARILYN J. LUNDBERG

Lion of Wrath → Pesharim

Literacy and Reading

Early Judaism was characterized by an immense diversity in types and purposes of literacy and reading. This can be illustrated by two descriptions of reading at different ends of the chronological spectrum of the Second Temple period. Nehemiah 8 depicts Ezra reading the Torah during the Persian period to people who had returned to Jerusalem from Babylon. It describes how Ezra "the scribe" stood on a pedestal while Levites and others "read from the scroll of the Torah of God, translating and explaining so that the people understood the recitation." Probably written in the late Persian period, this text depicts Aramaic-speaking returnees who neither read nor understood Hebrew (Schaper 1999: 17). It was the job of priestly officials to read the text aloud and to translate and explain it to them. In the first century C.E., approximately 400 years later, we see quite different depictions of literacy and reading in the writings of Philo and Josephus. For example, in his polemical work *Against Apion,* Josephus maintains that all children are taught to read at home (*Ag. Ap.* 1.60), so that all Jews can recite the laws of the Torah "more readily than their own name" (*Ag. Ap.* 2.178).

Neither of these texts can be taken at face value, yet they communicate valuable information about what their authors thought they could and should claim about reading and literacy in their communities. Nehemiah 8 has no apparent interest in claiming universal literacy among Jews, but instead depicts a situation in which priests and related officials are the literate segment of the population, with most people dependent on them for access to the text of the Torah. Not only can they not read, at least an extensive text such as the Torah, but they do not even understand the Hebrew in which it is written. The narrative stresses that, once exposed for the first time to the Torah, the people were dismayed and had to be told to respond with joy rather than weeping (Neh. 8:9-12). In contrast, by the time we get to Josephus, there is much interest in claiming universal literacy for the Jewish people. Josephus is writing in Greek to defend the Jewish faith in a first-century-C.E. social context where claims for universal literacy among Greeks were common. In response to such statements, Josephus asserts universal learning among Jews, insisting that Jews could both read and recite their Torah as readily as any Greek-educated pagan could read and recite Homer.

Social Contexts for Literacy and Claims about It

These examples point to the social contexts for literacy and reading, and for claims about them. Scholars have pointed out in recent years that "literacy" is a highly variable competence. Some people might gain enough basic alphabetic literacy to read and write their own names but be unable to read or write more extensive documents. Others might gain the literacy to read sacred texts such as the Torah but have no occasion to learn how to write either literary or practical texts. Still others might gain training in practical literacy to maintain business or governmental accounts but have minimal competence in either writing or reading literary-theological texts. These and still other groups should be distinguished from experts capable of both reading and creating literary-theological texts, often writing in archaizing dialects and drawing deeply on an extensive textual tradition that they had memorized.

Social context has also been important in shaping claims about literacy and reading. Whatever the actual situation of literacy obtaining in the Persian period, the author of Nehemiah 8 evidently felt no need to claim that Ezra's audience was literate and thoroughly educated in the Torah. In contrast, writing in the above-described situation of Greek-Jewish interchange about levels of literacy, both Philo and Josephus take pains to stress the importance of education to Jews and their thorough immersion in Torah texts through family education and regular study at Sabbath assemblies. This may well reflect a growth in Jewish literacy in Torah texts in comparison with the Persian period. Nevertheless, it may also reflect new pressures on those, like Philo or Josephus, who make claims about literacy in a context where such claims can influence the social standing of their group.

Contemporary scholars are not immune to such pressures. Much contemporary scholarship about literacy has been shaped by a continuing cultural emphasis on the value of universal literacy along with a redefinition of literacy as a basic ability to read and write. Such contemporary minimal definitions of literacy contrast strongly with discussions of education such as that in Josephus, which are focused on an individual's ability to read and recite entire ancient books. Yet some treatments of literacy have attempted to build a case for widespread literacy in early Judaism based on supposed evidence of such minimal "literacy" found across a broad range of early Jewish texts. Other treatments, however, have pointed out that these examples of literacy in Judaism are set in highly varied and specific contexts. Despite the polemical claims of an author such as Josephus, it appears that only a minority of early Jews gained one of a variety of "literacies" (cf. Millard 2000: 154-84).

Types of Literacy and Reading in Early Judaism

Within early Judaism, "literacies" are distinguished by the language of the texts involved, their purpose, and whether one learns to read or (also) write them. Throughout the Hellenistic and early Roman periods, Aramaic and Hebrew were the primary languages used for literary-theological texts such as the Torah or the books related to Enoch. The Aramaic traditions in Daniel and Ezra, the *Targum of Job,* and other Aramaic texts found at Qumran testify to a rich tradition of writing and reading literary Aramaic in the Hellenistic age. Meanwhile, Ben Sira is but one example of a literary-theological text written in Hebrew during the Hellenistic period. Soon after Ben Sira, the emergence of a nationalistic celebration of Hebrew as the "ancestral tongue" in the Maccabean Revolt led to an expansion of the production of many more texts written in imitation classical Hebrew. These included both literary-theological texts and some documentary and correspondence texts as well. Finally, as Greek gained importance in Israel and became the dominant spoken and literary language in the Diaspora, Jews educated in Greek translated older Hebrew texts, while also producing highly sophisticated new works in Greek, such as the Wisdom of Solomon.

As already hinted in the example of Nehemiah 8, priests appear to have been the primary ones who gained the ability to read and reproduce literary theological texts such as the Torah (Carr 2005: 201-27). Even later references to more general education, such as Philo's description of weekly Sabbath education in the Torah, often emphasize the role of priests in communicating this literacy in classical texts (*Hypoth.* 7.10-13). With time, there probably was an increase in the ability of nonpriests to read ancient literary-theological texts, possibly in response to Greek ideals of more general education. In addition, it is likely that nonpriestly literati played a greater role in the production of Greek literary-theological texts and translations. Nevertheless, at least up through the early Roman period, priests and groups associated with them appear to have been the primary readers, writers, and teachers of early Jewish classical literature. Many of the nonpriestly, lay people who gained a level of literacy in such texts, gained passive, reading literacy, but probably had no reason to get training in copying sacred texts or writing in classical Hebrew (Hezser 2001: 72-88).

The linguistic and demographic picture is different for the variety of literacies used in commerce and government of this time. Near the beginning of the Hellenistic period, Aramaic, the language used across the Persian Empire, appears to have been the primary language used in early Jewish legal and other documentary texts, both in the Diaspora and in Israel. Then, from the Hellenistic period into the Roman period, Greek became the dominant language for such everyday use, and many Jews working in governmental and many trade contexts would have had to gain at least the basic rudiments of Greek. As in much of the rest of the eastern part of the Roman Empire, Latin was used only rarely in texts, mostly in display inscriptions.

An ostracon in Jewish-Aramaic script giving a dated receipt for flour (7.0 × 3.5 cm., Idumea, 344 B.C.E.) *(The Shøyen Collection, MS 206/1)*

"Literacy" in such business and documentary texts involved the ability both to read and to write a limited range of materials and genres. Many such texts were short, and their contents were similar. Someone learning to write an Aramaic ostracon with a list of provisions would not necessarily have any competence to read, let alone expand upon or compose, a sophisticated text in classical Hebrew. Instead, they would have practice in processing and reproducing textual products as part of ongoing social processes of law, commerce, government, and display. Within the Greek world, this more limited set of clerical competencies was often associated with the office of "scribe" *(grammateus),* in contrast to the older understanding of "scribe" *(sōper)* seen in Nehemiah 8 and later early Jewish texts, where Ezra and others are depicted as consummate masters of the ancient textual tradition in Hebrew (and Aramaic).

BIBLIOGRAPHY

P. S. ALEXANDER 2003, "Literacy among Jews in Second Temple Palestine: Reflections on the Evidence from Qumran," in *Hamlet on a Hill: Semitic and Greek Studies Presented to Professor T. Muraoka on the Occasion of His Sixty-Fifth Birthday,* ed. M. F. J. Baasten and W. T. Van Peursen, Leuven: Peeters, 3-25. • D. M. CARR 2005, *Writing on the Tablet of the Heart: Origins of Scripture and Literature,* New York: Oxford. • C. HEZSER 2001, *Jewish Literacy in Roman Palestine,* Tübingen: Mohr-Siebeck. • A. MILLARD 2000, *Reading and Writing in the Time of Jesus,* Sheffield: Sheffield Academic Press. • J. SCHAPER 1999, "Hebrew and Its Study in the Persian Period," *Hebrew Study from Ezra to Ben-Yehuda,* ed. W. Horbury, Edinburgh: T&T Clark 15-26.

See also: Aramaic; Education; Greek; Hebrew; Inscriptions; Papyri; Scribes and Scribalism; Writing

DAVID M. CARR

Liturgical Works from Qumran

Introduction

The liturgical works from the Qumran library have received increasing attention in recent years. Their crucial importance for our understanding of the Qumran community and of the religious life of ancient Judaism is now widely recognized. "Liturgy" may be defined as any set of rituals (voluntary, repeated bodily actions that are assigned spiritual or cosmic significance) meant for public or communal performance. Liturgies can be part of a calendrical cycle of rites, or mark key turning points in the life of a community or an individual in relation to the community. Liturgies provide time with a structure, give the community an identity, coordinate different types of experience in order to present reality as a unified and comprehensible whole, and serve as paradigmatic patterns of action that may be drawn on even outside the sacral or religious sphere. The Qumran texts covered here are judged to be liturgical because their contents indicate that they were used in the corporate ritual life of an early Jewish group, in the calendrical realm (Sabbath, festivals, covenant renewal, and daily prayers), the realm of cleansing from ritual impurity, the realm of rites of passage such as marriage, and the apotropaic realm of the exorcism of malign spiritual influences. They constitute our earliest examples of fixed Jewish liturgical texts and are thus extremely important for the history of the Jewish liturgy

A fixed Jewish liturgy developed quite late; the earliest complete prayer books survive only from the ninth and tenth centuries C.E. Nevertheless, scattered elements of these later liturgical traditions are found in the Qumran texts, demonstrating that the late traditions drew at times on much earlier ones. Like the later liturgy, many of the Qumran texts open with headers or rubrics giving the time of recitation. The body of their texts follows fixed structures and patterns, they include formulaic blessing of God, and they close with a collective response. Some themes, such as the worship of the angels on the Sabbath, are also shared with the later liturgy. Likewise, elements of the pre-Kabbalistic Jewish mystical texts known as the Hekhalot literature (the literature of the heavenly "palaces") or merkavah mystical literature (pertaining to God's "throne-chariot") appear in a surprisingly high density in some Qumran documents.

Major Liturgical Texts

The major liturgical texts found in the Qumran library are discussed below. Unless otherwise indicated, they are in Hebrew and the titles have been assigned to them by modern scholars. Some other poorly preserved Qumran texts (e.g., 4Q291-293; 4Q392-393; 4Q440; 4Q443; 4Q445; 4Q456; 4Q476) may also have had a liturgical function, but they are too damaged for their context and use to be certain.

Festival Prayers (1Q34 + 1Q34[bis], 4Q507, 4Q508, 4Q509 + 4Q505)

Several fragmentary manuscripts consist of prayers to be recited during many and perhaps most or all of the Jewish festivals. The prayers are not obviously sectarian. They mention the Day of Atonement, the New Moon celebration, the Day of First Fruits (i.e., the Festival of Weeks or *Shavuʿot*), and probably the New Year. In addition, there may be mention of Passover and the First Fruits of New Wine or Oil.

4QBerakot (4Q286-90, 4Q280?)

The work conventionally known as 4QBerakot ("blessings") also contains curses. It is a liturgy for the sectarian covenant renewal ceremony that is summarized in the *Community Rule* (1QS 1–2). It contains laws of the covenant, a communal confession or review of the sect's history, hymns praising and blessing God that have striking similarities to both the near contemporary hymns in the New Testament book of Revelation and the much later hymns of the merkavah mystics; curses on Belial and his followers, and reference to a census of the sect for the half-shekel tax. Form-critical parallels with ancient Near Eastern covenant renewal ceremonies suggest that blessings may also have been recited over the sectarian community, but if so, these are entirely lost. 4Q280 is a liturgy for the same ceremony, but it may not belong to the same document as the other manuscripts.

The Songs of the Sabbath Sacrifice (4Q400-407, 11Q17, Mas1K)

The *Songs of the Sabbath Sacrifice* (sometimes referred to as the *Angelic Liturgy*) is a well-preserved work describing the angelic liturgy of the Sabbath holocaust offerings during the first quarter (thirteen weeks) of the Jewish year according to the sectarian solar calendar, with the Festival of Weeks occurring in week twelve. (The recitation of songs alongside holocaust offerings is mentioned in 2 Chron. 29:27-30, but none of these songs survives.) The heading of each song refers to the *maśkîl* or "sage," the title of an important office in the Qumran sectarian texts. The thirteen songs do not actually give any of the words of the angels, but rather describe the worship of the angels and include detailed descriptions of the macrocosmic Temple based on creative exegesis of Ezekiel 1 and related scriptural passages, many of which were later associated with Jewish worship during the Festival of Weeks. This work may be sectarian, although a copy was also found at Masada, indicating dissemination outside Qumran for reasons that remain debated. In any case, the Qumran sectarians kept many copies of the work. It, too, has strong parallels with the merkavah mystical literature and also with the New Testament book of Revelation.

Times for Praising God (4Q409)

4Q409 is a poorly preserved hymn that invokes God's praise and alludes to a number of biblical festivals (Weeks, Wood Offering, the autumn New Year, Booths, and perhaps First Fruits). Too little survives for its purpose to be clear, but it is not obviously sectarian.

LITURGICAL WORKS FROM QUMRAN

4QBarki Nafshi (4Q434-438) [Now Subsumes Grace after Meals (4Q434a)])

4QBarki Nafshi is a collection of hymns of thanksgiving that open with the phrase "Bless, O my soul, the Lord," an invocation modeled after a biblical phrase in Psalms 103 and 104. The same phrase is picked up independently in the later Jewish liturgy. The protagonists of the hymns are the "poor," who are a community preserved and protected among the Gentiles. The text draws on a wealth of metaphorical bodily imagery to express God's bestowing of devout qualities upon these protagonists. One passage in 4Q434 has numerous parallels with later liturgies for grace after meals, especially in the context of mourning a recent death. But, apart from this, the life situation and function of the liturgy are not clear from the content of the work, which does not show evidence of sectarian origin.

A Lamentation (4Q501)

Only one of at least two columns of 4Q501 survives. It is a communal lament in the first-person plural that calls on God to deliver the reciters from their oppressors. Its life situation is uncertain, but it may be connected with the fast mentioned in Zech. 7:1-5, which later developed into the commemoration of the destructions of the First and Second Temples on the Ninth of Av. It is not obviously sectarian.

A Wedding Ceremony? (4Q502)

4Q502 is an exceedingly fragmentary papyrus manuscript that presents a sectarian ritual of celebration and joy with people of all ages present. It includes a passage found also in 1QS 4:4b-6. References to a "man and his wife," a man and woman standing in a council of elders, fertility, and other hints led the original editor to suggest this is a liturgy for a marriage ceremony, and this remains possible. Other suggestions are that it is a ceremony welcoming older married couples into the celibate Qumran community or a ceremony celebrating the Spring New Year.

Daily Prayers (4Q503)

4Q503 is a very poorly preserved papyrus manuscript containing a liturgy of evening and morning prayers for a single month (perhaps the first month of the year), keyed according to both the phases of the moon and the movements of the sun and thus combining the lunar and solar calendars. Each day begins at sundown, as it does in the Priestly source of the Pentateuch. The connection with the solar calendar raises the possibility of a sectarian origin, but there are no other indications of this.

The Words of the Luminaries (4Q504, 4Q506)

The Words of the Luminaries is a collection of prayers for each day of the week. Those for the first six days are formally communal laments. Each seems to have begun with a title, most of which are lost; then it asks God to remember his wonderful deeds of old, surveys some part of scriptural history, petitions for God's deliverance and mercy, and closes with a benediction to God and a double amen. The Sabbath prayer(s) call on the angels to praise God likewise. It is not obviously a sectarian work, although one copy is very old and the other much younger, which may hint that the Qumran sectarians used it for a long time. The life situation of the work is uncertain; it seems to have been intended for use in daily prayer by some Jewish group. It has also been speculated that it may be a levitical liturgy or may have been used in the lay *mā'ămādôt* services in the Temple, known from the Mishnah. Unusually, the title of the work survives on the outside of the scroll. The meaning of this title is unclear; it may refer to prayers set for daily periods that were marked out by heavenly luminaries (i.e., the sun and the stars), although one of the Sabbath prayers also seems to refer to the praise of the angels, so angelic luminaries may be implied as well.

Purification Liturgies (4Q512, 4Q414)

4QPurification Liturgies offers a collection of ceremonies for cleansing people of ritual impurities. It survives in two very fragmentary manuscripts that overlap to a large extent, although the two do not necessarily represent the same recension of the work. The reconstruction of 4Q512 is facilitated to some degree by the fact that it is written on the back of 4Q503. Unlike Leviticus (although cf. Lev. 5:5; Num. 5:19-22; 6:23-27; and 2 Chron. 5:11-13), this work includes prayers to be recited with the rituals — usually, and somewhat unexpectedly, recited by the person being purified rather than by the officiating priest. The damaged state of the manuscripts makes it impossible to identify many of the rituals or the impurities they address, but one deals with purification from corpse impurity using the ashes of the red heifer (Numbers 19). An extra, nonbiblical ablution is added on the third day of the seven-day process, as in the *Temple Scroll*. Other passages in the work deal with purification from a discharge and with purificatory holocaust offerings. One passage mentions the Sabbath and some other festivals, perhaps including the first day of the four seasons of the year according to the sectarian solar calendar, so sectarian composition is possible but not certain. Many other passages are too fragmentary for their subject to be identifiable with any confidence.

Several apotropaic liturgies and rites may be grouped together:

The Songs of the Sage (4Q510-511)

The *Songs of the Sage* is a collection of songs of the sage *(maśkîl)* that offer praise to God for the purpose of subjugating evil spirits during the current, preeschatological age. A reference to "the lyre of saving acts" in 4Q511 frg. 10, line 8 may indicate instrumental accompaniment. These songs have parallels with the *Berakot*, the *Songs of the Sabbath Sacrifice*, and the hymns of the Merkavah mystics. A sectarian origin seems likely.

An Aramaic Magic Book (4Q560)

4Q560 is a very fragmentary Aramaic scroll containing exorcistic material, apparently belonging to a manual of incantations. Such Jewish incantation manuals are otherwise known only in medieval copies, especially from the Cairo Geniza. Similar exorcisms are known from late-antique Aramaic incantation bowls and amulets. There is no indication of sectarian origin.

Psalms of Exorcism (11QApocryphal Psalms^{a}/11Q11)

11QApocryphal Psalms^{a} contains three or four hymns of protection from demons, the last hymn being the biblical Psalm 91, which was traditionally used as an incantation against demons in later Jewish magic. At least one of the hymns is attributed to David, and another mentions Solomon. It has been speculated that these hymns have some connection with the four songs "to perform over the ones smitten (by demons)" mentioned in 11QPs^{a} 27:9-10, although their contents show no evidence of sectarian composition.

4QIncantation (4Q444)

4QIncantation is a very fragmentary manuscript that included a hymn and some curses, both in opposition to evil spirits. It has a high density of parallels to the *Songs of the Sage*. Although it is not explicitly a sectarian text, it does have some thematic parallels to sectarian dualism.

Liturgy in Other Texts

A number of the major Qumran texts of other genres include references to liturgical rites. For example, the *Damascus Document* (4Q266 frg. 11, lines 16-18/4Q270 7 ii 11-12) may refer to the same covenant renewal ceremony as that found in 4QBerakot and the *Community Rule* (1QS 1–2), mentioned above; the *War Rule* includes liturgies recited by the officers (1QM 10:2-3) and the high priest, the priests, and Levites (13:1-2; 15:4-7; 16:13-15) to the troops before battle and after it (1QM 18:5-6; 19:9-13); and the *Hodayot* manuscripts include some community hymns that contain hints of liturgical usage such as headers referring to the *maśkîl;* first-person plural verbal forms; calls to praise; and the mention of musical instruments and times for praise (see esp. 4QH^{a}).

BIBLIOGRAPHY

J. R. DAVILA 2000, *Liturgical Works,* Grand Rapids: Eerdmans. • J. R. DAVILA 2000, "The Dead Sea Scrolls and Merkavah Mysticism," in *The Dead Sea Scrolls in Their Historical Context,* ed. T. H. Lim et al., Edinburgh: Clark, 249-64. • I. ELBOGEN 1993, *Jewish Liturgy: A Comprehensive History,* Philadelphia: Jewish Publication Society; New York: Jewish Theological Seminary of America (German original, 1913). • D. FALK 1998, *Daily, Sabbath, and Festival Prayers in the Dead Sea Scrolls,* Leiden: Brill. • B. NITZAN 1994, *Qumran Prayer and Religious Poetry,* Leiden: Brill. • B. NITZAN 2003, "The Dead Sea Scrolls and the Jewish Liturgy," in *The Dead Sea Scrolls as Background to Postbiblical Judaism and Early Christianity,* ed. J. R. Davila, Leiden: Brill, 195-219. • S. C. REIF 1993, *Judaism and Hebrew Prayer: New Perspectives on Jewish Liturgical History,* Cambridge: Cambridge University Press. • M. D. SWARTZ 2001, "The Dead Sea Scrolls and Later Jewish Magic and Mysticism," *DSD* 8: 182-93.

JAMES R. DAVILA

Lives of the Prophets

The Lives of the Prophets recounts the life and death of the prophets of the Hebrew Scriptures to whom individual books are ascribed (Major Prophets, Book of the Twelve, Daniel) as well as seven prophets whose works are recounted in various narrative portions of Scripture. The work is of disputed origin (both in terms of date and provenance), but it may have been composed as early as the first century C.E.

Each prophet is treated in turn, and, as one might suspect, some at much greater length than others. Isaiah, Jeremiah, Ezekiel, Daniel, Elijah, and Elisha each receive between thirteen and twenty-one verses, whereas others receive as few as two or three verses (e.g., Hosea, Micah, Amos, Joel). The nonliterary prophets treated, in addition to Elijah and Elisha, include Nathan, Ahijah, Joad (the unnamed prophet of 1 Kings 13:1-32), Azariah, and Zechariah son of Jehoiada. In some cases, it is not so much the lives of the prophets that occupies the narrative but their deaths, a fact that has led to the general position that the work reflects veneration of the dead, although whether Jewish or Christian remains inconclusive. Amid the review of the prophets, the theological commitments of the author or community can also be discerned (such as belief in future resurrection, angels, and the "presence" of the dead prophets).

Original Language and Extant Manuscripts

The Lives of the Prophets survives in numerous Greek manuscripts as well as versions in Syriac, Armenian, Ethiopic, Arabic, and Latin. Portions were also translated into Hebrew during the medieval period for Jewish use. The most important Greek manuscript is Codex Marchalianus, also referred to as Q. This anonymous work dates to the sixth century and is the source of a group of subsequent manuscripts. There are also longer and shorter versions of the book (thirteenth and tenth centuries, respectively), which are attributed to Epiphanius of Salamis. Another recension is attributed to Dorotheus and is best represented in a thirteenth-century manuscript. Q, however, is routinely considered to be the oldest and best representative of the Greek text, although this does not mean that it is free from textual corruptions (e.g., 1:10; 2:5).

The original language, however, is still a debated issue. One cannot isolate this matter from the date and provenance of the book. Furthermore, since determinative evidence is lacking, one must be content to speak of possibilities and probabilities. As for the language of origin, some have argued for a Semitic (most often, Hebrew) original. Cited as arguments for a Hebrew original are mistranslations in the Greek and the author's apparent Judean setting, particularly his familiarity with Jerusalem. Counterarguments abound, particularly the fact that a Palestinian provenance does not commit one to a Hebrew original, since many first-century Jews could have moved effortlessly between Greek, Hebrew, and Aramaic. None of this precludes the possibility that there were Semitic traditions, either written or oral, from which *Lives* eventually developed (or upon which it was dependent), but this is a very different matter than positing a Semitic original from which a Greek *translation* was produced (e.g., Ben Sira). As with other books of Greek provenance (e.g., Wisdom of Solomon), whatever Semitic antecedents or influence there might have been, there is no compelling reason to doubt that *Lives* is an originally Greek literary composition. A Greek original is even more compelling if one accepts arguments for the book's Christian, Byzantine provenance (see below). Regardless, a Hebrew (or Semitic) original has not persuaded contemporary scholars.

Date and Provenance

The issues of date and Jewish or Christian province are intertwined. All theories rely, on some level, on conjecture and conclusions drawn on related matters. It is extremely difficult to determine the date of *Lives.* The manuscripts themselves are of no help, since the earliest dates to the sixth century. There are certainly elements in *Lives* that are reflected in older, Jewish midrashic traditions, but this tells us nothing about when the work was composed. There are also clear Christian elements (e.g., 2:8), but whether they are original or belong to a later stage of the book's tradition history remains debated. The absence of any clear reference to the events of 70 C.E. is notable but does not necessitate a date before the destruction of the Temple. Moreover, possible allusions to the events of 70 C.E. (12:11 and 10:11) may be of a more general nature and so do not require a post-70 date (Hare 1985: 380-81).

Other circumstantial evidence includes 1:1-8, where the Spring of Siloam is located outside the wall of Jerusalem, a point that may require a date before Herod Agrippa (41-44 C.E.) built the new south wall. Yet it may simply mean that the Herodian wall was a very recent addition (Hare 1985: 381). The reference in 21:1 to "Elijah, a Thesbite from the land of the Arabs" seems to imply a time when the Nabateans controlled this area, which came to an end under Trajan in 106 C.E. (Hare 1985: 381). But the reference may simply be evoking a more ancient time.

The issue of how and when the prophets came to be venerated is also contested. One view is that the prophets in *Lives* are not yet regarded as saints but as miracle-workers and figures worthy of emulation (Schwemer 1995 and 1996). A rival view is that the burial traditions in the work have much more in common with Byzantine Christian practices (Satran 1995).

Recent discussion of the *Lives* has centered on the issue of Jewish or Christian authorship. Most scholars assign the work a Palestinian provenance, but this does not settle the question of whether it is of Christian or Jewish origin. Accepting the language of origin as Greek allows for both possibilities, and the influence of extrabiblical traditions in *Lives* is hardly a mark of Second Temple Jewish literature alone, as the New Testament and subsequent Christian literature demonstrate.

The question of Jewish or Christian provenance can be addressed only by offering plausible arguments that best account for the existing — and ambiguous — data. In relatively recent scholarship, the issue has been addressed in two significant monographs, one by Anna Maria Schwemer (1995 and 1996) and the other by David Satran (1995). Schwemer argues at length that *Lives* is a Greek document of Jewish Judean provenance from the first century C.E. Satran argues with equal rigor that the most likely setting for *Lives* is Byzantine Christianity in the fourth century. That two such strikingly different conclusions can be reached on the basis of a relatively brief work (180 verses) attests to the inherent difficulties presented by this text.

For Satran, discontinuities between *Lives,* on the one hand, and both Second Temple and rabbinic literature, on the other, suggest that its setting should be sought elsewhere. The burial sites can be more convincingly placed during the Byzantine period. The expansion of Nebuchadnezzar's punishment (Daniel 4) employs concepts and vocabulary attested in Christian sources from the fourth century onward but not in Hellenistic Jewish literature. The force of Satran's argument is cumulative, but some of this evidence might reflect later Christian reworking. One of his more penetrating observations, however, is that discerning Christian interpolations may not be as straightforward as isolating explicitly christological statements, so reconstructing a Jewish original may require more than simply excising such statements. A more developed and nuanced understanding of the transmission and transposition of Jewish works, traditions, and themes into Christian literature is called for.

Schwemer's two-volume work argues that *Lives* is a Jewish work with Christian interpolations, some of which may be as early as the second century. She also argues for the book's Palestinian provenance on the basis of the author's frequent reference to Palestinian place names and local traditions. Here, though, one must consider whether these factors are simply traditions that persisted until Byzantine times (a possibility by no means precluded by Satran's argument). Perhaps Schwemer's strongest argument for a Jewish origin and early date centers on traditions in *Lives* that seem to antedate their presence in rabbinic sources, although no firm case can be made on this basis.

Both positions have merit and represent two competing paradigms: (1) whether the Jewish material reflects the text's origin and Christian elements are later additions, or (2) whether the Jewish material represents older traditions that persisted into the Byzantine era and formed a "basis" of sorts for an essentially Christian document. At least on this point we must be content with an answer as ambiguous as the evidence itself.

Relation to Extrabiblical Sources

Although the author is clearly dependent upon and knowledgeable of the biblical portrayals of the prophets, he does not restrict his comments to biblical material, but seems conversant with Jewish interpretive traditions and legends. Some of these traditions and legends are subtle, while others are clear. Some examples include: Isaiah being sawed in two (1:1), which is apparently alluded to in Heb. 11:37, thus suggesting the tradition's pre-Christian origins; Daniel's membership in the royal family (4:1); Daniel's prayer that Nebuchadnezzar's punishment be reduced from seven years to seven months (4:13); Jonah as the son of the widow of Zarephath (10:6); the naming of the unnamed prophet of 1 Kings 13:1-22 (Joad, 19:1); Elijah as a priest from the tribe of Aaron (21:1). The *Lives* was not written in isolation from the rich developments in biblical interpretation in the Second Temple period and beyond. Hence, it stands not only as a product of what a particular community valued, but as a window into the varied Jewish and Christian understandings of their Scriptures and their faith.

BIBLIOGRAPHY
D. R. A. HARE 1985, "The Lives of the Prophets," in *OTP* 2.379-99. • M. DE JONGE 1961-1962, "Christelijke Elementen in de Vitae Prophetarum," *Neues theologisches Journal* 16: 161-78. • D. SATRAN 1995, *Bibical Prophets in Byzantine Palestine: Reassessing the Lives of the Prophets,* Leiden: Brill. • A. M. SCHWEMER 1995-1996, *Studien zu den frühjüdischen Prophetenlegenden Vitae Prophetarum,* Tübingen: Mohr-Siebeck. • C. C. TORREY 1946, *The Lives of the Prophets: Greek Text and Translation,* Philadelphia: Society of Biblical Literature and Exegesis.

PETER ENNS

Logos

The ancient Greek word *logos* has a wide variety of meanings and is common to virtually all periods of Greek literature. It can mean computation, accounts, measure, esteem, ratio; explanation, argument, rule of conduct, hypothesis, definition, narrative, oration, dialogue, oracle, or saying. *Logos* can also mean the process of human reasoning, human rationality, and more broadly rationality or the rational principle of the universe. These latter meanings are important in Greek philosophy.

Logos in Greek Philosophy

Logos was used by the pre-Socratic philosopher Heraclitus (ca. 500 B.C.E.). Most often he used it in its more common meanings of proportion, account, and explanation. But he may also have used *logos* in the sense of an underlying cosmic principle of order coextensive with the primary cosmic element of fire. For Plato (429-347 B.C.E.) *logos* was associated with the rational or, in contrast to myth *(mythos),* was a rational account (*Phaedrus* 61b). Aristotle (384-322 B.C.E.) often used the term *logos* to refer to rational speech and rationality. Reason *(logos)* also distinguished human beings from lower animals (*Politica* 1332b). The concept of *logos* was also central to Stoicism and played a cosmological role. For the Stoics, *logos,* God, and nature were in reality one (Diogenes Laertius 7.135). *Logos* was the rational element that pervades and controls the universe (*SVF* 1:87) and was ultimately material. *Logos* was used in Middle Platonism (the Platonic tradition from ca. 80 B.C.E.to ca. 220 C.E.) in the sense of rational discourse and human rationality. At the level of cosmology, it also sometimes played an important role in relation to other concepts in Middle Platonism. Middle Platonism, unlike Stoicism, emphasized the reality of the immaterial, intelligible realm. One characteristic of Middle Platonism was its distinction between two aspects of the divine. The first was essentially transcendent and inner-directed. The second was an active power responsible for the ordering of everything else. Early Middle Platonists sometimes adopted the Stoic *logos* into their systems as the term for this active force of the divine in the world. More often, however, they gave this aspect of the divine a different name (e.g., idea, mind). This early Middle Platonic outlook influenced Hellenistic Judaism and particularly Philo of Alexandria.

Logos in the Septuagint

Logos is used frequently in the Septuagint. Over 90 percent of the time *logos* is a translation of the Hebrew word *dābār* (word). *Logos* in the Septuagint, like the Hebrew *dābār,* has a wide range of meanings including narrative, speech, dialogue, oracle, or proverb. Because Hebr. *dābār* and Gr. *logos,* however, did not have the identical range of meanings, the use of *logos* as a translation of Hebr. *dābār* inevitably influenced the way in which *logos* was understood. *Logos* often took on a more dynamic meaning than it originally had in Greek (Isa. 2:3). Particularly the plural *logoi* was used to refer to the Mosaic Law (Exod. 19:1). In the Psalms (Ps. 33:6) and in Sirach (39:17, 31), *logos* is associated with God's act of creation and his maintenance of cosmic order. In this way, *logos* also played a role similar to that played by wisdom in other biblical texts (Prov. 8:22-31; Sirach 24) and influenced Hellenistic Jewish literature.

Logos in Hellenistic Jewish Speculation

Logos became a much more important concept in Hellenistic Judaism and reached its climax in the writings of the Hellenistic Jewish exegete Philo of Alexandria (ca. 10 B.C.E.–50 C.E.). Fragments from the Hellenistic Jewish writer Aristobulus (ca. 150 B.C.E.) indicate that this process had begun by the middle of the second century B.C.E. Aristobulus claimed that Moses called the whole genesis of the world the words *(logoi)* of God (Eusebius, *Praep. Evang.* 13.12.3-4). He also connected the seventh day in Genesis with the sevenfold *logos* that is the principle of order in the world (13.12.13).

The connection between wisdom and *logos* is also made in the Wisdom of Solomon, a Hellenistic Jewish text from late first-century-B.C.E. or early first-century C.E. Egypt. God's word and God's wisdom are used in this text as two parallel ways of describing God's creation of the world and of human beings (Wis. 9:1-2).

It was, however, in the works of Philo of Alexandria that *logos* found its full flowering in Hellenistic Jewish literature. In his interpretations of the LXX of the Pentateuch, he sought to interpret the Mosaic Law in the light of Greek, primarily Middle Platonic, philosophy. Philo identified wisdom *(sophia)* with *logos* (*Leg. Alleg.,* 1.65) and gave both some of the same attributes (e.g., image of God [*Conf.* 146]).

For Philo the *logos* was the intermediate reality between God, who was essentially transcendent, and the universe. While he could use the Stoic concept of the *logos* as the principle of rationality that pervades the universe (*Her.* 188), Philo's *logos* primarily fits into the pattern of the intermediate figure found in most Middle Platonic systems. Philo depicted the *logos* in a variety of ways, and the figure had a number of different functions.

The first general function is cosmological. The *logos* is the image of God, the one closest to God, the only truly existent (*Fug.* 101). This image, the *logos,* also served as the model for the ordering of the rest of the universe (*Somn.* 2.45). The *logos* is also the instrument *(organon)* through which the universe was originally ordered and sustained (*Cher.* 127). The second function of the *logos* is anthropological. The *logos* is the paradigm according to which human beings were made, not the human being as a whole but only the human mind (*Opif.* 24–25). For Philo this paradigm was the *logos,* and man was an expression at third hand (God–*logos*–human mind) from the Maker (*Her.* 231). The third function of the *logos* is anagogical: that which guides the human soul to the realm of the divine (*Deus* 143). Like many Middle Platonists, Philo thought that God in his essence could not be implicated in the material universe. Yet the relative order of the material universe had to derive at least indirectly from God. For Philo the *logos* served as the intermediate reality through which the universe was originally ordered and by which it continued to be sustained.

Logos in the New Testament in General

Logos is used 331 times in the New Testament, and in most of the same ways in which it is used in the Septuagint and in Greek literature in general. What characterizes the use of *logos* in the New Testament is not some new meaning for the word beyond what is found in the Septuagint but its reference specifically to the divine revelation of God through Jesus Christ and his messengers. In many cases the "word of God" is simply the Christian message, the gospel (Acts 4:31).

Logos in the Prologue of the Gospel of John

The most striking use of the term *logos* in the New Testament is found in the hymn that is part of the Prologue to the Gospel of John (John 1:1-18). According to the hymn's first strophe (1:1-5), the *logos* was with God at the beginning, and was God, and was the means through which the universe and life came to be. In the second (1:10-12b), the *logos* came to its own, was not received by its own, but to those who received it, the *logos* gave the power to become children of God. In the third (1:14, 16), the *logos* became flesh in Jesus of Nazareth, and the glory of the *logos* was experienced by those who believe. There are various proposals for the intellectual background of the hymn (e.g., targums, midrashim, Gnosticism), but the closest parallels to the use of *logos* in the hymn are found in Jewish wisdom literature, especially Prov. 8:22-31 and Sirach 24. The various attributes and activities ascribed to wisdom in Jewish wisdom literature are ascribed to the *logos* in the hymn in the Prologue.

In Jewish wisdom literature, however, the figure of wisdom was never displaced by the *logos* as it was in the hymn. This striking difference indicates that the type of speculation found in the hymn has moved beyond Proverbs, Sirach, or the Wisdom of Solomon. Such a displacement of wisdom by *logos* is found in Philo, whose conception of the *logos* has some striking parallels with the *logos* in the hymn.

Both Philo and the hymn use *logos* as the equivalent of *wisdom* in Jewish wisdom literature. In both cases, *logos* overshadows the figure of wisdom in importance. Both Philo (*Opif.* 17, 24) and the hymn (John 1:1-2) understand the *logos* as a reality that existed with God before creation. Both Philo (*Somn.* 1.228-30) and the hymn (John 1:1) use the anarthrous *theos* (God) to refer to the *logos.* Both Philo (*Conf.* 146) and the hymn (John 1:1-2) connect the *logos* with the "beginning" *(archē)* of Gen 1:1. Both Philo (*Cher.* 127) and the hymn (John 1:3) think of the *logos* as the instrument through which *(di' hou)* the universe was created. Like the hymn, Philo (*Somn.* 1.75; *Opif.* 33; *Conf.* 60–63) associates the *logos* with light. Finally, both Philo (*Conf.* 145–46) and the hymn (John 1:12) connect the *logos* with becoming sons or children of God.

While the parallels between Philo and the hymn are important, it is also clear that the *logos* in Philo is developed far more philosophically than it is in the hymn. Philo's *logos* is rooted in the metaphysics of Middle Platonism in a way that the *logos* in the hymn is not. But both are part of the larger movement of Hellenistic Jewish wisdom/*logos* speculation. The use of *logos* in the hymn, however, moves beyond Hellenistic Jewish speculations about *logos*/wisdom in that it identifies the *logos* with Jesus of Nazareth.

Logos in Second-Century Christian Literature

The use of *logos* was widespread and played a diverse role in second-century Christian literature. It played only a minor role in the writings of Ignatius of Antioch (*Magn.* 8:2). It was important, however, for the *Odes of Solomon.* In the *Odes* the *logos* is the mediation of creation (*Odes of Solomon* 16), of God's self-revelation (*Odes Sol.* 7:7), and of salvation (*Odes Sol.* 46:11), and became incarnate (*Odes Sol.* 7:4). *Logos* was also important in Gnostic writings such as the *Gospel of Truth,* the *Tripartite Tractate,* and the *Trimorphic Protennoia* and in writers such as Justin Martyr, Theophilus of Antioch, and Irenaeus. There is, however, no clear reference to the *logos* from the Gospel of John in "orthodox" Christian writers until Theophilus of Antioch and Irenaeus of Lyons in the late second century.

BIBLIOGRAPHY

D. BOYARIN 2004, *Border Lines: The Partition of Judeo-Christianity,* Philadelphia: University of Pennsylvania Press. • R. E. BROWN 1966, *The Gospel according to John,* vol. 1, Garden City, N.Y.: Doubleday, 3-37. • J. DILLON 1996, *The Middle Platonists,* rev. ed., Ithaca, N.Y: Cornell University Press. • C. H. DODD 1968, *The Interpretation of the Fourth Gospel,* Cambridge: Cambridge University Press, 263-85. • A. A. LONG 1986, *Hellenistic Philosophy,* 2d ed., London: Duckworth. •

D. T. Runia 2001, *Philo of Alexandria, On the Creation of the Cosmos according to Moses: Introduction, Translation and Commentary*, Leiden: Brill. • D. Winston 1985, *Logos and Mystical Theology in Philo of Alexandria*, Cincinnati: Hebrew Union College. Thomas H. Tobin, S.J.

Luke-Acts

In his two-volume narrative, the Gospel of Luke and the book of Acts (referred to by modern scholars as Luke-Acts), Luke presents Jews who believe that Jesus is Israel's messiah in a dynamic of "engaged disengagement" with fellow disbelieving Jews at a time when Roman authority was beginning to distinguish them as two variant groupings. Luke reconfigures the Jesus material known as the Synoptic tradition and continues the story of the witnesses authenticated from "the beginning" in order to convince Jews, Jewish-Christians, Gentile believers, and all who are interested that Jesus is Israel's "Lord and Christ" (Luke 1:1-4; Acts 2:36) and thus "Savior" of all (Luke 2:11; Acts 13:23, 47). By opening up Israel's Scriptures with the new hermeneutic passed on to the twelve apostles by the crucified and risen Jesus himself, Luke depicts Jesus Messiah as Israel's true legacy and the fulfillment of God's plan for Israel to establish the one God's justice and release of sin for all times, peoples, and places.

Jews and Judaism in Luke-Acts

Luke provides more details about various Jewish beliefs and practices than any of his contemporaries with the exception of Josephus, who was probably writing his *Jewish Antiquities* at a slightly later time. Luke not only sketches the earliest profile of synagogue worship (Luke 4:16-20; Acts 13:14-41), but also distinguishes between Sadducees and Pharisees in the formers' lack of belief in the existence of spiritual beings as well as in life after death through resurrection of the body. Resurrection from the dead was one of the distinctive marks of Pharisaic appropriation of the oral teachings of the "elders" and became pivotal in early Christian belief that Jesus had been raised from the dead.

Sadducees

Luke divulges considerable information about the Sadducees from which the high priests and prominent chief priests were drawn. Together with their scribes and elders or "leaders of the people," they appear to hold the majority in the rulings of the Jewish council or Sanhedrin, which meets in the Temple precincts, and commands the Temple police charged to protect those environs (Luke 19:47–20:2, 19, 27-47; 22:2-4, 47-54, 66-71). The high priest presides over the Sanhedrin's deliberations, and in Acts the high priest, Annas, infuriated over the teaching that Jesus had been raised from the dead, instigates the arrest of the twelve apostles, along with their interrogation and punishment (Acts 4:5-6; 5:17-18, 21-28; cf. 6:7b). The high priest also leads the interrogation of Stephen and apparently allows the mob-style execution of this member of "the seven" to proceed, with a young man named Saul actively participating in Stephen's stoning (Acts 7:58–8:3) and catalyzing a vigorous persecution of any belonging to "the way" of Jesus, even requesting letters from the high priest authorizing Saul/Paul to bind followers of this way in the synagogues of Damascus (Acts 8:1-3; 9:1-2). In an ironic turnabout, another high priest, Ananias, will later order Paul to be struck on the face when Paul himself is escorted in for questioning before the Sanhedrin. Paul returns the favor with a verbal equivalent, and then apologizes when he realizes he has reviled the high priest. This is the same encounter in which Paul claims himself to be a Pharisee and divides the Sadducees and Pharisees against each other over the hope of the resurrection of the dead, with Pharisaic scribes coming to Paul's defense (Acts 23:1-10).

Pharisees

As in Matthew and Mark, Jesus also utters harsh words against "the hypocrisy of the Pharisees" (Luke 12:1), singling out their zealous adherence to the minutiae of oral traditions while passing by the weightier matters of God's justice ensconced in the Law and now more poignantly pitched in the speech and actions of Jesus himself. Unlike his Synoptic counterparts, Luke portrays Jesus as a guest of Pharisees, who challenges their notion of God's holiness (Luke 7:36-50; 11:37-54; 14:1-24). Jesus journeys from town to town, healing, and eating and drinking with "sinners" and other expendables in the streets and inns of Galilee, Transjordan, and Judea. He warns people against the "leaven" of the Pharisees. They entertain Jesus publicly, but behind the scenes they effectively impede God's love and justice.

This serious engagement of the Pharisees with Jesus and the shared belief in the resurrection may explain why Luke does not mention Pharisees explicitly when the attempts to arrest Jesus begin (last reference = Luke 19:39; cf. Matt. 27:62), and also why some of the Pharisees defend and even join the messianic way of Jesus in Acts. In the second arrest of the Twelve instigated by the Sadducees (Acts 5:17-40), Gamaliel, a Pharisee scribe/teacher of the Law, introduced as "well respected by the whole people [Gr. *laos*]," warns the council of Israel's leaders that they might just be "fighting against God" in opposing the new movement. Ironically, Gamaliel speaks prophetically, if unwittingly, about God's plan, which might just be enacted through those who proclaim "in Jesus the resurrection from the dead" (Acts 4:1-2; 5:33-39).

More than irony, this wisdom prepares the way for Saul/Paul, one of Gamaliel's most zealous students (Acts 22:3-5), to carry the banner of Jesus to Diaspora Jews and through them to the Gentile nations at the end of the earth (Acts 1:8; 13:46-47; 28:28). For Luke, Paul the Pharisee becomes the witness of witnesses as he, and not the Twelve (Acts 1:6-8), fulfills Jesus' command to extend the messiah's forgiveness of sins to all the "unclean Gentiles" of the earth (Acts 22:15; 26:16; cf. 11:8-9). It is noteworthy that in his final defense speech before both Jewish and Roman authorities (Acts 26:1-23), Paul claims that he, up to that very moment, "had lived his whole life according to the strictest party/grouping of our religion as a Pharisee." In his hope for the resurrection of the dead, he had "turned" to "the first to be raised from the dead," even "the suffering messiah" Jesus who, now through Paul's witness, "was proclaiming the light" of this fulfilled salvation "to the people [of Israel] and to the nations" (Acts 26:5-8, 16-18, 23; cf. 23:6!).

Luke's portrayal of the Pharisees' interactions with Jesus and with the first Jesus-messianic believers, then, reflects continuing engagement but also the ever increasing separation between nonbelieving Jews and Jewish believers in Messiah Jesus at the time when Luke was completing his two volumes. By the end of Acts, even the half-Jewish, half-Roman "king" Agrippa understands some difference between Paul's beliefs as "one associated with Christ/Christian" and those of Pharisaic Judaism (Acts 11:26; 26:26-29).

The People

The Greek word *laos* ("people") is the term that the LXX chooses to translate the Hebrew word *ʿam.* Luke's use of *laos* is probably the most revealing of his terms for the relationship between the Jesus movement and the Jewish people. He uses it thirty-six times in the Gospel and some forty-eight times in Acts (compare Matthew at fifteen times and Mark at three times). Luke echoes the main LXX meaning quite consistently to denote the chosen and covenanted people/tribes of Israel, especially as they are gathered as God's people. They come out to be baptized by John (Luke 3:15-16, 21), and Jesus calls out disciples from their ranks (Luke 6:17–7:1), directing the disciples to feed them in the wilderness (Luke 9:13-17). They praise God for visiting His people in the mighty prophet Jesus (Luke 7:16; 24:19), causing fear among the "leaders of the people," lest the people stone them for their lack of response to Jesus' (and John's) authority (Luke 19:47-48; 20:1-8, 9, 19, 26; 22:2). Yet like the synagogue worshipers in Nazareth (Luke 4:16-30), they can turn precipitously on Jesus, from glowing praise to feckless condemnation (Luke 19:48; 21:38; 23:13-16). Before Pilate the *laos* joins their leaders to cry out for Jesus' crucifixion (Luke 23:18-25).

This pattern largely repeats itself in Acts. The first believers come from the *laos* gathered for Pentecost (Acts 2:41-47). More and more of the *laos* join the Jesus movement and hold these "brothers and sisters" of "the way" with the highest respect, over against the Temple establishment, which actively resists (Acts 2:47; 4:2, 13-22; 5:12, 13, 26, 33-34). But with the unleashing of persecution against the Jerusalem church sparked by Stephen's "witness" (Acts 6:12, 8:1; cf. 22:20), *laos* becomes more of a neutral term vis-à-vis the Jesus movement until it represents a group who become, at best, ambivalent to Paul and eventually seek to kill him at his final Pentecost (Acts 21:27-40). From Acts 12 on, Luke employs the term "the Jews" more frequently and more negatively than *laos,* but at the assembly of Acts 15 James defines *laos* by appealing to the prophets and recalling Peter's visit to Cornelius in support of the Pauline mission that Gentiles not be required to be circumcised as they "turn to [the] God" of the Jesus-Messiah way (Acts 15:13-18). Now the term takes on for the first time explicitly the radical notion that God's messianic plan establishes both Jews and non-Jews as full members of God's eschatological "people" (Acts 15:14). Yet when Paul turns to the leaders of the *people* in Rome at the end of Acts, he continues to refer to disbelieving Jews as the *laos* and even cites Isaiah 6 to depict a *people* whose stubborn refusal to believe in Jesus Messiah is actually fulfilling Isaiah's prophetic end-horizon (Acts 28:17, 25-28). Thus out of the matrix of the *laos* of Israel a messianically fulfilled *laos* of both Jews and Gentiles is being constituted (e.g., Acts 18:10) which will eventually redound to Israel's "glory" (Luke 2:28-32; Acts 28:30-31).

Israel

Israel is God's specially chosen nation with a unique history of promise and expectation, of blessing and judgment to accomplish God's special purposes for the whole of creation. Israel remains Israel throughout Luke-Acts, both divided and disobedient, whole and faithful to God's calling in patterns that repeat Israel's past. There is no notion of a new Israel or parallel Israel, nor even of a true Israel. Rather, from the beginning of the call to Abraham, Israel has always disobeyed and resisted God's special gestures of forgiveness and restoration, while at the same time producing patriarchs, judges, prophets, kings, Messiah Jesus, and apostles specially appointed by God to be witnesses to God's grand scheme of salvation and blessing to all nations. Luke is intent to demonstrate that Israel's rejection of Messiah Jesus continues its disobedience to God's will (Torah/Scriptures) but precisely through this opposition also eschatologically fulfills the "plan" of God's reign/kingdom to bring eternal life to the whole world.

The Jews

Luke uses the plural *hoi Ioudaioi* some five times in the Gospel and seventy-two in Acts to signify all those who worship the one God of Israel as revealed in the Torah, their sacred Scripture, and for whom Jerusalem and especially the holy place, the Temple, was the religious, ethnic, political, and geographical center of their allegiance. The term distinguishes those who are aligned with the beliefs and practices of the "people of Israel" (Acts 4:27) — whether living in "the land of the Jews" or the Diaspora — over against non-Jews, "those of the nations"/"Gentiles," as well as the "Samaritans," yet a third grouping or "other race" of "foreigners." From Acts 12 onward, "the Jews" takes on a decidedly negative role; they are frequently hostile to Paul and his associates, some even pursuing Paul from city to city, with a group from Asia/Ephesus accusing Paul to the Sanhedrin of defiling their holy place, which leads to his arrest by the Romans. The parting scene in Rome, however, breaks this pattern, with "brother Jews" agreeing to disagree about Jesus, as Paul welcomes "all" (Acts 28:17, 19-22, 23-28, 30-31).

The Relation of Believing and Non-believing Jews

Luke's writing portrays, therefore, a time of "engaged disengagement" between non-believing and believing Jews, reflecting the period shortly before and especially after the First Jewish Revolt when the Temple lay in ruins (67-73 C.E.). Luke may be appealing, in part, to Jews at a critical juncture when the future of Judaism resided largely in the lay Pharisee movement — whose authority among the people was not as formally or visibly tied to the Temple establishment — and when Jewish believers were under considerable pressure to align solidly with Torah observance and community boundary markers such as circumcision, Sabbath, and dietary regulations. The strictures of the Pharisaic party within the Judean church (Acts 15:5) and the resulting rules of engagement — especially involving table fellowship between believing Jews and Gentiles — hashed out at the apostolic assembly of Acts 15 (Acts 15:28-29) not only point back to Pharisaic disgruntlement with Jesus' meal behavior, but also to that period of intense opposition to all Jewish social intercourse with Gentiles etched so graphically in Paul's final journey to Jerusalem (Acts 21:15-36). Instead of settled conventions for life together, in Acts an overwhelming number of Jewish believers are convinced that Paul is a traitor to Jewish messianic faith, which should continue practicing the "customs" taught by Moses and the circumcising of their children (Acts 21:21). Luke is silent about any solidarity from these "myriads of believers" among "the people" when Paul is accused by Diaspora Jews of defiling the Temple and is nearly killed by the *laos* gathered for Pentecost (Acts 21:20–22:24). Paul's third and final declaration, that the "salvation of God" has been sent to the Gentiles precisely as Jews continue to reject it (Acts 28:28), augurs a new period when Gentile believers will form the majority.

Diverging Interpretations

The historical-critical approaches that flourished through the Enlightenment and into the twentieth century emphasized how different Luke's understanding of Israel and Judaism was from Paul's theology. Coming at least a generation later than Paul, Luke was attempting to trace the roots of the Jesus movement into the flowering of a new universal religion in many ways better suited to the fertile soil of Roman expansion and domination than parochial Judaism(s). Luke was the evangelist *of* and *for* the Gentiles when Judaism had rejected the Jesus movement, leaving the new "Christian" religion to incorporate but also to progress beyond the Judaism that had given it birth. F. C. Baur and the Tübingen School, along with other scholars of the nineteenth century, showcased Acts as the synthesis of an early Catholic Church that had essentially superseded any universalistic appeal of Judaism.

Though interpreters from this trajectory in the twentieth century like Hans Conzelmann (1982) and Ernst Haenchen (1971) discounted supersessionist motives for Luke's enterprise, they nevertheless charted the still popular view that Luke-Acts essentially replaces Judaism with Christianity (cf., e.g., Sanders 1987; Tyson 1992).

Yet in the last few decades critical scholarship has challenged this scheme with alternative construals. Jacob Jervell (1979 and 1992) argues that Luke himself champions an extensive overlap of the first believers with the Jewish people as the fulfillment of Israel and the necessary scriptural foundation for worldwide expansion to non-Jews. This notion of "Israel alongside Israel" — with Gentile converts added on or forming a fulfilled Israel with believing Jews — when the vast majority of Jews were dissociating themselves from the Jesus messianists, has prompted a variety of critiques of the supersessionist model.

A view much in the minority and presented above is that Israel, both fulfilled and disobedient, remains a divided Israel throughout Luke-Acts (see further Moessner 1999). On this reading of Luke-Acts, Jesus is the crowning of God's way with the world through the covenant people of Israel. Through Jesus' rejection by his own people and his rising from the dead, the new life of the new covenant is unleashed for a repentant Israel and through their witness to the peoples of the nations (Luke 22:14-38). This messianic "way" is the plot of the whole of Israel's Scriptures as opened and exposited by the crucified and risen messiah himself (e.g., Luke 24:25-27). Even the apostles have to attain a new grasp of the scriptural whole. Thus this new mindset toward the scriptural plan of salvation entails at its core a turning around or transformed mind that perforce becomes the thrust of the apostolic message to Israel and the nations.

It is no wonder that Luke weaves into his new narrative proposal citations, allusions, mini-plots, and types from Scripture that focus upon a suffering righteous figure who, precisely through shame and maltreatment from his own people of Israel, is accomplishing God's bidding in a larger plan for the universal remission of sins. From the outset, the vocation of the Servant of the Lord in Isaiah is evoked to describe Jesus' sending to Israel; Jesus will be the source of a great contention that will nevertheless lead to the illumination of the Gentiles and ultimately to Israel's praise (Luke 2:29-35). Jesus recalls this vocation at his final eating and drinking with "sinners" before being handed over by them to be crucified (Luke 22:37, citing Isa. 53:12).

As Israel's servant, Jesus both recapitulates and consummates the vocation of "Moses and all the prophets." The mantle of this apostolic word is passed on to Paul and colleagues by the Servant himself, who continues through them the anointed mission of "release to the captives," first to Israel, and, through Israel's opposition, to the nations.

When in Rome Paul utters for the third time that the "salvation of God" is for the Gentiles (Acts 13:46; 18:6; 28:28), the servant pattern is broken. No longer does Paul then first turn to Israel, and the Jewish leaders do not attempt to discredit Paul. By preaching openly to "all" Paul fulfills Jesus' mandate of witness in Acts 1:8, when "you nations who are at the end of earth" — under Rome's mighty power — may now "turn and be saved" (Isa. 45:22; 49:6). As the Jewish leaders and Paul part ways (Acts 28:25), synagogue and church part company

LUKE-ACTS

in the ways they read the whole of their Scriptures and understand the messianic way of "the light of revelation to the nations, and glory to your people Israel!"

BIBLIOGRAPHY

R. L. BRAWLEY 1987, *Luke-Acts and the Jews: Conflict, Apology, and Conciliation,* Atlanta: Scholars Press. • J. JERVELL 1979, *Luke and the People of God: A New Look at Luke-Acts,* Philadelphia: Fortress. • J. JERVELL 1992, "God's Faithfulness to the Faithless People: Trends in Interpretation of Luke-Acts," *Word and World* 12: 29-36. • D. MARGUERAT 2002, *The First Christian Historian,* Cambridge: Cambridge University Press. • D. P. MOESSNER, ED. 1999, *Jesus and the Heritage of Israel,* Harrisburg, Penn.: Trinity Press International. • J. T. SANDERS 1987, *The Jews in Luke-Acts,* Philadelphia: Fortress Press. • G. E. STERLING 1992, *Historiography and Self-Definition: Josephos, Luke-Acts and Apologetic Historiography,* Leiden, Brill. • J. B. TYSON, ED. 1988, *Luke-Acts and the Jewish People: Eight Critical Perspectives,* Minneapolis: Augsburg. • J. B. TYSON 1992, *Images of Judaism in Luke-Acts,* Columbia: University of South Carolina Press.

DAVID P. MOESSNER

M

Maccabean Revolt

The Maccabean Revolt encompassed a series of events during the mid-second century B.C.E. by which the Maccabee family gained political, military, and religious power in Judea. The name "Maccabees" is taken from the nickname applied to Judas in 1 Macc. 2:4, which is usually interpreted as "the hammer."

Sources

The major literary sources for the Maccabean Revolt are 1 and 2 Maccabees, as well as Daniel. None of these books provides a thoroughly objective report of the events, though it is possible to derive from them an outline of the major developments. The book of Daniel combines Aramaic court tales and a Hebrew apocalypse that were put together ca. 165 B.C.E., before or in the very early stages of the revolt. Set in the sixth century B.C.E., the book first describes conflicts and contests at the royal court in Babylon (chaps. 1–6), and then supplies visions of the future (chaps. 7–12). The style of the second half of the book is imaginative and allusive, but it does show how one Jewish group regarded the threat to traditional Jewish life posed by Antiochus IV Epiphanes and his Jewish collaborators.

Second Maccabees describes how in the face of various threats God repeatedly defended the Jerusalem Temple and his people. It is important because it supplies precious information about the intrigues surrounding the Jewish high priesthood before the Maccabean Revolt and about Judas Maccabaeus' successes and failures as its leader. First Maccabees reports the achievements of three generations of the Maccabee family: the priest Mattathias; his sons Judas, Jonathan, and Simon; and Simon's son, John Hyrcanus. While sometimes called "dynastic propaganda," 1 Maccabees provides the most detailed and reliable account of the Maccabean Revolt from beginning to end.

Major Events

From these and other sources it is possible to discern an outline of the major events in the Maccabean Revolt. The dates are approximate, and some are disputed among scholars.

175 B.C.E.	Antiochus IV as Seleucid king
175-172	Jason as Jewish high priest
172-163	Menelaus as Jewish high priest
169	Antiochus IV's first Egyptian campaign; plunder of the Jerusalem Temple
168	Antiochus IV's second Egyptian campaign; founding of the citadel in Jerusalem
167	Desecration of the Jerusalem Temple and persecution of Jews
165	Judas leads the revolt
164	Rededication of the Temple; death of Antiochus IV
162-159	Alcimus as the Jewish high priest
161	Judas' victory over Nicanor and alliance with the Romans
160	Death of Judas and succession of Jonathan
159	Death of Alcimus
159-152	Jewish high priesthood vacant
152	Jonathan as Jewish high priest
142	Death of Jonathan and accession of Simon
141	Conquest of the Jerusalem citadel
134	Death of Simon and accession of John Hyrcanus

Beginnings

During the third century B.C.E. Judea was administered by the Ptolemaic dynasty based in Egypt. Around the year 200 Judea and its capital Jerusalem came under the control of the Seleucid dynasty based in Antioch of Syria. Throughout the second century the Seleucid kingdom passed among the descendants of Antiochus III (223-187). These dynastic struggles provide the background for the events described in 1 and 2 Maccabees.

When Antiochus IV Epiphanes gained control of the Seleucid Empire in 175, he allowed Jason to outbid his brother Onias III for the Jewish high priesthood

(2 Macc. 4:7-8). Jason then established Greek institutions at Jerusalem (most notably a gymnasium) and tried to make it into a Hellenistic city. In 172 Jason was outbid and replaced by Menelaus, who had no legitimate claim to the Jewish high priesthood.

By 167 Antiochus IV, with the help and encouragement of some Jewish collaborators (1 Macc. 1:11-15), had despoiled the Temple and its treasury, set up a military garrison or citadel near the Temple (the Akra), abolished the traditional Jewish law as the law of Judea, and established a new order of worship (the cult of the "Lord of Heaven"). Why Antiochus IV intervened in Jewish affairs is not clear. He may have merely needed money quickly to pay his soldiers and to keep himself in power. Or he may have planned to develop an eastern equivalent to the nascent Roman Empire in the west. Or he may have drifted or been invited into a socioeconomic, cultural, and/or religious civil war among factions in Judea. Some combination of these factors is also possible.

The roots of the Maccabean Revolt can be traced back to the high priesthoods of Jason and Menelaus. Their efforts at buying the high priesthood introduced instability into Judean religious life and society, and turned control of the Jerusalem Temple into a political and cultural struggle. In 2 Maccabees Jason is portrayed as a "Hellenizer," and Menelaus is viewed as an unscrupulous temple robber who turns traitor. That neither Jason nor Menelaus won out was due to Judas Maccabaeus and his supporters.

It is always difficult to pinpoint the beginnings of a revolution. The author of 1 Maccabees places it in 166 or 165 at Modein (near Lydda) with the bold resistance to forced pagan worship shown by Mattathias and his sons (1 Maccabees 2). The author of 2 Maccabees attributes the leadership in the revolt to Judas Maccabaeus (2 Macc. 5:27; 8:1-7) and says little or nothing about his father and brothers and nothing about the incident at Modein. The book of Daniel seems to dismiss the early Maccabean movement as at best "a little help" (Dan. 11:34).

Not all Jews supported the Maccabean Revolt. Even though 1 Maccabees tends to equate the Maccabean movement with Israel and to dismiss other Jews as "certain renegades" (1:11), it is clear that there were several parties in Judea besides the Maccabees. Both Jason and Menelaus had Jewish supporters. Some Jews at Jerusalem seem to have welcomed Antiochus' entrance into Jewish affairs (1:11-15). The pious observers of the Sabbath (1:29-38) and the Hasideans (7:12-18) were two more Jewish groups outside the Maccabean circle. And at least some of the Seleucid troops stationed at the citadel in Jerusalem seem to have been Jews.

Judas

The course of the Maccabean Revolt was neither sudden nor smooth. Judas and his supporters achieved dramatic military victories at the start, due in part to their familiarity with the landscape and the people. The capture of the Jerusalem Temple and the restoration of traditional Jewish worship there (1 Macc. 4:36-61; 2 Macc. 10:1-9), along with the death of Antiochus IV in late 164, solidified the Maccabean movement and gave it popular credibility.

Antiochus IV died in connection with an attempt at robbing a temple in Persia. Both 1 Macc. 6:1-16 and 2 Macc. 9:1-29 seek to connect his death with the Temple at Jerusalem. It appears that his death took place about the same time as the rededication of the Jerusalem Temple (the first Hanukkah). Although both writers insisted that Antiochus died for his sins against the Temple and the Jewish people, it is unlikely (given the state of communications at the time) that the Jews knew about the death of Antiochus IV before the rededication, or that Antiochus IV knew about the events in Jerusalem before his death. At any rate, by late 164 the persecutor of the Jews was dead and the Jerusalem Temple was in the hands of Judas Maccabaeus and his Jewish supporters.

The symbolic significance of Maccabean control of the Temple and the celebration of its rededication must have sent a very powerful message. Indeed, the message was so powerful that many modern readers suppose that the revolt reached its successful conclusion with the events of late 164. However, the ancient sources tell the story of further attacks by and against Judas, his defeat in battle, and his tragic death. With the arrival of Alcimus as the Jewish high priest in 162 and the death of Judas in 160, it seemed that the Maccabean Revolt was finished and had accomplished all that could be expected of it.

Jonathan and Simon

The sudden death of the high priest Alcimus in 159 B.C.E. (1 Macc. 9:54-57) left the high priesthood vacant (the *intersacerdotium*), and it apparently remained so until 152 when Judas' brother Jonathan got himself appointed as high priest. Some scholars have suggested that the Teacher of Righteousness known from the sectarian Qumran Scrolls had a legitimate claim to the high priesthood at this time but was pushed aside by Jonathan. In this theory the Teacher became part of the Qumran group, and this community came to view itself increasingly in opposition to those (Maccabean) Jews who assumed control of the Temple. Whereas the halakic document known as 4QMMT can be interpreted as a rather irenic statement of the legal differences between the Qumran group and the Jerusalem Temple authorities, the *Pesher on Habakkuk* (1QpHab) portrays in a very negative way a figure called "the Wicked Priest," who is generally identified as either Jonathan or his brother Simon.

What helped greatly to revive the Maccabean movement was further internal struggle for the Seleucid throne. The section devoted to Jonathan in 1 Macc. 9:23–12:53 describes in fascinating detail how he combined political shrewdness and military activity to gain ever more power and territory. The death of Alcimus and the vacancy in the high priesthood until 152 left Jonathan as the only serious Judean political and military figure with whom the various Seleucid claimants could deal. Jonathan succeeded by letting one Seleucid claimant outdo the other in promising him rewards for his support.

Jonathan made deals with the Seleucids Demetrius I (162-150), Alexander I Balas (150-145), and Antiochus VI (145-142), as well as the Egyptian Ptolemies, the Romans, and the Spartans. By supporting Alexander I Balas against Demetrius I, Jonathan gained the high priesthood at Jerusalem despite not belonging to the proper Zadokite family. The Maccabees were a priestly family from the "sons of Joarib" (1 Macc. 2:1; 1 Chron. 24:7; Neh. 11:10). But the high priesthood should have remained within the family of Onias III (2 Maccabees 3–4). While much that went on between 159 and 152 is unclear, at the end the author of 1 Maccabees could describe Jonathan's accession to the Jewish high priesthood without explanation or apology.

After Jonathan's capture and death in 142, his brother Simon gained control and leadership of the Maccabean movement. The section about Simon in 1 Macc. 13:1–15:41 describes his military and political successes, and tells how he secured the independence of the Jewish people and renewed its alliance with Rome. According to the decree quoted in 1 Macc. 14:41-45, Simon and his descendants were to occupy the offices of high priest, military commander, and leader of the people (ethnarch) "until a trustworthy prophet should arise" (14:41). When the Seleucid Antiochus VII (138-129) broke his alliance with Simon, he and his generals were defeated by Simon and his son John Hyrcanus. The story of the Maccabean Revolt according to 1 Maccabees closes with Simon's death in 134 and the accession of John Hyrcanus (16:1-24).

Endings

Just as it is difficult to know when a revolution begins, so it is difficult to know when one ends. A successful revolution results in a stable government and the restoration of civil life ("business as usual"). The appointment of Simon as the sole religious, military, and political leader in Judea (1 Macc. 14:41-45), and the succession of his son John Hyrcanus, were signs that the Maccabean Revolt had succeeded well beyond whatever its founders ever imagined.

One clear marker for both the beginning and the end of the Maccabean Revolt was the fate of the citadel (Akra) in Jerusalem. From its founding in 168 (1 Macc. 1:33) to its dissolution in 141 (13:50), this citadel was a remarkably persistent institution. The citadel was a fortress in Jerusalem, close to the Temple area. It was manned by troops loyal to the Seleucid rulers and governors. Some of the troops may have been Jewish, though most were Syrians and Gentile inhabitants of Palestine. The citadel survived for over twenty-five years and caused the Maccabees and other Jews a good deal of trouble. Only when the citadel was captured and dissolved could the revolt undertaken by the Maccabees be called a real success.

Before the Maccabean Revolt the province of Judea was administered by the Jewish high priest Onias III under the supervision of a Seleucid governor (2 Macc. 3:1-5). At the end of the revolt Judea was ruled directly by the Maccabean high priest, John Hyrcanus I. The chief difference was the increase in Jewish political independence from the Seleucids that the Maccabees had gained.

This increase in political independence was enormously significant. The Jews of Palestine went from being a small client people first in the Persian and Ptolemaic Empires and then in the Seleucid Empire to being an independent political entity tied by treaties to the Romans and the Spartans. They gained control over large areas of the land of Israel and rekindled the sense of national identity that had been dormant since the exile in the sixth century.

Revolutions often contain the seeds of their own destruction. One such seed was the Maccabees' reliance on Rome as their protector. The Romans were eager to make treaties but slow to follow through on them unless it suited their own interests. Nevertheless, the treaties between the Romans and the Jews existed because Judas, Jonathan, and Simon entered into relationships with the Romans. In the short run these official links suited both parties well. The Jews had a powerful defender against both the Seleucids and the Ptolemies. And with their client state in Judea, the Romans had a foothold in the Near East.

Another seed of destruction was the concentration of powers in the Maccabean dynasty. Though such a concentration was probably necessary if the revolt was to succeed, the result was that one family had all the religious, political, and military power in Judea. That family soon fell victim to the kind of dynastic struggles that had also plagued the Ptolemies and Seleucids.

The two seeds of destruction came together in 63 B.C.E. when the Roman general Pompey intervened in order to settle a Maccabean family dispute about who was to succeed Queen Salome Alexandra. Power eventually came to reside in Herod and his family, which married into the Maccabean family and gained control over the privileges and powers that the Maccabees had amassed under Judas, Jonathan, and Simon.

Bibliography

B. Bar-Kochva 1988, *Judas Maccabaeus: The Jewish Struggle against the Seleucids,* Cambridge: Cambridge University Press. • E. Bickerman 1979, *The God of the Maccabees,* Leiden: Brill. • E. J. Bickerman 1988, *The Jews in the Greek Age,* Cambridge, Mass.: Harvard University Press. • K. Bringmann 1983, *Hellenistische Reform und Religionsverfolgung in Judäa,* Göttingen: Vandenhoeck & Ruprecht. • J. J. Collins 2001, "Cult and Culture: The Limits of Hellenization in Judea," in *Hellenism in the Land of Israel,* ed. J. J. Collins and G. E. Sterling, Notre Dame, Ind.: University of Notre Dame, 38-61. • D. J. Harrington 1988, *The Maccabean Revolt: Anatomy of a Biblical Revolution,* Wilmington, Del.: Glazier. • M. Hengel 1974, *Judaism and Hellenism,* Philadelphia: Fortress. • J. Sievers 1990, *The Hasmoneans and Their Supporters,* Atlanta: Scholars Press. • V. Tcherikover 1959, *Hellenistic Civilization and the Jews,* Philadelphia: Jewish Publication Society.

See also: Hasmoneans; Judas Maccabaeus

Daniel J. Harrington, S.J.

Maccabees, First Book of

First Maccabees is one of the four books that are entitled Maccabees and one of the two among them that deals with the Maccabean Revolt. It is a work of historiography that surveys the history of Judea from the ascendancy of Antiochus IV (175 B.C.E.) to the murder of Simon son of Mattathias (134 B.C.E.). First Maccabees is preserved in the Greek Bible, the Septuagint. Its Greek text is a translation of a lost Hebrew book. Though the Hebrew original text cannot be reconstructed from the Greek translation, it is evident that the translator of the Greek version had it before him. 1 and 2 Maccabees are the last surviving Jewish historical books written before the works of Flavius Josephus.

Contents

Most of 1 Maccabees deals with the exploits of Mattathias and his sons, but the book opens with a concise introductory section that covers the century and half between Alexander the Great and Antiochus IV (1:1-9). It follows with a description of Antiochus' policy and that of his Jewish supporters, the Hellenizers, and dwells on the decree on the persecution of Jewish worshipers (1:10-64) and its execution. Antiochus IV is called "a scion of this stock [Alexander and his successors]," which "brought untold miseries upon the world." This is the same view of the Hellenistic regime proposed in the book of Daniel (Dan. 7:8). Then begins the narrative about the Hasmoneans:

2:1-70	Guerrilla warfare under the leadership of Mattathias; his deathbed testament
3:1–9:22	The revolt under the leadership of Judas Maccabaeus; first battles; the rededication of the Temple; wars against the neighboring peoples; the treaty with Rome; Judas' death on the battlefield
9:23–12:53	The survival of the rebels after Judas' death under the leadership of Jonathan; his appointment by Seleucid kings to be high priest and governor; his involvement in the affairs of the Seleucid kingdom; his battles and his fall at the hands of Tryphon
13:1–16:24	Simon's succession of Jonathan as the leader of the Jews; his appointment by the Seleucid king Demetrius I as high priest and governor; his conquest of the Akra, Jaffa, and Gezer; his appointment by the people's assembly to rule the people; his murder; the succession of his son John

Sources

The sources used by the anonymous author of 1 Maccabees are of major importance for appreciating the veracity of his narrative and the aims of his book. They can be classified under five headings: personal knowledge, data from informants, written sources, documents, and poetic passages.

If 1 Maccabees was written in the last decade of John's rule by a member of the Hasmonean court, the author could have participated in some of the battles and/or diplomatic missions and gathered personal information about the events from the time of Jonathan (ca. 160 B.C.E. or bit later) onward.

About events in which he did not participate or that happened before his coming of age, the author was evidently able to gather testimonies from participants or information and stories kept by their families.

He used some written sources, at least for the narrative about non-Jewish history, such as the internal affairs of the Seleucids, their relations with the Ptolemies, and the encomium of Rome. This kind of information could not be based on oral traditions or hearsay but must have derived from written sources unknown to us. The information in chap. 1 concerning Alexander, the Diadochi, and Antiochus IV is reminiscent of Daniel 11, but its sources are likewise unknown (Rappaport 1993).

The most important sources preserved in 1 Maccabees are the documents it presents. These contain royal letters, the treaty between Judea and Rome, and a decision of the people's assembly to appoint Simon high priest and ruler. Almost all scholars agree that most of these documents are authentic. A probable assumption is that they were kept in an archive, either of the Hasmoneans rulers themselves or of the Jerusalem Temple, of which the Hasmoneans were the high priests, and that they were available to the author of 1 Maccabees.

Apart from Mattathias' testament, there are few poems in 1 Maccabees: the lament over the suffering and destruction in Judea (2:7-13) and the praise of Simon (14:4-15). There is no way of knowing whether the author of 1 Maccabees wrote these poems and some other poetic sections, or whether they were among his sources. Some scholars tend to attribute the poetic sections to the author himself (e.g., Neuhaus 1974; Goldstein 1976: 30-31). The short speeches in 1 Maccabees, such as Judas' speech (3:18-22), Antiochus' speech (6:10-13), and the speech of Simon (13:3-6), were probably composed by the author.

The style of the original Hebrew of 1 Maccabees, as far as it can be appreciated through its Greek translation, is influenced by Biblical Hebrew, and especially by that of the historical books of the Bible. It includes verbal translation of many Hebrew idioms and expressions that can be detected behind the Greek, which resembles the Septuagint's Greek translation of the Bible.

The influence of Hellenistic culture can be also detected in the book, as in the importance of the individual heroes compared to the relatively minor role of the deity in human affairs (Rappaport 1998). The citation of documents, noted already in the book of Ezra, is also a change from the form of the biblical books of Samuel and Kings (Momigliano 1977: 31-33).

The influence of the Bible on the author of 1 Maccabees can be seen in his use of anachronistic ethnic and geographical names, such as Canaan (9:37), Ammon (5:6), and Esau (5:3, 65). The author also imitates the deathbed testament of Jacob to his sons (Genesis 49) in the testament ascribed to Mattathias (2:49-70).

Ideology

The views of the author of 1 Maccabees relate a variety of subjects, including obedience to the Law, one's attitude to other peoples and to paganism, the validity of historical rights, and the proper constitution for the Judean state.

The Jewish laws should be obeyed unconditionally. Most important are the ones that the persecutors forced the Jews to transgress: those pertaining to circumcision, Sabbath, diet, and the purity of the Temple and its cult. At a later stage came concern with the purity of the Holy Land, which includes Jewish attitudes toward neighboring Gentile peoples.

The attitude of the Hasmoneans to Gentiles was based on two considerations: religious-national sentiment and *Realpolitik.* The first one dictated purifying the land of all traces of pagan cults and taking vengeance on those Gentile enemies who injured the Jews. The author justifies the harsh treatment of the Gentiles roundabout by citing Simon on the historical right of the Jews to restore the inheritance that had been taken from them by their enemies (15:33-34). Yet political considerations demanded friendly relations with states and regimes at a distance from Judea (Rome, Sparta, the Ptolemies) and with the neighboring Nabateans, who opposed Seleucid dominion and temporarily helped the Hasmoneans.

Among those who should be punished, the author of 1 Maccabees also includes the Jewish Hellenizers, who should be annihilated following the example of Mattathias, who slaughtered the Jew who stepped forward to sacrifice on the pagan altar (2:23-26). The model for this idea is the zeal of Phineas, whom Mattathias calls "our father" (2:54).

The author's view of the proper constitution for the Judean state is expressed by both his supportive presentation of the decree of the people's assembly and his enthusiastic appraisal of the Roman republican constitution. Obviously this ideal Judean regime is combined with the author's full support of the Hasmonean dynasty, and more specifically of Simon and his offspring. This idea can be traced in the literary testament of Mattathias, in which Simon is given preference over his brothers (2:65).

Historical Setting

1 Maccabees was written at a time when an independent Jewish state was just being founded in the land of Israel. It was a new experience for the Jews in Judea that was triggered by religious persecution, by conflicts within Judean society, and by the disintegration of the Seleucid Empire. The future of the new state was not assured, and its constitution was contested from various directions. The persecution of the Jewish religion was a decisive event in the history of Judaism and of monotheism at large. The cause of this act by Antiochus IV Epiphanes is debated by historians and turns on two explanations or combinations of them. One ascribes the initiative to the Jewish Hellenizers (Bickerman 1979), the other to Antiochus himself (Tcherikover 1959: 175-203). Two generations later the memories of the persecution were still alive and influenced both the policy of the Hasmoneans and the author of 1 Maccabees.

First Maccabees preserves the text of an alliance between Judea and Rome. The authenticity of this document has been verified by comparing it to inscriptions of similar content. Both the citation of this document and the chapter about Rome (chap. 8) reflect sympathy toward Rome in the court of John Hyrcanus, but also the insecurity of Judea in the face of the dwindling power of both the Seleucid and Ptolemaic empires. The decision of the great assembly to appoint Simon as the head of the new state (14:25-49) was a result of a compromise among various Jewish groups. The rulers that came after Simon did not abide by it and changed the constitution that had been confirmed by the people's assembly. The most drastic change was the usurpation of kingship by Alexander Jannaeus. 1 Maccabees came at the earlier stages of this development and aimed to support the stabilization and legitimacy of the ruling Hasmonean dynasty.

Thus 1 Maccabees appeared at a time when a statement about the leadership and constitution of Judea was vital. The purpose of 1 Maccabees is to declare that the ruling dynasty is legitimate and its record impeccable. The state is militarily and politically secure because of the wise and courageous leadership of the Hasmoneans, exemplified by Simon, the father of the present ruler (John).

Date and Provenance

The *terminus post quem* of 1 Maccabees is the ascendancy of John Hyrcanus, the son of Simon. Scholars debate whether it was composed during John's rule or the beginning of the reign of Alexander Jannaeus (103-69 B.C.E.). The most probable date is sometime during the last decade of John's rule.

1 Maccabees was written in the land of Israel. Its anonymous writer was an admirer of the Hasmonean family who supported John as the legitimate ruler of Judea and who belonged to the Hasmonean court circle. Considering the author's familiarity with the Bible and with the history and political and diplomatic affairs of the Hellenistic kingdoms, it is reasonable to suppose that he was one of the messengers sent by the Hasmonean rulers on diplomatic missions from the time of Judas Maccabaeus, or perhaps a counselor at their court. It is also very probable that he came from one of the noble families that sided with the revolt against the Seleucids and the Hellenizers.

Bibliography

F.-M. ABEL 1949, *Les livres des Maccabées,* Paris: Gabalda. • E. BICKERMAN 1979, *The God of the Maccabees,* Leiden: Brill. • J. GOLDSTEIN 1976, *I Maccabees,* New York: Doubleday. • A. MOMIGLIANO 1976, "The Date of the First Book of Maccabees," in *Mélanges offerts à J. Heurgon,* Rome: École francaise, 657-61. A. MOMIGLIANO 1977, "Eastern Elements in Post-Exilic Jewish and Greek Historiography," in idem, *Essays in Ancient and Modern Historiography,* Oxford: Blackwell, 25-35. • G. O. NEUHAUS 1974, *Studien zu dem poetischen stücken im 1 Makkabäerbuch,* Würzburg: Echter. • U. RAPPA-

PORT 1993, "The Hellenistic World as Seen by the Book of Daniel," in *Rashi, 1040-1990: Hommage à Ephraim E. Urbach*, ed. G. Sed-Rajna, Paris: Cerf, 71-79. • U. RAPPAPORT 1998, "A Note on the Use of the Bible in 1 Maccabees," in *Biblical Perspectives: Early Use and Interpretation of the Bible in Light of the Dead Sea Scrolls*, ed. M. E. Stone and E. G. Chazon, Leiden: Brill, 175-79. • U. RAPPAPORT 2004, *The First Book of Maccabees: Introduction, Hebrew Translation, and Commentary*, Jerusalem: Yizhak Ben-Zvi (in Hebrew). • V. TCHERIKOVER 1959, *Hellenistic Civilization and the Jews*, trans. S. Appelbaum, Philadelphia: Jewish Publication Society.

See also: Antiochus IV; Hasmoneans; Judas Maccabaeus; Maccabean Revolt; Seleucids

URIEL RAPPAPORT

Maccabees, Second Book of

Canonical Status

2 Maccabees, a Jewish work in Greek preserved as part of the Septuagint, is a full-fledged member of the Catholic Old Testament, while Protestants relegate it, along with other works not found in the Hebrew Bible, to the Apocrypha. It has no status at all in Jewish tradition, which did not preserve it any more than the rest of Hellenistic Jewish literature. Apart from the ancient author of 4 Maccabees and the tenth-century author of *Josippon*, who used it extensively, there is little trace of any Jews reading 2 Maccabees prior to the modern period.

Contents and Structure

2 Maccabees is devoted to an eventful decade and a half (ca. 175-161 B.C.E.) in the relations of the Jews and the Seleucid kingdom, which, after being founded by one of Alexander the Great's successors in the fourth century and a series of wars with its Ptolemaic counterpart (based in Egypt) during the third, had annexed Palestine at the very beginning of the second. The story, which opens at 3:1, divides easily into two parts. The first part goes downhill, presenting the problem: after an idyllic opening with everything peaceful in Jerusalem, the city and Temple enjoying the respect of kings, we read of institutionalized Hellenization in Jerusalem with the encouragement of King Antiochus IV Epiphanes (chap. 4); of Antiochus' attack upon Jerusalem and robbery of the Temple (chap. 5); and of his infamous decrees against Judaism (chap. 6), which engendered some famous scenes of martyrdom (chaps. 6–7).

The second half of the book recounts the solution: Judas Maccabaeus' first victories (chap. 8) are followed by Antiochus' death (chap. 9); by the Jewish reconquest of Jerusalem and rededication of the Temple (10:1-8); by further Jewish victories and the revocation of the decrees against Judaism (10:9–11:38); and by yet more Jewish victories (chaps. 12–13), culminating in the defeat of the Seleucid general Nicanor and the institution of an annual holiday commemorating it (chaps. 14–15). That concludes the book, for, as the author puts it in 15:37, it is *because* "the Hebrews" took over Jerusalem, and retained rule there, that he may end his story. Thus, the story has a clear structure, from an idyllic "once upon a time" at 3:1 to an idyllic "happily ever after" at 15:37.

The first two chapters of the book are not part of the story: 1:1-10a and 1:10a–2:18 are letters from the Jews of Jerusalem inviting those of Egypt to celebrate Hanukkah in memory of the rededication of the Temple, and the rest of chap. 2 constitutes a preface by an anonymous "epitomator" (abridger) who explains that he created the book by condensing a longer work by one Jason of Cyrene (Lybia); that work, and its author, are otherwise unknown.

Thus, 2 Maccabees as we have it is comprised of two letters with a long attachment; the latter was used by the letter writers to give the background of the holiday they call upon the addressees to celebrate.

A Hellenistic Work

The book is not a general history of the Jews in the period concerned. Rather, it focuses upon Jerusalem, as is shown clearly by the opening and closing brackets of the story: it opens with "the holy city" (3:1) and closes with "the city" (15:37). The Hellenistic Jewish author thus indicated to his readers that the Jews are a civilized and respectable people organized around a *polis*, the central bearer of Greek culture. Correspondingly, the book terms Jews "citizens" (*politai;* e.g., 4:5, 50; 5:6, 8), complains that a villain changed Jerusalem's "constitution" (4:11), summarizes persecutions as prohibitions "to live as citizens (*politeuesthai;* 6:1) according to the laws of God," and contrasts the "urbane" Jews with their "barbarian" enemies (2:21; 5:22; 10:4; 13:9; 15:2). That is, good Jews are a type of good Greeks. The same point is made in many other ways as well, such as the author's concern to underline his heroes' "virtue" (6:31), "nobility" (6:18, 28, 31; 7:5, 11, etc.), and "manliness" (8:7; 10:35; 14:18, 43; 15:17); his interest in Hellenistic geography (note "Tripolis" in 14:1 as opposed to merely "a coastal city" in 1 Macc. 7:1); his application of standard Greek motifs (such as Scythian cruelty and Xerxes' arrogance; 4:47 and 5:21); and his sovereign play with the Greek language, such as his usage of puns and paronomasia. The book is a good example of contemporary Hellenistic prose; its language is quite comparable to that of Polybius, although its "pathetic" style, aimed at exciting readers and making them share the feelings of the story's characters, was the kind Polybius liked to scorn.

A Diaspora Work

Apart from the Greek language and Hellenistic nature, four factors point to the book's background in the Diaspora:

First, Gentiles kings, and Gentiles in general, are usually good and respect the Jews. Thus, a villain can kill a Jewish hero in Antioch only if the king is out of town (4:30-38). The king is of course outraged at the murder and executes the villain forthwith. Only misunderstandings lead to clashes (5:11), and Greeks by and large respect the Jews (4:35-36, 49; 12:30). All this is to assert that Jews can live just fine under Gentile rule and alongside Gentile neighbors, since after all they are all "men" (4:35!).

MACCABEES, SECOND BOOK OF

Second, the Temple and the sacrificial cult are not of great interest. Although Antiochus' persecutions involved the desecration of its cult (6:4-5; cf. 1 Macc. 1:54; 4:43-44), our book clearly views the Temple as of only secondary importance. This is explicit at 5:19, where the author pedantically explains that God's choice of the Temple is secondary to his choice of the people, so when the people sin the Temple, too, suffers. This statement reflects a Diaspora perspective, for the people are all over and the Temple is only in Jerusalem. The same orientation is also reflected in the emphasis that, although God protects the Temple, he resides in heaven (3:39); in the characterization of those who complained about theft of vessels from the Temple as "those who had spoken for the city and the villages and the holy vessels" — significantly, the city is mentioned first and the vessels last (4:48); and in the summary description of what was stolen from the Temple merely as "holy vessels" (5:16; contrast the detailed list in 1 Macc. 1:21-23) — even though many words are used in 5:16 to report that Antiochus also stole gifts from foreign kings. All these features prove again that Antiochus was an exception to the generally benign and respectful foreign rule. Lack of interest in the Temple and the sacrificial cult is natural for Jews of the Diaspora, who could only rarely participate in them.

Third, martyrdom is very important in this work. As noted, the story's turning point comes after the long and detailed martyrdoms of chaps. 6–7. Indeed, the beginning of chap. 8 has Judas Maccabaeus and his men praying to God to take heed to the suffering, and to hearken to the blood calling out to him from the ground (8:3). And God did. That is, the martyrs' suffering had been very effective, just as the seventh son had hoped (7:38). Similarly, the final victory, in chap. 15, is preceded by another long martyrdom scene (14:37-46). But the valuation of martyrdom — the willingness to die rather than violate one's religion — is a phenomenon characteristic of the Diaspora, as a comparison with 1 Maccabees shows. There, the book's heroes are willing not so much to die as to fight. As a particular case of this distinction, note that while 1 Maccabees emphasizes that Jews *must* fight on the Sabbath because otherwise they will die (2:40-41; 9:43-44), 2 Maccabees, though repeatedly underlining the sanctity of the Sabbath (6:6, 11; 8:26; 12:38), twice (5:25 and 15:1) comes very near to saying that Jews may *not* fight on it even at the cost of their lives. Such a position is to be expected from Jews who cannot fight anyway.

Fourth, nothing really changes in this book. True, in the "once upon a time" opening the city is ruled by the Seleucids, while in the "happily ever after" closing it is ruled by "the Hebrews" (15:37). But the impression is clearly that the end merely restores the beginning. Threats have been averted and enemies have been overcome, but no attention is given to anything new, such as Jewish rule established in their stead. This is typical for Diaspora historiography, as we see in such works as Esther, 3 Maccabees, and Philo's *Legatio ad Gaium;* everything is fine at the beginning and at the end, while the story has some interesting ups and downs in between. This perspective stands in stark contrast to 1 Maccabees, a dynastic history in which the point is to show just how much the Hasmoneans *changed* things, from wicked Seleucid rule to beneficent Hasmonean rule. In contrast, in 2 Maccabees the point is to show the reader just how it happened that, after the Jews' sins moved God to turn away his face (5:17) and thus allow the Seleucids to persecute them, the Jews' atonement, expressed especially by their suffering, moved God to "reconciliation" with the Jews and so to allow Judas Maccabaeus to *restore* the idyllic *status quo ante.* Indeed, "reconciliation" (*katalassō:* 1:5; 5:20; 7:33; 8:29) is our book's leitmotif, that is, the *restoration* of the proper relationship with God, who is, of course, unchanging. In developing this motif, the book makes much use of Deuteronomy 32 (quoted explicitly at 7:6 and alluded to elsewhere), which, too, is quite cyclical. Thus alongside the dichotomy of armies versus martyrs, we have a distinction between Jews who have the power to change their own lives (1 Maccabees) versus those who do not (2 Maccabees). Accordingly, 2 Maccabees is full of prayers, miracles, angels, apparitions, and divinely engineered poetic justice. It is very much a story of God's providential involvement.

Composition History of the Book

As we have noted, in chap. 2 an anonymous "epitomator" presents the work as his abridgement of a longer work by one Jason of Cyrene. That the book is an abridgement may be confirmed both by some stylistic peculiarities and by the fact that a few times (4:45; 8:33; 10:37; 12:36) new characters are mentioned as if they are known to the reader. Various indications show that the abridger — who also addresses the readers in a few theological excursuses (5:17-20; 6:12-17; cf. 4:16-17) — undertook some very substantial editing.

But it seems also to be the case that the book underwent some revision in order to put it to its present use as the underpinning of the Jerusalemites' invitation, in the opening letters, to celebrate Hanukkah. This determination derives from two complementary observations. On the one hand, the book ends with the establishment of Nicanor's Day (15:36), and normally we should assume that, like Esther and 3 Maccabees, the book was written to explain the holiday. Indeed, Nicanor's prominence in the book is obvious since he is the adversary in the only two military campaigns described in any detail (chaps. 8 and 15). On the other hand, it is fairly obvious that the passage of our book that explains Hanukkah, 10:1-8, is a secondary insertion, for it separates the end of chap. 9 from 10:9. Similarly, note the way 10:1 mentions the Temple before the city, although certainly the city was taken prior to the Temple; in this detail we have a Palestinian point of view, precisely the opposite of the Diasporan point of view we noted at 4:48, where the city was first mentioned although the topic was the temple vessels (see also 15:17). Note, too, in further contrast to what is usual for our book, the cultic detail in 10:3 and the antipathy to Gentiles in 10:2, 4. In sum, it seems that the Judeans who wanted to invite their Egyptian "brethren" to celebrate Hanukkah adapted a Hellenistic Jewish work dedicated to explaining the origin of Nicanor's Day, which told the basic story well enough but which they had to edit in order to include something explaining Hanukkah itself.

Date

Given the book's complex literary history (composition, abridgement, Jerusalemite editing), its dating, too, is complex. One important datum concerning the original composition would seem to be the original focus upon the victory over Nicanor. Given that Judas Maccabaeus was himself killed a year later (160 B.C.E.; 1 Maccabees 9) and that the next years saw the Hasmonean movement forced underground (1 Macc. 9:62-73) and then subject to various vicissitudes, it seems difficult to imagine that the book was written much later than the defeat of Nicanor. The more time that went by, the less significant that victory — and the festival commemorating it — would have seemed. On the other hand, the first Jerusalemite letter accompanying the book is dated no later than 124 B.C.E. (and perhaps as early as 143, depending upon issues of text and interpretation in 1:7-10). Thus, the book as we have it reflects a three-stage process of composition between 160 and 124 B.C.E., perhaps somewhat earlier than its Judean competitor, 1 Maccabees, which was composed sometime after John Hyrcanus' accession to power in 135/4 B.C.E. (1 Maccabees 16).

Text and Translations

The main witnesses to the text of 2 Maccabees are the Alexandrinus and Venetus manuscripts of the Septuagint, of the fifth and eighth centuries respectively. Apart from those two uncials (written in capital letters), there are also more than thirty manuscripts in miniscule script, just as there are also secondary translations, of which the most important is the Old Latin version edited by De Bruyne. The standard Greek edition of the book is by Robert Hanhart (2d ed. 1976).

BIBLIOGRAPHY

B. BAR-KOCHVA 1989, *Judas Maccabaeus: The Jewish Struggle against the Seleucids,* Cambridge: Cambridge University Press. • R. DORAN 1981, *Temple Propaganda: The Purpose and Character of 2 Maccabees,* Washington, D.C.: Catholic Biblical Association of America. • J. W. VAN HENTEN 1997, *The Maccabean Martyrs as Saviours of the Jewish People: A Study of 2 and 4 Maccabees,* Leiden: Brill. • M. HIMMELFARB 1998, "Judaism and Hellenism in 2 Maccabees," *Poetics Today* 19: 19-40. • A. MOMIGLIANO 1975, "The Second Book of Maccabees," *Classical Philology* 70: 81-88. • G. W. E. NICKELSBURG 1971, "1 and 2 Maccabees — Same Story, Different Meaning," *Concordia Theological Monthly* 42: 515–26. • D. R. SCHWARTZ 1998, "On Something Biblical about 2 Maccabees," in *Biblical Perspectives: Early Use and Interpretation of the Bible in Light of the Dead Sea Scrolls,* ed. M. E. Stone and E. G. Chazon, Leiden: Brill, 223-32. • D. R. SCHWARTZ 2008, *2 Maccabees,* Berlin: de Gruyter. • V. A. TCHERIKOVER 1959, *Hellenistic Civilization and the Jews,* Philadelphia: Jewish Publication Society. • D. S. WILLIAMS 2003, "Recent Research in 2 Maccabees," *CBR* 2: 69-83. • R. D. YOUNG 1991, "The 'Woman with the Soul of Abraham': Traditions about the Mother of the Maccabean Martyrs," in *"Women Like This": New Perspectives on Jewish Women in the Greco-Roman World,* ed. A.-J. Levine, Atlanta: Scholars Press, 67–81.

See also: Maccabees, First Book of

DANIEL R. SCHWARTZ

Maccabees, Third Book of

Although clearly the work of a Jewish author from the Hellenistic or early Roman period, 3 Maccabees is not found in the Hebrew Bible. It is universally agreed that the work was composed in Greek, and there is no evidence that it was translated into Hebrew or Aramaic. 3 Maccabees is found in only one of the three major uncial manuscripts of the Septuagint (the Alexandrinus, mid-fifth century C.E.). Like 4 Maccabees, but unlike 1 and 2 Maccabees, it was apparently not in the version of the Septuagint translated by Jerome into Latin (the Vulgate, fourth century C.E.), and thus is not included in the Roman Catholic Bible or the Protestant Apocrypha (although it is included in the Eastern Orthodox canon). It is therefore traditionally classified by Christian scholars among the pseudepigrapha. Although it has left no trace of influence on later Jewish tradition, it is of great interest for understanding the culture of the Jewish Diaspora in the Hellenistic and early Roman periods.

Date and Provenance

As noted above, the original language is evidently Greek, written in a particularly artificial and florid style. It appears that the author aimed to be considered among the literary elite of his time. The language points to an origin in the Diaspora, and the predominant focus of the text on the Jews of Alexandria suggests that the author was an Egyptian Jew, most likely an Alexandrian. Up to this point there is unanimous agreement in the scholarship.

The date of the work is more controversial. The narrative takes place under Ptolemy IV Philopator (221-204 B.C.E.), and appears to regard the Temple as still standing, thus putting the outside limits at 217 B.C.E. and 70 C.E., but no scholar since the eighteenth century has suggested that the text was actually composed during the reign of Philopator. Since the text appears to contain a verbal echo of the Greek translation of Daniel (3 Macc. 6:6; cf. v. 27 of the Prayer of Azariah, a Septuagint addition to the third chapter of Daniel), and makes no explicit reference to Roman rule, it is generally dated either to the late Hellenistic (Ptolemaic) period (first century B.C.E.) or to the early Roman period (27 B.C.E.–40 C.E.). However, there is a strong division between the Hellenistic and Roman camps. In general, those who favor a Hellenistic date stress the points of contact with other late Hellenistic texts such as Greek Esther and the *Letter of Aristeas,* and emphasize the elements in the text which encourage cooperation between Jews and non-Jews. Those who favor a Roman date tend to stress the confrontational aspects of the narrative. Since the narrative certainly has both confrontational and conciliatory aspects, and there is insufficient evidence conclusively to rule out either a late Hellenistic or an early Roman date, the question remains open for debate, with the balance of scholarly opinion tilting slightly to the Hellenistic side.

Ideological Message

The controversy over the date of the text is inextricably linked with the controversy over its interpretation. It is generally acknowledged that the challenges faced by the Jews of Roman Egypt were greater than those faced by the Jews of Hellenistic Egypt. Under the Ptolemies, a number of Jews occupied positions of prominence in the government, and there are few, if any, documented examples of persecution or serious ethnic conflict between the Jews and their neighbors. Under Roman rule, the situation appears to have worsened. Under Augustus (27 B.C.E.), the Jews were subjected to a much-hated tax, the *laographia*, which had previously been applied only to native Egyptians (i.e., non-Greeks). Under Caligula (38 C.E.), tensions in Alexandria culminated in one of the first pogroms in recorded Jewish history.

There has thus generally been a distinct difference in interpretation between those who see the text as Roman, and those who see it as Hellenistic. (Whether the interpretation is affected by the choice of date, or whether the choice of date is influenced by the interpretation, is an open and probably unanswerable question.) Those who see the text as Roman stress the elements in the story which depict the Jews as a persecuted minority, tormented by the cruel king, hated by their enemies, bitterly hostile toward apostates in their own community. Those who view the text as Hellenistic stress the possibilities for peaceful compromise found in the story, wherein the Jews prove themselves faithful, their enemies are confounded, the king is reformed, and the Jews are restored to favor. Both interpretations are possible, and ultimately readers must decide for themselves whether the text works more effectively as a model for life in a time of cooperation and compromise, or life in a time of crisis and conflict. In either case, heavy stress is laid on the importance of maintaining a life of integrity and fidelity to God's Law.

Both scholarly interpretations of the text would generally agree on two things: cooperation between the Jews and their Gentile neighbors, however attractive it might be, is permissible only within set limits that do not violate the Law, and apostasy (as it is understood by the author of the text) is utterly unacceptable as a solution to the challenges of maintaining a distinctive Jewish identity under a non-Jewish governing authority. Like a number of other Second Temple Jewish texts, such as Esther, Daniel, the *Letter of Aristeas*, and 2 Maccabees, it can thus be understood as a guide to life in the Diaspora, at a time when the Temple was still standing but many Jews lived and often prospered outside the land.

Historical Problems

Like many Second Temple Jewish texts, particularly those written in Greek, 3 Maccabees has long raised perplexing problems for those who seek to treat it as a historical source. The text can certainly be treated as a source for understanding the cultural identity and ideological outlook of Second Temple Jews in the Egyptian Diaspora (though, again, scholars may differ on the conclusions that they draw about the precise date and ideological orientation of the text). It is more difficult to identify with confidence any "historical kernel" in the narrative itself.

With very few exceptions (the most notable recent exception being Kasher 1985), scholars have long since ceased to regard the text as evidence of an actual persecution in the time of Ptolemy Philopator. However, many scholars are willing to contemplate the possibility that it can be traced back to a historical persecution at some other period of Ptolemaic rule. Josephus (*Ag. Ap.* 2.53-55) reports a similar (but not identical) incident, in which the Jews of Alexandria were gathered into the hippodrome and prepared for elephantine extinction, only to be spared at the eleventh hour. Josephus, however, places the incident in a different historical context, that of the civil war between Ptolemy VIII Physcon and Cleopatra II in 145 B.C.E. Both Josephus and 3 Maccabees claim to be explaining the origin of a festival celebrated by the Jews of Alexandria in their own time. Since the political context in which Josephus places the story is, on the surface, more plausible than the scenario envisioned by the author of 3 Maccabees, it has often been claimed that Josephus preserves the "true" origin of the festival. However, the version reported by Josephus is as sensational and as ideologically colored as the version in 3 Maccabees, and he records it, not in his more scholarly historical narrative, the *Jewish Antiquities*, but in the highly rhetorical context of the speech against Apion. There is simply not enough evidence to connect the persecution of 3 Maccabees with any historical persecution of the Jews of Alexandria in the Hellenistic period. We cannot even prove that any persecution ever took place in Egypt before the end of the Ptolemaic era. As in the case of the festival of Purim associated with the story of Esther, it is not now possible to explain what gave rise to the elephant festival celebrated by the Jews of Alexandria. Like Esther, like Daniel, and indeed like the much older narrative of the exodus from Egypt, it is probably better understood as a perennial fable about the uncertainties of life under foreign rule.

Bibliography

H. ANDERSON 1985, "3 Maccabees," in *OTP* 2:509-29. • J. M. G. BARCLAY 1996, *Jews in the Mediterranean Diaspora*, Edinburgh: Clark, 192-203. • J. J. COLLINS 2000, *Between Athens and Jerusalem: Jewish Identity in the Hellenistic Diaspora*, 2d ed., Grand Rapids: Eerdmans, 122-31. • N. C. CROY 2006, *3 Maccabees*, Leiden: Brill. • N. HACHAM 2002, "The Third Book of Maccabees: Literature, History and Ideology," Dissertation, Hebrew University of Jerusalem (in Hebrew). • M. HADAS 1953, *The Third and Fourth Books of Maccabees*,

New York: Harper. • S. R. JOHNSON 2004, *Historical Fictions and Hellenistic Jewish Identity,* Berkeley: University of California Press, 121-216. • A. KASHER 1985, *The Jews in Hellenistic and Roman Egypt,* Tübingen: Mohr-Siebeck, 211-32. • J.-M. MODRZEJEWSKI 1995, *The Jews of Egypt,* Philadelphia: Jewish Publication Society, 146-53. • J.-M. MODRZEJEWSKI 2008, *Troisième livre des Maccabées,* Paris: Cerf. • L. M. WILLS 1995, *The Jewish Novel in the Ancient World.* Ithaca.: Cornell University Press, 201-6. SARA RAUP JOHNSON

Maccabees, Fourth Book of

The anonymous writing 4 Maccabees is one of four early Jewish books that are named after the Maccabean heroes who stood up against the Greek king Antiochus IV (175-164 B.C.E.). Despite its title, the work has little to do with the Maccabees or the armed revolt they waged against the Seleucids. Instead, it elaborates the stories of martyrdom in 2 Macc. 6:18–7:42. The mother of the seven brothers receives much more attention than in 2 Maccabees. 4 Maccabees is a work with a mixed genre; its martyrdom reports and martyrs' eulogies (chaps. 4–8) function as proof of its philosophical treatise on the autonomy of devout reason (chaps. 1–3).

Textual Transmission

Several Septuagint manuscripts transmit the Greek text of 4 Maccabees. Some manuscripts of Josephus' writings also transmit the text in its original Greek version. Eusebius attributes the work to Josephus (*Hist. Eccl.* 3.10.6). However, the style and vocabulary of 4 Maccabees are quite different from those of Josephus' works. Therefore, scholars sometimes refer to the author as Pseudo-Josephus.

Date and Provenance

There are only general indications for the date and provenance of 4 Maccabees. The author largely neglects the actual history of Judean Jews. Jerusalem figures in the summary of the martyrdoms' prehistory in 3:20–4:26 (cf. 18:5) but is not mentioned in the descriptions of the martyrdoms themselves. The general character of the references to Jerusalem and Judea and occasional mistakes in them (e.g., the location for Jason's gymnasium in Jerusalem given in 4:20) make a Diaspora origin plausible. Scholars have argued for Alexandria or Antioch, but a city in Asia Minor would also be possible. The majority opinion favoring a first-century C.E. date (esp. Bickerman 1976) has been criticized since the 1980s, and later dates around 100 C.E. or even in the second to third century C.E. have recently been defended.

Sources

It has been suggested that 4 Maccabees is a copy of a commemorative speech given on the occasion of the Jewish holiday of Hanukkah (cf. 4 Macc. 1:10) or a composite work deriving from two sources, a popular philosophical discourse or diatribe on the autonomy of reason and a funeral oration *(epitaphios logos)* in the classical Greek tradition. The majority view, however, is that 4 Maccabees was never presented orally and that the correspondences with oral speeches are literary motifs. The text offers no indications pointing to longer sources, although elements of one written source have been incorporated in 4 Maccabees. The setting and vocabulary of the martyrdom accounts closely correspond to the report in 2 Maccabees 3–7, which renders it probable that 4 Maccabees has made use of 2 Maccabees.

Literary Unity and Rhetorical Style

Rhetorical parallels in the narrative demonstrate that the book is a coherent work. The detailed descriptions of the martyrdoms and their setting (4 Macc. 3:19–18:24) substantiate 4 Maccabees' philosophical proposition about the autonomy of devout reason; they can be considered the demonstration (*apodeixis,* 3:19) of the philosophical thesis presented in 1:1–3:18 (cf. Aristotle, *Rhetoric* 1414a lines 31-37). The coherence between the two main sections (4 Macc. 1:1–3:18 and 3:19–18:24) and the similarities of vocabulary and style in the two parts indicate that 1:1–3:18 and 3:19–18:24 belong together from the outset. After 1:1–3:18, various passages repeat the thesis in connection with the acts of the martyrs in highly rhetorical formulations (6:31-5; 7:16-23; 13:1-5; 16:1-4; 18:2). The discourse's composition and content match in particular the guidelines and practices of laudatory rhetoric, and the work's literary form and rhetorical style may best be explained by analogies with forms of laudatory speeches (e.g., *encomium, epitaphios logos*) or, perhaps, deliberative speeches *(logos protreptikos).*

Contents

The book can be divided into the following sections:

1:1–3:18	philosophical thesis: the autonomy of devout reason
3:19–4:26	the historical setting of the martyrdoms
5:1–7:23	martyrdom and praise of Eleazar
8:1–14:10	martyrdom and praise of the seven brothers
14:11–17:1	self-killing and praise of the mother
17:2–18:2	summary and consolation of the survivors

The philosophical proposition specified in 4 Macc. 1:1–3:18 concerns a basic problem of Greco-Roman philosophy: the antithesis of reason and emotions. 4 Maccabees does not focus on stamping out the emotions, as advocated by philosophers belonging to the Stoa, but on controlling them with the help of reason based on religion. The work incorporates various traditions from the ancient philosophical schools but reinterprets them from a Jewish perspective based upon belief in the God of Israel and the Jewish Law. It promotes a Jewish philosophy of its own, which is apparent from explicit references to such a philosophy (5:22, 35; 7:9, 21; 8:1) as well as from a small but important shift in the presentation of the famous four cardinal virtues. In 1:18, the author mentions these virtues in line with non-Jewish philosophical traditions (prudence, courage, self-control, and justice); but in 5:23-24 he lists them again in Eleazar's discussion with the Greek king. Prudence is replaced by piety *(eusebeia),* the belief in the Jewish God, and piety is presented as the foundation of Jewish philosophy (cf. 1:4, 6; 2:6, 23; 13:24; 15:10).

The historical setting (3:19–4:26) presents the martyrdoms as God's punishment for the disobedience to him by representatives of the Jewish people, in line with a Deuteronomistic view of history. 2 Maccabees presents a similar scenario for the martyrdoms. The prehistory of the martyrdoms in 4 Maccabees culminates in Antiochus IV's decision to force the Jews to switch to a Greek way of life by compelling them one by one to eat meat sacrificed to idols (4:26; 5:2).

The ninety-year-old priest Eleazar (5:4; 7:6, 12; 17:9; 2 Macc. 6:18-31 calls him a scribe) is the first Jew to refuse to obey the king's command. 4 Maccabees elaborates his subsequent martyrdom in three steps: (1) a long dialogue between Eleazar and the king precedes the martyrdom (chap. 5); (2) the martyrdom is depicted in all its horrible details (chap. 6); (3) an extensive eulogy concludes Eleazar's martyrdom (chap. 7).

The presentation of the martyrdoms of the seven brothers (8:1–14:10) follows the same structure: (1) dialogue with the king (8:1–9:9); (2) description of the seven martyrdoms (9:10–12:19); (3) eulogy (13:1–14:10).

The section about the mother (14:11–17:6) is composed differently. It recalls her brave encouragement of her seven sons, ending with a brief note that she threw herself into the fire after her sons' death (16:12–17:1). The remaining parts praise the mother for enduring her terrible torture of watching her sons being martyred, emphasizing that she disregarded her maternal love for them with the help of devout reason.

The last section (17:6–18:24) offers the conclusion according to the conventions of laudatory speeches. It summarizes the martyrs' accomplishments and consoles those who stayed behind, including a flashback to the ideal life of the martyrs' family in the spirit of scriptural passages and biblical heroes.

Purpose

The role of the martyrs in 4 Maccabees may be the key for determining its purpose. There are no indications that 4 Maccabees commemorates a recent persecution of the Jews. The Maccabean heroes died more than two centuries before the work was written. External political and cultural issues are unimportant in the perspective of 4 Maccabees; only the proper Jewish way of life counts. The martyrs function as models in their statements and behavior. The conflict between Antiochus IV and the Jewish people is reconfigured as a prestigious competition between the martyrs and the king; the martyrs bring about the reestablishment of the Jewish way of life after the king's defeat (1:11; 17:15; 18:4-5).

The martyrs thus represent the uniqueness of the Jewish people and function as models for the proper behavior of the Jewish minority in its interactions with non-Jewish culture. The martyrs' ideal behavior constructs Jewish identity in terms of a Torah obedience that is friendly to the non-Jewish world as long as the practice of Jewish Law is not endangered. Food is the most important boundary marker; Jews willing to forego the food laws in their contacts with non-Jews are considered outsiders. The martyrs also demonstrate to insiders and outsiders, pagans and Christians, that the Jews had their own famous model figures, who sacrificed their lives for the practices and beliefs of Judaism. Possibly, the author of 4 Maccabees has chosen martyrs as model figures in response to the new phenomenon of Christian martyrs.

BIBLIOGRAPHY

D. E. AUNE 1994, "Mastery of the Passions: Philo, 4 Maccabees and Earliest Christianity," in *Hellenization Revisited,* ed. W. Helleman, Lanham, Md.: University Press of America, 125-58. • E. J. BICKERMAN 1976, "The Date of Fourth Maccabees," in idem, *Studies in Jewish and Christian History,* Leiden: Brill, 1: 275-81. • U. BREITENSTEIN 1976, *Beobachtungen zu Sprache, Stil und Gedankengut des Vierten Makkabäerbuchs,* Basel/Stuttgart: Schwabe. • A. DUPONT-SOMMER 1939, *Le quatrième livre des Maccabées: Introduction, traduction et notes,* Paris: Champion. • J. W. VAN HENTEN 1997, *The Maccabean Martyrs as Saviors of the Jewish People,* Leiden: Brill. • J. W. VAN HENTEN 2002, "Martyrdom and Persecution Revisited: The Case of 4 Maccabees," in *Märtyrer und Märtyrerakten,* ed. W. Ameling, Stuttgart: Steiner, 59-75. • H.-J. KLAUCK 1989, "4. Makkabäerbuch," *JSHRZ,* 3.6: 645-763. • J. C. H. LEBRAM 1974, "Die literarische Form des vierten Makkabäerbuches," *VC* 28: 81-96. • R. RENEHAN 1972, "The Greek Philosophic Background of Fourth Maccabees," *Rheinisches Museum für Philologie* 115: 223-38. • D. A. DESILVA 2006, *4 Maccabees: Introduction and Commentary on the Greek Text in Codex Sinaiticus,* Leiden: Brill. • H. THYEN 1955, *Der Stil der Jüdisch-Hellenistischen Homilie,* Göttingen: Vandenhoeck & Ruprecht.

See also: Martyrdom JAN WILLEM VAN HENTEN

Magic Bowls and Incantations

Magic bowls are a form of amulet that consists of an incantation written upon an unglazed domestic pottery utensil. Produced in Mesopotamia from the fourth to seventh centuries C.E., they represent an aspect of popular religion exemplified by the belief that humanity shares the world with a multitude of supernatural beings that have an impact on its fate and well-being. The use of magic bowls was a common device available to help people cope and deal with misfortune and strife, whether of supernatural or human origin. Many people in late antiquity thought that the supernatural hindrances could be combated only within their own realm, which was otherwise inaccessible to mortals. The extraordinary technology by which one could rally supernatural forces to fight the battle in that inaccessible realm was what we call magic and is precisely what we find in the bowls. Indeed, each magic bowl was tailor-made for specific clients. The incantation in the bowl took the form of a legal document in which the name of the client, his/her adversaries (supernatural or human), and enforcing authority were usually stated. It operated on the premise that, provided

MAGIC BOWLS AND INCANTATIONS

it was properly written and set out, a chain of effective events would ensue — the appropriate forces would click into action, and the demons or evil spirits would have no choice but to depart.

History of Research

The first editions of magic bowl texts were produced by the British scholar Thomas Ellis and published in 1853 in Austin Layard's book *Discoveries in the Ruins of Nineveh and Babylon.* In 1898 Henri Pognon published a volume of Mandaic magic bowls. Although other texts were edited in the following years, it was only in 1913 that James A. Montgomery set the agenda for the future study of these texts in his book *Aramaic Incantation Texts from Nippur.* His student, Cyrus Gordon, also published a considerable number of bowl texts and supervised several dissertations relating to the subject. Another significant contribution to the study of the magic bowls was made by Joseph Naveh and Shaul Shaked (1985, 3d ed. 1998), who edited twenty-six bowls in two volumes. Other collections of texts have been prepared by McCullough (1967), Segal (2000), Levene (2003), and Müller-Kessler (2005). There are a significant number of magic bowls in both private and public collections that await publication and that will no doubt significantly contribute to our understanding of the life, language, and literature of the communities who wrote them.

Types of Magic Bowls

Incantations were most commonly written upon earthenware pots, most of which are of roughly the size and shape of an average cereal bowl. Others, however, range between the size and shape of a small saucer to that of a big salad bowl. Unusual shapes also include that of a goblet and jug. The layout of the incantations that are inscribed upon the bowls also varies. By far, the most common of them is that of a spiral, usually starting at the bottom of the concave side of the bowl flowing in a clockwise fashion toward its outer edge. One of the most eye-catching aspects of the bowls are the drawings found in many of them, which occur mostly inside the bowl at its center. Most frequently, these are depictions of bound demons, shackled hand and foot. This could be understood as being a form of sympathetic magic: just as the demon is bound in the drawing on the bowl, so, too, it is bound in real life and thus rendered harmless.

The Language of the Bowls

Most magic bowls are written in Jewish Babylonian Aramaic and often include some portions of Hebrew that consist, most commonly, of biblical citations. A variety of styles of script can be observed. These differences might be indicative of either regional variations or express the styles of different training schools or ateliers. The bowls constitute one of the richest sources for the study of late Aramaic dialects. The bowl texts have widened our lexical knowledge of Aramaic, increased our knowledge of the grammar of these dialects, and expanded our understanding of the relationships of the dialects to each other. The second largest group of texts is written in a Mandaic script that was used by the Gnostic Mandeans to write their dialect of Aramaic. The third group in size is made up of bowls written in Syriac. Some of these were written in Estrangelo by Christians, while others were composed in the proto-Manichean used by the Manicheans. The smallest language groups represented are Pahlavi and Arabic. A final group that deserves to be noted are those adorned by pseudo-script.

The Placement of the Bowls

Magic bowls were buried in and around the house in strategic positions that could include the threshold, any of the rooms of the house, or its four corners. They were usually placed there upside down, pressed into the ground. In some cases bowls were also deposited in graveyards. Unfortunately, the provenance of the great majority of bowls that are in museum and private collections is unknown. This is to be lamented, since most of them bear the names of their owners, of which we have whole family groups and indeed communities; this means that their location in a settlement could have been recorded.

An Aramaic incantation bowl from Mesopotamia, fifth–sixth century C.E.
(The Schøyen Collection, MS 1911/1)

Cross-Cultural Aspect of the Jewish Bowls

The population of the Jewish communities in Mesopotamia has been estimated to have reached close to a million in late antiquity. The bowls demonstrate that people did not always choose practitioners according to their cultural affiliation. Indeed, they contain much evidence of cross-cultural fertilization. References to non-Jewish gods and other powers in the Jewish Aramaic magic bowls raise interesting questions about how such foreign elements came to be included in ostensibly Jewish texts. It is not always easy to identify the processes of transmission by which such elements crossed cultural and linguistic boundaries to be used by the Jewish practitioners. Needless to say, we know from the Mandaic and Syriac Manichean bowls, as well as the Greek magical papyri, that this phenomenon of cross-cultural exchange was not unique to the Jewish magical texts, but was a common feature of the magical products of the late-antique Near East in general.

Other Content within the Bowls

The magic bowls provide information about a variety of issues besides the study of magic, folklore, and popular religion. In the Jewish bowls alone we find references to mythical stories drawn from a wide variety of both Jewish and non-Jewish materials, as well as fragments of liturgical, mystical, and biblical texts.

BIBLIOGRAPHY

H. JUUSOLA 1999, *Linguistic Peculiarities in the Aramaic Magic Bowl Texts*, Helsinki: Finnish Oriental Society. • A. H. LAYARD 1853, *Discoveries among the Ruins of Nineveh and Babylon*, New York: Harper & Brothers, 434-48. • D. LEVENE 2002, *Curse or Blessing, What's in the Magic Bowl? The Ian Karten Lecture*, Southhampton: University of Southampton. • D. LEVENE 2003, *A Corpus of Magic Bowls: Incantation Texts in Jewish Aramaic from Late Antiquity*, London: Kegan Paul. • W. S. MCCULLOUGH 1967, *Jewish and Mandean Incantation Bowls in the Royal Ontario Museum*, Toronto: University of Toronto Press. • J. A. MONTGOMERY 1913, *Aramaic Incantation Texts from Nippur*, Philadelphia: University of Pennsylvania Museum. • C. MÜLLER-KESSLER 2005, *Die Zauberschalentexte in der Hilprecht-Sammlung, Jena*, Wiesbaden: Harrassowitz. • J. NAVEH AND S. SHAKED 1993, *Magic Spells and Formulae: Aramaic Incantations of Late Antiquity*, Jerusalem: Magnes. • J. NAVEH AND S. SHAKED 1998, *Amulets and Magic Bowls: Aramaic Incantations of Late Antiquity*, 3d ed., Jerusalem: Magnes; Leiden: Brill. • H. POGNON 1898, *Inscriptions Mandaites des Coupes de Khouabir*, 2 vols., Paris: F. Vieweg (rpt. Amsterdam: Philo, 1979). • W. H. ROSSEL 1953, *A Handbook of Aramaic Magical Texts*, Ringwood, N.J.: Shelton College Press. • J. B. SEGAL 2000, *Catalogue of the Aramaic and Mandaic Incantation Bowls in the British Museum*, London: British Museum. • E. M. YAMAUCHI 1967, *Mandaic Incantation Texts*, New Haven, Conn.: American Oriental Society.

See also: Amulets; Divination and Magic

DAN LEVENE

Manasseh, Prayer of

The Prayer of Manasseh is a pseudonymous text that contains a prayer attributed to King Manasseh which he offered when exiled and imprisoned by the king of Assyria (2 Chron. 33:12-13). The prayer survives in Syriac in the *Didascalia Apostolorum* (third century C.E.), and in Greek in the *Apostolic Constitutions* (fourth century C.E.) and three manuscripts of the Septuagint, of which the oldest and most important is Codex Alexandrinus (fifth century C.E.). The "Prayer of Manasseh" found among the Dead Scrolls (4Q381 33.8-11) is not the same as the prayer found in these texts. In the Septuagint, the prayer has been placed among the Odes that are appended to the Psalms. While the prayer contains some Semiticisms, it was probably composed in Greek. Though the prayer survives only in Christian sources, it nevertheless remains unclear whether a Jewish or Christian author composed the piece. No uniquely Christian themes appear in the prayer, though Nickelsburg has noted that the prayer shares certain details with its context in the *Apostolic Constitutions* (Nickelsburg 2001). The date of the prayer is also uncertain. A Jewish origin could allow a date as early as the first century B.C.E. Several examples of prayers added to narratives come from this period (e.g., the Prayer of Azariah and the Additions to Esther). A Christian origin would not permit a date before the late second century C.E. The prayer appears in modern translations of the Apocrypha because of its inclusion in the canon of the Eastern Orthodox Church.

In the prayer, King Manasseh confesses his sins, petitions for forgiveness, and asks for his release from prison. The prayer's outline is as follows: (1) vv. 1-4, invocation to God; (2) vv. 5-10, appeal for mercy and confession; (3) vv. 11–15, further petitions for forgiveness and confession and plea for deliverance. This basic form places the prayer within the category of penitential prayers, though the prayer shares almost no verbal features with the penitential prayers clearly datable to the Second Temple period (Ezra 9:5-15; Neh. 1:4-11; 9:6-37; Dan. 9:3-19; Bar. 1:15–3:8; Prayer of Azariah; Tob. 3:1-6; 3 Macc. 2:1-10; 4Q504). In the invocation, the author refers to God as *pantokratōr*, a title that frequently occurs in both Jewish and Christian prayers (cf. 3 Macc. 2:9; Acts 4:24). The prayer contains many verbal allusions to biblical texts and weaves details from the narrative of Manasseh's reign, as described in 2 Kings 21 and 2 Chronicles 33, into the confessions and petitions: for example, the designation of the king's actions as "abominations" (v. 10; cf. 2 Kings 21:2, 6; 2 Chron. 33:2); the reference to the king's "fetters" (v. 10; cf. 2 Chron. 33:11); and the promise to offer praise with the "hosts of heaven" (v. 15; cf. 2 Kings 21:5; 2 Chron. 33:5) (see Nickelsburg 2001). Besides the obvious influence of Psalm 51 upon the king's words (e.g., v. 12, cf. Ps. 51:3; v. 14, cf. Ps. 51:1), the confessional statement in Exod. 34:6 also functions as a foundation for the king's appeal to God's mercy (vv. 7, 14). Similar to several Hebrew Bible psalms, the prayer ends with a promise from the suppliant that he will continuously praise God upon God's fulfillment of his requests (v. 15, cf. Ps. 51:15).

BIBLIOGRAPHY

J. H. CHARLESWORTH 1985, "Prayer of Manasseh," in *OTP* 2:625-37. • J. H. NEWMAN 2007, "Form and Function in the Prayer of Manasseh," in *Seeking the Favor of God,* vol. 2, *The Development of Penitential Prayer in Second Temple Judaism,* ed. M. Boda, D. Falk, and R. Werline, Atlanta: Scholars Press. • G. W. E. NICKELSBURG 2001, "The Prayer of Manasseh," in *The Oxford Bible Commentary,* ed. J. Barton and J. Muddiman, Oxford: Oxford University Press, 770-73.

RODNEY A. WERLINE

Manetho

Born at Sebennytos, Egypt, in the third century B.C.E., Manetho, a priest of the Greco-Egyptian god Serapis, is the first Egyptian historian to write a history of Egypt, translating into Greek holy priestly writings composed in hieratic script. This history was soon lost; what we have today are fragments extant in the works written by Josephus (first century C.E.) and by later Christian authors such as Sextus Julius Africanus (third century) and Eusebius (fourth century). The Jews are mentioned, albeit in a confused fashion, in two accounts quoted by Josephus. These accounts constitute a point of departure in contemporary Greek literary tradition where the Jews were portrayed in a somewhat idealized and complimentary fashion, and deeply influenced later Greek, Greco-Egyptian, and also Roman literature, as Tacitus' *Histories* (5.3.1–5.4.2) witness.

The first report in Josephus (*Ag. Ap.* 1.73-91) deals with the oppressive domination of Egypt by the so-called Shepherds, identified with the Hyksos, who "conquered Egypt, burned its cities, destroyed the temples of the gods, and dealt very cruelly with the native population." After years of harsh domination, the Egyptian king succeeded in defeating them and obliged them to leave Egypt. They left the country and journeyed over the desert into Syria, where they built a town named Jerusalem in the country called Judea.

The second tradition (*Ag. Ap.* 1.228-52) deals with Egyptian lepers, who were segregated by the Egyptian ruler and forced to work in the quarries east of the Nile. Their leader, Osarsiph, decreed that "they should neither worship the gods nor abstain from the flesh of animals reverenced by the Egyptians, and be in connection only with members of their own people." At this point, a reversal of the situation takes place. The lepers ally themselves with the inhabitants of Jerusalem, who return to Egypt and together take possession of the country under the leadership of Osarsiph, who then changes his name to Moses, behaving toward the inhabitants far worse than the Hyksos in former times. In the end, the Egyptian king defeats the lepers and their allies, pursuing them to the frontiers of Syria.

Some scholars think that the references to the Jews may be later additions. In this case, Manetho would not have mentioned the Jews at all, and the emergence of anti-Jewish views would belong to a later historical period, being possibly a consequence of the Maccabean Revolt. The question of the authenticity of these passages, therefore, is crucial for an understanding of the beginnings of anti-Jewish attitudes in the ancient world.

In the first account, the identification Shepherds-Hyksos-Jews has been attributed to a Jewish hand for apologetic purposes, namely, the desire to prove the antiquity of the existence of the Jewish people. However, the tone of the narrative is too negative to serve apologetic purposes. Moreover, a connection between Shepherds and Jews is implied also in Manetho's summaries extant in the works of Africanus and Eusebius, where the Jews are said to have left Egypt precisely after the end of the Shepherds' dynasties (Jacoby, *Fragmenta der griechischen Historiker,* 609, F2 and F3b).

In the second account, dealing with the lepers, the identification Osarsiph-Moses has been regarded as a later interpolation made by a Greco-Egyptian author, motivated by social and political competition and strife. However, an expulsion from Egypt of strangers, Greeks, and Jews caused by a pestilence is also mentioned by a contemporary of Manetho, Hecataeus (*Aegyptiaca apud* Diodorus Siculus, *Bibliotheca Historica,* 4.3.2). Moreover, the same mixture of history and fiction in this report also characterizes other literary works composed in Egypt at this time, such as the *Prophecy of the Lamb* and the *Potter's Oracle.*

It is therefore not improbable that tales of an expulsion of Jews from Egypt, perhaps dating back to the time of the Persian domination in the fifth century B.C.E., circulated in Egypt and may have gained momentum in the third century as a response to the biblical book of Exodus, which was being translated into Greek at the time.

BIBLIOGRAPHY

J. J. COLLINS 2000, "Reinventing Exodus: Exegesis and Legend in Hellenistic Egypt," in *For a Later Generation: The Transformation of Tradition in Israel, Early Judaism, and Early Christianity,* ed. R. A. Argall et al., Harrisburg, Penn.: Trinity Press International. • E. S. GRUEN 1998, "The Use and Abuse of the Exodus Story," *Jewish History* 12: 93-122, with responses by L. H. Feldman, "Did Jews Reshape the Tale of the Exodus?" (123-32); J. G. Gager, "Some Thoughts on Greco-Roman Versions of the Exodus Story" (129-32); and J. Mélèze Modrzejewski, "The Exodus Traditions: Parody or Parallel Version?" (133-36). • L. RASPE 1998, "Manetho on the Exodus: a Reappraisal," *Jewish Studies Quarterly* 5: 124-55. • M. STERN 1974, *Greek and Latin Authors on Jews and Judaism,* vol. 1, Jerusalem: Israel Academy of Sciences and Humanities, 62-86. • G. P. VERBRUGGHE AND J. M. WICKERSHAM 1996, *Berossos and Manetho: Introduced and Translated,* Ann Arbor: University of Michigan.

MIRAM PUCCI BEN ZEEV

Man of Lies → Pesharim

Mark, Gospel of

The Gospel of Mark is the shortest and, in the opinion of most scholars, the earliest of the New Testament gospels. It is usually dated to the period of the First Jewish Revolt against Rome (66-73 C.E.) or shortly thereafter. Early Christian tradition from the second century onward identified the anonymous author as John Mark, a sometime traveling companion of the apostle Paul (Philemon 24; Col. 4:10; 2 Tim. 4:11; Acts 12:12, 25; 13:13; 15:36-41) and protégé of the apostle Peter who composed the work in Rome (Papias in Eusebius, *Hist. Eccl.* 3.39.15). Some scholars accept this tradition as reliable, but many do not, and the gospel may have been written somewhere in Syria-Palestine. The Gospel of Mark seems to be directed toward a predominantly non-Jewish readership (e.g., in 7:3-5 it must explain the Jewish-Pharisaic custom of ritual hand washing), but it presupposes the world of Palestinian Judaism throughout. Its portrait of Judaism includes references to the Jewish people, to Jewish territories, parties, and figures, and to important aspects of Jewish religion and tradition. Though often accused of being anti-Semitic or anti-Jewish, Mark is better understood to reflect intramural debates and competition in first-century Judaism.

References to Jewish Land, People, Parties, and Figures

The evangelist refers to the "Jews" in 7:3, in reference to the custom of washing hands. The remaining five occurrences of the word appear in chap. 15, as part of the political title "king of the Jews." The territory of Judea is mentioned four times, once in reference to the crowds that followed John the Baptist (1:5), twice in reference to the crowds that followed Jesus (3:7; 10:1), and once in the eschatological discourse, as part of a warning to flee approaching danger (13:14). Galilee is mentioned several times, as the place of Jesus' origin (1:9) and as the venue for most of his public ministry (1:14, 28, 39; 3:7; 9:30; 15:41). In the same way the Sea of Galilee is mentioned (1:16; 7:31). In Jerusalem, in the courtyard of the high priest's house, Simon Peter is identified as a "Galilean" (14:70). There are no references to Samaria or Samaritans in the Gospel of Mark.

There are a number of references to Jewish priests. In a Galilean context Jesus orders a cleansed leper to show himself to a (local) priest, as the Law of Moses requires (1:44). In a dispute Jesus refers to Abiathar, a priest in the bygone days of David (2:26). All other references are to the ruling priests located in and around Jerusalem (8:31; 10:33; 11:18, 27; 14:1, 10, 43, 47, 53-55, 60-61, 63, 66; 15:1, 3, 10, 11, 31). The evangelist also refers several times to elders (7:3, 5; 8:31; 11:27; 14:43, 53; 15:1) and scribes (1:22; 2:6, 16; 3:22; 7:1, 5; 8:31; 9:11, 14; 10:33; 11:18, 27; 12:28, 32, 35, 38; 14:1, 43; 15:1, 31), again mostly in the vicinity of Jerusalem. Several times the ruling priests, scribes, and elders are grouped together, always as deadly opponents of Jesus (8:31; 11:27; 14:43, 53; 15:1).

Religious parties also make appearances in the Markan narrative. There is one reference to the Sadducees (12:18-27) and several to the Pharisees (2:16, 18, 24; 3:6; 7:1, 3, 5; 8:11, 15; 10:2; 12:13). On two of these occasions, the Pharisees are said to be in the company of the Herodians (3:6; 12:13).

Many Jewish persons are mentioned by name in Mark. Besides Jesus himself the first person named is John the Baptist (1:4, 6, 9, 14; cf. 6:14, 16-18, 20, 24-25; 8:28; 11:30, 32). The evangelist names various disciples many times (esp. Simon Peter, James, and John, sons of Zebedee), along with a complete roster of the twelve disciples (3:16-19). The evangelist names Mary, the mother of Jesus, and his brothers James, Joses, Judas, and Simon (6:3). Named women include Mary Magdalene and Mary the mother of James the Little and Joses, and Salome (15:40, 47; 16:1). Other named figures include Jairus, a ruler of one of the synagogues (5:22), Bartimaeus (10:46), Simon the leper (14:3), Simon of Cyrene, father of Alexander and Rufus (15:21), and Joseph of Arimathea (15:43, 45-46). Several biblical characters are named, including Moses (1:44; 7:10; 9:4-5; 10:3-4; 12:19, 26), David (2:25; 10:47-48; 11:10; 12:35-37), Elijah (6:15; 8:28; 9:4-5, 11-13; 15:35-36), and Abiathar (2:26).

Portrait of Jewish Religion and Tradition

Many times synagogues are mentioned in the Gospel of Mark (1:21, 23, 29, 39; 3:1; 5:22, 36, 38; 6:2; 12:39; 13:9). Readers are left with the impression that Jesus habitually preached in synagogues (cf. 1:39), oftentimes healing or exorcizing there (1:23, 39; 3:1).

Aspects of Jewish law are sometimes at issue. Disputes arise because the actions of Jesus and/or his disciples are seen as violations of the prohibition of work on the Sabbath (2:23-27; 3:2-5). Questions of purity sometimes lie in the background of a story, as in the touching and healing of the leper (1:40-45) and the woman with the hemorrhage who touched Jesus (5:28-34). Sometimes purity issues are hotly debated, as in the dispute over washing hands and defilement (7:1-23). The editorial comment "thus he declared all foods clean" (7:19) can be fully understood only in the light of Jewish food laws. In this lengthy passage, the Law of Moses is debated (7:10; cf. Exod. 20:12; 21:17), the prophet Isaiah is appealed to (7:6-7; cf. Isa. 29:13), and the *corban* tradition is challenged (7:11-13).

In Mark Jesus disputes some Jewish interpretations and practices, but he clearly presupposes the authority of the Torah. He commands the cleansed leper to show himself to the priest and to make an offering for his cleansing, as Moses commanded (1:43-44; cf. Lev. 14:2-20). He calls the Pharisees "hypocrites" for nullifying the command to honor one's parents (7:9-13; cf. Exod. 20:12). He also rejects the Pharisees' more lenient interpretation of divorce law (10:2-9; cf. Deut. 24:1-4). Jesus does this, not because he questions Moses, but because he thinks Pharisaic interpretation is at odds with other passages in the Torah, such as Gen. 1:27 and 2:24. In his dispute with the Sadducees, Jesus again appeals to Moses (Mark 12:18-27; cf. Exod. 3:6). When questioned about the greatest commandment, Jesus affirms the Shema and the command to love one's neighbor (Mark 12:28-34; cf. Deut. 6:4-5; Lev. 19:18).

When criticized for eating with "sinners," Jesus retorts that "those who are well have no need of a physician, but those who are sick" (2:15-17). This answer clearly implies that Jesus, like the Pharisees, regarded "sinners" as sinners indeed. The difference between Jesus and the Pharisees lay in how to respond to sinners.

Jesus enters Jerusalem amid shouts of Hosanna and other allusions to Psalm 118 (Mark 11:1-11), a psalm sung by visitors to the Holy City. He enters the Temple precincts and teaches (11:15-19, 27; 12:38). He makes preparations to celebrate the Passover (14:12-16). The evangelist refers to the feasts of Passover (14:1, 12, 14, 16) and Unleavened Bread (14:1, 12). Throughout the narrative the evangelist presupposes Jewish faith and life.

After his arrest by officers dispatched by the ruling priests, Jesus is brought before the Jewish council or Sanhedrin (14:53-65). Although the ruling priests try to solicit testimony against Jesus, the evangelist notes that the testimony did not agree (14:59). While it is not the purpose of the evangelist, this comment shows that the basic law pertaining to incriminating testimony was observed (cf. Deut. 17:6; 19:15). The testimony against Jesus was somehow inconsistent and so was dropped.

The evangelist Mark says that Pilate the Roman governor referred to Jesus as "king of the Jews" (15:2, 9, 12, 18, 26), the epithet Marc Antony and the Roman Senate bestowed upon Herod the Great (Josephus, *J.W.* 1.282; *Ant.* 14.36; 15.373, 409; 16.291, 311). However, the evangelist reports that the ruling priests and scribes mocked Jesus as the messiah, the "king of Israel" (15:32). This suggests that the evangelist knows that "king of Israel" was the authentic Jewish epithet of the messiah, not the Roman "king of the Jews."

References to Non-Jews

Non-Jews appear in the Gospel of Mark. On the eastern side of the Sea of Galilee, in the district of Gerasa, Jesus and his disciples encounter a demonized man (Mark 5:1-20). Presumably the man is a Gentile (given the geography, the proximity of a herd of swine, and the epithet "Most High God"). Of course, his demonic name "Legion" would have called to mind the Roman army. A few times mention is made of Herod Antipas (6:14, 16-18, 20-22; 8:15), son of Herod the Great and his Samaritan wife Malthace (Josephus, *J.W.* 1.562). Also mentioned is Philip's ex-wife Herodias (Mark 6:17, 19), niece, part-Jewish, and second wife of Herod Antipas (Josephus, *Ant.* 18.110, 136).

Jesus encounters an unnamed Syro-Phoenician woman, who begs for help for her daughter (Mark 7:24-30). Her location, as well as the manner in which she is addressed, makes it clear that she is a non-Jew. Initially Jesus refuses to help her, declaring that "the children [Israelites] first be fed, for it is not right to take the children's bread and throw it to the dogs [Gentiles]" (7:27-28). There is no hint in the Markan narrative of discomfort with this comment. Evidently the evangelist has assumed a Jewish perspective. The epithet "dogs" need not be taken as an insult; it may apply only to the metaphor, reflecting actual eating practice, in which people were served first and scraps were later thrown to the dogs. Nevertheless, such a comparison would be offensive to non-Jewish ears. It is not surprising that the very Jewish Matthean evangelist retains it (and even finds it necessary to enhance the woman's qualities of faith, thus making her more deserving of Jesus' beneficence), while the non-Jewish Lukan evangelist omits the story altogether.

Caesar is mentioned only in the context of the question regarding taxes (12:13-17). Pilate is mentioned only in connection with the hearing and execution of Jesus (15:1-20) and the subsequent burial (15:42-47). The centurion overseeing the crucifixion is mentioned but not named (15:39-45). Pilate is neither lionized nor demonized.

The Question of Anti-Semitism

A few scholars have argued that the Gospel of Mark is anti-Semitic. According to Samuel Sandmel (1978a: 48): "In short, Mark is a tract on behalf of gentile Christianity, contending that Christianity has only negative connections with the Judaism into which it had been born." Elsewhere Sandmel avers (1978b: 351): "Whatever the full range of the purpose of Mark, the denigration of Jews, especially the Jewish disciples, is a leading motif. So extreme is this denigration that it appears to suggest a disconnection between Christianity and the Judaism in which it was born."

But the data hardly support Sandmel's interpretation. The Markan Jesus is critical of his obtuse disciples, to be sure; and he is critical, even threatening of the priests, elders, and scribes who plot against him. But taken as a whole, the view of the Jewish people seems rather positive. Jesus ministers to the crowds, almost always to be understood as Jewish. Jesus heals many and empowers his disciples to do so. The evangelist states that Jesus "saw a great throng, and he had compassion on them, because they were like sheep without a shepherd" (6:34; cf. 14:27). These words may allude to the prayer of Moses, who petitioned God to "appoint a man over the congregation . . . who shall lead them . . . that the congregation of the LORD may not be as sheep which have no shepherd" (Num. 27:15-17). In no sense does this material denigrate the Jewish people.

The Markan Jesus expresses exasperation over Israel's lack of faith (e.g., 6:6; 9:19), but individual Israelites are also commended for their faith (e.g., 2:5; 5:34; 10:52). Only the ruling elites are threatened in Mark, as seen especially in the allusion to Jer. 7:11 in Mark 11:17 and in the Parable of the Vineyard in Mark 12:1-12 (cf. Isa 5:1-7). The Markan Jesus is hardly anti-Semitic, any more than was Jesus son of Ananias, who according to Josephus wandered about the city of Jerusalem in the 60s and, alluding to Jeremiah 7, warned of coming destruction (*J.W.* 6.300-309). Like Jesus of Nazareth, Jesus son of Ananias was violently opposed by Jerusalem's elites and was handed over to Roman authorities with demands that he be put to death.

The polemic in Mark no doubt was misused in Christian anti-Jewish polemic in later generations, but it scarcely rises to the level of the heated intramural Jewish polemic we see in the Dead Sea Scrolls, some pseudepigrapha, and some early rabbinic literature (see Johnson 1989). Indeed, the polemic of Mark hardly rises to the level of the Old Testament prophets themselves, some of whom called the Israelites "sons of the sorceress, offspring of the adulterer and the harlot" (Isa. 57:3) and begged God not to forgive them (Isa. 2:6; Jer. 18:23).

Even the threat at the conclusion of the Parable of the Vineyard, that God will "destroy the tenants, and give the vineyard to others" (12:9), is directed against the Jerusalem elite, not Jews in general (12:12). The "multitude," which is without question Jewish, fully supports Jesus and prevents the leaders from moving against Jesus openly.

Beck (1985: 100) comments that the "Marcan community may be described, therefore, as a sect over against Judaism." This is true only if carefully qualified. There was no single "Judaism" in the first century. The Judaism over against which the Markan community stands is the Judaism centered in Jerusalem and in many synagogues that rejected Jesus and his followers. This is the same Judaism rejected by the authors of some of the Dead Sea Scrolls. The Markan community affirmed the messiahship and divine sonship of Jesus in the face of both threats from Rome and resistance from synagogues. The people of Israel as a whole, however, remain "sheep that have no shepherd." For them the Markan community competes.

Hare (1979: 35) is closer to the truth when he says that in the Gospel of Mark we find "only the barest traces of prophetic and Jewish-Christian anti-Judaism, and not the slightest evidence of that Gentilizing anti-Judaism that was later to dominate Christian theology." So also Guelich (1993: 101), who concludes that a "careful, historical, literary reading of Mark's narrative will demonstrate that one can in no way speak of 'anti-Semitism' and only in a highly qualified manner of 'anti-Judaism' in Mark's Gospel." Like the other canonical gospels, the Gospel of Mark reflects the give-and-take of Jewish intramural debate, competition, and conflict in the first century.

Bibliography

N. A. Beck 1985, *Mature Christianity: The Recognition and Repudiation of the Anti-Jewish Polemic of the New Testament,* Selinsgrove, Penn.: Susquehanna University Press. • M. J. Cook 1978, *Mark's Treatment of the Jewish Leaders,* Leiden: Brill. • R. A. Guelich 1993, "Anti-Semitism and/or Anti-Judaism in Mark?" in *Anti-Semitism and Early Christianity: Issues of Polemic and Faith,* ed. C. A. Evans and D. A. Hagner, Minneapolis: Fortress, 80-101. • D. R. A. Hare 1979, "The Rejection of the Jews in the Synoptic Gospels and Acts," in *Anti-Semitism and the Foundations of Christianity,* ed. A. T. Davis, New York: Paulist Press, 27-47. • L. T. Johnson 1989, "The New Testament's Anti-Jewish Slander and the Conventions of Ancient Polemic," *JBL* 108: 419-41. • D. Lührmann 1987, "Die Pharisäer und die Schriftgelehrten im Markusevangelium," *ZNW* 78: 169-85. • S. Sandmel 1978a, *Anti-Semitism in the New Testament?* Philadelphia: Fortress Press. • S. Sandmel 1978b, *Judaism and Christian Beginnings,* Oxford: Oxford University Press. • A. Yarbro Collins 2007, *Mark: A Commentary on the Gospel of Mark,* Minneapolis: Fortress.

Craig A. Evans

Marriage and Divorce

Marriage underwent a revolution during the Second Temple period. The two main changes were the payments made at the time of marriage (which also affected payments to a divorcee or widow), and the obligations within marriage (which were also grounds for divorce when these obligations were neglected). During this period the link between obligations and divorce was broken by the introduction of a no-fault divorce, which made divorce easier and increased the importance of support for divorced wives. These changes affected the marriage contract *(ketubbah),* which is concerned mainly with payments, obligations within marriage, and the rights of a widow.

Marriage Payments

The payment made at the start of a marriage was called in the Torah a *mōhar* and appears to have been given by the groom to the bride's father (Gen. 34:12; Exod. 22:17; cf. payments to Laban by Abraham and Jacob), though the father also gave dowry gifts to his daughter (Gen. 24:59, 61; 29:24, 29). This practice was still reflected in the fifth-century-B.C.E. marriage contracts from Elephantine. By the early second century C.E. (the next earliest date from which any marriage contracts have survived), the bride's father was still paying a dowry, but the groom no longer paid anything to the bride's father. Instead he made a promissory payment to the bride, which came to be called the *ketubbah* payment after the name of the contract.

Rabbinic traditions honor Simeon b. Shetah with the rulings that caused this change (*t. Ketub.* 12:1), while acknowledging that his was merely the culmination of a series of changes (*b. Ketubbot* 82b; *y. Ketub.* 8:11, 32b). These accounts are much later than Simeon himself, who lived in the first century B.C.E., a fact that makes some scholars (e.g., Satlow 1993) doubt that these rulings originated in the Second Temple period. Yet the changes they describe mirror similar developments in Egyptian marriage law in the last two centuries B.C.E. (Pestman 1961). The reason for these changes were both to help grooms get married without first having to save up the minimum bride price (200 *zuz* = 200 *denarii,* almost a year's wages for a laborer) and to prevent divorce. The changes discouraged divorce, because the payment was now purely theoretical unless a man divorced a bride who had not broken any marriage vows, in which case he had to pay it to her in full, as well as returning her dowry.

Marital Obligations and Grounds for Divorce

Up to about the first century B.C.E., divorce was normally based on broken marriage vows. These vows were sexual faithfulness (based on Deut. 24:1) and the provision of food, clothing, and marital love (based on Exod. 21:10-11). The vow of faithfulness is rarely mentioned explicitly, but the other three are found in many ancient *Ketubbot,* either by citing the Exodus text (as in Karaite documents) or by paraphrasing it (as, e.g., in Papyrus Yadin 10: "I will feed you and clothe you and I will bring you [into my house] . . . together with the due amount of your food and your clothes and your bed"). Both men and women had to supply these three needs, as they were often called; the husband had to provide food and cloth or the money to purchase them; the wife had to cook and sew or provide a servant to do it; and they both had to offer marital love. The schools of Hillel and Shammai debated the minimum amounts that could be grounds for divorce (*m. Ketub.* 5:5-8). Other matters such as cruel behavior or repulsiveness (which prevented marital love) were also grounds for divorce and were presumably related to these categories (cf. *m. Ketub.* 7:2-6, 9-10).

On the basis of these grounds, both men and women could initiate a divorce and, although only a man could enact it (by writing out the divorce certificate), a rabbinic court could force the man to do so if the wife had sufficient grounds (*m. Giṭ.* 9:8; *m. ʿArak.* 5:6). The need for this largely disappeared after the Second Temple period, when all except Karaite divorces followed a new Hillelite no-fault procedure that could be initiated only by a man. However, a divorce certificate has survived which was written on behalf of a woman in 134 C.E. (Papyrus Se'elim 13; cf. Ilan 1996), showing that Jewish women were able to initiate divorces at a later period than rabbinic sources suggest.

The no-fault divorce introduced by the school of Hillel, probably in the first century B.C.E., could be called an "any-cause" divorce (as in Philo, *Spec. Leg.* 3.30; Josephus, *Ant.* 4.253; Matt. 19:3, though with a different Greek phrase in each case). The Hillelites argued that the phrase "a cause of indecency" in Deut. 24:1 represented *two* grounds for divorce: "indecency" (i.e., adultery) and "a cause" (i.e., any cause). It is likely that this type of divorce was much older, because both men and women of the fifth-century-B.C.E. Jewish community at Elephantine were able to divorce each other by a simple public declaration, without citing reasons. However, basing this type of divorce on the Deuteronomy text made it available only to men, because that passage refers only to a man divorcing his wife. The Shammaites (and Jesus) disagreed with this interpretation, insisting that the phrase "a cause of indecency" meant "nothing but adultery" (*m. Giṭ.* 9:10; *Sifre Deut.* 269; *y. Soṭah* 1:2, 16b; Matt. 19:9; cf. Instone-Brewer 2002: 133-88).

Other Aspects of Marriage

Other aspects of marriage remained as they had been in previous centuries, though some aspects changed soon after the destruction of the Temple in 70 C.E.

The law of levirate marriage (based on Deut. 25:5-10) continued to be followed, though there was an increasing uneasiness concerning it, so that it was already ignored in some Christian circles (1 Cor. 7:39-40); and the school of Hillel made it easier for a widow to refuse it (*m. Yebam.* 13:1). The degrees of relationships defining whom one could marry (based on Leviticus 18) remained the same, though the *Damascus Document* and the *Temple Scroll* forbid marriage to a niece (CD 5:9-11; 11QT 66:16-17).

Polygamy was still allowed throughout the Second Temple period, as illustrated in the Babatha family document. Yet the *Damascus Document* outlaws it (CD 4:20–5:6), and Roman law permitted it only within Palestine, so it became increasingly uncommon. The *Damascus Document* forbids marriage to two women "in their lifetime" (masculine suffix). It is disputed whether this prohibits remarriage after divorce.

Marriage and procreation were regarded as compulsory because of the first commandment in the Torah (Gen. 1:28; cf. *t. Yebam.* 8:4; *m. Yebam.* 6:6), perhaps even among the Essenes (see Isaksson 1965, who argues that Essenes married for a few years and then divorced). The courts could theoretically impose a divorce on both partners after ten years of infertility, though this was questioned in the first century (cf. Philo, *Spec. Leg.* 3.35) and increasingly later (cf. *b. Ketubbot* 77ab).

BIBLIOGRAPHY

J. J. COLLINS 1997, "Marriage, Divorce and Family in Second Temple Judaism," in *Families in Ancient Israel,* ed. L. G. Perdue et al., Louisville: Westminster John Knox, 104-62. • T. ILAN 1993, "Premarital Cohabitation in Ancient Judea: The Evidence of the Babatha Archive and the Mishnah (Ketubbot 1.4)," *HTR* 86: 247-64. • T. ILAN 1996, "Notes and Observations on a Newly Published Divorce Bill from the Judean Desert," *HTR* 89: 195-202. • D. INSTONE-BREWER 1999, "Jewish Women Divorcing Their Husbands in Early Judaism: The Background of Papyrus Se'elim 13," *HTR* 92: 349-57. • D. INSTONE-BREWER 2002, *Divorce and Remarriage in the Bible,* Grand Rapids: Eerdmans. • A. ISAKSSON 1965, *Marriage and Ministry in the New Temple,* Lund: Gleerup. • C. S. KEENER 1991, *And Marries Another: Divorce and Remarriage in the Teaching of the New Testament,* Peabody, Mass.: Hendrickson. • P. W. PESTMAN 1961, *Marriage and Matrimonial Property in Ancient Egypt,* Leiden: Brill, 15-20, 108-14. • M. SATLOW 1993, "Reconsidering the Rabbinic *ketubah* Payment," in *The Jewish Family in Antiquity,* ed. S. J. D. Cohen, Atlanta: Scholars Press, 133-51. • M. SATLOW 2001, *Jewish Marriage in Antiquity,* Princeton: Princeton University Press.

See also: Family; Sexuality

DAVID INSTONE-BREWER

Martyrdom

The origin of martyrdom is debated because scholars apply different definitions. A broad definition implies that various forms of heroic death among ancient Greeks and Romans can already be considered martyrdom. This explains why Socrates is sometimes called a martyr. More strict definitions raise the question whether there were cases of Jewish martyrdom before Christianity arose. Scholars have argued that the phenomenon of martyrdom arose only in the early years of the Roman Empire (Bowersock 1995; Shepkaru 2006).

However, Daniel and his companions as well as the heroes of 2 Maccabees and 4 Maccabees have been commemorated as martyrs by Jews and Christians from the ancient period onward.

Definitions

The term "martyr" is a fixed expression for a person who dies a heroic death for a specific cause. Scholarly definitions often highlight the aspect of witness or confession as the main characteristic of martyrdom, by focusing upon the Greek term *martys* ("witness, testimony"), which developed into the title "martyr" in early Christian writings. The first occurrence of the term comes in the *Martyrdom of Polycarp,* written ca. 160 C.E. (1:1; cf. 2:1; 14:2). Pre-Christian Jewish documents lack this terminology, but other technical terms are found in rabbinic writings from the third century C.E. onward: *Qiddush ha-Shem (Sanctification of God's Name)* for martyrdom, and *Asarah Haruge Malkhut (Ten Killed by the [Roman] Government)* for a specific group of martyrs. Earlier cases of Jewish martyrdom did occur if one defines a martyr as a person who prefers a violent death to compliance with an oppressive demand of hostile authorities. Both Daniel and his companions and the so-called Maccabean martyrs are confronted with a command by a foreign king that conflicts with their Jewish way of life. They decide to sacrifice their lives in order to remain faithful to their Jewish practices. Being executed or killing oneself in such a hostile situation was considered a heroic way of dying, although suicide is, in principle, an offense in the Jewish tradition (based on interpretations of Gen. 9:5).

Relevant Passages

The main passages about Jewish martyrdom until ca. 250 C.E. are found in Daniel 3 and 6 (Aramaic original and expanded Greek versions), 2 Macc. 6:18–7:42 (ca. 125 B.C.E.), and 4 Maccabees (first-second century C.E.). A specific genre of martyrdom writings is absent in this period, but the passages mentioned share the following pattern of narrative elements: (1) an enactment issued by the (pagan) authorities causes a conflict of interest for Jews; (2) they are forced to choose between complying with the laws of the non-Jewish government and maintaining Jewish practices; they decide to remain faithful to their Jewish way of life during the examination by the non-Jewish officials; (3) their examination is sometimes accompanied by torture; and (4) their execution is described.

The order of execution is followed in Daniel 3 and 6 by a miraculous deliverance, so Daniel and his companions are not martyrs in the strict sense. Nevertheless, they appear as famous forerunners of later martyrs (4 Macc. 16:3, 21; 18:12-33). They are considered martyrs themselves in later Jewish and Christian tradition (Van Henten and Avemarie 2002: 114-16, 144-55, and 149-50). Several rabbinic martyrdom stories show a similar narrative pattern (*b. Berakot* 61b about the martyrdom of R. Aqiva and *b. ʿAbodah Zarah* 17b–18a about R. Ḥanina ben Teradyon). Related passages describing heroic deaths of Jews and expressing martyrdom motifs include 1 Macc. 6:43-46; 2 Macc. 14:37-46; Philo, *Every Good Person Is Free* 88–91; *Assumption of Moses* 9:1–10:10, and Josephus, *J.W.* 7.389-406.

Content and Function

The court tales of Daniel 3 and 6 present religion as the central element of Jewish identity for Daniel and his companions. Their monotheism causes a conflict of loyalties at the moment that the king's policy and the Judeans' religious practice collide with each other. Daniel's companions refuse to pay tribute to Nebuchadnezzar's golden statue (Dan. 3:18). Daniel himself doesn't give up his prayers three times a day to God, even though his practice leads to his being thrown to the king's lions. The Maccabean martyrs refuse to give in to the king's command to eat pork during a sacrificial meal (2 Macc. 6:18; 7:2; 4 Macc. 5:2). Such a choice between faithfulness to God or to the secular authorities underlies most ancient Jewish and Christian martyr texts. In the Jewish passages there is also an ethnic dimension to the conflict. Shadrach, Meshach, and Abednego are accused as Judeans (Dan. 3:12) by colleagues who are identified as "Chaldeans" (3:8). The name "Chaldeans" refers in the book of Daniel to a professional class of sages (e.g., Dan. 1:4) and/or an ethnic group (5:30; 9:1). Daniel 3 therefore contrasts Judeans who obey the God of Israel with Chaldeans who venerate the king's statue. The outcome of the stories of Daniel 3 and 6 shows that the king's power is ultimately subordinate to that of the God of Daniel and his companions.

The books of 2 and 4 Maccabees also highlight a multilayered conflict: the wicked Greek king attempts to force the Jews to abandon their Jewish practices and switch to the Greek way of life. The king succeeds in executing the martyrs but ultimately suffers a defeat caused by God, who acts upon the martyrs' intercession (2 Maccabees 8–9; 4 Macc. 17:17–18:5). The martyrs' deaths lead to the reestablishment of the Jewish way of life and the restoration of the Jewish polity.

The Maccabean martyrs had an important social and patriotic function within the communities that decided to transmit the stories of their deaths. The martyrs are presented as model figures and indicate the proper way of life for other Jews (2 Macc. 6:28, 31; 4 Macc. 6:19; 17:23). They represent the Jewish people in the martyrdom passages, which demonstrate that the Jews had their own famous heroes who were willing to sacrifice their lives for their practices and belief. The martyrs' statements and exemplary acts also indicate the boundaries for social and cultural interaction with outsiders, by constructing a Torah-obedient Jewish group that is not hostile to the non-Jewish world as long as the observance of the laws is not endangered.

Theological Significance

New Testament scholars have scrutinized Jewish martyrdom passages because of their relevance for the genesis of the early Christian concepts of atonement and resurrection. Jewish traditions about the beneficiary death and resurrection of the martyrs were probably incorporated into the early believers' response to Jesus' execution and vindication.

The Maccabean martyrdoms result in the restoration of the covenant relation between God and the Jewish people that was violated by the transgression of God's laws by godless Jewish leaders (2 Macc. 4:7–10:9; 4 Maccabees 4–18). The martyrs suffer in solidarity with the others during God's temporary punishment of the people, through the agency of the Greek king. Their intercessory prayer just before dying invokes God's mercy for the people as well as his punishment of the foreign king. The martyrs' appeal to God's mercy hints at atonement (2 Macc. 7:33, 37-38; cf. Dan. 3:39-40 LXX). The more elaborate intercessory prayer of the martyrs in 4 Maccabees expresses the propitiatory and substitutionary functions of martyrdom (4 Macc. 6:28-29; 9:24; 12:17; 17:20-22).

The posthumous vindication of the martyrs is indicated in statements that hint at a resurrection without much detail (2 Macc. 7:9, 11, 14, 23, 29, 36), probably implying an immediate re-creation in heaven by God. 4 Maccabees attributes several forms of afterlife to the martyrs: they live on with the patriarchs near God (4 Macc. 7:19; 13:27; 16:25), receive immortal souls (18:23), and stand in heaven before God (17:5). 4 Macc. 18:17 points to a bodily resurrection of the martyrs, quoting Ezek. 37:3. In both Maccabean books the postmortem vindication of the martyrs goes hand in hand with the deliverance of Jews on earth.

The *Assumption of Moses* (or *Testament of Moses*), a work written in the first half of the first century C.E., has also frequently been discussed in connection with early Christian views about the end of time. The relevant passage (9:1–10:10) implies that the death of Jewish heroes leads to the inauguration of God's kingdom at the end of the age. Chapter 9 focuses on a Levite called Taxo and his seven sons, who are presented as the only Israelites who remain after an incredibly harsh oppression of the people. They retreat to a cave and await their death, because they refuse to transgress the Lord's commandments (9:4). Their prayer is full of allusions to scriptural passages and is followed by a description of the end in 10:1-10. The death of Taxo and his sons, therefore, inaugurates salvation for Israel and eternal punishment for its enemies.

BIBLIOGRAPHY

G. W. BOWERSOCK 1995, *Martyrdom and Rome,* Cambridge: Cambridge University Press. • D. BOYARIN 1999, *Dying for God: Martyrdom and the Making of Christianity and Judaism,* Stanford: Stanford University Press. • J. J. COLLINS 1993, *Daniel: A Commentary on the Book of Daniel,* Minneapolis: Fortress. • M. DE JONGE 1988, *Christology in Context: The Earliest Response to Jesus,* Philadelphia: Westminster/John Knox. • D. A. DESILVA 2006, *4 Maccabees: Introduction and Commentary on the Greek Text in Codex Sinaiticus,* Leiden: Brill. • A. J. DROGE AND J. D. TABOR 1991, *A Noble Death: Suicide and Martyrdom among Christians and Jews in Antiquity,* San Francisco: Harper. • J. W. VAN HENTEN 1997, *The Maccabean Martyrs as Saviors of the Jewish People,* Leiden: Brill. • J. W. VAN HENTEN AND F. AVEMARIE 2002, *Martyrdom and Noble Death: Selected Texts from Graeco-Roman, Jewish and Christian Antiquity,* London: Routledge. • T. RAJAK 1997, "Dying for the Law: The Martyr's Portrait in Jewish-Greek Literature," in *Portraits: Biographical Representation in the Greek and Latin Literature of the Roman Empire,* ed. M. J. Edwards and S. Swain, Oxford: Clarendon Press. • D. R. SCHWARTZ 2008, *2 Maccabees,* Berlin: de Gruyter. • S. SHEPKARU 2006, *Jewish Martyrs in the Pagan and Christian Worlds,* Cambridge: Cambridge University Press.

See also: Daniel, Book of; Maccabees, Second Book of; Maccabees, Fourth Book of

JAN WILLEM VAN HENTEN

Masada

Masada is a fortress located at the edge of the Judean Desert on the western shore of the Dead Sea, approximately 25 km. south of ʿEin Gedi. It sits atop a plateau measuring approximately 800 m. (N-S) by 300 m. (E-W) that rises nearly 440 m. above the Dead Sea. Masada is best known from Josephus' account of the Roman siege that took place there during the First Jewish Revolt against Rome. The battle ended when Masada's 960 defenders committed suicide (*J.W.* 7.252-406).

History of Excavations

In 1838 the American explorer Edward Robinson identified the site es-Sebba as the fortress of Masada mentioned in Josephus' writings. Since then, the location has attracted the attention of many explorers and archaeologists. The American missionary S. W. Wolcott was the first to climb to the summit in 1842. Félicien de Saulcy excavated the mosaic floor of a Byzantine chapel at the site in 1851. Claude R. Conder (1875) undertook the first extensive survey of the summit's archaeological remains. Alfred von Domaszewski (1897) mapped the siege works. Adolf Schulten visited Masada for a month in 1932 and produced the most detailed plans of the archaeological remains, which laid the foundation for later full-scale excavations.

In 1953 the Israel Exploration Society, the Israel Department of Antiquities and Museums, and the Hebrew University of Jerusalem conducted the first comprehensive study and mapping of Masada's plateau. Shmarya Gutmann (1954) discovered the "snake path," conducted a survey of the summit, and later restored the gatehouse and a Roman camp. Yigael Yadin excavated nearly 97 percent of Masada's summit in two seasons from 1963 to 1965. Scholars continue to debate whether his findings support Josephus' account of the Roman general Flavius Silva's siege of the site and the mass suicide of its defenders. A few additional expeditions explored areas excavated by Yadin, or aspects related to the Roman siege. Ehud Netzer conducted small excavations atop the summit from 1994 to 1996. Gideon Foerster, Benny Arubas, Haim Goldfus, and Jodi Magness excavated the Roman siege camp F.

Hasmonean Occupation

Archaeologists have uncovered evidence of human activity at Masada as early as the Chalcolithic period. Josephus claims that "Jonathan the high priest" built the fortress of Masada (*J.W.* 7.285). Most scholars believe that this refers to Alexander Jannaeus (103-76 B.C.E.), the first to build on the site. An assemblage of coins from the time of Alexander Jannaeus, and plaster in some of the site's many cisterns, show that Masada was occupied during the Hasmonean period. Some archaeologists suggest that several buildings, including the site's four small palaces, a small bathhouse, and three columbaria towers at its southern edge, incorporate earlier Hasmonean structures. Yadin, however, did not find any definitive architectural evidence of the Hasmonean period. Ehud Netzer's short excavation in 1989 to explore this issue failed to locate any Hasmonean remains. Because Herod's construction apparently destroyed earlier Hasmonean structures, the nature and size of the site before his reign are uncertain.

Herodian Fortification

The majority of the extant buildings on Masada's summit date to the period of Herod the Great. Herod fortified the site after rescuing his family there from the army of the Hasmonean Mattathias Antigonus, whom the Parthians had made king (*Ant.* 14.390-91). From approximately 37 to 31 B.C.E. he undertook a massive construction project atop the summit. He built twelve large cisterns, which were fed by floods from the wadis to the north and south of the mountain, to provide water year-round. A casemate wall (ca. 1,400 m. long) surrounds the plateau. It is approximately 6.5 m. wide, and contains nearly seventy rooms and more than thirty towers. Herod's northern palace, built atop three natural terraces, is the most prominent feature at the site. The upper terrace includes living quarters and a semicircular porch, while the middle terrace contains a circular building with associated rooms. The lower terrace contains a small bathhouse with a paved mosaic floor and rooms with decorated plaster walls. Herod's western palace (4,340 m.) near the casemate wall is Masada's largest residential building. It contains apartments, workshops, storerooms, and a large service wing. This building's plaster, mosaics, and possible indentations where a throne may have once sat, attest to its grandeur. Archaeologists have uncovered numerous objects from Herod's storerooms, including dates, olive pits, cloth, and an amphora inscribed in Latin, "to Herod, King of Judea."

Sicarii Occupation during the First Revolt

According to Josephus, the Sicarii took possession of Masada during the First Revolt. During their occupation, they modified many of Herod's palatial quarters and resided in the palaces and casemate wall. Yadin discovered extensive evidence throughout the site of their presence, including squatter's residences, ovens, and gendered objects such as spindle whorls, showing that their families resided there during the Roman siege. The discovery of several *mikva'ot* (ritual baths), stone vessels, ostraca with Jewish names, and a prayer shawl provide archaeological evidence that these families were Jewish. The Sicarii modified a preexisting building, likely a stable, into a synagogue with the addition of benches to accommodate up to 250 persons. Yadin found fragments of scrolls containing Deuteronomy and Ezekiel in a back room of this building. An ostracon in the synagogue containing the Hebrew words "priest's tithe" may have been part of a jar containing a tithe for a synagogue attendant or priest.

View of Masada showing Herod's western palace on the left and his northern palace with associated buildings at top *(Phoenix Data Systems / Neal and Joel Bierling)*

Written Remains

A few literary discoveries may provide additional information about Masada's occupants during the First Revolt. Yadin found a fragment of *The Songs of the Sabbath Sacrifice,* a document previously discovered among the Dead Sea Scrolls in caves near Qumran. This may indicate that members of the Qumran community were at Masada. A paleo-Hebrew papyrus fragment from Masada likely contains a Samaritan prayer, which could indicate the presence of some Samaritans. Others, however, question these interpretations, arguing that these documents were merely popular writings in the Second Temple period. A Herodian jar bears the inscription, "Ananias the high priest and Aqaviah his son." Ananias bar Nebedaeus served as high priest from 48 to 59 C.E., and Josephus (*J.W.* 2.409) tells us that his son Eleazar's refusal to offer sacrifices on behalf of the Roman emperor precipitated the First Revolt. This inscription, and the "priest's tithe" ostracon, may indicate that priests were among the site's defenders.

The Roman Siege

Archaeological excavations at Masada have uncovered extensive evidence of the Roman siege. Yadin discovered numerous ballista stones atop Masada. A group of over 200 arrowheads, some with shafts, were found in two rooms (442 and 456) in the western palace and were likely manufactured there. A considerable number of weapons was discovered at Masada, including hundreds of bronze armor scales, remains of at least ten shields, fragments of four iron swords, spears, javelins, helmets, riding equipment, knives, and military footwear. Latin papyri found at the site indicate that the Romans occupied Masada following its destruction.

The Roman soldiers who occupied the summit for a short time lived in the site's open spaces. This suggests that most of Masada's buildings were destroyed during the battle; otherwise, they would have used them. Because not all the rooms and storerooms at the site show evidence of burning, the Sicarii must have dismantled the ceilings of some structures to build their defensive wall. The extensive evidence of burning in other structures may support Josephus' claim that the Sicarii set Masada's buildings on fire. Following the siege, Roman soldiers likely looted the site and damaged many structures. Masada was partly destroyed by an earthquake sometime during the second to fourth centuries. The site remained unoccupied until the Byzantine period (fifth-sixth centuries), when monks constructed an apsidal church there as part of a monastic complex.

Josephus' Account of Mass Suicide

Josephus includes a lengthy account of Masada's siege in book 7 of his *Jewish War.* He writes that in the midsummer of 66 C.E. Menahem the Galilean seized the fortress at the outbreak of the First Revolt. It later fell into the hands of his relative Eleazar ben Ya'ir, a leader of the Sicarii. His men took much of Masada's vast stores of arms to Jerusalem to use against the Romans. The Sicarii occupying Masada raided neighboring settlements including ʿEin Gedi, where they killed 700 Jews. Flavius Silva, commander of the tenth legion, laid siege to Masada. The Sicarii unsuccessfully attempted to halt the Roman onslaught with the construction of a wooden wall that the Romans set on fire.

The highlights of Josephus' narrative are two lengthy speeches by Eleazar Ben Ya'ir urging his fellow defenders to commit suicide rather than fall into the hands of the Romans. Ten men were chosen by lot to slaughter the others. They in turn drew lots to determine who would kill the other nine before committing suicide. When Silva's troops stormed Masada, they found the bodies of 960 men, women, and children. Only two women and five children, who had hidden below ground, survived to report the tragic story of Masada's final hours and the circumstances behind the mass suicide.

Yadin largely accepted Josephus' account of Masada's siege as reliable. He identified eleven ostraca, one with the name "Ben Ya'ir," as one of the lots mentioned by Josephus. Yet several scholars have compared the literary details of the *Jewish War* with Yadin's findings to challenge the historicity of Josephus' narrative (Cohen 1982; Eshel 1999). Other experts have examined Josephus' works in light of Roman traditions about noble death to propose that he made up his account of the mass suicide to portray Jews as courageous warriors who do not fear death.

Date of Masada's Downfall

The recent publication of Yadin's excavations and other studies of the site have furnished new information about the battle, including the likely date of the Roman siege and the fate of the Sicarii. Masada's downfall is traditionally dated to 73 C.E. Two inscriptions recording the career of the Roman general L. Flavius Silva, and papyri found during excavations, suggest that it fell in the Spring of 74 C.E. If a divorce document found in Wadi Murabbaʿat (Mur 19), written "in year six at Masada," has been correctly dated to 71 C.E., it may furnish additional evidence about the Jews who occupied the site. The "year six" apparently refers to the sixth year of the revolt, which shows that Masada's defenders continued to date events from the beginning of the First Revolt even after the Temple's destruction in the year 70.

Skeletal Remains

Yadin found skeletons of men, women, and children in two locations: the bathhouse in the northern palace (three skeletons) and the southern cave (twenty-five skeletons). He identified these skeletons as Masada's defenders. They were buried with full military honors in 1969 near the foot of the siege ramp. Joseph Zias' subsequent examination of these remains has challenged Yadin's interpretation (Zias 1998). All the bones show signs of predation, and it is very likely that animals carried them to the locations of their discovery. Pig bones — a common feature of Roman burials — were found in the burial cave and may indicate that the remains belonged to pagans. The absence of mass graves suggests that the Romans likely captured the majority of Masada's defenders. A Latin papyrus found at Masada, dated to 73 or 74 C.E., may have been written by one of the site's besiegers. It contains portions of Virgil's *Aeneid* (4.9) describing the Carthaginian queen Dido's nightmares, and may allude to the horrors a Roman soldier witnessed during the siege.

The Siege Ramp and Weapons

The Roman siege ramp is the most dominant feature at Masada. It is located atop a natural spur (*J.W.* 7.305). Although an impressive achievement, it was not exceptional by Roman standards. Jonathan Roth estimates that it would have taken a force of only 2,400 men working in shifts around the clock, in three shifts of 800 men each, less than sixteen days to build. There is little evidence that Masada's defenders had the resources or weaponry to hinder the construction of this ramp. Numerous ballista balls were discovered atop Masada. Because two of the eight Roman camps were within the range of Roman ballista (Camps F and E), Masada's defenders can have had no artillery. The ballista stones discovered inside the fortress where likely shot there by the Romans. Archaeological evidence indicates that the Romans built a second ramp on top of Masada by the upper terrace after they had breached the site's walls. It is 20 m. long and 15 m. wide, with a height of nearly 2.5 m. A fragment of a scroll of Leviticus was found in the earth used for its construction. Because the twenty-six coins in it predate Masada's fall, some of the site's defenders must have continued fighting after the Romans stormed the site.

Roman Occupation of the Site

The Roman fortifications suggest that Masada's siege was of a short duration. Masada's eight camps lack ditches, which indicates either that the legions did not expect to stay long or that they were built after the winter rains had abated. Jodi Magness's study of the ceramics in Masada's camps reveals that most are locally made storage jars that would have been used for transporting and storing food and liquids and not for cooking. There is a notable absence of vessels for the preparation and serving of food, which is a characteristic of temporary military encampments. The use of tents rather than barracks also suggests that the Romans did not remain at Masada for long. Jonathan Roth's extensive study of the Roman camps and circumvallation wall has revealed that they are not unusual by ancient standards, and were actually unnecessary. He suggests that the Romans constructed them largely as busy work, or as a training exercise for the army, and that the entire siege lasted between seven and nine weeks.

Bibliography

K. Atkinson 2006, "Noble Deaths at Gamla and Masada?: A Critical Assessment of Josephus's Accounts of Jewish Resistance in Light of Archaeological Discoveries," in *Making History: Josephus and Historical Method,* ed. Z. Rogers, Leiden: Brill, 349-71. • S. J. D. Cohen 1982, "Masada: Literary Tradition, Archaeological Remains, and the Credibility of Josephus," *JJS* 33: 385-405. • H. M. Cotton 1989, "The Date of the Fall of Masada: The Evidence of the Masada Papyri," *Zeitschrift für Papyrologie und Epigraphie* 78: 157-62. • H. Eshel 1999, "Josephus' View on Judaism without the Temple in Light of the Discoveries at Masada and Murabba'at," in *Gemeinde ohne Tempel: Zur Substituierung und Transformation des Jerusalemer Tempels und seines Kults im Alten Testament, antiken Judentum und frühen Christentum,* ed. B. Ego, A. Lange, and P. Pilhofer, Tübingen: Mohr-Siebeck, 229-38. • J. Magness 2009, "The Pottery from Camp F at Masada," *BASOR* 353: 75-107. • J. Roth 1995, "The Length of the Siege of Masada," *SCI* 14: 87-110. • S. Talmon 1996, "Hebrew Written Fragments from Masada," *DSD* 3: 168-77. • Y. Yadin 1966, *Masada: Herod's Fortress and the Zealots' Last Stand,* New York: Random House. • Y. Yadin et al., eds. 1989-2007, *Masada 1–8: The Yigael Yadin Excavations 1963-1965: Final Reports,* Jerusalem: Israel Exploration Society/Hebrew University of Jerusalem. • J. Zias 1998, "Whose Bones? Were They Really Jewish Defenders? Did Yadin Obfuscate? *BAR* 24: 40-45, 64-66.

Kenneth Atkinson

Mastema → Satan and Related Figures

Matthew, Gospel of

The Gospel of Matthew is the first, in canonical order, of the four New Testament gospels. It is sometimes said that it is both the most Jewish and the most anti-Jewish of the four.

The Most Jewish of the Gospels

Matthew may be considered the most Jewish because he demonstrates the greatest knowledge of and interest in core features of Second Temple Judaism. For example, Matthew maintains that the followers of Jesus should keep fundamental Jewish laws pertaining to practices like the Sabbath (12:1-8), ritual purity and kashrut (15:1-20), divorce (19:3-9), and limited commerce with non-Jews (10:5, 17-23; 15:24). This position stands in stark contrast to Matthew's major source, the Gospel of Mark, which rejects such halakic positions (Mark 2:27; 7:19; 10:11-12). Matthew supports paying the double drachma or Temple tax as an acceptable *modus vivendi* or way of "avoiding offense," whereas the single Jesus logion Mark utilizes on the subject of taxes remains at best ambiguous (Matt. 17:24-27; Mark 12:17). And Matthew explicitly grounds Jesus' actions and speech in the broader context of enacting promises from the Hebrew Bible.

Far from abrogating the Torah, Matthew's Jesus claims that it can and must be fulfilled in its entirety (5:17-20). In Matthew, Jesus does not deliver a *lex nova* but the Mosaic Torah authoritatively interpreted, and his followers both understand and enact the Torah fully and in a manner superior to their opponents (5:19; 23:13-15; etc.). Matthew's Jesus lays particular stress on the "golden rule" or love command as the guiding principle of Torah interpretation (5:43-48; 7:12; 18:35; 22:34-40). Much of chap. 5, which is the first part of the Sermon on the Mount and contains the so-called Antitheses, can be viewed as a kind of midrash on the love command's hermeneutical role as the guiding interpretive principle for understanding and enacting the Torah. A number of scholars now find in this use of the love command an early tradition that Matthew shares with the *Didache* and several other early Jewish-Christian texts (Van de Sandt 2005). Jesus' interpretation of Torah is of course polemical, but Matthew's Jesus insists that it is perfectly consistent with the history and hopes of Israel as found in the Hebrew Bible. Matthew contends that Jesus reflects the true traditions of Israel and Israel's relationship with God, while many of the leaders contemporaneous with Jesus exploit and manipulate these traditions for their own gain (9:9-13; 15:6; 23:23). Jesus, by contrast, "teaches as one having authority and not as *their* scribes" (7:29).

In Matthew Jesus takes care to explain why it is that his disciples do not break the Torah. Matthew has long been recognized for its elaboration on Mark's legal material. Matthew's editorial activity is frequently devoted to emphasizing the legal precision of Jesus and the disciples and to correcting earlier portrayals of Jesus as potentially antinomian or the disciples as a group that fail to follow the Law or understand the teaching of their leader, Jesus. In Matthew the disciples are good students. Quite unlike the portrait of the disciples in Mark, in Matthew Jesus' followers do understand. They are true followers of Torah. This characterization reflects well on Jesus as a teacher but also underscores the importance and obtainable goal of fulfilling Torah (Overman 1990). Halakic debates place Matthew squarely in the midst of typical Jewish sectarian arguments in the Second Temple period.

The Most Anti-Jewish of the Gospels

Matthew, however, can also justifiably be described as the most anti-Jewish of the gospels. It is in Matthew more than any other gospel that Jewish leaders are singled out and denounced in hyperbolic and caustic terms (Saldarini 1994). Matthew alone is responsible for making the terms "Pharisee" and "hypocrite" virtual synonyms in Western vernacular. The disturbing language that Matthew's Jesus levels at the local Jewish leadership, concentrated especially in chap. 23, found an afterlife in early Christian anti-Jewish literature. Moreover, Matthew inserts the terms "scribes and Pharisees" whenever possible into passages where they can be denounced or utilized as legal whipping boys. And in Matthew it is the chief priests and Pharisees who begin the plotting and process of bringing Jesus to trial and his death (21:45).

The "synagogue" (Gr. *synagōgē*) is the common venue in Matthew for conflicts between Jesus and local leaders, whom Matthew almost always calls "scribes and Pharisees." Matthew alone affixes the possessive pronoun "their" to the term "synagogue" (4:23; 9:35; 10:17; 12:9; 13:54; cf. 23:34). This language of opposition captures the Gospel's prominent theme of division within and competition among Palestinian Jewish communities at the close of the first century C.E. Significantly, Matthew avoids this term as the name for his community's gathering, settling instead on the term "church" (Gr. *ekklēsia*), which, while a very common Greek term, was relatively rare nomenclature among both early Christians and Jews in this period (16:18; 18:18). Thus the term "synagogue" takes on the freight of an emerging institution at odds with the group of Matthean Jews gathered around Jesus.

Taken together, the harsh denunciation of certain Jewish leaders, the opposition to "their synagogue," and the claim that the Matthean community alone possesses the true interpretation of Torah are responsible for Matthew's reputation for anti-Semitism." This reputation is also based on Matthew's treatment of the passion of Jesus. Most notably, Matthew alone among the gospels supplies a conversation between Pontius Pilate and the people gathered around the cross, an exchange that has come to be known as "the cry of all the people." According to 27:24-25, Pilate believed Jesus was innocent of the charges against him but, sensing the beginnings of a riot, took water, washed his hands, and declared, "I am innocent of this man's blood; see to it yourselves. And all the people answered and said, 'His blood be upon us and our children.'"

The theme of "innocent blood" has a long history in the Hebrew Bible, and a number of relevant passages pertain to the destruction of the first Jerusalem Temple. The theme understandably rose to prominence again in the wake of the destruction of the Second Temple in 70 C.E. The distinctively Matthean feature of this passage is the addition of the clause "and upon our children," most likely a thinly veiled reference to the destruction of Jerusalem, which would have occurred during the lifetime of the Matthean community a generation after the death of Jesus. Further, while extreme to most modern ears, the charge concerning "innocent blood" was a stock feature of the volatile internal and sectarian rhetoric in Second Temple Judaism (Overman 1990b; Saldarini 1994). For most of subsequent church history, Christian leaders interpreted this passage as proof of Jewish culpability in the death of Jesus and as a warrant for persecuting Jews. Since the Second Vatican Council, however, the Roman Catholic Church has gradually tried to distance itself from this historic position.

The traditional interpretation of this text by Christians is wildly anachronistic, lacking any sense of its original context, in which it is only the local, largely Jerusalem-based leadership who are made responsible for Jesus' death and the city's destruction. In earlier portions of his story, Matthew subtly blames the destruction of Jerusalem and the loss of land to Rome on the corrupt leaders (Overman 1996). Matthew shares this placing of blame with Josephus, who also regards the destruction as an apocalyptic event and attributes it to Jewish division and poor leadership in the period leading up to the Jewish war of 66-70 C.E. Thus Matthew is employing stock language, imagery, and biblical themes against other Jewish groups in its milieu, in a dispute over leadership, authority, and responsibility for recent traumatic events.

Of course, this newer understanding of the setting and purpose of a passage like Matt. 27:25 does not overcome nearly two millennia of its misappropriation and application by Christians. However, a far more informed reading of such a passage sensitive to the real situation in which it was written may help, over time, to counter deeply prejudiced interpretations of the Matthean story.

Date and Provenance

While complete unanimity on the date and provenance of the Gospel of Matthew does not exist, a consensus has emerged recently on some fundamental questions. The date of the Gospel is nearly universally held to be sometime at the end of the first century C.E., with a few scholars holding open the possibility of an early second-century date. The place of origin remains disputed. The traditional location has been Antioch-on-the-Orontes on the Syrian/Turkish border. This view relies in part on a few instances where the early second-century author Ignatius of Antioch appears to be using Matthean material. Yet Matthean material was used by several early second-century authors, so Ignatian usage alone is not determinative. More recently, urban centers in the Galilee (e.g., Caesarea, Sepphoris) and in the Decapolis (e.g., Bet She'an/Scythopolis) have emerged as possible candidates. Locations in southern Lebanon such as Tyre, Baalbek, or even Damascus — so close to the northeast corner of Upper Galilee and to Caesarea Philippi, where Matthew's greatly expanded version of Peter's important confession occurs (16:16-19) — are also possibilities. Presumably the place in question enjoyed some measure of literacy, a reasonable level of Greek language, a mixed population of Jews and Gentiles, and a robust enough Jewish community to have division and competition. This seems to point to a locale in or near Palestine. Such a phenomenon would mirror in certain respects developments within early rabbinic Judaism following the First Revolt. In the period after 70, the nascent rabbinic movement went north into Galilee and slowly developed institutions, halakic conventions, and modes of authority that ultimately flowered in the late second and third centuries C.E.

The Jewish Author and His Jewish Community

A consensus has emerged slowly over the last two decades about the nature of the author and his community. That the author of Matthew was Jewish is rarely disputed now. To call him and the members of his community "Christians" because of their devotion to Jesus would be anachronistic and misleading. Neither the author nor his community members would have been familiar with the term. They considered themselves Jews. D. Sim (1998) has referred to Matthew as "the Gospel of Christian Judaism," A. J. Saldarini (1994) calls Matthew's audience a "Christian-Jewish community," and J. A. Overman (1996) refers to the Matthean Jews as adherents of "Jesus-Centered Judaism." Whatever hyphenated terminology is used, it is clear that Matthew's community was a Jewish group that struggled to remain true to the Torah and historic Israel, competed with other post-70 Jewish groups, and considered Jesus to be the true way for all Jews.

In the period after 70, Pharisaism, Jesus-centered Judaism, and nascent rabbinism mingled and quarreled in rather close proximity to one another. The type of Judaism represented by the Gospel of Matthew did not endure beyond the third century C.E. (Overman 1996). As Christianity became a thoroughly Gentile phenomenon, the Gospel of Matthew had to be read and reinterpreted in a way that made it more cogent to Christians and finally alien to Jews. Recent scholarship has recognized these historic developments and has made strides toward placing Matthew more squarely within its appropriate historical setting.

BIBLIOGRAPHY

D. BALCH, ED. 1991, *Social History of the Matthean Community: Cross-Disciplinary Approaches,* Minneapolis: Fortress. • W. D. DAVIES AND D. C. ALLISON 1988, *A Critical and Exegetical Commentary on the Gospel according to Saint Matthew,* 3 vols., Edinburgh: Clark. • U. LUZ 2001-2007, *Matthew,* 3 vols., Minneapolis: Fortress. • J. A. OVERMAN 1990, *Matthew's Gospel and Formative Judaism: The Social World of the Matthean Community,* Minneapolis: Fortress. • J. A. OVERMAN 1996, *Church and Community in Crisis: The Gospel According to Matthew,* Valley Forge, Penn.: Trinity Press International. • A. J. SALDARINI 1994, *Matthew's Christian-Jewish Community,* Chicago: University of Chicago Press. • D. SIM 1998, *The Gospel of Matthew and Christian Judaism: The History and Social Setting of the Matthean Community,* Edinburgh: Clark. • H. VAN DE SANDT 2005, *Matthew and the Didache: Two Documents from the Same Jewish-Christian Milieu?* Minneapolis: Fortress.

ANDREW J. OVERMAN

Meals

Meals had special significance in Second Temple Judaism in both domestic and cultic settings. They were characterized both by features that were common to the culture and by features that were distinctive, such as dietary restrictions.

Similarities with Greco-Roman Banquets

The Jewish table in the Second Temple period shared features with Greco-Roman banquet customs, especially as elaborated in the Greek symposium tradition. Like the Greeks, Jews in this period, when they ate a formal meal, normally reclined on couches (evidenced as early as Amos 6:4-7; see also Tob. 9:6; *m. Ber.* 6:6; *m. Pesaḥ.* 10:1). The reclining banquet included a whole range of accompanying customs that are reflected in early Jewish sources. For example, at the meals described by Ben Sira there is a "master of the feast" who, like the typical Greek *symposiarch,* presided over the dinner (Sir. 32:1-2; cf. Plato, *Symposium* 213e). Like the Greeks, who typically had music, particularly that of a flute girl, at their banquets (Plutarch, *Quaestionum Convivialum* 712f–713f), Ben Sira has high praise for "music at a banquet of wine" (Sir. 32:5-6). Ben Sira's rules for proper behavior at the banquet closely parallel the rules of Greek moralists. For example, one's behavior should reflect concern for the needs of the tablemate (Sir. 31:15-17, 41:19; compare Plutarch, *Quaest. Conv.* 614d-e), and one's speech should be appropriate to the occasion (Sir. 32:3-9; compare Plutarch, *Quaest. Conv.* 613c–614b; 629c-d).

In some cases, Greco-Roman banquet customs were adapted to fit the distinctive needs of the Jewish context. For example, it was common to pray at meals, but whereas the Greeks offered libations to Zeus and to Dionysus, the god of wine (Athenaeus, *Deipnon* 15, 675b-c), the Jews gave thanks to the one God, "creator of the fruit of the vine" (*m. Ber.* 6:1). Elevated discourse at the table is a particular marker of the symposium tradition. In the Greek philosophical tradition, it became customary to "dismiss the flute girl" and devote the symposium entertainment to philosophical conversation (Plato, *Symposium* 176e); at the Jewish table such table talk was to be about the Law (Sir. 9:15-16; *m. 'Abot* 3:3). At festival meals, such as the Passover meal, the conversation was specifically devoted to themes associated with the festival (*m. Pesaḥ.* 10:4-6).

Jewish Dietary Restrictions

The practice of dietary laws was distinctive to Jewish tradition and made it difficult for Jews to eat at a non-Jewish table. The cultural tension caused by dietary laws is evidenced in both non-Jewish and Jewish sources. Non-Jewish sources indicate that Greeks and Romans tended to characterize Jews by their food traditions, especially by the fact that they did not eat pork, which to many was merely considered an oddity (Plutarch, *Quaest. Conv.* 669e–671c). Others, however, agreed with Diodorus, who attributed Jewish refusal to eat with Gentiles to their "hatred of humanity" (34.1.2; see also Tacitus, *Historiae* 5.4-5).

The Jewish novelistic tradition idealized figures who stood their ground and would not eat non-kosher food, even in the face of persecution (Dan. 1:8-16; Tob. 1:10-12; 1 Macc. 1:62-63; cf. also the mention of Judith's diet in Jdt. 10:5; 12:19). Nevertheless, because of the importance of table fellowship with outsiders as a means for Jews, especially those of the Diaspora, to survive and prosper, we cannot conclude that they never ate at a Gentile table. Various levels of compromise and accommodation must have been practiced, ranging from the request for a special diet (*Letter of Aristeas* 181–86), to the apparent absence of diet as an issue at all. Ben Sira, for example, makes no mention of dietary laws as a hindrance to eating at a ruler's table (Sir. 31:12-16; 38:34–39:4).

As in the Greco-Roman banquet tradition, table fellowship was understood to be an activity that defined and celebrated community identity. When dietary laws and other distinctive Jewish practices were featured, the table became a focal point for Jewish identity vis-à-vis the outside world. In addition, the Jewish religious calendar included numerous feasts that ritualized the shared history and traditions of Judaism.

Jewish Meals in Sectarian Settings

Meals also provided a means for sectarian groups within Judaism to define a separate identity for themselves over against Judaism as a whole. In this practice, they took on characteristics modeled after the clubs and associations in the Greco-Roman world, which organized themselves according to common goals and beliefs and centered their gatherings on communal meals. For example, many scholars consider the Pharisees to have been primarily a table fellowship group who, like the rabbinic *havurot* (fellowships), set themselves apart based on issues of purity and celebrated their sectarian identity by means of their communal meals. Their table piety is thought to be reflected in *b. Berakot* 55a: "So long as the Temple stood, the altar made atonement for Israel. Now a man's table makes atonement for him."

Another such group is the community of Jews at Qumran, identified by most scholars as a group of Essenes. They regularly celebrated a communal meal ("they shall eat in common and bless in common and deliberate in common," 1QS 6:2-3) that was open only to initiates who had become sufficiently pure to share the "pure meal" (1QS 5:13-14). As with the Greek associations, at their meals they followed elaborate rules of protocol and behavior (1QS 5:24–6:13) and practiced religious rituals specific to their sectarian identity, for example, the so-called messianic banquet (1QSa 2:11-22).

Similarly, the Therapeutae, a Jewish group in Egypt, were primarily identified by their communal meal, which contrasted with the "unrestrained merry making" of the Greek symposia. Instead, the Therapeutae conducted themselves with orderly solemnity and centered their table talk on "some question arising in the Holy Scriptures" (Philo, *De Vita Contemplativa* 64–78).

Meals in the Early Jesus Movement

Jesus' followers typically met in one another's homes for prayer, worship, and fellowship in the context of a meal. When Gentiles began to join the predominantly Jewish movement in increasing numbers, issues over Jewish dietary scruples began to create problems.

In his letter to the Galatians, the apostle Paul recounts an episode in Antioch in which Cephas (probably Simon Peter) and other Jewish believers in Jesus withdrew from communal meals with Gentile adherents under pressure from "men from James," the brother of Jesus and a leader in the Jerusalem congregation (Gal. 2:11-13). Paul opposed this separation into two separate table fellowship groups because it implied that "Gentile [Christians] should live like Jews" and follow dietary laws, a position with which Paul disagreed (2:14-21). Paul's view of the gospel, as he told the Galatians, was that "in Christ . . . there is no longer Jew or Greek" (3:28), a principle that should be mirrored in their communal meals.

In the house churches that Paul established elsewhere in Asia Minor and Greece, it appears to have been the norm for both Jew and Gentile to share a common table. But tensions continued to arise, and Paul began to argue for a more diplomatic position than the one he had taken in Antioch. In addressing a tense situation in Rome, for example, Paul enjoined a compromise position in which those who differed over dietary issues should not "pass judgment on one another" (Rom. 14:13). He himself was "persuaded in the Lord Jesus that nothing is unclean in itself, but it is unclean for anyone who thinks it unclean" (14:14). Nevertheless, he urged, "It is good not to eat meat or drink wine or do anything that makes your brother or sister stumble" (14:21).

The Synoptic Gospels, written in the decades after Paul, reflect a continuation of the tensions between Jewish and Gentile believers. Jesus is depicted being criticized by scribes and Pharisees for sharing meals with impure outcasts such as "tax collectors and sinners" (Mark 2:13-17//Matt. 9:9-13//Luke 5:27-32) and for disregarding Pharisaic traditions of ritual hand washing before meals (Mark 7:1-23//Matt. 15:1-20; cf. Luke 11:37-41). The Gospel of Mark goes so far as to add the editorial comment, "Thus he [Jesus] declared all foods clean" (Mark 7:19). This remark, however, is noticeably dropped in Matthew's redaction of the Markan passage (Matt. 15:17), reflecting the extent to which the community of Matthew was more closely tied to Jewish traditions than that of Mark. Eventually, however, the Jesus movement would become predominately Gentile and the issue of dietary laws would fade in importance.

BIBLIOGRAPHY

J. D. BRUMBERG-KRAUS 2005, "Meals as Midrash: A Survey of Ancient Meals in Jewish Studies Scholarship," in *Food and Judaism: Studies in Jewish Civilization*, ed. L. J. Greenspoon et al., Omaha: Creighton University Press, 297-317. • J. NEUSNER 1963, *Fellowship in Judaism: The First Century and Today*, London: Vallentine, Mitchell & Co. • J. NEUSNER 1979, *From Politics to Piety: The Emergence of Pharisaic Judaism*, Englewood Cliffs, N.J.: Prentice-Hall. • D. E. SMITH 2003, *From Symposium to Eucharist: The Banquet in the Early Christian World*, Minneapolis: Fortress. • J. TABORY 1999, "Towards a History of the Paschal Meal," in *Passover and Easter: Origin and History to Modern Times*, ed. P. F. Bradshaw and L. A. Hoffman, Notre Dame: University of Notre Dame Press.

DENNIS E. SMITH

Mediator Figures

The term "mediator" in everyday usage refers to someone who reconciles two parties at variance with each other. In Hellenistic and Jewish Greek usage, the term *mesitēs* could represent the same sort of function, but also had a wider usage meaning "negotiator" or "intercessor/advocate" between humans or between God and humans. This wider range of connotations in Second Temple Jewish sources, such as the LXX rendering of Job 9:33 (Hebr. *môkîaḥ*) and writers such as Philo (*Mos.* 2.166; *Som.* 1.142) and Josephus (*Ant.* 7.193), is also reflected in New Testament usage (Gal. 3:19-20; 1 Tim. 2:5; Heb. 8:6; 9:15; 12:24). But in scholarly discussion of early Judaism, the term is often applied to various beings portrayed as having some special role as agents of divine purposes. That is, these figures do not typically function to reconcile God and humans or negotiate between them, but instead operate more as elect vehicles of God's revelatory, ruling, or redeeming actions.

The most interesting figures are those depicted as what we may call God's chief agent, distinguished from all of God's other servants and ascribed a distinctive status and role, and sometimes even an appearance like God's. The figure can sometimes be said to bear the divine name, or in other ways can be portrayed as a kind of heavenly vizier. In some cases, a principal angel (e.g., Michael) or a personified attribute of God (Wisdom or Word) is ascribed this sort of role. In other cases, a human worthy from the Bible such as Moses or Enoch is portrayed as exercising unique authority and exalted to a supreme position that is second only to God's. (Messiahs, which can overlap with the categories of heavenly figure, principal angel, and exalted patriarch — as, for example, in the case of Enoch in the *Similitudes of Enoch* — are another important type of divine agent, but they are treated in a separate article.) The obvious key questions are what prompted ancient Jews to attribute such a status to particular figures, and what it meant.

The proliferation of interest in such chief agents of God seems to have begun sometime in the postexilic period, and is likely related to wider speculations about God's heavenly host. In various biblical texts, God is depicted as presiding over a large body of other heavenly beings who function as God's servants (e.g., 1 Kings 22:19-22; Job 1:6), and the biblical title "LORD of hosts" reflects this notion. But this heavenly multitude remained basically anonymous until the Hellenistic period or perhaps a bit earlier. In this time there emerges a remarkable interest in the heavenly hosts, involving speculations about various ranks and orders (e.g., cherubim, seraphim, ophanim), and also the names (always theophoric, typically ending in *-el:* Michael, Gabriel, Yahoel, etc.) and functions of particular prominent angels (Olyan 1993; Mach 1992).

Within the Hebrew Bible, the earliest references to named angels with a particular prominence and role are in Daniel. Here, along with the memorable scene of God enthroned with "ten thousand times ten thousand" attending him (7:9-10), we also have specific identification of individual angels: Gabriel (Dan. 8:15-18; 9:21) and Michael, the latter described variously as "one of the chief princes" (10:13), "your prince" (10:21), and "the great prince, the protector of your people" (12:1).

In other texts as well, various named angels appear. *1 Enoch* features Michael, Gabriel, Suriel, and Uriel, a group of high-ranking angels with special responsibility (see esp. 9:1-11). In the book of Tobit, the angel Raphael is portrayed as one of a select group of seven angels who have a special standing and access to God (Tob. 12:15).

Principal Angels

The idea that God has one particular angel as chief agent may have derived in part from the references to "the angel of the LORD," found especially in Pentateuch passages (e.g., Gen. 16:7-14; 22:22-18; Exod. 14:19-20). Yet other biblical passages were also likely influential, such as Exod. 23:20-21, which refers to a figure (MT: *mal'āk;* LXX: *angelos*) to be sent by God who will be indwelt by God's name, and also Josh. 5:13-15; Ezek. 8:2-4; Dan. 7:9-14; 10:4-11. Of these latter passages, Dan. 7:9-14 was particularly significant, for it portrays a figure of human-like appearance ("one like a son of man") to whom God gives universal dominion. That is, although the passage does not explicitly picture this figure enthroned with God, he is given an incomparable status, ruling on God's behalf, functioning as God's vizier. It is possible that this human-like figure is an angelic being who acts here as the heavenly representative of the elect (Collins 2000), perhaps even the high angel Michael, who is referred to in Dan. 12:1 as "the great prince who has charge of your people." In Jewish and Christian tra-

MEDIATOR FIGURES

dition, this figure came to be identified with the Davidic messiah (e.g., *4 Ezra* 13; R. Akiba in *b. Ḥagigah* 14a; Mark 15:61-62).

Michael appears in other texts, either influenced by Daniel or independently attesting interest in this sort of figure. For example, the Qumran *War Scroll* (1QM) predicts the overthrow of "the kingdom of wickedness" and "eternal help" for the elect "by the might of the princely angel of the kingdom of Michael." At that same time, God will establish "the kingdom of Michael in the midst of the gods *(ʾēlîm),* and the realm of Israel in the midst of all flesh" (1QM 17:6-8). The mention earlier in this text of "the Prince of Light" (1QM 13:10), who has divine appointment to come to the aid of the elect in the last days, is likely another reference to Michael.

We have further mention of Michael in later texts, such as *2 Enoch,* where he is often called the "chief officer" of God (22:6; 33:10; 71:28; 72:5). He bears a similar title in recension A of the *Testament of Abraham* (e.g., 1:4; 2:2-12), and in the Greek version of *3 Baruch* (11:6); and it is probably Michael who appears in *Jos. & As.* 14:4-7, identifying himself as God's chief officer. All these titles may well derive from the description of the mysterious figure in Josh. 5:13-15 who declares himself to be "the captain of God's army."

In still other texts we have references to a figure described in a similar manner as having a special status. In the *Melchizedek Scroll* from Qumran (11Q13), there are references to a Melchizedek who functions as leader and defender of the elect in the last days. The elect are there characterized as "the men of the lot of Melchizedek," who will "restore them and proclaim liberty to them, relieving them . . . of all their iniquities" and will "exact the vengeance of God's judgments," protecting and rescuing the elect from "the hand of Belial" (11Q13 2:4-25). This same text interprets the words of Ps. 82:1-2, "*ʾElōhim* has taken his place in the council of God *(ʾEl);* in the midst of the gods *(ʾĕlōhîm)* he holds judgment," as predicting Melchizedek's eschatological activity. Remarkably, a biblical passage that originally referred to God's greatness is used here to assert Melchizedek's supremacy over all the rest of God's heavenly host. It is possible that this Melchizedek is the angel Michael of other Qumran texts.

In the *Apocalypse of Abraham,* God sends to Abraham a heavenly being named Yahoel with the order, "Through the mediation of my ineffable name, consecrate this man for me and strengthen him against his trembling" (10:3-4). This figure, whose name obviously combines YHWH and El, then refers to himself as empowered by God's "ineffable name in me" to exercise great authority, including control over the "living creatures" before God's throne and also over "Leviathan" (*Apoc. Abr.* 10:8-17; cf. 18:1-12). In light of the enormous significance of God's name in ancient Judaism, the reference to this figure as indwelt by the name surely indicates his exceptional status in the divine hierarchy. This is also reflected in his appearance in 11:1-4, his body like sapphire, his face like chrysolite, his hair like snow, his headdress like a rainbow, attired in purple garments and holding a golden staff in his hand. These visual details combine echoes of biblical epiphanic scenes such as Ezek. 1:26-28 and Dan. 7:9; 10:5-6 in order to depict a being of glorious stature.

In the *Apocalypse of Zephaniah* (originally of Jewish provenance but preserved and transmitted in Christian circles), there is yet another angelic figure, Eremiel, whose appearance is so glorious that the seer initially assumes him to be God (6:11-15). This angel's face shines like the sun, and he wears a golden sash on his breast; his feet are "like bronze melted in a fire," and he holds appointment over all the souls in "the abyss and hell" In view of his divine-like appearance, it is all the more significant that this angel forbids the seer from offering him worship and directs him to offer worship to God alone.

In *Joseph and Aseneth* (also likely of Greek-speaking Jewish origin, but preserved and edited by Christians), there is a scene where a remarkable heavenly being appears. Man-like in form, but with a face "like lightning and his eyes like sunshine," his hair "like a flame of fire," his hands and feet shooting sparks and "like iron shining forth from a fire" (14:8-10), he identifies himself as "the chief of the house of the Lord and commander of the whole host of the Most High" (14:7).

From this brief review several observations can be made. On the one hand, the identity of the principal angel varies; Michael appears more often than any other, but not consistently. On the other hand, all these texts reflect the notion that God has a particular angel who is appointed over all the others, exercising a role like that of a vizier of an Oriental monarch: God's chief agent. Also, even though the chief agent figure can be described visually with features drawn from biblical theophanies, the texts permit no confusion of this figure with God (Hurtado 1988: 22-35, 82-90). Instead, interest in such figures went hand in hand with a strong commitment to God's uniqueness and a distinction between God and all God's servants, even such glorious chief agent figures.

Personified Divine Attributes

Another interesting use of chief-agent language comes with reference to personified attributes of God, especially Wisdom and Word. The personification of Wisdom in several passages in Proverbs is no doubt the most familiar instance (Prov. 1:20-33; 3:13-18; 8:1–9:12). Dame Wisdom invites readers to learn from her, and in 8:22-31 she speaks of herself as having been created before all else and having been present at God's creation of the world, acting as God's "architect" or "master workman" (*ʾāmôn,* 8:30).

In later texts, this personification continues. In the Wisdom of Solomon, Dame Wisdom is "the fashioner of all things" (7:22), an "associate" in all God's works (8:4), the one by whom God formed humans (9:1-2), her influence extending to all things (8:1). Moreover, she is "a pure emanation of the glory of the Almighty," "a spotless mirror of the working of God and an image of his goodness" (7:25-26), sitting beside God's throne (9:4). Sirach 24 is another extended passage where Dame Wisdom declares her high status. Created "from eternity, in the beginning," she is now eternal (24:9), and her purview extends to the whole of creation (24:4-6).

Another interesting feature of these texts is the identification of Wisdom with Jewish religious life and its basis in Torah. In Proverbs, Wisdom is linked with reverence for God and obedience to his commands (1:7, 29; 2:1-6), and in Sir. 24:8 Wisdom is still more directly linked with Israel (24:8) and the Jerusalem Temple (24:10-12), this all reaching an explicit identification of Wisdom as Torah in 24:23. This is affirmed emphatically also in Baruch (3:9–4:4): "She is the book of the commandments of God" (4:1). Though not as explicit, Wisdom of Solomon still has the same outlook, connecting Wisdom with the history of Israel (esp. Wis. 6:1–12:2). Later, in rabbinic texts, the identification of Wisdom with Torah is replaced by the personification of Torah (e.g., *Midr. Ber. Rab.* 1:1, 4), which takes on much of the role of Wisdom reflected in the earlier texts.

We also have interesting instances of the personification of God's Word (*logos* in Greek). Philo of Alexandria gives the most extensive evidence. In some references, Philo's language is so vivid that it could easily be taken to indicate the belief that the Logos is an actual intermediary being, a lesser deity, through whom God conducts his relationship with the world. For example, in *QG* 2.62 Philo calls the Logos "the second god," also stating that the god in whose image Adam was created (Gen. 1:27) is actually this Logos. In *QE* 2.13 Philo appears to identify the Logos with the "angel" sent by God to lead Israel (Exod. 23:20-21), and Philo here calls the Logos "mediator" *(mesitēs).* Philo also applies a number of other honorific terms to the Logos: "firstborn" *(prōtogonon)* and elder among all the angels, "their ruler as it were," "archangel," "Name of God" (*De Confusione Linguarum* 146), and "governor and administrator of all things" (*QG* 4.110-11).

There is a certain similarity to the role of Philo's Logos in the targumic references to God's Memra *(mêmrâʾ)* and perhaps also in the rabbinic references to God's Shekinah (*šĕkînâ;* cf. Goldberg 1969). The Logos functioned to satisfy Philo's concern to affirm both God's transcendence and the reality of God's engagement with creation, and the references to God's Memra and Shekinah seem to have had a somewhat similar purpose.

Contrary to some earlier scholarly views (e.g., Ringgren 1947), however, this elaborate and vivid personification of Wisdom and Logos (and also God's Memra and Shekinah) does not comprise the formation of new divine entities ("hypostases") with independent or even semiindependent existence apart from God. Instead, in these cases the personification represents a vivid way of depicting the centrality of particular attributes or powers of God in the nature and operation of the world (Hurtado 1988: 42-50). It is a kind of poetic theological discourse, reflecting the boldness and vividness of all good poetry (and of all good theology!). The clearest indication of this is the complete absence of any evidence that any of these figures was ever the recipient of worship.

Exalted Human Heroes

Lauding biblical heroes is standard fare in postexilic Judaism. Adam, Seth, Enoch, Abraham, Jacob, and especially Moses are cited. In Sirach 44–49 a whole string of such figures is recited in praise. For the present purpose, it will suffice to review briefly references to Enoch and Moses, probably the two who figure most prominently in Second Temple Jewish texts in the role of God's chief agent (see Hurtado 1988: 51-69 for further discussion and references).

Though mentioned only briefly in Gen. 5:18-24, Enoch has a remarkable place in these texts. In *1 Enoch* 71:14-17, he is retroactively identified as the "Chosen One" and "Anointed One" who is portrayed in preceding passages in exalted terms. He surpasses all others in righteousness (46:3-4), will execute eschatological judgment upon the wicked (46:4-8; 63:11-12), was designated and chosen before creation (48:2-3, 7; 62:7-8), will receive the obeisance of all humankind (48:4-6; 62:9), and will be enthroned by God to exercise his role as vehicle of divine justice and redemption (51:3; 55:4; 61:8-9; 62:1-3; 69:26-29).

This interest in Enoch continues in later texts. In *2* (Slavonic) *Enoch* he is called by God to stand before him forever, and Enoch here seems to be transformed into an angelic being (22:5-10). In *2 Enoch* 24:1-3, God invites Enoch to sit beside him and orders that he be made privy to heavenly secrets kept from other angels. In *3* (Hebrew) *Enoch* 10–12, he is identified as Metatron (4:2-3), a powerful heavenly being referred to in other Jewish texts as well (Lieberman 1980), and who sits on a heavenly throne, is clothed in a majestic robe, wears a crown, and, astonishingly, is even titled by God "the lesser YHWH" (12:5).

It is no surprise that Moses is given similar attention. In LXX Sir. 45:1-5, God makes Moses "equal in glory to the holy ones [angels]." Although the extant Hebrew text of this verse is defective, it appears to compare Moses to *ʾĕlōhîm,* which typically refers to God but can sometimes refer to other heavenly beings (e.g., Ps. 82:1). It is therefore possible that the original sense was to liken Moses to God. This passage also says that Moses was chosen "out of all humankind" (Sir. 45:4).

In the *Testament of Moses,* the lawgiver is said to have been chosen and appointed "from the beginning of the world, to be the mediator [Lat. *arbiter*]" of God's covenant (1:14; cf. 3:12). He is also heralded as "that sacred spirit, worthy of the Lord . . . the lord of the word . . . the divine prophet throughout the earth, the most perfect teacher in the world," the "advocate" and "great messenger" whose prayers while on earth were Israel's great security (11:16-19).

The *Exagōgē,* a fragmentary play about the exodus from Egypt by the Egyptian Jewish author Ezekiel the Tragedian, includes a scene where Moses is given a scepter and crown, and instructed to sit on a throne in the heavens by a figure who may be God. Seated on this throne, Moses views the whole of creation, and a "multitude of stars" make obeisance and pass before him in ranks. The import of the text is disputed, but in view of other speculations about biblical heroes (esp. Enoch), it is plausible that Ezekiel the Tragedian either promotes or at least reflects knowledge of the idea that Moses held a uniquely exalted place in God's purposes, and that this could include his taking a role as chief agent acting on God's behalf.

The fullest witness to ancient Jewish interest in Moses as God's chief agent, however, is Philo, but we can note only a few passages as examples here. The *Vita Mosis* says that God appointed Moses "partner" in God's own possessions, and placed in Moses' hands "the whole world as a portion for [God's] heir" (*Mos.* 1.155). In another passage, Philo refers to Moses as "chief prophet and chief messenger" (*QG* 4.8).

Meaning and Function

It is reasonable to ask what all this rich and bold speculation about chief agents or mediator figures represents, and what impetus there was for it. In some earlier scholarship, it was asserted that this interest reflected a greater existential sense in the postexilic period of God as distant and less accessible, but several studies have shown that this is an error (e.g., Mach 1992). Instead, references to angels as set over various operations of nature or areas of the world were intended to depict God's power reaching all spheres and operations of creation. Over against their own earthly powerlessness and insignificance under various imperial regimes, ancient Jews portrayed their God as the ultimate monarch with a massive retinue to serve his will. In short, the projection of God's vast retinue was intended to relativize the earthly structures of authority and power under which the Jews lived as a subject people, and to assert the supremacy of their God. Studies of the depiction of God in Second Temple texts (e.g., Wicks 1915) have shown no reference to God as inaccessible or remote; in fact, quite the opposite.

Moreover, early Jewish worship and prayers in Second Temple texts reflect a rather consistent practice of addressing God directly, with no mediatorial figure invoked. It is especially significant to find this even in texts that also exhibit an interest in God's angelic hierarchy. Tobit is a ready example; despite the prominent place of Raphael (e.g., 12:12), the prayers in the book are exclusively directed to God (3:1-6, 11-15; 8:5-8; 13:1-17).

The same observation applies to personalized divine attributes and to exalted human heroes; none is a recipient of worship or petitionary prayer, and there is no basis for assuming that they emerged in early Jewish thought to help bridge the distance between humans and a remote and less accessible God. Instead, they functioned theologically, as ways of portraying God's greatness, imagining how God ordered the world, and of making other affirmations about the true significance of Israel and the sources of her traditions.

BIBLIOGRAPHY

G. H. Box 1932-1933, "The Idea of Intermediation in Jewish Theology," *JQR* 23: 1-3-19. • J. J. Collins 2000, "Powers in Heaven: God, Gods, and Angels in the Dead Sea Scrolls," in *Religion in the Dead Sea Scrolls*, ed. J. J. Collins and R. A. Kugler, Grand Rapids: Eerdmans, 9-28. • P. G. Davis 1994, "Divine Agents, Mediators, and New Testament Christology," *JTS* 45: 479-503. • A. M. Goldberg 1969, *Untersuchungen über die Vorstellung von der Schekinah in der frühen rabbinischen Literatur*, Berlin: de Gruyter. • L. W. Hurtado 1988, *One God, One Lord: Early Christian Devotion and Ancient Jewish Monotheism*, Philadelphia: Fortress. • R. Lesses 1998, *Ritual Practices to Gain Power: Angels, Incantations, and Revelation in Early Jewish Mysticism*, Harrisburg, Penn.: Trinity. • S. Lieberman 1980, "Metatron, the Meaning of His Name and His Functions," in I. Gruenwald, *Apocalyptic and Merkavah Mysticism*, Leiden: Brill, 235-41. • M. Mach 1992, *Entwicklungsstadien des jüdischen Engelglaubens in vorrabinischer Zeit*, Tübingen: Mohr-Siebeck. • G. F. Moore 1922, "Intermediaries in Jewish Theology," *HTR* 15: 41-85. • S. Olyan 1993, *A Thousand Thousands Served Him: Exegesis and the Naming of Angels in Ancient Judaism*, Tübingen: Mohr-Siebeck. • H. Ringgren 1947, *Word and Wisdom: Studies in the Hypostatization of Divine Qualities and Functions in the Ancient Near East*, Lund: Hakan Oholsson. • L. T. Stuckenbruck 2004, "'Angels' and 'God': Exploring the Limits of Early Jewish Monotheism," in *Early Jewish and Christian Monotheism*, ed. L. T. Stuckenbruck and W. E. S. North, London: Clark, 45-70. • E. E. Urbach 1987, "The Shekina — The Presence of God in the World," in idem, *The Sages: Their Concepts and Beliefs*, Cambridge: Harvard University Press, 37-65. • A. Yarbro Collins and J. J. Collins 2008, *King and Messiah as Son of God: Divine, Human, and Angelic Messianic Figures in Biblical and Related Literature*, Grand Rapids: Eerdmans.

See also: Angels; Enoch; Logos; Messianism; Metatron; Michael; Monotheism; Moses; Wisdom (Personified)

Larry W. Hurtado

Medicine and Hygiene

The Greco-Roman World

People of the Greco-Roman world, especially those inhabiting cities and towns, lived in a filthy environment. Except for a few affluent dwellings, the private residences of the multitudes (the *plebs urbana*) suffered from poor sanitary conditions. Overly crowded, damp, and improperly maintained, most also lacked running water, ventilation, and sewage disposal. The streets were no better. Despite some improvements introduced by the Romans — including public latrines (also known as *foricae*) and subterranean drainage systems *(cloacae)* that also functioned as sewers — towns and cities lacked adequate street cleaning and effective methods of discarding human and animal waste. Prohibitions against dumping excrement, corpses, and animal skins in the streets (e.g., Ulpian, *Digest* [of the *Corpus Iuris Civilis* or *Codex Justinianus*] 43.10.4-5) testify to the common habits of the day. Tossing out vessels with dung, urine, and garbage, especially during the night, was not unheard of (Juvenal, *Satirae* 3.268-77; *b. Megillah* 16a). Such unhealthy conditions facilitated the spread of diseases and resulted in life expectancy of a mere thirty to forty years for men and women, and in some places even shorter than that.

Medical inquiry and treatment emerged as people

strove to cope with illness, injuries, and death. Stretching back to ancient Mesopotamia and Egypt, medical practices blended empirical, if rudimentary, scientific knowledge with magic and religious beliefs. Despite some attempts to delineate the boundaries between these three categories (see, e.g., Ulpian's attempt in *Digest* 50.13.3), they regularly overlapped, and distinctions between them remained blurred and subjective. Healers, doctors, exorcists, peddlers of medicinal products, wandering miracle workers, as well as deities (such as Apollo, but mainly Asclepius and his entourage) with their priests and cults — men and women, slaves, and freedmen — all offered their expertise to a society scourged by illness and disease.

Building on ancient traditions, Greek and later Roman medical knowledge extended to anatomy, pharmacology, the treatment of certain types of wounds and illness, and various forms of surgery. Schools for the training of physicians functioned in Greece, Asia Minor, and Egypt, in particular Alexandria. Scholars, going back to the legendary Hippocrates who taught in Athens ca. 420 B.C.E., and other famous figures in the Roman period, such as Galen in the second century C.E., produced an extensive medical literature in different genres, from the diagnostic to the practical to the philosophical. To these one must add the paranormal material — magical bowls with incantations, charms, amulets, recipe books of spells and enchantments — all of which functioned seamlessly, and frequently simultaneously, with the more "scientific" practices. Hospitals and accessible medical care for the general public, known only on a small scale in the Roman world, mainly in army camps of the legions and in sanctuaries of the healing gods, developed gradually and spread widely with the rise of Christianity.

Early Judaism

Jews were part and parcel of this illness-infused Mediterranean world. Many of the purity laws — found already in the Pentateuch and systemized in various Second Temple texts and in later, rabbinic literature — may be seen as an effort to cope with the polluted environment in which people lived. Decrees to separate people with skin diseases (e.g., Leviticus 13–14), to wash hands before meals (Mark 7:1-4; Luke 11:37-38; *b. Šabbat* 14b) and after bowel movements (*m. Yoma* 3:2; Josephus, *J.W.* 2.149), or to withdraw from animal corpses (Lev. 5:2), although presented in religious terminology, also aimed to promote personal and communal hygiene as well as sanitation. But the common view that Jews widely followed these directives, and thus were less vulnerable to the harsh conditions of their insalubrious environment, has yet to be proven, at least with regard to the ancient world. Rather, Jewish sources from Roman Palestine depict the same urban landscape typical of other places in the Mediterranean world, including filthy alleys and habitual encounters with foul smells and remnants of cadavers, manure, and musty puddles (e.g., *y. Berakot* 3 [6d]; *b. Berakot* 24b). Priests in the Jerusalem Temple handling and consuming unrefrigerated meat on a daily basis were susceptible to harsh intestinal illnesses (*m. Šeqal.* 5:1-2), and the Temple itself was swamped with flies and bad odors (*m. 'Abot* 5:5).

Doctors and medicine in all its varieties were regular components of Jewish life throughout antiquity. Many Jewish texts betray a tension between the belief that ultimate cure lay only in the powers of the God of Israel, articulated in numerous biblical statements like "I am the LORD who heals you" (Exod. 15:26), or in the rabbinic proclamation "the best of the physicians [is destined] to hell" (*m. Qidd.* 4:14), and the daily experience of being treated by these very same caregivers. But such theological uncertainties did not preclude Jews from becoming doctors or prevent the populace from seeking their help. Chapter 38 in the book of Sirach, along with testifying that Jews in the second century B.C.E. already held the medical vocation in high esteem, also presents the common formula that bridged the conflict between faith in God and the need for human doctors: "Honor physicians for their services, for the Lord created them; for their gifts of healing come from the Most High" (Sir. 38:1-2). The rabbis, despite their unease with doctors, nevertheless depict them as necessary citizens of the ideal city (*b. Sanhedrin* 17b).

Ancient sources frequently refer to Jewish doctors and healers, designating them either by Hebr. *rōfê'*, Aram. *'āsyâ'*, or the common Gr. *iatros*. Of the miracle-healer type, the traditions about Jesus offer clear examples. They present Jesus as curing Peter's mother of her fever (Mark 1:29-31 and pars.), restoring the health of a paralytic, an invalid, the blind, and the mute (Mark 2:1-12; John 5:20; 9:1-7; Matt. 9:32-33), treating a leper (Mark 1:40-45) and a woman suffering from hemorrhages (Matt. 9:20-22), casting out evil spirits and demons (e.g., Mark 1:34), and even raising a few people from the dead (e.g., Mark 5:21-24, 35-43 and pars.; Luke 7:11-17).

More "scientific" examples are also numerous. The first-century-C.E. Latin encyclopedist Celsus ascribes a formula for a lotion that treats fractured skulls to a certain *Iudaeus* (*De Medicina* 5.19.11). Josephus reports of doctors attending King Herod's maladies (Josephus, *Ant.* 15.246), and he himself benefited from a physician's care after falling off a horse in Galilee and breaking his wrist (*Vita* 404). Rabbinic literature knows a few doctors by name, such as Tuvya, who witnessed the new moon and testified about it before the Temple court (*m. Roš Haš.* 1:7), or Teodoros, a second-century-C.E. doctor who advised the rabbis on medical matters, and on one occasion is even presented with a cohort of doctors, probably students, following him (*t. Ohol.* 4:2). A third-century rabbi, the Persian Mar Shemuel, was himself a well-known physician versed in astronomy and astrology (*b. Berakot* 58b), and the Talmud conveys many of his prescriptions and treatments. The Christian doctor Marcellus Empiricus, a Gallic high official in the court of Theodosius I, reported that the Jewish Patriarch Gamaliel (probably the VI) developed a special medicine for the spleen (*De Medicamentis* 23.77 [*Corpus Medicorum Latinarum* 5, ed. Niedermann and Liechtenhan, p. 408]), and the sixth-century Neoplatonic philosopher Damascius, the last head of the academy in Athens, knew of a Jewish doctor by the name of Domnus (*Vita Isidori Reliquiae*, ed. Zintzen, frg. 335).

Jewish literature from the Greco-Roman period, including Philo and Josephus, but most of all rabbinic literature, is a treasure trove of medical information. Although not organized in any systematic way, these texts demonstrate acute knowledge of human and animal anatomy, medicinal plants and herbs, as well as treatment procedures of the time, especially those that emerged from the Hippocratic School in Alexandria. Books of remedies and medicine were known to Jews already in the early days of the Second Temple (*Jub.* 10:13, and see *Sefer Noah* in *Beit Ha-Midrash*, vol. 3, ed. Jellinek, pp. 155-60), and they are also mentioned in the Talmud (e.g., *b. Berakot* 10b). The most comprehensive medical document that survived from ancient Jewish circles is the text known as *Sefer Refuot (Book of Remedies)*, attributed to the mysterious, perhaps legendary figure "Asaph the Jew." Written in biblical Hebrew, the book surveys the various branches of medicine and includes a discussion of 123 medicinal plants. The author also formulated a Jewish oath for doctors, which closely resembles the famous Hippocratic pledge. Unfortunately, the text does not provide clear evidence as to its dating or place of origin.

Magical practices dealing with illness and disease were also very popular among ancient Jews. Beyond the evidence relating to the figure of Jesus (discussed above), one needs only to survey the hundreds of incantations — inscribed on bowls, incised on metal sheets, or written as amulets — that were found in Jewish centers in Babylonia and Palestine, or the hundreds of pages devoted to magical spells and recipes that were uncovered in the Cairo Geniza, to realize that Jews did not refrain from magic. Second Temple Jewish literature frequently alludes to magical remedies (e.g., 4Q560; *T. Job* 47; Ps.-Philo, *Bib. Ant.* 25:12), as do the rabbis, although some of them voice their objection to certain methods (e.g., *m. Šabb.* 6:10; similar to their dissatisfaction with a total reliance on medicine).

BIBLIOGRAPHY

H. AVALOS 1995, *Illness and Health Care in the Ancient Near East*, Atlanta: Scholars Press. • H. AVALOS 1999, *Health Care and the Rise of Christianity*, Peabody, Mass.: Hendrickson. • H. C. KEE 1986, *Medicine, Miracle, and Magic in the New Testament*, Cambridge: Cambridge University Press. • J. PREUSS 1978, *Biblical and Talmudic Medicine*, trans. F. Rosner, New York: Sanhedrin. • L. P. HOGAN 1992, *Healing in the Second Temple Period*, Göttingen: Vandenhoeck & Ruprecht. • I. AND W. JACOB, EDS. 1993, *The Healing Past: Pharmaceuticals in the Biblical and Rabbinic World*, Leiden: Brill. • S. S. KOTTEK 1994, *Medicine and Hygiene in the Works of Flavius Josephus*, Leiden: Brill. • S. KOTTEK ET AL., EDS. 2000, *From Athens to Jerusalem: Medicine in Hellenized Jewish Lore and in Early Christian Literature*, Rotterdam: Erasmus. • O. RIMON, ED. 1996, *Illness and Healing in Ancient Times*, Haifa: Hecht Museum. • F. ROSNER 2000, *Encyclopedia of Medicine in the Bible and the Talmud*, Jerusalem: Jason Aronson. • W. HAASE, ED. 1994-1996, *Aufstieg und Niedergang der römischen Welt (ANRW)* II.37, vols. 1-3, *Wissenschaften (Medizin und Biologie)*, Berlin and New York: de Gruyter.

See also: Demons and Exorcism; Divination and Magic; Healing; Magic Bowls and Incantations; Sickness and Disease

YARON Z. ELIAV

Melchizedek

Melchizedek is an enigmatic priestly figure who appears only twice in the Hebrew Bible, in Gen. 14:18 and Ps. 110:4. In Gen. 14:18-20 Melchizedek is introduced as the king of Salem and the priest of God Most High. He brings out bread and wine to Abraham after the defeat of the eastern kings, blesses him, and receives from the patriarch a tithe of all his possessions. The designation of Melchizedek as priest of the Most High points to a Canaanite origin for this character. His name means "my king is Zedek" and may derive from the name of a Canaanite deity (Zedek). Yet later traditions often interpret Melchizedek's name as "king of righteousness." In Ps. 110:4 Melchizedek is mentioned in the context of the enthronement of a new king. Scholars believe that here it represents a title rather than a personal name. The psalm links the motifs of priesthood and kingship, envisioning Melchizedek as an archetype of royal priesthood.

Due to the scarcity of information about Melchizedek in biblical tradition and his enigmatic priestly identity, his story became a locus of extensive exegetical elaborations in Jewish and Christian literature. In the *Melchizedek Scroll* from Qumran (first or second century B.C.E.), Melchizedek is portrayed as a celestial being, one of the *ʾĕlōhîm*, who will be the eschatological judge on the Day of Atonement at the end of the tenth jubilee. The text describes him as a liberator of the righteous and a heavenly adversary of Belial and the spirits of his lot.

In contrast to 11QMelchizedek, neither Philo (*De Abrahamo* 253; *De Congressu* 99; *Leg. Alleg.* 3.79-82) nor Josephus (*J.W.* 6.438; *Ant.* 1.179-81) provides any hints about the heavenly status of Melchizedek but instead view him as a historical person, "a king peaceable and worthy of his priesthood."

In the late Second Temple period, Melchizedek's priesthood became attractive to some Jewish groups who sought to use his status as a mysterious sacerdotal figure for legitimating their priestly claims. Thus 2 (Slavonic) *Enoch*, a Jewish pseudepigraphon composed in the first century C.E., attempts to incorporate the enigmatic royal priest into the framework of a priestly Noachic tradition by transferring to him some priestly features of Noah and, more specifically, the sacerdotal characteristics of Noah's miraculous birth. Enochic authors utilize Melchizedek's priestly credentials in order to insert him into the priestly genealogy of Enoch's descendants. The ancient priestly status of Melchizedek suits well the anti-Mosaic agenda of the Enochic authors, since he held his office long before Moses received sacerdotal prescriptions on Mt. Sinai. In the Nag Hammadi tractate *Melchizedek* (NHC IX,1), a Christian work that contains originally pre-Christian Melchizedek speculation overlaid with christological reinterpretation, the name Melchizedek is again incorporated into the list of Noah's priestly descendants.

Later rabbinic tradition was likely aware of these early Enochic-Noachic adaptations of Melchizedek. They try to reinsert him into the "official" sacerdotal line by identifying him with Noah's son Shem. Theological deliberations about Shem-Melchizedek are attested in targumic, talmudic, and midrashic materials (e.g., *Tg. Ps.-J.* and *Tg. Neof.* on Gen. 14:18; *b. Nedarim* 32b; *Gen. Rab.* 43:1; 44:7; *'Abot de Rabbi Nathan* 2; *Pirqe Rabbi Eliezer* 7; 27). These passages seek to bolster the priestly antecedents of Shem-Melchizedek by transferring his priestly line to Abraham. The texts reinterpret Gen. 14:19-20 by claming that the priesthood was taken from Shem-Melchizedek and given to Abraham because the former gave precedence in his blessing to Abraham over God. The tradition also reinterprets Ps. 110:4 by translating the verse, "You [Abraham] are a priest forever because of the words of Melchizedek." Thus *b. Nedarim* 32b says of Shem-Melchizedek, "He was a priest, but not his seed."

The New Testament Epistle to the Hebrews portrays Melchizedek as a priest without parents or lineage, using him to create a heavenly and eternal priesthood to which Christ belongs. Similar to *2 Enoch,* the epistle co-opts Melchizedek to form an alternative priestly trajectory more ancient than and superior to the one stemming from Moses, Aaron, and Levi. Yet even though the comparison between Christ and Melchizedek is clear in the epistle, the precise nature of that comparison and the status it assigns to Melchizedek himself remain obscure (Attridge 1989). The author appears to be deliberately noncommittal about the enigmatic priest, perhaps because he was aware of the extensive scope of Melchizedek's nonbiblical sacerdotal portfolio.

BIBLIOGRAPHY

H. W. ATTRIDGE 1989, *The Epistle to the Hebrews,* Philadelphia: Fortress. • M. DELCOR 1971, "Melchizedek from Genesis to the Qumran texts and the Epistle to the Hebrews," *JSJ* 2: 115-35. • C. GIANOTTO 1984, *Melchizedek e la sua tipologia: Tradizioni giudiche, cristiane e gnostiche* (sec II a.C.–sec.III d.C), Brescia: Paideia. • F. HORTON 1976, *The Melchizedek Tradition: A Critical Examination of the Sources to the Fifth Century A.D. and in the Epistle to the Hebrews,* Cambridge: Cambridge University. • P. KOBELSKI 1981, *Melchizedek and Melchireša',* Washington, D.C.: Catholic Biblical Association of America. • E. F. MASON 2008, *"You Are a Priest Forever": Second Temple Jewish Messianism and the Priestly Christology of the Epistle to the Hebrews,* Leiden: Brill.

See also: Hebrews, Epistle to the; Melchizedek Scroll (11Q13)

ANDREI A. ORLOV

Melchizedek Scroll (11Q13)

The *Melchizedek Scroll* (11Q13) is a fragmentary text from Cave 11 near Qumran. It features a heavenly figure named Melchizedek who executes divine judgment and deliverance in the context of an eschatological jubilee and Day of Atonement.

Disposition of the Fragments

Discovered in 1956, the *Melchizedek Scroll* consists of between ten and fourteen parchment fragments. Scholarly assessments of how to count and configure these fragments vary, but the consensus is that portions of three columns are extant. Of these, col. 1 is represented by only a few fortuitously placed letters. Traces of at least three letters from a supralinear notation in col. 1 remain in the right margin of col. 2 between its lines 11 and 12. This notation then continues vertically down the margin to at least line 14 of col. 2. Significantly more text of col. 3 is extant; the destruction of Belial is mentioned, but little else can be deduced about its contents. Only materials from the beginning of each line (ranging from isolated letters to several words) are preserved intact, and it is unclear whether several of the remaining fragments of the manuscript preserve portions of col. 3 or other columns. Column 2 also suffers from multiple lacunae and spans numerous fragments, yet significantly more can be said about its contents. Portions of twenty-five lines remain; none are complete, but several are missing only a few words and are easily reconstructed. Also, portions of all four margins have survived. The DJD editors estimate that the column measured 12.5 cm. high and 14 cm. wide, averaging seventy-three letter spaces per line (García Martínez et al. 1998).

Date

The *editio princeps* of 11Q13 was published by Adam S. van der Woude in 1965; he argued that the hand was Herodian and thus the manuscript should be dated to the first half of the first century C.E. Józef Milik (1972), also appealing to paleography, argued instead for a first-century-B.C.E. date, specifically 75 to 50 B.C.E. Milik further asserted that the text was part of a longer "Pesher on the Periods" (concluding 4Q180-181) written by the Teacher of Righteousness himself and thus must be dated ca. 120 B.C.E., but few scholars have concurred. Similarly, Émile Puech (1987) proposed the second half of the second century B.C.E. as the date of composition, arguing that it was penned as a polemic against Hasmonean appropriation of Melchizedek's title "priest of God Most High."

Genre

The genre of the *Melchizedek Scroll* has been variously defined as midrash or pesher. Jean Carmignac (1970) labeled the text a "thematic pesher" because it employs a number of biblical quotations while addressing a single subject, the deliverance of God's people via Melchizedek from Belial. Quotations of Scripture are numerous; in col. 2 alone, three clusters of quotations are evident, each typically concluding with a pesher on its first cited text (lines 2-9: Lev. 25:13; Deut. 15:2; lines 10-14: Pss. 7:8-9; 82:1; 82:2; lines 15-25: Isa. 52:7; Dan. 9:25; Lev. 25:9). Numerous scholars have also detected ele-

MELCHIZEDEK SCROLL (11Q13)

ments of Isa. 61:1-3 in the column, but Paul Kobelski (1981) notes that these verses are never cited with introductory formulas and instead appear as allusions.

The Identity and Role of Melchizedek

The text's presentation of Melchizedek is its most striking feature. The overwhelming scholarly consensus is that the words *mlky ṣdq* (always written separately) are to be understood as the name Melchizedek. Others, though, have interpreted the phrase as another name for the Davidic messiah (Rainbow 1997); a title for an eschatological figure — a "king of righteousness" — with no connection at all to the biblical Melchizedek (Cockerill 1991); or an honorific for God (Manzi 1997).

Melchizedek is mentioned in the Hebrew Bible only in Gen. 14:18-20 and Ps. 110:4. Most Second Temple period discussions of the figure draw only on Genesis 14 and offer relatively mild rewritings (or for Philo, the expected allegorizations) of the Canaanite priest-king's encounter with Abram (1QapGen 22:12-17; Pseudo-Eupolemus, frg. 1 [Eusebius, *Praep. Evang.* 9.17.5-6]; Josephus, *J.W.* 6.438; *Ant.* 1.179-81; Philo, *Abr.* 235; *Congr.* 99; *Leg.* 3.79-82; cf. *Jub.* 13:25-27, where the encounter is retold but Melchizedek's name has been lost, most likely through haplography in the Hebrew textual tradition). In contrast to this, Melchizedek is presented in various Dead Sea Scrolls as an angelic figure, but no exegesis grounding this heavenly understanding of the figure in the biblical discussion is extant. The best scholarly explanation for this connection is that the Qumran community apparently read Ps. 110:4 as investing Melchizedek with an eternal priesthood, in contrast to its more common interpretation as an oath granting a priesthood like that of Melchizedek to a Davidic king (Flusser 1966; VanderKam 2000).

The relevant Qumran texts discussing Melchizedek are fragmentary, but the heavy reconstructions involved are consensus positions in most cases. In the *Songs of the Sabbath Sacrifice,* Melchizedek is an angelic "priest in the assembly of God" (4Q401 frg. 11 line 3) who serves in the heavenly sanctuary. This reference appears in the context of a song describing an eschatological war in heaven, and Melchizedek may be mentioned later in 4Q401 22 3 in the context of a priestly installation ceremony (Davila 2000). Melchizedek is thought to be correlated in 4Q544 frg. 3 col. iv line 3 with Michael and the Prince of Light (in contrast to Belial, the Prince of Darkness, and Melchiresha' in 4Q544 2 iii 13) but only Melchiresha' is preserved.

The conception of Melchizedek in these texts corresponds with that of 11Q13, where Melchizedek is *'lwhym* in the service of *'l*. This is conveyed in the author's recasting of biblical quotations in which God clearly is *'lwhym* in the original context (Ps. 82:1 in line 10 [first occurrence only]; Isa. 52:7 in lines 16, 23, and 24). The author consistently refers to God as *'l* in his composition and preserves that identification in his interpretation of biblical quotations. Also, in two quoted passages in which the MT preserves the Tetragrammaton (Deut. 15:2 in line 4; Ps. 7:9 in line 11), the citation in 11Q13 instead reads *'l*. The author may be drawing on alternate textual traditions rather than adapting the quotations personally, since he does allow other inconsistencies to remain; unfortunately, neither cited text is extant in Qumran biblical manuscripts. Other figures in the divine court are identified as *'ly hṣdq* (line 14, perhaps influenced by Isa. 61:3) or *'lwhym* (line 10, quoting Ps. 82:1). Overall this careful use of terminology implies that Melchizedek as *'lwhym* is a heavenly figure, consistent with the broader use of the term in poetic texts in the Hebrew Bible.

This interpretation is supported by the responsibilities afforded Melchizedek in col. 2. The extant columns likely are from the latter part of the manuscript, since col. 2 addresses events of a tenth, climactic jubilee period. The author understands history as consisting of ten jubilee units concluding with an eschatological Day of Atonement (line 7). In lines 2-9, Melchizedek acts to deliver the "captives" (line 4; translations from the DJD edition), presumably the same persons as "the inheritance of Melchizedek" (line 5); he proclaims liberty to them and frees them "from the debt of all their iniquities" (line 6). This last phrase has cultic overtones, and the next line mentions the Day of Atonement. Melchizedek appears to be the agent executing God's pronouncement (lines 3-4). Melchizedek announces liberty in the first week of the tenth jubilee (line 6), but it is unclear if liberation actually occurs at that time or if this is a proleptic announcement of liberation that occurs in conjunction with the eschatological Day of Atonement at the end of the tenth jubilee (line 8). This Day of Atonement appears to be the "year of grace of Melchizedek" (line 9). Melchizedek is the active figure thus far in the passage; since he is presented as a priest in Genesis 14, Ps. 110:4, and the *Songs of the Sabbath Sacrifice,* presumably the author of 11Q13 envisions him as the high priest conducting this eschatological atonement. Line 9 also speaks "of the administration of justice," thus introducing the theme of judgment. The extant text of line 8 implies that the righteous benefit from this judgment.

The mention of judgment smoothes the transition to the quotations of Ps. 82:1, Ps. 7:8-9, and Ps. 82:2 in lines 10-11. Here the emphasis clearly is on God's judgment of the wicked (with overtones of theodicy in the Ps. 82:2 quotation), administered by Melchizedek with the aid of other members of the heavenly court against Belial and those of his lot. Deliverance is again stressed in lines 15-25. The major text under consideration is Isa. 52:7, where a messenger announces peace and salvation and speaks of the kingship of the *'lwhym* of Zion. The messenger is identified with the prince anointed by the Spirit from Dan. 9:25; perhaps the identity of this messenger was further clarified in lines 21-22, but few words remain there. Perhaps also the messenger was correlated with the figure who blows the horn (presumably to announce the Day of Atonement, as in Lev. 25:9) in line 25, but the subsequent text has not survived. Melchizedek seems to have a role in proclamation in the early lines of the column, leading some scholars to identify him as the messenger (others propose the Teacher of Righteousness, the eschatological Prophet expected in other Dead Sea Scrolls texts, or the Davidic messiah). Presumably, though, the messenger is not Melchizedek, because he likely is the aforementioned *'lwhym* in lines 24-25 whom the messenger announces.

Relevance to the Epistle to the Hebrews

Beyond its significance for discussions of eschatology and ideas about Melchizedek in the Dead Sea Scrolls, 11Q13 has fueled much debate about the use of Melchizedek in the New Testament book of Hebrews, in which Jesus is described as a heavenly high priest. Early discoveries of Qumran texts that discuss a messianic priest sparked numerous theories about connections between the Scrolls community and either the author or recipients of Hebrews, but sober reassessments in the early 1960s did much to quell such enthusiasm. In his initial publication of 11Q13, van der Woude (1965) asserted the interpretation of Melchizedek as a heavenly figure in 11Q13; the following year in an article coauthored with Marinus de Jonge (1966) he proposed that the Scrolls and Hebrews had affinities in their presentations of Melchizedek. Most scholars have been reticent about the latter proposal, preferring to admit only that both the Qumran texts and Hebrews exhibit speculations about Melchizedek that go beyond those present in the Hebrew Bible. In recent years, though, several scholars have called for a reconsideration of potential conceptual ties between these texts.

BIBLIOGRAPHY

J. CARMIGNAC 1970, "Le document de Qumrân sur Melkisédeq," *RevQ* 7:343-78. • G. L. COCKERILL 1991, "Melchizedek or 'King of Righteousness,'" *EvQ* 63: 305-12. • J. R. DAVILA 2000, *Liturgical Works,* Eerdmans Commentaries on the Dead Sea Scrolls, Grand Rapids: Eerdmans. • J. A. FITZMYER 1967, "Further Light on Melchizedek from Qumran Cave 11," *JBL* 86: 25-41. • D. FLUSSER 1966, "Melchizedek and the Son of Man," *Christian News from Israel,* 23-29. • F. GARCÍA MARTÍNEZ, E. J. C. TIGCHELAAR, AND A. S. VAN DER WOUDE 1998, *Qumran Cave 11.II: 11Q2-18, 11Q20-30,* DJD 23, Oxford: Clarendon, 221-41. • F. L. HORTON 1976, *The Melchizedek Tradition: A Critical Examination of the Sources to the Fifth Century* A.D. *and in the Epistle to the Hebrews,* Cambridge: Cambridge University Press. • M. DE JONGE AND A. S. VAN DER WOUDE 1966, "11Q Melchizedek and the New Testament," *NTS* 12: 301-26. • P. J. KOBELSKI 1981, *Melchizedek and Melchireša',* Washington: Catholic Biblical Association of America. • F. MANZI 1997, *Melchisedek e l'angelologia nell'Epistola agli Ebrei e a Qumran,* Rome: Editrice Pontifico Instituto Biblico. • E. F. MASON 2008, *"You Are a Priest Forever": Second Temple Jewish Messianism and the Priestly Christology of the Epistle to the Hebrews,* Leiden: Brill. • J. T. MILIK 1972, "*Milkî-sedeq* et *Milkî-reša'* dans les anciens écrits juifs et chrétiens," *JJS* 23: 95-144. • C. A. NEWSOM 1997, *"Shirot 'Olat Hashabbat,"* in *Qumran Cave 4.VI: Poetical and Liturgical Texts, Part 1,* DJD 11, Oxford: Clarendon, 173-401. • É. PUECH 1987, "Notes sur le manuscrit de XIQMelkîsédeq," *RevQ* 12: 483-513. • P. RAINBOW 1997, "Melchizedek as a Messiah at Qumran," *BBR* 7: 179-94. • J. C. VANDERKAM 2000, "Sabbatical Chronologies in the Dead Sea Scrolls," in *The Dead Sea Scrolls in Their Historical Context,* ed. T. H. Lim, Edinburgh: Clark, 159-78. • A. S. VAN DER WOUDE 1965, "Melchisedek als himmlische Erlösergestalt in den neugefundenen eschatologischen Midraschim aus Qumran Höhle XI," *OTS* 14: 354-73.

See also: Hebrews, Epistle to the; Melchizedek

ERIC F. MASON

Menander, Sentences of the Syriac

The Syriac collection of sentences attributed pseudonymously to the Attic playwright Menander (ca. 340-290 B.C.E.) is an anthology of gnomic wisdom sayings written by an early Jewish or Christian author of the second century C.E. Although few of the work's sayings are distinctively Jewish and none of them is overtly Christian, many of them do have parallels in several early Jewish sapiential materials.

Manuscripts

The work is found in two manuscripts located at the British Library. The larger collection, Or. Add. 14.658, fols. 163v.-167v., was published in 1862 by J. P. N. Land and dates to approximately the seventh century C.E., while the smaller collection, Or. Add. 14.614, fols. 116v.-117v., thought to be based on a different recension of the text, was published by E. Sachau in 1870 and dates to the eighth or ninth century C.E.

The only publications of the Syriac texts are those of Land in1862 (a rather faulty transcription corrected by Wright in 1863 and by Land in his second volume in 1868) and Sachau in 1870. In 1912, F. Schulthess published the first German translation of the text and was able to improve on the prior work on the text through the use of a photographic reproduction of the manuscript. In 1952, J.-P. Audet did the same during the course of his translation into French.

Original Language and Date

The dating of the text is problematic. The difficulty is not so much the Syriac as the antiquity of the original text, which was probably in Greek. There are, however, indications in the text which could give parameters within which the original may be situated. Lines 164r.I.20, which refers to the profession of a gladiator, and 166r.II.15, which refers to the punishment of crucifixion for theft, seem to place the text squarely in the Roman era. Roman law, then, may offer both a *terminus ad quem* and a *terminus post quem* for the text. While some restrictions predate a general prohibition, it was in 325 C.E. that Constantine enacted the first such measure against gladiatorial contests. Lines 165r.I.27-29 presuppose the illegality of killing a slave, which would postdate the law enacted by Hadrian and strengthened by Antoninus Pius. Hence, it would appear reasonable to date the underlying text from the mid- to late-second century C.E.

Provenance

There does not seem to be enough evidence in the work to establish its provenance. Audet suggested Egypt, and the manuscripts were indeed purchased there in the nineteenth century from the monastery of St. Mary Deipara. Nonetheless, a good portion of that collection was brought there from elsewhere, so the question of place of origin remains open.

Structure

It is equally difficult to try to distinguish any clear structure to the work. There are several places in which groups of sayings are thematic, but most scholars do not find any systematic approach to the text. Baumstark suggested that the *Sentences* followed the course of a human life (Baumstark 1922: 488). Certainly, the framing of "begetting children" (163v.II.14) at the beginning and the theme of death at the end of the text merit notice. Yet these passages are not precise. For example, although the advice concerning respect for the words of parents in lines 163v.II.33-35 would fit a section on childhood early in the text, they could also be taken as obedience in later life to the teachings of one's parents. The admonishment against dishonoring parents in 163v.II.35-36 could also refer to dishonoring their memory in later life.

Jewish or Christian Authorship

While the text claims to have been written by Menander, Land and Baumstark appear to be the only scholars to consider this claim plausible. Based on the dating and the closest parallels to the text, it appears likely that the author comes from a Jewish or Christian background. Given that there are no overtly Christian allusions in the text, it is generally presumed that the author was Jewish, although the reference to Homer in 164r.II.34–164v.I.14 and the mention of the plural "gods" in lines 166r.I.13 and 15 has led some scholars to be reticent to place the text into a strictly Jewish context. Audet suggested that the author is not a Jew but a "God-fearing Gentile" (Audet 1952: 80). Nonetheless, the affinity between the Sentences and early Jewish writings, particularly wisdom writings, would seem to justify the opinion of Baarda that "Syriac Menander should be included among the Pseudepigrapha until there is decisive proof that it ought to be dealt with under another heading" (Baarda 1985: 589).

The Sentences have parallels in biblical materials, particularly Proverbs and also Qoheleth; in apocryphal Jewish works, particularly Ben Sira; and in early Jewish Pseudepigrapha, particularly Pseudo-Phocylides. The negative form of the so-called Golden Rule most closely parallels its form in the Babylonian Talmud (*b. Šabbat* 31a).

BIBLIOGRAPHY

J.-P. AUDET 1952, "La sagesse de Ménandre l'Égyptien," *RB* 59: 55-81. • T. BAARDA 1985, "The Sentences of the Syriac Menander," *OTP* 2: 583-606. • A. BAUMSTARK 1922, *Geschichte der syrischen Literatur,* Bonn: Marcus and Webers Verlag. • W. FRANKENBERG 1895, "Die Schrift des Menander (Land, *Anec. Syr.* I, 64ff.) ein Produkt der jüdischen Spruchweisheit," *ZAW* 15: 226-77. • A. KIRK 1997, "The Composed Life of the *Syriac Menander,*" *SR* 26: 169-83. • J. P. N. LAND 1862-1868, *Anecdota Syriaca,* 2 vols., Leiden: Brill. • E. SACHAU 1870, *Inedita Syriaca,* Vienna: Verlag der Buchhandlung des Waisenhauses in Halle. • F. SCHULTHESS 1912, "Die Sprüche des Menanders," *ZAW* 32: 199-224. • W. WRIGHT 1863, "Anecdota Syriaca," *The Journal of Sacred Literature and Biblical Record* 3: 115-130.

DAVID G. MONACO

Merkabah → Hekhalot Literature; Mysticism

Mesopotamia, Media, and Babylonia

According to 2 Kings 17 the inhabitants of the Northern Kingdom of Israel were taken captive to Mesopotamia about 720 B.C.E. Actually, only a small portion of the population was taken to Mesopotamia, and it is not clear that they retained their identity. More than a century later several thousand Judeans were taken to Babylonia in 597 B.C.E. and then, two decades later, when Jerusalem fell in 587/586. Those taken to Babylonia settled down, built up their communities, and became integrated into the society, as is indicated by personal names in such sources as the Murashu documents. The result was a community with two centers, one in Palestine and one in Mesopotamia. The exact size of the community in Babylon is difficult to determine, though judging from the situation in later centuries under the Parthians and Sassanians, it was a large and thriving one. If so, only a small part of this community returned to Palestine in the early Persian period.

Jews under Persian and Parthian Rule

During the Second Temple period the Jews in Mesopotamia were under Parthian rule much of the time. There is now some evidence about the Jews who settled in the region. This includes three tablets from the early Persian period (Joannès-Lemaire 1999). One has twelve Hebrew names and claims to have been written in the "city of Judah" *(uru ia-a-hu-du)* about 498 B.C.E. This does not appear to be Jerusalem but a place in Babylonia, though several sites in Mesopotamia are known to have been named for the geographical origins of the exiles who lived there. We now apparently have about ninety further texts in a private collection that relate to exiled Jews in the sixth century (Pearce 2006). The tablets range in date from Nebuchadnezzar (year 33 = ca. 572 B.C.E.) to Xerxes (year 13 = ca. 473 B.C.E.). They also contain references to the "city of Judah" or "city of the Jews." Some sixty names contain a form of YHWH. The Jewish settlers were apparently engaged mainly in agricultural activities.

The Murashu archive from Nippur, with tablets ranging from ca. 454-404 B.C.E., is another source that seems to mention Jews in Mesopotamia (Stolper 1985). The Murashu house was a business and financial establishment that made loans and managed estates for absentee landlords. It employed a number of servants and agents, some of whom seem to have been Jewish, judging from the form of their names. Several of the names have a form of YHWH, which is a good indication that they were Jewish. Genealogical relations signify, how-

MESOPOTAMIA, MEDIA, AND BABYLONIA

ever, that Jews did not necessarily take "Jewish" names, and there may be many more named individuals who were Jews than it is possible to recognize now.

As far as we can tell from the few individuals with Yahwistic names, Jews were well integrated into the society in which they lived. They do not appear to have inhabited only a "Jewish quarter" but had settled in various villages in the Nippur area. As far as occupations are concerned, the Jews were small landholders and lower-rank officials. Nothing clearly distinguishes them from other members of the Babylonian society in which they seem to have functioned comfortably. This general satisfaction with the situation, if correctly interpreted, is no doubt why few felt the need to return to the homeland of their ancestors.

Jews in the Hellenistic and Roman Periods

Occasional References to Jews

We have little information on the Jews in Mesopotamia through most of the Second Temple period. We have occasional references to the Jews "on the other side of the Euphrates" in sources from the Hellenistic and early Roman eras. According to Philo of Alexandria, many Jews lived beyond the Euphrates, in Babylon and other satrapies, and every year they sent a great deal of gold and silver in Temple dues to Jerusalem (*Legatio ad Gaium* 216; 282). Philo makes no specific reference to the "ten tribes," but for others these tribes still existed in their own right, as well as Jewish communities in Mesopotamia. Josephus also claims that at the time of the siege of Jerusalem by the Romans, some expected that their "fellow countrymen beyond the Euphrates" would come to join them (*J.W.* 1; Preface 2 §5; cf. 6.343). In *Ant.* 11.133 he refers to the "ten tribes beyond the Euphrates," with two tribes in Asia and Europe. *4 Ezra* 13:39-47 prophesies the return to Zion of the "ten tribes" taken into captivity beyond the Euphrates.

We have other occasional references. Josephus also tells us about a Jew named Zamaris who came from Babylonia leading a band of 500 mounted archers, whom Herod was able to persuade to settle in the Trachonitis (*Ant.* 17.23-31). Perhaps one of the most curious episodes relates to the Jews in the cities of Nearda and Nisibis, where the half-shekel Temple tax was collected from the region (Josephus, *Ant.* 18.310-79). Two Jewish brothers apparently established an independent kingdom in the region for about fifteen years in the early first century C.E., though naturally it could not last.

The Royal House of Adiabene

Josephus reports that in the first century C.E. the royal house of Adiabene in Mesopotamia was converted to Judaism (*Ant.* 20.17-53), apparently by Jewish merchants. We have no information on whether Jews settled in his kingdom. In the mid-40s C.E. a famine arose over a large area of the eastern Mediterranean. Helena, the queen mother of Adiabene and a convert to Judaism, was in Jerusalem at the time and spent a considerable sum in importing grain from Egypt and figs from Cyprus to distribute to the needy (*Ant.* 20.49-53). In addition, her son Izates, king of Adiabene and a convert as well, sent money to the leaders of Jerusalem to help with the famine.

Jewish Uprising in Mesopotamia in 116 C.E.

Jews are mentioned in passing in reference to Trajan's invasion of Armenia and Mesopotamia in 114-117 C.E. Jewish revolts had broken out in Cyrenaica, Egypt, and Mesopotamia during the years 115-117 C.E. The revolt in Mesopotamia seems to have occurred only in 116, after Trajan achieved submission of various cities and regions and then sailed down the Tigris to the Persian Gulf. His absence evidently encouraged this violent response among native peoples, of whom the Jews were only one. Trajan decided to devote his resources to suppressing the revolts in the west, but he died shortly afterward in 117, leaving Hadrian to establish peace in the region. Jewish participation seems only part of a broader backlash against the Roman conquest of Mesopotamia, which included the Parthians and other native inhabitants. Other than the brief knowledge that Jews were among those trying to throw off the recently acquired Roman yoke, we know nothing about it. To what extent the Jewish uprisings in Mesopotamia should be directly connected with the ones in the Mediterranean is debatable.

Early Rabbinic Sages

The final source for Jews in Babylonia is rabbinic literature, which has scattered references to sages who supposedly lived in Babylonia before the completion of the Mishnah in about 200 C.E. (references collected in Neusner 1965: vol. 1). These stories are very difficult to evaluate since they come from sources many centuries after the figures referred to, but it seems likely that regular travelers and even immigrants moved between Palestine and Babylonia. For example, the famous Rabbi Hillel, a Pharisaic leader according to scholarly deduction, is supposed to have been born in Mesopotamia in the late first century B.C.E. Stories are told that Rabbi Judah ben Bathyra lived in Nisibis but kept communications with Judah (*b. Pesaḥim* 3b). As noted above, Josephus affirms that Nisibis was one of the cities in which Jews paid the Temple half-shekel. A nearby city was Nearda, where Rabbi Nehemiah b. Beth Deli lived. He is alleged to have communicated with Rabbi Akiba in the late first century C.E. (*m. Yebam.* 16:7). He may have been a Palestinian Jew who migrated to Mesopotamia. These are just some examples of the stories in rabbinic literature which might help to fill out our picture of Jewry in Mesopotamia. Although the Mishnah was compiled in Palestine, the center of Judaism moved to Babylonia, where much rabbinic literature was composed, the most important being the Babylonian Talmud, which is still the basis of modern Orthodox Judaism.

BIBLIOGRAPHY

T. D. BARNES 1989, "Trajan and the Jews," *JJS* 40: 145-62. • J. L. BERQUIST, ED. 2007, *Approaching Yehud: New Approaches to the Study of the Persian Period,* Atlanta: Society of Biblical Literature. • F. JOANNÈS AND A. LEMAIRE 1999, "Trois tablettes cunéiforme à onomastique ouest-sémitique (collection Sh. Moussaïeff)," *Transeuphratène* 17: 17-34. •

J. NEUSNER 1965-1970, *A History of the Jews in Babylonia*, 5 vols., Leiden: Brill. • L. E. PEARCE 2006, "New Evidence for Judeans in Babylonia," in *Judah and the Judeans in the Persian Period*, ed. O. Lipschits and M. Oeming, Winona Lake, Ind.: Eisenbrauns, 399-411. • M. W. STOLPER 1985, *Entrepreneurs and Empire: The Murašû Archive, the Murašû Firm, and Persian Rule in Babylonia*, Leiden: Nederlands Historisch-Archaeologisch Instituut te Istanbul. • R. ZADOK 1979, *The Jews in Babylonia during the Chaldean and Achaemenian Periods according to the Babylonian Sources*, Haifa: University of Haifa.

See also: Adiabene; Babylonians; Diaspora Uprisings; Parthians LESTER L. GRABBE

Messianic Apocalypse (4Q521)

Modern interpreters have given the title *Messianic Apocalypse* to a fragmentary Hebrew text recovered from Qumran Cave 4 (4Q521). The work survives in some seventeen fragments dated paleographically to ca. 100-80 B.C.E. The fragments belong to a single copy of a work composed sometime in the second century B.C.E. It is unclear whether 4Q521 was composed or only copied by the Qumran sectarians, since it contains no distinctive sectarian terminology and since its possible echoes of terms and themes in the Qumran *Thanksgiving Hymns* or *Hodayot* are more readily explained as evocations of biblical texts. Its use of the word *Adonai* and avoidance of the Tetragrammaton, however, do agree with Qumran usage. The sparseness of the preserved text makes a determination of its genre difficult. Because nothing in it is presented as divine revelation mediated to a human recipient, the label *Apocalypse* is unwarranted. It would be more accurate to call it an eschatological midrash in hortatory style. Though poorly preserved like most Cave 4 texts, 4Q521 is an important witness to messianic ideas and to belief in resurrection in early Judaism.

Contents

Fragment 2 is the most substantially preserved part of the work. The extant portion of its second column, which consists of fourteen lines, describes the eschatological blessings that will come upon the faithful in the messianic age, in words that recall Ps. 146:6-8 and a few passages in Isaiah. Lines 1 and 2 affirm that "[the heav]ens and the earth will listen to his messiah *(mšyḥw)*, [and all] that is in them will not turn away from the precepts of the holy ones." An exhortation follows:

> Strengthen yourselves, you who seek the Lord, in his service! [*vacat*] Will you not find the Lord *(ʾdny)* in this, all those who hope in their heart? For the Lord will care for the pious *(hsdym)* and call the righteous by name, and his Spirit will hover over the poor *(ʿnwym)*, and he will renew the faithful with his strength. For He will honor the pious upon the throne of an eternal kingdom, freeing prisoners, granting sight to the blind, lifting up those bow[ed down]. (2 ii 3-8)

Lines 11-12 go on to declare,

> the Lord will perform glorious deeds such as have never been, just as he sa[id], [for] He will heal the wounded, give life to the dead *(wmtym yḥyh)*, and preach good news to the poor.

These words are a pastiche of allusions to Isaiah: 35:5-6 ("the eyes of the blind shall be opened"); 61:2 ("preach good news to the poor"); and perhaps 26:19 ("your dead shall live; their bodies shall rise"). The most striking element is the mention in line 12 of resurrection, which is rare in the Hebrew Bible and the Dead Sea Scrolls.

Scholarly discussion of 4Q521 has centered especially upon the messianism of frg. 2 col. ii. One issue concerns whether one or more messiahs are in view. Although it is possible that *mšyḥw* in line 1 refers to "his messiahs *(mĕšîḥaw)*" — especially since frg. 8 mentions "all its anointed ones" *(wkl mšyḥyh)* — more likely a single messiah (*mĕšîḥô*, "his messiah") is in mind. Another matter has to do with the character and role of the messianic figure, specifically, what sort of messiah is doing the work. God, presumably working through the messiah, is the clear and fitting subject of the healing of the wounded and raising of the dead, but a rather unlikely candidate for proclaiming good news, a job more suited to a prophetic herald or messenger. Indeed, the prophet of Isa. 61:1 claims to be anointed for such a task: "The Spirit of YHWH is upon me because YHWH has anointed me . . . to bring good news to the poor"). The messiah of 4Q521 is therefore most likely a prophetic messiah, one modeled, moreover, after Elijah, whose activity is evoked in frg. 2 col. iii with the words "the fathers will return to the sons" (cf. Mal. 4:5-6 [Hebr. 3:23-24]).

The second largest extant portion of 4Q521 comes in frgs. 5 + 7 col. ii, lines 1-3 of which reprise and expand upon the opening words of frg. 2 col. ii: "[. . .] see all [that has made] [the Lord: the ear]th and all that is in it [*vacat*], the seas [and all] [they contain] and all the reservoirs of waters and torrents." As an eschatological counterpart to God's work in creation, the succeeding lines focus on resurrection and final judgment:

> [. . .] those who do the good before the Lord [. . .] like these, the accursed. And to death shall they be [. . .] [. . .] he who gives life to the dead of his people [*vacat*]. (5 + 7 ii 4-6)

Together with frg. 2 ii, these lines suggest that 4Q521 anticipates the bodily resurrection of individuals in a restored nation.

The ill-preserved frg. 8 mentions "all the holy vessels" and "all its anointed ones *(mšyḥyh)*" who "will speak the word of the Lord." The mention of sacred vessels evidently presumes a restored (or new) Temple and might also imply that the anointed ones are priests. Yet elsewhere in the scrolls, the phrase "anointed ones" refers to prophets.

Affiliations and Significance

Expectation of an Elijah-like prophetic messiah who raises the dead is not attested elsewhere in the scrolls. The Qumran *Community Rule* briefly mentions "the

Prophet" alongside the Messiahs of Aaron and Israel (1QS 9:10-11) but does not speak of resurrection at all. 4Qpseudo-Ezekiel (4Q386), which is probably a nonsectarian work, speaks of "a great crowd of people" who have loved YHWH's name being raised up and given life, but their resurrection is a direct act of God.

Later Jewish tradition associated Elijah with raising the dead in the messianic age: "the dead will first come to life in the time of the Messiah" (*y. Ketub.* 12:3), and "the resurrection of the dead comes through Elijah" (*m. Soṭah* 9; *y. Šeqal.* 3:3). According to *Pesikta de Rab Kahana* 76a, "Everything that the Holy One will do, he has already anticipated by the hands of the righteous in this world, the resurrection of the dead by Elijah and Ezekiel."

The most illuminating parallels to 4Q521 come in New Testament traditions that conceive of Jesus as Israel's prophet-messiah and depict him bringing dead people back to life. In a Q passage, John the Baptist sends emissaries to ask Jesus, "Are you the one who is to come, or are we to wait for another?" Jesus replies by recounting his messianic deeds in a litany that contains a patchwork of phrases from Isa. 29:18; 42:18; 26:19; 35:5-6; and 61:1:

> "Go and tell John what you have seen and heard: the blind receive their sight, the lame walk, the lepers are cleansed, the deaf hear, the dead are raised, the poor have good news brought to them. And blessed is anyone who takes no offense at me." (Luke 7:18-23//Matt. 11:2-6).

As with 4Q521, the most notable feature of the Q pericope is the addition of resurrection to the Isaianic litany. In the Matthean redaction of Q (Matt. 11:2), resurrection of the dead is reckoned among the "deeds of the messiah" *(ta erga tou christou),* and in Luke the Q logion is preceded by a uniquely Lukan tradition about Jesus raising a widow's son in Nain, with Jesus' activity clearly modeled on the work of Elijah and Elisha (cf. 1 Kings 17:17-24; 2 Kings 4:32-37). In another tradition unique to Luke (4:16-30), Jesus also speaks of himself in prophetic-messianic terms: in his hometown synagogue in Nazareth, he takes a scroll of Isaiah, unrolls it, finds his text, reads it, and in his exposition of it claims himself as its fulfillment. The text he cites is Isa. 61:1-2, and in his commentary he explicitly mentions the work of Elijah before embarking on a ministry of authoritative teaching and miracle working (Luke 4:25-27, 31-44). Together, then, 4Q521 and various gospel passages demonstrate that at least some Jews in the late Second Temple period awaited an eschatological prophet-messiah, either Elijah or one like Elijah, among whose works would be raising the dead.

Bibliography

M. Becker 1997, "4Q521 und die Gesalbten," *RevQ* 18: 73-96. • J. J. Collins 1995, *The Scepter and the Star,* New York: Doubleday, 117-23. • J. Duhaime 1995, "Le messie et les saints dans un fragment apocalyptique de Qumrân (4Q521 2)," in *Ce Dieu qui vient: Mélanges offerts à Bernard Renaud,* ed. R. Kuntzmann, Paris: Cerf. • S. Hultgren 2008, "4Q521, the Second Benediction of the *Tefilla,* the *ḥăsîdîm,* and the Development of Royal Messianism," *RevQ* 91: 313-40. • M. Labahn 2004, "The Significance of Signs in Luke 7:22–23 in the Light of Isaiah 61 and the Messianic Apocalypse," in *From Prophecy to Testament: The Function of the Old Testament in the New,* ed. C. A. Evans, Peabody, Mass.: Hendrickson, 146–68. • É. Puech 1992, "Une Apocalypse messianique (4Q521)," *RevQ* 15: 475-519. • É. Puech 1993, *La croyance des Esséniens en la vie future: Immortalité, résurrection, vie éternelle?,* Paris: Gabalda, 627-92. • É. Puech 1998, *Qumran Cave 4.XVIII: Textes hébreux (4Q521–4Q528, 4Q576–4Q579),* DJD 25, Oxford: Clarendon, 1-39 + plates i-iii.

Daniel C. Harlow

Messianism

In the Hebrew Bible, "messiah" (Hebr. *māšîaḥ* = "anointed one") refers to persons serving in divinely ordained positions of authority, most often Israelite kings (e.g., 2 Sam. 23:1; Ps. 2:2) but also high priests (e.g., Lev. 4:3; Dan. 9:25) and, in one case, a foreign king (Isa. 45:1). Prophets were also anointed to office (1 Kings 19:16; Isa. 61:1) and could collectively be called "anointed ones" (Ps. 105:16). In early Jewish literature, the term "messiah," though used infrequently, is applied to royal, priestly, and heavenly eschatological figures (e.g., *Pss. Sol.* 17:32; 1QS 9:10-11; *1 Enoch* 48:10). In light of this usage, scholars use the term "messiah" broadly to refer to any eschatological figure, whether royal, priestly, prophetic, or heavenly, who serves as an agent of God's purposes in the world. Accordingly, messianism can be defined as the set of ideas associated with the identity and activity of divinely appointed eschatological agents of God's judgment, salvation, or rule.

Early Jewish messianism was characterized by significant diversity, depending on the type of messiah envisioned and the kind of transformation expected, whether national restoration or cosmic renewal. There existed no unified or synthetic concept of "the Messiah." It must be recognized, too, that many Jews held no messianic expectations, since such expectations are absent in much of early Jewish literature, from the early portions of *1 Enoch* and Ben Sira (ca. 200 B.C.E.) to Philo and Josephus (first century C.E.). Nevertheless, significant numbers of Jews — undoubtedly because they believed God was sovereign and just, but perceived a world marked by injustice and sin — embraced hopes that God would ultimately intervene to judge, redeem, and rule the world. And because they also believed God was transcendent, they envisioned God acting through some kind of eschatological agent, a messiah.

Royal Messianism

Royal messianism is the most widely attested type in early Judaism and is rooted in biblical ideas about kingship. In ancient Israel, as throughout the ancient Near East, kings were believed to represent divine rule and to mediate divine blessings to their people. Such a royal ideology is reflected in a number of biblical texts

(2 Samuel 7; Isa. 8:23–9:6 [Eng. 9:1-7]; Psalms 2, 45, 89, 110, 132), often in explicit reference to Davidic kings, whereby the king is characterized as the (adopted) son of God who, along with his descendants, would rule forever, bring victory over his enemies, and reign in peace and righteousness. Related to this royal ideology are texts indicating that kingship had been foreseen in Israel's ancestral past (Gen. 49:10; Num. 24:15-19), as well as passages of uncertain date that anticipated an ideal Davidic king (e.g., Mic. 5:2-5 and Isaiah 11). After the fall of the Judean monarchy in 586 B.C.E., some exilic and postexilic prophecies expressed hope for its restoration (e.g., Ezek. 34:23-24; Hag. 2:20-23; Jer. 33:14-26), though others envisioned theocratic rule (e.g., Isaiah 40–66) — without a king — probably to be mediated by priests, which is the form of governance actually attested in postexilic Judah.

From ca. 500 to 100 B.C.E., there is no clear evidence of hope for the restoration of the monarchy or royal messianism (though some interpret Chronicles in this way or point to the continued use of royal psalms in the liturgy of the Second Temple). Royal messianism, however, emerges ca. 100 B.C.E. in response to new social and political circumstances and continued for more than two centuries. To articulate and legitimate their views, advocates of royal messianism were able to draw on a rich array of scriptural texts embodying the preexilic Israelite royal ideology and later hopes for the restoration of the monarchy. The most common form of royal messianism focused on an expected Davidic king.

The fullest expression of such a Davidic messianic hope is found in *Psalms of Solomon* 17, which speaks of a coming Son of David who is specifically designated "messiah" (Gr. *christos*) (v. 32). Hope for this figure is based on an explicit appeal to God's promise of eternal Davidic rule as expressed in 2 Samuel 7 and Psalm 89; the passage also draws heavily on Psalm 2 and Isaiah 11. Thus, the messiah will destroy the unrighteous — both the Gentiles and Jewish "sinners" — though strikingly this warrior king will accomplish his mission by the word of his mouth. The Jewish exiles will be gathered, and the Son of David will rule in righteousness over a perfected Israel as well as the nations. He will be appointed, empowered, and instructed by God through his Spirit and will not only be mighty, but wise, compassionate, and just — wholly devoted to God and, indeed, the representative of God's kingship on earth. Altogether, then, the Davidic messiah is a militant figure who brings political change — judgment against enemies and deliverance for Israel — but also a virtuous and godly figure, one supremely equipped for righteous rule. It is clear, too, that this expression of Davidic messianism was formulated in response to the perceived unrighteousness of Hasmonean rule and the subsequent takeover of the Hasmonean kingdom by the Roman general Pompey (63 B.C.E.). In short, these illegitimate rulers — whether Jewish or foreign — would be replaced by a divinely sanctioned king, the Son of David.

Several sectarian documents from Qumran — all biblical commentaries or pesharim — also refer to a Davidic messiah (4Q252 col. v 1-4; 4QFlor i 10-13; 4QpIsa[a] frgs. 8-10 11-24; 4Q285 v 1-6), here named the "Branch of David," a title drawn from Jer. 23:5; 33:15. Further characterization of this royal messiah is derived from interpretations of Gen. 49:9-10, 2 Sam. 7:11-14, Amos 9:11, and especially Isa. 10:34–11:5. Accordingly, several Qumran references appeal to the Davidic covenant to affirm that God would raise up the Branch of David in the last days. The description of this figure, however, is fairly limited: he is called the "messiah of righteousness" and said to be sustained by a spirit of might, an attribute admittedly fitting for this king's task of saving Israel from its enemies. He therefore plays a key role in defeating the Kittim, Israel's eschatological enemy in Qumran texts and a clear reference to the Romans. In fact, in one fragmentary text, it appears that in the aftermath of his victory the Branch of David executes the king of the Kittim (4Q285 v 4). He then would rule over the nations and judge the peoples with the sword. But his judging would be done in accordance with the instructions of the priests. In this regard, perhaps the most striking feature of the Davidic messiah at Qumran is that he routinely appears alongside and is subordinated to priestly figures. Thus, the Branch of David, while first and foremost a military figure of considerable power, is also a limited figure, since he is firmly under the supervision of the priests. Nonetheless, according to these Roman-era texts, the Qumran sectarians saw a key role for a Davidic messiah in God's final victory over the enemies of his people.

Two other royal-messianic labels feature in Qumran texts, the Messiah of Israel and the Prince of the Congregation, titles regarded by most scholars as alternative designations for the Davidic messiah. The Messiah of Israel is mentioned in several of the earliest sectarian texts (1QS 9:10-11; CD 12:23; 1QSa 2:20) and is always paired with the Messiah of Aaron, a priestly messiah. The coming of the royal and priestly messiahs, along with an eschatological prophet, will mark the end of the age of wickedness, when some are given over to the sword and apostates are excluded from Israel. The Messiah of Israel also plays a role at the eschatological banquet. The Prince of the Congregation is understood as the fulfillment of Baalam's prophecy in Num. 24:17 that "a scepter shall rise out of Israel," who will strike violently the sons of Seth (CD 7:19-20). In the *War Scroll* (1QM 5:1-2) the Prince's shield bears the names of the tribes of Israel, though nothing is said about his role in the war, which is under the direction of the priests. 1QSb 5:20-29 offers a blessing for the Prince in which he is depicted as a figure possessing superior spiritual endowments who will judge righteously, defeat the ungodly, and establish the kingdom of God's people — though his blessing comes only after the blessing for the high priest. Finally, in 4Q285 the Prince of the Congregation is identified with the Branch of David, who defeats the Kittim in the eschatological battle (cf. also 4QpIsa[a] frgs. 2-6 15). One other text from Qumran, 4Q246, may also refer to a Davidic messiah under the title "Son of God" and "Son of the Most High," but the text is fragmentary and the messianic interpretation of the "Son of God" figure is debated.

Another reference to a Davidic messiah appears in *4 Ezra,* an apocalypse from ca. 100 C.E. In its interpretation of a vision about a lion from the forest that passes judgment on an eagle who has oppressed the earth (11:1–12:3), it states that the lion is "the messiah [Lat. *unctus;* Syr. *mšḥ*] whom the Most High has kept until the end of days, who will arise from the seed of David" (12:32), while the eagle is clearly a symbol for the Roman Empire. The image of the lion recalls Gen. 49:9-10, where it describes Judah as the forefather of kings. Moreover, this messiah is preexistent — an idea the author finds compatible with Davidic genealogical descent. This figure will judge and destroy the Roman Empire and then gather the Jewish remnant; he has no role, however, in a universal judgment or ruling a future Jewish kingdom. This sharp focus on the destruction of the Roman Empire and restoration of the Jewish nation is nevertheless understandable in the aftermath of the First Jewish Revolt against Rome. The messiah's actions are couched not in military terms but in legal ones, a formulation reminiscent of the context in which "one like a son of man" appears in Daniel 7. In this regard, the Davidic messiah of *4 Ezra* 11–12 shares features with the "man from the sea" described in *4 Ezra* 13, a heavenly redeemer figure modeled on the Danielic son of man (see below). Here, then, ideas about a Davidic messiah have been fused with those about a heavenly savior. *4 Ezra* 7:28-30 refers to the messiah, called "my son" or "my servant," who will be revealed with his people. They will rejoice for 400 years, after which the messiah dies and the world returns to primeval silence for seven days until the final judgment. The messiah's role, therefore, appears limited to an earthly kingdom and distinct from the final judgment.

In New Testament writings, Jesus is described as a Davidic messiah: in Rom. 1:3, a pre-Pauline unit, he is said to descend from the seed of David; in the Synoptic Gospels and Acts, he is regularly called the Son of David (Mark 10:47-48; Matt. 1:1-17; 9:27; 15:22; 21:9, 15; Luke 1:32; 2:4; 3:23-28; Acts 13:22-23); and in Revelation he is designated the lion of Judah, the root and descendant of David (Rev. 5:5; 22:16). Other gospel traditions suggest broader Jewish expectations for a Davidic messiah (Mark 12:35; John 7:41-43). Some have observed, however, that Jesus fits the picture of a Davidic messiah poorly, given his nonviolent ministry, seeming acceptance of Roman rule, and eventual suffering and death. On the other hand, Jesus shares characteristics with the ideal figure in *Psalm of Solomon* 17 and his identification with the Son of Man is similar to the Davidic figure in *4 Ezra.* Also, in Revelation Jesus is depicted as a militant figure — a warrior and judge who brings an end to Roman power.

Davidic messianism is more widely attested than other forms; nevertheless, other royal messiahs are found in early Judaism. First, the *Testaments of the Twelve Patriarchs,* drawing on Gen. 49:9-10, speaks about a royal messiah from Judah (*T. Jud.* 21:4-6) who is nonetheless subordinated to a priestly figure from Levi. The final form of the *Testaments* is Christian, but most scholars agree it is based on earlier Jewish material, which includes the reference to the messiah from Judah. (Of course, a Davidic messiah could reasonably be described as a messiah from Judah.) Second, *Sib. Or.* 3.652-56, a product of second-century B.C.E. Egyptian Judaism, states that God will send a King from the Sun, an Egyptian king from the Greek race (3.191-94), to restore the Jewish people and usher in the messianic age. This conception is analogous to the identification of Cyrus, the Persian king who released Judah from exile, as YHWH's messiah in Isa. 44:28–45:7. Third, several popular royal messiahs emerged in Palestine around the time of Herod's death (e.g., Simon, a slave of King Herod, and Athronges, a shepherd) and the Jewish revolt against Rome (e.g., Simon bar Giora). These royal figures, who sought to liberate the Jews from foreign oppression, embodied the model of popular kingship known from biblical accounts about Saul, Jeroboam, and David during his rise to power. Simon bar Kosiba, leader of the Jewish Revolt in 132-135 B.C.E., who bore the messianic title Bar Kokhba ("son of the star," based on Num. 24:17), also reflects this model, although he reportedly was hailed as a Davidic messiah by Rabbi Aqiba (*y. Taʿanit* 68d).

Priestly Messianism

Compared to royal messianism, priestly messianism represented a minor trend during the Second Temple period, though it, too, could draw on scriptural resources. In ancient Israel, the high priest was called "the anointed priest" (Lev. 4:3, 5, 16; 16:5), a usage still reflected in Dan. 9:26 (ca. 165 B.C.E.), where a historical high priest is called "an anointed one." During the postexilic reconstruction of Judah, Joshua the high priest served as leader of the community alongside the civil ruler Zerubbabel. In fact, the characterization of these leaders in Zech. 4:14 as "two sons of oil" suggests anointed status, though not in an eschatological context. Subsequently, the high priest served as the sole leader of Judah, as illustrated by Ben Sira (ca. 180 B.C.E.), who praised the glorious rule of his contemporary, the high priest Simon II (50:1-21). In the *Aramaic Levi Document* (ca. 200-150 B.C.E.), Levi is exalted above all and given the anointing of eternal peace (1Q21 frgs. 3-4). This fragmentary text further states that "the sovereignty of the priesthood is greater than the sovereignty of . . . ," presumably, the kingship (1Q21 frg. 1), while Levi is described in terms taken from Isa. 11:2, which originally applied to an ideal Davidic king. *Jubilees* (ca. 120 B.C.E.) also narrates a special blessing for Levi and his sons to become rulers (31:11-17), though this is followed by a blessing for Judah that he and one of his sons will be princes in Israel (31:18-20). Thus, *Jubilees* envisions dual leadership — priestly and civil — modeled on the leadership structure of early postexilic Judah, but no doubt in reaction to the Hasmonean collapse of priestly and civil duties into one office. Even so, none of these expressions of priestly rule speaks specifically about a messianic figure.

Sectarian texts from Qumran do, however, specify a

priestly messiah. In the *Damascus Document* he is named the "Messiah of Aaron" and is always mentioned in a phrase along the lines of "the Messiah of Aaron and Israel" (CD 12:23–13:1; 14:19; 19:10-11; 20:1). Some scholars have argued that this formulation refers to one figure with both priestly and royal characteristics, but the case for separate figures is clear: the Hebrew grammar allows for the distributive use of the singular "messiah"; the phrase "the messiahs of Aaron and Israel" occurs in 1QS 9:10-11; and, most importantly, in some texts separate priestly and royal eschatological figures appear (1QSa 2:11-15; CD 7:18-20; 4QFlor i 11-12). Little is said about the Messiah of Aaron except that the community must remain obedient until he arrives together with the Messiah of Israel. Their arrival would mark the end of the "age of wickedness," when some would be saved, others put to the sword, and atonement for sins would be made, presumably by the priestly messiah. The priestly messiah is also called the "Interpreter of the Law" (CD 7:18; 4QFlor i 11-12), a title indicative of the role he would play. Moreover, at the eschatological banquet, this messiah — here simply called "the Priest" — is the first to enter, and the first to extend his hand to bless the bread and the wine, followed by the Messiah of Israel (1QSa 2:11-15). Hence, as in other Qumran texts, the priestly figure takes precedence over the royal figure. Scriptural grounds adduced for the concept of a priestly messiah included Num. 24:17, where the "star" was taken to represent the priestly messiah (CD 7:18-19), and Deut. 33:8-11, the Blessing of Levi, cited in 4Q175, a catenae of messianic proof texts. It goes without saying that hopes for a priestly messiah expressed dissatisfaction with the currently ruling high priest in Jerusalem.

Another Qumran text, 4Q541, refers to an eschatological high priest who will make atonement, teach according to the will of God, and banish darkness from the earth with "his eternal sun," though he will meet opposition in an evil generation (frg. 9 col. i). This Aramaic document is not overtly sectarian and is a likely source for the Greek *Testament of Levi,* which in its current form is Christian. Nevertheless, *T. Levi* 18:2-5 reflects its Jewish source in speaking about one eschatological figure, a priestly messiah, associating him with the symbol of the star (cf. Num. 24:17). Still, within the *Testaments* as a whole, this priestly messiah shares the stage with the Messiah of Judah (*T. Jud.* 24:4-6). It should also be noted that the author of the New Testament book of Hebrews did not link the eschatological high priesthood of Jesus with Levi or Aaron, stating instead that God had designated Jesus high priest according to the order of Melchizedek (Heb. 5:5-10; 7:1-28; cf. Ps. 110:4).

Prophetic Messianism

Prophetic messianism constitutes another minor development in early Judaism, perhaps because the tradition of an anointed prophet, while present in the Hebrew Scriptures (1 Kings 19:16; Isa. 61:1), is not strongly attested. Two passages, however, had the potential to stimulate hope for a future, ideal prophetic figure: Deut. 18:15-18, where God declares that he will raise up a prophet like Moses, and Mal. 4:5-6, where God promises to send Elijah before the day of the Lord. Ben Sira (ca. 180 B.C.E.) alludes to this future Elijah, but not as a messianic figure (48:10); nor is the unnamed future prophet invoked in 1 Macc. 14:41 messianic. At Qumran, an eschatological prophet was expected to appear along with the Messiahs of Aaron and Israel (1QS 9:11), but he is not given the title "messiah" and nothing is said about his role. On the other hand, 4QTestimonia cites Deut. 18:18-19 alongside proof texts for a royal and priestly messiah. Perhaps the most important Qumran text for prophetic messianism is 4Q521, a Hasmonean-era text without apparent sectarian features. A fragment of this text begins, "[the heav]ens and the earth will listen to his (God's) messiah" (frg. 2), and goes on to announce that God will release captives, give sight to the blind, heal the wounded, give life to the dead, and preach good news to the poor (cf. Ps. 146:7-8; Isa. 61:1). The interpretation of this text is disputed, but it is reasonable to believe that God's work would be enacted through the aforementioned messiah and that this messiah would be a prophet, especially because he *preaches* good news, a role ill suited to God. In fact, 4Q521 may envision a new Elijah, since its profile of the messiah fits that of the prophet Elijah, who is said to have shut up the heavens and raised the dead (1 Kings 17:1, 17-24).

Several New Testament passages indicate Jewish expectations for an eschatological Elijah (Mark 9:11; Matt. 17:10; John 1:21), but it is not clear how representative these are of broader Jewish beliefs. Nevertheless, in some passages John the Baptist is identified as the new Elijah (Matt. 11:14; 17:10-13; Mark 9:13), though in another this is denied (John 1:21). Jesus is also depicted as a type of Elijah: the story of Jesus raising the son of the widow of Nain (Luke 7:10-17) parallels the story of Elijah raising the son of the widow of Zarephath (1 Kings 17:17-24), and the Gospels report that some thought Jesus to be Elijah (cf. Mark 6:14; 8:27). Moreover, there is a striking correspondence between the description of Jesus' ministry as messianic in Matt. 11:2-5 and Luke 7:22 — "the blind receive their sight, the lame walk . . . the dead are raised, and the poor have good news brought to them" — and works of the prophetic messiah, perhaps the new Elijah, in 4Q521. Beyond this, Jesus is also presented as a prophet like Moses: in the book of Acts, Deut. 18:15 is cited in reference to Jesus (3:22-23; 7:37), and in the Gospel of John, Jesus is hailed as "the prophet" after reenacting the miracles of manna (6:14) and water from a rock (7:40).

Josephus tells of other prophetic figures from the first century C.E. who sought to bring deliverance by reenacting miracles from Israel's past. Theudas called the masses to take their property and follow him to the Jordan River, where he would part the waters (*Ant.* 20.97), and "the Egyptian" summoned the common people to the Mount of Olives, from where he would command the walls of Jerusalem to fall so that the people could enter the city (*Ant.* 20.169-70). Whether these prophets should be designated "messiahs" depends in large measure on whether the divine deliverance they promised is considered eschatological.

Heavenly Figures

A final category of eschatological agents includes various heavenly figures. The idea of God acting through angels is common in the Hebrew Bible, but these were not eschatological figures. In Daniel 7 (ca. 165 B.C.E.), however, an eschatological heavenly deliverer is clearly in view. In the context of a vision about four beasts who represent oppressive earthly kingdoms, "one like a son of man" comes from the heavenly throne and receives "dominion, glory, and kingship" (Dan. 7:13-14). The precise identity of the "son of man" figure is a matter of long-standing scholarly discussion. The traditional interpretation, rarely defended today, asserted that this figure was the Davidic messiah. Another view holds "one like a son of man" to be no more than a symbol of the Jewish people, noting that the Jewish people also receive dominion and kingship (7:27). A more likely interpretation, however, sees "one like a son of man" as an angelic figure who serves as the heavenly representative and advocate of the Jewish people, probably to be identified with the archangel Michael. This last view is supported not only by Michael's role in Dan 12:1 (cf. also 10:13), but by the fact that in apocalyptic literature angels are regularly depicted as human beings ("son of man" = human being) and that the role of "one like a son of man" parallels that of the angels, called "the holy ones of the most high" (7:18). In any event, God's redemption does not come through a human agent but a heavenly being.

The angel Michael plays an analogous role in the Qumran *War Scroll*, which states that in the eschatological war against the Children of Darkness, God will raise up the kingdom of Michael and kingdom of Israel (1QM 17:7-8). Similarly in 1QM 13:10, the Prince of Light — a designation for Michael — assists the Children of Light against Belial and his lot. But in contrast to Daniel 7, in the *War Scroll* the archangel Michael works in concert with human agents, the Children of Light. In another Qumran text, 11QMelchizedek, a heavenly figure named Melchizedek plays a role in the eschatological scenario. Based on the jubilees legislation in Lev. 25:13 and its prophetic interpretation in Isa. 61:1, the text states that Melchizedek will proclaim liberty and forgiveness of sins — a Day of Atonement — for the Sons of Light. Then on the basis of Ps. 82:1-2, which states that *'ĕlōhîm* will hold judgment, it asserts that Melchizedek will judge and destroy Belial and his lot. Here Melchizedek has both royal and priestly characteristics and is probably to be identified as the archangel Michael.

Two further heavenly figures, specifically called messiahs and modeled on the Danielic son of man, are found in the *Similitudes of Enoch* (*1 Enoch* 37–71) and *4 Ezra* 13. The *Similitudes* (first century C.E.) refer to a heavenly judge and redeemer variously called Son of Man, Chosen One, Righteous One, and Messiah. This figure is angelic (46:1-2) and appears to be preexistent (48:3). His role is to represent and vindicate the righteous and to condemn the wicked (cf. 62:1-15). The characterization of this figure draws on Daniel 7 and the texts about Davidic kingship (Psalm 2; Isaiah 11) and the Servant of the Lord (Isaiah 42; 49; 52–53). It is often held that Enoch, the recipient of the apocalyptic revelation, is identified with the Son of Man (*1 Enoch* 71:14). But since earlier passages distinguish these figures (cf. 70:1), the matter remains under debate. *4 Ezra*, an apocalypse composed in the aftermath of the destruction of Jerusalem in 70 C.E., presents a vision of a Man from the Sea (chap. 13) who flies on the clouds of heaven and with a fiery stream from his mouth destroys all those assembled against him (cf. Isa. 11:4). He then gathers a peaceable people. In the interpretation of the vision, this figure is identified as "he whom the most high has been keeping for many ages, who will himself deliver his creation" (*4 Ezra* 13:26). Standing on Mt. Zion, this heavenly messiah will judge and destroy the nations (cf. Ps. 2:4-9) and gather in the exiles of Israel.

In the Gospels, Jesus refers to himself as the Son of Man, often in a context of eschatological judgment and deliverance (cf. Mark 13:26-27; Matt. 10:23). He is therefore characterized as a heavenly figure whose identity and role are similar to those of the son of man figures in Daniel 7, *1 Enoch* 37–71, and *4 Ezra* 13. Moreover, like the figures in the *Similitudes of Enoch* and *4 Ezra*, Jesus is identified as both "messiah" and "Son of Man." On the other hand, Rev. 14:14 reflects a tradition in which "one like a son of man" is clearly an angel and distinct from Jesus.

BIBLIOGRAPHY

J. J. COLLINS 2010, *The Scepter and the Star: Messianism in Light of the Dead Sea Scrolls*, 2d ed., Grand Rapids: Eerdmans. • J. H. CHARLESWORTH, ED. 1992, *The Messiah*, Minneapolis: Fortress. • J. A. FITZMYER 2007, *The One Who Is to Come*, Grand Rapids: Eerdmans. • R. A. HORSLEY AND J. S. HANSON 1985, *Bandits, Prophets, and Messiahs*, San Francisco: Harper & Row. • J. NEUSNER, W. S. GREEN, AND E. S. FRERICHS, EDS. 1987, *Judaisms and Their Messiahs at the Turn of the Christian Era*, Cambridge: Cambridge University Press. • G. W. E. NICKELSBURG 2003, "Agents of God's Activities," in idem, *Ancient Judaism and Christian Origins*, Minneapolis: Fortress, 89-117. • G. S. OEGEMA 1998, *The Anointed and His People*, Sheffield: Sheffield Academic Press. • K. E. POMYKALA 1995, *The Davidic Dynasty Tradition in Early Judaism*, Atlanta: Scholars Press. • S. SCHREIBER 2000, *Gesalbter und König*, Berlin: de Gruyter. • A. YARBRO COLLINS AND J. J. COLLINS 2008, *King and Messiah as Son of God: Divine, Human, and Angelic Messianic Figures in Biblical and Related Literature*, Grand Rapids: Eerdmans. • M. ZETTERHOLM, ED. 2007, *The Messiah in Early Judaism and Christianity*, Minneapolis: Fortress.

See also: Mediator Figures

KENNETH E. POMYKALA

Metatron

Metatron is the name of a principal angel that in Jewish angelology occupies a unique place: the divine vicegerent and the lesser manifestation of the divine name (YHWH *ha-qāṭôn*, "the lesser YHWH"). *3* (Hebrew) *Apocalypse of Enoch*, also known as *Sefer Hekhalot*, portrays

Metatron as the replica of the Deity whose crown, garments, throne, and even corporeality imitate the divine attributes. The Babylonian Talmud (*b. Ḥagigah* 15a) accentuates the uniqueness of Metatron's position by noting that he alone is allowed to be seated in heaven because he is the celestial scribe who records the good deeds of Israel. According to this talmudic passage, a vision of the seated Metatron led R. Elisha b. Avuyah to the erroneous belief that there are "two powers in heaven" because he mistook the angel for a second deity.

The origin of the Metatron tradition is shrouded in mystery. Some scholars trace it back to Enochic lore, noting that in rabbinic and Hekhalot materials many early roles and titles attributed to Enoch in apocalyptic writings have been transferred to Metatron. Metatron's origins, however, cannot be explained solely with reference to Enoch, because Metatron also assumed many of the titles and functions assigned to Michael, Yahoel, Melchizedek, and other exalted angelic figures in early Jewish apocalyptic writings.

A classical study by Gershom Scholem (1971) distinguishes two basic strands of Metatron speculation that were fused in rabbinic and Hekhalot literature. These include lore relating to Enoch and lore associated with Yahoel and Michael. One strand, which is reflected in talmudic passages, identifies Metatron with Yahoel as the representation of the divine name and knows nothing of his transfiguration from a human being into an angel. The other identifies Metatron with the figure of Enoch. This identification is made in *Sefer Hekhalot* (also known as *3 Enoch*), which offers the most detailed description of the transformation of Enoch into the principal angel Metatron. *Sefer Hekhalot* gives Enoch-Metatron the title *naʿar*, "youth," because he was transformed by God into a celestial creature and thus became the youngest of the angels. Metatron's scribal duties and judicial functions also reflect a connection with Enoch.

No scholarly consensus exists about the etymology of the name Metatron, which occurs in two forms in rabbinic literature, one written with six letters, *Mṭṭrwn*, and the other with seven, *Myṭṭrwn*. One suggestion is that the name derives from Lat. *metator* ("leader, guide"). Since talmudic materials identify Metatron with the "angel of the LORD" mentioned in Exod. 23:21, some scholars believe that the appellation may originally have been given to this angel, who led the Israelites through the wilderness like a Roman army *metator*. Another suggestion is that the name is based on Gr. *tetra* (four), construed as related to the four letters of the divine name, the Tetragrammaton. Still other suggestions relate the name to Gr. *metatyrannos* ("the one next to the ruler") or Gr. *(ho) meta thronou* ("next to the [divine] throne").

Metatron's proximity to the Deity is expressed in his appellation the "Prince of the Countenance" *(śar ha-pānîm)*. He is the only one allowed to behold the divine face and go behind the heavenly curtain. In some Hekhalot and Shiʿur Qomah materials, Metatron is depicted either as a celestial choirmaster or a heavenly priest who has his own celestial tabernacle.

Metatron's leading role in heaven as God's secretary and vice-regent, and possibly his demiurgic role, is expressed through another prominent office, the Prince of the World *(śar hā-ʿôlam)*, who is responsible for conveying divine decisions to the seventy (sometimes seventy-two) princes controlling the seventy nations of the earth. In Hekhalot and Shiʿur Qomah tradition, Metatron also functions as a heavenly guide, protector, and agent of revelation to the famous tannaim, R. Akiva and R. Ishmael.

Although scholars usually date the origins of speculation about Metatron to the rabbinic period, it is possible that the shaping of the exalted profile of this principal angel began already in the Second Temple period as a polemical response to traditions about exalted patriarchs and prophets.

BIBLIOGRAPHY

P. S. ALEXANDER 1985, "3 (Hebrew Apocalypse) of Enoch," in *OTP* 1: 223-315. • J. DAN 1993, *The Ancient Jewish Mysticism*, Tel Aviv: MOD Books, 108-24. • I. GRUENWALD 1980, *Apocalyptic and Merkavah Mysticism*, Leiden: Brill, 195-206. • M. IDEL 1990, "Enoch Is Metatron," *Immanuel* 24/25: 220-40. • S. LIEBERMAN 1980, "Metatron, the Meaning of His Name and His Functions," in I. Gruenwald, *Apocalyptic and Merkabah Mysticism*, Leiden: Brill, 235-41. • C. MOPSIK 1989, *Le livre hébreu d'Hénoch ou livre des palais*, Paris: Verdier. • H. ODEBERG 1928, *3 Enoch, or the Hebrew Book of Enoch*, Cambridge: Cambridge University Press. • A. ORLOV 2005, *The Enoch-Metatron Tradition*, Tübingen: Mohr-Siebeck. • P. SCHÄFER 1993, *The Hidden and Manifest God*, Albany: State University of New York Press. • G. SCHOLEM 1971, "Metatron," *EncJud* 11: 1443-46.

ANDREI A. ORLOV

Mezuzot → Phylacteries and Mezuzot

Michael, the Archangel

The only explicit reference to the angel Michael (Hebr. *mikāʾēl*, "who is like God?") in the Hebrew Bible occurs in the book of Daniel (written between 167 and 164 B.C.E.), where he functions as the angelic patron and protector of Israel. Thus in Daniel 10 Michael assists the angel Gabriel in fighting the angelic prince of Persia; he is called "one of the chief princes" (10:13) and "your [Daniel's] prince" (10:21). Similarly, Dan. 12:1 declares that "at that time Michael, the great prince, the protector of your people, shall arise."

Postexilic Jewish Literature

The earliest postexilic reference to the archangel Michael outside the Hebrew Bible appears in the *Book of the Watchers* (*1 Enoch* 1–36, ca. third century B.C.E.). Michael is identified as one of the archangels, whose number in early Jewish texts is usually four (e.g., *1 Enoch* 9:1; 40:9; 54:6; 71:8-9; 1QM 9:14-16; *Sib. Or.* 2.215; *Apoc. Mos.* 40:2). In several texts, he continues his biblical role as the angelic guardian of Israel (e.g., *1 Enoch* 20:5; 1QM 17:6-8).

A few texts assign Michael the role of *archistratēgos* or "chief captain" of the angelic host (*3 Bar.* 11:4; *2 Enoch* 22:6; 33:10; *Testament of Abraham* [often in recension A; only once, at 14:7, in recension B]). This military epithet is applied to an unnamed angel in LXX Josh. 5:13-15, whom later traditions identify with Michael (cf. Origen, *Commentary on Joshua* 5:14 and *Selecta in Jesum Nave* [*PG* 12.821]; *Gen. Rab.* 97:3; *Exod. Rab.* 32:2-3). Indeed, there is a widespread tendency in later Jewish and Christian tradition to identify Michael with virtually all of the unnamed angelic figures in the Hebrew Bible, including the "angel of the LORD."

Michael also functions at times as major domo and high priest in the heavenly temple, where he prays and performs liturgical functions on behalf of the righteous. Thus in *1 Enoch* 9:1-11 he intercedes along with the three other archangels, Gabriel, Sariel, and Raphael, for those dying at the hands of the giant offspring of the Watchers (cf. *T. Abr.* 14:6, 12-13; *1 Enoch* 68:2-5). In *3 Baruch* 11–16, he descends to the fifth heaven to receive the prayers of humanity and returns to the highest heaven to offer them on the altar of the heavenly temple.

Michael also serves as psychopomp, the guide of the righteous dead into paradise. So in the *Testament of Abraham* he joins other angels in burying the body of Abraham by the oak of Mamre and then escorts his soul into paradise. He performs a similar task for the body and soul of Adam in the *Life of Adam and Eve* 47, where the Lord hands Adam over to Michael to keep until the Day of Judgment. In *1 Enoch* 24–25, Michael is identified as the angel who watches over paradise. In *3 Bar.* 11:2, he is called "the holder of the keys of the kingdom of heaven" (cf. *4 Bar.* 9:5, "the archangel of righteousness who opens the gates for the righteous"). Michael also plays the role of *angelus interpres* as he guides visionary heroes during their heavenly journeys; in *1 Enoch* 71, for example, he shows Enoch the secrets of mercy and righteousness. He is not, however, unique in this task; in *1 Enoch* 21–37, for instance, he performs it alongside Uriel and Raphael.

Dead Sea Scrolls

Despite the prominent role of angelology at Qumran, the archangel Michael appears by name only about ten times in the Dead Sea Scrolls. Two of these occurrences are in fragments of *1 Enoch* (4Q101-202). According to the *War Scroll,* Michael's name, along with those of the archangels Gabriel, Sariel, and Raphael, is to be written on the shields of the sons of light in the eschatological battle (1QM 9:15-16). Later, he comes to their aid and is exalted above the gods even as the dominion of Israel is exalted above all flesh (1QM 17:6-7). Michael is also mentioned in a fragment of the *War Rule* (4Q285 frg. 10 line 3). In the fragmentary text 4Q470, he speaks to Zedekiah (presumably the last king of Judah) and makes a covenant with him before the congregation. In 4Q529, a fragmentary Aramaic text, he addresses a group of angels and recounts to them the contents of a vision. Michael is probably identical to the angelic "prince of light" mentioned in various Qumran texts (1QS 3–4; 1QM 13:9-12) and may also be the heavenly figure who appears under the name "Melchizedek" in the *Melchizedek Scroll* (11Q13).

Rabbinic Literature

In rabbinic literature, Michael appears mainly in midrashim from the amoraic period (third to fourth century C.E.) and in talmudic passages. His role is similar to what we find in early Jewish apocalyptic texts and the Qumran material. Thus he is the protector of Israel (*Exod. Rab.* 18:5; *b. Sanhedrin* 26ab; *Gen. Rab.* 44:15; *Cant. Rab.* 1:12); he defends Israel against the accusations of Satan (*Exod. Rab.* 18:5; *Deut. Rab.* 11:10; *Pirqe de Rabbi Eliezer* 27); he fills the role of intercessor (*Exod. Rab.* 18:5; *b. Yoma* 77a); and he serves as high priest in the heavenly sanctuary (e.g., *b. Ḥagigah* 12b; *b. Taʿanit* 5a).

New Testament

In the New Testament, the angel Michael is identified explicitly only twice, in Rev. 12:7 and Jude 9. However, it is possible that Michael is the unnamed angel described in Rev. 20:1-3 who descends from heaven with the key to the abyss and the chain to bind Satan (cf. Rev. 19:17). This task is similar to that performed by Michael in *1 Enoch* 10:11-12, where he binds the rebellious Watchers in Tartarus.

In Rev. 12:7-9, Michael and his angels fight against the dragon (Satan) and his angels, defeating them and throwing them down to the earth. The hymn beginning in the next verse (12:10) celebrates the advent of God's kingdom and "the authority of his messiah." Jude 9 (with its possible reference to the lost ending of the *Assumption of Moses*) portrays Michael disputing with Satan for the body of Moses (see Origen, *On First Principles* 3.2.1).

BIBLIOGRAPHY

M. J. DAVIDSON 1992, *Angels at Qumran,* Sheffield: Sheffield Academic Press. • D. D. HANNAH 1999, *Michael and Christ: Michael Traditions and Angel Christology in Early Christianity,* Tübingen: Mohr-Siebeck. • W. LUEKEN 1898, *Michael: Eine Darstellung und Vergleichung der judischen and morgenländischen-christlichen Tradition vom Erzengel Michael,* Göttingen: Vandenhoeck und Ruprecht. • M. MACH 1992, *Entwicklungsstadien des judischen Engelglaubens in vorrabbinischer Zeit,* Tübingen: Mohr-Siebeck. • S. M. OLYAN 1993, *A Thousand Thousands Served Him: Exegesis and the Naming of Angels in Ancient Judaism,* Tübingen: Mohr-Siebeck. • J. P. ROHLAND 1977, *Der Erzengel Michael, Arzt und Feldherr: Zwei Aspekte des vor- und frühbyzantinischen Michaelkultes,* Leiden: Brill.

See also: Angels — ARCHIE T. WRIGHT

Midrash, Midrashim

From the Hebrew root *drš,* "to investigate, seek, search out, examine" (cf. Lev. 10:16; Isa. 34:16; 1 Chron. 28:8), "midrash" refers to a form and method of scriptural interpretation, and to compilations of rabbinic exegesis. In its broadest sense, the term is often used to refer to an interpretation of any text, sacred or secular, ancient or contemporary. For the purposes of clarity, however, the term should be limited to a process of exegesis that betrays specific features that are not exclusively rabbinic but nonetheless characterize rabbinic interpretation, and to the vast corpora of rabbinic biblical interpretation of the ancient and early medieval periods. Although midrashic collections were written down and edited from approximately the fifth to the thirteenth centuries C.E., they represent traditions that circulated in oral form prior to their redaction. Midrash, both the process and the very fruit of that process, grew out of an attempt to understand laconic or obscure biblical verses, to make biblical ordinances relevant to the contemporary Jewish community, to teach moral lessons, and to maintain the Jewish metanarrative that shaped and continues to sustain the Jewish people.

Rabbinic compilations of this period are ordered either according to a verse-by-verse exegesis or are a series of sermons based on the verse at hand. Compilations ordered according to a verse-by-verse framework are categorized as exegetical midrashim, whereas collections of sermons are known as homiletical midrashim. The earliest midrashic collections, often referred to as halakic midrashim, since they deal primarily with issues of halakah, rabbinic law, are also exegetical by nature and thus often provide word-by-word explications on verses in Exodus, Leviticus, Numbers, and Deuteronomy. Redacted in the land of Israel, these compilations are also known as tannaitic midrashim because the language of the halakic texts is mishnaic Hebrew and the sages mentioned are both Tannaim, rabbis of the period from the turn of the century to the third century of the Common Era, and first generation Amoraim, rabbis of the third and fourth centuries of the Common Era.

Underlying Principles and Hermeneutical Methods

Rabbinic interpretation exhibits a number of distinct features that are also found in early Jewish writings. In fact, midrash and inner-biblical exegesis, in their attempts to resolve seeming contradictions, share affinities. The New Testament also displays earmarks of midrashic method. Moreover, the *pĕšārîm* (sg. *pešer*) of the Dead Sea Scrolls, which begin with a biblical lemma, followed by an interpretation, and often allude to the present and future, similarly demonstrate characteristics of rabbinic exegesis. But while midrash exhibits characteristics akin to other forms of Jewish and non-Jewish interpretation of the Greco-Roman period, it is nonetheless *sui generis.*

Midrash is verso-centric and philologically focused. That is, biblical words and phrases are the starting point of the midrashic process, a process that sought to uphold the themes and structure of the biblical narrative. Early Jewish and rabbinic expositors dealt with the burning issues of the day. They had theological axes to grind and sought to guide their own generation, to address religious concerns, and to promulgate their beliefs by means of explicating biblical verses.

Moreover, every letter of a word, every phrase, was open to interpretation, for the Bible, God's Word, was expressed in a certain way to teach or explain something. Nothing in Scripture is superfluous and every word has many meanings, some more apparent than others. That verses may be elucidated in multiple ways is adduced in the fact that often midrashic collections provide several interpretations of the same verse. Indeed, one will often find contradictory statements from various rabbis about the meaning of a word, and one interpretation is not more acceptable than another.

Another postulate of rabbinic exegesis is the unity and self-referential nature of Scripture. The rabbis regard the Bible as a seamless whole such that a verse in the Prophets *(Nevi'im)* or the Writings *(Ketuvim)* throws light on a verse in Torah, and a verse from Psalms, for example, supports a rabbinic reading of a verse in Genesis. Indeed the *pĕtiḥtâ,* or proem, of the haggadic compilations (see below), best exemplifies the interconnectedness of biblical verses. The interrelatedness of biblical verses and the rabbis' painstaking attempts to elucidate the word of God attest to the unalloyed authority of Scripture.

The midrashic presuppositions outlined above are implicit in many of the exegetical methods employed by the rabbis, such as the seven *middôt* (rules) attributed to Hillel and the thirteen *middôt* attributed to R. Ishmael, which are attested in the *Sifra,* and are illustrated in tannaitic midrashim, that is, those dating from ca. 20 to 200 C.E. Another set of hermeneutical principles, thirty-two canons, is attributed to Eliezer b. Yose the Galilean, a fourth-generation tanna. Some of the more common exegetical rules found in these midrashim are as follows:

1. *Qal waḥōmer* (literally, "light and heavy"; *argumentum a minori ad majus* or inference *a fortiori*) — one of the most common exegetical principles, also found in haggadic, nonlegal midrashim, and in the New Testament. An argument from the lesser to the greater, or vice versa: "If that is true, how much more is this true."
2. *Gĕzērâ šawâ* ("comparison of equals") — an inference from the similarity of words or expressions between two biblical passages. By means of analogy, a particular detail of a biblical law in one verse is derived from the meaning of the word or phrase in the other.
3. *Binyan 'ab* ("building a family") — A specific law in one verse may be applied to all other similar cases. Here, as in the case of the *qal waḥōmer* and the *gĕzērâ šawâ,* we have analogous reasoning. Whereas the *qal waḥōmer* analogizes using the logic of *a fortiori,* and in the case of the *gĕzērâ šawâ,* the analogy is based on the similarity of language or form, here the analogy is based on comparable features.
4. *Kĕlal ûpĕraṭ* ("general and specific"); *peraṭ ûkĕlal* ("specific and general"); *kĕlal ûpĕraṭ ûkĕlal* ("general and specific and general") — rules of inference between general and specific statements. When a general rule is followed by a specific statement, then the rule is applied only to the specific statement *(kĕlal ûpĕraṭ).* The converse is true when a

specific statement is followed by a general statement; thus the specific does not limit the general *(peraṭ ûkĕlal)*. When a general statement is followed by a specific statement and then in turn by another general statement *(kĕlal ûpĕraṭ ûkĕlal)*, the rule is applied to matters similar to the specific statement, but not necessarily the specific matter. Unlike the above canons, these rules of legal interpretation govern the derivation of law within a single textual context. There are other principles of this type dealing with acceptable inferences between generalizations and specifications.

5. *Dābār lāmēd mē-ʾinyānô wĕdābār hălāmēd mîsôpô* ("something learned from the context and something learned from a later reference in the same passage") — ambiguity is resolved by noting the context or examining a nearby text.
6. *Šĕnê kĕtûbîn ha-makšîšîn zeh et zeh* ("two passages compared with a third") — a contradiction between two verses must be resolved by a third verse.
7. *Hekkeš* ("analogy") — inference by analogy, whether explicit or implicit between two subjects within the same or similar context. Rather than relating two verses by means of a common word or expression, *hekkeš* links texts by means of a common subject.

These are just some of the various methods that the rabbis employed in deriving halakah, which illustrate the interpretative assumptions sketched above such as the perfection of Torah, and the interconnectedness of the verses. The rabbis strive to maintain consistency within a single verse and between passages. These methods also call our attention to the heart of the rabbinic enterprise, namely, to make obsolete ordinances efficacious, and thus to maintain the covenantal relationship.

Many of the methods and literary forms used in interpreting nonlegal biblical verses have to do with philological play, for indeed the play on words is one of the main features of rabbinic exegesis. The rabbis were punsters par excellence, and their aural acuity allowed them to move with great facility from one end of the biblical canon to the other in order to voice theological beliefs, to provide fanciful details to laconic biblical stories, to flesh out a patriarch's or matriarch's moral character, or bring out the immoral character of the likes of Esau and Pharaoh. Wordplay also takes the form of *gematria*, whereby the arithmetical value of Hebrew letters is used to interpret a word or verse, and *notaricon*, shorthand writing whereby individual letters are used to signify words. In other words, Hebrew words are understood as acronyms so that each letter stands for another word, which in turn forms a phrase or sentence.

In addition to wordplays, we find stories, maxims, and parables, *mĕšālîm* (sg. *māšāl*). The Hebrew parables about kings are the signal form of narrative in rabbinic exegetical literature. Nearly all rabbinic *mĕšālîm* consist of a bipartite structure — the fictional narrative, that is, the *māšāl* proper, and its application, the *nimšal*, which usually concludes with a biblical verse serving as the *māšāl*'s proof text. Formulaic phrases mark the two parts: *māšāl lĕ*, "it is like" (also, *māšāl lĕmâ hadābār dômê lĕ* or simply *lĕ*) and *kak*, "so too, similarly" (Stern 1991: 8).

Midrashic Compilations

Rabbinic biblical interpretation of the late-antique period is marked by a series of exegetical and homiletic collections of midrashim. As we move into the early medieval period, we notice the emergence of an innovative form of biblical interpretation, one that integrates the structure of classical rabbinic midrashim within the framework of retelling biblical history. Later midrashic works such as the *Yalkut Shimʿoni* and the *Midrash Ha-Gadol* not only anthologize earlier midrashim, but also supplement traditional material.

One can only speculate as to what prompted the interest in collating sage sayings, rabbinic homilies, and rabbinic scriptural interpretation in general. Possibly, the decline of Palestine as the center of intellectual activity may have given rise to the need and interest in compiling such works. It may be, too, that Christian claims to the biblical heritage also factored into the need to preserve rabbinic discourse in writing, but again such statements are only suggestive, since the rabbis made no effort to state explicitly their priorities, concerns, and desiderata. We therefore have no way of knowing why the rabbis collected midrashim, discrete units of rabbinic musings and teachings on legal and nonlegal matters, into massive volumes. What we can safely say, however, is that the compilations reflect an ordering based on Scripture, that scriptural verses serve as proof texts, and that even though we must shy away from depicting the "rabbis" as a monolithic group, the compilations, certainly on a *prima facie* level, give the impression of concordance, despite the multiple and varying voices found within rabbinic literature.

Aware that the medieval transmission of rabbinic texts is a complex process that calls into question endeavors to establish authentic texts and create critical editions, scholars are therefore confronted with the nettlesome, and according to some insoluble, problem of dating rabbinic texts. Indeed, scholarly wrangling over the question of how to define a rabbinic text as "early" or "late," and the issue of the ways in which textual transmission calls into question the very value of rabbinic texts as historical sources, is far from over. Because rabbinic writings were transmitted gradually in a cumulative manner, they are resistant to fixed dating. Yet wide acceptance of a basic chronology, based on comparative philological and literary analyses, makes it possible to use these rabbinic works for historical purposes. One can assume that, as Sacha Stern notes, "redacted works began to emerge and to be treated, if only by name, as single identifiable entities. Thus the *Talmud* itself treats the *Mishna*, if not as a finished product, at least as an identifiable work around which its argumentation can revolve. In this respect it may be possible to assign approximate dates to these redacted works, even if the continuous process of multilayer redaction did not entirely cease thereafter, and even if we find that variations between different manuscript traditions and early printed editions can be quite considerable" (Stern 1994: xxiii).

Tannaitic Compilations

Also known as the *midrĕšê hălākâ* (halakic midrashim), these compilations (unlike the other major works of the tannaitic period — Mishnah and Tosefta — which are arranged according to subject) are arranged according to the order of verses in the four books of Torah — Exodus, Leviticus, Numbers, and Deuteronomy. The major midrashic works of this period are the *Mekilta de Rabbi Ishmael* on Exodus, *Sifra* on Leviticus, *Sifrei* on Numbers, and *Sifre* on Deuteronomy. These compilations are commonly considered the products of two distinct midrashic modes of exegesis — those stemming from R. Ishmael and those from R. Aqiba. The *Mekilta* and *Sifrei on Numbers* belong to the school of R. Ishmael, whereas the *Sifra* and *Sifre on Deuteronomy* belong to R. Aqiba. These two types of tannaitic compilations exhibit methodological and terminological distinctions. Whether the rabbis are deriving law by means of biblical exegesis, or deriving biblical support for rabbinic ordinances, tannaitic midrashim are generally speaking rarely less than complicated texts where various verses and halakic issues intersect.

Divided into nine tractates, *Mekilta de Rabbi Ishmael* is a verse-by-verse exposition of Exod. 12:1–23:19, and often it expounds every word of the verse. The collection also includes interpretation of Exod. 31:12-17 and 35:1-3. Although the *Mekilta* concentrates on the halakic portions of Exodus, it contains extensive narrative sections. The *Sifra* ("Book"), a running exegetical commentary on Leviticus in its entirety, is a collection of midrashim that overwhelmingly, almost exclusively, discusses halakic matters. Portions of the *Sifra* do not refer to Leviticus but have been included because of linguistic and thematic affinities. Like the *Mekilta* its language is mishnaic Hebrew, but it also contains several Greek words.

Sifre on Numbers deals primarily with halakic passages but also includes several portions of the biblical narrative such as the grousing of the Israelites in the wilderness. The work is divided into sections, *pîsqāʾôt* (sg. *pîsqâ*), as is the *Sifrei on Deuteronomy*, which is divided into 357 *pîsqaʾôt* that vary in length and cover most of the book of Deuteronomy. The central division of *Sifre on Deuteronomy* expounds Deut. 12:1–26:15, but also includes midrashim on Deut. 1:1-30; 3:23-29, 32:1–34:2, for example. As mentioned above, *Sifre on Deuteronomy*, like the other tannaitic midrashim, includes nonlegal material, such as the rich and moving midrashim on the death of Moses.

Haggadic Compilations: Midrash Rabbah

The *Midrash Rabbah* ("The Large Midrash"), a major compilation of rabbinic interpretations of the books of Torah and the five *megillot* (scrolls) — Lamentations, Esther, Ruth, Song of Songs, and Ecclesiastes — is a collection of *haggadic* literature, for the most part composed in Palestine over a period of several hundred years. Based on internal evidence, *Genesis Rabbah* dates from the fifth century, and the latest, *Numbers Rabbah*, is from the twelfth century.

The premier example of a haggadic exegetical compilation, *Genesis Rabbah* comprises commentaries on almost the entire book of Genesis. Here we find both simple and elaborate explanations of words and phrases of the verse at hand and often in Aramaic. *Pārāšîyôt*, or chapters (sg. *pārāšâ*), except for 13, 15, 17, 18, 25, 35, and 37, contain one or more proems, *pĕtiḥtôt* (sg. *pĕtiḥtâ*), a verse usually from the Writings, especially from Psalms or the Wisdom literature, sometimes from the Prophets, but rarely from the Torah, that is seemingly extraneous but through a chain of interpretations is connected to the verse at the beginning of the section. So, for example, on the second half of Gen. 7:1 ("And the LORD said to Noah: 'Come, you and your entire household, unto the ark; for you I have seen righteous before Me in this generation'"), *Gen. Rab.* 33:2 opens: "For the LORD is righteous, He loves righteousness; the upright shall behold his face" (Ps. 11:7). And how is Ps. 11:7 related to the Gen. 7:1? The midrash continues:

> R. Tanhuma in R. Judah's name and R. Menahem in R. Eleazar's name said: No man loves his fellow craftsman, but a sage loves his companion. R. Hiyya loves his fellow craftsmen and R. Hoshaya loves his. The Holy One, blessed be He, also loves His [in the sense that God is righteous and loves those who are also righteous, and in that respect they are God's fellow craftsmen]. Therefore, "For the LORD is righteous, He loves righteousness; the upright shall behold his face" (Ps. 11:7) applies to Noah, as it is written, "for you I have seen righteous before Me in this generation."

The verse in Psalms is quoted to explicate Gen. 7:1 by showing that God actually loves to see the righteous. Because they are righteous like him, they are in a sense God's companions.

Homiletic Midrashim

In addition to verse-by-verse collections of midrashim, such as *Genesis Rabbah* and *Lamentations Rabbah*, several collections (e.g., *Leviticus Rabbah* and *Pesikta de Rab Kahana*) are arranged homiletically; that is, they are arranged as chapters of homilies that cluster around a particular topic. The collections of homilies share a structural arrangement: a series of proems *(pĕtiḥtôt)*, the body *(gûfâ)* of the homily, and an eschatological ending or peroration. As mentioned above, the *pĕtiḥtâ*'s structure exemplifies a fundamental aspect of midrash, namely, the desire to unite the diverse parts of the tripartite canon — Torah, Prophets, and Writings — into a harmonious, seamless whole that reflects the oneness of God's Word. As David Stern notes, "each and every verse is simultaneous with every other, temporally and semantically; as a result, every verse, no matter how remote, can be seen as a possible source for illuminating the meaning of any other verse. While this tendency is manifest throughout midrash — every place two otherwise unconnected verses are joined in order to reveal new nexuses of meaning — the *pĕtiḥtâ* is undoubtedly its most sophisticated literary expression" (Stern 1986: 108). In his general discussion of the midrashic proem, Martin Jaffee locates its *Sitz im Leben* in the rabbinic house of study, for its sophisticated literariness is "hardly suited for oral presentation" (Jaffee 1983: 167).

Given the formal structure of the homilies of *Leviticus Rabbah,* they were likely composed of various parts of sermons delivered in the synagogue that were welded together to create what Joseph Heinemann terms the "literary homily" (Heinemann 1986: 143). Thus, while homilies were delivered publicly, they nonetheless bear the characteristics of well-crafted works of literature.

In addition to *Leviticus Rabbah, Deuteronomy Rabbah,* and *Numbers Rabbah,* there are several compilations that employ the framework of the homiletical midrashim. *Pesiqta de Rab Kahana,* dating from 500 to 700 C.E., is arranged according to selected passages or sections read on special Sabbaths or festal days. Each *piska,* "section," has a unified theme that is appropriate to the scriptural reading of the day, which is arranged according to the Palestinian reading cycle.

Comprising various sermons on diverse themes, *Pesiqta de Rab Kahana* nonetheless maintains an underlying thread throughout the *pesiktas,* namely, the chosenness of Israel as God's people to whom God bestowed the gift of Torah. Moreover, it deals with biblical narratives and espouses fundamental rabbinic articles of faith, yet at the same time retells anecdotes about notable rabbis such as R. Aqiba (second century), R. Simeon bar Yohai (second century), and R. Abbahu (third century), and their legendary ways. The bulk of these stories, sources of purportedly biographical data, illustrate virtuous, exemplary conduct, most especially their dedication to Torah.

Leviticus Rabbah and *Pesiqta de Rab Kahana* have five chapters in common (see Stemberger and Strack 1996: 315), which provides scholars with ample fodder to discuss the relationship between the two, that is, whether or not one adopted some or all the chapters from one source or vice versa. Later compilations, which are more difficult to date, include *Midrash Psalms, Exodus Rabbah,* and the Tanḥuma-Yelamdenu literature. Since it incorporates earlier material, it is difficult to pinpoint the date of redaction of *Midrash Psalms,* also called *Shocher Tov,* from the opening words of Prov. 11:27. As Stemberger and Strack note (1996: 351), we must assume an extended period of development from the talmudic period to the thirteenth century. *Exodus Rabbah,* like *Psalms Rabbah,* is composed of two parts; the first is an exegetical midrash on Exodus 1–10, the second a homiletic midrash on Exodus 12–40. The work has been dated variously by modern scholars to the tenth, eleventh, or twelfth centuries (Stemberger and Strack 1996: 335-37).

Tanḥuma or Yelamdenu midrashim, according to Stemberger and Strack, "are a group of homiletic midrashim on the Pentateuch which are transmitted in many versions" and include not only the two editions of Tanḥuma, the Ordinary Edition and the Buber, but also various handwritten recensions. This literature also comprises *Exodus Rabbah II, Numbers Rabbah II, Deuteronomy Rabbah,* parts of *Pesiqta de Rab Kahana,* and other midrashim. Its commonly held date is the early ninth century (see Stemberger and Strack 1996: 331).

Given the complex textual transmission of *Deuteronomy Rabbah,* it is difficult to date it with a modicum of certainty. Given its language and reference to Palestinian rabbis and locations, it more likely than not originated prior to the Babylonian Talmud, but its textual history makes it impossible to date as early as the fifth century. Zunz dates it to the tenth century, although Lieberman disagrees with this late dating.

Traditionally ascribed to the first-century tanna Rabbi Eliezer ben Hyrkanos, *Pirqe de Rabbi Eliezer* ("Chapters of Rabbi Eliezer") is an eighth- or early ninth-century work that draws on the classical rabbinic texts, while at the same time it expands and develops its sources' motifs and narratives. Its author's retelling of biblical stories, which incorporates mystical language and imagery as well as fairly detailed discussions of astronomy and the calendar, makes it unlike earlier rabbinic works.

The intention of *Tanna de-be Eliyahu,* also known as *Seder Eliyahu,* is expressed at the outset: to urge right moral conduct *(derek ʾereṣ)* and to glorify the study of Torah. It contains interpretations of legal issues by means of parables and stories derived from the author's adventurous peregrinations. While there is no scholarly consensus as to its final redaction, it seems likely that the work was composed after the Babylonian Talmud and before the ninth century, even though it is often considered a tenth-century work (Stemberger and Strack 1996: 269-71).

As this brief survey of some of the well-known compilations attests, further work in the field of dating rabbinic texts is sorely needed.

Midrashic Anthologies

Thesaurus-like collections characterize the post-classical, mid-late medieval period of rabbinic literature. Noteworthy are the *Yalkut Shimʿoni* (known simply as the *Yalkut*), *Yalkut ha-Makhiri,* and the *Midrash ha-Gadol.* The *Yalkut,* compiled from more than fifty works and covering the entire span of Tanak, is one of the most well-known and comprehensive anthologies. The compiler, Shimʿon Ha-Darshan, availed himself of the wealth of rabbinic literature and amassed rabbinic sayings into an exhaustive collection ordered according to the verses of the Bible. The work is dated to the thirteenth century, but it was at the end of the fifteenth century that it circulated widely and received popular attention.

Compiled by Makhir ben Abba Mari in Spain, *Yalkut ha-Makhiri,* unlike the *Yalkut Shimʿoni,* deliberately excludes writings in the *Midrash Rabbah* and focuses primarily on the Prophets, Job, Psalms, and Proverbs. A late-thirteenth- or fourteenth-century work, the *Yalkut ha-Makhiri* uses early as well as late sources such as *Tanhuma, Midrash Job, Seder Eliyahu Rabbah,* and *Midrash Mishle (Proverbs).* It also preserves work not found in its sources, a feature which makes it a valuable resource.

The largest collection of midrash is the Yemenite anthology on the Pentateuch, the *Midrash ha-Gadol,* almost universally attributed to David ben Amram of Aden. Dated to the fourteenth century, *Midrash ha-Gadol* is divided according to the annual reading cycle. Its sources are extensive, including not only the classical and later midrashic works, but also both the Babylonian and Palestinian Talmuds, writings of the geonic period (sixth to eleventh century), the works of Alfasi, and Maimonides. In this case, the compiler may be regarded as author, for he "frequently inserts his own explanatory glosses." As Stemberger and Strack write, "Thus there results a mosaic-like composition, an entirely new work with its own style, whose sources can often no longer be reconstructed" (1996: 387).

There are several other collections of midrashic works of this period, collections that blend collation and commentary. In this later period, we also notice a rise in Bible commentaries, but this did not preclude an interest in midrash. The biblical interpretations of the rabbis as we find them in compilations of the early medieval period, *au contraire,* were often mentioned or alluded to in Bible commentaries, and even today find their way in contemporary sermons, for they are part of the very bedrock of the Jewish tradition.

BIBLIOGRAPHY

C. BAKHOS, ED. 2006, *Current Trends in the Study of Midrash,* Leiden: Brill. • D. BOYARIN 1990, *Intertextuality and the Reading of Midrash,* Bloomington: Indiana University Press. • M. FISHBANE 2003, *Biblical Myth and Rabbinic Mythmaking,* Oxford: Oxford University Press. • S. FRAADE 1991, *From Tradition to Commentary in the Midrash Sifre to Deuteronomy,* Albany: State University of New York. • G. HARTMAN AND S. BUDICK, EDS. 1986, *Midrash and Literature,* New Haven: Yale University Press. • G. HASAN-ROKEM 2000, *Web of Life: Folklore and Midrash in Rabbinic Literature,* trans. B. Stein, Stanford: Stanford University Press. • G. HASAN-ROKEM 2003, *Tales of the Neighborhood: Jewish Narrative Dialogues in Late Antiquity,* Berkeley: University of California Press. • J. HEINEMANN 1986, "The Nature of Aggadah," in *Midrash and Literature,* ed. G. Hartman and S. Budick, New Haven: Yale University Press. • M. HIRSHMAN 2000, "Theology and Exegesis in Midrashic Literature," in *Interpretation and Allegory: Antiquity and the Modern Period,* ed. J. Whitman, Leiden: Brill. • M. JAFFEE 1983, "'The Midrashic' Proem: Towards the Description of Rabbinic Exegesis," in *Approaches to Ancient Judaism,* vol. 4, *Studies in Liturgy, Exegesis and Talmudic Narrative,* ed. W. S. Green, Chico, Calif.: Scholars Press. • J. L. KUGEL 1990, *In Potiphar's House: The Interpretive Life of Biblical Texts,* New York: Harper Collins. • J. L. KUGEL 1998, *Traditions of the Bible: A Guide to the Bible As It Was at the Start of the Common Era,* Cambridge: Harvard University Press. • J. NEUSNER 1988, *Midrash in Context,* Atlanta: Scholars Press. • G. PORTON 1981, "Defining Midrash," in *The Study of Ancient Judaism,* ed. J. Neusner, New York: Ktav. • A. SHINAN AND Y. ZAKOVITCH 1986, "Midrash on Scripture and Midrash within Scripture," *Scripta Hierosolymitana* 31: 259-77. • G. STEMBERGER AND H. L. STRACK 1996, *Introduction to the Talmud and Midrash,* 2d ed., Minneapolis: Fortress. • D. STERN 1986, "Midrash and the Language of Exegesis: A Study of Vayikra Rabbah, Chapter I," in *Midrash and Literature,* ed. Hartman and Budick, New Haven: Yale University Press. • D. STERN 1991, *Parables in Midrash,* Cambridge: Harvard University Press. • D. STERN 1996, *Midrash and Theory: Ancient Jewish Exegesis and Contemporary Literary Studies,* Evanston, Ill.: Northwestern University Press. • S. STERN 1994, *Jewish Identity in Early Rabbinic Writings,* Leiden: Brill. • L. TEUGELS AND R. ULMER, ED. 2005, *Recent Developments in Midrash Research: Proceedings of the 2002 and 2003 SBL Consultation on Midrash,* Piscataway, N.J.: Gorgias Press. • B. VISOTZKY 2003, *Golden Bells and Pomegranates: Studies in Midrash Rabbah,* Tübingen: Mohr-Siebeck. • A. YADIN 2004, *Scripture as Logos: Rabbi Ishmael and the Origins of Midrash,* Philadelphia: University of Pennsylvania Press.

CAROL BAKHOS

Military, Jews in

First Temple Period

Biblical accounts of premonarchic times envisage the existence of an Israelite army based on tribal organization and mobilized for action each time there was need to fight the enemies of Israel. This was a militia-type army in which every able-bodied adult was expected to serve. Under the monarchy there came to be established a standing army composed mainly of Israelite soldiers, but also of foreign mercenaries, with the king protected by the royal guard. Recourse to call-up of the militia was maintained in emergency times. Swords were widely used and the infantry included spearmen, archers, and slingers. Reports of the use of chariots are corroborated by a document of Shalmaneser III, recording that Ahab king of Israel had 2,000 chariots and 10,000 infantry. With the destruction of the kingdoms of Israel (721 B.C.E.) and of Judah (586 B.C.E.) their armies disintegrated, but notions of their composition, weaponry, and exploits continued to have an impact during the Second Temple period.

Persian and Hellenistic Times

The Persian Empire used native troops, and in the province Judah the local garrisons responsible for internal security included Jews; the same holds true for Samaria with its Yahweh-worshiping Samaritan population. Given their small size, the military contribution of both provinces to major campaigns of the empire was clearly negligible, and it is never mentioned in the sources. According to Josephus (*Ant.* 11.317-21), Alexander the Great failed to receive military help from the Jewish high priest, and the Samaritan leader Sanballat put 8,000 men at Alexander's disposal during the siege of Tyre. Yet the authenticity of this report, as well as of other information on the participation of Jews in the campaigns of Alexander (Josephus, *Ag. Ap.* 1.192, 200-204) is disputed.

The Aramaic papyri of Elephantine, on the southern border of Egypt, attest the existence of a Jewish military colony in the late fifth century B.C.E. that apparently had been established in the Saite period and passed into the service of the Persian Empire after the conquest of Cambyses in 525 B.C.E. The report that Jews fought under Psammetichus against the Ethiopians (*Letter of Aristeas* 13) probably refers to a major duty of this colony. The same source relates that, of the Jews he transported to Egypt, Ptolemy I armed 30,000 men to garrison fortresses — to guard against the Egyptian population — and to serve in the army (*Letter of Aristeas* 13 and 36–37; Josephus, *Ant.* 12.8; *Ag. Ap.* 2.44). It is likely that under that king Jewish soldiers were stationed in Alexandria and Cyrene.

Josephus (*Ant.* 14.133) and other sources relate the existence of Jewish military camps, two of which were located on the western and eastern sides of the Delta. One district with Jewish military settlers was "the Land of Onias," east of the Delta, granted to Onias IV (or III) by Ptolemy VI in the 160s (Josephus, *J.W.* 1.190; 7.421-26), and later a Jewish force was posted at Pelusion to guard the entrance to the country from Palestine (*J.W.* 1.175). Papyrological evidence, notably from the Fayum, confirms that Jews served in the infantry and the cavalry of the Ptolemaic regular and reserve army. Jewish soldiers were enrolled in ethnically mixed units, and some evidence suggests that there also existed separate Jewish units, at least from the mid-second century B.C.E.

The cleruchs or military settlers of Tobias, a Ptolemaic official and head of a Jewish family with large estates in Transjordan in the mid-third century B.C.E., were a mixed unit. On the whole, Jews did not differ from other foreign mercenary soldiers and, like them, they were allotted plots of land for living; the Ptolemaic regime, suspicious of the native population, reckoned this system useful to secure their allegiance. Jews were trusted to hold commanding positions; two notable examples from the second century B.C.E. are the Jews Chelkias and Ananias, who commanded the army of Cleopatra III in the war against her son Ptolemy IX (Josephus, *Ant.* 13.348-51).

Little is known about Jewish soldiers in the service of the Seleucids, the other great Hellenistic kingdom with a large Jewish population. 2 Maccabees attributes a major role to Jews in a battle between the Macedonians (= Seleucids) and the Galatians in Babylonia (2 Macc. 8:20), and Josephus cites a letter of Antiochus III from the late third century B.C.E. ordering the establishment of a military colony of 2,000 Babylonian Jews in Phrygia, a region with other Seleucid military colonies (*Ant.* 12.147-53). These colonies served to check the rebellious native population, and the settlers formed the reserve Seleucid army. Josephus' report of the settlement of the Babylonian Jewish chieftain Zamaris with his 500 mounted archers and kinsmen in Batanea, at the invitation of Herod (*Ant.* 17.24), is telling of the military potential of the Jews of Babylonia. Presumably more important was the fighting of the Hasmoneans Jonathan, Simon, and John Hyrcanus for several Seleucid kings. The Seleucids evidently were willing to recruit Jewish manpower for their military needs, and prevailing conditions made it possible for Jews to join the Seleucid army.

The Hasmonean and Herodian Armies

Judas Maccabaeus won his first battles by guerrilla tactics. Later, either under Judas or Jonathan, the tactics, weaponry, and methods of fighting of the Hellenistic armies were introduced into the Hasmonean army. The standing army, composed of light and heavy infantry and cavalry, was strengthened by general mobilization in cases of major wars and included foreign mercenaries from the time of John Hyrcanus. It was equipped with Hellenistic artillery and siege machines, and the various fortresses that were constructed throughout the country, both for internal security and against foreign invasions, had much in common with Hellenistic fortifications. While 2 Maccabees testifies to Hellenistic influence on the Hasmonean army, both 1 and 2 Maccabees are inspired in their writing by biblical military accounts. It is significant for understanding the level of military knowledge current in Judea during the Herodian period that biblical, Hellenistic, Hasmonean, and Roman elements, as well as imaginary details, characterize the army envisaged in the Qumran *War Scroll*.

Herod's army was composed of Jewish and non-Jewish soldiers, with the royal guard consisting only of foreigners (notably Thracians, Germans, and Gauls). The standing army was stationed in cities and fortresses throughout the country to control the Jewish and Hellenistic population, because Herod was haunted by fears of rebellions and conspiracies. The safeguard of the country was also served by discharged soldiers sent to colonize Sebaste, Gaba, Esebonitis, and perhaps Idumea; these veterans may be regarded as reserve forces. Military settlers were employed in Batanea, Trachonitis, and Auranitis to suppress the brigandage that was endemic there. Herod, who had experience of fighting with and commanding Roman troops and was supported by large Roman forces in his war against the last Hasmonean king Antigonus (40-37 B.C.E.), based his army on the Roman model. The Roman cohort formed the basic tactical unit, with the light-armed soldiers and heavy infantry fighting in the manner of the Roman *auxilia* and the Roman legionaries, respectively. His army thus enhanced Herod's usefulness to the Roman government.

Under Roman Rule

Hellenistic rulers apparently found solutions to let Jewish soldiers observe the Law (Josephus, *Ant.* 13.251-52; *Ag. Ap.* 1.192), but service in the Roman army entailed participation in the festivals of the Roman state religion; the military oath and the worship of the standards were anathema to Jews. Thus Jews were deterred from joining the Roman army not merely by the problem of bearing arms or marching on the Sabbath and of obtaining kosher food, the specific religious reasons given by Roman magistrates for their exempting Jewish Roman citizens from military service in 49 and 43 B.C.E. (Josephus, *Ant.* 14.223-40). In the imperial period, when voluntary military service prevailed, only renegade Jews would have enlisted. Also, the Roman government distrusted Jewish soldiers. Most of Herod's Jewish soldiers joined the rebellion that erupted after his death. After the annexation of Judea to direct Roman rule in 6 C.E., the *auxilia* units that garrisoned the province consisted of pagan soldiers only. Given the chronic Jewish riots and revolts in Judea and elsewhere, it must have been too risky to enlist Jews into the army. All in all, Jewish service in the Roman army was very rare.

BIBLIOGRAPHY
B. BAR-KOCHVA 1989, *Judas Maccabaeus,* Cambridge: Cambridge University Press. • A. KASHER 1985, *The Jews in Hellenistic and Roman Egypt,* Tübingen: Mohr-Siebeck, 38-48. • I. SHATZMAN 1991, *The Armies of the Hasmonaeans and Herod,* Tübingen: Mohr-Siebeck. • I. SHATZMAN 2007, "The Military Aspects of the *War Rule,*" in *The Qumran Scrolls,* ed. M. Kister et al., Jerusalem: Yad Izhak Ben-Zvi (in Hebrew). • V. TCHERIKOVER 1957, *Corpus Papyrorum Judaicarum,* vol. 1, Cambridge: Harvard University Press, 11-16, 147-78. • Y. YADIN 1963, *The Art of Warfare in Biblical Lands,* Jerusalem: International Publishing Company.

ISRAEL SHATZMAN

Minor Prophets

The Minor Prophets are the twelve short prophetic books grouped together as the fourth book of the Latter Prophets (following Isaiah, Jeremiah, and Ezekiel) in the Jewish Tanak and as the fifth book of the Prophets (following Isaiah, Jeremiah, Ezekiel, and Daniel) in the Christian Old Testament. The Minor Prophets include Hosea, Joel, Amos, Obadiah, Jonah, Micah, Nahum, Habakkuk, Zephaniah, Haggai, Zechariah, and Malachi.

The designation "Minor Prophets" is due to the relative shortness of these books in relation to the Major Prophets. They are more properly designated "the Book of the Twelve Prophets." Jewish tradition designates them as *Tĕrê ʿaśar,* Aramaic for "the Twelve," and treats them as one book, although the Talmud specifies that each of the Twelve be separated by three blank lines instead of the usual four lines commonly employed to set off biblical books (*b. Baba Batra* 13b). Christian tradition commonly designates them as the *Dōdekaprophēton,* Greek for "the Twelve Prophets," and treats them as twelve separate books.

The books are generally read individually in both ancient and modern times, although modern scholars increasingly read the Book of the Twelve as a whole. Some (e.g., Nogalski 1993a; 1993b) maintain that additions to individual books were employed in the redaction of the Book of the Twelve, but such hypotheses do not account for the textual versions of the Book of the Twelve.

The Versions

Masoretic Text

The Book of the Twelve Prophets appears in two major versions. The Masoretic Text (MT) is the standard Hebrew version of the book employed in Jewish Bibles and frequently in Christian tradition. The order of the books, namely, Hosea, Joel, Amos, Obadiah, Jonah, Micah, Nahum, Habakkuk, Zephaniah, Haggai, Zechariah, Malachi (see also Sir. 49:10), presupposes reflection on the experience of Jerusalem from the Assyrian invasions of the late eighth century, through the Babylonian Exile of the sixth century, and the Persian-period restoration of the sixth-fourth centuries B.C.E. (Sweeney 2000). Some consider the order to be chronological, but this is impossible since Joel, Obadiah, and Jonah — and possibly Malachi — would be viewed as ninth-century books in the premodern tradition.

Septuagint

The Septuagint version (LXX) was originally produced in Alexandrian Jewish circles before it was adopted as sacred Scripture by early Christianity. The order of the books in early LXX manuscripts (see also *2 Esdras* 1:39-40) includes Hosea, Amos, Micah, Joel, Obadiah, Jonah, Nahum, Habakkuk, Zephaniah, Haggai, Zechariah, and Malachi. This order presupposes reflection on the fate of the northern kingdom of Israel as a paradigm for that of Jerusalem and the southern kingdom of Judah (Sweeney 2000). Other orders appear in *Mart. & Ascen. Isa.*

Fragments of the Greek Minor Prophets Scroll from Naḥal Ḥever (8ḤevXIIgr) *(Courtesy Israel Antiquities Authority)*

4:22 (Amos, Hosea, Micah, Joel, Obadiah, Jonah, Nahum, Habakkuk, Zephaniah, Haggai, Zechariah, Malachi); the *Lives of the Prophets* (Hosea, Micah, Amos, Joel, Obadiah, Jonah, Nahum, Habakkuk, Zephaniah, Malachi); and 4QXII[a] (see below).

Manuscripts from the Judean Desert

The earliest copies of the Twelve Prophets appear among the manuscripts of the Judean Desert. Fragments of eight Hebrew manuscripts of the Twelve Prophets, designated as 4QXII[a-g] (4Q76–4Q82 and 4QMicah) and dating from the mid-second century B.C.E. through the late first century C.E., were found in Qumran Cave 4.

4QXII[a] (4Q76), dated to ca. 150 B.C.E., begins with Zech. 14:18 and includes portions of Malachi and Jonah. It appears to be an independent textual witness, and it is unique insofar as Jonah follows Malachi.

4QXII[b] (4Q77), dated to the mid-second century B.C.E., is proto-MT and contains fragments of Zephaniah and Haggai.

4QXII[c] (4Q78), dated to ca. 75 B.C.E., represents the presumed LXX *Vorlage* and contains portions of Hosea, Joel, Amos, Zephaniah, and Malachi.

4QXII[d] (4Q79), dated to the second half of the first century C.E., contains proto-MT fragments of Hosea.

4QXII[e] (4Q80), dated to ca. 75 B.C.E., contains fragments of Haggai and Zechariah that resemble the LXX *Vorlage.*

4QXII[f] (4Q81), dated to ca. 50 B.C.E., contains proto-MT fragments of Jonah.

4QMicah is a single fragment that contains Micah 5:1-2 and may be a part of 4QXII[f]. 4QXII[g] (4Q82), dated to the latter half of the first century B.C.E., contains portions of Hosea, Joel, Amos, Obadiah, Jonah, Micah, Nahum, Habakkuk, Zephaniah, and Zechariah, and resembles the MT.

The Murabbaʿat Scroll of the Twelve Prophets (Mur 88) contains a Hebrew text virtually identical with the MT (apart from orthographic variations) that dates to the early second century C.E. Due to damage, the scroll now contains only portions of Joel, Amos, Obadiah, Jonah, Nahum, Micah, Habakkuk, Zephaniah, Haggai, and Zechariah.

The Naḥal Ḥever Greek Twelve Prophets Scroll (8ḤevXIIgr) is the oldest known witness to the Greek text of the Twelve Prophets and represents a rather crude translation of a proto-MT version of the Twelve. It includes portions of Jonah, Micah, Nahum, Habakkuk, Zephaniah, and Zechariah. Some consider it to be a proto-Theodotion or *kaige*-Theodotion version that represents an early attempt to revise the original LXX text.

BIBLIOGRAPHY

B. A. JONES 1995, *The Formation of the Book of the Twelve: A Study in Text and Canon,* Atlanta: Scholars Press. • J. D. NOGALSKI 1993A, *Literary Precursors to the Book of the Twelve,* Berlin: de Gruyter. • J. D. NOGALSKI 1993B, *Redactional Processes in the Book of the Twelve,* Berlin: de Gruyter. • J. D. NOGALSKI AND M. A. SWEENEY, EDS. 2000, *Reading and Hearing the Book of the Twelve,* Atlanta: Society of Biblical Literature. • P. L. REDDITT AND A. SCHART, EDS. 2003, *Thematic Threads in the Book of the Twelve,* Berlin: de Gruyter. • M. A. SWEENEY 2000, *The Twelve Prophets,* Collegeville: Liturgical Press. • E. TOV 1990, *The Greek Minor Prophets Scroll from Naḥal Ḥever,* Oxford: Clarendon. • J. W. WATTS AND P. R. HOUSE, EDS. 1996, *Forming Prophetic Literature: Essays on Isaiah and the Twelve in Honor of John D. W. Watts,* Sheffield: Sheffield Academic Press.

MARVIN A. SWEENEY

Miqṣat Maʿaśê ha-Torah (MMT)

Miqṣat Maʿăśê Ha-tôrâ ("Some of the Works of the Torah") is a fragmentary halakic document found in Cave 4 at Qumran. It is also known by the acronym 4QMMT or MMT. The expression "works of the Law" is found in the text's epilogue. The appearance of this expression in Hebrew has been of particular interest to New Testament scholars, being the only occurrence in early Jewish literature of a term comparable to Paul's Greek phrase *erga nomou.* The document is significant for understanding the history of the Qumran movement and the development of Jewish halakah during the late Second Temple period.

Manuscripts and Date

The official edition of 4QMMT was published in 1994 by Elisha Qimron and John Strugnell in DJD 10. The composition is dated by the editors to around 150 B.C.E., and it is generally considered one of the earliest Qumran writings or else a pre-Qumran work. (This assessment of the date presupposes a particular view of the history of the community, and is not required by the manuscript evidence.) It is preserved in six or seven late Hasmonean and early Herodian manuscripts (4Q394-399). In addition, a manuscript of MMT in cryptic script has been tentatively identified by Stephen Pfann, labeled 4QCryptA Miqṣat Maʿaśe Ha-Torah[g] (4Q313). None of the extant manuscripts preserves the whole document; most of them contain only fragments from either of the two main sections.

Problems with the Composite Text

The editors have created a composite text of the manuscripts of MMT. In spite of the substantial contribution by the initial editors, the composite text of the DJD edition is not entirely unproblematic. Already in the official edition and in the various appendices published with it, it becomes clear that the editors disagree concerning the textual basis of the document, specifically, the arrangement of the fragments of the last section of MMT, the epilogue. In the DJD edition, the composite text is arranged by Elisha Qimron. John Strugnell and Hartmut Stegemann have proposed an alternative placement for the fragments of the epilogue (esp. 4Q398 frgs. 11-13), but they have never published their alternative reconstruction.

Another problem with the composite text is that we have no evidence of the transition between the halakic section and the epilogue, since neither the ending of the

MIQṢAT MAʿAŚÊ HA-TORAH (MMT)

4Q394 MMT[a] and 4Q395 MMT[b], fragments from the "Some of the Works of the Torah" document *(Courtesy Israel Antiquities Authority)*

halakic section nor the opening section of the epilogue is preserved in any of the manuscripts. In addition, MMT was apparently copied in slightly differing forms. In at least one manuscript (4Q394), there was a calendrical section of some kind before the halakot, but this calendar was not necessarily incorporated into all manuscripts of MMT. It seems that the halakic section was transmitted rather faithfully, since the manuscripts contain hardly any indications of redactional activity. However, all manuscripts attesting the epilogue contain variant readings that do reflect such activity for this section. For these reasons, the composite text should never be used alone as an authoritative edition of the composition, but always together with the individual manuscripts.

Contents

The extant document can be divided into three literary divisions. Section A is a calendrical section representing a 364-day solar calendar, known, for instance, from the book of *Jubilees, 1 Enoch,* and the *Temple Scroll.* The very short calendrical reference of three lines is preserved in only one of the manuscripts (4Q394 frgs. 3a-4, col. i, lines 1-3). It appears that the calendar did not constitute a part of the original document. Section B consists of the halakot and contains regulations related to priestly concerns: sacrifice and (profane) slaughter, ritual purity, priestly marriages, people excluded from the community, and other boundary-marking issues. It is likely that the halakic section reflects inner-priestly disputes. Some of the legal interpretations of MMT resemble the opinions attributed to the Sadducees in later rabbinic literature (e.g., *m. Parah* 3:7). The laws of the legal section are mostly based on laws in Leviticus and Numbers, but in two cases the basic commandment of cultic centralization (Deut. 12:5) is cited in order to justify a legal interpretation. This is an indicator of the importance of Jerusalem and the Temple for the authors of MMT.

Section C is a concluding epilogue. The terms "admonition," "exhortation," or "hortatory conclusion" have also been used to describe this final section. In the epilogue, historical and theological references (e.g., to the kings and the exile) are used to exhort the readers to follow the correct interpretation of the Law and to enforce the purity of the cult. The emphasis is on repentance, return, and faithfulness to the covenant. This faithfulness requires the acceptance of the legal interpretation as presented in the halakic section.

The emphasis on covenant is further reflected in the structure of the document. The first words of the halakic section of MMT look like the incipit of a collection of laws, perhaps consciously modeled after the first words of Deuteronomy. In the epilogue, covenantal blessings and curses are mentioned several times (cf. Deuteronomy 27, 28). For the structure of the document, the authors of MMT adopted and adjusted the covenantal pattern known from biblical law collections: an incipit, legal statements, and a parenetic conclusion woven together with references to blessings and curses.

Literary Genre

The editors of MMT initially identified it as a letter written by the leader of the Qumran community — possibly even by the Teacher of Righteousness himself — to the leader of the community's opponents, a high priest in Jerusalem, possibly Jonathan or Simon. The reference in the *Commentary on Psalm 37* (4QpPs[a]) to the "precepts and law" sent by the Teacher of Righteousness to the Wicked Priest was adduced to substantiate this identification. Since the publication of the DJD edition, however, the genre of MMT has become a debated issue, and clearly the document contains hardly any of the formal characteristics of a personal letter (see already Strugnell 1994).

It is easier to reject the genre of personal letter for MMT than to make a strong case for an alternative generic identification. The fragmentary state of the manuscripts, especially the loss of the opening section of the document, has deprived us of conclusive evidence. Apparently, however, the document is not a pure representation of any genre but a mixture of elements of various genres, including legal and epistolary. In addition to adapting features of these genres, the authors introduced innovative elements suitable for their purposes.

Nonsectarian Character

It is generally agreed that MMT was authored by members of the Qumran group or its predecessors, members of a larger pre-Qumranic movement. However, it appears that the focus of the halakic section is not necessarily sectarian; it is not concerned with governing the life of a particular group but is rather addressed to Israel as a whole. Apart from the stringency of the purity regulations, there is nothing in the legal section of MMT that points to a sectarian community, nor can the generally assumed Qumranic equation of ritual impurity and sin be detected there. Furthermore, there is nothing in the theology of the epilogue typical of the Qumran community. The understanding of the covenant in MMT is not exclusivist as it is, for instance, in the Qumran *Community Rule.* In addition, the exhortations to repentance and return in the epilogue contrast with the determinism of much distinctive Qumran theology.

Regardless of whether MMT was written by members of the Qumran movement or not, the large number of first-century-B.C.E. copies of the work found at Qumran witness to its significance for the community. Furthermore, these late copies indicate the continuing importance of the Jerusalem Temple for the Qumran community.

BIBLIOGRAPHY

J. M. BAUMGARTEN 1994, "Sadducean Elements in Qumran Law," in *The Community of the Renewed Covenant: The Notre Dame Symposium on the Dead Sea Scrolls,* ed. E. Ulrich and J. VanderKam, Notre Dame: University of Notre Dame Press, 27-36. • G. J. BROOKE 1997, "Explicit Presentation of Scripture in 4QMMT," in *Legal Texts and Legal Issues: Proceedings of the Second Meeting of the International Organization for Qumran Studies, Cambridge 1995,* ed. M. J. Bernstein, F. García Martínez, and J. Kampen, Leiden: Brill, 67-88. • J. D. G. DUNN 1997, "4QMMT and Galatians," *NTS* 43: 147-53. • J. KAMPEN AND M. J. BERNSTEIN, EDS. 1996, *Reading 4QMMT: New Perspectives on Qumran Law and History,* Atlanta: Scholars Press. • L. H. SCHIFFMAN 1994, "Pharisaic and Sadducean Halakhah in the Light of the Dead Sea Scrolls: The Case of Tevul Yom," *DSD* 1: 285-99. • E. QIMRON AND J. STRUGNELL 1994, *Qumran Cave 4.V: Miqṣat Ma'aśe Ha-Torah,* DJD 10, Oxford: Clarendon. • J. STRUGNELL 1994, "MMT: Second Thoughts on a Forthcoming Edition," in *The Community of the Renewed Covenant: The Notre Dame Symposium on the Dead Sea Scrolls,* ed. E. Ulrich and J. VanderKam, Notre Dame: University of Notre Dame Press, 57-73. • E. ULRICH 2003, "The Non-attestation of a Tripartite Canon in 4QMMT," *CBQ* 65: 202-14. • H. VON WEISSENBERG 2009, *4QMMT: Reevaluating the Text, the Function, and the Meaning of the Epilogue,* Leiden: Brill.

HANNE VON WEISSENBERG

Miqva'ot

Miqva'ot are water installations built and used by Jews of the Second Temple period for purposes of achieving and/or maintaining ritual purity by immersion in water, in keeping with religious customs based on interpretation of biblical law. The Hebrew plural noun *miqwā'ôt* (the singular form is *miqweh*) comes from the verb *qwh,* "to gather." The word group is infrequent in the Bible, appearing prominently only at Gen. 1:9-10, where *miqveh* denotes the "gathering" of the waters in the Priestly (P) creation narrative. It is much more common in the Mishnah, where an entire tractate of its sixth division is devoted to the subject of *miqva'ot.*

Typical Features

A typical early Jewish *miqveh* is a pool carved down into bedrock with steps in one side for entry and exit. Because they were built to contain water, the interior surfaces of *miqva'ot* are heavily plastered, but they do not have drains. Some *miqva'ot* are accompanied by a second plastered pool that lies directly alongside. This additional pool, when present, typically has no steps and is connected to the *miqveh* by a narrow channel or pipe, through which water could flow from the second pool into the *miqveh.* The presence of these features helps to distinguish *miqva'ot* from other water installations, such as tubs for ordinary bathing and washing.

Miqva'ot are commonly found in early Jewish archaeological contexts, either in homes — during the Second Temple period, many Jewish houses in Jerusalem and Zippori contained more than one *miqveh* — or in locations near olive presses, wine presses, pottery kilns, synagogues, or the Temple Mount. A few isolated specimens have been found near cemeteries. The average size of a *miqveh* from the Second Temple period is approximately 2 by 4 m., but those in private homes may be smaller than average, holding only a few cubic meters of water. *Miqva'ot* located outside of private homes, by contrast, are often larger than average, and sometimes significantly so. In the vicinity of the ancient entrances to the Temple Mount, for example, some *miqva'ot* extend up to several meters on a side, and one *miqveh* at Qumran (L71) is extremely large, measuring nearly 20 m. long, 6 m. wide, and 5 m. deep at its deepest point.

The configuration of the steps going into and out of a *miqveh* also frequently varies. Many *miqva'ot* have only one set of steps going down one side, but others have two completely separate sets of steps. Still others have one very wide set of steps along an entire side, and sometimes these wide steps are divided by a wall or a low partition down the middle. The tread of the steps in a *miqveh* often varies as well, so that a series of steps with shallow tread will be followed by a step with a much deeper tread.

Modern archaeological interest in *miqva'ot* was first aroused after Yigael Yadin found several specimens during his excavations at Masada in the early 1960s. Since that time more than 300 *miqva'ot* have been uncovered in early Jewish contexts at archaeological sites in Judea (e.g., Jerusalem, Qumran), the Galilee (e.g., Zippori), and the Golan (e.g., Gamla). They are not as common in the coastal plain or in the hill country of the West Bank.

Archaeologists regard the presence of *miqva'ot* in sites from the Second Temple period as a sign of Jewish ethnicity. In particular, when *miqva'ot* are found as part of a constellation of material indicators of Jewish culture (other markers include stone vessels and an absence of pig bones), excavators feel confident in concluding that the inhabitants of the site were Jewish.

Attaining and Maintaining Ritual Purity

Ritual purity was an influential concept in early Judaism; it gave symbolic and practical expression to the centrality of the Temple and its cult during the Second Temple period. Early Jewish concerns about purity were primarily related to ideals about the Temple, rather than to norms of hygiene or morality. Ritual impurity thus did not make a Jew filthy or diseased or sinful but simply unfit to participate in the Temple ritual. The Torah called for priests in the Temple to be free of ritual impurity, and during the Second Temple period many Jews who were not priests nonetheless also sought to avoid and/or remove those same forms of impurity. According to the Mishnah, the use of a *miqveh* was central to this endeavor. As a result, rabbinic discussions of *miqva'ot* often go into considerable detail about how to achieve and maintain ritual purity.

Of course, it cannot be assumed that the Mishnah accurately reflects the everyday practices of all Jews during the Second Temple period. It records many Pharisaic traditions that may go back to that period, but it was not written until much later. As a result, in some cases, other sources provide more appropriate background. The *miqva'ot* at Qumran, for example, are better understood in the light of the Dead Sea Scrolls, which evince a distinctive interest in a very high degree of ritual purity that better accounts for the number and size of the *miqva'ot* at Qumran, along with the elaborate aqueduct system by which they were filled with water. With these reservations in mind, then, some rabbinic traditions can be of help in understanding and interpreting early Jewish *miqva'ot.*

Rabbinic Principles

Several basic principles recur in the mishnaic tractate *Miqva'ot.* Ritual impurity can be removed, for example, by disrobing and immersing oneself in "living water," that is, in water that has not been drawn by human effort. Natural bodies of water, such as lakes or seas, are thus ritually pure (*m. Miqw.* 5:4 refers to the use of the word *miqveh* in Gen. 1:10), as are ponds or streams or pools formed by the runoff of rainwater. Since it was hardly practical for everyone to immerse themselves in a sea, lake, or pond, the *miqveh* emerged as an alternative. In order to be able to wash away impurity, the Mishnah says, a *miqveh* should be dug into bedrock, and should hold at least forty *seahs* (about a cubic meter) of ritually pure water, that is, rainwater which has collected in the *miqveh* by natural means. Of particular interest in the rabbinic traditions is the fact that under certain conditions, ritually pure water can pass that purity on to other water. A pool of forty *seahs* of ritually pure water, for example, would purify any water that might later be added to it. In addition, any body of water that is physically connected to a ritually pure *miqveh* is rendered pure by that connection.

These rabbinic traditions cohere rather well — but not completely — with the current state of the archaeological evidence. Second Temple *miqva'ot* are, as a general rule, rarely so small as to have contained less than a cubic meter of water. Thus in most cases, after forty *seahs* of rainwater had collected naturally in a *miqveh,* it could have been conveniently refilled without altering its ritual purity. In addition, some *miqva'ot* were connected to adjacent plastered pools by a small pipe or channel, through which water could flow from the adjacent pool into the *miqveh.* The Mishnah discusses this arrangement, referring to the adjacent pool as an *'ôṣar* ("treasury"), and in rabbinic opinion, the use of an *'ôṣar* would have preserved the ritual purity of the *miqveh.*

By contrast, the Mishnah and Tosefta have rather little to say about the steps by which one entered and exited a *miqveh.* This relative silence in the literature is generally in accord with the extent of the variety of configurations for steps in the archaeological record. The

View of the miqveh in L48-L49 at Qumran. Notice the low, plastered partitions on the steps and the earthquake damage which has caused the left-hand side of the steps to drop. *(Jodi Magness)*

various arrangements of the steps in early Jewish *miqva'ot* do, however, appear to be consistent with the idea that most forms of impurity could be communicated by touch. Separate steps, or divided steps, would have addressed this concern by creating different points of entry and exit, significantly reducing the possibility that persons coming up from the *miqveh* in a state of ritual purity might accidentally contract the impurity of others who were in the process of going down into the *miqveh.*

Floruit and Decline

Miqva'ot are plentiful in early Jewish contexts during the Second Temple period, but their frequency in the archaeological record declines sharply after the destruction of the Temple during the Jewish War of 66-72 C.E. With the disappearance of the Temple, ritual purity became a less pressing concern for most Jews, and the number of *miqva'ot* fell off accordingly.

BIBLIOGRAPHY

D. AMIT 1999, "Ritual Baths (Mikva'ot) from the Second Temple Period in the Hebron Mountains," in *Judea and Samaria Research Studies,* ed. Z. H. Ehrlich and H. Eshel, Kedumim-Ariel: Research Institute, College of Judea and Samaria, 75-84 (in Hebrew). • J. MAGNESS 2002, *The Archaeology of Qumran and the Dead Sea Scrolls,* Grand Rapids: Eerdmans, 134-62. • E. NETZER 1982, "Ancient Ritual Baths (Miqva'ot) in Jericho," in *The Jerusalem Cathedra,* vol. 2, ed. L. I. Levine, Detroit: Wayne State University Press, 106-19. • E. REGEV 1996, "Ritual Baths of Jewish Groups and Sects in the Second Temple Period," *Cathedra* 79: 3-30 (in Hebrew). • R. REICH 1988, "The Hot Bath-House *(balneum),* the Miqveh, and the Jewish Community of the Second Temple Period," *JJS* 39: 102-7. • R. REICH 1990, *Miqva'ot (Jewish Ritual Immersion Baths) in Eretz-Israel in the Second Temple and Mishnah and Talmud Periods,* 3 vols., Dissertation, Hebrew University of Jerusalem (in Hebrew with Eng. abstract). • R. REICH 1997, "Miqwa'ot (Ritual Baths) at Qumran," *Qadmaniot* 114: 125-28. • R. REICH 2002, "They Are Ritual Baths: Immerse Yourself in the Ongoing Sepphoris Miqveh Debate," *BAR* 28/2, 50-55. • E. P. SANDERS 1992, *Judaism: Practice and Belief 63 BCE–66 CE*, Philadelphia: Trinity Press International, 214-30. • B. G. WRIGHT III 1997, "Jewish Ritual Baths — Interpreting the Digs and the Texts: Some Issues in the Social History of Second Temple Judaism," in *The Archaeology of Israel: Constructing the Past, Interpreting the Present,* ed. N. A. Silberman and D. Small, Sheffield: Sheffield Academic Press, 192-214.

See also: Purity and Impurity

BYRON R. MCCANE

Miracles and Miracle Workers

In ancient Israelite and early Jewish tradition, there is no sharp distinction between the constant miraculous character of God's providence (Job 37:5-22) and the special mighty acts that God performs for his people. While miracles are special and exceptional, they are not "against nature," since there is no conception of "nature" in the Hebrew Bible. Neither is there a special term for "miracle" in Scripture, though there are "signs" (Hebr. sg. *'ôt*), that is, extraordinary events through which people experience the sovereign power of God. R. Joshua ben Levi maintained that "The earning of our daily bread is an even greater wonder than the parting of the sea" (*Gen. Rab.* 20:22; *b. Pesaḥim* 118a). Similarly, Rabbi Joshua ben Levi is also remembered as having said that "when a person is healed from a sickness the wonder is greater than the rescue of the three men from the fiery furnace [Daniel 3]" (*b. Nedarim* 41a). In early Judaism, the paradigmatic miracle workers whose activities are narrated in the Tanak are Moses, Elijah, and Elisha, figures remembered as combining prophetic gifts with the performance of wonders (see Koskenniemi 2005). However, a qualitative line was drawn between the biblical period and the postbiblical period, for one strand of early rabbinic thought maintained that miracles of the sort narrated in the Tanak are no longer granted to later generations because of their unworthiness and lack of piety (*b. Berakot* 20a).

Miracles and miracle workers are found in two types of literary sources: those in which the performance of miracles and the activity of miracle workers have a historical core even though embellished with legendary accretions, and those in which miracle workers and the wonders they perform are purely fictional.

Miracles in 2 and 3 Maccabees

Both 2 and 3 Maccabees narrate fictional divine interventions that turned the tide of battle against the enemies of the Jews. 2 Maccabees, an abbreviation of a five-volume historical work by Jason of Cyrene (2 Macc. 2:19-32), was written in 124 B.C.E. about events that occurred a generation earlier (180-160 B.C.E.). According to the narrative, in response to the prayers of the people of Jerusalem, the Syrian emissary Heliodorus, who intended to remove the treasures stored in the Temple, was attacked while in the Temple by a heavenly horse and rider and two handsome young men (2 Macc. 3:22-28). Through the prayer of the high priest, Heliodorus recovered and the two young men again appeared to him and explained to him why God had spared his life (3:31-34). During the expedition of Antiochus IV Epiphanes against Egypt, apparitions of battling swordsmen and cavalry were seen in the sky over Jerusalem with no clear meaning (5:1-4), though later it became clear that Antiochus' siege of Jerusalem was meant (5:11-14). Later, Antiochus was on his way to Jerusalem to slaughter the inhabitants when he was struck down by God with a painful sickness of the bowels and was eaten by worms, eventually dying painfully (9:11-29). During a clash between the forces of Timotheus the Syrian and Judas Maccabaeus, five heavenly cavaliers appeared in the sky to protect Judas (10:29-31). Similarly when Lysias invaded Judea, a heavenly cavalier appeared at the head of Judas and his forces (11:8), who soundly defeated Lysias and his huge army.

In 3 Maccabees, a pro-Jewish piece of propaganda probably written in Egypt during the late second century B.C.E., the prayer of the high priest Simon results in God's striking Ptolemy IV Philopater with paralysis (3 Macc. 2:21). The whole plot of 3 Maccabees turns on the prayer of Eleazar, in response to which two glorious angels descend from the gates of heaven confusing and terrifying the army of Ptolemy IV (6:18-21), who repents and becomes a patron of the Jews.

Exorcists

Turning to historical evidence for miracles and miracle workers in early Judaism, there are a number of tantalizing references to exorcists and exorcism based on the widespread ancient view that demonic possession and demonic influences were a major cause of bizarre behavior and certain types of illness. While Jesus is certainly the most famous exorcist of the late Second Temple period, Mark preserves a brief narrative, often entitled "The Strange Exorcist," mentioning an exorcist casting out demons in the name of Jesus who did not belong to the circle of the followers of Jesus (Mark 9:38; Luke 9:49). Though the disciples reportedly tried to stop the man, Jesus disagreed with them. Acts 9:13-17 mentions seven Jewish exorcists, sons of Sceva a Jewish chief priest, who attempted to cast out demons "by Jesus whom Paul proclaims." These exorcists were overpowered, beaten up, and had their clothes torn off by the person who was demon possessed. While the historicity of this comic story is doubtful (no Jewish chief priest named Sceva is known), it does attest to the existence of itinerant Jewish exorcists who were active during the middle of the first century C.E.

The book of Acts narrates several other miracles and exorcisms, many of them punitive in nature. Some of these occur through direct divine or angelic intervention, such as the death of Herod Agrippa I (12:20-23; cf. Josephus, *Ant.* 19.346). Others occur through the actions of the apostles, such as Paul's blinding of the magician Bar-Jesus/Elymas (13:6-12) and exorcism of the slave girl with a "Pythian spirit" (16:16-24).

Josephus (*Ant.* 8.45-49) tells the story of a Jewish exorcist names Eleazar who possessed a ring with a root prescribed by Solomon under the stone who was able to pull the demon out of the nostrils of a demon-possessed person, and then demonstrate the reality of the exorcism by having the exiting demon tip over a basin full of water set up for the purpose of proving the reality of the exorcism (see Duling 1985).

Miracle Stories in Rabbinic Literature

In the early twentieth century, Paul Fiebig and Adolf Schlatter debated whether or not the miracles of Jesus had relevant rabbinic parallels. Fiebig (1911), who focused much of his career on emphasizing the importance of rabbinical studies for understanding the New Testament, argued for close parallels between the miracle working of Jesus and the rabbis. Adolf Schlatter (1912), on the other hand, argued against Fiebig, maintaining that neither Josephus nor the Mishnah contained any miracle story that originated in the first century C.E., concluding that the miracles of Jesus narrated in the canonical Gospels have no parallel in contemporary Judaism (and so were unique). Morton Smith (1945: 81), in agreement with Schlatter, argued that there were almost no stories of miracles performed by the Tannaim. More recently, Michael Becker (2002) has reexamined the role of miracle workers and miracle stories in rabbinic literature. He argues that interest in miracles and miracle workers is minimal among the Tannaim; there is a dearth of miracle terminology in the Mishnah and a generally low interest in the phenomena of miracles and miracle workers. The Tosefta exhibits a reserved, critical attitude toward the miraculous. Further, while early traditions were critical of charismatics such as Ḥoni and Ḥanina (see below), later rabbinic traditions transformed them from "magicians" to miracle workers.

Ḥoni the Circle Drawer and Ḥanina ben Dosa

The earliest nonrabbinic miracle workers whose names and activities are preserved in rabbinic literature are Ḥoni the Circle Drawer and Ḥanina ben Dosa. In *m. Taʿan.* 3:8 (repeated and increasingly embellished in subsequent rabbinic sources; see Goldin 1963 and Becker 2002: 291-378), the story is told of how Ḥoni *ha-Mĕʿaggel* ("the Circle-Drawer"), a first-century-B.C.E. holy man, prayed for rain. When his prayer was not answered, he drew a circle (Hebr. *mĕʿaggel*), swearing an oath by God's great name that he would not step outside the circle until God would send rain. When a few drops fell, he complained that this was not enough. When it rained torrentially, he complained that it was too much. It then began to rain moderately, and Ḥoni was satisfied. This story is summarized in Josephus (*Ant.* 14.22), who calls him Onias. The fact that he is referred to in rabbinic sources as "the circle-drawer" suggests that this epithet reflected a fixed feature of his prayer ritual.

Ḥanina ben Dosa, a Galilean from Arav, flourished during the middle third of the first century C.E. and is remembered in the Mishnah as both a *ḥāsîd* and a "man of deed" or miracle worker (*m. Soṭah* 9:15). Miracle stories associated with him, however, tend to be found in the Babylonian Talmud and later rabbinic literature. A cycle of stories that relate several miracles performed by Ḥanina ben Dosa is preserved in the Babylonian Talmud (*b. Taʿanit* 24b–25a). The miracles in this small cycle, which have parallels with those performed by Elisha (see Blenkinsopp 1999), include: (1) starting and stopping rain, (2) the multiplication of freshly baked loaves of bread, (3) making vinegar burn like oil, (4) instantaneous house repairs, (5) poisonous snakebite made ineffective, (6) a healing miracle, and (7) the rescue of Nehuniah's daughter. There are also several traditions in these cycles that are obviously legendary additions to the collection: (1) Ḥanina's poverty alleviated by the gift of the golden leg of a table; (2) a prediction that his goats, wrongly accused of damaging property, would return home with bears on their horns; (3) Ḥanina's votive offering transported to Jerusalem by five angels (*Cant. Rab.* 1:4). Two stories from this cycle can serve to represent the rest. The first is the story about Ḥanina's starting and stopping of rain (*b. Taʿanit* 24b; trans. Blenkinsopp 1999: 71-72):

> Rabbi Ḥanina ben Dosa was going on his way when it started to rain. He exclaimed, "Lord of the universe, the whole world is entirely at ease while Ḥanina is in distress." The rain stopped. When he reached home he exclaimed, "Lord of the universe, the whole world is entirely in distress while Ḥanina is at ease." It started to rain again.

The second is a healing story (*b. Berakot* 34b; trans. Blenkinsopp, pp. 75-76):

> Our rabbis taught: it happened that R. Gamaliel's son took ill. He sent two disciples to R. Ḥanina ben Dosa with the request that he pray for him. As soon as he saw them, he went up into an upstairs room and prayed for him. When he came down he told them, "Go, for the fever has left him." They said to him, "Are you a prophet?" "I am not a prophet," he replied, "nor am I the son of a prophet, but I have been granted this prerogative: if my prayer is fluent in my mouth, know that the sick person is favored; if not, I know that he will perish." They sat down and made a note in writing of the exact time. When they returned to R. Gamaliel, he said to them, "by the temple service! It happened exactly as you describe it, neither more nor less; the fever left him at exactly that time, and he asked us for a drink of water."

Rabbi Simeon bar Yoḥai

A notable rabbinic miracle worker, Rabbi Simeon bar Yoḥai, flourished ca. 140-70 C.E. Active primarily in Upper Galilee (see Rosenfeld 1999), he was an eminent sage (under whom Rabbi Judah the Prince studied) as well as a wonder worker and a righteous man. R. Simeon is not reported in tannaitic literature to have performed miracles, but he is described frequently as a wonder worker in the Talmuds and the midrashim. In one early tradition, a saying is preserved in which he extols the healing powers of a certain gemstone used as an amulet (*t. Qidd.* 5:17). According to *y. Ber.* 9:2 (13d) (cf. *b. Ketubbot* 77b; *Gen. Rab.* 35:2), "R. Hezekiah [said] in the name of R. Jeremiah: a rainbow never appeared during the lifetime of R. Simeon b. Yoḥai" — that is, the rainbow as a sign of heavenly protection was unnecessary during the lifetime of R. Simeon because he himself was a *ṣaddîq* capable of protecting the entire world.

A tradition of R. Simeon as a healer is found in *Pesiq. Rab Kah.* 22:2, where R. Simeon meets a couple who had been childless for ten years: "He [R. Simeon] prayed on the couple's behalf, and they were remembered with children. For, even as the Holy One remembers barren women, righteous men also have the power to remember barren women." Here a Palestinian source characterizes R. Simeon as a *ṣaddîq* who has the power to "remember" (i.e., heal) barren women like God himself. According to *b. Meʿilah* 17a-b, R. Simeon and another sage were sent to Rome to seek the annulment of some anti-Jewish decrees. On the way, they were greeted by a demon named Ben Temalion, who had been sent to aid them from heaven:

> Thereupon [Ben Temalion] advanced and entered into the Emperor's daughter. When [R. Simeon] arrived there, he called out: "Ben Temalion, leave her! Ben Temalion, leave her!" and as he proclaimed this he left her. [The Emperor] said to them: Request whatever you desire. They were led into the treasure house to take whatever they chose. They found that bill, took it, and tore it to pieces.

BIBLIOGRAPHY

P. W. BARNETT 1981, "The Jewish Sign Prophets — A.D. 40-70: Their Intentions and Origin," *NTS* 27: 679-97. • M. BECKER 2002, *Wunder und Wundertäter im frührabbinischen Judentum,* Tübingen: Mohr-Siebeck. • O. BETZ 1974, "Das Problem des Wunders bei Flavius Josephus im Vergleich zum Wunderproblem bei den Rabbinen und im Johannesevangelium," in *Josephus-Studien,* ed. O. Betz, K. Haacker, and M. Hengel, Göttingen: Vandenhoeck & Ruprecht, 23-44. • J. BLENKINSOPP 1999, "Miracles: Elisha and Ḥanina ben Dosa," in *Miracles in Jewish and Christian Antiquity: Imagining Truth,* ed. J. C. Cavadini, Notre Dame: University of Notre Dame, 57-81. • B. M. BOKSER 1985, "Wonder-Working and the Rabbinic Tradition: The Case of Ḥanina ben Dosa," *JSJ* 16: 42-92. • D. DULING 1985, "The Eleazar Miracle and Solomon's Magical Wisdom in Flavius Josephus's Antiquities Judaicae 8:42-49," *HTR* 78: 1-25. • P. FIEBIG 1911, *Jüdische Wundergeschichten des neutestamentlichen Zeitalters,* Tübingen: Mohr-Siebeck. • J. GOLDIN 1963, "On Ḥoni the Circle-Maker: A Demanding Prayer," *HTR* 56: 233-37. • B. KOLLMANN 1996, *Jesus und die Christen als Wundertäter: Studien zu Magie, Medizin und Schamanismus in Antike und Christentum,* Göttingen: Vandenhoeck & Ruprecht. • E. KOSKENNIEMI 2005, *Old Testament Miracle-Workers in Early Judaism,* Tübingen: Mohr-Siebeck. • B.-Z. ROSENFELD 1999, "R. Simeon b. Yoḥai — Wonder Worker and Magician, Scholar, *Saddiq* and *Hasid,*" *REJ* 158: 349-84. • A. SCHLATTER 1912, *Das Wunder in der Synagoge,* Gütersloh: Bertelsmann. • K. SCHUBERT 1982, "Wunderberichte und ihr Kerygma in der rabbinischen Tradition," *Kairos* 24: 31-37. • M. SMITH 1945, *Tannaitic Parallels to the Gospels,* Philadelphia: Society of Biblical Literature. • E. SORENSEN 2002, *Possession and Exorcism in the New Testament and Early Christianity,* Tübingen: Mohr-Siebeck. • D. L. TIEDE 1972, *The Charismatic Figure as Miracle Worker,* Missoula, Mont.: Scholars Press. • G. VERMES 1973, "Ḥanina ben Dosa: A Controversial Galilean Saint from the First Century of the Christian Era," *JJS* 23: 28-50.

See also: Demons and Exorcism; Divination and Magic; Healing

DAVID E. AUNE

Mishmarot

The Hebrew term *mišmārôt* ("guards") denotes an administrative division of personnel in the Jerusalem Temple. The priestly workforce was divided into twenty-four "families," each serving for one week. Levites were also divided into *mišmārôt* and so were lay Israelite males, whose units are designated *māʿămādôt* ("stands" or "posts"). The *mišmārôt* system was devised in order to supply an equal term of office for a growing priestly population, since a week of Temple service entailed material income in the form of sacrificial meat and offerings, as well as ownership of lands (*m. ʿArakin* 7). The priestly watches switched on the Sabbath, with the daily sacrifices divided between the outgoing and incoming *mišmārôt*. Each *mišmar* had its own compartment and utensils in the Temple to tend the sacrifices and accommodate various facilities (*t. Sukk.* 4:24-28).

In biblical Hebrew the courses are called "divisions" *(maḥlāqôt)*. The terms *mišmar* and *māʿămad* first appear in the *War Scroll* (1QM 2:2-3). These terms are not used in the calendrical scrolls from Qumran, despite the recurrent naming of priestly families in them. Greek Jewish authors use the term *ephēmeria, ephēmerides* (Josephus, *Life* 2; *Ant.* 7.67; Luke 1:5).

Priests were divided according to family eponyms. Four families are counted in Ezra 2:36-39 (= Neh. 7:39-41; cf. *t. Taʿan.* 2:1), but further organization work took place in early Second Temple times. A list of twenty-four priestly families appears in 1 Chronicles 24, dated roughly from the late Persian to the early Hellenistic period. The family name Yehoyarib heads the list, followed by the traditionally authoritative family of Yedaiah. In contrast, Qumran lists of *mišmārôt* commence with the family of Gamul. The Hasmonean clan descended from Yehoyarib (1 Macc. 2:1), hence its particular esteem in various sources, but possibly also the reason why it does not open the Qumran lists. Other prominent families are those of Yedaiah, Jeshebab, and Haqqoz. The clan of Bilgah was known as highly Hellenized (Stern 1976).

The Qumran *War Scroll* (1QM 2:1-6) describes the participation of priests, Levites, and Israelites in the sacrifices (cf. *m. Taʿan.* 4:3), with the community divided into twenty-six *mišmārôt*. 1QM thus provides evidence for the relative antiquity of *mišmārôt* and *māʿămādôt* (however, cf. 4QM manuscripts). The appearance of twenty-six *mišmārôt* in 1QM is puzzling, since only twenty-four such divisions appear elsewhere. This number is used as a convenient division of the 364-day year into two halves of twenty-six weeks each. Since there is no trace of the two additional families, the count in 1QM probably reflects only a future ideal.

The calendrical aspect of *mišmārôt* is apparent in the 364-day calendar tradition, which was inherently structured on units of weeks. A cycle of six years was devised in which each *mišmar* served for exactly thirteen weeks. Although several (earlier?) works from the 364-day calendar tradition do not mention *mišmārôt* (notably the *Temple Scroll* and *Jubilees*), they are still a part of most calendrical works from Qumran.

Various calendrical lists were found among the Dead Sea Scrolls. Each scroll may contain several lists with various contents. The classification is as follows (excluding several too fragmentary scrolls):

A. Calendrical documents without *mišmārôt* notations (4Q324b; 4Q324d; 4Q324e; 4Q326; 4Q337; 4Q394 1-2; 4Q394 3–7 i 1-3; 6Q17).

B. Mishmarot

- B 1. Festival Calendars (4Q319 frgs. 12-13, 77; 4Q320 frg. 4; 4Q321 4ff.; 4Q329a): a list of pentateuchal festivals in each year of the six-year cycle.
- B 2. Master list of the *mišmārôt* cycle (4Q319 7ff.; 4Q328; 4Q329; 4Q324j): a list of *mišmārôt* names followed by the names of *mišmārôt* serving at the beginning of years, quarters, months, and weeks.
- B 3. Detailed course of the year (4Q322, 4Q323, 4Q324, 4Q324a, 4Q324c, 4Q324i[?], 4Q325): a running account of the six-year cycle, noting sabbatical switches of *mišmārôt,* festivals (including the "sectarian" harvest festivals), and beginnings of months. Some of the documents (4Q322–4Q324) note additional dates in the six-year cycle, which resemble the notations in group E below.

C. Synchronistic lists of lunar phenomena (4Q320 1-2; 4Q321 1-4; 4Q321a): an alignment of the *mišmārôt* cycle with a set of three monthly lunar phenomena (see Ben-Dov 2008).

D. *ʾOtot* (4Q319 4-6): a "sign" at the beginning of each new triennial cycle is assigned to the *mišmārôt* Gamul and Shekaniah, respectively.

E. Additional texts that note the dates by *mišmārôt,* although they are not strictly calendars, are the historical texts (4Q322a, 4Q331, 4Q332, 4Q332a, 4Q333).

The Dead Sea Scrolls date the *mišmārôt* service to the very beginning of time, when the luminaries were created. The prologues of 4Q319 and 4Q320 anchor the *mišmārôt* service in creation, thus linking the concepts of creation and priesthood. A similar link is found in the mishnaic *māʿămādôt* liturgy (Tabory 2003).

Calendrical calculations of *mišmārôt* are less common in the rabbinic system, where the year lengths are constantly changing. It is unclear how the service of twenty-four *mišmārôt* fit the lunisolar year of ca. 50.5 weeks (nearly 55 when intercalated). It is possible that the *mišmārôt* followed one another in unbroken succession, but also that the cycle began anew every year in the month of Tishri (Beckwith 1996). In the three pilgrimage festivals, all the *mišmārôt* served together (*t. Sukk.* 4:15-23). There is scarcely a trace of the inclusion of *mišmārôt* in the actual rabbinic calendar tradition, despite late hints for this practice in *y. Sukk.* 55:4 and *Midrash Leviticus* 28.

The institution of *mišmārôt* and *māʿămādôt* did not cease with the destruction of the Temple in 70 C.E. According to a well-founded tradition, the priestly families survived and moved to various towns in the Galilee. This tradition was preserved in lists of *mišmārôt* and their dwelling places that were copied in synagogue inscriptions and either quoted or interpreted in later Palestinian sources. The *māʿămādôt* liturgy continued in Jewish liturgy into talmudic and medieval times.

Bibliography

R. T. Beckwith 1996, *Calendar and Chronology, Jewish and Christian,* Leiden: Brill. • J. Ben-Dov 2008, *Head of All Years: Astronomy and Calendars at Qumran in Their Ancient Context,*

Leiden: Brill • M. STERN 1976, "Aspects of Jewish Society: The Priesthood and Other Classes," in *The Jewish People in the First Century,* vol. 2, Assen: Van Gorcum; Philadelphia: Fortress, 580-96. • J. TABORY 2003, "*Ma'amadot:* A Second Temple Non-Temple Liturgy," in *Liturgical Perspectives: Prayer and Poetry in Light of the Dead Sea Scrolls,* ed. E. G. Chazon et al., Leiden: Brill, 235-61. • J. C. VANDERKAM 1998, *Calendars in the Dead Sea Scrolls: Measuring Time,* London: Routledge.

See also: Calendars; Priests

JONATHAN BEN-DOV

Mishnah

The Mishnah ("repetition" or "teaching") is the first rabbinic book, composed in Hebrew in the land of Israel and edited around 200 C.E. The Mishnah is primarily a collection of rulings about matters of practice, custom, ritual, and law. The rulings are sometimes presented anonymously, sometimes ascribed to named individuals; often the Mishnah presents two or more conflicting rulings on the same question. Aside from this legal material, the Mishnah also contains anecdotes, maxims, exhortations, scriptural exegesis, and descriptions of the rituals of the Jerusalem Temple. The sages named in the Mishnah (called collectively *tanna'im,* "teachers") are customarily assigned by modern scholars to distinct generations; the bulk of the named mishnaic sages belong to either the generation of Yavneh (ca. 80-120 C.E.) or the generation of Usha (ca. 140-180 C.E.). (Yavneh and Usha are the names of towns in which the sages are said to have gathered.) Relatively little material is ascribed to named figures who lived before the destruction of the Jerusalem Temple in 70 C.E.

The Mishnah covers a broad range of topics and is divided into six sections known as "orders" *(sedarim);* each order in turn is divided into "tractates" *(massektot).* There are sixty-three tractates in all. The six orders are: *Zera'im* ("Seeds"), on the disposition of the agricultural products of the land of Israel; *Mo'ed* ("Feasts" or "Appointed Times"), on Sabbath, festivals, and pilgrimage to the Temple; *Nashim* ("Women"), on marriage, divorce, and family law; *Neziqin* ("Damages"), on civil and criminal law, and judicial procedure; *Qodashim* ("Holy Things"), on Temple sacrifices and rituals; and *Toḥarot* ("Purities"), on the maintenance of ritual purity and the removal of ritual impurity.

The Mishnah is full of legal material but is not a law code, or at least is not obviously a law code. It contains numerous disputes and unresolved arguments; it does not usually state the penalty for the violation of its prescriptions; it is not complete, omitting many vital aspects of its subjects; at no point, except perhaps for the famous opening chapter of *'Abot,* which depicts a chain of tradition from Moses at Mt. Sinai to the mishnaic sages, does the Mishnah advance a global claim for its authority. If the Mishnah is a law code, it is an odd one.

Another odd feature of the Mishnah is its seeming obliviousness to its time and place. It seldom mentions the destruction of the Temple in 70 C.E. (or, for that matter, the defeat of Bar Kokhba in 135 C.E.); in fact, the Mishnah seems to be in denial of this event. It treats at great length the rituals of the Temple; it discusses priests and their prerogatives but never discusses rabbis and their prerogatives; it sets out in great detail the requirements of ritual purity, the sources of impurity, and the modes of purification, even though most of the purity system no longer had a raison d'être after the destruction of the Temple, and even though purification from the most severe forms of impurity was impossible without the Temple system being in place. The Mishnah more or less ignores the fact that its composers were living in Palestina, a province of the Roman Empire. Whatever replacements Jewish society was developing for the Temple, its rituals, and its personnel (e.g., synagogues, prayer, rabbis), are of no interest to the Mishnah. The Mishnah is not living in real time and does not seem interested in the affairs of its own time.

If the Mishnah is not a law code, and is not interested in the events of its own time, what is it? Who wrote it, why, and for whom? The answers to these questions are much debated, and no consensus has been reached. Three points, however, seem certain. First, whatever other purpose it may have been designed to serve, the Mishnah certainly was intended to be studied, and indeed it actually was studied: succeeding generations of sages studied the Mishnah, and the result of their work is incorporated in the first layer of the Talmuds of Babylonia and the land of Israel. Second, the Mishnah is a highly stylized summary of the opinions of sages over a period of more than a century. The Mishnah is anthological, produced by a "school" or movement, and its final editors used sources in its creation. Whether these sources were written or oral, and whether these sources can now be reconstructed, are questions of ongoing discussion, but the existence of these sources is certain. Third, although the Mishnah nowhere identifies its authors or editors, both Talmuds — and virtually all modern scholars — assume that Rabbi Judah the Patriarch, also known simply as Rabbi, was its editor. There is some connection, then, between the promulgation of the Mishnah and the office of the patriarch, although the nature of that connection is not clear.

What is the origin of the Mishnah's laws? One obvious source is Scripture. Like the Hebrew literature of the later Second Temple period, the Mishnah is based on Scripture, specifically the Torah. The rabbinic sages, like all other Jews of antiquity, looked first and foremost to the Torah for knowledge of religious law and practice. Other Jews did the same: prerabbinic writings of the Second Temple period, such as *Jubilees,* the *Temple Scroll,* the *Covenant of Damascus,* and the essays of Philo of Alexandria, all relate to the Torah in different ways for different purposes but all use the Torah, whether explicitly or implicitly, as the basis for their presentations of Jewish law.

One of the striking features of the Mishnah, however, is its relative independence from the Torah. The Mishnah is neither a commentary on, nor a paraphrase of, the Torah. It does not, as a rule, cite the Torah or speak in Biblical Hebrew. Nor is it organized along the lines of the Torah. And yet the Mishnah remains tightly bound to the Torah. Some sections of the Mishnah stand in such close relationship with the Torah that barely a line of the former can be understood without knowledge of the relevant verses of the latter. These verses, although essential to understanding the text, are not quoted; the editor of the Mishnah assumes that the reader will supply what is missing. Every so often, for reasons that are not clear, the Mishnah departs from its usual practice and explicitly adduces Scripture, usually the Torah, in order to buttress a legal ruling. The talmudic discussions of the Mishnah will usually try to attach the Mishnah's laws to scriptural verses, since the Mishnah itself usually fails to do so.

The Mishnah drew on other sources beyond Scripture. Some mishnaic laws seem to be of "sectarian" provenance, while others are part of the "common Judaism" of all Jews; some seem to derive from the priesthood, others from the scribes. Reflecting the fact that the rabbinic movement itself derived from various groups, the Mishnah, too, derived its laws from various sources. The common scholarly view that mishnaic law is somehow Pharisaic is not baseless but cannot be sustained. Gamaliel the Pharisee is mentioned by the New Testament (Acts 5:34; 22:3), Simon ben Gamaliel the Pharisee by Josephus (*Vita* 191–92). The Rabban Gamliel who became the leader of the rabbis of the Yavneh generation surely is a scion of this line; Rabbi Judah the Patriarch, the putative editor of the Mishnah, is his grandson. So there is an important link between the Pharisees of the Second Temple period and the rabbinic sages of the post-70 era, but this hardly means that all Pharisees became rabbis or that all rabbis were latter-day Pharisees. It is significant that the Mishnah in various passages sees the Sadducees as Other (e.g., *m. Parah* 3:7), and that in the mishnaic debates between Pharisees and Sadducees (e.g., *m. Yad.* 4:6-7) the winners are always the Pharisees, as seen from the fact that mishnaic law always agrees with them against the Sadducees. Hence we may say that the Mishnah is anti-Sadducean (*m. Sanh.* 10:1), but otherwise it has no pharisaic self-consciousness. No doubt some of the laws of the Mishnah derive from the Pharisees of the Second Temple period, but mishnaic law cannot be regarded *tout court* as Pharisaic.

What is new in the Mishnah? (1) The Mishnah is the first Jewish book to ascribe conflicting legal opinions to named individuals and groups, (2) who, in spite of their differences of opinion, remain members of the same social network. (3) Some earlier Hebrew works, like *Jubilees* and the *Covenant of Damascus,* had departed from the sequence of Scripture in order to arrange legal material thematically; writing in Greek, Philo and Josephus had done the same. But the Mishnah's abandonment of the scriptural sequence is total; its thematic arrangement is pursued on a much grander scale, covering many more topics in much greater detail, than in any earlier text. (4) The Mishnah contains abundant case law; there is nothing remarkable or novel about that. But the Mishnah also has numerous examples of abstract thinking, where it posits legal categories, analyzes them in detail, contrasts one category with another, and connects (contrasts) one law with another on the basis of their thematic similarity (dissimilarity). This is new. (5) The Torah distinguishes murder from manslaughter on the basis of the intention of the assailant (Exod. 21:12-14; Numbers 35). In the Mishnah the intention of the actor is taken into account far more often and in a far wider range of contexts than in any earlier Jewish document. In sum, the Mishnah represents not just a new literary form in the history of Judaism but also a new way of thinking and ultimately a new religiosity.

BIBLIOGRAPHY

A. AVERY-PECK AND J. NEUSNER, EDS. 2006, *Mishnah in Contemporary Perspective,* Leiden: Brill. • S. J. D. COHEN 2007, "The Judaean Legal Tradition and the Halakhah of the Mishnah," in *The Cambridge Companion to the Talmud and Rabbinic Literature,* ed. C. Fonrobert and M. Jaffe, Cambridge: Cambridge University Press, 121-43. • H. DANBY 1933, *The Mishnah,* Oxford: Clarendon. • A. GOLDBERG 1987, "The Mishna," in *The Literature of the Sages,* Part I, ed. S. Safrai, Assen: Van Gorcum; Philadelphia: Fortress, 211-62. • J. LIGHTSTONE 2002, *Mishnah and the Social Formation of the Early Rabbinic Guild,* Waterloo, Ont.: Wilfrid Laurier University Press. • J. NEUSNER 1981, *Judaism: The Evidence of the Mishnah,* Chicago: University of Chicago Press. • J. NEUSNER, ED. 1988, *The Mishnah: A New Translation,* New Haven: Yale University Press. • H. L. STRACK AND G. STEMBERGER 1992, *Introduction to the Talmud and Midrash,* Minneapolis: Fortress, 119-66.

SHAYE J. D. COHEN

Monotheism

The word "monotheism" appears to have been first used as Europeans sought to categorize the various forms of religion encountered in their colonial expansion. As typically defined in textbooks on religion, the term refers to the belief that one deity is the creator and ruler of all things, in distinction from "polytheism," belief in multiple deities with their individual roles and powers. Yet two important points need to be made. First, monotheism does not involve denying the *existence* of such beings, only that they properly cannot be compared with the one deity in status and significance, and even in nature. Second, ancient Jewish monotheism involved worship as much as, or even more than, doctrine. The uniqueness of the one deity is guarded most zealously in worship. Judaism, Christianity, and Islam are usually identified as the three great monotheistic traditions. Historically, however, Judaism in the Second Temple period presents us with the earliest popularly embraced form of genuine monotheism.

Historical Origins and Developments

Scholars recognize that in the preexilic period an exclusive devotion to YHWH was not widely or consistently embraced in Israel and Judah, and that their worship included other deities as well (M. S. Smith 2001), as is reflected in the complaints in biblical texts (e.g., Jer. 7:18; Hos. 11:2; Judg. 10:6). Some scholars have proposed that in this period there was a "Yahweh-alone" party; but if so, it was most definitely a minority. It is commonly agreed that it was only sometime in the postexilic period that a recognizable monotheism came to be widely affirmed, the Exile itself perhaps providing the social circumstances in which advocates of an exclusive reverence of YHWH were able to win wider favor for their position. In any case, by the Hellenistic period Judaism's most defining feature was its fiercely monotheistic stance.

Among the historical factors that likely had a role in monotheism coming to have such a dominant place in ancient Jewish religion was the attempt by the Seleucid king, Antiochus Epiphanes (ca. 215-164 B.C.E.), to coerce a cultural and religious assimilation on Judea, and the violent backlash that it generated under Maccabean leadership. This coercion surely made devout Jews thereafter much more sensitive about preserving their religious distinctives, and emphatic in their exclusive commitment to the one God of the biblical tradition.

As noted above, however, early Jewish monotheism always made ample room for other heavenly beings. The biblical epithet "YHWH of hosts" presumes that YHWH presides over a vast entourage of heavenly beings who serve him; and in other texts God is portrayed with a heavenly council of subordinates (e.g., 1 Kings 22:19; Job 1:6; Ps. 82:1). This view reflects the common ancient Near Eastern notion of a number of divine beings presided over by a high god who can be thought of as their father and king (M. Smith 1952; Nilsson 1963).

From this basic belief structure, the early Jewish monotheistic stance reflects a distinctive development. Granted, the God of biblical tradition presides over a court of heavenly beings who are in some sense likened to him, as is reflected in the term given to them in some texts, "sons of God" (e.g., Job 1:6). In pagan versions of this pattern, however, the high god is typically not the focus of religious devotion and may even not be known (and in some cases, particularly Greek philosophical tradition, *cannot* be known). Instead, one more typically addressed and directed worship to particular members of the pantheon of second-level deities, usually in relation to favors sought, for which they had the appropriate powers. In early Jewish tradition, by contrast, the high god is known explicitly as YHWH, the God of Israel, whose purposes and acts are declared in her Scriptures, and who is addressed directly in prayer and worship. Indeed, in early Jewish religious practice, petition and worship were to be directed *exclusively* to the one God.

By the Roman period, there had developed among Jews a rich body of speculation about God's heavenly host, involving various named principal angels (e.g., Gabriel and Michael, Dan. 8:16; 9:21; 12:1) and various ranks or orders (e.g., seraphim, cherubim), as well as speculation about hostile and disobedient spiritual beings (fallen angels, demons, Satan, etc.). But they were all emphatically treated as inferior and subservient to the one God, and fundamentally were within God's power. Contrary to some past assumptions among scholars, the proliferation of interest in God's entourage in the Second Temple period does not reflect a sense of God as remote and inaccessible. Instead, the aim seems to have been to portray God's greatness by ascribing to him a vast retinue that included high-ranking servants. This scheme was likely modeled after the grand structures of royal administration in the Persian and subsequent empires, and intended to depict God as the ultimate and highest ruler.

The evidence of early Jewish worship and prayer nevertheless indicates that this exalted representation of God did not prevent a strong sense of God's accessibility to the devout. As several studies of the prayers that feature in Second Temple Jewish texts have shown, when ancient Jews prayed, they addressed themselves directly to the one God, as reflected even in those texts in which principal angels figure prominently (e.g., Tob. 12:11-15; and see Hurtado 1988: 22-27). Though they allowed that God might well answer prayers by means of an angel (as, e.g., Raphael sent to Tobit), they considered it improper to pray or offer worship to any being other than the one God.

It appears, however, that the beliefs and practices of some Jews developed in directions that were seen by others as dangerous for the religious integrity of Judaism, particularly threatening God's uniqueness. An important study of rabbinic criticism of heresies associated with the belief that there are "two powers in heaven" (Segal 1977) argues that by the late first or early second century C.E. some Jewish religious leaders were reacting against what they saw as such dangerous developments. These probably included Jewish-Christian reverence of Jesus (which was viewed by Jewish critics as making Jesus a second god) and (perhaps a bit later) Gnostic speculations about a demiurge creator-deity. In any case, the condemnations of "two powers" heresies in early rabbinic circles may also have generated an even stricter emphasis on God's uniqueness and may have dampened somewhat the interest in angels and other heavenly beings that had proliferated previously.

Monotheistic Affirmations

Whatever developments there were, however, Second Temple Judaism was always characterized by emphatic and frequent professions of a monotheistic stance. We may take Philo of Alexandria's statement in his discussion of the first commandment as illustrative: "Let us, then, engrave deep in our hearts this as the first and most sacred of commandments: to acknowledge and honor one God who is above all, and let the idea that gods are many never even reach the ears of the man whose rule of life is to seek for truth in purity and guilelessness" (*De Decalogo* 65, more broadly 52–81; also *QG* 4.8; *Mos.* 1.75; *Spec. Leg.* 1.1-52; *Leg. Alleg.* 3.97-99, 436-38). In his study of Josephus' view of God, Shutt concluded that, despite the presence of Hellenistic ideas and terms in Josephus' writings, "the sovereignty of the one God of Israel over all" remained dominant (Shutt 1980: 172).

A lengthy survey of references more broadly in Second Temple Jewish and non-Jewish texts showed that monotheistic rhetoric characterized both Jewish affirmations of their religion and the representations of them by Gentiles (Cohon 1955). For example, the *Letter of Aristeas* emphasizes that "God is one," his power and sovereignty extending over all the earth, and portrays Moses as having taught Jews to worship "the only God omnipotent over all creation." Among non-Jewish writers, Tacitus' comment is illustrative: "The Jews acknowledge one God only, and conceive of Him by the mind alone" (*Histories* 5.3).

A number of older studies yielded the same results (e.g., Wicks 1915; Marcus 1931-1932). Most recently, the unpublished dissertation of Rainbow (1987) surveys some 175 passages in Jewish texts where he finds obvious monotheistic expressions. On the basis of his linguistic analysis of these passages, he identified ten "forms of explicit monotheistic speech" characteristic of the texts of the Greek and Roman eras: (1) phrases linking a divine title such as "God" or "Lord" with adjectives such as "one," "only," "sole," and "alone"; (2) God pictured as monarch over all; (3) a divine title linked with "living" and/or "true"; (4) confessional formulas such as "Yahweh is God" and the like; (5) explicit denial of other gods as real or as worthy of worship; (6) God's glory as not transferable to others; (7) God described as without rival or equal; (8) God referred to as incomparable; (9) use of scriptural passages as expressions of monotheism, for example, the Shema; and (10) restrictions on worship as rightfully due to the one God alone.

There are two major emphases in this early Jewish monotheistic rhetoric (see, e.g., Amir 1978; 1987). First is the assertion of God's universal sovereignty in statements insisting that the one God created and rules all things, even the nations that do not acknowledge this one God, and even the evil and rebellious spiritual powers (often a feature of apocalyptic texts). The second major emphasis is on God's uniqueness, which characteristically involves a contrast with the other deities of the ancient religious environment. This ridicule of other deities and the reverence given them is classically expressed in Isaiah (e.g., 40:18-20; 41:21-24; 45:20-21; 46:5-7), a writing that certainly remained influential throughout the Second Temple period. The criticism is also echoed in texts composed in the Hellenistic and Roman periods (e.g., Wisdom of Solomon 13–15).

Worship Practice

The crucial distinction, however, between the one God and all other heavenly beings (whether God's own entourage or the beings worshiped by others as deities) was expressed in worship, which was to be restricted to God alone. Although principal angels and other exalted figures feature prominently in some early Jewish texts, they were not treated as rightful recipients of worship in either the Jerusalem Temple or synagogue settings (Hurtado 1988). For instance, there was no altar to them, and no sacrifice directed to any of them, in the Temple. Even sectarian groups such as the Qumran community exhibited a similarly exclusivist devotional orientation. In the Qumran texts, as in Second Temple Jewish literature more widely, prayers are directed solely to the one God, and songs of worship likewise.

In fact, in the ancient setting generally, the key expression of one's religion, and the key differentiation of religious stances, was in worship. Devout Jews (and Christians) took a strongly exclusivist position, restricting their own worship to the one God, and also typically condemning as idolatry the worship of any other deity by others, a position that gave a universalizing force to their particularist stance. In one of the most lengthy condemnations of idolatry in the Second Temple period (Wisdom of Solomon 13–14), it is ascribed to human foolishness and error (in confusing creatures with their creator), and consists in worshiping lifeless images. In other cases, however, the *existence* of other deities is not denied; instead, they are presented as inferior (sometimes malevolent) beings and are certainly not to be worshiped. In Deut. 32:16-17, for example, the gods of other nations are "demons" (a view echoed in 1 Cor. 10:19-20). In some texts they are portrayed as disobedient spirits who deceived the nations into giving them worship, usurping the honor rightfully due to God alone (e.g., *1 Enoch* 19:1-2).

This exclusivist stance (often expressed rather pugnaciously) distinguished early Jewish practice in the Hellenistic and Roman religious environments; and Gentiles regarded Jews (and Christians subsequently) as singularly strange and even antisocial in their refusal to share in the worship of the other deities of the time. Devout Jews and non-Jews therefore agreed in treating worship as the key issue. So, for example, in 1 Macc. 1:41–2:26, the Seleucid ruler seeks to persuade or coerce Jews to participate in sacrifice offered to other deities, thereby promoting what the author regards as apostasy (2:15), and it is a fellow Jew's acquiescence that enflames Mattathias to violent action and to issue a summons to other devout Jews to engage in militant resistance. In the Roman period, Gaius Caligula's attempt to set up his image for worship in the Jerusalem temple precipitated sharp Jewish resistance that threatened to break out into war, and also generated Philo's heated protestation and reaffirmation of Jewish scruples in *Embassy to Gaius*.

The concern of Jews to affirm God's uniqueness in their piety extended well beyond the operations of the Temple. Various kinds of evidence suggest that profession of God's uniqueness in the words of the Shema was a familiar and widely used affirmation of faith, and may have featured as part of private devotional life and in synagogue services as well. The Nash Papyrus (second century B.C.E.?) likely shows the Decalogue and the Shema used for instructional and/or liturgical purposes. Josephus (*Ant.* 4.212) ascribes to devout Jews the practice of beginning and ending each day with prayers of thanksgiving to God, which may also have included the recitation of the Shema. The discovery of phylacteries at Qumran containing copies of the Shema further shows its importance and ritual function.

In texts such as *Apoc. Zeph.* 6:11-15, we have additional indication of Jewish scruples about worship.

Here the human seer is portrayed as confronted by a great angel, so glorious in appearance that the seer mistakes him for God and moves to worship him; but the angel sharply forbids this, making his identity as a high-ranking servant to the one God clear (a motif reflected also in Rev. 19:10; 22:8-9).

Social and Historical Significance

Ancient Jewish religious belief and practice had major social consequences. The monotheistic stance of early Judaism distinguished the Jewish people religiously and, thus, socially and contributed to their sense of being a distinctive people with a shared identity. Josephus wrote that "as God is one, also the Hebrew race is one" (*Ant.* 4.201). Especially in Diaspora locations, their refusal to share in the worship of other deities marked them off and could generate varying degrees of disdain and antagonism.

Early Jewish monotheism is also arguably a notable intellectual development. Ancient philosophical critiques of polytheism seem to have had little effect beyond small circles of sophisticates, with scant impact upon the ritual life of people generally (even among philosophers!). Jewish monotheistic belief and practice, however, characterized the daily life of a whole people. Moreover, in arguing for discrimination between valid and invalid deities and forms of religious devotion, exponents of Jewish monotheism such as Philo laid down a distinctive line of thought (subsequently taken up in early Christian apologists) that involved a critical engagement with religious beliefs and practices in the name of devout religious faith.

Bibliography

Y. Amir 1978, "Die Begegnung des biblischen und des philosophischen Monotheismus als Grundthema des jüdischen Hellenismus," *EvT* 38: 2-19. • Y. Amir 1987, "Der Jüdische Eingottglaube als Stein des Anstoßes in der hellenistisch-römischen Welt," *JBT* 2: 58-75. • P. Athanassiadi and F. Michael, eds. 1999, *Pagan Monotheism in Late Antiquity,* Oxford: Clarendon. • S. Cohon 1955, "The Unity of God: A Study in Hellenistic and Rabbinic Theology," *HUCA* 26: 425-79. • R. M. Grant 1986, *The Gods and the One God,* Philadelphia: Westminster. • P. Hayman 1991, "Monotheism — A Misused Word in Jewish Studies?" *JJS* 42: 1-15. • L. Hurtado 1988, *One God, One Lord: Early Christian Devotion and Ancient Jewish Monotheism,* Philadelphia: Fortress. • L. Hurtado 1998, "First-Century Jewish Monotheism," *JSNT* 71: 3-26. • J. P. Kenney 1986, "Monotheistic and Polytheistic Elements in Classical Mediterranean Spirituality," in *Classical Mediterranean Spirituality,* ed. A. H. Armstrong, New York: Crossroad, 269-92. • M. Mach 1999, "Concepts of Jewish Monotheism in the Hellenistic Period," in *The Jewish Roots of Christological Monotheism: Papers from the St. Andrews Conference on the Historical Origins of the Worship of Jesus,* ed. C. Newman, J. R. Davila, and G. S. Lewis, Leiden: Brill, 21-42. • R. Marcus 1931-1932, "Divine Names and Attributes in Hellenistic Jewish Literature," *PAAJR* 3: 43-120. • M. P. Nilsson 1963, "The High God and the Mediator," *HTR* 56: 101-20. • E. Peterson 1926, *Eis Theos: Epigraphische, formgeschichtliche und religionsgeschichtliche Untersuchungen,* Göttingen: Vandenhoeck & Ruprecht. • P. A. Rainbow 1987, "Monotheism and Christology in 1 Corinthians 8:4-6," Ph.D. dissertation, Oxford University. • A. F. Segal 1977, *Two Powers in Heaven: Early Rabbinic Reports about Christianity and Gnosticism,* Leiden: Brill. • R. J. H. Shutt 1980, "The Concept of God in the Works of Flavius Josephus," *JJS* 31: 171-89. • M. Smith 1952, "The Common Theology of the Ancient Near East," *JBL* 71: 135-47. • M. S. Smith 2001, *The Origins of Biblical Monotheism: Israel's Polytheistic Background and the Ugaritic Texts,* Oxford: Oxford University Press. • L. T. Stuckenbruck 2004, "'Angels' and 'God': Exploring the Limits of Early Jewish Monotheism," in *Early Jewish and Christian Monotheism,* ed. L. T. Stuckenbruck and W. E. S. North, London: Clark, 45-70. • H. J. Wicks 1915, *The Doctrine of God in the Jewish Apocryphal and Apocalyptic Literature,* London: Hunter & Longhurst.

See also: Mediator Figures LARRY W. HURTADO

Moore, George Foote

George Foote Moore (1851-1931) was a historian of religion best known for his three-volume work, *Judaism in the First Centuries of the Christian Era: The Age of the Tannaim* (1927-1930). He was born in West Chester, Pennsylvania, and educated at Yale University (1872) and Union Theological Seminary (1877). He was ordained a Presbyterian minister (1878) and served a congregation in Zanesville, Ohio (1878-1883), before teaching at Andover Theological Seminary (1883-1901) and Harvard University (1902-1931). He wrote dozens of articles and books, especially focusing on early Judaism and Christian representations of it.

In his seminal article "Christian Writers on Judaism" (1921), Moore surveyed nearly two millennia of Christian constructions of Judaism and demonstrated that this discourse had taken a crucial turn in the nineteenth century. Prior to this time, Christians who studied Judaism did so in order to defend Christian doctrines, especially the Trinity, from Jewish interlocutors whose arguments for rigorous monotheism required a response. However, modern scholars such as Emil Schürer and Wilhelm Bousset shifted their focus from doctrine to history, seeking to contrast the "spirit" of the teachings of Jesus to the supposed "legalism" of the early rabbis. The error of this method was compounded, in Moore's view, by a pietistic tendency to conflate modern forms of Christianity with the primeval religiosity of Jesus.

Moore's magnum opus, *Judaism in the First Centuries of the Christian Era* (1927-1930), sought to correct Christian scholars' ignorance of the rabbinic materials. He reconstructed early Judaism from the texts modern Judaism considered authoritative, just as early Christianity had most often been reconstructed from the New Testament. Most of the citations in Judaism come from traditions in the two talmudim attributed to rabbis of the first two centuries C.E., with some citations from the Mishnah and from the midrashim. Few Christian scholars were even able to read these texts in the original languages in Moore's time. Many later Christian scholars simply relied on his summaries, which had been conveniently organized by topic, while continuing to use Schürer's and Bousset's dichotomy of law versus spirit. From the rabbinic sources, Moore reconstructed what he called the "normative Judaism" of the first centuries C.E. By "normative Judaism" he meant Pharisaism, which he understood to be the dominant form of Jewish religiosity by the middle of the second century B.C.E. and the direct forebear of rabbinic Judaism.

Over the last quarter century or so, Moore's concept of "normative Judaism" has been subjected to criticism on two main points. First, the period in Judaism that he focused on closes with the redaction of the Mishnah, ca. 200 C.E. However, as Jacob Neusner (1980) has noted, Moore was little concerned with the legal disputations that occupy the main part of the Mishnah's bulk. Indeed, Moore rarely provided examples of such "casuistry," but rather defended the attention to legal details as the logical consequence of a "revealed religion" whose every detail is divine. Moore was more interested in what he called "the religious and moral element" of religion than in the details of its daily practice. In this sense, Moore has been called an apologist for rabbinic Judaism, in contrast to the Christian scholars he took so sternly to task for their apologetics on behalf of Christianity.

Second, as Shaye Cohen (1981), following Moore's student E. R. Goodenough, has argued, to consider proto-rabbinic Judaism "normative" accords the rabbis far more authority than they actually had. Scholars of early Jewish sectarianism like Cohen and Albert Baumgarten (1999) now consider the Tannaim to have been one group among others. E. P. Sanders (1992) has preferred the term "common Judaism" to refer to observances followed by the majority of Jews around the turn of the era, such as circumcision and kashrut, which were not restricted to proto-rabbinic Judaism. However, even these practices were subjects of debate in early Judaism, and scholars do not agree on how nearly the tannaitic practice approximated the practice of the majority of Jews.

If Moore's reconstruction of early Judaism must be revised, through greater attention to the rabbinic legal argumentation and to the history of other contemporary Jewish groups, his work still stands as a monument to the study of early Judaism as a subject in its own right, and to the ethical concerns that Christian scholars need to take into account in order to avoid studying Judaism as a mere context — or, worse — foil for Jesus and early Christianity.

BIBLIOGRAPHY

A. I. BAUMGARTEN 1999, "Marcel Simon's 'Verus Israel' as a Contribution to Jewish History," *HTR* 92: 465-78. • S. J. D. COHEN 1981, "Epigraphical Rabbis," *JQR* 71: 1-17. • G. F. MOORE 1910, *A Critical and Exegetical Commentary on Judges*, New York: Scribner's. • G. F. MOORE 1913-1919, *History of Religions*, New York: Scribner's. • G. F. MOORE 1921, "Christian Writers on Judaism," *HTR* 14: 192-254. • G. F. MOORE 1923, *The Birth and Growth of Religion: Being the Morse Lectures of 1922*, New York: Scribner's. • G. F. MOORE 1927-1930, *Judaism in the First Centuries of the Christian Era: The Age of the Tannaim*, 3 vols., Cambridge: Harvard University Press. • G. F. MOORE 1948, *The Literature of the Old Testament*, 2d ed., rev. L. H. Brockington, London: Oxford University Press. • J. NEUSNER 1980, "'Judaism' after Moore: A Programmatic Statement," *JJS* 31: 141-56 • E. P. SANDERS 1992, *Judaism: Practice and Belief: 63 BCE–66 CE*, Philadelphia: Fortress.

STEWART MOORE

Mosaics

Mosaics are artistic compositions made by inlaying small cubes of differently colored materials such as stone or glass into a wall or floor in order to form pictures or patterns. Walls and floors in early Jewish palaces and synagogues that were decorated with mosaics provide important examples of how early Jewish art and architecture were influenced by both biblical tradition and Greco-Roman culture. The ancient Jewish mosaics found in the land of Israel so far date from the third century B.C.E. to the eighth century C.E., that is, from the Hellenistic to the Umayyad period.

Hellenistic to Herodian Period

The first traces of mosaic floors in the land of Israel have been found in the excavations of Tell Hanafa and are dated by archaeologists to the third-second centuries B.C.E. Only fragments are left of a composition that included plants, animals, and human figures together with geometric motifs. The geometric motif decorating the

A mosaic floor from a first-century-C.E. mansion in Jerusalem's Jewish Quarter *(Institute of Archaeology, Hebrew University, Jerusalem)*

One of the well-preserved polychrome mosaics in the lower bathhouse at Herodium, showing a rosette in the center, three balls in two corners, and pomegranates in the other corners *(www.HolyLandPhotos.org)*

apodyterium or primary entry of the bath in the Hasmonean palace of the northern mound at Jericho has been dated to the beginning of the first century B.C.E.

Several mosaics with the same technical and stylistic characteristics have been found in the Hasmonean-Herodian palaces at Masada, Herodium, Jericho, Cypros, and Machaerus and in mansions of the same period excavated in the Jewish Quarter of Jerusalem. They can be divided into two main groups: black-and-white mosaics and polychrome ones. Both are geometrical and have a rosette as a central motif. The main geometrical patterns used in these first-century mosaics are the straight-tongued double *guilloche* or interlace pattern, the swastika-meander motif, the band-of-wave pattern, the black-and-white serrated sawtooth pattern, and the chessboard pattern. In the promontory palace at Caesarea, a second-century mosaic was added to decorate the *triclinium* or reception hall; a frame of square and swastika motifs surrounds a central composition of intertwined dodecangle circles.

Floral motifs such as vine leaves, pomegranates, and ivy leaves decorate the large bands that surround mosaics. A sophisticated example is the mosaic in the antechamber of the reception hall in the western palace at Masada. The materials used in this mosaic are stone for white, black and red tesserae, and green and blue glass tesserae for the palmettes in the corners. Pomegranates also decorate a square panel added at the corners of the great pool complex at Lower Herodium.

Roman Period

Among the mosaic floors dated by archaeologists to the third century C.E., those found in Nablus in Samaria and at Sepphoris in Galilee deserve special mention for including Dionysus/Bacchus in their subject matter. With their scrolls on a black background in the surrounding frame, and with their figurative scenes in the central carpet, these two mosaics are connected technically and stylistically with mosaics from the same period found at Jerash in Arabia and at Maryamin in Syria. A third mosaic floor of the same type has been found at Shaikh Zuwaydeh on the border between Palestine and Egypt. A fragmentary composition also found at Nablus near a previously discovered mosaic floor depicts mythological scenes associated with the boy Achilles presented to Chiron and Achilles disguised as a woman.

Byzantine Period

Most of the mosaic floors discovered in Palestine are dated to the Byzantine period (fourth to seventh centuries C.E.). They mainly decorate synagogues and ecclesiastical edifices such as churches and monasteries. One of the earliest church mosaic floors can be dated tentatively to the late fourth or early fifth century C.E. It was found in the lower pavement of the five aisles in the Basilica of the Nativity in Bethlehem, a church built by order of Constantine after 325 C.E. While the side aisles and the western narthex are decorated with a plain white mosaic floor enclosed in a simple band of black lines, the central nave is decorated with a rich geometrical composition surrounded by an acanthus frame filled with fruits and flowers. With the addition of a few animal motifs, the same patterns decorate the octagonal *presbyterium.*

The lower mosaic floor of the synagogue in Ḥammath Tiberias dates to the same period. This mosaic features three motifs that were later used in the decoration of the Samaritan and Jewish synagogues of the region: (1) the Ark of the Covenant, covered with an embroidered curtain and set between two menorahs; (2) the zodiac wheel, with Helios in the center accompanied by personifications of the four seasons and of the zodiac signs identified by their names written in Greek, Aramaic, or Hebrew; and (3) two lions depicted on either side of a dedicatory inscription with the names of the donors.

The fine mosaics that decorate the floors of the Samaritan synagogues discovered at el-Khirbet and Khirbet Samara in Samaria also belong to the Byzantine period. At el-Khirbet the central rectangular carpet is surrounded by a black-and-red *guilloche* followed by a large band of acanthus medallions decorated with animal representations and floral motifs. The main carpet is divided into three sections: two squares with a rectangular panel in the center that depicts the table of showbread situated between a menorah and the Ark of the Covenant. The large frame of acanthus scrolls is repeated in the mosaic floor of Khirbat Samara, which gives a natural representation of grapevines, a pomegranate tree, a palm tree, sheaves of wheat or barley, a birdcage, and metal objects. The intertwined geometrical motifs of the carpet repeat the same motifs used in the floor of the Basilica of the Nativity in Bethlehem and in the Church of Lazarus at Bethany.

Besides having distinctively Jewish and Christian symbols, mosaics in Byzantine-era churches and synagogues share many of the same decorations. Both churches and synagogues used the same geometric compositions (with or without isolated floral and animal motifs) in still-life representations of fruits and fruit baskets, birds and fish, and vessels of various types, and in complex compositions such as scrolls with vine shoots coming out of a jar. The scrolls themselves are decorated with hunting, pastoral, and agricultural scenes.

In synagogues, Jewish symbols are accompanied by biblical scenes: Daniel in the lions' den (at Naʿaran and Khirbet Susiyah); the binding of Isaac (at Beth ʾAlpha and Sepphoris); and King David depicted as Orpheus (at Maioumas in Gaza).

The most impressive mosaic in the land of Israel was discovered in 1993. It is a 44 × 15 ft. carpet that covered the floor of a fifth-to-seventh-century synagogue in Sepphoris. The mosaic is made up of seven wide bands, some of which are divided into smaller panels. The badly damaged first panel inside the entrance probably depicted the visit of the three angels to Abraham and Sarah (Gen. 18:1-15). The next band portrays the binding and near sacrifice of Isaac (Genesis 22). In the next band is a circular zodiac measuring 11 by 11 feet, with the sun god Helios in his horse-drawn chariot at its center. The next three bands, located above the zodiac, depict objects and rituals associated with the wilderness Tabernacle, the Jerusalem Temple, and the Jewish festivals.

In the mosaics found in Israel, the zodiac remains exclusive to synagogues. In churches, the zodiac is replaced by personifications of the months, as in the courtyard of the monastery of Lady Mary at Beth Shean and in the al-Hammam chapel in the same city. Personifications of the earth are found in Beth Guvrin and in Jerusalem (Mt. Zion). Some edifices are decorated with Nile landscape scenes, as in the Constantinian villa of Beth Guvrin, the church of Tabgha, the chapel of Haditha, the synagogue of Kyrios Leontis at Beth Shean, and the civic building in Sepphoris. The scenes are characterized by aquatic motifs of flora and fauna accompanied by walled cities representing Aegyptus and Alexandria and the Nilometer (a device used to measure the level of the Nile River).

Scenes from Greco-Roman mythology feature in various mosaics. Examples include Orpheus playing a lyre among animals in a mosaic in Jerusalem, Odysseus and the sirens in the prayer hall of Kyrios Leontis at Beth Shean, and the Indian triumph of Dionysus at Erez.

Inscriptions

Some mosaics include inscriptions with the names of the donors and artists, sometimes with the date and a benediction. The synagogue mosaic in ʿEin Gedi, for example, lists the names of the benefactors. In a few instances, the names of the artists survive, such as Marianos and his son Aninas in the Beth Alpha and Beth Shean synagogues, Antonius Galoga at Battir, and Alexander at Kissufim. In synagogue mosaics, inscriptions are written in Greek, Hebrew, or Aramaic. In Christian inscriptions, other languages are used such as Greek, Syriac, Armenian, Georgian, and in rare cases Latin.

BIBLIOGRAPHY

M. DOTHAN 1983, *Hammath Tiberias: Early Synagogues and the Hellenistic and Roman Remains,* Jerusalem: Israel Exploration Society. • S. FINE 2005, *Art and Judaism in the Greco-Roman World: Toward a New Jewish Archaeology,* Cambridge: Cambridge University Press. • R. HACHLILI 1987, *Ancient Jewish Art and Architecture in the Land of Israel,* Leiden: Brill. • L. I. LEVINE, ED. 1981, *Ancient Synagogues Revealed,* Jerusalem: Israel Exploration Society. • Y. MAGEN 1993, "Samaritan Synagogues," in *Early Christianity in Context: Monuments and Documents,* ed. F. Manns and E. Alliata, Jerusalem: Franciscan Printing Press, 193-230. • E. NETZER 2001, *The Palaces of the Hasmoneans and Herod the Great,* Jerusalem: Yad Ben-Zvi. • R. AND A. OVADIAH 1987, *Mosaic Pavements in Israel,* Rome: Bretschneider. • E. T. RICHMOND 1936, "Basilica of the Nativity," *Quarterly of the Department of Antiquities in Palestine* 5: 75-81. • E. L. SUKENIK 1932, *The Ancient Synagogue of Beth Alpha,* Jerusalem: Hebrew University Press. • R. TALGAM AND Z. WEISS 2004, *The Mosaics of the House of Dionysos at Sepphoris,* Jerusalem: Hebrew University Institute of Archaeology. • S. TALMON AND Y. YADIN 1999, *Masada VI: Yigael Yadin Excavations 1963–1965, Final Reports,* Jerusalem: Israel Exploration Society and Hebrew University of Jerusalem. • Z. WEISS AND E. NETZER 1996, *Promise and Redemption: A Synagogue Mosaic from Sepphoris,* Jerusalem: Israel Museum.

See also: Architecture; Art; Fortresses and Palaces; Synagogues MICHELE PICCIRILLO†

Moses

In the Second Temple period, the figure of Moses was not of equal importance for all expressions of Judaism. There are references to Jews who did not give much heed to the Mosaic Torah (e.g., 1 Macc. 1:52). And even among some pious groups who rigorously observed divine Torah, other figures, notably Enoch, seem to have been more prominent. In the literature of the period, there are two main developments. (1) The biblical roles of Moses are enhanced and amplified; for example, he is predestined from creation to be mediator, he continually intercedes for Israel, and he receives revelation about all things to the last days. (2) In the apologetic of Hellenistic Jewish writers (esp. Aristobulus, Artapanus, Philo, and Josephus), Moses conforms to Greek ideals: he is a great civilizer, philosopher, and inventor; an ideal king embodying the offices of legislator, high priest, and prophet; and a "divine man."

Palestinian Sources

Ben Sira (44:23–45:5; ca. 180 B.C.E.) praises Moses as a godly man who was equal in glory to the angels, a mira-

A wall painting from the third-century-C.E. synagogue at Dura Europos in Syria showing Moses and the burning bush. Notice that Moses wears a tunic with colored stripes *(clavi)* and a mantle *(Yale University Art Gallery, Dura-Europos Collection)*

cle worker and law-giver, chosen by God out of all humans for his faithfulness and humility. He was a holy man and prophet (45:6; 46:1).

The book of *Jubilees* (ca. 150 B.C.E.) emphasizes Moses' role as intercessor (*Jub.* 1:19) and lawgiver, and amplifies the extent of the revelation: God reveals to Moses knowledge of all times, from creation to the new creation (*Jub.* 1:4, 29; cf. 6:22). On the other hand, the status of Moses is distinctly attenuated in that the revelation to Moses is only partial and mediated by an angel from the heavenly tablets (*Jub.* 4:5, 32; 6:35; 23:32; 30:9; 50:13). Moses is not the incomparable recipient of revelation since earlier patriarchs, especially Enoch, had access to the heavenly tablets (*Jub.* 4:17-25; 7:38-39; cf. 10:10-14), and books of this revelation were passed down through the patriarchs to Levi, not Moses (12:25-27; 21:10; 45:16; cf. *Aramaic Levi Document, Testament of Qahat* [4Q542], and *Visions of Amram* [4Q543-548]).

In the Qumran texts, Moses is mostly associated with the authority of the Torah. Joining the sectarian community is tantamount to "taking upon oneself (an oath) to return to the Torah of Moses" (CD 15:9, 12; 16:1-2, 4-5; 1QS 5:8). Violations of Mosaic Torah willfully or through negligence are punished by permanent expulsion (1QS 8:21-27). It is forbidden to make oaths by the Torah of Moses, as also with the divine name (CD 15:2; cf. Josephus, *J.W.* 2.145, 153).

The most distinctive feature in the portrait of Moses in the Dead Sea Scrolls is his role as prophet *par excellence.* As in *Jubilees,* the Mosaic Torah is a prophetic text (cf. 1QS 1:3) and includes eschatological revelation, foretelling the sins and punishment of the Israelites until the last days (*Florilegium* [4Q174 1-3 i 2-3]; MMT [4Q394-399] C; *Apocryphon of Moses* [1Q22 1 i 7-12]; *Commentary on Genesis A* [4Q252 1 iv 2]; *Words of the Luminaries* [4Q504 1-2 iii 11-14]). According to the sectarian *Damascus Document,* even the ordinances of the community belong to the "Torah of Moses" (4Q266 11 5-6//4Q270 7 i 20), "for in it everything is specified" (CD 16:2). That is, Mosaic revelation is comprehensive; inherent in Mosaic Torah are the "hidden things" that are discernible only by inspired exegesis. Such an assumption lies behind the exposition of new laws as Mosaic in 4QMMT, the *Temple Scroll,* and *Reworked Pentateuch.* Moses is called God's "anointed one" in *Apocryphal Pentateuch B* (4Q377 2 ii 5), highlighting his role as one of the prophets (cf. CD 6:1; 1QM 11:7). Furthermore, the prophet like Moses of Deut. 18:15-19 is regarded as an eschatological figure (4QTestimonia; 11QMelchizedek 2:17-18; *Apocryphon of Moses*) along with the messiahs of Israel and Aaron.

Numerous Qumran texts emphasize Moses' role as mediator and intercessor. The *Apocryphon of Joshua*[a] describes Moses as the "man of God" who possesses the knowledge of the Most High, sees the vision of the Almighty, and whose voice is heard in the council of the Most High ([4Q378 frgs. 3, 26]). According to *Apocryphal Pentateuch B,* Moses was covered by the cloud because of his sanctity and was an incomparable herald of glad tidings through whom God would speak "as though he were an angel" (4Q377 2ii). There is no reference to Moses as king, and only brief mention of his priestly role of atonement in a nonsectarian prayer (4Q504 1-2 ii 9-10).

The *Testament of Moses* (first century C.E.) especially develops traditions surrounding the death of Moses. Moses indicates that God prepared him from creation to be mediator of the covenant (1:14) and revealed all secrets to him, including the eschaton. Moses passes on to Joshua a book with this revelation (10:11). Joshua is distraught at the loss of Moses as compassionate leader, untiring intercessor, wise judge, "master of the word," "faithful in all things," "divine prophet for the whole world," "perfect teacher," and "great messenger" (11:9-19). No place is appropriate for his burial since "the whole world is your sepulcher." A broken passage might indicate that Moses will continue beyond death as perpetual intercessor for the sins of Israel (12:6).

The *Biblical Antiquities* of Pseudo-Philo (first century C.E.) closely follows the biblical story of the exodus and Moses' roles in the exodus, but it includes significant additional traditions (chaps. 9–19): Moses' sister Miriam had a dream about the birth of Moses to be a great leader. Moses was born circumcised. On Mt. Sinai, Moses took a cutting from the tree of life, which he used to cure the waters of Marah. On the mountains of Moab, God revealed to Moses mysteries of sacred places and the end times. The reason he was not allowed to enter the promised land was to spare him from witnessing idolatry. When Moses died, the angels mourned and refrained from their heavenly songs. God buried Moses, and the place is not known to angels or humans.

In *2 Baruch* (early second century C.E.), God reveals to Moses information about future generations, the heavenly city, the eschatological judgment, and the mysteries of the cosmos (3:9; 4:5; 59:3-12). The Torah is eternal and was known by patriarchs before Moses, but with Moses the lamp of the Law was lit to illuminate all (17:4; 59:1-2; cf. 57:2).

Hellenistic Jewish Writers

The figure of Moses was known in the Greco-Roman world, and garnered both respect (e.g., Hecataeus of Abdera, ca. 300 B.C.E.) and mockery (e.g., Manetho, Lysimachus, Apollonius Molon, Posidonius, Tacitus, Galen, Celsus; cf. Josephus, *Ag. Ap.* 1.279-309; 2.145). Apologetic treatments of Moses are common among Hellenistic Jewish writers conscious of critiques of Judaism. In response, they tended to omit or reinterpret negative aspects of the story and to portray Moses positively according to Greco-Roman heroic ideals: an extraordinary birth, upbringing and beauty that foreshadow greatness, and the virtues of wisdom, courage, temperance, justice, and piety. The main sources from Alexandria are Aristobulus, Ezekiel, and Artapanus (all second century B.C.E.), and Philo (early first century C.E.). Eupolemus (second century C.E.) and Josephus (late first century C.E.) were Palestinian Jews writing in Greek. They share many panegyrical traditions about Moses; for example, Moses was the original philosopher, and Greek philosophy drew on Moses (Aristobulus; Artapanus; Philo; Josephus). He was a bringer of culture and civilization and invented the alphabet (Eupolemus; Artapanus). Moses was identified with the legendary Greek poet Mousaios, teacher of Orpheus (Artapanus; Aristobulus), and also with Hermes, the messenger of the gods, because of his renowned skill at interpreting sacred texts (Artapanus). He organized the political administration and religious cults of Egypt (Artapanus). He was a brilliant military commander in Egypt (Artapanus; Josephus). He avoided luxury and exercised complete mastery of his passions (Philo; Josephus; 4 Macc. 2:17). Moses received knowledge about all things from the past to the future (Ezekiel the Tragedian).

In his *Life of Moses,* Philo presents Moses as the "greatest and most perfect of men" (1.1-2), who combined in his character the ideal king, legislator, high priest, and prophet (2.1-7; treated respectively in 1.5-334; 2.8-65; 2.66-165; 2.187-287). He was a philosopher, a living embodiment of law and justice, an interpreter of sacred mysteries, and a mystic who underwent heavenly ascent and deification. Moses was not only beyond all others, his qualities were superhuman; for example, he had perfect command of his passions (*Mos.* 1.27). In this, Philo portrays Moses in the category of "divine man," but in one extraordinary passage he goes further to claim that Moses shared the nature of God and came from and returned to God (*On the Sacrifices of Cain and Abel* 8–10).

Josephus tells the story of Moses at length (esp. *Ant.* 2.205–4.331; *Ag. Ap.* 2.145-74). Despite his promise to neither add nor omit anything (*Ant.* 1.17), he embellishes Moses' biography with many extra traditions and regularly omits episodes that might reflect negatively on Moses (e.g., Moses slaying the Egyptian taskmaster, God's attempt to kill Moses, Moses striking the rock). He emphasizes Moses as the most ancient legislator, a brilliant general, a philosopher, teacher, an incomparable prophet, and a poet who invented a musical instrument. He had greater understanding than any other human and had complete control of his passions; he was modest, just, and merciful. Egyptian priests predicted his birth and future exploits over Egypt. In contrast to Artapanus and Philo, though, Josephus is more restrained in his exaltation of Moses, and explicitly counters traditions that exalted Moses to divine status (*Ant.* 4.326).

New Testament

There are diverse appropriations of the figure of Moses in the New Testament. Much of the presentation is consistent with treatments that enhance his biblical roles, as typical in Palestinian Jewish sources. He is so closely associated with the Law that "Moses" can be shorthand for the Torah of Moses (2 Cor. 3:15; Acts 15:21). Moses is also the interpreter of the Law, so that Pharisaic sages sit in the "seat of Moses" (Matt. 23:2). He is God's servant, messenger, mediator, and prophet. The motif of Moses writing about Christ (e.g., Luke 24:27, 44; Acts 3:22-26) is but a particular application of the motif of Moses as revealer of eschatological knowledge. There are only a few reflections of the apologetic traditions found in Hellenistic Jewish writers; for example, he was beautiful at his birth (Acts 7:20; Heb. 11:23), was instructed in the wisdom of Egypt (Acts 7:22), was appointed by God as ruler (Acts 7:35), and spurned the luxurious life of the Egyptian court (Heb. 11:24-25).

Particularly distinctive is the presentation of Moses as a type of Christ. Positively, Moses is a model of faith (Heb. 11:23-28) and a messenger who suffered rejection (Acts 7:35). In the Gospels, Jesus is often described in terms modeled on Moses in Scripture and legend; for example, in his birth, teaching, and rejection (esp. Matthew 1–2; 5–7) and in his role as prophet, priest, and king (esp. John). In Revelation, the exodus is a type of eschatological salvation through Jesus, and the angels sing the Song of Moses in praise of Christ (Rev. 15:3). Negatively, and especially in Paul and Hebrews, Moses is a transitional figure contrasted with Christ: Moses belonged to the old order, whose fading glory was temporary (2 Cor. 3:7, 13; Rom. 10:4-7); Jesus as God's son is superior to Moses as God's servant (Heb. 3:1-6); Jesus is the mediator of the new covenant (12:24).

There are some reflections of traditions about Moses as an eschatological figure. The appearance of Moses alongside Elijah in the transfiguration scene (Mark

9:2-8 and pars.) assumes an assumption of Moses and expectation of an eschatological Moses. John 5:45 alludes to Moses as eschatological intercessor and judge. John 6:30-35 may portray Jesus refusing to fulfill popular expectation by performing a repeat of the giving of manna.

Jude 9 refers to a tradition from a lost *Assumption of Moses* mentioned by Origen, according to which Michael and Satan argued over the body of Moses.

Rabbinic Judaism

In early rabbinic sources, Moses is by far the most important figure as the greatest teacher of Torah and thus the paradigm for the rabbi. This is ultimately reflected in the ubiquitous title *Moshe Rabbenu* ("Moses our Master," although it does not appear in the Mishnah). According to the rabbinic concept of Oral Torah, Moses received on Mt. Sinai not only the written Torah but also a comprehensive body of oral instruction, and this was transmitted through Joshua and the prophets eventually to the rabbis (*m. ʾAbot* 1:1; cf. *m. Yad.* 4:3; *m. Peʾah* 2:6). In this way, the rabbinic sages dealing with the aftermath of the loss of the Temple in 70 C.E. sought to ground their teachings in a chain of authority extending back to Moses on Mt. Sinai: all subsequent law was deemed inherent in Mosaic Torah. The point is illustrated in a famous story told in relation to R. Akiva (mid-second century C.E.): Moses listening in on R. Akiva teaching in his academy was distressed that he couldn't understand, until Akiva said that he received the teaching as tradition from Moses at Sinai (*b. Menaḥot* 29b).

Many of the traditions about Moses' biography seen in earlier writings continue in haggadic texts of the rabbis, and are developed much further. These are particularly concerned with fleshing out details about Moses' life, clarifying ambiguities, and explaining potentially troubling stories. For example, Moses was born circumcised; as a baby he took Pharaoh's crown and placed it on his own head; he was not allowed to enter Canaan to prevent him from witnessing idolatry which would lure the Israelites; he continues to intercede for Israel. Nevertheless, the rabbis avoid overly exalting Moses; in contrast to the Hellenistic Jewish writings, they resist attributing divine qualities to him, and Moses remains a thoroughly human figure with flaws.

BIBLIOGRAPHY

R. BLOCH 1954, "Quelques aspects de la figure de Moïse dans la tradition rabbinique," *Cahiers Sioniens* 8: 211-85. • J. BOWLEY 2001, "Moses in the Dead Sea Scrolls: Living in the Shadow of God's Anointed," in *The Bible at Qumran: Text, Shape, and Interpretation,*" ed. P. Flint, Grand Rapids: Eerdmans, 159-81. • L. FELDMAN 1992-1993, "Josephus' Portrait of Moses," *JQR* 82: 285-328; 83: 7-50, 301-30. • L. H. FELDMAN 2007, *Philo's Portrayal of Moses in the Context of Ancient Judaism,* Notre Dame: University of Notre Dame Press. • J. L. KUGEL 1998, *Traditions of the Bible: A Guide to the Bible as it Was at the Start of the Common Era,* Cambridge: Harvard University Press, 501-888. • W. MEEKS 1967, *The Prophet King: Moses Traditions and the Johannine Christology,* Leiden: Brill.

DANIEL K. FALK

Moses, Assumption of

The *Assumption of Moses* (also designated as the *Testament of Moses*) is a first-century-C.E., fragmentarily preserved writing in which Moses is pictured as delivering a farewell speech to his successor Joshua, shortly before the former's departure from earthly life. In his speech, Moses prophetically describes the history of the people of Israel from their entrance into the land, up to and including the reign of King Herod and his sons, followed by a description of eschatological events expected soon after that. Following this speech, Joshua is described as expressing his despair over having to lead the people into the promised land; he asserts that he does not have capacities similar to those of Moses, but his predecessor reassures him that, if he will remain loyal to the covenant, he will succeed, thanks to the providential care of God's Holy Spirit. The final part of the writing, of which only quotations in early Christian literature are extant, probably described how Moses was assumed into heaven, after the archangel Michael and the Devil had a discussion about the legitimacy of that event. The *Assumption of Moses* is one of the most important witnesses to the early Jewish eschatological worldview.

Transmission, Title, Origin

The fragments of the *Assumption of Moses* were discovered in the Milan Ambrosian Library, and published in 1861 by its librarian, A.-M. Ceriani. The writing, preserved in Latin on a fifth- or sixth-century palimpsest, could be identified as the *Assumption of Moses,* because it contains a number of lines that correspond exactly to a Greek quotation in the work of the Christian historian Gelasius of Cyzicus. On account of its testamentary form (see below), it is often also identified as the *Testament of Moses* (both titles, *Assumption* and *Testament of Moses,* occur in ancient lists of apocryphal works). It is likely that the Latin text was a translation from Greek, because it contains several expressions that can only be understood when retroverted into Greek. That the Greek model was a translation from Hebrew or Aramaic has often been argued, but is difficult to prove. Interpretations of the *Assumption of Moses* based on a hypothetical Hebrew original should be regarded as highly speculative. The almost exclusive attention of the author to people and events occurring in Jerusalem and Judea makes it virtually certain that the *Assumption of Moses* was written in that area.

Form and Contents

The form of the writing, insofar as it is extant, is that of a "farewell scene," a literary form that is defined as a speech delivered by someone who is about to die. Such persons are described as summoning their children (or, in this case, his successor) to their deathbed; a discourse on any subject (the future, or moral instruction, or both) is made, and usually the death and burial of the speakers are also described.

In the *Assumption of Moses,* the last hours of the earthly life of Moses are described, with explicit reference to the final chapters of Deuteronomy (chap. 31 in particular). Moses is portrayed as pronouncing to his successor Joshua a prophecy concerning the fate of Israel from its entrance into the promised land until the end of time (chap. 1). The (pseudo-)prophecy consists of three main parts: a description of Israel's history from the entrance into the land until the return from the Babylonian Exile (chaps. 2–4); a description of the following period, until the rule of a petulant king and his sons (chaps. 5–6); and a description of the real author's own time, and of the tribulations he expected for the near future, leading up to the ascension of Israel into heaven (chaps. 7–10). The prophecy is followed by a dialogue between Joshua and Moses. After Moses has instructed his successor to be strong, Joshua is portrayed as shrinking back from the difficult task that lay before him, and doubting whether he would be capable of fulfilling Moses' role (chap. 11; Joshua's eulogy of Moses far transcends the usual). Moses responds to Joshua's despair by telling him that he himself has had no merits of his own, but only achieved what God granted him; Joshua, too, should succeed only if he keeps to the commandments of the Lord (chap. 12).

After this, the manuscript breaks off. It is likely that a passage followed that contained a description of Moses' death and ascension into heaven, and also included a debate between the archangel Michael and the Devil about the legitimacy of Moses' ascension. The Devil would have resisted that honor, possibly because of Moses' human, that is, corruptible nature.

Unity and Date

It is generally agreed that the "petulant king" in chap. 5 is to be identified with Herod the Great (37-4 B.C.E.); it is likely, therefore, that the *Assumption of Moses,* insofar as it has been preserved, should be dated after that king's (and his sons') rule. However, no scholarly consensus exists as to whether the *Assumption of Moses* as we now know it reproduces an originally intended unity. It has been argued that the description, in chap. 8, of the horrors of the final age is a direct reflection of the persecution of Judaism by Antiochus IV Epiphanes in ca. 165 B.C.E. In that case, chaps. 5–6 would have been added to the writing at a later stage. Others have rejected this hypothesis as unnecessary, and have maintained that the description of the final age is intended as real prophecy of things soon expected; that the author for his scenario made use of traditions connected with Antiochus IV in, for example, First and Second Maccabees, would be no objection to that. It is commonly agreed, then, that the *Assumption of Moses* in its present form postdates the reign of Herod the Great by a few years, somewhere in the early first century C.E.; if one accepts the hypothesis of later additions, there may have been an earlier stage of the writing, to be dated to about 165 B.C.E.

Message

The author of the *Assumption of Moses* had but little appreciation for the society he was living in. As a lively portrait of the ruling classes illustrates (in chap. 6 and esp. chap. 7), he regarded the ruling class of his day as corrupt, hypocritical, and unjust, living for their bellies, and forgetful of the Lord's commandments. An admittedly somewhat cryptic note in 4:7-9 may suggest that the author also rejected the priestly class in Jerusalem, as well as the way in which they administered the sacrificial cult. In contrast to rulers and priests stands a Levite called Taxo, who together with his sons retreats from society into the desert, saying that they would rather die than transgress the commandments of the Lord (chap. 9). Interest in priestly matters is also expressed in chap. 10, where it is said that, at the breakthrough of God's kingdom, a heavenly messenger's "hands will be filled," an idiom indicating priestly ordination. Whereas it remains unclear who is intended with this Taxo, or with the messenger in heaven, all indications together suggest that the author of the *Assumption of Moses* was preoccupied with the priesthood in Jerusalem that malfunctioned, in his opinion, on a catastrophic scale. He seems to have regarded the priesthood's behavior as the culmination of the evil, sinfulness, and apostasy that characterized the history of his people as a whole (described in the pseudo-prophecy in chaps. 2–6).

Apparently, the author had lost all hope of an amelioration of the state of degradation to which the world had come. Salvation could only be expected from God himself, who must arise from his throne to establish his kingdom and make an end to diabolical powers and sadness (10:1-3). The direct cause for the divine intervention will be the attitude of the few who remain faithful (exemplified by Taxo and his sons), whose suffering amid impurity and sin cannot remain unavenged. This last point is also made in the dialogue between Moses and Joshua in chaps. 11–12: over against Joshua's despair of leading a sinful people to their destination is placed Moses' reassurance that God will never leave his people altogether, and that he will eventually act on behalf of those who are faithful to his covenant (12:13).

The author of the *Assumption of Moses* is a representative of an important current in early Judaism: eschatological apocalypticism, which also produced the book of Daniel (with a similar emphasis on cult and covenant) and many of the so-called sectarian writings among the Qumran Scrolls. This worldview, with its low esteem for the moral quality of humankind as a whole, and its utter dissatisfaction with the ruling classes in society, including the priesthood in Jerusalem, fits in with the chaotic state in which late Hellenistic and Roman Palestine found itself.

Bibliography

K. A. Atkinson 2004, "Herod the Great as Antiochus Redivivus: Reading the Testament of Moses as an Anti-Herodian Composition," in *Of Scribes and Sages: Early Jewish Interpretation and Transmission of Scripture,* vol. 1, ed. C. A. Evans, London: Clark, 134-49. • K. A. Atkinson 2006, "Taxo's Martyrdom and the Role of the *Nuntius* in the *Testament of Moses:* Implications for Understanding the Role of Other Intermediary Figures," *JBL* 125: 453-76. • J. W. van Henten 2003, "Moses as Heavenly Messenger in *Assumption of Moses* 10:2 and Qumran Passages," *JJS* 54: 216-27. • N. J. Hofmann 2000,

Die Assumptio Mosis: Studien zur Rezeption massgültiger Überlieferung, Leiden: Brill. • E. M. LAPERROUSAZ 1970, "Le Testament de Moïse (généralement appelé 'Assomption de Moïse')," *Semitica* 19 (includes a reprint of Ceriani's edition). • G. W. NICKELSBURG, ED. 1973, *Studies on the Testament of Moses,* Cambridge, Mass.: Society of Biblical Literature. • S. SCHREIBER 2001, "Hoffnung und Handlungsperspektive in der *Assumptio Mosis,*" *JSJ* 32: 252-71. • J. TROMP 1993, *The Assumption of Moses: A Critical Edition with Commentary,* Leiden: Brill. • J. TROMP 2003, "Origen on the *Assumption of Moses,*" in *Jerusalem, Alexandria, Rome: Studies in Ancient Cultural Interaction in Honour of A. Hilhorst,* ed. F. García Martínez and G. P. Luttikhuizen, Leiden: Brill, 323-40.

JOHANNES TROMP

Moses, Testament of → Moses, Assumption of

Moses Texts from Qumran

Due to the towering stature of Moses in Judaism as the prophet par excellence, new instruction during the Second Temple period is often presented as part of Mosaic discourse to ground it in the authority of Moses and Torah. Much of this occurs in the form of anecdotes or citations of his authority embedded in larger works, but a number of writings are devoted primarily to the figure of Moses as the central subject or putative author. Besides *Jubilees, Testament of Moses,* and Philo's *On The Life of Moses,* the largest body of Moses texts is known only from Qumran, although numerous of them are so fragmentary that the character of the work as a whole is unclear. In contrast to a large body of Enochic pseudepigrapha in Aramaic, all of the Moses works at Qumran are in Hebrew and none of them are Moses pseudepigrapha in the fullest sense, like Deuteronomy.

The Authority of the Mosaic Torah

Jubilees

The book of *Jubilees* retells the story of Genesis and Exodus from creation to Moses' reception of the Torah on Mt. Sinai. It is not a Moses pseudepigraphon in the strict sense, but told from the perspective of an angel relating the revelation to Moses. By showing the patriarchs observing festivals and laws, it systematically writes distinctive calendrical and halakic positions into the narrative. Although *Jubilees* originated around 150 B.C.E., before the settlement at Qumran and certain sectarian developments, it was an authoritative work at Qumran, as attested by its influence on other writings (e.g., CD 16:3-4), the large number of copies, and three or four related works (4Q225-227).

Temple Scroll

The large *Temple Scroll* re-presents Deuteronomy, systematically incorporating and harmonizing the laws from Exodus through Numbers. Effectively, then, it picks up where *Jubilees* leaves off. It, too, gives Torah a different voice, but here it is cast as the direct speech of God in the first person. Whether this intends to be a new Torah direct from God without Mosaic mediation or a rewritten Torah attempting to elucidate the true meaning of the laws received by Moses is unclear. At many points the *Temple Scroll* reads a distinctive halakic position into its version, for example, with regard to festivals and purity laws. The *Temple Scroll* is known only from Qumran, where three or four copies survive (11Q19-20, 4Q524, 11Q21?), but it, too, was edited before the settlement at Qumran (no later than about 150 B.C.E.), drawing on even earlier sources.

Reworked Pentateuch

If the five Hebrew manuscripts from the first century B.C.E. (4Q158, 4Q364-367) are copies of the same work, the so-called *Reworked Pentateuch* would be a version of the entire Pentateuch with rearrangement, harmonizing juxtapositions, and exegetical additions. It is based on a text similar to that used by the Samaritan Pentateuch, especially evident in the harmonizing juxtaposition of Deuteronomy 5 and Exodus 20. There are also similarities to the *Temple Scroll,* for example, the inclusion of festivals of New Oil and Wood Offering. Whether this work was intended as a revised edition of the Mosaic Torah or an interpretive harmony of it for study purposes is unclear. There is no special emphasis on the figure of Moses as either author or central subject.

The Authoritative Figure of Moses

Apocryphon of Moses

Five very fragmentary manuscripts are tentatively grouped under the designation *Apocryphon of Moses* due to points of contact, although it is not at all certain that they are copies of the same text. They all rework material from Deuteronomy about future leadership issues. What survives of 4Q375 seems to be an address by Moses based on Deut. 13:1–6 (Eng. 12:32–13:5) and Deut. 18:15–22, urging obedience to the prophet like Moses that God will raise up, but that any false prophet who preaches apostasy be put to death. Next, the text details a ritual of discernment in the case of appealing a charge as false prophet, involving sacrifices, consulting "hidden" laws in the Holy of Holies, and a presentation before the assembly. The rest of the ritual is lost from 4Q375, but if 1Q29, 4Q376, and 4Q408 are indeed copies of the same work, it involved an oracular use of two stones by the high priest to reveal God's will. The fragments of 1Q22 also contain a rewriting of Moses' address to the congregation of Israel from Deuteronomy to keep God's commandments, warning against apostasy and the consequent judgment, and instruction to appoint wise leaders to teach them God's laws. All of the manuscripts date to the latter half of the first century B.C.E. There are some concerns and language with similarities to Qumran sectarian texts, but no certain evidence of a Qumran origin.

Apocryphal Pentateuch A and B

4Q368 and 4Q377 are both texts about Moses, reworking material from Exodus, Numbers, and Deuteronomy. The former includes conversations between Moses and God and exhortations by Moses to the people of Israel, similar to 1Q22. The latter focuses on the special status of Moses as intermediator, and his uniqueness, comparing him to an angel. They both date from the first century B.C.E., respectively the latter and early halves.

Other Texts

4Q374 narrates episodes from the exodus from Egypt and settlement in Canaan, and in what survives focuses especially on the figure of Moses as a mediator and his stature "like God" to the Egyptians. 2Q21 contains narrative about Moses and the sons of Aaron, and recounts a prayer of Moses. 4Q390 and certain fragments of 4Q385a, 4Q387a, 4Q388a, and 4Q389 were previously identified as Moses pseudepigrapha but are now regarded as more likely associated with Jeremiah.

BIBLIOGRAPHY

M. BERNSTEIN 1999, "Pseudepigraphy in the Qumran Scrolls: Categories and Functions," in *Pseudepigraphic Perspectives: The Apocrypha and Pseudepigrapha in Light of the Dead Sea Scrolls,* ed. E. G. Chazon and M. Stone, Leiden: Brill, 1-26. • G. BRIN 1994, "Issues concerning Prophets (Studies in 4Q375)," in idem, *Studies in Biblical Law: From the Hebrew Bible to the Dead Sea Scrolls,* Sheffield: Sheffield Academic Press, 128-63. • H. NAJMAN 2003, *Seconding Sinai: The Development of Mosaic Discourse in Second Temple Judaism,* Leiden: Brill. • C. NEWSOM 1995, "Discourse on the Exodus/Conquest Tradition," in *Qumran Cave 4.XIV: Parabiblical Texts, Part 2,* ed. M. Broshi et al., DJD 19, Oxford: Clarendon, 85-110. • A. STEUDEL 2000, "4QApocryphon of Moses[c]?" in *Qumran Cave 4.XXVI: Cryptic Texts and Miscellanea, Part 1,* ed. P. Alexander et al., DJD 36, Oxford: Clarendon, 298-315. • J. STRUGNELL, 1995, "Apocryphon of Moses," in *Qumran Cave 4.XIV: Parabiblical Texts, Part 2,* ed. M. Broshi et al., DJD 19, Oxford: Clarendon, 111-36. • S. WHITE CRAWFORD 2000, *Temple Scroll and Related Texts,* London: Continuum. • J. VANDERKAM 2001, *The Book of Jubilees,* Sheffield: Sheffield Academic Press. • J. VANDERKAM AND M. BRADY 2001, "4QApocryphal Pentateuch A" and "4QApocryphal Pentateuch B," in *Wadi Daliyeh II and Qumran Cave 4.XXVIII,* ed. D. Gropp and M. Bernstein et al., DJD 28, Oxford: Clarendon, 131-49, 205-17.

DANIEL K. FALK

Multilingualism

One can ascertain only imperfectly the ability of Jews in the Second Temple period to communicate in more than one language. To what extent were they able to understand, speak, read, and write Greek, Hebrew, Aramaic, and Latin? William F. Mackey, in an important article, states that bilingualism is "not a phenomenon of language; it is a characteristic of its use" (Mackey 1968: 554). In sociolinguistic terminology, it belongs to the domain of the individual and not the property of the group; it is a person's speech *(parole)* rather than the language *(langue)* of his community. It is assumed that a bilingual person must belong to two different language communities, the majority of whom are monolingual, since a closed group that "is fluent in two languages could get along just as well with one language" (555).

Limits of the Evidence

Unlike the study of its modern counterpart, research on ancient Jewish multilingualism is limited to the written evidence. There is no preserved oral and aural evidence to corroborate or disprove the degree of proficiency and descriptions of "code switching." Take, for instance, the well-known account of the Assyrian representative who insisted on speaking to all in the palace "in Judean," that is, the local Hebrew dialect, rather than the official language of diplomacy, Aramaic, because both he and King Hezekiah's officials knew that the latter language would not be understood (2 Kings 18:26-37). If the passage of 2 Kings provides an accurate description, one wonders whether "the people on the wall" could have understood some Aramaic if it had been spoken more slowly rather than at its natural speed of royal discourse? Would they have grasped the warning had Rabshakeh spoken without the official jargon of diplomacy, sprinkled his speech with loanwords, and adapted his syntax to Hebrew? Would they have been able to read the declaration, had it been written down in Aramaic? Bilingualism, as it is now understood, is not limited to the near native fluency in two or more languages. It has been broadened to mean the basic ability to speak in complete, meaningful sentences in the other language and even the passive understanding of another written language. Language usage depends upon the role of the speaker or listener and his function in each case.

Postexilic Judah

The issue of the degree of linguistic proficiency arises prominently with the return to Yehud from the Babylonian Exile. On the first day of the seventh month, the Jews, men and women alike, gathered in the square before the Water Gate while Ezra read the scroll of the teaching of Moses to them. Then Ezra's helpers and the Levites explained the Mosaic teaching to them, reading, translating, and giving the sense "so that they understood" (Neh. 8:8). No language is specified, but later Jewish tradition (*b. Megillah* 3a; *b. Nedarim* 37b; *Gen. Rab.* 36:8) understands this as the origin of the targum, the translation of the Hebrew sacred text into Aramaic. The use of the verb "they read" is particularly significant, as it indicates that at least some, if not all of the Jews there, knew Hebrew, albeit poorly. Had they been monolingual, there would have been no need for the Levites "to read" the original Hebrew to them; the Aramaic translation would have sufficed. The Jews were not fluent enough, however, to understand the reading in Hebrew without the help of translators and expositors.

Elephantine

Within the period of the Second Temple, evidence of Jewish multilingualism varied in time and place. The Aramaic papyri of the military colony on the island of Yeb show a significant number of borrowings; there are loanwords of titles, technical terms, and topography from Old Persian, Egyptian, Akkadian, and Greek. Presumably, the Jewish inhabitants of Elephantine were multilingual, given the society in which they lived, but it is difficult to know to what extent they were so.

Alexandria

In Alexandria of the third century B.C.E., the Pentateuch was translated into Greek. While there are three overlapping, yet distinctive, accounts of the circumstances leading to the translation, they all indicate that there were at least some among the Jewish community who were bilingual. Otherwise, how would the community and its leaders know that the Greek version "has been well and piously made and is in every respect accurate" (*Letter to Aristeas* 310), that "the Greek words used corresponded literally with the Chaldean, exactly suited to things they indicated" (Philo, *Mos.* 2.38), or that "if anyone saw any further addition made to the text of the Law or anything omitted from it, he should examine it and make it known and correct it" (Josephus, *Ant.* 12.108)? The attestation to the accuracy of the translation and, in Josephus' case additionally (and not wholly consistently), the admonition to make private emendations in the event of additions or omissions presuppose some in the community who were bilingual (Baumgarten 2002: 13-20). The prologue to the Wisdom of Ben Sira likewise implies the presence of bilinguals among the community in Egypt when it questions the Septuagint translation ("even the law itself, the prophecies, and the rest of the books differ not a little as originally expressed") and when it admits the inadequacies of the grandson's Greek translation of his grandfather's Hebrew book.

Qumran

There is also evidence of multilingualism among members of the Qumran community. In the *Damascus Document,* it is stated that the Guardian of all the camps must be between thirty and fifty years of age, and have mastered all the secrets of men and "the languages of all their clans" (CD 14:9-10 and parallels in two 4QD manuscripts). The presence of Hebrew, Aramaic, and Greek manuscripts in the Qumran "library" is suggestive of the community's linguistic usage (Lim 2000; VanderKam 2001). The sectarian author of the *Habakkuk Pesher* knew of variants preserved in the Septuagint tradition, and 4QMMT testifies to the survival of Hebrew as a living, spoken language (Lim 2000: 67-72). The attestation of "the holy tongue" in 4Q464 has been interpreted to reflect sectarian belief in the eschatological reunification of all human language (Eshel and Stone 1993) or as an indication that Hebrew was the language of the Temple (Schwartz 1995: 33; Spolsky and Cooper 1991: 21).

Saul/Paul of Tarsus

In the first century C.E., the Jew turned Christian, Saul/Paul of Tarsus, was notable for his bilingualism. He wrote his letters in Greek but was likely to have known Hebrew and/or Aramaic, since according to his own letters his zeal for the "traditions of his fathers" went beyond those of his contemporaries (Gal. 1:14). He was a "Hebrew of Hebrews" (Phil. 3:5) whose training must have included the traditional Jewish education of his day and rudimentary forms of Greco-Roman rhetoric (Lim 1997: 161-64). According to Acts 22:3, he sat at the feet of no less a teacher than Rabban Gamaliel, grandson of Hillel, in Jerusalem. Paul demonstrated his bilingualism when he asked in Greek the tribune who was about to bring him to the barracks for permission to speak to the people in Hebrew or Aramaic, prompting the astonished guard to remark, "Do you speak Greek?" (Acts 21:37–22:21). This account in Acts is likely to have been embellished, but the Lukan portrayal of Paul's bilingualism is supported by the textual nature of the biblical quotations in Paul's letters. While they were all written in Greek, Paul was evidently aware of variants found in the Septuagint, (proto-) Masoretic Text, and Qumran biblical scrolls (Lim 1997: 146-60).

Inscriptions

But what was the typical situation of language usage? Drawing on the copious epigraphic and lapidary evidence of Jewish Palestine, Pieter van der Horst has calculated the overall average of inscriptions written in Greek to be 53 percent (Van der Horst 2001: 157). Many of the inscriptions, representing a wide range of Jewish Palestinian society, are bilingual, written as they were in Hebrew or Aramaic with Greek translation and signifying that "for many Greek was more understandable than the other two languages" (161). Stanley Porter further suggests a refinement to the analysis by applying the combined methods developed in diglossic and register studies. Palestinian inscriptions should be distinguished from those that have a formal or "high" register and those that have a casual style or "low register" (Porter 2000: 61-65).

Bar Kokhba and Babatha Archives

Multilingualism is further attested in the late Second Temple period and beyond by the Bar Kokhba and Babatha archives. In both these collections, documents and letters were written in Greek, Hebrew, and Aramaic. Among Babatha's records are to be found legal papers written in Greek but signed in Hebrew and/or Aramaic. Yet, the ascendancy of the Greek language is unmistakable. In one of the Greek papyri, a letter (P. Yadin 52) by a certain Soumaios to Jonathe and Masabala, the author states that he wrote in Greek either because the will or occasion to draft in Hebrew or Aramaic was not to be found. This is all the more remarkable in the context of the Bar Kokhba archive, in which 90 percent of the documents were deliberately penned in Hebrew and Aramaic for nationalist reasons.

Necessity and Ideology

Multilingualism was a prominent feature of early Judaism, but was it practiced out of practical necessity or ideologically motivated? Seth Schwartz has advanced a provocative thesis that combines both elements. He focuses on the changing role of Hebrew as part of the Jewish response to imperial domination: in the first stage (until 300 B.C.E.), Hebrew was commonly spoken by Jews in Palestine, but it was not considered "an essential component of their corporate identity"; in the second stage (300 B.C.E. to 70 C.E.), Hebrew was replaced by Aramaic as the spoken language but retained a symbolic role as the language of the Temple and Scripture; and in the third stage (after 70 C.E. to the fourth century), Hebrew maintained its "evocative power" but lost its practical significance of curatorial role and was marginalized.

BIBLIOGRAPHY

A. I. BAUMGARTEN 2002, "Bilingual Jews and the Greek Bible," in *Shem in the Tents of Japhet: Essays on the Encounter of Judaism and Hellenism,* ed. J. L. Kugel, Leiden: Brill, 13-30. • E. ESHEL AND M. E. STONE 1993, "The Holy Tongue at the End of Days in Light of a Fragment from Qumran," *Tarbiz* 62: 169-78. • C. HEZSER 2001, *Jewish Literacy in Roman Palestine,* Tübingen: Mohr-Siebeck, 243-47. • G. H. R. HORSLEY 1989, *New Documents Illustrating Early Christianity,* vol. 5, North Ryde: Macquarie University, 5-48. • P. W. VAN DER HORST 2001, "Greek in Jewish Palestine in Light of Jewish Epigraphy," in *Hellenism in the Land of Israel,* ed. J. J. Collins and G. E. Sterling, Notre Dame: University of Notre Dame Press, 154-74. • J. JOOSTEN 2000, "The Knowledge and Use of Hebrew in the Hellenistic Period: Qumran and the Septuagint," in *Diggers at the Well: Proceedings of a Third International Symposium on the Hebrew of the Dead Sea Scrolls and Ben Sira,* ed. T. Muraoka and J. Elwolde, Leiden: Brill, 115-30. • T. H. LIM 1997, *Holy Scripture in the Qumran Commentaries and Pauline Letters,* Oxford: Clarendon, 146-60, 161-64. • T. H. LIM 2000, "The Qumran Scrolls, Multilingualism, and Biblical Interpretation," in *Religion in the Dead Sea Scrolls,* ed. J. J. Collins and R. A. Kugler, Grand Rapids: Eerdmans, 57-73. • W. F. MACKEY 1968, "The Description of Bilingualism," in *Readings in the Sociology of Language,* ed. J. A. Fishman, The Hague: Mouton, 554-84. • J. M. MODRZEJEWSKI 1992, *Les juifs d'Egypte, de Ramses II à Hadrien,* Paris: Armand Colin. • T. MURAOKA AND B. PORTER 1998, *A Grammar of Egyptian Aramaic,* Leiden: Brill. • S. E. PORTER, ED. 2000, *Diglossia and Other Topics in New Testament Linguistics,* Sheffield: Sheffield Academic Press. • S. SCHWARTZ 1995, "Language, Power and Identity in Ancient Palestine," *Past and Present* 148: 3-47. • S. SCHWARTZ 2001, *Imperialism and Jewish Society, 200 B.C.E. to 640 C.E.,* Princeton: Princeton University Press. • B. SPOLSKY AND R. L. COOPER 1991, *The Languages of Jerusalem,* Oxford: Clarendon. • E. ULLENDORF 1961-1962, "The Knowledge of Languages in the Old Testament," *Bulletin of the John Rylands Library,* 44: 455-65. • J. C. VANDERKAM 2001, "Greek at Qumran," in *Hellenism in the Land of Israel,* ed. J. J. Collins and G. E. Sterling, Notre Dame: University of Notre Dame Press, 175-181.

See also: Aramaic; Babatha Archive; Bar Kokhba Letters; Greek; Hebrew; Inscriptions; Papyri

TIMOTHY H. LIM

Murabbaʿat, Wadi

The caves of Wadi Murabbaʿat lie in a deep ravine descending from Herodium (east of Bethlehem) to the Dead Sea. They are situated approximately 18 km. (11 miles) south of Qumran. Both the presence of water during the winter months and the wadi's remoteness from any permanent settlements made its caves an ideal refuge place throughout history. These caves contained important remains from the Chalcolithic period, the end of the Iron Age, the Second Temple period, the First Jewish Revolt, the Bar Kokhba Revolt, and the Middle Ages. Four of the caves, which are on the northern slope of the wadi, were discovered by Bedouin at the end of 1951; the fifth cave, on the southern slope, was discovered by Bedouin in 1955. The four caves were excavated by G. L. Harding and Roland de Vaux in 1952.

Documents dated to various periods, beginning with the end of the First Temple period and ending with the Middle Ages, were discovered in Wadi Murabbaʿat. From the seventh century B.C.E. a palimpsest (a document that was used twice) was found. First a list of names common in the kingdom of Judah at the end of the First Temple period were written on the papyrus, and then a two-line letter. This document is one of the earliest papyri ever found in the land of Israel.

From the beginning of the first century B.C.E. an ostracon recording decisions of a court was found. This document mentions Masada, which proves that the fortress was built during the Hasmonean period.

Another document from the Second Temple period is an I.O.U. from 55/56 C.E. that mentions sites west of Jerusalem. Six documents written during the First Jewish Revolt were brought to the caves in Wadi Murabbaʿat. Five of those documents were written in Jerusalem (and dated to between year one and year four of the revolt). The last one is a bill of divorce written in year six at Masada, in which Joseph son of Naksan divorced Miriam daughter of Jonathan. This document was dated according to the era initiated at the beginning of the First Jewish Revolt. Miriam left Masada in 71 C.E., one year after the fall of Jerusalem, and took her bill of divorce to Wadi Murabbaʿat.

Most of the documents found in Wadi Murabbaʿat were brought to the caves at the end of the Bar Kokhba Revolt (135/36 C.E.). These documents belonged to a group of people who had escaped from the region of Herodium and brought with them to the caves leather scrolls with religious texts (biblical scrolls, phylacteries, a mezuzah, and a prayer mentioning Zion), as well as papyri upon which were written financial documents and letters. Most of the documents found in the caves were written before the Bar Kokhba Revolt. Among those documents are four marriage contracts. Two are written in Aramaic and formulated in a way similar to those documented in the Mishnah. The two other documents are written in Greek. One of the Greek marriage documents is dated to 124 C.E., and in it a man named Elias son of Simon remarried his divorced wife Salome daughter of Vanus Galgula, who lived in the village of Beit Bassi in the district of Herodium.

Significant among the documents written during the Bar Kokhba Revolt are deeds of lease written in Hebrew. They document a series of transactions signed in the winter of "year two of the redemption of Israel by Simeon ben Kosiba (Bar Kokhba) in a camp situated in Herodium." In these transactions, plots of land were leased by the administrator of Herodium during the Bar Kokhba Revolt to a dozen people in the city of Nahash. The payment for the lease was not to be made by money but with grain that had to be tithed and weighed on the roof of the treasury of Herodium. The lease would last until the sabbatical year.

An interesting document has an intermediate status between a letter and a financial document. This is a letter from the two administrators of the village of Beit Mashiko to Yeshu'a son of Galgula, who bore the title of head of the camp. The administrators verified that a cow which a man named Joseph had confiscated belonged to Jacob son of Judah. The administrators attempted to write Hebrew but integrated Aramaic words into their letter — evidence for how difficult it was for some people in Judea to express themselves in Hebrew during the rebellion.

Two letters sent from Simeon bar Kokhba to Yeshu'a son of Galgula were found in Wadi Murabbaʿat. In the first letter Bar Kokhba vows that he will imprison whoever harms the Galileans. Some scholars have claimed that these are people from the Galilee, while others have suggested that the people under discussion were Christians. The second letter deals with the supplying of grain; in it Bar Kokhba requests that Yeshu'a accommodate on the Sabbath the people who were coming to gather wheat.

The textual finds at Murabbaʿat indicate that the refugees who fled to these caves during the First Jewish Revolt came from Jerusalem and from villages west of the city, while those of the Bar Kokhba Revolt came from Herodium.

BIBLIOGRAPHY

P. BENOIT, J. T. MILIK, AND R. DE VAUX, EDS. 1961, *Les Grottes de Murabbaʿât*, DJD 2, Oxford: Clarendon. • H. ESHEL 2002, "Documents of the First Jewish Revolt from the Judean Desert," in *The First Jewish Revolt: Archaeology, History and Ideology*, ed. A. M. Berlin and J. A. Overman, London: Routledge, 157-63. • E. KOFFNAHN 1968, *Die Doppelurkunden aus der Wüste Juda*, Leiden: Brill. • R. YARON 1960, "The Murabbaʿat Documents," *JJS* 11: 57-171.

See also: Bar Kokhba Letters; Contracts from the Judean Desert

HANAN ESHEL†

Music

The study of music in early Judaism encounters problems common to the study of other ancient practices. There are no explicit treatises on music extant from this time period. The few textual references, scattered among a large corpus, are not substantial descriptive accounts. Rather, they are oblique references to the occasional performance of music, sometimes including catalogues of the musical instruments used in these instances. One must attempt to correlate the archaeological sources with the literary and documentary record, and the relationships of text and artifact are often provided by educated guesswork and analogy to neighboring cultures. Nonetheless, a sketch can be made of music in early Judaism, when one considers the extant literary and archaeological evidence from the Persian, Hellenistic, and early Roman periods. The limited evidence suggests that there was nothing particularly unusual about musical performance or attitudes toward music in early Judaism. Music was a normal part of daily life, especially during the frequent liturgies of the Second Temple.

Literary Sources

Our chief literary sources are the biblical texts of the Persian period and the Mishnah. Passages from Ezra and Nehemiah recount the magnificent return of musicians and singers from the Babylonian Exile (Ezra 2; Nehemiah 7). These trained professionals supplied music during the rebuilding of the Second Temple and for its subsequent liturgical activity (Ezra 3; Nehemiah 12). Musical performance was the specific task of the Levites, who sang and played instruments. Priests played trumpets for certain occasions. The Mishnah supplements our literary evidence for music during the Second Temple period, both within and outside of the Temple itself. It describes the number and use of particular instruments, such as harps, flutes, pipes, cymbals, and trumpets (*m. ʿArak.* 2:3). Especially noteworthy is a powerful percussion instrument called the *magrephah* (literally, "the spoon"), whose sound and characteristics are obscure to us (*m. Tamid* 3:8; 5:6). The Levites and their assistants are depicted as the Temple's resident musicians, although the Tannaim disagreed about exactly who played which instruments during the Temple liturgy (*m. ʿArak.* 2:4-6). The Mishnah (*m. Tamid* 7:3-4) describes the musical accompaniment of the daily offering in the following manner: the priests contributed two different tones (prolonged and wavering) on their trumpets, and the Levites recited or sang a specific psalm for each day of the week (cf. also Sir. 50:11-20). The Mishnah also records one of the two extant named musicians from Jewish antiquity: Hogras ben Levi was in charge of "singing" in a list of Temple officers (*m. Šeqal.* 5:1), even though he was remembered dishonorably for not teaching his method of singing to others (*m. Yoma* 3:11). Other mishnaic tractates describe musical performance during Temple liturgies particular to a variety of Jewish festivals (*m. Sukk.* 5:4; *m. Roš Haš.* 3:2).

Outside of the Temple liturgies, the Mishnah attests to the performance of music at both wedding feasts (*m. Soṭah* 9:11) and funerals (*m. Šabb.* 23:4; cf. Matt. 9:23-24). Concerning music at feasts, Rabbi Aqiba (early second century C.E.) is quoted as condemning one particular practice: "Rabbi Aqiba said, 'He who modulates his voice when reciting the Song of Songs in a banquet hall and makes it like a musical performance has no share in the world to come'" (*t. Sanh.* 12:10). Although the Tosefta offers no context to interpret this teaching and the Talmuds do not explain it, we can infer that guests at wedding feasts would often sing a spirited rendition of the famous love poem, known for its erotic imagery. Regarding music at funerals, a statement attributed to Rabbi Judah (mid-second century

C.E.) indicates its continued importance in the period following the destruction of the Temple: "even the poorest man in Israel should not hire fewer than two flutes and one professional wailing woman" (*m. Ketub.* 4:4). The other named Jewish musician from antiquity was probably one such professional flute player: a certain Egyptian Jew, named Jakoubis, is identified as a flute *(aulos)* player in a second-century-B.C.E. papyrus list of cattle and their owners (*CPJ* 1:171).

The literary evidence is silent about music in the ancient synagogue. Music historians have often presumed that musical instruments were banned not long after 70 C.E. as a sign of mourning for the loss of the Jerusalem Temple, but no ancient sources actually refer to such a ban. Furthermore, there is no positive evidence that even *a cappella* singing occurred in the ancient synagogue; none of the meager descriptions of ancient synagogue services refers to the performance of music (Philo, Josephus, Luke-Acts). Some texts from the Dead Sea Scrolls and Philo have tantalized music historians looking for evidence of Jewish music outside the Temple liturgies. For example, the musical life of the Qumran community may be represented by their collection of psalms (1QH^{a}) and other hymnic compositions (1QS 10–11). Philo depicts the weekly all-night gathering of the Therapeutae (*De Vita Contemplativa* 79–90), which involved hymns newly composed by their leader, older songs sung antiphonally by men and women, and a concluding unison song to greet the sunrise.

In general, the literary sources rarely demonstrate evaluative judgments of music. Some texts do imagine music, especially instrumental music, as corrupting or seductive. For example, the author of Daniel uses the pomp of musical instruments to represent debauchery or idolatry (Dan. 3:5, 7, 10, 15; cf. also Philo, *Spec. Leg.* 1.28; 2.193; and Ps.-Philo, *Biblical Antiquities* 2). Most authors, however, associate music with happiness and celebration: "Joy was taken from Jacob; the flute and the harp ceased to play" (1 Macc. 3:45; 2 Macc. 10:38; cf. Sir. 32:3-6).

Archaeological Evidence

The archaeological data for the study of music in ancient Judea/Palestine have been compiled and analyzed by Joachim Braun. Though archaeological sources are sparse for the Persian period, some discoveries illuminate the musical tendencies of Jews during the Hellenistic and Roman periods. For example, a stone was found near the Temple wall with the inscription "at the house of blowing" for the trumpet or shofar (IAA 78.1415). The terminology for this "blowing" matches the "prolonged" tone from our literary sources (*m. Roš Haš.* 3:3-4; cf. also 1QM). Some scholars have argued that the Arch of Titus depicts trumpets being carried off from the destroyed and pillaged Jerusalem Temple, although it is possible that these images are Roman *tubae* belonging to the Roman soldiers.

Some coin types of Bar Kokhba (ca. 132-135 C.E.) reinforce the importance of music for the cultural identity of Jews during the Roman era. The reverse images depict two different kinds of lyres (three-string and four-string) and a pair of unidentified wind instruments (probably the trumpets of Numbers 10 and the Jerusalem Temple). The obverse images on these coins depict the Temple and legends such as "For the freedom of Jerusalem." Therefore, in the second century C.E., musical performance was remembered as a hallmark of the lost Temple services. Musical imagery was one component of the cultural matrix used to inspire Jews toward Judean self-governance.

Finally, some scholars have used discoveries in Judea/Palestine from the Roman and Byzantine periods to reevaluate a connection between musical performance and the cult of Dionysus. However, the ancient comparison made between some Jewish and Dionysiac rituals (Plutarch, *Quaestionum Convivialum* 4.6.2; Tacitus, *Historiae* 5.5; Philo, *De Vita Contemplativa* 12, 85) cannot be confirmed simply by the discoveries of mosaics with Dionysiac imagery or Dionysiac altars in the geographical region of Galilee. Other scholars have interpreted Roman (Dura-Europos) and Byzantine (Gaza) synagogue art to argue that Jews themselves imagined the music of David in connection with the iconographic typology of Orpheus.

Despite the influence of archaeological discoveries on the study of ancient Jewish music, the literary sources are at present the data most often interpreted. Though some scholars question the veracity of the biblical and tannaitic sources, these sources still provide the depictions against which other texts and archaeological data are tested. They portray early Jewish music chiefly in the service of Temple liturgies and other occasions of prayer or celebration.

Bibliography

J. Braun 2001, "Jewish Music II: Ancient Israel/Palestine," in *New Grove Dictionary of Music and Musicians,* 2d ed., Oxford: Oxford University Press, 13: 34-37. • J. Braun 2002, *Music in Ancient Israel/Palestine,* Grand Rapids: Eerdmans. • K. E. Grözinger 1982, *Musik und Gesang in der Theologie der frühen jüdischen Literatur,* Tübingen: Mohr-Siebeck. • A. Idelsohn 1929, *Jewish Music in Its Historical Development,* New York: Holt. • F. Leitner 1906, *Der gottesdienstliche Volksgesang im jüdischen und christlichen Altertum,* Freiburg: Herder. • J. McKinnon 1979-1980, "The Exclusion of Musical Instruments from the Ancient Synagogue," *Proceedings of the Royal Musical Association* 106: 77-87. • J. Smith 1984, "The Ancient Synagogue, the Early Church and Singing," *Music and Letters* 65: 1-16. • E. Werner 1959, *The Sacred Bridge: The Interdependence of Liturgy and Music in Synagogue and Church during the First Millennium,* London: Dobson.

Michael Peppard

Mystery

The term "mystery" most often denotes something that is inaccessible to human understanding or imagination. In the study of religion, its meaning often depends upon the context in which it appears; in some instances, it is employed in its general sense, and in others it bears a specific, technical meaning. Many religious systems of the world have some notion that there is a fundamental disconnection between the realm of human affairs and that of the world beyond, a separation that compromises the human ability to gain true knowledge about the nature of the universe and the divine reality. Thus, the category of mystery is often an epistemological one, and many traditions display practices and beliefs that attempt to create a space in which a mystery can become knowable, and known, to their respective adherents. In some manifestations of Second Temple Judaism, the concept of mystery is an important feature of religious and social sensibility and cosmology. Needless to say, there is often a corresponding element of secrecy — itself a social category — that accompanies a mystery, so that its authenticity is vouchsafed at least in part by its esoteric nature.

Second Temple Judaism

Prophetic Roots

Early Jewish ideas about mystery and about the proper means of gaining access to mysterious knowledge have roots in the prophetic tradition of ancient Israel. According to the conventions of Israelite prophecy, the prophet stands in the breach between God and the material world, receiving in revelatory forms (visions, auditions, etc.) the necessary information about the divine will. The content of such revelation pertains both to the nature of divine reality and to the course of mundane history, and the prophet is charged both to experience and to transmit (or translate into human language) ineffable truths and otherwise hidden matters of ultimate import. The work of the prophet also pertains to salvation, insofar as the message he bears aims to keep Israel on the path of its covenant obligations and aware of its true identity as the people of God.

The Divine Council (sôd)

One important aspect of the biblical precedent for the Second Temple Jewish concept of mystery is the divine "council" (Hebr. *sôd*) in which the God of Israel deliberates with the heavenly assembly about the maintenance of the created order, the results of which are the "secret" *(sôd)* purposes of the Lord that are revealed to the prophets (e.g., Jer. 23:18; Amos 3:7; cf. 1 Kings 22:19). Though more prominent in the prophetic literature, this scenario also finds expression in wisdom writings such as the book of Job, which itself displays considerably more skepticism about the possibility of gaining access to such secrets (e.g., Job 15, 38; cf. Sir. 34:1-8), even while it presents Job as one with whom God speaks directly.

Revealed Wisdom

The wisdom tradition — which is predicated in part upon the acquisition of knowledge through observation of the natural world, pedagogical instruction, and contemplation of prior revelation (the Torah) — also informs the concept of mystery in Second Temple Jewish thought. The notion of *revealed wisdom,* which is a later development in the wisdom tradition, is especially relevant insofar as it involves the revelation of mysteries to the sage, mysteries that in turn become part of the acquired wisdom (see esp. Daniel 2–4; *1 Enoch* 82, 105; 4QInstruction). Such a confluence of sapiential and prophetic themes into the concept of revealed wisdom is part of a broader dynamic that includes the rise of apocalyptic groups and traditions during the Second Temple period.

Apocalyptic Revelation

It is not surprising that the concept of mystery is especially to be found in texts and traditions of an apocalyptic bent, since these are inherently oriented toward the reception and interpretation of revelatory phenomena that address what is hitherto unknown about creation, the cosmos, and the course of human history. Extant Jewish texts of the Second Temple period that display a marked interest in mystery include Daniel, *1 Enoch,* the *Genesis Apocryphon,* and a number of the "sectarian" compositions found in the caves near Qumran (see below).

Rāz

Sustained contact with Persian and Greek (Hellenistic) societies and cultures seems also to have had its effect on Jewish notions of mystery. The Persian religion of Zoroaster appears to have had an operative religious category of mystery expressed by the word *rāz,* a term that was taken into Aramaic usage and can be found in the books of *1 Enoch* and the Aramaic portion of Daniel (chaps. 2 and 4), among other compositions. Perhaps because of its function in those Jewish texts, *rāz* was also deployed in some roughly contemporaneous Hebrew compositions such as 4QInstruction as well as later Qumran texts. It is possible that the term *rāz* came to overlap, or perhaps in some cases to replace, the use of *sôd* as an expression for the content of revelatory experience in the Second Temple period. By the time the targums were written, *rāz* was the word of choice for most any kind of secret or mystery.

Mystērion

The Greek word used to translate *rāz* in the LXX is usually *mystērion,* from which the English word "mystery" derives. This word has important connotations in Greco-Roman literature, especially because of its associations with the mystery religions. But in Jewish Greek texts, *mystērion* refers to those things known by God, secrets of creation and of the afterlife (e.g., Wis. 2:22; 6:22), or to the results of allegorical interpretation of Scripture (esp. throughout the works of Philo; cf. Josephus, *Ag. Ap.* 2.189).

The Dead Sea Scrolls

The word *rāz* is the primary vehicle for ideas about mystery in Qumran literature; *sôd* also occurs, but not exclusively as "mystery" or "secret." Additionally, *nistārôt* seems always to refer to "secrets" of the Law, that is, those hidden matters of Torah that proper interpretation brings into view. The word *rāz* occurs in a variety of texts but seems to receive added emphasis in sectarian and related compositions like the *Community Rule,* the

Damascus Document, the 4QInstruction texts (and related literature such as the 1QMysteries texts), the *Songs of the Sabbath Sacrifice,* the *Habakkuk Pesher,* and the *Hodayot.* Its exact meaning depends upon the context in which it is used, but in general it signifies mysteries of cosmological and/or eschatological import. In recent years the concept of mystery has received increased scholarly attention, especially regarding the meaning of the term *rāz nihyeh,* "the mystery that is to be," which appears to have been an important reference point for the sectarians who composed and/or preserved the Qumran texts (1QS 11:3; 4QInstruction and related texts).

Early Christianity

The concept of mystery constitutes a central aspect of early Christian theology. While Christian notions about mystery grow out of prior Jewish traditions (see especially Brown 1968 and Bockmuehl 1997), they also reflect an awareness, if not the influence, of Greco-Roman ideas and practices. Perhaps the most famous mystery passage in the New Testament is Mark 4:10-12 (pars. Matt. 13:10-13; Luke 8:9-10), in which Jesus explains that those who understand the parables are "granted the mystery *(mystērion)* of the kingdom of God." Drawing on Isa. 6:9, this Synoptic tradition emphasizes Jesus' role in human salvation and presents Jesus as the interpretive key for understanding the mystery of divine providence (cf. Rom. 11:25; Col. 1:27). In the letters of Paul, the concept of mystery includes not only God's work of salvation but also the "mystery of lawlessness" (2 Thess. 2:7; 2 Thessalonians is widely believed to be pseudonymous), by which evil is part of the overall providential plan of God (cf. 1QM 14:9; 1QH[a] 13:36). In the Pauline letter to the Colossians, the "knowledge of the mystery of God" pertains to "Christ, in whom all the treasures of wisdom and knowledge are hidden" (Col. 2:4-5). In other contexts, Paul defines "mystery" variously in terms of the scandal of a crucified messiah (1 Cor. 2:6-10), the eschatological resurrection of believers (1 Cor. 15:50-55), and the salvation of "all Israel" at the end of the age (Rom. 11:25-27). In the Pauline letter to the Ephesians, the mystery or hidden plan of God revealed in Christ is the union of Jews and Gentiles in the one people of God (3:1:13; cf. 1:9).

Early Rabbinic Judaism

The concept of mystery is not a prominent feature of rabbinic thought and self-understanding, and despite their ready adoption of other Aramaic terms the Tannaim avoided the use of the word *rāz* almost entirely. This is due no doubt to the association of the concept with apocalyptic ideas about revelation, ideas that were generally looked upon with suspicion within Torah-oriented rabbinic circles. Revelation, according to the early rabbis, was indeed an ongoing phenomenon through the process of rabbinic interpretation (Oral Torah), but was no longer granted in the form of immediate numinous experiences such as visions and auditions, at least not until the advent of the eschatological age. Some rabbinic texts use the word *misṭêrîn* (which is probably a transliteration of the Greek *mystērion* rather than a nominal form of the Hebr./Aram. *satar* = hide, keep secret) to signify the contents of *mišnâ* (e.g., *Pesiq. Rab.* 5:1), that is, the Oral Torah available only to Israel, and first and foremost to the prophets.

BIBLIOGRAPHY

M. BOCKMUEHL 1997, *Revelation and Mystery in Ancient Judaism and Pauline Christianity,* Grand Rapids: Eerdmans. • R. E. BROWN 1968, *The Semitic Background of the Term 'Mystery' in the New Testament,* Philadelphia: Fortress. • J. J. COLLINS 2003, "The Mysteries of God: Creation and Eschatology in 4QInstruction and the Wisdom of Solomon," in *Wisdom and Apocalypticism in the Dead Sea Scrolls and in the Biblical Tradition,* ed. F. García Martínez, Leuven: Leuven University Press. • M. J. GOFF, 2003, "The Mystery of Creation in 4QInstruction," *DSD* 10: 163-86. • A. E. HARVEY 1980, "The Use of Mystery Language in the Bible," *JTS* 31: 320-36. • R. KITTEL 1924, *Die hellenistiche Mysterienreligion und das Alte Testament,* Stuttgart: Kohlhammer. • I. WILLI-PLEIN 1977, "Das Geheimnis der Apokalyptik," *VT* 27: 62-81.

See also: Mystery Religion, Judaism as; Mysticism

SAMUEL THOMAS

Mystery Religion, Judaism as

Scholars have long debated whether and in what sense certain manifestations of early Jewish religious thought and practice might properly fall into the category of "mystery religion" when compared with other mystical traditions and practices of Mediterranean antiquity. This question has received a significant amount of attention during the past century, and in two distinct phases roughly corresponding to the first and second halves of the century. In the first, the question was put to the extant Jewish sources written in Greek — Philo, Josephus, and others — and the material remains of synagogues such as the one at Dura Europos in modern-day Syria. This first phase more or less corresponds to the period during which the comparative methodology of *Religionsgeschichte* (history of religions) was in fashion in European and American academies, and new archeological discoveries brought fresh and intriguing materials forward for consideration. The second phase began with the discovery and early publication of the Dead Sea Scrolls in the late 1940s and early 1950s, when several Second Temple Hebrew and Aramaic texts with a mystical bent became available for the first time.

Roughly corresponding to these phases of scholarship, then, are the two primary linguistic and cultural contexts out of which one might consider the possibility of an ancient Jewish mystery religion: the former is the Hellenized Judaism of Greco-Roman antiquity, and the latter deals with the Hebrew and Aramaic sources of Second Temple Palestine, which may also show distinct lines of influence by, or resistance to, Hellenism and its associated religious ideas and practices. A third element, the Persian tradition of Zoroaster and its Mithraic offshoot, must be considered as another potential

MYSTERY RELIGION, JUDAISM AS

source for understanding the nature of Jewish mysteries, even if scholars continue to debate the extent to which Zoroastrian ideas and practices penetrated Jewish (and Greco-Roman) religion and culture. There is broad agreement, however, that whatever "foreign" elements may have become part of Jewish religious expression, they were usually adapted to fit into the particular system of Israel's religious inheritance.

Any answer to the question of whether ancient Judaism might be characterized as a mystery religion must be a highly qualified one. The Jewish sources are variegated and complex and reflect diverse beliefs and practices among Jews of Mediterranean antiquity, and the data for other mystery religions do not often provide a solid basis for sufficient reconstruction and comparison. In any case, as Gary Lease has written, there is "a profound and substantial difference between a Judaism nurtured by its historical traditions [of collective salvation by the God of Israel] . . . and the major mystery cults which promised an individual liberation and a final union with a divinity on the basis of certain acts and representations," and it is with this basic distinction in view that we must consider the question of Judaism as a mystery religion (Lease 1972: 860-61).

Another distinction that may help to clarify the issue is the difference between a mystery religion as a whole cultic system and mystery as a theological category expressed in different ways in Second Temple Judaism and in early Christianity. Indeed, mystery theology was an important part of the Jewish religious landscape in late antiquity and was in considerable continuity with the traditions of Israel, but this need not imply that Judaism was therefore analogous to contemporaneous mystery cults.

What Is a Mystery Religion?

Discerning and applying a consistently useful definition of a mystery religion is a notoriously difficult task. Initiates were typically pledged to secrecy, outsiders were not allowed to observe and record ritual practices and their religious underpinnings, the material and textual sources are either silent or allusive in the extreme (and are fragmentary and temporally and geographically scattered), and thus any conclusions about the precise contours of a mystery religion must be drawn indirectly and by inference. Added to these difficulties is the fact that mystery religions were practiced in geographically and culturally distinct expressions over a long period of time. Reducing the mysteries of Isis, Dionysus, Cybele, Hermes, Orpheus, and Mithras to a common set of parallels to be used as comparative data is itself a dubious practice, and its usefulness in assessing the nature of early Jewish religion is rather limited, however appealing it may be to find parallels and draw corresponding conclusions. Finally, a significant portion of the evidence for mystery religions dates from several centuries after the fall of the Jerusalem Temple in 70 C.E., and we cannot assume that the beliefs and practices of these mysteries would have been in perfect continuity with those that existed during the Second Temple period.

Given these caveats, the following are usually thought to be typical features of ancient mystery religions (Argus 1975): (1) They are highly symbolic systems that employ myth, iconic representation, allegories, and liturgies to create symbolic space conducive to mystical experience, or union with the divine, and in this way they are redemptive. (2) They have a sacramental aspect; that is, they are rites whose purpose is the emotional exaltation of the participant through dramatic enactments. (3) They are systems of esoteric knowledge given only to the initiated, knowledge that is inherently tied to salvation and that derives from direct participation in the rites of the group. (4) They are concerned with eschatology, or the relationship between this life and the hereafter. (5) They are highly personal and volitional; that is, the participant's status in the group is not determined by heredity or nationality. And (6) they are shaped by a cosmic interest that seeks to orient human life to the order of the universe, an interest that includes cosmological speculation.

Some Similarities and Differences

Some of these aspects are consistent with what we find in certain strains of Second Temple Judaism, and others are not. For example, there is an increasing emphasis on eschatology in most expressions of Jewish religion in late antiquity, which appears to be tied to changing views about the afterlife and God's plan for the elect — developments that were surely related to the political and military vicissitudes of the Jewish people under Greek and Roman rule. Such an emphasis on eschatology and salvation is also found among many of the Greco-Roman mystery religions.

On the other hand, for most Jews of the period, Jewishness was determined by heredity and nationality, and Judaism was a religion of practices and beliefs in substantial continuity with Israel's religious past. It was not, in other words, personal and volitional but rather collective and historical, and in this way was substantially different from the surrounding religious milieux. In this way, too, salvation was tied not to personal choice but to ethnic membership in the covenant people of Israel's God.

Although there are signs that some Jews embraced practices of esoteric knowledge and special initiation (such as the *Yaḥad* ["community"] of the Qumran sectarian literature; see below), we know frustratingly little about Jewish liturgical practices during late antiquity, and whether and in what ways they provided for mystical experience or dramatic reenactments of divine myths — most likely they did not. However, because of restricted access to the Jewish Temple cult (which allowed Gentiles only on the periphery and maintained a strict hierarchy among Jews), some classical authors associated Jewish worship with Dionysiac religion (Plutarch, *Moralia* 671c; cf. Tacitus, *Historiae* 5.2-5) and accused the Jews of secretive cultic acts like human ritual sacrifice (Josephus, *Ag. Ap.* 2.8) — an accusation with no factual support.

In short, while there may indeed be some intriguing overlaps between early Judaism and the ancient

MYSTERY RELIGION, JUDAISM AS

mystery religions, there is little basis to consider Judaism to have been a mystery or a mystery cult, as some scholars have argued.

Second Temple Judaism and *Religionsgeschichte*

The first modern scholar to posit a direct correlation between early Judaism and the mystery religions of Greco-Roman antiquity was F. C. Conybeare in his edition of Philo's *On the Contemplative Life.* In this work, Conybeare proposed that the Therapeutae — the group of pious Jews near Alexandria, about whom Philo's treatise is written — were engaged in "a system of mysteries, perhaps in imitation of the Greek mysteries of Demeter which were celebrated year by year on the hill of Eleusis close to Alexandria" (Conybeare 1895: 303). However, very little is known about the Therapeutae apart from Philo's presentation of them, and in any case they would have comprised a very small and local manifestation of Jewish religious experience. Although Philo's description of this group — and the variety of Judaism it may represent — is intriguing, it does not allow for any broad statements about Judaism as a mystery religion.

Perhaps the most famous attempt to present Hellenistic Judaism as a mystery religion was mounted by E. R. Goodenough, whose massive thirteen-volume work *Jewish Symbols in the Greco-Roman World* (1953-68) was directed toward this end. Goodenough combined his early work (1935) on Philo (*By Light, Light*) with his study of Jewish monumental artifacts to provide a sweeping revision of Jewish religion during the Greco-Roman period. Goodenough's analysis led him to conclude that as early as two centuries before Philo of Alexandria, Judaism was already being transformed into a mystery religion replete with its own sacramental practices and systems of esoteric knowledge. But it was Philo's allegorical representation of Judaism that reflected the religion's culmination into a mystery, a possibility that was, in Goodenough's mind, only bolstered by the nontextual material data. But as most scholars now agree, Philo's presentation of Judaism as a mystery religion was more metaphorical and anagogical than directly analogical; that is, while he used mystery language to describe the lesser (literal) and greater (allegorical) aspects of Torah-centered Judaism, we should not read behind his words to reconstruct a corresponding sacramental and liturgical practice. Such a picture of Jewish religion is ultimately not supported by the textual sources and material remains.

Dead Sea Scrolls

The discovery of the Dead Sea Scrolls in late 1940s to mid 1950s and their subsequent publication brought a renewed interest in the topic of mysteries and early Judaism. One of the reasons for this is the prevalence among the Qumran texts of mystery terminology — especially *rāz* — and corresponding ideas about esoteric knowledge, religious experience, and special initiation of the elect into an exclusive conventicle of worship and belief. Indeed, the features of mystery religions given above can all be found in the Qumran literature in one form or another, and yet this seems to be mostly coincidental and not due to the direct influence of other mystery religions.

The members of the Qumran sect appear to have participated in some kind of mystical liturgy in which the goal was union with God in worship with the angels. This sort of practice is reflected especially in the *Songs of the Sabbath Sacrifice.* Although the sources do not indicate the means by which this mystical union was achieved, communal prayer was most likely involved in some form. The group maintained a rigorous process of initiation (e.g., 1QS 1:1-11; 3:6-12; cf. Josephus, *J.W.* 2.237-42), and claimed for itself exclusive and esoteric knowledge of God's purposes (e.g., 1QS 3–4; 1QpHab 7:5), purposes which would vindicate the sect in the eschatological confrontation between good and evil (e.g., *War Scroll; Pesher Habakkuk*). Although one presumably had to be Jewish (a "son of Israel") to enter into the community — and had also to manifest the right proportion of "parts of light" to "parts of darkness" — membership was evidently voluntary. Finally, there was among the members of the Qumran sect a rather profound cosmological interest, in terms of both the structures of the created order and the relationship between the human and the divine (e.g., the *Hodayot;* copies of the Enochic *Book of the Watchers* and *Astronomical Book*).

Christianity as a Mystery Religion

The many references to the term "mystery" in the New Testament writings, and especially in some of Paul's formulations (1 Cor. 15:51; Rom. 11:25, 16:25; Col. 1:26-27), have generated a vast literature on the question of whether early Christianity was understood, presented, and practiced as a mystery religion (on Paul, see Wedderburn 1987). It appears from the gospel accounts that Jesus had little contact with Gentiles or pagans (and their religious beliefs and cultic practices), but that Paul may have been more conscious of the fact that some of his audiences would have included Greco-Roman mystery adherents and would thus be sympathetic to parallel elements in the Christian *kerygma* ("proclamation") such as the dying and rising God, darkness and light imagery, eschatology, and initiation by baptism (e.g., Rom. 6:1-11). While there are in all likelihood genuine reflections of mystery religions in earliest Christianity (however they may be characterized), the degree to which Christianity was itself a mystery religion has been significantly downgraded.

Current Status of the Question

In the words of one recent commentator, "the existence of a peculiarly Jewish mystery cult, conceptualized and patterned after the Hellenistic mystery cults, is without evidence and unsupportable" (Lease 1972: 874). On the other hand, the evidence from Qumran points to a group that had a lively mystery theology replete with practices and beliefs that resembled the mystery cults in some important ways, such as being "defined in terms of *yiḥud* ('union') with the transcendent reality" (Alexander 2006: 103) — but that were more continuous with their Israelite predecessors than influenced by any Greco-Roman paradigm. Overall, the current consensus is that early Judaism was not a mystery religion, properly speaking, but that it displayed several intriguing parallels whose elucidation helps us better understand the nature and variety of Jewish practice and belief in the Temple period.

BIBLIOGRAPHY
P. ALEXANDER 2006, *The Mystical Texts,* London: Continuum/Clark. • S. ARGUS 1975, *The Mystery-Religions: A Study in the Religious Background of Early Christianity,* New York: Dover. • F. C. CONYBEARE, ED. 1895, *Philo: About the Contemplative Life,* Oxford: Clarendon Press. • E. R. GOODENOUGH 1935, *By Light, Light: The Mystical Gospel of Hellenistic Judaism,* New Haven: Yale University Press. • E. R. GOODENOUGH, 1953-1968, *Jewish Symbols in the Greco-Roman Period,* 13 vols., New York: Pantheon. • H.-J. KLAUCK 2003, *The Religious Context of Early Christianity: A Guide to Graeco-Roman Religions,* London: T&T Clark. • G. LEASE 1972, "Jewish Mystery Cults since Goodenough," *ANRW* II.20.2: 858-80. • M. MEYER, ED. 1987, *The Ancient Mysteries: A Sourcebook,* San Francisco: Harper & Row. • A. D. NOCK 1972, "The Question of Jewish Mysteries," in idem, *Essays on Religion in the Ancient World,* ed. Z. Stewart, Oxford: Clarendon, 1: 459-68. • J. PETUCHOWSKI 1981, "Judaism as 'Mystery' — The Hidden Agenda?" *HUCA* 52: 141-52. • A. J. M. WEDDERBURN 1987, *Baptism and Resurrection: Studies in Pauline Theology against Its Graeco-Roman Background,* Tübingen: Mohr-Siebeck.

See also: Goodenough, E. R.; Mystery

SAMUEL THOMAS

Mysticism

Mysticism is a scholarly construct based on the religious experience of Greece and early Christianity. The Greeks spoke of a *mystērion,* a secret personal experience of the divine, from the Greek verb, *myein,* "to close the eyes." When Western scholars began to theorize about religion, they often put mysticism in the center of their study, as the central experience of religion in general. The reasons to do so were many. Prominent among the reasons is the Christian tradition that mysticism is *scientia dei experimentalis,* the knowledge of God from experience. With this definition, all prophecy would certainly qualify as mysticism. It was a short hop to the idea that mysticism is the essence of religion. Since that time, a number of scholars have pointed out that this definition is too dependent on Western and specifically Christian definitions of mysticism. Prophecy, apocalypticism, spirit possession, and a variety of other traditions may be called "mystical" with the correct scholarly arguments and nuancing. But it is no longer clear that mysticism must be the central or essential definition of religion.

The Mystical Dimension of Apocalypticism

What if anything counts for mysticism in Second Temple Judaism? The answer must be closely associated with prophecy, which is one way in which the knowledge of God was obtained in biblical tradition. In the Second Temple period, classical prophecy waned, while a great many prophetic insights were caught up in a relatively new religious form called "apocalypticism." The apocalypticist, like the prophet, sought the knowledge of God from experience, which came through various techniques. Many apocalypticists received their visions through dreams, but others experienced revelations directly through waking visions. The techniques are not well described, but they and the visions may have been taught through small groups or guilds, just as prophecy itself was taught by guilds. After the destruction of the Second Temple, a number of techniques arose, including night vigils mourning for the Temple and the use of mantra-like prayers and hymns.

Apocalypticism had many characteristics. But those with the most mystical content concerned the secrets of how to achieve exaltation in this life and life after death. It is this tradition that flows into Jewish merkavah mysticism and later into medieval Kabbalah, early modern Lurianic (messianic) Kabbalah, and even Hasidism. The mysticism and esotericism of Jewish apocalypticism in the late Second Temple period greatly influenced Christianity, especially through the figure of Paul, who relates that he has received many different visions *(optasiai)* and revelations *(apocalypseis).*

Resurrection as Angelic Exaltation in Daniel

The first clear reference to resurrection can be defined exactly; both its date and circumstances can be fixed accurately. This is to be combined with the important reference to the Son of Man, who is God's primary intermediary.

> At that time Michael, the great prince, the protector of your people, shall arise. There shall be a time of anguish, such as has never occurred since nations first came into existence. But at that time your people shall be delivered, everyone who is found written in the book. Many of those who sleep in the dust of the earth shall awake, some to everlasting life, and some to shame and everlasting contempt. Those who are wise shall shine like the brightness of the sky, and those who lead many to righteousness, like the stars forever and ever. But you, Daniel, keep the words secret and the book sealed until the time of the end. Many shall be running back and forth, and evil shall increase. (Dan. 12:1-3)

Some of the language in Dan. 12:1-3 is taken directly from Isa. 26:19, which says that the dead will "awaken." The writer of Daniel has taken the ambiguous prophecy of Isaiah in a literal sense, saying that "the sleepers in the dust" will literally arise. He has also used Isa. 66:24 to great advantage, even taking the vocabulary of "contempt" from the last verse in Isaiah, the only other place in the Bible that it appears. But he has not taken the writing literally in every respect because he has some innovative notions about the identity of the resurrected and the process of resurrection.

The rest of Isaiah 66 is also important. In verses 18-

19, the nations will soon know of the Lord's power because He himself will show them His glory. Daniel interprets this passage to mean that the "son of man," the manlike figure of Dan. 7:13, is appointed the glory of the Lord. Daniel probably has the archangel Michael in mind for the position of "glory of the Lord," because his name means "he who is like God." The "son of man" is enthroned next to God in Dan. 7:13-14. It is quite possible, in fact likely, that this is meant to depict how God will exalt those "wisdom-givers" who become "angels" or "stars." Thus, inherent in this short notice is the basis for Jewish ascent mysticism in all the later mystic literatures: apocalypticism, merkavah, and Kabbalah, which takes one of its primary intuitions into reality from this passage. The word used for the brightness of the sky in Daniel *(zohar)*, becomes a technical term in later Jewish mysticism.

The Roots of Merkāvāh Mysticism

Merkavah or "chariot vision literature," named after the vision of Ezekiel in chap. 1 of his prophetic book, is the first great movement in Jewish mysticism. Apocalypticism and merkavah mysticism were not quiet contemplation. Instead they both witness to the active desire to journey to heaven, and not merely out of curiosity about what was there. It was to verify that God's promises to the apocalypticists were true and reliable: not only could one go to heaven at the end of one's life, but some people actually went while alive, as Paul's report in 2 Corinthians 12 shows. The importance of going during life was to demonstrate to the community by eyewitness that humans go to heaven and receive their just reward after death.

Going to heaven also conferred a number of other powers, as will be evident later. All this lies behind the mystic vocabulary for the goal of the journey: to gaze on the "King in His Beauty." This figure on the throne, already well known to us, was a sophisticated blending of all the notions of the glory of the Lord, the Shekinah, and the Angel of the LORD. This enigmatic human appearance of God, discussed with appropriate self-consciousness in the Bible, is related to the son of man. The preeminence of this angel is due primarily to the description of the angel of the LORD in Exodus. Exodus 23:20-21 states: "Behold, I send an angel before you, to guard you on the way and to bring you to the place which I have prepared. Give heed to him and hearken to his voice, do not rebel against him, for he will not pardon your transgression; for my name is in him." The Bible expresses the unique status of this angel by means of its participation in the divine name.

Thereafter in Exod. 33:18-23, Moses asks to see the *glory (kābôd)* of God. In answer, God makes "his goodness" pass in front of him, but He cautions, "You cannot see my face; for man shall not see me and live. . . . Behold, there is a place by me where you shall stand upon the rock; and while my glory passes by I will put you in a cleft of the rock, and I will cover you with my hand until I have passed by; then I will take away my hand and you shall see my back; but my face shall not be seen." Yahweh himself, the angel of God, and his glory *(kābôd)* are melded together in a peculiar way, which suggested to its readers a deep secret about the ways God manifested himself to humanity.

The Septuagint version of Ezekiel identifies the figure on the throne in Ezek. 1:26 with the form of man with various terms like *doxa, homoiōma, eidos,* and *eikōn.* The term *eidos* also has a philosophical history starting in Plato's *Parmenides* (130c), where it means the *idea* of man. Because of Plato's fortunate use of language, Hellenistic Jews like Philo could understand the phrase "form of man" — which describes man's resemblance to God in Gen. 1:26 and also occurs in biblical theophanies like Ezek. 1:26 — as referring to the platonic *eidos,* or idea of man, which inevitably meant for Platonists the unchanging immortal idea of man which survives death. So for Hellenistic Jewish mystics like Philo, the figure of man on the divine throne described in Genesis, Exodus, Ezekiel, Daniel, and the Psalms (and which formed the basis of the "son of man" speculation) was also understood as the ideal and immortal, platonic man. His immortality and glorious appearance were something Adam possessed in the Garden of Eden and lost when he sinned. Paul uses all these traditions to good advantage. In this form, the traditions are centuries older than Christianity.

Speculation on a Principal Angelic Mediator

In the Hellenistic period many new interpretations of Exodus 23–24, Ezekiel 1, and Daniel 7 grew up. The various descriptions of the angels were all melded into a single principal angelic mediator. Foremost among the various names given to this angel in various Jewish sects and conventicles is Yahoel in the first-century apocalyptic work, the *Apocalypse of Abraham.* The name Yahoel illustrates one interpretation of carrying the divine name, since it is a combination of the Tetragrammaton and a suffix denoting angelic stature. Yahoel first appears in chaps. 10–11, where he is described as the one "in whom God's ineffable name dwells." Other titles for this figure included Melchizedek, Metatron, Adoil, Taxo, Eremiel, and preeminently in Christianity but also perhaps elsewhere, "the son of man," or the manlike figure.

For instance, Melchizedek appears at Qumran, in the document called 11QMelchizedek, where he is identified with the "Elohim" of Ps. 82:1, thus giving us yet another variation on the theme of carrying the name of God. This same exegesis is applied to Christ in chap. 1 of the Epistle to the Hebrews. Metatron is called YHWH *hāqātōn,* or YHWH Junior, and sits on a throne equal to God's in *3 Enoch* 10:1. Typically, the name of the angel varies from tradition to tradition. Elsewhere, Michael is God's "mediator" and general (*archistratēgos, 2 Enoch* 33:10; *T. Dan* 6:1-5; *T. Abr.* 1:4; cf. *Life of Adam and Eve* 14:1-2). Eremiel appears in the *Apoc. Zeph.* 6:1-15, where he is mistaken for God. In *Asc. Isa.* 7:2-4, an angel appears whose name cannot be given.

Chief angelic mediators appear throughout Jewish literature of the first several centuries. The chief angelic mediator, whom we may call by a number of terms — God's vice-regent, his vizier, his gerent, or other terms expressing his status as principal angel — is easily distinguished from the plethora of divine creatures, for the principal angel is not only head of the heavenly hosts but sometimes participates in God's own being or divinity: "My name is in him" (Exod. 23:21). In dualistic contexts he is the angel who opposes Satan as "Prince of the World" (e.g., *Apoc. Abr.* 13–14, 20, 22, 23, 29).

Speculation on Exalted Patriarchs

Alongside these traditions lies the relevant notion to Christianity in some apocalyptic-mystical groups that certain heroes can be transformed into angels as part of their ascension. Amazingly, some patriarchs are exalted as angels. In the *Testament of Abraham* 11 (Recension A), Adam is pictured with a terrifying appearance and adorned with glory upon a golden throne. In chaps. 12–13 Abel is similarly glorified, acting as judge over creation until the final judgment. *2 Enoch* 30:8-11 also states that Adam was an angel: "And on earth I assigned him to be a second angel, honored and great and glorious." In the *Prayer of Joseph,* found in Origen's *Commentary on John* 2:31, with a further fragment in *Philocalia* 23:15, Jacob describes himself as "an angel of God and a ruling spirit," and claims to be the "firstborn of every living thing," "the first minister before the face of God," "the archangel of the power of the Lord," and "the chief captain among the sons of God."

Enoch and Moses, however, are the most important non-Christian figures of divinization or angelic transformation. The biblical figure of Enoch in Genesis 4 and 5 seems to be parallel to the Mesopotamian traditions of Enmeduranki and Adapa, wise men who traveled to heaven and founded divinatory priesthoods and ecstatic prophetic guilds. In the biblical account, Enoch alone, of all the members of the genealogy in Genesis 5, has no death notice. Instead, the text twice says that Enoch "walked with God" (Gen. 5:22, 24), and, at the end of the second, that "he was not, for God took him." These enigmatic statements gave later writers the freedom to speculate about Enoch's heavenly journey and also about his final disposition in heaven. The authors of the composite *1 Enoch* introduce the notions of translation, heavenly transformation, angelification, and even messianic redemption. According to *Jubilees,* Enoch undertakes a night vision in which he sees the entire future until the judgment day (4:18-19). He spends six jubilees of years with the angels of God, learning everything about the earth and heavens, from their composition and motion to the locations of hell and heaven (4:21). When he finally ascends, he takes up residence in the Garden of Eden "in majesty and honor," recording the deeds of humanity and serving in the sanctuary as priest (4:23-26); he writes many books (21:20), and there are indeed references to his writings in many other pseudepigrapha.

Philo describes Moses as divine, based upon the word *God* used of him in Exod. 4:16 and 7:1. Thus Sir. 45:1-5 compares Moses to God in the Hebrew or "equal in glory to the holy ones" in the Greek version of the text. Philo and the Samaritans also expressed Moses' preeminence in Jewish tradition essentially by all but deifying him. In the *Testament of Moses,* Moses is described as the mediator or "arbiter of his covenant" (1:14) and celebrated as "that sacred spirit, worthy of the Lord . . . the Lord of the Word . . . the divine prophet throughout the earth, the most perfect teacher in the world," the "advocate," and "the great messenger" (11:16-19). Indeed, Wayne Meeks concluded that "Moses was the most important figure in all Hellenistic Jewish apologetic."

Another important and rarely mentioned piece of evidence of the antiquity of mystical speculation about the *kābôd* is from the fragment of the tragedy *Exagōgē* written by Ezekiel the Tragedian. There, in a document of the second century B.C.E. or earlier, Moses is depicted as seeing a vision of the throne of God with a figure seated upon it. The figure on the throne is called *phōs gennaios,* "a venerable man," which is a double *entendre* in Greek, since *phōs* can mean either "light" or "man" depending on the gender of the noun.

The surviving text of Ezekiel the Tragedian also hints at a transformation of an earthly hero into a divine figure when he relates that the venerable man handed Moses his scepter and summoned him to sit upon the throne, placing a diadem on his head. Although there is no explicit proof that Ezekiel meant this to be a starry or angelic existence, both notions are consonant with his description. The stars bow to Moses and parade for his inspection, suggesting that he is to be their ruler. Since throughout the biblical period the stars are thought to be angels (Job 38:7), there is little doubt that Moses is here depicted as being leader of the angels and, hence, above the angels.

This enthronement scene with a human figure being exalted as a monarch or divinity in heaven resembles the enthronement of the "son of man"; the enthronement helps us understand some of the traditions which later appear in Jewish mysticism and may have informed Paul's ecstatic ascent (2 Corinthians 12). The identification of Jesus with the manlike appearance of God is both the central characteristic of Christianity and understandable within the context of Jewish mysticism and apocalypticism.

Philo speaks of Moses as being made into a divinity *(eis theon)* in several places (e.g., *Sacrifices* 1–10; *Moses* 1.155–58). In interpreting the Exodus account of Moses' receiving the Ten Commandments, Philo envisions an ascent, not merely up the mountain but to the heavens, possibly describing a mystical identification between God and Moses by suggesting that Moses attained to a divine nature through contact with the *logos.* In *QE* 1.29 and 40, Philo writes that on Sinai Moses was changed into a divinity. In *Moses* 1.155-58, he says that God placed the entire universe into Moses' hands and that all the elements obeyed him as their master; then God rewarded Moses by appointing him a "partner" *(koinōnon)* of His own possessions and gave into his hand the world as a portion well fitted for His heir (155). In the *Sacrifices of Cain and Abel* 8–10, Philo refers to Deut. 5:31 as proof that certain people are distinguished by God to be stationed "beside him." Moses is preeminent among these people for his grave is not known, which for Philo allegorically signifies that Moses was transported to heaven.

Judaism and Christianity differ strongly in how they absorb these traditions. Many of these themes surface in Christianity and are reapplied to Jesus, but the term "partner" (Hebr. *shutaf*) for any of God's helpers will become the rabbinic code-word for heresy. Thus, the sides were set for a great conflict in first- and second-century Judaism, all concerned with the existence, nature, status, and meaning of God's primary angelic mediator.

Later Developments

Techniques for Heavenly Ascent

In the ninth century, Hai Gaon recounts that the journey to view this divine figure was undertaken by mystics who put their heads between their knees (the posture Elijah assumed when praying for rain in 1 Kings 18:42), reciting repetitious psalms, glossolalic incantations, and mantra-like prayers, which are recorded in abundance in the Hekhalot literature. When he seeks to behold the merkavah and the palaces of the angels on high, he must follow a certain procedure. He must fast a number of days, place his head between his knees, and whisper many hymns and songs whose texts are known from tradition. Then he perceives the chambers as if he saw the seven palaces with his own eyes, and it is as though he entered one palace after another and saw what was there. And there are two *mishnayot* which the Tannaim taught regarding this topic, called *Hekhalot Rabbati* and *Hekhalot Zutreti.*

The Gaon is aware of the mystical techniques for heavenly ascent and describes them as "out-of-the-body" experiences or "soul flight," where the adept ascends to heaven while his body stays on earth. The Hekhalot texts themselves sometimes mention the transformation of the adept into a heavenly being, whose body becomes fire and whose eyes flash lightning, a theme which is repeated in the Paris Magical Papyrus.

The vision of the throne-chariot of God in Ezekiel 1, along with the attendant vocabulary of glory or *kābôd* for the human figure described there as God's glory or form, has also been recognized as one of the central themes of Jewish mysticism, which is closely related to the apocalyptic tradition. There is no doubt that this was an actual vision. The very name "merkavah" — that is, throne-chariot — mysticism, which is the usual Jewish designation for these mystical traditions even as early as the Mishnah (ca. 220 C.E.: see *m. Ḥag.* 2:1) — is the rabbinic term for the heavenly conveyance described in Ezekiel 1.

Speculation on Metatron

The rabbis most often call God's principal angel Metatron. The term "Metatron" in rabbinic literature and Jewish mysticism is probably not a proper name but a title adapted from the Greek word *Metathronos,* meaning "one who stands *after* or behind the throne." If so, it represents a rabbinic softening of the more normal Hellenistic term, *synthronos,* meaning "one who is *with* the throne," sharing enthronement or acting for the properly throned authority. The rabbis would have changed the preposition from one connoting equality (*syn-,* "with") to one connoting inferiority (meta-, "after or behind") in order to reduce the heretical implications of calling God's principal helping angel his *synthronos.*

Within the mystical documents themselves, the principal angel on the throne is called by a bewildering number of different names, many of which directly suggest that the figure participates somehow in the identity of God. Throughout the later Jewish mystical corpus, the figure on the throne, the figure called Metatron by the rabbis, is repeatedly called Zoharariel, YHWH, the God of Israel, a term which means "Brilliant-Lion-Angel, the Lord, the God of Israel." Elsewhere in the corpus we find *Shatqiel,* a construction based on the silence of God, as well as *Katzpiel,* based on the anger of God, and a great many titles for the principal, enthroned angel.

In *3 Enoch,* a Hebrew work which actually calls itself "The Book of Palaces" *(Sēfer Hēkhālôt),* we enter immediately into an ascension discourse. It is introduced explicitly as a commentary on Gen. 5:24: "Enoch walked with God, and he was no more, for God took him." Rabbi Ishmael is introduced as the speaker, and he explains the peculiar text. He reports his ascension through the six palaces and into the seventh, evidently the lower spheres, but depicted as fortified palaces with doors or gates. Rabbi Ishmael has qualified for this honor because of his great piety and because he is high priest, though this tradition may in fact be conflating the Ishmael who was a contemporary of Rabbi Akiba in the second century with a previous first-century Ishmael who was a priest. In any event, this Rabbi Ishmael is the narrator of a number of other merkavah texts, including *Hekhalot Rabbati* and *Ma'aśēh Merkavah.*

The Seven Palaces (Hēkhālôt)

Essentially Ishmael becomes an ascender, a heavenly traveler who narrates his experience in the heavens and, at the same time, speaks from within the rabbinic tradition. The heavens are divided into seven "palaces" or *hēkhālôt,* which Scholem thought were all to be found in the last sphere of the heavens. They are stacked, one outside the other, like a heavily fortified city with fierce gatekeepers at each of the seven concentric defense walls. The adept shows a charm at each guardhouse, answers a question, and is conveyed into the next inner court until he reaches the throne room, just as he might be conveyed through a high-security fortress. There is some evidence that Arsacid Persian capital cities were laid out in this concentric form, with seven sets of walls. The Arsacid throne room was also based on a celestial model, containing in the center a fixed throne with depictions of heavenly bodies actually revolving around the throne, some at relatively great distances, powered by animals treading on machinery hidden on the floor below.

The seven palaces seem to be the heavenly spheres themselves, and the *sēferôt* of Kabbalah are a later development, even though the name already exists in the early text *Sēfer Ha-yeṣîrāh.* The angel Metatron, the Prince of the Presence, becomes his angelic guide to the very throne of the Holy One. When Rabbi Ishmael recovers enough strength, he opens his mouth and sings the *Kedušāh,* which is exactly the appropriate prayer to say in the presence of the divine throne. The text is obviously making a point about the origin of Jewish liturgy in the heavenly throne room, and conversely the attempt of the synagogue service (and the Temple service before it, no doubt) to pattern itself on the supposed heavenly service. The Dead Sea Scroll texts, particularly the *Songs of the Sabbath Sacrifice,* make the same claim.

Sometimes the throne is empty, but usually Metatron himself sits on it as God's regent. There are places in the text where the divine voice emanates from behind the *pargōd,* the embroidered curtain behind the throne. Other times the text states that God sits on the throne, though in this case, His presence is not described in any detail. Metatron or Zoharariel is God's regent or gerent, standing in for God himself, who is beyond figuration.

Metatron explains why he is called "Youth" or *Naʿar.* Though he has seventy different names, the King of the King of Kings calls him "youth" because he is actually Enoch, the son of Jared and hence young in their eternal company (4:10). Here, a link with the merkavah mystics and Enoch is established, a relationship which is furthered by the story of Enoch in the Bible: Enoch's father's name, Jared, means "he goes down," and is exactly the same verb used for the mystical ascent into the heavens, *yerîdāh lamerkābāh.* So when Enoch is listed as "ben Yarad," he is both "the son of Jared" and "a person who descends." At first blush, this seems a peculiar epithet for an exemplar of heavenly ascent. But this paradox is typical of the merkavah mystics, who often said that they "went down" into the merkavah.

The best explanation for why an ascent to heaven should be called a "descent to the chariot" is to be found in the biblical story of Elijah. In 1 Kings 18:42 Elijah prays by putting his head between his legs, the same posture which merkavah mystics assume when they ascend to heaven. Moreover, this body position is known to aid in achieving ecstasy, especially when combined with repetitious prayers and meditation, exactly as in the Hekhalot literature. So whatever its origin, the parentage of Enoch (Jared) becomes a clue to the mystic techniques of ascent. The combination of themes yields a new cultural form. The exaltation form, which stresses the adept's trip to heaven, often shows how humans become divine and also demonstrates that the prophecies of the resurrection of believers can be demonstrated as true by the mystical ascenders, even though these trips to heaven happen in small esoteric groups.

Bibliography

P. Alexander 2006, *The Mystical Texts: Songs of the Sabbath Sacrifice and Related Manuscripts,* London/New York: Continuum. • J. J. Collins and M. Fishbane, eds. 1995, *Death, Ecstasy and Otherworldly Journeys,* Albany: SUNY Press. • J. J. Collins 1998, *The Apocalyptic Imagination,* 2d ed., Grand Rapids: Eerdmans. • J. R. Davila 2001, *Descenders to the Chariot: The People behind the Hekhalot Literature,* Leiden: Brill. • A. DeConick, ed. 2006, *Paradise Now: Essays on Early Jewish and Christian Mysticism,* Atlanta: Society of Biblical Literature. • I. Gruenwald 1980, *Apocalyptic and Merkabah Mysticism,* Leiden: Brill. • I. Gruenwald 1988, *From Apocalypticism to Gnosticism: Studies in Apocalypticism, Merkavah Mysticism, and Gnosticism,* Frankfurt: Lang. • D. Halperin 1988, *The Faces of the Chariot: Early Jewish Responses to Ezekiel's Vision,* Tübingen: Mohr-Siebeck. • M. Himmelfarb 1993, *Ascent to Heaven in Jewish and Christian Apocalypses,* Oxford: Oxford University Press. • S. T. Katz, ed. 1978, *Mysticism and Philosophical Analysis,* Oxford: Oxford University Press. • C. R. A. Morray-Jones 2002, *A Transparent Illusion: The Dangerous Vision of Water in Hekhalot Mysticism,* Leiden: Brill. • G. W. E. Nickelsburg 2006, *Resurrection, Immortality, and Eternal Life in Intertestamental Judaism,* 2d ed., Cambridge: Harvard University Press. • C. Rowland 1982, *The Open Heaven: A Study of Apocalyptic in Judaism and Early Christianity,* New York: Crossroad. • P. Schäfer 1988, *Hekhalot-Studien,* Tübingen: Mohr-Siebeck. • P. Schäfer 2009, *The Origins of Jewish Mysticism,* Tübingen: Mohr-Siebeck. • G. G. Scholem 1954, *Major Trends in Jewish Mysticism,* New York: Schocken, 40-79. • G. G. Scholem 1965, *Jewish Gnosticism, Merkabah Mysticism, and Talmudic Tradition,* New York: Jewish Theological Seminary of America. • A. F. Segal 2004, *Life after Death: A History of the Afterlife in Western Religion,* New York: Doubleday. • E. R. Wolfson 1995, *Through a Speculum That Shines: Vision and Imagination in Medieval Jewish Mysticism,* Princeton: Princeton University Press. • A. Yarbro Collins 1996, *Cosmology and Eschatology in Jewish and Christian Apocalypticism,* Leiden: Brill, 1996.

See also: Apocalypticism; Ascent to Heaven; Hekhalot Literature; Mediator Figures; Metatron

Alan F. Segal

N

Nabatea

The Nabateans (Aram. *Nabaṭû*) were an Arab people who established a kingdom centered at Petra in southern Transjordan that played an important role in the history of Palestine from at least the second century B.C.E. until its annexation by Rome in 106 C.E. Their territory embraced parts of what are today southern Syria, Jordan, the northwest of Saudi Arabia, the Negev of Israel, and the Sinai and eastern deserts of Egypt. Their rule stretched from Damascus to Mada'in Salih and Al-ʿUla in the northern Hijaz in the south, and from Dumah (Jauf) in the Wadi Sirhan of the Syrian Desert west to the Suez region of Egypt. The kingdom prospered as a result of the aromatics trade with Yemen. The history of the Nabateans must be compiled from classical Greek, Latin, and Jewish literary sources and an expanding corpus of Nabatean Aramaic inscriptions now exceeding 6,000 texts, most of which are graffiti. Their distinctive painted "eggshell" pottery has made it possible to identify over a thousand archaeological sites in the Levant.

Origins and Early History

The prehistory of the Nabateans remains obscure. Their connections with the Arabs known in Neo-Assyrian as the *Nabaiati* (and various other variants), the Nebaioth *(Nabayôt)* of the Hebrew Bible, and the Nabayat in early North Arabian texts remain linguistically difficult, but the Nabatean onomasticon and cultic life reflect North Arabia as their original homeland. It is generally assumed that Nabatean society was nomadic until ca. 100 B.C.E., when the first sign of Nabatean material culture begins, with the appearance of their distinctive pottery, dynastic coins, and monumental architecture. New Idumean ostraca from the Negev dating to the fourth and third centuries B.C.E. reveal a significant number of Arabs already occupying the region as farmers and as an integral part of the sedentary population. Many bear traditional Nabatean names, and their cults reflect those of the North Arabian sphere, suggesting that a "Nabateanized" Arab population was part of the indigenous population of Palestine already in the late Achaemenid and early Hellenistic period. In ca. 257 B.C.E., the Zenon Papyri of the Ptolemaic dynasty in Egypt also refer to the Nabateans as part of the regular Transjordan landscape and the people of Rabbel in the Hauran.

Nabatean Relations with Hasmonean and Herodian Judea

During the five known centuries of the Nabatean dynasty, its kings were involved peacefully and militarily with the Hasmonean and Herodian dynasties of Judea. Aretas I (fl. 170-160 B.C.E.) was friendly with the Maccabean rulers Judas and Jonathan (1 Macc. 5:24-28; 15:22; cf. 2 Macc. 12:10-12) and probably is to be identified with the "Aretas King of the Nabateans" mentioned in an early second-century-B.C.E. inscription from Elusa (Khalutza) in the Negev. Afterward, there is a gap of several generations before another Nabatean king is mentioned.

Under Aretas II (ca. 120-96 B.C.E.), the Nabateans were in conflict with the Hasmonean kings, particularly Alexander Jannaeus, for control of the major port city of Gaza. He is perhaps to be identified with the Arab king "Herotimus" who led campaigns into Syria and Egypt.

The conflict with Jannaeus continued in the reign of Obodas I (ca. 93-85 B.C.E.), who defeated the Hasmonean ruler in ca. 90 B.C.E. (Josephus, *Ant.* 13.375) and seized territories in Moab and Galaaditis from him (*Ant.* 13.382). In ca. 87 B.C.E., Obodas' army defeated and killed the Seleucid king Antiochus XII at the Battle of Cana in southern Syria (*Ant.* 13.387-91; *J.W.* 1.99-102). The royal cult of Obodas known from Nabatean inscriptions at the city in the Negev that bears his name (ʿAvdat, Oboda) is probably to be associated with this ruler; the inscriptions celebrate his victories over Jannaeus and Antiochus XII.

The great expansion of the Nabatean realm is associated with Aretas III (85-62 B.C.E.), who extended the borders of the kingdom to Damascus (*Ant.* 13.392; *J.W.* 1.103), but appears to have lost Gaza and northern Moab to Jannaeus (*Ant.* 13.395-97; cf. 14.18). The coins that designate Aretas III as "philhellene" were probably restricted to the region of Damascus. A coin minted in

The treasury at Petra, capital of the Nabatean Kingdom *(Phoenix Data Systems / Neal and Joel Bierling)*

Rome and issued by Scarus in ca. 58 B.C.E. depicts Aretas kneeling by his camel, which suggests that after Pompey's expedition the kingdom was regarded as a client state of Rome. The region provided shelter to Jannaeus' successors (*Ant.* 13.414; *J.W.* 1.125-26).

The reign of a king Obodas II (62-60 B.C.E.) is hypothesized on the basis of coins, but this is not certain; his reign must be squeezed into the narrow silent gap between Aretas III and Malichus I.

The long rule of Malichus I (61-30 B.C.E.) coincided in part with the tumultuous years of the civil wars in Rome. In 55 B.C.E., Gabinius, the Roman governor of Syria, exacted tribute from Malichus (*Ant.* 14.103), and later the king supplied military aid to Caesar at Alexandria in 47 B.C.E. During the Parthian invasion in 40 B.C.E., he supported the Iranian invaders. After their withdrawal, he drew the wrath of Rome and was forced to pay a large indemnity (Dio Cassius 48.41.5). Antony also exacted revenues from the territories of Malichus at the request of Cleopatra in 34 B.C.E. (49.32.5; Josephus, *Ant.* 15.92-96; *J.W.* 1.360). In 31 B.C.E. Malichus defeated Herod, the recently appointed king of Judea, in a battle in the Hauran of Syria (*Ant.* 15.108-12). Herod later defeated Malichus in a conflict near Amman, winning recognition as the "protector" of Nabatea (*Ant.* 15.159; cf. *J.W.* 1.385). Afterward, Malichus attempted to befriend the Hasmonean Hyrcanus II, but Herod intervened and executed the aged priest (*Ant.* 15.161-79).

Under Octavian (later, Augustus), the victor of Antony and Cleopatra at Actium in 31 B.C.E., the Nabateans enjoyed better relations with Rome. In 26-35 B.C.E., Obodas III (30-9 B.C.E.) supported the Roman prefect in Egypt, Aelius Gallus, in his campaign into south Arabia, supplying him with 1,000 Nabatean troops led by his vizier Syllaeus, accompanied by 500 troops of Herod the Great (Strabo 16.4.23 [780]). The Jewish troops of Herod are praised by Josephus (*Ant.* 15.317), but Syllaeus' reputation suffered at the hands of Strabo and Josephus' hostile sources. The failure of the campaign is assigned to Syllaeus by Strabo and led to his execution (Strabo 16.4.24 [782]), although the cities conquered in the campaign are listed elsewhere (Pliny, *Natural History* 6.32.160-61), and Augustus regarded Arabia as one of his victories (*Res Gestae* 26.5).

Syllaeus later appeared at the Herodian court, where Herod's sister Salome fell in love with the "clever and handsome" Nabatean administrator (*Ant.* 16.220). She even attempted to marry him with the support of the Roman empress Livia (*J.W.* 1.566; cf. *Ant.* 17.10), until Herod requested that Syllaeus convert to Judaism, which the Nabatean refused to do out of fear "he would be stoned to death by the Arabs" (*Ant.* 16.220-26). Subsequently Herod and Syllaeus were embroiled in conflict (ca. 21 B.C.E.), with Herod even invading Arabia and complaining to the Syrian governor about Syllaeus' behavior and attacks on his realm (*Ant.* 16.271-81). Both Herod and Syllaeus then departed to Rome to complain to Augustus about each other, but the arguments of the Nabatean were found compelling (*Ant.* 16.286-91).

At Obodas' death in 9 B.C.E., Syllaeus attempted to seize control of Nabatea, but a man named Aeneas, perhaps from a collateral branch of the royal house and not a direct royal descendant, seized the throne without the approval of Augustus (*Ant.* 16.294). After hearing their counterclaims, the Roman emperor appointed Aeneas, known now as Aretas IV, as king of the Nabateans. He was perhaps persuaded to make the appointment by Herod's advisor Nicolaus of Damascus, who was sent to Rome to counter Syllaeus' claim to the throne (*Ant.* 16.299, 335-54).

Aretas and Herod's son Antipater later brought new accusations against Syllaeus, forcing him to sail in ca. 6 B.C.E. to Rome again and defend himself (*J.W.* 1.574). In retaliation, Syllaeus allegedly attempted through associates to have Herod assassinated and successfully had Herod's brother poisoned (*Ant.* 17.62-63). How Syllaeus could survive for two decades after a series of such imperial affronts and court intrigues remains inexplicable. In any case, the sources are contaminated with bias.

Under Aretas IV (9 B.C.E.–40 C.E.), the Nabatean realm reached its greatest prominence. During his

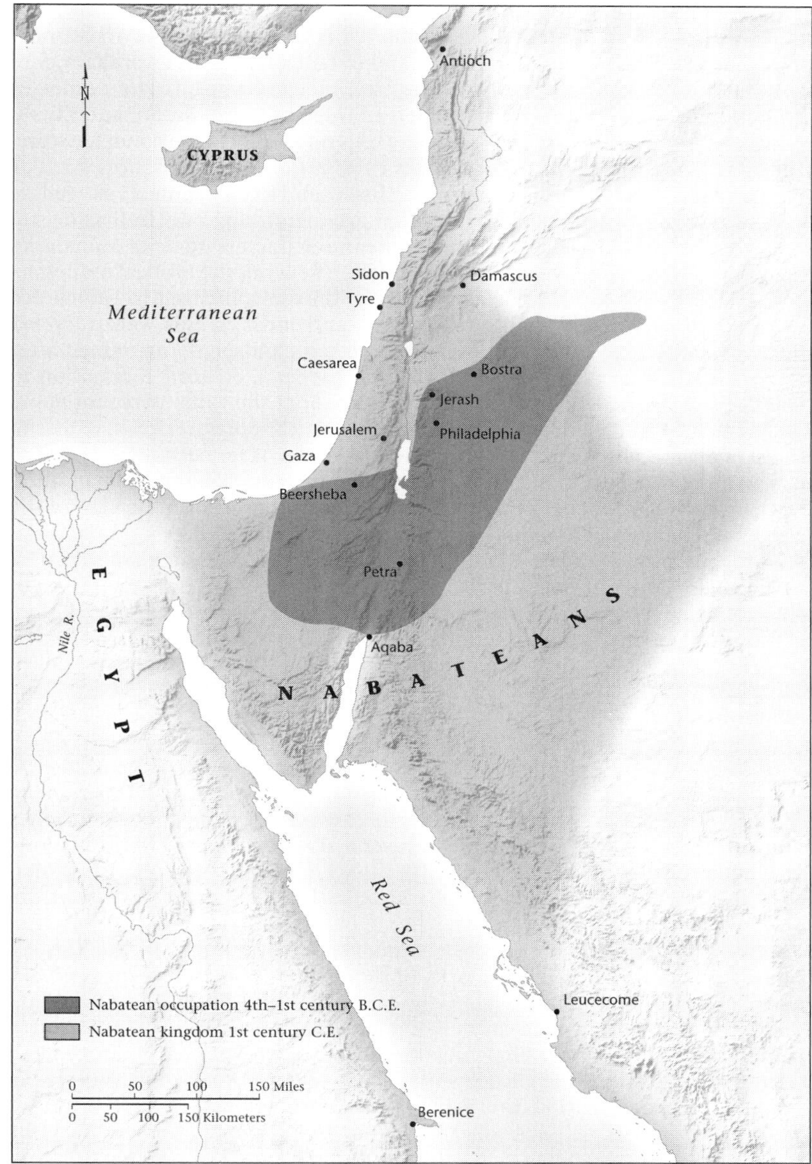

THE NABATEAN EMPIRE AT ITS GREATEST EXTENT

reign, the Nabatean capital at Petra was enhanced by a number of constructions, including temples. A theater at Hegra (Mada'in Salih) in the Ḥijāz was developed as an entrepôt. The kingdom appears to have flourished, as indicated by the abundant coinage and inscriptions dated to his reign.

A daughter of Aretas IV, identified as Shaʿudat, married Herod Antipas, but when he divorced her to marry Herodias, the wife of his half-brother Herod Philip, he drew the wrath of John the Baptist (Mark 6:17-29 and pars.) and the anger of Aretas IV, who launched a military campaign against Antipas. This action drew the condemnation of the emperor Tiberius, but the emperor's death in 37 C.E. prevented any Roman punitive action (*Ant.* 18.109-25). The other New Testament allusion to the Nabateans is connected to the apostle Paul's escape from the ethnarch Aretas IV in Damascus (2 Cor. 11:32-33; cf. Acts 9:23-25) and his withdrawal to some unknown location in Arabia (Gal. 1:17).

The reign of Malichus II (40-70 C.E.) is normally characterized as one of political and economic decline, based on the sparse literary references to his rule and the debasement of his coins. Still, the aromatics trade was flourishing through the port of Leuke Kome on the Red Sea and overland to Petra (*Periplus Maris Erythraei* 19). The epigraphic remains from Hegra also continue in his reign; one inscription indicates that a Jewish merchant resided at the oasis in 43 C.E. (*CIS* 2:219), and another at Dumah (Jauf) in the Wadi Sirhan indicates that it served as a military outpost in 45 C.E. A Nabatean inscription at Rome dating to Malichus II's reign is also now known, suggesting that the silence of the literary tradition about him may be accidental. In the Judean revolt of 66 C.E., Malichus provided 1,000 cavalry and 5,000 infantry to Titus to help Rome quell the uprising (*J.W.* 3.68).

Rabbel II (70-106 C.E.) began his rule in his minority, with his mother Shuqailat serving as regent until possibly 75 C.E. It appears that his rule was initially contested by Damasi, the scion of a powerful aristocratic family at Hegra, supported even by tribes in the far north in Syria.

Annexation to Provincia Arabia

In 106 C.E., Trajan ordered Cornelius Palma to annex the Nabatean kingdom and create the province of Arabia. The rapid transition to Roman rule is marked by the construction of the major highway known as the *Via Nova Traiana* between the capital at Bostra and Aila (ʿAqaba) on the Red Sea, the drafting of six auxiliary military units named the *Cohortes Ulpiae Petraeoreum* from the Nabatean army, and the organization of the realm for administration and taxation. Archives from the Cave of Letters in Judea furnish documentation for this transition. Especially revealing are the archives of a Jewish woman named Babatha, which contain Nabatean Aramaic, and Greek documents extending from 93 C.E. to the outbreak of the Bar Kokhba Revolt in 132 C.E. Although there are hints that the incorporation of Nabatea into the Roman provincial sphere was not without some opposition (Ammianus Marcellinus 14.8.13), the failure of Trajan to take the title *Arabicus* and the declaration of *Arabia adquisita* on coins suggests that the annexation was rather peaceful.

BIBLIOGRAPHY
D. F. GRAF 1988, *Rome and Its Arabian Frontier from the Nabataeans to the Saracens,* Burlington, Vt.: Ashgate. • U. HACKL, H. JENNI, AND C. SCHNEIDE 2003, *Quellen zur Geschichte der Nabatäer: Textsammlung mit Übersetzung und Kommentar,* Göttingen: Vandenhoeck & Ruprecht. • J. F. HEALEY 2001, *The Religion of the Nabataeans: A Conspectus,* Leiden: Brill. • A. KASHER 1988, *Jews, Idumeans, and Ancient Arabs,* Tübingen: Mohr-Siebeck. • Y. MESHORER 1975, *Nabatean Coins,* Jerusalem: Hebrew University of Jerusalem. • J. PATRICH 1990, *The Formation of Nabataean Art,* Jerusalem: Magnes. • R. WENNING 1987, *Die Nabatäer — Denkmäler und Geschichte,* Göttingen: Vandenhoeck & Ruprecht.

DAVID F. GRAF

Nabonidus, Prayer of → Daniel, Pseudo-Texts

Names

In Second Temple times, biblical names were well established as the definitive pool of Jewish names. People bearing names deriving directly from the Hebrew Bible were considered carriers of distinctively Jewish names, and often the Jewishness of persons mentioned in ancient sources is decided by scholars based on the fact that they have a biblical name. However, it is obvious that biblical names themselves are not, in a narrowly defined way, Hebrew but derive from various, non-Jewish sources. The name Moses, for example, is clearly of Egyptian origin. The names Mordecai and Esther are Babylonian, deriving from the names of the Babylonian divinities Marduk and Ishtar.

Throughout the ages, Jews often chose to adopt the names of the peoples among whom or under whose rule they lived. In the Second Temple period this was mainly Greek culture and, as time went by, Jews tended to adopt Greek names, often with no interest in the meaning of the name. Thus, we find Second Temple Jews being called by names such as Apollonius (after the Greek god Apollo), Demetrius (after the goddess Demeter), Athenaius (after the goddess Athene), and Isidorus (after the Egyptian goddess Isis). In what follows, the main tendencies in name-giving among Second Temple Jews will be outlined.

Biblical Names

Particularly among Jews in the land of Israel in the Second Temple period, biblical names remained the largest pool of useable and popular names. However, it is interesting to note which biblical names were most popular. In the land of Israel the names Abraham, Moses, and David were never used at all. The names of other biblical heroes, such as Isaac, Aaron, and Elijah, were also only very seldom employed. Instead, Jews preferred to use names of minor biblical figures such as Saul, Benjamin, Elisha, and even Ishmael, as well as biblical names that are mentioned only in lists or stories about insignificant characters such as Menahem, Yoezer, Yair, or Hillel. In general, the biblical names actually used were very limited compared to the choice available to parents, and most names were recycled over and over again (often children being named after grandparents or even parents), creating a situation in which so many persons bore the same personal name that a complex system of nicknames designed to distinguish one Shimeon from the other became necessary.

This concentration of persons under a small number of names is particularly manifest in the case of the Hasmoneans. The biblical names of this family of father (Mattathias) and five sons (Yohanan, Shimeon, Judah, Eleazar, and Jonathan) inspired over 30 percent of male name-giving during the Second Temple period. This phenomenon can be explained only as resulting from the popularity of this family's military and political success in the land of Israel during the Second Temple period. Two other biblical names are almost as popular as the Hasmonean ones. The first is Joseph, which is the second most popular of all names (after Shimeon) and may perhaps also be interpreted as a Hasmonean name. According to 2 Macc. 8:22, a Hasmonean brother by the name of Joseph also participated in the exploits of his family. If this is a reliable source, then men named Joseph were also thus designated after a Hasmonean hero.

The other equally popular name is Joshua (Jesus). The popularity of this name needs to be explained differently from the case of Joseph. Perhaps it was so popular because of the meaning of the name ("salvation"), but since meaning seems to have played a minor role in the choice of names by Jews in the Second Temple period, this explanation is problematic.

A similar, if more distinctive phenomenon can be identified with regard to the names of women. Here we discover that three names (only one of them, Miriam, biblical; the other two, Shalom and Shelamzion, Hebrew or Aramaic) account for over 50 percent of named women known to us from Second Temple times. Two of these names (Shelamzion and Miriam), incidentally, are also recorded for Hasmonean women, albeit not in the first generation. Shelamzion was the name of a Hasmonean queen (76-67 B.C.E.), and Miriam was the name of the Hasmonean wife of Herod (died 27 B.C.E.). Although this phenomenon is somewhat similar to what we saw for men, this huge concentration of women with such a small pool of names obviously has also something to do with conceptions of womanhood at the time, touching on the construction of female individuality.

In the Diaspora a similar phenomenon of a small

pool of Hebrew names is observable, but it is slightly different. In Egypt and other Diaspora centers, it seems that the names Moses and Abraham, which were avoided in the land of Israel, were sometimes used. The names Samuel and Jacob, also used in the land of Israel but infrequently, were exceptionally popular in all Diaspora communities. Also the name Shabtai (Sambathius), almost completely absent from the name pool of Jews in the land of Israel, was very popular in the Greco-Roman Diaspora.

Greek Names

Jews in the land of Israel used a much larger variety of Greek names than they did Hebrew ones, but much less frequently. Thus, only 14 percent of the population actually used Greek names. It is usually argued that these were mainly members of the ruling elite, but a more thorough study is required before this could be definitively established. The most popular name was clearly Alexander. In the Diaspora, the situation was reversed. Many more Jews bore Greek names than Hebrew ones. This situation was probably even more extreme than our sources show, because while people bearing biblical names are identified as Jewish by their name, Jews bearing Greek names who did not wish their ethnic or religious identity to be known remain indistinguishable from their Gentile counterparts in the historical record.

It has often been suggested that Greek names used by Jews were modeled after biblical Hebrew ones either by translation (e.g., Isaac/Gelasius; Jonathan/Dositheus) or by similar sounds (e.g., Shimeon/Simon; Jesus/Jason), but there is no evidence for such a phenomenon.

Other Names

In Second Temple times Jews in the land of Israel were strongly influenced by names in the Aramaic language used by their neighbors in the land such as Nabateans and Edomites. Thus, names like Abba and Martha became popular. However, Aramaic was mainly used for nicknames, which were bestowed on people in order to distinguish them from other people bearing the same biblical name, because Aramaic was the spoken languages of the masses.

On the other hand, Jews in the land of Israel were much less influenced by Latin names, which the Romans brought with them, despite the length and influence of Roman rule. Nevertheless some traces of the use of Latin names can be found, again mainly among the ruling classes. Thus we find Jews with names such as Justus, Julius, and Gaius.

In the Diaspora this situation is manifestly different. In the eastern Diaspora, primarily in Babylonia, Aramaic and Persian names (and sometimes Hebrew names that have undergone Aramaization, such as Hanina, deriving from Hananiah) are very common for Jews. In the western Diaspora, beginning with Rome, Latin names are very common. In Egypt it can be shown that, despite the deep Hellenization of the country, some Jews actually adopted Egyptian names, or Greek names in an Egyptian garb.

Bibliography

N. G. Cohen 1976, "Jewish Names as Cultural Indicators in Antiquity," *JSJ* 7: 97-128. • N. G. Cohen 1999, "The Name 'Shabtai' in the Hellenistic-Roman Period," in *These Are the Names: Studies in Jewish Onomastics,* ed. A. Demski, Ramat Gan: Bar-Ilan University Press, 11*-28* (in Hebrew). • M. Heltzer and M. Ohana, 1978, *The Extra-Biblical Tradition of Hebrew Personal Names (From the First Temple Period to the End of the Talmudic Period,* Haifa: University of Haifa (in Hebrew). • S. Honigman 2004, "Abraham in Egypt: Hebrew and Jewish-Aramaic Names in Egypt and Judea in Hellenistic and Early Roman Times," *Zeitschrift für Papyrologie und Epigraphik* 146: 279-97. • T. Ilan 2002, *Lexicon of Jewish Names in Late Antiquity, Part I: Palestine 330 BCE–200 CE,* Tübingen: Mohr-Siebeck. • H. Misgav 1997, "Nomenclature in Ossuary Inscriptions," *Tarbiz* 66: 123-30 (in Hebrew). • G. Mussies 1994, "Jewish Personal Names in Some Non-Literary Sources," in *Studies in Early Jewish Epigraphy,* ed. J. W. van Henten and P. W. van der Horst, Leiden: Brill, 242-76. • J. Naveh 1990, "Nameless People?" *IEJ* 40: 108-29. • A. Schlatter 1913, *Die Hebräischen Namen bei Josephus,* Gütersloh: Gütersloher Verlag. • V. Tcherikover 1957, "Introduction," in *Corpus Papyrorum Judaicarum,* vol. 1, ed. V. Tcherikover and A. Fuchs, Cambridge: Harvard University Press, xvii-xx. • M. Williams 1997, "Jewish Use of Moses as a Personal Name in Graeco-Roman Antiquity — A Note," *Zeitschrift für Papyrologie und Epigraphik* 118: 274. • L. Zunz 1837, *Namen der Juden: Eine Geschichtliche Untersuchung,* Leipzig: L. Fort.

Tal Ilan

Naphtali, Testament of (4Q215)

The title 4QTestament of Naphtali or 4Q215 designates three fragments of a Qumran manuscript. The three pieces are from the upper righthand portion of a single column; frg. 1 shows upper and righthand margins; frg. 2 comes from the left side of the piece and shows a small portion of the upper margin; frg. 3 is situated at the lower lefthand corner of the surviving text and comes from the inner portion of the column. The three fragments provide evidence of eleven lines of text, although line 6 is blank and only a few letters are visible on line 11. Lines 1-5 address the genealogy of Bilhah and lines 7-11 recall Laban's bringing of Hannah, Bilhah's mother, to Jacob; the assignment of Bilhah and Zilpah to Rachel and Leah; and Dan's birth. The text was assigned its name because of its similarity to Greek *Testament of Naphtali* 1:6-12 and because it is reported in the first-person singular by someone who refers to Bilhah and Jacob as his parents (lines 4, 7, 8, 10) and to Dan as his brother (line 10).

Part of the Cave 4 cache discovered in 1952, 4Q215 was initially associated with what is now known to be a separate work, 4Q215a (4QTime of Righteousness [DJD 36: 172-84]; see Chazon 1999). Pieced together by J. T. Milik between 1952 and 1960, 4Q215 was published by M. E. Stone in DJD 22 (1997). Stone also provided previews, updates, and related discussions of the text in several journal articles (1996a; 1996b; 1998a; 1998b).

Because the left margin is missing, we cannot be

entirely sure of the text's contents, but comparison with related texts provides assistance in this regard and permits a reasonable estimate of what the complete text reported. Lines 1-5 report Bilhah's genealogy and parallels the Greek *T. Naph.* 1:9-12 (cf. the *Midrash Bereshit Rabbati,* an eleventh-century-C.E. work attributed to a R. Moses; see Himmelfarb 1984). There we learn that a certain Rotheus, of the family of Abraham, had been redeemed from captivity by Laban, and that Rotheus was brother to Deborah, Rebecca's nurse. Laban gave Aina (Hannah in the Hebrew of 4Q215 and *Midrash Bereshit Rabbati*) to Rotheus as a wife; to Aina and Rotheus were born Bilhah and Zilpah; and to Bilhah were born Naphtali and Dan by Jacob (*T. Naph.* 1:6; cf. Gen. 30:1-8). Apart from naming Bilhah's father Ahiyot in line 1 (cf. Rotheus in *T. Naph.* 1:10; but he is called Ahotay in *Midrash Bereshit Rabbati*), the first episode preserved in 4Q215 matches Bilhah's genealogy in *T. Naph.* 1:9-12 perfectly.

Lines 7-11 lack a clear parallel in the Greek *Testament of Naphtali,* but *Midrash Bereshit Rabbati* preserves related material that permits one to reconstruct the content of this section (see esp. Himmelfarb 1984). Line 7 reports Jacob's flight from Esau to Laban (Gen. 27:40–28:4; 29:1). Line 8 mentions the father of Bilhah (Ahiyot/Rotheus) and tells how Laban brought forth Hannah, Bilhah's mother. The rest of line 8 and the first half of line 9 apparently report that Bilhah and Zilpah, the daughters of Ahiyot and Hannah, went to Rachel and Leah as handmaidens (cf. Gen. 29:24, 29). Lines 9-11 then recall Rachel's barrenness and the birth of Dan and Naphtali to Bilhah and Jacob (Gen. 30:1-8).

4Q215 offers firm evidence of a Semitic tradition that reappears in the Greek *Testaments of the Twelve Patriarchs* (cf. Hebr. *Testament of Naphtali; Midrash Bereshit Rabbati*). Oddly, although the Greek *Testament of Naphtali* states unequivocally that Bilhah's descent from Rotheus/Ahiyot ensures her place in the bloodline of Abraham (thereby ensuring an Abrahamic origin for all of Jacob's sons on the maternal and paternal sides [Stone 1997: 75]), 4Q215 in its extant form does not seem to have made this point.

BIBLIOGRAPHY

E. G. CHAZON 1999, "A Case of Mistaken Identity: 'Testament of Naphtali, 4Q215' and 'Time of Righteousness,'" in *The Provo International Conference on the Dead Sea Scrolls: Technological Innovations, New Texts, and Reformulated Issues,* ed. D. W. Parry and E. Ulrich, Leiden: Brill, 110-25. • M. HIMMELFARB 1984, "R. Moses the Preacher and the Testaments of the Twelve Patriarch," *AJS Review* 9: 55-78. • W. NEBE 1994, "Qumranica 1: Zu unveröffentlichen Handschriften aus Höhle 4 vom Qumran," *ZAW* 106: 317-19. • M. E. STONE 1996A, "The Genealogy of Bilhah (4QTNaph-4Q215," *DSD* 3: 20-36. • M. E. STONE 1996B, "Testament of Naphtali," *JJS* 47: 311-21. • M. E. STONE 1997, "215. 4QTestament of Naphtali," in *Qumran Cave 4: XVII, Parabiblical Texts, Part 3,* ed. G. Brooke et al., DJD 22, 73-84. • M. E. STONE 1998A, "Some Further Readings in the Hebrew Testament of Naphtali," *JJS* 49: 346-47. • M. E. STONE 1998B, "Warum Naphtali? Eine Diskussion im Internet," *Judaica* 54: 188-91.

See also: Patriarchs, Testaments of the Twelve

ROBERT A. KUGLER

Nash Papyrus → Papyri

Nebuchadnezzar

Nebuchadnezzar II (605-562 B.C.E.) was the second Chaldean monarch of Babylonia. A brilliant diplomat and military leader, Nebuchadnezzar (Akk. *Nabû-kudurri-uṣur,* "Nabû, protect my offspring") continued the military success of his father Nabopolassar, founder of the Chaldean dynasty. In his own accounts (the best known is the *Babylonian Chronicle*), Nebuchadnezzar tells of his military expeditions to the West. In 605 B.C.E. he defeated Egyptian armies at Carchemish and subsequently led the Neo-Babylonian Empire to its greatest extent. In classical sources, Nebuchadnezzar is remembered for his extensive building projects, such as the fortifications of Babylon, the impressive ziggurat, and the legendary Hanging Gardens.

Not surprisingly, the emphasis in Jewish reflections on Nebuchadnezzar (Hebr. *nĕbûkadne'ṣṣar;* variant: *nĕbûkadre'ṣṣar*) is on his campaigns against Jerusalem, the destruction of Solomon's Temple, and the Babylonian Exile. These texts reflect diverse attempts to wrestle with the memory of the worst calamity in ancient Israel. The sheer magnitude of the destruction, physical and psychological, and the mastermind behind it commanded attention and respect. It should be emphasized that early Jewish literature represents only a small part of a continuing fascination with Nebuchadnezzar in Judaism.

In March of 597 B.C.E. Nebuchadnezzar besieged Jerusalem and put Zedekiah on the throne (2 Kings 24:10-17). The biblical author stresses that the Babylonian advance, long since predicted by the prophets, happened "at the command of the LORD" (2 Kings 24:3, 4). In 587 B.C.E. King Zedekiah revolted against Nebuchadnezzar. Jerusalem was promptly besieged again and burned to the ground, the priests and civic leaders were executed, and the people were led into exile (2 Kings 25:1-21; 2 Chron. 36:5-21). Again the biblical authors emphasize that the Babylonians were victorious not of their own doing but because they were the instruments of the God of Israel (2 Kings 24:20; 2 Chron. 36:17; Ezra 5:12; cf. Ezek. 26:7; 29:18-19; Ep. Jer. 6:2; *2 Bar.* 79:1; *3 Bar.* 1:1; *4 Bar.* 5:21; 7:14, 25). The same events are related in the book of Jeremiah, albeit with some modifications. There God calls Nebuchadnezzar "my servant" (Jer. 27:6; cf. 25:9) and decrees that all nations, and even the wild animals, shall serve the Gentile king. Nebuchadnezzar, in turn, stipulates that Jeremiah, who has always advocated a pro-Babylonian position, be released from confinement and treated kindly (Jer. 39:11-14).

Jewish literature of the Second Temple period remembers Nebuchadnezzar as the architect of the Babylonian Exile. References to him range from cursory mention to sophisticated interpretations. What is missing, surprisingly, is an outright condemnation of Israel's worst enemy. 1 Esdras contains a retelling of the Babylonian invasion of Judah (1 Esdr. 1:40, 41, 45, 48; 2:10; 5:7; 6:15, 18, 26). In Ezra-Nehemiah each reference to Nebuchadnezzar is promptly followed by a remark that the Persian king Cyrus undid what the Babylonian monarch had done (Ezra 1:7; 2:1; 5:14; 6:5; Neh. 7:6), as if to claim that Nebuchadnezzar and the calamity he brought upon Israel were fully reversed by Cyrus. The book of Esther mentions Nebuchadnezzar twice in the context of the lineage of Mordecai (Esth. 2:6; Add. Esth. [Addition A] 11:4).

Nebuchadnezzar plays a most prominent role in Daniel and Judith. Whereas the Gentile kingdoms turn into apocalyptic nightmares in the second half of the book of Daniel (chaps. 7–12), initially Daniel and his three companions enjoy rather amicable relations with the foreign monarchs, including Nebuchadnezzar, at whose courts they serve and prosper (chaps. 1–6). Twice Daniel interprets Nebuchadnezzar's troubling dreams (Daniel 2 and 4), showing obvious affection for the Babylonian king (Dan. 4:27). Such heartfelt concern, which later greatly troubled the rabbis (*Midrash Tanḥuma* 4), is reminiscent of a passage in the apocryphal book of Baruch. In a letter sent to Jerusalem shortly after the Babylonian destruction of the city, Baruch asks the high priest to "pray for the life of King Nebuchadnezzar" and for his welfare (Bar. 1:10-12; cf. Jer. 29:4-9). The author may hope that the Babylonian monarch will treat the Jews as kindly as he treated Jeremiah. More likely, however, such affection is a literary strategy to cope with Nebuchadnezzar's villainy by subordinating him to the will of God, the real actor. The court tales in Daniel are conversion narratives that culminate in Nebuchadnezzar's conversion and his doxologies to the God of Daniel (Dan. 2:47-48; 3:28-29; 4:34-35). The book of Judith consistently misidentifies Nebuchadnezzar as the "king of the Assyrians" (Jdt. 1:7, 13; 2:1; etc.) and states that he resided "in the great city of Nineveh" (1:1). History and chronology are here deliberately confused. No longer a historical figure, Nebuchadnezzar has become a literary cipher, a pseudonym for "Israel's enemy." Regardless of the true identity of the villain in Judith (Antiochus IV Epiphanes?), Judith demonstrates that this enemy can be defeated.

Bibliography

M. Henze 1999, *The Madness of King Nebuchadnezzar*, Leiden: Brill. • R. H. Sack 2004, *Images of Nebuchadnezzar*, Selinsgrove: Susquehanna University Press. • D. J. Wiseman 1985, *Nebuchadrezzar and Babylon*, Oxford: Oxford University Press.

Matthias Henze

Nehemiah, Book of

The book of Nehemiah is the second part of Ezra-Nehemiah, although in the Masoretic text it is a separate book. Following ancient sources (*b. Baba Batra* 14b–15a; Eusebius, *Hist. Eccl.* 4.26.14), modern biblical research typically reads the books as parts of a unified project. Especially since the work of Japhet (1969), the two books are also read as a separate work from 1 and 2 Chronicles, even though there is some overlap between the end of 2 Chronicles and the beginning of Ezra, and despite the fact that the two short books are often associated with Chronicles in canonical arrangement. The book of Ezra-Nehemiah deals with successive returns of groups of Judeans from the Babylonian Exile, and with aspects of community life in postexilic Judah — Ezra with religious issues, Nehemiah mostly with social and structural issues such as reforming the economy, repopulating Jerusalem, and rebuilding the city walls.

The Missions of Ezra and Nehemiah

There is a strong link between the events described in the books of Ezra and Nehemiah, even though the precise sequence of those events remains controversial. Perhaps the oldest of these controversies concerns the question of who went to Jerusalem first: Ezra or Nehemiah? Williamson (1985), who believes Ezra's mission lasted a single year, has nonetheless argued strongly for the current consensus that Ezra preceded Nehemiah. In support of this, one may note, for example, that Nehemiah deals with mixed marriages among the upper classes (e.g., the case of Tobiah) that evidently escaped Ezra's broader reform. Further, Nehemiah's approach to interpreting law in Neh. 13:25 seems to follow the method introduced earlier by Ezra in 9:1-2. And although Ezra himself appears to have had a more informal relationship with the Persian authorities, the book of Nehemiah suggests that Nehemiah acted in an official capacity, perhaps even serving as a local governor of the community of Jews in the vicinity of Jerusalem. Nehemiah apparently had more official backing in his reforms than did Ezra, and in the text Nehemiah accomplishes all that he set out to do, while many of Ezra's anticipated changes are either left inconclusive or are absent entirely. Although the evidence remains inconclusive, Ezra's chronological priority is the dominant view. Thus, the book of Ezra-Nehemiah is our main source in the Bible for the years immediately following the conquest of Babylon by the Persian Empire under Cyrus until the years of Artaxerxes I (roughly 539-425 B.C.E.).

Structure and Purpose

Three units of text are normally distinguished for analysis in Ezra-Nehemiah: (1) Ezra 1–6, the correspondence surrounding the earlier returns of former exiles in the years immediately following Cyrus' conquest of Babylon and the accession of Darius I (ca. 539-515 B.C.E.); (2) the so-called Ezra Memoir, which consists of Ezra 7–10 and Ezra's prayer in Nehemiah 8; and (3) the Nehemiah Memoir, comprised of Neh. 1:1–7:4 and 11:1–13:31. One of the main purposes of the work is to assert the importance of political and religious leadership by highlighting the styles of Nehemiah the governor and Ezra the priest. Some interpreters suggest that the books intend to *contrast* the leadership styles of the two

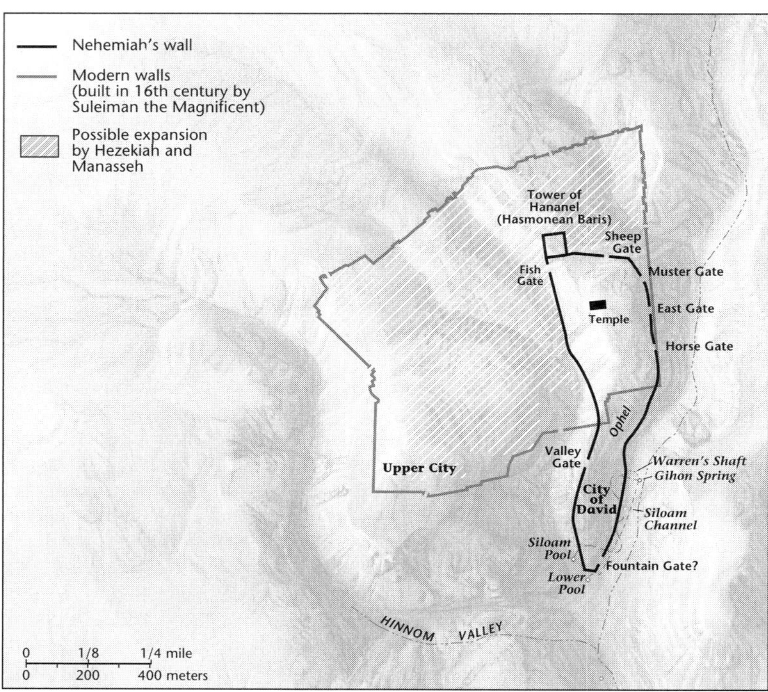

JERUSALEM IN THE POSTEXILIC PERIOD

figures, in favor of Ezra's religious leadership over Nehemiah's political leadership (see esp. Ezkenazi 1988). Noteworthy in this respect are Ezra's refusal of an armed Persian escort on religious grounds (Ezra 8:22), in contrast to Nehemiah's guard (Neh. 2:9); and the frequency with which the third-person narrator honors Ezra (7:6), in contrast to Nehemiah's frequent requests for God to "remember" his accomplishments (Neh. 5:19; 13:14, 22, etc.). The book of Ezra-Nehemiah certainly contributes to the ideal of dual leadership in the postexilic Judean community, as the book of Zechariah does in its portrayal of Zerubbabel the political leader and Jeshua the priest.

The Nehemiah Memoir

Most scholars think that the Nehemiah material is based on the historical experiences of a real person, whose eyewitness reports form the basis of a "Nehemiah Memoir." According to Blenkinsopp (1988), the book of Nehemiah consists of this putative eyewitness material (1:1–2:20; 3:33–7:5; 12:31-43; 13:4-31) combined with third-person narration (3:1-32; 11:1-2; 12:27-30, 44-47; 13:1-3) and supplemented with lists and genealogies (11:3–12:16).

The nature of the Nehemiah Memoir has been the subject of intense debate. The influential study of Kellerman (1967) compared the Nehemiah material to psalms of vindication (or "prayers of the accused") in which a person justifies his actions before God (e.g., Psalm 109), but Blenkinsopp (1988) has highlighted parallels in late Egyptian "votive texts addressed to a deity and deposited in a temple," such as those associated with an official named Udjahorresnet. The opening sequences of the Nehemiah Memoir, however, picture Nehemiah speaking intimately with the Persian emperor himself, suggesting parallels with the legendary stories of Daniel and Esther. Grabbe (1998) points out other texts (e.g., 2 Macc. 1:18–2:15) that represent Nehemiah accomplishing tasks that the Hebrew Bible assigns to Ezra, suggesting a diverse historical tradition for both figures and a good deal of variability in the textual tradition before the Hebrew and Aramaic texts were fixed in their final form.

Nehemiah the Governor

The precise nature of Nehemiah's political authority is also debated. If he was a governor, did he administer an ethnic enclave known as Yehud, with a status equal to other authorities mentioned in the book (e.g., Sanballat as governor of Samaria in Neh. 2:10)? It is clear that he would have required significant authority locally, and according to Neh. 2:9 he brought with him not only authorizing documentation but a contingent of Persian soldiers. Some scholars suggest that Nehemiah's wall building and military activity may reflect Persian interest in establishing a series of fortresses on the western front to deal with potential rebellions in Egypt and invasions of the Greeks (e.g., Hoglund 1992). Others, however, have raised serious questions about how strategically valuable to the Persians Jerusalem would have been, since it is situated in the hills of Judea; fortresses on the coast, outside of Nehemiah's area of authority, would arguably have been far more important (Briant 2002; Lipshits and Oeming 2006).

Based on widely varied evidence that includes jar impressions and seals as well as textual references, Eric and Carol Meyers (1993) have tried to reconstruct the series of governors over the area of Yehud as follows:

538	Sheshbazzar (Ezra 1:8; 5:14)
520-510?	Zerubbabel (Hag. 1:1, 14)
510-490?	Elnathan (seal impression)
490-470?	Yehoezer (jar impression)
470- ?	Ahzai (jar impression)
445-433	Nehemiah

After Nehemiah, the next governor indicated in the Elephantine Papyri is Bagavahya (Porten 1996, citing *TAD* A4.7 [dated 407 B.C.E.] = *CAP* 30). This is an Old Persian name and may suggest that Nehemiah and Sanballat's quarrels brought a Persian intervention and appointment, though Jews could certainly carry non-Hebrew names (e.g., Zerubbabel and Mordecai).

Nehemiah the Reformer

Nehemiah is presented as a political reformer who oversaw the repopulation of Jerusalem and the rebuilding of the city's infrastructure, particularly its outer wall. He is also portrayed as a social reformer who cancelled debts and saw to the care of the poor. And he is depicted as a nationalist who broke up foreign marriages when political power was at stake (Smith-Christopher 1994; Janzen 2002) and opposed local officials who were clearly jealous of his rising influence in the region surrounding Jerusalem. Thus, the Nehemiah story shares some of the same themes as the material in Ezra, including reforms conducted against local and even internal opposition as well as the generally bleak state of the community before these "heroes of the faith" arrived from the Diaspora. Given the many details it provides, Ezra-Nehemiah remains a significant source for knowledge of the Judean community in this rather obscure period of early Jewish history.

BIBLIOGRAPHY

R. ALBERTZ 2003, *Israel in Exile: The History and Literature of the Sixth Century B.C.E.*, Atlanta: Society of Biblical Literature. • J. BLENKINSOPP 1988, *Ezra-Nehemiah: A Commentary*, London: SCM. • P. BRIANT 2002, *From Cyrus to Alexander: A History of the Persian Empire*, Winona Lake, Ind.: Eisenbrauns. • T. ESKENAZI 1988, *In an Age of Prose: A Literary Approach to Ezra-Nehemiah*, Atlanta: Scholars Press. • L. GRABBE 1998, *Ezra-Nehemiah*, London: Routledge. • K. HOGLUND 1992, *Achaemenid Imperial Administration in Syria-Palestine and the Missions of Ezra and Nehemiah*, Atlanta: Scholars Press. • D. JANZEN 2002, *Witch-hunts, Purity and Social Boundaries: The Expulsion of the Foreign Women in Ezra 9–10*, Sheffield: Sheffield Academic Press. • S. JAPHET 1969, "The Supposed Common Authorship of Chronicles and Ezra-Nehemiah Investigated Anew," *VT* 18: 330-71. • O. LIPSHITS AND M. OEMING, EDS. 2006, *Judah and the Judeans in the Persian Period*, Winona Lake, Ind.: Eisenbrauns. • E. M. MEYERS AND C. L. MEYERS 1993, *Zechariah 9–14*, New York: Doubleday. • J. PAKKALA 2004, *Ezra the Scribe: The Development of Ezra 7–10 and Nehemia 8*, Berlin: de Gruyter. • B. PORTEN, ED. 1996, *The Elephantine Papyri in English*, Leiden: Brill. • D. SMITH-CHRISTOPHER 1994, "The Mixed Marriage Crisis in Ezra 9–10 and Nehemiah 13," in *Second Temple Studies*, ed. T. Eskenazi and K. Richards, Sheffield: Sheffield Academic Press, 243-65. • J. WATTS 2001, *Persia and Torah: The Theory of Imperial Authorization of the Pentateuch*, Atlanta: Society of Biblical Literature. • H. G. M. WILLIAMSON 1985, *Ezra, Nehemiah*, Waco, Tex.: Word. • J. L. WRIGHT 2004, *Rebuilding Identity: The Nehemiah-Memoir and Its Earliest Readers*, Berlin: de Gruyter.

See also: Ezra, Book of; Persian Period

DANIEL L. SMITH-CHRISTOPHER

Neusner, Jacob

Jacob Neusner (1932-) is a leading U.S. scholar whose work on rabbinic literature has revolutionized the study of classical Judaism and made the study of Judaism a central field within the modern, academic study of religion. Educated at Harvard University, the Jewish Theological Seminary, Oxford University, and Columbia University, Neusner has held teaching positions at Dartmouth College, Brown University, the University of South Florida, and Bard College. He is a member of the Institute of Advanced Study, Princeton, New Jersey, a life member of Clare Hall, Cambridge University, and has received numerous academic awards and honorary degrees. Neusner has written or edited over a thousand books on all aspects of ancient through modern Judaism, including textbooks on Judaism and world religions.

Neusner's earliest research followed a pattern common to the precritical study of rabbinic Judaism. He collected and assembled into logical sequence the talmudic stories about the life of the rabbinic sage Yohanan ben Zakkai as well as statements various rabbinic documents attribute to Yohanan (*A Life of Yohanan ben Zakkai*, 1962). He fleshed out and presented as "historical" the composite story that emerged. Neusner's break with such uncritical use of rabbinic sources came eight years later, when he noted the dramatic growth that occurred between earlier and later sources in both the quantity of materials about Yohanan and in the sorts of details that began to appear. This study resulted in a revision of the original biography (*Development of a Legend: Studies on the Traditions concerning Yohanan ben Zakkai*, 1970), in which Neusner showed that the "life" of Yohanan that emerged from the rabbinic literature was a legend, the product of centuries of literary accretions.

This recognition led to conclusions that became foundational to all subsequent study of classical Judaism. That rabbinic texts cannot be read as "history" is now a given. Equally important is Neusner's recognition of the significance of the boundaries of individual texts, that is, the understanding that each rabbinic document is a product of its own historical and geographic setting and authorship and must be interpreted as such. Each text, Neusner has proven, reveals a program of Judaism that responds to its own authors' needs and ideals. As a result of Neusner's work, the idea of a single, monolithic "rabbinic Judaism" has yielded to a conception of multiple "Judaisms," distinctive systems that responded to the situation of Jews living in different ages and locations.

Neusner saw that only with the ideals, values, and purposes expressed in individual documents in hand could researchers hope, later, to develop larger conclusions regarding rabbinic Judaism as an encompassing phenomenon. To reveal these distinctive programs, Neusner translated or retranslated all of the documents of rabbinic Judaism, which he evaluated anew as independent artifacts of their particular age and authorship. The work began with the Mishnah. Neusner revealed its traits of formal composition and social ideology and showed that what had been seen only as a compilation of arcane rules and legal debates revealed a program of religious and social reconstruction that responded to the destruction of the Second Temple and the failed Bar Kokhba Revolt.

Neusner additionally produced the first English translation of the Talmud of Israel as well as translations of the Talmud of Babylonia and the entire corpus of midrashic texts of the first eight centuries C.E. Even as he made these texts of Judaism available to the broader academy, his own exegesis and analysis established the distinctive focuses and sets of theological and social concerns that marked the rabbinic movement from its inception to its classical statement within the Babylonian Talmud.

Neusner's work in describing the systemic worldview of each rabbinic document made possible a second stage of his work. This is represented in his studies of the fundamental categories of rabbinic Judaism (e.g., Torah, merit, purity). In identifying and studying these categories, Neusner again moved beyond prior conceptualizations (e.g., those of G. F. Moore and E. E. Urbach), which examined Judaism through the prism of extrinsic categories, taken, for instance, from Christianity, thus obscuring Judaism's own native and distinctive characteristics and traits. Constructing approaches to the central ideas of Judaism across its documents has led to Neusner's most recent work, which describes the normative categories of rabbinic law and theology (e.g., *The Theological Grammar of the Oral Torah,* 1999).

This study has also enabled Neusner to compare Judaism with other religions, notably Christianity. His work in this area is most famously represented by his *A Rabbi Talks with Jesus* (1993), which has been translated into numerous European languages and which earned the praise of Pope Benedict XVI. Neusner sets out an imagined response of a first-century rabbi who hears Jesus' teaching, thus elaborating exactly those points on which first-century Jews and the earliest Christians would have agreed and disagreed. The result, developed in other studies of Judaism and Christianity, is to establish a coherent framework for dialogue between Jews and Christians, in which each side can take seriously the beliefs of the other and in which points of theological disagreement, rather than being ignored, become a focus of honest debate that clarifies each side's own distinctive theology.

Neusner depicts rabbinic Judaism as the product of Jews' reaction to what God demands of them in Torah. Evolving to meet the challenge of changing historical circumstances, Judaism reveals Jews' imagination in responding to what is often unimaginable. Neusner's conclusions regarding the nature and message of Judaism have shaped almost all contemporary understandings of that religion. Alongside this stands the impact of his critical methodology. Neusner has reshaped the entire enterprise of talmudic studies and given it a place within the critical academy. He has, at the same time, had a profound impact on the study of Judaism in the Hellenistic and Roman periods and of the New Testament. Scholars in these disciplines no longer may uncritically assert that beliefs and practices discussed only in the later talmudic literature were current among Jews of earlier times. In these ways, Jacob Neusner's work has significantly enhanced all contemporary study of Judaism in late antiquity.

BIBLIOGRAPHY

J. NEUSNER 1962, *A Life of Yohanan ben Zakkai,* Leiden: Brill. • J. NEUSNER 1965-1970, *A History of the Jews in Babylonia,* Leiden: Brill, 1965-1970. • J. NEUSNER 1970, *Development of a Legend: Studies on the Traditions concerning Yohanan Ben Zakkai,* Leiden: Brill. • J. NEUSNER 1971, *The Rabbinic Traditions about the Pharisees before 70,* 3 vols., Leiden: Brill. • J. NEUSNER 1983, *Judaism: The Evidence of the Mishnah,* Chicago: University of Chicago Press. • J. NEUSNER 1986, *Judaism: The Classical Statement.* • J. NEUSNER 1993, *A Rabbi Talks with Jesus: An Intermillennial, Interfaith Exchange,* New York: Doubleday. • J. NEUSNER 1999, *The Theological Grammar of the Oral Torah,* 3 vols., Binghamton: Dowling College Press. • J. NEUSNER, ED. 2005, *The Theological Dictionary of Rabbinic Judaism,* 3 vols., Lanham: University Press of America.

ALAN AVERY-PECK

New Jerusalem Text

The Aramaic *New Jerusalem* text is preserved in seven fragmentary manuscript copies from Qumran: 1Q32, 2Q24, 4Q554, 4Q554a, 4Q555, 5Q15, and 11Q18. Although all the copies date from the Roman era, the work was probably composed in the initial decades of the second century B.C.E.

The text describes, in precise, blueprint-like detail, the dimensions and structures of an enormous city, which, although unnamed (contrast Ezek. 48:35; Rev. 3:12; 21:2), can only be the New Jerusalem. The city is magnificent. Rectangular in shape, it is protected by high-towered walls dozens of kilometers long. Twelve massive gates pierce the walls, three to a wall; each gate is named after one of the tribes of Israel. Inside the walls are innumerable blocks of houses and rows of streets, arranged in a rigid orthogonal pattern. Broad boulevards cut through the city blocks at right angles, augmenting the sense of grandeur. Certain fragments, mostly from 11Q18, tell us that the city contains a New Temple and depict its implements, offerings, and rituals. Other fragments, from the 4Q copies, situate the city in its future sociopolitical context, when all its enemies have been humbled and the city is wealthy, strong, and at peace. The net effect is one of an immense, splendid New Jerusalem, brilliantly fashioned from marble and sapphire and adorned with fine gold, the center of the world.

The expectation for the New Jerusalem appears throughout the later prophetic books of the Hebrew Bible and the literature of early Judaism and Christianity. Its diverse examples permit multiple classifications, although a general distinction may be drawn between terrestrial cities and heavenly cities, and also between idealized and ideal ones. Ideal cities characteristically exhibit regular dimensions and colossal proportions. The most famous examples are those portrayed in Ezekiel 40–48 and Revelation 21–22, but the type appears elsewhere, including the *Reworked Pentateuch*

(4Q365a) and, as it applies to the New Temple, the *Temple Scroll.* Much has been made of the *New Jerusalem* text's apparent similarities with the *Temple Scroll,* but a close examination reveals little correspondence at any level, which suggests that they do not rely on a common source, and that one does not depend on the other. Although Ezekiel 40–48 is the principal antecedent of all subsequent illustrations of the ideal city in early Jewish literature, the Aramaic text was possibly also influenced by Hellenistic concepts of planned urban design. It is unlikely that the gridiron plan of the camp *(castrum)* of the Roman legions would have been a factor before the first century B.C.E.

The New Jerusalem of the Aramaic text neither descends from heaven, as it does in Revelation, nor is located in heaven. Rather, it exists on earth, and although its size is extraordinary, its interior structures are humanly proportioned: the city was intended to be used. Scholars have proposed various purposes for the city, including a mustering ground for the faithful during the final battle with the forces of evil, or a gathering place for pilgrims during the great festivals. Yet its civic design elements, the implicit utility and permanence of its structures, and the lavish use of precious stones and metals denote that the chief function of the text was urban. It is the embodiment of the perfect city of the future, the permanent dwelling place for the faithful people of God.

In terms of genre, the *New Jerusalem* text is likely an apocalypse. It discloses information via a third-person revelatory vision that is mediated by an otherworldly figure to the unnamed seer (not necessarily Ezekiel). The long walls, while not entirely without precedent in the ancient world, are an element of a suprahistorical perspective, as are the city's regimented design features, superlative splendor, and static, idealistic sociopolitical context. Its concern with the Temple and the central placement of the Gate of Levi in the east wall imply that the text was composed in priestly circles, while the homogeny of its houses might anticipate an egalitarian society. But this is not a sectarian document. It is composed in Aramaic, exhibits no distinctive sectarian ideas or terminology, and promulgates a pan-Israel view (indicated by the names of the gates and by the phrase "all Israel" at 11Q18 frg. 27 line 1). However, the eschatological horizon of the document was not too far removed from that of the Qumran sectarians, who, given the number of the surviving copies and their distribution among the Qumran caves, clearly valued this text.

BIBLIOGRAPHY

L. DITOMMASO 2005, *The Dead Sea New Jerusalem Text: Contents and Contexts,* Tübingen: Mohr-Siebeck. • F. GARCÍA MARTÍNEZ ET AL. 1998, *Qumran Cave 11.II: 11Q2-18, 11Q20-32,* DJD 23, Oxford: Oxford University Press, 305-55. • F. GARCÍA MARTÍNEZ 1999, "The Temple Scroll and the New Jerusalem," *The Dead Sea Scrolls after Fifty Years,* 2 vols., ed. P. W. Flint and J. C. VanderKam, Leiden: Brill, 2: 431-59. • É. PUECH 1995, "À propos de la Jérusalem nouvelle d'après les manuscrits de la mer Morte," *Semitica* 42/43: 87-102.

See also: Jerusalem, New

LORENZO DITOMMASO

New Year → Festivals and Holy Days

Nicolaus of Damascus

Nicolaus of Damascus was a highly educated, well-traveled, politically influential, and prolific author of the first century B.C.E. He is notable, among other things, for having been the court historian of Herod the Great and a major source for the historical writings of the Jewish historian Flavius Josephus.

Born around 64 B.C.E. to wealthy aristocratic parents of Damascus, a leading city in the Roman province of Syria with a thriving Greek populace and opportunity for Greek and then Roman culture, Nicolaus received a formal Greek education and in philosophy was a dedicated Peripatetic. Making his way to Rome, he served and became associate and friend of many of Rome's most influential citizens. During the period of the Triumvirate, he was a tutor for the children of Cleopatra and Antony, and became a close confidant of Augustus. According to Plutarch (*Moralia, Quaestionum Convivialum* 8.4.1) Augustus was so delighted with the type of delicious dates that Nicolaus would send him from Judea, especially Jericho, that he named that particular type *nicolai,* because they reminded him of his friend's sweetness and beautiful reddish cheeks.

By 14 B.C.E. Nicolaus had become an associate, counselor, and representative of Herod the Great, the Roman client king of Judea. Nicolaus traveled with Herod, and as Herod defended Jewish interests in his travels, such as in Ionia, Nicolaus, too, spoke on their behalf (Josephus, *Ant.* 16.27-30). Nicolaus' intimacy with Caesar Augustus aided Herod tremendously when Nicolaus interceded with the *princeps,* after Herod angered Augustus by his invasion of Arabia in 6 B.C.E. According to Josephus, Nicolaus was Herod's "most honored" friend (*J.W.* 2.21). Upon Herod's death in 4 B.C.E., Nicolaus argued on behalf of Herod's son Archelaus, who was named in Herod's will as successor. He likely spent the last years of his life in Rome.

Nicolaus wrote many works on a variety of subjects, including *Collections of Ethnic Customs,* tragedies and comedies, a panegyric biography of Augustus, philosophical works in the Aristotelian school, and an autobiography, one of the first known. In the study of early Judaism, he is most important for having written a biography of Herod the Great.

His magnum opus was a massive 144-book universal history, which now survives only in scattered fragments quoted by later authors. Beginning with mythology, it traced events down to the author's own time and may have been the longest history written in Greek (Wacholder 1962: 65). The first seven books, which are the best known, included a history of Assyria, Babylonia, and Media, pre–Trojan War Hellas, Lydia, and Arcadia. Books 123-44 dealt with the rise and reign of Herod the Great and with Herod's negotiations on behalf of the Jews in Asia Minor. Josephus took extracts from these books for his *Jewish Antiquities,* books 14-17.

Josephus refers to Nicolaus more than thirty times,

either as a historical figure or source. Nicolaus' history is widely thought to have been Josephus' major source for his *Jewish War* for the period between Antiochus IV Epiphanes and the kingship of Herod's son Archelaus in 4 B.C.E. Josephus also relied on Nicolaus for his *Jewish Antiquities*, though he criticizes him for being encomiastic toward Herod (*Ant.* 16.184-85).

Judging from Josephus' work, it is clear that Nicolaus referred to the Jews in various places in his massive history, in addition to books 123-24. In his understanding, Jews were part of Aramaic and Damascus history, since Abram, a Chaldean, was once a king there (*Ant.* 1.159) and David, "king of Judea," was attacked by a later king (*Ant.* 7.101-3). He also knew that they figured in Parthian, Hellenistic, and Roman campaigns and conquests. He refers to Moses, the "Jewish lawgiver," as the author of a book about "a man transported upon an ark" that parallels a story from Armenia (*Ant.* 1.95).

Nicolaus was clearly using Jewish sources and integrating them with others for his own universal history. For Jewish history of the first century B.C.E., it is hard to overestimate, but also difficult to grasp, the extent of the historical and literary importance of this non-Jewish international figure.

BIBLIOGRAPHY
E. SCHÜRER 1986, *The History of the Jewish People in the Age of Jesus Christ*, vol. 1, rev. and ed. G. Vermes et al., Edinburgh: Clark, 28-32.• M. STERN 1976, *Greek and Latin Authors on Jews and Judaism*, vol. 1, Jerusalem: Israel Academy of Sciences and Humanities, 227-60. • B. Z. WACHOLDER 1962, *Nicolaus of Damascus*, Los Angeles: University of California Press.

JAMES E. BOWLEY

Noah

The Bible calls Noah "a righteous man, blameless in his generation" (Gen. 6:9), although not a word is mentioned to demonstrate his righteousness. For this and other reasons, Noah became an object of much speculation during the Second Temple period. This was especially true for early Jews who felt that they, like Noah, lived amid an utterly wicked generation in which they alone found favor in the sight of the Lord. As a result, biblical stories about the tenth patriarch often invited creative interpretations. Many of these can be linked to the thorny etymology of Noah's name, which was alternately taken to mean "comfort," "salvation," "righteousness," and "remainder."

Judean Sources

Jubilees

Dating from the early to mid-second century B.C.E., the book of *Jubilees* adds a great deal of information to what we learn of Noah in Genesis. Details in the biblical text account for some of the supplementary material, such as the name of Noah's wife (4:33) and daughters-in-law (7:13-17), the years of his sons' births (4:33), his interfamilial marriage (4:33; cf. 1QapGen 6:7-10; Tob. 4:12), the sacrifices he offered upon leaving the ark (6:3), his harvesting his vineyard (7:3-6), the uttering of solemn oaths (6:10; 7:14), the later Israelite festivals and intercalary days grounded in specific Noachic events (6:15-31), and the name of the mountain (Lubar) upon which the ark alighted (5:28; 7:1; cf. 1QapGen 12:14; 4Q244 8). Many of these additions fit the tendencies of the author, who integrated genealogical, calendrical, and exegetical traditions. Upon Noah's drunken exposure and curse of Canaan (7:7-12), his three sons spread out and built cities around Mt. Lubar, Shem alone remaining near his father on its eastern side. The placement of each son's city foreshadows the portion of the earth that he will later be allotted by Noah in *Jubilees* 8–9. Noah's role as founder of cities is also present in 1QapGen 12:8 and 4Q244 8.

Another development is Noah's hortatory teaching, aimed toward his sons and their continued favor before God (7:20-39). In this first-person discourse, Noah implores them not to fall into the sins that first brought the flood, confessing that he already spots the beginnings of such base conduct. Especially important are the charges to refrain from murder, eating blood, and transgressing certain agricultural laws. Noah concludes by appealing to his great-grandfather Enoch, who originally received these commands and handed them down by way of Methuselah and Lamech.

A significant role of Noah in *Jubilees* is his oversight of the earth's allotment between his sons and grandsons (8:11–9:15). Following notification that his sons had divided the earth "in a bad way," Noah redivides the earth with the aid of a book, thereby adding an aura of divine sanction to the task. The detailed geographic description is based on concurrent Hellenistic notions of the inhabited earth *(oikoumenē)*, with Asia falling to Shem, Libya (modern Africa) to Ham, and Europe to Japheth. In contrast to Genesis 10, Noah's grandson Arpachshad receives the entire Levant. Therefore, according to *Jubilees* it is only because Canaan illegally settled in an allotment not originally granted him that this region is called "the land of Canaan" elsewhere in the Torah. From a broader perspective, Noah's activity as apportioner of the earth supplies a mandate for later Jewish claims on the land of Israel — an apparent concern for the author.

The Noah section ends with an apotropaic prayer aimed against a hoard of demons that survived the flood and were afflicting Noah's grandchildren (10:1-7). Noah's plea is 90 percent successful, since Mastema, the leader of spirits, persuades the Lord to leave one-tenth of them unbound and active. In order to counteract the effect of the remaining demons, however, God commands the angels to reveal all the secrets of herbal medicine to Noah, which he in turn records in a book. Books are again associated with Noah (and Enoch) in *Jub.* 21:10, where Abraham tells Isaac that by them he learned of an injunction against eating three-day-old meat. Alongside other references to "books" of Noah in the *Genesis Apocryphon*, *1 Enoch*, a single manuscript of the *Testament of Levi*, and later rabbinic works, some have argued that an independent *Book of Noah* lies behind much of the early Jewish material concerning Noah.

Many of the above elements are best understood as *Jubilees'* attempt to portray Noah as a *de facto* priest. He is an exceedingly righteous individual who preserved all that was right about the antediluvian era and stood against all that was wrong. This he accomplished by adhering perfectly to correct ancestral custom and ritual, and by preserving divinely revealed wisdom through teaching and writing. In *Jubilees* such wisdom is especially concerned with issues of calendar, sacrifice, and the treatment of blood.

Genesis Apocryphon (1QapGen)

Although fragmentary, the *Genesis Apocryphon* preserves the most extensive nonbiblical portrait of Noah from the Second Temple period. Dating from the first to second centuries B.C.E., the Aramaic text contains a great deal of unique information. Near the beginning of what remains of the scroll, we find a story about Noah's miraculous birth. The plot revolves around Noah's father Lamech, who, based on the child's spectacular appearance, suspects that Noah may be the fruit of an illicit union between his wife, Batenosh, and an angelic Watcher. In response, Lamech's father Methuselah runs to Enoch, who reassures him that Noah is indeed Lamech's son and that his countenance merely affirms his chosen status to render judgment on impiety and plant a new, righteous generation following the flood. This story may represent a form of the lost *Apocalypse of Lamech* mentioned in an ancient list of pseudepigraphic works. It has a shorter parallel in *1 Enoch* 106–7.

What follows is a long, first-person account of Noah headed by the rubric "the book of the words of Noah" (5:29). Noah begins by describing how he "became a man," was married, and had children, after which he received apocalyptic dream visions containing divine "secrets." These pertain to such matters as the upcoming flood and the divine calendrical cycle. A final vision in cols. 13-15 is probably meant to coincide with Noah's drunken sleep in Gen. 9:20-24, and cryptically relates portions of world history to Noah through a succession of trees. The interaction of the offshoots representing Noah's sons suggests that part of the dream deals with a future conflict destined to take place between the descendants of Shem and Ham.

Among the last tasks of Noah is his direction of the earth's division among his sons and grandsons. The account is similar to that in *Jubilees* 8–9, although there are numerous differences in order and detail. Based on the allotment of Arpachshad, it appears that the author, like *Jubilees,* wished to argue that the land of Israel originally belonged to the descendants of Shem, not Ham.

The *Genesis Apocryphon*'s view of Noah is utterly positive. Noah is portrayed as the visionary seer *par excellence* who is blameless and chosen by God from birth to reestablish righteousness on the earth. His role in dividing the earth is more heavily emphasized than in *Jubilees.* There may also be a subversion of Noah's drunken exposure, turning it instead into a locus of divine revelation.

1 Enoch

A number of fragments dealing with Noah are embedded within the book of *1 Enoch,* although the presence of pro-Enoch editing at times makes Noachic material difficult to discern. While this same factor makes dating difficult, a date before the Common Era is probable for all passages, with some quite possibly originating from the second or third centuries B.C.E.

Chapters 6–11 are part of the *Book of the Watchers* and focus largely on the grievous transgressions of the angelic "Watchers" (cf. Gen. 6:1-2). Responding to a plea for justice by the four archangels, the Lord proclaims judgment on the Watchers and assigns each angel a specialized task. The first archangel, Sariel, is commissioned to visit Noah and tell him to hide from the coming catastrophe (10:1-3). He is also instructed to reveal to Noah what is about to happen, and how to preserve himself. Finally, he is to make known that from Noah a "plant will be planted," the seed of which will endure forever. The equation of Noah or his sons with a plant is repeated often in Judean sources (e.g., *1 Enoch* 84:6; 1QapGen 6:1; *Jub.* 7:34).

1 Enoch 65–69 collect a group of Noachic traditions around a traumatic visit of Noah to his great-grandfather Enoch at the ends of the earth. Enoch reveals to Noah the extreme corruption of humanity, impending destruction, the fate and names of the sinful angels, and Noah's chosen and blameless status. The section contains a number of distinctive ideas, such as the ark being constructed by angels. *1 Enoch* 68:1 relates that the explanation of "all the secrets" was passed from Enoch to Noah in a book.

In the *Animal Apocalypse* (*1 Enoch* 85–90) Noah is portrayed as a white bull (i.e., elect descendant of Adam) who unexpectedly "became a man." This may refer to a turning point in Noah's life (cf. 1QapGen 6:6) and typically denotes elevation to angelic status in this part of *1 Enoch* (87:2-3; 90:17-21). If such is the case here, we find a startlingly high view of Noah.

1 Enoch 106–7 contains a version of the miraculous birth of Noah reminiscent of the early columns of the *Genesis Apocryphon.* Noah is described as being born with white skin and hair, luminous eyes, and the ability to stand up and speak. Enoch goes on to highlight Noah's special role and blameless status, as well as revealing to Methuselah what the child's name is to be. This portion of *1 Enoch* is attested at Qumran in 4Q204.

1 Enoch depicts Noah as an ultra-righteous harbinger of divine judgment on the Watchers and humanity. From birth he is preordained for survival in order to be "planted" on the renewed earth, and through him the divine secrets of the prediluvian patriarchs, primarily Enoch, are preserved.

Other Dead Sea Scrolls

A few other works among the Dead Sea Scrolls deal with Noah. 1QNoah (1Q19) recounts the impending judgment of God on the earth and Noah's miraculous birth, noting that his appearance was "like the glorious ones" (i.e., angels) and that his eyes lit up the house in which he was born. 4Q534-536 have also been identified as texts referring to Noah's birth, although this identification remains uncertain. If Noah is the subject, these Aramaic fragments represent a more extensive meditation on his birth and physical traits than the stories in the *Genesis Apocryphon* and *1 Enoch.* 4Q252 and 4Q254 provide interpretations of Noah's curse of Canaan, explaining why he was cursed for Ham's wrongdoing. Indeed, this exegetical crux garnered attention throughout the period (e.g., *Jubilees,* 1QapGen, Josephus, and Philo). A secondary reference to Noah is found in 4QTanḥumim (4Q176), which quotes Isa. 54:8-9, "As in (the) days of Noah will this be for me; as [I swore] that the waters of Noah would not flood the earth, so have I sworn not to become angry with you. . . ." Unfortunately, the interpretation of this verse is not fully preserved.

It is sometimes suggested that the various Noachic fragments in the Pseudepigrapha and Dead Sea Scrolls derive from a lost *Book of Noah* (see, e.g., García Martínez, 1992), but this remains hypothetical.

Diaspora Sources

Sibylline Oracles

Some of the earliest *Sibylline Oracles,* written in the regions of Phrygia and Alexandria between the third century B.C.E. and first century C.E., betray an intense interest in the figure of Noah. This attention appears to stem from the strong typological parallel that the sibyl senses between her own plight and that of the patriarch, whom she identifies as her father-in-law in *Sib. Or.* 3.823-29 and 1.288-90.

Sib. Or. 3.110-55 describes the division of the earth between the Greek mythical figures Cronos, Titan, and Iapetus, after which their father imposes oaths on them to stay within their shares. Upon their father's death, however, the sons transgress their oaths, and Cronos and Titan begin to war with each other. This is a transparent parallel to the tradition of the earth's division in *Genesis Apocryphon* 16–17 and *Jubilees* 8–9, in which Cronos, Titan, Iapetus, and their father equate to Shem, Ham, Japheth, and Noah respectively. The sibyl's use of this tradition reflects a fascinating combination of Hesiod's *Theogony* and a Jewish tradition otherwise known only from Palestinian sources.

Sib. Or. 1.125-290 is a treatment of Noah's activities and the flood. In the opening section Noah is bidden by God to preach repentance to the people of the earth in hopes that they might be spared. This appears to be the earliest attestation of the "preacher of repentance" motif, which becomes standard in subsequent Jewish and Christian portrayals of Noah (e.g., 2 Pet. 2:5; *Gen. Rab.* 30:7; *1 Clem.* 7:6; *Sepher ha-Yashar* 5:7-10). Upon his proclamation the people reproach Noah as demented, a plight with which the third sibyl empathizes (3.815-18). Following the flood section, which diverges in several respects from the biblical narrative and follows instead parallel Babylonian accounts, Noah is emphasized as the righteous founder of a golden and excellent generation.

Philo of Alexandria

Philo utilizes Noah primarily as a point of departure for his Hellenized, allegorical interpretations of Genesis. In his *Quaestiones et Solutiones in Genesin,* Philo draws the general from the specific by using many of the details associated with Noah to expound upright conduct or universal principles. In general, references to Noah's righteous character are cast according to Philo's deeply Hellenized ideal of the "virtuous man," who employs the laws of philosophy liberally. Other notable aspects of the *Quaestiones* are the equation of Noah's name with the word "righteous(ness)" or "justice," and secondarily with "rest" (*QG* 1.87; 2.45; cf. Gen. 5:29), the opinion that Noah and his family practiced abstinence while on the ark (*QG* 2.49), a description of Noah as the second Adam (*QG* 2.56, 66), and a defense of Noah's drunkenness as a type of becoming the virtuous, wise man (*QG* 2:68).

A long succession of Philo's so-called allegorical treatises center specifically on Noah: *De Gigantibus/Quod Deus Immutabilis Sit, De Agricultura/De Plantatione,* and *De Ebrietate/De Sobrietate.* These discourses expand significantly on allegorical themes already present in the *Quaestiones,* but add little regarding the "literal" view on Noah's character and activities. The most extensive treatments are in *De Gigantibus/Quod Deus,* in which Philo betrays his primary concern over Noah's ontological relationship to the rest of humanity. One novel detail is Philo's explanation of why Noah fathered only sons (*Gigantibus* 1).

The few mentions of Noah in Philo's later *Expositions of the Law* are in *De Abrahamo* 27 and 31–39, and *De Praemiis et Poenis* 23. In the former, Philo anticipates subsequent rabbinic debate by suggesting that the phrase "in his generation" (Gen. 7:1) indicates that Noah was not good absolutely, but only in comparison with the people of his time (32–33). The latter equates Noah with the Greek flood-hero Deucalion.

Josephus

In his *Jewish Antiquities* 1.72-108 Josephus tells his own version of the earth's moral decay, Noah's contrasting righteousness, and the related deluge. Like the *Sibylline Oracles,* he includes a number of details garnered from Babylonian and other flood stories, which he acknowledges as independent witnesses to people and events in the Bible. Josephus echoes the first sibyl's depiction of Noah as one who unsuccessfully urged his compatriots to amend their ways (*Ant.* 1.74), after which he fled the country. As in Philo, Josephus casts Noah's righteousness in terms of Greco-Roman ideas of "virtue."

The chronologies of the patriarchal generations and flood are emphasized by Josephus and follow the LXX rather than the MT. After the flood, Noah's sacrifices are presented as a reaction to his fear that a second deluge would again destroy the created order (*Ant.* 1.96-98). This unique explanation is apparently intended to anticipate God's covenant of the bow in Gen. 9:15, which includes a promise never again to send such a deluge.

Summary

Judean sources display interest in some aspects of Noah's life and character not present in more Hellenized accounts. These include his birth and physical traits, apocalyptic visions containing divine secrets, books given to or written by him, his role as divider of the earth, and his prominent role in the judgment of wickedness and reestablishment of righteousness. It is worth noting that the majority of these sources were originally written in Aramaic. In contrast, there are a number of motifs that arise only in texts originating outside Judea. These include Noah's role as preacher of repentance, his explicit association with related Babylonian and Greek myths, and his construal as the Hellenistic "virtuous man." A general concern with biblical chronology permeates a number of the works from both the land of Israel and the Diaspora. Besides the extended treatments of Noah listed above, he appears in a number of patriarchal lists (e.g., Tob. 4:12; Sir. 44:17-18; 4Q508; 5Q13; cf. Heb. 11:7), where his righteousness and receipt of the Lord's covenant (Gen. 9:8-17) are often emphasized.

Bibliography

M. Bernstein 1999, "Noah and the Flood at Qumran," in *The Provo International Conference on the Dead Sea Scrolls,* ed. D. W. Parry and E. C. Ulrich, Leiden: Brill, 199-231. • F. García Martínez 1992, "4QMess Ar and the Book of Noah," in idem, *Qumran and Apocalyptic,* Leiden: Brill, 1-44. • G. W. E. Nickelsburg 2003, "Patriarchs Who Worry about Their Wives: A Haggadic Tendency in the Genesis Apocryphon," in *George Nickelsburg in Perspective,* ed. J. Neusner and A. J. Avery-Peck, Leiden: Brill, 177-99. • D. Peters 2006, "Noah in the Dead Sea Scrolls," Dissertation, University of Manchester. • M. E. Stone 2006, "The Book(s) Attributed to Noah," *DSD* 13: 4-23. • J. C. VanderKam 1980, "The Righteousness of Noah," in *Ideal Figures in Ancient Judaism,* ed. J. J. Collins and G. W. E. Nickelsburg, Chico, Calif.: Scholars Press, 13-32. • J. C. VanderKam 1992, "The Birth of Noah," in *Intertestamental Essays in Honour of Józef Tadeusz Milik,* ed. Z. J. Kapera, Kraków: Enigma, 213-31. • C. Westermann 1984, *Genesis 1–11,* Minneapolis: Augsburg, 478-530.

See also: Flood

Daniel A. Machiela

Novels

The somewhat controversial term "novel" is widely used to refer to the genre of a number of Jewish (as well as classical and Christian) texts that include apparently deliberate fictional elements. Some scholars prefer to use the terms "romance" or "fiction" with virtually the same meaning. The early Jewish texts most often referred to as novels are Esther (both Hebrew and Greek), Daniel (both Hebrew and Greek), Judith, Tobit, and, above all, *Joseph and Aseneth.* Other texts which contain apparently fictional elements, but are more difficult to classify, include the *Letter of Aristeas,* 2 Maccabees, 3 Maccabees, the fragments of Artapanus, certain narratives contained within Josephus' *Jewish Antiquities* (notably the "Tobiad Romance," the tales of Alexander's visit to Jerusalem, and the story of the Royal Family of Adiabene), and the *Testament of Abraham.* Due to the fluidity and uncertainty of the genre, this is by no means an exhaustive list.

The term "novel" has gained considerable currency in Second Temple scholarship as a result of the publication of the most complete study to date, *The Jewish Novel in the Ancient World* (Wills 1995), and also through the research and collaboration of scholars in the Ancient Fiction and Early Christian and Jewish Narrative Group of the Society for Biblical Literature. The definition of the word "novel," the use of that word and other related terms such as "novelistic," "fiction," and "romance," and the problem of classifying texts under this genre continue to be debated by scholars, but there is a broad consensus that the texts mentioned above share many common features and can profitably be considered as a group, even though they are far from being generically identical to each other.

Classical Context: Greek and Roman Fictions

The problem of terminology has been complicated by the fact that discussion of the genre of the ancient novel is somewhat more advanced in the area of classical studies, but in that field the language used tends to be slightly different from that used in Second Temple scholarship. Many (though not all) classical scholars restrict the use of the term "novel" to a canon of five sentimental Greek novels and two satirical Latin novels, and refer to all other texts containing fictional elements as "fictions" (e.g., Reardon 1989; Stephens and Winkler 1995). In the oft-quoted words of J. R. Morgan (1993), "Whereas all novels are fiction, not all fictions are novels." In classical scholarship, the designation "novel" is generally rejected when referring to texts, such as the *Alexander Romance* and Lucian's *True Stories,* that contain fictional elements but do not closely resemble the canonical novels. In Second Temple scholarship, by contrast, the term "novel" is much more freely used, although none of the Jewish texts (except perhaps *Joseph and Aseneth*) can be said closely to resemble either the Greek sentimental or the Latin satirical novel. For this reason the term "Jewish fiction" is preferable to the term "Jewish novel," but in this article the terms "fiction" and "novel" will be used interchangeably unless otherwise indicated.

The Greek novel canon comprises five major surviving texts: Chariton's *Callirhoe,* Xenophon of Ephesus' *Ephesiaca,* Achilles Tatius' *Leucippe and Clitophon,* Longus' *Daphnis and Chloe,* and Heliodorus' *Ethiopica.* All are of the type known as the sentimental or ideal romance, centering on the adventures and ultimately the happy reunion of a beautiful young couple madly in love with each other. This appears to have been the predominant but not the only type written in Greek; some Greek fragments, if they had been fully preserved, would almost certainly be classified with the sentimental romances (e.g., the *Ninus Romance*), but others appear to have been satirical and ribald in nature, much more like the surviving Latin examples (e.g., Iamblichus' *Babyloniaca*). The Greek novels and fragments have been dated to a range between 100 B.C.E. and 500 C.E., making them for the most part later than the Jewish fictions, which range from 400 B.C.E. to 100 C.E. The only Jewish novel that closely resembles the pattern of the sentimental romance, with its focus on a young couple in love, is *Joseph and Aseneth,* but it seems more concerned about Aseneth's conversion than the couple's love affair. Other Jewish texts have notable elements that resemble the sentimental novels but do not follow the same plot line.

The Latin canon comprises two texts surviving in whole or in part: Petronius' *Satyricon* (mid-first century C.E.) and Apuleius' *Metamorphoses,* more popularly known as the *Golden Ass* (mid-second century C.E.). The Latin novels appear to have been inspired by the Greek tradition, but the surviving examples are more mocking than sentimental, drawing heavily on the native Latin tradition of satire *(satura)* to poke fun at the clichés of the sentimental romance. Scatological and sexual humor is rife. There is little trace in any of the Jewish novels of the ribald, satirical type of fiction, although it has been argued that some (Esther, Daniel) have a mildly satirical attitude toward Persian rule. If so, the satire in Jewish fictions is more likely drawn from native Jewish traditions that maintain a healthy skepticism toward the wielders of secular power than from Latin or Greek satirical models.

There are a number of other Greek and Latin fictional texts that are harder to classify. Oft-cited examples are Xenophon's *Cyropedia* (a heavily fictionalized biography of the Persian king Cyrus the Great), the *Alexander Romance* (loosely based on the career of Alexander the Great, but including such details as the fathering of Alexander by the last Egyptian pharaoh and Alexander's journey to the bottom of the sea), and Lucian's *True Stories,* which purports to give a serious account of the author's journey to (among other places) the moon and the belly of a whale. Although such texts do not follow the pattern of the canonical Greek or Roman novels, it seems clear that their authors intended them to be read as fiction, at least in part. Like many such classical fictions, most of the Jewish novels do not follow the plot line of the typical sentimental novel, but they do walk a fine line between the categories of history and fiction. It is characteristically difficult, with the Jewish fictions more so than the classical, to understand where the author intended the line between fiction and history to be drawn, how the texts were meant to be understood by the audience, and how they were in fact understood by successive generations.

History and Fiction

The problem of drawing a line between history and fiction is at the heart of much of the unresolved debate over the genre of these texts. By definition, the term "fiction" implies that (a) the author has chosen to produce a narrative that, in some part at least, does not correspond to reality as he understands it to be, and that (b) the author expects at least some part of his audience to perceive the same gap between the narrative and reality. In the case of the Jewish novels, all deal to some extent with the real or imagined past. If (a) does not apply, the author may be delusional or mistaken (i.e., a bad historian), but he is not writing fiction. If (a) applies, but (b) does not, the author is engaging in deliberate fraud (an accusation that has been leveled against the *Letter of Aristeas* in particular). Because every Jewish text that has been identified as a novel contains a significant element of historical narrative that, even by ancient reckoning, is blatantly at variance with historical reality, the authors of these texts have in fact in the past often been charged with being careless historians, or perpetrators of fraud, or both. The trend in modern scholarship, by contrast, is to assume that the authors of such texts were intentionally creating narratives that were in part fictional, and that they expected some part of the audience to share that understanding. (This does not exclude the possibility that a significant portion of the intended audience was naive enough to read fiction as history, or the possibility that the audience's reception of a text may have changed over time, with a text that was originally intended to be fictional coming to be read as history. Judging from Josephus' *Antiquities,* the latter appears to have occurred in the case of the *Letter of Aristeas,* and possibly in the case of Daniel and Esther as well.) However, the difficulty in arriving at any secure conclusion about ancient authorial intent and ancient reader response is great, and it is to be expected that scholars will continue to draw radically different conclusions, both about this issue in general and the historicity and purpose of specific texts in particular. Perhaps the most that can be said without controversy is that although every Jewish "novel" deals with the past, all present very serious problems of interpretation if read as straightforward historical narratives, and the modern tendency is to treat them instead as narratives about an imagined or idealized past.

Novelistic Elements

While the question of whether a particular text was intended to be read as historical or fictional is of central importance, efforts have also been made to define the genre of the Jewish novel descriptively by identifying one or more points of resemblance between certain Jewish texts and the novels and fictions found in the classical tradition.

Certainly, when similarities of form are sufficiently numerous to virtually guarantee that a given author was attempting to make his work conform to a recognized pattern, this approach to defining genre can be fruitful. In the case of the Greek ideal/sentimental novel, it appears that precisely this was occurring. The authors of each of the canonical Greek novels were clearly aware of conforming to a pattern, although each experimented with the genre in their own way (e.g., only Longus combines the genre of the sentimental novel with the genre of the pastoral idyll). With the exception of *Joseph and Aseneth,* which does appear to conform to the expectations of the genre of the sentimental novel, it is much more difficult to argue the case for the genre of the Jewish novels along these lines. The generic differences between (say) Daniel, Judith, Esther, 3 Maccabees, the *Letter of Aristeas,* and the narratives contained within Josephus' *Antiquities* are greater than the similarities, and it could reasonably be argued that each of the Jewish "novels" is in fact *sui generis,* not easily classifiable under any recognized genre. Most of the classical fictions, as opposed to the canonical Greek and Roman novels, are likewise *sui generis.*

If, however, one grants that it is not reasonable to expect genre uniformity from the Jewish fictions, it can profitably be observed that a number of individual characteristics reminiscent of the Greek novel do occur in Hellenistic Jewish texts with notable frequency. These are often described as "novelistic" elements.

Novelistic elements have never been definitively enumerated, but among those commonly cited are:

Popular Appeal

Ancient fictions circulated widely, and may have appealed more to the broader population than to the elite. It is not uncommon to find multiple manuscript variants (e.g., *Joseph and Aseneth*), or evidence of the redaction of previous oral and/or written traditions into the surviving texts (e.g., Daniel and Esther, among others). Some may have been read aloud in a festival or other popular setting, as Esther certainly was, and likely 3 Maccabees as well. Folklore may be a significant element, as especially in the case of Tobit.

Entertainment Value

To speak of entertainment value does not necessarily imply that such works were written exclusively to entertain. A number of serious purposes have been identified for particular texts, including concerns about proselytism, advocacy of a particular model of life in the Diaspora, valorization of the Greek translation of the Hebrew Bible, and castigation of apostasy, to name only a few. However, it is fair to say that amusing, fantastic, exotic, racy, or exciting elements are generally emphasized to increase the work's popular appeal.

Narrative Pattern

Although most of the Jewish fictions do not follow the typical pattern of the young couple in love, separated and tested by fate before being reunited, the narrative typically does follow the pattern of a life-or-death crisis culminating in a happy ending. The protagonist(s) may be a young couple *(Joseph and Aseneth),* an individual hero (Daniel, Tobit), a heroine (Esther, Judith), or an entire people (2 and 3 Maccabees).

Public Spectacle

At some point in the narrative, the protagonists are exposed to the intense interest of the public eye. Public trials and public (near) executions are common. There is great popular interest in the fate of the protagonist(s) and the outcome of the event, whether rejoicing or grieving over the prospect.

Historical and Geographical Inaccuracies

As noted above, Jewish novels are in part identified and defined by the extent to which they depart from historical reality, *as that reality was understood by the authors and their intended audience.* Some errors may have been unintentional, and many may have gone unnoticed by naive readers, but most readers could reasonably be expected to know that Nebuchadnezzar was Babylonian, not Assyrian, and did not rule *after* the destruction of the First Temple and the return of the Jews from exile (Judith); that Darius was a Persian, not a Mede, and that the Medes never ruled over Babylon (Daniel); or that the Persian Empire did not have hundreds of satrapies (it had about twenty), nor would a Persian king have been permitted to marry a Jewish queen (Esther). Such distortions were therefore presumably intentional and purposeful.

Citation of Documents and Evidence

Carelessness about historical detail is often curiously combined with intense concern for "proving" the verisimilitude of the account, by citing names, dates, facts, and especially verbatim documents. The documents generally appear to have been forged (e.g., the letters in Greek Esther and 3 Maccabees), with an apparent lack of concern for the reader's ability to detect the forgery. It was more important that the story *seem* to be verifiably true than that it actually *be* true and verifiable as such.

Characterization and Psychology

In comparison with modern novels, characterization and psychological development in ancient novels were relatively crude, but ancient fictions in general do show an unusual degree of interest in the interior life and motivation of characters, particularly the female characters. Prayers, laments, and interior monologues are common.

Emphasis on Female Characters

Female characters often assume a leading role (Esther, Judith, Aseneth), and priority is given to their concerns, such as marriage, family, and sexuality. This is paralleled in the Greek sentimental novel, where heroines take priority, while heroes tend to be colorless and passive.

Since no definitive list of novelistic elements has ever been compiled, this must be considered a partial list. Moreover, a significant problem with attempting to categorize the genre in this way is that while all of these elements parallel features of the Greek sentimental novel, and all appear to some degree in one or another of the Jewish fictions, not all Jewish "novels" carry all of these characteristics. A definitive study of the Jewish "novel" genre, to correspond with the ground-breaking work done on the definition of the genre apocalypse, has yet to be done (cf. Collins, ed. 1979). While the study of such Jewish texts as a group has proved fruitful in many ways, it is not yet clear what the final conclusion of a definitive study of the genre would be, or whether the genre is even capable of being definitively studied in the same way that apocalypses have been.

Origin of the Jewish Novels

The origin of the ancient novel has long been debated in the area of classical studies, with few conclusive results. An early view of the novel as a type of narrative which "evolved" from sensational historiography into prose fiction, or as a pastiche of borrowings from Hellenistic poetry and travel narratives, has now been discarded in favor of B. E. Perry's insistence upon the importance of conscious authorial intent. In his oft-quoted words: "The first romance was deliberately planned and written by an individual author, its inventor. He conceived it on a Tuesday afternoon in July, or some other day or month of the year" (Perry 1967: 175). Although the origin of the ancient novel remains an intriguing question, the present tendency in classical scholarship is to favor research into the nature and purpose of surviving texts over speculation about what might have preceded them.

The origins of the "Jewish novel," by contrast, have barely been explored. Because the parallels between the Greek sentimental novels and the Jewish fictions are particularly obvious in Jewish texts in Greek (Greek Esther, for instance, is noticeably more novelistic than Hebrew Esther), the usual assumption among scholars of Second Temple literature has been that novelistic elements in Jewish texts are a direct result of Greek influence. This may be a misconception, however. The earliest surviving Greek sentimental novel fragments are dated no earlier than 100 B.C.E., while a number of Jewish fictions in Greek are at least that early and may be earlier (e.g., the *Letter of Aristeas,* often dated to the mid-second century B.C.E.). The Hebrew versions of Daniel and Esther, already identified by Wills as "novels," are certainly earlier than 100 B.C.E.; Hebrew Esther may go back to the late Persian period. While it is certainly true that the mingling of Greek and Jewish cultural influences in the Hellenistic period was an important influence on the development of later Hellenistic-Jewish fictions, equal consideration ought to be given to the possibility of earlier influences dating back into the postexilic period.

Later Developments

Mention should be made of another important category of ancient fictions that lies largely beyond the scope of this article, that of Christian fictions such as the *Acts of Paul and Thecla* and the *Pseudo-Clementine Recognitions* (among many others). Although later in date than most Jewish fictions (excluding the canonical book of Acts itself, analyzed by Pervo 1987 as a novelistic composition), most Christian fictions are dated to the third century C.E. or later, and most of them are in many ways more similar to Jewish fictions than either are to the classical novels to which they are often compared. As with the Jewish fictions, there is a strong tendency in Christian fictions to promote a particular social or religious ideal, and it is difficult to draw a clear line between history and fiction.

The influence of the early Jewish novel upon later Jewish tradition is difficult to trace. Since the bulk of the Jewish novels were composed in or translated into and circulated primarily in Greek, the Greek versions have had more influence upon Christian than on rabbinic Jewish tradition, by way of the Septuagint and the translation of the Septuagint into the Latin Vulgate. Some texts, such as 3 Maccabees, have left no trace of later influence in Jewish tradition at all. Daniel and Esther influenced Jewish tradition only through the transmission of the Hebrew versions, which lack some of the later novelistic enhancements (e.g., the letters in Greek Esther, the tale of Susanna in Daniel). Others have left traces in Jewish tradition only in the form of variant narratives. The *Letter of Aristeas* was last cited in Jewish tradition by Josephus, but other tales of the miraculous translation of the Hebrew Bible into Greek are told by the rabbis; no reference is found to *Joseph and Aseneth,* but there is an alternate account of Aseneth's parentage in the midrash (which seeks to prove that Aseneth was not an Egyptian princess, but the product of Dinah's rape and thus a Hebrew maiden). How these variant narratives are related to the surviving Greek texts remains an open question; they may represent the continuation and ongoing evolution of purely oral traditions rather than any line of textual influence. It is also possible that some novelistic elements or narrative techniques continued to operate in rabbinic midrash in a more general way, but very little research has been done along these lines, making this a promising area for future research.

Bibliography

G. Bowersock 1994, *Fiction as History: Nero to Julian,* Berkeley: University of California Press. • J. A. Brant, C. Hedrick, and C. Shea, eds. 2005, *Ancient Fiction: The Matrix of Early Christian and Jewish Narrative,* Atlanta: Society of Biblical Literature. • J. J. Collins, ed. 1979, *Apocalypse: The Morphology of a Genre,* Semeia 14, Missoula, Mont.: Scholars Press. • R. F. Hock, J. B. Chance, and J. Perkins, eds. 1986, *Ancient Fiction and Early Christian Narrative,* Atlanta: Scholars Press. • S. R. Johnson 2004, *Historical Fictions and Hellenistic Jewish Identity,* Berkeley: University of California Press. • S. R. Johnson 2005, "Novelistic Elements in Esther: Persian or Hellenistic, Jewish or Greek?" *CBQ* 67: 571-89. • J. R. Morgan 1993, "Make-Believe and Make Believe," in *Lies and Fiction in the Ancient World,* ed. C. Gill and T. P. Wiseman, Austin: University of Texas Press, 175-229. • B. E. Perry 1967, *The Ancient Romances,* Berkeley: University of California Press. • R. I. Pervo 1987, *Profit with Delight: The Literary Genre of the Acts of the Apostles,* Philadelphia: Fortress. • R. I. Pervo 2008, *Acts: A Commentary,* Minneapolis: Fortress. • B. P. Reardon 1989, *Collected Ancient Greek Novels,* Berkeley: University of California Press, 1-16. • S. J. Stephens and J. J. Winkler 1995, *Ancient Greek Novels: The Fragments,* Princeton: Princeton University Press, 3-19. • S. Swain, ed. 1999, *The Greek Novel,* Oxford: Oxford University Press. • C. Thomas 2003, *The Acts of Peter, Gospel Literature, and the Ancient Novel,* Oxford: Oxford University Press. • L. M. Wills 1995, *The Jewish Novel in the Ancient World,* Ithaca: Cornell University Press.

Sara Raup Johnson

O

Oaths and Vows

Oaths *(šĕbuʿôt)* and vows *(nĕdārîm)* refer to legally binding statements that invoke the name of God. In ancient Judaism, the two most common types of oaths were (1) assertory oaths, in which one testifies regarding some factual matter — usually exculpatory professions of nonguilt; and (2) promissory oaths, in which a party obligates himself or herself to observe a certain course of conduct in the future. Vows involve the dedication of persons or property to God and thus are similar to a promissory oath, except that the oath-taker promises his or her obligation only conditionally.

Biblical Background

Assertory oaths are used in Exod. 22:7, 10, which discuss cases involving damage to or theft of deposited property. When no witnesses are available, the bailee must clear his name by means of an oath, namely, swearing his innocence before God. Another type of oath that is associated with legal testimony is the oath of imprecation (*šĕbuʿat ʾālâ;* these oaths are usually referred to by the term *ʾālâ* alone, but cf. Num. 5:21). Such oaths are used to compel testimony from recalcitrant witnesses by pronouncing curses upon anyone who does not come forward with information about a crime. References to this practice are made in Lev. 5:1, Judg. 17:1-3, 1 Kings 8:31, and Prov. 29:24.

Promissory oaths can take many forms. The obligations that an oath taker assumes can either be to perform a specified action or to refrain from doing something that is normally permitted. Respective examples of each can be seen in 1 Kings 1:30 (see also vv. 13, 17), where David swears that Solomon will succeed him as king, and in Ps. 132:2-5, wherein David swears an oath of self-denial, promising not to rest until he has found a proper home for the Ark of the Lord.

While oaths are offered unconditionally, in a vow, one's obligations become operative only after another party has fulfilled their end of the arrangement. Thus, in Gen. 28:20-21, while en route to Haran, Jacob vows to worship YHWH exclusively, but only if God is able to return him safely from this journey. In Judg. 11:30-31, Jephthah famously vows to offer as a sacrifice whatever comes out the door of his house, provided that YHWH grants him victory over the Ammonites. Vows to set aside property for the sanctuary are known as dedicatory vows, and the regulations for such vows are outlined in Leviticus 27. These vows are sometimes referred to as "positive" vows, with vows of self-denial (e.g., the Nazirite vow) being termed "negative" vows. Earlier studies differentiated positive and negative vows by defining the former as conditional and the latter as unconditional, but the evidence for such a distinction is problematic.

The Nazirite vow, the most well-known vow of self-denial, took two forms: lifelong and temporary. For those taking lifelong Nazirite vows, such as Samson and Samuel, the only clear obligation was to refrain from cutting one's hair (Judg. 13:5; 1 Sam. 1:11). For temporary Nazirite vows, the terms of which are delineated in Numbers 6, the votary had not only to refrain from cutting his or her hair but also avoid intoxicants (and grape products in general) and corpse contamination. In addition, the votary was to offer an animal sacrifice at the end of his or her time as a Nazirite. Because Samson's mother had to refrain from intoxicants, it has been suggested that lifelong Nazirites also were to avoid strong drink, but the text is not clear on this point (Cartledge 1992: 19-20).

The Torah warns repeatedly against swearing falsely in God's name, most prominently in the Decalogue itself (Exod. 20:7; Deut. 5:11; see also Lev. 19:12 and Deut. 23:22-24). Those who failed to uphold an oath, even inadvertently, were required to perform certain expiatory sacrifices (Lev. 5:4-13). Numbers 30, which begins by reiterating the binding nature of all vows and oaths, discusses the responsibilities a male head of household had regarding any vows and oaths made by women under his authority (e.g., wives and daughters).

Second Temple Literature

Because of its serious nature, Second Temple literature reflects a common sentiment against oaths and vows. Wisdom literature — both biblical and postbiblical —

often admonished against making them at all. Ecclesiastes 5:1-6 and 8:2-3 warn against excessive oath taking, a theme echoed in Sir. 23:9-11. 4QInstruction, multiple copies of which were found among the Dead Sea Scrolls, goes even further, suggesting that husbands annul all of their wives' oaths and vows (4Q416 frg. 2 col. iv line 10; 4Q418 frg. 10 lines 8-10). In two separate discussions on the commandment against taking God's name in vain, Philo argues that it is best to avoid oaths and vows whenever possible (*Spec. Leg.* 2:1-38; *De Decalogo* 82–95). Despite this sentiment, the practice of Nazirite vows (the temporary variety, at least) continued well into the Second Temple Period, as attested in both Josephus (*Ant.* 19.292-93; *J.W.* 2.313) and the New Testament (Acts 18:18; 21:23-24).

Josephus also notes that the Essenes eschewed oaths altogether (*J.W.* 2.135), and that when Herod attempted to impose loyalty oaths on certain segments of society, he exempted the Essenes, because of his good relations with them (*Ant.* 15.368-71). The *Damascus Document* contains similar prohibitions against swearing by the name of God (CD 15:1-5). The one exception to the Essenes' prohibition against oath taking was for new initiates entering the sect. According to Josephus, Essene proselytes were required to take "tremendous oaths" as part of their initiation process (*J.W.* 2.139-42). Among the sectarian literature from Qumran, these oaths have analogues in initiation procedures described both in the *Community Rule* (1QS 5:8-10) and in the *Damascus Document* (CD 15:5-6, 12-13).

The most extensive discussions of vows and oaths in Qumran literature are in the *Temple Scroll* and the *Damascus Document.* The *Temple Scroll* (11Q19 53:11–54:5) mostly follows the biblical text, combining material from Numbers 30 and Deut. 23:22-24, though it sometimes alters the biblical sources in subtle ways. The *Damascus Document* broaches halakic issues not explicitly considered in the Torah, such as whether an oath to violate the Torah is binding (CD 16:8-9) or the permissibility of prohibitive vows. The main section in the *Damascus Document* that deals with oaths and vows, CD 16:7-12, only mentions oaths yet begins by quoting Deut. 23:24, a verse that deals exclusively with vows. Either the *Damascus Document* expresses a general disapproval of vows or else seeks to treat them as halakically equal to oaths. Finally, CD 9:8-12 affirms the use of the oath of adjuration but restricts it to the congregation's jurisdiction.

Early Christianity

Among early Christian writings, Matt. 5:33-37 and Jas. 5:12 oppose oath-taking altogether. These passages not only disallow oaths sworn by the name of God, but those sworn on any other basis, including heaven, earth, Jerusalem, or one's own person. Matt. 23:16-22 elaborates on this topic by accusing the Pharisees and scribes of making inappropriate legal distinctions in such cases (e.g., ruling that an oath sworn by the Temple's altar is not binding, but one sworn by the offering on the altar is; cf. Josephus, *Ag. Ap.* 1.167).

Elsewhere in the New Testament, as mentioned above, Acts mentions two instances of Paul taking a Nazirite vow. In Matthew's account of Jesus' trial before the Sanhedrin (26:63), the high priest Caiaphas adjures Jesus to testify whether he is the Messiah. Finally, in describing when the end times will occur, Rev. 10:5-6 refers to a prophecy in Dan. 12:7 about a figure clad in linen who swears by "the one who lives forever."

Rabbinic Judaism

In tannaitic literature, much of the discussion of vows focuses on prohibitive vows. These vows merely likened property to temple property without actually dedicating it. The effect of this vow, however, was to consecrate this property and prohibit its use either by its owner or by anyone else. Such vows are forbidden by the *Damascus Document* (CD 16:13-15) and are critiqued in Mark 7:9-13 (Benovitz 1998: 9-40). With regard to women's vows, tannaitic halakah restricted the types of vows that fathers and husbands were allowed to annul, limiting it only to vows of self-denial and to vows that affected marital duties (see *m. Nedarim* 11; Lieberman 1965: 115-43).

BIBLIOGRAPHY

M. Benovitz 1998, *Kol Nidre: Studies in the Development of Rabbinic Votive Institutions,* Atlanta: Scholars Press. • J. Berlinerblau 1996, *The Vow and the "Popular Religious Groups" of Ancient Israel: A Philological and Sociological Inquiry,* Sheffield: Sheffield Academic Press. • T. Cartledge 1992, *Vows in the Hebrew Bible and the Ancient Near East,* Sheffield: JSOT Press. • B. Levine 1993-2000, *Numbers 1–20; 21–36,* New York: Doubleday. • S. Lieberman 1965, *Greek in Jewish Palestine: Studies in the Life and Manners of Jewish Palestine in the II–IV Centuries* C.E., New York: Feldheim. • J. Milgrom 1990, *Numbers,* Philadelphia: Jewish Publication Society. • L. H. Schiffman 1991, "The Law of Vows and Oaths (*Num.* 30, 3-16) in the *Zadokite Fragments* and the *Temple Scroll,*" *Revue de Qumran* 15: 199-214. • H. Tita 2001, *Gelübde als Bekenntnis: Eine Studie zu den Gelübden im Alten Testament,* Freiburg: Universitätsverlag; Göttingen: Vandenhoeck & Ruprecht.

Andrew Gross

Oniads

The Oniads were a dynasty of high priests in the Second Temple period, at a time when the high priesthood was seen both by the Jews and by their non-Jewish rulers (the Ptolemies and then the Seleucids) as the position of supreme leadership over the entire Jewish nation.

The Oniads traced the origins of their dynasty's lineage all the way back to Zadok, who served already under King David (e.g., 2 Sam. 15:24), and clearly enjoyed much prestige in the Jewish society of the third and early second century B.C.E. The most common names within the Oniad family were Onias (Ḥoni, or Ḥonio) and Simon. The first Onias was the son of Yaddua, who was high priest in Jerusalem at the time of Alexander the Great (Josephus, *Ant.* 11.347), and he was succeeded by his son, Simon I. Simon was followed first by his brother Eleazar (in whose time, says Josephus, *Ant.*

12.44ff., the Septuagint translation was produced), then by Eleazar's uncle, Manasse, and then by Simon's own son, Onias II (*Ant.* 12.157), who ingratiated himself with the Ptolemaic court (*Ant.* 12.158-159). He was succeeded by his son, Simon II, whose praises were sung at some length by Ben Sira (*Ant.* 12.224; Sirach 50). While his term of office may have been a time of relative calm and prosperity, the conquest of Palestine by the Seleucid rulers in 200 B.C.E. brought about many important changes, and his son, Onias III, served at a time of growing inner-Jewish tensions and much scheming by ambitious priests and parties in Jerusalem and by the imperial court at Antioch.

These maneuvers culminated in the deposition of Onias III by Antiochus IV, and the granting of the Jerusalem high priesthood to his brother Jason, in 175 B.C.E., and in the subsequent replacement of the latter by Menelaus, who came from the priestly "tribe" of Bilgah and thus was not an Oniad at all. Onias III went to Antioch to plead his cause, and apparently was murdered there while seeking refuge in a pagan temple in Daphne, a suburb of the Seleucid capital (2 Macc. 4:34; the event might be alluded to in Dan. 9:26 and 11:22, in *1 Enoch* 90:8, and perhaps even in *y. Sanh.* 10:6 [29c]). His son, Onias IV, fled to Egypt, and subsequently built an alternative temple in, or near, Heliopolis (Josephus, *Ant.* 13.62-73). (A different reconstruction of these events, whereby Onias III was not murdered, but fled to Egypt and established the temple there, is much less likely.)

Apparently coming to Egypt with a large following of Jews who fled the turmoil, and the persecutions in Jerusalem, Onias IV established several Jewish military colonies in and around Heliopolis. He also became an important military figure in the Ptolemaic court, much involved in the civil strife and court intrigues of Alexandria of the mid-second century B.C.E. (Josephus, *Ag. Ap.* 2.49-56). His two sons, Ananias and Chelkias, apparently inherited this high-ranking status and remained involved in Ptolemaic intrigues and warfare to the end of the second century B.C.E. In 103 B.C.E., when Cleopatra III was campaigning in Palestine and Syria, Chelkias lost his life in battle, and Ananias subsequently convinced the queen not to attack Jerusalem, thus missing the last chance of any Oniad to dislodge the Hasmoneans from the high priesthood they had forcefully usurped and return the Oniads to their former glory (Josephus, *Ant.* 13.285-87, 351-55).

Although the Oniad temple in Egypt apparently continued to function until its closure by the Romans in 73 or 74 C.E. (Josephus, *J.W.* 7.420-36), it is not really clear if the Oniad dynasty itself survived the turbulent events that convulsed the Ptolemaic kingdom until its conquest by the Romans in 31 B.C.E. Thus a dynasty of much respected high priests in the Jerusalem Temple of the fourth and third centuries B.C.E. ended up establishing a competing temple in Egypt in the mid-second century B.C.E., at about the same time that the Teacher of Righteousness and his followers established the Essene community at Qumran, and it finally sank into oblivion at about the same time that Herod the Great was decimating the remains of the Oniads' Hasmonean rivals. The temple they had founded in Egypt outlived the Jerusalem Temple by only three or four years, and just as its founding was prompted by events in Jerusalem in the 160s B.C.E., so its destruction was the by-product of events in Judea and Jerusalem in the late 60s C.E.

BIBLIOGRAPHY

L. CAPPONI 2007, *Il tempio di Leontopoli in Egitto: Identità politica e religiosa dei Giudei di Onia (c. 150 a.C.–73 d.C),* Pisa: ETS. • G. BOHAK 1996, *Joseph and Aseneth and the Jewish Temple in Heliopolis,* Atlanta: Scholars Press. • F. PARENTE 1994, "Onias III's Death and the Founding of the Temple of Leontopolis," in *Josephus and the History of the Greco-Roman Period: Essays in Memory of Morton Smith,* ed. F. Parente and J. Sievers, Leiden: Brill, 69-98. • M. STERN 1960, "The Death of Onias III," *Zion* 25: 1-16 (in Hebrew).

See also: Heliopolis; High Priests

GIDEON BOHAK

Ordinances (4QOrdinances)

The group of scrolls from Cave 4 Qumran designated 4QOrdinances consists of three manuscripts: 4Q159, 4Q513, and 4Q514 (4QOrd[a,b,c]). 4QOrd[a] was published by John Allegro, first in a preliminary edition and then in DJD 5. 4QOrd[b] and 4QOrd[c] were published by Maurice Baillet in DJD 7; he is responsible for the grouping of the three manuscripts and for giving two manuscripts the titles 4QOrd[b-c]. He did so due to a partial overlap between one fragment of 4QOrd[b] and one of 4QOrd[a]. In fact, however, this is no more than a shared halakic tradition between these two scrolls (see below).

4QOrd[a] contains legal and nonlegal materials. Though some of the details discussed in the scroll are relatively clear, its overall structure and intention remain obscure. Nevertheless, there is no justification for the claim that frg. 5 was misidentified and does not belong to this composition because it is a pesher and contains no ordinances. 4QOrd[a] is not the only scroll that combines halakic instructions with other literary genres (see, e.g., 4Q265 [*Miscellanies Rules*]). Furthermore, frg. 5 mentions Moses twice, and so does the last line of frg. 1. Therefore, the possibility that frg. 5 is the direct continuation of frg. 1 should not be ruled out.

Some of the halakic issues 4QOrd[a] refers to are unique; others are mentioned in other compositions as well. The latter is the case with the half-shekel payment required by the Torah from "everyone who is entered in the records" (Exod. 30:13). 4QOrd[a] stresses that this is a one-time payment and not a yearly tax, as was the view of the Pharisees. This law is also referred to in the *Temple Scroll* (39:7-11). The scroll prohibits women and any young man under the age of twenty (which according to Qumran halakah is the age of maturity) who had not yet paid his half-shekel dues from entering the inner courts of the Temple.

A similar (though slightly different) account is to be found in 4QOrd[b], which was the initial reason for Baillet's joining the two scrolls under the same title. Especially interesting is the rule referring to the case of the accused bride in Deut. 22:13-21. According to the biblical passage, in response to the husband's accusation that he found her not to be virgin, the girl's parents should display the sheet from the wedding night, thereby proving that this was their daughter's initial sexual encounter. The innovative element in 4QOrd[a] is the replacing of this problematic proof with another method: "trustworthy [women] shall examine her" (frgs. 2-4 lines 8-9). The same procedure is mentioned in 4QD as a precautionary measure. If a young girl has acquired a bad name in her maidenhood, she is not to be married unless she is first "examined by trustworthy [women] of repute selected by command of the supervisor over [the many]" (4Q271 frg. 3 lines 14-15). The other rulings in the scroll do not have parallels in the Qumran corpus, but they also without exception allude to specific injunctions in the Torah.

The content of 4QOrd[b] is more difficult to discern due to the poor condition of its remains. Baillet joined frgs. 3 and 4 even though they do not match physically. Nevertheless, some of its subject matter is discernible, and its overall character may be described as having a sectarian and polemical nature. In frg. 2 the author complains about some wrongdoings involving fornication. Fragment 4 mentions the waving of the Omer with an allusion to Lev. 23:38, using the sectarian phrase "error of blindness" and the words "not from the Torah of Moses." The passage is probably directed against the Pharisees and their view that the Omer is to be brought on the day after the Passover (which might fall on a Sabbath) and not always on Sunday.

4QOrd[c] has only one readable fragment and deals with procedures for purification. The scroll expresses the view known from other Qumran Scrolls, that every impure person whose period of impurity lasts more than one day should wash twice. As explained by Jacob Milgrom, the ablution on the first day is required to remove one layer of impurity so that the impure person may eat ordinary food. Only after the completion of the impurity period and the second ablution is he allowed to partake of the sacred food.

BIBLIOGRAPHY

J. M. ALLEGRO 1961, "An Unpublished Fragment of Essene Halakhah (4Q Ordinances)," *JSS* 6-7: 71-73. • J. M. ALLEGRO WITH A. A. ANDERSON 1968, *Qumrân Cave 4.I (4Q158-4Q186),* DJD 5, Oxford: Clarendon, 6-9. • M. BAILLET 1982, *Qumrân grotte 4.III (4Q482-4Q520),* DJD 7, Oxford: Clarendon, 287-98. • J. BAUMGARTEN 1985, "Halakhic Polemics in New Fragments from Qumran Cave 4," in *Biblical Archaeology Today: Proceedings of the International Congress on Biblical Archaeology,* ed. J. Amitai, Jerusalem: Israel Exploration Society and Israel Academy of Sciences and Humanities, 390-99. • M. J. BERNSTEIN 2003, "4Q159 fragment 5 and the 'Desert Theology' of the Qumran Sect," in *Emanuel: Studies in the Hebrew Bible, Septuagint and Dead Sea Scrolls in Honor of Emanuel Tov,* ed. S. Paul et al., Leiden: Brill, 43-56. • J. MILGROM 1994, "Purification Rule (4Q514 = 4QOrd[c])," in *The Dead Sea Scrolls: Hebrew, Aramaic and Greek Texts with English Translation,* vol. 1, *Rule of the Community and Related Documents,* ed. J. H. Charlesworth, Tübingen: Mohr-Siebeck; Louisville: Westminster John Knox, 177-79. • L. H. SCHIFFMAN 1994, "Ordinances and Rules," in *The Dead Sea Scrolls: Hebrew, Aramaic and Greek Texts with English Translation,* vol. 1, *Rule of the Community and Related Documents,* ed. J. H. Charlesworth, Tübingen: Mohr-Siebeck; Louisville: Westminster John Knox, 145-57. • A. SHEMESH 1998, "4Q271.3: A Key to Sectarian Matrimonial Law," *JJS* 49: 244-63.

AHARON SHEMESH

Orpheus, Pseudo-

Among the numerous poems ascribed to the mythological singer Orpheus belong fragments of a text that is most likely of Jewish origin: *Poetae Epici Graeci* frgs. 377 and 378. Verses from or traces of this brief poem can be found in the following authors between the second century B.C.E. and ca. 500 C.E.: (in chronological order) Aristobulus frg. 4 (in Eusebius, *Praep. Evang.* 13.12.4-5); Pseudo-Justin, *De Monarchia* 2.4; Theophilus, *Autolycum* 3.2; Clement of Alexandria, *Protreptikos* 4.3-5; *Stromateis* 5.78.4-5; 123.1–124.1; 126.5; 127.2; 133.2; Pseudo-Justin, *Ad Graecos de Vera Religione* (or *Cohortatio ad Graecos*) 15.1; Cyril of Alexandria, *Contra Julianum* 1.35; Theodoret, *Graecarum Affectionum Curatio,* 2.30-31; *Theosophia Tubingensis* 55–56.

Textual Transmission, Date, Origin

The textual transmission is very complex, and there is no scholarly consensus on a *stemma* (the more recent discussion is summarized in Holladay 1996: 43-91 and Bernabé 2004: 296). According to Riedweg (followed by Bernabé), the poem was transmitted in two versions only: in an *Urfassung* (twenty-one verses) dating from the late third century B.C.E. and in a longer revision (forty-one verses) which goes back to Aristobulus (ca. 150 B.C.E.; the Greek text of both versions is in Bernabé: 299-309). All other testimonies may indeed derive from these two versions. Other scholars, such as Walter and Holladay, suggest the existence of four recensions.

The chronological setting of the poem is debated as well. Most scholars place the beginnings of the text in the late third century or early second century B.C.E. (Walter 1983: 229, who argues for the first century B.C.E. or C.E., is an exception). The content of the fragments fits the literary and cultural context of ancient Jewish Alexandria very well, but there can be no certainty as to where the poem was originally written.

Contents

In the poem Orpheus calls upon his student Musaios to leave behind his former (polytheistic) beliefs and to follow the one and only God exclusively. Thus the text has Orpheus write a monotheistic manifesto. Very much as in Ezekiel's *Exagōgē* (vv. 68-70), God sits on a golden throne and reaches up to the sky while stretching his hand to the end of the *okeanos.* In the earlier version (Riedweg's *Urfassung*), God is invisible to human beings; in the later version, only the "Chaldean" master of astrology (probably Abraham) is able to see God.

Parallels between Jewish Hellenistic and pagan Hellenistic ways of speaking about God make the author's pretense that this poem was of pagan origin more plausible. The poem opens with the Orphic mystery formula saying that the uninitiated should shut their doors. The poem might more correctly be understood as a *hieros logos* introducing an initiate into the true doctrine rather than as another literary example of a Jewish testament. Insofar as this pseudo-Orphic poem postulates the righteousness and originality of Jewish wisdom, it belongs to a large group of Jewish-Hellenistic texts that trace aspects of pagan culture back to Jewish origins or confirm Jewish culture by referring to pagan beliefs. The content of the poem resembles the forged citations of Greek poets, the (more polemical) *Sibylline Oracles,* and the Jewish "history" of Artapanus. The latter equates Moses with Musaios and makes him the teacher of Orpheus (Eusebius, *Praep. Evang.* 27.4).

The poem is written in Greek hexameters and shows great familiarity with Homer and Hesiod as well as Orphic poetry. The author seems to have sympathized with the philosophy of the Stoa, while in Aristobulus' revision it is rather Platonic and Aristotelian thinking that prevails (God is understood as the origin of good things only).

Like the *Sibylline Oracles* and other Jewish-Hellenistic texts, the poem speaks in pointedly monotheistic language but also reflects images of Greek mythology (in addition to Orpheus and Musaios, also the moon goddess Mene and Okeanos). Orpheus of Greek myth apparently received a fairly important Jewish reception. In late antiquity King David is iconographically equated with Orpheus, for example, in the synagogue of Dura-Europos and the synagogue of Gaza (Walter 1984: 230-32; Kippenberg 1990).

Other Orphic fragments have also been understood by some scholars as possibly Jewish, such as *Orphicorum Fragmenta* 248 and 299 (Kern 1922; see Holladay 1996: 233-41).

BIBLIOGRAPHY

A. BERNABÉ 2004, *Poetae Epici Graeci: Testimonia et Fragmenta, Pars II, Orphicorum et Orphicis Similium Testimonia et Fragmenta. Fasciculus I,* Munich and Leipzig: K. G. Saur, 296-309. • J. J. COLLINS 2000, *Between Athens and Jerusalem: Jewish Identity in the Hellenistic Diaspora,* 2d ed., Grand Rapids: Eerdmans, 219-24. • A.-M. DENIS 2000, *Introduction à la littérature religieuse judéo-hellénistique,* Turnhout: Brepols, 1086-1101. • C. R. HOLLADAY 1996, *Fragments from Hellenistic Jewish Authors,* vol. 4, *Orphica,* Atlanta: Scholars Press. • O. KERN 1922, *Orphicorum Fragmenta,* Berlin: Weidmann. • H. G. KIPPENBERG 1990, "Pseudikonographie: Orpheus auf jüdischen Bildern," in *Visible Religion: Annual for Religious Iconography 7,* Leiden: Brill, 233-49. • G. S. OEGEMA 2002, "Poetische Schriften," in *Supplementa: Einführung zu den jüdischen Schriften aus hellenistisch-römischer Zeit,* ed. H. Lichtenberger and G. S. Oegema, Gütersloh: Gütersloher Verlagshaus, 76-85. • R. RADICE 1994, *La filosofia di Aristobulo e i suoi nessi con il "De mundo" attribuito ad Aristotele: Con due Appendici contenenti i frammenti di Aristobulo, traduzione a fronte e presentazione delle varianti,* Milano: Vita e Pensiero, 121-54, 213-27. • C. RIEDWEG 2007, "Literatura órfica en ámbito judío," in *El orfismo reencontrado,* ed. A. Bernabé and F. Casadesús, Madrid: Akal, 379-92. • C. RIEDWEG 1993, *Jüdisch-hellenistische Imitation eines orphischen Hieros Logos: Beobachtungen zu OF 245 und 247 (sog. Testament des Orpheus),* Tübingen: Gunter Narr. • N. WALTER 1983, "Pseudepigraphische jüdisch-hellenistische Dichtung: Pseudo-Phokylides, Pseudo-Orpheus, Gefälschte Verse auf Namen griechischer Dichter," *JSHRZ,* IV,3, Gütersloh: Gütersloher Verlagshaus, 173-276. • M. L. WEST 1983, *The Orphic Poems,* Oxford: Oxford University Press, 33-35.

RENÉ BLOCH

Ossuaries

An ossuary is a chest or box, usually made of stone but occasionally of clay or wood, used for secondary burial, that is, the reburial of human bones after the flesh of a corpse has decayed. Ossuaries are commonly found in Jewish tombs of the early Roman period (63 B.C.E.–35 C.E.) near Jerusalem.

A typical ossuary is hollowed out from a single block of limestone, which is so common in the area around Jerusalem, and is proportionate in size to the large and long bones of the body (i.e., skull and femur). Thus an average ossuary for an adult measures about 60 by 35 by 30 cm., with smaller measurements for the ossuaries of children. Ossuaries have removable lids, most of which are flat, although some are domed or gabled. Most ossuaries are totally plain, but many are decorated with motifs typical of Jewish art in this period. Geometric designs appear very frequently, the most common of which is the six-petaled rosette, which was chip-carved into the face of the ossuary using a chisel and a compass. Representations of Jewish religious themes are also frequent, including Torah shrines, palm branches, and menorahs. Although a few ossuary ornamentations are executed in high relief, most are created by a technique known as "chip-carving," by which the decoration is cut or chiseled into the face of the stone. Decorations often appear only on one long side of an ossuary.

Many (but not most) ossuaries are inscribed, either in Hebrew, Aramaic, or Greek. At present, slightly more than 40 percent of the known ossuary inscriptions are in Greek. Some ossuaries feature inscriptions in more than one language. Inscriptions are scrawled with charcoal or scratched with a sharp object, presumably by family members at the time of secondary burial. As a result, the reading of ossuary inscriptions can often be rather difficult, and misspellings are very common. Inscriptions may appear virtually anywhere on an ossuary — on the sides, ends, lid, or even along the inside edge. Ossuary inscriptions typically record only the name of the deceased, occasionally also adding a nickname, patronymic, place of origin, or distinguishing fact about the deceased.

Ossuaries are found in Jewish tombs from the early Roman period in and around the city of Jerusalem. A typical tomb with ossuaries is a nearly square underground chamber (approximately 3.5 m. on a side) cut

The ossuary of Joseph Caiaphas, the Jewish high priest from 18 to 37 C.E. Discovered in Jerusalem in 1990, the limestone ossuary has Caiaphas's name inscribed in Aramaic on its back and one of the sides, "Yehosef bar Qayafa'/Qafa'" *(Photo © The Israel Museum, Jerusalem)*

from bedrock, with a shallow rectangular pit in the floor creating a low shelf around the walls. Burial niches known as *loculi* (Hebr. *kōkhîm*) — narrow niches large enough to hold one human body — are carved into the walls above the shelf. The openings of *loculi* that contain human remains are often found to have been covered by flat stone slabs. In such tombs ossuaries may be found in whole or in part in many locations, including on the shelf, in the niches, or on the floor. Other typical finds from these tombs include human bones on the shelf and in the niches, perfume bottles *(unguentaria)*, juglets, cooking pots, and lamps. Coins, by contrast, are very rare.

Skeletal analysis shows that many ossuaries contain the bones of more than one individual, usually members of the same family group. The distribution of these skeletal remains is significantly affected by gender. Adult females, for example, are more likely to be found in an ossuary with an adult male than in an ossuary by themselves. Ossuaries containing the bones of both a male and a female are more likely to be inscribed with the name of the male than with the name of the female. Adult males, in other words, appear to be more fully individuated than adult females and children. These observations are consistent with the patrilineal kinship systems of Jewish society in Jerusalem during the early Roman period.

Based on the archaeological evidence, the ritual process of secondary burial in ossuaries appears to have taken place in two stages. First, at the time of death, the body was placed in the tomb, either on the shelf or in a niche. Later, probably several months (at least) after primary burial, when decomposition of the flesh was complete (or nearly so), family members returned to the tomb for the ritual of secondary burial. In this ritual, the bones of the deceased were taken from their resting place on the shelf or in a niche and were collected in an ossuary. The ossuary, which might or might not be marked with the name of the deceased, was then positioned in its final resting place, either on the shelf, on the floor, or in a niche. A *loculus* filled with ossuaries — and some *loculi* have been found to contain as many as five or six — was often sealed with a stone slab.

Although clay ossuaries had appeared in Syria-Palestine during the Chalcolithic period (4500-3400 B.C.E.), limestone Jewish ossuaries were unknown before the early Roman period. The reasons for their emergence during this period are uncertain. An earlier generation of scholars thought that ossuaries were associated with Pharisaic beliefs about bodily resurrection. On this view, bones gathered into an ossuary were purified from sin and prepared for the resurrection. Yet no early Roman sources connect ossuaries with belief in bodily resurrection, and rabbinic literary texts have been shown to be too unreliable to be taken as uncorroborated evidence for early Roman customs. Another view is that ossuaries were motivated by more practical concerns: they are sometimes regarded as the product of an effort to conserve limited space inside a tomb. Yet in most archaeological contexts, ossuaries are found stacked up on shelves or in niches, where they consume rather than conserve space. A more recent suggestion is that ossuaries might reflect the rising status of the individual in Jewish society. Unlike earlier forms of Jewish secondary burial, ossuaries preserved individual identity after death. Thus they may have risen from the encounter between traditional Jewish customs of secondary burial and newer Hellenistic conceptions of human personhood. At present no one of these theories can be said to command broad scholarly support.

Although they continued to be used sporadically into the late Roman period (250-363 C.E.), the frequency of the appearance of ossuaries in the archaeological record drops off precipitously in the early second century C.E. The most likely explanation for this rapid decline is that the violence of the Bar Kokhba Revolt (132-135 C.E.), along with the exclusion of Jews from the city of Jerusalem after the revolt, must have effectively ended both the demand for and the supply of ossuaries. The stone-carving industry that had previously been producing ossuaries apparently collapsed.

BIBLIOGRAPHY

S. FINE 2000, "A Note on Ossuary Burial and Resurrection of the Dead in First-Century Jerusalem," *JJS* 51: 69-76. • R. HACHLILI 1988, *Jewish Ornamented Ossuaries of the Late Second Temple Period,* Haifa: University of Haifa. • B. R. MCCANE 2003, *Roll Back the Stone: Death and Burial in the World of Jesus,* Harrisburg, Penn.: Trinity Press International. • Y. PELEG 2002, "Gender and Ossuaries: Ideology and Meaning," *BASOR* 325: 65-73. • L. Y. RAHMANI 1994, *A Catalogue of Jewish Ossuaries in the Collections of the State of Israel,* Jerusalem: Israel Antiquities Authority.

See also: Burial Practices BYRON R. MCCANE

Ostia

Ostia lies some eighteen miles downriver from Rome at the mouth the Tiber and is generally called "Rome's first colony." Throughout antiquity, it served as the principal ocean port for Rome, although some shipping was diverted to nearby Portus beginning in the early second century C.E. Because of Ostia's geographical, political, and economic relationship to Rome, the evidence for a large, thriving synagogue community is important for our understanding of the diffusion of Judaism in Rome and Italy. New work on this site is helping to clarify its history and significance.

The Synagogue

The Ostia synagogue site was first discovered in 1959-1960 and excavated in 1961-1962. The excavations revealed a large complex lying near the ancient shoreline and along the *Via Severiana,* the major Roman coastal road constructed under the emperor Septimius Severus in ca. 200 C.E. Situated in an area of suburban expansion, the synagogue complex (IV.17) contains two edifices: Building 1 is the synagogue proper; Building 2 is a small contiguous edifice containing several rooms and a courtyard with *nymphaeum.* The main hall of the synagogue (14) measures 14.31 × 12.5 m. with a curved wall and low bema on its western end. To the east stands a series of three entry rooms (7-9) that lead to a central colonnade (12) as the entrance to the hall of assembly. At the back of the hall, an apsidal *aedicula* (13) was installed as the Torah shrine or "ark" for the synagogue, and the corbels of its architrave bear reliefs of menorah with *ethrog* and *lulav.* On the south side of the complex stands a rectangular room (10) measuring 11.2 × 6 m.; it originally served as a dining room but was later converted into a kitchen or bakery with a large oven in the southwest corner. Room 18 was originally an open courtyard between Buildings 1 and 2. It was later closed off on its west end and converted into a dining room with wide benches or dining couches around the walls in the form of a typical Roman triclinium. In this form it measures 10.3 × 13.4 m. overall.

The building described above represents the last major phase of the synagogue's history and use. Its architecture and internal configuration reflect a major renovation and rebuilding of the complex in the early fourth century C.E., probably under the emperor Constantine (313-337 C.E.). The renovation project was evidently prompted by some sort of damage; evidence of an earthquake at Ostia in ca. 275 C.E. has recently come to light. The remodeled edifice was elaborate and ornate: the interior walls were decorated with painted plaster. The floors of the main hall, as well as the bema and Torah niche, were paved in *opus sectile* (cut marble in various colors set in geometric patterns), also typical of the fourth century at Ostia. The benches of the new triclinium were covered with marble, and the floor was paved with a black-and-white geometric mosaic. The entry areas (1-6) were augmented at this time with a new entry porch facing the street, and several of the rooms were reconstructed to create a more restrictive access to the main hall.

The initial excavator, Maria Floriani Squarciapino, dated the original building to the middle of the first century C.E. This date was based almost exclusively on the type of masonry found in the shell (or inner walls) of the main building and on architectural comparisons with then-known synagogues from the Galilee, many of which were erroneously dated to the first century C.E. Squarciapino also identified what she thought was a second or intermediate phase of renovation. This project mainly involved internal modifications, including the construction of an earlier Torah ark. She dated this project to the late second or early third century C.E. The third and final phase of occupation came with the fourth-century renovation described above.

Two new field projects have examined the Ostia synagogue in recent years. The first was conducted in 1997-1998 by a team from Lund University, the second by a team from the University of Texas in 2001 to the present. The Lund project mainly focused on published reports and the visible remains of the synagogue; it reaffirmed the early date and architectural progression proposed by Squarciapino but with some modifications. The Texas team raised questions regarding Squarciapino's dating of the edifice (White 1997b; 1999) and has yielded new, more accurate physical plans of the existing buildings.

Detailed masonry analysis has shown that the type of construction in the earlier shell of the synagogue edifice continued in use at Ostia to the beginning of the third century C.E. Hence, the masonry alone does not provide a narrow window for dating the initial construction. Stratigraphic excavations from 2002 through 2007 have unearthed previously excavated areas and several new ones, including an unexcavated section beneath the floor of the main hall. Ceramics and coins show that the synagogue hall was not constructed prior to about 170 C.E., and new evidence of lower constructions in the area has come to light. Some of the previous assumptions regarding the shape of the building have required revision: there were no benches around the walls of the main hall and no lower floor in that area; the marble colonnade comes from a later phase of construction; and an earlier Torah shrine has been found beneath the later *aedicula*. Taken together, the recent archaeological evidence yields the following provisional chronology of the synagogue building's construction and use:

1. ca. 100 C.E.: construction of an earlier edifice in the eastern half of the area of Building 1.
2. ca. 110-140: initial construction of Building 2.
3. ca. 170-190: initial construction of the first synagogue edifice.
4. ca. 210-225: first major renovation of the synagogue edifice, including installation of the marble colonnade with Corinthian capitals and mosaic floors. This phase may represent the building at its grandest in terms of size and decoration, but it also suggests a greater degree of integration with the surrounding neighborhood.
5. ca. 210-225: renovation of Building 2, including construction of new entry rooms facing the *Via Severiana* and installation of the *nymphaeum* facing onto its interior courtyard.
6. ca. 275: earthquake damage at Ostia.
7. ca. 315-337: renovation and reinforcement of the synagogue building; creation of new entry porch, kitchen/bakery, and dining area.
8. mid-4th century: construction of *aedicula* for the Torah shrine.
9. later 4th century: expansion of the Torah shrine and decoration with marble and *opus sectile*. (Items 7-9 may be thought of as one project continued over several stages.)
10. mid to late 6th century: final abandonment of the building.

Although the new archaeological discoveries have significantly redated the first phase of use as a synagogue, the Ostia synagogue complex remains the oldest known archaeologically in continental Europe. It is also likely that the Jewish congregation was already present at Ostia for at least some years before construction of this particular building; however, where it met is not known. Nonetheless, the decision to build such a large building and the role of a major donor in the project suggest that the Jewish community enjoyed some degree of acceptance at Ostia. The extent and opulence of the second and third phases of renovation are further testimony to their social and economic position.

The Jewish Inscriptions

To date only five Jewish inscriptions are known from Ostia, while two more were discovered at Portus. Most of these are funerary epitaphs. Of these, two are important here because they mention local synagogue officials and may thus shed more light on the organization of the local congregation. Of the nonfunerary inscriptions, one records honors for an acclaimed pantomimist of the third century C.E. who was from the Province of Judea; he was probably not Jewish. The other nonfunerary inscription is the donor plaque from the synagogue itself. We give here the translation of the three most important.

1. Donor plaque on marble in Greek with Latin introductory formula, discovered in the Ostia synagogue excavations in 1961, reused as a paver in the latest floor. Date: late second century C.E., partly reinscribed in the third century C.E.

> For the well-being of the Emperor.
> Mindi(u)s Faustus, together with his family,
> built and made (it) from his own gifts, and
> set up the ark for the Holy Law.

The original form of the inscription corresponds to the construction of the first synagogue edifice; however, the name of the original donor (underlined) was chiseled off and reinscribed. In its secondary form, which may correspond to the intermediate phase of renovation, it was used to commemorate the gifts of a later donor, Mindius Faustus. The name Mindius is a common family name at Ostia and may well reflect a Jewish freedman.

2. Latin epitaph on white marble discovered just south of Ostia in 1969 in the area of an ancient necropolis. Date: mid-second century C.E. or later.

> For Plotius Fortunatus, *archisynagōgos*, Plotius Ampliatus, (Plotius) Secundinus, and (Plotia) Secunda made (this monument) for their father (? or patron), and Ofilia Basilia (made it) for her well-deserving husband.

The plaque employs typical wording and would have been mounted above the door of a freestanding "house tomb." The title *archisynagōgos* is the most common title for synagogue officials in the Diaspora. The family name Plotius is common at Ostia, while the family name of the wife, Ofilia, is less so; however, her given name Basilia was common at Rome.

3. Latin epitaph on marble discovered at Castelporziano (south of Ostia) in 1906, probably from a necropolis closer to Ostia. Date: late second or early third century C.E.

> The Community (? or Congregation) of the Jews dwelling in the colony of Ostia (?), who acquired the plot from the collection, gave it to the *gerousiarch* Gaius Julius Justus to build a (tomb) monument, on the motion of Livius Dionysius, the father (of the synagogue) and . . . *gerousiarch* and Antonius . . . for life, in the year of their service, with the agreement of the *gerousia*. Gaius Julius Justus the *gerousiarch* made (the monument) for himself and his wife, and for his freedmen and freedwomen and their descendants. In width 18 feet; in depth 17 feet.

This elaborate funerary plaque was meant to adorn the entrance to the tomb of Julius Justus and his family. The first part of the text reports the decision of the *gerousia* (the board of elders for the congregation) to honor its chairperson, Julius Justus, by giving him a cemetery plot owned or acquired by the congregation, on which to build a tomb for himself. The second part is

'OTOT

typical of the wording for such epitaphs in that it specifies the legal ownership of the tomb, its size, and other provisions. Justus was a common Roman name among Jews as a translation of Tzaddiq. The family name C. Julius derives from the family of Julius Caesar but was common among imperial freedmen in later generations. The family name of Livius Dionysius is also prominent at Ostia.

The *gerousia* was probably the governing board of a particular Jewish congregation rather than for the whole city. The gift awarded to Julius Justus by the *gerousia* most likely recognizes his efforts as *gerousiarch* (leader of the *gerousia* for a specific term) in service to the community. Thus, Julius Justus was being honored following his term as *gerousiarch* by his successors and Livius Dionysius. It would be tempting to imagine that his service included construction of the synagogue or some specific project, but there is no direct evidence. Also, we cannot be sure that the two funerary epitaphs — one for an *archisynagōgos* (no. 2) and one for a *gerousiarch* (no. 3) — come from the same congregation, even though nothing prevents both titles from being used. Like *archisynagōgos,* the title "father of the synagogue" (here given to Livius Dionysius) typically designates those who serve as major patrons to the congregation. Still, uncertainty remains whether there were more synagogues at Ostia other than the one presently known archaeologically.

BIBLIOGRAPHY

M. FLORIANI SQUARCIAPINO 1963, "The Synagogue at Ostia," *Archaeology* 16: 194-203. • M. FLORIANI SQUARCIAPINO 1965, "La Sinagoga di Ostia, Secondo campagna di scavo," in *Atti del VI congresso internazionale di archeologia cristiana,* Vatican City: Pontifical Institute of Archaeology, 299-315. • R. MEIGGS 1973, *Roman Ostia,* 2d ed., Oxford: Clarendon. • B. OLSSON, D. MITTERNACHT, AND O. BRANDT, EDS. 2001, *The Synagogue of Ancient Ostia and the Jews of Rome,* Stockholm: Swedish Institute at Rome. • C. PAVOLINI 2006, *Ostia,* Rome: Guide Archeologiche Laterza. • A. RUNESSON 1999, "The Oldest Original Synagogue Building in the Diaspora: A Response to L. M. White," *HTR* 92: 409-34. • L. M. WHITE 1997A, *The Social Origins of Christian Architecture,* 2 vols., Harrisburg: Trinity Press International. • L. M. WHITE 1997B, "Synagogue and Society in Imperial Ostia: Archaeological and Epigraphic Evidence," *HTR* 90: 23-58. • L. M. WHITE 1999, "Reading the Ostia Synagogue: A Reply to A. Runesson," *HTR* 92: 435-64.

L. MICHAEL WHITE

'Otot

The word *'Ôtôt* ("signs") is a modern name for a Hebrew manuscript from Qumran (4Q319), copied between 50 and 25 B.C.E. It has a separate number now but was originally part of a copy of the *Rule of the Community* from Cave 4 (4Q259). The text started in col. 4 line 9 or 10 (after what was preserved of 1QS 9:24 in 4Q259) and continued until 6:18. From 6:19 onward the text has various *mišmārôt* rosters similar to those in the calendar texts 4Q320, 321, and 321a.

The *'ôtôt* roster integrates (1) the triennial lunar cycle, (2) the six-year *mišmārôt* cycle of priestly courses, (3) the seven-year cycle of *shemiṭṭah* or release (see Deut. 15:1; cf. also Exod. 23:10-11; Lev. 25:4-5), and (4) the forty-nine-year jubilee cycle (Lev. 25:8). The text records the occurrence of a sign of the priestly course of Gamul or Shekaniah after every three years (years 1, 4, 7, 3, 6, 2, 5, 1, etc.). The numbers are based on the seven-year cycle of *shemiṭṭah,* seven of which build a jubilee. The seventh year is referred to as "the release," and the first year as "after the release." A concluding summary formula records for each jubilee the number of signs (sixteen or seventeen) that occurred in it, specifying the number of signs in a release year (two or three). The use of *'ôtôt* ("signs") in Gen. 1:14 serves as the basis for the term *'ôt* in 4Q319, possibly also combining the meaning of *'ôt* in Jer. 10:2 and the meaning "standard" from the *War Scroll* (1QM 3–4): heavenly phenomena serve as standards for Gamul and Shekaniah, with each sign as a "leader" of the next three years until the appearance of the following sign.

After 294 years (six jubilees of forty-nine years each) the six-year *mišmārôt* cycle, the seven-year *shemiṭṭah* cycle, and the jubilee return to their initial position with the sign of Gamul in year one of the jubilee. This beginning is regarded as the very beginning of time. 4Q319 4:10-11 records Gamul for the fourth day of creation, when the luminaries were created (Gen. 1:14-19; 4Q320 1 i 1-5). The reference to a seventh jubilee (6:17) implies a cycle of seven jubilees. However, only six jubilees are listed, being numbered two to seven. It is not clear why these numbers were used. Some scholars suggest that this was done to emphasize the number "seven," or that it may imply a previously unknown concept of primordial time, or that the first jubilee was not listed due to the use of a larger sequence of apocalyptic heptadic chronology.

While the structure of the *'Ôtôt* text is transparent, its purpose is not yet fully comprehended. There are basically two interpretations for the 294-year *'ôtôt* roster. (1) It is a mechanism to harmonize different sacred time-schemes, synchronizing the lunar and solar calendars within the *mišmārôt* system of the 364-day calendar, counting the signs for doing so, and integrating them in the jubilee system. The sign refers to an astronomical configuration: the relation of the sun and moon at the time of creation, which repeats itself after every three years. Some scholars understand this to be close to the new moon at the vernal equinox, while others take it to be the full moon (cf. the lunar phenomena in 4Q320-321). A sign indicates when an additional thirty-seventh month of thirty days must be added to the lunar ephemeris for the lunar (354-day year) and solar cycle to run equally again in a 364-day year. (2) Uwe Gleßmer suggests instead that the *'ôtôt* roster was used for purposes of intercalation of the 364-day year with the tropical year of 365.25 days. After six years an extra week would be added, reducing the difference with the tropical year to 0.5 days. This would become a full week after fourteen six-year cycles, meaning that after eighty-four years another extra week needs to be added. Important

'OTOT

are the signs counted in the release years. These occur every twenty-one years, and only after forty-two years is the same priestly course recorded in a release year. The sexennial cycle controls the insertion of a "regular" extra week, while each second occurrence of Gamul in a release year would dictate the insertion of an "irregular" extra week. According to Gleßmer the regular triennial recordings of signs have to do with tithing (Deut. 24:28; 26:12). Other intercalation calculations are possible, but the fact is that all intercalation proposals remain without clear textual expression for the rules they suppose.

BIBLIOGRAPHY

J. BEN-DOV 2001, "319. 4QOtot," *Qumran Cave 4.XVI: Calendrical Texts,* DJD 21, Oxford: Clarendon, 195-244. • U. GLEßMER 1996, "The Otot-Texts (4Q319) and the Problem of Intercalations in the Context of the 364-Day Calendar," in *Qumranstudien,* ed. H.-J. Fabry et al., Göttingen: Vandenhoeck & Ruprecht, 124-64. • U. GLEßMER 1999, "Calendars in the Qumran Scrolls," in *The Dead Sea Scrolls after Fifty Years: A Comprehensive Assessment,* vol. 2, ed. P. W. Flint and J. C. VanderKam, Leiden: Brill, 213-78.

MLADEN POPOVIĆ

P

Pacifism → Peace

Pagan Religions

Biblical Perspectives

The Scriptures of ancient Israel express a variety of opinions with respect to the religious traditions of other peoples. It is taken for granted that no Israelite may take part in the religious practices of outsiders; on this point the Scriptures are fiercely unanimous. It is not clear, however, whether other nations may be left alone to maintain their own traditions. Some passages, most famously in the latter portion of the book of Isaiah (e.g., Isa. 44:6-20), subject the nations' gods to withering scorn and by implication extend that scorn to the people who worship them. Other writings, however, seem content to leave those people alone, and Deut. 4:19 even appears to suggest it was God's own intention that other nations could worship the heavenly bodies if they wished; only Israel was to avoid such practices, and only Israel's land had to be free of them. Later generations seeking to live according to their scriptural heritage could combine or select among these different attitudes as their own circumstances led them to do.

Early Jewish Attitudes

In the Jewish homeland, the need to adopt a stand toward other religions was one of the causes in the 160s B.C.E. of the Maccabean uprising against a priestly regime eager to bring Judaism closer to the mainstream of Hellenistic religious practice (1 Macc. 1:11-15). In contrast to this, and in keeping with the strongly exclusionary posture of the later prophets, the new Hasmonean leaders established the principle that Judaism must resist imitation of other religions. To this principled rejection, later rabbinic thinking added the pragmatic consideration that nothing of value can be derived from Gentile religions in any case; that was why "Amorite customs" could be embraced when they served a practical need (*t. Šabbat* 6–7), but Gentile religious customs could never be adopted: they never worked!

As the Jewish Diaspora continued to spread, a growing proportion of the nation lived outside the land of Israel. Surrounded by beliefs and practices they were forbidden to share, Jews had to find modes of adjustment to social realities the Torah had not anticipated. These modes of adjustment varied. Some Jewish writers sought opportunities to attack their neighbors' religions as stupid and corrupt beyond repair: "the worship of idols not to be named is the beginning and cause and end of every evil" (Wis. 14:27 [first century B.C.E.]). Others sought a more ingratiating approach, depicting the best features of pagan religions as ultimately derived from the same source as the teachings of Moses, though of course the true Mosaic teaching as preserved by Israel was free of the many defects to be found in these other versions. The Greek (LXX) translation of Exod. 22:27 (LXX 22:28) reads "thou shalt not revile the gods," taking Hebr. *'ĕlōhîm* as plural. More accommodating still, the *Testament of Abraham* (first century C.E.?) seems to lack any conception that Jews are necessarily more virtuous than others, a stance that implies that other religions are legitimate (and perhaps equally reliable) paths to righteousness. The first-century-C.E. Alexandrian writer Philo was more nuanced. For the native religions of Egypt he had nothing but scorn, but he spoke of the Greek heritage, or at least of its best exemplars, with ungrudging respect. Moreover, he endorsed the LXX reading, "thou shalt not revile the gods" as a precaution, lest Gentiles be moved to profane the true God (*Spec. Leg.* 1.53).

Proselytism and Conversion

Over a period of several centuries spanning the turn of the eras, a steady flow of outsiders found ways of joining the Jewish people. In Judea some of the early Hasmonean high priests forcibly annexed nearby territories to the growing Judean state and compelled the residents of these areas to adopt the Jewish way of life, but their motives in doing so remain poorly understood. Probably aggressive disdain for idolatry was mixed with a desire to increase the size of the kingdom and increase the financial resources of the Temple. In the Diaspora, however, the absence of Jewish military power meant that all newcomers to Judaism had to join up voluntarily. There is no early evidence of an organized Jewish campaign or "mission" to attract such proselytes. Such a campaign may have started in the third and fourth centuries C.E., perhaps in response to the growing success of Christian missionizing, but it appears that individuals in earlier times were attracted to Jewish life on their own and found their own way to join the local Jewish community. It appears that such proselytes were numerous; Jewish writings make frequent reference to them, and Roman authors of the first two centuries C.E. deplore their widespread presence with equal frequency.

Rabbinic Perspectives

As with most issues, the rabbinic materials display a great variety of attitudes toward Gentile religions. There is much hostile polemic, stressing the absurdity and the uselessness of idol worship. One striking passage takes for granted that Gentiles overall, since they live without effective religious restraint, are prone to violence and depravity (*m. ʿAbod. Zar.* 2:1-2). Other texts, however, acknowledge that individual non-Jews, despite their deplorable religious habits, can be upright and trustworthy, even admirable. One remarkably brief rabbinic discussion (the question was apparently not very interesting) reaches the conclusion that "the righteous of the nations [can] have a place in the world to come" (*t. Sanh.* 13:1).

This conclusion helps explain the ancient rabbis' lack of interest in attracting converts. From the close of antiquity, the Babylonian Talmud (earlier rabbinic attitudes cannot be ascertained) requires that would-be converts must be repeatedly discouraged before they are admitted into the community, but it also makes full provision for those individuals who successfully withstand such discouragement (*b. Yebamot* 47a). Rabbinic literature is full of encounters — sometimes friendly, sometimes hostile — between rabbis and Gentile interlocutors, and many of these conversations touch on fundamental religious questions, but the rabbinic participant in these discussions is never depicted as having begun the conversation. It appears that the ancient rabbis preferred to have as little to do with non-Jews as possible; Gentile righteousness, such as it was, could fend for itself.

Jewish-Gentile Relations

Ancient Jewry constituted an *ethnos* as well as a religious community, and the question of Jewish attitudes toward pagan religions cannot be separated from the question of their social, political, and material relations with their neighbors. These, too, were highly varied over the course of ancient history. Terrible explosions of violence in the first and second centuries C.E. led to the obliteration of Alexandrian Jewry, once the jewel of the Hellenistic Diaspora. In Judea, two huge uprisings against the Roman Empire, in 66-70 C.E. and 132-135 C.E., left the Jerusalem Temple in ruins and the country devastated. On the other hand, the Jews of Rome seem to have maintained a stable community, without such clashes, from the end of the Republic at the latest through the close of antiquity. In the East, Christian preachers (most famously John Chrysostom in Antioch around 387) often lamented the readiness of Christian laity to visit synagogues, especially on the great festivals, and to join in Jewish celebrations. Evidently such visitors were numerous and more than welcome.

The ancient rabbis recognized that Jewish attitudes toward paganism contained a strong social component. They tried to limit Jewish participation in pagan celebrations, both public and private (see *m. ʿAbodah Zarah* 1), but it appears that such participation on the part of private individuals must have been common or at least familiar. Rabbinic law contains many restrictions on Jewish use of Gentile foodstuffs (wine, bread, etc.), but the authorities acknowledge that the real aim of such rules was to prevent excessive contact with Gentile women (see *b. Šabbat* 17b). In a striking expression of this concern, the third-century Babylonian master Rav is reported to have taught that, when the Israelites joined the Moabite women in forbidden worship (see Numbers 25), they knew perfectly well that idol worship has no correspondence with reality, but they wanted an excuse to engage in public licentiousness (*b. Sanhedrin* 63b).

These rabbinic opinions cannot simply be projected onto the Second Temple period, but in all likelihood they do represent a crystallization of earlier attitudes. They display confidence that, in strong contrast to their biblical forebears, Jews now felt little religious attraction to the worship of their neighbors' gods. They also express, however, anxiety that ordinary Jews might nevertheless be so interested in social comity (and sexual opportunity?) that they might be drawn into pagan celebrations. The fear was that such participation could wean them altogether from their Jewish origins, and that danger had to be avoided at all costs.

Bibliography

J. G. Barclay 1996, *Jews in the Mediterranean Diaspora from Alexander to Trajan (323 BCE–117 CE)*, Berkeley: University of California Press. • J. J. Collins 1998, *Between Athens and Jerusalem: Jewish Identity in the Hellenistic Diaspora*, 2d ed., Grand Rapids: Eerdmans. • R. Goldenberg 1998, *The Nations That Know Thee Not: Ancient Jewish Attitudes toward Other Religions*, New York: New York University Press. • M. Goodman 1994, *Mission and Conversion: Proselytizing in the Religious History of the Roman Empire*, Oxford: Clarendon Press. • E. S. Gruen 2002, *Diaspora: Jews amidst Greeks and Romans*, Cambridge: Harvard University Press. • M. Hadas-Lebel 1990, *Jérusalem contre Rome*, Paris: Cerf. • P. W. van der Horst 1994, "'Thou Shalt Not Revile the Gods': The LXX Translation of Ex. 22:28 (27), Its Background and Influence," in idem, *Hellenism, Judaism, Christianity: Essays on Their Interaction*, Kampen: Kok Pharos. • J. Lieu et al., eds. 1992, *The Jews among Pagans and Christians in the Roman Empire*, London: Routledge. • G. N. Stanton and G. Stroumsa, eds. 1998, *Tolerance and Intolerance in Early Judaism and Christianity*, Cambridge: Cambridge University Press.

See also: Animal Worship; Conversion and Proselytism; Gentile Attitudes toward Jews and Judaism;

Gentiles, Jewish Attitudes toward; Hellenism and Hellenization; Idols and Images; Universalism

ROBERT GOLDENBERG

Palaces → Fortresses and Palaces

Paleo-Hebrew Scrolls

The term "paleo-Hebrew" is sometimes used to refer to the old Hebrew script based on Phoenician letter forms, first attested in the tenth century B.C.E. and continuing until today as the Samaritan script. Within the field of paleography, however, paleo-Hebrew is often used in a more narrow sense to describe the conscious use of the older Hebrew script after the loss of Judean national sovereignty, at a time when the Hebrew script was being pushed aside by the Jewish script. Outside of the Dead Sea Scrolls, the paleo-Hebrew script is attested in a few inscriptions (e.g., the Abba inscription), on Hasmonean coins and coins of the First and Second Jewish Revolts, and on a few ostraca from Masada.

The majority of scrolls found at Qumran, both biblical and nonbiblical, are written in Jewish script; however, seventeen texts were found that were written in paleo-Hebrew script (possibly eighteen, if the fragments from Cave 1 are from four, rather than three different scrolls): three (or four?) from Cave 1 (1Q3 paleoLev[a], paleoLev[b], and paleoNum); one from Cave 2 (2Q5 paleoLev); nine from Cave 4 (4Q11 paleoGen-Exod[l], 4Q12 paleoGen[m], 4Q22 paleoExod[m], 4Q45 paleoDeut[r], 4Q46 paleoDeut[s], 4Q101 paleoJob[c], 4Q123 paleoparaJosh, 4Q124 paleo-unid 1, and 4Q125 paleo-unid 2); two from Cave 6 (6Q1 paleoGen and 6Q2 paleoLev); and two, including the most extensive of the paleo-Hebrew scrolls, from Cave 11 (11Q1 paleoLev[a] and 11Q22 paleo-Unid.).

The paleo-Hebrew texts are for the most part biblical manuscripts, with the majority preserving portions of the Torah, the exceptions being 4Q101 paleoJob[c] and 4Q123 paleoparaJosh (plus, possibly, three fragmentary and therefore unidentified texts). While all five books of Torah are attested among the Qumran Scrolls, the best and most extensive portions come from Exodus and Leviticus.

All but one of the scrolls (4Q45 paleoDeut[r]) share in common the use of dots or short strokes that function as word dividers, a feature which is not true of the Qumran biblical scrolls in Jewish script. Various methods are used within the scrolls to mark paragraphs or sections, although the divisions in the Qumran Scrolls do not consistently match the divisions found in the Masoretic tradition (Ulrich 1999: 141).

Many of the scrolls have been dated on paleographical grounds by McLean (1982). The two oldest, according to his analysis, are 4Q46 paleoDeut[s] and 4Q101 paleoJob[c], dated to the last part of the third to the mid-second century B.C.E. 4Q12 paleoGen[m] dates to the mid-second century B.C.E., with 4Q123 paleoparaJosh around the same period. The majority of texts are dated to the first three quarters of the first century B.C.E. McLean places 11Q1 paleoLev[a] in the first half of the first century C.E., although Hanson (1985) earlier dated it to around 100 B.C.E.

The orthography of the scrolls ranges from quite conservative (4Q101 paleoJob[c]) to full (4Q22 paleoExod[m] and 6Q2 paleoLev). Most of the scrolls, like the MT, display a mixed, and not altogether consistent, orthography.

Many of the manuscripts are quite fragmentary. Four, however, are extensive enough that observations about their extent and text type can be made with some degree of confidence.

4Q11 paleoGen-Exod[l]

4QpaleoGen-Exod[l] consists of forty-one fragments containing what is probably the final verse of Genesis (Gen. 50:26) and portions of Exodus 1–36, up to 36:36 (one fragment possibly cites 40:15), which may indicate that the scroll originally included both Genesis and Exodus. The text, generally conservative in nature, falls into the tradition represented by the Masoretic text and the Samaritan text-base, agreeing at times with one, at times with the other, at times disagreeing with both. It is described by Ulrich (1999) as "edition I," the earliest extant tradition of Exodus.

4Q22 paleoExod[m]

4Qpaleo-Exod[m] preserves fragments of forty-three columns out of a consecutive forty-five, with portions of Exod. 6:25–37:16, making it one of the most extensive biblical manuscripts from Cave 4. Variants from the MT place the text within the Samaritan tradition. The extant portions of paleoExod[m] preserve twelve major expansions of the Samaritan tradition over against the MT, as well as one difference in the order of verses (26:35 before 30:1-10). The one expansion of the Samaritan text not present in 4QpaleoExod[m] is the commandment (composed from Deut. 11:20-30 and 27:2-7) to build an altar on Mt. Gerizim. In the Samaritan text that commandment appears as 20:17b. The presence of 4QpaleoExod[m] among the Qumran Scrolls thus indicates that the later Samaritan text is descended from a text that was at one time in wider use (Skehan, Ulrich, and Sanderson 1992).

4Q45 paleoDeut[r]

4Q45 includes fifty-nine fragments preserving small portions (some 85-94 verses in all plus unidentified fragments) of Deut. 1:8 to 34:1, although the identification of some fragments is questionable. The text does not show distinctive Samaritan features, being closer to the MT and LXX text traditions, although in minor variants the scroll does follow the Samaritan against the MT. Twelve readings are unique to the scroll.

11Q1 paleoLev[a]

11Q1 is by far the most extensive of the paleo-Hebrew scrolls. It consists of sixteen fragments and a scroll of seven columns (the bottom portion of the original) plus "miscellaneous, useless bits" (Freedman and

Mathews 1985). An additional fragment (L), which fits between frg. K and col. 1, is reportedly in France. The fragments cover portions of Leviticus from 4:24 to 22:27, while the scroll contains parts of 22:21 through 27:19. The scroll has two sheets sewn together: cols. 1-3 on one sheet and cols. 4-6 on the other, with a final blank column.

The text is described by Freedman (1974) as "mixed" in terms of the major text traditions (MT, Samaritan, LXX), but leaning toward the MT and Samaritan traditions. He classifies it as "Palestinian, or proto-Samaritan." Tov (2001), however, calls paleo-Leviticus a "non-aligned" text, noting that the patterns of agreement and disagreement with the major traditions are inconsistent.

While the number of scrolls written entirely in paleo-Hebrew is limited, paleo-Hebrew names for God appear in a number of other scrolls from the area of the Dead Sea. The Tetragrammaton is written in paleo-Hebrew in several other scrolls, for example, 11Q5 Psalms[a] and the Greek Minor Prophets Scroll from Naḥal Ḥever (8ḥevXIIgr). The divine name *ʾl* appears in several manuscripts, for example, 4Q183 Historical Work, and *ʾlwhym* in 4Q57 Isa[c].

Comparison with the Qumran biblical manuscripts in Jewish script indicates that, aside from the script and use of dots as word dividers, the paleo-Hebrew manuscripts show no distinctive characteristics in physical features, date, orthography, or character of text.

BIBLIOGRAPHY

M. BAILLET, J. T. MILIK, AND R. DE VAUX 1962, "Lévitique en écriture paléo-hébraïque," 56-57, pl. XII; "Genése en écriture paléo-hébraïque," 105-6, pl. XX; "Lévitique en écriture paléo-hébraïque," 106, pl. XX, in *Les 'petites grottes' de Qumran,* DJD 3, Oxford: Clarendon. • D. BARTHÉLEMY AND J. T. MILIK 1955, "Lévitique et autres fragments en écriture 'phénicienne,'" in *Qumran Cave 1,* DJD 1, Oxford: Clarendon, 51-54, pls. VIII-IX. • D. N. FREEDMAN 1974, "Variant Readings in the Leviticus Scroll from Qumran Cave 11," *CBQ* 36, 525-34. • D. N. FREEDMAN AND K. A. MATHEWS, WITH R. S. HANSON 1985, *The Paleo-Hebrew Leviticus Scroll (11QpaleoLev),* Philadelphia: American Schools of Oriental Research; Winona Lake, Ind.: Eisenbrauns. • F. GARCÍA MARTÍNEZ, E. J. C. TIGCHELAAR, AND A. S. VAN DER WOUDE 1998, *Qumran Cave 11: II. 11Q2-18, 11Q20-31,* DJD 23, Oxford: Clarendon Press. • M. D. MCLEAN 1982, "The Use and Development of Palaeo-Hebrew in the Hellenistic and Roman Periods," Dissertation, Harvard University. • P. W. SKEHAN, E. ULRICH, AND J. E. SANDERSON 1992, *Qumran Cave 4 IV: Palaeo-Hebrew and Greek Biblical Manuscripts,* DJD 9, Oxford: Clarendon. • E. TOV 2001, *Textual Criticism of the Hebrew Bible,* 2d rev. ed., Minneapolis: Fortress; Assen: Van Gorcum. • E. ULRICH 1999, *The Dead Sea Scrolls and the Origins of the Bible,* Grand Rapids: Eerdmans, 121-47.

MARILYN J. LUNDBERG

Palestinian Talmud

The Palestinian and Babylonian Talmuds are late-antique anthological compilations of Jewish religious and civil law organized as commentaries to the six orders and sixty-three tractates of the Mishnah. The Mishnah, a legal compendium edited, according to tradition, by Rabbi Judah ha-Nasi around 220 C.E., contains the teachings of Palestinian sages (*tannaim;* sg. = *tanna*) who flourished after the destruction of the Temple until the early third century. As one of the earliest formulations of what came to be known as Oral Torah, the Mishnah and related tannaitic traditions were transmitted and studied by rabbinic sages known as *amoraim* (sg. = *amora*) beginning in the early third century C.E. (the amoraic period). The comments and teachings generated by these sages were ultimately organized into a *gemara* (Aramaic for "learning") commentary to the Mishnah found in the Palestinian and Babylonian Talmuds (Mishnah + *gemara* commentary = Talmud). Since scholars traveled between the two centers, traditions and teachings of Palestinian sages were transmitted to Babylonia and appear in the Babylonian Talmud, while Babylonian teachings transmitted to Palestine are to be found in the Palestinian Talmud. Traditional texts refer to the Palestinian Talmud as "the Talmud of the West," "the Talmud of the land of Israel," or "the gemara of the land of Israel." The term *Yerushalmi* ("Jerusalem [Talmud]") found in medieval texts is a misnomer, since the work was not produced in Jerusalem.

The Two Talmuds

The Palestinian and Babylonian Talmuds differ from one another in significant ways. The gemara of the Palestinian Talmud is more concise, more disjointed, and less discursive than that of its Babylonian counterpart. While the growth of the Yerushalmi appears to have stopped abruptly in the latter part of the fourth century, amoraic activity continued in Babylonia for at least another 100 to 150 years. The traditions produced in this period tended toward greater argumentation and abstraction. This later amoraic stage was followed in Babylonia by a further period of approximately 150 years traditionally referred to as the savoraic period, when earlier teachings and sources were more fully embedded in the complex rhetorical and dialectical framework so characteristic of the Babylonian Talmud. In addition to this fundamental difference in character, the Babylonian Talmud contains much more haggadah (nonlegal material) than the Palestinian Talmud. Haggadah constitutes one-third of the former but only one-sixth of the latter. Magic, sorcery, demons, and angels appear often in the Palestinian Talmud, but with far less frequency than in the Babylonian Talmud.

Contents

The Palestinian Talmud covers thirty-nine of the sixty-three tractates of the Mishnah, almost all of which are from the first four of the Mishnah's six orders: *Zeraʿim* ("Seeds," containing the tractate on blessings as well as tractates on agricultural laws of particular interest to those residing in the land of Israel); *Mo'ed* ("Appointed Time," containing tractates pertaining to the Sabbath and festivals); *Našim* ("Women," containing tractates dealing with matters of betrothal, marriage, divorce, vows, etc.); and *Neziqin* ("Torts," containing tractates dealing with torts, lost property, the judicial system, etc.). In addition, the Palestinian Talmud covers the first three chapters of tractate *Niddah* ("Menstruant") from the fifth order of *Toḥorot* ("Purities"). There is no Palestinian gemara for tractate *'Abot* or *'Eduyyot* (in order *Neziqin*), tractate *Šabbat* chaps. 21–24, or *Makkot* chap. 3. Scholars surmise that Palestinian gemara for the missing chapters of *Šabbat* and *Makkot* existed at one time, but has been lost. By contrast, most scholars believe there never was organized Palestinian gemara for the orders *Toḥorot* (with the exception of *Niddah*) and *Qodašim* ("Holy Things"), even though these subjects were studied and generated traditions preserved elsewhere in talmudic literature.

The Palestinian Talmud was originally a continuous text of gemara without a Mishnah text. Only later was the gemara divided by tractate, chapter, and halakah, and the Mishnah text inserted chapter by chapter at the head of the relevant gemara. However, the Mishnah inserted into our Palestinian Talmud manuscripts and printed editions is not identical to the Mishnah upon which the Palestinian gemara was originally based. The Mishnah upon which the comments of the Palestinian Amoraim are based can often be inferred from an analysis of the comments.

Relation to the Mishnah

The Mishnah text that formed the basis of the Palestinian Talmud is also different from that of the Babylonian Talmud, as may be inferred from a comparison of their respective gemaras. Two talmudic stories indicate that R. Judah the Patriarch produced two editions of his Mishnah. L. Ginzberg surmised that the first edition became established in Babylonia while the second, revised edition prevailed in Palestine, but D. Rosenthal has argued the opposite. He follows S. L. Rapoport's view that it was the second edition of the Mishnah that became established in Babylonia; Palestinian Amoraim reverted to the teachings in the first edition. According to Epstein, however, there was no single recension of the Mishnah in Palestine in amoraic times, a function of the oral nature of the Mishnah's transmission and study. The Palestinian gemara seems to show an awareness of the fluid state of the text and alters and emends the Mishnah somewhat freely. Z. Frankel contrasts this Palestinian situation with the situation in Babylonia, where there was, in his view, only one recension of the Mishnah. This may account for the Babylonian Talmud's tendency to engage in text-critical discussion of the Mishnah, trying to justify and account for the text by suggesting ellipses and omissions and resorting less frequently to emendation or source criticism.

Sources

The Palestinian Talmud draws on many sources in its discussion of the Mishnah. Most prominent are related tannaitic teachings, both internal to the Mishnah and external to it. External tannaitic teachings, known as *beraitot* (sing. = *beraita*), are usually cited anonymously *(stam),* but many are attributed. The *beraitot* of three sages in particular, later contemporaries of R. Judah ha-Nasi, are identified: R Hiyya, R. Hoshayah, and Bar Qappara (cited about 200, 80, and 60 times respectively). Many of the *beraitot* cited in the Palestinian Talmud are found in the Tosefta, halakic midrashim, and Babylonian Talmud, a fact suggesting their wide circulation. Despite divergences there is often remarkable similarity. Whether the Palestinian Talmud drew from the Tosefta as a source or both works drew from a common third source is a debated question deeply connected with diverse theories regarding the composition, redaction, transmission, and study of rabbinic texts.

The Palestinian Talmud also contains well over one thousand midrashim attributed to Amoraim, mostly haggadic in nature. Some are paralleled in amoraic midrash and in the Babylonian Talmud, but again the relationship among these various works is a matter of some debate. Finally, Babylonian teachings appear in the Palestinian Talmud often prefaced with phrases like "there they say" or "the rabbis from there say." In many instances the teaching does not appear, or appears in a different form, in the Babylonian Talmud. Traditions are generally cited in Hebrew, whereas discussions and narratives are generally in western Aramaic. The Palestinian Talmud contains much more Greek than does the Babylonian Talmud, though many Greek terms have become seriously corrupted at the hands of uncomprehending scribes.

Centers of Palestinian Amoraic Activity

Several centers of Palestinian amoraic activity were involved in generating the constitutive materials of the Palestinian Talmud — Tiberias and Sepphoris in the Galilee, and Caesarea and (to a far lesser degree) Lydda in the south. Some scholars suppose that complete *sugyot* (passages) emanated from these centers to be compiled finally in Tiberias in a process that is not fully understood. It was once thought that oppression and persecution in Palestine during the third and fourth centuries prompted the hasty compilation of the Palestinian Talmud, a circumstance that would account for its brevity and lack of polish, but there is little evidence to support such a theory. The date of the Palestinian Talmud's redaction, like its motivating circumstances, is somewhat obscure. Five generations of Amoraim are mentioned, and many discussions end with the view of R. Yosi ben R. Bun, who was active in the last half of the fourth century. The last identifiable historical events mentioned in the Palestinian Talmud occurred in the time of Gallus (ca. 351) and possibly Julian (ca. 363). This suggests a date of redaction in the last decades of the fourth century C.E. (The traditional date of 425 assumes an unproven connection between the redaction of the Palestinian Talmud and the demise of the Patriarchate.) The prominence of Tiberian sages, particularly in the later strata of the text, suggests that the redaction took place in Tiberias, the seat of the patriarchate.

Composition and Redaction

The unfinished and disorderly quality of the Palestinian Talmud leads some scholars to posit a simple collection of material rather than a comprehensive final redaction. Thus, contradictions within a *sugya* are to be understood as arising from the simple juxtaposition of diverse sources. The characteristic phenomenon of parallel *sugyot* — lengthy sections of identical or nearly identical material copied from one place to another because of some thematic link — is also taken as a sign of minimal or haphazard redactional activity. These parallels are generally not adapted to their new context and may contain much that is irrelevant.

The *Babot* Tractates

It has long been noted that the first three tractates of *Neziqin (Baba Qamma, Baba Meṣiʿa,* and *Baba Batra)* differ markedly from the rest of the Palestinian Talmud in style, terminology, substance, and sages named. Specifically, these *Babot* tractates are briefer and even less "finished" than the rest of the Palestinian Talmud; they employ many older Hebrew words and many Greek words not used, or used differently, elsewhere; *sugyot* from these tractates diverge from their parallels elsewhere in the Palestinian Talmud; and finally, sages of the first two amoraic generations predominate in these chapters, as well as sages identified elsewhere as "rabbis of Caesarea." S. Lieberman concluded that the *Babot* tractates derive from a slightly earlier period (mid-fourth century) and from a different school, namely, that of Caesarea rather than Tiberias. Against this, J. N. Epstein argued that Caesarean material is found throughout the Palestinian Talmud. According to Epstein there was no single Palestinian Talmud subject to a single editing in a single center, but many different traditions and editings of which the three *Babot* tractates are but one example. Recently, G. Wewers has attempted to confirm the earlier dating of these tractates, while C. Heszer has tried to show that a Caesarean provenance can be neither proven nor excluded.

Relation to the Babylonian Talmud

Each of the two Talmuds contains teachings and sometimes entire passages from the other. Nevertheless, the relationship between the two is not clearly understood. Despite traditional apologetic claims that the redactors of the Babylonian Talmud were familiar with the Palestinian Talmud, critical scholars have by and large rejected the idea that one Talmud saw the other. Epstein allowed that individual Palestinian *sugyot* — taught orally and stemming from various recensions — may have been known in Babylonia, but the redactors of the Babylonian Talmud did not know our Palestinian Talmud. An important challenge to this long-standing consensus is the recent work of A. Gray, whose detailed study of tractate *ʿAbodah Zarah* argues for the Babylonian Talmud's dependence on, and amplification of, a redacted Palestinian tractate.

The Palestinian Talmud was authoritative for Jews in Palestine, Egypt, Kairowan, and southern Italy as late as the seventh century. With the establishment of the Abassid Caliphate and the extension of Islamic rule, Babylonian Jewish traditions gained ascendancy. Eventually, the Babylonian Talmud eclipsed the Palestinian Talmud. The latter was widely neglected in medieval times, except in Spain.

Manuscripts and Printed Editions

Although fragments of the Palestinian Talmud have been found in the Cairo Genizah, the only complete manuscript of the Palestinian Talmud — and thus our sole link to that Talmud's redactors — is Leiden, Scaliger no. 3, completed in 1289 by Yehiel b. Yekutiel of Rome, a careful scribe who complains in the colophon of the corrupt nature of the text from which he copied. The Leiden manuscript was the basis for the first printed edition in Venice, 1522-1523, by Daniel Bomberg. The manuscript contains marginal and interlinear additions and emendations, including the many corruptions and erroneous alterations of the printing house compositor. All subsequent modern editions, despite further corruptions and alterations to harmonize the text with the Babylonian Talmud's style and substance, are based on the Venice printed edition; these include the Krotoschin edition of 1886, the Zhitomer edition of 1860-1867, the Peterkov edition of 1898, and the Vilna edition of 1922. Thus the Leiden manuscript stands at the base of every known edition of the Palestinian Talmud. Another important manuscript is the Spanish Escorial manuscript G-1-3 of the three *Babot* tractates of *Neziqin* (*Baba Qamma* 3–*Baba Batra* 9). Escorial preserves Galilean Hebrew and Aramaic more accurately than does Leiden, and it exhibits strong affinities with the Geniza fragments.

Significance

The Talmuds are important sources for knowledge of Jews and Judaism in late antiquity, and the Palestinian Talmud is a critically important source for what would prove to be a period of extraordinary transformation for Palestinian Jewish society: the first four centuries of the Common Era.

Bibliography

B. Bokser 1981, "An Annotated Bibliographical Guide to the Palestinian Talmud," in *The Study of Ancient Judaism,* vol. 2, ed. J. Neusner, New York: Ktav. • J. N. Epstein 1962, *Introductions to Amoraic Literature: Bavli and Yerushalmi,* Jerusalem: Magnes (in Hebrew). • L. Ginzberg 1941-1961, *A Commentary on the Palestinian Talmud: A Study of the Development of the Halakhah and Haggadah in Palestine and Babylonia,* New York: Jewish Theological Seminary (in Hebrew; Introduction in English). • A. Goldberg 1987, "The Palestinian Talmud," in *The Literature of the Sages: First Part: Oral Torah, Halakhah, Mishna, Tosefta, Talmud, External Tractates,* ed. S. Safrai, Assen: Van Gorcum; Philadelphia: Fortress. • A. Gray 2005, *A Talmud in Exile: The Influence of Yerushalmi Avodah Zarah on the Formation of Bavli Avodah Zarah,* Providence, R.I.: Brown University Press. • S. Lieberman 1995, *HaYerushalmi Kif-*

shuto, 2 vols., New York and Jerusalem: Darom. • E. S. ROSENTHAL, ED. 1983, *Yerushalmi Neziqin: Edited from the Escorial Manuscript with an Introduction by E. S. Rosenthal, Introduction and Commentary by S. Lieberman,* Jerusalem: The Israel Academy. • P. SCHÄFER, ED. 1998-2000, *The Talmud Yerushalmi and Graeco-Roman Culture,* 3 vols., Tübingen: Mohr-Siebeck. • P. SCHÄFER AND H.-J. BECKER, EDS. 1991-1992, *Synopse zum Talmud Yerushalmi,* Tübingen: Mohr-Siebeck. • G. STEMBERGER AND H. L. STRACK 1996, *Introduction to the Talmud and Midrash,* 2d ed., Minneapolis: Fortress.

See also: Babylonian Talmud

CHRISTINE HAYES

Paneion

A large natural cave located in the side of a cliff at modern-day Banias (Arabic for Panias), the Paneion served for more than six centuries as a sanctuary for the god Pan. The cave was located at the foot of Mt. Hermon, originally in a rural setting. From its base poured forth springs that formed one of the sources of the Jordan River (see a description in Josephus, *Ant.* 15.10.3). As the result of an earthquake, the floor of the cave is now filled with rock rather than water.

While some scholars suggest an original connection of the place with the Canaanite god Baʿal, worship of Pan at the Paneion seems to have originated in the third century B.C.E., perhaps at the same time as the renewal of interest in the nearby sanctuary at Dan. The careers of the two sacred places may have been in some way linked. Around 200 B.C.E. the Paneion was the location of the defeat of the Ptolemaic army by Antiochus III, which transferred control of the Galilee and Judea to the Seleucids. Appropriately, the elephants of the Seleucid cavalry sent the Ptolemaic forces into a panic.

Before the rise of Herod the Great, the rural setting shaped the worship of Pan at the Paneion. Ceramic evidence points to the offering of meals and "picnicking" at the location, probably by residents of neighboring sites like Tel Anafa. In 20 B.C.E. Augustus gave the region to Herod the Great, who built a temple in the vicinity of the cave of Pan to honor his new patron, thus introducing the cult of the emperor to the Paneion and transforming the rural shrine into a royal sanctuary. There is some dispute over whether this Augustaeum was located immediately in front of the cave of Pan or elsewhere, perhaps at Omrit, a short distance to the south where a tetrastyle temple from the period is under excavation.

Upon Herod's death, his son Philip inherited the region, founding his capital, Caesarea Philippi, below the Paneion in 3 B.C.E. In 53/54 C.E. Agrippa II inherited the kingdom and built a massive and magnificent royal palace, recently excavated, near the Paneion. In 61 C.E. he renamed the city Neronias in honor of his new patron, but the name did not survive the death of Nero. During the First Revolt against Rome (66-70 C.E.), the Jewish population of the region remained loyal to Rome, although at the beginning of the revolt members of the community had been imprisoned and executed by the surrounding pagan population. Caesarea Philippi was the site of games celebrating the fall of Jerusalem in 70 C.E., in which many Jewish prisoners perished. By the end of the first century, Herodian rule ended with the death of Agrippa II, and the Paneion became the civic shrine of the city of Panias.

In the period following the end of Herodian rule, the sacred precinct of the Paneion expanded along the terrace upon which the cave opened, with the addition of a temple to Zeus and other courts and buildings associated with the worship of Pan and related deities. From this period one inscription on the cliff face, dedicating a statue to the nymph Echo as the result of a dream, indicates the possibility of an incubation oracle at the site. The inscription provides a potential parallel to *1 Enoch* 13, which depicts Enoch engaging in an incubation oracle at nearby Dan. Ceramic evidence, including small lamps, suggests that over time worshipers became more affluent and less likely to spend a lot of time at the cave. The remains of marble statuary, apparently of Anatolian origin, indicate that the Paneion had become highly Romanized, in contrast to the Semitic background of the surrounding population. During this period Pan evolved from the goat-footed god of shepherds into a more universal deity appropriate for the name Pan, "All," who could be identified with Zeus.

Evidence exists for a Jewish presence in the area. A mosaic inscription on a synagogue floor at Rehob near Scythopolis/Beth Shean (cf. *t. Šebu.* 4:11; *y. Šebuʿot* 36c) suggests that among other locations

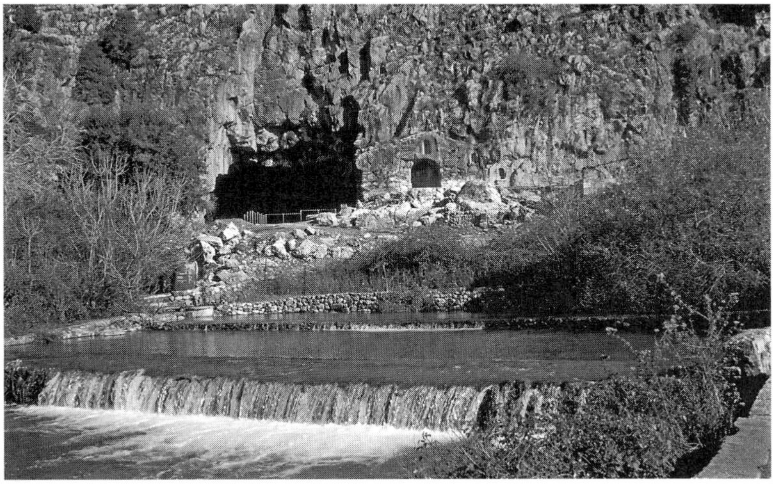

Paneion (Banias) at the foot of Mt. Hermon *(Phoenix Data Systems / Neal and Joel Bierling)*

Panias was on the boundary of the traditional area of Jewish habitation. The boundary issue complicated the application of rules pertaining to tithes and the sabbatical year. Archaeologists have discovered what may be a synagogue built on the ruins of Agrippa's palace.

In the New Testament, Matthew 16 identifies the villages of Caesarea Philippi as the location for Peter's confession of Jesus as the Messiah, although the "rock" to which Peter is implicitly compared may be Mt. Hermon rather than the cliff in which the Paneion is located. Later evidence exists for both a Gentile-Christian and a Jewish-Christian presence at the location. Interest in the Paneion seems to have waned in the fifth century, after the ascendancy of Christianity over paganism. Yet there is no evidence that the shrine was actively suppressed or deliberately destroyed.

BIBLIOGRAPHY

A. M. BERLIN 1999, "The Archaeology of Ritual: The Sanctuary of Pan at Banias/Caesarea Philippi," *BASOR* 315: 27-45. • E. LIPIŃSKI 1971, "El's Abode: Mythological Traditions Related to Mount Hermon," *OLP* 2: 13-69. • Z. U. MAʿOZ 1993, "Banias," in *The New Encyclopedia of Archaeological Excavations in the Holy Land,* ed. E. Stern, New York: Simon and Schuster, 1: 136-43. • G. W. E. NICKELSBURG 2001, *1 Enoch,* vol. 1, Minneapolis: Fortress, 238-47. • V. TZAFERIS 1992, "Cults and Deities Worshipped at Caesarea Philippi–Banias," in *Priests, Prophets and Scribes,* ed. E. Ulrich et al., Sheffield: Sheffield Academic Press. • J. W. WILSON 2004, *Caesarea Philippi: Banias, the Lost City of Pan,* London: Tauris. • J. F. WILSON AND V. TZAFERIS 1998, "Banias Dig Reveals King's Palace," *BAR* 24: 54-61, 85.

DAVID W. SUTER

Papyri

Writing in the ancient world that was not intended to last indefinitely was usually done on papyrus, a writing material made from the pith of a plant indigenous to the Nile River Valley. Papyrology is the study of nonliterary writing on papyrus and other temporary materials such as potsherds (ostraca), parchment, and wood. Most papyri come from Egypt and are written in Greek. Within Egypt, most papyri have been found in the Fayûm and the Nile Valley further south, not in the Nile Delta. Published papyri are normally referred to by a system of abbreviations listed in Oates et al. 2005; there has, however, been difficulty in establishing a standard system for referring to papyri from Judea.

Papyri from Egypt

The standard collection of papyri relating to Jews in Ptolemaic and Roman Egypt, *Corpus Papyrorum Judaicarum (CPJ),* was published in three volumes, the last of which appeared in 1964. A fourth volume with more recently published papyri has been planned, and Fikhman (1997) lists ninety-seven papyri that will be included.

Elephantine Papyri

Porten (1996) has English translations of the Aramaic papyri from Elephantine, which concern a Jewish garrison on the southern border of Egypt while it was under Persian rule (sixth-fourth centuries B.C.E.). Among the papyri are letters (both private and communal), contracts, a literary text *(Words of Aḥiqar),* historical texts, and accounts. The archive provides valuable insight into the religious and social life of the Jewish colonists who lived there. They established their own temple to YHW (an abbreviation of YHWH), whom they worshiped alongside a female consort (Anat-yhw) and other deities, in a cultic system that included meal offerings, incense burning, and animal sacrifice. Two pieces of official correspondence are particularly noteworthy. The first is a letter from Hananiah addressed to Jedaniah and his colleagues in the "garrison of the Jews." It was written in the fifth year of the reign of Darius II (419 B.C.E.) and contains regulations for the observance of *Maṣṣôt* (Unleavened Bread). The second is a letter of 408 B.C.E. written by Jedaniah and his colleagues, the priests at Elephantine, and addressed to Bagoas, the governor of Judea (cf. Neh. 12:22; Josephus, *Ant.* 11.297-301). The letter recounts the destruction of the Elephantine temple by Egyptians two years earlier, mentions an unsuccessful appeal for help to the Jerusalem high priest Yoḥanan, and requests the assistance of Bagoas in rebuilding it.

The Nash Papyrus

One exceptional papyrus, surviving in four contiguous fragments and known as the Nash Papyrus (text and photograph in Würthwein 1995), contains a Hebrew text including the Decalogue, in a form which contains elements from both the Exodus and Deuteronomy versions and has similarities to the Hebrew text underlying the Septuagint, and the beginning of the Shemaʿ prayer. It was acquired in Egypt from an antiquities dealer in 1902 and may have originated from the Fayûm. Dating the papyrus is very difficult because there is nothing from Egypt to compare it with, and until the discovery of the Dead Sea Scrolls it was the earliest known biblical text in Hebrew. The original editors thought it was from the first or second century C.E., but recent studies influenced by comparison with the Dead Sea Scrolls have favored the second century B.C.E. A fragmentary Hebrew prayer after meals was also found at Dura-Europos in Mesopotamia (P. Dura 10). These papyri thus provide some evidence for the use of Hebrew as a liturgical language in places where it does not otherwise appear to have been spoken. With these exceptions, however, all the Hebrew papyri from Egypt date to late antiquity.

Identifying Jewish Papyri

Identifying Jews in papyri and ostraca where there is no specific designation of an individual as "Jew" depends on various criteria. Aramaic was used in Egypt by people other than Jews during the Persian period, and does not in itself indicate Jewishness. The use of recognizably Jewish names has been the most important criterion, particularly for periods where there is no risk of confusion with Christians. For example, a series of documents shows the existence of four generations of a family in second-century-B.C.E. Thebes, including two people called Joseph and one Isaac, as well as two with the non-Jewish name Straton (Clarysse 2002). The broad definition of Jewish names in *CPJ* led to the identification of some individuals as Jewish whose names were also used by other Semitic groups. There was a fondness for Greek theophoric names such as Theodorus, Theodotus, and Dositheus, all meaning "God-given," but these were not necessarily exclusive to Jews.

The Label Ioudaios in Papyri

The label *Ioudaios* originally meant "from Judea" in a strictly geographical sense, but it gradually came to denote a religious rather than regional affiliation (Kraemer 1989). Its earliest use in a papyrus is dated to 260 B.C.E. (*CPJ* 18). A number of documents from the village of Samaria in the Fayûm, dated to 232 B.C.E., including a lease and negotiations about a dowry, designate people as *Ioudaios* or *Ioudaia,* only one of whom, Jonathas, has a clearly Jewish name (*Corpus Papyrorum Raineri* XVIII 7-9, 11). Some of these are styled "Jew of the Epigone," meaning that they had been born in Egypt but retained an ethnic identity from immigrant ancestors. *Ioudaios* is fairly rare in papyri after the second century B.C.E. because an individual's Jewishness was not relevant to most of the transactions that papyri record.

Evidence for Jews in Various Occupations

Papyri provide evidence for Jews in the Ptolemaic army, including a list where the names of "Jews" and "Macedonians" are mixed (*CPJ* 30). Some were cleruchs (military settlers with substantial allotments of land); others worked in an agricultural context or lived in predominantly agricultural villages. Some Jews who describe themselves as *taktomisthoi* (an army rank) made an agreement with a contractor to undertake work in a vineyard at Alexandrou Nesos in the Fayûm in 152 B.C.E. (P. Köln 3.144), and three other Jews were accused of stealing the grapes from ten vines (*CPJ* 21). There is also evidence for Jewish artisans including potters and weavers, Jews involved in transport by land and river, and Jews in royal service such as tax collectors and police. These are all the sorts of people who would not be mentioned in literary sources. Dositheus son of Drimylus, who appears in 3 Maccabees as a leading official at the court of Ptolemy IV (222-205 B.C.E.), is mentioned in papyri of approximately the right date, but with no indication of Jewish origin apart from his name, and in fact he is recorded as priest of the royal cult (*CPJ* 127).

Jews and the Ptolemaic Legal System

Papyri usually show Jews operating within the general legal system of Ptolemaic Egypt. A complaint by a woman named Helladote about her husband Jonathas the Jew appears to say that he "agreed in accordance with the law of the Jews to hold me as wife," but the restoration of the text is uncertain (*CPJ* 128). A papyrus from Alexandrou-Nesos dated to 218 B.C.E. (*CPJ* 129) deals with a woman's complaint about Dorotheus, who took her cloak and fled with it to the Jewish prayer house *(proseuchē).* Both these documents are addressed to the king, showing that Jews, like other inhabitants of Egypt, habitually referred legal problems to him. A dispute between two Jews about an assault was settled by a local court at Arsinoe in 226 B.C.E. (*CPJ* 19; it has, however, been claimed that this was a court of the Jewish community) and followed the procedure of Ptolemaic law to such an extent that the Jewish woman Heracleia appeared in court with her male guardian *(kyrios)* — a requirement of the Ptolemaic system — who is described as "Athenian of the Epigone." An interest-free loan of money from one Jew to another with penalties for late repayment was recorded in standard Ptolemaic style with a dating formula naming the rulers as gods (*CPJ* 23).

Papyri from Herakleopolis

There is a collection of documents from Herakleopolis, datable between 144/3 and 133/2 B.C.E. and published by Cowey and Maresch (2001), who argue that they prove the existence of a Jewish *politeuma* (self-governing community of aliens) in this Fayûm town. Previously there was considerable doubt about whether Jewish communities had this status, although it was attested from the second century B.C.E. for other groups such as the Idumeans at Memphis. Jews appear to have come to Herakleopolis as military settlers, which was the normal basis for a *politeuma.* Their organization included a *politarch,* probably a leader chosen annually, and *archontes,* officials who dealt with legal disputes between local Jews and were able to make decisions according to "ancestral custom," which appears to have been a fusion of Jewish and Ptolemaic law. Jews from other villages in the Herakleopolite district were able to appeal against their own elders *(presbyteroi)* to the *archontes.* There was a community archive *(archeion)* and a scribe *(grammateus).* This terminology may give some indication of how the Jewish settlement at Leontopolis (known from Josephus and from inscriptions) was organized, but there is no papyrological evidence as such for Leontopolis, although a letter to an official named Onias (*CPJ* 132) dated to 164 B.C.E. could be addressed to Onias IV, who founded the settlement.

Evidence for Jews in the Roman Period

There is substantial papyrological evidence for the Jews in Egypt after it became a Roman province in 30 B.C.E. For the first century of Roman rule, Jewish activities continued in much the same way in rural Egypt. Egyptian Jews had to deal with the question of how to refer to the emperor, a potential difficulty because most emperors from Augustus onward designated themselves "son of a god." For example, Augustus was officially designated *divi filius,* meaning adoptive son of the deified Julius Caesar. Such nomenclature could be offensive to Jews, and this is confirmed by a contract of 3 C.E. (*CPJ* 411), in which the borrower, Sambathion son of Dionysius, is assumed to be a Jew because of his name;

the lender, Heracles, is apparently not Jewish. The first part, written for or on behalf of Heracles, uses the expression "Caesar, son of the god" in the dating formula, but only "Caesar" is used in the date in Sambathion's part. On the other hand, in a notification of death from the Fayûm dated 101 C.E. (*CPJ* 427), Soteles, son of Joseph and husband of Sarah, reports the death of his son Joseph. The names leave no doubt about the family's Jewishness. The papyrus is written in three different hands. The third hand, which the editors take as Soteles' own, reads: "Soteles, son of Joseph, the abovementioned, I swear by the Emperor Caesa[r Nerva] Trajan Augu[stus]. . . ." Soteles did not take advantage of the exemption from the imperial cult that normally applied to Jews. Another papyrus from near the Dead Sea records a Jew swearing by the fortune *(tychē)* of the emperor in 127 C.E. (Cotton 1995, no. 2).

Papyri concerning Alexandria

Papyri do not normally survive from Alexandria because of the physical conditions there, but some found elsewhere in Egypt are informative about the situation in the city when read in conjunction with the literary evidence of Philo and Josephus. In particular, a petition to the governor from a Jew named Helenus son of Tryphon (*CPJ* 151, 5/4 B.C.E.) claims exemption from the poll tax (which was paid by Jews but not by Alexandrian citizens) on the grounds that Helenus' father was an Alexandrian citizen and he himself had a Greek education, presumably in the gymnasium. The letter was written by a scribe who changed the original designation of Helenus, "Alexandrian," to "Jew from Alexandria." Thus it seems that Helenus was not entitled to citizenship himself, presumably because his mother was not a citizen. Another papyrus about a legacy (*CPJ* 143, 13 B.C.E.) refers to a will being kept "in the archive *(archeion)* of the Jews" at Alexandria. A woman assumed to be Jewish from her name, Theodote daughter of Dositheus, was engaged as a wet nurse for a foundling baby (*CPJ* 146, 13 B.C.E.). A private letter of 41 C.E. (*CPJ* 152) tells the recipient to "beware of the Jews," a warning that has been interpreted in the context as a reference to moneylenders. Both Claudius' letter to the city of Alexandria about the status of the Jews in the city (*CPJ* 153) and the so-called *Acta Alexandrinorum* (Musurillo 1954), which record various events in the communal strife between Greeks and Jews at Alexandria from a Greek perspective, are preserved on papyrus.

Jewish Presence along the Nile

Papyri and ostraca illustrate the presence of Jews in various places along the Nile during the Roman period. There is a list of payers of the Jewish tax at Arsinoe (*CPJ* 421, 73 C.E.), where the oldest is a woman of sixty-one and the youngest is aged three. A list of people and institutions paying for water supply at Arsinoe in 113 C.E. (*CPJ* 432) indicates that there were two synagogues there: "the *proseuchē* of the Jews of the Thebaid" and the *eucheion.* One prayer house or synagogue *(proseuchē)* seems to have been the venue for meetings of a burial club (*CPJ* 138). A record of the sale of a house in the Jewish street or quarter *(amphodos)* of Oxyrhynchus names the purchasers as "Jews of Oxyrhynchus" (*CPJ* 423).

Taxation of Jews after 70 C.E.

Papyri do not provide any evidence for the impact which the Jewish Revolt of 66-70 C.E. had in Egypt, but they are very informative about its later effects. Most of our knowledge of how Vespasian's Jewish tax worked comes from a large number of ostraca from Apollinopolis Magna (Edfu), mostly dated to 70-116 C.E. *CPJ* 160-229 are receipts for payments of the tax, showing that it was enforced (retrospectively) in Vespasian's second year, which in Egypt ran from September 69, before the fall of Jerusalem. A typical record (*CPJ* 170) reads: "Theodorus son of Antonius Rufus, in respect of the 2-denarii tax on the Jews for the 7th year of Vespasian, 8 drachmai 2 obols; in respect of the *aparchai* 1 drachma." Egyptian Jews often had to pay two obols on top of the basic rate of the tax, as well as a further payment for *aparchai* ("firstfruits") levied in many cases. The tax was paid by (or on behalf of) males and females between the ages of two and sixty-three, including slaves belonging to Jewish owners. Some of the same people are recorded as paying other taxes too, and in most cases the Jewish tax represented the biggest part of their tax bill. The poll tax of sixteen drachmae would have been less of a burden in most cases as it was only levied on adult males, not on all household members.

Paucity of Papyri after 117 C.E.

One of the consequences of the Diaspora Revolt of 115-117 C.E. is the almost complete disappearance of papyrological evidence for Jews in Egypt for a lengthy period afterward. Some payments of the Jewish tax are recorded at Karanis in 145/6 or 168/9 (*CPJ* 460), but nowhere else. Papyri provide some indirect evidence for the history of the revolt itself, mainly through letters by people involved on the anti-Jewish side.

Papyri from Judea

The Zenon Archive

Until relatively recently, not many papyri from outside Egypt were known. A few from Egypt refer to people and events in Judea. The Zenon Archive, belonging to a finance minister of Ptolemy II (ruled 283-246 B.C.E.) whose secretary was named Zenon, includes some references to dealings with Toubias, a powerful Jewish figure in the Transjordan region whose family is known from Josephus (*CPJ* 1-5). The archive includes letters, accounts, lists, receipts, and memoranda. Though the documents reveal little about Judaism, they are a valuable source of information for the social, economic, and political conditions of the Ptolemaic dynasty, revealing much about trade relations between Palestine and Egypt and about taxes on land and agricultural products.

Recent Finds

With the publication of the Discoveries in the Judaean Desert series (DJD) and excavation reports for various

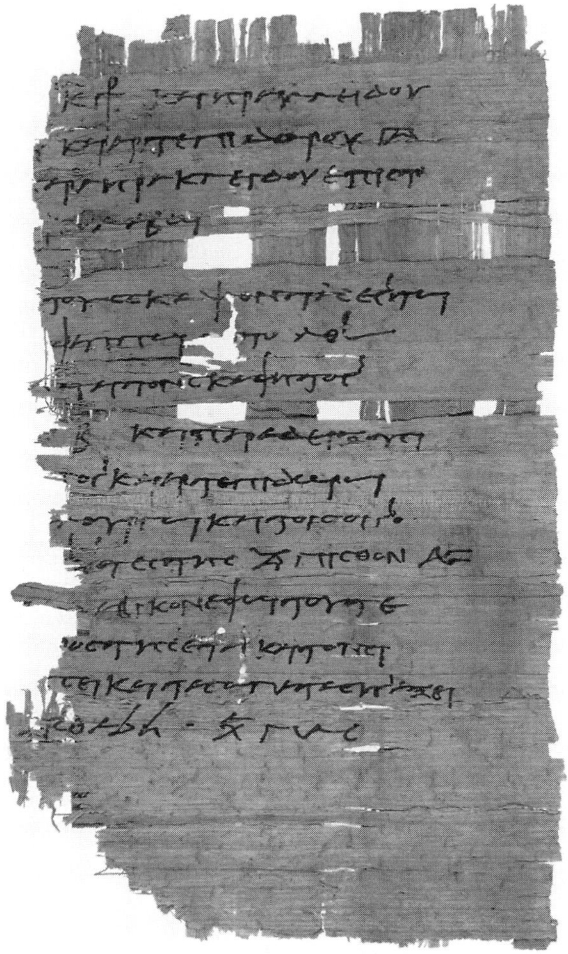

Fragment of a papyrus contract written in Greek from the Zenon Archive *(University of Michigan)*

Judean sites, a greater number of papyri have come to light. In some circumstances, the dry conditions of the Judean Desert proved favorable to the preservation of papyri. Cotton et al. (1995) give a survey of the extent of non-Egyptian papyri, but publications have continued since their article. Texts and English translations of most Judean Desert papyri are now available in Yardeni (2000).

Masada

The excavations at Masada produced many documents (primarily ostraca), and those concerning Jewish rather than Roman occupants were mainly published by Yadin and Naveh (1989). About 275 ostraca with one to three Hebrew or Greek letters and about 700 with names in Hebrew script may have been used as food-rationing tokens during the siege. Some ostraca with names on them, including "Ben Yair," could be the lots described by Josephus (*J.W.* 7.395) that were used for the final suicide pact. About fifteen fragments of parchment with Hebrew biblical or other literary texts were also found at Masada, and may have originated at Qumran. There were also abecedaries (exercises by scribes to practice writing individual letters of the alphabet), which have been found at other sites as well. Latin papyri found at the site were left by the Roman army and include a fragmentary pay record. A bilingual Latin and Greek papyrus with a list of apparently Jewish names may be a record of Jews working for the Romans (Masada II 748 in Cotton and Geiger 1989). The papyri have not settled the debate about whether Masada fell in Spring 73 or 74 C.E. (Cotton 1989).

The Babatha Archive

The most extensive collection of documents from in and around Judea is the Babatha Archive, which preserves some three dozen documents dated from 94 to 132 C.E. They belonged to a Jewish woman who was apparently caught up in the Bar Kokhba Revolt (132-135 C.E.) and hid her archive for future retrieval. The archive was found in the so-called Cave of Letters in Naḥal Ḥever and includes texts written mostly in Greek but also in Aramaic and Nabatean. They pertain to Babatha's private legal and financial matters and provide valuable insight into marriage and divorce, widowhood, the payment of dowries and inheritance rights, and the rights of orphans.

The Salome Komaïse Archive

A smaller archive belonging to Salome Komaïse, daughter of Levi, and her family (Cotton 1995) includes documents in Greek, Aramaic, and Nabatean. Greek was the language of the Roman administration, whereas Aramaic and Nabatean were the local languages, but Greek was used in personal documents, too. The area around the Dead Sea in the provinces of Judea and Arabia (which was the kingdom of Nabatea until 106 C.E.) was clearly multilingual. Salome's documents cover the period 125-131 C.E. and were lost in the same circumstances as Babatha's; both women came from the village of Mahoza in Arabia. The documents include a receipt for tax on dates, the end of a declaration of land made for a provincial census in 127 C.E., a deed of the gift of a date orchard to Salome from her mother, and the marriage contract for Salome's second marriage in which her husband agrees "to feed and clothe both her and her children to come in accordance with Greek custom and Greek manners."

The Bar Kokhba Letters

More than twenty letters from the leader of the Second Revolt have been found in the caves of Wadi Murabbaʿat and Naḥal Ḥever. Eleven of the letters are in Hebrew, eight are in Aramaic, and two are in Greek. Most of them were sent by Bar Kokhba himself and concern various logistical matters such as the sending and receipt of food and other supplies. The letters show that Bar Kokhba's real name was Shimon bar Kosiba. They also reflect his concern for observing the Jewish festivals; one letter (Ḥev. 15), for instance, concerns arrangements for gathering the four "species" for the celebration of Sukkot; it was written in Aramaic by Kosiba and addressed to Yehudah bar Manasseh.

Other Papyri

A number of papyri found near Jericho also appear to have been hidden in a cave at the time of the revolt. They concern business transactions, but there is also a list of names with sums of money (apparently loans and repayments) dated to the fourth century B.C.E. (DJD 38: 21-30). Other Judean papyri have extended knowledge about matters such as marriage, divorce, and loans, although there is often controversy about their interpretation. Papyrus Se'elim 13 (Instone-Brewer 1999) seems to be a divorce certificate sent by a Jewish wife, Shelamzion of ʿEin Gedi, to her husband Eleazar, during the Bar Kokhba Revolt. It does not give any indication of the grounds for the divorce, but it does show that it was possible for a Jewish woman to divorce her husband at this date. Papyrus Murabbaʿat 2.18 (published in DJD 2), an Aramaic text dated 54/55 C.E., gives details of a loan with a penalty clause if it is not repaid in time "even though this is a year of release." The text provides an example of the *prosbul* in action by which debtors agreed to forego the cancellation of debts that should have happened in sabbatical years. Papyrus Yadin 36 (reconstructed by Yardeni 2001), written in Nabatean in about 60 C.E., shows a creditor seizing and selling off some property including a palm grove, which the debtors' heir was later able to redeem; the surviving document is classified as a "redemption of a writ of seizure."

BIBLIOGRAPHY

W. CLARYSSE 2002, "A Jewish Family in Ptolemaic Thebes," *Journal of Juristic Papyrology* 32: 7-9. • H. M. COTTON 1989, "The Date of the Fall of Masada: The Evidence of the Masada Papyri," *Zeitschrift für Papyrologie und Epigraphik* 78: 157-62. • H. M. COTTON AND J. GEIGER 1989, *Masada II: The Latin and Greek Documents*, Jerusalem: Israel Exploration Society. • H. M. COTTON 1995, "The Archive of Salome Komaise, Daughter of Levi," *Zeitschrift für Papyrologie und Epigraphik* 105: 171-208. • H. M. COTTON ET AL. 1995, "The Papyrology of the Roman Near East: A Survey," *Journal of Roman Studies* 85: 214-35. • H. M. COTTON AND A. YARDENI, EDS. 1997, *Aramaic, Hebrew, and Greek Documentary Texts from Naḥal Ḥever and Other Sites*, Seiyal Collection 2, DJD 27, Oxford: Clarendon. • J. COWEY AND K. MARESCH, EDS. 2001, *Urkunden des Politeuma der Juden von Herakleopolis (144/3-133/2 v.Chr.)*, Wiesbaden: Westdeutscher Verlag. • I. FIKHMAN 1997, "L'état des travaux au *Corpus Papyrorum Judaicarum* IV," *Archiv für Papyrusforschung* 3.1: 290-96. • D. INSTONE BREWER 1999, "Jewish Women Divorcing Their Husbands in Early Judaism: The Background to Papyrus Se'elim 13," *HTR* 92: 349-57. • R. KRAEMER 1989, "On the Meaning of the Term Jew in Graeco-Roman Inscriptions," *HTR* 82: 35-53. • N. LEWIS 1989, *The Documents from the Bar Kochba Period in the Cave of Letters: Greek Papyri*, Jerusalem: Israel Exploration Society. • H. MUSURILLO 1954, *Acts of the Pagan Martyrs*, vol. 1, Oxford: Clarendon. • J. OATES ET AL. 2005, *Checklist of Greek, Latin, Demotic and Coptic Papyri, Ostraca and Tablets*, http://scriptorium.lib.duke.edu/papyrus/texts/clist.html. • B. PORTEN 1979, "A New Look: Aramaic Papyri and Parchments," *BA* 42: 74-104. • B. PORTEN 1996, *The Elephantine Papyri in English*, Leiden: Brill. • V. TCHERIKOVER, A. FUKS, AND M. STERN 1957-1964, *Corpus Papyrorum Judaicarum*, 3 vols., Cambridge, Mass.: Harvard University Press. • E. WÜRTHWEIN 1995, *The Text of the Old Testament*, 2d ed., Grand Rapids: Eerdmans. • Y. YADIN AND J. NAVEH 1989, *Masada I: The Aramaic and Hebrew Ostraca and Jar Inscriptions*, Jerusalem: Israel Exploration Society. • A. YARDENI 2000, *Textbook of Aramaic, Hebrew and Nabataean Documentary Texts from the Judaean Desert and Related Materials*, 2 vols., Jerusalem: Hebrew University. • A. YARDENI 2001, "The Decipherment and Restoration of Legal Texts from the Judaean Desert: A Reexamination of Papyrus Starcky (P.Yadin 36)," *CSI* 20: 121-37.

See also: Babatha Archive; Bar Kokhba Letters; Daliyeh, Wadi, ed-; Elephantine, Elephantine Papyri; Ḥever, Naḥal; Masada; Murabbaʿat, Wadi

DAVID NOY

Papyri from Qumran Cave 7

Cave 7 at Qumran is unique in two respects: all the fragments found there are in Greek, and all are written on papyrus. In the critical edition by Maurice Baillet (1962), nineteen fragments are numbered, but there are twenty-four altogether, with 7Q1, 7Q4, and 7Q6 comprising two fragments each, and 7Q19 comprising three more. The first two fragments (7Q1 and 7Q2) were identified by Baillet as containing text from the Septuagint: Exod. 28:4-7 and the Letter of Jeremiah 43–44, respectively. The remaining pieces, most containing only a few letters, were not identified.

New Testament Texts?

In 1972 J. O'Callaghan announced he had found several New Testament writings among the Cave 7 Greek Scrolls. With a focus on 7Q3–7Q18, he claimed that, with varying degrees of certainty, nine fragments contain text from six New Testament books: Mark, Acts, Romans, 1 Timothy, James, and 2 Peter. O'Callaghan's thesis found few followers, with the vast majority deeming it highly unlikely that any New Testament writing is represented among the Cave 7 fragments (e.g., Enste 2000; but cf. Thiede 1995 for a notable exception). There are three main problems with it. First, the physical evidence is flimsy indeed, with only five complete words in 7Q3–7Q18. Second, he dates all nine fragments to the Common Era. Third, his identifications seem very speculative. For example, line 4 of 7Q5 is too long for the traditional text of Mark 6:53, which forces him to omit the Greek *epi tēn gēn* ("to the land") so that the words on lines 3-5 line up correctly. This shorter reading is not supported by any significant manuscript of the New Testament.

Septuagint Texts?

Several scholars have proposed that 7Q3–7Q18 preserve parts of the Septuagint, which seems logical since 7Q1 and 7Q2 contain text from Exodus and the Letter of Jeremiah. V. Spottorno (1995) identifies 7Q5 as containing text from Zech. 7:3b-5; however, this reading involves the dubious identification of several Greek letters and variations from all known Greek texts of Zech. 7:3-5.

Portions of 1 Enoch?

In the 1980s and 1990s, three scholars concluded that several of the fragments are not from the Septuagint or the New Testament, but from *1 Enoch*. W. Nebe (1988) proposed that 7Q4 frg. 1 is part of *1 Enoch* 103:3-4, that 7Q4 frg. 2 is from 98:11, and that 7Q8 is possibly from 103:7-8. E. A. Muro (1997) took into consideration both the Greek letters and the physical characteristics of the papyrus fragments, piecing together 7Q4 frg. 1, 7Q8, and 7Q12 into one ensemble belonging to *1 Enoch* 103:3-8. É. Puech (1996, 1997) concurred with Nebe that 7Q4 frg. 1 contains text from *1 Enoch* 103:3-4 but preferred to place 7Q4 frg. 2 at *1 Enoch* 105:1. He further proposed that 7Q11 is part of *1 Enoch* 100:12, that 7Q13 belongs to 103:15, and that 7Q14 preserves traces of 103:12.

G. W. E. Nickelsburg (2004) disputes that the Cave 7 fragments contain any text from *1 Enoch*, for two reasons. First, he points to the meager size of the fragments involved; for example, the ensemble (103:3-8) pieced together by Muro and accepted by Puech presumes twenty-four lines of Greek, including eight that must be completely reconstructed, and preserves only thirty-four letters (or seven percent) of roughly 470 letters. Second, Nickelsburg observes that the "massive reconstruction" of *1 Enoch* 103:3-12 in 7Q4 frg. 1, 7Q8, 7Q12, and 7Q14 raises a major text-critical problem, since it depends on the Greek form preserved in the Chester Beatty Papyrus. This text is notoriously corrupt and has a propensity for shorter readings. In the case of 103:3-8, the papyrus has two shorter readings (in vv. 3 and 5) when compared with the corresponding Ethiopic text, which is longer. Nickelsburg's case is quite compelling, although it could be argued that 7Q4 frg. 1, 7Q8, 7Q12, and 7Q14 provide evidence that the defective text found in CBM existed in the first century C.E., or that the Ethiopic text is expansionistic for vv. 3 and 5 of *1 Enoch* 103.

BIBLIOGRAPHY

M. BAILLET 1962, "Grotte 7: B. Fragments non Identifiés," in *Les 'Petites Grottes' de Qumran,* 2 vols., DJD 3, Oxford: Clarendon Press, 1.143-45 (text) + 2.pl. xxx. • S. ENSTE 2000, *Kein Markustext in Qumran,* Freibourg: Universitätsverlag; Göttingen: Vandenhoeck & Ruprecht. • P. W. FLINT 2005, "The Greek Fragments of Enoch from Qumran Cave 7," in *Enoch and Qumran Origins: New Light on a Forgotten Connection,* ed. G. Boccaccini, Grand Rapids: Eerdmans, 224-33. • E. A. MURO 1997, "The Greek Fragments of Enoch from Qumran Cave 7 (7Q4, 7Q8, & 7Q12 = 7QEn gr = Enoch 103:3-4, 7-8)," *RevQ* 18: 307-12. • G. W. NEBE 1988, "7Q4 — Möglichkeit und Grenze einer Identifikation," *RevQ* 13: 629-33. • G. W. E. NICKELSBURG 2004, "The Greek Fragments of *1 Enoch* from Qumran Cave 7: An Unproven Identification," *RevQ* 22: 631-34. • J. O'CALLAGHAN 1972, "Papiros neo-testamentarios en la cueva 7 de Qumrân?" *Bib* 53: 91-100. • É. PUECH 1996, "Notes sur les fragments grecs du manuscrit 7Q4 = 1 Hénoch 103 et 105," *RB* 103: 592-600. • É. PUECH 1997, "Sept fragments de la Lettre d'Hénoch (1 Hén 100, 103 et 105) dans la grotte 7 de Qumrân (= 7QHén gr)," *RevQ* 18: 313-23. • V. SPOTTORNO 1995, "Una nueva posible identificacion de 7Q5," *Sefarad* 52: 541-43. • C. P. THIEDE 1995, *Rekindling the Word: In Search of Gospel Truth,* Valley Forge, Penn: Trinity, 189-97.

PETER W. FLINT

Paradise → Garden of Eden — Paradise

Parthians

Relations with the Seleucid Empire

The Parthians originated among the Parni, a group of Iranian-speaking tribes, nomadic horsemen who apparently originated in Central Asia. Much is still not known about the migration of the Parni into the region of Parthia. The general view has been that by about 240 B.C.E. the Parthians had taken away the northeast part of the Seleucid Empire once and for all. This historical reconstruction has severe weaknesses (Sherwin-White/Kuhrt 1993: 84-90). Arsaces took control of the provinces of Parthia and Hyrcania. The earliest area occupied by the Parthians under Arsaces I, the founder of a new dynasty about 238 B.C.E., was in fact north of the Elburz and thus outside the Seleucid realm. Seleucus II led a campaign against them ca. 230 B.C.E. but had to break off and return to put down a revolt in Asia Minor. The Parthians made raids into Seleucid territory, but occupation south of the Elburz did not take place until the middle of the second century. The Parthians were still vassals under Antiochus III (223-187 B.C.E.) and seemed to recognize this status themselves.

Movement into Seleucid territory began after the death of Antiochus III. It was Mithridates I (170-134 B.C.E.) who completed the process that had been begun by his predecessors. By 140 B.C.E. he had displaced the Seleucids from Iran and was making incursions into Babylonia. Demetrius II (145-140 B.C.E.) marched east against the Parthians but was taken captive by them. His successor, Antiochus VII (138-129 B.C.E.), made major efforts against the Parthian incursions, but his defeat and death at the hands of Phraates II opened the way for Parthian occupation of Babylonia. The Seleucid ruler Demetrius III, known in Jewish history because of the battle between him and Alexander Jannaeus, was taken captive by the Parthians in 87 B.C.E., perhaps by Mithridates II (c. 123-87 B.C.E.).

Relations with the Hasmoneans, the Romans, and Herod

Contact with Rome had been made toward the beginning of the first century B.C.E., but it was in 65-63 B.C.E. that Pompey helped to broker a peace between Phraates III of Parthia and Tigranes II of Armenia. The new governor of Syria, Crassus, attacked the Parthians in 53 B.C.E. but was defeated and killed. During the Roman Civil War Pompey attempted to form an alliance

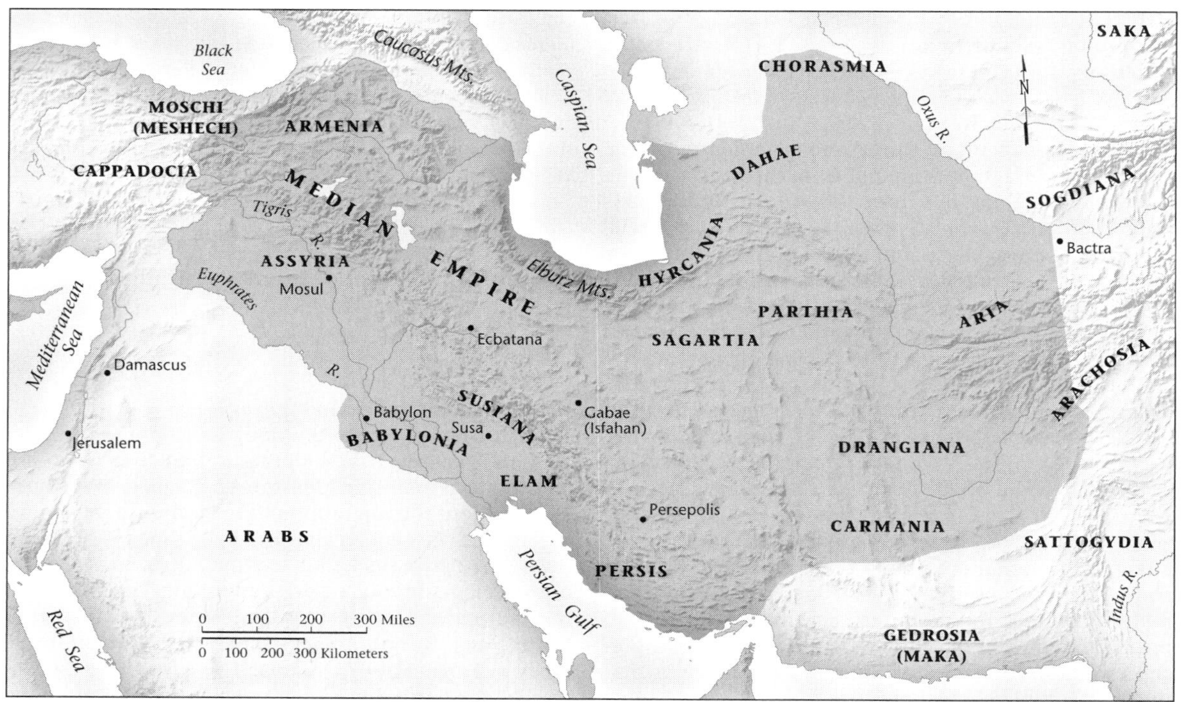

The Parthian Empire

with the Parthians but was killed before it came to anything, while a plan by Julius Caesar to wage war against the Parthians also came to nothing because of his assassination. Against the backdrop of conflicts between the Hasmoneans and other Jewish factions, the Parthians invaded Syria-Palestine in 40 B.C.E. Antigonus, the son of the Hasmonean king Aristobulus II, was allied with them in hopes of reestablishing the Hasmonean throne. Although the Parthians killed his brother, Herod escaped to Rome and gained Roman support to retake Palestine. However, the Parthians did not remain long in the region; perhaps they always intended their occupation of Syria-Palestine to be a temporary measure. In any case, they left Antigonus to face Herod and his Roman legions alone. In 39 B.C.E. Marc Antony pushed the Parthians back beyond the Euphrates. With Cleopatra's financial support he then invaded Parthia in 36 B.C.E. in a disastrous campaign which cost him a third of his force. His successful invasion and capture of Armenia in 34 B.C.E. hardly made up for this.

The Parthians were able to avert a war with Augustus by returning the captured standards of Crassus and Marc Antony in 20 B.C.E. The temporary peace established allowed trade to flourish between the two spheres of influence. But further treaties were signed between the two powers in 1 C.E., in 18 or 19 C.E., and in 37 C.E. Parthia itself was riven by internal disputes over the throne (with Rome occasionally intervening in its own interests, usually to keep the region unstable). Armenia stayed mostly under the domination of Rome, though this continued to create tension between the Romans and Parthians. In the mid-first century C.E., friction developed between Rome and Parthia over Armenia, since Rome traditionally had to approve any candidate for the throne of that country. The Roman commander Corbulo invaded and enthroned the Romans' own choice of candidate in 58 C.E., Corbulo himself becoming the governor of Syria. A few years later the Roman puppet king provoked the Parthians and then requested Roman aid. The Roman commander sent by Nero in 62 C.E. was defeated and captured by the Parthians. When Corbulo came too late to rescue him, he was still able to negotiate a settlement in which both the Romans and Parthians would withdraw from Armenia, while the Parthian candidate would become king of Armenia but go to Rome to be crowned.

The treaty signed in 63 C.E. established a peace between Rome and Parthia that lasted the next half century. Yet a curious tradition developed that we find in several Jewish apocalyptic writings, with a similar idea taken up in Christian writings on the Antichrist. This is the concept of *Nero redivivus* ("Nero resurrected"). After the death of Nero in 69 C.E., rumor had it that he had not actually died but was still alive and living secretly in the East. It was only a matter of time before he would gather an army of Parthian soldiers and return in triumph to take up his throne again. Originally, no actual "resurrection" was envisaged — only the return of Nero who had not actually died — until after the time of Nero's expected life span.

In the early second century C.E., the Romans attempted to extend their border eastward, which once again brought them into conflict with the Parthians. In 106 C.E. the emperor Trajan annexed Arabia to form a new province, but this was only a prelude to his campaigns to the East. His invasion of Mesopotamia was undoubtedly undertaken primarily out of strategic motives, since developments in Parthia were problematic from the Roman point of view. When the Parthian king Pacorus II died in 109/110 C.E., the Parthian throne was taken by his brother Chosroes. Pacorus had intended that the throne of Armenia go to his younger son Axidares, with Roman approval, but Chosroes now supported Pacorus' other son, Parthamasiris (Axidares' elder brother), who had seized the Armenian throne. Trajan set out in the Spring of 114 C.E. for Armenia. Parthamasiris submitted, but the crown was removed from him and Armenia — or at least the western part of it — made into a Roman province.

In the Autumn of 114 Trajan turned south into Mesopotamia. The precise course of events for the next year is uncertain, but he obtained the submission of various territories, including Nisibis, Edessa, Singra, and even territory beyond the Tigris. He did not return until late in 115. There was now a new province of Mesopotamia, but Trajan was not finished. In the spring of 116 he set out for the conquest of Assyria and Babylonia. He took Adiabene, Seleucia, and Ctesiphon by the Summer, establishing the new province of Assyria. After Trajan moved to the site of ancient Babylon to spend the Winter, a general revolt took place in the newly created provinces of Mesopotamia and Assyria. This appears to have included a Parthian counterattack. The emperor effectively suppressed the revolt and most of the conquered areas remained under Roman control, but Trajan died soon afterward.

Although Hadrian (117-138 C.E.) had to put down revolts in the Mediterranean, under him relations between Rome and Parthia seem to have been peaceful. The same applied to his successor Antoninus Pius (138-161 C.E.). Shortly after Marcus Aurelius (161-180 C.E.) began his reign, however, the Parthians broke the peace to attempt to remove the Roman-supported king of Armenia. The first Roman army sent against them was severely beaten. As usual, the Romans responded in force and made considerable advances eastward, taking the Parthian capital and replacing the Parthian king. The peace established in 166 C.E. lasted for the quarter of a century. In the civil turmoil that initiated the reign of Septimius Severus (193-211 C.E.), the Parthians took advantage of the situation and made advances into Roman-controlled territory. After Severus defeated his rival Pescennius Niger, he began his First Parthian War and won back territory in Mesopotamia, gaining the title *Parthicus Arabicus.* He launched his Second Parthian War in 197, capturing the Babylonian center of Ctesiphon and creating a province of Mesopotamia, but he failed to take the city of Hatra. Severus' son Caracalla (officially Aurelius Antonius, 211-217 C.E.) managed to gain the throne and sought a pretext to attack the Parthians. When his request to marry a Parthian princess was refused, he invaded Mesopotamia. He was assassinated shortly afterward, and his successor Macrinus offered peace to the Parthians. They refused until the Battle of Nisibis, at which point they concluded a treaty in which the Romans paid an indemnity. Not long afterward, about 225 C.E., the Sassanians overthrew the Parthians and established their own ruling dynasty.

BIBLIOGRAPHY

R. N. FRYE 1984, *History of Ancient Iran,* Berlin: de Gruyter. • S. SHERWIN-WHITE AND A. KUHRT 1993, *From Samarkhand to Sardis: A New Approach to the Seleucid Empire,* London: Duckworth. • E. YARSHATER, ED. 1983, *Cambridge History of Iran,* vol. 3, parts 1-2, *The Seleucid, Parthian, and Sasanian Periods,* Cambridge: Cambridge University Press.

LESTER L. GRABBE

Parting of the Ways

Most scholars today agree that Judaism played a formative role in the origins and early history of Christianity. What is debated, however, is when, why, and how Christianity emerged as a religion distinct from Judaism. The "Parting of the Ways" is one of the models and metaphors that scholars have used to explore these questions.

From Supersession to Separation

In the nineteenth and early twentieth centuries, scholarship on Judaism and Christian origins mirrored theological concerns. Consistent with the Protestant settings of the earliest historical-critical scholarship on the New Testament, the story of the rise of Christianity was told in supersessionist terms. Jesus was described as rejecting the legalism and ritualism of his Jewish contemporaries, transcending particularistic ideas about salvation, and recovering the prophetic heritage of ancient Israel. Paul was celebrated for actualizing Christianity's universalistic potential by rejecting the Law and by spreading the gospel to Gentiles. Implicit in this description of Christian origins was the characterization of Judaism as a dead religion, rendered irrelevant by the rise of Christianity.

In nineteenth- and early twentieth-century Jewish historiography, accounts of Christian origins were also shaped by apologetics. Jesus was often understood as a Jew, whether in the positive sense of a radical reformer or in the negative sense of a well-meaning but wayward sage. Typically, Paul was held responsible for the foundation of Christianity as a religion in conflict with Judaism. When his fellow Jews were unconvinced by his preaching of Jesus as messiah, Paul is said to have reinterpreted Jesus' teachings to appeal to Gentiles; not only did he sever them from Torah observance, but he mixed them with Hellenistic ideas. Implicit in this description of Christian origins was thus an understanding of Christianity as a corrupted form of Judaism.

The idea of the Parting of the Ways emerged as part of the search for more ecumenical models. Critiques of supersessionist views of Christian origins were voiced already in the 1920s and 1930s by George Foote Moore and James Parkes. It was not until after the Holocaust, however, that alternate models began to proliferate. Parkes's theories about the post-70 "separation" of Judaism and Christianity formed the basis for new theories about the "Parting of the Ways," which flourished in the wake of the establishment of secular institutional settings for the study of religion in the 1960s and 1970s.

In contrast to older supersessionist models, theories about the Parting of the Ways seek to understand Christian origins in a manner sensitive to Jewish history. To ask *when* and *why* Christianity "parted" from Judaism is to accept that Christianity was once a part of Judaism. Rather than dismissing either religion as a corrupted form of the other, the metaphor of "parted ways" characterizes Judaism and Christianity as separate entities with a shared prehistory. It also allows for the acknowledgement of Judaism's rich and vibrant post-Christian history.

Theories about the Parting of the Ways have thus gained popularity during the last twenty years, particularly in North America. Many scholars have embraced the idea of a decisive historical moment in the late first or early second century, after which Judaism and Christianity became separate religions and developed along different trajectories. It has been surprisingly difficult, however, to find primary evidence that firmly supports this idea. Allusive, moreover, has been a consensus on the precise timing of the "parting" and its precipitants.

The First and Second Centuries C.E.

Following Parkes, early articulations of the Parting of the Ways focused on three events: the flight of the Jerusalem church to Pella during the First Jewish Revolt of 66-70 C.E., the rise of rabbis to a position of leadership in Jewish society after the destruction of the Temple in 70 C.E., and the expulsion of Christians from synagogues after the so-called "council" of Yavneh in 90 C.E. These events were thought to mark the demise of "Jewish Christianity," the resultant severing of Christianity from its Jewish roots, and the demographic shift of the Jesus movement from Jews to Gentiles.

Research on the relevant sources, however, has shed doubt on the historicity of all three. Our earliest evidence for the "flight to Pella" is found in Eusebius' *Ecclesiastical History* (3.5.3); inasmuch as his account of the Jerusalem church is plagued by internal inconsistencies and shaped by his own concerns, the historical value of this tradition may be minimal. Also questionable is the image of the rabbis as the spiritual leaders of the Jewish people immediately after 70 C.E. Recent research has shown that it took several centuries for the rabbinic movement to establish any sort of hegemony. The notion of a "council" of Yavneh is a retrospective myth of rabbinic origins, developed in later sources. Our earliest evidence for the *birkat ha-minîm* is a *baraita* in the Babylonian Talmud (*b. Berakot* 28b–29a). Yet there is no early evidence to support the view that rabbis controlled synagogues at the end of the first century or even in the second.

Although some accounts of the Parting of the Ways still appeal to these events in attenuated fashion, the focus has largely shifted to other factors. One line of inquiry emphasizes theological factors (e.g., Dunn 2006). For some, the Parting of the Ways was an inevitable development from Jesus' own teachings. For others, it was Paul's preaching of a law-free gospel and/or his missionary efforts among Gentiles that paved the way for Christianity's emergence as a non-Jewish movement. Still others point to the articulation of high Christologies as determinative.

Another line of argument focuses on historical events and their social effects (e.g., Wilson 1995). Central to such accounts are the First Jewish Revolt of 66-70 C.E. and the Bar Kokhba Revolt of 132-135 C.E. The two revolts catalyzed a geographical shift, which may have facilitated the Jesus movement's transformation into a predominantly Gentile religion. Whether or not Christians fled Jerusalem during the First Revolt, ethnically Jewish members of the church would have been forced to leave the city after the second. By 135, the center of the movement may have thus shifted toward communities elsewhere in the Roman Empire. Some scholars further speculate that differences between followers of Jesus and other Jews were exacerbated by the Roman imposition of the *fiscus Iudaicus* after the First Revolt and/or by the messianic fervor surrounding Bar Kokhba. In addition, the rise in Roman anti-Judaism after the revolts may have contributed to the development of negative views of Jews and Judaism among Gentile converts like Justin and Marcion.

These approaches also have their critics. Theological interpretations of the Parting of the Ways have been questioned, for instance, for their echoes of older supersessionist views (Fredriksen 2003). Their assertions about the uniqueness of Jesus, Paul, and New Testament Christology have also been countered with Jewish parallels (e.g., Boyarin 2004). Likewise, doubts have been raised about the degree to which the First Revolt or the Bar Kokhba Revolt marked an irreparable "parting." To see the severing of the church's connections to Palestine as a primary catalyst for the Parting of Ways is to suggest that Christianity's connections to Judaism were limited to Palestinian Judaism. That the situation was more complex, however, is suggested by our ample evidence for the influence of forms of Judaism in the Diaspora — which flourished, perhaps not coincidentally, in many of the same cities where Christian communities were first established (Himmelfarb 1993).

Theories about the Parting of the Ways have also come under fire for their fixation on a single determinative moment and for their lack of sensitivity to local difference (Lieu 1994). Until recently, moreover, discussions of the Parting of the Ways rarely considered evidence for Jewish/Christian relations after the second century C.E. (Becker and Reed 2003).

Critiques of the "Parting" Model

Increasingly, questions about Christianity's relationship to Judaism are being discussed, not just by scholars of the New Testament, but also by scholars of rabbinics, patristics, and late antiquity. As a result, a broader range of textual and material data has been brought to bear on the question of the Parting of the

Ways. With the intensification of interdisciplinary discussion have come new ideas, critiques, and perspectives.

Doubts about an early and decisive Parting of the Ways have been voiced in recent studies of Christian writings penned after the second century. Far from confirming Christianity's separation from Judaism, some sources from the third and fourth centuries point to continued overlaps and ambiguities. Certain Christian authors proclaim the clear boundaries between Christian and Jew (e.g., Ignatius, *Magn.* 10:3); they often do so, however, in response to members of their communities who do not share their views about the mutual exclusivity of these identities (e.g., Chrysostom, *Homilies against the Jews*). Such sources may point to a gap between the rhetoric of separation and the reality of fluid boundaries and intercredal interactions, at least in some locales.

Rabbinic and patristic evidence also attests the lively interchange of exegetical and other traditions, particularly in the third and fourth centuries (Becker and Reed 2003). This evidence suggests that Jews and Christians did not go their separate ways after the second century; if anything, they may exhibit more concern for one another. Furthermore, it is in the third, fourth, and early fifth centuries that we find the most evidence for "Jewish-Christians" and "Judaizers." Accordingly, some scholars have proposed that we cannot speak of any decisive Parting of the Ways prior to the Christianization of the Roman Empire (Boyarin 2004).

Diversity and Definition

Studies of early Judaism and early Christianity have increasingly called our attention to the internal diversity of both traditions. In the first centuries of the Common Era, each encompassed a rich range of local specificities. Consequently, it is perhaps not surprising that different scholars see the Parting of the Ways as having occurred at different times and for different reasons. One finds different answers to the question of Christianity's relationship with Judaism depending on where one looks.

On one level, the continued debates about the Parting of the Ways may thus reflect the inherent limitations of a linear and global account (Petersen 2005). From a modern perspective, it makes sense to speak of a clear-cut "Christianity" that separated from a clear-cut "Judaism" at a specific point in time. The diversity of our ancient evidence, however, resists such reduction. Accordingly, it may not be possible to pinpoint the historical moment that shaped "Christianity" and "Judaism" in all their diverse forms and regional expressions — either before the fourth century or after (Becker and Reed 2003).

Nevertheless, theories about the Parting of the Ways have served an important function in modern scholarship. They have offered much-needed alternates to older supersessionist models. Debates surrounding the Parting of the Ways have also helped to break down the disciplinary boundaries between the study of the New Testament, rabbinics, patristics, and late antiquity.

Debates about the Parting of the Ways continue to rage today. Some scholars defend the model, albeit in an attenuated form that allows for a longer and more complex process of differentiation (e.g., Dunn 2006). Others call for more sophisticated models for understanding Jewish and Christian self-definition, drawing from the rich body of research on identity formation in other fields (e.g., Boyarin 2004). Only time can tell whether the idea of the Parting of the Ways will continue to hold sway.

BIBLIOGRAPHY

A. H. BECKER AND A. Y. REED, EDS. 2003, *The Ways That Never Parted: Jews and Christians in Late Antiquity and the Early Middle Ages,* Tübingen: Mohr-Siebeck. • D. BOYARIN 2004, *Border Lines: The Partition of Judeo-Christianity,* Philadelphia: University of Pennsylvania Press. • J. D. G. DUNN, ED. 1992, *Jews and Christians: The Parting of the Ways, A.D. 70 to 135,* Grand Rapids: Eerdmans, 1-25. • J. D. G. DUNN 2006, *The Partings of the Ways,* 2d ed., London: S.C.M. • P. FREDRIKSEN 2003, "What 'Parting of the Ways'? Jews, Gentiles, and the Ancient Mediterranean City," in *The Ways That Never Parted: Jews and Christians in Late Antiquity and the Early Middle Ages,* ed. A. H. Becker and A. Y. Reed, Tübingen: Mohr-Siebeck, 35-63. • M. HIMMELFARB 1993, "The Parting of the Ways Reconsidered: Diversity in Judaism and Jewish-Christian Relations in the Roman Empire," in *Interwoven Destinies: Jews and Christians through the Ages,* ed. E. Fisher, New York: Paulist, 47-61. • J. LIEU 1994, "The Parting of the Ways: Theological Construct or Historical Reality?" *JSNT* 56: 101-19. • A. K. PETERSEN 2005, "At the End of the Road: Reflections on a Popular Scholarly Metaphor," in *The Formation of the Church,* ed. J. Ådna, Tübingen: Mohr-Siebeck, 45-72. • S. G. WILSON 1995, *Related Strangers: Jews and Christians 70 C.E.–170 C.E.,* Minneapolis: Fortress.

ANNETTE YOSHIKO REED

Passover → Festivals and Holy Days

Patriarchs, Testaments of the Twelve

In their received form the *Testaments of the Twelve Patriarchs* are a second-century-C.E. Christian composition. They present the fictional valedictory speeches of Jacob's sons. Each testament includes an introduction in which the patriarch summons his children to his premortem speech; he then offers autobiographical reflections, exhorts his children to avoid his vices and/or pursue his virtues, and predicts their descendants' future; finally, his death and burial are recorded.

Contents

Seven patriarchs' autobiographical accounts depend directly on the book of Genesis (Reuben [Gen. 35:22]; Levi [Genesis 34]; Judah [Genesis 38]; Issachar [Gen. 49:14-15 LXX]; Zebulun [Gen. 49:13]; Gad [Gen. 37:2]; Joseph [Gen. 39:6b-18]). Five accounts build from other sources and interpretive readings of Genesis (Simeon, Dan, Naphtali, Asher, and Benjamin).

 PATRIARCHS, TESTAMENTS OF THE TWELVE

The patriarchs' biographical accounts trigger their moral exhortation: right action equals pleasing God and opposing Beliar (e.g., *T. Levi* 18:12; *T. Zeb.* 9:8; *T. Naph.* 2:6; *T. Benj.* 6:1), keeping the twofold commandment to love God and one's neighbor (*T. Benj.* 5:3), avoiding traditional Greco-Roman vices (e.g., *porneia* [*T. Jud.* 18:2]), and embracing virtues (e.g., *haplotēs* [*T. Iss.* 4:1]). Individually the patriarchs' accounts address the pitfalls of failing to exercise self-control over strong drink (Judah), attractive women (Reuben; Judah), envy (Simeon), greed (Judah), falsehood (Dan), anger (Simeon; Gad), temptations to unjust violence (Simeon; Judah; Dan; Gad), and double-mindedness (Asher); they praise the virtues of zeal for the Lord (Levi), temperance and purity (Judah), simplicity of life (Issachar), merciful warmheartedness (Zebulun), harmony with the natural order (Naphtali), single-mindedness (Asher), and chastity, endurance, and mercy (Joseph).

The eschatological sections call upon various sources to predict the future of the patriarchs' descendants (Enoch: *T. Levi* 10:5; 14:1; 16:1; *T. Jud.* 18:1; the fathers: *T. Levi* 10:1; the fathers' writings: *T. Zeb.* 9:5; and the heavenly tablets: *T. Ash.* 7:5). There are several types of future-oriented passages. Sin-Exile-Return (S.E.R.) sections foretell the sins of the patriarchs' descendants, the tribes' exile among the Gentiles as punishment, and God's restoration of the tribes (*T. Levi* 10; 14–15; 16; *T. Jud.* 18:1; 23; *T. Iss.* 6; *T. Zeb.* 9:5-7, 9; *T. Dan* 5:4a, 6-9; *T. Naph.* 4:1-3, 5; *T. Gad* 8:2; *T. Ash.* 7:2-3, 5-7; *T. Benj.* 9:1-2; the testaments of Reuben, Simeon, and Joseph lack S.E.R. passages).

Levi-Judah (L.J.) passages bemoan the rebellion of the patriarchs' descendants against Levi's and Judah's descendants and their defeat, but they also look forward to the descendants' loyalty to the tribes of Levi and Judah out of respect for their provision of priests, kings, and the messiah of Israel (*T. Reub.* 6:5–7:8, 10-12; *T. Levi* 2:11; *T. Sim.* 5:4-6; 7:1-2; *T. Jud.* 21:1-6a; *T. Iss.* 5:7-8a; *T. Dan* 5:4, 6-7, 10; *T. Naph.* 8:2; *T. Gad* 8:1-2; *T. Jos.* 19:6; the testaments of Zebulun, Asher, and Benjamin lack L.J. passages).

Ideal savior passages are related to the L.J. passages and refer to Jesus (*T. Levi* 18; *T. Jud.* 24; *T. Zeb.* 9:8; *T. Dan* 5:10-13). A final group of future-oriented passages announce that the patriarch — along with Abraham, Isaac, Jacob, Enoch, Noah, and Shem, and any whose observance of the Law or acceptance of Jesus as messiah made them righteous — will be resurrected to rule over his tribe at the messiah's second coming (*T. Sim.* 6:7; *T. Levi* 18:14; *T. Jud.* 25; *T. Zeb.* 10:1-4; *T. Benj.* 10:6-10).

Main Themes

The *Testaments'* main themes are ethics and eschatology: they urge modes of living critical to one's fate in the age to come. The *Testaments* assert an equivalency between the Israelite ancestors' teaching and the keeping of the twofold commandment of love for God and neighbor (Deut. 6:5; Lev. 19:18; *T. Iss.* 5:2; 7:6-7; *T. Dan* 5:2-3; *T. Gad* 4:1-2; *T. Jos.* 11:1; *T. Benj.* 3:1-3). They also correlate these Israelite values with Greco-Roman standards of conduct embodied in the classical vices and virtues (e.g., *sōphrosynē* in *T. Jos.* 9:1-3; *porneia* in *T. Jud.* 14:1-3; *phthonos* in *T. Sim.* 3:1-4; *hyperēphanos* in *T. Levi* 17:1; *andreios* in *T. Jud.* 15:6; *thymos* and *misos* in *T. Dan* and *T. Gad* 13:2-3; *taxis physeōs* in *T. Naph.* 3:4-5).

That such a life is possible is exemplified especially in the figure of Joseph, who functions as a type of Jesus and a model for the Christian life (*T. Levi* 16:3; cf. *T. Zeb.* 2:2; 3:3; *T. Gad* 2:3; *T. Benj.* 3:8). The *Testaments* praise Joseph's sexual self-restraint, emotional equilibrium, compassion for his enemies, and lack of envy, anger, and vengefulness against those who wronged him. The *Testament of Benjamin* foregoes biographical details of Benjamin for a panegyric on Joseph as the quintessential good man *(agathos anēr)* with a good mind *(agathē dianoia)* who achieved what the patriarchs asked, what Greco-Roman society requires, and what God's twofold commandment demands (*T. Benjamin* 4–5).

The *Testaments'* eschatological theme follows from the ethical exhortation. The patriarchs predict that when the tribes heed their forefathers' advice they will fare well (*T. Sim.* 6:2-4), but when they ignore the patriarchs' instructions they will be punished (*T. Sim.* 5:4-6). Doing well depends on fleeing Beliar to live under God's care (*T. Sim.* 2:4-6); conversely, those who remain under the sway of Beliar also remain under the spell of their vices (*T. Iss.* 6:1).

Christian elements are introduced when the patriarchs predict that their descendants will fail to heed their advice, succumb to Beliar's influence, and rebel against the tribes of Judah and Levi (*T. Reub.* 6:5-8; *T. Sim.* 5:4-6); some will also rebel against the Messiah (*T. Levi* 10:1-5; 14:1-8). The tribes will appear doomed, but Israel's God will intervene through a savior who will destroy the power of Beliar and his spirits (*T. Levi* 18:12; *T. Jud.* 25:3; *T. Zeb.* 9:8; *T. Dan* 5:10-11) and offer salvation at his second coming, even to those who fail to attain virtue through heeding the patriarchs' advice and keeping the double commandment (*T. Levi* 16:5; *T. Ash.* 7:7).

Textual Witnesses

Fourteen Greek manuscripts dating from the tenth to the eighteenth centuries C.E. divide into two manuscript families. Manuscripts *bk* of family I are the oldest available witnesses, and manuscript *b* best facilitates reconstructing an archetype. There are also Armenian, Slavonic, Serbian, and Latin versions of the *Testaments.* All but the Latin (Robert Grosseteste's translation from the Greek manuscript *b* made in 1242) belong to family II. Only the Armenian text is a potential resource for reconstructing an archetype. The majority view is that the earliest attainable text of the *Testaments* is little younger than the ninth century C.E.

Original Language

Several factors speak against the *Testaments'* original language having been Semitic: many of the purported indicators of a Hebrew or Aramaic original derive their Semitic flavor from Septuagint Greek (cf. *T. Jud.* 24:1

and Num. 24:17 LXX); few of the *Testaments* exhibit hints of Semitisms; and much of their vocabulary depends on Greek Stoic writings and Septuagint wisdom books for which there were no Hebrew originals. The Testaments were therefore probably composed in Greek.

Source Criticism

Some late Hebrew texts reflecting material in the speeches of Judah and Naphtali hint at the possibility of pre-Christian, Semitic-language precursors, but their uncertain provenance makes their value negligible. The Hebrew *Testament of Naphtali* 2–6 gives two visions, as does *T. Naph.* 2–5; and 10:5-7 of the Hebrew work describes the human body's organization as evidence of God's ordered creation, as does *T. Naph.* 2:8. *Midrash Wayissa'u* recalls a war against the Amorites similar to that related in *T. Judah* 3–7 (see also *Jub.* 34:1-9).

Some Dead Sea Scrolls are possible sources for the *Testaments.* The document 4Q538 has been linked with the story of Jacob's sons' second trip to Egypt in *T. Jud.* 12:11-12 (cf. Gen. 44:1–45:10; *Jub.* 43:1-13). The fragments 4Q539 1 and 2 may reflect elements of *T. Jos.* 14:4-5 (frg. 1) and 15:1–17:2 (frg. 2). 4Q215 1:2-5 and *T. Naph.* 1:11-12 are both accounts of Bilhah's birth and genealogy. More significant are 1Q21 and 4Q213-214b, which give Aramaic texts related to *T. Levi* 8–9 and 11–14, as well as biographical, prayer, and wisdom material not known from the Greek *Testament of Levi.* There are also two large fragments of an early medieval manuscript from the Cairo Geniza that preserve Aramaic parallels for *T. Levi* 6–7; 8–9; 11–13; and supplements to the Greek *Testament of Levi* in the Mt. Athos manuscript of the *Testaments* at *T. Levi* 2:3; 5:2; 18:2 that parallel portions of the Qumran manuscripts and the Cairo Geniza fragments. Like the evidence related to Judah, Naphtali, and Joseph, the Levi materials only prove that the *Testaments* incorporate some earlier Jewish traditions.

Form Criticism

The *Testaments* are farewell discourses (cf. Genesis 49; Deuteronomy 33), and they exhibit the formal literary characteristic of the testamentary genre: an introduction in which the testator gathers family or friends to hear his near-death speech, and a conclusion that narrates the speaker's death.

The biographical sections of the *Testaments* adapt many subgenres: synagogue homilies (*T. Judah* 13–17), hymns (*T. Sim.* 6:2-7), visions (*T. Levi* 2:5–5:7; *T. Naphtali* 5–6; 7), prayers (*T. Levi* 4:2), instructions (*T. Levi* 9), battle accounts (*T. Judah* 3–7), seriatim memoirs (*T. Levi* 11; *T. Judah* 2), paronomasia (*T. Iss.* 1:3-15; *T. Zeb.* 1:2-3), etiologies (*T. Zeb.* 6:1-3), and "rewritten Bible" (*T. Levi* 6:3–7:4; *T. Jos.* 3:1–9:5; 11:2–16:6). The parenetic sections draw forms from disparate sources including the Septuagint wisdom books and non-Jewish Hellenistic authors from Teles (third century B.C.E.) to Musonius (first century C.E.).

Tradition Criticism

The *Testaments* echo a wide range of traditions, including Jewish pseudepigraphic and rabbinic folklore (e.g., *T. Iss.* 1:3–2:5; cf. *Gen. Rab.* 72:3, 5; Gen. 30:14-16 for the mandrakes-for-sex story); the rhetoric and content of the Septuagint (e.g., *T. Jud.* 1:3; *T. Iss.* 1:15 for etymologies of names; *T. Naph.* 2:3; cf. Wis. 11:20 for sapiential hortatory material); the New Testament (e.g., *T. Jud.* 24:1-2; cf. Matt. 3:16; Mark 1:10 for a messiah who sees the heavens open); and Cynic-Stoic philosophy (e.g., *T. Reub.* 2:3-8; cf. Aetius 4.21.1-4 on what motivates human action).

Jewish or Christian Authorship

Many scholars have tried to posit the existence of a collection of original Jewish *Testaments.* The modern quest began in 1884 when F. Schnapp proposed a three-stage compositional history, the last of which introduced Christian material. The best-known successors to Schnapp include R. H. Charles, J. Becker, A. Hultgård, J. H. Ulrichsen, and J. Kugel. They offer differing hypotheses regarding the work's origins, from Charles's pro-Levi, then anti-Levi Pharisaic group to Ulrichsen's original Levi apocryphon (see also A. Dupont-Sommer and M. Philonenko, who argued for Essene authorship). By contrast, M. de Jonge acknowledges that the *Testaments* incorporate Jewish source materials but insists that they must otherwise be viewed as a Christian composition datable to the second century C.E. As such the *Testaments* are largely a parenetic composition dedicated to instructing Christians and potential Jewish converts in keeping God's universal law, which, communicated by the patriarchs and reaffirmed by Jesus, is the path to salvation. After decades of being a minority position, de Jonge's view has been gaining increasing acceptance in recent years.

Bibliography

J. Becker 1970, *Untersuchungen zur Entstehungsgeschichte der Testamente der Zwölf Patriarchen,* Leiden: Brill. • R. H. Charles 1908, *The Testaments of the Twelve Patriarchs: Translated from the Editor's Greek Text,* London: Blackwell. • A. Dupont-Sommer 1953, *Nouveaux aperçus sur les manuscrits de la mer morte,* Paris: Maisonneuve. • H. W. Hollander and M. de Jonge 1985, *The Testaments of the Twelve Patriarchs: A Commentary,* Leiden: Brill. • A. Hultgård 1977-1982, *L'eschatologie des Testaments des Douze Patriarches,* 2 vols., Uppsala: Almqvist & Wiksell. • J. L. Kugel 1998, *Traditions of the Bible: A Guide to the Bible as It Was at the Start of the Common Era,* Cambridge: Harvard University Press. • R. Kugler 2001, *The Testaments of the Twelve Patriarchs,* Sheffield: Sheffield Academic Press. • M. Philonenko 1960, *Les interpolations chrétiennes des Testaments des Douze Patriarches et les manuscrits de Qoumrân,* Paris: Presses universitaires de France. • J. H. Ulrichsen 1991, *Die Grundschrift der Testamente der Zwölf Patriarchen,* Uppsala: Almqvist & Wiksell.

See also: Testaments

Robert A. Kugler

Paul

Saul of Tarsus, who become known as Paul the Apostle (ca. 5-65 C.E.), was a pivotal figure in the early Jewish context of the Christian movement. While Paul regarded Christian faith as the fullness of Judaism, his missionary activity and letters facilitated Christianity's eventual transition from being a sect within early Judaism to becoming a separate (largely non-Jewish) religion.

Paul's Early Life in Judaism

Paul was a Diaspora Jew. According to Acts, he was born in Tarsus of Cilicia (Acts 9:11; 21:39; 22:3) in the early years of the Common Era (Acts 7:58). He claims to have been "circumcised on the eighth day, a member of the people of Israel, of the tribe of Benjamin" (Phil. 3:5). In Tarsus (a cosmopolitan city on the southeastern coast of Asia Minor), Paul was raised in a Jewish family, presumably heard and read the Bible in Greek, and was part of the local Jewish community. There he apparently also received a Greek rhetorical education on which he later drew in writing his letters. Two passages in Acts (22:3; 26:4-5) claim that Paul was then educated more intensively in Judaism at Jerusalem under the Pharisee Gamaliel. There he became proficient in Pharisaic lore ("as to the law, a Pharisee," Phil. 3:5), though his family may have been associated already with the Pharisee movement ("a son of Pharisees," Acts 23:6; the phase may, however, may simply be a Semitic locution for "member of the Pharisees").

The Judaism (Gal. 1:13) into which Paul was born was international and diverse. What we call "Judaism" (derived from "Judah/Judea") had long since been extended into Galilee and spread all over the Mediterranean world. In Paul's time there were substantial Jewish communities in Damascus, Antioch, Ephesus, Rome, Alexandria, and Tarsus. Since Diaspora Jews could not easily travel to the Jerusalem Temple, the local gathering places or synagogues became the centers of Jewish community life, culture, and religion. There Jews heard and read the Bible in Greek and gave special attention to practices that differentiated Jews from other peoples: circumcision, Sabbath observance, food laws, and ritual purity.

The diversity within Second Temple Judaism made it possible to practice Judaism in various ways: as a Pharisee, Sadducee, Essene, Samaritan, Christian, and so on. Paul claims that as a Pharisee in Jerusalem he persecuted the Jewish Jesus movement (the *ekklēsia,* "assembly, congregation, church") "out of zeal" (Phil 3:6), perhaps because he felt that Hellenistic Jews like Stephen who had become followers of Jesus were testing the outer limits of Judaism with their radical ideas about the Jerusalem Temple and observance of the Torah (Acts 7). According to Acts 8:1-3, Paul took part in the stoning of Stephen at least as a sympathetic observer and was active in the "severe persecution" that followed. The fact that the "apostles" (presumably Aramaic-Hebrew speakers native to Israel) were exempted suggests that his targets were Greek-speaking Jewish believers in Jesus. Paul may then have been sent to Damascus by the Greek-speaking synagogue in Jerusalem to investigate what Christian Hellenistic Jews were doing there and to do something about stopping them as he had done in Jerusalem.

Paul's "Conversion" or Call

What happened to Paul on the way to Damascus in 33 (or 36) C.E. is usually described as his "conversion." He refers to it in passing in Gal. 1:13-17 and Phil. 3:7-9. The event is presented in much greater detail three times in Acts (chaps. 9, 22, 26). Paul claims that before this event he had advanced in Judaism beyond his contemporaries and was far more zealous than they were for "the traditions of my ancestors" (Gal. 1:14), and that he was "as to righteousness under the Law, blameless" (Phil. 3:6). While many modern interpreters have tried to explain Paul's conversion on psychological grounds, the ancient texts point primarily to the categories of religious experience and theology. The assumptions that Paul felt inadequate in his religious observance or had a tender conscience seem ruled out by his own boasts about the high quality of his life in Judaism.

On the road to Damascus, according to Paul, God "was pleased to reveal his Son to me" (Gal. 1:15-16), with the result that he came to regard his credentials and accomplishments as a Jew now to be a "loss because of Christ" (Phil. 3:7). His experience involving the risen Jesus totally changed Paul's outlook and values. While his resumé as a Jew was the strongest imaginable, that no longer seemed important to him. Indeed, he even described it as "rubbish" (*skybala,* Phil. 3:8).

What was now most important to Paul was his new relationship with God made possible through his faith in the saving power of Jesus' death and resurrection. In the light of Paul's own description in Phil. 3:9 ("a righteousness . . . that comes through faith in [or, the faith of] Christ, the righteousness from God based on faith"), it is possible to trace what is often described as the center of Paul's theology — justification by faith — to his initial experience of the risen Christ on the way to Damascus. That experience is also at the root of Paul's Christ-mysticism, expressed most powerfully in Phil. 3:10-11: "I want to know Christ and the power of his resurrection and the sharing of his sufferings by becoming like him in his death if somehow I may attain the resurrection from the dead" (cf. Gal. 2:20, "I have been crucified with Christ; it is no longer I who live but Christ who lives in me; and the life that I now live in the flesh I live by faith in [or: the faith/faithfulness of] the Son of God, who loved me and gave himself for me").

The customary designation of Paul's Damascus Road experience as his "conversion" needs to be qualified. In Paul's context it was not so much a conversion from one religion (Judaism) to another religion (Christianity) as a move from one form of Judaism (Pharisaic) to another form of Judaism (Christian). Moreover, Paul insisted that his encounter with the risen Jesus involved a call or commission: "that I might proclaim him among the Gentiles" (Gal 1:16), and he described his experience in terms derived in part from the call narratives of the Hebrew prophets: God "set me apart before I was born" (Gal. 1:15; cf. Isa. 49:1; Jer. 1:5). Even the more embellished accounts in Acts agree that Paul's conversion experience brought with it a special vocation to bring the good news of Jesus' death and resurrection to non-Jews (Acts 9:15; 22:15; 26:17). It should be noted that the Christian-Jewish mission to the Gentiles seems to have already begun apart from and before Paul's apostolic activity commenced (see Acts 10–11, esp. 11:19-21).

After his conversion-call experience, Paul went to Arabia (probably the area east of Damascus) and then returned to Damascus (Gal. 1:17), where he had been received before with some suspicion (Acts 9:13-14). Only three years afterward did Paul confer with Cephas/Peter and James the brother of Jesus in Jerusalem and get their approval (Gal. 1:18-19). However, Paul repeatedly insisted that his call was directly by way of a revelation "through Jesus Christ and God the Father" (Gal. 1:1; cf. 1:12), and not from the apostles or any other human intermediary. Then he went "into the regions of Syria and Cilicia" (Gal. 1:21), where he seems to have borne witness to his revelatory experience and carried out his activity as apostle to the Gentiles.

Paul the Apostle

The years between Paul's conversion and the first accounts of his missionary activities remain obscure. But from roughly 46 C.E. onward there is evidence that Paul traveled around the Mediterranean world, trying to fulfill his commission as the apostle to the Gentiles. Modern readers of Acts have divided Paul's missionary career into three journeys or phases: Acts 13:1–14:28 (46-49 C.E.), 15:30–18:17 (50-52 C.E.), and 18:18–21:16 (54-58 C.E.). The geographical range of these journeys is remarkable, with stops at Cyprus, Antioch of Pisidia, Iconium, Lystra and Derbe, Antioch in Syria, Jerusalem, Philippi, Thessalonica, Berea, Athens, Corinth, Antioch in Syria again, Ephesus, Macedonia and Greece, Troas, Miletus, Ephesus again, Jerusalem again, and Rome. Whether he ever got to Spain (Rom. 15:24) and thus fulfilled his dream to bring the gospel to "the ends of the earth" (Acts 1:8) is not clear.

In early Judaism an apostle was an emissary who was sent from one community to another. According to Acts 13:1-4, Paul and Barnabas were initially commissioned by the Christian community in Antioch of Syria to go to Cyprus. Paul was convinced that God's promises to Israel were being fulfilled in "our Lord Jesus Christ," and that it was his vocation to bring this "good news" (gospel) to non-Jews also. Whereas the prophets envisioned all the nations coming to Jerusalem (Isa. 2:2-4; Zech. 8:20-23), Paul regarded himself as bringing this more perfect form of Judaism to the Gentiles. He came to view his mission as founding new congregations rather than building on "someone else's foundation" (Rom. 15:20; cf. 1 Cor. 3:5-15; 2 Cor. 10:13-16).

According to Acts, Paul's custom on entering a city was to go to the local synagogue and make contact with the Jewish community. There he often got a mixed or even hostile reception, and would then turn to the Gentiles, where he had much more success. There are, however, few indications of this practice in Paul's own letters, which indicate rather that he evangelized over the workbench as he plied his trade (according to Acts 18:3, he was a tentmaker). In both Acts and his letters, Paul assumes some familiarity with the Jewish Scriptures and customs. This suggests that the Gentiles to whom Paul preached and wrote may have come from those already familiar with Judaism through contact with the local Jewish community. Judaism was attractive to non-Jews for its monotheism, high ethical standards, and active community life. Those Gentiles who frequented synagogues without undergoing circumcision and full conversion are described in Acts as "God-fearers." Such persons would have been well prepared and most amenable to Paul's apostolic preaching.

Paul was a pastoral theologian, and his letters were extensions of his apostolic ministry. He developed much of his theology in response to problems that arose in communities that he had founded (Thessalonica, Galatia, Corinth, and Philippi) and from which he had moved on to other places. Paul did not work alone. Rather, he developed a network of coworkers, some of whom were Jews by birth and others who were Gentiles (Rom. 16:1-17). Paul was arrested in Jerusalem while bringing the proceeds of a financial contribution to the Christian community there, and was sent to Rome as a prisoner where, according to Christian tradition, he died a martyr's death in the mid-60s C.E., during the emperor Nero's persecution.

Paul's Christian-Jewish Opponents

In his earliest extant letter from 51 C.E., Paul in 1 Thess. 2:14-16 writes some harsh words about the Jews in Judea "who killed both the Lord Jesus and the prophets and drove us out." He also accuses "Jews" of trying to prevent the mission to the Gentiles.

One pastoral-theological problem that appears in several of Paul's letters concerned whether Gentile Christians needed to become full-fledged Jews by undergoing circumcision and taking upon themselves the obligation to obey the precepts of the Torah. Paul vigorously resisted all efforts by other Christian Jewish missionaries to impose full conversion to Judaism upon Gentile Christians. It is important always to keep in mind that Paul's often heated rhetoric about his opponents in Galatians, 2 Corinthians, and Philippians was directed not to Jews in general but specifically to Christian Jewish missionaries who criticized Paul for his Torah-free gospel for Gentiles.

Paul's objection was primarily theological. He was convinced that Jesus' death and resurrection had accomplished what observing the Torah could never do, that is, bring about right relationship with God (righteousness or justification) and impart the gift of the Holy Spirit. He was also convinced that, through Jesus, Gentile Christians could become full members of the people of God. He believed that God's promises to Israel were being fulfilled among them, and so he sprinkled his letters with biblical quotations and allusions, often drawing on midrashic traditions of interpretation.

Galatia

Paul founded the Gentile Christian communities in Galatia (in central Asia Minor). After he moved on to other places, Christian Jewish missionaries apparently arrived and tried to convince the Galatian Christians that Paul's gospel was inadequate, and that they needed to be circumcised and convert to Judaism and observance of the Jewish Law (6:11-13). News of these events infuriated Paul to the extent that he omitted the customary thanksgiving from his letter, and insisted that the gospel that he had preached to them was from God and that there is no other gospel. In the body of his letter, Paul first appealed to his own conversion-call experience, the approval that he received from the apostles in Jerusalem, and his confrontation with Peter in Antioch over equality between Jewish and Gentile Christians (1:11–2:21). Then after reminding the Galatian Christians that they had already received the Holy Spirit and so did not need circumcision and the Law (3:1-5), Paul constructed an elaborate scriptural argument that all those who are in Christ through faith and baptism are "Abraham's offspring" (3:6-29). For them to go through formal conversion to Judaism was in Paul's mind the equivalent of denying the salvation and freedom that Christ had won for them (5:1-26). For Paul, circumcision had become a matter of indifference, and what really mattered for "the Israel of God" was the new creation brought about by Jesus' life, death, and resurrection (6:15-16).

Corinth

Paul founded the church at Corinth (a port city in southern Greece). While 1 Corinthians is mainly concerned with problems facing Gentile Christians, in 2 Corinthians 3 Paul argues that when non-Christian Jews (and perhaps Law-observing Christian Jews) read the Jewish Scriptures, they fail to understand them because "their minds are hardened" and "a veil lies over their minds." He also contends that "when one turns to the Lord (Christ), the veil is removed" (3:14-16). For Paul, Christ is the key to the Scriptures. He suggests that the Sinai covenant consisted of types and shadows pointing to Christ, and was at best of temporary historical value and at worst an ally of sin and death.

In 2 Corinthians 10–13, Paul again defended himself against attacks from fellow Christian Jewish missionaries who not only criticized Paul's Law-free gospel for Gentiles but also denigrated his person. They were saying that Paul's "letters are weighty and strong, but his bodily presence is weak, and his speech contemptible" (10:10). Paul's rhetorical strategy was to accept the truth of their charges and to insist that his case only proves the truth of the paradox that God's "power is made perfect in weakness" (12:9). In the course of what he refers to as his "fool's speech," Paul restates his credentials as a Jew ("Are they Hebrews? So am I") and lists his many personal sufferings for the sake of the gospel (11:21-29). When appealing to his weaknesses in 12:1-10, he notes his own mystical experiences but prefers to dwell on his "thorn in the flesh" and his other sufferings on the grounds that "whenever I am weak, I am strong" (12:10). The point of Paul's impassioned discourse was to establish that he was in no way inferior to his Christian Jewish rival missionaries, whom he mocked as "super-apostles" (12:11).

Philippi

According to Phil. 3:1-11, the same or a similar group of Christian Jewish missionaries made their way to Philippi (in northern Greece) after Paul's departure. They, too, attacked Paul's credentials as a Jew and his Torah-free gospel for Gentiles, and insisted that Gentile members of the Jesus movement be circumcised. In response Paul first dismisses them as "dogs" (echoing a pejorative Jewish term for Gentiles; see Matt. 15:26-27), "evil workers" (for their insistence on the "works" of the Law), and "those who mutilate the flesh" (for their insistence on circumcision). Next Paul lists his own credentials as a Jew: "circumcised on the eighth day . . . under the law, blameless" (3:4-6). Then he attests to the "surpassing value of knowing Christ Jesus my Lord" (3:8) and dismisses his own superlative status as a Jew to be "loss" and even "rubbish."

In all three letters Paul responded in very strong language to fellow Christian Jewish missionaries by attesting to his own identity as a Jew and to the superiority of his present identity "in Christ" as one freed from the power of sin and made an instrument of the Holy Spirit.

Paul and the Law

Whether Paul himself continued to observe the Jewish Law habitually or only periodically depending on his circumstances, and whether he allowed, expected, or encouraged other Christian Jews to observe it, is not entirely clear. Since his letters were addressed mainly to Gentile Christians, he does not explicitly take up those issues. In reflecting on his "rights" as an apostle and on how he had not made use of those rights, he told his Corinthian converts,

> For though I am free with respect to all, I have made myself a slave to all, that I might win the more. To the Jews I became as a Jew, in order to win Jews; to those under the Law I became under the Law — though not being myself under the Law — that I might win those under the Law. To those outside the Law I became as one outside the Law — not being without Law toward God but under the Law of Christ — that I might win those outside Law. (1 Cor. 9:19-21).

What is clear is that Paul was convinced that only Jesus' death and resurrection could bring about right relationship with God, and that Christ and the Law are not on the same level of importance.

Letter to the Romans

Paul did not found the Christian community at Rome. Rather, it developed quite early within the large Jewish community there. Paul hoped to stop at Rome on his way to found new communities in Spain. But first he had to bring the proceeds of the collection taken up among Gentile Christian churches to Jerusalem for the support of the "saints" there. His letter to the Romans was his way of introducing himself and his gospel to the Roman Christians, and perhaps to prepare for his appearance before the Christian leaders in Jerusalem and for his missionary activity in Spain. There were also tensions at Rome between Gentile Christians and Jewish Christians, and so Paul the pastoral theologian was eager to help both groups toward greater understanding and mutual respect. Written around 57 C.E., his letter to the Romans stands as Paul's great theological synthesis. And one of its major topics is the Torah.

The thesis of Romans is that the gospel is "the power of God for salvation to everyone who has faith, to the Jew first and also the Greek" (1:16). The gospel is the proclamation of the saving significance of Jesus' death and resurrection (1:2-4; 3:25-26). Faith is the way by which all — Jew and Gentile alike — may share in this salvation, though the traditional order of salvation history — Jew and then Greek — is respected.

In Rom. 1:18–3:20 Paul argues that all persons — Gentiles and Jews — need the revelation of God's righteousness in Christ, since "all have sinned and fall short of the glory of God" (3:23). Paul proclaims that one is "justified by faith apart from works prescribed by the Law" (3:28), the point made in various polemical contexts in earlier letters. Then, as in Gal 3:6-29, Paul holds up Abraham as the model of justification by faith (4:1-25) — making the new point that God credited Abraham's faith as righteousness before and apart from Abraham's circumcision — and explains how believers have been liberated from domination by sin, death, and the Law (5:1–7:25) and freed for life in the Spirit (8:1-39).

In developing his theological vision, Paul had to find a place for the Torah. His basic conviction was that Jesus' death and resurrection did what the Torah could never do, that is, bring about right relationship with God (righteousness or justification). Moreover, he contends that even Jews who had the Law failed to observe it (2:17-29) and so showed the need for the revelation of God's righteousness in Christ (1:17). In Gal. 3:19-25 he had already assigned several different roles to the Mosaic Law: witness to Christ, help toward recognizing sin, and guide or pedagogue until Christ came. In Romans Paul often places the Law as a personified figure alongside sin and death: the Law makes people conscious of sin, stimulates them to sin, and imprisons them under the powers of sin and death (7:7-25).

Nevertheless, Paul insists that the Law bears witness to Christ (3:21), that "the Law is holy, and the commandment is holy and just and good" (7:12), and that those who have faith in Jesus do not overthrow the Law but rather uphold it (3:31). He goes on to say that "Christ is the end of the Law" (10:4), with the word *telos* to be taken in its sense of goal or purpose. In other words, Christ has carried out the task (righteousness or justification) that had proved impossible for the Mosaic Law. And in Rom. 13:10 (cf. 8:4) he proclaims that one who truly and consistently acts out of love and according to the Spirit will naturally perform whatever is important and essential in the Law.

The Mystery of Israel

In Romans 9–11 Paul tries to discern the relationship among three groups in God's plan of salvation: Christian Jews like himself, Gentiles who had become Christians, and Jews who had not. This theological exercise had pastoral implications for Christians at Rome who were divided along Jewish and Gentile lines. Paul wanted to show that both groups were important in God's plan and so deserving of mutual respect.

In Rom. 9:1-5 Paul begins his meditation by expressing sorrow that not all Jews have accepted the gospel and by listing the salvation-historical prerogatives of Israel: "to them belong the adoption, the glory of the covenants, the giving of the Law, the worship, and the promises, to them belong the patriarchs, and of their race according to the flesh is the Christ." At the end he affirms that "the gifts and the calling of God are irrevocable" (11:29). Throughout he proudly affirms his own identity as a Jew.

According to Paul, the role of believing Jews like himself was to provide the continuity between God's promises to Israel and their fulfillment through Jesus Christ. He acknowledges that many Jews (indeed, the majority of his contemporaries) had not accepted the gospel, and that he had his greatest apostolic success among non-Jews. He attributes this turn of events to the divine plan. According to Paul, nonbelieving Jews were still pursuing righteousness based on the works of the Law (9:30-33). Paul hoped that when his fellow Jews witnessed the astounding results of his work among the Gentiles, they would become jealous and eagerly embrace the gospel. He was confident that God had not rejected Israel as his people and pointed to himself as proof: "I myself am an Israelite, a descendant of Abraham, a member of the tribe of Benjamin" (11:1).

As a way of clarifying and summarizing these relationships, Paul uses the analogy of the olive tree in Rom. 11:17-24. The olive tree represents the one people of God, and the root of the olive tree is constituted by Christian Jews like himself. The Gentile Christians are branches from a wild olive tree grafted onto the tree and now animated by the root, while non-Christian Jews are branches cut off from the olive tree. Paul assumed that the Christian movement now represents the main line of the historic people of God. He could not imagine the church apart from Israel. The Gentile Christians are now honorary members of God's people by God's grace. Paul was concerned to increase respect among Gentile Christians for Christian Jews in Rome. This analogy reminded both groups of their connections to Israel as the people of God.

What is the destiny of non-Christian Jews? Paul introduces his answer in a solemn way: "I want you to understand this mystery" (11:25). In this context "mystery" refers to the unfolding of the divine plan and carries a future, eschatological sense. The mystery that Paul announces is a summary of this entire meditation: "A hardening has come upon part of Israel, until the full number of Gentiles has come in. And so all Israel will be saved" (11:25b-26a). Paul first used the biblical image of divine "hardening" (Isa. 6:9-10) to explain why not all Israel had accepted the gospel. Then he adopted the idea of a fixed number of non-Jews being allowed to become members of God's people. Finally, he affirms that "all Israel will be saved."

Paul's solemn affirmation leaves open some important questions. Is "all Israel" a collective expression (like "all Israel has a portion in the world to come," *m. Sanh.* 10:1), or does it include each and every Jew? Is Israel's salvation dependent on an explicit connection with Christ, or does God have a separate way for Israel? Will this salvation take place by missionary activity, or will it be the result of a divine, eschatological action? A few prominent scholars maintain that Paul envisioned two paths to salvation: Torah observance for Jews and faith in Christ for Gentiles. Most interpreters, though, understand Paul to mean that, in the end, non-Christian Jews will come to acknowledge Jesus as their messiah. On the whole, Paul's effort at discerning God's plan in Romans 9–11 remains a bold moment in the history of Christian theology, and served as the basis for Vatican II's 1965 statement on the Church's relation to the Jewish people (*Nostra aetate* 4).

BIBLIOGRAPHY

D. BOYARIN 1994, *A Radical Jew: Paul and the Politics of Identity,* Berkeley: University of California Press. • D. A. CARSON, P. T. O'BRIEN, AND M. SIEFRID, EDS. 2004, *Justification and Variegated Nomism,* vol. 2, *The Paradoxes of Paul,* Tübingen: Mohr-Siebeck; Grand Rapids: Baker Academic. • J. D. G. DUNN, ED. 2001, *Paul and the Mosaic Law,* Grand Rapids: Eerdmans. • J. D. G. DUNN 2006, *The Partings of the Ways between Christianity and Judaism and Their Significance for the Character of Christianity,* 2d ed., London: SCM. • J. G. GAGER 2000, *Reinventing Paul,* Oxford: Oxford University Press. • D. J. HARRINGTON 1992, *Paul on the Mystery of Israel,* Collegeville: Liturgical Press. • M. HENGEL 1990, *The Pre-Christian Paul,* London: SCM. • W. A. MEEKS 1983, *The First Urban Christians,* New Haven: Yale University Press. • E. P. SANDERS 1977, *Paul and Palestinian Judaism,* Philadelphia: Fortress. • E. P. SANDERS 1983, *Paul, the Law and the Jewish People,* Philadelphia: Fortress. • A. F. SEGAL 1990, *Paul the Convert: The Apostolate and Apostasy of Saul the Pharisee,* New Haven: Yale University Press. • K. STENDAHL 1976, *Paul among Jews and Gentiles and Other Essays,* Philadelphia: Fortress. • T. H. TOBIN 2004, *Paul's Rhetoric in Its Contexts: The Argument of Romans,* Peabody, Mass.: Hendrickson. • S. WESTERHOLM 2004, *Perspectives Old and New on Paul: The "Lutheran" Paul and His Critics,* Grand Rapids: Eerdmans. • N. T. WRIGHT 1991, *The Climax of the Covenant: Christ and the Law in Pauline Theology,* Minneapolis: Fortress.

DANIEL J. HARRINGTON, S.J.

Peace

The directive to "seek peace and pursue it" appears in the Hebrew Bible (Ps. 34:14), the New Testament (1 Pet. 3:11), and early rabbinic literature (e.g., *Pirqê 'Abot* 1:12). Much of the recent discussion of peace in biblical and early Jewish studies has been driven by contemporary motivations as well as purely historical or academic interests. Studies of warfare have tended to focus on the First Temple period (ca. 950-587 B.C.E.), under the assumption that biblical books such as Samuel and Kings reliably reflect the history of the time. In recent work, however, the study of these narratives has been radically rethought, on the view that they were likely the product of the postexilic period. Thus, to take just one feature, the miraculous element in biblical narratives may actually reflect the same Second Temple ethos that one perceives in postexilic narratives of miraculous delivery from danger, such as the stories in Daniel 3 and 6.

Peace and Rest

Other approaches to the idea of peace in the Bible begin with the analysis of terms. In Hellenistic Jewish texts, the Greek term *eirēnē* normally translates the Hebrew word *šālôm,* and it often stands for the concept of well-being: "The fear of the LORD is the crown of wisdom, making peace and perfect health to flourish" (Sir. 1:18). However, in later Hebrew usage, the term for "rest," *šeqet,* is arguably even more closely associated with cessation of conflict and can refer to disarmament, negotiations, and freedom from international conflict. The postexilic books of 1 and 2 Chronicles, for instance, not only suggest that David was denied the privilege of building the Temple because he was a man of war (1 Chron. 22:8) but also praise Solomon as a man of peace (1 Chron. 22:9). Similarly, Ben Sira commends Solomon for presiding over an age of peace (Sir. 47:13-16). Somewhat ironically, decidedly violent narratives like 1 Maccabees and Judith also contain some of the most explicit references to "peace negotiations" (1 Macc. 6:49, 58, 60, 61; 7:13, 15; 11:51; 13:37; cf. "words of peace" in Jdt. 3:1; 7:24). There are also references to treaties (2 Macc. 13:25) and permanent bronze tablets to commemorate peace treaties (1 Macc. 8:22). Such explicit references to negotiations, processes, and memorials to peace are much rarer in older texts of the Hebrew Bible.

Mixed Marriages and International Relations

One of the most widely pressing social issues facing the postexilic Judean community was mixed marriage (Ezra 9–10; see Janzen 2002). Although this situation is usually understood as a social concern about assimilation on the part of a minority culture, it is clear that there are other aspects of the issue that relate to questions of international relations. Ezra 9:12 speaks of mixed marriage by stating that one should not "seek peace" with enemies (i.e., foreign marriage partners). This stance must be seen in the context of mixed marriages as a political tool of international relations. Nehemiah speaks, for example, of the dangers of Solomon's mixed marriages, clearly seeing political significance to unexamined practices of mixed marriage.

All the more significant, then, is that many modern scholars date the book of Ruth to the Persian period and suggest that it reflects a counterview to Ezra's narrow definitions of acceptable marriage. Ruth is a Moabite, and Ezra explicitly excludes Moabites from the community. Furthermore, Joseph's marriage to the Egyptian

Aseneth in *Joseph and Aseneth* may intend in part a positive commentary on Jewish-Egyptian relations. If mixed marriage was seen as having potentially important political significance, then the debates evident in the postexilic literature may well have been fueled by contrasting attitudes toward international relations.

Apocalypticism and Nonviolent Resistance

Many scholars have pronounced apocalyptic literature as inherently violent and vengeful because of the imagery of war and bloodshed so often associated with it. Others, however, have pointed out that angry *rhetoric* can coexist with decidedly nonmilitant *behavior* in some apocalyptic literature. Collins (1993), for example, famously argued that the book of Daniel represents a "pacifist manifesto" and that the critique of "little help" in Dan. 11:34 and the rejection of the "violent ones" in Dan. 11:14 offer a negative assessment of the Maccabean Revolt. Licht (1961) similarly suggested that the story of Taxo in the *Testament of Moses* represents an intentionally nonmilitant form of resistance. And the Enochic *Book of the Watchers* associates weaponry and warfare with the other horrible lessons taught to humanity by fallen angels (*1 Enoch* 8:1). Leaving punishment to God, so the argument goes, may not be thought of as "peaceful," but neither is it "pro-war," especially if militancy is critiqued in apocalyptic texts. In any case, the desire for "peace" would have taken shape in the context of imperial domination by the Persian, Greek, and Roman Empires (Zerbe 1993).

The debate involves New Testament literature as well. In an influential article, Stendahl (1962) discussed Paul's quotation of Prov. 25:21 in Rom. 12:20, especially the reference to "burning coals on their heads." He suggested that Paul's pacifism (which is evident throughout Romans 12) was actually based on an apocalyptic view of God's ultimate violent overthrow of evil: one can treat enemies graciously because God will eventually punish them. The same issue emerges in the alleged contradiction between the pacifism of Jesus and the violence of the Apocalypse of John. Yet since those who want "peace" must also engage in resistance to imperial domination in ways that are consistent with peacefulness (i.e., nonviolently), there is no necessary contradiction in the rhetoric of Paul, the violence of Revelation, and the pacifism of Jesus, whose own rhetoric could, after all, be both apocalyptic and violent.

Wisdom and Pacificism

The wisdom tradition represents yet another type of reflection on peace. Proverbs calls for calm and self-restraint (17:27), the prevention of conflict (17:9, 14), and concern for the welfare of enemies (17:13). Wisdom is even contrasted with power and fortifications (Prov. 16:32; 21:22). Ecclesiastes carries this even further: "wisdom is better than might" (9:16) and "wisdom is better than weapons of war" (9:18; cf. Prov. 24:5-6). Quietism is also reflected in the antiwar ethos of the New Testament Epistle of James, where the Jewish wisdom tradition is most obviously the major influence: "Let everyone be quick to listen, slow to speak, slow to anger; for your anger does not produce God's righteousness. . . . But the wisdom from above is first pure, then peaceable, gentle, willing to yield, full of mercy and good fruits, without a trace of partiality or hypocrisy. And a harvest of righteousness is sown in peace for those who make peace" (Jas. 1:19-20; 3:17-18). One may compare Sirach's references to the dangers of the tongue in sowing discord (Sir. 28:9, 13) with the same emphasis in James (Jas. 3:5-8).

Jewish scholars have long noted the significant ethos of peacefulness that was characteristic of Pharisaic thought (Genot-Bismuth 1981), which even led to an aversion toward judicial killing. Josephus famously commented that "Pharisees are naturally lenient in the matter of punishments" (*Ant.* 17.288-98). The widely noted quietism of the early rabbinic teachers is arguably rooted in the wisdom tradition's emphasis on self-control and peacefulness, as expressed in the traditions surrounding Rabbi Yoḥanan ben Zakkai. Ben Zakkai's opposition to the First Jewish Revolt led to his escaping Jerusalem to make a separate peace with Rome, and many of his teachings are notably quietist if not directly pacifist.

Giving Voice to "Silenced" Perspectives

Finally, it is important to note that recent studies of biblical narrative have sought to read texts "against the grain" by paying attention ("giving voice") to minor or silent characters as a strategy of questioning previous perceptions of the significance of particular texts. Such an approach raises questions about Second Temple attitudes to war and peace as well. For example, the charge of treason directed against fellow Jews in the nationalist literature of Maccabees effectively silences those who, for their own perceived legitimate reasons, opposed the militancy of the Hasmoneans (1 Macc. 7:13). We hear such voices opposing violent factions in other periods as well. Jeremiah, for example, opposed the resistance to Babylon and faced accusations of treason; Yoḥanan b. Zakkai opposed the revolt against Rome; and Christian Jews supposedly fled Jerusalem for Pella in order to escape the same revolt. Such examples caution against hearing Maccabean violence as the only or dominant voice in that period, especially if Daniel 7–12 represents precisely such a critique of Maccabean militancy.

Bibliography

D. Boyarin 1999, *Dying for God: Martyrdom and the Making of Christianity and Judaism,* Stanford: Stanford University Press. • J. J. Collins 1993, *Daniel,* Minneapolis: Augsburg Fortress. • J. Genot-Bismuth 1981, "Pacifisme pharisien et sublimation de l'idée de guerre aux origines du rabbinisme," *Etudes théologiques et religieuses* 56: 73-89. • D. Janzen 2002, *Witch-Hunts, Purity and Social Boundaries: The Expulsion of the Foreign Women in Ezra 9–10,* Sheffield: JSOT Press. • J. Licht 1961, "Taxo, or the Apocalyptic Doctrine of Vengeance," *JJS* 12: 95-103. • M. Polnar and N. Goodman 1994, *The Challenge of Shalom: The Jewish Tradition of Peace and Justice,* Philadelphia: New Society. • K. Stendahl 1962, "Hate, Non-Retaliation, and Love: 1QS x,17-20 and Rom.

12:19-21," *HTR* 55: 343-55; G. Zampaglione 1973, *The Idea of Peace in Antiquity,* Notre Dame: University of Notre Dame Press. • G. Zerbe 1993, "'Pacifism' and 'Passive Resistance' in Apocalyptic Writings: A Critical Evaluation," in *The Pseudepigrapha and Early Biblical Interpretation,* ed. J. H. Charlesworth and C. A. Evans, Sheffield: JSOT Press, 65-95.

See also: Violence

Daniel L. Smith-Christopher

Penitential Prayer

Penitential prayers are a type of petitionary prayer in which an individual, a group, or an individual on behalf of a group confesses sins and petitions God for forgiveness as an act of repentance. The texts that arose during the Second Temple period that fall within this grouping are the following: Ezra 9:5-15; Neh. 1:4-11; 9:6-37; Dan. 9:3-19; Bar. 1:15–3:8; Prayer of Azariah; Tob. 3:1-6; 3 Macc. 2:1-10; *The Words of the Heavenly Lights* (4Q504); and perhaps 4Q393, although it is extremely fragmentary.

Form

These prayers typically contain the following features: (1) address to God in the second person; (2) the use of *ydh,* "confess," in the *Hitpaʿel;* (3) a pronouncement of God's righteousness, "You are righteous, O Lord," in punishing the people; (4) a confession of sin, of which the most frequent is a form of "We have sinned, we have done wrong, we have acted wickedly"; and (5) a petition that usually begins with the words "and now" for the removal of the sin and punishment.

Origin

The presence of Deuteronomic language and ideology in the prayers is immediately recognizable and suggests that the prayers in part arose among or under the influence of the Deuteronomistic interpreters. These interpreters held that the people's sins brought punishment upon them in the form of the covenantal curses, the worst of which was exile (Deuteronomy 28). Deuteronomy taught that in their exile the people would repent and that God would then restore them to the land (Deuteronomy 4 and 30). Solomon's prayer in 1 Kings 8, which develops the ideas of Deuteronomy 4 and 30, seems to remove any ambiguity about the way in which this repentance and subsequent restoration will take place; the people will repent and confess their sins (cf. 1 Kings 8:47). Solomon's prayer in 1 Kings 8, along with the prayers in Ezra 9 and Nehemiah 9, also shows signs of priestly influence (Boda 1999). This is especially visible in Ezra 9 in the use of language from the *ʾašam* offering in Leviticus 5, in which people are to "confess" *(ydh)* upon recognizing and feeling remorse for wrongs that they have committed. Influenced by Ezekiel and priestly accounts of Israel's wilderness period, Nehemiah 9 recounts Israel's history of sin in the form of a penitential prayer, similar to Psalm 106. The relationship between penitential prayer and lament is much less clear. Some have proposed that lament transformed into penitential prayer in the Second Temple period, but this position remains a matter of debate.

Development

In the second and first centuries B.C.E., the place and role of penitential prayer grew and expanded. Various groups continued to utilize penitential prayer as a lens through which to view the Jews' many problems during this era (Dan. 9:3–19; Bar. 1:15–3:8). However, a shift took place as some groups began to see themselves as the penitential movement that they understood to be promised by Deuteronomy. Combining their group ideology with the language of Deuteronomy, they now distinguished between righteous and wicked groups within the Jewish people, instead of applying these terms to the people as a whole. Penitence or the penitential prayer tradition probably combined with apocalyptic determinism to form views of the authors of the *Apocalypse of Weeks* (*1 Enoch* 93:1-10; 91:11-17), the *Animal Apocalypse* (*1 Enoch* 85–90), and *Jubilees* (*Jubilees* 1, 23). Each group identified itself with the promised future group of penitents.

The Qumran Scrolls clearly base their version of this identification on an interpretation of Deuteronomy 4 and 30; the community is distinguishable from the rest of Israel because the community "seeks" *(drš)* God, that is, it is penitent. The *Words of the Heavenly Lights* (4Q504), which may predate the community, contains a weekly cycle of daily prayers that take the form of a penitential prayer extended through the entire week. The climax of the cycle comes on Friday in preparation for the Sabbath. These daily prayers resemble the recounting of Israel's history as a history of sin in Nehemiah 9 and Psalm 106. The community's annual covenant renewal ceremony (1QS 1:16–2:18) adapts the elements of penitential prayer into a liturgy in which the various components of a typical penitential prayer have been assigned to the various participants in the ceremony.

The connection between penitential prayer and the acquisition of various kinds of knowledge is a significant development in this period. Daniel's penitential prayer (Dan. 9:3–19) functions as part of his quest to understand Jeremiah's prophecy concerning the length of the Exile — seventy years (Jer. 25:11-12; 29:10). At the conclusion of the prayer, Gabriel arrives with the interpretation of the text and its application to the time of the author, who lived during Antiochus IV's reign of terror. "Seventy years" is now "seventy weeks of years." The pattern in Daniel resembles Ben Sira's description of the activity of the scribe, who rises early and confesses sins in order to understand various forms of wisdom (Sirach 38–39) and then teaches their meanings to his students. The present structure of the book of Baruch leaves a similar impression that penitential prayer leads to wisdom; the editor of the book follows the prayer in Bar. 1:15–3:8 with a poem about wisdom. Understanding repentance and studying Torah as primary roles of the community, the Qumran sect read the word *drš* in Deut. 4:29-30 as not simply "to seek" God, but "to seek" God in a text, through interpretation. Thus, the community made reading and interpreting Torah a constituent of repentance. The Qumran *Hodayot* also contain several reflections on sin, confessional statements, and declarations of God's righteousness in bringing or threatening punishment (e.g., 1QH 4, 5, 7, 9, 11, 12, 19). The author often connects the acquisition of special knowledge to his penitential practice.

BIBLIOGRAPHY

R. J. BAUTCH 2003, *Developments in Genre between Post-Exilic Penitential Prayers and the Psalms of Communal Lament,* Atlanta: Scholars Press. • M. J. BODA 1999, *Praying the Tradition: The Origin and the Use of Tradition in Nehemiah 9,* Berlin: de Gruyter. • R. A. WERLINE 1998, *Penitential Prayer in Second Temple Judaism: The Development of a Religious Institution,* Atlanta: Scholars Press.

RODNEY A. WERLINE

Pentateuch

The Pentateuch (from Gr. *pente teuchos,* "five scroll") or Torah (Hebr. "instruction, Law") is comprised of the first five books of the Bible, Genesis through Deuteronomy. It was the most consistent object of reverence and study in early Judaism. From Jewish philosophers such as Philo to groups such as the Sadducees, Pharisees, and Essenes, virtually all Jews in the Hellenistic and Roman periods honored the Pentateuch as their most central text. To be sure, some early pseudepigraphic books, particularly those associated with Enoch, may intend their teachings as an alternative to the Mosaic Torah (Nickelsburg 1998); and others, such as the book of *Jubilees* and the *Temple Scroll,* evidently intended at the very least to supplement the written Torah, standing alongside the written Torah as part of a dynamic process of Mosaic discourse (Najman 2003). Moreover, classical rabbinical texts speak of an "oral Torah" of teachings that circulated among rabbis of the Second Temple period (e.g., *b. Giṭṭin* 60b; *y. Meg.* 4:74a; *b. Yoma* 28ab; *y. Pe'ah* 2:17a). Nevertheless, such oral teachings are not attested in written form until decades after the revolt of Bar Kokhba in 132-135 C.E. (Jaffee 2001). With a few possible exceptions, then, the extant evidence points resolutely to widespread veneration of the Pentateuch across the diverse groups of Second Temple Judaism.

Final Literary Formation

Though the Pentateuch had already reached something like its present form by the early Second Temple period, there are several signs that its process of formation was not yet complete. For example, the early Greek translation of the Pentateuch presents versions of Genesis 1 and the Tabernacle narrative in Exodus 25–40 that diverge from and may be earlier than those found in the Masoretic version of these texts. In addition, the dating system in the Pentateuch is different in the Septuagint (LXX), Samaritan Pentateuch (SP), and Masoretic Text (MT).

For a time, however, a few Jewish groups appear to have worked with other textual forms and literary editions of the Pentateuch, and some even appear to have attempted further revisions. Study of pentateuchal texts among the Dead Sea Scrolls (e.g., 4QpaleoExodus^{m}) indicates that some books of the Pentateuch circulated in different literary editions during the Second Temple period (Ulrich 1999). Several Pentateuchal manuscripts contain harmonizations of laws in Exodus and Numbers with laws in Deuteronomy. This type of harmonization was the basis for the Samaritan edition of the Pentateuch, which contained still other additions. The Qumran finds also include another expanded edition of the Pentateuch, *Reworked Pentateuch* (4QRP), which includes features such as speeches by Rebecca and Miriam (Tov and White 1994). The *Temple Scroll* at Qumran represents a yet more radical presentation of pentateuchal themes, giving in the first person a revelation at Sinai of God's instructions for the Temple and a fluid conflation of Deuteronomy and other legal texts afterward (Swanson 1995). These finds indicate that at least some Jews continued to revise and circulate different textual and literary forms of the Pentateuch late into the Second Temple period.

Nevertheless, aside from the SP and the LXX, these alternative forms of the Pentateuch did not prevail. Instead, a proto-Masoretic form of the Pentateuch gained virtually total dominance within Hebrew-reading, non-Samaritan Jewish groups in the early Roman period. The triumph of this relatively early textual tradition of the Pentateuch contrasts with the situation for some other biblical books. For example, in the case of the book of Jeremiah, it appears that the rabbis of the early Common Era preferred a later, significantly longer edition of Jeremiah than the one reflected in the Old Greek and some Qumran manuscripts.

Significance

Though Jewish groups appear to have disagreed over which prophetic and other books were sacred, virtually all accorded a sacred status to the books of the Pentateuch (Carr 1996: 34-39). Narratives from the Second Temple period assume reverence for the Torah. Especially notable is the depiction in 1 and 2 Maccabees of the Hasmoneans as Torah-observant Jews (e.g., 1 Macc. 3:48; 14:14; 2 Macc. 10:25-26) and their war as a fight to defend the twin values of Torah and Temple (e.g., 1 Macc. 1:56-57; 14:29; 2 Macc. 6:1-2). Further, most nonnarrative texts from the Hellenistic and early Roman periods feature some kind of focus on pentateuchal texts. Ben Sira describes how the scribe studies "the law of the Most High" along with the "wisdom of the ancients" and other teachings (Sir. 39:1-5), and his "praise of the fathers" starts with an extended review of major figures in the Torah (Sirach 44–45). Almost half of the Wisdom of Solomon is a wisdom-focused retelling of the story recounted in the Torah (Wisdom 10–19). Similarly, the community texts from Qumran focus on the importance of constant recitation and correct interpretation of the Torah (1QS 6:6-8; 8:14-16; note also CD 14:6-8), and the bulk of the Qumran collection of parabiblical texts features works related in some way to the Torah. Even pseudepigraphic texts almost always are attributed to figures in the Torah narrative (e.g.,

Enoch, the twelve patriarchs, and Moses), and they often feature retellings of events narrated in the Torah (e.g., *Jubilees* and *Genesis Apocryphon*).

Some early Jewish texts see the Torah as equivalent to the figure of personified divine Wisdom so prominent in earlier Hebrew instructional texts (e.g., Proverbs 8). Ben Sira praises Wisdom as a female figure who came to dwell amidst humanity as the Jewish Torah (Sir. 24:23-29). Several Qumran texts likewise identify Wisdom and Torah (4Q525 2 ii 1-6; and 11QPs[a] 18:10-13 [//Ps. 154:12-15]). Likewise, a hymn in the book of Baruch equates wisdom with "the book of the commandments of God, the law that endures forever" (Bar. 4:1 NRSV; see 3:9–4:4).

This sapiential valuation of the Pentateuch probably reflects its foundational role in Jewish literary education throughout the Second Temple period (Carr 2005: 206-78). Many Jews of this period never learned to write or read, but those who did gain a Hebrew education probably started with and focused on texts from the Torah. We see this educational focus on Torah in Ben Sira's endorsement mentioned above. For him and other Jews in the Second Temple period, the Torah served a role in Hebrew education much like the Homeric writings did in Greek education. They were the writings that each student learned early on to read, write, and memorize. Moses was the Jewish Homer. This foundational role only continued and expanded with time. By the first century C.E., Philo (*Hypoth.* 7.10-13) and Josephus (*Ag. Ap.* 2.175) explicitly describe Torah-based education on the Sabbath. Early rabbinic texts suggest that the first text to be learned by the student should be Leviticus (*ʾAbot R. Nat.* 6 and 15; *Lev. Rab.* 7:3), followed by other Torah texts.

The Torah was also important on a communal level (Baumgarten 1985). It helped define "Israel" as a cultic community centered on the Temple. The highly varied groups of the Second Temple period disagreed about many things (including their evaluation of the existing Jerusalem Temple), but they agreed on the central importance of the Temple and the Torah (Schwartz 2001: 1-62). This is one reason why the books of the Maccabees depict the rise of the Hasmonean kings as a fight to defend Temple and Torah. These two pillars of identity persisted after the demise of the short-lived Hasmonean monarchy. In 70 C.E. the Temple was destroyed, leaving only the Torah as a tangible orientation point for later Judaism. Yet it was prominent enough by then to serve that role. Even as rabbinic Judaism revered other, non-Torah biblical texts along with the emerging traditions of the "oral Torah," the Pentateuch remained a central pillar of Jewish worship, study, and life.

BIBLIOGRAPHY

A. I. BAUMGARTEN 1985, "The Torah as Public Document in Judaism," *SR* 14: 17-24. • D. M. CARR 1996, "Canonization in the Context of Community: An Outline of the Formation of the Tanakh and the Christian Bible," in *A Gift of God in Due Season: Essays on Scripture and Community in Honor of James A. Sanders,* ed. D. M. Carr and R. D. Weis, Sheffield: JSOT Press, 22-65. • D. M. CARR 2005, *Writing on the Tablet of the Heart: Origins of Scripture and Literature,* New York: Oxford University Press. • M. JAFFEE 2001, *Torah in the Mouth: Writing and Oral Tradition in Palestinian Judaism, 200 BCE–400 CE*, New York: Oxford University Press. • H. NAJMAN 2003, *Seconding Sinai: The Development of Mosaic Discourse in Second Temple Judaism,* Leiden: Brill • G. W. E. NICKELSBURG 1998, "Enochic Wisdom: An Alternative to the Mosaic Torah?" in *Ḥesed ve-Emet: Studies in Honor of Ernest S. Frerichs,* ed. J. Magness, Atlanta: Scholars Press, 123-32. • J. SANDERS 2005, *Torah and Canon,* 2d ed., Eugene, Ore.: Wipf & Stock. • S. SCHWARTZ 2001, *Imperialism and Jewish Society, 200 B.C.E. to 640 C.E.*, Princeton: Princeton University Press. • D. D. SWANSON 1995, *The Temple Scroll and the Bible: The Methodology of 11QT,* Leiden: Brill. • E. TOV AND S. A. WHITE 1994, "Reworked Pentateuch," in *Qumran Cave 4, VIII: Parabiblical Texts, Part 1,* DJD 13, Oxford: Clarendon, 187-351 with pls. XIII-XXXVI. • E. ULRICH 1999, *The Dead Sea Scrolls and the Origins of the Bible,* Grand Rapids: Eerdmans.

See also: Reworked Pentateuch; Samaritan Pentateuch; Temple Scroll (11QTemple); Torah and Tradition

DAVID M. CARR

Pentecost, Festival of → Festivals and Holy Days

People of the Land

ʿAm hā-ʾāreṣ ("People of the Land") is a Hebrew phrase that was used for different groups of people in the course of ancient Jewish history.

Biblical Usage

In the Hebrew Bible, the term refers sometimes to a certain group within the population and denotes a representative upper-class group such as landowners (Gen. 23:13). Usually the term refers to a group of the population that is geographically or ethnically defined, sometimes pagan but usually Israelite. The term *ʿammê hā-ʾāreṣ* in the plural refers to various other sorts of people or to the people of a particular country. In the books of the Bible that deal with the beginning of the Second Temple period, the phrase refers to the inhabitants of the land of Israel who interfered with the process of the return to Zion.

Second Temple Usage

ʿAm hā-ʾāreṣ la-miṣwôt ("people of the land with respect to the commandments") was the term referring to those who were careless about the observance of the *miṣwôt* (commandments) relating to ritual purity and the separating of tithes. Thus it became a term of abuse for the lowest stratum of society, in contradistinction to the *ḥābēr* (member) of the elite Pharisee *hăbūrôt* (fellowships) that were extremely strict in these matters. According to the halakah, a person who did not observe these *miṣwôt* was not only committing a sin himself but was also liable to lead others to become impure or eat *tebel* (produce that had not been tithed). Hence it is clear why the *ʿammê hā-ʾāreṣ* were characterized by reference to these particular *miṣwôt,* rather than, for example, by strict Sabbath observance. The latter is, of course, a central commandment but not observing it does not necessarily involve one's fellow Jew. Furthermore, the *miṣwôt* of ritual purity and tithes were related to the Temple, the place where purity was to be observed more than anywhere else, and the place to which the tithes were brought, to distribute them to the priests and Levites, who took their turns in serving in the rites. The *ʿam hā-ʾāreṣ la-miṣwôt* was a stratum of society that was excluded from the community only insofar as it was necessary to avoid eating untithed produce or contracting impurity.

Mishnaic and Early Amoraic Usage

After the destruction of the Temple, the observance of ritual purity and tithes lost its importance, although it continued to be observed, and the study of Torah became the central value in Judaism instead of the Temple and its rites. As a result of this, the term *ʿam hā-ʾāreṣ* lost its social application and became *ʿam hā-ʾāreṣ la-Tôrâ* ("people of the land with respect to Torah"), in other words, an ignoramus who does not take any part in studying Torah. Such a person is at the bottom of the social scale, while the rabbinic leadership was at the top. The new term expressed the wish of the sages to unite the people behind them, and at the same time to exclude from the normative community those who had not joined in this unity, such as the *ʿammê hā-ʾāreṣ* or the Jewish-Christian sects. The fate of the *ʿammê hā-ʾāreṣ* was different from that of the Christians, for the latter crystallized an ideology and a religion separate from Judaism, while the *ʿammê hā-ʾāreṣ* continued a social trend without a unifying framework. In the Ushan period (ca. 180-220 C.E.), a negative attitude developed toward the *ʿammê hā-ʾāreṣ* because of the desire to rehabilitate the study of Torah, which was endangered following the failure of the Bar Kokhba Revolt and the subsequent repressive legislation.

Not only were the *ʿammê hā-ʾāreṣ* excluded from rabbinic communities but a simmering hatred developed between them and the sages, expressed in halakot such as the instruction not to return lost articles to them, or in statements that it is permissible to kill an *ʿam hā-ʾāreṣ* as one slaughters a pig, even on a Yom Kippur (Day of Atonement) that falls on the Sabbath.

It should be noted that these virulent statements against the *ʿam hā-ʾāreṣ* are found only in the Babylonian Talmud, and most of them are concentrated in one place: *b. Pesaḥim* 49a-b. It may be that the picture of simmering hatred between the sages and the *ʿammê hā-ʾāreṣ* reflects more the views of the editors of the Babylonian Talmud than the actual situation in land of Israel after the Destruction and in the Ushan period. Indeed, it is possible that such statements were invented by later Babylonian editors or sages and attributed to certain Tannaim (rabbinic sages who lived ca. 70-200 C.E.) without any real historical basis. However, this comment does not deny the trends already noted for the sages of Usha, although it helps explain the excessive virulence of the statements and halakot relating to the *ʿam hā-ʾāreṣ la-Tôrâ*.

By the time of Rabbi Judah ha-Nasi, study of the Torah was firmly established. Now, because of his wish to associate with the urban aristocracy, who were for the most part *ʿammê hā-ʾāreṣ la-Tôrâ*, a change began in the attitude to the *ʿam hā-ʾāreṣ*, and their rights were made equal to those of Jews in general. At the beginning of the Amoraic period (ca. 220-370 C.E.), the opinion crystalized that a population is made up of different elements, among which there was room for *ʿammê hā-ʾāreṣ*, and indeed some of them were worthy people. In the second half of the Amoraic period (ca. 370-500 C.E.), the term *ʿam hā-ʾāreṣ* disappeared from the social scene.

BIBLIOGRAPHY

A. BÜCHLER 1906, *Der galiläisch ʿAm ha-ʾAres des zweiten Jahrhunderts*, Vienna: Israelitisch-theologische Lehranstalt; rpt. Olms, 1968. • A. OPPENHEIMER 1977, *The ʿAm ha-Aretz: A Study in the Social History of the Jewish People in the Hellenistic-Roman Period*, Leiden: Brill. • D. ROKEAH 2005, *Am ha-Aretz: The Ancient Pious Men, Jesus, and Christians*, in *Mehqerei Talmud*, vol. 2, ed. Y. Sussmann and D. Rosenthal, Jerusalem: Magnes, 876-903 (in Hebrew).

AHARON OPPENHEIMER

Persecuted Righteous Person

References to the unjust suffering of the innocent in the literature of early Judaism are ubiquitous. In a world dominated by foreign powers and beset with intra-Jewish rivalries, the righteous are often portrayed as oppressed by Gentile overlords, Jewish opponents, even evil spirits, or Satan. The authors of such texts employ many different genres and literary forms to press their case and implore God for judgment in the expressed hope that the wicked will be punished and the righteous saved. Such stories derive from three models known from folklore: tales of court conflict, martyr legends, and chastity stories.

Tales of Court Conflict

Tales of court conflict, such as those in the Joseph narratives of Genesis 37–50, the book of Esther, and Daniel 3 and 6, share a structure with a folkloric type known as "The Disgrace and Rehabilitation of a Minister." In this type of story, set in a royal court, a wise or righteous person is the victim of an unjust plot or conspiracy, is condemned to death or prison, then is released and exalted to a position of honor. There is no unanimity among scholars as to the number of narrative elements in the Jewish version of this story-type; proposals range from five to as many as twenty-one elements. The variety of proposals testifies to the richness and complexities of the literary texts. At a minimum, the basic plot structure includes one or more protagonists who move through the following stages: (1) initial prosperity; (2) endangerment, often in the form of a conspiracy; (3) condemnation; (4) rescue; and (5) exaltation. In the last stage, the protagonist's wisdom or righteousness is recognized.

In the stories listed above, the protagonist is a Jew in a foreign court who excels because of his administrative skills, which, unfortunately, also brings him to the attention of an antagonist. In the book of Genesis, Joseph is both a skilled overseer of Potiphar's house and a righteous man who resists the sexual advances of Potiphar's wife. In the book of Esther, Mordecai is a courtier who displays his righteousness by reporting a plot to assassinate the king and refusing to bow to Haman, who then plots against him. Daniel and his three companions practice the Torah in a foreign land and are portrayed as being ten times better than foreign officials. Some of these officials then conspire to use their devotion to God's Law as a means to get rid of them. While the circumstances vary greatly, in each of these stories the hero is the victim of a plot and is threatened with imprisonment or execution for his faithfulness. The rescue takes place through a providential orchestration of events or more directly by a divine intervention in the form of an angel. The rescue always takes place before death, and the protagonist is vindicated and exalted in the royal court.

Martyr Legends

In the literature of early Judaism, stories of martyrdom appear to be a variant version of tales of court conflict. Two changes are especially significant. First, it is characteristic of martyr legends that the heroes are questioned directly by a tyrant before their death. Second, the heroes die, and their rescue and exaltation takes place after death in the heavenly court or realm. Examples of martyr stories in early Judaism are the martyrdoms of Eleazar, and the seven brothers and their mother (2 Macc. 6:18–7:42), the martyrdom of Isaiah (*Ascen. Isa.* 1:1–3:12 and 5:1-16), and the story of the persecution and exaltation of the righteous one (Wis. 1:16–2:20; 4:16–5:13).

2 Maccabees

The author of 2 Maccabees describes the persecution of Jews who refused to abandon the practices of Torah as ordered by Antiochus IV Epiphanes. The elderly Eleazar refuses to eat swine's flesh. Those in charge of the sacrifice advise him to pretend to be eating, but Eleazar replies that he will be faithful to God and leave an example for the young. He is then tortured and dies. The seven brothers and their mother are also compelled to eat swine's flesh and, in this case, converse directly with King Antiochus. They express their willingness to die for the laws of God and their confidence that their vindication will take place after death when God raises their bodies from the dead.

Martyrdom of Isaiah

The *Martyrdom of Isaiah* is an early Jewish text in which Isaiah prophesies his own death, which then unfolds as he predicted. Beliar or Satan dwells in the heart of King Manasseh, and the persecution of the righteous increases during his reign. This may indicate that the author's real-time opponents were Jewish and not Gentile. Because of the persecution, Isaiah and the prophets flee to the wilderness, but they are discovered there by Belkira, a lying prophet of Samaritan origin. Belkira accuses Isaiah of being a false prophet, and Manasseh has him seized and sawed in half. A verbal exchange between Belkira and Isaiah takes place in the death scene. Belkira mocks Isaiah and tempts him to prophesy falsely like him, but Isaiah responds by cursing him. In this story, the real opponent of the righteous prophet is Satan — Manasseh and Belkira are merely his agents. The rescue after the execution is implied by the comment that Isaiah had a vision of the Lord at the time he was sawed in half.

Wisdom of Solomon

The Wisdom of Solomon begins by exhorting the rulers of the earth to love righteousness and then proceeds to summarize a story about the oppression of a righteous person by the wicked (chaps. 2, 4–5). The text offers the musings of the persecutors before and after the righteous one is killed. Beforehand, the wicked conspire against the righteous one because he reproves them for sin and calls himself a servant of the Lord. They decide to put the latter claim to the test and condemn him to a shameful death to see if God will deliver him. In the afterlife, at the final judgment, the wicked see the salvation of the righteous one and speak to one another in repentance. In this author's summary of the martyr story, there is no mention of the righteous one addressing his adversaries at the time of his death. The rescue takes place because the soul is immortal and God rewards the righteous with eternal life.

Gospel Passion Narratives

Before considering the third type of story of the persecuted righteous person, we should note that these first two types are regarded by many scholars as providing a basis for the passion narratives found in the four gospels of the New Testament, if not for the gospel genre itself. Highly speculative is the suggestion (Crossan 1991) that the two types should be kept distinct, that the first is the organizing principle of a primitive passion narrative detectable in the *Gospel of Peter*, and that the second type is found in the Gospel of Mark's passion narrative. The two story types coalesced in early Jewish texts before the time of Jesus. The narratives of Jesus' death in the Gospels, along with the earlier Jewish martyr stories, supply a pattern for subsequent Christian martyrdoms, such as those of Stephen (Acts 6–7) and Polycarp (*Martyrdom of Polycarp*).

Chastity Stories

Another story type of the persecution of the righteous person derives from a type known in folklore as chastity stories. The elaboration of the story of Joseph and Potiphar's wife in the *Testaments of the Twelve Patriarchs* is attributable to the influence of this type. Joseph recounts several attempts of Potiphar's wife to seduce him — all in an effort to assure the righteous that the Lord will rescue and exalt them, too, if they exercise self-control and keep themselves pure (*T. Jos.* 2:1–10:3).

Susanna

The book of Susanna provides an example of a folktale type known as the falsely accused chaste wife. This particular Jewish adaptation of the type follows the basic structure of tales of court conflict, although the royal court setting has been dropped in favor of a local Jewish court of elders. Susanna is a beautiful woman who fears the Lord. She is espied by two elders as she walks in her husband's garden. When she later refuses to lie with them, they conspire to ruin her by testifying falsely that they found her with a young man. Susanna's rescue by God comes from the intervention of Daniel, who is able to expose the wicked lies of the two elders and confirm the innocence of Susanna.

Apocryphal Acts of Apostles

Adaptations of chastity stories become very significant in recounting the exploits of women in early Christian apocryphal acts of apostles. While early Christian versions of such stories exhibit variations with as many as fourteen structural elements, five functions are fairly consistent: (1) woman vows chastity; (2) husband, fiancé, or suitor attempts to violate vow; (3) husband, suitor, fiancé, or governor persecutes woman; (4) woman is rescued; (5) woman is allowed to remain chaste.

This structure can be illustrated from two incidents in the story of Thecla in the *Acts of Paul and Thecla*. In the first, Thecla vows chastity after hearing the apostle preach in Iconium. She then breaks off her engagement to her financé Thamyris, who plots against her until she is condemned to be burned. She is rescued when God sends a miraculous thunder shower over the pyre. Thecla is free and continues to follow Paul. In a second incident in the city of Antioch, an influential citizen named Alexander becomes enamored of Thecla and attempts to take her by force. Thecla resists him and tears his cloak (cf. Gen. 39:12-18). Alexander then leads her to the governor, who condemns her to the wild beasts. Thecla experiences a miraculous deliverance in the arena. The governor acknowledges that she is the servant of God, and Paul himself commissions Thecla to teach the Word of God. The scenes of rescue in the two incidents involving Thecla employ imagery and terminology that recalls the rescues in Daniel 3 and 6.

BIBLIOGRAPHY

V. BURRUS 1987, *Chastity as Autonomy*, Lewiston: Mellen. • J. J. COLLINS 1984, *Daniel, with an Introduction to Apocalyptic Literature*, Grand Rapids: Eerdmans. • J. D. CROSSAN 1991, *The Historical Jesus*, New York: HarperCollins, 383-91. • G. W. E. NICKELSBURG 1980, "The Genre and Function of the Markan Passion Narrative," *HTR* 73: 153-84, rpt. in *George W. E. Nickelsburg in Perspective*, ed. J. Neusner and A. J. Avery-Peck, Leiden: Brill, 2003, 2:473-503. • V. PROPP 1968, *Morphology of the Folktale*, 2d ed., Austin: University of Texas Press. • L. M. WILLS 1990, *The Jew in the Court of the Foreign King*, Minneapolis: Fortress. • L. M. WILLS 2003, "Response to 'The Genre and Function of the Markan Passion Narrative,'" in *George W. E. Nickelsburg in Perspective*, ed. J. Neusner and A. J. Avery-Peck, Leiden: Brill, 2003, 2:504-12.

See also: Martyrdom RANDAL A. ARGALL

Persian Period

The Persian period represents a seminal era in Jewish history. Most of the elements that characterized Second Temple Judaism had their origin under Persian rule. Persian administration is often pictured as being different — usually as much more benevolent — from Assyrian and Neo-Babylonian rule. This is partly because Jewish literature itself seems to reflect such a state of affairs. The effect is illusory, however; the Persians ruled much as the previous ancient Near Eastern empires.

The Persians governed by means of a few major divisions of the empire (conventionally called "satrapies"). The satrapies were in turn divided into provinces, of which Judah (Aram. *Yehud*) was only a small one on the edge of the empire. Throughout most or all of its time under the Persians, Judah had a governor; this person was frequently Jewish but not necessarily so. All indications are that the Judeans (or Jews) initially hoped for a return to the status quo before the destruction of Jerusalem in 587/586 B.C.E., that is, the restoration of the monarchy. There are indications that some Jews saw Zerubbabel as the scion of David who would eventually take up his vacant throne (cf. Hag. 2:20-23; Zechariah 3–4). This was not to be, and Judah remained a small province in a much larger empire for almost another four centuries.

Judah *(Yehud)* in the Persian Period

Much of the history of Persian *Yehud* is a blank. Inscriptions and archaeology help us to fill this in, as do literary sources. Unfortunately, even for periods where the biblical text ostensibly gives information, this is not necessarily reliable. Specialists differ in their assessment of the biblical text for this period, of course, but there is considerable skepticism about much of the book of Ezra at the moment, both about the early years of the province and about the mission of Ezra itself. On the other hand, Haggai, Zechariah 1–8, and much of Nehemiah are treated as more reliable by a majority of scholars (if not by everyone). There is fairly wide agreement that a writing by Nehemiah himself (though in edited form) lies behind Nehemiah 2–6, 13, and some verses in chaps. 1, 7, and 12. This does not mean that we can accept this narrative at face value, since Nehemiah had strong views and strong prejudices, and the historian has to take these into account in evaluating his version of events.

Contrary to the books of Ezra, Esther, and other biblical passages, it is unlikely that the Persians favored the Jews or treated them in any way differently from other minorities or remote provinces. Thus, the passages that suggest that the Persians issued special decrees on behalf of the Jews or provided funding for Jewish projects or exempted Jews from taxation are likely to be only propaganda in their present form; on the contrary, the Persians taxed temples and only exceptionally provided state funding for cult sites. On the other hand, toleration for local religions was standard, and there is evidence that permission would have readily been given

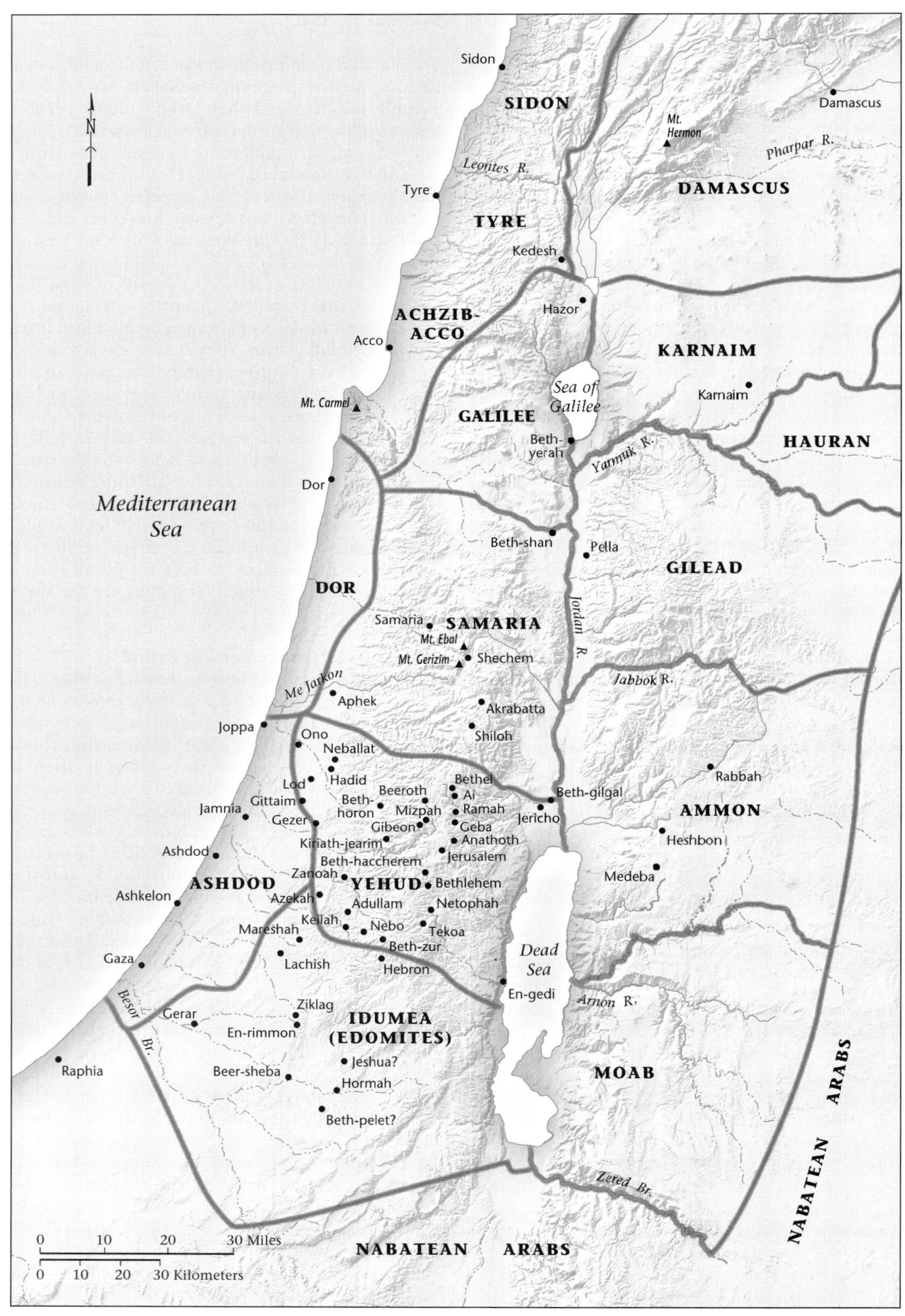

Palestine under Persian Rule

PERSIAN PERIOD

to allow Jews in Babylon to return to Judah or to rebuild their ruined Temple. Thus, when Haggai and Zechariah suggest that some prominent Jews (such as Zerubbabel and Joshua) had returned from exile to Judah and that work was going on to rebuild the Temple in the early decades of the Persian period, this is entirely believable. The date of completion of the Temple given in Ezra 6:15 (ca. 516 B.C.E.) is unlikely to be correct, since the resources are not likely to have been sufficient to finish it so quickly, but the Jews probably had a functioning Temple in the late sixth or early fifth century B.C.E.

Some scholars have pictured the Persian kings as closely supervising and controlling their subject people, often hypothesizing that events in Judah were the result of "Persian policy." Although much remains to be learned about Persian administration, the evidence from the wider imperial rule suggests that the area ruled was too large and diverse to allow tight supervision from the center. It seems, rather, that much was left up to the decisions of individual satraps and even governors. As long as the required taxes were paid and there seemed to be no threat of rebellion, a fair amount of leeway appears to have been allowed at the local level. Thus, Cyrus (539-530 B.C.E.), Cambyses (530-522 B.C.E.), and also Darius (522-486 B.C.E.) seem to have allowed Jews to return from Mesopotamia to Judah, though not ordering it or providing financial support.

The book of Ezra and other passages give the impression that the land was empty, except for some foreign "peoples of the land" who caused trouble, and the land was resettled by returnees from the Babylonian Exile. In actual fact, the figures in the Bible itself (e.g., 2 Kings 24:13-16; Jer. 52:27-30) suggest that only a small portion of the people was deported, and a substantial population remained in the land. The fighting with the Babylonians and the hardships and disease that followed the fall of Jerusalem reduced the population considerably, but the land was by no means empty. Furthermore, those returning from exile appear to have been only a trickle over the years and were absorbed into the population without leaving any clear mark in the archaeological record. Many of those labeled as "foreigners" in such passages as Ezra 9:1-2 were in all likelihood Jews, descended from those left in the land after the deportations.

We seem to know little, then, until the middle of the fifth century B.C.E. Nehemiah's mission raises a number of questions. It took place in 445 B.C.E., according to the usual reckoning. If Jerusalem had been inhabited for close to a century, why had the walls not been built? But if there was no problem, why the sudden need to undertake such a project? According to the book of Ezra, Ezra had come only a few years earlier (in 458 B.C.E., if the king in question is Artaxerxes I) and sorted out the city and province. His commission from Artaxerxes was wide ranging and gave him great authority in the local area (Ezra 7). So why did Nehemiah need to come and do a similar job?

Some resolve the problem by dating Ezra's mission to Artaxerxes II, long after Nehemiah (in 398 B.C.E.). Others argue that Ezra's mission could have been accomplished in only a year's time, but this must assume that it was ultimately a failure. When the Ezra story is examined in detail, however, there is much that is problematic in it. The decree of Artaxerxes confers powers on Ezra that many argue are incredible and which the Ezra story indicates he did not exercise. The historical Ezra seems to be buried in a heavily edited and legendary account.

Persian Empire (all dates B.C.E.)

550-530	Cyrus rules Persia
539	Cyrus captures Babylon; end of Neo-Babylonian Empire; beginning of Persian Empire
538	Edict of Cyrus allows Judeans to return to Judah
530-522	Cambyses extends Persian Empire to include Egypt
522-486	Darius I
516/515	Traditional date of rebuilding of Jerusalem Temple
490	Persia invades Greece; defeated at Battle of Marathon
486-465	Xerxes I
480-479	Second Persian invasion of Greece
465-424	Artaxerxes I
458	Ezra's arrival in Jerusalem
445	Nehemiah's arrival in Jerusalem
423	Xerxes II
423-404	Darius II
404-358	Artaxerxes II
398	Alternate date for Ezra's arrival in Jerusalem
358-338	Artaxerxes III
338-336	Arses
336-331	Darius III
333	Darius III defeated at Battle of Issus by Alexander of Macedon
333-330	Alexander's conquest of Near East brings end to Persian Empire

Why Jerusalem's walls needed repairing is not clear. There is no indication of a threat of armed attack; on the other hand, to be in charge of a walled city with gates guarded by one's own men would give great power and control over the population of the city. This was precisely Nehemiah's position in chap. 13 when he attempted to enforce his view about the Sabbath. He was able to stop traders by shutting the gates before the Sabbath and not allowing them in. The implication is that Jerusalemites were also prevented from going out of the city to trade with them outside the walls. Whether this was Nehemiah's original intent for building the walls or not, it was certainly a convenient consequence of his repair work.

Apart from Ezra-Nehemiah and the prophetic books of Haggai and Zechariah 1–8, we have little other biblical information on the Persian period. Other sources of information are documents from the Jewish colony in Elephantine in Egypt and papyri originating in the province of Samaria found in Wadi Daliyeh. These tell us a bit about the Jews of Judah. But only archaeology (including coins) covers much of the fourth century, which is otherwise mainly a blank for Yehud (though we have a good deal of information about events elsewhere in the empire). We seem to have the names of some of the high priests and also the coins of "Hezekiah the governor."

Yet in spite of the large gaps in our knowledge, there is much about the Persian period that was extremely significant for the development of later Judaism. We find the first emphasis on keeping the Sabbath, the development of written Scripture, the concept of a religious community rather than a state, the rise of apocalypticism, and the high priest rather than a monarch as the main representative of the Jewish community. Persian rule — perhaps in spite of itself — seems to have fostered these developments.

BIBLIOGRAPHY
J. BERQUIST 1995, *Judaism in Persia's Shadow: A Social and Historical Approach,* Minneapolis: Fortress. • P. BRIANT 2002, *From Cyrus to Alexander: A History of the Persian Empire,* trans. P. T. Daniels, Winona Lake, Ind.: Eisenbrauns (French original: *Histoire de l'empire perse de Cyrus à Alexandre,* vols. 1 and 2, Leiden: Nederlands Instituut voor het Nabije Oosten, 1996). • W. D. DAVIES AND I. FINKELSTEIN, EDS. 1984, *The Cambridge History of Judaism,* vol. 1, *Introduction; the Persian Period,* Cambridge: Cambridge University Press. • L. L. GRABBE 2004, *A History of the Jews and Judaism in the Second Temple Period,* vol. 1, *Yehud: A History of the Persian Province of Judah,* London: Clark. • K. HOGLAND 1992, *Achaemenid Imperial Administration in Syria-Palestine and the Missions of Ezra and Nehemiah,* Atlanta: Scholars Press. • S. JAPHET 2006, *From the Rivers of Babylon to the Highlands of Judah: Collected Studies on the Restoration Period,* Winona Lake, Ind.: Eisenbrauns. • O. LIPSCHITS 2006, *Judah and Judeans in the Persian Period,* Winona Lake, Ind.: Eisebrauns.

See also: Daliyeh, Wadi ed-; Elephantine, Elephantine Papyri; Ezra, Book of; Nehemiah, Book of; Joshua (Yeshua), the High Priest; Zerubbabel

LESTER L. GRABBE

Persian Religion

Influence on Early Judaism

The question of Persian or Iranian influence on early Judaism has been an object of scholarly discussion for more than a century and is still a debated issue. The discovery of the Qumran texts caused a renewed interest in the problem. Early Judaism was a diversified religion that was not limited to a particular country and culture. Diaspora Jewish communities were found all over the Mediterranean world and farther to the east in Mesopotamia and Iran. The Jews were not isolated from the societies in which they lived, and they were exposed to a broad spectrum of cultural and religious influences that affected groups and individuals in varying degrees. Iranian religion or Zoroastrianism has been considered one of the more important contexts for understanding some characteristic features of early Judaism. Zoroastrianism was not a uniform phenomenon in antiquity, and a more normative form did not impose itself until the late Sassanian period (fifth to sixth century C.E.). One of the early variant forms considered Zurvan and not Ahura Mazda to be the supreme deity, but the latter was the god who created the world and protected it from destruction by the evil powers. The notices of Iranian religion given by classical authors (e.g., Strabo and Plutarch) often differ from traditional Zoroastrian sources, thus underlining the variety of religious expression in Iran.

For more than 200 years Palestine was under Persian rule, and contacts between Jews and Iranians continued in the Hellenistic and Roman periods accompanied by political sympathy. Persian sovereignty paved the way for a cultural encounter that included knowledge of Persian kings, administration and court life, and other aspects of Iranian culture (reflected in the books of Ezra, Esther, and Daniel). The Jewish communities of Iran and neighboring Mesopotamia probably played an important role in conveying information on Iranian religion to other Jews. Many Iranian words were adopted by the Jews directly or indirectly, and the number of such loanwords has increased through the discovery of the Qumran texts. The significance of these borrowings for the question of a parallel religious influence is a matter of controversy. In any case, they enhance the possibility of such an influence.

Since a detailed presentation of all themes and aspects of Persian influence cannot be given here, the reader is referred to more comprehensive surveys and discussions (Winston 1966; Hultgård 1979; Shaked 1984; Boyce and Grenet 1991; cf. also Barr 1985). In view of its importance, the complex of eschatological and apocalyptic ideas needs to be discussed, as also the tendency toward a dualistic worldview found especially in the Qumran texts. Examples of mythic and ritual detail that suggest Iranian influence will also be given.

Eschatology

One of the main characteristics of early Judaism is the emergence of a complex of ideas that deals with the future of the Jewish people and with the history and end of the world and humanity. The history of the world is linked to that of the Jewish people and their hopes for a restoration of Israel, which is often expected to be ushered in by messianic figures. The great turning point of world history will involve both destruction and renewal and will be announced by various signs and cataclysms. A final battle between Good and Evil is also predicted in several Jewish texts and is in fact described in the *War Scroll* from Qumran (1QM and related fragments), where the Sons of Light will fight the Sons of Darkness. To this universal eschatology, which is often colored by apocalyptic ideas, corresponds an individual eschatology that distinguishes between righteous and wicked human beings who on the Day of Judgment will face different destinies in the afterlife, either in paradise or hell.

Both the whole complex of eschatological ideas and particular beliefs within it, such as the bodily resurrection of the dead and the final battle between Good and Evil at the end of time, have counterparts in Zoroastrianism (overview in Hultgård 1998), and some sort of connection is usually assumed. In Zoroastrianism, universal and individual eschatology date from an early period (fifth century B.C.E. at the latest) and are well integrated, forming an essential element of its worldview, cult, and mythology. In Judaism, by contrast, these ideas evolved at a later date and only gradually forced their way into the center of the religion. The priority is thus on the Iranian side, but that does not imply that the eschatological complex was simply taken over by Judaism. Instead, Iranian influence exerted itself by providing a stimulus for developing eschatological ideas that to a certain extent were rooted in Jewish traditions, but which until then had not ripened or been fully conceptualized.

Early Jewish eschatology was transmitted in different forms, the most important being prophecies, dream visions, apocalyptic accounts, otherworldly journeys, and oracles. Some of these forms and the details they include may partly owe their origin to Iranian religion. The otherworldly journey described in *2 Enoch*, for instance, has much in common with the one undertaken by Arda Wiraz and other Iranian visionaries (Boyce and Grenet 1991). In the book of Daniel, the great image shown to King Nebuchadnezzar, with its head in gold, breast and arms in silver, belly and thighs in bronze, legs in iron, and feet in part iron and part clay, represents different kingdoms that will be replaced by the kingdom of God (Dan. 2:31-45). Similarly, the Zoroastrian myth of the tree with metallic branches symbolizing ages of the world and kingdoms leads up to the end of time (*Bahman Yasht* 1.1-5; 2.14-22 and passages in the *Denkard*). The background of the Daniel text is debated (Persian, Greek, and Mesopotamian have been suggested), but the closest parallel is found in Iranian tradition. Several Jewish passages in the *Sibylline Oracles* (e.g., *Sib. Or.* 3.388-95; 2.252-55, 313-20) are considered to reflect Iranian ideas.

Critics of the notion of Iranian influence often point to the late date of the Zoroastrian Pahlavi texts, which transmit the bulk of Iranian eschatological doctrine. Although mainly compiled in the ninth century C.E., these texts are based on much earlier tradition, to which they also refer. The *Avesta* has preserved a passage (*Yasht* 19.88-96) that describes the coming defeat of the evil powers and the renovation of the world. Greek authors mention elements of Iranian eschatology such as the resurrection of the dead, and Plutarch (*De Iside et Osiride* 46–47) gives a summary of cosmogony and universal eschatology that draws much from Theopompus' writing in the early fourth century B.C.E. Details in Plutarch's account correspond precisely with what is known from the Pahlavi texts, and this shows that the Iranian eschatological tradition goes far back in time.

Dualism

Closely related to eschatology are the dualistic features common to Zoroastrianism and early Judaism. Second Temple Judaism, especially in its later phase (second century B.C.E. onward), included the belief in a personified evil power who is called by various names, such as Belial, Mastema, and Satan, and who rules over a multitude of demons. He is the great adversary of God and humanity, and the enemies of Israel and wicked people in general are thought to serve in his ranks. The tendency for such a dualistic conception is more or less pronounced among different Jewish groups but is most clearly seen among the Qumran Essenes. The Dead Sea Scrolls reveal a dualistic worldview with two opposing forces personified as the Spirit of Truth and the Spirit of Falsehood, who are integrated into an elaborated system of good and evil, often expressed in the symbolism of light versus dark. God has instituted them to rule over the righteous and the wicked respectively until the time of His "visitation," but humankind has to choose between them (1QS 3:18–4:26; 4QAmram). The affinities with Iranian dualism, including its emphasis on the choice between good and evil and its eschatological outlook, are striking. These similarities are interpreted by most scholars as resulting from Iranian influence.

Myth and Ritual

Iranian mythic and ritual elements appear also to have found their way into Second Temple Judaism. Iranian demonology probably explains the name *Asmodaios* (Old Iranian *aēšma daēva*) in Tob. 3:8, and the detail of the dog accompanying Tobias and Raphael (Tob. 6:1) is more in line with the Zoroastrian religious esteem for that animal than with the contempt usually shown for it in Semitic cultures. The exhortation in Tob. 4:7-18 compares almsgiving with the laying up of treasure in the afterlife for the "day of tribulation," which is an old and well-known idea in Zoroastrianism.

The legend of Noah's birth found in *1 Enoch* 106, which is also attested in Qumran fragments (e.g., 1QNoah; 1QapGen), presents some features that recall the myth of Zarathustra's birth. Noah was born as a white shining child, the house was filled with light, and he rose from the hands of the midwife and uttered a blessing to the Lord. According to Iranian legend, the village where Zarathustra's mother lived was all shining the three last nights before he was born. At his birth a light shone forth over him and he started to speak and bless Ahura Mazdā. The legend is based on ancient tradition, and some traits of it are mentioned by Pliny.

Jewish descriptions of humanity's fate after death sometimes display details that most probably have their origin in Iranian traditions. A Qumran fragment describing the Day of Judgment (4Q521) refers to the "bridge of the abyss," which clearly is inspired by the Cinvat bridge of Iranian eschatology over which righteous and wicked alike have to pass. The righteous succeed in reaching the other side, whereas the impious fall down into the abyss. In the *Testament of Abraham* 17 it is said that Death personified meets the righteous in a beautiful and peaceful appearance but the wicked in a decayed and grim appearance. The different shapes taken on by Death are further explained as a result of the good or evil deeds that people performed in their lives. The idea is not found elsewhere in early Judaism and is apparently a Jewish adoption of the ancient Iranian idea of the *daēna,* who encounters the dead in a changing shape depending on their status as just or impious (*Hadoxt Nask* 2).

A peculiar statement on the souls of animals and their place in the world to come appears in *2 Enoch* 58–59. At the Last Judgment the souls of animals will accuse those who treated them ill, and this will have bad consequences for their own human souls. The statement is followed by praise for those who perform a right sacrifice because it gives them "healing" in the afterlife. The passage clearly reflects the Iranian idea that animals have a soul that ascends in the sacrifice to the abode of Ahura Mazdā, and it corresponds to the repeated exhortations in religious texts to protect and care for animals. One of the oldest texts, a *Gāthā* (Y. 29), has the "soul of cattle" accuse those who treat them ill.

With respect to ritual, reference has been made to the festival of Purim, which according to the book of Esther was instituted in memory of the liberation of the Jews from the evil plot of Haman. The feast seems originally to have been a Jewish adaptation of the popular Iranian feast called *Fravardigān* in Middle Iranian. The name given to the Jewish feast in the Greek versions of Esther, *frouraia* or *fourdia,* hints more clearly at an Iranian background.

An interesting case is the cult legend told in 2 Macc. 1:18-36, which reports that the priests hid part of the Jerusalem Temple fire in a dry well before they went into exile. When the Jews returned, Nehemiah ordered the Temple fire to be recovered but only a thick liquid was found. He then enjoined the priests to sprinkle the liquid over the sacrificial wood, and when the sun shone out again, the altar burst miraculously into a great blaze. On hearing this, the Persian king ordered the place where the fire had been hidden to be made sacred. It is further said that Nehemiah and his companions called the liquid *nephthar,* "purification," but most people called it *naphtha.* The explanation attributed to Nehemiah is obviously secondary. The word *naphtha* is of Babylonian origin *(naptu)* but is also attested in Old Iranian. The background of the legend is to be found in the Iranian fire cult and fire legends linked with the worship of the goddess Anāhita. In one of her fire temples in northern Mesopotamia, there was a well with *naphtha* in close proximity to the sacrificial fires (Strabo, *Geography* 15.1.4). Legend also records that the cult in a Zoroastrian fire temple in Lydia was characterized by an automatic flashing up of the sacrificial wood when the magi recited the ritual texts (Pausanias 5.27.6).

BIBLIOGRAPHY

J. BARR 1985, "The Question of Religious Influence: The Case of Zoroastrianism, Judaism, and Christianity," *JAAR* 53: 201-35. • M. BOYCE AND F. GRENET 1991, *A History of Zoroastrianism,* vol. 3, Leiden: Brill. • J. J. COLLINS 1997, *Apocalypticism in the Dead Sea Scrolls,* London: Routledge. • J. DUCHESNE-GUILLEMIN 1982, "Apocalypse juive et apocalypse iranienne," in *La soteriologia dei Culti Orientali nell'Impero Romano,* ed. U. Bianchi and M. Vermaseren, Leiden: Brill, 753-59. • J. R. HINNELLS 1994, "Zoroastrian Influence on Judaism and Christianity: Further Considerations," in *Agathe Elpis: Studi storico-religiosi in onore di Ugo Bianchi,* ed. G. Sfameni Gasparro, Rome: Bretschneider, 305-22. • A. HINZE 1999, "The Saviour and the Dragon in Iranian and Jewish/Christian Eschatology," in *Irano-Judaica,* vol. 4, ed. S. Shaked and A. Netzer, Jerusalem: Ben Zvi Institute, 72-90. • A. HULTGÅRD 1979, "Das Judentum in der hellenistisch-römischen Zeit und die iranische Religion: Ein religionsgeschichtliches Problem," *ANRW* I.19.1, 512-90. • A. HULTGÅRD 1988, "Prêtres juifs et mages zoroastriens: influences religieuses à l'époque hellénistique," *RHPR* 68: 415-28. • A. HULTGÅRD 1998, "Persian Apocalypticism," in *The Encyclopedia of Apocalypticism,* vol. 1, ed. J. J. Collins, New York: Continuum, 39-83. • A. HULTGÅRD 2000, "Das Paradies: Vom Park des Perserkönigs zum Ort der Seligen," in *La Cité de Dieu, Die Stadt Gottes,* ed. M. Hengel, S. Mittmann, and A. M. Schwemer, Tübingen: Mohr-Siebeck, 1-43. • M. PHILONENKO 1994, "Le pont de l'abîme," *Le signe, le symbole et le sacré: Cahiers internationaux de symbolisme* 77-79: 181-86. • S. SHAKED 1984, "Iranian Influence on Judaism: First Century B.C.E. to Second Century C.E.," in *Cambridge History of Judaism,* vol. 1, *Introduction; The Persian Period,* ed. W. D. Davies and L. Finkelstein, Cambridge: Cambridge University. Press, 308-25. • S. SHAKED 1994, *Dualism in Transformation: Varieties of Religion in Sasanian Iran,* London: School of Oriental and African Studies, University of London. • G. WIDENGREN, A. HULTGÅRD, AND M. PHILONENKO 1995, *Apocalyptique iranienne et dualisme qoumrânienne,* Paris: Maisonneuve. • D. WINSTON 1966, "The Iranian Component in the Bible, Apocrypha, and Qumran: A Review of the Evidence," *History of Religions* 5: 183-266.

See also: Dualism; Eschatology

ANDERS HULTGÅRD

Pesharim

Overview

The Hebrew term *pesher* (Hebr. *pešer;* pl. *pĕšārîm*) means "interpretation" and is used to denote both a particular kind of contemporizing biblical interpretation found in some of the Dead Sea Scrolls, and a type of Qumran composition that is comprised of such exegesis. The "continuous pesharim" consist of a series of sequential biblical citations, each followed by a formulaic phrase that includes the word *pesher* (e.g., "its pesher [*pišrô*] concerns . . ."). The linking phrase introduces an interpretation in which the text is applied to the author's own historical context, which is believed to be situated in the "end of days."

There are fifteen compositions among the Qumran corpus that are recognized as "continuous pesharim": five pesharim on Isaiah (4Q161, 4Q162, 4Q163, 4Q164, 4Q165), three on the Psalms (1Q16, 4Q171, 4Q173), and seven on books of the Minor Prophets (1QpHab on Habakkuk; 1Q14 on Micah; 1Q15 and 4Q170 on Zephaniah; 4Q166 and 4Q167 on Hosea; 4Q169 on Nahum). 3Q4 appears to be another pesher on Isaiah; 4Q168 has been designated as a pesher on Micah; and it is possible that 5Q10 (Commentary on Malachi A) and/or 4Q253a (Commentary on Malachi B) may reflect remnants of continuous pesharim on Malachi. The siglum 4QUnidentified Pesharim Fragments (4Q172) has been assigned to a group of fourteen fragments, some of which have now been associated with known pesher manuscripts, while others may represent otherwise lost pesher compositions.

Unlike many other Qumran compositions, which have been preserved in multiple manuscripts and various recensions, each of the pesharim is extant in only a single copy. Most of the existing manuscripts of continuous pesharim have been dated paleographically to the first century B.C.E. (the Hasmonean and Herodian periods).

Related works include 4QCommentary on Genesis A-D (4Q252–4Q254a) and a number of texts that have been designated "thematic pesharim": 4QFlorilegium (4Q174), 4QCatena A (4Q177), 4QCatena B (4Q182), and 11QMelchizedek (11Q13). Like the continuous pesharim, each of the thematic pesharim features a series of biblical citations along with contemporizing eschatological interpretations; they employ set formulas for citation and identification, including formulas containing the word "pesher." Unlike the continuous pesharim, in which the literary framework is determined by the particular biblical base-text, the thematic pesharim are structured around a concept, with eclectic citations of different biblical sources functioning as "prooftexts" for the author's assertions.

The word "pesher" also appears in 1Q22Words of Moses, 1Q30Liturgical Text (?), 4QOrdinances (4Q159), 4Q180Ages of Creation[a], 4Q464Exposition on the Patriarchs, and CD 4:14. The employment of the term *pesher* in CD to introduce an extended interpretation of Isa. 24:17 is in keeping with the usage familiar from the pesher compositions. In some of the other instances of "isolated pesher," the term seems to be used with citations of the Pentateuch rather than of prophetic texts. CD is replete with additional examples of pesher-like interpretations, in which prophetic texts are cited and applied to sectarian contexts but without the use of the term "pesher."

The continuous pesharim are the earliest known works of biblical interpretation to feature a systematic commentary structure. The explicit citation of the base-texts in these compositions has been contrasted with alternative implicit forms of early biblical interpretation, such as "rewritten Bible."

Pesher interpretation does not aim simply to explicate the biblical text or expand upon it, as is generally the case with early biblical exegesis of legal or narrative texts. Rather, it aims to identify the "true" historical setting for biblical prophecies. Etymologically, the word "pesher" is associated with dream interpretation, and this is how the Aramaic cognate is used in the book of Daniel. Just as dreams function in the Bible as sources of revelation when interpreted by specially endowed individuals, so too pesher treats biblical prophecy as a repository of divine messages that can be deciphered by an inspired human agent. Perhaps the most effective description of pesher comes from a pesherist himself, in 1QpHab 7:1-5, commenting upon Hab. 2:2,

> "YHWH said to me, 'Write the vision and make it plain upon the tablets so that he who reads it can run.'"

The interpretation supplied is:

> God told Habakkuk to write down the things that are going to come upon the last generation, but the fulfillment of the end-time He did not make known to him. . . . Its interpretation concerns the Teacher of Righteousness, that God made known to him all the mysteries of the words of his servants the prophets.

The above citation not only points up the nature of pesher interpretation but also illustrates its hallmark tripartite structure: (1) citation of the prophetic biblical text; (2) introductory formula typically using a form of the word "pesher"; and (3) an application of the text to a contemporary reality outside its original context. Each of these distinctive elements of Qumran pesher is indicative of a sphere in which the pesharim advance our understanding of early Judaism: the transmission of biblical texts, early biblical interpretation, and the history of the Second Temple period.

Text and Canon Criticism

Since each pesher interpretation is preceded by the citation of the biblical text (the lemma), the pesharim serve as witnesses to textual variants. Some of these are considered textually or exegetically significant, though many simply reflect typical Qumran spelling, pronunciation, or grammar, and others appear to have arisen due to scribal error. An interesting focus case for this discussion is 1QpHab 11:8-15, the citation and interpretation of Hab. 2:16. The MT reads "Drink then yourself, and be uncircumcised [Hebr. *wĕhēʿārēl*]." Although the lemma in 1QpHab reads "and stagger" (*wĕhērāʿēl,* a variant that is similar to MT, but with two letters transposed), the pesher comment on this phrase states, "he did not circumcise the foreskin of his heart," indicating an awareness of the MT reading. There is some debate as to whether pesherists created variants, altering texts to suit their interpretations. Thus, for example, when 1QpHab 8:3 cites Hab. 2:5 as "wealth [Hebr. *hôn*] betrays a haughty man," in contrast to MT "wine" *(hayyayin),* this may either attest to a preexisting variant in the pesherist's biblical text, or it may reflect his intentional modification of a text, in order to accommodate the ensuing pesher interpretation about the corruption and greed of the Wicked Priest.

With respect to canonical criticism, the systematic citation and interpretation of selected works is an indication of their authoritative status for the Qumran community. In a different way from the cited biblical texts, it is clear that the pesher compositions themselves were viewed as authoritative, in that they were believed to have been composed by means of divine revelation, and that acceptance of these texts served as a boundary marker differentiating members of the Community from outsiders.

Early Biblical Exegesis

The introductory formula bridging the lemma and its interpretation points to the close connection that was perceived between the biblical text and the application. This correspondence, the relationship between the lemma and its application, is important for both the derivation and expression of pesher. As products of inspired exegesis, pesharim have often been compared to rabbinic midrash. In pesher, as in midrash, multivalence is significant for the formation and formulation of the interpretation. Thus textual variants, wordplay, allegory, and symbolism are essential techniques in the pesherist's recontextualization of his base-text to reflect his own circumstances and concerns. Another similarity to midrash, in some pesharim, is the use of additional biblical texts besides the primary base-text.

Unlike rabbinic midrashim, continuous pesharim are not expressed in free-flowing prose, but are formulated as identifications of specific elements in the lemma, or of the general context in which the lemma is believed to be applicable. In *Pesher Habakkuk, Pesher Nahum,* and *Pesher Psalms*[a], the pesherist maintains close correspondence between the lemma and his interpretation, often paraphrasing the base-text in a manner that reflects aspects of the original context and literary structure. Early studies of pesher emphasized the tendency of the pesharim toward "atomization," or focusing upon isolated details in the lemma, but it is now recognized that pesher exhibits a high degree of sensitivity to the broader context of the base-text.

In addition to specific exegetical techniques, much emphasis has been placed on the underlying presuppositions or "hermeneutics" of pesher exegesis. As formulated by K. Elliger (1953), pesher interpretation is predicated upon the belief that the content of biblical prophecy concerns the end time, and that the end time is the time of the author.

Ideology, Socioreligious Realities, and Historical Events

As "fulfillment literature," pesharim offer evidence of the beliefs, values, and experiences of the Qumran community, to be extrapolated from the content and tone of the pesher applications. Most significant among the beliefs is a strong concern with theodicy in the context of a worldview of dualistic determinism. Thus, the pesharim substantiate the conviction that outsiders were doomed to perdition, whereas the members of the Community were elected for divine revelation and ultimately for eternal salvation. In addition to illuminating ideological aspects of sectarianism, the pesharim also offer a picture of some of the social realities reflected in the verbal polemic, especially in the opposition to the Jerusalem establishment. The Community's sense of alienation and persecution is vividly illustrated by references to attacks by the "Wicked Priest" against the Community and its leader: "he pursued the Teacher of Righteousness to his house of exile to swallow him up with his poisonous vexation. At the appointed time of the repose of the Day of Atonement he (the Wicked Priest) appeared to them to swallow them up and make them stumble on the fast day, their restful Sabbath" (1QpHab 11:4-8). And again, "the Wicked Priest, who [lay in ambush for the Teache]r of Righteousn[ess and sought to] murder him . . . and the Torah that he sent to him." These passages also hint at the centrality of halakic concerns, including calendrical issues, in sectarian disputes.

The usefulness of the pesharim as a source for historical information is the subject of debate. In general, the pesharim employ oblique and often stereotyped language, and tend to use sobriquets rather than actual names to refer to historical figures. Thus, they do not enable the modern reader to uncover new historical data, but they do allow for an enhanced picture of information already known from other sources, especially Josephus and rabbinic writings. Since the historical events are described in veiled terms, modern researchers differ in their interpretations of the specific historical contexts and figures. Some of the proposed historical contexts are discussed below, in reference to individual pesharim. Here we present a brief overview of some of the key sobriquets found in the pesharim.

Kittim

The term "Kittim" represents mighty Gentile adversaries in a number of early Jewish writings, and may variously refer to Greeks or Romans. The biblical roots of the sobriquet are associated with Greece (Gen. 10:4; 1 Chron. 1:7). It is generally agreed that the epithet is used in the pesharim to refer to the Romans. The Kittim appear prominently in 1QpHab, where they serve as the contemporary equivalent and identification of the biblical text's Chaldeans (i.e., Babylonians.) The term appears also in 4QpNah, 1QpPs, and 4QpIsa[a] as well as in the *War Scroll* and *War Rule.*

The Teacher of Righteousness

References to the Teacher of Righteousness appear in the *Damascus Document* as well as in the pesharim (1QpHab, 4QpPs[a], 4QpPs[b], 1QpMic). This figure is usually understood to be the founder of the Qumran community. 1QpHab presents him as the inspired revealer and interpreter of the *Pesher to Habakkuk,* and modern scholars have frequently speculated about his authorship of other Qumran scrolls (especially the *Thanksgiving Scroll,* 4QMMT, and the *Community Rule*).

The biblical source for this epithet is Joel 2:23, "for he has given you the early rain [Hebr. *môreh*] for your vindication *(liṣdākāh).*" Through wordplay and symbolism, this verse was associated with the Teacher of Righteousness, the *Môreh Ha-ṣĕdāqāh* (or *Môreh Ṣedeq*), who would educate and enlighten the people in order to teach them righteousness and prepare them to merit salvation in the final judgment. Additional epithets for this figure also stress his educational role: Teacher of the Community, Interpreter of the Torah, and Interpreter of Knowledge. Since the Teacher was a priest,

PESHARIM

there have been attempts to identify this figure as a Jerusalem high priest, whether Onias III (high priest prior to the Maccabean Revolt) or an unknown high priest holding office during the Maccabean Revolt. There have also been a few anachronistic and unconvincing attempts to identify the Teacher as a Christian figure. Most likely, this figure is not to be identified with any individual known from sources outside the Dead Sea Scrolls.

The Wicked Priest

The Wicked Priest is the arch-opponent of the Community and the nemesis of the Teacher of Righteousness. This figure appears in *Pesher Habakkuk* and *Pesher Psalms.* He was the head of the Jerusalem establishment and presumably a high priest (*kōhēn hārōʾš,* thus engendering the epithet Wicked Priest, *kōhēn hārāšāʿ*, through wordplay). It is generally accepted that the Wicked Priest designates a Hasmonean, but there is debate as to the specific identification, whether Jonathan or Simon of the first generation of Hasmonean high priests and rulers, or the later figure of King Alexander Jannaeus, or others. The "Groningen Hypothesis" is a proposal that this epithet was not a static appellation for a single figure but was used at different times to refer to successive high priests. According to 1QpHab, the Wicked Priest was initially perceived as a legitimate and promising ruler but was corrupted by greed and later abused his power, oppressing the people and persecuting the Community. 1QpPs[a] relates his attempt to murder the Teacher of Righteousness to the sending of "torah," which some scholars have identified with 4QMMT. The pesharim assert that the Wicked Priest received due punishment.

The Man of Lies

The Man of Lies, also "Spouter (or Preacher) of Lies" or "Man of Scoffing," is portrayed as a demagogue opposed to the Teacher of Righteousness. This opposition is highlighted by the term "spouter," a means of dispensing liquid that contrasts with the desirable "rain" implicit in the name of the Teacher of Righteousness. The imagery of "dripping lies" is found Mic. 2:6, 11 and Amos 7:16; 9:13. This figure appears in *Pesher Habakkuk* and the *Damascus Document.* A community of "scoffers" is also mentioned in *Pesher Isaiah[b]*, and related terms appear in the *Thanksgiving Scroll.* The role of the Man of Lies as a religious leader and (mis)interpreter of Torah is distinguished from the portrayal of the Wicked Priest as a political figure, but it has been suggested that the epithets may describe different facets of opposition to a single individual.

The Lion of Wrath

The Lion of Wrath appears in *Pesher Nahum* and *Pesher Hosea,* in each case prompted by references to "lions" in the biblical base-text. In both compositions, it probably designates King Alexander Jannaeus, ostensibly the first Hasmonean ruler to have designated himself as "king" as well as "high priest" on his coins. Alternative proposals have focused upon Gentile rulers, including Antiochus IV, Titus, or Pompey. The context in both of the pesharim is opposition to "Ephraim," and the context in *Pesher Hosea* also refers to "the last priest." In *Pesher Nahum,* the Lion of Wrath is said to "hang men alive," which is generally understood as a reference to Alexander Jannaeus' crucifixion of his Jewish opponents as described by Josephus. This controversial and fragmentary passage has stirred much debate about attitudes toward crucifixion in ancient Judaism, and the Community's attitude toward Alexander Jannaeus. The latter question remains unresolved, even with recourse to the Qumran *Prayer for King Jonathan.* This text has been identified as a Qumran prayer for Alexander Jannaeus, but it has alternately been described as a prayer for Jonathan the Hasmonean, a prayer against Alexander Jannaeus, or a prayer of non-Qumranic origin. As for crucifixion, the pesher is unlikely to attest to either approval or disapproval of crucifixion as a legitimate penalty for traitors, but rather expresses the author's sense of vindication in the punishment of his opponents.

Ephraim, Manasseh, Judah; Seekers after Smooth Things

Pesher Nahum, Pesher Psalms[a], Pesher Hosea, and the *Damascus Document* identify Jewish factions as "Ephraim" and "Judah." In *Pesher Nahum* and *Pesher Psalms[a],* Manasseh appears as well. Modern scholarship has aligned these epithets with the three major sects named by Josephus as comprising ancient Jewish society: Pharisees, Sadducees, and Essenes. Both the hypothesis identifying the Qumran Community as Essenes and the simple three-sect model have been challenged in recent years, but the general identifications retain wide acceptance.

The term "Judah" in the Dead Sea Scrolls sometimes seems to refer to the Community or part of the Community (CD 4:11; 1QpHab 8:1), and at other times to the Jewish nation as a whole, or to the geographic region of Judea.

The use of the term "Ephraim" to delegitimize opponents may have some roots in anti-Samaritan polemic, such as that probably found in 4Q372. In *Pesher Nahum,* "Ephraim" is used interchangeably with the epithet "Seekers after Smooth Things" (Hebr. *dōršê haḥălāqôt*) to designate the Jerusalem leadership. A biblical basis for the latter epithet is found in Isa. 30:10, which describes the people of Israel as rejecting legitimate prophets, turning instead to those who "speak smooth things" and offer comforting delusions. It is likely that the term is a derisive rejection of these opponents' lenient halakic rulings, associated with misguided legal exegesis, via wordplay between *ḥălāqôt* and *ḥălākôt* (laws, legal rulings). The term "Seekers after Smooth Things" appears in the *Damascus Document, Thanksgiving Scroll,* and some wisdom texts (4Q184, 4Q185) to denote religious opponents of the Community, depicted as having great influence over the populace through demagoguery and deception. If the identification of this group as Pharisees is correct, then *Pesher Nahum* corroborates images of the Pharisees as having enjoyed the following of the masses.

In *Pesher Nahum,* the downfall of "Manasseh" is said to foreshadow that of "Ephraim." This is generally viewed as a reference to the decline of the Sadducees and defeat of Aristobulus II, preceding the anticipated eradication of Hyrcanus II and the Pharisees.

Pesher on Micah

The surviving fragments of *Pesher Micah* (1Q14) contain citations from chaps. 1 and 6 of Micah pertaining to divine retribution. Sectarian terminology includes "the Council of the Community" and the "Righteous Tea[ch]er."

Pesharim on Zephaniah

The pesharim on Zephaniah (1Q15 and 4Q170) are poorly preserved. The extant fragments comment upon chap. 1 of Zephaniah, in which the subject is the "Day of the Lord." 1Q15 seems to contain a quotation of Zeph. 1:18–2:2. The word "pesher" has survived, along with only a few words of the comment. In 4Q170, bits of Zeph. 1:12-13 remain, along with the word *pišrô* and just two words of commentary.

Pesharim on Isaiah

The Isaiah commentary from Qumran Cave 3 is too fragmentary to characterize definitively. Parts of Isa. 1:1 and 1:2 have survived, along with some bits of words that are not citations, including what seems to be the phrase "[Da]y of Judgme[nt]." The structure of interspersed citation and commentary, and the eschatological content, seem indicative of pesher.

As a group, the Isaiah pesharim seem less developed than *Pesher Habakkuk* or *Pesher Nahum,* featuring lengthy citations with short pesher identifications rather than full paraphrases or elaborations of the lemma.

Extant portions of 4Q161 comment upon chaps. 10 and 11 of Isaiah, which concern, respectively, a promise of divine salvation for Israel from the military threat posed by Assyria, and the messianic prophecy of the "shoot of Jesse." A reference to a battle originating in the Valley of Akko probably alludes to a Ptolemaic campaign against Judea in the time of Alexander Jannaeus. Sobriquets include "Prince of the Congregation," the "Kittim," and "the Poor Ones."

The base-text of 4Q162 is Isaiah 5 (perhaps chap. 6), which describes God's wrath against his sinful people. In terse comments, the pesherist identifies the sinners as the Jerusalem establishment of his own time. Verses 15-23 are not cited or addressed by the pesher, and there is some debate as to whether this reflects the pesherist's selective use of the biblical text, or his dependence upon a variant version of Isaiah that lacked these verses.

The sixty-one extant fragments of 4Q163 include citations of verses from a number of chapters of Isaiah (8–10; 14; 19; 29–31) as well as from Zechariah, Hosea, and possibly Jeremiah. Among the terse identifying comments that have survived, we find some typical sectarian phrases such as "Sons of Zadok" and "Seekers after Smooth Things."

4Q164 relates the description of the rebuilding of Jerusalem in Isaiah 54 to the Community, applying the prophetic imagery of precious stones to the community's leadership, including a twelve-member council.

Like 4Q163, 4Q165 is another Isaiah pesher characterized by terse identifying comments upon verses from a range of chapters in the biblical book (chaps. 11, 14, 15, 21, 32, and 40).

Pesharim on Psalms

Three documents from the Qumran caves are pesharim on the Psalms: 1Q16, 4Q171, and, 4Q173. 1Q16 is very fragmentary. Legible remains include parts of citations of Psalm 68, a few occurrences of the word *pišrô,* and the words "Jerusalem" and "[K]ittim."

The extant portions of 4Q171 address Psalms 37, 45, and 60. The message of Psalm 37 is well suited to the dualistic eschatological mind-set of pesher — assuring the ultimate triumph of the righteous despite the current flourishing of the wicked. The pesher makes clear that the righteous are "the chosen ones," those in the "council of the community" who observe the Torah. Sobriquets include the "Man of Lies," the "Interpreter of Knowledge," and "the Priest, the [Righteous] Teacher," as well as "Ephraim," "Manasseh," and "Judah."

In 4Q173, a citation of Psalm 129 is preserved, preceded by some fragments in which the word *pesher* survives and the Righteous Teacher is named.

Pesher on Habakkuk

The best preserved of the Qumran pesharim is 1QpHab, one of the original seven scrolls found in Cave 1. It contains thirteen mostly intact columns that comment upon chaps. 1 and 2 of Habakkuk. The focus of the biblical book is theodicy. God initially assures the concerned prophet that punishment will befall the prospering sinners of Judah, through the instrument of the Chaldeans (i.e., Babylonians); he then assures Habakkuk that the Babylonians themselves will be punished for their harshness. The *Pesher on Habakkuk,* dated to the latter half of the first century B.C.E., adapts this message of retribution to the Jewish leadership of the Second Temple period and to the Romans (termed "Kittim"). The author opposes groups that he terms "Traitors" aligned with "the Man of Lie" and with "the House of Absalom," and particularly "the Wicked Priest" and the "last priests."

Pesharim on Hosea

The surviving fragment of 4QPesher Hosea[a] (4Q166) contains one poorly preserved column and one well-preserved column, with citation of and commentary on Hos. 2:8-14. The author of the pesher uses some stock Qumranic idioms in applying the biblical descriptions of Israel as a faithless wife, liable to punishment, to his own contemporary society. Much of the language pertains to time ("time of their treachery"; "generation of visitation"; "times of wrath"), and particularly noteworthy is the phrase "appointed times of the Gentiles," which is also found in *Jubilees* 6:35 in the context of sectarian calendrical disputes.

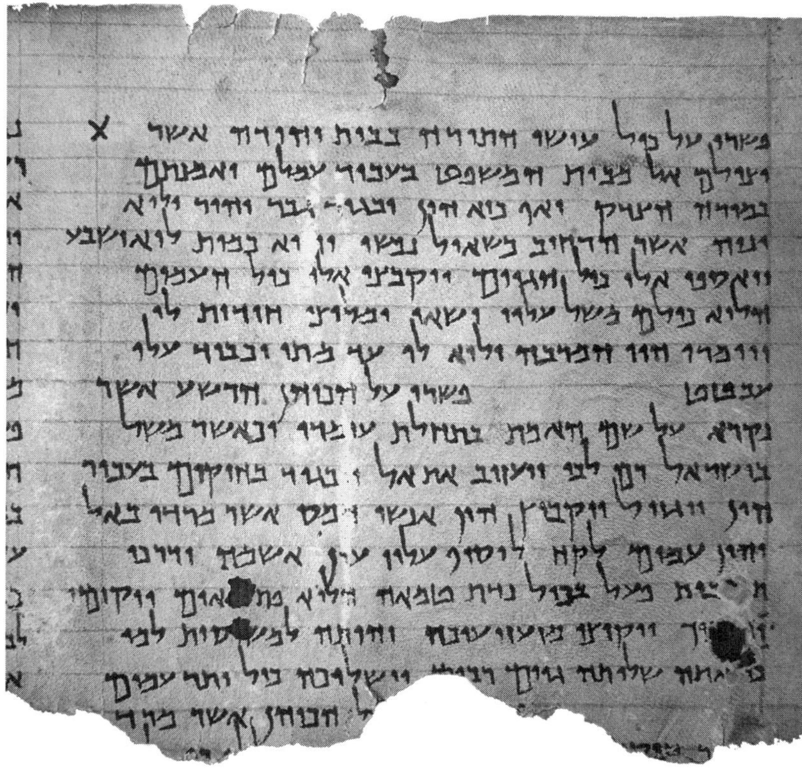

Column 8 of the Pesher on Habakkuk (1QpHab) found in Cave 1 near Qumran *(John C. Trever)*

In 4QPesher Hosea[b] (4Q167), citations and interpretations of Hosea 5, 6, and 8 have been preserved. The biblical texts are concerned with divine retribution, focusing upon Ephraim and Judah, which lends itself to pesher interpretations pertaining to sectarian controversy. In addition to Ephraim, the pesher features references to the Lion of Wrath and the last priest.

Pesher on Nahum

The six surviving columns of the *Pesher Nahum* (4Q169) contain comments upon all three chapters of the short biblical book of Nahum. Nahum predicts the impending downfall of mighty Assyria as punishment for its oppression. The author of this pesher indicates that the true message of Nahum's prophecies is the triumph of his community over its evil opponents, who include the Gentile "Kittim" and internal opponents termed "Ephraim" and "Manasseh." An unusual feature of the *Pesher on Nahum* is that it explicitly names specific historical figures, the Greek kings Demetrius and Antiochus, in addition to relying upon the more typical use of epithets. It is widely accepted that the *Pesher on Nahum* includes references to the reign of the Hasmonean king Alexander Jannaeus (ruled 103-76 B.C.E.), and that of his wife and successor Salome Alexandra (76-67 B.C.E.), and to the civil war between their sons that led to the Roman takeover of Judea under Pompey (63 B.C.E.). The most controversial portion of the pesher is the passage stating that the Lion of Wrath would "hang men alive," as noted above.

Bibliography

J. D. Amusin 1977, "The Reflection of Historical Events of the First Century B.C. in Qumran Commentaries (4Q161; 4Q169; 4Q166)," *HUCA* 48: 123-52. • S. L. Berrin 2004, *The Pesher Nahum Scroll from Qumran: An Exegetical Study of 4Q169*, Leiden: Brill. • S. L. Berrin 2005, "Qumran Pesharim," in *Biblical Interpretation at Qumran*, ed. M. Henze, Grand Rapids: Eerdmans, 110-33. • W. H. Brownlee 1979, *The Midrash Pesher of Habakkuk*, Missoula, Mont.: Scholars Press. • G. J. Brooke 1981, "Qumran Pesher: Toward the Re-definition of a Genre," *RevQ* 10: 483-503. • G. J. Brooke 1987, "The Biblical Texts in the Qumran Commentaries: Scribal Errors or Exegetical Variants?" in *Early Jewish and Christian Exegesis: Studies in Memory of William Hugh Brownlee*, ed. C. A. Evans and W. F. Stinespring, Atlanta: Scholars Press, 85-100. • J. Carmignac 1969-1971, "Le Document de Qumrân sur Melkisédek," *RevQ* 7: 343-78. • J. H. Charlesworth 2002, *The Pesharim and Qumran History: Chaos or Consensus?* Grand Rapids: Eerdmans. • M. Collins 2009, *The Use of Sobriquets in the Qumran Dead Sea Scrolls*, London: Clark. • G. L. Doudna 2001, *4Q Pesher Nahum: A Critical Edition*, London: Sheffield Academic Press. • K. Elliger 1953, *Studien zum Habakuk-Kommentar vom Toten Meer*, Tübingen: Mohr-Siebeck. • M. P. Horgan 1979, *Pesharim: Qumran Interpretations of Biblical Books*, Washington: Catholic Biblical Association of America. • M. P. Horgan 2002, *The Dead Sea Scrolls: Hebrew, Aramaic, and Greek Texts with English Translations*, vol. 6B, *Pesharim, Other Commentaries, and Related Documents*, Tübingen: Mohr-Siebeck. • J. Jokiranta 2005, "Pesharim: A Mirror of Self-Understanding," in *Reading the Present in the Qumran Library: The Perception of the Contemporary by Means of Scriptural Interpretations*, ed. K. de Troyer and A. Lange, Atlanta: Society of Biblical Literature, 23-34. • T. Lim 2002a, "Biblical Quotations in the Pesharim and the Text of the Bible: Methodological Considerations," in *The Bible as Book: The Hebrew Bible and the Judaean Desert Discoveries*, ed. E. D. Herbert and E. Tov, London: British Library. • T. Lim 2002b, *Pesharim*, London: Sheffield. • B. Nitzan 1986, *Pesher Habakkuk (1QpHab), A Scroll from the Wilderness of Judaea: Text, Introduction and Commentary*, Jerusalem: Bialik Institute and Tel-Aviv University (in Hebrew).

Shani Berrin Tzoref

Pesher on the Periods (4Q180)

The fragmentary Qumran document 4Q180 is a thematic commentary that describes history as a sequence of precisely defined periods. Although the extant fragments of this sectarian work deal only with episodes related to antediluvian and postdiluvian events, the original work may have included details about other, later periods, perhaps even of the entire historical sequence.

The first editor of this manuscript labeled it *Ages of Creation* (Allegro 1969), but the text itself offers a more appropriate title, *Pesher on the Periods* (4Q180 frg. 1 line 1). Only eight decipherable fragments and four tiny, barely readable ones have survived. They stem from at least four columns of a scroll written in a late Herodian formal hand (Strugnell 1970).

The largest and best preserved fragment is frg. 1. The column it preserves contains only eleven lines, ten inscribed and one blank in the middle of the column (frg. 1 line 6); it thus has a smaller format than other texts from Qumran. In addition to the blank line 6, other blanks of a word or two remain elsewhere (joined frgs. 2–3 col. ii line 3). These uninscribed spaces mark distinct literary units, a scribal practice well known from other manuscripts of Qumran. Another scribal convention used by the nonsectarian texts from Qumran and appearing in this text is the writing of the Tetragrammaton in Paleo-Hebrew characters (frg. 1 line 1).

Pesher on the Periods clearly belongs to the specific literature of the Qumran community; it employs locutions typical of these writings and cites biblical passages in a manner typical of the pesharim (3–4 i 3-5, quoting Gen. 17:3-4; 3–4 ii, quoting Gen. 13:8; 18:20-21; and 5–6 line 6, quoting Gen. 12:17). Nevertheless, the work is unique among Qumran pesharim in commenting on a conceptual theme — the periods of sacred history — rather than on biblical prophecies.

The first five lines of frg. 1 offer introductory matter. The following lines reproduce the sequence of biblical chronology starting with the flood (frg. 1 lines 7-10; cf. Gen. 6:1-4) and continuing with the later events of Abraham's career (2–4 i-ii; cf. Gen. 17:3; 18:20-21; 19:1). The first paragraph opens with the title, followed by a general description of the periods of history as divinely preordained and engraved on the heavenly tablets. Similar formulations are found in frg. 4 line 2; 1QH[a] 9(1):7, 19; and CD 2:7. This description of history as a sequence of precisely defined periods is known from other community writings (1QS 3:15, 23; 4:13; 1QH[a] 9[1]:24; 1QpHab 8:13) and from early Jewish apocalypses (e.g., Dan. 9:24-27; the *Animal Apocalypse* [*1 Enoch* 85–90]; the *Apocalypse of Weeks* [*1 Enoch* 91:11-17; 93:1-10]; and the so-called *Pesher of the Apocalypse of Weeks* [4Q247]).

The general description of the periods concludes with a reference to a sequence or order (frg. 1 line 4, where the term *serekh* is employed), after which the text breaks. The following line speaks of "twenty," probably the twenty generations from Adam to Abraham that represent the first two periods. The events alluded to in the surviving fragments concern episodes that fall within these two periods: the sin of the angels (frg. 1 lines 7-8; see Gen. 6:1-4); the change of Abraham's name (2–3 i 3-10; see Gen. 17:3-5); the visit of the three angels to Abraham's abode (2–3 ii 34; see Gen. 18:2); and the destruction of Sodom and Gomorrah (2–3 ii 5-7; see Gen. 18:20-21).

Because of the close similarity between 4Q180 frg. 1 lines 5-9 and 4Q181 frg. 2 lines 1-4, both of which refer to the birth of giants, J. T. Milik (1976) considered 4Q180 and 4Q181 to be two copies of the same work. He therefore produced a composite text to create one document, a combination adopted by other scholars (Puech 1987; Roberts 1995; Wise, Abegg, and Cook 2005). In Milik's opinion 11QMelchizedek (11Q13) constitutes a third copy of the same work.

A connection between 4Q180, 4Q181, and 11Q13, however, should be discarded on material and contextual grounds (Puech 1987). Considerations of a similar nature refute the proposed identity of 4Q180 and 4Q181 (see Dimant 1979: 89-91; Huggins 1992). The documents represented in 4Q180 and 4Q181 have distinct subject matters as well as distinct literary structures and forms. 4Q180 is constructed as a thematic pesher, whereas 4Q181 is written in a style reminiscent of the *Hodayot*. The material combination of the two manuscripts attempted by Milik is also problematic. The close parallel line concerning the giants is well integrated into the context of 4Q180, whereas it stands out in 4Q181 frg. 2 lines 1-4. The latter appears to cite the former, rather than the reverse. Perhaps both cite a third source, or a biblical episode well known in the circles of Qumran. At any rate, 4Q180 and 4Q181 should be treated as two distinct works.

BIBLIOGRAPHY

J. M. ALLEGRO 1969, *Qumrân Cave 4. I (4Q158-4Q186)*, DJD 5, Oxford: Clarendon, 77-79 (pl. XXVII). • D. DIMANT 1979, "The 'Pesher on the Periods' (4Q180) and 4Q181," *Israel Oriental Studies* 9: 77-102. • R. V. HUGGINS 1992, "A Canonical 'Book of Periods' at Qumran?" *RevQ* 15: 421-36. • J. T. MILIK 1972, "*Milkî-sedeq* et *Milkî-reša'* dans les anciens écrits juifs et chrétiens," *JJS* 23: 95-144. • J. T. MILIK 1976, *The Books of Enoch*, Oxford: Clarendon, 248-52. • É. PUECH 1987, "Notes sur le manuscrit de XIQMelkîsédeq," *RevQ* 12: 483-513. • É. PUECH 1993, *La Croyance des esséniens en la vie future*, 2 vols., Paris: Gabalda, 2: 526-29. • J. J. M. ROBERTS 1995, "Wicked and Holy (4Q180-4Q181)," in *The Dead Sea Scrolls: Hebrew, Aramaic, and Greek texts with English Translations*, vol. 2, *Damascus Document, War Scroll, and Related Documents*, ed. J. H. Charlesworth, Tübingen: Mohr-Siebeck; Louisville: Westminster John Knox, 204-13. • J. STRUGNELL 1970, "Notes en marge du volume V des 'Discoveries in the Judaean Desert of Jordan,'" *RevQ* 7: 252-54. • M. O. WISE, M. G. ABEGG, AND E. M. COOK 2005, *The Dead Sea Scrolls: A New Translation*, 2d ed., San Francisco: Harper, 209-10.

See also: Wicked and Holy (4Q181)

DEVORAH DIMANT

Peshiṭta

The Peshiṭta is a translation of the Bible into Syriac, a form of late Eastern Aramaic. It is the second oldest of the ancient versions of Scripture and one of the earliest works of Syriac literature. Although the earliest attestations of the word "Peshiṭta" to designate the main Syriac version of the Bible occur in the writings of the West Syrian author Moshe bar Kepha (ca. 813-903), where he uses it to distinguish this version from the Syro-Hexapla (the other main Syriac translation, of seventh-century origin), there is general agreement that the origins of the Peshiṭta reach back to the second, if not the first, century of the Common Era. Whether these earliest initiatives were the work of Jewish or Christian translators, or a combination of the two, continues to provoke scholarly debate. Indeed, central to Peshiṭta origins is the nature of the links it has to both Jewish and Christian traditions. Beyond dispute, however, are two distinguishing Peshiṭta features: it is the earliest translation of the whole scriptural corpus into another Semitic language, and it was handed down exclusively by the Eastern churches. Representing a compilation and careful reworking of earlier materials, the Peshiṭta Bible was firmly established by the fifth century, an achievement linked with the name of Bishop Rabbula.

The Term *Peshiṭta*

There are varying views on the precise meaning of the term Peshiṭta. In form, it is a passive participle of the root *p-š-t,* and feminine in gender (in agreement with the Syriac for "version"). In Syriac, as in Jewish Aramaic, the participle from this root developed from meaning "stretched out" to "straightforward," and then to what is "simple" or "obvious." In similar fashion, its counterpart in mishnaic Hebrew came to mean "straightforward." Thus the name "Peshiṭta" can be taken to mean "the simple (version)." An alternative view is that the participle came to mean "widespread," also derived from "stretched out," but since no parallel can be found for such usage in Syriac, the meaning "simple" is probably the closer to the truth.

Origin and Date

The place of origin for the Peshiṭta, though uncertain, is usually identified as Edessa, where the Syriac dialect is already attested at the turn of the era. Capital of the small principality of Osrhoene, east of the Euphrates, and situated on one of the great trade routes to the East, Edessa was destined to become a major center of learning, producing a number of eminent Syriac writers in the centuries to follow. It is also possible that Peshiṭta origins might lie further east in Adiabene, as a consequence of its king, Izates, having converted to Judaism during the reign of Emperor Claudius (41-54 C.E.). If this latter view could be verified, it might lend support for a possible first-century date.

Whereas the Septuagint has a clear Jewish origin, the Peshiṭta's roots are more complex. Jewish influence is clearly present and is variously accounted for. Joosten (1996: 390), along with many other scholars, notes that the Peshiṭta's translation from a Hebrew *Vorlage* constitutes a strong argument for an origin in the Jewish Diaspora. Yet others see the situation as more complicated, the evidence of date and transmission history possibly allowing for a Christian origin in the case of some of the later books (Dirksen 1993). At the latest, the translation most likely predates the fourth century, since both Aphrahat and Ephrem cite a form of the text almost identical to it. Because it uses a particle that Ephrem no longer understood, namely, the particle *yt* (as in Gen. 1:1), it can hardly be later than 200 C.E. While preachers from Palestine (whether Jewish or Christian) may have initiated translation processes as early as the end of the first century or the beginning of the second century in the district of Adiabene in general and in Edessa in particular, internal evidence might suggest that the work spanned one or two generations at the end of the second century C.E. It is also possible that the first Christian converts in the region may have come from Jewish communities, and may have had much closer ties with their Jewish neighbors in these early formative years than was later to be the case. Weitzman (1999: 258-62) argues that internal evidence would suggest that, while the translators valued prayer and faith, they were less than enthusiastic for sacrifice or the other ritual demands of Judaism, and that in some books they appear more identified with the Jews as a people, while in others they appear more inward looking. His conclusion, that they belonged to a nonrabbinic Jewish community which eventually accepted Christianity, although attractive, remains nonetheless hypothetical.

While many scholars urge caution in looking to the early Syriac versions of the New Testament in order to throw some light on the date and milieu of Peshiṭta origins, Joosten (1996: 390-91) maintains that the use of the Peshiṭta in *Diatessaron* Old Testament quotations implies not only the Peshiṭta's prior existence but also its enjoyment of a certain prestige in the infant Syriac-speaking church before Tatian composed his *Diatessaron* ca. 170 C.E. This in turn could provide a chronological foothold, since it is reasonably certain that Tatian's *Diatessaron* was the first attempt to render the Gospels in Syriac. Because it would be inconceivable that the Syriac church would have translated the majority of the Old Testament books before undertaking a translation of the Gospels, Joosten concludes that the Peshiṭta must be Jewish and pre-Christian in origin. However, not all scholars are as confident that Old Testament *Diatessaron* quotations can be thus identified.

In sum, Peshiṭta origins continue to be debated (Jenner 2005: 243-44), with the balance of evidence favoring a Jewish origin. Whereas Christian links and a Christian transmission context are relatively clear, the silence of Jewish sources regarding Peshiṭta origins until the Middle Ages demands explanation. The most probable one would seem to be that, as the Peshiṭta quickly became the Bible of the Syriac-speaking churches, it became less valued and indeed less needed by Syriac-speaking Jews.

Textual Features and Affiliations

Relation to the Masoretic Text (MT)

There is scholarly consensus, however, that the Peshiṭta is an ancient and independent translation of a proto-Masoretic *Vorlage.* Analysis of its textual transmission history reveals three levels within the Peshiṭta manuscript tradition, indicating a decline in closeness to the MT (Koster 1977). There seems to have been a watershed around the ninth century, after which almost all Peshiṭta manuscripts reflect what is variously called the Standard Text (Gelston 1987), or Textus Receptus (Koster 1977). To describe the Peshiṭta as a daughter version of the MT is overly simplistic. Yet, even if, as Jenner (2005) maintains, its birth was a complex affair, and its natural father *(Vorlage)* and mother (translators) as well as its birthplace were unknown, nevertheless the relationship between the Peshiṭta and the MT is close enough to warrant a "second-degree familial relationship." Apart from Sirach, the deuterocanonical books were translated from the Septuagint.

Translation Techniques

As in the case of the Septuagint, the Peshiṭta was probably not translated as a whole, but rather book by book. Analysis of translation techniques indicates that there was more than one translator, and, allowing for some individual features characterizing some books, the overall degree of consistency in the version as a whole suggests a common approach to the task of translation, some scholars proposing perhaps even a single school (Greenberg 2002; Weitzman 1999: 203-5). Excluding Chronicles, the Peshiṭta's rendering of the various books of the Hebrew Bible is almost verbatim for the most part, and reasonably accurate otherwise, with just a minority of unique readings. The translators generally aimed at providing an idiomatic but faithful translation, combining fidelity with intelligibility (Weitzman 1999: 61).

Relation to the Septuagint (LXX)

There is also consensus that influence from the LXX is secondary, and can be seen in some books more than others, usually in order to resolve difficulties presented by the Hebrew text. Such consultation of the LXX appears particularly in those books most used in the liturgy (Isaiah, Psalms). The secondary nature of LXX influence is, in Jenner's view, "astonishing" since he maintains that, in the initial period of Syriac Christianity, official church exegesis was explicitly based on the Greek version (2005: 244).

Parallels with the Targums

There have been numerous attempts to account for the many parallels that exist between the Peshiṭta and the targums, especially in the Torah, an issue by no means entirely resolved. At one end of the scale lies the hypothesis that the Peshiṭta derives from a lost Palestinian targum rather than from a Hebrew text. This is a theory that can be quickly put to rest when viewed in the wider context of the Peshiṭta's quantitative literalism, when contrasted with the more expansive and periphrastic renderings of the extant Palestinian targums. As a refinement of this theory, some scholars propose that the Peshiṭta was translated for the most part from a Hebrew original, but that the translators also consulted a written copy of the targum, more specifically *Targum Onqelos,* since the Peshiṭta exhibits most parallels with this targum. However, standing against such theories of literary dependence of the Peshiṭta on the targums, is the fact that many of the alleged parallels can be explained either through polygenesis or coincidence, particularly since both sets of texts represent in fact two dialects of the same language. Indeed, a volume of essays entitled *Targum and Peshiṭta* (ed. Flesher 1998) is remarkable for the fact that all the contributors independently came to the conclusion that the Peshiṭta did not originate as a targum.

Recent scholarship acknowledges that the only book where the parallels between the Peshiṭta and the targums are indeed so close as to imply literary dependence is Proverbs. But, here it is the targum which has drawn upon the Peshiṭta, and not the reverse. Indeed, as Weitzman (1999: 91) maintains, "there is no reason to posit the Peshiṭta's dependence upon any written targum, extant or otherwise." Accordingly, for the rest of the Scriptures, he considers it more likely that, where Peshiṭta and targum attest some form of agreement in both sense and wording, the ultimate source of this agreement most probably lies in some preexisting exegetical tradition, and possibly even in a translational tradition, or in a combination of both.

For those renderings shared by both Peshiṭta and targum which yield clear sense, and are also consistent with the Masoretic vocalization, Weitzman's hypothesis (1999: 101-3) of a common exegetical and translational tradition in oral circulation, the former in the house of study and the latter in the synagogue, is attractive. It would explain how, if translators felt free to draw upon it as suited their needs, various allegiances would have come into play, now agreeing with one or other targum, now disagreeing. It would also explain the Peshiṭta's acquaintance with some interpretations that are to be found in the rabbinic sources, and not in any known targum.

Textual History

Compared with the textual history of the Septuagint, that of the Peshiṭta is relatively stable. Textual witnesses, though not abundant, may be divided into three categories: (i) the biblical manuscripts, lectionaries, and Masoretic Syriac manuscripts; (ii) the commentaries and liturgical hymns; (iii) theological treatises, sermons, and other such writings. The earliest extant biblical manuscripts (5b1 and 5ph1) date to the fifth century and are incomplete (the former contains the Torah, the latter Ezekiel). The oldest complete Peshiṭta manuscript is 7a1 (Codex Ambrosianus), which is somewhat later, possibly seventh century (Joosten 1996: 390-91), though Jenner places it earlier (2005: 247). It was first edited by A. Ceriani in 1876-1883. A corrected form of this manuscript has been adopted as the basis for the

Leiden Peshiṭta Institute editions. Many volumes in this series have already been published, each accompanied by a detailed apparatus containing other early manuscript readings.

That the Leiden Peshiṭta edition has been very successful can be demonstrated by the amount of research it has stimulated in recent years. This research has given rise to several monographs on individual books. These focus in particular on the textual history of the Peshiṭta, and on the way in which it was received and preserved in the patristic literature of the Syrian churches. As a result, the translation techniques of the Peshiṭta's individual books can be identified more clearly within the context of their reception history, and isolated readings, unique to the Peshiṭta, can be interpreted with greater confidence.

Bibliography

P. B. Dirksen 1993, *La Peshiṭta dell'Antico Testamento,* Brescia: Paideia. • P. V. M. Flesher, ed. 1998, *Targum and Peshiṭta,* Atlanta: Scholars Press. • A. Gelston 1987, *The Peshiṭta of the Twelve Prophets,* Oxford: Clarendon. • G. Greenberg 2002, *Translation Technique in the Peshiṭta to Jeremiah,* Leiden: Brill. • K. D. Jenner 2005, "La Peshiṭta: fille du texte massorétique?," in *L'enfance de la Bible hébraïque: Histoire du text de l'Ancien Testament,* ed. A. Schenker and P. Hugo, Geneva: Labor et fides, 238-63. • J. Joosten 1996, "La Peshiṭta de l'Ancien Testament dans la recherche récente," *RHPR* 76: 385-95. • M. D. Koster 1977, *The Peshiṭta of Exodus,* Assen: Van Gorcum. • M. P. Weitzman 1999, *The Syriac Version of the Old Testament: An Introduction,* Cambridge: Cambridge University Press.

Carmel McCarthy

Peter, Epistles of

The New Testament contains two letters attributed to the apostle Simon Peter. According to the Gospels, Simon was a Galilean fisherman who was in the inner circle of Jesus, from whom he received the Aramaic nickname Kephas/Cephas, meaning "Rock" (Gr. *Petros,* "Peter"; cf. Mark 1:16-18 and pars.; cf. John 1:35-42). As Paul tells it, Peter came to be known after Jesus' death as the "apostle to the circumcised" in particular (Gal. 2:7-9). Yet it is very doubtful whether either of the New Testament letters bearing Peter's name was actually composed by the apostle. It is much more likely that they were written in his name by different authors in the late first or early second century. The suggestion that they were produced within an enduring "Petrine School" preserving authentic teachings of the apostle is entirely conjectural.

1 Peter

The text now known as 1 Peter presents itself as a circular letter sent from Rome (called "Babylon" in 5:13) to Christian communities in five regions of Asia Minor (1:1-2). The letter assumes an audience of Gentiles (e.g., 4:3-4; cf. 1:18; 2:10) — or, as the text itself would have it, former Gentiles who are now part of a new "race" of Christians (cf. 2:12; 4:3 with 2:9-10; 4:16).

Underlying the letter as a whole is a perception of hardships suffered by the intended audience as an identifiable and apparently aloof cultic minority (1:6; 2:12; 3:14-15; 4:3-4, 12-19; cf. 5:9-10). Whether the text assumes persecution of Christians on the part of local governments is unclear; but much of what is said is in any case well understood in light of the more informal social tensions that could be expected to arise within Greco-Roman society when some segment of the population became unwilling to participate in dominant social and cultural practices as a result of their adoption of a foreign deity (Achtemeier 1996: 28-36).

The driving concern of the letter is to provide consolation, encouragement, and moral exhortation to a minority group experiencing this kind of social pressure. Much of "Peter's" advice turns on the idea that they are only sharing in the long-anticipated, eschatological suffering that he also saw Christ experience (4:12-5:1; cf. 1:11; 2:19-23; 3:17-18; 4:1), and that it will ultimately work to their advantage at Christ's final revelation *(apokalypsis)* (1:5-9, 13, 20-21; cf. 2:19-20; 3:14; 5:8-10). In the meantime, the group is exhorted to "accept the authority of every human institution," whether the imperial and local governments (2:13-17), slavery (2:18-25), or the patriarchal family (3:1-7), in the hopes that they may allay some hostility if they "conduct [themselves] honorably among the Gentiles" (2:12; cf. 3:13). At the same time, they are told to set aside the illicit desires taken to be generally definitive of Gentile existence, even if doing so generates tensions on the part of those Gentiles among whom they are living (1:14, 18; 4:1-4). They are in any case not to repay evil for evil when treated unjustly (3:9, 15-18), and should strive to maintain the solidarity of the group above all (3:8; 4:8-10; cf. 5:1-5). The general thrust of the letter, then, is summed up in a concluding exhortation: "Therefore let those suffering in accordance with God's will entrust themselves to a faithful Creator, while continuing to do good" (4:19).

It is striking that this text, while clearly written to non-Jews, nonetheless considers its audience to be something other than Gentiles. By virtue of the "new birth" they are understood to have experienced through baptism (1:3; 3:21) and, perhaps more specifically, through their reception of a divine Spirit (1:2; 2:5; 3:18; 4:6, 14), they now represent a distinct "race" *(genos),* "nation" *(ethnos),* and "people" *(laos)* (2:9). While the text can use the novel term "Christian" to carve out this new identity — as in 4:16, the only occurrence of the term in the New Testament apart from Acts 11:26; 26:28 — in the main it arrogates the traditional discourse of Jewish identity to itself. God's declaration in Exod. 19:6 that Israel represents "a priestly kingdom and a holy nation," along with Isaiah's description of Israel as an "elect race" (LXX Isa. 43:20), is appropriated for this Gentile group (1 Pet. 2:9). A scriptural rationale for this appropriation is apparently found in the text of Hos. 2:23 (LXX 2:25: "I will say to Not-my-people, 'You are my people'"), now read, in a manner reminiscent of Rom. 9:25-26, with reference to Gentiles who have come to align themselves with Israel's God through Christ

(1 Pet. 2:10). In any event, these non-Jews are now themselves styled as "exiles" (1:1, 17; 2:11), living "among the Gentiles" (2:12) in "the Diaspora" (1:1). The "inheritance" from which they are exiled, however, has been relocated to the heavenly realm (1:3-4).

As all this makes clear, Israel's Scriptures have been appropriated and read in light of an apocalyptic worldview, including the assumption that the suffering, resurrection, and future "revelation" of Christ represent the foreordained culmination of Israel's ancient prophecies (1:10-12, 20). The text is quite explicit that "it was revealed to [the prophets] that they were serving not themselves but you [Christians]" (1:12), who are living near "the end of all things" (4:7), the final judgment (4:5, 17). The very Spirit that allowed them to prophesy is understood to have been the Spirit of Christ (1:11).

1 Peter gives no indication that it was written in a situation in which the Jewish communities of Asia Minor figured in any significant way. At no point does the question of the relation of this Gentile community to neighboring Jews surface as even a theoretical issue, let alone a pressing, social one. The letter's wholesale appropriation of the basic terms of Jewish identity occurs seemingly without apology. This state of affairs is remarkable in light of the ascription of the work to the one whom Paul called the "apostle to the circumcised" (Gal 2:8).

2 Peter

The letter known as 2 Peter actually frames itself in just this way: as "the second letter" Peter wrote to its audience (3:1). Whether what we now know as 1 Peter is in the background as the "first" letter, however, is an open question. 2 Peter identifies a more general audience of "those who have received a faith as precious as ours through the righteousness of our God and Savior Jesus Christ" (1:1). Written in the fictive setting of Peter's last days (1:12-15), the work presents what can fairly be considered a "testament of Peter" analogous to the pseudonymous Jewish testaments of the Hellenistic period, only packaged — characteristically for the Christian literature — in epistolary form.

The broad aim of this (and, ostensibly, the earlier) letter is to serve as a "reminder" of what the author assumes the audience should already know (1:12-15; 3:1). This has to do primarily with a Hellenistic dichotomy, with a Christian twist, between "the corruption that is in the world because of desire" and the "divine nature" *(theias physeōs)* in which they can participate thanks to the power made available by the knowledge of Christ (1:3-4). "Peter" urges his audience to "confirm your call and election" by matching an ethic of self-control, endurance, and love to their faith in order to ensure "entry into the eternal kingdom of our Lord and Savior Jesus Christ" (1:5-11).

More immediately, however, "Peter" is concerned to warn his audience regarding "false teachers" who, he "predicts," will arise among them and lead many astray (2:1-3; 3:3-4). It is difficult to move from the author's invective to a clear profile of the teachers that lie behind it. The problem is complicated by the fact that much of what is said in this connection has been taken over from the Letter of Jude. The opponents are clearly members of the author's group: they have "knowledge of our Lord and Savior Jesus Christ" (2:20) and participate in the group's communal meals (2:13). At the same time, the charge that they "deny the Master who bought them" (2:1) indicates that they are working with an understanding of Christ that the author considers problematic. The complaints that they "speak bombastic nonsense" (2:18) and "slander the glorious ones" (2:10, apparently referring to angels; cf. 2:11) suggest that this view of Christ functions within a larger mythic framework that is at odds with the one espoused by the author. Specifically, it seems to have lacked the apocalyptic elements on which 2 Peter insists (3:3-13). Particularly distressing to the writer in any case is his perception that the false teachers' ethic, under the banner of a promise of "freedom," amounts to a return to the desires and "defilements of the world" about which he is so concerned (2:18-22; cf. 2:2, 12-14; 3:3).

Basic to the strategy of 2 Peter is the drawing of a contrast between the "cleverly devised myths" presented by the ostensibly future rivals and the eyewitness account of Peter himself, of which the letter is intended as reminder (1:16-19; 3:1-2). The text presents its own apocalyptic teaching as conforming not only to "the commandment of the Lord and Savior spoken through your apostles," but also to "the words spoken in the past by the holy prophets" (3:2; cf. 1:19-21). In fact, while 2 Peter is remarkable among New Testament works in that it explicitly counts early Christian writings — specifically, a collection of Paul's letters — as "Scripture" (3:15-16), it is primarily the Jewish Scriptures that are used to contextualize, and thus make sense of, his group's situation. The rivals are said to conform to stock types attested already in the Jewish Scriptures: false prophets (2:1); Balaam (2:15-16; cf. Num. 22:21-35); the proverbial dog who "turns back to its own vomit" (2:22; cf. Prov. 26:11). What is more, moments from Israel's mythic past — when God cast wicked angels, in chains, into hell to await the final judgment (2:4; cf. *1 Enoch* 10); when he destroyed the earth, while saving Noah and his family, with water (2:5; cf. Genesis 6–9); when he destroyed Sodom and Gomorrah with fire, saving only Lot (2:6; 3:6; cf. Gen. 18:16–19:29) — are said to provide examples of God's unsparing wrath on those who pursue corrupting desires, and his protection, on the other hand, of "the pious" (2:6, 9-10). As in 1 Peter, the authorial voice of 2 Peter shows no explicit concern regarding its relationship to the Jewish community to whose mythic past it lays claim.

Bibliography

P. J. Achtemeier 1996, *1 Peter,* Minneapolis: Fortress. • M. Eugene Boring 1999, *1 Peter,* Nashville: Abingdon. • R. J. Bauckham 1983, *Jude, 2 Peter,* Waco: Word. • J. H. Elliott 2000, *1 Peter,* New York: Doubleday. • J. Neyrey 1993, *2 Peter, Jude,* New York: Doubleday. • R. L. Webb 2004, "The Petrine Epistles: Recent Developments and Trends," in *The Face of New Testament Studies,* ed. S. McKnight and G. R. Osborne, Grand Rapids: Baker.

Matt Jackson-McCabe

Pharisees

No Jewish group of the Second Temple period is mentioned more often in the New Testament (ninety-nine times vs. fourteen for the Sadducees) and Josephus (forty-four times; Sadducees, thirteen) than the Pharisees. Yet there is no generally accepted position regarding them. Although nearly all would agree that they played a major role in shaping the identity of rabbinic, medieval, and modern Judaism, their precise role in Jewish society and religious life before 70 C.E. and between the destruction of the Temple and the Bar Kokhba Revolt is disputed in nearly every aspect. This is mainly because there is no agreement about which sources should be used, and because for the agreed sources (Josephus and the New Testament) there is no consensus about how they should be used.

Debated Issues

The most important question is how trustworthy Josephus is in his accounts of the Pharisees as the leading party within the three mentioned by him in some detail (*J.W.* 2.119-66; *Ant.* 13.171-73; 18.12-22; *Life* 10–11). What can be made of his claim that he himself belonged to the Pharisees (*Life* 12)? What in his description of the Pharisees reflects his own opinion, and what has to be attributed to his sources? Does his account picture the Pharisees as they were before 70 C.E., or as he saw them retrospectively while writing in Rome near the end of the first century? Do the Gospels contain reliable historical information about the Pharisees before 70, or are they mainly polemical in their portrayal?

Another question concerns the use of texts in which the Pharisees are not named as such. Especially important is whether there are references to the Pharisees in the Dead Sea Scrolls under the nickname of "the seekers after smooth things." Also debated is whether the *Psalms of Solomon* (first century B.C.E.) can be taken as Pharisaic.

Other disagreements center on the religious character of the Pharisees and their place and function in Jewish society. Were they primarily a religious or a political interest group? Were they a lay scribal movement in competition with the priesthood, middle-class urban artisans, or members of the "retainer" class? Connected to the question of their aims and status is their relation to the synagogue, the priests and the Temple, and the scribes with whom they are so often mentioned in the New Testament.

Despite these open questions, a careful analysis of the sources reveals more consistency than one would expect from this quantity of varied source material. Especially noteworthy is that there is no contradictory information (Deines 2001).

The Pharisees in the Sources

The earliest use of Gr. *pharisaios* (derived from the Semitic root *p-r-š*, whose meaning can be "to separate, discriminate or specify" or, in later texts, also "to explain"), is in Phil. 3:5 (written between 50 and 60 C.E.), where Paul claimed that he was "according to the Law a Pharisee" (cf. Acts 23:6; 26:5; in 22:3 Luke has Paul describe himself as a disciple of Gamaliel, "educated according to the strict manner of the Law of our fathers"; cf. Gal. 1:14). The Lukan references in Acts reveal that the designation "Pharisee" could be exchanged with circumlocutions not using this specific label (as in 22:3).

Throughout the sources there are certain characteristics associated with Pharisaism, namely their exactness and precision (Gr. *akribeia*) regarding the Torah (*J.W.* 1.110; 2.162; *Ant.* 17.41; *Vita* 191; Acts 22:3; 26:5); their striving for righteousness and piety (*J.W.* 2.163; *Ant.* 13.289-91; 14.176; Matt. 5:20; Luke 16:15; 18:14; 20:20; cf. CD 1:18-9; *Pss. Sol.* 1:2-3; 2:15); their adherence to "certain regulations handed down by former generations and not recorded in the Laws of Moses" (*Ant.* 13.297, 408; cf. *b. Qiddušin* 66a; Gal. 1:14; Mark 7:1-5; Matt. 23:2-3; cf. *m. ʾAbot.* 1:1); and their influence on and support of the people (*J.W.* 1.107-12). These characteristics can be used to form a profile of Pharisaism even if the persons concerned are not *expressis verbis* designated as Pharisees.

It is not known whether the Pharisees called themselves by the Greek name *pharisaioi* or its rabbinic equivalent *pĕrušîm/n*, or whether it was applied to them by others. The only uses of "Pharisee" as a self-designation come from Paul and Josephus; both made this claim in a context where they needed to demonstrate their adherence to the most respected form of Judaism since their Jewishness had been put in question through the changes in their biographies. But obviously both expected their readers to understand the high and positive Jewish profile connected to this term (cf. Acts 26:5). This might hint at the acceptance and positive interpretation of the name at least around the middle of the first century C.E.

Most scholars accept as the meaning of the name "separatists" (alternatively "specifiers," i.e., precise interpreters of the sacred texts), although they disagree over whether this epithet was used initially in a positive sense (by themselves) or a negative one (by others, then perhaps later adopted positively by themselves). The use of the root *p-r-š* in 4QMMT C 7 for separation "from the majority of the people" might hint at a conflict between once closely related groups over who the "real" separators were, thus indicating a positive understanding of separation. "Separation" would then mean distancing oneself from all those kinds of impurities and transgressions of the Torah against which the Hasmoneans and their supporters fought.

History

Origins

The origin of the Pharisees is unknown, but there are good reasons to suppose that their roots go back to pious circles in the postexilic era whose religious program had a strong Deuteronomistic influence combined with apocalyptic elements. It is no longer popular in scholarship to posit the origin of the Pharisees and the Essenes within the social milieu that also brought forward the Hasideans (1 Macc. 2:42; 7:12; 2 Macc. 14:6) and similar groupings (like the strict observers of the

Sabbath in 1 Macc. 2:29-38) who supported the Hasmoneans to a certain point. But this view is still able to integrate most of the available information. The development of different Jewish parties in the wake of the Hasmonean success can thus be seen as a result of their different levels of active participation in the makeup of the emerging new Jewish state, based on varying interpretations of the Torah and their application to the social, religious, and political agendas.

Josephus mentions the Pharisees for the first time together with the other two of the three Jewish *haireseis* ("party, philosophical school, sect"; *Ant.* 13.171-73; cf. Acts 15:5; 26:5) in the context of the rule of the Hasmonean Jonathan (161-143 B.C.E.). This accords with the proposed date of 4QMMT as a document from the formative period of the three major Jewish parties. In *Ant.* 13.171-73 Josephus does not describe how these three groups came into being (it is otherwise with the so-called Fourth Philosophy; cf. *J.W.* 2.117-18; *Ant.* 18.1-10) but confines himself to a short description of their different views regarding fate. This strangely dislocated description should be taken as a literary device indicating to the reader that the following history is not understandable without keeping these three parties in mind.

Under Hasmonean Rule

Under Hasmonean rule the Pharisees were able to maintain some public influence through their popular support by the people, although their relation with the Hasmonean rulers changed quite often over time. According to Josephus, these rulers vacillated in their attitude toward the Pharisees between active support (John Hyrcanus at the beginning of his rule: *Ant.* 13.288-98; cf. *b. Berakot* 29a; Alexandra Salome: *J.W.* 1.108-14; *Ant.* 13.405-10; possibly Hyrcanus II) and rejection and even military conflict resembling civil war (Alexander Jannaeus: *Ant.* 13.372-83, 398-405; cf. *J.W.* 1.88-98). Herod and his successors adopted similarly changeable attitudes (*J.W.* 1.571-72; *Ant.* 14.172-76; 15.1-4, 368-71; 17.41-49).

Under Roman Rule in the First Century

The Gospels and Josephus contain further references to Pharisaic connections to the ruling and administrative bodies of Judea in the first century C.E. (Mark 3:6; 12:13; Matt. 21:45; 27:62; John 7:32, 45; 11:47, 57; 18:3; Acts 5:37; 23:6-8; *J.W.* 2.411; cf. 4.158-61; *Life* 17–23, 189–98). The emergence after Herod's death (4 B.C.E.) of the Fourth Philosophy, which Josephus describes as a nationalist and anti-Roman variant of the Pharisees (*Ant.* 18.4, 9, 23; cf. *J.W.* 2.117-18; 1.648-55 par. *Ant.* 17.149-67), can be taken as indicative of the Pharisees' having a rather shallow political agenda. They used political influence to implement their religious program, but they did not depend on political support for it. So their participation in daily politics (which quite often was a form of invited participation (*Ant.* 13.289-90, 402-8; cf. *J.W.* 1.111; *Ant.* 14.176; 15.3, 370; even in *J.W.* 1.571 par. *Ant.* 17.41-49 the initiative is not from the Pharisees' side) was a means to attain their religious goals but not a goal in itself. They obviously had fewer conflicts with the Herodian rulers and the Romans than with the Hasmoneans. The reason for this seems to be a conflicting religious agenda with the Hasmonean priest-kings, whereas a rule without religious ambitions allowed them greater influence.

According to the traditional (and in the main correct) view, the Pharisees were, in the decades after the First Jewish War, absorbed into the emerging rabbinic movement, which they shaped decisively. The Pharisaic heritage is therefore incorporated into rabbinic literature, although the latter cannot be taken as a whole and without careful analysis as a source for Pharisaism.

A Torah-based Movement for Sanctification

Josephus' designation of the Jewish parties (for mainly non-Jewish readers) as *haireseis* and as *philosophiai* reflects his understanding of the Jewish parties as philosophical schools of thought with corresponding ways of life and the idea of a choice (cf. *Life* 10–12). Understood this way, they should be seen primarily neither as political interest groups nor as closed "sects." For the Pharisees the latter was argued in scholarship quite often with reference to the few *havurot*-texts in rabbinic literature (cf. Schürer 1973-1987: 2.386-88, 398-400) and/or the Essenes as described in *J.W.* 2.122, 137-44, 150. Especially with the discovery of the Dead Sea Scrolls and their inner-sectarian rules, the Pharisees were seen as a comparable religious grouping. The mention of 6,000 Pharisees in *Ant.* 17.42 (as compared with the 4,000 Essenes; *Ant.* 18.20) was taken as additional support for this. But the close relation between the Pharisees and the people as described in the sources, and their total ignorance of any insider rules or membership regulations, makes it unlikely that Pharisaism as a movement should be seen first and foremost as a closed sect (this does not, however, exclude the possibility of some more sectarian-like factions within the wider movement).

Pharisaism can more adequately be understood as a movement promulgating and developing a specific understanding of the Torah in which the nonwritten traditions ("the traditions of the elders" [Mark 7:3-5] or "the fathers" [*Ant.* 13.297, 408]), which were regarded as similarly authoritative and based on God's revelation to Moses (Matt. 23:2; *Ant.* 13.297), served as essential elements.

The aim of Pharisaism can be described as sanctification: the whole nation (not just the priests) stands under the command to be holy (cf. Exod. 19:6). The way to holiness is a life according to the Torah. Therefore *all* Israel should know the Law and be encouraged to keep it. This can be seen as a result of the Hellenistic crisis in the second century B.C.E., when many priests failed to maintain their Jewish identity and led many to give up their Jewish way of life as well. For Pharisaism, the priests alone could no longer be responsible for the holiness of Israel; rather, every household stands under this obligation through which it may contribute to Israel's standing before God.

The elements of specific Pharisaic halakah point in this direction. Their aim was to shape the Torah tradition so that it could be practiced by as many people as possible during their daily routine. The rabbinic concept of *tevul yom* (cf. the Mishnah tractate of the same name and *t. Parah* 3.8; its root can be traced back to 4QMMT) might serve as a good example. It allows keeping the purity commandments without preventing peasants, tradesmen, and merchants from doing their regular work. Among the matters of daily concern to the Pharisees were:

- purity (Mark 7:1-5; Matt. 23:25-26 par. Luke 11:39; cf. the sixth order of the Mishnah);
- tithing (Luke 11:42; 18:12; cf. the Mishnah tractates *Demai, Maʿaśer, Maʿaśer Šeni*);
- fasting (Mark 2:18; Luke 18:12; cf. also *Megillat Taʿanit* and the Mishnah tractate *Taʿanit*);
- Sabbath observance (Mark 2:23-28; 3:1-6; cf. the Mishnah tractates *ʿErubin* and *Šabbat*);
- proper religious behavior in public (Mark 2:14-16; Matt. 23:5-7; cf. also 23:27-33); and
- teaching others (their disciples are mentioned in Mark 2:18 par. Luke 5:33; Matt. 22:16; *Ant.* 13.289; 15.3; cf. also John 9:28; Matt. 16:12).

This last concern reflects the interest of the Pharisees in educating and encouraging the whole nation to live according to God's commandments as a way of securing God's blessing of Israel. The partial terminological overlap between scribes and Pharisees (at least all the individual Pharisees in Josephus and in John function in the way scribes in the Synoptic Gospels do) is a hint of their Scripture-based scholarly and educational aims.

Other Pharisaic Doctrines

For Josephus and the New Testament the Jewish parties differed mainly in their teachings about the afterlife (*J.W.* 2.163; *Ant.* 18.14; Mark 12:18; Acts 23:6; cf. *m. Sanh.* 10:1-3) and the related doctrine of fate (Gr. *heimarmenē;* cf. *J.W.* 2.162; *Ant.* 13.172; 18.13). The Pharisees' doctrine of a cooperation between God's providence and humanity's free will made the individual responsible for his deeds without denying God's direct involvement. The Pharisees believed in the resurrection of the dead with a related judgment, and angels (Acts 23:8), which hints at apocalyptic elements in their religious worldview. Early Christianity was in this respect very close to Pharisaism. Their messianic beliefs can be traced only vaguely, but there are some indications of messianic (*Ant.* 17.43-45; Matt. 22:41-42; their general interest in Jesus has to be taken into account as well; cf. further *Psalms of Solomon* 17–18 and the messianic elements within the Fourth Philosophy) and eschatological (Luke 17:20) expectations. None of these doctrines is Pharisaic in an exclusive sense, and this is why Pharisaism should be understood as a nonexclusive religious movement whose adherents wanted to be nothing other than proper Jews (cf. Gal. 1:13).

Epilogue

Rabbinic and medieval Judaism and their various modern offspring have seen themselves as legitimate heirs of the Pharisees and as a continuation of the Pharisaic way of connecting Torah and tradition. Inner-Jewish critics of this Pharisaic-rabbinic tradition were polemically called "Sadducees" (which in the rabbinic view have no part in salvation; cf. *m. Sanh.* 10:1). Because of this self-identification with the Pharisees by a Jewish majority following the rabbinic form of Judaism, Christians, too, saw their Jewish contemporaries as the descendants of the Pharisees of the New Testament and therefore as Jesus' declared enemies who wanted him dead (cf. Mark 3:6). This reductionist view of the relationship between Jesus and the Pharisees created agelong tensions and hostilities between Judaism and Christianity and overlooked completely the many elements Jesus and the Pharisees had in common.

Bibliography

A. I. Baumgarten 1983, "The Name of the Pharisees," *JBL* 102: 411-28. • A. I. Baumgarten 1997, *The Flourishing of Jewish Sects in the Maccabean Era: An Interpretation,* Leiden: Brill. • R. Deines 1997, *Die Pharisäer: Ihr Verständnis im Spiegel der christlichen und jüdischen Forschung seit Wellhausen und Graetz,* Tübingen: Mohr-Siebeck. • R. Deines 2001, "The Pharisees between 'Judaisms' and 'Common Judaism,'" in *Justification and Variegated Nomism: A Fresh Appraisal of Paul and Second Temple Judaism,* vol. 1: *The Complexities of Second Temple Judaism,* ed. D. A. Carson et al., Tübingen: Mohr-Siebeck, 443-504. • R. Deines 2007, "Die Pharisäer und das Volk im Neuen Testament und bei Josephus," in *Josephus und das Neue Testament,* ed. C. Böttrich and J. Herzer, Tübingen: Mohr-Siebeck, 147-80. • M. Hengel and R. Deines 1995, "E. P. Sanders' 'Common Judaism', Jesus, and the Pharisees: A Review Article," *JTS* 46: 1-70. • S. Mason 1991, *Flavius Josephus on the Pharisees,* Leiden: Brill, 1991. • J. P. Meyer 2001, *A Marginal Jew,* vol. 3, *Companions and Competitors,* New York: Doubleday, 289-388. • J. Neusner 1973, *From Politics to Piety: The Emergence of Pharisaic Judaism,* Englewood Cliffs, N.J.: Prentice-Hall (rpt. New York: KTAV, 1979). • J. Neusner and B. D. Chilton, eds. 2007, *In Quest of the Historical Pharisees,* Waco, Tex.: Baylor University Press. • A. J. Saldarini 1988, *Pharisees, Scribes and Sadducees in Palestinian Society,* Wilmington, Del.: Michael Glazier (rpt. Grand Rapids: Eerdmans, 2001). • E. Schürer 1987, *A History of the Jewish People in the Time of Jesus Christ,* 2d ed., Edinburgh: Clark. • M. Smith 1987, *Palestinian Parties and Politics That Shaped the Old Testament,* 2d ed., London: SCM. • G. Stemberger 1995, *Jewish Contemporaries of Jesus: Pharisees, Sadducees, Essenes,* Minneapolis: Fortress.

Roland Deines

Philo

Philo of Alexandria (ca. 20 B.C.E.–ca. 50 C.E.) is one of the most important witnesses to Jewish exegetical traditions and practices of the Second Temple period. He was a prominent figure in the large Alexandrian Jewish community, coming from one of the wealthiest and most distinguished families. He is a good example of a writer from the East who used allegorical interpretation to find common ground between his ancestral tradition and Hellenistic philosophy. His impact on ancient Judaism appears to have ended with the destruction of the Alexandrian Jewish community in 115-117 C.E. At least direct awareness of his works is not discernible until Azariah dei Rossi (1513-1578) summarized some of his views in *Me'or 'Einayim,* and he was ambivalent about Philo's status. Philo's legacy did not, however, end with the destruction of his community; his achievement had such enormous appeal to early Christians that they preserved his writings and claimed him as one of their own, giving him a posthumous baptism (Prochurus, *Acts of John*) and even introducing him as a "bishop" in some Byzantine catenae (e.g., *Fragmenta Graeca, QG* 1.55).

Overview of His Life

We know very little about Philo's life. We have more contemporary evidence for his brother Gaius Julius Alexander, an exceptionally wealthy customs official in Alexandria, and his nephew Tiberius Julius Alexander, an ambitious social climber who gave up his ancestral traditions to make his way through the *cursus honorum,* than we do about Philo. Our evidence for Philo consists of the autobiographical asides that he makes in his writings and the tendentious *testimonia* of later Christians. The one exception is his role in the embassy to Gaius following the pogrom of 38 C.E.

Philo was born into a family with multiple citizenships: he was a citizen of the Jewish *politeuma* of Alexandria, the Greek city of Alexandria, and Rome. At least his brother and nephew must have held these citizenships, and it is likely that they were hereditary. His world was therefore complex. The complexities began with education. Philo received a thorough Jewish education, as his intimate familiarity with the LXX attests. It does not appear that he knew Hebrew or Aramaic; his Jewish education was apparently in Greek, as would have been true for most Diaspora Jews. It may have taken place in his home or perhaps in a house of prayer, although firm evidence for the latter is from a later period. He would also have received a standard Greek education. He would have attended a gymnasium for his primary training in grammar, mathematics, and music (*Preliminary Studies* 74–76). When he was thirteen, he would have officially enrolled in the gymnasium for the ephebate, a Greek cultural tradition carried over from the days when Greek city-states required it as preparation for military service. Its later Hellenistic form required training in literature and athletics, the latter as a remnant of its former function. It served as the right of entry to citizenship in Alexandria. Later in Philo's life, Claudius shut the door on Jewish claims to Alexandrian citizenship, a decision that closed the ephebate to them as well (*CPJ* 153 lines 83-95).

Philo's Jewish and Greek educations are reflected in his lifestyle. He was unambiguously committed to Jewish *halakot.* He criticized fellow Jews who thought that the underlying meaning of Jewish rituals negated the necessity of their observance. Philo argued that they were essential markers of community identity (*Migration* 89–93). In particular, he emphasized the importance of circumcision (*Spec. Laws* 1.1-12), Sabbath observance (*Dreams* 2.123), the celebration of Yom Kippur (*Spec. Laws* 1.186), dietary regulations (*Spec. Laws* 4.100), and endogenous marriage (*Spec. Laws* 3.29) as essential markers of Jewish identity. On one occasion he made a pilgrimage to the Jerusalem Temple (*Providence* 2.64). At the same time, he did not think that Jewish *halakot* prevented him from enjoying Hellenistic culture. He appears to have enjoyed a lifelong love of athletics, first as a participant while in the gymnasium and then as an observer (*Spec. Laws* 2.230 and *Agriculture* 113–15; *Good Person* 26, 110; *Providence* 2.58). He commented on what he saw at the theater on at least two occasions (*Drunkenness* 177; *Good Person* 141). While plays such as Ezekiel's *Exagōgē* may suggest that there was a Jewish theater in Alexandria, Philo explicitly commented on a Euripidean play, which indicates that he attended either a Greek theater or Jewish productions of Greek tragedies (*Good Person* 141). He also speaks of his attendance at banquets where he found it necessary to exercise moderation (*Alleg. Interp.* 3.156). In sum, Philo did not feel restricted from participating in Hellenistic culture. The exception to this was participation in a pagan cult.

The pattern evident in his mores is also evident in his thinking. Philo went on to receive advanced training in rhetoric and philosophy. We are not certain how he acquired his advanced philosophical training. He may have read on his own as Augustine did centuries later or, like Cicero, hired a tutor and attended the lectures of well-known philosophers. We know of a number of philosophers who were active in Alexandria toward the end of the first century B.C.E., but we do not know with whom Philo studied. What is certain, however, is that he read and digested some of the most important works in the Platonic tradition. The two most important Platonic treatises for him were the *Timaeus* and the *Phaedrus.* He also appears to have known the *Laws,* the *Phaedo,* the *Republic,* the *Symposium,* and the *Theaetetus.* He undoubtedly knew the works of other philosophers such as Aenesidemus, but it is often difficult to know whether he read them firsthand or in fragmentary form as they were cited in a doxography.

Philo put his education to good use in his writings. An important question is the social location of his writing. As was true for his education, all of the evidence is indirect. It is hard to imagine that his works were private, intended solely for his own benefit as some have argued that Seneca's letters to Lucilius were and as Marcus Aurelius' *Meditations* were in fact. The variation in the nature of his treatises suggests that he was not their implied reader; the works assume multiple audiences. There are several possibilities for the social location. Some think that they reflect participation in a house of prayer, whether through worship or education or both. Philo described services in houses of prayer as if they were schools (e.g., *Moses* 2.216; *Spec. Laws* 2.62). Perhaps Philo taught in an Alexandrian house of prayer. Another possibility is that he owned a private school where he taught young Jews exegesis and philosophy.

There is one statement in his treatises that assumes a school setting, but it is difficult to know whether we should read this literally or as verisimilitude for the dialogue setting (*Animals* 6). It is clear that

Philo worked in an exegetical tradition and not as an isolated interpreter. He is keenly aware of other Jewish interpreters and includes their views in his commentaries, a fact that agrees with but does not require a school setting. The format of two sets of his commentaries, *The Questions and Answers* and the *Allegorical Commentary,* parallel the type of works that circulated in philosophical schools. More importantly, the preservation of his treatises through Origen suggests that they were part of a Jewish library.

Sometime prior to the destruction of the Alexandrian Jewish community in 115-117 C.E., the works of Philo and other Jewish authors such as Aristobulus passed into Christian hands. Since Clement and Eusebius knew Aristobulus directly rather than through an intermediate source, it is likely that the works of Aristobulus and Philo were part of a common library. While it is possible that both were incorporated into the famous Alexandrian library and then copied by Christians, it is more reasonable to believe that a Jewish library that contained the works of Aristobulus and Philo passed into Christian hands. If Philo had a library for his school, he, like Aristotle (Strabo, *Geography* 13.1.54), would probably have made provisions for its transmission when he died. Either a later head of the school converted to Christianity and brought the library with him, or a well-to-do Christian attended the school and made copies of some of the most important works. Either way, it seems likely that the works of Aristobulus and Philo were transmitted together and belonged to a school library.

We are certain of one event in Philo's life. He served on the first Jewish embassy to Caligula following the pogrom in Alexandria that broke out during Agrippa I's visit in 38 C.E. The delegation left Alexandria in the fall of 39 C.E. and arrived in Rome in 40. According to Philo, there were five members of the delegation (*Embassy* 370; Josephus, *Ant.* 18.257-60, says that there were three). Josephus informs us that Philo was the head of the Jewish delegation (*Ant.* 18.259), a position probably due to his age and education (Philo, *Embassy* 182). The selection of Philo for this role suggests that he was a prominent and respected member of the Alexandrian Jewish community. E. R. Goodenough thought that Philo must have served on the Jewish senate in Alexandria prior to this. While this is possible, Philo's own description of his appointment suggests that he was taken from his intellectual work and thrust into the maelstrom of politics (*Spec. Laws* 3.1-6). As is well known, the embassy enjoyed less success than they had hoped. Philo returned to Alexandria to his school. He probably died in the next decade.

Overview of His Writings

Philo was a voluminous author. Eusebius provided a list of his works that serves as a useful starting point but must be supplemented (*Hist. Eccl.* 2.18.1-9). Philo organized his commentaries into three major series: the *Questions and Answers on Genesis and Exodus,* the *Allegorical Commentary,* and the *Exposition of the Law.* Modern scholarship generally recognizes two other groups of treatises: the philosophical and the apologetic works.

Philo's works have come down to us largely in Greek, although some are preserved in a rather literal sixth-century Armenian translation, and some material is extant only in Latin. The chart below assumes that the work is extant in Greek unless otherwise specified. It is important to note that the textual base of a number of treatises is problematic. There are times when treatises have been separated into two distinct works (e.g., *Alleg. Interp.* 2 = the current *Alleg. Interp.* 1 and 2; *Giants* = the current *Giants* and *Unchangeable*) and one case where short treatments have been clustered (*Virtues* = *Spec. Laws* 4.133-238; *Virtues;* and lost *Piety*). In other cases, we have only part of a treatise: sometimes the majority of the treatise (*Planting* and possibly *Sobriety*) and sometimes only fragments (*God, Hypothetica, Numbers*). There are a significant number of lost treatises. We know about them when either Philo or Eusebius mentioned them explicitly or when there is an obvious lacuna in a series of sequential treatises (labeled "significant lacuna"). There were undoubtedly other treatises that disappeared at an early date; for example, the *Questions and Answers on Genesis* may well have included a treatment of Genesis 1 and the *Questions and Answers on Exodus* probably dealt with Exodus 1–5, but we have not included any speculations about these.

We thus have thirty-six treatises fully or mainly extant in Greek, with fragments of another; plus an additional thirteen treatises fully or mainly extant in Armenian, with fragments of two others. This gives us a total of forty-nine fully or mainly preserved treatises and fragments of three others. We know or can reasonably speculate that Philo wrote another twenty-three treatises. We thus have approximately two-thirds of his work.

The Three Commentary Series

(1) *The Questions and Answers on Genesis and Exodus.* This is a zetematic (questioning) work named for the format of the commentary. The series goes sequentially through the texts of Gen. 2:4–28:9 and Exod. 6:2–30:10 posing questions and providing answers for difficulties in the text. The form of the commentary goes back to Aristotle's *Homeric Problems* and had became a fixture in the philosophical tradition, as Plutarch's zetematic works demonstrate (e.g., *Platonic Questions*). Jewish interpreters such as Demetrius (frgs. 2 and 5) and Aristobulus (frg. 2) show that the practice passed into Jewish circles at an early date. Philo's *Questions and Answers* are, however, the first full zetematic work that we have in Jewish circles. Since the answers offer literal, allegorical, or both literal and allegorical options and rarely make a case for a specific reading, this commentary series was probably intended for beginning students in Philo's school or for Jewish readers more generally who wanted an orientation to the text.

(2) *The Allegorical Commentary.* Philo is most famous for this series of treatises, which proceed sequentially through the text of Gen. 2:1–41:24. The commentary provides an allegorical reading of Genesis, largely

Treatise	Biblical Text	Textual Base
Questions and Answers		
QG 1	Gen. 2:4–6:13	Armenian *QG* 1
QG 2	Gen. 6:14–11:32	Armenian *QG* 2 + additions
QG 3	Gen. 12:1–17:27	Armenian *QG* 3 + additions
QG 4	Gen. 18:1–22:24	Armenian *QG* 4.1-70 + additions
QG 5	Gen. 23:1–25:18	Armenian *QG* 4.71-153 + additions
QG 6	Gen. 25:19–28:9	Armenian *QG* 4.154-95 + Latin 1-11 + Armenian *QG* 4.196-245
QE 1	Exod. 6:2–9:35	Lost (Eusebius, *Hist. Eccl.* 2.18.5)
QE 2	Exod. 10:1–13:16	Additions + Armenian *QE 1* + additions
QE 3	Exod. 13:17–17:16	Lost (Eusebius, *Hist. Eccl.* 2.18.5)
QE 4	Exod. 20:25b–4:18	Armenian *QE* 2.1 + additions + Armenian *QE* 2.2-49
QE 5	Exod. 25:1–27:19	Armenian *QE* 2.50-102 + additions
QE 6	Exod. 27:20–30:10	Armenian *QE* 2.103-24 + additions
Allegorical Commentary		
	Gen. 1:1-31	Lost (*Alleg. Interp.* 1.1-2; significant lacuna)
Allegorical Interpretation 1	Gen. 2:1–3:1a	*Alleg. Interp.* 1–2
Allegorical Interpretation 2	Gen. 3:1b-8a	Lost (significant lacuna)
Allegorical Interpretation 3	Gen. 3:8b-19	*Allegorical Interpretation* 3
Allegorical Interpretation 4	Gen. 3:20-23	Lost (*Sacrifices* 51; significant lacuna)
Cherubim	Gen. 3:24; 4:1	*Cherubim*
Sacrifices	Gen. 4:2-4	*Sacrifices*
	Gen. 4:5-7	Lost (significant lacuna)
Worse	Gen. 4:8-15	*Worse*
Posterity	Gen. 4:16-25	*Posterity*
	Gen. 5:32	Lost (*Sobriety* 52?)
Giants and *Unchangeable*	Gen. 6:1-12	*Giants* and *Unchangeable*
Covenants 1	Lost	(*Names* 53; Eusebius, *Hist. Eccl.* 2.18.3)
Covenants 2	Lost	(*Names* 53; Eusebius, *Hist. Eccl.* 2.18.3)
Agriculture	Gen. 9:20a	*Agriculture*
Planting	Gen. 9:20b	*Planting*
		End of treatise lost
Drunkenness 1	Gen. 9:21	*Drunkenness*
		(Note: This could be vol. 2 and vol. 1 could be lost.)
Drunkenness 2	Gen. 9:21b-23	Lost (Eusebius, *Hist. Eccl.* 2.18.2; Philo, *Sobriety* 1)
Sobriety	Gen. 9:24-27	*Sobriety*
		End of treatise lost (?)
Confusion	Gen. 11:1-9	*Confusion*
Migration	Gen. 12:1-4, 6	*Migration*
Rewards	Gen. 15:1	Lost (*Heir* 1)
Heir	Gen. 15:2-18	*Heir*
Preliminary Studies	Gen. 16:1-6a	*Preliminary Studies*
Flight	Gen. 16:6b-9, 11-12	*Flight*
Names	Gen. 17:1-5, 15-22	*Names*
God	Gen. 18:2	Armenian Fragment

Treatise	Biblical Text	Textual Base
Dreams 1	Gen. 20:3 (?)	Lost (Eusebius, *Hist. Eccl.* 2.18.4)
Dreams 2	Gen. 28:10-22; 31:10-13	*Dreams* 1
Dreams 3	Gen. 37:8-11; 40:9-11, 16-17; 41:17-24	*Dreams* 2
Dreams 4	Lost	(Eusebius, *Hist. Eccl.* 2.18.4)
Dreams 5	Lost	(Eusebius, *Hist. Eccl.* 2.18.4)
Exposition of the Law		
Creation	Gen. 1:1–2:5	*Creation*
Abraham	Genesis 4–25	*Abraham*
Isaac	Genesis 25–28, 35	Lost (*Joseph* 1)
Jacob	Genesis 25–50	Lost (*Joseph* 1)
Joseph	Genesis 37–50	*Joseph*
Decalogue	Deut. 5:1-20 (cf. Exod. 20:1-17)	*Decalogue*
Special Laws 1	Polytheism and idolatry	*Special Laws* 1
Special Laws 2	Oaths, Sabbath, parents	*Special Laws* 2
Special Laws 3	Adultery and murder	*Special Laws* 3
Special Laws 4	Stealing, false witness, and covetousness	*Special Laws* 4
Virtues:		
Justice		*Special Laws* 4.133-238
Courage		*Virtues* 1–50
Philanthropy		*Virtues* 51–227
Piety		Lost
Passions		Lost (*Alleg. Interp.* 3.139)
Rewards		*Rewards*
Introductory Work		
Moses 1		*Moses* 1
Moses 2		*Moses* 2
Philosophical Treatises		
Bad Person		Lost (*Good Person* 1)
Good Person		*Good Person*
Providence 1		Armenian *Providence* 1
Providence 2		Armenian *Providence* 2 + Greek fragments in Eusebius, *Praep. Evang.* 7.21; 8.14
Animals		Armenian *Animals*
Eternity 1		*Eternity*
Eternity 2		Lost (*Eternity* 150)
Numbers		Armenian Fragment
Apologetic Treatises		
Essenes		Lost (*Contemplative Life* 1)
Contemplative Life		*Contemplative Life*
Hypothetica		Fragments in Eusebius, *Praep. Evang.* 8.6.1-7.20 and 8.11.1-18
Virtues 1		Lost (Eusebius, *Hist. Eccl.* 2.5.1; 2.6.3)
Virtues 2		Lost (Eusebius, *Hist. Eccl.* 2.5.1; 2.6.3)
Virtues 3		*Flaccus*
Virtues 4		*Embassy*
Virtues 5		Lost (*Embassy* 373; Eusebius, *Hist. Eccl.* 2.5.1; 2.6.3)

dedicated to the ascent of the soul. The form of these treatises is closest to some of the commentaries in the philosophical tradition, especially the anonymous *Theaetetus Commentary*, Plutarch's *On the Generation of the Soul in the Timaeus*, and Porphyry's *On the Cave of Nymphs*. The basic difference is that Philo linked a series of treatises together in a single large enterprise. The series uses questions and answers — although not always explicitly formulated as questions — but expands allegorical interpretations through secondary and tertiary texts that are thematically or verbally related. The sophisticated nature of this commentary series suggests that it was intended for advanced students in Philo's school or other Jewish exegetes.

(3) *The Exposition of the Law*. The third commentary series is quite different. It is a systematic explanation of the law that spans the entire Pentateuch from creation to the blessings and curses of the final speech of Deuteronomy (*Abraham* 1-6; *Moses* 2.45-47; *Decalogue* 1; *Rewards* 1-3). Unlike the treatises in the other two commentary series, those in this one do not cite the biblical text and then comment on it but retell the biblical story and interpret it. In this sense they are much less like a commentary and more similar to the works in Jewish circles that we call "rewritten Bible." They deal largely with the literal meaning of the text, although they can alternate back and forth between literal and allegorical interpretations. The *Exposition* is broad enough in scope and straightforward enough in explanation that it could have served both Philo's students and any interested Jewish readers in the community.

There are also two volumes on Moses (*Moses* 1-2). These appear to be related in some way to the Exposition (*Rewards* 52-56); however, they do not fit within it. The best explanation of their relationship to the commentaries is to understand them as an introductory biography on the work of Moses, in much the same way that Arrian wrote a biography of Epictetus and Porphyry wrote a *Life of Plotinus*. In both cases, the biography was intended to orient the reader to the thought of the philosopher. The *Life of Moses* was thus probably intended for any curious reader. While the audience was presumably Jewish, the work does not require a background in Judaism.

The Philosophical Treatises

Philo also wrote a number of treatises that we can call philosophical. They cite Greek sources rather than Jewish Scripture and use genres that are common in the philosophical tradition. Among them is an arithmology (*Numbers*); two dialogues (*Providence* 1-2 and *Animals*); a thesis, a work that sets out a position and the supporting as well as the counterarguments (*Eternity* 1 [pro] and 2 [con]); and a discourse, a work that argues a thesis, in this instance a paradox (the lost *Bad Person* and the *Good Person*). The treatises assume an audience that knows and appreciates Hellenistic philosophy. In two cases (*Providence* 1-2 and *Animals*), Philo attempted to overturn the unacceptable views of his nephew, Tiberius Julius Alexander. The treatises were probably intended for students in Philo's school and, in some cases, made explicit cases for common Jewish beliefs in order to keep young Jews within their ancestral faith.

The Apologetic Treatises

Finally, Philo wrote a series of treatises in the aftermath of the pogrom in Alexandria in 38 C.E. These treatises address contemporary events and openly situate Jews in the larger Greco-Roman world. The lost treatise on the *Essenes* and the presentation of the Therapeutae in *The Contemplative Life* describe two Jewish groups whom Philo could hold up to the larger world as "athletes of virtue." The fragmentary *Hypothetica* was probably intended to prepare Philo for his exchanges with his opponents — including Apion (Josephus, *Ant.* 18.257-59) and Chaeremon (*CPJ* 153) — when he went to Rome. Philo also wrote a five-volume treatment of the fates of the opponents of the Jewish people demonstrating the reversal of fortunes that each opponent of the Jewish people experienced. These included Sejanus (lost), Pilate (lost), Flaccus (*Flaccus*), and Caligula (*Embassy*). The implied audiences of these treatises are non-Jewish, although this would not exclude Jewish readers from reading and using them in apologetic contexts.

Achievement

Philo was not a systematic thinker, although there have been noble attempts to make him one. He was first and foremost an exegete or interpreter of Moses. He called himself "an interpreter" (*Animals* 7, 74; cf. also *Creation* 5). This does not mean that he did not have a comprehensive understanding of the cosmos, but that he did not work out a systematic presentation of it. He wrote commentaries and works that addressed specific issues. His lifelong project was to interpret the Jewish Scriptures allegorically through the lens of Hellenistic philosophy. In this regard his project was similar to Chaeremon's interpretation of Egyptian texts through Stoic philosophy or Plutarch's allegory of Egyptian myths through Middle Platonic thought (*Isis and Osiris*) or Numenius of Apamea's explanations of oriental traditions via Platonism (*On the Good*).

Philo did have a specific lens through which he read his ancestral Scriptures. It was captured in antiquity by the *bon mot:* "Either Plato philonizes or Philo platonizes" (Jerome, *On Famous Men* 11). Philo's task may have been to interpret Moses, but the Moses he read was a Platonized Moses. Unlike a number of Jews and later Christians who constructed a history of culture in which they subordinated Hellenistic thought to Jewish thought by making the "theft of philosophy" argument, Philo, who knew the argument and referred to it on occasion, appears to have believed that Moses and Plato had seen the same realities. Philo did not believe that he needed to read Plato into Moses, but out of Moses. For example, he argued that the "pattern of the tent" that Moses saw before he constructed the Tabernacle demonstrated the presence of Platonic ideas (Exod. 25:9, 40 in *Moses* 2.74, 76; Exod. 25:9 in *QE* 2.52; Exod. 25:40 in *QE* 2.82; and Exod. 26:30 in *QE* 2.90). It was from such a perspective that he interwove Plato's *Timaeus* into his treatises, especially *Creation* and the *Allegorical Interpretations* 1–3.

This does not mean that Philo was a Platonist; he was not if we understand him on his own terms. Nor does it mean that he restricted his philosophical lens to Platonism; he did not. Like most Hellenistic thinkers, he was eclectic. For thinkers like Antiochus of Ascalon, Eudorus, Arius Didymus, and many others, different systems of thought contributed to the understanding of reality. The best course of action was to draw the best from each tradition, even if a single tradition served as the overarching *Weltanschauung*. Philo falls easily into this perspective. He incorporated into his treatises not only Middle Platonic perspectives but also Stoic and Neopythagorean ones. Stoicism was the common coin of the Hellenistic and Roman worlds. Philo drew from a significant number of Stoic concepts, including cosmological, anthropological, and ethical views. His arguments for providence are largely Stoic. Similarly, he adopted Neopythagorean arithmology. His basic frame of thought was Platonic, but this was not an exclusive commitment for him.

Assessments of his contribution have been extreme. H. A. Wolfson thought that he created the system of thought that became the basis for medieval philosophy and theology until Spinoza deconstructed it. On the other end of the spectrum, R. Goulet considered him to be a hack who spoiled a far more brilliant allegorical commentary on the entire Pentateuch. Most scholars fall between these two poles in their assessment, although there is no unanimity on specifics. One critical area where Philo did make a lasting contribution was in theology proper: he considered God to be ontologically prior to everything else that was good. He identified the *ho ōn* of Exod. 3:14 with the *to on* of Platonism and emphasized divine transcendence (*Worse* 160; *Names* 11–15). Like other Middle Platonists, he posited an intermediary who was God's face to the cosmos and humanity's access to God, that is, the Logos. He thought that the Logos was God's image based on his interpretation of Gen. 1:27. In his thought there is God, the Image of God (the Logos), and human beings who were created in the image of God's Image (the Logos) (*Creation* 24–25). Humanity can ascend to God through the Logos. The Scriptures are the key to understanding this reality. He understood that philosophy and the Scriptures taught the same thing about the Ultimate Cause (*Virtues* 65). Philosophy provided an intellectual framework, but it did not displace the legislation of Moses as the authoritative statement of the divine realities.

An assessment of Philo depends on how he is measured. If he is measured by the impact of his work on subsequent thinkers, then we may call this Jewish writer "the first Christian theologian." If, on the other hand, he is measured by what he accomplished, we may say that he is the most important representative and apex of the rich Jewish exegetical tradition that flourished in Alexandria from the end of the third century B.C.E. to the beginning of the second century C.E.

BIBLIOGRAPHY

Text

L. COHN, P. WENDLAND, S. REITER, AND I. LEISEGANG, EDS. 1896-1930, *Philonis Alexandrini opera quae supersunt*, 7 vols., Berlin: Reimer (2d ed. 1962).

Translations

R. ARNALDEZ, C. MONDÉSERET, AND J. POUILLOUX 1961-1992, *Les Œuvres de Philon d'Alexandrie*, 34 vols., Paris: Cerf. • L. COHN, I. HEINEMANN, M. ADLER, AND W. THEILER 1909-1938, *Philo von Alexandria: Die Werke in deutscher Übersetzung*, 7 vols., Breslau: Marcus (2d ed. Berlin: de Gruyter, 1962-1964). • F. H. COLSON, G. H. WHITAKER, AND R. MARKUS 1929-1962, *Philo*, 10 vols. and 2 supp. vols., LCL, Cambridge: Harvard University Press.

Bibliographies

R. RADICE AND D. T. RUNIA 1988, *Philo of Alexandria: An Annotated Bibliography 1937-1986*, Leiden: Brill. • D. T. RUNIA 2000, *Philo of Alexandria: An Annotated Bibliography 1987-1996*, Leiden: Brill (updated each year in *Studia Philonica Annual*).

Reference Works

D. T. RUNIA AND G. E. STERLING, EDS. 1989-, *The Studia Philonica Annual*, Atlanta: Society of Biblical Literature.• G. E. STERLING, ED. 2001-, The Philo of Alexandria Commentary Series, Leiden: Brill. • P. BORGEN, K. FUGLSETH, AND P. SKARSTEN 2000, *The Philo Index: A Complete Greek Word Index to the Writings of Philo of Alexandria*, Grand Rapids: Eerdmans; Leiden: Brill.

Studies

P. BORGEN 1997, *Philo of Alexandria: An Exegete for His Time*, Leiden: Brill. • É. BRÉHIER 1950, *Les Idées philosophiques et religieuses de Philon d'Alexandrie*, Paris: Vrin. • J. M. DILLON 1996, *The Middle Platonists, 80 B.C. to A.D. 220*, rev. ed., Ithaca: Cornell University Press. • E. R. GOODENOUGH 1935, *By Light, Light: The Mystic Gospel of Hellenistic Judaism*, New Haven: Yale University Press. • R. GOULET 1987, *La philosophie de Moïse: Essai de reconstitution d'un commentaire philosophique préphilonien de pentateuque*, Paris: Vrin. • I. HEINEMANN 1973, *Philons griechische und jüdische Bildung: Kulturvergleichende Untersuchungen zu Philons Darstellung der jüdischen Gesetze*, Hildesheim: Olms. • V. NIKIPROWETZKY 1977, *Le commentaire de l'écriture chez Philon d'Alexandrie: Son caractère et sa portée; observations philologiques*, Leiden: Brill. • D. T. RUNIA 1986, *Philo of Alexandria and the Timaeus of Plato*, Leiden: Brill. • D. T. RUNIA 1993, *Philo in Early Christian Literature: A Survey*, Assen: Van Gorcum; Minneapolis: Fortress. • T. H. TOBIN 1983, *The Creation of Man: Philo and the History of Interpretation*, Washington, D.C.: Catholic Biblical Association of America. • D. WINSTON 1985, *Logos and Mystical Theology in Philo of Alexandria*, Cincinnati: Hebrew Union College Press; Hoboken, N.J.: KTAV. • H. A. WOLFSON 1948, *Philo: Foundations of Religious Philosophy in Judaism, Christianity, and Islam*, 2 vols., Cambridge: Harvard University Press.

See also: Philo, Apologetic Treatises; Philo, Exposition of the Law; Philo, Philosophical Works; Philo, Questions and Answers on Genesis and Exodus

GREGORY E. STERLING

Philo, Allegorical Commentary

In modern scholarship the title *Allegorical Commentary* is applied to all the exegetical treatises of Philo of Alexandria that are included neither in his *Exposition of the Law* nor in his *Questions and Answers on Genesis and Exodus.* According to Eusebius, Philo himself gave to these treatises the title *Allegory of the Sacred Laws* (*Hist. Eccl.* 2.18.1). The treatises in the *Allegorical Commentary* numbered thirty-one; the following works survive in Greek but are usually referred to by their Latin titles:

1. *Legum Allegoriae (Allegory of the Law)* books I–III on Gen. 2:1-7; 2:18–3:1a; 3:8b-19
2. *De Cherubim (On the Cherubim)* on Gen. 3:24 and 4:1
3. *De Sacrificiis Abelis et Caini (On the Sacrifices of Abel and Cain)* on Gen. 4:2-4
4. *Quod Deterius Potiori Insidiari Soleat (The Worse Attacks the Better)* on Gen. 4:8-15
5. *De Posteritate Caini (On the Posterity and Exile of Cain)* on Gen. 4:16-25
6. *De Gigantibus (On The Giants)* on Gen. 6:1-4
7. *Quod Deus Sit Immutabilis (On the Unchangeableness of God)* on Gen. 6:4-12
8. *De Agricultura (On Husbandry)* on Gen. 9:20a
9. *De Plantatione (On Noah's Work as a Planter)* on Gen. 9:20b
10. *De Ebrietate (On Drunkenness)* on Gen. 9:21
11. *De Sobrietate (On Sobriety)* on Gen. 9:24-27
12. *De Confusione Linguarum (On the Confusion of Tongues)* on Gen. 11:1-9
13. *De Migratione Abrahami (On the Migration of Abraham)* on Gen. 12:1-6
14. *Quis Rerum Divinarum Heres Sit? (Who Is Heir of Divine Things?)* on Gen. 15:2-18
15. *De Congressu Eruditionis Gratia (On the Preliminary Studies)* on Gen. 16:1-6
16. *De Fuga et Inventione (On Flight and Finding)* on Gen. 6:6-14
17. *De Mutatione Nominum (On the Change of Names)* on Gen. 17:1-22
18. *De Deo (On God)* on Gen. 18:2 (all that remains of this work is a small fragment in Armenian)
19. *De Somniis (On Dreams)* books I–II on Gen. 28:12-17; 31:10-13 (Jacob's two dreams) and Genesis 37 and 40–41 (the dreams of Joseph)

The *Allegorical Commentary* constitutes the most voluminous part of Philo's oeuvre. The treatises within the series cover important passages in Genesis 2–41 in a verse-by-verse commentary. In them Philo adapts the question-and-answer format. The questions, however, emerge from the exegesis of the passage, and the answers are lengthier and more complex than in his *Questions and Answers on Genesis and Exodus.* This series is of particular importance because it constitutes the first extant systematic inquiry into the book of Genesis, providing an in-depth analysis of each verse in light of its allegorical dimension as well as scholarly questions on the literal meaning. Philo addresses here a highly educated Jewish audience able to follow complicated discussions of minute details.

Exegetical Approach

The style of the *Allegorical Commentary* often strikes the modern reader as difficult and convoluted. It does not make for a fluent reading but demands the same kind of attention as rabbinic midrash, which similarly disregards the flow of the biblical stories and creatively engages each verse in its own right. Philo's style in the *Allegorical Commentary* is properly appreciated if we consider that he wished to put allegory on an academic footing, thus combining two genres which had hitherto not been connected. Academic investigations into foundational texts had a long tradition in Alexandria, having been practiced by both Homeric scholars and Jewish exegetes in the spirit of the *Aporemata Homerica* (works dealing with interpretive "difficulties" raised by Homer's epic poems, the *Iliad* and the *Odyssey*). In the second century B.C.E., the Jewish writer Demetrius provides crucial glimpses into this world of Jewish scholarship, which identified and solved problems of the biblical text, especially apparent contradictions between verses (Eusebius, *Praep. Evang.* 9.21.1-9; 9.29.1-3). This kind of literal and surprisingly critical scholarship on the biblical text became established in Alexandria at a very early stage, when Jewish exegesis in the land of Israel still proceeded in the style of "rewritten Bible" and the pesher commentaries from Qumran.

Philo was well aware of the scholarly enterprise of his colleagues, embracing some of it while vehemently opposing its more critical varieties. Overall he considered it very seriously, attempting to show that his own favored approach, namely spiritual allegory, was consistent with academic inquiry and even a natural continuation of it. This was a revolutionary step because allegorical interpretations had thus far been suggested rather freely, being justified at the most by etymological references. Philo's Jewish predecessors in the allegorical mode, such as Aristobulus and Aristeas, started with a question but offered their solution without providing an in-depth study of the literal meaning of the text. This is precisely what Philo aimed at in his *Allegorical Commentary,* thus setting new standards for allegorical interpretation.

The nature and origin of the allegorical method among Jews and Greeks are debated in modern scholarship. It is disputed whether allegory served merely as an apologetic means of defending a canonical text or whether it had a more creative function. Scholars have often identified allegory as a method invented by the Stoics, who sought ways of defending Homer's epics and thus suggested a more elevated, philosophical meaning to replace the literal, mythical level. This approach has been challenged with the observation that the Stoics did not introduce allegory, but were rather concerned with etymology, which investigated the root meanings of key words and eventually also led to allegory (Long 1992). Similarly, Philo has often been seen as adopting Stoic allegory in order to defend Scripture and render it more philosophical as well as Greek. This approach, too, has been challenged, with the counterclaim that Philo's method rather subjects Greek culture to the Jewish Scriptures (Dawson 1992). While Philo's allegory was conservative in the sense that it solved problems of the biblical text without considering radical literary solutions, such as emending the text, it is clear that he maintained the literal meaning of Scripture as far as the Law was concerned. It is well known that Philo opposed radical colleagues who substituted allegory for observance of laws like those pertaining to circumcision (*De Migratione Abrahami* 89–94). In his interpretations of the narrative parts of Scripture, the role of allegory varies: sometimes he offers an additional meaning, enriching Scripture by a further dimension (e.g., *De Abrahamo* 68–80), while on other occasions he follows Aristobulus and uses allegory in order to uproot the mythological level of Scripture (e.g., *Leg. Alleg.* 2.19).

Place in Philo's Corpus

The precise place of the *Allegorical Commentary* among Philo's works is still disputed today. Special attention has been given to the question of its relationship to Philo's *Questions and Answers,* which is most similar to it, because here, too, biblical verses are systematically quoted and then interpreted both literally and allegorically. It has been asserted that *Questions and Answers* is Philo's earliest work and that in it he was trying out ideas that he subsequently developed in the *Allegorical Commentary* (Terian 1991). Yet one could equally interpret the *Questions and Answers* as an abbreviation of thoughts presented in the *Allegorical Commentary.* The difference between the works is best understood as a difference of audience: while the *Allegorical Commentary* addresses specialized and highly educated readers, the *Questions and Answers* aims at more primary education, perhaps of young students in the Jewish community.

The *Allegory of the Law* as a Representative Treatise

The three books of the *Allegory of the Law* are the central piece of Philo's *Allegorical Commentary.* Philo presents here a close reading of clusters of running verses from the first two chapters of Genesis. Somewhat surprisingly he starts with Gen. 2:1, leaving out the creation of the world as described in Genesis 1. Either Philo's commentary on that chapter is lost (so Tobin 2000), or Philo decided not to comment on it allegorically because he considered it to be a separate unit (Praem. 1). Indeed, when treating it in his *Exposition of the Law,* he insisted that it may not be interpreted allegorically (*De Opificio Mundi* 1–28). Philo's *Allegory of the Law* thus seems to have focused on the stories of the early heroes, which he regarded as belonging to the second part of the Torah dealing with "history" (Praem. 1).

Philo proceeds verse by verse in the *Allegory of the Law,* quoting a biblical passage, identifying a particular problem or question raised by it, and then discussing and ultimately resolving it on the allegorical level. A good example is *Leg. Alleg.* 1.101-2, where Philo comments on Gen. 2:17, "But of the tree of knowledge of good and evil ye shall not eat." Using classical Greek terminology, Philo raises the difficulty why the command is here formulated in the plural, while in the previous verse God had addressed a single person, saying, "you may eat of every tree of the garden" (Gen. 2:16). Having defined the problem, Philo states his allegorical solution, again using standard academic terminology. He suggests that different forms of address have been chosen because the good is scarce but evil abounds.

Similar questions are raised in connection with the creation of man. Commenting on Gen. 2:7, Philo lines up several of them (*Leg. Alleg.* 1.33):

> Someone may inquire why God generally considered worthy of the divine spirit the earthborn and body-loving mind . . . ; secondly, what is the precise meaning of the expression "breathed into"; thirdly, why was it breathed "into the face"; fourthly, why does he mention the word "breath" rather than "spirit" even though he knows the latter word, as when he said "and the spirit of God was lying upon the water"? (LXX Gen. 1:2)

Philo initially provides elaborate literal answers before embarking on the allegorical level. He thus insists, in response to the first query, that God is generous and happily provides good things to everyone; in response to the second, that the expression "breathed into" is the same as "blew into" or "put a soul into soulless things"; and, in response to the third, that there is a difference between "breath" and "spirit": the latter implies strength and vigor, while the former is like air. These explanations show how important the literal level was for Philo and how eager he was to integrate his allegorical approach with proper scholarship.

In terms of content, the *Allegory of the Law* covers some of the same ground that is treated in *De Opificio Mundi.* Most important of these is the issue of the double creation of man. Philo, for the first time in Jewish exegesis, addresses the question of why there are two creation stories that apparently convey contradictory accounts of man's creation. Philo solves this problem by arguing that the two stories refer to two types of man (*Leg. Alleg.* 1.31; *Opificio Mundi* 34). Gen. 1:26 speaks of man's creation in the image of God, thus implying an ideal form of man who has nothing terrestrial about him, while Gen. 2:7 mentions man's creation out of the earth and thus speaks about a material creature. The ideal man was created first, serving as a model for his terrestrial equivalent. Philo thus adopts the Platonic notion of ideal forms, which are perfect and absolutely transcendental, serving as models for material creations. Although Plato himself did not yet speak about an ideal form of man, his students systematized his thought. Arius Didymus, an Alexandrian Platonist living a generation before Philo, is the first extant writer to mention an ideal form of man (Eusebius, *Praep. Evang.* 11.23).

When Philo dwells on the second account of creation, he gives special attention to the notion of divine breath entering the dust from the ground (Gen. 2:7). This gives him the opportunity to dwell on the relationship between mind and body. Philo assumes with Plato that the mind at first existed independently in a spiritual realm before it descended into the body, thus being imprisoned in the material world. Biblical writers still conceived of man in a holistic fashion and did not strongly distinguish his "spiritual" faculties from his material characteristics. A Jewish contemporary of Philo, however, as well as many rabbinic teachers, expressed similar notions of a body-mind dichotomy (Wis. 8:19; *Gen. Rab.* 34:10; *b. Sanhedrin* 71).

Other Treatises

Each of the treatises in Philo's *Allegorical Commentary* treats a particular passage in Genesis, focusing each time on a central subject or problem. Some even postulate an overall solution, such as the treatise *On the Unchangeableness of God,* which argues that the biblical indication of God's regret about the creation of man must not be read in an anthropomorphic vein, but taken allegorically as an affirmation of God's transcendence. Similarly, the treatises *On the Confusion of Tongues* and *On the Giants* treat biblical stories that appeared to many of Philo's Jewish contemporaries as mythological and parallel to stories in Greek literature. Applying both literal and allegorical methods, Philo aimed at showing that Scripture does not contain myth but only metaphysical truth.

BIBLIOGRAPHY

P. BORGEN 1997, *Philo of Alexandria: An Exegete of His Time,* Leiden: Brill. • D. DAWSON 1992, *Allegorical Readers and Cultural Revision in Ancient Alexandria,* Berkeley: University of California Press, 73-126. • A. A. LONG 1992, "Stoic Readings of Homer," in *Homer's Ancient Readers,* ed. R. Lamberton and J. J. Keaney, Princeton: Princeton University Press, 41-66. • J. MORRIS 1987, "The Jewish Philosopher Philo," in E. Schürer, *The History of the Jewish People in the Age of Jesus Christ,* rev. and ed. G. Vermes and F. Millar, Edinburgh: Clark, 3.2.840-68. • D. T. RUNIA 1990, "The Structure of Philo's Allegorical Treatises," in idem, *Exegesis and Philosophy: Studies on Philo of Alexandria,* Aldershot: Variorum, 202-56. • A. TERIAN 1991, "The Priority of the Quaestiones among Philo's Exegetical Commentaries," in *Both Literal and Allegorical: Studies in Philo of Alexandria's Questions and Answers on Genesis and Exodus,* ed. D. M. Hay, Atlanta: Scholars Press, 29-46. • T. H. TOBIN 2000, "The Beginning of Philo's Legum Allegoriae," *SPhA* 12: 29-43. • D. WINSTON AND J. DILLON 1983, *Two Treatises of Philo of Alexandria: A Commentary on De Gigantibus and Quod Deus Sit Immutabilis,* Chico, Calif.: Scholars Press.

See also: Allegory MAREN R. NIEHOFF

Philo, Apologetic Treatises

Philo appears to have written at least eight treatises that are generally considered to be apologetic. Unfortunately, only three of these and fragments of a fourth are preserved. As with the three commentary series (*Questions and Answers on Genesis and Exodus,* the *Allegorical Commentary,* and the *Exposition of the Law),* Philo did not conceive of these treatises as a single unit. While he grouped some of them into larger units, the category of apologetic treatises is a modern construct. Scholars apply it to these treatises because they situate Judaism in the Roman Empire. In some cases the treatises are direct responses to criticisms; in other cases, the works champion Jewish values in the context of the larger world. The implied audiences are non-Jewish, although this would not exclude Jewish readers from using them in their attempts to situate themselves in a Greco-Roman context.

Setting

While Philo might have written some of the treatises early in his life, the bulk of the treatises — and all those extant — were associated with the pogrom that broke out in Alexandria in 38 C.E. and its aftermath. The explosion occurred when Agrippa I visited Alexandria on his way to claim the kingdom that Gaius had given him. A group of Alexandrians mocked the king, and riots broke out. Two leading Alexandrians, Isodorus and Lampo, promised the governor Flaccus support with the new emperor if he, in turn, would support their efforts against the Jews. Flaccus, whose standing with the new emperor was shaky because of his ties to Tiberius, agreed, and the pogrom was on. He had, however, misread the political landscape. He was summoned to Rome, accused in part by none other than Isodorus and Lampo, and exiled. The new prefect, C. Vitrasius Pollio, moved the issue from the streets into the courtroom. Two embassies set out for Rome: an Alexandrian headed by Isodorus and Apion and a Jewish headed by Philo. After two hearings, it was apparent that the emperor favored the Alexandrians. Philo described the second reception of the Jewish delegation in these words: "When we entered, we immediately knew on the basis of his glance and body language that we had not come to a judge, but to an accuser, more hostile than those who opposed us" (*Embassy* 349). Following the assassination of Gaius on 24 January 41 C.E., hostilities broke out again. Claudius quickly suppressed them, heard both delegations, and issued a decree that attempted to reestablish the policies of Julius Caesar and Augustus (Josephus, *Ant.* 19.279). However, neither group of antagonists was ready to give up: both the Alexandrians and Jews sent second delegations (*CPJ* 153 lines 87-92). Claudius settled the matter with a famous letter that gave the Jewish community in Alexandria the right to practice their ancestral religion but closed the door for them to have more (*CPJ* 153).

Philo described his being thrust into these events in a famous passage: "There was once a time when by pursuing the study of philosophy and the contemplation of the cosmos and its contents, I enjoyed the beautiful, desirable, and truly blessed mind." These days were gone. "But the most troublesome of evils, good-hating envy, lay in wait for me. Suddenly it fell on me and did not stop pulling me down until it cast me down into a great sea of civil cares in which I am carried along

— unable even to keep my head above water" (*Spec. Laws* 3.1-6). While this might refer to a more general role that Philo played in the community, it probably alludes to his appointment as a member of the Jewish delegation that left Alexandria in the winter of 39 and arrived in Rome the next spring (Philo, *Embassy* 355; Josephus, *Ant.* 18.257-60). Philo suffered through the indignities of Gaius and the arrival of a second Jewish delegation. Philo probably returned to Alexandria following Claudius' letter. It was in the maelstrom of these "civil cares" that Philo wrote his apologetic treatises.

The *Hypothetica*

One of the most enigmatic works attributed to Philo is the *Hypothetica*. While Eusebius knew and accepted the work as Philonic, some modern scholars have registered doubts. The ambiguous position of the work is represented by its place in the standard critical edition: Cohn and Wendland omitted the fragments in their *editio major* but included it in their *editio minor*. Although the work is poorly preserved and has some unusual features, the majority of scholars consider it authentic.

Eusebius preserved two fragments. He attributed the first fragment to the first scroll of a work entitled the *Hypothetica* that "argued on behalf of the Jews against their accusers" (*Praep. Evang.* 8.5.11–8.7.20). Later the bishop quoted a fragment "from his apology on behalf of the Jews" (*Praep. Evang.* 8.10.19–8.11.18). The two excerpts are probably from the same work: Eusebius dropped the opaque title *Hypothetica* when he introduced the second fragment and repeated his description of the work as an apology. This is confirmed by his division of the Jewish people into two groups in his preface to the second fragment: the multitudes follow the literal meaning of the Law (first fragment), while the philosophical group of Essenes (second fragment) move to higher forms of contemplation (8.10.18-19). The relationship between the fragments is complicated by Eusebius' catalogue of Philo's works in the *Historia Ecclesiastica*, where the bishop does not mention the *Hypothetica* but includes a one-volume work *Concerning the Jews* (*Hist. Eccl.* 2.18.6). This title is a common heading for works that deal with the Jewish people and was probably a secondary title. While it is possible that *Concerning the Jews* refers to the *Hypothetica*, the fact that it is listed among the single-scroll works of Philo, while the *Praeparatio Evangelica* suggests that the *Hypothetica* contained at least two scrolls, makes the identification problematic.

The title *Hypothetica* does not help us understand the work. It has been taken variously to mean "Suppositions," based on the hypothetical approach of the opening of fragment 1; "Counsels or Admonitions," based on the use of *hypothēkē* elsewhere in Philo; "Imputations" in the sense of false opinions about Jews; or "Hypothetical Propositions," based on the use of the term in Stoic logic. While certainty is not possible, the last possibility would explain the setting of the work: it was probably intended to prepare Philo for his exchanges with his Alexandrian opponents who were influenced by Stoicism — in particular, Chaeremon (*CPJ* 153). Philo used Stoic logic to deflect the criticisms about Jewish origins.

The work deals with the exodus and settlement in the land (8.6.1-9), the law code (8.7.1-20), and the Essenes (8.11.1-18). The treatment of historical issues plays freely with biblical traditions in an effort to exonerate the Jews and Moses by arguing on the basis of logical probabilities rather than historical evidence. The fivefold epitome of the Law is similar to the summaries in Pseudo-Phocylides and Josephus' *Against Apion* 2.145-219, esp. 190-219. While there have been different explanations for the relationships among these treatments, it is likely that they drew from a common tradition, perhaps from common thematic treatments in Jewish ethical instruction. The treatment of the Essenes is similar to but not identical with Philo's treatment of them in other treatises.

On the Contemplative Life

Philo gave another brief account of the Essenes in *Quod Omnis Probus Liber Sit* 75–91. He also referred to a treatise devoted fully to them in the opening of his treatment of the Therapeutae (*Vita Contemplativa* 1). Since the statement presupposes an entire treatise, it cannot refer to the account in *Probus*. If the account of the Essenes in *Praep. Evang.* 8.11.1-18 is from the second book of the *Hypothetica*, it could refer to it. The alternative is that it refers to a lost treatise.

Philo treated the Essenes and Therapeutae similarly. Aristotle distinguished four eudaemonistic lives, of which the active and contemplative were the most important (*Ethica Nicomachea* 1.5.1-8). Stoics picked up Diogenes Laertius 7.92, while others added a third, the rational (Diogenes Laertius 7.130). Philo knew this discussion and, like the Stoics, thought that the active and contemplative lives could be united (*Moses* 1.48). In his treatments of the Essenes and Therapeutae, he suggested that the Essenes were an example of the active life and the Therapeutae a model of the contemplative life.

Philo held both groups of Jewish philosophers out to the larger world as "athletes of virtue." The descriptions stand in the same tradition as the depictions of Egyptian priests in Chaeremon (in Porphyry, *De Abstinentia* 4.6-8), the Indian sages in Arrian (*Indica* 11.1-8) and Philostratus (*Vita Apollonii* 3.10-51), the naked Egyptian sages in Philostratus (*Vita Apollonii* 6.6), the Neopythagoreans in Iamblichus (*Vita Pythagorae* 96–100), and the Essenes in Pliny (*Naturalis Historia* 5.73) and Josephus (*J.W.* 2.120-61 and *Ant.* 18.18-22). While Philo may have known the Therapeutae personally, his account is shaped by the concern to present a Jewish counter to these other groups. He discussed the meaning of their name (2–12) and their lifestyle (13–39), and contrasted their symposium with those of the Greeks (40–90).

The most likely time for the composition of this work is in the aftermath of the pogrom. Philo may have written the treatise for the benefit of a Roman audience and could have thought of it as a counter to Chaeremon's presentation of the Egyptian priests.

On the Virtues

The setting for Philo's treatise *On Virtues* is suggested by the subtitle given in most of the manuscripts that refer to it as the fourth book of *Concerning the Virtues.* Some of the same manuscripts refer to the *Embassy to Gaius* as the first book of *Concerning the Virtues.* The relationship between the two is confused in the ancient sources. Eusebius mentioned that Philo had "related what happened to the Jews in the time of Gaius in five books" (*Hist. Eccl.* 2.5.1). He went on to mention the *Embassy* (2.5.6) and without indicating any shift in the work under consideration, the second book, *Concerning the Virtues* (2.6.3). When the bishop gave his catalogue of Philo's works, he said that "he came to Rome in the time of Gaius and in the time of Claudius is said to have read before the full Roman Senate the account that he wrote about Gaius' impiety that he — with tactful irony — entitled *Concerning the Virtues*" (2.18.8).

There are a number of ways to reconstruct the data from Eusebius and the manuscripts. If we follow the lead of the texts themselves, the following is reasonable. Philo opened his work *Against Flaccus* with "the next after Sejanus to continue his plot against the Jews was Flaccus Avillius" (*Flaccus* 1). This suggests that Philo wrote an earlier treatise about Sejanus. Eusebius tells us that this was the second book of *Concerning the Virtues* (*Chronicle;* cf. *Hist. Eccl.* 2.5.6-7). If the bishop is correct, our *Flaccus* would be the third treatise in the series. Philo ended the *Embassy* with a reference to the *Palinode* or *Reversal* (*Embassy* 373). If *Flaccus* and the *Embassy* belong to the same series, the first two volumes have been lost, the third is *Flaccus,* the fourth the *Embassy,* and the fifth has been lost. The association of *On the Contemplative Life* with this series correctly recognizes the social setting of the treatise, but appears to have associated it with *Concerning the Virtues* incorrectly.

Against Flaccus* and *Embassy to Gaius

The two treatises, *Against Flaccus* and the *Embassy to Gaius,* share a common perspective: they demonstrate how God has protected the Jewish people through crises and reversed the fortunes of those who have persecuted them. The structures of the two works make the point unambiguously: *Flaccus* 1–96 relates the pogrom in Alexandria and 97–191 narrates Flaccus' exile and eventual execution; the *Embassy* relates Gaius' insane opposition to the Jews while the missing *Palinode* related his assassination. Eusebius says that Philo read his account of Gaius to the Roman Senate (*Hist. Eccl.* 2.18.8). While this stretches credibility, the works were undoubtedly intended to demonstrate the folly of persecuting the Jews to any outsiders and the protection of God to insiders.

BIBLIOGRAPHY

Hypothetica

J. M. G. BARCLAY 2007, *Against Apion,* Leiden: Brill, 353-61. • K.-W. NIEBUHR 1987, *Gesetz und Paränese: Katechismusartige Weisungsreihen in der frühjüdischen Literatur,* Tübingen: Mohr-Siebeck, 6-72. • G. E. STERLING 1990, "Philo and the Logic of Apologetics: An Analysis of the *Hypothetica,*" *SBLSP,* Atlanta: Scholars Press, 412-30. • G. E. STERLING 2003, "Universalizing the Particular: Natural Law in Second Temple Jewish Ethics," *SPhA* 15: 61-76.

On the Contemplative Life

F. C. CONYBEARE 1895, *Philo about the Contemplative Life,* Oxford: Clarendon; rpt. New York: Garland, 1987. • P. GRAFFIGNA 1992, *Filone d'Alexandria, De vita contemplative,* Genova: Melangelo. • J. E. TAYLOR 2003, *Jewish Women Philosophers of First Century Alexandria: Philo's Therapeutae Reconsidered,* Oxford: Oxford University Press.

Against Flaccus

H. BOX 1939, *Philonis Alexandrini In Flaccum,* Oxford: Oxford University Press. • P. W. VAN DER HORST 2003, *Philo's Flaccus: The First Pogrom,* Leiden: Brill.

Embassy to Gaius

E. M. SMALLWOOD, *Philonis Alexandrini Legatio ad Gaium,* Leiden: Brill, 1961.

GREGORY E. STERLING

Philo, Exposition of the Law

Exposition of the Law is a designation given by scholars to a series of treatises by Philo of Alexandria that can be distinguished on grounds of style and content from his other two series of exegetical works, the *Allegorical Commentary* and *Questions and Answers on Genesis and Exodus.* The works included in the *Exposition* are Philo's treatise *On the Creation of the World (De Opificio Mundi),* his lives of the Israelite patriarchs Abraham and Joseph *(De Abrahamo* and *De Iosepho),* his treatise on the Ten Commandments *(De Decalogo),* and his four-volume commentary *On the Special Laws (De Specialibus Legibus).* Two other treatises function as an epilogue to his treatment of the Mosaic Law: *On the Virtues (De Virtutibus)* and *On Rewards and Punishments (De Praemiis et Poenis).* These works are Philo's most accessible writings, in which he explains the principles of Jewish religion and history. While it has sometimes been assumed that the exoteric character of these writings presupposes a Gentile audience, it is now generally accepted that Philo primarily addressed fellow Jews in the community of Alexandria. Faced with multiple approaches and lively controversies, Philo aimed at expounding his own position. He hoped to gain a wider following and to expand his circle of students, who would ultimately also be able to read his more complicated works.

Stylistically, the *Exposition* clearly differs from Philo's other exegetical works. In his *Allegorical Commentary* and *Questions and Answers on Genesis and Exodus* he quotes Bible verses, offering respectively either an allegorical interpretation or a solution to a particular question. In the *Exposition,* by contrast, Philo freely paraphrases and rearranges biblical material, both in Genesis and in the legal passages of the Pentateuch. It is this style of "rewritten Bible" that makes these writings easily accessible to both ancient and modern readers.

PHILO, EXPOSITION OF THE LAW

In terms of contents, Philo pointed to a significant connection between the creation of the world, the lives of the patriarchs, and the specific laws. He wanted his treatises to be read in that order so that the discussion of the creation directly precedes the *Life of Abraham* (*Abr.* 2–3). This order is important and has been preserved in the Modern Hebrew edition of Philo's works, while the English edition interrupts the flow of the *Exposition,* introducing the *Allegorical Commentary* after the treatise on the creation.

The intended sequence of the *Exposition* rests on the notion that the Mosaic Law reflects the law of nature, which had already been enacted by the patriarchs even before the specific laws were given. Philo stresses that "Moses wished to show initially that the ordinances laid down are not at variance with Nature and, secondly, that it is not hard for those who wish to live in accordance with the established laws, seeing that . . . the forefathers readily and easily lived under them" (*Abr.* 5). The thread running through the whole *Exposition* is thus the coherence of norms attested in nature by the creation of the world, in history by the lives of the patriarchs, and in legislation by the specific laws of the Pentateuch.

The precise scope and place of the *Exposition* within Philo's overall work are still disputed today. It is difficult, for example, to know how Philo's two-volume *Life of Moses* relates to the *Exposition.* The second part in particular deviates significantly from the genres of the rewritten Bible and biography. This treatise, moreover, takes into account a wider, apparently also non-Jewish audience (*Mos.* 1:1-2). For these reasons it is usually not included in the *Exposition,* but E. R. Goodenough's plea to consider it as a "companion piece" has gained wide acceptance (Goodenough 1933; Morris 1987).

The place of the *Exposition* within Philo's overall work also remains a matter of debate. The question usually asked is whether it should be seen as the fruit of his ripe old age or as the precursor to his *Allegorical Commentary.* Formulated thus, the question probably misses the point, as it presupposes that Philo wrote each series *in toto* before approaching the other. The question also implies that the different series reflect an intellectual development on the part of Philo. According to some, he started as an allegorist and subsequently became a more literal expounder of the Torah, while others argue that he started with a more general type of exegesis, becoming more text-oriented and allegorical in his old age. It is, however, far more likely that Philo pursued different aims with different audiences, working alternatively on various kinds of treatises. He wanted each reader to be aware of the other works in the series without, however, intending a complete separation. Indeed, Philo freely introduced allegorical passages in his *Exposition* and *Questions and Answers on Genesis and Exodus,* while both questions-and-answers and literal paraphrases appear as well in his *Allegorical Commentary.*

De Opificio Mundi

The first part of Philo's *Exposition* is his treatise *On the Creation of the World,* which sets the tone for the whole series. Taking the story of creation as a fundamental theological issue (*De Opificio Mundi* 170–72), Philo defines his own understanding over against other prevalent opinions. He fervently rejects a metaphorical reading of the creation, as offered by students of Plato and Aristotle as well as some fellow Jews, who all believed in the eternity of the world (*Opif.* 7–8, 26–28; *De Aeternitate Mundi* 10–17). Insisting on the literal meaning of Genesis as well as Plato's *Timaeus,* Philo stresses that Moses and the Greek philosopher perceived the true nature of the creator God, who is active and transcending the material world, but taking providential care of His creation (*Opif.* 8–22). Most scholars today recognize that, according to Philo, God's creation of the world was not *ex nihilo.* Living in an age when this notion did not yet exist, Philo rather assumed that God's creation consists in actively shaping the preexistent, passive material (*Opif.* 8–12).

Another issue of fundamental importance is discussed in the treatise on the creation: the nature and origin of mankind. Philo is the first known exegete to give serious attention to the crux of the two creation stories: one depicts man created together with woman in the image of God, while the other envisions man as having been created from the earth, but endowed with the divine spirit, while Eve was created secondarily, being molded from Adam's ribs. Philo suggests a reconciliation of these two stories, arguing that they refer to different types of man. While the first story describes, in his view, the ideal type of man, perfectly rational and sexless, the second speaks about the earthly type as a copy of the ideal man (*Opif.* 69–71, 134–35). While it is generally agreed that Philo employs the Platonic categories of ideal and copy, it is still disputed to what extent his exegesis betrays a particularly misogynist perspective. Does his discussion of the ideal type not imply male categories, constructing the archetype of man in masculine terms? Furthermore, does his praise of the earthly Adam, before "woman becomes for him the beginning of blameworthy life" (*Opif.* 51), not indicate a substantial rejection of women and femininity? Winston has countered these interpretations by proposing that we interpret such passages in their proper context. Philo, he stresses, also praises the "fellowship" between husband and wife (*Opif.* 152), while, more generally, his views on women are shared by many ancient writers (Winston 1998).

De Abrahamo and *De Iosepho*

The second part of Philo's *Exposition* is devoted to a biographical treatment of the major Israelite patriarchs. Philo's lives of the patriarchs are no longer fully extant. While the biographies of Abraham and Joseph are still available, those of Jacob and Isaac have unfortunately not survived. In telling the lives of the patriarchs, Philo was intrigued by the connection between a person's character and his actions. He was keen to show how traces of character visible in early infancy subsequently reach maturity and enable the hero to play his destined role in life. In Philo's view, all the forefathers, starting from Enosh, were men "yearning after virtue" (*Abr.* 48). Each did so in his own particular way, Enosh, for example, by setting his hope on the Creator. The exemplary triad, Abraham, Isaac and Jacob, however, were of an exceptionally high order, embodying virtue to such an extent that they practically transcended their human status and represented the pure virtues of teaching, nature, and practice (*Abr.* 54). Joseph, by contrast, is an appendix personifying the politician compromising virtue because of pressing circumstances.

The *Life of Abraham* is famous for its interpretation of Abraham's migration to the land of Canaan (*Abr.* 62–80). Philo offers two complementary perspectives, one literal and the other allegorical. Abraham's migration in the literal sense, Philo explains, was "more of the soul than of the body," because the patriarch showed an exceptional degree of detachment from earthly things, while proving to be wholly devoted to the divine command (*Abr.* 66). This attitude enabled him to take a solitary step, leaving behind all his material attachments. On the allegorical level, Abraham's migration signifies the path of a "virtue-loving soul in its search for the true God" (*Abr.* 69). The different stages of the journey thus represent different stages of spiritual development, Chaldea signifying reliance on visible phenomena and Haran trust in the senses, while the land of Canaan/Israel symbolizes the soul's ascent to God himself. In a passage that has sometimes been identified as descriptive of a mystical experience, Philo explains how God in his love for humankind does not turn away his face "when the soul approaches" (*Abr.* 79). The literal and the allegorical interpretation thus complement each other, one presenting a historical example of the correct spiritual attitude, the other envisioning any soul on its path to God.

De Decalogo, De Specialibus Legibus, De Virtutibus, De Praemiis et Poenis

The third part of Philo's *Exposition* is devoted to a treatment of the Mosaic legislation itself. His discussion is divided into five books, one treating the Decalogue *(De Decalogo),* the other four dealing with the specific laws *(De Specialibus Legibus).* Two additional treatises function as an epilogue: one treating the virtues *(De Virtutibus),* the other the rewards and punishments resulting from observance or nonobservance of the Law *(De Praemiis et Poenis).* Philo argues that the Decalogue introduces the main categories underlying the specific laws, which are accordingly collected under the headings of the Ten Commandments. While in Philo's view all of Mosaic Law is a reflection of the law of nature and thus anchored in the creation of the world, it nevertheless distinguishes the Jews as a nation of spiritual pioneers. Following the Law, Jews implement the most stringent values and set a moral example for the world. The overall marker of Mosaic Law is its call to transcend the material world in the fields of cultic worship, sexuality, and food. Mosaic stringency isolates the Jews, clearly defining their identity vis-à-vis the Egyptians, Persians, Greeks, and Romans.

Philo's approach is decidedly different from that of the rabbis. Unlike them, he neither knows of the Mishnah nor considers the application of Mosaic Law to specific cases. He does not deal with halakic issues or reflect the hypothetical decisions of local Alexandrian law courts, as Goodenough suggested in a controversial argument. Philo's discussion of the Torah instead relies on a philosophical approach similar to that of Saadja Gaon in the Middle Ages. He attempts to categorize the laws and to explain their underlying meaning. He does not distinguish between rational and revealed commandments, as later Jewish philosophers do, but argues for the rationality of all the commandments. In his view, even the food laws were set up in order to teach spiritual values. Pork, for example, was forbidden precisely because it is the most delicious of meats. Abstinence from it is thus a perfect way of inculcating self-restraint.

Today it is widely recognized that both Philo's approach and the details of his discussion differ from the rabbinic discourse in the land of Israel. Ignorant of Hebrew and Aramaic, he was not inspired by contemporary teachers in Jerusalem. As a proud Diaspora Jew living in the cultural metropolis of Alexandria, Philo apparently saw no reason to seek instruction in Jerusalem.

BIBLIOGRAPHY

P. BORGEN 1997, *Philo of Alexandria: An Exegete for His Time,* Leiden: Brill, 65-77. • E. R. GOODENOUGH 1933, "Philo's Exposition of the Law and His De Vita Mosis," *HTR* 25: 109-251. • J. MORRIS 1987, "The Jewish Philosopher Philo," in E. Schürer, *The History of the Jewish People in the Age of Jesus Christ,* rev. and ed. G. Vermes et al., Edinburgh: Clark, 3.1: 840-68. • M. R. NIEHOFF 2001, *Philo on Jewish Identity and Culture,* Tübingen: Mohr-Siebeck. • D. T. RUNIA 2001, *Philo of Alexandria: On the Creation of the Cosmos according to Moses: Introduction, Translation and Commentary,* Leiden: Brill. • D. WINSTON 1998, "Philo and the Rabbis on Sex and Body," *Poetics Today* 19: 41-62.

MAREN R. NIEHOFF

Philo, Philosophical Works

Philo, whose works have been transmitted by early Christianity rather than Judaism, represents a high point in the long-established Greek Jewish tradition of the Diaspora. This tradition, which produced the Greek translation of the Hebrew Bible, connected Greek education and philosophy with Jewish culture, and it adapted many elements of the surrounding culture, perhaps most importantly allegorical interpretation. This technique had been used by Stoics in their interpretation of mythology, but it has been questioned whether or not they influenced Philo directly. Earlier Jewish-Greek authors whose writings are almost entirely lost may also have had significance for the author. Other influences came from contemporary Platonism. Philo perceived the human soul as the central element in the ascent to divine contemplation. He considered the divine revelation manifest in the Scriptures equal to the highest form of philosophy. Another distinctive element of his thought was his perception of the divine Logos and its role in the creation of the world. The Logos, the active principle of God's thought, was at times perceived as the creator of the cosmos and at other times as the mediator between God and the world.

Scholars have debated at length which of the two, the philosophical or the exegetical aspects, were more dominant in Philo's writing. The question as formulated is overly simplified and therefore difficult to answer. Both aspects are important for Philo, but most of his treatises are allegorical commentaries on the Pentateuch, which may be considered the basis of his interests.

Most of Philo's treatises have been preserved, and the philosophical works represent only a small part. The works include *On the Eternity of the World, That Every Good Man Is Free, On Providence 1 and 2,* and *Whether Animals Have Reason.* The two former have been transmitted in the original Greek. The latter three are known through Armenian translations from the sixth century, although fragments of *On Providence* are extant in Greek.

Although Philo's writing shows a strong philosophical orientation in general, the five above-mentioned treatises have been singled out as "philosophical" because of the prevalence of philosophical argumentation and the lack of allegorical interpretation in them; in fact, they hardly contain any direct references to the Scriptures. For this and other reasons these works have often been treated as stepchildren in Philo's oeuvre. To explain the absence of scriptural references and some inconsistencies in Philo's philosophical views, scholars have argued that these treatises could have stemmed from his youth before he was fully immersed in his Jewish heritage. This argument, however, is problematic, contradicts details within Philo's works, and in the end has proven untenable.

In addition, some scholars have tried to dismiss these works as altogether inauthentic. In the last twenty-five years, however, closer attention has been given to the literary structure and the content of these treatises in an effort to explain their idiosyncrasies. New editions and translations have been published — some of the works, such as *About Animals,* had never been translated into a modern language. Scholars have also advanced specific reasons why these works appeared in their particular format and why they should be considered genuine.

The philosophical works are important in their own right, because they show that Philo was well acquainted with certain aspects of Hellenistic philosophy. They also provide valuable insight into the contemporary culture and the study of ancient philosophy in the first century. The five treatises deal with a variety of subjects that were common topics in ancient philosophy of the time.

On the Eternity of the World (De Aeternitate Mundi)

The main proposition in this work is the question of whether the world is destructible or not. The question is also raised whether the world came into existence or was uncreated. The work is typical of its time in linking the notions of coming into existence and ceasing to exist.

The treatise consists of an introduction, followed by a sequence of arguments which present various, often opposing, philosophical views. Philo offers arguments in favor of one or another position, although these may not necessarily reflect his personal views and may even be contrary to his own position. One section of the work is no longer extant, and there has been much speculation about what it would have contained. The most probable solution seems to be that the missing part reflected Philo's own position on the question of the indestructibility of the world.

After the introduction, in which he defines the meanings of the words for "world" and "destruction," Philo lists three main positions among philosophical schools: (1) The cosmos (or a plurality of worlds) is created and destructible, a view ascribed to Democritus, Epicurus, and most of the Stoics. Philo adds that the Stoics accept God as cause of the genesis of the world but not of its destruction; this is supposedly an editorial comment on Philo's part. (2) The cosmos is uncreated and indestructible — the Aristotelian position and that of certain Pythagoreans. Philo agrees with Aristotle on the perfection of the cosmos and its indestructibility, but disagrees that the world is uncreated. (3) The cosmos is created and indestructible — a view attributed to Plato and possibly Hesiod before him. This view also agrees with the biblical narrative in the book of Genesis. Philo maintains that long before Hesiod Moses was the source of inspiration for this doctrine and gives a (rare) biblical reference to the book of Genesis.

The doxographic sequence above shows that Philo envisioned an ascending order that finds its high point in Moses as the ultimate guarantee of the doctrine that the cosmos is created and indestructible. In his other major work, *On the Creation of the World* (7-12), Philo gives clarifications to the doxography outlined here. Together with most Platonists and against the Aristotelians, he accepts the view that the world is created. In theory it should come to an end, but it is preserved from destruction by the will and providence of the Creator. It remains unclear whether Philo thought that God created matter, out of which the world is fashioned, or that matter preceded the creation of the world. Moreover, Philo did not perceive creation as a creation in time, since time only originated with the world, but rather as depending for its existence on an external cause.

The exposition sets the stage for the remainder of the work, in which Philo continues at length arguing the three positions outlined above.

That Every Good Man Is Free (Quod Omnis Probus Liber Sit)

That Every Good Man Is Free is about the freedom of the just according to Stoic principles. At the beginning of the treatise Philo informs his readers that it is the sequel of another work (now lost), entitled *That Every Bad Person Is a Slave.* Philo develops the Stoic paradox that only the wise person is free. The paradox states that things generally considered desirable belong only to the virtuous. The premise of this thought is that the only good is that which is morally good.

After a general introduction and praise of wisdom and the soul, Philo comes to his main point: that of true freedom. True freedom, like true sovereignty, means following God and freeing oneself from passions and desires. It can be postulated that in his previous work on slavery Philo would have argued the converse: that being a slave is being dependent on passions and desires. The idea is that wise persons alone master their emotions, desires, and fears. After some digressions on contempt of death, bravery, and obedience, Philo gives examples of free persons who, like Moses, are happy and friends of God. They are free because of their voluntary actions and because they cannot be compelled to do wrong. They also treat indifferent things with indifference; this refers to the Stoic concept of *adiaphora:* things that do not carry any positive or negative value in moral terms.

The remainder of the treatise deals with stories of people who are exemplary for the subject. Philo refers to traditional tales, such as of Calanos, Anaxarchos, Zeno, and Diogenes. He also includes a lengthy account of the Essenes; their ascetic way of life earns them a place in this treatise. He accentuates their innocence, rejection of slave labor, study of the law, devotion to God and neighbors, sharing of goods, and providing help for the sick and the poor. This account, which is quoted by the church historian Eusebius, is one of our few sources of knowledge about the Essenes.

On Providence 1 and 2 (De Providentia)

These treatises on divine providence are stylized dialogues between Philo and his apostate nephew Alexander. The works are transmitted in an Armenian translation; a substantial part of the second book is extant in Greek. The first book offers an extensive account of the workings of God's providence. Alexander has doubts about the concept and brings in multiple objections, while Philo believes that it governs the world. Like other Platonists of his time, Philo tries to find a balance between an absolute free will and inflexible determinism. He maintains the autonomy of the will as a basis for ethical judgment, while at the same time preserving the doctrine of divine providence.

The second book continues the discussion. Starting with the problem of retribution, Alexander argues that wicked people often fare well and good people fare badly. Polycrates and Socrates are cases in point for Alexander. Philo responds that God does not necessarily punish evil immediately and that the wicked are never really happy. External goods have no value in the presence of God, and the true philosopher despises them. Sages defy poverty and ill-treatment — Socrates, Zeno, and Anaxarchos being the examples.

Other arguments deal with the theory of creation and the order of the world, all in the context of providence. The problem of evil in nature is part of the dialogue as well; natural nuisances, such as bad weather and savage animals, or disasters, such as earthquakes and floods, are discussed. Philo stresses the value of temperance, which is not dependent on natural causes but on moral behavior.

Whether Animals Have Reason (De Animalibus)

Like the previous treatises, this work has been transmitted in Armenian. It again reflects a discourse between Alexander and Philo, but a third person is also involved, Lysimachus, a nephew of Alexander. In the first part of the work Alexander argues for the rationality of animals; the second part carries Philo's refutation. It again shows that Philo is heavily indebted to Stoic and Platonic points of view. He draws on Stoicism to prove the distance between humans and animals. An elaborate scheme of all existence lies in the background: divisions exist between corporeal and incorporeal, animate and inanimate, rational and irrational, mortals and divine beings, and ultimately between male and female. The discourse is, however, less about animals than about humans in their relationship with other beings. The divide between man and all other beings is the ability to reason. In his closing arguments Philo maintains that it would be unjust to grant equality to unequal entities. Philo considers it an insult to treat those endowed with reason in the same way as irrational creatures. In spite of Philo's preoccupation with human superiority, the treatise provides a wealth of information for zoological and botanical studies of early imperial times.

Bibliography

R. Arnaldez and J. Pouilloux 1969, *Philon d'Alexandrie, De aeternitate mundi,* Paris: Cerf. • M. Baldassari 1993, "Le opere filosofiche di Filone Alessandrino," in *La filosofia antica,* vol. 2, Como: Luca della Robbia, 173-202. • J. M. Dillon 1996, *The Middle Platonists, 80 B.C. to A.D. 220,* rev. ed., Ithaca, N.Y.: Cornell University Press. • F. Frick 1999, *Divine Providence in Philo of Alexandria,* Tübingen: Mohr-Siebeck. • M. Hadas-Lebel 1973, *Philon d'Alexandrie, De providentia I et II,* Paris: Cerf. • M. Petit 1974, *Philon d'Alexandrie, Quod omnis probus liber sit,* Paris: Cerf. • G. Reale 1990, *A History of Ancient Philosophy,* vol. 4, Albany: State University of New York Press. • D. T. Runia 1981, "Philo's De Aeternitate Mundi: The Problem of Its Interpretation," *Vigiliae Christianae* 35: 105-51. • D. T. Runia 1996, "Philon von Alexandrien," in *Philosophie der Antike,* vol. 2, ed. F. Ricken, Stuttgart: Kohlhammer, 128-45. • A. Terian 1981, *Philonis Alexandrini, De Animalibus,* Chico, Calif.: Scholars Press. • D. Winston 1996, "Hellenistic Jewish Philosophy," in *History of Jewish Philosophy,* ed. D. H. Frank and O. Leaman, London: Routledge, 38-61.

Annewies van den Hoek

Philo, Questions and Answers on Genesis and Exodus

The *Questions and Answers on Genesis and Exodus* (Greek title, *Zētēmata kai lyseis eis tēn Genesin kai tēn Exodon;* Latin title, *Quaestiones et Solutiones in Genesin et Exodum*) is the third and least well-known of Philo of Alexandria's great scriptural commentaries. It is an exposition of the first two books of the Pentateuch but does not treat them in their entirety. It consists of lengthy series of questions that stay close to the biblical

PHILO, QUESTIONS AND ANSWERS

text, the answers to which form a kind of running commentary.

Text and Versions

The original work, written in Greek, consisted of six books for Genesis and five (or perhaps six) books for Exodus. The part on Exodus is recorded as such in the catalogue of Eusebius, but less than a century later only two of the five books had survived. The original Greek text of the work has been lost. For our knowledge of the surviving work, we are chiefly dependent on an Armenian translation made in sixth-century Byzantium.

Because the Armenian translators of the so-called Hellenizing school made a word-for-word translation, their version can give us a reasonably accurate impression of the original. In the edition of the Armenian text (with Latin translation) by Aucher (1826) and in modern translations, the *Questions on Genesis* has four books, but the fourth book contains books 4, 5, and 6 of the original division. There is also a rather idiosyncratic Latin translation of book 6 dating to the late fourth century, which contains twelve sections missing in the Armenian version. Numerous fragments of the original Greek have been preserved in patristic excerpt collections such as the *Catenae* and the *Florilegia*. These have been expertly collected and edited by Petit (1978), who also edited the Latin translation (1973). Two short extracts have been preserved in Greek manuscripts (*QG* 2.1-7; *QE* 2.62-68).

Contents

Genesis is dealt with as follows: book 1 treats Gen. 2:4–6:13 (100 questions); book 2, Gen. 6:14–10:9 (82); book 3, Gen. 15:7–17:27 (62); book 4 (Armenian 4.1-70), Gen. 18:1–22:18 (70); book 5 (Armenian 4.71-153), Gen. 23:1–25:18 (83); book 6 (Armenian 4.154-245 and Latin additions), Gen. 25:19–28:9 (92 + 12). The remains of the Exodus commentary are: book 1 on Exod. 12:2-23 (23 questions); book 2 on Exod. 20:25–28:34 (124 questions). Marcus (1953), followed by Royse (1976-1977), has noted the remarkable parallels between the scriptural coverage of Philo's books and the weekly readings *(parašiyyôt)* of the Pentateuch in the annual cycle of the Babylonian synagogue. This suggests similar readings in the Alexandrian synagogues; that is, Philo's work may have covered six weekly readings for Genesis and five (or six) for Exodus. There is no evidence that the work extended to the remaining books of the Pentateuch.

Method of Interpretation

The method used by Philo in this work is straightforward and fairly uniform. A lengthy series of questions that closely follow the biblical text is followed by answers. Most questions begin with "why" *(dia ti)* or "what" *(ti estin)* and often incorporate direct quotes from the text. The length of the answers varies considerably, ranging from a few lines to more than five pages. Both literal and allegorical exegesis are practiced, with the exegete often explicitly moving from the literal *(to rhēton)* to the deeper sense *(to pros dianoian)*, for example in *QG* 3.50; *QE* 2.21. There is a greater focus on the exposition of numbers through arithmology than elsewhere in Philo.

Exegetical Origins, Affinities, and Context

The origin of the exegetical method employed in the *Questions and Answers* can partly be sought in Greek literature (*Peripatos*, Alexandrian Homeric exegesis), but there is no precedent for the practice of making a running commentary.

There are considerable parallels between the *Questions and Answers* and Philo's *Allegorical Commentary*. Scholars have pointed out that the questions posed in the former work often form the nucleus of the more sophisticated allegorical work. It has been argued that the work can be seen as a kind of prolegomenon to the other commentary (Sterling 1991), but this view may not do justice to the role of the literal exposition. It also has been argued that it precedes the other commentaries chronologically (Terian 1991), but this cannot be considered certain.

When describing the meetings of the community of Therapeutae, Philo tells us that their leader asks a question of Scripture or resolves a problem posed by another (*On the Contemplative Life* 75). The correspondence of the commentary's form with the *parašiyyôt* may also suggest a synagogal context. Nevertheless, given the scholastic form of the work, its social and intellectual context is more likely to have been a school of exegesis or a circle of exegetes. This does not preclude its use as a fund of material for preaching and exposition in the synagogue.

Influence

The legacy of the work is to be sought in early Christian rather than Jewish exegesis. Its contents were used by church fathers such as Origen, Didymus, Ambrose, and Augustine. Christians also took over the form of the question and answer, but they did not use it for running commentaries. Because of the poor transmission of the text, the *Questions and Answers* have been studied less intensively than other Philonic works. Much further research needs to be carried out on both form and content.

Bibliography

Armenian Text and Latin Translation

J. B. Aucher 1826, *Philonis Judaei Paralipomena Armena, Libri Videlicet Quatuor in Genesin, Libri Duo in Exodum*, Venice: Typis Coenobii PP. Aremnorum in Insula S. Lazari.

English Translation

R. Marcus 1953, *Philo of Alexandria*, Suppl. vols. 1 and 2, LCL, Cambridge, Mass.: Harvard University Press.

French Translation

C. Mercier and A. Terian 1979-1992, *Quaestiones in Genesin* and *Quaestiones in Exodum*, 2 vols., Les Œuvres de Philon d'Alexandrie, Paris: Cerf.

Greek Fragments

F. Petit 1978, *Quaestiones Fragmenta Graeca*, Les Œuvres de

Philon d'Alexandrie, Paris: Cerf. • J. PARAMELLE 1984, *Philon d'Alexandrie: Questions sur la Genèse II 1–7: Texte grec, version arménienne, parallèles latins,* Geneva: Patrick Cramer.

Ancient Latin Translation

F. PETIT 1973, *L'ancienne version latine des Questions sur la Genèse de Philon d'Alexandrie,* Berlin: Akademie Verlag.

Studies

J. R. ROYSE 1976-1977, "The Original Structure of Philo's *Quaestiones," Studia Philonica* 4: 41-78. • D. M. HAY, ED. 1991, *Both Literal and Allegorical: Studies in Philo of Alexandria's Questions and Answers on Genesis and Exodus,* Atlanta: Scholars Press. • G. E. STERLING 1991, "Philo's *Quaestiones:* Prolegomena or Afterthought?" in *Both Literal and Allegorical: Studies in Philo of Alexandria's Questions and Answers on Genesis and Exodus,* ed. D. M. Hay, Atlanta: Scholars Press, 99-123. • A. TERIAN 1991, "The Priority of the *Quaestiones* among Philo's Exegetical Commentaries," in *Both Literal and Allegorical: Studies in Philo of Alexandria's Questions and Answers on Genesis and Exodus,* ed. D. M. Hay, Atlanta: Scholars Press, 29-46.

DAVID T. RUNIA

Philo the Epic Poet

Three fragments survive of a Greek epic poem, *Peri Hierosolyma,* "On Jerusalem," by one Philo, of whom nothing else is known. They are cited by Eusebius (*Praep. Evang.* 9.20.1; 9.24.1; 9.37.1-3), from the work of Alexander Polyhistor, a freedman and scholar who flourished in the middle of the first century B.C.E. Philo evidently wrote sometime before Alexander the Great. The three fragments deal with Abraham, Joseph, and the water supply of Jerusalem. The fragment on Joseph is said to be from the fourteenth book. The epic seems to have consisted primarily of a recitation of biblical history. Philo shows his affinity with Hellenistic literature by giving the work a geographical focus. Hellenistic poems were often concerned with the founding of cities. They were also characterized by obscure and recherché language. In Philo's case, many passages are ambiguous and barely intelligible.

The third fragment praises the beauty of the city in summer when the streams are flowing. Joseph is said to have sat on the throne of Egypt "spinning secrets of time in a flood of fate." The most controversial passage is the one on Abraham. While the understanding of almost every phrase has been disputed, the passage on Abraham may be translated as follows:

> Ten thousand times have I heard in the ancient laws how once Abraham abounded in glorious reasonings, in respect of the famous, surpassing, splendid cord of bonds, spells pleasing to God. For when he left the splendid enclosure of the awesome race, the praiseworthy thunderer prevented the burnt offering and made his reputation immortal. Thenceforward the offspring of that awesome-born one obtained much-hymned praise . . . as the strong-handed one, bearing a sharp sword, made ready with firm resolve, and a rustle at one side became stronger — but he placed in his hand the horned ram.

The passage clearly refers to the Binding of Isaac, which is called "a splendid cord of bonds." The most startling item is the phrase *theophilē thelgētra,* "spells pleasing to God." Translators have shied away from the literal sense, and substituted such phrases as "divinely pleasing gestures" or "god-beloved prayers." But *thelgētra* means spells, and binding was often used in magic rituals. It would seem, then, that Philo was construing the binding of Isaac as a ritual wherein the binding itself was pleasing to God. We cannot infer too much about the magical implications of the ritual in view of the author's penchant for bombastic language.

Philo was one of many Jewish Hellenistic authors who tried to present the biblical story in the genres of Greek literature. A certain Ezekiel wrote a tragedy about the exodus. Theodotus wrote an epic poem that seems to be mainly about Shechem. The themes of this Greco-Jewish literature were all derived from the Bible. Whether the authors hoped to reach a Gentile readership is unclear. The incessant recitals of the biblical story in inelegant Greek are most likely to have been of interest to Hellenized Jewish readers. The attempt to express Jewish tradition in Greek literary forms is significant, however. Philo construes the Torah as a collection of "ancient laws" *(thesmoi)* rather than as unique revelation. The attempt to find a common cultural basis with the Greeks is characteristic of Alexandrian Judaism.

BIBLIOGRAPHY

H. W. ATTRIDGE 1985, "Philo the Epic Poet," in *OTP* 2: 781-84. • J. J. COLLINS 2005, "Spells Pleasing to God: The Binding of Isaac in Philo the Epic Poet," in idem, *Jewish Cult and Hellenistic Culture,* Leiden: Brill, 99-111. • C. R. HOLLADAY 1989, *Fragments from Hellenistic Jewish Authors,* vol. 2, *Poets,* Atlanta: Scholars Press, 205-99.

JOHN J. COLLINS

Phocylides, Pseudo-

Pseudonymous Authorship

The *Sentences* of Pseudo-Phocylides comprise a gnomic poem of 230 lines written in dactylic hexameters and in the Ionic dialect. The work was composed pseudonymously under the name of Phocylides, a Greek poet who lived in Miletus in the sixth century B.C.E. The prologue of lines 1-2 identifies Phocylides as "the wisest of men" and claims that he has been inspired by "divine secrets." In spite of its archaizing style, however, this collection of sayings cannot be attributed to the original Phocylides. Its language and meter reflect a later period, it depends upon the Septuagint, and it knows Stoic ethics. It therefore cannot have been written before ca. 200 B.C.E. The authenticity of the poem is no longer defended, and its date of composition is widely held to fall between the first century B.C.E. and the first century C.E., and more precisely before the destruction of the Second Temple in 70 C.E.

Except for a few fragments of gnomic wisdom regularly beginning with the words *Kai tode Phōkylidēs,* the work of Phocylides had already disappeared by the Hellenistic and Roman periods, a fact that facilitated use of his name by a later poet. The attribution to Phocylides could also have been influenced by the negative judgment that the Greek poet may have made on Nineveh (frg. 4D). On the other hand, the consistency of style and versification and the sufficiently coherent structure of the poem show it to be the work of an individual author and not an anonymous anthology to which the name of Phocylides was attached afterward.

Pseudepigraphy was a very frequent phenomenon in Hellenistic Jewish literature and one that bears upon the genre of the work. The authors of sapiential and gnomological texts frequently adopted pseudonyms in order to lend their work authority. By using the name of a Greek poet universally appreciated for his ethical and pedagogical values, the author could also show that the Greeks were inspired by biblical sources and that Mosaic tradition predated the Greeks. For Hellenized Jews, adopting a Greek pseudonym was also a way to affirm their belonging to Hellenistic culture. Accordingly, Pseudo-Phocylides omits any explicit reference to Jewish religious practices or moral principles (Sabbath, circumcision, condemnation of idolatry), preferring rules compatible with moral standards of the pagan world. Finally, by imitating an ancient poet, Pseudo-Phocylides followed a classicism frequent in the Greco-Roman world. Its multicultural nature renders the poem particularly difficult to situate literarily and philosophically.

Literary Genre

Entitled *gnōmai* or *poiēsis ōphelimos* in the main manuscripts, the poem is constituted of short sentences or *gnomae* of one or two verses. It resembles the gnomologies or collections of sentences that flourished from the fourth century B.C.E. under the influence of Cynic and Stoic philosophy. These new schools attached increasing importance to moral philosophy and to the attainment of happiness by the acquisition of wisdom. The gnomologies established an inventory of vices and virtues accessible to all. Their thematic organization, which goes back to Chrysippus (third century B.C.E.), was taken up in the *Anthology* of Stobaeus (fifth century C.E.), the first writer to quote Pseudo-Phocylides. Jews and Christians also adapted them for their own use. Because the sentences of Pseudo-Phocylides are not an anthology, they are best compared to gnomic texts transmitted under the name of an author, real or supposed (e.g., Theognis of Megara, Menander's *Sententiae Monosticae,* Sextus' *Sententiae*), and to the moral instructions of a master to a pupil (Chares' *Iambi,* Isocrates' *Ad Nicoclem,* and *Ad Demonicum,* Pythagoras' *Golden Verses*).

Pseudo-Phocylides is also connected with the genre of didactic poetry (e.g., Hesiod's *Works and Days*). Since gnomologies were frequently used as schoolbooks, helping pupils to learn the rudiments of writing and reading while teaching them the principles of morality, it is unlikely that Pseudo-Phocylides had only a scholarly use. In Near Eastern literature, one can find similar genres in wisdom instructions and sapiential collections of sayings (e.g., the Egyptian *Instructions of Amenemope;* Proverbs; Ben Sira). Finally there are some similarities between Pseudo-Phocylides and the genre of the epitome (Wilson 1994), which underwent a remarkable development in the Greco-Roman era. The epitomes introduced new pupils in philosophical and religious schools to a complex system of beliefs, and they provided more advanced students with practical training in moral action and responsibility.

Sources and Parallels

Pseudo-Phocylides presents himself as a Greek poet whose maxims are in accordance with the Hellenistic Jewish moral tradition. Whereas the Greek character of the work is evident and constant, its Jewishness is more concealed. Pseudo-Phocylides borrows many words or expressions from Homeric epic poetry, from Hesiod's *Works and Days* and *Theogony,* and of course the fragments of the original Phocylides. The verses frequently have parallels in Greek gnomic texts and have also been influenced directly or indirectly by biblical texts. In particular, there are analogies with the book of Proverbs, Ben Sira, and sections of the Pentateuch (Exodus 20–23; Leviticus 17–26; Deut. 5:20-24, 27). Pseudo-Phocylides probably relied on a lost Jewish gnomic source. Lines 175-227 have significant similarities to passages in Philo's *Hypothetica* (7.1-9) and Josephus' *Against Apion* (2.190-219). A common source probably lies behind Pseudo-Phocylides, the *Didache,* and the *Doctrine of the Twelve Apostles,* a Christian apocryphon of the first century C.E. For a list of parallels, see Derron 1986: 35-54.

Literary Structure

Between a prologue (vv. 1-2) and an epilogue (vv. 228-30) that identifies the author and the aim of the work, Pseudo-Phocylides offers a summary of the Decalogue (vv. 3-8) and deals with the topics of traditional moral practice typically found in gnomologies: justice, welfare, wealth, moderation, envy, death and afterlife, fortune, speech and wisdom, work, marriage, family, and responsibilities toward kin. The sayings are organized in a loose manner, thanks to transitions by catchwords, associations of ideas, and alternating positive and negative precepts. Yet the poem can be divided into two main parts (Wilson 1994); one is organized around the cardinal virtues (vv. 9-131), while the other is arranged according to the relationships in which one lives (vv. 132-227). The four cardinal virtues as they had been fixed since Plato (justice, moderation, courage, and wisdom) are not always explicitly mentioned but are at issue in several verses. On justice, for example, depend pity, charity, and the good use of riches. Courage is not named but expresses itself in the attitude toward death and the afterlife. In the second part, there is a clearer arrangement of sayings, which deal with social life outside the family, the nature and importance of work, and duties toward kin.

Morality and Social Context

Ideologically, Pseudo-Phocylides fits in the context of Cynic-Stoic philosophy in the first century B.C.E. Like other gnomic literature, the work adapts principles belonging to unwritten laws — universal truths that were the first philosophical verities taught in the schools, including respect toward God and one's parents, family duties, duties toward the dead, and the practice of hospitality. It promotes a traditional morality with a pragmatic character, as was common in the Greco-Roman period. Certain sentences have no parallels in Jewish texts (e.g., help for the shipwrecked, v. 25; the irreversibility of the past, vv. 55-56; the versatility of people, vv. 95-96). Other lines include allusions to Jewish tradition, as in the attention given to the poor and the weak, to the practice of almsgiving (vv. 9-41), and to sexual morality (vv. 186-90). Other sentences belong exclusively to Jewish wisdom (e.g., resurrection of the dead, vv. 103-4; prohibition of meat slain by a wild animal, vv. 147-48).

The God of Pseudo-Phocylides is primarily a God of justice and guarantor of the social order. The precepts have as their aim the living of a harmonious life until the end of the age (v. 230), which only the gift of the secrets of God makes possible (v. 2). Belief in a single God does not exclude references to allegory and mythology (Eros, Cypris, Peitho, Eris, Hades). The religious terminology remains unclear, and *theos* coexists with *theoi* (honor moderately the gods, v. 98, emended variously; the resurrected become gods, v. 104).

In vv. 103-15, Pseudo-Phocylides describes only vaguely the role of the body *(sōma)*, the soul *(psychē)*, and the spirit *(pneuma)*. After affirming the resurrection of the body, he locates the soul with the deceased, while the spirit (and not the soul as expected), on loan from God, returns to the air after death.

By mixing Cynic-Stoic and Jewish thought, Pseudo-Phocylides wanted to present moral principles that were useful to both pagans and Jews, with the aim of bringing them together while enabling Jews to maintain their Jewish identity in a Hellenistic environment.

By participating in Gr. *paideia*, Jews possess an instrument of social progress. In addressing his poem to a free man at the head of a patriarchal household, Pseudo-Phocylides guides him on the way of wisdom by showing him the moral obligations tied to his social position. In view of the political and economical importance of the Jewish community of Alexandria, and the similarities with Philo, the author may have lived in Alexandria, a location that may be confirmed by the allusion to the practice of dissecting the human body (v. 102; but perhaps this verse simply alludes to burial in an ossuary). Yet the parallels with the *Didache* suggest that Pseudo-Phocylides may be of Syrian origin.

Influence of the Poem

The sentences of Pseudo-Phocylides were very popular. The poem was adopted early on by Christians, as seen in the insertion of vv. 5-79 into a family of manuscripts of the *Sibylline Oracles* (2.56-148). The interpolator omitted the "polytheistic" verses (vv. 70-75) but added twenty verses sometimes drawn from the *Didache*. The Suda believes our poem issued from the *Sibylline Oracles*. Pseudo-Phocylides was used as a schoolbook throughout the Middle Ages, in both the East and the West. The work has been preserved in 157 manuscripts. The authenticity of the poem was challenged only in 1606 by Joseph Scaliger *(Animadversiones in Chronologia Eusebii)*, who thought that Pseudo-Phocylides was a Christian author.

BIBLIOGRAPHY

J. J. COLLINS 1997, *Jewish Wisdom in the Hellenistic Age*, Louisville: Westminster John Knox, 158-77. • J. J. COLLINS 2005, *Jewish Cult and Hellenistic Culture*, Leiden: Brill, 128-42. • A.-M. DENIS 2000, *Introduction à la littérature religieuse judéo-hellénistique*, vol. 2, Turnhout: Brepols, 1037-61. • P. DERRON 1986, *Pseudo-Phocylide: Sentences*, Paris: Belles Lettres. • P. W. VAN DER HORST 1978, *The Sentences of Pseudo-Phocylides*, Leiden: Brill. • P. W. VAN DER HORST 1988, "Pseudo-Phocylides Revisited," *JSP* 3: 3-30. • J. THOMAS 1992, *Der jüdische Phokylides*, Göttingen: Vandenhoeck & Ruprecht. • W. T. WILSON 1994, *The Mysteries of Righteousness*, Tübingen: Mohr-Siebeck. • W. T. WILSON 2005, *The Sentences of Pseudo-Phocylides*, Berlin: de Gruyter.

PASCALE DERRON

Phoenicia

"Phoenicia" (Gr. *Phoinikē*) comprises roughly the northern half of the Levantine coast (Canaan), as distinct from the southern coastal plain extending from Carmel to Gaza (Palestine/Philistia). Pressed against the Mediterranean by the slopes of Mt. Lebanon, a string of maritime city-states has occupied this narrow strip of land since the Bronze Age. The two most important Phoenician cities were Sidon and Tyre. Other significant centers included Aradus (Arwad), Tripolis, Byblos, and Berytus (modern Beirut). The ancient port town of Akko was the southernmost city of the Phoenician heartland from the sixth through fourth centuries B.C.E., but may have lost its Phoenician character by the time of its refounding as Ptolemais in the early third century B.C.E.

In fact, the extent to which any of these cities or their hinterlands retained identifiably "Phoenician" features — ethnic, religious, linguistic — into the Greco-Roman period has yet to be adequately elucidated. Coins minted in the second century B.C.E. exalt Berytus as "Metropolis of Canaan," signaling continuity with an indigenous past. On the other hand, virtually no writing in Phoenician script has materialized from the first century C.E., raising the possibility that the language was no longer spoken by that time. Hellenistic- and Roman-era temples abound on both sides of the Lebanon range, some deliberately located at pre-Hellenic cult sites; yet it is not always clear whether the devotees conceptualized their deities in Semitic, Greek, or Roman terms. The ambiguities of Phoenician identity are aptly captured in the Gospel tradition of Jesus' sojourn in the region of Tyre; the evangelists alternately label the woman he encounters there as "a Greek, a

Syro-Phoenician by birth" (Mark 7:26) and "a Canaanite" (Matt. 15:22).

The cities of Phoenicia were important for three reasons. Their possession of the principal harbors of the Levant, along with landward routes connecting them to the interior, enabled the Phoenicians to dominate long-distance trade with the Mediterranean, which they amplified by founding colonies as far west as North Africa and Spain. Their proximity to Mt. Lebanon gave them direct access to its fabled cedar forests (along with substantial iron mines); the coast yielded murex and vitreous sand, essential components for Phoenicia's lucrative textile and glass exports. But until the advent of Roman rule, the most influential determinant of the region's fortunes was its strategic value to Egyptian- and Mesopotamian-based imperial powers: control of the Levant conferred security from invasion as well as the ability to invade. Taken together, these factors made Phoenicia a coveted prize for conquerors.

From Cyrus to Augustus

In the sixth century B.C.E., the lands of the Near East were brought, for the first time, under the sway of a single regime: the Achaemenids of Persia. A key ingredient to their success was the creation of an expeditionary fleet capable not only of maintaining a firm grip on the Nile Valley, but also of projecting naval power into the Aegean. Phoenicia (together with Cilicia and Cyprus) facilitated this, supplying timber and craftsmen to build the Persian fleet and rowers to man it. In return for these invaluable services, the Achaemenids not only allowed Phoenician monarchs to retain their local sovereignty, but expanded their territories as well.

A mid-fourth-century-B.C.E. navigation manual documents a chain of Palestinian harbors, controlled by Tyre or Sidon, extending as far south as Ashkelon. A famous (though undated) inscription on the sarcophagus of King Eshmunazzar of Sidon specifies that the Persian suzerain "gave us Dor and Joppa, the mighty grain lands which are in the Plain of Sharon." This region has yielded varying concentrations of Phoenician artifacts and architectural elements dating to the Persian period, but whether these remains point to actual colonization (as distinct from a mere administrative or commercial presence) is unclear.

Efforts to dominate the eastern Mediterranean brought the Achaemenids into conflict with mainland Greece as well as secessionist forces in Egypt. As collaborators with Persia, Phoenicians sometimes found themselves the target of these opposing powers. But on one occasion, at least, the city of Sidon made common cause with Egypt against Achaemenid rule and was severely punished. Tyre met with a similar fate as a consequence of its refusal to abandon the Persian side during Alexander the Great's invasion in 332 B.C.E. Yet both cities reemerged — with the assistance of the conqueror — soon after these debacles. The Phoenicians' acumen as merchants and mariners made them too valuable an asset to completely subjugate or permanently eliminate.

Territorial fallout from the wars of Alexander's successors left Phoenicia (with the exception of Aradus) in the hands of the Ptolemaic dynasty, transforming the littoral into a garrisoned frontier. The Ptolemaic period (ca. 287-198 B.C.E.) witnessed a gradual replacement of the Phoenician monarchies by Greek-style civic institutions (councils, assemblies, magistrates), though the office of "judge" *(shofet?)* may hearken back to earlier Semitic traditions of governance. The advent of Seleucid rule at the beginning of the second century B.C.E. brought a respite to the Levantine coast, but deterioration of Seleucid control during the latter half of the same century triggered a vicious competition for territory between the Phoenician cities and their neighbors. Roman intervention temporarily curtailed this, only to plunge the region anew into political chaos during its own destructive civil wars (49-31 B.C.E.).

The Mediterranean having become a pacified "Roman lake" under the Julio-Claudians, Phoenicia's strategic importance shifted from the naval to the terrestrial sphere. With Rome's legionary might concentrated in northern Syria, the road running along the Phoenician coast became instrumental for military access to Palestine. To cement loyalties, the emperor Augustus planted a Roman colony at Berytus (in 30 or 15 B.C.E.). Half a century and more later (ca. 52-54 C.E.), the emperor Claudius repeated this move at the former Phoenician city of Ptolemais. Auxiliaries from both colonies would take part in the suppression of the Judean Revolt of 66-70 C.E.

Phoenicia and Judea

Lebanese timber is a recurrent motif in accounts of the Second Temple. The book of Ezra claims that both Tyrians and Sidonians, by imperial decree, provided cedar for the Temple's construction (Ezra 3:7). A century later, Nehemiah petitions the custodian of Lebanon's forests (evidently claimed by the Achaemenids as a royal domain) to supply timber "to make beams for the gates of the temple fortress, and for the wall of the city, and for the house that I shall occupy" (Neh. 2:8). At the dawn of Seleucid dominion over Palestine, Antiochus III placed himself in continuity with this tradition of imperial beneficence by exempting Phoenician timber designated for the Temple's repair from transit tolls (*Ant.* 12.141). On the eve of the Temple's destruction, the Herodian king Agrippa II footed a sizable bill for the felling and transportation of such beams to Jerusalem (*J.W.* 5.36).

The Phoenician contribution to the Second Temple went beyond matters of construction and repair. At some point — most likely during the late second or early first century B.C.E., after the Seleucids had ceased to subsidize the Temple's expenses — the Tyrian half-shekel came to serve as the exclusive medium for the annual Temple tax. This unique silver coinage was minted by Tyre from 126 B.C.E. until the late 50s C.E., when it was supplanted by a Roman provincial issue from Antioch. Lack of written testimony breeds speculation as to how and why the Tyrian standard was adopted by the Jews for this purpose, but the custom clearly had broad economic consequences for both regions. Tyrian silver is among the most frequently attested coin types found in late Hellenistic and early Roman Palestine, notably along the Tyrian frontier of Upper Galilee.

Judea itself was not contiguous with Phoenicia. At the beginning of the Persian period, landlocked Yehud bordered the Palestinian domains of Tyre and Sidon; but by the time the Hasmoneans reached the coast at Joppa, that zone of Phoenician control had long since receded. The situation was otherwise in the Galilee. Jews dwelt there in substantial numbers prior to Hasmonean penetration of the region. The Maccabean Revolt elicited a hostile reaction from the Galilean Jews' Phoenician neighbors (1 Macc. 5:15). This might suggest that the later conquests of John Hyrcanus I and his sons exacerbated border tensions. However, the fact that the Itureans — themselves predators of Phoenician territory — were among the Hasmoneans' targets (*Ant.* 13.318-19) may have mitigated apprehensions.

The only portion of Tyre's Galilean border explicitly attested in Second Temple sources is the village of Qedesh (Kedasa, Kydissa), which appears to have functioned successively as a Persian and Seleucid administrative center. Distribution of Phoenician semifine pottery at Qedesh and other sites in the Hula Valley (Ulatha) indicates the presence of a self-consciously Tyrian population. A similar demographic situation seems to have existed in Hellenistic times on the plain of Ptolemais adjacent to Mt. Carmel (cf. Josephus' cryptic remark that Carmel still belonged to Tyre in his day; *J.W.* 3.35). Josephus also comments that the Galilean village of Kabul (Chabulon), bordering Ptolemais' territory, possessed houses "built like those in Tyre and Sidon and Berytus" (*J.W.* 2.504). Hellenization of an urban center did not necessarily entail the erasure of Phoenician elements in its vicinity.

Evidence for outright warfare between Phoenicians and Jews is confined to periods of more general upheaval. During Rome's civil war, Julius Caesar issued a series of decrees transferring to John Hyrcanus II unspecified agricultural domains formerly tributary to "the kings of Syria and Phoenicia" (*Ant.* 14.209). A desire to reclaim these usufructs may form part of the background to a Tyrian invasion of Galilee five years later, when the Levant had fallen into the hands of Caesar's assassins. Marion, the military strongman at Tyre, briefly captured and garrisoned three fortresses in Galilee before being expelled by Jewish forces (*Ant.* 14.208). In fact, the engagement was not so decisive, for in the very next year the triumvir Marc Antony dispatched an edict to the Tyrians, commanding them to relinquish Hyrcanus' territories (*Ant.* 14.314-18). Belligerence also flared up in 66 B.C.E. at Qedesh (*J.W.* 2.458) and at Gush Halav (Gischala) in Upper Galilee. Josephus' nemesis, John b. Levi, fortified the latter and gathered an armed following that appears to have included Phoenicians as well as Jews and other Syrians (*J.W.* 2.588, 625; *Vita* 372). A joint raid launched against Gush Halav by Tyre, Gadara, and Aganaea (*Vita* 44) confirms that John's band posed a threat to more than one community — not just Phoenicians.

Violence in Judean-Phoenician relations was the exception rather than the rule; nevertheless, it is the occasion of our most direct evidence for Jewish settlement in Phoenicia. At the outbreak of the First Revolt, Jews suffered attacks in cities throughout the Levant. From Josephus' body count we learn of extensive Jewish communities at Tyre and Sidon (the latter spared its Jewish inhabitants; *J.W.* 2.477-79). Josephus' account of the Gush Halav episode may also imply that Jews lived in rural villages across the Tyrian border (*J.W.* 2.588). The antiquity of these communities is unknown. The claim of the Hellenistic Jewish author writing in the name of Hecataeus of Abdera — that a mass Jewish exodus to the Phoenician coast took place during the late fourth-century wars of the Diadochoi (*Ag. Ap.* 1.94) — is implausible and may safely be discounted. Explicit allusions to Jews living in Phoenician cities occur only in first-century-C.E. sources (Philo, *Legatio ad Gaium* 281; Acts 11:19; 15:3; 21:1-7; 27:3).

Population movements went both ways. Already in Nehemiah's day, Tyrian merchants possessed a trading station in Jerusalem (Neh. 13:16). Inscriptions dating to the second century B.C.E. attest Sidonian communities on the coast at Jamnia (*SEG* 41.1556) and inland at Idumean Mareshah (*OGIS* 593). A similar enclave resided at Shechem in Samaria (*Ant.* 12.257-64). All these communities appear to have been sedentary. Itinerant Phoenician entrepreneurs could also be found in the train of Hellenistic armies, profiting from the trade in war captives (Joel 3:4-8; cf. 1 Macc. 3:41; 4.23; *Ant.* 14.321).

Greco-Roman culture and building supplied a further medium for interaction. In the second century B.C.E., the Jewish high priest Jason sent a delegation with a dedicatory gift to the quinquennial games at Tyre (2 Macc. 4:18-20), and we may infer that Phoenicians likewise took part in Herod the Great's Augustan games (*Ant.* 15.269). Both Herod and his descendants engaged in lavish architectural patronage of the Phoenician coast (*J.W.* 1.422; *Ant.* 19.335-37; 20.211). At times the citizens of Tyre and Sidon relied upon the Herodian dynasty (and thus on Palestine) for grain (Acts 12:20; cf. *Ant.* 15.305-16). The connection between Berytus and the House of Herod was especially close — not accidentally, as support for Rome's first military colony in the Levant was an implicit display of imperial loyalty. The Julio-Claudian emperors rewarded that allegiance with lands adjoining Phoenicia. Agrippa II, who received territory on both sides of Mt. Lebanon itself (*Ant.* 19.275; *J.W.* 3.57; 7.97), embodies the tightly interwoven nature of Judean and Phoenician history.

BIBLIOGRAPHY

D. BARAG 1982-1983, "Tyrian Currency in Galilee," *INJ* 6-7: 7-13. • A. BEN-DAVID 1969, *Jerusalem und Tyros: Ein Beitrag zur palästinensischen Münz- und Wirtschaftsgeschichte 126 A.C.–57 P.C.*, Basel/Tübingen: Kyklos. • A. BERLIN 1997, "From Monarchy to Markets: The Phoenicians in Hellenistic Palestine," *BASOR* 306: 75-88. • D. EDELMAN 2006, "Tyrian Trade in Yehud under Artaxerxes I: Real or Fictional? Independent or Crown Endorsed?" in *Judah and the Judeans in the Persian Period*, ed. O. Lipschits and M. Oeming, Winona Lake, Ind.:

Eisenbrauns, 207-46. • J. D. GRAINGER 1991, *Hellenistic Phoenicia,* Oxford: Clarendon. • R. S. HANSON 1980, *Tyrian Influence in the Upper Galilee,* Cambridge: American Schools of Oriental Research. • S. C. HERBERT AND A. M. BERLIN 2003, "A New Administrative Center for Persian and Hellenistic Galilee: Preliminary Report of the University of Michigan/University of Minnesota Excavations at Kedesh," *BASOR* 329: 13-59. • A. KASHER 1990, *Jews and Hellenistic Cities in Eretz-Israel,* Tübingen: Mohr-Siebeck. • F. MILLAR 1993, *The Roman Near East: 31 BC–AD 337,* Cambridge: Harvard University Press. • E. STERN 2000, *Dor: Ruler of the Seas,* Jerusalem: Israel Exploration Society. CHRIS SEEMAN

Phoenix

The phoenix is a fabulous bird of the sun that features widely in the mythology of Greco-Roman, Jewish, and Christian antiquity. It makes an appearance in three early Jewish texts: the drama on the Exodus by Ezekiel the Tragedian, *3 Baruch,* and *2 Enoch.*

Greco-Roman Sources

In the diverse classical formulations of the myth, beginning with Herodotus, the phoenix has a fantastically long life span of 500 years (in some sources 1,461 or even 12,954 years). It resembles the eagle in appearance but is much larger and is adorned with brilliantly colored plumage. The myth centered chiefly on the death and rebirth of the phoenix, about which there were two main traditions. According to the first, as its time to die nears, the bird builds a nest of aromatic spices and sets fire to it. A new phoenix then emerges from the ashes of its predecessor. In the second tradition, the phoenix impregnates the nest, the sun ignites both the pyre of spices and the phoenix, and a successor arises. The new phoenix collects the remains of its predecessor in a hollow log or egg of myrrh and deposits them in the temple of the sun in Heliopolis. The new phoenix returns to Ethiopia, its point of origin, and lives on incense until its life runs its course. Ancient astrologers associated the life span of the phoenix with the Great Year, a cycle in which the astral bodies complete their movements and return to their original positions, after which history would repeat itself.

Ezekiel the Tragedian

In the historical drama *Exagōgē* by Ezekiel the Tragedian (second century B.C.E.; in Eusebius, *Praep. Evang.* 9.29.242, 254-69), the bird's appearance in the story of the exodus is occasioned by the mention of the palm trees at Elim; the Greek word *phoinix,* which is used in LXX Exod. 15:27, can mean either "phoenix" or "date palm." Though the bird is not explicitly called the phoenix, the identification is clear enough from the description and from a parallel passage in Pseudo-Eustathius that does name it (*Commentarius in Hexaemeron* [PG 18.729d]). Ezekiel gives an elaborate description of the bird's physical features. The bird's appearance in the drama symbolizes the beginning of a new era in (salvation) history.

3 Baruch

The visionary hero of the Greek *Apocalypse of Baruch (3 Baruch),* a work that most interpreters think originated in the Hellenistic Jewish Diaspora of the late first or early second century C.E., encounters the phoenix in the third heaven (chaps. 6–8). The bird accompanies the sun as "the guardian of the world," protecting humanity from the sun's rays. On its right wing is an inscription in letters of gold: "Neither the earth nor the heaven bear me, but the wings of fire bear me." Neither the bird's life span nor its death and rebirth are described. It is said to eat "the manna of heaven" and drink "the dew of the earth" and to excrete cinnamon in the form of a worm. At the end of each day, the sun's crown must be removed and renewed because its rays are defiled by the unrighteous acts of humanity. For its part, the phoenix is exhausted from checking the rays of the sun, which would otherwise destroy humanity in punishment for their sins.

2 Enoch

The longer recension of *2 Enoch,* another ascent apocalypse usually thought to be of approximately the same date and provenance as *3 Baruch,* departs from classical tradition by featuring not just one but several phoenixes. They appear in the fourth heaven along with companion solar elements called *khalkedras* (brass serpents), carrying heat and dew as they accompany the sun (12:1-3), at whose appearance they burst into song (15:1-4). Later, in both the long and short recensions of *2 Enoch,* mention is made of seven phoenixes and seven cherubim in the sixth heaven (19:6).

Later Jewish and Christian Sources

In rabbinic Jewish tradition, the phoenix has its counterpart in the giant sun bird *ziz* (e.g., *Tg. Ps.* 50:11; *b. Baba Batra* 25a; 73b; *b. Giṭṭin* 31b; *Lev. Rab.* 22:10; *Gen. Rab.* 19:4). This creature is as large as Leviathan, with its ankles resting on earth and its head reaching to the sky. Its wings are so huge that they block the rays of the sun and protect the earth against storms from the south.

The phoenix also resembles the sun bird griffin in the Byzantine Christian *Physiologus.* Like the phoenix in *3 Baruch,* the griffin prevents the sun's rays from destroying the world and has on its wings the words "Light giver, give light to the world" (cf. *3 Bar.* 6:14). When the *Physiologus* describes the phoenix itself, it takes the bird's rising to new life as a sign of Christ's death and resurrection. In this symbolic association it is joined by other early Christian sources such as the Coptic *Sermon on Mary* (fifth-sixth century). Other Christian texts extend the analogy and treat the bird as a symbol of life after death or the eschatological resurrection of believers (e.g., *1 Clement* 24, 25–26; *Didascalia* 40; Lactantius, *De Ave Phoenice; Apostolic Constitutions* 5.7; Tertullian, *Resurrection of the Flesh 13*).

BIBLIOGRAPHY

J. HUBAUX AND M. LEROY 1939, *Le mythe du phénix dans les littératures grecque et latine,* Paris: Droz. • H. JACOBSON

1983, *The Exagoge of Ezekiel,* Cambridge: Cambridge University Press, 157-64. • R. van den Broek 1972, *The Myth of the Phoenix according to Classical and Early Christian Tradition,* Leiden: Brill.

DANIEL C. HARLOW

Phylacteries and Mezuzot

The term "phylacteries" refers to box-like leather capsules containing biblical passages that are worn on one's arm and head. This practice is informed by Deut. 6:8 — "Bind them [i.e., these words] as a sign [*'ôt*] on your hand, and let them be as a symbol [or: frontlet, headband, *ṭōṭâpōt*] on your forehead [literally, "between your eyes"]" — and by the parallel formulation at Deut. 11:18 (cf. Exod. 13:9, 16). Though some scholars have argued that these verses are figurative in nature, archaeological and literary data indicate that headbands were worn by the inhabitants of Syria-Palestine and that various peoples in the ancient Near East did indeed observe practices in which the words (i.e., terms) of the treaty with the sovereign were worn on one's body. The combined evidence of the *Letter of Aristeas* (159), the writings of Philo (*Spec. Leg.* 4.137) and Josephus (*Ant.* 4.213), the exemplars uncovered at Qumran, and rabbinic sources suggests that the practice was reasonably widespread by the (late) Second Temple period. At the same time, some Second Temple and medieval groups, such as Samaritans and Karaites, rejected the literalist approach to the passages from both Exodus and Deuteronomy.

The term "phylactery" is taken from the Greek word *phylaktērion* (Matt. 23:5), meaning "charm, amulet," and has been taken to indicate that some Jews in antiquity attributed apotropaic qualities to the donning of phylacteries. The rabbinic term for phylacteries is *tĕfillîn.* Some exegetes maintain that the lexeme indicates a connection with liturgical practice, inasmuch as the singular form, *tĕfillâ,* also means "prayer." Yet others maintain, on the basis of Aramaic and Syriac usage, that the term simply means "ornament" or "pendant." It is unknown whether Second Temple circles used the biblical term *ṭ(w)ṭpt,* which was variously interpreted (e.g., LXX renders it "immovable"; Philo, "moving"), or some other term to denote this ritual artifact.

The term "mezuzah," whose meaning in biblical Hebrew is simply "doorpost," was applied by rabbinic tradents to pieces of leather containing biblical passages that are placed on the doorpost of homes and gates (*Sifre Deuteronomy* 36). This practice is informed by Deut. 6:9 and 11:20. Similar, though not identical, practices are attested among the Samaritans and may have been observed elsewhere in the ancient Near East (see, e.g., the Arslan Tash incantation).

Phylacteries

Description

Like the Hebrew Bible, Second Temple literary sources attest virtually no prescriptions governing the production and use of phylacteries. Rabbinic sources, by contrast, record numerous traditions. These concern, *inter alia,* the materials used for the capsules and leather slips containing biblical passages, the shape of the capsules, the scope and sequence of biblical passages to be included, the ink, the proper formation of letters, the spacing and paragraphing, the sequence of passages, the number of columns, the language, the correction of mistakes and/or omissions, and the times during which phylacteries are worn. Most of the relevant discussion, however, is found in the Talmudim and in other sources of relatively late provenance. This state of affairs, along with the presence of differing traditions in each of the rabbinic compositions, renders an exact reconstruction of early rabbinic praxis tentative.

Phylactery cases from Qumran. The top two cases (2-3 cm. × 1 cm.) contain four compartments and were worn on the forehead. The bottom case (2.2 cm. × 1.2 cm.) is a single-compartment case and was worn on the arm. *(Courtesy Israel Antiquities Authority)*

The earliest empirical evidence is afforded by the exemplars uncovered at Qumran, the oldest of which are dated to the second century B.C.E. These ancient exemplars may be roughly divided into two categories: those corresponding, more or less, to later rabbinic norms, and those displaying "Qumran-type" features. Other exemplars, whose dates extend up to the early second century C.E., were preserved at Wadi Murabbaʿat, Naḥal Ḥever, and Naḥal Se'elim; these display, in large measure, what would become rabbinic norms.

Shape and Contents

Rabbinic tradition prescribes that tefillin consist of leather capsules resting upon a broader base. While the capsules and bases were not to be circular in shape, it is possible that rectangular tefillin were acceptable (see *m. Meg.* 4:8; *b. Megillah* 42b; *b. Menaḥot* 35a; cf. *y. Meg.* 4:9 [75c]). The arm-phylactery consists of one compartment in which four biblical passages, generally written on a single piece of processed leather (see *Mekhilta de Rabbi Ishmael Pisḥa* 17; cf. *y. Meg.* 1:9 [71c]; *b. Menaḥot* 34b), are placed; the head-phylactery consists of four compartments, each housing a leather strip bearing a different biblical passage. The capsules are bound to one's arm and forehead by means of a leather strap that passes through the base of the phylactery. Rabbinic sources do not prescribe the size of capsules, stipulating only that there be sufficient room on the forehead for two phylacteries (*b. ʿErubin* 95b). The leather employed must be made from the hide of a "pure" (i.e., kosher) animal (see Lev. 11:2-8; Deut. 14:3-8). Rabbinic sources suggest that some "sectarian" groups may have insisted on additional stringencies in this last matter (see *b. Šabbat* 108a; cf. *b. Sop.* 1:2).

The tefillin capsules and writing slips uncovered at Qumran are indeed made of leather from the hide of pure animals. The head-capsules are rectangular in shape, ranging in size from roughly 19-30 mm. wide and 9-25 mm. from front to back. The exemplars consisting of one compartment range from 41 mm. × 11 mm. to roughly 11 mm. × 11 mm. While most of the capsules consist of four compartments, most of the leather slips correspond to rabbinic arm-phylacteries, in which all of the biblical passages appear on one piece of leather. This begs the question of whether the Qumran community employed different designs for the head- and arm-phylacteries — or at least the leather strips contained therein — or rather made them in interchangeable fashion. The uncertainty surrounding this issue is further demonstrated by the head-phylactery studied by Yigael Yadin, in which each of the leather strips contains more than one biblical passage.

The vague formulations of Deut. 6:8 and 11:18 left unclear precisely which passages are to be placed in the phylacteries. Rabbinic sources prescribe the use of four passages, Exod. 13:1-9; 13:10-16; Deut. 6:4-9; and 11:13-21. The rabbinic-type phylacteries from Qumran conform to this norm. The Qumran-type exemplars display an expanded form of this same selection of passages, adding to them the following: Exod. 12:43-51; Deut. 5:1-6:3; 10:12–11:12. Deuteronomy 32, or a part thereof, may also have been employed at Qumran, but this is not certain. Rabbinic sources allude to the illicit practice of making (head-) phylacteries with five *ṭōṭâpōt* (*m. Sanh.* 11:3; *y. Sanh.* 11:3 [30b]). It is not clear, however, whether the Qumran-type phylacteries are the intended referent of these discussions.

In contrast to rabbinic norms, the Qumran-type exemplars employ both sides of the leather for writing. They also display the *plene* (full) orthography associated with Qumran Hebrew as well as textual features differing from those of the proto-Masoretic text. Some of the textual variants are attested in the ancient witnesses, while others are "unaffiliated."

Arrangement of Biblical Passages

Some rabbinic sources indicate that the sequence of passages (and, in the case of head tefillin, the placement of slips in their respective compartments), follows the biblical order, beginning with Exod. 13:1-9 and concluding with Deut. 11:13-21 (*Mekhilta de Rabbi Ishmael Pisḥa* 17–18; *b. Menaḥot* 34b). *B. Menaḥot,* however, cites a variant custom, which tradents then attempt to reconcile with the first tradition. (The resulting harmonization was itself the subject of four post-talmudic interpretations.) This attempt at harmonization notwithstanding, it is possible that the two traditions cited by *b. Menaḥot* point to the existence of competing traditions within rabbinic circles. Indeed, rabbinic tradents also differ regarding the acceptability of phylacteries in which the sequence of passages diverges from that prescribed: one amoraic figure deems some types of divergence acceptable, while other tradents disallow any divergence (*b. Menaḥot* 34b; cf. *Mekhilta de Rabbi Ishmael, Pisḥa* 18). It is noteworthy that while the rabbinic-type ancient exemplars reflect the biblical sequence, the Qumran-type exemplars attest various arrangements. Most of the latter place the Deuteronomic passages, in sequence, first; the Exodus passages, also arranged in order, follow. Other exemplars, however, follow the biblical sequence. At least one set of exemplars, examined by Yadin, reflects an even more loosely defined arrangement. It is not certain what reasoning informs the various arrangements. Finally, Josephus alludes to the inclusion of the Deuteronomic passages, but the scope of these is not specified; he makes no clear allusion to the Exodus passages. The biblical passages in the ancient exemplars are arranged in one column. This practice, which eventually gave way to a competing custom, is likewise attested in rabbinic literature (*y. Meg.* 1:9 [71c]).

Wearing Phylacteries

Second Temple sources are silent regarding the precise time(s) governing the donning of phylacteries. Rabbinic sources attest some, albeit partial, guidelines. Thus, some Amoraim maintained that tefillin are to be worn during the morning recitation of the Shema, while others disagreed (*y. Ber.* 2:2 [4c]; cf. *b. Berakot* 14b). In addition, rabbinic sources attest the view that they need not (or, possibly, ought not) be worn on the Sabbath and biblically mandated festivals (*Mekhilta de Rabbi*

Ishmael, Pisḥa 17; *b. ʿErubin* 96a; *b. Menaḥot* 36b). Finally, rabbinic tradents debated the propriety of wearing tefillin at night (*b. Menaḥot* 36a-b).

The employment in Qumran-type phylacteries of the Decalogue (Deut. 5:6-18) along with the first two paragraphs of the Shema (Deut. 6:4-9; 11:13-:1), passages which appear in other Second Temple and rabbinic sources as part of the daily prayer, bolsters the likelihood of some sort of relationship between phylacteries and early Jewish prayer forms. The possible use of Deuteronomy — which, according to rabbinic tradition, was recited in the Jerusalem Temple (*b. Roš Haššanah* 31a; cf. *y. Meg.* 3:7 [74b]) — in one Qumran phylactery might strengthen the connection between early prayer forms and the practice of donning phylacteries.

Mezuzot

Once again, Second Temple sources do not address the ritual details known from later rabbinic texts, such as the proper placement of mezuzot, the types of structures requiring mezuzot, and the production of the mezuzot themselves. Rabbinic laws governing the production of mezuzot slips bear many similarities to those governing phylacteries, but differ in various respects (see e.g., *m. Menaḥ.* 3:7; *Sifre Deuteronomy* 36; *y. Meg.* 1:9 [71c]; *y. Šab.* 8:3 [11b]; *b. Menaḥot* 29a–36b). Rabbinic sources prescribe the inclusion of Deut. 6:4-9 and 11:13-21, arranged sequentially. The eight extant Qumran-type mezuzot, although fragmentary, reflect use of the same biblical passages found in the Qumran-type phylacteries. It remains unclear what considerations inform the inclusion of the Exodus passages.

Bibliography

G. J. Brooke 2003, "Deuteronomy 5–6 in the Phylacteries from Qumran," in *Emanuel: Studies in Hebrew Bible, Septuagint, and Dead Sea Scrolls in Honor of Emanuel Tov,* ed. S. M. Paul et al., Leiden: Brill, 57-70. • N. G. Cohen 1986, "Philo's Tefillin," in *Proceedings of the Ninth World Congress of Jewish Studies, Division A: The Period of the Bible,* Jerusalem: World Union of Jewish Studies, 199-206. • J. T. Milik 1977, "II. Tefillin, Mezuzot et Targums (4Q218–4Q157)," in *Qumrân Grotte 4.II,* ed. R. de Vaux and J. T. Milik, DJD 6, Oxford: Clarendon, 34-79, 80-85. • M. Morgenstern and M. Segal 2000, "XḤev/SePhylactery," in *Miscellaneous Texts from the Judaean Desert,* ed. J. H. Charlesworth et al., DJD 38, Oxford: Clarendon, 183-91. • D. Rothstein 1992, "From Bible to Murabbaʿat: Studies in the Literary, Textual and Scribal Features of Phylacteries and Mezuzot in Ancient Israel and Early Judaism," Ph.D. dissertation, University of California at Los Angeles. • J. H. Tigay 1978, "On the Term Phylacteries (Matt 23:5)," *HTR* 72: 45-52. • J. H. Tigay 1982, "On the Meaning of *Ṭ(W)ṬPT,*" *JBL* 101: 321-31. • E. Tov 1997, "*Tefillin* of Different Origin from Qumran?" in *A Light for Jacob: Studies in the Bible and the Dead Sea Scrolls in Memory of Jacob Shalom Licht,* ed. Y. Hoffman and F. H. Polak, Jerusalem: Bialik Institute; Tel Aviv: Tel Aviv University, 44-54. • M. Weinfeld 1991, *Deuteronomy 1–11,* New York: Doubleday, 340-54. • Y. Yadin 1969, *Tefillin from Qumran* (XQPhyl 1-4), Jerusalem: Israel Exploration Society and the Shrine of the Book.

David Rothstein

Physiognomies → Horoscopes

Pilgrimage

The practice of traveling to Jerusalem to celebrate important turning points in the Jewish calendar and to commemorate significant historical events in Israelite-Jewish history has its basis in biblical texts dealing with the festivals of Passover *(Pesaḥ),* Weeks *(Shevuʿot),* and Tabernacles *(Sukkot).* Exod. 23:17 states, "Three times in the year all your males shall appear before the Lord God" (cf. Exod. 34:23). Deut. 16:16 expands upon this injunction by mentioning the festivals, the place that God will choose (Jerusalem), and the obligation not to appear empty-handed.

The Practice of Pilgrimage

In the Second Temple period, pilgrimage to Jerusalem was deemed an important act of piety but was evidently not an absolute requirement. Passages in the Mishnah and Talmud indicate that the biblical verses pertaining to pilgrimage were not understood to mean that pilgrimage three times a year was obligatory, but rather that pilgrimage was associated with these three festivals. As the Mishnah puts it, "The following do not have a prescribed measure . . . appearing (before the Lord)" (*m. Pe'ah* 1:1). One might go on pilgrimage annually, as did the parents of Jesus who "went up to the Temple every year at the feast of Passover" (Luke 2:41), or every few years, or perhaps even only once in a lifetime. Rabbinic sources regard as righteous those individuals or families who were strict about making pilgrimage once a year (*Tanḥuma Tesaveh* 13; *Midr. Sam.* 1:7 [Buber 23a] and *Yalqut Shimoni* #77 [to Shilo]). Even those who were not particularly observant occasionally went on pilgrimage, perhaps encouraged by the policy of the rabbis to be lenient during festival times on certain matters related to ritual purity (*m. Ḥag.* 3:7–8; *b. Ḥagigah* 26a). National and religious unity superseded ritual purity at these times. Increased pilgrimage also strengthened the status of Jerusalem. The rabbis, however, were not lenient regarding the requirement not to come "empty-handed"; they stipulated that pilgrims should come "with sacrifices" (*Mekhilta de Kaspa* 2 [p. 333], *b. Hagigah* 7a) and perhaps even "alms" (*Sifre Deut.* #143, p. 196).

Exemptions

According to the Bible, however, only men were obligated to go on pilgrimage, women and children being exempt. The rabbis also exempted deaf-mutes, "imbeciles," those of doubtful sex, slaves, the lame, the blind, those who were sick and aged, and even those who could not walk. Male children were obligated to join their fathers only if they were old enough to ride upon their shoulders, according to one view, or to hold their father's hands, according to another (*m. Ḥag.* 1:1). Other exemptions tended to reduce the number of potential males on pilgrimage. In relation to Passover, Num. 9:1-14 exempts men who have contracted corpse uncleanness and those who are "on a journey afar off." *Mishnah Pesaḥim* 9:2 cites the view of R. Akiba that "a journey afar off" was beyond Modiith, identified with Modiin in the Shephelah east of Lod (ca. 27 km. west of Jerusalem), and the same distance in any direction. This distance was apparently the limit of the direct influence of the Jerusalem Temple on the everyday life of Jews in the surrounding area, including matters of pilgrimage, although pilgrims did come from regions farther away in the land of Israel (e.g., Luke 13:1 on Galileans; Jesus from Galilee in John 2:13; 4:43; 5:1; 7:10; 10:22 [Hanukkah]). The second view cited in the Mishnah is attributed to R. Eliezer and specifies that the distance was "the threshold of the Temple Court." This passage likewise indicates a low number of participants in the Passover festival and consequently on pilgrimage, or at least a lower number than might be imagined and in spite of traditions recording fantastic numbers of pilgrims (*t. Pesaḥ.* 4:3; Josephus, *J.W.* 6.423–25).

Pilgrimage in the Land of Israel

In spite of all the exemptions, however, pilgrimage was apparently not limited in the environs of Jerusalem to individual males. Men of the family could not leave the women, children, and the infirm alone; and in spite of the exemptions, it was usually families and not individuals who went up on pilgrimage together with their friends, neighbors, and relatives. The return trip was also often communal (Luke 2:42). The journey to Jerusalem was accompanied by joyful ritualized singing and dancing (*m. Bik.* 3:2ff.; *Lam. Rab.* 1:16, p. 80).

The pilgrimage of families often left the homes of those going to Jerusalem empty, and their property and crops unprotected and at the mercy of their (non-Jewish) neighbors, particularly since pilgrims would have stayed in Jerusalem or the immediate area throughout the entire week of Passover or Sukkot (*m. Zebaḥ.* 11:7; *b. Zebaḥim* 97a). Rabbinic sources tell of miraculous protection of this property, but these traditions probably reflect exactly the opposite (*y. Pe'ah* 3.17d).

While the major purpose of pilgrimage was to bring sacrifice and participate in the Temple cult, Torah study was also important. Seeing the sages on the Temple Mount engaging in Torah study could inspire the pilgrim to similar study (*Midr. Taʿanit* on Deut. 14:23).

Pilgrimage from the Diaspora

Although pilgrimage was apparently not obligatory upon the Jews of the Diaspora, it was not uncommon, especially in the late Hasmonean and Herodian periods. Philo (*Spec. Leg.* 1.69) mentions "innumerable companies of men from a countless variety of cities, some by land and some by sea, from east and from west, from the north and from the south" who came to the Temple at every festival, seeking refuge and asylum from their busy lives, and desiring to serve God and form new friendships.

Pilgrimage from the Diaspora was connected to annual collections of the half-shekel and other monies sent to the Temple by Diaspora Jews, such as the sums contributed by the Jews of Asia Minor in 88 B.C.E. (Strabo *apud* Josephus, *Ant.* 14.110-18) or the sums that Flaccus would not allow to be sent from Asia (61-62 C.E.) when he served as procurator there (Cicero, *Pro Flacco* 28). Large sums of money were also sent from Babylonia (Josephus, *Ant.* 18.310-17), and pilgrimage increased from there after Herod set up a military colony in Bathyra to pacify Trachonitis and to guard the pilgrimage routes of Babylonian Jews coming from the east (Josephus, *Ant.* 17.26).

To help the pilgrims, the rabbis ruled that pilgrimage routes were to remain clean and not be defiled by Gentile impurity (*t. Ahilot* 18:3). The number of Diaspora pilgrims, especially from Babylonia, increased, a circumstance that led the rabbis to take the return of pilgrims to Babylonia into consideration when determining when to begin prayers for rain; they decided to postpone them until the last pilgrims had reached the Euphrates (*m. Taʿan.* 1:3).

Pilgrims came from most parts of the Diaspora. Acts 2:5 tells us that in Jerusalem there were devout Jews "out of every nation under heaven," and many of these undoubtedly came to Jerusalem first as pilgrims. Some even died there, as we learn from funerary inscriptions (*CIJ* 2:244ff. [#1210-1414]). Acts 6:9 mentions the synagogues of the Freedmen (= Romans), the Cyrenians, and the Alexandrians, and of Jews from Cilicia and Asia. These Diaspora communities also undoubtedly began as pilgrimage communities, and the same is probably true for those foreign Jews buried in Jerusalem during the Second Temple period. Rabbinic literature mentions Alexandrian and Tarsian synagogues in Jerusalem (*t. Meg.* 3:6; *y. Meg.* 3.73d; *b. Megillah* 26a). Some scholars identify the synagogue that housed the "guest-chamber and the rooms and the water installation for lodging for those needing them from abroad" (*CIJ* 2:1404) with the synagogue of the Freedman. Other synagogues probably also maintained hostels for pilgrims from the Diaspora.

Finding Lodging

Although pilgrims sought to spend as much time in Jerusalem and on the Temple Mount as possible, not all slept in Jerusalem. Jesus, after spending the day on the Temple Mount, returned to sleep in the village of Bethany, east of Jerusalem (Matt. 21:17; Mark 11:12). And while rabbinic law preferred that worshipers stay in Jerusalem during the entire pilgrimage festival, it mandated that they stay in the city only on the day of sacrifice, permitting them to sleep at other times in the suburbs (*Sifre Deut.* #134, p. 190). The rich sometimes maintained "pilgrimage houses" in Jerusalem, but this was not possible for most pilgrims. Finding lodging was not always easy since there were no hotels as such. Rabbinic law forbade householders and others from taking rent or fees from pilgrims for lodging, because technically Jerusalem and its houses belonged to "all the tribes." Pilgrims got around that restriction, however, by offering their hosts the skins of sacrifices (*'Abot de Rabbi Nathan* Version A, chap. 35 and pars.; *t. Maʿaś. Š.* 1:12).

The Temple Mount

Upon arrival in Jerusalem, groups of pilgrims, if they were ritually pure (ideally purification was to take place a week before their arrival) would have gone straight up to the Temple Mount (*m. Bik.* 3:4). They would probably have entered from the southern gates, proceeding northward through the eastern courts and circled around the Temple, exiting from the southern gates from a westerly direction (*m. Mid.* 2:2). One of the high points of the visit to the Temple complex was to bow before the gates of the Temple courtyard or Azarah (*m. Mid.* 2:3). The pilgrims probably returned to the mount as often as possible to see the priests officiate in the daily sacrifice or Tamid service and to listen to songs of the Levites (Ben Sira 20:15-18; *m. Mid.* 5:4). Although the Temple was destroyed in 70 C.E., going on pilgrimage to Jerusalem, visiting the Temple Mount, and circling its walls continued intermittently for hundreds of years afterward.

BIBLIOGRAPHY

M. FRIEDMAN 1996, "Jewish Pilgrimage after the Destruction of the Second Temple," in *City of the Great King: Jerusalem from David to the Present,* ed. N. Rosovsky, Cambridge Harvard University Press, 136-46. • M. GOODMAN 1999, "The Pilgrimage Economy of Jerusalem in the Second Temple Period," in *Jerusalem: Its Sanctity and Centrality to Judaism, Christianity, and Islam,* ed. L. I. Levine, New York: Continuum, 69-76. • S. SAFRAI 1965, *Pilgrimage at the Time of the Second Temple,* Tel-Aviv: Am Hassefer (in Hebrew). • S. SAFRAI 1981, *Die Wallfahrt im Zeitalter des Zweiten Tempels,* Neukirchen-Vluyn: Neukirchener Verlag. • S. SAFRAI 1996, *In Times of Temple and Mishnah: Studies in Jewish History,* Jerusalem: Magnes, 1:43-102 (in Hebrew). • S. SAFRAI 2006, "Early Testimonies in the New Testament of Laws and Practices Relating to Pilgrimage and Passover," in *Jesus' Last Week: Jerusalem Studies in the Synoptic Gospels,* vol. 1, ed. S. Notley, M. Turnage, and B. Becker, Leiden: Brill, 41-51.

JOSHUA J. SCHWARTZ

Politeuma Papyri, Jewish → Herakleopolis Papyri

Popular Religion

"Popular religion" is a useful term, but it can cause misunderstanding. It might seem to imply that there was an official religion for the people and that this differed from popular religion. In fact, in most nations of the ancient Near East, we should probably think of several religious spheres. The ruler often had a favored cult or deity, which he would promote by founding or supporting temples and cult sites, but this cult was not necessarily the only national cult, nor was it necessarily the one worshiped by most inhabitants of the country. Indeed, in a polytheistic society, a number of cults would usually be given state sponsorship. There might also be other cults or religious structures — those favored by the ruling class, those favored by the dominant ethnic group, even the religion of a conqueror.

A Variety of Phenomena

These cults — which can sometimes, but not always, be designated the "official religion" — are often at a certain remove from the religion as practiced by the common people. The phrase "popular religion" is commonly used to designate several different things. It might refer to popular cults that are ignored or even discouraged by the ruling class; it might refer to quasi-religious practices that were popular but perhaps frowned on by the upper classes or central temple personnel (e.g., magic, curses, good luck charms, divination); or it might refer to family religion as practiced in the home. In many cultures, there is also a gender issue; there are cults primarily or even exclusively for women. Also, many people had personal deities (these might well be chosen for ethnic or gender reasons) to whom they appealed for personal favors and help in time of trouble. This is not to suggest that there is necessarily a sharp divide between "popular" and "official" religion or that popular religion is somehow inferior or less religious or different phenomenologically. What recent studies recognize, however, is that the piety, rites, and beliefs carried on in the family and home and other private spheres sometimes have significant variants from or additional elements not normally attested for the "official" or dominant religion.

Popular Religion and Monotheism

The question of popular religion impinges on the issue of monotheism. Monotheism had apparently developed in Judaism by the Persian period, but we cannot be sure that it was the view of everyone. In the early exilic period there is evidence that the common people found cults such as the "Queen of Heaven" appealing (Jer. 44:15-19). Monotheism was probably the position of the Temple leadership, yet this is no guarantee that all Jews believed likewise. The Jewish colony at Elephantine had a temple to *Yhw,* probably a variant of YHWH, the deity of Israel. But *Yhw* may have had a consort; although only he is referred to in the documents, some offering lists include the names Eshem-Bethel and Anat-Bethel, and in one document a man swears by Anat-Yahu. Bethel was probably seen as another name of *Yhw,* but was Anat seen as his consort? This is possible, but equally possible is that Anat-Bethel and Anat-Yahu were seen only as hypostases of *Yhw* by this time.

Private Vows

Private vows were an important feature of popular religion (Berlinerblau 1996). They could not be controlled very easily by others, and women could participate as well as men. This is probably the reason for the long regulation about vows in Num. 30:2-17, much of which is about vows taken by a woman. If she is under the authority of a man (father, husband), he can annul the vow; otherwise, it stands. The example of Hannah in 1 Samuel (1:11) suggests that many of the vows by women related to children — to become pregnant, to have a successful birth, for health for the child, for success for children when they grow up, and so on. In polytheistic contexts, the vow might be made to a deity thought to give particular favor to women.

Divination and Magic

The traditional practices of astrology, extispicy (divining by the entrails), and related means of divination were well known in the Assyrian and Babylonian periods and continued into the Persian. Isaiah 65:1-12 covers a whole range of activity that may be magical, divinatory, and/or cultic. One interpretation is that this passage refers to sacrificing on incense altars associated with high places *(bāmôt),* which included a sacred grove and worship of Asherah as YHWH's consort (Ackerman 1992: 165-94). The problem with finding cult places, such as *bāmôt,* in this passage is the lack of any attestation from archaeology by this time (probably the Persian period). Cult objects (such as figurines, common for Judah in the Assyrian period) are completely absent for the Persian period in both Judah and Samaria, as are temples and tombs containing such objects (Stern 1999: 254; 2001: 478-79, 488). If *bāmôt* flourished during the Babylonian or Persian period, we should expect some evidence in the archaeology. This might suggest the passage is referring to some sort of magical practice. On the other hand, we find plenty of incense altars in Judah, which possibly suggests some sort of cultic celebrations among the populace.

In a number of passages in Second Isaiah, usually dated to the exilic period, criticisms are directed at certain practices. YHWH emphasizes that only he knows the end from the beginning (Isa. 41:21-29; 42:9; 43:9; 44:7-8; 45:20-21; 46:10; 48:3-8, 14-16), the very sort of esoteric knowledge promised by divination. The LORD states that he annuls the omens of the diviners *(ʾôtôt baddîm),* makes fools of the augurs *(qōsĕmîm),* and makes foolish the knowledge of the sages (44:25). As for Babylon, the daughter of the Chaldeans, her spells *(kĕšāfayim)* and enchantments *(ḥăbārîm),* her scanners of the heavens *(hōbĕrê šāmayîm)* and her stargazers *(ḥōzîm bakkôkābîm)* will not help her in her time of trouble (47:9, 12-13). This sustained polemic suggests that all these practices were in common existence among the people at the time.

The Cult of the Dead

A number of the divinatory and other practices hinted at by some texts may have had a connection with the cult of the dead, which apparently had already existed under the monarchy. In several Third Isaiah passages (conventionally dated to the Persian period) are some references to what seem to be secret cults, some of which apparently have the aim of deriving esoteric knowledge from the dead (cf. Lewis 1989; Ackerman 1992). A passage condemning the religious practices of the people (Isa. 57:3-13) is addressed to "sons of a sorceress" (v. 3: *bĕnê ʿōnĕnāh*). It speaks of worshiping among the terebinths and slaughtering children in the wadis (v. 5) and sacrificing on the hills (v. 7). The people provoke YHWH to anger by sacrificing in the gardens, burning incense on bricks, passing the night in tombs, and eating unclean things (65:1-7). Although the rites mentioned here are somewhat obscure, the suggestion of some sort of cult of the dead is plausible. Similar is Isa. 66:3-4, which speaks of sacrificing dogs and swine's blood, and 66:17, which talks of eating unclean animals in a ritual context.

Apotropaism

There is considerable archaeological evidence of "apotropaic" practices, to ward off curses, demons, and bad luck. These often took the form of faces and figurines representing Egyptian deities such as Bes, Ptah, and Pataikos. A popular practice was the wearing of necklaces with faience or glass beads, and pendants and amulets with images or symbols of the protective deities. The necklaces seem to have been worn particularly by children. Also a part of this tradition were masks, often made of clay, and jars and vases with faces incised in the clay. This includes "Janus-faced" vases with two faces. The Bes image was particularly popular, but a variety of grotesque faces are attested, including strange bird figures. These were found in Jerusalem and ʿEin Gedi from the sixth and especially the fifth century B.C.E. As time went on, some common practices dropped out of use, but others were added, such as pilgrimages to holy sites.

BIBLIOGRAPHY

S. ACKERMAN 1992, *Under Every Green Tree: Popular Religion in Sixth-Century Judah,* Atlanta: Scholars Press. • J. BERLINERBLAU 1993, "The 'Popular Religion' Paradigm in Old Testament Research: A Sociological Critique," *JSOT* 60: 3-26. • J. BERLINERBLAU 1996, *The Vow and the "Popular Religious Groups" of Ancient Israel: A Philological and Sociological Inquiry,* Sheffield: Sheffield Academic Press. • T. J. LEWIS 1989, *Cults of the Dead in Ancient Israel and Ugarit,* Atlanta: Scholars Press. • E. STERN 1999, "Religion in Palestine in the Assyrian and Persian Periods," in *The Crisis of Israelite Religion: Transformation of Religious Tradition in Exilic and Post-Exilic Times* , ed. B. Becking and M. Korpel, Leiden: Brill, 245-55. • K. VAN DER TOORN 1996, *Family Religion in Babylonia, Syria and Israel: Continuity and Change in the Forms of Religious Life,* Leiden: Brill.

See also: Divination and Magic; Family Religion

LESTER L. GRABBE

Pottery

Potsherds, or pieces of ceramic vessels, are the most ubiquitous objects discovered in archaeological excavations of ancient sites. Their importance to the archaeologist lies in the fact that, other than breakage, this material is nearly indestructible, and a comparison of the shape and decoration of ceramic vessels found in excavation can be used to date archaeological strata and ancient structures.

Sir Flinders Petrie (1853-1942) was one of the first archaeologists to recognize the value of potsherds and whole ceramic vessels for dating archaeological strata. In this system of sequence dating, ceramic vessels are classified by types and grouped into assemblages.

Since types of vessels tend to seriate, or change, over generations, it is possible to obtain a relative date of the archaeological strata in which they are uncovered. Archaeologists compare vessel types with those discovered at other sites in order to find parallels from the same period.

Depositional processes must be taken into account in order to judge the value of potsherds and whole vessels in the archaeological record. Archaeological strata are often damaged by later construction, so potsherds from more than one period may be found in mixed contexts. Whole vessels are usually discovered in graves, caves, or cisterns that were used over several generations. Archaeologists place a high value on vessels that are discovered *in situ* as foundation deposits or in destruction layers that can be firmly dated.

Ceramic assemblages are primarily made up of fine wares, coarse wares, and oil lamps. Fine wares are usually table wares, such as dishes, cups, and jugs used for dining, while coarse wares, such as cooking pots and jars, were used for transport, storage, and food preparation as well as for plain table wares. Fine wares and lamps have distinctive shapes and surface treatments and were often imported. Coarse, or utilitarian, wares were usually produced locally although heavy storage jars, or amphorae, were used to transport wine and other commodities from foreign lands.

Ceramic assemblages from the same period tend to vary from region to region. The presence or absence of particular types of vessels in assemblages from the Second Temple period is an important indication of the ethnicity of the inhabitants of a site as well as evidence of trade with neighboring or foreign countries. The regional divisions in that period include the coastal region, the interior region surrounding Jerusalem, the Judean Desert and the Dead Sea coast, the northern region of the Galilee and the Golan, and the southern region of the Negev.

Early Hellenistic Pottery

The early Hellenistic period (third century B.C.E.) was an important transitional era in the history of ancient Israel that witnessed the penetration of Hellenic influence into the region on a large scale. In spite of this, ceramic finds that can be absolutely dated to the third century are elusive. Difficulties exist in assigning local types to either the Ptolemaic or the Seleucid periods, and imported wares, such as Attic black-glazed and "West Slope" wares, apparently remained in use for several generations, probably because of their relatively high cost as compared to local products (Tal 2006: 284). Sites with pottery dated to the period include Shiqmona, Dor, Apollonia, Tel Michal, and Joppa as well as the Idumean/Sidonian city of Maresha and the Nabatean fort of 'Ein Rahel in the Arabah. Oil lamps include a local type of globular, wheel-made lamp called the "Shephelah" lamp that was produced in the coastal plain at the end of the fourth and early third centuries (Rosenthal and Sivan 1978: 78) and mold-made lamps from Maresha (Levine 2003: Fig. 6.15.154). The Rhodian wine amphora was the predominant imported jar in the region during the better part of the third and second centuries (Ariel and Finkielsztejn 2003: 138).

Middle Hellenistic Pottery

Pottery vessels from contexts dated to the first half of the second century B.C.E. have been discovered at sites in northern Israel and along the coast. Locally produced plain ware vessels were influenced to a great extent by Greek forms. Common vessels include shallow bowls with a central depression, commonly called "fish plates," bowls with in-turned rims, out-curved carinated bowls, mortaria, skyphoi, kraters, lekanai, jugs, juglets, lagynoi, unguentaria, bag-shaped storage jars, globular cooking pots, and flasks. Coastal sites, such as Dor and Akko-Ptolemais, tend to have a wider variety of vessels, including different types of cooking wares, as compared to sites from the central and northern interior probably due to their access to foreign markets, mixed populations, and affluence (Berlin 1997: 44). In the Galilee, the excavations at Kadesh have produced evidence of a strong Phoenician influence on the material culture (Herbert and Berlin 2003: 48). Casseroles appear in Phoenician-dominated sites along the coast, in northern Israel and in the non-Jewish site of Samaria in the interior but are absent in Judea until the mid first century (Berlin 2006: 140). In the second century hemispherical, moldmade relief bowls (formerly called "Megarian" bowls) became the common drinking vessel, replacing the kantharos and skyphos produced in Attic ware and West Slope technique. Vessels used for perfumed oils include Phoenician semifine amphoriskoi and fusiform unguentaria, or "spindle" bottles.

Locally produced wheelmade lamps and the moldmade Delphiniform lamp were the common types in this period (Rosenthal and Sivan 1978: 13, 78) Delphiniform lamps are decorated with a variety of molded designs and most have a characteristic S-coil on one side and elongated nozzles.

Late Hellenistic Pottery

The cosmopolitan character of pottery assemblages of the Middle Hellenistic period continued unabated among non-Jewish populations along the Mediterranean coast. In regions with mixed populations such as the Galilee and the Golan, the insistence on ritual purity penetrated the region later, and those populations appear to have been more open to foreign influences until the end of the first century (Berlin 2006: 21, 142).

Imported hemispherical moldmade relief bowls and other fine wares continued to appear in archaeological contexts of the late second and early first centuries, particularly among populations along the coast and in inland cities such as Marisa and Samaria that were open to Greek influence. Other types of imported fine-ware vessels also began to flow into the region from Italy, the Greek islands, Cyprus, and Asia Minor. Tableware with a red lustrous sheen, Eastern Sigillata A (ESA), is the most important diagnostic ware in the Late Hellenistic and Roman periods with the latest ESA forms appearing in the third century C.E. (Hayes 1985: 13). It developed out of BSP wares (Black Slipped Predecessor), probably in the region of North Syria sometime after 144 B.C.E., and it was widely distributed by Phoenician merchants (Berlin 1997: 25; Berlin 2006: 14).

The most common cooking vessel in the eastern Mediterranean was the closed globular cooking pot suited for the slow cooking of soups and legumes (Berlin 1993: 41). Open cooking vessels, or casseroles, have a long history in the Greek world, and they became popular in this period among both Hasmonean and non-Jewish populations (Bar-Nathan 2006: 151). Ceramic cooking braziers, probably used to heat casseroles, are a Greek innovation found in Late Hellenistic assemblages, particularly in the coastal cities such as Dor and also at Tel Anafa (Berlin 1993: 42).

Imported Rhodian amphoras began to be replaced to a large extent by wine amphoras with double-barreled handles imported from Cos. In turn, in the first century the Koan amphoras were replaced by imitation wine amphoras produced in Italy. Northern sites exhibit a full range of Phoenician semifine ware storage jars and serving vessels (Berlin 1997: 44). Bag-shaped storage jars produced locally throughout the region continued to be used for storing and transporting wine, oil, and other commodities.

Hasmonean Pottery

The pottery assemblages from the Hasmonean-controlled regions of Judea and Samaria are quite different from the cosmopolitan composition of assemblages in the rest of the country. The inhabitants tended to produce a limited repertoire of rather crudely made local vessels that are rarely decorated, and they adopted only a few Hellenistic forms. They also appear to have imported very few luxury wares and commodities. For example, there is a complete absence of ESA wares at Jericho in Hasmonean contexts, but these were replaced with locally produced red-slipped vessels (possibly from Jerusalem) (Hayes 1985: 183; Bar-Nathan 2002: 121). Key sites with Hasmonean assemblages include Jerusalem, the Hasmonean palaces at Jericho, Tell el-Ful, Cypros, Beth Zur, and Machaerus. Hasmonean pottery workshops were discovered at Qumran and possibly at Jericho, and Hasmonean pottery is found beyond the boundaries of the kingdom, particularly during the reign of Alexander Jannaeus (Bar-Nathan 2002: 195-96). It was produced with minor changes until the end of the first century but was increasingly supplanted by the new Herodian forms and Roman imports (Bar-Nathan 2002: 199).

The Hasmonean pottery assemblage of the second and first centuries B.C.E. includes local red-slipped fine tableware, cups with flaring walls, bowls with drooping rims, coarse, shallow plates with a flat or ring base, bowls and cups with flattened, string-cut bases and in-curved walls, deep bowls with out-curved rims, mortaria, kraters, narrow-necked, ridged globular jugs with cup mouths, biconical jugs, carinated lagynoi, small "Judean" flasks, flasks with an asymmetrical globular body, bag-shaped storage jars with upright necks, and large storage jars with everted rims. For unknown reasons numerous small bowls and plates were found in association with the many *mikva'ot* at Jericho (Bar-Nathan 2002: 196). A small number of vessels have crudely executed, painted geometric decoration. Globular juglets with cup mouths were apparently produced to store perfumed oils and possibly the expensive Judean balsam cultivated around the Dead Sea. In addition to globular cooking pots (the main cooking vessel in the region from the fifth through the first centuries), casseroles became an important addition to Jewish kitchens (Berlin 2006: 140; Bar-Nathan 2006: 151). Locally produced lamps include wheelmade "saucer lamps" and pinched lamps that had a long tradition in Palestine from the Late Iron Age period, and the mold-made radial lamps that imitated the common Hellenistic molded lamps.

One important type of jar that began to appear in the Hasmonean periods is the "Genizah" or "Scroll" jar: a hole-mouth storage jar with a vertical neck, an ovoid or cylindrical body, and a wide ring base with a concave bottom (Bar-Nathan 2002: 23-27; pls. 1-2, nos. 2-11). These jars were usually covered with a lid in the form of an inverted bowl. The jars were discovered in the Qumran caves storing scrolls belonging to the Dead Sea Scrolls archive. They were produced throughout the first century B.C.E. until 70 C.E. in the Dead Sea area and have been discovered primarily at Qumran and the winter palaces at Jericho (and possibly at Tell el-Ful), but they have not been discovered in Jerusalem (Lapp 1961: 154, Type 14; Bar-Nathan 2002: 26-27).

Herodian Pottery

The ceramic vessels that developed during the reign of Herod in the second half of the first century B.C.E. had a high degree of uniformity and were the dominant types that were used throughout Judea and Samaria well into the first century C.E. (Bar-Nathan 2002: 200-201). Key sites include Jerusalem and the surrounding area, Qumran, Samaria, Caesarea, Tel Anafa, as well as the royal Herodian palaces at Masada, Jericho, Machaerus, and Herodium. When compared to Hasmonean pottery, Herodian pottery includes new types that appear to have been influenced by Roman pottery of the Augustan period. Roman fine wares, imported mainly from the

A set of Eastern Sigillata A dishes from the "Herodian Residence" in Jerusalem's Jewish Quarter *(Institute of Archaeology, Hebrew University, Jerusalem)*

Jerusalem painted or "pseudo-Nabatean" bowls from the first-century-C.E. mansions in Jerusalem's Jewish Quarter *(Institute of Archaeology, Hebrew University, Jerusalem)*

West, such as Pompeian Red Ware, Thin-walled ware, and Western Terra Sigillata began to appear in Herodian contexts. ESA wares did not appear at either Jericho or Masada before 30 B.C.E. (Bar-Nathan 2006: 368). At Masada, Herod's palaces were supplied with wine imported mainly from Italy and also from Knidos, Chios, and Rhodes, and amphorae were also used to transport apples from Italy and fish sauce (garum) from Spain (Bar-Nathan 2006: 313). The amphorae imported to Masada inscribed with *tituli picti* in Latin include the name "Herod, King of Judea" and indicate two dated series of consignments: 27/26 and 19 B.C.E. (Bar-Nathan 2006: 307-8).

The plain, utilitarian wares of the Herodian assemblage differ from the Hasmonean wares in being more levigated with a metallic quality and petrographic analysis of storage jars found at Jericho, showing that they were produced from different clays (Bar-Nathan 2006: 199). The Herodian repertoire includes many older forms such as the ubiquitous globular perfume juglets, globular jugs, asymmetrical flasks, and more refined (usually thinner) versions of cups and bowls with ring bases. A variation of the globular cooking appears with a short neck and triangular rim at the end of the period. New forms include: carinated plates, globular lagynoi, barrel-shaped jugs, cooking ware jugs, casseroles with carinated shoulders, one-handled jugs of cooking ware fabric, and a tall, ridged-neck storage jar. Painted fineware vessels (Jerusalemite Painted Pottery) similar to Nabatean painted wares began to be produced in Jerusalem at the end of the century (Hershkovitz 2003: 31*). Large storage jars and handmade pithoi, or *dolia*, probably used for storing grain, were discovered at the Herodian palaces (Bar-Nathan 2006: 39, 377). In the Galilee, the most common type of cooking wares began to be produced at Kfar Hananya while the Galilean village of Shikhin near Sepphoris produced large storage jars admired by rabbinic sources throughout the first century (Adan-Bayewitz 1987; 1989; 1993: 23-26). In the second half of this century, piriform unguentaria superseded the Hellenistic fusiform unguentaria. The Hasmonean radial moldmade lamps appeared until the beginning of the first century C.E., while toward the end of the period knife-pared "Herodian Lamps" with saptulate nozzles began to be produced.

First Century C.E. until the Year 70

From the mid first century B.C.E. there appears to have been an increase in piety and influence of Jewish sects such as the Pharisees, who transmitted a rigorous ideal of ritual purity, formerly a monopoly of the priestly class, to the common people. This ideal of ritual purity was manifested materially in the increased construction and use of *mikva'ot* or ritual baths, the production of stone (chalk) vessels for storing water, earthen and dung vessels for storing dry goods, and locally produced pottery vessels and utensils. Key sites include Jerusalem, Gamla, Masada, Herodium, Macherus, Callirrhoe, Qumran, ʿEin Gedi, ʿEin Boqeq, and Caesarea.

Imported fine wares and amphorae are found in Judea and Samaria in rather limited quantities. The same may be said of Italian cooking vessels such as Pompeian Red Ware and *orlo bifido* pans. These were found in cities and in the Herodian palaces throughout the Herodian realm as late as the First Revolt but are rarely found in rural areas (Bar-Nathan 2006: 358-59). Imported wares were probably purchased primarily by the wealthier classes, and religious considerations prevented higher demand. This is particularly apparent in regard to oil lamps, with the plain, undecorated "Herodian lamp" (probably produced in Jerusalem) the most common lamp throughout Palestine, even among pagan populations (Barag and Hershkovitz 1994: 4). "Citadel lamps" (a type of gray ware lamp with molded floral designs similar to those found on Jerusalemite Painted Pottery) were produced in Jerusalem late in the period, several of which were discovered at Masada (Hershkovitz 2003: 32*-33*). Imported Roman lamps, with their molded depictions of pagan gods, mythology, and erotic scenes are rare. These lamps, usually produced in Imperial workshops, may have been introduced into the area by Roman soldiers (Bar-Nathan 2002: 188).

Many ceramic vessel forms of the Herodian period continued to be produced in Judea as late as the destruction of the Second Temple in 70 C.E. The production of plain ware bowls appears to have declined during this period (Bar-Nathan 2002: 202). Fine "Jerusalemite painted pottery" decorated with painted floral designs, found in Jerusalem and the Judean Desert, was probably a special tableware used for the Sabbath and high holy days (Hershkovitz 2003: 33*). At Masada few ceramic cups were found in Zealot contexts, possibly due to the use of glass cups toward the end of this period (Bar-Nathan 2006: 374).

Globular pots, carinated casseroles, and cooking jugs continued to appear throughout this period. A new type of cooking pot with carinated shoulders appeared toward the end of the period. Casseroles dishes *(kdera)* were important kitchen implements used for cooking both solids and liquids (*m. Ned.* 6:1-2), and, according to Jewish sources, in the case of divorce even the poor were required to supply their wives with this kind of vessel (*t. Ketub.* 5:8; Zevulun and Olenik 1979: 68-71; Bar-Nathan 2002: 68). Cooking ware jugs with one or two handles were abundant in Judea and spread to the Galilee. This was probably a vessel that Jewish sources call the *yorah,* used for heating and boiling liquids (Bar-Nathan 2002: 68, 177). Red ware kraters (*tamkui* in Jewish sources) were used to serve cooked food to diners or as vessels to collect food that could be distributed daily to the destitute (Zevulun and Olenik 1979: 24; Bar-Nathan 2002: 179). Three ceramic ladles (the *tarvad* referred to in Jewish sources) used as pouring and measuring utensils were found at Masada (*t. Baba Batra* 7; Bar-Nathan 2006: 231). Globular jugs with triangular rims were the dominant type, and toward the end of the period ridged-neck jugs and jugs with sieves and spouts began to appear.

Bag-shaped storage jars with a capacity of 20 to 29 liters continued to be the most widely used type of jar throughout the region in this period (Bar-Nathan 2006: 371). Ovoid storage jars were discovered in Jerusalem and sites around the Dead Sea (Bar-Nathan 2006: 47-50). At Masada storage jars were found with inscriptions in Hebrew, Aramaic, and Greek *(tituli picti)* of the names of the owners, the contents, or the amount (Bar-Nathan 2006: 44-45). A variety of convex ceramic funnels were discovered in Zealot contexts at Masada, a number of which were found together with vessels apparently used for purification (Bar-Nathan 2006: 228). Some unusual vessels used by the Zealots (66-73/74 C.E.) discovered at Masada include a jar (or jug) used as a spindle for holding balls of thread during spinning and hand basins or washstands used for ritual purification (Bar-Nathan 2006: Fig. 75; p. 235, Fig. 74). The hand basins are flaring, crater-like vessels attached to a globular body supported by tall, cylindrical stands. Jewish sources indicate that these may have been in widespread use in Jewish households, particularly before partaking in meals and before morning prayers (*t. Ber.* 4:8; Zevulun and Olenik 1979: 8).

Ceramic perfume containers (globular juglets, pirifom unguentaria, pyxides, and alabastra) were popular and have been found both in tombs and in settlements throughout the region. A surprising number of these were discovered at Masada in Zealot contexts (Bar-Nathan 2006: 35). The globular juglets with rounded or flattened bases (*ṣĕlôḥît*) have cup mouths that can be sealed, an indication of the value and care of the contents. Jewish sources refer to a number of different liquids that these vessels contained, including spikenard oil, balsam oil, and wine, and juglets of Judean balsam were often placed in tombs (*Gen. Rab.* 30:10; Bar-Nathan 2002: 51). The sources refer to their use in the bathhouse for cleansing one's body (*y. Šeb.* 8:2) and also for placing near the fire in one's home (*t. Šab.* 3[4]:5). Piriform unguentaria have a wide distribution in Judea, Galilee, and Nabatea and have also been found Europe. However, many of those found throughout the region may have been produced at Petra. The locally produced pyxides discovered in the industrial area at Jericho may have also contained balsam (Bar-Nathan 2002: 64). Small, tubular containers called "Kohl bottles" used for cosmetics or medicinal preparations were discovered in the Zealots' dwellings at Masada and at Gamla (Berlin 2006: 57, figs. 2.30, nos. 24-33). One such vessel was found with a wooden stopper (Bar-Nathan 2006: 206, fig. 67, nos. 21-30).

"Genizah" or "scroll" jars from this period have been discovered in the Qumran caves and in small quantities at Masada, where they may have been brought by Essenes who joined the Zealots (Bar-Nathan 2006: 72). Bowl lids were apparently common at Qumran in this period, and one was discovered in the Western Palace at Masada together with a Genizah jar (Bar-Nathan 2002: 26-27; 2006: 72).

Between the First and Second Jewish Revolts

The traumatic events of the First Jewish Revolt brought about the destruction of many key sites in Judea and the Galilee, and fewer well-dated pottery assemblages have been found in this period than in the preceding one. Initially, the pottery repertoire remained relatively unchanged, but by the time of the Second Revolt in 132 C.E. new vessel forms appeared. The Roman occupation was a factor influencing local tastes. Pottery from this period has been found mainly in tombs and in caves used by the Jewish rebels in the Second Revolt. Key sites include Jerusalem, Jericho (the Roman villa), the Cave of Letters in the Judean Desert, and Cave 2 in Wadi Daliyeh.

Imported fine wares include ESA wares and a small amount of Eastern Sigillata B vessels. The gray knife-pared Herodian lamps continued to appear alongside a new type of moldmade lamp with spatulate nozzles ("southern lamps") found mainly in Judea, some of which have molded Jewish symbols (Rosenthal and Sivan 1978: 82). Imported and local imitations of Roman round lamps with a decorated discus were in common use after the First Revolt throughout the region (Bar-Nathan 2002: 190). During the second century C.E., workshops in Gerasa (Jerash) produced distinctive types of lamps such as polilychnoi (multinozzled) lamps with leaf-shaped handles and lamps with high arched handles (Rosenthal and Sivan 1978: 90-95). Basins and heavy deep bowls, or mortaria (extensively used in Roman cooking), became important in food preparation. Cooking wares include an increasingly popular type with carinated shoulders and globular pots with high necks, as well as cooking jugs. Bag-shaped storage jars continued to be produced with minor variations, and the earliest form of the Gaza wine jar began to appear.

In Jerusalem, Roman legionary kilns belonging to the Tenth Roman Legion operated from this period and produced a variety of imitation red-slipped wares, thin-walled wares with relief decoration, anthropomorphic and zoomorphic vessels, as well as imitation Roman oil lamps, cooking cauldrons, cooking pans, lids, and mortaria (Magness 2005).

BIBLIOGRAPHY

D. ADAN-BAYEWITZ 1987, "Notes and News: Kefar Hananya 1986," *IEJ* 37: 178-79. • D. ADAN-BAYEWITZ 1987, "Notes and

News: Kefar Hananya 1987," *IEJ* 39: 98-99. • D. Adan-Bayewitz 1993, *Common Pottery in Roman Galilee: A Study of Local Trade,* Ramat Gan: Bar Ilan University Press. • D. T. Ariel and G. Finkielsztejn 2003, "Amphora Stamps and Imported Amphoras," in *Maresha Excavations Final Report I. Subterranean Complexes 21, 44, 70, IAA Reports 17,* ed. A. Kloner, Jerusalem: Israel Antiquities Authority, 137-151. • R. Bar-Nathan 2002, *Hasmonean and Herodian Palaces at Jericho,* vol. 3, *The Pottery,* Jerusalem: Israel Exploration Society. • R. Bar-Nathan 2006, *Masada VII: The Pottery of Masada.* Jerusalem: Israel Exploration Society. • D. Barag and M. Hershkovitz 1994, "Lamps from Masada," in *Masada IV: The Yigael Yadin Excavations, 1963-1965. Final Reports,* eds. J. Aviram, G. Foerster and E. Netzer, Jerusalem: Israel Exploration Society, 7-78. • A. M. Berlin 1993, "Italian Cooking Vessels from Tel Anafa," *IEJ* 42: 35-44. • A. M. Berlin 1997, "Archaeological Sources for the History of Palestine: Between Large Forces: Palestine in the Hellenistic Period," *BA* 60: 2-51. • A. M. Berlin 2006, *Gamla I: The Pottery of the Second Temple Period,* Jerusalem: Israel Antiquities Authority. • J. W. Hayes 1985, "Sigillate Orientali," in *Atlante delle forme ceramiche II: Ceramica fine romana nel bacino mediterraneo,* ed. A. Carandini, Rome: Istituo della Enciclopedia Italiana, 1-96. • H. and A. M. Berlin 2003, "A New Administrative Building for Persian and Hellenistic Galilee: Preliminary Report of the University of Michigan and the University of Minnesota Excavations at Kadesh," *BASOR* 329: 13-59. • M. Hershkovitz 2003, "Jerusalemite Painted Pottery from the Late Second Temple Period," in *The Nabateans in the Negev,* ed. R. Rosenthal-Heginbottom, Haifa: Haifa University, 31*-34*. • P. W. Lapp 1961, *Palestinian Ceramic Chronology 200 BC–70 AD,* New Haven: Yale University Press. • T. Levine 2003, "Pottery and Small Finds from Subterranean Complexes 21 and 70," in *Maresha Excavations Final Report I: Subterranean Complexes 21, 44, 70, IAA Reports 17,* ed. A. Kloner, Jerusalem: Israel Antiquities Authority, 73-130. • J. Magness 2005, "The Roman Legionary Pottery," in *Excavations on the Site of the Jerusalem International Convention Center (Binyanei Ha'uma),* ed. B. Arubas and H. Goldfus, Portsmouth, R.I.: Journal of Roman Archaeology, 69-191. • R. Rosenthal-Heginbottom 1995a, "Moldmade Relief Bowls from Tel Dor, Israel — A Preliminary Report," in *Hellenistic and Roman Pottery in the Eastern Mediterranean — Advances in Scientific Studies,* ed. H. Meyza and J. Mlynarezyk, Warsaw: Warsaw University Press, 365-396. • R. Rosenthal-Heginbottom 1995b, "Imported Hellenistic and Roman Pottery," in *Excavations at Dor, Final Report,* vol. 1B, ed. E. Stern, Jerusalem: Hebrew University, 183-288. • R. Rosenthal and R. Sivan 1978, *Ancient Lamps in the Scholessinger Collection,* Jerusalem: Institute of Archaeology, Hebrew University. • K. W. Slane 1997, *Tel Annafa II, i: The Fine Wares,* Ann Arbor: University of Michigan Press. • O. Tal 2006, *The Archaeology of Hellenistic Palestine: Between Tradition and Renewal,* Jerusalem: Bialik (in Hebrew). • U. Zevulun and Y. Olenik 1979, *Function and Design in the Talmudic Period,* Tel Aviv: Haaretz Museum.

Tali Erickson-Gini

Priests

The story of the priesthood during the Second Temple era is complex. For much of the period the high priest's office was a locus not only of religious authority but also of political power. As a result, it drew many claimants. The literature pertaining to it only occasionally reflects what actually happened and more often presents what its authors wished had happened, or hoped would be the case. Further, the literature often focuses not on the priesthood as a whole but on the high priesthood alone. We do know, however, that throughout the Second Temple period priests exercised the traditional roles of making sacrifice (Sir. 50:1-21), teaching and interpreting the Torah (Josephus, *Ag. Ap.* 2.184-87), and giving oracles (Zech. 7:3). In the Hasmonean period those basic tasks were augmented, and in some respects eclipsed, by the high priests' royal and military powers.

Persian Period

Of the Persian period sources, Haggai and Zechariah 1–8 are the earliest, datable to around 520 B.C.E. Haggai identifies Joshua, from the line of Aaron, as the returnees' high priest (Hag. 1:1, etc.; cf. 1 Chron. 5:27-41 [Eng. 6:1-15), and he certifies that the priests of the postexilic period were teachers of Torah (Hag. 2:10-19; Zech. 7:3 denotes their oracular role). Interested in legitimating the sacerdotal leadership for postexilic Judah, Zechariah 3 describes Joshua's purification and reinvestment by the angel of the Lord and other heavenly beings. This reinvestment was perhaps intended to ascribe to Joshua civil authority, a notion reinforced by Zech. 6:9-15, where he is crowned and takes his place alongside (or as?) the one called "Branch" (cf. Isa. 11:1).

The Priestly portion of the Pentateuch (P) articulates a division between the sons of Aaron as altar priests (Exodus 28–29) and the Levites as lower-status Temple servants (Num. 3:12-13; 8:16-19; etc.). P acknowledges the Aaronites' descent from Levi (Exod. 6:16-20; Num. 18:2) but stoutly defends their privileges among Levites (e.g., Numbers 16–18). That this class distinction among Levites was contested and required grounding in the Mosaic period is evident from the repeated narrative (e.g., Numbers 16–17; 25:6-13) and legislative (e.g., Numbers 18) gestures P makes toward affirming Aaronite ascendance and entitlement. If dated late, Exod. 32:25-29 signals the competing perspective.

Chronicles and Ezra-Nehemiah also divide the priesthood into "priests and Levites" (e.g., Ezra 6:20; Neh. 12:1; 1 Chron. 13:2). As in P, the priests descend from Aaron (Neh. 10:38; 12:47; 1 Chron. 5:27-29; 15:4), and the Levites are Temple servants. The roles of Levites are further defined as singers, gatekeepers, and "the descendants of Solomon's servants" (Ezra 2:41-43, 55). They are reluctant at first to fulfill such secondary roles in the Second Temple (Ezra 8:15). Nehemiah 12:10-11 reports a succession of six high priests in the Persian period (a plausibly low number; see VanderKam 2004: 99).

Ezekiel 44:10-16 should be seen against the backdrop of P, since it is likely a postexilic passage. It explains the origins of P's second-class priesthood as punishment for cultic infidelities, and it grants the altar priesthood exclusively to the Zadokites, who did remain faithful (Ezek. 44:15). That this prescription conflicts with P's (and the Chronicler's) identification of the altar priests as Aaronites suggests authorship by a perspective dissenting from P. On this reading, Ezek. 44:10-16 counted P's Aaronites among the Levites.

Malachi and Third Isaiah also dissent from P, decrying the priests' cultic and moral corruption (Mal. 1:6-13; Isa. 56:10-11) and announcing their rejection (Mal. 2:1-3; Isa. 56:9). Malachi declares the corrupt priests' replacement with pure priests from Levi, the original priest and Torah teacher (Mal. 2:4-7; 3:1-4; the rhetoric of Mal. 3:1-4 echoes Num. 25:6-13, showing that it knows P). Third Isaiah prophesies that Judea's oppressed will become priests and that Diaspora Jews will return to be made priests and Levites by God (Isa. 61:6; 66:21).

Although writing much later, Josephus offers a historically plausible explanation of Nehemiah's ill treatment of the priest Manasseh and gives insight into the origin of the sanctuary at Gerizim (Neh. 13:28; *Ant.* 11.302-12; Cross 1966). Manasseh, brother of Jaddua the high priest, married Nikaso, daughter of Sanballat, the Persian-appointed governor of Samaria. When Manasseh was pressured to forego his foreign marriage to preserve his priesthood, Sanballat promised him a temple on Mt. Gerizim to sustain the marriage alliance.

Hellenistic Period

The sources for the period from Alexander the Great to the Hasmoneans are few but vigorous in representing the history of the (high) priesthood from Onias I (ca. 320-290 B.C.E.) to Alcimus (161-159 B.C.E.). Some of these reports are of doubtful authenticity. For example, Hecataeus of Abdera, quoted by Josephus, identifies a high priest in Alexander's day as "Hezekiah." Yet he observes, probably accurately, that priests then exercised civic and ritual authority (*Ag. Ap.* 1.187-88). Josephus also presents a clearly legendary account of Alexander sparing Jerusalem and paying homage to the high priest Jaddua because of a vision he had about the high priest (*Ant.* 11.325-36; cf. *b. Yoma* 69a, where the meeting takes place in Antipatris, and the high priest is Simon the Just). Still, many sources do offer plausible information. 1 Maccabees records a letter from Arius I of Sparta to Onias I expressing the Lacedemonians' affiliation with the Jews (1 Macc. 12:7, 19-23; cf. *Ant.* 12.225-27). Josephus abbreviates Aristeas' account of the exchange between Ptolemy II Philadelphus and Eleazar (Simon I's successor) that led to the production of the Septuagint (*Ant.* 12.44-56). Although he likely oversimplifies Onias II's resistance to paying annual dues to Ptolemy III as a matter of greed — it was more likely a gesture of alliance with the Seleucids in the Third Syrian War — Josephus plausibly shows that Onias' tax dodging facilitated the appointment of the Tobiad Joseph (Onias' nephew by marriage) as the Ptolemies' tax farmer and that Joseph competed with the Oniads for control of the region (*Ant.* 12.157-85). Josephus identifies Onias' successor, Simon the Just, and ascribes to him participation in the armed opposition to Hyrcanus (Joseph's son), which drove Hyrcanus to establish the Tobiads' desert retreat and consolidate Tobiad power (*Ant.* 12.228-29).

Not coincidentally, Sir. 50:1-21 adds to our knowledge of Simon and of the high priest's power, praising him not only for his priestly service (vv. 5-21) but also for his efforts to strengthen the Temple, build a reservoir, and fortify the city's walls (vv. 1-4). 2 Maccabees 3:1 describes Simon's successor, Onias III, as a pious man and a worthy but unsuccessful opponent of the Hellenizers. 2 Maccabees 3 reports that his first opponent, the extremist Hellenizer Simon, brother of Menelaus and an ally of the Tobiads, sought twice to overthrow him. Jason, Onias' Hellenizing brother, succeeded in buying the office from Antiochus IV Epiphanes. Menelaus (Simon's brother) later outbid Jason for the office. Onias publicly accused Menelaus of pilfering Temple vessels for his own enrichment, so Menelaus had him assassinated (2 Maccabees 4). Both 1 and 2 Maccabees as well as Josephus report that the Seleucids assigned Alcimus to the high priesthood after Menelaus (1 Macc. 7:5, 14; 2 Macc. 14:3; *Ant.* 12.387-93; 20.237). They also note that he held the office for two years through his alliances with Hellenizing forces, including the Seleucids. Onias III's son, Onias IV, fled to Egypt and is said by Josephus to have established a temple at Leontopolis (*Ant.* 13.62-73; cf. *J.W.* 1.33; 7.423).

Reaction to the priesthood's long-standing corruption, which intensified under Jason, Menelaus, and Alcimus, prompted responses in the *Aramaic Levi Document*, *Jubilees* 30 and 32, and *1 Enoch* 12–16. *Aramaic Levi* imagines an ideal priesthood by reconstructing its origins through a sanitized expansion of the biblical portrait of Levi (Genesis 34; 49:5-70). Dating to the third century B.C.E., *Aramaic Levi* retells Genesis 34 to prove Levi's zeal for the purity of God's people. It narrates Levi's elevation to the priesthood in the heavens and on earth, Isaac's sacerdotal instructions to him, and his exemplary life. It also attributes to him a wisdom hymn celebrating his excellence as a teacher and judge. *Aramaic Levi* may not have been intended as a polemical work, but its antiquarianism certainly argued that a "pure priesthood" could be found in Levi's story retold. The same may be said of *Jubilees* 30 and 32, which closely resemble *Aramaic Levi.* Written in the mid-second century B.C.E. as a traditionalist counterbalance to the policies of the Hasmoneans, *Jubilees* also idealizes the origins of the priesthood by reworking Levi's story. *1 Enoch* 12–16, a third-century-B.C.E. text that implicitly equates the sinful Watchers with errant priests, was surely written with a polemical aim (*1 Enoch* 15:3-4; cf. *Ps. Sol.* 8:13; CD 5:6-7; Nickelsburg 2001: 271-72).

Hasmonean Period

Many suppose that after Alcimus' death in 159 B.C.E. there was a seven-year period without a high priest, but the evidence is not conclusive. Josephus reports that Judas Maccabee took the office at Alcimus' death (*Ant.* 12.414), and many speculate that the Teacher of Righteousness could have been the high priest in this period. At the same time, 1 Macc. 10:15-21 seems to indicate that the office was vacant after Alcimus died and until Jonathan assumed it.

Whatever the truth about an *intersacerdotium,* the high priesthood resumed with Jonathan as its first undisputed Hasmonean possessor (152-142 B.C.E.). He was able to secure his position thanks to the competition between Demetrius and Alexander, rival claimants to the Seleucid throne (1 Macc. 10:15-21; *Ant.* 13.44-46). Simon followed his brother Jonathan (142-135 B.C.E.; 1 Macc. 14:35–16:22; *Ant.* 13.213-29) and won Hasmonean autonomy from the Seleucids. He firmly combined royal, military, and sacerdotal powers in a single person. His son, John Hyrcanus, succeeded him (135-104 B.C.E.; 1 Macc. 16:23-24; *Ant.* 13.230-99), making both secular rule and the high priesthood hereditary and strengthening the Hasmonean double claim to royal and sacerdotal power (*Ant.* 13.230). Also noteworthy is Hyrcanus' encounter with the Pharisees. The Pharisee Eleazar suggested that Hyrcanus' pontificate was illegitimate because his mother had been a captive among the Seleucids and could have been defiled there, making Hyrcanus an offspring of a polluted woman (*Ant.* 13.288-92). Legendary or not, this episode reflects the natural tension between the Hasmoneans and pious Jews over the dynasty's stewardship of the high-priestly office. Yet it is not a denial of the legitimacy of their priestly lineage (Schofield and VanderKam 2005).

After Aristobulus (104-103 B.C.E.; *Ant.* 13.301-18), Alexander Jannaeus strove to survive among the competing Seleucids and Romans (103-76 B.C.E.; *Ant.* 13.320-407), egregiously violating the purity of the priesthood and the nation along the way (e.g., *Ant.* 13.372, 380). On his deathbed he chose as his successor Alexandra, his wife (76-67 B.C.E.; *Ant.* 13.405-32); she in turn appointed as high priest her son Hyrcanus II over his brother Aristobulus II (76-63 B.C.E.; *Ant.* 13.408). The feud between the two drew Rome into Palestinian affairs and brought an end to independent Hasmonean rule (*Ant.* 14.95-96). After that, the office of the high priesthood was little more than a concession traded freely among parties at the whim of the Romans and their proxies.

The Dead Sea Scrolls join other sources in voicing dissatisfaction with the Temple priesthood during this period. *Pesher Habakkuk* and *Psalms Pesher*[a] refer to a "Wicked Priest" widely believed to be one of the Hasmoneans. Many texts idealize Levi and his descendants as the true priests (Levi: 4QpsJub[a] 2 ii 11-12; 4Q PsalmsJosh[b] 1:5; 5QS 2:7; 4QTestament 14–20; *Aramaic Levi;* Levites: 11QT 21:1; 22:10-12; 44:5, 14; 57:12; 60:6-7, 12, 14; 61:8; 1QM 13:1; 18:5-6; 4QM[a] 1-3 9; 4QM[c] 9-10; CD 13:3; 1QS 1:18-19; 1QS 2:11; Kugler 1999). The group conceived itself as having the atoning function and holy status of priests (1QS 5:1-7; 8:5-6, 8-9; 9:6; 10:4; CD 3:18-4:4; 4QFlor 1:3-4) and being subject to priestly purity and age rules (1QS 5:13; 6:16-17; 1QSa 1:8-17; 2:3-10; CD 10:6-8; 15:15-17). Community members even identified themselves as Ezekiel's Zadokites (1QS 5:2, 9; 9:14 [?]; 1QSa 1:2, 24; 2:3), yet they seem to have made no distinction between Aaronites and Zadokites (cf. 1QS 5:2, 9; 9:7). In a variety of ways, the community constructed its life as a polemic against an impure priesthood.

The Early Roman Period

From 63 B.C.E. to 70 C.E. the Temple priesthood was subject to the whims of Roman rule under procurators and Herodians. The power the office enjoyed under the Persians, Greeks, and Hasmoneans was virtually absent. Indeed, a dizzying succession of no fewer than thirty high priests occupied the office during these years, and few of them received appointment for any other reason than their political value to the competing powers in the Levant.

Literary reflections on the priesthood are fewer for this period, perhaps in part because of the declining influence of the Temple and sacrifice at a time when alternative forms and forums for religious expression, such as the synagogue, blossomed in early Judaism. To be sure, some of the Dead Sea Scrolls mentioned above were composed in this era, testifying at least to the Qumran group's enduring concern for the office. But even this evidence should be considered in its proper context: the group evidently adopted the title "Zadokite" only for themselves (Kugler 2000), a move that likely reflected their view that the Temple priesthood was corrupt beyond saving and could be replaced only by their extra-Temple embodiment as God's true Temple servants. With the Roman destruction of the Second Temple, however, the priesthood came to an end, and not even the vision of the people of Qumran could bear that final blow to the institution.

The Priests at Work within and outside the Temple

In the first century C.E., there were probably around 20,000 priests and Levites (Josephus, *Ag. Ap.* 2.108; Sanders 1992: 78). They served for a week at a time on a rotating basis in twenty-four "courses" called *mišmārôt* (1 Chron. 24:4; *Ant.* 7.365; *m. Sukkah* 5:6). No more that twenty or thirty priests would have been standing and sacrificing in the Temple at any moment on an average day, though double or triple that number would have been on active duty during the three annual pilgrimage festivals.

The main task of priests was expert butchery: slaughtering animals, flaying them, cutting up the meat and distributing it, sprinkling and pouring blood on and around the altar, and putting fat and fatty pieces of meat on the altar. In most cases, the priests ate most of the meat, though in some sacrifices the worshiper who brought the animal received most of it. In certain sacrifices, all the meat was burned completely on the altar, as the Lord's portion. Priests also inspected animals to make sure they were unblemished, heard "confessions," accepted sacrifices and offerings, burned incense, and offered prayers, Scripture readings, and singing (Exod. 30:1-8; Lev. 16:13; Isa. 56:7; Sir. 50:16-18; Philo, *Spec. Leg.* 1.195). They also joined Levites in collecting agricultural tithes from farmers around the country (Neh. 10:37-38; Josephus, *Life* 29, 63; cf. *t. Pe'ah* 4:3; Sanders 1992: 149).

Since most priests and Levites were not aristocrats,

they had to work for a living; the support they received for working in the Temple in the form of food and animal hides was not enough to live on (Sanders 1992: 170-89). When they were not on duty in the Temple, they were busy with their everyday occupations. They were not allowed to grow their own crops, and so could not be farmers, but they could have other jobs. Many but not all of them lived in and around Jerusalem. In their towns and villages, they probably served as teachers, Torah interpreters, scribes, magistrates, and judges (Josephus, *Ag. Ap.* 2.187; Mark 1:40-45). Some may have had lowly occupations such as masons and ironmongers.

BIBLIOGRAPHY

F. M. CROSS 1966, "Aspects of Samaritan and Jewish History in Late Persian and Hellenistic Times," *HTR* 59: 201-11. • A. HUNT 2006, *Missing Priests: The Zadokites in Tradition and History,* New York: T&T Clark. • R. A. KUGLER 1999, "The Priesthood at Qumran: The Evidence of References to Levi and the Levites," in *The Provo International Conference on the Dead Sea Scrolls,* ed. D. W. Parry and E. Ulrich, Leiden: Brill, 465-79. • R. A. KUGLER 2000, "The Priesthood at Qumran," in *The Dead Sea Scrolls after Fifty Years: A Comprehensive Assessment,* vol. 2, ed. P. W. Flint and J. C. VanderKam, Leiden: Brill, 93-116. • G. W. E. NICKELSBURG 2001, *1 Enoch 1: A Commentary on the Book of 1 Enoch Chapters 1–36, 81–108,* Minneapolis: Fortress. • D. W. ROOK 2000, *Zadok's Heirs: The Role and Development of the High Priesthood in Ancient Israel,* Oxford: Oxford University Press. • E. P. SANDERS 1992, *Judaism: Practice and Belief: 63 BCE–66 CE,* London: SCM; Philadelphia: Trinity Press International. • J. SCHAPER 2000, *Priester und Leviten im achämenidischen Juda: Studien zur Kult- und Sozialgeschichte Israels in persischer Zeit,* Tübingen: Mohr-Siebeck. • A. SCHOFIELD AND J. VANDERKAM 2005, "Were the Hasmoneans Zadokites?" *JBL* 124: 73-87. • J. C. VANDERKAM 2004, *From Joshua to Caiaphas: High Priests after the Exile,* Minneapolis: Fortress.

See also: High Priests; Levites

ROBERT A. KUGLER

Prophecy

Prophecy, the inspired proclamation of the will of God, was an important institutional feature of preexilic Israelite religion. Though the more characteristic features of Israelite prophecy, such as the prophetic speech forms preserved in written form in the collected oracles of the Latter Prophets, are largely missing from mid- to late-Second Temple Judaism, new forms of revelatory speech and writing developed in changing political and social circumstances in early Judaism. There are four major types of revelatory speech and writing during this period: (1) apocalyptic vision reports, (2) eschatological prophecy (a primarily oral phenomenon), (3) clerical prophecy (also primarily oral), and (4) sapiential prophecy (both oral and written).

Apocalyptic Vision Reports

The primary revelatory medium in apocalyptic literature (from the Greek word *apokalyptikos,* meaning "revelatory") is the vision, the meaning of which is typically explained to the apocalyptic seer by an *angelus interpres* ("interpreting angel"). Visions had been a traditional revelatory medium among Israelite prophets, and in later prophetic books, sometimes labeled "proto-apocalyptic" literature, the literary device of the interpreting angel is used with greater frequency (Zech. 1:7–6:8). Unlike the authors of the prophetic books of the Hebrew Bible, apocalyptists concealed their identities by writing under the names of ancient Israelite worthies such as Enoch, Abraham, Baruch, and Ezra. Prophecy is one of the major antecedents of apocalyptic literature.

Eschatological Prophecy

Eschatological prophecy is a revelatory phenomenon that occurred within the context of apocalyptic or millennial movements in early Judaism. Josephus informs us of a number of millenarian movements that were predicated on the destruction of the present order as a necessary prelude to arrival of full and final salvation (Horsley and Hanson 1985; Gray 1993). Barnett (1981) has appropriately labeled the leaders of these movements "sign prophets" since they sought to validate their prophetic claims by replicating miraculous deeds performed by Israelite prophets of the past. Theudas (ca. 44-46 C.E.), who reportedly regarded himself as a prophet, intended to lead a band of 400 followers dryshod across the Jordan River in replication of a similar feat by Joshua narrated in Joshua 3, which was itself a mini-Exodus (*Ant.* 20.97-98; Acts 5:36). He and his followers were attacked and slaughtered by the Romans before he could pull his enterprise off. Josephus also reports the activities of an unnamed Egyptian Jew in ca. 50 C.E. who led a large band of followers into the wilderness, from where he intended to proceed to the Mount of Olives. From there he expected to witness the collapse of the walls of Jerusalem, which would allow him and his followers to invade the holy city (*Ant.* 20.169-72; *J.W.* 2.261-63; Acts 21:38). His act was probably a replication of the feat of Joshua in the conquest of Jericho (Josh. 6:1-21). This person, like Theudas, regarded himself as a prophet, though Josephus pointedly labels him a false prophet and a charlatan.

It is possible that both Theudas and the unnamed Egyptian Jew regarded themselves as the "prophet like Moses" referred to in Deut. 18:15-18, that is, Joshua *redivivus.* These two prophetic movements, and similar movements, linked the role of a prophet with that of a miracle worker, following the biblical precedent of the roles of Moses, Elijah, and Elisha. Josephus includes the following two elements in a summary of such religious movements of restoration in *J.W.* 2.259 (LCL trans.): "Deceivers and imposters, under the pretence of divine inspiration, fostering revolutionary changes, persuaded the multitude to act like madmen, and led them out into the desert under the belief that God would there give them tokens of deliverance" (see also *Ant.* 20.167-68).

There is evidence (primarily from Josephus) that there were also some freelance eschatological prophets in early Judaism, those not associated with apocalyptic or millennial movements. One such enigmatic figure is Joshua (Jesus) ben Ananiah, one of the pilgrims who came to Jerusalem to celebrate the festival of Sukkot in the fall of 62 C.E. Josephus describes the bizarre career of Joshua and also records the oracle of doom that he repeatedly proclaimed in the Temple (*J.W.* 6.300-309; LCL trans.):

> A voice from the east,
> A voice from the west,
> A voice from the four winds.
> A voice against Jerusalem and the temple,
> A voice against the bridegroom of the bride,
> A voice against all the people.

In this poetic oracle, the term "voice" probably refers to the "voice of God," an idiom used with some frequency during the Second Temple period. Joshua ben Ananiah was reportedly arrested and interrogated by the Roman procurator Albinus (61-62 C.E.) but then released on the grounds of insanity. Joshua reportedly reiterated the lament, "Woe to Jerusalem," for seven years until he was finally killed by a Roman missile during the last days of the Roman siege of Jerusalem.

Josephus also mentions the outbreak of prophecy during several military sieges of Jerusalem. He tells us, for instance, that when Herod was besieging Jerusalem in 37 B.C.E. in an attempt to recapture it, "throughout the city the agitation of the Jewish populace showed itself in various forms. The weaker gathered near the Temple and became divinely possessed and composed many oracles fit for the crisis" (*J.W.* 1.347). Josephus, however, does not provide any information about the form or content of these oracles.

Joshua ben Ananiah was not the only one to prophesy during the Roman siege of Jerusalem. During the last days of the siege, in August-September of 70 C.E., Josephus explains how it was that 6,000 people who had taken refuge in the porticoes of the Temple were incinerated when the building was torched by the Romans (*J.W.* 6.285; LCL trans.): "They owed their destruction to a false prophet who had on that day proclaimed to the people in the city that God commanded them to go up into the temple court, to receive there the signs of deliverance."

The most famous prophetic figure of early Judaism is John the Baptist, whose activities are reported in both Josephus (*Ant.* 18.116-19, where he is not called a prophet but a proclaimer of repentance) and the New Testament, and who was apparently part of a larger "baptist movement" in Syria and Palestine from the second century B.C.E. through the third century C.E. John proclaimed the imminent eschatological judgment and administered a ritual washing (probably a novel adaptation of Jewish proselyte baptism) for those who repented and changed their way of life. The Gospels often label John a prophet, sometimes suggesting his identification as Elijah *redivivus* (Mark 11:32 pars. Matt. 21:26; Luke 20:6; Matt. 14:5; Luke 1:76; 7:26 and par.; Matt. 11:9; John 1:21, 25). According to Matt. 11:13-14, Jesus said, "For all the prophets and the law prophesied until John; and if you are willing to accept it, he is Elijah who is to come" (see also Matt. 17:10-13).

Though little is known about the mysterious figure called the "Teacher of Righteousness," who apparently founded the Qumran community sometime in the middle of the second century B.C.E., some modern scholars (e.g., Jeremias 1963) think that he regarded himself as the Mosaic eschatological prophet, though he is never explicitly designated a prophet in the surviving literature. Yet if he authored some of the Qumran *Hodayot,* he did claim to possess the Holy Spirit (1QH[a] 15:6-7), which gave him knowledge and insight (1QH[a] 20:11-12; 13:18-19), particularly in the understanding of mysteries (1QH[a] 9:21; cf. 1QpHab 7:1-5).

Clerical Prophecy

In ancient Israel priests were associated with noneschatological oracular activity, particularly in connection with mysterious divination devices called Urim and Thummim, associated with the priestly garment called the ephod. The *Vitae Prophetarum* (which may be a first-century-C.E. Jewish work) attributed the cessation of prophecy in Israel to the cessation of the priests' ability to see visions of the angels of God, give forth visions of God from the inner sanctuary, or inquire of God by means of the ephod of Urim and Thummim. A prophecy attributed to the high priest Caiaphas (18-36 C.E.) is mentioned in John 11:49-52, where the author explains the high priest's words "it is expedient for you that one man should die for the people, so that the whole nation should not perish," as a statement that the high priest did not make of his own accord but because as high priest he had the ability to prophesy. This anecdote indicates the close connection in popular thought between the office of the high priest in Judaism and the gift of prophecy. The Jewish historian Josephus, though he never calls himself a prophet, was a descendant of a priestly family and saw a close correlation between his priestly status and his prophetic gifts (*J.W.* 3.351-54; see Blenkinsopp 1974). After being captured by the Romans, Josephus famously predicted that Vespasian, the Roman general in charge of suppressing the Jewish rebellion (66-73 C.E.), would become emperor, an event that occurred on 1 July 69 (*J.W.* 3.400-402; 6.312; Suetonius, *Vespasian* 5–6; Dio Cassius 65.1.4).

Sapiential Prophecy

Like clerical prophecy, sapiential prophecy is noneschatological and is connected with the faculty of wisdom, the specialty of the holy man or sage. Rabbi Yoḥanan ben Zakkai, who like Josephus reportedly predicted Vespasian's elevation to the principate (*'Abot R. Nat.* [A] 4:5), is also remembered for having predicted the doom of Galilee, since he had also been consulted twice during his eighteen-year stay at Arav (*y. Šabb.* 16:15d). According to *Midrash Rabbah* Lam. 2:2, at the beginning of the Second Jewish Revolt, Rabbi Aqiba said of Bar Kosiba (nicknamed Bar Kokhba or "son of a star" with reference to the messianic prediction in Num. 24:7), "This is the king Messiah" (but cf. *y. Taʿan.* 4:6 [68d] for a conflicting tradition).

There was a view in some strands of rabbinic Judaism that prophecy had ceased in Israel. According to *t. Soṭah* 13.2: "When the last of the prophets [i.e., Haggai, Zechariah, and Malachi] died, the holy spirit ceased in Israel. Despite this they were informed by means of oracles *(bat qôl).*" A similar view is expressed in *Seder Olam Rabbah* 30, though here the role of the rabbis as the spiritual successors of the prophets is emphasized: "Until then, the prophets prophesied by means of the holy spirit. From then on give ear and listen to the words of the sages." These and other passages suggest that for the rabbis, the phrase "holy spirit" was virtually synonymous with prophecy (Levison 1997b). However, the evidence for various forms of prophetic activity surveyed above suggests that prophecy was alive and well during the Second Temple period. The Spirit and prophecy have a close association in Philo and Josephus, both from the first century C.E. (Levison 1997a). Philo's conception of prophetic inspiration exhibits a strong Hellenistic influence, an influence evident in this statement in *Quis Rerum Divinarum Heres Sit* 265 (LCL trans.): "This is what regularly befalls the fellowship of the prophets. The mind is evicted at the arrival of the divine Spirit, but when that departs the mind returns to its tenancy." Philo read prophetic texts and narrative in the Jewish Scriptures from this perspective. In *De Vita Mosis,* he systematically presents Moses as prophet, priest, and king. Moses must be considered a prophet, for he spoke "when possessed by God and carried away out of himself," experiencing "that divine possession in virtue of which he is chiefly and in the strict sense considered a prophet (*Mos.* 2.188, 191). Josephus' views on prophecy are frequently read into his rewritten versions of the Hebrew Bible (Feldman 1990). So, for example, 1 Sam. 16:13, which states that "the spirit of the LORD came mightily upon David from that day forward," is revised by Josephus to read "when the divine spirit had moved him, he began to prophesy" (*Ant.* 6.166).

BIBLIOGRAPHY

D. E. AUNE 1983, *Prophecy in Early Christianity and the Ancient Mediterranean World,* Grand Rapids: Eerdmans. • L. W. BARNETT 1981, "The Jewish Sign Prophets — A.D. 40-70 — Their Intentions and Origin," *NTS* 27: 679-97. • J. BARTON 1986, *Oracles of God: Perceptions of Ancient Prophecy in Israel after the Exile,* London: Darton, Longman, and Todd. • J. BLENKINSOPP 1974, "Prophecy and Priesthood in Josephus," *JJS* 25: 239-62. • L. H. FELDMAN 1990, "Prophets and Prophecy in Josephus," *JTS* 41: 386-42. • R. GRAY 1993, *Prophetic Figures in Late Second Temple Jewish Palestine: The Evidence of Josephus,* New York and Oxford: Oxford University Press. • R. A. HORSLEY AND J. S. HANSON 1985, *Bandits, Prophets, and Messiahs: Popular Movements in the Time of Jesus,* San Francisco: HarperSanFrancisco. • A. P. JASSEN 2007, *Mediating the Divine: Prophecy and Revelation in the Dead Sea Scrolls and Second Temple Judaism,* Leiden: Brill. • G. JEREMIAS 1963, *Der Lehrer der Gerechtigkeit,* Göttingen: Vandenhoeck & Ruprecht. • J. R. LEVISON 1997A, *The Spirit in First-Century Judaism,* Leiden: Brill. • J. R. LEVISON 1997B, "Did the Spirit Withdraw from Israel? An Evaluation of the Earliest Jewish Data," *NTS* 43: 35-57. • R. MEYER 1990, "Jüdische Charismatiker und Propheten in hellenistisch-römischen Zeit," in *Erfüllung und Erwartung: Studien zur Prophetie auf dem Weg von Alten zum Neuen Testament,* ed. G. Wallis, Berlin: Evangelische Verlaganstalt. • B. D. SOMMER 1996, "Did Prophecy Cease? Evaluating a Reevaluation," *JBL* 115: 31-37.

See also: Jesus of Nazareth; John the Baptist

DAVID E. AUNE

Prophets, Pseudo-

"Pseudo-prophetic texts" is the general rubric under which a collection of Hebrew fragments from Qumran Cave 4 has come to be classified. The fragments comprise a previously unknown work or works related to the biblical books of Jeremiah and Ezekiel. Paleographically, most of the fragments date to the second half of the first century B.C.E. (except 4QpapPseudo-Ezekiel[e], whose script dates to the second century B.C.E.), although their content (especially the Jeremiah material) may suggest an earlier date of composition.

Classification and Publication

The use of the general classification "pseudo-prophetic texts" hints at one of the larger problems associated with these texts — that of defining them more precisely. Part of the difficulty owes to the deplorable physical condition of most of the fragments, and to the prevalence of language that is broadly biblical and prophetic. Another difficulty has come from a complicated history of scholarship.

All of these fragments have now been published under more precise titles in the series Discoveries in the Judaean Desert (DJD). In those editions, fragments from the manuscripts numbered 4Q383-391 are divided into three separate Jeremiah works (one of them in six copies) and an Ezekiel work preserved in six copies.

The Jeremiah texts are as follows: 4QApocryphon of Jeremiah A, 4QpapApocryphon of Jeremiah B?, and 4QApocryphon of Jeremiah C (in six copies, Apocryphon of Jeremiah C[a-f]). Based upon a reference to Tahpanhes (a city in Egypt where Jeremiah reputedly ended his career; cf. Jer. 42:19; 43:7) and use of other Jeremianic language, the editor of 4QpapApocryphon of Jeremiah B(?) (M. Smith 1995a) published those papyrus fragments as a possible apocryphal Jeremiah text. 4QApocryphon of Jeremiah A and C were published later (D. Dimant 2001) as distinct works related to Jeremiah, although their editor allows that A may be another copy of C.

The texts pertaining to Ezekiel are as follows: 4QPseudo-Ezekiel[a-d], 4QPseudo-Ezekiel Unidentified Fragments (all published by D. Dimant 2001), and 4QpapPseudo-Ezekiel[e] (published separately by M. Smith 1995b). An overlapping fragment connects 4QPseudo-Ezekiel[a], 4QPseudo-Ezekiel[b], and 4QPseudo-Ezekiel[d]. There are no overlaps of the leather fragments with the papyrus manuscript.

Prior to the publication of the DJD editions, the

fragments of 4Q383-391 were reclassified several times. At first, the entire body of fragments that now comprise *Pseudo-Ezekiel* and the *Apocryphon of Jeremiah* was given the title *Pseudo-Ezekiel* (and sometimes *Second Ezekiel*). This was done by J. Strugnell (the original editor of the texts), with the understanding that the fragments represented one work pertaining to both prophets. Later, D. Dimant assumed editorial responsibility and subdivided those fragments into three distinct works. The first was a *Pseudo-Ezekiel* text containing the largest number of fragments and preserved in several copies. Somewhat smaller was a *Pseudo-Moses* composition (in multiple copies) which contained a review of history through divine revelation to Moses. And an *Apocryphon of Jeremiah* was represented by only a few clear fragments.

By the time 4Q383 and 4Q385-390 were published in DJD 30, the fragments had undergone a substantial reclassification. 4Q383 became 4QApocryphon of Jeremiah A, while the majority of fragments from 4Q385-390 (including what was previously the Moses composition) were assigned to the copies of the work labeled *Apocryphon of Jeremiah C*. The remainder was presented as belonging to five of the six copies of *Pseudo-Ezekiel*. 4Q384, which is 4QpapApocryphon of Jeremiah B(?), and 4Q391, or 4QpapPseudo-Ezekiel[e] (both in DJD 19), kept their previous designations.

Fragments Related to Jeremiah

Although it is difficult to speak with much clarity or certainty about a cohesive work or group of compositions, some qualities, particularly those pertaining to connections to the biblical books, can be described. Most of the fragments clearly related to Jeremiah are small and damaged, with some differences in hand and material aspect. No large sections of continuous unbroken text are preserved. The fragments of *Apocryphon of Jeremiah* share no overlaps with the biblical book itself, but do share language and details, particularly biographical, concerning the prophet and his activities surrounding the Exile (esp. Jeremiah 40–44 and 52). These are reminiscent of other works related to Jeremiah, such as the *Epistle of Jeremiah, 2 Baruch,* and *4 Baruch (Paraleipomena Ieremiou)*. Other fragments rework biblical details into surveys of events in Israel's history (primarily exilic and postexilic times), using chronological frameworks like those found in *Jubilees, 1 Enoch,* and the *Damascus Document* (with references to "seventy years," "weeks of years," and "jubilees"). The composition likely attempts to address matters of sin, exile, and the hope of return in ways similar to the wider body of Jewish apocrypha and pseudepigrapha of the Second Temple period.

Fragments Related to Ezekiel

Similarly, although the fragments assigned to *Pseudo-Ezekiel* do not quote the biblical book of Ezekiel, they do draw heavily on it, reworking passages such as the vision of the dry bones (Ezekiel 37), the chariot vision (Ezekiel 1), and the prophecy against Egypt (Ezekiel 30). Unfortunately, these fragments are also rather broken. Qumranic sectarian terminology does not appear in them, although there are many similarities of grammar, vocabulary, and theme. In general, the larger fragments convey a concern for the themes of punishment of the wicked, reward of the righteous, and hastening of time toward a final, redemptive era, similar to a wider body of Jewish writings, including *4 Ezra* and *2 Baruch*. There also appears to be a connection (most likely due to access to common traditions) between *Pseudo-Ezekiel's* exegesis of Ezekiel 37 and some early Christian writings concerned with resurrection. These include the *Epistle of Barnabas* (12:1), the *Apocalypse of Peter* (4:7-9), and *1 Clement* (50:4). Aside from their shared association with the prophet Ezekiel, the fragments appear to be unrelated to the *Apocryphon of Ezekiel* known to early church fathers.

The physical condition of these fragments may leave many of the issues pertaining to their precise categorization unresolved. And it may be that a coherent understanding of the larger composition(s) will continue to be elusive. Still, this intriguing group of "pseudo-prophetic texts" provides us with a window into some of the ways biblical prophetic material was understood and reinterpreted in early Judaism.

BIBLIOGRAPHY

M. BRADY 2000, "Prophetic Traditions at Qumran: A Study of 4Q383-391," Dissertation, University of Notre Dame. • D. DIMANT 2001, *Qumran Cave 4.XXI, Parabiblical Texts, Part 4: Pseudo-Prophetic Texts,* DJD 30, Oxford: Clarendon. • M. SMITH 1995A, "4QpapApocryphon of Jeremiah B?," in *Qumran Cave 4.XIV, Parabiblical Texts, Part 2,* DJD 19, Oxford: Clarendon, 137-52. • M. SMITH 1995B, "4QpapPseudo-Ezekiel[e]," in *Qumran Cave 4.XIV, Parabiblical Texts, Part 2,* DJD 19, Oxford: Clarendon, 153-93.

MONICA L. W. BRADY

Proselytism → Conversion and Proselytism

Proverbs, Book of

The book of Proverbs is the clearest example of instructional literature in the Hebrew Bible. It is an anthology of sayings, admonitions, and longer discourses on how to succeed in life and maintain proper reverence before God. The basic point of orientation in Proverbs is human behavior and its consequences.

Structure

The traditional Hebrew version of the book (Masoretic text or MT) consists of thirty-one chapters. The first major section, 1:1–9:18, has a more unified message than do subsequent sections. These chapters warn of specific temptations and encourage the youthful addressee to seek wisdom. Chapters 10–30 contain the following collections of sayings: 10:1–22:16; 22:17–24:22; 24:23-34; 25:1–29:27; 30:1-14; 30:15-33; 31:1-9; 31:10-31. In these units, there is a mixture of explicit commands or prohibitions and simple declarative statements. Many contiguous proverbs have no identifiable connection

PROVERBS, BOOK OF

and are grouped together based on catchwords. In terms of length, the two-line saying is the most common form.

Authorship and Setting

Several headings in Proverbs mention King Solomon (e.g., 10:1), who is associated with the authorship of sayings. The historical reliability of these attributions is now questioned by most scholars; few would accept Solomonic authorship for any of this material. In actuality, the diverse content of Proverbs probably comes from a variety of sources. Some of the sayings have a "folk" origin and reflect the observations of farmers, artisans, and other sectors of ancient Israelite society. Many proverbs undoubtedly come from literate classes, including royal administrators.

A number of the book's features adhere to an established wisdom tradition in the ancient Near East, most notably in Egypt. One passage (22:17–23:11) demonstrates dependence on the Egyptian *Instruction of Amenemope* (ca. twelfth century B.C.E.). Since Egyptian instructions were copied in scribal schools, Proverbs could also have been compiled in such a setting. Even though the existence of organized schools in Israel is debated, it is likely that the preserved form of Proverbs comes from scribal officials who were responsible for cataloguing maxims. There is a reference in 25:1 to the sayings "that the officials of King Hezekiah of Judah copied."

Date

Pinpointing a precise date of composition for Proverbs is an impossible task. The text is largely devoid of historical markers, and the process of collecting sayings was an ongoing one in ancient Israel. Many observations in the book assume kingship to be a present reality, and this suggests a preexilic date for at least some of the content. Most commentators assume that this collection continued to evolve after the Exile. The discourses in Proverbs 1–9 are thought by many interpreters to be later, perhaps from the Persian period.

Content and Message

Much of Proverbs is cast as advice from a father to his son, a common motif for ancient instructional literature. The young pupil is supposed to learn proper comportment, and the advice is generally pragmatic. Sayings offer simple observations about life and how to avoid various pitfalls. Favorite topics include relationships between superiors and inferiors, honest business dealings, familial relations, and the need to control one's temper. The book is notable for its lack of interest in the Torah and the national destiny of Israel.

A thesis statement for Proverbs is set forth in the initial prologue: "The fear of the LORD is the beginning of knowledge; fools despise wisdom and instruction" (1:7). The "fear of the LORD" concept has the connotation of reverential awe: the young man who is the target of this advice should develop an obedient mind-set, with the understanding that he will be called to account for the content of his character. Many of the sayings in Proverbs affirm a consistent relationship between act and consequence. The righteous will enjoy earthly rewards based on their good deeds, and the wicked will suffer a terrible fate. For example, "Those who are attentive to a matter will prosper" (16:20). Conversely, "The evil are ensnared by the transgression of their lips" (12:13). In such sayings, the sages seek to convey the benefits of living a righteous life (although they do not promise eternal life). Sometimes God is mentioned as the arbiter of human conduct, but in other sayings events seem to happen automatically. It has been argued that later (postexilic) editors added God language to a largely secular instruction, but this is uncertain.

Lady Wisdom and the Strange Woman

In Proverbs 1–9, two female figures are depicted as personified agents and juxtaposed with one another. Lady wisdom represents the correct path, and her instruction is accessible to all who will listen. By reaching out to her, pupils can find meaning and success in life. In contrast, the strange woman (presented as an adulteress) symbolizes the reckless and destructive course.

LXX Proverbs

The ordering of material in the Greek version (LXX) of Proverbs is different from that in the MT, particularly in chaps. 24–31. In addition, textual variants throughout the book raise the question of whether the Greek translator intentionally changed the meaning of certain sayings, did not understand the point of the Hebrew phrase, or had a different *Vorlage* (parent text). Many scholars claim that LXX Proverbs should be examined in its own right, as a sapiential document from the Hellenistic period.

Reactions to Proverbs

The ethical understanding found in Proverbs, particularly the affirmation of an act-consequence relationship, would be questioned by later sages of the Second Temple period (e.g., Qoheleth). In addition, Ben Sira (second century B.C.E.) made an explicit link between Wisdom and Torah. Finally, certain instructional texts from the Hellenistic period moved beyond the earthly focus in Proverbs to offer eternal life as a reward for righteousness (e.g., Wisdom of Solomon).

BIBLIOGRAPHY

L. BOSTRÖM 1990, *The God of the Sages: The Portrayal of God in the Book of Proverbs*, Stockholm: Almqvist and Wiksell. • R. CLIFFORD 1999, *Proverbs*, Louisville: Westminster John Knox. • M. FOX 2000, *Proverbs 1–9*, New York: Doubleday. • M. FOX 2005, "LXX Proverbs as a Text-Critical Resource," *Text* 22: 95-128. • W. MCKANE 1970, *Proverbs*, Philadelphia: Westminster. • R. MURPHY 1998, *Proverbs*, Dallas: Word. • H. WASHINGTON 1994, *Wealth and Poverty in the Instruction of Amenemope and the Hebrew Proverbs*, Atlanta: Scholars Press.

SAMUEL L. ADAMS

Psalm 151

Psalm 151 is preserved in two editions and four ancient languages. The most familiar edition is the Greek (Septuagint) version, on which the Latin and Syriac translations are based. The original Hebrew edition became known only with the publication of the large Psalms scroll from Cave 11 at Qumran (11QPs[a]) in 1961. Although Jews, Protestants, and Catholics do not regard Psalm 151 as part of the book of Psalms, it is viewed as Scripture by the Greek and other Eastern Orthodox churches. For these churches the canonical text that concludes the Psalter is the Septuagint version (or translations made from the Greek).

The Greek version consists of one psalm of seven verses with a single superscription, which ends the Book of Psalms in the Septuagint. In 11QPs[a], however, the "Qumran Psalter" ends with two separate Hebrew Psalms 151A and 151B, each with its own superscriptions. This shows that the Psalm 151 in the Greek Bible is an amalgamation of the two Hebrew psalms. It appears that these Hebrew psalms were composed well before the Christian era, most likely in the Hellenistic period, and that the translation into Greek was made at the beginning of the second century C.E.

Psalm 151 (or 151A and 151B) is the only Psalm where both superscription(s) and content are *unambiguously* autobiographical with respect to David. While the superscriptions of several other biblical psalms clearly refer to events in David's life (e.g., Psalm 57, "a *miktam* of David, when he fled from Saul, in the cave"), in all such cases the body of the psalm cannot specifically be linked to David but expresses heartfelt sentiments of the pious (cf. Ps. 57:1, "Be merciful to me, O God . . . ; in the shadow of your wings I will take refuge, until the destroying storms pass by").

In contrast, events in David's life are unambiguously evident in both the superscription(s) and contents of Psalm 151. In the Greek version, the superscription includes "truly ascribed to David" and "after he had fought in single combat with Goliath," and the psalm itself refers to David's brothers ("I was small among my brothers"), David as shepherd ("I tended my father's sheep"), his musical prowess ("my hands made a harp"), his being chosen ("and took me from my father's sheep"), his anointing ("and anointed me with his anointing oil"), and his victory over Goliath ("I went out to meet the Philistine . . . but I drew his own sword; I beheaded him").

The Hebrew original is even more Davidic, with Psalm 151A titled "a hallelujah of David the son of Jesse," and the superscription to Psalm 151B denoting the Goliath incident: "At the beginning of God's power after the prophet of God had anointed him. Then I [saw] a Philistine uttering defiances from the r[anks of the enemy]"). Unfortunately, the rest of 151B is not preserved in the Cave 11 *Psalms Scroll.*

Psalm 151A is longer than the Greek version, with additional details about David (v. 1: the LXX reads, "I tended my father's flock"; 11QPs[a] adds, "So he made me shepherd of his flock and ruler over his kids"), or more information on certain themes (compare v. 2: the LXX reads, "My hands made a harp; my fingers fashioned a lyre"; 11QPs[a] adds, "and I have rendered glory to the Lord, thought I, within my soul" plus another verse expressing David's hymnody [v. 3, "The mountains do not witness to him . . . the trees have cherished my words and the flock my works"). Unlike the Greek edition, the Hebrew version makes specific reference to the covenant in a longer form of v. 7 that describes the purpose of David's anointing by Samuel: "and he made me leader to his people, and ruler over the sons of his covenant."

BIBLIOGRAPHY

M. G. ABEGG, P. W. FLINT, AND E. ULRICH 1999, *The Dead Sea Scrolls Bible,* San Francisco: HarperSanFrancisco, 585-86. • W. BAARS 1972, "Psalmi Apocryphi," in *The Old Testament in Syriac according to the Peshiṭta Version,* Part 4.6, Leiden: Brill, i-x + 1-12, esp. 2-4. • J. H. CHARLESWORTH WITH J. A. SANDERS 1985, "More Psalms of David," in *OTP,* 2:609-24, esp. 612-15. • P. W. FLINT 1998, "The Book of Psalms in the Light of the Dead Sea Scrolls," *VT* 48: 453-72, esp. 467-69. • F. GARCÍA MARTÍNEZ, E. J. C. TIGCHELAAR, AND A. S. VAN DER WOUDE 1998, "11QPs b," in *Qumran Cave 11.II,* DJD 23, Oxford: Clarendon, 37-47 + pl. iii. • A. PIETERSMA 2000, *A New English Translation of the Septuagint, and the Other Greek Translations Traditionally Included under That Title: The Psalms,* Oxford: Oxford University Press, 147-48. • J. A. SANDERS 1965, *The Psalms Scroll of Qumrân Cave 11 [11QPs[a]],* DJD 4, Oxford: Clarendon, 49, 53-64 + pl. xvii. • J. C. VANDERKAM AND P. W. FLINT 2002, *The Meaning of the Dead Sea Scrolls,* San Francisco: HarperSanFrancisco, 189-91, 447.

PETER W. FLINT

Psalms, Apocryphal

The designation "Apocryphal Psalms" is used in various ways. Most broadly, it can include any religious poetry that has been preserved from the Second Temple period, apart from those 150 poems that were collected into what became the biblical (Masoretic) Psalter. There were poetic compositions written in Greek and preserved in Septuagint manuscripts (Psalm 151, The Prayer of Manasseh), and other psalms preserved by the Syriac church (Syriac Psalms 151–155). Sometimes the authors and communities that produced such religious poetry are very difficult to determine *(Psalms of Solomon);* in other cases, the theology, vocabulary, and worldview of certain collections of poems link them clearly to a specific sectarian group (the *Thanksgiving Psalms* or *Hodayot* stem from the same Jewish community at Qumran that produced the *Rule of the Community* and the *War Scroll*).

More narrowly, the term "Apocryphal Psalms" is restricted to poetic texts preserved in the manuscripts found at Qumran, especially those compositions that were totally unknown before the discovery of the Dead Sea Scrolls. From Cave 4, there are two collections of psalms (discussed below), as well as some more fragmentary collections. For example, 4Q448 includes a psalm that mentions King Jonathan plus another psalm related to what was preserved in Syriac as Psalm 154, and 4Q409 is a psalm-type summons to praise God at the time of various festivals. In addition, a few damaged manuscripts have been designated as "psalm," "hymn," or "prayer" because the few words that have survived seem to address God directly or preserve some poetic language or parallel expressions. Although much of this material is very fragmentary and there are many unanswered questions, it is an important witness to an ongoing tradition of composing religious poetry in the Second Temple period.

Noncanonical Psalms A and B

"Noncanonical Psalms A and B" is the title given to a collection of psalms in Hebrew, preserved only in two manuscripts, 4Q380 and 4Q381, both copied in the first century B.C.E. There is no overlapping text between the two scrolls, and so it is not certain if they are copies of the same collection or if there were two distinct collections. Portions of at least fifteen psalms are preserved, some with headings that follow the pattern of the biblical psalm titles; for example, "The Prayer of Manasseh, king of Judah when the king of Assyria took him prisoner" (4Q381 frg. 33 line 8). Where the psalms are attributed to specific figures, all are either royal or prophetic. In addition to King Manasseh, there is a psalm of "the man of God" (4Q318 frg. 24 line 4), a "king of Judah" (4Q381 frg. 31 line 4), and Obadiah (4Q380 frg. l col. ii line 18); no psalm is specifically attributed to David by name.

The psalms are clearly modeled on the biblical psalter in content, theme, and structure. In addition to the biblical-style titles noted above, two psalms preserve the biblical term *selah* at the end (4Q381 frg. 24 line 3; frg. 33 line 6). Some of the distinctive themes include: a psalm about Zion (4Q380 frg. 1 col. i lines 1-11), a recounting of creation (4Q381 frg. 1 lines 1-12), a covenant lawsuit exhortation (4Q381 69 76-77), and lamentation and petition for forgiveness of sins (4Q318 frg. 33 lines 4-5). Certain compositions seem to be built around allusions to, and even direct quotation of, biblical psalms (e.g., 4Q381 frg. 24 lines 2-7 quotes Ps. 86:16-17 and Ps. 89:7-14). There is virtually no distinctive sectarian vocabulary, and the Tetragrammaton is used frequently.

Barki Nafshi

The *Barki Nafshi* is a collection of psalms that has been named from the phrase "Bless, O my soul" that begins one of the better-preserved psalms. These psalms have no title and are not attributed to any specific biblical figure. There are five manuscripts at Qumran (4Q434-438); all are probably copies of a single collection, though there is only a small amount of overlapping of text.

Since only the beginning of one psalm is preserved, it is not clear if this exhortation "Bless the Lord, O my soul" (as in Ps. 103:1, 2, 22 and Ps. 104:1, 35) was a standard opening formulary and a defining feature of these psalms. These are all psalms of praise for God's mercy, kindness, and favor in delivering the poor and afflicted from their enemies and from various perils. The language is very general; the poetic style is traditional with short parallel lines. There are many citations of and allusions to biblical phrases and even complete lines, most often from Isaiah or the Psalms.

Some scholars have suggested that these psalms were composed by the same sectarian community at Qumran that wrote the *Rule of the Community*, the *Hodayot*, and the *War Scroll*. But others judge that the vocabulary and themes are not really distinctive, and could reflect the much more general piety of Second Temple Judaism. It is difficult to find any hint of a specific context for either the composition or the ongoing use of these psalms.

BIBLIOGRAPHY

E. SCHULLER, 1998, "Non-Canonical Psalms, 4Q380 and 4Q381," in *Qumran Cave 4.VI, Poetical and Liturgical Texts, Part 1*, DJD 11, Oxford: Clarendon, 75-172. • M. WEINFELD AND D. SEELY 1999, "Barkhi Nafshi," in *Qumran Cave 4.XX, Poetical and Liturgical Texts, Part 2*, ed. E. G. Chazon et al., DJD 29, Oxford: Clarendon, 255-334.

See also: Barki Nafshi (4Q434-438); Hodayot (1QH and Related Texts); Hymns, Prayers, and Psalms; Manasseh, Prayer of; Psalm 151 EILEEN SCHULLER

Psalms, Book of

The psalms played an indisputably important role in early Jewish ritual life and in the composition of Scripture. Although the book of Psalms is sometimes referred to as the "Songbook of the Second Temple," the precise role of the psalms in Temple worship during the Persian and Greco-Roman eras is unclear, but the psalms were likely used in both public and private worship, for praying and for studying.

Structure and Contents

The medieval Masoretic text of the book of Psalms found in most Bibles offers a division of the 150 psalms into five "books" (1–41, 42–72, 73–89, 90–106, 107–150) that have been thought to correspond in some way to the five books of the Pentateuch. Scholars continue to debate the precise rationale for this grouping and the internal organization of the book. Psalm 1 is a wisdom psalm that seems to introduce the collection of psalms as instruction (torah) that should be studied; the second psalm is a royal psalm that has been interpreted to refer to a future messiah. The book of Psalms ends with a crescendo of intensifying praise to God (Psalms 145–150) so that by the end of the book, everything that breathes is called upon to render praise to God as king, creator, and redeemer, ending with the final word, *Hallelujah* ("Praise the LORD!"). In addition to these bookends, the shaping of the Psalter can be seen in various ways, including the punctuation at the end of the second book of the Psalms, Ps. 72:20, with the phrase, "The prayers of David, son of Jesse, are complete." Some scholars have suggested that one rationale for the shap-

PSALMS, BOOK OF

ing of the collection is to shift attention from human kings to the divine king, nonetheless retaining the expectation of a future messianic king. Yet that is just one interpretation isolating one theme in a complex collection of poems.

There are subcollections within the book of Psalms that seem to predate their division into five books. The largest comprises Psalms 42–83. It has been called the "Elohistic Psalter" by modern scholars because of its preference for the use of the generic term *Elohim* for God rather than the Tetragrammaton, YHWH or "LORD." The collection may have been used in the worship of the northern kingdom of Israel. Psalms 120–134 all have the title "A Song of Ascent" and are thought to have been used by pilgrims on their way up to the Temple in Jerusalem for the major festivals. Twelve psalms are attributed to the "sons of Asaph," perhaps a guild of Temple singers (Psalms 50, 73–83), and eleven psalms are attributed to "the sons of Korah" (Psalms 42, 44–49, 84–85, 87–88), also members of a musical guild (2 Chron. 20:19).

Modern form-criticism of the Psalms classifies them into five major types: individual laments (the largest category), communal laments, individual thanksgivings, communal thanksgivings, and hymns. In addition, there are a number of smaller subtypes, such as songs celebrating the city of Jerusalem, enthronement psalms which extol God as king, royal psalms which focus on the human king of Israel, and wisdom psalms that are didactic and show similarities to the biblical wisdom literature. There are many variations among these types, and often individual psalms contain mixed forms. In terms of theme, the book of Psalms is representative of the Tanak as a whole, characterized by great variety. Some psalms emphasize the divine role as creator of the good cosmos (Psalm 104), and some stress the role of divine action in Israel's history (Psalm 105). Others focus on the divine covenant with the Davidic king (Psalm 89). The Psalms include both a high view of humans as "little less than gods" (Ps. 8:5) and a low view of the psalmist as "a worm and no man" (Ps. 22:6).

Psalms Elsewhere in the Bible

Psalms also appear outside the book of Psalms. Their appearance in narrative settings provides clues both about how psalms may have been used by individuals and in corporate worship, but also about the composition of the psalms and their ongoing process of transmission. Exodus 15:1-18, the song of the Israelites commemorating their liberation from the Egyptians, is thought to be one of the oldest compositions in the Bible. It is an individual thanksgiving that became a model for later victory hymns, such as Judith 16. The Song of Hannah in 1 Sam. 2:1-10 is a corporate thanksgiving that served as a model for the Magnificat in Luke 1:46-55. The duplication of the same psalm in different books also occurs. 2 Samuel 22:1-51 is almost identical to Psalm 18, providing a narrative context in the life of David (cf. Isa. 38:10-20 and Psalms 30 and 107.)

The addition of psalm-like compositions to the Greek books of Esther and Daniel suggests that psalm composition continued throughout the Greco-Roman period, perhaps even as a part of the oral performance of these books in Hellenized Jewish circles. 1 Chronicles 16:8-36 is a thanksgiving that combines reworked excerpts from Psalms 105, 96, and 106. The appearance of this alternate psalm suggests that creative and interpretive reuse of the psalms was an acceptable way of composing new scripture.

Evidence from the Dead Sea Scrolls

With the exception of Psalm 137, which explicitly mentions the Babylonian Exile, the Psalms cannot be dated with certainty, but psalms manuscripts from the Dead Sea Scrolls have provided more evidence concerning the development of the book of Psalms. Thirty-nine scrolls incorporate psalms, a number that makes the "book" of Psalms the most frequently represented among the Scrolls, yet it is also apparent that there was no one fixed "canonical" collection of psalms in the first century B.C.E. The great Psalms Scroll found at Qumran (11QPs[a]) has a different ordering from the Masoretic Psalter. 11QPs[a] also includes seven compositions not found in the Masoretic Psalter, three of which are known from Syriac sources; four of these were previously unknown. While the scroll was most likely copied at Qumran for the community's use, the collection as a whole likely predates the community and was probably used by a segment of Judaism, such as the Essenes, that followed the solar calendar. All told, the evidence from Qumran points to a gradual stabilization of the book of Psalms. One hundred sixteen psalms in the received Masoretic text have superscriptions. Twenty-eight of the thirty-four psalms that do not have a superscription occur in the last two books of psalms, a point that suggests the earlier crystallization of the first three books of psalms.

The Dead Sea Scrolls contain many other psalms or psalm-like compositions, including the *Hodayot,* a sectarian collection of hymns, many of which begin with "I thank the Lord" or the blessing formula, "Blessed are you, Lord." In addition to manuscripts of psalms known from the Bible and extracanonical psalms, the Dead Sea Scrolls also include a pesher commentary on the Psalms (4Q171) that interprets Psalms 37 and 45 by relating their contents directly to the life of the Qumran community.

David and the Psalms

By the first century B.C.E., the Psalms were considered authored by King David, an understanding rooted in various traditions about his life as a poet and musician (1 Sam. 16:16-16; 2 Sam. 1:17-27) as well as someone with prophetic gifts (2 Sam. 23:1-2). His portrayal in the fourth-century-B.C.E. book of Chronicles greatly emphasizes his role as sponsor of the Jerusalem Temple and its worship (1 Chron. 28:11-19; 1 Chron. 29:1-5). The evolution of increasing Davidic attribution of the Psalms can be seen in the Masoretic text of the Psalms, in which seventy-three psalms contain the Hebrew superscription *lĕ-Dāwîd* in the heading (sixty-nine occur in the first three books). In the Septuagint, twelve more are ascribed to David, for a total of eighty-five. The view of David as inspired author of psalms is most clearly evident in one of the compositions found in 11QPs[a] in which God is said to have given him a "discerning and brilliant spirit," and he is credited with 4,050 compositions, including 3,600 psalms and 364 songs to sing before the altar for the daily sacrifice.

The New Testament Gospels, among other early Jewish writings, understand the Psalms as prophetic speech of David (Matt. 22:44/Mark 12:36/Luke 20:42; Acts 1:16-17, 20; 2:25). Jesus' words on the cross from Ps. 22:1 (Matt. 27:46; Mark 15:34) may thus not simply lament divine abandonment, but point to the end of the psalm with its praise for divine restoration. The view of David as prophetic author of the Psalms continued not only in early Christianity but in rabbinic Judaism, underlying the classic rabbinic commentary, *Midrash Tehillim.*

BIBLIOGRAPHY

P. W. FLINT 1997, *The Dead Sea Psalms Scroll and the Book of Psalms,* Leiden: Brill. • E. GERSTENBERGER 1988-2001, *Psalms, Part 1, with an Introduction to Cultic Poetry; Psalms, Part 2, and Lamentations,* Grand Rapids: Eerdmans. • S. GILLINGHAM 1994, *The Poems and Psalms of the Hebrew Bible,* Oxford: Oxford University Press. • E. MENN 2003, "Sweet Singer of Israel," in *Psalms in Community: Jewish and Christian Textual, Liturgical, and Artistic Traditions,* ed. H. W. Attridge and M. Fassler, Atlanta: Society of Biblical Literature, 61-74. • J. A. SANDERS 1967, *The Dead Sea Psalms Scroll,* Ithaca: Cornell University Press. • E. SCHULLER 1986, *Non-Canonical Psalms from Qumran: A Pseudepigraphic Collection,* Atlanta: Scholars Press. • G. WILSON 1985, *The Editing of the Hebrew Psalter,* Chico, Calif.: Scholars Press.

See also: Hodayot (1QH and Related Texts); Hymns, Prayers, and Psalms; Psalms, Apocryphal; Psalms Scrolls; Worship JUDITH H. NEWMAN

Psalms Scrolls

Among the almost 900 scrolls found in the Judean Desert, no book is represented by more copies than the book of Psalms. The Dead Sea Scrolls include thirty-nine Psalms scrolls: thirty-six from Qumran, one from Naḥal Ḥever, and two from Masada. At least one more scroll from Qumran incorporates a psalm, and there are three pesharim on the book of Psalms. Of the 150 psalms found in the "MT 150 Psalter" (i.e., the Masoretic book of Psalms), 126 are represented in the thirty-nine Psalms scrolls or other relevant manuscripts such as the three pesharim. The remaining twenty-four psalms were all most likely included but are now lost due to damage and the deterioration of the scrolls. Of Psalms 1–89, nineteen no longer survive, and of Psalms 90–150 five are not represented, a discrepancy explained by the fact that scrolls usually begin on the outside, which is more easily damaged and thus more prone to deterioration.

At least fifteen "apocryphal" psalms or compositions are included among four manuscripts (4QPs[f], 11QPs[a], 11QPs[b], 11QapocPs). Six were previously familiar to scholars: Psalms 151A, 151B, 154, and 155; David's Last Words (= 2 Sam. 23:1-7); and Sir. 52:13-30. The other nine (or ten?) were unknown prior to the discovery of the Scrolls: Apostrophe to Judah, Apostrophe to Zion, David's Compositions, Eschatological Hymn, Hymn to the Creator, Plea for Deliverance, three Songs against Demons, and possibly the Catena of Psalm 118.

In decreasing order, the manuscripts with the highest number of verses represented are 11QPs[a], 4QPs[a], 5/6ḤevPs, 4QPs[b], 4QPs[c], and 4QPs[e]. At least ten manuscripts are arranged stichometrically, while twenty-one are in prose format: two from Cave 1, two from the Minor Caves, fourteen from Cave 4, and three from Cave 11. One scroll (11QPs[a]) is a prose collection with a single psalm written in stichometric format.

The extant superscriptions reveal little variation in comparison with the MT Psalter, but with two exceptions: 11QPs[a] has a title for Psalm 123 ("A Song of Ascents. Of David") where the MT has no superscription, and a different title for Psalm 145 ("A Prayer. Of David") from that found in the MT.

At least thirteen manuscripts were copied before the Common Era. The oldest of these are 4QPs[a] and 4QPs[w], from the second century B.C.E.; ten were copied in the first century B.C.E.; and the final one (4QPs[v]) is more loosely classified as Hasmonean. A further six scrolls are generally classified as Herodian, and four are assigned to the first century C.E. More specifically, ten others are dated to the early to mid-first century C.E. and five to the mid-first century C.E. onward.

Scrolls Diverging from the Masoretic Psalter

Twelve scrolls contain two types of disagreement from the Masoretic Psalter: in *arrangement* of psalms (seven scrolls from Cave 4: e.g., Psalm 31 → 33 in 4QPs[a] and 4QPs[q]); and in *content,* that is, the inclusion of compositions not found in the MT (two from Cave 4 and one from Cave 11; e.g., the Apostrophe to Zion in 4QPs[f]). Both types of difference are present in two more scrolls from Cave 11 (11QPs[a] and 11QPs[b]).

The Psalms scrolls contain hundreds of individual readings, of two kinds: orthographic (spelling) differences and textual variants that extend from single words to entire verses. Many textual variants are minor, but several are significant for our understanding of the text of the Psalter. One example is in Psalm 145, an acrostic poem that lacks the *nun* verse in the Masoretic Psalter. In 11QPs[a] the psalm has the missing *nun* verse at the end of v 13: "God is faithful in his ways, and gracious in all his deeds" (col. 17:2-3). This reading is supported by one medieval Hebrew manuscript, the Septuagint (but with "the Lord" instead of "God") and the Peshiṭta.

Contents of the Psalms Scrolls

While most Psalms scrolls are very fragmentary and were much larger when copied, some never contained more than a few compositions or part of a Psalter (e.g., 4QPs[h] and 5QPs probably contained only Psalm 119). Only five scrolls (1QPs[a], 4QPs[e], 4QPs[f], 11QPs[b], and 11QPs[d]) preserve material from both Psalms 1–89 and

Psalms Scroll from Qumran (11QPs[a]) *(Courtesy Israel Antiquities Authority)*

90–150; most likely, some originally contained psalms from the earlier part of the Psalter while others comprised psalms from the later part.

The great *Psalms Scroll* (11QPs[a]), copied about 50 C.E., preserves forty-nine compositions, with at least one more (Psalm 120) now missing but originally present. In the following list, the symbol → indicates that the second composition in a sequence directly follows the first.

> Psalm 101 → 102 → 103; 109; 118 → 104 → 147 → 105 → 146 → 148 [+ 120] → 121 → 122 → 123 → 124 → 125 → 126 → 127 → 128 → 129 → 130 → 131 → 132 → 119 → 135 → 136 → Catena → 145 (with postscript) → 154 → Plea for Deliverance → 139 → 137 → 138 → Sirach 51 → Apostrophe to Zion → Psalm 93 → 14 → 133 → 14 → 155 → 142 → 143 → 149 → 150 → Hymn to the Creator → David's Last Words → David's Compositions → Psalm 140 → 134 → 151A → 151B → blank column [*end*]

This arrangement differs greatly from the one found in the Masoretic and Septuagint Psalters, in both the different order of material and the presence of additional compositions.

The Qumran Psalms Hypothesis

The first Psalms manuscripts to be discovered were fragmentary and seemed largely similar to the Masoretic Psalter, but this changed decisively with J. A. Sanders's publication of 11QPs[a] in 1965. In a series of articles (e.g., Sanders 1974), Sanders developed four theses that challenged traditional views on the text and canonization of the book of Psalms, formulating what may be labeled the Qumran Psalms Hypothesis: (1) 11QPs[a] witnesses to a Psalter that was being gradually stabilized from beginning to end. (2) Two or more Psalters are represented among the Psalms scrolls. (3) 11QPs[a] contains the latter part of a true scriptural Psalter and is not a secondary collection dependent upon Psalms 1–150 as found in the Received Text. (4) 11QPs[a] was compiled at Qumran and thus may be termed the "Qumran Psalter."

Stabilization of the Psalter

Sanders proposed that 11QPs[a] witnesses to a Psalter that was being gradually stabilized, from beginning to end. Study of groupings of Psalms in 11QPs[a], other Psalms scrolls, and the Masoretic Psalter shows that agreements between the MT and the scrolls can be regarded as indicative of stability (e.g., Psalms 49 → 50 in 4QPs[c]), while disagreements in order (e.g., Psalms 103 → 112 in 4QPs[b]) or content (e.g., Psalm 109 → Apostrophe to Zion in 4QPs[f]) provide evidence of fluidity. Focusing on adjoining psalms, G. H. Wilson (1983) proposed two bases for comparison between Psalms 1–89 and Psalms 90–150: order and content. Of Psalms 1–89, thirty-six are found in the same order as in the MT (92 percent of the total), while only three are in a conflicting order (8 percent). Of Psalms 90–150 only thirty-one support the Masoretic arrangement (39 percent), while forty-nine are in a conflicting order (61 percent). With respect to *content,* additional compositions are never joined with any of Psalms 1–89 but are linked thirteen times with compositions that appear in Psalms 90–150 of the MT Psalter.

These statistics suggest little variation from the MT-150 Psalter for Psalms 1–89, but many divergences for Psalm 90 and beyond. The evidence from Qumran indicates that Psalms 1–89 were stabilized over time, but Psalm 90 onward remained fluid (the precise cutoff point being uncertain). Furthermore, comparison of the older and later Psalms scrolls further indicates that this stabilization did not take place gradually, but in two distinct stages: Psalms 1–89 (or so) prior to the first century B.C.E., and 90 onward toward the end of the first century C.E.

Two or More Editions of the Book of Psalms

Sanders also proposed that the Psalms scrolls attest to more than one edition: the 11QPs[a] Psalter, probably the MT 150 collection, and possibly others besides. Here a (literary) edition is understood as "an intentional reworking of an older form of the book for specific purposes or according to identifiable editorial purposes" (Ulrich 1999: 89). Whether a particular book or passage constitutes a literary edition entails an assessment of variant readings, involving either key passages or different arrangements of material. Several of the Psalms scrolls differ from the Masoretic Psalter in two prominent ways: in the order of adjoining psalms, and in the presence or absence of entire compositions. A comparative analysis indicates three major editions and other collections:

Edition I: An Early Psalter The arrangement of this psalter was virtually stabilized before the second century B.C.E. and comprised Psalms 1 to 89 or thereabouts. (The cutoff point is uncertain; it may have ended with another psalm such as 72.)

Edition IIa: The 11QPs[a] Psalter This psalter contained Psalms 1–89 followed by the arrangement preserved in 11QPs[a]. The collection is discernible in two or three manuscripts on the basis of common juxtaposition of key compositions: 11QPs[a], 11QPs[b], and maybe 4QPs[e]. While the earlier part of the 11QPs[a] Psalter is not found in 11QPs[a], material from Psalms 1–89 is also preserved in 11QPs[b] (77:18-21; 78:1) and in 4QPs[e] (e.g., 76:10-12; 89:44-48, 50-53).

Edition IIb: The MT 150 Psalter Although several scrolls found at Qumran support the general arrangement of Psalms 1–89, none unambiguously confirms the longer order of the received Masoretic Text against 11QPs[a]. Firm evidence of the MT 150 collection is found only at Masada, where MasPs[b] (second half of the first century B.C.E.) ends with Psalm 150 against 11QPs[a] (Psalm 150 followed by the Hymn to the Creator). It is possible that some scrolls from Qumran supported the MT 150 Psalter when fully extant, but these are either very fragmentary (e.g., 1QPs[b]) or do not preserve material beyond Book II of the Psalter (4QPs[c], 5/6ḤevPs).

Additional Collections Further arrangements of psalms appear in several manuscripts from Qumran (4QPs[b], 4QPs[d], 4QPs[f], 4QPs[k], 4QPs[n], 11QapocPs). It is doubtful that any represents another edition of the book of Psalms.

Secondary Collections Some Psalms scrolls most likely contain secondary collections (i.e., compositions selected from a fixed scriptural collection). Two examples are 4Q522 (*Prophecy on Joshua,* with apocryphal compositions followed by Psalm 122) and 11QapocPs (Psalm 91 excerpted from a larger collection of psalms).

11QPs[a] as Part of a Scriptural Psalter

The third component of the Qumran Psalms Hypothesis is that 11QPs[a] contains the latter part of a true scriptural Psalter, and is not a secondary collection dependent upon Psalms 1–150 as found in the Masoretic Text. Reactions to this proposal by Sanders have been sharp and widespread. In 1966, M. H. Goshen-Gottstein and S. Talmon published articles asserting that 11QPs[a] is not part of a true scriptural Psalter, but a secondary liturgical compilation selected from the finalized arrangement of 150 Psalms as found in the received Psalter. Goshen-Gottstein argued that David's Compositions (the prose composition in col. 27 of 11QPs[a]) is incompatible with a scriptural Psalter, while Talmon posited that 11QPs[a] contains material supplementary to Scripture itself. In a series of articles, P. Skehan argued for the secondary status of 11QPs[a] (e.g., Skehan 1973). Reiterating the arguments put forward by his two Israeli counterparts, Skehan also sought to demonstrate that the MT 150 Psalter is chronologically prior to 11QPs[a]. In his assessment, the large Psalms scroll evolved over time, from a "library edition," to an "instruction book" containing the supposed works of David, to "an instruction book for budding Levite choristers" at the Temple, during the Oniad high priesthood (ca. 200 B.C.E.). Over the years, most scholars have supported the view that 11QPs[a] contains a rearrangement or supplementation of the MT 150 Psalter (e.g., Haran 1993).

G. H. Wilson (1985) took into consideration not only 11QPs[a], but almost all of the Cave 4 scrolls. His conclusions support several elements of the Qumran Psalms Hypothesis, especially those of stabilization over time and the status of 11QPs[a] as a true scriptural Psalter rather than a secondary collection. For example, Wilson showed that the collection in 11QPs[a] is structured in accordance with principles that govern Books IV and V in the MT 150 Psalter (e.g., the juxtaposition of superscripts and postscripts highlighting different groupings in 11QPs[a]).

P. Flint (1997) examined all the Psalms scrolls from Qumran and other Judean sites, noting that different editions of scriptural books are attested in antiquity (e.g., the two editions of Exodus in 4QExod[m] and the MT), as well as secondary liturgical compilations (e.g., 4QDeut[j] with its liturgical reordering of poetic texts from Exodus and Deuteronomy). Thus the textual evidence allows for both possibilities: that 11QPs[a] belongs to an edition of the book of Psalms, or is a collection drawn from a Psalter that had previously been finalized.

Attempts to show that 11QPs[a] represents a secondary liturgical compilation are unconvincing because they erroneously presume that the arrangement of the MT 150 Psalter had been finalized and was accepted by virtually all Jews well before the second century B.C.E. The 11QPs[a] collection should instead be regarded as a true scriptural Psalter, on three main grounds: attribution to David, structural principles, and usage (i.e., quotations and allusions in other writings found at Qumran). The Davidic character of this edition is especially evident from the arrangement of compositions in 11QPs[a], forming clusters dominated by psalms with Davidic titles, and the statement in David's Compositions (col. 27:11) that 4,050 compositions — undoubtedly including those in 11QPs[a] — were spoken by David "through prophecy." Such evidence, plus the absence of any Psalms scroll from Qumran clearly confirming the longer order of the MT 150 Psalter against 11QPs[a], suggests that the 11QPs[a] Psalter is the foremost representative of the book of Psalms in the Dead Sea Scrolls.

Provenance of the 11QPs[a] Psalter

The fourth component of the Qumran Psalms Hypothesis is that 11QPs[a] was compiled at Qumran and may thus be termed the "Qumran Psalter." Several arguments have been used in support, but these are not convincing. Other factors indicate that the collection was compiled and used by wider Jewish circles, including those at Qumran, that embraced the 364-day solar calendar — all the individual compositions in 11QPs[a] seem to predate the Qumran period, and the absence of explicitly sectarian features in 11QPs[a] suggests that none of its component pieces was composed there.

11QPs[a] Psalter most likely originated prior to the Qumran period; Sanders later stated (1993) that 11QPs[a] was brought to Qumran from outside, possibly as the *hôn* offered as surety by a novice on entering the community. The notion of an 11QPs[a] Psalter used at Qumran and among other Jewish circles advocating the solar calendar suggests a more widespread appeal to various Jewish groups, possibly including the Sadducees. This wide appeal stands in marked contrast to the Pharisees and rabbis with their 354-day lunar calendar, and cannot be viewed as sectarian. To restrict the solar calendar to "Qumran or other sects" (so Goshen-Gottstein 1966) is to make a false retrospective judgment.

Yet a distinction must be drawn between the origin of *collections* and the production of individual *scrolls*. While the 11QPs[a] Psalter was compiled among wider circles embracing the 364-day solar calendar, it seems likely that some or all copies (11QPs[a], 11QPs[b], 4QPs[e]?) were copied at Qumran in view of the apparent popularity of this Psalter among the covenanters.

On the question of provenance, then, Sanders's earlier thesis that 11QPs[a] was compiled at Qumran is found wanting, but his later proposal that it was brought there from outside is a step in the right direction. While 11QPs[a] itself was more likely copied at Qumran, asserting that the 11QPs[a] Psalter was compiled before the Qumran period supports Sanders's overall vision by affirming that this edition of the book of Psalms was used by wider Jewish circles than one small group living in the Judean Desert.

BIBLIOGRAPHY

Editions

M. BAILLET, J. T. MILIK, AND R. DE VAUX 1962, *Les "Petites Grottes" de Qumrân*, DJD 3, Oxford: Clarendon. • D. BARTHÉLEMY AND J. T. MILIK 1955, *Qumran Cave 1*, DJD 1, Oxford: Clarendon. • P. W. FLINT 2000, "The Biblical Scrolls from Naḥal Ḥever (including 'Wadi Seiyal')," in *Qumran Cave 4.XXVI, Miscellaneous Texts, Part 2*, DJD 36, Oxford: Clarendon. • F. GARCÍA MARTÍNEZ, E. TIGCHELAAR, AND A. VAN DER WOUDE 1998, "Four Psalms Scrolls from Cave 11," in *Qumran Cave 11, II: 11Q2-18, 11Q20-31*, DJD 23, Oxford: Clarendon. • J. A. SANDERS, ED. 1965, *The Psalms Scroll of Qumrân Cave 11 (11QPs[a])*, Oxford: Clarendon. • P. W. SKEHAN, E. ULRICH, AND P. W. FLINT 2000, "The Cave 4 Psalms Scrolls," in *Qumran Cave 4.11: Psalms to Chronicles*, ed. E. Ulrich, DJD 16, Oxford: Clarendon. • S. TALMON 1999, "The Psalms Scrolls from Masada," in *Masada VI: The Yigael Yadin Excavations 1963-1965, Final Reports: Hebrew Fragments from Masada*, ed. S. Talmon and Y. Yadin, Jerusalem: Israel Exploration Society.

Studies

P. W. FLINT 1997, *The Dead Sea Psalms Scrolls and the Book of Psalms*, Leiden: Brill. • M. H. GOSHEN-GOTTSTEIN 1966, "The Psalms Scroll (11QPs[a]): A Problem of Canon and Text," *Textus* 5: 22-33. • M. HARAN 1993, "11QPs[a] and the Canonical Book of Psalms," in *Minḥah le-Nahum: Biblical and Other Studies Presented to Nahum M. Sarna*, ed. M. Brettler and M. Fishbane, Sheffield: Sheffield Academic Press, 93-201. • J. A. SANDERS 1974, "The Qumran Psalms Scroll (11QPs[a]) Reviewed," in *On Language, Culture and Religion: In Honor of Eugene A. Nida*, ed. M. Black and W. A. Smalley, Paris: Mouton, 79-99. • J. A. SANDERS 1993, "Psalm 154 Revisited," in *Theologie und gesellschaftlicher Wandel*, ed. G. Braulik et al. Freiburg: Universitätsverlag, 296-306. • P. W. SKEHAN 1973, "A Liturgical Complex in 11QPs[a]," *CBQ* 34: 195-205. • S. TALMON 1966, "Pisqah Beʿemṣa' Pasuq and 11QPs[a]," *Textus* 5: 11-21. • E. ULRICH 1999, *The Dead Sea Scrolls and the Origins of the Bible*, Grand Rapids: Eerdmans. • B. Z. WACHOLDER 1988, "David's Eschatological Psalter: 11QPsalms[a]," *HUCA* 59: 23-72. • G. H. WILSON 1983, "The Qumran Psalms Manuscripts and the Consecutive Arrangement of Psalms in the Hebrew Psalter," *CBQ* 45: 377-88. • G. H. WILSON 1985, *The Editing of the Hebrew Psalter*, Chico, Calif.: Scholars Press.

PETER W. FLINT

Pseudepigrapha, Old Testament

Introduction

In modern scholarly usage the label "Old Testament Pseudepigrapha" refers to writings composed in the Hellenistic and early Roman periods (ca. 200 B.C.E.–200 C.E.) and fictionally attributed or otherwise related to characters from the time of the Hebrew Bible or Old Testament, but not included in the Jewish canon or the major Christian canons of Scripture. The category is a modern creation, and even as such it identifies no definite corpus of writings but a variety of collections with different criteria for inclusion.

The label "Old Testament Pseudepigrapha" is a problematic and in some cases an inaccurate one. To begin with, the term "Old Testament" is a Christian label that sits uncomfortably with Jews; a more ecumenical label, especially for writings composed and transmitted in Jewish circles, would be "Jewish Pseudepigrapha" or "Pseudepigrapha of the Hebrew Bible." The latter label itself would be anachronistic, however, since many of the writings in question (e.g., *1 Enoch; Jubilees*) were written when the Hebrew Bible did not yet exist as a fixed, close collection. Indeed, a few works reckoned among the Old Testament Pseudepigrapha (e.g., *1 Enoch*) seem to have been regarded as Scripture by at least some Jews in the Second Temple period. Moreover, some works eventually canonized in the Hebrew Bible (e.g., Daniel) are themselves pseudepigrapha from the Second Temple period.

Yet another problem is that some of the writings generally grouped with the Pseudepigrapha (e.g., 3, 4 Maccabees) do not employ the literary convention of pseudepigraphy (writing in the name of a revered figure of the past). Others (e.g., *Story of Ahiqar; Sibylline Oracles*) employ it but in relation to figures not found in the Hebrew Bible. Still others (e.g., the *Biblical Antiquities* of Pseudo-Philo) are pseudonymous only by way of secondary, mistaken attribution.

Despite these problems with the label "Old Testament Pseudepigrapha," its usage is so entrenched that it would be difficult to abandon it and replace it with a better one. Scores of pseudepigrapha relating in one way or another to the Hebrew Bible survive from antiquity, some complete and some only in fragments. The focus of this article is on Jewish pseudepigrapha composed before the time of the Bar Kokhba Revolt (132-135 C.E.).

Pseudepigrapha Mentioned in the Hebrew Bible and New Testament

The Hebrew Bible itself not only contains pseudonymously attributed books (most notably Deuteronomy and Daniel), it quotes from a number of lost texts that might be regarded as Jewish pseudepigrapha if they were ever to be recovered. The writer of the book of Kings mentions the "Book of the Words (or Acts) of Solomon" (1 Kings 11:41). The Chronicler refers to a dozen or so works, including the "Words (or Acts) of Samuel the Seer" and the "Words (or Acts) of Gad the Seer" (1 Chron. 29:29-30); the "Words (or Acts) of Nathan the Prophet" (1 Chron. 29:29-30; cf. 2 Chron. 9:29); and the "Prophecy of Ahijah the Shilonite" and the "Visions of Jeddo (Iddo?) the Seer concerning Jeroboam the son of Nebat" (2 Chron. 9:29). At least some of these lost works attributed to much earlier prophets and kings may well have been pseudepigraphic. Indeed, there is debate on whether the sources cited by the Chronicler actually existed at all.

The New Testament seems to quote or allude to a number of Old Testament Pseudepigrapha. Jude 14-15 quotes the *Book of the Watchers* (*1 Enoch* 1:8). 2 Timothy 3:8 alludes to the legend of the magicians Jannes and Jambres, who opposed Moses. Fragments survive of a pseudepigraphon about them which is of uncertain origin. The quotation in Jude 9 may be from a *Testament of Moses,* but it is unclear whether this was the same work that survives in a fragmentary Latin manuscript and is today called the *Testament* or *Assumption of Moses.* The quotations in Eph. 5:14 and Jas. 4:5 may come from lost pseudepigrapha.

Pseudepigrapha in the Dead Sea Scrolls and Other Jewish Manuscripts

Recently Discovered Pseudepigrapha

Traditionally, works known only from the Dead Sea Scrolls have not been counted among or grouped with the Old Testament Pseudepigrapha, but a number of them fit the definition given above. There are Aramaic works assigned to Jacob (4Q537), Amram (4Q543-548), Qahat (4Q542), and the archangel Michael (4Q529). The Aramaic *Genesis Apocryphon* (1Q20) retells the story of Genesis, and other Aramaic works have some relationship with the book of Daniel (notably the *Prayer of Nabonidus* [4Q242] but also 4QAramaic Apocalypse [4Q243-245], 4Q246, and 4Q552-553) and the book of Esther (4Q550; 4Q550a-e). Several fragmentary Hebrew works seem to assign prophecies to Moses (1Q22; 2Q21; 4Q385a, 387a, 388a, 389, 390) and Ezekiel (4Q385-386, 388, 391), and to pertain to Jeremiah (4Q383-384, 385c, 387b, 389a) and Joshua (4Q378-379, also quoted in 4Q175). Exorcistic psalms are attributed to David and perhaps Solomon (11Q11). Obadiah and Manasseh each have one psalm assigned to them (4Q380-381). (The second is unrelated to the better-known *Prayer of Manasseh,* a work sometimes placed in the Old Testament Apocrypha and sometimes among the Old Testament Pseudepigrapha.) Psalms are also attributed to a king of Judah (the name is lost) and an unnamed "man of God" in 4Q381. The *Temple Scroll* (11Q19-20) is an unusual case; it is set in the time of Moses and retells the revelation of the Mosaic Torah, but its authorial voice is that of God. Many other Qumran texts may be relevant but are too fragmentary for their contents to be clear.

Previously Known Pseudepigrapha

A number of Jewish pseudepigrapha were preserved complete only in Christian circles, usually in translation, but fragmentary copies of their originals survive among the Dead Sea Scrolls. This is true of most of the book of *1 Enoch,* a collection of early apocalypses in the name of Enoch preserved in part in Greek and complete only in an Ethiopic translation of the Greek. Aramaic fragments of the *Book of the Watchers* (*1 Enoch* 1–36), the *Astronomical Book* (*1 Enoch* 72–82), the *Book of Dreams* (*1 Enoch* 83–90), and the *Epistle of Enoch* (*1 Enoch* 91–107) were preserved at Qumran. Likewise, fragments of the Hebrew original of the book of *Jubilees* (a paraphrase and expansion of Genesis and part of Exodus) survive only among the Dead Sea Scrolls. Fragments of *Jubilees* also survive in translations into Greek, Syriac, and Latin, but the whole work is preserved only in Ethiopic. Aramaic fragments of the *Book of Giants* survive at Qumran; otherwise, the work is known only through much later fragments of a Manichean version in Iranian and Turkic. *Aramaic Levi* is known from medieval fragments from the Cairo Geniza (a vast repository of medieval Jewish manuscripts associated with a synagogue in Cairo), but also from fragments from Qumran. It served as a source for *The Testament of Levi* in the Greek *Testaments of the Twelve Patriarchs.* Much of *Hebrew Naphtali* survives in medieval traditions that have some relationship to the Greek *Testament of Naphtali,* although neither the surviving Hebrew material nor the surviving Greek text seems to preserve the text of the original Second Temple–era work. A Qumran fragment (4Q215) preserves related Hebrew material. Other Aramaic Qumran fragments may be related to the Greek *Testament of Judah* (3Q7, 4Q484, 4Q538) and *Testament of Joseph* (4Q539). The Hebrew originals of the Greek Psalm 151 and of some Syriac Psalms of David also survive in 11Q5. Finally, a *Book of Noah* is cited in *Genesis Apocryphon* 29, and it also seems to be quoted in various later sources.

Pseudepigrapha Preserved in Late Jewish Manuscripts

It has sometimes been argued that a number of Jewish pseudepigrapha preserved only in much later Jewish manuscripts go back to the Second Temple period. These include the oracular *Words of Gad the Seer,* which survives in Hebrew in one eighteenth-century Indian manuscript; the *Aramaic Song of the Lamb,* an acrostic poetic retelling of the battle of David and Goliath quoted in the late Tosefta Targum to 1 Sam. 17:8, 43 and perhaps in *Targum Jonathan* to 2 Sam. 23:8; a Hebrew sapiential text in a medieval manuscript from the Cairo Geniza; and the *Treatise of Shem,* which survives complete in a fifteenth-century Syriac manuscript, but medieval fragments of a rather different version in Jewish Aramaic and Judeo-Arabic have been recovered from the Cairo Geniza. It is possible, although by no means certain, that these works are early enough to be of interest to students of Second Temple Judaism.

There is also the special case of the *Ladder of Jacob,* a work of rewritten scripture that survives complete only in medieval manuscripts in Old Church Slavonic, with Hebrew fragments of it also preserved in a tenth-century-C.E. manuscript from the Cairo Geniza. It is possible that this is a Jewish work that was translated into Slavonic, perhaps via a Greek version, but it is also possible that a now lost Christian Greek original was translated independently into Hebrew and Slavonic. Its date of composition is very uncertain.

Pseudepigrapha Transmitted by Christians: Methodological Issues

The most difficult pseudepigrapha to evaluate are those preserved solely in Christian manuscript traditions. They survive in many ancient church languages, including Arabic, Armenian, Coptic, Ethiopic, Georgian, Greek, Latin, Old Church Slavonic, and Syriac. Most seem to have existed in a Greek version at some stage. At least one (Pseudo-Philo's *Biblical Antiquities*) was clearly composed in Hebrew before being translated into Greek, and others were composed in Greek. Often all or most of the Greek translation has been lost, so some of these texts survive only or mainly in secondary and tertiary translations into other languages. This refracting through multiple translations combined with frequently very narrow manuscript bases should urge caution about assuming that one can know the correct sense of the original in any given passage of one of these works. Any conclusions drawn about such works should be based on general themes and frequently repeated ideas in them rather than on individual proof texts.

It is tempting to assume that, when pseudepigrapha preserved only in a Christian context show no obvious signs of Christian authorship (such as references to Jesus, the virgin birth, crucifixion and resurrection, the apostles, the church), they must be Jewish compositions that have merely been transmitted by Christians. This has often been taken for granted, as has been the assumption that pseudepigrapha that contain only a few, peripheral references to overtly Christian matters are actually Jewish works that have been touched up by Christians during transmission, and that removing these supposed interpolations recovers the pristine Jewish document.

There are serious difficulties with these assumptions. In principle, ancient Old Testament Pseudepigrapha could have been composed by many different sorts of people, including Jews, Jewish-Christians, Gentile Christians, Samaritans, Gentile God-fearers, Gentiles sympathetic to Judaism, and pagans with some interest in Jewish traditions. Christians transmitted a great deal of otherwise lost Jewish literature (notably the many works by the first-century-C.E. Jewish philosopher Philo of Alexandria and his later contemporary, the Jewish historian Flavius Josephus), but also a vast corpus of Greco-Roman literature and, of course, an enormous amount of Christian literature of various genres. In addition, some Old Testament Pseudepigrapha were clearly composed by Christians (e.g., the *Odes of Solomon* and some of the *Sibylline Oracles*), and Christians sometimes heavily modified and Christianized the Jewish pseudepigrapha they passed down (the use of *Aramaic Levi* in the Greek *Testament of Levi* is an example).

Moreover, it is clear that Christian texts sometimes were made more explicitly Christian over time as they were copied and translated (e.g., Basil of Caesarea's *Hexaemeron*), and sermons by well-known Christian authors from late antiquity (e.g., John Chrysostom and Augustine of Hippo) sometimes retold Old Testament stories with few and peripheral references to explicitly Christian matters, so that if one did not know better, one might be tempted to treat these references as secondary additions. It is difficult in principle to establish that ancient Christian authors actually retold stories from the Old Testament without referring explicitly to Christian matters at all, since one can always challenge whether a work without Christian references was actually composed by a Christian. Nevertheless, Ephrem the Syrian, for example, does retell some Old Testament stories at length in his commentaries on Genesis and Exodus without introducing any Christian elements. Likewise, a late-antique Latin epic poem of nearly 400 lines known as *De Martyrio Maccabaeorum* retells the story of the Maccabean martyrs (2 Maccabees 6–7) without introducing any Christian content; and yet there are compelling reasons for regarding it as a Christian composition. (For more on the texts mentioned in this paragraph, see chap. 2 of Davila 2005c.)

It is clear, then, that pseudepigrapha with little or even no explicitly Christian material may nevertheless have been composed by Christians. And to make matters more confusing, Jews sometimes wrote works that could easily be mistaken for Christian compositions. An example is the Qumran *Hodayot* (1QH[a]). This work survives in the original Hebrew, was discovered in a Jewish archaeological context, and is clearly a Jewish composition. But if it were preserved only in a Syriac translation in medieval manuscripts, it would probably be identified as a product of late-antique Syriac-speaking Christianity.

All this being the case, how can one tell whether a given Old Testament pseudepigraphon transmitted only in Christian manuscripts is a Christian composition or a Jewish one that was adopted by Christians and dropped by Jews? A viable way forward has been proposed by Robert A. Kraft, who argues that interpreters must begin with the language and social context of the earliest manuscripts of the work and try to understand the work first in that context (Kraft 1994; Kraft 2001; for

PSEUDEPIGRAPHA, OLD TESTAMENT

examples of Kraft's methodology being employed, see Satran 1995; Harlow 1996; Kraemer 1998). Someone in this context actually copied and presumably read it, so it is a matter of fact rather than inference that the work once existed in this context. If the internal evidence (the content) of the text fits this context comfortably, then there is no reason to look for an earlier or different context for it. This does not rule out the possibility that it actually arose in an earlier and different social situation; it merely admits that, in the absence of evidence for an earlier origin, the best way to proceed is to study the work in the context in which it existed. Caution is in order even when working with these texts under these limitations. Often it is unclear how many people actually used such works or how carefully they read them. Readers of Scripture can tolerate a great deal of cognitive dissonance when studying a text, especially when they are interested in a particular point that may or may not have been the central concern of the author or the original audience. This is all the more true for quasi-scriptural books like the Pseudepigrapha, whose authority would have been far more open to dispute.

In some, perhaps many cases it becomes clear that the context of the surviving manuscripts is not the original context. The work may have been composed in earlier, different Christian circles or in a range of other contexts as noted above. In such cases a Jewish origin can only be established on the basis of positive evidence. It may be clear on philological grounds that the work, whatever the language(s) in which it now survives, was translated from Hebrew or Aramaic. The content may show that the work was composed before the rise of Christianity, in which case it cannot be a Christian composition (although it could still have been written by a Samaritan, a God-fearer, or a Jew). Or the text may show a sympathetic concern with the Jewish ritual cult, Jewish legal tradition, Jewish ethnic and national interests, and even Jewish eschatological speculation of a sort incompatible with Christianity. If so, this combination may be best explained by Jewish authorship. The best arguments for Jewish composition involve multiple converging lines of evidence rather than one or two apparently Jewish features.

Jewish Pseudepigrapha Transmitted Only by Christians

Works That Are Probably Jewish

When this methodology is applied to the extant corpus of Old Testament Pseudepigrapha, one can identify a fairly substantial number of texts safely regarded as Jewish beyond reasonable doubt in addition to those works already noted above. These include the apocalypses *4 Ezra, 2 Baruch,* and the *Similitudes of Enoch* (*1 Enoch* 37–71); works of rewritten scripture, such as the *Assumption* or *Testament of Moses,* Pseudo-Philo's *Biblical Antiquities,* and 4 Maccabees; and the liturgical poems known as the *Psalms of Solomon.* In addition, 3 Maccabees and the *Letter of Aristeas* (the latter claims to be written by a Gentile but has long been recognized as a Jewish composition) tell stories about important events in the Second Temple period and are traditionally classed as pseudepigrapha as well. One might also note the sermons on Jonah, Samson, and Gad preserved in Armenian, which seem also to be of ancient Jewish origin, if not strictly speaking pseudepigrapha. Most, if not all, of these works were composed in the Greek and early Roman periods and are therefore useful sources for reconstructing early Judaism.

Works of Uncertain Jewish Origin

A Jewish origin has also been argued for a number of other pseudepigrapha, but reasonable doubt remains for them. These include the apocalypses *2 Enoch* (whose social context and even text remain to be reconstructed satisfactorily), the *Apocalypse of Abraham,* and *3 Baruch;* the oracular works *Sibylline Oracles* books 3, 4, and 5; the sapiential text *Pseudo-Phocylides;* the well-known works of rewritten scripture *Testament of Job* and *Joseph and Aseneth;* and the lesser-known Syriac *History of Joseph,* Coptic *Apocryphon of Jeremiah,* and Coptic *Narrative of Joseph.* Until more conclusive arguments are presented for regarding these as Jewish texts, it would be safest to use them as ancillary evidence to support evidence drawn from the texts already regarded as Jewish beyond reasonable doubt, but not to use them on their own to reconstruct aspects of ancient Judaism. The *Prayer of Manasseh* is too brief for its origins to be at all certain. Arguments advanced for the Jewish origin of other pseudepigrapha (e.g., *Testament of Abraham, Life of Adam and Eve, Testaments of the Twelve Patriarchs, Lives of the Prophets,* some of the remaining *Sibylline Oracles,* and *Story of Zosimus*) are not convincing, and these are best regarded as Christian compositions unless and until better cases are made for them.

Pseudepigrapha of Pagan Origin

It is interesting to note that some of the earliest-attested Pseudepigrapha are pagan compositions. The *Balaam Text from Deir ʿAlla* (which recounts a calamitous vision of the biblical figure Balaam, here "the seer of the gods") is known from a Jordanian inscription in a non-Israelite Northwest Semitic dialect and can be dated epigraphically and stratigraphically to about 700 B.C.E. The *Story of Ahiqar* is a pagan work about a sage in the court of the early seventh-century-B.C.E. Assyrian King Esarhaddon, but it is first attested in a fifth-century-B.C.E. Aramaic manuscript from the Jewish colony in Elephantine, Egypt, and the story became popular among Jews, Christians, and even Muslims in subsequent centuries. There are fragments of pagan *Sibylline Oracles.* Although the surviving books of *Sibylline Oracles* are attributed to legendary pagan prophetesses, they appear to have been composed by Christians and perhaps Jews, but not pagans.

Generalizations about Extant Jewish Pseudepigrapha

One may make a few generalizations about the surviving works that can be regarded as Jewish pseudepigrapha beyond reasonable doubt and that are likely to have been composed by the time of the Bar Kokhba Revolt. They were written in Hebrew, Aramaic, and Greek. Most of them clearly stem from a form of Judaism for whom the Mosaic Torah was of central importance. The acceptance of the Mosaic Torah in the works found in *1 Enoch* is much less clear, and it has been argued that they represent a form of Judaism that looked to Enoch rather than Moses as its founding sage. Many, if not most of the surviving Jewish pseudepigrapha seem to have been composed in Palestine, but this is in part an accident of discovery, since many come from the discoveries in the Judean Desert. The geographical provenance of many of the rest is uncertain, and it is hard to say whether Diaspora works are actually poorly represented and, if so, what should be made of the fact. As already noted, these documents come in a wide variety of genres and with a wide range of agendas and, properly understood, they are a precious resource for understanding Judaism in the Greek and early Roman eras.

Later Pseudepigrapha

Old Testament pseudepigrapha continued to be composed by Jews, Christians, and pagans throughout antiquity. In addition to those already mentioned, more than thirty more pseudepigrapha composed before the rise of Islam (early seventh century C.E.) survive completely or nearly intact, along with dozens of fragmentary texts and quotations of otherwise lost works, as well as some references to works that are lost entirely apart from their titles. (Those pseudepigrapha not already published in Charlesworth, ed., 1983, 1985 are being translated for the More Old Testament Pseudepigrapha Project, underway at the University of St. Andrews. The project is also republishing some texts from the Charlesworth volumes with new manuscript evidence.) Moreover, the composition of Old Testament pseudepigrapha continued unabated through the Middle Ages and even into the modern era. Many of these later texts await thorough study by scholars.

BIBLIOGRAPHY

M. J. BERNSTEIN 1999, "Pseudepigraphy in the Qumran Scrolls: Categories and Functions," in *Pseudepigraphic Perspectives: The Apocrypha and Pseudepigrapha in Light of the Dead Sea Scrolls,* ed. M. E. Stone, Leiden: Brill, 1-26. • R. H. CHARLES, ED. 1913, *The Apocrypha and Pseudepigrapha of the Old Testament in English,* vol. 2, *Pseudepigrapha,* Oxford: Clarendon. • J. H. CHARLESWORTH, ED. 1983-1985, *The Old Testament Pseudepigrapha,* vol. 1, *Apocalyptic Literature and Testaments,* vol. 2, *Expansions of the "Old Testament" and Legends, Wisdom and Philosophical Literature, Prayers, Psalms, and Odes, Fragments of Lost Judeo-Hellenistic Works,* New York: Doubleday. • E. G. CHAZON AND M. E. STONE, EDS. 1999, *Pseudepigraphic Perspectives: The Apocrypha and Pseudepigrapha in Light of the Dead Sea Scrolls,* Leiden: Brill. • J. R. DAVILA 2005A, "(How) Can We Tell if a Greek Apocryphon or Pseudepigraphon Has Been Translated from Hebrew or Aramaic?" *JSP* 15: 3-61. • J. R. DAVILA 2005B, "The Old Testament Pseudepigrapha as Background to the New Testament," *ExpTim* 117: 53-57. • J. R. DAVILA 2005C, *The Provenance of the Pseudepigrapha: Jewish, Christian, or Other?* Leiden: Brill. • M. DE JONGE 2003, *Pseudepigrapha of the Old Testament as Part of Christian Literature: The Case of the Testaments of the Twelve Patriarchs and the Greek Life of Adam and Eve,* Leiden: Brill. • D. C. HARLOW 1996, *The Greek Apocalypse of Baruch (3 Baruch) in Hellenistic Judaism and Early Christianity,* Leiden: Brill. • R. S. KRAEMER 1998, *When Joseph Met Aseneth: A Late Antique Tale of the Biblical Patriarch and His Egyptian Wife, Reconsidered,* Oxford: Oxford University Press. • R. A. KRAFT 1994, "The Pseudepigrapha in Christianity," in *Tracing the Threads: Studies in the Vitality of Jewish Pseudepigrapha,* ed. J. C. Reeves, Atlanta: Scholars Press, 55-86. • R. A. KRAFT 2001, "The Pseudepigrapha and Christianity Revisited: Setting the Stage and Framing Some Central Questions," *JSJ* 32: 371-95. • H. F. D. SPARKS, ED. 1984, *The Apocryphal Old Testament,* Oxford: Clarendon. • DAVID SATRAN 1995, *Biblical Prophets in Byzantine Palestine: Reassessing the Lives of the Prophets,* Leiden: Brill. • M. E. STONE 1996, "The Dead Sea Scrolls and the Pseudepigrapha," *DSD* 3: 270-95.

See also: Pseudepigraphy JAMES R. DAVILA

Pseudepigraphy

Pseudepigraphy refers to the ancient practice of textual composition in the name of a revered figure of the past, whether legendary or historical. In part, the term is designed to explain a similarly named corpus of noncanonical works connected to the Hebrew Bible (the Old Testament Pseudepigrapha) as well as a corpus of noncanonical writings ascribed to New Testament figures (variously referred to as the New Testament Apocrypha or Pseudepigrapha). It is often difficult to ascertain whether the so-called Old Testament Pseudepigrapha are of Jewish or Christian provenance, making it difficult to separate the study of Jewish and Christian pseudepigraphy (Davila 2005).

The idea of pseudepigraphy, etymologically understood (i.e., from Gr. *pseudēs,* "false," and *epigraphē,* "inscription" or "attribution"), implies a theory of authorship involving deception or even forgery. Although many studies have emphasized the transgression involved, more culturally sensitive approaches explain the production of pseudepigraphic texts as a re-creation of the discourse of the esteemed figures of the past (Najman 2003) or as an accepted mode of composition for a tradition that discouraged individual authorial glory (Wyrick 2004).

Pseudepigraphy in the Hebrew Bible

Other than the authentic utterances of the prophets, most of the books of the Hebrew Bible appear to have been originally either anonymous or pseudepigraphical. An exception may be the book of Nehemiah, perhaps a genuinely ascribed work composed by Nehemiah himself. Other biblical books were attributed long after their composition, through editorial intervention or by superscription (the affixing of a title to a work or section).

In the Pentateuch, some passages (especially legal materials) are presented as the exact words of Moses or even God Himself and might be assessed as pseudepigraphical (Smith 1972: 200-206). While Genesis, Exodus, Leviticus, and Numbers as a whole are connected

PSEUDEPIGRAPHY

to Moses only by subsequent traditions, the book of Deuteronomy, which features a framing narrative that presents the work as the farewell testament of Moses before his death, is often considered pseudepigraphic in its entirety (Smith 1972: 191-215; Najman 2003: 19-40). However, the impression that the text as a whole was composed in the voice of Moses might also be the result of editorial intervention. In any event, later traditions acknowledge Moses as the textualizer or prophetic scribe rather than the author of these books (e.g., *b. Baba Batra* 14b–15a; see Wyrick 2004: 21-79).

Scholars often consider the titles of biblical books to be the work of editors who sought to label a book by its author or subject matter (cf. Joshua, Samuel, Ruth, and Job) rather than authorial signatures. With regard to the "Classical" or "Latter Prophets," the prophetic utterances themselves mostly do not name the prophet who spoke them. In fact, the names of several of the minor prophets are found only in a superscription; these include the books of Joel, Obadiah, Nahum, Habakkuk (with the exception of the poem in Hab. 3:1-9, thought to be dependent on the superscription in 1:1), and Zephaniah. Malachi may be a fictitious individual, unless the name was intended as a sobriquet of a legendary, known individual (such as Ezra, the view of later Jewish tradition). The name Micah is found in Jer. 26:17-19 but nowhere in the prophetic book by that name other than in the superscription. Presumably, third-person biographical passages in these works were not composed by the prophets themselves. Further, the editors often mistakenly or intentionally include additional passages deriving from later periods and different individuals. Significant sections of both Isaiah (chaps. 24–27, 40–55, 56–66) and Zechariah (chaps. 9–14) might be seen as pseudepigraphic, although they are in some sense the product of editorial additions and are possibly the literary creations of traditions that emulated both prophets.

The remaining books of the Hebrew Bible (the *ketuvim,* "Writings") contain a variety of authorial and attributive strategies (see Wyrick 2004: 80-110). The Psalms appear to be attributed (in some fashion) to David and other illustrious individuals by means of superscriptions (e.g., "A Psalm of/to/for David"), although it is uncertain whether these were originally intended as indications of their authorship. The book of Proverbs is attributed to Solomon (as well as to Asaph, Lemuel, and Augur) by superscription alone; the text itself makes no claim to authorship. The Song of Songs consists of poetry that includes Solomon as one of its characters and was possibly therefore attributed to him by superscription (the editor was here guided by 1 Kings 4:32, which speaks of the 1,005 songs composed by Solomon). In contrast, the writer known as Qohelet son of David, King in Jerusalem (Ecclesiastes), is a clear pseudonym that can only imply Solomon, and yet it, too, appears in a superscription and is thus an example of pseudepigraphy and reveals a certain hesitancy on the part of the editor applying the attribution. The book of Daniel includes sections about the career of the legendary individual Daniel (chaps. 1–6), as well as pseudepigraphal apocalyptic visions composed in his voice (chaps. 7–12). Job, Ruth, Lamentations, Esther, Ezra, and 1-2 Chronicles are anonymous; however, eventually all biblical books became attached to an appropriate textualizer (see *b. Baba Batra* 14b–15a).

Noncanonical Jewish Works

A threefold scheme has been suggested as a typology from which to examine the extent to which works can be evaluated as pseudepigraphic (Bernstein 1997: 1-26). The least pseudepigraphic works are those attributed to a legendary author merely by their superscription or title (or sometimes by an allegedly authoritative tradition) and not by any suggested authorship in their content, such as the *Prayer of Manasseh* or the *Psalms of Solomon.* Next, a variety of works, though largely anonymous, exhibit individual pseudepigraphic voices as a result of editorial intervention or compositional allusion and thus do not exhibit evidence of an intent to deceive. The category might include the Wisdom of Solomon, the book of Baruch, the *Testaments of the Twelve Patriarchs,* and the *Testaments of Job, Abraham,* and *Moses.* Finally, the speaker of the work may be understood as a legendary figure of antiquity. This category includes purportedly autobiographical works like *1* and *3 Enoch, Jubilees, 2* and *3 Baruch, 4 Ezra,* and the *Apocalypses of Abraham, Zephaniah, and Elijah,* as well as some works found at Qumran, such as the *Aramaic Levi Document,* the Hebrew *Testament of Naphtali,* the *Temple Scroll,* Psalm 151A, and the *Genesis Apocryphon.* As is evident, apocalyptic works were especially susceptible to this last and strongest form of pseudepigraphic composition. Some scholars have gone so far as to suggest that pseudepigraphy is largely a phenomenon associated with the apocalyptic genre (Stone 2006: 8). Indeed, the valuation of pseudepigraphy in scholarship since the Enlightenment has often been tied to the perceived worth of the genre apocalypse in general and its canonical representatives (Daniel in the Hebrew Bible and Revelation in the New Testament) in particular.

The above scheme ignores both imagined first-person speeches and cited fictitious letters (e.g., Ezra 1:2-4; 1 Macc. 8:23-20), considering that such literary conceits were accepted in antiquity even by traditions that decried forgery. In so doing, it does not consider the obvious analogy between inserted passages and larger works composed in the same vein. In addition, it may overly emphasize the notion of person, considering that some texts switch from first to third person at will, while others employ first person as a literary device to lend immediacy to the account. Moreover, legendary authorial ascription by the composer could equally be intended in works composed in the third person.

It may also be worth making a distinction between pseudonymity and pseudepigraphy, where texts characterized by pseudonymity are not attributed to authoritative figures (Bernstein 1997: 7). Possible examples of pseudonymity more narrowly understood include the *Letter of Aristeas* or Tobit, both first-person works attributed to figures who are fictional, historical, or legendary, but not strictly authoritative. Some anonymous works were mistakenly attributed to historical figures, such as the *Biblical Antiquities* credited to Philo of Alexandria. There are also Jewish and Christian works composed in the name of legendary figures that one would expect to be more authoritative in a pagan context, such as the *Sibylline Oracles* or the *Pseudo-Orphic Hymns*. These works, as well as those composed in the name of historical literary figures of Gentile origin (such as Pseudo-Phocylides, the Syriac Menander, Pseudo-Hecataeus, and the fragments credited to Aeschylus, Sophocles, Euripides, and others) appeal to the universal rather than specifically Jewish authority of their pseudonyms in the strongest way, despite not being first-person accounts.

Attribution Analysis and the History of Scholarship

Attribution analysis, the philological technique of assessing the authenticity of the attribution of texts and passages to individuals, was perfected in Hellenistic Alexandria in the third century B.C.E. (Speyer 1971: 112-31; Wyrick 2004: 220-23, 282-90). There is some evidence of a parallel but contrasting assessment of attribution in Second Temple Judaism: works of the Hebrew Bible were judged to be authoritative if they were considered to derive from a "succession of prophets" stretching from Moses to Ezra and his near contemporary Nehemiah (Wyrick 2004: 159-85). Practically speaking, only works preserved in the Jerusalem Temple by the priestly class were held in common as authoritative by most Jewish religious factions.

Many works not collected in the Temple were also linked to legendary figures from Moses to Ezra. Such attribution might indicate that they aspired to the authoritative status of the books kept at the Temple. Still other texts were composed in the name of figures who preceded Moses (i.e., Adam, Seth, Enoch, Noah, Abraham, Jacob, or the twelve patriarchs). This form of pre-Mosaic ascription likely indicates their reliance on a form of divinely issued knowledge thought to predate the revelation to Moses at Mt. Sinai. Such additional revelations challenge, supplement, and sometimes draw their legitimacy from the authority of the Mosaic Torah (Najman 1999: 388 and 2003: 43-60).

The early Christian practice of attribution analysis, derived from Alexandrian scholarly techniques, was employed as a means of testing the authenticity and inspiration of purported scriptural records or revelations associated with Jesus and his disciples (Speyer 1971: 179-217). The debate over authenticity often amounted to a battle over the definition of Christianity, as many works under discussion contained beliefs and teachings that contradicted the practices of the leading churches of "orthodox" Christianity. The location of forgery and interpolation, initially undertaken in the pursuit of recovering the true wisdom of the ancients, returned in full force during the Renaissance to dominate philological scholarship thereafter. Recognition of these and other strands in the history of scholarship can help contemporary studies to avoid the assumption, common since the Renaissance, that pseudepigraphic texts are fraudulent on multiple levels. It can also enable scholars to recognize that the question of whether a falsely attributed work can be inspired, still asked in many modern studies of pseudepigraphy, is a resumption of early Christian theological debate and outside the realm of secular academic study.

Attribution Practices and Literary Discourse

The practice of pseudepigraphy should not be divorced from the history of attribution practices in the literary culture of Israel, early Judaism, ancient Greece and Rome, and early Christianity (Wyrick 2004: 80-110, 282-315). Legendary authorship (the crediting of works simultaneously composed and performed to Homer, Hesiod, and other culture heroes) was the norm in Greece until sometime in the sixth century when individuals began to attribute their own compositions to themselves (e.g., Archilochus, Pindar). Even after this point, some discourses in Greek culture continued to tolerate legendary composition (e.g., attributing medical works to Hippocrates).

The notion of composing in one's own name never became the norm in Israel, despite the example of the named prophets of the Hebrew Bible. These did not in any case admit to composing their prophetic utterances but rather credited them to God. Jewish works composed in the Greek orbit could be attributed to the individual composing them; such is the case with the writings of Philo and Josephus. With the well-known exception of Sirach or Ecclesiasticus, virtually signed by its real author (Jesus Ben Sira), most works composed in a biblical mode do not admit to authorship by a historical individual, as was the norm in Hellenistic and Hellenized circles.

Attributions were often made on the basis of the genre of a work: proverbs or wisdom utterances were assigned to Solomon, psalms to David, and legal materials or authoritative legal interpretations to Moses. It has been proposed that the name of the legendary hero (such as Moses, David, or Solomon) indicates a literary discourse, a form of communication in which developments of thought are considered to be elaborations of the paradigm created by a founder figure and are thus attributed to this figure (Najman 2003: 1-40). According to this model, the text reworks and expands older traditions and claims for itself the authority of those traditions, even as it claims to be produced by or associated with the founding figure, sanctioning the new interpretations or visions and extending the earlier ancestral tradition. Research on pseudepigraphic discourse therefore should focus on the discursive quality of the biblical figures credited for these new works, as well as on the biblical passages and conceptual premises upon which such discourses were based (see, e.g., Stone and Bergren 1998).

In the various traditions collectively grouped together under the rubric "rabbinic Judaism," there are few literary works that claim (correctly or falsely) to be "authored" by an individual. Exceptions may be *3 Enoch* or *Sefer Hekhalot* (styled as the revelation of R. Ishmael) and the *Pirqe de Rabbi Eliezer* (although the attribution to Eliezer ben Hyrcanus and its first two biographical chapters could conceivably belong to an editor). Rabbinic collections as a whole were often attributed to the editorial work of individuals (such as the Mishnah to Rabbi Judah ha-Nasi, the Tosefta to R. Hiyya bar Abba, the Babylonian Talmud to Rab Ashi, or the thirteenth-century Zohar to Simeon bar Yochai). Within rabbinic works, considerable attention is paid to the status of the individual rabbi credited with a tradition. Some texts attempt a thoroughgoing resolution of all ambiguities of provenance, attributing anonymous statements and collections on the basis of allegedly implied clues (e.g., *b. Sanhedrin* 17b and the Geonic *Letter of Sherira Gaon*). However, the authenticity of even the most straightforward individual attributions is often challenged in modern scholarship. Legal rulings attributed to a rabbinic sage may actually refer to a disciple, a later tradent, or even some earlier authority. In general, statements in rabbinic works attributed to biblical figures or even God may express what it is possible to infer or imagine the speaker to have said (Bregman 1997: 36-38).

Acknowledging the role of sincere belief is crucial in the study of Jewish attribution and legendary composition practices, as it is in the study of all religious phenomena. An evaluation of the practice of pseudepigraphy as forgery or literary imposture would impose a culturally foreign concept of writing in one's own name as a standard by which to evaluate Jewish culture, which largely stood aloof from this norm.

Bibliography

A. D. Baum 2001, *Pseudepigraphie und literarische Fälschung im frühen Christentum,* Tübingen: Mohr-Siebeck. • J. R. Davila 2005, *The Provenance of the Pseudepigrapha: Jewish, Christian, or Other?* Leiden: Brill. • M. Bernstein 1997, "Pseudepigraphy in the Qumran Scrolls: Categories and Functions," in *Pseudepigraphic Perspectives,* ed. E. G. Chazon and M. E. Stone, Leiden: Brill, 1-26. • M. Bregman 1997, "Pseudepigraphy in Rabbinic Literature," in *Pseudepigraphic Perspectives,* ed. E. G. Chazon and M. E. Stone, Leiden: Brill, 27-41. • E. G. Chazon and M. E. Stone, eds. 1997, *Pseudepigraphic Perspectives: The Apocrypha and Pseudepigrapha in Light of the Dead Sea Scrolls,* Leiden: Brill. • D. G. Meade 1986, *Pseudonymity and Canon,* Tübingen: Mohr-Siebeck. • B. M. Metzger 1972, "Literary Forgeries and Canonical Pseudepigrapha," *JBL* 91: 3-24. • H. Najman 1999, "Interpretation as Primordial Writing: Jubilees and Its Authority Conferring Strategies," *JSJ* 30: 379-410. • H. Najman 2003, *Seconding Sinai: The Development of Mosaic Discourse in Second Temple Judaism,* Leiden: Brill. • M. Smith 1972, "Pseudepigraphy in the Israelite Tradition," in *Pseudepigrapha I,* ed. Kurt von Fritz, Vandoeuvres-Geneva: Fondation Hardt, 191-215. • W. Speyer 1971, *Die Literarische Fälschung im Heidnischen und Christlichen Altertum: Ein Versuch Ihrer Deutung,* Munich: Beck'sche Verlagsbuchhandlung. • M. E. Stone 2006, "Pseudepigraphy Reconsidered," *Review of Rabbinic Judaism* 9: 1-15. • M. E. Stone and T. Bergren, eds. 1998, *Biblical Figures outside the Bible,* Harrisburg, Penn.: Trinity Press International. • J. Wyrick 2004, *The Ascension of Authorship: Attribution and Canon Formation in Jewish, Hellenistic, and Christian Traditions,* Cambridge: Harvard University Press.

Jed Wyrick

Pseudo-Philo → Biblical Antiquities (Pseudo-Philo)

Ptolemies

The Ptolemies were the kings of Hellenistic Egypt. They were the descendants of Ptolemy Lagos (ruled 305-282 B.C.E.), one of Alexander the Great's successors, who in 305 B.C.E. became king with the name of Ptolemy I Soter ("savior"). The Ptolemies imposed an absolute rule on Egypt, inheriting most of the pharaonic bureaucratic organization. Exception was made for the three cities of Alexandria, Naucratis, and Ptolemais, which were granted the status of a Greek city-state. The Ptolemies were also able to establish a strong hegemony in the eastern Mediterranean, which remained unchallenged until the end of the third century B.C.E.

Their Dynastic Ruler Cult

The Ptolemies presented themselves as both Egyptian and Greek rulers to address the expectations of all of their subjects. They legitimized their kingship by declaring themselves dynastic successors of Alexander the Great, the only Greek ruler the Egyptians had ever seen and already a myth for their Greek subjects. Their iconography portrays them wearing either the diadem, the head fillet of the Hellenistic kings, or the double pharaonic headdress, in attitudes required by both royal protocols. They introduced their dynastic ruler cult, by which they integrated their divine royal personae into both the Greek and the Egyptian religious traditions. Their statues portraying them as gods were in-

Ptolemy II with his sister and wife Arsinoë II. Ptolemaic cameo (278 B.C.E.) cut out of the nine layers of an Indian sardonyx; Kunsthistorisches Museum, Vienna *(Erich Lessing / Art Resource, N.Y.)*

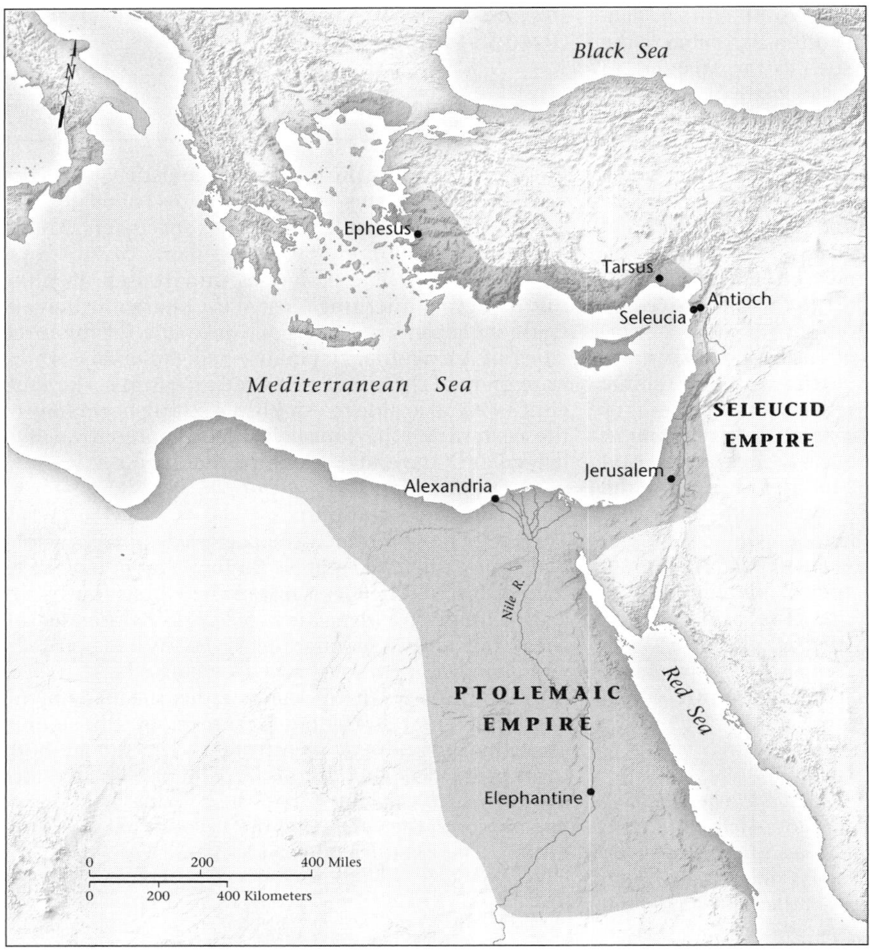

THE NEAR EAST UNDER PTOLEMAIC RULE

stalled in Greek and Egyptian temples alike, next to other Greek and Egyptian gods. By exhibiting Alexander's mummified body in Alexandria for worship, and by declaring his divine ancestors Heracles and Zeus to be theirs as well, the Ptolemies entered the Greek pantheon. By acquiring an Egyptian royal name, they put themselves politically and religiously in the footsteps of the Egyptian Pharaohs; by marrying their siblings, they recurrently staged the Egyptian mythological union of Osiris and Isis. In both cases they reinforced their power through religion, while keeping it within the dynasty.

Their Cultural Patronage

Culturally, the Ptolemies defined themselves as the patrons of the library and museum of Alexandria. The two institutions were closely connected architecturally and aimed to offer a learning environment to scholars. The library collected Greek and foreign works in translation; at its peak in the first century B.C.E. it is said to have contained 700,000 scrolls. The custom of cataloguing books by author and title to facilitate library search was first introduced in Alexandria in the third century B.C.E. The museum was a boarding institution for scholars who used the library for their study. It hosted scholars of both literary and scientific disciplines. Other Hellenistic rulers, such as the Seleucids in Antioch and the Attalids in Pergamon, imitated Ptolemaic cultural patronage.

The Ptolemies had to negotiate with the traditionally powerful Egyptian priestly class on land and tax privileges in the legitimation of royal power. This relationship proved not to be easy. Documents show that the Ptolemies were able to contain the influence of the priestly class until the end of the third century B.C.E., after which they had to concede more power and privileges, mainly regarding ownership and tax exemptions on temple land. The priestly class may have played an active role in the Delta disturbances and in the Ptolemies' loss of control of part of the country at the end of the third century B.C.E., when Upper Egypt detached into a pharaonic independent kingdom that lasted twenty years.

Seleucid Wars and Dynastic Disputes

On the external front, the Ptolemies waged six wars with the Seleucids for the control of Coele-Syria, a conflict which occasionally they tried to solve, unsuccessfully, with interdynastic marriages. The origin of the conflict dates back to the formation of both the Ptolemaic and the Seleucid kingdoms at the end of the fourth century B.C.E. The Ptolemies held the region until the Fifth Syrian War in 202-195 B.C.E., when they lost it to the Seleucid Antiochus III (223-187 B.C.E.). The interdynastic marriage between Ptolemy V (204-180 B.C.E.) and Cleopatra I, daughter of Antiochus III, sealed the peace agreement.

In the second century B.C.E. succession disputes fueled by court intrigues tore the dynasty apart. Ptolemy VI (180-145 B.C.E.) and his siblings Cleopatra II and Ptolemy VIII fought for the succession upon the death of their father Ptolemy V. This internal dispute factored into the Sixth Syrian War, which brought the Seleucid army into Egypt at the gates of Alexandria twice in 169 and 168 B.C.E. The interdynastic marriage between the Seleucid Cleopatra I and Ptolemy V resolved for the time being the disagreement about sovereignty over Coele-Syria. At the death of both sovereigns, the regents appointed on behalf of the underage heir managed Ptolemaic affairs in a way that threatened Antiochus IV (175-164 B.C.E.), who exploited the instability of the Ptolemaic kingdom by invading Egypt. The Romans, who were present in the eastern Mediterranean to wage war against the Macedonian king Perseus (179-168 B.C.E.), had already established their supremacy over the Seleucids with the Peace of Apamea in 188 B.C.E. and therefore did not look favorably on a Seleucid attempt at expansion into Egypt. In 168 B.C.E. the Roman legate in the region, C. Popilius Laenas, forced Antiochus IV, who was besieging Alexandria allegedly in support of Ptolemy VI against his brother Ptolemy VIII, to leave Egypt immediately and to abandon any designs on Egypt. With Egypt thus endangered, Ptolemy VI, his sister-wife Cleopatra II, and their brother Ptolemy VIII agreed to reign jointly, a solution that lasted only a few years. The following twenty years saw dynastic struggle, exile, civil war, and economic hardship. When Ptolemy VI died in 145 B.C.E., Ptolemy VIII returned to Egypt and ruled together with his sister Cleopatra II, whom he married, and with their daughter Cleopatra III until 116 B.C.E.

Ptolemaic Rulers (all dates B.C.E.)
Ptolemy I Soter (305-282)
Ptolemy II Philadelphus (284-286); ruled jointly with Ptolemy the Son (267-259)
Ptolemy III Euergetes (246-222)
Ptolemy IV Philopator (222-204)
Ptolemy V Epiphanes (204-180)
Ptolemy VI Philometor (180-164, 163-145); ruled jointly with Ptolemy Eupator in 152
Ptolemy VIII Euergetes II (Physcon) (170-163, 145-116)
Cleopatra II Philometora Soteira (131-127), in opposition to Ptolemy VIII
Cleopatra III Philometor Soteira Dikaiosyne Nikephoros (Kokke) (116-101); ruled jointly with Ptolemy IX (116-107) and Ptolemy X (107-101)
Ptolemy IX Soter II (Lathyros) (116-107, 88-81 as Soter II); ruled jointly with Cleopatra III in his first reign
Ptolemy X Alexander I (107-88); ruled jointly with Cleopatra III till 101
Berenice III Philopator (81-80)
Ptolemy XI Alexander II (80)
Ptolemy XII Neos Dionysos (Auletes) (80-58, 55-51)
Cleopatra V Tryphaena (58-57) ruled jointly with Berenice IV Epiphaneia (58-55)
Cleopatra VII Philopator (51-30); ruled jointly with Ptolemy XIII (51-47), Ptolemy XIV (47-44), and Ptolemy XV Caesarion (44-30)
Arsinoe IV (48-47) opposed Cleopatra VII

Embroilment in Roman Politics

The years of Ptolemy VI, Ptolemy VIII, and their wife-sisters set a pattern for the remaining decades of the Ptolemaic rule in Egypt, inasmuch as unsolvable dynastic disputes and court intrigues invited Rome's increasing incursions into Egyptian affairs. From the second century B.C.E. on, Roman senators regularly visited Egypt, and Egyptian affairs were discussed in the Roman senate. Egypt became an integral part of Roman politics when the struggle over succession between Cleopatra VII and her siblings became entwined in the Roman civil wars. Caesar's defeat of Pompey determined the fall of Ptolemy XII's supporters and the coronation of his sister Cleopatra VII. Cleopatra's later sentimental involvement with Marc Antony put her on the wrong side of the second round of civil wars. She eventually lost her kingdom to Octavian in 31 B.C.E., an event that brought the Ptolemaic dynasty and political independence of Egypt to an end.

Relations with the Jews

The history of the Ptolemies is intimately connected with that of the Jews, both in Judea and in Egypt. The earliest episode recorded in the sources occurred in 312/311 B.C.E., when the *diadochos* Ptolemy Lagos, later Ptolemy I, deported part of the population from Samaria and Judea to Egypt, in the wake of his military expedition in Coele-Syria against Demetrius, the future Antigonid dynast. The sources report two contrasting stories. According to the *Letter of Aristeas,* Ptolemy led a brutal campaign in the region, of which the deportation of the Jews was just one of the consequences. Josephus knows a consonant version, whereby the Samaritans and the Jews suffered imprisonment during war and consequent deportation. The Satrap Stela may confirm this evidence in the mention of the capture and deportation of monotheistic, Aramaic-speaking people from the region, which cannot exclude Samaritans and Jews. Josephus knows also the account of Hecataeus of Abdera, according to whom the Jews under the leadership of a high priest voluntarily followed Ptolemy; they were presented with the description of their future settlement in Egypt, encompassing the sharing of the country government. This story is doubted today, mostly on account of its pseudonymous authorship but also its disputable assertions, which cannot stand comparison with external historical evidence.

Ptolemy Lagos' military needs recommended the relocation of part of the deported Jews in the garrisons of the country upon their arrival in Egypt in 311 B.C.E. These Jews would be the core of later Egyptian Jewish communities, particularly of the community in Alexandria. Papyri relating to royal control of the slave market may suggest that some of the deported Jews were enslaved for a portion of the third century B.C.E., to be eventually freed by royal decree, as also the *Letter of*

Aristeas, although in a strongly apologetic manner, purports.

The endemic fighting between the Seleucids and the Ptolemies for control of Coele-Syria involved Judea as well. After the military campaign in 311 B.C.E., Ptolemy I invaded the region again in 301, this time annexing it to his kingdom. On this occasion he took Jerusalem; according to the sources, he did so treacherously on the Sabbath. Ptolemy imposed garrisons, governmental control, and fiscal duties, but there is no evidence that he interfered with the religious apparatus.

A second consistent migration of Jews from the Levant occurred in the mid-second century B.C.E. In the wake of Antiochus IV's desecration of the Temple in 167 and the consequent Maccabean Revolt, Onias IV, descendant of the high priest Onias III, decamped to Egypt with his followers. Ptolemy VI allowed the Oniads to establish a settlement in Leontopolis with a temple; there is, however, no evidence that the temple of Leontopolis was ever a religious point of reference for Egyptian Jews. The Oniads, on the other side, provided high-level military assistance to Ptolemy VI in his fight against his brother Ptolemy VIII. The Ptolemies could count on the allegiance of the Oniads until the end of their reign, when they, together with the Alexandrian Jews, sided instead with the Romans.

The Ptolemies allowed the Jews complete religious autonomy. They did not require the Jews to participate in the ruler cult, which would have been an open breach of Jewish law. Epigraphical evidence shows that the Ptolemies patronized the building and dedications of Jewish houses of prayers. With the exception of some individuals, the Ptolemies did not grant citizenship to the Jews but only residence linked to their initial military status. To other Jews who reached Egypt independently, the Ptolemies probably also granted residence on an individual basis, but this is uncertain. Unauthorized residence, of Jews and others, cannot be excluded. The Jews were subject to taxation, or exemption therefrom, according to their status, as was the case with other inhabitants.

Starting from the mid-second century B.C.E., the Ptolemies instituted *politeumata* in Egypt, territorially based ethnic groups to which they granted relative civic independence. The Jewish communities of Herakleopolis and Alexandria were organized as *politeumata* with their own magistrates, who were petitioned on legal matters. It is unclear whether those magistrates applied the Jewish Law, that is, whether the Ptolemies ever recognized the Jewish Law as part of the Egyptian legal system. Resolving this issue involves considering the origin of the Septuagint. The translation of some of its books has been dated to the end of the third century B.C.E., but the *Letter of Aristeas* dates it to the early third century B.C.E. by the agency of Ptolemy II. Some scholars reject both dates on historical grounds in favor of a date in the later mid-second century B.C.E. The issue is of utmost importance, since the Ptolemies' direct involvement, or lack thereof, in the translation of the Torah would clarify not only their relationship with the Egyptian Jews but also the nature of the Ptolemaic legal system. Of particular importance in this matter are the recently edited papyri from the Jewish *politeuma* of Herakleopolis, which date to the mid-second century B.C.E. and contain important information on the local administration of justice. The study of these documents has only just begun.

Jewish Life in Ptolemaic Egypt

Discussion of Jewish life in Ptolemaic Egypt, and especially the relationship with the governing authority, cannot ignore some important literary texts. At the beginning of the third century B.C.E., the Egyptian priest Manetho included in his Greek translation of the Egyptian antiquities addressed to Ptolemy II a variation of the exodus story that was derogatory to the Jews. Although there is no evidence that these tales ever caused problems for the Jews in the Ptolemaic period, they survived with enrichment through the Roman period. The discourse in the *Letter of Aristeas* and 3 Maccabees is different. As already mentioned, the former work chronicles the events promoting the Greek translation of the Torah. According to this text, the head of the library recommended that Ptolemy II order the translation in order to have the Torah shelved among the other masterpieces already housed in the library. The king proceeded through official diplomatic channels, inviting the Jerusalemite high priest to send to Alexandria the most accredited intellectuals, who would produce the best possible translation. The account portrays a king who held the Jews, their religion, their culture, and their book in the highest esteem.

A contrasting picture comes in 3 Maccabees, where Ptolemy IV (221-205 B.C.E.) persecutes the Egyptian Jews because he was forbidden to enter the Temple of Jerusalem after his victory in the Fourth Syrian War in 217 B.C.E. The tale describes an initial imposition of Greek citizenship limited to the Alexandrian Jewish community, followed by a punishment extending to all the Jews of the country who, after a compulsory registration, were deported to Alexandria to be stampeded by elephants. Josephus also knows of the elephant episode but attributes it to Ptolemy VIII (145-116 B.C.E.) under unclear circumstances.

Both stories contain folkloric themes that raise doubts about their historicity, doubts that only compound the question of their date, occasion, and purpose. Scholars have proposed several interpretations ranging chronologically from the second century B.C.E. — when Ptolemaic dynastic struggles brought political instability and a new wave of Jewish immigration may have affected adversely the relationship between the Ptolemies and the Jews — to the early Roman period, when Jewish persecution is actually documented.

Bibliography

P. Green 1990, *Alexander to Actium: The Historical Evolution of the Hellenistic Age,* Berkeley: University of California Press. • G. Hölbl 2001, *A History of the Ptolemaic Empire,* London: Routledge. • J. M. S. Cowey and K. Maresch, eds. 2001, *Urkunden der Politeuma der Juden von Herakleopolis (144/3–133/2 v. Chr.) (P.Polit.Iud.),* Wiesbaden: Westdeutsches. •

J. Frey, J. Herzer, M. Janssen, and C. K. Rothschild, eds. 2009, *Pseudepigraphie und Verfasserfiktion in frühchristlichen Briefen*, Tübingen: Mohr-Siebeck. • E. S. Gruen 1998, *Heritage and Hellenism: The Reinvention of Jewish Tradition*, Berkeley: University of California Press, 189-245. • V. Tcherikover 1959, *Hellenistic Civilization and the Jews*, Philadelphia: Jewish Publication Society.

See also: Seleucids SANDRA GAMBETTI

Purim → Festivals and Holy Days

Purity and Impurity

Purity in early Jewish tradition usually refers to a state of ritual fitness necessary for the people of Israel to enjoy the holy presence and power of God. Impurity describes not only a lack of purity but a threatening force generated primarily by the human being. Less often, purity denotes physical cleanliness or the clarity of refined metals. The Hebrew words *ṭāhôr* and *ṭāmēʾ* are the principal terms for "pure" and "impure," respectively. Also prominent are *brr*, "purify, clean, polish"; *zkh*, "innocent"; *zqq*, "pure"; *ṭbl*, "immerse"; *kbs*, "launder"; *lbn*, "turn white"; *nqh*, "innocent"; *qdš*, "sanctify by bathing"; *rḥṣ*, "wash." The most prominent Greek terms are *katharos*, "pure"; *akathartos*, "impure"; and *miainō*, "stain, defile."

Hebrew Bible

Despite differences in custom and interpretation, the Pentateuch remained foundational for purity practices in all varieties of early Judaism. In the priestly corpus there is an implicit system of purity and impurity. The terms "moral" and "ritual," although imperfect categories, help to differentiate between types of impurity. Moral impurities such as idolatry, murder, and sexual sins are capital violations of God's Law.

Ritual Impurity

Ritual impurities are not due to transgression but simply result from the human condition, more specifically, from the physical processes of death, scale disease, and sexual discharges. Anyone with these conditions is labeled "impure" and is forbidden to come to the sanctuary or handle any holy objects. Certain objects, such as earthenware, clothes, and vessels of wood, skin, and metals are also susceptible to impurity (Lev. 11:32-35; Num. 31:20, 22-23). Individuals who touch an impure person or object become impure secondarily to a lesser degree.

For major impurities, for example, scale disease or gonorrhea, a person must be healed before any purification ritual may begin. Minor impurities are routine and last anywhere from one day (e.g., for impurity resulting from sexual intercourse) to one week (e.g., after menstruation or burial of the dead). Purification involves bathing in water and waiting for sunset but can also include more complex rituals. Unlike ritual impurity, moral impurity is not physically contagious. Both kinds of impurity threaten Israel's relationship with God, preventing worship and contaminating the sanctuary and land.

Forbidden Foods

Impure, forbidden foods form an interesting juncture between ritual and moral impurity. Israel's diet (Leviticus 11; Deuteronomy 14), like the purity rituals, symbolizes and reinforces her separation from other nations. However, these laws are prohibitions, not unavoidable facts of life like menstruation or corpse contamination. In the Second Temple period, the kosher diet became a sticking point among Jews under Hellenistic rule where pork was a food of choice.

Moral Impurity

Outside the Pentateuch, the biblical emphasis is primarily on purification from sin. The language of ritual purification is often used metaphorically to describe the removal of guilt (cf. Ps. 51:9: "Purge me with hyssop [used for corpse impurity], and I shall be clean," Isa. 4:4).

Second Temple Archaeology: Ritual Baths and Stone Vessels

Anthropologists have demonstrated that, in a period of persecution or cultural upheaval, a group will reinforce its boundaries and identity by increasing and intensifying its purity laws. In the Second Temple era the crisis in Judaism brought about by Hellenization and foreign domination may have caused the emphasis on purification among Jews. Issues of cult and purity engaged and divided Jews more so in this period than at any other time in antiquity.

Jewish purity during this time is marked by several trends. Jerusalem was regarded as a holy city restricted by purity regulations. Ritual purity was observed by many laity as well as priests, and ordinary food was often eaten in a state of purity. Purity rituals frequently accompanied prayer and moral purification. Gentiles were increasingly labeled impure.

The archaeological record supports a heightened concern for ritual purity in Second Temple times. The excavation of the Upper City of Jerusalem, for instance, yielded many *miqvaʾot* (ritual baths), at least one *miqveh* in every house in the Herodian Quarter. Also, a cave for manufacturing vessels of stone, a substance insusceptible to impurity, was discovered.

It is unlikely that purity of food and vessels was just the concern of priests. Ritual baths, some attached to synagogues, have been found in Galilee as well as Jerusalem. They also adjoin cave-tombs in this period in Jerusalem, Jericho, and probably Hebron. Their presence suggests that Jews were concerned to purify themselves from corpse contamination immediately, as the sources attest. Domestic vessels made of stone, including mugs, pitchers, and bowls for daily meals, have been discovered in rural settlements throughout the country.

Second Temple Literature

Gentile Impurity

Already in late biblical texts the concern for purity intensifies. For the first time in Jewish history, Gentiles are considered impure. Ezra forces divorce from pagan spouses to insure the purity of holy seed (Ezra 9:2). Nehemiah expels Tobias the Ammonite from the Temple and orders his rooms to be purified (Neh. 13:8-9). *Jubilees* regards both marrying and eating with Gentiles as defiling (*Jub.* 22:17; 30:10).

Moral Impurity

Moral purification is sometimes accompanied by ritual ablutions. Adam repents by standing in river water up to his neck (*Life of Adam and Eve* 6–7). Similarly, *Sibylline Oracles* 4.165 exhorts: "Wash your whole bodies in perennial rivers" to plead for divine forgiveness (cf. *T. Levi* 2:3).

Dead Sea Scrolls

The Dead Sea Scrolls reflect a maximalist interpretation of purity. Several texts require purity of body as well as spirit in an effort to live in a community of "perfect holiness." The site at Qumran supports the description of the Scrolls with evidence of an ancient aqueduct connecting several ritual baths and cisterns as well as 200 fragments of stone vessels. The Qumran sectarians were careful to maintain the purity of their communal food and drink, "the purity." Members bathed before eating (1QS 5:13; 4Q514 frg. 1 cols. i–ii lines 2-4; 4Q274 1 i 3-9). Food had to be harvested in a state of purity lest it transmit impurity to produce by the liquid of its juice (4Q284a frg. 1 lines 2-8). Outsiders, even Jews, were considered impure along with their belongings and forbidden to eat with the sect. The holiness of the Temple is extended to the entire city of Jerusalem (cf. 4Q399 frg. 3 lines 10-13). The *Temple Scroll* describes a three-day process with two baths before the impure can enter the Temple city, and sexual intercourse is prohibited (11Q19 45:11-12; cf. CD 12:1-2).

Philo and Josephus

Philo and Josephus confirm the rigor of their contemporaries in matters of purity. After sexual intercourse and corpse impurity, Jews would supposedly touch nothing until they had immersed in water (Philo, *Spec. Leg.* 3.206, 363; cf. Josephus, *Ag. Ap.* 2.199, 203). According to Josephus, the purity of Jerusalem in Second Temple times was not limited to holy feasts. Antiochus III supported a ban on impure animals and hides in Jerusalem and restricted Gentile access to the Temple complex (*Ant.* 12.145-46 [12.3.4]; 14.285). Josephus also claims that persons with severe impurities were excluded from the entire city (*J.W.* 5.227-32; cf. *m. Kelim* 1:6-9) and that menstruants were secluded even in ordinary cities (*Ant.* 3.261-62; cf. *m. Ned.* 7:4).

Josephus' description of the Essenes' purity is close to that of the Dead Sea Scrolls, supporting the large consensus that the Qumran sectarians were Essenes. In the initiation process of the Essenes, a candidate was allowed to eat the pure food of the community after one year of examination, and after two more years, drink the pure drink (*J.W.* 2.138; cf. 1QS 6:16-22; 7:20-23). Essenes required baths and clothing changes before meals (*J.W.* 2.129-31). Quite possibly, they did not defecate in Jerusalem but at a place outside the city wall on account of the city's holiness (*J.W.* 2.147-49; 5.144-45; cf. Deut. 23:15; 11Q19 46:15; 4Q472a). Purification also accompanied Torah study in anticipation of prophetic revelation (*J.W.* 2.159).

Rabbinic Literature

Although compiled at a later date, rabbinic literature continues the Pharisaic tradition and reports the strictness of earlier sages in matters of purity. "The impurity of a knife was more distressing to Israel than murder" (*t. Yoma* 1:12; *y. Yoma* 2:1, 39d; *b. Yoma* 23b). Some rabbis immersed every morning before prayer (*t. Yad.* 2:20; later rabbinic practice was simply to wash hands; cf. *b. Šabbat* 13b–14b). At the same time, the Pharisees adopted the lenient practice of *tebul yôm,* by which a person who had immersed after impurity could function immediately within society as long as he kept away from holy things until completely pure.

The Pharisaic *Havurot* (fellowships) ate ordinary food in a state of purity, and this is the expectation of the Mishnah for all Jews (*m. Ḥul.* 2:5; *m. Zabim* 3:2; cf. *t. Miqw.* 6:7). A statement attributed to Simeon b. Eleazar notes that a ruling prohibiting men from even eating meals with their wives during menstruation was unnecessary because this was already widely observed (*t. Šabb.* 1:7; *b. Šabbat* 13a; *y. Šabbat* 3ab). The Mishnah requires purity before pressing, but not harvesting, grapes and olives (*m. Tohorot* 9–10).

The Mishnah provides a systematic organization of the laws of ritual purity in a section entitled *Toḥorot* (Purities). Original sources of impurity are called "fathers of impurity," and persons/objects who are contaminated secondarily are "offspring of impurity." Usually, impurity can contaminate persons and vessels one remove from its original source, but it can affect food, especially holy food, as far as four steps away from the source.

New Testament

Most of the teaching on purity in the New Testament centers around moral purity, but some passages reveal the concern of Jews in this period to maintain ritual purity as well. The Synoptic Gospels support the notion that many Jews bathed or at least washed their hands before eating. Mark states this was a "tradition of the elders" passed down from earlier generations (Mark 7:3; cf. Luke 11:38). Cups, pitchers, kettles, and earthenware were often ritually purified (Mark 7:3-4; Matt. 23:25). Also, the notion of Gentile impurity was active (Acts 10:38).

The early church wrestled with its heritage of purity laws from ancient Judaism. Since they were a marker of Jewish identity, purity rituals became problematic when Gentiles were included. The Apostolic Decree settled the matter temporarily by requiring a minimum standard of cultic purity (Acts 15:28-29; 21:25). In the end, moral purity was affirmed, but ritual purity (except for Christian baptism) was set aside.

Rationale and Significance

In ancient Israel purity was connected to the holiness of YHWH. Israel's moral purity is an attempt to emulate the ethical character of YHWH (Leviticus 19; cf. *Leviticus Rabbah* 23). Ritual purity is an important marker separating Israel from pagans and maintaining the distinctiveness of Israel's lifestyle (Lev. 20:24b-25). Israel's diet, particularly, inhibits social intercourse with Gentiles and thus precludes intermarriage (cf. Exod. 34:15-16).

While it is a physical condition, ritual purity is not concerned with hygiene (cf. *b. Šabbat* 14a). Indeed, ritual impurity can be transferred to an individual who is simply in the same room as a corpse without any physical contact. Also, houses and fabrics which have no connection to germs or disease can be affected.

Scholars have noticed a common thread among the purity laws: they emphasize the separation of life and death. The most impure item in the system is the corpse. Lepers, with their flaking skin and open sores, visually illustrate the process of decay. Impure animals convey contamination only when they are dead, and most of them are carnivorous. Even the discharge of genital fluids may represent death since there is a loss of life-giving forces (Milgrom 1991: 733).

By labeling contact with dead items impure, biblical authors emphasize that Israel serves a living God, not a lifeless image or a dead ancestor. Items associated with death must be restricted because they are incompatible with worship of the God who gives life (Ps. 115:17; cf. Deut. 30:15-20). In anthropological terms, those who are at the margins of death and life are in a liminal state and must perform prescribed rituals to reenter the community. Theologically, the distinction between God and humanity is accentuated. To be human is to participate in processes which generate life but ultimately end in death, whereas YHWH, the source of life, is not subject to death.

BIBLIOGRAPHY

G. ALON 1977, *Jews, Judaism and the Classical World,* Jerusalem: Magnes. • M. DOUGLAS 1966, *Purity and Danger: An Analysis of the Concepts of Pollution and Taboo,* London: Routledge. • T. FRYMER-KENSKY 1983, "Pollution, Purification, and Purgation in Biblical Israel," in *The Word of the Lord Shall Go Forth: Essays in Honor of David Noel Freedman,* ed. C. L. Myers and M. O'Connor, Winona Lake, Ind.: Eisenbrauns, 399-414. • H. K. HARRINGTON 1993, *Impurity Systems of Qumran and the Rabbis,* Atlanta: Scholars Press. • H. K. HARRINGTON 2004, *The Purity Texts,* London: Clark. • C. HAYES 2002, *Gentile Impurities and Jewish Identities,* New York: Oxford University Press. • J. KLAWANS 2000, *Impurity and Sin in Ancient Judaism,* Oxford: Oxford University Press. • J. NEUSNER 1994, *Purity in Rabbinic Judaism,* Atlanta: Scholars Press. • H. MACCOBY 1999, *Ritual and Morality: The Ritual Purity System and Its Place in Judaism,* Cambridge: Cambridge University Press. • J. MILGROM 1991, *Leviticus 1–16,* New York: Doubleday. • J. C. POIRIER 2003, "Purity beyond the Temple in the Second Temple Era," *JBL* 122/1: 247-65. • E. REGEV 2000, "Non-Priestly Purity and Its Religious Aspects according to Historical Sources and Archaeological Findings," in *Purity and Holiness: The Heritage of Leviticus,* ed. M. J. H. M. Poorthuis and J. Schwartz, Leiden: Brill, 223-44. • R. REICH 1987, "Synagogue and Ritual Bath during the Second Temple and the Period of the Mishnah and Talmud," in *Synagogues in Antiquity,* ed. A. Kasher, A. Oppenheimer, and U. Rappaport, Jerusalem: Yad Izhak Ben Zvi, 205-12 (in Hebrew).

HANNAH K. HARRINGTON

Q

Qahat, Admonitions (Testament) of

Qumran Cave 4 yielded one manuscript (4Q542) of a hitherto unknown priestly composition, the main narrator of which identifies himself as the son of Levi (4Q542 frg. 1 ii 11) and father of Amram (4Q542 frg. 1 ii 9). Since his name is not expressly mentioned, this self-presentation allows for the identification of the speaker as Qahat, who appears in biblical genealogies (Gen. 46:11; Exod. 6:16, 18; Num. 3:17, 19, 27, 29, etc.) but does not play any significant role in the Hebrew Bible. The language of the composition is Aramaic, and the manuscript is composed of one large, two-column fragment (4Q542 frg. 1) and two smaller fragments with little text preserved (4Q542 frgs. 2 and 3). The editor dated it paleographically to the last quarter of the second century B.C.E., or its end at the latest (Puech 2001: 262-64).

When J. T. Milik published the first fragment of the *Admonitions,* he suggested that the *Admonitions of Qahat* together with the *Visions of Amram* and *Visions of Levi* (or *Aramaic Levi Document*) form a literary trilogy of the patriarchs of the priestly tribe. His first intuition has been confirmed by further studies, but his opinion that these three literary works should be called "testaments" has been subject to criticism. These priestly compositions are, in fact, didactic texts that form priestly school literature influenced by Babylonian scribal practices (Drawnel 2004; Drawnel 2006b). Their setting is probably the levitical priestly family.

Qahat in his *Admonitions* addresses his sons in a speech that concentrates on the transmission of priestly traditions and on taking care of the books that contain it. The author maintains the hortatory tone throughout the preserved text, hence this composition can be properly called Qahat's *Admonitions.*

The *Admonitions* can be divided into three sections. In the first part (4Q542 1 i 1-4a) Qahat addresses his sons and describes their future graces bestowed upon them by the God of gods. The knowledge of God's great name leads to the recognition of his omnipotence in the work of creation and his benevolence toward successive generations of priestly descendants. Then the bright priestly future is shortly hinted at with the assurance of joy and gladness prepared for priestly truthful generations.

The second section (4Q542 1 i 4b–1 ii 8) concentrates on Qahat's exhortations and assurance of future blessings. His address to his children (4Q542 1 i 4b–1 ii 1) intends to protect the priestly inheritance handed down to priestly descendants from being transmitted by half-breeds and strangers. A similar contempt for the same two groups of people may be found in the *Visions of Levi* (v. 91), where the glorious fate of the wisdom teacher is contrasted with the rejection of those qualified as strangers and half-breeds. The *Admonitions* adduces the example of the patriarchs and their moral virtues of justice and uprightness followed by the exhortation to be pure and saintly. Qahat's sons are a source of joy to the patriarchs, for they keep and carry on the patriarchal inheritance in their life. There follow seven qualities that make up this patriarchal and priestly inheritance: truth, justice, uprightness, perfection, innocence, holiness, and priesthood. Qahat then changes the topic and speaks again about the future of his sons, stressing God's eternal blessings that will dwell upon them and the future role of those who participate in the judgment of all the sinners (4Q542 1 ii 2-8). The left part of the column is, however, torn off, and thus a good part of the text is lost.

The third literary section of the manuscript (4Q542 1 ii 9-13) directly addresses Qahat's son, Amram, with an instruction to keep all the books that Qahat received from his ancestors and that he indicates as his own writings. Caring for Qahat's writings and carrying them along are seen as meritorious acts. Here the manuscript ends, and the next two fragments (4Q542 frgs. 2 and 3) contain only a few words concerning the contrast between light and darkness (4Q542 frg. 2 11-12) and fornication (4Q542 frg. 3 ii 12).

The *Admonitions* share several literary and thematic elements with the *Visions of Levi* and *Visions of Amram:* the narration uses the first-person singular, giving an autobiographical character to the whole work; a priestly patriarch speaks to his children, instructing them in matters that deal with priestly inheritance; the transmission of the priestly lore falls on the shoulders of successive generations of priestly descendants; knowledge contained in the priestly books is to be jealously kept for priestly eyes only and becomes a criterion of correct behavior. To this priestly didactic trilogy one should add the Aramaic *Book of Enoch,* which, like the *Visions of Levi* (vv. 31-47), teaches arithmetical knowledge for astronomical calculations (Drawnel 2006a).

BIBLIOGRAPHY

H. DRAWNEL 2004, *An Aramaic Wisdom Text from Qumran: A New Interpretation of the Levi Document,* Leiden: Brill. • H. DRAWNEL 2006A, "Priestly Education in the *Aramaic Levi Document* (*Visions of Levi*) and *Aramaic Astronomical Book* (4Q208–211)," *RevQ* 22: 547-74. • H. DRAWNEL 2006B, "The Literary Form and Didactic Content of the Admonitions (Testament) of Qahat," in *From 4QMMT to Resurrection: Mélanges qumraniens en hommage Émile Puech,* ed. F. García Martínez et al., Leiden: Brill, 55-73. • J. T. MILIK 1978, "Écrits preesséniens de Qumrân: d'Hénoch à Amram," in *Qumrân: Sa piété, sa théologie, son milieu,* ed. M. Delcor, Leuven: Leuven University Press, 91-106. • J. T. MILIK 1972, "4QVisions d'Amram et une citation d'Origène," *RB* 79: 77-97. • É. PUECH 1991, "Le Testament de Qahat en araméen de la grotte 4 *(4QTQah),*" *RevQ* 15: 23-54. • É. PUECH 2001, *Qumrân Grotte 4 — XXII: Textes araméens. Première partie: 4Q529-549,* DJD 31, Oxford: Clarendon.

HENRYK DRAWNEL

Qoheleth

The book of Qoheleth, also known by its Greek title "Ecclesiastes," is a literary classic among ancient Near Eastern instructional texts and throughout all of world literature. In this text, the author presents a series of timeless reflections on the fleeting and inconsistent nature of life. Qoheleth works as an empiricist to "search out by wisdom all that is done under heaven" (1:13). He returns repeatedly to the topic of death and his belief that all perceived gains are nullified at the end of a person's earthly days.

Structure and Literary Integrity

There is no consensus on a coherent structure for Qoheleth. Some scholars find an identifiable pattern; others are inclined to view the book as a loose cluster of sentences. A superscription (1:1) and two epilogues (12:9-11, 12-14) frame the main portion of text (1:3–12:7). These chapters contain a series of units on the human experience, primarily in relation to death, and are punctuated by the famous refrain, "vanity of vanities." The text seems to contain several insertions by one or more later editors who wanted to weaken the penetrating observations of the original sage (e.g., 3:17; 8:5).

Title and Authorship

The Hebrew title of the book, *Qoheleth,* is a feminine participle used in reference to a male author; its precise meaning remains obscure. The author is identified in the superscription as "the son of David, king in Jerusalem," which is a reference to Solomon. This traditional designation cannot be maintained as historically accurate. The author is described in the first epilogue as someone who "taught the people knowledge, weighing and studying and arranging many proverbs" (12:9). This career summary implies a teacher involved in the type of instruction found in the book of Proverbs. Qoheleth does take on the persona of Solomon in the first two chapters, describing himself as a person of considerable means. Even if the details are embellished, this text almost certainly comes from a well-educated individual with status in the postexilic society, a teacher who insists on verifying life's vicissitudes for himself.

Date

There is no consensus on the exact time period for Qoheleth, although two Persian loanwords, *pardes* ("garden," 2:5) and *pitgam* ("sentence," 8:11), preclude a date prior to the Exile. Proposals range from the fifth to the second century B.C.E., with the late third century being the most popular choice. The language in the book is Late Biblical Hebrew. The influence of Aramaic is apparent, and there are linguistic features that also appear in the Mishnah. In addition, the author takes up the issue of life after death (3:21) in a manner that is not attested prior to the Hellenistic period (compare the lack of interest in Proverbs).

Message

Qoheleth is a complex text, full of contradictory assertions. For example, the author cites the benefits of Wisdom in one verse (2:13), only to bemoan the possibility that a fool can inherit a wise man's property (2:18-21). Despite this enigmatic style, there are central themes. First is the author's insistence on the transitory nature of earthly existence. The term *hebel* is usually translated as "vanity" and quite literally means "breath" or "vapor." In Qoheleth, "vanity of vanities" relates to the brevity of life, which is a source of great frustration for this author. He categorically rejects the possibility of the individual soul surviving after death.

In addition, Qoheleth contests the more optimistic understanding of human potential found in the book of Proverbs. Like Job, he posits a vast gulf between God and the created order; Qoheleth does not believe that individuals can accurately discern the divine will for their lives. There may be "a time for every matter under heaven" (3:11), but humanity does not have access to such information. In addition, this book does not promise consistently favorable outcomes for the righteous and sure punishment for the wicked. The most intelligent person does not always become wealthy (9:11), and death strikes everyone in equal measure (9:2-3). Within this framework, no lasting profit is possible for anyone (2:11).

Another theme relates to memory. Life on earth follows a cyclical pattern, and no one should think that his acts will be remembered, since "there is nothing new under the sun" (1:9). Yet Qoheleth is not thoroughly pessimistic in his outlook; he affirms the possibility of present joy through a *carpe diem* mentality (e.g., 9:7-10). Even if one fate awaits all persons, individuals should utilize their existing resources to seek happiness. This is especially important in youth, before one's faculties begin to fail (12:1-8).

Influences

Some commentators believe that Qoheleth was influenced by the philosophical systems taking root during the Hellenistic age. Epicureanism and Stoicism are the most common suggestions, although this is disputed. Qoheleth was also indebted to more long-standing cultural traditions, particularly from Egypt and Mesopotamia.

Reactions to Qoheleth

The incisive commentary in this book and the author's radical questioning of the tradition proved to be controversial and almost kept Qoheleth from being canonized. The command of the second epilogist to "keep the commandments" (12:13) was probably designed to align the book more closely with official religion and mitigate some of the original sage's daring statements on uncertainty and transitoriness. In addition, the issue of death and the afterlife would be taken up by later sages during the Hellenistic period. While some figures shared Qoheleth's belief in the finality of death (e.g., Ben Sira), others maintained that the righteous soul lives on forever (e.g., Wisdom of Solomon).

BIBLIOGRAPHY

S. BURKES 1999, *Death in Qoheleth and Egyptian Biographies of the Late Period,* Atlanta: Society of Biblical Literature. • J. CRENSHAW 1987, *Ecclesiastes,* Philadelphia: Westminster. • M. FOX 1999, *A Time to Tear Down and a Time to Build Up: A Rereading of Ecclesiastes,* Grand Rapids: Eerdmans. • T. KRÜGER 2004, *Qoheleth,* Minneapolis: Fortress. • N. LOHFINK 2003, *Qoheleth,* Minneapolis: Fortress. • T. LONGMAN III 1998, *The Book of Ecclesiastes,* Grand Rapids: Eerdmans. • R. MURPHY 1992, *Ecclesiastes,* Waco: Word.• L. SCHWIENHORST-SCHÖNBERGER 1994, *'Nicht im Menschen gründet das Glück' (Koh 2,24): Kohelet im Spannungsfeld jüdischer Weisheit und hellenistischer Philosophie,* Freiburg: Herder. • C. L. SEOW 1997, *Ecclesiastes,* New York: Doubleday.

SAMUEL L. ADAMS

Qumran

Identification and History of Exploration

Khirbet Qumran (or Kumran or Gumran) is the modern Arabic name of a site located on the northwest shore of the Dead Sea. Although some scholars have identified Qumran with Ir ha-Melaḥ (the City of Salt) mentioned in Josh. 16:61-62, the *Copper Scroll* (3Q15) indicates that Qumran should be identified with Secacah, another desert town mentioned in this passage.

Early explorers who visited Qumran included Louis-Felicien Caignart de Saulcy (1850-1951); Claude R. Condor and Charles Tyrwhitt-Drake (1873); Charles Clermont-Ganneau (1874), who excavated one of the graves in the cemetery; and Gustaf Dalman (1914). However, Qumran attracted little attention before the discovery of the first Dead Sea Scrolls in 1946-1947. In February-March 1949 Roland de Vaux of the École Biblique et Archéologique Française de Jérusalem and G. Lankester Harding, the chief inspector of antiquities in Jordan, conducted excavations in Cave 1 and confirmed that this was the cave from which the first scrolls had been removed. De Vaux and Harding also surveyed Qumran and excavated two graves in the cemetery. Two years later (1951) they conducted a first season of excavations at Qumran, followed by large-scale excavations from 1953 to 1956. Recently other expeditions have explored different parts of the site, including the settlement and cemetery (Yitzhak Magen and Yuval Peleg), residential caves to the north of the settlement (Magen Broshi and Hanan Eshel), and the cemetery (Broshi, Eshel, and Richard Freund).

Description of the Settlement and Occupation Phases

De Vaux divided the sectarian settlement at Qumran into three phases, which he termed "Period Ia," "Period Ib," and "Period II." De Vaux dated Period Ia to the third quarter of the second century B.C.E. (ca. 130-100 B.C.E.), Period Ib from ca. 100 B.C.E. to 31 B.C.E., and Period II from ca. 4-1 B.C.E. to 68 C.E. A late Iron Age settlement preceded Period Ia, and Period II was followed by a brief phase of Roman occupation (Period III).

Iron Age

Qumran was first inhabited during the late Iron Age (eighth-seventh century B.C.E.). The Iron Age settlement consisted of a rectangular building with a row of rooms along the east side of an open courtyard. An enclosure attached to the west side of the building contained a large round cistern (L110; L refers to a locus, an archaeological division of space). The cistern, which was filled by surface runoff, remained in use until the destruction of the sectarian settlement at the end of Period II (in later phases it was fed by water channels connected to an aqueduct). The long wall running southward from the southeast corner to the settlement to Wadi Qumran, which encloses the esplanade to the south of the site, belongs to this phase and remained in use until the end of Period II. This phase ended with the fall of the kingdom of Judah ca. 586 B.C.E.

Period Ia

Qumran had been abandoned for several hundred years when the sectarian settlement was established. This occupation phase was modest in size and short-lived. Parts of the ruined Iron Age building were rebuilt and reoccupied. A new channel was built to supply the Iron Age cistern and two new rectangular pools (L117-L118) nearby. Rooms were constructed around the cistern, and some of the walls in the area of the central courtyard were reused. De Vaux attributed to this phase two side-by-side potters' kilns (L66) in the southeast part of the site. Since coins of Alexander Jannaeus (103-76 B.C.E.) were plentiful in the next phase (Period Ib), de Vaux dated Period Ia to the reign of John Hyrcanus I (135-104 B.C.E.).

Overview of Khirbet Qumran and surrounding area. A number of the caves where the Dead Sea Scrolls were found can be seen left of the ravine. *(Werner Braun)*

Period Ib

According to de Vaux, the sectarian settlement at Qumran acquired its definitive form during the reign of Alexander Jannaeus, when it expanded greatly in size. The main entrance to the settlement was through a gate to the north of a two-story watchtower (L9-L11). Two more entrances to the site were located by a small stepped pool to the northwest (L138) and in the area of the potters' workshop on the southeast side of the settlement. A staircase consisting of wooden steps winding around a square pillar occupied the southwest corner of the tower and provided access to storage rooms at the ground-floor level. The entrance to the tower was from a wooden gangway at the second-story level.

The tower guarded the main point of entry into the settlement, giving access to a passage that divided the site into two main parts: an eastern sector dominated by the tower (de Vaux called this the "main building"), and a western sector centered on the round Iron Age cistern (referred to by de Vaux as the "secondary building"). The main building incorporated remains of the Iron Age building and consisted of rooms grouped around a central, open-air courtyard.

The largest room in the settlement (L77) is located on the south side of the main building. It functioned as an assembly hall and communal dining room, as indicated by the adjacent pantry (L86 in Period Ib) with over 1,000 dishes.

A toilet was found in a room (L51) to the east of the central courtyard in the main building. This room opened onto two adjacent stepped pools (L49, L50). A potters' workshop (L64 and L84) and large stepped pool (L71) were located in the southeast part of the main building.

The rooms in the western sector (secondary building) included storerooms, industrial installations, and workshops. An open-air courtyard to the west of the round cistern (L111) gave access to two rooms (L120 and L121) that apparently were used for storage. A hoard of silver Tyrian tetradrachmas was discovered buried beneath the floor of L120. A large stone mortar found in association with the Period Ib floor in L105 suggests that some of the rooms in this area were used for food preparation, as in Period II. De Vaux identified a long, narrow lean-to overlooking the ravine at the southwest edge of the site (L97) as a stable for pack animals.

The hydraulic system was greatly expanded in Period Ib. De Vaux described this elaborate water system as the most striking feature of Qumran. It remained in use with some modifications until the destruction of the sectarian settlement at the end of Period II. The water was brought by aqueduct from Wadi Qumran, which flows into the Dead Sea to the south of the marl terrace on which the settlement sits. Branches of the aqueduct wound through the settlement and supplied all of the pools. Decantation basins in front of each pool or group of pools served as settling tanks, catching the silt carried by the floodwaters.

The aqueduct entered the settlement at its northwest corner, where there was a sluice gate to break the rapid flow of the floodwaters (L137). From here the water spread out into a shallow decantation basin adjoined by a small stepped pool (L138). From the decantation basin the water flowed south through a channel, filling the round Iron Age cistern (L110) and the two rectangular stepped pools nearby (L117 and L118).

From the area of the round cistern, the water was channeled to a large rectangular pool (L85, L91) and from there to a large stepped pool (L56, L58) between the main building and the dining hall/assembly room (L77). From the eastern end of this pool a channel branched off to stepped pools to the northeast (L49, L50) and the south, through a breach in the southeast corner of the main building and into a small stepped pool (L68). From here the channel flowed through a basin serving the potters' workshop (L75) and into a large stepped pool at the southeast corner of the site (L71). The overflow was carried by gutters southward onto the esplanade.

According to de Vaux, the end of Period Ib was marked by an earthquake and a fire. Evidence for earthquake destruction was found throughout the settlement but is perhaps clearest in the case of one of the pools (L49), where the steps (L48) and floor had split and the eastern half had dropped about 50 cm. This crack continues through the small pool just to the north and can be traced to the north and south. The wooden shelves with stacks of dishes in the pantry (L86) collapsed onto the floor. Earthquake damage is also evident in the tower, where the lintel and ceiling of one of the rooms at the ground level (L10A) collapsed. The northwest corner of the secondary building was damaged, as indicated by another earthquake crack running diagonally through L111, L115, L118, and L126. The western edge of the large decantation basin (L132) slid into the ravine below.

Site plan of the settlement at Qumran

The testimony of Flavius Josephus (*J.W.* 1.370-80; *Ant.* 15.121-47) enabled de Vaux to date the earthquake to 31 B.C.E. In addition to the earthquake damage, a layer of ash that had blown across the site when the wood and reed roofs burned indicates there had been a fire. De Vaux concluded that the earthquake and fire were simultaneous but admitted that there was no evidence to confirm this.

Period II

De Vaux relied on numismatic evidence to date the beginning of Period II to the time of Herod's son and successor, Herod Archelaus (4 B.C.E.-6 C.E.). According to de Vaux, the buildings damaged by the earthquake and fire were not repaired immediately. Because the water system ceased to be maintained, the site was flooded and silt accumulated to a depth of 75 cm. The silt overflowed the large decantation basin at the northwest corner of the site and spread up to the north wall of the secondary building, growing thinner toward the east. The silt overlay the layer of ash from the fire, indicating that the period of abandonment was subsequent to the fire.

Following the abandonment the site was cleared and reoccupied by the same community that had left it, as indicated by the fact that the general plan remained the same and many of the buildings seem to have been used for the same purposes as before. Some of the damaged structures in the settlement were strengthened while others were left filled with debris and abandoned. The dishes in the pantry, which had fallen and broken in the earthquake, were left lying on the floor at the back of the room. This area, now designated L89, was sealed off by a low wall. The northwest corner of the secondary building, which had begun to slide into the ravine, was buttressed. The pools that had been split by the earthquake (L48-L49, L50) and the toilet to the north (L51) went out of use. This area seems to have become an open-air courtyard in Period II. The potters' workshop continued in use with no significant modifications.

The tower on the northern side of the site was reinforced by the addition of a sloping stone rampart or "glacis." The rampart blocked two narrow windows at the ground floor level on the tower's north side and obstructed the open passages around it. In the secondary building, the eastern wall of open-air courtyard L111 was doubled in thickness, and it was now roofed over. A staircase installed in L113 led to a dining room on the west side of the secondary building (above, L111, L120-L123). Workshops, ovens, and silos were installed in many of the rooms in the secondary building in Period II. Millstones from a mill for grinding grain were found in L100, where they were dumped during Period III.

After the earthquake the roof of the dining room (L77) was rebuilt. Square, plastered mud-brick bases were erected in a row on top of the Period Ib floor at the eastern end of the room. Wooden posts placed on these bases supported the ceiling beams. The dining room was now moved to the second-story level.

De Vaux identified a large room in the center of the

main building (L30) as a "scriptorium." The debris of the collapsed second-story level yielded a long, narrow, mud-brick table covered with plaster and fragments of two smaller tables. A low mud-brick bench covered with plaster was attached to the east wall of the room. The debris also included a plastered platform with a raised border and two cup-shaped depressions, and inkwells. De Vaux's interpretation of this room as a scriptorium has been challenged, because there is no evidence that scribes at this time wrote at a table while seated on a bench (instead they squatted or sat with the material on their laps). One alternative proposal is that this room was a tricilinium in which the diners reclined on the benches, as was customary in the Greco-Roman world. However the benches, which are only 40 cm. wide, are too narrow for reclining. Furthermore, the presence of inkwells, which are not a common find in archaeological excavations in Israel, suggests that some sort of writing activity took place in this room.

The water system was also modified during Period II. The large decantation basin at the northwest corner of the site (L132) silted up and was replaced by a small basin by the sluice-gate (L137). The large pool to the south of the main building was now divided into two (L56, L58).

A cemetery containing about 1,100 graves is located fifty m. to the east of the site. The graves, which are marked by heaps of stones, are arranged in neat rows along the top of the plateau and on hills to the north and east. The bodies were placed in a loculus or niche at the bottom of a rectangular cavity dug into the marl of the plateau. All but one of the burials are oriented so that the feet of the deceased face north and the head faces south. Other graves located on hills to the south do not have the same regular alignment and orientation. Of the forty-three graves that de Vaux excavated on the plateau and on hills to the north and east, all but three contained adult male burials (the three exceptions are adult females). Graves on hills to the south that included large numbers of women and children apparently represent Bedouin burials that are unrelated to the sectarian settlement.

The Period II settlement suffered a violent destruction by fire, which de Vaux attributed to the Roman army at the time of the First Jewish Revolt. Since Josephus mentions that Vespasian occupied Jericho in June of 68 C.E., de Vaux concluded that the Romans must have destroyed Qumran at that time. This marks the end of the sectarian settlement at Qumran.

Period III

Following the destruction in 68 C.E., Qumran seems to have been occupied by a small garrison of Roman soldiers who were probably members of the Tenth Legion. They inhabited only part of the main building, including the ground floor rooms of the tower that were still accessible. The soldiers dumped the debris they cleared to the north of the main building and in the cisterns to the south. They renovated a small part of the water system, using only one large cistern that had suffered little damage (L71). The numismatic evidence and historical considerations led de Vaux to suggest that this phase ended with the fall of Masada in 73 or 74 C.E.

A Revised Chronology for Qumran

That Period Ia yielded no coins and only a few potsherds that are indistinguishable from those of Period Ib suggests that de Vaux's Period Ia might not exist. Instead, most of the architectural remains attributed to Period Ia might belong to Period Ib. On the other hand, in a few places de Vaux distinguished architectural remains that he believed postdated the Iron Age but that were covered by Period Ib structures. For example, two potters' kilns (L66) in the southeastern part of the settlement were covered by a stepped pool that was destroyed by the earthquake of 31 B.C.E. (L48-L49).

De Vaux's Period Ib should be subdivided into a pre-31- and a post-31-B.C.E. phase (see below). Most if not all of the architectural remains attributed to Period Ia could belong to the pre-31-B.C.E. phase of Period Ib, while de Vaux's Period Ib includes both pre-31-B.C.E. and post-31-B.C.E. remains. If de Vaux's Period Ia does exist, the currently available evidence suggests that it should be dated to the early first century B.C.E. instead of ca. 130-100 B.C.E.

According to de Vaux, Qumran lay in ruins and was unoccupied for about thirty years after the earthquake of 31 B.C.E. This period of abandonment ended when the site was reoccupied between 4 and 1 B.C.E. Most scholars have accepted de Vaux's chronology, though many have grappled with the problems raised by the thirty-year gap in occupation. Attributing the burial of the hoard of Tyrian tetradrachmas from L120 to the end of Period Ib instead of the beginning of Period II (as de Vaux suggested) means that the site was not abandoned after the earthquake of 31 B.C.E. The inhabitants immediately repaired or strengthened many of the damaged buildings but did not bother to clear those beyond repair.

The settlement of Period Ib continued without interruption until 9/8 B.C.E. or sometime thereafter, when Qumran suffered a deliberate, violent destruction by fire, as indicated by the layer of ash which de Vaux associated with the earthquake. The site was reoccupied early in the reign of Herod Archelaus in 4 B.C.E. or shortly afterward. The fact that the water system fell into disrepair and silt covered the site indicates that the abandonment lasted for at least one winter season. Since it is impossible to pinpoint the date, the causes leading to the destruction must remain unknown, though it is tempting to associate them with the revolts and turmoil that erupted after the death of Herod the Great in 4 B.C.E.

The Nature of the Qumran Community

The Qumran community probably consisted of about 150-200 members, although this number could have fluctuated. Most of the members of the community apparently lived outside the settlement, in tents, huts, and some of the nearby caves. The rooms inside the settlement seem to have been used for communal purposes: dining rooms, assembly rooms, kitchens, workshops, and industrial installations.

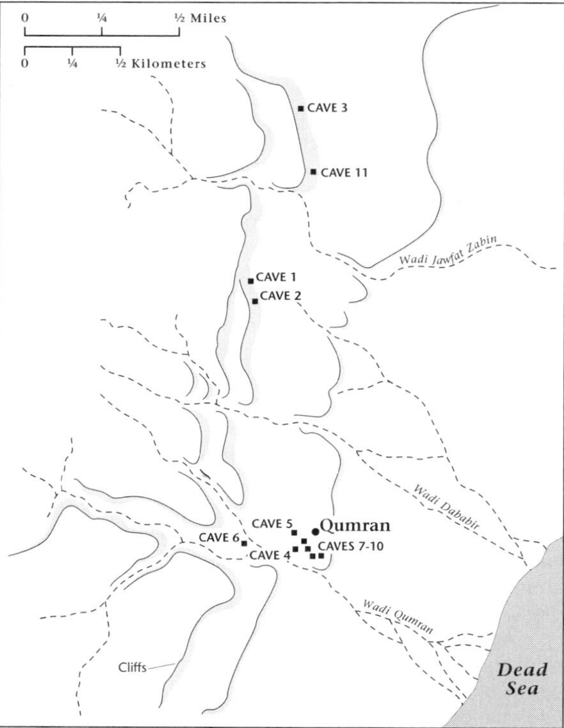

Location of the Qumran Caves

Archaeological and literary evidence indicates that Qumran was inhabited by the same Jewish sect that deposited the scrolls in the nearby caves. Apparently this sect was founded by one branch of the Zadokite priesthood, although not all members (or even leaders) were Zadokites. They called themselves by various names, including the *yaḥad* and the "Sons of Light." Our ancient sources (Flavius Josephus, Philo Judaeus, and Pliny the Elder) refer to them in Greek and Latin as Essenes. Some members of the sect lived in towns and villages around the country while others practiced desert separatism. Qumran was one such desert community; we do not know whether there were others.

The sect considered the current priesthood of the Jerusalem Temple illegitimate and refused to participate in the sacrifices offered there. Instead the sectarians viewed themselves as a replacement for the Temple and created by means of the sect a substitute for the sacrificial cult, extending the Temple regulations to all full members. For example, male members wore white linen garments, including a linen loincloth similar to those worn by the priests serving in the Temple.

The high degree of ritual purity required for the sectarian lifestyle finds physical expression in the archaeological remains at Qumran. For example, the presence of ten *miqva'ot* (ritual baths) can be understood in light of references in the Dead Sea Scrolls to purification by immersion in water. The *miqva'ot* at Qumran are characterized by their broad sets of steps and other features such as low partitions on the steps and deep basins at the bottom. Their large number and sizes were necessary to accommodate a community, as opposed to individuals or a family.

Communal meals that may have had a sacral or religious character were a hallmark of the sectarian lifestyle. This explains the presence of two communal dining rooms at Qumran, one at the southern end of the main building (L77) and the other on the western side, in the secondary building (above, L111; L120-L123). Animal bones representing the remains of kosher species (sheep, cows, goats) that had been butchered, cooked, and eaten were deposited under potsherds or inside pots in the open-air spaces outside the dining rooms. These bones apparently represent the remains of animals consumed at the communal meals and perhaps reflect a sectarian belief that these meals were a substitute for participation in the Temple sacrifices.

Both dining rooms had adjacent pantries stocked with hundreds of dishes consisting mainly of plates, cups, and bowls (L86; L114). The large number of dishes should probably be understood in light of the sectarian belief that impurity could be transmitted through food and drink. For this reason the sectarians were served individual portions instead of dining from common dishes, as was customary in the Greco-Roman world. The sectarian concern with the transmission of impurity also explains the presence of a potters' workshop at Qumran, which enabled the community to assure the purity of the pottery by manufacturing it themselves. The pottery types manufactured at Qumran include the tall cylindrical jars (or "scroll jars") that reportedly contained some of the scrolls found in Cave 1 and which were found in great numbers in other caves around Qumran as well as inside the settlement. These distinctive jars, which are virtually unique to Qumran, may have been used as storage containers for the pure goods of the sect (food, drink, and perhaps scrolls).

Recent Controversies about Qumran

Some scholars have suggested that Qumran was not a sectarian settlement but a villa, manor house, fort, commercial entrepôt, or pottery-manufacturing center, thereby rejecting the archaeological evidence for the association of the scrolls with the site. In de Vaux's time Qumran appeared to be unique because few sites had been excavated in the Dead Sea region. The fact that many more sites have been excavated and published since then — including Herodian Jericho, Ein Boqeq, ʿEin Gedi, Herodium, Masada, Kallirrhoe, and Machaerus — only highlights the unique nature of the settlement at Qumran. None of the anomalous features at Qumran is paralleled at any other site. These include the large number of *miqva'ot* (and their large sizes), the animal bone deposits, the large adjacent cemetery, the communal dining rooms with adjacent pantries of dishes, the numerous workshops, and an unusual ceramic repertoire (including the distinctive cylindrical jars). Therefore, the alternative interpretations of Qumran (e.g., Cansdale 1997; Hirschfeld 2004) are contra-

Cylindrical pottery jars with lids ("scroll jars") found in caves near Qumran (height: 40-50 cm.) *(Courtesy Israel Antiquities Authority)*

dicted by the archaeological evidence, even without taking the scrolls into account.

Qumran's unusual features are all physical expressions of this community's halakah, which involved maintaining the highest possible level of ritual purity. This accounts for the absence of these features at other sites. Qumran provides a rare case in which archaeological remains clearly reflect a system of religious beliefs and practices.

BIBLIOGRAPHY

L. CANSDALE 1997, *Qumran and the Essenes: A Re-Evaluation of the Evidence,* Tübingen: Mohr-Siebeck. • K. GALOR, J.-B. HUMBERT, AND J. ZANGENBERG, EDS. 2006, *Qumran: The Site of the Dead Sea Scrolls: Archaeological Interpretations and Debates,* Leiden: Brill. • Y. HIRSCHFELD 2004, *Qumran in Context: Reassessing the Archaeological Evidence,* Peabody, Mass.: Hendrickson. • J.-B. HUMBERT AND A. CHAMBON, EDS. 1994, *Fouilles de Khirbet Qumrân et de Aïn Feshkha I: Album de photographies, repertoire du fonds photographique, synthese des notes de Chantier du P. Roland de Vaux OP,* Fribourg: Editions Universitaires. • J.-B. HUMBERT AND A. CHAMBON, EDS. 2003, *Excavations of Khirbet Qumran and Ain Feshka: Synthesis of Roland de Vaux's Notes,* trans. S. J. Pfann, Fribourg: Academic Press (Eng. trans., with corrections, of the 1994 French volume). • J.-B. HUMBERT AND J. GUNNEWEG, EDS. 2003, *Khirbet Qumran et 'Ain Feshkha II: Studies of Anthropology, Physics and Chemistry,* Fribourg: Academic Press. • J. MAGNESS 2002, *The Archaeology of Qumran and the Dead Sea Scrolls,* Grand Rapids: Eerdmans. • R. DE VAUX 1973, *Archaeology and the Dead Sea Scrolls,* Oxford: British Academy. • M. O. WISE ET AL., EDS. 1994, *Methods of Investigation of the Dead Sea Scrolls and the Khirbet Qumran Site: Present Realities and Future Prospects,* New York: New York Academy of Sciences.

See also: Dead Sea Scrolls; Essenes

JODI MAGNESS

R

Rabbis

The rabbis were Jewish sages who flourished after the destruction of the Second Temple in 70 C.E. Most of them lived in Palestine under Roman domination until the editing of the Mishnah, the earliest rabbinic compilation, in the early third century C.E. At this time, a rabbinic community developed in Babylonia, between the Tigris and Euphrates Rivers, which in the early Second Temple period was part of the Persian Empire. The Babylonian Talmud, or Bavli, is the only classical rabbinic work composed outside of Palestine. Several rabbinic works were composed in Palestine, among them the Palestinian Talmud, or Yerushalmi, as well as several collections of midrash, rabbinic commentaries on the Bible.

Several factors establish continuities between rabbinic sages and sages of the Second Temple period. For example, beginning in approximately the fifth century B.C.E., Jewish sages created a literature based on the study and reinterpretation of Scripture, the record of divine revelation, rather than on the experience of direct divine revelation. After the Roman conquest of Judea in 70 C.E., the rabbis were the major Jewish heirs and continuators of this scribal, scholarly tradition.

Other factors as well establish continuities between rabbis and sages of the Second Temple period. It would be a mistake to characterize the rabbis as the direct successors of the Pharisees, but of the three major sects described by Josephus (Essenes, Pharisees, and Sadducees; *J.W.* 2.162-63, 166; *Ant.* 13.297-98; 18.12-15), the rabbis bear the closest resemblance and have the strongest ties to the Pharisees. Rabbinic texts feature and cite as authoritative individuals identified as Pharisees in nonrabbinic sources such as the New Testament. For the Pharisees and for the rabbis after them, teachings based on the study of Scripture were, at least in theory, accessible to all, in contrast to the esotericism of the Essenes, whom many scholars still believe collected and contributed to the library of Qumran. The Pharisees and the rabbis after them, unlike the Sadducees as described by Josephus, carefully transmitted and adhered to a body of tradition attributed to authoritative sages and transmitted independently of the Torah of Moses.

Pre-70-C.E. Sages in Rabbinic Literature

Scholars are divided on the question of whether or not rabbinic traditions provide accurate information about sages in the Second Temple period. It is undeniable that the rabbis routinely altered reality and the earlier traditions at their disposal for polemical, didactic, and moralistic purposes, but not all rabbinic literature does so to the same extent. More nuanced distinctions need to be made since there are important differences in the degree to which rabbinic sources distort the past, as well as in the nature of the distortions.

For example, Babylonian rabbis tended to depict the Jewish past, in particular Second Temple Jewish society, as dominated by sages, in contrast to Palestinian rabbis, who were more willing to depict Jewish history as dominated by priests and kings, in conformity with historical reality during the Second Temple period. This differing tendency was not the result of a greater desire for historical verisimilitude on the part of Palestinian rabbis. Rather, they were more attuned than their Babylonian counterparts to the larger world outside the study house and tended to be involved personally in relationships other than those between rabbis. When Palestinian rabbis told stories about the Second Temple period, features other than those characteristic of rabbis often came to mind. An important factor influencing the Babylonian rabbinic tendency to depict virtually everyone as a rabbi is their relatively narrow focus on the scholarly world immediately around them and their tendency to ignore the larger world outside. The task of study and the master-disciple relationship occupied a particularly prominent place in their experience, and so they relegated virtually everything else to secondary importance. They portrayed the past in terms familiar to them from personal experience. Their universe of experience extended beyond the walls of the study house, and these diverse experiences often found expression in their stories and statements. In addition, it is possible that Babylonian rabbis told stories emphasizing the importance of rabbis in the distant past in order to strengthen their belief and the belief of their disciples that rabbis were entitled to be the leaders of Babylonian Jewish society.

Another important factor influencing rabbinic depictions of sages during the Second Temple period is that some Second Temple traditions were unavailable to certain rabbis living in certain times and in certain localities. One interesting illustration of this point is that one of Josephus' famous descriptions of Pharisees and Sadducees (*Ant.* 13.297) has a clearly recognizable parallel in the Babylonian Talmud (*b. Qiddušin* 66a) but is not found in Palestinian rabbinic literature. Josephus' description is as follows:

The Pharisees passed on to the people certain ordinances from a succession of fathers, which are not written down in the laws of Moses. For this reason the party of the Sadducees dismisses these ordinances, averring that one need recognize only the written ordinances, whereas those from the tradition of the fathers need not be observed.

This tradition significantly affected the Bavli's portrayal of the Second Temple period, since it is a fundamental tenet of rabbinic thought that the rabbis possessed traditions that were authoritative despite their independence from Scripture. As a result, traditions in the Bavli tend to be hostile toward the Sadducees, while traditions in Palestinian compilations tend to reflect a more neutral perspective; and Babylonian rabbis, more than Palestinian rabbis, tended to see themselves as the descendants of the Pharisees.

Exegetical factors also colored rabbinic portrayals of sages during the Second Temple period. A story depicting Hillel's rise to the patriarchate illustrates this point. This story has been the basis for elaborate theorizing about the relationship between Hillel, a well-known Pharisaic sage, and the Bathyrans, important military allies of King Herod. Comparison between the various versions of the story demonstrates that the earliest version does not depict an encounter between Hillel and allies of the king. In the earliest version, Hillel's interlocutors are nameless and listen silently while Hillel solves a legal problem using rabbinic techniques of scriptural interpretation.

How did the Bathyrans make their way into later versions of the story of Hillel's rise to the patriarchate? Very likely another ancient rabbinic tradition about Hillel is the source. According to this second tradition, "Hillel the elder expounded seven things before the Bathyrans." A list of seven exegetical techniques follows, although this tradition provides no examples of the content of Hillel's exegesis. The Bathyrans were probably added to the story of Hillel's rise to power based on the second tradition's report of his use of exegetical arguments in their presence. Whoever connected these two traditions satisfied two storytelling needs: the need to identify anonymous characters, and the need to elaborate upon the insufficiently explained. Who is Hillel speaking to in the story of Hillel's rise to power? The second tradition supplies the answer. What did Hillel say to the Bathyrans in the second tradition? The story of Hillel's rise to power supplies the answer.

Significantly, then, the original version of the story of Hillel's rise to the patriarchate contained no mention of Herod's allies, the Bathyrans. They were added to the story not for any polemical purpose, but because of the storytelling requirements described above. There is thus no evidence in this case that the rabbis were, or even attempted to depict themselves, as superior to royal officials.

Subtle distinctions need to be drawn, therefore, between early and later, and Palestinian and Babylonian traditions about and attributed to ancient rabbis, since some traditions tend to be more accurate than others or to distort reality in particular ways but not in others. Editors and storytellers in Babylonia were particularly willing to emend earlier sources to reflect realities and attitudes in third- to seventh-century Babylonia. In addition, the modern critic needs to be sensitive to exegetical and storytelling factors that often motivated tradents and editors to introduce changes into the traditions at their disposal. Our ability to make more refined distinctions will improve our ability to predict which kinds of distortions are likely to be present in a particular source found in a particular compilation, and better equip us to make use of rabbinic sources as historical evidence.

As noted above, the tendency of Babylonian rabbis to see rabbis virtually everywhere is due in part to their greater detachment from society, in contrast to Palestinian rabbis, who are more integrated into society. This distinction is in turn linked to tendencies in the contemporary non-Jewish world, with Babylonian rabbinic detachment corresponding to strict hierarchical divisions within Persian society, and Palestinian rabbinic integration corresponding to the somewhat more permeable boundaries between classes in the Roman Empire. Differences between Palestinian and Babylonian rabbinic storytelling, therefore, have much to do with the larger cultural context within which these two literatures were produced and nothing to do with a greater or lesser desire to avoid anachronisms or distortions in the narration of past events.

Bibliography

S. J. D. Cohen 2006, *From the Maccabees to the Mishnah,* 2d ed., Louisville: Westminster John Knox. • M. Fishbane 1990, "From Scribalism to Rabbinism: Perspectives on the Emergence of Classical Judaism," in *The Sage in Israel and the Ancient Near East,* ed. J. G. Gammie and L. G. Perdue, Winona Lake, Ind.: Eisenbrauns, 439-56. • S. D. Fraade 1991, *From Tradition to Commentary: Torah and Its Interpretation in the Midrash Sifre to Deuteronomy,* Albany: State University of New York. • Y. Heinemann 1970, *Darkhei ha-Aggadah,* 3d ed., Jerusalem: Magnes (in Hebrew). • R. Kalmin 2004, "Hillel and the Soldiers of Herod: Sage and Sovereign in Ancient Jewish Society," in *Jewish Religious Leadership: Image and Reality,* vol. 2, ed. J. Wertheimer, New York: Jewish Theological Seminary, 91-126. • R. Kalmin 2006, *Jewish Babylonia between Persia and Roman Palestine,* Oxford: Oxford University Press. • S. Mason 2001, *Flavius Josephus on the Pharisees: A Composition-Critical Study,* rpt., Boston: Brill. • J. Neusner 1999, *Rabbinic Traditions about the Pharisees before 70,* 3 vols., rpt. Atlanta: Scholars Press. • S. Schwartz 2001, *Impe-*

REPENTANCE

rialism and Jewish Society, 200 B.C.E. to 640 C.E., Princeton: Princeton University Press. RICHARD KALMIN

Repentance

Repentance is a religious concept that embraces a variety of actions and attitudes such as returning to a previous commitment, turning aside from a path of behavior, showing regret or remorse for misdeeds, and having a change of mind. Discussing the history of such a religious concept presents certain difficulties. Because of the prominent place of repentance in Western theology, it can be hard to recognize that there might not have always been a concept of repentance as such. While repentance as an emotion is undoubtedly experienced everywhere, its positive evaluation and the efficacy accorded it are not. It is not simply a question of there being variations on an essentially universal concept. Rather, the history of repentance as a religious or moral ideal is bound up in particular cultural systems.

Hebrew Bible

Most interpreters understand prophetic use of the root *šûb,* as in the phrase "return to the LORD," to signify repentance. Yet Amos, Hosea, and First Isaiah employ the term with something closer to a sense of appeal, perhaps better translated: "turn aside to the LORD." It is therefore the assumed response to affliction and appears parallel to other verbs of appeal. The point is that the God of Israel wants his people to turn to him for sustenance rather than to other sources like the foreign nations (e.g., Hos. 5:13–6:3, Isa. 9:12). In the oracles of Jeremiah, the phrase becomes something like an invitation, a basis for a reunion between God and people that no longer entails appeal, but is also not to be equated simply with renewed obedience (e.g., Jer. 3:22). It is only in the prose sermons of Jeremiah and biographical notices of his life, and then in a host of relatively late exilic and postexilic texts, that one finds *šûb* focused on the cessation of sin. This change is usually accompanied by a new negative formulation: "to turn away from" a bad path or sin (e.g., Jer. 18:11). The Deuteronomistic History maintains that Israel's failure to "turn" despite prophetic warnings was largely responsible for its exile (e.g., 2 Kings 17:13). The book of Deuteronomy suggests that this "turn" will occur in future days (Deut. 4:30; 30:1-8). Unlike other works, the book of Jonah seems to regard "turning" as a present-day possibility for averting judgment (Jonah 3:8-10).

Greco-Roman Literature

There are a number of key differences between biblical turning and the notion of repentance as we find it throughout early Christian and rabbinic literature. In the later sources, the act has a strong mental component of regret and repudiation that is absent in the biblical sources, where behavioral change proves to be of primary importance. For this reason, in Biblical Hebrew, one does not "turn away" from a single sin but only from a general pattern of behavior, though one can surely repent of a particular sin in current usage! Indeed, the Latin term *paenitentia,* "repentance," has no direct connection to Hebr. *šûb* and corresponds rather to Gr. *metanoia,* which means "regret." In classical usage, *metanoia* is a moral or intellectual failing: the wise need not regret their actions, for they always act appropriately.

The denigration of repentance in Greek philosophical literature, especially Stoic circles, led scholars to believe that the notion of *metanoia* could not have influenced later usage, despite the fact that its sense of regret fits quite well. Thus, studies exploring the widespread use of "repentance" in Philo's writings have concluded that its presence there should be attributed to Jewish influences on his work that prevailed despite his Hellenistic philosophical training. But there is reason to doubt this conclusion. Aside from Philo, we find the first-century-C.E. Greek writer Plutarch making ample use of *metanoia* in a positive light. Against Stoic principles, both Philo and Plutarch argue that the wise are those who recognize their errors, those whom the pain of regret holds back from future mistakes (e.g., Philo, *On Flight and Finding* 157; Plutarch, *On Compliancy* 536). It seems likely that the elevation of *metanoia* was part of a counter-Stoic movement whose thought was preserved in both Philo and Plutarch. A few allusions to *metanoia* among other Hellenistic authors hint at its potential significance. It is worth noting that *metanoia* was not the translation adopted by the Septuagint for *šûb.* Philo's insistence on that term suggests that it was influenced by the Greek to which he was accustomed.

Second Temple Judaism

The picture that emerges within late Second Temple Judaism is quite mixed. Contrary to certain scholarly accounts, there was no apparent expectation of a nationwide repentance that would usher in redemption. That redemption is premised on human repentance is a tenet in later Judaism and Christianity. Rather, only divine transformation of the world order and even human nature can secure a significant change in national circumstance. The important allusion in Deuteronomy to Israel's eventual turning is interpreted in the first chapter of *Jubilees* and end of 4QMMT as a preordained turn toward sectarian practice that does not, properly speaking, entail moral introspection or an effort at religious transformation. The sectarians at Qumran evidently viewed joining their sect as a fulfillment of this process.

The situation differs considerably when we consider individual piety. There are spotty indications of an emerging notion of repentance. In the book of *Jubilees,* Israel is to turn away from its errors once each year (*Jub.* 5:17-18), a suggestion not found in the biblical account of Yom Kippur, and Judah "mourns over" his sin with Tamar and thereby indicates that he did not willfully sin (*Jub.* 41:23-25). The old terminology of "turning away" from sin still appears but is now applied to specific sins and with an emotion of regret, "mourning," an emphasis found in the *Testaments of the Twelve Patriarchs* as well. Ben Sira also applies *šûb* to individual sins. For his part, Josephus presents regret as a failing, but he can also view *metanoia* as a sort of ideal for individuals.

New Testament

Both early Christianity and rabbinic Judaism tended to enshrine words that were significant but not central in the general culture and turn them into technical terms. Why certain words were chosen over others is not always clear, but "repentance" was certainly among them. What is remarkable is how precisely the meaning and use of repentance overlap in the lexicons of these two emerging religions. For both, repentance has a largely negative valence, as a rejection of specific past sins. It plays a role for inveterate sinners and the righteous. Both cases can be found in the Hellenistic writings, where "sinners" are exhorted to convert to philosophy and the righteous must hold in check their baser impulses. The increasing interest in repentance in late antiquity may have accorded with an emerging focus on interiority, a need for alternatives to the sacrificial cult in thinking about atonement, and the exigencies of communal maintenance.

Scholarship has often had a skewed picture of the role of *metanoia* in the New Testament. First of all, there has been a tendency to view Jesus' preaching on the topic — of necessity — as innovative. This has led to the claim that *metanoia* goes beyond the repentance found in Jesus' Jewish background, that it means something more like "change of mind" rather than "regret," "conversion" rather than "repudiation of sins." This is unlikely. In Luke-Acts, the desideratum of repentance focuses on regret for sins of financial misappropriation, bloodshed (the Jews' "murder" of Jesus), and idolatry. Second, there has been a tendency to overemphasize the importance of repentance in Jesus' preaching. Most attestations of *metanoia* are found in Luke-Acts, and the argument that it is present elsewhere, even when not mentioned, is not compelling. Rather, we can see the Lukan editor introducing repentance into his source materials (e.g., compare Luke 5:32 to Mark 2:17). Paul lacks any real focus on repentance. On the whole, early Christian material is similar to its Second Temple Jewish background in not emphasizing repentance as a precondition for redemption. Later writers, concerned with rapidly expanding Christian communities, introduced the concept as a method of establishing clear but relatively porous lines for joining the group, as well as dealing with infractions in a less than draconian fashion. It therefore came to be seen as a necessary component of redemption and became an important trope of moral exhortation.

Rabbinic Judaism

The fact that the rabbis used a noun, *tešûbâ*, etymologically related to biblical *šûb* has significantly complicated efforts at definition. Scholars have sometimes suggested that it be understood as something closer to the Hebrew "return" than the Latinate "repentance." The rabbis did undoubtedly employ this root because of its prestigious origins, but origins do not determine eventual meanings. In mishnaic Hebrew, *šûb* was no longer the root used for indicating "return," and, partially under the influence of Aramaic, it could be seen, among other things, as closer to "regret." This semantic shift coincided with the ascendancy of "repentance" as a Hellenistic philosophical ideal to create the rabbinic concept of *tešûbâ*. And indeed, as stated earlier, its meaning and usage are significantly similar to those of *metanoia*. Thus, in both rabbinic literature and Plutarch, the opinion is expressed that the penitent is on a higher plane than one who has never sinned. Interestingly, the opposite opinion (the traditional Stoic view) is also expressed (*b. Berakot* 34b). This tension within rabbinic literature plays itself out in the interpretation of Scripture: there are frequent disputes over whether Israel's biblical ancestors sinned and repented or never really sinned at all (e.g., *b. Šabbat* 56b with regard to Josiah). Thus, in terms of definition and the genealogy of the concept, "repentance" would appear to be the perfect translation of *tešûbâ*.

"Repentance" appears as a central concept throughout all periods and corpora of rabbinic literature. Midrash consistently casts a variety of biblical figures as penitent sinners and presents them as exemplars for contemporary transgressors. In homiletical literature, there is a very strong focus on the openness and constant opportunity for reconciliation with God that is presented by *tešûbâ*, an insistence that probably served to keep alive the possibility for integration in rabbinic communities. In certain circumstances, legal literature more sharply delineates the efficacy of repentance, combining it with other forms of atonement and insisting that actual heretics do not qualify for forgiveness. The notion that it is the wise who repent receives expression as the commandment for all to repent each year on Yom Kippur (*m. Yoma* 9:8)

BIBLIOGRAPHY

W. L. HOLLADAY 1958, *The Root Šûb in the Old Testament*, Leiden: Brill. • D. LAMBERT 2006, "Did Israel Believe that Redemption Awaited Their Repentance? The Case of *Jubilees* 1," *CBQ* 68: 631-50. • G. D. NAVE JR. 2002, *The Role and Function of Repentance in Luke-Acts*, Atlanta: Society of Biblical Literature. • B. NITZAN 1999, "Repentance in the Dead Sea Scrolls," in *The Dead Sea Scrolls after Fifty Years: A Comprehensive Assessment*, ed. P. W. Flint and J. C. VanderKam, Leiden: Brill, 145-70. • E. P. SANDERS 1985, *Jesus and Judaism*, Philadelphia: Fortress Press, 106-13. • E. E. URBACH 1970, "Redemption and Repentance in Talmudic Judaism," in *Types of Redemption*, ed. R. J. Z. Werblowsky and C. J. Bleeker, Leiden: Brill, 190-206. • D. WINSTON 1995, "Philo's Doctrine of Repentance," in *The School of Moses: Studies in Philo and Hellenistic Religion*, ed. J. P. Kenney, Atlanta: Scholars Press, 29-40.

DAVID LAMBERT

Resistance Movements

The history of the Jewish homeland in the late Hellenistic and early Roman periods is often noted for the number of major military conflicts that took place. There were at least three substantial wars: the Maccabean Revolt (168/7-164 B.C.E.) against the Seleucid ruler Antiochus IV; the so-called First Revolt (66-70 C.E.) against Roman rule; and the so-called Second Revolt (132-135 C.E.), also against Roman rule, often referred to as the Bar Kokhba Revolt. To this list other conflicts can be added, such as the struggles led by various members of the Maccabean family against the successors of Antiochus IV in the mid-second century B.C.E.; the campaign of Pompey in 63 B.C.E.; the Parthian invasion of 40 B.C.E.; and the campaign of Varus in 4 B.C.E. It is also possible that the 115-117 C.E. uprisings that centered around Egypt and Cyrene spread to the Jewish homeland. It is therefore understandable that the large number of conflicts has attracted much comment and discussion in scholarship as an ongoing, prominent feature of the period. Indeed, a significant amount of attention has been devoted to exploring what link may exist between these various conflicts. There has been a dominant underlying assumption that these are not isolated, unrelated conflicts with at best a casual connection, but that they are linked as part of an era of persistent Jewish aspiration for political independence. The claim by Josephus that there was a specific school of thought, dubbed the "fourth philosophy," whose central point of definition was that it urged Jews to accept God alone as their ruler, has been widely used as the thread by which the various conflicts have been woven together (*J.W.* 2.118; *Ant.* 18.23-24). For some the reconstruction has involved showing how such an ideology underpinned all the attempts to assert Jewish autonomy, while for others it has also involved proposing the existence of a formal organization or movement instigating and fostering the cause of resistance to foreign rule, at least from the establishment of the Roman province of Judea in 6 C.E. onward.

Although such a reconstruction might appear attractive given the number of wars that can be listed and the explicit commentary offered by Josephus as a contemporary witness, it is important to proceed with far more caution when exploring these occasions of armed conflict. Three initial notes of caution need to be kept in the foreground of any discussion. First, the period of history under examination spans almost 300 years. It is not unusual that the study of any society or region covering three centuries should include among its list of events wars and other military conflicts. Indeed, the choice of start date and end date will have a significant bearing on the nature of the inquiry. Hence, the use of the Maccabean Revolt and the Bar Kokhba Revolt as the two bookends implicitly encourages an investigation that views the period as a time during which Jews actively sought to obtain political independence. However, there is no intrinsic reason to opt for such a set of dates as defining the period. Second, the limited and inconsistent nature of the available source material means it is difficult to avoid reconstructing the history of the period beyond what those sources want to describe. Not all groups and individuals active in the period have left their own testimony, while those who have left an account have done so in order to present a particular interpretation of what happened. For example, Josephus provides a very detailed narrative of the First Revolt, but it is one constructed after the event that does not seek to do justice to the motivation of all the participants. Josephus has his own interests to serve through the narrating of the years leading up to the conflict and of the actual war. Third, it is important to remember the very limited nature of the extant source material. There is a natural tendency for attention to focus on the situation in the first century C.E. because of the account rendered by Josephus, and for that discussion to be dominated by a sense of increasing tension and conflict through which resistance to Roman rule intensified over time. The lack of a narrative source for the years between 70 and 132 C.E. means it is not possible to make any comparative assessment of these years as opposed to those in the time leading up to the First Revolt. It is important that the absence of a narrative source for that period is not presumed to mean it was a more peaceful era.

The label "resistance movements" offers a way to begin exploring the various armed conflicts without adopting the presumption of a tangible link connecting all such expressions of opposition. Adopting a case-by-case approach that commences from the principle of each instance of resistance being a discrete occasion prompts the question, Resistance against what? Foreign rule in general or certain types of rule in particular? Furthermore, was the focus of the resistance on removing the current ruler(s), or was there a declared intention to introduce a new type of leadership, or simply an alternative ruler? The following discussion focuses on those instances of active resistance where the existing mechanisms of authority were openly opposed. It will also be restricted to the examples of resistance to foreign rule in the first century C.E., in the time leading up to and during the First Revolt. Although not discussed here, it is important to note that there were also Jewish resistance movements against Jewish rulers during this period (e.g., Alexander Jannaeus and Herod the Great).

Drawing upon the narratives of Josephus, the following warrant comment: the "fourth philosophy"; bandits, both named and unnamed; Sicarii; priests; Zealots; and named individuals with followers.

The Fourth Philosophy

According to Josephus, a new school of thought, separate from the three other known schools, was entirely responsible for any ideological opposition to Roman rule (*J.W.* 2.118, 433; *Ant.* 18.4-10, 23-25; 20.102). At the time of the initial census in Judea (6 C.E.) Judas "the Galilean" called upon Jews not to register. According to Judas, to do so would be an act of slavery, since the Jews should have no master other than God (*J.W.* 2.118). Beyond reiterating that what Judas founded had nothing to do with the thinking of all other Jews, Josephus provides no further detail in the account of the Jewish War. In *Jewish Antiquities* he offers a much expanded and different version of the story. Judas is from Gamala; he and a person named Zadok, identified as a Pharisee, founded the school of thought, which was exactly the same as the Pharisees in every respect other than its ideological opposition to Rome. Most important of all, Josephus provides an extensive commentary on how this school of thought was responsible for the war that commenced some sixty years later (*Ant.* 18.5-10). In other words, rather than diminish the role played by this "fourth philosophy," Josephus actually increases the effort to apportion responsibility to it in his later work.

The relevance of this "fourth philosophy" for understanding Judaism in the first century C.E. is difficult to establish. There are a number of unusual features in the description of this group: it has a named founder(s); it is identified only by a specific political doctrine; and the geographical origin of the founder is identified, even if Josephus is inconsistent about the actual location. Further complicating the situation is the fact that Josephus goes on to refer to several descendants of Judas as being actively involved in resistance against Roman rule: two sons, James and Simon (*Ant.* 20.102); a son (or grandson?), Menahem (*J.W.* 2.433; 7.253); and a further relative, Eleazar ben Ya'ir (or son of Jairus; *J.W.* 2.447; 7.253). Although this information has often been viewed as evidence for hereditary leadership of an organized group actively opposing Roman rule, it could also be a case of Josephus anachronistically assigning the origin of ideological opposition to Rome to a family of his own generation that was known to be unpopular (Menahem and many of his followers were murdered [*J.W.* 2.443-48]). Josephus' desire to exonerate most Jews from opposing Rome was facilitated by attributing all ideological opposition to a single person who was not directly linked to Jerusalem or even Judea and who lived some sixty years before the war began. Any attempt to maintain that the reference to Judas being active in 6 C.E. is historical must address the as-yet-unexplained question of why it was someone from Galilee, where the census was not yet imposed, who led such a movement. The whole notion of a distinct "fourth philosophy," devoted entirely to the cause of ideological opposition to Roman rule, is best viewed as part of Josephus' elaborate effort to shift responsibility for the war from those who were most directly involved in its commencement (see further below, under priests).

There are four further aspects of the so-called fourth philosophy to note. First, there is a partially contradictory reference to Judas in Acts 5:37. At the time of the census, Judas the Galilean led an uprising in which he and many of those who followed him were killed. For those who consider the reference to Judas historical, debate continues over whether there was armed resistance associated with the protest against the census. Second, although lacking any explicit evidence, some scholars have suggested that Judas the Galilean was the same person as Judas son of Hezekiah, who led a revolt after the death of Herod (*J.W.* 2.56; *Ant.* 17.271-72). Both the third and fourth features are concerned with nomenclature. Third, one of the descendants of Judas, Eleazar, is identified as a leader of the Sicarii (*J.W.* 7.252). Fourth, at one point in the narrative some of Menahem's followers are described as "armed zealots" (*J.W.* 2.444). Both references have been used to argue that there was one formal revolutionary group that went by various names. Again, caution is warranted. In *Jewish War* 2.444 Josephus refers to the attitude of the followers, not the name of the group: they are zealous in behavior, "armed fanatics." The reference in *Jewish War* 7.252 needs to be placed alongside *Jewish War* 2.425, where the Sicarii are named but not connected with Menahem or his relative Eleazar. Indeed, when those two individuals are named, along with their followers, Josephus does not refer to them as Sicarii.

Bandits (Named and Unnamed)

Josephus refers to bandits (*lēstēs*) being a constant presence in the events leading to the First Revolt (*J.W.* 2.228, 235, 253, 254, 264, 271, 275, 278; *Ant.* 20.121, 124, 160, 163-65, 168, 185-86, 210, 215, 256). Many of these references lack specific information and may be best understood as part of the attempt by Josephus to construct a picture of the sociopolitical situation in Judea before the war as one of ever increasing trouble. At the same time, it is likely that Josephus used "bandit" to label people who had an agenda beyond simply engaging in robbery as a living. One such possible example is Eleazar son of Deinaeus (*J.W.* 2.235, 253; *Ant.* 20.121, 161). At no stage does Josephus ascribe an agenda to the activity of Eleazar. However, if he were only a self-serving robber, it is curious that he came to the aid of Jews in their dispute with Samaritans after the latter had killed Galilean pilgrims traveling to Jerusalem, and that when he was finally captured after some twenty years of activity, the Roman governor of Judea, Felix, sent him to Rome for trial.

The Sicarii

The term "Sicarii" is another label that Josephus uses in a derogatory sense for people he wanted to blame for bringing about the war and its disastrous consequences (*J.W.* 2.254; *Ant.* 20.163). It is clear that Josephus viewed the Sicarii, so named because of their use of a dagger (*sica*) as a weapon of choice (*J.W.* 2.255), as a discrete group that originated while Felix was governor (52–ca. 59 C.E.). Furthermore, this group was active in Jerusalem, using a variety of tactics to achieve their aims, including kidnapping and assassination. As described by Josephus, Romans were not the direct target of the activity of the Sicarii; indeed, the Sicarii apparently worked with Felix to assassinate the high priest Jonathan (*Ant.* 20.163). The corresponding account in *Jewish War,* however, does not claim that Felix hired the Sicarii to dispose of Jonathan. At the outbreak of the First Revolt, Sicarii became involved (*J.W.* 2.425), apparently managing to enter the Temple complex in disguise in order to join forces with those Jews who had decided to rebel against Roman rule. In other words, they are not identified as being part of the group that actually started the revolt.

Although the Sicarii are often identified in scholarship as being led by Menahem, Josephus never makes this claim. As noted above, it is only when introducing

RESISTANCE MOVEMENTS

Jewish Resistance to Roman Rule

50s-30s B.C.E.	Social banditry arises in Syria and Palestine
4 B.C.E.	Herod the Great dies; Herod Archelaus massacres Jewish pilgrims in Jerusalem during Passover; Varus, Roman legate of Syria, quells unrest in Judea
6 C.E.	Judas the Galilean and Zadok the Pharisee found "fourth philosophy" and lead revolt in protest of a Judean census
ca. 36 C.E.	Anonymous Samaritan leads followers to Mt. Gerizim; Roman prefect of Judea, Pontius Pilate, sends in contingent of cavalry to rout and kill them; standards incident
40	Emperor Caligula attempts to install statue of himself in Jerusalem Temple; Petronius, governor of Syria, delays executing order, which is eventually rescinded on urging of Agrippa
44	Agrippa, the last Jewish king, dies
44-46	Roman procurator Fadus attempts to purge Judea of brigands
ca. 45	Jewish prophet Theudas takes followers to Jordan River to await its miraculous parting; Fadus routs and kills many, has Theudas executed
48-52	Roman procurator Cumanus takes aggressive military action against the brigands
50s	An anonymous Egyptian Jew leads followers to Mount of Olives to witness miraculous fall of Jerusalem's walls; Roman governor Felix sends in troops; Sicarii and "false prophets" emerge
60-66	Brigandage and revolution mark the procuratorships of Festus, Albinus, and Florus
66	Florus plunders Temple treasury and violently quells Jewish resistance; Eleazar b. Ananias and Temple priests terminate sacrifices on behalf of Rome and emperor; Menahem breaks into arsenal at Masada and joins insurrection in Jerusalem
August 66	Jewish insurgents capture Antonia Fortress in Jerusalem; Cestius Gallus, legate of Syria, attacks Jerusalem but withdraws and suffers defeat
66-68	Simon bar Giora takes control of Jerusalem with royal pretentions; later surrenders and is taken to Rome for execution
Spring-Fall 67	Roman army under Vespasian subdues Galilee
Winter 67-68	Zealot party forms under Eleazar son of Simon; eventually comes under leadership of John of Gischala
Spring-Fall 70	Titus takes Jerusalem and destroys Temple and city
73/74	Roman Tenth Legion storms Masada, the last refuge of Jewish rebels under Eleazar ben Ya'ir; rebels commit mass suicide
115/116-117	Diaspora Jews in Egypt, Cyrene, Cyprus, and Mesopotamia stage uprisings during reign of Emperor Trajan
132-135	Simon ben Kosiba (Bar Kokhba) leads failed revolt during reign of Emperor Hadrian

the siege of Masada that Josephus, in providing a summary of the various groups on which he wants to lay blame for the war, names Eleazar son of Jairus as leader of the Sicarii (*J.W.* 7.252). There is no particular reason why Josephus should have thought it expedient to leave out naming the Sicarii as the followers of Menahem. It is possible that Josephus simply forgot.

However, it is also possible that, in writing *Jewish War* book 7 several years after the completion of books 1–6, Josephus created a connection that never actually existed in order to provide a label for the defenders of Masada. The detail of what Josephus offers regarding the Sicarii in book 7 of *Jewish War* is intriguing. Eleazar's first speech echoes the ideas Josephus identifies as being unique to the fourth philosophy, that life under Rome is one of slavery, and the importance of having no master other than God (*J.W.* 7.323-24, 29, 36). Then, when referring to the fate of Sicarii who had fled to Egypt (*J.W.* 7.410-19), Josephus claims that they extolled the idea of having God alone as their master, even under pain of torture and death (*J.W.* 7.411). It is important to note the implications here in what Josephus has narrated: either not all Sicarii were under the leadership of Eleazar, or some of the defenders at Masada escaped and fled to Egypt. In determining what credence, if any, should be given to the Sicarii actually upholding such ideological principles, it is necessary also to explain how such a group could work in the employment of a Roman governor.

Priests

Josephus never identifies priests as a resistance movement. This is a deliberate ploy to avoid placing any blame upon himself and his immediate colleagues. Instead, Josephus explicitly depicts the leading priests as people who advocated peace (*J.W.* 2.301, 316, 320-24, 410-11, 422). Only once the war had commenced did the priests allegedly take over leadership of the revolt (*J.W.* 2.562-69, 647-51). Once in charge, their plan was to offer effective resistance in order to sway the Romans to sue for peace (*J.W.* 4.319-25). However, there are sufficient indicators in what Josephus narrates to show that at

RESISTANCE MOVEMENTS

least some of the leading priests were crucial in bringing about the war. The key passage is the point at which the war began, the cessation of sacrifices offered on behalf of Rome and the emperor (*J.W.* 2.409-10). Although he does not explain why the decision was made, Josephus does identify a key figure in the process: Eleazar son of Ananias. Josephus does not recognize Eliezar's associates as priests, yet their participation in physically helping to stop the practice of sacrifices, and the absence of criticism directed at them by Josephus for defying the sanctity of the Temple, are strong indicators that these associates must have been priests. That some priests had a key role in starting the revolt does not necessarily mean they were part of a long-standing group committed to the removal of Roman rule. The decision to oppose Roman rule in 66 C.E. may have been triggered by the specific circumstances of life during the governorship of Florus, such as his demand that arrears in taxes be paid from Temple funds (*J.W.* 2.293-94).

It is possible that some priests had previously expressed views or undertaken actions not deemed legitimate by the Romans. Josephus explained that his trip to Rome in 63/64 C.E. was to plead the case of some priests previously sent to Rome for trial (*Life* 13). The involvement of some priests at the outset of the revolt readily explains how priests were able to assume positions of leadership. Moreover, the silver coinage issued during the first year of the revolt (up to Passover in 67 C.E.) may offer some insight into their motivation, particularly given that Josephus deliberately avoids offering such information (McLaren 2003).

The Zealots

Josephus is very clear in asserting that a group known by the name Zealots came into existence during the First Revolt in 67-68 C.E. (*J.W.* 4.161). The name of the group was a reflection of the zeal with which they supported their cause. This group became embroiled in a dispute with other rebels regarding the course of the war. They opposed the apparent lack of activity displayed by the administration of Ananus and his supporters (*J.W.* 4.162-313). Enlisting the aid of Idumeans, they managed to overthrow Ananus and temporarily take on the leadership of the defense of Jerusalem. Josephus then presents a picture of increasing civil war in which the Zealot group eventually came under the leadership of John of Gischala (*J.W.* 5.98-105). Their original leader was Eleazar son of Simon (*J.W.* 5.5), who had been active in the war from the outset (*J.W.* 2.564-65). Having taken control of the Temple, one of their first actions was to propose the appointment of a new high priest, to be selected by lot (*J.W.* 4.153-54). It is clear that the Zealots were a new coalition of people drawn together by a sense of frustration and dissatisfaction at the way the war was unfolding. But individuals before 67-68 C.E. who displayed zeal in their behavior cannot be identified as members of a group known as the Zealots. Instead, they were simply people who were given the nickname "zealot" because they exhibited enthusiasm for a particular cause (e.g., Simon the Zealot, one of Jesus' followers; cf. Luke 6:15).

Named Individuals with Followers

In the context of the war itself, Josephus identifies two individuals with large followings who played a major role in the siege of Jerusalem: John of Gischala (*J.W.* 4.121-28) and Simon son of Giora (*J.W.* 4.503-13). Although the Zealots eventually come under the leadership of John, neither he nor Simon is identified as being connected with any of the named groups. John first appears in the account of the Galilean campaign (*J.W.* 2.585-94; *Life* 43–45). He was a rival of Josephus who apparently fled while his hometown was under attack to Jerusalem, where he became one of the leading figures in the rebel forces during the siege. After his capture by the Romans, John was imprisoned for life (*J.W.* 6.434). Josephus offers a contrasting picture of how and why John became involved in the war. In the *Jewish War* account John was a "bandit" eager for self-gain, who used the war as a pretext to increase his wealth. In the later *Life* version, John was initially opposed to the war and became involved only after the non-Jewish population of the surrounding towns attacked his hometown of Gischala. Importantly, the one common point in these two accounts is that John was not part of an organization devoted to removing Roman rule; his involvement arose out of unusual circumstances.

The other named individual leader was Simon son of Giora. From the Roman perspective Simon was deemed to be the most prominent leader of the rebels. He was captured and had the distinction of being executed at the culmination of the triumph (*J.W.* 7.153-57). Simon was involved in fighting against the Romans from the very beginning of the war (*J.W.* 2.521). He was, however, not part of the initial leadership, and Josephus describes his activity in the region of Acrabatene as that of a bandit (*J.W.* 2.652-54). Simon is then named as trying to align himself with the bandits who had occupied Masada, namely, the group under the leadership of Eleazar son of Jairus (*J.W.* 4.503-6). Josephus depicts this as no more than an alliance of convenience, and one that did not last. Although there is no detailed explanation offered of why he fought against the Romans, Josephus does claim that Simon gathered a large following by declaring slaves free and offering rewards (*J.W.* 4.508). For whatever reason, Simon appears to have been strongly in favor of offering armed resistance against Roman rule. However, this was not because he was a member of one of the named groups.

Assessment

The only definite point of connection between the many resistance groups and individuals was that at some stage they engaged in opposition to Rome. As such, the traditional picture that all expressions of open resistance to Roman rule were the work of one revolutionary group, usually identified with the Zealots (Hengel 1976), is wrong. Although that picture has been thoroughly critiqued (Horsley 1986; Smith 1971 and 1996), a widely espoused compromise position has emerged: that there was a shared ideology motivating those who opposed foreign rule. Even this position is questionable, though. All of the people who engaged in direct opposition to Rome found it useful to provide some explanation of why they chose that particular course of action. It is also likely that, in searching for a means of justifying their decision, reflection on the meaning of the first commandment featured prominently. This, however, does not mean that the ideological basis for all opposition to Roman rule should be traced to one group, to one particular founding teacher, or even to one ideology. To do so would be to adopt the interpretation Josephus constructed after the war, when it was necessary to marginalize a notion that had been central to the conflict, that God alone should be the ruler of the Jewish people.

BIBLIOGRAPHY

S. APPLEBAUM 1971, "The Zealots: The Case for Reevaluation," *Journal of Roman Studies* 61: 155-70. • W. R. FARMER 1956, *Maccabees, Zealots, and Josephus: An Inquiry into Jewish Nationalism in the Greco-Roman Period,* New York: Columbia University Press • D. GOODBLATT 2006, *Elements of Ancient Jewish Nationalism,* Cambridge: Cambridge University Press. • M. HENGEL 1976, *Die Zeloten: Untersuchungen zur jüdischen Freiheitsbewegung in der Zeit von Herodes I. bis 70 n. Chr.,* 2d ed., Leiden: Brill; trans. D. Smith, *The Zealots: Investigations into the Jewish Freedom Movement in the Period from Herod I until A.D. 70,* Edinburgh: Clark, 1989. • R. A. HORSLEY 1986, "The Zealots: Their Origin, Relationships and Importance in the Jewish Revolt," *NovT* 28: 159-92. • R. A. HORSLEY AND J. S. HANSON 1985, *Bandits, Prophets and Messiahs: Popular Movements in the Time of Jesus,* Minneapolis: Winston. • B. ISAAC 1984, "Bandits in Judaea and Arabia," *HSCP* 88: 171-203. • G. JOSSA 1994, "Josephus' Action in Galilee during the Jewish War," in *Josephus and the History of the Greco-Roman Period: Essays in Memory of Morton Smith,* ed. F. Parente and J. Sievers, Leiden: Brill, 265-78. • J. KAMPEN 1988, *The Hasideans and the Origins of Pharisaism: A Study in 1 and 2 Maccabees,* Atlanta: Scholars Press • J. S. MCLAREN 2003, "The Coinage of the First Year as a Point of Reference for the Jewish Revolt (66-70 CE)," *SCI* 22: 135-52. • J. S. MCLAREN 2004, "Constructing Judaean History in the Diaspora: Josephus's Accounts of Judas," in *Negotiating Diaspora: Jewish Strategies in the Roman Empire,* ed. J. M. G. Barclay, London: Clark, 90-108. • V. NIKIPROWETZKY 1973, "Sicaires et Zélotes — une réconsidération," *Semitica* 23: 51-64 • J. J. PRICE 1992, *Jerusalem under Siege: The Collapse of the Jewish State 66-70 C.E.,* Leiden: Brill. • D. M. RHOADS 1976, *Israel in Revolution: 6-74 C.E.: A Political History Based on the Writings of Josephus,* Philadelphia: Fortress. • P. SCHÄFER, ED. 2003, *The Bar Kokhba War Reconsidered: New Perspectives on the Second Jewish Revolt against Rome,* Tübingen: Mohr-Siebeck. • B. D. SHAW 1984, "Bandits in the Roman Empire," *Past and Present* 105: 3-52. • M. SMITH 1971, "Zealots and Sicarii: Their Origins and Relation," *HTR* 64: 1-19. • M. SMITH 1996, "The Troublemakers," in *The Cambridge History of Judaism,* vol. 3, *The Early Roman Period,* ed. W. Horbury et al., Cambridge: Cambridge University Press, 501-68.

JAMES S. MCLAREN

Restoration

Restoration denotes the attempt of individuals or groups in a society to reestablish in whole or in part conditions that prevailed before a major change took place. With respect to early Judaism, the term "restoration" is used by scholars in several senses: (1) the postexilic restoration as described principally in Ezra-Nehemiah; (2) the Jews' liberation from an ongoing "exile," or at least the ongoing effects of the Exile that lasted for centuries even after the so-called postexilic period; and (3) the return to some kind of golden age.

Restoration in the Hebrew Bible

The Torah contains several restoration texts, most of them founded on the Sinaitic covenant, which shaped Israel's consciousness of its own history and destiny. The northern kingdom of Israel and later the southern kingdom of Judah were sent into their respective exiles because they had failed to meet their covenantal obligations. Furthermore, this covenantal thinking fostered the expectation that a change in Israel's behavior (repentance) would lead to a restoration of Israel's national fortunes (e.g., Lev. 26:40-45; Deut. 30:1-10). God's promise to give Abraham's descendants the promised land was also a popular theme in the postexilic period (e.g., Isa. 41:8; 51:2; 63:16; Neh. 9:7). The Abrahamic covenant was unconditional and eternal and therefore still in effect, despite the Exile and the fact that Jews both inside and outside the land of Israel continued to live under foreign powers. Another example of this kind of reading of the Torah is Jacob's deathbed blessing of his twelve sons in Genesis 49. Genesis 49:10 in particular came to be read as a prediction of the restoration of kingship to Judah: "the scepter shall not depart [forever] from Judah."

The Hebrew prophets assure Israel of restoration because of the covenant. Particularly in times of national crisis, the prophets offered fantastic visions of future restoration that were largely unfulfilled in the people's subsequent history (cf., e.g., Isa. 2:1-4; 4:2-6; 35:1-10; 54:1-17; Jer. 31:38-40; Ezek. 39:25-29; Mic. 5:7-9). Some of these visions resemble those in later apocalypses. An important text in this respect is Isa. 65:17-25, which envisions an earthly life such as we know, but longer and free of pain and care. Although this prophetic text is oriented toward a restored earthly society in a way that has very much in common with earlier prophets, it also overlaps significantly with later apocalyptic visions. For example, the apocalypse in *Jubilees* 23 specifically alludes to Isa. 65:17-25, especially with regard to the expected increased longevity in the latter days.

The move from increased human longevity at the time of national restoration to a concept of personal resurrection from the dead seems to have been a small step. The metaphor of national restoration as resurrection from the dead had already been used in Ezek. 37:1-14 and Isa. 26:19. In the context of Ezekiel's vision for the restoration of Israel in 36:16–37:14, once the land and the people are cleansed, God will provide "a new heart" and "a new spirit" (36:26-27; cf. 11:19; 18:31; Jer. 31:31-34) that will prompt the people to live a holy life in accordance with God's commandments. Since obedience is the condition for "long life" in the land (cf. Deut. 30:20; 32:47), and the life-giving spirit reinforces this interpretation, the prophet's vision of the revivified dry bones could easily be taken, as indeed it later was, as a literal resurrection of corpses. Daniel 12:1-4 makes the final step of actually positing a resurrection of the dead, which can be seen as part of the book's vision for the restoration of Israel.

Restoration in Early Judaism

Restoration and Covenant

Under the rubric of "common Judaism," E. P. Sanders (1992: 289-98) gives a succinct summary of Jewish "positive hopes" for the future according to the following four categories, distinguishing in each case between Palestinian and Diaspora sources, as well as between pre-Roman and Roman: (1) the twelve tribes of Israel will be assembled; (2) the Gentiles will be converted, destroyed, or subjugated; (3) Jerusalem will be made glorious and the Temple will be rebuilt, made more glorious, or purified; (4) in the time to come worship will be pure and the people will be righteous. Despite this synthesis, it should not be assumed that in early Judaism the ideas of covenant and restoration were everywhere and always fundamental to Jewish thinking. Not every Jewish text that refers, for example, to the twelve tribes of Israel has the restoration of Israel in view. Nevertheless, there are many texts in the Second Temple period that do evidence a strongly covenantal orientation, often a Deuteronomic one, and such texts frequently include hopes of restoration.

Diaspora and Exile

An interesting question in this regard is whether some Diaspora Jews at some times and in some places may have considered themselves to be in a state of ongoing "exile" and therefore in need of restoration (cf. Scott, ed. 1997: 173-218; see, however, Gruen 2002). A case can be made, for example, that even the inveterate etymologizer and allegorizer of biblical texts, Philo of Alexandria, had an expectation for the eventual return of Diaspora Jews to the Jewish homeland. Septuagint translations have been adduced to reinforce such arguments (e.g., Scott, ed. 1997: 178-200). The question of whether Jews of the Second Temple period had a conception of an ongoing "exile" has been extremely controversial in the field of New Testament studies, where it is sometimes correlated with early Christian perspectives on restoration (Pitre 2005).

Restoration in the Enochic Tradition

Although the Enoch tradition does not feature the Sinaitic covenant in any prominent way, there is nevertheless a strong sense of restoration in the Enochic corpus of the *Urzeit-Endzeit* sort, which is quite common in apocalyptic literature (cf. Scott, ed. 2001: 147-77). In the booklets that make up *1 Enoch*, the present age is wicked and in need of renewal; divine judgment will eradicate evil and injustice from the earth and return the world to God's original created design. The authority for such a claim rests on the receipt of divine revelation by Enoch.

Restoration in the Maccabean-Hasmonean Era

The book of Daniel constitutes the main apocalyptic reaction to the Maccabean crisis, and the desecration of the Temple under Antiochus IV Epiphanes is a central preoccupation in this apocalypse. The author wants to know how long the Temple will continue to lie in a profaned state (Dan. 8:13), which is caused by the "abomination of desolation" (Dan. 9:27; 11:31; 12:11). Whereas according to the books of Maccabees, Judas Maccabaeus had restored the Temple exactly three years after it had been desecrated (1 Macc. 4:52-54; 2 Macc. 10:5), all the predictions in Daniel expect a longer period of profanation (Dan. 8:14; 12:11-12). The author of Daniel apparently did not recognize the restoration by Judas Maccabaeus and continued to look for a more spectacular restoration, which would include the resurrection of the dead. Nevertheless, the restoration by Judas Maccabaeus laid the groundwork for the conception of restoration in the Hasmonean dynasty that included, for example, territorial expansionism to fulfill biblical prophecies about the expected extent of the restored land of Israel.

Restoration in the Dead Sea Scrolls

The apocalyptic perspectives in Daniel were appropriated by the Qumran community. A great variety of restoration perspectives is represented in the Scrolls; they include, for example, the restoration of "all the glory of Adam"; the restoration of the land of Israel, the Jewish people, Jerusalem, and its Temple; and the restoration of sacrificial worship and ritual purity. In general, the community, with its strongly apocalyptic orientation, saw itself in the situation of "already–not yet" with respect to restoration: from their perspective, the end times had already begun to dawn, and some of the events leading up to the consummation had already taken place (and continued to take place), while others were yet to be accomplished by the time of the new creation. From the priestly perspective of the community, all things would finally become as God had originally intended them from the creation of the world, so that in the end the earthly and the heavenly cultus would correspond precisely. Indeed, as the *Songs of the Sabbath Sacrifice* shows, the community understood itself to be participating already in the heavenly liturgy, even if only mystically or proleptically. As in Daniel, various timetables were devised to show where the community stood in relationship to the final events, revisions being necessary in the course of time as set dates inevitably slipped by.

The Influence of Greco-Roman Tradition

Both Palestinian and Diaspora forms of Judaism were immersed to one degree or another in the Greco-Roman world in which Jews unavoidably lived and moved. In light of this fact, we must reckon with the possibility —

indeed, the probability — of reciprocal influence between Jewish conceptions of restoration and widespread Greco-Roman traditions about the return of the golden age. The Jewish *Third Sibylline Oracle* (767–95), for instance, contains a description of the eschatological kingdom — a golden age in which the world will revert to its original, pristine state (note the reference to "the one who created heaven and earth" [785–86]), and the Jerusalem Temple ("the house of the great God") will be the exclusive center of universal worship (772–74). With its expectation of universal peace between human beings and also between humans and animals (780, 788–95), the text clearly alludes to the restoration depicted in Isaiah 11, albeit without the latter passage's reference to a perfect Davidic king who will reign in Jerusalem. At the same time, the Sibyl's description of the eschatological kingdom has similarities to other texts that look forward to the return of the golden age, such as Vergil's *Fourth Eclogue*. Indeed, the parallels are so close that it has frequently been discussed which way the influence might have run: from the *Third Sibyl* to the *Fourth Eclogue* or vice versa.

Restoration in Judaism and "Christianity"

It would be misleading to say that Jews in the Second Temple period envisioned redemption or restoration as something that would be strictly historical and public, whereas early Christians conceived of restoration as spiritual and private. Such a generalization fails to take into account the tremendous diversity within Judaism of the Second Temple period. Some Jews like Josephus actively suppressed biblical expectations of restoration at every turn, and others omitted traditionally key aspects of the restoration such as the Temple. The generalization also ignores that Jesus and his earliest followers were all Jews. In the teaching of Jesus, when the kingdom of God arrives, it will come in a public, visible way. Both Jesus and his followers appropriated the rich diversity of Israel's hopes for restoration, often adding their own interpretations to the received tradition.

BIBLIOGRAPHY

D. DIMANT 2000, "Resurrection, Restoration, and Time-Curtailing in Qumran, Early Judaism, and Christianity," *RevQ* 76: 527-48. • L. FRIED 2003, "The Land Lay Desolate: Conquest and Restoration in the Ancient Near East," in *Judah and the Judeans in the Neo-Babylonian Period*, ed. O. Lipschitz and J. Blenkinsopp, Winona Lake, Ind.: Eisenbrauns, 21-54. • E. GRUEN 1998, "Jews, Greeks, and Romans in the Third Sibylline Oracle," in *Jews in a Graeco-Roman World*, ed. M. Goodman, Oxford: Clarendon, 15-36. • E. S. GRUEN 2002, "Diaspora and Homeland," in idem, *Diaspora: Jews amidst Greeks and Romans*, Cambridge: Harvard University Press, 232-52. • B. PITRE 2005, *Jesus, the Tribulation, and the End of Exile: Restoration Eschatology and the Origin of the Atonement*, Tübingen: Mohr-Siebeck. • E. P. SANDERS 1992, *Judaism: Practice and Belief, 63 BCE–66 CE*, London: SCM. • J. M. SCOTT, ED. 1997, *Exile: Old Testament, Jewish, and Christian Conceptions*, Leiden: Brill. • J. M. SCOTT, ED. 2001, *Restoration: Old Testament, Jewish, and Christian Perspectives*, Leiden: Brill. • J. M. SCOTT 2005, *On Earth as in Heaven: The Restoration of Sacred Space and Sacred Time in the Book of Jubilees*, Leiden: Brill.

See also: Eschatology — JAMES M. SCOTT

Resurrection

Resurrection is the eschatological act in which God brings the dead to life in order to recompense them for the righteous or sinful deeds that they committed during their lives. In addition to a resurrection of the body, biblical and Jewish texts also speak of the ascent of the spirit or of one's (immortal) soul to heaven and of exaltation among the angelic host. The relevant texts are usually set in times of distress.

The Biblical Prophets

Several texts from the prophetic corpus employ resurrection language in a literal or metaphorical sense. Ezekiel 37 describes Israel's restoration from the Babylonian Exile as a bodily resurrection. Isaiah 52:13–53:12, a text that will echo through the Jewish and Christian tradition, speaks vividly of the suffering, death, burial, and heavenly exaltation of the prophetic Servant of YHWH. Although scholars dispute its original meaning(s), its paradigm of life from death is clear (Baltzer 2001).

Isaiah 24–27 derives from a time of deep distress, perhaps the aftermath of the destruction of Jerusalem in 587 B.C.E. Chapter 26:13-19 focuses on the dead and specifically on the issue of Israel and its enemies. The lords who have oppressed the nation are now dead shades in Sheol and will remain there (26:14). However, the author's people, who alone have acknowledged YHWH, but who dwell in the dust, will awake and come to life, and their bodies will rise to the light (26:19).

Early Jewish Texts

Chapters 20–36 of *1 Enoch* (ca. 225 B.C.E.) recount Enoch's journeys across the face of the earth. In chap. 22 he sees the equivalent of Sheol, a mountain with three or four caves that contain the souls or spirits of all the dead, sorted according to kind until the final judgment. The righteous dwell in a bright place, refreshed by a fountain of water. Another compartment contains the spirits of persons (epitomized by Abel) who were murdered and cry out for divine vengeance. Their ultimate fate is not mentioned. The sinners are of two kinds. Those who were not recompensed for their sins during their lives suffer torment and will be resurrected and dispatched to everlasting torment. Other sinners will remain where they presently are. In Enoch's vision of Jerusalem (chaps. 26–27), the righteous, including presumably those in the first compartment who will have been raised, will live incredibly long lives, finding nourishment for their bodies in the fruit of the tree of life next to the sanctuary. The sinners who have blasphemed the divine glory will be pitched into the cursed Valley of Hinnom. The double vision expands on elements in Isa. 65:17-25; 66:14, 24. This section of *1 Enoch* is noteworthy in several respects. It focuses on the fate of "all" humanity and their situation in the interim before the judgment. This universal perspective notwithstanding, it also reflects the plight of those who have been persecuted unto death.

Written during the persecution of the Jews by Antiochus Epiphanes (167-164 B.C.E.), Dan. 10:1–12:4 is a historical apocalypse that recounts Israelite history from the Persian period to the imminent eschaton. Its climax (12:1-3) is a brief description of the coming judgment. According to v. 2, "many of those who sleep in the land of dust will awake, some to everlasting life, and some to everlasting contempt." Different from Isa. 26:19 and like *1 Enoch* 26–27, both of whose language it appears to echo, Dan. 12:2 anticipates a double resurrection. The righteous who have died because of their faithfulness to the Torah will be given back the life they forfeited and will live for an extraordinarily long time in the new Jerusalem, while the apostates who saved their lives by capitulating to the decrees of Antiochus will suffer everlasting contempt after they have been hurled into the fires of Hinnom. Verse 3 expands the scenario; the wise teachers, who have led many to righteousness by encouraging their faithfulness to the Torah, will be elevated to heaven, where they will share the glory of the angels, shining like the stars and the firmament. The language of this verse echoes the wording of Isa. 52:13 and 53:11.

Chapters 92–105 of *1 Enoch* (second century B.C.E.) reflect the perceived absence of divine justice. Rich and powerful "sinners" prosper although they oppress the righteous, who think they are suffering the curses of the covenant. The author promises the souls of the righteous dead in Sheol and their friends who are still alive that God's judgment will reverse the situation. Their sinful oppressors will receive the just recompense they have thus far eluded when they descend into the dark and fiery regions of Sheol, now turned into hell. The souls of the righteous dead, however, will come to life and ascend to heaven, where they will shine like the luminaries and enjoy the company of the angels. The imagery of Dan. 12:3 has been democratized to include all the righteous and not just their leaders. According to *Jub.* 23:22, an interpretation of Isaiah 65–66 written between 170 and 150 B.C.E., there will be no resurrection; but while their bones rest in the earth, the spirits of the righteous will have great joy (in heaven).

Second Maccabees 7 (early first century B.C.E.) is the story of a mother and her seven sons put to death during the Antiochan persecution. Here God's vindication of the persecuted righteous involves a bodily resurrection. The protagonists' obedience to the Torah that leads to their condemnation in the king's court will be set right in the supreme court of "the king of the world." In the resurrection, they will receive back the bodies that were tortured and destroyed. The imagery of the story, set forth especially in the speeches of the sons and their mother, draws on Second Isaiah's oracles about Mother Zion receiving back her lost sons, God's acts of new creation, and the prophet's songs about the suffering and vindicated servant and spokesman of YHWH. Roughly a century later, the story is retold in 4 Maccabees. Here the reward of the sons and their mother involves the eternal life of their immortal souls rather than the resurrection of their bodies. A similar notion of immortality appears in the Wisdom of Solomon 2 and 5, an interpretation of Isa. 52:13–53:12, set in two speeches that recount a story about the persecution of the righteous spokesman of YHWH, who is vindicated in God's court, where he is exalted as the judge of his enemies. Stories about Joseph (Genesis 37–50), Mordecai (Esther), the three young men and Daniel (Daniel 3, 6), and Susanna provide a model for this interpretation of the last Servant song.

In the *Hymn Scroll* from Qumran (ca. 100 B.C.E.), language about resurrection is applied not to a future event but to the present circumstances of the sectarians. Their entrance into the community has already effected their passage from the realm of death and Sheol into the company of the angels and the blessings of everlasting life (1QH 11[3]:19-36; 19[11]:3-14).

Most of the texts discussed above depict resurrection or its equivalent as God's act of judgment in the context of persecution or suffering. Other texts from the first centuries B.C.E. and C.E. posit such postmortem retribution regardless of whether or not a person has been recompensed during that person's life (*Psalms of Solomon* 3, 13, 14, 15; *1 Enoch* 51:1; Ps.-Philo, *Bib. Ant.* 3:10; *4 Ezra* 7:32-37; *2 Baruch* 49–51). Thus, resurrection is becoming a standard topic in Jewish texts, cut off from its roots in times of persecution and oppression.

The New Testament

New Testament texts about resurrection and its equivalents draw on most of the nuances and literary forms in Jewish texts discussed above (Nickelsburg 2006: 227-47). The principal factor that differentiates the early Christian texts from their Jewish counterparts is the unique and universal claim that the eschaton has begun to break in with the resurrection of Jesus of Nazareth. For most of these texts, the resurrection of Jesus itself is the central issue. Dealing with the problematic fact of the Messiah's death, early creeds and hymns portray his death and resurrection as the persecution and vindication of the righteous one. God set right the death wrongly carried out by sinful humans. The passion narratives in all four Gospels are governed by the structure of such texts as the Joseph and Daniel stories and their reshaping in Wisdom of Solomon 2 and 5 (Nickelsburg 2006: 249-79). Jesus' death, moreover, is often depicted as his exaltation to the status of Son of God or the glorified Son of Man in Daniel 7 and the *Parables of Enoch.* Again reflecting variations in the Jewish tradition, although the empty tomb traditions presume a bodily resurrection, the stories of his postresurrection appearances are more ambiguous (Nickelsburg 2006: 246-47). He is not recognized by those who knew him, or he is mistaken for someone else. He can materialize through closed doors or appear in a heavenly glorified form. These postresurrection appearance stories usually imitate biblical stories about the call of the prophets, in which Jesus now plays the role of the deity, calling apostles to carry out his mission.

If Jesus' resurrection is important for himself (the vindication of a wrongful death), it has broader consequences for the believing community and, indeed, for the cosmos. He is exalted as the Son of Man who will judge his enemies and humanity in general. His resurrection is the first fruits of those who sleep (1 Cor. 15:1-28), and believers will be raised not in the glory of the angels, but in the likeness of the exalted Christ (Phil. 3:20-21; 1 Cor. 15:35-57; contrast 2 *Baruch* 49–51).

Two other aspects of Jewish resurrection theology appear in the New Testament texts, although they are rarely recognized or acknowledged. First, as in the Qumran *Hymns Scroll,* the central part of Paul's letter to the Romans (chap. 6) posits a kind of realized eschatology. Entrance into the community through baptism effects one's transition from death to life, even though the believer's resurrection is an event of the future (6:5, 8; contrast Col. 3:1; see Nickelsburg 2006: 233-36). The Fourth Gospel has a similar emphasis; through faith one already has been raised and judged and granted eternal life (Nickelsburg 2006: 242-44). Secondly, the final judgment is based not simply on faith in Christ or the lack of it, as is often averred, but on one's good or evil deeds, and this even in the Pauline epistles that celebrate "justification by faith" (Gal. 6:7-8; Rom. 2:4-11; 14:10-12; cf. 2 Cor. 5:10).

BIBLIOGRAPHY

A. J. AVERY-PECK AND J. NEUSNER, EDS. 2000, *Judaism in Late Antiquity, Part 4, Death, Life-after-Death, Resurrection and the World-to-Come in the Judaisms of Antiquity,* Leiden: Brill. • K. BALTZER 2001, *Deutero-Isaiah: A Commentary on Isaiah 40–55,* Minneapolis: Fortress. • H. C. C. CAVALLIN 1974, *Life after Death: Paul's Argument for the Resurrection of the Dead in 1 Cor 15; Part I: An Enquiry into the Jewish Background,* Lund: Gleerup. • R. MARTIN-ACHARD 1960, *From Death to Life: A Study of the Development of the Doctrine of the Resurrection in the Old Testament,* Edinburgh: Oliver & Boyd. • G. W. E. NICKELSBURG 2006, *Resurrection, Immortality, and Eternal Life in Intertestamental Judaism and Early Christianity,* expanded ed., Cambridge: Harvard University Press. • P. PERKINS 1984, *Resurrection: New Testament Witness and Contemporary Reflection,* Garden City: Doubleday. • É. PUECH 1993, *La croyance des Esséniens en la vie future: Immortalité, résurrection, vie éternelle? Histoire d'un croyance dans le judaïsme ancien,* 2 vols., Paris: Gabalda. • A. F. SEGAL 2004, *Life after Death: The History of the Afterlife in Western Religion,* New York: Doubleday. • N. T. WRIGHT 2003, *The Resurrection of the Son of God,* Minneapolis: Fortress.

See also: Death and Afterlife

GEORGE W. E. NICKELSBURG

Revelation → Apocalypse, Prophecy

Revelation, Book of

The book of Revelation is an apocalypse in the Christian New Testament. It was composed in Asia Minor in the last half of the first century C.E. by a figure named John (1:1, 4, 9; 22:8). The periods of the First Jewish Revolt against Rome (66-70 C.E.) and late within the reign of Domitian (81-96 C.E.) are the most common specific proposals for the date of Revelation (Marshall 2001: 88-97; Yarbro Collins 1984: 54-62). Most scholars opt for the latter date. Though the author makes no claim to be one of Jesus' twelve disciples, nor the figure to whom tradition attributes the Fourth Gospel, later Christian tradition has conflated these figures. The name "John" indicates that the writer was Jewish. For many scholars, the peculiar character of John's Greek suggests a Semitic mother tongue, and they therefore propose that John was born in Judea/Palestine rather than in the Diaspora (e.g., Aune 1997: xlix-l). The only other historical figure named in the text is Antipas (2:13). Aune surveys the prosopographical data and gives examples of Jewish men bearing the longer form Antipatros, but it is much more commonly attested for Gentiles. Other names of individuals in the text, Jezebel (2:20) and Balaam and Balak (2:14), are clearly metaphorical, even if in the case of Jezebel the name is being applied to a rival teacher in John's own time (Duff 2000). These metaphorical names are drawn from Jewish tradition.

Explicit Mention of Jews and Aspects of Jewish Tradition

Traditionally, Revelation has been interpreted as a Christian text and usually within a theological construct of Christianity's supersession over Judaism. This Christian theological construct also usually entails an understanding of Judaism as rejected by God inasmuch as Jews have not accepted Jesus, whose saving death and resurrection have abrogated the significance of the Mosaic Law, in a manner consistent with the traditional interpretation of Paul.

Many interpreters have seen an animus against Jews and Judaism as a driving force in Revelation. This interpretation of the book is deeply conditioned by a Christian interpretive framework (Marshall 2001). As scholars move away from a Christian hermeneutic, the anti-Jewish reading of Revelation loses some of its force.

The explicit data concerning Jews and Judaism in Revelation consist mainly of four passages. The first is Rev. 2:9 (cf. 3:9), in which John lashes out against "those who say that they are Jews and are not, but are a synagogue of Satan." This verse has been interpreted traditionally as referring to Jews who are not Christians (Yarbro Collins 1984: 68, 75-76). On the other hand, John's declaration that they are not Jews ought to be taken seriously. No differentiator between Judaism and Christianity is in view; instead, the concern is with eating food offered to idols, an issue that often functioned in Judaism's distinction of itself from other religions (Marshall 2001: 124-34; Frankfurter 2001).

The second passage is the mention of 144,000 individuals drawn from the twelve tribes of Israel or stand-

Asia Minor with the Churches Addressed in the Book of Revelation

ing on Zion (Rev. 7:4-9; 14:1-6), a group that has traditionally been taken to represent different portions or modes of the Christian church. Yet these representations may be understood as instantiations of Judaism's traditional ethnic mapping of Jews and Gentiles (Marshall 2001: 149-63).

Two verses that designate the members of the author's community as those who "keep the commandments of God" (Rev. 12:17; 14:12) constitute the third textual complex. This designation has received very little attention in trying to understand the attitude of Revelation toward Jews and Judaism, but it may indicate a Jewish concern with Torah observance (Marshall 2001: 134-48).

The fourth relevant passage is Rev. 11:1-14, which narrates the protection of the "temple of God" in the holy city (Jerusalem) and the destruction of the "great city" (Rome), and which culminates in a vision of the Ark of the Covenant. This passage has usually been read as an indictment of Jerusalem (and by implication of Judaism) involving an appropriation of the Ark of the Covenant as a heavenly and Christian (as opposed to earthly and Jewish) artifact. Yet the correspondence between heavenly and earthly realities that characterizes the bulk of the work should be understood to operate here as well, so that the Ark of the Covenant retains its straightforward association with Israel's history (Marshall 2001: 163-72).

Implicitly Jewish Features

In addition to these specific mentions of Jews and Judaism, it is widely recognized that Revelation is deeply immersed in the literary and cultural heritage of Judaism. That the apocalypse is steeped in the Hebrew prophets, especially Ezekiel, has long been noted. Moreover, John considers himself to be a prophet in the tradition of Israel's prophets (1:3; 10:11). John's cosmology is also thoroughly Jewish, consisting of a heavenly throne room for the God who was, who is, and is to come; creatures singing the trishagion (4:8); attending angels; and the Ark of the Covenant in the heavenly temple (11:19).

Most Christian interpretation has treated the ostensibly Jewish character of Revelation in two ways. One approach embraces some of the Jewish elements as marks of Christian supersessionism, while regarding other elements as "Jewish-Christian" and therefore, in effect, sub-Christian. The other approach attributes the Jewish elements to hypothetical sources underlying the final document; the scene in which Michael instead of Christ defeats Satan (Rev. 12:7-9), for instance, is assigned to an earlier Jewish or Jewish-Christian stage of development.

Beyond explicit and implicit references to Jews and Judaism, it is worth noting the end of Revelation, in which the protagonists are rewarded and the antagonists punished. Put simply, Jews and Judaism are nowhere among the antagonists. Conversely, John's evident concern is that people who integrate too closely with the apparatus of Roman imperial rule, especially in cultic observance, should be definitively punished.

Clarifying the Jewish Character of the Work

There is no doubt that the religious commitments of John include understanding Jesus as the messiah. John's Christology, however, is only one element of his religious identity. It is necessary to understand Revelation as Jewish unless the reading strategy itself is to be Christian (Marshall 2001; 2007). So understood, Revelation provides a singularly rich source of data on Judaism in Asia Minor in the first century C.E. Contrary to the Judaism of Asia Minor witnessed by archaeological and epigraphic remains, the Judaism of Revelation stands opposed to a *modus vivendi* with Greco-Roman culture. Revelation's understanding of Jesus as the means of Gentile integration into a covenant with the God of Israel represents a specific but explicable phenomenon within the larger pattern in Asia Minor of

Jews welcoming Gentile participation in Jewish communities as God-fearers and patrons. Conversely, Revelation's evident antagonism toward Rome need not be regarded as simply a Christian development of Jewish literary traditions of resistance to Rome (Yarbro Collins 1984: 89-94), but as a further example of Jewish resistance to foreign political domination. If Revelation is dated to the period of the First Jewish Revolt, it becomes a crucial source for the variety of Diaspora Jewish attitudes to that war. Contrary to Josephus' general pronouncements of *quietus* in the Diaspora, the book of Revelation reflects a community intensely preoccupied with maintaining the purity of their religion specifically as a means of assisting in the revolt against Roman domination.

BIBLIOGRAPHY

D. E. AUNE 1997-98, *Revelation,* 3 vols., Dallas: Word. • R. H. CHARLES 1920, *A Critical and Exegetical Commentary on the Revelation of St. John,* 2 vols., Edinburgh: Clark. • P. B. DUFF 2000, *Who Rides the Beast? Prophetic Rivalry and the Rhetoric of Crisis in the Churches of the Apocalypse,* Oxford: Oxford University Press. • D. FRANKFURTER 2001, "Jews or Not? Reconstructing the 'Other' in Rev. 2:9 and 3:9," *HTR* 94: 403-25. • P. HIRSCHBERG 1999, *Das eschatologische Israel: Untersuchungen zum Gottesvolkverständnis der Johannesoffenbarung,* Neukirchen-Vluyn: Neukirchener Verlag. • J. W. MARSHALL 2001, *Parables of War: Reading John's Jewish Apocalypse,* Waterloo, Ont.: Wilfrid Laurier University Press. • J. W. MARSHALL 2007, "John's Jewish (Christian?) Apocalypse," in *Jewish Christianity Reconsidered: Rethinking Ancient Groups and Texts,* ed. M. Jackson-McCabe, Minneapolis: Fortress, 233-56. • P. L. MAYO 2006, *"Those Who Call Themselves Jews": The Church and Judaism in the Apocalypse of John,* Eugene, Ore.: Wipf & Stock. • A. YARBRO COLLINS 1984, *Crisis and Catharsis: The Power of the Apocalypse,* Philadelphia: Westminster.

JOHN W. MARSHALL

Revolt, First Jewish

The First Jewish Revolt is the name given the insurrection against Roman rule that broke out in the Spring of 66 C.E. (in the month of *Iyyar = Artemisios*). The revolt took place in Judea and involved the Transjordan, the Galilee, and the Golan — but not Diaspora Jewry to any significant degree, even though the rebels appealed to Diaspora communities to join. It ended four years later, in the Autumn of 70 C.E. *(Elul = Gorpiaios),* with the complete suppression of the region, the destruction of Jerusalem and the Second Temple, the transformation of Judaism from a temple-based to a community-based religion, new disabilities imposed on Jews across the empire (the *fiscus Iudaicus*), and still-simmering flames of resistance that broke out sixty years later in the full-scale rebellion led by Simon Bar Kokhba (sometimes called the Second Revolt).

Sources

Relatively little would be known about the war without the first-person account of Yosef ben Matityahu, later (Titus) Flavius Josephus, who wrote a remarkably full factual history of the conflict in Greek, the *Bellum Judaicum (Jewish War),* a work which follows the conventions of classical historiography and is marked by keen observation, tendentious shading, personal bias, and a Jewish theological outlook. Josephus' record of events is what informs and makes comprehensible the other sources, which include Tacitus and Cassius Dio, rabbinic legends, archaeological excavations, and the silver and bronze coins that the revolutionary government minted throughout the revolt. All these sources confirm the basic outline and many of the small details of Josephus' full if tendentious record.

Remains of the Burnt House in Jerusalem, evidence of the destruction of the city by the Romans in the year 70 C.E. *(Phoenix Data Systems / Neal and Joel Bierling)*

Background and Causes

The deepest roots of the war may be found in the practically uninterrupted agitation against Rome that followed the conquest of Jerusalem by Pompey the Great in 63 B.C.E., when he caused irreparable offense by entering the Temple sanctuary. Popular resistance against Rome's presence in the area was fomented by the last Hasmonean princes and then, when they died out, by militant revolutionary, often messianic, groups. The main groups began forming with the imposition of direct Roman rule on Judea in 6 C.E., the year of Quirinius' census in Syria and Judea.

During the next sixty years there arose in Judea and Galilee many other messianic and apocalyptic figures who attracted large numbers of followers who were hopeful of change and who clashed with both the Roman government and local Jewish leaders. Most of the many groups are not distinguished with names in the hostile sources, which also obscure theology and political ideology. The most militant of them attacked not Roman officials but Jewish leaders regarded as Roman collaborators.

Outrageous abuses by the Roman procurators, some of whom harbored personal animosity against the Jews, especially during the twenty years running up to the war, made open rebellion seem ever less impracticable or inadvisable even to Jewish upper-class priestly

Chronology of the First Jewish Revolt

Spring 66	Roman procurator Gessius Florus plunders Temple treasury and permits troops to massacre Jewish protestors; priests terminate sacrifices on behalf of the emperor; Sicarii under Eleazar b. Yair seize Masada
Fall 66	Jewish insurgents capture Antonia Fortress in Jerusalem; Cestius Gallus, Roman legate of Syria, attacks Jerusalem but retreats and suffers defeat at Beth Horon; Jews form coalition government led by priests, aristocrats, and rebel leaders
Dec. 66–Dec. 68	Vespasian and son Titus subdue Galilee and western Palestine; Josephus surrenders at Jotapata; Zealot party forms under Eleazar b. Simon
67–68	End of coalition government and priesthood: Jewish militants seize Temple Mount, appoint a new high priest, and kill Ananus son of Ananus, Jesus son of Gamala, and other leaders of coalition
68–69	Year of the four emperors (Galba, Otho, Vitellius, Vespasian)
Spring 69	Three Jewish rebel factions led by John of Gischala, Eleazar b. Simon, and Simon bar Giora, respectively, vie for control of Jerusalem in a civil war
Spring–Fall 70	Titus lays siege to Jerusalem with four legions and auxiliaries; captures Temple Mount and destroys Temple
73/74	Roman Tenth Legion under Flavius Silva, governor of Judea, storms Masada, last holdout of Sicarii, who commit mass suicide

and lay leaders, on whom the Romans relied to maintain order. Once the Romans lost the support of the local aristocracy, all was lost. Yet the increasing radicalization of all segments of the Jewish population, as well as the spreading messianic fervor, did not unite the Jewish population but rather served further to sharpen the competition and internal conflicts. The disparate militants struggled with each other, and the different upper-class factions competed both with each other and with the militant revolutionaries for control of the approaching rebellion.

The match that lit the tinder box was a clash between the Jewish and Greek inhabitants of Caesarea, which the last procurator, Gessius Florus, who, Josephus says, "abstained from no form of robbery or assault," deliberately mishandled. There followed a quick sequence of conflicts that brought the rebellion past the point of no return. Florus ignored the righteous indignation over the Caesarea incident, appropriated seventeen talents from the Temple, and in response to the predictable protest allowed his troops, in two separate attacks, to plunder and massacre. After attempts at intercession by King Agrippa II and a Roman envoy failed, a group of priests cut off the sacrifices on behalf of the Roman emperor, an act which laid "the foundation of the war," in Josephus' words. At the same time, Jews throughout Syria and in Alexandria suffered brutal attacks by their Greek neighbors, whose hands were more free because of the spreading Jewish rebellion; as Josephus later wrote, these attacks in turn made war "a necessity."

The Course of the Revolt

Finally Nero sent Cestius Gallus, the governor of Syria, to quash the nascent uprising. Cestius marched quickly to Jerusalem without securing the rest of the country, but as he was on the brink of taking the Temple Mount he suddenly and inexplicably withdrew, drawing the Jewish forces after him. His army was cut to pieces in the pass of Beth Horon. This victory was the cause of delirious jubilation by the Jews and reinforced confidence in divine help. Comparison to the Maccabees was inevitable. All segments of the Jewish population joined the war, or at least were sympathetic to it at first; only certain upper-class individuals fled the country. But the Roman disgrace at Beth Horon ensured a more massive and better planned military response.

In Jerusalem, the victorious Jews formed a government led by high priests and other aristocrats. The militant rebel groups apparently agreed to provide the army of the new independent state. This government organized the defense of the country, minted coins, and fortified Jerusalem, but it launched only one operation from Jerusalem, a disastrous assault on Ashkelon. Leaders and army remained bound to the city by mutual suspicion and factional disputes. Josephus was sent as governor/general of the Galilee, about which he wrote two contradictory accounts (in the *Bellum Judaicum* and *Vita*), but it is clear that he was occupied as much with fending off internal attacks as with organizing the defense against the Romans. When Vespasian attacked from the north with a huge force, Josephus staged a valiant defense but was eventually captured at the Lower Galilean town of Jotapata, after which he served the Romans as an advisor, translator, and spokesman through the end of the war.

In less than two years, Vespasian succeeded in systematically subduing most parts of the country and drawing a tight ring around Jerusalem. He was occasionally aided by the factional wars afflicting the various cities and towns that he assaulted. But he had to suspend operations while the status of the emperorship remained uncertain during "the year of the four emperors," 68-69 C.E. Eventually he was declared emperor and returned to Rome, leaving his son Titus to finish the war with the capture of Jerusalem. Yet by the time of Titus' siege in 70, things had radically changed in Jerusalem.

The militant revolutionaries, who had both weapons and experience in using them, frustrated by their own subordinate role and dissatisfied with the unwillingness or inability of the first government to score any

REVOLT, FIRST JEWISH

Silver denarius minted by Vespasian to celebrate supression of the Judean revolt. Judea is personified as a woman seated in mourning beneath a Roman victory trophy, with IVDAE[A] written underneath. *(Richard Cleave)*

successes against the Romans, staged a violent coup d'état in the Winter of 67/68, seizing the Temple Mount, appointing a new high priest, and killing the high priests Ananus son of Ananus, Jesus son of Gamala, and other leaders of the first government. The rebels were aided briefly by an Idumean force as well as by the armed revolutionaries who streamed into the capital from the regions occupied by the Romans, although along with these refugees came a large population of noncombatants who had to be sheltered and fed, thus straining the city's resources.

Once in control, the militants began systematically eliminating opponents, but the two main rebel leaders, John b. Levi of Gischala and the Zealot leader Eleazar b. Simon, soon quarreled. The internal rivalry became only more destructive when Simon bar Giora forced his way into Jerusalem in Spring 69 with his large, ragtag group of followers. The city was divided into three areas, and in the factional battles many Jews were killed and the city's food reserves were destroyed. Thus the city and its swollen population were severely weakened when Titus began the siege during Passover, 70 C.E.

Within six months after arriving at Jerusalem with four legions and a huge auxiliary force, Titus succeeded in piercing the city's three walls, capturing the Temple Mount and burning the Temple. Some Jews lost hope with each Roman victory and tried to elude the rebel guards and flee the city, and the widening famine drove many others to despair. But many Jews stubbornly clung to the belief that God would save the Temple and Holy City and protect the most faithful defenders, and some even were convinced that the entire Roman Empire, the fourth and last empire in Daniel's prophecy, would fall, ushering in a new historical age. Josephus reports that more than one million Jews died in the Jerusalem siege, but actual casualty rates are unknowable.

The Romans had been harsh with cities that resisted, such as Jotapata and Gamla, but did not pursue a scorched-earth policy. A traveler passing from northern Galilee to Jerusalem in the Winter of 70 would not have seen any sign of the war at all in some areas — unlike the wasteland that the Romans made of Judea after the Bar Kokhba Revolt. Jerusalem, however, was a smoking pile of ruins: the Romans took extra measures to destroy thoroughly large sections of the city, and to make sure no stone remained on top of another on the Temple Mount, which had served as a magnet for ideological opposition to Rome. Josephus, in perhaps his most bald-faced lie, wrote that Titus controverted the advice of his generals and ordered that the edifice be spared, but that a firebrand thrown by an overenthusiastic soldier caused the Temple to burst into flames. This account not only required Josephus to introduce a supernatural intervention (such spontaneous combustion was impossible in a metal and stone structure), but it also contradicts standard Roman procedure. For although the Romans generally respected religious structures, and made no assault on Judaism per se in either of the Jewish rebellions, it was consistent policy to eliminate the focus of dangerous political agitation. Josephus' story was, moreover, meant to serve Titus' efforts to erase his reputation for cruelty and to enhance his message of *clementia*.

The Aftermath

The war was not completely over with the destruction of Jerusalem. Mopping-up operations continued for the next three years, culminating in the fall of Masada in 73 or 74, which has become famous for the suicide of the nearly 1,000 Sicarii and their families there. It should be remembered, however, that the only source, Josephus, tries to present the entire episode as a fitting end to Jewish extremism, in a manner that is much less heroic and attractive than modern generations have made it.

The Flavians celebrated their victory with a lavish triumph, massive issues of coins, victory arches (of which the Arch of Titus in Rome is only one), the *Templum Pacis* where the spoils of Jerusalem were exhibited, and other monuments (e.g., the Coliseum). The Flavian message proclaimed not only the consequences of rebellion against Rome, but also the glorious inauguration of the new dynasty of Caesars. For the Jews, the

Ballista balls used in the Roman siege of Masada *(Phoenix Data Systems / Neal and Joel Bierling)*

Replicas of the Roman siege engines used at Masada in the mopping-up operations of the First Revolt *(Phoenix Data Systems / Neal and Joel Bierling)*

fall of the Temple caused a traumatic shock whose depth is hard to measure today. Some apocalyptic works written soon afterward, like *4 Ezra, 2 Baruch,* and the *Fifth Sibylline Oracle,* envisioned swift, righteous divine vengeance, but other Jewish circles saw in recent events a sign that the apocalypse was still a long way off and that God's intention was for the Jews to live peacefully with Rome.

BIBLIOGRAPHY

A. M. BERLIN AND J. A. OVERMAN, EDS. 2002, *The First Jewish Revolt: Archaeology, History, and Ideology,* London: Routledge. • M. GOODMAN 1987, *The Ruling Class of Judaea: The Origins of the Jewish Revolt against Rome A.D. 66-70,* Cambridge: Cambridge University Press, 1987. • M. HENGEL 1989, *The Zealots: Investigations into the Jewish Freedom Movement in the Period from Herod I until 70 A.D.,* trans. D. Smith, Edinburgh: Clark. • U. RAPPAPORT, ED. 1983, *Judea and Rome: The Jewish Revolts,* Jerusalem (in Hebrew). • J. J. PRICE 1992, *Jerusalem under Siege: The Collapse of the Jewish State, 66-70 C.E.,* Leiden: Brill. • D. M. RHOADS 1976, *Israel in Revolution: 6-74 C.E.,* Philadelphia: Fortress, 1976.

See also: Arch of Titus; Josephus; Josephus, Jewish War; Resistance Movements JONATHAN J. PRICE

Reworked Pentateuch (4QRP)

Reworked Pentateuch is the collective title for five manuscripts from Qumran Cave 4: 4Q158 and 4Q364-367. Two other manuscripts, 4Q368 and 4Q377, belong to a work known as *Apocryphal Pentateuch,* which may be related to the *Reworked Pentateuch.* The five manuscripts are grouped together under a common rubric not because they are copies of the same composition, but because they are examples of the same scribal tradition and therefore very similar to one another. The scribal tradition they represent is characterized by intervention into the text for the purpose of exegesis. In these manuscripts, the intervention takes the form of a running text taken from the five books of the Pentateuch (Genesis, Exodus, Leviticus, Numbers and Deuteronomy). When the texts of the manuscripts of 4QRP are compared to other textual witnesses (e.g., the Masoretic Text), it is apparent that 4QRP's texts are greatly expanded, characterized by harmonizations, exegetical comments, the regrouping of passages from different books around a common theme, and especially the addition of new material into the text, material not found in other pentateuchal witnesses. The scribal tradition reflected in the manuscripts of 4QRP is a continuation of the scribal tradition behind the proto-Samaritan family of manuscripts (i.e., the manuscript family to which the Samaritan Pentateuch belongs), but goes beyond the proto-Samaritan tradition in its use of new or added material.

All five manuscripts were copied in the first century B.C.E. 4Q364 and 4Q365, the best preserved, appear to have contained a complete copy of all five books of the Pentateuch, possibly on one scroll. The other three manuscripts are preserved only in fragments, but it is unlikely they were complete Torah scrolls. The examples of the types of scribal interventions found in 4QRP are taken from 4Q364 and 4Q365.

Contents

4QRP contains many small exegetical comments or explanatory notes. One example from 4Q364 (frg. 1) is found at Gen 25:19, which reads: "[And these are the descendants of I]saac, the son of Abraham; [he begat Isaac] *whom Sarah [his] wife b[ore] to him.*" The phrase in italics is not found in any other textual witness. Its purpose is to remind the reader that Isaac is the son of Sarah as well as Abraham (and not, e.g., Hagar). This exegetical comment may have been prompted by the fact that in Gen. 25:12 Ishmael is identified as the son of Hagar as well as Abraham. This type of small, harmonizing note is common in 4QRP.

Larger-scale harmonizations occur in 4QRP as well. Harmonization is defined as the importation of words from one text into a parallel text to bring the two texts into conformity with each other. Harmonizations often occur in narrative contexts, to make uniform two parallel accounts of the same event. 4QRP shares several large-scale harmonizations with the proto-Samaritan textual family but preserves others as well. A harmonization unique to 4Q364 (frg. 23a-b, col. 1) occurs at Deut. 2:8-14, the speech in which Moses recounts the Israelites' journey through Transjordan and their avoidance of Edom and Moab. Immediately before Deut. 2:8, 4Q364 inserts text from Num. 20:14-18, the parallel account of the same event. The Numbers account includes Moses' negotiation with the king of Edom, which is missing in the Deuteronomy passage. The importation of Num. 20:14-18 into Deuteronomy 2 resolves the difference and brings the two accounts into harmony.

Two major examples of the addition of new material, one from a narrative and one from a legal context, come from 4Q365. The first occurs at the end of Exodus 15, the Song of the Sea. In 4Q365 (frgs. 6a-b), Exod. 15:16-20 is extant. The fragment is broken, but it is probable that it continued with verse 21. Verses 20-21 are known as "The Song of Miriam": "Then Miriam the prophet, the sister of Aaron, took her timbrel in her hand and led out all the women after her, with timbrels and dances. And Miriam responded to them: 'Sing to the LORD, for he has gloriously triumphed; the horse and its rider he has hurled into the sea.'" Until the discovery of 4Q365, all textual witnesses to Exodus 15 contained only v. 21, the incipit from the Song of Moses earlier in the chapter (15:1). 4Q365, however, continues with seven fragmentary lines of text, extending Miriam's recital into a song in its own right:

1. you despised [
2. for the majesty of[
3. You are great, O deliverer [
4. the hope of the enemy has perished, and he has cea[sed/is forgotten . . .
5. they perished in the mighty waters, the enemy[
6. Extol the one who raises up, [a ra]nsom you gave[
7. [do]ing gloriously[

After the seven lines, the running text resumes with Exod. 15:22. The additional material echoes the language of Moses' song, but fills a perceived gap in the text of Exodus by placing a complete song in Miriam's mouth.

4Q365 also contains an example of the addition of otherwise unknown material into the pentateuchal text in a legal context. Fragment 23 preserves Lev. 23:42–24:2, the end of the festival calendar in Leviticus. However, after the beginning of verse 24:2, the text continues with legislation for festivals not found in other witnesses to Leviticus or the other books of the Pentateuch. The fragment reads as follows, beginning with line 4:

4. and the LORD spoke to Moses, saying, "Command the children of Israel, saying, when you come to the land which
5. I am giving to you for an inheritance, and you dwell upon it securely, you will gather wood for the burnt offering and for all the wor[k] of
6. [the h]ouse which you will build for me in the land, to arrange them upon the altar of the burnt offering [and] the calv[e]s
7. . . .] . . . for Passover sacrifices and for whole burnt-offerings and for thank offerings and for free-will offerings and for burnt offerings, daily[
8. . . .] . . . and for the d[o]ors and for all the work of the house, [they] will brin[g . . .
9. . . . fe]stival of New Oil, they will bring the wood two[. . .
10. . . .] those who bring on the fir[s]t day, Levi [. . .
11. . . . Reu]ben and Simeon[and on the] four[th] day [. . .

The two "new" festivals commanded are the Festival of New Oil (line 9) and the Wood Festival (lines 5-11). The Festival of New Oil is a harvest festival, a natural continuation of the harvest festivals already enumerated in this chapter of Leviticus: the Firstfruits of Barley (Lev. 23:10-14) and Wheat (23:15-21). The Wood Festival is for the offering of wood for the Temple sacrifices, a necessity for the continuation of the Temple cult. During the Second Temple period mechanisms were put in place to collect this wood; for example, in Neh. 10:35 and 13:31 prominent families or citizens, including Nehemiah himself, provide wood for the Temple service.

Although these two festivals were not originally part of the Mosaic festival legislation, it is easy to see how they would have been derived through exegesis of the Torah; if the firstfruits of barley and wheat are offered during a festival, so should the firstfruits of oil. And the wood was a necessary component of the cult; surely it should be hallowed by a festival as well. This is an example of the growth of the tradition through scribal exegesis, the hallmark of 4QReworked Pentateuch.

Other evidence for the celebration of these festivals is found in other words from the Qumran collection: 4QCalendrical Document E, 4QMMT, and the *Temple Scroll.* In addition, Josephus (*J.W.* 2.425) and *m. Taʿan.* 4:5 mention a wood offering for the Temple. Thus, we know that these festivals were being observed by at least some groups of Jews in the Second Temple period; 4Q365 provides us with evidence for the exegetical activity that led to these observances.

Scriptural Status

An unresolved question concerning this group of manuscripts is whether or not they were accorded the same scriptural authority as other, less expanded texts of the Pentateuch. That they present themselves as copies of the Torah is beyond question; there is no observable physical indication, such as paragraph markings or line indentations, to show that the content of these manuscripts is in any way "different" from other manuscripts of the Pentateuch. Further, the expansions in these manuscripts are a continuation of the scribal exegetical tradition found in the proto-Samaritan manuscript family. Finally, similar exegetical conclusions are found in parallel passages in *Jubilees* and the *Temple Scroll.* However, since definitive evidence such as direct quotation is lacking, the question of the authoritative status of 4QReworked Pentateuch (as a group or as single manuscripts) remains unresolved. 4QReworked Pentateuch seems to be the chronologically latest example of this type of scriptural exegesis, in which the exegetical conclusions are incorporated into the sacred text itself. During this same period the exegetical style familiar to us as "lemma plus comment" gained ascendancy, and soon would completely dominate the practice of exegesis.

BIBLIOGRAPHY

J. M. ALLEGRO 1968, *Qumrân Cave 4, I (4Q158-4Q186),* DJD 5, Oxford: Clarendon. • S. WHITE CRAWFORD 2008, *Rewriting Scripture in Second Temple Times,* Grand Rapids: Eerdmans. • E. TOV AND S. WHITE 1994, "Reworked Pentateuch," in *Qumran Cave 4, VIII, Parabiblical Texts, Part 1,* DJD 13, Oxford: Clarendon, 187-352.

SIDNIE WHITE CRAWFORD

Righteousness/Justice

Early Jewish views of the cosmological order are conveyed by the Hebrew word *ṣĕdāqâ,* usually translated either "righteousness" or "justice." Its Greek counterpart is the word *dikaiosynē. Ṣĕdāqâ* embodies the ground rules that govern the relationship between YHWH and his people, as well as between people. It is manifested in YHWH's character and the Jewish social ideal, focusing on the ethical and theological norms established by God. It is also associated with truth (Tob. 1:3, 4:6; Wis. 5:6), mercy (Bar. 5:9), uprightness (Wis. 9:3), and faithfulness (Zech. 8:8; 1 Macc. 14:35). The righteous person engages in charitable acts (Tob. 2:14; Sir. 32:16; 44:10), and is taught to be kind (Wis. 12:29). Since they oppose the ungodly and reproach sins against the Torah (Wis. 2:12), the righteous are given to righteous anger (1 Macc. 2:24). They observe the Year of Release (*Jub.* 7:37) and intercede in prayer (2 Esdr. 7:111). To observe righteousness is also to cover nakedness, bless the Creator, honor father and mother, love one's neighbor, and guard against fornication, uncleanness, and all iniquity (*Jub.* 7:20).

Covenant and Election

God elected Abraham and made a covenant with him (2 Macc. 1:2, 25) "to the end that he may command his children and his household after him that they may keep the way of the LORD, to do righteousness and justice" (Gen. 18:19; cf. *Jub.* 16:26; 21:24; 22:11-12; 24:29; *Pss. Sol.* 9:16-19; 4 Macc. 18:1; *1 Enoch* 93:5). The covenant between YHWH and Israel calls for observance of the Torah (cf. Sir. 24:23-25; 44:19-22; *Pss. Sol.* 14:1-3; Add. Esth. 16:15; Sus. 1:3). God elects and saves the righteous because of his mercy (Sir. 27:3-4; *Pss. Sol.* 14:6; 16:15; Pr. Azar. 1:12). Israel is elected by God in remembrance of his covenant with the patriarchs (2 Macc. 1:25; *Pss. Sol.* 7:8-9; 11:2; Pr. Man. 1:1).

The Commandments

"If we diligently observe this entire commandment before the LORD our God, as he has commanded us, we will be in the right" (Deut. 6:25; cf. Bar. 4:13; 4 Macc. 15:10). The Torah gives some concrete instructions on how to practice *ṣĕdāqâ,* such as judging impartially in court, practicing charity, and avoiding idolatry. Deuteronomy boasts, "What great nation is there, that has statutes and ordinances so righteous as all this law, which I set before you this day?" (4:8). Israel inherited the land despite its stubbornness because of God's righteousness, and must not think that the divine intervention was earned by its own righteousness or uprightness of heart (Deut. 9:4-6; 16:20).

Salvation and Retribution

The criterion for salvation for the righteous and punishment for the wicked is based on one's actions (*Pss. Sol.* 9:9-10). Salvation is bestowed on the basis of individual merit. "[Noah, Daniel, and Job] would save neither son nor daughter; they would save only their own lives by their righteousness" (Ezek. 14:14, 20). Ben Sira warns not to assert one's righteousness before God (7:5). Ultimately, God alone is the source of righteousness (Sir. 18:2; Bar. 5:9; *Jub.* 16:26). God grants righteousness and salvation to whomever he wishes. He judges the world with righteousness (Pss. 96:13; 98:9), and blesses the righteous when they repent (*Pss. Sol.* 9:14-15). God loves those who pursue righteousness (Prov. 15:9), for he prefers righteousness and justice to sacrifice (Prov. 21:3; cf. Mal. 3:3; Sir. 35:8-9). In the eschaton, those saved will praise God in righteousness as they dwell in Jerusalem forever, while those who commit sin and injustice will vanish from the earth (Tob. 14:7; cf. 2 Esdr. 9:13; Wis. 5:14-15). The enemies of the righteous — "the sinners" — will be delivered into the hands of the righteous for judgment (*1 Enoch* 95:3; 96:1). Indeed, the wicked will perish forever (*Pss. Sol.* 15:13b). The righteous may not always receive their due but suffer afflictions on this earth (cf. 4 Esdr. 4:39; 7:18; 8:57; 10:22; 4 Macc. 15:10; 18:15). Divine retribution may tarry (4 Esdr. 4:27, 35).

New Testament Understanding

The apostle Paul took Gen. 15:6, "Abraham believed God, and it was reckoned to him as righteousness," to mean that Abraham's faith, and not Torah observance, made him right with God (Gal. 3:6; Rom. 4:3, 9; cf. Jas. 2:23). According to Paul, the righteousness of God — his act of putting human beings into right relationship with him in a way that demonstrates his own justice or integrity or faithfulness — is revealed through faith in Jesus and his atoning death (Rom. 3:20-25; cf. Rom. 1:17; 1 Cor. 1:30; 1 Pet. 2:24; 2 Pet. 1:1). For the sake of salvation, Jesus was made to be sin though he knew no sin, so that those who have faith in him might become the righteousness of God (2 Cor. 5:21). "They are now made righteous by his grace as a gift, through the redemption that is in Christ Jesus" (Rom. 3:24). Christ's death, an act of righteousness, leads to righteousness or justification and to eternal life for all (Rom. 5:17-18). "Christ is the end of the law so that there may be righteousness for everyone who has faith" (Rom. 10:4). No human being is righteous in the eyes of God by the observance of the Torah (cf. Gal. 3:21-26; Phil. 3:9). Salvation owes to God's mercy, not to people's works of righteousness (Titus 3:5). On the final day, the world will be judged in righteousness by Christ, and the dead will be raised (Acts 17: 31). Works of righteousness come through Christ (Phil. 1:11).

Bibliography

G. BRIN 1992, "The Development of Some Laws in the Book of the Covenant," in *Justice and Righteousness: Biblical Themes and Their Influence,* ed. H. G. Reventlow and Y. Hoffman, Sheffield: JSOT Press, 60-70. • J. H. CHARLESWORTH 2003, "Theodicy in Early Jewish Writings," in *Theodicy in the World of the Bible,* ed. A. Laato and J. C. De Moor, Leiden: Brill, 470-508. • W. HOUSTON 2006, *Contending for Justice: Ideologies and Theologies of Social Justice in the Old Testament,* London: Clark. • J. KRAŠOVEC 1988, *La justice (ṢDQ) de Dieu dans la Bible hébraique et l'interpretation juive et chrétienne,* Göttingen: Vandenhoeck & Ruprecht. • E. P. SANDERS 1977, *Paul and Palestinian Judaism: A Comparison of Patterns of Religion,* Philadelphia: Fortress Press. • M. A. SEIFRID 2001, "Righteousness Language in the Hebrew Scriptures and Early Judaism," in *Justification and Variegated Nomism,* vol. 1, ed. D. A. Carson, P. T. O'Brien, and M. A. Seifrid, Grand Rapids: Baker Academic, 415-42. • M. WEINFELD 1995, *Social Justice in Ancient Israel and in the Ancient Near East,* Jerusalem: Magnes.

KYONG-JIN LEE

Rights of Jews in the Roman World

No comprehensive legislation concerning the Jews living under Roman rule has been preserved, and one may reasonably doubt if such legislation ever existed. About the legal status of the Jews we have only scraps of information, found in the works of Philo and Josephus and in a number of Greek and Roman documents. They consist of decrees issued by the councils of Asian Greek cities, letters written to them by Roman local officials, decisions taken by Roman statesmen and by the Roman senate (the so-called *senatus consulta*), and edicts issued by Roman emperors.

A Problem of Sources

Unfortunately, the documents themselves are no longer extant; we have only quotations from them in the work of Josephus, who is known to have been a highly partisan author. Their authenticity, therefore, has often been questioned in modern scholarship, the more so because they are often quoted only partially, lack numbers and dates, and at times have duplications and textual corruptions. However, parallels in structure, phraseology, and content can readily be found in authentic contemporary Greek and Roman documents (preserved on stone, bronze, or papyrus) that deal with other peoples. Paradoxically, it is the very confusion of these texts and their errors that constitute a strong argument for their authenticity; an informed forger would have taken pains to replicate standard formulas and conventional structures correctly. Their content may therefore by regarded as substantially genuine.

Jewish Rights in Judea and in the Diaspora

From extant source material we learn that the Romans allowed the Jews to live according to their own traditions. The custom of sending their sacred monies to Jerusalem "from Italy and from all the provinces" is attested already by Cicero in the middle of the first century B.C.E. (*Pro Flacco* 28, 67). Some years later, a decree issued by Julius Caesar concerning Judean Jews states that "if . . . any question shall arise concerning the Jews' manner of life, it is my pleasure that they shall have the decision" (Pucci Ben Zeev 1998: 1, 47 B.C.E.). In the Diaspora, the Jews were allowed to assemble (ibid. 7, 9, 14, 19, 20), feast and hold common meals (ibid. 7), perform their cult, observe their Sabbaths, perform their rites, and offer their ancestral prayers (ibid. 17-22, 24). They also had a certain amount of autonomous internal administration, which meant the permission to manage their own revenues (ibid. 18) and to collect contributions of money (ibid. 7, 9) to be sent to Jerusalem (ibid. 22-27). Jews enjoyed autonomous internal jurisdiction, being granted a place "in which they decided their affairs and controversies with one another" (ibid. 14, 20); they were entitled to a special, separate place to live in (ibid. 20), to build sacred buildings in accordance with their native custom (ibid. 19), and to have "suitable food for them," namely, kosher food, in the local markets (ibid. 20).

Were Jewish Rights Common Rights or Privileges?

The right to follow traditional customs and laws was not exceptional. From inscriptions, papyri, and literary sources concerning other peoples living in the Roman world, spanning the period from the second century B.C.E. to the imperial age, we learn that the Romans usually gave back to conquered peoples the right to live by their own laws, a right which in theory they had lost at the time of the Roman conquest. By preserving the existing frameworks, the Romans were able to keep local order without much expense and have a ready-made organization through which levies could be raised.

It has often been claimed that Jewish rights were exceptional because some of them were different from those enjoyed by most peoples; such, for example, were the exemption from taxes in the sabbatical years in Judea (Pucci Ben Zeev 1998: 5); in Rome, the permission to have the distribution of grain kept for the next day when they happened to be distributed on the Sabbath (Philo, *Legatio ad Gaium* 158); and in Syria, at Antioch on the Orontes, the cash payment received in lieu of the oil distributed free to the citizens (Josephus, *Ant.* 12.120). However, these permissions were necessary if the Jews were allowed to follow their traditional customs and laws. The exemption from taxes in the sabbatical years was due to the fact that "in this time they neither take fruit from the trees nor do they sow" (Pucci Ben Zeev 1998: 5) and at Rome the grain was kept for the next day since, as Philo observes, on the Sabbath "no one is permitted to receive or give anything or to transact any part of the business of ordinary life." Similarly, the exemptions of the Jews from military service in Judea (ibid. 1; 5) and in Asia (ibid. 9-13; 15-16) were due to the fact, acknowledged by the Roman authorities themselves, that the Jews "cannot undertake military service because they may not bear arms or march on the days of the Sabbath; nor can they obtain the native foods to which they are accustomed" (ibid. 9). At Rome, the Jews were exempted from the bans issued against the rights of assembly. Julius Caesar "by edict forbade religious societies to assemble in the cities, but these people alone he did not forbid to do so," and this permission was confirmed some years later (ibid. 7). Philo observes that Augustus "ordered that the Jews alone should be permitted to assemble in synagogues. These gatherings, he said, were not based on drunkenness and carousing to promote conspiracy and so to do grave injury to the cause of peace, but were schools of temperance and justice" (*Legatio* 312–13).

As for the imperial cult, the Jews had their own way to perform it. Philo (*Legatio* 157; 232; 317) and Josephus (*J.W.* 2.197; *Ag. Ap.* 2.77-78, 196-99) tell us that in the

Temple of Jerusalem the Jews honored the emperor by offering sacrifices on his behalf, while in the Diaspora they showed their loyalty by offering prayers for his welfare. These forms of devotion cannot be regarded as exceptional since the imperial cult was not monolithic but allowed for notable differences in various places. Inscriptions from all over the western and eastern provinces unambiguously attest that sacrifices "on behalf" of the emperor existed side by side with the well-known sacrifices "to" the emperor.

Did the Jews enjoy privileges at all? Very few, it appears: among them, some minor honorific rights granted in Judea by Caesar to Hyrcanus II, his children, and the envoys sent by him (Pucci Ben Zeev 1998: 5) and, in Egypt, the right of being punished like Alexandrian citizens when guilty of a crime, namely, not scourged with whips, which were used on slaves, but beaten with blades (Philo, *In Flaccum* 78-80).

There is no doubt that the Jews, with their monotheistic faith and strong attachment to their laws, constituted a special phenomenon in the ancient world, but this does not mean that they enjoyed a special status.

Geographical and Chronological Limitations

Some of the rights accorded to the Jews seem to have applied only to a given place at a given time. Such, for example, were the right to be scourged with blades in Egypt and to receive cash to pay for their own oil in Syria.

As for the right to follow Jewish laws and customs, even if extant sources concern a particular issue and cover a particular geographical place, their homogeneity in content, both geographically and chronologically, suggests uniformity. It therefore appears that the Jews were entitled to live according to their traditional laws and customs both in Judea and in the Diaspora, in the republican and in the imperial eras. This right, however, cannot be regarded as necessarily permanent; the historical period under examination also witnesses episodes such as those taking place under Emperors Caligula and Hadrian. As happened also in the case of other peoples, the Romans never accorded absolute and permanent rights.

Jewish Rights at Work

In spite of the rights accorded to the Jews by the Romans, in different places of the Diaspora Asian, Libyan, Alexandrian, and probably other Greeks too, had their own reasons for objecting to Jewish traditional practices. It therefore happened that the Jews were prevented by their neighbors from observing the Sabbath, performing their sacred rites, and sending their sacred monies to Jerusalem (Pucci Ben Zeev 1998: 7, 17-27). The Jews applied to the local Roman officials and often received more decrees and more supporting letters, which, however, were often ignored and had little practical consequences. Such an apathetic attitude on the part of the Romans does not surprise us, since they seem to have had a very limited interest in what happened in the provinces, and perhaps they themselves did not expect their decisions to be implemented.

In many centers of the Mediterranean, therefore, Jewish religious freedom was somewhat theoretical, and it appears that — often or sometimes; it is difficult to establish — the Jews had to face hard times trying to follow their ancestral customs and laws.

Bibliography

J. M. G. Barclay 1998, *Jews in the Mediterranean Diaspora: From Alexander to Trajan (323 BCE–117 CE)*, Edinburgh: Clark. • E. S. Gruen 2002, *Diaspora: Jews amidst Greeks and Romans*, Cambridge: Harvard University Press. • M. Pucci Ben Zeev 1998, *Jewish Rights in the Roman World: The Greek and Roman Documents Quoted by Josephus Flavius*. Tübingen: Mohr-Siebeck. • P. Trebilco 1991, *Jewish Communities in Asia Minor*, Cambridge: Cambridge University Press.

Miriam Pucci Ben Zeev

Roman Emperors

The English term "emperor" comes from Lat. *imperator*. The ancient Romans used *imperator* in connection with the military realm. During the Republic a victorious general would be acclaimed *imperator* by his troops, or receive the honorific title from the Senate. The chaotic atmosphere of the civil wars at the end of the first century B.C.E. saw a debilitated Senate grant Octavian, Caesar's adoptive son and self-proclaimed political heir, the title of *imperator*, not on account of his military valor but in order to restore the Republic. The additional honors and powers which Octavian, later Augustus, received from the Senate in the following years and the constitutional reforms he later promoted changed the weight of the *imperator* on the Roman institutional scale, to the extent that already during Augustus' lifetime the *imperator* was clearly an independent figure interacting with the ancestral institutions still active in Rome — the Senate and the *comitia* — but having *de facto* absorbed some of their characteristics. *Imperator*, together with *Caesar* and *Augustus*, becomes a fundamental component of the official title of the emperor thereafter.

The available sources, almost invariably favorable to a strong independent and deliberative Senate, depict a contentious relationship between the Senate and the

Emperors in the Early Roman Period

Augustus (31 B.C.E.–14 C.E.)
Tiberius (14-37)
Gaius Caligula (37-41)
Claudius (41-54)
Nero (54-68)
Galba, Otho, and Vitellius (68-69)
Vespasian (69-79)
Titus (79-81)
Domitian (81-96)
Nerva (96-98)
Trajan (98-117)
Hadrian (117-138)

emperor, with the Senate striving to keep traditional influence against an emperor who allegedly collaborates with the Senate only in appearance, but in reality manages to concentrate all institutional powers, especially legislative and judicial ones, in his own hands. On the other side, the Senate could no longer claim its independence as in the golden age of the Republic, since periodically the Senate body was replenished with imperial nominees and not through the traditional process including completion of the *cursus honorum* and census ratification.

Historical analysis distinguishes two phases in the development of the power of the emperor *vis-à-vis* the Senate. The term "principate" refers to a constitutional arrangement where the emperor still recognizes the institutional role of the Senate, with which he tries, at least in appearance, to collaborate. The term "dominate" refers to a phase in which the emperor becomes autocratic and the Senate plays a subservient role; the beginning of this period is generally identified with the reign of the emperor Diocletian in 284 C.E.

One of the most contentious issues was the choice of the successor to the ruling emperor. Augustus had inaugurated the process by appointing to the throne his adoptive son Tiberius before his death. Later, the promotion of troops became the key to imperial designation. The role of the Senate was limited to the ratification of the designee; any dissent was cleared through political action. In both cases the principle of the enthronement of the best so dear to senatorial historiography was undermined.

Other than in Judea and surrounding Levantine territories, written sources and archaeological excavations reveal for the dawn of the Roman Empire the existence of a consistent Diaspora, with Jewish communities in Alexandria, Cyrene, Antioch, Ephesus, Sardis, Delos, Thessaloniki, Athens, Corinth, Rome, just to mention the most important cities. In the first two centuries of the Roman Empire the emperors never issued any charter for the Jews living in the empire, but established a relationship with each community on an individual basis. This was the case also for Jewish communities located in provinces under senatorial jurisdiction.

Augustus

In the Levant, Augustus granted Herod the title of king with authority over Judea, Samaria, Idumea, Galilee, Perea, Gaulanitis, Batanea, and Trachonitis. At Herod's death, Augustus divided the kingdom among some members of the Herodian family, but annexed Judea, Samaria, and Idumea into the empire. Augustus is said never to have interfered with the Temple authority, and to have made personal offerings, together with his wife Livia, for maintaining the rituals in Jerusalem. The Herodians were for the Roman emperors client kings; the extension, composition, or even existence of their kingdom was subordinated to Roman interests in the region. Agrippa II was the last Herodian to rule over part of the region until 53 C.E., when Claudius incorporated all the territories of Palestine into the Roman Empire.

In the Diaspora, Augustus granted the Jewish com-

Augustus of Prima Porta, a 2.04-m. statue discovered in 1863 in the Villa of Livia (Augustus's wife) at Prima Porta, near Rome *(FollowTheMedia / Till Niermann)*

munities the right of residence in the cities where they had settled, the possibility to follow their ancestral laws and customs, and the right to send annually the tithe to Jerusalem for the maintenance of religious rituals at the Temple. The better-documented cases are Rome, Alexandria, Cyrene and Ephesus. According to Philo of Alexandria, Augustus granted the Jews of Rome citizenship; the Jews of Alexandria and Cyrene were not citizens, but they equally benefited from Augustus' benevolence.

Tiberius

The sources mention an incident in 19 C.E. when Tiberius ordered the Roman Jews to be expelled. The accounts, mainly in Josephus and Tacitus, are utterly unclear about the causes of the incident and the extent of the Jewish population involved. Also under Tiberius, Philo mentions a persecution the prefect Sejanus allegedly organized against the Jews in 31 C.E., which was suspended only through his condemnation to death. Also in

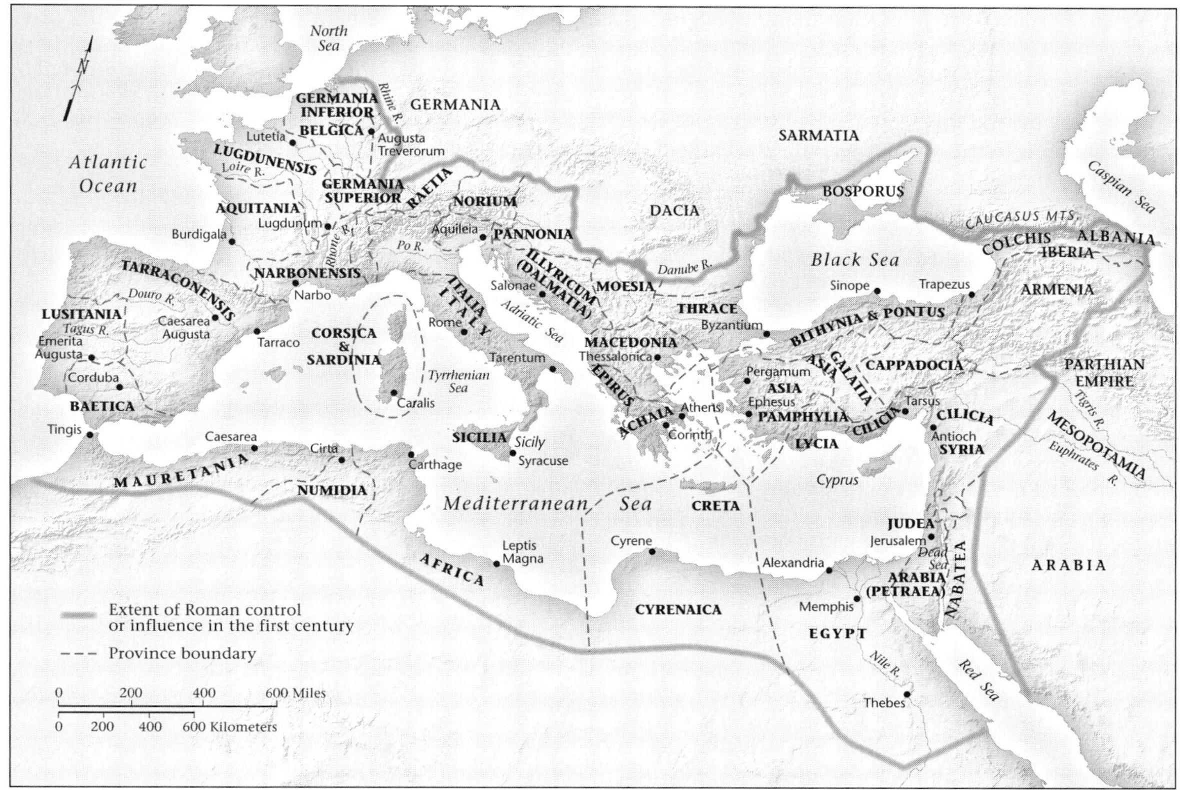

The Roman Empire in the First Century C.E.

this case the source does not explain the reason for the persecution and whether it targeted the Jews in Rome, or those living in Italy, or throughout the empire. In any case, Tiberius annulled Sejanus' undertaking before it was fully implemented. Sejanus' unfriendliness towards the Jews may also be reflected in Pontius Pilate's disputable attitudes at the beginning of his governorship in Judea, when he upset the local population by disrespecting their customs. The fact that Pilate was appointed under Sejanus' aegis, while Tiberius was in almost permanent retreat in Campania, may suggest that the prefect was imposing a hostile direction onto the imperial policy vis-à-vis the Jews independently from Tiberius' policy.

Gaius Caligula

More historically compelling is Gaius' attitude between 38 and 41 C.E. According to Philo, in 38 Gaius deprived most of the Jews living in Alexandria of their rights of residence. In 39 Gaius ordered Petronius, the governor of Syria, to set up his own statue in the Temple of Jerusalem, de facto canceling the Jewish monotheistic cult. While Petronius' diplomacy and Gaius' assassination prevented the implementation of the emperor's order in Jerusalem, it can be doubted that the Alexandrian Jews were able to recover their rights of residence even after an embassy to Claudius in 41 — it is possible that they never recovered them.

Nero

General uproar occurred in the Diaspora Jewish communities in 66 C.E. when Nero's imperial legion reacted to the Jews' conquest of Jerusalem. In Alexandria the Roman legions were led by the prefect Tiberius Julius Alexander, himself an apostate Jew.

Vespasian and Titus

The revolt in Judea lasted until 70 C.E., when Titus Flavius Vespasian, son of the ruling emperor Vespasian, reconquered Jerusalem and destroyed the Temple. The sack of Jerusalem, particularly the taking of the Temple menorah, is represented on Titus' triumphal arch in Rome. The destruction of the Temple marks the end of the Jerusalem sacrificial cult and its religious hierarchy. Vespasian did not order the destruction of the Jewish communities, either in Palestine or in the Diaspora, or forbid the observance of Jewish monotheism; yet he introduced the *fiscus iudaicus,* a special tribute each Jew in the empire had to pay to the temple of Jupiter Capitolinus in Rome — the same amount that was sent to Jerusalem when the Temple was still standing.

Trajan

The humiliation Vespasian's measure produced among the Jews is probably among the reasons for the revolts in Egypt, Cyrenaica, Cyprus, Judea, and Mesopotamia during the reign of Trajan between 115 or 116 and 117 C.E. Scattered sources make historical analysis difficult; recent research has denied the existence of a larger Jewish plan for the revolt in favor of independent regional uprisings. In Egypt, a revolt for unclear reasons developed, probably because of chronic distrust between Greeks and Jews. Trajan's legions intervened, and crushed the Jews of Egypt and Alexandria, destroying the main house of prayer there and killing the majority of the Egyptian Jews. Hadrian later ordered the confiscation of the property of those who had died, making it impossible for the Egyptian Jewish communities to recover. In Mesopotamia the Jews revolted in protest against Trajan's conquest of the region, which would have imposed on them the *fiscus iudaicus.* In Judea the evidence is very inconclusive, but it seems that the change of the status of the *provicia Iudea* from praetorian to consular at the beginning of the second century C.E. was the consequence of an uprising at the end of the reign of Trajan. The cause of the uprising remains unknown.

Hadrian

Trajan's successor Hadrian took a tough initiative against the last Jewish attempt at independence for Judea in 132-135 C.E. The outcome of the Bar Kokhba Revolt was the expulsion of the Jews from Jerusalem and the destruction of the city, which was followed by the beginnings of the Roman colony Aelia Capitolina. On the larger scale, Hadrian abolished circumcision, a prohibition reversed by Antoninus Pius.

With the exception of Gaius' attempt to abolish Jewish monotheism, Vespasian's *fiscus iudaicus,* and Hadrian's short-lived prohibition of circumcision, no emperor ever intervened against the Jews *qua* Jews across the empire with the intention of eliminating the group. Even after the Diaspora and the Bar Kokhba Revolt, after which the Jewish communities of Cyprus, Cyrene, Alexandria, and Jerusalem almost ceased to exist, other communities continued their legacy and sometimes flourished. With the proclamation of the *Constitutio Antoniniana* in 212 C.E. all the Jews of free status acquired Roman citizenship, putting an end to any threat to the very existence of their communities. In the second and third century C.E. the Jews could serve in the public administration, and were exempted from those civic duties that violated their religion. They maintained the autonomy of their judicial courts, as well as the religious organization around their synagogues.

Judaism remained a *religio licita* under the early Christian empire, as it had been under the pagan. However, between the fifth and the sixth century a galvanized Christian orthodoxy, which saw its role grow in the repression of heresy promoted by Theodosius I, put pressure on the Roman emperors to redefine the relationship between the Roman state and the Jews. Initially state control was limited to the Jewish religious hierarchy, then extended to the limitation of Jewish legal autonomy, eventually preventing the growth of Jewish communities throughout the empire, curtailing privileges and the legal and political capacity of the Jews. Under the legal codification of Roman law promoted by Justinian, a Jew could no longer serve in the imperial administration or testify in court if the accused was neither a heretic nor a Jew.

BIBLIOGRAPHY

F. MILLAR 1977, *The Emperor in the Roman World,* London: Duckworth. • E. M. SMALLWOOD 1976, *The Jews under Roman Rule: From Pompey to Diocletian,* Leiden: Brill, 1976. • A. LINDER, ED. 1987, *The Jews in Roman Imperial Legislation,* Detroit: Wayne State University Press.

SANDRA GAMBETTI

Roman Generals

Most of Rome's subjects had been subjugated through military conquest and settled down fairly quickly under Roman rule. The Jews were an exception. Although those residing in the western and central Mediterranean were quiescent, farther east that was not the case. Resistance to Roman rule in Judea, suppressed but not eliminated during the long and brutal reign of the client king, Herod the Great (37-4 B.C.E.), intermittently flared into revolt, as in 66 and 132 C.E. The Roman provinces of Egypt, Cyrene (which included Cyprus), and Mesopotamia also were the scene of serious uprisings in the early second century C.E. Such rebellions necessitated military action on the part of Rome. More often than not the generals sent to suppress them were the best that Rome had at the time, as the following chronologically organized discussion of generals shows.

Gnaeus Pompeius "Magnus"

Pompey's brutal conquest of Judea, which culminated in the capture of the Temple and his sacrilegious penetration of the Holy of Holies (63 B.C.E.), an act never forgiven or forgotten by the Jews, came about more through force of circumstance than through deliberate intent. Sent to the East in 66 B.C.E. to deal with the threat posed to Roman interests by the Pontic king, Mithridates VI, and his son-in-law and ally, Tigranes II, ruler of Armenia and Syria, Pompey, at that time Rome's premier general, found himself drawn into Judean affairs through a quarrel between the Hasmonean princes, Aristobulus and Hyrcanus, sons of the late queen, Alexandra Shelamzion (died 67 B.C.E.). Each of them believed that by appealing to the Romans for military help he could win the throne for himself. Thanks to Pompey's support Hyrcanus eventually won, but the price he had to pay was heavy: Pompey reduced his rank from that of king to ethnarch, refused to allow him to refortify Jerusalem, considerably reduced the size of his territory, and placed it under the general oversight of the Roman governor of Syria (Smallwood 1981: 21-30). Pompey gained great glory at Rome for his conquest of Judea — Jews featured conspicuously in the triumph he celebrated there in 61 B.C.E. His memory, however, was reviled by Jews, as the hostile allusions to him in such works as the *Psalms of Solomon* reveal (Schürer 1973: 193-94).

Marcus Aemilius Scaurus

Scaurus was a subordinate officer *(quaestor)* to Pompey in the East (66-63 B.C.E.) and the first Roman governor of the province of Syria (ca. 63-61 B.C.E.). He first came into contact with the Jews in 65 B.C.E. after being dispatched to Syria by Pompey to sort out that region for Rome. Hastening from Damascus to Judea, where an armed struggle for the throne was in progress between the Hasmonean brothers, Aristobulus and Hyrcanus, he found himself lobbied for military aid by both parties to the conflict. Although Scaurus himself was inclined to support Aristobulus, Pompey subsequently (63 B.C.E.) chose to back Hyrcanus, who, as a result, secured the throne. Scaurus' name tantalizingly appears in a fragmentary calendrical document from Cave 4 at Qumran (4Q324a), where he is referred to as Aemilius *('Mlyws)*. It would seem that at some point he carried out a massacre of Jews sufficiently serious for it to be deemed worthy of annual memorialization. Whether that otherwise unattested event, the extent of which is wholly irrecoverable, occurred before Hyrcanus' triumph over Aristobulus and the fall of Jerusalem (63 B.C.E.) or during Scaurus' subsequent governorship of Syria cannot be determined (Schwarz 2002). One of his duties as governor of that province would have been to see that law and order prevailed in Hyrcanus' ethnarchy.

Gaius Sosius

Gaius Sosius was a subordinate officer *(quaestor)* to Marc Antony in the East ca. 39 B.C.E. and subsequently (38-37 B.C.E.) his appointee as governor of Syria. Ordered by Antony in 38 B.C.E. to eject the Parthian puppet-ruler Antigonus from Judea and to install Herod (later, the Great) as king, Sosius led a large Roman army to Judea the following year, captured the Temple after a protracted siege, placed Herod on the throne, and dispatched Antigonus in chains to Antony. For recovering Judea from the Parthians Sosius was awarded a triumph at Rome, which he celebrated in 34 B.C.E. Probably it was to mark his reconquest of Judea that he undertook to rebuild the temple of Apollo near the Circus Flaminius, subsequently known as the Temple of Apollo Medicus Sosianus (Claridge 1998: 245-47). His victory over the Jews was also celebrated on Roman coinage.

Publius Quinctilius Varus

Varus was favorite of the emperor Augustus, with whom he was connected by marriage and for whom he governed the province of Syria (7/6-4 B.C.E.) and commanded the Rhine army (9 C.E.). Vilified in Roman sources as the author of one of Rome's worst military defeats, the loss in Germany in a single day of three whole legions, Varus is presented by the Jewish historian Josephus as an effective governor of Syria whose best efforts in a difficult situation not of his own making were undermined by the incompetence of others, most notably the imperial finance officer Sabinus. Forced to intervene militarily in Judea in 4 B.C.E. on account of the widespread revolts that erupted there during the power vacuum that followed Herod's death, Varus rapidly restored law and order, enslaving many of the defeated rebels and crucifying thousands of others. That operation was no small-scale affair; the entire military complement of the province of Syria (three legions) had to be deployed in Judea, the Roman veteran colony at Beirut was pressed into providing 1,500 recruits, and local client kings were required to furnish troops on an unprecedented scale. Small wonder that this episode impressed itself on Jewish memory; the War of Asveros, listed in *Seder Olam* as the most significant Romano-Jewish conflict between Pompey's conquest and that of the Flavians, is generally regarded as an allusion to it (Schürer 1973: 332 n. 9).

Titus Flavius Vespasianus

Vespasian was a Roman Senator of undistinguished origins and modest achievements who was appointed by the emperor Nero toward the end of 66 C.E. to put down the revolt in Judea, the recently expired governor of Syria, Cestius Gallus, having signally failed to do so. Despite the fact that Vespasian had last seen serious fighting in the 40s C.E. as a legionary commander in Britain during the Claudian conquest, he turned out to be an able commander-in-chief. With the help of his elder son Titus and a force of some 60,000 men that included one of the legions based in Egypt, he set about systematically defeating the rebels and restoring Roman authority in Judea. During 67 C.E. he reduced Galilee, and by the time of Nero's death in the middle of 68 C.E. he had confined the resistance largely to Jerusalem and the three Herodian fortresses, Machaerus, Herodium, and Masada. Nero's death, the subsequent civil wars, and Vespasian's own decision to bid for the throne (he was acclaimed emperor by the troops on July 1, 69 C.E.) meant that he played no further part in the suppression of the Jewish Revolt, which was temporarily put on hold.

Titus Flavius Vespasianus

Titus was the elder son of Emperor Vespasian and was entrusted early in the latter's reign (Spring of 70 C.E.) with completing the suppression of the ongoing revolt in Judea. After a five-month siege of Jerusalem, Titus effectively achieved that task — with the sack of the Temple in August (on the Ninth of Ab, according to Jewish calculations) the revolt was all but crushed. Only three fortresses remained in rebel hands, and their capture was left to subordinate officers such as L. Flavius Silva. Titus meanwhile proceeded to tour Rome's eastern provinces where he milked his victory over the Jews for all it was worth. Jewish prisoners of war in their thousands were slaughtered in the amphitheaters of the area in celebration of it, and permanent memorials were erected in Antioch, the capital of the province of Syria. Rome, too, became a showcase for the Flavian conquest of the Jews. An elaborate triumph there in 71 C.E., the only one ever to be celebrated over the population of an existing province rather than an external enemy (Millar 1993: 79), was followed by the minting of coins celebrating Judea's capture and by the erection of a whole clutch of buildings and monuments, whose purpose was to impress contemporaries and to keep the memory of the conquest forever green (Millar 2005). These included the still extant Arch of Titus near the eastern end to the main forum. Erected in Titus' memory in 81 C.E., the year in which he died, it contains, *inter alia,* a relief depicting his triumphal procession with Roman soldiers carrying aloft the looted Temple treasures which subsequently (75 C.E.) were put on public display in Vespasian's new Temple, or Forum, of Peace at Rome (Claridge 1998: 116-18).

Lucius Flavius Silva

Silva was the Roman general who captured the fortress of Masada from Jewish rebels in either 73 or 74 C.E. and so ended the revolt begun in 66. The remains of his extensive siege works (circumvallation wall and ramp) and eight camps can still be clearly seen in the Judean Desert (Yadin 1966).

Quintus Marcius Turbo

Turbo rose to prominence during the reign of the emperor Trajan (98-117 C.E.). He was dispatched in 116 C.E. to put down the serious Jewish uprising that had broken out the previous year in Cyrene (modern Libya) and then spread to Egypt and Cyprus. He suppressed the revolt with such efficiency that Trajan's successor, Hadrian (117-138 C.E.), gave him further special commands in other parts of the empire.

Lusius Quietus

Lusius Quietus was a Moorish chieftain who rose to prominence under the emperor Trajan (98-117 C.E.) on account of his sterling service with the Roman army in Dacia and Parthia. Appointed in 116 C.E. to crush the general uprising in Trajan's newly created province of Mesopotamia, he did so with great efficiency and brutality, slaughtering many Jews in the process. Subsequently (117 C.E.?) he was made governor of Judea, at that time in a state of unrest, if not outright revolt. Whether the "War of Quietus" mentioned in the Mishnah and *Seder Olam* refers to his military activities in Mesopotamia or in Judea is a matter of dispute, but the latter seems more likely (Smallwood 1981: 421-27). Whatever the truth, the coining of the phrase testifies to Quietus' powerful but negative impact upon the Jews.

Sextus Julius Severus

Severus was the leading Roman general of the emperor Hadrian (117-38 C.E.), for whom he governed several important frontier provinces. Transferred from Britain to Judea to deal with the revolt of Bar Kokhba (132-135 C.E.), he suppressed the uprising systematically and ruthlessly, not stopping even at using starvation to break Jewish resistance. For his success in ending the rebellion, the most serious ever mounted by the Jews against Rome, he was immediately awarded *ornamenta triumphalia* (triumphal decorations), the highest military honor then available to men below the rank of emperor, and was subsequently promoted to the governorship of Syria, Rome's most important eastern province.

BIBLIOGRAPHY

A. CLARIDGE 1998, *Rome: An Oxford Archaeological Guide,* Oxford: Oxford University Press. • F. MILLAR 1993, *The Roman Near East (31 BC–AD 337),* Cambridge, Mass.: Harvard University Press. • F. MILLAR 2005, "Last Year in Jerusalem: Monuments of the Jewish War in Rome," in *Flavius Josephus and Flavian Rome,* ed. J. Edmondson, S. Mason, and J. Rives, Oxford: Oxford University Press, 101-28. • E. SCHÜRER 1973, *The History of the Jewish People in the Age of Jesus Christ,* vol. 1, rev. and ed. G. Vermes and F. Millar, Edinburgh: Clark. • E. M. SMALLWOOD 1981, *The Jews under Roman Rule from Pompey to Diocletian,* Leiden: E. J. Brill. • Y. YADIN 1966, *Masada: Herod's Fortress and the Zealots' Last Stand,* London: Weidenfeld & Nicolson.

See also: Roman Governors

MARGARET H. WILLIAMS

Roman Governors

The establishment of Roman hegemony over the Mediterranean in the last two centuries B.C.E. inevitably brought the Jews settled throughout that area under Roman control. Whether they resided in a client state or in one of Rome's many provinces made little difference: everywhere, even in nominally independent Judea, the power of the local provincial governor was paramount. Confusingly, not all Rome's governors bore the same title; *proconsul, legate, prefect,* and *procurator* are among the terms most commonly found. There are various reasons for this terminological variety, a key one being the type of province governed. Since that is the case, the discussion below is organized along provincial lines. Only the four provinces for which there is a significant amount of evidence (Asia, Egypt, Judea, and Syria) are considered. Under each province, general remarks about the area and its governance are followed by brief discussions, chronologically ordered, of its most significant governors.

Province of Asia

Consisting of the territory once ruled by the Attalid dynasty in what is now northwest Turkey, the province of Asia had no military garrison on account of its generally peaceful character. In normal circumstances it was governed by men of senatorial rank (i.e., from the top tier of Roman society) entitled *proconsuls.* Their main duties were judicial, and it is in that capacity that we mostly see them interacting with the Jews of their province. Generally this interaction took the form of upholding Jewish complaints against local Greek attempts to frustrate the observance of the Sabbath and/or the dispatch to Jerusalem of monies collected for the Temple tax. Not all proconsuls, however, were supportive of the Jews, as the case of Asia's best-known governor, L. Valerius Flaccus, shows.

Lucius Valerius Flaccus

Proconsul of the province from 62-61 B.C.E., Lucius Valerius Flaccus was subsequently (59 B.C.E.) put on trial at Rome for extortion. He was accused, among other things, of illegally seizing large sums of Jewish gold amassed for the purpose of paying the Temple tax (Cicero, *Pro Flacco* 66–69). Although Flaccus was acquitted and his confiscation of the Temple tax money implicitly upheld, the right of adult male Jews in Asia and other parts of the Roman world to collect and send their half-shekel dues annually to Jerusalem does not seem to have been affected by his activities. Documentary evidence from the second half of the first century B.C.E. shows several Roman officials upholding Jewish rights in this matter, among them two proconsuls of Asia (Philo, *Legatio ad Gaium* 315; Josephus, *Ant.* 16.172-73).

Province of Egypt

Created in 30 B.C.E. by Octavian (later, Augustus) after the defeat and suicide of Cleopatra VII, the province of Egypt from the outset was always governed by a prefect of equestrian rank (i.e., from the second tier of Roman society), supported by a large legionary garrison. This arrangement was anomalous since provinces containing legions normally were governed by men of senatorial rank. Egypt, however, was a special case on account of its political importance to the emperor; he used its corn to feed the Roman populace. Consequently, senators (since they were potential political rivals) were not allowed to set foot in it without imperial permission.

Jews had been settled in Egypt since the time of Ptolemy I. They were particularly numerous in Alexandria, where their relations with the Greek population were often tense. On several occasions tension between the two ethnic groups reached such a peak that violence broke out and military intervention by the prefect was required. Usually he could cope on his own, as the discussion below concerning Avillius Flaccus and Tiberius Julius Alexander shows. However, in 116 C.E., when fighting between Jews and Greeks spread all over Egypt in the course of the general uprising of North African Jews against Rome, a special commander with additional troops had to be sent in.

Aulus Avillius Flaccus

When Aulus Avillius Flaccus was prefect of Egypt (32-38 C.E.), the simmering tension between the Jews and Greeks in Alexandria boiled over, resulting in the first recorded pogrom in Jewish history (38 C.E.). Neither the precise sequence of events nor the exact motives for Flaccus' anti-Jewish stance can be recovered from Philo's highly partisan and inconsistent accounts in his *In Flaccum* and *Legatio ad Gaium.* Although Philo represents the Greeks as solely to blame for the breakdown in law and order, the actions taken by Flaccus against the Jews — reducing their civic status from that of resident aliens to foreigners, arresting and publicly scourging thirty-eight leading lights of the Jewish community, and getting his troops to search Jewish houses for arms — suggests that he did not view them as wholly innocent. If, as some have argued, Flaccus' motive for turning against the Jews was to protect his position vis-à-vis the new emperor Gaius (Caligula), it did not work. Before the year was out, Flaccus was arrested, found guilty (probably of treason), and banished to a Greek island where he was later murdered on imperial orders. His anti-Jewish measures were reversed by the emperor Claudius shortly after Gaius' own murder in 41 C.E.

Tiberius Julius Alexander

Nephew of the writer Philo and an apostate Jew, Tiberius Julius Alexander was prefect of Egypt from 66 to 69 C.E. He had already governed Judea in the 40s C.E. with some success. In his new province he dealt no less firmly with disturbers of the Roman peace. In 66 C.E., in response to a Jewish uprising against the Greeks of Alexandria, he sent in two of the legions under his command. Peace was restored, but only at the price of heavy Jewish casualties. A fervent supporter of Vespasian in the civil wars of 68-69 C.E., he was subsequently made Titus' chief-of-staff in Judea.

Province of Judea

Created by the emperor Augustus in 6 C.E. after the deposition of the ethnarch Archelaus, Judea was a minor province, at that stage comprising only Idumea, Samaria, and Judea proper. Placed under the general oversight of the Syrian legate, Rome's principal governor in the East, its day-to-day running was entrusted to a prefect of equestrian rank. His chief duty, as with all provincial governors, was to maintain law and order. For that purpose he had a small garrison force of locally recruited auxiliary soldiers, conservatively estimated at around 3,000 men. Its precise composition in the first phase of the province's history (6-41 C.E.) is not known but was probably made up mostly of troops formerly in the service of Archelaus and, before him, Herod the Great (Millar 1993: 45). Traditionally recruited from the pagan cities Caesarea Maritima and Sebaste (Samaria), these non-Jewish soldiers caused immense trouble in the second phase of the province's history (44-66 C.E.) on account of their blatant anti-Semitism. Most of them were based at Caesarea Maritima, where the prefect had his headquarters, but one unit was always on duty in Jerusalem in the Antonia fortress overlooking the Temple complex.

The arrangements put in place in 6 C.E. largely endured down to the outbreak of the Jewish Revolt in 66 C.E., but two changes are to be noted. While the earlier governors (6-41 C.E.) were called *prefects,* a title with military overtones, those who ran the province in its second phase (44-66 C.E.) after the brief interlude of Agrippa I's reign (41-44 C.E.) were styled *procurators,* a more managerial-sounding term. That change in title, an empire-wide phenomenon, did not mean that the duties of the Judean governor had changed in character. They maintained law and order and judged cases not involving Jewish religious law. But if the character of the duties had not changed, their scope had, for the post-44-C.E. province was double the size of the earlier one, Galilee and Perea now being among the areas included in it.

ROMAN GOVERNORS

The inadequacy of the above arrangements was brought home to the Romans by Judea's inexorable slide, first into anarchy and then into revolt (66 C.E.). Once the back of that rebellion had been broken with the destruction of the Temple in 70 C.E., major reforms were introduced. Henceforth the province was to be administered by legates of senatorial rank and proven military competence and security entrusted to legionaries, not locally recruited auxiliary forces. Prewar auxiliary units such as the Sebastenians were now transferred to other provinces, and the Legio X Fretensis began its long occupation of Jerusalem.

Judean Prefects (6-41 C.E.)

With the exception of Pontius Pilatus (26-36 C.E.), little is known about the prefects, their names, dates of office, and even their number being far from certain. About the three who held office under Augustus (i.e., down to 14 C.E.), namely, Coponius, Marcus Ambibulus (perhaps Ambivius), and Lucius (?) Annius Rufus, nothing definite is known. Valerius Gratus (15-26 C.E.), the first of the emperor Tiberius' two appointees, clearly experienced difficulties working with the high priests, three of whom he deposed in the early stages of his governorship, but the nature of those difficulties remains unknown. Whether the Marcellus who was made interim governor of Judea after the deposition of Pilate in 26 C.E. is to be identified with the Marullus whom Tiberius' successor, the emperor Gaius, appointed prefect of Judea in 37 C.E. is a matter of debate.

Pontius Pilate, however, is well attested: Philo, Josephus, Tacitus, and the authors of the four Gospels all refer to him; his name also occurs on coins that he struck during his governorship; additionally, he is mentioned in a dedicatory inscription from a building that he erected in the emperor Tiberius' honor in Caesarea Maritima (Lehmann and Holum 2000: no. 43). Christian and Jewish sources invariably show Pilate in a bad light. In the Gospels, where he figures as judge in the trial of Jesus, he is mostly depicted as weak and malleable. Philo accuses him, among other things, of venality, violence, robbery, and endless savage ferocity, charges which he signally fails to substantiate. His narrative reveals, at worst, insensitivity on Pilate's part; he had installed in his palace in Jerusalem shields honoring the emperor by name. Josephus also cannot find a good word to say for Pilate, whom he portrays as deliberately provocative and brutal to boot. Under cover of darkness he had introduced into Jerusalem troops carrying standards topped with graven images. When the Jews had protested vigorously at this break with tradition, he had broken up their demonstration by force.

An inscription found in the theater at Caesarea Maritima: "Pontius Pilatus, Prefect of Judea, has presented the Tiberieum to the Caesareans" *(Phoenix Data Systems / Neal and Joel Bierling)*

But each of these writers had an agenda that required him to present Pilate in a less than favorable light (Bond 1998). Once that is appreciated and the facts soberly examined, Pilate emerges as a competent operator. He was conspicuously loyal to the emperor who had appointed him, as the dedication at Caesarea Maritima and the episode of the shields show. He had good relations with the Jewish authorities; during his tenure no changes were made to the high priesthood, Joseph Caiaphas remaining in office throughout. He improved the infrastructure of his province by building an aqueduct. Above all, he maintained law and order, dealing firmly with public protests, lawbreakers such as the brigand Barabbas, and potential revolutionaries (most notably Jesus of Nazareth). Not once during his whole ten years as governor were the backup services of Syrian legions required. In the end it was Pilate's determination to preserve law and order at all costs that brought about his downfall. A too vigorous response to Samaritans gathering on Mt. Gerizim led to complaints being lodged with the legate of Syria and Pilate's removal by the latter from office.

Judean Procurators (44-66 C.E.)

Altogether there were no fewer than seven procuratorial governors of the enlarged Judean province: Cuspius Fadus (44-ca. 46 C.E.), Tiberius Julius Alexander (ca. 46-48 C.E.), Ventidius Cumanus (48–ca. 52 C.E.), Antonius Felix (ca. 52-60 C.E.), Porcius Festus (ca. 60-62 C.E.), Lucceius (?) Albinus (62-64 C.E.), and Gessius Florus (64-66 C.E.). As can be seen from these dates, apart from Felix, who was in office for about eight years, the rest held office on average for two to three years only — clearly an undesirable situation given the grave problems now facing the Roman administration. Inevitably, there was widespread resentment at the reimposition of direct Roman rule after the benign interlude of Agrippa I's reign (41-44 C.E.). That resentment, exacerbated by famine and economic hardship and inflamed by the preaching of those Josephus calls "false prophets," "impostors," and "pseudo-messiahs," promising, among other things, liberation from Roman rule and the establishment of the kingdom of God, rapidly reduced the province to a state of ungovernability that criminal elements were not slow to exploit.

Not all of the governors sent out from Rome were incompetent. Fadus took a tough line with the first of the "false prophets," an "impostor" called Theudas, killing Theudas himself and butchering his followers. Alexander (later promoted to the governorship of Egypt)

Roman Governors of Judea to the First Revolt

Prefects
Coponius (6-9 C.E.)
Marcus Ambibulus (9-12)
Annius Rufus (13-15)
Valerius Gratus (15-26)
Pontius Pilatus (26-36)
Marcellus (36-38)
Marullus (38-41)
[41-44: Judea ruled by King Agrippa I]

Procurators
Cuspius Fadus (44-46)
Tiberius Julius Alexander (46-48)
Ventidius Cumanus (48-52)
M. Antonius Felix (52-60)
Porcius Festus (60-62)
Albinus (62-64)
Gessius Florus (64-66)

was similarly firm with militants from Galilee, crucifying two sons of Judas of Gamla, leader of the uprising over the census of Quirinius in 6 C.E. Felix, a far abler governor than Tacitus, who despised his servile origins, can bring himself to admit that he was ruthless in suppressing both religious extremists (Zealots) and yet another popular movement headed by a "false prophet," this time hailing from Egypt, for whom Paul of Tarsus was at one point mistaken (Acts 21:38). Festus likewise dealt successfully with an "impostor." (It was in their judicial capacity that both these prefects encountered the apostle Paul.)

But other governors were less competent. Cumanus, dismissed from his post by the Syrian legate Ummidius Quadratus and sent to Rome to stand trial before the emperor, was found guilty of negligence and exiled. To incompetence Albinus and Gessius Florus added gross venality, the former accepting bribes from both pro-Roman and anti-Roman factions, the latter "stripping whole cities and ruining entire populations" (Josephus, *J.W.* 2.278) in his zest for personal enrichment. By 66 C.E. Judea was beyond the control of the procurators, and not even the forces of the Syrian legate Cestius Gallus could retrieve the situation for Rome.

Province of Syria

Consisting of the territory centered on Antioch on the Orontes, the former western capital of the Seleucid dynasty, Syria was the most heavily garrisoned of Rome's eastern provinces (usually having three or four legions). From the time of its creation by Pompey in 63 B.C.E., it was always governed by senior politicians of proven military competence and senatorial rank. In the imperial period (i.e., from 27 B.C.E. onward) these officials, now regularly entitled legates, were appointed by the emperor, to whom they were directly answerable. Among the duties of the governor of Syria was the general oversight of Judea, whether the latter was a client state or a province under direct Roman rule. Since Judea was often in a turbulent state, military intervention there by the governor of Syria was not uncommon. But that official did more than march his legions into Judea. Occasionally, he might involve himself in administrative or cultic matters, or even take disciplinary action against the prefects and procurators in charge of the area. (The two governors of Syria who had to fight significant wars in Judea, Gaius Sosius and P. Quintilius Varus, are discussed in this volume in the entry "Roman Generals.") Those whose dealings with the area were generally of a more pacific nature are considered below. Although many Jews were settled in Syria itself, little is known about their relationship with the governors of that province.

Aulus Gabinius

Aulus Gabinius (57-55 B.C.E.) was forced to intervene militarily in Judea in 57 B.C.E. on account of a challenge to the rule of Rome's Hasmonean client Hyrcanus II by his nephew Alexander. Gabinius came to the conclusion that stability in the area would best be achieved by dispensing with the services of the Hasmoneans. Five regional councils composed of aristocrats were set up instead, Hyrcanus being allowed to retain only his high priestly title and duties. Although an imaginative response to a difficult situation, Gabinius' administrative experiment did not bring stability to Judea, nor did it long survive his governorship; under Julius Caesar, Hyrcanus regained his title of ethnarch and presumably his secular powers as well.

Publius Sulpicius Quirinius

Following the emperor Augustus' decision to depose the Judean ethnarch Archelaus and to turn his former territory into a province, Quirinius (6 C.E.), lately appointed to the governorship of Syria, was required to prepare Judea for direct Roman rule by conducting a census there. This involved drawing up a register of its inhabitants and their taxable assets. Inevitably there was resistance, some of it armed (Acts 5:37), which Quirinius had to put down by force. A garbled reference to the census occurs in Luke 2:1, where it is erroneously made to coincide with the birth of Jesus (Schürer 1973: 399-427).

Lucius Vitellius

Lucius Vitellius (35-39 [?] C.E.) was a leading politician of the early imperial period who governed the province of Syria for the emperors Tiberius and Gaius (Caligula). He is not to be confused with his son, Aulus Vitellius, who ruled briefly as emperor in 69 C.E. Famed for the high quality of his administration, Lucius Vitellius showed himself to be unusually sensitive to Jewish feelings. It was he who restored to them the custody of the high-priestly vestments, hitherto kept by the Romans in the Antonia fortress and released to the Jews only at the major festivals and at Yom Kippur. Aware of the Jews' aversion to the presence on their soil of the Romans' military standards (traditionally surmounted by a bust of the emperor), he also agreed to reroute his proposed march into Nabatean Arabia, thereby avoiding areas of dense Jewish settlement. Nor was it only the Jewish residents of Judea whose concerns he took seriously. In response to Samaritan complaints, he dismissed the local governor, Pontius Pilate, from his post and sent him to Rome to stand trial before the emperor Tiberius.

Publius Petronius

Publius Petronius (39 [?]–41/2 C.E.) was legate of Syria under the emperors Gaius (Caligula) and Claudius. It was during Petronius' governorship that Caligula conceived the outrageous idea of having a cult statue of himself set up in the temple at Jerusalem. Petronius, as the commander of the main Roman force in the area (the four legions based in Syria), was given the unenviable task of seeing that the emperor's orders were carried out. Through skillful diplomacy, masterly procrastination, and, in the end, a stroke of luck (Caligula's assassination), Petronius managed to thwart the insane project and so saved the Romans from having to deal with a major revolt in Judea. Nor was this the only occasion on which he showed himself supportive of the Jews. When some Greek youths in Dora, a city in the south of his province, desecrated the local synagogue by putting up in it a statue of the emperor Claudius, he ordered the city authorities to arrest and hand over the culprits for trial before himself.

BIBLIOGRAPHY

J. M. G. BARCLAY 1996, *Jews in the Mediterranean Diaspora,* Edinburgh: Clark. • H. K. BOND 1998, *Pontius Pilate in History and Interpretation,* Cambridge: Cambridge University Press. • E. S. GRUEN 2002, *Diaspora: Jews amidst Greeks and Romans,* Cambridge: Harvard University Press. • C. M. LEHMANN AND K. G. HOLUM 2000, *The Greek and Latin Inscriptions of Caesarea Maritima,* Boston: American Schools of Oriental Research. • F. MILLAR 1993, *The Roman Near East (31 BC–AD 337),* Cambridge: Harvard University Press. • E. SCHÜRER 1973, *The History of the Jewish People in the Age of Jesus Christ,* vol. 1, rev. and ed. G. Vermes and F. Millar, Edinburgh: Clark. • E. M. SMALLWOOD 1981, *The Jews under Roman Rule from Pompey to Diocletian,* Leiden: Brill.

See also: Julius Caesar, Gaius; Roman Generals

MARGARET H. WILLIAMS

Romanization

"Romanization" can be defined in the broadest sense as the varied processes of interaction between Roman and local cultures during the period of the Roman Empire (Chancey 2005). More nuanced and narrowly defined models for understanding these processes have been proposed; they have been explained as the imposition of an "urban overlay" of Roman-style monumental architecture on a foundation of local culture, with a new culture resulting from the mixture (Strange 1992); as a veneer over indigenous cultures (Ball 2001); as a replacement of local cultures (Millar 1993); as the willing acculturation to Roman culture by locals, with commoners emulating elites in their appropriation of Roman ways (Millett 1990); and as "Creolization," the resistant adaptation of Roman culture (Webster 2001). The interactions of Roman and indigenous cultures were too complex and varied across different regions, time periods, spheres of culture (language, architecture, religion, philosophy, economics, civic organization, etc.), and social settings for any one of these models to be regarded as universally applicable, but each model might have utility in evaluating particular sets of data.

In the eastern Mediterranean region, an additional cultural influence was already present when the Romans arrived: Hellenism. Because the Romans encouraged the further adoption of aspects of Hellenistic culture there, Romanization is inextricably interwoven with Hellenization. Some scholarly studies treat Romanization as an aspect of Hellenization (Hengel 1989; Levine 1998; Bowersock 1990). The mixing of Roman and Hellenistic culture is often referred to as "Greco-Roman" culture.

Herod and His Dynasty

The client king Herod the Great may not have been the first individual to undertake widespread construction projects in the Roman East; according to Josephus, the Roman general Gabinius (mid-first century B.C.E.) had sponsored the rebuilding of several cities in Syria and Palestine (*J.W.* 1.165-66; *Ant.* 14.88). It is Herod, however, who deserves primary credit for introducing Roman-style architecture to the Levant. Influenced by his own visits to Rome (Roller 1998), he sponsored the building of Hellenistic and Roman structures (bathhouses, fountains, peristyles, gymnasia, stoas, temples, theaters) in cities throughout the region and as far west as Greece (*J.W.* 1.422-25; *Ant.* 16.146-48). Within his own territory, he constructed two new cities and named them both in honor of the emperor Sebaste (a Greek equivalent for the Latin title *Augustus*) and Caesarea Maritima. Both foundations displayed the orthogonal planning characteristic of Greco-Roman cities and were amply endowed with monumental buildings. Caesarea Maritima, for example, had a Roman-style theater, amphitheater, aqueduct, harbor, and a temple dedicated to the emperor and the goddess Roma. Herod celebrated its completion in 10 B.C.E. with games that included Hellenistic musical and athletic competition and Roman animal and gladiatorial shows. In or near Jerusalem, Herod constructed an amphitheater and theater; most famously, he thoroughly expanded and renovated the Temple complex, endowing it with massive porticoes. He also rebuilt or constructed fortresses and palaces at Alexandreion, Cypros, Herodium, Hyrcania, Jericho, Machaerus, and Masada, sometimes adding Roman-style baths and utilizing Roman construction methods such as *opus incertum, opus reticulatum,* and *opus sectile* and Roman decorative techniques such as frescoes, mosaics, and stucco moldings (MacMullen 2000; Richardson 1996; Roller 1998).

Other members of Herod's dynasty followed his example to varying degrees. Thus, Antipas renamed Sepphoris as Autocratoris, probably in honor of the imperial title Autocrator, and dubbed the Perean city of Betharamphtha as Julias, after Augustus' wife (*Ant.* 18.27). He built a new city, Tiberias, to serve as capital of Galilee (*Ant.* 18.36-38; *J.W.* 2.168). In Philip's territory, Bethsaida became Julias and Paneas became Caesarea Philippi (*Ant.* 18.28). Sepphoris, Tiberias, and Caesarea Philippi all displayed basic organizational and architectural elements of the eastern Roman city, though considerably less so in the first century C.E. than in later centuries.

Roman Troops

For the most part, only small contingents of locally raised Roman auxiliary troops were regularly assigned to Palestine in the period between Herod the Great and the First Revolt. In 70 C.E., however, the Legio X Fretensis was stationed in Judea as a long-term garrison. By the early decades of the second century, it had been joined by the Legio VI Ferrata, stationed in the Jezreel Valley and southern Galilee. Unsurprisingly, Roman cultural influence in Palestine grew with the arrival of thousands of Roman soldiers and support personnel. The sole prerevolt Roman colony at Ptolemais was joined by sister colonies at Caesarea Maritima and in 132 C.E. at Jerusalem, renamed Aelia Capitolina. Epigraphic evidence shows that Caesarea adopted a Roman-style government with decurions and *duumviri*, and the other Roman colonies probably did likewise. In the late second and the third centuries, other major cities also received the status of colony. Numerous cities adopted honorific names, such as Joppa, which added the name Flavia in honor of the emperor, and Sepphoris, which became Diocaesarea, honoring both the emperor and Zeus.

Urban Architecture and Planning

In the second and later centuries C.E., Greco-Roman-style urban architecture and civic planning flourished in the region's larger cities. The layout of several cities, such as Ashkelon, Sepphoris, and Neapolis, included cardos and decumani, the major north-south and east-west thoroughfares typical of the Roman city. Roman-style theaters, bathhouses, nymphea (monumental fountains), and basilical buildings appeared at many cities, and some also received sports architecture such as Roman circuses and amphitheaters or Hellenistic stadiums and hippodromes (Segal 1997). Roman soldiers likely did much of the construction work for these structures; financial sponsors may have ranged from local and provincial elites to Roman governors. In some cases, the benefactor was the emperor himself (e.g., Hadrian's sponsorship of an aqueduct at Caesarea Maritima).

Synagogue Design

Local benefactors were behind the wave of synagogue construction that began in the late second and the third centuries and lasted until the Muslim conquest in the seventh century. Various sources of architectural inspiration for these synagogues have been suggested, such as temples, triclinia, and basilicas. Identifying a specific progenitor is less important than recognizing the general influence of Greco-Roman culture on their design (i.e., the rectangular shape, the extensive use of columns, and decoration with mosaics, carved stone, and stucco moldings).

Coins

Coinage increasingly reflected Roman sensibilities as the centuries progressed. Although Hasmonean coins had borne both Greek and Hebrew inscriptions, those of Herod the Great had only Greek, as was the norm in the eastern Mediterranean. Herod's coins avoided depicting busts of either the emperor or the king himself as well as images of other living things, such as animals or deities. These choices differentiated Herod's coins from those of many other minting authorities. Although Herod struck his coins on Hellenistic weight standards, other members of the dynasty utilized Roman standards. While some, such as Antipas and Archelaus, avoided human portraits and figural representations, most allowed the use of such images. Images of the emperor and members of his family were common, and coins of Agrippa II, struck at the pagan city of Paneas, went so far as to depict deities. City coins in Palestine likewise reflected the numismatic conventions of the Roman East, with imperial busts, deities, pagan temples, and Greek inscriptions. By the mid-second century C.E., coins of the Jewish cities of Sepphoris and Tiberias were virtually indistinguishable from those of pagan cities.

The coinage of the two Jewish revolts illustrates how a local people might adopt, adapt, and reject aspects of Roman culture. Rather than bearing Greek inscriptions, they bore Hebrew, utilizing an archaic script that symbolically connected the rebels with the ancient Jewish past. Their dating formulas referred not to the year of the current emperor's reign but to the year of the revolt. Inscriptions on coins from the First Revolt also identified their values — shekel, half-shekel, and quarter-shekel — employing a standard that differentiated them from those struck on Roman and Hellenistic standards and establishing them as an alternative to the widely known shekels and half-shekels struck at Tyre. Coins of both revolts bore nonfigural imagery. Those on First Revolt coins included a chalice, amphora, or palm tree; some issued during the Bar Kokhba Revolt depicted a stylized image of the façade of the Jerusalem Temple, probably symbolizing the hope to rebuild it. The designs of the Bar Kokhba coins were struck on coins issued by other authorities; thus, portraits of the emperor were obliterated and Jewish imagery literally replaced pagan imagery (Meshorer 1985 and 2001).

Inscriptions

Palestine reflects the same epigraphic trends as other parts of the empire, with the number of inscriptions rising alongside the increase of Roman cultural influence in general and the presence of Roman troops in particular. As was the norm, the single largest category of inscriptions was apparently that of burial inscriptions. In the early Roman period, most burial inscriptions were in Aramaic or Hebrew, but by the third century C.E., Greek had come to predominate. Thus, at the third- and fourth-century-C.E. Jewish burial complex of Beth She'arim approximately 80 percent of the inscriptions are in Greek. Other types of inscription — civic inscriptions, donor and dedicatory inscriptions, mosaic inscriptions — became more numerous in the second and later centuries, with Greek as the language of choice. Most likely, however, these trends do not fully represent Palestine's linguistic environment, since the language(s) chosen for inscriptions may reflect epigraphic custom and convention more than they reflect the common spoken language(s) of the masses (Chancey 2005). Aramaic, for example, is on the whole underrepresented in Palestine's Roman-period epigraphic corpus, but few scholars would question that it was widely spoken among the Jewish population.

Rome's Economic Impact

The nature of Rome's economic impact on local cultures is contested (Harland 2002). Some scholars have argued that Rome imposed a heavy tax burden, increased the supply of coinage to facilitate collection of those taxes and to encourage debt, and aided the growth of cities to foster the exploitation of peasants and their produce (Crossan and Reed 2001; Horsley 1989 and 1996). Others have questioned whether the economic picture was so bleak (Jensen 2006), citing, for example, a lack of explicit evidence for excessive taxation (Udoh 2005).

Jewish Cultural Resistance

Some developments in Jewish culture might be interpreted at least in part as resistance to Roman culture (Berlin 2002; Richardson and Edwards 2002). Continuation of customs such as circumcision, Sabbath observance, and kashrut helped to foster a distinctive Jewish identity, as did the creation of distinctive artifacts (ossuaries, *mikva'ot,* and stone vessels) and the practices associated with them. The emphasis on halakah throughout Judaism (albeit expressed in often differing interpretations) might be considered an effort to construct and maintain a Jewish identity in an imperial culture, and developments in apocalyptic thought reflected hope for an age in which Roman rule would be no more.

BIBLIOGRAPHY

W. BALL 2001, *Rome in the East: The Transformation of an Empire,* London and New York: Routledge. • A. M. BERLIN 2002, "Romanization and Anti-Romanization in Pre-Revolt Galilee," in *The First Jewish Revolt: Archaeology, History, and Ideology,* ed. A. M. Berlin and J. A. Overman, London and New York: Routledge, 57-73. • G. W. BOWERSOCK 1990, *Hellenism in Late Antiquity,* Ann Arbor: University of Michigan Press. • M. A. CHANCEY 2005, *Greco-Roman Culture and the Galilee of Jesus,* Cambridge: Cambridge University Press. • J. D. CROSSAN AND J. L. REED 2001, *Excavating Jesus: Beneath the Stones, Behind the Texts,* New York: HarperSanFranciso. • P. A. HARLAND 2002, "The Economy of First-Century Palestine: State of the Scholarly Discussion," in *Handbook of Early Christianity: Social Science Approaches,* ed. A. J. Blasi, J. Duhaime, and P.-A. Turcotte, Walnut Creek, Calif.: AltaMira, 511-27. • M. HENGEL 1989, *The "Hellenization" of Judaea in the First Century after Christ,* trans. J. Bowden, London: SCM; Philadelphia: Trinity Press International. • R. A. HORSLEY 1989, *Sociology and the Jesus Movement,* New York: Crossroad. • R. A. HORSLEY 1996, *Archaeology, History, and Society in Galilee: The Social Context of Jesus and the Rabbis,* Valley Forge, Penn.: Trinity Press International. • L. I. LEVINE 1998, *Judaism and Hellenism in Antiquity: Conflict or Confluence?* Peabody, Mass.: Hendrickson. • M. H. JENSEN 2006, *Herod Antipas in Galilee,* Tübingen: Mohr-Siebeck. • R. MACMULLEN 2000, *Romanization in the Time of Augustus,* New Haven: Yale University Press. • Y. MESHORER 1985, *City-Coins of Eretz Israel and the Decapolis in the Roman Period,* Jerusalem: Israel Museum. • Y. MESHORER 2001, *A Treasury of Jewish Coins,* Jerusalem: Yad Ben Zvi; Nyack, N.Y.: Amphora Books. • F. MILLAR 1993, *The Roman Near East: 31 BCE–337 CE,* Cambridge, Mass.: Harvard University Press. • M. MILLETT 1990, *The Romanization of Britain: An Essay in Archaeological Interpretation,* Cambridge: Cambridge University Press. • P. RICHARDSON 1996, *Herod: King of the Jews and Friend of the Romans,* Columbia: University of South Carolina Press. • P. RICHARDSON 2004, *Building Jewish in the Roman East,* Waco, Tex.: Baylor University Press. • P. RICHARDSON AND D. EDWARDS 2002, "Jesus and Palestinian Social Protest," in *Handbook of Early Christianity: Social Science Approaches,* ed. A. J. Blasi, J. Duhaime, and P.-A. Turcotte, Walnut Creek, Calif.: AltaMira, 247-66. • D. W. ROLLER 1998, *The Building Program of Herod the Great,* Berkeley: University of California Press. • S. SCOTT AND J. WEBSTER, EDS. 2003, *Roman Imperialism and Provincial Art,* Cambridge: Cambridge University Press. • A. SEGAL 1997, *From Function to Monument: Urban Landscapes of Roman Palestine, Syria and Provincia Arabia,* Oxford: Oxbow Press. • J. F. STRANGE 1992, "Some Implications of Archaeology for New Testament Studies" in *What Has Archaeology to Do with Faith?* ed. J. H. Charlesworth and W. P. Weaver, Philadelphia: Trinity Press International, 25-39. • J. WEBSTER 2001, "Creolizing the Roman Provinces," *American Journal of Archaeology* 105: 209-225. • F. UDOH 2005, *To Caesar What Is Caesar's: Tribute, Taxes, and Imperial Administration in Early Roman Palestine (63 BCE–70 CE),* Providence, R.I.: Brown Judaic Studies.

MARK A. CHANCEY

Rome

The city of Rome had the largest Jewish community in the western part of the Mediterranean. As early as the first century B.C.E. Jews settled across the Tiber, in Trastevere, Rome's immigrant quarter. From there they spread over the city, with separate communities springing up in the Suburra, the Campus Martius, near the Porta Capena, as well as in the northeastern part of town. Literary and archaeological evidence attests to a continued Jewish presence in Rome well into the fifth century C.E.

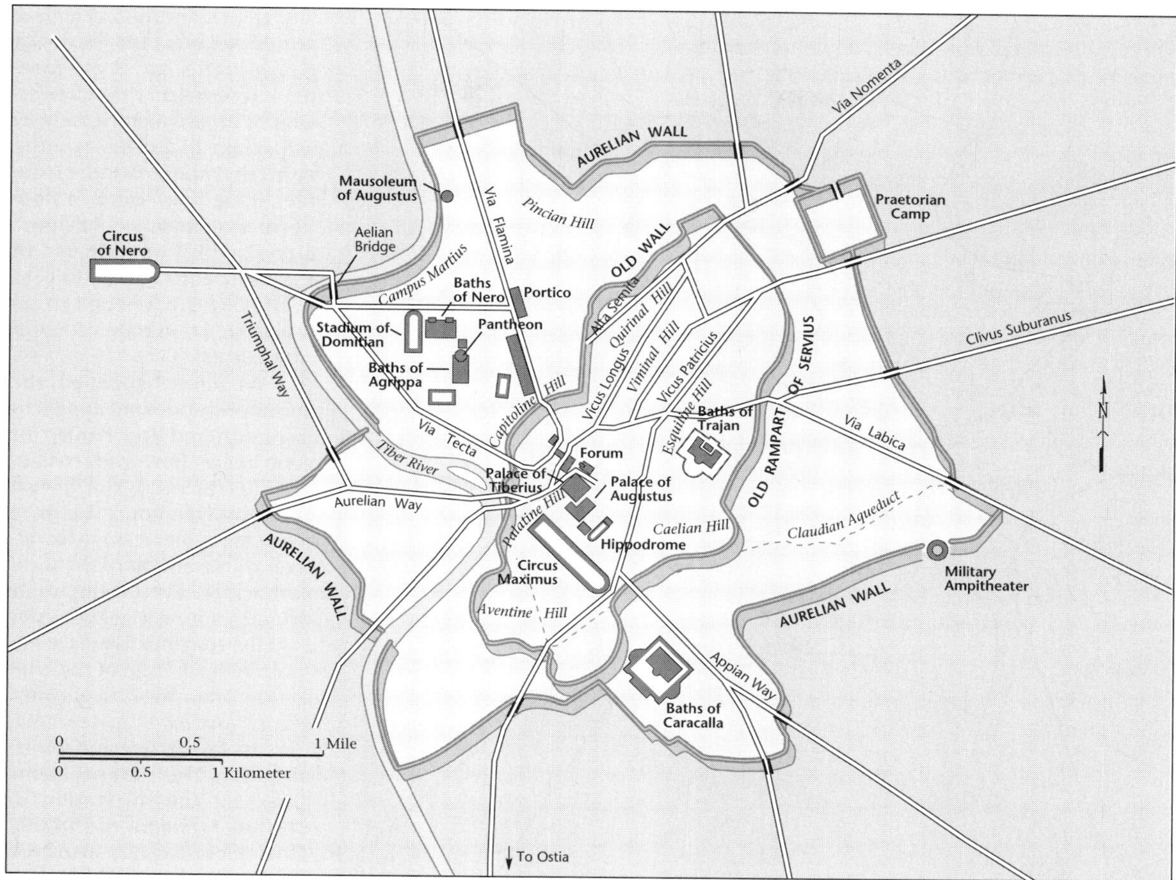

Ancient Rome

Origins of the Jewish Community

The origin of the community is shrouded in mystery. At first, Jews probably came to Rome of their own free will. Later, as a result of Roman military campaigns in the East, Jews also came to Rome as slaves. The funerary inscriptions discovered in the Jewish catacombs of Rome, however, indicate that voluntary immigration to Rome by Jews from all over the Roman Empire continued throughout antiquity. These same funerary inscriptions attest to the existence of no fewer than thirteen distinctive Roman Jewish communities — communities that may or may not all have existed at the same time. The names given by Roman Jews to their respective communities were varied; while some reflect the community's religious composition, others reflect the place of origin or the occupation of its members. Still others reflect the community's topographic location. Estimates of the size of this community have traditionally ranged from 10,000 to 60,000. Recent research carried out in the Jewish catacombs suggests, however, that the average size of the community was considerably lower, at least during the third and fourth centuries C.E. (around 5,000 at best, and possibly even less than that).

To date, no architectural remains bearing on any of these communities have been uncovered in Rome (in nearby Ostia, however, a fairly monumental synagogue, which may have originated in the late first century C.E., was excavated in the 1960s). Still, much Jewish archaeological and epigraphic evidence survives in the form of four Jewish catacombs and two Jewish hypogea (underground buildings) that were constructed by Jews along the city's main arteries including the Via Portuensis, the Via Appia, and the Via Nomentana. Even though most of this highly significant funerary evidence dates to the third and fourth centuries C.E., recent radiocarbon dates from one of the Jewish catacombs suggest that these catacombs may have originated in the first century C.E.

Early History of Jewish Community

As for the community's earliest history, much of our evidence is literary and was mostly produced by non-Jews. It seems that Jews were generally able to live peaceful lives in Rome. Visiting the city in the early first century C.E., the Jewish Alexandrian philosopher Philo reports that Roman Jews were accustomed to gather in *proseuchai* (houses of prayer) and that they were permitted to practice the laws of their fathers (*Legatio ad Gaium* 156). In Rome, Judaism was considered a *religio licita*

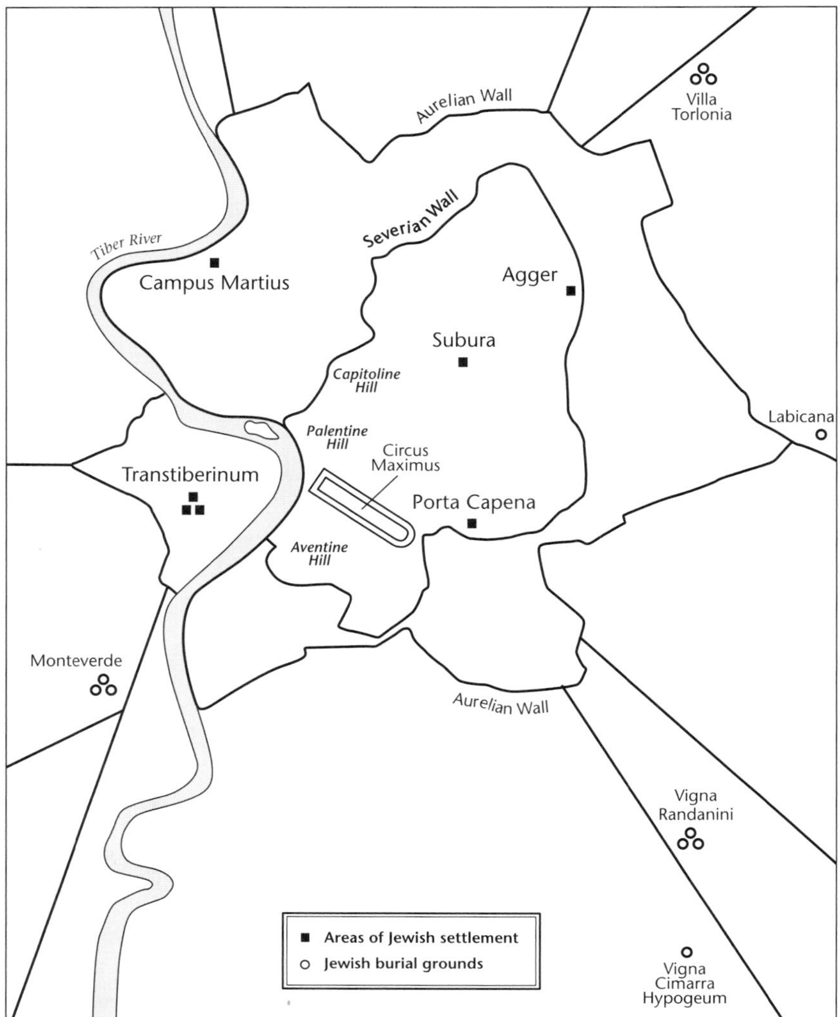

JEWISH COMMUNITIES IN ANCIENT ROME

(tolerated religion) with all that this status entailed. This also follows from an early non-Jewish source indicating that Jews were normally free to send money to the Temple in Jerusalem (Cicero, *Pro Flacco* 66–69). During the first centuries of its existence, the Roman Jewish community was integrated into contemporary society to the extent that some of their communities carried the name of Roman patrons. During this time Roman Jews are even reported to have grieved "for nights on end" at Julius Caesar's bier on the Forum (Suetonius, *Divus Iulius* 84.5).

Conflict with Roman Authorities

In the course of the first century C.E., the Roman Jewish community came into conflict with the Roman authorities twice. The first of these conflicts took place in the reign of Tiberius (14-37 C.E.). Primary sources disagree slightly over what happened and why (Tacitus, *Annales* 2.85:4-5; Suetonius, *Tiberius* 36.1; Josephus, *Ant.* 18.81-85; Cassius Dio 57.18.5). Josephus reports that the conversion of an aristocratic lady by the name of Fulvia was the event that started all the trouble. Some Jews seem to have been expelled to Sardinia, along with worshipers of Egyptian cults (according to Tacitus, this happened to no less than 4,000 men of freedman status).

Whatever happened, the community does not appear to have suffered too badly, for soon thereafter, under Claudius (41-54 C.E.), the Jewish community in Rome was once more tangible enough to attract the attention of the local authorities. Even though our primary sources again differ slightly, religious issues seem again to have been at the core of the conflict (Suetonius, *Divus Claudius* 25.4; Acts 18:2; Cassius Dio 60.6.6; and Orosius 7.16.5). This time problems arose "at the instigation of Chrestus" *(impulsore Chresto).* This reference has attracted an enormous amount of scholarly attention. While some scholars believe that the name Chrestus belongs to a person whose particulars are otherwise lost to history, others have argued that it is a variant of *Christos,* "Christ." Proponents of the latter view thus consider the rise of Christianity to have caused the trouble that then attracted the attention of the Roman authorities. Certainty is impossible. Although a reference to Christianity here is surely conceivable, the matter depends to a great extent on how one evaluates the significance of Rome's early Christianity community (a community about which we know excruciatingly little during this period). However this may be, Jews were once more expelled from Rome. Again, we do not know how many people were involved, or for how long a period of time they were forced into exile. Not all Jews appear to have left the city. Interestingly enough, this time, too, expulsion of Jews coincided with measures against the adherents of other non-Roman cults and creeds.

Jews and Christians in Rome

For the Romans it was the large fire in 64 C.E. that destroyed so much of the city that became the defining

ROME

The Forum in Rome

moment in how to view the Jews and Christians, not only in the capital but elsewhere: while the fire was blamed on the city's Christian population, who then suffered persecution, the Jews were left in peace. By this time, Romans were apparently cognizant of the fact that as groups Jews and Christians were not interchangeable. They apparently also knew how to distinguish the one from the other. Thus the measures of Roman policymakers attest to an awareness of a process of separation between these communities that had been in the making for some time.

Scholars have long argued that contacts between Christians and Jews in Rome continued in a fairly intensive fashion long after the first century C.E. Even though this is correct to some extent, recent research has also revealed that it was during the mid-first century C.E. that Jews and Christians *as social groups* began going their own separate paths: while the Jewish community organized itself around certain social practices and issues of faith that connected it to the other Jewish communities around the Mediterranean, the early Christian community of Rome developed into a separate and different kind of community, one dominated by worshipers with a strong penchant for things Greco-Roman. Thus Rome's early Christian community came to constitute a group of people with different social practices and with different core beliefs.

Later Evidence for the Jewish Community

In the later first century C.E. and beyond, the Roman Jewish community continued to attract the attention of their non-Jewish contemporaries. After the First Jewish Revolt, 700 prisoners of war were paraded through the streets of Rome (Josephus, *Vita* 522–23), and Josephus himself came to the capital as well. Satirists such as Persius, Juvenal, and Martial refer to the community on more than one occasion, suggesting that Roman Jews continued to be part of Rome's cultural cityscape. Toward the end of the first century, the emperor Domitian executed some of his closest relatives and expelled others, the charge being that they had "drifted into Jewish ways" (Cassius Dio 67.14.1-3). Unfortunately, we do not know what precisely is meant by that phrase: does it indicate that a general sympathy for Jewish religious practices had now reached the higher echelons of Rome society?

In the course of the second century, the Jewish community of ancient Rome no longer crops up in pagan literary sources. Early Christian literary sources are also quite reticent. When they are not, their historiographic import is severely limited. Rabbinic literature refers to the Roman Jewish community more than once, but many of these references may not reliably reflect the realities of the daily life of Roman Jews. A rabbinic kind of Judaism did of course manifest itself at Rome, but we do not know when exactly this happened; the evidence from the catacombs seems to suggest that it did not occur in any substantial fashion until the very end of antiquity.

The lack of literary references to the Jews of ancient Rome should not be taken to mean, however, that the Roman Jewish community ceased to exist during this period. Archaeological evidence from Jewish catacombs and hypogea indicates quite clearly that Jews continued to live and thrive throughout the city, well into the early fifth century C.E. The archaeological evidence is particularly important in that it helps to document, once again, the high level of cultural integration of the community on the one hand, and its strong sense of Jewish self-identity on the other.

Jewish Catacombs, Tombs, and Funerary Inscriptions

The Jewish catacombs of Rome may have originated as early as the first century C.E., sometime before their Christian counterparts came into being. Jews began constructing large underground communal cemeteries for the purpose of laying Jews — and Jews only — to rest in a community setting that was specifically Jewish. Most of the tombs in the Jewish catacombs were plain, carrying a simple carved or painted inscription at best. A few more elaborately rendered tombs, however, have also survived. They received wall paintings that are explicitly Jewish in their iconography. Still other members of the community ordered sarcophagi. Some of these were once again decorated with Jewish themes; others display the kind of decorative motifs one commonly encounters on non-Jewish sarcophagi of the period.

Despite their unpretentious formal appearance, the roughly 600 funerary inscriptions constitute a major source of information concerning Roman Jews in late antiquity. These inscriptions tend to celebrate values and ideas that are specifically Jewish. Even so, almost all of them were carved in Greek and Latin rather than in Hebrew or Aramaic. Such inscriptions thus help to document the extent to which the Jewish community of ancient Rome as a whole adapted to Greco-Roman culture, both linguistically and onomastically.

Throughout antiquity, the Jews of Rome never lived in cultural isolation. Even in late antiquity, when the Christianization of the Roman Empire was well underway, Judaism in Rome continued to attract proselytes who were then laid to rest in the Jewish catacombs. While contacts were clearly not one-way, we know very little of how many Jews left the community to become "Romans" instead. However this may be, virtually all the evidence we have suggests that both Roman society and the Roman Jewish community were fairly open for a long period of time. It was only with the rise of Christianity that this began to change.

BIBLIOGRAPHY

J. M. G. BARCLAY 2006, "Reflections on the Demography of the Jewish Community of Ancient Rome," in *Les cités de l'Italie tardo-antique (IVe-VIe siècle)*, ed. M. Ghilardi et al., Rome: École Française de Rome, 345-58. • O. BIRGER ET AL., EDS. 2001, *The Synagogue of Ancient Ostia and the Jews of Rome*, Stockholm: Svenska Institutet i Rom. • H. BOTERMANN 1996, *Das Judenedikt des Kaiser Claudius: Römischer Staat und Christiani im 1. Jh.*, Wiesbaden: Steiner. • S. CAPPELLETTI 2006, *The Jewish Community of Rome from the Second Century B.C. to the Third Century C.E.*, Leiden: Brill. • K. P. DONFRIED AND P. RICHARDSON, EDS. 1998, *Judaism and Christianity in First Century Rome*, Grand Rapids: Eerdmans. • H. J. LEON 1960, *The Jews of Ancient Rome*, Philadelphia: Jewish Publication Society. • M. NANOS 1996, *The Mystery of Romans: The Jewish Context of Paul's Letter*, Minneapolis: Fortress. • D. NOY 1995, *Jewish Inscriptions of Western Europe*, vol. 2, *The City of Rome*, Cambridge: Cambridge University Press. • P. LAMPE 2003, *From Paul to Valentinus: Christians at Rome in the First Two Centuries*, Minneapolis: Fortress. • L. V. RUTGERS 1995, *The Jews in Late Ancient Rome*, Leiden: Brill. • H. D. SLINGERLAND 1997, *Claudian Policy-Making and the Early Imperial Repression of Judaism at Rome*, Atlanta: Scholars Press. • S. SPENCE 2004, *The Parting of the Ways: The Roman Church as a Case Study*, Leuven: Peeters. • M. H. WILLIAMS 2001, "Alexander, Bubularus de Macello: Humble Sausage Seller or Europe's First Identifiable Purveyor of Kosher Meat?" *Latomus* 61: 122-33. • M. H. WILLIAMS 2004, "Being a Jew in Rome: Sabbath Fasting as an Expression of Romano-Jewish Identity," in *Negotiating Diaspora: Jewish Strategies in the Roman Empire*, ed. J. M. G. Barclay, London: Clark, 8-18.

See also: Catacombs LEONARD V. RUTGERS

Rule of Blessings (1QSb)

The *Rule of Blessings* from Qumran (1QSb or 1Q29) is a collection of blessings on different groups and functionaries in Israel. It survives in a single copy of five columns (there was at least one further column), as one of two appendices to the Cave 1 copy of the *Rule of the Community* (1QS), along with the *Rule of the Congregation* (1QSa). Both of these appendices apparently pertain to life in the messianic age following the eschatological restoration. All three texts are sectarian writings of the Qumran community, and this scroll dates to 100-75 B.C.E.

Literary Structure

Much of the content is lost due to the poor condition of this part of the scroll, but the basic structure is clear. The work is a series of blessings on different groups and individuals in ascending hierarchical status, each introduced by the formula "Words of blessing for the Maskil (Instructor), to bless. . . ." As apparent from other texts, the Maskil was a chief functionary in the sectarian community, a master of liturgy, lore and law, whose duty was to instruct community members and perform rituals. The first blessing is on "those who fear God" (1:1), the general membership of the community. After several blessings on unidentified recipients (probably including priests and Levites and tribal leaders) is a blessing on "the Zadokite priests" (3:22). These blessings are based on the priestly blessing of Num. 6:22-27. Next is a blessing on what must be the high priest, since he is dedicated "for the Holy of Holies" (4:28), where only the high priest may enter on the Day of Atonement. In col. 5 is a blessing on an unidentified individual of high status, upon whom is God's Spirit (5:6), and his utterances and splendor inspire fear in those who hear him (5:18-19). This could still be part of the blessing on the high priest, or, if a different individual, perhaps the eschatological prophet like Moses (cf. Deut. 18:15-22). Lastly is a blessing upon "the Prince of the Congregation" (5:20), evidently the royal messiah. The blessing is based on the description of the ideal king in Isaiah 11 who will judge justly and destroy the wicked, and the blessing of Judah as lion and ruler in Gen. 49:9-10. It speaks of the establishment of a kingdom of the people forever, exalting the prince to the eternal heights.

Purpose

The blessings are best interpreted in light of the scroll as a whole. The *Community Rule* describes an annual renewal of the covenant in which the sectarian community is mustered by rank, and blessings are recited over them as the "lot of God" and curses pronounced on apostates and the "lot of Belial" (1QS 2:2-18). The *Rule of the Congregation* (1QSa) depicts the eschatological assembly, seated in hierarchical order before the high priest and royal messiah. In this context, in which there is no lot of Belial to curse, 1QSb gives blessings to be recited over each group and functionary in the eschatological assembly, in hierarchical order. It is unclear whether the blessings are to be recited in the present, in anticipation of the eschatological assembly, much as the community liturgically acted out its union with the heavenly community in the present. There is a possible anti-Hasmonean polemic in the blessing of the high priest, "not by the hand of a prince" (4:24).

Messianism

The blessings in cols. 4-5 are important for understanding the messianic views of the sect, but the evidence is ambiguous. Does the order suggest that the royal messiah has higher status than the eschatological priest, and does this contrast with the apparent precedence of the priest over the Messiah of Israel in 1QSa 2:11-22? Is the unidentified blessing in col. 5 part of the high priest's blessing, so that there are only two messianic figures as also in 1QSa? Or is it a blessing on a third messianic figure between the high priest and the Prince of the Congregation, probably the prophet like Moses?

BIBLIOGRAPHY

J. H. CHARLESWORTH AND L. STUCKENBRUCK 1994, "Blessings (1QSb)," in *Rule of the Community and Related Documents,* Tübingen: Mohr-Siebeck; Louisville: Westminster John Knox, 119-131. • F. GARCÍA MARTÍNEZ 1995, "Messianic Hopes in the Qumran Writings," in *The People of the Dead Sea Scrolls,* ed. F. García Martínez and J. Trebolle Barrera, Leiden: Brill, 159-89. • J. T. MILIK 1955, "Recueil des Bénédictions (1QSb)," in *Qumran Cave I,* ed. D. Barthélemy and J. T. Milik, DJD 1, Oxford: Clarendon, 118-29. • L. SCHIFFMAN 1989, *The Eschatological Community of the Dead Sea Scrolls: A Study of the Rule of the Congregation,* Atlanta: Scholars Press, 72-76. • H. STEGEMANN 1996, "Some Remarks to 1QSa, to 1QSb, and to Qumran Messianism," *RevQ* 17: 479-505.

DANIEL K. FALK

Rule of the Community (1QS + fragments)

The *Rule of the Community* (Hebr. *Serek ha-Yaḥad*) is a document found in caves near Khirbet Qumran off the northwest shore of the Dead Sea. It describes the religious beliefs and practices and organizational rules of a community that called itself the *yaḥad.* The community that produced it is widely identified as belonging to the ancient Jewish movement of the Essenes, some members of which inhabited the site from about 150 B.C.E. (or, as recently argued, ca. 100 B.C.E.) to 68 C.E.

Manuscripts

The *Rule of the Community* is preserved in multiple manuscript copies. A virtually intact manuscript was found in Cave 1 (1QS), ten fragmentary manuscripts in Cave 4 (4QS[a-j]), a pair of small fragments in Cave 5 (5Q11), and possibly a tiny fragment in Cave 11 (11Q29). The manuscripts exhibit both essential agreement and variations in structure and contents, which point not so much to carelessness as to deliberate development in the growth of the work. We will follow the practice of most scholars who typically use the best-preserved manuscript, 1QS, for a comprehensive description of the work, but it is by no means certain that the precise form of the work in this document would have been used widely in the community.

Genre and Contents

Though the title in the first line of 1QS, "Rule of the Community," might suggest that it contains only legal material, it is in fact a composite of various genres, including a theological exposition, liturgical and hymnic sections, and even calendric material. The structure of 1QS is as follows:

1:1-15	Introduction
1:16-3:12	Liturgy for the Renewal of the Covenant
3:13-4:26	Treatise on the Two Spirits
5:1-6:23	Rules for Community Life
6:24-7:25	Penal Code
8:1-9:26a	Segments of Early Rules or "Manifesto"
9:26b-11:22	Final Psalm

1:1-15

The document opens with an introduction emphasizing the Law and the Prophets as the basis for the community's life and teachings. The community, members of which are called "the sons of light," are contrasted with those outside, who are called "the sons of darkness." The members form a covenant community, aiming at "perfection of the way" in its obedience to the To-

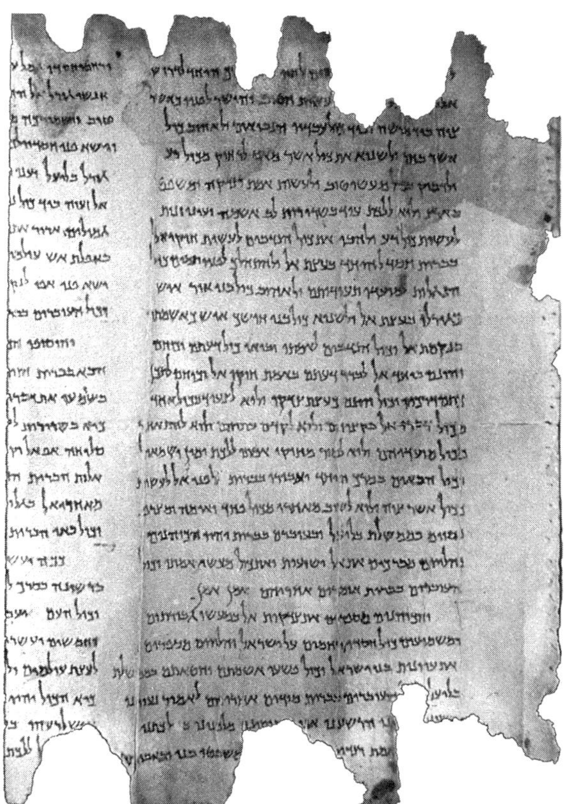

The beginning of the Cave 1 copy of the *Rule of the Community* (1QS) *(John Trever)*

RULE OF THE COMMUNITY (1QS + FRAGMENTS)

rah. They adhere to a solar calendar for their liturgical festivals (which have been "revealed concerning their appointed times") as opposed to the Jerusalem Temple community, which followed a lunar calendar. Another manuscript of the *Rule* (4QS^d) does not have this introduction nor, in fact, any of the material in the first four columns of 1QS.

1:16–3:12

The next section details the annual renewal of the covenant and the entrance ceremony for new members' admission. Blessings and curses, the latter for those who refuse to enter the covenant or do so with an impure heart, structure a ceremony that has been creatively remodeled after scriptural precedents.

3:13–4:26

A section often referred to as the "Treatise on the Two Spirits" — an atypical theological passage — articulates the community's dualistic worldview. Two overlapping and seemingly contradictory frameworks of thought are visible: a cosmological framework, according to which a person belongs either to the realm of the spirit of light or the realm of the spirit of darkness, but also an anthropological or psychological framework, in which a person is simultaneously influenced by both spirits struggling in the heart of each individual. An apocalyptic dimension is evident in the description of the end of the dominion of the spirit of darkness, after which those chosen for the eternal covenant will inherit "the glory of Adam," the paradisiacal condition of the first creation.

5:1–7:25

The next section may be divided into two subsections. The first (5:1–6:23) begins with a rule that provides a window on the ideals and everyday practices of the community. The covenanters take an oath, committing themselves "to return to the Torah of Moses," the proper interpretation of which has been revealed to the priests, the "sons of Zadok," and the "the multitude of the men of the community." The specific rules that follow stipulate separation from outsiders and present regulations for the meetings of the full members of the community (*ha-rabbîm,* "the many") and for acceptance of new members. The manuscripts 4QS^b and 4QS^d provide a shorter and perhaps more original form of the text for these columns.

The second subsection (6:24–7:25) contains a casuistic penal code detailing the rules that govern the life of the community. This collection of rules is heterogeneous, apparently collected incrementally, and compiled from individual judicial proceedings in the meetings of "the many." The offenses listed incur penalties ranging from ten days to permanent expulsion.

8:1–9:26a

Early scholars called the next section a "manifesto" or "program" of the community, arguing that it originated in the period before the community was established and that it formed the nucleus around which the remainder of the material in the document accumulated. The evidence from Cave 4, however, now complicates that interpretation of this section, for 4QS^e does not contain the material in 1QS 8:15–9:11. The section begins with an introduction comparable to the one in col. 5 and is followed by a penal code exhibiting some differences from the one in col. 6. The latter part of col. 9 includes two sections addressed to a community official called "the wise leader" *(ha-maśkîl).*

9:26b–11:22

The Cave 1 manuscript closes with a hymn that provides an intimate portrait of the piety of the community. A calendric section cataloguing the times of prayer turns into a prayer reminiscent of the community's *Thanksgiving Hymns.* 4QS^e, however, has an alternate calendric text, called *'Ôtôt* ("signs"), in place of the entire calendar-hymn in 1QS.

Textual Development and Relationship to History

Evidence of parallel editions and developing editorial stages can be detected within and among the preserved copies of the *Community Rule.* The variants in the diverse manuscripts provide a key for tracing developments in the history of the community. The analytical process is complicated, however, by the observation that even the earliest forms of the document are already compilations of various passages that apparently originated in different settings at different times. Thus, it is difficult to use any particular form of the document as a reliable historical source for the community's ideas and practices at any given time.

The best-preserved manuscript, 1QS, is dated to ca. 100-75 B.C.E. The manuscripts 4QS^b and 4QS^d, which were copied around a half century later, preserve a shorter version of the document than 1QS. The direction of textual development — whether a shorter version developed into a longer one, or vice versa — has been a subject of lively debate. For example, Philip Alexander (1996) assumes that the order in which the manuscripts were copied reflects the order in which the different recensions were produced. Thus, he considers 4QS^{b,d} the result of intentional omissions from the longer document. Most scholars, however, agree with the view originally expressed by J. T. Milik that the shorter text as in 4QS^{b,d} represents an earlier form of the document from which 1QS developed. This means that the earlier versions (in 4QS^{b,d}) continued to be copied long after the later version (in 1QS) had been produced, and there never existed a single, up-to-date, authoritative version of the *Community Rule* that supplanted all other versions. Thus, the transmission process of community manuscripts paralleled that of biblical manuscripts, which allowed the coexistence of older textual traditions side by side with newer ones.

Indicators within the text also do not support the notion of a single accepted version of the work. 1QS, for example, contains three different penal codes and two sections describing the admission of new members. The disparity between different regulations and punishments indicates that older sections were not omitted from the composition as new rules were created. In this respect, the work was "cumulative" rather than "current." It is difficult to know which regulation or punishment was followed at any particular time, although redaction-critical analysis occasionally provides an indication of the comparative age of each practice.

Close analysis of the texts reveals the existence of parallel editions, developing editorial stages, and cross-influence among different Essene documents. These features make it difficult to link the text with the precise historical realities lying behind it. Though not all agree, it appears that the *Community Rule* was "postscriptive" rather than "prescriptive": it was not a law code of prescribed behavior but a postfactum record of accumulating judicial decisions. It is possible that the primary form of transmitting the community traditions was oral, entrusted to the priests and the *rabbîm,* and that the written forms were secondary. The traditions may have been written down for archival purposes and for the education of new members. This hypothesis could explain the presence of parallel and contradictory regulations even within a single manuscript.

Relationship with Other Writings

A number of other Essene writings show a cross-influence with the *Rule of the Community.* Sections of the work are quoted in Cave 4 manuscripts of the *Damascus Document* (4Q266 frg. 10 and 4Q270 frg. 7), the *Miscellaneous Rules* (4Q265), a manuscript entitled simply the *Rule* (5Q13), and possibly the *Ritual of Marriage* (4Q502 frg. 16). Other manuscripts related to the *Community Rule* are *Rebukes Reported by the Overseer* (4Q477), *Communal Ceremony* (4Q275), and *Four Lots* (4Q279). Attached to the scroll of 1QS were two other texts, the *Rule of the Congregation* (1QSa) and the *Words of Blessing* (1QSb), which may be seen either as two independent works or as appendices to 1QS.

The ethos of the Hebrew Bible permeates the entire Qumran corpus, so it is not surprising that the *Community Rule* is thoroughly imbued with biblical diction and concepts. This "anthological style" — the result of constant study and meditation on the Scriptures by those who authored this document — is common in Second Temple period literature. When a direct quotation of Scripture does appear, it usually acts as a kind of proof text, and this is the case with the three quotations we find in the *Community Rule:* 1QS 5:13b-16a; 6:16b-19a; 8:12b-16a. They are used to bolster and justify the need for separation from outsiders. Surprisingly, the three quotations present in 1QS are not found in 4QS[b,d].

Although the question of possible direct influence between the *Rule of the Community* and other ancient writings has received little study so far, scholars have pointed out indirect affinities with Josephus' description of the Essenes as well as with the language, practice, and thought of the early Christians. The parallels between 1QS and Josephus number over thirty (most of them are in *J.W.* 2.119-61), among them detailed descriptions of the procedure of entry into the community, the pooling of wealth, strict hierarchical order, common meals, and ritual washings. The parallels are such that the burden of proof rests with those who argue that the Qumran group was not Essene. With the writings of the New Testament, similarities can be seen in the areas of community structures and practices (e.g., *ha-rabbîm,* "the many"; *ha-mĕbaqqer/episkopos,* "overseer/bishop"; ritual washings/baptisms; pooling of wealth; and communal meals); Greek equivalents of Hebrew and Aramaic expressions (e.g., "the works of the law" and "the righteousness of God"); literary forms (e.g., lists of virtues and vices); and certain concepts and theological ideas (esp. dualism and messianism). Particularly striking is the use of Isa. 40:3 as a motivational passage from Scripture, by the Essenes for withdrawal into the desert to live a life of perfection according to the Torah, by the evangelists for John the Baptist in the desert proclaiming a baptism for the forgiveness of sins and the advent of the kingdom of God.

BIBLIOGRAPHY

P. S. ALEXANDER 1996, "The Redaction-History of Serekh ha-Yaḥad: A Proposal," *RevQ* 17: 437-56. • P. S. ALEXANDER AND G. VERMES 1998, *Qumran Cave 4,XIX: Serekh ha-yaḥad and Two Related Texts,* DJD 26, Oxford: Clarendon. • S. D. FRAADE 1993, "Interpretive Authority in the Studying Community at Qumran," *JJS* 44: 46-69. • C. HEMPEL 1999, "Community Structures in the Dead Sea Scrolls: Admission, Organization, Disciplinary Procedures," in *The Dead Sea Scrolls after Fifty Years,* vol. 2, ed. P. W. Flint and J. C. VanderKam, Leiden: Brill, 67-92. • M. A. KNIBB, *The Qumran Community,* Cambridge: Cambridge University Press, 77-144. • A. R. C. LEANEY 1966, *The Rule of Qumran and Its Meaning: Introduction, Translation and Commentary,* London: SCM. • S. METSO 1997, *The Textual Development of the Qumran Community Rule,* Leiden: Brill. • S. METSO 2007, *The Serekh Texts,* London: Clark. • C. A. NEWSOM 2004, *The Self as Symbolic Space: Constructing Identity and Community at Qumran,* Leiden: Brill. • E. QIMRON AND J. H. CHARLESWORTH 1994, "Cave IV Fragments (4Q255-264 = 4QS MSS A-J)," in *The Dead Sea Scrolls,* vol. 1, *Rule of the Community and Related Documents,* Tübingen: Mohr-Siebeck; Louisville: Westminster John Knox, 53-103. • M. WEINFELD 1986, *The Organizational Pattern and the Penal Code of the Qumran Sect: A Comparison with Guilds and Religious Associations of the Hellenistic-Roman Period,* Göttingen: Vandenhoeck & Ruprecht.

SARIANNA METSO

Rule of the Congregation (1Q28a)

The *Rule of the Congregation* or *Serekh ha-ʿEdah* (1Q28a or 1QSa) is an early Jewish rule text fragmentarily preserved in the library of the Qumran community. It is part of the same scroll that contains the *Rule of the Community* (1QS). Eight or perhaps nine fragments of the work, written in cryptic script, have been identified among the remains of Cave 4 (Pfann 2000: 36). However, these fragments are so sparse that their identification must remain hypothetical.

The work is sometimes called the *Messianic Rule* because the perspective of the text is markedly more eschatological than that of the *Rule of the Community.* The title used by the original editor (Barthélemy 1955), *Rule of the Congregation,* is better since it is used in the text itself ("and this is the rule for all the congregation of Israel," 1Q28a 1:1).

The manuscript 1Q28a dates paleographically to about 100-75 B.C.E. (Barthélemy 1955: 107-8). The alleged Cave 4 fragments of the work have been dated to the second century B.C.E. (Pfann 2000), but caution is necessary because neither the relationship of these fragments to 1Q28a nor the absolute chronology of the cryptic script at Qumran is settled.

Provenance

In its present form, 1Q28a is a so-called sectarian composition, the product of the Qumran community. Some think that 1:6–2:10 is pre-Qumranic and that it underwent a Zadokite recension when accepted by the sectarians at Qumran. Most scholars, however, content themselves with a broader, paleographical dating. We may note the relationship of this writing with the *Rule of the Community;* some passages of 1QS are clearly alluded to or reworked here. The relationship of 1Q28a with such sectarian compositions as the *War Scroll* or the *Damascus Document* is also important.

Contents

The introduction of the text (1:1-5) declares that it sets forth the "rule of the congregation of Israel in the last days." All those who join the community pledge to abide by the law of the sons of Zadok, the priests. The assembly includes women and children. The next section (1:6-19) outlines the stages of life of the members of the community. At the age of twenty, a man is old enough to have sexual relations and to assist in hearing cases. At age twenty-five, he can serve in the community, and at age thirty he can assume a position of leadership. The next section (1:19-22) lists those who are disqualified from service in the community for reasons of age or mental incompetence. The text then designates the Sons of Levi as the leaders of the community (1:22-25a) before describing the convocation of the entire assembly in the presence of the priestly and royal messiahs (1:25–2:10). The text ends with a description of the eschatological banquet (2:11-22).

Interpretation and Importance

In the first four decades of Qumran research, scholars interpreted 1Q28a nearly unanimously as an eschatological composition. However, recent research assumes that the work had a rather complicated prehistory. It seems that 1Q28a in its present form was compiled from two originally distinct parts and that its primitive form lacked any eschatological emphasis (Hempel 1996). In 1:6–2:11 the organization and customs of an existing community are treated without any eschatological allusion. This material has close connections with the legislative part of the *Damascus Document* and is a very early work, perhaps even antedating the emergence of the *Rule of the Community.* The rest of the document should be divided into two parts. 1Q28a 1:1-3 + 2:11-22 is an independent treatise on the eschatological banquet, while 1Q28a 1:4-5 originated when the two main parts were compiled. The two main parts of the work were not originally connected, and the part that contains the general communal legislation was not an eschatological document.

The eschatological part of the text that describes the "messianic meal" presents two eschatological protagonists, both called "anointed one" *(mašiaḥ).* One of these is a royal figure, the other a priest. The priestly protagonist appears as the head of the eschatological community and presides over the cultic assembly of the community. The royal figure is portrayed as having a subordinate rank, at least in cultic matters.

The text applies the language of procreation (*yôlîd,* "begets") to the relationship between the royal protagonist and God (but the reading is disputed). In doing so, it appears to use the adoptionist language of an Israelite royal coronation formula (cf. Psalm 2). The royal figure, the protagonist in 2:12, is called *hammašiaḥ* ("the anointed one"). By labeling him in this way, the author of the text uses the word *mašiaḥ* in a titular sense to refer to an eschatological royal figure — the very first such usage in the entire history of the term.

BIBLIOGRAPHY

D. BARTHÉLEMY 1955, "Règle de la Congrégation," in *Qumran Cave 1,* DJD 1, Oxford: Clarendon, 108-18. • J. H. CHARLESWORTH AND L. T. STUCKENBRUCK 1994, "Rule of the Congregation," in *The Dead Sea Scrolls: Hebrew, Aramaic, and Greek Texts with English Translations,* vol. 1, *Rule of the Community and Related Documents,* Tübingen: Mohr-Siebeck; Louisville: Westminster John Knox, 108-17. • C. HEMPEL 1996, "The Earthly Essene Nucleus of 1QSa," *DSD* 3: 253-69. • S. PFANN 2000, "4Q249a-z and 4Q250a-j: Introduction" and "4Qpap cryptA 4QSerekh ha-ʿEdah[a-i]," in *Qumran Cave 4.XXVI: Cryptic Texts and Miscellanea, Part 1,* DJD 36, Oxford: Clarendon, 515-74. • L. H. SCHIFFMAN 1989, *The Eschatological Community of the Dead Sea Scrolls: A Study of the Rule of the Congregation,* Atlanta: Scholars. • G. G. XERAVITS 2003, *King, Priest, Prophet: Positive Eschatological Protagonists of the Qumran Library,* Leiden: Brill.

GÉZA G. XERAVITS

Ruth, Book of

In the Hebrew Bible, Ruth belongs to the writings *(Ketuvim).* In the Jewish tradition, Ruth is one of the five Festival Scrolls *(Megillot)* used as readings at Jewish festivals. While one strand of tradition presents the festival scrolls chronologically starting with Ruth (*b. Baba Batra* 14b, slightly varied in ms. B 19[A] Leningrad and *Biblia Hebraica Stuttgartensia*), the liturgical ordering positions Ruth in second place after the Song of Songs (cf. *Miqra'ot Gedolot*). The Old Greek translation, Josephus (*Ag. Ap.* 1.8; *Ant.* 5.9), and the Christian canon place Ruth among the historical writings after the book of Judges. Reasons for this location are the introductory note that situates the story in premonarchic times (1:1), the genealogy that mentions Ruth's husband Boaz as great-grandfather of David (4:18-22), and the ancient ascription of Ruth to Samuel (*b. Baba Batra* 14b). Despite this early dating, the plot, theology, and use of legal traditions suggest a later formation.

The Postexilic Origin of the Book

Since the dating of Ruth is highly disputed among modern scholars, a summary of the most relevant arguments for a postexilic dating seems appropriate. The note in 1:1 presupposes the Deuteronomistic terminology and idea of premonarchic Israel (cf. 2 Kings 23:22). The note on former custom in 4:7 attests to a gap between the alleged time of the story and the time of the author. The genealogy of King David in 4:18-22 uses the term *tôlĕdôt,* a keyword of the exilic priestly strand in the Pentateuch. The artful prose and congruent plot of the story distinguish Ruth from the narratives in Genesis, Judges, and 1-2 Samuel. As a novel, Ruth resembles writings such as Jonah and Esther. Contrary to other narratives, the female main characters, their dialogues, and actions in Ruth mark out an unusual female perspective on matters of family ties and survival.

The main reasons for a late dating, however, are the extent of Ruth's allusions and literary parallels to other stories of Israel's origin as well as the book's interpretation of the legal stipulations in Deuteronomy 22–25. The book of Ruth explicitly alludes to Gen. 33:9 (2:13) and Genesis 38 (4:12) in order to add Ruth to the Israelite matriarchs (cf. also 4:11). In 2:11, Boaz describes Ruth's journey in wording that reminds the reader of God's call to Abraham (Gen. 12:1). Naomi's blessing of Boaz (2:20) parallels the blessing in Gen. 24:27. Moreover, literary parallels to the book(s) of Samuel equate Ruth's pledge of love (1:16-17) and Jonathan's (1 Sam. 20:12-13, 17) and correlate the encounter of Ruth and Boaz (2:10; 3:10) with the meeting of David and Abigail (1 Sam. 25:23, 32-33). Deuteronomy 23:4-7 excludes the Moabites from the Israelite assembly because they did not feed Israel but hired Balaam to curse them. In contrast, Ruth provides the daily bread for Naomi and is a blessing to her Israelite mother-in-law through her care and love. The book of Ruth creatively combines the levirate duty (Deut. 25:5-10) and the duty of redemption (Deut. 25:23-34). While Naomi sends Ruth to the threshing floor in order to seduce Boaz into marriage, Ruth confronts him as a *gô'ēl,* "redeemer" (3:9), and Boaz connects both legal issues in the presence of the elders (4:1-10). Thus, the author of Ruth presents levirate marriage and redemption as a duty of solidarity for women (Fischer in Brenner 1999: 24-49, 47).

The Discourse on Foreignness and Proselytism

Ruth offers a short story of homecoming and new beginnings. The two female protagonists manage to reclaim Naomi's inherited land at Bethlehem and to found a new family that carries on the lineage of Naomi. Ruth is characterized as an agile Moabite who clings to her Judean mother-in-law, venerates the God of Israel, and endorses Judean family values. Because of Ruth's care for Naomi, the law against Moabites (Deut. 23:4-7) no longer applies to her. Therefore, Ruth is admitted to the group of praiseworthy matriarchs. By means of a highly positive portrait of the faithful and God-fearing Moabite woman, the story counters the claim that postexilic Judeans should separate from foreigners and divorce their foreign wives (cf. Ezra 8–10; Nehemiah 13). Later Jewish interpretations of Ruth confirm foreignness and conversion to the Torah as main issues of the book.

Reception and Use as a Festival Scroll

The Old Greek translation of Ruth generally conforms to the Hebrew text attested in the MT. Most variants are due to the translator's orientation toward the receptor language. The canonical status of Ruth is asserted in *b. Megillah* 7a and reaches back to the second century C.E. Ruth is also attested in four fragmentary Hebrew manuscripts of Qumran, which mainly concur with the consonantal text of the MT. Although the medieval Aramaic translation (Targum) of Ruth paraphrases and expands the story, it affirms the MT. Both the Targum and *Ruth Rabbah,* an exegetical midrash compiled in the sixth century C.E., treat the Moabite woman as a model proselyte and perfect example of loyalty, modesty, and integrity. From the fact that Naomi asks Ruth three times to return to Moab (1:8-15), the rabbis drew the idea that a proselyte should be repulsed three times.

The earliest witness to the use of Ruth as a festival scroll consists in the posttalmudic tractate *Soferim* 14:18. The association of Ruth with the Festival of Weeks (Shavuʿot) is based on the mentioning of the grain harvest (1:22; 2:23), the traditional belief that David was born and died on Shavuot (*t. Ḥagigah* 17a; *y. Beṣah* 2:4) as well as the idea that Israel accepted the Torah on Shavuot and thus parallels Ruth's claim to the Torah. In modern Jewish liturgy, Ruth is read on Shavuot at the *shakharit* service prior to the reading of the Torah; in Diaspora synagogues, it is read on the second day of Shavuot.

BIBLIOGRAPHY

D. R. G. BEATTIE 1977, *Jewish Exegesis of the Book of Ruth,* Sheffield: JSOT Press. • A. BRENNER 1999, *Ruth and Esther: A Feminist Companion to the Bible,* Sheffield: Sheffield Academic Press. • E. F. CAMPBELL 1975, *Ruth,* Garden City, N.Y.: Doubleday. • D. N. FEWELL AND D. M. GUNN 1990, *Compromising Redemption: Relating Characters in the Book of Ruth,* Louisville: Westminster John Knox. • I. FISCHER 1999, "The Book of Ruth: A 'Feminist' Commentary on the Torah," in A. Brenner, *Ruth and Esther, a Feminist Companion to the Bible,* 24-49. • A. LACOCQUE 2004, *Ruth,* Minneapolis: Augsburg Fortress. • K. NIELSEN 1997, *Ruth: A Commentary,* Louisville: Westminster John Knox. • J. M. SASSON 1989, *Ruth: A New Translation with a Philological Commentary and a Formalist-Folklorist Interpretation,* 2d ed., Sheffield: Sheffield Academic Press.

CHRISTL M. MAIER

S

Sabbath

In biblical law, the seventh day of the week is a holy day and appointed time, to be observed as a complete rest from work for all Israelites, slaves, resident aliens, and livestock (Exod. 20:8-11; 23:12; Deut. 5:12-15). The humanitarian orientation of Sabbath — freedom from exploitation — is grounded theologically in the nature of God's creation (Gen. 2:2-3; Exod. 20:11; 31:17) and historically in God's redemption of Israel from slavery (Deut. 5:12-15). It is said to be a "sign" of God's covenant with Israel (Exod. 31:13-17; Ezek. 20:12), and in this way sets Israel apart. The penalty for profaning it is death (Exod. 31:15; 35:2; Num. 15:32-36). But the Torah gives very little guidance about what constitutes work forbidden on the Sabbath. The laws expressly forbid only the kindling of fire (Exod. 35:3) and work related to plowing and harvesting (Exod. 34:21). One case treats the gathering of wood as profaning the Sabbath (Num. 15:32-36), and from the narrative about manna (Exod. 16:5, 22-30) one might infer a prohibition on travel and food preparation on the Sabbath. The prophets and Nehemiah specify further acts that profane the Sabbath: selling (Amos 8:5), pursuing personal interests (Isa. 58:13-14), carrying burdens in or out of a house or city (Jer. 17:19-27), treading wine presses, loading and transporting goods, and selling goods (Neh. 13:15-22). Biblical passages attest regular disregard of the Sabbath during the time of the monarchy and the postexilic community, which they regard as a major breach of Israel's covenant contributing to the Exile (Jer. 17:27; Neh. 13:18). Isaiah declares that the Sabbath is to be honored as a delight (Isa. 58:13) and welcomes proselytes and eunuchs who keep it (Isa. 56:3-7).

In the Temple, the Sabbath was marked by special offerings in addition to the daily offerings (Num. 28:9-10) and a fresh batch of twelve loaves of bread (Lev. 24:8; 2 Chron. 9:32). The Chronicler mentions songs of praise by the Temple singers on the Sabbath as well as festivals (1 Chron. 23:30-31), and the heading for Psalm 92 designates it as "A Song for the Sabbath."

Sabbath Observance in the Greco-Roman Period

During the Greco-Roman period, observance of Sabbath was one of the most prominent boundary markers setting Jewish communities apart from Gentiles, along with circumcision and food laws. There is fairly consistent testimony throughout the Mediterranean world of local assemblies on Sabbath for reading and study of Torah and praise to God (Philo, *Moses* 2.215; Ps.-Philo, *Bib. Ant.* 11:8; Josephus, *Ag. Ap.* 1.209; 2.175; cf. *Ant.* 12.4-6; Luke 4:16-17; Acts 13:14-15). The synagogue could be called a "Sabbath house" (Josephus, *Ant.* 16.164). Sabbath was well known among Gentiles, so that attacks on Jews were often timed to the Sabbath, when Jews would be at rest and not fight (e.g., 1 Macc. 9:32; 2 Macc. 5:25-26; Josephus, *Ag. Ap.* 1.209). Sabbath observance was a source of considerable tension with Gentiles. Jewish communities throughout the Mediterranean world went to great lengths to gain exemptions from work and rights to observe Sabbath, including freedom from military service and appearing in court, restrictions on travel and preparation of food, and right to assemble (e.g., a papyrus from mid-third-century-B.C.E. Egypt, *CPJ* 10; Agatharchides [second century B.C.E.] quoted by Josephus [*Ag. Ap.* 1.209]; *Ant.* 13.249-52; 14.225-27, 241-46, 257-58, 263-64; 16.27-28, 45, 163, 168). Greco-Roman writers frequently lampooned Sabbath rest as evidence that the Jews were lazy (e.g., Tacitus, *Histories* 5.4.3; Juvenal, *Satires* 14.96-106). Sabbath was also a major source of disputes among Jewish groups. Some advocated lessening or even abolishing Sabbath strictures that made life difficult in the Hellenistic world, but others sought to strengthen Sabbath laws. The books of Maccabees (e.g., 1 Macc. 1:43-45; 2 Macc. 6:6) describe this division reaching a crisis during the reign of Antiochus IV Epiphanes (175-164 B.C.E.). When Antiochus outlawed Sabbath observance, the pious traditionalists who rallied around the Maccabees at first refrained from self-defense on the Sabbath. After devastating losses they established a precedent that defense of life — as distinct from offensive military action — is not a desecration of the Sabbath (1 Macc. 2:31-41; 9:32, 43-46). This precedent was widely accepted (*Ant.* 12.277; 14.63).

Throughout the Greco-Roman period, there was considerable effort to define Sabbath laws more precisely.

Sabbath in the Book of Jubilees

The book of *Jubilees* (ca. 150 B.C.E.) makes the Sabbath a central concern and is framed with instructions about Sabbath (chaps. 2 and 50). It presents Sabbath as the basic unit of God's time. The angels observe Sabbath with God in heaven. Sabbath is the basis of both the seasons of the year in the 364-day solar calendar and the flow of history in the chronology of jubilee periods. The author systematically dates festivals and activities of the patriarchs to avoid conflict with the Sabbath. Transgressing God's time — Sabbaths and festivals — is the cardinal sin, and profaning Sabbath merits the death penalty.

The Sabbath laws in *Jubilees* (2:17-32; 50:6-13) are very strict. In addition to prohibitions mentioned or implied in Scripture (pursuing one's own interests, preparing food or drink, carrying items in or out of a city or dwelling, setting out on a journey, selling or buying, tilling, kindling a fire), they prohibit lifting a load, drawing water, eating or drinking anything not prepared the preceding day, riding an animal, sexual intercourse, talking about work, traveling by ship, striking or killing, slaughtering or trapping an animal, fasting, and making war. The ban on sexual intercourse is probably due to concerns of ritual purity (cf. Exod. 19:14-15); by contrast, the rabbis later viewed sexual intercourse as an appropriate Sabbath activity. Besides the ban on fasting, *Jubilees* emphasizes positively that the Sabbath is a feast day, for eating and drinking and praise to God as creator (2:21; 50:10; cf. Jdt. 8:6; *Apocalypse of Moses* 43). Festival offerings are not allowed on the Sabbath, only the daily and Sabbath offerings. The Sabbath is especially associated with God's kingdom (50:9) and is for Israel alone, not Gentiles (2:31).

Qumran and Dead Sea Scrolls

Incorporated into the *Damascus Document* (CD 10:14–11:18, with fragmentary parallels in 4Q266, 267, 270, 271) is a code of Sabbath laws that shows strong continuity with *Jubilees* but that is more developed and has some different positions. There is an evident attempt to develop a systematic application of laws in each category based on interpretation of the scriptural data, but the distinctive Sabbath laws belong to the "hidden things" revealed only to the sect (CD 3:12-16), which other Jews transgress. The strict laws seem generally in line with the testimony of Philo (*Quod Omnis Probus Liber Sit* 81) and Josephus (*J.W.* 2.147) on the Essenes. Within the sect, offenders of Sabbath law are not to be put to death but kept in custody; they can be rehabilitated after seven years of probation (CD 12:3-6).

According to this code, labor is to cease about thirty minutes before sunset on Friday, presumably to guard against accidental infraction. The ban includes discussing or planning work, and even handling stones or earth. The prohibition of work for servants is extended to forbid provoking an employee or servant, a nurse carrying an infant from one domain to another, or sending a Gentile to do business on one's behalf. The ban on transporting burdens prohibits moving items into or out of temporary shelters as well as houses, and even carrying a perfume bottle on one's person. Concerning food, one is to eat only what is prepared beforehand, and only in the camp. It is thus forbidden to open a sealed container or draw water with a vessel. It is permissible to eat what is fallen in the field and to drink directly from a source. The limit a person may travel on the Sabbath is 1,000 cubits, although it is permissible to go as far as 2,000 cubits to let an animal graze (one cannot drive it). Apparently, this law is based on defining one's "place" (Exod. 16:29) from the description of the levitical cities (Num. 35:4). Beyond working to earn money, lending and making judgments concerning wealth are also prohibited. It is not permissible to profane the Sabbath for the sake of property or gain, nor assist an animal giving birth or rescue an animal from a pit. One may rescue a person from a pit, but one must not use a tool (cf. 4Q265 frg. 6 lines 6-8). In contrast to Num. 28:10 and *Jubilees*, this code limits Temple sacrifices on the Sabbath to the Sabbath offerings alone. It also forbids vulgar and empty speech, the wearing of filthy clothes, voluntary intermingling (?), and resting in a place near Gentiles.

Four other fragmentary texts (4Q251, 4Q264a, 4Q265, 4Q274, 4Q421) contain some additional Sabbath laws. A restriction on priests from examining skin impurity or sprinkling seems to suggest that the sect believed work by priests on the Sabbath should be limited to tasks specifically for the Sabbath. There are also restrictions on expounding or reading a scroll. A restriction on speech about profane matters clarifies that the Sabbath is for holy words and praise of God.

That praise is the appropriate speech on Sabbath is also reflected in a collection of prayers for days of the week (*Words of the Luminaries*, from ca. mid-second century B.C.E.). There are petitions for each day of the week, but on the Sabbath there is instead a song of praise to God. A collection of mystical songs to accompany the sacrificial service on Sabbaths (*Songs of the Sabbath Sacrifice*) is motivated by the view that the Sabbath is a special day of praise for the angels and that the human community joins this heavenly worship.

Philo

Philo attests that the Sabbath was observed throughout the Diaspora with assembly for reading and study of the Torah, but he also knows of Jews who did not observe Sabbath. He shows knowledge of a body of prohibited activities derived from Scripture, in continuity with those of general Jewish tradition, such as kindling fire, handling wood for fire, picking fruit or leaves, tilling land, carrying burdens, going to court, demanding repayment of deposit or debt, making art, conducting business, and engaging in strenuous mental activity (*Spec. Laws* 2.65-68; *Moses* 2:21-22, 211, 219-220, 251; *Migration of Abraham* 91; *Creation* 128). But he stresses the positive purpose of the Sabbath for assembly, joy, relaxation, study, and reflection (*Spec. Laws* 2.56-139; cf. also *Contemplative Life* 30–36). For Philo as well as

Aristobulus, Sabbath is a universal principle of nature, and Gentiles are welcome to keep it.

Early Christianity

The New Testament Gospels report disputes between Jesus and Pharisees over the observance of Sabbath. The issue was not whether Sabbath should be observed. Consistent with common Jewish practice, Jesus and his followers are presented as observing Sabbath as a day of rest with restrictions on travel (Luke 23:56; Matt. 24:20; Acts 1:12) and for assembling at the synagogue for reading of Scripture and prayer (Mark 1:21; 6:2; Luke 4:16, 31). The dispute was whether acts of helping — specifically healing and feeding — overrule Sabbath even in cases that are not life-threatening (Mark 1:21-34; 2:23–3:6; Matt. 12:1-14; Luke 6:1-11; 13:14-16; 14:1-6). Jesus argues for this extension on the basis of the rescue of animals (Matt 12:11), the priority of human life and the precedent of David (Mark 2:25-27), an extension from preventing death to enhancing life (Mark 3:4), and exemption for circumcision (John 7:22). All of these arguments are within the range of Pharisaic/rabbinic discussion of Sabbath laws, although his conclusion allows more freedom than elsewhere attested.

The author of Acts also attests the centrality of Sabbath assembly for Scripture, instruction, and prayer (Acts 15:21; 16:13; 17:2), but in Gentile contexts Paul treats Sabbath — with holy days in general — as a matter of personal conscience (Rom. 14:5; Gal. 4:10; cf. Col. 2:16).

Early Rabbinic Judaism

The early rabbis were concerned to define and quantify precisely what constitutes a violation of Sabbath and to enunciate underlying principles of law. A lengthy tractate of the Mishnah *(Šabbat)* is devoted to this task, systematically asking for every facet: How much? How far? What kind? It lists thirty-nine classes of prohibited work with many similarities to *Jubilees* and the Dead Sea Scrolls, although showing a tendency toward greater leniency. A major principle is the necessity of preparation before the Sabbath. The Mishnah also defines various mechanisms and legal fictions to make Sabbath law practical, for example the combining of Sabbath limits, treated at length in a separate tractate *(ʿErubin)*. That saving life overrules the Sabbath is attested as an accepted principle among rabbis of the second century (*Mek. Rabbi Ishmael, Shabbat* 1). Early rabbinic sources attest rituals marking out the Sabbath in the home, including the lighting of a Sabbath lamp, prayers to dedicate the start of Sabbath and its end, and a festive meal (*m. Šabbat* 2; *m. Ber.* 8:5; *t. Ber.* 3:7). A special short version of the *ʿAmidah* prayer that replaces the middle supplications with praise for Sabbath is assumed in a debate attributed to the houses of Shammai and Hillel in the first century C.E. (*t. Ber.* 3:12, 13).

BIBLIOGRAPHY

J. M. BAUMGARTEN 2004, "Some Theological Aspects of Second Temple Shabbat Practice," in *Sabbath: Idea, History, Reality,* ed. G. J. Blidstein, Beer Sheva: Ben Gurion University of the Negev Press, 35-41. • D. A. CARSON 1982, *From Sabbath to Lord's Day: A Biblical, Historical, and Theological Investigation,* Grand Rapids: Zondervan. • L. DOERING 1999, *Schabbat: Sabbathalacha und -praxis im antiken Judentum und Urchristentum,* Tübingen: Mohr-Siebeck. • R. GOLDENBERG 1979, "The Jewish Sabbath in the Roman World up to the Time of Constantine the Great," *ANRW* 2.19.1, Berlin and New York: de Gruyter, 414-47. • J. MANN 1914, "The Observance of the Sabbath and the Festivals in the First Two Centuries of the Current Era according to Philo, Josephus, the New Testament and the Rabbinic Sources," *The Jewish Review* 4: 433-56, 498-532. • H. A. MCKAY 1994, *Sabbath and Synagogue: The Question of Sabbath Worship in Ancient Judaism,* Leiden: Brill. • E. P. SANDERS 1990, *Jewish Law from Jesus to the Mishnah: Five Studies,* Philadelphia: Trinity Press International, 6-23. • L. H. SCHIFFMAN 1975, *The Halakhah at Qumran,* Leiden: Brill, 77-133. • H. WEISS 1991, "Philo on the Sabbath," *SPhA* 3: 83-105. • H. WEISS 1998, "The Sabbath in the Writings of Josephus," *JSJ* 29, 4: 363-90.

DANIEL K. FALK

Sacrifices and Offerings

Temples were conceived in the ancient Near East as sanctified loci where deities resided on earth and received their due from worshipers. They were attended by priests and other cultic servants who were responsible for their day-to-day functioning and upkeep. Among the many responsibilities of priestly and nonpriestly temple personnel were the collection, processing, and redistribution of sacrifices and offerings brought to the temple by or on behalf of worshipers.

Persian-Era Biblical Representations

Biblical sources of the Persian period (e.g., the priestly passages [including Holiness materials] in the Pentateuch, Ezra-Nehemiah, and Malachi) are rich in representations of sacrifice. They are a valuable source of information regarding the sacrificial cult during the Second Temple period, given the limitations of other textual corpora and the scant material evidence that survives. We begin with them, though the following three caveats should be noted. First, it is important to keep in mind that such texts vary in their provenance and purpose (e.g., some are prescriptive, some focus on criticizing alleged practices, and some are simply narrative descriptions). Second, they tend to present an image of what sacrificial practice ought to be according to the authors of the texts, an image whose relationship to actual, historical practice remains unclear. Thus, they are anything but an unproblematic window into the day-to-day workings of the cult. Third, a minority of scholars argue that much of the core material of the priestly material in the Pentateuch antedates the sixth century and is therefore not to be dated to the Persian period. According to their viewpoint, priestly representations of cult would not be directly relevant to a discussion of sacrifices and offerings during the Second Temple period.

Purposes for Offering Sacrifice

Biblical texts of the Persian period suggest that worshipers of YHWH might bring him sacrifices and offerings for any number of reasons: because they are required to do so on account of a particular pilgrimage feast such as Shavuot ("Weeks") or Sukkot ("Booths"); because they wish to approach the deity with petitions; because they seek to purify themselves after having become polluted, and sacrifices are mandated as a final component of the purification process; or because they wish to have their transgressions forgiven, to fulfill a vow, to express thanks to YHWH, to honor the deity, or to obtain blessing in exchange for a freely offered gift.

Types of Offerings

Cattle, sheep, and goats without physical defect are represented in biblical texts as the central, and most valuable, offerings of the Judean sacrificial system; clean birds such as the dove, turtledove, and pigeon are also to be brought as offerings, as are grain in various forms, oil, wine, and incense. Salt is mentioned among offerings in several texts (Ezra 6:9; 7:22), as is wood (Neh. 10:35). In some instances, precious metals might be contributed to the sanctuary.

Different types of offerings are attested in biblical sources of the Persian period, among them the firstfruits and firstlings of sacrificial animals; tithes; grain offerings; the whole burnt offering; the purification (or, sin) offering; the reparation (or, guilt) offering; and the well-being (or, peace) offering. Each of these has its appropriate context. For example, both a whole burnt offering and a purification offering are required of a woman completing her purification from the pollution of childbirth according to Lev. 12:6-8; in contrast, a well-being offering is presented by a worshiper who wishes to give thanks to YHWH, as in Lev. 7:12-15.

Levitical Prescriptions

Prescriptive texts in the first seven chapters of Leviticus describe in detail the manner in which each type of offering is to be presented and processed. An example is the well-being offering. The priestly writing in the Pentateuch divides the well-being offering into three subtypes: thanksgiving, vow, or freewill offering. Leviticus 3 and 7 describe its required rites: the worshiper slaughters the defect-free animal, which may be from the herd or flock, male or female, and the priests manipulate its blood and burn its fat and organ meat to the deity. Both the worshiper and the priests share in the cooked meat of the well-being offering, with particular portions reserved for each (the priest receives the right thigh and breast). Thanksgiving offerings require a grain and oil component to accompany the meat sacrifice (e.g., oiled cakes and wafers). Blood manipulation and fat and organ burning take place on the altar of burnt offerings, which stands within the sanctuary precinct. Some sacrifices are to be eaten only by males of the priestly line (e.g., the purification offering); others are to be shared by all members of priestly households (e.g., the elevation offering or firstfruits); still others are to be shared by priest and worshiper (e.g., the well-being offering); finally, there are sacrifices which are the preserve of the deity alone (the whole burnt offering). In all cases, sacrificial blood, fat, and organ meat are set aside for YHWH, the blood to be manipulated by priests, the fat and organ meat to be burned by them on the altar of burnt offerings.

Texts such as Num. 18:19-20 suggest that sacrifices and offerings reserved for priests and their dependents were their primary source of sustenance. In all cases, only persons who were ritually clean or about to complete their purification through sacrifices could enter the sanctuary and participate in its sacrificial rites. Polluted persons, in contrast, are to be excluded from sanctuary space, conceived as holy, and therefore to be protected from all forms of defilement.

Elephantine

Aside from Persian-era biblical representations of the Judean sacrificial cult, several other textual corpora and individual sources contribute significantly to our knowledge of sacrifices and offerings during the Second Temple period. Primary among these are the Elephantine Papyri, from fifth-century-B.C.E. Egypt, the Dead Sea Scrolls of the last centuries B.C.E. and the first century C.E., and the works of the Jewish historian Josephus (first century C.E.).

The Elephantine Papyri, a diverse corpus of documents mainly written in Imperial Aramaic, provide us with a wealth of textual material concerning the offerings and sacrifices of a Judean military colony posted on an island (Elephantine or Yeb) in Upper (or southern) Egypt. This community of Judeans supported its own temple of YHWH, which may have been founded before the Persian king Cambyses' invasion and conquest of Egypt in 525 B.C.E., and remained in operation until it was destroyed by local rivals in 410 B.C.E. (Several documents in the archive claim that the temple was founded before the Persian conquest.) Elephantine texts indicate that the temple was staffed by Judean priests and other, nonpriestly cultic servants. Several letters written after the temple's destruction suggest that animal sacrifices (cattle, goats, sheep), grain offerings, and incense had been presented to YHWH there. These texts use the Hebrew technical vocabulary of sacrifice familiar from biblical sources (e.g., *ʿolâ,* "whole burnt offering"; *minḥâ,* "grain offering"; *lĕbonâ,* "frankincense") as well as their Aramaic equivalents. Gold and silver bowls used in temple rites are also mentioned. One text refers to the Elephantine temple as "the house of the altar of the God of Heaven," alluding indirectly to offering rites performed on the altar; another describes YHWH as "the god who dwells in Elephantine the fortress," indicating the temple's function as the deity's dwelling place on earth.

Other documents in the archive mention offerings of silver from both men and women for YHWH and for several divinized temple attributes (Ishumbaytil, "The Name of the House of God," and Anatbaytil, "The Sign [?] of the House of God"). Many aspects of the Elephantine temple cult resemble those of the cult of YHWH as it is represented in biblical sources of the Persian period such as the priestly strand of the Pentateuch, though distinctive characteristics are also in evidence (e.g., the presence in the Elephantine cult of "temple servitors" [*lahinayya'*], who are not mentioned in biblical sources; and the storing of leaven in sealed containers during Passover, a nonbiblical practice). Unfortunately, no relevant archaeological evidence from the temple cult at Elephantine survives.

The founding of a temple of YHWH in a land other than Israel, likely during the sixth century B.C.E., is a striking thing and worthy of comment, given the strong biblical tradition that alien lands defile ritually, making the establishment of sanctuaries in them theoretically impossible, since the temple sphere is holy space, and what is holy must be guarded from any kind of pollution (see Hos. 9:3; Amos 7:17; Ezek. 4:12-15). A second biblical tradition also militates against the establishment of temples to YHWH in the Diaspora. This is the notion of cult centralization in Jerusalem, promulgated successfully by the end of the seventh century by the Deuteronomistic school, the circle responsible for the book of Deuteronomy and the Deuteronomistic History (Joshua–2 Kings). According to the Deuteronomists, the Temple in Jerusalem was the only legitimate place for the offering of sacrifices to YHWH. Several Judean kings are said to have shut down the other sanctuaries of the land, following the Deuteronomistic program of reform. The very existence of the Elephantine temple of YHWH is therefore most interesting given the strong tradition that alien lands defile ritually, and given the Deuteronomistic ideology of centralization, which evidently had its supporters during the sixth and fifth centuries B.C.E.

The descendants of Judean exiles in Babylon, contemporaries of the Jews at Elephantine, built no temple to YHWH that we know of, and a number of their texts allude to the problematic nature of erecting such a sanctuary and worshiping YHWH in it (e.g., Ps. 137:4: "How do we sing a song of YHWH in an alien land?"). It would seem that the Jews of Elephantine were not Deuteronomists, nor were they constrained by the old tradition that alien lands are polluting. Their temple was only one of several Jewish sanctuaries to be built in Egypt during the Second Temple period (note also the temple of Onias IV built during the second century B.C.E. in Leontopolis, and mentioned by Josephus, *Ant.* 13.72).

Qumran

Conflicting Evidence

The place of sacrifice among the sectarians of Qumran remains a debated topic among scholars. No unambiguous archaeological evidence survives for the performance of sacrifices at the site of Qumran, though it seems clear that the sectarians ate meat as part of their diet, given the bones of sheep, goats, and cows buried in clay vessels in various locations at the site. Yet Josephus claims that the Essenes offered their own sacrifices apart from the Temple in Jerusalem (*Ant.* 18.19), and if the Qumran sectarians were Essenes, as many scholars continue to believe, the communal locus would be the place where such sacrifices would most likely have occurred.

Some texts among the Dead Sea Scrolls seem to suggest that the sectarians sent offerings to the Jerusalem Temple, including the whole burnt offering, grain offerings, frankincense, and wood (e.g., CD 11:18-21), though they were apparently forbidden to go there themselves (CD 6:11-14); other texts demonstrate a serious concern for the manner in which sacrifices are offered (e.g., 4QMMT, 4QJubilees[d, e]). Yet the *Community Rule* (1QS 9:4-5), using sacrificial idiom, states that prayer (*tĕrûmat śĕpātayim,* literally "offering of the lips") and exemplary actions (*tĕmîm derek,* literally "perfection of way") substitute for sacrifices.

In short, given the conflicting witnesses, it is difficult to reach any definitive conclusions about the role of sacrifice among the Qumran sectarians, and we ought also to keep in mind that attitudes toward sacrifice may have changed during the lifetime of the community. What seems clear, however, is that members of the sect expected a future, eschatological cult in Jerusalem in which they could participate fully. As many have noted, the *Temple Scroll* provides a blueprint for that future cult.

The Temple Scroll

Much about the temple cult of the future as described in the *Temple Scroll* resembles ritual practice as it is represented in biblical materials, particularly the priestly portion of the Pentateuch. The *Temple Scroll* presents prescriptions for sacrificial rites, including those of the Sabbath and the festivals. Among the sacrifices and offerings mentioned are unblemished sacrificial animals to be offered as whole burnt offerings, purification offerings, reparation offerings, and well-being offerings; grain, oil, and drink offerings; tithes; and the firstfruits. Both blood manipulation by priests and fat and organ burning on the altar are also components of sacrificial ritual mentioned by the *Temple Scroll.*

For all its similarity to biblical representations of sacrifice, the *Temple Scroll* is also characterized by many interesting departures from priestly and other biblical norms. At times, the author of the *Temple Scroll* must choose between contradictory biblical sources in order to present a coherent picture. Many of the innovations of the *Temple Scroll* are discussed in detail by Milgrom (2000), but several are worth mentioning here. Perhaps most striking is the expansion of the festival calendar in the *Temple Scroll.* Festivals for New Wine and New Oil are described, as is a six-day festival dedicated to the collection of the wood for the altar. A departure from priestly requirements is the use of a bronze altar (11Q19 12:13), in contrast to the altar of acacia wood overlaid with bronze specified in Exod. 27:1-2 and 38:1-2. (Other, earlier biblical materials require an altar of earth or fieldstones.) An example of the author choosing between contradictory biblical sources is the observance of the rites of the Passover at the Temple by all males twenty years of age and older. This presentation of the Passover follows Deut. 16:1-8, except for the age requirement — an innovation building on Deut. 16:16

— and a few other details. But it departs from priestly texts such as Exod. 12:1-20, 43-49, which represent the Passover sacrifice and meal as domestic rites rather than rites of the Temple.

Josephus

The works of the Jewish historian Josephus (first century C.E.), particularly his *Jewish Antiquities*, constitute a fourth major source of material on sacrifices and offerings in the Second Temple period. The *Antiquities* contains detailed descriptions of the Temple and its sacrificial rites. In *Ant.* 3.223-39, Josephus provides a review of sacrificial practice, deriving much of his content from a variety of priestly materials in Leviticus as well as other biblical sources.

His treatment of the whole burnt offering illustrates well both his method and the nature of the content found in his larger presentation of the sacrifices. According to Josephus, the Hebrews offered three males of the flock and herd for the whole burnt offering: a kid, a lamb, and a bull. The kid and lamb from the flock must be one year old, though the bull from the herd may be older. After the worshiper has slaughtered the sacrificial animals, the priests sprinkle their blood on the altar, wash their bodies, divide them into sections, and salt the sections. They then lay the sections of the animal on the altar to be burned, and take the hides for themselves. Much of the content of this description is based on Leviticus 1, including the following details: the choice of male sacrificial animals; the worshiper performing the slaughter (as in the Hebrew Masoretic Text); and the priests manipulating the sacrificial blood.

Some other details of the description are evidently derived from other biblical texts. One example is the salting of the whole burnt offering, which is not mentioned in Leviticus 1, and seems to be based on the last phrase of Lev. 2:13 and Ezek. 43:24, the latter stating that priests salt the burnt offering in that dedicatory context. Another example is the statement that the priests receive the hides, a practice which is not discussed in Leviticus 1 but is mentioned in Lev. 7:8. Some of the details of Leviticus 1 are omitted in Josephus' description for reasons that are unclear (e.g., the laying of the worshiper's hand upon the head of the sacrificial animal, the flaying of the animal's body, and the option of a bird as a whole burnt offering instead of a quadruped).

Finally, there are details that are not directly derived from biblical descriptions of the rites of the whole burnt offering (e.g., the age specifications for the bull, the sheep, and the goat, though these may have been influenced in part by texts such as Lev. 9:3; Num. 28:11, 19, 27; 29:2, 8, 13; and the fact that three animals are required for the offering). As with biblical texts, caution is necessary when we consider such representations of sacrifice, since it remains unclear exactly what their relationship might have been to the practices of the Temple in Josephus' time.

BIBLIOGRAPHY

G. A. ANDERSON 1987, *Sacrifices and Offerings in Ancient Israel*, Atlanta: Scholars Press. • L. H. FELDMAN 2000, *Flavius Josephus: Translation and Commentary*, vol. 3, *Judean Antiquities 1–4*, Leiden: Brill. • J. KLAWANS 2005, *Purity, Sacrifice, and the Temple: Symbolism and Supersessionism in the Study of Ancient Judaism* • R. KUGLER 2000, "Rewriting Rubrics: Sacrifice and the Religion of Qumran," in *Religion in the Dead Sea Scrolls*, ed. J. J. Collins and R. A. Kugler, Grand Rapids: Eerdmans, 90-112. • J. MILGROM 1991, *Leviticus 1–16*, New York: Doubleday. • J. MILGROM 2000, "Sacrifice," in *Encyclopedia of the Dead Sea Scrolls*, vol. 2, ed. L. H. Schiffman and J. C. VanderKam, Oxford: Oxford University Press, 807-12. • M.-Z. PETROPOULOU 2008, *Animal Sacrifice in Ancient Greek Religion, Judaism, and Christianity, 100 BC to AD 200*, Oxford: Oxford University Press. • B. PORTEN 1996, *The Elephantine Papyri in English*, Leiden: Brill.

SAUL M. OLYAN

Sadducees

The Sadducees were a Jewish group of the Second Temple period, according to Josephus one of three "sects" or "parties" *(haireseis)*. Some derive their name from *ṣaddîq*, "just," and think of a deliberate distortion of the name by their opponents; most commonly, however, it is derived from Zadok, the Davidic priest.

Sources

The Sadducees have left no writings; attempts to attribute to them 1 Maccabees, Ben Sira, Judith, the Targum of Ruth, and other writings on the basis of their general outlook or of doctrines contained in them fail to convince. All the texts on them at our disposal were written by outsiders and are tendentious. The main witness is Flavius Josephus, who says that in his youth he tested the Sadducean teaching and way of life (*Vita* 11); but his writings betray no special knowledge. The New Testament names the Sadducees among the opponents of Jesus. There may be allusions to them in the Qumran writings, mainly in the *Pesher on Nahum*, where "Manasseh" is frequently understood as an allusion to them. The *Temple Scroll* and 4QMMT have become important in the discussion of the Sadducean halakah and may contribute to our understanding of the Sadducees, but only indirectly. A number of rabbinic texts, beginning with the Mishnah, relate controversies with the Sadducees and/or Boethusians and stories about them. The halakic views attributed to them may reflect reality, but the narrative framework cannot be used for historical reconstructions. This holds true even for the few relevant tannaitic texts. Later texts are full of clichés and do not reveal reliable new information. The scholion to the *Megillat Taʿanit* has recently been reevaluated as a source for the Jewish groups of the Second Temple, but it remains problematic. The church fathers who speak of the Sadducees follow the New Testament and Josephus and offer no trustworthy traditions unknown from elsewhere. Later Karaite traditions on the Sadducees depend on rabbinic texts or on the *Damascus Document*, which was discovered in ca. 780 and was thought to be a Sadducean writing.

History

The origins of the Sadducees are unknown. Josephus first mentions them in the context of the Maccabee Jonathan as one of three Jewish schools of thought (*Ant.* 13.171). As historical actors they first appear under John Hyrcanus (135-104 B.C.E.), who is said to have deserted the Pharisees, abrogated their regulations, and joined the Sadducees (*Ant.* 13.288-98). The Talmud (*b. Qiddušin* 66a) knows this story but places it under Alexander Jannaeus (103-77 B.C.E.). After the reconciliation of Jannaeus' widow Salome Alexandra with the Pharisees, the Sadducees lost their influence. They are mentioned again only after Coponius' appointment as procurator of Judea in C.E. 6 (*J.W.* 2.118, 164-66). These notices do not allow a reconstruction of the history of the Sadducees.

The Sadducees might go back, in whatever form and degree of organization, to pre-Maccabean times, but as a group they became relevant only during the last century of the Second Temple. Herod appointed a high priest from Egypt, Boethus, certainly a member of the Zadokite line at Leontopolis (*Ant.* 15.320-22). His family brought forth several high priests. This might explain the rabbinic tradition (*'Abot de Rabbi Nathan* A 5; B 10) that Zadok and Boethus, distant disciples of Antigonos of Sokho, founded the Sadducees and the Boethusians. The two groups, frequently interchangeable in rabbinic sources, may therefore be considered as closely related. The Boethusians were perhaps a group around the dynasty of the high priest Boethus, the inner circle of the larger Sadducean group. As a whole they cannot simply be identified as a party of priests.

The only high priest explicitly called a Sadducee was Ananus, the son of Ananus, who had James, the brother of Jesus, sentenced to death in 62 C.E. (*Ant.* 20.199-200; cf. Acts 4:1, which allies "the priests and the captain of the Temple and the Sadducees"). There have been attempts to identify the Boethusians with the Essenes; some would see them as Qumran Sadducees, to be distinguished from the Jerusalem Sadducees known from Josephus and the New Testament. But in spite of striking parallels based on common priestly traditions, these movements should be kept apart.

Josephus writes that the Sadducees "have the confidence of the wealthy alone but no following among the populace" (*Ant.* 13.298). "There are but few men to whom this doctrine has been made known, but these are men of the highest standing"; but "whenever they assume some office . . . they must submit to the formulas of the Pharisees" (*Ant.* 18.17). This last point is supported by rabbinic texts that also say that the Sadducean priests conduct the cult according to the rules of the Pharisees or the sages; but this claim is certainly highly tendentious. Whenever Sadducees became high priests, they wielded considerable power. In the revolt against Rome, the priesthood at the Temple was of particular importance. We have no information of how involved the Sadducees were in the First Revolt, but it is certainly a distortion to depict them as collaborators with the Roman occupants. After the fall of the Temple in 70 C.E., they disappeared with their base of power. No Sadducees are known to have joined the rabbinic movement. It is probable that their way of thinking rather contributed to the people's long-lasting resistance to the rabbinic leadership.

Doctrines

Denial of Resurrection and Angels

According to Acts 23:8, "the Sadducees say that there is no resurrection, neither angel, nor spirit." This fits the notice of Josephus that they deny the persistence of the soul after death, penalties in the underworld, and rewards (*J.W.* 2.164-65). The Sadducean denial of the resurrection, known also from rabbinic sources, may have been due to the fact that it was a comparatively new doctrine not backed by the main body of the Bible. That they should have denied the existence of angels is strange, since angels are mentioned in the Torah. But they might have opposed later developments of this doctrine, or the idea that in the resurrection the righteous "shall be made like unto angels" (e.g., *2 Bar.* 51:10).

Denial of Fate

Josephus adds that the Sadducees do away with fate; for them, all people are responsible for their own wellbeing (*Ant.* 13.173). Josephus depicts the Sadducees in Hellenistic terms (elsewhere he attributes the denial of fate to the Epicureans), which need not reflect precisely the views of the Sadducees themselves. These tenets of the Sadducees have in common the rejection of later developments in biblical religion. This is not surprising, since traditionalism is typical of groups led by priests.

Rejection of Pharisaic Traditions

Josephus also observes that the Sadducees do not accept the regulations of the Pharisees that are not recorded in the laws of Moses, but only those regulations that were written down (*Ant.* 13.297). This is frequently understood as a kind of *sola scriptura,* but from the halakic disputes reported in early rabbinic texts, it becomes clear that the Sadducees had their own interpretative tradition of the Torah. For the implementation of the Torah in daily life, especially in the cult, the Sadducees had to rely on traditions not contained in the Bible itself; the question was only what authority to attribute to these traditions.

Acceptance of the Torah

Patristic traditions claim that the Sadducees accepted only the Pentateuch and rejected the Prophets. The Pentateuch certainly had a special place in Sadducean thinking, but this does not distinguish them from the Pharisees and the rabbis. They could not have totally rejected the Prophets and the Writings (except perhaps Daniel with its doctrine of resurrection); the Psalms, after all, were used in the daily liturgy of the Temple! It is only that for them the Prophets and the Writings did not enjoy the same degree of authority as the Torah.

Halakah

Josephus mentions the halakic positions of the Sadducees only in passing. The New Testament totally ignores them. Only rabbinic texts report some details. The Sadducees are said to have followed divergent halakot mainly regarding the Temple service and ritual purity, but also in some points of Sabbath, criminal, and civil law.

Temple Service

An outstanding dispute concerned the Day of Atonement. When the high priest entered the Holy of Holies to offer the incense, according to Sadducean tradition he had to place the incense on the coals before he entered, whereas the Pharisees claimed that this had to be done within (*t. Yoma* 1:8). The dispute is based on differing understandings of Lev. 16:2. Other differences regarded the financing of the daily sacrifices (by individual contributions or from the Temple tax; *b. Menaḥot* 65a) and certain meal offerings.

Ritual Purity

The Sadducees did not accept the purity of a *ṭebul yom*, a person who had immersed during the day and not waited until sunset for the priest who burnt the red heifer. They did not restrict the impurity of a *niddah* to menstruation (they ignored its cycle) but extended it to observing any blood. They considered the bones of clean animals as unclean. Regarding a liquid flowing from a pure vessel into an impure one, they assumed the lower vessel's impurity to climb to the higher one; the Pharisees assumed this only in the case of a thick liquid.

Sabbath Law

Other differences concerned the Sabbath law. The Sadducees did not accept the *ʿerub haṣerot* (mixing or blending of courtyards), which allows the use of the common courtyard on Sabbath. They also opposed striking the willow on Hoshanah Rabbah (the seventh and last day of Sukkot) when it fell on a Sabbath, or harvesting the Omer grain offering on a Sabbath. They understood Lev. 23:11 to refer not to the day after the "festival" of Pesaḥ but to the Sabbath in the week of Pesaḥ; Pentecost thus always fell on a Sunday.

Criminal and Civil Law

In the field of criminal law, the Sadducees were said to be more severe regarding death penalties. In civil law, they restricted even more than the Pharisees the inheritance rights of a daughter (Num. 27:8) and declared a master not responsible for damages caused by his servants (*m. Yadayim* 4).

Relation to Pharisaic, Rabbinic, and Qumran Halakah

The Sadducean halakah as described in rabbinic sources is for the most part stricter than that of the Pharisees or the rabbis. On some issues Sadducean and Qumran halakot are identical, but in other matters (e.g., meal offerings, Temple tax) they contradict each other. The halakic systems of the Sadducees and of the group at Qumran are based on common earlier traditions, but the groups cannot be equated.

The halakic and doctrinal positions of the Sadducees are frequently explained by their literal exegesis and rejection of tradition. In reality they are founded on tradition, although one different from that of the Pharisees. The genuine religious zeal of the Sadducees cannot be doubted; they adhered strictly to what they thought right and considered themselves loyal to biblical traditions, which they tried to hand on in their own time.

Bibliography

G. Baumbach 1989, "The Sadducees in Josephus," in *Josephus, the Bible and History*, ed. L. H. Feldman and G. Hata, Leiden: Brill, 173-95. • A. I. Baumgarten 1997, *The Flourishing of Jewish Sects in the Maccabean Era: An Interpretation*, Leiden: Brill. • J. M. Baumgarten 1980, "The Pharisaic-Sadducean Controversies about Purity and the Qumran texts," *JJS* 31: 157-70. • Y. Erder 1994, "The Karaites' Sadducee Dilemma," *IOS* 14: 195-226. • M. Goodman 1994, "Sadducees and Essenes after 70 CE," in *Crossing the Boundaries*, ed. S. E. Porter, P. Joyce, and D. E. Orton, Leiden: Brill, 347-56. • J. LeMoyne 1972, *Les Sadducéens*, Paris: Gabalda. • E. Main 1996, "Les Sadducéens et la résurrection des morts: Comparaison entre Mc 12,18-27 et Lc 20,27-38," *RB* 103: 411-32. • H. Newman 2006, *Proximity to Power and Jewish Sectarian Groups of the Ancient Period*, Leiden: Brill. • V. Noam 2003, *Megillat Taʿanit: Versions, Interpretation, History with a Critical Edition*, Jerusalem: Yad Ben-Zvi (in Hebrew). • A. Paul 1969, *Écrits de Qumran et sectes juives aux premiers siècles de l'Islam: Recherches sur l'origine du Qaraïsme*, Paris: Letouzey et Ané. • E. Regev 2005a, *The Sadducees and Their Halakhah*, Jerusalem: Yad Ben-Zvi (in Hebrew). • E. Regev 2005b, "Were the Priests all the Same? Qumranic Halakhah in Comparison with Sadducean Halakhah," *DSD* 12: 158-88. • E. Regev 2006, "The Sadducees, the Pharisees, and the Sacred: Meaning and Ideology in the Halakhic Controversies between the Sadducees and Pharisees," *Review of Rabbinic Judaism* 9: 126-40. • A. J. Saldarini 1988, *Pharisees, Scribes and Sadducees in Palestinian Society*, Wilmington, Del.: Michael Glazier; rpt. Grand Rapids: Eerdmans, 2001. • Y. Sussman 1994, "The History of the Halakha and the Dead Sea Scrolls: Preliminary Talmudic Observations on *Miqṣat Maʿaśê ha-Torah* (4QMMT)," in E. Qimron and J. Strugnell, *Qumran Cave 4.V: Miqṣat Maʿaśê ha-Torah*, DJD 10, Oxford: Clarendon, 179-200.

Günter Stemberger

Salome Komaïse Archive → Papyri

Salvation → Eschatology

Samaria

Israelite and Assyrian Periods

Samaria (Hebr. *Šōmrôn*) is the name of a city and a province. According to the Bible's etymology, Omri, king of Israel (ca. 882/878 [as sole ruler]-871 B.C.E.), bought the hill of Samaria from a man by the name of Shemer and called it after the original owner (1 Kings 16:24). In the opinion of most scholars, however, the word *Šōmrôn* is derived from the root *šmr,* meaning "to guard, to watch." Thus the name "Samaria" would reflect the strategic location of the city on a hill (430 m. above sea level), close to the intersections of major roads in the four directions of the compass. Its site was near the modern village of Sebastiyeh, which preserves the name Herod the Great gave to the city to honor Augustus (Hellenized as Sebastos).

In the second year of his rule as sole king, Omri moved the capital of the Northern Kingdom from Tirzah (modern Tell el-Farʿah North) to his new foundation of Samaria (1 Kings 16:23-24). It remained the capital until it was conquered and destroyed by the Assyrians in 722/721 B.C.E. Thousands of its inhabitants were deported, new settlers from the Assyrian Empire were brought in, and the city was rebuilt and made the capital of the province of Samaria (Assyrian Samerina), which extended from Bethel in the south to the Valley of Jezreel in the north, and from the Sharon in the west to the Jordan Valley in the east. Despite the Assyrian resettlement policy, the majority of the population remained Israelite. In the Babylonian and Persian periods, the city of Samaria was also the capital of the province of the same name.

Archaeological finds from the Assyrian, Babylonian, and Persian periods are not abundant. Apart from a few traces of buildings which survived from the Persian period, the small objects excavated include pottery, coins, and fragments of a bronze throne that may have been used by a governor in the city of Samaria. Archaeological surveys, however, have shown that the northern and western zones of Samaria soon recovered from the ravages of the Assyrian attacks and prospered during the Persian period. Settlements increased greatly in numbers, and the system of roads was expanded. Although evidence for the city of Samaria is very sparse, from the fact that the region around it was densely populated, it may be inferred that it was one of the most eminent cities in Palestine. In comparison with Jerusalem and Judea, the region and the city of Samaria were not only larger but also more densely settled and enjoyed greater material wealth. Language and scripts known from papyri, coins, and bullae were substantially the same in Persian Judea and Samaria. Similarly, the two regions shared common proper names.

Persian Period

During the Persian period, the province of Samaria was part of the satrapy "Beyond the River" (Abar Nahara), whose governors resided in the city of Samaria and probably had authority over Jerusalem as well at the beginning of Persian rule. A number of governors of the province are known by name from biblical and extrabiblical sources. Most prominent were Sanballat the Horonite and, according to the reconstructions by F. M. Cross, his descendants. From the book of Nehemiah, the Elephantine Papyri, the Wadi ed-Daliyeh Papyri, coins, bullae, and Josephus, the following series has been postulated: Sanballat I the Horonite (born ca. 485 B.C.E.; book of Nehemiah; Elephantine Papyrus *CAP* [Cowley, ed., *Aramaic Papyri*] 30 line 29 = *TAD* [*Textbook of Aramaic Documents*] A4.7 line 29); his son Delaiah (born ca. 460 B.C.E.; Elephantine Papyri *CAP* 30:29; 31:28; 32:1 = *TAD* A4.7.29; 4.8.28; 4.9.1); Sanballat II, possibly the son of Delaiah (born 435 B.C.E.; Wadi Daliyeh Samaria Papyri [= WDSP] 11:13 [front] and seal no. 22 attached to WDSP 16); his son [Yesh]uaʿ/[Yeshaʿ]yahu or [Yad]uaʿ (born ca. 410 B.C.E.; WDSP 12:13 and seal no. 22); his brother Hananiah (born ca. 410 B.C.E.; WDSP 7:17; 9:14); and Sanballat III, possibly the son of Hananiah (born ca. 385, died 332 B.C.E.; Josephus, *Ant.* 11.302-45).

Although Sanballat was an Akkadian name (Sin-uballiṭ = "[the moon god] Sin gives life"), the sons of Sanballat mentioned in the Elephantine Papyri (*CAP* 30:29) had Yahwistic names — Delaiah and Shelemiah — as did the governor Hananiah. However, not all scholars are in agreement with Cross's conjecture of a dynasty of Sanballats, and some note that only one governor by the name of Sanballat is documented, namely, the Sanballat mentioned in Nehemiah and Elephantine Papyrus 30:29. Josephus wrongly placed him in the time of Alexander the Great. Others think there may have been two Sanballats — one at the time of Nehemiah and another in the time of Alexander the Great. Uncertainties exist also with regard to the exact reading of some of the names in the papyri from Wadi ed-Daliyeh.

Except for the names of the governors of Samaria, very little is known about the fate of Samaria during the Persian period from literary sources, such as the books of Ezra and Nehemiah and the *Antiquities* of Josephus. Sanballat the Horonite, together with the Ammonite and Arab neighboring governors, opposed the rebuilding of the walls of Jerusalem during the time of Nehemiah, who came to Jerusalem as governor of Judea in 445 or 444 B.C.E. (Neh. 3:33–4:17; Eng. 4:1-23); however, they were not able to stop the building activities. Whether this account depicts historical reality or reflects only the view of Nehemiah is impossible to tell, and the date of the book of Ezra-Nehemiah as well as the authenticity of the documents contained in it are a matter of debate. Some of the letters cited in the book of Ezra are certainly later than the Persian period. A particular problem is Neh. 13:28, which states that "one of the sons of Jehoiada, son of the high priest Eliashib, was the son-in-law of Sanballat the Horonite" and that Nehemiah chased him away. A similar incident is described by Josephus in *Ant.* 11.302-45 but is set in the time of Alexander the Great. According to Josephus, Manasseh, the brother of the high priest Jaddua, married Nikaso, the daughter of Sanballat. Because the latter was a foreigner, the elders of Jerusalem demanded that Manasseh divorce Nikaso or stay away from the altar. Manasseh informed his father-in-law of this, and Sanballat promised to build him a temple on Mt. Gerizim where he could be high priest. With the permission of Alexander the Great, Sanballat did build the temple and appointed Manasseh high priest. Scholars are divided over the reliability of Josephus' account. Some believe that the historian modified a version of Neh. 13:28; others think that his story is trustworthy.

In a letter of 408 B.C.E., the Jews of Elephantine in Egypt turned not only to the governor of Judea, Bagohi, but also to the authorities in Samaria, the sons of Sanballat, Delaiah, and Shelemiah. They informed Bagohi (Bagoas) that they had written earlier to the high priest and the other priests in Jerusalem but had received no answer.

Archaeological excavations carried out since 1982 suggest that the temple to YHWH on Mt. Gerizim was built in the Persian period (middle or second half of the fifth century B.C.E.) rather than in the time of Alexander the Great, as Josephus claims (*Ant.* 11.321-24). It is the only cultic site uncovered in Persian-period Samaria. No pagan temple was found. In the Hellenistic period, the temple on Mt. Gerizim was enlarged, and a sizable city around it was erected at that time.

The finds in the Abu Shinjeh cave in Wadi ed-Daliyeh (halfway between Samaria and Jericho), discovered by Bedouin in 1962, include human skeletons and papyri as well as pottery, coins, textiles, bullae, jewelry, and glass vessels. The dates on the papyri, written in the city or province of Samaria, place most of them in the reign of the Persian king Artaxerxes III Ochus (358-337 B.C.E.). The documents were written in official Aramaic, the same language that was used in the Elephantine Papyri of the fifth century B.C.E. The majority are deeds of sale of slaves, houses, and other (unknown) objects. In the texts, the city of Samaria is sometimes called a "city" *(qîryātā')*, sometimes a "citadel" *(bîrtā')* in the "province" *(mĕdintā')* of Samaria. Both a governor *(paḥat šômrāyin)* and, under him, a prefect *(sĕgānā')* ruled the province. From the finds it can be deduced that the people whose skeletons and belongings were found in the cave were wealthy citizens of Samaria. The greater part of the names mentioned in the papyri are Yahwistic.

By combining the evidence from Wadi ed-Daliyeh with a report in Curtius Rufus (*Historiae Alexandri Magni* IV, 8.34.9-11), we may infer the plight of the people who hid in the cave. Curtius Rufus relates that the inhabitants of Samaria burned alive the Macedonian governor of Syria, Andromachus. When Alexander the Great learned of the deed, he marched against the Samarians to avenge the murder. At his approach, prominent citizens of Samaria must have fled and hid in the cave in Wadi ed-Daliyeh, but apparently they were discovered and suffocated when the Macedonians lit a fire at the entrance of the cave. According to Eusebius, *Chronicle* ad annum Abr. 1680 (ed. A. Schoene [Berlin, 1868], 2:114), Alexander not only punished the perpetrators of the murder of Andromachus but also settled Macedonians in the city of Samaria, which now took on a Greek character.

It seems that many of the inhabitants of Samaria fled to the second main city of the region, Shechem, which was rebuilt at that time. In the opinion of the excavators, Shechem was rebuilt as a Samaritan city, but the new excavations on Mt. Gerizim suggest that it was instead reestablished as a Greek city.

Hellenistic Period

Whereas in the Persian period the number of settlements in the region of Samaria had increased considerably, the Hellenistic period saw a sharp decline. To the end of the fourth century B.C.E. belong the round towers, still visible today, that were part of the fortifications of the city of Samaria, which also included a city wall. Probably in the second century B.C.E. the acropolis was fortified by a thick wall. In the course of John Hyrcanus' (134-104 B.C.E.) conquests, Samaria was completely destroyed in 108/107 B.C.E. after it had been besieged for a year (Josephus, *Ant.* 13.275-81; *J.W.* 1.64-65). In 112/111 B.C.E. Hyrcanus destroyed Shechem and the city on Mt. Gerizim (*Ant.* 13.254-56; *J.W.* 1.63). They were never to be rebuilt. Emperor Vespasian (69-79 C.E.) founded a new Roman city, Flavia Neapolis, approximately one and a half km. to the west of Shechem. The name of the Arab city of Nablus, which occupies the site of the Roman city, is derived from Neapolis.

Early Roman Period

In 63 B.C.E. Pompey incorporated Samaria into the province of Syria and separated it from Judea (*J.W.* 1.155-56; *Ant.* 14.74-75). Gabinius, governor of Syria from 57 to 54 B.C.E., rebuilt the city (*Ant.* 14.88; *J.W.* 1.166). In ca. 27 B.C.E. Emperor Augustus (27 B.C.E.–14 C.E.) granted Samaria to Herod (37-4 B.C.E.; cf. *Ant.* 15.217, 292-98; *J.W.* 1.396), who restored it to a magnificent city and called it "Sebaste" in honor of the emperor (from Gr. *Sebastos* = Lat. *Augustus;* cf. *Ant.* 15.296). From then on, the name "Samaria" was used for the area of the former Northern Kingdom of Israel. Herod settled 6,000 colonists in it (*J.W.* 1.403); rebuilt a wall around the city; and erected temples to Augustus and Kore, a stadium, a theater, a forum, and a basilica. Shechem and the city on Mt. Gerizim, on the other hand, were not rebuilt.

In 6 C.E. Samaria became part of the Roman province of Judea. In the First Jewish Revolt against Rome (66-70 C.E.), Samaria was among the cities that were devastated by Jewish rebels (*J.W.* 2.460). In the second century C.E., it was rebuilt on a grand scale by Emperor Septimius Severus (193-211 C.E.), and it is to this period that most of the remains visible today are to be dated.

Throughout the Second Temple period, the majority of the inhabitants of the region of Samaria continued to be worshipers of YHWH. This becomes clear from a critical study of biblical and extrabiblical sources, including archaeological excavations and surveys. The city of Samaria, on the other hand, became a Greek city when Alexander settled Macedonians there in 331 B.C.E. Later, Herod the Great settled mercenaries "of the neighboring populations" (*J.W.* 1.403; *Ant.* 15.296). Toward the end of the Second Temple period, in the second/first century B.C.E., Samarian Yahwists rejected the authority of Jerusalem and recognized the temple on Mt. Gerizim as the only legitimate cult place. They thus became Samaritans; that is, from this point on, Yahwistic Samarians whose center was Mt. Gerizim are properly called Samaritans.

BIBLIOGRAPHY
A. ALT 1934, "Die Rolle Samarias bei der Entstehung des Judentums," in *Festschrift Otto Procksch zum sechzigsten Geburtstag am 9. August 1934*, ed. A. Alt et al., Leipzig: Deichert, 5-28; rpt. in idem, *Kleine Schriften zur Geschichte des Volkes Israel* (Munich: Beck, 1953), 2: 316-37. • A. ALT 1954, "Der Stadtstaat Samaria," *Berichte über die Verhandlungen der Sächsischen Akademie der Wissenschaften zu Leipzig, Philologisch-historische Klasse,* Band 101, Heft 5, Berlin: Akademie-Verlag; rpt. in idem, *Kleine Schriften zur Geschichte des Volkes Israel* (Munich: Beck, 1959), 3: 258-302. • A. E. COWLEY 1923, *Aramaic Papyri of the Fifth Century B.C.*, Oxford: Clarendon; rpt. 2005. • F. M. CROSS 1966, "Aspects of Samaritan and Jewish History in Late Persian and Hellenistic Times," *HTR* 59: 201-11 (rpt. in *Emerging Judaism: Studies on the Fourth and Third Centuries B.C.E.*, ed. M. E. Stone and D. Satran [Minneapolis: Fortress, 1989], 49-59 and in F. Dexinger and R. Pummer, eds., *Die Samaritaner* [Darmstadt: Wissenschaftliche Buchgesellschaft, 1992], 312-32). • F. M. CROSS 1998, "Samaria and Jerusalem in the Era of the Restoration," in idem, *From Epic to Canon: History and Literature in Ancient Israel,* Baltimore: Johns Hopkins University Press, 173-202. • J. DUŠEK 2007, *Les manuscrits araméens du Wadi Daliyeh et la Samarie vers 450-332 av. J.-C.,* Leiden: Brill. • H. ESHEL 2007, "The Governors of Samaria in the Fifth and Fourth Centuries B.C.E.," in *Judah and the Judeans in the Fourth Century B.C.E.,* ed. O. Lipschits, G. N. Knoppers, and R. Albertz, Winona Lake, Ind.: Eisenbrauns, 223-34. • L. L. GRABBE 1992, *Judaism from Cyrus to Hadrian,* 2 vols., Minneapolis: Fortress. • D. M. GROPP 2001, *Wadi Daliyeh II and Qumran Miscellanea, Part 2: The Samaria Papyri from Wadi Daliyeh,* DJD 28, Oxford: Clarendon, 1-117 • M. KARTVEIT 2009, *The Origins of the Samaritans,* Leiden: Brill. • Y. MESHORER AND S. QEDAR 1999, *Samarian Coinage,* Jerusalem: Israel Numismatic Society. • B. PORTEN AND A. YARDENI 1986, *Textbook of Aramaic Documents from Ancient Egypt,* vol. 1, *Letters,* Jerusalem: Hebrew University. • E. STERN 2001, *Archaeology of the Land of the Bible,* vol. 2, *The Assyrian, Babylonian, and Persian Periods: 732-332 BCE*, New York: Doubleday. • A. ZERTAL 1990, "The Pahwah of Samaria (Northern Israel) during the Persian Period: Types of Settlement, Economy, History and New Discoveries," *Transeu* 3: 9-30.

See also: Daliyeh, Wadi ed-; Gerizim, Mount; Samaria-Sebaste; Samaritan Pentateuch; Samaritanism; Sanballat; Seals and Seal Impressions

REINHARD PUMMER

Samaria Papyri → Daliyeh, Wadi ed-

Samaria-Sebaste

Samaria, the ancient capital of the northern kingdom of Israel, was founded by King Omri in the first half of the ninth century B.C.E. on top of a hill 430 m. above sea level. It had a royal citadel surrounded by a lower city. Surrounded by fertile land and situated at a major crossroads, it became a flourishing city. Even after its conquest in 722 B.C.E. by the Assyrian king Sargon II, who deported much of its population and settled others in their place, it retained its function as a capital of the province of Samaria and served as the seat of the Assyrian, Babylonian, and Persian governors of that region.

Hellenistic and Hasmonean Periods

A Samaritan delegation led by Sanballat, the Persian satrap of Samaria, submitted its capitulation to Alexander the Great in 332 B.C.E., when he was just starting the siege of Tyre. But later, when Alexander was in Egypt, the Samarians killed Andromachus, his commander in Syria. When he returned from Egypt, the perpetrators were executed. Two hundred skeletons found in the caves of Wadi ed-Daliyeh in the desert of Samaria seem to reflect these events. Papyri from the last years of the Persian regime along with coins, Aramaic seals, and other objects found with the skeletons indicate that they belonged to Samarian refugees of high social rank.

A Macedonian colony was established at the site, transforming it into a Greek city. Under the Diadochi and thereafter the city changed hands, each time resulting in further ruin. In ca. 296 B.C.E. the city came under Ptolemaic control. However, no debris associated with these events was found in the excavations. In 200 B.C.E. Coele-Syria, Samaria included, fell into the hands of the Seleucids. In the second half of the second century, the acropolis, occupying an area of ca. 230 × 120 m., received a new massive wall, around four m. wide with rectangular towers. In ca. 107 B.C.E. the city fell to Antigonus and Aristobulus, the sons of the Hasmonean John Hyrcanus I, after a year of siege that caused heavy famine. The city was surrounded by a ditch and by double siege walls some eighty stades (ca. 15 km.) long. The Seleucid king, who was called twice to assist the besieged city, failed to raise the siege. The city was entirely razed, and its inhabitants were sold as slaves.

The city of Samaria differed in its ethnic composition, cultural affiliation, and religion from the other towns and villages of the indigenous Samaritans, whose political and religious center was the temple on top of Mt. Gerizim and the town that had developed around it. These were destroyed by the Hasmoneans already in 112-111 B.C.E. The Hellenized pagan character of the city during the Hellenistic period is reflected in a temple of Isis and Serapis, which was built in the third century north of the acropolis, and by a plethora of small finds including two bronze statuettes of Heracles, terracotta figurines, around 2,000 stamped handles of wine amphorae from Rhodes and from other Greek islands, clay lamps decorated by various figurative motifs, and Greek inscriptions.

Herod's Rebuilding of the City

In 63 B.C.E. Pompey freed Samaria from Jewish dominion and set it under the new Roman province of Syria. In 57-55 the city was rebuilt and repopulated by Gabinius, the Roman governor of Syria, and hence the name Gabinians that was given to its inhabitants. A new residential quarter of dwellings with shops and streets arranged orthogonally were built on the acropolis.

In 47 B.C.E. Herod was appointed *stratēgos* of Coele-Syria and Samaria by Sextus Julius Caesar, the

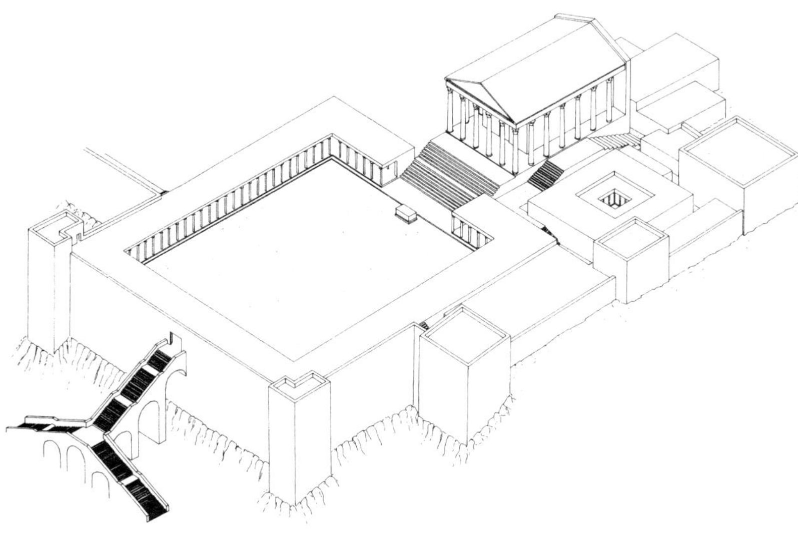

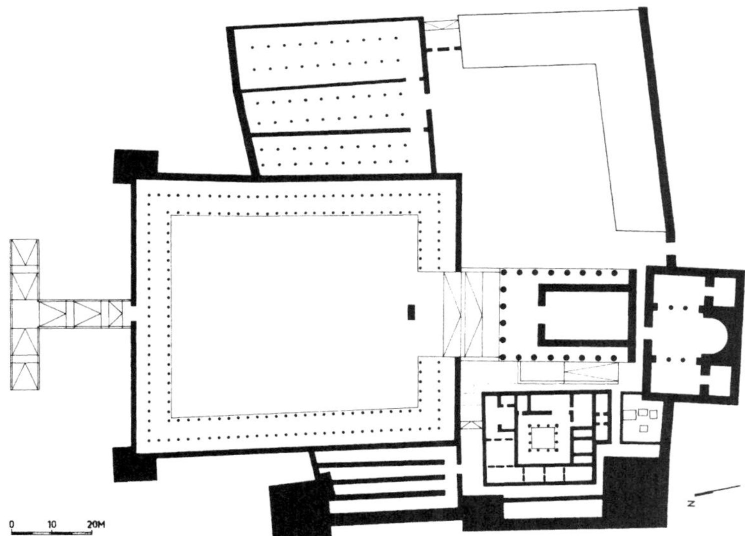

Isometric view (from northwest) and reconstructed plan of the temple complex and its surroundings at Sebaste *(Ehud Netzer)*

governor of Syria, on behalf of Caesar (*J.W.* 1.213). In 43 he retired to the city after the assassination of his father by Malichus, made repairs in the city, granted it an "excellent constitution" (*J.W.* 1.403), and succeeded in bringing peace among quarreling parties there. The city was loyal to him in his struggle against Antigonus for the kingship over the country during the years 39-37 B.C.E., and Herod made the city his stronghold.

After the Battle of Actium in 30 C.E., Augustus granted the city to the kingdom of Herod, who contrived to make it a fortress. He enlarged the city beyond its former boundaries and surrounded it by a new wall twenty stades (ca. 3.7 km.) long. The area of the fortified city had maximal diameters of around a kilometer from east to west and slightly less so from north to south. The west gate received two round towers set on top of the square Hellenistic foundations that flanked the gate. Another round Herodian tower enforced the wall about sixty m. farther to the northwest. The acropolis was enlarged by retaining walls, converted to a royal citadel, and fortified with a new wall and square towers. A monumental entrance with a staircase 7.5 m. wide led up to the more official part of the citadel. A villa (32.5 × 24.4 m.) with a peristyle courtyard built on the western end of this part served as a small palace. It had a bathroom and a water cistern, and was decorated by typical Herodian mosaic floors, frescoes, and stucco. A structure with four plastered pools, three of them graded, located to its south, may have served as a bathhouse or a service installation. An apsidal building (25 × 34.4 m.) on the southern extension of the acropolis, retained by massive walls, may have served as a royal reception hall. But the larger part of the royal citadel was occupied by a large hexastyle or octastyle Corinthian temple (35 × 24 m.) oriented on a north-south axis with a deep portico in front. The temple, located on top of the hill and set on top of a platform 4.5 m. high, dominated the entire city and its countryside. A vast forecourt (83 × 72 m.) extended north beyond the former wall of the acropolis. This part was retained on three sides by two massive walls, with a fill and an underground corridor in between. A row of square piers divided the corridors lengthwise. Above, a double portico surrounded the court on the west, north, and east. Access to the forecourt was from the north, evidently by a monumental T-shaped staircase that rested on arches, similar to Robinson's Arch in Jerusalem.

An altar (3.6 × 1.8 × 1.74 m.) was built in front of a broad staircase that led from the forecourt to the temple. The temple was dedicated to the cult of Emperor Augustus. Herod had also changed the name of the city to Sebaste in honor of the emperor, who in 27 B.C.E.

had assumed the name Augustus (the Greek equivalent of which is *Sebastos*). The southern part of the forecourt was flanked by ten corridor-type warehouses resembling those of Masada, three on the west (30 m. long and 2.5 to 3 m. wide) and seven on the east (68-75 m. long and 3-4 m. wide; the four easternmost were evidently divided lengthwise by a row of columns).

A large hall (Herodian or Gabinian) oriented west to east was uncovered under the later north-south forum-basilica. Its function is unknown. The Herodian building projects included also a stadium with a rectangular racecourse (194.5 × 58 m.) surrounded by porticos. It seems that the theater (ca. 65 m. in diameter) also had a Herodian phase.

Herod settled 6,000 colonists in Sebaste — veterans of his army and others from among the locals, granting each an extramural agricultural estate. The Gabinian colonists, who were evicted from the acropolis in order to make way for the temple, may have been compensated at that occasion. Herod had also established a mint in the city in 27 or 25 B.C.E. Its date of foundation, which marked a new local era, was recorded in city coins. Eighty-seven coins found at the site are from Herod's reign; thirty-nine are from the first century up to 69 C.E.

After Herod's death, Sebaste sided with the Romans, who therefore canceled one quarter of its taxes. It was included in the ethnarchy of Archelaus. At the outbreak of the Great Revolt in 66 C.E., after a massacre of the Jews of Caesarea, Sebaste was attacked and burned by the Jews. Being a pagan city, it sided again with the Romans, unlike the local Samaritans of the countryside.

Second through Fourth Centuries

Sebaste became a Roman colony during the reign of Septimius Severus (193-211 C.E.), when the city enjoyed its second peak of urban building. The temple to Augustus was restored, the theater and stadium were rebuilt, and a forum with a splendid basilica was erected. To the north of the acropolis, on the site of the Hellenistic temple of Serapis and Isis, a much vaster temple, dedicated to Kore, was constructed in this period. In the fourth century the city started to decline. Eusebius in his *Onomastikon* refers to Sebaste as a small town *(polichnē)* of Palestine. According to Christian tradition, John the Baptist was buried there, as well as the prophet Elisha and Obadiah, who was in charge of Ahab's palace (1 Kings 18:3).

BIBLIOGRAPHY

D. BARAG 1993, "King Herod's Royal Castle at Samaria-Sebaste," *PEQ* 125: 3-18. • B. BAR KOKHBA 2003, "The Conquest of Samaria by John Hyrcanus: The Pretext for the Siege, Jewish Settlement in the ʿAkraba District, and the Destruction of the City of Samaria," *Cathedra* 106: 7-34 (in Hebrew). • J. W. CROWFOOT, K. M. KENYON, AND E. L. SUKENIK 1942, *Samaria-Sebaste 1: The Buildings at Samaria,* London: Palestine Exploration Fund. • J. W. CROWFOOT, G. M. CROWFOOT, AND K. M. KENYON 1957, *Samaria-Sebaste 3: The Objects of Samaria,* London: Palestine Exploration Fund. • A. FRUMKIN 2002, "The Water Supply Network of Samaria-Sebaste," in *The Aqueducts of Israel,* ed. D. Amit, J. Patrich, and Y. Hirschfeld, Portsmouth, R.I.: Journal of Roman Archaeology, 267-77. • J. MAGNESS 2001, "The Cults of Isis and Kore at Samaria-Sebaste in the Hellenistic and Roman Periods," *HTR* 94, 2: 157-77. • Y. MESHORER AND S. QEDAR 1991, *The Coinage of Samaria in the 4th Century BCE,* Los Angeles: University of California Press. • E. NETZER 2006, *The Architecture of Herod, The Great Builder,* Tübingen: Mohr-Siebeck, 81-93. • G. A. REISNER, C. S. FISHER, AND D. C. LYON 1924, *Harvard Excavations at Samaria,* 2 vols., Cambridge: Harvard University Press. • F. ZAYADINE 1966, "Samaria-Sebaste, le theatre," *RB* 73: 562-85.

JOSEPH PATRICH

Samaritanism

Samaritanism is a religion that developed from the Israelite tradition and shares with Judaism the beliefs and practices of the Torah (Pentateuch). According to the Samaritans' own understanding, they, rather than the Jews, are the true Israelites. They maintain that at the time of Eli (1 Sam. 1:9; 2:11) a schism occurred because he left Mt. Gerizim, went to Shiloh, and gathered around himself the apostates from the true Israelite religion, that is, the Jews (see the Samaritan Arabic *Book of Joshua,* chap. 43). Although these traditions are preserved in medieval Samaritan sources only, two second-century-B.C.E. inscriptions from the Greek island of Delos have the Samaritans referring to themselves as "Israelites who make offerings to the hallowed *Argarizein* [Mt. Gerizim]."

Except for the Samaritan Pentateuch, none of their writings from the early, that is, pre-fourth-century-C.E. period have survived. The reconstruction of Samaritan history, beliefs, and practices during their formative years therefore depends heavily on archaeological, Greco-Roman, Jewish, and Christian sources.

Varying Perspectives in Ancient Sources

For a long time, Jewish and Christian authors saw the Samaritans as semipagans. The earliest documented expression of this view comes in the writings of the Jewish historian Josephus, who wrote in the first century C.E. In *Ant.* 9.288-91 he gives his reading of 2 Kings 17:24-41. Applying the passage to the Samaritans of his own day, he emphasizes the replacement of the Israelite population by new settlers brought by the king of Assyria from the interior of Persia and Media in the eighth century B.C.E. Similarly, in *Ant.* 10.183-85, a summary statement by Josephus without a biblical equivalent, it appears from his wording that *all* Samaritans after Shalmaneser's deportation of *the* Israelites were settlers from Persia and Media. Josephus calls the Samaritans "Cutheans" from the city of Cuthah (2 Kings 17:24) in Mesopotamia, and this became the pejorative term that later Jewish authors used to refer to the Samaritans.

For a long time modern scholars also took 2 Kings 17 at face value and saw the birth of Samaritanism in the events surrounding the destruction of the Northern Kingdom. This has now changed, and the origin of Samaritanism is dated to a much later period. Research has also shown that there was no sudden schism between Jews and Samaritans but rather a gradual separation that culminated in the formation of two distinct religions only in the second-first century B.C.E. To avoid confusion, a distinction should be made between *Samarians* as inhabitants of the region of Samaria in general and *Samaritans* as members of the religious community that accepts only Mt. Gerizim as its sacred center to the exclusion of Jerusalem.

Biblical Sources

Both biblical and extrabiblical sources indicate that the inhabitants of Samaria who worshiped YHWH were still considered members of Israel in the Persian and Hellenistic periods, and not pagans or semipagans. Various biblical passages presuppose that the inhabitants of Samaria are part of the people of Israel and that the inhabitants of the North share a common faith with those of the South (Isa. 11:12-13; Jer. 23:5-6; 31:17-20; 41:5; Ezek. 37:15-28; Zech. 8:13; 9:13; 10:6-12). This perspective inspired the hope that one day the unity of Ephraim and Judah would be restored. Had the Northerners been seen as pagans, such prophecies would not have been enunciated.

The author of Chronicles certainly took the existence of YHWH worshipers in the North for granted. According to him, priests, Levites, and people "from all the tribes of Israel [came] to Jerusalem to sacrifice to the LORD" (2 Chron. 11:13-17). The Judahite King Abijah addresses the northern Israelites in 2 Chronicles 13 in a major speech, holding out the possibility of repentance for them. Under King Asa "great numbers had deserted to him from Israel when they saw that the LORD his God was with him" (2 Chron. 15:9). They gathered around him in Jerusalem, sacrificed to YHWH, and "entered into a covenant to seek the LORD, the God of their ancestors, with all their heart and with all their soul" (2 Chron. 15:9-15). During the reign of Ahaz, Oded, a prophet of YHWH, spoke to the Israelites in Samaria, persuading them to release the Judahite prisoners they had taken (2 Chron. 28:8-15). King Hezekiah "sent word to all Israel and Judah, and wrote letters also to Ephraim and Manasseh, that they should come to the house of the LORD at Jerusalem, to keep the Passover to the LORD the God of Israel" (2 Chron. 30:1).

Clearly, the inhabitants of Samaria are addressed as Israelites; there is no trace in the text of forced emigrations or settlements of foreigners. The cultic reforms carried out by Hezekiah extended to Ephraim and Manasseh (2 Chron. 31:1). Similarly, Josiah implemented his reforms in "the towns of Manasseh, Ephraim, and Simeon, and as far as Naphtali" (2 Chron. 34:6) and "made all who were in Israel worship the LORD their God" (2 Chron. 34:33). Thus, for the Chronicler, the Northerners were YHWH worshipers, not foreign pagans.

In line with the view reflected in 2 Kings 17, the adversaries of the returnees from Babylonia are also described in Ezra-Nehemiah as descended from semipagans (esp. Ezra 4:1-5). It is now clear that this presentation is mistaken. In 2 Macc. 5:22 Samaritans are considered to be of the same *genos* as the Jews. A passage usually cited as being anti-Samaritan is Ben Sira 50:25-26: the "people that live in Shechem" are called "foolish." If the remark is in fact directed at the Samaritans, it remains unclear why they are labeled "foolish."

Papyri and Inscriptions

As for extrabiblical sources, in the fifth century B.C.E. the Jews of Elephantine in Egypt addressed a letter to the governor in Judah and to the one in Samaria. They also wrote to the high priest and other priests in Jerusalem, but they do not mention a high priest or priests in Samaria or on Mt. Gerizim. Furthermore, in the papyri found in Wadi ed-Daliyeh north of Jericho, which date to the middle of the fourth century B.C.E., the great majority of the wealthy inhabitants of the city of Samaria who left the documents behind bore Yahwistic names. In the third and second centuries B.C.E., pilgrims to Mt. Gerizim from the city of Samaria presented votive inscriptions that were unearthed recently. These inscriptions show that in the Hellenistic period the names of the persons who worshiped and made donations on Mt. Gerizim are indistinguishable from the names in vogue in contemporary Jerusalem.

Josephus

Hostility to the Samaritans is evident in the first century C.E. in Josephus' work *Antiquities of the Jews* and in the New Testament. As noted above, Josephus sees the Samaritans as descendants of settlers brought to Israel by the Assyrians, and he accuses them of duplicity because, so he writes, they sometimes claim that they are Jews but sometimes deny it. Because of his animosity, Josephus' accounts have to be used with caution for the reconstruction of early Samaritan history. He is more trustworthy when it comes to events that took place during his own lifetime. Several incidents are mentioned by him in which the Samaritans clashed with the Judeans and the Romans. One occurred in 8 C.E. when Samaritans scattered human bones in the Jerusalem Temple precincts (*Ant.* 18.29-30). On another occasion the Samaritans killed one (or several) Galileans who were on their way to Jerusalem through Samaritan territory (*J.W.* 2.232-46//*Ant.* 20.118-136). In 36 C.E., under Pontius Pilate, a Samaritan led members of his group up Mt. Gerizim to show them the sacred vessels (of the Tabernacle) buried there (*Ant.* 18.85-89). At stake was the Samaritan belief that in the end times the prophet promised in Deut. 18:18 would return and reestablish the sacrificial cult on Mt. Gerizim. Later, this figure was called the Taheb, the "Returning/Restoring One"; he is the Samaritan eschatological prophet. The Romans' violent handling of the situation cost Pilate his office. A similar incident is recounted in *J.W.* 3.307-15, where over 10,000 Samaritans are said to have been massacred on Mt. Gerizim by the Romans.

New Testament

The pericopes in the New Testament that deal with Samaritans see them as related to the Jews but locate them somewhere between Jews and Gentiles. The most important passages are the following: Luke 10:25-37 (the Parable of the Good Samaritan); Luke 17:11-19 (the healing of the lepers, in which only the Samaritan returns to thank Jesus); and John 4:4-42 (the Samaritan woman at the well). There are also shorter references: Matt. 10:5-6 (Jesus' instruction to the Twelve, "Go nowhere among the Gentiles and enter no town of the Samaritans"); Luke 9:52-56 (a Samaritan village refuses to give hospitality to Jesus on his way to Jerusalem); and John 8:48 (the Jews accuse Jesus of being a Samaritan and having a demon). All of these texts, however, must be used with caution in any attempt at historical reconstruction, because Christian theology and missionary interests have influenced the authors in their depictions of the Samaritans.

Rabbinic References

Rabbinic sources display an ambivalent attitude toward the Samaritans. On the one hand, the Samaritans are recognized as devout followers of the Torah. On the other, they are considered semi- or even full pagans. In many cases, however, they are used as a foil to clarify certain points of halakah, and what is said about them does not necessarily, and certainly not always, reflect historical circumstances. The different attitudes may also be due to differences of opinion among the rabbis.

The Schism in the First-Second Century B.C.E.

All indications are that the rift between the two branches of Israelite religion occurred in the second-first century B.C.E. It was then that the Samaritans introduced their specific readings into a version of the Pentateuch that was current at that time among worshipers of YHWH in both the South and the North. The decisive event that alienated the Samaritans and caused them to recognize Mt. Gerizim as the only legitimate place of worship was the destruction of their temple by John Hyrcanus (134-104 B.C.E.) in 112-111 B.C.E. From then on, Samaritanism and Judaism went their own ways, separate from each other.

Differences between Samaritanism and Judaism

Among the outstanding differences between Samaritanism and Judaism are the following: (1) the central cult place of the Samaritans is Mt. Gerizim, not Mt. Zion; (2) the Prophets and Writings of the Jewish Bible are not part of the Samaritan sacred canon; (3) the community is led by a high priest (the office of rabbi did not develop among the Samaritans); (4) Samaritanism developed its own traditions of biblical exegesis, halakah, liturgy, and historiography; (5) even after the destruction of their temple, the Samaritans continued to offer a yearly animal sacrifice at Passover by slaughtering, roasting, and eating sheep as prescribed in Exodus 12; and (6) in general, they continued to celebrate those feasts that are commanded in the Pentateuch.

Later History

Despite the separation, contacts between Samaritanism and Judaism continued throughout the centuries. The late dates of the Samaritan sources make it difficult to be more precise about the state of the religion at its beginnings. Early in their history, that is, shortly before and after the turn of the era, Samaritans experienced the development of sects; the best known were the Dositheans. These sects eventually disappeared and left only scant traces in the literature.

Various epigraphic, archaeological, and literary sources show that there was a Samaritan diaspora in antiquity in several countries of the Mediterranean region. It is probable that where there were Jews in that region, there were also Samaritans. Eventually, the numbers of the Samaritans dwindled due to persecutions and conversions. This caused them to concentrate in the area of their origin, where they live today. Now half of the Samaritan population lives in Palestine, that is, in Nablus and on Mt. Gerizim, and half in Israel, that is, in Holon, south of Tel Aviv.

BIBLIOGRAPHY

Bibliography

A. D. CROWN AND R. PUMMER 2005, *A Bibliography of the Samaritans, Third Edition: Revised, Expanded, and Annotated,* Lanham, Md.: Scarecrow.

Reference Work

A. D. CROWN, R. PUMMER, AND A. TAL, EDS. 1993, *A Companion to Samaritan Studies,* Tübingen: Mohr-Siebeck.

History of Research

F. DEXINGER AND R. PUMMER, EDS. 1992, *Die Samaritaner,* Darmstadt: Wissenschaftliche Buchgesellschaft.

Studies

R. J. COGGINS 1975, *Samaritans and Jews: The Origins of the Samaritans Reconsidered,* Oxford: Blackwell. • A. D. CROWN, ED. 1989, *The Samaritans,* Tübingen: Mohr-Siebeck. • F. DEXINGER 1981, "Limits of Tolerance in Judaism: The Samaritan Example," in *Jewish and Christian Self-Definition,* ed. E. P. Sanders, Philadelphia: Fortress, 2:88-114. • S. J. ISSER 1998, "The Samaritans and Their Sects," in *Cambridge History of Judaism: The Early Roman Period,* ed. W. Horbury, W. D. Davies, and J. Sturdy, Cambridge: Cambridge University Press, 569-95. • M. KARTVEIT 2009, *The Origin of the Samaritans,* Leiden: Brill. • G. KNOPPERS 2005, "Mt. Gerizim and Mt. Zion: A Study in the Early History of the Samaritans and the Jews," *SR* 34: 309-38. • A. LEHNARDT 2002, "The Samaritans (Kutim) in the Talmud Yerushalmi: Constructs of 'Rabbinic Mind' or Reflections of Social Reality?" in *The Talmud Yerushalmi and Graeco-Roman Culture,* ed. P. Schäfer, Tübingen: Mohr-Siebeck, 3: 139-60. • J. MACDONALD 1964, *The Theology of the Samaritans,* London: SCM. • J. A. MONTGOMERY 1907, *The Samaritans, The Earliest Jewish Sect: Their History, Theology and Literature,* Philadelphia: Winston. • R. PUMMER 1987, *The Samaritans,* Leiden: Brill. • R. PUMMER 2005, *Early Christian Authors on Samaritans and Samaritanism: Texts, Translations and Commentary,* Tübingen: Mohr-Siebeck. • L. M. WHITE 1987, "The Delos Synagogue Revisited: Recent Field-work in the Greco-Roman Diaspora," *HTR* 80: 133-60.

See also: Gerizim, Mount; Samaria; Samaritan Pentateuch

REINHARD PUMMER

Samaritan Pentateuch

The Samaritan Pentateuch is the sacred scripture of the Samaritans; the Prophets and Writings of the Jewish Bible are not part of the Samaritan canon.

Relation to the Masoretic Text (MT)

The text of the Samaritan Pentateuch (SP) is essentially the same as that of the Masoretic text (MT), although traditionally it has been said that there are 6,000 differences between the two. However, this number goes back to a list in the London Polyglot of 1657 and is inaccurate for several reasons. First of all, it is based on only one manuscript, which was acquired by Pietro della Valle in 1616 and was first published, with numerous mistakes, in the Paris Polyglot (1629) and republished, albeit with corrections, in the London Polyglot. Second, most of the differences concern *scriptio plena* and *scriptio defectiva* ("full" spelling with the use of consonants to represent vowels vs. "defective" spelling that does not use vowel letters). Yet it is now clear that Samaritan scribes followed no specific norm in this regard. The many manuscripts that have come to the attention of scholars since the days of the Paris and London Polyglots show that individual scribes exercised great freedom in copying the Pentateuch. Uniformity exists rather in the oral transmission, that is, in the recitation of the Torah. Therefore, to assess the text of the Pentateuch properly it is necessary to take into account the reading of the Pentateuch as practiced by the Samaritans. This reading reveals that in many cases which in the past were considered instances of *scriptio plena,* the letters in question do not function as vowel letters or *matres lectionis* ("mothers of reading") but rather as consonants.

Other differences between the SP and the MT have been categorized by a number of scholars from Wilhelm Gesenius (1815) to Emanuel Tov (2001). It is evident that all classifications select certain characteristics without being exhaustive, which would be an unachievable task. In the last analysis, it is impossible to quantify the differences between the two versions.

Religiously Significant Readings in the SP

Certain readings in the Samaritan Pentateuch are religiously significant in that they express specific Samaritan beliefs. Especially prominent in this regard are those passages that have a bearing on the holiness of Mt. Gerizim. The cardinal importance of the mountain is revealed in the form of the Decalogue contained in the Samaritan Pentateuch. The Samaritans considered the Jewish first commandment an introduction and inserted after Exod. 20:17 (MT) and Deut. 5:18 (21) a number of verses, or parts thereof, that highlight the importance of Mt. Gerizim in the history of Israel. These inserted verses constitute the Samaritan tenth commandment: Exod. 13:11a; Deut. 11:24b; 27:2b-3a, 4a, 5-7; and 11:30. According to the Samaritans, the mountain was chosen by God from the beginning to be the only place of sacrifice. Thus all twenty-one occurrences of the Deuteronomic formula "the place that the LORD your God *will* choose" were allegedly changed to "the place that the LORD your God *has* chosen." The changes were made in each case by omitting one Hebrew letter from one word (MT *ybḥr* [imperfect "will choose"] to SP *bḥr* [perfect "has chosen"]). Whereas the unnamed place in the MT was eventually understood to refer to Jerusalem (which was not yet conquered in the lifetime of Moses and could therefore not be named), the Samaritans claim that the "place" is Mt. Gerizim. In Deut. 27:4 the SP reads "Gerizim" instead of MT "Ebal," a reading which is also found in the *Vetus Latina* and is probably older than that of the MT. Another possibly "sectarian" reading that emphasizes that Mt. Gerizim had been selected from the days of the Patriarchs is found in Exod. 20:24 (21), where the SP reads, "in *the* place where I *have* caused my name to be remembered I will come to you and bless you," whereas the MT reads, "in *every* place where I *will* cause my name to be remembered I will come to you and bless you." For the Samaritans there is only *one* such place: Mt. Gerizim. Additional ideological changes are often enumerated by scholars, but in many cases they may go back to pre-Samaritan texts and not be specific to the Samaritans. The same is true for phonological and orthographic changes.

Nature and Origin of the SP in Light of the Dead Sea Scrolls

Thanks to the Qumran Scrolls, the nature and origin of

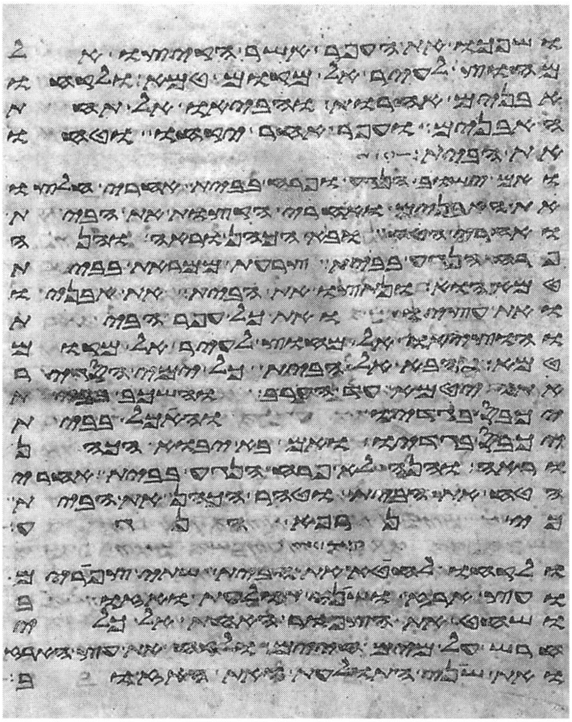

A page from Leviticus in a medieval copy of the Samaritan Pentateuch (Ascalon, Israel, 1189 C.E.) *(The Schøyen Collection, MS 201)*

the SP have become clearer. It has emerged that the SP is based on a text type that was current during the last two centuries B.C.E. Texts of this group are called pre-Samaritan or harmonistic texts because they do not contain any readings distinctive to Samaritan theology and their main characteristics are harmonizing readings that try to make the pentateuchal text "consistent" from one passage to another. The primary example is 4QpaleoExod^{m}. In this pre-Samaritan manuscript written in Paleo-Hebrew characters, longer and shorter passages from Deuteronomy as well as from Exodus itself were inserted into the text to make Exodus and Deuteronomy conform to each other (e.g., after Exod. 18:24, in v. 25, Deut. 1:9-18 was inserted) or to relate the carrying out of a command (e.g., after Exod. 8:19 an addition taken from Exod. 8:16-19 was inserted).

Other differences between the MT on the one hand and pre-Samaritan texts and the SP on the other concern linguistic features and the content of certain passages. Because none of the pre-Samaritan texts exhibits readings that reflect Samaritan ideology, above all the sanctity and centrality of Mt. Gerizim, scholars have discarded the earlier designation "proto-Samaritan." In modifying the text slightly to make it conform to their beliefs and practices, the Samaritans applied the same method as the scribes of the pre-Samaritan texts, that is, they copied from other passages of the Bible and inserted the text where they thought it should be. By inserting their tenth commandment, they defined and asserted their identity and established their own version of Scripture. There is now a consensus among scholars that the SP is an adaptation of a pre-Samaritan or harmonistic text known from Qumran that was made in the second or first century B.C.E. when the Samaritans emerged as a distinct religion separate from that of Judahite Israel. Older views of the nature and origin of the SP are thereby superseded, and earlier discussions concerning the superiority or inferiority of the SP as compared to the MT are now proven to be immaterial.

Manuscripts of the SP

Although early Jewish and Christian writings as well as Samaritan epigraphic sources from the Byzantine period testify to the special form of the Pentateuch among the Samaritans already in antiquity, extant Samaritan Pentateuch manuscripts do not predate the tenth or eleventh centuries C.E. For the Samaritans the most revered copy of the Torah is the Abisha Scroll, so called because, according to Samaritan beliefs, it was written by Abisha, the great-grandson of Aaron at the entrance of the Tent of Meeting in the thirteenth year after the entry of the Israelites into Canaan. Recent analysis, on the other hand, has concluded that the oldest part of the scroll goes back to the twelfth century C.E.

Samaritan Pentateuch manuscripts are not vocalized but contain only the consonantal text. Except for recent editions, prepared primarily for non-Samaritans, vowel signs were used only rarely and inconsistently. The pronunciation of the text was passed on orally. An analysis of the recitation of the Torah as practiced by the Samaritans confirms the dating of the origin of their version in the second or first century B.C.E.

The Samaritan Script

The script in which the Pentateuch has been and still is being written by Samaritan scribes is special to the Samaritans and is therefore called Samaritan script. Although it resembles the so-called Paleo-Hebrew script, it is not the same as the latter, but is derived from the late Second Temple Hebrew script.

BIBLIOGRAPHY

Editions

A. VON GALL 1918, *Der Hebräische Pentateuch der Samaritaner,* Giessen: Töpelmann, rpt. 1966 (lists variants from numerous manuscripts but presents an eclectic text). • A. TAL, ED. 1994, *The Samaritan Pentateuch Edited according to MS 6 (C) of the Shekhem Synagogue,* Tel Aviv: Tel Aviv University, Chaim Rosenberg School of Jewish Studies (a diplomatic edition of one of the most important extant manuscripts from the year 1204 C.E.). • A. N. TSEDAKA AND R. TSEDAKA 1964-1965, *Jewish Version–Samaritan Version of the Pentateuch with Particular Stress on the Differences between Both Texts,* Tel Aviv and Holon (the SP and the MT are in parallel columns with the differences highlighted; it is not a critical edition but useful for a first orientation).

Studies

F. DEXINGER 1977, "Das Garizimgebot im Dekalog der Samaritaner," in *Studien zum Pentateuch: Walter Kornfeld zum 60. Geburtstag,* ed. G. Braulik, Vienna: Herder, 111-33. • W. GESENIUS 1815, *De pentateuchi samaritani origine, indole et auctoritate: Commentatio philologico-critica,* Halle: Impensis librariae Rengerianae. • M. KARTVEIT 2009, *The Origin of the Samaritans,* Leiden: Brill, 259-312. • R. PUMMER 2007, "The Samaritans and Their Pentateuch," in *The Pentateuch as Torah: New Models for Understanding Its Promulgation and Acceptance,* ed. G. N. Knoppers and B. M. Levinson, Winona Lake, Ind.: Eisenbrauns, 237-69. • J. D. PURVIS 1968, *The Samaritan Pentateuch and the Origin of the Samaritan Sect,* Cambridge: Harvard University Press. • J. E. SANDERSON 1986, *An Exodus Scroll from Qumran: 4QpaleoExod^{m} and the Samaritan Tradition,* Atlanta: Scholars Press. • S. SCHORCH 2004, *Die Vokale des Gesetzes: Die samaritanische Lesetradition als Textzeugin der Tora,* vol. 1, *Das Buch Genesis,* Berlin: de Gruyter. • E. TOV 2001, "Pre-Samaritan Texts and the Samaritan Pentateuch," in idem, *Textual Criticism of the Hebrew Bible,* Minneapolis: Fortress, 80-100.

See also: Gerizim, Mount; Samaria; Samaritanism

REINHARD PUMMER

Sanballat

Sanballat (Hebr. *sanballaṭ;* Akk. *Sîn-uballiṭ,* "May Sin [the moon god] give him life") was the name of three governors of Samaria during the Persian period. Sanballat I, the Horonite, was a leader of Samaria and the founder of a dynasty that controlled the city and surrounding area for six generations. The practice of pap(p)onymy (naming the son after the grandfather) helps us trace the dynasty as follows: Sanballat I (mentioned in Nehemiah), third quarter of the fifth century B.C.E.; his son Delaiah (mentioned in the Elephantine Papyri), end of the fifth century; Sanballat II (mentioned in the Samaritan Papyri), early fourth century; Yaddua/Yeshua (mentioned in the Samaritan Papyri), second quarter of the fourth century; Hananiah (mentioned in the Samaritan Papyri), end of the fourth century. Another Sanballat (III) is also mentioned by Josephus and dated to the last half of the fourth century B.C.E.

In the Bible, Sanballat I is associated with Tobiah the Ammonite (Neh. 2:10) in showing displeasure with Nehemiah's efforts at rebuilding the walls of Jerusalem; he is also associated with "Tobiah the Ammonite official, and Geshem the Arab" (Neh. 2:19) in mocking and ridiculing Nehemiah and accusing him of rebellion against the king; and with Tobiah and the Arabs and the Ammonites and the Ashdodites (Neh. 4:7) in reacting with anger as the walls of Jerusalem were being repaired. He is listed again with Tobiah, Geshem the Arab, and "the rest of our [the restoration community's] enemies" (Neh. 6:1), who were intending to harm Nehemiah. He seems to have sent several letters to Nehemiah threatening to denounce his activities as an open rebellion to the king (Neh. 6:4), and he also appears in complicity with Tobiah in hiring a prophet to speak against Nehemiah (Neh. 6:12).

Both Tobiah and Sanballat I seem to have been members of the group repatriated under the leadership of Zerubbabel. Nehemiah prayed, "Remember Tobiah and Sanballat, O my God, according to these things that they did, and also the prophetess Noadiah and the rest of the prophets who wanted to make me afraid" (Neh. 6:14). Sanballat I's ethnic identification as "the Horonite" (Neh. 2:10) has proven not to be an easy puzzle to solve. He has been related to Ben Ḥoron (10 miles northwest of Jerusalem), Horonaim (Moab), and Harran (by the Balikh River). A recent alternative is to read "Horonite" as "Hauranite," making him a "feudal" lord of the south. Despite the adversarial nature of all of the references to Sanballat I in the book of Nehemiah, his children bear Yahwistic names and his family seems to have had close connections with the leadership of the Jewish community in Jerusalem, as is attested by the marriage of one of his daughters to a member of the family of the Jerusalem high priest Eliashib (Neh. 13:28).

In a petition sent by Jedaniah and the Jewish leaders of the Elephantine colony (a draft has been preserved among the Elephantine Papyri) to Bagavahya, governor of Judah, requesting permission to rebuild their temple that had been destroyed by Vidranga, there is mention of a previous letter sent to Sanballat's (written *Sinuballit*) sons Delaiah and Shelemiah. The letter implies that the sons were in charge of affairs by the time the petition was written. The petition refers to Sanballat as "governor *(pḥt)* of Samaria," which included both the city and the province of the same name (335 B.C.E.). A later memorandum written by Bagavahya and Delaiah provided endorsement for Jedaniah's claim and support for the rebuilding of the temple in Elephantine as "was formerly before Cambyses."

The name Sanballat (II), the grandson of the Sanballat of the Elephantine Papyrus, is attested as a patronymic in a papyrus document from Wadi ed-Daliyeh dated to the reign of Artaxerxes, probably in 375-338 B.C.E. The position of the name in the documents suggests that he was the governor of Samaria at that time. The name also appears in a Hebrew seal (Wadi ed-Daliyeh Seal 22) as the patronymic of Samaria's governor.

Josephus mentions a Sanballat (*Sanaballetēs; Ant.* 11.311) who was appointed "satrap" of Samaria by Darius III and whose daughter Nikaso was married to Manasseh, brother of Jaddua the high priest of Jerusalem (*Ant.* 11.302-3). Josephus reports that Sanballat negotiated with Darius III for the building of a temple on Mt. Gerizim and had promised his son-in-law the position of high priest (*Ant.* 11.310-11; 11.315). When Alexander the Great's armies were advancing into Palestine, Sanballat changed allegiances and supported Alexander. In return, he received Alexander's support for the construction of the temple and the appointment of his son-in-law as high priest (*Ant.* 11.321-24; 11.342). Josephus' lack of precise knowledge of the Persian period, however, has caused scholars to doubt his account of Sanballat's political dealings with Darius III and Alexander the Great.

BIBLIOGRAPHY

F. M. CROSS 1975, "A Reconstruction of the Judean Restoration," *Int* 29: 187-201. • R. EGGER 1986, *Josephus und die Samaritaner,* Freiburg: Universitätsverlag. • D. M. GROPP 2001, *The Samaria Papyri from Wadi Daliyeh: Wadi Daliyeh II and Qumran Miscellanea,* Part 2, DJD 28, Oxford: Clarendon. • S. MITTMANN 2000, "Tobia, Sanballat und die persische Provinz Juda," *Journal of Northwest Semitic Languages* 26: 1-50. • B. PORTEN ET AL., 1996, *The Elephantine Papyri in English,* Leiden: Brill. • K. D. SCHUNCK 1998, *Nehemia,* Neukirchen-Vluyn: Neukirchener Verlag. • D. R. SCHWARTZ 1990, "On Some Papyri and Josephus' Sources and Chronology for the Persian Period," *JSJ* 21: 175-99.

ALEJANDRO F. BOTTA

Sanders, Ed Parish

E. P. Sanders (1937-) earned his Th.D. at Union Theological Seminary in 1966 under W. D. Davies and taught at McMaster University (1966-1984), Oxford University (1984-1990), and Duke University (1990-2005). His research has focused on the nature of early Judaism and on Jesus and Paul within their Jewish contexts. Sanders has insisted that New Testament scholars must understand Judaism on its own terms and be familiar with ancient Jewish sources. He has devoted considerable energy to correcting inaccurate Christian characterizations of Judaism as a legalistic religion of "works-righteousness."

Sanders has argued that most forms of early Judaism agreed on key theological points: God chose the Jews as his elect people and gave them the Torah to live by as their covenant obligation. God rewards obedience and punishes transgression. The Torah includes provisions for forgiveness and atonement. Those who maintain their covenant membership through obedience to Torah will be saved by God's grace. Thus, while Jews affirmed the necessity of Torah observance, they did not believe that works made them righteous before God. Salvation came only through God's grace and mercy. Sanders calls this theological framework "covenantal nomism." Some scholars have faulted Sanders for downplaying strands of Judaism that do not neatly fit within his paradigm, though many have granted that his overall model is basically correct.

Although Sanders acknowledges the diversity of early Judaism, he rejects the idea that it was so fragmented that it must be regarded as multiple "Judaisms." In addition to sharing a belief in covenantal nomism, most Jews held many practices in common (e.g., observance of the Sabbath and festivals, the kosher dietary system, circumcision), were loyal to the Jerusalem Temple (with the obvious exception of the Qumran community), and felt a sense of worldwide solidarity with other Jews. Thus, most varieties of early Judaism can be subsumed within what he calls "Common Judaism." In his view, the sects were minority movements; most Jews would not have identified themselves as Pharisees, Sadducees, or Essenes. Scholars have been misled by the Gospels and summary passages in Josephus to think that the Pharisees exercised greater power and influence in the pre-70 era than they actually did. He also argues that much scholarship (particularly within New Testament studies) has misunderstood the purity system as oppressive. Impurity was a natural part of life and was not regarded as sinful. Sanders also suggests that Greco-Roman culture was less widespread in first-century-C.E. Palestine than is sometimes supposed.

Sanders argued in his influential *Jesus and Judaism* (1985) that Jesus is best understood as a Jewish apocalyptic prophet. Jesus, according to him, believed that the arrival of the kingdom of God was imminent. When he overturned the tables of the money changers in the temple, it was not a "cleansing" (as the act has often been called in Christian scholarship) to protest the sacrificial cult or its administration by priests but a symbolic act prophesying the Temple's imminent destruction and its replacement by the eschatological temple. Sanders points to passages in Isaiah, Tobit, *1 Enoch, Jubilees, Psalms of Solomon,* the *Temple Scroll,* and other texts to suggest that expectations of a new temple were widespread. Jesus' twelve disciples symbolized the tribes of Israel, which would be reunited in the eschaton. Jesus thought that he himself would play a key role in the kingdom, though exactly what he perceived that role to be is difficult to determine. Sanders's emphasis on the Jewishness of Jesus' message contrasts sharply with earlier reconstructions that had portrayed Jesus as attacking Judaism and with certain more recent reconstructions that argue that Jesus was not apocalyptically oriented.

Sanders's *Paul and Palestinian Judaism* (1977) is regarded as a milestone in Pauline studies. His survey of Palestinian Jewish texts from 200 B.C.E. to 200 C.E. (i.e., early rabbinic literature, the Dead Sea Scrolls, certain books from the Apocrypha and Pseudepigrapha) demonstrates that with the exception of *4 Ezra,* all assume a theology of covenantal nomism.

Traditional Protestant scholarship, which argued that Jews were insecure about their ability to live by Torah or arrogant about their accomplishments, was thus misguided. Paul's break from Judaism was not prompted by earlier frustration with the Torah; rather, he reevaluated the Law after he came to believe that Jesus was the risen Messiah. In Paul's revised view, because Jesus died, his death must have been necessary for salvation, and if his death was necessary, then the Law must have been inadequate. For Paul, the Law could indeed lead to righteousness, but not the higher righteousness achieved by faith in Christ.

The rejection of the scholarly view of Judaism as a religion of works-righteousness came to be known as the "New Perspective on Paul" (a phrase coined by James D. G. Dunn). Though the New Perspective has been generally accepted, it has had both its refiners (e.g., Dunn, N. T. Wright, Daniel Boyarin) and detractors, especially from Evangelical and Reformed sectors of New Testament scholarship concerned that it undermines the Protestant understanding of justification by faith alone (see, e.g., the arguments that some forms of Judaism were legalistic in Carson, O'Brien, Seifrid, eds. 2001-2004). Few scholars, however, would question its impact on the field.

BIBLIOGRAPHY

D. A. CARSON, P. T. O'BRIEN, AND M. A. SEIFRID, EDS. 2001-2004, *Justification and Variegated Nomism,* 2 vols., Grand Rapids: Baker Academic. • J. D. G. DUNN 2005, *The New Perspective on Paul: Collected Essays,* Tübingen: Mohr-Siebeck. • E. P. SANDERS 1969, *The Tendencies of the Synoptic Tradition,* Cambridge: Cambridge University Press. • E. P. SANDERS 1977, *Paul and Palestinian Judaism: A Comparison of Patterns of Religion,* Philadelphia: Fortress. • E. P. SANDERS 1983, *Paul, the Law, and the Jewish People,* Philadelphia: Fortress. • E. P. SANDERS 1985, *Jesus and Judaism,* Philadelphia: Fortress. • E. P. SANDERS 1990, *Jewish Law from Jesus to the Mishnah,* London: SCM Press; Philadelphia: Trinity Press International. • E. P. SANDERS 1991, *Paul,* Oxford: Oxford University Press. • E. P. SANDERS 1992, *Judaism: Practice and Belief: 63 BCE–66 CE,* London: SCM; Philadelphia: Trinity Press International. • E. P. SANDERS 1993, *The Historical Figure of Jesus,* London: Penguin. • E. P. SANDERS AND M. DAVIES 1989, *Studying the Synoptic Gospels,* London: SCM. • F. UDOH ET AL., EDS. 2008, *Redefining First-Century Jewish and Christian Identities: Essays in Honor of E. P. Sanders,* Notre Dame: University of Notre Dame Press. • N. T. WRIGHT 1991, *The Climax of the Covenant: Christ and the Law in Pauline Theology,* Edinburgh: Clark, 1991.

See also: Covenantal Nomism; Grace

MARK A. CHANCEY

Sanhedrin

The Greek word *Sanhedrin* (from *syn,* "together," and *hedra,* "seat") is usually translated "council." It occurs about one dozen times in the Septuagint, with a variety of meanings (such as assembly or court), translating at least four different Hebrew words (e.g., *din* in Prov. 22:10; *qāhāl* in Prov. 26:26). The Greek *synedrion* appears as a loanword in the Mishnah with the meaning "council" (cf. *m. Soṭah* 9:11).

Most occurrences of *synedrion* in the Gospels are in reference to the Council of Jerusalem, before which Jesus appeared (Matt. 26:59; Mark 14:55; 15:1; Luke 22:66; John 11:47). After the emergence of the church, the apostles also will appear before this *synedrion* (Acts 4:15; 5:21, 27, 43, 41). Josephus refers to this body of elders (*Ant.* 14.167-80; *Life* 62, "the Sanhedrin at Jerusalem").

There is related terminology that probably refers to the same body. The word *gerousia,* which occurs frequently in the Septuagint, can be translated "senate" or "council of elders" (Exod. 3:16, 18; 4:29; 12:21; 24:9; Lev. 9:3; Num. 22:4; 2 Macc. 11:27; Jdt. 4:8). The term occurs in Josephus more than two dozen times (*Ant.* 4.186, 218, 220, 222, 255) and about ten times in Philo (*De Ebrietate* 14; *De Migratione Abrahami* 168; *Mos.* 1.73; 2.153). Philo also refers to the "council of elders [*gerousia*], which our savior and benefactor Augustus elected to manage the affairs of the Jewish nation after the death of the king of our own nation" (*In Flaccum* 74).

The word *presbytērion* refers to a council of elders, whether the Sanhedrin of Jerusalem (Luke 22:66; Acts 22:5), or a council of Christian leaders (1 Tim. 4:14; Ignatius, *Eph.* 2:2; 4:1; *Magn.* 2:1; 13:1; *Trall.* 2:2; 7:2; *Phld.* 4:1). Josephus employs the word *boulē* in reference to the Jerusalem Sanhedrin (*J.W.* 5.532) and the word *bouleutērion* in reference to the Sanhedrin's place of meeting (*J.W.* 5.144). Philo also uses *boulē* in reference to the Roman Senate (*In Flaccum* 40).

These many references, from diverse authors and traditions, support the historicity of the Sanhedrin, yet at the same time demonstrate fluidity of terminology and hint at its changing roles and powers. Jewish and Christian writers knew of the existence of this political and judicial body, but did not necessarily understand well its function or how it was assembled. Scholarly discussion should take into account the limitations of the available sources.

Scholars have debated the origin, function, and even number of Sanhedrin bodies that existed in the Second Temple period (for a survey, see Mantel 1961). S. B. Hoenig (1953), for example, argues for three Sanhedrins consisting of political, priestly, and scribal councils, the last constituting the so-called Great Sanhedrin. But this complicated hypothesis relies too heavily on rabbinic traditions that in all probability have indulged in midrashic hagiography and tend to read rabbinic ideals back into earlier periods. Nevertheless, it may be admitted that the tradition that the "Great Sanhedrin" comprised seventy (or seventy-one) members, based on Num. 11:16 ("Gather to me seventy men of the elders of Israel"), may be credible (*m. Sanh.* 1:6; cf. Josephus, *J.W.* 2.482). Other biblical passages speak of "seventy elders" (Exod. 24:1, 9; Num. 11:24-25; Deut. 27:1; Ezek. 8:11), which probably provided a template on which the *synedrion* of the time of Jesus was based.

The origins of the Sanhedrin may be hinted at in the reference to the "great assembly" *(qāhāl gĕdōlâ)* that Nehemiah convened, in order to investigate and bring charges against those practicing usury (Neh. 5:7-8). The references to the "elders of the Jews" in Ezra may also refer to this assembly (Ezra 5:5; 6:7-8, 14). According to the fourth-century writer Hecataeus of Abdera, the Jewish people were governed by priests, chosen by Moses, who served as judges, over whom a high priest presided (*apud* Diodorus Siculus 40.3.4–5). Behind this artificial and collapsed summary of the history of Israel may be a fairly accurate description of the existence and function of the Jewish Council in the approximate time of Alexander the Great. We are told by Josephus that Antiochus III (223-187 B.C.E.) decreed that the Jewish "nation live according to the laws of their own country; and let the senate [*gerousia*] and the priests, and the scribes of the temple, and the sacred singers, be relieved from poll tax and the crown tribute, and other taxes also" (*Ant.* 12.142). In the Hasmonean period we hear of Jewish government comprised of "the high priest, the senate of the nation [*gerousia tou ethnous*], the priests" (1 Macc. 2:6).

From the time of Alexander to the time of Roman authority, the power of the Sanhedrin waxed and waned. With the rise of the Hasmonean dynasty, the power of the Sanhedrin was diminished (1 Macc. 14:41–49, esp. v. 44, with reference to Simon: "None of the people or priests shall be permitted to nullify any of these decisions or to oppose what he says, or to convene an assembly in the country without his permission . . ."). From Simon to Alexander Jannaeus the authority of the high priest was almost absolute. Under Alexandra Salome the Sanhedrin regained some of its authority, especially under Pharisaic influence (Josephus, *Ant.* 13.408: "She made Hyrcanus high priest because he was the elder, but much more because he cared not to meddle with politics, and permitted the Pharisees to do everything and also ordered the multitude to obey them . . ."). In the Roman period the high priest, Sanhedrin, and Roman-appointed governors shared power. But under the rule of Herod the Great the power of the high priest and Sanhedrin was greatly diminished. After the death of Herod the high priest and Sanhedrin regained much of its authority (*Ant.* 20.251: ". . . after their death, the government became an aristocracy, and the high priests were entrusted with a dominion over the nation"; cf. Philo, *In Flaccum* 74).

The shared authority of high priest, Sanhedrin, and Roman governor is seen in the trial and execution of Jesus of Nazareth in the time of Pilate the prefect (Mark 14:43–15:45; *Ant.* 18.64-65) and in the trial, punishment, and release of Jesus, son of Ananias, in the time of Albinus (62-64 C.E.) the procurator (*J.W.* 6.300-309). The convening of the "sanhedrin of judges" and the condemnation of James the brother of Jesus, without the authorization of the Roman procurator, resulted in the removal of Ananus from the office of high priest (*Ant.* 20.200-203). The lack of capital authority on the part of the Sanhedrin is assumed in the Synoptic Gospels and is explicitly stated in the Fourth Gospel (John 18:31).

BIBLIOGRAPHY

E. BAMMEL, ED. 1970, *The Trial of Jesus: Cambridge Studies in Honour of C. F. D. Moule,* London: SCM. • D. R. CATCHPOLE 1971, *The Trial of Jesus,* Leiden: Brill. • S. B. HOENIG 1953, *The Great Sanhedrin,* Philadelphia: Dropsie College. • J. S. KENNARD 1962, "The Jewish Provincial Assembly," *ZNW* 53: 25-51. • H. MANTEL 1961, *Studies in the History of the Sanhedrin,* Cambridge: Harvard University Press. • P. WINTER 1961, *On the Trial of Jesus,* Berlin: de Gruyter. • P. WINTER 1964, "The Trial of Jesus and the Competence of the Sanhedrin," *NTS* 10: 494-99. • S. ZEITLIN 1946, "Synedrion in Greek Literature, the Gospels and the Institution of the Sanhedrin," *JQR* 37:189-98.

See also: Elders CRAIG A. EVANS

Sardis

Early History

The earliest Jewish presence at Sardis remains largely unknown, although it has been argued (A. T. Kraabel in Hanfmann 1983: 178-79) that some Jewish families reached this ancient Lydian city in western Asia Minor shortly after the Babylonian destruction of Jerusalem in 587 B.C.E. In the Hebrew Bible, Obadiah 20 mentions "the exiles of Jerusalem who are in Sepharad," Sepharad being the Semitic name for the city of Sardis. This biblical reference, therefore, suggests a Jewish presence in the area dating back to the late sixth century. Of Jewish settlers in and around Sardis nothing more is known for several hundred years.

Jewish Settlement in the Hellenistic Period

The first clear reference to Jewish settlement in the area in and around Sardis comes from the Jewish historian Josephus. Writing in Rome at the end of the first century C.E., Josephus cites a letter from the Hellenistic king Antiochus III to his governor in Babylonia ordering the resettlement of some 2,000 Jewish families from Mesopotamia and Babylonia to locations in Lydia and Phrygia (*Ant.* 12.147-52). His account further states that these settlers were given land for homes and vineyards, as well as exemption from taxes for a period of ten years.

That Sardis received a significant portion of these Jewish families is emphatically confirmed by a group of early second-century-B.C.E. inscriptions, public letters from Antiochus III and his wife, Queen Laodice, to the recently devastated city of Sardis authorizing supplies for its reconstruction and emphasizing the royal desire for the city's repopulation as soon as possible. It can be inferred from the inscriptions that the majority of these Jewish settlers were farmers brought in to stabilize the regions that surrounded cities such as Sardis during the waning years of Seleucid control. Nevertheless many of these Greek-speaking Jews were also known to have flourished in urban occupations such as skilled artisans and craftsmen, physicians, shopkeepers, scholars, and petty public officials.

It is certainly noteworthy that the Sardis Jews of late antiquity continued to regard this royal mandate outlining the city's resettlement as a seminal event in the history of their community. Indeed, the community pointedly incorporated these Hellenistic inscriptions into the foundational piers of its late-antique synagogue, a monumental structure that was not completed until the final decades of the fourth century C.E.

The Jewish Community of Roman Sardis

Although Jewish settlement in Sardis thus received its first major impetus from a Hellenistic monarch, the community continued to grow and subsequently to flourish under the protection of Rome. Elsewhere in the *Antiquities,* Josephus takes note of the Sardian Jews in late Hellenistic and early Roman times. His primary intention is to illustrate consistent Roman affirmation of Jewish religious freedom in Sardis and indeed throughout Greece and Asia Minor.

Beginning with Julius Caesar, Roman rulers granted the Jews of Sardis and Jewish communities throughout the region the right to collect common funds, to assemble for worship and common meals, and to follow all the requirements of Jewish law. Later these rights were expanded to include exemption from military service and from participation in the imperial cult.

Josephus, however, probably exaggerates the civic status of Jews living in Greek cities when he refers to them as full citizens *(politai).* On the contrary, what Josephus actually describes as the civic status of the Jewish communities in Sardis and throughout the region appears to be that of a *politeuma* (an autonomous social and civic entity), which ought not to be confused with full Greek citizenship. Furthermore, it should be noted that even the affirmation of the many rights and privileges accorded these Jewish communities appears to have taken place within a context of intermittent civic tension with the local Greek majorities.

In fact, Josephus inadvertently documents this tension when quoting from a number of official decrees to various Jewish communities in western Asia Minor, including that of Sardis. He cites a decree from the Sardis council and people (*Ant.* 14.259-61), for example, that begins by affirming the "long history" of communal rights and privileges which the Jewish community residing in that city had enjoyed, rights which were now being *restored* following an unspecified period in which they had apparently been abrogated.

Nor was the political status of Jews significantly different with respect to rights conferred on them directly by Rome. Although some Jews clearly were Roman citizens as early as the time of Julius Caesar, if not before (*Ant.* 14.228-29), prior to the third century of the Common Era the vast majority of Jews residing in the cities of western Asia Minor, including Sardis, held neither full local citizenship nor Roman citizenship. Indeed, the decline of Roman imperial power and the increasing instability of the Greek upper classes that occurred during the third century formed the background and created the historical conditions for the dramatic rise of Jewish communities throughout the region, giving them a new voice in civic affairs. In Sardis, in particular, the Jewish community became a more visible presence in civic life during the latter part of the third century. Prior to that time, however, there is scant evidence of such a presence.

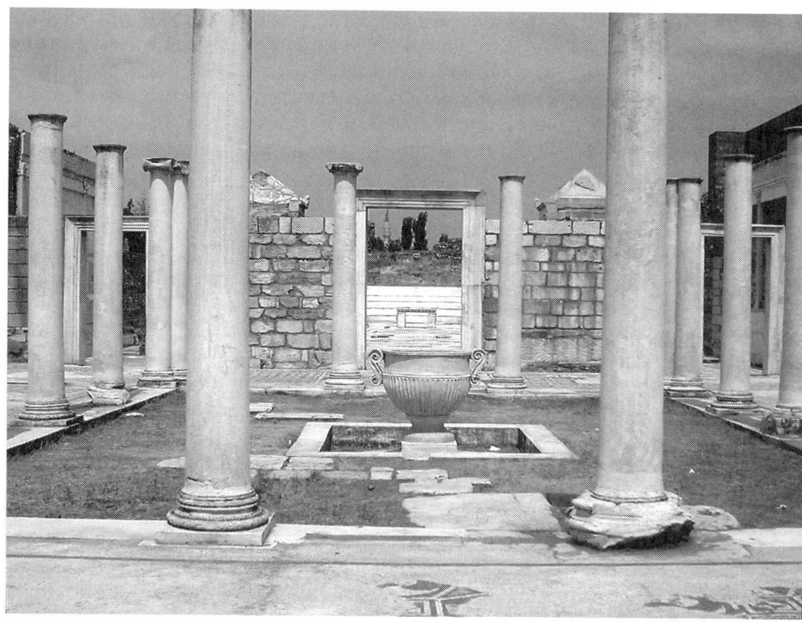

Forecourt of the Jewish synagogue at Sardis, looking west *(www.HolyLandPhotos.org)*

The Rise and Evolution of the Synagogue at Sardis

The early Roman decree of the Sardis city council, which was cited by Josephus as restoring certain longstanding rights to the Sardis Jewish community, also granted to the community several new privileges. Among these were guaranteed access to kosher foods to be sold in the city markets and the acquisition of public space for the erection and maintenance of a synagogue.

The earliest material evidence for a synagogue at Sardis, however, can be traced only to the early third century C.E. An inscription listing the city's public fountains indicates the existence of a synagogue, supplied with water by local authorities and functioning as a public place of worship. This otherwise unknown third-century synagogue was replaced a century later by the late-antique synagogue, the imposing structure that became a city landmark.

The conversion to a synagogue of the south hall of one of the city's two monumental bath-gymnasium complexes may have begun as early as the late third century, when the archaeological evidence suggests the beginnings of such a conversion. The tentative nature of this evidence, however, indicates that if such a late third-century renovation was initiated, work did not progress immediately thereafter; indeed, the synagogue's main hall was not completed before the middle of the fourth century, with work continuing on the synagogue forecourt even into the final decades of the fourth century.

The late-antique synagogue at Sardis is the largest synagogue ever found outside of Palestine, its main hall and forecourt forming a combined length of eighty m. Moreover, its architecture and sophisticated interior detail indicate a high level of prosperity for the community that built and maintained it, apparently making modest repairs even into the sixth century.

The forecourt consisted of a peristyle courtyard, roofed around the periphery. The central portion of the courtyard, which was open to the sky, boasted a large marble fountain served by an elaborate water system. The courtyard floor was paved in colorful mosaics, with a number of donor inscriptions incorporated into their multicolored geometric patterns.

Three doors at the west end of the forecourt marked the entrance to the main hall, which is of monumental size and estimated to hold a thousand people. Flanking the central door on the east wall stood two shrines crowned with pediments and mounted on masonry platforms. The west end of the main hall is enclosed by a semicircular apse, which is lined with marble benches stacked in three tiers.

A notable feature of this apse is the beautiful peacock-and-crater mosaic that covers its floor and is dated by its excavators to the early fourth century. Aside from the dramatic apse mosaic, however, the floor of the main hall is paved in mosaic panels executed in multicolored geometric patterns, some of which incorporate a small number of inscriptions.

Perhaps the most remarkable aspect of the main hall's décor was the iconic quality of its surviving furnishings. Lion statues and an eagle table, emblematic of the city's ancient Lydian and Roman imperial rulers, respectively, were pointedly reappropriated and employed anew to adorn the hall's central interior space.

The long north and south walls of the main hall are divided architecturally into seven bays, the upper portions of which were decorated with panels of marble inlay; the lower portions of these walls were covered with donor inscriptions, which were cut into plaques of marble revetment and mounted on the walls. The vast majority of the approximately eighty inscriptions found in the synagogue were located on these two walls. On the basis of both style and quality of workmanship, most of them have been dated to the second half of the fourth century, with the remainder dated to the fifth and even sixth centuries. Indeed, the lengthy time span represented by the synagogue's rich catalogue of inscriptions is only one of several reasons why a recent attempt to date the synagogue itself to the mid-sixth century is highly unlikely (Magness 2005: 443-75).

Jewish Believers and Gentile Sympathizers at Sardis

Among the synagogue's eighty Greek inscriptions, six refer to their donors by the term *theosebēs* (God-fearer), a term that can refer either to a pious Jewish believer or to a Gentile sympathizer or adherent to Judaism. Given the brevity of these *theosebēs* inscriptions and the location of several of them in the synagogue forecourt, the suggestion (Kraabel) that they refer to Gentile sympathizers is not without merit.

On the other hand, at least one of these inscriptions refers to a member of a Sardis Jewish family of long standing. Moreover, because of the dating of all six inscriptions to the later fourth through early sixth centuries, it is more likely that most, if not all, of them refer to pious Jewish believers rather than to Gentile sympathizers.

The Sardis Jewish Community in Late Antiquity

It is also from the many inscriptions adorning the synagogue's interior space and spanning several centuries that a picture emerges of a robust and socially secure community in the Sardis of late antiquity. One particularly noteworthy aspect of that picture is that nine of these inscriptions attest to members of the synagogue as having been members of the Sardis city council. Even in the fourth and fifth centuries this rank indicates a relatively high level of economic prosperity for the individuals who held it, since substantial property requirements remained the defining qualification for membership in that body. And even though in this later period service on the city council may have held little appeal for well-to-do Greek citizens, particularly those who had converted to Christianity and were being lured into more rewarding opportunities in the church and in the imperial bureaucracies, Jewish citizens may have recognized that council representation would create for their community a countervailing power to the rise of the Christian imperium.

In addition to these nine references to the civic honor of council membership, some of the synagogue inscriptions identify their donors as skilled craftsmen (including several goldsmiths, a marble sculptor, and some mosaic workers). Further material evidence, including inscriptions found in the fifth-century shops that adjoin the synagogue's south wall, identify Jewish owners of several small paint and dye shops, and of a glass shop.

That Sardis Jews were well represented in occupations such as skilled craftsmen and tradesmen is also noteworthy, for if it can be shown that the prestige of civic offices such as that of town council was in fact declining, it can also be argued that the importance of artisans and successful tradesmen was, relatively speaking, rising. This is true particularly in the larger cities such as Sardis. Indeed, the emperor Constantine, needing skilled labor for the rebuilding of the empire, granted personal exemptions from costly compulsory public service to many skilled workers, including painters, sculptors, stone carvers, mosaicists, plasterers, gilders, metal workers, potters and glass workers, fullers, and those engaged in purple dying (*Codex Theodosianus* 13.4.2).

Surprisingly, the synagogue inscriptions also attest to a Jewish presence within the governing elite of the new Christian imperial bureaucracy. Two donor inscriptions, one identifying a former procurator and the other a *comes* (a term referring to a senior officeholder in the imperial service), strongly suggest that at least some Sardian Jews had achieved unequivocal social and political prominence. Within this context it is indeed noteworthy that the Jewish community of Sardis appears to have remained secure and prosperous throughout this tumultuous early Christian period, retaining its monumental synagogue and even continuing to make modest renovations in the fifth and sixth centuries, apparently ignoring with impunity the hostile imperial rulings now being issued from nearby Constantinople with increasing force and frequency.

BIBLIOGRAPHY

M. P. BONZ 1993, "Differing Approaches to Religious Benefaction: The Late Third-Century Acquisition of the Sardis Synagogue," *HTR* 86.2: 139-54. • M. P. BONZ 1994, "The Jewish Donor Inscriptions from Aphrodisias: Are They Both Third-Century, and Who Are the *Theosebes?*" *HSCP* 96: 281-99. • M. P. BONZ 1999, "The Jewish Community of Ancient Sardis," in *Evolution of the Synagogue: Problems and Progress*, ed. H. C. Kee and L. H. Cohick, Harrisburg, Penn.: Trinity Press International, 106-22. • G. M. A. HANFMANN 1983, *Sardis: From Prehistoric to Roman Times*, Cambridge, Mass.: Harvard University Press. • J. H. KROLL 2000, "The Greek Inscriptions of the Sardis Synagogue," *HTR* 94.1: 1-127. • J. MAGNESS 2005, "The Date of the Sardis Synagogue in Light of the Numismatic Evidence," *AJA* 109: 443-75. • J. REYNOLDS AND R. TANNENBAUM 1987, *Jews and Godfearers at Aphrodisias: Greek Inscriptions with Commentary*, Cambridge: Cambridge Philological Society. • L. ROBERT 1964, *Nouvelles inscriptiones de Sardis*, Paris: Librarie d'Amerique et d'Orient Adrien Maisonneuve. • A. R. SEAGER 1983, "The Building History of the Sardis Synagogue," *AJA* 76: 423-35. • P. TREBILCO 1991, *Jewish Communities in Asia Minor*, Cambridge: Cambridge University Press.

See also: Asia Minor; Synagogues

MARIANNE PALMER BONZ

Satan and Related Figures

Hebrew Bible

Satan as a proper name stems from the Hebrew noun *śāṭān*, meaning "adversary" or "opponent," and is possibly derived from the Hebrew verb *śṭn*, although this point has been debated. In the Hebrew Bible, the root *śṭn* is most often used as a common noun referring to a

SATAN AND RELATED FIGURES

political or military adversary or legal accuser. The secondary form of this root, *śṭm,* is used to produce the name *maśṭēmâ* (see below).

In the Hebrew Bible, the noun *śāṭān* denotes both human and heavenly figures who act as accusers or adversaries, either as agents or enemies of God. Often the human *śāṭān* is portrayed as a military rival. Certain Philistines worried that David would become a *śāṭān* or adversary during their battle with the Israelites (1 Sam. 29:4). 1 Kings names two of Solomon's military adversaries as *śāṭān* (11:14, 23, 25). And in Ps. 109:6, the psalmist beseeches God to raise up a *śāṭān* (accuser) to bring his abuser to trial. Here the meaning of *śāṭān* denotes the role of prosecutor.

The noun *śāṭān* is used of a celestial figure twenty-six times in four different contexts of the Hebrew Bible (Numbers 22; Job 1, 2; Zechariah 3; 1 Chronicles 21). In Num. 22:22, 32 an angel of the LORD *(mal'āk yhwh),* referred to as a *śāṭān,* is sent by God to be an "adversary" on the road in order to block Balaam's sinful journey. The *śāṭān* in this story clearly acts as a messenger, not enemy, of God. The *śāṭān* acts only within the will of God and therefore could be understood as an extension of YHWH himself.

Both Job and Zechariah add the definite article to the noun *śāṭān (ha-śāṭān),* indicating that the term in these contexts does not denote a proper name. Nor does this form necessarily refer to a specific angelic being whose constant role is to be "the accuser." Rather, the use of the definite article deemphasizes the precise identity of the angelic being and stresses its current but temporary status. Therefore, *ha-śāṭān* in these passages refers to a celestial being who has been assigned the temporary role of adversary or accuser in order to keep a watchful eye on humanity or to accuse and test God's people. The stories in both Job and Zechariah are set in the divine council or heavenly court, raising the question of whether the *ha-śāṭān* intrudes upon the council or is a member of it.

Job 1 and 2 portray *ha-śāṭān* as standing among the sons of God in the divine council. In Job 1:7 and 2:2, God asks *ha-śāṭān,* "From where have you come?" This question could signify YHWH's surprise at the satan's presence in heaven; more likely, though, God is simply asking *ha-śāṭān* where his divinely appointed responsibilities have taken him. In this case *ha-śāṭān* is not roaming the earth in order to cause trouble but to fulfill the directives given to him by God.

God holds up his servant Job to *ha-śāṭān* as an example of upright fidelity. Responding to *ha-śāṭān's* challenges, God gives the accuser permission to remove the blessings Job has received due to his righteousness in order to test the motives for his piety. Thus, the figure of *ha-śāṭān* in Job appears to be a celestial being who has access to the divine council, travels the earth on divinely appointed missions, and has the ability to challenge God. Similar to Numbers 22, *ha-śāṭān* in Job acts within the will of God and is subject to his power. He is not yet an independent and rival force of evil.

Zechariah 3 also depicts *ha-śāṭān* participating in the divine council. Joshua, the high priest, is seen before the angel of the LORD in a vision of the heavenly courtroom. Standing on Joshua's right, *ha-śāṭān* functions as his accuser. Although he does not speak in this story, the setting implies that *ha-śāṭān* is challenging Joshua's high priesthood. Eventually, *ha-śāṭān* is rebuked by the angel of the LORD and Joshua's guilt is taken away.

Since in Zechariah, as in Job, the noun occurs with the definite article, it remains unlikely that *ha-śāṭān* is a proper name. But, whereas *śāṭān* in Numbers 22 is identified as the angel of the LORD, in Zechariah 3 *ha-śāṭān* is rebuked by the angel of the LORD. Whether or not the *śāṭān* figures in Zechariah and Job are identical is unclear.

It is possible that Joshua, as high priest, represents the unified postexilic community. In this understanding, *ha-śāṭān* opposes the Judeans' return due to their continued sinfulness. Yahweh overrules *ha-śāṭān,* and the angel of the LORD gives Joshua new priestly garments, symbolizing the forgiveness of the postexilic community as a whole (Zech. 3:3-5).

Others, however, have suggested that this interpretation is based upon a faulty assumption concerning the level of religious and political unity in postexilic Judah. Within a fractious postexilic community, *ha-śāṭān* could be a cosmic personification of Judeans who oppose Joshua's high priesthood, probably in favor of another. Zechariah's vision, then, concludes that God has sided with Joshua. This interpretation lends support to Pagels' (1991) theory that *śāṭān* is a celestial embodiment of a division within the Judean community.

The final reference to a *śāṭān* in the Hebrew Bible occurs in 1 Chron. 21:1, which portrays him rising up against Israel and causing David to take a census of the people. This is the only reference in the Hebrew Bible where *śāṭān* without the definite article is used for a figure that could be considered an adversary of God; as such, it could be the first attestation of the proper name Satan. However, if *śāṭān* is not being used as a proper name, then the adversary could refer to any unnamed terrestrial or celestial being who urged David to take the census.

The earlier account of this event in 2 Samuel 24 depicts YHWH himself encouraging David to number the people of Israel. Therefore somewhere between the composition of 2 Samuel and 1 Chronicles, responsibility for David's perceived sin shifted from Yahweh to *śāṭān.* Two main theories have emerged for this alteration. First, the Chronicler shifted the responsibility for YHWH's instruction to *śāṭān* in order to distance God from what appears to be sinful counsel. However, in other places, such as the account of Rehoboam and his advisors, comparable episodes are retained by the Chronicler without similar concern (2 Chron. 10:15; 18:18-22). Second, the Chronicler has shifted the incitement from Yahweh to *śāṭān* in order to preserve the positive relationship between God and King David (Day 1988: 36-37). Since Chronicles wishes to portray David as an idealized king, stories that cast him in a negative light are often altered or deleted altogether. The events recorded in 1 Chronicles 21 could not be deleted because they would result in the building of what was at least thought to be the altar of the Solomonic Temple.

Current scholarly consensus dates the book of Chronicles to the Persian period. The first unquestionable references to Satan as a proper name for God's evil archenemy do not occur until the second century B.C.E. (*Jub.* 23:29; *As. Mos.* 10:1). Those who argue that *śāṭān* in Chronicles is not a proper name contend that the time period between Chronicles and these other texts, with no occurrence in between, is too great to necessitate a similar meaning. The Hebrew Bible, then, contains no indisputable reference to Satan as an autonomous, celestial enemy of God. Eventually, though, biblical ideas about *śāṭān* as an agent of God evolved into an understanding of *śāṭān* as an autonomous enemy of God and leader of a celestial demonic kingdom. Precisely when and why this shift occurred remains unclear.

Second Temple Literature

Early Jewish and Christian literature contains many references to evil celestial beings who battle against God's people, often by causing violence or leading humans astray. Surprisingly few occurrences name this adversary Satan (1QH 4:6; 45:3; 1QSb 1:8; *T. Job* 3:6 and 6:1–8:3 are exceptions), preferring names such as Devil, Belial, and Mastema, among others. Although the rise of an evil enemy of God stems from a number of different factors, two appear to have played significant roles.

First, the development of a celestial enemy was heavily influenced by the Jews' experience under Babylonian and Persian rule. Exposure to Zoroastrianism with its emphases on cosmic dualism played a fundamental role in the expansion of the good versus evil dichotomy found in early Judaism. Similar to the rival gods in Persian literature, Jewish tradition never gives Satan equal status with God. YHWH alone is God, with no evil equivalent.

The dichotomy of good and evil found its personified counterpart in unequal leaders in the respective figures of God and Satan. Accordingly, the idea in the Hebrew Bible of a sovereign God responsible for all things, both good and evil, was replaced with a celestial conflict between God and Satan as the leaders of two distinct warring camps. Thus, Satan may have partly evolved from those attributes earlier assigned to God that appeared questionable to both Jews and Christians of the Second Temple period.

Second, the concept of Satan as a personification of evil solidified with the rise of brutal enemies who oppressed Israel. Israel's battles against foreign enemies (especially Antiochus IV) eventually became cosmically represented in a heavenly war between God and his angels against Satan and his minions. Thus, the clash between Israel's theology of election and the reality of its foreign oppression aided in the development of Satan as an autonomous figure.

One of the earliest references to an angel of God "falling" and becoming an enemy of God can be found in the composite book of *1 Enoch.* In the *Book of the Watchers* (*1 Enoch* 1–36) at least two traditions are woven together to describe a cosmic rebellion. Shemihaza and his followers descend from heaven and impregnate human women, who give birth to the giants (*1 Enoch* 6:1–7:8). In *1 Enoch* 8:1-4 Asael and his followers are punished for revealing the secrets of heaven (including metallurgy and cosmetics) to the inhabitants of earth. These references are the first examples in early Jewish literature of divine agents openly rebelling against God, resulting in sin and destruction in the world.

Belial

The personification of evil continued in early Jewish literature in the figure of Belial. Hebr. *bĕliyyaʿal* means "wickedness." Although the etymology of the word is still debated, the Hebrew Bible uses *bĕliyyaʿal* in a compound form to describe a wicked person or people (e.g., the "sons of Belial" in Deut. 13:13 [14 Eng.]), or in concert with mythological concepts such as death and Sheol (Ps. 18:5-6 [4-5 Eng.]; 2 Sam. 22:5-6; 41:9 [8]). The Hebrew Bible also uses *bĕliyyaʿal* to refer to those individuals or groups who are harmful to God's intended social order (Judg. 19:22; 20:13; 1 Kings 21:10-13). Despite Belial's later association with wickedness, rebellion, and death, the Hebrew Bible and the LXX use this term only in its more general sense of "wickedness."

Early Jewish and Christian literature expanded the meaning of the word *bĕliyyaʿal* from wickedness to the proper name of God's celestial enemy. The earliest suggested attestation of Belial as a proper name can be found in the book of *Jubilees,* which was written in the mid-second century B.C.E. However, while Belial in *Jubilees* may be the proper name of an evil agent, it is also possible to translate the term in its generic sense ("spirits of wickedness," 1:20; "sons of wickedness," 5:33). So it is difficult to ascertain with certainty if *Jubilees* is the first work to use Belial as a proper name or if it continues the more general usage commonly found in the Hebrew Bible.

References to Belial as God's evil enemy are well attested at Qumran, especially in the major sectarian scrolls 1QH, 1QS, and 1QM. Belial is described as an evil angel and the Prince of Wickedness (cf. 1QM 13:11, which also states that God appointed Belial to corrupt the children of light; 17:5-6). The later title implies that Belial is now considered a leader of evil forces ("the lot of Belial") who oppose God and his people. He is typically associated with the forces of darkness, waging war against the sons of light and combating the sons of God (1QM 1:1; 13:12; 1QS 2:2; 16-2:8), often by leading God's people astray (CD 5:18; 1QS 3:21). The earthly conflicts between the Wicked Priest and the Teacher of Righteousness are reflected in the heavenly struggle between Belial and Michael. At Qumran, the word "Belial" is used for the leader of God's cosmic enemy more often than any other name.

The proper name Belial (and its Greek form Beliar) is also used in other early Jewish and Christian pseudepigraphic works. As in the scrolls, Belial is described as an angel of wickedness (*Mart. Isa.* 2:4); his angels battle against the angels of the Lord (*T. Asher* 6:4); he is the master of the spirits of error (*T. Judah* 25:3); he is the head of demonic powers (*Mart. Isa.* 1:8); and he at-

SATAN AND RELATED FIGURES

tempts to lead God's people astray (*T. Reu.* 4:7; *Liv. Pro.* 4:6). Despite its use throughout early Jewish and Christian literature for God's celestial enemy (see also *Sib. Or.* 2.67; 3.63, 73), Belial as a proper name did not retain its popularity in either tradition.

The New Testament contains only one reference to Beliar, in the rhetorical "what agreement does Christ have with Beliar?" (2 Cor. 6:15). The context of this verse contrasts righteousness with lawlessness and light with darkness, making it probable that Paul (or the Pauline scribe who inserted the intrusive and rather un-Pauline-sounding passage in 2 Cor. 6:14–7:1) is utilizing common traditions about Belial.

Mastema

Mastema is another name used in Second Temple literature for God's celestial enemy and the leader of evil forces. The name appears to derive from a secondary form of *śṭn,* the Hebrew root for both the noun *śāṭān* and the proper name Satan. In the Hebrew Bible *maśṭēmâ* means "hostility" (Hos. 9:7-8). At Qumran, *maśṭēmâ* often describes the hostility of Belial, the common name in the DSS for the chief agent of evil (1QS 3:23; 4Q286 10 ii 2; 1QM 13:4; 1QM 14:9; CD 16:5).

Like Belial, *maśṭēmâ* evolved from meaning "hostility" to being associated with an evil angel (Belial) to becoming the personification of hostility and the proper name of an evil angel (Mastema). Mastema as a proper name is found most prominently in the book of *Jubilees,* where he is described as the chief of the evil spirits and appears to be equated with Satan (*Jub.* 10:8, 11). He beseeches God to spare one tenth of the evil spirits who, under Mastema's command, will continue to fulfill their created task of leading humanity astray (*Jub.* 10:8). As with Satan's role in Job 1 and 2, *Jub.* 17:15-18 portrays Mastema encouraging God to direct Abraham to sacrifice his son in order to test his faith, although the motives for his doing so remain unclear. Prince Mastema stands as an adversary to Moses, trying to kill him (*Jub.* 48:1-4) and assisting the Egyptian magicians so that Moses will fall into Pharaoh's hand (*Jub.* 48:9-10). Mastema also stirs the Egyptian army to pursue the Hebrews until God defeats it (*Jub.* 48:12). Yet, while Mastema often stands as an adversary against Moses and the Israelites, the powers of Mastema are also the ones responsible for executing God's judgment against the firstborn of the Egyptians on the night of Passover (*Jub.* 49:2). These varying portraits reflect the problem of viewing Mastema as an evil figure acting either against or within the will of God.

New Testament

Satan

Satan as a proper name for God's evil enemy is used thirty-five times in the New Testament. The New Testament writers often use a variety of other terms for God's celestial enemy, including "Beelzebul" *(beelzebul)* or "prince of demons" (Mark 3:22; Matt. 12:24-27; Luke 11:15-19); "the evil one" (Matt. 5:37; 13:19, 38; John 17:15; Eph. 6:16; 2 Thess. 3:3; 1 John 2:13, 14); "the tempter" (Matt. 4:3); "the enemy" (Matt. 13:39); and "ruler of this world" (John 16:11). In addition to Satan, the name for God's enemy most often used in the New Testament is "the Devil" (*ho diabolos,* 32 times).

Satan is generally characterized as the ruler of a kingdom of darkness and the adversary of God. Similar to Belial at Qumran, he controls a certain lot of demons and evil spirits who afflict the world with illness (Luke 13:16) and lead humanity astray (1 Cor. 7:5). At times Satan's demons "possess" humans, causing both physical and psychological impairment (Matt. 15:22). John 13:27 notes that Satan entered *(eisēlthen)* Judas, causing him to betray Jesus.

Satan's activities often place him at odds with Jesus. The Gospels portray Satan and his demons experiencing some sort of defeat at the hand of Jesus. Christ's ministry, which inaugurates the kingdom of God on the earth, begins the overthrow of Satan's kingdom and the victory of God's rule (Luke 10:18). Jesus' authority is reflected in his ability to cure illnesses and cast out demons (Luke 11:20; Matt. 12:28). Despite the apparent overthrow of the kingdom of darkness in the Gospels, the rest of the New Testament continues to portray Satan as God's adversary leading the righteous astray, practicing deceit, and causing illness (Rom. 16:20; 1 Cor. 7:5; 2 Cor. 12:7).

Even though Satan is portrayed as the enemy of God in the New Testament, there are still echoes of him acting within the will of God. Satan is used by God to test Jesus (Matt. 4:1). In humans, he destroys the flesh so that the spirit can be saved (1 Cor. 5:1-5). He also appears to help sinners by chastising them so that they learn not to blaspheme (1 Tim. 1:20).

Devil

The word "Devil" is an English translation of the Greek word *diabolos,* meaning "adversary," "accuser," or "slanderer." The LXX uses *diabolos* to translate *śāṭān* in the Hebrew Bible. As with the noun *śāṭān* in the Hebrew Bible, of the twenty-one occurrences of Devil in the LXX, only four do not posses the definite article. In Greek literature, *diabolos* is most often used as an adjective describing a human slanderer. *Diabolos* is also used as a noun or adjective in the context of encouraging God's people not to be slanderous (1 Tim. 3:11; 2 Tim. 3:3; Titus 2:3).

Most often in the New Testament, as well as in some early Christian and Jewish literature, the noun *diabolos* is used for the proper name "Devil," the supernatural enemy of God. The names "Satan" and "Devil" thus appear to be used interchangeably, and the aliases for Satan mentioned above also are used for the Devil. Further, the Devil is associated with both the great dragon and the serpent, an apparent reference to the deceiver and tempter of Eve in Genesis 3 (Rev. 12:9). He is also called a murderer and a liar (John 8:44; Rev. 12:9). Whereas *ha-śāṭān* is an angel of God in the Hebrew Bible, the New Testament claims that the Devil merely disguises himself as an angel of light (2 Cor.11:14).

The New Testament portrays the Devil performing two main functions. First, he is the ruler of the kingdom of darkness, which includes both powerful evil angels and evil spirits who possess individuals, causing disease and insanity (Mark 9:25). Thus, he is given the title "ruler of powers of the air" (Eph. 2:2). Second, the Devil is responsible for attempting to sever the connection between God and his people by endeavoring to lead humanity, and even Jesus, astray through trial and temptation (Luke 8:12; Matt. 4:1; John 13:2).

Thus the Devil becomes known as the "ruler" or "god" of this world (John 12:31; 14:30; 2 Cor. 4:4). He rules over the earth and its inhabitants who have yet to acknowledge the true God (Acts 28:16; Col. 1:13). Those under his power are called his "children" (Acts 13:10; 1 John 3:10). He keeps the gospel from unbelievers (Luke 8:12) and oppresses humanity (Acts 10:38). True to his name, the Devil is an adversary to humanity, trapping them in sin (1 Pet. 5:8).

Rabbinic Literature

Satan as an autonomous celestial opponent of God is rare in rabbinic literature when compared with the New Testament; evidently, Satan did not play a large role in early rabbinic theology. However, there are several references to Satan in rabbinic literature that cohere with other early Jewish and Christian concepts. Satan is associated with the serpent in Genesis 3 (*b. Soṭah* 9b; *b. Sanhedrin* 29a). He is associated with the "angel of death" and the "evil inclination" (*b. Baba Batra* 16a). Satan is also made responsible for instigating the sin and trouble recorded in biblical episodes such as the death of Moses (*Deut. Rab.* 13:9), David's sin with Bathsheba (*b. Sanhedrin* 95a), and Haman's plot to kill the Jews (*Esth. Rab.* 3:9). However, Satan's power remains limited by God, and he is rendered powerless on the Day of Atonement (*b. Roš Haššanah* 16b; *b. Yoma* 20a).

The Defeat of Satan

Although the names for God's celestial enemy are diverse in early Jewish and Christian literature, the characteristics and functions of a supreme evil being are similar. Most texts agree that although this world, or at least a segment of it, is under the rule of an evil entity, eventually God will again bring order to the earth. God will restore his rule as king in the earth, which often entails a defeat of the evil kingdom, including its celestial leader. So in the Qumran *War Scroll,* God will eventually destroy Belial and his evil forces in a cosmic battle ending his wicked rule (1QM 1:4-5, 13-16).

In the New Testament, Christ's ministry begins the process of defeating Satan and bringing an end to his reign through the inauguration of the kingdom of God. The death and resurrection of Christ render the Devil powerless (Heb. 2:4). John 16:11 claims that Satan has already been judged and cast out of the world (John 12:31, 32). Yet Jesus' death, resurrection, and ascension do not bring about a definitive end to Satan's influence (John 15:18-19; Eph. 6:16; 1 Pet. 5:8-9). Early Christian theology affirms that Christ's death and resurrection assure God's victory over Satan, but the effects of that victory are slowly occurring. Final victory will occur only at the second coming of Christ, when Satan will be utterly destroyed (2 Thess. 2:8; Rev. 20:7-10).

BIBLIOGRAPHY

P. L. DAY 1988, *An Adversary in Heaven: Satan in the Hebrew Bible,* Atlanta: Scholars Press. • N. FORSYTH 1989, *The Old Enemy: Satan and the Combat Myth,* Princeton: Princeton University Press. • P. D. HANSON 1975, *The Dawn of Apocalyptic,* Philadelphia: Fortress Press. • V. MAAG 1965, "Belijaʿal im Alten Testament," *TZ* 21: 287-99. • P. VON DER OSTEN SACKEN 1969, *Gott und Belial,* Göttingen: Vandenhoeck & Ruprecht. • S. H. T. PAGE 1995, *Powers of Evil: A Biblical Study of Satan and Demons,* Grand Rapids: Baker Books. • E. PAGELS 1995, *The Origin of Satan,* New York: Random House. • A. Y. REED 2005, *Fallen Angels and the History of Judaism and Christianity: The Reception of Enoch Literature,* Cambridge: Cambridge University Press. • J. S. RUSSELL 1977, *The Devil: Perceptions of Evil from Antiquity to Primitive Christianity,* Ithaca: Cornell University Press. • N. J. TROMP 1969, *Primitive Conceptions of Death and the Nether World in the Old Testament,* Rome: Pontifical Biblical Institute. • A. T. WRIGHT 2005, *The Origin of Evil Spirits,* Tübingen: Mohr-Siebeck.

See also: Angels; Dualism; Fallen Angels; Sons of God

CHAD T. PIERCE

Schürer, Emil

Emil Schürer (1844-1926) was a Lutheran theologian and inaugurator of the *Wissenschaft des Judentums* or scholarship on Judaism in German Protestant theology. From 1862 to 1866 he studied theology in Erlangen, Berlin, and Heidelberg, where he was inspired by the theologians R. Rothe and A. Ritschl and by the leading historical-critical scholar, H. J. Holtzmann. In 1868 he finished his doctorate in Leipzig with a dissertation on Schleiermacher's idea of religion. In 1869 he received his licentiate in theology with a dissertation (in Latin) on the debate over the date of Easter in the second century. In 1873 he began teaching in Leipzig, where he made friends with the young Adolf Harnack. He later went to Giessen (1878), Kiel (1890), and finally Göttingen (1895), where he stayed until his death.

The work that made Schürer famous was published in 1874 under the title *Lehrbuch zur neutestamentlichen Zeitgeschichte.* With this work, written before he turned thirty, Schürer made a major contribution not only to the historical study of the New Testament but also to scholarly research on early Judaism. The second edition of this work, in two volumes, came out in 1886-1890 under the title *Geschichte des jüdischen Volkes im Zeitalter Jesu Christi.* The third and fourth editions, in three volumes, were often reprinted and then translated into English in 1890-1893. A fully revised and updated English edition of this monumental work was published in 1973-1987 under the editorship of G. Vermes, with the title *The History of the Jewish People in the Age of Jesus Christ.*

In 1876 Schürer and Harnack founded the *Theologische Literaturzeitung,* which became the major journal for Protestant theology. As editor (until 1910) he was feared for his devastating reviews of the work of others. In spite of the suspicions of orthodox Lutherans,

Schürer understood himself to be a faithful Christian with both a liberal and critical attitude.

In his work Schürer applied the historical-critical methods used in the study of the New Testament to early Jewish literature. In his reconstruction of early Jewish history, at that time misleadingly and rather derogatorily called *Spätjudentum* (Late Judaism), he basically drew on Josephus for Jewish political history and the Mishnah for Jewish belief and practice. He took additional information from the Synoptics and works like the *Psalms of Solomon*. In the later editions of his *Geschichte des jüdischen Volkes*, he broadened his attention to apocalyptic literature and the Pseudepigrapha.

Schürer interpreted the Pharisees as a narrow, legalistic group. According to him, they approached the Law of Moses with a eudemonistic striving for divine reward. In his view, Jewish life under the Torah became a casuistic and ultimately selfish ethic. Here Schürer's Lutheran and liberal dogmatic viewpoint is clearly visible, and it provoked criticism, not least from Jewish interpreters. In early Jewish apocalypticism and messianic expectations, he saw a preparation for the Gospel.

Schürer's interest in early Jewish history and literature was thus largely inspired by the New Testament and largely determined by his Lutheranism, and this orientation resulted in a one-sided selection and biased interpretation of themes and parallels. Nevertheless — and in spite of his largely negative verdict on early Jewish religion — Schürer's work long remained the most detailed introduction to early Judaism, exerting an enormous influence on subsequent scholarship.

BIBLIOGRAPHY

Major work

E. SCHÜRER 1874, *Lehrbuch zur neutestamentlichen Zeitgeschichte*, Leipzig: Hinrichs; 2d ed. published under the title *Geschichte des jüdischen Volkes im Zeitalter Jesu Christi*, 2 vols., 1886-1890; 3d ed., 3 vols., 1898-1901; 4th ed., 1901-1909, with index volume, 1911; Eng. trans. of 3d ed.: *A History of the Jewish People in the Time of Jesus Christ*, 3 vols., Edinburgh: Clark, 1890-1893; newly revised and expanded Eng. ed.: *The History of the Jewish People in the Age of Jesus Christ*, 3 vols., vol. 3 in two parts, rev. and ed. G. Vermes et al., Edinburgh: Clark, 1973-1987.

Other Works

E. SCHÜRER 1879, *Die Gemeindeverfassung der Juden in Rom in der Kaiserzeit*, Leipzig: Hinrichs. • E. SCHÜRER 1882, *Die Predigt Jesu Christi in ihrem Verhältniß zum Alten Testament und zum Judentum*, Darmstadt: Wissenschaftliche Buchgesellschaft. • E. SCHÜRER 1903, *Das messianische Selbstbewußtsein Jesu Christi*, Göttingen: Dieterichs. • E. SCHÜRER 1913, *Verzeichnis der Personennamen in der Mischna*, Leipzig: Hinrichs.

On Schürer

S. J. D. COHEN 1986, "The Political and Social History of the Jews in Greco-Roman Antiquity: The State of the Question," in *Early Judaism and Its Modern Interpreters*, ed. R. A. Kraft and G. W. E. Nickelsburg, Philadelphia: Fortress; Atlanta: Scholars Press, 33-56. • M. HENGEL 1990, "Der alte und der neue Schürer," *JSS* 35: 19-64. • R. DEINES 1997, *Die Pharisäer*, Tübingen: Mohr-Siebeck, 68-95. • A. OPPENHEIMER, ED. 1999, *Jüdische Geschichte in hellenistisch-römischer Zeit. Wege der Forschung: Vom alten zum neuen Schürer*, München: Oldenbourg. • H.-G. WAUBKE 1998, *Die Pharisäer in der protestantischen Bibelwissenschaft des 19. Jahrhunderts*, Tübingen: Mohr-Siebeck, 226-50.

JÖRG FREY

Scribes and Scribalism

The importance of scribes cannot be doubted when considering the immense literary production of Second Temple Judaism and the formative significance of the period for the textual development and transmission of the Hebrew Bible. Yet a number of issues render an assessment of "scribes" and the correlate "scribalism" problematic. The evidence is, above all, complex, opaque, and disparate, and this complexity is compounded by the breadth and diversity of the phenomena that scholars have typically associated with the "scribal" rubric. This has resulted in widely divergent conclusions regarding the identity, functions and status of Jewish scribes during the Second Temple period. In these circumstances, much depends on preliminary conceptual decisions and methodological assumptions.

Problems of Definition

Scribes

One of the basic difficulties lies in determining what constitutes a scribe — and similarly what qualifies as "scribal" — during the period, and what evidence should be taken into account in a description of the concept. Here scholars have taken both narrow and broad approaches.

A narrow, exclusive approach begins with the fundamental assumption that all scribes are professional writers. Evidence should therefore be restricted to sources in which professional writers are explicitly referred to, either by a title or with a function pertaining to professional writing (e.g., Schams 1998). Terms designating such a role include, among others, Hebr. *sōfēr* and Gr. *grammateus*. However, apart from the fact that such titles appear to have been used rather flexibly, a major difficulty for this approach lies in coming to terms with the variety of other functions frequently associated with these titles in the sources that are not strictly related to writing skills (e.g., legal expertise, instruction, interpretive authority). Moreover, given the "rhetoric of anonymity" characteristic of scribal literary culture (Jaffee 2001), it stands to reason that limiting the evidence to overt references would result in the exclusion of much data relevant to scribes and scribal approaches.

By contrast, a broad, inclusive definition takes as its starting point the wider constellation of skills and aptitudes associated with textual study and scholarly culture. According to this approach, Second Temple

SCRIBES AND SCRIBALISM

Jewish scribes were essentially "Torah scholars" (Ger. *Schriftgelehrten;* so Hengel 1969; Schürer 1979; Orton 1989). Specific titles and even professional writing as such are less significant for a definition than scholarly attributes like scriptural knowledge, legal skills, wisdom, religious leadership, teaching, or authority. Yet the resulting conflation of activities, titles, roles, and literatures under a single heading tends to obscure the fact that not all literate, educated persons were professional writers, nor were they labeled as such, just as not all professional writers were legal experts or sages occupied with scholarly pursuits. It is important to keep in mind that the term *Schriftgelehrte* represents a modern, synthetic concept without equivalent in early Jewish sources (Sanders 1992; Schams 1998).

The variety of conceptual approaches has resulted both in and from a lack of clarity regarding the object of study: does the term "scribe" denote a specific societal role — either a *profession* (such as an official writer/copyist/reader or an expert in law, whether in a small village, in the military, or in a royal court), membership in a *political faction,* or perhaps a *class* or *status?* Or does it describe a person with a *set of skills* (technical competence in writing; knowledge of specific texts; mastery of conventions for drafting official documents), or a person with a *level of expertise* in these skills, regardless of professional or ideological affiliation? Does the term entail a specific hermeneutical outlook or religious mode ("scribalism")? Answers to these questions are often assumed, but rarely are they articulated in a clear way. In any case, it is clear that there was no uniform definition of a "scribe" in the period; it varied according to time, location, and individual usage. The plurality and adaptability of scribal attributes must be considered alongside the fact that extant sources often do not permit a precise determination of what specific conception is intended in a given instance.

Scribalism

Contributing to the conceptual confusion is the widespread appeal to an ill-defined notion of "scribalism" as a phenomenon in Second Temple Judaism. Generally, this term is used to describe an approach to revelation reflecting the increasingly text-oriented character of Jewish religious experience, the effects of which are evident in the formation of the Hebrew scriptures and other literature of the period. This process of textualization is often associated with broader trends in literacy (Schniedewind 2004; Carr 2005), and with a transformation of prophecy into exegesis (Fishbane 1989; Sommer 1996). Frequently the concept is bound up with other presuppositions, whether explicit or implicit. For example, the term "scribalism" has been contrasted with notions like "popular piety" (Wilhelm Bousset) or "free prophecy" (Max Weber), and at times — particularly in older scholarship — it bears a marked pejorative sense (parallel to "legalism"), indicating an institutional rigidity combined with a secondary, epigonal character. More popularly of late, the label has been widely employed to describe the putative social setting of books like *1 Enoch* and *Jubilees.* The valorization of writing and physical documents in this literature, together with the attribution of scribal titles and characteristics to prestigious figures of biblical antiquity, are taken to imply a social setting within "scribal circles," though the nature of such "circles" and the relationship to other contemporaneous scribes and other groups remains altogether uncertain. Along similar lines, the Qumran group is referred to by some as a "scribal community," but presumably without any implication that all its members were professional writers. In sum, the vague and indiscriminate use of the terms "scribalism" and "scribal" has rendered them problematic for an assessment of scribes in the period, particularly in view of the plurality of scribal models and behaviors attested.

Evidence

In the absence of any scribal self-description, information about the role and character of scribes in the period must be deduced from two types of evidence: (1) descriptive statements about scribes (reports of various kinds in literary, documentary, and epigraphic materials which mention scribes); (2) the remains of scribal literary activity itself (i.e., literary phenomena and what is known about the physical and social realities of book production).

Descriptive Statements

The majority of the evidence consists of incidental references to "scribes" of various kinds. Such reports are shaped and limited by the interests and biases of the authors. None of these statements was intended to present a complete picture of the identity or function of scribes. For a full analysis of the data, see Schams 1998 and Saldarini 1989.

While there are definite continuities, it is difficult to establish a precise relationship between Jewish scribes in the Second Temple period and the rich background of ancient Near Eastern scribal traditions, traces of which are also found within the Hebrew Bible. Here scribes appear in various capacities, but usually as elite, highly educated officials in royal service. This is supported by scattered references to preexilic scribes in the Hebrew Bible who appear to function as diplomats, high-level cabinet officials, and military officers (e.g., 2 Kings 12:11; 18:18, 37; 22:3, 8-12; Jeremiah 36).

Persian Period

Scribes appear to have functioned as officials in all levels of government at this time. Ezra is the most prominent scribal figure of the period to be mentioned in the Hebrew Bible, though his exact status and position in relation to the Achaemenid administration are debated. In Ezra 7:6 he is not only an "expert scribe" *(sōfēr mahîr)* but also a priest, a scholar and teacher of the law of Moses, and a leader who possesses divine wisdom and administrative authority. It is not clear, however, to what extent the characteristics of this exemplary figure represent the specific conception of what a scribe was in the period, particularly given overlapping priestly, levitical, and scribal functions. Levitical or priestly

SCRIBES AND SCRIBALISM

scribes are also mentioned in the book of Chronicles (1 Chron. 24:6; 2 Chron. 34:13) and much later in *T. Levi* (8:17; cf. 13:1-2), while another scribe mentioned in Ezra-Nehemiah, Zadok, is paired with a priest and a Levite when appointed over the Temple treasuries (Neh. 13:13).

Hellenistic Period

The increase in number and broader distribution of professional writers attested in the Hellenistic period owes in part to increased bureaucracy set in motion by Ptolemaic policies, a trend continued in successive administrations. Other factors influencing this change may have included a greater interest in and availability of written texts (including sacred scrolls), itself related to economic factors like the accessibility of writing materials, and cultural factors such as Hellenization (Schams 1998: 315-16). Scribes apparently performed a variety of official functions (mostly documentary, archival, and legal). Some were employed by the Jerusalem temple, as indicated by the "Seleucid Charter" of Antiochus III, which exempted the "scribes of the temple" *(grammateis tou hierou)* from taxes, together with elders, priests and sacred singers (Josephus, *Ant.* 12.138-44).

In Ben Sira, if there are boundaries between sage, scholar, and scribe, they are difficult to discern (compare Sir. 38:32–39:11 to the "wisdom of the scribe" mentioned in 38:24). All three roles appear to combine skill, wisdom, and piety. On the other hand, whether this key passage reflects the social reality of a defined class in Ben Sira's day is not as straightforward as often assumed (Schams 1998: 100-104).

Some scribes appear in 1 Macc 7:12 as a group seeking justice from the high priest Alcimus. This "group of scribes" *(synagōgē grammateōn)* is then referred to in the following verse as "the Hasideans." This difficult text poses more questions than answers about the nature of these scribes and their affiliation. Similarly, the brief mention in 2 Macc. 6:18 of the forced degradation of a certain Eleazar, "one of the foremost among the scribes," offers little certain data beyond the notion that some scribes were held in high regard for their piety and character.

Another important feature of the Hellenistic period is the trend evident in numerous texts to describe biblical figures as "scribes." For example, though no scribal traits are attributed to the figure of Enoch in the biblical text of Genesis, certain passages in the books of *1 Enoch* and the *Book of Giants* explicitly designate him as such. His titles include "scribe of righteousness" (*1 Enoch* 12:4; 15:1), "skilled scribe" (*1 Enoch* 92:1), and "distinguished scribe" (4QEnGiants[a] 8:4). In a similar way, David is referred to as a "scribe" in 11QPs[a] 27:2, in a list extolling his wisdom, piety, and literary productivity. Yet, important though this scribalizing trend is for understanding scribal perceptions in the period, the specific social context in which such traditions developed remains unclear.

Roman Period

The Roman period presents a complicated array of testimony regarding scribes. On the one hand, Josephus depicts scribes as government officials functioning in a range of capacities, including high-level bureaucrats (*J.W.* 1.529), temple affiliates (*J.W.* 5.532), and low-level village officials (*J.W.* 1.479). The same perspective is also evident in his additions or clarifications while retelling the biblical narrative in the *Antiquities* (e.g., *Ant.* 6.120; 7.364). On the other hand, scribes appear as a distinct group in the New Testament, as well as in the Mishnah and the Tosefta. In addition, scribes are clearly associated with legal expertise and the teaching of Scripture. This tension between the depiction of Josephus and that of the New Testament and rabbinic literature apparently results from the selective interests of the authors. Though scribes are portrayed as a group in the Synoptic Gospels (e.g., Mark 11:18; Luke 6:7; Matt. 5:20), the nature of their affiliation is never explained. In light of other witnesses (esp. Josephus), it appears historically unlikely that scribes formed a unified faction or political party. Instead, their portrayal in the New Testament as a group has been either flatly rejected or attributed to other unifying factors such as common opposition to the authority of Jesus (Saldarini 1989) or common scribal occupation (Schams 1998).

In certain passages in the Mishnah and Tosefta "the scribes" are portrayed as a distinct group of the past and the source of certain legal rulings (cf. Urbach 1958; Saldarini 1989). However, the issues involved in relating this rabbinic conception to historical social realities are extremely complex, and little can be determined about the nature of Second Temple scribes from this testimony.

In addition to descriptive statements, the absence of scribes where they might be expected also requires explanation (Schams 1998: 251-73). For example, one finds no mention of scribes in Qumran sectarian literature dealing with the community itself, though there were certainly scribes among the community's membership (e.g., the individual copyist of 1QS, 1QSa, 1QSb, 4QSam[c], and some corrections in 1QIsa[a]). Moreover, the absence of any specific mention of the copyists of scriptural scrolls in extant reports from the Second Temple period is remarkable indeed, particularly in light of the material remains from the period. Thus the composite picture that emerges from these statements is quite limited and far less clear than would be desired. What is certain is that multiple and diverse conceptions of scribes existed, and that they functioned in a variety of different social roles.

Remains of Scribal Literary Activity

A different order of information about scribes in the period can be deduced from the remains of scribal literary activity itself. One type of such data derives from internal literary and textual phenomena. Scribal involvement is evident on many levels of the development of the biblical text and the production of other Jewish literature from the post-exilic period. For example, a variety of inner-biblical exegetical strategies can be discerned in textual alterations in the form of glosses, corrections, supplements, and specifications, as well as higher-level editorial and compositional activity (Fishbane 1985; Zakovitch 1992). Whether such activity is properly designated "scribal" relates to the vexed issues of definition referred to above. In any case, while many of these are based on conjecture, others are supported by textual evidence, so that in most cases we can make no firm distinction between authorial and scribal activity (Talmon 1975). This is particularly the case in "harmonizing" scribal approaches. Another type of data relates to external aspects of textual production such as scripts, handwriting styles, and writing materials (Tov 2004).

The existence of different scribal models or approaches (not to say "schools") is evident from the primary textual witnesses. However, though correlations between scribal approaches and specific social groups have been postulated (e.g., Pharisees, Sadducees, Qumran sectarians; cf. Tov 2004: 248, 261-76), the evidence is insufficient to demonstrate any exclusive affiliation of scribal approach with social setting during the period of the Second Temple. Scribes of various kinds were apparently found among a variety of factions and levels within Second Temple Jewish society.

Thus, evidence deduced from the remains of scribal literary activity reveals little about the specific social background or affiliation of scribes. It does, however, confirm the general diversity and absence of any consistent scribal profile indicated by the reports reviewed above. This apparent scribal pluriformity accords well with what is otherwise known regarding the range of early Jewish belief and practice.

BIBLIOGRAPHY

J. BLENKINSOPP 1990, "The Sage, the Scribe, and Scribalism in the Chronicler's Work," in *The Sage in Israel and the Ancient Near East,* ed. J. G. Gammie and L. G. Purdue, Winona Lake, Ind.: Eisenbrauns, 307-15. • D. CARR 2005, *Writing on the Tablet of the Heart: Origins of Scripture and Literature,* Oxford: Oxford University Press. • P. R. DAVIES 1998, *Scribes and Schools: The Canonization of the Hebrew Scriptures,* Louisville: Westminster John Knox. • M. FISHBANE 1985, *Biblical Interpretation in Ancient Israel,* Oxford: Clarendon. • M. FISHBANE 1989, "From Scribalism to Rabbinism: Perspectives on the Emergence of Classical Judaism," in idem, *The Garments of Torah: Essays in Biblical Hermeneutics,* Bloomington: Indiana University Press, 64-78. • M. HENGEL 1969, *Judentum und Hellenismus,* Tübingen: Mohr-Siebeck. • M. S. JAFFEE 2001, *Torah in the Mouth: Writing and Oral Tradition in Palestinian Judaism, 200 BCE–400 CE,* Oxford: Oxford University Press. • D. E. ORTON 1989, *The Understanding Scribe: Matthew and the Apocalyptic Ideal,* Sheffield: JSOT Press. • A. J. SALDARINI 1989, *Pharisees, Scribes and Sadducees in Palestinian Society,* Wilmington, Del.: Michael Glazier; rpt. Grand Rapids: Eerdmans, 2001. • E. P. SANDERS 1992, *Judaism: Practice and Belief 63 BCE–66 CE,* London: SCM Press. • C. SCHAMS 1998, *Jewish Scribes in the Second-Temple Period,* Sheffield: Sheffield Academic Press. • W. M. SCHNIEDEWIND 2004, *How the Bible Became a Book: The Textualization of Ancient Israel,* Cambridge: Cambridge University Press. • E. SCHÜRER 1979, *The History of the Jewish People in the Age of Jesus Christ,* rev. and ed. G. Vermes, F. Millar, and M. Black, Edinburgh: Clark, 2: 322-36. • B. D. SOMMER 1996, "Did Prophecy Cease? Evaluating an Evaluation," *JBL* 115: 31-47. • S. TALMON 1975, "The Textual Study of the Bible — A New Outlook," in *Qumran and the History of the Biblical Text,* ed. F. M. Cross and S. Talmon, Cambridge, Mass.: Harvard University Press, 321-400. • K. VAN DER TOORN 2007, *Scribal Culture and the Making of the Hebrew Bible,* Cambridge, Mass.: Harvard. • E. TOV 2004, *Scribal Practices and Approaches Reflected in the Texts Found in the Judean Desert,* Leiden: Brill. • E. URBACH 1958, "Interpretation as the Basis for the Halakhah and the Problem of the *Soferim,*" *Tarbiz* 27: 166-82 (in Hebrew). • Y. ZAKOVITCH 1992, *Introduction to Inner-Biblical Interpretation,* Even-Yehuda: Reches (in Hebrew).

See also: Literacy and Reading; Scripts and Scribal Practices; Writing D. ANDREW TEETER

Scripts and Scribal Practice

Scribal Materials and Practice

Various forms and means of writing were employed during the late Second Temple period, each with its own tools, inscription surface, and guidelines. The primary form of writing preserved from this period is in ink applied by pen to papyrus or animal skins, largely in Hebrew, Aramaic, and Greek. The second major group of preserved inscriptions were done on stone and metal foils (e.g., the *Copper Scroll*), which were chiseled or etched with metal points. (The recently published "Vision of Gabriel" is exceptional insofar as it is written in ink on stone.) This type of writing often entailed its own unique adaptation of the lettering of the inscription, called "lapidary script," to suit the medium and the tools. Wax tablets were also in common use but have been less well preserved. Nonprofessional writing like tomb inscriptions and graffiti could be done with any number of media, including ink, paint, or charcoal, or it could be etched with a sharp point.

The manuscripts from the Judean Desert show that various scribal guidelines were followed when producing a scroll. These include the production of the skin or papyrus (with margins and dry lines), the preparation of ink, and the procedure for writing onto the scroll's surface. For Hebrew biblical manuscripts, the external Mishnah tractate *Maseket Soferim* presents a detailed set of guidelines that are similar to the varied practices reflected in the Dead Sea Scrolls.

Inks tended to be carbon-based, derived from lampblack and ground charcoal obtained from fine plants and roots. According to Latin sources, agents such as oven soot and acacia-based gum Arabic helped to bind the ink paste together and fix it to the writing surface. However, no evidence of their use has been found among the scrolls from the Judean Desert.

The pen or stylus was normally made of reed with a carefully cut tip, though iron-tipped pens were also used. The width and the shading of individual strokes were determined by the angle and width of the nib, which was regularly honed and trimmed with a razor or knife, and by the angle at which the pen was held by the scribe.

SCRIPTS AND SCRIBAL PRACTICE

Spaces were generally used to indicate word divisions, although in Paleo-Hebrew texts dots served the same purpose. Greek monumental inscriptions and uncial literary texts were often written in *scriptio continua* with no word divisions. As a result, words would sometimes be broken at the column edge and continue to the next line. In some biblical manuscripts, punctuation and pauses were signified by additional marks or spaces of varying widths between words at the end of a line or clause.

Script Types

Formal

Formal scripts were developed for the writing of literary and official documents, generally by professional scribes trained by the government or other institutions. Typically, numerous strokes were made to form each letter, in a manner similar to those of monumental lapidary inscriptions. Accidental ink trails — the bane of writing with pen and ink — were tolerated and even incorporated as part of the script by forming them into thickened ornamental details at the ends of strokes called "serifs." The varied width of strokes became formalized as proportionate shading, which tended to be limited to strokes going in one direction (horizontal, vertical, or diagonal) or broadly curved.

Semiformal

The subsequent development of semiformal scripts simplified the formation of each letter by minimizing the use of serifs and shading, thus decreasing the effort required to form each letter. Cursive tendencies also decreased the labor by reducing the number of times that the pen had to be lifted from the writing surface. Eventually, pen strokes were developed that connected two letters as ligatures and even the letters of entire words. In general appearance and in number of strokes, however, the letter forms themselves remained the same.

Semicursive

Semicursive scripts reduced the number of separate strokes needed to form each letter, while maintaining the general squared appearance of letters of the formal and semicursive scripts. At certain points, the reduction entailed the slight rounding of a stroke that would appear in a formal or semiformal script as two strokes intersecting at an acute angle.

Cursive

Cursive scripts ignored the demand for or desirability of straight, uniform strokes, preferring to round off intersections between strokes into single looping curves and at times eliminating strokes altogether. Although originally developed for simplicity and speed, these scripts also came to include substyles that emphasized the beauty of rounded, flowing strokes.

Mixed

The mixing of script styles was common. Often, a more formal script might appear alongside letters and ligatures from the cursive form of the script, sometimes sporadically, at other times consistently. In such cases, an inscription or document might be described as having a "formal script with semiformal tendencies" or being "semiformal with cursive influences."

Lapidary

For monumental inscriptions, stone artisans of various cultures adapted contemporary formal scripts to the straight lines or simple, graduated curves that could be produced by hammer and chisel on hard stone. This lapidary script became a standard that influenced the style of inscriptions etched or carved with a metal stylus or knife onto wood and stone. Its influence can be seen also in other mediums such as formal inscriptions handwritten in ink on papyrus or skin. Yet the additions of stylized serifs at the tips of strokes were introduced to simulate natural tendencies, such as ink trails, that were common to the pen and ink medium. The lapidary squared scripts appear to have been limited for the most part to Western alphabets (including Greek and Latin). The West Semitic alphabets did not develop a true lapidary script during the first millennium B.C.E., with the exception of Aramaic (e.g., the Uzziah inscription and the *Copper Scroll*). Instead the Semitic alphabets, when applied to stone, were etched to mimic the fluidity of the contemporary cursive handwritten script.

Lingua Franca and National Scripts

In antiquity the Phoenician, Aramaic, and Greek languages each had the status of a *lingua franca* thanks to their respective influences on international communication and commerce. In the case of Phoenicia, this prevalence was due to the region's dominance in international trade. With Aramaic and Greek, the prevalence owed to military conquest and the need to control communication and trade throughout the conquered lands of the Persian and Hellenistic empires. In each case, as universal control waned, the script (and language) developed local variants known as "national scripts." This was particularly the case during the ninth century B.C.E. with respect to the Phoenician family of scripts, which includes the early Hebrew, Hebrew Hieratic (Cryptic A), Aramaic, and Greek scripts. It is also the case at the beginning of the third century B.C.E. for the Aramaic family of scripts, which includes the Jewish Square, Nabatean, Syriac, Palmyrene, and other Northern Mesopotamian scripts.

Paleo-Hebrew Scripts

The Hebrew script of the First Temple Period apparently continued in use in various locales throughout the Second Temple Period. This is especially evident in late fourth-century-B.C.E. coins, seals, and stone inscriptions from Mt. Gerizim. Later uses of the script, especially in Judea, appear to have arisen out of a resistance to the scripts that Gentiles used: Aramaic and Greek. This is evidenced in a series of sixteen, mainly pentateuchal manuscripts found at Qumran dating from the late third century B.C.E. (4QpaleoDeut and 4QpaleoJob) to the first half of the first century C.E. (11QpaleoLev^{a}). It is possible that these scrolls are of Sadducean or early

Samaritan origin, since they are confined primarily to the books of the Pentateuch. In some biblical manuscripts (e.g., 11QPsalms[a]) and commentaries (1QpHab) written in standard Jewish square script, Paleo-Hebrew was also used for writing the divine name. In addition, apparently for nationalistic reasons, many issues of Jewish coins were written primarily in Paleo-Hebrew throughout most of the Hasmonean dynasty from John Hyrcanus I (135-106 B.C.E.) until Mattathias Antigonus (40-37 B.C.E.), and again on coins of the First and Second Revolts against Rome (66-70 C.E. and 132-135 C.E.). Among the daughter scripts of early Phoenician, this script evolved relatively slowly over the course of a millennium. However, varied styles did coexist in contemporary settings throughout the period of its use.

A standard lapidary form of Paleo-Hebrew script was never actually invented. The numerous surviving Hebrew inscriptions and seals in stone from both the First and Second Temple periods were generally inscribed or etched in the contemporary form of the handwritten script, with the notable but rather late local exceptions of various Samaritan monumental inscriptions and certain Jewish coins of the First and Second Revolts.

The ink-inscribed Paleo-Hebrew script developed slowly and continuously from the earlier cursive/semicursive form of the First Temple period to its development and use as a formal or semiformal script during the Second Temple period. This also formed the basis of the Samaritan script used until today. Over the centuries the script maintained a vertical (or rightward-sloping diagonal) shading.

Hebrew Hieratic (Cryptic A) Scripts

Priestly castes from various surrounding societies wrote in esoteric or cryptic scripts, dubbed "hieratic scripts." Notable examples are Egypt (e.g., Egyptian hieratic script) and Delphi (at the temple of Apollo) in Greece. It should not be surprising, therefore, that the various styles of esoteric or cryptic scripts in the caves of Qumran are connected with certain Jewish priestly groups of the Second Temple period. It appears that the Cryptic A script of Qumran is based upon an alphabet that derived from the early Phoenician script, as do Paleo-Hebrew, Aramaic, and Greek. Nor is it surprising that no inscriptions in stone survive, since the texts produced in this script were not initially intended to be read by the public. Approximately 10 percent of the extant nonbiblical manuscripts from Qumran were written in this script and date primarily from the second century B.C.E. A number of texts originally written in the Cryptic A script were eventually copied in the current Jewish Aramaic "square script," apparently once the perceived need or popularity of writing in the esoteric style had waned or the concern for secrecy abated. This transition is found in manuscripts of foundational documents of diverse priestly communities, as is reflected in the *Midrash Sefer Moshe* (4Q249 cryptA MSM[a] and 4Q249a[a] cryptA MSM[b]?; cf. 4Q445 frgs. 4-6 MSM[c]), the *Rule of the Congregation* (4Q249[a]–4Q249[i] cryptA Serekh ha-ʿEdah[a–i]; cf. 1QSa), *Miqṣat Maʿaśê ha-Torah* (4Q313 cryptA MMT[g]; cf. 4Q395-399 MMT[a–f]), and the *Pentacontad Liturgical Calendar* (4Q324[c–h] cryptA Liturgical Calendar[a–e]; cf. 4Q326 Cal Doc. C and 4Q394 1-2 Cal Doc. D). Characteristics of the evolving Cryptic A scripts include (1) a rotation of each letter of the alphabet between 15 to 70 degrees counterclockwise; (2) the development of a tendency toward horizontal rather than vertical shading; (3) the general shortening of extended lines (e.g., ascenders and descenders); and (4) additional form of the script classified as "miniscule."

Jewish Aramaic Scripts

The Aramaic language with its script was first propagated as a *lingua franca* among the Semitic-speaking peoples of the Near East by the Assyrians (cf. the Adon Papyrus). This practice was carried forward through the Persian period. Aramaic and its script, termed "Imperial Aramaic," were deemed a more efficient form of communication than the more difficult cuneiform-scripted languages of the Assyrians, Babylonians, and Persians. Soon after the dissolution of the Persian Empire, local or national Aramaic scripts and dialects developed, including Syriac, Hatran, Palmyrene, Nabatean, Egyptian, and Judean Aramaic. Since most of these daughter scripts and languages were expressed in writing with pen and ink on papyrus or parchment, the scripts tended to evolve at a more accelerated rate than the other scripts of the region. A lapidary form of the script also developed. From the second century B.C.E. onward, the form of the Jewish script used in literary documents began to favor horizontal shaded strokes rather than the vertical shaded strokes of the earlier periods. Also, uniform letter heights began to develop, so that by the Herodian period the formal Jewish script quickly developed (1) a squared "book hand" appearance of each letter; (2) increasingly pronounced serifs at the tips of the letters; and (3) a "baseline" delimiting the bottoms of the letters (apparently keeping in step with the squared forms of Greek and Latin scripts used in literary documents in the West). The less formal forms of the script, especially the cursive, developed more slowly.

Greek Scripts

The Greek language and script were introduced to the regions of Judea, Samaria, and the Galilee after the acquisitions of those lands by the Seleucid Greeks from the beginning of the second century B.C.E. Imperial Greek steles began to appear almost immediately during the reign of Antiochus III (cf. the Hephzibah inscription) and Seleucus IV (cf. the Heliodorus inscription) as part of a concerted effort to introduce Hellenistic culture and to establish Greek as the *lingua franca* of the empire. A beautifully inscribed Greek votive plaque from Tel Dan, roughly contemporary with the Hephzibah and Heliodorus inscriptions, was found bearing a translation scrawled in Aramaic in the bottom margin. The secondary inscription bears witness to the current struggle with the new language. Such lapidary forms of the Greek script remained fairly static, with only minor

SEALS AND SEAL IMPRESSIONS

formal developments discernible until the end of the Second Temple period (e.g., the Temple warning inscription and the Theodotos inscription from first century C.E.). The straight lines of lapidary scripts highly influenced the formal scripts used for penning literary works (e.g., manuscripts of the Septuagint from the Judean wilderness) whose letter forms tended to develop very slowly when compared with other, less formal, writing styles. This includes scribal hands that were utilized in archival documents and in the public sphere, where cursive forms of letters and ligatures evolved. The handwritten forms of the script varied slightly between the Diaspora and Judea. Judean forms of the script — as utilized on papyrus documents and ostraca at Masada, documents of the Bar Kokhba period, and the ossuaries of Jerusalem — lagged behind somewhat in the evolution of letter forms and especially in the use of ligatures and connected writing that was prominent in Egypt and Syria. One explanation for this has been that, as long as there was still an active contemporary use of Aramaic and Hebrew scripts (which were very slow to allow connections between the letters), this was also reflected in the writing of the Greek scripts.

BIBLIOGRAPHY

F. M. CROSS 1965, "The Development of the Jewish Scripts," in *The Bible and the Ancient Near East: Essays in Honor of W. F. Albright*, ed. G. E. Wright, New York: Anchor Books, 133-202. • F. M. CROSS 1998, "Palaeography and the Dead Sea Scrolls," in *The Dead Sea Scrolls after Fifty Years*, vol. 1, ed. P. Flint and J. VanderKam, Leiden: Brill, 379-402. • N. LEWIS 1989, *The Documents from the Bar Kokhba Period in the Cave of Letters II: Greek Papyri*, Jerusalem: Israel Exploration Society. • M. D. MCLEAN 1982, "The Use and Development of Palaeo-Hebrew in the Hellenistic and Roman Periods," Dissertation, Harvard University. • Y. MAGEN, H. MISGAV, AND L. TSEFANIA 2004, *Mount Gerizim Excavations*, vol. 1, *The Hebrew, Aramaic and Samaritan Inscriptions*, Jerusalem: Israel Antiquities Authority. • J. NAVEH 1970, *The Development of the Aramaic Script*, Jerusalem: Israel Academy of Sciences and Humanities. • J. NAVEH 1982, *The Early History of the Alphabet: An Introduction to West Semitic Epigraphy and Palaeography*, Jerusalem: Magnes. • S. PFANN 2001, "The Character of the Early Essene Movement in the Light of the Manuscripts Written in Esoteric Scripts from Qumran," Dissertation, Hebrew University of Jerusalem. • E. TOV 2004, *Scribal Practices and Approaches Reflected in the Texts Found in the Judean Desert*, Leiden: Brill. • A. YARDENI 2000, *Textbook of Aramaic, Hebrew and Nabataean Texts from the Judaean Desert and Related Material*, Jerusalem: Hebrew University. • A. YARDENI 2002, *The Book of Hebrew Script: History, Palaeography, Script Styles, Calligraphy, and Design*, London: British Library.

See also: Writing

STEPHEN J. PFANN

Seals and Seal Impressions

Seals and seal impressions (imprints of seals in clay, also known as bullae) constitute one of the rare sources of data for the evolution of Yahwism as well as for political and economic issues in the Persian period. The synthesis of the archaeological record with the biblical text both complicates and enriches understanding of the religious and cultural landscape of this formative era. It is to this time and the subsequent Hellenistic age that the editing of the Pentateuch and other key portions of the biblical text is generally dated.

In both Judah and Israel before 586 B.C.E., the favored seal type had been the scarab or scaraboid, which was perforated for suspension from a string (Avigad and Sass 1997). The most familiar of the Judean and Israelite seals of the monarchic period are the two-line inscribed scarab or scaraboid bearing the owner's name and patronymic, sometimes decorated with a small floral flourish or a simple image — a lyre, for example, or a cricket, or occasionally an Egypto-Phoenician motif such as a ureaus (erect cobra) or winged griffin. Seals of this type may mention the public office of the owner. Also numerous, but less familiar to biblical scholars, are anepigraphic seals from both Israel and Judah displaying Egyptian motifs, especially symbols related to the sun. Keel and Uehlinger (1998) suspect that these seals, too, belonged to the elite of the two kingdoms.

Over the subsequent neo-Babylonian and Persian periods Samarians and, apparently, Judean exiles in Babylonia came to prefer the anepigraphic Greek-style signet ring with a classical Greek or Greco-Persian design. This type had spread eastward from the Greek city-states of Persian-controlled Asia Minor. Judah/Yehud, always more culturally isolated than the north, continued to favor the epigraphic scaraboid, inscribed now in Aramaic, but the neo-Babylonian faceted conoid stamp seal also appears.

Archaeological Sources

For the Persian period there are four important groups of seals or seal impressions from which the foregoing summary derives. Two of these come from Judea. The first, dated to the late sixth or early fifth century, is a collection of clay bullae and a few seals that were acquired

Bulla made of lead (1.2 × 1.1 cm.) stamped with an impression of a menorah, from the Dead Sea area, first century B.C.E–first century C.E. *(The Schøyen Collection, MS 1912)*

SEALS AND SEAL IMPRESSIONS

on the antiquities market but believed to originate in Jerusalem (Avigad 1976). On the basis of a bulla inscribed "Elnathan the Governor" and a seal belonging to "Shelomith the maidservant of Elnathan the Governor" it has been suggested (Meyers 1985) that this is the same Shelomith named as the daughter of Zerubbabel in 1 Chron. 3:19. If Shelomith, a Davidic princess, was also the wife of Elnathan the Governor, her royal pedigree likely strengthened Elnathan's claim to the Judean governorship.

The second group of Persian-period Judean bullae are impressions on storage jars discovered in controlled excavations in Jerusalem and various other sites in Judea (Carter 1999). These fall into two groups, the first of which are anepigraphic and come from nine sites. Most show an animal, usually a lion alone or with a Persian-style fire altar. Among the second group, the inscribed bullae, the earliest impressions bear the name *moṣah*. Likely originating during neo-Babylonian rule, these continue into the Persian period. Their find spots in the Bethel area, especially Tell en-Nasbeh, may indicate that Jerusalem had not yet resumed its role as capital of the Persian province of Yehud. It appears that these seal impressions relate to taxation or trade or both. The same is true for the impressions of inscribed seals on storage jars from six sites which read *Yehud* in various defective and full spellings. These bullae may include the name of an official or the title "governor" with a proper name. The largest number of this seal type comes from Ramat Rahel, just south of Jerusalem, followed by Jerusalem itself.

A number of conclusions have been drawn from these excavated Judean bullae. By mapping their distribution, historians have been able to speculate on the boundaries of the province of Judah in the Persian period, concluding that Persian Yehud was small, confined only to the central hills of Palestine, and excluding the Shephelah and coastal plain. Furthermore, the likely sequence of Judean governors has been reconstructed largely on the basis of the seals and similarly inscribed Judean coin issues. The coin and seal inscriptions have also strengthened the argument that throughout the Persian period Judah was an independent province and never subject to Samarian jurisdiction. Whether the Judean priesthood had achieved parity or superseded the office of governor remains an open question.

In chronological order, the third corpus of sealings comes from the city of Nippur in southern Mesopotamia, the home of the Murashu banking firm whose commercial archive of over 740 clay tablets was excavated in 1893. The cuneiform documents were written and sealed between 454 and 404 B.C.E. during the reigns of Artaxerxes I and Darius II. One or more communities of exiled Jews lived in the Nippur area in the Persian period, and many of the names in the tablets are identifiably Jewish. A recent analysis has successfully linked many of the 657 different seal images with the names of the seal owners, all of them officials and middle-rank men (Bregstein 1993). Whereas the Babylonians and Iranians at Nippur continued the centuries-old tradition of stamp or cylinder seals, people with West Semitic names (14 percent of the total) — including Jews — preferred rings with more "Western"-style images. Furthermore, unlike other West Semites, men with identifiably Jewish names never used a seal with a Babylonian worship scene.

The fourth group of sealings, all but two or three of them uninscribed, originated in Samaria although they were discovered in a cave in the Wadi ed-Daliyeh (Leith 1997). These date fairly securely between 375 and 335 B.C.E. and originally sealed a large number of private financial documents — the Samaria Papyri are the surviving remnants of these. Written in official Aramaic, these documents recorded the sale of slaves and other property by upper-class Samarians. Slaves, sellers, and many of the buyers bear Yahwistic or Hebrew names. The small number of sealings from diminutive cylinder seals with Persian Court–style images may represent seals used by Samarians with official status in the Persian provincial administration. Well known from this corpus of bullae is a traditional Israelite two-line name seal inscribed in Paleo-Hebrew, "Yeshayahu, son of Sanballat, Governor of Samaria," probably the great-grandson of the Samarian governor of the same name who locked horns with Nehemiah, governor of Judea. More than half of the bullae, however, attest to the Samarian elite's growing taste for Greek finger rings. The seal imagery suggests that despite the Samarians' ostensibly cosmopolitan outlook, their sense of religious and/or political identity may have constrained them from selecting ritual scenes including fire altars or any version of Egyptian or Egypto-Phoenician devices of the type found at Phoenician sites of this period. The fact that contemporary Samarian coins, a manifestly public and "official" medium under the Persians, featured Persian fire altars and Persian court style motifs reinforces the suspicion that elite Samarians exercised Yahwistic or at least ethnically informed scruples in their choice of private seals, consciously rejecting devices they deemed problematic. This phenomenon suggests that the Judean seals with fire altars may similarly have functioned in an official capacity, perhaps one related to taxation.

Biblical References

Biblical references to seals and sealing in texts generally assigned to the Persian or Hellenistic periods may be metaphorical or actual. Furthermore, they seem accurately to reflect what is known from archaeology about the development of seal types and from anthropology about the symbolic significance borne by one's seal. Haggai's encomium to Prince Zerubbabel (Hag. 2:23) as YHWH's seal (Hebr. *ḥôtām*) presupposes a stone scaraboid or stamp seal worn on a string around the wrist or neck, the most common seal type in preexilic Judah. Haggai explicitly reverses Jer. 22:24, where YHWH figuratively tears King Jehoiachin like a seal from his right hand (Hebr. *yad*) and throws him to the Babylonians. The lover in Song of Songs 8:6 longs to become a seal of the same type lying against the beloved's heart or dangling from the wrist.

A king's signet embodied his identity and hence the principle of royal power. In the book of Esther, access to the royal signet confers first upon Haman (Esth. 3:10, 12) and then upon Esther and Mordecai (Esth. 8:2, 8, 10) the authority to issue royal edicts. Job alludes to the process of pressing a seal into clay (38:14), to a sealing's function as an assertion of ownership (Job 37:7) and as a guarantee against tampering, theft, or escape (9:7; 14:17). The sealing of Jesus' tomb (Matt. 27:66; Gr. *sphragizō*) recalls Daniel's fate, sealed up in the lions' den by the signets of the king and his lords (Dan. 6:17 [MT 6:18]). In the Song of Songs, the metaphor for a woman's sexuality is a "sealed fountain" (4:12), an image that draws upon all these nuances of ownership, control, and containment.

English Bible translations generally render the Hebrew root *ḥtm* as "seal" or "to seal." The appearance in the Hebrew Bible of *ṭabbaʿat,* usually translated "signet" or "ring," may point to a postexilic date for a passage. As the archaeological record indicates, until the Persian and Hellenistic periods, rings were not used as seals to any significant degree in the territory of either Judea or Samaria. The word *ṭabbaʿat* appears almost exclusively in Esther, in the Joseph novella (Gen. 41:42), and in the Priestly account of the Tabernacle, where the term may refer to a finger ring (Exod. 35:22) but more often to a ring-shaped object such as the rings for the Ark's carrying poles (Exod. 25:12 and passim). If the Priestly writer[s] did originate in Babylonian exilic circles, it may be of relevance that Jews at Nippur differed from their Babylonian neighbors in preferring seal rings over stamps or cylinders.

BIBLIOGRAPHY

N. AVIGAD AND B. SASS 1997, *Corpus of West Semitic Stamp Seals,* Jerusalem: Israel Academy of Arts and Sciences. • N. AVIGAD 1976, *Bullae and Seals from a Post-Exilic Judean Archive, Qedem* 4, Jerusalem: Hebrew University. • L. B. BREGSTEIN 1993, *Seal Use in Fifth Century BC Nippur, Iraq: A Study of Seal Selection and Sealing Practices in the Murašu Archive,* Ph.D. dissertation, University of Pennsylvania. • C. E. CARTER 1999, *The Emergence of Yehud in the Persian Period,* Sheffield: Sheffield Academic Press. • J. CHRISTOPH 1993, *The Yehud Stamped Jar Handle Corpus: Implications for the History of Postexilic Palestine,* Ph.D. dissertation, Duke University. • O. KEEL AND C. UEHLINGER 1998, *Gods, Goddesses and Images of God in Ancient Israel,* Minneapolis: Fortress. • M. G. KLINGBEIL 1992, "Syro-Palestinian Stamp Seals from the Persian Period: The Iconographic Evidence," *Journal of Northwest-Semitic Languages* 18: 95-124. • M. J. W. LEITH 1997, *Wadi Daliyeh I, The Wadi Daliyeh Seal Impressions,* DJD 24, Oxford: Clarendon. • M. J. W. LEITH 2000, "Seals and Coins in Persian Period Samaria," in *The Dead Sea Scrolls Fifty Years after Their Discovery,* ed. L. Schiffman et al., Jerusalem: Israel Exploration Society, 691-707. • A. LEMAIRE 2001, "Épigraphie et religion en Palestine à l'époque achéménide," *Transeuphratène* 22: 97-113. • P. MACHINIST 1994, "The First Coins of Judah and Samaria: Numismatics and History in the Achaemenid and Early Hellenistic Periods," in *Continuity and Change: Proceedings of the Last Achaemenid History Workshop, April 6-8, 1990, Ann Arbor, Michigan,* ed. H. Sancisi-Weerdenburg et al., Leiden: Nederlands Instituut voor het Nabije Oosten, 365-80. • E. M. MEYERS 1985, "The Shelomith Seal and the Judean Restoration: Some Additional Considerations," *Eretz Israel* 18: 33*-38*. • M. PIELSTÜCKER AND B. SASS 2001, "A Hebrew Seal from Jaffa and the Hebrew Script of the Post-First Temple Period," *ʿAtiqot* 42: 199-209. • E. STERN 1982, *Material Culture of the Land of the Bible in the Persian Period 538-332 B.C.,* Warminster: Aris & Phillips; Jerusalem: Israel Exploration Society.

See also: Daliyeh, Wadi ed-

MARY JOAN WINN LEITH

Sectarianism

The Sociology of Sectarianism

The term "sect" is associated with the sociological work of Max Weber in the early 1900s and its further adaptations and applications (e.g., by Ernst Troeltsch). Weber saw "church" and "sect" as two polar types of social organization, the defining difference being the mode of membership: a church claims to be an institution for the salvation of those who are born to it, whereas a sect is a voluntary association, in which membership is achieved through qualification. Weber's ideas developed over time (see the survey by Chalcraft 2007), and he also applied them to ancient Judaism (Weber 1952). Although the terms "sect" and "church" are culturally specific, Weber did not mean for these types to be restricted to Christianity and to the Western world. In the secular and more universal sphere, he speaks of an *Anstalt-Verein* typology, a typology meant to illumine the impact of a sect or voluntary association on everyday conduct. The aspiration toward greater ideals typical of voluntary associations has implications for the individual, for the type of leadership in the group, and for the wider society.

An association was always more or less sect-like. However, in many later applications, a cluster of attributes for church and sect dominates: church is traditional, hierarchic, formal, inclusive, materialistic, appealing to the dominant classes, and large in size; sect, in contrast, is radical, egalitarian, informal, exclusive, ascetic, appealing to the outcast, and small, with a voluntary membership based on merit. Rather than given factors, these features should be seen as comparable variables. Troeltsch distinguished "mysticism" as a third category; it was characterized by radical individualism and indifference to dogmas. In the North American context, a "denomination" was seen as an evolution on the way from sect to church.

The sociology of sectarianism has largely been replaced or digested by the sociology of (new) religious movements and by the sociology of religion in general. The term "sect" has suffered from negative connotations (such as being heretical), and the expression "new religious movements" is thought to have a more neutral sense. From the 1960s onward, scholars stressed that such movements do not necessarily split off from a church but protest against the wider (secular) society or the state. Deviant ideas do not suffice to make a sect in the sociological sense; theological doctrines and beliefs are to be abandoned as a criterion for sectarianism. The organizational form and the socioeconomic status of members can also vary from sect to sect.

In modern sociology, one of the major defining features for sect-like groups has been tension toward the sociocultural environment. Church-like groups adapt to societal change, whereas sects wish to cause or prevent social change in opposition to the wider society, thus standing in high tension to it. Religious groups are seen on a continuum rather than in fixed categories. Tension has been measured, for example, by questionnaires about group members' difference (deviant norms) in a given context, their antagonism (claim for legitimacy, interest in proselytizing, political aims), and separation (restriction of social relations to mainly insiders; Stark and Bainbridge 1987). Deviance is defined by the interplay between the sect and those in power or the majority of the populace; sectarianism is thus always in a state of alteration according to the societal context. Sectarianism can be studied both at the level of the individual (modes of religiosity) and at the level of the collective.

Models of Sectarianism Applied to Biblical Literature

Biblical scholars use the term "sect" in a more technical sense. The usage varies according to the theoretical model, so there is no single application of the sociology of sectarianism. Labels like "reform movement," "faction," and "cult" have been used as technical terms to make distinctions between sect-like and other groups. Some scholars have distinguished between two kinds of high-tension groups: those that seek to restore traditional beliefs and practices (sects) and those that have novel beliefs and practices (cults; Stark and Bainbridge 1987). Bryan R. Wilson has been one of the sociologists to modify and expand the traditional church-sect typology. He conducted wide-ranging surveys of non-Christian religious sects and detected various patterns of sectarianism. To facilitate comparative study, he categorized seven different "responses to evil in the world" in sects: introversionist, conversionist, manipulationist, thaumaturgist, reformist, revolutionist, and utopian. These subtypes are again ideal types; they are not found in pure forms.

Wilson's typology has been especially popular among biblical scholars (see the application to early Judaism by Piovanelli in Chalcraft 2007). The reason may be that models of sectarianism are consulted in the first place in order to classify and describe different groups in relation to each other. This research tradition is indebted to New Testament scholarship, where applications and modifications of various sociological sect models are numerous (e.g., Holmberg 1990). The use of the sociology of sectarianism has also received criticism (Craffert 2001). Biblical scholars accept, for example, Wilson's responses but do not reflect on the cultural conditions that, according to the model, led to these responses. Some of the conditions might not have existed in the ancient world (e.g., individualism as a condition for conversionist sects). Forcing onto a group the label "sect" or "not a sect" and classifying groups into different kinds of sects can sometimes become the end rather than the means of understanding group dynamics and cultivating fruitful scholarly discussion.

Jewish Sectarianism in the Second Temple Period

The study of sectarianism in the Second Temple period is, to a large extent, an inquiry into the nature of early Judaism. The identification of a sect always deals in some way or other with its counterpart. A sect stands in tension with the society and reveals what the "normative" side (the elite, the establishment, the masses) values, promotes, or rejects. The notion of any single normative Judaism in the Second Temple period has been widely rejected, and even religion in preexilic Israel was perhaps not as monolithic as previously believed. However, without a cohesive and centralized power in Judaism, speaking of sects as high-tension groups is not very meaningful.

Nevertheless, sects and sectarianism are well-established concepts in the study of early Judaism. Often the term "sect" is used in the nontechnical sense and is considered suitable for describing the diversity and particularism of Judaism in the Second Temple period. The terms "party," "faction," "coalition," "(reform) movement," and "group" are some of the labels used side by side with "sect." Both the transformation from ancient Israelite religion to early Judaism and the intensification of social differentiation are viewed against the background of those events of the sixth and fifth centuries B.C.E. that led the dispersion of the people of Israel. Some Judeans returned to the land, but conflicts arose between the returnees and the locals (Talmon 1986).

The Elephantine community in Egypt and the Samaritans are often distinguished as being the first clear groups to break away from the Jerusalem community, although in the case of Elephantine the separation was primarily geographical. Some scholars distinguish between antecedents and mature forms of sectarianism (Baumgarten 1997).

In any case, sectarianism was full-blown by the beginning of the Common Era, as is clear, for example, from Josephus' account of the major Jewish groups: Pharisees, Sadducees, Essenes, and Fourth Philosophy. The term "sect" has traditionally served as the translation for the Greek label *hairesis* used by Josephus to describe these groups.

The actual flourishing of various distinct groups has been causally connected to differing reactions toward the Maccabean Revolt and the following Hasmonean state. The relations with and attitudes toward the Temple played a major role in the rise of sectarianism, as did urbanization, increased literacy, and millenarian hopes. Sects are considered to constitute the essence of early Judaism, not an aberrant phenomenon but a typical one. In addition to the major sects mentioned by Josephus, many more groups can be identified that have left distinct literature (e.g., Enochic Jews, Jesus' followers) or that had specific political or other social objectives reported by outside sources or inferred from them (e.g., Hellenizers).

The Qumran Sect

The movement responsible for preserving, copying, and composing the Qumran corpus is often considered the paradigm case of a sect in the Second Temple period (see Wassen and Jokiranta in Chalcraft 2007). Evidence for this evaluation is found in the group's rejection of the Temple (partly or wholly), its strict halakah, its preference for a different calendar, its concentration on purity rules, and the sometimes foreign elements in its beliefs. Asceticism, isolation or separation, exclusive membership, and strict discipline are also seen as characteristics of a sectarian organization. Clearly, some of the assumptions are made with the traditional sect-church model in mind and need further testing. Additionally, the stances reflected in different documents among the Dead Sea Scrolls may vary, due to developments in the movement, a limited amount of information derived from fragmentary documents, or the fact that documents represent various groups in various locations and/or times.

In any case, a sect in the sociological sense does not signify something utterly strange or distant; at best, sectarian models direct our attention to some central aspects in the interaction between a particular group and the surrounding groups in a given setting. Sects may reject common practices but also function as a pressure for change in society. Comparative studies between the Qumran community and early Christian groups, as well as modern religious movements, have demonstrated similar attitudes, needs, and relations within these groups. Models can serve as heuristic tools to view the evidence.

In Qumran studies, the term "sectarian" is also used to indicate the provenance of texts: sectarian writings are considered to be those not just copied but composed by members of the Qumran movement. However, not all the texts authored by the group have a clearly recognizable sectarian ideology (Newsom 1990). Moreover, a group may adopt texts from outside and use them for its own purposes in a sectarian fashion. All in all, a sect can own, copy, use, and compose texts that have (or had) a wider background or a wider audience than its own members. The label "sectarian text" is therefore not a sociological concept, and it confuses more than it clarifies. The rubric "sectarian provenance" is also misleading if it bears the assumption that nonsectarian texts were written by people without a community or developed organization.

Furthermore, the sociology of sects has always sought to explain and predict the development of religious groups, taking into account their environment. Accordingly, scholars of early Judaism have attempted to explain the successes and failures of various groups in the Second Temple period and to characterize their possible developments. Generally, the tendency to move from higher to lower tension is often the case in sectarian movements. However, a sect may also die or remain at the high-tension end. There is a temptation to use the model as a gap-filler, especially in cases where sources are fragmentary or inadequate. It must be remembered that ideal types do not exist in reality and cannot prove any scholarly constructions true or false.

New alternative classificatory systems for religious traditions have also emerged. The cognitive science of religion is one expanding field, which attempts to capture the universal in human cultures and distinguishes between different religious traditions according to their ritual systems and ways of transmitting the tradition (Whitehouse and Laidlaw 2004).

BIBLIOGRAPHY

A. BAUMGARTEN 2002, "'But Touch the Law and the Sect Will Split': Legal Dispute as the Cause of Sectarian Schism," *Review of Rabbinic Judaism* 5: 301-15. • A. BAUMGARTEN 1997, *The Flourishing of Jewish Sects in the Maccabean Era: An Interpretation,* Leiden: Brill. • J. CAMPBELL, W. LYONS, AND L. PETERSEN, EDS. 2005, *New Directions in Qumran Studies: Proceedings of the Bristol Colloquium on the Dead Sea Scrolls, 8-10 September 2003,* London: Clark. • D. CHALCRAFT, ED. 2007, *Sectarianism in Early Judaism: Sociological Advances,* London: Equinox. • S. J. D. COHEN 1999, *The Beginnings of Jewishness: Boundaries, Varieties, Uncertainties,* Berkeley: University of California Press. • P. CRAFFERT 2001, "An Exercise in the Critical Use of Models: The 'Goodness of Fit' of Wilson's Sect Model," in *Social Scientific Models for Interpreting the Bible: Essays by the Context Group in Honor of Bruce J. Malina,* ed. J. Pilch, Leiden: Brill, 21-46. • B. HOLMBERG 1990, *Sociology and the New Testament: An Appraisal,* Minneapolis: Fortress. • L. LAWRENCE AND M. AGUILAR LING, EDS. 2004, *Anthropology and Biblical Studies: Avenues of Approach,* Leiden: Deo. • C. NEWSOM 1990, "'Sectually Explicit' Literature from Qumran," in *The Hebrew Bible and Its Interpreters,* ed. W. Propp, B. Halpern, and D. Freedman, Winona Lake, Ind.: Eisenbrauns, 167-87. • E. REGEV 2007, *Sectarianism in Qumran: A Cross-Cultural Perspective,* Berlin: de Gruyter. • A. SALDARINI 1988, *Pharisees, Scribes, and Sadducees in Palestinian Society: A Sociological Approach,* Wilmington, Del.: Glazier. • R. STARK AND W. BAINBRIDGE 1987, *A Theory of Religion,* New York: Peter Lang. • S. TALMON 1986, "The Emergence of Jewish Sectarianism in the Early Second Temple Period," in idem, *King, Cult, and Calendar in Ancient Israel: Collected Studies,* Jerusalem: Magnes, 165-201. • E. TROELTSCH 1931, *The Social Teaching of the Christian Churches,* trans. O. Wyon, New York: Macmillan. • M. WEBER 1952, *Ancient Judaism,* trans. H. Gerth and D. Martindale, Glencoe: Free Press (original 1917-20). • M. WEBER 2002, *The Protestant Ethic and the Spirit of Capitalism: New Introduction and Translation by Stephen Kalberg,* London: Blackwell (original 1904-05). • H. WHITEHOUSE AND J. LAIDLAW, EDS. 2004, *Ritual and Memory: Toward a Comparative Anthropology of Religion,* Walnut Creek, Calif.: AltaMira. • B. WILSON 1973, *Magic and the Millennium: A Sociological Study of Religious Movements of Protest among Tribal and Third-World Peoples,* London: Heinemann. • B. WILSON 1990, *The Social Dimension of Sectarianism: Sects and New Religious Movements in Contemporary Society,* Oxford: Clarendon.

JUTTA JOKIRANTA

Seekers after Smooth Things → Pesharim

Seleucids

The Seleucids were a dynasty of Greek kings based in Syria during the Hellenistic period. They were the descendants of Seleucus I Nicator (312/11-281 B.C.E.), one of Alexander the Great's successors (the Diadochi). Upon Alexander's death in 323 B.C.E., no province was assigned to Seleucus at the Congress of Babylon, although he was invested with an important military role. Only in 321 B.C.E. at Triparadeisos did he receive the province of Babylon, which he was able to recover militarily only years later upon Antigonus' death in 311 B.C.E. With the annexation of Syria on that occasion, his territories extended from the Mediterranean to the Indus River. Like the other Hellenistic dynasts, the Seleucids initially concentrated their political and military attention on the Eastern Mediterranean and its direct or hegemonic control. For the Seleucids, this phase culminated in 281 B.C.E. when, at Lysimachus' death, Seleucus I annexed Anatolia. For most of the third century B.C.E., the Seleucids reigned over a region that at times included almost all of what had been Alexander's empire.

The Extent of Their Empire

The Seleucids' rule over their empire had to take into account the heterogeneous political and cultural traditions of different peoples. While Anatolia and the coastal region of the Levant were mostly familiar with the institution of the city-state, the easternmost territories, traditionally part of the Mesopotamian and later of the Persian empires, were accustomed to the rule of centralized governments, whose effects on the indigenous populations were mediated through the political and military power of local aristocrats loyal to the king. No evidence suggests that the Seleucids superimposed any changes on either political tradition. Rather, they kept the administrative organization Alexander had inherited from the previous rulers and instituted particular relationships, attested by a corpus of diplomatic correspondence, with the local communities and their political leaders — whether large regional provinces or small city-states. Only mistrust and open rebellion prompted the Seleucids to intervene militarily in order to avoid the territorial fragmentation or reduction of their empire — yet not always successfully.

Like all Hellenistic kings, the Seleucids introduced their ruler cult, by which they traced back their ancestry to the Greek god Apollo. It was through the members of the dynastic cult hierarchy, who were also administrative officials and whose names had to be mentioned in official documents, that the Seleucids introduced a unifying net all over the empire. This does not mean, however, that the ruler cult interfered with, or was imposed upon, local cults and religious hierarchies. Rather, the Seleucids respected and patronized the local cults, making sacrificial offerings and supporting the restoration and building of temples.

As the Ptolemies did in Egypt, the Seleucids promoted cultural patronage in Syria, particularly through a library in Antioch, following the example of the one in Alexandria. The library of Antioch never reached the size or fame of its Egyptian rival, although important intellectuals presided over it and worked there. Unfortunately the scarcity of available records does not allow a complete evaluation of its impact on the Hellenistic cultural environment.

The territorial extent of the Seleucid Empire experienced several peaks and setbacks. At the end of the third century B.C.E., Antiochus III (223-187 B.C.E.) recovered the Mesopotamian and Iranian provinces after some successful attempts at secession by local leaders — a massive victory that earned him the appellation "the Great." In the same period, after more than a century of endemic military confrontations, Antiochus III won the Fifth Syrian War and annexed Coele-Syria, snatching it for good from Ptolemaic control. At this moment the Seleucid Empire reached its largest extent. Yet a few years later, in 188 B.C.E., the eastern territories again withdrew their loyalty from the Seleucid dynasty.

The first decades of the second century B.C.E. saw the Seleucids clash with the Roman power in the Eastern Mediterranean. As a final halt to Seleucid ambitions, the Romans ended their war with Syria in 188 B.C.E. with the Peace of Apamea, which forced the Seleucids to abandon Anatolia, to limit drastically their military capability, and to pay a considerable fine. From that moment onward, the Seleucids became *de facto* client kings of the growing Roman Empire, with the obligation to send to Rome members of the royal family as hostages, as a token of respect for the signed treaties. Rome kept under strict diplomatic and military control any Seleucid attempt at expansion.

Territorial reductions continued with the final loss of the Mesopotamian and Iranian territory to the Parthians in the 160s B.C.E., when Antiochus IV's military expedition to recover them failed. In 140 B.C.E. Coele-Syria became an independent kingdom ruled by the Hasmonean priestly dynasty, who acquired their power in the wake of the Maccabean Revolt. From then on the Seleucid Empire would encompass only the Syrian territories from west of the Euphrates to the Mediterranean coast. This is the region that Pompey annexed to the Roman Empire in 63 B.C.E., putting an end to the Seleucid dynastic power.

Interactions with the Jews

The earliest evidence of interaction between the Seleucids and the Jews dates to 198 B.C.E., when Antiochus III deported 2,000 Jewish families from Mesopotamia and Babylon to some cities of Lydia and Phygia in Anatolia. Josephus provides a transcription of the official royal letter to the local governor ordering the transfer. He attributes the deportation to the king's need to inject a contingent of loyal people into cities otherwise hostile to him. According to the letter, the king allowed the transferred Jews to abide by their own laws and customs. Josephus remains silent about other

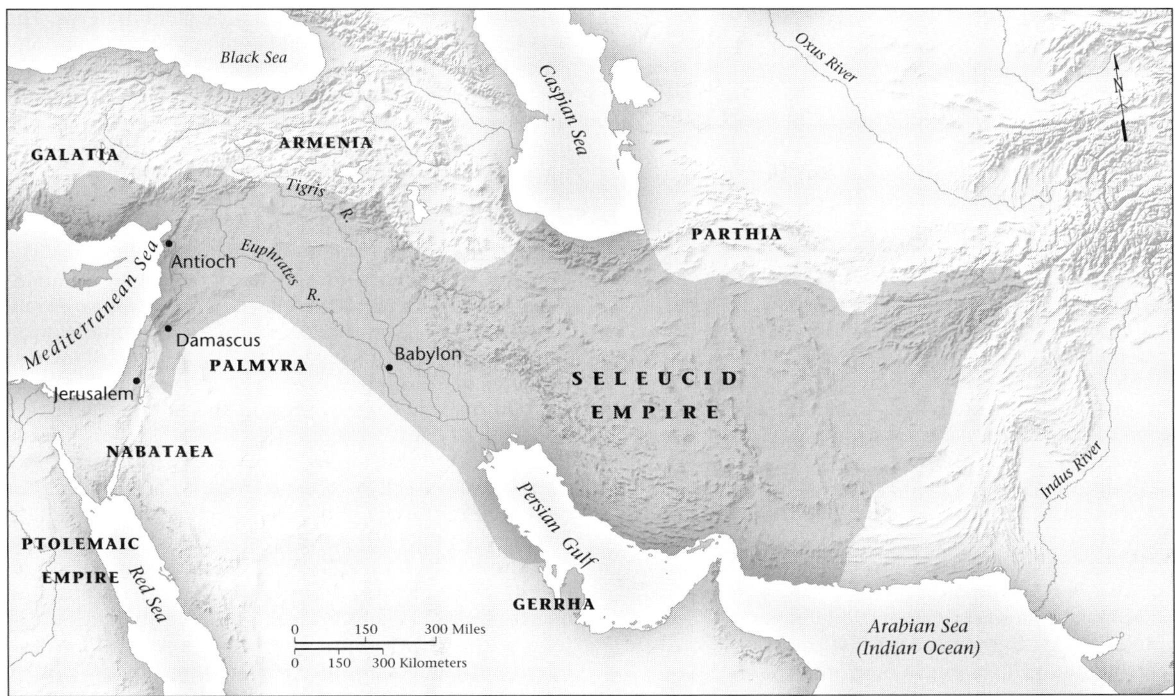

THE SELEUCID EMPIRE

conditions they may have agreed upon or been forced to accept. Together, the vagueness of Josephus' evidence about the final destination of those Jews and the absence of further records prevents further historical analysis.

With the conquest of Coele-Syria in 195 B.C.E. as the outcome of the Fifth Syrian War, the Seleucids became rulers of Judea. Josephus stresses the positive relationship the Seleucids established with the Jews, emphasizing, through the transcription of an official royal decree, Antiochus III's high esteem for the Jewish customs. Allegedly the king left the high priesthood alone and forbade Gentiles to enter Jerusalem as well as unclean animals to tread through its streets. Seleucus IV (187-175 B.C.E.), Antiochus III's son and successor, ratified this relationship with the Jews and added sacrificial offerings from his own treasury.

With Antiochus IV (175-164 B.C.E.), Seleucus IV's brother and successor, the good relationship between the Seleucids and the Jews abruptly terminated. He sacked and desecrated the Temple. These two acts are hard to interpret because the sources — mainly Josephus' *Antiquities,* 1 Maccabees, and 2 Maccabees — are apologetic, cryptic, and to some extent contradictory. In any case, it is clear that Jerusalem was run by the ruling priestly family (within which a Hellenizing faction played an important role) that was at odds with a rival priestly family. This situation must be seen against a complicated backdrop involving the uneasy diplomacy between the Seleucids and the Ptolemies from the 170s B.C.E., in combination with the problematic relationship between the Seleucids and the Romans, now constantly present in the Eastern Mediterranean.

Problems started already during the last years of Seleucus IV's reign. A feud within the Temple hierarchy prompted Simon, a member of a priestly family but not the ruling one, to alert the king's functionaries to the high priest Onias III's irregular custody of the Temple treasure. Some of it was not being used to fund the sacrifices and was therefore unaccounted for. The king, who was financing the sacrifices out of his own pocket and was having trouble paying the Romans the fine imposed by the Peace of Apamea, ordered the treasure to be confiscated, a move that Onias III's supporters prevented. Seleucus IV's death in 175 B.C.E. and struggles over succession delayed a response to the feud within the Jerusalem priestly hierarchy.

The new king, Antiochus IV, soon faced the difficult Judean situation he inherited from his predecessor. At this point Jason, Onias III's brother, had the king grant him the high priesthood by offering him a huge sum of money. In this context, the apologetic sources speak of Jason as a renegade, since he also offered to Hellenize Jerusalem, whose inhabitants would be enrolled as citizens of Antioch and would participate in all the political and social ceremonial that such a transformation entailed. Although the offer of Hellenizing Jerusalem did not include the abandonment of Jewish monotheism, the sources record a relaxation in the observance of rituals, due to the priestly class's attention to the Greek way of life, especially training in the gymnasium.

Seleucid Rulers

Seleucus I Nicator (Satrap 311-305 B.C.E., King 305-281 B.C.E.)
Antiochus I Soter (coruler from 291, ruled 281-261 B.C.E.)
Antiochus II Theos (261-246 B.C.E.)
Seleucus II Callinicus (246-225 B.C.E.)
Seleucus III Ceraunus (or Soter) (225-223 B.C.E.)
Antiochus III the Great (223-187 B.C.E.)
Seleucus IV Philopator (187-175 B.C.E.)
Antiochus IV Epiphanes (175-164 B.C.E.)
Antiochus V Eupator (164-162 B.C.E.)
Demetrius I Soter (161-150 B.C.E.)
Alexander I Balas (150-145 B.C.E.)
Demetrius II Nicator (first reign, 145-138 B.C.E.)
Antiochus VI Dionysus (or Epiphanes) (145-140 B.C.E.?)
Diodotus Tryphon (140?-138 B.C.E.)
Antiochus VII Sidetes (or Euergetes) (138-129 B.C.E.)
Demetrius II Nicator (second reign, 129-126 B.C.E.)
Alexander II Zabinas (129-123 B.C.E.)
Cleopatra Thea (126-123 B.C.E.)
Seleucus V Philometor (126/125 B.C.E.)
Antiochus VIII Grypus (125-96 B.C.E.)
Antiochus IX Cyzicenus (114-96 B.C.E.)
Seleucus VI Epiphanes Nicator (96-95 B.C.E.)
Antiochus X Eusebes Philopator (95-92 B.C.E. or 83 B.C.E.)
Demetrius III Eucaerus (or Philopator) (95-87 B.C.E.)
Antiochus XI Epiphanes Philadelphus (95-92 B.C.E.)
Philip I Philadelphus (95-84/83 B.C.E.)
Antiochus XII Dionysus (87-84 B.C.E.)
(Tigranes I of Armenia) (83-69 B.C.E.)
Seleucus VII Kybiosaktes or Philometor (70s B.C.E.–60s B.C.E.?)
Antiochus XIII Asiaticus (69-64 B.C.E.)
Philip II Philoromaeus (65-63 B.C.E.)

Jason sent money to the king for the sacrifices to Herakles at the quadrennial game in Antioch. The sources allege that the ambassadors in charge of the money decided to bring the money to Tyre instead and to use it to build triremes. The timing (war between Syria and Egypt was imminent) and the location (Tyre, the Seleucid port on the Mediterranean) make the gesture suspicious; the diversion of the money to Tyre may have been intended for building ships, in breach of the Peace of Apamea.

In 173 B.C.E., Menelaus, Simon's brother and a member of the rival priestly family, went on a mission to the king on behalf of Jason. Once in Antioch, though, he secured the high priesthood for himself by outbidding Jason. It is not clear whether Jason or Menelaus ever deposited the promised sums in the king's coffers, but in the same year Antiochus IV found the financial means to pay off the fine owed to the Romans.

The beginning of Antiochus IV's reign also coincided with the dawn of a new political era in Egypt. The Seleucid relationship with Egypt had previously improved through the marriage between Cleopatra, daughter of Antiochus III, and Ptolemy V. But now, upon both sovereigns' death, a court governing on behalf of the underaged Ptolemy VI showed a hostile disposition toward the Seleucids and a renewed ambition to recover Coele-Syria. This prompted Antiochus IV to invade Egypt for the first time in 170 B.C.E. — the Sixth Syrian War. The campaign did not last long because the Romans, who were interested in preserving Egyptian independence as well as limiting Seleucid expansion, interrupted it after only one year with the diplomatic intervention of C. Popilius Laenas at Eleusis, a small town at the gates of Alexandria.

On his way back to Syria in the fall of 169 B.C.E., Antiochus IV intervened directly in Jerusalem affairs. While some of the apologetic sources absolve the Jews of any responsibility, a cross-comparison with other historical narratives shows that the king intervened to resolve the feud within the Jerusalemite priestly hierarchy. During the king's Egyptian campaign Jason had retaken Jerusalem and confined Menelaus to the city citadel. It is very likely that Jason gathered the support of Jerusalem's inhabitants, not only those who had followed him in the Hellenization of the city but also more conservative ones, who saw in him the legitimate high priest and regarded Menelaus as a usurper. Antiochus intervened in favor of Menelaus, whom he had appointed some years earlier. The king's attack was not limited to Jason and his military contingent but extended to the city at large, since it supported Jason. He ordered the demolition of the walls, the killing of many citizens, and the desecration and ransacking of the Temple with its riches and sacred vessels. He also imposed a governor and a military contingent on Jerusalem. The punishment culminated with an intrusion into the religious realm, with the dedication of the Temple to Zeus and the order for Jews to forsake their ancestral laws. According to the sources, the king did not limit his religious measure to Judea but promoted a degree of religious homogenization through edicts sent all over the empire. Unfortunately it is not possible to confirm this allegation with corroborating evidence.

The harsh enforcement of these religious provisions sparked the Maccabean Revolt, which eventually caused the Seleucids in 140 B.C.E. to lose all of Coele-Syria, including Judea, Samaria, Galilee, and Phoenicia, to the independent kingdom ruled by Hasmoneans. Onias III's descendants found themselves cut out of the dispute and unable to reacquire the high priesthood. They emigrated to Egypt, where Ptolemy VI granted them permission to build a temple at Leontopolis.

BIBLIOGRAPHY

D. GERA 1998, *Judaea and Mediterranean Politics 219 to 161 BCE*, Leiden: Brill. • J. D. GRAINGER 1990, *Seleukos Nikator: Constructing a Hellenistic Kingdom*, London: Routledge. • J. MA 1999, *Antiochos III and the Cities of Western Asia Minor*, Oxford: Oxford University Press. • O. MØRKHOLM 1966, *Antiochus IV of Syria*, Copenhagen: Gyldendal. • S. SHERWIN-

White and A. Kuhrt 1992, *From Samarkhand to Sardis: A New Approach to the Seleucid Empire,* Berkeley: University of California Press.

See also: Diadochi, Maccabean Revolt

Sandra Gambetti

Self-Glorification Hymn

In the *Self-Glorification Hymn* from Qumran (4Q491 frg. 11, 4Q471b, 1QH[a] 26-27, 4QH[a] frg. 7 col. i and frg. 12), an anonymous figure describes his exalted status. He portrays himself as seated in heaven, sharing the lot of the angels. Various identifications have been proposed for the speaker of this hymn, among them the archangel Michael and King Herod the Great. It has also been suggested that it reflects an alleged mystical experience by a human figure, perhaps the Teacher of Righteousness. Comparison of this hymn to the *Rule of Blessing* (1QSb) suggests a possible identification of this figure with the eschatological high priest. In the *Rule of Blessing* this figure is described as sitting with the angels in the heavenly temple and taking part in angelic ceremonies, and as a teacher whose wisdom is a light that illumines the world with knowledge. In similar fashion, the speaker in the *Self-Glorification Hymn* "is reckoned with" the angels and claims to impart extraordinary teachings. The speaker's wisdom is alluded to in the statement "Neither] with gold will (I) cro[wn myself]" (4Q471b lines 8-9), words that evoke the search for wisdom in the book of Job: "The finest gold of Ophir cannot be weighed against it. . . . Nor vessels of fine gold be exchanged for it" (28:16-17).

The speaker's self-portrait in the hymn seems very close to the Qumran sect's perception of their own historical leader, the Teacher of Righteousness. Perhaps because of this literary resemblance, the Teacher's followers linked the *Self-Glorification Hymn* with their leader after his death. This correspondence perhaps inspired, in turn, the incorporation of the *Self-Glorification Hymn* into a copy of the *Hodayot* from Cave 4 (4QH[e]). This manuscript, which is preserved in only one fragment, contains a hymn that parallels the hymn that follows the *Self-Glorification Hymn* in 4QH[a] frg. 7, col. i and 1QH[a] 26-27.

Since the scripts of 4Q471b and 4QH[e] are identical, they can be identified as parts of one manuscript. Due to the special character of the two hymns — the *Self-Glorification Hymn* and the hymn following — one may argue that both originated in a collection of hymns that were incorporated into the *Hodayot.* Thus, the *Self-Glorification Hymn* is preserved in 4Q471b; in a second, similar hymn found in 4QH[e]; and in two other *Hodayot* scrolls (4QH[a] frg. 7, col. i; 1QH[a] 26-27). The second hymn, designated as a *Hymn of the Community,* also emphasizes communion with the angels. The four copies of the *Self-Glorification Hymn* can be divided into Recension A (4QH[a] frg. 7 col. i and frg. 12; 4Q471b; 1QH[a] 26-27) and Recension B (4Q491 frg. 11).

The description of a figure sitting in the company of the angels in the "holy dwelling" may be compared with early Jewish accounts of ascents to heaven, mainly in connection with Enoch (*1 Enoch* 17–36) and with Levi (*Testament of Levi).* Other accounts of heavenly enthronement, based on Daniel 7, are found in the *Similitudes of Enoch* (*1 Enoch* 37–71) and the *Testament of Abraham.* In the Qumran sectarian literature, one can find a similar description in the *War Scroll,* where "the chosen ones of the holy people" are described as seated with God and the angels in the holy dwelling (1QM 12:1). In a Hellenistic Jewish drama, the *Exagōgē* of Ezekiel the Tragedian, there is a dream of Moses in which he sees a great throne on Mt. Sinai where a noble man is seated, wearing a royal crown and holding a scepter. He then calls Moses and gives him the royal crown, which is later interpreted by Jethro as predicting that Moses will be a judge and leader of humankind (Eusebius, *Praep. Evang.* 9.24.4-6). Finally, the idea of enthronement in the *Self-Glorification Hymn* should be compared with gospel traditions that identify Jesus with the heavenly Son of Man figure (Mark 14:62; cf. *1 Enoch* 55:4; 62:3).

Bibliography

M. G. Abegg, Jr. 1997, "Who Ascended to Heaven? 4Q491, 4Q427, and the Teacher of Righteousness," in *Eschatology, Messianism, and the Dead Sea Scrolls,* ed. C. A. Evans and P. W. Flint, Grand Rapids: Eerdmans, 61-73. • P. Alexander 2006, *The Mystical Texts: Songs of the Sabbath Sacrifice and Related Manuscripts,* London: Continuum. • J. J. Collins 1995, *The Scepter and the Star: The Messiahs of the Dead Sea Scrolls and Other Ancient Literature,* New York: Doubleday, 136-53. • E. Eshel 1996, "4Q471b: A Self Glorification Hymn," *RevQ* 17, 176-203. • E. Eshel 1999, "The Identification of the 'Speaker' of the Self-Glorification Hymn," in *The Provo International Conference on the Dead Sea Scrolls,* ed. D. W. Parry and E. C. Ulrich, Leiden: Brill, 619-35. • I. Knohl 2000, *The Messiah before Jesus: The Suffering Servant of the Dead Sea Scrolls,* Berkeley: University of California. • M. Smith 1990, "Ascent to the Heavens and Deification in 4QM[a]," in *Archaeology and History in the Dead Sea Scrolls,* ed. L. H. Schiffman, Sheffield: JSOT Press, 181-88. • M. O. Wise 2000, "*My kmwni b'lym:* A Study of 4Q491c, 4Q471b, 4Q427 7 and 1QH[a] 25:35–26:10," *DSD* 7: 173-219.

Esther Eshel

Sepphoris

Sepphoris was a leading city in Lower Galilee called *Ṣippôrî* in Hebrew or *Sepphōris* in Greek. Its Greek name after Hadrian was Diocaesarea, especially in the later Christian authors. Sepphoris stood virtually in the geographic center of Lower Galilee, barely five miles north of Nazareth.

Josephus relates that Ptolemy Lathyrus of Egypt attacked the city unsuccessfully on a Sabbath (*Ant.* 13.338). That Ptolemy struck on a Sabbath implies that he knew that the city was Jewish; that he was unsuccessful suggests that it was already walled. This attack took place shortly after the accession of Alexander Jannaeus in 106 B.C.E. In 63 B.C.E. Sepphoris and all Galilee came under the severe rule of Rome. About 55 B.C.E. Gabinius, proconsul in Syria, set up one of the Roman *synedria* or councils in Sepphoris (*Ant.* 14.91; *J.W.* 1.170).

Sepphoris figures prominently in Josephus' narratives of the civil war between Herod the Great and Matthias Antigonus in 40-37 B.C.E. (*Ant.* 14.414; *J.W.* 1.304). Herod captured Sepphoris after Antigonus abandoned it during a snowstorm. The city remained in Herod's hands until his own death about 4 B.C.E. But when Herod died, the city rose in revolt under Judah ben Hezekiah and suffered the consequences. Varus, governor of Syria, marched from Antioch with two legions and two wings of Arab cavalry. Varus left the siege and punishment of Sepphoris to his own son and a friend. The razed and empty city soon passed to the new tetrarch, Herod Antipas, son of Herod the Great. Antipas ordered that it be rebuilt as his showcase (*Ant.* 17.289; *J.W.* 2.56).

Josephus describes the rebuilt Sepphoris as the "ornament of all Galilee" (*Ant.* 18.27) and claims that it was the "strongest city in Galilee" (*J.W.* 2.511; *Life* 232). Excavations in Sepphoris tend to confirm these lofty words. The city was laid out on a grid oriented with its hill, and its streets were paved with crushed limestone. A Roman theater stood partially cut into the hillside in Greek style on the north side of the city. Citizens of Sepphoris could repair to the theater for an evening's entertainment, probably of light comedy, mimes, or other fashionable amusements. Ordinary residences and elegant mansions stood here and there within the city blocks. Since Sepphoris was built on a hill, it was visible for miles. It may be the city that Jesus had in mind when he said, "A city set on a hill cannot be hidden" (Matt. 5:14).

According to *Life* 37–39, a certain Justus remarked that Herod Antipas had ordered that the archives and the treasury be brought from Sepphoris to Tiberias. But after Nero's accession, when Felix was procurator of Judea (52-60 C.E.), the archives and treasury reverted to Sepphoris.

Josephus became the Jewish commander of the Galilee in the war against Rome. He asserted that the citizens of Sepphoris were afraid of the other Galileans

Mosaic floor from Sepphoris dating to the third century C.E. The woman has been named "Mona Lisa of the Galilee." *(www.HolyLandPhotos.org)*

because of the city's friendship with the Romans and because of their pledge of loyalty to Cestius Gallus, legate of Syria (*Life* 30). As commander of Galilee Josephus attacked Sepphoris (the capital) successfully. The men of the city ran together into the (walled?) acropolis (*Life* 376).

In 66 B.C.E. the citizens of Sepphoris saluted the Roman general Vespasian in the field and petitioned for protection from their Jewish neighbors, who did not sympathize with the Sepphoreans because they openly sided with the Romans (*J.W.* 3.30-34; *Life* 411). Vespasian sent 1,000 cavalry and 6,000 infantry to Sepphoris under the command of Placidius (*J.W.* 3.59).

The earliest coins of Sepphoris are from the time of Nero (54-68 C.E.). The first type, minted in 68 C.E., honors Vespasian and Nero. The obverse inscription reads "In the time of Vespasian, City of Peace (Eirenopolis), Neronias Sepphoris."

The citizens of Sepphoris shared in the common culture of the Galilee. The social structure was organized more or less by wealth and by birth. At the apex of the social structure were the elites (the "rich" of the New Testament, called "great ones" in later Jewish sources), many of whom were Herod's retainers.

Sepphoris was also a major seat of Jewish learning. R. Halafta of the first and second centuries was an older contemporary of Gamaliel II and Yoḥanan b. Nuri (*t. Šabb.* 13[14]:2; *t. Maʿaś. Š.* 1:13), and had his own academy at Sepphoris (*y. Taʿan.* 2:5; *y. Roš Haššanah* 27a). His son, Yose ben Halafta of Sepphoris, a student of Akiba of the second century C.E., figures prominently in the Mishnah. Judah Ha-Nasi ("the Prince") lived the last seventeen years of his life at Sepphoris and redacted the oral law to form the Mishnah with his colleagues, including Gamaliel III.

Ḥanina bar Hama was head of the academy at Sepphoris in the third century C.E. with his colleague Jonathan ben Eleazar. Ḥanina's rival at Sepphoris was Yannai. Yoḥanan bar Nappacha, whom Rabbi Yannai had mentored, worked both at Sepphoris and later at Tiberias and is often credited with beginning the Palestinian Gemara. Rabbi Alexandri, trained at Lydda, moved to Sepphoris in the third century C.E., as did Rabbi Simlai, who came from Babylon. Probably the most celebrated rabbi of Sepphoris in the mid-fourth century C.E. was Hillel II, great-great-grandson of Gamaliel III of Sepphoris. Another illustrious rabbi was Resh Lakish ("Resh" = "Rabbi Shimon"), who lived most of his life in Sepphoris. His colleague was Yoḥanan, his brother-in-law and sometime halakic opponent.

We glean more about Sepphoris from the Mishnah. The rabbis knew of an "old fort" (*m. ʿArak.* 9:6) and an archive at Sepphoris (*m. Qidd.* 4:5), an institution noted by Josephus. The rabbis also spoke of two aqueducts that flowed from springs at Abel, three Roman miles to the east (*m. ʿErub.* 8:7). Archaeological surveys and excavations have confirmed that one was built in the first century B.C.E., and the second one later. Citizens could count on water even in times of drought because of their reservoir.

View looking southwest at the 4000-seat theater at Sepphoris, constructed in the late first century C.E. *(www.HolyLandPhotos.org)*

Sepphoris had at least one synagogue in the first century C.E., but none have been found. Remains of two synagogues of the fifth centuries C.E. are known. Yet Jewish texts mention synagogues at Sepphoris, including the "synagogue of the Babylonians" and the "synagogue of the Gophnites" (*y. Nazir* 56a; *m. Sanh.* 10:28). (Gophna ["vineyard"] is a village in Judea.) These texts and others imply that Sepphoris was an important economic center (*y. B. Meṣʿia* 5:6).

Archaeology tends to confirm that Sepphoris was largely Jewish. Beneath the floors of most of the excavated houses one finds Jewish ritual baths or *miqvāʾôt*. These were cut into bedrock and usually comprised one small, plastered pool with steps leading down to the water. Many pieces of stone vessels have also been found; since they were made of stone, they were not subject to ritual impurity (*m. Kelim* 10:1; *m. Yad.* 1:2).

The Roman architecture of Sepphoris is represented in civil basilicas, villas with mosaic floors, and a city plan with paved streets from the first century C.E. onward, especially the *cardo* and its main cross street, the *decumanus*. The Jerusalem Talmud (*y. Ketub.* 1:25d) mentions a fortified upper city and a colonnaded street, perhaps the cardo or main street. Sepphoris was also a major center with inns, synagogues, and schools or academies (*y. Peʾah* 20b, 27–31).

"Liturgies" were a form of service or taxation levied on all major cities and on guilds. Certain leading men of Sepphoris served on the city's *boulē* or council, which made them accountable to the government for the city's taxes (*y. Peʾah* 16a [1.1]). Oppressive liturgies may explain why Jewish land around the city was passing into Gentile hands, according to *y. Dem.* 5:8 and *y. Giṭ.* 4:9.

The Jerusalem Talmud (*y. Šabb.* 12:3) speaks of tensions between the *bulbatî* and *paganî* at Sepphoris over who would be the first to enter and leave the patriarch's house. These may be the names of two leading families in the city. Yet *bulbatî* may refer to members of the council *(boulēteroi)*, in which case the *paganî* would be farmers or landowners. The text then recalls a power struggle in which both groups appealed to R. Simeon b. Laqish, who inquired of R. Yoḥanan. The latter ruled in favor of the *paganî*. The language of the ruling suggests that the proper question was who was worthy by learning, not birth.

BIBLIOGRAPHY

R. A. BATEY 1991, *Jesus and the Forgotten City: New Light on Sepphoris and the Urban World of Jesus*, Grand Rapids: Baker. • E. M. MEYERS 1993, "Aspects of Roman Sepphoris in the Light of Recent Archaeology," in *Early Christianity in Context: Monuments and Documents*, ed. F. Manns and E. Alliata, Jerusalem: Franciscan Printing Press, 29-36. • R. M. NAGY ET AL. 1996, *Sepphoris in Galilee: Crosscurrents of Culture*, Raleigh: North Carolina Museum of Art. • J. F. STRANGE, T. R. W. LONGSTAFF, AND D. E. GROH 2006, *Excavations at Sepphoris*, vol. 1, *University of South Florida Probes in the Citadel and Villa*, Leiden: Brill. • Z. WEISS ET AL. 2005, *The Sepphoris Synagogue: Deciphering an Ancient Message through Its Archaeological and Socio-Historical Context*, Jerusalem: Israel Exploration Society. • Z. WEISS AND E. NETZER 1996, *Promise and Redemption: A Synagogue Mosaic from Sepphoris*, Jerusalem: Israel Museum.

See also: Galilee JAMES F. STRANGE

Septuagint

The term "Septuagint" applies to various Greek texts of the Jewish Scriptures. The label derives from the story in the *Letter of Aristeas* that seventy-two or seventy (hence the siglum LXX) translators rendered the Torah into Greek. Even before Alexander the Great's conquest of the Near East during the decade between 333 and 323 B.C.E., the influence of Greek language and culture had been felt in the land of Palestine and in the Diaspora communities where Jews had begun to dwell. It was in one of these communities — Alexandria, Egypt — that the first rendering of the Hebrew Bible into Greek took place.

Origins

As related in the *Letter of Aristeas*, Ptolemy II Philadelphus enlisted the expertise of seventy-two elders from Jerusalem to prepare a Greek version of the Torah (or Pentateuch) for inclusion in his library. With such grand royal patronage, these men, working through committees to arrive at consensus, rapidly completed their task, to the approval of Ptolemy and Alexandria's Jewish residents alike. In such high regard was this text held, so the author of the *Letter* relates, that any and all alterations were strictly forbidden. This would have happened around 275 B.C.E.

The accuracy of *Aristeas'* account, dated more than a hundred years after the events it claims to describe, has been questioned since the Renaissance. It is widely accepted that the date and location of this translation are correct. However, close analysis has demonstrated that each of the five books of the Pentateuch had a different translator (Exodus probably had two), although there are clear connections between the generally literal approach taken by all of them. Moreover, it can be doubted that royal initiative was the sole impetus for this translation; surely, it also met the needs of Alexandria's Jews, for whom Hebrew was becoming more and more a "foreign" tongue.

Contents and Character

The term "Septuagint" ultimately came to be applied to the Greek renderings of all of the books of what we call the Hebrew Bible and other materials originally composed in Hebrew or Aramaic, as well as to some books (or parts of books) that were not translations at all; that is, they were original, Greek compositions. Little is known about the circumstances under which the books in the Septuagint were translated or composed. Some, like Joshua, closely follow the Pentateuch's tradition of reasonable literalism. Others tend to occupy a place at either end of the literal-free continuum (e.g., Ecclesiastes and Proverbs, respectively). To some degree, these widely divergent approaches to their Semitic *Vorlagen* (i.e., the Hebrew or Aramaic texts that lay before the translators) indicate that there was apparently no overarching "philosophy" of translation that united those responsible for the Septuagint.

Page from a Greek papyrus codex of the fourth century C.E. found in Egypt showing the text of Exod. 6:28–7:12. Together with Codex Vaticanus, this is the oldest extant manuscript of Septuagint Exodus. *(The Schøyen Collection, MS 2649)*

It is, moreover, also the case that what we call the Septuagint is largely a matter of happenstance, reflecting whatever Greek text or texts were available to those who compiled the great codices (e.g., Vaticanus, Alexandrinus, Sinaiticus) of the third and fourth centuries C.E. Sometimes they had at least partial access to what the earliest translators had produced (as in the case of the Pentateuch); at other times the process of transmission (whereby the Greek text was repeatedly copied over decades and centuries) combined disparate textual traditions into one (see, e.g., Kingdoms [1 and 2 Samuel, 1 and 2 Kings]; in still other cases, the earliest renderings were lost and later ones were substituted (as is true, e.g., for Daniel). Uncritical use of the term "Septuagint," as if it were a unified document, is therefore ill advised.

These very facts lead to the observation that *Aristeas'* prohibition against textual change, whatever historical validity it may have, was widely and regularly ignored (although Josephus, implicitly, and Philo, explicitly, transmitted and even enlarged upon *Aristeas'* account). This may already have been the case as early as the mid-second century B.C.E. The primary impetus for revision of old(er) Greek texts would have been comparison with the "biblical" Hebrew text then in use (although some changes, purely for "stylistic" reasons, cannot be ruled out). It is clear that, for some material, the Hebrew (or Aramaic) *Vorlage* was very similar to the consonantal text that we now speak of as the Masoretic Text (MT). For other books, however, the Greek translators had before them Hebrew wording that varied, slightly or more extensively, from what became the MT. When readers detected what they thought of as discrepancies between the Greek "translation" and the Hebrew "original," they were on occasion motivated to change the Greek to reflect that Hebrew. Such activity, over an extended period of time, would naturally have occurred in Jerusalem, but it may have occurred in many other places as well.

All of this points to the singular importance of the Septuagint as the first recorded translation of the Hebrew Bible. But it also suggests another emphasis that has characterized Septuagint studies, namely, the consideration of changes made by the translators themselves, to reflect the historical (as in LXX Isaiah) or cultural (as in LXX Proverbs) context of their times. It is in such material that we gain insight into characteristic aspects of belief and practice among Hellenistic Jews.

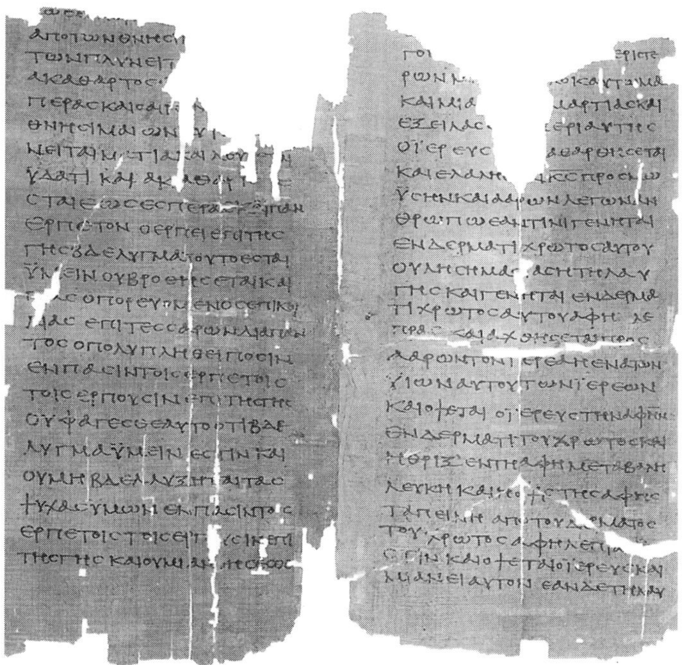

Two pages of a papyrus codex showing text from the book of Leviticus in Greek. Dating to ca. 200 C.E., this is one of the oldest Septuagint manuscripts extant for the book of Leviticus. *(The Schøyen Collection, MS 2649)*

As noted above, it is essential to avoid "global" characterizations, since each book or block of Septuagint material has unusual, if not unique features that should not be "universalized." It is impossible to know why the creators of some LXX books saw it as their role to update or otherwise modify their *Vorlagen* for the benefit of their intended audience, while others appear to have assiduously avoided any such modifications. Moreover, any comprehensive analysis of Hellenistic Jewish thought and practice must take into account the large amount of material that appears substantially the same in the Hebrew and the Greek.

Theodotion, Aquila, and Symmachus

The *Letter of Aristeas* provides the translators of the Septuagint with names, but in the last analysis those responsible for the oldest Greek as well as subsequent revisions and retranslations are for the most part anonymous figures. Such is not the case with "The Three" — Theodotion, Aquila, and Symmachus — whose works were known to Origen in the third century C.E. and preserved by him and in part in later editions of his justly famous Hexapla, a compilation of different ancient texts of the Hebrew Bible in six parallel columns. Even for these three individuals, we are without sure, uncontested biographical data. It does, nonetheless, seem likely that all three were Jewish and that they undertook their revision or rewriting within some Jewish communal context as early as the first century B.C.E. (for portions of Theodotion, whose text was already known to writers of the New Testament) and as late as the early third century C.E. (for Symmachus).

The very fact that these three translators were active well into the Common Era casts doubt on the often-cited assertion that Christian adoption (or cooption) of the Septuagint led to its speedy and complete rejection by Jews. It should also be pointed out that although "biblical" citations in the New Testament share the wording of known LXX renderings on occasion, in many other passages such citations reflect fresh translation from the Hebrew, hitherto unknown revisions of the older Greek, reliance on memory, or deliberate modification to accord with their new textual context.

Modern Study of the Septuagint

Modern study of the Septuagint has benefited greatly from publication of the Dead Sea Scrolls, which contain Hebrew texts similar to the *Vorlage* of the LXX (in addition to those that may be termed proto-MT), thus affirming the view that some Greek translators did in fact reliably and accurately reflect what lay before them when it differed from, as well as when it was similar to, what became the MT. Moreover, modern scholars have access to a wide array of ancient Greek texts as well as translations of the Greek into languages such as Armenian, Coptic, and Ethiopic. Computerized programs provide concordances and other aids, allowing for all sorts of comparisons and analyses that were either unimagined or impossibly time-consuming in earlier generations. Nonetheless, modern researchers should never allow contemporary technology to separate them entirely from the papyrus and leather with which the ancient scribes worked.

Additionally, the post–World War II period has facilitated the recognition of the importance of the Septuagint for Jewish studies. At a certain point, Jews (with the exception of Greek-speaking Jews) did lose interest in the Septuagint, and the copying and study of Greek manuscripts passed largely into Christian hands. In the early nineteenth century, a few Jewish scholars returned to the study of the LXX, appropriately emphasizing the Jewish origins and early history of this important document (or, better, collection of documents). From many directions, a full understanding of and appreciation for the accomplishments of Hellenistic Jews and Judaism is impossible without taking into account the Septuagint. As both a translation of earlier Hebrew and Aramaic texts and a witness to the vibrancy and vitality of early Jewish life, the Septuagint has a central role to play in documenting what it has meant to be Jewish and live Jewishly.

BIBLIOGRAPHY

A. AEJMELAEUS 1996, *On the Trail of the Septuagint Translators,* Kampen: Kok Pharos. • A. G. AULD 2005, *Joshua: Jesus Son of Nauÿ in Codex Vaticanus,* Septuagint Commentary Series, Leiden: Brill. • J. M. DINES 2004, *The Septuagint*, London: T&T Clark. • N. FERNÁNDEZ MARCOS 2000, *The Septuagint in Context*, Leiden: Brill. • L. GREENSPOON 2003, "Hebrew into Greek: Interpretation in, by, and of the Septuagint," in *A History of Biblical Interpretation*, vol. 1, *The Ancient Period*, ed. A. J. Hauser and D. F. Watson, Grand Rapids: Eerdmans, 80-113. • M. HARL 1994, *La Bible grecque des Septante*, Paris: Cerf. • M. HENGEL 2002, *The Septuagint as Christian Scripture: Its Prehistory and the Problem of Its Canon*, Grand Rapids: Baker Academic. • W. KRAUS AND G. R. WOODEN, EDS. 2006, *Septuagint Research: Issues and Challenges in the Study of the Greek Jewish Scriptures*, Atlanta: Society of Biblical Literature. • S. JELLICOE 1968, *The Septuagint and Modern Study*, Oxford: Oxford University Press. • K. H. JOBES AND M. SILVA 2000, *Invitation to the Septuagint*, Grand Rapids: Baker. • M. A. KNIBB, ED. 2006, *The Septuagint and Messianism*, Leuven: Peeters. • A. PIETERSMA AND B. WRIGHT, EDS. 2007, *A New English Translation of the Septuagint and Other Greek Translations Traditionally under That Title*, New York: Oxford University Press. • E. TOV 1997, *The Text-Critical Use of the Septuagint in Biblical Research*, 2d ed., Jerusalem: Simor. • R. L. TROXEL 2008, *LXX-Isaiah as Translation and Interpretation: The Strategies of the Translator of the Septuagint of Isaiah*, Leiden: Brill. • E. ULRICH 1999, *The Dead Sea Scrolls and the Origins of the Bible*, Grand Rapids: Eerdmans.

LEONARD J. GREENSPOON

Sermon → Homily

Serpent

The image of the serpent or snake is multidimensional in early Jewish literature, capable of symbolizing either good or evil. Although it is often associated with the Devil or Satan, for example, it can also have positive associations as a symbol of power, glory, wisdom, or immortality.

Greco-Roman Context

Serpents figure prominently in Greco-Roman mythology and iconography. Serpent symbolism reached its apex during the period ca. 300 B.C.E. to 200 C.E. During this period, images of Asclepius in the form of a serpent, or accompanied by a serpent usually curled around a staff, were known by Jews and Romans in Palestine. The image of Mercury with a caduceus (two serpents facing each other) was also familiar in the land of Israel. The caduceus denoted health, divine aid, rejuvenation, and perhaps resurrection. It appeared on coins of Herod the Great (40-4 B.C.E.), Herod Archelaus (4 B.C.E.–6 C.E.), and Valerius Gratus (15-26 C.E.). Positively, the serpent could be appreciated as the most beautiful of creatures. Rings, bracelets, and necklaces were sometimes fashioned as realistic or idealized serpents. At Pompeii, for example, the most attractive articles of gold jewelry were styled as serpents, and bronze bracelets appear in pre-70 Jerusalem.

Hebrew Bible

In the Hebrew Bible eighteen nouns are used to denote a serpent or snake; among these, the most prominent is the one that appears first: *naḥaš*, used of the beast of the field that talks to Eve (Gen. 3:1). Hebrew epic poetry owes the serpentine sea monster named Leviathan *(liwyātān)* as a symbol of primordial chaos to ancient Near Eastern creation mythology (Ps. 74:14, 12-17; Job 3:8; 41:1-34; cf. 26:13; Isa. 27:1). God's power is demonstrated when the rods of Moses and Aaron miraculously turn into snakes that devour the snakes magically produced by Pharaoh's wise men and sorcerers (Exod. 4:1-5; 7:8-13). According to Num. 21: 4-9, Moses fashioned a bronze serpent *(śārāp)* and placed it on a pole to heal the Israelites from a plague of poisonous serpents *(nĕḥāšîm)* that God had sent to punish the people. According to 2 Kings 18:4, this serpent was later installed in the Jerusalem temple and worshiped under the name *Nĕhuštān*. The prophet Isaiah's call vision (Isa. 6:2-3) features winged serpents *(sărāpîm)* around the divine throne that symbolize God's glory.

Early Jewish Texts

In the *Damascus Document* serpent imagery is applied negatively to the Greek invaders of the land of Israel and even the unfaithful in Judea (CD [A] 8:10; [B] 19:15, 22-23). The term "vipers" is used of those who profane the Torah in the land (CD [A] 5:14). The *Isaiah Pesher* presents numerous words for serpent, based on Isa. 14:28. The Hebrew noun *ptn*, "cobra," appears in the plural, *ptnym*, "cobras," in the *Thanksgiving Hymns*, where it denotes the poison spewed out by the men of Belial (1QH^{a} 13:27). The Hebrew *ʾpʿh*, "sand viper" (cf. Isa. 30:6; 59:5) also appears in the *Thanksgiving Hymns*. The symbolism of the passage is unclear, but most scholars assume that the viper is negative. It is likely also that "works of the viper" (1QH^{a} 11:17) denoted "offspring [or creatures] of the viper" since the next sentence refers to "the spirits of the viper."

In early Jewish apocalyptic literature, the serpent of Genesis 3 is often identified as Satan, the "accuser" (*Life of Adam and Eve* 33:3; *Liv. Pro.* 12:13; *Apoc. Mos.* 16:5; cf. *Sib. Or.* 1.1.38-64). The authors of *Jubilees* and Pseudo-Philo portray the serpent as the deceiver and tempter. The sea serpent Leviathan becomes food at the eschatological banquet (*1 Enoch* 60:7; *4 Ezra* 6:50-52; *2 Bar.* 29:1-8) or receives God's wrath (*Apoc. Abr.* 10:12; 21:4; cf. *Ladder of Jacob* 6:13). In Bel and the Dragon, a Greek addition to the book of Daniel, the image of a large dragon-serpent is worshiped by the Babylonians, but Daniel causes it to burst asunder. The author of the Wisdom of Solomon interpreted Moses' upraised serpent (Num. 21) as a "symbol of salvation" (15:6), but clearly God is "the savior of all" (16:7). *1 Enoch* depicts Gabriel as the archangel in charge of paradise, the serpents, and the cherubim. In the *Testament of Abraham*, Death is portrayed as a being of which one head is a serpent. According to the *Lives of the Prophets*, near Jeremiah's grave the dust healed snakebites, since the prophet had prayed so that the asps left. In Palestinian Jewish lore, Bar Kokhba's body or phallus was encircled by a snake that had killed him (*y. Ta'an.* 4:69a). The Greek version of *3 Baruch* depicts the serpent's body as Hades. 4 Maccabees calls the serpent "deceitful" and "the destroyer" (18:8).

Philo of Alexandria was familiar with Egyptian valuations of the serpent as a symbol of immortality and wisdom. Yet in his allegorical approach to interpreting Jewish Scripture, he takes the serpent of Genesis 3 to symbolize the temptation of sensual pleasure and the bronze serpent of Numbers 21 to represent the power of self-control (*Leg. Alleg.* 2.71-82). Josephus interpreted Genesis 3 so that the serpent is malicious (*Ant.* 1.1.4), cruel (*Ant.* 17.5.5), and the enemy of humans (*Ant.* 1.1.4). John the Baptizer assails the Pharisees and Sadducees as "offspring of vipers" (Matt. 3:7//Luke 3:7). In Matt. 10:16, Jesus sends out his disciples "among the wolves" and instructs them to "be wise as serpents." The Fourth Gospel draws a typological correspondence between the salvific effects of the bronze serpent of Moses in Numbers 21 and Jesus' being lifted up on the cross (John 3:14-15). Paul followed other early Jews in understanding the serpent of Genesis 3 as a liar (2 Cor. 11:3). Finally, the book of Revelation identifies the "great dragon who was thrown down" as "that ancient serpent, who is called the Devil and Satan, the deceiver of the whole world" (Rev. 12:9; cf. 12:14-15), and depicts its eschatological defeat (Rev. 20:2, 7-10).

BIBLIOGRAPHY

J. H. CHARLESWORTH 2010, *The Good and Evil Serpent*, New Haven: Yale University Press. • K. P. JOINES 1974, *Serpent Symbolism in the Old Testament: A Linguistic, Archaeological, and Literary Study*, Haddonfield, N.J.: Haddonfield House. • H. MANESCHG 1981, *Die Erzählung von der ehernen Schlange (Num 21,4-9) in der Auslegung der frühen jüdischen Literatur*, Frankfurt: Lang. • M. MARTINEK 1996, *Wie die Schlange zum Teufel Wurde: Die Symbolik in der Paradiesgeschichte von der hebräischen Bibel bis zum Koran*, Wiesbaden: Harrassowitz.

JAMES H. CHARLESWORTH

Seth

In biblical tradition, Seth is the third son of Adam and Eve. There are at least two different biblical traditions regarding him. One views him as the firstborn son of Adam and Eve and the explicit heir to Adam's rank of being "in the image and likeness of God" (Gen. 5:3-8; cf. 1 Chron. 1:1). The other attempts to integrate both him and his son Enosh within the formally separate narrative trajectory that posits Cain and Abel as the first male offspring of the protoplasts and Seth as a brother and substitute for the murdered Abel (Gen. 4:25). Neither interpretive stream is subject to further elaboration in the Hebrew Bible.

A curious reference to the future punishment of the "descendants of Seth" (*bĕnê Šēt*, literally "sons of Seth") occurs in an eschatological oracle placed in the mouth of Balaam (Num. 24:17) that is recycled almost verbatim in several Second Temple sources (CD 7:20-21 = 4Q266 3 iii 22; 1QM 11:6; 4Q175 line 13). The simplest interpretive solution, adopted by *Targum Onqelos* and the commentary of Abraham Ibn Ezra, is to view the label "descendants of Seth" as an alternative way of expressing the concept of postdiluvian humanity. More recent efforts to parse this phrase as a learned reference to a nomadic tribe named Šūtū fail to show how this solution could be meaningful in its present context.

On the basis of the redacted versions of the biblical text, which construct rival kinship lines for Seth and Cain, Christian sources effect a bifurcation of the early generations of humanity into the progeny of Seth and the progeny of Cain in order to confine the emergence of evil to the earthly plane. But an analogous distinction is occasionally visible in Jewish literature, where Seth is deemed the progenitor and ancestor of all the subsequent generations of the righteous, and Cain incurs condemnation for inaugurating all the generations of the wicked and the rebels who revolted against God (*Pirqe Rabbi Eliezer* §22). When the flood erases the posterity of Cain from the earth, God then uses the progeny of Seth *(šēt)* to reestablish *(hūštat)* the world (*Num. Rab.* 14:12; cf. *Midrash Bereshit Rabbati* [ed. Albeck, p. 57]), exploiting a wordplay to underscore Seth's importance for the history of the human race.

In contrast to the Hebrew Bible, other sources are replete with traditions that revolve around the figure of Seth. Most of this material is directly tied to the assertion of Seth's resemblance to his father Adam, who was in turn modeled after "the image and likeness of God" (Gen 1:26-27; 5:1-3). Seth becomes an important link in the chain of transmission of knowledge and divine secrets accumulated by his father, and he himself is alleged to have been favored with revelatory experiences.

Numerous writings purportedly authored by Seth surface in late antiquity and seem to have been especial favorites of those groups whom Christian heresiologists and modern scholars term "Gnostic." Epiphanius claims that the Borborite Gnostics possessed "many books in the name of Seth" (*Panarion* 26.8.1). The same authority provides a report about a group who were called "Sethians" who had "seven books called by the name of Seth" (*Panarion* 39.5.1). Among the Nag Hammadi Codices, several works bearing the name of Seth *(The Three Steles of Seth; The Second Treatise of the Great Seth)* are ascribed to him *(Gospel of the Egyptians)*, or have a strong interest in his character *(The Apocalypse of Adam; The Apocryphon of John)*.

Manicheism and Mandeism refer to Seth as Sethel, a linguistic indication that Seth's ascribed likeness to divinity has morphed into a type of modal identity. This apotheosis of Seth is also visible in certain schemes which posit a heavenly Seth who periodically visits earth in various human guises for the purpose of imparting revelation to humanity.

An early association of Seth with the preservation and transmission of primeval knowledge is already visible in Josephus. Seth and his immediate progeny are credited with the discovery and wider promulgation of the astronomical sciences thanks to their inscribing them upon two pillars of stone and masonry (*Ant.* 1.69-71). The same tradition surely lies behind the account of Seth's transcription of the testaments of Adam and Eve on clay and stone tablets in *Vita Adae et Evae* 49–51.

Eastern Christian sources amplify these traditions to make Seth in effect the literary executor of Adam's estate. Early Muslim tradents of prophetic lore, who rely largely on information gleaned from a wide variety of Jewish and Christian sources, attribute fifty works to the authorial and/or secretarial hand of Seth, whose name they often gloss in accordance with Gen. 4:25 as "a gift from God" (Hibat Allāh).

BIBLIOGRAPHY

L. GINZBERG, 1925, *The Legends of the Jews*, Philadelphia: The Jewish Publication Society of America, 5: 148-50. • A. F. J. KLIJN 1977, *Seth in Jewish, Christian and Gnostic Literature*, Leiden: Brill. • J. C. REEVES 1996, *Heralds of That Good Realm: Syro-Mesopotamian Gnosis and Jewish Traditions*, Leiden: Brill.

JOHN C. REEVES

Sexuality

Multiple difficulties beset any attempt to describe sexuality in early Judaism. The Hellenistic and early Roman periods belong to the long era "before sexuality," that is, before the construction of erotic experience and practice as central to identity and oriented on opposing poles of heterosexuality and homosexuality. It is always difficult to gauge the relationship between what people say about sex and what they do, and evidence that survives from the period is very limited. Celebrations of *erōs* comparable to those in Greek and Latin love poetry are rare. The highly colored description of Sarah in the *Genesis Apocryphon* (col. 20) and Philo's brief description of the creation of Eve (*De Opificio Mundi* 152) are passages that suggest a lost literature.

In early Jewish texts, sex is usually addressed in attempts to explain or regulate practice through engagement with biblical tradition or in apologetics that vilify unbelievers or defend Jewish practice against similar vilifications. As is the case with rabbinic texts (Satlow 1995), early Jewish texts are highly rhetorical. Further, as Roman domination of the Mediterranean grew, moral evaluations of sexual practice similar to those in contemporaneous Greek and Latin sources increasingly characterized early Jewish ones. Concerned with the obligations and rights of the free male head of the household, early Jewish writers promote marriage and childbearing, express anxiety over sexual contact with relatives, construct sex between males on the lines of pederasty, condemn males who allow themselves to be penetrated, express concern with self-control, and manifest the beginnings of interest in sexual asceticism as care of the self.

Hellenistic Period

From the late third century B.C.E. on, sex and the spirit world played an important mythic role in early Jewish apocalyptic tradition, particularly in the legend of the fallen angels or Watchers, which explained evil and sin as originating in the rape or seduction of human women by the Watchers and the illicit knowledge communicated by them and their offspring the Giants (Gen. 6:1-6; *1 Enoch* 1–36; *Jub.* 4:22; 5:1-11; 7:2-23; 20:3-5; *Book of the Giants* [4Q203 frg. 8]). Scholars explain the original function of the myth variously as a polemic against improper marriages (especially by priests), a protest against divination, or a parody of the wars among Alexander the Great's successors, the Diadochi, and their claims of divine origin (see Loader 2007: 43-49). In *Jubilees*, the legend is used against intermarriage (20:3-5). Fear of sexual contact with the spirit world appears in other texts of the era (*1 Enoch* 106–7; Tob. 6:14–8:4).

In *Jubilees* other important issues of sexual practice are grounded in a "rewriting" of the book of Genesis. Endogamy is warranted by Rebecca's complaints about Esau's Hittite wives (Gen. 26:34-35; 27:46; *Jub.* 25:1-23; 27:7-11) and by the rape of Dinah (Gen. 33:17–34:31; *Jub.* 30:1-17). The second creation account in Genesis 2 warrants purification after childbirth (*Jub.* 3:8-12; cf. Lev. 12:2-5), and forbidden relations are reinforced in *Jubilees'* version of the notice about Reuben having sex with his father's concubine Bilhah (Gen. 35:22; *Jub.* 33:1-20) and in its reworking of the Judah and Tamar episode (Genesis 38; *Jub.* 41:23-24). The (unspecified) fornication of the men of Sodom and Gomorrah (Gen. 19:1-29) and the sin of Lot and his daughters (Gen. 19:30-38) incur equal condemnation (*Jub.* 16:7-9).

Ben Sira (early second century B.C.E.) offers typically sapiential advice on avoiding sex with wicked women and prostitutes, temptations to incest, and the company of other men's wives (Sir. 9:1-9). The sage delineates and condemns the sexually profligate man and wife (23:16-27), contrasts bad women and good wives (25:15–26:17), and warns against the sexuality of daughters (7:23-26; 22:4-5; 26:10-12; 42:9-14). A reference to a wife's jealousy seems to imply polygamy (26:6).

The Rise of Rome: Pseudo-Aristeas and *Sibylline Oracles* 3

In other sources, apologetic motifs dominate. The *Letter to Aristeas* (late second century B.C.E.) contrasts the Jews with other nations who sexually approach (or, in one emendation, prostitute) males and who violate both mothers and their daughters (*Letter of Aristeas* 152). The third *Sibylline Oracle* (ca. 160-50 B.C.E.) "predicts" Roman war crimes, highlighting Romans' indulgence in male-male sex and the prostitution of boys in brothels (*Sib. Or.* 3.175-78, 182-87). This stigmatization of the Romans as prone to sex with boys appears at the same time that Romans were expressing their own anxieties about sex with boys in the *lex Sca(n)tinia*, which appears to have criminalized sex with a freeborn boy and sex between free males who submitted to penetration. By contrast, the "pious race" is concerned with holy unions and abstains from sex with boys (*Sib. Or.* 3.594-600). The Sibyl urges the Greeks to follow this Jewish example, abstaining from adultery and pederasty and rearing all their children (3.762-66).

SEXUALITY

After Augustus: Pseudo-Phocylides and Philo of Alexandria

Claims of sexual probity and charges of immorality played an important role in Roman politics of the later Republic and provided the context for Augustus' laws promoting marriage and child-rearing and criminalizing adultery and sex with a freeborn girl. The adultery law also seems to have reiterated the stipulations of the *lex Sca(n)tinia*. While the laws bound only Roman citizens (a limited category for Jews) and were aimed at the elite, their propagandistic effects were also felt by noncitizens. In the *Sentences* of Pseudo-Phocylides (a sapiential poem imitating a sixth-century-B.C.E. Greek poet, but widely read as the work of a Jewish author of the first century B.C.E. or C.E.) and the works of Philo of Alexandria, post-Augustan Roman moral propaganda, philosophical aspirations, and biblical heritage converge. Both Pseudo-Phocylides and Philo use the Septuagint, whose sixth commandment (or first of the second tablet) is the prohibition of adultery (LXX Exod. 20:2-17; Deut. 5:6-21). Both read the commandment as prohibiting pederasty (Pseudo-Phocylides 3; Philo, *De Decalogo* 168; *Hypoth.* 8.7.1).

In a lengthy inculcation of family values, Pseudo-Phocylides praises marriage and childrearing and prohibits sex with near relations (including a father's concubines), abortion or exposure, sex with a pregnant wife, castrating the young, and sex with animals. Both sex between males and the imitation of male sex by women transgress natural unions (175–206). The warning against prostituting one's wife may echo the stipulation that a complaisant husband could be charged with pandering under the Julian law on adultery (177). Phocylides urges protecting both sons (210–14) and daughters (215–16) from sexual predators. Unrestrained eros toward a wife (or woman) incurs the stern warning, "Eros is not a god but a passion destructive of all" (194).

Philo viewed sex as "natural" only in marriage and for procreation, a judgment he shared with first-century Roman philosophers (Seneca, *Helvia* 13.3; Musonius Rufus, *Diatribe* 12.86.4-10). The sixth commandment takes first place in the "second pentad" of the Decalogue because adultery is the worst of transgressions due to its noxious effect on families and city-states and to the destructive force of pleasure (*De Decalogo* 122, 168; *De Iosepho* 44; *Spec. Leg.* 3.8). On Philo's reading, this commandment also prohibits pederasty and submission to "something beyond the age," as well as seduction or rape of virgins (*De Decalogo* 168; *Hypoth.* 8.7.1). Under it are the biblical stipulations involving sex (*Spec. Leg.* 3.1-82). Pursuit of pleasure even in marriage is blameworthy and adultery unnatural (3.9-11). Forbidden relations (3.12-28) and marriage with foreigners (3.29) weaken social cohesion. Sex with a menstruating woman is unnatural because it frustrates conception. Philo's procreative imperative condemns men who marry women "proven" to be infertile (3.34-36). Similar but worse are a man who submits to sex and the pederast (3.37-42); worse still those who have sex with beasts (3.43-50). Prostitution is likewise absolutely excluded (3.51). Like Pseudo-Phocylides, Philo reflects Roman anxiety about complaisant husbands; a man who remarries an ex-wife divorced or widowed from another marriage is a "panderer" (*Spec. Leg.* 3.31; cf. Pseudo-Phocylides 177). The Septuagint's tenth commandment, "you shall not desire," includes all food laws, whose goal is the discipline of desire, especially *erōs* (*Spec. Leg.* 4.78-132).

In Philo's interpretation, the people of Sodom and Gomorrah sinned by luxury in food, drink, and illicit sex, specifically adultery and sex between males. Like other ancient authors, he saw adultery and male-male sex as continuous rather than opposed (cf. Dio Chrysostom, *Discourses* 7.139) and viewed the penetrated partner as especially degraded because he played a female role and in so doing ultimately became female (*De Abrahamo* 134–41). In his treatise *De Vita Contemplativa* (57-63) Philo explicitly rejects Plato's *Symposium* (and Xenophon's), condemning pederastic love in its own terminology, and proposes a banquet contemplating not *erōs* but the works of Moses.

Philo shows some consciousness of and discomfort with the role of slavery in sexual practice. Moses, he says, prescribed that a woman captive used for sex must be treated as a "lawful wife" or freed (*De Virtutibus* 109–14; cf. Deut. 21:10-13). Banquets of "Italic luxury" are served by the boy slaves available to guests; in contrast, the banquets of the Therapeutae are served by free (and therefore inviolate) youths (*De Vita Contemplativa* 48–52; 71–72).

After 70: Josephus

After the First Jewish Revolt in 66-73 C.E., slander against the Jews included charges of unbridled lust (Tacitus, *Histories* 5.5). Josephus summarizes the marriage laws as allowing sex only in marriage and for procreation, and so excluding adultery and male-male sex (*Ag. Ap.* 2.199-203). Although in Genesis 19 the men of Sodom and Gomorrah incite God's wrath by their hostility to guests, Josephus reads their ultimate crime in pederastic terms (*Ant.* 1.194, 200). Elsewhere he describes Antony as exploiting his extraordinary power to obtain sex with both women and boys (*Ant.* 15:29), and thus assumes the Roman perspective that sees hetero- and homoeroticism as continuous and predatory sex as metonymy for tyranny (see Cicero, *Against Verres* 2.1.24 §§62-69; Livy, *Epitomae* 39.42-43).

Assessment

Standard treatments of early Judaism tend to attribute to it an unqualified endorsement of heterosexual marriage and an implacable hostility to homoeroticism. A more diffuse and diverse picture emerges from the texts. Earlier texts show a sense of sex as a risky business; later texts evince philosophic suspicion of pleasure and emotion, while proffering Jewish "family values" to match and exceed the Roman defense and promotion of marriage. Pederasty and male-male sex emerge as a vice of the Roman overlords (who blamed these practices on the Greeks). The picture of ancient Jews as strictly heteroerotic enthusiasts is disturbed by the increasing interest that Second Temple texts show in sexual restraint and even renunciation. It is also called into question by a text like the Qumran *War Scroll,* which excludes women and boys from the eschatological camp, presumably because a youth or a woman might inspire lust and cause the holy warriors to have sex (or at least to ejaculate) and become ritually impure (1QM 7:3-4). What was practiced seems to have been more diverse than what was professed.

BIBLIOGRAPHY

M. D'ANGELO 2006, "Gender and Geopolitics in the Work of Philo of Alexandria: Jewish Piety and Imperial Family Values," in *Mapping Gender in Ancient Religious Discourse,* ed. T. Penner and C. Von Stichele, Leiden: Brill, 63-88. • K. GACA 2003, *The Making of Fornication: Eros, Ethics and Political Reform in Greek Philosophy and Early Christianity,* Berkeley: University of California Press. • J. L. KUGEL 2006, *The Ladder of Jacob: Ancient Interpretations of the Biblical Story of Jacob and His Children,* Princeton: Princeton University Press. • W. LOADER 2004, *The Septuagint, Sexuality, and the New Testament: Case Studies on the Impact of the LXX in Philo and the New Testament,* Grand Rapids: Eerdmans. • W. LOADER 2007, *Enoch, Levi, and Jubilees on Sexuality,* Grand Rapids: Eerdmans. • M. SATLOW 1995, *Tasting the Dish: Rabbinic Rhetorics of Sexuality,* Atlanta: Scholars Press.

See also: Family; Marriage and Divorce

MARY ROSE D'ANGELO

Shammai

Shammai was a prominent scholar of the Second Temple period who lived and worked with his colleague Hillel in the land of Israel during the second half of the first century B.C.E. Along with Hillel, Shammai was a disciple of the sages Shemaiah and Avtalyon. The honorary title *ha-Zāqēn,* "the Elder," is often appended to his name, which may be a derivative of the biblical name Shemaiah. Hillel and Shammai are named as the last of the "Pairs" of scholars *(Zûgôt):* Hillel functioned as *nāśî'* (president of the legal council), and Shammai was appointed his vice-president *('āb bêt dîn)* after Menahem (identified by some as Menahem the Essene mentioned by Josephus as living at the time of Herod) had left (*m. Ḥag.* 2:2). No other biographical details of Shammai's life are known. It has been suggested by some scholars that Shammai is to be identified with Samaias, a Pharisee mentioned by Josephus as a disciple of Pollion (Avtalyon?) during the reign of Herod, but most scholars identify this Samaias with Shemaiah (Feldman 1958).

Later lore emphasizes Shammai's irascibility and intransigence as opposed to the patience and flexibility of his colleague Hillel. For example, Shammai is reported to have chased away an impertinent potential proselyte with "the builder's rule in his hand," perhaps an allusion to the strict and unbending "canon" (= rule) of legal exegesis (*b. Šabbat* 31a; cf. *'Abot de Rabbi Nathan* A 16). Yet there is no indication of such strictness in the early sources. On the contrary, in his only reported nonlegal saying he instructs one to "receive every man with a friendly countenance" (*m. 'Abot* 1:15). It is true that his legal opinions, which deal with a range of topics typical of Second Temple period halakah (laws of the Sabbath, Sukkah, and the Day of Atonement, purities, the sabbatical year, civil and criminal law), show in some cases a tendency to conservatism and severity: he refused to feed his minor son on the Day of Atonement (but was overruled by other sages [*t. Yoma* 5:2]) and arranged a *sukkah* to be prepared in the bedchamber of his daughter-in-law who had just given birth to a son, so that the infant could eat in a *sukkah.* However, these are not legal rulings but instructions regarding family members. Shammai also ruled, against his contemporaries, that a person who had appointed an agent to execute a murder was himself liable for the death penalty.

On the other hand, despite a strong reverence for the sanctity of the Sabbath, Shammai ruled that an offensive war may be waged on the Sabbath (*t. 'Erub.* 3:7; *Sifre Deut.* 203). It has been suggested that his opinions conform to early rulings of the oral Torah from the beginning of the Hasmonean period that prized consistency (disregarding compromising situations and legal distinctions based on age or other methods of measurement) and emphasized the significance of the action itself over that of the intentions of the actor. Shammai has also been linked by some to uncompromising Jewish attitudes toward Rome (Ben Shalom 1993: 82-98 and *passim*).

In the three or four recorded disputes between Hillel and Shammai, however, it is difficult to distinguish consistent tendencies on either side. Nonetheless, Hillel and Shammai are noted for having created two factions (*m. 'Abot* 5:17; cf. *b. Šabbat* 17a), while their disciples are blamed for creating separate schools of legal teaching, due to slackness in their studies, that effectively split the Torah into "two Torahs" (*t. Ḥag.* 2:9; *t. Soṭah* 14:9). The activities of these schools, the "House of Hillel" *(Bêt Hillel)* and the "House of Shammai" *(Bêt Shammai),* ultimately generated hundreds of legal controversies; those of *Bêt Hillel* are often noted for their leniency as opposed to the greater stringency of the rulings of *Bêt Shammai.*

By the end of the Second Temple period, the rulings of *Bêt Hillel* had gained ascendancy, but this did not prevent the accurate transmission of many of the rulings of Shammai's disciples, whether transmitted in the name of *Bêt Shammai* or individually. There were still scholars of great standing, such as Rabbi Eliezer b. Hyrkanos, who were known to be disciples of Shammai (and thus called *Shamuti*). Indeed, it is a telling indication of the primacy of place given to the controversies between Hillel and Shammai by later generations, that in the wake of the destruction of the Temple, the scholars who congregated at Yavneh, expressing fear that the oral Torah might be forgotten, declared, "Let us begin (our testimonia) with (the controversies of) Hillel and Shammai" (*t. 'Ed.* 1:1).

BIBLIOGRAPHY
I. BEN-SHALOM 1993, *The School of Shammai and the Zealots' Struggle against Rome,* Jerusalem: Yad Izhak Ben-Zvi, 76-109 (in Hebrew). • L. FELDMAN 1958, "The Identity of Pollio, the Pharisee, in Josephus," *JQR* 49: 53-62. • L. GINZBERG 1955, "The Significance of the Halachah for Jewish History," in idem, *On Jewish Law and Lore,* Philadelphia: Jewish Publication Society, 75-124. • J. NEUSNER 1971, *The Rabbinic Traditions about the Pharisees before 70,* Leiden: Brill, 1: 184-211, 303-40; 3: 312-13. • E. SCHÜRER 1979, *The History of the Jewish People in the Age of Jesus Christ,* rev. and ed. G. Vermes, F. Millar, and M. Black, Edinburgh: Clark, 2: 363-66.

See also: Hillel PAUL MANDEL

Shemihazah → Fallen Angels

Sheol → Death and Afterlife

Sheshbazzar

Sheshbazzar is mentioned in the Hebrew Bible only in the book of Ezra-Nehemiah (Ezra 1:8-11; 5:14-16). The parallel accounts in 1 Esdr. 2:12-15; 6:18-20 contain no substantial additional information, except his name appears as "Sanabassaros," and he is clearly distinct from Zerubbabel, who is mentioned anachronistically during the time of Cyrus in the second passage. Josephus also mentions Sheshbazzar, although he is largely dependent on the tradition found in 1 Esdras (*Ant.* 11.11, 93, 101; Japhet 1982-83).

According to Ezra 1:8-11, this "prince of Judah" *(nāśîʾ yĕhûdâ)* received the Temple vessels by order of Cyrus king of Persia in order to bring them to Jerusalem as the initial action undertaken in the return from exile. Ezra 5:14-16 represents a reflection on the events recorded in the first unit. In this Aramaic account, the Persian leadership of the province Eber Nahara sends a letter to King Darius, which includes the claim of the Jerusalem leadership that Cyrus had previously entrusted the Temple vessels to a certain Sheshbazzar, who had been appointed governor *(peḥâ)* and had laid the foundations of the Temple. Thus, according to Ezra-Nehemiah, Sheshbazzar is notable for two reasons: he was the first governor of the new community in the restoration period, and he began the process of Temple reconstruction, having received the Temple vessels from the Persians (Japhet 1982-83). He is also apparently of the tribe of Judah, although his relationship to the Davidic dynasty is never made explicit in Ezra-Nehemiah.

Most discussions about Sheshbazzar have focused on his relationship to two other individuals: the governor Zerubbabel and Shenazzar, both associated with the Davidic line only in Chronicles (1 Chron. 3:17-19). However, several difficulties with both possibilities immediately arise. First, this brief genealogy in Chronicles is notoriously complicated, especially given the variant readings between the MT and the LXX (Pomykala 1995: 83-88). Apart from the textual problems, the Chronicler's account contains two important points: (1) Shenazzar is a son of Jeconiah the Davidide; and (2) Zerubbabel is the grandson of Jeconiah, through his son Pedaiah and through neither his brother Shenazzar nor through their brother Shealtiel. The other references in the Hebrew Bible to Zerubbabel present him as a descendant of Shealtiel (Ezra 3:2, 8; 5:2; Neh. 12:1; Hag. 1:1, 12, 14; 2:2, 23), but without any clarification of this Shealtiel's ancestry or an association with the Davidic line. As scholars have rejected more recently a relationship between the composition of Chronicles and Ezra-Nehemiah, the need to identify this otherwise unknown Sheshbazzar mentioned only in Ezra-Nehemiah with someone named in the Chronicler's postexilic Davidic genealogy (such as Shenazzar or Zerubbabel) has likewise been abandoned.

Second, despite the rendering of the name in 1 Esdras, the evidence for linguistic connections between Shenazzar and Sheshbazzar points against a view that would simply equate the two persons (Berger 1971). Thus, the weight of the evidence cannot be used to demonstrate that Sheshbazzar is Shenazzar; without this association, his heritage as a Davidide cannot be asserted.

Third, Ezra-Nehemiah claims that Zerubbabel also "laid the foundations" of the Temple some two decades after it had been accomplished by Sheshbazzar. Thus, some scholars used to argue that these two leaders were a single person known by two names. However, this view has been rejected (Ben Yashar 1981).

Fourth, the contention among some scholars that both of the titles, "prince" and "governor," should be understood as indications of a Davidic heritage for Sheshbazzar can no longer be sustained. Evidence from both the Hebrew Bible and extrabiblical documents (such as jar handles, seals, coins, and the Elephantine Papyri) demonstrate that several of the known governors of the territory designated as Yehud during the Persian period were in fact not of Davidic descent (Meyers and Meyers 1987: 13-16; VanderKam 2004: 99-111). In addition, the exact role or function of the governor during this early part of the Persian period continues to be unclear.

Therefore, the identity, precise ancestry, and political status of Sheshbazzar remain mysterious. Further, the nature of his mission and his apparent position as the civil authority continue to be shrouded in ambiguity. As a result, additional insight that could be gained from this evidence into the Persian Empire's involvement in the affairs of this region remains nebulous.

BIBLIOGRAPHY
M. BEN YASHAR 1981, "On the Problem of Sheshbazzar and Zerubbabel," *Beth Mikra* 27: 46-56 (in Hebrew). • P.-R. BERGER 1971, "Zu den Namen *ššbṣr* und *šnʾṣr,*" *ZAW* 95: 111-12. • S. JAPHET 1982-1983, "Sheshbazzar and Zerubbabel — Against the Background of the Historical and Religious Tendencies of Ezra-Nehemiah," *ZAW* 94: 66-98; 95: 218-29. • C. MEYERS AND E. MEYERS 1987, *Haggai, Zechariah 1–8,* Garden City, N.Y.: Doubleday. • K. POMYKALA 1995, *The*

Davidic Dynasty Tradition in Early Judaism, Atlanta: Scholars Press, 83-88. • J. VANDERKAM 2004, *From Joshua to Caiaphas,* Minneapolis: Fortress, 99-111.

See also: Zerubbabel STEVEN J. SCHWEITZER

Sibylline Oracles

The *Sibylline Oracles* are a collection of various Jewish and Christian prophetic utterances written in Greek hexameters and attributed to a pagan prophetess. The collection dates from the late Hellenistic to the early Byzantine periods. The earliest Jewish oracles, the core of the collection, are principally the products of the Egyptian Diaspora and date from the Maccabean era to the initial decades of the second century C.E. Some oracles exhibit a small measure of Christian interpolation, while others have been extensively reworked.

The Corpus

The standard collection of the *Sibylline Oracles* is constituted from two collations of books. The first collation, which contains books 1-8, is preserved in two groups of manuscripts. Group Θ includes an anonymous prologue and begins with the present book 1. Group Ψ commences with book 8, which displays a marked christological interest. Their texts also differ in minor respects; for example, *Sib. Or.* 2.56-148 reproduces, with additions, lines 5-79 from Pseudo-Phocylides. The second collation, which contains books 9-14, is preserved in a group of manuscripts designated Ω. Since books 9 and 10 reiterate material from the first collation, they are omitted from the standard collection, although the numbering of books 11-14 is retained. The *Sibylline Oracles* are quoted extensively by the church fathers, who in some cases cite material from oracles that are no longer extant.

Sibyls

A Sibyl is a woman, typically a crone, who utters ecstatic prophecies. The origins of the phenomenon are obscure. An Asian provenance is not impossible, although Greece, with an old autochthonous tradition of female oracles, is the probable source. Rome had a similarly ancient tradition, but Livy (1.7.8) writes of a time, in the days of Romulus, when the Sibyl had yet to arrive in Italy, and it is likely that she did so by way of the Greek colonists who settled Magna Graecia. Whatever the case, by the first century B.C.E. Sibyls had become associated with specific sites, notably in Italy and Asia Minor. Among the more famous Sibyls were the Erythrean, Tiburtine, and Cumaean, the last the subject of Virgil's classic description (*Aeneid* 6.1-155; cf. *Eclogue* 4). The Hebrew Sibyl, whose identification in the sources overlaps with that of the Babylonian and Persian Sibyls, is sometimes called Sambethe (*Sib. Or.* Prologue; 34) or Sabbe. In *Sib. Or.* 3.809-10 the Sibyl claims a Babylonian origin.

Development of the Tradition

Throughout classical antiquity, numerous oracles in Greek hexametric verse circulated under the sibylline rubric, the most celebrated of which were the *libri sibyllini.* These were kept in the temple of Jupiter Capitolinus at Rome and were said to have been purchased from the Sibyl by Tarquinius Priscus (*Sib. Or.* Prologue; 50–52) or Tarquinius Superbus (Aulus Gellius, *Noctes Atticae* 1.19, etc.), kings of Rome during its archaic pre-Republican period. After the temple burned down in 83 B.C.E., the *libri* were reconstituted by gathering oracles from other collections (Tacitus, *Annals* 6.12). They survived until the fifth century C.E., when they were finally extirpated by Flavius Stilicho (Rutilius Namatianus, *De Reditu Suo* 2.51-52). The *libri sibyllini* were consulted typically in instances when the state required insight pursuant to an urgent policy decision, as during a military or religious crisis or upon the manifestation of calamities or prodigies. The fact that the emperor Augustus collected and destroyed more than 2,000 copies of prophecies in private hands (Suetonius, *Augustus* 31.1) testifies to the popularity of such texts, and also to their potentially subversive use, since their commensurate appeal and uncomplicated form (see below) allowed oracles to serve a variety of purposes, including political propaganda. Indeed, it was in a political role that sibylline literature took root in Ptolemaic Egypt, where it fit well within an established backdrop of oracular resistance texts that looked to the downfall of the Macedonian Greek overlords and the restoration of indigenous Egyptian rule.

The Sibylline Tradition and Egyptian Judaism

This sibylline tradition was adopted during the middle of the second century B.C.E. by Egyptian Jews whose adaptations included a strong emphasis on moral exhortation (esp. regarding sexual conduct) and the rejection of idolatry, as well as a shift in focus toward the theme of the eschatological reversal of fortune, which to some degree alleviated the genre's characteristically gloomy tenor. Although oracles are not apocalypses, their political application broadly suited the functions of historical apocalypticism as it developed in Judaism during this period, while their forecasting capability ensured that they could readily accommodate the intromission of an eschatological horizon, which, while not unknown in the sibylline literature of classical antiquity, rarely occupies the interest of the oracle to the extent that it does in the ancient Jewish examples. On the other hand, the *Sibylline Oracles* are unconcerned with the heavenly world, angels, or other hallmarks of the vertical dimension of apocalypticism, and their interest in the postmortem fate of the individual surfaces more in the later oracles. Their theology of history, which is less complex than those that inform either the Deuteronomic or apocalyptic historiographies, seems to reflect elements from both. The *Sibylline Oracles* routinely structure their reviews of history into periods.

Book 3

The oldest Jewish sibylline text is the main corpus of *Sibylline Oracles* 3 (3.97-349, 489-829), which includes five oracles (3.97-161, 162-95, 196-294, 545-656, and 657-808) and assorted woes. Its date of composition is derived from the turning point from *vaticinium ex eventu* to future prediction, which occurs with the appearance of the seventh king of Egypt (3.193 and 318; cf. 3.608). Some scholars identify this figure with a first-century-B.C.E. monarch, but more probably he is either Ptolemy VI Philometor, who reigned for a second time from 163-145 B.C.E. and was favorably disposed toward his Jewish subjects, or his expected successor, Ptolemy Neos Philopator. It is this Greek figure, and not a Jewish king, who should be identified with the "king from the sun" who brings peace to the entire earth (3.652-56), since the appellation very much reflects its native Egyptian milieu; among other things, it appears in the *Potter's Oracle* in the service of Egyptian nationalism, while the association of the sun with kingship in Egypt is as old as the Pharaohs. Accordingly, these oracles reflect one of the most extraordinary attitudes expressed within the spectrum of Second Temple Judaism. They anticipate a vindication of Jewish ethics and an eschatological restoration of kingdom and Temple through the agency of Gentiles, namely, the Ptolemaic house and in particular its seventh king, who is understood in royal messianic terms. These data suggest that the oracles might have been composed in Egyptian circles closely associated with the legitimate heir to the high priesthood in Jerusalem, Onias IV, who fled to Egypt during the Maccabean Revolt, where he prospered under Philometor and was permitted to erect his own temple at Leontopolis.

The other portions of *Sibylline Oracles* 3 were written at a later time. Most are products of Egyptian Judaism, although the forecast of doom and woe of 3.401-88 features Asia Minor and was drawn perhaps from the Erythrean Sibyl. Its historical allusions imply that it was composed during the first quarter of the first century B.C.E. The oracle of 3.350-80 also might date from that period or, if the "lady" it mentions is the famous Cleopatra VII, some decades later. Its anti-Roman stance is an early example of what would become a persistent theme in later *Sibyllines*. Verses 1-96 are the remains of an originally separate book. They preserve an assortment of material, including oracles involving Cleopatra (3.46-62, 75-92), now called the "widow," and a description, written perhaps a century later, of the coming of the eschatological adversary, who is named Beliar but probably should be identified with Nero. This is another early occasion of a theme that gained prominence in subsequent oracles, as well as in medieval apocalyptic literature as a whole.

Book 4

Sibylline Oracle 4.49-101 is an anti-Macedonian political oracle that arranges history into ten generations, which are divided unequally among four kingdoms: Assyria, Media, Persia, and Macedon. Although the oracle is actually older than the main corpus of book 3, its Jewish authorship is unlikely. Schemata of ten or four periods, however, recur in later *Sibyllines* and other Jewish texts, notably in the dream of the four kingdoms of Daniel 2, which probably dates from the last half of the third century B.C.E. If the oracle's final verse alludes to the earthquake that devastated Rhodes in ca. 226 *B.C.E., then it also might date from this period. The rest of Sibylline Oracles* 4 updates the original oracle by grafting Rome onto its review of history and appending descriptions of Nero's return, eschatological woes, the final conflagration, and resurrection and judgment. The final redaction of *Sibylline Oracles* 4 occurred shortly after the eruption of Vesuvius in 79 C.E. (4.130-34).

Books 11-14

Sibylline Oracles 11-14 preserve an extended historical review from the flood to the Arab invasion of Egypt in the early seventh century. Opinions vary concerning the degree of Christianization in these books, as well as the nature of their mutual relationship. If book 11 was initially composed (or redacted) as a discrete collection, as seems likely, then it must be considered another pre-Christian Jewish sibylline book from Egypt, since its review of history begins with Egypt and terminates with the death of Cleopatra. But in its present form it is nothing more than a review: it lacks an eschatological section and is largely devoid of moral exhortation or theological content. *Sibylline Oracles* 11 also exhibits no enmity to Rome.

Book 5

The same cannot be said for *Sibylline Oracles* 5, whose six oracles (5.1-51, 52-110, 111-178, 179-285, 286-434, and 435-504) are cemented together by the mortar of their hostility to Rome. The empire's crimes include moral violations, hubris, and the destruction of Jerusalem and its Temple (5.150-61). Unlike *Sibylline Oracles* 3, this book does not expect salvation through Gentile agency, nor is it favorably disposed to Gentile rule. Instead, it looks to a Jewish savior who is called "king" (5.108-9) and "star" (5.155-61), and who will come from heaven (5.256-59, 414-25) to usher in a final destruction, although several oracles also include the hope for the New Jerusalem (5.249-55, 420-27). The Sibyl's attention is occupied by the advent of the eschatological adversary, identified here as Nero *redivivus*, a figure of great moral evil. In such themes and concerns, *Sibylline Oracles* 5 exhibits close parallels with its near contemporary, the New Testament book of Revelation. Revelation likely attained its final form near the close of the first century C.E., no more than a generation before the compilation of *Sibylline Oracles* 5, which, based on its internal allusions, transpired immediately prior to the Diaspora uprisings of 115/116-117 C.E., although the book underwent a final redaction slightly afterward.

Books 1-2

Sibylline Oracles 1 and 2, which are one book in the manuscripts, consist of an originally Jewish oracle that arranges history into ten periods. Its provenance and date of composition are obscured by its extensive Christian redaction and the excision of the eighth and ninth periods (and their historical data), although its lack of reference to the destruction of the Temple (an event mentioned at 1.393-96, but in a Christian passage) might denote a pre-70-C.E. date. An early Jewish substratum for the other *Sibylline Oracles* is difficult to establish.

Other Books

Books 12-14 have already been discussed. Books 6 and 7 are entirely Christian, while book 8, although as composite and anti-Roman as book 5, exhibits no substantive evidence of Jewish authorship. It does, however, contain the well-known Christian sibylline acrostic at 8.217-50.

Significance

The Jewish *Sibylline Oracles* are at once complex and simplistic. They preserve an array of perspectives and attitudes, but express them within a relatively narrow range of themes and expectations, which in turn are focused by an insistence on a universal code of ethical conduct and framed by a generic, uncomplicated oracular form. Their most remarkable characteristic, however, is their existence. The early *Sibylline Oracles* represent an attempt by ancient Judaism to relate to the Gentile world on its terms. The endeavor was at least moderately successful, if we consider the substantial influence of the *Sibylline Oracles* on the contours of late antique and medieval Christian apocalypticism.

BIBLIOGRAPHY

Editions

C. ALEXANDRE 1841-56, *Oracula Sibyllina I, II,* Paris: Didot. • A. RZACH 1891, *Oracula Sibyllina,* Wien: Tempsky. • J. GEFFCKEN 1902A, *Die Oracula Sibyllina,* Leipzig: Hinrichs.

Modern Translations (with Bibliographies and Extensive Introductions)

J. J. COLLINS 1983, "Sibylline Oracles," *OTP* 1:317-472. • H. MERKEL 1998, *Sibyllinen,* JSHRZ 5.8, Gütersloh: Gütersloher Verlag, 1043-1140.

Studies

R. BUITENWERF 2003, *Book III of the Sibylline Oracles and Its Social Setting,* Leiden: Brill. • J. J. COLLINS 1974, *The Sibylline Oracles of Egyptian Judaism,* Missoula, Mont.: Scholars Press. • J. GEFFCKEN 1902B, *Komposition und Entstehungszeit der Oracula Sibyllina,* Leipzig: Hinrichs. • M. GOODMAN 1986, "The Sibylline Oracles," in E. Schürer, *The History of the Jewish People in the Age of Jesus Christ,* vol. 3.1, Edinburgh: Clark, 618-54. • E. GRUEN, 1998, *Heritage and Hellenism,* Cambridge: Harvard University Press, 268-90. • J. L. LIGHTFOOT 2007, *The Sibylline Oracles: With Introduction, Translation, and Commentary on the First and Second Books,* Oxford: Oxford University Press. • V. NIKIPROWETZKY 1970, *La Troisième Sibylle,* Paris: Mouton. • H. W. PARK 1988, *Sibyls and Prophecy in Classical Antiquity,* ed. B. C. McGing, London: Routledge.

LORENZO DITOMMASO

Sicarii → Resistance Movements

Sickness and Disease

The study of ancient medicine has benefited from the insights of modern medical anthropology. In particular, anthropologists distinguish between disease as a biological condition and illness as a social-experiential condition (Kleinman 1980: 72). Cultural classifications of illness do not necessarily correspond to particular diseases. For instance, female infertility can have various underlying biological causes, not all of which are diseases; and ancient Hebrew culture regarded infertility as an illness, although many modern cultures do not. Yet rather than intruding insupportable distinctions between scientific medicine and religious beliefs, more accurate description can be achieved by investigating what counted as illness, what people believed about its etiology, and what a sick person would do in seeking relief.

Hebrew Bible

In addition to the most common generic terms *ḥlh,* "be weak, sick," *k'b,* "be in pain," and *nkh,* "to smite (with plague, etc.)," biblical Hebrew has a prolific vocabulary for specific physical and emotional sicknesses (see Preuss 1978; Rosner 2000). In Hebrew literature prior to the Second Temple period, the etiology of all illness was referred to God. Two key passages in the Torah articulate this medical theology:

> He [Moses] said, "If you will listen carefully to the voice of the LORD your God, and do what is right in his sight, and give heed to his commandments and keep all his statutes, I will not bring upon you any of the diseases *(hammaḥălāh)* of the Egyptians; for I am the LORD who heals you." (Exod. 15:26 [NRSV]; cf. Deut 7:15)

The blessings and curses in Deuteronomy 27–28 depict illnesses, of any kind, as penalties for noncompliance with divine commandments. In priestly literature, sickness renders one impure and is closely associated with sin. Nothing in early literature seriously modifies this view; even the book of Job maintains that God sends sickness, and questions only whether sin is the reason in all cases.

Second Temple Literature

Sin as a Cause of Disease

This traditional medical theology continues in the Second Temple period, as best exemplified in the *Testaments of the Twelve Patriarchs,* a work that is Christian in its present form but that many scholars regard as an early Jewish writing. For those patriarchs who suffer a disease, the condition is explicitly linked to sin. The document even equates specific sins with specific body parts. For example, Reuben has a disease in his loins because he desired a woman, and Gad contracts a liver disease on account of anger. The connection of sins to diseases in particular body parts does not occur in preexilic Hebrew literature, although it has other Near Eastern precedents; thus the traditional etiology of sickness has become more detailed, but the basic explanation remains the same.

SICKNESS AND DISEASE

New Etiologies of Sickness

Moreover, Second Temple literature also contains several new concepts about the etiology of sickness. First of all, sickness sent by God may occur in various ways. The *Prayer of Nabonidus* (4QPrNab) and the madness of Nebuchadnezzar in Daniel 4 both depict mental illnesses as sent by God and ascribed to the afflicted party's sins (Hogan 1992: 149-57). In its description of Antiochus' fatal illness, 1 Maccabees follows this traditional etiology by having Antiochus himself blame his sickness on his crimes against Jerusalem (1 Macc. 6:8-13). Wisdom literature asserts a more distant operation of divine action in its claim that immoderate habits lead to sickness. For instance, Ben Sira warns against overeating: "Do not be greedy for every delicacy, and do not eat without restraint; for overeating brings sickness, and gluttony leads to nausea. Many have died of gluttony, but the one who guards against it prolongs his life" (37:29-31).

Similarly, Philo interprets the serpent episode in Numbers 21 to refer to self-control *(sōphrosynē)* and the lack thereof. The attacking serpents represent the lack of self-control that causes sickness, and the bronze serpent is self-control, the means of health (Philo, *Leg. Alleg.* 2.79). Likewise, Paul attributes the sickness and death of certain members of the Corinthian congregation to their perpetrating social abuses at the Lord's Supper (1 Cor. 11:30). Whether punishment of sin operates directly or indirectly, it remains a major etiology of sickness in the period.

Intermediaries as Senders of Illness

Second Temple literature also contains various intermediaries as senders of illness. These can be malevolent figures or divine functionaries. For instance, the "Treatise on the Two Spirits" in the Qumran *Community Rule* explains sickness and disease as the action of evil spirits:

> But concerning the Spirit of Deceit (these are the principles): greed and slackness in righteous activity, wickedness and falsehood, great hypocrisy, fury, great vileness, shameless zeal for abominable works in a spirit of fornication, filthy ways in unclean worship, a tongue of blasphemy, blindness of eyes and deafness of ears, stiffness of neck and hardness of heart, walking all the ways of darkness, and evil craftiness. (1QS 4:9-11; trans. Qimron)

Other scrolls that contain prayers for warding off evil spirits and the illnesses they bring reflect the same belief about etiology (e.g., 11QapocPs[a] and the likely apotropaic liturgies in 11Q5 and 11Q6).

Sickness as Vicarious Suffering

Although it is safe to say that Second Temple literature ultimately attributes sickness to divine providence, one major new motif emerges: a person may suffer sickness and disease not for his or her own sins, but as a direct result of others' sins. At least one of the so-called servant songs in Second Isaiah reflects this concept and adds a vicarious dimension to it:

> He was despised and rejected by others;
> A man of suffering and acquainted with
> infirmity. . . .
> Surely he has borne our infirmities and carried
> our diseases;
> Yet we accounted him stricken struck down
> by God, and afflicted.
> But he was wounded for our transgressions. . . .
> (Isa. 53:3, 4-5a)

The passage is notable for its self-conscious contrast between the old idea (one's own sins cause sickness) and the new idea (a righteous person may suffer for others' sins). Several other texts demonstrate this development. The Qumran *Thanksgiving Hymns* vividly depict a righteous speaker who suffers injury and illness because of the evil actions of other human beings, though not vicariously. For instance,

> As for me, I am dumb . . .
> [my arm] is torn from its shoulder,
> and my foot has sunk in to the mire.
> My eyes are closed by the spectacle of evil,
> and my ears by the crying of blood. . . .
> All the foundations of my edifice totter,
> and my bones are pulled out of joint. . . .
> A whirlwind engulfs me
> because of the mischief of their sin.
> (1QH 7; trans. Vermes)

The case of Tobit's blindness is similar: in defiance of royal intimidation, he buries a murdered man and is mocked by his neighbors for doing so. Then,

> That same night, I washed myself and went into my courtyard and slept by the wall of the courtyard; and my face was uncovered because of the heat. I did not know that there were sparrows on the wall; their droppings fell into my eyes and produced white films. (Tob. 2:9-10)

Although this explanation is what we would call naturalistic, the narrator clearly associates Tobit's blindness with his good deeds. The *Testament of Job* provides a similar analysis: by having Job destroy an idol (a good deed), the *Testament* provides a rationale for Satan's hostility to Job. The book of Tobit, the Qumran Scrolls, and the *Testament of Job* share the belief that being a good person in an evil environment can make one sick.

Sickness as an Occasion for Divine Healing

A final new type of etiology appears in some of the gospel healing narratives. In John 9, the disciples ask Jesus whose sin caused a man's blindness. Jesus replies that sin was not the cause, but rather "he was born blind so that God's works might be revealed in him" (9:3). That is, the man became blind so that his healing might demonstrate God's presence and power. It is not clear to what extent this text reflects a common Jewish (or even Christian) idea about how illnesses occur, but it at least indicates the possibility of this kind of etiology.

In short, Second Temple literature contains two major trends beyond the earlier biblical traditions.

First, the earlier belief that God sends all diseases undergoes much elaboration. Punishment, for sin and for breach of the covenant, remains a prominent explanation for disease. Many narratives represent God's responsibility as a direct intervention, whereas wisdom literature depicts the association between sin and sickness as an observable pattern of the divinely ordered cosmos. In addition, God may send disease in order to demonstrate his glory or to effect some providential turn of events. The explanation for sin is itself elaborated by the role of evil spirits that bring about both evil deeds and diseases. As a cause of sickness, this type can occur both to sinful people who invite such influence, and to righteous people who attract the hostility of evil people or beings. With the latter explanation, Second Temple literature innovates with its traditions. If the canonical book of Job treated the righteous sufferer as a difficult special case, Second Temple literature suggests that such cases are not unusual. This belief corresponds to the apocalyptic worldview, in which the cosmos has fallen under the dominion of evil powers that persecute the righteous. Thus, just as apocalypticism proposed a new explanation for human suffering in general, so this type of explanation appears in beliefs about sickness.

Bibliography
H. Avalos 1995, *Illness and Health Care in the Ancient Near East: The Role of the Temple in Greece, Mesopotamia, and Israel,* Atlanta: Scholars Press. • L. P. Hogan 1992, *Healing in the Second Temple Period,* Göttingen: Vandenhoeck & Ruprecht. • A. Kleinman 1980, *Patients and Healers in the Context of Culture: Explorations of the Borderland between Anthropology, Medicine and Psychiatry,* Berkeley: University of California Press. • J. Preuss 1978, *Biblical and Talmudic Medicine,* trans. Fred Rosner, New York: Sanhedrin. • F. Rosner 2000, *Encyclopedia of Medicine in the Bible and the Talmud,* Jerusalem: Jason Aronson. • K. Seybold and U. B. Mueller 1981, *Sickness and Healing,* trans. D. W. Stott, Nashville: Abingdon. • J. Wilkinson 1998, *The Bible and Healing: A Medical and Theological Commentary,* Grand Rapids: Eerdmans.

See also: Demons and Exorcism; Divination and Magic; Healing; Magic Bowls and Incantations; Medicine and Hygiene

Rebecca Raphael

Sin

The preferred term for "to sin" in biblical Hebrew literature is *ḥāṭāʾ*. Judging from its Akkadian and Semitic cognates, the root means "to be mistaken, found deficient, or lacking; to be at fault; or to miss a specified goal or mark." Another root, *pšʿ*, signifies the violation of a norm, standard, or covenant and can be translated "to rebel, revolt, or transgress." Also common are *ʿāwōn,* "error, iniquity," from *ʿāwâ,* "to be bent, twisted"; and *ʿăbērâ,* "transgression," the preferred term in rabbinic literature, from *ʿābar,* "to cross [break]" the Law.

Hebrew Bible

Biblically, to sin is to be found lacking with regard to the requirements of God (cf. Exod. 20:20). Sin includes a range of offenses from inappropriate cultic procedures to violations of the dignity and rights of fellow human beings. Any of these offenses can break down mutual relations between God and his people, causing separation, wrath, and retribution (Jer. 14:20-21; Isa. 64:7; Ps. 51:11). God, who is the source of holiness, will not tolerate sin in his presence.

The Torah distinguishes between defiant and inadvertent sin. Penalties for the former are death or *karet,* extirpation of one's family line. Unintentional sins can be expiated by repentance, restitution, and atoning sacrifices (Lev. 4:2; 5:5, 20-26 [MT]; Num. 15:27-31).

Apocrypha and Pseudepigrapha

While the biblical notion of sin continues to dominate Jewish thinking in the postbiblical period, a tendency emerges to describe sin more abstractly, as a force or realm that is antagonistic to both God and humanity. Good and evil, usually configured in Scripture as two categories of people, are conceived of as two powers that control the world (*T. Jud.* 20:1). Nevertheless, the Law continued to be the measuring rod of good and evil (*Sir.* 35:1; 41:8; *Pss. Sol.* 14:2).

How did sin originate? There are two main explanations. One is that Adam and Eve brought evil into the world through their transgression of God's command (*Sir.* 25:24; *2 Bar.* 23:4; cf. *4 Ezra* 7:118-19: "O Adam, what have you done? For though it was you who sinned, the fall was not yours alone, but ours also who are your descendants"). The other is that the intercourse of (fallen) angels and women in the time of Noah was so heinous that it changed the moral nature of humanity (cf. *1 Enoch* 10:7-9; 64:1-2).

Dead Sea Scrolls

Sin is usually portrayed in the DSS as one of two forces controlling human destiny. In the Qumran *Community Rule* they are personified as the Angel of Darkness, who controls the children of darkness, and the Prince of Lights, who helps the children of light to overcome evil (1QS 3:20-24). The *War Scroll* describes the opposing angels as Belial and Michael (1QM 17:6-7; cf. CD 5:18; 4Q544 1-3). The resolution of this spiritual conflict will come in the eschatological age (1QH[a] 12:20; 1QM 1:8-10). Many scrolls describe sin as an inherent human condition in which each person must struggle from birth (1QH[a] 12:29-30). The *Hodayot* describe the human person as "a structure of dust shaped with water, his base is the guilt of sin, vile unseemliness, source of impurity, over which a spirit of degeneracy rules" (1QH[a] 5:20-21; cf. 1QS 11:9). The hapless human is completely dependent on God for atonement. In fact, the establishment of the community itself was an atoning act of God (CD 4:9-10; cf. 1QS 9:4).

Although God predestines some people for evil and others for good (1QS 3:17-21; 4:15-17; cf. 1QH[a] 7:17-21), individuals must still choose good over evil (1QS 3:18-19; 4:23; cf. also CD 2:14-16). Sinners must confess their sins, plead for mercy, swear never to sin again, and pray for divine aid in the future (1QH[a] 4:18-24; 6:17; 14:6; cf. CD 15:3). Since the sectarians opposed the current priesthood, the sacrificial cult was temporarily suspended; nevertheless, the study of the Law as mediated by the community and its teacher was a powerful weapon against sin (1QH[a] 4:23; 12:24-25).

Sin brings dire consequences to the offender. Sinners are barred from God's presence and covenant (1QH[a] 7:29; 12:35), delivered up to their enemies (CD 1:3-4), and will ultimately suffer "the gloom of everlasting fire" (1QS 2:8). At Qumran the sinner is ostracized with all his belongings; he is forbidden to enter the community's ritual baths, eat of its pure food, or join in any other of its activities (1QS 5:13-14). The unintentional sinner was separated for a time and given a separate food ration, while the defiant person was permanently expelled (1QS 8:21-26; cf. 3:4-7; CD 9:16-20).

Apparently, at Qumran sin caused ritual as well as moral defilement, requiring the penitent to immerse in water. The *Community Rule* requires sinners to undergo immersion at the time of their confession and entrance to the community (1QS 3:4-9; cf. CD 10:2). Not all impurity, however, is the result of sin.

New Testament

Like the Scrolls, the New Testament describes sin as a power that entraps all creation (Acts 26:18; Rom. 8:22). This power is often personified as Satan, the Devil or evil angel who constantly tries to lead Christians astray (1 Pet. 5:8). His successful temptation of Adam and Eve subjected all humanity to a mortal body and sinful nature (Rom. 5:12). The remedy for sin is the atonement, forgiveness, and cleansing made possible by the perfect life and sacrificial death of Jesus (Eph. 6:16; Heb. 10:10). In addition, Christians, as the holy people of God (Eph. 1:4), must resist selfish desires and activities, also called "works of the flesh" (Gal. 5:19-20). Attending to God's word and doing good deeds are effective weapons against temptation (Rom. 12:21; Heb. 4:12).

The antagonism between flesh and spirit, especially the tension between illicit sexual passions and holiness, is common in Pauline literature (Rom. 8:13; Gal. 5:17). Adultery is an affront to the Holy Spirit, who has been given by God to Christians to help them live the holy life (1 Thess. 4:4; cf. Matt. 5:27-28). A Christian who acts immorally must be shunned (1 Cor. 5:11), and those who insist on ungodliness must be expelled (1 Cor. 5:13; 3:17). Unrepentant sinners are liable to eternal torment by fire (Matt. 5:29-30; Rev. 21:8).

Rabbinic Literature

The rabbis regard sin as the violation of any of the commandments of the Torah, either by committing an act contrary to the divine will or omitting one in accord with it (*m. Yoma* 8:8). They rarely speak of sin in the abstract; an offense that was not an actual overt act was not subject to flagellation (*b. Šebiʿit* 4a). Sin ostracizes Israel from God until it is purified by repentance and restitution, and — while the Temple stood — by atoning sacrifices (*m. Yoma* 8:9; cf. Lev. 5:5-7; 6:5; Num. 15:30-31).

Sin and holiness are antithetical (cf. *Sifra Qedošim* 93b, "By separating oneself from sin, a person can become holy"). The biblical command to be holy as God is holy is interpreted by the sages: "As I am separated, so be ye separated: this means separation from things impure and defiling, foremost among which are idolatry, adultery, and other prohibited sexual relations, and murder" (*Sifra Qedošim* 57b; cf. 81a). In order to save his life a person may violate other laws of the Torah, but never these three prohibitions (*b. Sanhedrin* 74a).

The rabbis refer often to the *yēṣer hā-raʿ* or "evil inclination," that is, the innate human tendency to disobey God (*b. Sukkah* 52b; *b. ʿErubin* 13b). Rabbi Abin is reputed to have said that the angels were given only one portion of holiness since they are not subject to the evil *yeṣer* but that humanity was given two portions of holiness in order to resist it (*Lev. Rab.* 24:8). The chief temptation of the *yēṣer hā-raʿ* seems to be illicit sexual relations (*Gen. Rab.* 9:7).

The Talmud emphasizes that one must fight against the evil inclination in order to secure God's presence and warns that a final accounting will take place (*b. Berakot* 17a; cf. *m. ʾAbot* 2:1; 3:1). The most effective weapon against evil is study of the Torah; although God created the evil inclination, he created the Torah as its antidote (*b. Qiddušin* 30b; *b. Soṭah* 21a). The school of R. Ishmael advises: "My son, if this repulsive wretch [the *yēṣer hā-raʿ*] attacks you, lead him to the house of learning: if he is stone, he will dissolve; if iron, he will shiver into fragments" (*b. Qiddušin* 30b). Just as sin tears down integrity, so observance of the Torah and doing good deeds build up holiness (*b. Yoma* 39a; *Mekilta* 98a; *Sifra* 35a; 91d). Sometimes the rabbis enjoin extra proscriptions as a "fence" for protecting the "house" of the written Law (*m. ʾAbot* 1:1; *b. Yebamot* 20a); as *Leviticus Rabbah* puts it, "He who surrounds himself with a fence against anything unchaste is called holy" (*Lev. Rab.* 26:6).

Bibliography

G. A. Anderson 1995, "Intentional and Unintentional Sin in the Dead Sea Scrolls," in *Pomegranates and Golden Bells: Studies in Biblical, Jewish, and Near Eastern Ritual, Law, and Literature in Honor of Jacob Milgrom,* ed. D. P. Wright, D. N. Freedman, and A. Hurvitz, Winona Lake, Ind.: Eisenbrauns, 49-64. • G. A. Anderson 2009, *Sin: A History,* New Haven: Yale University Press. • J. J. Collins 2004, "Before the Fall: The Earliest Interpretations of Adam and Eve," in *The Idea of Biblical Interpretation: Essays in Honor of James L. Kugel,* ed. H. Najman and J. H. Newman, Leiden: Brill, 293-308. • H. K. Harrington 2001, *Holiness: Rabbinic Literature in the Graeco-Roman World,* London: Routledge. • J. Klawans 2000, *Impurity and Sin in Ancient Judaism,* Oxford: Oxford University Press. • J. Milgrom 1976, *Cult and Conscience: The ASHAM and the Priestly Doctrine of Repentance,* Leiden: Brill. • J. Milgrom 1991, 2000, *Leviticus 1–16; Leviticus 17–22,* New York: Doubleday.

See also: Atonement; Evil; Holiness; Purity and Impurity; Sacrifices and Offerings

Hannah K. Harrington

SLAVES, SLAVERY

Slaves, Slavery

Slavery as a dominant form of production appeared very late in ancient societies, and perhaps only ancient Greece and Rome can be considered slave societies. Slaves, that is, persons held in servitude whether by military conquest, birth, bondage to debt, or self-indenture, were ubiquitous in the ancient Near East. They were part of the social landscape of ancient Israel and Second Temple Judaism, in both the land of Israel and the Diaspora, as well of early Christianity. Various aspects of slavery in the ancient world continue to be debated. The evidence for slavery in the period covered by this volume comes from the Hebrew Bible, the papyri from Elephantine and Wadi ed-Daliyeh, literary texts of the Hellenistic and early Roman periods, and early rabbinic tradition.

Hebrew Bible

The Hebrew word for male slave is *ʿebed* (800 times in the Hebrew Bible; the Aramaic term in Dan. 24:7 is *ʿăbad*), which is also used to denote servants (e.g., Gen. 12:16; Deut. 23:16), military subordinates (e.g., Gen. 14:15; 2 Sam. 19:7), political subjects (Gen. 20:8; Judg. 3:24), civil servants (2 Kings 22:12; 24:10), and God's servants (Exod. 32:13; Isa. 41:8). It is translated in the LXX as *pais,* "child, young man, son, servant" (340 times); *doulos,* "slave, servant" (310 times); and *therapōn,* "attendant, servant" (42 times). A female slave is called *šipḥāh,* "slave girl" (Gen. 16:2-3; 25:12; LXX *paidiskē*) and *ʾāmāh* (56 times), "slave woman" (Gen. 20:17; 30:3; LXX *paidiskē*).

The Hebrew Bible's major regulations concerning servants are found in the Covenant Code (Exod. 21:1-11, 26-27; 22:1-4), Lev. 25:39-46, and Deut. 15:12-18. The Covenant Code establishes that the male Hebrew slave should serve only for six years and then have the option of becoming a permanent slave or being set free. The female Hebrew slave serves as a domestic servant, wife, or concubine and can be set free only if the master mistreats her. Deuteronomy erases that difference between male and female Hebrew slaves: both are to be offered the option of being set free after six years of service or of becoming permanent servants (Deut. 15:12, 17). While these texts do not address the issue of foreign slaves, Lev. 25:39-46 does. This text establishes that Israelites should not be bought or sold as slaves (Lev. 25:42). The Israelite who has to sell himself into serfdom should not be treated as a slave but as a hired or bound laborer (Lev. 25:40) and should be set free in the jubilee year. The text allows the acquisition of slaves from foreign nations or resident aliens, and they can be considered as property (Lev. 25:45). Fifteen percent of the population that returned from the Babylonian Exile were slaves (Ezra 2:64; Neh. 7:66).

Elephantine Papyri

In the nineteenth and twentieth centuries, archaeologists discovered a large number of Aramaic documents, mostly from the late fifth century B.C.E., at Elephantine in Egypt, the site of a Jewish military colony. All the slaves mentioned in the Elephantine Papyri have Egyptian names; these include the brothers Petosiri and Bela, sons of Tabi and slaves of Mibtahiah (*TAD* B2.11); and Ta(p)met (*TAD* B3.6), a handmaiden of Meshullam b. Zaccur. The only exception is Jedaniah b. Takhoi (*TAD* B3.9), a Jewish slave born of an Egyptian mother. Slavery was not necessarily a permanent status in Elephantine; serfdom may be a better word to describe it. Ta(p)met, a female servant mentioned in a marriage contract (*TAD* B3.3:7), was probably born free and seems to have become a free person later on (*TAD* B3.5; B3.6). Servants bore a brand on their right hands with the name of their master, as stated in *TAD* B2.11:4-5: "PN, a slave (. . .), branded on his right hand (with) a brand reading (in) Aramaic like this: (belonging) to Mibtahiah." Slaves in Elephantine were considered movable property and as such could be seized as security in case of unpaid debts (*TAD* B3.1:10; *TAD* B3.13:11).

Samaria Papyri

The Samaria Papyri from Wadi ed-Daliyeh came to light in 1962. These fragmentary texts are written in Aramaic and date to the fourth century (ca. 375-355 B.C.E.). Most of the eighteen or so legible fragments are deeds from the sale of slaves. The names of slaves are Yahwistic, but there are no provisions for manumission as regulated in Deut. 15:12 and Lev. 25:40. Slaves are sold "in perpetuity" and become part of the hereditary property of the family. The Samaria Papyri do not reflect any difference in the treatment of Samarian and foreign slaves. The documents sometimes describe the slave as "without defect" or "without a slave brand."

Texts of the Greco-Roman Period

The existence of slaves among the Essenes is a matter of debate. While Josephus (*Ant.* 18.21) and Philo (*Quod Omnis Probus Liber Sit* 12 [79]) state that the Essenes did not own slaves, the *Damascus Document* contains regulations forbidding masters from selling to Gentiles slaves who have joined the covenantal community (CD 12:10-11) and from making them work on the Sabbath (CD 11:12).

The writings of the Hellenistic and Roman periods do not differentiate between Israelite and foreign slaves except in commentaries or explanations of the biblical regulations concerning slavery (so Philo, *Spec. Leg.* 2.79). In Philo and Josephus slavery is not a natural state, as it is in Aristotle (*Politics* 1255a), but the consequence of divine punishment (Philo, *De Praemiis et Poenis* 164; Josephus, *Ant.* 20.166).

Both Jewish and non-Jewish texts urge masters to treat their slaves in a humanitarian way. Ben Sira advises that if you have only one slave you should "treat him as yourself" (Sir. 33:21). Yet he also says not to leave the hands of the slave idle because "he will seek liberty" (Sir. 33:26), and counsels not being ashamed of "drawing blood from the back of a wicked slave" (Sir. 42:5).

Slavery obliterated previous ethnicity and nationality, and in case of manumission freed persons would adopt the ethnicity or nationality of their former master. In the early Jesus movement, "conversion" of whole households, including slaves, was not uncommon

(John 4:53; Acts 10:2; 11:14; 16:15, 31, 32-34; 1 Cor. 1:16; 16:15). Slaves usually went through a name change, adding their masters' names to indicate who owned them. Slaves were circumcised in Jewish households until this practice was prohibited by Roman decrees in the third and fourth century C.E., but except for this practice, there was no significant difference between Jews and non-Jews in their implementation of slavery during the Greco-Roman period. In the *Institutes* of the Roman jurist Gaius (*fl.* 130-180 C.E.) the slave is considered a *res*, a thing that can be bought, owned, and sold at the will of the owner; slaves are denied the right to inherit property *(Testamentifactio)*, represent themselves in court, and get legally married *(Ius connubii)*. They are, however, allowed to usufruct (to use and derive profit or benefit from) a small amount of property *(peculium)* and to have an unofficial spouse *(contubernium)*.

Rabbinic Literature

In most cases, the Mishnah develops regulations concerning slavery independently of biblical traditions. The Mishnah establishes that a slave can become free if his master transfers the master's whole property to him, but he remains a slave if the master retains even "one ten-thousandth part" of it (*m. Pe'ah* 3:8). One tradition notes that priests' slaves were allowed to eat from the heave offerings only while their masters were alive but were forbidden to do so if the priests sold them or died (*m. Ter.* 8:1). The Mishnah also introduces the category of the half-slave, half-free person (*m. Pesaḥ.* 8:1) who "works for his master one day and for himself one day" (*m. Giṭ.* 4:5). It also provides regulations concerning slave girls: "These are the girls [invalid for marriage to an Israelite] who [nonetheless] receive a fine [from the man who seduces them]" (*m. Ketub.* 3:1). Slaves served variously as doorkeepers and personal attendants and performed menial tasks (*m. B. Bat.* 10:7), but some also served as teachers and tutors in philosophy. Masters, however, were not supposed to receive condolences for the death of a slave (*m. Ber.* 2:7). The emphasis on the origin of the slave is marginal in the Mishnah.

The various biblical regulations became integrated into one system in the Talmud (*b. Qiddušin* 14b–25b) and in the Midrash *(Mekhilta of Rabbi Ishmael, Neziqin)*. In these texts slaves are categorized as either Hebrew or non-Hebrew. Hebrew slaves are divided into those who became slaves by court order and those who sold themselves into slavery.

BIBLIOGRAPHY

R. S. BAGNALL 1993, "Slavery and Society in Late Roman Egypt," in *Law, Politics and Society in the Ancient Mediterranean World*, ed. B. Halpern and D. Hobson, Sheffield: Sheffield Academic Press, 220-40. • G. C. CHIRICHIGNO 1993, *Debt Slavery in Israel and the Ancient Near East*, Sheffield: Sheffield Academic Press. • M. I. FINLEY 1980, *Ancient Slavery and Modern Theology*, London: Chatto & Windus. • J. A. GLANCY 2002, *Slavery in Early Christianity*, Oxford: Oxford University Press. • D. M. GOLDENBERG 2003, *The Curse of Ham: Race and Slavery in Early Judaism, Christianity, and Islam*, Princeton: Princeton University Press. • D. GROPP 2000, "Slavery," in *Encyclopedia of the Dead Sea Scrolls*, ed. L. H. Schiffman and J. C. VanderKam, Oxford: Oxford University Press, 2: 884-86. • C. HEZSER 2006, *Jewish Slavery in Antiquity*, Oxford: Oxford University Press. • K. HOPKINS 1993, "Novel Evidence for Roman Slavery," *Past and Present* 138: 3-27. • B. S. JACKSON 1988, "Biblical Law of Slavery: A Comparative Approach," in *Slavery and Other Forms of Unfree Labour*, ed. L. Archer, London: Routledge, 86-102. • D. B. MARTIN 1989, "Slavery and the Ancient Jewish Family," in *The Jewish Family in Antiquity*, ed. S. J. D. Cohen, Atlanta: Scholars Press, 113-29. • E. E. URBACH 1964, "The Laws regarding Slavery as a Source for Social History of the Period of the Second Temple, the Mishnah, and Talmud," in *Papers of the Institute of Jewish Studies*, ed. J. G. Weiss, Lanham, Md.: University Press of America, 1-94.

See also: Daliyeh, Wadi ed-; Elephantine, Elephantine Papyri

ALEJANDRO F. BOTTA

Slavonic

Transmission of Jewish Pseudepigrapha

The majority of the early Jewish extrabiblical materials that circulated in Slavic regions came from Byzantium, a city that exercised an unmatched formative influence on the development of the Slavic literary heritage. An important witness can be found in the so-called *Lists of the True and False Books*, which are indexes of noncanonical works brought from Byzantium and then translated, revised, and incorporated into various Slavonic collections such as the *Izbornik (Florilegium) of Svjatoslav* (1073). The remarkable fluidity found in these lists can be explained by the peculiarities of dissemination of noncanonical materials in Eastern Orthodoxy.

Apocryphal texts and fragments were not sharply demarcated from ideologically mainstream materials and were preserved alongside them in the same collections. Many ancient Jewish documents and traditions were adopted into the framework of Eastern Orthodoxy in a new theological capacity. Thus, for example, some pseudepigraphic texts and fragments about such biblical figures as Adam, Enoch, Noah, Jacob, Abraham, and Moses were often viewed as lives of protological saints and were incorporated into hagiographical collections.

There were several types of collections of early Jewish pseudepigrapha and fragments that were transmitted in Slavic circles. Eastern Orthodoxy typically preserved and handed on early Jewish materials as part of larger historiographical, moral, hagiographical, liturgical, and other collections containing both ideologically marginal and mainstream contents. In these compilations, the Jewish materials were often rearranged, expanded, or abbreviated.

Historiographic compendiums known as *Palaeas* (from Gr. *palaea*, "ancient") played a major role in disseminating early Jewish materials. The *Palaeas* are historiographies in which canonical biblical stories are mixed with noncanonical elaborations and interpretations. The Slavic Orthodox literary heritage knew several versions of *Palaeas*, including the so-called *Explanatory Palaea (Tolkovaja Paleja)*, which cover biblical and

Israelite history from creation to the reign of Solomon, embellished with apocryphal stories about Adam, Eve, Abel, Cain, Noah, Isaac, and other figures of primeval and Israelite history. Another important witness to this historiographic genre is the so-called *Chronographical Palaea (Hronograficheskaja Paleja),* which includes extracanonical stories about Lamech, Melchizedek, Moses, and Solomon.

Yet another important category of historiographical writing that served as a vehicle for the preservation of early Jewish pseudepigraphical traditions was the chronograph. This category included Slavonic translations of the chronicles of universal history of such Byzantine authors as George Hamartolos, John Malalas, and George Synkellos, along with anonymous chronographic compilations that originated in Slavic lands on the basis of earlier sources. Similar to the *Palaeas,* the chronographs did not merely retell the canonical materials but compiled extensive extracanonical additions dealing with the characters of biblical and Israelite history.

Finally, early Jewish pseudepigraphic texts and traditions were also included in various collections of a moral and liturgical nature, such as the *Great Menologia (Velikie Chetii Minei)* and the *Just Balance (Merilo Pravednoe).*

The task of discerning the possible provenance and purposes of the original texts and fragments is made very difficult by the numerous editorial additions, abbreviations, and rearrangements. In recent years, however, several promising methodological approaches to the study of early Jewish texts preserved in the Slavonic language have been formulated (Kulik 2004). These studies help to distinguish between various levels of transmission and adaptation of the early Jewish materials in the Slavic literary environment.

Major Clusters of Pseudepigraphic Materials

A classic study by A. I. Jacimirskij, which still remains unsurpassed in its thoroughness, distinguishes more than twenty clusters of pseudepigraphical works and fragments organized around major biblical characters (Jacimirskij 1921). Most of these materials were also preserved in other Christian traditions and survive not only in Slavonic but in Greek, Latin, Syriac, Ethiopic, Georgian, Armenian, and other languages of the Christian East and West. Yet, among the great variety of materials that circulated in the Slavic literary environment, several documents survived solely in Slavonic translations. This distinctive class of writings includes 2 (Slavonic) *Enoch, Apocalypse of Abraham,* and the *Ladder of Jacob.*

Works Preserved Only in Slavonic

2 Enoch is a Slavonic translation of a Jewish pseudepigraphon usually dated to the first century C.E. The central theme of the text is the celestial ascent of the seventh antediluvian patriarch Enoch through the seven heavens and his luminous metamorphosis near the throne of glory. The book combines the features of an apocalypse and a testament, and can be divided into three parts. The first part (chaps. 1–38) describes Enoch's heavenly journey culminating in his encounter with the Deity, who reveals to the seer the secrets of creation. This part ends with Enoch's return to earth where he must instruct his children in the celestial knowledge received from God and the angels. The second part (chaps. 39–67) deals with Enoch's testamentary admonitions to his sons during his short visit to earth and ends with the second ascension of the patriarch. The third part (chaps. 68–73) describes the priestly functions of Enoch's family and the miraculous birth of Melchizedek, and ends with the flood. *2 Enoch* exists in longer and shorter recensions that differ not only in length but also in the character of the text. Both of them preserve original material. The majority of scholars think that the Slavonic version was translated from Greek. The Semitisms found in various parts of the text point to the possibility of a Semitic *Vorlage* behind the Greek version.

The *Apocalypse of Abraham,* another text preserved solely in its Slavonic translation, is a Jewish work that was probably composed in Palestine in the first or second century C.E. Some features of the text suggest a Semitic *Vorlage,* although a Greek stage of transmission should not be excluded. The Slavonic text of the apocalypse can be divided into two parts. The first part (chaps. 1–8) represents a haggadic elaboration of the story of Abraham's rejection of idols. The second, apocalyptic part (chaps. 9–31) depicts the patriarch's ascent to heaven, where he is accompanied by his angelic guide Yahoel and is initiated into heavenly and eschatological mysteries. According to some scholars, the two parts may originally have existed independently, yet they appear synthesized into a coherent unity, sharing common theological themes.

The *Ladder of Jacob,* which has also been preserved in its entirety solely in Slavonic, circulated in Slavic circles as a part of the *Explanatory Palaea.* This work is connected with Jacob's dream about the ladder and the interpretation of his vision. The text underwent extensive editing and rearrangement. Despite its afterlife inside the compendium of heterogeneous materials and its long history of transmission in Greek and Slavonic circles, the work seems to preserve several early traditions that can be safely placed within Judaism of the first century C.E. Scholars propose that the Slavonic *Ladder of Jacob* most likely derives from a Greek translation, which in turn appears to have been made from Hebrew or Aramaic.

Works Preserved in Languages alongside Slavonic

Besides these three works available exclusively in Slavonic, the Slavic Orthodox literary heritage has preserved a substantial number of texts and fragments attested elsewhere in other languages, including Greek. One of the most extensive clusters includes materials dealing with the stories of the creation and fall of Adam and Eve. The impressive bulk of materials pertaining to these biblical figures is represented by the Slavonic *Life of Adam and Eve,* a Slavonic version of the primary Adam books. It contains some material absent in other versions of the primary Adam books, including the story of

Satan's second deception of Adam and Eve and the legend of the contract or cheirograph that Satan made with the protoplasts. The *Slavonic Vita* is a translation from Greek and exists in longer and shorter recensions.

Another cluster of important Adam materials includes a fragment known as the *Adam Octipartite*, the so-called *Sataniel Text*, and the *Story of God's Creation of Adam*. The *Adam Octipartite* contains the tradition about the creation of Adam's body from eight elements. The *Sataniel Text* is an Adam fragment interpolated into the Russian manuscripts of the Slavonic version of *3 Baruch*. It attests to the tradition of Sataniel's refusal to venerate Adam and Sataniel's deception of Eve by using the serpent as a proxy. The *Story of God's Creation of Adam* exhibits strikingly dualistic tendencies, portraying the creation of the protoplast as the work of both God and Satan.

A number of significant early Jewish traditions pertaining to the story of the protoplasts were also incorporated into Christian Adamic writings that circulated in Slavic circles. Examples include the *Legend about the Wood of the Cross*, the *Struggle of the Archangel Michael with Sataniel*, the *Legend of the Tiberian Sea*, the *Discourse of the Three Hierarchs*, and the *Homily of Adam to Lazarus in Hell*. Although these works have distinctively Christian features, it is clear that they contain a wealth of early Jewish traditions. The themes of creation are also reflected in the fragmentary *Seventy Names of God* and *About All Creation*, both published by N. S. Tihonravov (1863).

A cluster of unique traditions about the flood is represented by the Enochic *Fragment about the Two Tablets* and the *Historical Palaea* and by the Noachic narrative known as the *Fragment about the Flood*.

Other pseudepigraphic works preserved in Slavonic but also in different versions in other languages include *Testament of Abraham*, *Joseph and Aseneth*, *Testaments of the Twelve Patriarchs*, *Testament of Job*, *Life of Moses*, *Ascension of Isaiah*, *3 Baruch*, *4 Baruch*, *Apocalypse of Zosimus*, *Ahiqar*, and the *Word of the Blessed Zerubbabel*. Despite the existence of the Greek and other versions of these works, the Slavonic materials sometimes attest to more ancient readings.

There are also quite extensive clusters of works and fragments pertaining to stories about biblical figures such as David, Solomon, Elijah, and Daniel. However, the large bulk of the materials pertaining to these clusters appear to derive from later medieval circles.

Slavonic Pseudepigrapha and the Bogomils

Several studies have attempted to explicate the theological tenets found in the Slavonic translations of some pseudepigraphical works, such as *2 Enoch*, *3 Baruch*, the *Apocalypse of Abraham*, and the *Slavonic Life of Adam and Eve*, through their alleged connections with the Bogomil movement, a dualistic sect that flourished in the Balkans in the Middle Ages. These studies have argued that the large number of Jewish pseudepigrapha preserved in Slavonic appear to contain Bogomil interpolations (Ivanov 1925). Some scholars have even proposed that works like *2 Enoch* were composed in the Slavonic language by the Bogomils between the twelfth and fifteenth centuries C.E. (Maunder 1918). Recent scholarship, however, is increasingly skeptical of such radical proposals and generally finds little or no connection between these works and the Bogomil movement (Turdeanu 1981; Andersen 1987).

BIBLIOGRAPHY

F. I. ANDERSEN 1987, "Pseudepigrapha Studies in Bulgaria," *JSP* 1: 41-55. • C. BÖTTRICH 1995, *Das slavische Henochbuch*, JSHRZ V.7, Gütersloh: Gütersloher Verlag. • L. DITOMMASO AND C. BÖTTRICH, EDS. FORTHCOMING, *Old Testament Apocrypha in the Slavonic Tradition: Continuity and Diversity*, Tübingen: Mohr-Siebeck. • H. E. GAYLORD 1982, "How Sataniel Lost His '-el,'" *JJS* 33: 303-9. • I. FRANKO 1896-1910, *Apokrifi i legendi z ukrains'kih rukopisiv*, Monumenta Linguae Necnon Litterarum Ukraino-Russicarum [Ruthenicarum], 1-5; 5 vols., L'viv: Shevchenka. • J. IVANOV 1925, *Bogomilski knigi i legendi*, Sofia: Pridvorna Pechatnica. • A. I. JACIMIRSKIJ 1921, *Bibliograficheskij obzor apokrifov v juzhnoslavjanskoj i russkoj pis'mennosti (Spiski pamjatnikov) Vypusk 1. Apokrify vethozavetnye*, Petrograd: RGAT. • V. JAGIC 1893, "Slavische Beiträge zu den biblischen Apocryphen, I, Die altkirchenslavischen Texte des Adambuches," *Denkschriften der kaiserlichen Akademie der Wissenschaften: Philosophisch-historische Classe* 42: 1-104. • A. KULIK 2004, *Retroverting Slavonic Pseudepigrapha: Toward the Original of the Apocalypse of Abraham*, Atlanta: Scholars Press. • A. S. D. MAUNDER 1918, "The Date and Place of Writing of the Slavonic Book of Enoch," *The Observatory* 41: 309-16. • A. ORLOV 2006, *From Apocalypticism to Merkabah Mysticism: Studies in the Slavonic Pseudepigrapha*, Leiden: Brill. • D. PETKANOVA AND A. MILTENOVA 1993, *Starob'lgarska Eshatologija. Antologija*, Sofia: Slavica. • I. J. PORFIR'EV 1877, *Apokrificheskie skazanija o vethozavetnyh licah i sobytijah po rukopisjam Soloveckoj biblioteki*, Sbornik Otdelenija Russkogo Jazyka i Slovesnosti Imperatorskoj Akademii Nauk, 17.1, St. Petersburg: Tipografija Imperatorskoj Akademii Nauk. • A. N. PYPIN 1862, *Lozhnye i otrechennye knigi russkoj stariny: Pamjatniki starinnoj russkoj literatury, izdavaemye Grafom Grigoriem Kushelevym-Bezborodko*, 3, St. Petersburg: Kulish • M. E. STONE 1992, *A History of the Literature of Adam and Eve*, Atlanta: Scholars Press. • N. S. TIHONRAVOV 1863, *Pamjatniki otrechennoj russkoj literatury*, 2 vols., St. Petersburg and Moscow: Obschevstvennaja Pol'za. • N. S. TIHONRAVOV 1894, *Apokrificheskie Skazanija*, Sbornik Otdelenija Russkogo Jazyka i Slovesnosti Imperatorskoj Akademii Nauk, 58: 4, St. Petersburg: Tipografija Imperatorskoj Akademii Nauk. • É. TURDEANU 1981, *Apocryphes slaves et roumains de l'Ancien Testament*, Leiden: Brill.

ANDREI A. ORLOV

Smith, Morton

Morton Smith (1915-1991) was born in Philadelphia and educated at Harvard (B.A. 1936; S.T.B. 1940; Th.D. 1957). At the advice of his Harvard teachers, Harry Wolfson (1887-1974) and Arthur Darby Nock (1902-1963), he completed a doctorate at the Hebrew University of Jerusalem in 1948. Their intention was to allow

Smith to master rabbinic literature, and to become one of the few New Testament specialists with firsthand knowledge of rabbinic works at the highest level. After returning to the United States he served as an Episcopal parish priest in Philadelphia, Baltimore, and Boston. His initial academic appointment was at Brown University (1950-1955), then at Drew University (1956-1957), and finally at Columbia University (1957-1985), where he continued as a Professor Emeritus until his death in New York in 1991.

A key event in Smith's life was his loss of faith, best recognized from his article, "Psychiatric Practice and Christian Dogma" (Smith 1949). Smith expounded a perfectionist theology whose objective was to make people permanently at war with their own failings. Psychiatry and Christianity, according to Smith, had diametrically opposite goals. As his critics charged (Bennett 1949), Smith's notions of Christianity were ones in which the sacraments were meaningless, grace useless. Whatever the case, it seems that Smith was unable to meet the absolute standards he set for himself. He drew the consequences in his academic publications but was never defrocked as a clergyman, and up to the end of his life he continued to supply information about his accomplishments and publications to the *Episcopal Clerical Dictionary.*

As a scholar, Smith promoted a position that he explicitly referred to as atheism and which he compared with the attitude of ancient Epicureans (Smith 1996: 1:7-11). God or gods might well exist, but that was not a matter for historians to consider. History was to be written in purely human terms, from which any hint of divine intervention or purpose was to be rigorously excluded.

In his earliest publications Smith insisted that the task of historians of religion was to describe each of the separate traditions as carefully as possible before making comparisons. Nevertheless, some of Smith's most important contributions were based on a wide comparative view of the ancient world. Examples of his achievements in this area include his doctoral thesis (Smith 1951), his analysis of the common theology of the ancient Near East (Smith 1996: 1:15-27), his study of Second Isaiah and the Persians (Smith 1996: 1:73-83), his discussion of Nehemiah as the tyrant of Jerusalem (Smith 1971: 126-47), and his detailed study of the Gospel accounts of Jesus in the context of ancient magic (Smith 1978).

One of Smith's articles, "Palestinian Judaism in the First Century" (Smith 1996: 1:104-15), became the basis of a whole generation of scholarship on Josephus and the Pharisees. He argued that Josephus' accounts of the Pharisees in the *Jewish War* and *Jewish Antiquities* should be evaluated against the background of the times when these works were written. On that basis he discounted Josephus' portrayal in the *Antiquities* of the Pharisees running Jewish life in the late Second Temple period years before the destruction of the Temple in 70 C.E. While Smith's conclusions were later challenged (see, e.g., Mason 1981), his insights remain significant and have been the point of departure for important later studies (e.g., Sanders 1992).

Smith delighted in discomfiting the conventionally pious, especially those of liberal Christian persuasion. He wrote numerous sharp reviews exposing the flaws of the work of other scholars and coined the term *pseudo-orthodoxy* for the stance of those who wanted to obscure the results of critical scholarship in their work (Smith 1996: 1:37-54; Smith and Hoffman 1983).

Throughout his life Smith had a close association with Gershom Scholem (1897-1982). He helped Scholem prepare the final version of *Major Trends in Jewish Mysticism* in 1937. The connection was strengthened further during Smith's years in Jerusalem. Guy Stroumsa has discovered extensive correspondence between Smith and Scholem, particularly concerning Smith's understanding of the Secret Gospel of Mark as it developed over the years (Stroumsa 2003).

One of Smith's students at Columbia was Jacob Neusner (1932-). For almost over two decades Smith suggested questions for Neusner to investigate and read drafts of works in progress. By 1984 Smith and Neusner had begun quarreling, with public and published critiques of each other's scholarship (Shanks 1985; Neusner 1993). Smith trained a generation of well-known historians of ancient Judaism, codirecting the dissertations of scholars such as Lee I. Levine, and solo-supervising those by Albert I. Baumgarten, Stanley J. Isser, Shaye J. D. Cohen, Joseph Sievers, Seth Schwartz, and Joseph Portanova (Smith 1996: 2:278).

In 1958 Smith claimed to have discovered, at the Greek Orthodox monastery of Mar Saba in the Judean Desert, a fragment of a letter of Clement of Alexandria that contained quotations from a Secret Gospel of Mark. He later published both a popular account of the find (Smith 1973a) and a detailed scholarly monograph (Smith 1973b). Smith was widely suspected of having forged the Secret Gospel, and he replied to his critics while still alive (Smith 1982). In recent years attention has returned to the topic, with some renewing the charge of forgery, with greater or lesser degrees of success (Carlson 2005; Jeffrey 2007; Piovanelli 2007), but with others still insisting that Smith found the work at Mar Saba, as he had claimed (Stroumsa 2003; Brown 2005).

BIBLIOGRAPHY

E. D. F. BENNETT 1949, "To the Editors," *Journal of Pastoral Care* 3.2: 17-18. • S. G. BROWN 2005, *Mark's Other Gospel: Rethinking Morton Smith's Controversial Discovery,* Waterloo, Ont.: Wilfrid Laurier University Press. • S. CARLSON 2005, *The Gospel Hoax: Morton Smith's Invention of Secret Mark,* Waco, Tex.: Baylor University Press. • P. JEFFREY 2007, *The Secret Gospel of Mark Unveiled,* New Haven: Yale University Press. • S. MASON 1981, *Flavius Josephus on the Pharisees: A Composition-critical Study,* Leiden: Brill. • J. NEUSNER 1993, *Are There Really Tannaitic Parallels to the Gospels?* Atlanta: Scholars Press. • P. PIOVANELLI 2007, *"L'évangile Secret de Marc* Trente-Trois ans Après," *RB* 114: 52-72, 237-54. • E. P. SANDERS 1992, *Judaism: Practice and Belief 63* BCE–*66* CE, London: SCM. • H. SHANKS 1985, "Annual Meetings Offer Intellectual Bazaar and Moments of High Drama," *BAR* 11, 2: 14-16. • M. SMITH 1949, "Psychiatric Practice and Christian Dogma," *Journal of Pastoral Care* 3.1: 12-20. • M. SMITH

1951, *Tannaitic Parallels to the Gospels,* Philadelphia: Society of Biblical Literature. • M. SMITH 1971, *Palestinian Parties and Politics That Shaped the Old Testament,* New York: Columbia University Press. • M. SMITH 1973A, *The Secret Gospel: The Discovery and Interpretation of the Secret Gospel according to Mark,* New York: Harper & Row. • M. SMITH 1973B, *Clement of Alexandria and a Secret Gospel of Mark,* Cambridge: Harvard University Press. • M. SMITH 1978, *Jesus the Magician: Charlatan or Son of God?* New York: Harper & Row. • M. SMITH 1982, "Clement of Alexandria and the Secret Mark: The Score at the End of the First Decade," *HTR* 75: 449-61. • M. SMITH 1996, *Studies in the Cult of Yahweh,* vol. 1, *Studies in Historical Method, Ancient Israel, Ancient Judaism;* vol. 2, *New Testament, Early Christianity, Magica,* ed. S. J. D. Cohen, Leiden: Brill. • M. SMITH AND R. J. HOFFMAN 1983, *What the Bible Really Says,* San Francisco: HarperSanFrancisco. • G. STROUMSA 2003, "Comments on Charles Hedrick's Article: A Testimony," *Journal of Early Christian Studies* 11: 147-53.

ALBERT I. BAUMGARTEN

Solomon

Hebrew Bible

The biblical story of King Solomon, David's son, appears in 1 Kings 1–12. He is described as the legitimate heir to David, a king endowed with divine wisdom, and the builder of the Temple. At the same time, his marriages to foreign women led him into idolatry, thereby making him indirectly responsible for the secession of the northern Israelite tribes. So from the very beginning of the tradition, his character is ambivalent and problematic. This ambivalence is already reflected in the sources used in 1 Kings, but it is eased in the parallel text of 2 Chronicles 2–11, which eliminates all references to the dubious aspects of Solomon.

Solomon's reputation for wisdom is developed in other places of the Hebrew Bible. His status as a revered sage appears indirectly in sapiential literature insofar as the books of Proverbs, Qohelet, and Song of Songs are pseudepigraphically ascribed to him. Psalm 72 and Psalm 127 are also attributed to him. The ascription to Solomon of the former likely originated in the association of the word "peace" (*šālôm,* Ps. 72:7) with the king's name *(šĕlōmô).* In the same way, the presence in the psalm of the word "loved one" *(yādîd),* which could be seen as an allusion to Solomon's second name, Jedidiah (2 Sam. 12:24-25), probably functioned as a motivation for the Solomonic attribution.

Greek Bible

The description of Solomon in the Septuagint presents new traits. Leaving aside that the Hebrew *Vorlage* of the LXX is different from the text preserved by the MT, the Greek translators present a more favorable characterization of Solomon. So, for example, the severe judgment of the MT on Solomon's love of foreign women is tempered in LXX 3 Kgdms. 10:1-13; 11:1-7. Similarly, the LXX applies to Solomon theories of Hellenistic kingship that were common in the second century B.C.E. Thus the Greek text understands the wisdom of Solomon as wisdom befitting a king, who is the incarnation of law and justice. This aspect appears especially in the so-called miscellanies (3 Kgdms. 2:35, 46).

Apocrypha and Pseudepigrapha

In the Wisdom of Ben Sira, mention of King Solomon occurs in the "Praise of the Ancestors" (44:1–50:24), a panegyric on the heroes and sages of Israel. The portrayal of Solomon (47:12-22) follows 1 Kings in its main traits; he is the wise king and builder of the Temple. However, Ben Sira does not ignore the darker aspects of Solomon, going against the general positive trend in postexilic literature represented by Chronicles and Psalm 72, which omit the negative characteristics. The main sin Ben Sira imputes to Solomon is lust and not idolatry.

Eupolemus, a Jewish historian of the mid-second century B.C.E., also describes Solomon's achievements, focusing on the construction of the Temple and the international relations with Egypt and Tyre (cited in Eusebius, *Praep. Evang.* 9.30.1–34.18). He goes beyond Chronicles in making clear that the preparations for the construction of the Temple were already completed in David's time, yet he emphasizes Solomon's superiority over Egypt and Tyre.

The Wisdom of Solomon is structured by the implicit pseudepigraphic attribution to the famed king; it does not mention him explicitly, but its complex system of allusions makes an explicit identification unnecessary. In Wis. 6:22 Solomon conveys his wisdom to the rulers of the earth, and in Wis. 7:15-22 his knowledge is reinterpreted in encyclopedic and esoteric terms. This rereading of the biblical source adds a new motif to Solomon's characterization that became very popular in later texts.

The "esoteric" characterization of Solomon, built on the biblical tradition of his extraordinary knowledge, became the basis for Solomon's growing reputation as an exorcist. Thus in Pseudo-Philo, *Biblical Antiquities* 60 David warns an evil spirit about a descendant of his who will rule over it. Solomon is no doubt alluded to here, so this tradition was well established by the first century C.E.

Aside from a few allusions to and quotations from the Hebrew Bible, the Dead Sea Scrolls scarcely mention Solomon The only exception is 11QApocryphal Psalms[a] (11Q11), a scroll that contains the remnants of Psalm 91 and three other compositions of exorcistic content. Solomon appears in the second of them. His role as an exorcist became very important from the first century C.E. onward in works like the *Testament of Solomon.* It proceeded to spark a debate between Jews and Christians over whether Solomon or Jesus was the greatest exorcist, echoes of which appear in works such as the *Questions of Bartholomew* and the *Dialogue between Timothy and Aquila.* Other works, such as the *Hygromanteia of Solomon,* combine astrology and demonology and show the vitality of these esoteric traditions. The medieval *Clavicula Salomonis,* translated into most vernacular European languages, would eventually transmit them to the modern age.

Josephus

Josephus' treatment of Solomon is extensive; almost half of book 8 of his *Jewish Antiquities* is devoted to the king. As usual, Josephus reworks his biblical sources and presents a clearly Hellenized king. He heightens the importance of Solomon, adding several magnifying details. In *Ant.* 8.44-49, he develops the traditional theme of Solomon's wisdom by changing it into the philosophical knowledge of natural phenomena and empirical data. He goes even further and uses non-biblical traditions that linked Solomon with esoteric knowledge and, above all, with exorcisms (*Ant.* 8.42-49). He also makes use of Hellenistic historians (Menander of Ephesus, Dios) who supplemented the biblical history of the relationship between Hiram king of Tyre and Solomon, presenting both kings on an equal footing. However, Josephus' view is tempered at the end by an ethical note about Solomon's excessive passion toward women, the ultimate cause of his final failure (*Ant.* 8.191-95).

Amulets and Bowls

Solomon's characterization as exorcist was evidently very popular among Jews and Christians alike. The motif of Solomon's magic ring recurs often, and his popularity went beyond the text and reached everyday life. He appears repeatedly in amulets found in the Cairo Genizah, in Jewish magic bowls, and in Christian amulets (Torijano 2002). Among them stand out the amulets in which Solomon is depicted as a horseman piercing a demon. These amulets, of Jewish origin, were used until the Middle Ages. It is quite likely that the Christian iconography of St. George and other military saints was inspired by them.

BIBLIOGRAPHY

D. C. DULING 1985, "The Eleazar Miracle and Solomon's Magical Wisdom in Flavius Josephus's *Antiquitates Judaicae* 8.42-49," *HTR* 78: 1-25. • L. H. FELDMAN 1970, "Josephus as an Apologist to the Greco-Roman World: His Portrait of Solomon," in *Aspects of Religious Propaganda in Judaism and Early Christianity,* ed. E. Schüssler-Fiorenza, Notre Dame: University of Notre Dame Press, 69-98. • P. A. TORIJANO 2002, *Solomon the Esoteric King: From King to Magus, Development of a Tradition,* Leiden: Brill.

See also: Demons and Exorcism; Divination and Magic; Magic Bowls and Incantations

PABLO A. TORIJANO

Solomon, Psalms of

The *Psalms of Solomon* is a collection of eighteen pseudonymous Jewish poems that recount an unknown community's response to a series of military attacks and political persecutions. The *Psalms of Solomon* were likely attributed to Solomon based on the similarity between canonical Psalm 72 and the reference to the "son of David" in *Pss. Sol.* 17:21. Preserved only in Greek and Syriac manuscripts, the *Psalms of Solomon* contain a mixture of historical reflections, halakic disagreements, and political disputes, all conveyed through the medium of poetry. The three longest poems in the collection (2, 8, 17) describe an invasion of Jerusalem by an unnamed foreign conqueror, who is widely identified as the Roman general Pompey. Because many of these poems describe Jewish halakic debates and political strife in Jerusalem during the late first century B.C.E., the *Psalms of Solomon* are an invaluable source for understanding religious and political disputes in Hellenistic Judaism at the time of the Roman conquest in 63 B.C.E. The *Psalms of Solomon* also contain the most detailed depiction of the Davidic messiah prior to the New Testament, making them an important text for understanding the historical development of messianism.

Contents

Psalm of Solomon 1 lacks a heading and was likely added to the collection to introduce the theme of warfare that dominates much of the corpus (*Psalms of Solomon* 1, 2, 7, 8, 13, 15, 17). The poem personifies Jerusalem as a woman who cries to the Lord for deliverance from foreign invaders (1:1). The psalmist concludes that God is justified in allowing Gentiles to attack Jerusalem (1:3-8) because of the sins of its inhabitants.

Psalm of Solomon 2 recounts the aftermath of a foreign attack upon Jerusalem (2:1-3). The psalmist blames "the sons of Jerusalem," who have defiled the offerings and committed sexual transgressions (2:3-4, 6, 11), for this disaster. The poet regards the subsequent death of the Gentile commander, called "the dragon" (2:25), in Egypt (2:26-27) as an answer to his prayer that this man be punished for considering himself equal to God (2:28-29). The writer concludes with a warning to both Jewish and Gentile sinners that they are bound for "eternal destruction in dishonor" (2:31) unless they recognize God's sovereignty over the universe (2:30-37).

Psalm of Solomon 3 is a short poem that contrasts the fates of the righteous and the sinner. The poet encourages the devout to pray and fast as a means to atone for sin (3:8). Unlike the pious, who have the assurance of eternal life (3:12), the psalmist concludes that sinners are destined to be forgotten when God visits the devout (3:11).

Psalm of Solomon 4 describes a political crisis in the "council of the pious" (4:1), where an unjust official continues to abuse his power (4:3-13). The psalmist asks that God punish this sinner and urges the pious to remain steadfast in their faith (4:14-25).

Psalm of Solomon 5 espouses the view that material poverty is a blessing because excessive wealth leads to sin (5:11-17). The author encourages the righteous to rejoice, despite their deprivations, and praise God as their king (5:18-19).

Psalm of Solomon 6 is a short poem that describes the benefits of prayer. The poet is confident that prayer protects the righteous from all dangers (6:3-6). Because the author believes that God fulfills all requests made by the devout, the writer urges the pious to pray constantly so that God will know their needs (6:5-6).

Psalm of Solomon 7 is a plea to God for protection

SOLOMON, PSALMS OF

from a military assault. The author is especially worried that Gentiles will desecrate the Temple (7:2), but does not believe that Jerusalem will be destroyed. He encourages the righteous to pray to God for protection from these invaders (7:7-8).

Psalm of Solomon 8 describes the aftermath of a foreign invasion of Jerusalem. The author blames the hidden sins of the people for this catastrophe. These sins included cultic violations, theft from the Temple, and sexual transgressions (8:9-13). The poet, although convinced that Jerusalem's inhabitants deserve this punishment, petitions God for mercy (8:25-32).

Psalm of Solomon 9 appeals to God's covenant with Abraham (9:8-10) to show that God has always had compassion for Israel. The author encourages the righteous to seek repentance for their transgressions (9:7) so that God may continue to bless them as He has in the past.

Psalm of Solomon 10 espouses the belief that God disciplines the devout to keep them away from sin (10:1-4). The poet concludes that although the Law limits God's discipline, it requires that the righteous be punished for their sins (10:1-5).

Psalm of Solomon 11 describes the author's hope that all Jews will return to Jerusalem. The author personifies Jerusalem as a woman, who prepares for the arrival of her children (11:7). She adorns special robes to proclaim God's blessings on the city and her offspring (11:2, 7).

Psalm of Solomon 12 is a plea for deliverance from a "wicked" man and his compatriots, whose crimes include slander, lying, and deceit (12:1). Because the poet believes that his devout community is powerless against these sinners, he appeals to God's past promises of protection and expects the Lord to save his community from their enemies (12:4-6).

Psalm of Solomon 13 describes the rescue of its author from "sword, "famine and the death of sinners" (13:2). The poet believes that God will protect him like a righteous son and destroy sinners (13:8-9).

Psalm of Solomon 14 urges the righteous to accept suffering as a sign of God's protection (14:1). The writer compares the pious to trees planted by God that are under divine care (14:3-4). The psalmist believes that the acceptance of God's discipline, and following the Law, is the only certain path to eternal life.

Psalm of Solomon 15 describes how God protected the author and his community from persecution (15:1). The psalmist writes not only to thank God, but also to explain why the Lord did not shield him from harm. He concludes that both he and his community survived because God had placed a protective "mark" upon them (15:6). The poet believes that on the Day of Judgment God will once again mark the devout to distinguish them from sinners (15:6-13).

Psalm of Solomon 16 is a psalm of thanksgiving that recounts God's deliverance of the author from some crisis (16:1-5). The psalmist pleads with God to protect him from both sexual temptation (16:7-10) and poverty (16:12-15).

Psalm of Solomon 17 recounts a military destruction of Jerusalem by a foreign conqueror (17:11-18). The psalmist blames Jewish sinners for Jerusalem's destruction. The poet pleads with God to send the only legitimate ruler, "the son of David" (17:21), who will purge Jerusalem of its Gentile and Jewish sinners (17:21-46). This king will be able to accomplish this feat because he will be the "Lord's messiah" (17:32) and without sin (17:36). His reign will not be peaceful, for the author expects the Davidic messiah to "smash the arrogance of the sinner like a potter's vessel" (17:23). The psalmist also believes that the messiah will protect his community, restore the lost tribes to Jerusalem, and rule forever as its king (17:26-46).

Psalm of Solomon 18 is a poem that describes the coming Davidic messiah. Its description of this messiah is very similar to the one in *Psalm of Solomon* 17 (17:24, 32; 18:5-9). The writer asks God to cleanse Israel in preparation for the messiah's arrival (18:5). The poem was likely added to the collection at a later date to provide it with a fitting conclusion.

Manuscripts, Original Language, and Date

There are only eleven Greek and five Syriac manuscripts of the *Psalms of Solomon,* all of which date to the medieval period. The Greek text is clearly translation Greek, and in numerous instances the translator has improperly vocalized the unvocalized Hebrew text or has attempted to adhere to Hebrew syntax. A few obscure passages in the Greek (e.g., *Pss. Sol.* 2:13; 4:6; 12:2-3) suggest that the translator was not fully conversant with the Hebrew language. Because the Syriac version attempts to smooth difficult Greek readings, and tends to gravitate toward the Greek 253 manuscript group, which represents the most reliable witnesses, the majority of scholars regard it as a secondary translation made from the Greek edition. Because no trace of the original Hebrew has been found, it is impossible to determine if the Greek edition is an accurate translation of the original, or whether it sometimes expands or paraphrases the Hebrew.

The absence of any references to historical events following 70 C.E., and the apparent quotation from *Psalm of Solomon* 11 in Bar. 4:36–5:9, suggests that the *Psalms of Solomon* were translated from Hebrew into Greek sometime prior to the first century B.C.E. Their listing in the index to the Codex Alexandrinus shows that the *Psalms of Solomon* were in circulation in Greek prior to the fifth century C.E. when this codex was produced.

The majority of scholars believe that the earliest direct historical allusion in the *Psalms of Solomon* is to the Roman general Pompey's invasion of Jerusalem in 63 B.C.E. (*Pss. Sol.* 2:1-2; 8:18-22; 17:7-9) and the latest to his assassination in Egypt in 48 B.C.E. (2:26-27). The collection was later edited, and possibly expanded to include new poems, between 48 and 42 B.C.E., following Pompey's death. Some scholars have proposed that *Psalm of Solomon* 17 may have been written, or redacted, during the Herodian period in reaction to the siege of Jerusalem by Herod the Great and the Roman general Sosius in 37 B.C.E.

Reception

Some manuscripts title the collection *Psalms of Solomon,* whereas others label it *Psalms of Salomon.* Three Greek manuscripts designate these poems as the *Wisdom of Solomon.* In two Syriac manuscripts the *Psalms of Solomon* follow the forty-two *Odes of Solomon,* and the first *Psalm of Solomon* is numbered as the forty-third Ode, suggesting that the collection was used in worship by Syriac-speaking Christians. The *Psalms of Solomon* are listed in several catalogues, such as pseudo-Athanasius' *Synopsis Scripturae Sacrae* (early sixth century C.E.), the ninth-century-C.E. *Sticometria* of Nicephorus, the Armenian Canon list transmitted by Mechitar of Ayrivank' (1285 C.E.), and six Slavic lists (eleventh-sixteenth centuries C.E.), all of which are likely copied from earlier catalogues. The *Psalms of Solomon* were unknown to scholars until their discovery (sometime before 1604) and publication (1626) in the seventeenth century.

Authorship

The *Psalms of Solomon* have been attributed to the Sadducees, the Pharisees, the Essenes, the Hasidim or a related Jewish sect, and the Christians. Because many theological themes in the *Psalms of Solomon,* such as the importance of the Law and a belief in resurrection, were held by such groups as the Pharisees and Essenes, they cannot be used to associate the *Psalms of Solomon* with one of these Jewish sects. Despite their apparent literary unity, due in part to their use of vocabulary drawn from Scripture, these poems were likely written by several authors.

BIBLIOGRAPHY

Editions

H. E. RYLE AND M. R. JAMES 1891, *Psalms of the Pharisees, Commonly Called the Psalms of Solomon,* Cambridge: Cambridge University Press. • R. B. WRIGHT 2007, *The Psalms of Solomon: A Critical Edition of the Greek Text,* New York: Clark.

Studies

K. ATKINSON 2004, *I Cried to the Lord: A Study of the Psalms of Solomon's Historical Background and Social Setting,* Leiden: Brill. • R. R. HANN 1982, *The Manuscript History of the Psalms of Solomon,* Chico, Calif.: Scholars Press. • J. SCHÜPPHAUS 1977, *Die Psalmen Salomos: Ein Zeugnis Jerusalemer Theologie und Frömmigkeit in der Mitte des vorchristlichen Jarhunderts,* Leiden: Brill. • J. L. TRAFTON 1985, *The Syriac Version of the Psalms of Solomon: A Critical Evaluation,* Atlanta: Scholars Press. • M. WINNINGE 1995, *Sinners and the Righteous: A Comparative Study of the Psalms of Solomon and Paul's Letters,* Stockholm: Almqvist & Wiksell.

KENNETH ATKINSON

Solomon, Testament of

Contents

The *Testament of Solomon* is a pseudepigraphic work that narrates how Solomon dealt with several demons and how those he subdued were employed in the construction of the Jerusalem Temple. The narrative begins with a plea for help by a young boy who is being harassed by Ornias, a malevolent demon. Solomon then prays fervently, asking God for the authority necessary to conquer the demon and rescue the boy. The divine help comes through the intermediation of the archangel Michael, who gives Solomon a special ring with the power to imprison demons and harness their powers for building the Temple. Solomon lends this ring to the young boy, who uses it to control Ornias and bring him to the king's presence. Solomon converses with him and gets to know his name, zodiacal sign, his specialty in doing evil, and the name of the archangel who opposes him. As a result, Solomon orders Ornias to submit to him and cooperate in the construction of the Temple.

This narrative structure works as a template for introducing some fifty-seven demons in the first eighteen chapters of the *Testament.* In the following chapters, the narrative develops into several haggadic stories. Sheba, the "Queen of the South," enters into the narrative. This story is followed by a tale about the failure of Solomon to prevent the death of a son at the hands of his evil father. Next, Adarkes, the king of Arabia, sends a letter to Solomon asking for his help in subduing a malevolent wind demon. After the demon is subdued by one of Solomon's servants, it is brought before Solomon, who commands it to put an immoveable cornerstone in place at the Temple. The text proceeds to describe how Solomon began to make use of his knowledge and power over the demons in incorrect ways, falling into all kinds of sins, especially those provoked by his lust for a Jebusite woman. This lust leads him to final failure and turns him into a "laughingstock to the idols and demons" (26:7). The *Testament* concludes with Solomon warning the reader about his bad end despite his promising beginnings.

Versions and Recensions

The *Testament of Solomon* went almost unnoticed until 1837, when F. F. Fleck edited a text based on a single sixteenth-century manuscript. F. C. Conybeare translated the text into English in 1898. Although Solomonic esoteric literature was very popular in late antiquity and into the modern age, as the different versions of the so-called *Clavicula Salomonis* attest, the textual evidence for the *Testament of Solomon* is limited to seventeen Greek manuscripts dated from the fifteenth to the eighteenth century. To these manuscripts we can add the so-called Vienna Papyrus, dated around the fifth or sixth century of our era, which contains parts of *Testament of Solomon* 18, the chapter in which Solomon interrogates and subdues thirty-six heavenly bodies who are divisions *(decans)* of the Zodiac. Several other Greek manuscripts also have part of the work, and an Arabic manuscript that contains a work with the same title but whose relationship to it is secondary.

Though most of our manuscripts are rather late, this lateness allows a rather complicated textual history to be reconstructed. C. C. McCown, the author of the eclectic critical edition of the text (1922), distinguished three different versions (A, B, C) and thought that the text was better represented by the so-called short recension (A). However, the complete edition of the fifth-century Vienna Papyrus by R. W. Daniel (1983), which preserves part of chap. 18, has made possible a better evaluation of the B or long recension. There is a clear relationship between the Vienna Papyrus, which seems to have been part of a *rotulus* (scroll that was unrolled vertically and not horizontally), and MS P, the main representative of the long recension. T. E. Klutz (2005) has clearly shown how the long recension explains the redaction history for the whole *Testament* better than the shorter recension does.

Redaction, Structure, Genre

The problems posed by the redaction history, structure, and genre of the *Testament of Solomon* are so interrelated that they have to be addressed together. The preference of scholars for recension B (Duling 1983; Torijano 2002; Klutz 2005) has proven valuable not only for the textual issues but also for the redactional and compositional questions that this work poses, since it provides a better explanation for the full form of the work. Equally, the *dekani* astrological material of the Vienna Papyrus and its early dating add new insight into the composition of the text. Therefore it is quite likely that the demonological and zodiacal material of chap. 18 constituted an independent unit and circulated as such from the first century C.E. at the very least; it shows no sign of Christianization and has a positive view of King Solomon. In a parallel way, the demonological passages in the first fifteen chapters of the work would have circulated independently at least from the second century C.E. on; they share with chap. 18 the zodiacal structure and the lack of Christian characteristics, but it is likely that both documents were autonomous for a time. At the end of the second century C.E. or perhaps during the third, a Christian editor merged both texts. This new version still had a positive view of Solomon's power but tried to show the supremacy of Jesus' power over Solomon's (by the inclusion of chaps. 16–17). Finally, the document underwent further Christianization as Jewish versus Christian polemic over Solomon and Jesus grew; in this final stage the whole pro-Solomonic orientation was changed by the addition of the last chapters (19–26) and the thematic revamping of the work. This last version agrees on the whole with the form of the *Testament* as it appears in the manuscripts of recension B; it reflects a Christian setting and has a very negative image of King Solomon, who is bested at the end by the same demons that he thought were under his command. Thus, the latest form of the *Testament* transformed the Jewish sources it used with a polemical twist.

In every single manuscript, the work is labeled a "Testament" *(diathēkē)* in the title and in several passages (1:1; 15:14; 25:8). The work does have a few elements of the testamentary genre (e.g., first-person retrospective narration), but it lacks some important ones (deathbed setting, moral exhortation, and future prediction). Further, the redaction history of the *Testament* shows that a progressively negative view of Solomon crept into the text as it was rewritten by successive Christian editors, a tendency that goes against the positive impression that a testament's main character usually conveys. Scholars therefore tend to understand the work as a repository of magical and demonological lore. However, given the redaction history of the work and its use of biblical tradition (1 Kings 4–11), it is quite likely that the work was understood as a testament in late antiquity, at least in its latest form, even if some of its features do not exactly fit the genre as it appears in other texts (e.g., *Testaments of the Twelve Patriarchs, Testament of Abraham*).

Traditions and Main Themes

The thematic interest of the *Testament of Solomon,* at least of its oldest parts, is centered on esoteric lore. The relationship between Solomon and exorcism is an old one in Judaism (cf. Josephus, *Ant.* 8.44-49). The *Testament* echoes those traditions, developing a complex and comprehensive demonology. It describes the physical appearance of each demon, its powers and evil inclinations, its zodiacal affiliation according to chorographic, (i.e., geographical and group-oriented) astrology, and the angels to be invoked against it. Although demonology itself is not distinctively Jewish, it appears in the *Testament* within a double framework that has a clearly Jewish origin. The first corresponds to the well-known Jewish tradition on the role of demons in the construction of the Temple. This tradition provides the general structure that gave some continuity to the general plot of the work in its early formulation. The second one is structured around the question "Who are you?" addressed to each demon; it constitutes an exorcistic formula that it is attested already in the first century C.E. in a psalm from Qumran (11QapocPs[a] or 11Q11). This exorcistic formula appears in the Christian *Questions of Bartholomew* in a context where Solomon and Jesus are compared. Both the haggadic narration and the exorcistic formula structured the medical folk traditions that constitute the oldest stage of the *Testament of Solomon.* In the first eighteen chapters, each demon is related to a particular illness or health problem, so thematically the *Testament* is a sort of medical handbook in which both demon-caused illnesses and their remedies are described. This kind of belief, which links illness and demonic possession, is well attested in Jewish magical bowls and amulets from late antiquity, and it appears in Jewish sources up to the modern period (e.g., *Sefer Raziel*).

If medical demonology was the main interest of the oldest parts of the work, this changed in the last redactional stages, which correspond to its present Christianized form. The *Testament of Solomon* rewrites its biblical sources to emphasize the dubious morality of the relationship between Solomon and the demons. Thus, it develops an ethical perspective and depicts Solomon's final failure as a direct consequence of his unrestricted sexual drive. This aspect is conspicuous in chaps. 19–26, where several stories change the overall tone. The whole *Testament* is reinterpreted from a moral point of view, and Solomon is represented as a character who should not be emulated.

Provenance and Date

As note above, recent research proposes a development of the document in four stages (Klutz 2005). A likely chronology for the successive phases would be the following: the material now in chap. 18 was written by a Jewish author between the first century B.C.E. and first century C.E. A second document (now in chaps. 1–15), also of Jewish origin, was produced by the end of the first century or the early second century C.E. Both stages share a positive attitude toward Solomon and an interest in combining zodiacal, demonological, and medicinal lore. They make use of an old exorcistic formula that can be identified as Jewish since it is attested at Qumran. Late in the second century C.E., these two documents were combined into a single one by a Christian editor; at this point Solomon's characterization was still positive, and the material now in chaps. 6–17 plus other Christian traits were added. Finally, perhaps in the third century C.E., the work was further Christianized with the addition of the material now in chaps. 19–26. At this stage a Christian editor gave the work a clear anti-Solomonic bias.

This chronology also gives some hints about the possible place of origin for the *Testament*. The dating of the fourth and last stage depends heavily on the fact that the work is quoted in the so-called *Dialogue of Timothy and Aquila*. This text quotes the *Testament* in a setting of polemical competition between Jesus and Solomon. Thus it may be dated around the third century C.E. and located in Egypt (the *dekani* might also point to the same setting), although Palestine and Asia Minor have also been proposed.

BIBLIOGRAPHY

P. S. ALEXANDER 2003, "Contextualizing the Demonology of the Testament of Solomon," in *Die Dämonen*, ed. A. Lange, H. Lichtenberger, and D. Römheld, Tübingen: Mohr-Siebeck, 613-35. • F. C. CONYBEARE 1898, "The Testament of Solomon," *JQR* 11: 1-45. • R. W. DANIEL 1983, "The Testament of Solomon XVIII 27–28, 33–40," in *Festschrift zum 100-jährigen Bestehen der Papyrussammlung der österreichischen Nationalbibliothek: Papyrus Erzherzog Rainer*, Vienna: Brüder Hollinek, 294-304. • D. C. DULING 1983, "The Testament of Solomon," in *OTP* 1: 935-88. • D. C. DULING 1988, "The Testament of Solomon: Retrospect and Prospect," *JSP* 2: 87-112. • F. F. FLECK 1837, *Wissenschaftliche Reise durch das südliche Deutschland, Italien, Sicilien und Frankreich 2/3, Anecdota Maxima Parte Sacra*, Leipzig: J. A. Barth, 112-40. • S. I. JOHNSTON 2002, "The *Testament of Solomon* from Late Antiquity to Renaissance," in *The Metamorphosis of Magic from Late Antiquity to the Early Modern Period*, ed. J. N. Bremmer and J. R. Veenstra, Leuven: Peeters, 35-50. • T. E. KLUTZ 2005, *Rewriting the Testament of Solomon: Tradition, Conflict and Identity in a Late Antique Pseudepigraphon*, London: Clark. • C. C. MCCOWN 1922, *The Testament of Solomon, Edited from Manuscripts at Mount Athos, Bologna, Holkham Hall, Jerusalem, London, Milan, Paris and Vienna*, Leipzig: Hinrichs. • P. A. TORIJANO 2002, *Solomon the Esoteric King: From King to Magus, Development of a Tradition*, Leiden: Brill.

PABLO A. TORIJANO

Solomon, Wisdom of

The Wisdom of Solomon (as the Septuagint calls it) or Book of Wisdom (as the Old Latin and Vulgate call it) is a Hellenistic Jewish writing from around the turn of the eras that encourages the pursuit of wisdom. The author assumes the identity of King Solomon, Israel's sage par excellence, although the book was actually written centuries later. The text survives in the Septuagint, for which the earliest manuscripts date to the fourth century C.E. The work is considered part of the Apocrypha in Protestant tradition but is included in the Roman Catholic and Orthodox canons of the Old Testament.

Contents and Structure

The contents fall naturally into three sections, although locating the breaks is imprecise because the sections overlap. The first (1:1–6:21), often designated the "Book of Eschatology," contrasts the destinies of the righteous and wicked and exhorts the reader to seek wisdom, live righteously, and thereby gain immortality. Those who suppose this life to be the whole of reality are gravely mistaken. In the first of two speeches placed on their lips (2:1-20), the ungodly advise doing as one pleases because death means annihilation. In the second speech (5:4-13), the ungodly, now facing judgment, realize their miscalculation and recant: they now see that the righteous are vindicated by God, while those who mocked and persecuted them are the ones facing annihilation. In his own rebuttal of a materialistic perspective (2:21–4:20), the author contrasts appearances and reality. Apparent injustices merely prepare the righteous for ultimate blessedness. Not even the death of the righteous supports the nihilist's case. Indeed, the righteous only appear to die; through physical death they actually pass into the fullness of immortality. The wicked, on the other hand — despite any apparent benefits of their behavior — are cursed to extinction.

The second section, the "Book of Wisdom" proper (6:22–9:18), describes the nature and benefits of wisdom and Solomon's quest for her. The search for wisdom is not futile; indeed, she seeks out those who desire her. The author adopts the persona of Israel's celebrated king most clearly in 7:1-22a, where he builds on the account of Solomon's attainment of wisdom in 1 Kings 3. In a litany of praise for his beloved wisdom (7:22b–8:1), he enumerates her qualities, balancing her transcendence and immanence; she is the fashioner of all things but also indwells human beings and enables them to know the workings of the universe. The author describes his quest for wisdom as the wooing of a bride and again extols her (8:2-16). The section ends with Solomon's prayer for wisdom; expanding upon 2 Kings 3 and 2 Chronicles 1, Solomon acknowledges his human limitations and prays that the wisdom present at creation be granted him as guide and guardian (8:17–9:18).

The allusion at the end of Solomon's prayer to those "saved by wisdom" (9:18) introduces the third section, the "Book of History" (chaps. 10–19). Here the emphasis is on wisdom as God's agent directing the course of Israel's history. Chapter 10 reviews wisdom's activity in the lives of seven righteous persons from Adam to Moses and their wicked counterparts. Chapter 11 begins a lengthy meditation on the exodus and desert wanderings with a focus on seven incidents wherein God's provision for the Israelites is contrasted with his punishment of the Egyptians. The guiding principle is that God uses the very things to bless the righteous that he uses to punish the ungodly, as, for example, when he provided Israel water in the desert but polluted the Egyptians' water. An excursus on God's mercy (11:15–12:27) contends that there is proportionality and harmony even in God's acts of punishment, and another long excursus (chaps. 13–15) ridicules idolatry, especially in its Egyptian forms. The remaining chapters complete the series of contrasts which show that God delivers Israel by the same means that he punishes Egypt. The book closes by reiterating the principle of cosmic harmony according to which the just are helped and the unjust are thwarted, and finally by praising God for his providence.

Authorship, Provenance, and Date

Earlier theories of multiple authorship have given way to a solid consensus that the Wisdom of Solomon is the work of a single author. Occasional suggestions of a Semitic original have likewise been displaced by agreement that the work was composed in Greek. The author assumes the identity of Israel's wise King Solomon, but only as a literary device. The book was actually written long after Solomon by an unknown Jew steeped in Greek language, philosophy, and rhetoric as well as Israel's biblical heritage.

The place of writing is uncertain, but cumulative evidence makes Alexandria a likely site. This center of Jewish life within a Hellenistic environment affords a viable setting for the social and religious tensions reflected in the book and the most probable matrix for the philosophical traditions it adopts. The focus on the exodus and hostility toward the Egyptians in chaps. 10–19, the polemic against Egyptian animal worship, and the affinities with the thought of Philo of Alexandria all suggest composition in Alexandria.

Suggested dates range from the second century B.C.E. to the mid-first century C.E. Dependence on the Septuagint rules out composition earlier than the second century B.C.E. The address to rulers of the far reaches of the earth (6:1-4) and the reference to the cult of monarchs who rule from a distance (14:16-20) more aptly describe Roman rulers, especially the early emperors, than the Ptolemaic kings who preceded them. Linguistic evidence favors the same time frame: a number of words and constructions in the book are not attested elsewhere prior to the first century C.E. The condemnation of rulers who oppress the righteous and the intense anti-Egyptian sentiments have suggested to some a date during the reign of the emperor Caligula (37-41 C.E.) and the prefecture of Flaccus in Egypt (32-38 C.E.). The aftermath of Flaccus' revocation of Jewish civic rights and the bloody pogrom against Alexandrian Jews in 38 C.E. provide a plausible backdrop for the book, but not necessarily the only one; Jews in Roman Egypt lived in constant tension with their Greek and Egyptian neighbors. The climate of religious and philosophical debate reflected in the book transcends any particular incident and precludes a more precise dating than sometime in the early Roman period (ca. 30 B.C.E.–40 C.E.).

Genre and Purpose

Two major views of the literary genre of the work, both based on Greek rhetorical models, have been proposed: the protreptic discourse, or didactic exhortation to pursue a particular course of action; and the encomium, an epideictic form of rhetoric designed to demonstrate and praise the glories of some figure or virtue rather than to exhort or persuade. In fact, various parts of the book reflect different genres: the "Book of Eschatology" is hortatory in nature and best fits the protreptic model; the "Book of Wisdom," with its sustained praise of wisdom, is most like an encomium; and the "Book of History" is epideictic, demonstrating the historical workings of wisdom. Moreover, the generic models are not discrete: epideictic oratory functions implicitly (sometimes explicitly) as exhortation, and protreptic discourse can praise and demonstrate as well as exhort. Standard rhetorical devices within these larger generic patterns, such as the diatribe (citation of a hypothetical speaker followed by a refutation), *synkrisis* (comparison of two things in order to show the superiority of one), and *soritēs* (a chain of propositions in which the predicate of one becomes the subject of the next) also appear throughout the Wisdom of Solomon.

The question of the book's purpose is linked to the question of its intended audience. The author explicitly addresses Gentile rulers (1:1; 6:1, 9, 21), but the contents are ill suited for instructing such an audience. There is much to suggest that the author had fellow Jews primarily in mind. In assuming Solomon's identity without actually naming him, and in appealing to key figures from the Pentateuch as paradigms of the righteous without actually naming them, the author presupposes extensive biblical knowledge. Inferring the many biblical names and episodes from allusive and disjunctive references would be easy enough for Jews familiar with the biblical narrative but impossible for outsiders unless they were already very knowledgeable about Judaism. The sharp polemic against idolatry may suggest Gentile recipients but could also serve to fortify Jews in their convictions and dissuade them from assimilating to the surrounding culture. While a mixed audience is possible, the primary target audience seems to have been Jews who were enticed by Hellenistic culture and who needed affirming in their own heritage. The wisdom that was present at creation, that worked continually to save the just and hinder the wicked, and that afforded the only path to immortality, operated precisely and paradigmatically in the foundational events of Israel's own history. Jews could draw strength and pride from a tradition that was superior to the idolatrous polytheism and immorality of their neighbors and that embodied the highest philosophical ideals of the day.

Sources of Thought

Naturally the author draws extensively on the wisdom traditions of Israel, both the narrative accounts of Solomon's wisdom and the wisdom writings themselves. The personification of wisdom builds on that in Proverbs 8 and Sirach 24. As already noted, the author deploys many characters and events from the biblical narratives to illustrate wisdom's workings in history. In contrasting the fates of the righteous and wicked he is influenced by Israel's apocalyptic tradition as well as the language of persecution and vindication in Isaiah's Servant poems.

Most distinctive of the Wisdom of Solomon, however, is the synthesis of these Jewish traditions with Hellenistic thought. The development of the cosmic dimension of wisdom beyond what is found in the earlier wisdom writings is heavily indebted to Stoicism. Wisdom, like the Stoic *logos/pneuma,* is the all-pervasive principle of order in the universe. As in Stoicism, the ideal is to live in harmony with this cosmic principle of order. The pursuit of wisdom leads to the four cardinal virtues of Stoic and Platonic thought (8:7). Platonic influence is evident in the emphasis on the immortality of the soul, the doctrine of the preexistence of souls (8:19-20), the understanding of wisdom as an emanation from the transcendent creator (7:25-26), and the view that God created the cosmos out of "formless matter" (11:17). The presentation of the materialist's perspective in chap. 2 may be indebted to Epicureanism, and certain qualities and epithets predicated of wisdom may be modeled on language used to praise Isis in the cult of that Egyptian goddess.

Significance and Influence

As a blending of Jewish tradition with Hellenistic philosophical thought and rhetorical technique, the Wisdom of Solomon represents an important development in Jewish religious thought. Here, under the influence of Stoicism, the figure of wisdom takes on cosmic dimensions that are not found in the Hebrew wisdom tradition but that enable the author to bridge the exclusive nationalist tradition of Israel and the universalistic impulses of Hellenistic philosophical thought; human beings gain immortality by living in harmony with the cosmic principle of order that is accessible to all people, even if Israel's history provides the only examples. In defending God's justice and insisting that innocent sufferers are ultimately vindicated, the Wisdom of Solomon also presents one of the earliest and most vigorous Jewish affirmations of the Platonic idea of the immortality of the soul. However, here the soul's immortality is not inherent, as most Platonists assumed, but conditional: a life of justice leads to immortality, whereas a life of wickedness leads to death. In the Wisdom of Solomon the Platonic doctrine of the preexistence of souls has its first known attestation in a Jewish text.

The book had little impact on subsequent Jewish literature but influenced early Christian thought in many ways. New Testament representations of Jesus as the "image of God" (Col. 1:15-20), the "Word" (John 1:1-18), and the "reflection of God's glory" (Heb. 1:3) are reminiscent of the portrayal of wisdom in the Wisdom of Solomon. The idea of wisdom as a spirit with cosmic, personal, and historical dimensions may have influenced Pauline and other early Christian conceptions of the Holy Spirit. Among other New Testament passages possibly influenced by the Wisdom of Solomon are Paul's "natural theology" and critique of human depravity in Rom. 1:18-27 (cf. Wis. 13:1-9; 14:22-31) and the description of the armor of God in Eph. 6:11-17 (cf. Wis. 5:17-20). Patristic writers used the work directly and extensively, especially in christological formulations. For example, Origen exploited the christological potential of wisdom's portrayal in Wis. 7:25-26, and Augustine read the book's portrayal of the persecuted righteous person as a prediction of Christ's passion.

BIBLIOGRAPHY

N. CALDUCH-BENAGES AND J. VERMEYLEN 1999, *Treasures of Wisdom: Studies in Ben Sira and the Book of Wisdom,* Leuven: Peeters. • J. J. COLLINS 1997, *Jewish Wisdom in the Hellenistic Age,* Louisville: Westminster John Knox, 178-221. • L. L. GRABBE 1997, *The Wisdom of Solomon,* Sheffield: Sheffield Academic Press. • H. HÜBNER 1999, *Die Weisheit Salomons/Liber Sapientiae Salomonis,* Göttingen: Vandenhoeck und Ruprecht. • M. KOLARCIK 1991, *The Ambiguity of Death in the Book of Wisdom 1–6,* Rome: Pontifical Biblical Institute. • M. KOLARCIK 1997, "The Book of Wisdom," in *The New Interpreter's Bible,* vol. 5, Nashville: Abingdon. • C. LARCHER 1969, *Études sur le Livre de la Sagesse,* Paris: Gabalda. • C. LARCHER 1983-1985, *Le Livre de la Sagesse ou la Sagesse de Salomon,* 3 vols., Paris: Gabalda. • A. PASSARO AND G. BELLIA 2005, *The Book of Wisdom in Modern Research,* Berlin: de Gruyter. • J. M. REESE 1970, *Hellenistic Influence on the Book of Wisdom and Its Consequences,* Rome: Pontifical Biblical Institute. • D. WINSTON 1979, *The Wisdom of Solomon,* New York: Doubleday.

RANDALL D. CHESNUTT

Some of the Works of the Law → Miqṣat Maʿaśê ha-Torah

Song of Songs

The Song of Songs (*Šir ha-Šîrîm;* cf. 1:1) belongs to the Hebrew writings *(Ketuvim)* and the festival scrolls *(Megillot).* In *Biblia Hebraica Stuttgartensia,* the standard critical edition of the Hebrew Bible, the book follows Ruth and precedes Ecclesiastes, while modern Hebrew Bibles present the liturgical ordering starting with Song of Songs. In the Greek and Latin Bibles, and thus the Christian canon, the book follows Ecclesiastes. The English name Canticle(s) is derived from the Latin title *Canticum Canticorum.* The often-used label "Song of Solomon" recalls the long-held view of Solomonic authorship.

Genre and Contents

The Song of Songs offers a collection of love lyrics, in which a woman and a man express to one another the delights of their mutual love. The book partakes in the continuous tradition of ancient Near Eastern love lyrics that mention both human and divine couples (cf. Hagedorn 2005: 105-259) and that persist in Arabic love songs *(waṣfs)*. Some stanzas are arranged as a dialogue between the two lovers, who seek each other's company but fail to meet. The eight chapters of the book do not provide a discernible course of events. Most of the descriptive poems are replete with erotic overtones; the metaphors of lavish gardens and vineyards filled with fruits and fragrances symbolize the lovers' yearning for sexual intercourse. The daughters of Jerusalem are occasionally mentioned as guardians of this love affair (2:7; 3:5; 5:8, 16; 8:4). While the male lover seems to lead the rural life of a herder, there are also references to the king's army (1:9; 2:7-8; 4:4; 6:4, 12) and court (1:4; 2:7; 6:8) as well as to the city and its buildings (2:4; 3:2-3). Wandering in the city's streets by night, the woman is violently treated by soldiers (5:7). Since the book abounds in bold imagery and striking hyperbole, extravagant expressions and many *hapax legomena,* it often appears surrealistic to modern readers. By pointing to ancient Near Eastern iconography, Keel (1994) demonstrates that the descriptions of the female and male aim at a dynamic perception of the person.

Date

On the basis of occurrences of Solomon's name (1:1, 5; 3:7, 9, 11; 8:11-12), references to a king (1:4, 12; 7:6), and a general inclusion of the book into the wisdom tradition, King Solomon has traditionally been regarded as the author of the book. One rabbinic tradition ascribes the collection of love poems to the "men of Hezekiah" (*b. Baba Batra* 15a; cf. Prov. 25:1). While a preexilic origin of some passages cannot be excluded, an exact dating of the poetry is highly disputed. Most modern scholars favor a postexilic date because of late linguistic features, several genuine Aramaisms and Persianisms (Dopps-Allsopp in Hagedorn 2005: 27-77), as well as references to imported fragrances that were traded in Palestine in Persian and Hellenistic times.

Reception in Antiquity

Song of Songs is attested in four fragmentary Qumran manuscripts (4QCant[a,b,c]; 6QCant) that were copied in the Herodian period (30 B.C.E. to 70 C.E.). They have few orthographic variants to the MT but shows signs of intentional omission of literary units. The function and use of these abbreviated manuscripts (Tov 2000) or shorter literary editions (Flint in Hagedorn 2005: 96-104) is unknown. In early Jewish and Christian communities, Song of Songs has mostly been interpreted as a praise of divine love for the chosen people, either YHWH and Israel or Christ and the church. In mystic traditions, the lovers are God or Christ and the soul of the individual believer. The Old Greek version, which is dated to the first century B.C.E. or C.E., however, does not corroborate such an allegorical intention or understanding. Besides giving an overtly literal translation, the Greek text replicates phrases used elsewhere in the book (1:3, 4; 2:9, 10; 8:2, 4) in order to clarify certain passages. The traditional interpretation of the lovers as God and Israel and thus of a divine-human relationship is attested in early Jewish midrashim (e.g., *Sifre Deut.* 344 [on Deut. 33:3]) and in the Mishnah (*m. Taʿan.* 4:8). The discussion about the canonical status of the book in rabbinic sources demonstrates that this allegorical interpretation was prevalent but not fully established in early Judaism (*m. Yad.* 3:5; *t. Yad.* 2:14; *b. Megillah* 7a). Rabbi Akiba warns against a profane use of the poems in banquet halls (*t. Sanh.* 12:10; cf. *b. Sanhedrin* 101a). A dramatic interpretation was first proposed by Origen in the third century C.E. The codices Sinaiticus and Alexandrinus follow this reading by indicating the identity and order of speakers in the margins.

Use as a Festival Scroll

The Targum, composed in the seventh or eighth century C.E., interprets Song of Songs as an allegory of the history of Israel from the exodus to the age of the messiah and the building of the third Temple by inserting a lot of haggadic material. On the basis of this interpretation, Song of Songs has since medieval times come to serve as the festival scroll *(Megillah)* for Passover, the remembrance of the exodus.

Modern Interpretations

Starting in the eighteenth century, scholarship has resorted to the literal interpretation of the Song of Songs as secular love poetry. Besides this predominant reading of the text, readings of the book as a drama or as cult lyric are marginal. In the first half of the twentieth century, some scholars compared the Song of Songs with cultic liturgies of Tammuz (Adonis) and assumed an Israelite fertility cult as the setting of the original poems (cf. Ezek. 8:14). The edited version of the biblical text, however, speaks of love between humans, and the short form of God's name *(yah)* is mentioned only once (8:6). With regard to the biblical tradition of God's love for Israel and the mythological background of the metaphors, however, one may acknowledge that the allegorical interpretation of ancient readers was not artificial but based on the ancient Near Eastern idea of a divine-human relationship, which was considered beneficial for humans.

BIBLIOGRAPHY

D. M. CARR 2003, *The Erotic Word: Sexuality, Spirituality, and the Bible,* New York: Oxford University Press. • M. V. FOX 1985, *The Song of Songs and Ancient Egyptian Love Songs,* Madison: University of Wisconsin Press. • A. HAGEDORN, ED. 2005, *Perspectives on the Song of Songs/Perspektiven der Hoheliedauslegung,* Berlin: de Gruyter. • O. KEEL 1994, *The Song of Songs: A Continental Commentary,* Minneapolis: Fortress. • R. E. MURPHY 1990, *The Song of Songs,* Minneapolis: Fortress. • M. H. POPE 1977, *Songs of Songs,* New York: Doubleday. • E. TOV 2000, "Canticles [4QCant[a-c] = 4Q106-108]," in *Qumran Cave 4.XI: Psalms to Chronicles,* ed. E. C. Ulrich et al., DJD 16, Oxford: Clarendon, 195-219.

CHRISTL M. MAIER

SONGS OF THE SABBATH SACRIFICE

Songs of the Sabbath Sacrifice

The *Songs of the Sabbath Sacrifice* (sometimes called the *Angelic Liturgy*) is a poetic cycle of thirteen individual compositions, each correlated with one of the first thirteen Sabbaths of the year. The title is derived from the heading that designates each composition: *šîr ʿôlat haššabbat,* "Song of the whole offering of the Sabbath." Although the content of the songs differs according to the place of each within the cycle, every one begins with an invocation to the angels to praise God and contains description of the angels, their praise, and the heavenly realm.

Date and Provenance

Ten fragmentary copies of the composition exist, eight from Qumran Cave 4 (4Q400-407), one from Qumran Cave 11 (11Q17), and one from Masada (Mas 1 k). Since there are no historical allusions in the text, the primary clues to the date are derived from paleographical analysis. According to the standard analysis, the manuscripts from Qumran are all written in late Hasmonean and early Herodian scripts (ca. 75 B.C.E.-1 B.C.E.), whereas the 11Q and Masada manuscripts are written in developed and late Herodian hands, respectively (ca. 20-50 C.E.). Dates derived from paleographical analysis alone must be taken very cautiously. Nevertheless, a second-century-B.C.E. date for the composition of the *Sabbath Songs* seems plausible.

Although the scholarly consensus is that the *Sabbath Songs* were composed by the religious movement to which the Qumran community belonged, the evidence supporting this conclusion is actually quite slim. The large number of copies attests to the significance of the *Sabbath Songs* at Qumran, but not necessarily their origin there, especially in light of the copy found at Masada. Internal evidence from the *Songs* themselves is slight but on balance probably points toward a Qumran origin. Given the focus of the songs on angelic worship, there is little occasion in the body of the texts for the kind of sectarian organizational terminology or specifically sectarian perspectives that would identify the text as deriving from Qumran. The headings, however, perhaps preserve such a clue in the directive phrase with which each begins, "For the maskil." While it is not impossible that the term *maśkîl* could be intended as a common noun ("for the wise person"), *maśkîl* was the title of an official functionary at Qumran, one associated with teaching and liturgical functions (see 1QS 3:13; 9:12; 1QSb 1:1; 3:22; 5:20).

Contents, Structure, and Function

Despite the fragmentary nature of all of the surviving manuscripts, physical reconstruction of the remains of the best-preserved scroll and the date headings allow one to grasp the overall structure of the work and the role of particular songs in it. Each song began with a standardized heading, consisting of a directive to the *maśkîl,* the descriptive heading, and the number and date of the Sabbath according to the solar calendar (e.g., "For the *maśkîl:* song of the sacrifice of the first Sabbath on the fourth of the first month"). Following the heading is a call to praise introduced by the imperative "praise" *(hallĕlû),* a direct object (an epithet of God), and a vocative (an angelic title). A second parallel imperative call to praise always follows, and in some cases an elaborated sequence of such calls to praise. Beyond the call to praise, there is no set structure for the body of the song. Both style and content differ depending on the place of the song within the cycle.

Concerning the structure of the cycle as a whole, changes in style and content suggest that it had three distinct sections: songs 1-5, songs 6-8, and songs 9-13. The cycle may be visualized as a pyramidal structure, in which the two points of climax are the central seventh song and the concluding twelfth and thirteenth songs.

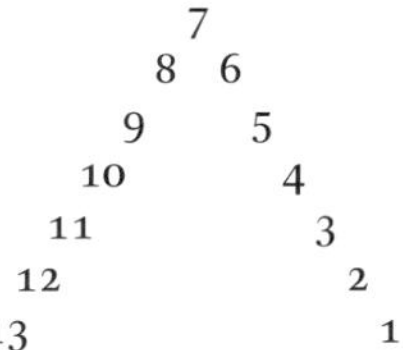

The first five songs are written in a parallel style, which can be described either as poetry or elevated prose. Grammatically, they contain ordinary syntax, including finite verbs. Although badly preserved, these songs appear to describe the establishment of the angelic priesthood and its duties, with particular attention given to describing the praise uttered by the angelic priests. The end of the fifth song contains eschatological and predestinarian themes, and refers to the role of the angels in the eschatological battle. The second song contains the only references to the human community (4Q400 frg. 2), whose own praise, priesthood, and holiness is modestly seen as incomparable to that of the angels.

The central section, songs 6-8, is strikingly different. Composed largely of repetitious literary units in which the number seven features prominently, the sixth and eighth songs are nearly mirror images of one another. These songs contain formulaic accounts of the praises and blessings of the "seven chief princes" (sixth song) and the "seven deputy princes" (eighth song). The central seventh song begins with an extended series of seven increasingly elaborate calls to praise addressed to the seven angelic councils. The rest of the song describes the way in which the parts and structures of the heavenly temple itself utter praise. Despite the broken condition of the end of the song, it appears to describe the "inner room" *(dĕbîr)* and the chariot throne of God, together with the praise of multiple chariots, cherubim, and *ʾôpannîm* ("wheels"), as well as that of godlike angels.

The description of the heavenly temple and its praise in the seventh song anticipates the content of the final group of songs 9-13. These appear to give a progressive description of the heavenly temple and its praise, culminating in an extended description of the divine chariot throne (twelfth song) and of the angelic high priests and their sacrifices (twelfth and thirteenth songs). Although only fragments of songs 9-11 remain,

SONGS OF THE SABBATH SACRIFICE

the ninth song contains references to "vestibules" and "entryways," whereas the tenth refers to the veil *(pārôket)* that separated the outer temple from the inner shrine. In the eleventh there are repeated references to the inner shrines *(dĕbîrîm)* of the heavenly temple and concludes with an account of multiple chariot thrones praising God. The twelfth song opens with an extended description of the chariot throne that bears the Glory, a description that draws exegetically on Ezekiel 1, 10 and 1 Kings 19 to explain how the chariot throne utters its praise. The song also includes an account of the praise of the angels who process in and out of the heavenly temple. Finally, in the thirteenth song comes an extended description of the appearance of the priestly angels and of their sacrificial service. In contrast to the more or less discursive style of songs 1-5 and to the highly formulaic repetition of songs 6-9, this final group of songs consists largely of nominal and participial sentences with sequences of elaborate construct chains. Thus in different ways the middle and final sections of the cycle attempt to create a numinous style.

How the *Sabbath Songs* were used remains uncertain. The numinous effect of the poetics of the cycle would be most intense if the songs were read or heard in a single encounter. While it is not impossible that the songs might have been used in such a meditative fashion, the date headings suggest that the songs were to be read individually on successive Sabbaths. The descriptive title *Songs of the Sabbath Sacrifice* might suggest either a liturgical accompaniment for the sacrificial act (cf. 2 Chron. 29:27-28; Sir. 50:22-28; *m. Tamid* 3:8; 7:3-4) or praise offered as a substitute for the *musaf* sacrifice of the Sabbath. The problem with that interpretation, however, is that there are only thirteen songs in the cycle, not the fifty-two required for a yearly cycle (cf. "David's Compositions," 11QPs[a] 17:2-11). While it has occasionally been argued that the songs might have been repeated quarterly, the numbering system (e.g., "the first Sabbath on the fourth of the first month," "the twelfth Sabbath on the twenty-first of the third month") appears to be specific to the first quarter of the year, with no indication that the songs would be repeated for the fourth through the twelfth months. Moreover, internal indications suggest a specific correlation between the content of the songs and the festival cycle of the first quarter of the year. In the Jewish calendar of the Second Temple period, the week of consecration of the priesthood is the first week of the year. Similarly, the first *Sabbath Songs* takes as its theme the establishment of the angelic priesthood. The twelfth song, with its exegetically based description of the chariot throne, occurs on the Sabbath immediately following Shavuʿot. According to evidence from manuscripts of the haftarot (liturgical readings from the Prophets), the synagogue reading for the festival of Shavuʿot included all or part of Ezekiel 1, plus Ezek. 3:12, although the date of origin for this practice cannot be determined. Nevertheless, these correlations suggest that the cycle of *Sabbath Songs* may have been shaped to coordinate with liturgical dates and readings specific to the first quarter of the year.

However the *Sabbath Songs* were recited, they served as a powerful means for cultivating the experience of communion with the angels that was vital to the religious self-understanding of the Qumran community. Deprived of access to the Jerusalem Temple because of their belief that it was polluted by improper practices, the members of the Qumran community could experience a connection with the heavenly temple through this liturgical cycle. The blessings uttered by the seven chief and deputy princes in the sixth and eighth songs also seem to be addressed not just to the angels but to a community of humans as well as angels.

Angelology and the Heavenly Temple

General terminology for the angels in the *Sabbath Songs* includes "divine beings" *(ʾēlîm),* "gods" *(ʾĕlôhîm),* "angels" *(malʾākîm),* "holy ones" *(qĕdôšîm),* and "spirits" *(rûḥôt/rûḥîm),* though these terms are often linked to descriptive attributes that underscore the knowledge, splendor, holiness, or everlastingness of the angels. Primary attention is given to the priestly functions of the angels, who are designated as "priests" *(kôhănîm)* and "ministers of the presence" *(mĕšārĕtê pānîm),* and whose functions include maintaining the purity of the heavenly temple, making propitiation for the repentant, teaching priestly Torah, pronouncing blessings, and conducting the heavenly sacrificial service. Particular attention is given to a description of the splendid angelic priestly garments.

The leadership of the angelic priests consists of seven hierarchically ranked "chief princes" *(nāśîʾê rôš)* and "deputy princes" *(nāśîʾê mišneh),* apparently corresponding to the chief and deputy high priests of the earthly priesthood (see 2 Kings 25:18; 1QM 2:1; *m. Tamid* 7:3). These leaders preside over seven angelic councils. A broken text (4Q401 frg. 11 line 3) may refer to Melchizedek as the highest ranking of the priestly angels (literally, "priest of the assembly of God").

As discussed above, the heavenly temple is described using architectural terms drawn from the biblical descriptions of the earthly sanctuaries. One of the most peculiar features of the *Sabbath Songs* is the vacillation between the depiction of the heavenly sanctuary as consisting of one or of seven sanctuaries (e.g., "the seven exalted holy places" and the antiphonal phrase that echoes from "inner room to inner room" in 4Q403 frg. 1 col. ii lines 11-15). Perhaps each of the seven angelic councils is understood to serve in a heavenly sanctuary, with the throne of Glory present in the highest-ranking sanctuary.

The traditions concerning angelic priests and the heavenly temple in the *Sabbath Songs* have significant parallels with other Second Temple literature, most significantly with *Jubilees, 1 Enoch,* and the *Aramaic Levi Document.* The depiction of heavenly worship in the early Christian book of Revelation is also strikingly similar. Yet the *Sabbath Songs* differ in being a liturgical work rather than an apocalypse or a testament. The motif of common praise of the angels, especially on the Sabbath, is also attested in the Sabbath prayer in the *Words of the Heavenly Luminaries* (4Q504-506), and with the development of the Qedushah in the synagogue liturgy, which describes angelic praise around the throne of God and which joins the earthly and heavenly communities in a common act of praise. Finally, while one cannot trace a direct line of influence, important parallels exist between the *Sabbath Songs* and the hymns found in later Jewish merkavah and Hekhalot mystical texts.

BIBLIOGRAPHY

P. ALEXANDER 2006, *The Mystical Texts: Songs of the Sabbath Sacrifice and Related Manuscripts,* London: Clark/Continuum. • J. DAVILA 2000, *Liturgical Works,* Grand Rapids: Eerdmans, 83-167. • C. H. T. FLETCHER-LOUIS 2002, *All the Glory of Adam: Liturgical Anthropology in the Dead Sea Scrolls,* Leiden: Brill, 252-394. • B. NITZAN 1994, *Qumran Prayer and Religious Poetry,* Leiden: Brill, 273-318. • C. A. NEWSOM 1987, *Songs of the Sabbath Sacrifice: A Critical Edition,* Atlanta: Scholars Press. • C. A. NEWSOM 1998, "Shirot ʿOlat Hashabbat," in *Qumran Cave 4. VI: Poetical and Liturgical Texts, Part I,* DJD 11, ed. E. Eshel et al., Oxford: Clarendon, 173-401, pls. xvi-xxxi. • C. A. NEWSOM 1999, "Angelic Liturgy: Songs of the Sabbath Sacrifice," in *The Dead Sea Scrolls: Hebrew, Aramaic, and Greek Texts with English Translations,* vol. 4B, Tübingen: Mohr-Siebeck; Louisville: Westminster John Knox.

CAROL A. NEWSOM

Son of God

Hebrew Bible

Some passages of the Hebrew Bible reflect the belief that certain figures have a special, filial relationship with God. These figures can be either individuals or a group. The Hebrew Bible occasionally refers in an honorific way to the Davidic king as God (Isa. 9:6, "Mighty God"; Pss. 45:6 and 89:28, "Highest One") or a person whose father is God (2 Samuel 7; Pss. 2:7; 89:27-28; 110:3). There are also a few passages where the people of Israel are called God's son (e.g., Exod. 4:22; Hos. 11:1). Furthermore, in Gen. 6:2, Ps. 89:7, and Dan. 3:25 heavenly beings are called "sons of God."

Dead Sea Scrolls

Some of the so-called messianic texts of the Qumran library contain the term "son of God." In these texts the phrase refers to an individual who has a preeminent role in eschatological events. In the *Rule of the Congregation* (1Q28a or 1QSa) "the messiah" is one whom God "begets." Despite the objections of some, the reading of *yôlîd* ("begets") in 1Q28a 2:11 is certain. The author of the text uses this language of begetting in much the same way that several biblical psalms do. In 4QFlorilegium, 2 Sam. 2:14 is used to describe the relationship between the "Branch of David" — the eschatological king — and God. In 4QAramaic Apocalypse (4Q246) the eschatological king is identified with the expressions "[. . . Gr]eat will he be called, and he will be designated by his name; he will be called son of God, and they will call him son of the Most High" (4Q246 i 9–ii 1). Finally, 4QPrayer of Enosh says, "You made him for you a firstbor[n] son [. . .] like him, for a prince and ruler in all your inhabited world [. . . on him] the c[row]n of the heavens and the glory of the clouds" (4Q369 1 ii 6-8). Several scholars interpret this passage collectively as referring to the people of Israel, but the text appears to have a royal individual in view.

Apocrypha and Pre-Christian Pseudepigrapha

The deuterocanonical books of the Old Testament and the pre-Christian documents among the Pseudepigrapha show little interest in using the term "son of God." Ben Sira (second century B.C.E.) calls God "my Father" (51:10) and "Father . . . of my life" (23:1, 4). In 4:10, Ben Sira says, "Be a father to orphans, and be like a husband to their mother; you will then be like a son of the Most High, and he will love you more than does your mother." According to the Wisdom of Solomon, which was composed around the turn of the era, the righteous man boasts that God is his father (2:16) and he can be called child *(pais)* of God. God is also "our Father" (14:3). These passages clearly regard the contemporary community of righteous Jews as God's sons. To these, one may add Wis. 5:5, "Why have they [the righteous] been numbered among the sons of God? And why is their lot among the holy ones?" This passage evidently envisions the righteous being elevated to angelic status, a notion found in various apocalypses.

Among the Pseudepigrapha, the *Third Sibylline Oracle* (mid-second century B.C.E.) calls God "the begetter" of "the people of God" (3:725-26). Similarly, in *T. Jud.* 24:3 (this chapter of the *Testaments of the Twelve Patriarchs* is pre-Christian) the addressees are told that they will become "sons to God." The same picture emerges in *Ps. Sol.* 13:9.

Besides the collective understanding of divine sonship, some passages of the Pseudepigrapha envisage individuals as God's sons. Ezekiel the Tragedian's drama *Exagōgē* (second century B.C.E.) describes Moses' exaltation to heaven and depicts God calling Moses "child" (line 100). According to some interpreters, the image of Moses' divine sonship is found also in Samaritan tradition, with the term "son of the house" in *Tibat Marqe.* In the ostensibly Jewish chap. 4 of the Greek *Testament of Levi,* the patriarch appears as a positive eschatological protagonist and is called "his [God's] son." Some scholars think that the phrase "I and my son" in *1 Enoch* 105:2 refers to God and his messiah, but the passage may concern Enoch and his son Methuselah. The early Jewish novella *Joseph and Aseneth* uses "son of God" and "firstborn of God" as recurrent titles for Joseph. It seems, however, that here the term is used in a more general sense, for Aseneth is called "daughter of God" (21:4), and the chosen ones of God are also referred to as "sons of God" (e.g., 16:14; 19:8). So the term may simply intend to say that Joseph is among the righteous.

New Testament

In the writings of nascent Christianity, one finds a widespread and central use of the title "son of God." Although several passages speak about humans as "sons of God" (e.g., Matt. 5:9; Luke 6:35), the main accent falls on Jesus' divine sonship. He is characterized as God's son in connection with important stages of his life: his birth (Luke 1:32, 35), his baptism (Mark 1:11 and pars.), his transfiguration (Mark 9:7 pars.), and his passion (Mark 15:39; 16:62; pars.). Most of these passages express God's granting authority to Jesus, whereas the gospel passion narratives reflect contemporary debates about Jesus' role in salvation history.

In the Pauline letters, "son" and "son of God" become key titles of Jesus (e.g., Rom. 8:3-4; Gal. 1:3-4). In Rom. 1:3-4 Paul, possibly drawing on an earlier traditional formula, refers to Jesus' divine sonship as originating in the fact of his resurrection. Other passages, however, affirm the preexistence, divinity, and incarnation of Christ (e.g., Phil. 2:6-11, though here the title "son of God" is not employed). Similar ideas are expressed in the Johannine literature (e.g., John 3:17; 1 John 4:7-16). It seems that early on the affirmation of Jesus as the Son of God became an important creedal confession.

Post-Christian Pseudepigrapha

Several Jewish pseudepigrapha postdate the birth of Christianity, and many of these texts underwent considerable Christian redaction. Hence it is not always easy to discern the distinctively Jewish elements. *Testament of Levi* 18:6 says that when a "new priest" appears "from the temple of the Glory there will come on him holiness by a voice of the Father." This verse evokes those passages in the Gospels that recount the baptism of Jesus at the Jordan. *Fourth Ezra,* a long and well-developed apocalypse from the end of the first century C.E., devotes several passages to a positive eschatological protagonist. He is sometimes called "my son, the Messiah" (7:28, 29; the word "Jesus" is a Christian addition in the Latin version of these verses) or simply "my son" (13:32, 37, 52; 14:9).

Summary

Early Jewish literature uses the term "son(s) of God" in a complex manner. It can denote both individuals and groups and refer to both earthly and transcendent figures. When it is used for denoting an individual, in most texts it refers to a positive eschatological protagonist. The title generally emphasizes the figure's authority and close relation to God.

BIBLIOGRAPHY

J. H. CHARLESWORTH ET AL., EDS. 1998, *Qumran Messianism: Studies on the Messianic Expectations in the Dead Sea Scrolls,* Tübingen: Mohr-Siebeck. • J. J. COLLINS 1995, *The Scepter and the Star: The Messiahs of the Dead Sea Scrolls and Other Ancient Literature,* New York: Doubleday, 154-72. • J. A. FITZMYER 2000, *The Dead Sea Scrolls and Christian Origins,* Grand Rapids: Eerdmans, 41-61, 63-72. • M. HENGEL 1976, *The Son of God,* Philadelphia: Fortress. • G. G. XERAVITS 2003, *King, Priest, Prophet: Positive Eschatological Protagonists of the Qumran Library,* Leiden: Brill. • A. YARBRO COLLINS AND J. J. COLLINS 2008, *King and Messiah as Son of God: Divine, Human, and Angelic Messianic Figures in Biblical and Related Literature,* Grand Rapids: Eerdmans.

GÉZA G. XERAVITS

Son of Man

Son of man, or son of a human being (Hebr. *ben 'ādām;* Aram. *bar 'ĕnāš;* Gr. [*ho*] *huios* [*tou*] *anthrōpou*), is a Semitic expression that individualizes a noun for humanity in general by prefacing it with "son of," thus designating a single member of the human species. Its meaning can be as indefinite as "someone" or "a certain person" (with "son" designating the individual as male). The term's use in Dan. 7:13-14 to refer to a humanlike figure borne on the clouds to the divine throne room became, paradoxically, the fountainhead of a multibranched Jewish and Christian tradition about a transcendental agent of God's eschatological reign and judgment.

"Son of Man" as a Human Being

The expression occurs in the Hebrew Bible thirteen times in synonymous poetic parallelism (Num. 23:19; Job 16:21; 25:6; 35:8; Ps. 8:4 [8:5 Hebr.]; 80:17 [18 Hebr.]; 146:3; Isa. 51:12; 56:2; Jer. 49:18, 33; 50:40; 51:43), always in the second member, as an emphatic counterpart for a word designating "man" or "human being" *(geber, 'îš, 'ĕnôš),* and in the Qumran Scrolls it is used in parallelism with "one born of a woman" (1QS 11:20-21). With the exception of Ps. 8:5, the term does not seem to be a "lofty" one for a human being, as is often claimed. In Ezekiel, God addresses the prophet as "son of man" *(ben 'ādām)* ninety-three times, but it is uncertain whether the expression emphasizes Ezekiel's mere human status before God, or whether he is being singled out among humans as one who is privileged to be God's messenger.

"Son of Man" as God's Transcendent Agent

Daniel 7

The night vision recounted in Daniel 7 is the end-product of a complex history of traditions with roots in ancient Near Eastern, and probably Canaanite, myth. In its present form it dates from the persecution of the Jews by Antiochus IV Epiphanes (167-164 B.C.E.). The chapter divides into two parts: the description of the vision itself (7:1-14, 19-22); and its interpretation (7:15-18, 23-27). The action in the vision is played out on two levels. Four fearsome beasts arise from the chaotic deep and carry out their activity *on earth,* where they are finally dealt with (7:1-8, 11-12). The court that judges them is *in heaven,* and it is there that the "one like a son of man" is exalted (7:9-10, 13-14).

After the heavenly court, convened by "one who is ancient of days" (the aged, white-haired deity), has judged the four beasts and burned the body of the last of them (7:9-12), "one like a son of man" *(kĕbar 'ĕnāš),* that is, a humanlike figure in contradistinction to the beasts, arrives in the heavenly court on a cloud chariot and approaches the deity, who bestows on him everlasting and indestructible "dominion, glory, and kingdom," so that "all peoples, nations, and languages will serve him" (7:13-14).

According to the interpretation, the beasts represent four kingdoms, the last of these being the Macedonian, which is making war against "the holy ones of the Most High" (7:23-25). The ten horns of the beast represent the Macedonian kings, with the tenth representing Antiochus IV and his blasphemy against the Most High. The enthronement of the "one like a son of man" means that the "kingdom and dominion and the greatness of the kingdoms under the whole heaven will be given to the people of the holy ones of the Most High; their kingdom will be an everlasting kingdom, and all dominions will serve and obey them" (7:27). The enthronement of the "one like a son of man" involves Israel's everlasting dominion over the nations of the earth. Thus the vision ends by resolving the problem with which it began: the kingdoms of the world, which have subjugated Israel, must now serve her.

The principal crux of interpretation in this vision is the identity of the "one like a son of man." The coincidence of the wording in vv. 14 and 27 suggests to many interpreters that this figure is a personification of the righteous of Israel, "the people of the holy ones of the Most High." More likely, this humanlike figure is a high angel. In 8:15 and 9:21, the angelic interpreter Gabriel is called "one having the appearance of a man *(kĕmarʾêh gāber)*" and "the man *(ʾîš)* Gabriel." That is, according to the author's apocalyptic worldview, in which events in heaven and earth correspond to one another, the righteous of Israel are the clients of the angelic host, "the holy ones of the Most High," with a special angelic patron who is the equivalent of, if not identical with, "Michael, the great prince" (Dan. 12:1). Thus the enthronement of this heavenly figure and the exaltation of Israel are heavenly and earthly counterparts of one another.

The Parables of Enoch (1 Enoch 37–71)

Composed between the late first century B.C.E. and the first half of the first century C.E., the *Parables of Enoch* focuses on the conflict between "the chosen and righteous" of Israel and their oppressors, "the kings and the mighty," who are probably the Roman rulers of Palestine. Like Daniel 7, it promises an imminent judgment; the oppressors, who now "possess the earth (or the land), will be punished, and the righteous will be vindicated and live in a transformed earth under a newly created heaven. As in Daniel 7, the righteous and chosen have their heavenly patron, who is designated variously as "the Chosen One," "the Righteous One," "the Anointed of the Lord," and "the/this/that son of man." This last designation appears first in chaps. 46–48, in a series of passages that interpret Dan. 7:9-10, 13-14. He is a transcendent heavenly figure who interacts with the deity.

However, he is not a carbon copy of Daniel's "one like a son of man." As his other designations indicate, he embodies characteristics that the Hebrew Bible ascribes to Second Isaiah's Servant of YHWH and to the Davidic king. Compare the naming scenes in *1 Enoch* 48:1-7 and Isa. 49:1-6; the nomenclature in *1 Enoch* 49:1-4 and Isa. 42:1; 49:7; the language in *1 Enoch* 48:8a, 10 and Ps. 2:2; and the imagery in *1 Enoch* 49:3-4; 51:3 and Isa. 11:3-4; and *Ps. Sol.* 17:35 (39). In addition, his existence prior to creation seems to reflect Israelite speculation about heavenly wisdom (*1 Enoch* 48:1-3, 6; cf. Prov. 8:22-31; Sir. 24:1-3).

The function of Enoch's protagonist also differentiates him from the Danielic figure. In Dan. 7:13-14, the "one like a son of man" arrives on the scene after the divine court has passed judgment on the four kingdoms, and he is enthroned as the executor of God's everlasting reign. In the *Parables,* the son of man figure is enthroned not to rule but to execute judgment against the kings and the mighty, and in this respect he is the heavenly vindicator of the righteous and chosen. The judgment scene, moreover, is described in an extensive interpretation of the last Servant song of Second Isaiah (compare *1 Enoch* 62–63 with Isa. 52:13–53:12; cf. Nickelsburg 2006: 83-107). Here the kings and the mighty, the counterparts of the astonished kings and the nations in Isaiah 52–53, are aghast when they recognize in their judge, the Chosen One, the chosen ones whom they have oppressed.

Thus, for the author of the *Parables of Enoch,* Daniel's "one like a son of man" is recast especially as the embodiment and fulfillment of Israel's messianic hopes, which were themselves reshaped in the Servant theology of Second Isaiah. Unlike Second Isaiah, however, the *Parables* do not portray a suffering figure but the heavenly patron of the suffering chosen and righteous. Hidden from their oppressors, he is the object of the faith of the chosen and righteous, to whom he is revealed in the oracles of the *Parables* (compare *1 Enoch* 48:6-7 with Isa. 49:2). His function as the executor of God's eschatological judgment reflects both the royal and Servant theologies of Isa. 11:3-4 and 42:1, 3.

4 Ezra 11–13 and 2 Baruch

The *Parables'* figure of the Chosen One makes his reappearance in two texts composed in the decades after the Roman destruction of Jerusalem in 70 C.E. *Fourth Ezra* 11–13 recasts Daniel's night vision as a pair of visions. Daniel's fourth beast (*4 Ezra* 12:11) is now an eagle representing Israel's current oppressor, the Roman Empire. The "one like a son of man" is now a "man" hidden in God's presence (*4 Ezra* 12:32; 13:26; cf. Isa. 49:3; *1 Enoch* 48:6; 62:7) but identified with the Davidic messiah (*4 Ezra* 12:31-32), who ascends from the sea on the clouds of heaven and torches Israel's enemies with the fiery breath of his mouth (*4 Ezra* 13:3-4; cf. Dan. 7:13; Isa. 11:4; *Ps. Sol.* 17:35 (39); *1 Enoch* 51:3). In *2 Baruch* 36–39 the messiah convicts and executes the leader of the fourth kingdom, and his transcendental character and function as the judge of Israel's enemies is described in chaps. 29–30 and in 53:9, 12; 72:1-6.

Wisdom of Solomon 2, 5

The Wisdom of Solomon, which dates from the early first century C.E., is relevant for our subject because it preserves an interpretation of Isaiah 52–53 akin to that in *1 Enoch* 62–63 (Nickelsburg 2006: 83-107). Here, more in keeping with the Isaianic text, the servant figure is not the heavenly patron of the suffering righteous but the suffering righteous spokesman of the Lord himself, who is put to death by his enemies but exalted to heaven, where he executes judgment on them. This variation on Second Isaiah's theme is relevant for New Testament theologies about the son of man.

"Son of Man" in the New Testament

With four exceptions (Acts 7:56; Heb. 2:6-8; Rev. 1:13; 14:14), the term "son of man" occurs in the New Testament only in the Gospels, and always on the lips of Jesus, almost exclusively with reference to himself. Scholars debate whether, and to what extent, these son of man sayings were, in some form or another, uttered by the historical Jesus, and, if so, whether they were self-referential.

The son of man sayings divide into three groups which refer, respectively, to the exalted, eschatological son of man; the death and resurrection of the son of man; and the earthly existence of Jesus *qua* human being. Sayings about the eschatological son of man often reflect the imagery and language of Dan. 7:13-14 but usually with judicial connotations or implications that suggest a tradition akin to the *Parables'* recasting of the Danielic passage. In the context of the Gospels, the eschatological son of man is always understood to be the resurrected and exalted Jesus, although Mark 8:38 may indicate that the saying originally referred to a figure other than Jesus. All four occurrences of "son of man" outside the Gospels refer to the exalted Jesus, with Heb. 2:6-8 quoting Ps. 8:5. Sayings about the death and resurrection of the son of man employ the formula of suffering and vindication that appears in the Wisdom of Solomon's recasting of Isaiah 52–53 and the variation of the judgment scene in *1 Enoch* 62–63. In keeping with the general Semitic use of the term, sayings about the earthly son of man focus on Jesus' humanity, but in some instances an allusion to this "son of man" as the future exalted son of man seems close at hand.

Although the apostle Paul never employs the expression "son of man," favoring "Lord" as a term more understandable in his Hellenistic environment, a number of his references to Jesus' future activity as God's judicial agent appear to know traditions now embedded in the Gospels.

Bibliography

D. Burkett 2000, *The Son of Man Debate: A History and Evaluation,* Cambridge: Cambridge University Press. • J. J. Collins 1993, *Daniel: A Commentary on the Book of Daniel,* Minneapolis: Fortress, 304-10. • C. Colpe 1972, *"ho huios tou anthrōpou,"* in *TDNT* 8:400-477. • D. R. A. Hare 1990, *The Son of Man Tradition,* Minneapolis: Fortress. • H. S. Kvanvig 1987, *Roots of Apocalyptic: The Mesopotamian Background of the Enoch Figure and of the Son of Man,* Neukirchen: Neukirchener Verlag. • G. W. E. Nickelsburg 2006, *Resurrection, Immortality, and Eternal Life in Intertestamental Judaism and Early Christianity,* expanded ed., Cambridge: Harvard University Press. • J. Theisohn 1975, *Der auserwählte Richter: Untersuchungen zum traditionsgeschichtlichem Ort der Menschensohngestalt der Bilderreden des Äthiopischen Henoch,* Göttingen: Vandenhoeck & Ruprecht. • E. Sjöberg 1946, *Der Menschensohn im äthiopischen Henochbuch,* Lund: Gleerup. • M. E. Stone 1990, *Fourth Ezra: A Commentary on the Book of Fourth Ezra,* Minneapolis, Fortress, 407-13. • A. Yarbro Collins 1993, "The Influence of Daniel on the New Testament," in J. J. Collins, *Daniel: A Commentary on the Book of Daniel,* Minneapolis: Fortress, 90-105. • A. Yarbro Collins and J. J. Collins 2008, *King and Messiah as Son of God: Divine, Human, and Angelic Messianic Figures in Biblical and Related Literature,* Grand Rapids: Eerdmans.

George W. E. Nickelsburg

Sons of God

Hebrew Bible

The Hebrew Bible employs the language of divine "sonship" in a number of contexts. The people of Israel are called God's son or sons (e.g., Exod. 4:22; Deut. 14:1; Hos. 1:10), and the relationship of God to the Davidic king is also described as that of a father to a son (e.g., 2 Sam. 7:14; Ps. 2:7). The expression "sons of God" or "sons of (the) gods," *bĕnê (ha)'ĕlōhîm,* however, occurs six times in the Hebrew Bible and seems without exception to refer to a class of divine beings who are subordinate to the God of Israel (Gen. 6:2, 4; Deut. 32:8; Job 1:6; 2:1; 38:7). The related expressions, "sons of the Most High/Elyon," *bĕnê ʿelyôn* (Ps. 82:6), and "sons of gods/El," *bĕnê 'ēlîm* (Pss. 29:1; 89:7 [Eng. 89:6]), are used in a similar fashion. In one Aramaic passage, the singular "son of God," *bar 'ĕlāhîn,* is also used in this manner with reference to a being who is identified as an angel of God (Dan. 3:25).

The most controversial of the occurrences of "sons of God" in the Hebrew Bible are those in the opening verses of Genesis 6. In this passage, certain "sons of God" intermingle sexually with "daughters of man" and beget children by them. The majority of critical scholars understand the expression "sons of God" in this passage as it is used elsewhere in the Hebrew Bible, with reference to divine beings. Genesis 6:1-4, when read in this way, speaks of a time when divine beings engaged in sexual intercourse with human women and spawned some impressive children. A handful of modern scholars who are uncomfortable with the presence of such a mythological account in the biblical literature have proposed some very creative alternative interpretations of this passage. Despite the ingenuity of some of these readings, that the "sons of God" in Genesis 6 are in fact divine beings makes the best sense of the passage in its ancient literary and theological context and accords best with the use of the expression "sons of God" elsewhere in the Hebrew Bible.

Second Temple Jewish Literature

In the Second Temple period, "sons of God" continued to denote divine beings, angels in particular (e.g., Wis. 5:5; cf. the singular "son of God" in Dan. 3:25). The LXX of Job 1:6; 2:1; 38:7, and Deut. 32:8 render *bĕnê (hā)'ĕlōhîm* as "angels of God" ("my angels" in Job 38:7, where the pronoun refers to God). The euphemistic "sons of heaven" also occurs with reference to these beings in several writings (e.g., *1 Enoch* 6:2; 14:3; 1QS 4:22; 11:8; 1QH 11:22; 4Q181 frg. 1 col. ii line 2). Aside from the superhuman "sons of God," the people of Israel could also be referred to as God's sons (e.g., *Jub.* 1:24, 25; *Pss. Sol.* 17:27; *1 Enoch* 62:11; Wis. 12:19-21). Similarly, the New Testament uses "sons of God" with reference to righteous individuals (Matt. 5:9; Rom. 8:14, 19; Gal. 3:26).

The earliest Jewish readers of Genesis 6:1-4 did not have the same misgivings as some of this passage's modern exegetes. For these ancient interpreters, the "sons of God" of this narrative were angelic beings, called "Watchers" or "sons of heaven" (e.g., *1 Enoch* 6:2; 14:3). According to several Jewish writings of the Second Temple period, the primary example of which is the *Book of the Watchers* (*1 Enoch* 1–36), these heavenly beings violated proper boundaries when they intermingled with human women (e.g., *1 Enoch* 15:2–16:1; Jude 6). In so doing, they created all sorts of problems for humanity. The children produced as a result of their mixed unions were a race of giants whose insatiable appetites led them to commit egregious acts of violence against humans. The Watchers also taught humans certain illicit arts by which humanity became morally corrupt. In response to the sins that were taking place on the earth, God had the Watchers imprisoned to await the final judgment and sent a great flood to destroy the transgressing angels' violent offspring along with corrupt humanity. This story functions in the early Jewish literature as a type for the eschatological era. The Watchers were sinners who received their just punishment from the deity, while Noah, the righteous man, was delivered. According to this pattern, sinners in the final age would be punished, and the righteous vindicated.

BIBLIOGRAPHY

P. S. ALEXANDER 1972, "Targumim and Early Exegesis of 'Sons of God,'" *JJS* 23: 60-71. • B. BYRNE 1979, *'Sons of God'—'Seed of Abraham': A Study of the Idea of the Sonship of God of All Christians in Paul against the Jewish Background,* Rome: Pontifical Biblical Institute. • J. J. COLLINS 2008, "The Sons of God and the Daughters of Men," in *Sacred Marriages: The Divine-Human Sexual Metaphor from Sumer to Early Christianity,* ed. Martti Nissinen and Risto Uro, Winona Lake, Ind.: Eisenbrauns, 259-74. • G. COOKE 1964, "The Sons of (the) God(s)," *ZAW* 76: 22-47. • R. S. HENDEL 1987, "Of Demigods and the Deluge: Toward an Interpretation of Genesis 6:1-4," *JBL* 106: 13-26. • G. W. E. NICKELSBURG AND J. C. VANDERKAM 2004, *1 Enoch: A New Translation,* Minneapolis: Fortress.

See also: Angels; Evil; Fallen Angels

RYAN E. STOKES

Spirit, Holy

Early Jewish texts that discuss the holy spirit reflect a vast range of concerns, including creation, purification, prophetic inspiration, and the interpretation of Scripture. This spirit, however, was not understood in static terms; it could be construed as a reality akin to the Stoic *pneuma,* the *pneumata* that inspired sibyls and priestesses, even Socrates' *daemon.* Though rooted in the Jewish Scriptures, in other words, conceptions of the spirit were fluid and indebted to Greco-Roman culture.

Dead Sea Scrolls and Early Pseudepigrapha

The Dead Sea Scrolls offer a range of contexts in which the holy spirit plays a significant role. In CD 7:4 and 5:11-13, "holy spirit" replaces the biblical term *nepeš* (Lev. 11:43; 20:25), in statements that the human spirit can be defiled. One wisdom author instructs, "Do not for any money exchange your holy spirit, for no price is adequate" (4Q416 frg. 2 col. ii lines 6-7).

Spirit and prophecy are aligned in some of the Dead Sea Scrolls. Following from Neh. 9:30 and Zech. 7:12, 1QH^a 8:15-16 roots study of Torah and right actions in "what the prophets have revealed through his holy spirit." In *Jub.* 31:12, "a spirit of prophecy came down upon" Jacob (see 25:14); and in *1 Enoch* 91:1, Enoch claims, "the spirit is poured over me so that I may show you everything that shall happen to you forever."

A principal work of the spirit is purification. The psalmist in the *Thanksgiving Hymns* praises God for choosing "to purify me with your holy spirit" (1QH^a 8:20). The *Community Rule* may provide the historical context of purification: an annual covenant renewal ceremony that may have included immersion of the purified initiates (1QS 3:7-8).

The spirit was also believed to inspire their particular interpretation of Scripture. A hymn writer, perhaps the Teacher of Righteousness, traces this interpretation to the spirit: "And I, the Instructor, have known you, my God, through the spirit which you gave (in)to me, and I have listened loyally to your wonderful secret through your holy spirit" (1QH^a 20:11-12). The content of such inspired interpretation may be evident in such texts as the *Habakkuk Commentary,* in which ancient Scripture is applied directly to the recent past and immediate future of the community.

The spirit also has a communal dimension: "And it is by the holy spirit of the community, in its truth, that he is cleansed of all his iniquities" (1QS 3:6). This is expressed by the image of a spirit-filled temple:

> When these exist in Israel in accordance with these rules in order to establish the spirit of holiness in truth eternal, in order to atone for the guilt of iniquity and for the unfaithfulness of sin, and for approval for the earth, without the flesh of burnt offerings and without the fats of sacrifice . . . in order to form a most holy community, and a house of the Community for Israel, those who walk in perfection. (1QS 9:3-6)

This communal dimension is apparent in *Jub.* 1:20-21, where Moses, recalling Psalm 51, intercedes for Israel, "Create a pure heart and a holy spirit for them." God responds in turn by recalling Psalm 51 and Ezek. 11:19-20, "And I shall create for them a holy spirit, and I shall purify them" (*Jub.* 1:22-25).

A distinctive portion of the Qumran *Community Rule* is the so-called "Teaching on the Two Spirits," which is spun from Gen. 2:7:

> God created humanity to rule the world and placed within him two spirits so that he would walk with them until the moment of his visitation: they are the spirits of truth and of deceit. From the spring of light stem the generations of truth, and from the source of darkness the generations of deceit. And in the hand of the Prince of Lights is dominion over all the sons of justice; they walk in paths of light. And in the hand of the Angel of Darkness is total dominion over the sons of deceit; they walk in paths of darkness. (1QS 3:17-21).

Three levels of struggle emerge from Gen. 2:7: anthropological (two spirits struggling within); collective (two opposing generations); and cosmic (the Prince of Lights and the angel of Darkness).

Philo Judaeus

Philo's various interpretations of the spirit are deeply indebted to popular Greco-Roman philosophies. The interpretation of the inbreathing of Gen. 2:7 as the impartation of the rational mind and the capacity for virtue reflects the influence of Stoicism. Seneca believed that a holy spirit resides within, providing the capacity for virtue if it is well-tended (*Leg. Alleg.* 1.31-42; Seneca, *Epistles* 41). The Stoic character of the spirit comes to fullest flower in Philo's interpretation of the spirit that inspired Bezalel (Exod. 31:3) as "susceptible of neither severance nor division, diffused in its fullness everywhere and through all things" (*De Gigantibus* 27). Alexander of Aphrodisias, summarizing the view of the renowned Stoic thinker Chrysippus, writes that *pneuma* is that "which wholly pervades it [the cosmos] and by which the universe is made coherent and kept together" (*On Mixture* 216.14-17).

The association of the spirit and prophecy evinces a decidedly popular Greco-Roman flair, in which loss of control is the unmistakable sign of inspiration. In his interpretation of the word *ekstasis* in LXX Gen. 15:12, Philo writes, "This is what regularly befalls the fellowship of the prophets. The mind is evicted at the arrival of the divine Spirit, but when that departs the mind returns to its tenancy" (*Her.* 265; see *Spec. Leg.* 1.65; 4.49; *QG* 3.9). Though Moses would differ from the prophetic race by his ability to speak without losing control of his mind, he too experienced "that divine possession in virtue of which he is chiefly and in the strict sense considered a prophet" (*Mos.* 2.191).

Inspiration also takes on the characteristics of a magnificent Roman rhetor. Abraham, though not of noble lineage,

> whenever he was possessed, everything in him changed to something better, eyes, complexion, stature, carriage, movements, voice. For the divine spirit which was breathed upon him from on high made its lodging in his soul, and invested his body with singular beauty, his voice with persuasiveness, and his hearers with understanding. In such a state, he was ranked among the prophets. (*Virt.* 217–19)

Philo even attributes his own interpretation of Scripture to inspiration. In *Spec. Leg.* 3.1-6, he is wafted upon the winds of knowledge through the ascent of his mind; during these episodes, he peers into the deepest meaning of Moses' writings. Philo claims to be taught, when he is *compos mentis,* the meaning of Scripture by his customary friend (*Spec. Leg.* 2.252; cf. *Cher.* 27–29; *Somn.* 1.164-65; and *Fug.* 53–58). The word "customary," which Philo uses to describe the divine spirit, is evocative of Socrates' daemon, which Plato refers to as "the customary prophetic inspiration of the daemon" (*Apology* 40A; see *Phaedrus* 242B; Plutarch, *Genius of Socrates* 589D).

Flavius Josephus

Like the authors of the DSS and Philo, Josephus associates the spirit and prophecy. In his *Antiquities of the Jews,* he adds references to prophecy in scriptural contexts that refer only to the spirit. For example, while 1 Sam. 16:13 recounts that "the spirit of the LORD came mightily upon David from that day forward," Josephus adds that David, "when the divine spirit had removed to him, began to prophesy" (*Ant.* 6.166; see also 8.408).

To a lesser extent than Philo, Josephus claims to be an inspired interpreter of Scripture. In an instance of self-exoneration, he explains why he surrendered to Rome: "and Josephus . . . was an interpreter of dreams and skilled in divining the meaning of ambiguous utterances of the Deity . . . not ignorant of the prophecies in the sacred books. At that hour he was inspired to read their meaning . . ." (*J.W.* 3.351-53).

Apocrypha

Wisdom Literature

Ben Sira associates a spirit of wisdom with interpretation when he describes the scribal calling: "he will be filled by a spirit of understanding/he will pour out his own words of wisdom" (Sir. 39:6). Although it sounds as if a scribe succumbs to the influence of an external spirit, as in Acts 2:4, it is more likely that Ben Sira urges his students to cultivate spirits of wisdom. Ben Sira repudiates visions and claims to revelation; disciplined study alone is the source of insight into Scripture. Such discipline is the path to being filled with a spirit of understanding.

In contrast, the later Alexandrian author of the Wisdom of Solomon regards the spirit as a gift: "I prayed . . . and the spirit of wisdom came to me" (7:7); and "Who has learned your counsel, unless you . . . sent your holy spirit from on high?" (9:17). Yet, as in Philo's writings, the spirit, at the book's beginning, is metamorphosed along Stoic lines: "the spirit of the Lord has filled the world, and that which holds all things together knows what is said . . ." (1:7-8).

Novellas

In Jdt. 16:14, Gen. 2:7, combined with Ps. 104:29-30, influences the depiction of the spirit: "You sent forth your spirit, and it formed [built] them." The verb "create" or "form" is supplanted in Judith by the verb "build," lifted from Gen. 2:22. Consequently, in a surprising exegetical move, the formation of woman, not man, becomes the paradigm of creation in the victory song of this Jewish heroine.

In the slender tale of Susannah, God raises up "the holy spirit" of a youthful Daniel (Theodotion 44/45). As in CD 7:4, 5:11-13, and 4Q416 2 ii 7, the spirit within a human being from birth is described as "the holy spirit."

4 Ezra

In response to Ezra's prayer for the holy spirit (*4 Ezra* 14:22), Ezra is given the promise that the lamp of understanding will remain lit throughout his experience, during which he dictates ninety-four books. When he drinks a cup given to him, his heart pours forth understanding, and wisdom increases within him. Following his experience, it is said that these ninety-four books contain "the spring of understanding, the fountain of wisdom, and the river of knowledge" (14:47). This is an experience of inspiration in which the mind is made more alert, not less — an impression confirmed by the significant detail that Ezra's own spirit retained its memory (14:40).

Later Pseudepigrapha

The association of the spirit with prophecy characterizes many Jewish pseudepigrapha. One statement of a sybil, the Greco-Roman counterpart of the Jewish prophet, sounds like the Stoic affirmation of Wis. 1:6-7: "the spirit of God which knows no falsehood is throughout the world" (*Sib. Or.* 3.696-701).

The *Biblical Antiquities* of Pseudo-Philo is replete with spirit references. The spirit, not surprisingly, inspires prophecy: Miriam is the recipient of a dream in which the birth of Moses is predicted (*Bib. Ant.* 9:10); Deborah is said to have predicted Sisera's demise by the inspiration of the spirit (31:9); to the military accomplishments of the first judge, Othniel (Judg. 3:9-10), are added a prophetic experience (28:6): "when they had sat down, a holy spirit came upon Kenaz . . . and he began to prophesy." Even an abbreviated account of Saul's pursuit of David contains an extrabiblical reference to prophecy: "And [a] spirit abided in Saul, and he prophesied" (62:2).

As in the writings of Philo and Josephus, inspired prophecy in *Biblical Antiquities* begins to look less like Israelite prophecy and more like the inspiration associated with Delphi and a variety of Greco-Roman prophetic figures. The inspiration of Joshua in *Bib. Ant.* 20:3, for example, melds biblical and Greco-Roman ingredients. To Deut. 34:9a, "Joshua son of Nun was full of the spirit of wisdom," the work adds, "his mind was afire and his spirit was moved, and he said . . ." (20:3). These added elements reflect the hallmarks of enthusiasm in a classic text, Cicero's *On Divination* 1.114, where the winged soul is "inflamed and aroused," or Plutarch's *De Defectu Oraculorum* 432E-F, in which the "soul becomes hot and fiery, and throws aside the caution that human intelligence lays upon it" (see also *Bib. Ant.* 28:10).

The novella *Joseph and Aseneth* spins from Gen. 41:45 a tale of love that culminates in Aseneth's conversion to Israelite faith. Prior to their marriage, "they kissed each other for a long time. . . . And Joseph kissed Aseneth and gave her spirit of life, and he kissed her the second time and gave her spirit of wisdom, and he kissed her the third time and gave her spirit of truth" (19:10-11).

Other pseudepigrapha root a vision of the messiah in Isaiah 11 (e.g., *1 Enoch* 49:2-3; *Ps. Sol.* 17:37). *T. Levi* 18:7, 10-12 predicts:

> And the glory of the Most High shall burst forth upon him. And the spirit of understanding and sanctification shall rest upon him. . . . And he shall open the gates of paradise; he shall remove the sword that has threatened since Adam, and he will grant to the saints to eat of the tree of life. The spirit of holiness shall be upon them. And Beliar shall be bound by him. And he shall grant to his children the authority to trample on wicked spirits.

Even if the *Testament of Levi* is not a Jewish but a Christian work, 11QMelchizedek is Jewish. Here the peaceful herald of Isa. 42:7 merges with the anointed one in Dan. 9:25, who is called "the anointed of the spirit."

In the Syriac *Apocalypse of Baruch,* Baruch prays, "you who created the earth, the one who fixed the firmament by the word and fastened the height of heaven by the spirit" (*2 Bar.* 21:4). God responds, "For my spirit creates the living" (23:5). As in Jdt. 16:14, the spirit becomes an active agent in creation.

Conclusion

For over a century, scholarship has perpetuated a reconstruction according to which Jews believed that the holy spirit had departed from Israel with the death of the classical (postexilic) Israelite prophets. This view was supported both by cobbling together diverse literary texts (Ps. 74:9; 1 Macc. 4:46, 9:27, and 14:41; Josephus, *Ag. Ap.* 1.37-41; *2 Bar.* 85:3; Prayer of Azariah 15; and *t. Soṭah* 13:2-4) and by putting undue weight upon a late saying from the Tosefta. This brief entry offers evidence to dispel this misperception that Judaism was spiritually arid. On the contrary, many quarters of Judaism were often swept up in the winds of inspiration.

BIBLIOGRAPHY

D. E. AUNE 1983, *Prophecy in Early Christianity and the Ancient Mediterranean World,* Grand Rapids: Eerdmans. • H. GUNKEL 1979, *The Influence of the Holy Spirit: The Popular View of the Apostolic Age and the Teaching of the Apostle Paul,* trans. R. A. Harrisville and P. A. Quanbeck II, Philadelphia:

Fortress. • J. R. LEVISON 1997A, "Did the Spirit Withdraw from Judaism? An Evaluation of the Earliest Jewish Data," *NTS* 43: 35-57. • J. R. LEVISON 1997B, *The Spirit in First-Century Judaism,* Leiden: Brill. • J. R. LEVISON 2009, *Filled with the Spirit,* Grand Rapids: Eerdmans. • R. P. MENZIES 1991, *The Development of Early Christian Pneumatology: With Special Reference to Luke-Acts,* Sheffield: JSOT. • G. T. MONTAGUE 1976, *Holy Spirit: Growth of a Biblical Tradition,* New York: Paulist. • P. SCHÄFER 1972, *Die Vorstellung vom heiligen Geist in der rabbinischen Literatur,* Munich: Kösel. • G. N. STANTON ET AL., EDS. 2004, *The Holy Spirit and Christian Origins,* Grand Rapids: Eerdmans. • M. M. B. TURNER 1996, *Power from on High: The Spirit in Israel's Restoration and Witness in Luke-Acts,* Sheffield: Sheffield Academic Press.

JOHN R. LEVISON

Stars

The night sky is a source of inspiration and awe, at the same time completely quiet yet teeming with activity. The sky and the celestial bodies in it are the only things that have been witnessed by all humans since the dawn of history. All human societies have gazed skyward and have tried to solve the mysteries of the cosmos "up there" and to divine what information it might reveal.

Ancient Near East and Hebrew Bible

Although they knew the sun, moon, planets and stars by different names, the people of the ancient Near East all viewed these celestial bodies as gods and accorded them the appropriate worship. Human reverence for these celestial bodies (stars) stems from the perception, in part correct, that they influence events on earth. The position of these bodies during the course of the year indicated seasons, and for agriculturalists this knowledge was essential for successful planting and harvesting. For this reason the ancients observed the location of the stars as they appeared on the horizon or moved in the sky during the year. But these observations quickly became the responsibility of the governing authorities, for information about the stars was thought to be valuable not only for guiding farmers but also for predicting coming events. The sheer number of astronomical texts that have survived from ancient Mesopotamia, Egypt, Greece, and Rome is enormous. Each of these cultures had skilled professionals who carefully recorded details about the relative positions, movements, and appearance of these bodies. Alongside detailed astronomical observations grew a literature interpreting the "meaning" of the various astronomical features such as the relative positions of stars, their position on the horizon at sunset or dawn, and their physical appearance. Astrology, therefore, was an integral part of astronomy in antiquity. The skilled astronomers, who were also astrologers, would consult vast records of astronomical details and accompanying accounts of associated events, and they would "predict" what might occur next. These predictions could pertain to individuals, the king, or the tribe or nation at large. Behind all this lies the belief that the stars are the physical manifestations of gods; and since the gods control events on earth, knowledge of the stars can provide insight into what might happen on earth. Even biblical tradition suggests that the outcome of human battles is merely the earthly manifestation of battles between the stars (gods) of the respective combatants in heaven (Judg. 5:19-20). As gods, therefore, the stars, indeed all celestial bodies, must be worshiped and appeased. This practice was also common in ancient Israel and Judah. Worship of the celestial bodies was a natural part of all religions in the ancient Near East. Nonetheless, this so offended the biblical editors that they record legislation against it (Deut. 4:19). The prophet Isaiah bemoans the worship of celestial bodies, mostly because this would detract from the worship of Yahweh, whom the biblical editors imagined as the creator and sustainer of all cosmic forces (Isa. 47:13). These two texts alone attest to the vitality of this practice in ancient Israel and Judah, although many religious officials found it offensive.

Early Judaism

During the Hellenistic era Jewish images of the cosmos and the power of the celestial bodies began to change as Jews interacted with Greco-Roman astronomy and religious ideas. *1 Enoch* 72–82, the Enochic *Astronomical Book,* continues a long astronomical tradition by providing detailed calculations for the movements of the celestial bodies (Albani 1994).

Stars also became a symbol of the heavenly realm and of the righteous who would one day ascend to heaven (Dan. 12:1-3; *2 Bar.* 51:10). This connection between humans and the celestial realm redefines humanity's relationship to the cosmos. The righteous could now hope to transcend the physical realm and be integrated to the vast divine realm "up there." This comports with aspects of Greco-Roman religion such as the various Gnostic religions that imagined the physical realm as something so thoroughly corrupt that it must be transcended.

Moreover, as they drew on biblical traditions, humans viewed stars as symbols or divine agents of punishment or deliverance (cf., e.g., *Sib. Or.* 5.155-60; *1 Enoch* 80:7-8; cf. Num. 24:17; Rev. 1:20). Tellingly, the leader of the second Jewish revolt against Rome was nicknamed Bar Kokhba ("son of the star").

Early Jewish communities also used stars and constellations in their iconography. The zodiac appears in several texts (e.g., *2 Enoch* 21; 4Q186, 318; *Treatise of Shem*) and in several early Palestinian synagogues (notably Beth Alpha and Hammat-Tiberias; cf. Fine 2005). The stars and the accompanying zodiac imagery became powerful symbols for these early Jewish communities, and they expressed Jewish religious ideals in a creative and meaningful blend of ancient and Hellenistic Jewish images of the celestial bodies. Thus, the stars and other celestial bodies continued to attract the fascination of the Jewish religious imagination.

BIBLIOGRAPHY

M. ALBANI 1994, *Astronomie und Schöpfungsglaube: Untersuchungen zum astronomischen Henochbuch,* Neukirchen-

Vluyn: Neukirchener Verlag. • J. EVANS 1998, *The History and Practice of Ancient Astronomy,* Oxford: Oxford University Press. • S. FINE 2005, *Art and Judaism in the Greco-Roman World,* Cambridge: Cambridge University Press.

See also: Astronomy and Astrology; Resurrection

J. EDWARD WRIGHT

Stone Vessels

Usage of limestone or "chalk" vessels was common among Jews throughout Palestine in the decades immediately preceding and following the destruction of the Second Temple. They have been found at dozens of sites in Judea and Galilee, as well as at Gamla in the Golan Heights and at Machaerus, ʿEin ez-Zara, and Mt. Nebo in the Transjordan. They are quite rare, however, in Samaria and in Diaspora settings. A variety of types were made, including jar stoppers, inkwells, mugs (often erroneously called "measuring cups" in older scholarly literature), goblets, trays, bowls, kraters, storage jars, and (less commonly) tables. Most types were produced using a lathe, some were carved entirely by hand, and some required both methods. Some forms are typologically similar to vessels made of clay, metal, or glass. Thus, kraters built with bases have been compared to the Greco-Roman washbasin (the labrum), and shallow bowls have been compared to imported *terra sigillata* wares. A few stone vessels have been found with inscriptions.

With obvious exceptions like tables and trays, stone vessels were designed to hold liquids. Literary sources (*m. ʾOhol.* 5:5; *b. Šabbat* 58a; John 2:6) indicate that they were regarded as unsusceptible to ritual impurity, along with vessels made of dung or of unfired earth (*m. Kelim* 4.4; *m. Yad.* 1:2; *m. Parah* 5:5). They were reportedly used at the Temple to mix the ashes created by the burning of the red heifer (*m. Parah* 3:2; 5:5).

The role of stone vessels in the purity system allows archaeologists to use their presence at a site as an indicator of Jewish inhabitants, and their widespread discovery in Galilee has played a major role in recent scholarly arguments that the region was predominantly Jewish. Some scholars, however, have downplayed their purity function, suggesting that their appeal was partly utilitarian, with their popularity due to sturdiness or stylistic trends.

Exactly when usage of stone vessels began is uncertain, but it clearly increased in the late first century B.C.E., when Herod's renovation of the Jerusalem Temple resulted in increased quarrying of limestone. The phenomenon of their usage is thus related to that of stone ossuaries, which also began at that time. Fragments of stone vessels are very common in mid-first-century-C.E. strata, especially in destruction layers from the First Jewish Revolt, suggesting that this was the apex of their usage. Manufacture and usage dwindled after the revolt, apparently ceasing altogether by the mid-second century C.E. Some have suggested that their disappearance was due to a decreased emphasis on ritual purity in the wake of the Temple's destruction; others have noted, however, that the Temple's demise did not diminish the interest in ritual purity among the rabbis and many other Jews.

Stone vessels have been found in both urban and rural settings and in homes both large and small. Aside from more expensive large storage jars, kraters, and tables, which appear primarily in homes of urban elites, their usage seems to have cut across class lines. Misshapen or partially formed pieces, cores removed during the manufacture of jars, chips, and/or quarries attest to the presence of significant workshops at numerous sites including Jerusalem (the southwest corner of the Temple Mount, the "City of David," Mt. Zion, the Jewish quarter, Mt. Scopus), Gethsemane, Jebel Mukkabar, Tell el-Ful, Hizma, and, in Galilee, Reina and Bethlehem. Lesser numbers of cores found at other sites indicate small-scale production by artisans.

The extent to which usage of stone vessels was associated with particular subgroups within Judaism is unclear. Priests had an obvious need to maintain purity, and many vessels, including some of the more expensive and elaborate forms, have been found in the homes of priestly elites in Jerusalem. Mugs and kraters have been found at Qumran, attesting to a place for them in that sect's understanding of the purity system. Some scholars have suggested that the widespread use of stone vessels is an indication of the strength of Pharisaic influence; alternatively, Pharisaic preference for such vessels might merely reflect larger social trends. Perhaps many users of stone vessels identified with no particular sect or party. It is also possible that some Jews found no place within their understanding of the purity system for the innovation of stone vessels. Our sources are too limited to allow confident answers to such questions.

BIBLIOGRAPHY

J. M. CAHILL 1992, "Chalk Vessel Assemblages of the Persian, Hellenistic and Early Roman Periods," in *Excavations at the City of David 1978-1985,* ed. A. de Groot and D. T. Ariel, Jerusalem: Israel Antiquities Authority, 3: 190-274. • R. DEINES 1993, *Jüdische Steingefäße und pharisäische Frömmigkeit,* Tübingen: Mohr-Siebeck. • S. GIBSON 2003, "Stone Vessels of the Early Roman Period from Jerusalem and Palestine: A Reassessment," in *One Land — Many Cultures: Archaeological Studies in Honour of Stanislao Loffreda OFM,* ed. G. C. Bottini, L. Di Segni, and L. D. Chrupcala, Jerusalem: Franciscan Printing Press, 287-308. • Y. MAGEN 1994, *"Purity Broke Out in Israel,"* Catalogue no. 9, the Reuben and Edith Hecht Museum, University of Haifa. • Y. MAGEN 2002, *The Stone Vessel Industry in the Second Temple Period: Excavations at Hizma and the Jerusalem Temple Mount,* Jerusalem: Israel Exploration Society and Israel Antiquities Authority. • E. M. MEYERS 2008, "Sanders's 'Common Judaism' and the 'Common Judaism' of Material Culture," in *Redefining First-Century Jewish and Christian Identities: Essays in Honor of Ed P. Sanders,* ed. F. E. Udoh et al., Notre Dame: University of Notre Dame Press, 153-74. • S. S. MILLER 2003, "Some Observations on Stone Vessel Finds and Ritual Purity in Light of Talmudic Sources," in *Zeichen aus Text und Stein: Studien auf den Weg zu einer Archäeologie des Neuen Testaments,* ed. S. Alkier and

J. Zangenberg, Tübingen and Basel: Francke, 402-20. • J. REED 2003, "Stone Vessels and Gospel Texts: Purity and Socio-Economics in John 2," in *Zeichen aus Text und Stein: Studien auf den Weg zu einer Archäologie des Neuen Testaments,* ed. S. Alkier and J. Zangenberg, Tübingen and Basel: Francke, 381-401. • J. ZANGENBERG 2008, "Common Judaism and the Multidimensional Character of Material Culture," in *Redefining First-Century Jewish and Christian Identities: Essays in Honor of Ed P. Sanders,* ed. F. E. Udoh et al., Notre Dame: University of Notre Dame Press, 175-83.

MARK A. CHANCEY

Suffering Servant

"Suffering Servant" has become a standard term for the anonymous "servant" (Hebr. *ʿebed;* Gk. *pais*) of the LORD who is the protagonist of the so-called fourth Servant Song in Isaiah 53 (Isa. 52:13–53:12). If the identity of the Servant is sought in the book of Isaiah itself, the two main candidates are the exiled nation of Israel or an anonymous individual, the prophet whom modern scholarship knows as Second Isaiah, eulogized in this poem after his death (cf. Isa. 53:7-9, 12), presumably by his disciples. The motif of vicarious suffering in Isaiah 53 was enormously influential in Christian tradition, which applied it to the ministry and passion of Jesus (e.g., Rom. 4:25; 1 Cor. 15:3b). In pre-Christian Judaism, however, Isaiah 53 was not understood in terms of vicarious suffering.

Isaiah 53

The Servant's suffering is *vicarious:* "upon him was the punishment that made us whole, and by his bruises we are healed" (Isa. 53:5); "the LORD has laid on him the iniquity of us all" (v. 6); *undeserved:* "he had done no violence, and there was no deceit in his mouth" (v. 9); and *divinely ordained:* "Yet it was the will of the LORD to crush him" (v. 10). Several additional ideas have influenced the text's diverse reception. These include the Servant's being exalted or glorified by God (52:13), seeing the "light" (53:11 according to 1QIsa^{a-b}, 4QIsa^{d}, LXX, against MT), benefiting others by making them righteous (53:11) and by interceding for them (53:12), and surprising others by appearing as their judge (52:15). Moreover, the text includes the voice of a minority "we" who want their message about the Servant to be "believed" (53:1) and who, after an initial hesitation or distancing of themselves from the Servant (53:2-3, 4b), have concluded that he bore divine punishment not for his own sins, as it first appeared (53:4b), but for theirs (53:4a, 5-6). These speakers are the beneficiaries of the Servant's work, identical with the "many" whom he makes righteous (53:11) and whose sins he bears (53:11, 12); by implication they could be called "believers" (cf. 53:1).

Echoes in Daniel 12

The Hebrew Bible's most identifiable echo of Isaiah 53 is found in Dan. 12:3b, which speaks of "the wise" *(maśkîlîm)* as "those who make the many righteous," parallel to Isaiah's Servant who will "make the many righteous" (Isa. 53:11). The wise and a portion of the many whom they benefit are promised resurrection and eternal life in Dan. 12:2, with an allusion to Isa. 26:19. Moreover, Daniel's wise ones will "shine like the brightness of the sky, like the stars forever and ever" (Dan. 12:3); in this respect, they resemble Isaiah's Servant, who is "raised to great heights" (Isa. 52:13, NJPS) and sees the "light" (Isa. 53:11; 1QIsa^{a-b}; 4QIsa^{d}; LXX).

Echoes in Wisdom of Solomon

The Wisdom of Solomon (ca. 30 B.C.E. to 70 C.E.) pits the wicked "we" against the individual righteous man or *dikaios* (Wis. 2:12, 18; cf. Isa. 53:11). The wicked condemn the righteous man to a shameful death in Wis. 2:20. At the final judgment, the wicked "will be amazed" *(ekstēsontai)* at the unexpected salvation of the righteous man (Wis. 5:2), just as Isaiah's many "will be amazed" *(ekstēsontai)* at the Servant (Isa. 52:14). Moreover, Wisdom's "we" confess, "it was we who strayed *(eplanēthēmen)* from the way *(hodos)* of truth" (Wis. 5:6), just as Isaiah's "we" confess, "All we like sheep have gone astray *(eplanēthēmen),* each . . . in his own way *(hodos)*" (Isa. 53:6). Both groups realize an error in their thinking and the correct alternative. Hence Wisdom's speakers exclaim, "This is the man whom we once held in derision . . . we fools! We thought *(elogisametha)* that his life was madness and that his end was without honor *(atimon),*" when in fact he is now numbered among the sons of God (Wis. 5:4-5; cf. Isa. 53:3-4). At this point, however the parallel breaks down: there is no vicarious suffering or sin-bearing of Wisdom's righteous man on behalf of sinners. Where the sinful "many" are made righteous in both Isaiah and Daniel (Isa. 53:11 MT; Dan. 12:3), Wisdom's "we" can only lament that "the light of righteousness did not shine on us" (Wis. 5:6).

Echoes in the Dead Sea Scrolls

The Dead Sea Scrolls offer parallels to the language of Isaiah 53 and are often appealed to in quests for a pre-Christian suffering Messiah. However, like the texts from Daniel and Wisdom, they tend to reproduce the suffering-plus-exaltation motif from Isaiah 53 without clearly reflecting Isaiah's language of vicarious suffering. Of the four manuscripts of the Qumran *Self-Glorification Hymn,* 4Q491c frg. 1 (= 4Q491 frg. 11) is the most relevant. In line 5 the anonymous narrator, evidently a now-exalted human being and not an originally divine figure, boasts of inhabiting "a mighty throne in the congregation of the gods" or angels *(ʾĕlōhîm).* In the next line he declares, "no one is exalted besides me" (cf. Isa. 52:13). The clearest allusion is in line 8, "who is esteemed despicable like me," which shares two terms with Isa. 53:3 *(ḥšb, bwz).* The borrowing, though, is very selective and falls short of reflecting the unique feature of vicarious suffering.

Scholars continue to discuss whether the Qumran Teacher of Righteousness saw himself in light of Isaiah's Servant passages. The debate centers on the so-called Teacher Hymns in the *Hodayot* (1QH^{a} cols. 10-

16), which he is thought to have written. The most telling verbal allusion comes with the collocation of the terms for being "despised" and not "esteemed" — words that are paired only once in the entire Hebrew Bible, in Isa. 53:3 — in 1QH[a] 12:22-23, "My hand succeeds against all those who despise me, for they do not esteem me" (cf. 12:8). The Teacher Hymns echo also the Servant's familiarity with sickness (16:26-27) and his role in making the many righteous (12:27), but they say nothing of vicarious suffering.

Similitudes of Enoch

The heavenly savior of the *Similitudes of Enoch* (*1 Enoch* 37–71, late first century B.C.E. or early first century C.E.) is referred to twice as the Messiah and repeatedly as the Son of Man of Dan. 7:13. He is also described in terms of Isaiah's Servant passages, most obviously as "the light of the Gentiles" (*1 Enoch* 46:3; cf. Isa. 42:6; 49:6; Luke 2:32), possibly also as the Chosen or Elect One (16 times in *1 Enoch* 39:6–62:1; cf. Isa. 41:8-9; 42:1; 43:10; 44:1-2; 45:4), and as the Righteous One (*1 Enoch* 38:2-3; cf. Isa. 53:11). In *1 Enoch* this language serves partly to establish a parallel between the Righteous and Elect One (53:6) and the "righteous and elect ones" whom he saves (38:2-3; 39:6-7; 48:1; etc.). These expressions, though, are too frequent and stereotyped to bear any close resemblance to the Servant. Moreover, Enoch's heavenly Righteous One is a preexistent figure (48:3, 6) who never suffers or dies.

New Testament

In the New Testament it is precisely the motif of vicarious suffering, never clearly affirmed in the early Jewish texts, that is emphasized. Two prime examples come in 1 Cor. 15:3-4, "that Christ died for our sins [cf. Isa. 56:4-6, 8, 11-12 LXX] in accordance with the scriptures, and that he was buried [cf. Isa. 53:9]" and Rom. 4:25, "who was delivered up [*paredothē*] for our transgressions [*paraptōmata;* cf. Isa. 53:12 LXX; 1QIsa[a-b]; 4QIsa[d]] and was raised for our justification" (cf. Isa. 53:11 MT).

At a very early stage in Christian tradition, the passive of *paradidōmi* (Isa. 53:12) was applied to Jesus' passion and its ambiguous instigation, as in the phrase "on the night on which he was *betrayed* [by Judas]" or "*delivered up* [by God]" (1 Cor. 11:23). The Synoptic passion predictions foretell the Son of Man being delivered into the hands of men (Mark 9:31 par.; 10:33 par.; cf. 14:41) or delivered up for crucifixion (Matt. 26:2; cf. Luke 24:7), while Acts specifies that God is the one who ultimately had Jesus "given up" *(ekdotos)* to the Jewish and Roman authorities (Acts 2:23; cf. Isa. 53:6, where God is the subject of *paradidōmi*). The ransom saying of Mark 10:45 shares three terms with Isa. 53:12 — *didōmi/paradidōmi, psychē,* and *polloi* — in the phrase "to give his life . . . for many" (cf. Mark 14:24, "poured out for many"), and for the term *allagma* in Isa. 43:3 it uses the synonym *lytron,* "as a ransom."

Several other applications of the Suffering Servant to Jesus may be noted. Matthew 8:17 quotes Isa. 53:4 in reference to Jesus' healing Peter's mother-in-law and other sick people (cf. also Matt. 12:18-21, paraphrasing Isa. 42:1-4). In Luke's passion narrative Jesus says that the scripture "And he was counted among the lawless" (Isa. 53:12) must be fulfilled in him (Luke 22:37; cf. Mark 15:28 NRSV mg.). The Servant Songs may have influenced the passion narratives also in the motifs of Jesus' silence before the high priest (Matt. 26:63/Mark 14:61; cf. Isa. 53:7), his being struck and having soldiers spit in his face (Matt. 26:67; 27:30; Mark 10:34; cf. Isa. 50:6), and his unexpected burial as a criminal in the tomb of a rich man (Mark 15:42-47 par.; cf. Isa. 53:9 MT). In Acts 3, Peter's sermon uses the term "servant" to present Jesus as the one who was "delivered up" but later "glorified" (Acts 3:13). Acts 8:26-40 quotes Isa. 53:7-8 and has the evangelist Philip apply it to Jesus. 1 Peter 2:21-25 speaks of Christ's innocence and vicarious suffering in language drawn from Isa. 53:9, 4 + 12, 5, 6. This is paralleled in Heb. 9:28 (cf. 1 Pet. 2:24), where Christ is said to have borne the sins of many (Isa. 53:12).

Targum of Isaiah

The classic interpretation favored by medieval and modern Jewish exegetes applies the singular language of suffering in Isaiah 53 to the whole nation of Israel. Yet in the *Targum of Isaiah* (second century C.E.), the Servant remains an individual, "my Servant, the Messiah" (*Tg. Isa.* 52:13; cf. 53:10; 42:1 mss.; 43:10). The targum, however, rejects the notion of a *suffering* Messiah. Vicarious sin-bearing is reserved for the Gentiles (53:8), or indeed for the Temple itself, which was "handed over" for Israel's iniquities (53:5). The singular "man of sorrows" applies collectively to the Gentile nations (*Tg. Isa.* 53:3). Other statements of individual suffering are also read collectively, recast as plural, and applied to the members of the house of Israel (*Tg. Isa.* 52:14; 53:4; 53:10).

BIBLIOGRAPHY

W. H. BELLINGER AND W. R. FARMER, EDS. 1998, *Jesus and the Suffering Servant: Isaiah 53 and Christian Origins,* Harrisburg, Penn.: Trinity. • J. J. COLLINS 2006, "A Messiah before Jesus?" and "An Essene Messiah? Comments on Israel Knohl, *The Messiah before Jesus,*" in *Christian Beginnings and the Dead Sea Scrolls,* ed. J. J. Collins and C. A. Evans, Grand Rapids: Baker, 15-35, 37-44. • E. R. EKBLAD 1999, *Isaiah's Servant Poems according to the Septuagint,* Leuven: Peeters. • M. HENGEL WITH D. P. BAILEY 2004, "The Effective History of Isaiah 53 in the Pre-Christian Period," in *The Suffering Servant: Isaiah 53 in Jewish and Christian Sources,* ed. B. Janowski and P. Stuhlmacher, Grand Rapids: Eerdmans, 75-146. • I. KNOHL 2000, *The Messiah before Jesus: The Suffering Servant of the Dead Sea Scrolls,* Berkeley: University of California Press. • A. NEUBAUER AND S. R. DRIVER 1876-1877, *The Fifty-Third Chapter of Isaiah according to the Jewish Interpreters,* 2 vols., Oxford: J. Parker; rpt. New York: KTAV, 1969. • G. W. E. NICKELSBURG 2006, *Resurrection, Immortality, and Eternal Life in Intertestamental Judaism and Early Christianity,* expanded ed., Cambridge: Harvard University Press. • M. O. WISE 1999, *The First Messiah: Investigating the Savior before Jesus,* New York: HarperSanFrancisco.

See also: Persecuted Righteous Person

DANIEL P. BAILEY

Sun and Moon

According to Gen. 1:14-19 God created the sun and moon on the fourth day of creation. These notions are attested in Second Temple period literature (Ben Sira; *Jubilees;* Philo; Josephus; 1QH 23:1; 4Q392 frg. 1 line 6; 4Q440 frg. 1 line 1; *4 Ezra* 6:45; *2 Enoch* 30:2). Following Gen. 1:16, the *Astronomical Book* (*1 Enoch* 72-82) calls the sun "the great luminary" and the moon "the smaller luminary" (*1 Enoch* 72:4, 35-36; 73:1; see also *Jub.* 2:9; *1 Enoch* 41:5). According to *3 Bar.* 9:5-8, the moon is inferior to the sun; she waxes and wanes and shines only at night due to God's anger with her for giving light to Samael when he took the shape of the serpent.

Their Nature and Function in Early Jewish Literature

Sun and moon regulate the day and the night, shining forth from their abode (*1 Enoch* 2:1; 17:3; 71:4; 1QS 10:3 [par. 4Q256 19:1; 4Q258 8:12; 4Q260 2:2]; 1Q34bis frg. 3 col. ii line 1; 1QH 20:4-9; 4Q392 1 6). Various texts emphasize that the luminaries do not alter their appointed order and course (Jer. 31:34-35; Bar. 6:60; *1 Enoch* 2:1; 41:5; 69:20; *T. Naph.* 3:2). This notion is vividly expressed in the *Astronomical Book* (*1 Enoch* 72–82, 4Q208-211) and various calendrical texts and hymns from Qumran (4Q317, 4Q318, 4Q319, 4Q320, 4Q321, 4Q321a, and 4Q503). These writings reflect an interest in the order and course of sun and moon and how they regulate priestly and liturgical rosters. (The title *Words of the Luminaries* [4Q504 8 *verso*] may refer to the sun, moon, and stars or to priests, but its precise meaning is uncertain.) Furthermore, the reverse situation — that the sun and moon may cease to follow their appointed order in accordance with God's decree — has strong implications. The confusion or reversal of the natural order may indicate the arrival of the messianic age, the end of the age, or the day of judgment (*2 Bar.* 10:12; *1 Enoch* 80:4-5; *4 Ezra* 5:4; 7:39; *Ascen. Isa.* 4:5; *T. Levi* 4:1; *T. Mos.* 10:5; *Sib. Or.* 3.88-92, 801-3; 4:56-57), a notion with roots in biblical tradition (Isa. 13:10; 24:23; Ezek. 32:7; Joel 2:10; 3:15; Amos 8:9; Zech. 14:7).

Israelite and early Jewish texts deny that the luminaries are deities (Gen. 1:14-19; Wis. 13:2) and also prohibit their worship (Deut. 4:19; 17:2-5; 11QT 55:16-21; Philo). Yet in a general sense God is at times referred to as a luminary (1QH 15:25), as are angels (1QSb 4:27). In *1 Enoch* 72–82 the angel Uriel controls the sun and moon. In *3 Baruch* the sun is located in the third heaven (7:1); drawing on Greco-Roman depictions of the sun, the text describes it as a crowned man being drawn by a chariot and four horses, accompanied by forty angels and a phoenix (6:1; 7:5; 8:3-7), while the moon has the form of a woman sitting on a chariot and also accompanied by angels (9:1-4). The sun could more specifically be regarded as a symbol of God or his majesty (Sir. 42:16; 43:2; 50:7; 1QH 12:5-6; *Odes Sol.* 15:1-2; Philo, *Embassy to Gaius* 191; *2 Enoch* 24:4; 39:4), or of the wise and just (cf. 11Q5 27:2; *1 Enoch* 58:3; 106; *T. Jud.* 24:1; *T. Levi* 4:3; 18:3-4; Latin *Life of Adam and Eve* 29:13; *4 Ezra* 7:97).

In this regard, the metaphorical connection between the sun and justice continues ancient Near Eastern and Old Testament traditions (e.g., Ps. 84:12 [Eng. 84:11]; Hos. 6:5; Zeph. 3:5; Mal. 3:20 [Eng. 4:2]). According to 1Q27 1 i 6 (par. 4Q300 3 6), justice will be revealed like the sun, which regulates the world. In the incantation in 11Q11 5 a demon is confined to Sheol, where the sun cannot shine upon him but rises upon the just man. In the Wisdom of Solomon, the unrighteous say that the light of righteousness did not shine upon them and that the sun did not rise upon them (5:6). Philo discusses four figurative senses for the sun (*Dreams* 1.77-92): the human mind (77–78; cf. *Leg.* 2.30; 3.35; *Posterity* 57–58; *Planting* 40; *Drunkenness* 44; *Heir* 89, 263, 307; *Dreams* 1.72, 118; *Spec. Laws* 4.192); sense perception (79–84, cf. 118); the divine word (85–86); and God (87–92). Philo presents the rising sun as an allegory of virtue arisen in the soul and associates virtue and truth with the sun (*Embassy* 1.46; *Names* 149; *Dreams* 2.134; *Spec. Laws* 4.52; *Virtues* 164).

Sun and Moon in Calendrical, Liturgical Reckoning

Despite syntactical and semantic difficulties with the Hebrew of Gen. 1:14, ancient Jewish writers understood the luminaries to serve as signs for the festivals. They differed on which luminary was most significant. Ben Sira accords the moon importance in calendrical matters, but not the sun (Sir. 43:2-8), mentioning the full moon on festival days (Sir. 50:6; see also Ezekiel the Tragedian, *Exagōgē* 157; Philo, *Spec. Laws* 1.189; 2.155, 210). *Jubilees* instead gives prime importance to the sun and expands the list of things in Gen. 1:14 for which the sun is significant, mentioning days, Sabbaths, months, feasts, years, Sabbaths of years, jubilees, and all seasons of the year (*Jub.* 2:8-10; 4Q216 6:5-10). Moreover, any lunar reckoning in calendrical matters is explicitly opposed as a great error (*Jub.* 6:36-37). The rule of the sun is singled out as being shown to Enoch, while the moon goes unmentioned (*Jub.* 4:21).

4QInstruction, a wisdom text from Qumran, possibly understands Gen. 1:14 in an astrological sense. 4Q416 1 is not concerned with the calendrical or liturgical significance of the luminaries' courses but with their function as signs of upcoming events. The luminaries disclose the fates of kingdoms, provinces, and individual people, but they also indicate the character of the coming seasons (cf. *Jub.* 12:16-17).

Philo

Philo seems constrained by Gen. 1:14 to ascribe to the sun and moon the function of revealing signs of future events. Their significance, however, is limited to predictions of mainly meteorological phenomena (*Creation* 53–61; *Spec. Laws* 1.92). Eclipses of the sun and moon have ominous significance (*Providence* 2.50), indicating general events on earth. Philo also notes the calendrical purpose of the luminaries to indicate divisions of time (*Spec. Laws* 1.90) and mentions the new moon as the beginning of the month (*Spec. Laws* 2.140). Created by God on the fourth day, the luminaries are superior to earthly beings, but they are not worthy of worship and do not have full autonomy (*Creation* 45–46; *Cherubim*

88; *Posterity* 19; *Agriculture* 51; *Drunkenness* 106, 110; *Confusion* 173; *Migration* 179; *Names* 59; *Decalogue* 53, 66; *Spec. Laws* 1.13-20, 34, 207; 2.255; 3.185-89; *Rewards* 41–42; *Contemplative Life* 5; *Eternity* 83; *QG* 2.34; 4.51). According to Philo, the luminaries received their light from the light created on the first day of creation (*Creation* 29, 31).

Josephus

In accordance with Jewish tradition, Josephus understands the sun and moon to have been created by God on the fourth day of creation (*Ant.* 1.31; *Ag. Ap.* 2.192), and they act according to God's will (*Ant.* 1.156; cf. *Ant.* 11.55). He also knows of Anaxagoras' notion that the sun was a white-hot mass and of the Athenians' belief that the sun was divine (*Ag. Ap.* 2.265). Josephus does not explain Gen. 1:14 in specific calendrical terms, but limits the luminaries' function to signifying the seasons (*Ant.* 1.31). He reckons with a lunar calendar (*Ant.* 2.318; 3.240; 4.78, 84), but also notes the sun's position in the zodiacal sign of Aries (*Ant.* 3.248). The moon's phases can have calendrical import (e.g., the new moon at the deaths of Mariamne and Aaron, *Ant.* 4.78, 84) or be inauspicious omens (e.g., the lunar eclipse noted in *Ant.* 17.167). Similarly, and like Virgil (*Georgics* 1.466-69) and Pliny (*Natural History* 2.30), Josephus mentions the sun's darkness or dimness at the time of the murder of Caesar, signaling an inauspicious omen (*Ant.* 14.309). Both Philo (*Moses* 2.21, 102–3; *Heir* 221–23) and Josephus (*Ant.* 3.145) explain the seven-branched candelabrum in comparison with the sun and the planets.

Ideas and beliefs about sun and moon were diverse in ancient Judaism. Although the evidence is meager, the possible worship of the sun by the Therapeutae and the Essenes, referred to by Philo (*Contemplative Life* 27) and Josephus (*J.W.* 2.128, 148), deserves mention. Solar cults were popular in the Greco-Roman world and are attested in the exilic period (Ezek. 8:16). Wisdom 16:27-28 witnesses to the importance of saying prayer at the time of the rising of the sun. Some scholars speak of sun worship among ancient Jewish groups or even in the Temple of Jerusalem, while others suggest that Jews simply prayed in the direction of the rising sun.

Bibliography

W. Fauth 1996, "Salutatio Solis orientis: Zu einer Form der Heliolatrie bei Pythagoreern, Manichäern, Therapeuten und Essenern," in *Geschichte–Tradition–Reflexion,* eds. H. Cancik, H. Lichtenberger, and P. Schäfer, vol. 1, Tübingen: Mohr-Siebeck, 41-54. • J. Maier 1979, "Die Sonne im religiösen Denken des antiken Judentums," *ANRW* 19.1: 346-412. • M. S. Smith 1982, "Helios in Palestine," *Eretz Israel* 16: 199-214. • M. S. Smith 1990, "The Near Eastern Background of Solar Language for Yahweh," *JBL* 109: 29-39. • E. J. C. Tigchelaar 2005, "'Lights Serving as Signs for Festivals' (Genesis 1:14b) in Enuma Elish and Early Judaism," in *The Creation of Heaven and Earth,* ed. G. H. van Kooten, Leiden: Brill, 31-48.

Mladen Popović

Synagogues

The ancient synagogue was a unique and innovative institution that played a central role in Jewish life, leaving indelible marks on Christianity and Islam as well. As the Jewish public space par excellence throughout the Roman world (excluding pre-70 Jerusalem and perhaps other Jewish cities), the synagogue was always the largest and most monumental building in any Jewish community and was often located in the center of the town or village. In comparison to the Jerusalem Temple, which it eventually came to replace as the central religious institution in Jewish life, the synagogue was revolutionary in a number of ways: (1) *Location:* The synagogue was universal in nature and enabled Jews to organize their communal life and worship ritual anywhere. (2) *Leadership:* Synagogue functionaries were not restricted to a specific socioreligious group, as was the case in the Temple, where only priests could officiate. With respect to the synagogue, anyone could hold a leadership position. (3) *Participation:* The synagogue involved its congregants in all aspects of its ritual. This stands in contrast to the Jerusalem Temple, where visitors remained in the outer, women's court unless they themselves were offering a sacrifice. They were unable to view what was transpiring in the inner, Israelite or priestly courts, in which the official sacrificial proceedings took place. (4) *Worship:* The most distinct aspect of the synagogue from a religious perspective was that it provided a context for additional forms of worship other than sacrifices. It eventually came to embrace a wide range of religious activities, including scriptural readings, targum (the translation of Scriptures), communal prayers, hymns, sermons, and *piyyut* (religious poetry).

Judean Synagogues in the Late Second Temple Period

The communal dimension was a prominent feature of the first-century-C.E. Judean synagogue, and buildings excavated to date reflect an architectural plan befitting such a community-oriented institution. The synagogues in Gamla (Golan), Masada, and Herodium (in the Judean Desert), as well as those in Qiryat Sefer and Modiʿin (in the western Judean foothills) are all square or rectangular spaces with columns and benches, an arrangement facilitating communal participation for political, religious, or social purposes. The model chosen for these settings approximated the Hellenistic *bouleutērion* or *ecclesiastērion,* which likewise catered to a group of people gathering for a variety of purposes.

Even in this early period, the religious dimension was an important component of the synagogue's agenda, although it should be placed in proper perspective given the nature of our literary sources (both Jewish and Christian), which have a clear propensity to emphasize this aspect of the synagogue's activities. The gospel accounts focus on Jesus' preaching and teaching in a synagogue setting, especially Luke's description of his Sabbath-morning appearance in a Nazareth synagogue (4:16-30); the Sabbath assembly of Caesarean Jews in their synagogue provides the setting for a provocative anti-Jewish act (Josephus, *J.W.* 2.285-88); and the Tiberian *proseuchē* ("house of prayer") was the scene of emergency town meetings following Sabbath and fast-day worship (Josephus, *Life* 277-98). The famous Theodotos inscription from first-century-C.E. Jerusalem mentions the social-communal aspects of the synagogue along with its religious-educational ones. Thus, archaeological remains provide an important corrective to the proclivity of the literary sources to highlight the religious dimensions of the institution. The buildings found to date are neutral communal structures with no notable religious components, such as inscriptions, artistic representations, or the presence of a Torah shrine. Scrolls were brought into the hall for the Torah reading and then removed. Architecturally speaking, the first-century synagogue did not have the decidedly religious profile that it would acquire in late antiquity.

Despite the relative paucity of material, enough has survived to enable us to appreciate the diversity that characterized the pre-70 Judean synagogue. Many Jerusalem synagogues were built by Jews hailing from various Diaspora communities, and these institutions probably maintained their own unique customs and practices. The *proseuchē* of Tiberias stands in striking contrast to other Judean synagogues in name (referred to as *proseuchē* [a house of prayer] and not *synagōgē* [a house of assembly]) and presumably in size as well. The Caesarea synagogue, located in the midst of buildings belonging to non-Jews, is clearly quite different from those of Gamla, Qiryat Sefer, Masada, or Herodium. And, of course, the Qumran worship setting was unique to itself, as indeed were most other aspects of this community. With regard to Jerusalem, there can be little doubt that — given the presence of the Temple — what were considered usual synagogue activities elsewhere may have found expression within the precincts of the Temple Mount. Moreover, at least some synagogues in Jerusalem assumed additional functions absent elsewhere, such as cultivating ties with other Diaspora communities and serving the needs of pilgrims to the city.

The differences among these buildings are quite significant with regard to the location of entrances, internal plans, position and number of benches, the shape of the hall, and the overall setting in the midst of surrounding structures. Even the two synagogues created by the Jewish rebels at Masada and Herodium following the outbreak of hostilities in 66 C.E. differ from one another, although this is primarily due to the plans and functions of the earlier buildings they replaced. It is therefore unwarranted to speak of a single model for Judean synagogues of the Second Temple period; attempts at trying to define one architectural typology for these buildings are unconvincing. Whatever elements were held in common can be attributed to Greco-Roman architectural traditions that were adopted by synagogue builders because of their utility. In effect, a variety of communal buildings shared certain basic characteristics that served the range of activities conducted in the first-century institution.

The Gospels mention healings and miracles being performed by Jesus in the synagogues of Galilee. Sources other than the New Testament ignore this aspect of synagogue life, possibly because healings and miracles were too common to require comment. Whatever the case, there can be little doubt that such activities took place in synagogues. However, it is difficult to assess the extent of such synagogue activity. Was it confined to first-century Galilee? To rural synagogues? To a particular stratum of society? This would seem doubtful, but owing to the limited evidence at our disposal, not much more can be said in this regard.

A topic that has received some attention in recent decades is the relationship between the Jerusalem Temple and the first-century synagogue. Some strikingly contrasting positions have been taken in this regard. On the one hand, a number of scholars have posited the influence of the Temple on the synagogue. Donald Binder (1999) has taken this line of argument to the extreme, claiming that the synagogue was an extension of the Temple and that the latter's functions, officials, liturgy, architecture, sanctity, and art shaped those of the former. However, evidence for such assertions is slim at best.

On the other hand, Paul Flesher (1995) suggests that the synagogue and Temple were diametrically opposed religious institutions representing two very different types of "Judaisms." However, if the "Judaisms" of the synagogue and Temple were indeed so different, it is surprising that no ancient source bothered to note this clash. Philo, the Gospels, Paul, and Josephus do not seem to have been aware of such a distinction, and it would seem that no such dichotomy existed in antiquity.

Indeed, we find in late Second Temple Judean society two contrasting, yet complementary, developments. The Temple, for its part, was assuming an ever more central role in Jewish religious life, not only because of the growth of Jerusalem as an urban center and focus of significant pilgrimage, but also because of the accruement of power by the priesthood and the enhanced role of the Temple Mount (at least since Herod's time) as the setting for a wide range of social, economic, religious, and political activities. The synagogue, in contrast, had evolved by this time into a distinct and defined institution in the center of communal activity throughout Second Temple Judea. Centralization of the Temple was paralleled by decentralization among the local synagogues. Prior to 70, the Temple was universally recognized as the central institution in Jewish life; nevertheless, the emerging synagogue had become the pivotal institution on the local scene. This parallel development in the first century was indeed fortuitous, and although no one could have foreseen the outcome, the seeds of Jewish communal and religious continuity had already been sown well before the destruction of the Temple.

Diaspora Synagogues in the Pre-70 Era

The range of sources relating to pre-70 Diaspora synagogues is varied. Three major categories are represented — literary, archaeological, and epigraphic —

and within each there are substantial differences in the nature of the evidence and its historical value. The literary material, for example, ranges from references in Philo's commentaries and treatises, to edicts cited by Josephus, to Acts' accounts of Paul's visits to Diaspora synagogues in Asia Minor and Greece.

Similarly with regard to the epigraphic material: some inscriptions are major communal documents (Berenice) or shorter contracts of manumission (Bosporus); others are brief statements of individual (Delos, Acmonia, Egypt) or communal (Egypt) benefactions; still others are epitaphs noting synagogue affiliation (Rome). On the archaeological plane, there are remains of two buildings, one dating to the first centuries B.C.E. and C.E. (Delos) and the other a fourth-century-C.E. structure that originated either in the first or, more probably, the second century C.E. (Ostia).

This broad range of primary material at our disposal points to a number of features common to the pre-70 Diaspora synagogue or *proseuchē* (both terms are widely used). All sources subscribe to the centrality of this institution among Jewish communities throughout the Roman world. As in Judea, this point is driven home by the fact that no other Jewish communal institution or building is ever noted in the sources. While several communities boasted larger communal institutions, such as a *politeuma* or *gerousia* (Berenice, Alexandria), no specific place is ever mentioned as housing these bodies, and it seems safe to assume that they met in the synagogue. Each locale may express the centrality of the synagogue differently, given the local context, but the implication is always the same.

Some Diaspora Jewish communities regarded their synagogues as holy places. The very term *proseuchē* may be indicative of this fact, as are specific references to the synagogue as a place of asylum, a "sacred precinct" (Egypt), or a "holy place" (Antioch; Philo's reference to Essenes). The ceremony for the manumission of slaves in the synagogues of the Bosporus kingdom may also indicate the degree of sanctity associated with these buildings, since it was carried out not only in the presence of the community, but often with specific reference to the God of the Jews (as was the case in Delphi, where the ceremony was performed in the presence of Apollo).

The reasons for the attribution of sanctity to some Diaspora synagogues are noteworthy. This status was an attempt on the part of Jewish communities to accord their synagogues and *proseuchai* the prestige enjoyed by temples throughout the Hellenistic and Roman worlds. In fact, it was precisely at this time that granting temples the title of "sacred and inviolable" *(hieros kai asylos)* increased dramatically and was viewed as a mark of high honor. Some Diaspora communities adopted this status (whether formally or not), thus enhancing, in their own eyes as well as in the eyes of others, the prestige of their main communal institution.

As the primary focus of every local community, the synagogue served as a setting for all facets of communal life. Most Jews in antiquity sought to preserve their Jewish identity, and however they might define that identity such an institution was a *sine qua non* in this endeavor. In the first place, it served to distinguish them from the surrounding society by fulfilling the multiple purposes — religious, educational, social, political, and economic — that a religious and ethnic minority such as the Jews would have needed. The Diaspora synagogue paralleled the contemporary Judean one in its myriad functions yet shared many characteristics with non-Jewish institutions in its immediate vicinity.

Although linked by a distinct (though not always easily defined) religious and ethnic heritage, these Diaspora communities exhibited a striking degree of diversity, stemming primarily from the fact that the Jews who established these early communities had no models of a community center facility from which to draw. Furthermore, powerful forces had an impact on each Diaspora community, resulting in the adoption of patterns taken from the wider culture. The names of members of the community often imitated those popular on the local scene. For instance, the contribution of a synagogue building in Acmonia, by Julia Severa, a prominent pagan, reflects a kind of patronage that may have been unique to this part of Asia Minor; the organization and functioning of the Jewish *politeuma* in Berenice may well have derived, in part at least, from Cyrenian models; the type of building used by Delian Jews bore similarities with other buildings on that island; and the manumission decrees from Bosporus, with their formulary components, are well known in that particular region.

Some scholars have suggested far more profound connections between the synagogue and the Greco-Roman world, namely that the Jews patterned this institution and its activities on Greco-Roman models, the one most frequently mentioned in this regard being the private association. These associations ranged from the more officially recognized *politeuma* and *collegium* to less-defined groups *(synodos, koinon, thiasos, communitas)* that may have been based on common geographical origins, commercial interests, religious affiliation, mutual aid, or dining and burial needs.

Nevertheless, the synagogue differed from these Greco-Roman institutions in many ways. The Jewish community undertook a far greater range of activities than the ordinary *collegium,* and the imperial authorities were far more tolerant of the Jewish *collegium* than of other religious or ethnic associations. For instance, *collegia* were often banned by the authorities while the Jewish community remained unaffected. The Jews had the right to maintain their own courts, attend to their own food requirements, and avoid worshiping the civic deities or appearing in court on Sabbaths and festivals; they were exempt from serving in the army, sent monies to Jerusalem, and conducted a wide range of communal affairs. In Alexandria and Berenice, the Jewish community was recognized as a *politeuma.* Most of the above rights and privileges were not applicable to contemporary *collegia* or *thiasoi.* Thus, application of the term *collegium* to the synagogue seems to have been one of Roman convenience and not necessarily reflective of a specific legal framework.

Pagan interest in the synagogue is indicative of the

SYNAGOGUES

institution's accessibility as well as importance and centrality in the Jewish community. Evidence for pagan sympathizers and converts throughout the Diaspora is well known, and in many instances these people were actively supportive of the local Jewish community. Examples include the God-fearers of Bosphorus and the benefactions of the above-noted pagan patroness Julia Severa. Also noteworthy in this regard is the attraction of women to Judaism, a phenomenon attested throughout the Roman world in a variety of sources.

Three extensive synagogue inscriptions from Cyrene attest to the Jewish community's attempt to navigate its way between integration and exclusivity. The community's award ceremony for a Roman official was conducted during Sukkot and included praise of the honoree and the presentation of a wreath at each meeting (on the Sabbath?) and on the New Moon. This award was the unanimous decision of the entire congregation and was memorialized on a stele erected in the synagogue. Moreover, both communal and religious aspects of the ceremony come into play in this inscription. It was initiated by the congregation, which decided whom to honor and how; all the events mentioned were conducted on dates from the Jewish calendar.

Together with these Jewish components, there were also very definite and discernible Greco-Roman influences. All the inscriptions are in Greek; the leaders all bore official Greek titles, and their personal names were almost all Greek as well. The same holds true of the communal institutions noted (i.e., *politeuma,* amphitheater). Moreover, the forms of bestowing honor (a wreath and woolen fillet, a public inscription) and the voting procedure adopted (casting white or black stones) are likewise well-attested Greek practices.

The Diaspora synagogue was indeed a creative synthesis of Jewish tradition, the specific requirements of each community, and the influence of the surrounding culture. Far from constituting an isolated and insulated minority, or the opposite — a people on the threshold of full assimilation — Diaspora Jews succeeded in creating an institution that expressed and reflected their needs both as individuals and as a community, and did so within the confines of the cultural and social contexts in which they found themselves.

Thus, for all its borrowing and diversity, the Jewish communal institution remained quintessentially Jewish. It served the Jewish community and housed its rites and observances, which were influenced first and foremost, though far from exclusively, by a common Jewish past and present. The Jews had brought their own *patria* to the Diaspora, a cultural and religious tradition that pagans could respect, resent, or ignore. The Jews were committed to honoring and perpetuating this heritage, and Roman society, for the most part, was supportive of a group's safeguarding and transmitting its traditional customs. On the communal level, the synagogue was the main vehicle for achieving this goal.

The Liturgy of Pre-70 Synagogues

The fundamental form of worship in synagogues at this time, the Torah reading liturgy, is explicitly mentioned in virtually every type of source from the Second Temple period in Judea and the Diaspora, in cities as well as villages. Josephus and Philo make this point clearly:

> He [Moses] appointed the Law to be the most excellent and necessary form of instruction, ordaining not that it should be heard once for all or twice or on several occasions, but that every week men should abandon their other occupations and assemble to listen to the Law and to obtain a thorough and accurate knowledge of it, a practice that all other legislators seem to have neglected. (Josephus, *Ag. Ap.* 2.175)

> He [Augustus] knew therefore that they [the Jews] have houses of prayer [*proseuchai*] and meet together in them, particularly on the sacred Sabbaths, when they receive as a body training in their ancestral philosophy. (Philo, *Embassy to Gaius* 156; cf. *Hypoth.* 7.12)

The New Testament preserves two very important accounts of first-century synagogue liturgy:

> And he [Jesus] came to Nazareth, where he had been brought up; and he went to the synagogue, as his custom was, on the Sabbath day. And he stood up to read; and there was given to him the book of the prophet Isaiah. He opened the book and found the place where it was written. . . . (Luke 4:16-17)

> But when they [Paul and his companions] departed from Perga, they came to Antioch in Pisidia, and went into the synagogue on the Sabbath day and sat down. And after the reading of the Law and the Prophets the rulers of the synagogue sent a message to them. . . . (Acts 13:14-15)

> For in generations past Moses has had in every city those who preach him, being read in the synagogues every Sabbath day. (Acts 15:21)

Thus, there can be no doubt that by the first century C.E. Torah reading had become the core of Jewish synagogue worship. Several related liturgical features, although not as well attested, accompanied the Torah reading. Both the Gospel of Luke (4:17-19) and the book of Acts (13:14-15), for example, refer to readings from the Prophets and to sermons that followed the scriptural reading. Philo notes more advanced study and instruction (*Moses* 2.215-16; *Spec. Laws* 2.62-64; *Hypoth.* 7.13). Later rabbinic literature mentions the targum.

The evidence shows that by the first century a weekly ceremony featuring communal reading and study of sacred texts was a universal Jewish practice. In fact, this liturgy was unique to the ancient world; no such form of worship featuring the recitation and study of a sacred text by an entire community on a regular basis was known in antiquity, although certain mystery cults in the Hellenistic-Roman world produced sacred texts that were read to initiates on occasion. The self-laudatory tone of the Jewish sources may indeed reflect their authors' intention to trumpet this form of worship, which set the Jewish community apart from the surrounding cultures.

Diaspora Synagogues in Late Antiquity

The evidence for the Diaspora synagogue in late antiquity (third to seventh centuries C.E.) lies in the material remains of some twelve buildings (and nine others of less certainty) and hundreds of inscriptions relating to the synagogue or its officials. Although literary sources note scores of synagogues throughout the Roman-Byzantine and Sassanian worlds, virtually nothing conclusive can be said about these institutions.

Archaeological finds of synagogue buildings derive from all parts of the Roman Empire, from Dura Europos (Syria) in the east to Elche (Spain) in the west. Between these geographical extremities, synagogue remains have been found at Gerasa in Provincia Arabia, Apamea in Syria, Sardis and Priene in Asia Minor, Aegina in Greece, Stobi in Macedonia, Plovdiv (ancient Philippopolis) in Bulgaria, Ostia and Bova Marina in Italy, and Hammam Lif (Naro) in North Africa. Inscriptions from these synagogues alone number well over 150, with the overriding majority coming from Sardis and Dura Europos. Taken together with inscriptions found elsewhere (e.g., Asia Minor), and especially those from the catacombs of Rome and Venusia that mention the titles of synagogue officials, the total number of synagogue-related inscriptions from the Diaspora amounts to well over 300. The two most important Diaspora synagogues discovered to date are Dura Europos in eastern Syria and Sardis in western Asia Minor.

Dura Europos

The most sensational synagogue find from antiquity is that of Dura Europos, located on the Euphrates River at the eastern extremity of the Roman Empire. First discovered in 1932, the Dura synagogue was quite modest on its exterior. It was located in a residential area and was originally a private home. In its later stage, the building was significantly expanded and the local community undertook an ambitious artistic program. From floor to ceiling, depictions of biblical episodes cover each of its four walls, resulting in paintings unmatched in any other synagogue from antiquity. Among the scenes preserved are the crossing of the Sea of Reeds, Pharaoh and the infancy of Moses, the return of the Ark from the land of the Philistines, the dedication of the Tabernacle with Aaron and his sons, Samuel anointing David, Ezekiel's vision of the dry bones, several Purim episodes in one panel, a series of scenes from the life of Elijah, and more.

Most of the scholarly literature on Dura has been devoted to interpreting these scenes, their placement, and sequence. While they clearly represent what the community considered the high points of the biblical narrative, opinion remains divided on a number of issues. Is there, for example, one dominant theme, or a series of themes, that dictated the selection of the various scenes, or were they selected at random? Were internal or external considerations uppermost in the selection process?

Immediately above the Torah shrine are new representations of the Temple menorah, the Temple façade, and the *'Aqedah* (the Binding of Isaac), and above them is a series of scenes: Jacob blessing his grandsons, Ephraim and Manasseh; Jacob blessing his sons; and David playing a lyre while enchanting a variety of animals. These scenes are crowned by a seated figure (a king? messiah?) surrounded by his court or the tribes of Israel. Flanking all these scenes are four large figures. On the top righthand side is Moses, as an inscription indicates. The identity of the other figures has been the subject of much scholarly dispute. E. R. Goodenough identified them all as Moses; E. L. Sukenik saw the two on the right as Moses and the two on the left as Joshua, while C. Kraeling associated each figure with a different biblical personality (Moses, Joshua, Ezra, and Abraham).

If there were any doubts before this discovery about whether such a Jewish art existed in antiquity, then Dura put them to rest. To date, however, nothing even remotely comparable has been recovered in any other Jewish setting. Thus, the wider implications of Dura have dimmed somewhat in the seventy-five years since the original discovery. Although many other Diaspora synagogues have come to light, these later finds seem to indicate that a similar highly developed pattern of Jewish artistic tradition did not exist elsewhere and that Dura was *sui generis* in this regard.

Sardis

The impressiveness of the Sardis synagogue, discovered in 1961, stems from its prominent location, large dimensions, and rich remains. Located on the city's main street, the synagogue was housed in what once was a wing of the municipal *palaestra* or gymnasium. The building itself measured about 80 m. in length; in its last stage it was divided into two parts, a 60 m.-long sanctuary and a 20 m.-long atrium.

Three portals — a large central entryway flanked by two smaller ones — led from the courtyard into the main sanctuary, immediately inside of which stood two *aediculae* (small shrine-like installations with columns supporting a pediment) flanking the main entrance. At least one of the *aediculae* — probably the southern one, which was of a better quality — was intended to house the Torah scrolls. The function of the second one remains unknown; additional scrolls or possibly a menorah might have been placed there, or it may have served as a seat for a community official. As was the case elsewhere in the synagogue, the stones used for these *aediculae* were taken from other buildings in the city.

A massive stone table, coined the "eagle table" because of the two large Roman eagles engraved in relief on each of its two supporting stones, stood at the western end of the sanctuary. The table was flanked by two statues of pairs of lions sitting back-to-back. Both the eagles and lions are in secondary use, the latter perhaps dating as far back as the city's Lydian period (sixth-fifth centuries B.C.E.).

Two rows of pillars divide the central nave of the main hall to create two side aisles. Because there are no traces of a balcony or stone benches, it appears that the congregation — which by some estimates might have numbered up to a thousand people — probably sat on mats or wooden benches, and some may have stood. The floor was decorated lavishly with geometric patterns and was divided into seven bays, while the lower parts of the walls were decorated with marble panels or revetments *(skoutlōsis),* and the upper parts featured panels of brightly colored marble inlay.

Interior of the third-fourth-century-C.E. synagogue at Capernaum *(www.HolyLandPhotos.org)*

Remains of some nineteen menorahs were found incised in stone, brick, metal, or pottery. The most impressive of these is an ornate stone menorah that bears the name "Socrates," probably its donor.

Eighty-five inscriptions, seventy-nine of which are in Greek (of the thirty names noted, only two are in Hebrew) and mostly in a fragmentary state, were found either on the mosaic floor or on plaques that were once part of the marble wall revetment. These inscriptions are almost always dedicatory in nature, naming the donor and his fulfillment of a vow. Sometimes they preserve additional information, such as one's profession, public office, or the fact that the donor was a God-fearer *(theosēbēs).* Of particular interest to the religious functioning of the synagogue is an inscription found in the center of the mosaic floor mentioning "Samoe, *hiereus* [priest] and *sophodidaskalos* [wise teacher or teacher of wisdom]."

These finds challenge some of the earlier negative assumptions concerning Jewish life in the Diaspora in late antiquity, demonstrating that at least some communities had achieved a high degree of recognition and status in their respective cities; in the case of Sardis, this prominence continued for three centuries after the Christianization of the empire, right up the Persian destruction of the city in 616.

Synagogue Architecture in Late Roman–Byzantine Palestine

Late antiquity witnessed a proliferation of synagogue construction. From the Golan and Galilee to the southern hills of Judea, Jewish communities built a variety of such structures, each according to its means and cultural-religious proclivities. Recognition of this heterogeneity has had an enormous impact on our understanding of Palestinian synagogues. A neat division of synagogue buildings into distinct architectural types — an "early" Galilean-type dating to the second-third centuries C.E.; a broadhouse- or intermediate-type dating to the fourth-fifth centuries; and a "late" basilica-type dating to the sixth-seventh centuries — was once the regnant conception. However, this view was seriously undermined by a series of excavations in the last third of the twentieth century:

(1) Most of the second- to third-century Galilean-type synagogues are now dated to the fourth to sixth centuries. While the most salient and best known of these sites is Capernaum, the group also includes Barʿam, Merot, Gush Halav, Meiron, Chorazim, and Nabratein. In fact, the lintel of the Nabratein building bears an inscription stating that the synagogue was built 494 years after the destruction of the Temple (i.e., 564 C.E.), a date that has been confirmed by recent excavations.

(2) The synagogues at Khirbet Shemaʿ and probably also Ḥammat Tiberias are often categorized as broadhouse buildings, but they were built in the latter third and fourth centuries, at the same time as several Galilean-type structures.

(3) All the excavated synagogues from the Golan date to the Byzantine period (fifth to seventh centuries). While these synagogues have a number of shared characteristics, they also have characteristics that can be associated with the Galilean-type synagogue.

The most widespread synagogue plan found in almost every part of the country is the basilica-type. It features three entrances on the wall opposite Jerusalem, often preceded by a narthex (an entrance corridor) and an outer atrium (courtyard). The main hall is usually divided by two rows of columns into a nave and side aisles; an apse, niche, or *bema* (platform) was built at the Jerusalem-oriented end of the building. Mosaic floors usually decorate these buildings.

The physical appearance of each of these synagogue types reflects significant Greco-Roman or Byzantine influences. The architecture and decoration of the

Galilean-type building drew heavily from Roman public buildings that flourished in the East in the early centuries C.E. and later reappeared in a somewhat modified form in the Byzantine churches of Syria. These buildings were often so similar to pagan edifices that one rabbinic source (*b. Šabbat* 72b) invoked the image of someone bowing before a building, thinking it was a synagogue, realizing only afterward that it was a pagan temple. Similarly, the plan, architecture, and art of the basilica-type building often resembled those of contemporary churches. The borrowing was so extensive that even certain details of church architecture that did not particularly serve synagogue needs were copied. For instance, the chancel screen in churches served to separate the clergy from the congregation, but even though such a hierarchical division was unknown in the ancient synagogue, this architectural element was nevertheless incorporated into the basilica-type synagogue.

Jewish Art in Byzantine Palestine

Artistic remains appear in dozens of Palestinian synagogues from this era. Usually, however, the art is limited in scope, displaying only geometric or floral designs and one or more Jewish symbols. The most notable exceptions to this rule from Byzantine Palestine are the synagogues in Ḥammat Tiberias (fourth century), Sepphoris (fifth century), and Bet Alpha (sixth century), which preserve fairly complete mosaic floors that afford some idea of the artistic proclivities of some Jewish communities in this period.

Ḥammat Tiberias

Excavated by Moshe Dothan in 1961, the building in Ḥammat Tiberias contained a series of strata ranging from the third to eighth centuries, the most impressive of which dates to the second half of the fourth century. The sanctuary was oriented southward, toward Jerusalem, and featured a nave with one aisle on the west and two on the east. While the mosaic floor in the eastern aisles bore only geometric designs and three inscriptions, the central nave boasted three striking panels. These included, in the order of one's progression through the hall from the north toward the *bema* in the south: (1) eight dedicatory inscriptions filling nine squares flanked by two lions in a heraldic posture; (2) a striking zodiac with the four seasons in its outer corners and a representation of the sun god Helios in the center; (3) Jewish symbols, including the Torah shrine and a pair each of *menorot, shofarot, lulavim, ethrogim,* and incense shovels — a cluster that would reappear frequently in synagogue art.

The benefactors of this building, clearly among the wealthy and acculturated residents of Tiberias, are readily identifiable by their Greek or Latin names (e.g., Ioullos, Zoilos, Maximos) appearing in the inscriptions. These benefactors were presumably responsible for financing the synagogue's construction, and several apparently held official positions in the synagogue community. The most prominent of these benefactors is Severus, identified in several inscriptions as a "disciple (or protégé) of the most illustrious patriarchs." The dominant role of Greek in this floor, together with its striking mosaic, clearly indicates the cosmopolitan cultural orientation of this synagogue's donors and probably many, if not most, of its members.

The panel depicting the zodiac and Helios is the centerpiece of this mosaic floor. While this particular design would reappear in other Palestinian synagogues in subsequent centuries, the Tiberias depiction remains the earliest such representation, and far and away the most impressive one artistically. It closely approximates the quality of the richly decorated mosaic floors in fourth-century Antioch. The Tiberias depiction of Helios in the form of Sol Invictus, with his full array of attributes, had become a widespread symbol in pagan circles by the third and fourth centuries, and was also associated with Jesus in several fourth-century representations. Such depictions were not only unknown in Jewish contexts prior to this time; Josephus reports that depicting the zodiac was categorically prohibited in the Jerusalem Temple centuries earlier (*J.W.* 5.213), and the Mishnah likewise forbids the display of several Helios-related symbols appearing here (*m. ʿAbod. Zar.* 3:1). Thus, the first appearance of such a blatantly pagan motif in the center of an important Tiberian syna-

Remains of the third-sixth-century synagogue at Gush Halav in Upper Galilee *(Hanan Isachar)*

SYNAGOGUES

gogue is as enigmatic as it is fascinating. No dearth of scholarly ink has been spilt in attempting to explain this phenomenon.

Sepphoris

In 1993, Ehud Netzer and Zeev Weiss of the Hebrew University of Jerusalem discovered a synagogue on the northern slopes of the important Galilean city of Sepphoris. The building itself is exceptional in that it is unusually narrow, having a main hall and only one side aisle, and faces northwest (away from Jerusalem).

The most impressive feature of this synagogue is its mosaic floor. In contrast to other decorated synagogue floors that were divided into three bands, or registers, this one was divided into seven, some of which were subdivided into smaller panels. Greek dedicatory inscriptions (and one, later two, in Aramaic) were integrated into most of the central panels, a practice unknown in other synagogues. The synagogue's remaining Aramaic inscriptions were located in the side aisle among more modest geometric designs; this is an interesting, though not surprising, sociocultural and economic distinction.

When entering the hall from the southeast, one would have encountered the following motifs in a southeast-northwest sequence. The first two, and most poorly preserved, registers depict scenes from the life of Abraham — the visit of the angels (Genesis 18) when Abraham is promised a son (conjectured on the basis of a parallel sequence of scenes from the sixth-century St. Vitale church mosaics in Ravenna), and the *ʿAqedah* (Genesis 22).

Beyond these two registers is the largest one, featuring the zodiac signs, the four seasons, and the sun in a chariot. The figure of Helios is not depicted here, but only the sun's rays extending in every direction, with one pointing downward into the chariot to give the impression that the sun is riding in it. The zodiac signs are accompanied mostly by young men, either naked or in simple cloaks covering only part of their bodies; all but one figure are barefoot; the Hebrew name of the month together with a star appears in each zodiac sign.

The next two registers revolve around the theme of the wilderness tabernacle. One features Aaron (almost totally obliterated) officiating at the altar surrounded by a number of cultic objects; a water basin appears on one side and two animals, a bull and a lamb, on the other. The second of these registers exhibits four objects: another lamb, a black jug (or amphora) identified as holding oil; a container with the word "flour," and two trumpets identified as such. In addition, the showbread table with twelve loaves of bread is depicted along with a wicker basket containing fruit, apparently the firstfruits *(bikkurim)* offering.

The next register is divided into three panels. Each of the outer two features a menorah flanked by a large shofar and tongs to the right, and a *lulav* and *ethrog* to the left. The central panel depicts the Temple façade with an incense shovel beneath it. The final register, nearest the *bema,* appears, ironically, to be the least fraught with religious significance. It, too, is divided into three panels; the central one depicts a stylized wreath enclosing a Greek inscription, while the two flanking panels display lions facing the central wreath, each clutching the head of a bull or ox in its paw.

The elaborate programmatic composition of Sepphoris is unique to synagogue mosaic art. Questions have been raised about whether these registers convey one overall message (eschatological? polemical?) and whether there is any connection between the artistic representations and the synagogue liturgy. It has also been suggested that many of the details in this mosaic possibly reflect significant priestly influence on the shaping of the particular artistic program and its details.

Beth Alpha

The third synagogue with a well-preserved mosaic floor is that of Beth Alpha, first discovered in late 1928 and excavated by Eleazar L. Sukenik in early 1929. The floor is divided into three panels; the one nearest the *bema* in the southern wall of the building contains the familiar cluster of Jewish symbols (Torah shrine, two menorahs, and so forth); a central panel depicts the zodiac signs and Helios riding in his chariot; a third panel displays the *ʿAqedah* scene. Two inscriptions greet the visitor to the synagogue just inside the northern entrance, one in Greek noting the artisans responsible for the mosaic, and the other in Aramaic recording the date of construction and the congregants' contributions.

Detail of the mosaic floor of the fifth-century Jewish synagogue at Beth Alpha showing the sun-chariot surrounded by the twelve constellations and signs of the zodiac *(Phoenix Data Systems / Neal and Joel Bierling)*

The Beth Alpha mosaic is far less sophisticated than the two examples presented above, insofar as its symbols and figures are depicted frontally, schematically, and with little attempt at realism. Whether this is due to its later sixth-century context or to the fact that it is the product of a rural as against an urban community is difficult to assess.

The Byzantine Context of Jewish Art

The increased use of Jewish art in synagogues, as well as in cemeteries and domestic settings, is rooted in a number of internal and external developments. To the former category belongs the profound change in attitude and behavior among Jews toward figural art. Beginning in the second century C.E., and with increased frequency in the third and fourth centuries, we are witness to a more receptive attitude toward art generally and figural art in particular. Whereas the motifs used by the Jews in the late Second Temple period were overwhelmingly geometric and floral, in the late Roman and Byzantine eras they seem to have expressed a greater openness to Greco-Roman culture, particularly in patriarchal circles and among the urban aristocracies in the Galilean cities. This more tolerant approach to figural art was undoubtedly an important factor that set the stage for the more significant revolution that would take place in late antiquity.

Two factors, both rooted in external stimuli, were likewise crucial to this transformation. One was the changing attitude to art generally in the ancient world, from a representative depiction to one conveying symbolic meaning. Art was becoming an expression of religious and philosophical ideas and values, and if this was true of paganism in late antiquity, it was especially the case with regard to Christianity and Judaism.

The other external factor is the emergence and representation of specific religious symbols. Christian art was inherently symbolic in late antiquity, and Jewish art did not lag far behind. Probably the most blatant example of Christian influence on the Jewish artistic scene is the emergence of the cross and menorah as preeminent symbols. The appearance of the menorah as a widespread Jewish symbol was part and parcel of the larger Byzantine-Christian context. The use of symbols was now more widespread than ever before, and while Christianity spearheaded this development, given the imperial and ecclesiastical means at its disposal, the Jews quickly followed suit. This use of symbols as a means of reinforcing group identity seems to have been a desideratum for both Christians and Jews in this period.

The Byzantine period also witnessed significant strides in the transformation of the synagogue building into a distinctively religious institution. The process that had begun in late Roman Palestine was now more fully realized. The Jerusalem orientation of synagogue buildings was, as noted, further emphasized by placing a *bema* (platform), niche, or apse for the Torah shrine against the Jerusalem-oriented wall. The emphasis on a Jerusalem orientation was even greater in synagogues that adopted the Christian basilical plan as well as the accompanying niche or apse that became part of the wall facing Jerusalem.

The appearance of a *bema, aedicula,* or apse as a fixture in most synagogues of this period was not simply an architectural addition. It signified that the Torah shrine was now accorded a permanent and central status within the hall. Second Temple synagogues had no such arrangement; the Torah scrolls were carried into the assembly hall only at an appointed time. By late antiquity, however, the presence of a Torah shrine had become the norm as well as an important component in determining the religious ambience of the synagogue's main hall.

The artistic dimension, with its rich repertoire of Jewish symbols and biblical representations, is another indication of the increased religious profile of the late antique synagogue. Furthermore, literary sources and a considerable number of inscriptions from this period refer to the synagogue as a "holy place" (*ʾatrâ qādîšâ* or *hagios topos*) and to the synagogue community as a "holy congregation" (*qĕhillâ qādîšâ*) or "holy *ḥavurah*" (*ḥāvurtâ qādîšâ*).

Thus, the synagogue of late antiquity came to be widely viewed as a holy place, a status already articulated in fourth-century Byzantine imperial legislation. Valentinian I (ca. 370 C.E.) referred to the synagogue as a *religionum loca* when prohibiting soldiers from seizing quarters there. Such a status was likewise assumed in other edicts issued over the next half century and was aimed at protecting synagogues from violent acts.

The tendency to link synagogue and Temple gained momentum in the Byzantine period. The appearance of plaques in synagogues containing lists of the twenty-four priestly courses — in Caesarea, Ashkelon, Reḥov, perhaps Kis-

Relief depiction of the Tabernacle and the Ark of the Covenant from the third-fourth-century synagogue at Capernaum *(www.HolyLandPhotos.org)*

sufim (near Gaza), Nazareth, and Yemen — may serve as evidence for the ties being forged at this time between these two institutions. Contemporary *piyyutim* (religious poetry of the synagogue) used the twenty-four priestly courses as a frequent motif. One Byzantine *paytan* (poet), Hadutha (or Hadutaha), wrote *piyyutim* for each of the twenty-four priestly courses, and other synagogue poets, themselves priests, also seem to have been focused on Temple-related matters.

In the third and fourth centuries, such themes were also being introduced into the synagogue liturgy. For example, the Additional Service on Sabbaths and holidays *(Mussaf ʿAmidah)* and the additional Torah portion for holidays *(maftir)* both focused on the Temple sacrifices. It was also about this time that the *ʿAvodah* service recalling the Temple ritual on Yom Kippur was added to that day's synagogue liturgy — as was the recitation of a psalm for each day of the week, a custom first documented for priests in the Temple. This latter practice is first explicitly mentioned as an element of synagogue worship only in a seventh- or eighth-century source, but it most probably originated before that. Moreover, we recall the claim usually ascribed to R. Joshua b. Levi (or, alternatively, to the sages generally) that the *ʿAmidah* prayer was introduced as a substitute for sacrifices.

Temple associations seem to have permeated other aspects of synagogue life too. A midrashic fragment on Deuteronomy found in the Cairo Genizah is telling in this regard:

> As long as the Temple existed, the daily offerings and sacrifices would atone for the sins of Israel. Nowadays, the synagogues of Israel replace the Temple, and as long as Israel prays in them, they, in effect, replace the daily offerings and sacrifices; and when prayers are recited [therein] at the proper times and [the Jews] direct their hearts [to God through their prayers], they gain merit and will see the rebuilding of the Temple and the sacrificing of the daily offering and [other] sacrifices, as it is written: "And I will bring them to My holy mountain, and I will rejoice in My house of prayer; their sacrifices and offerings are welcome on My altar, for My house will be called a house of prayer for all peoples." (Isa. 56:7)

Here the synagogue is accorded an elevated status: along with prayer, it replaces the Temple and sacrifices. Moreover, the passage claims that proper observance of prayer will lead to the reestablishment of the Temple, a situation that had been foreseen by the prophet Isaiah.

The reasons usually offered for the synagogue's evolution into an institution with a pronounced religious character include the enhanced association of the synagogue with the Temple; the permanent presence of the Torah scrolls in the main hall; the increased importance of public prayer; and the possible influence of Diaspora models, some of which, as we have seen, had already achieved a holy status. However, several additional factors appear to have played a significant role in this process.

The first was the remarkable development in the concept of holiness throughout the Byzantine-Christian world. "Holiness" as a religious category characterizing places, people, and objects was becoming an ever-greater concern in a wide variety of religious circles.

A second impetus may have been the dramatic development and growing presence of Christianity throughout much of Palestine at this time. We have suggested above that the increased use of Jewish symbols in the Byzantine period resulted, in large part, from this Christian ascendance, which stimulated the Jews to reassert and reestablish their own self-identity. Moreover, it may well be that the synagogue assumed an increased spiritual and religious role for the Jews as a result of Christianity's emphasis on the sanctity of the land in general and of specific sites in particular, not to speak of the many hundreds of churches that were now being built throughout the country. That churches were also being referred to as "holy" or compared to a temple *(naos)* in general, and to the Jerusalem Temple in particular, may have motivated Jews to make similar assertions regarding the synagogue's sanctity. The synagogue thus would have provided a setting for the Jewish community to express whatever disappointment and despair it felt over the loss of the Temple, on the one hand, and its longings and hopes for its rebuilding, on the other. What they were powerless to realize in the political realm, Jews may have hoped to achieve within the confines of their synagogues, albeit in an associative and symbolic vein. The *piyyut* is clearly a primary source for charting such sentiments.

Synagogue Liturgy in Late Antiquity

By late antiquity, a rabbinic synagogue liturgy had developed; if this liturgy was indeed embraced by a community at this time (which remains unknown), it would have offered a rich array of forms and expression. We have noted above that the early Second Temple synagogue liturgy focused on scriptural readings and related practices: the *haftarah* (reading from the Prophets), the sermon or instruction, and the targum. However, following the destruction of the Second Temple, the rabbis developed a public prayer service that they intended to be obligatory. The two basic morning and evening prayers were the *Shemaʿ* paragraphs (Num. 15:37-41; Deut. 6:4-9; 11:13-21), with their accompanying blessings, and the *ʿAmidah.* Regarding the *Shemaʿ*, the rabbis clearly adopted a Temple-based custom but reworked it by supplementing, amplifying, and eliminating material. While the three pentateuchal paragraphs retained their centrality, the sages added a second blessing before the *Shemaʿ* (and possibly changed the content of the first, which is left undefined in the Mishnah) and removed the Decalogue.

The second main component of the rabbinic prayer service was the *ʿAmidah,* whose rabbinic stamp is most evident. Two sources attest explicitly to the innovation at Yavneh immediately following the Temple's destruction in 70 C.E. The Babylonian Talmud (*Berakot* 28b) cites a tradition in which Simeon Hapaquli arranged eighteen benedictions before Rabban Gamaliel according to [their] order at Yavneh, and another source (*m. Ber.* 4:3-4a) deals with a dispute between Rabban Gamaliel and other Yavnean sages regarding which components of the *ʿAmidah,* if any, ought to be standardized.

Thus, by the end of the second century, the rabbinic Sabbath and holiday liturgy seems to have featured five elements, three of which occurred daily, one weekly, and one several times a week. The *Shemaʿ*, *ʿAmidah,* and priestly blessing (included as part of the *ʿAmidah,* but singled out here because of its uniqueness and importance) constituted the basic liturgical framework, with the Torah reading supplementing this basic ritual twice on the Sabbath (morning and afternoon) and once on Mondays and Thursdays. Reading the *haftarah* was a Sabbath and holiday addition.

Conclusion

In the millennium leading up to the end of late antiquity, Jewish society and its institutions underwent a total transformation. There is no example more illustrative of these far-reaching changes than the ancient synagogue. First crystallized in the Second Temple period, it became the communal center of each Jewish settlement and the Jewish public building par excellence. However, while maintaining its status as a communal center, the synagogue of late antiquity began to acquire an enhanced measure of sanctity, its liturgy was expanded, and its main hall assumed a marked degree of holiness. Far from being an age of decadence and decline, as had formerly been assumed, late antiquity was indeed a period of dynamic growth and continued development within Jewish communities in general, and with regard to the synagogue in particular.

"Exuberant diversity," a phrase coined by Peter Brown in another context, can easily be applied to the ancient synagogue. It makes little difference whether the discussion focuses on the nomenclature of the synagogue, officials, architecture, art, inscriptions, or liturgy. In each of these areas the ancient synagogue reflects a kaleidoscope of styles, shapes, customs, and functions that is best accounted for by two complementary factors: the influence of non-Jewish social and religious milieux on the synagogue and the fact that the institution was first and foremost a local one. The tastes and proclivities of each community governed all aspects of the local synagogue — physical, functional, cultural, and religious.

As a communal institution, the synagogue was all-inclusive. The entire range of communal needs was met within its framework, and the synagogue in turn mirrored the community's wishes in its physical appearance, functions, and leadership. However, the very essence and singularity of the synagogue lay in its dual focus on the communal and religious dimensions. On the one hand, the former came to be dominated and shaped in the course of time by the latter; whereas the main hall of the building was once neutral in decoration and function, it was eventually regarded as a sacred area, with its art highlighting ritual objects and symbols. On the other hand, this religious emphasis was rooted in the community that created it, and the religious functions were anchored in the will, participation, and resources of the community at large.

In a larger context, the synagogue's primary historical significance was that it constituted the core institution for Jews everywhere throughout late antiquity. Despite its many geographical, linguistic, cultural, and religious variations, this communal institution and the ongoing expansion of its religious component provided a common framework for Jewish communities everywhere. In a sense, the function fulfilled by the Jerusalem Temple in the pre-70 era was now achieved, *mutatis mutandis,* by this locally based, yet universally present, institution that Jews created wherever they lived — a "diminished sanctuary" that served their corporate and religious needs throughout late antiquity and beyond.

BIBLIOGRAPHY

M. AVI-YONAH 1961, "Synagogue Architecture in the Late Classical Period," in *Jewish Art: An Illustrated History,* ed. C. Roth, Greenwich: New York Graphic Society, 65-82. • D. D. BINDER 1999, *Into the Temple Courts: The Place of the Synagogues in the Second Temple Period,* Atlanta: Society of Biblical Literature. • I. ELBOGEN 1993, *Jewish Liturgy: A Comprehensive History,* trans. R. P. Scheindlin, Philadelphia: Jewish Publication Society. • S. FINE, ED. 1999, *Jews, Christians, and Polytheists in the Ancient Synagogue: Cultural Interaction during the Greco-Roman Period,* London: Routledge. • S. FINE 2005, *Art and Judaism in the Greco-Roman World: Toward a New Jewish Archaeology,* Cambridge: Cambridge University Press. • P. V. M. FLESHER 1995, "Palestinian Synagogues before 70 C.E.: A Review of the Evidence," in *Ancient Synagogues: Historical Analysis and Archaeological Discovery,* ed. D. Urman and P. V. M. Flesher, Leiden: Brill, 1.27-39. • E. R. GOODENOUGH 1953-1968, *Jewish Symbols in the Greco-Roman Period,* 13 vols., New York: Pantheon. • R. HACHLILI 1988, *Ancient Jewish Art and Archaeology in the Land of Israel,* Leiden: Brill. • R. HACHLILI 1998, *Ancient Jewish Art and Archaeology in the Diaspora,* Leiden: Brill. • R. HACHLILI 2002, "The Zodiac in Ancient Synagogal Art: A Review," *Jewish Studies Quarterly* 9: 216–58. • C. KRAELING 1956, *The Excavations at Dura-Europos,* vol. 8, part 1, *The Synagogue,* New Haven: Yale University Press; rpt. New York: KTAV, 1979. • L. I. LEVINE 1992, "The Sages and the Synagogue in Late Antiquity: The Evidence of the Galilee," in *The Galilee in Late Antiquity,* ed. L. I. Levine, New York: Jewish Theological Seminary, 291-322. • L. I. LEVINE 2000, "The History and Significance of the Menorah in Antiquity," in *From Dura to Sepphoris: Studies in Jewish Art and Society in Late Antiquity,* ed. L. I. Levine and Z. Weiss, Ann Arbor: Journal of Roman Archaeology, 131-53. • L. I. LEVINE 2003, "Contextualizing Jewish Art: The Synagogues at Hammat Tiberias and Sepphoris," in *Jewish Culture and Society under the Christian Roman Empire,* ed. R. Kalmin and S. Schwartz, Leuven: Peeters, 91-131. • L. I. LEVINE 2005, *The Ancient Synagogue: The First Thousand Years,* rev. ed., New Haven: Yale University Press. • S. C. REIF 1993, *Judaism and Hebrew Prayer: New Perspectives on Jewish Liturgical History,* Cambridge: Cambridge University Press. • Z. WEISS 2005, *The Sepphoris Synagogue: Deciphering an Ancient Message through Its Archaeological and Socio-Historical Contexts,* Jerusalem: Israel Exploration Society.

See also: Architecture; Art; Associations; Cyrenaica; God-fearers; Mosaics; Ostia; Sardis; Sepphoris; Tiberias; Worship LEE I. LEVINE

Syria

Early History

The history of human settlement in the region of Syria dates back several millennia. During its long history, the area has been dominated by different powerful civilizations. Being situated at a geographical point of transition between north and south, as well as east and west, the area was attractive for both economic and political reasons, leading to conflicts to gain and retain possession of this strategic crossroads.

During the third millennium B.C.E., various Semitic peoples migrated into the region of Syria. Excavations of the ancient city of Ebla *(Tell Mardikh),* in northwestern Syria, have revealed the existence of a thriving kingdom that dominated northern Syria, Lebanon, and parts of northern Mesopotamia during the period of ca. 2600 to 2240 B.C.E., and continued to exercise some influence over the region for several centuries. Other important cities were Ugarit, Hamath, Mari, and Kadesh.

In the subsequent period (ca. 2100 to 1600 B.C.E.), Syria was divided into several powerful states dominated by Amorites and Hurrians. The Hurrians were able to limit the influence of Egypt and formed the kingdom of Mittani around 1600 B.C.E. In the fourteenth century B.C.E. three powerful competitors, apart from the Hurrians, fought for control over the region. The Hittites conquered the kingdom of Mitanni around 1350 B.C.E., but parts of the kingdom were lost to a new contender — Assyria. Egyptians and Hittites continued to compete for the region until the thirteenth century B.C.E.

By the end of the thirteenth century B.C.E., large parts of Syria were under the control of the Arameans. Late in the eleventh century B.C.E., at the time when the Israelites were establishing a kingdom in Jerusalem, the Arameans founded their primary kingdom in Damascus. In the ninth and eighth centuries B.C.E., the Assyrian Empire expanded to the west, and in 732 B.C.E. Tiglath-pileser III captured Damascus. In subsequent centuries, the Assyrian Empire was, however, under strong pressure from Cimmerians, Scythes, and Medes, which invaded from the north and the west, resulting in the fall of Nineveh in 612 B.C.E. With the weakening of Assyria, Egyptian influence increased, and the western parts of Syria were dominated by Egypt until 604 B.C.E., when the Babylonian prince Nebuchadnezzar defeated the Egyptians at Carchemish. Thereafter, Syria was under the control of Nebuchadnezzar's successors for half a century, until the region was incorporated into the expanding Persian Empire. With Alexander's invasion of Asia Minor in 334 B.C.E., and his victory over the Persians at Issus the following year, a new era in the history of Syria began.

The Hellenistic and Roman Periods

After the death of Alexander in 323 B.C.E., his leading generals agreed, as a compromise, to adopt Alexander's half-brother, Philip Arrhidaeus (Philip III), and his still unborn child, if a boy, as kings, with the intention that they would rule jointly. Later the same year, Alexander's wife Roxana gave birth to a son who accordingly became Alexander IV. Perdiccas, one of Alexander's generals, was appointed guardian and regent of the entire empire, and Alexander's other generals, known as the *diadochoi,* "successors," doled out satrapies for themselves. Soon, however, war broke out, and borders and balances of power were constantly changing. Both kings were eventually murdered (Arrhidaeus in 317 B.C.E., and Alexander in 310/309 B.C.E.), and the satrapies became independent kingdoms.

When Alexander's empire was divided, the young officer Seleucus (from 305 B.C.E. called Seleucus I Nicator) was given a high administrative position in Babylonia but was later outmaneuvered and fled to Ptolemy (from 304 B.C.E. called Ptolemy I Soter) in Egypt. In 314 B.C.E., Antigonus (Antigonus I Monophthalmus), Alexander's general who originally had received Phrygia, Lycia, and Pamphylia, invaded Syria (under Ptolemy's control) and became the ruler of large portions of Alexander's empire. In 312 B.C.E., Seleucus was able to retake Babylon with troops borrowed from Ptolemy and eventually formed an alliance against Antigonus, with Cassander and Lysimachus in particular. Together they defeated Antigonus at Ipsus in 301 B.C.E.

Despite an earlier agreement, the victors agreed to assign the southern parts of Syria (Coele-Syria), including Palestine, to Ptolemy. Seleucus, who was greatly indebted to Ptolemy, did not engage him in battle but never gave up his claim to the territory. Dissension about this area gave rise to a series of wars between the Seleucids and Ptolemies. From ca. 200 B.C.E., the southern parts of Syria were finally conquered by the Seleucids when Antiochus III defeated Ptolemy V at Panium. These ongoing conflicts, however, significantly weakened both sides. In the north, the Seleucids retained control only of the areas of Antioch and Damascus. The rest of the region was divided into several independent states under various overlords, resulting in political instability. In the south, the area was divided between three kingdoms: the Hasmonean, Nabatean, and Iturean. In 83 B.C.E. the Armenian king Tigranes II seized Syria and ruled until he was defeated by the Romans. With the Roman assumption of power in 64-63 B.C.E., Syria was eventually turned into a Roman province, with Antioch as its capital.

This complicated political situation makes it hard to define Syria geographically. When the Seleucid kingdom was at its height of power during the reign of Antiochus III, Syria included all of Palestine. With the emergence of the Hasmonean kingdom under Simon in 142 B.C.E., that would of course change. Initially, the Romans preserved the distinction between Syria and Palestine but later allocated parts of the province to various Nabatean and Herodian rulers, and Judea became a separate province in 6 C.E. After the Jewish revolt in 66-70 B.C.E., Palestine was again incorporated into Syria, resembling the earlier situation at the height of the Seleucid era.

The Jewish Community in Syria

The sources for reconstructing the history of the Jewish community in Syria are very limited, confined mainly to the sixth-century chronicler John Malalas, the Jewish historian Josephus, and First and Second Maccabees. The evidence for synagogues in Syria is exclusively literary and is confined to Antioch, Damascus, and Dora.

Josephus (*J.W.* 7.43) states that Jews were numerous in Syria, especially in Antioch. For the Hellenistic period, regarding the portion held by the Seleucid dynasty, the sources are limited to describing Jews within this city. After the victory over Antigonus in 301 B.C.E., Seleucus I Nicator became the sole ruler over a vast kingdom that included Babylonia, Syria, and Mesopotamia, and he soon engaged in founding (or refounding) new cities as part of a strategic plan to colonize the new territory. According to Malalas (*Chronographia* 199-201), he founded Antioch in 300 B.C.E. Josephus claims that Jews were already among the original settlers (*Ant.* 12.119; *Ag. Ap.* 2.39), who may have been mercenary soldiers fighting in Seleucus' army (cf. 2 Macc. 8:20). Probably during the reign of Seleucus' son and successor, Antiochus I Soter (281/0-261 B.C.E.), the capital was transferred from Seleucia to Antioch, which contributed considerably to the city's development into one of the greatest cities of antiquity. The general importance of Antioch partly explains its attraction also for Jews, but Josephus (*J.W.* 7.43) mentions that the proximity of the city to the Jewish homeland was another factor. As Barclay has pointed out, during most of the Hellenistic-Roman period, the Jewish territory was in fact considered to be part of Syria, and Jews who moved from Judea to various Syrian cities, such as Antioch, Damascus, or Tyre, were considered to have moved only from one part of Syria to another. As for the portion controlled by the Ptolemies before 200 B.C.E., the situation probably resembled the one in Egypt, where Jews were found at diverse levels of administration (Barclay 1996).

Throughout the Hellenistic and early Roman periods, the Jewish community of Antioch, and probably Syria in general, flourished, relatively speaking, but from time to time it was also heavily affected by the general political turmoil in the region. There were two major political events that in particular affected the Jewish population in Syria: the Maccabean Revolt against the Seleucids, and the Jewish war against Rome. The effort to turn Jerusalem into a Greek polis, initiated by some radical Jewish groups with the support of Antiochus IV Epiphanes, eventually culminated in the outbreak of the Maccabean Revolt in 166 B.C.E. Even though the Maccabees themselves were profoundly Hellenized in many respects, the development enforced a socially constructed contrast between "Judaism" and "Hellenism." As a reaction to the Maccabean uprising, the Jewish population in some areas, such as Joppa, Jamnia, Tyre, Sidon, and Galilee, seems to have been under some pressure from the non-Jewish population to dissociate themselves from the revolt. This led in turn to virtual rescue parties arranged by the Maccabees, extending the fighting well beyond the borders of Judea (1 Macc. 5:1-68; 2 Macc. 12:2-31). Furthermore, in the aftermath of the formation of the Hasmonean state, a period of territorial expansion was initiated. This resulted in a systematic Judaization of numerous Greek cities in the costal plain up to Mt. Carmel, in Idumea, Samaria, Galilee, and in the region across the Jordan, where the non-Jewish population was violently removed or compelled to accept the introduction of Jewish customs (see, e.g., 1 Macc. 13:11, 43-48; Josephus, *Ant.* 13.395-97). These developments were reversed with the conquest by the Romans under Pompey.

In Antioch, internal struggles over the Seleucid throne further contributed to complicated relations between Jews and non-Jews. After having outmaneuvered his rival Alexander I Balas, Demetrius II was caught in a situation where his own troops raised a mutiny, putting the city in a state of civil war. Demetrius appealed for help from the Hasmonean leader Jonathan, who sent 3,000 Jewish soldiers to the city. They certainly helped suppress the revolt but also plundered and burned the city (1 Macc. 11:41-51; Josephus, *Ant.* 13.135-42).

There are also reports of disturbances in Syrian cities during 39-44 C.E., which may have been connected to the catastrophic situation in Alexandria in 38 C.E. Malalas (*Chronographia* 244–45) records a virtual pogrom in Antioch, with a subsequent intervention of Jewish troops. The story is full of obvious mistakes but may contain a kernel of truth. The outbreak of the revolt in 66 C.E. led to similar reactions, and it is even possible that an outburst of violence against the Jewish population in Caesarea (Josephus, *J.W.* 2.284-92, 457) was the direct cause of the revolt, which soon spread to numerous places (Josephus, *J.W.* 2.458–60). In Damascus, Josephus states (*J.W.* 2.559-61; 7.368), the Jewish population was slaughtered by the tens of thousands.

Antioch, Apamea, and Sidon were, at least in the beginning of the war, free from violence. As for Antioch, this can probably be explained by the presence of the Roman legions stationed in the capital of Syria. Josephus, however, reports that when Vespasian landed in Syria, a certain Antiochus, the son of the *archōn* of the Jews in Antioch, who evidently had renounced his Jewish identity, accused some Jews of planning to burn the city. In order to prove their loyalty, Jews were compelled to perform sacrifices to Greek deities. Those who refused were killed; faced with this option, some Jews submitted to performing what from a Jewish perspective was considered "idolatry." When a fire later actually broke out, Antiochus soon repeated his accusations, and only the instant intercession of the Roman authorities prevented a catastrophe (*J.W.* 7.46-62). In the aftermath of the war, according to Josephus (*J.W.* 7.100-111), the non-Jewish population of Antioch wanted the Jews expelled but were denied this request by Titus, who instead confirmed the special privileges of the Jews. It is not hard to grasp how this affected the relations between Jews and non-Jews in the city.

However, the situation in Syria was not altogether characterized by enmity between Jews and non-Jews. Josephus reports that the non-Jews of Antioch were especially attracted by Judaism (*J.W.* 7.45), and the same seems to have been true for Damascus, where the non-Jewish males did not trust their own wives, since almost all were profoundly involved in Judaism (so *J.W.* 2.559-60). In Acts 10, Luke describes the Roman officer Cornelius in Caesarea, who became involved with the Jewish Jesus movement, as "a devout man who feared God" *(eusebēs kai phoboumenos ton theon),* indicating his prior attachment to Judaism. Given the abundance of evidence for non-Jewish interest in Judaism (see, e.g., Murray 2004), it is reasonably safe to assume a similar situation in many other Syrian cities.

In general, the Jews of Syria were well integrated into Greco-Roman society. They had a legally well-defined position and were probably considered to be a kind of voluntary association. Their religious customs were normally tolerated and to some extent also respected. The authorities, whether Greek or Roman, on the whole confirmed the rights of the Jewish community to exist on its own terms, and the Jews usually found ways of expressing their loyalty to the non-Jewish society without engaging in non-Jewish cults (Harland 2003). There existed a mutual cultural exchange: the Jewish communities exercised a considerable influence on the Greco-Roman population and were themselves intensely influenced by Hellenism (Hengel 1974). At the same time, it is important to note that this situation sometimes proved to be rather fragile. In times of political turmoil, an underlying anti-Jewish attitude prevalent in both Greek and Roman culture could be expressed in riots and pogroms. In this respect, the situation in Syria probably mirrors the general, highly conflicting attitudes toward Jewish people — a mixture of admiration and fear, tolerance and suspicion.

Bibliography

J. M. G. Barclay 1996, *Jews in the Mediterranean Diaspora: From Alexander to Trajan (323 BCE–117 CE),* Edinburgh: Clark. • D. D. Binder 1999, *Into the Temple Courts: The Place of the Synagogue in the Second Temple Period,* Atlanta: Society of Biblical Literature. • K. Butcher 2003, *Roman Syria and the Near East,* London: British Museum Press. • G. Downey 1961, *A History of Antioch in Syria from Seleucus to the Arab Conquest,* Princeton: Princeton University Press. • P. Green 1990, *Alexander to Actium: The Hellenistic Age,* London: Thames and Hudson. • P. A. Harland 2003, *Associations, Synagogues, and Congregations: Claiming a Place in Ancient Mediterranean Society,* Minneapolis: Fortress. • M. Hengel 1974, *Judaism and Hellenism: Studies in Their Encounter in Palestine during the Early Hellenistic Period,* London: SCM. • H. Klengel 1992, *Syria: 3000 to 300 B.C.: A Handbook on Political History,* Berlin: Akademie Verlag. • C. H. Kraeling 1932, "The Jewish Community at Antioch," *JBL* 51: 130-60. • L. I. Levine 2000, *The Ancient Synagogue: The First Thousand Years,* New Haven: Yale University Press. • M. Murray 2004, *Playing a Jewish Game: Gentile Christian Judaizing in the First and Second Centuries CE,* Waterloo, Ont.: Wilfrid Laurier University Press. • G. Shipley 1999, *The Greek World after Alexander: 323-30 BC,* London: Routledge.

See also: Antioch (Syrian); Damascus

Magnus Zetterholm

Syriac

Syriac is an Eastern Aramaic dialect first attested in and around Edessa at the turn of the Christian Era. It soon spread over a large geographical area from Syria to Persia and reached its heyday from the third to the seventh century. A vast amount of literature was produced and preserved in Syriac, including numerous early Jewish works. The significance of the Syriac versions of the Jewish Apocrypha and Pseudepigrapha varies for each book. In some cases the Syriac translation is attested in a single manuscript only, but that version is part of the oldest and most important group of textual witnesses and hence is of great importance. In other cases, multiple Syriac translations of the same work are preserved, but they are derivative of other (mostly Greek) textual versions.

Early Jewish Literature Preserved in Syriac

A proper assessment of the Syriac translations of early Jewish literature is fraught with difficulties. First, the origins of the Syriac translations lie in obscurity. It is often impossible to ascertain the date of the translation (or, in some cases, of the multiple Syriac translations). The Peshiṭta, the standard version of the Bible of the Syriac Churches (Syrian Orthodox, Maronite, and Church of the East), which was completed by the third century C.E., was not translated as a whole but book by book. It remains unclear whether the Peshiṭta is a Jewish, Christian, or a Jewish-Christian translation, and it may well be that making such a distinction between Jews and Christians during the first and second centuries is anachronistic. Some scholars have argued that some books of the Old Testament Peshiṭta were translated by Jews and others by Christians (Dirksen 1988; Brock 1992). The situation is likely similar for the apocryphal and pseudepigraphic books.

Second, the uncertainty whether the Syriac translations of early Jewish texts were made by Jews or by Christians points to a larger problem. How we can tell with any confidence whether an ancient pseudepigraphon is in fact Jewish or Christian? While in some cases the evidence is unambiguous, there are numerous texts of doubtful origin (Davila 2005).

Third, Syriac translations of Jewish Apocrypha and Pseudepigrapha in general have received little scholarly attention (Duval 1907). Syriac literature includes a number of texts attributed to biblical figures as well as several anonymous and pseudepigraphic wisdom texts of uncertain origin, many of which remain unexamined and unedited (Bundy 1991).

The Peshiṭta

All the biblical books of the Peshiṭta Old Testament were translated from Hebrew, whereas the books of the

Apocrypha are translations from the LXX, with the exception of Sirach, which was also translated from Hebrew (Brock 1989). Only a few complete manuscripts of the Peshiṭta survive, and not all manuscripts include the same books. The famous Ambrosian Codex of the Peshiṭta (7aI in the Leiden Peshiṭta edition), the oldest complete Peshiṭta Old Testament manuscript, dating from the sixth or seventh century, contains a number of extracanonical books, including book 6 of Josephus' *Jewish War,* intermingled with the canonical books. It is therefore difficult to distinguish clearly between biblical, apocryphal, and pseudepigraphic books (Peshiṭta Institute 1961). The following works are part of the Peshiṭta manuscript tradition.

Wisdom of Solomon

The Wisdom of Solomon is a sapiential text that purports to be written by Solomon. The book, which was composed in Greek, survives in seven Peshiṭta manuscripts of which the Ambrosian manuscript is the most complete, and several lectionaries (Peshiṭta ed. 1959, reedited in 1979).

Letter of Jeremiah

The apocryphal Letter of Jeremiah is a polemical treatise against idolatry (cf. Ep. Jer. 10:1-16; 29). In LXX the Letter follows the book of Lamentations as a separate text, but in the Vulgate it appears as chap. 6 of Baruch. A small portion of the Greek text was found in Cave 7 of Qumran (7Q2). The Syriac is a close translation of the Greek.

Letter of Baruch

The Letter of Baruch purports to be a letter sent by Baruch, the scribe of Jeremiah, to the exiles in Assyria whom he first consoles and then admonishes to observe the Mosaic Torah. It is found at the end of the Syriac *Apocalypse of Baruch* (*2 Baruch* 78–87). Throughout *2 Baruch*'s history of transmission, however, the epistle was separated from the apocalypse, transmitted independently, and survives in thirty-six manuscripts and lectionaries. The Ambrosian Codex (7aI) includes two recensions of the epistle, the independent form and the epistle in chaps. 78–87 of *2 Baruch* (the Peshiṭta edition is forthcoming).

Book of Baruch

The apocryphal book of Baruch, composed in the wake of the desecration of the Temple by Antiochus IV in 167 B.C.E., is the oldest of a group of texts attributed to Baruch. Syriac Baruch, like the other versions, is a translation of the Greek, which in turn is a translation of a lost Hebrew original.

Additions to Daniel

The Greek versions of the book of Daniel include three extended "additions" not found in the Masoretic Text. They were likely composed in Aramaic during the second century B.C.E. The Prayer of Azariah and the Song of the Three Young Men, inserted between Dan. 3:23 and 3:24 (Peshiṭta Dan. 3:26-90), consists of two prayers. The story of Bel and the Dragon, a satirical polemic against idolatry, appears as an independent book after the book of Daniel. Susanna, the story of a devout Jewish woman wrongfully accused of adultery and rescued by Daniel, likewise follows biblical Daniel (Peshiṭta ed. 1980, albeit without Susanna; the Prayer of Azariah is also found in Peshiṭta ed. 1972).

Judith

The book of Judith is an early Jewish novel written in the late second century B.C.E. that relates how a Jewish widow rescues the Jewish people from an oppressive enemy. Composed in Hebrew, the book now survives in Greek, Latin, and Syriac. The most important Greek manuscripts are Alexandrinus (A) and Vaticanus (B). Jerome states that he used an Aramaic text (no longer extant) and older Latin texts (which are attested). Three Syriac translations survive, one in the Peshiṭta tradition, one in the Syro-Hexapla (on which, see below), and a third, late copy that was recently discovered in India.

Ben Sira

The textual history of the wisdom book of Ben Sira (Ecclesiasticus), written in Hebrew in the second century B.C.E., is complex. About two-thirds of the book survives in Hebrew in several manuscripts from the Judean Desert and in six manuscripts from the Cairo Geniza from the eleventh and twelfth centuries. Both the Greek and the Syriac versions go back directly to the Hebrew text, whereas the Latin translation is based on the Greek. The Syriac translation shows the influence of the Greek, presumably because it was later brought into conformity with the Greek. A second Syriac translation was produced by the West Syrian bishop Paul of Tella in ca. 613 C.E. as part of the Syro-Hexapla, a rendering of the Septuagint text found in the fifth column of Origen of Alexandria's Hexapla, which was a compilation of different ancient versions of the Hebrew Bible in six parallel columns.

4 Ezra and 2 Baruch

4 Ezra and *2 Baruch* are two pseudepigraphic apocalypses, composed in Hebrew during the late first century C.E. in response to the Roman destruction of Jerusalem. No Jewish manuscripts survive. Syriac translations of both texts are preserved in the Ambrosian Codex, supplemented with fragments of three Jacobite lectionaries (Peshiṭta ed. 1973). For both texts the Syriac version belongs to the most important textual witnesses.

Apocryphal Psalms

A few books present special cases. These include the Apocryphal Psalms, a collection of five Psalms attributed to David originally composed in Hebrew. The Psalms are preserved in a late (ca. 800 C.E.?) Syriac translation, and in some psalters appear as an addendum to the canonical Psalms. Psalm 151 is also attested in the LXX and, together with Psalms 154 and 155, at Qumran in 11QPs[a] (Peshiṭta ed. 1972).

Prayer of Manasseh
The Prayer of Manasseh is an apocryphal penitential prayer from the turn of the Common Era. It is preserved in Greek *(Didascalia Apostolorum)* and Syriac, and was probably composed in Greek. The Prayer is attested in the LXX manuscripts since the fifth century, among the poems appended to the Psalter. It is also attested in the Peshiṭta manuscripts since the ninth century. There are seven Syriac manuscripts and several manuscripts of the *Didascalia Apostolorum* in Syriac translation (Peshiṭta ed. 1972).

Psalms of Solomon
The *Psalms of Solomon* is a collection of eighteen psalms attributed to Solomon and composed in the first century B.C.E. The work survives in Greek and Syriac. Both are translations of a now lost Hebrew original, and the Syriac is influenced by the Greek. The Peshiṭta edition is based on four incomplete manuscripts, one of which (Rylands Syr. ms. 9) also includes the *Odes of Solomon* (Peshiṭta ed. 1972).

1 Esdas
1 Esdras, a retelling of the history of Israel from Josiah's reform to Ezra's public reading of the Torah, was initially not preserved in the Peshiṭta tradition. The only known Syriac version is a Syro-Hexaplaric manuscript, which later was adopted in a number of Peshiṭta manuscripts (first Syriac ed. P. A. de Lagarde 1861; Peshiṭta ed. 1972).

Tobit
The book of Tobit is an early Jewish novel of the third century B.C.E. whose textual history is similar to that of 1 Esdras. The Peshiṭta translation was lost and replaced by the Syro-Hexaplaric version that survives in its entirety in a single manuscript. All other manuscripts present a translation only of the second half of Tobit. The translation stems neither from the Syro-Hexapla nor from the Peshiṭta but is a rendering of the Greek that was possibly revised in light of an unknown Hebrew text. This mixed text is included in the Leiden Peshiṭta edition (first Syriac ed. P. A. de Lagarde, 1861; Peshiṭta ed. 1972).

1–4 Maccabees
A Syriac version of 1–4 Maccabees is attested in numerous manuscripts as part of the Peshiṭta tradition.

Pseudepigrapha
In addition to the early Jewish literature preserved in the Peshiṭta manuscript tradition, Syriac translations of some Pseudepigrapha survive.

Jubilees
The book of *Jubilees* is a pseudepigraphic retelling of Genesis and the first half of Exodus, composed in Hebrew in the second century B.C.E. The book was translated into Greek and possibly into Syriac, and from Greek into Latin and Classical Ethiopic. A total of fifteen Hebrew fragments of *Jubilees* were found among the Dead Sea Scrolls. Only two Syriac fragments survive. The first, published by A. M. Ceriani, is very short. The second is an anonymous Syriac chronicle that lists nineteen citations from *Jubilees* of various lengths. A Syriac translation of the entire work may have existed at one point but is now lost.

Joseph and Aseneth
Joseph and Aseneth, the story about Joseph and his marriage to Aseneth, daughter of the Egyptian priest Potiphera, was originally composed in Greek and survives in numerous recensions. Two Syriac manuscripts are preserved, of which the older, dating to the sixth century, is the oldest surviving text of the book. It remains unclear whether *Joseph and Aseneth* is an early Jewish work translated from Greek into Syriac or whether it is originally a (Christian) Syriac composition (Davila 2005).

Sentences of the Syriac Menander
The *Sentences of the Syriac Menander* is a collection of popular sapiential sayings ascribed to Menander the Sage, a third-century-B.C.E. Athenian author. The Syriac text survives in a longer recension and in an epitome. However, both its date of composition (third century C.E.?) and its origin (Jewish or pagan?) remain unclear (Bundy 1991).

BIBLIOGRAPHY
S. P. BROCK 1989, *The Bible in the Syriac Tradition,* Kerala, India: St. Ephrem Ecumenical Research Institute. • S. P. BROCK 1992, "Versions, Ancient (Syriac)," in *ABD* 6: 794-99. • D. BUNDY 1991, "Pseudepigrapha in Syriac Literature," *SBLSP* 30: 745-65. • J. R. DAVILA 2005, *The Provenance of the Pseudepigrapha,* Leiden: Brill. • P. B. DIRKSEN 1988, "The Old Testament *Peshiṭta,*" in *Mikra,* ed. M. J. Mulder, Minneapolis: Fortress. • P. B. DIRKSEN 1989, *An Annotated Bibliography of the Peshiṭta of the Old Testament,* Leiden: Brill. • R. DUVAL 1907, *La littérature syriaque,* Paris: Lecoffre. • G. W. E. NICKELSBURG 2005, *Jewish Literature between the Bible and the Mishnah,* 2d ed., Minneapolis: Fortress. • PESHIṬTA INSTITUTE 1961, *List of Old Testament Peshiṭta Manuscripts (Preliminary Edition),* Leiden: Brill. • M. WEITZMAN 1999, *The Syriac Version of the Old Testament: An Introduction,* Cambridge: Cambridge University Press.

MATTHIAS HENZE

T

Tabernacles, Feast of → Festivals and Holy Days

Table Fellowship → Meals

Tales of the Persian Court (4Q550)

Tales of the Persian Court (4Q550) is a modern title for a text among the Dead Sea Scrolls that recounts the experience of a group of Jews in the royal court of the Persian kings Darius and Xerxes. The fragments of 4Q550 are divided into six groups (a-f). Although scholars disagree on the order of the fragments, most concur that the first three, 4Q550^{a-c}, represent a portion of a distinct narrative. The next group, 4Q550^{d-e}, present a different plot line, and therefore most experts consider these fragments independently from 4Q550^{a-c}. The last fragment, 4Q550^{f}, is rarely included with the others as its subject matter and handwriting are distinctively different.

Scholars have long considered these fragments to be related, if not directly then at least in genre, to the court tales found in the Bible and pseudepigraphic literature. As early as 1956, J. Starcky recognized that he had in his set of fragments a text, possibly from the Persian period, that recalled the biblical books of Esther or Daniel. In 1992, J. T. Milik published the fragments along with a thorough transcription, translation, and discussion of the relationship of the fragments to other literatures. Milik supposed that 4Q550 was the model or prototype for the various versions of the book of Esther and titled the fragments 4QprEsther. Although Milik's conclusions regarding a direct relationship to the book of Esther have been largely contradicted, his ordering of the fragments, his transcription and translation, and his discussions have been invaluable to recent scholarship.

Fragments 4Q550^{a-c} present a tale of the Persian court. The king, who is either bored or unable to sleep, has the chronicles of his father, King Darius, read to him (4Q550^{a}). The chronicles relate that Patireza, a loyal servant in the royal wardrobe, is due some kind of reward or honor. It is possible that an injustice has been done to him or some special good deed of his has been overlooked. Fear grips the king for not having acted upon this information earlier (4Q550^{b}). He rewards Patireza's son with the father's position and gives the son many "possessions" (4Q550^{b}). A princess is introduced into the story, and it appears that Patireza "acted with truth" in regard to her as well (4Q550^{c}). In the next line, a herald speaks, but here the fragment ends except for the single word "purple." It is possible that Patireza's son is further rewarded by being clothed in purple, a common symbol of royalty, but it is just as likely that the herald is referring to some piece of the royal wardrobe.

Several scholars have noted the similarities of this narrative with the book of Esther. The king has the royal annals read to him during which recitation he discovers new information upon which he chooses to act. In both accounts, the king seeks to honor a member of his court who, until then, has been overlooked or mistreated. Also similar to Esther, a princess appears who is linked in some manner to the protagonist. Fragments 4Q550^{d-e} also recall Esther by introducing a subgenre of the court tale: the courtier conflict theme. Here the protagonist, Bagasri, is victorious over Bagoshi (4Q550^{d} col. 2). Both men serve in the court of the king, and it would seem that Bagasri is Jewish (4Q550^{d} col. 1). Although the specific events of the conflict are missing, several references recall other Jewish narratives of the foreign court type. The opening lines of 4Q550^{d} col. 1 not only describe a Jewish court official but also place the blame for the Jewish Diaspora on the Jewish community itself: ". . . for the sins of my fathers . . . that they sinned aforetime" (lines 1-3). In addition, as in the denouements found in Daniel 2–6, the king acknowledges the sovereignty of God: "The Most High whom you worship and serve, he is sovereign over the whole earth" (4Q550^{d} col. 3).

Although there is no direct connection between these narratives and those found in the Bible, these court tale fragments remind us of the large corpus of literature that must have existed in antiquity.

BIBLIOGRAPHY

J. J. COLLINS AND D. A. GREEN 1999, "The Tales from the Persian Court (4Q550[a-e])," in *Antikes Judentum und Frühes Christentum: Festschrift für Hartmut Stegemann zum 65. Geburtstag,* ed. W. Reinbold et al., Berlin: de Gruyter, 39-52. • S. W. CRAWFORD 1996, "Has *Esther* Been Found at Qumran? 4QProto-Esther and the *Esther* Corpus," *RevQ* 17: 307-25. • S. W. CRAWFORD 2002, "4QTales of the Persian Court (4Q550[a-e]) and Its Relation to Biblical Royal Courtier Tales, Especially Esther, Daniel and Joseph," in *The Bible as Book: The Hebrew Bible and the Judaean Desert Discoveries,* ed. E. D. Herbert and E. Tov, London: British Library, 121-37. • K. DE TROYER 2000, "Once More, the So-Called Esther Fragments of Cave 4," *RevQ* 19: 401-22. • J. T. MILIK 1992, "Les modèles Araméens du livre d'Esther dan la grotte 4 de Qumrân," *RevQ* 15: 321-406. • J. STARCKY 1956, "Le travail d'édition des fragments manuscrits de Qumrân: Communication de J. Starcky." *RB* 63: 66-67. • M. G. WECHSLER 2000, "Two Para-Biblical Novellae from Qumran Cave 4: A Reevaluation of 4Q550," *DSD* 7: 130-72.

DEBORAH A. GREEN

Tanḥumim (4Q176)

Tanḥumim (4Q176) comprises some fifty-four Hebrew fragments and is called "consolations" *(tanḥumim)* because of the words in the first extant column of text: "And from the book of Isaiah: Words of consolation. ['Be consoled, be consoled, my people!'] says your God . . ." (frgs. 1-2 col. i lines 4-5; cf. Isa. 40:1), and in the later fragmentary col. iii, where we find reference to "the words of consolation" (frgs. 8-11, line 13). The scroll, written by two hands, dates to the middle of the first century B.C.E.

Most of what survives consists of various biblical quotations or allusions: Ps. 79:2–3; Isa. 40:1-5; 41:8-9; 49:7, 13-17; 43:1-2, 4-6; 51:22-23; 52:1-2; 54:4-10 (followed by a few lines of commentary); Zech. 13:9 (followed by what appears to be more commentary in frgs. 16-18, 22-23, 33, 51, and 53). Against Allegro, fragments 19–21 have been identified as belonging to a Hebrew scroll of *Jubilees* and are now classified as 4Q176a (see Kister, Nebe). Recent study proposes fragments of five columns of text (Høgenhaven): frgs. 1–2 (= col. i), frgs. 3-5, 1-2, 6-7 (= col. ii), frgs. 8-11 (= col. iii), frgs. 14-15, 12-13, 42 (= col. iv?); and frgs. 16-18, 22-23, 33, 51, 53 (= col. v).

The quotations of Isaiah agree with several distinctive readings in 1QIsaiah[a] over against the MT. An eschatological orientation of the scroll is suggested at the outset by the expression of the hope that God will perform his marvelous work and do justice to his people (frgs. 1-2 col. i line 12) and by the later references to Belial, whose purpose is "to oppress his [God's] servants" (frgs. 8-11 col. iii line 15), and the anticipation that Israel(?) "will rejoice" and be raised up (ibid., line 16).

Stanley has suggested that Tanḥumim is a copy of an older notebook, in which a student of Scripture has copied a series of passages, chiefly from Isaiah 40–54, producing an anthology of consolations, perhaps to meet a personal need or a community need. Stanley cites the example of Pliny the Younger, who upon hearing of the death of his uncle (Pliny the Elder), read and extracted selections from Livy: "I called for a volume of Livy and went on reading. . . . I even went on with the extracts I had been making" (Pliny the Younger, *Epistles* 6.20.5).

Høgenhaven builds on Stanley's study, focusing on three significant nonbiblical sections of the scroll (though in fact these sections do allude to words and phrases drawn from Scripture). The first section (col. i lines 12-15) constitutes a prayer that makes use of imagery found in Psalm 79. Against Allegro, this material is not a pesher (for Psalm 79 is not interpreted); it is a prayer whose language and imagery are enhanced by the psalm. The second section (col. iii lines 13-17) is quite fragmentary and so is not easy to interpret. Expressions such as "desperate," "until words of consolation," "great glory," and "will rejoice" suggest that a turning point is envisioned, from calamities to redemption. The third section (col. v lines 1-8) seems to envision vindication for the righteous and punishment for the wicked.

Tanḥumim offers several verbal and thematic links to other Qumran texts, such as 4Q418 (4QInstruction) and 4Q215a (4QTime of Righteousness). 4Q418 frg. 81 presents several parallels with Tanḥumim col. v, particularly with respect to God's creation of the world and his determination of the respective states, or lots, of human beings. A similar theme is encountered in 4Q215a frg. 1 col. ii lines 8-10. What unites these three texts are notions of a divine plan from the beginning of time and an eschatological hope (Høgenhaven). It is in the light of this perspective that the "consolations" of Tanḥumim should be understood.

Tanḥumim also offers an interesting verbal parallel to Paul's assertion in Rom. 3:20, as seen in a woodenly literal rendering: "For by works of law all flesh shall not be justified before him [God]." Paul's *dioti . . . ou dikaiothēsetai pasa sarx enōpion autou* approximates Tanḥumim's *kî lô' yiṣdaq kōl 'îš milipnēyw* ("for all/every man is not justified before him") at col. v lines 1-2 (cf. Ps. 143:2; 1QH[a] 9:14). Of course, Paul's declaration that no one is justified before God "by works of law" does not reflect the perspective of Qumran.

BIBLIOGRAPHY

J. M. ALLEGRO 1968, *Qumrân Cave 4:I (4Q158–4Q186),* DJD 5, Oxford: Clarendon, 60–67. • J. HØGENHAVEN 2007, "The Literary Character of 4QTanḥumim," *DSD* 14: 99–123. • M. KISTER 1985-1987, "Newly Identified Fragments of the Book of Jubilees: Jub. 23:21-23, 30-31," *RevQ* 12: 529-36. • G.-W. NEBE 1989, "Ergänzende Bemerkung zu 4Q176, Jubiläen 23, 21," *RevQ* 14: 129-30. • C. D. STANLEY 1992, "The Importance of 4QTanḥumim (4Q176)," *RevQ* 15: 569-82. • J. STRUGNELL 1969-1971, "Notes en marge du volume V des 'Discoveries in the Judaean Desert of Jordan,'" *RevQ* 7: 163-276, esp. 229-36.

CRAIG A. EVANS

Targum, Targumim

The Hebrew word *targûm* (pl. *targûmîm*) is generally understood to refer to the ancient translations of the Hebrew Bible into Aramaic during the early centuries C.E., and possibly the late centuries B.C.E. Most of our extant targumim appear to go back to scriptural translations that were produced initially within the land of Israel (Palestine), having been transmitted mainly under rabbinic auspices. (Neither the *Samaritan Targum* nor the Syriac Peshiṭta is being considered here.) The term "targûm" is based on the quadriliteral verbal root *trgm*, which has cognates in other Semitic languages but is likely to have had an Indo-European origin. It originally appears to have denoted the translation of an administrative or commercial document from one language to another in the context of an international exchange. This appears to be the usage of the sole biblical appearance of the verb *trgm* in Ezra 4:17, with reference to a letter written by local Judean officials in Aramaic, but translated, or to be translated *(mĕtûrgām)*, for presentation to the Persian king Artaxerxes. The nominal form *targûm* is not evidenced prior to early rabbinic literature (beginning with the Mishnah, ca. 200 C.E.), where it is used principally for the translation of the Hebrew Bible, mainly into Aramaic, but also into other languages, especially Greek. However, it is also used in rabbinic literature for the Aramaic sections of the Hebrew Bible (e.g., in Daniel, Ezra, and Nehemiah), and for "internal translation" within Hebrew, whereby one person of lower status broadcasts or explains the words of another of higher status (Alexander 1985: 320-21; Safrai 2006: 244-45).

Targumic Origins

The origins of the practice of translating the Hebrew Bible, most likely beginning with the Torah (Pentateuch), into Aramaic is clouded in uncertainty. Some scholars (both modern critical and ancient rabbinic) see the practice first enacted or modeled in Ezra's reading of the Torah to the assembled masses in Jerusalem ca. 450 B.C.E., as described by Neh. 8:1-8, with the simultaneous (or interlinear) elucidation by the Levites so that the people would understand the reading: "They read from the scroll of the teaching *(tôrâ)* of God, translating it *(mĕpōraš)* and giving the sense, so they understood the reading" (v. 8 NJPS). At issue here is the meaning of *mĕpōraš*, which could mean anything from "distinctly" to "with explanation." The use of the same verbal form in Ezra 4:18, in which the Persian king Artaxerxes responds to the aforementioned letter from the Judean officials by referring to "the letter that you wrote me has been read to me in translation *(mĕpōraš)*" suggests that *mĕpōraš* and *mĕtûrgām* are synonymous expressions, denoting translation from one language (Hebrew/Aramaic) into another (Aramaic/Persian) but also entailing a degree of clarification and interpretation (in Neh. 8:8).

Whatever transpired at this event, we do not have a single mention of the translation of the Hebrew Bible into Aramaic in any source from the Second Temple period (unlike several accounts of the translation of the Torah into Greek in mid-third-century-B.C.E. Alexandria, Egypt). Thus, it is impossible to know whether Ezra's bilingual reading and rendering of Scripture represents or initiated a regular practice of public translation of the Hebrew Bible into Aramaic, say (as is commonly presumed), in the weekly readings of Scripture in Second Temple synagogues, whether orally or from established texts (Levine 2005: 159-62). Although we have several depictions (in Josephus, Philo, and the New Testament) of the public reading of the Torah and Prophets in Second Temple synagogues, not one of them refers to the practice of an accompanying recitation of an Aramaic translation, as described in rabbinic sources beginning with the Mishnah.

Although we have fragments of an Aramaic translation of two noncontinuous sections of Leviticus (4QTgLev [4Q156]) and parts of two copies of an Aramaic translation of the book of Job from Qumran (11QTgJob [11Q10] and 4QTgJob [4Q157]), both of these being fairly literal in their renderings, we have no way of knowing what their function was within that community or its larger movement. It would appear that they did not accompany the lectionary recitation of Scripture in a synagogue context, since we have no reason to presume that those texts had a place in the synagogue service (Shepherd 2004). Otherwise, we have no extant targumic texts, or knowledge of such, that can be dated confidently to prerabbinic (pre-70 C.E.) times. Our earliest extant targumic texts (outside of the Dead Sea Scrolls) date from no earlier than the third century C.E., although they likely draw on an earlier targumic substratum and certainly incorporate earlier exegetical traditions, as do all early rabbinic texts (Kaufman 1985; York 1974).

Targumic Social Practice: Synagogue

For the social practice of targumic scriptural translation in the synagogue setting, we are dependent on the laws and narratives of early rabbinic texts, beginning with the Mishnah. To what extent those rules and narratives are representative of what actually occurred in ancient synagogues is impossible to know, in part because the degree of rabbinic authority in the synagogues is uncertain, and because there is no reason to assume a common liturgical or lectionary practice in synagogues across time and place. Nevertheless, early rabbinic literature is our only extant source for the social practice of targum. In those texts we are told that a person called the *mĕtûrgĕmān* (or *tûrgĕmān*) was designated to follow the reading of each verse from the Torah, or up to three verses from the Prophets, with a rendering in Aramaic. While the scriptural text is to be read from a scroll, its targum was rendered orally, whether spontaneously, from memory, or, most likely, in some combination of the two. It is presumed that targumic texts circulated and were stored in synagogues, and that they shared some but not all of Scripture's sanctity. Their public performance was not from a written text, however, so as not to blur the distinction between written Scriptures and their oral explication, and the persons reading and

TARGUM, TARGUMIM

rendering were separate and distinct. Similarly, the higher status of the written text of Scripture over its oral targumic accompaniment was accentuated through the choice as *mĕtûrgĕmān* of someone of lower status than that of the scriptural reader. Unlike the ancient Jewish Greek translation of Scripture (the Septuagint), the recitation of the targum never, as far as we know, replaced the reading of the Hebrew Scriptures, but rather served as its accompaniment. Thus, what one heard in a synagogue, at least one that followed these early rabbinic rules, would have been a bilingual, interlinear reading/recitation of the Hebrew scriptural text and its Aramaic rendering (Alexander 1985; Fraade 1992; Levine 2005: 578-83; Smelik 1995: 31-41). There is, then, no evidence for an ancient "Aramaic Bible" (at least not of the rabbinic targumim) akin to the Greek Bible.

Targumic Social Practice: Study

While it is often presumed that the extant targumim reflect the practice of targum mainly in the synagogue and that they were intended thereby for a popular synagogue audience who lacked comprehension of the Hebrew Scriptures, we have strong evidence, once again from early rabbinic literature, that they may just as well reflect the practice of targum in the context of scriptural study, whether by individuals or small groups, at a wide range of educational levels, but including those who were learned in Scripture and rabbinic tradition and bilingual in Hebrew and Aramaic. As in the liturgical setting, the use of targum in the context of study accompanied rather than replaced Hebrew Scripture. This is confirmed by our earliest extant manuscripts of rabbinic targumim from the Cairo Geniza, in which at least the first few words of each verse in Hebrew precede their Aramaic rendering (Klein 1986, 2002). In the context of study, the Aramaic targum appears to have served both as a reinforcement for the learning of Scripture in Hebrew ("twice Scripture and once targum" [*b. Berakot* 8a-b]) and as a pedagogical bridge between the fixed "written Torah" and the more fluid "oral Torah" of scriptural interpretation ("Scripture leads to targum, targum leads to mishnah [oral teaching], mishnah leads to talmud [dialectical commentary]," *Sifre* Deuteronomy 161). The pedagogical settings and functions of targum remain largely unexamined except for some preliminary probes (Fraade 2006; Smelik 1995: 24-31; York 1979).

Targum and Ancient Jewish Multilingualism

The rabbinic emphasis on the accompanying function of targum with respect to Hebrew Scripture raises the question of the degree to which the targumic audience was multilingual, having access to the Hebrew original even as it relied on the Aramaic rendering for a fuller understanding of the Hebrew. Here it should be stressed that the common portrayal of the function of targum as serving those who had no comprehension of Hebrew, since Hebrew had died as a language of widespread comprehension in all but the limited scholastic circles of the rabbinic sages, does not find support within the ancient sources. However, caution is in order since the vast majority of those sources, in the centuries following the destruction of the Second Temple, come from rabbinic circles. Still, there is an ever-increasing corpus of nonrabbinic Hebrew texts from Hellenistic and Roman times, including the Dead Sea Scrolls, the documents found in the Bar Kokhba caves, and numerous inscriptions, mainly from synagogue remains, all of which suggest that Hebrew continued in use, at least in some locations and among some groups, well into late antiquity, alongside the use of Greek and Aramaic, albeit in different proportional and functional mixes (Smelik 1995: 2-23). Nor does Mishnaic Hebrew represent a largely dead, unspoken, scholastic language replaced by Aramaic for all nonscholastic uses. In short, it cannot be presumed, on the model of the Greek Jewish Scriptures, that the targumim in the early centuries C.E. were primarily intended for an audience that had no comprehension of the Hebrew "original" (Tal 2001).

Types of Translation

The universal dilemma of the translator, whether to bring the target audience to the source or vice versa — whether to aim for fidelity to the source language or fluency in the target language — is best expressed by a saying attributed to Rabbi Judah bar El'ai (mid-second century C.E.): "One who translates literally (according to its form) is a liar, while one who adds [to it] is a blasphemer" (*t. Meg.* 3:41). Presumably, the ideal lies somewhere between the two extremes, but how to locate it is not explained. Perhaps it is for this reason that a variety of targumim, especially for the Pentateuch, display varying solutions to this quandary, with some cleaving closely to the original Hebrew text, aiming for a word-for-word equivalency while still being interpretive in nature (e.g., *Targum Onqelos* to the Pentateuch and *Targum Jonathan* to the Prophets), and others being more paraphrastic and expansive of the Hebrew original, thereby aiming to convey the broad sense of Scripture as understood by the interpretive tradition of the translators (e.g., *Targum Pseudo-Jonathan* to the Pentateuch). However, neither of these are pure types; the former provide plenty of nonliteral explications, and the latter often begin with a close rendering of the scriptural base text before adding explanatory expansions. *Targum Pseudo-Jonathan* to the Pentateuch, for instance, is far more expansive than the other Palestinian targumim (Kasher 1988; Shinan 1979, 1992). For a descriptive survey of the extant targumim to the Pentateuch, Prophets, and Writings, see Safrai 2006: 263-78.

Form and Genre

The style and form of targum distinguish it both from prerabbinic forms of "rewritten Bible" (e.g., the *Genesis Apocryphon* from Qumran, the *Book of Jubilees*) and from forms of scriptural commentary (Philo's allegorical commentaries, the Qumran pesharim, and rabbinic midrash), even as it often shares exegetical methods and traditions with all of these. In its most expansive and paraphrastic forms (e.g., *Targum Pseudo-Jonathan* to the Pentateuch), it stretches the limits of targum as translation while still being clearly distinguishable from midrashic forms of scriptural commentary. Unlike midrash, targum does not employ technical terminology to differentiate between, or to link, the scriptural verse and its rendering. Nor does it juxtapose multiple, conflicting interpretations (although it does exhibit numerous "double translations"), or attribute its renderings to named authorities. Further, targum does not explicitly render one verse by means of another, is not explicit in its interpretive methods, and does not reflect upon or authorize its discourse. In all of these ways, targum is directly and continuously linked to the Hebrew text of Scripture that it accompanies in both textual and social practice (with the exception of the *Fragmentary Targum*).

Relation to Rabbinic Literature

The relation of targum to early rabbinic literature, and alternatively to late Second Temple Jewish literature and the New Testament, has long been a subject of debate. Although the extant targums have been preserved and transmitted through rabbinic channels (with the exception of those among the Dead Sea Scrolls), and all of our ancient references to and rules for the social practice of targum are to be found in early rabbinic literature, some scholars, especially from the 1930s through the 1980s, have sought to locate targumic renderings or their incorporated traditions in either pre- or extrarabbinic settings. Those who have argued for a prerabbinic provenance have sought thereby to find in targum a Jewish source for the exegetical teachings of the New Testament and early Christianity by locating them in the context of late Second Temple Judaism, especially in what is presumed to be the popular setting of the synagogue (e.g., McNamara 1972).

Such arguments are based largely on isolated affinities between targumic renderings and Second Temple Jewish and New Testament ideas and traditions of scriptural exegesis, and on equally isolated differences between the targumim and early rabbinic texts, especially in the case of halakah (rabbinic law). They likewise presume a linguistic situation that has been called into serious question, as noted above.

Like each branch of rabbinic literature, targum has its own distinctive generic features of terminology and form that are specific to its distinctive rhetorical and pedagogical purposes. For example, the targumim frequently employ terms such as *memra* (hypostasized divine speech), which does not correspond to any word in the scriptural base text, as a buffer between what might otherwise appear as direct divine-human contact. Nevertheless, the differences between targum and other forms of rabbinic literature hardly negate their abundant affinities.

Efforts to locate the extant targumim, or their traditions, in prerabbinic times and loci have not withstood the burden of scholarly scrutiny for a variety of reasons, not least of which is the difficulty of dating the targumim as early as some have sought. Nevertheless, a systematic study of the affinities and differences between the targumim, especially with respect to halakic traditions and interpretations and the varieties of early rabbinic literature, remains a serious desideratum. Only then will it be possible to evaluate the balance between such similarities and differences, and to determine whether the differences reflect social and ideological provenance or genre (Fraade 2006; Safrai 2006).

Purpose and Function

The purpose(s) of targum is not self-evident from the targumic texts themselves, but must be surmised from deductions of its setting and audience (e.g., synagogue/house of study, popular/scholarly) and from its manner of delivery and employment. There is no reason to presume that these were singular either synchronically or diachronically. In all contexts and usages, the targums sought to give their readers and auditors a better grasp of the Hebrew original which it accompanied, by rendering it in accord with the exegetical traditions current among their creators. By maintaining a clear linguistic demarcation between written Scripture in Hebrew and its orally delivered, interlinear recitation and explication, targum served to render Scripture comprehensible in new cultural settings without altering or displacing the iconic status of its sacred base text. In this way, targum itself became a model for Jewish scriptural translation through the ages, even as it acquired its own privileged place, in rabbinic Bibles, alongside Scripture long after Aramaic ceased to be a vernacular Jewish language.

Bibliography

P. S. Alexander 1985, "The Targums and Rabbinic Rules for the Delivery of Targum," in *Congress Volume: Salamanca, 1983*, ed. J. A. Emerton, Leiden: Brill, 14-28. • P. S. Alexander 1988, "Jewish Aramaic Translations of Hebrew Scriptures," in *Mikra: Text, Translation, Reading and Interpretation of the Hebrew Bible in Ancient Judaism and Early Christianity*, ed. M. J. Mulder, Assen: Van Gorcum, 217-53. • M. J. Bernstein 2000, "The Aramaic Targumim: The Many Faces of the Jewish Biblical Experience," in *Jewish Ways of Reading the Bible*, ed. G. J. Brooke, Oxford: Oxford University Press, 133-65. • S. D. Fraade 1992, "Rabbinic Views on the Practice of Targum, and Multilingualism in the Jewish Galilee of the Third-Sixth Centuries," in *The Galilee in Late Antiquity*, ed. L. I. Levine, New York: Jewish Theological Seminary of America, 253-86. • S. D. Fraade 2006, "Locating Targum in the Textual Polysystem of Rabbinic Pedagogy," *BIOSCS* 39: 69-91. • R. Kasher 1988, "The Aramaic Targumim and their Sitz im Leben," in *Proceedings of the Ninth World Congress of Jewish Studies*, vol. 9, *Panel Session: Bible Studies and the Ancient Near East*, ed. M. H. Goshen-Gottstein, Jerusalem: World Union of Jewish Studies and Magnes, 75-85. • S. A. Kaufman 1985, "On Methodology in the Study of the Targums and Their Chronology," *JSNT* 23: 117-24. • M. L. Klein 1986, *Genizah Manuscripts of Palestinian Targum to the Pentateuch*, 2 vols., Cincinnati: Hebrew Union College Press. • M. L. Klein 2002, "Targumic Studies and the Cairo Genizah," in *The Cambridge Genizah Collections: Their Contents and Significance*, ed. S. C. Reif, Cambridge: Cambridge University Press, 47-58. • L. I. Levine 2005, *The Ancient Synagogue: The First Thousand Years*, 2d ed., New Haven: Yale University Press. • M. McNamara 1972, *Targum and Testament:*

Aramaic Paraphrases of the Hebrew Bible — A Light on the New Testament, Shannon, Ireland: Irish University Press. • Z. SAFRAI 2006, "The Targums as Part of Rabbinic Literature," in *The Literature of the Sages: Second Part: Midrash and Targum, Liturgy, Poetry, Mysticism, Contracts, Inscriptions, Ancient Science and the Languages of Rabbinic Literature,* ed. S. Safrai et al., Assen: Van Gorcum, 243-78. • D. SHEPHERD 2004, *Targum and Translation: A Reconsideration of the Qumran Aramaic Version of Job,* Assen: Van Gorcum. • A. SHINAN 1979, *The Aggadah in the Aramaic Targums to the Pentateuch,* Jerusalem: Makor (in Hebrew). • A. SHINAN 1992, *The Embroidered Targum: The Aggadah in Targum Pseudo-Jonathan of the Pentateuch,* Jerusalem: Magnes (in Hebrew). • W. F. SMELIK 1995, *The Targum of Judges,* Leiden: Brill. • A. TAL 2001, "Is There a Raison d'être for an Aramaic Targum in a Hebrew-speaking Society?" *REJ* 160: 357-78. • A. D. YORK 1974, "The Dating of Targumic Literature," *JSJ* 5: 49-62. • A. D. YORK 1979, "The Targum in the Synagogue and in the School," *JSJ* 10: 74-86.

STEVEN D. FRAADE

Tcherikover, Victor (Avigdor)

Victor Tcherikover (1894-1959) was born in St. Petersburg and studied philosophy and ancient history at the University of Moscow. In 1921 he went to Germany and studied ancient history under Eduard Meyer in Berlin. In 1925 he moved to Palestine and became one of the first teachers at the Hebrew University; he taught until his death in 1959.

His first major work was a study of the foundation of Hellenistic cities, "Die Hellenistischen Städtegrundungen von Alexander der Grossen bis auf die Römerzeit," *Philologus Supplementband* 19,1 (1927) 1-216. His subsequent work, however, dealt primarily with Jewish topics. In 1930 he published in Hebrew a major study, *Ha Yehudim va-ha Yevanim ba Tekufah ha Helenistit* (Tel Aviv: Devir, 1930), which appeared in English only in 1959, the year of his death, as *Hellenistic Civilization and the Jews* (New York: Jewish Publication Society, 1959; rpt., Peabody, Mass.: Hendrickson, 1999).

This book combined two detailed studies, the first dealing with the events leading up to the Maccabean Revolt and the second dealing with the history of the Jews in Alexandria. He argued that the so-called Hellenistic reform in Jerusalem was political and economic in its goals. It "involved no principles." The initial fighting between Jason and Menelaus was a struggle for power within the ruling elite. The Syrian intervention, however, was provoked by a hypothetical revolt by the Hasidim, the nonpriestly scribes who were the forerunners of the Pharisees. So "it was not the revolt which came as a response to the persecution, but the persecution which came as a response to the revolt." Both of these positions remain controversial. Elias Bickerman and Martin Hengel argued that the reform was cultural and religious, and that primary responsibility for the persecution rests with Menelaus. Tcherikover's view reflects his own conviction of the primacy of economic and social considerations, but it requires little extrapolation beyond the sources, and has again found favor in recent years. The revolt of the Hasidim, however, has no basis in the ancient sources and is now regarded as an unnecessary hypothesis.

On the subject of Alexandrian Judaism, Tcherikover argued that the introduction of the *laographia,* or poll tax, by Augustus created a clear-cut division between citizens and noncitizens, as only the latter were liable for the tax. The Jews now found themselves classified with the Egyptians. Hence the Jews aspired to citizenship and tried to infiltrate the gymnasium with this end in view. Consequently, conflict developed both with the Alexandrian citizens, who resented their intrusion, and with the Egyptian masses, who resented their pretensions to superior status. This argument remains extremely controversial. Many scholars deny that the Jews would have sought Alexandrian citizenship, since it would have entailed some recognition of pagan gods. Others dispute whether Augustus made any drastic change in the system of taxation. The evidence for Tcherikover's interpretation lies in a few fragmentary papyri whose interpretation is open to dispute. Nonetheless, there is no evidence for such a poll tax before the reign of Augustus, and Tcherikover's theory remains the most compelling interpretation that has been proposed of the conflict between Jews and their neighbors in Alexandria in the first century C.E.

From 1935 on, a central place in Tcherikover's work was occupied by the preparation of the corpus of Jewish papyri, in collaboration with Alexander Fuks. The first volume appeared in 1957, prefaced by a book-length introduction to the Diaspora in Egypt. The second and third volumes appeared posthumously in 1960 and 1964. This multivolume work stands as Tcherikover's *magnum opus.* It remains the standard edition of the Jewish papyri from Hellenistic-Roman Egypt.

BIBLIOGRAPHY

V. TCHERIKOVER 1999, *Hellenistic Civilization and the Jews,* rpt. of 1959 edition with a preface by J. J. Collins, Peabody, Mass.: Hendrickson. • V. TCHERIKOVER AND A. FUKS 1957-1964, *Corpus Papyrorum Judaicarum,* 3 vols., Cambridge, Mass.: Harvard University Press.

JOHN J. COLLINS

Teacher of Righteousness → Pesharim

Tefillin → Phylacteries and Mezuzot

Temple, Jerusalem

Our information regarding the Jerusalem Temple throughout the Second Temple period is extremely uneven. The Persian period yields almost no data, the Hellenistic-Hasmonean period somewhat more but still extremely limited data, and the Herodian-Roman era an incredibly rich trove of information, both literary sources and archaeological finds.

Persian Era

King Cyrus of Persia set a pattern of tolerance for all imperial rulers of the Second Temple era — recognition of the sanctity of the Temple and its centrality to the Jewish population, and a willingness to contribute to its physical and ritual dimensions. In 539 B.C.E., the year he conquered Babylonia, Cyrus not only allowed the Jewish exiles to return to Jerusalem from Babylonia (Ezra 1:1-4) to rebuild their Temple, but also financed the project (Ezra 6:2-5). By the seventh month of the first year the altar was completed — despite opposition from the local population (the identity of which is unknown). The author of the book of Ezra tells us that divine worship was thus resumed several weeks later and that the altar was used for the Sukkot festival celebrations (Ezra 3:1-5).

A half year later, in the second month of the second year, work commenced on the Temple's foundations, but owing to frequent delays the building was completed only several decades later. This was celebrated by an elaborate ceremony replete with trumpets, cymbals, the recitation of psalms, and the wearing of priestly vestments (Ezra 3:8-11), yet it was received with mixed reactions. The elders wept over the modest dimensions of the new Temple in comparison with the one that had been destroyed by Nebuchadnezzar, while the younger generation rejoiced and regarded the construction of the Temple as the fulfillment of a dream (Ezra 3:12-13).

Hellenistic and Hasmonean Eras

In 198 B.C.E., the Seleucid king Antiochus III extended support to the Jewish people, similar to that of Cyrus, promising to restore the city and Temple, provide the necessary sacrificial and other ritual supplies, restore the traditional leadership, and grant it extensive tax exemptions (*Ant.* 12.138-44).

The Temple merited much attention under the Hasmoneans (141-63 B.C.E.), although our information in this regard is limited. The Hasmoneans themselves regularly officiated there and mobilized the funds necessary for the ongoing maintenance, refurbishing, rebuilding, and expansion of its facilities. Moreover, the Temple was not only revered as Judaism's single most holy site by an ever-growing population in Judea, but was also accorded much attention and debate among the newly established sects, each of which in its own way enhanced the centrality of Jerusalem's sacred site. No sect denied the sanctity of this site, although many were critical of the way in which the Temple was being managed.

Literary works such as 2 Maccabees, *Jubilees,* and the *Letter of Aristeas* give expression to the importance of the Temple at this time. In addition, a number of religious practices emphasizing its centrality now seem to have crystallized, or were revitalized, although much of the evidence in this regard derives only from the later, Herodian period. Pilgrimage, donating a half-shekel as well as giving the second tithe, the fourth-year vineyard produce, or the firstfruits to the Temple may well have been practiced at this time.

Herodian Era

It was Herod's enormous investment in rebuilding the Temple and Temple Mount, in addition to the dramatic increase in literary sources, that allows us to examine the institution, its functions, leadership, and importance in far greater detail. The rebuilding of the Temple and Temple Mount by Herod was a project of unparalleled size and magnificence, constituting the crowning jewel of Herod's reign. All sources describing this complex agree that it was an impressive edifice. Josephus notes: "For he [Herod] believed that the accomplishment of this task would be the most notable of all the things achieved by him, as indeed it was, and would be great enough to assure his eternal remembrance" (*Ant.* 15.380). Even rabbinic literature, which usually ignores, and on occasion disparages, Herod is most complimentary with regard to this undertaking: "Whoever has not seen Herod's building has not seen a beautiful building in his life" (*b. Baba Batra* 4a).

Popular imagination conjured an aura of sanctity around the construction of Herod's Temple, conferring upon it a divine hand that facilitated the project. Both

View looking west at the eastern facades of the Herodian Temple in Jerusalem. On the balustrade surrounding the whole was a series of inscriptions forbidding Gentiles from entering the more sacred areas of the Temple *(www.HolyLandPhotos.org)*

A Greek inscription from the Jerusalem Temple forbidding entry by Gentiles on pain of death *(Courtesy Israel Antiquities Authority)*

rabbinic literature and Josephus cite a similar tradition in this respect; *b. Taʿanit* 23a preserves the following: "And thus we have from the days of Herod, that when they were working on construction of the Temple, rains would fall at night. On the morrow the winds would blow and disperse the clouds and the sun would shine and the people would proceed with their work, and they knew that they were doing God's work." In the same vein, Josephus writes: "And it is said that during the time when the Temple was being built, no rain fell during the day, but only at night, so that there was no interruption of the work. And this story, which our fathers have handed down to us, is not at all incredible if, that is, one considers the other manifestations of power given by God" (*Ant.* 15.425).

Owing to the extreme sensitivity about everything associated with the building of the Temple, especially the fears of some that the old edifice might be torn down and not replaced due to the lack of funds, Herod took all possible precautions to gain widespread support from the populace at large no less than the priestly leadership. He promised to have all the materials required for the new building in place before the old one was destroyed. Preparing 1,000 wagons and 10,000 skilled workers for his massive undertaking, Herod had 1,000 priests trained as masons and carpenters to do the actual work in the Temple so as not to engage nonpriests, who were forbidden to enter the sacred area. Construction of the Temple edifice itself lasted eighteen months, and upon its completion (ca. 18 B.C.E.) the king organized lavish festivities (*Ant.* 15.388-90, 421-23).

The Temple Mount: Physical Dimensions and Functions

Although the sources attesting to the Temple complex are plentiful, those describing its physical dimensions often contradict one another, and the discrepancies between them are far from trivial. Detailed descriptions of the Temple and Temple Mount area are found primarily in Josephus' *War* and *Antiquities,* and Mishnah *Middot,* while archaeological data, as far as they exist, add important information about the western and southern areas of the Temple Mount.

The discrepancies among the sources touch on nearly every aspect of the Temple complex: the number of gates leading to the Temple Mount and those leading to the Temple precincts; the circumference of the Temple Mount; the dimensions of the gates leading into the Temple courts; the size of the stones that were used in its construction; and many other details. For example, both literary sources and archaeological remains inform us about the dimensions of the Temple Mount. Mishnah *Mid.* 2:1 notes that the Temple Mount had a circumference of 500 by 500 cubits (ca. 250 × 250 m.), while Josephus records two figures: *Ant.* 15.400 quotes the figure of four stades (ca. 800 m.), while *J.W.* 5.192 mentions six (ca. 1,200 m.). On the basis of the archaeological finds, the total circumference of the Temple Mount was approximately 1,550 m. — considerably greater than what is recorded in any of the written sources.

Not only do Josephus, the Mishnah, and archaeology exhibit factual contradictions, but even within Josephus' writings and the tractate *Middot* we find details that are at odds with each other. Many solutions have been offered, although very few have addressed the entire range of discrepancies. Scholars have tried to harmonize Josephus with the Mishnah (for the most part ignoring the internal contradictions within each), but not infrequently have preferred one source, usually Josephus, as more reliable historically. A widespread approach of late has been to assume that the different sources relate to different time periods, with the mishnaic description usually assigned to the pre-Herodian era.

A somewhat different approach resolves most, if not all, of these disparities, based on the following considerations: (1) Archaeological evidence regarding the Temple in its final mid-first-century-C.E. stages should take precedence. (2) In *Jewish War,* Josephus describes the Temple as Titus viewed it when approaching the city in the spring of 70 C.E. It is at this point in his narrative that Josephus introduces his detailed survey of Jerusalem, with special emphasis on the Temple. (3) Josephus' survey of the Temple in *Antiquities* describes Herod's original construction in 20/19 B.C.E. and probably reflects this initial stage. (4) We know from an array of sources that the Temple and Temple Mount underwent ongoing repairs and modifications over decades; this is attested in the New Testament (forty-six years according to John 2:20), rabbinic literature (at the time of Rabban Gamaliel the Elder, who flourished ca. 25-50 C.E.; *t. Šabb.* 13:2 [ed. Lieberman, p. 57]), and *Ant.* 20.219. This last-noted source informs us that work on the Temple Mount was finally completed in 64 C.E., leaving 18,000 people unemployed. (5) The differences between *Antiquities* and *War* may be explained best in light of the repairs, renovations, and additions made over the eighty-year period between the initial construction *(Antiquities)* and its completion *(War)*. (6) A substantial part of tractate *Middot* is in accord with *War*, and thus seems to reflect the very end of the Second Temple period.

If these points are accepted, one ought to be cautious when speaking of *the* Second Temple or *the* Temple Mount generally. Literary and archaeological sources describe a building complex that underwent a long series of substantial modifications. While relatively few of these changes seem to have affected the Temple building itself, the Temple courtyards and Temple Mount area were continuously being renovated in the post-Herodian period.

Herod's construction plans for the Temple Mount area, in its entirety, were indeed ambitious and far-reaching. Josephus' description of what was involved in building the artificial platform gives us a sense of the enormity of his undertaking (*J.W.* 5.184-89). Elsewhere, Josephus tells us that Herod doubled the size of King Solomon's Temple Mount (*J.W.* 1.401). Archaeological remains amply confirm the monumental nature of this project; Herod increased the area of the Temple Mount by extending it to the south, west, and north; only the eastern side, associated with Solomon's structure, remained in place since in this direction the earlier Hasmonean complex reached the crest of the slope, descending to the Qidron Valley, and did not offer much room for expansion.

Extensive archaeological excavations have been carried out in the western and southern areas of the Temple Mount wall. Among the significant finds were the remains of a gigantic arch located about thirteen meters north of the southwestern corner of the Western Wall. The discovery of a series of intact smaller arches descending southward, as well as a staircase with several steps, made it clear that a monumental staircase connected the Temple Mount with the valley below and was apparently used as a main entrance to the basilica located at the southern end of the Temple Mount.

At this very spot, the base of the southwestern corner of the Temple Mount, a remarkable Hebrew inscription was discovered on a stone block that probably fell from the top of the wall. It reads: "The place [literally, house] of trumpeting to announce. . . ." Josephus speaks of a tower that stood "at a point where it was the custom for one of the priests to stand and to give notice, by sound of trumpet, of the approach and close of every Sabbath, thereby indicating to Jerusalem's residents the respective hours for ceasing and resuming their labors" (*J.W.* 4.582). This inscription thus marked the spot where the priest stood when blowing the trumpet.

The southern Huldah Gates of the Temple Mount are of particular interest, since they offered the most direct access to the Temple area. An underground passageway leading toward the Temple courtyards was found inside the western Huldah Gate. Its huge columns, high ceilings, and elaborately decorated stone domes were an architectural masterpiece. Since the requirements for ritual purity upon entering the Temple precincts appear to have been scrupulously observed, the eastern Huldah Gate offered Temple-goers a last opportunity to purify themselves before entering (the western gate, with its monumental staircase, was used by those leaving the Temple area).

The southern area was apparently also used for religious and judicial purposes. As we read in several early rabbinic sources, if someone wished to appeal the verdict of a local court, he would first turn to the court that sat "atop the steps leading to the Temple Mount" (*t. Ḥag.* 2:9 [ed. Lieberman, p. 383]; *t. Sanh.* 7:1 [ed. Zuckermandel, p. 425]). While the precise location of this court remains unknown, it may well have been in the area of the Huldah Gates. Benjamin Mazar speculated that the Hebrew word *zĕqēnîm* (elders) appearing in several fragmentary inscriptions from this area (one found in the nineteenth century and the other in his Temple Mount excavations, both near the eastern Huldah Gate) possibly referred to members of this appellate court. However, this reading is extremely tentative. We also read about the Pharisaic leader Rabban Gamaliel the Elder who, while sitting with his colleagues on these same steps, dispatched letters to various regions of Judea and the eastern Diaspora, informing them about matters concerning tithes, sabbatical-year laws, and the intercalation of a leap year (*t. Sanh.* 2:6 [ed. Zuckermandel, p. 416]).

Herod's conceptualization of the Temple Mount as a whole followed a well-known Hellenistic architectural model, which called for an artificial platform surrounded on three sides by porticoes and on the fourth by a basilica or royal stoa (from Gr. *basileus*, meaning "king"). In such complexes, a temple stood in the center or, at times, off to one side. Similar sacred precincts, or *temenē*, have also been found in North Africa, Asia Minor, and Syria. The temples of Jupiter in Damascus and Bel in Palmyra have been relatively well preserved and therefore give us some notion of what such a setting might have looked like. Herod, however, outdid his contemporaries by constructing his platform and buildings on a far grander and more elaborate scale than others.

Those entering the Temple Mount in Jerusalem found themselves surrounded on three sides by nine-meter-high porticoes and on the fourth by an immense basilica hall, the largest known in the East at the time. It is probably these buildings that were decorated with barbarian and Nabatean spoils donated by Herod (*Ant.* 15.401). The entire Temple Mount, exclusive of the Temple precincts, functioned as the *agora* or forum of Jerusalem; the vast courtyard area outside the Temple precincts was called the Court of the Gentiles, for only here were they permitted to enter. Josephus reports that the basilica built by Herod along the southern part of the Temple Mount contained 162 colossal pillars arranged in four rows and decorated with Corinthian capitals. Together with the Temple Mount and the Temple structure itself, this basilica constituted in many ways a central institution in Jerusalem life, much as did such edifices in other Roman cities, where the basilica was often not only the most prominent building in the forum but also a counterpoint of the local temple(s); it served as the focal civic institution and, at the same time, complemented the religious dimension represented by the nearby Temple. From Josephus' description of the grandeur of this basilica (*Ant.* 15.411-17), this building may have had the same prominence in Jerusalem as well.

The Temple Mount as the Jerusalem Forum

Given the multifunctional nature of the Temple Mount, there were undoubtedly many occasions when the basilica and other parts of the Temple Mount hummed with activity. While the city's political agenda was managed by Jerusalem's city council *(boulē),* which met in its own building *(bouleutērion)* just west of the Temple Mount, meetings of smaller groups (e.g., members of sects) and assemblies of the people at large were held on the Temple Mount. Upon returning from one of his trips abroad, for instance, Herod convened the populace there to report on the outcome and to announce his sons' order of accession to the throne after his death (*J.W.* 1.457-66; *Ant.* 16.132-35); following the mourning ceremonies for his father in 4 B.C.E., Archelaus heard the greetings, acclamations, and grievances of his subjects in the Temple precincts while seated on a golden throne placed on a high platform (*J.W.* 2.1-7; *Ant.* 17.200-209).

Often packed with pilgrims during the festivals, this court also served as a convenient venue for the exchange of political views and the airing of declarations, criticisms, and grievances. Sometimes a particularly fervent speech might be delivered, inflaming passions and sparking violence. Josephus often depicts riots erupting in this setting, as in 4 B.C.E. following the death of Herod, during the procuratorship of Cumanus, and under the last procurators. It is not surprising, then, that the Antonia fortress was designed to provide military units with direct access to the porticoes of the Temple Mount. From Herod's reign onward, soldiers were often posted on the roofs around the Temple Mount during festivals to demonstrate their presence and hopefully prevent trouble (though, in fact, they sometimes incited it).

We have already mentioned an appellate court near the Huldah Gates, yet other judicial bodies also met on the Temple Mount and possibly also in the basilica hall. A supreme court (also referred to in rabbinic literature as the Sanhedrin) met in the Chamber of Hewn Stone, just south of the Temple itself. One rabbinic tradition (*b. Šabbat* 15a; *b. Roš Haššanah* 31a; *b. ʿAbodah Zarah* 8b) reports that prior to the destruction of the city (the forty-year figure is undoubtedly a symbolic number), the supreme court moved from its previous location to (the) Ḥanut (or *Ḥānûyôt,* literally "shop[s]"), the identity of which has eluded scholars. Mazar suggested that this term may refer to the basilica at the southern end of the Temple Mount that may have served, *inter alia,* as this court's place of meeting. In addition, a third court met on the *ḥēl* (rampart, embankment) just outside the Women's Court.

The economic activity on the Temple Mount, one of the largest markets in Jerusalem and undoubtedly centered in the basilica, focused on the needs of the Temple cult. This activity was substantial and carefully supervised. Animals had to be supplied for sacrifices and grain for meal offerings, while Jews coming from foreign lands had to exchange their money for local currency or tokens. This activity increased immeasurably during the three pilgrimage festivals, when people thronged to the city in large numbers. This lively commercial life, which was undoubtedly accompanied by great commotion, seems to have been at odds with the spiritual aura associated by many with this area. The description of Jesus overturning the tables of the moneychangers in Mark 11:15-17 (and parallels) may be somewhat exaggerated and theologically biased, but it may very well reflect mixed feelings of surprise and revulsion by those who confronted this reality for the first time. Undeniably, cultic activity in the Temple had a distinctly materialistic side that could not be ignored. The telling description in *m. Šeqal.* 5:4 details the kinds of transactions that took place here.

As was the case with other ancient sanctuaries, the Jerusalem Temple played an important role as a bank for both personal and public funds. The reason for this rather widespread practice is obvious; such funds would be safe in precincts protected by the gods and kept under the careful supervision of a sacred institution. Similarly, private monies were deposited in

View looking east at the whole of the reconstructed Temple Mount as it would have appeared in the late Second Temple period (18 B.C.E.–70 C.E.) *(www.HolyLandPhotos.org)*

the Temple too (2 Macc. 3:10-12; *m. ʿArak.* 9:4; *J.W.* 6.282), as were the annual half-shekel contributions.

In addition, valuable gifts were often given to the Temple. Votives offerings were common (*m. Šeqal.* 5:6; 6:5-6; *t. ʿArak.* 3:1 [ed. Zuckermandel, p. 545]), including a golden chain that Gaius Caligula gave to Agrippa I, who then donated it to the Temple (*Ant.* 19.294), and a golden lamp that Queen Helena gave to the Temple and hung over the entrance of the *hēkhāl* (*m. Yoma* 3:10). Several Alexandrians are also noted for their generous gifts: Nicanor donated a most impressive gate located between the Women's Court and the Israelite Court; Alexander, brother of Philo, plated the other nine Temple gates with gold and silver (*m. Mid.* 1:4; *J.W.* 5.205); and provisions were made to receive donations intended for the poor (*m. Šeqal.* 5:6). There is no question that enormous sums of money were deposited in the Temple; Josephus claims that at the time of Pompey's conquest the Temple in 63 B.C.E. held about 2,000 talents (*J.W.* 1.152; *Ant.* 14.72), and it is thus little wonder that these treasures were often plundered (*J.W.* 1.179; *Ant.* 17.264).

The Temple Mount also witnessed nonsacrificial religious activity (instructional and otherwise). It was here that leaders of the various sects congregated, taught their disciples, and preached to the masses. Josephus tells us that in the Hasmonean period Judas the Essene convened with "his disciples" on the Temple Mount (*Ant.* 13.311). Later on, Luke mentions that Jesus preached there, as did some of the apostles (Luke 2:46-47; 21:37; Acts 2–3), and the early Christians appear to have favored Solomon's portico on the eastern side of the Temple Mount for their gatherings (John 10:23-30; Acts 3:11-26; 5:12-16). Rabbinic literature speaks of many Pharisees who frequented the site, and Rabban Gamaliel the Elder is reported to have responded to the questions of Yoʿezer Ish-Habirah from the School of Shammai when standing by the Eastern Gate (*m. ʿOr.* 2:12). A late tradition claims that Rabbi Yoḥanan ben Zakkai "taught in the shadow of the sanctuary" (*b. Pesaḥim* 26a), while many debates between the Pharisees and Sadducees (if indeed they actually occurred) probably took place in these areas as well.

The Temple Buildings and Its Courts

The Temple building and its sacred courts stood on an artificially raised platform. It was not exactly in the center of the Temple Mount, as can be clearly discerned from the visible remains. According to an enigmatic report in the Mishnah, the open spaces that surrounded this complex varied in size, with the largest area to the south, then the east, north, and west, in descending order (*m. Mid.* 2:1). The sacred precincts were surrounded by a stone balustrade featuring Greek and Latin inscriptions warning Gentiles not to enter the Temple area. This warning, noted by Josephus (*J.W.* 5.194; *Ant.* 15.417), has also been preserved in several Greek inscriptions discovered in the nineteenth and twentieth centuries, one of which has remained fairly intact: "No foreigner is to enter within the forecourt and the balustrade around the sanctuary. Whoever is caught will have himself to blame for his subsequent death."

Beyond this balustrade, a stairway of fourteen steps led to an elevated area on which the Temple and its courtyards stood. At the top of the stairs was a level area, the *ḥēl* (rampart, embankment), which, as noted, was the site of an appellate court (*m. Mid.* 2:3). Beyond

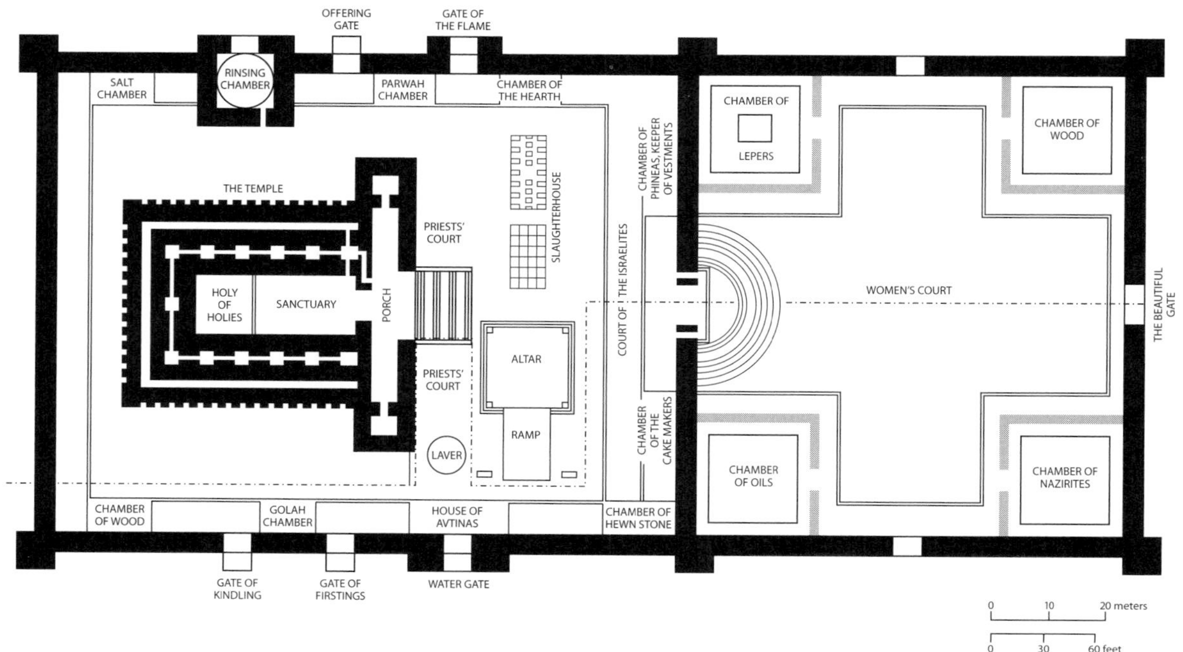

Floor plan of Herod's Temple *(Adapted from Encyclopedia Judaica)*

the *ḥēl* was a wall that encompassed the Temple courts; the main point of entry was from the Eastern Gate, perhaps that referred to in Acts 3:2 as the "Beautiful Gate." Secondary gates for entry were located to its north and south. Inside these gates, one reached the Women's Court. According to *m. Mid.* 2:5, four chambers occupied the four corners of this court, two for Nazirites and lepers and two for storing wood and oil.

Despite the term "Women's Court," the area was not used by women alone. In fact, every man, woman, or child who came to the Temple entered this precinct. Those not offering sacrifices would remain there; others with sacrifices, including women after childbirth and on some other occasions (*t. ʿArak.* 2:1 [ed. Zuckermandel, p. 544]), would proceed to the Israelite Court. The Women's Court was used for nonsacrificial ceremonies and rituals, such as the high priest reading from the Torah on Yom Kippur; the *Haqhel* ceremony on Sukkot at the end of every sabbatical year, which likewise involved reading from the Torah; and Simḥat Bet Ha-sho'evah, the Water-Drawing Festival (literally, the Rejoicing of the House of Water-Drawing), which was held annually on the intermediate days of Sukkot.

The Mishnah makes it quite clear that there was no separation between men and women in the Women's Court. This is indicated by the fact that a special balcony was erected to separate the sexes at the Simḥat Bet Ha-sho'evah festivities owing to the extreme levity and merrymaking on that occasion (*m. Mid.* 2:5). Thus, on the other 360 or so days of the year, there apparently was no balcony and thus no division between men and women. It should be pointed out, however, that in *J.W.* 5.198-99 Josephus notes that "a special place was walled off for the women" in this court, a general statement standing in stark contradiction to the Mishnah and to his own account, however brief, in *Ant.* 15.418-19. Again, Josephus' description in *War* may well be referring to the mid-first century C.E., when a stricter code for women and Gentiles was introduced into Jerusalem's religious life and other areas as well.

If indeed there was no gender separation, why was this area called the Women's Court? Three possibilities come to mind: (1) the name may reflect the very last stage before the destruction of the Temple, when, as noted, women were separated from men; (2) women who came to the Temple remained for the most part in this court; or (3) women may have constituted the majority of those who frequented the Temple year around, and thus this court's name reflects their dominant presence.

Beyond the Women's Court, to the west, were fifteen semicircular steps (*m. Mid.* 2:5) on which the Levites stood when they sang the Songs of Ascents (Psalms 120–134). Jews who came to offer sacrifices would ascend these steps and pass through the Nicanor Gate, which was considered the most magnificent of the Temple gates, and then enter the Israelite Court, from where those bringing sacrifices watched as the priests conducted the sacrificial ritual in silence (*Letter of Aristeas* 92 and 95). The priests officiated in the adja-

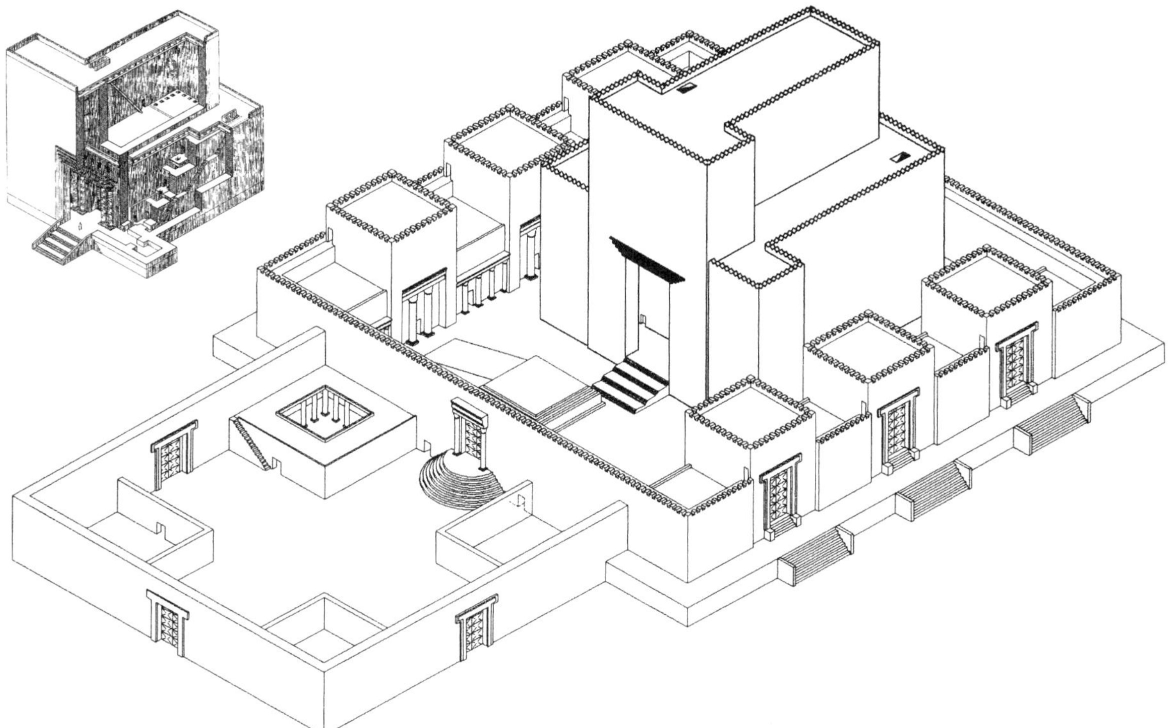

Isometric views of the temple (left: after Joseph Patrich; right: by Ehud Netzer) *(Ehud Netzer)*

cent Priestly Court, where the outside sacrificial altar, laver, and place of slaughter were located. There is some confusion in our sources over what separated these two courts. Josephus states that "a low stone parapet . . . separated the laity outside from the priests" (*J.W.* 5.226), while the Mishnah offers two other options: a different type of pavement or a series of stairs (*m. Mid.* 2:6). According to the Mishnah, the Levites would stand on a raised platform between these two courts and recite psalms during the daily sacrificial offering (*m. Mid.* 2:6; *m. Tamid* 7:3; see also 1 Chron. 23:30; 2 Chron. 29:25-29).

Around these two inner courtyards and among its many gates was a portico whose columns Josephus describes as being "exceedingly beautiful and lofty" (*J.W.* 5.200). Josephus also speaks about a series of chambers (generally mentioning the treasury chambers [*J.W.* 5.200; 6.282]), while the Mishnah mentions six rooms (*m. Mid.* 5:3-4). On the northern side were the Salt Chamber (for salting the sacrifices), the Hide Chamber (for salting the hides of the sacrificial animals), and the Rinsing Chamber (for cleaning the innards of the sacrifices); to the south were the Wood Chamber, the *Golah* Chamber (perhaps referring to a wheel, Hebr. *galgal,* where an apparatus for drawing water for the Temple precincts was located), and the Chamber of Hewn Stone where the high court sat. West of the Israelite and Priestly Courts was a flight of stairs leading to the raised platform on which the Temple stood. The Temple reached almost 120 cubits (60 m.) high, although it had reportedly sunk by the mid-first century C.E. and required restoration by Agrippa II (*Ant.* 15.391; *J.W.* 5.36).

One of the most enigmatic issues concerns how the façade of the Temple looked. The range of suggestions is great, from the simplest reconstruction to the most baroque. The problem, of course, is that while our sources cite explicit dimensions, they do not describe how the façade actually looked. Over the past decades, however, Michael Avi-Yonah's interpretation has gained a great deal of support. On the basis of a representation of the Temple appearing on Bar Kokhba coins and of a similar façade on a wall painting from the third-century-C.E. Dura Europos synagogue, Avi-Yonah (1968) suggested that the façade had four columns (two round and two square, the latter functioning as corner pilasters), a large rectangular opening, as well as a cornice and a series of spikes (against birds) at the top. The marble façade had many gold-plated components featuring, among other things, a golden vine with large grape clusters (*J.W.* 5.210; *Ant.* 15.395; Tacitus, *Histories* 5:5; *m. Mid.* 3:8).

The Temple itself was divided into three main rooms. The first one, called the *'ûlam* (porch) was entered from the east; it had no door and was wider than the other two rooms. Beyond the *'ûlam* was the sanctuary *(hēkhāl),* in the middle of which stood the golden altar for incense. To its right stood the showbread table, while to the left there was a golden menorah. Beyond the *hēkhāl* to the west, and separated from it by two curtains, was the Holy of Holies *(dĕbîr).* In the First Temple period, the Ark of the Covenant housing the two tablets of the Ten Commandments stood in the Holy of Holies (Exod. 25:10-22). The Ark disappeared when the First Temple was destroyed in 586 B.C.E., leaving this room empty throughout the Second Temple period (*J.W.* 5.219), except when the high priest would enter to offer prayers on Yom Kippur.

Temple Functionaries

The high priest was directly in charge of all activities relating to the Temple. He was aided in his various cultic responsibilities by an assistant or deputy, referred to as *segen* or *stratēgos.* By virtue of his position in the Temple, the high priest was considered the most important religious and political leader of the Jews throughout the Second Temple period — with the exception of the period of King Herod's rule. He officiated in the Temple on all major holidays, such as Yom Kippur and festivals, and on other days he generally conducted the sacrificial service; if necessary, others could do so on his behalf. Only the high priest wore gold vestments (those of ordinary priests were made of cloth), and he would conduct the reportedly infrequent red heifer ritual on the Mount of Olives as well as the reading of the Torah on Yom Kippur and the *Haqhel* ceremony.

Administration of the Temple required a large staff. Given the vast sums of money involved, it seems that the treasurers, together with the seven administrators who managed the finances and property, held important posts. In addition to being responsible for collecting the half-shekel donations, the treasurers were in charge of storing the holy vessels and priestly vestments, supplying wood, animals, flour, and oil, as well as collecting money from those seeking to make such offerings.

Many of the specific tasks performed in the Temple were divided among fifteen officers listed by name in *m. Šeqal.* 5:1, *m. Yoma* 3:11, and *t. Šeqal.* 2:14 (ed. Lieberman, pp. 210-11). It is not entirely clear whether these functionaries were the first to hold these positions in Second Temple times, or the last whose names the Mishnah was able to recall. The responsibilities mentioned relate to seals, libations, bird-offerings, curtains and vestments, treating intestinal maladies among the priests, supervising water sources, making announcements, locking the gates, preparing strips of cloth or leather (the use of which is unclear), and readying the showbread and frankincense.

Alongside the permanent officials, the Temple administration included the twenty-four priestly courses, a participatory rotation system requiring all priests, wherever they happened to live, to serve in the Temple for one week (from Sabbath to Sabbath) twice a year. The first mention of such an arrangement appears in 1 Chronicles 24, although only rabbinic literature spells out what may well have been the normative practice in the late Second Temple period (*m. Taʿan.* 4:2).

The Levites were distinctly inferior to the priests and are virtually ignored by Hellenistic and Hasmonean sources such as Ben Sira and 1 Maccabees. They, too, were divided into twenty-four courses and were in charge of security and music during the Temple rituals

(*Ant.* 7.367; *m. Taʿan.* 4:2). The Levites are described as the guardians of the Tabernacle (Num. 31:30, 47) and probably functioned in the same capacity in the Second Temple as well (*m. Mid.* 1:1). Philo notes that the Levites, charged with maintaining the Temple's purity, would patrol the area regularly to make sure that there were no ritual violations; they also were charged with opening and closing the Temple gates (*Spec. Leg.* 1.156). At the daily services, Levites would perform musically from a platform placed on the line separating the Priestly Court from the Israelite Court, and at the Simḥat Bet Hasho'evah ceremonies on Sukkot a choir of Levites would recite psalms from the steps leading into the Israelite Court. According to a later rabbinic tradition, the Levites were charged with humbler tasks as well: assisting a high priest with his vestments, reading the Torah, and preparing the *lulavim* and *ethrogim* for the Sukkot ceremony (*b. ʿArakin* 11b).

Above all, the Temple's personnel were charged regularly with caring for the needs of those coming to the Temple to offer sacrifices. This task demanded an enormous amount of administration and coordination, since large quantities of incense, salt, and wood were required daily the year round. The burning of incense on the golden altar in the *hēkhēl* accompanied the daily morning and evening rituals. For instance, some of the plants used for incense grew in the Jerusalem area, while others were brought from near and far; salt ("Sodom salt," brought from the Dead Sea region) was sprinkled on all of the sacrifices, and a special chamber was set aside in the inner courtyard for its storage; wood was needed not only for sacrifices but also for keeping the perpetual light burning in the "hearth chamber." The fire for the altar and the fire for cooking the priests' food were also taken from this chamber. Wood supplies were contributed by individuals who brought them to Jerusalem on specific days (according to Josephus, on the 14th and 15th of Av) or by certain families who brought them on fixed dates each year (*m. Taʿan.* 4:5). The custom of donating wood allegedly began in the Persian period and may have continued without interruption throughout the Second Temple period.

The Temple as a Religious Focus

The Temple throughout this period served first and foremost as a religious focal point for Jews in Judea and the Diaspora. For most people in antiquity, the offering of sacrifices was a quintessential expression of religious piety. Josephus notes: "Whoever was master of these (Jerusalem fortifications) had the whole nation in his power, for sacrifices could not be made without (controlling) these places, and it was impossible for any of the Jews to forgo offering these, for they would rather give up their lives than the worship which they are accustomed to offer God" (*Ant.* 15.248).

By the late Second Temple period, Jerusalem's Temple had come to symbolize the Jewish *locus sanctus* par excellence. Here was where God dwelled; this was the cosmic center of the universe *(axis mundi)*, the navel *(omphalos)* of the world that both nurtured and bound together earth and heaven, as well as past, present, and future. For Judaism, no less than for other religions of antiquity, space was not a homogeneous entity. The sacred was to be found in the midst of the profane (i.e., the ordinary), and the former, of course, is directly related to the presence of the divine. Such was Jacob's experience in Bethel (Gen. 28:17) and Moses' at the burning bush (Exod. 3:5); later on, this sacredness was embodied in the Temple from Solomon's time onward. For Jews, this sanctity was even more enhanced by their exclusive notion of only one temple. A poignant expression of this attitude in a halakic context is found in the Mishnah, which lists ten degrees of holiness, with Jerusalem and the Temple precincts at the very pinnacle (*m. Kelim* 1:6-9).

One means of demonstrating loyalty and support for the Temple was Diaspora Jewry's annual contribution of a half-shekel. The donation was intended to help pay for the maintenance of the Temple, the purchase of animals for the required daily offerings, as well as the renovation of the walls and towers, the water supply systems, and other municipal needs. Philo describes this observance in some detail:

> The revenues of the Temple are derived not only from landed estates but also from other and far greater sources that time will never destroy. For as long as the human race endures, and it will endure forever, the revenues of the Temple also will remain secure, coeternal with the whole universe. For it is ordained that everyone, beginning at his twentieth year, should make an annual contribution. . . . Because the nation is very populous, the offerings of first fruits are naturally exceedingly abundant. In fact, practically in every city there are banking places for the holy money where people regularly come and give their offerings. And at stated times there are appointed to carry the sacred tribute envoys selected on their merits, from every city those of the highest repute, under whose conduct the hopes of each and all will travel safely. For it is on these first fruits, as prescribed by the Law, that the hopes of the pious rest. (*Spec. Leg.* 1.76-78)

We have a great deal of evidence regarding these Diaspora contributions. Almost a dozen imperial and local decrees recognize their collection as a valid and legitimate practice (e.g., *Ant.* 16.160-72); in one case, the Jews of Asia Minor took the local Roman governor Flaccus to court (with none other than Cicero serving as the latter's defense lawyer) when he refused to allow the continuation of this privilege (Cicero, *Pro Flacco* 28–68). The sums enumerated in the trial were substantial — twenty pounds of gold from Laodicea and a hundred from Apamea.

We know very little about the scope of contributions made by the Jews of Judea. However, we do have quite a bit of information about other kinds of religious observances that expressed their ties and generosity toward the Temple and city. An important link between Judean Jewry and the Temple was the institution of the *māʿămādôt* (nonpriestly participants in ceremonies involving the priestly courses). Many brought their firstfruits to Jerusalem annually, a ritual often accompanied by pomp and ceremony (*m. Bikkurim* 3), and tithes were allotted to the priests, Levites, and poor. By the late Second Temple period, the second tithe (set aside four times in the course of a sabbatical-year cycle) became a widespread practice; this tithe either had to be eaten in Jerusalem or its monetary equivalent had to be spent in the city. The fourth year's fruits (the yield of a tree in the fourth year after its planting) were likewise either to be eaten in Jerusalem or their monetary equivalent had to be spent there.

Sacrifices were offered for a variety of reasons. Besides the expression of feelings of sin, guilt, and thanksgiving, a sacrifice might result from the taking of vows by a Nazirite, by mothers after childbirth, or by lepers upon the conclusion of their infirmity. Converts were required to offer sacrifices, and such people were probably not a rare sight in Jerusalem given that conversion was not uncommon at this time. Pilgrimage to Jerusalem was a popular phenomenon, as Jews streamed to the Temple to visit the holiest site of the Jewish people and to take part in its ceremonies with large numbers of their fellow Jews the world over.

Jerusalem was invariably filled with pilgrims during the three festivals: Passover, Shavuʿot (the Pentecost), and Sukkot (the Feast of Booths). Since it was "the navel of the world," one could sense the essence of the city as tens of thousands of pilgrims, from Judea and the Galilee and from all parts of the Diaspora, gathered there for a few days or weeks, thereby playing a not-inconsequential role in forging the city's character and economy. One can appreciate Philo's enthusiasm when he wrote: "Countless multitudes from countless cities come, some over land, others over sea, from west and east and north and south at every feast. They take the Temple for their port as a general haven and safe refuge from the bustle and great turmoil of life, and there they seek to find calm weather . . ." (*Spec. Leg.* 1.69). Jerusalem became the hub of Jewish life on these occasions, and many languages and dialects commonly spoken by Jews at the time could be heard in its streets. Luke may have exaggerated his description of the Pentecost celebrations in Jerusalem, but perhaps not by much (Acts 2:1-11).

Most pilgrims, however, came from Judea. It is reported that almost entire towns were emptied of their inhabitants during the three pilgrimage festivals. When the Roman army was advancing along the coast at the outbreak of the revolt in 66, it reportedly found the entire city of Lydda deserted except for some fifty people, since everyone had gone to Jerusalem for the Sukkot holiday (*J.W.* 2.515). Galilee, too, was a major contributor to the pilgrimage traffic. Luke (2:41) relates that "it was the practice of his [Jesus'] parents to go to Jerusalem every year for the Passover festival; and when he was twelve, they made the pilgrimage as usual." He also informs us that Galileans were killed by Pontius Pilate when they were in Jerusalem (Luke 13:1). Josephus tells of Galilean pilgrims being attacked and many killed in Samaria on their way to Jerusalem, and a riot ensued when the perpetrators went unpunished (*Ant.* 20.118-21). Rabbinic literature as well has preserved a number of accounts of pilgrimages from Galilee (e.g., *y. Maʿaś. Š.* 5:2, 56a).

The residents of Jerusalem, for their part, were encouraged to welcome the pilgrims and offer them food and lodging. Visitors arriving in Jerusalem found accommodations in hostels and inns, the homes of private residents, nearby villages such as Bethphage and Bethany, and tents on the outskirts of the city (*Ant.* 17.217). Landlords were forbidden (at least in theory) to charge money for lodgings, but in recompense received the hides of sacrificed animals. Pilgrims also stayed in synagogues, as attested by the Theodotos inscription. According to one rabbinic tradition, which may be more fantasy than fact, the laws of purity were relaxed during the three pilgrimage festivals in order to allow people to interrelate more easily (*m. Ḥag.* 3:6-7; *y. Ḥag.* 3:6-7, 79d).

The numbers of pilgrims arriving in Jerusalem on the festivals must have been enormous. Josephus writes in one place that 2.5 million pilgrims came to the city during Passover (*J.W.* 6.423-25), and in another he speaks of no fewer than 3,000,000 (*J.W.* 2.280). One rabbinic source quotes the figure of 12,000,000 people (*t. Pesaḥ.* 4:15 [ed. Lieberman, p. 166]). While these numbers are incredibly exaggerated, Joachim Jeremias (1969) relied on a mishnaic tradition (*m. Pesaḥ.* 5:5-6), where it is noted that the people who brought the Passover sacrifice filled the Israelite Court nearly three times over. By calculating the court's area and estimating its maximum capacity, tripling it, and then multiplying it by ten (according to Josephus and rabbinic literature, there were at least ten people per sacrifice), Jeremias estimated that there were about 180,000 pilgrims during a Passover festival. E. P. Sanders (1992) posits a number between 300,000 and 500,000; and Wolfgang Reinhardt (1995) opts for 1,000,000 on each festival. These higher estimates of hundreds of thousands of pilgrims appear exaggerated, and even though Jeremias' figure is mere conjecture (we cannot be sure of the areas included on these occasions, the precise density to be calculated, or the exact number of participants per sacrifice), his approach yields a cautious assessment and thus may not be far from the truth. If we estimate the permanent population of Jerusalem at the time to have been 60,000 to 70,000, then doubling or even tripling this number for the pilgrimage festivals may be reasonable. We would thus be talking about somewhere between 125,000 to 200,000. Of course, the number undoubtedly varied, depending on the holiday and political-religious climate at the time.

Feelings of joy and exultation permeated the pilgrimage experience to Jerusalem, as they did in all pilgrimage settings from time immemorial. Both Philo and Josephus describe that moment and its attendant feelings. In the context of discussing the biblical injunction of pilgrimage, Josephus certainly struck home when noting the religious component, but he especially focuses on the social aspect of pilgrimage, in particular the unity and camaraderie fostered by being together with masses of seemingly different but essentially like-minded coreligionists (*Ant.* 4.203-4). Philo, true to form as a philosopher and religious thinker, emphasizes a somewhat different perspective:

> There is also the temple made by hands; for it was right that no check should be given to the forwardness of those who pay their tribute to piety and desire by means of sacrifices either to give thanks for the blessings that befall them or to ask for pardon and forgiveness for their sins. But he provided that there should not be temples built either in many places or many in the same place, for he judged that since God is one, there should also be only one temple. (*Spec. Leg.* 1.67)

Philo here focuses on a cardinal distinction that set Jewish pilgrimage to Jerusalem's Temple apart from similar phenomena throughout the ancient world. Generally speaking, pilgrims came from nearby regions, as was the case with the sanctuaries of Asclepius at Pergamum or Artemis at Perge, even when those assembled comprised a large number. The reason for this is that each deity had many shrines, and his or her worship could take place in one of countless locales throughout the empire.

Judaism had but one God, and this God had but one shrine. Therefore, those wishing to visit his earthly abode and participate in public sacrificial ceremonies in his honor had to come to Jerusalem. The city thus became a pilgrimage site par excellence in the first-century Roman Empire. Josephus formulates this idea rather succinctly: "In no other city let there be either altar or temple; for God is one and the Hebrew race is one" (*Ant.* 4.201). There was one mother-city for the Jews or, as Philo puts it, the far-flung Diaspora Jewish communities functioned as colonies to their mother city, Jerusalem. Only Jerusalem could provide the most complete worship experience, and the centripetal pull of the city was perhaps the most significant factor in bonding Jews everywhere. Much as Rome functioned as the *urbs* par excellence for the empire as a whole (at least in Roman eyes), so, too, did the Jerusalem Temple cement the various disparate Jewish communities of Judea and the Diaspora into a unified whole.

BIBLIOGRAPHY

J. ÅDNA 1999, *Jerusalemer Tempel und Tempelmarkt im 1. Jahrhundert n. Chr.,* Wiesbaden: Harrassowitz. • M. BEN-DOV 1985, *In the Shadow of the Temple: The Discovery of Ancient Jerusalem,* Jerusalem: Keter. • T. A. BUSINK 1970, *Der Tempel von Jerusalem von Salomon bis Herodes: Einer archäologisch-historische Studie unter Berücksichtigung des westsemitischen Tempelbaus,* 2 vols., Leiden: Brill. • F. HOLLIS 1934, *Archaeology of Herod's Temple,* London: Dent. • J. JEREMIAS 1969, *Jerusalem in the Time of Jesus: An Investigation into Economic and Social Conditions during the New Testament,* Philadelphia: Fortress. • L. I. LEVINE 1994, "Josephus' Description of the Jerusalem Temple: *War, Antiquities,* and Other Sources," in *Josephus and the History of the Greco-Roman Period,* ed. F. Parente and J. Sievers, Leiden: Brill, 233-46. • L. I. LEVINE 2002, *Jerusalem: Portrait of the City in the Second Temple Period (538 B.C.E.–70 C.E.),* Philadelphia: Jewish Publication Society. • B. MAZAR 1975, *The Mountain of the Lord,* Garden City, N.Y.: Doubleday. • K. RITMEYER AND L. RITMEYER 1989, "Reconstructing Herod's Temple Mount in Jerusalem," *BAR* 15, no. 6: 23-42. • E. P. SANDERS 1992, *Judaism: Practice and Belief: 63 BCE–66 CE,* London: SCM; Philadelphia: Trinity Press International. • A. SCHALIT 1969, *König Herodes: Der Mann und Sein Werk,* Berlin: de Gruyter.

See also: Jerusalem; Pilgrimage; Sacrifices and Offerings; Worship LEE I. LEVINE

Temple Scroll (11QTemple)

Manuscripts

11QTemple, the longest preserved composition from Qumran, is perhaps the most important halakic composition known from the Second Temple period. Because a significant portion of this text is devoted to a detailed description of the Jerusalem Temple, it is commonly referred to as the *Temple Scroll.*

As many as five copies of this composition have been recovered, the most well-preserved of which is 11QTemple[a] (11Q19). The scroll is over twenty-six feet long and has sixty-six extant columns, though portions of it have significantly deteriorated and the top third of the scroll has been lost. 11QTemple[a] was discovered in 1956 by Bedouin in Qumran's Cave 11, but the scroll remained in the possession of an antiquities dealer in Bethlehem until 1967. In 1960, the scroll's existence had been brought to the attention of the Israeli scholar Yigael Yadin by an American go-between, but they were unable to work out an arrangement to purchase the scroll. After the 1967 war Yadin was able to acquire the scroll, and eventually he published a full Hebrew edition and commentary of it in 1977. A revised English edition later appeared in 1983. Paleographic analysis dates 11QTemple[a] to the end of the first century B.C.E. or beginning of the first century C.E.

In addition to 11QTemple[a], Cave 11 also yielded significant portions of a second copy and possibly a third. Forty-two fragments of 11QTemple[b] (11Q20) have been preserved, some of which are quite large. Though its text differs in small details from that of 11QTemple[a], the two manuscripts are clearly copies of the same composition. 11QTemple[b] appears to have been copied slightly later than 11QTemple[a], dating paleographically to ca. 25-50 C.E. The other manuscript from Cave 11 is tentatively labeled 11QTemple[c]? (11Q21). Because only three small fragments of it are extant, relatively little can be said about its relationship to the other manuscripts or even whether it is in fact a copy of the *Temple Scroll.*

Cave 4 at Qumran has yielded one — perhaps two — additional copies of the *Temple Scroll.* Because of the poor preservation of 4QTemple[b] (4Q524), which consists of thirty-nine small fragments, only a few clear overlaps with 11QTemple[a] can be established, but its contents do not seem to differ significantly from those of the other manuscripts. One noteworthy difference is that 4QTemple[b] appears to have a longer ending, continuing past the point where 11QTemple[a] ends. Accord-

Columns 43–44 of the Temple Scroll (11Q19 or 11QTemple[a]) *(Photograph by Bruce and Kenneth Zuckerman, West Semitic Research. Courtesy Shrine of the Book)*

ing to paleographic analysis, 4QTemple[b] is the oldest extant manuscript of the *Temple Scroll,* dating to the early Hasmonean period (ca. 150-125 B.C.E.).

As for the other Cave 4 manuscript, tentatively designated 4QTemple[a]? (4Q365a), its connection to the *Temple Scroll* remains an open question. Of its five fragments, only one clearly overlaps with 11QTemple[a], and it has been suggested that rather than being an actual copy of the *Temple Scroll,* this manuscript may have been a source used by its author or some other related composition.

Contents

The following summary of the *Temple Scroll's* contents is based on 11QTemple[a]. The first extant column, which is labeled col. 2 because at least one column has been lost from the beginning, contains standard Deuteronomistic warnings against forbidden religious practices. The rest of the text can be divided basically into four sections.

(1) Description of the Temple Precinct (cols. 3-13; 30-45): This section describes in detail the Temple precinct and its various constituent parts. The first half begins with the Temple itself and its inner sanctuaries, while the second half describes both the structures lying outside the Temple and the courtyards that concentrically surround it.

(2) The Festival Calendar (cols. 13-29): This section, which has been inserted into the description of the temple precinct, describes the various festivals throughout the year and details the sacrifices that are to be offered on each of them. This description begins with the daily sacrifices, continues with the additional sacrifices for the Sabbath and the new month, and then moves to the special pilgrimage festivals. Two factors that distinguish this festival calendar are its use of a 364-day solar calendar and the addition of several festivals not found in the canonical Torah.

(3) Purity Regulations (cols. 45-51): This section covers purity regulations for the Temple, the Temple city, as well as regulations for all of the cities throughout Israel.

(4) "Deuteronomic" Section (cols. 51-66): This final section restates the legal portions of Deuteronomy and can be further subdivided into three parts. First, cols. 51-57 mostly draw upon Deuteronomy 12–17, while mixing in and harmonizing this material with parallels from Exodus, Leviticus, and Numbers. Next, cols. 57-59, known as the "Law of the King," greatly expand Deut. 17:14-20 and place strict regulations on the king's behavior. Finally, cols. 60-66 correspond fairly closely to Deuteronomy 18–22.

Composition

The Torah obviously served as a most important source for the *Temple Scroll,* but the author also appears to have incorporated other preexisting sources into his work. These sources, which can be distinguished by linguistic and stylistic criteria, roughly correspond to the major sections outlined above. The first two-thirds of the scroll were compiled from two main sources, the "Temple Source" (cols. 3-13, 30-45) and the festival calendar (cols. 13-29), the latter of which was inserted within the former. The purity regulations in cols. 45-51 show more of the author's editorial hand, and it is unclear whether they were drawn from a single, coherent source. The "Deuteronomic" section at the end of the *Temple Scroll* also evinces a complex redactional history, harmonizing many of Deuteronomy's laws with similar regulations from the other books of the Torah. Many of these harmonizations, however, may have been adopted from a preexisting source. In addition, the text of Deuteronomy includes a few key expansions, the most extensive of which is the Law of the King. This particular expansion clearly derives from an independent source, and it has been suggested that other smaller expansions, such as the laws concerning treason in col.

64, derive from a common "Midrash to Deuteronomy" source.

Date

The *terminus ad quem* of the *Temple Scroll*'s date of composition is established by its oldest manuscript, 4QTemple[b]. Based on this manuscript's paleographically established date, the *Temple Scroll* was compiled no later than the mid-second century B.C.E. Attempts to establish a *terminus a quo* usually focus on known historical events that may have prompted one or another of the scroll's legal innovations. Because of the work's composite nature, however, these innovations may allow us only to establish the date of a particular source used by the *Temple Scroll* rather than that of the scroll itself. With that in mind, the most useful source in this regard appears to be the Law of the King — which is preserved in the extant portions of 4QTemple[b] — because it is usually interpreted as a polemic against the Hasmonean rulers. If the source from which the Law of the King was taken cannot antedate the era of Hasmonean rule, this would establish the composition of the *Temple Scroll* sometime in the mid-second century B.C.E.

Theology

The author of the *Temple Scroll* envisions an idealized version of Jewish life and worship, as exemplified by the unrealistically massive dimensions of the Temple precinct it describes. Despite the seemingly unrealistic nature of this vision, however, the author sees his version of Jewish life as what should be normative and not merely as something to be implemented at the end of days. The key clue in the text occurs at the very end of the description of the festival calendar, where 11QTemple[a] 29:8-10 states that God will replace the Temple being described in the scroll with a future, eternal temple (a similar temple is described in 4QFlorilegium). Thus, rather than describing the Temple that will be coming at the end times, the author of the *Temple Scroll* is describing what he believes should have been standing in Jerusalem all along. In the same way, the whole program of Jewish worship that he advocates in the *Temple Scroll* reflects what he believes should have been normative and proper since the revelation at Sinai.

Relation to Hebrew Bible and Qumran Sectarian Literature

The *Temple Scroll* falls within a larger category of Second Temple Jewish literature known rather anachronistically as "Rewritten Bible." This category encompasses texts that interpret Scripture by retelling, recasting, or embellishing parts of the biblical text to form a new composition. This raises the question of what relationship the author of the *Temple Scroll* believed his work to have with existing Scripture. There are some indications that the *Temple Scroll* was considered to be revealed Scripture and perhaps even was meant to replace or supersede the Torah. This issue, however, still remains in dispute.

One such indication is the scroll's tendency to have God refer to himself in the first person. Deuteronomy couches its legal provisions within speeches delivered by Moses, and therein God is referred to in the third person. When these provisions are incorporated into the *Temple Scroll*, however, the author often reformulates them as first-person pronouncements and thus as direct speech from God. The author of the *Temple Scroll* thereby removes Moses as the mediator between God and the Israelites and brings the reader one step closer to God than even the Torah itself does. The author, however, is somewhat inconsistent in this practice, and the *Temple Scroll* includes many third-person references to God as well.

Another indication of the scroll's scriptural status is its use of the Tetragrammaton. The Qumran sectarians tended to avoid using the Tetragrammaton in nonbiblical texts, often substituting a row of four dots or writing it in Paleo-Hebrew letters. The oldest manuscript of the *Temple Scroll*, 4QTemple[b], follows this practice, using four dots in place of the Tetragrammaton. Yet 11QTemple[a] and 11QTemple[b], both of which are later, Herodian manuscripts, freely use the Tetragrammaton throughout. Therefore, it is possible that the text was not considered to be Scripture when it was composed but may have been accorded this status at a later time.

This possibility, of course, raises the question of the *Temple Scroll*'s relationship with Qumran sectarian writings and whether its origin can be traced to the Qumran sect. When compared to writings from Qumran that are generally assumed to be sectarian, such as the *Damascus Document* (CD), the *Rule of the Congregation* (1QSa), and the *War Scroll* (1QM), the *Temple Scroll* exhibits a number of clear halakic parallels, especially with regard to purity regulations. On the other hand, clear halakic differences also exist among these texts, and these differences render problematic any attempt to define the *Temple Scroll* as a sectarian composition. The *Temple Scroll* also adheres to the 364-day calendar advocated in the literature of the Qumran sect as well as in *1 Enoch* and the *Book of Jubilees*.

BIBLIOGRAPHY

Major Editions of 11QTemple and Related Manuscripts

F. GARCÍA MARTÍNEZ ET AL. 1998, *Qumran Cave 11.II*, DJD 23, Oxford: Clarendon, 357-414, pls. XLI-XLVIII [11Q20-21]. • É. PUECH 1998, *Qumran Grotte 4.XVIII: Textes Hébreux (4Q521–4Q528, 4Q576–4Q579)*, DJD 25, Oxford: Clarendon, 85-114, pls. VII-VIII [4Q524]. • E. QIMRON 1996, *The Temple Scroll: A Critical Edition with Extensive Reconstructions*, Beer Sheva: Ben-Gurion University of the Negev Press. • S. WHITE 1994, "4QTemple?" *Qumran Cave 4.VIII: Parabiblical Texts, Part 1*, ed. H. Attridge et al., DJD 13, Oxford: Clarendon, 319-33, pl. XXXIII-XXXIV [4Q365a]. • Y. YADIN 1983, *The Temple Scroll*, 3 vols., Jerusalem: Israel Exploration Society.

Other Editions and Studies

G. BROOKE, ED. 1989, *Temple Scroll Studies: Papers Presented at the International Symposium on the Temple Scroll, Manchester, December 1987*, Sheffield: JSOT Press. • S. WHITE CRAWFORD 2000, *The Temple Scroll and Related Texts*, Sheffield: Sheffield Academic Press. • J. MEIER 1997, *Die Tempelrolle vom Toten Meer und das "Neue Jerusalem,"* 3d ed., Munich: Reinhardt. • L. H. SCHIFFMAN 1989, "The Law of the Temple Scroll and Its Provenance," *Folia Orientalia* 25: 85-98. • D. SWANSON 1995, *The Temple Scroll and the Bible: The Methodology of 11QT*, Leiden: Brill. • M. O. WISE 1990, *A Critical Study of the Temple Scroll from Qumran Cave 11*, Chicago: Oriental Institute of the University of Chicago. • Y. YADIN 1985, *The Temple Scroll: The Hidden Law of the Dead Sea Sect*, New York: Random House.

ANDREW GROSS

Temple Tax

The temple tax was an annual half-shekel tax paid to the Jerusalem Temple by Jewish males in the late Second Temple period. It was sometimes known as a didrachma tax (Matt. 17:24-27; cf. Josephus, *Ant.* 18.312). According to *m. Sheqalim*, a tractate devoted to describing it, the tax was used to pay for a variety of expenses, including daily communal sacrifices, festival sacrifices, drink offerings, the showbread, and the two loaves (4.1-4).

Philo (*Her.* 37.186) and Josephus (*Ant.* 3.194-96) indicate that the tax was already an established custom in their own day. Josephus regards its payment as a biblical mandate going back to Moses. The source for this belief is Exod. 30:11-16, which refers to a half-shekel census tax paid as an atonement by every Israelite over age twenty for the service of the Tent of Meeting (cf. Exod. 38:26). Though the biblical passage clearly refers to a one-time event, it nonetheless later served as the justification for a yearly tax. Other passages cited in the scholarly literature as possible inspiration for the tax include 2 Chron. 24:4-14, in which Joash orders the Levites to gather money each year from the cities of Judah for the repair of the Temple; and Neh. 10:32-33, in which Nehemiah institutes a one-third shekel tax to pay for communal offerings. *M. Sheqalim* 2:4 refers to payment of the tax by returnees from the Babylonian Exile. Many scholars believe, however, that the half-shekel tax was not instituted until the Hasmonean period, when it served both to bolster the Temple financially and (like the creation and celebration of Hanukkah) to increase support for the Hasmonean kingship and priesthood (Baumgarten 1996).

Payment of the tax appears to have been widespread in both Palestine and the Diaspora. According to *m. Sheqal.* 1:1-6, it was collected in the month of Adar and was required of males, including freed slaves and proselytes. Priests apparently were exempt, though Levites were not. The tax was optional for women, slaves, and children and not accepted if offered by Samaritans or Gentiles. *M. Sheqalim* 2:1-4 refers to its collection outside of Jerusalem, and Matt. 17:24-27 notes the presence in Galilee of collectors. Josephus indicates that Babylonian Jews paid it (*Ant.* 18.132). He also mentions "sacred monies" gathered by Jews in Asia and Cyrene to send to Jerusalem, citing documents that indicate that civic and provincial officials sometimes tried to prevent their Jewish inhabitants from sending the money (*Ant.* 16.160-73). Similarly, Cicero defends Flaccus, the Roman proconsul of Asia, against charges that he seized money gathered by the Jews of Apamea, Laodicea, Adramyttium, and Pergamum (*Pro Flacco* 28.66-69). According to Cicero, community sums were often shipped in the form of gold. The amounts of money involved were considerable — one hundred pounds of gold at Apamea, twenty at Laodicea.

Though payment was widespread, it was not universal. One of the Dead Sea Scrolls (4Q159) suggests that the Qumran sect opposed the annual tax, interpreting Exod. 30:11-16 as requiring only a one-time payment. *Mekilta* tractate *Baḥodesh* 1 also suggests that not all Jews favored the tax. Some have argued that Matt. 17:24-27, which reports a query about whether Jesus would pay it, indicates that Galileans were lax in observing the custom, though the passage itself is not clear on that point.

T. Ketubbot 13:20 specifies that any time a Pentateuchal passage mentions silver, it should be understood as Tyrian coinage, and *m. Bekorot* 8:7 also reflects a high view of Tyrian silver. These traditions are usually interpreted as suggesting that Tyrian coinage was required for payment of the tax, despite the fact that Tyre's shekels and half-shekels bore images of the city's patron deity, Melqart-Heracles, on their obverses and of an eagle on their reverses. Some have suggested that this preference is explained by the exceptionally pure silver content (95 percent) of Tyrian coinage (Meshorer 2001). Alternatively, the custom might have originated in the fact that Tyre provided most of Palestine's silver when the tax was created in the Hasmonean period and for the entirety of the time it was collected. Though some have argued that production of Tyrian half-shekels actually shifted to Jerusalem in c. 20 B.C.E. (Meshorer 2001), there is little evidence for this view.

After the destruction of the Temple, Vespasian dictated that a new tax of two denarii should be collected from Jews throughout the empire. This new tax went not to Jerusalem but to the temple of Jupiter Capitolinus in Rome (Josephus, *J.W.* 7.218; Dio Cassius 65.7.2; cf. Suetonius, *Domitian* 12.2). The *fiscus Iudaicus* seems to have been collected until at least the third century C.E. (Smallwood 2001; Ginsburg 1931).

BIBLIOGRAPHY

A. I. BAUMGARTEN 1996, "Invented Traditions of the Maccabean Era," in *Geschichte, Tradition, Reflexion: Festschrift für Martin Hengel zum 70. Geburtstag*, ed. H. Cancik, H. Lichtenberger, and P. Schäfer, Tübingen: Mohr-Siebeck, 1: 197-210. • E. J. BICKERMAN 1980, "La Charte Seleucide de Jerusalem," in idem, *Studies in Jewish and Christian History*, Leiden Brill, 2: 44-86. • M. S. GINSBURG 1931, "Fiscus Judaicus," *JQR* 21: 281-91. • J. LIVER 1963, "The Half-Shekel Offering in Biblical and Post-Biblical Literature," *HTR* 56: 173-98. • S. MANDELL 1984, "Who Paid the Temple Tax When the Jews Were under Roman Rule?" *HTR* 77: 223-32. • Y. MESHORER 2001, *A Treasury of Jewish Coins*, Jerusalem: Yad Ben Zvi; Nyack, N.Y.: Amphora Books. • E. P. SANDERS 1992, *Judaism: Practice and Belief: 63 BCE–66 CE*, London: SCM Press; Philadelphia: Trinity Press International. • E. M. SMALLWOOD 2001, *The Jews Under Roman Rule: From Pompey to Diocletian*, 2d ed., Leiden: Brill.

MARK A. CHANCEY

Testaments

Scholars define the genre "testament" by formal literary characteristics or by the nature of a document's content. The former is a simple narrative framework: an introduction in which the testator gathers family to hear his near-death speech and a conclusion that narrates the speaker's death (Collins 1984). Content definitions of the testamentary genre are not so straightforward. For some, a testament requires parenesis (Von Nordheim 1980), for others eschatological or apocalyptic discourse is necessary (Munck 1950), and still others require parenesis *and* eschatology to recognize a text as a testament (e.g., *Testament of Levi;* see Kolenkow 1975). The larger difficulty with content definitions is the common ground they share with other genres (e.g., apocalypses, wisdom writings), rendering them somewhat meaningless. Thus we rely on the presence of the narrative framework to declare a text of early Judaism to be a testament. By that reckoning only three Jewish texts of Greco-Roman and late antiquity represent the genre: *Testament of Moses, Testament of Job,* and *Testaments of the Twelve Patriarchs.* To be sure, other texts are dubbed "testaments" *(Testament of Adam, Testament of Abraham, Testament of Isaac, Testament of Jacob, Testament of Solomon).* However, they either lack the narrative framework of the genre or are of uncertain provenance (appearing to be Christian in origin or later than the period covered by this volume), and some labor under both disqualifiers.

Testament of Moses

The testament begins with Moses summoning Joshua to give him final instructions and concludes with Moses' death. (Because the sole surviving manuscript, a Latin palimpsest first published in 1861, is broken at the end, we do not have the end of the death narrative; there is little reason to believe, though, that anything else followed.) The opening scene recalls Deut. 31:7, 14 with Moses reassuring Joshua that all will be well for Israel beyond his death: God created the world for the people of Israel, and God had used Moses to mediate to Israel God's abiding covenant (1:1-14). Moses then predicts the future from the conquest to the Exile, blaming the eventual expulsion from the land on the last four kings of Judah, who would violate the "covenant and oath" (2:1–3:14). From their exile the people will implore God to recall the covenant with Abraham, Isaac, and Jacob, and an unnamed mediator (Daniel?) will appeal to God's pride by questioning whether a chosen people should suffer so in captivity (4:1-4). As a result God will raise up a foreign king to deliver the tribes from exile, although some will remain scattered and two will not take part in the restored cult (4:5-9). A new prediction passage recalls the Hasmoneans as apostates (5:1-6) whose sins against God and people are punished by the traumas imposed by Herod (6:1-7) and by Varus' campaign in 4 B.C.E. (6:8-9). Then follows another (undatable) cycle of apostasy and its consequences, this time a catalogue of priestly sins (7:1-10) punished by a cornucopia of sufferings (7:1–8:5). Paralleling the human intercessor of 4:1-4, 9:1-7 introduces Taxo, a mysterious figure who promises that he and his sons would even die as martyrs to prompt the advent of God's kingdom. Then Moses describes the future kingdom as destined to be established by God alone (10:1-10). Finished presaging the future, Moses admonishes Joshua to be a good leader (10:11-15), but Joshua voices his fear that without the mediation of Moses the people will not survive the predicted future, filled as it is with "tears and sobbings" (11:1-9). Moses reassures Joshua by repeating that God made the world from before time for Israel, so it is not human mediation or righteous deeds that assure Israel's glorious fate, but God alone who controls history in Israel's favor (12:1-9). Thus even if in the present age the righteous enjoy goodness and the wicked suffer (12:10-11), in the end God will vindicate all of Israel and remain true to God's "covenant and oath" (12:12-13).

Allusions to Herod (6:2-6) and his sons (who by the time of writing had not yet reigned longer than their father; 6:7), and to Varus, the Roman commander who put down a revolt in Palestine around 4 B.C.E. (6:9), prove that the testament was composed sometime between 4 B.C.E. and 30 C.E.. Given the familiarity with the campaign of Varus and the interest in the priesthood, a Palestinian provenance seems likely.

Assessments of the testament's purpose range widely. Some simply characterize its theology as Deuteronomic, but Collins (1984) considers the work to be a good example of "covenantal nomism" because it assumes election for Israel followed by God's requirement to keep the Law to retain God's favor, and others suggest the testament argues that God acts unilaterally on behalf of Israel, offering unconditional mercy for a sinful, punished, and only nominally repentant Israel (D. Harrington in Nickelsburg 1976). The concluding assurances Moses offers Joshua, as well as the "covenant and oath" language that echoes the unilateralism of Genesis 15, favors the latter view.

Testament of Job

Job, identified as a king of Egypt, summons his children to his deathbed to recount for them the events of his life before his second marriage (to Dinah, daughter of Jacob). He explains to them that the suffering of his earlier life was caused by his destruction of a temple of Satan. Even though an angel warned that destroying the temple would bring Satan's destructive wrath upon him, the messenger also said that if Job endured that suffering with patience all would be restored to him twofold and he would receive the gift of resurrection. The latter promise, together with his zeal to protect his neighbors from the temptation of Satan's temple, prompted Job to wreck the sanctuary (chaps. 1–5). An angry Satan came to his home disguised as a beggar and after an exchange in which Job outwitted Satan, God granted Satan permission to afflict Job (chaps. 6–8). But before relating the attack of Satan (chaps. 16–27), Job tells his children of the great wealth he possessed and his generous use of it to provide a full measure of the losses he and his neighbors endured at Satan's hands (chaps. 9–15). One special feature of chaps. 16–27 is the extended account of the pitiful fate of Job's first wife, Sitidos, and its contrast with Job's enormous patience (chaps. 21–26). Another is Satan's announcement that Job's patient endurance so exceeds his own superior strength that he concedes the contest to Job (chap. 27).

Job's fellow kings, Eliphaz, Bildad, and Zophar, arrive, remain silent for seven days in astonishment at Job's great reversal of fortunes, and subsequently take turns plaintively querying Job on how his great wealth and position were lost. Job's consistent response is that there is no cause for alarm, for the heavenly estate promised him far outweighs the one Satan had destroyed (chaps. 28–43). Folded into this long section is the final episode from the life of Job's wife wherein she receives at least the satisfaction of knowing that her dead children were received into God's kingdom (chaps. 39–40). As for himself, Job tells his children from his deathbed, his assurances for his friends were soon vindicated when his wealth was soon restored to him, as were the joy of family through his marriage to Dinah and the birth of his present addressees (chap. 44).

Returning to the present, Job urges his children to be generous to the poor and to avoid marrying foreign women, and he distributes his wealth to his sons (chap. 45). At this his daughters, Hemera, Kasia, and Amaltheia's Horn, complain that they have no inheritance so he gives them the sashes that God gave him to bind himself with when God commanded him to rise and gird his loins (Job 38:3; 40:2), sashes that cured his physical and emotional distress and gave him other miraculous benefits. Thus each woman has an ecstatic religious experience as she dons her sash (chaps. 46–50), so when Job dies, his daughters assist him into heaven with their songs, and his body is buried (chaps. 51–53).

Although it enjoys a weak consensus at best, a first-century-C.E. Egyptian provenance is generally assigned to the testament. A number of features suggest Egyptian provenance (e.g., Job's kingship), and the intense focus on loss of status and wealth may echo the Jewish experience in Egypt at the mid-first-century advent of Roman rule. Some have questioned the work's compositional unity, but most explain the text's unevenness as the result of a single author's use of disparate sources.

Regarding the religious perspective of the work, although most critics blandly ascribe the testament to a general "Hellenized Judaism," others, having noted its focus on the contrast between earthly and heavenly realities and the importance of heavenly insight, see it as having resonance with mystic forms of Jewish thought, or as addressing the anxieties of Jews who had experienced diminished social status under Roman rule. And regardless of commentators' level of insight on its overall purpose, everyone recognizes the puzzle in the testament's prominent, yet uneven, depiction of women (Sitidos the pitiful vs. Job's boldly demanding and spirit-inspired daughters).

Testaments of the Twelve Patriarchs

The deathbed speeches of the sons of Jacob, each testament in this collection follows more or less a familiar pattern: it begins with the patriarch's summons to his children to his bedside, continues with his autobiographical reflections, moral exhortation, and future prediction, and concludes with an account of the man's death and burial. Seven patriarchs' autobiographical accounts rely on Genesis (Reuben [Gen. 35:22]; Levi [Genesis 34]; Judah [Genesis 38]; Issachar [Gen. 49:14-15 LXX]; Zebulun [Gen. 49:13]; Gad [Gen. 37:2]; Joseph [Gen. 39:6b-18]), and five depend on other sources and interpretive readings of Genesis (Simeon, Dan, Naphtali, Asher, and Benjamin). The autobiographical accounts trigger moral exhortation: right action equals pleasing God and opposing Beliar, keeping the twofold commandment to love God and one's neighbor, and heeding traditional Greco-Roman vices. Individually the patriarchs' accounts address the pitfalls of failing to exercise self-control vis-à-vis strong drink (Judah), attractive women (Reuben; Judah), envy (Simeon), greed (Judah), falsehood (Dan), anger (Simeon; Gad), temptations to unjust violence (Simeon; Judah; Dan; Gad), and double-mindedness (Asher), and they praise the virtues of zeal for the Lord (Levi), temperance and purity (Judah), simplicity of life (Issachar), merciful warm-heartedness (Zebulun), harmony with the natural order (Naphtali), single-mindedness (Asher), and chastity, endurance, and mercy (Joseph).

Much attention has been lavished on the forms that appear in the concluding eschatological sections. They include (1) Sin-Exile-Return (S.E.R.) sections that describe the future sins of the patriarch's descendants, the tribe's exile among the Gentiles as punishment for their sin, and God's restoration of the tribe; (2) Levi-Judah (L.J.) passages wherein the patriarch bemoans his descendants' rebellion against Levi's descendants, as well as their certain defeat in such efforts, and/or looks forward to his descendants' loyalty and obedience to the tribes of Levi and Judah out of respect for their special roles; (3) ideal savior passages that look forward to a deliverer for Israel; and (4) resurrection-of-the-patriarch passages that anticipate his rule over his tribe in the future.

Largely because of the foregoing eschatological material and its occasional clear references to Jesus, establishing the date and provenance of *Testaments of the Twelve Patriarchs* is notoriously difficult, and it might seem better to some to disqualify it for the purposes of this article as a purely Christian composition dating no earlier than the second century C.E. However, its heavy reliance on quasi-testamentary material known from earlier Jewish works and traditions such as the *Aramaic Levi Document* and Hebrew traditions relating to Judah, Naphtali, and perhaps Joseph, virtually ensures that it was at one time either in parts or as a whole one or several Jewish compositions of testamentary character. As such it likely served a variety of purposes, from addressing concerns over the purity of the priesthood (Levi) to elaborating speculatively on curiosities in the biblical text (Naphtali). As a Christian composition of the second century C.E. it explains the consanguineous nature of adherence to the teachings of Israel's patriarchs, the moral norms of the Greco-Roman world, and trust in Jesus Christ as savior.

TESTIMONIA (4Q175)

Summary

This article began by defining the testamentary genre by the presence of a narrative framework. Discussion of the three exemplars of the genre, so defined, should make one thing abundantly clear: the narrative framework does not in any way constrain the purpose to which its corresponding genre may be put. Although they share the same narrative framework, the *Testaments of Moses, Job,* and *the Twelve Patriarchs* all serve different masters when it comes to constructing the religion of early Judaism. Moses argues that God acts unilaterally on Israel's behalf, Job declaims the balanced nature of God's justice for those who earn it by their endurance, and the patriarchs make being Israelite equitable with being a citizen of a Greek *polis* or of the Roman Empire (and with professing faith in Jesus Christ). It is a familiar lesson: genres are little more than vehicles for the ideas of their users.

BIBLIOGRAPHY

J. J. COLLINS 1984, "Testaments," in *Jewish Writings of the Second Temple Period,* ed. M. E. Stone, Assen: Van Gorcum; Philadelphia: Fortress, 325-56. • G. W. E. NICKELSBURG, ED. 1973, *Studies on the Testament of Moses,* Cambridge, Mass.: Society of Biblical Literature. • G. W. E. NICKELSBURG, ED. 1976, *Studies on the Testament of Job,* Missoula, Mont.: Scholars Press. • A. B. KOLENKOW 1975, "The Genre Testament and Forecasts of the Future in the Hellenistic Jewish Milieu," *JSJ* 6: 57-71. • R. A. KUGLER 2001, *Testaments of the Twelve Patriarchs,* Sheffield: Sheffield Academic Press. • R. A. KUGLER AND R. ROHRBAUGH 2004, "On Women and Honor in the *Testament of Job,*" *JSP* 14: 43-62. • J. MUNCK 1950, "Discours d'adieu dans le Nouveau Testament et dans la littérature biblique," in *Aux sources de la tradition chrétienne: Mélanges offerts à M. Goguel,* ed. O. Cullmann and P. Menoud, Neuchâtel and Paris: Delachaux & Nestlé, 155-70. • E. VON NORDHEIM 1980, *Die Lehre der Alten: Das Testament als Literaturgattung im Judentum der Hellenistischen-römischen Zeit,* Leiden: Brill, 1980.

ROBERT A. KUGLER

Testimonia (4Q175)

The Qumran text known as the *Testimonia* (4Q175) is a collection of biblical extracts collected around the theme of the eschatological age. This manuscript is highly distinctive because it is a single piece of parchment (9 × 15 cm.) inscribed with just one column of writing twenty-nine lines long. Widely thought to have been penned by the same scribe who copied out the Cave 1 copy of the *Rule of the Community* (1QS), the manuscript is to be dated approximately to the first quarter of the first century B.C.E. The damage patterns seem to indicate that it was folded in antiquity, perhaps so that it could be easily carried in a pouch. The scribe used four dots to represent the Tetragrammaton (as also in 1QS and 4Q53). Though this all indicates that the composition was copied within the Dead Sea sect, it does not necessarily make its contents sectarian.

The manuscript contains four authoritative scriptural extracts linked together by catchwords. After the first, second, and third a marginal mark in the shape of a hook separates each extract. The first extract is from Exod. 20:21 largely according to the Samaritan tradition. In the corresponding Masoretic Text, this represents a combination of Deut. 5:28b-29 with 18:18-19. The eschatological figure referred to is the prophet like Moses. This same passage is used in the New Testament, notably in Acts 3:22-23 and 7:37, to describe the prophetic status of Jesus; indeed, the whole composition has been used to revive the theory that early Christian preachers used testimonia, collections of proof texts.

The second extract is Num. 24:15-17. Though it can be construed as referring to the eschatological princely messiah under two guises, as star of Jacob and scepter of Israel, it is more commonly thought that the passage refers to two eschatological figures, the priest messiah (the star) and the royal messiah (the scepter); it could also be that the visionary's self-description (the man) develops the role of prophet as that has been described

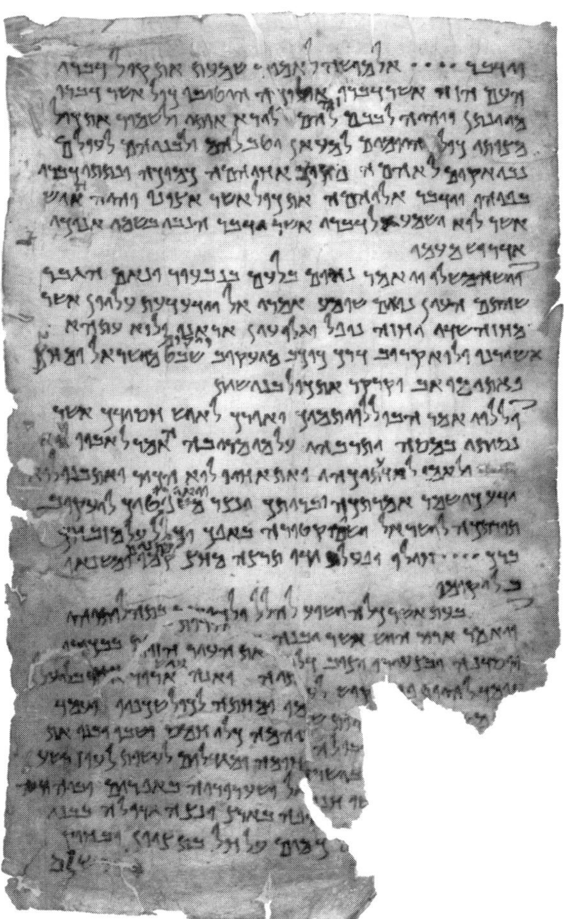

4Q175 Testimonia *(Photograph by Bruce and Kenneth Zuckerman, West Semitic Research, in collaboration with Princeton Theological Seminary. Courtesy Department of Antiquities, Jordan)*

in the first quotation of Exod. 20:21b. In that case Num. 24:15-17 would form a neat bridge between the first and the third quotations. The same passage is cited in the *Damascus Document* (CD 7:19), where the star is identified as the interpreter of the Law and the scepter as the prince of the whole congregation.

The third extract is Deut. 33:8-11, Moses' blessing of Levi. It most likely refers exclusively to the eschatological priest messiah as the opponent of idolatry, the keeper of the covenant, and the teacher of Torah. However, some modern interpreters have preferred to see here an allusion to the sectarian movement's so-called Teacher of Righteousness, known to have been a priest (4Q171), and his interpretation of the Law. The passage is also cited and commented upon in 4Q174.

The fourth extract is from the *Apocryphon of Joshua,* a rewritten form of the book of Joshua, which probably had scriptural authority for some Jews, which is known now from 4Q378-379, and which also contains many allusions to other scriptural passages. Most scholars understand this fourth extract to be a quotation from the *Apocryphon of Joshua,* though not from a known manuscript copy of it, since 4Q379 frg. 22 contains a scribal error; a minority view suggests that the relevant section of 4Q379 was copied from 4Q175. The extract begins with a piece of Josh. 6:26 that is then continued with a description of a man of Belial and what is best restored as a reference to his two sons. This threesome corresponds negatively to the eschatological prophet, king, and priest of the first three extracts. Several different identifications have been proposed, notably Simon Maccabee and his two sons Judas and Mattathias, all assassinated in 135 B.C.E.; John Hyrcanus I and his sons Aristobulus and Alexander Jannaeus; or Alexander Jannaeus and his sons Hyrcanus II and Aristobulus II. Some scholars have also argued that the father was the Wicked Priest, the Teacher's archenemy.

Overall, the single page seems to have contained four proof texts, three positive and one negative, concerning the cast of the eschatological age. The extracts appear to be cited in a protocanonical order. There is nothing to indicate that any of the first three eschatological figures had already arrived, but it is quite likely that the references to the evil figures in the fourth extract are best understood in relation to actual historical personages roughly contemporary with the composition's compiler.

BIBLIOGRAPHY

G. J. BROOKE 1985, *Exegesis at Qumran: 4QFlorilegium in Its Jewish Context,* Sheffield: JSOT Press; rpt. Atlanta: Society of Biblical Literature, 2006, 309-19. • G. J. BROOKE 2005, "Thematic Commentaries on Prophetic Scriptures," in *Biblical Interpretation at Qumran,* ed. M. Henze, Grand Rapids: Eerdmans, 138-40. • F. M. CROSS 2002, "Testimonia (4Q175 = 4QTestimonia = 4QTestim)," in *The Dead Sea Scrolls: Hebrew, Aramaic, and Greek Texts with English Translations,* vol. 6B: *Pesharim, Other Commentaries, and Related Documents,* ed. J. H. Charlesworth, Tübingen: Mohr-Siebeck; Louisville: Westminster John Knox, 308-27. • H. ESHEL 1992, "The Historical Background of the Pesher Interpreting Joshua's Curse on the Rebuilder of Jericho," *RevQ* 15: 409-20. • J. A. FITZMYER 1957, "'4QTestimonia' and the New Testament," *TS* 18: 513-37 (reprinted several times).

GEORGE J. BROOKE

Text Types, Hebrew

Since antiquity it has been recognized that the Hebrew Bible exists in a variety of forms. Of course there is the traditional Hebrew text, known as the Masoretic Text (MT) after the tradents, called Masoretes, who gave the text its final form in the Middle Ages (the Hebrew verb *māsar* means "hand down, transmit"). Beside the MT, Christians and Jews have long known of the Greek translation (the Septuagint or LXX), the Aramaic translations (the targumim), and a number of others. In the seventeenth century, another ancient Hebrew version of the Torah, the Samaritan Pentateuch (SP), was brought to the attention of Western scholars.

Although most of these versions are translations, in many cases differences among them can be traced back to different forms of the Hebrew text that served as the basis for the translation. These differences are sometimes substantial. They indicate that those responsible for producing new (Hebrew) copies of biblical books did not always see their task as simply the reproduction of the text in front of them, but rather felt authorized to make changes that clarified or otherwise improved the text. The different forms of the Hebrew text of the Bible that resulted from these scribal activities are known as text types. Prior to the discovery of the Dead Sea Scrolls, scholarship identified three major text types: the MT, the Samaritan, and the Hebrew text underlying the LXX. The wide variety of manuscripts of biblical books found at Qumran and at other sites in the Judean Desert since 1947 has forced a reappraisal of older views and has led to the conclusion that the Hebrew text of the Bible was likely transmitted in a much greater variety of forms than originally imagined.

Defining Text Types

The most useful definition of a text type is a group of texts that share major features, though they may disagree in minor details (Ulrich 1999). Such major features mainly consist of differences in content or sequence from other text types: one text type might contain a verse or passage absent in another text type, or present material in a different order. It is important to recognize that text types should generally be identified and discussed with reference to individual books of the Bible rather than all the books of a particular version. The individual books were circulated and developed independently for some time before a particular text of each became part of a larger authoritative collection. Therefore, the books in each version, such as MT or LXX, do not all share the same characteristics. For instance, the LXX version of 1 Kings contains a substantial amount of material that is absent in the MT version. The situation is reversed, however, for the book of Jeremiah, where LXX witnesses a shorter ver-

TEXT TYPES, HEBREW

sion while the text of MT is around 17 percent longer. Thus while it would be correct to describe both MT Jeremiah and LXX 1 Kings as "expanded" or "full" texts, it would be incorrect to characterize the entire MT or the entire LXX as "expanded."

The Scrolls from the Judean Desert and the Biblical Text

The discovery beginning in 1947 of biblical manuscripts dating from ca. 200 B.C.E.–150 C.E. at Qumran and other sites near the Dead Sea has revolutionized our understanding of the number and nature of Hebrew text types existing in that period. First, we have gained a better understanding of the text types behind all three of the major versions known prior to 1947. While some scholars in the nineteenth and early twentieth centuries argued that the MT went through a process of editing that brought it to its current form sometime after 70 C.E. (the date of the destruction of the Jerusalem Temple by the Romans), some copies of biblical books found at Qumran and dated up to 250 years earlier witness essentially the same consonantal text as the later MT, showing that the biblical books as transmitted in the MT derived directly from forms of the text current in the centuries prior to 70 C.E.

With regard to LXX, scholars had long debated how many of the differences between it and MT should be attributed to changes made by the Greek translators of each book and how many might rather attest to a different version of the Hebrew text, which was then translated faithfully into Greek. For instance, in the book of Jeremiah, which, as mentioned above, is substantially shorter in the LXX, many scholars attributed the differences vis-à-vis MT to abridgment by the Greek translator. However, two manuscripts of Jeremiah found at Qumran (4QJer[b], 4QJer[d]) contain a shorter text similar to that of the LXX, indicating that the Greek translation of Jeremiah was almost certainly based upon a short Hebrew text rather than the longer one witnessed by MT.

The status of SP prior to the Qumran discoveries was also unclear, with many scholars regarding its frequent harmonistic additions and other distinctive elements as sectarian changes made by the Samaritans after they had split off from the main body of Judaism. Some of the best-preserved copies of Exodus and Numbers at Qumran, however, contain nearly all the distinctive elements of SP, lacking only the explicitly sectarian features such as the new tenth commandment prescribing worship at Mt. Gerizim. These manuscripts show that the Samaritans in fact made only relatively few and minor changes to an expansive version of the Pentateuch that was already circulating in Second Temple Jewish communities.

Among the Dead Sea Scrolls were found numerous other biblical manuscripts that do not represent a text type already known from these versions. Often these manuscripts agree in some significant details with one of the known versions, but disagree in others. Many also contain unique readings not attested in any other known text. For example, one manuscript of the book of Samuel, 4QSam[a], contains an entire paragraph lacking in all other versions; by contrast, one manuscript of Judges (4QJudg[a]) lacks four verses present in all other versions. In a few cases, there is evidence that heavily revised and expanded versions of particular books also existed at Qumran. One scroll containing the latter part of the Psalter, 11QPs[a], presents what we know as Psalms 101–150 in a dramatically different sequence, interspersed with psalms otherwise attested only in the Greek or Syriac translations of Psalms as well as some poems that are otherwise completely unknown. Another fragmentary group of manuscripts, 4QReworked Pentateuch[a-e], covers parts of the Pentateuch but rearranges, adds, paraphrases, and possibly even omits material. Scholars have debated whether 11QPs[a] and especially the *Reworked Pentateuch* represent biblical manuscripts, as opposed to derivative or interpretive works of some sort. More and more scholars are coming to the conclusion that they are indeed manuscripts of the biblical books they reflect. Thus they may well indicate the degree to which the Hebrew text was still in flux during the Second Temple period. All these manuscripts, however, even those whose differences from known versions are less extensive, attest to previously unknown Hebrew text types that must have circulated simultaneously with those that were later preserved in MT, LXX, and SP.

Development and Transmission

It is unlikely that many books of the Bible existed in a single text type for longer than a very brief period. The majority show clear signs of gradual development over time. In the latter stages of composition, each book was probably already being read and recopied, with earlier forms circulating alongside later forms. The recopying itself was often responsible for the final stages of a text's composition. While some scribes simply copied what was in front of them as exactly as possible, many others felt free to introduce deliberate changes of various kinds into the text. Thus the processes of composition and copying overlapped considerably; this overlap explains, for instance, the occurrence of both the short form and the longer form of Jeremiah among the DSS. As each book gained wider circulation and was recopied in different places or by different groups, the changes continued and the number of text types likely increased.

The finds from Qumran, which preserve more than one text type for a number of biblical books, give us a window into this situation of textual pluriformity. They also indicate that it is not adequate to conclude, as one influential theory has suggested, that various text types exist because each developed in a particular geographic locale in isolation from all the others (Cross and Talmon 1975). While geography may well have been a factor in the development of some text types, other factors such as sociological or political divisions may also have been important. Furthermore, the presence of such a variety of text types at a single location, the library of the Qumran community, suggests that the members of that community, who otherwise appear to have been quite rigid in their practice of their particular version of Juda-

Folio 422v (Ruth 3:13b–4:13a) of the Leningrad Codex *(Photograph by Bruce and Kenneth Zuckerman, West Semitic Research, in collaboration with the Ancient Biblical Manuscript Center. Courtesy Russian National Library [Saltykov-Shchedrin])*

ism, do not seem to have been particularly troubled by discrepancies in biblical manuscripts. Although no clear proof is available, the evidence from Qumran suggests that other Jewish communities of the period likewise tolerated or accepted a number of text types simultaneously.

This situation of multiple coexisting Hebrew text types did not endure. By the time of the Bar Kokhba Revolt (132-35 C.E.), there is evidence that only one form of each book remained legitimate: the form now found in the MT. In striking contrast to the pluriformity of Qumran, all the biblical texts found at other sites in the Judean Desert contain a consonantal text virtually identical with that of the medieval manuscripts of the MT. While the majority of the Qumran texts date from ca. 150 B.C.E. to ca. 50 C.E., all of the other Judean Desert manuscripts date from between ca. 70 and 130 C.E. The evidence suggests that, after the First Jewish Revolt and the destruction of the Jerusalem Temple by the Romans in 70 C.E., a predecessor to the MT established itself as the official version of Jewish Scripture.

The exact processes by which other text types ceased to be copied and a proto-MT survived are not recoverable, but some suggestions can be made. Since the MT became the version of the Bible espoused by rabbinic Judaism, that version of the text was likely the one preserved and copied by the predecessors of rabbinic Judaism prior to the destruction of the Temple. Some other text types may have ceased to be copied for polemical reasons. If a certain shorter version of Jeremiah, for instance, was known to be related to the one in the Greek Bible that had by this time become the property of Christians, or if an expanded version of the Pentateuch was identified with the Torah of the Samaritans, that certainly would have discouraged the continued copying of those texts by Jews. On the other hand, it may be that groups that possessed other text types did not survive the war against Rome, or even that Jewish leaders after the revolt simply assembled or chose among whatever scrolls remained to them. Whatever the exact situation, the MT's transmission from that point on was marked by a concern for precise copying, without the freedom exercised by many earlier scribes. Comparison of the proto-MT manuscripts from Qumran and elsewhere in the Judean Desert with the extant manuscripts from the early medieval period illustrates the exactitude with which the text was copied. Only in the ninth and tenth centuries C.E. do we have the first evidence for the work of the Masoretes, who added vowel markings and an elaborate system of commentary to the consonantal text to create the true MT. It took another millennium to discover that the texts underlying the MT were each once only one of a variety of text types circulated and studied by Jews in the Second Temple period.

BIBLIOGRAPHY

F. M. CROSS AND S. TALMON, EDS. 1975, *Qumran and the History of the Biblical Text,* Cambridge: Harvard University Press. • M. J. MULDER 1988, "The Transmission of the Biblical Text," in *Mikra: Text, Translation, Reading, and Interpretation of the Hebrew Bible in Ancient Judaism and Early Christianity,* ed. M. J. Mulder, Philadelphia: Fortress, 87-135. • E. TOV 2001, *Textual Criticism of the Hebrew Bible,* 2d rev. ed., Minneapolis: Fortress. • E. TOV 2008, "Three Strange Books of the LXX: 1 Kings, Esther, and Daniel Compared with Similar Rewritten Compositions from Qumran and Elsewhere," in *Die Septuaginta: Texte, Kontexte, Lebenswelten,* ed. M. Karrer and W. Kraus, Tübingen: Mohr-Siebeck. • E. ULRICH 1999, *The Dead Sea Scrolls and the Origins of the Bible,* Grand Rapids: Eerdmans. • E. ULRICH 2002, "The Text of the Hebrew Scriptures at the Time of Hillel and Jesus," in *Congress Volume: Basel 2001,* ed. A. Lemaire, Leiden: Brill, 85-108. • J. VANDERKAM AND P. FLINT 2002, *The Meaning of the Dead Sea Scrolls,* San Francisco: Harper, 103-53.

See also: Samaritan Pentateuch; Septuagint

MOLLY M. ZAHN

Thallus

Thallus is a historian whose work has not survived and is known only through later Christian writers. When he lived is unknown. The name Thallus is so common as not to permit identification with others of that name. In the eighteenth century, John Hudson proposed that the word *allos* in Josephus, *Ant.* 18.167 be emended to *thallos,* but the change has no foundation. When he is referred to, he is often listed with other historians of the late first century B.C.E. or early first century C.E., but since he is first mentioned by the Christian apologist Theophilus, who wrote around 180 C.E., scholars have often given a large ballpark figure for when he lived. If the excerpt quoted below does refer to events at the death of Jesus, then he would have written after this event. Some have suggested he was a Samaritan, but on flimsy reasoning.

Thallus is said by Eusebius of Caesarea (Jacoby 1923-1958: 256 T1) to have composed in three volumes a compendium of history from the sack of Troy to the 167th Olympiad in 112/109 B.C.E. He also discussed the battle of the Titans with Zeus (Jacoby 1923-1958: 256 F2) and, in general, has a euhemeristic version of history whereby, for example, Saturn is said to have been a man (Jacoby 1923-1958: 256 F4).

Thallus is most well-known from a mention by the ninth-century Byzantine historian, George Syncellus (Jacoby 1923-1958: 256 F1). Syncellus quotes the third-century Christian writer Julius Africanus. Africanus ends his account of Jesus' death with a description of the darkness that accompanied it:

> Throughout the whole world a most fearful darkness was brought on and by an earthquake rocks were riven and most of Judea and of the rest of the earth was overthrown. This darkness Thallus, in the third of his histories, calls an eclipse of the sun.

Much depends on how one interprets the demonstrative pronoun *this.* Does it refer to a fearful darkness which covers the whole earth and call such a phenomenon an eclipse? Or does it refer specifically to the darkness at Jesus' death and say it was only an eclipse? Many commentators have opted for the latter reading, and have seen Thallus as the earliest non-Christian witness to Jesus and to the tradition of darkness at the crucifixion. However, Julius Africanus then appends an argument against calling the darkness at the death of Jesus an eclipse as he died at Passover, 14 Nisan, which is in the middle of the month, whereas an eclipse occurs only at the beginning or end of a month. Africanus further argues against identifying the darkness at Jesus' death with the eclipse which took place on 24 November 29 C.E., in the reign of Tiberius. Africanus quotes another historian, Phlegon of Tralles, who reports, according to Africanus, that this eclipse did occur in the middle of the month, but Africanus denies that this is the same as the eclipse at the death of Jesus, as Phlegon makes no mention of an earthquake and the other phenomena. It therefore seems likely that Africanus is refuting any attempt to say that the events surrounding Jesus' death were purely natural phenomena. Furthermore, not much later Syncellus quotes Eusebius of Caesarea writing about the same events surrounding the death of Jesus. Just before quoting Phlegon of Tralles, Eusebius mentions how, in other historical documents, it is recorded that there was a solar eclipse, an earthquake in Bithynia, and the collapse of many buildings in Nicea (Jacoby 1923-1958: 257 F16). These other historical documents could include Thallus. In conclusion, it seems that Thallus simply called any fearful darkness that covered the whole earth an eclipse and is not referring at all to the death of Jesus.

BIBLIOGRAPHY

W. ADLER AND P. TUFFIN 2002, *The Chronography of George Syncellus: A Byzantine Chronicle of Universal History from the Creation,* Oxford: Oxford University Press. • F. JACOBY 1923-1958, *Die Fragmente der griechischen Historiker,* 3 parts in 14 vols., Berlin: Weidmann. • C. R. HOLLADAY 1983, *Fragments from Hellenistic Jewish Authors,* vol. 1, *Historians,* Chico, Calif.: Scholars Press, 343-369. • G. THEISSEN AND A. MERZ 1998, *The Historical Jesus: A Comprehensive Guide,* Minneapolis: Fortress, 84-85.

ROBERT DORAN

Theaters

The theater was born on the soil of ancient Greece, progeny of the Greek mind and culture. The gods and heroes who populated the stage of the ancient Greek theater were taken directly from Greek epic literature and myth. To the Jewish and even the non-Jewish population of Roman Palestine, the Greek and Roman theaters were foreign not only in concept but also in content and language. Since this part of the Greco-Roman world lacked a classical tradition, the construction of dozens of theaters in a relatively short period of time raises a number of fundamental questions. Who built these theaters? When were they built? For whom were they built? What purpose were they intended to serve?

Roman Palestine and Provincia Arabia

Although the region had been exposed to classical culture as early as the latter part of the fifth century B.C.E., and it had been directly ruled by the Hellenistic kingdoms from the beginning of the fourth century B.C.E., the first theater in the region, at Caesarea, was not erected until 10 B.C.E. Thus far, twelve theaters have been found west of the Jordan River: at Sepphoris, Dor, Legio, Beth-Shean (two theaters), Shumi (Shuni), Caesarea, Sebaste, Shechem, Antipatris, Jericho, and Elusa. East of the river, eighteen theaters have been found: at Sahr, Gadara/Umm Qeis (two), Philipopolis, Kanawat/Canatha, Abila, Adraa, Bosra, Pella, Hammath-Gader, Birketein, Gerasa/Jerash (two), Philadelphia/Amman (two), Petra (two), and Wadi Sabra.

Chronological and Geographical Framework

Three theaters were erected in the kingdom of Herod the Great (37-4 B.C.E.): at Caesarea, in Jerusalem, and in Jericho. A fourth was presumably initiated by his son

View looking north at the northern *parados* — the vaulted entrance through which portions of the audience would enter and exit the theater at Caesarea. On the right side of the image a portion of the *cavea* (seating area) is visible. *(www.HolyLandPhotos.org)*

Antipas at Sepphoris. The theater at Caesarea was part of a very impressive urban complex intended to symbolize the Hellenistic character and spirit of Herod's kingdom. The theater in Jerusalem had not yet been located, but the theater in Jericho was built near the winter palace and was part of a complex that also included a hippodrome and, apparently, a gymnasium. The Herodian theaters were not intended to disseminate the culture of the classical theater to a new audience. The content and language of the Greek theater at that time were foreign to most of the population.

Between the latter part of the first century B.C.E. and the first century C.E., five theaters were erected in the Nabatean kingdom: at Sahr (Trachonitis), Elusa (the Negev), two at Petra (Edom), and in Wadi Sabra, near Petra. The theater at Sahr is part of a sanctuary, as is the theater in Wadi Sabra, whereas the one at Elusa is in an urban context. The large theater at Petra lies at the very heart of the necropolis, while the small one is in the city itself. There is no knowing what the specific functions of the Nabatean theaters were. It may be that, like the Herodian examples, they were built to demonstrate a political-cultural imperative; however, it is also possible that they served, at least in part, the need to worship in general and to worship the dead in particular.

The first theaters in the Hellenized cities were erected in the first century C.E. Most of these theaters were erected on the initiative of cities and funded by them. The first built in this period is the south theater at Gerasa (92 C.E.), erected near the temple of Zeus and part of the city's early sanctuary. The theaters at Pella and Bosra were erected subsequently, the latter at about the time it became the capital of *Provincia Arabia* (106 C.E.). Hence, it may be that the initiative for its construction was not municipal-local but governmental or provincial.

At the beginning of the second century C.E., the cities of Judea and the *Provincia Arabia* began to flourish. In the days of the Antonine emperors theaters were erected on municipal initiative for local audiences: two in Philadelphia, the north theater in Gerasa, and a theater each at Canatha and Shechem. Most of the theaters in Roman Palestine and in the *Provincia Arabia* were constructed in the latter part of the second century C.E. and the first half of the third. The region's cities reached the height of their prosperity during the Severan dynasty (193-235 C.E.). In this span of time, theaters were erected at Beth-Shean (two) and at Sebaste, Dor, Hammath-Gader, and Shumi (Shuni), and in Transjordan at Gadara (two), Abila, and Birketein, near Gerasa.

The Herodian theaters did not reflect the true cultural needs of most of Judea's population but were a foreign implant on its landscape. This also seems to have been the case in the Nabatean realm, where the theaters served as the architectural framework for mass gatherings for worship, and apparently for necrolatry. On the other hand, the theaters erected by the Hellenistic cities were mass-amusement installations that provided entertainment of the simplest sort. A check of the historical and literary sources, including talmudic ones, verifies that theaters served first and foremost an audience of a Hellenized oriental culture that was satisfied with presentations of mime and the like. It is reasonable to assume that it never saw a tragedy or comedy.

Typology and Architecture

The thirty theaters known in the region can be divided into two distinct groups: urban and extra-urban. Urban theaters were built for the citizenry, whereas those built outside the cities were intended to serve the pilgrims visiting the various sanctuaries. Most of the urban theaters were erected without considering the city's street network; instead, the site was generally selected for topographical reasons, as with the theaters in Beth-Shean, Sepphoris, Sebaste, and Gadara. On the other hand, the north theater at Gerasa is a fine example of a theater carefully integrated into the city's street network. In plan, the theaters in the region are Roman and not Hellenistic. Hence, their orchestra is a semicircle rather than a circle, and their seating, which partially rests on an artificial slope, does not extend beyond the orchestra semicircle.

At the same time, almost all the region's theaters were erected on the slopes of hills in order to avoid having to build artificial slopes. Thus in most instances the lower seating complex *(ima cavea)* is set on a natural slope, and the upper one *(summa cavea)* rests on an artificial slope. In keeping with the topography and constraints of a site, the upper sections of the *cavea* were erected in various ways. In most cases they were sloped, radial, barrel-vaulted passages *(vomitoria)* that intersected with a semicircular corridor roofed by a continuous barrel vault *(ambulacrum).* Sometimes the *summa cavea* rests on an artificial sloped mound of earth supported by two semicircular monocentric parallel walls covered by a continuous barrel vault *(ambulacrum)* or the entire seating complex rests on an artificial slope of pressed earth supported by two semicircular monocentric parallel walls whose interior space is filled with earth.

As was customary in Roman theaters, the stage structure *(scaena)* and seating complex *(cavea)* were turned into a unit by means of the *versurae,* or "wings." Typically there were three entrances in the stage's façade. The stage *(pulpitum)* extended to the foot of the *scaenae frons* and was separated from the orchestra by the low decorative wall *(proscaenium).* The region's theaters were built of local stone; only the *scaenae frons* decorations, including its three-dimensional sculpture, were marble. The construction and original architectural solutions of the thirty theaters thus far discovered are outstanding. The largest theater in Syria-Palestina, at Philadelphia, could hold about 8,000 spectators; the smallest (Sahr in Trachonitis) held about four hundred. On the average, this region's theaters held about 5,000 to 7,000 people. Their construction, location, and distribution confirm the cities' ability to meet the considerable cost and the engineering and architectural challenges entailed in erecting such complex installations. Most theaters continued to serve their original purpose until the end of the Byzantine period, a usage which attests to their having truly expressed the cultural needs of most of the urban population in this region of the Roman world.

BIBLIOGRAPHY

M. BIEBER 1961, *The History of the Greek and Roman Theater,* Princeton: Princeton University Press. • E. FREZOULS 1961, "Recherches sur les théâtres de l'Orient Syrien," *Syria* 36: 54-86. • G. IZENOUR 1992, *Roofed Theaters in Classical Antiquity,* New Haven: Yale University Press. • F. B. SEAR 1990, "Vitruvius and the Roman Theater Design," *AJA* 94: 249-258. • A. SEGAL 1995, *Theaters in Roman Palestine and Provincia Arabia,* Leiden: Brill.

See also: Entertainment Structures

ARTHUR SEGAL

Theodicy

Theodicy is the attempt to defend the justice of God in the face of the problem of evil in general and the suffering of the righteous in particular. It attempts to make evil or suffering rationally or emotionally intelligible. The religious and metaphysical assumptions that give rise to theodicy in early Judaism include the belief in a sovereign and good God who controls the processes of history and who dispenses justice to nations and to individuals. Although a concern with theodicy is implicit in many writings from the First Temple period — and in the ancient Near East in general — it becomes more explicit and widespread in Second Temple literature. The books of Job (fifth century B.C.E.) and 2 Esdras (late first century C.E.) are sustained explorations of the issues of theodicy, both constructed as dialogues in which a skeptical protagonist raises objections to traditional explanations for suffering and injustice. The reasons for the increased attention to theodicy in the Second Temple period may be sought both in the extraordinary national disasters that befell Judaism, exemplified in the destructions of the First and Second Temples, and in the broader cultural and religious changes of the second half of the first millennium B.C.E., when older patterns for locating the individual in a secure and orderly cosmos lost plausibility and were in part replaced by new views that saw the cosmos as an uncertain and even oppressive locus.

Retributivist Approaches

The repertoire of theodicies that address the individual's experience of evil and those concerned with national suffering are largely similar. By far the most pervasive is the retributivist theodicy, which attempts to explain suffering as the result of or a divine punishment for prior misconduct. With respect to the individual, it is grounded in the wisdom tradition's understanding of the "act-consequence" structure of reality, whereby good actions produce good and evil produces evil. This perspective is first systematically employed to account for national experience in the Deuteronomistic History (Joshua–2 Kings; late seventh to mid-sixth century B.C.E.), which explains the fate of Israel and Judah in relation to their obedience and disobedience to God's covenant. Essentially the same Deuteronomistically framed retributivist theodicy is employed both by *Psalms of Solomon,* to explain the Roman conquest of Judea in 63 B.C.E., and by *2 Baruch,* to explain the destruction of the Second Temple by the Romans in 70 C.E. The books of Chronicles refine the retributivist approach so as to avoid the issue of intergenerational retribution or the suffering of the people for the sins of its kings (cf. Ezekiel 18). Instead, the Chronicler demonstrates how each king and each generation was responsible for the fate that befell them.

The failure of the retributivist explanation to correspond with experienced reality provoked repeated objections. With respect to national experience, although Israel's sins could be acknowledged as relevant to episodes of destruction, the much greater evil perpetrated by the Romans was perceived as a scandal to divine justice (2 Esdr. 3:28-36). In general, the retributivist response to this problem was to project a future judgment, often envisioned as an eschatological or messianic era, in which God would punish the wicked and reward the righteous (e.g., *Psalms of Solomon* 17). In this literature the problematic reality is often as much about the unjust suffering of pious Jews and the well-being of the impious as about the problem of Gentile powers and was similarly resolved by a future judgment (e.g., *1 Enoch* 90). So, too, in the literature concerned with individual suffering (e.g., Job 5; 8; 11; Wisdom of Solomon 2–5), delayed retribution was a common explanation. Contextualizing the problem in this way constructs a narrative solution, such that the present sense of dissonance is resolved in the ultimate outcome of events, just as the conflicts in a plot are resolved in the denouement. Thus the incomprehensible suffering of the present is given meaning in an overarching story.

The death of the pious or the wicked before the outworking of justice presented a problem for the retributivist position. While the developing belief in the resurrection of the dead or the immortality of the soul is not entirely a response to the problems of theodicy, resurrection and immortality play a major role in reflections on theodicy, as tests as disparate as *1 Enoch* 22, Daniel 12, and Wisdom of Solomon 2–5 attest. The belief in resurrection was also significant in the developing theology of martyrdom and the voluntary submission to suffering and death in times of persecution (2 Maccabees 7).

Retributivist theodicies are often combined with those that operate on a different logic. Suffering might be interpreted as a warning or discipline to prevent mortal sin or as a process by which one's character is developed (Job 5:17-18; 33:14-18; *Pss. Sol.* 13:8-10). Unjust suffering might be envisioned as a test of righteousness (Job 1-2; Sir. 2:1-5; Wis. 3:5-6; *Pss. Sol.* 16:4). More complex is the assertion that one individual or group may be punished vicariously for the sins of another, an idea first attested in relation to the so-called "suffering servant" of Isa. 52:13–53:12. In 2 Macc. 7:38 the intense suffering and death of the martyrs is said to end the wrath of God, and so bring about God's intervention on behalf of the people. This theological interpretation is developed in 4 Maccabees, as the blood of the martyrs serves as "an atoning sacrifice" for the nation's sins (4 Macc. 17:21-22). Early Christianity similarly interpreted the death of Jesus (Rom. 3:25; Heb. 2:17).

Mythic Approaches

Second Temple Judaism also developed comprehensive mythic accounts of the origin and ultimate end of evil. *1 Enoch* 6–16; 85–90 interpreted the fall of the Watchers and their mating with human women, a myth that elaborated on Gen. 6:1-4, as the cause of evil upon the earth. Despite the cleansing effects of the flood, the evil spirits released by the death of the angelic offspring continued to attack humans and to lead them into sin. Other reflections on the origin of evil focus on the story of Adam and Eve, reading it through a dualistic metaphysical framework as the devil's corruption of humanity (Wis. 2:24; *2 Enoch* 31). The notion that Adam's sin doomed humankind to sinfulness and thus to suffering is articulated by 2 Esdr. 7:116-26 but disputed in *2 Bar.* 54:15. Sirach 15:11-20 interprets the creation story as an affirmation of individual human choice, which thus undergirds a fundamentally retributivist theodicy.

A different mythic approach from that of the Qumran community appears to be influenced by Zoroastrian dualism. The "Two Spirits" section of the *Community Rule* (1QS 3–4) describes the metaphysical opposition between the Prince of Light and the Angel of Darkness, whose enmity structures the conflict between good and evil not only in the course of history but also within the heart of every person. History and its evils are understood as predetermined by God as part of a cosmic drama that will, however, end in the triumph of the forces of good *(War Scroll)*. Thus the suffering of the righteous is again incorporated into a narrative that endows it with meaning. Similar dualistic mythic constructions of reality were common in late Second Temple Judaism.

Philosophical Approaches

Jewish literature that significantly engaged Greek philosophical thought brought a new set of resources to bear on the issues of theodicy. In the Wisdom of Solomon the author deflects the blame for all evil from God in keeping with the Platonic notion that the deity created a perfectly ordered world and always acts justly. The problem is with human perception. Wisdom of Solomon, however, attempts with some difficulty to incorporate apocalyptic perspectives into a largely philosophical framework in chaps. 1–5.

A more consistent philosophical response to the problems of theodicy is articulated in Philo. Philo makes use of the philosophical distinctions between apparent and real well-being and evil and between primary and secondary causality, as well as arguing for the providential uses of many things that seem like evils to human beings (*On Providence* 3–32; 82; 102). For both Philo and the author of the Wisdom of Solomon, the relative insignificance of the embodied life in comparison with the immortal soul relativizes the issues of theodicy.

Although most Second Temple Jewish literature attempts to provide answers to the problem of theodicy, other responses are occasionally apparent. Job at least provisionally considers the possibility that God is malevolent (Job 16:7-17). If the divine speeches (Job 38–41) are intended to provide a response to Job's questions, the response is an enigmatic one. Significantly, however, the divine speeches do not claim that God has created and maintains a properly moral order in the world, although the evils that exist are not allowed to go unchecked. The contrast between Job's demand for a just order and God's response creates something close to a tragic vision of human existence. Qohelet, too, is perplexed by the evident absence of a clear retributive order in the world. Although a divine order may exist, it cannot be grasped by humans (Qoh. 2:22; 3:11; 8:17). As in Job 28, divine wisdom is inaccessible. Thus in Qohelet's view, everything is absurd (Hebr. *hebel*). The skeptical perspective, however, remained a minority view and is not often present in the literature of the later Second Temple period, though it finds a partial representative in the persona of Ezra in 2 Esdras.

BIBLIOGRAPHY
J. J. COLLINS 1997, "The Problem of Evil and the Justice of God," in idem, *Jewish Wisdom in the Hellenistic Age,* Louisville: Westminster John Knox, 80-96. • J. L. CRENSHAW, ED. 1983, *Theodicy in the Old Testament,* Philadelphia: Fortress. • A. LAATO AND J. C. DE MOOR, EDS. 2003, *Theodicy in the World of the Bible,* Leiden: Brill. • C. A. NEWSOM 2003, *The Book of Job: A Contest of Moral Imaginations,* New York: Oxford University Press. • G. L. PRATO 1975, *Il problema della teodicea in ben Sira,* Rome: Biblical Institute Press. • J. A. SANDERS 1955, *Suffering as Divine Discipline in the Old Testament and Post-Biblical Judaism,* Rochester: Colgate Rochester Divinity School. CAROL A. NEWSOM

Theodotus

Author and Work

Theodotus was an epic poet of whose work eight fragments totaling forty-seven lines of hexameter verse are preserved by Eusebius in quotations from Alexander Polyhistor. The fragments concern Jacob and the events surrounding Shechem as related in Genesis 33–34. Fragment 1 describes the founding of Shechem by Sikimus, son of Hermes, and its geography. Fragment 2 notes that Shechem was ruled by Hamor and his son, Shechem, who are called stubborn. Fragment 3 provides a quick overview of Jacob's flight from Esau, and the birth of his eleven sons and only daughter, Dinah. Fragment 4 deals with the rape of Dinah by Shechem, the proposed marriage of Shechem and Dinah, and the demand of Jacob that all males in Shechem be circumcised, as intermarriage between Jews and non-Jews is not allowed. Fragment 5 gives the origin of circumcision among the Jews, recounting the covenant God made with Abraham (Gen. 17:9-22). Fragment 6 details how Levi and Simeon killed the men of Shechem, with Simeon appealing to an oracle from God (Gen. 15:18-21). Fragment 7 provides a very negative portrayal of the Shechemites as "godless." The final fragment describes the killing of Hamor by Simeon, Shechem by Levi, and the pillaging of the city and Dinah's rescue. The fragments are focused on Shechem, but since we do not know the length or have an outline of the whole poem, we do not know how far they are representative of the poem.

Alexander Polyhistor titles Theodotus' work *On the Jews,* while Eusebius has *Concerning Jacob.* Eusebius seems to be describing the content of the fragments rather than supplying a formal title. Polyhistor also uses the title *On the Jews* as the title for other works by Hellenistic Jewish authors. The actual title is unknown. Theodotus' poem has some very slight resonances with the LXX. Theodotus recasts the biblical account into a Homeric or epic style, which was popular during the Hellenistic period.

Scholars have debated whether Theodotus was a Samaritan or a Jew. One line of scholarship (Freudenthal 1875; Daise 1988), regards Theodotus as a Samaritan. The main arguments are the stress on Shechem, its designation as a sacred city, and the evidence of syncretism, specifically that Shechem was founded by a son of Hermes. In response, one does not know the extent of the poem, and the phrase "sacred city" is typical Homeric language to honor cities. Also, it is uncertain whether the text says "son of Hermes" or "son of Hamor." Even if "son of Hermes" is correct, this is no more syncretistic than what one finds in a Jewish writer such as Eupolemus. On the other hand, Collins (1980) has argued strongly for Jewish authorship, from the negative portrayal of Shechem as impious, from the fact that the Shechemites are not said to circumcise themselves, and from the positive portrayal of Jacob and his sons. The action of Simeon and Levi is portrayed as divinely sanctioned, and this interpretation of the action is in line with other Jewish traditions (*T. Levi* 5–7; *Jubilees* 30; Jdt. 9:2)

Date and Historical Setting

Theodotus wrote before Alexander Polyhistor (mid-first century B.C.E.). Some have argued for a date in the late third to mid-second century B.C.E. Theodotus' description of the wall surrounding Shechem, which began to fall into disrepair ca. 200 B.C.E., supports this early date.

A later date rests on a correlation between pro-Jewish themes in Theodotus and the policy of John Hyrcanus, who destroyed the temple at Mt. Gerizim in 112/111 B.C.E. and Shechem itself in 107 B.C.E. Since the poem presupposes that Shechem is still in existence, it would have been written before 107 B.C.E. Proponents of this later date hold that the archaeological evidence can be explained by memories of the earlier fortified wall, and warn that one should be hesitant in correlating too simplistically epic descriptions with archaeological *realia.*

BIBLIOGRAPHY
J. J. COLLINS 1980, "The Epic of Theodotus and the Hellenism of the Hasmoneans," *HTR* 73: 91-104. • M. DAISE 1988, "Samaritans, Seleucids, and the Epic of Theodotus," *JSP* 17: 25-51. • F. FALLON 1985, "Theodotus," in *OTP* 2:785-93. • J. FREUDENTHAL 1875, *Alexander Polyhistor und die von ihm erhaltenen Reste jüdaischer und samaritanischer Geschichtswerke,* Breslau: H. Skutsch, 99-101. • C. R. HOLLADAY 1989, *Fragments from Hellenistic Jewish Authors,* vol. 2, *Poets,* Atlanta: Scholars Press, 51-204. • R. PUMMER 1982, "Genesis 34 in Jewish Writings of the Hellenistic and Roman Periods," *HTR* 75: 177-88. • R. PUMMER AND M. ROUSSEL 1982, "A Note on Theodotus and Homer," *JSJ* 13: 177-82.

See also: Alexander Polyhistor ROBERT DORAN

Therapeutae

The Therapeutae were a group of celibate, philosophically minded Jewish ascetics, both male and female, who lived in a community close to Alexandria, Egypt, in the first century C.E. They are presented in Philo of Alexandria's *De Vita Contemplativa (On the Contemplative Life)* as an example of Jewish excellence on the basis of Stoic ideals. This treatise followed a lost work on the subject of the active life of philosophy in which the Essenes were defined as the perfect Jewish example (*Cont.* 1), and was the fourth of a five-part work called *On Virtues.*

The Term *Therapeutai*

Philo himself notes that the members of this group are called *therapeutai* (*Cont.* 2). In contemporaneous Greek literature and inscriptions, this word has a general meaning of "one who serves, attends [God/the gods]." In Philo's usage the term likewise means "devoted attendants," referring to priests and Levites, both metaphorical and actual, and in singular form to Moses (*Det.* 160; *Spec. Leg.* 3.135; *Sacr.* 13, 118–19, 127, cf. 120; *Post.* 182; 184; *Ebr.* 126; *Cont.* 11; *Fug.* 42; *Mos.* 2.135, 149, 274, cf. *Mos.* 2.67). Philo uses the word *therapeutēs* symbolically to refer to someone who "attends" God by means of a good, ascetic, wise, and devoted life, like that of Moses, thus one who "heals souls" (*Plant.* 60; *Ebr.* 69; *Mut.* 106; *Congr.* 105; *Fug.* 91; *Migr.* 124; *Sacr.* 127; *Cont.* 2, 90; *Spec. Leg.* 1.309; *Virt.* 185–86; *Praem.* 43–44, cf. *Prob.* 75). Yet Philo can also use the term negatively to refer to people who attend or serve false gods or concepts (*Ebr.* 210; *Legat.* 97).

Communal Life

In *De Vita Contemplativa* Philo defines the group as embracing a life of mystical, musical, and meditative endeavor, in which they are seized by a "heavenly passion" (*Cont.* 12), a phrase that may relate to aspects of early merkavah mysticism. Their asceticism is integrally connected with a desire to minimize aspects of the material world in order to concentrate on the spiritual. Accordingly, these devotees of God leave their city, family, and possessions to live together in a rural location, just south of Alexandria on the ridge between the Mediterranean Sea and Lake Mareotis, where there are farms and fresh breezes (*Cont.* 13, 18–23). Each devotee has his or her own simple hut with a front and back, the latter being called a *semneion,* "reverence place," or *monastērion,* "solitary place," where they study sacred literature, hymns, and philosophical writings (*Cont.* 25). They pray twice each day, at sunrise and sunset, and spend the rest of the day reading Scripture, interpreting it allegorically, and composing hymns (*Cont.* 28–29). They are defined as "students of Moses" (*Cont.* 63) since they "have dedicated their personal lives and themselves to the understanding and contemplation of the facts of Nature, according to the sacred instructions of the prophet Moses" (*Cont.* 64). Their work takes place for six days, and after sunset food is provided by people who are members of the community at a lower level named *ephēmereutai,* "dailies," or *diakonoi,* "servers" (*Cont.* 30, 34, 66, 75), though some eat only every three or six days (35).

On the seventh day, the Therapeutae assemble together in a strict hierarchy to hear the most senior *(presbytatos)* of the group, the president (*proedros, Cont.* 79–80), give a discourse (*Cont.* 30–31; cf. 75) in a large *semneion* divided into two parts — for men and women respectively — by a wall three to four cubits high (*Cont.* 33), after which they have a meal together in a *symposion* or "dining hall." This meal consists only of bread with a seasoning of salt (and hyssop) and spring water (*Cont.* 37). Their clothing consists of an *exomis* (simple work tunic for men) or linen cloth (for men and women) with a cloak of woolly skin in winter (38), but on the seventh day they assemble wearing white (probably linen) (38, 66).

On every seventh seventh (forty-ninth) evening, prior to the beginning of the fiftieth day at sunrise, the group has a special celebration (*Cont.* 65–89). This description defines them as following a solar calendar at some variance with that of mainstream Judaism. On this forty-ninth evening, they stand in a hierarchical row with their eyes and hands lifted to heaven and pray. They then recline at table in order, with men segregated on the right and women on the left, on simple wooden beds strewn with local papyrus. The president then delivers a discourse of allegorical interpretation, to which all listen very attentively and quietly, after which they clap. The president then sings a hymn, after which all the others sing in turn. A table is brought in on which are placed bread and water, meant to recall "the sacred table in the vestibule of the holy Temple sanctuary" (*Cont.* 81). The bread and water are allotted "to the most excellent portion of the priests, as a reward for services" (*Cont.* 82). When the meal is completed, both men and women stand up together in two choirs in the middle of the dining hall, each under the direction of a choral master or mistress in the place of Moses and Miriam respectively, who led choirs of men and women after the deliverance from Egypt (Exodus 15). They first sing separately and then sing and dance together all night long, "drunk until dawn with this beautiful drunkenness" (*Cont.* 89). At sunrise they turn to the east and stretch their hands to heaven to pray for a bright day and clearness of reasoning, after which they go back to their own huts.

Philo's Emphases

Philo clearly wished to emphasize aspects of the group that would impress those who followed Stoic philosophy, in which asceticism, detachment from the world, and intellectual clarity and concentration on the essence of the universe (Nature/God) were prime interests. He does not give a comprehensive picture of the group, leading scholars to speculate widely on where this community might fit within the context of early Judaism.

Given his interests in extolling the group as an example of Jewish excellence within the rubric of Greco-Roman philosophy, Philo downplays aspects of the group that were idiosyncratic (e.g., their heterodox calendar). The inclusion of women on an apparently equal footing to men is a matter Philo notes but in a slightly apologetic manner, continually emphasizing the modesty and self-control of the group so as not to lead anyone to imagine immorality. For example, when Philo notes that the women were "mostly aged virgins" (*Cont.* 68), the word "mostly" is designed to be ambiguous regarding whether the women were mostly older or mostly virginal or both. He thus draws the reader away from images of younger, nonvirginal women.

A large part of Philo's treatise is taken up with the description of the celebration of the Sabbath of Sabbaths: the forty-ninth evening. It is not improbable that Philo visited this group personally on this occasion and described what he saw. Like the Pythagoreans, the Therapeutae apparently venerated not only the number seven but its square. Their white clothing on this day recalls the attire of Egyptian cultic priests, as well as Levites, Pythagoreans, and Essenes, though the latter are said always to have worn white (Josephus, *J.W.* 2.123, 137).

Position in Early Judaism

Some scholars have questioned whether the Therapeutae actually existed (Engberg-Pedersen 1999), but since Philo locates them close to Alexandria, rather than in some remote location, it is unlikely that he invented them.

Overall, it makes sense to place the Therapeutae within the wider milieu of Alexandrian Judaism of the first century C.E. rather than link them with any better-known Judean schools of legal philosophy (e.g., the Essenes). In the larger exegetical and philosophical tradition of Alexandrian Judaism, a distinctive form of allegorical exegesis and asceticism, in line with currents of Greco-Roman philosophy — particularly Stoic practitioners such as Chaeremon — is attested in such authors as Aristobulus and Philo himself. Philo decries literalists as *mikropolitai,* "citizens of a small town," that is, parochials (*Somn.* 1.39) and shows an inherent sympathy with the Therapeutae, even though in their calendar and asceticism they appear closer to extreme allegorizers than to Philo. These extremists were criticized by Philo in another rhetorical context for inviting negative appraisals from their Jewish coreligionists despite their goodness (*Migr.* 86–93).

BIBLIOGRAPHY

F. C. CONYBEARE 1895, *Philo about the Contemplative Life,* Oxford: Clarendon; New York: Garland. • T. ENGBERG-PEDERSEN 1999, "Philo's De Vita Contemplativa as a Philosopher's Dream," *JSJ* 30: 40-64. • D. HAY 1992, "Things Philo Said and Did Not Say about the Therapeutae," *SBLSP* 31: 673-83. • D. HAY 1998, "The Veiled Thoughts of the Therapeutae," in *Mediators of the Divine: Horizons of Prophecy, Divination, Dreams and Theurgy in Mediterranean Antiquity,* ed. R. M. Berchman, Atlanta: Scholars Press, 167-84. • R. S. KRAEMER 1989, "Monastic Jewish Women in Greco-Roman Egypt: Philo Judaeus on the Therapeutrides," *Signs* 14: 342-70. • J. RIAUD 1987, "Les Thérapeutes d'Alexandrie dans la tradition et dans la recherche critique jusqu'aux découvertes de Qumran," in *ANRW* II.20.2, 1189-1295. • H. SZESNAT 1998, "'Mostly Aged Virgins': Philo and the Presence of the Therapeutrides at Lake Mareotis," *Neotest* 32: 191-201. • J. E. TAYLOR 2001, "Virgin Mothers: Philo on the Women Therapeutae," *JSP* 12: 37-63. • J. E. TAYLOR 2003, *Jewish Women Philosophers of First-Century Alexandria: Philo's 'Therapeutae' Reconsidered,* Oxford: Oxford University Press. • J. E. TAYLOR 2004, "The Women 'Priests' of Philo's *De Vita Contemplativa:* Reconstructing the Therapeutae," in *On the Cutting Edge: The Study of Women in Biblical Worlds: Essays in Honor of Elisabeth Schüssler Fiorenza,* ed. Jane Schaberg et al., New York: Continuum, 102-22. • J. E. TAYLOR AND P. R. DAVIES 1998, "The So-Called Therapeutae of *De Vita Contemplativa:* Identity and Character," *HTR* 91: 3-24.

JOAN E. TAYLOR

Tiberias

History

The Galilean city of Tiberias (Hebr. *Teberya;* Gr. *Tiberias*) was named after the Roman emperor Tiberius (14-37 C.E.; Josephus, *J.W.* 2.168; *Ant.* 18.36). It was founded by Herod Antipas, son of Herod the Great and governor of Galilee for forty-two years (4 B.C.E.–38 C.E.), with the intention of replacing Sepphoris as capital of Galilee. Josephus tells us that in order to populate the city as quickly as possible, Herod Antipas attracted residents "by equipping houses at his own expense and adding new gifts of land" (*Ant.* 18.36-38). In 54 C.E., the city became a Jewish *polis,* named Tiberias Claudiopolis Syria Palestina, most of the inhabitants of which were either Hellenized Jews or Gentiles of modest means. After the death of Agrippa I ca. 44 C.E., the city came under procuratorial rule and remained the capital of Galilee until 61 C.E., when the emperor Nero gave it to Agrippa II (*Life* 9.37-38). At the beginning of the Great Revolt in 66 C.E., the city was fortified with walls that remained standing even after the city had surrendered to the Romans (*J.W.* 2.57-73; 3.460-61). After Agrippa II's death (ca. 100 C.E.), the city was incorporated into the province of Syria and placed under direct Roman control. According to Epiphanius, bishop of Salamis (*Adversus Haereses* 30.12) some time during the reign of the emperor Hadrian, "a very great temple" was built in his honor. In the second century C.E., Tiberias, considered unclean by rabbinic sages because of the numerous old graves it contained, was purified by Rabbi Simeon bar-Yohai (*Gen. Rab.* 79:18; *y. Šeb.* 9:1, 38d). Toward the beginning of the third century, the city was granted the status of a Roman colony. Tiberias gradually became a center of Jewish learning and a spiritual capital, not only of Jewish Palestine but also of the Diaspora. All institutions of Jewish leadership were transferred from Sepphoris to Tiberias — first the Sanhedrin and soon after the Patriarchate. The Mishnah was edited in the city ca. 200 C.E., and the Jerusalem Talmud in the early fourth century C.E. In the sixth century (520 C.E.), the Academy (*Pirka*) of Eretz-Israel, located in Tiberias and headed by the Babylonian Mar Zutra, succeeded the Sanhedrin as the highest authority of the Jewish people. Jewish institutions maintained their seat in Tiberias after the Arab conquest in 635 C.E., probably until the tenth century C.E.

Archaeology

The city's location, on the western shore of the Sea of Galilee (ca. 206 m. below sea level), was south of present-day Tiberias and north of the hot springs of Hammath. To the west, the steep, basaltic scarp of the Jordan Rift Valley rises to a peak known as Mt. Berenice, whose summit is almost at sea level. At Hammath

Tiberias, about a mile south of Tiberias, are hot mineral springs that are thought to have curative properties, particularly for skin diseases. Some thirteen kilometers further south are the freshwater springs of Nahal Yavne'el. An aqueduct was most likely constructed during the Roman period to divert some of this springwater to Tiberias.

The Cardo

Much of the city's urban development was determined by the shoreline of the Sea of Galilee, along which the quays and wharfs of the harbor were built for the fishing industry, the main local source of livelihood. A broad paved promenade ran along the harbor. At a distance of 150 meters west of and parallel to the shore are traces of a colonnaded main street, the so-called *cardo*. B. Rabani and G. Foerster exposed various sections of the street, which bisected the city from north to south and determined the focus of Tiberias' commercial and public life in the shops and buildings erected along its sides. The date of construction at the southern extremity of Tiberias, near one of the city's gates, goes back to the first century C.E. This, and most other sections of the *cardo,* although mostly later in date, were paved with diagonal basalt slabs. Its approximate width (33 m.), including the colonnades and shops on both sides, was typical of a city street in the Roman period. Later repairs and possible northern extensions indicate that this route was maintained as the city's main thoroughfare until the abandonment of Tiberias in the early twelfth century.

Fortifications

Josephus (*J.W.* 3.447-61) informs us that the city was fortified during the Great Revolt. A wall is explicitly mentioned in relation to the events that transpired in 67 C.E., when Vespasian commanded his forces to conquer the city. Although no remains of this early wall have been uncovered, the city's first-century-C.E. southern gate was discovered during Foerster's excavations.

The Southern Gate

The arch of this gate, built of well-dressed basalt, spanned four meters and was supported on either side by rectangular towers. Round towers partially attached to the arch and to the rectangular ones projected southward. The bottom exterior part of the towers was carved with a *cyma-recta* profile, exhibiting a double curvature with a concave projection at the top and a convex surface below. Two ornamental columns flanked the entrance, each set on a pedestal decorated with rhombuses in relief. The area below the arch was paved with parallel rectangular slabs. The archaeological evidence and architectural style indicate that the gate was built when the city was founded or shortly after. As it was freestanding, its primary function was to mark the southern boundaries of the city.

The Palace

Dating to approximately the same time as the city gate, the remains of a private dwelling were uncovered in the course of an excavation conducted by Y. Hirschfeld and K. Galor (2007). Given its location beneath a basilica complex originally built during the fourth century, the exposed area is rather limited. As a result, neither the building's extent nor its plan can be determined. However, enough evidence is available to date its construction to the early first century C.E. The quality and nature of the finds, including typical Herodian-style ashlars, column drums, *opus sectile* floors, and bright red fresco fragments, suggest that these are the remains of Herod Antipas' palace mentioned by Josephus (*Life* 12.64-66). A fine but clear layer of ash on top of the building's ruins and beneath the early Byzantine basilica may point to its destruction during the First Revolt against Rome.

A Monumental Wall

Among the most monumental remains dating to the early second century and uncovered in Hirschfeld and Galor's excavation is an enormous wall running in an east-west direction. In spite of its impressive width of 2.75 meters, the location almost certainly excludes the possibility of its being a city wall. It could be a contender for a *temenos* of the city's unfinished Hadrianeum.

The Theater

Although no traces of the stadium mentioned by Josephus (*Life* 17.92; *J.W.* 3.539) have been uncovered, another monument used for public events was identified within the boundaries of ancient Tiberias. A Roman-style theater, not mentioned in any of the ancient sources, was partially excavated by Y. Hirschfeld (1991-1992) at the foot of Mt. Berenice. The few exposed building sections allow us to determine its original size, shape, and date. Constructed sometime in the second century C.E., it probably had a seating capacity similar to the Roman theater in Beth Shean, which is estimated to have held 5,000 people.

Synagogues

We learn in the Babylonian Talmud (*b. Berakot* 8a) that toward the end of the third and beginning of the fourth centuries C.E., there were thirteen synagogues in the city. According to Josephus (*Life* 54.277-80), the earliest was built during the Second Temple era. However, the remains of only one sixth- or seventh-century synagogue have been unearthed so far in a salvage excavation conducted by A. Berman (1981-1982). Two additional synagogues were uncovered within the bounds of Hammath Tiberias. The southern one, excavated by M. Dothan (1961-1963), consists of two building phases, one dating to the first half of the third century and the other to the early fourth century. The synagogue of the second stage, which can still be seen today, is decorated with a magnificent polychrome mosaic pavement and is considered one of the finest found in ancient Palestine. The synagogue in the center of the settlement was excavated by E. Oren (1969) and contains a seven-branched menorah carved in stone and a stone seat, the so-called "Seat of Moses."

A Roman Tomb

A two-storied Roman tomb from the late first and early second centuries C.E. was excavated by F. Vitto (1976) in one of the modern neighborhoods of Tiberias. The tomb was surrounded by a wall made of basalt ashlars, and the entrance to the burial structure was blocked by a basalt door. The two burial chambers, one above ground and the other below, has numerous loculi.

Later Building Activity

Additional remains of monumental architecture uncovered in the ancient city center include a bathhouse, the so-called marketplace, the basilica complex, and a market street (running parallel to and east of the *cardo*). A public building was exposed at the foot of Mt. Berenice, about 250 meters west of the Sea of Galilee. Finally, a Byzantine-period church was found and excavated on the summit of the mountain.

In contrast to the view taken by the bathhouse's original excavator, B. Rabani (1954-1955), that it was built as early as the first century C.E., additional work carried out by Hirschfeld and Galor concluded that it was built no earlier than the fourth century C.E., with additional renovations and modifications made in the sixth century C.E. Unlike Rabani, who believed that the colonnaded structure functioned as a marketplace in the Byzantine period, G. Foerster and K. Cytryn-Silverman have suggested identifying the building as an Umayyad mosque. The basilica building, originally exposed by A. Druks (1963, 1968) and identified as a church, has been exposed and examined more recently by Y. Hirschfeld (1993, 2005-2006) and by Hirschfeld and Galor, maintaining that the basilica complex was built in the fourth century and continued to be used — with various alterations and additions carried out in the following centuries. The latter also exposed an Ayyubid market street (1993, 2005-2006) typical of this period throughout the region. The remains of the third-century public building were excavated by Y. Hirschfeld (1989), who believed that the Byzantine phase of the exposed structure should be identified with the Great Academy founded in the city by Rabbi Yohanan in the third century C.E. The sixth-century church on Mt. Berenice, built in conjunction with the city wall that ran to the top of the summit and was protected by it, was fully excavated by Y. Hirschfeld (1990-1992). The walls were made of large basalt stones, and the floor was covered with a polychrome mosaic and marble tiles. A smoothened stone block with a circular hole in its center was found beneath the altar in the central apse. The so-called Anchor church derives its name from this relic.

Following the earthquake of 749 C.E., most of the city's buildings were rebuilt and remained in use until the Crusader conquest in 1099 C.E. It was then that the city center shifted northward to form the nucleus of modern Tiberias.

BIBLIOGRAPHY

M. AVI-YONAH 1950-1951, "The Foundation of Tiberias," *IEJ* 1: 160-69. • M. AVI-YONAH 1967, "Tiberias in the Roman Period," in *All the Land of Naphtali,* ed. H. Hirschberg, Jerusalem: Israel Exploration Society, 154-62. • M. DOTHAN 1983, *Hammath Tiberias: Early Synagogues and the Hellenistic and Roman Remains,* Jerusalem: Israel Exploration Society. • M. DOTHAN 2000, *Hammath Tiberias,* vol. 2, *Late Synagogues,* ed. B. L. Johnson, Jerusalem: Israel Exploration Society. • Y. HIRSCHFELD 1992, *A Guide to Antiquity Sites in Tiberias,* Jerusalem: Israel Antiquities Authority. • Y. HIRSCHFELD 1993, "The Anchor Church at the Summit of Mt. Berenice, Tiberias," *BA* 57: 122-34. • Y. HIRSCHFELD 2004, *Excavations at Tiberias, 1989-1994,* Jerusalem: Israel Antiquities Authority. • Y. HIRSCHFELD AND K. GALOR 2007, "New Excavations in Roman, Byzantine, and Early Islamic Tiberias," in *Ancient Galilee in Interaction: Religion, Ethnicity, and Identity,* ed. H. Attridge, D. Martin, and J. Zangenberg, Tübingen: Mohr-Siebeck, 207-29. • D. STACEY 2004, *Excavations at Tiberias, 1973–1974: The Early Islamic Periods,* Jerusalem: Israel Antiquities Authority.

KATHARINA GALOR

Tiberius Julius Alexander

Tiberius Julius Alexander (ca. 20–post 71 C.E.) was a member of one of the wealthiest and most distinguished families of the Jewish community in Alexandria, Egypt. His father, Gaius Julius Alexander, was known for his immense wealth (Josephus, *Ant.* 20.100). His uncle was Philo of Alexandria, the famous Jewish exegete. One of the sources of Alexander's wealth was his appointment as alabarch or arabarch of Alexandria, the customs official who was responsible for the collection of tariffs on goods coming from the East, by Tiberius (Josephus, *Ant.* 18.159, 259; 19.276-77; 20.100). In gratitude Alexander named his oldest son, Tiberius Julius Alexander, after the emperor. This places Tiberius Julius Alexander's birth sometime during Tiberius' principate. Given his later career, this must have been early ca. 20 C.E.

Early Life

We can reconstruct Tiberius Julius Alexander's early life on the basis of what is generally known of elite Jews in Alexandria. He would have received a Jewish education either at home or in a private setting. He would also have gone through the standard rounds of a Greek education: preliminary studies, the ephebate, and — in his case — some additional training in philosophy. The former two would have been required for anyone from a family that held Greek and Roman citizenships in Alexandria, as his family did. His advanced training may have occurred in his uncle's school, although this is speculative. Philo addressed the views of his nephew in two treatises: *On Providence* 1–2 and *Whether Animals Have Reason.* In both cases, Tiberius is presented as holding an unacceptable view: he questioned God's providence and thought that animals had reason. Tiberius' place in these dialogues has led others to suggest that Tiberius authored Philo's *On the Eternity of the World* 1 and was the Alexander to whom the Pseudo-Aristotelian *On the Cosmos* was dedicated, but these speculations have been widely rejected.

Military and Political Career

Tiberius is best known for his ascent of the *cursus honorum,* the sequence of public offices that aspiring Roman politicians held. As the son of Alexander, he held equestrian rank and was eligible to hold numerous posts, an eligibility on which he capitalized. He began humbly as a junior member of the first Jewish embassy to Gaius (39-41 C.E.) following the pogrom in Alexandria (Philo, *Animals* 54). His first administrative post was district governor of the Thebaid in Upper Egypt (*OGIS* 663). He was promoted to a far more significant post when he became the procurator of Judea (46-48 C.E.). He appears to have handled his position with aplomb, managing a severe famine (Josephus, *Ant.* 20.49-53, 101; Acts 11:28-30) and executing two revolutionaries, James and Simon, the sons of Judas the Galilean (Josephus, *Ant.* 20.102). His ability to keep the Jews at peace (Josephus, *J.W.* 2.220) led to his appointment as governor of Syria by Nero (as evidenced in an unpublished inscription). This, in turn, led to his service as an officer on Corbulo's staff; he was charged with escorting Tiridates, the king of Armenia, to the Roman lines (Tacitus, *Annals* 15.28.3). His skill in these various appointments led to his tenure as prefect of Egypt in 66-69 C.E. (*CPJ* 418b; Josephus, *J.W.* 2.309; Tacitus, *Annals* 11.1) where he adroitly maneuvered through the "year of the emperors" following Nero's death. After waiting to express support for Galba, Otho, and Vitellius, he decided to be the first to have his troops acclaim Vespasian as emperor on 1 July 69 C.E. (Josephus, *J.W.* 4.616-18; 5.45-46; Tacitus, *Histories* 2.74, 79; Suetonius, *Vespasian* 6.3). Vespasian and Titus did not overlook this show of support: Tiberius became Titus' chief of staff during the siege of Jerusalem (Josephus, *J.W.* 5.45-46; 6.237; *OGIS* 586). Following the destruction of Jerusalem, he traveled to Rome with Titus and participated in his triumph (Juvenal, *Satires* 1.127-31). Like Josephus, he appears to have settled in Rome. Although it is contested, it is likely that Vespasian appointed him prefect of the praetorian guard (*CPJ* 418b). The date of his death is unknown.

Religious Practices

Tiberius' participation in the government and Roman army created tensions with his Jewish faith. Josephus says bluntly: "he did not maintain his ancestral traditions" (*Ant.* 20.100). Like an earlier Jew from Egypt, Dositheus, he appears to have placed social advancement above his religious observance (3 Macc. 1:3). He could not have practiced Jewish rituals and maintained Jewish beliefs in all of the positions that he held. His role as a high-ranking officer on the staffs of Corbulo and Titus would have required that he offer sacrifices on behalf of his men. His role as prefect of Egypt would have involved participation in cultic activities designed to guarantee the flooding of the Nile. He represents a Jew who had fully assimilated to the larger culture, although this does not mean that he forgot his origins. According to Josephus, Tiberius supported Titus' decision to preserve the Temple (*J.W.* 6.236-43). Further, if the Lysimachus of *Whether Animals Have Reason* was Tiberius' nephew and son-in-law, then Tiberius' daughter married into an observant Jewish family (*Animals* 2). While Tiberius forsook his ancestral customs and unambiguously cast his lot with Rome, there are some hints that he did not entirely forget his Jewish origins.

BIBLIOGRAPHY

A. LEPAPE 1934, "Tiberius Iulius Alexander, Préfet d'Alexandrie et d'Egypte," *Bulletin de la Société Royale d'Archeologie d'Alexandrie* 8: 331-41. • E. G. TURNER 1954, "Tiberius Julius Alexander," *Journal of Roman Studies* 44: 54-64. • V. BURR 1955, *Tiberius Julius Alexander,* Bonn: Habelt. • S. ETIENNE 2000, "Réflexion sur l'Apostasie de Tibérius Julius Alexander," *SPhA* 12: 122-42.

GREGORY E. STERLING

Tithing

Biblical Basis

Jewish literature in the Second Temple period teaches the obligation to set aside a tenth of various types of property for different beneficiaries. This obligation is based on the biblical laws of tithes. Genesis relates that Abraham gave "a tenth of everything" to Melchizedek king of Salem (14:20). Jacob vows to YHWH: "of all that you give me, I will set aside a tithe for you" (28:22). This becomes a duty in Leviticus, which prescribes tithes from whatever grows in the earth (27:30) and from the herd or flock (v. 32), both of which are "holy to the LORD." Numbers attests to this kind of tithe, "the tithes set aside by the Israelites as a gift to the LORD" (Num. 18:24), but with a change: it is now given to the Levites, who may eat it "anywhere" (18:31), as wages "in return for the Temple services that they perform" (18:21). This leads to the additional "tithe of a tithe": the Levites must give one tenth of their tithes "as a gift to the LORD," to the priests (18:26-28), thereby preserving the original nature of the tithe in its entirety as "holy to the LORD." The tithe from produce is mentioned in Deuteronomy but is transformed: no longer given to others, it is now eaten by its owner, "in the presence of the LORD your God, in the place where he will choose" (14:23), as an annual obligation (v. 22).

First Tithe

Literary sources of the Second Temple period resolve the basic issue of whether the tithe is to be given to others or eaten by its owner: two tithes must be set aside, one to be given to the Levites or priests, and the other to be eaten by the owner in Jerusalem. This latter, "second tithe" already appears in LXX (Deut. 26:12; see below); *Jubilees* (32:10); Tobit (1:7); and in the Mishnah (an entire tractate: *Ma'aśer Šeni*). The duality of tithes is also indicated in the *Temple Scroll* (60:6-7; 43) and is so understood by Josephus (*Ant.* 4.205).

Despite this general consensus, there were numerous disagreements. First tithe was taken during the Second Temple period, not only by Levites as mandated in Numbers, but also (and at times exclusively) by priests (see Oppenheimer 1977: 38-42). This disagreement is reflected in the sources: Tobit (1:7) and possibly *Miqṣat*

Ma'aśê ha-Torah (4QMMT B 3-5; see Elman 1999: 152) allocate tithes to the Levites, and even Josephus, while admitting that the priests actually took the tithe (*Ant.* 20.181, 207) says that in principle the Levites were to receive it (*Ant.* 4.240; see 67, 205). Levite eligibility is emphasized in the *Temple Scroll* (60:6-7), which explains that the tithe was initially for YHWH (as in Genesis and Leviticus), but was transferred (in Numbers) to the Levites, when they became the servants of the Temple (see Baumgarten 1985: 6-7). This two-phase explanation also appears in tannaitic literature (Henshke 2003), based on the agreement that it is for the Levites (see, e.g., *m. Ma'aś. Š.* 5:9-10). According to one view in the Talmuds, however, in this respect the priest is subsumed under the category of Levite (*y. Ma'aś. Š.* 5:5 [56b]; *b. Ketubbot* 27a), or the Levites were fined for not returning to Zion in the time of Ezra, with the tithes transferred to the priests. *Jubilees,* in contrast, relying as usual on the actions of the patriarchs, ignores the law of the Levites in Numbers, and awards the tithe to the priests "for eternal generations" (13:26-27; 32:1-8; Henshke 2003: 90).

The tithes were initially brought to the Temple treasury, as documented in the Bible (Amos 4:4; Mal. 3:8-10; 2 Chron. 31:5-6; Neh. 10:38-39; 12:44; 13:5), and in the Second Temple period literature (see LXX to 1 Sam. 1:21; Tob. 1:6-7; Jdt. 11:13; see *y. Ma'aśer Šeni,* end). Later on, the owners gave the tithes directly to those entitled (see, e.g., *m. Ma'aś. Š.* 5:9; see Alon 1957: 83-92).

Second Tithe

The second tithe is defined as "consecrated" (Deut. 26:13), which prohibits its consumption while impure (v. 14), but the level of its sanctity is debatable. Rabbinic halakah permits its consumption in all Jerusalem (see, e.g., *Sifre* on Deuteronomy 106; cf. Henshke 1997: 5-17), a view that Josephus, too, seems to indicate (*Ant.* 4.205). *Jubilees,* in contrast, permits its eating only in the Temple (32:14). The time of its eating is also a subject of debate. The *Temple Scroll* permits eating the second tithe only "on the holy days" (43:15-17), while this limitation is absent from the other sources. Another limitation, shared by the *Temple Scroll* (43:4-12) and *Jubilees* (32:11), is that the tithe must be eaten within a year and is forbidden if it remains for the next year. Rabbinic halakah, in contrast, also requires the removal of tithes, but only after three years, when all the accrued tithe obligations have to be fulfilled. This act, the "removal of tithes," is performed on the eve of Passover of the fourth and seventh years (*m. Ma'aś. Š.* 5:6; see Henshke 2007: 154-56).

The second tithe loses its sanctity when exchanged for money, which must be spent on food and drink in the place chosen by YHWH (Deut. 14:24-26). The *Temple Scroll* (43:14) calls this a "sale," the rabbis a "redemption." The latter, however, included a sale (*m. Ma'aś. Š.* 4:6), which the rabbis prohibited only when the produce retained its second-tithe status and merely changed hands (*m. Ma'aśer Šeni,* beginning). If the redemption was effected with the owner's money, rabbinic halakah required the addition of a fifth, following Lev. 27:31 (*m. Ma'aś. Š.* 4:3; see Henshke 2003: 88 n. 18, 97).

Third or "Poor Man's" Tithe

Deuteronomy mandates that an additional tithe be given "after a period of three years" to the Levite, the stranger, the fatherless, and the widow (Deut. 14:28-29). Tobit 1:8 (Vatican Codex) calls this the "third tithe," implying that it is added in the third year (see also the Sinaiticus Codex version) to the second tithe, which it does not replace. Josephus confirms this (*Ant.* 4.240). LXX Deuteronomy (26:12), however, implies that the second tithe is abrogated in this year, to be replaced by the tithe for the needy. This is also the approach of rabbinic halakah, which calls it the "poor man's tithe" and requires it in the third and sixth years of the sabbatical year cycle (see, e.g., *Sifre* on Deuteronomy 109).

"In the third year," following the above "removal of tithes," the owner must state "before the LORD your God" a formulaic declaration of the fulfillment of the obligations of tithing, and a prayer for YHWH's blessing (Deut. 26:12:15). Rabbinic literature (*m. Ma'aś. Š.* 5:10, 15) calls this a "confession" or "avowal." Josephus states that it was uttered in the Temple (*Ant.* 4.242-43); the medieval sages said this as well, but it is not explicit in rabbinic literature (see Henshke 2007: 151-53). According to the Mishnah, Jonathan the high priest canceled the avowal of the tithe (*m. Ma'aś. Š.* 5:15), an act that was censured by some Amoraim (*y. Ma'aśer Šeni,* end). Several reasons, none of them decisive, were offered for the cancellation (see Alon 1957: 89-91). Later on, the avowal apparently was reinstituted (Albeck 1957, n. 5).

Other Issues Disputed in the Sources

The tithe from the herd or flock mentioned in Leviticus was offered on the altar (*Jub.* 32:8; Tob. 1:6-7; *m. Zebaḥ.* 5:8), but the question of eligibility to eat it was the subject of debate. According to the Mishnah, the owner ate it after it was sacrificed (*m. Zebaḥ.* 5:8; see Henshke 2006: 57-65), while in various Second Temple sources it is earmarked for the priests (4QMMT B 63-64; Philo, *Virtutibus* 95; *Jub.* 13:25-26; 32:15; Tob. 1:6-7; 4Q270; 11QT 60:2). Deuteronomy (which specifies that it is "holy to the LORD") supports the latter position, while the rabbinic interpretation was seemingly influenced by the concept of the sanctity of the second tithe (indicated by Deuteronomy) that was eaten by its owner.

Genesis specifies tithes "of everything," but despite echoes of tithing from property that is neither produce nor beast (see Alon 1957: 294), there is no unequivocal provision in the sources for such a formal obligation. 2 Chronicles 31:5 mentions *debaš* in the context of tithes, which rabbinic halakah understands as dates (*y. Bik.* 1:3:63d), while the *Temple Scroll* (60:9) requires the tithing of *debaš* (understood as honey). An additional tithe appears in the "practice of the king" passage in Samuel: "He will take a tenth part of your grain and vintage"; "he will take a tenth part of your flocks" (1 Sam. 8:15, 17). The Tannaim disagreed whether these were actual royal prerogatives or whether this was stated only as a threat (*t. Sanh.* 4:5). The *Temple Scroll* grants the king a tithe from the spoils of war, possibly following the tithe that Abraham gave Melchizedek; the Tannaim, however, affirmed the king's special rights to plunder but not to a tithe (*m. Sanh.* 2:4).

The tithes were a heavy economic burden, and one of the main distinctions between the *haverim* ("fellows, associates," who were precise in their observance, or scholars) and *ʿam hā-ʾāreṣ* ("people of the land," those who were not exacting in their observance, or ignorant) was the former's proper observance of this obligation (see Oppenheimer 1977: 69-79). Uncertainty regarding the fulfillment of this duty led to the concept of *demai* (questionably tithed produce) and the manifold halakic literature regarding it, which was centered in the mishnaic tractate of *Demai* and its parallels.

BIBLIOGRAPHY

C. ALBECK 1957, "Introduction to the Tractate of Maʿaser Sheni," in *Six Orders of the Mishnah, Order of Zeraim,* Jerusalem: Bialik, 243-45 (in Hebrew). • G. ALON 1957, *Studies in Jewish History,* vol. 1, Tel Aviv: Ha-Kibuts ha-meuḥad (in Hebrew). • J. M. BAUMGARTEN 1985, "The First and Second Tithes in the *Temple Scroll,*" in *Biblical and Related Studies Presented to Samuel Iwri,* ed. A. Kort and S. Morschauer, Winona Lake, Ind.: Eisenbrauns, 5-15. • J. ELMAN 1999, "MMT B 3-5 and Its Ritual Context," *DSD* 6: 148-56. • D. HENSHKE 1997, "The Sanctity of Jerusalem: The Sages and Sectarian Halakhah," *Tarbiz* 67: 5-28 (in Hebrew). • D. HENSHKE 2003, "On the History of the Exegesis of the Pericopes concerning Tithes: From the Temple Scroll to the Sages," *Tarbiz* 72: 85-111 (in Hebrew). • D. HENSHKE 2006, "Tithing of Livestock: The Roots of a Second Temple Halakic Controversy," *Megillot* 4: 55-87 (in Hebrew). • D. HENSHKE 2007, *Festival Joy in Tannaitic Discourse,* Jerusalem: Magnes (in Hebrew). • Y. KAUFMANN 1937, *The Religion of Israel,* vol. 1, Tel Aviv: Bialik (in Hebrew). • A. OPPENHEIMER 1977, *The Am Ha-Aretz,* Leiden: Brill.

DAVID HENSHKE

Tobiads

Various sources of the third and second centuries B.C.E. refer to a Jewish clan that played a role in the struggles between the Ptolemaic and Seleucid monarchies. Given the fact that the family's estate was in the Ammonite region of Transjordan, however, it is likely that already two centuries earlier the "Tobiah the Ammonite slave" mentioned in Neh. 2:19 was a member of the same clan. Whatever "slave" means here (high title? deprecation?), this Tobiah seems already then to have enjoyed prominence in Jerusalem as well (see Neh. 6:17-18 and 13:7). The Zenon Papyri document the activities of a Tobias of the third century B.C.E., who was a wealthy landowner and businessman engaged in trade with Egypt. He resided in Transjordan, in "the Land of Tobias," which was apparently organized as something of a military colony; thus, for example, a papyrus of 259 B.C.E., testifying to the sale of a slave girl, is witnessed by "cavalrymen of the troop of Tobias," and a letter Tobias sent two years later to an Egyptian official, which begins with a standard Greek greeting formula invoking the blessing of the gods upon the recipient, lists the physical details of slaves he was exporting.

This papyrological evidence dovetails with that supplied by Josephus, who preserves, in the twelfth book of his *Antiquities,* a long and romantic tale of one Joseph, son of Tobias, who was a tax-farmer in Palestine for the Ptolemies, who ruled the region until the beginning of the second century B.C.E. According to Josephus, Joseph's mother (Tobias' wife) was a sister of the high priest, Onias II, and hence the family serves as an example of Hellenization in the highest and most central circles of Judean society during this early period. Josephus also reports that Joseph's son Hyrcanus lived as a baron at his estate in Transjordan. Josephus describes his residence, of which the impressive remains at ʿAraq el-Emir have been excavated. According to Josephus, Hyrcanus was at odds with his brothers, whom Josephus terms "the Tobiads." Indeed, it seems that Hyrcanus maintained his father's pro-Ptolemaic orientation while his brothers moved over to supporting the Seleucids; this presumably has to do with the fact (according to Josephus, *Ant.* 12.236) that, although Hyrcanus maintained his status until the days of Seleucus IV (so too 2 Macc. 3:11), he committed suicide upon Antiochus IV Epiphanes' ascent to the throne in 175 B.C.E. Similarly, such alignments would explain Josephus' report (*Ant.* 12.239-40) that the Tobiads supported Menelaus in his struggle against the preceding high priest, Jason, who, when forced out of the city, appropriately fled first to Ammonitis, where Hyrcanus had maintained his stronghold, and thence to Egypt itself (2 Macc. 5:7-8). The assumption that the Tobiads supported Seleucid rule also goes hand in hand with Josephus' statement (*J.W.* 1.32) that they urged Antiochus IV to invade Judea and offered to serve as his guides, and with his statement in *Ant.* 12.240 that they urged Antiochus IV to foster Hellenism in Jerusalem. Thus, they were among the Hasmoneans' main opponents in their early years, after which they disappear from our sources.

It is true that Josephus' testimony about the Tobiads is afflicted by two serious difficulties. First, he places his long account of Joseph, son of Tobias, *after* he reports the Seleucid conquest of Palestine in 200 B.C.E., although Ptolemaic taxation of Palestine is the premise of the story. While many scholars hold, accordingly, that Josephus erred and that the story in fact belongs to the third century B.C.E., others give more credence to Josephus' own explanation for the anomaly (*Ant.* 12.154), namely, that despite his conquest of Palestine Antiochus III had allowed the Ptolemies to continue to collect its tax revenues in the context of his daughter's marriage to Ptolemy V. Second, there are various contradictions and improbabilities among Josephus' statements about the rivals for the high priesthood in the early years of Antiochus IV, and also discrepancies between Josephus' evidence and that of 2 Maccabees. These limit our ability to follow the details of party politics during this crucial period. Much ink has been spilt about both issues. Nevertheless, the picture of the Tobiads as a highly Hellenized and influential Jewish family, with a base of power in Ammonitis but active in Jerusalem and with ties to the capitals of the two Hellenistic kingdoms that bracketed Palestine, remains intact.

BIBLIOGRAPHY

G. FUKS 2001, "Josephus' Tobiads Again: A Cautionary Note," *JJS* 52: 354-56. • D. GERA 1990, "On the Credibility of the History of the Tobiads (Josephus, *Antiquities* 12, 156-222, 228-236)," in *Greece and Rome in Eretz Israel: Collected Essays,* ed. A. Kasher et al., Jerusalem: Yad Izhak ben Zvi, 21-38. • J. A. GOLDSTEIN 1975, "The Tales of the Tobiads," in *Christianity, Judaism and Other Greco-Roman Cults: Studies for Morton Smith at Sixty,* vol. 3, ed. J. Neusner, Leiden: Brill, 85-123. • C. C. JI 1998, "A New Look at the Tobiads in ʿIraq al-Amir," *Liber Annuus* 48: 417-40. • B. MAZAR 1957, "The Tobiads," *IEJ* 7: 137-45, 229-38. • S. G. ROSENBERG 2006, *Airaq al-Amir: The Architecture of the Tobiads,* Oxford: Hedges. • D. R. SCHWARTZ 1998, "Josephus' Tobiads: Back to the Second Century?" in *Jews in a Graeco-Roman World,* ed. M. Goodman, Oxford: Clarendon, 47-61. • D. R. SCHWARTZ 2002, "Once Again on Tobiad Chronology: Should We Let a Stated Anomaly Be Anomalous? — A Response to Gideon Fuks," *JJS* 53: 146-51. • M. STERN 1962-1963, "Notes on the Story of Joseph the Tobiad," *Tarbiz* 32: 35-47 (in Hebrew). • V. A. TCHERIKOVER 1959, *Hellenistic Civilization and the Jews,* Philadelphia: Jewish Publication Society, 126-42, 392-95. • V. A. TCHERIKOVER AND A. FUKS 1957, *Corpus Papyrorum Judaicarum,* vol. 1, Cambridge: Harvard University Press, 115-29. • J. C. VANDERKAM 2004, *From Joshua to Caiaphas: High Priests after the Exile,* Minneapolis: Fortress, 168-226. • E. WILL ET AL. 1991, *ʿIraq al-Amir: Le château du tobiade Hyrcan,* Paris: Geuthner.

See also: ʿAraq el-Amir DANIEL R. SCHWARTZ

Tobiah

There are three individuals named Tobiah in the MT of the Hebrew Bible, all or some of whom may be related to one another genealogically. The first refers to a member of the community in Yehud who had returned from exile and who played a role in the crowning ceremony mentioned in Zech. 6:9-15. No patronym or other type of designation is recorded for this individual, but his association in this text with the restoration leadership, the community's wealth, and service as guardian of the memorial crown suggests a high status and prestige.

The second refers to the head of a family who returned at the time of Zerubbabel from the Babylonian Exile, but could not prove Israelite ancestry (Ezra 2:60// Neh. 7:62//1 Esdr. 5:37). The names of two of the three families mentioned in these verses appear subsequently as opponents of the governor Nehemiah: Tobiah and Delaiah (Neh. 6:10-14). It is possible, perhaps even likely, that this family's inability to prove their Israelite heritage had repercussions in subsequent power struggles in Yehud.

Thus, the third individual known as Tobiah is this (in)famous person who appears consistently to be in conflict with Nehemiah, according to Neh. 2:10, 19-20; 4; 6; 13:4-9. Tobiah is further declared to be "the Ammonite official," which may imply that he was a foreigner rather than an Israelite. However, his name and the name of his son Jehohanan both reflect Yahwistic connections (Neh. 6:18). He may have been an Israelite who rose to a position of power in Ammon. This would probably place him on equal footing with Sanballat the Horonite, who served as governor in Samaria, and with Nehemiah, who served as governor over Yehud. Regardless of his nationality and possible connection to the individual of the same name mentioned just above, this Tobiah wielded significant influence within the territory of Yehud. This conclusion is based on two statements: many people were bound to him by oath through his marriage and his son's marriage into prominent Judean families (Neh. 6:19), and the priest Eliashib — to whom Tobiah was related in some unspecified way — had prepared a large room for him within the Temple precincts during Nehemiah's absence from Yehud (Neh. 13:4-9).

This Tobiah harasses Nehemiah and his counterparts in Yehud repeatedly. Tobiah and his cohorts accuse Nehemiah of rebellion (Neh. 2:19; 6:6), attempt to dissuade the people from rebuilding through demoralizing rhetoric and the exhibition of a military threat (Nehemiah 4), and instigate prophets to lure Nehemiah within the Temple precincts (Neh. 6:10-15). Whatever the nature of these claims made against Tobiah, the book of Nehemiah presents evidence of tensions both within the restoration community and between the community and surrounding entities. Thus, Tobiah represents an element that was resistant to the policies instituted by Nehemiah in Persian period Yehud.

In addition to these three Tobiahs in the MT of the Hebrew Bible, Josephus mentions the Tobiad family of landowners located in the Ammonite region of the Transjordan during the third century B.C.E. (*Ant.* 12.154-236). Supporters of the Ptolemies, this family was connected with the high priest Onias via marriage, operated as tax collectors throughout the region, and became involved in the Maccabean Revolt during the mid-second century B.C.E. (cf. 2 Macc. 3:11). It is also possible that this Tobiah is the same person as the Tobiah associated with the region of Ammon who is mentioned in the Zenon Papyri of the mid-third century. The narrative section in Josephus concerning the family of Tobiah and the priest Onias is often referred to as the "Tobiad Romance," and the historicity of the account has been the subject of much scholarly debate, especially in light of the obvious chronological difficulties in this section of the *Antiquities.*

The issue of relationships with foreigners arises again in connection with these Tobiads, as it does for the two individuals named Tobiah discussed above. The son of the namesake of this family, named Joseph, rises to power and pursues a dancing girl of foreign descent. However, Joseph's brother Solymius prevents Joseph from having sexual relations with this woman by substituting his own daughter (and thus Joseph's niece) instead (*Ant.* 12.168-89). Thus, it is better for this prominent individual to engage in a suspect sexual encounter (but one not explicitly prohibited in the Torah) rather than disgrace himself through such involvement with a foreign woman.

BIBLIOGRAPHY
A. BÜCHLER 1975 [1899], *Die Tobiaden und die Oniaden im II. Makkabäerbuche und in der verwandten jüdisch-hellenistischen Litteratur,* Hildesheim: Olms. • D. GERA 1990, "On the Credibility of the History of the Tobiads," in *Greece and Rome in Eretz Israel,* ed. A. Kasher, U. Rappaport, and G. Fuks, Jerusalem: Israel Exploration Society, 21-38. • B. MAZAR 1957, "The Tobiads," *IEJ* 7: 137-45, 229-38. • J. VANDERKAM 2004, *From Joshua to Caiaphas,* Minneapolis: Fortress, 168-81.

STEVEN J. SCHWEITZER

Tobit, Book of

The book of Tobit is an early Jewish novella with folktale motifs that is included in the Apocrypha. The story is set in the Assyrian exile of the seventh to eighth centuries B.C.E. It relates how young Tobiah, aided and abetted by the disguised angel Raphael, cures his father Tobit of blindness caused by bird dung and delivers his cousin and bride Sarah of the jealous demon that has murdered all her prior husbands. Intermixed into the narrative are numerous instructions about proper behavior, of which burial of the dead, almsgiving, and endogamy are given significant attention. The book is as full of scholarly uncertainties as it is engaging. Some debates have been largely settled, in light of Dead Sea Scrolls material, while others remain unresolved. Tobit is notable both for drawing upon non-Jewish themes and characters and being an invaluable source for a wide variety of topics in Judaism during the Second Temple period.

The Texts of Tobit

There is no one text of Tobit, nor can a single original text be reconstructed. The oldest manuscripts, 4Q196-199 (Aramaic) and 4Q200 (Hebrew) are fragmentary and exhibit minor disagreements. One must turn to other witnesses, of which the Greek text type G^2 (Sinaiticus codex and minuscule 319) and various OL manuscripts (esp. Regius) are closer to the scrolls. But two other Greek text types (G^1 and G^3) may at times share readings in the scrolls not found in G^2 and must at the very minimum also be consulted. Most other versions, including the Vulgate, are of limited text-critical value.

Language

The Dead Sea Scrolls demonstrate that Tobit was written in a Semitic language. Though many assume it to have been Aramaic, this remains to be proved. The separate question of whether an Aramaic or Hebrew text was used as a basis for the Greek has also not been satisfactorily determined, although a number of scholars favor Hebrew.

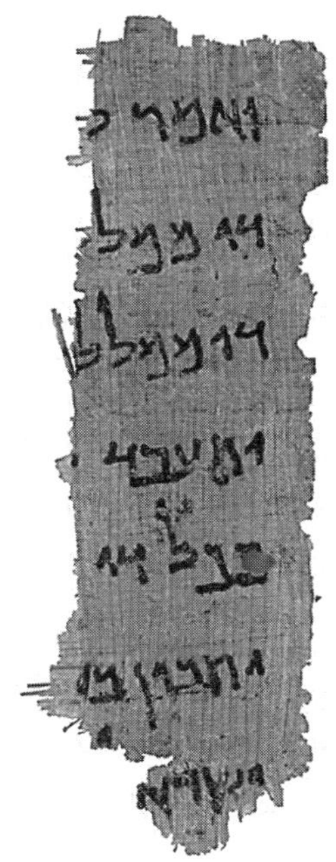

Fragment of an Aramaic papyrus manuscript of Tobit (4Q196) from Qumran (ca. 50 B.C.E.) *(The Schøyen Collection, MS 5234)*

Literary Integrity

The compositional unity of Tobit has been widely debated. Opinions range from a single author to as many as four datable layers. Tensions between the themes and content of the frame (chaps. 1, 13–14) and the body of the story are often noted, along with numerous discontinuities and problems from minor points (Is the character Nadin good or bad?) to major ones (Why does Raguel marry his daughter and send seven men to their deaths if he knows that she is destined for Tobiah?).

Date and Provenance

The date and provenance of Tobit also remain uncertain. The story is dated by consensus to 225-175 B.C.E. However, the latest possible date is based upon an argument from silence, the absence of any reference to the persecutions of Antiochus Epiphanes (175-164 B.C.E.). And the earliest possible date is postulated on the basis of citations from the Prophets as scripture. Paleography dates the Dead Sea Scroll fragments to between 100 B.C.E. and 25 C.E. As for provenance, some interpreters argue for an origin in the Diaspora, others in Judea (or even Samaria). Geographical errors may work against an origin in the eastern Diaspora, while the use of a Semitic language may rule out Egypt. Antioch has been also suggested.

Genre

Within the frame of the classic heroic fairy tale (slay monster, marry woman, obtain wealth), Tobit contains a variety of subgenres, including prayer, testament, court tale, apocalypse, proverbs, instructions, and medical recipes.

The Worlds of Tobit

Tobit operates simultaneously in three worlds: (1) its ostensible setting in the eighth to seventh centuries B.C.E. in Assyria; (2) the world of the matriarchs and patriarchs, whose behavior is particularly echoed by the story's characters; and (3) the world(s) of its authors and perhaps redactors. The result is not a straightforward depiction of Judaism at any particular time, although certain details, such as the practice of reclining, may be accurate. It is this mix of reality, fantasy, and sacred literature brought to life that makes Tobit a rich story that can both instruct and entertain.

Use of Non-Jewish Themes and Characters

The classic fairy tale is ancient and widespread. Some scholars have connected Tobit in particular to later stories involving the "Grateful Dead" (the ghost of a dead person coming back to help someone who buried him) and a "Monster in the Bedroom." Most clear, however, is Tobit's debt to the story and proverbs of Ahiqar. Tobit mimics the use of the first person in the *Tale of Ahiqar* for part of the narrative, includes proverbs with direct parallels to those attested in later versions of *Ahiqar,* and even incorporates the figure of Ahiqar in the story, transforming him into a Jewish relative of Tobit. It has also been suggested that Tobit relies either directly or indirectly on the *Odyssey,* although in most instances this is difficult to prove.

Tobit as a Source for Second Temple Judaism

The book of Tobit resists transparent historical analysis. Attempts have been made to correlate the dangers in Tobit with the difficulty of Diaspora life or other problematic times, but it is worth noting that readers of gruesome pagan Hellenistic tales could be happy and secure. The multivalent nature of the narrative, however, opens up other forms of analysis. Precisely those points in the story in which differences and discontinuities occur may indicate that certain issues were considered so important that it was worth disrupting the narrative.

Tobit may also be analyzed for its wealth of data on a wide variety of topics. It contains one of the most complete accounts of tithing practices, is a source on dietary regulations, has highly developed material on angelology and demonology, and provides the earliest account of the observance of Shavuot without a Temple and of a postexilic Jewish wedding, including a wedding contract. It refers to both ancient medical treatments and attitudes toward doctors. It is a valuable source on the class and gender roles in narrative. Its numerous specific teachings on right and wrong conduct include an early Jewish account of the famous "silver rule," the first Jewish instruction against binge drinking, and an intriguing reference to placing consumable substances on graves. The story also contains a wealth of liturgical material, including one passage (11:14-15) very similar to lines 4-6 of 11Q14. Tobit is also an important source for studying such phrases as "Lord of Heaven" and "the Book of Moses" and attitudes toward Gentiles in the eschaton. It is also a prime example of how food and eating may be used to tell a story.

BIBLIOGRAPHY

P. DESELAERS 1982, *Das Buch Tobit: Studien zu seiner Entstehung, Komposition und Theologie,* Göttingen: Vandenhoeck & Ruprecht. • B. EGO 1999, *Buch Tobit,* JSHRZ II. • J. A. FITZMYER 2003, *Tobit,* Berlin: de Gruyter. • R. HANHART 1984, *Text und Textgeschichte des Buches Tobit,* Göttingen: Vandenhoeck & Ruprecht. • P. J. MILNE 1986, "Folktales and Fairy Tales: An Evaluation of Two Proppian Analyses of Biblical Narratives," *JSOT* 34: 35-60. • C. A. MOORE 1996, *Tobit: A New Translation with Introduction and Commentary,* New York: Doubleday. • M. RABENAU 1994, *Studien zum Buch Tobit,* Berlin: Walter de Gruyter. • C. J. WAGNER 2003, *Polyglotte Tobit-Synopse: Griechisch, Lateinisch, Syrisch, Hebräisch, Aramäisch; mit einem Index zu den Tobit-Fragmenten vom Toten Meer,* Göttingen: Vandenhoeck & Ruprecht. • S. WEEKS, S. J. GATHERCOLE, AND L. T. STUCKENBRUCK 2004, *The Book of Tobit: Ancient and Medieval Versions,* Berlin: de Gruyter. • S. WEEKS 2006, "Some Neglected Texts of Tobit: The Third Greek Version," in *Studies in the Book of Tobit: A Multidisciplinary Approach,* ed. M. R. J. Bredin, London: Clark, 12-42. • L. M. WILLS 1995, *The Jewish Novel in the Ancient World,* Ithaca: Cornell University Press, 68-92. • G. XERAVITS AND J. ZSENGELLER, ED. 2005, *The Book of Tobit: Text, Tradition, Theology,* Leiden: Brill. • F. ZIMMERMANN 1958, *The Book of Tobit,* New York: Harper & Brothers.

NAOMI S. JACOBS

Tohorot (4Q274, 276-277, 278)

Several fragments of the Dead Sea Scrolls found in Qumran Cave 4 have been titled *Tohorot,* "Purities," because they discuss various matters of ritual purity. They are labeled with alphabetic sigla: Tohorot A (4Q274), Tohorot B (4Q276-77), and Tohorot C (4Q278). Sectarian antagonism is not evident in these texts, and some of the laws concern purity issues relating to women. Thus, they probably date back to the second century B.C.E., before the community's formal withdrawal to Qumran. The legal perspective of the author(s) is priestly and stringent like that found in other Qumran texts.

The concern among many Jews in Second Temple Judaism to be ritually pure before eating is apparent in 4QTohorot A (4Q274 frg. 1 col. i lines 3-9; cf. 1QS 5:13; Josephus, *J.W.* 2.129; Luke 11:38). Surprisingly, the text requires even Jews in a state of ritual impurity to bathe before eating (4Q274 1 i 3-9).

The potential of liquids to convey impurity is treated in 4QTohorot A (4Q274 3 ii 4-9). Crops wetted even by rain are considered susceptible to impurity, and harvesters must be in a state of ritual purity so as not to cause contamination. Even the juice of fruit oozing from the baskets could potentially transmit impurity from the harvester or other source (e.g., a dead rodent) to the produce. Food must be pure from the time of harvesting to the point of consumption. In contrast, the rabbis did not require purity while gleaning fruit, but they did require it during the pressing of oil and even quarantined workers at the olive presses (*m. Tohorot* 9–10).

The concern over the susceptibility of liquids to impurity is attested in other documents from Qumran as well. Access to the community drink was allowed to novices only after two years of examination (1QS 6:20; 7:20; cf. Josephus, *J.W.* 2.123). Liquid stains in the house of the dead had to be removed so that corpse impurity would not spread (CD 12:15-17; 11Q19 frg. 49 lines 8-11). Liquid could even transfer impurity backward into a vessel from which it had been poured out (4Q394 frg. 3 lines 5-8)

4QTohorot A forbids purification rituals on the Sabbath. The author discusses the case of a person purifying from corpse impurity whose sprinkling rites fell on the Sabbath (4Q274 2 i 2-3). The individual must make sure not to touch purities during the Sabbath and perform purification rites after the holy day (cf. also *m. Pesaḥ.* 6:1-2).

According to 4QTohorot A, semen is as impure as the flux of the *zab,* whose bed or chair defiles even without direct contact. Those who handle anything which has been in contact with semen either directly or indirectly, for example, by carrying a soiled garment or mattress, become impure and must launder their clothes (4Q274 2 i 8; cf. the stringencies of 11Q19 frg. 45 11-12). For the rabbis, semen does not have the potency to defile individuals without direct contact (*b. Nazir* 66a; *m. Zebaḥ.* 5:11).

Another principle which comes into relief in 4QTohorot A is the difference in status of an ordinary person and one who has decided to live at a higher standard of purity (cf. the distinction between "camps" in CD 7:4-7). Like the *Temple Scroll,* 4Q274 suggests that a purer person will not eat the contents of even a sealed vessel in the house of the dead (4Q274 3 ii 4; 11Q19 frg. 49 line 8).

4QTohorot B discusses the rite of the red cow, which was burned to produce ashes for purification from corpse contamination (Num. 19:17-21). The text authenticates the ritual for the period of the Second Temple for which the only evidence had heretofore been later rabbinic documents (200 C.E. at the earliest). The Pharisees and Sadducees of the Mishnah argued over the correct standard of purity for those who participated in the red cow rite. 4QTohorot B agrees with the Sadducees, who would not allow the priest to burn the cow if his purification was still in process (*m. Parah* 3:7; 4Q277 1 ii 2; cf. also 4Q266 9 ii 1-4; 4Q394 3-7 i 13-16; 11Q19 51:2-5). Another sign of the priestly attitude typical at Qumran is that the author allows only a mature priest to sprinkle purgation water over the one who has contracted corpse impurity (4Q277 1 ii 6-7; cf. *m. Parah* 3:4).

Since little of the nine lines of 4QTohorot C has been preserved, its contribution is negligible.

BIBLIOGRAPHY

J. M. BAUMGARTEN 1999, *Qumran Cave 4 XXV: Halakhic Texts,* DJD 35, Oxford: Clarendon. • H. K. HARRINGTON 2004, *The Purity Texts,* London: Clark.

HANNAH K. HARRINGTON

Torah and Tradition

The lexical meaning of the Hebrew word "Torah" *(tôrâ)* is instruction or teaching. Used in a wide variety of contexts, the term had a rich set of connotations in early Judaism. Torah could signify traditions as well as texts, and its meanings ranged from the particular to the universal.

On the one hand, Torah could signify the Mosaic Torah, a particular tradition embodied in specific texts, especially the Pentateuch. But it could also refer to authoritative interpretations of biblical law and narrative. Moreover, while Mosaic Torah as embodied in the Pentateuch was certainly authoritative and definitive in early Judaism, additional authoritative texts — both legal and narrative — continued to be written throughout the Second Temple period, before the Hebrew Bible was canonized, and these texts too may be called Torah. In addition, Torah sometimes signified Wisdom, or the law of the cosmos, both of which have universal significance. In general, Torah was not limited to a particular corpus of texts but was inextricably linked to a broader tradition of extrabiblical law and narrative, interpretation, and cosmic wisdom. Without reference to this highly variegated tradition, the Torah of early Judaism cannot be understood.

Torah in Greek-Speaking Judaism

In the Septuagint, the Hebrew word *tôrâ* is almost always translated as *nomos,* a word that typically signifies the law of a particular city or state. Thus the Torah of Moses is the traditional law of Israel, as the *Nomos* of Solon is the traditional law of Athens. However, the Stoics understand the cosmos to have a *nomos,* a natural law with universal significance. Against this philosophical background Philo of Alexandria presents the Torah of Moses, because it is the only *nomos* given by the divine creator of nature, as the perfect copy of the law of nature, with which it is uniquely consistent. Accordingly, Philo understands the Law of Moses not only as a particular set of laws for Jewish observance but also as possessing universal significance. Either through adherence to the Law of Moses or through philosophical reflection, one can attain a vision of God, as did the most perfect exemplars: Moses, Abraham and Socrates.

To be sure, Philo understands the Law of Moses to be embodied by the Pentateuch, and he distinguishes between the text of the Law of Moses and its interpretation far more clearly than texts found at Qumran and other Second Temple traditions. He knows and often records traditions of interpretation that are inherited from the priests and elders of Israel. However, since Philo takes the Law of Moses to be the perfect copy of the law of nature, Philo's Torah cannot be reduced to a corpus of texts, regardless of how perfect that corpus might be. Indeed, the authority of the texts rests ultimately, not only on the fact that they originate in divine revelation, but also on their intimate relation to God and the law of nature, a law which is essentially unwritten.

Torah as Wisdom

In early Jewish texts, Torah is sometimes synonymous with Wisdom (e.g., Psalm 119, Proverbs, Ben Sira). According to this understanding too, Torah or Wisdom is not limited to any particular textual tradition, though it may include such traditions. Rather, Torah has the same status as Wisdom, which has heavenly origins and is said to originate at the time of the creation of the world. For example, the book of Ben Sira develops a relationship between wisdom and law, drawing extensively on the language of Deuteronomy and Proverbs. In chap. 24, Lady Wisdom speaks of herself in the first person and explains that Wisdom *is* the Torah of Israel. Here Torah is knowledge of the cosmos, understanding of the divine in the world, and a higher moral sensibility.

Torah as "Rewritten Bible" and New Law Codes

Texts that have been labeled "Rewritten Bible" by scholars, such as *Commentary on Genesis A* (4Q252), *Jubilees,* and the *Temple Scroll,* often refer to themselves as Torah. These texts rework older textual traditions (e.g., Genesis and Exodus) or incorporate them into a new context that is supposed to establish their interpretation. They draw both on traditions that were later canonized and on others that were not. For their intended communities, or at least for their authors, these texts seem to have authoritative or even "scriptural" status. Here Torah expands to include newly authored texts.

The extensive paraphrasing of the Bible at Qumran suggests that the Pentateuch may be comfortably revised and updated without undermining its authority. Taken together, *Jubilees,* the *Temple Scroll,* and the *Words of Moses* constitute an almost fully rewritten Pentateuch, with an emphasis on levitical preeminence and a particular interpretation of legal and cultic texts. There is a real possibility that this other Torah could have become the authoritative text for the early Jewish community. This would have produced a significantly different Torah from the corpus that was later canonized. Nevertheless, the biblical texts, and the versions and paraphrases found at Qumran, all appear to have had authority within their communities. They also differ on many points, yet the close proximity in which they were found seems to imply the possibility of coexistence within a single group.

There are other texts that do not explicitly call themselves Torah but implicitly claim that the new laws within them are part of the Torah (e.g., the Qumran *Community Rule*). Such texts reflect an understanding of Torah that at times included particular reference to the Pentateuch, but did so within a larger context of constructing a new law code for the intended community. This understanding of Torah is presented as definitive. It includes the biblical legal traditions and other legal traditions that we know, in many cases, only from Qumran.

The Torah understood as Pentateuch eventually assumed an exclusive, canonical, and privileged status within rabbinic Judaism, but the interpretive traditions (Oral Torah) continued to be considered part of what is understood to be Torah, a text that is inextricably bound to its traditions of interpretation. In early Judaism, then, the Torah was repeatedly redefined or sometimes radically transformed in the context of a particular interpretive community and its tradition of reading and interpretation. In the Second Temple period, there was thus no Torah apart from its tradition. Neither was there a concept of *sola scriptura.*

BIBLIOGRAPHY

G. J. BROOKE 1993, "Torah in the Qumran Scrolls," in *Bibel in jüdischer und christlicher Tradition: Festschrift für Johann Maier zum 60. Geburtstag,* ed. H. Merklein et al., Frankfurt: Anton Hain, 97-120. • M. HIMMELFARB 1999, "Torah, Testimony, and Heavenly Tablets," in *A Multiform Heritage: Studies on Early Judaism in Honor of Robert A. Kraft,* ed. B. G. Wright, Atlanta: Scholars Press, 19-29. • H. NAJMAN 1999, "The Law of Nature and the Authority of Mosaic Law," *SPhA* 11: 55-73. • H. NAJMAN 2000, "Torah of Moses: Pseudonymous Attribution in Second Temple Writings," in *The Interpretation of Scripture in Early Judaism and Christianity,* ed. C. A. Evans, Sheffield: Sheffield Academic Press, 202-16 • J. T. SANDERS 2001, "When Sacred Canopies Collide: The Reception of the Torah of Moses in the Wisdom Literature of the Second Temple Period," *JSJ* 32: 121-36. • E. ULRICH 2003, "From Literature to Scripture: Reflections on the Growth of a Text's Authoritativeness," *DSD* 10: 3-25. • C. WERMAN 2002, "'The Torah and the Teudah' Engraved on the Tablets," *DSD* 9.1: 75-103. • S. WHITE CRAWFORD 2008, *Rewriting Scripture in Second Temple Times,* Grand Rapids: Eerdmans.

See also: Pentateuch HINDY NAJMAN

Tosefta

The Tosefta (Hebrew for "supplement" or "collection") is a rabbinic work that parallels and supplements the Mishnah. Most of the Mishnah's sixty-three tractates have a corresponding tractate in the Tosefta. As rule the Tosefta is much longer than the Mishnah. The relationship of the Tosefta to the Mishnah is a difficult, as yet unsolved, synoptic problem. Most scholars agree that the Tosefta as we have it is later than, and a response to, the Mishnah as we have it; the Tosefta often quotes and explicates our Mishnah, and often explicates our Mishnah without quoting it. Thus the Tosefta is a real supplement to the Mishnah. But the Tosefta also has other material whose relationship to the Mishnah is not clear. The Tosefta often repeats the Mishnah's words verbatim without explication; contains material not found in our Mishnah; presents Mishnaic material in different form (sometimes using different language to make the same point as the Mishnah, sometimes disagreeing with the Mishnah). Numerous theories have been advanced to make sense of the Tosefta's relationship to the Mishnah, but none has proved convincing. Many scholars now agree that there is no single relationship between the Mishnah and the Tosefta, as the relationship can vary from one paragraph to another. There is growing consensus, too, that some Toseftan material is earlier than the Mishnah, that is, that the Tosefta in various places contains the literary stuff out of which the Mishnah was created. Hence the Tosefta is both earlier and later than the Mishnah.

BIBLIOGRAPHY

S. J. D. COHEN, ED. 2000, *The Synoptic Problem in Rabbinic Literature,* Providence: Brown University Press. • H. FOX AND T. MEACHAM, EDS. 1999, *Introducing Tosefta,* New York: Ktav. • A. GOLDBERG 1987, "The Tosefta," in *The Literature of the Sages,* Part I, ed. S. Safrai, Assen: Van Gorcum; Philadelphia: Fortress, 283-302. • J. NEUSNER 1977-1986, *The Tosefta Translated from the Hebrew,* 6 vols., New York: Ktav; rpt. Peabody, Mass.: Hendrickson, 2002. • H. L. STRACK AND G. STEMBERGER 1992, *Introduction to the Talmud and Midrash,* Minneapolis: Fortress, 167-81.

See also: Mishnah SHAYE J. D. COHEN

Transjordan

The region of Transjordan is roughly equivalent to the modern kingdom of Jordan. The term "Transjordan" indicates the region of Palestine east of the Jordan River, including the following territories, from north to south: Trachonitis, Batanea, Auranitis, the Decapolis ("Ten Cities"). The region included a fertile plain (Bashan), highlands (Gilead), and steppes (Moab and Ammon). Though the cities of the Decapolis were Greek, the territory of Perea was mainly inhabited by Jews.

The earliest Israelite settlement of Canaan included regions east of the Jordan River. The tribes of Manasseh, Gad, and Reuben all occupied regions east of the river. The kingdom of Saul also extended east, though it was expanded under the empire of David and Solomon. At its greatest extent, the territory of David extended south to the Gulf of Aqaba and north into Syria. Three of Solomon's twelve districts were located in Transjordan. A portion of the kingdoms of Israel and Judah extended east, bordered by the foreign kingdoms of Ammon to the east and Moab to the south.

The Hasmonean and Herodian Eras

Maccabean Judea grew in the second century B.C.E. under various leaders. The region to the north of the Dead Sea was added in 160-142 B.C.E., the region east of the Dead Sea in 134-104, and then regions both to the north (Galladitis and Gaulanitis) and to the south of those already added were conquered in 103-76.

Josephus gives us the account of the land holdings of Herod the Great, which included Trachonitis (the lava plate), Auranitis (the Hauran), and Batanea (*J.W.* 1.398-400). In the first century B.C.E. Augustus augmented Herod's landholdings, which already included Galilee, Hippos, and Gadara, to the east and southeast of the Sea of Galilee. According to Josephus, Augustus ceded to Herod Batanea, Auranitis, and Trachonitis, all regions east of the Sea of Galilee, because he opposed banditry (*Ant.* 15.343-49; *J.W.* 1.398-99). The major trade routes in this region, the King's Highway from Aqaba and the Wadi Sirhan from Arabia, were especially subject to bandits, and the control of Herod over the region did little to stabilize it. The result of these bequests allowed Herod and his dynasty to rule all of the districts south of the Golan Heights until almost the end of the first century C.E.

The region of the northern Hauran and the Nabatean kingdom were separate entities that were to fall later under Roman rule. The northern Hauran, which includes Auranitis, was leased to the "Arabs" by Zenodorus, the leader of a band of robbers antagonistic toward the Roman government in 24 B.C.E. (so Josephus, *J.W.* 1.399-400; *Ant.* 15: 354-64). The Arab rulers of Auranitis, most likely the Nabatean kings, held the region for only a few years before 23 B.C.E., when it was passed into Herodian control. At this point, Herod controlled Idumea, Judea, Samaria, Galilee, Batanea, Auranitis, Trachonitis, and a stretch of territory east of the Jordan River and the Dead Sea as far south as Perea.

In 20 B.C.E., on the occasion of Augustus' visit to Syria, the people of Gadara sought emancipation from Herod's kingdom and attachment to the province (*Ant.* 15: 354-59). Augustus' high opinion of Herod was upheld, and Gadara, Hippos, and Kanatha in the Hauran remained under Herod's control, but many of the cities included in the Decapolis — Scythopolis, Pella, Abila, Dium, Adraa, Gerasa, and Philadelphia — formed an enclave of Roman provincial territory surrounded by the two kingdoms.

War erupted between the two kingdoms in 9 B.C.E. Our record of the events comes from Josephus, whose account derives from the contemporary narrative of Nicolaus of Damascus (*Ant.* 16.271-99; 9.335-55; Nicolaus in *Fragmente der griechischen Historiker* 90, F.136[5]). In 12 B.C.E. Herod was absent from the region, and the Nabateans encouraged the residents of Trachonitis to revert to banditry and gave their chief bandits refuge in Nabatean territory. The bandits raided Judea and "Coele Syria" (perhaps meaning the Decapolis). When Herod returned, he was able to regain control of Trachonitis. Without Roman intervention, the Nabateans were forced to pay a debt to Herod, and both sides released their refugees. After these actions were completed, Herod invaded Nabataea successfully and established a colony of Idumeans to control Trachonitis.

Further complications arose between the two kingdoms when Aretas IV succeeded to the throne in 9/8 B.C.E. without the permission of Augustus (*Ant.* 16.295). The emperor briefly considered granting the Nabatean kingdom to Herod but was deterred upon hearing about the conflicts between Herod and his sons. Upon Herod's death in 4 B.C.E., revolts broke out throughout the Diaspora, including the destruction of Herod's palace at Betharamphtha in Perea, across the river from Jericho (*J.W.* 2.59; *Ant.* 17.277). Three of Herod's sons were made heirs: Archelaus was made king, and Herod Antipas and Philip became tetrarchs (*J.W.* 1.664; *Ant.*

17.188-90). Antipas ruled Galilee and Perea, and Philip had Gaulanitis, Trachonitis, Batanea, and the city of Paneas. Gadara and Hippos finally escaped Herodian rule and became provincial cities and thus had to pay tribute to Rome. In 6 C.E. Archelaus was deposed and the province of Judea was created, including the territories of Idumea, Judea, and Samaria.

When Herod's son Philip died in 33 or 34 C.E., his territory became part of Syria before being given in 37 C.E. to Agrippa I, Herod's grandson, along with the tetrarchy of Lysanias located in the Anti-Lebanon. Also in the 30s Herod Antipas became engaged in a conflict with Aretas IV over territorial borders. This resulted in a war in which Antipas was defeated. Upon the death of Aretas in 40 C.E., the Nabatean dynasty passed into the hands of his son, Malichus II, who continued his father's policy of urban growth. The kingdom of Herod was briefly reunified from 41 to 44 C.E. under the reign of Agrippa I, who received Galilee from Caligula (*Ant.* 18.252). Upon Agrippa I's death in 44 C.E., Philip's territory was given to Agrippa II, although he did not receive Batanea, Trachonitis, and Auranitis until 53.

During the Revolts

Roman intervention in the territories of Herod's successors did not become substantial until the second half of the first century C.E. With the First Jewish Revolt in Judea from 66 to 70 C.E., the Roman army made its most significant intervention to date in the region. The Syrian general of Agrippa II killed Babylonian Jews in Transjordan territories and the Jewish colony in Caesarea Philippi (Neronias), while Jews killed Gentiles in Transjordan. With Vespasian's triumph in Judea, the population was subjugated to Roman rule in the Roman province of Judea. The dispersion of Jews into adjacent non-Jewish regions was extensive. In 106 C.E. most of the territory in the region became the Roman province of Arabia under the emperor Trajan, and many Jews found themselves living within this new Roman territory.

The Second Jewish Revolt, also known as the Bar Kokhba Revolt, forced even more Jews to flee east of the Jordan River. Under the emperor Hadrian in the second century C.E. Jewish practices were made illegal and Jews rebelled against the Roman incursions into Jerusalem. As a result of the persecution, many Jews were relocated to North Africa and many others fled into Arabia, so the Diaspora spread well beyond the Jordan River.

Architectural Evidence

It is difficult to identify specifically Jewish buildings outside of Jerusalem, partially due to the largely aniconic nature of artistic and architectural representations. Synagogues identified in Diaspora regions (in Transjordan and elsewhere) were important centers of Jewish organization. The structures contained features necessary for religious and domestic activity, including kitchens, dining rooms, and even living quarters to support and house the local community. Because the religion of Jews was not part of the entire community, the synagogue itself became the community.

One of our only surviving synagogues in Transjordan is located at Gerasa (Jerash). Constructed in the third century C.E., the structure was later surmounted by a Christian church in the sixth or seventh century. The remains of the synagogue are meager, but an early sixth-century mosaic floor in the narthex of the structure depicting the great flood could have been part of the earlier Jewish structure.

Where synagogues were not present, Jewish religion was expressed mainly in the domestic sphere. Because most Jewish religious artifacts are indistinct from domestic artifacts, it is almost impossible to identify homes built specifically for Jews, though there is one major exception. In the first quarter of the second century B.C.E. the Tobiads, a priestly Jewish landowning family in Transjordan, built a monumental "palace" at modern ʿAraq el-Emir, complete with stone lions and leopard-shaped fountains.

Textual Evidence

The most significant source of information on Jews living in Transjordan comes to us from an important group of documents deposited in the Cave of Letters at the time of the Bar Kokhba Revolt. Discovered by Yigael Yadin in his excavations in the Judean Desert in 1960 and 1961, the Babatha Archive contains various legal contracts and deeds concerning the legal affairs of a Jewish woman, Babatha, daughter of Simeon.

Twenty-seven of the sixty documents discovered have been published and reveal much about the life of a woman in second-century Judea. Babatha was from the village of Moaza, located between ʿEin Gedi and Masada south of the Dead Sea. She was twice married and widowed, and wealthy. Her documents reveal issues concerning marriage, divorce, and women's legal issues in the Roman judicial system. The date of the last document indicates that Babatha died shortly after August 132 C.E.

The language of the Babatha Archives highlights the progression of language during the second century as well as some of the Roman administrative issues she had to face. The region of Moaza had been part of the Nabatean territory but was integrated into Arabia in 106. The earliest documents in the collection are dated to shortly before the annexation, in the years 94 and 99, under the reign of Rabbell II. These early documents, written in Nabatean, are concerned with property rights. Another document in the collection, dated to shortly afterward annexation in 110, is a deed of deposit and is written in Greek. A series of documents dated between 119 and the early 120s C.E. are written in Aramaic.

A linguistic transformation occurs within the archive's last phase, which dates from the mid-120s to 19 August 132, the latest datable document. This last phase is written in Greek, with a few personal comments and signatures in Aramaic, which indicates that Nabatean was not a language in common use among the population of this area. These texts document transactions that took place with the Roman provincial administration. Some of these papyri are concerned with

TRIBUTE AND TAXES

the return of land in the census of 127 C.E. under Titus Aninius Sextius Florentinus, the *legatus Augusti pro praetore* of Arabia. Information regarding taxation is also found in the archives, in a document clearly indicating that each plot of land was subject to a new fixed tax as registered at the administrative center at Petra. This document dates to 127 C.E. and concludes with a statement of subscriptions made by Babatha and the *praefectus alae* of Rabbath-moab. The oath made by Babatha in Aramaic and the subscription of the *praefectus* in Latin are both translated into Greek. The five witnesses who signed the document added their names in Nabatean.

BIBLIOGRAPHY

G. BOWERSOCK 1983, *Roman Arabia,* Cambridge: Harvard University Press. • H. COTTON 1994, "A Cancelled Marriage Contract from the Judaean Desert (XḤev/Se Gr. 2)," *JRA* 84: 64-86. • J. CROWFOOT AND R. HAMILTON 1930, "The Discovery of a Synagogue at Jerash," *PEQ* 1930. • M. GRANT 1973, *The Jews in the Roman World,* New York: Dorset. • C. KRAELING 1938, *Gerasa — City of the Decapolis,* New Haven: ASOR. • N. LEWIS, ED. 1989, *The Documents from the Bar Kokhbah Period in the Cave of Letters: Greek Papyri,* ed. Y. Yadin and J. Greenfield, Jerusalem: Israel Exploration Society. • P. RICHARDSON 2004, *Building Jewish in the Roman East,* Waco, Tex.: Baylor University Press. • Y. YADIN, J. GREENFIELD, A. YARDENI, AND B. LEVINE 2002, *The Documents from the Bar Kokhbah Period in the Cave of Letters: Hebrew, Aramaic and Nabataean-Aramaic Papyri,* Jerusalem: Israel Exploration Society.

See also: ʿAraq el-Emir; Babatha Archive; Decapolis; Nabatea; Tobiads SUSAN GELB ROSENBERG

Tribute and Taxes

The term "tribute" refers to imposts paid by subjects to a foreign power either directly on an annual basis or indirectly, for instance, in the form of tolls and duties. "Taxes" are payments made to local authorities of a state or subject state. Following the defeat of the Persian Empire by Alexander the Great, the Jews paid tribute to the Ptolemies, then to the Seleucids, and afterward to the Romans. There is little information about Ptolemaic taxation of Palestine, and not very much more is known of Seleucid taxation. In 142 B.C.E. Simon the Hasmonean freed the Judeans from subjection and tribute to the Seleucids. Even prior to this liberation, the Judeans must have paid taxes, first to the high-priestly aristocracy and, afterward, to the Hasmoneans. With these taxes the Hasmoneans amassed their personal wealth, administered the large territory that they conquered from the surrounding city-states, and maintained effective armies, which had become quite vast by the time of Alexander Jannaeus. No record exists of what these taxes were. It is, however, certain that the Hasmoneans did not rely either on the Temple tax, established for the upkeep of the Jerusalem Temple and its cult, or on tithes, which were paid to the Temple, the priests, and the Levites.

From Pompey to Marc Antony (63-41 B.C.E.)

Pompey, after he conquered the Jewish state in 63 B.C.E., deprived it of the territories previously conquered by the Hasmoneans. This reduced state, comprising eastern Idumea, Judea proper, Perea, and Galilee, was incorporated into the province of Syria and was for this reason tributary to Rome (*J.W.* 1.154-57; *Ant.* 13.395-97; 14.74-77; Cassius Dio, *Historia Romana* 39.56.6). The Senate contracted the tribute imposed by Pompey to one of Rome's public companies, the *societas publicanorum* (Cicero, *De Provinciis Consularibus* 5.10; *Pro Flacco* 69).

Three general observations should be made regarding the taxation of Palestine from 63 to 47 B.C.E. First, we cannot determine the type of tribute imposed by Pompey. Second, on account of the numerous revolts in Palestine and Rome's inability to pacify Palestine and Syria, the *publicani* were unable to collect tribute for much of the territory and for much of the time. Third, consequently and also because of the instability of the Roman state during the late Republic and early Principate, "Roman tribute" in practice consisted of "exactions," that is, amounts extracted from the Judeans as "gifts," war contributions and indemnities, advance taxation, and open robbery. Subsequently, the system of taxation in Palestine depended on the political status of the Jewish state and on the extent of the territory controlled by the Judeans. The political status determined what tribute, if any, the Judeans paid; the extent of the territory determined the kinds and amounts of revenue they could raise and the tribute they paid.

The decrees issued by Julius Caesar and the Senate confirming grants made to the Jewish state, Hyrcanus II, and Antipater (Herod's father) give the most direct information about taxation in Jewish Palestine under the Romans. The grants comprised favors and privileges given to the Judeans and their rulers by Caesar, as rewards for the services they rendered to him in the Winter of 47 B.C.E. during his Alexandrian campaign against Pompey's partisans. Josephus cites these decrees, in fragmentary and disorderly fashion, in *Ant.* 14.190-95, 200-210.

Caesar reorganized and regulated the hitherto chaotic regime in Palestine and established a rational tax system that was beneficial to the Romans and, considered together with other grants and exemptions, to the Judeans. When he appointed Hyrcanus II ethnarch, Caesar recognized the Judeans as an *ethnos* with the legal right to live according to their customs (*Ant.* 14.194-96). With this came the *de iure* right of the Jewish authorities to raise the Temple tax even from Jews living outside of Judea. Caesar also granted Roman citizenship to Antipater with exemption from taxation everywhere and appointed him procurator *(epitropos)* of Judea (*Ant.* 14.137, 143; *J.W.* 1.194, 199). Further, Caesar restored the seaport city of Joppa to the Judeans, together with the fertile and strategic land between Joppa and Lydda in the "Great Plain" of Sharon. Treating Judea as a city-state comprising two principal cities, Caesar imposed a tribute "for the city of Jerusalem" to be paid "every year except in the seventh year. . . . And

TRIBUTE AND TAXES

that in the second year they shall deliver the tribute at Sidon, consisting of one-fourth of the produce sown" (*Ant.* 14.202-3). Caesar and the Senate, in other words, established a tax cycle for Judea consisting of six taxable years and recommencing at the end of each sabbatical year. Hyrcanus was to deliver to the seaport at Sidon one-quarter of the produce of his territory in the second, fourth, and sixth years. It is not known whether Hyrcanus demanded from his subjects 25 percent of the produce biannually or collected half that amount annually (except the seventh year), as *Ant.* 14.202 seems to stipulate. Further, Hyrcanus was to deliver 20,670 *modii* of grain every year at Sidon, except on the sabbatical year, for the "city of Joppa." This was tribute "on the land, the harbor, and exports" (*Ant.* 14.205-6), that is, compensation to the Romans for the loss of the tolls and duties *(portoria)* from the seaport at Joppa and the overland trade route. In 44 B.C.E. the Senate granted a reduction of "one (?) *kor*" from the biannual tribute, which makes it impossible to know how much the Judeans subsequently paid (*Ant.* 14.200-201).

Both provincial tribute and the various indirect taxes are thought to have been considerable, and they varied widely during the Republic and early Principate. More onerous were the exactions, corvées, and requisitions that were part of the Roman provincial administration. Caesar exempted the Jews from the most notorious of these: billeting, military service, and "molestation" (*Ant.* 14.204), including the requisition of transport animals for soldiers and officials *(angareia),* and the confiscation of the temple tax.

According to Cicero (*In Verrem* 3.6.12-15), direct provincial tribute was divided into *vectigal certum* (or *stipendium*) and *censoria locatio.* The *stipendium,* being a fixed yearly amount, would have been easy to collect by either local authorities or Roman governors and quaestors. When assessed as a percentage of the total valuation of landed property, it was profitable to the Romans but disastrous for farmers in the event of a bad harvest. Tribute in Asia and Sicily was a *decuma* ("tithe"), a variable percentage of the annual harvest. Whereas the right to collect the tithes in Sicily was sold by Roman quaestors to private contractors *(decumani)* in Sicily itself, C. Gracchus' law of 123 B.C.E. gave the collection of the Asian tithes to the *societates publicanorum,* who bid for and bought the right from censors in Rome. The province of Asia is the only example of the *censoria locatio,* that is, of direct tribute contracted out to the *publicani* by censors in Rome. Caesar reformed the taxation in Asia by turning over to the local authorities the collection of tribute from the farmers (Appian, *Bella Civilia* 5.4; Dio, *Historia Romana* 42.6.3; Caesar, *Bellum Civile* 3.3, 31, 103).

There is no evidence that, before 47 B.C.E., tribute for Judea was contracted out in Rome. However, Caesar did for Judea what he had done for Asia: he required the Jews to pay a *decuma* and abolished the *publicani,* turning over collection and delivery to the Jewish authorities. The local authorities in Asia probably contracted with Roman quaestors the amounts due for each year. There was no Roman quaestor in Judea with whom a contract could be made, though Hyrcanus' *epitropos,* Antipater, may have represented Roman financial interests in the region. As in Asia, Caesar's tax reform in Judea was a favor, with the added bonus that for Judea the Romans had to be content with what the Jewish leaders collected and delivered as tribute.

Rome expected allied peoples to pay for the administration of their territories. The inhabitants of Judea paid local taxes to Hyrcanus (*Ant.* 14.196), including tolls and duties at Joppa. Caesar's arrangement was interrupted by the civil war that followed his assassination in 44 B.C.E. Arriving in Syria in 43 B.C.E., Cassius imposed a tribute of 700 talents on the Jewish state (*Ant.* 14.272-76; *J.W.* 1.218-22). Although Cassius exacted this sum in one year, and it was probably exorbitant, this was an instance of extraordinary exaction that must be put in the context of his and Brutus' treatment of other cities of Syria and of the East in general. After the *Triumviri* defeated Brutus and Cassius in the Autumn of 42 B.C.E., the Jewish authorities, portraying themselves as victims of Cassius' brutality, secured from Antony (who dominated the East until his defeat in 31 B.C.E.) confirmation that the Jewish state would continue to pay the same tribute that Caesar had demanded (*Ant.* 14.304-23, 217-27).

Under Herod and Sons (40 B.C.E.–6 C.E.)

The subject of Herodian taxation has long been debated. Negative assessments of its impact are based on three aspects of his reign: Rome's continued exaction of tribute from his kingdom, Herod's largesse and extensive building programs, and Josephus' negative statements. The situation, however, was complex and more nuanced than is usually assumed.

There is preponderant evidence that the Jewish state paid no tribute to Rome while it was ruled either by Herod himself or by his scions. Two factors are decisive: First, with Herod's appointment in 40 B.C.E. Judea for the first time became one of Rome's client kingdoms. In spite of Appian's garbled account of Herod's appointment (*Bella Civilia* 5.75), in the Republic and early Principate no Roman client kingdom was tributary. Second, Antipater's descendants, by virtue of the hereditary grant made to him by Caesar, were Roman citizens with immunity from taxation everywhere. Thus the territories ruled by the Herods were free from tribute as such, and their revenues, considered the income of full Roman citizens, were also free from taxation. Consequently, the Herods ruled with complete financial independence (within the limits of Rome's hegemony).

Herodian taxation fell on landed property and was paid in produce. It is uncertain, however, whether this tax was a percentage of the harvest or on the land itself. Attempting to extract cash in an agricultural economy was recognized to be futile. However, the Herods may occasionally have imposed taxes, besides tolls and duties, that required cash payments, but they did not exact a poll tax. Herod imposed taxes "upon public purchases and sales." There were demands at his death that Archelaus remove these taxes (*Ant.* 17.205). We do not know the rate that was assessed, or what kinds of sales and which parts of Herod's kingdom were affected. Thus, when in 37 C.E. Vitellius (governor of Syria) "remitted to the inhabitants of the city [Jerusalem] all taxes on the sale of agricultural produce" (*Ant.* 18.90), these taxes are best considered to have been imposed by the Roman *praefecti,* who governed Archelaus' former ethnarchy after 6 C.E. Herod derived his tax income mostly from tolls and duties. These were paid for trade within and for goods transiting through the many semiautonomous cities in his kingdom, some of which he either founded or rebuilt. Much more income came from the control he exercised over seaports and the overland, long-distance trade routes that traversed his vast kingdom, particularly the southern trade routes on which frankincense and myrrh, spices, cotton, and silk were transported through Nabatean Arabia and Idumea to Gaza, where the southern routes met the coastal route on the Mediterranean coast. When Octavian added Gaza to Herod's kingdom in 30 B.C.E., he gave Herod full control over the trade routes together with the vast income that came from them. After Herod died, Gaza was reannexed to the province of Syria and the income reverted to the Romans (Pliny, *Naturalis Historia* 12.65). Meanwhile, Herod strengthened his hold over the coastal route and greatly increased his tax income by rebuilding Antipatris and Caesarea. Moreover, when in 23 B.C.E. Octavian (now Augustus) added Auranitis, Batanea, and Trachonitis to Herod's kingdom, he granted him control over the trade route that went north across Transjordania to Damascus.

Herod did not pay, and could not have paid, for his buildings (including the Temple) and benefactions from the direct taxes he imposed on Jewish peasants. In 28/27 B.C.E., he received no direct tax revenue because of the drought and famine that devastated his kingdom (*Ant.* 15.303-6). In 20 B.C.E., while his building program was approaching its zenith, he reduced the taxes paid by his Jewish subjects by one third (*Ant.* 15.365). In 14 B.C.E., he further reduced them by a quarter (*Ant.* 16.62-65). Thus, unless the latter reduction was only for that year, Herod reduced the taxes paid by the Judeans by 50 percent in the six-year period. The reductions suggest that the Judeans paid less, rather than more, direct taxes as Herod's reign progressed. Nevertheless, because of the bitter and persistent opposition among some of his Jewish subjects, Herod's tax policies failed to achieve the political results that he desired (*Ant.* 16.63-65): to avert the kind of charges that were later brought against him, namely, that he taxed the Judeans to "helpless poverty" and despoiled them to enrich Greek cities (*Ant.* 16.154-55; etc.)

Under the Roman Governors (6-70 C.E.)

The region of Judea became tributary when Archelaus was banished and his territory was annexed in 6 C.E. Agrippa I, who had been granted Galilee by Gaius in 39 C.E., was appointed king over Herod's entire former kingdom by Claudius in 41 C.E. After Agrippa died in 44 C.E., the whole of Jewish Palestine was reannexed into a province. The annexation of 6 C.E. was accompanied by a provincial census, conducted by Quirinius. In the early Principate, provincial censuses were conducted haphazardly and without a fixed form. They were used at the annexation of a new territory or in order to assess the revenues of a province. Quirinius' census, being of the first category, led to a revolt. Our sources are completely silent about any other census in Palestine, even after the annexation of 44 C.E., when a census would have been expected.

The form of census determined the kind of tribute resulting from it. Quirinius' census consisted in "an assessment of the property of the Jews," that is, a survey of landed property (*Ant.* 18.1-2). Although Josephus twice refers to the census as a "registration" (*Ant.* 18.3; *J.W.* 7.253), it was not a population census, that is, a registration of persons together with their property.

Outside of Egypt, Roman provinces in the early Principate paid two forms of direct tribute: the *tributum soli* or tax on landed property and the *tributum capitis* or tax on individuals. Ulpian (*De Censibus* 3) and Appian (*Syrian Wars* 11.8.50) suggest that the *tributum soli* could be assessed (after a census) as a percentage of the total valuation of landed property, that is, a fixed amount similar to Cicero's *stipendium.* However, it could also be assessed as a percentage of the annual yield *(decumae).* Since Quirinius' census was a valuation of property, the Jews paid a *tributum soli* (see, e.g., *Ant.* 18.273-75; *Life* 71). It is uncertain, however, whether they paid a variable percentage of their annual yield or a fixed percentage of the total valuation of their landed property.

The *tributum capitis* was generally paid in cash. In the late Republic such imposts were local and ad hoc exactions by Roman magistrates. These should be distinguished from the poll tax (*phoros tōn sōmatōn,* "tax on persons/bodies"; *laographia* in Egypt), levied from the early Principate onward, the imposition of which required a regular population census. There is no evidence that a registration of persons (known, e.g., from Egypt) was ever conducted in Judea from 6 to 66 C.E. Thus, contrary to what might be suggested by some literary sources (e.g., Appian, *Syrian Wars* 11.8.50; Mark 12:13-17 and par.; Luke 2:1-7), the Jews did not pay a poll tax under the governors. The only mention of a *per capita* tribute paid by the Jews of Judea is the Temple tax, converted by Vespasian after 70 C.E. into a head tax imposed on all Jews. In the long list of peoples and their subjection to Rome that Josephus puts in the mouth Agrippa II (*J.W.* 2.380-87), it is only Egypt that is explicitly said to have paid both a poll tax (in cash) and a land tax.

Tolls and duties continued to be significant. Roman magistrates, as elsewhere in the empire, also occasionally levied "extraordinary taxes" (*J.W.* 2.272-73). Among these was the "house tax" remitted by Agrippa I in 41 C.E. (*Ant.* 19.299) and the duties remitted by Vitellius. The Jews found these exactions onerous; when they involved the diversion of Temple funds, bloody revolts ensued (*Ant.* 17.264; 18.60-62; *J.W.* 2.50; etc.).

The *tributum soli* was most likely paid in produce,

though cash payment cannot be excluded. The "imperial corn" found in the villages of the Upper Galilee during the First Revolt was probably from such payment (*Life* 70–73). Josephus' only account of a collection does not allow us to determine whether payment was in produce or in cash: in the crisis situation of 66 C.E., the Jewish authorities "rapidly collected" the arrears of tribute from the villages around Jerusalem. He gives the amount in talents, but payments made in produce could be assessed in cash, and tribute raised in produce could be converted into cash (*Life* 70–73). Other (indirect) taxes, particularly tolls and duties, were levied mostly in cash.

Herod and his sons collected taxes through "slaves" (*Ant.* 17.308). We do not know exactly how Rome later collected direct tribute. Josephus' description above implies that responsibility for collection fell on Jewish magistrates and members of the Sanhedrin. It is uncertain how, in this event, the Jewish authorities reached an agreement with the governors on the annual tribute due. The high-priestly aristocracy collected tithes through their "slaves" and "servants" (*Ant.* 20.181, 206-7). These or others like them could also have collected the tribute from farmers, and the authorities thereafter delivered it to the governor. Apparently, Agrippa II sent a Jewish delegation in 66 C.E. to appeal to the governor to "appoint some of their number to collect the tribute in the country [i.e., outside of Jerusalem and its environs]." This would indicate that the Revolt had rendered the usual system of collection impracticable (*J.W.* 2.407).

Since Caesar had abolished the *publicani* in 47 B.C.E., there were no Roman tax collectors in Jewish Palestine. The *telōnai* of the Gospels were not collectors of (direct) tribute but collectors of tolls and duties. The collectors known to us by name are all Jews: Levi/Matthew (Mark 2:17//Luke 5:27-32; Matt. 9:9-13); Zacchaeus, the *architelōnēs* (Luke 19:1-10); and the leader and toll collector, John of Caesarea (*J.W.* 2.287, 292). A collector in Antipas' Galilee (as Levi/Matthew might have been) did not collect Roman taxes, and John could have collected taxes for the city of Caesarea. If the collection of tolls and duties was farmed out by the governor, this system would have been similar to what obtained elsewhere in the empire, and both the leasing contractors and their agents were apparently Jews.

The Impact of Tribute and Taxation on the Jews

In assessing the extent and impact of Herodian taxes and Roman tribute, we must be aware that impositions by a colonial authority, or by an unpopular and tyrannical ruler, are by definition oppressive. Charges of maladministration and excessive taxation are, in these cases, more than economic statements; they are political. Besides, tax-related revolts were not caused solely by the rate of taxation. Those who opposed Quirinius' census and the tribute it presaged did so because paying tribute amounted to their "tolerating mortal masters, after having God for their lord" (*J.W.* 2.118). The problem was not that the rate of taxation was onerous, but that the Romans were taxing at all. The issue is similarly framed by the Gospels: "Is it lawful to pay taxes (*kēnson*) to Caesar, or not? Should we pay them or should we not?" (Mark 12:14 and par.; cf. Luke 23:2). Scholars are divided about whether provincial taxes were on the whole heavy in the Principate. Our evidence does not allow a complete picture of taxation in Judea from 6 to 70 C.E. We cannot establish the rates that were applied and therefore cannot compare them to what obtained in other provinces; nor do we know how they affected people's lives.

BIBLIOGRAPHY

S. APPLEBAUM 1989, *Judaea in Hellenistic and Roman Times: Historical and Archeological Essays,* Leiden: Brill. • E. BADIAN 1968, *Roman Imperialism in the Late Republic,* Ithaca, N.Y.: Cornell University Press. • D. BRAUND 1984, *Rome and the Friendly King: The Character of the Client Kingship,* London: Helm. • D. BRAUND 1988, "Client Kings," in *The Administration of the Roman Empire, 241 BC–AD 193,* ed. D. Braund, Exeter: University of Exeter Press, 69-96. • P. BRUNT 1981, "The Revenues of Rome," *Journal of Roman Studies* 71: 161-72. • P. BRUNT 1990, *Roman Imperial Themes,* Oxford: Clarendon. • D. JACOBSON 2001, "Three Roman Client Kings: Herod of Judaea, Archelaus of Cappadocia and Juba of Mauretania," *PEQ* 133: 22-38. • N. LEWIS 1985-1988, "A Jewish Landowner in the Province of Arabia," *SCI* 8-9: 132-37. • A. MOMIGLIANO 1934, *Ricerche sull'organizzazione della Giudea sotto il dominio romano, 63 a.C.–70 d.C.,* Bologna: Annali della R. Scuola Normale Superiore di Pisa. • D. OAKMAN 1986, *Jesus and the Economic Questions of His Day,* Lewiston, N.Y.: Mellen. • M. PUCCI BEN ZEEV 1998, *Jewish Rights in the Roman World: The Greek and Roman Documents Quoted by Josephus Flavius,* Tübingen: Mohr-Siebeck. • F. UDOH 2005, *To Caesar What Is Caesar's: Tribute, Taxes, and Imperial Administration in Early Roman Palestine (63 B.C.E.–70 C.E.),* Providence, R.I.: Brown University Press.

See also: Economics; Temple Tax; Tithing

FABIAN E. UDOH

Trumpets, Feast of → Festivals and Holy Days

U

Universalism

Universalism is the idea that God has a concern for all human beings, even if God has entered into a covenant relationship with one particular people, the people of Israel. It is a problematic notion. It is often opposed to particularism, a word that generally has negative overtones. But this is a simplistic and misleading opposition, because every culture retains some particular features, whereas universality is an ideal that inspires people rather than an actual fact. Universalism has also been contrasted with relativism, sometimes to the detriment of the former. Ethnology, especially in the postcolonial era, has shown that the idea of universal values is less self-evident than previously thought. Universalism has even been associated with Western ethnocentrism and cultural imperialism. In this context, Jewish particularism — or the very fact that many aspects of Judaism are relevant only for Jews — has been reassessed positively. It has been argued that the genius of Judaism lies precisely in its ability to combine a particular dimension with a universal one. Universalism, then, is closely linked to the recognition that human beings share common features or a common nature beyond the diversity of their particular cultures.

In the study of ancient Judaism, emphasis has traditionally been put on the prophetic books of the Hebrew Bible, which were thought to convey a message that, from an ethical point of view, embodied the universal dimension of Judaism better than did the legal texts of the Torah. Moreover, from a Christian perspective, universalism has traditionally been linked to the issue of salvation. However, the possibility for Gentiles to be saved or have a share in the world to come is only one possible criterion that helps to assess the universal dimension(s) of Judaism. Other notions, such as Covenant, Law, and Temple, are probably more relevant.

Early Jewish Perspectives

Jewish writers from the Hellenistic and Roman period hold differing views about these issues. Some of these sources are particularistic (e.g., *Jubilees;* the *War Scroll* from Qumran), whereas others are universalistic (e.g., Philo). But they all share a common perception of God as creator of the whole world and judge over all humankind. In contrast to some biblical texts, no current of early Judaism believes that God is the national deity of Israel only. However, this does not imply that God cares for all human beings in the same way. A universal God can still elect a particular people.

Theoretically, nearly every aspect of Judaism can be assigned a universal value or, on the contrary, be considered something strictly peculiar to the Jewish people. The Sabbath, for instance, may have a cosmic and universal significance as well as a particular one. The biblical texts pertaining to the Sabbath already justify it in two different ways, by referring either to God's rest on the seventh day after the creation of the world, a universal event (Exod. 20:8-11), or to the liberation of the Hebrews from Egypt, a particular event (Deut. 5:15). Among early Jewish authors, Philo holds a universalistic understanding of the Sabbath, implying that it is natural and commendable for every human being to rest on the seventh day. Before Philo, Aristobulus seems to have professed a similar theory. Conversely, most rabbinic authorities think that the Sabbath is to be observed by Jews only.

Conversion of Non-Jews and Jewish Philanthrōpia

More generally, in early Jewish texts there are at least four different ways of attributing a universal dimension to the Torah. First, non-Jews can be allowed to join the Jewish people through a process of conversion. Judaism, then, has a universal dimension insofar as every human being can become a Jew, and the Sinai covenant is open to all. If proselytes are to be treated as native Israelites (as the biblical and most of the rabbinic texts affirm), this is a fundamental point, since it implies that there is no difference of nature between Jews and non-Jews, and thus that they belong to a single humankind beyond their religious and cultural differences. Philo and Josephus even see in the fact that Judaism welcomes proselytes a mark of Jewish love toward all human beings *(philanthrōpia).* But what about non-Jews who do not convert? The possibility of conversion will be perceived differently depending on whether it represents the only access to God, or other ways are granted to the Gentiles to partake in God's revelation, as with the rabbinic notion of Noahide commandments.

The Torah as Universal Law

Second, the Torah may be seen as a Law given to all humankind, without Gentiles being asked to convert. The fact that non-Jews observe some of the commandments without formally becoming Jews meets with approval. This was probably the case in many Jewish communities in the Diaspora, in which God-fearing Gentiles participated in synagogue life. This view is best represented by Philo but is also found in some tannaitic texts. Most of the rabbis, however, resented the fulfillment of certain parts of the Torah by non-Jews. In rabbinic thought, the Torah became the *ketubbah,* or marriage contract, between God and his people, and a way to exalt the merits of the latter in opposition to the nations. As a matter of fact, the idea that the Law was given to Israel alone and that no other people received it can already be found in several early Jewish texts (e.g., Baruch 3).

The Universal Benefit of Jewish Observances

Third, the Jewish cult at the Jerusalem Temple and the Jewish observance of the commandments can be considered to have positive effects for all humankind, even for those who do not acknowledge the divine origin of the Law and do not recognize the God of Israel. This idea has biblical roots and is linked to the notion of divine providence for all humankind, as well as to the promise made to Abraham that his seed would be a blessing to the nations. In early Judaism, Philo, for instance, writes that the Jewish people serve God as a priest whose offerings and prayers benefit all human beings (*Spec. Leg.* 2.163-67). In this case, the particular status of Jews becomes the very means through which a universal blessing can be granted to humankind.

The Universal Dimensions of Jewish Values

Fourth, the universal dimension of Jewish customs or laws may be emphasized through a comparison with the laws of other peoples. For example, the prohibition of murder, which can be found in most legal systems, can be considered not only a particular commandment of the Torah but also a natural law common to all human beings, or a divine law given by God to all humankind. In this case, Jews and non-Jews share common values that are universal, either because one notices empirically that people from different cultures adhere to them, or because God is conceived of as providentially educating humankind through revelations, laws, or wisdom that all people can receive, even though they do not belong to the people of Israel.

This line of thought can be found to some extent in sapiential literature. It also characterizes Jewish philosophers like Aristobulus or Philo, who postulate a fundamental agreement between the Torah and the law of nature, the former being the most perfect expression of the latter in a written form. Since all human beings are rational, at least theoretically, they are able to follow the law of nature, and thus some universal norms of human behavior can be established. True, Jewish writers in the Diaspora also tend to claim that pagan lawgivers drew inspiration from the Mosaic Law, and that the agreement between Jewish and pagan laws or customs demonstrates the superior wisdom of the Torah. Still, beyond this apologetic discourse, they state that Jews and Gentiles share common values or laws, and this affirmation is yet another type of universalism.

BIBLIOGRAPHY

T. L. DONALDSON 2007, *Judaism and the Gentiles: Jewish Patterns of Universalism (to 135 C.E.),* Waco, Tex.: Baylor University Press. • J. D. G. DUNN 1999, "Was Judaism Particularist or Universalist?" in *Judaism in Late Antiquity,* vol. 3, part 2, ed. J. Neusner and A. J. Avery-Peck, Leiden: Brill, 57-73. • M. HIRSHMAN 2000, "Rabbinic Universalism in the Second and Third Centuries," *HTR* 93: 101-15. • J. D. LEVENSON 1996, "The Universal Horizon of Biblical Particularism," in *Ethnicity and the Bible,* ed. M. G. Brett; Leiden: Brill, 143-69. • R. LOEWE, ED. 1966, *Studies in Rationalism, Judaism and Universalism in Memory of Leon Roth,* London: Routledge. • D. NOVAK 1983, *The Image of the Non-Jew in Judaism: An Historical and Constructive Study of the Noahide Laws,* New York: Edwin Mellen, 1983. • S. TALMON 1992, "Partikularität und Universalismus aus jüdischer Sicht," in *Juden und Christen im Gespräch: Gesammelte Aufsätze,* ed. H. Frankemölle, Neukirchen-Vluyn: Neukirchener Verlag, 159-65. • L. M. WILLS 2008, *Not God's People: Insiders and Outsiders in the Biblical World,* Lanham, Md.: Rowman & Littlefield.

KATELL BERTHELOT

Unleavened Bread, Festival of → Festivals and Holy Days

Violence

Jews in the Second Temple period were both the victims of violence and the perpetrators of it. They lived under foreign empires that sometimes resorted to force, or the threat of force, to control their populations, and some of the violence inflicted by these rulers — the Babylonians' destruction of the First Temple; the violent sacrileges of Antiochus IV; the Roman destruction of the Second Temple in 70 C.E. — have attracted much scholarly attention as pivotal events in early Jewish history. But Jews were also capable of violence themselves, and it is that behavior which is the focus of this entry.

Defining "Violence"

The term "violence" often denotes acts that cause physical injury and destruction, but some would expand its definition to include slavery, poverty, prostitution, and other harmful behavior that affects its victims in indirect or unconscious ways and whose harmful effects may be more psychological than physical. By almost any definition, however, violence encompasses a wide range of behaviors at every level of social organization: inter- and intracommunal warfare, violent protest, executions, torture, banditry, vigilantism, rape, domestic violence, and self-killing, not to mention violence perpetrated against animals (as in sacrifice) or targeted against objects (as in iconoclasm and vandalism). There is evidence for many of these kinds of violence in Jewish culture of the Second Temple period, with most of the documentation pertaining to Judea but some of it also bearing on Jewish communal and ethnic violence in Diaspora settings such as Alexandria.

Textual Evidence

The evidence for ancient Jewish violence is different from that available to social scientists and anthropologists focused on modern violence. It comes not from observation or interviews but chiefly from ancient texts that yield only some of their secrets to modern scholarship. Such texts do offer a substantial amount of evidence. Narratives like 1-4 Maccabees and Josephus' *Jewish War* enable historians to investigate the motives and causes of specific moments of violence like the Maccabean Revolt and the Jewish War of 66-70 C.E. (cf. Goodman 1987). Ritual and legal texts like the *War Rule,* which offers description of how to fight an eschatological war, seem written to encourage and direct violent behavior. Through apocalyptic texts like 2 (Syriac) *Baruch* and the *Assumption of Moses,* scholars can glimpse the role of imagined violence in religious and political fantasy. Ultimately, however, our ability to understand early Jewish violence is restricted by the paucity and obscurity of such sources and the difficulty of sorting out fact from fiction in the claims they make — and as one might expect, the evidence is even scarcer for less visible forms of violence like domestic abuse than for public and large-scale events like the Jewish War (although see Ilan 2001: 195-214). What data there are have been interpreted in widely divergent ways, as illustrated by recent debate over whether infanticide was an accepted and widespread practice among early Jews (Schwartz 2004).

The Role of Religion

One point that seems clear is that religion played an important role in motivating and legitimating early Jewish violence. Scholars like Girard have argued that religious practice itself is rooted in and responds to violent impulses, giving expression to them but also redirecting them against surrogate victims. Whether there is anything to this or similar theories, early Jewish literature complicates an irenic view of religion as an antidote to violence. Far from counteracting aggression and rivalry, religion often seems to have sanctioned and even kindled violent behavior in early Jewish culture.

Religious motives lie behind many of the best-documented examples of Jewish violence from the Second Temple period. A good deal of the factionalism in Judea of the late Second Temple period was fueled by the question of who controlled the cult, and major Jewish wars like the Maccabean Revolt and the First Jewish Revolt were piously motivated as a defense of religious tradition, or so it is claimed by sources like 1 Maccabees and Josephus.

Violence was a frequent part of Jewish religious experience as well. The Temple's ritual proceedings were organized around animal sacrifice, and its sanctity depended on the threat of violence against would-be intruders. In the Roman period the warning was asserted explicitly in Greek and Latin inscriptions that lined the sanctuary's perimeter. The memory of violence, of Jews striking back at their enemies, was also at the center of holidays like Purim and Hanukkah originating in the Second Temple period.

The Influence of the Hebrew Bible

What was it about Jewish religious belief and practice that engendered such violence and made it so central to Jewish memory and imagination? Some scholars argue that violence is inherent in monotheism, but religious violence is by no means limited to monotheistic cultures. A more specific precipitant was the Hebrew Bible, which legitimized certain kinds of violence even as it prohibited others. Biblical law and narrative allow for and sometimes call for destruction and killing: execution for certain crimes and sins, the prosecution of war, the destruction of idols, even the wholesale extermination of foes like the Amalekites (Exod. 17:14-16). The violence of biblical figures like the priest Phinehas in Numbers 25 was seen as a model of zealous righteousness (cf. 1 Macc. 2:23-29), and God Himself is often depicted using violence to accomplish His goals. The Bible's role as a catalyst for violence depended on how it was interpreted. When readers were so inclined, they could recast its contents in ways that softened or delimited its apparent endorsement of violence, but it clearly played an influential role in sanctioning violence as a defense against religious threats and as a form of fealty to God.

New Forms of Religious Violence

Martyrdom

While biblical precedent was important, early Jewish culture also gave rise to new forms of religious violence. The origins of martyrdom, the choice to die rather than renounce one's religion, can be traced to the age of Antiochus' persecution. As depicted in sources like 2 and 4 Maccabees, such behavior called to mind the voluntary sacrifice of Abraham and Isaac, but it was in fact a postbiblical innovation with no clear biblical precedent, possibly arising under the influence of Hellenistic and Roman cultures, which had their own ideals of heroic voluntary death.

Public Violence

The Hellenistic and Roman period also saw an increase in religious rioting and other publicly staged violence in Jerusalem during the festivals of Passover, Shavuot, and Sukkot, moments fraught with sacred resonance and eschatological expectation. This trend, too, can be linked to larger changes in Jewish culture: the growing popularity of festival pilgrimage after the second century B.C.E., the immense and unruly crowds this created in Jerusalem during festival time, deepening resentment against Roman rule in the first century, and the rise of sectarian antagonism among Jews. Jewish violence as depicted in Second Temple period texts was often motivated by religious conservatism, a commitment to preserving the traditions inherited from ancient Israel, but like Jewish culture in general, it was also adaptive, changing under the impact of foreign rule and other historical and cultural experiences.

Assessment

Violence was one of the most important instruments of social transformation in early Jewish culture. It may not be a coincidence that what often brings about the dramatic changes in reality described in Second Temple period apocalyptic texts is violence — the destruction of the Temple, and God's final battle against His enemies. Early Jews lived in a world shaped by violence inflicted by others and by themselves, and that has clearly left an imprint on the development of early Jewish literature and how it depicts political, religious, and even eschatological change.

The study of early Jewish violence is sensitive because accusations of Jewish violence, of sacrilege, ritualistic murder, and deicide, have long been a justification for anti-Jewish violence, going back to the Hellenistic and Roman period (Frankfurter 2006). There is no way to measure the extent of violence in early Jewish culture, but there is no reason to think that it was any worse than that of other ancient peoples like the Celts, who also lived under the duress of foreign rule. Indeed, the picture sketched here has to be balanced against the alternatives to violence also articulated in Second Temple period texts — acquiescence to foreign rule, passive suffering, and nonviolent protest. If the literary sources are any indication, however, it is impossible to understand early Jewish culture fully without recognizing the many roles that violence played in its development as a tactic of self-defense, as an instrument of social and political control, as a focus of group memory and literary imagination, and as a way of expressing religious commitment.

BIBLIOGRAPHY

J. J. COLLINS 2003, "The Zeal of Phinehas: The Bible and the Legitimation of Violence," *JBL* 122: 3-21. • D. FRANKFURTER 2006, *Evil Incarnate: Rumors of Demonic Conspiracy and Satanic Abuse in History,* Princeton, Princeton University Press. • R. GIRARD 1977, *Violence and the Sacred,* Baltimore: Johns Hopkins University. • M. GOODMAN 1987, *The Ruling Class of Judaea: The Origins of the Jewish Revolt against Rome A.D. 66-70,* Cambridge: Cambridge University Press. • R. HAMERTON-KELLY, ED. 1987, *Violent Origins,* Stanford: Stanford University Press. • J. W. VAN HENTEN 2002, *Martyrdom and Noble Death: Selected Texts from Graeco-Roman, Jewish and Christian Antiquity,* London: Routledge. • R. HORSLEY 1993, *Jesus and the Spiral of Violence,* Minneapolis: Fortress. • T. ILAN 2001, *Integrating Women into Second Temple History,* Peabody, Mass.: Hendrickson. • D. SCHWARTZ 2004, "Did the Jews Practice Infant Exposure and Infanticide in Antiquity?" *SPhA* 16: 61-95. • T. SELAND 1995, *Establishment Violence in Philo and Luke,* Leiden: Brill. • S. WEITZMAN 1999, "From Feasts into Mourning: The Violence of Early Jewish Festivals," *JR* 79: 545-565.

See also: Peace

STEVEN WEITZMAN

War, Book of (4Q285, 11Q14)

Although the two Qumran documents known as the *Book of War (Sefer ha-Milḥamah)* have been discussed in the secondary literature since the late 1960s, a consensus was not reached concerning their import until the full textual evidence became available nearly twenty-five years later. 11Q14 was early on considered to be a blessing text similar to 4Q Blessings[a] (van der Woude 1968). An early assessment of 4Q285 suggested that it was the lost end of the *War Scroll* (Milik 1972: 143).

The public became aware of 4Q285 in 1991 as articles in the popular press announced that a fragmentary manuscript dating to the first century B.C.E. had been discovered revealing a pre-Christian expectation of a crucified messiah. After a year of debate it was determined that the messiah was rather the executioner and the victim was probably the king of the enemies of Israel in the context of an eschatological war. It was also in 1991 that scholars became aware of parallel passages in 4Q285 and 11Q14 that revealed that they were witnesses to the same book.

The official editions of 4Q285 and 11Q14 are in agreement as to the order of the fragments and thus the events witnessed therein (but see Norton 2003). The strength of the evidence — fragmentary overlaps and damage patterns — is most convincing. On the basis of this order the document can be reconstructed to reveal the following events: 4Q285 appears to describe a campaign beginning in the mountains of Israel (frg. 4 line 4). The final battle is then fought on the Mediterranean (?) Sea (frg. 4 line 6). The evil forces are routed, evidently with the help of the angelic hosts (frg. 1 line 3), and the wicked leader is brought before the Prince of the Congregation (the Messiah) for judgment (frg. 4 line 10). This wicked leader is found guilty and put to death in fulfillment of Isaiah 10:33–11:5 (frg. 7 line 4). The daughters of Israel then celebrate with timbrel and dance (frg. 7 line 5), and the high priest orders the cleansing of the land from the corpses of the Kittim (4Q285 frg. 7 line 6; frg. 10 lines 5-6). Finally the high priest blesses God before the assembly, reflecting the imminent age of peace and prosperity (4Q285 frg. 8 and 11Q14 frg. 1 col. ii). This messianic age is apparently inaugurated following the victory over the Kittim.

Although it is clear that the language and subject matter of 4Q285 and 11Q14 are reminiscent of the *War Scroll,* there is no overlapping text among the extant fragments and the *War Scroll.* The *War Scroll* itself exhibits a complex character that reflects at least three ancient end-time war traditions: a war against the Kittim (1QM 1), a universal war of divisions (1QM 2), and a universal war against the Kittim (1QM 15-19). The first two traditions are complementary: a whirlwind battle to overthrow the Kittim and capture Jerusalem is followed by a forty-year campaign against the nations of the world. The third tradition combines the first two traditions and envisages a universal war fought against the Kittim. This third tradition has confused what would otherwise be a coherent composition and has made the composite nature of the *War Scroll* clearly evident. It is also this third tradition that the *Book of War* reflects. However, the overtly messianic nature of 4Q285 and 11Q14 stands in contrast to the almost complete lack of messianic presence in the *War Scroll.* There are two possible solutions: first, the *Book of War* is a witness to the lost end of the *War Scroll* when the Messiah arrives and brings the universal war against the Kittim to its end. Or, second, the *Book of War* is an explicit and unique messianic recension of the *War Scroll.*

BIBLIOGRAPHY

M. G. ABEGG JR. 1994, "Messianic Hope and 4Q285 — A Reassessment," *JBL* 113: 81-91. • P. ALEXANDER AND G. VERMES 2000, "4QSefer ha-Milḥama," in *Qumran Cave 4 XXVI: Cryptic Texts and Miscellanea, Part 1,* ed. S. J. Pfann et al., DJD 36, Oxford: Clarendon, 228-46. • F. GARCÍA MARTÍNEZ 1998, "4QSefer ha-Milḥamah," in *Qumran Cave 11.II: 11Q2-18, 11Q20-30,* ed. F. García Martínez, E. J. C. Tigchelaar, and A. S. van der Woude, DJD 23, Oxford: Clarendon, 243-51. • J. T. MILIK 1972, "*Milkî-sedeq* et *Milkî-rešaʿ* dans les anciens écrits juifs et chrétiens," *JJS* 23: 95-144. • J. NORTON 2003, "Observations on the Official Material Reconstructions of Sefer ha-Milḥamah (11Q14 and 4Q285)," *RevQ* 21: 3-27. • B. SCHULTZ 2009, *Conquering the World: The War Scroll (1QM) Reconsidered,* Leiden: Brill. • A. S. VAN DER WOUDE

WAR SCROLL (1QM)

1968, "Ein neuer Segensspruch aus Qumran (11QBer)," in *Bibel und Qumran: Beiträge zur Erforschung der Beziehungen zwischen Bibel und Qumranwissenschaft,* ed. S. Wagner, Leipzig: Evangelische Haupt-Bibelgesellschaft zu Berlin, 253-58.

MARTIN G. ABEGG JR.

War Scroll (1QM)

Manuscripts

The *War Scroll,* a manuscript found in 1947 in Qumran Cave 1, depicts the preparation for, and the various phases of, the eschatological battle (Hebr. *milḥāmāh*) between the "Sons of Light" and the "Sons of Darkness." This manuscript, known as 1QMilḥamah (1QM), was prepared for publication by E. L. Sukenik. A fragment of the same scroll was found *in situ* in 1949 by a team of archaeologists under R. de Vaux and G. L. Harding (1Q33). Between 1952 and 1956, several other manuscripts related to the *War Scroll* were discovered in Caves 4 and 11. They are either (a) copies of a similar recension of the work (4Q492 M^{b}, 4Q494 M^{d}, 4Q495 M^{e}, 4Q496 M^{f}); (b) copies of different recensions of the work (4Q471 War Scroll–like Text B, 4Q491a M$^{a/a}$, 4Q491b M$^{a/b}$, 4Q493 M^{c}, 4Q497 War Scroll–like Text A); (c) copies of a separate work (a *Book of the War* or *Sefer ha-Milḥamah* = 4Q285, 11Q14); or (d) an independent hymnic composition (4Q491c M$^{a/c}$ and other copies of a *Self-Glorification Hymn* in 1QH^{a} 26:6-17, 4Q427 H^{a} frg. 7 col. 1, 4Q431 H^{e} frg. 1 = 4Q471b). All these manuscripts were copied either in the first century B.C.E. or the early first century C.E.

Contents

1QM has been preserved on nineteen columns containing fourteen to nineteen lines of text each (the end of the columns is lost). There are also a few letters from a twentieth column, but the last sections of the scroll are missing. The main topic of 1QM is the eschatological war to be fought by the Sons of Light, the faithful remnant of Israel, against their enemies. Led by their religious and secular leaders, they are to be an instrument of God and His heavenly hosts to bring an end to wickedness and to establish Israel's domination forever. The text contains an apocalyptic overview of the war (col. 1), instructions to prepare the war and to direct the troops (col. 1 end to col. 9 bottom), a collection of prayers and hymns (col. 9 end to col. 14 bottom), and a description of the ultimate military engagements after speeches of encouragement (col. 14 end to col. 20?).

The material found in similar recensions comes from all parts of the text. It provides elements missing in 1QM, as well as a few significant variants such as the mention of the "prince" in the rule for the standards (4Q496 M^{f} frg. 10). Fragmentary copies of other recensions of the *War Scroll* or related compositions provide a few additional parallels, illumine the redactional history of the text, offer hints of what might have stood in the lacunae of 1QM, or add relevant details (e.g., additional types of trumpets or war machines, a reference to the collection of booty, and the gathering in Jerusalem after victory). The two copies of *Sefer ha-Milḥamah* (4Q285 and 11Q14) describe the final victory over the Kittim, including the capture, trial, and execution of their king by the Prince of the Congregation, and the blessing of the eschatological community in the purified land. The *Self-Glorification Hymn* found in 4Q491c M$^{a/c}$ (frg. 11 col. 1 and frg. 12) reports the exceptional claim of a speaker to have been exalted among divine beings, eventually sitting on a throne for a judgment; three copies of a similar text in manuscripts of the *Hymns* (1QH^{a} 26:6-17; 4Q427 H^{a} frg. 7; and 4Q431 H^{e} frg. 1 = 4Q471b) demonstrate that it was also used in other contexts.

Composition and Genre

1QM has achieved its current form through some kind of literary growth. Tensions and duplications in the main parts of the document (cols. 1; 2-9; 10-14; 15-19) indicate that these may have developed separately before being brought together. Some parts of the document (especially cols. 2-9 and 10-14) integrate elements that may have circulated independently. In almost every instance where 1QM has been compared with the related texts from Cave 4, the latter provide a text shorter and probably earlier than their parallels in 1QM (compare 4Q491a M$^{a/a}$ frg. 11 col. 2, lines 8-24 and 1QM 16:11–17:15; 4Q491b M$^{a/b}$ frgs. 1-3 and 1QM 7:3b-7; 4Q492 M^{b} frg. 1 and 1QM 12:7-16 and 19:1-8).

In its current form, 1QM is an eschatological rule that parallels, in a religious and utopian way, the genre of the Greco-Roman tactical treatise. The people who put it together adapted and shaped collections of rules, prayers, and speeches into a sort of guidebook for the priests and Levites in charge of leading the eschatological war, so that they could work out their future duties and perform them properly when these unprecedented events took place.

What the precise usage of 1QM and other war texts was in the Qumran community remains unknown. These texts define the present and future in terms of a conflict between two clearly identified camps and leave no doubt about its final outcome. This powerful and encompassing vision certainly helped legitimize the decision of the sectarians to cut themselves off from a corrupted environment; it also provided them with a strong sense of identity as the true remnant of Israel and helped them consolidate their commitment to the Mosaic Law as interpreted and enforced in the community by its religious authorities. During the group's final years of existence, 1QM may also have motivated part of the congregation to join the Great Revolt against Rome, interpreted as the real and ultimate confrontation with evil, in the feverish expectation of God's final act of salvation.

Date

One of the most debated issues about 1QM is its date of composition. The only data that one really can take for granted about it are an upper date *(terminus a quo)* around 164 B.C.E., based on the dependence of 1QM 1 on Daniel 11–12 and the events of the Maccabean pe-

WAR SCROLL (1QM)

riod related there; and a lower date *(terminus ad quem)* around the middle of the first century B.C.E., derived from the paleography of the manuscript.

Detailed studies have confirmed the dependence of 1QM 1 upon the great vision of Daniel 11–12. But the text of Daniel has been reinterpreted in such a way that it is not easy to determine how 1QM stands in relation to the Maccabean period. Attempts to identify the Kittim in 1QM are inconclusive; the term was probably used to designate the Seleucids in certain documents from Qumran and the Romans in others, as in external sources. The fact that many copies of this text were in circulation during the Roman period certainly suggests, however, that the latter were considered at that time as the enemy to be defeated.

Yigael Yadin's examination of the military equipment and tactics in 1QM led him to conclude that they reflect the Roman art of war and, consequently, that the text is to be dated after the Roman takeover of Palestine in 63 B.C.E. This conclusion has been challenged by R. Gmirkin, who has argued that the Roman parallels to 1QM 3–9 better fit the Roman art of war of the second century B.C.E. Gmirkin has extended this date to the whole manuscript; but Davies, who also dates this part of 1QM to about the same period, argues for a much longer redactional history of 1QM and thinks that its final composition did not take place before the Roman period.

Relation to the Hebrew Bible and Other Writings

Various texts found in books that are now parts of the Hebrew Bible articulate a vision of the final struggle resulting in the eradication of wickedness and the establishment of the kingship of God and Israel forever. The authors of the *War Scroll* attempted to deduce from these writings rules to be applied and procedures to be followed in order to ensure the proper participation of their community in this decisive event. Their beliefs and hopes were shaped by the memory of historical antecedents of salvation as well as by prophetic expectations of victory.

In 1QM, five explicit biblical quotations are formally introduced at the beginning of the war prayers (1QM 9 end to 11:12). They recall essential features of the war. Laws of purity are to be strictly enforced because God stands in the midst of the camps (1QM 10:1-2 = Deut. 7:21-22). Israel should not be afraid of her enemy, since God himself does battle on her behalf (1QM 10:2-5 = Deut. 20.2-5). Blowing trumpets is a way to be remembered before God and saved from the enemy (1QM 10:6-8 = Num. 10:9). The oracles of Num. 24:17-19 and Isa. 31:8 are quoted as proof that the enemies are to be destroyed by the power of God (1QM 11:6-7, 11-12).

Besides these, some 200 implicit biblical quotations or allusions have been identified in the 280 lines or so preserved in 1QM. There are quotations from almost every part of the Hebrew Bible, but especially from the books of Numbers, Deuteronomy, Isaiah, Ezekiel, Daniel, and Psalms. Several elements in the *War Scroll* are echoed in other Jewish writings as well, especially in the two books of the Maccabees (organization and practices of the armies, use of trumpets, banners, slogans, etc.) and in the Pseudepigrapha (angelology, cosmic battles, etc.). Various connections have also been suggested between the *War Scroll* and the New Testament: the contrast between Christ and Beliar in 2 Cor. 6:14–7:1 has been compared with 1QM 13; the opposition between light and darkness is also found in the Gospel of John; and the book of Revelation is framed around a similar vision of the eschatological war between good and evil in which human and supernatural beings take part together.

BIBLIOGRAPHY

Major Editions of 1QM and Related Manuscripts

M. BAILLET 1982, *Qumrân Grotte 4.III (4Q482–4Q520)*, DJD 7, Oxford: Clarendon, 2-72, pls. V-XXVI (4Q491-497). • D. BARTHÉLEMY AND J. T. MILIK 1955, *Qumran Cave I*, DJD 1, Oxford: Clarendon, 135-36, pl. XXXI (1Q33, additional fragment of 1QM). • E. CHAZON ET AL. 1999, *Qumran Cave 4 XX: Poetical and Liturgical Texts, Part 2*, DJD 29, Oxford: Clarendon, 77-123, pls. IV-VI (4Q427), 199-205 (4Q431 frg. 1 = 4Q471b), 421-32, pl. XXVIII (4Q471b). • F. GARCÍA MARTÍNEZ ET AL. 1998, *Qumran Cave 11.II*, DJD 23, Oxford: Clarendon, 243-51, pl. XXVIII (11Q14). • S. J. PFANN ET AL. 2000, *Qumran Cave 4.XXVI*, DJD 36, Oxford: Clarendon, 228-46, pls. XII-XIII (4Q285), 439-45, pl. XXX (4Q471). • É. PUECH 1988, "Quelques aspects de la restauration du Rouleau des Hymnes," *JJS* 39: 38-55 (reconstruction of 1QH^a 26). • E. L. SUKENIK 1955, *The Dead Sea Scrolls of the Hebrew University*, Jerusalem: Magnes (Hebrew 1954), transcription and pls. 16-34, 47 (1QM), and 58 (fragments of 1QH^a 26).

Other Editions and Studies

P. S. ALEXANDER 2003, "The Evil Empire: The Qumran Eschatological War Cycle and the Origins of Jewish Opposition to Rome," in *Emanuel: Studies in Hebrew Bible, Septuagint, and Dead Sea Scrolls in Honor of Emanuel Tov*, ed. S. M. Paul et al., Leiden: Brill, 17-31. • J. J. COLLINS 1997, "The Eschatological War," in idem, *Apocalypticism in the Dead Sea Scrolls*, London: Routledge, 91-109. • P. R. DAVIES 1977, *1QM, the War Scroll from Qumran: Its Structure and History*, Rome: Pontifical Biblical Institute. • J. DUHAIME 1995, "War Scroll," in *The Dead Sea Scrolls: Hebrew, Aramaic, and Greek Texts with English Translations*, vol. 2, *Damascus Document, War Scroll and Related Documents*, ed. J. H. Charlesworth, Louisville: Westminster John Knox, 80-203. • J. DUHAIME 2004, *The War Texts*, London: Clark. • F. GARCÍA MARTÍNEZ AND E. J. C. TIGCHELAAR 2000, *The Dead Sea Scrolls Study Edition*, 2 vols., Leiden: Brill, 1: 112-44; 2: 640-43, 950-53, 970-91, 1208-11. • R. GMIRKIN 1996, "The War Scroll and Roman Weaponry Reconsidered," *DSD* 3: 89-129. • B. SCHULTZ 2009, *Conquering the World: The War Scroll (1QM) Reconsidered*, Leiden: Brill. • G. VERMES 1998, *The Complete Dead Sea Scrolls in English*, New York: Penguin, 161-89. • D. O. WENTHE 1998, "The Use of Scripture in 1QM," *DSD* 5: 290-319. • M. O. WISE, M. ABEGG, AND E. COOK 1996, *The Dead Sea Scrolls: A New Translation*, San Francisco: HarperSanFrancisco, 150-72, 291-94, 403-5. • Y. YADIN 1962, *The Scroll of the War of the Sons of Light against the Sons of Darkness*, Oxford: Oxford University Press.

JEAN DUHAIME

Washing, Ritual

Washing in water for ritual purposes is widely attested in the ancient world, particularly in Christian baptism and its antecedents in Jewish ritual bathing. Washing terminology appears in many contexts and is often linked to purification in the Bible and other literature.

Terminology and Usage

In the Hebrew Bible, the primary terms for washing are *rḥṣ* for bathing and *kbs* for washing objects. These terms are often associated with the purity terms *ṭhr* and *qdš*. The Dead Sea Scrolls and rabbinic literature continue the distinction between *rhṣ* and *kbs,* adding *ṭbl* for immersion, including the *ṭebul yom,* a person who has bathed but remains unclean until sunset. The Septuagint and Second Temple literature use many terms for washing, such as *niptō, plynō,* and *louō,* translating both *rhṣ* and *kbs* as *plynō.* The New Testament uses these terms as well, along with frequent references to *baptizō,* only occasionally associated with purification terms such as *katharizō* and *hagnizō.*

While washing terminology appears primarily in ritual contexts, a consideration of other uses uncovers a broader spectrum of washing. In the Hebrew Bible, most references to washing deal with ritual purity and are located almost entirely in Leviticus and other Priestly texts. Some texts discuss general purity issues that involve all Israelites, while many others focus on special purity requirements for the priests. A few passages, such as Exod. 19:10-15, describe purification in preparation for theophany. Outside of the Torah, few references combine washing and purity, and some of these uses seem more metaphorical than literal, as in Isa. 4:3-4. Some of these texts even use *kbs* for washing the body, as in Ps. 51:2, 7, a reversal of the pattern described above. Unlike certain rituals in the ancient Near East that required washing before healing disease, such washing in the Hebrew Bible is performed only after healing has occurred, possibly to avoid the appearance of incantations and magic.

The Dead Sea Scrolls and other Second Temple literature witness ritual and metaphorical uses, as well as washing for initiation or conversion. Many of the ritual contexts are handled in the same way as in the Torah, with a few added situations, including prayer (*Letter of Aristeas* 304b–6), Sabbath (2 Macc. 12:38), and gleaning (4Q284a 1 2-5). In some cases, the details of ritual washing have been clarified or standardized in comparison to the Hebrew Bible, for example, whether women needed to immerse after menstruation. Metaphorical uses from this period include controlling the passions (Philo, *Spec. Leg.* 1.257-58) and repentance (4Q393).

In the New Testament, references to washing can be divided between mention of Jewish ritual washing, often polemical (e.g., Mark 7), and statements regarding Christian practices and beliefs about baptism. These Christian references rarely combine washing and purity as in the previous texts. Instead, they emphasize initiation with the addition of several new metaphorical uses, such as forgiveness of sins in the case of John the Baptist (Mark 1:1-18), rebirth (1 Cor. 6:11), or dying and rising with Christ (Rom. 6:3-5).

Rabbinic literature emphasizes the ritual aspect of washing, again connecting washing and purity. Initiation appears as well, along with occasional metaphorical references. While these texts discuss many of the same ritual contexts and concerns as the Hebrew Bible and other texts, there are some significant differences. There are extensive discussions of the structure and operation of *miqva'ot* (ritual baths) and continued standardization of the sort noted above. There are also debates over the use of public baths, concluding for instance that immersion is needed after using a public hot bath (*b. Šabbat* 13b–14a) and that the presence of statues in baths does not constitute idolatry since users disrespect the statues by performing bodily functions in front of them (*m. ʿAbod. Zar.* 3:4).

The Chronology of Ritual Washing

Dating these developments depends partly on dating the composition of the Priestly source of the Pentateuch. An early date for P suggests that ritual washing existed in the First Temple period, a view that is challenged by the relative silence of the historical books. Such arguments from silence are problematic, but they still raise important questions. A postexilic or later date for P correlates with this historical silence and with the archaeological evidence below, but it does not account for the sudden emphasis on ritual washing in the Second Temple period. Regardless of the date for P, since the J source is presumed to be earliest, it may be that washing in the Priestly source was inspired by J's use of washing for theophany as in Exodus 19.

Similarly, dating the origins of the Dead Sea Scrolls community affects the chronology of ritual washing. Parallels between washing in the Dead Sea Scrolls and in rabbinic literature suggest a shared tradition predating the sectarians' split from the Jerusalem Temple, presumably after the Maccabean Revolt. Even so, the dates for these precursor traditions are unclear. This is further complicated by the fact that the Mishnah was not compiled until 200 C.E., long after the destruction of the Second Temple in 70 C.E., so mishnaic references to practices in the Second Temple period may be more idealized than actual.

Proselyte Baptism

The debate over proselyte baptism illustrates the problem of using the Mishnah and later rabbinic writings as evidence for Second Temple practices. As described above, some Second Temple texts include washing as part of conversion to Judaism or initiation into a community. Judith 14:10 focuses on Achior's circumcision, while Aseneth washes her face and hands but does not fully immerse (*Jos. & Asen.* 14:12-13, 15). The Babylonian Talmud recounts a debate between R. Eliezer ben Hyrcanus and R. Joshua ben Hananiah which suggests that by the end of the first century conversion required immersion and offering a sacrifice in the Temple, along with circumcision for men (*b. Yebamot* 46a). Further, the use of immersion in the Dead Sea Scrolls and by the followers of John the Baptist and Jesus suggests that immersion was becoming a requirement for initiation and/or conversion earlier in the first century C.E. Thus proselyte baptism likely existed during this period, but we cannot tell when or how it began. In Jewish tradition, immersion for conversion does not seem to have held any unique significance apart from the expectation that a convert would now be expected to maintain purity through future immersions. The New Testament and early Christian literature challenge this expectation that washing was repeatable by making baptism a singular, nonrepeatable event, as Justin Martyr emphasizes (*Dialogue with Trypho* 13, 166).

Bathing Practices

Many texts require bathing for purification, but few of them describe how bathing was performed. The absence of prayers for bathing may reflect an avoidance of incantations and healing rituals from other cultures in the ancient Near East. There are only a few fragmentary references to washing in the Dead Sea Scrolls (e.g., 4Q414). According to the *Letter of Aristeas*, the translators of the Septuagint washed and raised their hands to heaven in prayer (*Letter of Aristeas* 304b–6), and the New Testament attests to a baptismal formula "in the name of the Father, and of the Son, and of the Holy Spirit" (Matt. 28:20), presumably a later addition.

Similarly, little is said in early texts about the kind of water or structures in which bathing must occur. To date archaeologists have not found any *miqva'ot* dated prior to the second century B.C.E. However, we can assume that initially such washing was done in rivers or other available water, as in Naaman's immersion (2 Kings 5:1-19). Leviticus 14 and a few other texts mention *mayyim ḥayyim*, "living water" — springs or flowing water. Later texts develop a hierarchy of water sources leading up to living water (*m. Miqw.* 1:1-8; *Didache* 7).

Although many supposed *miqva'ot* have been discovered, few texts actually discuss their structure, apart from references to forty *seahs* of water (*m. Miqw.* 1:7) and the use of an attached reservoir to help maintain the necessary volume of suitable water (*m. Miqwa'ot* 6). This paired structure is still reflected in modern Jewish practices, but whether it was required in the Second Temple period is debated, especially given the number of single baths found at a site like Sepphoris.

Similarly, it appears that the first Christians were baptized in streams or other available water, after the example of John the Baptist (see Acts 8:36). The earliest known baptismal font was found at Dura Europos, dating to the mid-third century C.E. This font and other early fonts were fairly simple in shape and large enough for full immersion. Over time, Christian fonts became smaller to reflect the shift to infant baptism and more elaborate with various geometric forms and decorations. Given the wide range of functions and the difficulty in using later texts to describe earlier practices, we may never be able to describe the actual practice of ritual washing at the turn of the eras.

BIBLIOGRAPHY

J. KLAWANS 2000, *Impurity and Sin in Ancient Judaism*, Oxford: Oxford University Press. • J. D. LAWRENCE 2006, *Washing in Water: Trajectories of Ritual Bathing in the Hebrew Bible and Second Temple Literature*, Atlanta: Society of Biblical Literature. • P. LARERE 1993, *Baptism in Water and Baptism in the Spirit: A Biblical, Liturgical, and Theological Exposition*, Collegeville, Minn.: Liturgical Press. • J. MAGNESS 2002, *Archaeology of Qumran and the Dead Sea Scrolls*, Grand Rapids: Eerdmans. • J. MILGROM 1991, *Leviticus 1–16: A New Translation with Introduction and Commentary*, New York: Doubleday. • E. P. SANDERS 1992, *Judaism: Practice and Belief: 63 B.C.E.–66 C.E.*, London: SCM. • J. E. TAYLOR 1997, *The Immerser: John the Baptist within Second Temple Judaism*, Grand Rapids: Eerdmans. • A. YARBRO COLLINS 1996, "The Origin of Christian Baptism," in eadem, *Cosmology and Eschatology in Jewish and Christian Apocalypticism*, Leiden: Brill, 218-38.

See also: Conversion and Proselytism; Miqva'ot; Purity and Impurity JONATHAN D. LAWRENCE

Watchers, Book of the (1 Enoch 1–36)

In the opening verses of Genesis 6, one reads the strange story of certain "sons of God" who cohabit with the "daughters of man." Although much about this brief biblical account remains a mystery, the story of these divine beings who intermingled with human women became the fundamental theological paradigm for many Jews of the Second Temple period. The *Book of the Watchers* (*1 Enoch* 1–36) contains the earliest and most extensive elaboration of the "sons of God" story and, in fact, derives its name from its designation of these heavenly beings, "Watchers." This work also tells of the antediluvian patriarch Enoch and his fantastic tours of the mythical world.

Composition and Content

The *Book of the Watchers* is the first work in the larger collection known as the *First Book of Enoch*. The *Book of the Watchers* is itself a composite work, but, in its present form, it is arranged in three major sections: an introduction (chaps. 1–5), the sons of God story (chaps. 6–16), and a description of Enoch's travels (chaps. 17–36). Chapters 1–5 set the stage for the work that follows with a pseudonymous oracle of judgment placed on the lips of the primeval patriarch Enoch. Enoch announces that God will one day appear with his heavenly army to execute judgment on all the wicked of humanity (1:2-9). Unlike nature, which does not deviate from the order God established for it, wicked humanity has strayed from keeping God's commandments (2:1–5:4). Therefore, all humanity will be judged, except for the elect, who will receive forgiveness and salvation (5:5-9).

Chapters 6–16 retell and expand upon the sons of God story of Gen. 6:1-4. In this retelling, two hundred heavenly beings, called "watchers," conspire together to take wives from among the human women and beget children by them (6:1-8). Their leader is a Watcher by the name of Shemihazah. When the Watchers descend,

WATCHERS, BOOK OF THE (1 ENOCH 1–36)

they cause a number of problems for humanity. The children born from their mixed unions with human women are gigantic and have insatiable appetites. Desperate for food, the Watchers' giant offspring resort to eating humans (7:1-5). The Watchers also worsen the human predicament by teaching a number of illicit crafts to humans, including magic and divination (7:1; 8:1-3). One Watcher in particular, Asael, is singled out for introducing humans to metalwork, showing them how to manufacture implements of war, cosmetics, and jewelry (8:1-2). When the earth cries to heaven for relief, the holy ones Michael, Sariel, Raphael, and Gabriel bring the matter before the Most High (9:1-11). The Most High commissions the four holy ones to imprison the sinful Watchers until the final judgment, to destroy all the wicked, including the cannibalistic giants, from the earth, and to restore the earth to its former state of purity and righteousness (10:1–11:2).

Enoch reenters the story at this point and is given the task of informing the Watchers of the judgment against them (12:1–13:3). The Watchers, in return, request that Enoch petition the Lord of heaven for forgiveness on their behalf (13:4-7). Then, in a vision, Enoch is caught up into heaven, where he sees the Great Glory enthroned in the heavenly temple and surrounded by thousands of heavenly attendants (13:8–14:23). The Great Glory commissions Enoch to assure the watchers of their coming doom, explaining that immortal, spiritual beings are not to mix with mortal flesh (14:24–15:7). At this point in the discourse, there appears an etiology of evil spirits. As a result of their mixed, spiritual and fleshly parentage, when the giants' flesh is destroyed, they will continue to exist and create all sorts of ills for humanity in the form of evil spirits (15:8–16:1).

Chapters 17–36 continue the vision account begun in the preceding chapters. In this final section of the book, Enoch, guided by seven archangels, receives a tour of the mythical world. His itinerary includes the prison for disobedient angels (18:10; 19:1; 21:7-10), the holding places for dead humans (22:1-14), the mountain of God and the tree of life (24:2–25:7), the garden of Eden and the tree of wisdom (32:3-6), and, finally, the ends of the earth (33:1–36:3). At the conclusion of his journey, Enoch blesses the Lord of glory who created all of these great and glorious wonders (36:4).

Message

Given the diverse origins of the material which this composite work comprises, identifying one central theme in the *Book of the Watchers* is difficult. Much of the book, however, centers on the promise of an eschatological judgment, in which the righteous will be delivered and the wicked punished. The *Book of the Watchers* opens with a prediction of eschatological judgment (chaps. 1–5). Although the Watcher story (chaps. 6–16) has some clear etiological components, the narrative functions first and foremost as a paradigm for the postdiluvian period. Just as sin multiplied in the days before the flood and the righteous suffered, so at present sin is multiplying and the righteous are suffering. Just as God destroyed the wicked and rewarded the righteous of the flood generation, so God one final time will destroy the wicked and deliver the righteous. (A typological understanding of the flood was shared by several authors of the Second Temple period [e.g., CD 2:17-21; Matt. 24:36-41; 2 Pet. 2:4-5].) Even the journeys of Enoch in the final section of the work (chaps. 17–36) contribute to its end-time thrust. That many of the sights Enoch beholds are of eschatological significance (e.g., the tree of life and the holding places for the dead) would assure the reader of the future that is in store.

The Shemihazah and Asael Narratives

Scholars have long regarded chaps. 6–11 as a distinct unit in the *Book of the Watchers.* Several significant incongruities set this section apart from the material that surrounds it. In addition to the fact that these chapters constitute a self-contained narrative, the figure Enoch, around whom the rest of the work centers, is nowhere to be found in them. Within these chapters, scholars typically further distinguish between two strands of material. The oldest is the Shemihazah narrative. This version of the story has Shemihazah, the Watchers, and their violent children as the culprits. Humanity, in contrast, is merely the victim of the Watchers' sexual immorality and their powerful offspring's violence. The Watchers' corrupt teaching does not figure prominently in this earlier form of the narrative. At a later date, a redactor complicated the story by adding material concerning the watcher Asael. In this later tradition, the Watchers' evil teaching comes to the fore, and humanity is implicated in the antediluvian sin. Through Asael's teaching, humans, not merely Watchers and giants, become violent and sexually immoral.

The *Book of the Watchers* and Genesis 6

Although J. T. Milik hypothesized that the author of Genesis 6:1-4 relied on the story of the divine transgressors found in the *Book of the Watchers* (Milik 1976: 31-32), virtually all scholars hold that the *Book of the Watchers* expands on the biblical account. In the later reworking of the story, the obscure and laconic reference to the "sons of God" who take human wives is filled out with details not provided in the earlier version. The "sons of God" receive names, and the significance of their interaction with humans is made explicit. While Genesis reports these events in a largely neutral manner, the *Book of the Watchers* clearly condemns the Watchers' deed as sin. The later expansion also links the activity of these beings with the flood that follows in the Genesis narrative, though its various literary layers do so in different ways. The Shemihazah narrative explains the flood as a response to the violence perpetrated against humanity by the watchers' children. The Asael narrative, on the other hand, explains the flood as a response as well to the sins of humans. Interestingly, the *Book of the Watchers* contains a third explanation for the flood, which credits it to the sin of Cain in murdering his brother Abel (22:5-7). These various explanations of the flood are not necessarily exclusive of one another, but they represent the diverse interpretive traditions of the various contributors to the book.

Date and Provenance

The pseudepigraphic nature of the *Book of the Watchers* conceals much about the historical situation of its composition. Some of its traditions may be Galilean in origin (Nickelsburg 2001: 65). Scholars agree that the book probably took shape sometime during the third century B.C.E. An Aramaic manuscript of the *Book of the Watchers* dated to the first half of the second century B.C.E. demonstrates that this work had reached its final form by this time (Milik 1976: 25, 140). Some scholars have suggested that a very specific historical reference lies behind the Watcher narrative in the *Book of the Watchers,* such as the wars of the Diadochoi (Nickelsburg 2001: 169-71) or disputes concerning priestly purity (Suter 1979: 115-35). Whether or not such a specific historical situation lies behind the story, the narrative has been crafted in such a way that it can easily be applied to any number of situations (Collins 1982: 97-98).

Language and Transmission

Since the discovery of Aramaic manuscripts of the *Book of the Watchers* among the Dead Sea Scrolls, scholarly consensus has regarded this language as that in which the *Book of the Watchers* was originally composed. Unfortunately, only fragmentary bits of the work were preserved in the caves near Qumran. At some point, perhaps before the turn of the era, the work was translated into Greek (Nickelsburg 2001: 14). A substantial portion of this translation is preserved in the fifth- or sixth-century Codex Panopolitanus (*1 Enoch* 1:1–32:6a) and in the ninth-century chronographic work of George Syncellus, which quotes three excerpts from the *Book of the Watchers* (6:1–9:4; 8:4–10:14; 15:8–16:1). The *Book of the Watchers* was translated from Greek into Classical Ethiopic (Ge'ez) sometime between the fourth and sixth centuries (Knibb 1978: 2:21-22). Only in Ethiopic is the work preserved in its entirety. The earliest copies of this translation, however, date from the fifteenth and sixteenth centuries.

BIBLIOGRAPHY

S. BHAYRO 2005, *The Shemihazah and Asael Narrative of 1 Enoch 6–11,* Münster: Ugarit Verlag. • K. C. BAUTCH 2003, *A Study of the Geography of 1 Enoch 17–19: "No One Has Seen What I Have Seen,"* Leiden: Brill. • M. BLACK 1970, *Apocalypsis Henochi Graece,* Leiden: Brill. • M. BLACK 1985, *The Book of Enoch* or *1 Enoch: A New English Edition with Commentary and Textual Notes,* Leiden: Brill. • G. BOCCACCINI, ED. 2002, *The Origins of Enochic Judaism* (= *Henoch* 24,1-2), Turin: Zamorani. • G. BOCCACCINI AND J. J. COLLINS, EDS. 2007, *The Early Enochic Literature,* Leiden: Brill. • J. J. COLLINS 1982, "The Apocalyptic Technique: Setting and Function in the Book of the Watchers," *CBQ* 44: 91-111. • D. DIMANT 1978, "1 Enoch 6–11: A Methodological Perspective," *SBLSP* 13, ed. P. Achtemeier, Missoula: Scholars Press, 1:323-39. • P. D. HANSON 1977, "Rebellion in Heaven, Azazel, and Euhermeristic Heroes in 1 Enoch 6–11," *JBL* 96: 195-233. • M. A. KNIBB 1978, *The Ethiopic Book of Enoch: A New Edition in the Light of the Aramaic Dead Sea Fragments,* 2 vols., Oxford: Oxford University Press. • J. T. MILIK 1976, *The Books of Enoch: Aramaic Fragments of Qumrân Cave 4,* Oxford: Oxford University Press. • C. A. NEWSOM 1980, "The Development of *1 Enoch* 6–19: Cosmology and Judgment," *CBQ* 42: 310-29. • G. W. E. NICKELSBURG 1977, "Apocalyptic and Myth in 1 Enoch 6–11," *JBL* 96: 383-405. • G. W. E. NICKELSBURG 2001, *1 Enoch 1: A Commentary of the Book of 1 Enoch Chapters 1–36; 81–108,* Minneapolis: Fortress. • G. W. E. NICKELSBURG AND J. C. VANDERKAM 2004, *1 Enoch: A New Translation,* Minneapolis: Fortress. • D. W. SUTER 1979, "Fallen Angel, Fallen Priest: The Problem of Family Purity in 1 Enoch 6–16," *HUCA* 50: 115-35.

RYAN E. STOKES

Wealth and Poverty

The use of the words "wealth" and "poverty" depends on the social systems in which they occur and on the social location of a particular author. In the world of the Bible and early Judaism, being wealthy or poor involved more than just economic dimensions. It involved political and social aspects as well, since the poor were also generally politically powerless and socially marginalized. In addition, these aspects were interconnected with religious thought. Theological dimensions found in the Hebrew Bible lay the groundwork for the developments in Second Temple texts.

The Hebrew Bible

As background to developments in the Second Temple period, there are two different approaches to wealth and poverty in the Hebrew Bible that merit attention. The first operates on the idea of retributive justice, in which wealth is a sign of God's blessing and poverty is characterized as the consequence of immoral or unwise behavior. Although the most cogent representative of this view is the book of Proverbs (e.g., 10:4, 22), the idea surfaces in other writings as well (e.g., 1 Sam. 2:7). However, later writers in the sapiential tradition began to question the adequacy of this explanation (Eccl. 9:15-16).

The second approach to wealth and poverty is closely associated with the idea that goods are limited and therefore the rich have attained their wealth at the expense of the poor. In this view, providing social justice for the poor is a necessary corrective. It is particularly prominent in legal and prophetic passages but can also be found in wisdom writings. In conjunction with the exodus tradition, YHWH is understood as the defender and advocate of the poor (e.g., Exod. 22:20; Lev. 25:35-55; Prov. 14:31; 17:5). In Deutero-Isaiah and Zephaniah, poverty begins to be applied to Israel typologically as she looks for a "new exodus" from her oppressors (Isa. 41:17; Zeph. 3:12).

Over time this second view came into greater prominence. In the Psalms the poor *(ʿănāwîm)* represent YHWH's faithful people and anticipate their vindication (9:13; 147:6; 149:4; cf. 1QH 2:31-33; 5:13-22), and in Deutero-Zechariah poverty in the sense of humility is a characteristic of the messianic king (Zech. 9:9).

Second Temple Literature

Social Location and Socioeconomic Rhetoric

An important influence on a given work's rhetoric of

wealth and poverty is the social location of the author, as can be illustrated from a comparison of *1 Enoch* and Sirach. The *Epistle of Enoch* (*1 Enoch* 92–105) reflects a marginalized social setting and attacks the rich for unjustly oppressing the poor. The author acknowledges that some might conclude that riches are a reward for righteousness but then proceeds to attack this view (96:4). Throughout the *Epistle* the rich are always and only associated with wicked oppressors of the righteous (96:4-8; 97:7–98:4; 102:4-9; 103:5-15). Although the righteous are never called "poor," they are clearly the objects of the oppression of the wealthy. In order to compensate for this breakdown in retributive justice, the author appeals to the idea of divine judgment whereby there will be a great socioeconomic reversal in the afterlife. In the *Apocalypse of Weeks* (*1 Enoch* 91:11-17; 93:1-10) this hope is transposed into an apocalyptic temporal dualism so that in the new world order the correlation between wealth and righteousness found in the model of retributive justice will be reestablished.

Ben Sira, who was a member of the retainer class of the Jerusalem elite, had a more complicated view of wealth. On the one hand, wealth and poverty are part of the created order and operate under God's providence (Sir. 11:14; cf. Prov. 22:2). Wealth is functionally neutral and is considered a good thing if acquired rightly (Sir. 13:24; 31:8-11), and it should be enjoyed (14:3-19). Sin and foolishness can lead to poverty (18:30–19:1). Wealth can also function positively as a symbol of the surpassing value of wisdom/fear of God, health, or friendship (1:16-17; 7:18-19; 30:14-16; 40:25-27; cf. Prov. 8:18-21; Wis. 7:8-13; 4Q185; 4Q525). On the other hand, Ben Sira is well aware that retributive justice is not always or consistently reflected in social reality (Sir. 13:1-23; 31:1-7). It is possible to be righteous and poor, either because the student is being tested (2:1-9) or because justice has been providentially delayed (11:20-28). Thus Ben Sira is also an advocate of social justice (34:21-27) and affirms that God is particularly close to the poor (4:1-10; 21:5; 35:14-26). In the meantime, those who are righteous and poor are compensated with the alternative currency of honor (10:19–11:6), especially that associated with an enduring good name (41:6-13).

Heavenly Treasuries

On the conviction that there was a particularly close relationship between YHWH and the poor, there developed a triangular theological construct whereby the poor person functioned as a proxy for YHWH. Proverbs 19:17 had stated that whoever gives to the poor has loaned to God, and He will repay. This concept, in conjunction with the lexical development of *ṣedāqāh ṣidqāh* in Hebrew and Aramaic meaning "almsgiving," became highly significant in the understanding of the functionality of wealth during the Second Temple period. By giving to the poor or engaging in other meritorious acts, one was essentially making a deposit in one's heavenly treasury. This heavenly wealth shows up in a variety of texts with different functions. In both Tobit and Sirach, the deposit provides future deliverance from death or trouble (Tob. 4:5-11; Sir. 29:8-13; cf. 1 Tim. 6:18-19). Likewise, in Tobit, Sirach, and Daniel, almsgiving substitutes for sacrifice and thus can have atoning benefits (Tob. 4:11; Sir. 3:30; 35:1-4; Dan. 4:24), though it is useless when accompanied by acts of social injustice (Sir. 34:21-27; cf. *T. Ash.* 2:5-7).

In the New Testament the notion of a heavenly treasury occurs in several places and can refer to rewards or punishments in this life or in the hereafter (Matt. 6:19-21; 19:21; Jas. 5:3; 1 Pet. 1:4). The triangular construct between the giver, the poor, and God/Christ also underlies passages such as Matt. 25:31-46 and Phil. 4:18-19.

Theological Use of Poverty and Wealth

Through a fusion of the themes of God's special relationship with the poor, the breakdown of the model of retributive justice, and the socially marginalized location of certain authors, some texts reflect metaphorical understandings of wealth and poverty that transcended socioeconomic issues. This understanding is especially prominent in the Dead Sea Scrolls. While some texts still speak of the poor as a socioeconomic group (e.g., CD 6:14-22; 14:14), others use "the poor" in a more religious-communal sense. In the *War Scroll* they are the ones whom God will avenge (1QM 11:13; 13:12-14), and the pesher on Psalm 37 refers to the "congregation of the poor ones," a phrase best understood as a self-designation of the Qumran sect (4QpPs^{a} 1–10 ii 10; cf. 1QpHab 12:3-6). Likewise, in 4QInstruction there is a connection between the addressee's poverty and his elect status. This is not a spiritualized, idealized view of poverty insofar as it is still grounded in socioeconomic marginalization and in need of reversal. As is evident from *1 Enoch,* the correlation between poverty and the righteous on the one hand and wealth and the wicked on the other is most clear in apocalyptic texts from socially marginalized groups who yearned for the cataclysmic intervention of God to set right the present social order (cf. *T. Jud.* 25:4; *Pss. Sol.* 10:5-8; 16:13-15).

The New Testament also uses the notions of poverty and wealth in metaphorical ways. Most notable is the reference to the "poor in spirit" in Matthew's version of Jesus' Beatitudes (5:3), which applies the neediness and dependence characteristic of the poor to the disposition of the messianic community. There are also several references in the New Testament to being "rich in faith" (1 Cor. 4:8; 2 Cor. 6:10; 8:9; Jas. 2:5; Rev. 2:9; 3:18).

BIBLIOGRAPHY

G. ANDERSON 2007, "Redeem Your Sins by the Giving of Alms: Sin, Debt, and the 'Treasury of Merit' in Early Jewish and Christian Tradition," *Letter and Spirit* 3: 37-67. • L. HOPPE 2004, *There Shall Be No Poor among You: Poverty in the Bible,* Nashville: Abingdon. • B. MALINA 1987, "Wealth and Poverty in the New Testament and Its World," *Int* 41: 354-67. • C. MURPHY 2001, *Wealth in the Dead Sea Scrolls and in the Qumran Community,* Leiden: Brill. • G. W. E. NICKELSBURG 1998, "Revisiting the Rich and the Poor in *1 Enoch* 92–105 and the Gospel According to Luke," *SBLSP* 37: 579-605. • B. WRIGHT 2004, "The Categories of Rich and Poor in the

Qumran Sapiential Literature," in *Sapiential Perspectives: Wisdom Literature in Light of the Dead Sea Scrolls,* ed. J. J. Collins et al., Leiden: Brill, 101-23. • B. WRIGHT AND C. CAMP 2001, "'Who Has Been Tested by Gold and Found Perfect?' Ben Sira's Discourse of Riches and Poverty," *Henoch* 23: 153-73.

BRADLEY GREGORY

Weeks, Apocalypse of → Enoch, Epistle of

Weeks, Festival of → Festivals and Holy Days

Wicked and Holy (4Q181)

The Qumran text 4Q181 is a fragmentary work that develops a series of contrasts between wicked and righteous beings, both angelic and human, in the time of the flood and at the end of the age. It is written in the style, vocabulary, and thought peculiar to the writings stemming from the Qumran community and was copied in the last third of the first century B.C.E.

4Q181 has survived in three fragments, two legible ones of medium size and a tiny piece with only one letter visible. The fragment numbered 1 by Allegro comes from the upper section of the column. This column was obviously preceded by another, not preserved except for a single surviving letter from the end of the top line. Thus frg. 1 cannot have stood at the beginning of the manuscript. It is rather frg. 2, with its large margin, that comes from the first column of the scroll and forms the opening of the work.

This datum sheds light on the nature and position of the first four lines in frg. 1, which introduce the composition. These lines allude to the angels that sired giants from mortal women, an episode told in Gen. 6:1-4. Genesis 6:4 is, in fact, cited in abbreviated form in line 2. Lines 1-4 closely resemble and are partly identical to 4Q180 frg. 1 lines 5, 8-9. This resemblance led J. T. Milik to argue that 4Q180 and 4Q181 are copies of the same work. He therefore produced a composite text combining the two manuscripts. Several recent editions adopt his view and his composite edition (e.g., Puech 1987; Roberts 1995). However, the similar lines in the two texts are not entirely identical, nor can the corresponding lines in 4Q180 be easily fitted into 4Q181 to create a single text. Further, the position of the biblical episode in the two manuscripts is different. In 4Q180 the episode is well integrated into the coherent thematic and stylistic sequence of the pesher on the historical periods. In 4Q181, by contrast, the episode is dissimilar both thematically and stylistically to the other surviving sections of the manuscript. A plausible explanation for this situation would therefore be that 4Q181 cites one section of 4Q180. Alternatively, both 4Q180 and 4Q181 may depend on a third source describing the well-known biblical episode, which was the object of keen interest among the Qumran sectaries.

The sinful angels and giants described at the beginning of the work seem to serve as the paradigm for evildoers. The following phrases about God's mighty and wondrous works (frg. 2 lines 5-10) may suggest that the evil brought about by their misdeeds was justly punished by annihilation in the flood. The sin of the angels may be referred to again in the next fragment's emphasis on the impurity caused by the "iniquity of men" (frg. 1 line 1), which will be brought to end (frg. 1 line 3). Thus frg. 1 lines 1-2 may also apply to the events connected with the flood. However, the description in frg. 1 is formulated in language that would apply equally well to the wicked of the last generations and their final judgment and destruction. That these final circumstances are also meant here becomes clear from the following depiction, which contrasts the punishment and destruction of sinners (frg. 1 lines 1-2) with the clearly eschatological reward awaiting the righteous, everlasting life in the company of angels (frg. 1 lines 3-6).

The clear eschatological overtones of both the punishment of sinners and the reward of the righteous (frg. 1 lines 3-6) may be connected with the reference to a period of seventy weeks of years mentioned at the beginning of the work (frg. 2 line 3). This number is incorporated into the passage about the sinful angels and significantly is not mentioned in the parallel section of 4Q180 frg. 1 lines 5-9. Since the number is introduced in a context describing iniquity, it may refer to the final historical period of evil (cf., e.g., Dan. 9:24-27; *1 Enoch* 89:39–90:19) or to the entire sequence of history calculated in units of weeks and years (cf., e.g., *1 Enoch* 11:12; the *Apocalypse of Weeks* [*1 Enoch* 91:11-17; 93:1-10]; and the so-called *Pesher on the Apocalypse of Weeks* [4Q247]).

The wicked against whom the author levels his strictures may belong to the apostates of Israel. If so, their iniquity is comparable to that of the evil angels and giants. Such a parallelism would account for the similarity in vocabulary and tone between the depiction of the angels in frg. 2 line 4 and the reference to the evildoers' iniquity and their punishment in frg. 1 lines 1-2. The reward of the righteous described in the following passage (frg. 1 lines 3-6) may then refer to the elect among the people of Israel, although this is not explicitly stated. The link between the generation that perished in the flood and the wicked of the end time echoes a widespread analogy drawn in early Jewish writings between the primordial catastrophe and the eschatological judgment (cf., e.g., *1 Enoch* 10:11-22; 93:4; 91:14; Luke 17:26).

Another remarkable aspect of 4Q181 that clearly distinguishes it from 4Q180 is the particular affinity it displays to specific formulations and ideas of the *Hodayot*. Of particular interest is the striking resemblance of the formulation in 4Q181 frg. 1 lines 3-4 to several unique expressions in the so-called *Self-Glorification Hymn* (cf. 4Q491 frg. 11 col. i line 14; 4Q471b frg. 1 line 1). These affinities suggest that 4Q181 belongs to a genre close to that of the *Hodayot*. In the light of such literary features, lines 1-4 of frg. 2 appear to stand out in style and in subject matter alike, and must therefore quote another source, perhaps 4Q180 or a similar text.

BIBLIOGRAPHY

J. M. ALLEGRO 1969, *Qumran Cave 4. I (4Q158-4Q186)*, DJD 5, Oxford: Clarendon, 77-79 (pl. XXVII). • D. DIMANT 1979, "The 'Pesher on the Periods' (4Q180) and 4Q181," *IOS* 9: 77-102. • R. V. HUGGINS 1992, "A Canonical 'Book of Periods' at Qumran?" *RevQ* 15: 421-36. • J. T. MILIK 1972, "*Milkî-ṣedeq* et *Milkî-rešaʿ* dans les anciens écrits juifs et chrétiens," *JJS* 23: 95-144. • J. T. MILIK 1976, *The Books of Enoch*, Oxford: Clarendon, 248-52. • É. PUECH 1987, "Notes sur le manuscrit de XIQMelkîṣédeq," *RevQ* 12: 483-513. • É. PUECH 1993, *La Croyance des esséniens en la vie future*, 2 vols., Paris: Gabalda, 2: 526-29. • J. J. M. ROBERTS 1995, "Wicked and Holy (4Q180–4Q181)," in *The Dead Sea Scrolls: Hebrew, Aramaic, and Greek Texts with English Translations*, vol. 2, *Damascus Document, War Scroll, and Related Documents*, ed. J. H. Charlesworth, Tübingen: Mohr-Siebeck; Louisville: Westminster John Knox, 204-13. • J. STRUGNELL 1970, "Notes en marge du volume V des 'Discoveries in the Judaean Desert of Jordan,'" *RevQ* 7: 252-54. • M. O. WISE, M. G. ABEGG, AND E. M. COOK 2005, *The Dead Sea Scrolls: A New Translation*, 2d ed., San Francisco: Harper, 209-10.

See also: Pesher on the Periods (4Q180)

DEVORAH DIMANT

Wicked Priest → Pesharim

Wilderness

Literally and symbolically, the wilderness has been an important backdrop for the development of Jewish identity. From the early biblical narratives, frequently set in the wilderness, to Second Temple literature, the wilderness becomes a theologically charged image, (re)used and thematized by various Jewish groups.

Defining Wilderness

The "wilderness" (Hebr. *midbār;* cf. *ʿărābâ;* Gr. *erēmos*) generally describes an uninhabited region (1 Macc. 3:45; Philo, *Mos.* 1.167), but frequently it connotes an arid environment, hostile to human habitation and cultivation (*Mos.* 1.192) and therefore is synonymous with "desert." In geographical references, *midbār* occurs before other place names ("Wilderness of Zin," Num. 13:21; "Wilderness of Paran," Gen. 21:21; "Wilderness of Sinai," Exod. 19:1; etc.). In postbiblical texts, the designation *midbār* alone almost always refers to the Judean Wilderness, bounded on the east by the Dead Sea (Judg. 1:16; Matt. 3:1).

Wilderness as Biblical Motif

Later writers draw heavily on biblical motifs of the wilderness, both as time (the "wandering" period) and place. For instance, the wilderness is the setting of many patriarchal/matriarchal narratives, and most notably, this landscape hosts the formative events of the exodus from Egypt and the giving of the Law at Mt. Sinai. Because of this association, some early scholars found Israelite religion to be essentially a desert cult that later idealized the nomadic way of life. The characterization of Israel as practicing a desert religion has been contested (Talmon 1966), but the desert is associated with key events in Israelite history, and, as such, symbolized for later Jewish writers rebellion, hardship, and preparation, as well as divine providence and revelation.

The Wilderness as a Place of Rebellion and Danger

During the "wandering period," the wilderness forms the backdrop for Israel's murmuring (Exod. 16:2) and rebellion (Num. 27:14), including the subsequent punishment of forty years in the desert (Num. 14:32-33; cf. Job 12:24; Ps. 106:26; Ezra 20). This era becomes the time of Israel's sinfulness *par excellence*, both in the Bible (e.g., Exod. 16:2; Numbers 14, 16; Deut. 9:7; Ezra 20; Psalm 78) and in later texts, where Israel's ordeal was understood to be God punishing the Israelites for their unfaithfulness (e.g., Acts 7:36-40) or testing and teaching them in the desert (Philo, *Congr.* 1.165, 170; 1QM 1:3; Heb. 3:8-10).

The wilderness is a dreadful place, a windy, "howling waste" (Deut. 32:10; Job 1:19) with "poisonous snakes and scorpions" devoid of human habitation (Deut. 8:15; Philo, *Alleg. Interp.* 2.84). Later traditions also note that it is an unpredictable place where wild animals live and beasts threaten or brigands may attack (Sir. 8:16; 13:19). Frequently, then, the wilderness is associated with chaos, those forces threatening to undo creation and civilization, for it always threatens to overtake cities and choke out cultivated vines and vegetation (cf. Isa. 5:6; Zeph. 2:9).

Later writers rework this wilderness motif to mean metaphorically a "trackless" place of chaotic lawlessness, where God is not known (Wis. 5:7; 11:2); others find it to be the symbol of desolation or even spiritual emptiness, as Jerusalem herself becomes a "wilderness" according to the Scrolls (1QM 1:3; 4Q179; cf. Luke 21:20; Matt. 24:15; Mark 13:14). In light of the Greek persecutions, 1 Maccabees figuratively describes Jerusalem "as a wilderness" (3:45), whose sanctuary became "desolate like a desert" (1:39).

Wilderness as Liminal Space

The wilderness is also the natural habitation of demons and spirits, such as Lilith and satyrs (Isa. 13:21; 34:14; cf. Matt. 12:43; Luke 8:29). Azazel, an old desert deity (cf. the scapegoat ritual in Lev. 16:10, 22), is a full-fledged demonic being in later literature (*1 Enoch*, Ethiopic text, 8:1; 9:6; 10:4-8; *Apoc. Abr.* 13:6-14; 14:4-6; 20:5-7; etc.). Yet while closer to the chaotic forces and otherworldly beings, this place is at the same time closer to God, a liminal space of permeability between heaven and earth where one may be allowed closer access to the divine.

Redeeming Aspects of the Wilderness

Some prophetic traditions remember the wilderness wandering period as the golden age, or honeymoon period, when Israel was joined to YHWH with marital devotion (Jer. 2:2-3; Hos. 2:14-15). These texts, as well as the related idea that those living in the wilderness are closer to God and are forced to trust in God's provision, were catalysts for others who found the desert to be an ideal place to practice piety (e.g., 4Q434; 4Q504; cf. Philo, *Alleg. Interp.* 1.34; *Mos.* 1.225). As it was for some later Christians, the wilderness could be a place of self-denial and fasting, where one could avoid the tumult of the city and the temptation to sin (Philo, *Sacrifices* 1.50; *Decalogue* 1.2). For some, the desert was where one could communicate with God, particularly in the context of efficacious prayer (Najman 2006).

In the biblical narratives, the wilderness was frequently the place of divine self-revelation (Isa. 40:3; cf. Moses, Elijah, Hagar, etc.) and was the setting of the greatest revelatory event: the giving of the Law at Sinai. The latter paradigmatic event probably encouraged those at Qumran, among others, to thematize the desert as the ideal access point for divine (self)-revelation. Later, some rabbis conclude that the wilderness is the symbol of universalism and therefore the ideal place for God's revelation. It is no-man's-land, and equally it is everyman's land; therefore, the Torah was given here so that all of the nations could have a portion of it (*Mekilta Baḥodesh* 1).

Wilderness in the Dead Sea Scrolls

As their many legal and exegetical texts suggest, the authors of the Dead Sea Scrolls were a pious group who avidly studied Scripture. As such, it is no surprise that the Qumran community sought the desert as a backdrop where they could seek piety and divine revelation. Whether they withdrew to the wilderness by choice or by necessity, they interpreted their move to be divinely inspired, drawing on the predictive language of Isa. 40:3, "In the wilderness prepare the way of the LORD" (1QS 8:13-16; 9:19b; 4Q176 frg. 1 lines 5-9; cf. John the Baptist in Mark 1 and pars.). The sectarians may have even chosen the particular site at Qumran based on the prediction in Ezekiel 47 where a verdant river was said to flow from the new Temple into the Dead Sea (VanderKam 1999: 162).

The authors of the scrolls appropriate and reconfigure many thematic usages of the wilderness found elsewhere. The *Damascus Document* recalls the negative associations of the wilderness generation, who "murmured in their tents" and were judged by God "face to face" (CD 3:7-9; cf. 1QM 1:3; Ezek. 20:35-38); accordingly, Talmon labels the wilderness in the Scrolls, as in the Bible, as a negative motif, associated with punishment and transition (Talmon 1966). Yet elsewhere the sectarians celebrate God's provision in the wilderness (4Q504 frg. 6 lines 6-8) and even identify with the Israelites by describing themselves in the language of Exodus (18:21-22; cf. CD 13:1; 1QS 2:21-22). Like those at Sinai, the sectarians understood themselves to be the recipients of divine revelation, guided by a Moses-like leader, the Teacher of Righteousness. As the "(re)turnees/penitents of the wilderness" (4Q171 frg. 3 line 1), they may have played on the words "to return" and "to repent" to suggest that by returning to the wilderness they could redeem the very disobedience of the earlier wilderness generation (cf. 1QS 8:8-10; Schofield 2008). At the very least, they must have viewed the desert to be an ideal place to abide by their stringent purity laws and live a life devoted to study and prayer.

The Historical/Classical Sources

Historically, the wilderness served as a place of refuge, as it was for Elijah and David. During the political tumult of Second Temple times, "many who were seeking righteousness and justice went down to the wilderness to live there . . . because troubles pressed heavily upon them" (1 Macc. 2:29-30). The desert was a refuge for the Maccabees themselves (1 Macc. 2:31; 9:33, 62; 2 Macc. 5:27). Josephus also notes that the wilderness was where "deceivers and imposters, under the pretence of divine inspiration . . . persuaded the multitude to act like madmen, and led them out into the desert under the belief that God would give them tokens of deliverance" (*J.W.* 2.259; cf. *Ant.* 20.97, 188; *J.W.* 2.252-65; 1 Macc. 2:31).

For Philo, the wilderness was a place of spiritual refuge. He idealizes it as the home of the Therapeutae, a pious group of Jews who avoided the tumult of the city and dwelt in a desert place (*Contempl. Life* 1.19-20). Not unlike the Essenes, they fled "the ungodliness among town-dwellers" where there is ill for body and soul (*Good Person*). He himself speaks of withdrawing into the desert to ponder lofty things (*Alleg. Interp.* 2.85; *Decalogue* 10; cf. Nikiprowetzky 1996). For Philo, as for his contemporaries, the wilderness functioned as an almost mythical place, one of both physical and spiritual refuge.

BIBLIOGRAPHY

G. BROOKE 1994, "Isaiah 40:3 and the Wilderness Community," in *New Qumran Texts and Studies,* ed. G. Brooke and F. García Martínez, Leiden: Brill, 117-32. • R. W. FUNK 1959, "The Wilderness," *JBL* 78: 205-14. • H. NAJMAN 2006, "Towards a Study of the Uses of the Concept of the Wilderness in Ancient Judaism," *DSD* 13: 99-113. • V. NIKIPROWETZKY 1996, "Le thème du desert chez Philon d'Alexandrie," in idem, *Études philoniennes,* Paris: Cerf, 293-308. • A. SCHOFIELD 2008, "The Wilderness Motif in the Dead Sea Scrolls," in *Israel in the Wilderness: Interpretations of the Biblical Narratives in Jewish and Christian Tradition,* ed. K. E. Pomykala, Leiden: Brill, 37-53. • D. SCHWARTZ 1992, "Temple and Desert: On Religion and State in Second Temple Period Judea," in idem, *Studies in the Jewish Background of Christianity,* Tübingen: Mohr-Siebeck, 29-43. • S. TALMON 1966, "The 'Desert' Motif in the Bible and in Qumran Literature," in *Biblical Motifs,* ed. A. Altmann, Cambridge: Harvard University Press, 31-64. • J. C. VANDERKAM 1999, "The Judean Desert and the Community of the Dead Sea Scrolls," in *Antikes Judentum und Frühes Christentum: Festschrift für Hartmut Stegemann zum 65. Geburtstag,* ed. B. Kollmann et al., Berlin: de Gruyter, 159-71.

ALISON SCHOFIELD

Wisdom (Personified)

The roots of Wisdom's personification in Second Temple Judaism lie in a number of OT passages, especially in Proverbs. Because the Hebrew word for "wisdom," *ḥokmâ,* is feminine, Wisdom is invariably a woman. She is depicted as a preacher of the truth, more precious than earthly valuables, and, having been the first creation, she is then an assistant to God in the rest of creation (Prov. 8:1-11, 22-31). Job 28 by contrast emphasizes her inaccessibility.

Ben Sira 24 and Bar. 3:9–4:4 are important early expansions of her *curriculum vitae.* According to the former, she indwells the whole world (Sir. 24:3-6). However, Adam did not truly know her (24:28), and she is associated particularly closely with Israel (24:8). As such, she is in some sense identified with the Torah (24:23). She also serves in the Tabernacle (24:10), and so has a priestly role such that the high priest loosely embodies her in his service (Sirach 50). Baruch continues in the same vein, associating Wisdom with the Torah (Bar. 3:9; 4:1). The dominant emphasis, however, is on her inaccessibility or humanity's willful ignorance of her (3:15, 29-31). The *Similitudes of Enoch* similarly emphasize her rejection by humanity: "Wisdom found no place in which she could dwell, and her dwelling was in heaven. Wisdom went out in order to dwell among the sons of men, but did not find a dwelling; Wisdom returned to her place and took her seat in the midst of the angels" (*1 Enoch* 42:1-2; trans. Knibb).

Her most extensive characterization comes in the Wisdom of Solomon. The traditional motifs of her role in creation (Wis. 9:9) and her encompassing of all knowledge (9:11; cf. 8:2) are present. She also plays an important part in biblical history: she preserved Adam after his transgression (10:1), helped Noah steer the ark (10:4), rescued Lot (10:6), and even delivered the Israelites from Egypt (10:13), thus playing a similar role to that of the angel of the LORD in some literature (e.g., Exod. 14:19; 23:20). She is also, as in other places, the inspirer or sender of the prophets (Wis. 7:27; cf. Luke 11:49-51). Her principal function in the Wisdom of Solomon is probably as giver of immortality (Wis. 8:13, 17). Particularly interesting is the description of her nature, and the way the book relates her attributes to her functions. She never fades or fails (6:12; 7:14) and is "more mobile than all motion, and passes and moves through all things on account of her purity" (7:24). In relation to God, she is "the breath of the power of God, and an emanation of the pure glory of the almighty" (7:25), the effulgence, image, and mirror of his glory and goodness (7:26). She is omnipotent by virtue of the simplicity of her essence and has the power to renew creation because of her self-existence (7:27). Wisdom is a holy spirit *(pneuma)* that "holds all things together," like the Stoic Logos. The analogies with the Stoic Logos are especially evident in the list of the attributes of Wisdom in 7:22b-24.

In the Mishnah and Talmud, we see more continuity with the themes of Ben Sira. In *m. 'Abot* 6:10, Wisdom is identified with Torah (Prov. 8:22 is cited here). Elsewhere she is its source, since she has, in an interpretation of Prov. 9:1, "hewn out the seven pillars" of the Torah (*b. Šabbat* 116a; Numbers is divided into three books in this context).

A good deal of New Testament scholarship has seen Jesus portrayed as Wisdom incarnate (e.g., Burnett 1979). Matthew's Gospel is regarded as particularly important here (Matt. 11:19, 25-30; 23:34-39), as is Paul (1 Cor. 8:6; Col. 1:15-20). However, in general the New Testament uses wisdom motifs without a straightforward identification of Jesus with wisdom. The presentation of Jesus as the Logos, in the prologue of the Gospel of John, is at least indirectly indebted to the traditional depictions of personified Wisdom, in view of the identification of Wisdom with the Logos/Pneuma in the Wisdom of Solomon.

Lady Wisdom went on to have an extensive career in Gnostic literature. Her "fall" was an integral part of many systems (e.g., Irenaeus, *Against Heresies* 1.2.2; 1.29.4), and in some works there is an explicitly evil Sophia, "the Sophia of death" (*Gospel of Philip* 60, 12), or "corruptible Sophia" (*Gospel of Judas* 44, 4). It is questionable, however, whether any of this goes back to pre- or non-Christian Judaism.

There is considerable debate within scholarship as to whether Wisdom is ever regarded in early Judaism as a power or person in her own right, or whether she is rather a literary motif. The dominant view is probably the latter, though the Wisdom of Solomon contains language that is perhaps open to being read as suggesting that Lady Wisdom has become a hypostasis of some sort; the "emanation" language in Wis. 7:25 and her redemptive activity in chap. 10 may be the strongest evidence.

BIBLIOGRAPHY

F. W. BURNETT 1979, *The Testament of Jesus-Sophia: A Redaction-Critical Study of the Eschatological Discourse in Matthew,* Washington, D.C.: University Press of America, 1979. • J. J. COLLINS 1997, *Jewish Wisdom in the Hellenistic Age,* Louisville: Westminster John Knox. • H. VON LIPS 1990, *Weisheitliche Traditionen im Neuen Testament,* Neukirchen: Neukirchener Verlag. • R. E. MURPHY 1995, "The Personification of Wisdom," in *Wisdom in Ancient Israel: Essays in Honour of J. A. Emerton,* ed. J. Day et al., Cambridge: Cambridge University Press, 222-33. • A. M. SINNOTT 2005, *The Personification of Wisdom,* Aldershot: Ashgate. • G. C. STEAD 1969, "The Valentinian Myth of Sophia," *JTS* 20: 75-104.

SIMON J. GATHERCOLE

Wisdom Literature

Wisdom literature is a category used to classify a wide range of texts from the ancient Near East. Wisdom (or sapiential) writings are often composed by teachers for students. These writings typically instill a desire to acquire knowledge and an understanding of the world so that one can make sound judgments and lead a successful and fulfilling life. Sapiential literature contains practical advice regarding ordinary spheres of activity such as marriage and finances.

WISDOM LITERATURE

Biblical Texts

Five documents constitute the biblical corpus of Jewish wisdom literature: Proverbs, Job, Ecclesiastes, the Wisdom of Solomon, and Ben Sira. Of these five, the last two deuterocanonical works are early Jewish compositions. Ben Sira's instruction is dated to around 175 B.C.E. on the basis of the prologue to its Greek translation, which was done by his grandson, who reports that he moved to Egypt in 132 B.C.E. The Wisdom of Solomon is often dated to around the turn of the Common Era. It was probably composed in Alexandria, Egypt, and may have been written during the reign of the Roman emperor Caligula (37-41 C.E.).

Ben Sira and Wisdom of Solomon

Ben Sira and the Wisdom of Solomon have traditionally been almost the only available Jewish wisdom texts from the late Second Temple period. One could also appeal to Bar. 3:9–4:4, which associates wisdom with the Torah. For early Jewish sapiential literature written in Greek in a Diaspora context, the Wisdom of Solomon remains the core evidence at our disposal. The differences between the Greek translation of Ben Sira and its Hebrew original can also shed light on the Jewish sapiential tradition in its broader Hellenistic setting. The sayings of Pseudo-Phocylides, a Hellenistic Jewish composition which contains ethical advice and practical instruction, can be related to the wisdom tradition as well (Collins 1997).

Dead Sea Scrolls

Before the discovery of the Dead Sea Scrolls, Ben Sira was the only extant Palestinian wisdom text from the late Second Temple era written in Hebrew. (Several Hebrew manuscripts of this work were discovered in a synagogue in Cairo in the late nineteenth century.) The Dead Sea Scrolls contain fragments of several compositions often considered to be wisdom texts: 4QInstruction (1Q26; 4Q415-418, 423), the book of Mysteries (1Q27; 4Q299-301), 4QWiles of the Wicked Woman (4Q184), 4QSapiential Work (4Q185), 4QWords of the Maskil (4Q298), 4QWays of Righteousness (4Q420-421), 4QInstruction-like Composition B (4Q424), and 4QBeatitudes (4Q525). The Scrolls include other works that can be related to the wisdom tradition, such as the "Treatise on the Two Spirits," which is part of the *Community Rule* (1QS 3:13–4:26).

Diversity in Forms, Ideas, and Themes

The wisdom texts from Qumran indicate that there was more diversity within the early Jewish sapiential tradition than previously realized. These compositions contain a variety of forms, ideas, and themes. The Qumran wisdom texts confirm some sapiential developments that are evident from Ben Sira and the Wisdom of Solomon. Others that one would expect based on these two texts are either not found or are muted in the Qumran material. The Torah, apocalypticism, and piety are important issues in the sapiential tradition during the late Second Temple period.

Several aspects of early Jewish wisdom are in continuity with the traditional wisdom of Proverbs. Like sapiential literature in general, that of early Judaism is pedagogical and eudaemonistic. The wisdom texts of this period contain exhortations that urge one to acquire knowledge (e.g., Sir. 6:32-37; 4Q298 3-4 ii 3-6). 4Q185 and 4Q525 encourage the pursuit of wisdom, and Proverbs, Ben Sira, and the Wisdom of Solomon have the same general goal. Some of the early Jewish sapiential texts offer practical instruction on common-sense topics that is consistent with Proverbs 10–31. 4Q424 describes unreliable people who should not be hired. 4QInstruction considers indebtedness a serious problem, as does Proverbs (e.g., 4Q416 2 ii 4-6; 4Q417 2 ii 18-27; Prov. 6:3-4). Proper speech and filial piety are prominent topics in both early Jewish and older wisdom (for the former, see Sir. 11:7-8; 4Q525 14 ii 18-28; for the latter, 4Q416 2 iii 15-19; Sir. 3:1-16).

In terms of form, there are connections between early Jewish wisdom and older sapiential traditions. Ben Sira and 4QWords of the Maskil to All Sons of Dawn are instructions written by teachers for students (e.g., Sir. 24:33-34; 4Q298 1-2 i 1), and 4QBeatitudes is written for people in training to become teachers of some sort (4Q525 14 ii 16-18). The "Treatise on the Two Spirits" is also an instruction (1QS 3:13; cf. 4Q418 81 17; 4Q418 221 2-3). The early Jewish wisdom texts contain sequences of admonitions, as in 4Q416 2 ii 14-21 and Sir. 8:1-19. Many passages in Ben Sira and the Wisdom of Solomon include didactic poetry in the tradition of Proverbs 1–9, and 4QSapiential Work and 4QBeatitudes contain similar material. 4Q185 and 4Q525 use the beatitude form to praise wisdom, as does Ben Sira and Proverbs (4Q185 1-2 ii 8-12; 4Q525 2 ii + 3 1-6; Sir. 14:20; Prov. 3:13).

Wisdom Personified

The theme of wisdom personified as a woman is an important element in Ben Sira and the Wisdom of Solomon. In Proverbs Lady Wisdom urges people to heed her teachings and testifies to the divine creation of the world. Ben Sira depicts the Torah as a consequence of her descent to Israel (24:23). The Wisdom of Solomon combines the personified wisdom of Proverbs with Hellenistic philosophical ideas, such as the *pneuma* (spirit) of the Stoic tradition, a rational world-soul that emanates throughout the world and pervades all things (cf. Wis. 1:7; 7:22-24; 8:1). Given the prominence of personified wisdom in Ben Sira and the Wisdom of Solomon, it is somewhat unexpected that this tradition does not play a major role in the sapiential texts from Qumran. This corpus, like the Dead Sea Scrolls in general, contains no portrait of Lady Wisdom as lengthy and developed as those of Proverbs 8 or Sirach 24. Many Qumran wisdom texts, such as 4QInstruction, 4Q298, the Book of Mysteries, and 4Q424, show no interest in personified wisdom whatsoever. Several Dead Sea wisdom compositions do, however, reflect some knowledge of this tradition. 4Q185 and 4Q525 constantly use feminine language in their exhortations to acquire wisdom, as in 4Q185 1-2 ii 12: "Find her and [hold fast] to her and get her as an inheritance. With her are [length of d]ays, fatness of bone, joy of heart, rich[es, and honor]" (cf. Prov. 3:16; 4Q525 2 ii + 3 1-6). Lines 13-15 of 4Q185 1-2 ii portray the search for wisdom in romantic terms, urging one not to "play tricks" against wisdom or attain her with "flatteries." Though highly fragmentary, 4Q525 24 ii describes a female speaker who exhorts people to hear her words. This may have been a poem uttered by Lady Wisdom. Column 21 of the Cave 11 *Psalms Scroll* includes a hymn that is influenced by the wisdom tradition. This work, another version of which is in Sir. 51:13-30, personifies wisdom and likens the search for it to that of a man in love with a woman: "I was a young man before I had erred when I looked for her. She came to me in her beauty and up till the end I searched for her" (11QPs[a] 21:11-12).

Wisdom and Torah

Torah piety is a prominent aspect of early Jewish wisdom. Ben Sira represents a merging of the covenantal and sapiential traditions. He teaches that wisdom can be acquired through observance of the Torah (e.g., 1:26). Ben Sira praises the Torah and appeals to it as an authoritative source. The Wisdom of Solomon does not celebrate the Torah in the manner of Ben Sira but nevertheless uses it as a basis of instruction. This is exemplified by Wisdom of Solomon 11–19, which retells the story of the exodus. Baruch 3:9–4:4, and perhaps some of the putative wisdom psalms of the Bible such as Psalms 1 and 119, also attest a combination of wisdom and Torah themes. Some Qumran sapiential texts venerate the Torah in a manner similar to Ben Sira. 4QSapiential Work endorses following the Torah (4Q185 1-2 iii 9). 4QBeatitudes associates wisdom with the Torah: "Happy is the man who has obtained wisdom and follows the Torah of the Most High" (4Q525 2 ii + 3 3-4). 4Q185 and 4Q525 confirm the view attested in Ben Sira that in the late Second Temple period wisdom texts could appeal to the Torah as an authoritative source of revelation.

Elsewhere in the Qumran wisdom corpus the Torah is utilized but not invoked or praised in the manner of Ben Sira. 4QInstruction best illustrates the issue. This work clearly shows familiarity with the Torah. The composition draws on the story of the rebellious Korah from Numbers 16 (4Q423 5 1-2). The addressee's elect status is depicted as God granting him possession of the Garden of Eden (4Q423 1). But 4QInstruction never makes the Torah a theme in its own right. The word never occurs in the text. Rather the author constantly invokes the apocalyptic *rāz nihyeh,* which can be translated as "the mystery that is to be" as an authoritative source of supernatural revelation (see below). In early Judaism the Torah could be incorporated into sapiential instruction in different ways. Not every wisdom text from this period is as "Torah-centric" as Ben Sira. 4QWays of Righteousness includes halakah, legal guidelines for Jewish daily life that presume the authority of the Torah (4Q421 11-13). Halakah is rare in early Jewish wisdom, occurring also in 4QInstruction (4Q416 2 iv 7-9; 4Q418 103 ii). 4QWays of Righteousness reflects a way in which veneration of the Torah influenced the sapiential tradition that is not attested in Ben Sira.

Wisdom and Apocalypticism

Apocalypticism is another major issue in early Jewish wisdom. Ben Sira, in his singular devotion to the Torah, dismisses esoteric sources of speculation: "Reflect upon what you have been commanded, for what is hidden is not your concern" (3:22; cf. 34:1-8). Access to secret sources of divine revelation is a core feature of the apocalyptic tradition, which flourished in Palestine during the time of Ben Sira. Other common features of an apocalyptic worldview include the proclamation of eschatological judgment, a conviction that the present world order is sinful or corrupt, the allocation of rewards and punishments after death, and a concern with the angelic world. The Wisdom of Solomon demonstrates that apocalyptic ideas can be incorporated into a sapiential text. It describes the divine judgment of the wicked and postulates that the righteous will enjoy a blessed afterlife (3:7; 4:20–5:23). Ben Sira, despite his mistrust of non-Torah sources of divine knowledge, includes teachings that are compatible with apocalypticism, such as the imagery of theophanic judgment in 16:18.

The Qumran wisdom texts illustrate the extent to which the apocalyptic tradition influenced early Jewish wisdom. Apocalyptic features are not widespread throughout this corpus, but they are paramount in 4QInstruction and the Book of Mysteries. 4QInstruction, in a complete reversal of Sir. 3:21-24, upholds the *rāz nihyeh* as the chief means of acquiring wisdom. This phrase signifies a divinely revealed deterministic divine plan that guides history and creation (cf. 4Q417 1 i 10-12). The addressee (called the *mēbîn,* or "understanding one") is to study the mystery that is to be: "[Day and night meditate upon the mystery that is] to be. Inquire constantly. Then you will know truth and iniquity, wisdom and [foll]y you will [recognize]" (4Q417 1 i 6-7).

4QInstruction is the best example available of a wisdom text with an apocalyptic worldview. The *mēbîn* is part of an elect group that is in the lot of the angels (4Q418 81 4-5). There is also instruction on the final judgment (4Q416 1; 4Q418 69 ii). Eschatological judgment is important in the Book of Mysteries as well, and is associated with the *rāz nihyeh* (1Q27 1 i 3-4).

The "Treatise on the Two Spirits" offers a deterministic understanding of the natural order and attributes human conduct to the powers of angelic forces of light and darkness (1QS 3:13-22). After God's judgment the righteous will be rewarded with eternal life and the wicked with eternal punishment (1QS 3:23–4:26). Like Mysteries, the Treatise can be understood as a wisdom text with an apocalyptic worldview. These two compositions demonstrate that 4QInstruction is not an isolated phenomenon but rather exemplifies a type of early Jewish wisdom that is characterized by influence from the apocalyptic tradition.

This trajectory is also evident in the Wisdom of Solomon to a limited extent. Ben Sira represents another type of wisdom from this period in which the defining feature is Torah piety, a category that is also represented by 4Q185 and 4Q525. The distinction between these two types of wisdom should not be made too rigidly; texts that utilize the Torah can be found in both categories, as can passages that are reminiscent of the apocalyptic tradition (e.g., 4Q185 1-2 i 8-9). The core elements of some early Jewish wisdom texts derive from their incorporation of apocalyptic themes, as is the case in 4QInstruction, and the characteristic features of others relate to their appeals to the Torah as an authoritative source, as in Ben Sira.

Piety and Praise of God

Piety and the praise of God are prominent in early Jewish wisdom. Proverbs assumes participation in the sacrificial cult (cf. 15:8), but many of its sayings discuss ordinary and practical aspects of human life rather than the worship of God. By contrast, most of the wisdom texts of early Judaism emphasize the veneration of the deity. Ben Sira teaches that the wise person has a full understanding of God's role in the world, to which praise is a natural response (e.g., 15:10; 42:16). The *mēbîn* of 4QInstruction is taught to "praise his name constantly" (4Q416 2 iii 11).

In the late Second Temple period the traditional wisdom of Israel was transformed by the influence of traditions that are alien to the book of Proverbs such as apocalypticism and Torah piety. The wisdom texts from Qumran, when examined in relation to Ben Sira and the Wisdom of Solomon, provide a rich impression of the sapiential literature of early Judaism.

BIBLIOGRAPHY

J. J. COLLINS 1997, *Jewish Wisdom in the Hellenistic Age,* Louisville: Westminster John Knox. • J. J. COLLINS ET AL., EDS. 2004, *Sapiential Perspectives: Wisdom Literature in Light of the Dead Sea Scrolls,* Leiden: Brill. • T. ELGVIN ET AL. 1997, *Qumran Cave 4.XV: Sapiential Texts, Part 1,* DJD 20, Oxford: Clarendon. • F. GARCÍA MARTÍNEZ, ED. 2003, *Wisdom and Apocalypticism in the Dead Sea Scrolls and in the Biblical Tradition,* Leuven: Leuven University Press. • M. J. GOFF 2006, *Discerning Wisdom: The Sapiential Literature of the Dead Sea Scrolls,* Leiden: Brill. • D. J. HARRINGTON 1996, *Wisdom Texts from Qumran.* London: Routledge. • C. HEMPEL ET AL., EDS. 2002, *The Wisdom Texts from Qumran and the Development of Sapiential Thought,* Leuven: Leuven University Press. • J. STRUGNELL AND D. J. HARRINGTON 1999, *Qumran Cave 4.XXIV: Sapiential Texts, Part 2. 4QInstruction (Mûsār lĕ Mēvîn),* DJD 34, Oxford: Clarendon.

MATTHEW GOFF

Wisdom Literature at Qumran

Wisdom or sapiential literature is a modern scholarly category that encompasses a wide range of ancient writings from Israel and the ancient Near East in general. Wisdom compositions are often written by a teacher to students and characterized by a search for order in the natural world and human society, a eudemonistic devotion to the addressee, and practical advice.

Overview

The Dead Sea Scrolls contain eight compositions that are widely considered to be wisdom texts: 4QInstruction (1Q26; 4Q415-18, 423), the Book of Mysteries (1Q27; 4Q299-301), 4QWiles of the Wicked Woman (4Q184), 4QSapiential Work (4Q185), 4QWords of the Maskil (4Q298), 4QWays of Righteousness (4Q420-21), 4QInstruction-like Composition B (4Q424), and 4QBeatitudes (4Q525). Other texts can be understood as sapiential texts or units that are part of larger compositions. In this category one can place the "Treatise on the Two Spirits" of the *Community Rule* (1QS 3: 134:26), the first two columns of the *Damascus Document,* several hymns of the Cave 11 *Psalms Scroll* (cols. 18, 21, and perhaps 26 of 11QPs[a]), and the final poem of the Aramaic Levi Document.

Biblical and Deuterocanonical Works

There are also Qumran manuscripts of biblical and deuterocanonical wisdom texts, such as Proverbs (4Q102–3), Job (4Q99–101), Qoheleth (4Q109–10), and Ben Sira (2Q18). The Scrolls may include other wisdom compositions, as reflected in their official titles, such as 4Q411 (4QSapiential Hymn) and 4Q425 (4QSapiential-Didactic Work B), but they are often too fragmentary to decide their genre conclusively. Because of the fragmentary nature of these Scrolls and the broad scope of wisdom as a genre, there is no consensus on the precise number of wisdom texts among the Dead Sea Scrolls. It is generally agreed that the Scrolls include sapiential literature, and many scholars would consider the first eight texts enumerated above to be wisdom texts. This material was probably written in the second and first centuries B.C.E.

4QInstruction

The largest wisdom text from Qumran is 4QInstruction (1Q26; 4Q415–418, 423). There are remnants of at least six copies of this text. 4QInstruction is written by a teacher to a student, who is constantly referred to as a *mēbîn,* or "understanding one." He is told to acquire learning on numerous topics through contemplation of the *rāz nihyeh,* an expression that can be translated "the mystery that is to be." This is an appeal to supernatural revelation that discloses a divine plan structuring history and creation. The *rāz nihyeh* reflects the influence of the apocalyptic tradition and constitutes a departure from the traditional wisdom of Israel, as exemplified by Proverbs.

Eschatological judgment is also a topic of 4QInstruction (4Q416; 4Q418 69 ii). The *mēbîn* is part of an elect community that has affinities with the angels (4Q418 81). He is told that he has authority over the Garden of Eden, a metaphor for his elect status (4Q423). The *mēbîn* is also poor.

Several passages in 4QInstruction assume that the addressee is a farmer (e.g., 4Q423 3-5), and the work frequently gives advice regarding indebtedness, suggesting that many members of the intended audience were forced to borrow.

WISDOM LITERATURE AT QUMRAN

Book of Mysteries

Portions of several copies of the Book of Mysteries (1Q27; 4Q299–301) were found among the Dead Sea Scrolls. Scholars are divided as to whether 4Q301 should be associated with this composition. The modern title of the work derives from its frequent use of "mystery" *(rāz)* terminology. Mysteries uses the phrase *rāz nihyeh* in relation to eschatological judgment and the eradication of the wicked: "They do not know the mystery that is to be, and the former things they do not understand. . . . They will not save their lives from the mystery that is to be" (1Q27 1 i 3-4). The composition is addressed to "those who hold fast to mysteries," which suggests they believed that they possessed revealed knowledge (4Q299 43 2; 4Q300 8 5; cf. 4Q299 8 7). The work polemicizes against a rival group, the "magicians" *(ḥartumîm),* a word used to describe the Babylonian wise men in the book of Daniel (4Q300 1a ii-b). The "magicians" possess knowledge that Mysteries disdains. They are "skilled in transgression" and know the "parable" and "riddle" (line 1). Their teachings cannot be sufficiently reconstructed.

The Book of Mysteries is generally considered a wisdom text, but its genre is ambiguous. A limited degree of its content is reminiscent of traditional wisdom (e.g., 1Q27 1 ii), but its themes of revelation and eschatological judgment are more in keeping with the apocalyptic tradition. The apocalyptic worldview of the Book of Mysteries evokes 4QInstruction, and the two works have much in common in terms of theme and vocabulary, such as the mystery that is to be. This helps establish the two works as part of the same sapiential tradition.

4QWiles of the Wicked Woman

4QWiles of the Wicked Woman (4Q184) describes a woman who leads men to sin and death. The composition is reliant on the account of the "Strange Woman" *(iššâ zarâ)* from the book of Proverbs. She is a promiscuous and immoral female who lurks in city streets and attempts to seduce young men. The dependence on Proverbs is a chief reason 4Q184 is considered a wisdom text. 4Q184 transforms the "Strange Woman" of Proverbs into a mythological figure of evil. She no longer merely leads sinners to Sheol (an ancient Hebrew term for the location of the dead), as in Prov. 2:18. The woman of 4Q184 is a resident of the underworld. Her "beds" and "tents" are there (lines 5, 7). Sheol is said to contain "eternal flames" (line 7), which suggests it was viewed as a place of punishment after death, a concept not found in Proverbs. While the woman represents a way of life that leads to death, what constitutes such behavior is not described in detail. She signifies wickedness in a general sense.

4QSapiential Work

4QSapiential Work (4Q185) encourages the acquisition of wisdom. One should "Find her and [hold fast] to her and get her as an inheritance. With her are [length of d]ays, fatness of bone, joy of heart, rich[es, and honor]" (4Q185 1-2 ii 12; cf. Prov 3:16). Proverbs 8 includes an elaborate depiction of wisdom personified as a woman. 4Q185 offers no vivid account of personified wisdom, but its use of feminine language implies some familiarity with this tradition. 4Q185 1-2 ii 13-14 states that one should "not play tricks ag[ainst her, nor] with [a spirit] of deceit seek her, nor hold fast to her with flatteries." This employs a romantic metaphor to describe the search for wisdom. 4Q185 also encourages one to observe "the words of [his] covena[nt]" (4Q185 1-2 iii 9; cf. 4Q185 1-2 ii 3). The composition combines Torah piety with traditional wisdom that is reminiscent of Proverbs, as does Ben Sira.

4QWords of the Maskil to All Sons of Dawn

4QWords of the Maskil to All Sons of Dawn (4Q298) urges one to acquire learning and be ethical. 4Q298 3-4 ii 3-6 reads: "And now give ea[r, O wise ones]; and you who know, listen! And men of understanding, in[crease learning]; and you who see[k] justice, (add) modesty." Often the work encourages moral conduct without providing instruction on specific topics, although there is a lesson on the eschatological future in 4Q298 3-4 ii 8-10. The composition is reasonably attributed to the Dead Sea sect. The instructor of 4Q298 is called a *maśkîl,* a term for a key pedagogical functionary in the sectarian rulebooks (cf. 1QS 3:13; 9:18-19; CD 13:22-23). The students of 4Q298 are referred to as "sons of dawn," an expression found in the *Damascus Document* (CD 13:14-15). 4Q298, with the exception of its title, is written in an esoteric script known as Cryptic A, a scribal practice of the Dead Sect. 4QWords of the Maskil probably was used to inspire members of this group in their pursuit of wisdom and righteousness.

4QWays of Righteousness

4QWays of Righteousness (4Q420-21) is often viewed as a wisdom text, but some scholars dispute this classification. (See the article by Hempel in Lange et al. 2002.) 4Q421 11-13 contains halakah (detailed guidelines for daily life and religious practices grounded in the Torah) regarding the Sabbath, a rarity in wisdom literature. 4QWays of Righteousness mentions a "yoke of wisd[om]" (4Q421 1a ii-b 10), which is an allusion to the Torah as in the sapiential text Ben Sira (6:30; 51:26). The metaphor describes one's acceptance of a life guided by the Torah. 4QWays of Righteousness teaches that one's speech should be cautious and deliberate (4Q420 1a ii-b 1-2; cf. 4Q421 1a ii-b 13-14), a commonplace lesson in the wisdom tradition (cf. Prov. 18:13). 4Q421 1a i has several affinities with the *Community Rule* (compare line 3 with 1QS 5:23), and the Sabbath legislation of the work is similar to that of the *Damascus Document* (cf. CD 11:9). The Dead Sea sect probably wrote parts of 4Q420-21. 4QWays of Righteousness is plausibly considered a composite work, a wisdom text redacted with material that resembles the Qumran rulebooks.

4Q424

4Q424, which has the cumbersome title 4QInstruction-like Composition B, is a work of practical wisdom consistent with Proverbs 10–31. 4Q424 contains instruction regarding negative and positive types of people. Several negative personalities are discussed, such as "a slothful man," "a man who murmurs," and "a man with devious lips" (4Q424 1 6-8). The addressee is to avoid such people in his selection of employees who will have responsibility regarding money and legal affairs. 4Q424 1 10 reads, for example: "A greedy man do not put in a position of authority over [your] we[alth]" (cf. Prov. 28:22; Sir. 14:3). This implies that the composition was written for a person of means. This is different from 4QInstruction (despite the official title of 4Q424), which emphasizes the poverty of the *mēbîn.* The addressee of 4Q424 is affluent, but he does not appear to be in training to become a scribe, as is the case with Ben Sira's students. 4Q424 3 7-10 is the only section of this Qumran text that gives attention to positive types of people. They are ideal and general figures, such as "a prudent man" who "will receive knowledge" (line 7).

4QBeatitudes

The title of 4QBeatitudes derives from its collection of beatitudes in 4Q525 2 ii + 3 1-6. Beatitudes are statements that describe an ideal person, often beginning with phrases such as "Happy is the one who. . . ." This collection combines wisdom and the Torah: "Happy is the man who has obtained wisdom and follows the Torah of the Most High" (lines 3-4). The fragment considered the beginning of the work (4Q525 1) stresses the importance of learning, much like the prologue to Proverbs (1:1-7).

4Q525 contains no full-blown portrait of personified wisdom but displays some knowledge of this motif. The fragmentary text 4Q525 24 ii includes statements from a female speaker and may have been a poem uttered by Lady Wisdom. 4Q525 14 ii gives instruction on proper speech that assumes the addressee is in training to become a teacher (lines 15-16). He is to "answer correctly among princes" (line 25).

The intended audience of 4Q525 is probably in training to become scribes and teachers who will work for nobles or aristocrats. The social setting of 4QBeatitudes is similar to that of Ben Sira.

Wisdom Passages Embedded in Larger Works

Several Qumran texts can be considered sapiential works that are part of larger compositions. First and foremost in this category is the "Treatise on the Two Spirits," which is a section of the *Community Rule* (1QS 3:13–4:26). The Treatise identifies itself as an instruction taught by a *maśkîl* that regards the "nature of the sons of man" (3:13). The lesson includes a highly deterministic and dualistic conception of the world and attributes human conduct to the machinations of angels of light and darkness. This continues until an eschatological moment of divine judgment, after which eternal rewards are allocated to the righteous and punishments to the wicked. This apocalyptic perspective has little in common with the traditional wisdom of Proverbs but resonates with 4QInstruction and Mysteries. The Treatise is probably a product of the same trajectory of the sapiential tradition that produced these two works.

Column 2 of the *Damascus Document* contains an exhortation that puts forward a deterministic understanding of the history of Israel (lines 9-10), stating that God "has established wisdom and counsel before him" (line 3).

The poem that concludes the Aramaic *Levi Document,* which is attested at Qumran and in other ancient sources, encourages the acquisition of wisdom and praises the one who can teach it (4Q213 1 i).

Psalms Scroll

The massive *Psalms Scroll* from Cave 11 (11QPs[a]) contains three hymns that are often associated with the wisdom tradition. A version of Psalm 154, previously available in a Syriac manuscript, is in col. 18 of 11QPs[a]. This work presents wisdom as the recognition of God's grandeur: "For to make known the glory of the Lord is wisdom given" (lines 3-4). The poem personifies wisdom as a woman to a limited extent, depicting the righteous praising God as the sound of "her voice" (line 10), which is also described as the reading of the Torah (lines 11-12).

11QPs[a] 21:11-17 and 22:1 attest an acrostic version of Sir. 51:13-30. This poem is erotically charged: "I kindled my desire for her and would not turn away my face. I bestirred my desire for her, and on her heights I would not waver. My hand op[ened her gates]. . . . I perceived her unseen parts" (lines 15-17).

The sexual dimension of the hymn expresses the speaker's passion of his love for wisdom. 11QPs[a] 26:9-15 preserves an otherwise unknown work known as "Hymn to the Creator." The psalm praises God's creation of the world: "Blessed be he who makes the earth by his power, establishing the world with his wisdom. By his understanding he stretched out the heavens" (lines 13-14; cf. Prov. 3:19: Jer. 10:12).

These three compositions of 11QPs[a] can be understood as "wisdom psalms" in that they reflect substantial influence from the wisdom tradition, although "Hymn to the Creator" may be better categorized as a creation psalm along the lines of Psalm 104.

The Dead Sea Scrolls expand the corpus of wisdom texts from the late Second Temple period and thus make an important contribution to our knowledge of the early Jewish sapiential tradition.

Bibliography

J. J. Collins et al., eds. 2004, *Sapiential Perspectives: Wisdom Literature in Light of the Dead Sea Scrolls,* Leiden: Brill. • T. Elgvin et al. 1997, *Qumran Cave 4.XV: Sapiential Texts, Part 1,* DJD 20, Oxford: Clarendon. • F. García Martínez, ed. 2003, *Wisdom and Apocalypticism in the Dead Sea Scrolls and in the Biblical Tradition,* Leuven: Leuven University Press. • M. J. Goff 2006, *Discerning Wisdom: The Sapiential Literature of the Dead Sea Scrolls,* Leiden: Brill. • D. J. Harrington 1996, *Wisdom Texts from Qumran.* London: Routledge. • C. Hempel et al., eds. 2002, *The Wisdom Texts from Qumran and the Development of Sapiential Thought,* Leuven: Leuven University Press. • A. Lange 1995, *Weisheit und Prädestination,* Leiden: Brill. • J. B. Rey 2009, *4QInstruction: Segasse et eschatologie,* Leiden: Brill. • J. Strugnell

AND D. J. HARRINGTON 1999, *Qumran Cave 4.XXIV: Sapiential Texts, Part 2. 4QInstruction (Mûsār lĕ Mēvîn)*, DJD 34, Oxford: Clarendon.

MATTHEW GOFF

Wisdom of Solomon → Solomon, Wisdom of

Wolfson, Harry Austryn

Harry Austryn Wolfson (1887-1974) was a historian of philosophy whose controversial two-volume study of Philo of Alexandria (1947) made him one of the most notable modern interpreters of early Judaism. Wolfson was born in Ostrin, Lithuania, whence the middle name Austryn that he later chose for himself, and educated at the renowned Slabodka Yeshiva. He emigrated in 1903 with his parents to the United States and studied briefly at the Rabbi Isaac Elchanan Yeshiva on the lower East Side of New York. In 1905 he left the Yeshiva to teach at a new Hebrew school in Scranton, Pennsylvania. Here, in his spare time, he enrolled in elementary school, completing his "degree" there in three months and graduating three years later from Central High School with an average of nearly 100. Fortuitously, he learned of scholarship aid available from Harvard, for which he applied, and was admitted. He took his degree in three years and, in 1912, also his M.A.

With the recommendations of Professors George Foot Moore and George Santayana, Wolfson was awarded the Sheldon Traveling Fellowship for a year's study abroad (extended in his case for a second year) to carry out research on Hasdai Crescas, who had located the cause of all the errors of Maimonides in the latter's Aristotelian science, which he subjected to a thorough critique in book 1 of his *Light of the Lord* (written in Hebrew in 1410). At the Bibliothèque Nationale in Paris, Wolfson found manuscripts not only of Crescas and Averroës' commentaries on Aristotle, which formed an essential part of Crescas' intellectual background, but even more important, a Hebrew supercommentary on Averroës by Moses of Narbonne (or Narboni), whose work is mentioned and used by Crescas and which later helped to clear up many problems. At the Hofbibliothek in Vienna, he copied another Crescas manuscript, as well as manuscripts of Narboni's commentary on the twenty-five propositions that Maimonides placed at the beginning of the second part of his *Guide of the Perplexed.*

Wolfson's findings were well received by Professor Moore, and he was awarded the doctorate at the 1915 commencement. However, his Crescas manuscript of almost a thousand handwritten pages, completed in 1917, would, for lack of funding, not be published until 1929, when the costs were underwritten by a Harvard graduate, Lucius Littauer, who in 1925 had endowed the establishment of a chair for the Nathan Littauer Professor of Hebrew Literature and Philosophy, the first of its kind at any American or European university, to which Wolfson was appointed as the first incumbent. The investigation of the sources of Crescas' thought entailed intensive study by Wolfson of the many commentaries on Aristotle's works written by the great Islamic commentator Averroes. Since most of these existed only in manuscripts, Wolfson proposed the publication of a *Corpus Commentariorum Averrois in Aristotelem* and was appointed as its editor in chief.

Impressive as Wolfson's *Crescas' Critique of Aristotle* was, it was only the prelude to much greater achievements. He contributed five studies on Spinoza to the *Chronicon Spinozanum* that were published between 1921 and 1926 and that culminated in his two-volume work on *The Philosophy of Spinoza: Unfolding the Latent Processes of His Reasoning* (1934), probably the most dazzling of all his writings.

By 1937 Wolfson had assembled all the material from Plato to Spinoza and was ready to convert it into books. The projected series of no fewer than twelve books (only seven of which were subsequently published, although at least drafted manuscripts of all of them were prepared), under the general title "Structure and Growth of Philosophical Systems from Plato to Spinoza," reveals "the prodigious scope of Wolfson's learning and the single-minded dedication with which he pursued his goal" (Runia 1990: 10, 113-14).

In 1947 Wolfson published his two-volume study of Philo of Alexandria, in which he attempted to refute the conventional portrait of him as a weak-minded eclectic who lacked independent judgment and establish him instead as a philosopher in the grand manner, a profound critic of all the Greek schools of philosophy, and the founder of a system of religious thought that became the common philosophy of the three religions with cognate scriptures, Judaism, Christianity, and Islam (Wolfson 1961: Preface). In this novel conception of the history of Western philosophy, Philo is seen as one who had sought to adapt Greek philosophy to Scripture.

Wolfson's study on Philo is by far the most controversial of all his works. His representation of Philo's position as one of virtual "orthodoxy," however, is illuminated to some extent by his personal preference for the Orthodox over the Reform and Conservative reinterpretations of Jewish tradition. It is rooted in his own firm conviction that the Greek philosophers had "made quibbling about the meaning of God one of their chief occupations." The gods of the philosophers, he thought, were mostly "only polite but empty phrases for the honest atheism of the fool in Scripture," who was at least "a downright honest and plain-spoken fellow." (Wolfson 1961: 270-71). Twin drives would thus seem to motivate Wolfson's idiosyncratic interpretation of the history of philosophy. A Judeo-centric tendency moved him to assign the highest priority to the Jewish component in medieval philosophy, and his strong preference for either straightforward theism or an honest atheism, accompanied by a similarly straightforward reading of texts, drove him to force Philo into an "orthodox" mold. There were certainly enough traditional religious formulas in Philo's frequently ambiguous writings to make such a procedure possible, and Wolfson's keen intellect did the rest.

Wolfson's innovative study of Philo was followed

by his impressive *Philosophy of the Church Fathers* (1956; 3d ed. 1970), and finally by *The Philosophy of the Kalam* (1976) and *Kalam Repercussions in Jewish Philosophy* (1979) (the latter two posthumously).

BIBLIOGRAPHY

AMERICAN ACADEMY FOR JEWISH RESEARCH 1965, *Harry Austryn Wolfson Jubilee Volume on the Occasion of His Seventy-fifth Birthday*, 3 vols., Jerusalem: American Academy for Jewish Research. • J. COHEN 1997, *Reason and Change*, Jerusalem: Bialik Institute, 41-115 (in Hebrew). • H. GOLDBERG 1989, *Between Berlin and Slobodka*, Hoboken, N.J.: Ktav, 37-62. • J. GOLDIN 1980, "On the Sleuth of Slabodka," *The American Scholar* 49, no. 3: 391-404. • W. HARVEY 1982, "Hebraism and Western Philosophy in H. A. Wolfson's Theory of History," *Immanuel* 14: 77-85. • D. RUNIA 1990, "History of Philosophy in the Grand Manner: The Achievement of H. A. Wolfson," in *Exegesis and Philosophy: Studies on Philo of Alexandria*, Aldershot: Variorum. • L. SCHWARTZ 1978, *Wolfson of Harvard*, Philadelphia: Jewish Publication Society. • M. SCHWARTZ 1978, Review of H. A. Wolfson, *The Philosophy of the Kalam, Hamizrah Heḥadash* 27: 89-96 (in Hebrew). • L. WIESELTIER 1976, "Philosophy, Religion, and Harry Wolfson," *Commentary* 61, no. 4: 57-64. • D. WINSTON 1994, Review of David Runia, *Exegesis and Philosophy, Ancient Philosophy* 14: 224-31. • H. A. WOLFSON 1934, *The Philosophy of Spinoza: Unfolding the Latent Processes of His Reasoning*, Cambridge: Harvard University Press. • H. A. WOLFSON 1947, *Philo: Foundations of Religious Philosophy in Judaism, Christianity and Islam*, 2 vols., Cambridge: Harvard University Press. • H. A. WOLFSON 1956, *The Philosophy of the Church Fathers*, Cambridge: Harvard University Press. • H. A. WOLFSON 1957, *Crescas' Critique of Aristotle: Problems of Aristotle's Physics in Jewish and Arabic Philosophy*, Cambridge: Harvard University Press. • H. A. WOLFSON 1961, *Religious Philosophy*, Cambridge: Harvard University Press, 270-71. • H. A. WOLFSON 1973-1977, *Studies in the History of Philosophy and Religion: Harry A. Wolfson*, 2 vols., ed. I. Twersky and G. H. Williams, Cambridge: Harvard University Press. • H. A. WOLFSON 1976, *The Philosophy of the Kalam*, Cambridge: Harvard University Press.

DAVID WINSTON

Women

A discussion of Jewish women in the Second Temple period must first of all take into account the fact that it falls between the biblical and talmudic periods. In both biblical and talmudic times, laws were formulated governing the position and expected behavior of Jewish women, and both were canonized. In some respects these differed one from the other. From the Second Temple period we have some documents reflecting attempts to construct and regulate Jewish women's lives, but these were not canonized. Thus, this period should be viewed as the "missing link" between the two canonical periods in Jewish history, and it serves as such for many issues relevant to women in Judaism.

The literature about Jewish women in the Second Temple period can be roughly divided into three types: fiction, wisdom texts, and halakah. The following discussion will follow these three branches and then conclude with a few remarks about the historical reality of women.

Heroines in Fiction

Beginning in the Persian period, a new phenomenon developed that made women into the chief protagonists in works of fiction. While the Hebrew Bible does include female heroines such as the matriarchs of Genesis and the women of the book of Judges, they are usually auxiliary figures to the male heroes of these stories. In Second Temple literature this changes. Already two late biblical books are named after women — Ruth and Esther. This phenomenon is further developed with the books of Judith and Susanna. In the book *Joseph and Aseneth* we find a strong female protagonist, but there is some debate about the date and Jewish or Christian provenance of this book. These women not only give the books their names but are also themselves the heroines and are unexpectedly located at their center. A good example is Susanna. In this book the hero is the young Daniel and the main issue at hand is miscarriage of justice by a corrupt judicial system and leadership. The story of the attempted seduction of Susanna is a subplot within the main story. Yet in this subplot the woman is the virtuous heroine. Neither a women as heroine nor seduction as a topic of miscarriage of justice is necessary, however. A similar story is told in the Bible about Naboth the Jezreelite and his vineyard (1 Kings 21). It employs neither a woman nor seduction as its topic. The choice of a woman heroine and the topic specifically relevant to her are unique to the new interests of Second Temple literature.

The heroines of Second Temple books are some of the most memorable women figures in world literature. Ruth is the widowed, non-Jewish, loyal daughter-in-law who chooses to follow her mother-in-law Naomi into the unknown. Susanna is the virtuous wife who is willing to die rather than compromise her sexual virtue. Esther is the woman who compromises her Judaism and infiltrates the Persian court in order to save her people from annihilation. Judith is the prototype of the zealot, a virtuous widow who changes into a seductress and single-handedly assassinates the enemy general in order to save her city from destruction.

Meaningful female heroines also appear in Second Temple literature in works besides those to which they give their name. In 2 Maccabees 7 the nameless mother of seven sons is one of the first and most memorable Jewish martyrs. Like Judith, she serves as a role model for both men and women, fulfilling the nationalist and religious ideals of Second Temple Judaism. Further, in the book of Tobit we find Sarah, who becomes the ultimate prototype of the killer wife by indirectly causing her seven husbands to die on their wedding night (Tob. 3:7-9).

Many suggestions have been made in order to explain this unusual phenomenon of the new female heroine. A contributing factor was surely the influence of the Greek literary genre of the novel, which became widespread throughout the Hellenistic world from the

WOMEN

third century B.C.E. and which indulged in portrayals of powerful women in historical, semihistorical, and purely fictional settings.

Idealization in Wisdom Literature

While the heroines discussed above are, on the whole, virtuous women, Second Temple literature in general views women much more systematically than do biblical texts. Early Jewish writings are inclined to make general, and often very negative, observations on their character. Negative comments of this sort are mainly found in what is usually designated wisdom literature. Much has been said about the biblical book of Proverbs and its portrayal of women. In its first chapters it juxtaposes the highly positive figure of Lady Wisdom, who is a suitable companion to a Jewish man, with the strange, seductive Dame Folly, who is dangerous and should be shunned. At the end of the book, Proverbs presents the woman of valor, who is a diligent and efficient housewife, provider, and paragon of virtue. She is an ideal woman, but it is nowhere suggested that such women do not and cannot exist.

This many-faceted feminine image in Proverbs is condensed in the wisdom literature of Second Temple times to yield the negative, human seductress who represents everywoman. Already in the pessimistic biblical book of Qohelet we read, "and I find woman more bitter than death" (7:26). A similar sentiment is expressed by Jesus Ben Sira, who lived toward the end of the third and beginning of the second centuries B.C.E. He maintained that women in general constitute a threat to the dignity and well-being of men and that the most dangerous threat comes from a man's own daughter.

Another composition of the same cloth was found among the Dead Sea Scrolls and has come to be known as *Wiles of the Wicked Woman* (4Q184). Here a Second Temple author elaborates on and greatly extends the dangers described in Proverbs as those of the foreign seductress.

Portrayal in Philosophically Oriented Works

This pessimistic and negative assessment of women is also found in Jewish literature that is overtly indebted to Hellenistic philosophical discourse. It is already voiced in the *Letter of Aristeas* (250), but its main propagator is Philo of Alexandria. As has often been shown, Philo accepted the Aristotelian judgment that the female is, in and of herself, inferior to the male. He used this to explain the biblical narratives allegorically. The women of the Bible represent inferior aspects of a person's psyche, namely the senses, while the male figures represent the superior mind. The creation of woman, for example, is explained as a corruption of the mind by the senses (*Opificio Mundi* 59).

This short review presents a literature that is indebted to an intensive and unsympathetic male discourse on the very nature and essence of womanhood. Second Temple literature thus displays a sort of internal contradiction where, alongside a large number of virulent diatribes against females and the feminine, we find powerful and sympathetic female figures, some of whom actually save the Jewish people. A middle ground between the two comes in the legal discourse about women evident in Second Temple literature.

Women in Halakah

A large number of issues concerning women, which are clearly formulated in the Mishnah but which have no antecedent in the Bible, have their roots in Second Temple times and are reflected in the literature and documents preserved from this period. This is true of Josephus' reworking of the biblical laws, Philo's philosophical discourse on the *Special Laws*, the reworked Genesis of the book of *Jubilees*, the New Testament, and the halakic texts from Qumran.

Marriage Contracts

The Mishnah includes an entire tractate devoted to women's marriage contracts, *Ketubbot*, even though a marriage contract is nowhere mentioned in the Bible itself. Does this mean that ancient Israelites did not know such a document? A straightforward answer to such a question is not forthcoming, but Aramaic documents from the Jewish settlement at Elephantine in Egypt, dated firmly to the Persian period, include marriage contracts belonging to Jewish women. These documents do not fit the halakic description of a Jewish marriage contract as it appears in the Mishnah (the Mishnah specifies, e.g., that a wife can initiate her own divorce), but they may serve as evidence for a stage in the development of the latter. Another such stage is the marriage contract mentioned in the book of Tobit, written by Sarah's father to Tobias, giving him his daughter as wife "according to the decree of the law of Moses." This document is very different from the rabbinic *ketubah*, because it represents an agreement between father and son-in-law rather than between husband and wife. Yet a similar formulation to the words "according to the decree of the Law of Moses" is found also in the rabbinic *ketubah*.

Divorce

A similar issue is the question of divorce. Deuteronomic law mentions a bill of divorce which a man writes a woman (Deut. 24:1-4), but this law is not formulated so as to advise male Jews about how to divorce their wives. Instead, it emphasizes a unique case of a man who divorces a woman who in turn goes and marries another man from whom she is then also divorced. The Bible rules that, in such a case, the first husband cannot take her back. Thus, the mention of the divorce document is incidental and does not describe the document or how it functioned as a rule. For example, it does not imply that only a man could write such a document to a woman, but not vice versa. Thus, Josephus informs us that the sister of King Herod, Salome, wrote a divorce bill and sent it to her husband. Josephus is quick to add that this is against Jewish custom, and modern scholars have universally adopted his judgment, claiming that the woman had done this in her capacity as a Roman citizen but not as a Jew. It turns out, however, that Josephus here is voicing his opinion in a debate that was raging at the time, about a woman's right to divorce her husband, and which was not yet definitively concluded 160 years later, when a certain Jewish woman, Shelamzion daughter of Joseph, wrote a divorce bill to her husband, a document preserved among the scrolls from the Judean Desert. Josephus' view here probably reflects the fact that he was a Pharisee, as were the forefathers of the rabbis.

Testimony in Court

Divorce is not the only issue on which Josephus agrees with the rabbis against other voices preserved in Second Temple literature. Thus, without having any biblical basis, Josephus states explicitly that women are barred from serving as witnesses in Jewish courts of law "because of the levity and temerity of their sex" (*Ant.* 4.219). The rabbis, too, exempted women from giving evidence (*m. Roš Haš.* 1:8); and elsewhere, in another context, also concluded that women are light-headed (*b. Qiddušin* 80b). Yet this unity of opinion between Josephus and the rabbis is interrupted by the evidence from the Dead Sea Scrolls. In the Qumran *Rule of the Congregation,* or *Messianic Rule* (1QSa), we are informed that at the age of twenty, once members of the sect marry, their wives are called upon to bear witness against them in cases where they transgress the ruling of the community (1QSa 1:11). The simple meaning of the text is that in the Qumran community, where members were constantly expected to testify against their fellow members, women were expected to participate in the system as well. This text shows that the exclusion of women from giving evidence was, in Second Temple times, anything but universal.

Presence in Public

One of the issues hotly debated in Second Temple literature is the question of women's presence in public. Ben Sira maintained that a person should keep his daughter under lock and key. Philo agreed, claiming, "Market places and council halls and law courts and gatherings and meetings . . . are suitable for men. . . . Women are best suited to the indoor life which never strays from the house, within which the middle door is taken by the maidens as their boundary and the outer door by those who have reached full womanhood" (*Special Laws* 31). The ideal voiced by these two Second Temple Jewish thinkers is realized and glorified in the book of Judith. Although Judith is a very public heroine, when she is not required to act in an emergency she secludes herself on her roof, away from the public eye. Rabbinic literature, however, contains no such strictures against women's freedom of movement. In this respect, the rabbis proved more lenient than their Second Temple predecessors.

Participation in Ritual Life

The issue of women's position within Jewish society can serve as a test case for the assertion that the rabbis are the direct heirs of the opponents of the Dead Sea sect (Pharisees?). In most halakic cases we find the Qumran covenanters and the rabbis on two sides of the divide. However, when it comes to the position of women, this is not always true. Thus, in rabbinic literature women are often lumped together with slaves, minors, and other underprivileged individuals, such as the bodily impaired, as exempt from performing certain commandments. A closer look at these commandments shows that they exclude women from a significant percentage of Jewish ritual life. This categorization and exemption is a complete novelty. Nothing even remotely resembling it is found in the Bible. Here, however, the Qumran material constitutes a middle ground between the Bible and the rabbis. Thus, in the *Damascus Document* we find a list that includes fools, the mentally sick, and the bodily disabled together with minors as forbidden entry into the congregation of the elect "because holy angels are present" (CD 15:15-17; 4Q266). Women are not mentioned in this list, an omission probably indicating that they were allowed to participate in the life of the congregation. However, women are excluded in a similar list found in the Qumran *War Scroll,* one that itemizes all those who may not enter the camp of war, for the same reason of the presence of angels (1QM 7). Also, in a fragment from Cave 4 minors and women are excluded from partaking in the Pesach sacrifice. As in rabbinic literature, so here women are lumped together with minors. In this the Qumran community resembles the rabbis conceptually. However, it may be of interest to note that the rabbis do not exempt, but rather include, both women and minors in the celebration and consumption of the Pesach sacrifice. This is probably an indication of how the rabbis and the Jews of Qumran differed on minor (and sometimes major) points of law but held a common assumption about gender hierarchy, the partial participation of women in Jewish life, and their affinity to both minors and to deformed and maimed individuals. Although the rabbis do not explain the exclusion of persons mentioned in these lists from ritual as the Qumranites do, as a result of the presence of angels in their midst, they find such lists useful.

Women in History

Some of the most powerful historical female figures feature in the writings of Josephus. These include Miriam the Hasmonean, the wife of King Herod, who was tragically executed by her husband in his fight against her royal house; Berenice, the daughter of King Agrippa, who enticed the Roman general Titus while he was laying siege to Jerusalem; and, most importantly, Queen Shelamzion Alexandra, who ruled the Hasmonean kingdom single-handedly for nine years (76-67 B.C.E.). To these portraits one may also add the figure of the scheming Herodias of the New Testament, who through her machinations has John the Baptist beheaded (Mark 6:14-28; Matt. 14:1-11).

The various literary creations discussed thus far show the Second Temple period as a time of dynamic changes in the perception of gender within Judaism. Ideas were tested and discarded or altered and adopted. Various groups voiced differing opinions on women, their worth, and their place in society. What does this say about the real women of the time? It seems that the

WORDS OF THE LUMINARIES (4Q504-506)

most we can say is that the Second Temple period was characterized by a fragmentation of Jewish society and by sectarianism, which had a major impact on women's lives. Sects by their very nature are more egalitarian than established society and more readily welcome women's participation. Thus, we know that the Jesus movement included female members. The philosophical conclave of the Therapeutae in Egypt described by Philo counted women among its members. It can be argued that the Pharisees, the Dead Sea sect, and even various military zealot organizations counted women among their ranks. It should also not be forgotten that Second Temple times saw the only legitimate queen in Jewish history. It is a great mystery how this ever came about. Obviously such historical realities may have had some impact on the way women were discussed in and presented by the literature surveyed above.

BIBLIOGRAPHY

A. BRENNER, ED. 1995, *A Feminist Companion to Esther, Judith and Susanna,* Sheffield: Sheffield Academic Press. • B. J. BROOTEN 1982, *Women Leaders in the Ancient Synagogue,* Chico, Calif.: Scholars Press. • L. J. ERON 1991, "'That Women Have Mastery over Both King and Beggar' (*T. Jud.* 15.5): The Relationship of the Fear of Sexuality to the Status of Women in Apocrypha and Pseudepigrapha: 1 Esdras (*3 Ezra*) 3–4, Ben Sira and the *Testament of Judah,*" *JSP* 9: 43-66. • B. HALPERN-AMARU 1999, *The Empowerment of Women in the Book of Jubilees,* Leiden: Brill. • T. ILAN 1999, *Integrating Jewish Women into Second Temple History,* Tübingen: Mohr-Siebeck. • T. ILAN 2006, *Silencing the Queen: The Literary Histories of Shelamzion and Other Jewish Women,* Tübingen: Mohr-Siebeck. • A.-J. LEVINE, ED. 1991, *"Women Like This": New Perspectives on Jewish Women in the Greco-Roman World,* Atlanta: Scholars Press. • B. MAYER-SCHÄRTEL 1995, *Das Frauenbild des Josephus: Eine sozialgeschichtliche und kulturanthropologische Untersuchung,* Stuttgart: Kohlhammer. • E. SCHULLER 1999, "Women in the Dead Sea Scrolls," in *The Dead Sea Scrolls after Fifty Years: A Comprehensive Assessment,* ed. P. W. Flint and J. C. VanderKam, Leiden: Brill, 117-44. • D. SLY 1990, *Philo's Perceptions of Women,* Atlanta: Scholars Press. • A. STANDHARTINGER 1995, *Das Frauenbild in Judentum der hellenistischen Zeit: Ein Beitrag anhand von 'Joseph und Aseneth,'* Leiden: Brill. • J. E. TAYLOR 2003, *Jewish Women Philosophers of First Century Alexandria: Philo's 'Therapeutae' Reconsidered,* Oxford: Oxford University Press. • W. C. TRENCHARD 1983, *Ben Sira's View of Women: A Literary Analysis,* Chico, Calif.: Scholars Press. • L. M. WILLS 1999, *The Jewish Novel in the Ancient World,* Ithaca: Cornell University Press.

TAL ILAN

Words of the Luminaries (4Q504-506)

The *Words of the Luminaries (Dibrê Hamme'ôrôt)* is the name of a liturgy (in Hebrew) comprising seven prayers, one for each day of the week. The title is written on the back of the first column of 4Q504, the best-preserved and oldest manuscript, which is dated on paleographic grounds to the mid-second century B.C.E. This early date virtually guarantees the liturgy's origin prior to the sectarian settlement at Qumran, begun about 100 B.C.E. Accordingly, no distinctively Qumranic ideas and terminology are in evidence. At least one more copy of this text survives: 4Q506 is dated to the first century C.E. and attests this liturgy's long life at Qumran, where it would have been integrated into the daily prayer ritual of the Qumran community that served as the sect's alternative to the sacrifices in what they considered to be a defiled Jerusalem Temple. The DJD 7 edition of 4Q504–4Q506 (Baillet 1982) is updated in Parry and Tov 2005.

Form and Content

The six weekday prayers are communal supplications (for the genre see, for example, Neh. 9:6-37, Bar. 1:15–3:8, *m. Ta'an.* 2:1-4, and the entry "Penitential Prayer" in this volume). Each weekday prayer has a heading indicating on which day of the week the prayer is to be said and then opens with the introductory formula, "Remember, Lord," followed immediately by a lengthy prologue (one to two columns long) of historical recollections that leads into and serves to justify the petition. The Sunday and Thursday petitions are requests for forgiveness, knowledge of Torah, and strengthening in its observance. The petitions on Tuesday, Wednesday, and Friday are for physical deliverance. (Monday's prayer is hopelessly fragmentary.) A brief concluding benediction summarizes the main theme of the day's petition, for example, "Blessed is God who gave us rest . . ." (Tuesday) and "[Blessed is God], who has delivered us from every distress" (Friday). The response, "Amen, Amen," then closes the prayer. A *vacat* (blank space) is left before the heading of the next prayer.

There is a chronological progression in the historical recollections over the course of the six weekdays that draws these prayers into a weekly scheme: the creation and fall of Adam are recalled on Sunday, the revelation at Sinai on Wednesday, from the Wilderness experience to the glory of the First Temple on Thursday, and the Second Temple period on Friday. The scheme indicates that this liturgy is a deliberate literary composition by a single author rather than a random collection of prayers. The work provides an important model for early liturgical composition as well as an important precedent for fixed, daily communal prayer (see below).

The purely doxological and hymnic "Thanksgiving (Song) on the Sabbath," which concludes this weekly liturgy (on the final columns of 4Q504 *recto* plus an additional eleven lines on the *verso*) stands apart generically owing to the special, holy character of the Sabbath day. The Sabbath hymn features invitations to praise God, has neither petitions nor a historical prologue, and is, therefore, not technically part of the historical scheme although its creation theme does bring this weekly liturgy full circle.

Significance

The chief significance of the Words of the Luminaries as a liturgical work is its attestation of fixed, daily communal prayers *outside* of the sectarian Qumran community during the latter half of the Second Temple period, and its continuity of tradition with the later rabbinic liturgy and the first Jewish prayer books (ninth to tenth centuries C.E.) in such details as the distinction between Sabbath and regular weekday prayer, the wording of petitions for knowledge, forgiveness and repentance, and the use of concluding benedictions. The rabbinic development of a fixed liturgy as a replacement for sacrifices after the Second Temple's destruction now finds a precedent in the appropriation of daily liturgies like the Words of the Luminaries by the separatist Qumran community.

BIBLIOGRAPHY

M. BAILLET 1982, *Qumrân Grotte III (4Q482-4Q520)*, DJD 7, Oxford: Clarendon. • E. G. CHAZON 1991, *A Liturgical Document from Qumran and Its Implications: "Words of the Luminaries" (4QDibHam)*, Dissertation, Hebrew University of Jerusalem; Leiden: Brill, forthcoming. • E. G. CHAZON 1991-1992, "4QDibHam: Liturgy or Literature?" *RevQ* 15: 447-55. • E. G. CHAZON 1992, "Is Divrei ha-Me'orot a Sectarian Prayer?" in *The Dead Sea Scrolls: Forty Years of Research*, ed. D. Dimant and U. Rappaport, Leiden: Brill • J. R. DAVILA 2000, *Liturgical Works*, Grand Rapids: Eerdmans. • H. ESHEL 2004, "*Dibre Hame'orot* and the Apocalypse of Weeks," in *Things Revealed: Studies in Early Jewish and Christian Literature in Honor of Michael E. Stone*, ed. E. G. Chazon, D. Satran, and R. A. Clements, Leiden: Brill. • D. K. FALK 1998, *Daily, Sabbath, and Festival Prayers in the Dead Sea Scrolls*, Leiden: Brill. • D. W. PARRY AND E. TOV 2005, *The Dead Sea Scrolls Reader*, Part 5, *Poetic and Liturgical Texts*, Leiden: Brill.

See also: Penitential Prayers

ESTHER G. CHAZON

Works of the Law →
Miqṣat Maʿaśê Ha-Torah (MT)

Worship

Worship is a modern term with no exact equivalent in the lexicons of the Hebrew, Greek, or Aramaic, used in the texts of early Judaism. *ʿAbodah*, the Hebrew word meaning "service" or "bondage," perhaps comes closest to expressing the contemporary concept of worship. For the purposes of this essay, worship is understood to involve formalized human communication with Israel's God involving three dimensions of human experience — space, time, and energy — which also serves the purpose of reinforcing an understanding of and commitment to God either by an individual or by a community. Human discourse, understood to comprise both language and ritual action, is the means of such communication. Study of the sacred text can also be considered a form of worship, not to mention revelation in early Judaism. Although the means and mediatorial agents are different, there is a continuum between petitionary prayer and the invocation of God or heavenly beings that is found in "magical" invocations to the degree that both seek to communicate with powerful beings in an immaterial or spiritual realm in order to cause some change in the present or immediate future. Early Jewish worship should also be seen as connected to the requirements of the developing legal tradition that governed all aspects of Jewish life.

Sacred Locations for Worship

In preexilic Israel, there were numerous ancient cult sites where Israelites gathered to offer sacrifices which were mediated by local priests. With the institution of Israelite kingship and construction of a central Temple in Jerusalem to unify the polity, rival cult sites were eclipsed though never entirely displaced as places for local worship. Archaeological and epigraphic sources make clear that Jerusalem was not an unrivalled center of sacrificial worship in the Persian period and beyond. The account of Ezra-Nehemiah portrays the exiles who returned from Babylon in the late sixth century B.C.E. in conflict with the *ʿam hāʾāreṣ* ("people of the land") who had not left the land (Ezra 4:1-5) over rebuilding the Jerusalem Temple. The archaeological record suggests continued use of Lachish, Bethel, and Mizpah as cult sites in the Persian period. Moreover, during the Second Temple period, the existence of three rival temples suggested diverse perspectives on the centrality of Jerusalem. By the fifth century Egyptian Jews in a military colony had constructed a temple in Elephantine on the Nile in Upper Egypt with its own priests and worship of "Yahu" and other gods. Worship there included offering of prayers for the government, Sabbath observance, and Passover celebration. The Elephantine temple was destroyed in 411 B.C.E. In Judah proper, a Samaritan temple on Mt. Gerizim near Shechem seems to have stood for about two centuries until it was destroyed by John Hyrcanus in 112/111 B.C.E. (2 Macc. 5:23; 6:2). Another Egyptian Jewish temple was built in the second century B.C.E. in Leontopolis in Lower Egypt, where it stood until its closure by the Romans in 73 C.E.

One rival Jewish temple did not involve a physical building. In the second century B.C.E., a nascent Essene community broke with the Temple leadership of Jerusalem, later to settle in the wilderness near the Dead Sea as mentioned in the Qumran community's rules (1QS 9:3-4 and CD 6:11-15). Instead of a physical temple in which were offered daily sacrifices of grain and animals, the sectarians substituted an understanding of the purified community constituting a "temple of men" who offered "works of the Law" in their entire manner of life and its disciplined practices of prayer and interpretation of Torah (4QFlorilegium, 4Q175). The priests themselves figured as the "holy of holies," the most sacred center of the community.

In spite of its contested place, the Temple in Jerusalem nonetheless seems to have played a central unifying role for the Jewish community, not only in Palestine but in the Diaspora as well. Some texts indicate that praying in the direction of the Jerusalem Temple was particularly efficacious (1 Kings 8:29, 38, 42; 2 Chron. 6:20, 29, 32, 34). Idealized depictions of the Temple and its functioning appear in Priestly texts of the Pentateuch, Ezekiel 40–48, the *Letter of Aristeas* 83–90, and the *Temple Scroll* from Qumran (11Q19). The author of Deutero-Isaiah goes so far as to envision the Temple in

Jerusalem as a "house of prayer for all peoples" (Isa. 56:7).

There are no contemporaneous sources that describe the procedures for daily sacrifice in the Jerusalem Temple during the Greco-Roman period, and the description of the sacrificial system in the Mishnah should be considered with caution as representing an idealized viewpoint from a rabbinic (Pharisaic) perspective which casts a jaded eye on the practices of alternate strands of Judaism. As with other ancient temples, daily offerings of animal and vegetable sacrifice served both individual and communal purposes in the worship of the deity. In any case, the Alexandrian Jew Philo understood sacrifice in allegorical terms, with sacrificial actions representing the interior transformations of the soul (*Mos.* 2.106-8). Private worship, that is, the offering of prayers, hymns, and blessings by individuals, could occur anywhere, if we can accept descriptions of individuals praying in narratives as verisimilar to actual practice. Judith, covered in ashes and sackcloth as a sign of lament, offers a long prayer near her home at the time of the evening incense sacrifice (in the Temple) before she sets off to assassinate Holofernes (Jdt. 9:2-14). Daniel is described as praying, praising, and seeking mercy from God on his knees three times a day in the direction of Jerusalem (Dan. 6:10-13).

The synagogue also served as a location for Jewish worship through prayer and study. The origins, architecture, and exact social role of the synagogue continue to be debated. The early postexilic scrolls of Ezra-Nehemiah, Haggai, Zechariah, and Chronicles make no mention of synagogues but rather focus on the rebuilding of the Jerusalem Temple. Although the first synagogue buildings are not found until the late Second Temple period, the social roots of the synagogue likely date to the exilic period, with community gatherings focused on prayer and the public reading of Scripture functioning as a way to maintain traditions and preserve cohesive community when expelled Judeans settled in Egypt and Babylon. Two different terms designate the synagogue, the *proseuchē,* meaning "house of prayer," which was a Diaspora term, and *synagōgē,* meaning "house of assembly," which seems to be a Judean designation.

Writing in the first century C.E., Josephus affirms the importance of reading and studying Scripture in the synagogue as central to Jewish practice (*Ag. Ap.* 2.175), synagogue practices also reflected in the New Testament descriptions (Luke 4:16-22; Acts 13:13-16). There is also evidence for synagogue buildings both within and outside the Levant beginning in the latter part of the Second Temple period. The oldest synagogue discovered so far in Palestine is in Jericho. It was used from roughly 130 to 30 B.C.E. and was apparently a part of the winter palace of the Hasmonean rulers. In the Diaspora, the first-century-B.C.E. synagogue on the Aegean island of Delos housed Greek-speaking Samaritans. The earliest Jewish synagogue buildings share no common architectural style. Indeed, the third-century-C.E. synagogue at Dura-Europos in the region of Syria was anomalously decorated with many frescoes illuminating biblical and extrabiblical scenes which no doubt served to enrich Jewish liturgical observances and may have served a didactic purpose as well. Some early synagogues (Hammath-Tiberias, Sepphoris) had mosaic floors featuring a zodiac circle with the sun god Helios in the center, evidence of syncretistic worship.

Sacred Times for Worship

It was of crucial importance to mark time correctly in ritual observance in order to worship the God Jews considered the creator of the cosmos and the redeemer of His people Israel, indeed, the creator of time and seasons themselves. God was understood to have created the sun, moon, and stars as a means of distinguishing days and seasons (Gen. 1:14-16), so proper observance of the ordained calendrical cycle was important. Sabbaths were a way of observing divine sovereignty over the created order by ceasing work and devoting time to praise and thanks to God for creation as well as rest, study, and recuperation in *imitatio dei* (Gen. 2:3; Exod. 20:8-11). As a "temple in time" that did not require a designated sacred space, the Sabbath could be observed anywhere in the Diaspora.

At some point in the postexilic period, after the Temple's reconstruction in the fourth century B.C.E., the daily sacrificial system was resumed. Priests played an essential role in offering sacrifice. In the exilic and postexilic period, the priestly house of Aaron, part of the tribe of Levi, seems to have claimed special rights to maintain the system of sacrifices with the majority of the tribe of Levi relegated to a custodial role, but the role of the priesthood was contested during the Hellenistic period, likely exacerbated by shifting allegiances to the Seleucid government during the period of Hasmonean independence in Yehud.

In addition to Sabbaths, which could be observed anywhere by all Jews, and daily sacrifice, which required priestly mediation, yearly observance of the three chief festivals of Passover, Weeks, and Booths, ordained already in the Bible, was mandated and drew pilgrims to the Temple in Jerusalem. The Jewish new year of Rosh Hashanah and the Day of Atonement, Yom Kippur, were also required observances.

A major calendrical dispute in early Judaism involved whether to calculate time and cyclical worship observances according to the 354-day lunar calendar or the 364-day solar calendar, or perhaps even more likely an intercalated solar-lunar calendar observed by the Essenes at Qumran. Some literature presents an idealized picture of worship according to the solar calendar (*Jubilees* 2, 6; *1 Enoch* 72–82). The many calendrical texts found at Qumran suggest that establishing holy time was essential to their priestly orientation and ritually dense community life, yet the calendrical materials at Qumran include calendars for not only the 364-day year but also a 360-day calendar. The Essene community at Qumran also observed an expanded number of festivals and holy days including the First Fruits of New Wine, Oil, and Wood, with the feast of Shavuʿot (Pentecost) playing a central role in their festival observance, tied as it was to the sect's annual covenant renewal ceremony. The end of the Qumran *Community Rule* (1QS) contains a description of the calendrical observances of the community as well as a first-person poem that describes the leader's regular worship obligations.

Forms of Worship

Prayers, hymns, and psalms are found in abundance in early Jewish literature, included both as part of narrative compositions and as independent compositions. The Greek versions of several books of scripture contain prayers and hymns as additions (Esther, Daniel). A consistent feature of all these prayers is their reuse of Scripture in multiple ways, whether modeled after earlier prayers in Scripture (e.g., the hymns of triumph in Exodus 15 and Judith 16) or woven through with interpreted scriptural language. Many figures in narratives are depicted as praying. Josephus' *Jewish Antiquities*, for instance, contains over a hundred prayers put in the mouths of biblical characters, whereas the Greek histories after which he patterned his work display very little interest in prayer. It is thus clear that prayer became an essential part of Jewish worship during the Second Temple period. Long confessional prayers appear in a number of postexilic and Second Temple books, suggesting an important development in Jewish piety and theology.

Roughly one-quarter of the 850 texts found in the caves around the Dead Sea have been identified as prayers, hymns, psalms, and liturgies, only a minority of which are explicitly sectarian in their language and ideas. These texts have yet to be fully integrated into a comprehensive understanding of the development of early Jewish worship patterns because few have any direct connection with developed Jewish liturgies of the rabbinic era. They nonetheless share some common themes, scriptural phraseology, and forms. Blessing formulas, for example, which became a rabbinic prayer staple, are evidenced increasingly in the Qumran literature. Complicating assessment of the Qumran material is the difficulty of distinguishing between those prayers used only by the Essene group at Qumran and those prayers and hymns that may have been used by other Jews generally throughout Judea and the Diaspora. The precise ritual practices associated with these prayers and liturgies are even more difficult to assess because these are generally transmitted orally and not described in narratives.

In terms of understanding communal worship, the historical end point is the fixed daily prayer comprising the recitation of the Shema (Deut. 6:4-9; 11:13-21; Num. 15:37-41) and the *Amidah*, or Eighteen Benedictions. The daily recitation of the Shema and *Amidah* by adult males became a halakic obligation in the rabbinic era, but the degree to which Jewish liturgical texts became fixed both in terms of a daily prayer requirement and the prayers' fixed wording remains an open question. Joseph Heinemann, a preeminent scholar of Jewish liturgy, argued for a gradual process of stabilization for the *Amidah* and Jewish liturgy, with the destruction of the Second Temple in 70 C.E. and the failure of the Jewish revolt in Palestine in 132-135 C.E. as accelerating the shift to fixity. More recently, Ezra Fleischer has argued for a sharp delineation in 70 C.E. and the creation *de novo* of the statutory prayers. It is not clear whether the Shema was recited at Qumran, but the fact that *tefillin* (leather straps with boxes containing scripture for use during prayer) and *mezuzot* (containers holding parchments of the Shema to be placed on doorposts) were found there suggests that this is a real possibility, since these reflect ritual enactments of Deut. 6:7-8 and 11:18-20.

BIBLIOGRAPHY

E. CHAZON 1994, "Prayers from Qumran and Their Historical Implications," *DSD* 1: 265-84. • D. K. FALK 1998, *Daily, Sabbath, and Festival Prayers in the Dead Sea Scrolls*, Leiden: Brill. • E. FLEISCHER 1990, "On the Beginnings of Obligatory Hebrew Prayer," *Tarbiz* 59: 397-441 (in Hebrew). • L. I. LEVINE 1987, "The Second Temple Synagogue: The Formative Years," in *The Synagogue in Late Antiquity*, ed. L. I. Levine, Philadelphia: American School of Oriental Research. • R. SARASON 2001, "The 'Intersections' of Qumran and Rabbinic Judaism: The Case of Prayer Texts and Liturgies," *DSD* 8: 169-81. • J. C. VANDERKAM 2004, *From Joshua to Caiaphas: High Priests after the Exile*, Minneapolis: Fortress. • S. REIF 1993, *Judaism and Hebrew Prayer*, New York: Cambridge University Press.

JUDITH H. NEWMAN

Writing

Writing in early Judaism involved the production of quite different sorts of texts, and Jews drew on different writing systems and sets of practices in producing them. Generally, Jewish texts can be divided into documentary texts of various kinds and the reproduction and production of literary-theological texts. The category of documentary texts includes the vast variety of texts used in everyday social transactions: deeds, receipts, records, letters, and the like. The category of literary-theological texts comprises cultural texts that were passed down through generations as the heritage of the Jewish people as a whole or a subgroup within it. It includes the sorts of texts now found in the Hebrew Scriptures, along with many other texts regarding communal identity, proper behavior, and divinity.

Writing Materials

Before looking in more detail at the production of documentary and literary-theological texts, we should note the different kinds of materials in which such texts could be written. Papyrus was used from very early on in Israel, continuing into the Second Temple period. Most papyrus in Israel probably was imported from Egypt, where the reeds used to make it grew. Some have argued that it was the most common writing material in preexilic Israel (Haran 1982). In the Second Temple period, we see increasing dominance of the use of parchment for writing all kinds of texts, but particularly literary-theological ones. Parchment is a writing material made out of animal hides scraped clean of hair, cured, and cut into strips on which columns of text could be written. Longer texts could be written on papyrus or parchment through the sewing together of separate sheets. Shorter letters, student exercises, and administrative documents often were written on potsherds, pieces of broken pottery, a common and relatively disposable medium of writing. Display and funerary writings often were inscribed in stone. Finally, several other types of materials are less frequently attested, such as silver, copper, wood, and wax boards.

Documentary Texts

At the beginning of the Second Temple period, Jews in Israel appear to have moved from a Hebrew writing system for documentary texts to an Aramaic one. We have examples of earlier, preexilic Israelite documentary texts written in Hebrew, using Paleo-Hebrew script and the word dividers typical of such texts, on papyri (e.g., Murabbaʿat 17A and 17B) and potsherds (e.g., from Samaria, Arad, and Lachish). This script and writing system in classical Hebrew appears connected to the monarchical systems of Judah and Israel. During the Persian period and afterward, however, we find documentary texts written on the same materials, papyri (e.g., from Elephantine and Wadi ed-Daliyeh), and ostraca, but many of them are written in Aramaic, and even many Hebrew texts are written in the square Aramaic script, using word spacing typical of Imperial and later Aramaic texts. Aramaic was the language used for commerce and administration across the Persian Empire, and it may also have been the primary tongue for Judean exiles returning from Babylon. Apparently, within Israel of the postexilic period, Aramaic and the Aramaic script (and writing system) supplanted the earlier Hebrew writing system of the Israelite and Judean monarchies as the means for everyday, written transactions.

As the Second Temple period continued, however, another shift in writing systems for documentary texts occurred in Israel. To be sure, we still see some Aramaic documentary texts, for example, in the composition of more traditional legal forms such as marriage contracts. Nevertheless, Greek begins to rise to prominence as a language for documentary texts. Greek was the standard language for Greeks and others working in Greek government, and it increasingly took the place of Aramaic as the written lingua franca for other sorts of documentary transactions as well. Papyrus was still used for many such documentary texts, as in the Greek papyri found in Egypt preserving the files of an official named Zenon and dating to the third century B.C.E. Documentary texts on ostraca also were produced. But we also start to see some use of parchment for documentary texts; for example, a Greek documentary text was found in Cave 4 at Qumran (4QAccount gr [4Q350]).

Near the beginning of the second century B.C.E., Hebrew appears to have experienced a revival, largely due to an emergent linguistic nationalism associated with the Maccabean Revolt. The texts of 1 and 2 Maccabees both refer proudly to rebels who spoke in their ancestral tongue, probably Hebrew (van Henten 1999), and some smaller Maccabean coins feature Hebrew inscriptions in Paleo-Hebrew script, in contrast to earlier ones inscribed exclusively in Greek. The Maccabees appear to have presented themselves as defenders of traditional Judaism against Hellenistic incursions, and this celebration of Hebrew and older Hebrew script probably was part of a reassertion of Jewish culture in response to what was depicted as a Hellenistic threat.

Literary-Theological Texts

The writing of literary-theological texts is often more conservative than the writing of documentary texts, and this is reflected in the various ways that Second Temple Jewish texts reflect the impact of much more ancient writing systems, such as that of Egypt. For example, several literary-theological texts found near Qumran (2QPs; 4QNum^{b} and 4QD^{e}) still show the use of red lettering for new sections, a practice that was widespread in ancient Egyptian documents and attested as well in the Deir ʿAlla inscriptions and several Phoenician inscriptions (Tov 2004: 54). Moreover, in the Second Temple period we still see some literary-theological texts written on papyrus, again showing links to Egypt (Tov 2004: 44-53). Egypt's ancient writing practices had a major impact on the writing systems of Phoenicia and neighboring countries, such as Judah and Israel, which adopted Phoenicia's form of the alphabet and other aspects of its writing system. The impact is still evident centuries later in some aspects of early Jewish writing.

Nevertheless, early Jewish writing also shows influ-

A bronze inkwell from the Scriptorium at Khirbet Qumran
(The Schøyen Collection, MS 1655/2)

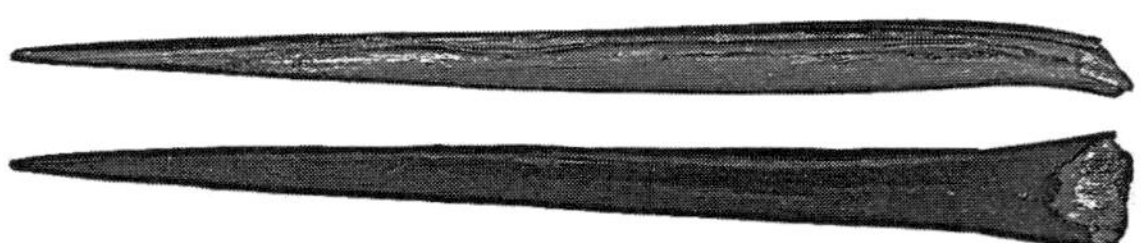

A stylus of palm leaf, with natural ink groove, found at Qumran (first century B.C.E. to 68 C.E.) *(The Schøyen Collection, MS 1655/2)*

ence from the writing systems of Mesopotamia and Persia, particularly the Aramaic writing system that was widely used across the Neo-Assyrian, Neo-Babylonian, and Persian empires. During the Second Temple period, the square Aramaic script becomes more common than the Paleo-Hebrew script of the Judean and Israelite monarchies. Moreover, the majority of early Jewish scrolls, particularly of literary-theological texts, are written on parchment, the material commonly used for writing Aramaic texts throughout the East (Tov 2004: 31-53). These elements associated with imperial Aramaic writing systems persisted well after Alexander's conquest of the area and the beginning of Hellenistic rule.

The influence of Greek writing systems on early Jewish literary-theological writing is more complex, partly because of the diverse responses of early Jews to the encounter with Hellenism. Jews in the Diaspora and Israel both were heavily influenced by the Greek literary system, a system focused on Homeric writings and a defined set of tragedies, histories, and other works by approved, pre-Hellenistic authors. Within this context, some early Jews — both in the Diaspora and in Israel — wrote new works in Greek and produced Greek translations of older Hebrew and Aramaic works. Some of these new works and translations of older ones found their way into the early church's Greek Old Testament (often labeled the "Septuagint"), while others were preserved separately.

Other Jews, however, responded in a more hostile way to Greek textual culture, especially after the confrontation with Hellenism around the Maccabean Revolt. For example, there are indirect signs that the Hasmonean kings promoted a defined corpus of Hebrew "Torah and Prophets," all books ostensibly written before a newly defined "end of prophecy" that came with the onset of Hellenism (1 Macc. 4:44-46; 9:27; 14:41). Though this Hebrew corpus was an alternative to the Greek literary corpus predominant at the time, its definition in terms of pre-Hellenistic chronological limits also shows an influence from the Greek corpus it opposed (Carr 2005: 253-72). Meanwhile, just as Greek authors often attempted to insert their works into the Greek literary tradition by ascribing them to pre-Hellenistic authors, so early Jews often took over this practice of pseudepigraphy to assure the place of their works in the Jewish literary tradition. This practice shows that, however much some may have promoted a set of Hebrew "Torah and Prophets" texts as a defined, pre-Hellenistic corpus, these efforts at circumscribing scriptures were not successful with all Jewish groups (including and especially the Qumran community).

After the Maccabean Revolt there are signs of a revival of older Hebrew writing practices, perhaps as part of a broader Hebrew linguistic nationalism. The Hasmoneans used the older Paleo-Hebrew script on some smaller coins. An account of their rise (1 Maccabees) was written in an archaizing Hebrew that is evident in the extant Greek versions. And several biblical manuscripts in Paleo-Hebrew script have been found at Qumran. Whether or not these latter manuscripts are products specifically of the Sadducees (cf. Tov 2004: 246-48), they are important witnesses to early Jewish revival of classical Hebrew and older Hebrew writing practices that were not widespread in the earlier half of the Second Temple period.

Student Exercises

Student exercises do not fit easily in either of the above categories (documentary and literary-theological), but do well illustrate the mix of cultural streams discussed above. The finds in the Judean Desert have revealed a number of student exercises. Some are abecedaries, apparently reflecting students' learning of the alphabet. Some others appear to be lists of words, mainly names, in alphabetical order, reflecting a student's progression to the formation of larger units. And scholars have speculated that several poorly written copies of biblical and other literary-theological texts may have been written by students as well (Tov 2004: 13-14). All of these are texts written in Aramaic letters, often featuring Hebrew words. Yet the progression from alphabet to alphabetized lists to literary sections is most typical of Hellenistic period education in Greek (Morgan 1998: 59-73). These fragments may show the adaptation in Hebrew education of educational phases from Greek education. Many, however, do not appear to have progressed far through this curriculum. Several documents found at Naḥal Ḥever and Wadi Murabbaʿat feature a contrast between the professional polish of the documents themselves and the crudeness of the handwritten signatures on them (Tov 2004: 13).

BIBLIOGRAPHY

D. M. CARR 2005, *Writing on the Tablet of the Heart: Origins of Scripture and Literature,* New York: Oxford. • M. HARAN 1982, "Book Scrolls in Israel in Pre-Exilic Times," *JSJ* 33: 161-73. • M. HARAN 1983, "Book-Scrolls at the Beginning of the Second Temple Period," *HUCA* 44: 111-22. • C. HEZSER 2001, *Jewish Literacy in Roman Palestine,* Tübingen: Mohr-Siebeck. • A. MILLARD 2000, *Reading and Writing in the Time of Jesus,* Sheffield: Sheffield Academic Press. • T. MORGAN 1998, *Literate Education in the Hellenistic and Roman Worlds,* Cambridge: Cambridge University Press. • E. TOV 2004, *Scribal Practices and Approaches Reflected in the Texts Found in the Judean Desert,* Leiden: Brill. • J. W. VAN HENTEN 1999, "The Ancestral Language of the Jews in 2 Maccabees," in *Hebrew Study from Ezra to Ben-Yehuda,* ed. W. Horbury, Edinburgh: T&T Clark, 53-68. • M. O. WISE 1994, *Thunder in Gemini and Other Essays on the History, Language and Literature of Second Temple Palestine,* Sheffield: JSOT Press.

See also: Literacy and Reading; Scripts and Scribal Practices

DAVID M. CARR

Y

Yavneh

Yavneh (in Hebrew), or Jamnia (in Greek), is a town located west by northwest of Jerusalem near the Mediterranean coast. The name Yavneh is regularly used by modern scholars in connection with the first generation of mishnaic sages, who allegedly met there after the destruction of the Temple in 70 C.E. (these sages are "Yavnean," as is the layer of the Mishnah which they composed or in which they are cited), and, by extension, to the efforts of the sages in the land of Israel to reconstitute their religion and society in the wake of the destruction (these efforts are the work of "the council [in some modern accounts: synod] of Yavneh"). Modern scholarly usage is based in the first instance on the following six sources: (1) the legend of Yoḥanan ben Zakkai's escape from Jerusalem, in which (at least according to some versions) he asks of Vespasian, and receives, "Yavneh and its sages" (*b. Giṭṭin* 56b); (2) several rabbinic traditions which locate "R. Gamaliel and his court" at Yavneh (*t. Ber.* 2:6), R. Gamaliel being the putative successor to R. Yoḥanan b. Zakai; (3) R. Yoḥanan b. Zakkai's self-conscious transfer of the ritual blowing of the shofar on Rosh Hashanah from the Temple to the court at Yavneh (*m. Roš Haš.* 4:1-2); (4) the story in the Tosefta that "When the sages gathered at the vineyard in Yavneh, they said, 'The time will come when a person will seek a word of the words of Torah and will not find it, of the words of the scribes and will not find it . . .' so they said, 'Let us begin with Hillel and Shammai'" (here follow the opening words of *m. ʿEduyyot; t. ʿEd.* 1:1); (5) the talmudic report that R. Gamaliel and his court established the central prayer of the daily liturgy, the "Eighteen Benedictions," including the benediction against heretics (*b. Berakot* 28b–29a); (6) the talmudic report that the disputes between the Houses of Hillel and Shammai came to an end at Yavneh (*b. ʿErubin* 13b). Of these, numbers (1), (2), (4), and (5) support the idea that there was a gathering or council or court or school at Yavneh, an idea that seems to be confirmed by many other texts that feature sages of the Yavnean period. Numbers (1), (3), (4), (5), and (6) support the idea that the Yavnean sages were establishing the basis for a new Judaism for a temple-less world. In addition, the debates among some sages of the Yavnean period about the status of some biblical books (*m. Yad.* 3:5) has suggested to some modern scholars that the council of Yavneh was responsible for the "canonization" of the Hebrew Bible.

Much of this reconstruction has unraveled in recent years, as there is substantial debate about the dating, historicity, and interpretation of these traditions. In particular, the legend about R. Yoḥanan ben Zakkai seems to be just that, a legend of dubious historicity; the blessing against heretics, in all likelihood, was not originally an anti-Christian prayer, contrary to a widespread view, and has nothing to do with the expulsion of Christians from the synagogue (John 9:22, 12:42, 16:2); the canonization of the Hebrew Bible was probably complete generations before the Yavnean sages.

The significance of Yavneh lies in the fact that the rabbinic sages after the destruction of the Temple began the process that would, about a century later, produce the Mishnah. That book became the basis of a new and distinctive kind of Judaism, a Judaism that would endure one way or another from that day to this. Synod or no synod, this is an accomplishment.

Bibliography

D. Boyarin 2004, *Border Lines: The Partition of Judaeo-Christianity,* Philadelphia: University of Pennsylvania Press. • S. J. D. Cohen 1986, "The Significance of Yavneh: Pharisees, Rabbis, and the End of Jewish Sectarianism," *HUCA* 55: 17-53. • W. Horbury 1983, "The Benediction of the Minim and Early Christian Controversy," *JTS* 33: 19-61. • R. Kimelman 1981, "Birkat ha Minim and the Lack of Evidence for an Anti-Christian Jewish Prayer in Late Antiquity," in *Jewish and Christian Self-Definition,* vol. 2, *Aspects of Judaism in the Greco-Roman Period,* ed. E. P. Sanders, Philadelphia: Fortress, 226-44.

Shaye J. D. Cohen

Yoḥanan Ben Zakkai

Yoḥanan ben Zakkai belonged to the generation of Judean Jews that experienced firsthand the Jewish Revolt against Rome in 66-74 C.E. He is remembered in rabbinic tradition as having been instrumental in reconstituting Judaism as a viable postsacrificial religion in the wake of the destruction of the Jerusalem Temple. But while rabbinic sources offer a profusion of traditions concerning his words and deeds, they also highlight the profound empirical and epistemological impediments to writing traditional rabbinic biography and history.

Evidence for the life of Yoḥanan ben Zakkai is exclusively literary and rabbinic. In the chain of tradition in *Pirqe ʾAbot,* he is named as the recipient of the traditions of Hillel and Shammai and credited with having been the teacher of five important tannaitic sages (2:8). He is thus imagined as the bridge between the "named pairs" of sages *(zuggôt)* who flourished during the Second Temple period and the *tannaim* of second-century Palestine. Tannaitic and later rabbinic sources describe him as a leader of the Pharisees prior to the Destruction, actively opposing the teachings of both Sadducees and priests regarding cultic practice (e.g., *m. Šeqal.* 1:4; *m. ʿEd.* 8:3; *m. Yad.* 4:6; *t. Para* 3:8; *b. Baba Batra* 115b; *b. Menaḥot* 65a). A couple of passages suggest, however, that he may himself have been of priestly stock (*t. Ohol.* 16:8; *t. Para* 3:7), a possibility affirmed by some modern historians (Schwartz 1980-1981). Yoḥanan ben Zakkai is thus a liminal figure: while his social and ideological profiles bear a resemblance to those of various Jerusalem-based scribal and perhaps sectarian groups, he does not fit comfortably into existing taxonomies. Nor is it certain that, in the period after the revolt, he can properly be considered a "rabbi" as that term would later be defined within the rabbinic movement.

Yet, despite these considerable uncertainties, tannaitic texts do provide clear and consistent testimony for a series of ordinances *(taqqānôt)* enacted by Yoḥanan ben Zakkai that aimed at altering Jewish ritual practices in response to the loss of the Temple (*Sifra, ʾEmor* 16.9; *m. Sukk.* 3:12; *m. Roš Haš.* 4:1-4; *m. Menaḥ.* 10:5; *t. Roš. Haš.* 2:9). Significantly, these *taqqānôt* did not address matters of purity law, which hold a central place in Pharisaic and early tannaitic legal discourse. Rather, they ordained that certain practices that had been restricted to the Temple precincts — such as blowing the *shofar* when the New Year falls on the Sabbath — could also be performed elsewhere. It is not certain whether Yoḥanan ben Zakkai and his colleagues initially envisioned these innovations merely as stopgap measures, though later rabbinic tradition would present them as the foundation for a new post-Temple Judaism.

Indeed, rabbinic literature provides far more than merely a series of tantalizing biographical details and isolated legal rulings. Yoḥanan ben Zakkai is the hero of a rich vein of rabbinic narrative tradition that recounts his flight from Jerusalem to Yavneh during the revolt (*ʾAbot R. Nat.* A 4; *ʾAbot R. Nat.* B 6; *Lam. Rab.* 1:5; *b. Giṭṭin* 56a-b; *Midrash Proverbs* 15). Having been carried out of the besieged city in a coffin by his disciples, the sage is taken to the Roman camp, where he prophesies the ascension of Vespasian to the imperial office and receives permission from the flattered general to establish an "academy" at the coastal town of Yavneh (Jamnia) under Roman auspices. Earlier generations of scholars sought to determine the precise historical events and intentions from this cycle of stories (Alon 1977). But Jacob Neusner and others have convincingly argued that the narrative underwent considerable literary expansion and differentiation during subsequent centuries and therefore cannot be dissected for the purposes of naïve historical reconstruction (esp. Neusner 1970). In recent years, even the basic historical significance of the "council" at Yavneh has been subject to revisionist interpretations and remains hotly debated (compare Cohen 1984 and Boyarin 2000).

Rather, these narratives of escape and foundation can be better read as reflecting the historical perceptions of crisis and renewal on the part of the generation of those who lived through the Destruction, as filtered through a rabbinic worldview (Schäfer 1979). It has similarly been argued that these stories not only reflect the ideology of rabbinic elites, but also encode folkloric elements that illuminate the process by which the continuity between Second Temple Jerusalem and post-destruction Judaism was crystallized in the Jewish imagination (Hasan-Rokem 2000: 171-89).

BIBLIOGRAPHY

G. ALON 1977, "R. Joḥanan b. Zakkai's Removal to Jabneh," in *Jews, Judaism and the Classical World,* trans. I. Abrahams, Jerusalem: Magnes, 269-313. • D. BOYARIN 2000, "A Tale of Two Synods: Nicaea, Yavneh, and Rabbinic Ecclesiology," *Exemplaria* 12: 21-62. • S. J. D. COHEN 1984, "The Significance of Yavneh: Pharisees, Rabbis, and the End of Jewish Sectarianism," *HUCA* 55: 27-53. • G. HASAN-ROKEM 2000, *Web of Life: Folklore and Midrash in Rabbinic Literature,* trans. B. Stein, Stanford: Stanford University Press. • J. NEUSNER 1970, *Development of a Legend: Studies on the Traditions concerning Yohanan ben Zakkai,* Leiden: Brill. • P. SCHÄFER 1979, "Die Flucht Joḥanan b. Zakkais aus Jerusalem und die Gründung des 'Lehrhauses' in Jabne," *ANRW* 2.19/2: 43-101. • D. SCHWARTZ 1980-1981, "Was Rabban Yoḥanan ben Zakkai a Priest?" *Sinai* 88: 32-39 (in Hebrew).

RA'ANAN BOUSTAN

Yom Kippur → Festivals and Holy Days

Z

Zadokites

The Zadokites are a group of priests associated with the Jerusalem Temple who appear in the book of Ezekiel, in a Hebrew fragment of the Wisdom of Ben Sira, and in about half a dozen of the Qumran documents.

Origins

In Ezekiel's vision for the newly built Second Temple, the "sons" or "seed" of Zadok are portrayed as the only ones among the priestly tribe of Levi who will have the right to approach the altar of the Jerusalem Temple (Ezek. 40:46; 43:19), in order to burn on the altar the holy sacrificial portions of fat and blood (Ezek. 44:15). They have earned this right by remaining faithful when the rest of the Levites, along with the people of Israel, went astray (Ezek. 48:11). The term "sons of Zadok" thus appears to indicate a subgroup of Levitical priests who claimed descent from Zadok, one of David's priests in Jerusalem. However, this picture of the Zadokites as part of the ancient Israelite priestly tribe of Levi is not substantiated by the earliest material about Zadok himself. Zadok appears without preamble in a list of officials in 2 Sam. 8:17, where his father is said to be Ahitub, a priest descended from the levitical line of Eli at Shiloh (1 Sam. 14:3). Yet 2 Sam. 8:17 is widely considered to be corrupt because it appears to be a garbled version of information given previously in 1 Sam. 22:20, and to contradict the surrounding narrative and a subsequent list of officials in 2 Sam. 20:25. This means that although Zadok's priestly colleague Abiathar (1 Sam. 22:20-23; 2 Sam. 15:24-29, 35-36; 17:15; 19:11; 20:25) is shown as being of levitical descent, Zadok himself is not. Furthermore, in 1 Kings 2:26-27 Solomon retains Zadok but expels Abiathar from being priest in Jerusalem because Abiathar supported Solomon's elder brother Adonijah as the heir to the throne instead of Solomon. The Zadokite priesthood is thus shown as supplanting the levitical priesthood in Jerusalem in accordance with the divine will (see 1 Sam. 2:27-35), which makes Ezekiel's description of the Zadokites as Levites problematic. Either the term "Levite" must be understood as functional rather than genealogical, or Ezekiel is attempting to justify the inclusion of an outside faction in the priesthood by claiming Israelite priestly ancestry for them.

Zadokites in Later Biblical Material

It has often been assumed that the chief priests of the First Temple, and subsequently the high priests of the Second Temple, were lineal descendants of Zadok. Although there is no evidence to this effect for the First Temple (Bartlett 1968), there is slightly more indication that the high priests in the Second Temple may have been regarded as Zadokites. The main evidence comes from the books of Chronicles; there, in a retrospective rewriting of First Temple history, Zadok is firmly incorporated into the tribe of Levi as one of the sons of Aaron, who are a subgroup of the tribe of Levi and in the eyes of the Chronicler the only legitimate holders of priestly office. This is an extension of the priestly ideology set out in the Priestly writings of the Pentateuch, whereby Aaron is depicted as high priest and his sons as the only legitimate priests (Exodus 28), and the high priesthood passes hereditarily to the eldest son (Lev. 21:10; Num. 3:2-4; 20:25-28). In Chronicles Zadok is incorporated into the priestly genealogies in 1 Chron. 6:1-15 (Hebr. 5:27-41) and 1 Chron. 6:49-53 (Hebr. 6:34-38) that begin with Aaron and cover the First Temple period, and in 1 Chron. 24:1-3 Zadok appears as a direct descendant of Aaron's eldest son Eleazar. Zadok is therefore depicted as a high priest, with the implication that all subsequent holders of the same office were his direct descendants. However, the genealogy in 1 Chron. 6:1-15 appears to be largely schematic rather than an accurate record of chief priests in the First Temple, because there are repeated groups of names, and very few of the names that are given coincide with the names of chief priests in the subsequent narrative. Additionally, in the subsequent narrative only one of the chief priests is actually specified as being of the house of Zadok (Azariah in 2 Chron. 31:10), which is quite surprising if there was indeed both a concern for the purity of descent and an awareness of the priests' Zadokite lineage during the First Temple period. The genealogies therefore suggest that by the time Chronicles was written, some time in the early to mid–Second Temple period, the claim of descent from Zadok had become important for the Jerusalem high priests. Even so, none of the high priests from the Second Temple period who are mentioned in the Hebrew Bible are specifically associated with Zadok, with the possible exception of Seraiah in Neh. 11:11; nor is there any mention outside Ezekiel of the sons of Zadok as a group.

Evidence from Other Sources

Evidence outside the Hebrew Bible for Zadokites is limited. In Josephus, the picture of an unbroken Zadokite line of chief priests in the First Temple is taken over from Chronicles (*Ant.* 7.56, 110; 8.11-12; 10.152-53), but none of the priests for the Second Temple period is explicitly associated with Zadok, and the "sons of Zadok" as a group never appear. The Hebrew version of the Wisdom of Ben Sira (second century B.C.E.) includes a benediction between 51:12 and 51:13 that praises God for choosing the sons of Zadok to be priests, although the status of this benediction is uncertain. It does not appear in the Greek or Syriac versions of the book, and on the basis of its ideology and vocabulary, it has been suggested that it was composed and inserted into the text by a member of the Qumran sect, where the Zadokites were revered as the only faithful priests (Skehan and Di Lella 1987). Certainly the sons of Zadok figure in the Qumran community's literature, although their precise status in the community is debated. The first known Qumran-related document containing references to the sons of Zadok was the so-called *Damascus Document* (CD), discovered in the Cairo Genizah in 1896 and published in 1910 by Solomon Schechter under the title *Fragments of a Zadokite Work.* Fragments of the work were then discovered among the Dead Sea Scrolls. The *Damascus Document* contains a midrashic interpretation of Ezek. 44:15, according to which the sons of Zadok are "the elect of Israel . . . who shall stand at the end of days" (CD 4:5). Among the Qumran materials themselves, the *Rule of the Community* (1QS), the *Rule of the Congregation* (1QSa), and the *Rule of the Blessings* (1QSb) present "the sons of Zadok, the priests" as an authoritative group who are lawgivers and guardians of the covenant (1QS 5:1-3, 8-10; 1QSa 1:1-3, 23-25; 2:2-3; 1QSb 3:22-25). Further, the *Damascus Document* speaks of the book of the Law being hidden and not revealed until the coming of Zadok (CD 5:2-5).

Scholars have taken this material to mean that Zadokite priests founded the Qumran community and played a leading role in it. This would have occurred in the mid-second century B.C.E. when the Zadokites lost control of the Jerusalem high priesthood and sought another setting in which to exercise their religious prerogatives, either with the murder of the (Zadokite) high priest Onias III (171 B.C.E.) or with the installation of Jonathan the Hasmonean as high priest (152 B.C.E.). Some have also suggested that the figure of Zadok in CD 5:2-5 refers to the sect's (Zadokite) founder and leader, identified in 4Q171 lines 14-16 as "the priest, the Teacher of Righteousness." However, other versions of the *Rule of the Community* that were found in Cave 4 do not mention the sons of Zadok. Nor are the Zadokites the only priests in the Qumran documents; the sons of Aaron appear as authoritative priests, sometimes in documents that also refers to the sons of Zadok (e.g., 1QS 9:7; 1QSa 1:14-16, 22-25; 2:11-16), although never in direct conjunction with them. These peculiarities have led scholars to question whether Qumran was indeed a fundamentally Zadokite community. An influx of Zadokites may have come later, as a secondary development, or the term "Zadokite" may be only an honorific, symbolic, epithet for the community.

The Zadokites are also traditionally associated with the Sadducees, a lay group within Judaism that emerged during the second century B.C.E. The association seems to have arisen because of the etymological correspondence between the names "Zadokite" and "Sadducee," but the nature of the relationship between the two groups is unclear.

BIBLIOGRAPHY

J. R. BARTLETT 1968, "Zadok and His Successors at Jerusalem," *JTS* 19: 1-18. • P. R. DAVIES 1987, *Behind the Essenes: History and Ideology in the Dead Sea Scrolls,* Atlanta: Scholars Press, 51-72. • A. HUNT 2006, *Missing Priests: The Zadokites in Tradition and History,* New York: T&T Clark. • J. LIVER 1967, "The 'Sons of Zadok the Priests' in the Dead Sea Sect," *RevQ* 6: 3-30. • D. W. ROOKE 2000, *Zadok's Heirs: The Role and Development of the High Priesthood in Ancient Israel,* Oxford: Oxford University Press. • P. W. SKEHAN AND A. DI LELLA 1987, *The Wisdom of Ben Sira,* New York: Doubleday, 568-71. • G. VERMES 1996, "The Leadership of the Qumran Community: Sons of Zadok-Priests-Congregation," in *Geschichte-Tradition-Reflexion: Festschrift für Martin Hengel zum 70. Geburtstag,* ed. H. Cancik et al., Tübingen: Mohr-Siebeck, 1:375-84.

See also: High Priests; Priests

DEBORAH W. ROOKE

Zealots → Resistance Movements

Zenon Papyri → Archives and Libraries; Papyri

Zephaniah, Apocalypse of

The *Apocalypse of Zephaniah* is an early Christian work, perhaps of Jewish origin, that narrates the otherworldly journey of a seer in the company of an angel who explains scenes relating to the postmortem fate of individuals. The work has survived in a short quotation in Clement of Alexandria's *Stromateis* (5.11.77) and in two fragmentary Coptic manuscripts of the fourth century C.E., a long fragment in Akhmimic, and a short one in Sahidic. Altogether, only about a fourth of the work has been preserved. It may have been written in Greek in Egypt, probably in the second or third century C.E., and may have originated in either a Jewish or a Christian setting. Nothing can be said with certainty here, since there is no mention of Jewish customs and traditions and no distinctively Christian elements. The work's greatest affinities are found in the Coptic *Apocalypse of Paul, 1 Enoch,* the *Apocalypse of Abraham, 2 Enoch,* and the *Testament of Isaac.* Recent scholarship suggests that the work was originally composed in a Coptic-speaking Christian monastery in second-century Egypt, where an interest in Jewish apocalyptic thinking was especially present.

In the passage quoted by Clement, a "spirit" takes the unnamed seer up into the fifth heaven, where he sees many angels called "lords" crowned by the Holy Spirit with diadems. They have thrones sevenfold more brilliant than the sun and dwell in "temples of salvation" from which they sing hymns to the "ineffable God." In the Sahidic fragment, the seer is in the company of an *angelus interpres* and sees the soul of a lawless person in Hades being punished by 5,000 angels. It was taken from its body before it had time to repent. The angel then takes the visionary to a "great broad place," where he sees thousands of figures (presumably more souls) of various appearances. The fragment closes with the words, "Truly, I, Zephaniah, saw these things in my vision."

In the much lengthier Akhmimic text, the unnamed seer witnesses the death of a righteous person at whose burial psalms and odes are chanted (presumably by angels). He also is granted a vision of the inhabitants of his native city going about their business, and of the entire inhabited world "hanging like a drop in a bucket" drawn from a well. From there he is taken to Mt. Seir and shown a vision of angels recording the deeds of human beings; other angels carry off the souls of the ungodly. After a brief glimpse of the gates of a beautiful city, he sees an angelic accuser and the angel Eremiel. This is followed by a vision of two manuscripts, the first one recording the bad deeds of the seer, the second presumably recording his good deeds (two pages of Akhmimic text are missing here). He is put in a boat and then given an angelic garment, praying with the angels in their own language. Two trumpet blasts signal the triumph of the righteous and the torment of the damned, respectively. The righteous dead intercede for the damned, and a final trumpet blast signals the coming wrath of God.

The main theme of the apocalypse is the coming death of the individual and the question of how to prepare oneself for the journey of the soul into the afterlife. Behind these motives is the ancient Egyptian interest in life after death. This interest continued in late-antique Christian monastic circles, with their strong focus on apocalyptic imagery and thinking, as is evidenced by such works as the Coptic *Apocalypse of Elijah,* the *Apocalypse of Peter,* and the *Gospel of Peter,* all of which were discovered during archaeological expeditions in Egypt.

The apocalypse's focus on postmortem judgment is underlined in the detailed description of the punishments of hell. However, the possibility of repentance and a turning away from sin is stressed again and again. There is no interest in the history of Israel or world history. The interest falls instead on the postmortem fate of the individual, with a strong emphasis on the possibility of repentance.

The allusions to biblical tradition include mention of the liberation of Israel from Egypt, of Susanna from the elders, and of Daniel's friends from the fiery furnace. Other biblical figures mentioned are Abraham, Isaac, Jacob, Enoch, Elijah, and David. There may be one allusion to the Temple in Jerusalem with the mention of Mt. Seir, and the description of the beautiful city may represent an idealization of Jerusalem. Whereas the image of God in the apocalypse is that of a *pantokratōr* who dwells in heaven, God is foremost the eschatological judge. More detailed, however, is the description of the angels, which are divided into bad angels, angels who accompany Zephaniah on his journey, and angels who act as the accusers of humans.

BIBLIOGRAPHY

Edition

A.-M. DENIS 1970, "Apocalypsis Sophoniae," in *Apocalypsis Henochi Graece,* Leiden: Brill.

Translations

B. J. DIEBNER 2003, "Zephanjas Apokalypsen," *JSHRZ* V.9, Gütersloh: Gütersloher Verlagshaus. • K. H. KUHN 1984, "The Apocalypse of Zephaniah and an Anonymous Apocalypse," in *AOT,* 915-25. • G. STEINDORFF 1899, *Die Apokalypse des Elias, eine unbekannte Apokalypse und Bruckstücke der Sophonias-Apokalypse: Koptische Texte, Übersetzung, Glossar,* Leipzig: Hinrichs. • O. S. WINTERMUTE 1983, "Apocalypse of Zephaniah," in *OTP,* 1.497-515.

Studies

M. HIMMELFARB 1993, *Ascent to Heaven in Jewish and Christian Apocalypses,* Oxford: Oxford University Press, 51-55. • G. S. OEGEMA 2001, *Apokalypsen,* JSHRZSup. 6.3, Gütersloh: Gütersloher Verlagshaus, 182-91. GERBERN S. OEGEMA

Zerubbabel

The information in the Hebrew Bible concerning the postexilic figure Zerubbabel comes largely from sources dated to the Persian or early Hellenistic periods: the books of Ezra-Nehemiah, Haggai, Zechariah, and Chronicles. In 1 Chron. 3:19, his father is stated to be Pedaiah, son of Jeconiah the Davidide. All other references declare him to be the "son of Shealtiel" (Ezra 3:2, 8; 5:2; Neh. 12:1; Hag. 1:1, 12, 14; 2:2, 23), but without any further information. His ancestry is not stated in Zechariah (4:6-10). Suggestions to resolve this discrepancy of his father's name have been offered, but not without difficulty. Regardless, it should be noted that the Davidic heritage of Zerubbabel is known only because of the otherwise problematic text in Chronicles; there is no hint of a Davidic ancestry for Zerubbabel or Shealtiel in the other books.

Some scholars have understood Zerubbabel to be the same individual as Sheshbazzar, the first leader of the returnees from the Babylonian Exile, who is described in much the same way as the later Zerubbabel (Ezra 1:8-11; 5:14-16). However, this possible connection has been rejected (Ben Yashar 1981).

According to Ezra-Nehemiah, Haggai, and Zechariah, Zerubbabel functioned as one of the two main leaders of the postexilic community during the Persian period. He and Joshua the high priest worked to rebuild the Temple during the restoration process at the time of King Darius. However, Haggai alone declares that Zerubbabel was the governor *(peḥah)* of the territory known as Yehud during the Persian period (1:1, 14; 2:2, 21) and God's chosen "signet ring" (2:20-23). Ezra-Nehemiah presents Zerubbabel as one of the leaders of the restoration in general without any particular concern for political associations. Zechariah reflects Zerubbabel's importance only as it relates specifically to the Temple reconstruction and not to any other aspects of the community's restoration (4:6-10).

The distancing of Zerubbabel from possible political dimensions may be understood in light of messianic aspirations during this time period. If Zerubbabel was a Davidide, and was the governor, this may have promoted the belief among some elements in the community during this period that the Davidic dynasty might once again be restored. This possibility is often read against the problematic text in Zech. 6:9-14, which relates the crowning of the high priest Joshua. Several features may indicate that the text once included a reference to Zerubbabel: there are two crowns rather than one; someone is called "the Branch" (a term used in the prophetic literature in the context of hope for the restored Davidic dynasty; cf. Isa. 11:1-5; Jer. 23:5-6; 33:14-16; cf. Isa. 4:2-6); and this "Branch" will have "a priest by his throne," which suggests that the Branch should not be identified with the high priest Joshua even though he is the antecedent in the text's present form. The identification of the "Branch" as someone distinct from Joshua is also apparently reflected earlier in Zech. 3:6-10. However, any *emphatic* conclusion that Zerubbabel, who does disappear from the biblical narrative, was removed by the Persians amidst a context of fervent messianic hopes or even potential revolt cannot be sustained given this meager evidence, as suggestive as such a possibility might seem.

Apart from the hypothetical nature of Zerubbabel's demise, the Hebrew Bible does convey the view that Zerubbabel was a primary leader in the community — the governor according to Haggai — and that he rebuilt the Temple with Joshua and others in the face of opposition (Ezra 3; 5–6).

In addition to these texts in the Hebrew Bible, Zerubbabel appears in 1 Esdras in another episode that further serves to enhance his prestige. While 1 Esdras largely parallels the material from 2 Chronicles 35–36, almost all of Ezra, and Nehemiah 8, Zerubbabel appears in the unparalleled account of the bodyguards (1 Esdr. 3:1–4:63). At a banquet held by King Darius, Zerubbabel demonstrates his superior wisdom over the other sages in debating who or what is the strongest in the world. Darius rewards Zerubbabel's answer by granting his request to return to Jerusalem to rebuild the Temple. This court tale explains how this special individual was chosen to perform this exceedingly important task.

The New Testament refers to Zerubbabel only in Jesus' genealogies (Matt 1:12-13; Luke 3:27). The unexpected appearance of Zerubbabel and his father Salathiel in both the Matthean and Lukan versions is the only commonality occurring between David and Joseph, which serves only to complicate the relationship of these two lists, which are otherwise independent.

BIBLIOGRAPHY

M. BEN YASHAR 1981, "On the Problem of Sheshbazzar and Zerubbabel," *Beth Mikra* 27: 46-56 (in Hebrew). • S. JAPHET 1982, "Sheshbazzar and Zerubbabel — Against the Background of the Historical and Religious Tendencies of Ezra-Nehemiah," *ZAW* 94: 66-98; 1983, *ZAW* 95: 218-29. • K. POMYKALA 1995, *The Davidic Dynasty Tradition in Early Judaism*, Atlanta: Scholars Press, 45-60, 69-111. • J. VANDERKAM 2004, *From Joshua to Caiaphas*, Minneapolis: Fortress, 10-42, 99-111.

STEVEN J. SCHWEITZER